ISBN 978-0-332-54348-2
PIBN 11239028

1 MONTH OF
FREE
READING

at

www.ForgottenBooks.com

By purchasing this book you are eligible for one month membership to ForgottenBooks.com, giving you unlimited access to our entire collection of over 1,000,000 titles via our web site and mobile apps.

To claim your free month visit:
www.forgottenbooks.com/free1239028

English
Français
Deutsche
Italiano
Español
Português

www.forgottenbooks.com

Mythology Photography **Fiction**
Fishing Christianity **Art** Cooking
Essays Buddhism Freemasonry
Medicine **Biology** Music **Ancient
Egypt** Evolution Carpentry Physics
Dance Geology **Mathematics** Fitness
Shakespeare **Folklore** Yoga Marketing
Confidence Immortality Biographies
Poetry **Psychology** Witchcraft
Electronics Chemistry History **Law**
Accounting **Philosophy** Anthropology
Alchemy Drama Quantum Mechanics
Atheism Sexual Health **Ancient History**
Entrepreneurship Languages Sport
Paleontology Needlework Islam
Metaphysics Investment Archaeology
Parenting Statistics Criminology
Motivational

378.73
Un32Ir

✓

RACIAL, ETHNIC AND SEX ENROLLMENT DATA FROM INSTITUTIONS OF HIGHER EDUCATION

492-32

c|

RACIAL, ETHNIC AND SEX ENROLLMENT DATA FROM INSTITUTIONS OF HIGHER EDUCATION

492-32

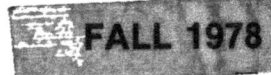

U.S. DEPARTMENT OF EDUCATION/Office for Civil Rights

U.S. DEPARTMENT OF EDUCATION
OFFICE FOR CIVIL RIGHTS

RACIAL, ETHNIC AND SEX
ENROLLMENT DATA
FROM INSTITUTIONS
OF HIGHER EDUCATION

FALL 1978

M,

AUGUST 1981

INTRODUCTION

This publication presents summations of the data collected through the survey "Fall Enrollment and Compliance Report of Institutions of Higher Education, 1978". This survey is part of the Higher Education General Information Survey (HEGIS XII) conducted by the National Center for Education Statistics.

Racial, ethnic and sex enrollment data were included by the Office for Civil Rights under authorization of Section 80.6(b) of the Regulations implementing Title VI of the Civil Rights Act of 1964 and similar provisions implementing Title IX of the Education Amendments of 1972.

Institutions receiving Federal financial assistance in the 50 States, the District of Columbia and outlying areas of the United States were surveyed for this study.

Requirements for reporting and definitions of terms are found in the Instruction Sheets for 1974, 1976 and 1978 survey instruments (APPENDICES A, B and C). Technical notes are covered in APPENDIX D.

For further information regarding the survey and the availability of data file tapes and microfiche, write or call:

Office of Special Concerns
Office for Civil Rights
400 Maryland Ave., S.W.
Washington, D.C. 20202
(202) 245-0015

TABLE OF CONTENTS

Page

INTRODUCTION

SECTION 1: TOTAL ENROLLMENT BY INSTITUTION

Table 1 — Total Undergraduate Enrollment in Institutions of Higher Education
by Race, Ethnicity and Sex: Institution, State and Nation, 1978   1

Table 2 — Total Graduate Enrollment in Institutions of Higher Education by
Race, Ethnicity and Sex: Institution, State and Nation, 1978   134

Table 3 — Total First Professional Enrollment in Institutions of Higher Education
by Race, Ethnicity and Sex: Institution, State and Nation, 1978   189

SECTION II: TOTAL ENROLLMENT BY STATE

Table 4 — Total Undergraduate Enrollment in Institutions of Higher Education by Race,
Ethnicity and Sex: State and Nation, 1978   213

Table 5 — Total Graduate Enrollment in Institutions of Higher Education by Race,
Ethnicity and Sex: State and Nation, 1978   217

Table 6 — Total First Professional Enrollment in Institutions of Higher Education
by Race, Ethnicity and Sex: State and Nation, 1978   220

SECTION III: TOTAL ENROLLMENT BY TYPE OF INSTITUTION

Table 7 — Total Enrollment in Two Year Institutions of Higher Education by Race,
Ethnicity and Sex: State and Nation, 1978   223

Table 8 — Total Enrollment in Four Year Institutions of Higher Education by Race,
Ethnicity and Sex: State and Nation, 1978   226

SECTION IV: COMPARISONS OF FULL-TIME ENROLLMENT 1974, 1976, 1978

Table 9 — Comparisons of Full-Time Undergraduate Enrollment in Institutions of
Higher Education by Race and Ethnicity: State and Nation, 1974, 1976, 1978   230

Table 10 — Comparisons of Full-Time Graduate Enrollment in Institutions of Higher
Education by Race and Ethnicity: State and Nation, 1974, 1976, 1978   237

Table 11 — Comparisons of Full-Time First Professional Enrollment in
Institutions of Higher Education by Race and Ethnicity:
State and Nation, 1974, 1976, 1978   244

SECTION V: COMPARISONS OF FULL-TIME ENROLLMENT BY CONTROL
OF INSTITUTION

Table 12 — Comparisons of Full-Time Enrollment in Publicly Controlled
Institutions of Higher Education by Race and Ethnicity:
State and Nation, 1974, 1976, 1978   250

Table 13 — Comparisons of Full-Time Enrollment in Privately Controlled
Institutions of Higher Education by Race and Ethnicity:
State and Nation, 1974, 1976, 1978   257

TABLE OF CONTENTS (continued)

		Page
SECTION VI: COMPARISONS OF TOTAL ENROLLMENT 1976, 1978		
Table 14 — Comparisons of Full- and Part-Time Undergraduate Enrollment in Institutions of Higher Education by Race, Ethnicity and Sex: State and Nation, 1976, 1978		263
Table 15 — Comparisons of Full- and Part-Time Graduate Enrollment in Institutions of Higher Education by Race, Ethnicity and Sex: State and Nation, 1976, 1978		272
Table 16 — Comparisons of Full- and Part-Time First Professional Enrollment in Institutions of Higher Education by Race, Ethnicity and Sex: State and Nation, 1976, 1978		281
SECTION VII: ENROLLMENT BY MAJOR FIELD OF STUDY		
Table 17 — Total Enrollment in Institutions of Higher Education for Selected Major Fields of Study and Level of Enrollment by Race, Ethnicity and Sex: State, 1978		289
Table 18 — Comparisons of Enrollment in Institutions of Higher Education For Selected Fields of Study and Level of Enrollment by Race, Ethnicity and Sex: State, 1978		702
SECTION VIII: TOTAL ENROLLMENT BY CLASS LEVEL		
Table 19 — Total Enrollment of Undergraduates by Class Level in in Institutions of Higher Education by Race, Ethnicity and Sex: State and Nation, 1978		790
Table 20 — Total Enrollment of Graduates by Class Level in Institutions of Higher Education by Race, Ethnicity and Sex: State and Nation, 1978		805
APPENDIX A: 1974 SURVEY INSTRUMENT AND INSTRUCTION SHEET		
APPENDIX B: 1976 SURVEY INSTRUMENT AND INSTRUCTION SHEET		
APPENDIX C: 1978 SURVEY INSTRUMENT AND INSTRUCTION SHEET		
APPENDIX D: TECHNICAL NOTES		

TABLE 1 - TOTAL UNDERGRADUATE ENROLLMENT IN INSTITUTIONS OF HIGHER EDUCATION BY RACE, ETHNICITY AND SEX:
INSTITUTION, STATE AND NATION, 1978

	AMERICAN INDIAN ALASKAN NATIVE		BLACK NON-HISPANIC		ASIAN OR PACIFIC ISLANDER		HISPANIC		TOTAL MINORITY		WHITE NON-HISPANIC		NON-RESIDENT ALIEN		TOTAL
	NUMBER	%	NUMBER	%	NUMBER	%	NUMBER	%	NUMBER	%	NUMBER	%	NUMBER	%	NUMBER
ALABAMA															
ALABAMA A & M UNIVERSITY															
AL TOTAL	3	.1	2,452	74.6	2	.1	5	.2	2,462	74.9	217	6.6	607	18.5	3,286
AL FEMALE	1	.1	1,318	90.8	2	.1	3	.2	1,324	91.2	76	5.2	51	3.5	1,451
AL MALE	2	.1	1,134	61.8	0	.0	2	.1	1,138	62.0	141	7.7	556	30.3	1,835
ALABAMA CHRISTIAN COLLEGE															
AL TOTAL	1	.1	544	48.9	3	.3	1	.1	549	49.4	550	49.5	1	1.2	1,112
AL FEMALE	0	.0	177	50.3	1	.3	0	.0	178	50.6	170	48.3	2	1.1	352
AL MALE	1	.1	367	48.3	2	.3	1	.1	371	48.8	380	50.0	9	1.2	760
ALA LUTH ACAD AND COLLEGE															
AL TOTAL	0	.0	228	100.0	0	.0	0	.0	228	100.0	0	.0	0	.0	228
AL FEMALE	0	.0	170	100.0	0	.0	0	.0	170	100.0	0	.0	0	.0	170
AL MALE	0	.0	58	100.0	0	.0	0	.0	58	100.0	0	.0	0	.0	58
ALABAMA STATE UNIVERSITY															
AL TOTAL	0	.0	3,923	98.8	2	.1	8	.2	3,933	99.0	8	.2	30	.8	3,971
AL FEMALE	0	.0	2,268	99.4	1	.0	5	.2	2,274	99.6	5	.2	3	.1	2,282
AL MALE	0	.0	1,655	98.0	1	.1	3	.2	1,659	98.2	3	.2	29	1.6	1,689
ALEXANDER CITY STATE JC															
AL TOTAL	1	.1	407	33.9	0	.0	1	.1	409	34.1	791	65.9	0	.0	1,200
AL FEMALE	1	.2	204	34.6	0	.0	0	.0	205	34.8	384	65.2	0	.0	589
AL MALE	0	.0	203	33.2	0	.0	1	.2	204	33.4	407	66.6	0	.0	611
ATHENS STATE COLLEGE															
AL TOTAL	2	.2	73	6.5	4	.4	1	.1	80	7.1	1,037	92.3	6	.5	1,123
AL FEMALE	0	.0	27	6.2	3	.7	1	.2	31	7.1	405	92.5	2	.5	438
AL MALE	2	.3	46	6.7	1	.1	0	.0	49	7.2	632	92.3	4	.6	685
AUBURN U MAIN CAMPUS															
AL TOTAL	19	.1	285	1.9	34	.2	31	.2	369	2.4	14,932	97.3	44	.3	15,345
AL FEMALE	10	.2	130	2.0	15	.2	15	.2	170	2.6	6,258	97.2	8	.1	6,436
AL MALE	9	.1	155	1.7	19	.2	16	.2	199	2.2	8,674	97.4	36	.4	8,909
AUBURN U AT MONTGOMERY															
AL TOTAL	0	.0	338	12.5	25	.9	0	.0	363	13.4	2,347	86.6	0	.0	2,710
AL FEMALE	0	.0	220	15.5	12	.8	0	.0	232	16.4	1,186	83.6	0	.0	1,418
AL MALE	0	.0	118	9.1	13	1.0	0	.0	131	10.1	1,161	89.9	0	.0	1,292
BIRMINGHAM STHN COLLEGE															
AL TOTAL	0	.0	160	12.8	8	.6	1	.1	169	13.5	1,068	85.5	12	1.0	1,249
AL FEMALE	0	.0	118	19.4	3	.5	1	.2	122	20.1	482	79.4	3	.5	607
AL MALE	0	.0	42	6.5	5	.8	0	.0	47	7.3	586	91.3	9	1.4	642
BOOKER T WASHINGTON BUS C															
AL TOTAL	0	.0	325	100.0	0	.0	0	.0	325	100.0	0	.0	0	.0	325
AL FEMALE	0	.0	269	100.0	0	.0	0	.0	269	100.0	0	.0	0	.0	269
AL MALE	0	.0	56	100.0	0	.0	0	.0	56	100.0	0	.0	0	.0	56
BREWER STATE JR COLLEGE															
AL TOTAL	0	.0	416	23.3	2	.1	0	.0	418	23.4	1,371	76.6	0	.0	1,789
AL FEMALE	0	.0	283	28.0	0	.0	0	.0	283	28.0	729	72.0	0	.0	1,012
AL MALE	0	.0	133	17.1	2	.3	0	.0	135	17.4	642	82.6	0	.0	777
CHATTAHOOCHEE VALLEY CC															
AL TOTAL	9	.4	755	30.8	14	.6	13	.5	791	32.2	1,655	67.4	8	.3	2,454
AL FEMALE	5	.4	370	32.6	3	.3	-6	.5	384	33.9	749	66.0	1	.1	1,134
AL MALE	4	.3	385	29.2	11	.8	7	.5	407	30.8	906	68.6	7	.5	1,320
ENTERPRISE ST JR COLLEGE															
AL TOTAL	1	.1	142	7.7	13	.7	3	.2	159	8.6	1,692	91.4	0	.0	1,851
AL FEMALE	0	.0	84	8.1	11	1.1	1	.1	96	9.3	937	90.7	0	.0	1,033
AL MALE	1	.1	58	7.1	2	.2	2	.2	63	7.7	755	92.3	0	.0	818
FAULKNER STATE JR COLLEGE															
AL TOTAL	2	.1	257	15.3	5	.3	6	.4	270	16.1	1,393	82.8	19	1.1	1,682
AL FEMALE	1	.1	174	20.0	2	.2	1	.1	178	20.5	684	78.8	6	.7	868
AL MALE	1	.1	83	10.2	3	.4	5	.6	92	11.3	709	87.1	13	1.6	814
GADSDEN STATE JR COLLEGE															
AL TOTAL	26	.7	511	14.2	0	.0	9	.2	546	15.1	2,874	79.6	191	5	3,611
AL FEMALE	9	.5	264	15.5	0	.0	4	.2	277	16.3	1,397	82.0	30	1	1,704
AL MALE	17	.9	247	13.0	0	.0	5	.3	269	14.1	1,477	77.5	161	5¦8	1,907
GEO C WALLACE ST CC-DOTHN															
AL TOTAL	7	.4	243	12.3	10	.5	8	.4	268	13.6	1,702	86.2	4	.2	1,974
AL FEMALE	3	.3	154	14.4	4	.4	3	.3	164	15.3	909	84.7	0	.0	1,073
AL MALE	4	.4	89	9.9	6	.7	5	.6	104	11.5	793	88.0	4	.4	901
GEO C WALLACE ST CC-HNCV															
AL TOTAL	0	.0	21	2.0	0	.0	0	.0	21	2.0	1,000	97.6	4	.4	1,025
AL FEMALE	0	.0	13	2.1	0	.0	0	.0	13	2.1	614	97.9	0	.0	627
AL MALE	0	.0	8	2.0	0	.0	0	.0	8	2.0	386	97.0	4	1.0	398
GEO C WALLACE ST CC-SELMA															
AL TOTAL	0	.0	739	40.6	0	.0	0	.0	739	40.6	1,074	59.0	6	.3	1,819
AL FEMALE	0	.0	298	38.4	0	.0	0	.0	298	38.4	478	61.6	0	.0	776
AL MALE	0	.0	441	42.3	0	.0	0	.0	441	42.3	596	57.1	6	.6	1,043
HUNTINGDON COLLEGE															
AL TOTAL	1	.2	70	11.3	0	.0	2	.3	73	11.8	532	85.8	15	2.4	620
AL FEMALE	0	.0	37	10.4	0	.0	1	.3	38	10.7	311	87.4	7	2.0	356
AL MALE	1	.4	33	12.5	0	.0	1	.4	35	13.3	221	83.7	8	3.0	264
JACKSONVL ST UNIVERSITY															
AL TOTAL	7	.1	766	12.8	33	.5	38	.6	844	14.1	5,161	85.9	0	.0	6,005
AL FEMALE	3	.1	452	14.8	14	.5	13	.4	482	15.8	2,573	84.2	0	.0	3,055
AL MALE	4	.1	314	10.6	19	.6	25	.8	362	12.3	2,588	87.7	0	.0	2,950
JEFFERSON DAVIS STATE JC															
AL TOTAL	0	.0	121	19.0	0	.0	0	.0	121	19.0	515	81.0	0	.0	636
AL FEMALE	0	.0	61	16.3	0	.0	0	.0	61	16.3	313	83.7	0	.0	374
AL MALE	0	.0	60	22.9	0	.0	0	.0	60	22.9	202	77.1	0	.0	262
JEFFERSON ST JR COLLEGE															
AL TOTAL	3	.0	1,170	18.5	7	.1	8	.1	1,188	18.8	5,083	80.6	37	.6	6,308
AL FEMALE	2	.1	746	22.8	3	.1	4	.1	755	23.0	2,514	76.7	7	.2	3,276
AL MALE	1	.0	424	14.0	4	.1	4	.1	433	14.3	2,569	84.7	30	1.0	3,032
JOHN C CALHOUN ST CC															
AL TOTAL	15	.3	441	9.6	9	.2	15	.3	480	10.4	4,065	88.2	62	1.3	4,607
AL FEMALE	6	.3	231	11.6	4	.2	6	.3	247	12.4	1,735	86.8	16	.8	1,998
AL MALE	9	.3	210	8.0	5	.2	9	.3	233	8.9	2,330	89.3	46	1.8	2,609

TABLE 1 - TOTAL UNDERGRADUATE ENROLLMENT IN INSTITUTIONS OF HIGHER EDUCATION BY RACE, ETHNICITY AND SEX: INSTITUTION, STATE AND NATION, 1976

	AMERICAN INDIAN ALASKAN NATIVE		BLACK NON-HISPANIC		ASIAN OR PACIFIC ISLANDER		HISPANIC		TOTAL MINORITY		WHITE NON-HISPANIC		NON-RESIDENT ALIEN		TOTAL
	NUMBER	%	NUMBER	%	NUMBER	%	NUMBER	%	NUMBER	%	NUMBER	%	NUMBER	%	NUMBER
ALABAMA								CONTINUED							
JUDSON COLLEGE															
AL TOTAL	0	.0	16	5.0	0	.0		.0	16	5.0	301	95.0	0	.0	317
AL FEMALE	0	.0	16	5.0	0	.0		.0	16	5.0	301	95.0	0	.0	317
AL MALE	0	.0	0	.0	0	.0	8	.0	0	.0	0	.0	0	.0	0
LAWSON STATE CMTY COLLEGE															
AL TOTAL	0	.0	1,241	98.1	0	.0		.0	1,241	98.1	2	.2	22	1.7	1,265
AL FEMALE	0	.0	905	99.8	0	.0		.0	905	99.8	0	.0	2	.2	907
AL MALE	0	.0	336	93.9	0	.0	8	.0	336	93.9	2	.6	20	5.6	358
LIVINGSTON UNIVERSITY															
AL TOTAL	1	.1	251	24.3	2	.2	1	.1	255	24.7	768	74.3	11	1.1	1,034
AL FEMALE	1	.2	135	28.2	1	.2	0	.0	137	28.7	338	70.7	3	.6	478
AL MALE	0	.0	116	20.9	1	.2	1	.2	118	21.2	430	77.3	8	1.4	556
LOMAX-HANNON JC															
AL TOTAL	0	.0	160	100.0	0	.0		.0	160	100.0	0	.0	0	.0	160
AL FEMALE	0	.0	89	100.0	0	.0		.0	89	100.0	0	.0	0	.0	89
AL MALE	0	.0	71	100.0	0	.0	8	.0	71	100.0	0	.0	0	.0	71
LURLEEN B WALLACE ST JC															
AL TOTAL	0	.0	126	15.6	0	.0		.0	126	15.6	677	84.0	3	.4	806
AL FEMALE	0	.0	82	17.8	0	.0		.0	82	17.8	377	82.0	1	.2	460
AL MALE	0	.0	44	12.7	0	.0	8	.0	44	12.7	300	86.7	2	.6	346
MARION MILITARY INSTITUTE															
AL TOTAL	0	.0	8	3.6	1	.4	2	.9	11	4.9	207	92.0	7	3.1	225
AL FEMALE	0	.0	0	.0	0	.0	0	.0	0	.0	0	.0	0	.0	0
AL MALE	0	.0	8	3.6	1	.4	2	.9	11	4.9	207	92.0	7	3.1	225
MILES COLLEGE															
AL TOTAL	0	.0	1,246	99.4	0	.0	0	.0	1,246	99.4	8	.6		.0	1,254
AL FEMALE	0	.0	687	100.0	0	.0	0	.0	687	100.0	0	.0		.0	687
AL MALE	0	.0	559	98.6	0	.0	0	.0	559	98.6	8	1.4	8	.0	567
MOBILE COLLEGE															
AL TOTAL	2	.2	65	7.5	0	.0	5	.6	72	8.3	800	91.7		.0	872
AL FEMALE	1	.2	53	9.2	0	.0	1	.2	55	9.5	523	90.5		.0	578
AL MALE	1	.3	12	4.1	0	.0	4	1.4	17	5.8	277	94.2	8	.0	294
NTHEST ALA ST JR COLLEGE															
AL TOTAL	2	.1	39	2.6	0	.0	1	.1	42	2.8	1,384	93.8	49	3.3	1,475
AL FEMALE	1	.1	15	2.2	0	.0	0	.0	16	2.4	646	96.6	7	1.0	669
AL MALE	1	.1	24	3.0	0	.0	1	.1	26	3.2	738	91.6	42	5.2	806
NTHWST ALA ST JR COLLEGE															
AL TOTAL	0	.0	95	9.7	0	.0		.0	95	9.7	868	88.7	1	1.6	979
AL FEMALE	0	.0	66	11.4	0	.0		.0	66	11.4	514	88.6		.0	580
AL MALE	0	.0	29	7.3	0	.0	8	.0	29	7.3	354	88.7	16	4.0	399
OAKWOOD COLLEGE															
AL TOTAL	0	.0	1,240	99.1	0	.0		.0	1,240	99.1	11	.9		.0	1,251
AL FEMALE	0	.0	642	99.2	0	.0		.0	642	99.2	5	.8		.0	647
AL MALE	0	.0	598	99.0	0	.0	8	.0	598	99.0	6	1.0	8	.0	604
PATRICK HENRY STATE JC															
AL TOTAL	0	.0	147	19.8	0	.0	4	.5	151	20.3	592	79.7		.0	743
AL FEMALE	0	.0	100	22.8	0	.0	2	.5	102	23.3	336	76.7		.0	438
AL MALE	0	.0	47	15.4	0	.0	2	.7	49	16.1	256	83.9	8	.0	305
S D BISHOP ST JR COLLEGE															
AL TOTAL	0	.0	1,193	89.0	0	.0		.0	1,193	89.0	117	8.7	30	2.2	1,340
AL FEMALE	0	.0	857	93.1	0	.0		.0	857	93.1	56	6.1	8	.9	921
AL MALE	0	.0	336	80.2	0	.0	8	.0	336	80.2	61	14.6	22	5.3	419
SAMFORD UNIVERSITY															
AL TOTAL	5	.2	172	6.6	3	.1	8	.3	188	7.2	2,426	92.4	11	.4	2,625
AL FEMALE	0	.0	138	9.1	3	.2	5	.3	146	9.7	1,364	90.2	2	.1	1,512
AL MALE	5	.4	34	3.1	0	.0	3	.3	42	3.8	1,062	95.4	9	.8	1,113
SELMA UNIVERSITY															
AL TOTAL	0	.0	632	100.0	0	.0	0	.0	632	100.0	0	.0		.0	632
AL FEMALE	0	.0	371	100.0	0	.0	0	.0	371	100.0	0	.0		.0	371
AL MALE	0	.0	261	100.0	0	.0	0	.0	261	100.0	0	.0	8	.0	261
SNEAD STATE JR COLLEGE															
AL TOTAL	0	.0	12	1.0	0	.0	1	.1	13	1.0	1,243	98.7	3	.2	1,259
AL FEMALE	0	.0	3	.4	0	.0	0	.0	3	.4	668	99.4	1	.1	672
AL MALE	0	.0	9	1.5	0	.0	1	.2	10	1.7	575	98.0	2	.3	587
STHESTN BIBLE COLLEGE															
AL TOTAL	0	.0	2	.9	1	.4		.0	3	1.3	226	97.8	2	.9	231
AL FEMALE	0	.0	0	.0	0	.0		.0	0	.0	98	100.0	0	.0	98
AL MALE	0	.0	2	1.5	1	.8	8	.0	3	2.3	128	96.2	2	1.5	133
STHN BENEDICTINE COLLEGE															
AL TOTAL	1	.3	16	4.1	2	.5	4	1.0	23	5.9	368	93.6	2	.5	393
AL FEMALE	1	.6	3	1.7	0	.0	1	.6	5	2.9	169	97.1	0	.0	174
AL MALE	0	.0	13	5.9	2	.9	3	1.4	18	8.2	199	90.9	2	.9	219
SOUTHERN BUSINESS COLLEGE															
AL TOTAL	0	.0	856	69.9	0	.0		.0	856	69.9	368	30.1		.0	1,224
AL FEMALE	0	.0	636	70.0	0	.0		.0	636	70.0	273	30.0		.0	909
AL MALE	0	.0	220	69.8	0	.0	8	.0	220	69.8	95	30.2	8	.0	315
STHN UNION ST JR COLLEGE															
AL TOTAL	0	.0	217	14.1	0	.0		.0	217	14.1	1,316	85.5	7	.5	1,540
AL FEMALE	0	.0	100	14.2	0	.0		.0	100	14.2	599	85.2	4	.6	703
AL MALE	0	.0	117	14.0	0	.0	8	.0	117	14.0	717	85.7	3	.4	837
STHN VOCATIONAL COLLEGE															
AL TOTAL	0	.0	373	96.4	0	.0		.0	373	96.4	14	3.6	0	.0	387
AL FEMALE	0	.0	216	100.0	0	.0		.0	216	100.0	0	.0	0	.0	216
AL MALE	0	.0	157	91.8	0	.0	8	.0	157	91.8	14	8.2	0	.0	171
SPRING HILL COLLEGE															
AL TOTAL	0	.0	21	2.5	1	.1	16	1.9	38	4.5	793	94.3	10	1.2	841
AL FEMALE	0	.0	10	2.7	1	.3	2	.5	13	3.5	360	96.0	2	.5	375
AL MALE	0	.0	11	2.4	0	.0	14	3.0	25	5.4	433	92.9	8	1.7	466
STILLMAN COLLEGE															
AL TOTAL	0	.0	578	98.0	0	.0	4	.7	582	98.6	4	.7		.7	590
AL FEMALE	0	.0	349	99.1	0	.0	2	.6	351	99.7	1	.3		.0	352
AL MALE	0	.0	229	96.2	0	.0	2	.8	231	97.1	3	1.3	4	1.7	238

TABLE 1 - TOTAL UNDERGRADUATE ENROLLMENT IN INSTITUTIONS OF HIGHER EDUCATION BY RACE, ETHNICITY AND SEX: INSTITUTION, STATE AND NATION, 1978

	AMERICAN INDIAN ALASKAN NATIVE		BLACK NON-HISPANIC		ASIAN OR PACIFIC ISLANDER		HISPANIC		TOTAL MINORITY		WHITE NON-HISPANIC		NON-RESIDENT ALIEN		TOTAL
	NUMBER	%	NUMBER	%	NUMBER	%	NUMBER	%	NUMBER	%	NUMBER	%	NUMBER	%	NUMBER
ALABAMA CONTINUED															
TALLADEGA COLLEGE															
AL TOTAL	0	.0	638	98.6	0	.0	0	.0	638	98.6	5	.8	4	.6	647
AL FEMALE	0	.0	438	99.1	0	.0	0	.0	438	99.1	4	.9	0	.0	442
AL MALE	0	.0	200	97.6	0	.0	0	.0	200	97.6	1	.5	4	2.0	205
TROY STATE U MAIN CAMPUS															
AL TOTAL	5	.1	746	13.3	26	.5	37	.7	814	14.6	4,766	85.2	11	.2	5,591
U FEMALE	2	.1	377	14.7	6	.2	10	.4	395	15.4	2,160	84.4	4	.2	2,559
AL MALE	3	.1	369	12.2	20	.7	27	.9	419	13.8	2,506	85.9	7	.2	3,032
TROY ST U ODTHN-FT RUCKER															
AL TOTAL	1	.1	55	6.2	0	.0	7	.8	63	7.	818	92.7	1	.1	882
AL FEMALE	0	.0	26	7.6	0	.0	1	.3	27	7.	314	92.1	0	.0	341
AL MALE	1	.2	29	5.4	0	.0	6	1.1	36	6.4	504	93.2	1	.2	541
TROY STATE U MONTGOMERY															
AL TOTAL	2	.1	369	21.7	7	.4	8	.5	386	22.7	1,311	77.1	3	.2	1,700
AL FEMALE	1	.2	181	32.2	1	.2	3	.5	186	33.1	376	66.9	0	.0	562
AL MALE	1	.1	188	16.5	6	.5	5	.4	200	17.6	935	82.2	3	.3	1,138
TUSKEGEE INSTITUTE															
AL TOTAL	0	.0	2,599	88.5	59	2.0	32	1.1	2,690	91.6	13	.4	233	7.9	2,936
AL FEMALE	0	.0	1,471	94.6	12	.8	7	.5	1,490	95.8	7	.5	58	3.7	1,555
AL MALE	0	.0	1,128	81.7	47	3.4	25	1.8	1,200	86.9	6	.4	175	12.7	1,381
UNIVERSITY OF ALABAMA															
AL TOTAL	0	.0	1,412	10.8	0	.0	109	.8	1,521	11.6	11,495	87.5	114	.9	13,130
AL FEMALE	0	.0	872	13.9	0	.0	46	.7	918	14.7	5,315	84.9	30	.5	6,263
AL MALE	0	.0	540	7.9	0	.0	63	.9	603	8.8	6,180	90.0	84	1.2	6,867
U ALABAMA IN BIRMINGHAM															
AL TOTAL	13	.2	1,880	22.0	40	.5	14	.2	1,947	22.8	6,534	76.6	49	.6	8,530
AL FEMALE	9	.2	1,287	28.3	19	.4	11	.2	1,326	29.1	3,216	70.6	11	.2	4,553
AL MALE	4	.1	593	14.9	21	.5	3	.1	621	15.6	3,318	83.4	38	1.0	3,977
U ALABAMA IN HUNTSVILLE															
AL TOTAL	3	.1	179	5.4	30	.9	24	.7	236	7.2	3,015	91.8	35	1.1	3,286
AL FEMALE	2	.1	108	6.4	12	.7	11	.6	133	7.8	1,564	92.0	3	.2	1,700
AL MALE	1	.1	71	4.5	18	1.1	13	.8	103	6.5	1,451	91.5	32	2.0	1,586
UNIVERSITY OF MONTEVALLO															
AL TOTAL	2	.1	166	6.7	0	.0	0	.0	168	6.7	2,281	91.6	41	1.6	2,490
AL FEMALE	1	.1	117	7.7	0	.0	0	.0	118	7.7	1,392	91.3	14	.9	1,524
AL MALE	1	.1	49	5.1	0	.0	0	.0	50	5.2	889	92.0	27	2.8	966
U OF NORTH ALABAMA															
AL TOTAL	2	.0	363	8.7	6	.1	4	.1	375	9.	3,796	90.7	14	.3	4,185
AL FEMALE	2	.1	216	9.7	4	.2	0	.0	222	9.0	2,011	89.9	5	.2	2,238
AL MALE	0	.0	147	7.6	2	.1	4	.2	153	7.9	1,785	91.7	9	.5	1,947
U OF SOUTH ALABAMA															
AL TOTAL	35	.6	534	9.3	45	.8	17	.3	631	11.0	5,046	87.9	65	1.1	5,742
AL FEMALE	21	.7	327	11.7	13	.5	10	.4	371	13.2	2,426	86.5	7	.2	2,804
AL MALE	14	.5	207	7.0	32	1.1	7	.2	260	8.8	2,620	89.2	58	2.0	2,938
WALKER COLLEGE															
AL TOTAL	0	.0	52	7.4	0	.0	0	.0	52	7.	641	91.4	8	1.1	701
AL FEMALE	0	.0	34	8.6	0	.0	0	.0	34	8.8	357	90.4	4	1.0	395
AL MALE	0	.0	18	5.9	0	.0	0	.0	18	5.8	284	92.8	4	1.3	306
ALABAMA TOTAL (58 INSTITUTIONS)															
AL TOTAL	171	.1	32,086	23.6	394	.3	448	.3	33,099	24.3	101,281	74.4	1,813	1.3	136,193
AL FEMALE	83	.1	18,995	27.8	150	.2	176	.3	19,404	28.4	48,679	71.2	304	.4	68,387
AL MALE	88	.1	13,091	19.3	244	.4	272	.4	13,695	20.2	52,602	77.6	1,509	2.2	67,806
ALASKA															
ALASKA BIBLE COLLEGE															
AK TOTAL	4	30.8	0	.0	0	.0	0	.0	4	30.8	9	69.2		.0	13
AK FEMALE	1	12.5	0	.0	0	.0	0	.0	1	12.5	7	87.5	0	.0	8
AK MALE	3	60.0	0	.0	0	.0	0	.0	3	60.0	2	40.0	0	.0	5
ALASKA PACIFIC UNIVERSITY															
AK TOTAL	12	32.4	4	10.8	2	5.4	0	.0	1	48.6	19	51.4		.0	37
AK FEMALE	8	50.0	1	6.3	0	.0	0	.0		56.3	7	43.8	0	.0	16
AK MALE	4	19.0	3	14.3	2	9.5	0	.0	8	42.9	12	57.1	0	.0	21
SHELDON JACKSON COLLEGE															
AK TOTAL	167	56.2	0	.0	0	.0	1	.3	168	56.6	126	42.4	3	1.0	297
AK FEMALE	104	59.4	0	.0	0	.0	1	.6	105	60.0	69	39.4	1	.6	175
AK MALE	63	51.6	0	.0	0	.0	0	.0	63	51.6	57	46.7	2	1.6	122
U ALASKA FAIRBANKS CAMPUS															
AK TOTAL	254	12.2	48	2.3	37	1.8	10	.5	349	16.7	1,725	82.6	15	.7	2,089
AK FEMALE	152	16.1	22	2.3	11	1.2	4	.4	189	20.1	747	79.3	6	.6	942
AK MALE	102	8.9	26	2.3	26	2.3	6	.5	160	13.9	978	85.3	9	.8	1,147
U OF ALASKA TANANA VLY CC															
AK TOTAL	150	7.4	63	3.1	25	1.2	22	1.1	260	12.9	1,749	86.8	6	.3	2,015
AK FEMALE	101	8.3	33	2.7	11	.9	13	1.1	158	12.9	1,061	86.8	3	.2	1,222
AK MALE	49	6.2	30	3.8	14	1.8	9	1.1	102	12.9	688	86.8	3	.4	793
U ALAS ANCHORAGE CAMPUS															
AK TOTAL	119	4.8	88	3.5	53	2.1	36	1.4	296	11.8	2,194	87.7	13	.5	2,503
AK FEMALE	75	4.8	44	2.8	30	1.9	20	1.3	169	10.8	1,394	88.9	5	.3	1,568
AK MALE	44	4.7	44	4.7	23	2.5	16	1.7	127	13.6	800	85.6	8	.9	935
U OF ALASKA ANCHORAGE CC															
AK TOTAL	342	5.4	381	6.0	167	2.6	128	2.0	1,018	16.1	5,289	83.8	7	.1	6,314
AK FEMALE	206	5.6	184	5.0	90	2.5	68	1.9	548	15.0	3,104	84.9	3	.1	3,655
AK MALE	136	5.1	197	7.4	77	2.9	60	2.3	470	17.7	2,185	82.2	4	.2	2,659
U OF ALASKA KENAI CC															
AK TOTAL	72	5.1	5	.4	7	.5	8	.6	92	6.5	1,318	92.9	9	.6	1,419
AK FEMALE	39	4.8	1	.1	3	.4	4	.5	47	5.7	768	93.5	6	.7	821
AK MALE	33	5.5	4	.7	4	.7	4	.7	45	7.5	550	92.0	3	.5	598
U OF ALASKA KUSKOKWIM CC															
AK TOTAL	199	77.1	1	.4	2	.8	2	.8	204	79.1	53	20.5	1	.4	258
AK FEMALE	122	77.2	1	.6	2	1.3	2	1.3	127	8.4	30	19.0	1	.6	158
AK MALE	77	77.0	0	.0	0	.0	0	.0	77	78.0	23	23.0	0	.0	100

TABLE 1 - TOTAL UNDERGRADUATE ENROLLMENT IN INSTITUTIONS OF HIGHER EDUCATION BY RACE, ETHNICITY AND SEX:
INSTITUTION, STATE AND NATION, 1978

	AMERICAN INDIAN ALASKAN NATIVE		BLACK NON-HISPANIC		ASIAN OR PACIFIC ISLANDER		HISPANIC		TOTAL MINORITY		WHITE NON-HISPANIC		NON-RESIDENT ALIEN	
	NUMBER	%	NUMBER	%	NUMBER	%	NUMBER	%	NUMBER	%	NUMBER	%	NUMBER	%
ALASKA		CONTINUED												
U ALAS MATANUSKA-SUSITNA														
AK TOTAL	7	2.6	1	.4	0	.0	0	.0	8	3.0	262	97.0	0	.0
AK FEMALE	4	2.9	0	.0	0	.0	0	.0	4	2.9	135	97.1	0	.0
AK MALE	3	2.3	1	.8	0	.0	0	.0	4	3.1	127	96.9	0	.0
U ALAS STHESTN SENIOR C														
AK TOTAL	10	7.1	4	2.9	2	1.4	1	.7	17	12.1	123	87.9	0	.0
AK FEMALE	7	8.5	1	1.2	1	1.2	1	1.2	10	12.2	72	87.8	0	.0
AK MALE	3	5.2	3	5.2	1	1.7	0	.0	7	12.1	51	87.9	0	.0
U OF ALAS JUNEAU-DGLS CC														
AK TOTAL	62	10.1	6	1.0	10	1.6		.5	81	13.1	535	86.9	0	.0
AK FEMALE	34	9.9	3	.9	6	1.7	3	.6	45	13.1	298	86.9	0	.0
AK MALE	28	10.3	3	1.1	4	1.5	1	.4	36	13.2	237	86.8	0	.0
U OF ALASKA KETCHIKAN CC														
AK TOTAL	108	16.1	0	.0	16	2.	6	.9	130	19.4	538	80.4	1	.1
AK FEMALE	67	16.2	0	.0	11	2.4	4	1.0	82	19.9	331	80.1		.0
AK MALE	41	16.0	0	.0	5	2.0	2	.8	48	18.8	207	80.9	8	.4
U OF ALASKA SITKA CC														
AK TOTAL	7	43.8	1	6.3	0	.0	0	.0	8	50.0	7	43.8	1	6.3
AK FEMALE	5	45.5	0	.0	0	.0	0	.0	5	45.5	5	45.5	1	9.1
AK MALE	2	40.0	1	20.0	0	.0	0	.0	3	60.0	2	40.0	0	.0
ALASKA		TOTAL (	14 INSTITUTIONS)											
AK TOTAL	1,513	9.1	602	3.6	321	1.9	217	1.3	2,653	15.9	13,947	83.7	56	.3
AK FEMALE	925	9.7	290	3.0	165	.7	119	1.2	1,499	15.7	8,028	84.0	26	.3
AK MALE	588	8.3	312	4.4	156	2.2	98	1.4	1,154	16.2	5,919	83.3	30	.4
ARIZONA														
ARIZONA STATE UNIVERSITY														
AZ TOTAL	291	1.1	678	2.6	293	1.1	1,256	4.8	2,518	9.7	23,022	88.9	361	1.4
AZ FEMALE	172	1.5	307	2.6	136	1.2	540	4.6	1,155	9.9	10,485	89.5	74	.6
AZ MALE	119	.8	371	2.6	157	1.1	716	5.0	1,363	9.6	12,537	88.4	287	2.0
ARIZONA WESTERN COLLEGE														
AZ TOTAL	99	5.0	128	6.4	120	6.0	470	23.5	817	40.9	1,154	57.8	27	1.4
AZ FEMALE	69	8.0	32	3.7	112	13.0	213	24.7	426	49.4	414	48.0	23	2.7
AZ MALE	30	2.6	96	8.5	8	.7	257	22.6	391	34.4	740	65.2	4	.4
CENTRAL ARIZONA COLLEGE														
AZ TOTAL	171	13.4	66	5.2	8	.6	249	19.5	494	38.7	784	61.3	0	.0
AZ FEMALE	82	17.6	14	3.0	3	.6	98	21.1	197	42.4	268	57.6	0	.0
AZ MALE	89	10.9	52	6.4	5	.6	151	18.6	297	36.5	516	63.5	0	.0
COCHISE COLLEGE														
AZ TOTAL	23	.7	164	4.7	56	1.6	550	15.9	793	22.9	2,527	73.0	143	4.1
AZ FEMALE	15	.9	52	3.1	36	2.2	263	15.8	366	22.0	1,241	74.7	55	3.3
AZ MALE	8	.4	112	6.2	20	1.1	287	15.9	427	23.7	1,286	71.4	88	4.9
COLLEGE OF GANADO														
AZ TOTAL	208	83.9	0	.0	2	.8	2	.8	212	85.5	36	14.5	0	.0
AZ FEMALE	148	83.1	0	.0	0	.0	1	.6	149	83.7	29	16.3	0	.0
AZ MALE	60	85.7	0	.0	2	2.9	1	1.4	63	90.0	7	10.0	0	.0
DEVRY INST OF TECHNOLOGY														
AZ TOTAL	25	1.1	70	2.9	31	1.3	101	4.3	227	9.6	2,147	90.4	0	.0
AZ FEMALE	0	.0	4	4.7	1	1.2	7	8.2	12	14.1	73	85.9	0	.0
AZ MALE	25	1.1	66	2.9	30	1.3	94	4.1	215	9.4	2,074	90.6	0	.0
EASTERN ARIZONA COLLEGE														
AZ TOTAL	276	7.7	139	3.	15	.4	653	18.1	1,083	30.0	2,478	68.8	43	1.2
AZ FEMALE	149	8.3	14	.	7	.4	287	19.1	457	25.6	1,322	74.1	6	.3
AZ MALE	127	7.0	125	6.4	8	.4	366	20.1	626	34.4	1,156	63.6	37	2.0
GRAND CANYON COLLEGE														
AZ TOTAL	33	3.6	36	3.9	8	.9	33	3.6	110	12.0	793	86.6	13	1.4
AZ FEMALE	21	4.9	13	3.0	4	.9	12	2.8	50	11.5	381	87.4	5	1.1
AZ MALE	12	2.5	23	4.8	4	.8	21	4.4	60	12.5	412	85.8	8	1.7
GLENDALE CMTY COLLEGE														
AZ TOTAL	49	.4	290	2.4	143	1.2	1,044	8.7	1,526	12.7	10,398	86.4	111	.9
AZ FEMALE	28	.5	99	1.6	76	1.2	506	8.3	709	11.7	5,319	87.4	55	.9
AZ MALE	21	.4	191	3.2	67	1.1	538	9.0	817	13.7	5,079	85.3	56	.9
MARICOPA TECH CC														
AZ TOTAL	135	4.0	460	13.6	27	.8	549	16.3	1,171	34.7	2,200	65.3	0	.0
AZ FEMALE	72	5.4	246	18.5	11	.8	190	14.3	519	39.0	811	61.0	0	.3
AZ MALE	63	3.1	214	10.5	16	.8	359	17.5	652	31.9	1,395	68.1	0	.3
MESA COMMUNITY COLLEGE														
AZ TOTAL	104	1.6	215	3.3	53	.8	560	8.	932	14.2	5,549	84.8	63	1.0
AZ FEMALE	62	1.9	90	2.7	32	1.0	285	8.6	469	14.3	2,790	85.1	21	.6
AZ MALE	42	1.3	125	3.8	21	.6	275	8.4	463	14.2	2,759	84.5	42	1.3
PHOENIX COLLEGE														
AZ TOTAL	311	2.0	568	3.	143	.9	3,122	19.8	4,144	26.3	11,560	73.2	82	.5
AZ FEMALE	196	2.5	253	3.3	73	.9	2,265	28.4	2,787	35.0	5,138	64.5	37	.5
AZ MALE	115	1.5	315	4.8	70	.9	857	11.0	1,357	17.3	6,422	82.1	45	.6
SCOTTSDALE CMTY COLLEGE														
AZ TOTAL	115	1.9	55	.9	34	.6	99	1.6	303	4.	5,805	94.7	19	.3
AZ FEMALE	79	2.2	12	.3	22	.6	41	1.1	154	4.	3,434	95.5	8	.2
AZ MALE	36	1.4	43	1.7	12	.5	58	2.3	149	5.2	2,371	93.7	11	.4
MOHAVE COMMUNITY COLLEGE														
AZ TOTAL	142	4.2	2	.1	18	.5	54	1.6	216	6.3	3,191	93.6	1	.0
AZ FEMALE	80	4.0	1	.0	10	.5	32	1.6	123	6.1	1,897	93.9	1	.0
AZ MALE	62	4.5	1	.1	8	.6	22	1.6	93	6.7	1,294	93.3	0	.0
NAVAJO COMMUNITY COLLEGE														
AZ TOTAL	789	97.5	0	.0	1	.1	4	.5	794	98.1	14	1.7	1	.1
AZ FEMALE	544	97.8	0	.0	0	.0	2	.4	546	98.2	10	1.8	0	.0
AZ MALE	245	96.8	0	.0	1	.4	2	.8	248	98.0	4	1.6	1	.4
NORTHERN ARIZ UNIVERSITY														
AZ TOTAL	377	3.6	114	1.1	54	.5	512	4.9	1,057	10.	9,326	89.	48	.5
AZ FEMALE	209	4.1	36	.7	25	.5	213	4.2	483	9.	4,551	90.	10	.2
AZ MALE	168	3.1	78	1.4	29	.5	299	5.6	574	10.4	4,775	88.8	38	.7

	AMERICAN INDIAN ALASKAN NATIVE		BLACK NON-HISPANIC		ASIAN OR PACIFIC ISLANDER		HISPANIC		TOTAL MINORITY		WHITE NON-HISPANIC		NON-RESIDENT ALIEN		TOTAL
	NUMBER	%	NUMBER	%	NUMBER	%	NUMBER	%	NUMBER	%	NUMBER	%	NUMBER	%	NUMBER
ARIZONA CONTINUED															
NORTHLAND PIONEER COLLEGE															
AZ TOTAL	821	21.4	175	4.6	0	.0	204	5.3	1,200	31.2	2,641	68.8	0	.0	3,841
AZ FEMALE	330	14.0	71	3.0	0	.0	70	3.0	471	20.0	1,883	80.0	0	.0	2,354
AZ MALE	491	33.0	104	7.0	0	.0	134	9.0	729	49.0	758	51.0	0	.0	1,487
PIMA COMMUNITY COLLEGE															
AZ TOTAL	518	2.4	867	4.0	233	1.1	3,513	16.3	5,131	23.8	15,708	73.0	682	3.2	21,521
AZ FEMALE	293	2.6	381	3.4	134	1.2	1,801	16.3	2,609	23.6	8,222	74.3	232	2.1	11,063
AZ MALE	225	2.2	486	4.6	99	.9	1,712	16.4	2,522	24.1	7,486	71.6	450	4.3	10,458
PRESCOTT CENTER COLLEGE															
AZ TOTAL	0	.0	0	.0	0	.0	1	1.5	1	1.5	66	98.5	0	.0	67
AZ FEMALE	0	.0	0	.0	0	.0	0	.0	0	.0	38	100.0	0	.0	38
AZ MALE	0	.0	0	.0	0	.0	1	3.4	1	3.4	28	96.6	0	.0	29
STHWSTN BAPT BIBLE C															
AZ TOTAL	1	.6	1	.6	2	1.2	1	.6	5	2.9	165	97.1	0	.0	170
AZ FEMALE	0	.0	0	.0	1	1.4	1	1.4	2	2.8	69	97.2	0	.0	71
AZ MALE	1	1.0	1	1.0	1	1.0	0	.0	3	3.0	96	97.0	0	.0	99
UNIVERSITY OF ARIZONA															
AZ TOTAL	118	.6	221	1.2	153	.8	770	4.2	1,262	6.8	16,618	90.0	575	3.1	18,455
AZ FEMALE	59	.7	99	1.2	70	.8	330	4.0	558	6.7	7,679	91.9	116	1.4	8,353
AZ MALE	59	.6	122	1.2	83	.8	440	4.4	704	7.0	8,939	88.5	459	4.5	10,102
YAVAPAI COLLEGE															
AZ TOTAL	74	7.0	7	.7	4	.4	64	6.1	149	14.2	867	82.3	37	3.5	1,053
AZ FEMALE	46	8.8	0	.0	2	.4	39	7.4	87	16.6	434	82.7	4	.8	525
AZ MALE	28	5.3	7	1.3	2	.4	25	4.7	62	11.7	433	82.0	33	6.3	528
ARIZONA TOTAL (22 INSTITUTIONS)															
AZ TOTAL	4,680	3.3	4,256	3.0	1,398	1.0	13,811	9.6	24,145	16.8	117,055	81.6	2,206	1.5	143,406
AZ FEMALE	2,654	3.8	1,724	2.5	755	1.1	7,196	10.4	12,329	17.7	56,488	81.3	647	.9	69,464
AZ MALE	2,026	2.7	2,532	3.4	643	.9	6,615	8.9	11,816	16.0	60,567	81.9	1,559	2.1	73,942
ARKANSAS															
AMERICAN C OF COMMERCE															
AR TOTAL	0	.0	16	8.3	0	.0	0	.0	16	8.3	176	91.7	0	.0	192
AR FEMALE	0	.0	10	8.1	0	.0	0	.0	10	8.1	114	91.9	0	.0	124
AR MALE	0	.0	6	8.8	0	.0	0	.0	6	8.8	62	91.2	0	.0	68
ARKANSAS BAPTIST COLLEGE															
AR TOTAL	0	.0	389	90.7	0	.0	0	.0	389	90.7	40	9.3	0	.0	429
AR FEMALE	0	.0	176	98.9	0	.0	0	.0	176	98.9	2	1.1	0	.0	178
AR MALE	0	.0	213	84.9	0	.0	0	.0	213	84.9	38	15.1	0	.0	251
ARKANSAS COLLEGE															
AR TOTAL	2	.4	45	9.4	3	.6	1	.2	51	10.7	418	87.4	9	1.9	478
AR FEMALE	1	.4	20	7.4	3	1.1	0	.0	24	8.9	244	90.7	1	.4	269
AR MALE	1	.5	25	12.0	0	.0	1	.5	27	12.9	174	83.3	8	3.8	209
ARKANSAS STATE U MAIN CAM															
AR TOTAL	44	.7	777	12.6	14	.2	21	.3	856	13.8	5,330	86.1		.1	6,190
AR FEMALE	22	.7	440	13.6	8	.2	9	.3	479	14.9	2,746	85.1	4	.1	3,225
AR MALE	22	.7	337	11.4	6	.2	12	.4	377	12.7	2,584	87.2		.1	2,965
ARKANSAS STATE U BEEBE BR															
AR TOTAL	1	.1	47	7.0	1	.1	1	.1	50	7.4	626	92.6	0	.0	676
AR FEMALE	0	.0	17	5.8	1	.3	0	.0	18	6.1	277	93.9	0	.0	295
AR MALE	1	.3	30	7.9	0	.0	1	.3	32	8.4	349	91.6	0	.0	381
ARKANSAS TECH UNIVERSITY															
AR TOTAL	16	.6	133	5.2	6	.2	7	.3	162	6.4	2,364	93.0	15	.6	2,541
AR FEMALE	6	.5	49	4.3	3	.3	4	.4	62	5.5	1,065	94.2	4	.4	1,131
AR MALE	10	.7	84	6.0	3	.2	3	.2	100	7.1	1,299	92.1	11	.8	1,410
CAPITAL CITY BUS COLLEGE															
AR TOTAL	0	.0	324	53.6	0	.0	0	.0	324	53.6	280	46.4	0	.0	604
AR FEMALE	0	.0	164	55.0	0	.0	0	.0	164	55.0	134	45.0	0	.0	298
AR MALE	0	.0	160	52.3	0	.0	0	.0	160	52.3	146	47.7	0	.0	306
CENTRAL BAPTIST COLLEGE															
AR TOTAL	0	.0	1	.5	2	.9	0	.0	3	1.4	212	98.6	0	.0	215
AR FEMALE	0	.0	0	.0	0	.0	0	.0	0	.0	88	100.0	0	.0	88
AR MALE	0	.0	1	.8	2	1.6	0	.0	3	2.4	124	97.6	0	.0	127
COLLEGE OF THE OZARKS															
AR TOTAL	5	1.0	40	7.7	58	11.1	0	.0	103	19.8	418	80.2	0	.0	521
AR FEMALE	3	1.3	14	5.9	13	5.5	0	.0	30	12.7	206	87.3	0	.0	236
AR MALE	2	.7	26	9.1	45	15.8	0	.0	73	25.6	212	74.4	0	.0	285
CROWLEY'S RIDGE COLLEGE															
AR TOTAL	0	.0	1	1.6	0	.0	0	.0	1	1.6	62	98.4	0	.0	63
AR FEMALE	0	.0	0	.0	0	.0	0	.0	0	.0	44	100.0	0	.0	44
AR MALE	0	.0	1	5.3	0	.0	0	.0	1	5.3	18	94.7	0	.0	19
EAST ARK CMTY COLLEGE															
AR TOTAL	0	.0	253	34.0	4	.5	0	.0	257	34.5	487	65.5	0	.0	744
AR FEMALE	0	.0	187	38.5	0	.0	0	.0	187	38.5	299	61.5	0	.0	486
AR MALE	0	.0	66	25.6	4	1.6	0	.0	70	27.1	188	72.9	0	.0	258
GARLAND CO CMTY COLLEGE															
AR TOTAL	2	.1	118	8.7	17	1.2	5	.4	142	10.4	1,203	88.4	16	1.2	1,361
AR FEMALE	2	.2	61	7.4	10	1.2	5	.6	78	9.4	748	90.3	2	.2	828
AR MALE	0	.0	57	10.7	7	1.3	0	.0	64	12.0	455	85.4	14	2.6	533
HARDING COLLEGE MAIN CAM															
AR TOTAL	7	.2	37	1.3	8	.3	13	.5	65	2.3	2,728	96.7	27	1.0	2,820
AR FEMALE	2	.2	12	.8	2	.1	4	.3	20	1.4	1,423	97.6	15	1.0	1,458
AR MALE	5	.4	25	1.8	6	.4	9	.7	45	3.3	1,305	95.8	12	.9	1,362
HARDING GRAD SCH RELIGION															
AR TOTAL	0	.0	0	.0	0	.0	0	.0	0	.0	1	100.0	0	.0	1
AR FEMALE	0	.0	0	.0	0	.0	0	.0	0	.0	1	100.0	0	.0	1
AR MALE	0	.0	0	.0	0	.0	0	.0	0	.0	0	.0	0	.0	0
HENDERSON ST UNIVERSITY															
AR TOTAL	4	.1	551	20.6	15	.6	5	.2	575	21.5	2,101	78.5	0	.0	2,676
AR FEMALE	2	.1	329	21.3	6	.4	2	.1	339	21.9	1,207	78.1	0	.0	1,546
AR MALE	2	.2	222	19.6	9	.8	3	.3	236	20.9	894	79.1	0	.0	1,130

TABLE 1 - TOTAL UNDERGRADUATE ENROLLMENT IN INSTITUTIONS OF HIGHER EDUCATION BY RACE, ETHNICITY AND SEX: INSTITUTION, STATE AND NATION, 1978

	AMERICAN INDIAN ALASKAN NATIVE		BLACK NON-HISPANIC		ASIAN OR PACIFIC ISLANDER		HISPANIC		TOTAL MINORITY		WHITE NON-HISPANIC		NON-RESIDENT ALIEN	
	NUMBER	%	NUMBER	%	NUMBER	%	NUMBER	%	NUMBER	%	NUMBER	%	NUMBER	%
ARKANSAS — CONTINUED														
HENDRIX COLLEGE														
AR TOTAL	1	.1	51	5.2	12	1.2	3	.3	67	6.8	911	92.7	5	5
AR FEMALE	0	.0	28	6.0	6	1.3	2	.4	36	7.8	427	92.0	.	2
AR MALE	1	.2	23	4.4	6	1.2	1	.2	31	6.0	484	93.3	4	18
JOHN BROWN UNIVERSITY														
AR TOTAL	11	1.6	5	.7	4	.6	1	.1	21	3.0	661	95.2	12	1.7
AR FEMALE	8	2.2	1	.3	4	1.1	1	.3	14	3.9	336	94.7	5	1.4
AR MALE	3	.9	4	1.2	0	.0	0	.0	7	2.1	323	95.8	7	2.1
MISS CO CMTY COLLEGE														
AR TOTAL	0	.0	161	16.0	0	.0	22	2.2	183	18.2	825	81.8	0	.0
AR FEMALE	0	.0	100	16.3	0	.0	12	2.0	112	18.2	502	81.8	0	.0
AR MALE	0	.0	61	15.5	0	.0	10	2.5	71	18.0	323	82.0	0	.0
NORTH ARKANSAS CC														
AR TOTAL	0	.0	0	.0	0	.0	0	.0	0	.0	765	100.0	0	.0
AR FEMALE	0	.0	0	.0	0	.0	0	.0	0	.0	477	100.0	0	.0
AR MALE	0	.0	0	.0	0	.0	0	.0	0	.0	288	100.0	0	.0
OUACHITA BAPT UNIVERSITY														
AR TOTAL	0	.0	107	7.5	0	.0	6	.4	113	8.0	1,282	90.2	26	1.8
AR FEMALE	0	.0	53	7.2	0	.0	3	.4	56	7.6	668	90.8	12	1.6
AR MALE	0	.0	54	7.9	0	.0	3	.4	57	8.3	614	89.6	14	2.0
PHILANDER SMITH COLLEGE														
AR TOTAL	0	.0	516	97.5	6	1.1	3	.6	525	99.2	4	.8	0	.0
AR FEMALE	0	.0	236	98.3	0	.0	2	.8	238	99.2	2	.8	0	.0
AR MALE	0	.0	280	96.9	6	2.1	1	.3	287	99.3	2	.7	0	.0
PHILLIPS CO CMTY COLLEGE														
AR TOTAL	56	3.7	570	38.1	6	.4	4	.3	636	42.5	862	57.5	0	.0
AR FEMALE	25	3.0	359	43.6	1	.1	2	.2	387	47.0	437	53.0	0	.0
AR MALE	31	4.6	211	31.3	5	.7	2	.3	249	36.9	425	63.1	0	.0
SHORTER COLLEGE														
AR TOTAL	0	.0	169	98.3	0	.0	0	.0	169	98.3	2	1.2	1	.6
AR FEMALE	0	.0	92	100.0	0	.0	0	.0	92	100.0	0	.0	0	.0
AR MALE	0	.0	77	96.3	0	.0	0	.0	77	96.3	2	2.5	1	1.3
STHN ARK U MAIN CAMPUS														
AR TOTAL	2	.1	388	22.1	6	.3	3	.2	399	22.7	1,350	76.7	1	.6
AR FEMALE	1	.1	236	23.7	3	.3	2	.2	242	24.3	752	75.7	0	.0
AR MALE	1	.1	152	19.9	3	.4	1	.1	157	20.5	598	78.2	10	1.3
STHN ARK U EL DORADO BR														
AR TOTAL	0	.0	95	24.0	2	.5	0	.0	97	24.5	299	75.5	0	.0
AR FEMALE	0	.0	69	25.2	1	.4	0	.0	70	25.5	204	74.5	0	.0
AR MALE	0	.0	26	21.3	1	.8	0	.0	27	22.1	95	77.9	0	.0
STHN ARK U STHWST TECH														
AR TOTAL	0	.0	80	13.2	0	.0	0	.0	80	13.2	524	86.6	1	.2
AR FEMALE	0	.0	27	15.4	0	.0	0	.0	27	15.4	148	84.6	0	.0
AR MALE	0	.0	53	12.3	0	.0	0	.0	53	12.3	376	87.4	1	.2
SOUTHERN BAPTIST COLLEGE														
AR TOTAL	1	.2	13	3.1	0	.0	0	.0	14	3.3	384	91.9	20	4.8
AR FEMALE	1	.5	2	.9	0	.0	0	.0	3	1.4	207	97.2	3	1.4
AR MALE	0	.0	11	5.4	0	.0	0	.0	11	5.4	177	86.3	17	8.3
U OF ARKANSAS MAIN CAMPUS														
AR TOTAL	98	.9	525	4.6	82	.7	47	.4	752	6.6	10,375	91.1	266	2.3
AR FEMALE	34	.7	253	5.4	25	.5	16	.3	328	7.0	4,292	92.1	40	.9
AR MALE	64	1.0	272	4.0	57	.8	31	.5	424	6.3	6,083	90.3	226	3.4
U OF ARK AT LITTLE ROCK														
AR TOTAL	44	.6	991	14.2	35	.5	18	.3	1,088	15.6	5,889	84.3	8	.1
AR FEMALE	17	.5	644	17.5	16	.4	8	.2	685	18.6	3,004	81.4	0	.0
AR MALE	27	.8	347	10.5	19	.6	10	.3	403	12.2	2,885	87.5	8	.2
U OF ARK MEDL SCI CAMPUS														
AR TOTAL	0	.0	24	4.5	3	.6	1	.2	28	5.2	507	94.8	0	.0
AR FEMALE	0	.0	17	4.7	2	.6	0	.0	19	5.3	341	94.7	0	.0
AR MALE	0	.0	7	4.0	1	.6	1	.6	9	5.1	166	94.9	0	.0
U OF ARKANSAS-MONTICELLO														
AR TOTAL	4	.2	278	16.3	4	.2	3	.2	289	16.9	1,417	83.0	1	.1
AR FEMALE	1	.1	145	16.2	2	.2	2	.2	150	16.8	743	83.2	0	.0
AR MALE	3	.4	133	16.3	2	.2	1	.1	139	17.1	674	82.8	1	.1
U OF ARKANSAS PINE BLUFF														
AR TOTAL	5	.2	2,504	85.5	6	.2	47	1.6	2,562	87.5	326	11.1	39	1.3
AR FEMALE	3	.2	1,474	87.9	3	.2	23	1.4	1,503	89.6	170	10.1	4	.2
AR MALE	2	.2	1,030	82.4	3	.2	24	1.9	1,059	84.7	156	12.5	35	2.8
U OF CENTRAL ARKANSAS														
AR TOTAL	0	.0	553	12.1	0	.0	0	.0	553	12.1	4,006	87.6	13	.3
AR FEMALE	0	.0	337	12.2	0	.0	0	.0	337	12.2	2,412	87.5	6	.2
AR MALE	0	.0	216	11.9	0	.0	0	.0	216	11.9	1,594	87.7	7	.4
WESTARK COMMUNITY COLLEGE														
AR TOTAL	81	2.5	129	4.0	88	2.7	16	.5	314	9.8	2,858	89.3	29	.9
AR FEMALE	44	2.9	69	4.5	22	1.4	9	.6	144	9.4	1,379	90.3	4	.3
AR MALE	37	2.2	60	3.6	66	3.9	7	.4	170	10.2	1,479	88.4	25	1.5
ARKANSAS TOTAL (34 INSTITUTIONS)														
AR TOTAL	384	.6	9,891	16.2	382	.6	227	.4	10,884	17.8	49,693	81.4	502	.8
AR FEMALE	172	.6	5,621	18.0	131	.4	106	.3	6,030	19.3	25,101	80.4	97	.3
AR MALE	212	.7	4,270	14.3	251	.8	121	.4	4,854	16.3	24,592	82.4	405	1.4
CALIFORNIA														
ALLAN HANCOCK COLLEGE														
CA TOTAL	75	1.4	304	5.7	225	4.2	661	12.4	1,265	23.7	4,078	76.3	0	.0
CA FEMALE	40	1.4	134	4.7	105	3.7	354	12.4	633	22.1	2,229	77.9	0	.0
CA MALE	35	1.4	170	6.9	120	4.8	307	12.4	632	25.5	1,849	74.5	0	.0
AMER ACAD DRAMATIC ARTS-W														
CA TOTAL	1	.5	9	4.3	0	.0	9	4.3	19	9.0	189	89.6	3	1.4
CA FEMALE	0	.0	4	3.9	0	.0	5	4.9	9	8.8	93	91.2	0	.0
CA MALE	1	.9	5	4.6	0	.0	4	3.7	10	9.2	96	88.1	3	2.8

	AMERICAN INDIAN ALASKAN NATIVE		BLACK NON-HISPANIC		ASIAN OR PACIFIC ISLANDER		HISPANIC		TOTAL MINORITY		WHITE NON-HISPANIC		NON-RESIDENT ALIEN		TOTAL
	NUMBER	%	NUMBER	%	NUMBER	%	NUMBER	%	NUMBER	%	NUMBER	%	NUMBER	%	NUMBER
CALIFORNIA	**CONTINUED**														
ANTELOPE VALLEY COLLEGE															
CA TOTAL	139	3.1	210	4.7	81	1.8	287	6.4	717	15.9	3,774	83.8	13	.3	4,504
CA FEMALE	77	3.1	92	3.8	45	1.8	144	5.9	358	14.6	2,089	85.2	4	.2	2,451
CA MALE	62	3.0	118	5.7	36	1.8	143	7.0	359	17.5	1,685	82.1	9	.4	2,053
ARMSTRONG COLLEGE															
CA TOTAL	0	.0	35	19.0	14	7.6	4	2.2	53	28.8	61	33.2	70	38.0	184
CA FEMALE	0	.0	22	27.8	8	10.1	2	2.5	32	40.5	33	41.8	14	17.7	79
CA MALE	0	.0	13	12.4	6	5.7	2	1.9	21	20.0	28	26.7	56	53.3	105
ART CTR COLLEGE OF DESIGN															
CA TOTAL	5	.5	8	.7	79	7.2	35	3.2	127	11.5	897	81.5	77	7.0	1,101
CA FEMALE	3	.7	5	1.2	29	7.2	8	2.0	45	11.2	340	84.4	18	4.5	403
CA MALE	2	.3	3	.4	50	7.2	27	3.9	82	11.7	557	79.8	59	8.5	698
AZUSA PACIFIC COLLEGE															
CA TOTAL	7	.6	67	5.6	37	3.'	45	.7	156	13.0	967	80.3	81	6.7	1,204
CA FEMALE	3	.5	30	4.5	22	3.	23	.5	78	11.8	556	83.9	29	4.4	663
CA MALE	4	.7	37	6.8	15	2.8	22	8.1	78	14.4	411	76.0	52	9.6	541
BAKERSFIELD COLLEGE															
CA TOTAL	171	1.9	639	7.2	210	2.	1,454	16.4	2,474	27.9	6,338	71.6	40	.5	8,852
CA FEMALE	85	1.9	350	7.7	109	2.	720	15.9	1,264	27.9	3,254	71.8	14	.3	4,532
CA MALE	86	2.0	289	6.7	101	2.4	734	17.0	1,210	28.0	3,084	71.4	26	.6	4,320
BARSTOW COLLEGE															
CA TOTAL	17	1.9	79	8.6	10	1.'	137	15.0	243	26.6	612	67.0	59	6.5	914
CA FEMALE	12	2.8	43	10.1	3	.	66	15.5	124	29.0	300	70.3	3	.7	427
CA MALE	5	1.0	36	7.4	7	1.4	71	14.6	119	24.4	312	64.1	56	11.5	487
BETHANY BIBLE COLLEGE															
CA TOTAL	6	1.3	9	1.9	11	2.3	30	6.3	56	11.7	420	87.5	4	.8	480
CA FEMALE	3	1.5	2	1.0	1	.5	12	5.8	18	8.7	188	91.3	0	.0	206
CA MALE	3	1.1	7	2.6	10	3.6	18	6.6	38	13.9	232	84.7	4	1.5	274
BIOLA COLLEGE															
CA TOTAL	8	.4	51	2.2	50	2.2	57	2.5	166	7.3	2,064	90.6	47	2.1	2,277
CA FEMALE	3	.2	23	1.8	32	2.5	26	2.1	84	6.7	1,157	92.2	14	1.1	1,255
CA MALE	5	.5	28	2.7	18	1.8	31	3.0	82	8.0	907	88.7	33	3.2	1,022
BROOKS COLLEGE															
CA TOTAL	10	1.5	61	8.9	27	3.	42	6.1	140	20.3	519	75.4	29	4.2	688
CA FEMALE	10	1.5	59	8.8	27	4.	42	6.2	138	20.5	507	75.3	28	4.2	673
CA MALE	0	.0	2	13.3	0	.0	0	.0	2	13.3	12	80.0	1	6.7	15
BROOKS INSTITUTE															
CA TOTAL	0	.0	0	.0	0	.0	0	.0	0	.0	0	.0	0	.0	0
CA FEMALE	0	.0	0	.0	0	.0	0	.0	0	.0	0	.0	0	.0	0
CA MALE	0	.0	0	.0	0	.0	0	.0	0	.0	0	.0	0	.0	0
BUTTE COLLEGE															
CA TOTAL	77	1.2	78	1.2	56	.9	249	4.0	460	7.3	5,791	92.4	19	.3	6,270
CA FEMALE	35	1.1	24	.7	29	.9	110	3.4	198	6.1	3,045	93.8	5	.2	3,248
CA MALE	42	1.4	54	1.8	27	.9	139	4.6	262	8.7	2,746	90.9	14	.5	3,022
CABRILLO COLLEGE															
CA TOTAL	75	1.4	50	.9	154	2.8	325	5.9	604	10.9	4,808	87.1	106	1.9	5,518
CA FEMALE	46	1.5	15	.5	82	2.7	154	5.1	297	9.9	2,682	89.4	20	.7	2,999
CA MALE	29	1.2	35	1.4	72	2.9	171	6.8	307	12.2	2,126	84.4	86	3.4	2,519
CAL BAPTIST COLLEGE															
CA TOTAL	8	1.1	51	7.1	6	.8	20	2.	85	11.	602	83.7	32	4.5	719
CA FEMALE	2	.6	23	6.7	1	.3	7	2.	33	9.	299	86.9	12	3.5	344
CA MALE	6	1.6	28	7.5	5	1.3	13	3.8	52	13.8	303	80.8	20	5.3	375
CALIFORNIA CHRISTIAN C															
CA TOTAL	0	.0	0	.0	0	.0	1	4.3	1	4.3	22	95.7	0	.	23
CA FEMALE	0	.0	0	.0	0	.0	1	10.0	1	10.0	9	90.0	0	.0	10
CA MALE	0	.0	0	.0	0	.0	0	.0	0	.0	13	100.0	0	.0	13
CAL COLLEGE ARTS & CRAFTS															
CA TOTAL	17	1.8	50	5.4	91	9.9	33	.	191	20.8	654	71.2	74	8.1	919
CA FEMALE	7	1.2	26	4.6	47	8.4	9	.	89	15.9	429	76.5	43	7.7	561
CA MALE	10	2.8	24	6.7	44	12.3	24	6.8	102	26.5	225	62.8	31	8.7	358
CALIFORNIA INST OF ARTS															
CA TOTAL	1	.2	31	5.8	10	1.	19	5	61	11.3	450	83.6	27	5.0	538
CA FEMALE	0	.0	9	4.3	5	2.	4	1.9	18	8.6	181	86.2	11	5.2	210
CA MALE	1	.3	22	6.7	5	1.5	15	4.6	43	13.1	269	82.0	16	4.9	328
CAL INST OF TECHNOLOGY															
CA TOTAL	1	.1	13	1.6	62	7.8	20	2.5	96	12.0	643	80.4	61	7.5	800
CA FEMALE	0	.0	1	1.1	8	9.1	3	3.4	12	13.6	69	78.4	7	8.0	88
CA MALE	1	.1	12	1.7	54	7.6	17	2.4	84	11.8	574	80.6	54	7.6	712
CAL LUTHERAN COLLEGE															
CA TOTAL	3	.2	38	3.1	12	1.0	23	1.9	76	6.2	1,123	92.0	22	1	1,221
CA FEMALE	2	.3	16	2.6	10	1.6	7	1.1	35	5.6	586	93.5	6	1	627
CA MALE	1	.2	22	3.7	2	13	16	2.7	41	6.9	537	90.4	16	2.8	594
CALIFORNIA MARITIME ACAD															
CA TOTAL	0	.0	8	1.7	17		16	3.3	41	8.5	443	91.5	0	.	484
CA FEMALE	0	.0	0	.0	0		0	.0	1	5.9	16	94.1	0	.0	17
CA MALE	0	.0	8	1.7	16		16	3.4	40	8.6	427	91.4	0	.0	467
CAL ST COLLEGE-BAKERSFLD															
CA TOTAL	54	2.4	170	7.7	77	3.	267	12.0	568	25.6	1,598	72.0	52	2.3	2,218
CA FEMALE	30	2.5	93	7.7	40	3.	130	10.8	293	24.4	885	73.6	25	2.1	1,203
CA MALE	24	2.4	77	7.6	37	3.6	137	13.5	275	27.1	713	70.2	27	2.7	1,015
CAL STATE C-SN BERNARDINO															
CA TOTAL	64	2.1	379	12.4	59	1.	480	15.7	982	32.1	2,045	66.8	36	1.2	3,063
CA FEMALE	38	2.4	209	13.1	30	1.	236	14.8	513	32.2	1,064	66.9	14	.9	1,591
CA MALE	26	1.8	170	11.5	29	2.8	244	16.6	469	31.9	981	66.6	22	1.5	1,472
CAL ST COLLEGE-STANISLAUS															
CA TOTAL	41	1.7	142	6.0	65	2.7	259	11.0	507	21.4	1,800	76.1	57	2.4	2,364
CA FEMALE	16	1.3	63	5.3	32	2.7	121	10.1	232	19.3	947	79.0	20	1.7	1,199
CA MALE	25	2.1	79	6.8	33	2.8	138	11.8	275	23.6	853	73.2	37	3.2	1,165
CAL POLY ST U-SN LUIS OB															
CA TOTAL	235	1.6	257	1.8	653	4.5	470	3.2	1,615	11.0	12,947	88.3	106	.7	14,668
CA FEMALE	82	1.5	78	1.4	179	3.2	134	2.4	473	8.4	5,163	91.4	13	.2	5,649
CA MALE	153	1.7	179	2.0	474	5.3	336	3.7	1,142	12.7	7,784	86.3	93	1.0	9,019

TABLE 1 - TOTAL UNDERGRADUATE ENROLLMENT IN INSTITUTIONS OF HIGHER EDUCATION BY RACE, ETHNICITY AND SEX: INSTITUTION, STATE AND NATION, 1978

	AMERICAN INDIAN ALASKAN NATIVE		BLACK NON-HISPANIC		ASIAN OR PACIFIC ISLANDER		HISPANIC		TOTAL MINORITY		WHITE NON-HISPANIC		NON-RESIDENT ALIEN	
	NUMBER	%	NUMBER	%	NUMBER	%	NUMBER	%	NUMBER	%	NUMBER	%	NUMBER	%
CALIFORNIA CONTINUED														
CAL STATE POLY U-POMONA														
CA TOTAL	210	1.6	485	3.8	698	5.4	1,269	9.8	2,662	20.7	9,322	72.3	901	7.0
CA FEMALE	84	1.8	201	4.2	192	4.0	426	8.9	903	19.0	3,689	77.5	171	3.6
CA MALE	126	1.6	284	3.5	506	6.2	843	10.4	1,759	21.7	5,633	69.4	730	9.0
CAL STATE U-CHICO														
CA TOTAL	78	.7	265	2.3	235	2.1	460	4.0	1,038	9.1	10,110	88.4	293	2.6
CA FEMALE	38	.7	108	1.9	108	1.9	189	3.3	443	7.8	5,185	91.0	69	1.2
CA MALE	40	.7	157	2.7	127	2.2	271	4.7	595	10.4	4,925	85.7	224	3.9
CAL STATE U-DOMINGUEZ HLS														
CA TOTAL	53	1.0	2,055	40.2	458	9.0	357	7.0	2,923	57.1	2,087	40.8	107	2.1
CA FEMALE	32	1.2	1,193	44.3	220	8.2	166	6.2	1,611	59.9	1,047	38.9	33	1.2
CA MALE	21	.9	862	35.5	238	9.8	191	7.9	1,312	54.1	1,040	42.9	74	3.1
CAL STATE U-FRESNO														
CA TOTAL	106	.9	463	3.9	723	6.1	1,423	12.0	2,715	22.9	8,590	72.4	553	4.7
CA FEMALE	48	.8	259	4.5	352	6.1	625	10.8	1,284	22.2	4,352	75.3	144	2.5
CA MALE	58	1.0	204	3.4	371	6.1	798	13.1	1,431	23.5	4,238	69.7	409	6.7
CAL STATE U-FULLERTON														
CA TOTAL	166	1.0	561	3.4	598	3.6	1,458	8.8	2,783	16.8	13,462	81.4	297	1.8
CA FEMALE	72	.9	301	3.7	302	3.7	678	8.4	1,353	16.7	6,616	81.5	109	1.3
CA MALE	94	1.1	260	3.1	296	3.5	780	9.2	1,430	16.9	6,846	80.9	188	2.2
CAL STATE U-HAYWARD														
CA TOTAL	105	1.4	1,149	15.1	638	8.4	450	5.9	2,342	30.9	4,980	65.6	266	3.5
CA FEMALE	48	1.2	661	16.7	322	8.1	223	5.6	1,254	31.7	2,589	65.4	113	2.9
CA MALE	57	1.6	488	13.4	316	8.7	227	6.3	1,088	30.0	2,391	65.8	153	4.2
CAL STATE U-LONG BEACH														
CA TOTAL	270	1.1	2,300	9.5	2,546	10.5	2,035	8.4	7,151	29.6	16,384	67.9	606	2.5
CA FEMALE	141	1.1	1,340	10.8	1,305	10.5	914	7.4	3,700	29.8	8,530	68.6	203	1.6
CA MALE	129	1.1	960	8.2	1,241	10.6	1,121	9.6	3,451	29.5	7,854	67.1	403	3.4
CAL STATE U-LOS ANGELES														
CA TOTAL	112	.7	2,617	16.0	3,222	19.7	3,821	23.3	9,772	59.7	5,903	36.0	706	4.3
CA FEMALE	54	.6	1,600	18.7	1,709	20.0	1,909	22.3	5,272	61.7	3,056	35.8	218	2.6
CA MALE	58	.7	1,017	13.0	1,513	19.3	1,912	24.4	4,500	57.4	2,847	36.3	488	6.2
CAL STATE U-NORTHRIDGE														
CA TOTAL	536	2.5	1,671	7.7	1,676	7.7	1,850	8.5	5,733	26.3	15,592	71.6	441	2.0
CA FEMALE	269	2.5	895	8.2	763	7.0	894	8.2	2,821	26.0	7,914	72.9	128	1.2
CA MALE	267	2.4	776	7.1	913	8.4	956	8.8	2,912	26.7	7,678	70.4	313	2.9
CAL STATE U-SACRAMENTO														
CA TOTAL	262	1.7	1,083	7.0	1,215	7.8	890	5.7	3,450	22.2	11,516	74.0	606	3.9
CA FEMALE	123	1.6	558	7.3	569	7.5	375	4.9	1,625	21.3	5,884	77.1	125	1.6
CA MALE	139	1.8	525	6.6	646	8.1	515	6.5	1,825	23.0	5,632	70.9	481	6.1
HUMBOLDT STATE U														
CA TOTAL	96	1.5	47	.7	143	2.3	160	2.5	446	7.0	5,823	92.0	62	1.0
CA FEMALE	52	1.9	17	.6	60	2.1	55	2.0	184	6.6	2,604	92.8	19	.7
CA MALE	44	1.2	30	.9	83	2.4	105	3.0	262	7.4	3,219	91.3	43	1.2
SAN DIEGO STATE U														
CA TOTAL	454	1.9	1,204	5.1	1,063	4.5	2,045	8.6	4,766	20.1	18,496	77.9	496	2.1
CA FEMALE	224	1.9	645	5.5	489	4.2	1,033	8.9	2,391	20.5	9,149	78.4	127	1.1
CA MALE	230	1.9	559	4.6	574	4.7	1,012	8.4	2,375	19.6	9,347	77.3	369	3.1
SAN FRANCISCO STATE U														
CA TOTAL	141	.8	1,902	10.7	3,391	19.1	1,160	6.5	6,594	37.1	10,581	59.5	619	3.5
CA FEMALE	69	.7	1,063	11.1	1,881	19.7	588	6.2	3,601	37.7	5,692	59.6	251	2.6
CA MALE	72	.9	839	10.2	1,510	18.3	572	6.9	2,993	36.3	4,889	59.3	368	4.5
SAN JOSE STATE U														
CA TOTAL	355	1.7	1,893	9.2	2,367	11.5	1,975	9.6	6,590	31.9	13,309	64.5	739	3.6
CA FEMALE	206	2.1	1,053	10.5	1,114	11.2	937	9.4	3,310	33.2	6,488	65.0	185	1.9
CA MALE	149	1.4	840	7.9	1,253	11.8	1,038	9.7	3,280	30.8	6,821	64.0	554	5.2
SONOMA STATE UNIVERSITY														
CA TOTAL	59	1.4	155	3.7	89	2.2	181	4.4	484	11.7	3,618	87.5	33	.8
CA FEMALE	28	1.2	74	3.2	49	2.1	86	3.7	237	10.2	2,074	89.4	9	.4
CA MALE	31	1.7	81	4.5	40	2.2	95	5.2	247	13.6	1,544	85.1	24	1.3
CENTER FOR EARLY ED														
CA TOTAL	0	.0	2	14.3	0	.0	0	.0	2	14.3	12	85.7	0	.0
CA FEMALE	0	.0	2	14.3	0	.0	0	.0	2	14.3	12	85.7	0	.0
CA MALE	0	.0	0	.0	0	.0	0	.0	0	.0	0	.0	0	.0
CERRITOS COLLEGE														
CA TOTAL	132	1.2	549	4.9	319	2.9	1,840	16.6	2,840	25.5	7,090	63.8	1,187	10.7
CA FEMALE	62	1.1	292	5.1	145	2.5	896	15.7	1,395	24.5	3,777	66.2	531	9.3
CA MALE	70	1.3	257	4.7	174	3.2	944	17.4	1,445	26.7	3,313	61.2	656	12.1
CERRO COSO CMTY COLLEGE														
CA TOTAL	43	1.6	213	7.8	52	1.9	106	3.9	414	15.2	2,290	84.3	12	.4
CA FEMALE	27	1.9	77	5.5	31	2.2	51	3.6	186	13.2	1,212	86.2	8	.6
CA MALE	16	1.2	136	10.4	21	1.6	55	4.2	228	17.4	1,078	82.3	4	.3
CHABOT COLLEGE														
CA TOTAL	411	2.5	1,082	6.5	1,226	7.3	1,276	7.6	3,995	23.9	12,614	75.6	76	.5
CA FEMALE	235	2.5	576	6.2	588	6.3	671	7.2	2,070	22.3	7,206	77.5	23	.2
CA MALE	176	2.4	506	6.9	638	8.6	605	8.2	1,925	26.1	5,408	73.2	53	.7
CHAFFEY COLLEGE														
CA TOTAL	108	1.3	326	3.9	129	1.5	1,228	14.6	1,791	21.3	6,540	77.7	81	1.0
CA FEMALE	65	1.4	161	3.4	65	1.4	630	13.5	921	19.7	3,713	79.5	34	.7
CA MALE	43	1.1	165	4.4	64	1.7	598	16.0	870	23.2	2,827	75.5	47	1.3
CHAPMAN COLLEGE														
CA TOTAL	24	.7	216	6.7	142	4.4	110	3.4	492	15.3	2,555	79.3	173	5.4
CA FEMALE	12	.7	113	6.6	68	4.0	63	3.7	256	15.0	1,424	83.4	27	1.6
CA MALE	12	.8	103	6.8	74	4.9	47	3.1	236	15.6	1,131	74.8	146	9.6
CHRIST COLLEGE IRVINE														
CA TOTAL	0	.0	0	.0	2	1.7	0	.0	2	1.7	113	94.2	5	4.2
CA FEMALE	0	.0	0	.0	1	1.9	0	.0	1	1.9	51	96.2	1	1.9
CA MALE	0	.0	0	.0	1	1.5	0	.0	1	1.5	62	92.5	4	5.0
CHRISTIAN HERITAGE C														
CA TOTAL	2	.4	1	.2	5	1.0	8	1.7	16	3.3	466	96.3	2	.4
CA FEMALE	1	.5	0	.0	3	1.4	6	2.8	10	4.6	206	95.4	0	.0
CA MALE	1	.4	1	.4	2	.7	2	.7	6	2.2	260	97.0	2	.7

TABLE 1 - TOTAL UNDERGRADUATE ENROLLMENT IN INSTITUTIONS OF HIGHER EDUCATION BY RACE, ETHNICITY AND SEX: INSTITUTION, STATE AND NATION, 1978

	AMERICAN INDIAN ALASKAN NATIVE		BLACK NON-HISPANIC		ASIAN OR PACIFIC ISLANDER		HISPANIC		TOTAL MINORITY		WHITE NON-HISPANIC		NON-RESIDENT ALIEN		TOTAL
	NUMBER	%	NUMBER	%	NUMBER	%	NUMBER	%	NUMBER	%	NUMBER	%	NUMBER	%	NUMBER
CALIFORNIA CONTINUED															
CITRUS COLLEGE															
CA TOTAL	56	1.0	283	5.0	111	2.0	660	11.6	1,110	19.6	4,455	78.5	107	1.9	5,672
CA FEMALE	20	.7	143	4.9	61	2.1	314	10.7	538	18.4	2,353	80.4	37	1.3	2,928
CA MALE	36	1.3	140	5.1	50	1.8	346	12.6	572	20.8	2,102	76.6	70	2.6	2,744
CLAREMONT MEN'S COLLEGE															
CA TOTAL	1	.1	29	3.4	44	5.1	31	3.6	105	12.1	724	83.7	36	4.2	865
CA FEMALE	0	.0	10	6.4	11	7.0	6	3.8	27	17.2	129	82.2	1	.6	157
CA MALE	1	.1	19	2.7	33	4.7	25	3.5	78	11.0	595	84.0	35	4.9	708
HARVEY MUDD COLLEGE															
CA TOTAL	0	.0	5	1.1	76	16.0	9	1.9	90	19.0	370	78.1	14	3.0	474
CA FEMALE	0	.0	2	3.4	10	17.2	0	.0	12	20.7	45	77.6	1	1.7	58
CA MALE	0	.0	3	.7	66	15.9	9	2.2	78	18.8	325	78.1	13	3.1	416
PITZER COLLEGE															
CA TOTAL	0	.0	53	6.7	28	3.5	56	7.1	137	17.3	636	80.5	17	2.2	790
CA FEMALE	0	.0	36	7.3	19	3.8	34	6.9	89	18.0	395	80.0	10	2.0	494
CA MALE	0	.0	17	5.7	9	3.0	22	7.4	48	16.2	241	81.4	7	2.4	296
POMONA COLLEGE															
CA TOTAL	2	.1	46	3.4	113	8.4	87	6.5	248	18.5	1,056	78.7	37	2.8	1,341
CA FEMALE	0	.0	25	3.9	62	9.6	47	7.3	134	20.7	496	76.7	17	2.6	647
CA MALE	2	.3	21	3.0	51	7.3	40	5.8	114	16.4	560	80.7	20	2.9	694
SCRIPPS COLLEGE															
CA TOTAL	1	.2	18	3.2	25	4.5	35	6.3	79	14.1	457	81.8	23	4.1	559
CA FEMALE	1	.2	18	3.2	25	4.5	35	6.3	79	14.1	457	81.8	23	4.1	559
CA MALE	0	.0	0		0		0	.0	0	.0	0	.0	0	.0	0
COASTLINE CMTY COLLEGE															
CA TOTAL	199	1.1	96	.6	590	3.4	463	2.7	1,348	7.7	16,061	92.3	0	.0	17,409
CA FEMALE	116	1.0	51	.4	375	3.2	291	2.5	833	7.1	10,956	92.9	0	.0	11,789
CA MALE	83	1.5	45	.8	215	3.8	172	3.1	515	9.2	5,105	90.8	0	.0	5,620
GOLDEN WEST COLLEGE															
CA TOTAL	304	1.9	181	1.2	793	5.1	788	5.0	2,066	13.2	13,563	86.6	40	.3	15,669
CA FEMALE	155	1.8	80	.9	395	4.6	406	4.7	1,036	12.0	7,567	87.8	16	.2	8,619
CA MALE	149	2.1	101	1.4	398	5.6	382	5.4	1,030	14.6	5,996	85.0	24	.3	7,050
ORANGE COAST COLLEGE															
CA TOTAL	472	3.0	171	1.1	994	6.4	867	5.6	2,504	16.0	13,014	83.4	90	.6	15,608
CA FEMALE	236	3.1	65	.8	365	4.7	376	4.9	1,042	13.5	6,623	86.0	35	.5	7,700
CA MALE	236	3.0	106	1.3	629	8.0	491	6.2	1,462	18.5	6,391	80.8	55	.7	7,908
COGSWELL COLLEGE															
CA TOTAL	2	.5	21	5.1	65	15.9	23	5.6	111	27.1	130	31.7	169	41.2	410
CA FEMALE	1	3.3	1	3.3	4	13.3	2	6.7	8	26.7	16	53.3	6	20.0	30
CA MALE	1	.3	20	5.3	61	16.1	21	5.5	103	27.1	114	30.0	163	42.9	380
COLLEGE OF THE CANYONS															
CA TOTAL	16	.7	83	3.8	30	1.4	117	5.3	246	11.2	1,936	88.1	16	.7	2,198
CA FEMALE	8	.7	18	1.5	15	1.3	57	4.8	98	8.2	1,088	91.1	8	.7	1,194
CA MALE	8	.8	65	6.5	15	1.5	60	6.0	148	14.7	848	84.5	8	.8	1,004
COLLEGE OF THE DESERT															
CA TOTAL	30	.7	159	3.6	61	1.4	584	13.3	834	18.9	3,522	79.9	51	1.2	4,407
CA FEMALE	19	.8	61	2.6	36	1.5	304	12.8	420	17.7	1,930	81.5	19	.8	2,369
CA MALE	11	.5	98	4.8	25	1.2	280	13.7	414	20.3	1,592	78.1	32	1.6	2,038
COLLEGE OF MARIN															
CA TOTAL	59	1.2	185	3.8	115	2.4	152	3.1	511	10.6	4,241	87.6	88	1.8	4,840
CA FEMALE	20	.8	47	1.8	61	2.3	78	3.0	206	7.9	2,386	91.1	28	1.1	2,620
CA MALE	39	1.8	138	6.2	54	2.4	74	3.3	305	13.7	1,855	83.6	60	2.7	2,220
COLLEGE OF NOTRE DAME															
CA TOTAL	0	.0	69	8.3	35	4.2	30	3.6	134	16.1	537	64.5	162	19.4	833
CA FEMALE	0	.0	43	8.0	25	4.6	20	3.7	88	16.4	376	69.9	74	13.8	538
CA MALE	0	.0	26	8.8	10	3.4	10	3.4	46	15.6	161	54.6	88	29.8	295
COLLEGE OF THE REDWOODS															
CA TOTAL	260	3.2	54	.7	68	.8	204	2.5	581	7.1	7,579	92.9	0	.0	8,160
CA FEMALE	177	3.9	20	.4	37	.8	95	2.1	329	7.2	4,242	92.8	0	.0	4,571
CA MALE	83	2.3	34	.9	26	.7	109	3.0	252	7.0	3,337	93.0	0	.0	3,589
COLLEGE OF THE SEQUOIAS															
CA TOTAL	108	2.0	176	3.3	58	1.1	731	13.6	1,073	20.0	4,118	76.7	176	3.3	5,367
CA FEMALE	50	1.7	86	2.9	26	.9	370	12.5	532	17.9	2,347	79.1	89	3.0	2,968
CA MALE	58	2.4	90	3.8	32	1.3	361	15.0	541	22.6	1,771	73.8	87	3.6	2,399
COLLEGE OF THE SISKIYOUS															
CA TOTAL	31	2.5	33	2.6	16	1.3	34	2.7	114	9.0	1,096	87.0	50	4.0	1,260
CA FEMALE	21	3.3	9	1.4	7	1.1	15	2.3	52	8.1	581	90.9	6	.9	639
CA MALE	10	1.6	24	3.9	9	1.4	19	3.1	62	10.0	515	82.9	44	7.1	621
COLUMBIA COLLEGE															
CA TOTAL	30	1.5	6	.3	11	.6	37	1.9	84	4.2	1,885	95.3	10	.5	1,979
CA FEMALE	18	1.5	1	.1	6	.5	27	2.3	52	4.4	1,118	95.2	4	.3	1,174
CA MALE	12	1.5	5	.6	5	.6	10	1.2	32	4.0	767	95.3	6	.7	805
COMPTON CMTY COLLEGE															
CA TOTAL	14	.4	3,026	76.5	41	1.0	162	4.1	3,243	81.9	186	4.7	529	13.4	3,958
CA FEMALE	6	.3	1,847	86.7	22	1.0	77	3.6	1,952	91.6	91	4.3	87	4.1	2,130
CA MALE	8	.4	1,179	64.5	19	1.0	85	4.6	1,291	70.6	95	5.2	442	24.2	1,828
CONTRA COSTA COLLEGE															
CA TOTAL	83	1.3	2,130	33.2	390	6.1	506	7.9	3,109	48.4	3,261	50.8	53	.8	6,423
CA FEMALE	43	1.2	1,230	34.5	198	5.5	260	7.3	1,731	48.5	1,823	51.1	16	.4	3,570
CA MALE	40	1.4	900	31.5	192	6.7	246	8.6	1,378	48.3	1,438	50.4	37	1.3	2,853
DIABLO VALLEY COLLEGE															
CA TOTAL	158	1.1	403	2.7	432	2.9	521	3.5	1,514	10.3	13,112	89.2	79	.5	14,705
CA FEMALE	56	.8	151	2.0	193	2.6	241	3.3	641	8.7	6,714	90.9	32	.4	7,387
CA MALE	102	1.4	252	3.4	239	3.3	280	3.8	873	11.9	6,398	87.4	47	.6	7,318
LOS MEDANOS COLLEGE															
CA TOTAL	45	1.2	349	9.7	71	2.0	388	10.7	853	23.6	2,757	76.3	4	.1	3,614
CA FEMALE	23	1.1	203	10.1	32	1.6	202	10.0	460	22.9	1,550	77.0	2	.1	2,012
CA MALE	22	1.4	146	9.1	39	2.4	186	11.6	393	24.5	1,207	75.3	2	.1	1,602
CRAFTON HILLS COLLEGE															
CA TOTAL	26	1.1	48	2.0	32	1.3	148	6.1	254	10.5	2,165	89.2	7	.3	2,426
CA FEMALE	15	1.1	26	1.9	12	.9	69	5.1	122	9.0	1,236	90.9	1	.1	1,359
CA MALE	11	1.0	22	2.1	20	1.9	79	7.4	132	12.4	929	87.1	6	.6	1,067

TABLE 1 - TOTAL UNDERGRADUATE ENROLLMENT IN INSTITUTIONS OF HIGHER EDUCATION BY RACE, ETHNICITY AND SEX:
INSTITUTION, STATE AND NATION, 1978

	AMERICAN INDIAN ALASKAN NATIVE		BLACK NON-HISPANIC		ASIAN OR PACIFIC ISLANDER		HISPANIC		TOTAL MINORITY		WHITE NON-HISPANIC		NON-RESIDENT ALIEN		TOT
	NUMBER	%	NUMBER	%	NUMBER	%	NUMBER	%	NUMBER	%	NUMBER	%	NUMBER	%	NUM
CALIFORNIA CONTINUED															
CUESTA COLLEGE															
CA TOTAL	52	1.3	53	1.3	132	3.4	225	5.7	462	11.8	3,402	86.5	67	1.7	3,
CA FEMALE	30	1.4	12	.6	74	3.5	102	4.9	218	10.4	1,863	88.6	21	1.0	2,
CA MALE	22	1.2	41	2.2	58	3.2	123	6.7	244	13.3	1,539	84.1	46	2.5	1,
CYPRESS COLLEGE															
CA TOTAL	81	1.4	90	1.5	227	3.9	464	7.9	862	14.6	4,982	84.5	52	.9	5,
CA FEMALE	36	1.1	39	1.2	95	3.0	237	7.5	407	12.8	2,751	86.7	16	.5	3,
CA MALE	45	1.7	51	1.9	132	4.8	227	8.3	455	16.7	2,231	82.0	36	1.3	2,
D-Q UNIVERSITY															
CA TOTAL	60	37.7	0	.0	0	.0	99	62.3	159	100.0	0	.0	0	.0	
CA FEMALE	45	41.7	0	.0	0	.0	63	58.3	108	100.0	0	.0	0	.0	
CA MALE	15	29.4	0	.0	0	.0	36	70.6	51	100.0	0	.0	0	.0	
DEEP SPRINGS COLLEGE															
CA TOTAL	0	.0	1	4.2	0	.0	0	.0	1	4.2	23	95.8		.0	
CA FEMALE	0	.0	0	.0	0	.0	0	.0	0	.0	0	.0		.0	
CA MALE	0	.0	1	4.2	0	.0	0	.0	1	4.2	23	95.8		.0	
DOMINICAN C OF SAN RAFAEL															
CA TOTAL	1	.3	10	2.7	9	2.4	16	4.3	36	9.7	298	80.5	36	9.7	
CA FEMALE	1	.3	8	2.8	6	2.1	9	3.1	24	8.4	244	85.3	18	6.3	
CA MALE	0	.0	2	2.4	3	3.6	7	8.3	12	14.3	54	64.3	18	21.4	
DOMINICAN SCH PHIL & THEO															
CA TOTAL	1	5.6	0	.0	1	5.6	3	16.7	5	27.8	13	72.2		.0	
CA FEMALE	0	.0	0	.0	0	.0	0	.0	0	.0	1	100.0		.0	
CA MALE	1	5.9	0	.0	1	5.9	3	17.6	5	29.4	12	70.6	0	.0	
DON BOSCO TECHNICAL INST															
CA TOTAL	0	.0	4	1.2	19	5.8	141	43.1	164	50.2	159	48.6		1.2	
CA FEMALE	0	.0	0	.0	0	.0	0	.0	0	.0	0	.0		.0	
CA MALE	0	.0	4	1.2	19	5.8	141	43.1	164	50.2	159	48.6		1.2	
EL CAMINO COLLEGE															
CA TOTAL	337	1.2	4,855	17.6	2,128	7.7	1,960	7.1	9,280	33.6	18,162	65.7	182	.7	27,
CA FEMALE	168	1.1	2,833	19.3	1,024	7.0	933	6.3	4,958	33.7	9,677	65.8	73	.5	14,
CA MALE	169	1.3	2,022	15.7	1,104	8.5	1,027	8.0	4,322	33.5	8,485	65.7	109	.8	12,
FASH INST DESIGN & MERCH															
CA TOTAL	0	.0	223	11.8	93	4.9	165	8.7	481	25.5	1,363	72.3	42	2.2	1,
CA FEMALE	0	.0	210	11.9	87	4.9	157	8.9	454	25.6	1,280	72.2	38	2.1	1,
CA MALE	0	.0	13	11.4	6	5.3	8	7.0	27	23.7	83	72.8	4	3.5	
DE ANZA COLLEGE															
CA TOTAL	430	4.3	316	3.2	680	6.9	557	5.6	1,983	20.1	7,863	79.5	44	.4	9,
CA FEMALE	237	4.4	156	2.9	326	6.0	295	5.4	1,014	18.7	4,407	81.1	13	.2	5,
CA MALE	193	4.3	160	3.6	354	7.9	262	5.9	969	21.7	3,456	77.6	31	.7	4,
FOOTHILL COLLEGE															
CA TOTAL	78	1.0	342	4.5	565	7.4	404	5.3	1,389	18.3	6,117	80.5	91	1.2	7,
CA FEMALE	34	.8	150	3.5	267	6.3	204	4.8	655	15.5	3,532	83.6	39	.9	4,
CA MALE	44	1.3	192	5.7	298	8.8	200	5.9	734	21.8	2,585	76.7	52	1.5	3,
FRESNO PACIFIC COLLEGE															
CA TOTAL	1	.3	11	3.0	9	2.4	32	8.6	53	14.3	287	77.4	31	8.4	
CA FEMALE	0	.0	5	2.5	6	3.0	15	7.4	26	12.9	161	79.7	15	7.4	
CA MALE	1	.6	6	3.6	3	1.8	17	10.1	27	16.0	126	74.6	16	9.5	
FULLERTON COLLEGE															
CA TOTAL	200	1.4	196	1.4	415	3.0	1,249	14.7	2,060	14.7	11,753	83.8	208	1 5	14,
CA FEMALE	85	1.2	86	1.2	195	2.8	557	7.9	923	13.1	6,041	85.8	77	1 1	7,
CA MALE	115	1.6	110	1.6	220	3.2	692	9.9	1,137	16.3	5,712	81.8	131	1 8	6,
GAVILAN COLLEGE															
CA TOTAL	25	1.2	38	1.9	65	3.2	556	27.5	684	33.8	1,227	60.6	113	5.6	2,
CA FEMALE	13	1.2	10	.9	31	2.9	283	26.0	337	31.0	687	63.2	63	5 8	1,
CA MALE	12	1.3	28	3.0	34	3.6	273	29.1	347	37.0	540	57.6	50	5(3)	
GLENDALE CMTY COLLEGE															
CA TOTAL	67	1.0	68	1.1	323	5.0	763	11.9	1,221	19.1	4,875	76.2	305	4	6,
CA FEMALE	41	1.2	22	.6	154	4.5	400	11.6	617	17.9	2,742	79.8	79	2	3,
CA MALE	26	.9	46	1.6	169	5.7	363	12.3	604	20.4	2,133	72.0	226	718	2,
GOLDEN GATE UNIVERSITY															
CA TOTAL	1	.0	117	4.2	137	4.9	61	2.2	316	11.2	2,452	87.0	51	1.8	2,
CA FEMALE	0	.0	40	3.6	59	5.3	26	2.3	125	11.2	961	86.4	26	2.3	1,
CA MALE	1	.1	77	4.5	78	4.6	35	2.1	191	11.2	1,491	87.3	25	1.5	1,
GROSSMONT COLLEGE															
CA TOTAL	67	1.2	98	1.7	113	2.0	360	6.3	638	11.2	4,986	87.3	88	1.	5,
CA FEMALE	28	.9	43	1.4	59	2.0	177	5.9	307	10.3	2,625	88.1	46	1.8	2,
CA MALE	39	1.4	55	2.0	54	2.0	183	6.7	331	12.1	2,361	86.4	42	1.8	2,
HARTNELL COLLEGE															
CA TOTAL	141	3.4	161	3.8	179	4.3	932	22.3	1,413	33.7	2,704	64.6	70	1.7	4,
CA FEMALE	66	3.2	53	2.6	91	4.4	455	21.9	665	32.0	1,391	67.0	19	.9	2,
CA MALE	75	3.6	108	5.1	88	4.2	477	22.6	748	35.4	1,313	62.2	51	2.4	2,
HEALD ENGR COLLEGE															
CA TOTAL	1	.1	65	8.5	129	16.8	27	3.5	222	28.9	442	57.5	105	13.7	
CA FEMALE	0	.0	9	10.6	13	15.3	4	4.7	26	30.6	42	49.4	17	20.0	
CA MALE	1	.1	56	8.2	116	17.0	23	3.4	196	28.7	400	58.5	88	12.9	
HOLY FAMILY COLLEGE															
CA TOTAL	1	1.4	0	.0	1	1.4	2	2.9	4	5.7	66	94.3	0	.0	
CA FEMALE	1	1.4	0	.0	1	1.4	2	2.9	4	5.7	66	94.3	0	.0	
CA MALE	0	.0	0	.0	0	.0	0	.0	0	.0	0	.0	0	.0	
HOLY NAMES COLLEGE															
CA TOTAL	6	1.7	32	8.8	16	4.4	25	6.9	79	21.8	169	46.6	115	31.7	
CA FEMALE	5	1.8	28	10.0	16	5.7	22	7.9	71	25.4	155	55.6	53	19.0	
CA MALE	1	1.2	4	4.8	0	.0	3	3.6	8	9.5	14	16.7	62	73.8	
HUMPHREYS COLLEGE															
CA TOTAL	3	1.1	12	4.3	7	2.5	26	9.3	48	17.2	186	66.7	45	16.1	
CA FEMALE	3	1.5	8	4.1	7	3.6	22	11.3	40	20.5	146	74.9	9	4.6	
CA MALE	0	.0	4	4.8	0	.0	4	4.8	8	9.5	40	47.6	36	42.9	
IMMACULATE HEART COLLEGE															
CA TOTAL	3	.8	39	9.9	7	1.8	84	21.3	133	33.7	238	60.3	24	6.1	
CA FEMALE	3	1.0	32	10.8	7	2.4	61	20.5	103	34.7	188	63.3	6	2.0	
CA MALE	0	.0	7	7.1	0	.0	23	23.5	30	30.6	50	51.0	18	18.4	

TABLE 1 - TOTAL UNDERGRADUATE ENROLLMENT IN INSTITUTIONS OF HIGHER EDUCATION BY RACE, ETHNICITY AND SEX: INSTITUTION, STATE AND NATION, 1978

	AMERICAN INDIAN ALASKAN NATIVE		BLACK NON-HISPANIC		ASIAN OR PACIFIC ISLANDER		HISPANIC		TOTAL MINORITY		WHITE NON-HISPANIC		NON-RESIDENT ALIEN		TOTAL
	NUMBER	%	NUMBER	%	NUMBER	%	NUMBER	%	NUMBER	%	NUMBER	%	NUMBER	%	NUMBER
CALIFORNIA CONTINUED															
IMPERIAL VALLEY COLLEGE															
CA TOTAL	19	1.0	91	4.7	207	10.8	730	38.1	1,047	54.6	805	42.0	66	3.4	1,918
CA FEMALE	9	.9	43	4.3	132	13.2	452	45.2	636	63.7	334	33.4	29	2.9	999
CA MALE	10	1.1	48	5.2	75	8.2	278	30.3	411	44.7	471	51.3	37	4.0	919
INDIAN VALLEY COLLEGES															
CA TOTAL	35	1.6	51	2.3	51	2.3	72	3.3	209	9.5	1,974	89.5	23	1.0	2,206
CA FEMALE	19	1.4	26	1.9	28	2.0	46	3.3	119	8.6	1,261	91.0	5	.4	1,385
CA MALE	16	1.9	25	3.0	23	2.8	26	3.2	90	11.0	713	86.8	18	2.2	821
INTERNATIONAL COLLEGE															
CA TOTAL	0	.0	0	.0	0	.0	0	.0	0	.0	14	93.3	1	6.7	15
CA FEMALE	0	.0	0	.0	0	.0	0	.0	0	.0	12	100.0	0	.0	12
CA MALE	0	.0	0	.0	0	.0	0	.0	0	.0	2	66.7	1	33.3	3
JOHN F KENNEDY UNIVERSITY															
CA TOTAL	1	.8	3	2.4	1	.8	2	1.6	7	5.6	117	92.9	2	1.6	126
CA FEMALE	0	.0	2	3.2	0	.0	1	1.6	3	4.8	60	95.2	0	.0	63
CA MALE	1	1.6	1	1.6	1	1.6	1	1.6	4	6.3	57	90.5	2	3.2	63
LAKE TAHOE CMTY COLLEGE															
CA TOTAL	6	.8	4	.6	8	1.1	18	2.5	36	5.0	688	94.9	1	.1	725
CA FEMALE	2	.5	2	.5	5	1.1	9	2.1	18	4.1	420	95.9	0	.0	438
CA MALE	4	1.4	2	.7	3	1.0	9	3.1	18	6.3	268	93.4	1	.3	287
LASSEN COLLEGE															
CA TOTAL	122	5.9	62	3.0	12	.6	80	3.9	276	13.4	1,683	81.5	105	5.1	2,064
CA FEMALE	77	6.9	21	1.9	5	.5	42	3.8	145	13.1	936	84.4	28	2.5	1,109
CA MALE	45	4.7	41	4.3	7	.7	38	4.0	131	13.7	747	78.2	77	9.1	955
LIFE BIBLE COLLEGE															
CA TOTAL	6	1.2	42	8.4	11	2.2	34	6.8	93	18.5	402	80.1	7	1.4	502
CA FEMALE	2	1.1	12	6.9	4	2.3	13	7.4	31	17.7	142	81.1	2	1.1	175
CA MALE	4	1.2	30	9.2	7	2.1	21	6.4	62	19.0	260	79.5	5	1.5	327
LINCOLN UNIVERSITY															
CA TOTAL	0	.0	2	.8	6	2.3	1	.4	9	3.5	0	.0	249	96.5	258
CA FEMALE	0	.0	0	.0	3	4.8	0	.0	3	4.8	0	.0	59	95.2	62
CA MALE	0	.0	2	1.0	3	1.5	1	.5	6	3.1	0	.0	190	96.9	196
LOMA LINDA UNIVERSITY															
CA TOTAL	3	.1	281	10.0	271	9.7	234	8.3	789	28.1	1,818	64.8	197	7.0	2,804
CA FEMALE	3	.2	163	9.9	148	9.0	127	7.7	441	26.8	1,105	67.1	102	6.2	1,648
CA MALE	0	.0	118	10.2	123	10.6	107	9.3	348	30.1	713	61.7	95	8.2	1,156
LONG BEACH CITY COLLEGE															
CA TOTAL	293	1.0	2,637	9.3	1,283	4.5	1,528	5.4	5,741	20.2	22,414	79.0	231	.8	28,386
CA FEMALE	173	1.0	1,210	6.9	563	3.2	689	3.9	2,635	15.0	14,805	84.4	105	.6	17,545
CA MALE	120	1.1	1,427	13.2	720	6.6	839	7.7	3,106	28.7	7,609	70.2	126	1.2	10,841
LOS ANGELES BAPT COLLEGE															
CA TOTAL	1	.3	9	2.4	4	1.1	12	3.2	26	7.0	341	91.9	4	1.1	371
CA FEMALE	0	.0	4	2.1	1	.5	3	1.6	8	4.3	179	95.7	0	.0	187
CA MALE	1	.5	5	2.7	3	1.6	9	4.9	18	9.8	162	88.0	4	2.2	184
EAST LOS ANGELES COLLEGE															
CA TOTAL	167	1.3	690	5.6	1,322	10.7	8,751	70.6	10,930	88.1	1,428	11.5	43	.3	12,401
CA FEMALE	77	1.2	392	6.0	677	10.3	4,551	69.3	5,697	86.8	853	13.0	15	.2	6,565
CA MALE	90	1.5	298	5.1	645	11.1	4,200	72.0	5,233	89.7	575	9.9	28	.5	5,836
LOS ANGELES CITY COLLEGE															
CA TOTAL	223	1.5	6,307	41.9	2,829	18.8	2,900	19.3	12,259	81.5	2,771	18.4	11	.1	15,041
CA FEMALE	99	1.2	3,419	43.0	1,366	17.2	1,502	18.9	6,386	80.3	1,567	19.7	4	.1	7,957
CA MALE	124	1.8	2,888	40.8	1,463	20.7	1,398	19.7	5,873	82.9	1,204	17.0	7	.1	7,084
LOS ANG HARBOR COLLEGE															
CA TOTAL	207	2.3	1,756	19.5	1,254	13.9	1,820	20.2	5,037	56.0	3,937	43.8	16	.2	8,990
CA FEMALE	120	2.4	993	20.2	592	12.0	939	19.1	2,644	53.7	2,272	46.1	8	.2	4,924
CA MALE	87	2.1	763	18.8	662	16.3	881	21.7	2,393	58.9	1,665	40.9	8	.2	4,066
LOS ANGELES MISSION C															
CA TOTAL	38	1.8	255	11.9	55	2.6	903	42.3	1,251	58.5	879	41.1	7	.3	2,137
CA FEMALE	27	1.9	163	11.6	31	2.2	551	39.1	772	54.8	635	45.1	2	.1	1,409
CA MALE	11	1.5	92	12.6	24	3.3	352	48.4	479	65.8	244	33.5	5	.7	728
LOS ANG PIERCE COLLEGE															
CA TOTAL	390	2.3	607	3.5	708	4.1	1,125	6.6	2,830	16.5	14,224	83.0	77	.4	17,131
CA FEMALE	199	2.2	272	3.0	311	3.4	567	6.2	1,349	14.7	7,779	85.0	25	.3	9,153
CA MALE	191	2.4	335	4.2	397	5.0	558	7.0	1,481	18.6	6,445	80.8	52	.7	7,978
LOS-ANG SOUTHWEST COLLEGE															
CA TOTAL	19	.4	5,152	96.1	91	1.7	26	.5	5,288	98.7	72	1.3	0	.0	5,360
CA FEMALE	12	.3	3,348	97.2	28	.8	23	.7	3,411	99.0	33	1.0	0	.0	3,444
CA MALE	7	.4	1,804	94.2	63	3.3	3	.2	1,877	98.0	39	2.0	0	.0	1,916
LOS ANG TR TECH COLLEGE															
CA TOTAL	222	1.7	7,231	55.7	902	6.9	2,816	21.7	11,171	86.0	1,660	12.8	157	1.2	12,988
CA FEMALE	59	1.2	3,630	71.4	253	5.0	746	14.7	4,688	92.2	349	6.9	47	.9	5,084
CA MALE	163	2.1	3,601	45.6	649	8.2	2,070	26.2	6,483	82.0	1,311	16.6	110	1.4	7,904
LOS ANG VALLEY COLLEGE															
CA TOTAL	513	3.0	1,079	6.3	1,182	6.9	2,223	13.0	4,997	29.2	12,038	70.4	62	.4	17,097
CA FEMALE	292	3.0	550	5.6	589	6.0	1,127	11.5	2,558	26.0	7,261	73.8	20	.2	9,839
CA MALE	221	3.0	529	7.3	593	8.2	1,096	15.1	2,439	33.6	4,777	65.8	42	.6	7,258
WEST LOS ANGELES COLLEGE															
CA TOTAL	90	1.2	3,947	53.8	486	6.6	433	5.9	4,956	67.5	2,380	32.4	3	.0	7,339
CA FEMALE	69	1.5	2,352	52.4	234	5.2	241	5.4	2,896	64.6	1,589	35.4	1	.0	4,486
CA MALE	21	.7	1,595	55.9	252	8.8	192	6.7	2,060	72.2	791	27.7	2	.1	2,853
AMERICAN RIVER COLLEGE															
CA TOTAL	265	1.5	1,270	7.2	464	2.6	820	4.7	2,819	16.1	14,670	83.7	35	.2	17,524
CA FEMALE	145	1.6	586	6.3	241	2.6	429	4.6	1,401	15.2	7,820	84.7	15	.2	9,236
CA MALE	120	1.4	684	8.3	223	2.7	391	4.7	1,418	17.1	6,850	82.6	20	.2	8,288
COSUMNES RIVER COLLEGE															
CA TOTAL	62	1.5	617	14.6	306	7.2	320	7.6	1,305	30.9	2,893	68.5	23	.5	4,221
CA FEMALE	33	1.3	314	12.6	145	5.8	184	7.4	676	27.1	1,820	72.8	3	.1	2,499
CA MALE	29	1.7	303	17.6	161	9.3	136	7.9	629	36.5	1,073	62.3	20	1.2	1,722
SACRAMENTO CITY COLLEGE															
CA TOTAL	147	1.3	2,007	17.5	1,277	11.1	1,406	12.3	4,837	42.2	6,236	54.4	388	3.4	11,461
CA FEMALE	85	1.4	1,046	17.5	612	10.2	772	12.9	2,515	42.0	3,367	56.3	103	1.7	5,985
CA MALE	62	1.1	961	17.5	665	12.1	634	11.6	2,322	42.4	2,969	52.4	285	5.2	5,476

11

TABLE I - TOTAL UNDERGRADUATE ENROLLMENT IN INSTITUTIONS OF HIGHER EDUCATION BY RACE, ETHNICITY AND SEX: INSTITUTION, STATE AND NATION, 1978

	AMERICAN INDIAN ALASKAN NATIVE		BLACK NON-HISPANIC		ASIAN OR PACIFIC ISLANDER		HISPANIC		TOTAL MINORITY		WHITE NON-HISPANIC		NON-RESIDENT ALIEN	
	NUMBER	%	NUMBER	%	NUMBER	%	NUMBER	%	NUMBER	%	NUMBER	%	NUMBER	%
CALIFORNIA CONTINUED														
LOYOLA MARYMOUNT U														
CA TOTAL	15	.4	258	7.5	139	4.9	603	17.4	1,015	29.4	2,286	66.1	156	4.5
CA FEMALE	7	.4	151	9.1	62	3.7	283	17.0	503	30.3	1,094	65.9	63	3.8
CA MALE	8	.4	107	6.0	77	4.3	320	17.8	512	28.5	1,192	66.3	93	5.2
MARYMOUNT PALOS VERDES C														
CA TOTAL	4	1.1	37	10.6	17	4.9	38	10.9	96	27.6	150	43.1	102	29.3
CA FEMALE	2	.9	32	13.8	8	3.4	29	12.5	71	30.6	108	46.6	53	22.8
CA MALE	2	1.7	5	4.3	9	7.8	9	7.8	25	21.6	42	36.2	49	42.2
MELODYLAND SCH THEOLOGY														
CA TOTAL	0	.0	10	4.0	3	1.2	7	2.8	20	8.1	212	85.8	15	6.1
CA FEMALE	0	.0	4	5.2	2	2.6	1	1.3	7	9.1	64	83.1	6	7.8
CA MALE	0	.0	6	3.5	1	.6	6	3.5	13	7.6	148	87.1	9	5.3
MENDOCINO COLLEGE														
CA TOTAL	83	4.9	22	1.3	12	.7	44	2.6	161	9.5	1,515	89.3	21	1.2
CA FEMALE	59	5.5	7	.7	6	.6	34	3.2	106	9.9	960	89.4	8	.7
CA MALE	24	3.9	15	2.4	6	1.0	10	1.6	55	8.8	555	89.1	13	2.1
MENLO COLLEGE														
CA TOTAL	1	.2	4	.6	10	1.6	3	.5	18	2.9	461	73.9	145	2.2
CA FEMALE	1	.5	1	.5	4	2.1	1	.5	7	3.7	145	76.3	38	2.0
CA MALE	0	.0	3	.7	6	1.4	2	.5	11	2.5	316	72.8	107	28.7
MERCED COLLEGE														
CA TOTAL	72	1.2	621	10.2	187	3.1	819	13.4	1,699	27.8	4,282	70.1	131	2.1
CA FEMALE	36	1.2	315	10.4	101	3.3	393	13.0	845	27.9	2,158	71.1	31	1.0
CA MALE	36	1.2	306	9.9	86	2.8	426	13.8	854	27.7	2,124	69.0	100	3.2
MILLS COLLEGE														
CA TOTAL	5	.6	85	10.0	63	7.	26	3.1	179	21.0	610	71.7	62	7.3
CA FEMALE	5	.6	85	10.0	63	7.4	26	3.1	179	21.0	610	71.7	62	7.3
CA MALE	0	.0	0	.0	0	.0	0	.0	0	.0	0	.0	0	.0
MIRA COSTA COLLEGE														
CA TOTAL	49	1.2	364	8.5	122	2.9	435	1.2	970	22.8	3,289	77.2		.0
CA FEMALE	25	1.2	130	6.1	63	2.9	198	.2	416	19.4	1,726	80.6	8	.0
CA MALE	24	1.1	234	11.1	59	2.8	237	18.2	554	26.2	1,563	73.8	8	.0
MODESTO JUNIOR COLLEGE														
CA TOTAL	187	2.1	184	2.1	264	3.0	880	1.1	1,515	17.3	7,221	82.7		.0
CA FEMALE	109	2.4	92	2.0	118	2.6	417	.2	736	16.2	3,818	83.8	8	.0
CA MALE	78	1.9	92	2.2	146	3.5	463	19.1	779	18.6	3,403	81.4	8	.0
MNTREY INST FORGN STUDIES														
CA TOTAL	0	.0	2	2.4	1	1.2	4	4.8	7	8.3	69	82.1	8	9.5
CA FEMALE	0	.0	0	.0	1	1.8	0	.0	1	1.8	49	86.0	7	12.3
CA MALE	0	.0	2	7.4	0	.0	4	14.8	6	22.2	20	74.1	1	3.7
MONTEREY PEN COLLEGE														
CA TOTAL	48	.9	659	13.0	437	8.6	236	.7	1,380	27.3	3,677	72.7		.0
CA FEMALE	24	.9	281	10.4	247	9.2	117	.3	669	24.8	2,028	75.2		.0
CA MALE	24	1.0	378	16.0	190	8.1	119	8.0	711	30.1	1,649	69.9	8	.0
MOUNT SNT MARY'S COLLEGE														
CA TOTAL	2	.2	58	6.2	64	6.	151	1.2	275	29.5	645	69.1	1	1.4
CA FEMALE	2	.2	56	6.1	64	7.0	148	16.1	270	29.4	634	69.1	1	1.4
CA MALE	0	.0	2	12.5	0	.0	3	18.8	5	31.3	11	68.8	8	.0
MOUNT SAN ANTONIO COLLEGE														
CA TOTAL	118	.8	1,180	7.9	499	3.	2,797	18.7	4,594	30.7	10,360	69.1	33	.2
CA FEMALE	58	.7	715	8.7	257	3.2	1,446	17.6	2,476	30.1	5,744	69.8	7	.1
CA MALE	60	.9	465	6.9	242	.6	1,351	20.10	2,118	31.3	4,616	68.3	26	.4
MT SAN JACINTO COLLEGE														
CA TOTAL	57	2.7	79	3.7	19	.9	188		343	16.0	1,794	83.4	13	.6
CA FEMALE	33	2.9	29	2.6	12	1.1	97	8.7	171	15.2	955	84.7	2	.2
CA MALE	24	2.3	50	4.9	7	.7	91	8.8	172	16.8	839	82.1	11	1.1
NAPA COLLEGE														
CA TOTAL	67	1.5	123	2.7	121	2.7	248	5.5	559	12.3	3,919	86.4	58	1.3
CA FEMALE	33	1.3	63	2.4	66	2.5	144	5.6	306	11.8	2,274	87.8	11	.4
CA MALE	34	1.7	60	3.1	55	2.8	104	5.3	253	13.0	1,645	84.6	47	2.4
NATIONAL UNIVERSITY														
CA TOTAL	20	1.0	237	11.7	73	3.	104	5.1	434	21.4	1,562	76.9	5	1.7
CA FEMALE	5	1.0	60	12.2	17	3.	27	5.5	109	22.2	376	76.4	7	1.4
CA MALE	15	1.0	177	11.5	56	3.6	77	5.0	325	21.1	1,186	77.1	28	1.8
NEW COLLEGE OF CALIFORNIA														
CA TOTAL	8	1.4	95	16.4	5	.9	16	2.	124	21.4	445	76.7	11	1.9
CA FEMALE	2	.7	48	16.0	4	1.3	8	2.6	62	20.7	231	77.0	7	2.3
CA MALE	6	2.1	47	16.8	1	.4	8	2.9	62	22.1	214	76.4	4	1.4
NORTHROP UNIVERSITY														
CA TOTAL	1	.1	8	1.1	0	.0	0	.0	9	1.3	437	61.1	269	37.6
CA FEMALE	0	.0	4	10.8	0	.0	0	.0	4	10.8	27	73.0	6	16.2
CA MALE	1	.1	4	.6	0	.0	0	.0	5	.7	410	60.5	263	38.8
OCCIDENTAL COLLEGE														
CA TOTAL	4	.2	81	4.9	112	6.8	94	5.7	291	17.7	1,316	80.0	37	2.3
CA FEMALE	1	.1	42	5.2	64	8.0	42	5.2	149	18.6	640	79.8	13	1.6
CA MALE	3	.4	39	4.6	48	5.7	52	6.2	142	16.9	676	80.3	24	2.9
OHLONE COLLEGE														
CA TOTAL	64	1.0	170	2.6	411	6.2	522	7.9	1,167	17.6	5,406	81.7	42	.6
CA FEMALE	33	.9	88	2.4	198	5.3	264	7.1	583	15.7	3,114	83.9	14	.4
CA MALE	31	1.1	82	2.8	213	7.3	258	8.4	584	20.1	2,292	78.9	28	1.0
OTIS ART INST LOS ANG CO														
CA TOTAL	0	.0	4	4.7	8	9.4	5	5.9	17	20.0	56	65.9	12	14.1
CA FEMALE	0	.0	1	2.2	6	13.0	3	6.5	10	21.7	30	65.2		13.0
CA MALE	0	.0	3	7.7	2	5.1	2	5.1	7	17.9	26	66.7	8	15.4
PACIFIC CHRISTIAN COLLEGE														
CA TOTAL	7	1.2	47	8.0	11	1.9	25	2.0	90	15.3	493	83.6	7	1.2
CA FEMALE	2	.6	27	7.9	7	2.7	14	4.1	50	14.7	289	84.8	2	.6
CA MALE	5	2.0	20	8.0	4	1.6	11	4.4	40	16.1	204	81.9	5	2.0
PACIFIC OAKS COLLEGE														
CA TOTAL	0	.0	8	9.3	1	1.2		4.7	13	15.1	69	80.2	4	4.7
CA FEMALE	0	.0	8	10.7	1	1.3		5.3	13	17.3	59	78.7	3	4.0
CA MALE	0	.0	0	.0	0	10	0	.0	0	.0	10	90.9	1	9.1

	AMERICAN INDIAN ALASKAN NATIVE		BLACK NON-HISPANIC		ASIAN OR PACIFIC ISLANDER		HISPANIC		TOTAL MINORITY		WHITE NON-HISPANIC		NON-RESIDENT ALIEN		TOTAL
	NUMBER	%	NUMBER	%	NUMBER	%	NUMBER	%	NUMBER	%	NUMBER	%	NUMBER	%	NUMBER

ORNIA CONTINUED

IC UNION COLLEGE
OTAL	15	.7	58	2.8	135	6	71	3.4	279	13.4	1,659	79.5	150	7.2	2,088
MALE	10	1.0	34	3.3	67	61	34	3.3	145	13.9	826	79.2	72	6.9	1,043
MALE	5	.5	24	2.3	68	6.8	37	3.5	134	12.8	833	79.7	78	7.5	1,045

AR COLLEGE
OTAL	249	2.1	313	2.7	348	3.0	806	6.9	1,716	14.7	9,814	84.3	115	1.0	11,645
MALE	136	2.3	100	1.7	156	2.7	400	6.9	792	13.7	5,000	86.2	10	.2	5,802
MALE	113	1.9	213	3.6	192	3.3	406	6.9	924	15.8	4,814	82.4	105	1.8	5,843

VERDE COLLEGE
OTAL	1	.2	24	5.6	10	2.4	110	25.9	145	34.1	269	63.3	11	2.6	425
MALE	1	.4	17	6.3	2	.7	68	25.2	88	32.6	179	66.3	3	1.1	270
MALE	0	.0	7	4.5	8	512	42	27.1	57	36.8	90	58.1	8	5.2	155

ENA CITY COLLEGE
OTAL	66	.4	2,147	1.4	1,175	7.9	1,563	10.5	4,951	33.3	9,555	64.3	364	2.4	14,870
MALE	32	.4	1,167	1.4	615	7.6	827	10.2	2,641	32.5	5,325	65.6	150	1.8	8,116
MALE	34	.5	980	14.5	560	8.3	736	10.9	2,310	34.2	4,230	62.6	214	3.2	6,754

N BIBLE COLLEGE
OTAL	1	1.2	30	37.0	3	3.7	3	3.7	37	45.7	38	46.9	6	7.4	81
MALE	1	2.2	17	37.0	0	.0	0	.0	18	39.1	23	50.0	5	12.	46
MALE	0	.0	13	37.1	3	8.6	3	8.6	19	54.3	15	42.9	1	2.9	35

RDINE UNIVERSITY
OTAL	20	.7	358	12.8	79	2.	112	4.0	569	20.4	1,895	67.8	331	11.8	2,795
MALE	10	.7	210	15.3	42	3.0	40	2.9	302	22.0	982	71.6	88	6.4	1,372
MALE	10	.7	148	10.4	37	2.6	72	5.1	267	18.8	913	64.2	243	17.1	1,423

GE OF ALAMEDA
OTAL	83	1.4	2,703	46.6	566	9.	339	5.8	3,691	63.6	2,087	36.0	27	.5	5,805
MALE	46	1.5	1,560	49.5	250	7.	173	5.5	2,029	64.4	1,111	35.2	13	.4	3,153
MALE	37	1.4	1,143	43.1	316	11.9	166	6.3	1,662	62.7	976	36.8	14	.5	2,652

ER RIVER COLLEGE
OTAL	14	2.2	34	5.4	3	.5	15	2.4	66	10.5	557	88.7	5	.8	628
MALE	6	1.7	7	1.9	3	.8	9	2.5	25	6.9	335	92.3	3	.8	363
MALE	8	3.0	27	10.2	0	.0	6	2.3	41	15.5	222	83.8	2	.8	265

COLLEGE
OTAL	78	1.0	4,208	55.0	588	7.7	519	6.8	5,393	70.6	2,144	28.0	107	1.4	7,644
MALE	37	1.1	2,013	58.3	231	6.7	190	5.5	2,471	71.6	953	27.6	26	.3	3,450
MALE	41	1.0	2,195	52.3	357	8.5	329	7.8	2,922	69.7	1,191	28.4	81	1.9	4,194

TT COLLEGE
OTAL	76	1.3	2,542	43.3	494	8.4	275	.7	3,387	57.7	2,435	41.5	49	.8	5,871
MALE	39	1.2	1,477	46.5	226	7.1	146	4.6	1,888	59.4	1,278	40.2	12	.4	3,178
MALE	37	1.4	1,065	39.5	268	10.0	129	4.8	1,499	55.7	1,157	43.0	37	1.4	2,693

COLLEGE
OTAL	28	1.3	584	27.7	79	3.7	147	7.	838	39.8	1,267	60.1	3	.1	2,108
MALE	18	1.2	468	30.0	46	2.9	103	6.0	635	40.7	924	59.2	3	.2	1,562
MALE	10	1.8	116	21.2	33	6.0	44	8.8	203	37.2	343	62.8	0	.0	546

LOMA COLLEGE
OTAL	3	.2	23	1.4	19	1.2	38	2.4	83	5.2	1,528	94.8		.0	1,611
ALE	0	.0	14	1.5	14	1.5	26	2.8	54	5.8	883	94.2	0	.0	937
MALE	3	.4	9	1.3	5	.17	12	1.8	29	4.3	645	95.7	0	.0	674

RVILLE COLLEGE
OTAL	27	1.4	48	2.	46	2.	380	20.1	501	26.5	1,358	71.9	31	1.6	1,890
MALE	10	1.0	10	1.1	25	2.4	202	19.2	247	23.5	797	75.8	7	.7	1,051
MALE	17	2.0	38	4.8	21	2.4	178	21.2	254	30.3	561	66.9	24	2.9	839

ONDO COLLEGE
OTAL	229	2.0	114	1.	346	3.0	4,453	38.6	5,142	44.6	6,277	54.4	114	1.0	11,533
MALE	105	2.0	52	1.0	157	3.0	2,188	41.7	2,502	47.7	2,690	51.3	52	1.0	5,244
MALE	124	2.0	62	1.0	189	3.0	2,265	36.0	2,640	42.0	3,587	57.0	62	1.0	6,289

SIDE CITY COLLEGE
OTAL	245	2.0	1,144	.2	144	1.2	1,014	8.1	2,547	20.4	9,717	77.9	211	1.7	12,475
MALE	132	2.0	606	9.1	70	1.1	502	7.	1,310	19.7	5,312	79.8	35	.5	6,657
MALE	113	1.9	538	9.2	74	1.3	512	8.8	1,237	21.3	4,405	75.7	176	3.0	5,818

EBACK CMTY COLLEGE
OTAL	138	1.0	198	1.5	334	2.5	470	3.5	1,140	8.5	12,156	90.7	102	.8	13,398
MALE	76	1.0	85	1.1	167	212	243	3.1	571	7.4	7,161	92.4	22	.3	7,754
MALE	62	1.1	113	2.0	167	3.0	227	4.0	569	10.1	4,995	88.5	80	1.4	5,644

JOHN'S COLLEGE
OTAL	0	.0	2	1.	4	.7	17	15.7	23	21.3	84	77.8	1	.9	108
MALE	0	.0	0	.0	0	3.0	0	.	0	.0	0	.0	0	.0	0
MALE	0	.0	2	1.8	4	.7	17	15.9	23	21.3	84	77.8	1	.9	108

ARY'S COLLEGE OF CAL
OTAL	4	.3	100	6.	27	1.8	96	.5	227	15.3	1,114	75.2	140	9.5	1,481
MALE	1	.1	42	7.4	10	1.4	44	6.2	97	13.7	566	80.1	44	6.2	707
MALE	3	.4	58	7.8	17	2.2	52	6.7	130	16.8	548	70.8	96	12.4	774

PATRICK'S COLLEGE
OTAL	0	.0	0	.0	4	11.1	6	16.7	10	27.8	26	72.2	0	.0	36
MALE	0	.0	0	.0	0	.0	0	.0	0	.0	0	.0	0	.0	0
MALE	0	.0	0	.0	4	11.1	6	16.7	10	27.8	26	72.2	0	.0	36

RNARDINO VLY COLLEGE
OTAL	182	1.4	1,692	13.5	168	1.3	1,727	13.7	3,769	30.0	8,730	69.5	69	.5	12,568
MALE	77	1.2	822	12.9	89	1.4	823	12.9	1,811	28.4	4,538	71.2	22	.3	6,371
MALE	105	1.7	870	14.0	79	1.3	904	14.6	1,958	31.6	4,192	67.8	47	.8	6,197

IEGO CITY COLLEGE
OTAL	38	.9	1,423	33.5	141	.3	611	14.4	2,213	52.1	1,969	46.4	65	1.5	4,247
MALE	25	1.2	728	35.3	63	3.1	316	15.3	1,132	54.8	905	43.8	27	1.3	2,064
MALE	13	.6	695	31.8	78	.6	295	13.5	1,081	49.5	1,064	48.7	38	1.7	2,183

IEGO EVENING C
OTAL	148	.9	2,531	15.1	562	.4	1,502	9.0	4,743	28.3	11,824	70.5	205	1.2	16,772
MALE	62	.8	1,156	14.7	240	3.0	620	7.9	2,078	26.4	5,731	72.8	67	.9	7,876
MALE	86	1.0	1,375	15.5	322	.6	882	9.9	2,665	30.0	6,093	68.5	138	1.6	8,896

IEGO MESA COLLEGE
OTAL	41	.5	569	7.2	257	.2	451	5.7	1,318	16.6	6,495	81.9	122	1.	7,935
MALE	19	.5	273	6.6	132	3.2	220	5.3	644	15.6	3,425	83.2	48	1.	4,117
MALE	22	.6	296	7.8	125	.3	231	6.1	674	17.7	3,070	80.4	74	1.9	3,818

TABLE 1 - TOTAL UNDERGRADUATE ENROLLMENT IN INSTITUTIONS OF HIGHER EDUCATION BY RACE, ETHNICITY AND SEX: INSTITUTION, STATE AND NATION, 1978

	AMERICAN INDIAN ALASKAN NATIVE		BLACK NON-HISPANIC		ASIAN OR PACIFIC ISLANDER		HISPANIC		TOTAL MINORITY		WHITE NON-HISPANIC		NON-RESIDENT ALIEN	
	NUMBER	%	NUMBER	%	NUMBER	%	NUMBER	%	NUMBER	%	NUMBER	%	NUMBER	%
CALIFORNIA CONTINUED														
SAN DIEGO MIRAMAR COLLEGE														
CA TOTAL	7	.8	56	6.6	31	3.7	59		153	18.1	687	81.4	4	
CA FEMALE	5	1.3	22	5.6	17	4.3	27	710	71	18.1	320	81.4	2	
CA MALE	2	.4	34	7.5	14	3.1	32	8.4	82	18.2	367	81.4	2	;8
SAN FRANCISCO ART INST														
CA TOTAL	14	2.1	13	1.9	19	2.8	27	4.	73	10.9	505	75.6	90	13.
CA FEMALE	7	2.4	4	1.4	7	2.4	8	2.0	26	9.0	240	83.3	22	7.
CA MALE	7	1.8	9	2.4	12	3.2	19	5.8	47	12.4	265	69.7	68	17.6
CITY COLLEGE SN FRANCISCO														
CA TOTAL	128	.6	3,823	17.5	6,194	2 .3	1,027	8.3	11,972	54.7	9,479	43.3	433	2 0
CA FEMALE	59	.5	2,040	18.1	2,999	26.6	893	7.9	5,991	53.1	5,082	45.1	201	1 8
CA MALE	69	.7	1,783	16.8	3,195	30.1	934	8.8	5,981	56.4	4,397	41.4	232	212
SAN FRANCISCO CONSV MUSIC														
CA TOTAL	2	1.3	8	5.1	13	8.2	6	3.8	29	18.4	117	74.1	12	7.6
CA FEMALE	0	.0	3	4.7	7	10.9	1	1.6	11	17.2	47	73.4	6	9.4
CA MALE	2	2.1	5	5.3	6	6.4	5	5.3	18	19.1	70	74.5	6	6.4
SAN JOAQUIN DELTA COLLEGE														
CA TOTAL	766	4.9	1,288	8.2	1,363	8.7	2,373	15 2	5,790	37.0	9,119	58.3	727	4 6
CA FEMALE	358	4.5	632	7.9	666	8.4	1,164	14 6	2,820	35.4	4,845	60.8	302	3 8
CA MALE	408	5.3	656	8.6	697	9.1	1,209	1518	2,970	38.7	4,274	55.7	425	515
SAN JOSE BIBLE COLLEGE														
CA TOTAL	1	.4	12	5.0	3	1 3	8	3	24	10.1	213	89.5	1	4
CA FEMALE	0	.0	3	3.4	2	2 3	0		5	5.7	82	93.2	1	1 1
CA MALE	1	.7	9	6.0	1	17	8	518	19	12.7	131	87.3	0	10
EVERGREEN VALLEY COLLEGE														
CA TOTAL	30	.6	272	5.3	276	.3	527	1 .2	1,105	21.4	3,952	76.5	107	2.'
CA FEMALE	10	.4	147	5.3	140	.0	259	0.3	556	19.9	2,208	79.1	29	1.
CA MALE	20	.8	125	5.3	136	9.7	268	18.3	549	23.2	1,744	73.6	78	3.8
SAN JOSE CITY COLLEGE														
CA TOTAL	141	1.2	468	3.8	692	5 7	1,138	3	2,439	20.0	9,707	79.5	67	5
CA FEMALE	64	1.3	216	4.5	269	5 6	492	1o 2	1,041	21.5	3,779	78.0	22	5
CA MALE	77	1.0	252	3.4	423	517	646	818	1,398	19.0	5,928	80.4	45	16
CANADA COLLEGE														
CA TOTAL	27	.5	404	8.1	143	2.9	512	10 2	1,086	21.7	3,796	75.9	120	2
CA FEMALE	15	.5	224	7.0	87	2.7	277	8 7	603	18.9	2,546	79.6	49	1
CA MALE	12	.7	180	10.0	56	3.1	235	1310	483	26.8	1,250	69.3	71	31?
COLLEGE OF SAN MATEO														
CA TOTAL	68	.6	444	4.2	742	7.'	781	7.	2,035	19.4	8,345	79.5	122	1.2
CA FEMALE	33	.6	175	3.4	365	7.	357	6.4	930	17.9	4,212	81.2	47	.9
CA MALE	35	.7	269	5.1	377	7.8	424	8.0	1,105	20.8	4,133	77.8	75	1.4
SKYLINE COLLEGE														
CA TOTAL	56	1.0	571	10.1	654	11.	792	1 0	2,073	36.5	3,523	62.1	79	1
CA FEMALE	39	1.1	336	9.6	338	9.	479	14 6	1,192	33.9	2,291	65.1	35	1
CA MALE	17	.8	235	10.9	316	11.5	313	1415	881	40.8	1,232	57.1	44	210
SANTA ANA COLLEGE														
CA TOTAL	192	1.7	574	5.1	264	2	1,506	13 4	2,536	22.6	8,204	73.1	487	4 3
CA FEMALE	91	1.7	257	4.7	116	213	700	12 9	1,164	21.4	4,117	75.8	148	2 7
CA MALE	101	1.7	317	5.5	148	2.8	806	1319	1,372	23.7	4,087	70.5	339	518
SANTA BARBARA CTY COLLEGE														
CA TOTAL	115	2.2	148	2.8	144	2 7	508	.6	915	17.3	4,369	82.7	0	.
CA FEMALE	51	2.0	47	1.8	59	213	240	0.2	397	15.3	2,204	84.7	0	.
CA MALE	64	2.4	101	3.8	85	3.2	268	180	518	19.3	2,165	80.7	0	.0
SANTA MONICA COLLEGE														
CA TOTAL	156	1.1	1,397	10.1	858	6.2	1,193	8 6	3,604	25.	9,872	71.0	423	3.0
CA FEMALE	80	1.0	638	8.2	422	5.4	596	7 7	1,736	82.9	5,822	75.2	189	2.4
CA MALE	76	1.2	759	12.3	436	7.1	597	917	1,868	0.4	4,050	65.8	234	3.8
SANTA ROSA JUNIOR COLLEGE														
CA TOTAL	125	1.2	185	1.8	180	1.7	440	.2	930	8	9,431	90.1	112	1.1
CA FEMALE	80	1.3	70	1.2	83	1.4	215	4.5	448	7 9	5,555	91.7	54	.9
CA MALE	45	1.0	115	2.6	97	2.2	225	8.1	482	1019	3,876	87.8	58	1.3
SHASTA COLLEGE														
CA TOTAL	326	3.3	76	.8	81	.8	417	.2	900	0	9,066	91.0	0	.0
CA FEMALE	184	3.2	45	.8	45	.8	236	4.1	510	9 0	5,183	91.0	0	.0
CA MALE	142	3.3	31	.7	36	.8	181	4.2	390	911	3,883	90.9	0	.0
SIERRA COLLEGE														
CA TOTAL	105	1.8	30	.5	73	1.	218	-8	426	4	5,353	92.4	14	.2
CA FEMALE	48	1.6	4	.1	38	1.3	96	3.2	186	2	2,808	93.8	1	.0
CA MALE	57	2.0	26	.9	35	1.	122	4.4	240	816	2,545	91.0	13	.5
SIMPSON COLLEGE														
CA TOTAL	0	.0	9	4.1	8	3.7	5	2.3	22	1 .0	194	88.6	3	1
CA FEMALE	0	.0	1	1.1	2	2.1	1	1.1	4	0.2	89	93.7	2	2 1
CA MALE	0	.0	8	6.5	6	4.8	4	3.2	18	14.5	105	84.7	1	18
SOLANO COMMUNITY COLLEGE														
CA TOTAL	88	1.3	977	14.9	364	.	362	.5	1,791	27.4	4,572	69.9	176	2.7
CA FEMALE	42	1.4	427	14.4	146	.6	161	.4	776	26.2	2,090	70.5	98	3.3
CA MALE	46	1.3	550	15.4	218	8.9	201	5.6	1,015	28.4	2,482	69.4	78	2.2
SOUTHERN CAL COLLEGE														
CA TOTAL	3	.5	12	2.1	21	3 7	33	8	69	12.1	477	83.8	23	.0
CA FEMALE	1	.4	6	2.2	8	310	16	10	31	11.6	228	85.1	9	4.9
CA MALE	2	.7	6	2.0	13	4.3	17	8.6	38	12.6	249	82.7	14	4.7
STHN CAL INSTITUTE ARCH														
CA TOTAL	0	.0	2	.8	9	3.6	12	4.8	23	9.2	178	71.5	48	19.3
CA FEMALE	0	.0	0	.0	2	6.3	0	.0	2	6.3	24	75.0	6	13.9
CA MALE	0	.0	2	.9	7	3.2	12	5.5	21	9.7	154	71.0	42	19.4
SOUTHWESTERN COLLEGE														
CA TOTAL	78	.8	434	4.5	883	9.2	2,021	21.1	3,416	35.7	5,784	60.4	375	3.
CA FEMALE	39	.8	187	3.9	327	6.9	1,055	22.3	1,608	33.9	2,978	62.8	155	3.0
CA MALE	39	.8	247	5.1	556	11.5	966	20.0	1,808	37.4	2,806	58.0	220	4.8
STANFORD UNIVERSITY														
CA TOTAL	38	.6	356	5.4·	374	5.7	385	5.9	1,153	17.6	5,246	80.0	159	2.
CA FEMALE	14	.5	169	6.1	174	6.3	156	5.7	513	18.6	2,179	79.1	62	2.4
CA MALE	24	.6	187	4.9	200	5.3	229	6.0	640	16.8	3,067	80.6	97	2.8

E.1 - TOTAL UNDERGRADUATE ENROLLMENT IN INSTITUTIONS OF HIGHER EDUCATION BY RACE, ETHNICITY AND SEX: INSTITUTION, STATE AND NATION, 1978

	AMERICAN INDIAN ALASKAN NATIVE		BLACK NON-HISPANIC		ASIAN OR PACIFIC ISLANDER		HISPANIC		TOTAL MINORITY		WHITE NON-HISPANIC		NON-RESIDENT ALIEN		TOTAL
	NUMBER	%	NUMBER	%	NUMBER	%	NUMBER	%	NUMBER	%	NUMBER	%	NUMBER	%	NUMBER
FORNIA CONTINUED															
NO CITY COLLEGE															
TOTAL	163	1.3	912	7.2	411	3.3	2,879	22.9	4,365	34.7	8,089	64.3	128	1.0	12,582
EMALE	101	1.5	507	7.7	209	3.2	1,376	21.0	2,193	33.5	4,317	66.0	33	.5	6,543
MALE	62	1.0	405	6.7	202	3.3	1,503	24.9	2,172	36.0	3,772	62.5	95	1.6	6,039
LEY COLLEGE															
TOTAL	22	.9	60	2.4	112	4.5	744	30.1	938	37.9	1,497	60.5	39	1.6	2,474
EMALE	9	.7	11	.9	62	5.0	384	31.1	466	37.7	762	61.7	7	.6	1,235
MALE	13	1.0	49	4.0	50	4.0	360	29.1	472	38.1	735	59.3	32	2.6	1,239
COLLEGE															
TOTAL	17	2.3	28	3.7	3	.4	20	2.7	68	9.1	655	87.7	24	3.2	747
EMALE	7	1.7	0	.0	1	.2	12	2.9	20	4.8	391	94.2	4	1.0	415
MALE	10	3.0	28	8.4	2	.6	8	2.4	48	14.5	264	79.5	20	6.0	332
NTERNATIONAL U															
TOTAL	7	.8	57	6.3	51	5.7	19	2.1	134	14.9	379	42.2	386	42.9	899
EMALE	2	.6	23	7.3	13	4.1	7	2.2	45	14.2	176	55.5	96	30.3	317
MALE	5	.9	34	5.8	38	6.5	12	2.1	89	15.3	203	34.9	290	49.8	582
CAL-BERKELEY															
TOTAL	100	.5	695	3.5	3,054	19.3	699	3.5	5,348	26.7	14,195	71.0	456	2.3	19,999
EMALE	53	.6	357	4.2	1,709	19.9	264	3.1	2,383	27.8	6,068	70.8	124	1.4	8,575
MALE	47	.4	338	3.0	2,145	18.8	435	3.8	2,965	26.0	8,127	71.1	332	2.9	11,424
CAL-DAVIS															
TOTAL	71	.6	371	2.9	1,164	9.2	443	3.5	2,049	16.3	10,333	82.0	224	1.8	12,606
EMALE	36	.6	190	3.0	578	9.3	199	3.2	1,003	16.1	5,167	82.8	68	1.1	6,238
MALE	35	.5	181	2.8	586	9.2	244	3.8	1,046	16.4	5,166	81.1	156	2.4	6,368
CAL-IRVINE															
TOTAL	29	.4	359	4.7	756	9.9	615	8.0	1,759	23.0	5,586	73.0	312	4.1	7,657
EMALE	12	.3	205	5.8	348	9.8	277	7.8	842	23.7	2,633	74.0	84	2.4	3,559
MALE	17	.4	154	3.8	408	10.0	338	8.2	917	22.4	2,953	72.1	228	5.6	4,098
CAL-LOS ANGELES															
TOTAL	83	.4	1,034	5.1	2,860	14.2	1,295	6.4	5,272	26.1	14,345	71.1	550	2.7	20,167
EMALE	33	.3	613	6.1	1,431	14.3	608	6.1	2,685	26.8	7,188	71.7	158	1.6	10,031
MALE	50	.5	421	4.2	1,429	14.1	687	6.8	2,587	25.5	7,157	70.6	392	3.9	10,136
CAL-RIVERSIDE															
TOTAL	31	1.0	229	7.1	204	6.3	297	9.1	761	23.4	2,457	75.7	29	.9	3,247
EMALE	13	.8	134	8.6	96	6.2	131	8.4	374	24.0	1,172	75.3	11	.7	1,557
MALE	18	1.1	95	5.6	108	6.4	166	9.8	387	22.9	1,285	76.0	18	1.1	1,690
CAL-SAN DIEGO															
TOTAL	39	.5	371	4.4	699	8.3	489	5.8	1,598	18.9	6,673	78.9	191	2.3	8,462
EMALE	17	.5	241	6.6	313	8.5	204	5.6	775	21.1	2,844	77.4	55	1.5	3,674
MALE	22	.5	130	2.7	386	8.1	285	6.0	823	17.2	3,829	80.0	136	2.8	4,788
CAL-SAN FRANCISCO															
TOTAL	0	.0	17	4.6	60	16.3	15	4.1	92	25.1	273	74.4	2	.5	367
EMALE	0	.0	15	4.7	55	17.1	12	3.7	82	25.5	237	73.8	2	.6	321
MALE	0	.0	2	4.3	5	10.9	3	6.5	10	21.7	36	78.3	0	.0	46
CAL-SANTA BARBARA															
TOTAL	105	.8	252	2.0	614	4.9	786	6.2	1,757	13.9	10,695	84.8	160	1.3	12,612
EMALE	48	.7	117	1.8	294	4.5	369	5.7	828	12.8	5,619	86.6	40	.6	6,487
MALE	57	.9	135	2.2	320	5.2	417	6.8	929	15.2	5,076	82.9	120	2.0	6,125
CAL-SANTA CRUZ															
TOTAL	26	.5	131	2.4	189	3.4	357	6.5	703	12.8	4,757	86.4	44	.8	5,504
EMALE	10	.3	79	2.7	108	3.7	180	6.2	377	13.0	2,493	86.2	22	.8	2,892
MALE	16	.6	52	2.0	81	3.1	177	6.8	326	12.5	2,264	86.7	22	.8	2,612
ERSITY OF JUDAISM															
TOTAL	0	.0	0	.0	0	.0	0	.0	0	.0	92	100.0	0	.0	92
EMALE	0	.0	0	.0	0	.0	0	.0	0	.0	61	100.0	0	.0	61
MALE	0	.0	0	.0	0	.0	0	.0	0	.0	31	100.0	0	.0	31
ERSITY OF LA VERNE															
TOTAL	6	.4	103	7.6	24	1.8	197	14.6	330	24.4	870	64.3	153	11.3	1,353
EMALE	0	.0	64	8.4	11	1.4	132	17.3	207	27.2	504	66.1	51	6.7	762
MALE	6	1.0	39	6.6	13	2.2	65	11.0	123	20.8	366	61.9	102	17.3	591
ERSITY OF THE PACIFIC															
TOTAL	8	.2	95	2.6	392	10.9	115	3.2	610	16.9	2,745	76.1	250	5.9	3,605
EMALE	4	.2	50	2.8	165	9.4	51	2.9	270	15.3	1,406	79.8	86	4.9	1,762
MALE	4	.2	45	2.4	227	12.3	64	3.5	340	18.4	1,339	72.7	164	8.9	1,843
ERSITY OF REDLANDS															
TOTAL	12	.5	177	7.8	114	5.0	103	4.5	406	17.9	1,839	80.9	28	1.2	2,273
EMALE	4	.4	70	6.9	51	5.0	49	4.8	174	17.1	831	81.9	10	1.0	1,015
MALE	8	.6	107	8.5	63	5.0	54	4.3	232	18.4	1,008	80.1	18	1.4	1,258
ERSITY OF SAN DIEGO															
TOTAL	9	.4	76	3.4	75	3.3	193	8.6	353	15.7	1,797	79.9	100	4.4	2,250
EMALE	2	.2	32	2.7	37	3.2	107	9.2	178	15.3	945	81.0	43	3.7	1,166
MALE	7	.6	44	4.1	38	3.5	86	7.9	175	16.1	852	78.6	57	5.3	1,084
SAN FRANCISCO															
TOTAL	16	.4	272	7.1	509	13.3	281	7.4	1,078	28.2	2,134	55.8	611	16.0	3,823
EMALE	6	.3	168	8.4	280	14.0	149	7.4	603	30.1	1,209	60.4	189	9.4	2,001
MALE	10	.5	104	5.7	229	12.6	132	7.2	475	26.1	925	50.8	422	23.2	1,822
ERSITY OF SANTA CLARA															
TOTAL	7	.2	79	2.3	261	7.6	277	8.1	624	18.2	2,609	76.3	187	5.5	3,420
EMALE	3	.2	37	2.5	116	7.8	123	8.3	279	18.7	1,144	76.8	66	4.4	1,489
MALE	4	.2	42	2.2	145	7.5	154	8.0	345	17.9	1,465	75.9	121	6.3	1,931
SOUTHERN CALIFORNIA															
TOTAL	68	.5	1,081	7.2	1,698	11.4	1,056	7.1	3,903	26.1	9,054	60.6	1,989	13.3	14,946
EMALE	26	.4	627	10.3	737	12.1	459	7.5	1,849	30.3	3,612	59.2	641	10.5	6,102
MALE	42	.5	454	5.1	961	10.9	597	6.8	2,054	23.2	5,442	61.5	1,348	15.2	8,844
WEST LOS ANGELES															
TOTAL	3	2.2	23	16.9	6	4.4	6	4.4	38	27.9	98	72.1	0	.0	136
EMALE	2	1.6	20	16.1	6	4.8	6	4.8	34	27.4	90	72.6	0	.0	124
MALE	1	8.3	3	25.0	0	.0	0	.0	4	33.3	8	66.7	0	.0	12
PARK COLLEGE															
TOTAL	70	1.1	94	1.5	83	1.3	509	8.0	755	11.9	5,564	87.7	26	.4	6,346
EMALE	39	1.1	37	1.1	38	1.1	260	7.5	374	10.7	3,109	89.1	6	.2	3,489
MALE	31	1.1	57	2.0	45	1.6	249	8.7	382	13.4	2,455	85.9	20	.7	2,857

15

TABLE I - TOTAL UNDERGRADUATE ENROLLMENT IN INSTITUTIONS OF HIGHER EDUCATION BY RACE, ETHNICITY AND SEX: INSTITUTION, STATE AND NATION, 1978

	AMERICAN INDIAN ALASKAN NATIVE		BLACK NON-HISPANIC		ASIAN OR PACIFIC ISLANDER		HISPANIC		TOTAL MINORITY		WHITE NON-HISPANIC		NON-RESIDENT ALIEN	
	NUMBER	%	NUMBER	%	NUMBER	%	NUMBER	%	NUMBER	%	NUMBER	%	NUMBER	%
CALIFORNIA CONTINUED														
OXNARD COLLEGE														
CA TOTAL	35	1.0	324	9.6	227	6.7	1,009	29.9	1,595	47.3	1,755	52.0	22	.7
CA FEMALE	22	1.3	166	9.5	86	4.9	473	27.0	747	42.7	997	57.0	5	.3
CA MALE	13	.8	158	9.7	141	8.7	536	33.0	848	52.2	758	46.7	17	1.0
VENTURA COLLEGE														
CA TOTAL	110	1.2	300	3.3	304	3.3	1,569	17.1	2,283	24.9	6,858	74.8	27	.3
CA FEMALE	50	1.0	150	3.0	147	3.0	751	15.1	1,098	22.1	3,855	77.7	6	.1
CA MALE	60	1.4	150	3.6	157	3.7	818	19.4	1,185	28.2	3,003	71.3	21	.5
VICTOR VALLEY COLLEGE														
CA TOTAL	39	1.5	280	10.9	52	2.0	133	5.2	504	19.6	2,056	80.1	7	.3
CA FEMALE	18	1.3	119	8.9	25	1.9	61	4.6	223	16.7	1,110	83.1	2	.1
CA MALE	21	1.7	161	13.1	27	2.2	72	5.8	281	22.8	946	76.8	5	.4
WEST COAST BIBLE COLLEGE														
CA TOTAL	0	.0	0	.0	4	2.0	14	7 0	18	9.0	166	83.4	15	7.5
CA FEMALE	0	.0	0	.0	2	2.0	6	8 1	8	8.1	86	86.9	5	5.1
CA MALE	0	.0	0	.0	2	2.0	8	810	10	10.0	80	80.0	10	10.0
WEST COAST U MAIN CAMPUS														
CA TOTAL	0	.0	39	9.5	20	.9	23	5 6	82	20.0	190	46.5	137	3.5
CA FEMALE	0	.0	8	10.4	4	.2	0	0	12	15.6	40	51.9	25	2.5
CA MALE	0	.0	31	9.3	16	1.6	23	619	70	21.1	150	45.2	112	3.7
W COAST U ORANGE CO CTR														
CA TOTAL	0	.0	1	.4	5	1.9	10	.9	16	6.2	221	85.3	22	8.5
CA FEMALE	0	.0	0	.0	1	3.7	0	.0	1	3.7	25	92.6	1	3.7
CA MALE	0	.0	1	.4	4	1.7	10	4.3	15	6.5	196	84.5	21	9.1
WSTN STATES COLLEGE ENGR														
CA TOTAL	0	.0	18	17.5	21	20.4	10	9.7	49	47.6	27	26.2	27	26.2
CA FEMALE	0	.0	1	50.0	0	.0	1	50.0	2	100.0	0	.0	0	.0
CA MALE	0	.0	17	16.8	21	20.8	9	8.9	47	46.5	27	26.7	27	26.7
WSTN ST U C LAW ORANGE CO														
CA TOTAL	4	1.5	8	3.0	7	2.6	24	8 9	43	15.9	228	84.1	0	.0
CA FEMALE	0	.0	3	3.2	2	2.1	7	7 4	12	12.8	82	87.2	0	.0
CA MALE	4	2.3	5	2.8	5	2.8	17	916	31	17.5	146	82.5	0	.0
WSTN ST U C LAW SAN DIEGO														
CA TOTAL	4	1.9	12	5.6	5	2.3	12	5 6	33	15.3	183	84.7	0	.0
CA FEMALE	1	1.3	6	7.7	2	2.6	4	5 1	13	16.7	65	83.3	0	.0
CA MALE	3	2.2	6	4.3	3	2.2	8	518	20	14.5	118	85.5	0	.0
WEST HILLS COLLEGE														
CA TOTAL	31	2.0	93	6.1	53	3.5	208	13.6	385	25.2	1,130	73.9	15	1.0
CA FEMALE	12	1.7	34	4.7	19	2.6	103	14.3	168	23.3	547	75.9	6	.8
CA MALE	19	2.3	59	7.3	34	4.2	105	13.0	217	26.8	583	72.1	9	1.1
WESTMONT COLLEGE														
CA TOTAL	0	.0	3	.3	19	1.9	18	1.8	40	4.0	960	95.1	9	.9
CA FEMALE	0	.0	1	.2	8	1.5	9	1 6	18	3.3	531	96.4	2	.4
CA MALE	0	.0	2	.4	11	2.4	9	210	22	4.8	429	93.7	7	1.5
MISSION COLLEGE														
CA TOTAL	73	3.2	48	2.1	164	7 1	249	1 8	534	23.1	1,776	76.8		.2
CA FEMALE	52	3.5	27	1.8	70	4 7	163	1 9	312	20.8	1,186	79.2		.0
CA MALE	21	2.6	21	2.6	94	1115	86	10.5	222	27.2	590	72.3		.5
WEST VALLEY COLLEGE														
CA TOTAL	298	2.2	186	1.4	688	5.2	838	6.3	2,010	15.1	11,168	83.9	130	1.0
CA FEMALE	173	2.3	93	1.3	330	4.4	432	5.8	1,028	13.8	6,357	85.6	39	.5
CA MALE	125	2.1	93	1.6	358	6.1	406	6.9	982	16.7	4,811	81.8	91	1.5
WHITTIER COLLEGE														
CA TOTAL	4	.4	89	8.3	61	5.7	200	18 8	354	33.2	608	57.0	104	9.8
CA FEMALE	1	.2	45	8.4	32	5.9	106	19 7	184	34.2	307	57.1	47	8.7
CA MALE	3	.6	44	8.3	29	5.5	94	1718	170	32.2	301	57.0	57	10.8
WOODBURY UNIVERSITY														
CA TOTAL	1	.1	52	4.5	31	2.7	43	3 7	127	11.0	292	25.2	740	63.8
CA FEMALE	1	.2	30	5.7	23	4.4	25	4 7	79	15.0	221	41.9	227	43.1
CA MALE	0	.0	22	3.5	8	1.3	18	218	48	7.6	71	11.2	513	81.2
WORLD COLLEGE WEST														
CA TOTAL	0	.0	2	4.3	1	2.2	1	2.2	4	8.7	42	91.3	0	.0
CA FEMALE	0	.0	0	.0	1	4.3	0	.0	1	4.3	22	95.7	0	.0
CA MALE	0	.0	2	8.7	0	.0	1	4.3	3	13.0	20	87.0	0	.0
YUBA COLLEGE														
CA TOTAL	163	3.1	227	4.3	135	2.5	467	8.8	992	18.7	4,263	80.3	51	1.0
CA FEMALE	90	3.2	94	3.4	80	2 9	248	8.9	512	18.4	2,258	81.1	13	.5
CA MALE	73	2.9	133	5.3	55	212	219	8.7	480	19.0	2,005	79.5	38	1.5
CALIFORNIA TOTAL (226 INSTITUTIONS)														
CA TOTAL	17,638	1.4	116,371	9.2	82,558	6.6	123,430	9.8	339,997	27.0	890,490	70.7	28,598	2.3
CA FEMALE	9,014	1.4	62,099	9.5	39,449	6.1	60,144	9°2	170,706	26.2	471,342	72.4	9,223	1.4
CA MALE	8,624	1.4	54,272	8.9	43,109	7.1	63,286	10.4	169,291	27.9	419,148	69.0	19,375	3.2
COLORADO														
ADAMS STATE COLLEGE														
CO TOTAL	15	.9	56	3.3	43	2.6	470	28.0	584	34.7	1,082	64.4	15	.9
CO FEMALE	8	.9	27	3.2	21	2.5	239	28.0	295	34.5	553	64.7	7	.8
CO MALE	7	.8	29	3.5	22	2.7	231	28.0	289	35.0	529	64.0	8	1.0
AIMS COMMUNITY COLLEGE														
CO TOTAL	25	.9	19	.7	23	.9	268	10.2	335	12.7	2,268	86.0	33	1.3
CO FEMALE	6	.4	8	.6	11	.8	115	8.3	140	10.1	1,242	89.4	7	.5
CO MALE	19	1.5	11	.9	12	1.0	153	12.	195	15.6	1,026	82.3	26	2.1
ARAPAHOE CMTY COLLEGE														
CO TOTAL	46	.7	139	2.2	36	.6	276	3	497	7 7	5,742	89.3	189	2.9
CO FEMALE	26	.7	63	1.6	21	.5	153	10	263	6 8	3,532	91.3	74	1.9
CO MALE	20	.8	76	3.0	15	.6	123	4.8	234	911	2,210	86.4	115	4.5
COLORADO COLLEGE														
CO TOTAL	13	.7	49	2.6	27	1.5	81	4.4	170	9.1	1,659	89.2	30	1.6
CO FEMALE	5	.5	25	2.7	16	1.7	45	4.9	91	9.9	816	89.2	8	.9
CO MALE	8	.8	24	2.5	11	1.2	36	3.8	79	8.4	843	89.3	22	2.3

16

W VE	BLACK NON-HISPANIC		ASIAN OR PACIFIC ISLANDER		HISPANIC		TOTAL MINORITY		WHITE NON-HISPANIC		NON-RESIDENT ALIEN		TOTAL
	NUMBER	%	NUMBER	%	NUMBER	%	NUMBER	%	NUMBER	%	NUMBER	%	NUMBER
TINUED													
	0	.0	1	.4	22	8.1	31	11.4	238	87.2	4	1.5	273
	0	.0	0	.0	10	8.8	17	15.0	96	85.0	0	.0	113
	0	.0	1	.6	12	7.5	14	8.8	142	88.8	4	2.5	160
	3	.4	1	.1	13	1.9	62	9.1	613	90.4	3	.4	678
	1	.3	1	.3	5	1.4	18	5.1	335	94.6	1	.3	354
	2	.6	0	.0	8	2.5	44	13.6	278	85.8	2	.6	324
	26	1.5	0	.0	1	.1	27	1.6	1,666	97.7	12	.7	1,705
	1	.1	0	.0	1	.1	2	.2	866	99.7	1	.1	869
	25	3.0	0	.0	0	.0	25	3.0	800	95.7	11	1.3	836
	3	.1	21	1.0	31	1.5	55	2.6	1,931	92.6	99	4.7	2,085
	0	.0	1	.3	7	2.4	8	2.7	282	94.9	7	2.4	297
	3	.2	20	1.1	24	1.3	47	2.6	1,649	92.2	92	5.1	1,788
	151	1.0	176	1.1	303	2.0	676	4.4	14,588	95.1	82	.5	15,346
	73	1.0	94	1.3	120	1.6	303	4.1	7,027	95.4	38	.5	7,368
	78	1.0	82	1.0	183	2.3	373	4.7	7,561	94.8	44	.6	7,978
	12	3.3	2	.6	17	4.7	33	9.2	316	87.8	11	3.1	360
	1	3.6	0	.0	1	3.6	2	7.1	26	92.9	0	.0	28
	11	3.3	2	.6	16	4.8	31	9.3	290	87.3	11	3.3	332
	36	8.4	11	2.6	16	3.7	73	17.0	347	80.9	9	2.1	429
	36	8.4	11	2.6	16	3.7	73	17.0	347	80.9	9	2.1	429
	0	.0	0	.0	0	.0	0	.0	0	.0	0	.0	0
	511	16.2	83	2.6	387	12.3	1,047	33.2	1,821	57.7	288	9.1	3,156
	246	15.5	33	2.1	180	11.4	497	31.4	1,042	65.7	46	2.9	1,585
	265	16.9	50	3.2	207	13.2	550	35.0	779	49.6	242	15.4	1,571
	112	2.7	69	1.7	396	9.7	620	15.2	3,415	83.6	49	1.2	4,084
	54	2.5	36	1.7	175	8.2	288	13.4	1,846	86.1	9	.4	2,143
	58	3.0	33	1.7	221	11.4	332	17.1	1,569	80.8	40	2.1	1,941
	53	1.3	33	.8	236	5.	359	8.5	3,775	89.9	65	1.5	4,199
	13	.7	15	.8	61	3.	107	5.7	1,768	93.5	15	.8	1,890
	40	1.7	18	.8	175	7.8	252	10.9	2,007	86.9	50	2.2	2,309
	19	.7	12	.4	107	3.9	313	11.3	2,440	87.8	26	.9	2,779
	2	.2	6	.5	44	3.5	169	13.4	1,090	86.2	6	.5	1,265
	17	1.1	6	.4	63	4.2	144	9.5	1,350	89.2	20	1.3	1,514
	0	.0	0	.0	1	1.3	1	1.3	78	98.7	0	.0	79
	0	.0	0	.0	0	.0	0	.0	35	100.0	0	.0	35
	0	.0	0	.0	1	2.3	1	2.3	43	97.7	0	.0	44
	15	3.8	3	.8	38	9.6	56	14.1	340	85.6	1	.3	397
	3	1.4	3	1.4	17	7.9	23	10.6	193	89.4	0	.0	216
	12	6.6	0	.0	21	11.6	33	18.2	147	81.2	1	.6	181
	20	3.2	10	1.6	28	4.	65	10.3	551	87.0	17	2.7	633
	12	2.3	9	1.7	24	4.	51	9.9	461	89.2	5	1.0	517
	8	6.9	1	.9	4	3.4	14	12.1	90	77.6	12	10.3	116
	11	.3	12	.4	46	1.4	91	2.8	3,102	97.2	0	.0	3,193
	0	.0	6	.4	19	1.1	37	2.2	1,660	97.8	0	.0	1,697
	11	.7	6	.4	27	1.8	54	3.6	1,442	96.4	0	.0	1,496
	633	8.1	64	.8	713	9.1	1,475	18.8	6,344	80.8	31	.4	7,850
	302	8.5	17	.5	329	9.2	680	19.1	2,883	80.8	6	.2	3,569
	331	7.7	47	1.1	384	9.0	795	18.6	3,461	80.8	25	.6	4,281
	6	2.4	3	1.2	36	14.1	45	17.6	155	60.8	55	21.6	255
	0	.0	1	1.0	13	13.5	14	14.6	79	82.3	3	3.1	96
	6	3.8	2	1.3	23	14.5	31	19.5	76	47.8	52	32.7	159
	23	5.1	0	.0	10	2.2	36	8.0	404	90.2	8	1.8	448
	7	14.0	0	.0	2	4.0	11	22.0	36	72.0	3	6.0	50
	16	4.0	0	.0	8	2.0	25	6.3	368	92.5	5	1.3	398
	26	2.6	2	.2	30	3.0	60	6.0	937	93.5	5	.5	1,002
	10	2.1	1	.2	12	2.5	24	5.0	455	95.0	0	.0	479
	16	3.1	1	.2	18	3.4	36	6.9	482	92.2	5	1.0	523
	28	3.9	3	.4	165	22.9	203	28.1	507	70.2	12	1.7	722
	15	3.8	1	.3	93	23.4	111	28.0	285	71.8	1	.3	397
	13	4.0	2	.6	72	22.2	92	28.3	222	68.3	11	3.4	325
	388	9.5	59	1.4	277	6 8	766	18.8	3,227	79.1	89	2.2	4,082
	136	8.6	25	1.6	94	5 9	270	17.0	1,285	80.9	34	2.1	1,589
	252	10.1	34	1.4	183	713	496	19.9	1,942	77.9	55	2.2	2,493
	90	6.4	16	1.1	31	2 2	144	10.2	1,246	88.4	19	1.3	1,409
	12	2.9	6	1.4	6	1 4	31	7.5	383	92.1	2	.5	416
	78	7.9	10	1.0	25	215	113	11.4	863	86.9	17	1.7	993
	3	1.3	2	.9	11	4.8	17	7.4	209	90.9	4	1.7	230
	0	.0	2	1.9	2	1.9	4	3.8	100	95.2	1	1.0	105
	3	2.4	0	.0	9	7.2	13	10.4	109	87.2	3	2.4	125

TABLE 1 - TOTAL UNDERGRADUATE ENROLLMENT IN INSTITUTIONS OF HIGHER EDUCATION BY RACE, ETHNICITY AND SEX: INSTITUTION, STATE AND NATION, 1978

	AMERICAN INDIAN ALASKAN NATIVE		BLACK NON-HISPANIC		ASIAN OR PACIFIC ISLANDER		HISPANIC		TOTAL MINORITY		WHITE NON-HISPANIC		NON-RESIDENT ALIEN	
	NUMBER	%	NUMBER	%	NUMBER	%	NUMBER	%	NUMBER	%	NUMBER	%	NUMBER	%
COLORADO	CONTINUED													
SAINT THOMAS SEMINARY														
CO TOTAL	0	.0	1	1.9	1	1.9	2	3.8	4	7.7	48	92.3	0	.0
CO FEMALE	0	.0	0	0	0	.0	0	.0	0	.0	1	100.0	0	.0
CO MALE	0	.0	1	2.0	1	2.0	2	3.9	4	7.8	47	92.2	0	.0
TRINIDAD STATE JR COLLEGE														
CO TOTAL	39	4.8	29	3.5	21	2.6	200	24.4	289	35.2	425	51.8	107	13.0
CO FEMALE	14	5.4	10	3.9	15	5.8	92	35.7	131	50.8	111	43.0	16	6.2
CO MALE	25	4.4	19	3.4	6	1.1	108	19.2	158	28.1	314	55.8	91	16.2
U OF COLORADO AT BOULDER														
CO TOTAL	88	.5	401	2.3	398	2.3	626	3.6	1,513	8.7	15,664	89.9	247	1.4
CO FEMALE	59	.8	197	2.5	173	2.2	276	3.5	705	9.0	7,043	90.2	59	.8
CO MALE	29	.3	204	2.1	225	2.3	350	3.6	808	8.4	8,621	89.6	188	2.0
U O[r] COLO COLO SPRINGS														
CO TOTAL	6	.2	97	3.8	66	2.6	113	.4	282	11.0	2,267	88.6	10	.4
CO FEMALE	1	.1	52	4.1	26	2.1	59	4.7	138	10.9	1,125	88.8	4	.3
CO MALE	5	.4	45	3.5	40	3.1	54	4.2	144	11.1	1,142	88.4	6	.5
U OF COLO AT DENVER														
CO TOTAL	41	.9	172	3.9	149	3.4	219	4.9	577	13.1	3,703	83.8	138	3.1
CO FEMALE	19	1.0	91	4.6	58	2.9	112	5.6	280	14.1	1,690	85.1	17	.9
CO MALE	22	.9	81	3.3	91	3.7	103	4.2	297	12.2	2,013	82.8	121	5.0
U OF COLD MEDICAL CENTER														
CO TOTAL	2	.5	9	2.2	20	4.8	21	5.1	52	12.6	362	87.4	0	.0
CO FEMALE	2	.5	8	2.1	18	4.8	19	5.1	47	12.6	326	87.4	0	.0
CO MALE	0	.0	1	2.4	2	4.9	2	4.9	5	12.2	36	87.8	0	.0
UNIVERSITY OF DENVER														
CO TOTAL	40	1.0	100	2.5	68	1.7	75	1.9	283	7.0	3,408	84.9	325	8.1
CO FEMALE	14	.8	60	3.3	41	2.3	35	1.9	150	8.3	1,566	86.4	97	5.4
CO MALE	26	1.2	40	1.8	27	1.2	40	1.8	133	6.0	1,842	83.6	228	10.3
U OF NORTHERN COLORADO														
CO TOTAL	29	.3	252	2.8	77	.9	300	3.3	658	7.3	8,302	92.2	45	.5
CO FEMALE	14	.3	144	2.7	49	.9	174	3.3	381	7.2	4,908	92.5	15	.3
CO MALE	15	.4	108	2.9	28	.8	126	3.4	277	7.5	3,394	91.7	30	.8
U OF SOUTHERN COLORADO														
CO TOTAL	34	.8	168	3.9	24	.6	840	1,7	1,066	25.0	2,984	69.9	217	5.1
CO FEMALE	17	.9	55	3.0	8	.4	397	21.9	477	26.4	1,319	72.9	14	.8
CO MALE	17	.7	113	4.6	16	.7	443	18.0	589	24.0	1,665	67.8	203	8.3
WESTERN BIBLE COLLEGE														
CO TOTAL	2	1.0	2	1.0	0	.0	4	1.9	8	3.8	199	95.2	2	1.0
CO FEMALE	1	1.1	0	.0	0	.0	0	3.0	1	1.1	92	96.8	2	2.1
CO MALE	1	.9	2	1.8	0	.0	4	15	7	6.1	107	93.9	0	.0
WESTERN ST COLLEGE COLO														
CO TOTAL	8	.3	17	.6		.1	49	1.7	78	2.7	2,808	97.0	9	.3
CO FEMALE	3	.3	5	.4	4	.3	15	1.3	27	2.3	1,151	97.4	4	.3
CO MALE	5	.3	12	.7		.0	34	2.0	51	3.0	1,657	96.7	5	.3
YESH TORAS CHAIM TALMUD														
CO TOTAL	0	.0	0	.0	0	.0	0	.0	0	.0	24	100.0	0	.0
CO FEMALE	0	.0	0	.0	0	.0	0	.0	0	.0	0	.0	0	.0
CO MALE	0	.0	0	.0	0	.0	0	.0	0	.0	24	100.0	0	.0
COLORADO	TOTAL (	39 INSTITUTIONS)												
CO TOTAL	976	.9	3,680	3.2	1,540	1.3	6,455	5.7	12,651	11.1	99,195	86.9	2,256	2.0
CO FEMALE	506	.9	1,669	3.1	729	1.3	2,962	5.4	5,866	10.8	48,055	88.3	511	.9
CO MALE	470	.8	2,011	3.4	811	1.4	3,493	5.9	6,785	11.4	51,140	85.7	1,745	2.9
CONNECTICUT														
ALBERTUS MAGNUS COLLEGE														
CT TOTAL	0	.0	29	7.1	8	2.0	9	2.2	46	11.2	354	86.6	9	2.2
CT FEMALE	0	.0	29	7.1	8	2.0	9	2.2	46	11.3	353	86.5	9	2.2
CT MALE	0	.0	0	.0	0	.0	0	.0	0	.0	1	100.0	0	.0
ANNHURST COLLEGE														
CT TOTAL	0	.0	12	3.8	1	.3	5	1.6	18	5.6	288	90.3	13	4.1
CT FEMALE	0	.0	9	3.8	0	.0	2	.8	11	4.6	220	91.7	9	3.8
CT MALE	0	.0	3	3.8	1	1.3	3	3.8	7	8.9	68	86.1	4	5.11
ASNUNTUCK CMTY COLLEGE														
CT TOTAL	2	.2	61	6.4	4	.4	7	.7	74	7.7	884	92.2	1	.1
CT FEMALE	2	.4	5	.9	3	.6	2	.4	12	2.2	521	97.6	1	.2
CT MALE	0	.0	56	13.2	1	.2	5	1.2	62	14.6	363	85.4	0	.0
BAIS BINYOMIN ACADEMY														
CT TOTAL	0	.0	0	.0	0	.0	0	.0	0	.0	43	100.0	0	.0
CT FEMALE	0	.0	0	.0	0	.0	0	.0	0	.0	0	.0	0	.0
CT MALE	0	.0	0	.0	0	.0	0	.0	0	.0	43	100.0	0	.0
BRIDGEPORT ENGR INSTITUTE														
CT TOTAL	0	.0	15	3.3	5	1.1	0	.0	20	4.4	429	94.3	6	1.3
CT FEMALE	0	.0	2	9.5	0	.0	0	.0	2	9.5	19	90.5	0	.0
CT MALE	0	.0	13	3.0	5	1.2	0	.0	18	4.1	410	94.5	6	1.4
CENTRAL CONN ST COLLEGE														
CT TOTAL	15	.2	194	2.1	48	.5	80	.9	337	3.6	9,000	96.4	0	.0
CT FEMALE	8	.2	101	2.4	17	.4	45	1.1	171	4.1	3,992	95.9	0	.0
CT MALE	7	.1	93	1.8	31	.6	35	.7	166	3.2	5,008	96.8	0	.0
CONNECTICUT COLLEGE														
CT TOTAL	2	.1	54	3.1	5	.3	14	.8	75	4.3	1,633	93.5	38	2.2
CT FEMALE	2	.2	34	3.2	3	.3	9	.8	48	4.5	987	92.8	29	2.7
CT MALE	0	.0	20	2.9	2	.3	5	.7	27	4.0	646	94.7	9	1.3
EASTERN CONN ST COLLEGE														
CT TOTAL	22	.8	76	2.9	9	.3	26	1.0	133	5.1	2,467	94.9	0	.0
CT FEMALE	14	1.0	39	2.7	4	.3	13	.9	70	4.9	1,371	95.1	0	.0
CT MALE	8	.7	37	3.2	5	.4	13	1.1	63	5.4	1,096	94.6	0	.0
FAIRFIELD UNIVERSITY														
CT TOTAL	0	.0	55	1.5	4	.1	42	1.2	101	2.8	3,518	97.0	9	.2
CT FEMALE	0	.0	33	1.7	2	.1	20	1.1	55	2.9	1,829	96.9	4	.2
CT MALE	0	.0	22	1.3	2	.1	22	1.3	46	2.6	1,689	97.1	5	.3

18

AN VE	BLACK NON-HISPANIC		ASIAN OR PACIFIC ISLANDER		HISPANIC		TOTAL MINORITY		WHITE NON-HISPANIC		NON-RESIDENT ALIEN		TOTAL
	NUMBER	%	NUMBER	%	NUMBER	%	NUMBER	%	NUMBER	%	NUMBER	%	NUMBER
TINUED													
	862	28.5	10	.3	267	8.8	1,161	38.4	1,847	61.1	16	.5	3,024
	580	27.8	3	.1	198	9.5	799	38.3	1,278	61.3	7	.3	2,084
	282	30.0	7	.7	69	7.3	362	38.5	569	60.5	9	1.0	940
	16	8.2	2	1.0	3	1.5	21	10.8	165	85.1		4.1	194
	16	8.2	2	1.0	3	1.5	21	10.8	165	85.1	8	4.1	194
	0	.0	0	.0	0	.0	0	.0	0	.0	8	.0	0
	84	6.8	22	1.8	26	2.1	132	10.7	1,090	88.0	1	1.3	1,238
	11	8.7	3	2.4	5	4.0	19	15.1	107	84.9		.0	126
	73	6.6	19	1.7	21	1.9	113	10.2	983	88.4	18	1.4	1,112
	0	.0	0	.0	0	.0	0	.0	40	95.2	2	4.8	42
	0	.0	0	.0	0	.0	0	.0	8	100.0	0	.0	8
	0	.0	0	.0	0	.0	0	.0	32	94.1	2	5.9	34
	364	20.2	5	.3	141	7.8	510	28.3	1,281	71.1	11	.6	1,802
	224	22.9	4	.4	86	8.8	314	32.0	666	68.0	0	.0	980
	140	17.0	1	.1	55	6.7	196	23.8	615	74.8	11	1.3	822
	150	3.3	26	.6	47	1.0	233	5.2	4,243	94.5	14	.3	4,490
	76	2.9	14	.5	26	1.0	121	4.6	2,485	95.1	6	.2	2,612
	74	3.9	12	.6	21	1.1	112	6.0	1,758	93.6	8	.4	1,878
	223	6.6	9	.3	53	1.6	289	8.6	3,066	91.3	5	.1	3,360
	151	6.7	6	.3	29	1.3	187	8.2	2,081	91.7	2	.1	2,270
	72	6.6	3	.3	24	2.2	102	9.4	985	90.4	3	.3	1,090
	70	4.0	5	.3	26	1.5	111	6.4	1,637	93.6	0	.0	1,748
	27	2.7	4	.4	15	1.5	52	5.3	932	94.7	0	.0	984
	43	5.6	1	.1	11	1.4	59	7.7	705	92.3	0	.0	764
	45	5.7	8	1.0	14	1.8	72	9.2	651	83.0	61	7.8	784
	23	6.5	4	1.1	7	2.0	35	9.9	312	87.9	8	2.3	355
	22	5.1	4	.9	7	1.6	37	8.6	339	79.0	53	12.4	429
	110	5.3	20	1.0	24	1.1	164	7.9	1,920	92.0	3	.1	2,087
	68	5.3	13	1.0	14	1.1	101	7.9	1,179	92.1	0	.0	1,280
	42	5.2	7	.9	10	1.2	63	7.8	741	91.8	3	.4	807
	0	.0	0	.0	0	.0	0	.0	19	100.0	0	.0	19
	0	.0	0	.0	0	.0	0	.0	19	100.0	0	.0	19
	0	.0	0	.0	0	.0	0	.0	0	.0	0	.0	0
	13	.5	11	.4	5	.2	35	1.4	2,467	98.5	2	.1	2,504
	7	.4	4	.2	2	.1	17	1.0	1,645	99.0	0	.0	1,662
	6	.7	7	.8	3	.4	18	2.1	822	97.5	2	.2	842
	274	12.8	19	.9	67	3.1	362	17.0	1,749	81.9	24	1.1	2,135
	176	14.3	11	.9	43	3.5	231	18.8	988	80.4	10	.8	1,229
	98	10.8	8	.9	24	2.6	131	14.5	761	84.0	14	1.5	906
	161	9.6	24	1.4	95	5.6	282	16.8	1,401	83.2		.0	1,683
	34	11.2	6	2.0	17	5.6	57	18.8	247	81.3		.0	304
	127	9.2	18	1.3	78	5.7	225	16.3	1,154	83.7	8	.0	1,379
	94	6.5	2	.1	37	2.6	137	9.5	1,309	90.5		.0	1,446
	53	6.1	0	.0	13	1.5	69	8.0	797	92.0		.0	866
	41	7.1	2	.3	24	4.1	68	11.7	512	88.3	8	.0	580
	3	.6	11	2.2	2	.4	27	5.3	482	94.7		.0	509
	2	.7	1	.3	2	.7	13	4.5	277	95.5		.0	290
	1	.5	10	4.6	0	.0	14	6.4	205	93.6	8	.0	219
	70	2.0	4	.1	22	.6	96	2.8	3,365	97.0	7	.2	3,468
	44	2.1	4	.2	13	.6	61	2.9	2,049	96.9	4	.2	2,114
	26	1.9	0	.0	9	.7	35	2.6	1,316	97.2	3	.2	1,354
	151	5.6	16	.6	124	4.6	291	10.8	2,383	88.7	13	.5	2,687
	99	6.1	13	.8	69	4.3	181	11.2	1,425	88.3	8	.5	1,614
	52	4.8	3	.3	55	5.1	110	10.3	958	89.3	5	.5	1,073
	0	.0	3	7.5	13	32.5	16	40.0	23	57.5	1	2.5	40
	0	.0	0	.0	0	.0	0	.0	0	.0	0	.0	0
	0	.0	3	7.5	13	32.5	16	40.0	23	57.5	1	2.5	40
	0	.0	0	.0	0	.0	0	.0	10	100.0	0	.0	10
	0	.0	0	.0	0	.0	0	.0	0	.0	0	.0	0
	0	.0	0	.0	0	.0	0	.0	10	100.0	0	.0	10
	15	2.0	2	.3	7	.9	24	3.1	739	96.7	1	.1	764
	15	2.0	2	.3	7	.9	24	3.2	735	96.7	1	.1	760
	0	.0	0	.0	0	.0	0	.0	4	100.0	0	.0	4
	0	.0	1	3.7	0	.0	1	3.7	25	92.6	1	3.7	27
	0	.0	0	.0	0	.0	0	.0	0	.0	0	.0	0
	0	.0	1	3.7	0	.0	1	3.7	25	92.6	1	3.7	27
	642	31.9	9	.4	77	3.8	732	36.4	1,261	62.7	17	.8	2,010
	437	34.3	3	.2	50	3.9	493	38.7	777	60.9	5	.4	1,275
	205	27.9	6	.8	27	3.7	239	32.5	484	65.9	12	1.6	735

TABLE 1 - TOTAL UNDERGRADUATE ENROLLMENT IN INSTITUTIONS OF HIGHER EDUCATION BY RACE, ETHNICITY AND SEX: INSTITUTION, STATE AND NATION, 1978

	AMERICAN INDIAN ALASKAN NATIVE		BLACK NON-HISPANIC		ASIAN OR PACIFIC ISLANDER		HISPANIC		TOTAL MINORITY		WHITE NON-HISPANIC		NON-RESIDENT ALIEN	
	NUMBER	%	NUMBER	%	NUMBER	%	NUMBER	%	NUMBER	%	NUMBER	%	NUMBER	%
CONNECTICUT CONTINUED														
SOUTHERN CONN ST COLLEGE														
CT TOTAL	5	.1	165	2.5	17	.3	45	.7	232	3.5	6,374	96.3	13	.2
CT FEMALE	4	.1	109	2.6	4	.1	25	.6	142	3.4	4,049	96.5	7	.2
CT MALE	1	.0	56	2.3	13	.5	20	.8	90	3.7	2,325	96.0	6	.2
THAMES VLY STATE TECH C														
CT TOTAL	0	.0	46	2.5	17	.9	44	2.4	107	5.7	1,756	94.3	0	.0
CT FEMALE	0	.0	8	1.9	5	1.2	11	2.7	24	5.8	388	94.2	0	.0
CT MALE	0	.0	38	2.6	12	.8	33	2.3	83	5.7	1,368	94.3	0	.0
TRINITY COLLEGE														
CT TOTAL	2	.1	55	3.1	10	.6	16	.9	83	4.7	1,656	93.8	27	1.5
CT FEMALE	2	.3	30	3.8	6	.8	5	.6	43	5.4	739	93.5	8	1.0
CT MALE	0	.0	25	2.6	4	.4	11	1.1	40	4.1	917	94.0	19	1.9
TUNXIS COMMUNITY COLLEGE														
CT TOTAL	1	.0	49	1.7	11	.4	27	.9	88	3.0	2,838	96.6	11	.4
CT FEMALE	0	.0	22	1.3	4	.2	12	.7	38	2.2	1,671	97.4	6	.3
CT MALE	1	.1	27	2.2	7	.6	15	1.2	50	4.1	1,167	95.5	5	.4
UNIVERSITY OF BRIDGEPORT														
CT TOTAL	2	.0	177	3.4	6	.1	39	.8	224	4.3	4,716	91.5	212	4.1
CT FEMALE	1	.0	128	4.2	4	.1	20	.7	153	5.0	2,821	93.1	56	1.8
CT MALE	1	.0	49	2.3	2	.1	19	.9	71	3.3	1,895	89.3	156	7.4
UNIVERSITY OF CONNECTICUT														
CT TOTAL	15	.1	509	3.5	106	.7	156	1.1	786	5.4	13,740	94.5	21	.1
CT FEMALE	4	.1	267	3.9	52	.8	70	1.0	393	5.7	6,467	94.2	3	.0
CT MALE	11	.1	242	3.1	54	.7	86	1.1	393	5.1	7,273	94.7	18	.2
UNIVERSITY OF HARTFORD														
CT TOTAL	11	.2	279	4.1	45	.7	58	.8	393	5.7	6,494	94.3	0	.0
CT FEMALE	5	.2	153	4.7	23	.7	26	.8	207	6.3	3,072	93.7	0	.0
CT MALE	6	.2	126	3.5	22	.6	32	.9	186	5.2	3,422	94.8	0	.0
UNIVERSITY OF NEW HAVEN														
CT TOTAL	0	.0	632	12.1	44	.8	106	2.0	782	15.0	4,323	82.7	120	2.3
CT FEMALE	0	.0	197	13.6	14	1.0	34	2.3	245	16.9	1,186	81.7	20	1.4
CT MALE	0	.0	435	11.5	30	.8	72	1.9	537	14.2	3,137	83.1	100	2.6
WATERBURY ST TECH COLLEGE														
CT TOTAL	1	.1	22	1.7	8	.6	13	1.0	44	3.4	1,253	96.4	3	.2
CT FEMALE	0	.0	7	2.7	1	.4	0	.0	8	3.1	251	96.9	0	.0
CT MALE	1	.1	15	1.4	7	.7	13	1.2	36	3.5	1,002	96.3	3	.3
WESLEYAN UNIVERSITY														
CT TOTAL	3	.1	150	6.0	32	1.3	52	2.1	237	9.5	2,237	89.4	29	1.2
CT FEMALE	1	.1	80	6.9	18	1.6	26	2.2	125	10.8	1,022	88.0	14	1.2
CT MALE	2	.1	70	5.2	14	1.0	26	1.9	112	8.3	1,215	90.5	15	1.1
WESTERN CONN ST COLLEGE														
CT TOTAL	54	1.5	97	2.7	6	.2	45	1.3	202	5.7	3,239	91.6	95	2.7
CT FEMALE	27	1.3	54	2.7	2	.1	28	1.4	111	5.5	1,845	91.7	56	2.8
CT MALE	27	1.8	43	2.8	4	.3	17	1.1	91	6.0	1,394	91.5	39	2.6
YALE UNIVERSITY														
CT TOTAL	8	.2	283	5.4	272	5.2	179	3.4	742	14.2	4,240	81.1	249	4.8
CT FEMALE	2	.1	134	6.6	131	6.5	61	3.0	328	16.2	1,626	80.2	74	3.6
CT MALE	6	.2	149	4.7	141	4.4	118	3.7	414	12.9	2,614	81.6	175	5.5
CONNECTICUT TOTAL (44 INSTITUTIONS)														
CT TOTAL	233	.2	6,307	5.6	867	.8	2,013	1.8	9,420	8.3	102,655	90.7	1,058	.9
CT FEMALE	128	.2	3,484	6.0	398	.7	1,017	1.8	5,027	8.7	52,601	90.7	355	.6
CT MALE	105	.2	2,823	5.1	469	.9	996	1.8	4,393	8.0	50,054	90.8	703	1.3
DELAWARE														
BRANDYWINE COLLEGE														
DE TOTAL	0	.0	78	7.0	0	.0	1	.1	79	7.1	1,037	92.6	4	.4
DE FEMALE	0	.0	60	8.9	0	.0	0	.0	60	8.9	613	90.9	1	.1
DE MALE	0	.0	18	4.0	0	.0	1	.2	19	4.3	424	95.1	3	.7
DELAWARE STATE COLLEGE														
DE TOTAL	0	.0	1,177	72.3	0	.0	0	.0	1,177	72.3	421	25.9	30	1.8
DE FEMALE	0	.0	602	74.3	0	.0	0	.0	602	74.3	192	23.7	16	2.0
DE MALE	0	.0	575	70.3	0	.0	0	.0	575	70.3	229	28.0	14	1.7
DEL TECH & CC STHN CAM														
DE TOTAL	1	.1	229	18.2	5	.4	4	.3	239	19.0	1,019	81.0	0	.0
DE FEMALE	1	.1	156	20.7	3	.4	2	.3	162	21.5	592	78.5	0	.0
DE MALE	0	.0	73	14.5	2	.4	2	.4	77	15.3	427	84.7	0	.0
DEL TECH & CC STANTON CAM														
DE TOTAL	7	.3	206	9.6	9	.4	5	.2	227	10.5	1,929	89.4	1	.0
DE FEMALE	4	.4	106	11.8	2	.2	3	.3	115	12.8	785	87.1	1	.1
DE MALE	3	.2	100	8.0	7	.6	2	.2	112	8.9	1,144	91.1	0	.0
DEL TECH & CC TERRY CAM														
DE TOTAL	5	.5	180	17.0	9	.9	11	1.0	205	19.4	852	80.6	0	.0
DE FEMALE	3	.5	98	17.5	4	.7	3	.5	108	19.3	451	80.7	0	.0
DE MALE	2	.4	82	16.5	5	1.0	8	1.6	97	19.5	401	80.5	0	.0
DEL TECH & CC WILMINGTON														
DE TOTAL	0	.0	425	40.4	16	1.5	53	5.0	494	47.0	551	52.4	6	.6
DE FEMALE	0	.0	277	41.3	7	1.0	33	4.9	317	47.3	349	52.1	4	.6
DE MALE	0	.0	148	38.8	9	2.4	20	5.2	177	46.5	202	53.0	2	.5
GOLDEY BEACOM COLLEGE														
DE TOTAL	1	.1	114	9.0	1	.1	6	.5	122	9.7	1,141	90.3	0	.0
DE FEMALE	1	.1	83	9.4	1	.1	6	.7	91	10.3	794	89.7	0	.0
DE MALE	0	.0	31	8.2	0	.0	0	.0	31	8.2	347	91.8	0	.0
UNIVERSITY OF DELAWARE														
DE TOTAL	16	.1	439	3.2	51	.4	48	.4	554	4.1	12,794	94.4	206	1.5
DE FEMALE	6	.1	253	3.5	30	.4	22	.3	311	4.3	6,806	94.6	81	1.1
DE MALE	10	.2	186	2.9	21	.3	26	.4	243	3.8	5,988	94.2	125	2.0
WESLEY COLLEGE														
DE TOTAL	1	.1	56	7.7	1	.1	1	.1	59	8.1	663	91.3	4	.6
DE FEMALE	0	.0	24	5.8	0	.0	1	.2	25	6.0	389	93.7	1	.2
DE MALE	1	.3	32	10.3	1	.3	0	.0	34	10.9	274	88.1	3	1.0

	AMERICAN INDIAN ALASKAN NATIVE		BLACK NON-HISPANIC		ASIAN OR PACIFIC ISLANDER		HISPANIC		TOTAL MINORITY		WHITE NON-HISPANIC		NON-RESIDENT ALIEN		TOTAL
	NUMBER	%	NUMBER	%	NUMBER	%	NUMBER	%	NUMBER	%	NUMBER	%	NUMBER	%	NUMBER
DELAWARE CONTINUED															
WILMINGTON COLLEGE															
DE TOTAL	2	.3	160	24.5	2	.3	18	2.8	182	27.9	464	71.2	6	.9	652
DE FEMALE	0	.0	86	29.6	2	.7	14	4.8	102	35.1	189	64.9	0	.0	291
DE MALE	2	.6	74	20.5	0	.0	4	1.1	80	22.2	275	76.2	6	1.7	361
DELAWARE TOTAL (10 INSTITUTIONS)															
DE TOTAL	33	.1	3,064	12.5	94	.4	147	.6	3,338	13.6	20,871	85.3	257	1.1	24,466
DE FEMALE	15	.1	1,745	13.3	49	.4	84	.6	1,893	14.4	11,160	84.8	104	.8	13,157
DE MALE	18	.2	1,319	11.7	45	.4	63	.6	1,445	12.8	9,711	85.9	153	1.4	11,309
DISTRICT OF COLUMBIA															
AMERICAN UNIVERSITY															
DC TOTAL	6	.1	732	13.4	67	1.2	66	1.2	871	15.9	4,050	74.0	554	10.1	5,475
DC FEMALE	3	.1	425	15.2	30	1.1	44	1.6	502	18.0	2,095	75.0	196	7.0	2,793
DC MALE	3	.1	307	11.4	37	1.4	22	.8	369	13.8	1,955	72.9	358	13.3	2,682
CAMPUS-FREE COLLEGE															
DC TOTAL	2	2.6	20	25.6	0	.0	2	2.6	24	30.8	49	62.8	5	6.4	78
DC FEMALE	1	3.0	1	3.0	0	.0	0	.0	2	6.1	31	93.9	0	.0	33
DC MALE	1	2.2	19	42.2	0	.0	2	4.4	22	48.9	18	40.0	5	11.1	45
CATHOLIC U OF AMERICA															
DC TOTAL	4	.2	146	5.5	34	1.3	45	1.7	229	8.7	2,186	82.9	221	9.4	2,636
DC FEMALE	1	.1	83	6.3	12	.9	21	1.6	117	8.9	1,122	85.6	72	5.5	1,311
DC MALE	3	.2	63	4.8	22	1.7	24	1.8	112	8.5	1,064	80.3	149	11.2	1,325
GALLAUDET COLLEGE															
DC TOTAL	7	.7	53	5.5	5	.5	16	1.7	81	8.4	767	79.4	118	12.2	966
DC FEMALE	3	.6	31	6.0	2	.4	6	1.2	42	8.1	423	81.7	53	13.2	518
DC MALE	4	.9	22	4.9	3	.7	10	2.2	39	8.7	344	76.8	65	14.5	448
GEORGETOWN UNIVERSITY															
DC TOTAL	9	.2	219	4.1	87	1.6	166	3.1	481	9.1	4,590	86.8	217	4.1	5,288
DC FEMALE	5	.2	128	4.5	50	1.8	68	2.4	251	8.9	2,463	87.1	115	4.1	2,829
DC MALE	4	.2	91	3.7	37	1.5	98	4.0	230	9.4	2,127	86.5	102	4.1	2,459
GEORGE WASH UNIVERSITY															
DC TOTAL	19	.3	492	7.6	165	2.6	168	2.6	844	13.1	4,681	72.5	932	14.4	6,457
DC FEMALE	10	.3	330	10.9	77	2.5	78	2.6	495	16.3	2,259	74.4	281	9.3	3,035
DC MALE	9	.3	162	4.7	88	2.6	90	2.6	349	10.2	2,422	70.8	651	19.0	3,422
HOWARD UNIVERSITY															
DC TOTAL	11	.2	5,790	84.3	18	.3	22	.3	5,841	85.0	97	1.4	931	13.6	6,869
DC FEMALE	8	.2	3,226	88.5	8	.2	12	.3	3,254	89.3	54	1.5	336	9.2	3,644
DC MALE	3	.1	2,564	79.5	10	.3	10	.3	2,587	80.2	43	1.3	595	18.4	3,225
MOUNT VERNON COLLEGE															
DC TOTAL	0	.0	37	7.7	2	.4	19	4.0	58	12.1	375	78.5	45	9.4	478
DC FEMALE	0	.0	37	7.7	2	.4	19	4.0	58	12.1	375	78.5	45	9.4	478
DC MALE	0	.0	0	.0	0	.0	0	.0	0	.0	0	.0	0	.0	0
SOUTHEASTERN UNIVERSITY															
DC TOTAL	3	.4	410	55.8	18	2.4	7	1.0	438	59.6	95	12.9	202	27.5	735
DC FEMALE	3	.8	237	64.6	6	1.6	1	.3	247	67.3	34	9.3	86	23.4	367
DC MALE	0	.0	173	47.0	12	3.3	6	1.6	191	51.9	61	16.6	116	31.5	368
STRAYER COLLEGE															
DC TOTAL	9	.5	1,259	73.7	10	.6	19	1.1	1,297	75.9	191	11.2	221	12.9	1,709
DC FEMALE	6	.5	866	77.7	6	.5	10	.9	888	79.6	116	10.4	111	10.0	1,115
DC MALE	3	.5	393	66.2	4	.7	9	1.5	409	68.9	75	12.6	110	18.5	594
TRINITY COLLEGE															
DC TOTAL	0	.0	44	9.6	8	1.8	21	4.6	73	16.0	380	83.2	4	.9	457
DC FEMALE	0	.0	43	9.4	8	1.8	21	4.6	72	15.8	380	83.3	4	.9	456
DC MALE	0	.0	1	100.0	0	.0	0	.0	1	100.0	0	.0	0	.0	1
UNIVERSITY OF DC															
DC TOTAL	222	1.7	10,894	84.3	531	4.1	140	1.1	11,787	91.2	549	4.2	590	4.6	12,926
DC FEMALE	37	.5	6,468	90.1	82	1.1	82	1.1	6,669	92.9	172	2.4	341	4.7	7,182
DC MALE	185	3.2	4,426	77.1	449	7.8	58	1.0	5,118	89.1	377	6.6	249	4.3	5,744
WASH INTRNATL COLLEGE															
DC TOTAL	0	.0	170	64.9	3	1.1	7	2.7	180	68.7	70	26.7	12	4.6	262
DC FEMALE	0	.0	95	79.8	0	.0	4	3.4	99	83.2	19	16.0	1	.8	119
DC MALE	0	.0	75	52.4	3	2.1	3	2.1	81	56.6	51	35.7	11	7.7	143
DISTRICT OF COLUMBIA TOTAL (13 INSTITUTIONS)															
DC TOTAL	292	.7	20,266	45.7	948	2.1	698	1.6	22,204	50.1	18,080	40.8	4,052	9.1	44,336
DC FEMALE	77	.3	11,970	50.1	283	1.2	366	1.5	12,696	53.2	9,543	40.0	1,641	6.9	23,880
DC MALE	215	1.1	8,296	40.6	665	3.3	332	1.6	9,508	46.5	8,537	41.7	2,411	11.8	20,456
FLORIDA															
BARRY COLLEGE															
FL TOTAL	5	.4	93	6.7	11	.8	212	15.2	321	23.0	975	69.7	102	7.3	1,398
FL FEMALE	3	.3	66	6.3	7	.7	169	16.2	245	23.5	721	69.1	78	7.5	1,044
FL MALE	2	.6	27	7.6	4	1.1	43	12.1	76	21.5	254	71.8	24	6.8	354
BETHUNE COOKMAN COLLEGE															
FL TOTAL	0	.0	1,698	95.4	2	.1	3	.2	1,703	95.7	16	.9	60	3.4	1,779
FL FEMALE	0	.0	991	95.6	0	.0	0	.0	991	95.6	7	.7	39	3.8	1,037
FL MALE	0	.0	707	95.3	2	.3	3	.4	712	96.0	9	1.2	21	2.8	742
BISCAYNE COLLEGE															
FL TOTAL	0	.0	110	5.5	6	.3	1,030	51.4	1,146	57.2	781	39.0	75	3.7	2,002
FL FEMALE	0	.0	56	6.7	3	.4	578	68.8	637	75.8	189	22.5	14	1.7	840
FL MALE	0	.0	54	4.6	3	.3	452	38.9	509	43.8	592	50.9	61	5.2	1,162
BREVARD CMTY COLLEGE															
FL TOTAL	34	.4	710	7.8	68	.7	141	1.5	953	10.5	7,943	87.2	218	2.4	9,114
FL FEMALE	20	.4	408	8.7	41	.9	61	1.3	530	11.3	4,072	87.0	78	1.7	4,680
FL MALE	14	.3	302	6.8	27	.6	80	1.8	423	9.5	3,871	87.3	140	3.2	4,434
BROWARD CMTY COLLEGE															
FL TOTAL	46	.3	956	6.4	22	.1	311	2.1	1,335	8.9	13,053	87.1	600	4.0	14,988
FL FEMALE	27	.3	632	7.6	8	.1	157	1.9	824	9.9	7,175	86.5	295	3.6	8,294
FL MALE	19	.3	324	4.8	14	.2	154	2.3	511	7.6	5,878	87.8	305	4.6	6,694

21

	AMERICAN INDIAN ALASKAN NATIVE		BLACK NON-HISPANIC		ASIAN OR PACIFIC ISLANDER		HISPANIC		TOTAL MINORITY		WHITE NON-HISPANIC		NON-RESIDENT ALIEN	
	NUMBER	%	NUMBER	%	NUMBER	%	NUMBER	%	NUMBER	%	NUMBER	%	NUMBER	%
FLORIDA CONTINUED														
CENTRAL FLA CMTY COLLEGE														
FL TOTAL	2	.1	388	17.2	6	.3	25	1.1	421	18.7	1,793	79.5	40	1.8
FL FEMALE	2	.2	270	21.1	4	.3	14	1.1	290	22.7	976	76.4	11	.9
FL MALE	0	.0	118	12.1	2	.2	11	1.1	131	13.4	817	83.6	29	3.0
CHIPOLA JUNIOR COLLEGE														
FL TOTAL	7	.7	194	19.0	1	.1	4	.4	206	20.2	815	79.7	1	.1
FL FEMALE	2	.4	113	20.5	0	.0	3	.5	118	21.5	431	78.4	1	.2
FL MALE	5	1.1	81	17.2	1	.2	1	.2	88	18.6	384	81.4	0	.0
CLEARWATER CHRISTIAN C														
FL TOTAL	0	.0	2	1.2	0	.0	4	2.3	6	3.5	160	92.5	7	4.0
FL FEMALE	0	.0	0	.0	0	.0	3	3.4	3	3.4	81	93.1	3	3.4
FL MALE	0	.0	2	2.3	0	.0	1	1.2	3	3.5	79	91.9	4	4.7
COLLEGE OF BOCA RATON														
FL TOTAL	0	.0	15	3.4	0	.0	21	4.7	36	8.1	374	84.4	33	7.4
FL FEMALE	0	.0	5	1.9	0	.0	10	3.7	15	5.6	242	90.6	10	3.7
FL MALE	0	.0	10	5.7	0	.0	11	6.3	21	11.9	132	75.0	23	13.1
DAYTONA BCH CMTY COLLEGE														
FL TOTAL	4	.1	523	13.3	14	.4	34	.9	575	14.6	3,322	84.2	50	1.3
FL FEMALE	2	.1	331	15.2	8	.4	20	.9	361	16.6	1,806	82.9	11	.5
FL MALE	2	.1	192	10.9	6	.3	14	.8	214	12.1	1,516	85.7	39	2.2
ECKERD COLLEGE														
FL TOTAL	1	.1	50	5.8	2	.2	34	3.9	87	10.0	713	82.3	66	7.6
FL FEMALE	0	.0	36	9.8	2	.5	15	4.1	53	14.5	292	79.8	21	5.7
FL MALE	1	.2	14	2.8	0	.0	19	3.8	34	6.8	421	84.2	45	9.0
EDISON COMMUNITY COLLEGE														
FL TOTAL	33	1.1	138	4.7	12	.4	50	1.7	233	8.0	2,679	91.9	2	.1
FL FEMALE	27	1.5	95	5.4	5	.3	26	1.5	153	8.7	1,614	91.3	0	.0
FL MALE	6	.5	43	3.7	7	.6	24	2.1	80	7.0	1,065	92.9	2	.2
EDWARD WATERS COLLEGE														
FL TOTAL	0	.0	610	95.3	0	.0	0	.0	610	95.3	5	.8	25	3.9
FL FEMALE	0	.0	380	96.7	0	.0	0	.0	380	96.7	2	.5	11	2.8
FL MALE	0	.0	230	93.1	0	.0	0	.0	230	93.1	3	1.2	14	5.7
EMBRY-RIDDLE AERON U														
FL TOTAL	24	.4	182	3.2	65	1.2	63	1.1	334	5.9	5,044	89.4	262	4.6
FL FEMALE	0	.0	9	4.9	0	.0	2	1.1	11	6.0	170	93.4	1	.6
FL MALE	24	.4	173	3.2	65	1.2	61	1.1	323	5.9	4,874	89.3	261	4.8
FLAGLER COLLEGE														
FL TOTAL	0	.0	14	2.0	1	.1	1	.1	16	2.3	689	96.9	6	.8
FL FEMALE	0	.0	6	1.5	0	.0	1	.3	7	1.8	390	97.7	2	.5
FL MALE	0	.0	8	2.6	1	.3	0	.0	9	2.9	299	95.8	4	1.3
FLORIDA BEACON COLLEGE														
FL TOTAL	0	.0	11	18.6	0	.0	2	3.4	13	22.0	38	64.4	8	13.6
FL FEMALE	0	.0	1	5.0	0	.0	1	5.0	2	10.0	17	85.0	1	5.0
FL MALE	0	.0	10	25.6	0	.0	1	2.6	11	28.2	21	53.8	7	17.9
FLORIDA COLLEGE														
FL TOTAL	0	.0	11	2.1	0	.0	6	1.2	17	3.3	493	95.9	4	.8
FL FEMALE	0	.0	1	.4	0	.0	1	.4	2	.8	257	98.1	3	1.1
FL MALE	0	.0	10	4.0	0	.0	5	2.0	15	6.0	236	93.7	1	.4
FLORIDA INST TECHNOLOGY														
FL TOTAL	1	.0	63	2.1	4	.1	49	1.6	117	3.9	2,527	83.8	372	12.3
FL FEMALE	0	.0	13	2.5	1	.2	3	.6	17	3.2	467	89.0	41	7.8
FL MALE	1	.0	50	2.0	3	.1	46	1.8	100	4.0	2,060	82.7	331	13.3
FLA JR COLLEGE JACKSONVL														
FL TOTAL	29	.2	2,369	19.8	83	.7	84	.7	2,565	21.4	9,393	78.5	13	.1
FL FEMALE	12	.2	1,701	24.9	30	.4	39	.6	1,782	26.1	5,042	73.8	4	.1
FL MALE	17	.3	668	13.0	53	1.0	45	.9	783	15.2	4,351	84.6	9	.2
FLORIDA KEYS CMTY COLLEGE														
FL TOTAL	4	.4	47	5.1	11	1.2	66	7.2	128	13.9	784	85.3	7	.8
FL FEMALE	3	.7	18	4.0	3	.7	35	7.9	59	13.3	381	85.6	5	1.1
FL MALE	1	.2	29	6.1	8	1.7	31	6.5	69	14.6	403	85.0	2	.4
FLORIDA MEMORIAL COLLEGE														
FL TOTAL	0	.0	514	88.3	0	.0	3	.5	517	88.8	0	.0	65	11.2
FL FEMALE	0	.0	271	92.2	0	.0	1	.3	272	92.5	0	.0	22	7.5
FL MALE	0	.0	243	84.4	0	.0	2	.7	245	85.1	0	.0	43	14.9
FLORIDA SOUTHERN COLLEGE														
FL TOTAL	4	.2	24	1.5	1	.1	33	2.0	62	3.8	1,531	94.5	27	1.7
FL FEMALE	1	.1	8	.9	1	.1	18	2.1	28	3.3	812	95.0	15	1.8
FL MALE	3	.4	16	2.1	0	.0	15	2.0	34	4.4	719	94.0	12	1.6
FORT LAUDERDALE COLLEGE														
FL TOTAL	0	.0	244	26.5	5	.5	54	5.9	303	32.9	597	64.8	22	2.4
FL FEMALE	0	.0	50	29.1	1	.6	10	5.8	61	35.5	106	61.6	5	2.9
FL MALE	0	.0	194	25.9	4	.5	44	5.9	242	32.3	491	65.5	17	2.3
GULF COAST CMTY COLLEGE														
FL TOTAL	8	.2	346	10.7	28	.9	22	.7	404	12.5	2,806	87.0	14	.4
FL FEMALE	4	.2	180	11.1	8	.5	7	.4	199	12.3	1,422	87.6	3	.2
FL MALE	4	.3	166	10.4	20	1.3	15	.9	205	12.8	1,384	86.5	11	.7
HILLSBOROUGH CMTY COLLEGE														
FL TOTAL	10	.1	1,432	13.1	105	1.0	336	3.1	1,883	17.2	8,935	81.8	99	.9
FL FEMALE	9	.2	924	15.7	48	.8	187	3.2	1,168	19.9	4,659	79.4	42	.7
FL MALE	1	.0	508	10.1	57	1.1	149	3.0	715	14.2	4,276	84.7	57	1.1
INDIAN RIVER CMTY COLLEGE														
FL TOTAL	7	.2	408	14.3	16	.6	32	1.1	463	16.2	2,345	82.2	46	1.6
FL FEMALE	5	.3	283	17.8	11	.7	13	.8	312	19.6	1,260	79.2	18	1.1
FL MALE	2	.2	125	9.9	5	.4	19	1.5	151	11.9	1,085	85.8	28	2.2
INTERNATIONAL FINE ARTS C														
FL TOTAL	0	.0	7	3.0	3	1.3	6	2.6	16	6.9	202	87.4	13	5.6
FL FEMALE	0	.0	7	3.0	3	1.3	6	2.6	16	7.0	201	87.4	13	5.7
FL MALE	0	.0	0	.0	0	.0	0	.0	0	.0	1	100.0	0	.0
JACKSONVILLE UNIVERSITY														
FL TOTAL	4	.2	102	5.4	15	.8	87	4.6	208	10.9	1,606	84.3	91	4.5
FL FEMALE	2	.3	54	7.1	6	.8	35	4.6	97	12.7	652	85.6	13	1.7
FL MALE	2	.2	48	4.2	9	.8	52	4.5	111	9.7	954	83.5	78	6.8

	BLACK NON-HISPANIC		ASIAN OR PACIFIC ISLANDER		HISPANIC		TOTAL MINORITY		WHITE NON-HISPANIC		NON-RESIDENT ALIEN		TOTAL
'E	NUMBER	%	NUMBER	%	NUMBER	%	NUMBER	%	NUMBER	%	NUMBER	%	NUMBER
'INUED													
	253	21.3	12	1.0	15	1.3	284	23.9	888	74.9	14	1.2	1,186
	86	33.7	1	.4	4	1.6	91	35.7	162	63.5	2	.8	255
	167	17.9	11	1.2	11	1.2	193	20.7	726	78.0	12	1.3	931
	182	14.7	9	.7	27	2.2	218	17.7	1,017	82.3	0	.0	1,235
	82	31.4	0	.0	5	1.9	87	33.3	174	66.7	0	.0	261
	100	10.3	9	.9	22	2.3	131	13.4	843	86.6	0	.0	974
	506	22.3	5	.2	23	1.0	537	23.7	1,721	76.0	6	.3	2,264
	151	18.9	2	.3	7	.9	161	20.2	635	79.7	1	.1	797
	355	24.2	3	.2	16	1.1	376	25.6	1,086	74.0	5	.3	1,467
	209	15.8	3	.2	13	1.0	231	17.4	1,093	82.5	1	.1	1,325
	80	13.1	3	.5	4	.7	89	14.6	520	85.2	1	.2	610
	129	18.0	0	.0	9	1.3	142	19.9	573	80.1	0	.0	715
	64	21.3	0	.0	3	1.0	301	100.0	0	.0	0	.0	301
	32	20.5	0	.0	2	1.3	156	100.0	0	.0	0	.0	156
	32	22.1	0	.0	1	.7	145	100.0	0	.0	0	.0	145
	9	8.7	0	.0	1	1.0	10	9.7	93	90.3	0	.0	103
	1	7.7	0	.0	1	7.7	2	15.4	11	84.6	0	.0	13
	8	8.9	0	.0	0	.0	8	8.9	82	91.1	0	.0	90
	202	5.5	16	.4	12	.3	238	6.5	3,376	92.4	4	1 1	3,654
	139	7.0	9	.5	5	.3	158	8.0	1,795	90.8	20	1 2	1,977
	63	3.8	7	.4	7	.4	80	4.8	1,581	94.5	16	110	1,677
	22	7.5	2	.7	16	5.4	40	13.6	255	86.4	0		295
	2	1.9	0	.0	5	4.6	7	6.5	101	93.5	0	0	108
	20	10.7	2	1.1	11	5.9	33	17.6	154	82.4	0	10	187
	5,991	17.5	288	.8	12,306	35.9	18,660	54.5	13,775	40.2	1,807	5	34,242
	4,028	21.4	133	.7	6,617	35.2	10,824	57.6	7,416	39.5	548	2	18,788
	1,963	12.7	155	1.0	5,689	36.8	7,836	50.7	6,359	41.1	1,259	81	15,454
	19	16.8	2	1.8	6	5.3	28	24.8	81	71.7	4	3 5	113
	19	20.0	2	2.1	5	5.3	26	27.4	65	68.4	4	4 2	95
	0	.0	0	.0	1	5.6	2	11.1	16	88.9	0	10	18
	102	18.1	1	.2	0	.0	105	18.6	387	68.5	73	12.9	565
	69	21.5	1	.3	0	.0	72	22.4	236	73.5	13	4.0	321
	33	13.5	0	.0	0	.0	33	13.5	151	61.9	60	24.6	244
	94	9.8	14	1.5	63	6.6	174	18.2	753	78.6	31	3.2	958
	67	15.1	5	1.1	23	5.2	97	21.8	339	76.4	8	1 8	444
	27	5.3	9	1.8	40	7.8	77	15.0	414	80.5	23	15	514
	209	6.2	40	1.2	50	1.5	309	9.2	3,063	90.8	0	.0	3,372
	110	6.8	16	1.0	15	.9	146	9.0	1,473	91.0	0	.0	1,619
	99	5.6	24	1.4	35	2.0	163	9.3	1,590	90.7	0	.0	1,753
	35	6.3	9	1.6	12	2.2	56	10.1	374	67.4	125	22.5	555
	18	7.3	2	.8	8	3.2	28	11.3	192	77.7	27	13.9	247
	17	5.5	7	2.3	4	1.3	28	9.1	182	59.1	98	31.8	308
	736	9.5	34	.4	268	3.5	1,049	13.6	6,605	85.3	86	1.1	7,740
	495	10.9	18	.4	152	3.3	674	14.8	3,829	84.3	38	.8	4,541
	241	7.5	16	.5	116	3.6	375	11.7	2,776	86.8	48	1.5	3,199
	82	5.1	5	.3	7	.4	105	6.5	1,512	93.5	0	.0	1,617
	38	4.3	3	.3	4	.4	52	5.8	838	94.2	0	.0	890
	44	6.1	2	.3	3	.4	53	7.3	674	92.7	0	.0	727
	867	12.2	88	1.2	44	.6	1,024	14.5	6,053	85.5	6	.1	7,083
	524	14.2	32	.9	21	.6	588	15.9	3,102	84.0	2	.1	3,692
	343	10.1	56	1.7	23	.7	436	12.9	2,951	87.0	4	.1	3,391
	428	13.6	5	.2	30	1.0	469	14.9	2,662	84.6	15	.5	3,146
	320	16.9	3	.2	17	.9	345	18.3	1,543	81.6	2	.1	1,890
	108	8.6	2	.2	13	1.0	124	9.9	1,119	89.1	13	1.0	1,256
	4	.8	0	.0	1	.2	5	1.0	499	98.4	3	.6	507
	1	.4	0	.0	0	.0	1	.4	278	98.9	2	.7	281
	3	1.3	0	.0	1	.4	4	1.8	221	97.9	1	.4	226
	147	4.4	15	.5	63	1.9	231	7.0	3,087	93.0	1	.0	3,319
	85	5.4	6	.4	32	2.0	125	8.0	1,437	92.0	0	.0	1,562
	62	3.5	9	.5	31	1.8	106	6.0	1,650	93.9	1	.1	1,757
	96	8.3	3	.3	5	.4	108	9.3	1,032	89.2	17	1.5	1,157
	61	9.5	1	.2	3	.5	66	10.2	574	89.0	5	.8	645
	35	6.8	2	.4	2	.4	42	8.2	458	89.5	12	2.3	512
	0	.0	0	.0	23	37.1	23	37.1	39	62.9	0	.0	62
	0	.0	0	.0	0	.0	0	.0	0	.0	0	.0	0
	0	.0	0	.0	23	37.1	23	37.1	39	62.9	0	.0	62
	109	11.0	0	.0	50	5.0	159	16.0	697	70.1	138	13.9	994
	48	11.7	0	.0	16	3.9	64	15.6	268	65.2	79	19.2	411
	61	10.5	0	.0	34	5.8	95	16.3	429	73.6	59	10.1	583

23

TABLE 1 - TOTAL UNDERGRADUATE ENROLLMENT IN INSTITUTIONS OF HIGHER EDUCATION BY RACE, ETHNICITY AND SEX: INSTITUTION, STATE AND NATION, 1978

	AMERICAN INDIAN ALASKAN NATIVE		BLACK NON-HISPANIC		ASIAN OR PACIFIC ISLANDER		HISPANIC		TOTAL MINORITY		WHITE NON-HISPANIC		NON-RESIDENT ALIEN	
	NUMBER	%	NUMBER	%	NUMBER	%	NUMBER	%	NUMBER	%	NUMBER	%	NUMBER	%
FLORIDA	CONTINUED													
SAINT PETERSBG JR COLLEGE														
FL TOTAL	74	.5	641	4.7	78	.6	159	1.2	952	7.0	12,092	89.4	475	3.5
FL FEMALE	43	.6	449	5.9	43	.6	90	1.2	625	8.2	6,960	91.3	42	.6
FL MALE	31	.5	192	3.3	35	.6	69	1.2	327	5.5	5,132	87.1	433	7.3
SANTA FE CMTY COLLEGE														
FL TOTAL	8	.1	1,150	16.9	75	1.1	153	2.2	1,386	20.4	5,194	76.3	226	3.3
FL FEMALE	2	.1	725	19.0	43	1.1	73	1.9	843	22.1	2,888	75.9	76	2.0
FL MALE	6	.2	425	14.2	32	1.1	80	2.7	543	18.1	2,306	76.9	150	5.0
SEMINOLE CMTY COLLEGE														
FL TOTAL	21	.6	318	8.7	38	1.0	73	2.0	450	12.2	3,217	87.5	9	.2
FL FEMALE	8	.4	194	10.9	15	.8	34	1.9	251	14.1	1,534	85.9	0	.0
FL MALE	13	.7	124	6.6	23	1.2	39	2.1	199	10.5	1,683	89.0	9	.5
STHESTN C ASSEMBLIES GOD														
FL TOTAL	6	.5	14	1.2	0	.0	32	2.7	52	4.4	1,121	94.8	10	.8
FL FEMALE	1	.2	3	.6	0	.0	19	3.9	23	4.8	456	94.4	4	.8
FL MALE	5	.7	11	1.6	0	.0	13	1.9	29	4.1	665	95.0	6	.9
SOUTH FLORIDA JR COLLEGE														
FL TOTAL	2	.3	55	7.9	1	.1	13	1.9	71	10.1	629	89.9	0	.0
FL FEMALE	0	.0	26	7.6	0	.0	5	1.5	31	9.1	310	90.9	0	.0
FL MALE	2	.6	29	8.1	1	.3	8	2.2	40	11.1	319	88.9	0	.0
FLA AGRICULTURAL & MECH U														
FL TOTAL	1	.0	4,411	90.5	2	.0	8	.2	4,422	90.7	311	6.4	140	2.9
FL FEMALE	0	.0	2,267	94.5	1	.0	2	.1	2,270	94.6	98	4.1	31	1.3
FL MALE	1	.0	2,144	86.7	1	.0	6	.2	2,152	87.0	213	8.6	109	4.4
FLA ATLANTIC UNIVERSITY														
FL TOTAL	9	.2	264	5.6	32	.7	195	4.1	500	10.6	4,093	86.9	116	2.5
FL FEMALE	3	.1	177	7.6	13	.6	89	3.8	282	12.1	2,012	86.4	34	1.5
FL MALE	6	.3	87	3.7	19	.8	106	4.5	218	9.2	2,081	87.4	82	3.4
FLORIDA INTERNATIONAL U														
FL TOTAL	5	.1	618	9.3	150	2.3	1,952	29.3	2,725	41.0	3,690	55.5	239	3.6
FL FEMALE	2	.1	340	10.8	42	1.3	939	29.7	1,323	41.9	1,735	55.0	99	3.1
FL MALE	1	.1	278	7.9	108	3.1	1,013	29.0	1,402	40.1	1,955	55.9	140	4.0
FLORIDA STATE UNIVERSITY														
FL TOTAL	14	.1	1,511	9.8	34	.2	247	1.6	1,806	11.7	13,481	87.6	106	.7
FL FEMALE	7	.1	980	12.0	20	.2	114	1.4	1,121	13.7	7,042	85.9	34	.4
FL MALE	7	.1	531	7.4	14	.2	133	1.8	685	9.5	6,439	89.5	72	1.0
FLORIDA TECHNOLOGICAL U														
FL TOTAL	7	.1	255	3.2	87	1.1	354	4.4	703	8.7	7,279	90.6	53	.7
FL FEMALE	0	.0	113	3.5	22	.7	118	3.6	253	7.8	3,001	92.0	9	.3
FL MALE	7	.1	142	3.0	65	1.4	236	4.9	450	9.4	4,278	89.6	44	.9
UNIVERSITY OF FLORIDA														
FL TOTAL	18	.1	1,222	5.2	213	.9	905	3.9	2,358	10.1	20,747	88.8	263	1.1
FL FEMALE	8	.1	701	7.1	77	.8	302	3.1	1,088	11.0	8,714	88.4	60	.6
FL MALE	10	.1	521	3.9	136	1.0	603	4.5	1,270	9.4	12,033	89.1	203	1.5
U OF NORTH FLORIDA														
FL TOTAL	5	.2	182	7.8	12	.5	23	1.0	222	9.5	2,104	90.3	5	.2
FL FEMALE	3	.3	106	9.1	4	.3	13	1.1	126	10.9	1,032	89.0	1	.1
FL MALE	2	.2	76	6.5	8	.7	10	.9	96	8.2	1,072	91.5	4	.3
U OF SOUTH FLORIDA														
FL TOTAL	20	.1	823	4.8	61	.4	700	4.1	1,604	9.4	15,342	90.0	95	.6
FL FEMALE	8	.1	519	6.4	31	.4	322	3.9	880	10.8	7,249	88.8	30	.4
FL MALE	12	.1	304	3.4	30	.3	378	4.3	724	8.2	8,093	91.1	65	.7
U OF WEST FLORIDA														
FL TOTAL	11	.3	235	6.7	24	.7	57	1.6	327	9.3	3,183	90.4	12	.3
FL FEMALE	8	.5	153	8.6	13	.7	21	1.2	195	11.0	1,577	88.7	5	.3
FL MALE	3	.2	82	4.7	11	.6	36	2.1	132	7.6	1,606	92.0	7	.4
STETSON UNIVERSITY														
FL TOTAL	3	.2	48	2.6	12	.7	9	.5	72	4.0	1,704	93.8	40	2.2
FL FEMALE	1	.1	28	3.3	7	.8	5	.6	41	4.9	785	93.1	17	2.0
FL MALE	2	.2	20	2.1	5	.5	4	.4	31	3.2	919	94.5	23	2.4
TALLAHASSEE CMTY COLLEGE														
FL TOTAL	10	.3	547	18.0	56	1.8	20	.7	633	20.8	2,410	79.2	0	.0
FL FEMALE	8	.5	333	19.0	29	1.7	10	.6	380	21.7	1,371	78.3	0	.0
FL MALE	2	.2	214	16.6	27	2.1	10	.8	253	19.6	1,039	80.4	0	.0
TALMUDIC C OF FLORIDA														
FL TOTAL	0	.0	0	.0	0	.0	0	.0	0	.0	53	100.0	0	.0
FL FEMALE	0	.0	0	.0	0	.0	0	.0	0	.0	0	.0	0	.0
FL MALE	0	.0	0	.0	0	.0	0	.0	0	.0	53	100.0	0	.0
TAMPA COLLEGE														
FL TOTAL	0	.0	74	8.7	3	.4	18	2.1	95	11.2	754	88.6	2	.2
FL FEMALE	0	.0	33	16.8	1	.5	10	5.1	44	22.4	152	77.6	0	.0
FL MALE	0	.0	41	6.3	2	.3	8	1.2	51	7.8	602	91.9	2	.3
UNIVERSITY OF MIAMI														
FL TOTAL	38	.4	684	7.2	219	2.3	1,784	18.8	2,725	28.7	6,757	71.2	4	.0
FL FEMALE	12	.3	381	9.4	57	1.4	814	20.1	1,264	31.2	2,781	68.7	1	.0
FL MALE	26	.5	303	5.6	162	3.0	970	17.8	1,461	26.9	3,976	73.1	3	.1
UNIVERSITY OF TAMPA														
FL TOTAL	1	.1	66	3.8	5	.3	36	2.0	108	6.1	1,488	84.6	162	9.2
FL FEMALE	1	.1	30	4.3	0	.0	11	1.6	42	6.1	595	85.7	57	8.2
FL MALE	0	.0	36	3.4	5	.5	25	2.3	66	6.2	893	83.9	105	9.9
VALENCIA CMTY COLLEGE														
FL TOTAL	31	.4	764	9.0	74	.9	152	1.8	1,021	12.1	7,384	87.3	55	.7
FL FEMALE	16	.4	519	11.6	32	.7	69	1.5	636	14.2	3,827	85.5	11	.2
FL MALE	15	.4	245	6.1	42	1.1	83	2.1	385	9.7	3,557	89.2	44	1.1
HARNER SOUTHERN COLLEGE														
FL TOTAL	0	.0	7	2.7	0	.0	0	.0	7	2.7	245	94.2	8	3.1
FL FEMALE	0	.0	4	2.9	0	.0	0	.0	4	2.9	126	92.6	6	4.4
FL MALE	0	.0	3	2.4	0	.0	0	.0	3	2.4	119	96.0	2	1.6
WEBBER COLLEGE														
FL TOTAL	0	.0	13	12.9	0	.0	0	.0	13	12.9	82	81.2	6	5.9
FL FEMALE	0	.0	2	4.3	0	.0	0	.0	2	4.3	44	93.6	1	2.1
FL MALE	0	.0	11	20.4	0	.0	0	.0	11	20.4	38	70.4	5	9.3

TABLE 1 - TOTAL UNDERGRADUATE ENROLLMENT IN INSTITUTIONS OF HIGHER EDUCATION BY RACE, ETHNICITY AND SEX: INSTITUTION, STATE AND NATION, 1978

	AMERICAN INDIAN ALASKAN NATIVE		BLACK NON-HISPANIC		ASIAN OR PACIFIC ISLANDER		HISPANIC		TOTAL MINORITY		WHITE NON-HISPANIC		NON-RESIDENT ALIEN		TOTAL
	NUMBER	%	NUMBER	%	NUMBER	%	NUMBER	%	NUMBER	%	NUMBER	%	NUMBER	%	NUMBER
FLORIDA															
FL TOTAL	916	.3	35,529	11.8	2,208	.7	22,641	7.5	61,294	20.4	232,041	77.3	6,721	2.2	300,056
TOTAL (74 INSTITUTIONS)															
FL FEMALE	470	.3	21,448	14.4	877	.6	11,421	7.7	34,216	23.0	112,721	75.7	2,034	1.4	148,971
FL MALE	446	.3	14,081	9.3	1,331	.9	11,220	7.4	27,078	17.9	119,320	79.0	4,687	3.1	151,085
GEORGIA															
ABRAHAM BALDWIN AGRL C															
GA TOTAL	0	.0	100	5.1	1	.1	2	.1	103	5.3	1,759	90.3	85	4.4	1,947
GA FEMALE	0	.0	61	8.0	0	.0	1	.1	62	8.1	699	91.1	6	.9	767
GA MALE	0	.0	39	3.3	1	.1	1	.1	41	3.5	1,060	89.8	79	6.7	1,180
AGNES SCOTT COLLEGE															
GA TOTAL	0	.0	12	2.3	4	.8	9	1.7	25	4.8	481	91.6	19	3.6	525
GA FEMALE	0	.0	12	2.3	4	.8	9	1.7	25	4.8	481	91.6	19	3.6	525
GA MALE	0	.0	0	.0	0	.0	0	.0	0	.0	0	.0	0	.0	0
ALBANY JUNIOR COLLEGE															
GA TOTAL	2	.2	184	15.1	0	.0	3	.2	189	15.5	1,025	84.3	2	.2	1,216
GA FEMALE	1	.1	133	18.9	0	.0	2	.3	136	19.3	565	80.4	2	.3	703
GA MALE	1	.2	51	9.9	0	.0	1	.2	53	10.3	460	89.7	0	.0	513
ALBANY STATE COLLEGE															
GA TOTAL	0	.0	1,605	96.6	1	.1	0	.0	1,606	96.7	51	3.1	4	.2	1,661
GA FEMALE	0	.0	994	97.6	0	.0	0	.0	994	97.6	23	2.3	1	.1	1,018
GA MALE	0	.0	611	95.0	1	.2	0	.0	612	95.2	28	4.4	3	.5	643
ANDREW COLLEGE															
GA TOTAL	0	.0	76	23.0	0	.0	0	.0	76	23.0	221	67.0	33	10.0	330
GA FEMALE	0	.0	42	22.1	0	.0	0	.0	42	22.1	141	74.2	7	3.7	190
GA MALE	0	.0	34	24.3	0	.0	0	.0	34	24.3	80	57.1	26	19.6	140
ARMSTRONG STATE COLLEGE															
GA TOTAL	5	.2	336	11.1	16	.5	14	.5	371	12.3	2,644	87.5	8	.3	3,023
GA FEMALE	0	.0	250	14.8	10	.6	2	.1	262	15.5	1,428	84.4	2	.1	1,692
GA MALE	5	.4	86	6.5	6	.5	12	.9	109	8.2	1,216	91.4	6	.5	1,331
ATLANTA CHRISTIAN COLLEGE															
GA TOTAL	0	.0	10	5.2	0	.0	0	.0	10	5.2	178	92.2	5	2.6	193
GA FEMALE	0	.0	1	1.3	0	.0	0	.0	1	1.3	76	98.7	0	.0	77
GA MALE	0	.0	9	7.8	0	.0	0	.0	9	7.8	102	87.9	5	4.3	116
ATLANTA COLLEGE OF ART															
GA TOTAL	1	.4	39	15.2	5	1.9	1	.4	46	17.9	209	81.3	2	.8	257
GA FEMALE	0	.0	11	8.1	3	2.2	0	.0	14	10.3	121	89.0	1	.7	136
GA MALE	1	.8	28	23.1	2	1.7	1	.8	32	26.4	88	72.7	1	.8	121
ATLANTA JUNIOR COLLEGE															
GA TOTAL	1	.1	1,401	87.5	3	.2	3	.2	1,408	87.9	48	3.0	145	9.1	1,601
GA FEMALE	0	.0	715	95.7	0	.0	0	.0	715	95.7	11	1.5	21	2.8	747
GA MALE	1	.1	686	80.3	3	.4	3	.4	693	81.1	37	4.3	124	14.5	854
AUGUSTA COLLEGE															
GA TOTAL	13	.4	443	14.1	41	1.3	22	.7	519	16.5	2,614	83.0	17	.5	3,150
GA FEMALE	4	.2	284	16.5	24	1.4	9	.5	321	18.7	1,395	81.1	5	.3	1,721
GA MALE	9	.6	159	11.1	17	1.2	13	.9	198	13.9	1,219	85.3	12	.8	1,429
BAINBRIDGE JUNIOR COLLEGE															
GA TOTAL	0	.0	96	20.3	0	.0	0	.0	96	20.3	376	79.7	0	.0	472
GA FEMALE	0	.0	57	24.6	0	.0	0	.0	57	24.6	175	75.4	0	.0	232
GA MALE	0	.0	39	16.3	0	.0	0	.0	39	16.3	201	83.8	0	.0	240
BERRY COLLEGE															
GA TOTAL	0	.0	36	2.7	5	.4	9	.7	50	3.7	1,284	95.5	10	.7	1,344
GA FEMALE	0	.0	26	3.3	5	.6	4	.5	35	4.5	743	95.1	3	.4	781
GA MALE	0	.0	10	1.8	0	.0	5	.9	15	2.7	541	96.1	7	1.2	563
BRENAU COLLEGE															
GA TOTAL	1	.1	38	4.6	1	.1	0	.0	40	4.8	782	93.9	11	1.3	833
GA FEMALE	1	.2	35	5.3	1	.2	0	.0	37	5.6	612	93.3	7	1.1	656
GA MALE	0	.0	3	1.7	0	.0	0	.0	3	1.7	170	96.0	4	2.3	177
BREWTON-PARKER COLLEGE															
GA TOTAL	0	.0	162	25.9	0	.0	0	.0	162	25.9	448	71.6	16	2.6	626
GA FEMALE	0	.0	41	19.0	0	.0	0	.0	41	19.0	174	80.6	1	.5	216
GA MALE	0	.0	121	29.5	0	.0	0	.0	121	29.5	274	66.8	15	3.7	410
BRUNSWICK JUNIOR COLLEGE															
GA TOTAL	1	.1	191	17.3	5	.5	0	.0	197	17.8	910	82.2	0	.0	1,107
GA FEMALE	1	.2	139	22.7	2	.3	0	.0	142	23.2	470	76.8	0	.0	612
GA MALE	0	.0	52	10.5	3	.6	0	.0	55	11.1	440	88.9	0	.0	495
CLARK COLLEGE															
GA TOTAL	0	.0	1,806	98.6	2	.1	5	.3	1,813	99.0	1	.1	18	1.0	1,832
GA FEMALE	0	.0	1,195	99.5	0	.0	2	.2	1,197	99.7	0	.0	4	.3	1,201
GA MALE	0	.0	611	96.8	2	.3	3	.5	616	97.6	1	.2	14	2.2	631
CLAYTON JUNIOR COLLEGE															
GA TOTAL	11	.4	206	6.9	8	.3	12	.4	237	8.	2,719	91.7	9	.3	2,965
GA FEMALE	6	.4	144	8.9	3	.2	5	.3	158	9.	1,455	90.0	4	.2	1,617
GA MALE	5	.4	62	4.6	5	.4	7	.5	79	5.8	1,264	93.8	5	.4	1,348
COLUMBUS COLLEGE															
GA TOTAL	5	.1	630	16.9	31	.8	45	1.2	711	19.1	2,971	79.8	41	1.1	3,723
GA FEMALE	3	.2	422	21.4	11	.6	23	1.2	459	23.3	1,506	76.3	8	.4	1,973
GA MALE	2	.1	208	11.9	20	1.1	22	1.3	252	14.4	1,465	83.7	33	1.9	1,750
COVENANT COLLEGE															
GA TOTAL	0	.0	12	2.3	2	.4	7	1.4	21	4.1	474	92.6	17	3.3	512
GA FEMALE	0	.0	3	1.2	1	.4	4	1.6	8	3.1	238	93.3	9	3.5	255
GA MALE	0	.0	9	3.5	1	.4	3	1.2	13	5.1	236	91.8	8	3.1	257
DALTON JUNIOR COLLEGE															
GA TOTAL	0	.0	41	2.9	5	.4	0	.0	46	3.3	1,346	96.6	1	.1	1,393
GA FEMALE	0	.0	20	2.8	4	.6	0	.0	24	3.4	691	96.6	0	.0	715
GA MALE	0	.0	21	3.1	1	.1	0	.0	22	3.2	655	96.6	1	.1	678
DEKALB COMMUNITY COLLEGE															
GA TOTAL	31	.3	1,744	18.0	53	.5	79	.8	1,907	19.7	7,673	79.2	107	1.1	9,687
GA FEMALE	19	.4	983	19.5	28	.6	37	.7	1,067	21.2	3,932	78.1	33	.7	5,032
GA MALE	12	.3	761	16.3	25	.5	42	.9	840	18.0	3,741	80.4	74	1.6	4,655

TABLE 1 - TOTAL UNDERGRADUATE ENROLLMENT IN INSTITUTIONS OF HIGHER EDUCATION BY RACE, ETHNICITY AND SEX: INSTITUTION, STATE AND NATION, 1978

	AMERICAN INDIAN ALASKAN NATIVE		BLACK NON-HISPANIC		ASIAN OR PACIFIC ISLANDER		HISPANIC		TOTAL MINORITY		WHITE NON-HISPANIC		NON-RESIDENT ALIEN	
	NUMBER	%	NUMBER	%	NUMBER	%	NUMBER	%	NUMBER	%	NUMBER	%	NUMBER	%
GEORGIA CONTINUED														
DRAUGHON'S JC BUSINESS														
GA TOTAL	0	.0	193	48.1	0	.0	0	.0	193	48.1	208	51.9	0	.0
GA FEMALE	0	.0	127	47.4	0	.0	0	.0	127	47.4	141	52.6	0	.0
GA MALE	0	.0	66	49.6	0	.0	0	.0	66	49.6	67	50.4	0	.0
EMANUEL CO JUNIOR COLLEGE														
GA TOTAL	0	.0	42	16.0	0	.0	0	.0	42	16.0	220	84.0	0	.0
GA FEMALE	0	.0	27	18.8	0	.0	0	.0	27	18.8	117	81.3	0	.0
GA MALE	0	.0	15	12.7	0	.0	0	.0	15	12.7	103	87.3	0	.0
EMMANUEL COLLEGE														
GA TOTAL	0	.0	12	3.3	0	.0	0	.0	12	3.3	350	96.2	2	.5
GA FEMALE	0	.0	3	1.6	0	.0	0	.0	3	1.6	180	98.4	0	.0
GA MALE	0	.0	9	5.0	0	.0	0	.0	9	5.0	170	93.9	2	1.1
EMMANUEL SCH MINISTRIES														
GA TOTAL	0	.0	0	.0	0	.0	0	.0	0	.0	52	100.0	0	.0
GA FEMALE	0	.0	0	.0	0	.0	0	.0	0	.0	15	100.0	0	.0
GA MALE	0	.0	0	.0	0	.0	0	.0	0	.0	37	100.0	0	.0
EMORY UNIVERSITY														
GA TOTAL	0	.0	104	2.6	22	.5	42	1.0	168	4.2	3,800	94.2	65	1.6
GA FEMALE	0	.0	73	3.9	13	.7	19	1.0	105	5.6	1,741	93.0	26	1.4
GA MALE	0	.0	31	1.4	9	.4	23	1.1	63	2.4	2,059	95.3	39	1.8
FLOYD JUNIOR COLLEGE														
GA TOTAL	2	.2	128	9.9	2	.2	1	.1	133	1.3	1,164	89.7	0	.0
GA FEMALE	1	.1	76	10.8	1	.1	0	.0	78	11.1	623	88.9	0	.0
GA MALE	1	.2	52	8.7	1	.2	1	.2	55	.2	541	90.8	0	.0
FORT VALLEY STATE COLLEGE														
GA TOTAL	0	.0	1,593	91.3	2	.1	3	.2	1,598	6	117	6.7	29	1.7
GA FEMALE	0	.0	861	96.5	0	.0	0	.0	861	91.5	29	3.3	2	.2
GA MALE	0	.0	732	85.9	2	.2	3	.4	737	86.5	88	10.3	27	3.2
GAINESVILLE JR COLLEGE														
GA TOTAL	4	.3	71	5.1	2	.1	2	.1	79	5.7	1,292	93.4	13	.9
GA FEMALE	2	.3	35	5.4	2	.3	1	.2	40	6.2	603	93.5	2	.3
GA MALE	2	.3	36	4.9	0	.0	1	.1	39	5.3	689	93.2	11	1.5
GEORGIA COLLEGE														
GA TOTAL	0	.0	497	18.0	2	.1	2	.1	501	18.2	2,237	81.1	21	.8
GA FEMALE	0	.0	366	22.9	1	.1	1	.1	368	23.0	1,224	76.5	7	.4
GA MALE	0	.0	131	11.3	1	.1	1	.1	133	11.5	1,013	87.3	14	1.2
GA INST OF TECHN MAIN CAM														
GA TOTAL	9	.1	550	6.2	92	1.0	119	1.3	770	8.7	7,689	86.8	401	4.5
GA FEMALE	2	.1	160	10.2	19	1.2	18	1.1	199	12.7	1,326	84.4	46	2.9
GA MALE	7	.1	390	5.4	73	1.0	101	1.4	571	7.8	6,363	87.3	355	4.9
GA INST TECHN-STHN TECH														
GA TOTAL	1	.0	192	8.3	7	.3	11	.5	211	9.2	1,986	86.2	107	4.6
GA FEMALE	0	.0	32	17.1	1	.5	2	1.1	35	18.7	149	79.7	3	1.6
GA MALE	1	.0	160	7.6	6	.3	9	.4	176	8.3	1,837	86.8	104	4.9
GEORGIA MILITARY COLLEGE														
GA TOTAL	31	2.3	472	34.8	13	1.0	75	5.5	591	43.5	757	55.7	10	.7
GA FEMALE	11	3.2	164	47.3	5	1.4	8	2.3	188	54.2	159	45.8	0	.0
GA MALE	20	2.0	308	30.5	8	.8	67	6.6	403	39.9	598	59.1	10	1.0
GEORGIA SOUTHERN COLLEGE														
GA TOTAL	1	.0	400	7.3	6	.1	2	.0	409	7.5	5,030	92.0	27	.5
GA FEMALE	0	.0	267	9.2	2	.1	0	.0	269	9.3	2,621	90.4	9	.3
GA MALE	1	.0	133	5.2	4	.2	2	.1	140	5.5	2,409	93.8	18	.7
GEORGIA SOUTHWESTERN COLLEGE														
GA TOTAL	0	.0	242	15.1	3	.2	5	.3	250	15.6	1,338	83.5	14	.9
GA FEMALE	0	.0	168	17.6	2	.2	2	.2	172	18.0	778	81.6	4	.4
GA MALE	0	.0	74	11.4	1	.2	3	.5	78	12.0	560	86.4	10	1.5
GEORGIA STATE UNIVERSITY														
GA TOTAL	29	.2	2,295	17.5	7	.6	57	.4	2,456	18.8	10,360	79.1	282	2.2
GA FEMALE	15	.2	1,452	20.7	3	.5	26	.4	1,529	21.8	5,368	76.4	132	1.9
GA MALE	14	.2	843	13.9	38	.6	31	.5	927	15.3	4,992	82.3	150	2.5
CORDON JUNIOR COLLEGE														
GA TOTAL	0	.0	200	19.0	1	.1	0	.0	201	19.1	848	80.7	2	.2
GA FEMALE	0	.0	125	23.1	1	.2	0	.0	126	23.2	414	76.4	2	.4
GA MALE	0	.0	75	14.7	0	.0	0	.0	75	14.7	434	85.3	0	.0
KENNESAW COLLEGE														
GA TOTAL	3	.1	38	1.2	6	.2	17	.5	64	2.0	3,104	95.6	78	2.4
GA FEMALE	2	.1	21	1.2	3	.2	10	.6	36	2.0	1,720	97.3	11	.6
GA MALE	1	.1	17	1.1	3	.2	7	.5	28	1.9	1,384	93.6	67	4.5
LA GRANGE COLLEGE														
GA TOTAL	4	.5	70	8.9	0	.0	0	.0	74	9.4	690	87.5	25	3.2
GA FEMALE	2	.5	42	9.6	0	.0	0	.0	44	10.1	386	88.5	6	1.4
GA MALE	2	.6	28	7.9	0	.0	0	.0	30	8.5	304	86.1	19	5.4
MACON JUNIOR COLLEGE														
GA TOTAL	6	.3	306	14.4	2	.2	8	.7	332	15.7	1,789	84.3	0	.0
GA FEMALE	5	.4	204	17.0	1	.1	8	.7	218	18.2	981	81.8	0	.0
GA MALE	1	.1	102	11.1	3	.3	8	.9	114	12.4	808	87.6	0	.0
MEDICAL COLLEGE OF GA														
GA TOTAL	1	.0	61	7.8	8	1.0	1	.1	71	9.0	714	90.7	2	.3
GA FEMALE	0	.0	55	8.3	5	.8	1	.2	61	9.2	601	90.6	1	.2
GA MALE	1	.8	6	4.8	3	2.4	0	.0	10	8.1	113	91.1	1	.8
MERCER U MAIN CAMPUS														
GA TOTAL	4	.2	234	12.6	1	.1	23	1.2	262	14.1	1,576	85.1	15	.8
GA FEMALE	2	.2	158	19.0	0	.0	9	1.1	169	2.3	659	79.3	3	.4
GA MALE	2	.2	76	7.4	1	.1	14	1.4	93	9.1	917	89.7	12	1.2
MERCER U IN ATLANTA														
GA TOTAL	3	.3	157	14.5	1	.1	10	1.0	171	15.8	899	83.2	11	1.0
GA FEMALE	1	.2	41	9.4	0	.0	6	1.0	48	11.0	388	88.8	1	.2
GA MALE	2	.3	116	18.0	1	.2	4	1.0	123	18.1	511	79.3	10	1.6
MERCER U STHN SCHOOL PHAR														
GA TOTAL	0	.0	9	2.8	4	1.3	5	1.	18	5.	287	90.0	14	4.4
GA FEMALE	0	.0	5	4.9	1	1.0	2	1.6	8	7.8	89	86.4	6	5.8
GA MALE	0	.0	4	1.9	3	1.4	3	1.4	10	4.8	198	91.7	8	3.7

	AMERICAN INDIAN ALASKAN NATIVE		BLACK NON-HISPANIC		ASIAN OR PACIFIC ISLANDER		HISPANIC		TOTAL MINORITY		WHITE NON-HISPANIC		NON-RESIDENT ALIEN		TOTAL
	NUMBER	%	NUMBER	%	NUMBER	%	NUMBER	%	NUMBER	%	NUMBER	%	NUMBER	%	NUMBER
GEORGIA	**CONTINUED**														
MIDDLE GEORGIA COLLEGE															
GA TOTAL	12	.8	182	12.2	2	.1	1	.1	197	13.2	1,225	82.4	65	4.4	1,487
GA FEMALE	4	.6	82	13.2	0	.0	0	.0	86	13.9	527	85.1	6	1.0	619
GA MALE	8	.9	100	11.5	2	.2	1	.1	111	12.8	698	80.4	59	6.8	868
MOREHOUSE COLLEGE															
GA TOTAL	0	.0	1,640	100.0	0	.0	0	.0	1,640	100.0	0	.0	0	.0	1,640
GA FEMALE	0	.0	0	.0	0	.0	0	.0	0	.0	0	.0	0	.0	0
GA MALE	0	.0	1,640	100.0	0	.0	0	.0	1,640	100.0	0	.0	0	.0	1,640
MORRIS BROWN COLLEGE															
GA TOTAL	0	.0	1,647	97.9	1	.1	0	.0	1,648	98.0	1	.1	33	2.0	1,682
GA FEMALE	0	.0	936	98.5	0	.0	0	.0	936	98.5	0	.0	14	1.5	950
GA MALE	0	.0	711	97.1	1	.1	0	.0	712	97.3	1	.1	19	2.6	732
NORTH GEORGIA COLLEGE															
GA TOTAL	0	.0	59	3.9	1	.1	3	.2	63	4.2	1,444	95.8	0	.0	1,507
GA FEMALE	0	.0	21	2.6	1	.1	1	.1	23	2.9	775	97.1	0	.0	798
GA MALE	0	.0	38	5.4	0	.0	2	.3	40	5.6	669	94.4	0	.0	709
OGLETHORPE UNIVERSITY															
GA TOTAL	0	.0	34	3.9	35	4.0	15	1.7	84	9.7	719	82.6	67	7.7	870
GA FEMALE	0	.0	17	3.8	11	2.5	2	.4	30	6.7	404	90.2	14	3.1	448
GA MALE	0	.0	17	4.0	24	5.7	13	3.1	54	12.8	315	74.6	53	12.6	422
PAINE COLLEGE															
GA TOTAL	1	.1	796	99.5	1	.1	0	.0	798	99.8	2	.3	0	.0	800
GA FEMALE	0	.0	551	99.8	0	.0	0	.0	551	99.8	1	.2	0	.0	552
GA MALE	1	.4	245	98.8	1	.4	0	.0	247	99.6	1	.4	0	.0	248
PHILLIPS COLLEGE															
GA TOTAL	0	.0	155	35.2	0	.0	8	1.8	163	37.0	277	63.0	0	.0	440
GA FEMALE	0	.0	25	15.2	0	.0	3	1.8	28	17.0	137	83.0	0	.0	165
GA MALE	0	.0	130	47.3	0	.0	5	1.8	135	49.1	140	50.9	0	.0	275
PHILLIPS COLLEGE															
GA TOTAL	0	.0	112	40.9	3	1.1	9	3.3	124	45.3	150	54.7	0	.0	274
GA FEMALE	0	.0	27	45.8	2	3.4	2	3.4	31	52.5	28	47.5	0	.0	59
GA MALE	0	.0	85	39.5	1	.5	7	3.3	93	43.3	122	56.7	0	.0	215
PIEDMONT COLLEGE															
GA TOTAL	0	.0	21	5.6	1	.3	1	.3	23	6.1	340	90.4	13	3.5	376
GA FEMALE	0	.0	9	5.7	0	.0	1	.6	10	6.3	146	92.4	2	1.3	158
GA MALE	0	.0	12	5.5	1	.5	0	.0	13	6.0	194	89.0	11	5.0	218
REINHARDT COLLEGE															
GA TOTAL	0	.0	17	3.2	0	.0	0	.0	17	3.2	481	91.1	30	5.7	528
GA FEMALE	0	.0	11	4.5	0	.0	0	.0	11	4.5	217	89.7	14	5.8	242
GA MALE	0	.0	6	2.1	0	.0	0	.0	6	2.1	264	92.3	16	5.6	286
SAVANNAH STATE COLLEGE															
GA TOTAL	13	.6	1,836	88.9	0	.0	0	.0	1,849	89.5	134	6.5	83	4.0	2,066
GA FEMALE	3	.3	1,134	97.0	0	.0	0	.0	1,137	97.3	27	2.3	5	.4	1,169
GA MALE	10	1.1	702	78.3	0	.0	0	.0	712	79.4	107	11.9	78	8.7	897
SHORTER COLLEGE															
GA TOTAL	0	.0	36	4.4	2	.2	0	.0	38	4.7	766	94.2	9	1.1	813
GA FEMALE	0	.0	17	3.7	1	.2	0	.0	18	3.9	434	95.0	5	1.1	457
GA MALE	0	.0	19	5.3	1	.3	0	.0	20	5.6	332	93.3	4	1.1	356
SOUTH GEORGIA COLLEGE															
GA TOTAL	1	.1	238	21.9	7	.6	0	.0	246	22.7	811	74.7	29	2.7	1,086
GA FEMALE	1	.2	157	26.1	5	.8	0	.0	163	27.1	434	72.1	5	.8	602
GA MALE	0	.0	81	16.7	2	.4	0	.0	83	17.1	377	77.9	24	5.0	484
SPELMAN COLLEGE															
GA TOTAL	0	.0	1,243	98.8	1	.1	0	.0	1,244	98.9	0	.0	14	1.1	1,258
GA FEMALE	0	.0	1,243	98.8	1	.1	0	.0	1,244	98.9	0	.0	14	1.1	1,258
GA MALE	0	.0	0	.0	0	.0	0	.0	0	.0	0	.0	0	.0	0
THOMAS COUNTY CC															
GA TOTAL	0	.0	47	26.6	0	.0	0	.0	47	26.6	126	71.2	4	2.3	177
GA FEMALE	0	.0	34	29.1	0	.0	0	.0	34	29.1	83	70.9	0	.0	117
GA MALE	0	.0	13	21.7	0	.0	0	.0	13	21.7	43	71.7	4	6.7	60
TIFT COLLEGE															
GA TOTAL	1	.1	94	12.7	0	.0	0	.0	95	12.9	641	86.9	2	.3	738
GA FEMALE	0	.0	48	8.0	0	.0	0	.0	48	8.0	553	91.7	2	.3	603
GA MALE	1	.7	46	34.1	0	.0	0	.0	47	34.8	88	65.2	0	.0	135
TOCCOA FALLS COLLEGE															
GA TOTAL	0	.0	2	.5	0	.0	2	.5	4	1.0	383	97.2	7	1.8	394
GA FEMALE	0	.0	0	.0	0	.0	1	.6	1	.6	161	98.2	2	1.2	164
GA MALE	0	.0	2	.9	0	.0	1	.4	3	1.3	222	96.5	5	2.2	230
TRUETT MCCONNELL COLLEGE															
GA TOTAL	0	.0	79	12.2	0	.0	0	.0	79	12.2	556	85.7	14	2.2	649
GA FEMALE	0	.0	18	5.9	0	.0	0	.0	18	5.9	279	91.8	7	2.3	304
GA MALE	0	.0	61	17.7	0	.0	0	.0	61	17.7	277	80.3	7	2.0	345
UNIVERSITY OF GEORGIA															
GA TOTAL	17	.1	747	4.4	57	.3	79	.5	900	5.3	15,968	93.9	134	.8	17,002
GA FEMALE	5	.1	420	5.1	28	.3	34	.4	487	5.9	7,752	93.6	47	.6	8,286
GA MALE	12	.1	327	3.8	29	.3	45	.5	413	4.7	8,216	94.3	87	1.0	8,716
VALDOSTA STATE COLLEGE															
GA TOTAL	2	.1	466	11.7	8	.2	8	.2	484	12.2	3,471	87.2	24	.6	3,979
GA FEMALE	1	.0	299	13.9	4	.2	3	.1	307	14.3	1,838	85.4	7	.3	2,152
GA MALE	1	.1	167	9.1	4	.2	5	.3	177	9.7	1,633	89.4	17	.9	1,827
WAYCROSS JUNIOR COLLEGE															
GA TOTAL	0	.0	41	11.4	0	.0	0	.0	41	11.4	319	88.6	0	.0	360
GA FEMALE	0	.0	27	13.2	0	.0	0	.0	27	13.2	177	86.8	0	.0	204
GA MALE	0	.0	14	9.0	0	.0	0	.0	14	9.0	142	91.0	0	.0	156
WESLEYAN COLLEGE															
GA TOTAL	0	.0	50	10.4	0	.0	3	.6	53	11.0	411	85.3	18	3.7	482
GA FEMALE	0	.0	50	10.4	0	.0	3	.6	53	11.0	411	85.3	18	3.7	482
GA MALE	0	.0	0	.0	0	.0	0	.0	0	.0	0	.0	0	.0	0
WEST GEORGIA COLLEGE															
GA TOTAL	4	.1	645	17.7	2	.1		.2	657	18.0	2,974	81.6	14	.4	3,645
GA FEMALE	3	.2	426	22.0	1	.1	4	.1	432	22.3	1,500	77.4	5	.3	1,937
GA MALE	1	.1	219	12.8	1	.1	4	.2	225	13.2	1,474	86.3	9	.5	1,708

	AMERICAN INDIAN ALASKAN NATIVE		BLACK NON-HISPANIC		ASIAN OR PACIFIC ISLANDER		HISPANIC		TOTAL MINORITY		WHITE NON-HISPANIC		NON-RESIDENT ALIEN	
	NUMBER	%	NUMBER	%	NUMBER	%	NUMBER	%	NUMBER	%	NUMBER	%	NUMBER	%
GEORGIA	CONTINUED													
YOUNG HARRIS COLLEGE														
GA TOTAL	0	.0	2	.4	0	.0	1	.2	3	.6	498	99.4	0	.0
GA FEMALE	0	.0	1	.4	0	.0	0	.0	1	.4	275	99.6	0	.0
GA MALE	0	.0	1	.4	0	.0	1	.4	2	.9	223	99.1	0	.0
GEORGIA	TOTAL (		68 INSTITUTIONS)											
GA TOTAL	220	.2	27,223	19.8	555	.4	738	.5	28,736	20.9	106,418	77.5	2,228	1.6
GA FEMALE	95	.1	15,583	22.9	243	.4	263	.4	16,184	23.7	51,407	75.4	561	.8
GA MALE	125	.2	11,640	16.8	312	.5	475	.7	12,552	18.1	55,011	79.5	1,667	2.4
HAWAII														
CHAMINADE U OF HONOLULU														
HI TOTAL	3	.2	79	5.0	296	18.6	41	2.6	419	26.4	1,168	73.6	1	.1
HI FEMALE	1	.2	20	4.1	97	19.8	13	2.6	131	26.7	359	73.1	1	.2
HI MALE	2	.2	59	5.4	199	18.1	28	2.6	288	26.3	809	73.7	0	.0
HAWAII LOA COLLEGE														
HI TOTAL	1	.4	2	.7	22	8.0	6	2.2	31	11.3	196	71.5	47	17.2
HI FEMALE	1	.7	2	1.3	15	10.0	1	.7	19	12.7	115	76.7	16	10.7
HI MALE	0	.0	0	.0	7	5.6	5	4.0	12	9.7	81	65.3	31	25.0
HAWAII PACIFIC COLLEGE														
HI TOTAL	0	.0	199	16.3	104	8.5	47	3.8	350	28.6	786	64.3	86	7.0
HI FEMALE	0	.0	12	8.2	42	28.8	4	2.7	58	39.7	63	43.2	25	17.1
HI MALE	0	.0	187	17.4	62	5.8	43	4.0	292	27.1	723	67.2	61	5.7
U OF HAWAII AT MANOA														
HI TOTAL	21	.1	66	.4	11,187	73.1	196	1.3	11,470	74.9	3,117	20.4	718	4.7
HI FEMALE	9	.1	28	.4	5,752	73.1	89	1.1	5,878	74.7	1,672	21.3	318	4.0
HI MALE	12	.2	38	.5	5,435	73.1	107	1.4	5,592	75.2	1,445	19.4	400	5.4
U OF HAWAII AT HILO														
HI TOTAL	12	.4	18	.6	1,771	61.6	168	5.8	1,969	68.5	731	25.4	176	1
HI FEMALE	8	.6	5	.4	847	62.9	75	5.6	935	69.5	330	24.5	81	.0
HI MALE	4	.3	13	.8	924	60.4	93	6.1	1,034	67.6	401	26.2	95	6.2
U OF HAWAII WEST OAHU C														
HI TOTAL	1	.5	9	4.5	112	55.7	5	2.5	127	63.2	74	36.8	0	.
HI FEMALE	0	.0	4	6.5	23	37.1	3	4.8	30	48.4	32	51.6	0	.
HI MALE	1	.7	5	3.6	89	64.0	2	1.4	97	69.8	42	30.2	0	.0
U OF HAWAII HONOLULU CC														
HI TOTAL	10	.2	70	1.7	3,100	73.5	163	3.9	3,343	79.3	708	16.8	165	3.9
HI FEMALE	0	.0	20	1.7	800	67.3	49	4.1	869	73.1	267	22.5	52	4.4
HI MALE	10	.3	50	1.7	2,300	76.0	114	3.8	2,474	81.7	441	14.6	113	3.7
U OF HAWAII KAPIOLANI CC														
HI TOTAL	6	.1	33	.7	3,583	80.9	95	2.1	3,717	84.0	568	12.8	142	2
HI FEMALE	2	.1	12	.5	2,152	80.8	64	2.4	2,230	83.8	345	13.0	87	3.3
HI MALE	4	.2	21	1.2	1,431	81.1	31	1.8	1,487	84.2	223	12.6	55	3.1
U OF HAWAII KAUAI CC														
HI TOTAL	3	.4	1	.1	497	61.1	88	10.8	589	72.4	198	24.3	27	3.3
HI FEMALE	1	.3	0	.0	217	60.4	30	8.4	248	69.1	98	27.3	13	3.6
HI MALE	2	.4	1	.2	280	61.5	58	12.7	341	74.9	100	22.0	14	3.1
U OF HAWAII LEEWARD CC														
HI TOTAL	12	.2	110	2.0	3,725	69.3	193	3.6	4,040	75.2	1,161	21.6	171	3.2
HI FEMALE	6	.2	60	2.4	1,607	65.5	86	3.5	1,759	71.6	612	24.9	84	3.4
HI MALE	6	.2	50	1.7	2,118	72.6	107	3.7	2,281	78.2	549	18.8	87	3.0
U OF HAWAII MAUI CC														
HI TOTAL	4	.3	3	.2	818	57.6	146	10.3	971	68.3	367	25.8	83	5.
HI FEMALE	1	.1	0	.0	376	52.4	83	11.6	460	64.1	231	32.2	27	3.8
HI MALE	3	.4	3	.4	442	62.9	63	9.0	511	72.7	136	19.3	56	8.0
U OF HAWAII WINDWARD CC														
HI TOTAL	5	.4	12	1.0	493	43.1	89	7.8	599	52.4	498	43.5	47	.1
HI FEMALE	4	.6	7	1.1	283	43.5	44	6.8	338	52.0	288	44.3	24	.7
HI MALE	1	.2	5	1.0	210	42.5	45	9.1	261	52.8	210	42.5	23	.17
HAWAII	TOTAL (		12 INSTITUTIONS)											
HI TOTAL	78	.2	602	1.5	25,708	66.2	1,237	3.2	27,625	71.1	9,572	24.6	1,663	3
HI FEMALE	33	.2	170	.9	12,211	67.5	541	3.0	12,955	71.6	4,412	24.4	728	4.0
HI MALE	45	.2	432	2.1	13,497	65.0	696	3.4	14,670	70.6	5,160	24.8	935	4.15
IDAHO														
BOISE STATE UNIVERSITY														
ID TOTAL	45	.6	67	.8	112	1.4	105	1.3	329	1	7,738	95.7	16	.2
ID FEMALE	28	.7	16	.4	63	1.6	55	1.4	162	4.1	3,809	95.9	2	.1
ID MALE	17	.4	51	1.2	49	1.2	50	1.2	167	4.11	3,929	95.6	14	.3
COLLEGE OF IDAHO														
ID TOTAL	2	.4	5	.9	36	6.7	9	1.7	52	.7	476	89.1	6	1.1
ID FEMALE	2	.9	1	.4	14	6.2	5	2.2	22	.7	204	89.9	1	.4
ID MALE	0	.0	4	1.3	22	7.2	4	1.3	30	7.0	272	88.6	5	1.6
COLLEGE OF SOUTHERN IDAHO														
ID TOTAL	1	.0	10	.4	26	.9	55	2.0	92	3.3	2,703	96.0	21	.7
ID FEMALE	0	.0	0	.0	12	.9	30	2.4	42	3.13	1,216	95.9	10	.8
ID MALE	1	.1	10	.6	14	.9	25	1.6	50	3.2	1,487	96.1	11	.7
IDAHO STATE UNIVERSITY														
ID TOTAL	20	.5	31	.7	55	1.3	41	1.0	147	3.4	4,151	96.6	1	.0
ID FEMALE	13	.6	16	.8	16	.8	19	.9	64	3.0	2,065	97.0	0	.0
ID MALE	7	.3	15	.7	39	1.8	22	1.0	83	3.8	2,086	96.1	1	.0
LEWIS-CLARK ST COLLEGE														
ID TOTAL	62	4.8	11	.9	8	.6	8	.6	89	6.9	1,178	91.7	18	1.4
ID FEMALE	42	5.7	2	.3	3	.4	3	.4	50	6.8	674	92.2	7	1.0
ID MALE	20	3.6	9	1.6	5	.9	5	.9	39	7.0	504	91.0	11	2.0
NORTH IDAHO COLLEGE														
ID TOTAL	16	1.1	9	.6	9	.6	15	1.0	49	3.3	1,430	95.8	13	.9
ID FEMALE	4	.5	0	.0	2	.3	7	.9	13	1.6	780	98.2	1	.1
ID MALE	12	1.7	9	1.3	7	1.0	8	1.1	36	5.2	650	93.1	12	1.7

28

	AMERICAN INDIAN ALASKAN NATIVE		BLACK NON-HISPANIC		ASIAN OR PACIFIC ISLANDER		HISPANIC		TOTAL MINORITY		WHITE NON-HISPANIC		NON-RESIDENT ALIEN		TOTAL
	NUMBER	%	NUMBER	%	NUMBER	%	NUMBER	%	NUMBER	%	NUMBER	%	NUMBER	%	NUMBER
IDAHO. CONTINUED															
NTHWST NAZARENE COLLEGE															
ID TOTAL	5	.4	5	.4	6	.5	7	.6	23	1.9	1,146	97.0	13	1.1	1,182
ID FEMALE	4	.6	1	.1	4	.6	5	.7	14	2.0	662	96.8	8	1.2	684
ID MALE	1	.2	4	.8	2	.4	2	.4	9	1.8	484	97.2	5	1.0	498
RICKS COLLEGE															
ID TOTAL	20	.3	1	.0	15	.2	28	.4	64	1.0	6,034	94.2	310	4.8	6,408
ID FEMALE	13	.3	0	.0	2	.1	16	.4	31	.8	3,722	94.3	192	4.9	3,945
ID MALE	7	.3	1	.0	13	.5	12	.5	33	1.3	2,312	93.9	118	4.8	2,463
UNIVERSITY OF IDAHO															
ID TOTAL	36	.6	35	.6	67	1.1	14	.2	152	2.4	5,970	96.1	88	1.4	6,210
ID FEMALE	20	.9	5	.2	24	1.0	5	.2	54	2.3	2,239	97.1	14	.6	2,307
ID MALE	16	.4	30	.8	43	1.1	9	.2	98	2.5	3,731	95.6	74	1.9	3,903
IDAHO TOTAL (9 INSTITUTIONS)															
ID TOTAL	207	.6	174	.5	334	1.0	282	.9	997	3.1	30,826	95.4	486	1.5	32,309
ID FEMALE	126	.8	41	.3	140	.9	145	.9	452	2.8	15,371	95.7	235	1.5	16,058
ID MALE	81	.5	133	.8	194	1.2	137	.8	545	3.4	15,455	95.1	251	1.5	16,251
ILLINOIS															
AERO-SPACE INSTITUTE															
IL TOTAL	0	.0	8	11.4	0	.0	2	2.9	10	14.3	16	22.9	44	62.9	70
IL FEMALE	0	.0	3	33.3	0	.0	1	11.1	4	44.4	0	.0	35	55.6	9
IL MALE	0	.0	5	8.2	0	.0	1	1.6	6	9.8	16	26.2	9	63.9	61
AMERICAN ACADEMY OF ART															
IL TOTAL	2	.2	80	9.2	20	2.3	93	10.7	195	22.3	675	77.3	3	.3	873
IL FEMALE	0	.0	34	9.2	10	2.7	34	9.2	78	21.1	291	78.6	1	.3	370
IL MALE	2	.4	46	9.1	10	2.0	59	11.7	117	23.3	384	76.3	2	.4	503
AMERICAN CONSV OF MUSIC															
IL TOTAL	0	.0	48	15.4	7	2.3	5	1.6	60	19.3	251	80.7		.0	311
IL FEMALE	0	.0	14	8.9	4	2.5	0	.0	18	11.5	139	88.5	0	.0	157
IL MALE	0	.0	34	22.1	3	1.9	5	3.2	42	27.3	112	72.7	0	.0	154
AUGUSTANA COLLEGE															
IL TOTAL	0	.0	99	4.4	5	.2	12	.5	116	5.2	2,115	94.2	15	.7	2,246
IL FEMALE	0	.0	58	5.0	2	.2	4	.3	64	5.5	1,082	93.8	8	.7	1,154
IL MALE	0	.0	41	3.8	3	.3	8	.7	52	4.8	1,033	94.6	7	.6	1,092
AURORA COLLEGE															
IL TOTAL	1	.1	80	10.6	5	.7	25	3.3	111	14.8	629	83.6	12	1.6	752
IL FEMALE	0	.0	43	12.8	2	.6	14	4.2	59	17.6	272	81.2	4	1.2	335
IL MALE	1	.2	37	8.9	3	.7	11	2.6	52	12.5	357	85.6	8	1.9	417
BARAT COLLEGE															
IL TOTAL	0	.0	20	3.4	7	1.2	9	1.5	36	6.1	530	89.1	2	4.9	595
IL FEMALE	0	.0	20	3.4	7	1.2	9	1.5	36	6.1	530	89.1	29	4.9	595
IL MALE	0	.0	0	.0	0	.0	0	.0	0	.0	0	.0	0	.0	0
BELLEVILLE AREA COLLEGE															
IL TOTAL	36	.5	364	5.1	44	.6	35	.5	479	6.7	6,647	93.3	0	.0	7,126
IL FEMALE	14	.4	177	5.3	23	.7	15	.4	229	6.8	3,137	93.2	0	.0	3,366
IL MALE	22	.6	187	5.0	21	.6	20	.5	250	6.6	3,510	93.4	0	.0	3,760
BLACKBURN COLLEGE															
IL TOTAL	0	.0	31	7.0	3	.7	2	.5	36	8.1	396	89.6	10	2.3	442
IL FEMALE	0	.0	15	6.1	1	.4	0	.0	16	6.5	227	92.7	2	.9	245
IL MALE	0	.0	16	8.1	2	1.0	2	1.0	20	10.2	169	85.8	8	4.1	197
BLACK HAWK C EAST CAMPUS															
IL TOTAL	3	.4	16	2.2	7	1.0	2	.3	28	3.8	702	96.2		.0	730
IL FEMALE	2	.7	8	2.6	4	1.3	1	.3	15	5.0	287	95.0	0	.0	302
IL MALE	1	.2	8	1.9	3	.7	1	.2	13	3.0	415	97.0	0	.0	428
BLACK HAWK C QUAD-CITIES															
IL TOTAL	10	.2	198	4.0	37	.8	137	2.8	382	7.8	4,531	92.2		.0	4,913
IL FEMALE	5	.2	111	4.1	13	.5	68	2.5	197	7.2	2,524	92.8	0	.0	2,721
IL MALE	5	.2	87	4.0	24	1.1	69	3.1	185	8.4	2,007	91.6	0	.0	2,192
BRADLEY UNIVERSITY															
IL TOTAL	2	.0	324	7.0	19	.4	19	.4	364	7.8	4,209	90.6	71	1.5	4,644
IL FEMALE	1	.1	194	9.8	5	.3	10	.5	210	10.6	1,747	88.5	17	.9	1,974
IL MALE	1	.0	130	4.9	14	.5	9	.3	154	5.8	2,462	92.2	54	2.0	2,670
BRISK RABBINICAL COLLEGE															
IL TOTAL	0	.0	0	.0	0	.0	0	.0	0	.0	34	100.0	0	.0	34
IL FEMALE	0	.0	0	.0	0	.0	0	.0	0	.0	0	.0	0	.0	0
IL MALE	0	.0	0	.0	0	.0	0	.0	0	.0	34	100.0	0	.0	34
CARL SANDBURG COLLEGE															
IL TOTAL	6	.3	65	2.9	5	.2	27	1.2	103	4.6	2,143	94.9	12	.5	2,258
IL FEMALE	2	.2	40	3.3	2	.2	14	1.1	58	4.7	1,164	95.0	3	.2	1,225
IL MALE	4	.4	25	2.4	3	.3	13	1.3	45	4.4	979	94.8	9	.9	1,033
CENTRAL YMCA CMTY COLLEGE															
IL TOTAL	34	.8	3,100	69.0	13	.3	359	8.0	3,506	78.0	548	12.2	438	9.8	4,492
IL FEMALE	20	.7	2,371	78.3	8	.3	239	7.9	2,638	87.1	320	10.6	69	2.3	3,027
IL MALE	14	1.0	729	49.8	5	.3	120	8.2	868	59.2	228	15.6	369	25.2	1,465
CHGO CONSERVATORY COLLEGE															
IL TOTAL	0	.0	36	62.1	2	3.4	0	.0	38	65.5	17	29.3	3	5.2	58
IL FEMALE	0	.0	17	65.4	1	3.8	0	.0	18	69.2	7	26.9	1	3.8	26
IL MALE	0	.0	19	59.4	1	3.1	0	.0	20	62.5	10	31.3	2	6.3	32
CHICAGO STATE UNIVERSITY															
IL TOTAL	5	.1	4,003	84.6	19	.4	97	2.1	4,124	87.2	587	12.4	18	.4	4,729
IL FEMALE	5	.2	2,651	89.3	13	.4	49	1.7	2,718	91.6	240	8.1	10	.3	2,968
IL MALE	0	.0	1,352	76.8	6	.3	48	2.7	1,406	79.8	347	19.7	8	.5	1,761
CTY C CHGO CITY-WIDE C															
IL TOTAL	0	.0	790	30.8	30	1.2	64	2.5	884	34.5	1,048	40.9	632	24.6	2,564
IL FEMALE	0	.0	499	33.4	21	1.4	20	1.3	540	36.1	628	42.0	326	21.8	1,494
IL MALE	0	.0	291	27.2	9	.8	44	4.1	344	32.1	420	39.3	306	28.6	1,070
CITY C CHGO KENNEDY-KING															
IL TOTAL	0	.0	9,045	97.8	35	.4	47	.5	9,127	98.7	84	.9	33	.4	9,244
IL FEMALE	0	.0	4,828	98.5	19	.4	2	.0	4,849	98.9	40	.8	14	.3	4,903
IL MALE	0	.0	4,217	97.1	16	.4	45	1.0	4,278	98.5	44	1.0	19	.4	4,341

ILLINOIS CONTINUED

	AMERICAN INDIAN ALASKAN NATIVE		BLACK NON-HISPANIC		ASIAN OR PACIFIC ISLANDER		HISPANIC		TOTAL MINORITY		WHITE NON-HISPANIC		NON-RESIDENT ALIEN		TOTAL
	NUMBER	%	NUMBER	%	NUMBER	%	NUMBER	%	NUMBER	%	NUMBER	%	NUMBER	%	NUMBER
CITY C CHICAGO LOOP C															
IL TOTAL	0	.0	4,638	68.1	175	2.6	447	6.6	5,260	77.2	848	12.4	706	10.4	6,814
IL FEMALE	0	.0	3,252	74.1	111	2.5	272	6.2	3,635	82.9	542	12.4	210	4.8	4,387
IL MALE	0	.0	1,386	57.1	64	2.6	175	7.2	1,625	67.0	306	12.6	496	20.4	2,427
CITY C CHGO MALCOLM X C															
IL TOTAL	0	.0	4,500	91.4	81	1.6	204	4.1	4,785	97.2	24	.5	116	2.4	4,925
IL FEMALE	0	.0	2,687	91.6	47	1.6	119	4.1	2,853	97.2	15	.5	67	2.3	2,935
IL MALE	0	.0	1,813	91.1	34	1.7	85	4.3	1,932	97.1	9	.5	49	2.5	1,990
CITY C CHGO OLIVE-HARVEY															
IL TOTAL	29	.6	4,550	93.4	10	.2	133	2.7	4,722	96.9	141	2.9	9	.2	4,872
IL FEMALE	18	.6	2,805	93.4	6	.2	83	2.8	2,912	97.0	86	2.9	4	.1	3,002
IL MALE	11	.6	1,745	93.3	4	.2	50	2.7	1,810	96.8	55	2.9	5	.3	1,870
CITY C CHICAGO DALEY C															
IL TOTAL	20	.3	459	7.3	43	.7	369	5.9	891	14.2	5,388	85.7	6	.1	6,285
IL FEMALE	12	.3	303	8.4	23	.6	198	5.5	536	14.9	3,050	85.0	2	.1	3,588
IL MALE	8	.3	156	5.8	20	.7	171	6.3	355	13.2	2,338	86.7	4	.1	2,697
CTY C CHGO TRUMAN C															
IL TOTAL	0	.0	1,271	17.1	336	4.5	1,030	13.9	2,637	35.5	4,671	62.9	123	1.7	7,431
IL FEMALE	0	.0	694	16.3	179	4.2	491	11.6	1,364	32.1	2,869	67.5	15	.4	4,248
IL MALE	0	.0	577	18.1	157	4.9	539	16.9	1,273	40.0	1,802	56.6	108	3.4	3,183
CITY C CHICAGO WRIGHT C															
IL TOTAL	10	.3	507	17.5	41	1.4	198	6.8	756	26.1	1,924	66.5	213	7.4	2,893
IL FEMALE	4	.3	208	18.0	15	1.3	80	6.9	307	26.6	761	65.9	86	7.5	1,154
IL MALE	6	.3	299	17.2	26	1.5	118	6.8	449	25.8	1,163	66.9	127	7.3	1,739
COLLEGE OF DUPAGE															
IL TOTAL	51	.5	139	1.5	186	2.0	121	1.3	497	5.2	8,970	94.8	0	.0	9,467
IL FEMALE	14	.3	61	1.3	89	1.8	54	1.1	218	4.5	4,612	95.5	0	.0	4,830
IL MALE	37	.8	78	1.7	97	2.1	67	1.4	279	6.0	4,358	94.0	0	.0	4,637
COLLEGE OF LAKE COUNTY															
IL TOTAL	26	.3	658	7.5	86	1.0	379	4.3	1,149	13.0	7,679	87.0	0	.0	8,828
IL FEMALE	13	.3	363	7.9	37	.8	156	3.4	569	12.3	4,047	87.7	0	.0	4,616
IL MALE	13	.3	295	7.0	49	1.2	223	5.3	580	13.8	3,632	86.2	0	.0	4,212
COLLEGE OF SAINT FRANCIS															
IL TOTAL	4	.1	126	4.1	33	1.1	19	.6	182	5.9	2,917	94.1	1	.0	3,100
IL FEMALE	3	.1	117	4.1	29	1.0	15	.5	164	5.8	2,674	94.2	1	.0	2,839
IL MALE	1	.4	9	3.4	4	1.5	4	1.5	18	6.9	243	93.1	0	.0	261
COLUMBIA COLLEGE															
IL TOTAL	24	.9	1,060	40.6	24	.9	94	3.6	1,202	46.1	1,400	53.6	8	.3	2,610
IL FEMALE	14	1.1	579	43.5	12	.9	54	4.1	659	49.5	668	50.2	4	.3	1,331
IL MALE	10	.8	481	37.6	12	.9	40	3.1	543	42.5	732	57.2	4	.3	1,279
CONCORDIA TCHRS COLLEGE															
IL TOTAL	0	.0	23	2.6	4	.5	4	.5	31	3.6	837	96.1	3	.3	871
IL FEMALE	0	.0	13	2.4	4	.7	3	.5	20	3.7	525	96.0	2	.4	547
IL MALE	0	.0	10	3.1	0	.0	1	.3	11	3.4	312	96.3	1	.3	324
DANIEL HALE WILLIAMS U															
IL TOTAL	0	.0	481	96.6	1	.2	16	3.2	498	100.0	0	.0	0	.0	498
IL FEMALE	0	.0	317	97.8	1	.3	6	1.9	324	100.0	0	.0	0	.0	324
IL MALE	0	.0	164	94.3	0	.0	10	5.7	174	100.0	0	.0	0	.0	174
DANVILLE JUNIOR COLLEGE															
IL TOTAL	7	.3	197	7.2	5	.2	13	.5	222	5.1	2,410	87.5	122	4.4	2,754
IL FEMALE	4	.3	122	8.2	3	.2	6	.4	135	9.1	1,344	90.6	4	.3	1,483
IL MALE	3	.2	75	5.9	2	.2	7	.6	87	6.8	1,066	83.9	118	9.3	1,271
DELOURDES COLLEGE															
IL TOTAL	0	.0	0	.0	1	1.0	0	.0	1	1.0	102	99.0		.0	103
IL FEMALE	0	.0	0	.0	1	1.0	0	.0	1	1.0	102	99.0		.0	103
IL MALE	0	.0	0	.0	0	.0	0	.0	0	.0	0	.0	0	.0	0
DEPAUL UNIVERSITY															
IL TOTAL	7	.1	783	13.4	118	2.0	268	4.6	1,176	20.2	4,606	79.0	47	.8	5,829
IL FEMALE	4	.1	529	18.8	68	2.4	154	5.5	755	26.8	2,046	72.6	16	.6	2,817
IL MALE	3	.1	254	8.4	50	1.7	114	3.8	421	14.0	2,560	85.0	31	1.0	3,012
DEVRY INST OF TECHNOLOGY															
IL TOTAL	5	.2	452	19.4	126	5.4	131	5.6	714	30.6	1,597	68.4	23	1.0	2,334
IL FEMALE	1	.8	65	54.6	5	4.2	1	.8	72	60.5	47	39.5	0	.0	119
IL MALE	4	.2	387	17.5	121	5.5	130	5.9	642	29.0	1,550	70.0	23	1.0	2,215
EASTERN ILL UNIVERSITY															
IL TOTAL	8	.1	590	6.5	16	.2	29	.3	643	7.1	8,317	91.9	88	1.0	9,048
IL FEMALE	3	.1	318	6.4	8	.2	11	.2	340	6.9	4,605	92.8	18	.4	4,963
IL MALE	5	.1	272	6.7	8	.2	18	.4	303	7.4	3,712	90.9	70	1.7	4,085
ELGIN COMMUNITY COLLEGE															
IL TOTAL	10	.2	120	2.4	32	.6	246	4.8	408	8.0	4,672	91.9	4	.1	5,084
IL FEMALE	6	.2	72	2.6	11	.4	107	3.9	196	7.1	2,562	92.8	2	.1	2,760
IL MALE	4	.2	48	2.1	21	.9	139	6.0	212	9.1	2,110	90.8	2	.1	2,324
ELMHURST COLLEGE															
IL TOTAL	12	.5	132	5.4	11	.4	128	5.2	283	11.5	2,074	84.6	95	3	2,452
IL FEMALE	8	.6	75	5.8	5	.4	79	6.1	167	13.0	1,068	83.0	51	4	1,286
IL MALE	4	.3	57	4.9	6	.5	49	4.2	116	9.9	1,006	86.3	44	31.0	1,166
EUREKA COLLEGE															
IL TOTAL	0	.0	70	16.8	0	.0	1	.2	71	17.0	338	81.1	8	1 9	417
IL FEMALE	0	.0	28	16.6	0	.0	1	.6	29	17.2	140	82.8	0	3 0	169
IL MALE	0	.0	42	16.9	0	.0	0	.0	42	16.9	198	79.8	8	12	248
FELICIAN COLLEGE															
IL TOTAL	0	.0	7	3.6	7	3.6	17	8.6	31	15.7	134	68.0	32	16.2	197
IL FEMALE	0	.0	7	4.4	3	1.9	17	10.8	27	17.1	117	74.1	14	8.9	158
IL MALE	0	.0	0	.0	4	10.3	0	.0	4	10.3	17	43.6	18	46.2	39
GEORGE WILLIAMS COLLEGE															
IL TOTAL	2	.3	151	20.7	7	1.0	28	3.8	188	25.8	532	73.1	8	1.1	728
IL FEMALE	2	.4	81	17.8	4	.9	15	3.3	102	22.5	349	76.9	3	.7	454
IL MALE	0	.0	70	25.5	3	1.1	13	4.7	86	31.4	183	66.8	5	1.8	274
GOVERNORS ST UNIVERSITY															
IL TOTAL	3	.2	397	32.1	4	.3	27	2.2	431	34.8	798	64.5		.7	1,238
IL FEMALE	2	.3	257	38.9	3	.5	16	2.4	278	42.1	377	57.1		.8	660
IL MALE	1	.2	140	24.2	1	.2	11	1.9	153	26.5	421	72.8		.7	578

TABLE 1 - TOTAL UNDERGRADUATE ENROLLMENT IN INSTITUTIONS OF HIGHER EDUCATION BY RACE, ETHNICITY AND SEX: INSTITUTION, STATE AND NATION, 1978

	AMERICAN INDIAN ALASKAN NATIVE		BLACK NON-HISPANIC		ASIAN OR PACIFIC ISLANDER		HISPANIC		TOTAL MINORITY		WHITE NON-HISPANIC		NON-RESIDENT ALIEN		TOTAL
	NUMBER	%	NUMBER	%	NUMBER	%	NUMBER	%	NUMBER	%	NUMBER	%	NUMBER	%	NUMBER
ILLINOIS CONTINUED															
GREENVILLE COLLEGE															
IL TOTAL	1	.1	40	5.1	5	.6	7	.9	53	6.8	720	91.8	11	1.4	784
IL FEMALE	1	.2	12	2.8	3	.7	5	1.2	21	4.9	404	93.7	6	1.4	431
IL MALE	0	.0	28	7.9	2	.6	2	.6	32	9.1	316	89.5	5	1.4	353
HEBREW THEOL COLLEGE															
IL TOTAL	0	.0	0	.0	1	.7	0	.0	1	.7	141	97.9	2	1.4	144
IL FEMALE	0	.0	0	.0	0	.0	0	.0	0	.0	61	100.0	0	.0	61
IL MALE	0	.0	0	.0	1	1.2	0	.0	1	1.2	80	96.4	2	2.4	83
HIGHLAND CMTY COLLEGE															
IL TOTAL	2	.1	63	3.8	2	.1	6	.4	73	4.4	1,590	95.6	0	.0	1,663
IL FEMALE	1	.1	37	4.2	0	.0	3	.3	41	4.7	836	95.3	0	.0	877
IL MALE	1	.1	26	3.3	2	.3	3	.4	32	4.1	754	95.9	0	.0	786
ILL BENEDICTINE COLLEGE															
IL TOTAL	0	.0	37	3.3	5	.4	5	.4	47	4.2	1,082	95.7	2	.2	1,131
IL FEMALE	0	.0	15	3.3	0	.0	1	.2	16	3.6	432	96.4	0	.0	448
IL MALE	0	.0	22	3.2	5	.7	4	.6	31	4.5	650	95.2	2	.3	683
ILLINOIS CENTRAL COLLEGE															
IL TOTAL	477	4.0	328	2.8	93	.8	119	1.0	1,017	8.6	10,748	91.2	19	.2	11,784
IL FEMALE	311	4.6	208	3.1	52	.8	63	.9	634	9.3	6,137	90.4	16	.2	6,787
IL MALE	166	3.3	120	2.4	41	.8	56	1.1	383	7.7	4,611	92.3	3	.1	4,997
ILLINOIS COLLEGE															
IL TOTAL	1	.1	11	1.5	1	.1	3	.4	16	2.1	730	97.2	5	.7	751
IL FEMALE	1	.3	2	.6	1	.3	1	.3	5	1.6	307	98.1	1	.3	313
IL MALE	0	.0	9	2.1	0	.0	2	.5	11	2.5	423	96.6	4	.9	438
ILL ESTN CC FRONTIER CC															
IL TOTAL	0	.0	4	.1	0	.0	0	.0	4	.1	2,876	99.9	0	.0	2,880
IL FEMALE	0	.0	3	.2	0	.0	0	.0	3	.2	1,741	99.8	0	.0	1,744
IL MALE	0	.0	1	.1	0	.0	0	.0	1	.1	1,135	99.9	0	.0	1,136
ILL ESTN LINCOLN TRAIL C															
IL TOTAL	0	.0	9	.5	1	.1	0	.0	10	.6	1,683	98.7	13	.8	1,706
IL FEMALE	0	.0	2	.2	1	.1	0	.0	3	.3	998	99.6	1	.1	1,002
IL MALE	0	.0	7	1.0	0	.0	0	.0	7	1.0	685	97.3	12	1.7	704
ILL ESTN CC OLNEY CEN C															
IL TOTAL	0	.0	0	.0	0	.0	3	.1	3	.1	2,138	99.0	19	.9	2,160
IL FEMALE	0	.0	0	.0	0	.0	2	.2	2	.2	1,280	99.7	2	.2	1,284
IL MALE	0	.0	0	.0	0	.0	1	.1	1	.1	858	97.9	17	1.9	876
ILL ESTN CC WABASH VLY C															
IL TOTAL	3	.1	44	1.5	1	.0	2	.1	50	1.7	2,969	98.3	2	.1	3,021
IL FEMALE	1	.1	11	.8	0	.0	0	.0	12	.9	1,291	99.1	0	.0	1,303
IL MALE	2	.1	33	1.9	1	.1	2	.1	38	2.2	1,678	97.7	2	.1	1,718
ILLINOIS INST TECHNOLOGY															
IL TOTAL	2	.1	511	14.1	252	7.0	127	3.5	892	24.6	2,504	69.1	228	6.3	3,624
IL FEMALE	1	.2	167	29.2	55	9.6	20	3.5	243	42.5	307	53.7	22	3.8	572
IL MALE	1	.0	344	11.3	197	6.5	107	3.5	649	21.3	2,197	72.0	206	6.7	3,052
ILLINOIS STATE UNIVERSITY															
IL TOTAL	51	.3	1,640	9.9	85	.5	93	.6	1,869	11.2	14,658	88.0	121	.7	16,648
IL FEMALE	32	.3	1,011	10.7	49	.5	54	.6	1,146	12.2	8,232	87.4	37	.4	9,415
IL MALE	19	.3	629	8.7	36	.5	39	.5	723	10.0	6,426	88.8	84	1.2	7,233
ILLINOIS VLY CMTY COLLEGE															
IL TOTAL	0	.0	21	.9	0	.0	0	.0	21	.9	2,283	99.1	0	.0	2,304
IL FEMALE	0	.0	9	.8	0	.0	0	.0	9	.8	1,129	99.2	0	.0	1,138
IL MALE	0	.0	12	1.0	0	.0	0	.0	12	1.0	1,154	99.0	0	.0	1,166
ILL WESLEYAN UNIVERSITY															
IL TOTAL	0	.0	70	4.3	10	.6	7	.4	87	5.4	1,518	94.1	9	.6	1,614
IL FEMALE	0	.0	42	4.7	5	.6	3	.3	50	5.6	846	94.1	3	.3	899
IL MALE	0	.0	28	3.9	5	.7	4	.6	37	5.2	672	94.0	6	.8	715
JOHN A LOGAN COLLEGE															
IL TOTAL	7	.4	113	7.1	17	1.1	9	.6	146	9.2	1,401	88.4	37	2.3	1,584
IL FEMALE	3	.4	63	7.5	10	1.2	4	.5	80	9.5	751	89.3	10	1.2	841
IL MALE	4	.5	50	6.7	7	.9	5	.7	66	8.9	650	87.5	27	3.6	743
JOHN WOOD CMTY COLLEGE															
IL TOTAL	9	.4	55	2.4	13	.6	4	.2	81	3.5	2,250	96.3	6	.3	2,337
IL FEMALE	4	.3	35	2.5	6	.4	2	.1	47	3.4	1,342	96.5	1	.1	1,390
IL MALE	5	.5	20	2.1	7	.7	2	.2	34	3.6	908	95.9	5	.5	947
JOLIET JUNIOR COLLEGE															
IL TOTAL	21	.3	560	7.0	50	.6	235	2.9	866	10.8	7,136	88.7	41	.5	8,043
IL FEMALE	13	.3	306	7.3	23	.5	100	2.4	442	10.5	3,733	89.0	21	.5	4,196
IL MALE	8	.2	254	6.6	27	.7	135	3.5	424	11.0	3,403	88.5	20	.5	3,847
JUDSON COLLEGE															
IL TOTAL	1	.2	11	2.6	1	.2	6	1.4	19	4.5	395	94.3	5	1.2	419
IL FEMALE	0	.0	7	3.3	1	.5	2	.9	10	4.7	201	94.4	2	.9	213
IL MALE	1	.5	4	1.9	0	.0	4	1.9	9	4.4	194	94.2	3	1.5	206
KANKAKEE CMTY COLLEGE															
IL TOTAL	11	.3	383	11.3	24	.7	21	.6	439	12.9	2,936	86.4	24	.7	3,399
IL FEMALE	3	.1	228	11.3	10	.5	13	.6	254	12.6	1,747	86.8	12	.6	2,013
IL MALE	8	.6	155	11.2	14	1.0	8	.6	185	13.3	1,189	85.8	12	.9	1,386
KASKASKIA COLLEGE															
IL TOTAL	13	.5	77	2.8	11	.4	7	.3	108	3.9	2,679	96.1	2	.1	2,789
IL FEMALE	7	.4	45	2.6	6	.3	3	.2	61	3.5	1,670	96.5	0	.0	1,731
IL MALE	6	.6	32	3.0	5	.5	4	.4	47	4.4	1,009	95.4	2	.2	1,058
KENDALL COLLEGE															
IL TOTAL	0	.0	67	20.7	0	.0	2	.6	69	21.3	240	74.1	15	4.6	324
IL FEMALE	0	.0	53	31.2	0	.0	2	1.2	55	32.4	106	62.4	9	5.3	170
IL MALE	0	.0	14	9.1	0	.0	0	.0	14	9.1	134	87.0	6	3.9	154
KISHWAUKEE COLLEGE															
IL TOTAL	51	1.5	104	3.1	35	1.1	71	2.1	261	7.8	2,991	89.8	80	2.4	3,332
IL FEMALE	15	.9	48	2.8	22	1.3	25	1.5	110	6.5	1,579	93.2	5	.3	1,694
IL MALE	36	2.2	56	3.4	13	.8	46	2.8	151	9.2	1,412	86.2	75	4.6	1,638
KNOX COLLEGE															
IL TOTAL	1	.1	31	3.1	13	1.3	6	.6	51	5.1	901	90.6	43	4.3	995
IL FEMALE	1	.2	19	4.4	8	1.9	3	.7	31	7.3	380	89.0	16	3.7	427
IL MALE	0	.0	12	2.1	5	.9	3	.5	20	3.5	521	91.7	27	4.8	568

TABLE 1 - TOTAL UNDERGRADUATE ENROLLMENT IN INSTITUTIONS OF HIGHER EDUCATION BY RACE, ETHNICITY AND SEX: INSTITUTION, STATE AND NATION, 1978

ILLINOIS   CONTINUED

	AMERICAN INDIAN ALASKAN NATIVE		BLACK NON-HISPANIC		ASIAN OR PACIFIC ISLANDER		HISPANIC		TOTAL MINORITY		WHITE NON-HISPANIC		NON-RESIDENT ALIEN	
	NUMBER	%	NUMBER	%	NUMBER	%	NUMBER	%	NUMBER	%	NUMBER	%	NUMBER	%
LAKE FOREST COLLEGE														
IL TOTAL	1	.1	71	6.7	8	.8	10	.9	90	8.5	953	90.2	14	1.3
IL FEMALE	0	.0	46	8.6	4	.7	4	.7	54	10.1	480	89.4	3	.6
IL MALE	1	.2	25	4.8	4	.8	6	1.2	36	6.9	473	91.0	11	2.1
LAKE LAND COLLEGE														
IL TOTAL	19	.5	109	3.1	5	.1	8	.2	141	4.0	3,251	93.4	90	2.
IL FEMALE	3	.2	12	.7	2	.1	2	.1	19	1.2	1,606	97.9	15	
IL MALE	16	.9	97	5.3	3	.2	6	.3	122	6.6	1,645	89.3	75	4:?
LEWIS AND CLARK CC														
IL TOTAL	4	.3	69	6.0	4	.3		.3	81	7.0	1,065	92.4	7	.6
IL FEMALE	2	.3	39	6.0	2	.3		.0	43	6.6	608	93.1	2	.3
IL MALE	2	.4	30	6.0	2	.4		.8	38	7.6	457	91.4	5	1.0
LEWIS UNIVERSITY														
IL TOTAL	1	.0	237	10.1	26	1.1	53	2.3	317	13.5	2,012	85.4	26	1.1
IL FEMALE	0	.0	136	15.2	12	1.3	20	2.2	168	18.8	720	80.4	8	.9
IL MALE	1	.1	101	6.9	14	1.0	33	2.3	149	10.2	1,292	88.6	18	1.2
LINCOLN CHRISTIAN COLLEGE														
IL TOTAL	0	.0	10	2.1	0	.0	0	.0	10	2.1	455	97.2	3	.6
IL FEMALE	0	.0	1	.4	0	.0	0	.0	1	.4	222	99.6	0	.0
IL MALE	0	.0	9	3.7	0	.0	0	.0	9	3.7	233	95.1	3	1.2
LINCOLN COLLEGE														
IL TOTAL	0	.0	179	28.1	10	1.6	1	.2	190	29.8	445	69.9	2	.3
IL FEMALE	0	.0	78	28.4	6	2.2	0	.0	84	30.5	190	69.1	1	.4
IL MALE	0	.0	101	27.9	4	1.1	1	.3	106	29.3	255	70.4	1	.3
LINCOLN LAND CMTY COLLEGE														
IL TOTAL	12	.2	240	4.5	21	.4	10	.2	283	5.4	4,968	94.1	31	.6
IL FEMALE	6	.2	134	4.7	8	.3	5	.2	153	5.3	2,712	94.1	16	.6
IL MALE	6	.2	106	4.4	13	.5	5	.2	130	5.4	2,256	94.0	15	.6
LOYOLA U OF CHICAGO														
IL TOTAL	11	.1	707	9.5	168	2.3	318	4.3	1,204	16.2	6,164	82.7	83	1 1
IL FEMALE	5	.1	473	12.1	92	2.4	177	4.5	747	19.2	3,104	79.7	45	1 2
IL MALE	6	.2	234	6.6	76	2.1	141	4.0	457	12.9	3,060	86.1	38	111
MACCORMAC COLLEGE														
IL TOTAL	0	.0	46	10.3	3	.7	17	3.8	66	14.7	377	84.2	5	1.1
IL FEMALE	0	.0	35	8.8	2	.5	16	4.0	53	13.3	343	85.8	4	.0
IL MALE	0	.0	11	22.9	1	2.1	1	2.1	13	27.1	34	70.8	1	2.1
MACMURRAY COLLEGE														
IL TOTAL	0	.0	67	11.0	7	1.1	8	1.3	82	13.5	527	86.5	0	
IL FEMALE	0	.0	37	9.4	6	1.5	2	.5	45	11.5	348	88.5	0	
IL MALE	0	.0	30	13.9	1	.5	6	2.8	37	17.1	179	82.9	0	:0
MALLINCKRODT COLLEGE														
IL TOTAL	1	.9	1	.9	6	5.1		5.1	14	12.0	94	80.3	9	7 7
IL FEMALE	1	.9	1	.9	6	5.7		4.7	13	12.3	89	84.0	4	3 8
IL MALE	0	.0	0	.0	0	.0		9.1	1	9.1	5	45.5	5	4515
MCHENRY COUNTY COLLEGE														
IL TOTAL	4	.2	5	.2	3	.1	11	.5	23	1.1	2,067	98.8	3	.1
IL FEMALE	3	.3	1	.1	2	.2	3	.3	9	.9	958	99.1	0	.0
IL MALE	1	.1	4	.4	1	.1	8	.7	14	1.2	1,109	98.5	3	.3
MCKENDREE COLLEGE														
IL TOTAL	4	.5	112	14.2	4	.5	11	1.4	131	16.7	652	83.0	3	.4
IL FEMALE	0	.0	52	14.9	1	.3	3	.9	56	16.1	292	83.9	0	.0
IL MALE	4	.9	60	13.7	3	.7	8	1.8	75	17.1	360	82.2	3	.7
MIDSTATE COLLEGE														
IL TOTAL	0	.0	38	11.8	3	.9	0	.0	41	12.8	279	86.9	1	.3
IL FEMALE	0	.0	22	10.8	3	1.5	0	.0	25	12.3	178	87.7	0	.0
IL MALE	0	.0	16	13.6	0	.0	0	.0	16	13.6	101	85.6	1	.8
MIDWEST COLLEGE OF ENGR														
IL TOTAL	0	.0	1	1.3	3	3.8	1	1.3	5	6.3	74	92.5	1	1.3
IL FEMALE	0	.0	0	.0	0	.0	0	.0	0	.0	1	100.0	0	.0
IL MALE	0	.0	1	1.3	3	3.8	1	1.3	5	6.3	73	92.4	1	1.3
MILLIKIN UNIVERSITY														
IL TOTAL	2	.1	92	6.3	1	.1	10	.7	105	7.2	1,341	92.2	9	.6
IL FEMALE	1	.1	48	7.0	0	.0	3	.4	52	7.6	531	92.0	3	.4
IL MALE	1	.1	44	5.7	1	.1	7	.9	53	6.9	710	92.3	6	.8
MONMOUTH COLLEGE														
IL TOTAL	0	.0	27	4.1	2	.3	6	.9	35	5.3	601	91.2	23	3.5
IL FEMALE	0	.0	12	3.8	1	.3	3	1.0	16	5.1	292	93.3	5	1.6
IL MALE	0	.0	15	4.3	1	.3	3	.9	19	5.5	309	89.3	18	5.2
MOODY BIBLE INSTITUTE														
IL TOTAL	3	.3	24	2.1	9	.8	11	1.0	47	4.1	1,044	90.2	66	5.7
IL FEMALE	1	.2	11	2.2	3	.6	5	1.0	20	4.0	454	90.1	30	6.0
IL MALE	2	.3	13	2.0	6	.9	6	.9	27	4.1	590	90.4	36	5.5
MORAINE VLY CMTY COLLEGE														
IL TOTAL	14	.1	230	2.2	88	.8	146	1.4	478	4.6	9,955	95.0	50	.5
IL FEMALE	10	.2	165	2.9	42	.7	78	1.4	295	5.1	5,440	94.4	25	.4
IL MALE	4	.1	65	1.4	46	1.0	68	1.4	183	3.9	4,515	95.6	25	.5
MORRISON INST OF TECHN														
IL TOTAL	3	1.7	9	5.2	0	.0	7	4.0	19	10.9	155	89.1	0	.0
IL FEMALE	0	.0	1	4.5	0	.0	0	.0	1	4.5	21	95.5	0	.0
IL MALE	3	2.0	8	5.3	0	.0	7	4.6	18	11.8	134	88.2	0	.0
MORTON COLLEGE														
IL TOTAL	2	.1	0	.0	4	.1	25	.8	31	1.0	3,083	99.0	0	.0
IL FEMALE	1	.1	0	.0	3	.2	10	.6	14	.8	1,698	99.2	0	.0
IL MALE	1	.1	0	.0	1	.1	15	1.1	17	1.2	1,385	98.8	0	.0
MUNDELEIN COLLEGE														
IL TOTAL	2	.1	242	16.5	24	1.6	75	5.1	343	23.3	1,097	74.6	31	2.1
IL FEMALE	2	.1	223	16.3	23	1.7	69	5.0	317	23.2	1,023	74.7	29	2.1
IL MALE	0	.0	19	18.6	1	1.0	6	5.9	26	25.5	74	72.5	2	2.0
NATL COLLEGE ED MAIN CAM														
IL TOTAL	1	.3	56	14.5	9	2.3		2.3	75	19.4	309	8C.1	2	.5
IL FEMALE	1	.3	49	13.8	9	2.5		2.5	68	19.2	285	80.3	2	.6
IL MALE	0	.0	7	22.6	0	.0		.0	7	22.6	24	77.4	0	.0

TABLE ,1 - TOTAL UNDERGRADUATE ENROLLMENT IN INSTITUTIONS OF HIGHER EDUCATION BY RACE, ETHNICITY AND SEX:
            INSTITUTION, STATE AND NATION, 1978

	AMERICAN INDIAN ALASKAN NATIVE		BLACK NON-HISPANIC		ASIAN OR PACIFIC ISLANDER		HISPANIC		TOTAL MINORITY		WHITE NON-HISPANIC		NON-RESIDENT ALIEN		TOTAL
	NUMBER	%	NUMBER	%	NUMBER	%	NUMBER	%	NUMBER	%	NUMBER	%	NUMBER	%	NUMBER
ILLINOIS		CONTINUED													
NATL COLLEGE ED URBAN CAM															
IL TOTAL	7	3.3	126	60.3	1	.5	46	22.0	180	86.1	28	13.4	1	.5	209
IL FEMALE	7	3.5	119	60.1	1	.5	43	21.7	170	85.9	27	13.6	1	.5	198
IL MALE	0	.0	7	63.6	0	.0	3	27.3	10	90.9	1	9.1	0	.0	11
NORTH CENTRAL COLLEGE															
IL TOTAL	2	.2	29	3.1	10	1.1	6	.6	47	5.1	873	94.5	4	.4	924
IL FEMALE	1	.3	13	3.4	3	.8	2	.5	19	5.0	357	94.7	1	.3	377
IL MALE	1	.2	16	2.9	7	1.3	4	.7	28	5.1	516	94.3	3	.5	547
NTHESTN ILL UNIVERSITY															
IL TOTAL	26	.4	916	12.5	252	3.4	838	11.4	2,032	27.7	5,170	70.5	133	1.8	7,335
IL FEMALE	12	.3	537	13.4	110	2.7	494	12.3	1,153	28.7	2,822	70.3	39	1.0	4,014
IL MALE	14	.4	379	11.4	142	4.3	344	10.4	879	26.5	2,348	70.7	94	2.8	3,321
NORTHERN ILL UNIVERSITY															
IL TOTAL	24	.1	1,122	6.7	144	.9	206	1.2	1,496	8.9	14,989	89.5	256	1.5	16,741
IL FEMALE	8	.1	700	7.9	74	.8	107	1.2	889	10.1	7,842	88.8	101	1.1	8,832
IL MALE	16	.2	422	5.3	70	.9	99	1.3	607	7.7	7,147	90.4	155	2.0	7,909
NORTH PARK C & THEOL SEM															
IL TOTAL	4	.3	79	6.8	19	1.6	26	2.2	128	10.9	1,030	88.1	11	.9	1,169
IL FEMALE	3	.5	33	5.0	13	2.0	13	2.0	62	9.5	588	89.8	5	.8	655
IL MALE	1	.2	46	8.9	6	1.2	13	2.5	66	12.8	442	86.0	6	1.2	514
NORTHWESTERN UNIVERSITY															
IL TOTAL	6	.1	671	8.7	157	2.0	92	1.2	926	12.0	6,608	85.7	177	2.3	7,711
IL FEMALE	4	.1	392	10.8	62	1.7	41	1.1	499	13.8	3,061	84.6	59	1.6	3,619
IL MALE	2	.0	279	6.8	95	2.3	51	1.2	427	10.4	3,547	86.7	118	2.9	4,092
OAKTON COMMUNITY COLLEGE															
IL TOTAL	5	.1	162	2.8	160	2.7	60	1.0	387	6.6	5,478	93.4	0	.0	5,865
IL FEMALE	1	.0	96	3.0	67	2.1	29	.9	193	6.0	3,047	94.0	0	.0	3,240
IL MALE	4	.2	66	2.5	93	3.5	31	1.2	194	7.4	2,431	92.6	0	.0	2,625
OLIVET NAZARENE COLLEGE															
IL TOTAL	3	.2	75	4.1	8	.4	8	.4	94	5.1	1,731	94.1	15	.8	1,840
IL FEMALE	1	.1	49	4.6	7	.7	4	.4	61	5.7	992	93.5	8	.8	1,061
IL MALE	2	.3	26	3.3	1	.1	4	.5	33	4.2	739	94.9	7	.9	779
PARKLAND COLLEGE															
IL TOTAL	8	.2	229	6.9	21	.6	15	.5	273	8.2	2,991	90.1	57	1.7	3,321
IL FEMALE	3	.2	124	6.9	9	.5	9	.5	145	8.1	1,629	91.1	15	.8	1,789
IL MALE	5	.3	105	6.9	12	.8	6	.4	128	8.4	1,362	88.9	42	2.7	1,532
PRAIRIE STATE COLLEGE															
IL TOTAL	14	.3	611	12.4	124	2.5	101	2.0	850	17.2	4,072	82.6	8	.2	4,930
IL FEMALE	7	.3	319	12.5	62	2.4	38	1.5	426	16.8	2,109	83.0	7	.3	2,542
IL MALE	7	.3	292	12.2	62	2.6	63	2.6	424	17.8	1,963	82.2	1	.0	2,388
PRINCIPIA COLLEGE															
IL TOTAL	0	.0	6	.8	0	.0	5	.6	11	1.4	759	95.7	23	2.9	793
IL FEMALE	0	.0	2	.5	0	.0	2	.5	4	.9	418	97.2	8	1.9	430
IL MALE	0	.0	4	1.1	0	.0	3	.8	7	1.9	341	93.9	15	4.1	363
QUINCY COLLEGE															
IL TOTAL	3	.3	24	2.7	3	.3	12	1.3	42	4.7	835	93.9	12	1.3	889
IL FEMALE	1	.2	13	2.8	3	.6	3	.6	20	4.2	450	95.3	2	.4	472
IL MALE	2	.5	11	2.6	0	.0	9	2.2	22	5.3	385	92.3	10	2.4	417
REND LAKE COLLEGE															
IL TOTAL	2	.1	27	1.4	4	.2	4	.2	37	1.9	1,854	97.1	18	.9	1,909
IL FEMALE	1	.1	12	1.6	4	.5	1	.1	18	2.4	737	97.1	4	.5	759
IL MALE	1	.1	15	1.3	0	.0	3	.3	19	1.7	1,117	97.1	14	1.2	1,150
RICHLAND CMTY COLLEGE															
IL TOTAL	2	.2	161	12.2	6	.5	3	.2	172	13.0	1,149	87.0	0	.0	1,321
IL FEMALE	0	.0	100	16.2	3	.5	2	.3	105	17.0	511	83.0	0	.0	616
IL MALE	2	.3	61	8.7	3	.4	1	.1	67	9.5	638	90.5	0	.0	705
ROCKFORD COLLEGE															
IL TOTAL	0	.0	27	4.0	14	2.1	14	2.1	55	8.1	622	91.9	0	.0	677
IL FEMALE	0	.0	13	3.6	9	2.5	9	2.5	31	8.5	334	91.5	0	.0	365
IL MALE	0	.0	14	4.5	5	1.6	5	1.6	24	7.7	288	92.3	0	.0	312
ROCK VALLEY COLLEGE															
IL TOTAL	13	.2	330	4.8	31	.4	86	1.2	460	6.6	6,353	91.7	112	1.6	6,925
IL FEMALE	5	.1	191	5.2	10	.3	31	.8	237	6.5	3,383	92.1	54	1.5	3,674
IL MALE	8	.2	139	4.3	21	.6	55	1.7	223	6.9	2,970	91.4	58	1.8	3,251
ROOSEVELT UNIVERSITY															
IL TOTAL	18	.4	1,685	41.3	78	1.9	132	3.2	1,913	46.9	1,882	46.1	288	7.1	4,083
IL FEMALE	10	.4	1,200	53.4	30	1.3	66	2.9	1,306	58.1	845	37.6	95	4.2	2,246
IL MALE	8	.4	485	26.4	48	2.6	66	3.6	607	33.0	1,037	56.5	193	10.5	1,837
ROSARY COLLEGE															
IL TOTAL	0	.0	78	8.9	7	.8	22	2.5	107	12.1	764	86.7	10	1.1	881
IL FEMALE	0	.0	60	8.6	5	.7	15	2.2	80	11.5	608	87.5	7	1.0	695
IL MALE	0	.0	18	9.7	2	1.1	7	3.8	27	14.5	156	83.9	3	1.6	186
RUSH UNIVERSITY															
IL TOTAL	0	.0	24	8.5	7	2.5	7	2.5	38	13.4	244	85.9	2	.7	284
IL FEMALE	0	.0	22	8.6	7	2.7	5	2.0	34	13.3	220	85.9	2	.8	256
IL MALE	0	.0	2	7.1	0	.0	2	7.1	4	14.3	24	85.7	0	.0	28
SAINT XAVIER COLLEGE															
IL TOTAL	1	.1	82	5.7	2	.1	9	.6	94	6.5	1,347	93.2	5	.3	1,446
IL FEMALE	0	.0	69	6.7	2	.2	7	.7	78	7.5	955	92.2	3	.3	1,036
IL MALE	1	.2	13	3.2	0	.0	2	.5	16	3.9	392	95.6	2	.5	410
SANGAMON STATE UNIVERSITY															
IL TOTAL	0	.0	78	5.4	13	.9	4	.3	95	6.5	1,344	92.3	17	1.2	1,456
IL FEMALE	0	.0	42	6.3	5	.8	2	.3	49	7.4	611	91.7	6	.9	666
IL MALE	0	.0	36	4.6	8	1.0	2	.3	46	5.8	733	92.8	11	1.4	790
SAUK VALLEY COLLEGE															
IL TOTAL	4	.2	19	.9	10	.5	79	3.9	112	5.5	1,907	94.5	0	.0	2,019
IL FEMALE	2	.2	11	1.0	6	.6	31	2.9	50	4.7	1,020	95.3	0	.0	1,070
IL MALE	2	.2	8	.8	4	.4	48	5.1	62	6.5	887	93.5	0	.0	949
SCH ART INSTITUTE CHICAGO															
IL TOTAL	1	.1	145	15.5	25	2.7	40	4.3	211	22.5	714	76.2	12	1.3	937
IL FEMALE	0	.0	85	14.9	17	3.0	16	2.8	118	20.6	445	77.8	9	1.6	572
IL MALE	1	.3	60	16.4	8	2.2	24	6.6	93	25.5	269	73.7	3	.8	365

33

TABLE 1 - TOTAL UNDERGRADUATE ENROLLMENT IN INSTITUTIONS OF HIGHER EDUCATION BY RACE, ETHNICITY AND SEX:
INSTITUTION, STATE AND NATION, 1978

	AMERICAN INDIAN ALASKAN NATIVE		BLACK NON-HISPANIC		ASIAN OR PACIFIC ISLANDER		HISPANIC		TOTAL MINORITY		WHITE NON-HISPANIC		NON-RESIDENT ALIEN		TOTAL
	NUMBER	%	NUMBER	%	NUMBER	%	NUMBER	%	NUMBER	%	NUMBER	%	NUMBER	%	NUMBER
ILLINOIS					CONTINUED										
SHAWNEE COLLEGE															
IL TOTAL	3	.1	320	15.6	5	.2	3	.1	331	16.1	1,722	83.9	0	.0	2,053
IL FEMALE	2	.1	245	17.4	2	.1	2	.1	251	17.8	1,161	82.2	0	.0	1,412
IL MALE	1	.2	75	11.7	3	.5	1	.2	80	12.5	561	87.5	0	.0	641
SHERWOOD MUSIC SCHOOL															
IL TOTAL	0	.0	10	32.3	2	6.5	0	.0	12	38.7	19	61.3		.0	31
IL FEMALE	0	.0	4	22.2	2	11.1	0	.0	6	33.3	12	66.7	0	.0	18
IL MALE	0	.0	6	46.2	0	.0	0	.0	6	46.2	7	53.8	0	.0	13
SHIMER COLLEGE															
IL TOTAL	1	.3	49	16.0	4	1.3	85	27.7	139	45.3	168	54.7		.0	307
IL FEMALE	0	.0	28	17.4	0	.0	40	24.8	68	42.2	93	57.8	0	.0	161
IL MALE	1	.7	21	14.4	4	2.7	45	30.8	71	48.6	75	51.4	0	.0	146
SOUTHEASTERN ILL COLLEGE															
IL TOTAL	11	.6	237	13.2	8	.4	9	.5	265	14.8	1,523	84.9	6	.3	1,794
IL FEMALE	2	.3	11	1.6	1	.1	2	.3	16	2.4	653	97.5	1	.1	670
IL MALE	9	.8	226	20.1	7	.6	7	.6	249	22.2	870	77.4	5	.4	1,124
STHN ILLINOIS U CARBONDL															
IL TOTAL	104	.6	1,377	7.4	345	1.8	100	.5	1,926	10.3	16,113	86.2	658	3.5	18,697
IL FEMALE	27	.4	684	9.7	171	2.4	22	.3	904	12.8	5,932	84.2	205	2.9	7,041
IL MALE	77	.7	693	5.9	174	1.5	78	.7	1,022	8.8	10,181	87.3	453	3.9	11,656
STHN ILLINOIS U EDWARDSVL															
IL TOTAL	15	~.2	1,757	21.0	38	.5	36	.4	1,846	22.0	6,329	75.6	198	2.4	8,373
IL FEMALE	11	.2	1,230	27.6	18	.4	13	.3	1,272	28.6	3,144	70.6	35	.8	4,451
IL MALE	4	.1	527	13.4	20	.5	23	.6	574	14.6	3,185	81.2	163	4.2	3,922
SPERTUS COLLEGE JUDAICA															
IL TOTAL	0	.0	17	4.4	0	.0	1	.3	18	4.7	363	94.8	2	.5	383
IL FEMALE	0	.0	3	1.4	0	.0	0	.0	3	1.4	211	97.7	2	.9	216
IL MALE	0	.0	14	8.4	0	.0	1	.6	15	9.0	152	91.0	0	.0	167
SPOON RIVER COLLEGE															
IL TOTAL	4	.5	12	1.5	3	.4	1	.1	20	2.6	752	96.2	10	1.3	1782
IL FEMALE	3	.7	9	2.1	1	.2	1	.2	14	3.3	412	95.8	4	.9	430
IL MALE	1	.3	3	.9	2	.6	0	.0	6	1.7	340	96.6	6	1.7	352
SPRINGFLD COLLEGE IN ILL															
IL TOTAL	3	.6	21	4.3	3	.6	4	.8	31	6.3	443	90.6	15	3.1	489
IL FEMALE	3	.9	10	3.0	2	.6	1	.3	16	4.8	315	94.6	2	.6	333
IL MALE	0	.0	11	7.1	1	.6	3	1.9	15	9.6	128	82.1	13	8.3	156
STATE COMMUNITY COLLEGE															
IL TOTAL	1	.1	1,158	95.0	0	.0	0	.0	1,159	95.1	59	4.8	1	.1	1,219
IL FEMALE	0	.0	718	95.2	0	.0	0	.0	718	95.2	35	4.6	1	.1	754
IL MALE	1	.2	440	94.6	0	.0	0	.0	441	94.8	24	5.2	0	.0	465
TELSHE YESHIVA-CHICAGO															
IL TOTAL	0	.0	0	.0	0	.0	0	.0	0	.0	58	98.3	1	1.7	59
IL FEMALE	0	.0	0	.0	0	.0	0	.0	0	.0	0	.0	0	.0	0
IL MALE	0	.0	0	.0	0	.0	0	.0	0	.0	58	98.3	1	1.7	59
THORNTON CMTY COLLEGE															
IL TOTAL	74	.9	1,341	16.3	98	1.2	180	2.2	1,693	20.6	6,518	79.4	0	.0	8,211
IL FEMALE	42	.9	869	17.7	53	1.1	81	1.7	1,045	21.3	3,863	78.7	0	.0	4,908
IL MALE	32	1.0	472	14.3	45	1.4	99	3.0	648	19.6	2,655	80.4	0	.0	3,303
TRINITY CHRISTIAN COLLEGE															
IL TOTAL	0	.0	18	4.5	3	.7	2	.5	23	5.7	326	81.1	53	13.2	402
IL FEMALE	0	.0	9	4.2	2	.9	1	.5	12	5.6	170	79.4	32	15.0	214
IL MALE	0	.0	9	4.8	1	.5	1	.5	11	5.9	156	83.0	21	11.2	188
TRINITY COLLEGE															
IL TOTAL	1	.1	24	3.2	7	.9	4	.5	36	4.9	697	94.2	7	.9	740
IL FEMALE	1	.2	17	4.1	4	1.0	3	.7	25	6.0	389	93.5	2	.5	416
IL MALE	0	.0	7	2.2	3	.9	1	.3	11	3.4	308	95.1	5	1.5	324
TRITON COLLEGE															
IL TOTAL	33	.2	1,191	6.1	282	1.5	455	2.3	1,961	10.1	17,407	89.5	76	.4	19,444
IL FEMALE	18	.2	689	6.3	136	1.2	186	1.7	1,029	9.4	9,949	90.4	25	.2	11,003
IL MALE	15	.2	502	5.9	146	1.7	269	3.2	932	11.0	7,458	88.4	51	.6	8,441
UNIVERSITY OF CHICAGO															
IL TOTAL	11	.4	94	3.5	136	5.1	45	1.7	286	10.7	2,354	88.2	28	1.0	2,668
IL FEMALE	3	.3	55	6.3	53	6.0	16	1.8	127	14.5	742	84.5	9	1.0	878
IL MALE	8	.4	39	2.2	83	4.6	29	1.6	159	8.9	1,612	90.1	19	1.1	1,790
U HLTH SCI-CHGO MEDL SCH															
IL TOTAL	0	.0	2	2.0	6	6.1	6	6.1	14	14.3	84	85.7	0	.0	98
IL FEMALE	0	.0	2	3.3	2	3.3	4	6.7	8	13.3	52	86.7	0	.0	60
IL MALE	0	.0	0	.0	4	10.5	2	5.3	6	15.8	32	84.2	0	.0	38
U OF ILL CHICAGO CIRCLE															
IL TOTAL	79	.5	3,224	19.3	958	5.7	1,477	8.9	5,738	34.4	10,442	62.6	508	3.0	16,688
IL FEMALE	37	.5	1,945	27.3	392	5.5	684	9.6	3,058	42.9	3,966	55.7	97	1.4	7,121
IL MALE	42	.4	1,279	13.4	566	5.9	793	8.3	2,680	28.0	6,476	67.7	411	4.3	9,567
U OF ILL HEOL CTR CHGO															
IL TOTAL	1	.1	98	5.7	97	5.6	32	1.9	228	13.2	1,495	86.5	5	.3	1,728
IL FEMALE	1	.1	83	6.4	72	5.6	28	2.2	184	14.3	1,101	85.5	2	.2	1,287
IL MALE	0	.0	15	3.4	25	5.7	4	.9	44	10.0	394	89.3	3	.7	441
U OF ILL URBANA CAMPUS															
IL TOTAL	83	.3	971	3.9	531	2.1	236	.9	1,821	7.3	23,100	92.0	181	.7	25,102
IL FEMALE	40	.4	530	5.1	220	2.1	84	.8	874	8.4	9,509	91.2	39	.4	10,422
IL MALE	43	.3	441	3.0	311	2.1	152	1.0	947	6.5	13,591	92.6	142	1.0	14,680
VANDERCOOK C OF MUSIC															
IL TOTAL	0	.0	22	29.3	0	.0	2	2.7	24	32.0	51	68.0	0	.0	75
IL FEMALE	0	.0	1	5.0	0	.0	1	5.0	2	10.0	18	90.0	0	.0	20
IL MALE	0	.0	21	38.2	0	.0	1	1.8	22	40.0	33	60.0	0	.0	55
WAUBONSEE CMTY COLLEGE															
IL TOTAL	4	.2	90	5.2	8	~.5	56	3.3	158	9.2	1,527	88.9	33	1.9	1,718
IL FEMALE	0	.0	52	6.2	5	.6	25	3.0	82	9.8	746	89.1	9	1.1	837
IL MALE	4	.5	38	4.3	3	.3	31	3.5	76	8.6	781	88.6	24	2.7	881
WESTERN ILL UNIVERSITY															
IL TOTAL	14	.1	665	6.2	21	.2	88	.8	788	7.4	9,762	91.1	165	1.5	10,715
IL FEMALE	3	.1	306	6.4	7	.1	43	.9	359	7.5	4,377	91.2	61	1.3	4,797
IL MALE	11	.2	359	6.1	14	.2	45	.8	429	7.2	5,385	91.0	104	1.9	5,918

TABLE 1 - TOTAL UNDERGRADUATE ENROLLMENT IN INSTITUTIONS OF HIGHER EDUCATION BY RACE, ETHNICITY AND SEX: INSTITUTION, STATE AND NATION, 1978

	AMERICAN INDIAN ALASKAN NATIVE		BLACK NON-HISPANIC		ASIAN OR PACIFIC ISLANDER		HISPANIC		TOTAL MINORITY		WHITE NON-HISPANIC		NON-RESIDENT ALIEN		TOTAL
	NUMBER	%	NUMBER	%	NUMBER	%	NUMBER	%	NUMBER	%	NUMBER	%	NUMBER	%	NUMBER
ILLINOIS CONTINUED															
WHEATON COLLEGE															
IL TOTAL	3	.2	21	1.1	21	1.1	13	.7	58	2.9	1,892	96.0	20	1.0	1,970
IL FEMALE	2	.2	13	1.3	11	1.1	4	.4	30	3.0	950	96.1	9	.9	989
IL MALE	1	.1	8	.8	10	1.0	9	.9	28	2.9	942	96.0	11	1.1	981
WM RAINEY HARPER COLLEGE															
IL TOTAL	27	.2	87	.8	84	.7	180	1.6	378	3.3	10,809	94.7	228	2.0	11,415
IL FEMALE	13	.2	54	.9	44	.7	78	1.2	189	3.0	6,001	95.0	124	2.0	6,314
IL MALE	14	.3	33	.6	40	.8	102	2.0	189	3.7	4,808	94.3	104	2.0	5,101
ILLINOIS TOTAL (135 INSTITUTIONS)															
IL TOTAL	1,667	.9	65,881	14.2	6,389	1.4	11,147	2.4	85,084	18.4	369,835	80.0	7,440	1.6	462,359
IL FEMALE	861	.4	39,704	16.5	2,985	1.2	5,427	2.3	48,977	20.4	189,258	78.6	2,434	1.0	240,669
IL MALE	806	.4	26,177	11.8	3,404	1.5	5,720	2.6	36,107	16.3	180,577	81.5	5,006	2.3	221,690
INDIANA															
ANCILLA DOMINI COLLEGE															
IN TOTAL	0	.0	0	.0	0	.0	5	2.4	5	2.4	203	97.1	1	.5	209
IN FEMALE	0	.0	0	.0	0	.0	3	1.9	3	1.9	154	97.5	1	.6	158
IN MALE	0	.0	0	.0	0	.0	2	3.9	2	3.9	49	96.1	0	.0	51
ANDERSON COLLEGE															
IN TOTAL	7	.4	98	5.3	3	.2	5	.3	113	6.1	1,707	92.5	25	1.4	1,845
IN FEMALE	3	.3	52	5.0	1	.1	5	.5	61	5.9	958	92.7	14	1.4	1,033
IN MALE	4	.5	46	5.7	2	.2	0	.0	52	6.4	749	92.2	11	1.4	812
BALL STATE UNIVERSITY															
IN TOTAL	27	.2	676	4.7	22	.2	58	.4	783	5.4	13,636	94.3	43	.3	14,462
IN FEMALE	18	.2	395	4.9	9	.1	30	.4	452	5.6	7,553	94.2	14	.2	8,019
IN MALE	9	.1	281	4.4	13	.2	28	.4	331	5.1	6,083	94.4	29	.5	6,443
BETHEL COLLEGE															
IN TOTAL	1	.2	11	2.6	4	1.0	3	.7	19	4.6	381	91.4	17	4.1	417
IN FEMALE	0	.0	7	3.3	3	1.4	2	.9	12	5.7	191	90.1	9	4.2	212
IN MALE	1	.5	4	2.0	1	.5	1	.5	7	3.4	190	92.7	8	3.9	205
BUTLER UNIVERSITY															
IN TOTAL	4	.2	38	1.7	18	.8	11	.5	71	3.2	2,150	96.4	9	.4	2,230
IN FEMALE	0	.0	23	1.8	12	1.0	3	.2	38	3.0	1,208	96.5	6	.5	1,252
IN MALE	4	.4	15	1.5	6	.6	8	.8	33	3.4	942	96.3	3	.3	978
CALUMET COLLEGE															
IN TOTAL	10	.7	143	10.6	9	.7	148	11.0	310	23.0	1,035	76.7	5	.4	1,350
IN FEMALE	1	.1	90	13.0	4	.6	85	12.3	180	26.0	511	73.8	1	.1	692
IN MALE	9	1.4	53	8.1	5	.8	63	9.6	130	19.8	524	79.6	4	.6	658
CLARK COLLEGE															
IN TOTAL	0	.0	256	43.5	2	.3	1	.2	259	44.0	326	55.4	3	.5	588
IN FEMALE	0	.0	126	43.0	1	.3	0	.0	127	43.3	165	56.3	1	.3	293
IN MALE	0	.0	130	44.1	1	.3	1	.3	132	44.7	161	54.6	2	.7	295
DEPAUW UNIVERSITY															
IN TOTAL	4	.2	41	1.9	7	.3	15	.7	67	3.1	2,122	96.6	7	.3	2,196
IN FEMALE	2	.2	19	1.6	3	.3	5	.4	29	2.5	1,143	97.3	3	.3	1,175
IN MALE	2	.2	22	2.2	4	.4	10	1.0	38	3.7	979	95.9	4	.4	1,021
EARLHAM COLLEGE															
IN TOTAL	0	.0	59	5.7	6	.6	0	.0	65	6.3	952	92.2	15	1.5	1,032
IN FEMALE	0	.0	30	5.5	2	.4	0	.0	32	5.8	509	92.9	7	1.3	548
IN MALE	0	.0	29	6.0	4	.8	0	.0	33	6.8	443	91.5	8	1.7	484
FORT WAYNE BIBLE COLLEGE															
IN TOTAL	0	.0	11	2.4	9	2.0	2	.4	22	4.8	425	93.4	8	1.8	455
IN FEMALE	0	.0	4	1.8	3	1.4	1	.5	8	3.6	208	94.1	5	2.3	221
IN MALE	0	.0	7	3.0	6	2.6	1	.4	14	6.0	217	92.7	3	1.3	234
FRANKLIN COLLEGE INDIANA															
IN TOTAL	1	.2	4	.6	1	.2	1	.2	7	1.1	621	96.1	18	2.8	646
IN FEMALE	0	.0	0	.0	1	.3	1	.3	2	.6	306	98.4	3	1.0	311
IN MALE	1	.3	4	1.2	0	.0	0	.0	5	1.5	315	94.0	15	4.5	335
GOSHEN COLLEGE															
IN TOTAL	1	.1	32	2.7	5	.4	25	2.1	63	5.3	1,048	88.9	68	5.8	1,179
IN FEMALE	1	.1	18	2.5	4	.6	13	1.8	36	5.1	632	89.1	41	5.8	709
IN MALE	0	.0	14	3.0	1	.2	12	2.6	27	5.7	416	88.5	27	5.7	470
GRACE COLLEGE															
IN TOTAL	1	.1	0	.0	1	.1	0	.0	2	.3	719	99.3	3	.4	724
IN FEMALE	0	.0	0	.0	0	.0	0	.0	0	.0	385	99.7	1	.3	386
IN MALE	1	.3	0	.0	1	.3	0	.0	2	.6	334	98.8	2	.6	338
HANOVER COLLEGE															
IN TOTAL	0	.0	9	1.0	7	.8	2	.2	18	2.0	863	96.4	14	1.6	895
IN FEMALE	0	.0	1	.2	4	1.0	1	.2	6	1.4	402	97.1	6	1.4	414
IN MALE	0	.0	8	1.7	3	.6	1	.2	12	2.5	461	95.8	8	1.7	481
HOLY CROSS JUNIOR COLLEGE															
IN TOTAL	0	.0	5	2.3	0	.0	0	.0	5	2.3	210	95.9	4	1.8	219
IN FEMALE	0	.0	2	2.2	0	.0	0	.0	2	2.2	87	97.8	0	.0	89
IN MALE	0	.0	3	2.3	0	.0	0	.0	3	2.3	123	94.6	4	3.1	130
HUNTINGTON COLLEGE															
IN TOTAL	0	.0	1	.2	1	.2	0	.0	2	.4	495	97.4	11	2.2	508
IN FEMALE	0	.0	1	.4	0	.0	0	.0	1	.4	252	99.2	1	.4	254
IN MALE	0	.0	0	.0	1	.4	0	.0	1	.4	243	95.7	10	3.9	254
INDIANA CEN UNIVERSITY															
IN TOTAL	8	.4	49	2.7	11	.6	8	.4	76	4.1	1,755	95.8	1	.1	1,832
IN FEMALE	4	.4	28	2.5	8	.7	3	.3	43	3.9	1,064	96.1	0	.0	1,107
IN MALE	4	.6	21	2.9	3	.4	5	.7	33	4.6	691	95.3	1	.1	725
INDIANA C MORTUARY SCI															
IN TOTAL	0	.0	10	13.7	0	.0	0	.0	10	13.7	63	86.3	0	.0	73
IN FEMALE	0	.0	3	60.0	0	.0	0	.0	3	60.0	2	40.0	0	.0	5
IN MALE	0	.0	7	10.3	0	.0	0	.0	7	10.3	61	89.7	0	.0	68
INDIANA INST TECHNOLOGY															
IN TOTAL	1	.2	22	5.5	3	.7	4	1.0	30	7.4	206	51.1	167	41.4	403
IN FEMALE	1	1.8	5	8.9	0	.0	0	.0	6	10.7	43	76.8	7	12.5	56
IN MALE	0	.0	17	4.9	3	.9	4	1.2	24	6.9	163	47.0	160	46.1	347

TABLE 1 - TOTAL UNDERGRADUATE ENROLLMENT IN INSTITUTIONS OF HIGHER EDUCATION BY RACE, ETHNICITY AND SEX: INSTITUTION, STATE AND NATION, 1978

	AMERICAN INDIAN ALASKAN NATIVE		BLACK NON-HISPANIC		ASIAN OR PACIFIC ISLANDER		HISPANIC		TOTAL MINORITY		WHITE NON-HISPANIC		NON-RESIDENT ALIEN		TOTAL
	NUMBER	%	NUMBER	%	NUMBER	%	NUMBER	%	NUMBER	%	NUMBER	%	NUMBER	%	NUMBER
INDIANA CONTINUED															
INDIANA STATE U MAIN CAM															
IN TOTAL	19	.2	800	8.3	32	.3	37	.4	888	9.2	8,563	88.7	200	2.1	9,651
IN FEMALE	8	.2	448	9.4	20	.4	16	.3	492	10.3	4,228	88.5	58	1.2	4,778
IN MALE	11	.2	352	7.2	12	.2	21	.4	396	8.1	4,335	89.0	142	2.9	4,873
INDIANA ST U EVANSVL CAM															
IN TOTAL	5	.2	99	3.5	13	.5	7	.2	124	4.3	2,720	94.8	24	.8	2,868
IN FEMALE	1	.1	60	4.2	4	.3	3	.2	68	4.8	1,349	94.8	6	.4	1,423
IN MALE	4	.3	39	2.7	9	.6	4	.3	56	3.9	1,371	94.9	18	1.2	1,445
INDIANA U BLOOMINGTON															
IN TOTAL	43	.2	1,183	5.2	153	.7	184	.8	1,563	6.9	20,885	91.6	363	1.6	22,811
IN FEMALE	24	.2	645	5.7	96	.8	84	.7	849	7.5	10,327	91.3	139	1.2	11,315
IN MALE	19	.2	538	4.7	57	.5	100	.9	714	6.2	10,558	91.8	224	1.9	11,496
INDIANA UNIVERSITY EAST															
IN TOTAL	2	.2	42	3.6	1	.1	2	.2	47	4.0	1,127	95.8	2	.2	1,176
IN FEMALE	1	.2	33	5.2	0	.0	1	.2	35	5.5	602	94.2	2	.3	639
IN MALE	1	.2	9	1.7	1	.2	1	.2	12	2.2	525	97.8	0	.0	537
INDIANA U AT KOKOMO															
IN TOTAL	3	.2	33	2.0	2	.1	6	.4	44	2.7	1,599	97.2	2	.1	1,645
IN FEMALE	1	.1	20	2.1	0	.0	4	.4	25	2.6	931	97.2	2	.2	958
IN MALE	2	.3	13	1.9	2	.3	2	.3	19	2.8	668	97.2	0	.0	687
INDIANA U NORTHWEST															
IN TOTAL	4	.1	911	27.9	7	.2	174	5.3	1,096	33.6	2,145	65.7	25	.8	3,266
IN FEMALE	3	.1	676	32.4	5	.2	112	5.4	796	38.1	1,276	61.1	17	.8	2,089
IN MALE	1	.1	235	20.0	2	.2	62	5.3	300	25.5	869	73.8	8	.7	1,177
IND-PURDUE U INDIANAPOLIS															
IN TOTAL	22	.2	1,380	11.1	76	.6	51	.4	1,529	12.3	10,774	86.7	128	1.0	12,431
IN FEMALE	9	.1	903	13.8	44	.7	27	.4	983	15.0	5,526	84.2	51	.8	6,560
IN MALE	13	.2	477	8.1	32	.5	24	.4	546	9.3	5,248	89.4	77	1.3	5,871
INDIANA U AT SOUTH BEND															
IN TOTAL	10	.3	221	5.6	13	.3	22	.6	266	6.8	3,641	92.7	21	.5	3,928
IN FEMALE	3	.1	139	6.3	7	.3	14	.6	163	7.4	2,030	92.2	8	.4	2,201
IN MALE	7	.4	82	4.7	6	.3	8	.5	103	6.0	1,611	93.3	13	.8	1,727
INDIANA U SOUTHEAST															
IN TOTAL	13	.4	68	2.2	6	.2	7	.2	94	3.0	3,003	96.8	6	.2	3,103
IN FEMALE	4	.2	42	2.5	2	.1	3	.2	51	3.0	1,623	96.8	3	.2	1,677
IN MALE	9	.6	26	1.8	4	.3	4	.3	43	3.0	1,380	96.8	3	.2	1,426
IND-PURDUE U FORT WAYNE															
IN TOTAL	6	.1	223	3.6	27	.4	29	.5	285	4.7	5,783	94.5	53	.9	6,121
IN FEMALE	3	.1	130	4.3	10	.3	16	.5	159	5.2	2,878	94.1	21	.7	3,058
IN MALE	3	.1	93	3.0	17	.6	13	.4	126	4.1	2,905	94.8	32	1.0	3,063
IND VOC TECH C-COLUMBUS															
IN TOTAL	11	.9	28	2.2	9	.7	11	.9	59	4.7	1,201	95.3	0	.0	1,260
IN FEMALE	9	1.4	15	2.3	4	.6	2	.3	30	4.6	623	95.4	0	.0	653
IN MALE	2	.3	13	2.1	5	.8	9	1.5	29	4.8	578	95.2	0	.0	607
IND VOC TECH C-EVANSVILLE															
IN TOTAL	7	.6	38	3.3	7	.6	4	.3	56	4.8	1,102	95.2	0	.0	1,158
IN FEMALE	3	.8	6	1.6	1	.3	2	.5	10	2.6	374	97.4	0	.0	384
IN MALE	6	.8	32	4.1	6	.8	2	.3	46	5.9	728	94.1	0	.0	774
IND VOC TECH C-FORT HAYNE															
IN TOTAL	18	.8	146	6.3	19	.8	24	1.0	207	8.9	2,108	91.1	0	.0	2,315
IN FEMALE	5	.6	67	7.9	6	.7	11	1.3	89	10.4	763	89.6	0	.0	852
IN MALE	13	.9	79	5.4	13	.9	13	.9	118	8.1	1,345	91.9	0	.0	1,463
IND VOC TECH-INDIANAPOLIS															
IN TOTAL	24	.7	995	27.0	16	.4	26	.7	1,061	28.8	2,618	71.2	0	.0	3,679
IN FEMALE	4	.3	466	31.8	3	.2	6	.4	479	32.7	985	67.3	0	.0	1,464
IN MALE	20	.9	529	23.9	13	.6	20	.9	582	26.3	1,633	73.7	0	.0	2,215
IND VOC TECH C-KOKOMO															
IN TOTAL	18	1.2	74	4.8	13	.8	15	1.0	120	7.7	1,434	92.3	0	.0	1,554
IN FEMALE	3	.6	26	5.1	6	1.2	3	.6	38	7.5	469	92.5	0	.0	507
IN MALE	15	1.4	48	4.6	7	.7	12	1.1	82	7.8	965	92.2	0	.0	1,047
IND VOC TECH C-LAFAYETTE															
IN TOTAL	6	.7	14	1.7	5	.6	1	.1	26	3.1	804	96.9	0	.0	830
IN FEMALE	4	1.0	6	1.6	2	.5	1	.3	13	3.4	370	96.6	0	.0	383
IN MALE	2	.4	8	1.8	3	.7	0	.0	13	2.9	434	97.1	0	.0	447
IND VOC TECH-SELLERSBURG															
IN TOTAL	5	.6	42	4.8	10	1.1	1	.1	58	6.6	817	93.4	0	.0	875
IN FEMALE	2	.8	7	2.7	1	.4	0	.0	10	3.8	254	96.2	0	.0	264
IN MALE	3	.5	35	5.7	9	1.5	1	.2	48	7.9	563	92.1	0	.0	611
IND VOC TECH C-SOUTH BEND															
IN TOTAL	12	.6	208	9.8	12	.6	33	1.6	265	12.5	1,848	87.5	0	.0	2,113
IN FEMALE	6	.6	115	12.2	7	.7	17	1.8	145	15.3	800	84.7	0	.0	945
IN MALE	6	.5	93	8.0	5	.4	16	1.4	120	10.3	1,048	89.7	0	.0	1,168
IND VOC TECH-TERRE HAUTE															
IN TOTAL	15	1.4	64	5.9	14	1.3	15	1.4	108	10.0	977	90.0	0	.0	1,085
IN FEMALE	4	1.1	6	1.6	7	1.9	1	.3	18	4.9	350	95.1	0	.0	368
IN MALE	11	1.5	58	8.1	7	1.0	14	2.0	90	12.6	627	87.4	0	.0	717
INTERNATIONAL BUSINESS C															
IN TOTAL	1	.3	33	8.4	2	.5	2	.5	38	9.6	356	90.4	0	.0	394
IN FEMALE	1	.4	11	4.9	1	.4	1	.4	14	6.2	212	93.8	0	.0	226
IN MALE	0	.0	22	13.1	1	.6	1	.6	24	14.3	144	85.7	0	.0	168
LOCKYEAR COLLEGE															
IN TOTAL	0	.0	142	22.0	2	.3	2	.3	146	22.7	493	76.6	5	.8	644
IN FEMALE	0	.0	94	24.0	2	.5	1	.3	97	24.7	293	74.7	2	.5	392
IN MALE	0	.0	48	19.0	0	.0	1	.4	49	19.4	200	79.4	3	1.2	252
MANCHESTER COLLEGE															
IN TOTAL	1	.1	32	2.9	2	.2	8	.7	43	3.9	1,052	94.9	14	1.3	1,109
IN FEMALE	1	.2	13	2.3	2	.4	5	.9	21	3.8	529	95.5	4	.7	554
IN MALE	0	.0	19	3.4	0	.0	3	.5	22	4.0	523	94.2	10	1.8	555
MARIAN COLLEGE															
IN TOTAL	0	.0	35	7.0	3	.6	4	.8	42	8.4	442	88.8	14	2.8	498
IN FEMALE	0	.0	22	6.9	2	.6	1	.3	25	7.8	292	91.3	3	.9	320
IN MALE	0	.0	13	7.3	1	.6	3	1.7	17	9.6	150	84.3	11	6.2	178

	AMERICAN INDIAN ALASKAN NATIVE		BLACK NON-HISPANIC		ASIAN OR PACIFIC ISLANDER		HISPANIC		TOTAL MINORITY		WHITE NON-HISPANIC		NON-RESIDENT ALIEN		TOTAL
	NUMBER	%	NUMBER	%	NUMBER	%	NUMBER	%	NUMBER	%	NUMBER	%	NUMBER	%	NUMBER
INDIANA	CONTINUED														
MARION COLLEGE															
IN TOTAL	1	.1	22	2.8	6	.8	5	.6	34	4.3	737	92.8	23	2.9	794
IN FEMALE	0	.0	8	1.5	4	.8	3	.6	15	2.9	488	94.2	15	2.9	518
IN MALE	1	.4	14	5.1	2	.7	2	.7	19	6.9	249	90.2	8	2.9	276
OAKLAND CITY COLLEGE															
IN TOTAL	0	.0	23	4.9	4	.9		.0	27	5	440	94.2	0	.0	467
IN FEMALE	0	.0	7	3.8	2	1.1	0	.0	9	4.8	177	95.2	0	.0	186
IN MALE	0	.0	16	5.7	2	.7	0	.0	18	6.8	263	93.6	0	.0	281
PURDUE U MAIN CAMPUS															
IN TOTAL	19	.1	856	3.5	158	.6	178	.7	1,211	4.	23,130	93.8	317	1.3	24,658
IN FEMALE	9	.1	401	4.0	60	.6	69	.7	539	5.0	9,301	93.7	90	.9	9,930
IN MALE	10	.1	455	3.1	98	.7	109	.7	672	4.6	13,829	93.9	227	1.5	14,728
PURDUE U CALUMET CAMPUS															
IN TOTAL	5	.1	421	9.0	38	.8	246	5.3	710	15.2	3,959	84.8	2	.0	4,671
IN FEMALE	4	.2	243	11.7	17	.8	104	5.0	368	17.7	1,714	82.3	0	.0	2,082
IN MALE	1	.0	178	6.9	21	.8	142	5.5	342	13.2	2,245	86.7	2	.1	2,589
PURDUE U NORTH CEN CAMPUS															
IN TOTAL	0	.0	41	3.1	8	.6	2	.2	51	3.9	1,264	96.0	1	.1	1,316
IN FEMALE	0	.0	24	3.4	7	1.0	1	.1	32	4.5	679	95.5	0	.0	711
IN MALE	0	.0	17	2.8	1	.2	1	.2	19	3.1	585	96.7	1	.2	605
ROSE-HULMAN INST OF TECHN															
IN TOTAL	1	.1	1	.1	12	1.0	3	.3	17	1 5	1,145	98.2	4	.3	1,166
IN FEMALE	0	.0	0	.0	0	.0	0	.0	0	0	0	.0	0	.0	0
IN MALE	1	.1	1	.1	12	1.0	3	.3	17	115	1,145	98.2	4	.3	1,166
SAINT FRANCIS COLLEGE															
IN TOTAL	1	.1	10	1.3	1	.1	2	.3	14	1.8	764	96.8	11	1.4	789
IN FEMALE	0	.0	7	1.3	0	.0	1	.2	8	1.5	529	98.0	3	.6	540
IN MALE	1	.4	3	1.2	1	.4	1	.4	6	2.4	235	94.4	8	3.2	249
SAINT JOSEPH'S COLLEGE															
IN TOTAL	0	.0	46	4.9	5	.5	15	1.6	66	7.1	869	92.9	0	.0	935
IN FEMALE	0	.0	15	4.4	1	.3	7	2.0	23	6.7	321	93.3	0	.0	344
IN MALE	0	.0	31	5.2	4	.7	8	1.4	43	7.3	548	92.7	0	.0	591
SAINT MARY'S COLLEGE															
IN TOTAL	0	.0	8	.5	7	.4		.5	23	1.3	1,689	97.9	14	.8	1,726
IN FEMALE	0	.0	8	.5	7	.4		.5	23	1.3	1,689	97.9	14	.8	1,726
IN MALE	0	.0	0	.0	0	.0	8	.0	0	.0	0	.0	0	.0	0
SAINT MARY-OF-THE-WOODS C															
IN TOTAL	0	.0	17	3.1	1	.2		1.1	24	4.3	497	89.9	32	5.8	553
IN FEMALE	0	.0	17	3.1	1	.2	6	1.1	24	4.3	497	89.9	32	5.8	553
IN MALE	0	.0	0	.0	0	.0	8	.0	0	.0	0	.0	0	.0	0
SAINT MEINRAD COLLEGE															
IN TOTAL	0	.0	4	2.1	3	1.6	3	1.6	10	5.3	177	94.7	0	.0	187
IN FEMALE	0	.0	0	.0	0	.0	0	.0	0	.0	0	.0	0	.0	0
IN MALE	0	.0	4	2.1	3	1.6	3	1.6	10	5.	177	94.7	0	.0	187
TAYLOR UNIVERSITY															
IN TOTAL	0	.0	9	.6	0	.0	5	.3	14	.9	1,478	98.4	10	.7	1,502
IN FEMALE	0	.0	2	.3	0	.0	3	.4	5	.6	789	98.7	5	.6	799
IN MALE	0	.0	7	1.0	0	.0	2	.3	9	1.3	689	98.0	5	.7	703
TRI-STATE UNIVERSITY															
IN TOTAL	4	.3	25	2.0	1	.1	5	.4	35	2.8	1,043	83.9	165	13.3	1,243
IN FEMALE	0	.0	6	2.7	0	.0	0	.0	6	2.7	209	92.5	11	4.9	226
IN MALE	4	.4	19	1.9	1	.1	5	.5	29	2.9	834	82.0	154	15.1	1,017
UNIVERSITY OF EVANSVILLE															
IN TOTAL	3	.1	171	4.6	4	.1	2	.1	180	4.8	3,432	92.1	116	3.1	3,728
IN FEMALE	1	.0	87	4.2	3	.1	1	.0	92	4.4	1,970	94.1	31	1.5	2,093
IN MALE	2	.1	84	5.1	1	.1	1	.1	88	5.4	1,462	89.4	85	5.2	1,635
UNIVERSITY OF NOTRE DAME															
IN TOTAL	5	.1	167	2.4	57	.8	201	2.9	430	6.3	6,395	93.5	18	.3	6,843
IN FEMALE	2	.1	64	4.0	22	1.4	44	2.8	132	8.3	1,451	91.6	1	.1	1,584
IN MALE	3	.1	103	2.0	35	.7	157	3.0	298	5.7	4,944	94.0	17	.3	5,259
VALPARAISO UNIVERSITY															
IN TOTAL	6	.2	100	3.0	13	.4	14	.4	133	3	3,208	95.1	31	.9	3,372
IN FEMALE	3	.2	53	2.9	7	.4	10	.5	73	4.0	1,756	95.8	4	.2	1,833
IN MALE	3	.2	47	3.1	6	.4	4	.3	60	310	1,452	94.3	27	1.8	1,539
VINCENNES UNIVERSITY															
IN TOTAL	2	.1	233	6.0	7	.2	7	.2	249	.5	3,423	88.7	186	4.8	3,858
IN FEMALE	1	.1	81	4.9	1	.1	2	.1	85	.2	1,536	93.2	27	1.6	1,648
IN MALE	1	.0	152	6.9	6	.3	5	.2	164	6.4	1,887	85.4	159	7.2	2,210
WABASH COLLEGE															
IN TOTAL	2	.2	11	1.4	5	.6	9	1.1	27	3	771	95.3	11	1.4	809
IN FEMALE	0	.0	0	.0	0	.0	0	.0	0	0	0	.0	0	.0	0
IN MALE	2	.2	11	1.4	5	.6	9	1.1	27	313	771	95.3	11	1.4	809
INDIANA		TOTAL (	60 INSTITUTIONS)												
IN TOTAL	359	.2	10,441	6.0	883	.5	1,664	1.0	13,347	7 7	158,830	91.1	2,217	1.3	174,394
IN FEMALE	147	.2	5,777	6.9	419	.5	742	.9	7,085	8 5	75,963	90.7	669	.8	83,717
IN MALE	212	.2	4,664	5.1	464	.5	922	1.0	6,262	619	82,867	91.4	1,548	1.7	90,677
IOWA															
AMERICAN INSTITUTE BUS															
IA TOTAL	3	.4	19	2.3	10	1.2	1	.1	33	3.9	804	95.9	1	.1	838
IA FEMALE	2	.3	7	1.1	1	.2	0	.0	10	1.5	639	98.5	0	.0	649
IA MALE	1	.5	12	6.3	9	4.8	1	.5	23	12.2	165	87.3	1	.5	189
BRIAR CLIFF COLLEGE															
IA TOTAL	3	.3	21	1.9	1	.1	6	.5	31	2.8	1,069	95.5	19	1.7	1,119
IA FEMALE	2	.3	10	1.3	1	.1	5	.7	18	2.4	722	97.4	1	.1	741
IA MALE	1	.3	11	2.9	0	.0	1	.3	13	3.4	347	91.8	18	4.8	378
BUENA VISTA COLLEGE															
IA TOTAL	0	.0	2	.2	0	.0		.0	2	.2	1,079	99.7	1	.1	1,082
IA FEMALE	0	.0	2	.4	0	.0		.0	2	.4	474	99.4	1	.2	477
IA MALE	0	.0	0	.0	0	.0	8	.0	0	.0	605	100.0	0	.0	605

	AMERICAN INDIAN ALASKAN NATIVE		BLACK NON-HISPANIC		ASIAN OR PACIFIC ISLANDER		HISPANIC		TOTAL MINORITY		WHITE NON-HISPANIC		NON-RESIDENT ALIEN		TOTAL
	NUMBER	%	NUMBER	%	NUMBER	%	NUMBER	%	NUMBER	%	NUMBER	%	NUMBER	%	NUMBER
IOWA CONTINUED															
CENTRAL U OF IOWA															
IA TOTAL	3	.2	30	2.4	10	.8	15	1.2	58	4.6	1,176	93.3	26	2.1	1,260
IA FEMALE	1	.2	11	1.7	6	.9	5	.8	23	3.6	611	95.3	7	1.1	641
IA MALE	2	.3	19	3.1	4	.6	10	1.6	35	5.7	565	91.3	19	3.1	619
CLARKE COLLEGE															
IA TOTAL	0	.0	2	.5	0	.0	2	.5	4	1.0	395	98.0	4	1.0	403
IA FEMALE	0	.0	2	.5	0	.0	2	.5	4	1.0	395	98.0	4	1.0	403
IA MALE	0	.0	0	.0	0	.0	0	.0	0	.0	0	.0	0	.0	0
COE COLLEGE															
IA TOTAL	1	.1	36	3.6	29	2.9	9	.9	75	7.6	894	90.3	21	2.1	990
IA FEMALE	1	.2	17	3.9	18	4.1	0	.0	36	8.2	394	89.5	10	2.3	440
IA MALE	0	.0	19	3.5	11	2.0	9	1.6	39	7.1	500	90.9	11	2.0	550
CORNELL COLLEGE															
IA TOTAL	7	.8	43	4.9	17	2.0	5	.6	72	8.3	771	88.5	28	3.2	871
IA FEMALE	6	1.5	25	6.1	9	2.2	2	.5	42	10.2	360	87.8	8	2.0	410
IA MALE	1	.2	18	3.9	8	1.7	3	.7	30	6.5	411	89.2	20	4.3	461
DES MOINES AREA CC															
IA TOTAL	29	.6	77	1.5	37	.7	32	.6	175	3.4	4,790	94.3	116	2.3	5,081
IA FEMALE	18	.6	40	1.4	11	.4	13	.4	82	2.8	2,774	96.0	33	1.1	2,889
IA MALE	11	.5	37	1.7	26	1.2	19	.9	93	4.2	2,016	92.0	83	3.8	2,192
DIVINE WORD COLLEGE															
IA TOTAL	0	.0	11	11.6	11	11.6	3	3.2	25	26.3	67	70.5	3	3.2	95
IA FEMALE	0	.0	0	.0	0	.0	0	.0	0	.0	1	100.0	0	.0	1
IA MALE	0	.0	11	11.7	11	11.7	3	3.2	25	26.6	66	70.2	3	3.2	94
DORDT COLLEGE															
IA TOTAL	2	.2	2	.2	2	.2	0	.0	6	.5	891	74.7	296	24.8	1,193
IA FEMALE	0	.0	0	.0	1	.1	0	.0	1	.1	498	73.8	176	26.1	675
IA MALE	2	.4	2	.4	1	.2	0	.0	5	1.0	393	75.9	120	23.2	518
DRAKE UNIVERSITY															
IA TOTAL	5	.1	266	6.1	55	1.3	28	.6	354	8.1	3,991	90.9	47	1.1	4,392
IA FEMALE	1	.0	144	6.8	27	1.3	10	.5	182	8.6	1,913	90.7	15	.7	2,110
IA MALE	4	.2	122	5.3	28	1.2	18	.8	172	7.5	2,078	91.1	32	1.4	2,282
CLINTON COMMUNITY COLLEGE															
IA TOTAL	0	.0	8	1.0	0	.0	2	.3	10	1.3	753	98.0	5	.7	768
IA FEMALE	0	.0	3	.8	0	.0	1	.3	4	1.1	355	98.9	0	.0	359
IA MALE	0	.0	5	1.2	0	.0	1	.2	6	1.5	398	97.3	5	1.2	409
MUSCATINE CMTY COLLEGE															
IA TOTAL	0	.0	6	.8	0	.0	19	2.7	25	3.5	685	96.1	3	.4	713
IA FEMALE	0	.0	2	.6	0	.0	9	2.7	11	3.3	322	96.1	2	.6	335
IA MALE	0	.0	4	1.1	0	.0	10	2.6	14	3.7	363	96.0	1	.3	378
SCOTT COMMUNITY COLLEGE															
IA TOTAL	37	2.7	45	3.3	14	1.0	28	2.1	124	9.2	1,227	90.6	3	.2	1,354
IA FEMALE	21	2.7	25	3.2	9	1.2	16	2.1	71	9.2	699	90.8	0	.0	770
IA MALE	16	2.7	20	3.4	5	.9	12	2.1	53	9.1	528	90.4	3	.5	584
ELLSWORTH CMTY COLLEGE															
IA TOTAL	1	.1	65	8.5	1	.1	2	.3	69	9.0	678	88.5	19	2.5	766
IA FEMALE	0	.0	6	1.9	1	.3	1	.3	8	2.6	301	97.1	1	.3	310
IA MALE	1	.2	59	12.9	0	.0	1	.2	61	13.4	377	82.7	18	3.9	456
FAITH BAPT BIBLE COLLEGE															
IA TOTAL	1	.2	2	.4	0	.0	1	.2	4	.8	478	99.2	0	.0	482
IA FEMALE	1	.4	1	.4	0	.0	0	.0	2	.8	236	99.2	0	.0	238
IA MALE	0	.0	1	.4	0	.0	1	.4	2	.8	242	99.2	0	.0	244
GRACELAND COLLEGE															
IA TOTAL	5	.4	22	1.8	19	1.5	5	.4	51	4.1	1,137	91.8	51	4.1	1,239
IA FEMALE	2	.3	5	.7	12	1.8	3	.4	22	3.3	632	93.9	19	2.8	673
IA MALE	3	.5	17	3.0	7	1.2	2	.4	29	5.1	505	89.2	32	5.7	566
GRAND VIEW COLLEGE															
IA TOTAL	0	.0	59	5.0	4	.3	4	.3	67	5.6	1,030	86.8	89	7.5	1,186
IA FEMALE	0	.0	32	4.3	3	.4	2	.3	37	4.9	702	93.4	13	1.7	752
IA MALE	0	.0	27	6.2	1	.2	2	.5	30	6.9	328	75.6	76	17.5	434
GRINNELL COLLEGE															
IA TOTAL	4	.3	42	3.4	15	1.2	7	.6	68	5.5	1,153	92.7	23	1.8	1,244
IA FEMALE	2	.4	25	4.6	10	1.9	3	.6	40	7.4	491	90.9	9	1.7	540
IA MALE	2	.3	17	2.4	5	.7	4	.6	28	4.0	662	94.0	14	2.0	704
HAWKEYE INST TECHNOLOGY															
IA TOTAL	3	.2	61	3.6	6	.4	0	.0	70	4.2	1,604	95.5	5	.3	1,679
IA FEMALE	2	.3	32	4.3	3	.4	0	.0	37	5.0	704	95.0	0	.0	741
IA MALE	1	.1	29	3.1	3	.3	0	.0	33	3.5	900	95.9	5	.5	938
INDIAN HLS CC-CENTERVILLE															
IA TOTAL	1	.3	15	4.9	0	.0	0	.0	16	5.2	289	93.8	3	1.0	308
IA FEMALE	0	.0	0	.0	0	.0	0	.0	0	.0	136	99.3	1	.7	137
IA MALE	1	.6	15	8.8	0	.0	0	.0	16	9.4	153	89.5	2	1.2	171
INDIAN HLS CC-OTTUMWA															
IA TOTAL	1	.1	2	.3	5	.7	3	.4	11	1.5	740	98.1	3	.4	754
IA FEMALE	1	.3	1	.3	0	.0	0	.0	2	.6	336	99.1	1	.3	339
IA MALE	1	.2	1	.2	5	1.2	3	.7	9	2.2	404	97.3	2	.5	415
IOWA CENTRAL CC															
IA TOTAL	0	.0	11	.5	1	.0	1	.0	13	.6	2,014	97.5	39	1.9	2,066
IA FEMALE	0	.0	0	.0	1	.1	1	.1	2	.2	939	99.1	7	.7	948
IA MALE	0	.0	11	1.0	0	.0	0	.0	11	1.0	1,075	96.2	32	2.9	1,118
IOWA LAKES CC NORTH CTR															
IA TOTAL	0	.0	15	3.1	1	.2	1	.2	17	3.5	468	96.1	2	.4	487
IA FEMALE	0	.0	0	.0	0	.0	1	.4	1	.4	258	99.2	1	.4	260
IA MALE	0	.0	15	6.6	1	.4	0	.0	16	7.0	210	92.5	1	.4	227
IOWA LAKES CC SOUTH CTR															
IA TOTAL	0	.0	1	.1	2	.3	1	.1	4	.6	695	99.4	0	.0	699
IA FEMALE	0	.0	0	.0	1	.4	1	.4	2	.8	249	99.2	0	.0	251
IA MALE	0	.0	1	.2	1	.2	0	.0	2	.4	446	99.6	0	.0	448
IOWA STATE U SCI & TECHN															
IA TOTAL	13	.1	209	1.1	100	.5	42	.2	364	1.9	18,219	95.7	462	2.4	19,045
IA FEMALE	6	.1	72	.9	36	.5	16	.2	130	1.7	7,452	97.1	94	1.2	7,676
IA MALE	7	.1	137	1.2	64	.6	26	.2	234	2.1	10,767	94.7	368	3.2	11,369

TABLE 1 - TOTAL UNDERGRADUATE ENROLLMENT IN INSTITUTIONS OF HIGHER EDUCATION BY RACE, ETHNICITY AND SEX: INSTITUTION, STATE AND NATION, 1978

	AMERICAN INDIAN ALASKAN NATIVE		BLACK NON-HISPANIC		ASIAN OR PACIFIC ISLANDER		HISPANIC		TOTAL MINORITY		WHITE NON-HISPANIC		NON-RESIDENT ALIEN		TOTAL
	NUMBER	%	NUMBER	%	NUMBER	%	NUMBER	%	NUMBER	%	NUMBER	%	NUMBER	%	NUMBER
IOWA	**CONTINUED**														
IOWA WESLEYAN COLLEGE															
IA TOTAL	0	.0	65	10.3	1	.2	4	.6	70	11.0	564	89.0	0	.0	634
IA FEMALE	0	.0	33	8.4	0	.0	2	.5	35	8.9	360	91.1	0	.0	395
IA MALE	0	.0	32	13.4	1	.4	2	.8	35	14.6	204	85.4	0	.0	239
IOWA WESTERN CMTY COLLEGE															
IA TOTAL	6	.3	10	.5	11	.5	2	.1	29	1.4	2,053	98.1	10	.5	2,092
IA FEMALE	4	.4	3	.3	2	.2	1	.1	10	1.0	991	98.9	1	.1	1,002
IA MALE	2	.2	7	.6	9	.8	1	.1	19	1.7	1,062	97.4	9	.8	1,090
KIRKWOOD CMTY COLLEGE															
IA TOTAL	66	1.4	78	1.6	3	.7	57	1.2	236	5.0	4,429	93.1	90	1.9	4,755
IA FEMALE	36	1.4	42	1.6	1	.7	31	1.2	128	5.0	2,423	94.0	27	1.0	2,578
IA MALE	30	1.4	36	1.7	1	.7	26	1.2	108	5.0	2,006	92.1	63	2.9	2,177
LORAS COLLEGE															
IA TOTAL	0	.0	3	.2	1	.1	2	.1	6	.	1,650	99.5	3	.2	1,659
IA FEMALE	0	.0	1	.2	1	.2	1	.2	3	.	653	99.5	0	.0	656
IA MALE	0	.0	2	.2	0	.0	1	.1	3	.4	997	99.4	3	.3	1,003
LUTHER COLLEGE															
IA TOTAL	0	.0	43	2.2	0	.0	0	.0	43	2.2	1,836	95.8	37	1.	1,916
IA FEMALE	0	.0	20	1.9	0	.0	0	.0	20	1.9	1,024	96.2	20	1.9	1,064
IA MALE	0	.0	23	2.7	0	.0	0	.0	23	2.7	812	95.3	17	2.0	852
MAHARISHI INTRNATL U															
IA TOTAL	2	.3		.7	9	1.5	12	2.0	27	.	529	89.7	34	8	590
IA FEMALE	2	1.1		.0	2	1.1	3	1.6	7	.	168	91.3	9	9	184
IA MALE	0	.0		1.0	7	1.7	9	2.2	20	.	361	88.9	25	12	406
MARSHALLTWN CMTY COLLEGE															
IA TOTAL	8	.7	14	1.2	25	2.1		.7	55	4.	1,130	95.4	0	.0	1,185
IA FEMALE	3	.5	0	.0	2	.3			6	.	658	99.1	0	.0	664
IA MALE	5	1.0	14	2.7	23	4.4	7	1.3	49	9.4	472	90.6	0	.0	521
MARYCREST COLLEGE															
IA TOTAL	0	.0	22	3.2	5	.7	6	.9	33	4.8	660	95.1	1	.1	694
IA FEMALE	0	.0	15	2.5	5	.8	4	.7	24	4.1	566	95.8	1	.2	591
IA MALE	0	.0	7	6.8	0	.0	2	1.9	9	8.7	94	91.3	0	.0	103
MORNINGSIDE COLLEGE															
IA TOTAL	12	1.0	23	2.0	12	1.0	5	.4	52	4.4	1,098	93.5	24	2.0	1,174
IA FEMALE	7	1.2	6	1.0	6	1.0	3	.5	22	3.8	552	95.0	7	1.2	581
IA MALE	5	.8	17	2.9	6	1.0	2	.3	30	5.1	546	92.1	17	2.9	593
MOUNT MERCY COLLEGE															
IA TOTAL	2	.2	9	1.0	2	.2	8	.9	21	2.3	883	97.6	1	.1	905
IA FEMALE	2	.3	7	1.1	0	.0	7	1.1	16	2.5	635	97.5	0	.0	651
IA MALE	0	.0	2	.8	2	.8	1	.4	5	2.0	248	97.6	1	.4	254
MOUNT SAINT CLARE COLLEGE															
IA TOTAL	0	.0	1	.6	0	.0		.0	1	.6	164	97.6	3	1.8	168
IA FEMALE	0	.0	0	.0	0	.0		.0	0	.0	117	98.3	2	1.7	119
IA MALE	0	.0	1	2.0	0	.0		.0	1	2.0	47	95.9	1	2.0	49
NORTHEAST IA VOC TECH SCH															
IA TOTAL	3	.3	0	.0	3	.3	0	.0	6	.6	1,075	99.4	0	.0	1,081
IA FEMALE	0	.0	0	.0	0	.0	0	.0	0	.0	590	100.0	0	.0	590
IA MALE	3	.6	0	.0	3	.6	0	.0	6	1.2	485	98.8	0	.0	491
N IOWA AREA CMTY COLLEGE															
IA TOTAL	4	.2	36	2.0	5	.3	13	.7	58	3 2	1,764	96.8	0	.0	1,822
IA FEMALE	3	.3	12	1.3	3	.3	3	.3	21	2 3	902	97.7	0	.0	923
IA MALE	1	.1	24	2.7	2	.2	10	1.1	37	4.1	862	95.9	0	.0	899
NORTHWESTERN COLLEGE															
IA TOTAL	2	.3	15	2.0	0	.0	0	.0	17	2.3	731	96.9	6	.8	754
IA FEMALE	0	.0	5	1.2	0	.0	0	.0	5	1.2	398	98.0	3	.7	406
IA MALE	2	.6	10	2.9	0	.0	0	.0	12	3.4	333	95.7	3	.9	348
OPEN BIBLE COLLEGE															
IA TOTAL	0	.0	0	.0	0	.0	2	1.9	2	1.9	102	98.1	0	.0	104
IA FEMALE	0	.0	0	.0	0	.0	0	.0	0	3.0	40	100.0	0	.0	40
IA MALE	0	.0	0	.0	0	.0	2	3.1	2	.1	62	96.9	0	.0	64
OTTUMWA HEIGHTS COLLEGE															
IA TOTAL	0	.0	6	2.1	0	.0	1	.3	7	2.4	273	95.5	6	2.1	286
IA FEMALE	0	.0	0	.0	0	.0	0	.0	0	.0	185	99.5	1	.5	186
IA MALE	0	.0	6	6.0	0	.0	1	1.0	7	7.0	88	88.0	5	5.0	100
PALMER JUNIOR COLLEGE															
IA TOTAL	7	1.0	33	4.6	0	.0	6	.8	46	.5	654	92.1	10	1.4	710
IA FEMALE	3	1.0	14	4.5	0	.0	2	.6	19	.1	293	93.3	2	.6	314
IA MALE	4	1.0	19	4.8	0	.0	4	1.0	27	6.8	361	91.2	8	2.0	396
SAINT AMBROSE COLLEGE															
IA TOTAL	3	.2	40	2.	2	.1	0	.0	45	2.7	1,586	96.6	10	.6	1,641
IA FEMALE	1	.2	15	2.4	1	.2	0	.0	17	2.7	602	96.6	4	.6	623
IA MALE	2	.2	25	2.5	1	.1	0	.0	28	2.8	984	96.7	6	.6	1,018
SIMPSON COLLEGE															
IA TOTAL	3	.4	60	7.	1	.1	3	.4	67	8.4	721	90.5	9	1.1	797
IA FEMALE	1	.3	18	4.	0	.0	0	.0	19	5.0	357	94.4	2	.5	378
IA MALE	2	.5	42	10.0	1	.2	3	.7	48	11.5	364	86.9	7	1.7	419
SIOUX EMPIRE COLLEGE															
IA TOTAL	20	5.0	18	4.5	0	.0	0	.0	38	.4	365	90.6	0	.0	403
IA FEMALE	9	10.5	3	3.5	0	.0	0	.0	12	1.0	74	86.0	0	.0	86
IA MALE	11	3.5	15	4.7	0	.0	0	.0	26	8.2	291	91.8	0	.0	317
SOUTHEASTERN CMTY COLLEGE															
IA TOTAL	0	.0	66	3.9	6	.4	21	1.2	93	5.5	1,573	93.4	19	1.1	1,685
IA FEMALE	0	.0	11	1.3	2	.2	9	1.0	22	2.5	839	97.2	2	.2	863
IA MALE	0	.0	55	6.7	4	.5	12	1.5	71	8.6	734	89.3	17	2.1	822
SOUTHWESTERN CMTY COLLEGE															
IA TOTAL	1	.2	12	2.	0	.0	0	0	13	2.	443	97.1	0	.0	456
IA FEMALE	0	.0	1	3.4	0	.0	0	0	1	.7	163	99.4	0	.0	164
IA MALE	1	.3	11	.8	0	.0	0	10	12	4.4	280	95.9	0	.0	292
UNIVERSITY OF DUBUQUE															
IA TOTAL	1	.1	34	3.8	1	.1	13	1.5	49	5.5	818	92.0	22	2.5	889
IA FEMALE	0	.0	15	3.4	1	.2	6	1.4	22	5.0	414	95.0	0	.0	436
IA MALE	1	.2	19	4.2	0	.0	7	1.5	27	6.0	404	89.2	22	4.9	453

	AMERICAN INDIAN ALASKAN NATIVE		BLACK NON-HISPANIC		ASIAN OR PACIFIC ISLANDER		HISPANIC		TOTAL MINORITY		WHITE NON-HISPANIC		NON-RESIDENT ALIEN		TOTAL
	NUMBER	%	NUMBER	%	NUMBER	%	NUMBER	%	NUMBER	%	NUMBER	%	NUMBER	%	NUMBER
IOWA CONTINUED															
UNIVERSITY OF IOWA															
IA TOTAL	50	.3	367	2.5	75	.5	86	.6	578	4.0	13,647	94.3	240	1.7	14,465
IA FEMALE	30	.4	190	2.6	37	.5	37	.5	294	.1	6,875	94.7	90	1.2	7,259
IA MALE	20	.3	177	2.5	38	.5	49	.7	284	1.9	6,772	94.0	150	2.1	7,206
U OF NORTHERN IOWA															
IA TOTAL	11	.1	165	1.8	21	.2	31	.3	228	2.5	8,692	97.2	24	.3	8,944
IA FEMALE	3	.1	94	1.9	8	.2	15	.3	120	2.4	4,851	97.4	10	.2	4,981
IA MALE	8	.2	71	1.8	13	.3	16	.4	108	2.7	3,841	96.9	14	.4	3,963
UPPER IOWA UNIVERSITY															
IA TOTAL	0	.0	25	4.7	0	.0	5	.9	30	5.6	495	93.0	7	1.3	532
IA FEMALE	0	.0	6	2.5	0	.0	2	.8	8	3.4	224	94.9	4	1.7	236
IA MALE	0	.0	19	6.4	0	.0	3	1.0	22	7.4	271	91.6	3	1.0	296
VENNARD COLLEGE															
IA TOTAL	1	.5	0	.0	0	.0	1	.5	2	1.0	184	94.4	9	4.6	195
IA FEMALE	1	1.0	0	.0	0	.0	0	.0	1	1.0	95	93.1	6	5.9	102
IA MALE	0	.0	0	.0	0	.0	1	1.1	1	1.1	89	95.7	3	3.2	93
WALDORF COLLEGE															
IA TOTAL	0	.0	29	5.8	2	.4	2	.4	33	6.7	461	92.9	2	.4	496
IA FEMALE	0	.0	0	.0	2	.9	0	.0	2	.9	223	98.2	2	.9	227
IA MALE	0	.0	29	10.8	0	.0	2	.7	31	11.5	238	88.5	0	.0	269
WARTBURG COLLEGE															
IA TOTAL	0	.0	12	1.1	10	.9	2	.2	24	2.2	1,071	97.8	0	.0	1,095
IA FEMALE	0	.0	6	1.0	3	.5	0	.0	9	1.6	571	98.4	0	.0	580
IA MALE	0	.0	6	1.2	7	1.4	2	.4	15	2.9	500	97.1	0	.0	515
WESTERN IOWA TECH															
IA TOTAL	20	1.4	10	.7	10	.7	22	1.5	62	4.2	1,406	95.4	6	.4	1,474
IA FEMALE	13	1.6	5	.6	5	.6	10	1.2	33	4.0	796	95.9	1	.1	830
IA MALE	7	1.1	5	.8	5	.8	12	1.9	29	4.5	610	94.7	5	.8	644
WESTMAR COLLEGE															
IA TOTAL	2	.3	51	8.3	1	.2	1	.2	55	9.	552	89.9	7	1.1	614
IA FEMALE	0	.0	13	4.5	0	.0	0	.0	13	4.0	272	95.1	1	.3	286
IA MALE	2	.6	38	11.6	1	.3	1	.3	42	12.8	280	85.4	6	1.8	328
WILLIAM PENN COLLEGE															
IA TOTAL	3	.5	84	14.0	2	.3	6	1.0	95	15.9	501	83.8	2	.3	598
IA FEMALE	0	.0	20	9.0	2	.9	3	1.4	25	11.3	196	88.3	1	.5	222
IA MALE	3	.8	64	17.0	0	.0	3	.8	70	18.6	305	81.1	1	.3	376
IOWA TOTAL (58 INSTITUTIONS)															
IA TOTAL	346	.3	2,407	2.3	580	.6	536	.5	3,869	3.7	99,207	94.5	1,851	1.8	104,927.
IA FEMALE	184	.4	1,017	2.0	251	.5	231	.4	1,683	3.2	49,700	95.6	599	1.2	51,982
IA MALE	162	.3	1,390	2.6	329	.6	305	.6	2,186	4.1	49,507	93.5	1,252	2.4	52,945
KANSAS															
ALLEN CO CMTY JR COLLEGE															
KS TOTAL	1	.1	14	1.8	3	.4	7	.9	25	3.2	716	91.7	40	5.1	781
KS FEMALE	0	.0	2	.5	1	.2	4	.9	7	1.6	418	97.0	6	1.4	431
KS MALE	1	.3	12	3.4	2	.6	3	.9	18	5.1	298	85.1	34	9.7	350
BAKER UNIVERSITY															
KS TOTAL	14	1.6	83	9.5	4	.5	5	.6	106	12.2	744	85.3	22	2.5	872
KS FEMALE	7	1.8	34	8.7	1	.3	1	.3	43	11.0	341	87.4	6	1.5	390
KS MALE	7	1.5	49	10.2	3	.6	4	.8	63	13.1	403	83.6	16	3.3	482
BARTON CO CMTY JR COLLEGE															
KS TOTAL	4	.2	14	.8	3	.2	6	.4	27	1.6	1,683	98.4	0	.0	1,710
KS FEMALE	1	.1	7	.7	2	.2	5	.5	15	1.5	974	98.5	0	.0	989
KS MALE	3	.4	7	1.0	1	.1	1	.1	12	1.7	709	98.3	0	.0	721
BENEDICTINE COLLEGE															
KS TOTAL	2	.2	42	4.6	7	.8	28	3.0	79	8.6	836	90.7	7	.8	922
KS FEMALE	2	.4	15	3.3	6	1.3	11	2.4	34	7.4	419	91.5	5	1.1	458
KS MALE	0	.0	27	5.8	1	.2	17	3.7	45	9.7	417	89.9	2	.4	464
BETHANY COLLEGE															
KS TOTAL	3	.4	20	2.7	1	.1	4	.5	28	3.8	708	95.0	9	1.2	745
KS FEMALE	0	.0	7	2.0	0	.0	1	.3	8	2.3	339	97.1	2	.5	349
KS MALE	3	.8	13	3.3	1	.3	3	.8	20	5.1	369	93.2	7	1.8	396
BETHEL COLLEGE															
KS TOTAL	2	.3	35	6.1	4	.7	3	.5	44	7.7	499	86.9	31	5.4	574
KS FEMALE	2	.8	10	3.8	4	1.5	0	.0	16	6.1	234	89.3	12	4.6	262
KS MALE	0	.0	25	8.0	0	.0	3	1.0	28	9.0	265	84.9	19	6.1	312
BUTLER CO CMTY JR COLLEGE															
KS TOTAL	19	1.2	99	6.2	9	.6	43	2.7	170	10.7	1,397	87.5	29	1.8	1,596
KS FEMALE	8	1.4	21	3.7	2	.3	8	1.4	39	6.8	532	93.0	1	.2	572
KS MALE	11	1.1	78	7.6	7	.7	35	3.4	131	12.8	865	84.5	28	2.7	1,024
CENTRAL BAPTIST THEOL SEM															
KS TOTAL	0	.0	0	.0	0	.0	0	.0	0	.0	6	85.7	1	14.3	7
KS FEMALE	0	.0	0	.0	0	.0	0	.0	0	.0	4	100.0	0	.0	4
KS MALE	0	.0	0	.0	0	.0	0	.0	0	.0	2	66.7	1	33.3.	3
CENTRAL COLLEGE															
KS TOTAL	1	.4	3	1.2	2	.8	1	.4	7	2.9	234	97.1	0	.0	241
KS FEMALE	0	.0	3	2.2	1	.7	0	.0	4	2.9	133	97.1	0	.0	137
KS MALE	1	1.0	0	.0	1	1.0	1	1.0	3	2.9	101	97.1	0	.0	104
CLOUD CO CMTY JR COLLEGE															
KS TOTAL	1	.1	13	1.1	2	.2	1	.1	17	1.4	1,154	98.4	2	.2	1,173
KS FEMALE	0	.0	1	.1	1	.1	1	.1	3	.4	732	99.5	1	.1	736
KS MALE	1	.2	12	2.7	1	.2	0	.0	14	3.2	422	96.6	1	.2	437
COFFEYV. CMTY JR COLLEGE															
KS TOTAL	0	.0	76	10.5	2	.3	12	1.7	90	12.4	577	79.5	59	8.1	726
KS FEMALE	0	.0	27	8.2	1	.3	2	.6	30	9.1	294	89.4	5	1.5	329
KS MALE	0	.0	49	12.3	1	.3	10	2.5	60	15.1	283	71.3	54	13.6	397
COLBY COMMUNITY COLLEGE															
KS TOTAL	2	.1	11	.7	1	.1	8	.5	22	1.5	1,477	98.4	2	.1	1,501
KS FEMALE	0	.0	1	.1	1	.1	1	.1	3	.3	987	99.6	1	.1	991
KS MALE	2	.4	10	2.0	0	.0	7	1.4	19	3.7	490	96.1	1	.2	510

KANSAS	AMERICAN INDIAN ALASKAN NATIVE		BLACK NON-HISPANIC		ASIAN OR PACIFIC ISLANDER		HISPANIC		TOTAL MINORITY		WHITE NON-HISPANIC		NON-RESIDENT ALIEN		TOTAL
	NUMBER	%	NUMBER	%	NUMBER	%	NUMBER	%	NUMBER	%	NUMBER	%	NUMBER	%	NUMBER
KANSAS CONTINUED															
COWLEY CO CMTY JR COLLEGE															
KS TOTAL	18	1.1	64	3.8	0	.0	25	1.5	107	6.3	1,597	93.7	1	.1	1,705
KS FEMALE	9	.9	24	2.4	0	.0	20	2.0	53	5.2	968	94.8	0	.0	1,021
KS MALE	9	1.3	40	5.8	0	.0	5	.7	54	7.9	629	92.0	1	.1	684
DODGE CTY CMTY JR COLLEGE															
KS TOTAL	9	.8	31	2.9	3	.3	33	3.0	76	7.0	1,007	92.6	4	.4	1,087
KS FEMALE	3	.5	9	1.6	1	.2	11	2.0	24	4.4	525	95.6	0	.0	549
KS MALE	6	1.1	22	4.1	2	.4	22	4.1	52	9.7	482	89.6	4	.7	538
DONNELLY COLLEGE															
KS TOTAL	1	.2	251	54.7	7	1.5	32	7.0	291	63.4	84	18.3	84	18.3	459
KS FEMALE	1	.4	188	73.7	2	.8	14	5.5	205	80.4	43	16.9	7	2.7	255
KS MALE	0	.0	63	30.9	5	2.5	18	8.8	86	42.2	41	20.1	77	37.7	204
EMPORIA STATE UNIVERSITY															
KS TOTAL	17	.4	177	4.3	12	.3	73	1.8	279	6.8	3,752	91.6	65	1.6	4,096
KS FEMALE	9	.4	90	4.0	3	.1	30	1.3	132	5.8	2,121	93.4	17	.7	2,270
KS MALE	8	.4	87	4.8	9	.5	43	2.4	147	8.1	1,631	89.3	48	2.6	1,826
FORT HAYS KANS ST COLLEGE															
KS TOTAL	31	.8	31	.8	14	.4	17	.4	93	2.4	3,773	95.9	67	1.7	3,933
KS FEMALE	15	.7	13	.6	7	.3	10	.5	45	2.2	1,958	97.4	7	.3	2,010
KS MALE	16	.8	18	.9	7	.4	7	.4	48	2.5	1,815	94.4	60	3.1	1,923
FT SCOTT CMTY JR COLLEGE															
KS TOTAL	0	.0	54	4.7	11	1.0	0	.0	65	5.6	1,015	88.0	74	6.4	1,154
KS FEMALE	0	.0	7	1.1	1	.2	0	.0	8	1.3	608	96.7	13	2.1	629
KS MALE	0	.0	47	9.0	10	1.9	0	.0	57	10.9	407	77.5	61	11.6	525
FRIENDS BIBLE COLLEGE															
KS TOTAL	1	1.0	0	.0	0	.0	0	.0	1	1.0	95	93.1	6	5.9	102
KS FEMALE	0	.0	0	.0	0	.0	0	.0	0	.0	53	94.6	3	5.4	56
KS MALE	1	2.2	0	.0	0	.0	0	.0	1	2.2	42	91.3	3	6.5	46
FRIENDS UNIVERSITY															
KS TOTAL	11	1.3	63	7.6	4	.5	7	.8	85	10.3	691	83.9	48	5.8	824
KS FEMALE	7	1.7	25	5.9	2	.5	3	.7	37	8.8	376	89.3	8	1.9	421
KS MALE	4	1.0	38	9.4	2	.5	4	1.0	48	11.9	315	78.2	40	9.9	403
GARDEN CITY COMMUNITY JC															
KS TOTAL	9	.9	57	5.4	8	.8	76	7.2	150	14.3	884	84.2	16	1.5	1,050
KS FEMALE	6	1.1	7	1.3	5	.9	47	8.7	65	12.0	474	87.6	2	.4	541
KS MALE	3	.6	50	9.8	3	.6	29	5.7	85	16.7	410	80.6	14	2.8	509
MASKELL INDIAN JR COLLEGE															
KS TOTAL	843	100.0	0	.0	0	.0	0	.0	843	100.0	0	.0	0	.0	843
KS FEMALE	425	100.0	0	.0	0	.0	0	.0	425	100.0	0	.0	0	.0	425
KS MALE	418	100.0	0	.0	0	.0	0	.0	418	100.0	0	.0	0	.0	418
HESSTON COLLEGE															
KS TOTAL	2	.3	7	1.1	2	.3	9	1.4	20	3.0	633	95.5	10	1.5	663
KS FEMALE	1	.3	5	1.4	1	.3	4	1.1	11	3.0	355	96.5	2	.5	368
KS MALE	1	.3	2	.7	1	.3	5	1.7	9	3.1	278	94.2	8	2.7	295
HIGHLAND CMTY JR COLLEGE															
KS TOTAL	86	6.6	294	22.5	0	.0	41	3.1	421	32.2	883	67.6	2	.2	1,306
KS FEMALE	39	11.0	30	8.4	0	.0	9	2.5	78	21.9	278	78.1	0	.0	356
KS MALE	47	4.9	264	27.8	0	.0	32	3.4	343	36.1	605	63.7	2	.2	950
HUTCHINSON CMTY JR COLLEGE															
KS TOTAL	11	.5	121	6.0	9	.4	49	2.4	190	9.4	1,820	90.2	8	.4	2,018
KS FEMALE	1	.1	22	2.7	4	.5	20	2.4	47	5.7	779	94.2	1	.1	827
KS MALE	10	.8	99	8.3	5	.4	29	2.4	143	12.0	1,041	87.4	7	.6	1,191
INDEPENDENCE COMMUNITY JC															
KS TOTAL	4	.4	87	8.9	1	.1	12	1.2	104	10.7	849	87.3	20	2.1	973
KS FEMALE	1	.2	18	3.4	0	.0	7	1.3	26	4.9	508	95.0	1	.2	535
KS MALE	3	.7	69	15.8	1	.2	5	1.1	78	17.8	341	77.9	19	4.3	438
JOHNSN CO CMTY JR COLLEGE															
KS TOTAL	5	.1	47	.9	19	.3	35	.6	106	1.9	5,328	97.9	6	.1	5,440
KS FEMALE	2	.1	22	.7	12	.4	24	.7	60	1.9	3,145	98.1	2	.1	3,207
KS MALE	3	.1	25	1.1	7	.3	11	.5	46	2.1	2,183	97.8	4	.2	2,233
KANSAS CITY KANS CMTY JC															
KS TOTAL	11	.4	579	19.6	9	.3	80	2.7	679	23.0	2,213	75.1	55	1.9	2,947
KS FEMALE	4	.3	348	21.8	6	.4	43	2.7	401	25.1	1,191	74.6	4	.3	1,596
KS MALE	7	.5	231	17.1	3	.2	37	2.7	278	20.6	1,022	75.6	51	3.8	1,351
KANSAS NEWMAN COLLEGE															
KS TOTAL	2	.3	44	6.9	2	.3	28	4.4	76	12.0	556	87.6	3	.5	635
KS FEMALE	1	.3	24	7.7	1	.3	15	4.8	41	13.1	271	86.9	0	.0	312
KS MALE	1	.3	20	6.2	1	.3	13	4.0	35	10.8	285	88.2	3	.9	323
KANSAS ST U AGR & APP SCI															
KS TOTAL	43	.3	349	2.5	67	.5	139	1.0	598	4.3	12,933	93.6	284	2.1	13,815
KS FEMALE	16	.3	140	2.3	25	.4	48	.8	229	3.7	5,821	95.3	59	1.0	6,109
KS MALE	27	.4	209	2.7	42	.5	91	1.2	369	4.8	7,112	92.3	225	2.9	7,706
KANSAS TECHNICAL INST															
KS TOTAL			4	1.5	7	2.6	4	1.5	15	5.6	250	93.6	2	.7	267
KS FEMALE	0	.0	0	.0	1	2.9			2	5.7	32	91.4	1	2.9	35
KS MALE	0	.0	4	1.7	6	2.6	3	1.3	13	5.6	218	94.0	1	.4	232
KANSAS WESLEYAN															
KS TOTAL	0	.0	19	5.1	1	.3	10	2.7	30	8.1	339	91.1	3	.8	372
KS FEMALE	0	.0	6	3.4	0	.0	5	2.8	11	6.2	166	93.8	0	.0	177
KS MALE	0	.0	13	6.7	1	.5	5	2.6	19	9.7	173	88.7	3	1.5	195
LABETTE CMTY JR COLLEGE															
KS TOTAL	4	.4	27	2.7	0	.0	16	1.6	47	4.7	926	92.4	29	2.9	1,002
KS FEMALE	3	.6	16	3.1	0	.0	1	.2	20	3.9	485	95.5	3	.6	508
KS MALE	1	.2	11	2.2	0	.0	15	3.0	27	5.5	441	89.3	26	5.3	494
MANHATTAN CHRSTN COLLEGE															
KS TOTAL	0	.0	8	4.0	0	.0	1	.5	9	4.5	189	95.5	0	.0	198
KS FEMALE	0	.0	2	2.2	0	.0	1	1.1	3	3.3	88	96.7	0	.0	91
KS MALE	0	.0	6	5.6	0	.0	0	.0	6	5.6	101	94.4	0	.0	107
MARYMOUNT COLLEGE KANSAS															
KS TOTAL	1	.1	45	6.3	10	1.4	21	2.9	77	10.7	640	89.0	2	.3	719
KS FEMALE	1	.2	14	3.0	9	1.9	12	2.6	36	7.7	432	92.3	0	.0	468
KS MALE	0	.0	31	12.4	1	.4	9	3.6	41	16.3	208	82.9	2	.8	251

TABLE 1 - TOTAL UNDERGRADUATE ENROLLMENT IN INSTITUTIONS OF HIGHER EDUCATION BY RACE, ETHNICITY AND SEX: INSTITUTION, STATE AND NATION, 1978

	AMERICAN INDIAN ALASKAN NATIVE		BLACK NON-HISPANIC		ASIAN OR PACIFIC ISLANDER		HISPANIC		TOTAL MINORITY		WHITE NON-HISPANIC		NON-RESIDENT ALIEN		TOTAL
	NUMBER	%	NUMBER	%	NUMBER	%	NUMBER	%	NUMBER	%	NUMBER	%	NUMBER	%	NUMBER
KANSAS	CONTINUED														
MCPHERSON COLLEGE															
KS TOTAL	2	.4	39	8.5	1	.2	7	1.5	49	10.7	391	85.2	19	4.1	459
KS FEMALE	0	.0	3	1.6	0	.0	3	1.6	6	3.3	174	95.1	3	1.6	183
KS MALE	2	.7	36	13.0	1	.4	4	1.4	43	15.6	217	78.6	16	5.8	276
MID-AMERICA NAZARENE C															
KS TOTAL	2	.2	19	1.8	1	.1	5	.5	27	2.5	1,030	96.1	15	1.4	1,072
KS FEMALE	0	.0	4	.7	1	.2	3	.5	8	1.4	548	97.9	4	.7	560
KS MALE	2	.4	15	2.9	0	.0	2	.4	19	3.7	482	94.1	11	2.1	512
NEOSHO CO CNTY JR COLLEGE															
KS TOTAL	2	.3	15	2.6	2	.3	11	1.9	30	5.2	509	88.4	37	6.4	576
KS FEMALE	0	.0	6	1.9	1	.3	7	2.2	14	4.3	308	95.1	2	.6	324
KS MALE	2	.8	9	3.6	1	.4	4	1.6	16	6.3	201	79.8	35	13.9	252
OTTAWA UNIVERSITY															
KS TOTAL	5	.7	105	13.8	3	.4	17	2.2	130	17.1	602	79.2	28	3.7	760
KS FEMALE	4	.9	41	9.4	2	.5	7	1.6	54	12.4	367	84.2	15	3.4	436
KS MALE	1	.3	64	19.8	1	.3	10	3.1	76	23.5	235	72.5	13	4.0	324
PITTSBURG ST UNIVERSITY															
KS TOTAL	38	1.1	123	3.5	20	.6	34	1.0	215	6.2	3,126	89.8	141	4.0	3,482
KS FEMALE	21	1.3	52	3.2	6	.4	17	1.0	96	5.9	1,523	92.9	20	1.2	1,639
KS MALE	17	.9	71	3.9	14	.8	17	.9	119	6.5	1,603	87.0	121	6.6	1,843
PRATT CMTY JUNIOR COLLEGE															
KS TOTAL	3	.8	32	8.3	0	.0	5	1.3	40	10.3	331	85.5	16	4.1	387
KS FEMALE	1	.6	6	3.7	0	.0	2	1.2	9	5.6	149	92.5	3	1.9	161
KS MALE	2	.9	26	11.5	0	.0	3	1.3	31	13.7	182	80.5	13	5.8	226
SAINT JOHN'S COLLEGE															
KS TOTAL	0	.0	3	1.4	1	.5	1	.5	5	2.4	197	95.2	5	2.4	207
KS FEMALE	0	.0	0	.0	0	.0	1	.8	1	.8	124	99.2	0	.0	125
KS MALE	0	.0	3	3.7	1	1.2	0	.0	4	4.9	73	89.0	5	6.1	82
SAINT MARY COLLEGE															
KS TOTAL	3	.7	43	10.0	10	2.3	13	3.0	69	16.0	338	78.2	25	5.8	432
KS FEMALE	2	.5	28	7.4	8	2.1	12	3.2	50	13.3	302	80.1	25	6.6	377
KS MALE	1	1.8	15	27.3	2	3.6	1	1.8	19	34.5	36	65.5	0	.0	55
SAINT MARY PLAINS COLLEGE															
KS TOTAL	1	.2	20	3.7	2	.4	21	3.9	44	8.2	486	90.2	9	1.7	539
KS FEMALE	1	.3	5	1.4	0	.0	11	3.1	17	4.8	334	94.6	2	.6	353
KS MALE	0	.0	15	8.1	2	1.1	10	5.4	27	14.5	152	81.7	7	3.8	186
SEWARD CO CNTY JR COLLEGE															
KS TOTAL	0	.0	20	2.1	1	.1	20	2.1	41	4.3	896	94.9	7	.7	944
KS FEMALE	0	.0	6	1.1	0	.0	9	1.7	15	2.8	530	97.2	0	.0	545
KS MALE	0	.0	14	3.5	1	.3	11	2.8	26	6.5	366	91.7	7	1.8	399
SOUTHWESTERN COLLEGE															
KS TOTAL	9	1.5	33	5.6	2	.3	9	1.5	53	9.0	520	87.8	19	3.2	592
KS FEMALE	8	2.7	8	2.7	0	.0	5	1.7	21	7.0	271	90.9	6	2.0	298
KS MALE	1	.3	25	8.5	2	.7	4	1.4	32	10.9	249	84.7	13	4.4	294
STERLING COLLEGE															
KS TOTAL	3	.6	27	5.3	4	.8	13	2.5	47	9.1	460	89.5	7	1.4	514
KS FEMALE	2	.8	6	2.3	1	.4	5	1.9	14	5.4	242	93.4	3	1.2	259
KS MALE	1	.4	21	8.2	3	1.2	8	3.1	33	12.9	218	85.5	4	1.6	255
TABOR COLLEGE															
KS TOTAL	1	.3	21	5.3	2	.5	3	.8	27	6.8	355	88.8	18	4.5	400
KS FEMALE	1	.5	5	2.5	0	.0	3	1.5	9	4.5	182	91.0	9	4.5	200
KS MALE	0	.0	16	8.0	2	1.0	0	.0	18	9.0	173	86.5	9	4.5	200
U OF KANSAS MAIN CAMPUS															
KS TOTAL	68	.4	539	3.3	90	.6	150	.9	847	5.2	14,788	91.4	551	3.4	16,186
KS FEMALE	35	.5	256	3.5	36	.5	59	.8	386	5.2	6,853	93.0	126	1.7	7,365
KS MALE	33	.4	283	3.2	54	.6	91	1.0	461	5.2	7,935	90.0	425	4.8	8,821
U OF KANS MEDICAL CENTER															
KS TOTAL	0	.0	6	1.5	1	.2	1	.2	8	2.0	395	97.8	1	.2	404
KS FEMALE	0	.0	4	1.2	1	.3	1	.3	6	1.9	318	98.1	0	.0	324
KS MALE	0	.0	2	2.5	0	.0	0	.0	2	2.5	77	96.3	1	1.3	80
WASHBURN U OF TOPEKA															
KS TOTAL	31	.7	312	7.4	16	.4	124	2.9	483	11.4	3,734	88.0	26	.6	4,243
KS FEMALE	18	.8	167	7.5	7	.3	46	2.1	238	10.6	1,989	88.9	10	.4	2,237
KS MALE	13	.6	145	7.2	9	.4	78	3.9	245	12.2	1,745	87.0	16	.8	2,006
WICHITA STATE UNIVERSITY															
KS TOTAL	99	1.0	627	6.2	104	1.0	165	1.6	995	9.8	8,974	88.4	177	1.7	10,146
KS FEMALE	54	1.2	361	7.7	35	.7	78	1.7	528	11.3	4,121	88.2	24	.5	4,673
KS MALE	45	.8	266	4.9	69	1.3	87	1.6	467	8.5	4,853	88.7	153	2.8	5,473
KANSAS	TOTAL (52 INSTITUTIONS)														
KS TOTAL	1,425	1.5	4,753	4.9	484	.5	1,425	1.5	8,087	8.3	87,620	89.6	2,092	2.1	97,799
KS FEMALE	711	1.5	2,096	4.3	198	.4	628	1.3	3,633	7.5	44,419	91.6	421	.9	48,473
KS MALE	714	1.4	2,657	5.4	286	.6	797	1.6	4,454	9.0	43,201	87.6	1,671	3.4	49,326
KENTUCKY															
ALICE LLOYD COLLEGE															
KY TOTAL	0	.0	7	4.2	0	.0	0	.0	7	4.2	157	94.6	2	1.2	166
KY FEMALE	0	.0	3	2.7	0	.0	0	.0	3	2.7	107	96.4	1	.9	111
KY MALE	0	.0	4	7.3	0	.0	0	.0	4	7.3	50	90.9	1	1.8	55
ASBURY COLLEGE															
KY TOTAL	1	.1	7	.6	8	.6	5	.4	21	1.7	1,230	97.6	9	.7	1,260
KY FEMALE	1	.2	4	.6	5	.8	2	.3	12	1.8	636	97.7	3	.5	651
KY MALE	0	.0	3	.5	3	.5	3	.5	9	1.5	594	97.5	6	1.0	609
BELLARMINE COLLEGE															
KY TOTAL	0	.0	58	4.1	9	.6	22	1.5	89	6.3	1,305	91.7	29	2.0	1,423
KY FEMALE	0	.0	38	4.5	4	.5	7	.8	49	5.8	782	92.7	13	1.5	844
KY MALE	0	.0	20	3.5	5	.9	15	2.6	40	6.9	523	90.3	16	2.8	579
BEREA COLLEGE															
KY TOTAL	0	.0	122	9.0	1	.1	0	.0	123	9.1	1,147	85.0	80	5.9	1,350
KY FEMALE	0	.0	77	10.1	1	.1	0	.0	78	10.2	654	85.8	30	3.9	762
KY MALE	0	.0	45	7.7	0	.0	0	.0	45	7.7	493	83.8	50	8.5	588

TABLE 1 - TOTAL UNDERGRADUATE ENROLLMENT IN INSTITUTIONS OF HIGHER EDUCATION BY RACE, ETHNICITY AND SEX: INSTITUTION, STATE AND NATION, 1978

	AMERICAN INDIAN ALASKAN NATIVE		BLACK NON-HISPANIC		ASIAN OR PACIFIC ISLANDER		HISPANIC		TOTAL MINORITY		WHITE NON-HISPANIC		NON-RESIDENT ALIEN		TOTAL
	NUMBER	%	NUMBER	%	NUMBER	%	NUMBER	%	NUMBER	%	NUMBER	%	NUMBER	%	NUMBER
KENTUCKY CONTINUED															
BRESCIA COLLEGE															
KY TOTAL	0	.0	16	2.1	0	.0	0	.0	16	2.1	740	95.6	18	2.3	774
KY FEMALE	0	.0	9	1.9	0	.0	0	.0	9	1.9	465	97.1	5	1.0	479
KY MALE	0	.0	7	2.4	0	.0	0	.0	7	2.4	275	93.2	13	4.4	295
CAMPBELLSVILLE COLLEGE															
KY TOTAL	1	.2	12	1.9	0	.0	0	.0	13	2.1	604	97.6	2	.3	619
KY FEMALE	0	.0	6	1.8	0	.0	0	.0	6	1.8	333	98.2	0	.0	339
KY MALE	1	.4	6	2.1	0	.0	0	.0	7	2.5	271	96.8	2	.7	280
CENTRE COLLEGE OF KY															
KY TOTAL	0	.0	19	2.5	2	.3	2	.3	23	3.1	722	96.4	4	.5	749
KY FEMALE	0	.0	9	2.9	1	.3	1	.3	11	3.5	299	96.5	0	.0	310
KY MALE	0	.0	10	2.3	1	.2	1	.2	12	2.7	423	96.4	4	.9	439
CUMBERLAND COLLEGE															
KY TOTAL	0	.0	88	4.4	0	.0	0	.0	88	4.4	1,873	94.1	30	1.5	1,991
KY FEMALE	0	.0	35	3.2	0	.0	0	.0	35	3.2	1,037	96.3	5	.5	1,077
KY MALE	0	.0	53	5.8	0	.0	0	.0	53	5.8	836	91.5	25	2.7	914
DRAUGHON'S BUSINESS C															
KY TOTAL	0	.0	30	9.4	0	.0	0	.0	30	9.4	288	90.6	0	.0	318
KY FEMALE	0	.0	23	15.2	0	.0	0	.0	23	15.2	128	84.8	0	.0	151
KY MALE	0	.0	7	4.2	0	.0	0	.0	7	4.2	160	95.8	0	.0	167
EASTERN KY UNIVERSITY															
KY TOTAL	6	.1	823	7.2	8	.1	14	.1	851	7.5	10,420	91.4	128	1.1	11,399
KY FEMALE	2	.0	430	7.1	2	.0	8	.1	442	7.3	5,598	92.2	31	.5	6,071
KY MALE	4	.1	393	7.4	6	.1	6	.1	409	7.7	4,822	90.5	97	1.8	5,328
GEORGETOWN COLLEGE															
KY TOTAL	2	.2	30	3.3	0	.0	3	.3	35	3.8	858	93.6	24	2.6	917
KY FEMALE	1	.2	7	1.6	0	.0	1	.2	9	2.0	427	97.0	4	.9	440
KY MALE	1	.2	23	4.8	0	.0	2	.4	26	5.5	431	90.4	20	4.2	477
KENTUCKY BUSINESS COLLEGE															
KY TOTAL	0	.0	126	15.2	1	.1	0	.0	127	15.3	702	84.6	1	.1	830
KY FEMALE	0	.0	68	18.1	0	.0	0	.0	68	18.1	306	81.6	1	.3	375
KY MALE	0	.0	58	12.7	1	.2	0	.0	59	13.0	396	87.0	0	.0	455
KY CHRISTIAN COLLEGE															
KY TOTAL	1	.2	2	.5	0	.0	1	.2	4	.9	421	99.1	0	.0	425
KY FEMALE	0	.0	0	.0	0	.0	0	.0	0	.0	206	100.0	0	.0	206
KY MALE	1	.5	2	.9	0	.0	1	.5	4	1.8	215	98.2	0	.0	219
KENTUCKY STATE UNIVERSITY															
KY TOTAL	3	.2	1,192	68.5	4	.2	2	.1	1,201	69.0	489	28.1	51	2.9	1,741
KY FEMALE	1	.1	555	66.9	4	.5	0	.0	560	67.6	262	31.6	7	.8	829
KY MALE	2	.2	637	69.8	0	.0	2	.2	641	70.3	227	24.9	44	4.8	912
KENTUCKY WESLEYAN COLLEGE															
KY TOTAL	0	.0	30	4.0	1	.1	2	.3	33	4.4	709	93.9	13	1.7	755
KY FEMALE	0	.0	13	3.0	0	.0	0	.0	13	3.0	422	96.8	1	.2	436
KY MALE	0	.0	17	5.3	1	.3	2	.6	20	6.3	287	90.0	12	3.8	319
LEES JUNIOR COLLEGE															
KY TOTAL	0	.0	8	2.7	0	.0	0	.0	8	2.7	279	93.3	12	4.0	299
KY FEMALE	0	.0	1	.6	0	.0	0	.0	1	.6	163	99.4	0	.0	164
KY MALE	0	.0	7	5.2	0	.0	0	.0	7	5.2	116	85.9	12	8.9	135
LINDSEY WILSON COLLEGE															
KY TOTAL	0	.0	27	7.3	0	.0	0	.0	27	7.3	335	91.0	6	1.6	368
KY FEMALE	0	.0	13	6.4	0	.0	0	.0	13	6.4	188	93.1	1	.5	202
KY MALE	0	.0	14	8.4	0	.0	0	.0	14	8.4	147	88.6	5	3.0	166
LOUISVILLE SCHOOL OF ART															
KY TOTAL	0	.0	9	10.7	0	.0	0	.0	9	10.7	75	89.3	0	.0	84
KY FEMALE	0	.0	3	5.5	0	.0	0	.0	3	5.5	52	94.5	0	.0	55
KY MALE	0	.0	6	20.7	0	.0	0	.0	6	20.7	23	79.3	0	.0	29
MIDWAY COLLEGE															
KY TOTAL	0	.0	13	4.2	0	.0	0	.0	13	4.2	290	93.5	7	2.3	310
KY FEMALE	0	.0	13	4.2	0	.0	0	.0	13	4.2	290	93.5	7	2.3	310
KY MALE	0	.0	0	.0	0	.0	0	.0	0	.0	0	.0	0	.0	0
MOREHEAD STATE UNIVERSITY															
KY TOTAL	20	.4	232	4.7	10	.2	12	.2	274	5.5	4,676	94.0	24	.5	4,974
KY FEMALE	10	.4	102	3.8	4	.1	6	.2	122	4.6	2,547	95.2	7	.3	2,676
KY MALE	10	.4	130	5.7	6	.3	6	.3	152	6.6	2,129	92.6	17	.7	2,298
MURRAY STATE UNIVERSITY															
KY TOTAL	16	.3	289	4.6	11	.2	17	.3	333	5.3	5,932	93.9	52	.8	6,317
KY FEMALE	8	.2	152	4.4	5	.1	8	.2	173	5.0	3,255	94.8	4	.1	3,432
KY MALE	8	.3	137	4.7	6	.2	9	.3	160	5.5	2,677	92.8	48	1.7	2,885
NORTHERN KY UNIVERSITY															
KY TOTAL	2	.0	65	1.1	12	.2	1	.0	80	1.4	5,565	98.1	28	.5	5,673
KY FEMALE	1	.0	31	1.1	7	.2	0	.0	39	1.4	2,829	98.4	8	.3	2,876
KY MALE	1	.0	34	1.2	5	.2	1	.0	41	1.5	2,736	97.8	20	.7	2,797
OWENSBORO BUSINESS C															
KY TOTAL	0	.0	37	10.4	0	.0	0	.0	37	10.4	317	89.3	1	.3	355
KY FEMALE	0	.0	25	15.5	0	.0	0	.0	25	15.5	136	84.5	0	.0	161
KY MALE	0	.0	12	6.2	0	.0	0	.0	12	6.2	181	93.3	1	.5	194
PIKEVILLE COLLEGE															
KY TOTAL	0	.0	21	3.6	0	.0	0	.0	21	3.6	564	95.4	6	1.0	591
KY FEMALE	0	.0	1	.3	0	.0	0	.0	1	.3	285	99.3	1	.3	287
KY MALE	0	.0	20	6.6	0	.0	0	.0	20	6.6	279	91.8	5	1.6	304
SAINT CATHARINE COLLEGE															
KY TOTAL	0	.0	10	6.3	0	.0	0	.0	10	6.3	146	91.8	3	1.9	159
KY FEMALE	0	.0	4	4.7	0	.0	0	.0	4	4.7	80	93.0	2	2.3	86
KY MALE	0	.0	6	8.2	0	.0	0	.0	6	8.2	66	90.4	1	1.4	73
SEMINARY OF SAINT PIUS X															
KY TOTAL	0	.0	1	.9	3	2.6	2	1.7	6	5.1	111	94.9	0	.0	117
KY FEMALE	0	.0	0	.0	0	.0	0	.0	0	.0	0	.0	0	.0	0
KY MALE	0	.0	1	.9	3	2.6	2	1.7	6	5.1	111	94.9	0	.0	117
STHESTN CHRISTIAN COLLEGE															
KY TOTAL	0	.0	5	5.7	1	1.1	0	.0	6	6.9	72	82.8	9	10.3	87
KY FEMALE	0	.0	2	4.1	1	2.0	0	.0	3	6.1	43	87.8	3	6.1	49
KY MALE	0	.0	3	7.9	0	.0	0	.0	3	7.9	29	76.3	6	15.8	38

TABLE 1 - TOTAL UNDERGRADUATE ENROLLMENT IN INSTITUTIONS OF HIGHER EDUCATION BY RACE, ETHNICITY AND SEX: INSTITUTION, STATE AND NATION, 1978

	AMERICAN INDIAN ALASKAN NATIVE		BLACK NON-HISPANIC		ASIAN OR PACIFIC ISLANDER		HISPANIC		TOTAL MINORITY		WHITE NON-HISPANIC		NON-RESIDENT ALIEN	
	NUMBER	%	NUMBER	%	NUMBER	%	NUMBER	%	NUMBER	%	NUMBER	%	NUMBER	%
KENTUCKY	CONTINUED													
SOUTHERN BAPT THEOL SEM														
KY TOTAL	0	.0	0	.0	0	.0	0	.0	0	.0	0	.0	0	.0
KY FEMALE	0	.0	0	.0	0	.0	0	.0	0	.0	0	.0	0	.0
KY MALE	0	.0	0	.0	0	.0	0	.0	0	.0	0	.0	0	.0
SPALDING COLLEGE														
KY TOTAL	2	.3	91	14.1	3	.5	3	.5	99	15.3	538	83.4	8	1.2
KY FEMALE	2	.3	85	14.1	3	.5	3	.5	93	15.5	500	83.2	8	1.3
KY MALE	0	.0	6	13.6	0	.0	0	.0	6	13.6	38	86.4	0	.0
SUE BENNETT COLLEGE														
KY TOTAL	0	.0	11	4.3	0	.0		.0	11	4.3	221	86.3	24	9.4
KY FEMALE	0	.0	6	4.3	0	.0	8	.0	6	4.3	131	94.2	2	1.4
KY MALE	0	.0	5	4.3	0	.0	8	.0	5	4.3	90	76.9	22	18.8
SULLIVAN JC BUSINESS														
KY TOTAL	0	.0	188	19.9	0	.0		.0	188	19.9	756	80.1	0	.0
KY FEMALE	0	.0	125	20.0	0	.0	8	.0	125	20.0	500	80.0	0	.0
KY MALE	0	.0	63	19.7	0	.0		.0	63	19.7	256	80.3	0	.0
THOMAS MORE COLLEGE														
KY TOTAL	2	.2	44	3.4	14	1.1	5	.4	65	5.1	1,205	94.4	6	.5
KY FEMALE	0	.0	27	4.0	3	.4	1	.1	31	4.6	637	95.1	2	.3
KY MALE	2	.3	17	2.8	11	1.8	4	.7	34	5.6	568	93.7	4	.7
TRANSYLVANIA UNIVERSITY														
KY TOTAL	0	.0	21	2.9	2	.3		.0	23	3.2	691	95.3	11	1.5
KY FEMALE	0	.0	12	3.3	2	.5	0	.0	14	3.8	351	95.6	2	.5
KY MALE	0	.0	9	2.5	0	.0	8	.0	9	2.5	340	95.0	9	2.5
UNION COLLEGE														
KY TOTAL	0	.0	34	7.1	2	.4	.	.2	37	7.8	434	91.0	6	1.3
KY FEMALE	0	.0	10	3.6	0	.0		.0	10	3.6	261	95.3	3	1.1
KY MALE	0	.0	24	11.8	2	1.0	8	.5	27	1.3	173	85.2	3	1.5
UNIVERSITY OF KENTUCKY														
KY TOTAL	51	.3	497	3.0	275	1.7	68	.4	891	5.4	15,332	93.5	172	1.
KY FEMALE	29	.4	250	3.3	120	1.6	32	.4	431	5 8	7,017	93.9	28	.0
KY MALE	22	.2	247	2.8	155	1.7	36	.4	460	512	8,315	93.2	144	1.8
U OF KENTUCKY CC SYSTEM														
KY TOTAL	36	.3	1,549	11.5	44	.3	27	.2	1,656	12.3	11,603	86.4	174	1 3
KY FEMALE	25	.3	993	12.4	22	.3	13	.2	1,053	13.2	6,894	86.2	47	16
KY MALE	11	.2	556	10.2	22	.4	14	.3	603	11.1	4,709	86.6	127	2.3
UNIVERSITY OF LOUISVILLE														
KY TOTAL	27	.2	1,093	8.8	84	.7	60	.5	1,264	10.1	10,962	87.9	239	1 9
KY FEMALE	12	.2	600	10.4	27	.5	29	.5	668	11.6	5,038	87.6	44	18
KY MALE	15	.2	493	7.3	57	.8	31	.5	596	8.9	5,924	88.2	195	2.9
WATTERSON COLLEGE														
KY TOTAL	2	.2	257	19.4	2	.2	6	.5	267	20.1	1,060	79.8	1	.1
KY FEMALE	0	.0	109	19.3	1	.2	4	.7	114	20.2	450	79.8	0	.0
KY MALE	2	.3	148	19.4	1	.1	2	.3	153	20.0	610	79.8	1	.1
WESTERN KY UNIVERSITY														
KY TOTAL	13	.1	826	8.2	1	.1	26	.3	878	8.8	8,984	89.6	170	1.7
KY FEMALE	3	.1	453	8.8		.1	6	.1	465	9.0	4,671	90.5	27	.5
KY MALE	10	.2	373	7.7	18	.2	20	.4	413	8.5	4,313	88.6	143	2.9
KENTUCKY	TOTAL (	39 INSTITUTIONS)												
KY TOTAL	185	.2	7,890	7.7	510	.5	279	.3	8,864	8.7	91,813	90.0	1,350	1.3
KY FEMALE	95	.2	4,294	8.1	215	.4	121	.2	4,725	8.9	47,980	90.5	297	.6
KY MALE	90	.2	3,596	7.3	295	.6	158	.3	4,139	8.4	43,833	89.4	1,053	2.1
LOUISIANA														
BOSSIER PARISH CC														
LA TOTAL	0	.0	128	8.6	15	1.0	13	.9	156	10.5	1,326	88.9	10	.7
LA FEMALE	0	.0	92	9.2	14	1 4	10	1.0	116	11.6	876	87.8	6	.6
LA MALE	0	.0	36	7.3	1	12	3	.6	40	8.1	450	91.1	4	.8
CENTENARY C OF LOUISIANA														
LA TOTAL	0	.0	39	5.2	9	1.2	1	.1	49	6.5	670	89.3	31	4.1
LA FEMALE	0	.0	22	6.1	5	1.4	0	.0	27	7.5	327	90.3	8	2.2
LA MALE	0	.0	17	4.4	4	1.0	1	.3	22	5.7	343	88.4	23	5.9
DELGADO COLLEGE														
LA TOTAL	27	.3	3,438	35.9	89	.9	268	2.8	3,822	39.9	5,436	56.7	325	4
LA FEMALE	12	.3	1,545	42.7	34	.9	105	2.9	1,696	46.8	1,815	50.1	111	3 11
LA MALE	15	.2	1,893	31.8	55	.9	163	2.7	2,126	35.7	3,621	60.7	214	.6
DILLARD UNIVERSITY														
LA TOTAL	0	.0	1,147	94.2	0	.0	0	.0	1,147	94.2	0	.0	70	5.8
LA FEMALE	0	.0	841	94.4	0	.0	0	.0	841	94.4	0	.0	50	5.6
LA MALE	0	.0	306	93.9	0	.0	0	.0	306	93.9	0	.0	20	6.1
GRAMBLING STATE U														
LA TOTAL	0	.0	3,261	98.0	4	.1	2	.1	3,267	98.2	3	.1	57	1.7
LA FEMALE	0	.0	1,757	99.4	0	.0	0	.0	1,757	99.4	2	.1	8	.5
LA MALE	0	.0	1,504	96.4	4	.3	2	.1	1,510	96.8	1	.1	49	3.1
LOUISIANA COLLEGE														
LA TOTAL	0	.0	77	6.5	1	.1	3	.3	81	6.8	1,102	92.9	3	.3
LA FEMALE	0	.0	43	6.8	0	.0	2	.3	45	7.1	585	92.9	0	.0
LA MALE	0	.0	34	6.1	1	.2	1	.2	36	6.5	517	93.0	3	.5
LA STATE U AND A&M C														
LA TOTAL	23	.1	914	4.7	23	.1	183	.9	1,143	5.8	17,473	89.2	973	5.0
LA FEMALE	12	.1	525	6.0	11	.1	78	.9	626	7.2	7,878	90.2	230	2.6
LA MALE	11	.1	389	3.6	12	.1	105	1.0	517	4.8	9,595	88.4	743	6.8
LA STATE U ALEXANDRIA														
LA TOTAL	5	.3	149	10.2	8	.5	10	.7	172	11.7	1,292	88.3	0	.0
LA FEMALE	4	.4	110	12.0	2	.2	5	.5	121	13.2	797	86.8	0	.0
LA MALE	1	.2	39	7.1	6	1.1	5	.9	51	9.3	495	90.7	0	.0
LA STATE U EUNICE														
LA TOTAL	3	.3	95	9.7	1	.1	1	.1	100	10.2	880	89.8	0	.0
LA FEMALE	3	.5	72	12.2	0	.0	1	.2	76	12.9	512	87.1	0	.0
LA MALE	0	.0	23	5.9	1	.3	0	.0	24	6.1	368	93.9	0	.0

44

DUATE ENROLLMENT IN INSTITUTIONS OF HIGHER EDUCATION BY RACE, ETHNICITY AND SEX:
TATE AND NATION, 1978

	BLACK NON-HISPANIC		ASIAN OR PACIFIC ISLANDER		HISPANIC		TOTAL MINORITY		WHITE NON-HISPANIC		NON-RESIDENT ALIEN		TOTAL
	NUMBER	%	NUMBER	%	NUMBER	%	NUMBER	%	NUMBER	%	NUMBER	%	NUMBER
TINUED													
	35	5.2	5	.7	5	.7	45	6.7	628	93.0	2	.3	675
	34	5.8	4	.7	4	.7	42	7.2	540	92.5	2	.3	584
	1	1.1	1	1.1	1	1.1	3	3.3	88	96.7	0	.0	91
	161	5.9	22	.8	11	.4	194	7.1	2,526	92.8	2	.1	2,722
	101	7.1	8	.6	3	.2	112	7.9	1,305	92.0	1	.1	1,418
	60	4.6	14	1.1	8	.6	82	6.3	1,221	93.6	1	.1	1,304
	2,029	16.9	179	1.5	348	2.9	2,572	21.4	9,233	76.7	228	1.9	12,033
	1,304	21.4	85	1.4	164	2.7	1,562	25.6	4,461	73.2	69	1.1	6,092
	725	12.2	94	1.6	184	3.1	1,010	17.0	4,772	80.3	159	2.7	5,941
	717	8.8	35	.4	40	.5	811	10.0	7,077	87.3	216	2.7	8,104
	377	11.4	11	.3	14	.4	409	12.4	2,861	86.5	36	1.1	3,306
	340	7.1	24	.5	26	.5	402	8.4	4,216	87.9	180	3.8	4,798
	258	10.8	21	.9	201	8.4	489	20.5	1,902	79.5	0	.0	2,391
	168	14.2	9	.8	107	9.0	289	24.4	896	75.6	0	.0	1,185
	90	7.5	12	1.0	94	7.8	200	16.6	1,006	83.4	0	.0	1,206
	571	13.3	19	.4	20	.5	619	14.4	3,661	85.0	26	.6	4,306
	365	16.1	11	.5	9	.4	390	17.2	1,872	82.6	5	.2	2,267
	206	10.1	8	.4	11	.5	229	11.2	1,789	87.7	21	1.0	2,039
	744	13.4	7	.1	31	.6	794	14.4	4,669	84.4	69	1.2	5,532
	474	16.6	3	.1	11	.4	495	17.4	2,338	82.1	14	.5	2,847
	270	10.1	4	.1	20	.7	299	11.1	2,331	86.8	55	2.0	2,685
	1,424	18.7	16	.2	13	.2	1,467	19.2	6,110	80.1	52	.7	7,629
	976	23.3	11	.3	5	.1	997	23.8	3,168	75.8	16	.4	4,181
	448	13.0	5	.1	8	.2	470	13.6	2,942	85.3	36	1.0	3,448
	823	17.8	22	.5	109	2.4	981	21.2	3,623	78.4	15	.3	4,619
	478	19.0	6	.2	53	2.1	552	21.9	1,958	77.8	6	.2	2,516
	345	16.4	16	.8	56	2.7	429	20.4	1,665	79.2	9	.4	2,103
	75	13.1	6	1.0	6	1.0	89	19.5	484	84.3	1	.2	574
	53	13.7	1	.3	4	1.0	60	15.5	326	84.2	1	.3	387
	22	11.8	5	2.7	2	1.1	29	15.5	158	84.5	0	.0	187
	62	25.3	0	.0	16	6.5	78	31.8	165	67.3	2	.8	245
	37	19.6	0	.0	15	7.9	52	27.5	135	71.4	2	1.1	189
	25	44.6	0	.0	1	1.8	26	46.4	30	53.6	0	.0	56
	2	.4	2	.4	3	.6	22	4.6	454	95.4	0	.0	476
	2	.6	2	.6	2	.6	17	4.9	329	95.1	0	.0	346
	0	.0	0	.0	1	.8	5	3.8	125	96.2	0	.0	130
	5	4.1	27	22.0	0	.0	32	26.0	91	74.0	0	.0	123
	0	.0	0	.0	0	.0	0	.0	0	.0	0	.0	0
	5	4.1	27	22.0	0	.0	32	26.0	91	74.0	0	.0	123
	52	7.5	2	.3	55	7.9	109	15.6	544	78.0	44	6.3	697
	47	7.7	1	.2	52	8.6	100	16.4	465	76.5	43	7.1	608
	5	5.6	1	1.1	3	3.4	9	10.1	79	88.8	1	1.1	89
	629	10.0	8	.1	19	.3	667	10.6	5,497	87.6	112	1.8	6,276
	433	12.5	6	.2	4	.1	450	13.0	2,984	86.4	18	.5	3,452
	196	6.9	2	.1	15	.5	217	7.7	2,513	89.0	94	3.3	2,824
	6,658	95.7	2	.0	1	.0	6,662	95.8	94	1.4	200	2.9	6,956
	3,669	98.5	2	.1	1	.0	3,673	98.6	25	.7	26	.7	3,724
	2,989	92.5	0	.0	0	.0	2,989	92.5	69	2.1	174	5.4	3,232
	2,681	98.9	0	.0	1	.0	2,683	99.0	16	.6	11	.4	2,710
	1,732	99.1	0	.0	0	.0	1,733	99.1	10	.6	5	.3	1,748
	949	98.6	0	.0	1	.1	950	98.8	6	.6	6	.6	962
	688	99.4	0	.0	0	.0	688	99.4	4	.6	0	.0	692
	477	99.2	0	.0	0	.0	477	99.2	4	.8	0	.0	481
	211	100.0	0	.0	0	.0	211	100.0	0	.0	0	.0	211
	255	4.2	63	1.0	286	4.7	637	10.6	5,031	83.4	365	6.1	6,033
	102	4.3	25	1.0	96	4.0	227	9.5	1,953	82.0	202	8.5	2,382
	153	4.2	38	1.0	190	5.2	410	11.2	3,078	84.3	163	4.5	3,651
	1,608	14.6	20	.2	24	.2	1,659	15.0	8,311	75.3	1,065	9.7	11,035
	1,020	18.9	7	.1	11	.2	1,042	19.3	4,185	77.4	181	3.3	5,408
	588	10.4	13	.2	13	.2	617	11.0	4,126	73.3	884	15.7	5,627
	1,642	93.7	18	1.0	4	.2	1,664	95.0	71	4.1	17	1.0	1,752
	1,040	97.9	2	.2	0	.0	1,042	98.1	18	1.7	2	.2	1,062
	602	87.2	16	2.3	4	.6	622	90.1	53	7.7	15	2.2	690
(30 INSTITUTIONS)													
	30,367	24.3	624	.5	1,674	1.3	32,899	26.3	88,373	70.6	3,896	3.1	125,168
	17,896	28.5	260	.4	756	1.2	19,026	30.3	42,625	68.0	1,042	1.7	62,693
	12,471	20.0	364	.6	918	1.5	13,873	22.2	45,748	73.2	2,854	4.6	62,475

	AMERICAN INDIAN ALASKAN NATIVE		BLACK NON-HISPANIC		ASIAN OR PACIFIC ISLANDER		HISPANIC		TOTAL MINORITY		WHITE NON-HISPANIC		NON-RESIDENT ALIEN		TOTA
	NUMBER	%	NUMBER	%	NUMBER	%	NUMBER	%	NUMBER	%	NUMBER	%	NUMBER	%	NUMB
MAINE															
ANDOVER COLLEGE															
ME TOTAL	1	.3	0	.0	1	.3	4	1.3	6	2.0	294	98.0	0	.0	3
ME FEMALE	0	.0	0	.0	1	.6	2	1.1	3	1.7	177	98.3	0	.0	1
ME MALE	1	.8	0	.0	0	.0	2	1.7	3	2.5	117	97.5	0	.0	1
BANGOR THEOLOGICAL SEM															
ME TOTAL	0	.0	0	.0	0	.0	0	.0	0	.0	23	100.0	0	.0	
ME FEMALE	0	.0	0	.0	0	.0	0	.0	0	.0	13	100.0	0	.0	
ME MALE	0	.0	0	.0	0	.0	0	.0	0	.0	10	100.0	0	.0	
BATES COLLEGE															
ME TOTAL	0	.0	27	2.0	6	.4	4	.3	37	2.7	1,301	96.3	13	1.0	1,3
ME FEMALE	0	.0	13	2.2	4	.7	1	.2	18	3.0	579	96.2	5	.8	6
ME MALE	0	.0	14	1.9	2	.3	3	.4	19	2.5	722	96.4	8	1.1	7
BEAL BUSINESS COLLEGE															
ME TOTAL	5	1.2	0	.0	1	.2	1	.2	7	1.7	413	98.1	1	.2	4
ME FEMALE	5	1.9	0	.0	1	.4	1	.4	7	2.7	256	97.0	1	.4	2
ME MALE	0	.0	0	.0	0	.0	0	.0	0	.0	157	100.0	0	.0	1
BOWDOIN COLLEGE															
ME TOTAL	0	.0	39	2.8	10	.7	4	.3	53	3.9	1,293	94.3	25	1.8	1,3
ME FEMALE	0	.0	18	3.2	6	1.1	0	.0	24	4.2	538	95.1	4	.7	5
ME MALE	0	.0	21	2.6	4	.5	4	.5	29	3.6	755	93.8	21	2.6	8
CASCO BAY COLLEGE															
ME TOTAL	0	.0	2	.8	1	.4	0	.0	3	1.2	238	98.8	0	.0	2
ME FEMALE	0	.0	0	.0	0	.0	0	.0	0	.0	184	100.0	0	.0	1
ME MALE	0	.0	2	3.5	1	1.8	0	.0	3	5.3	54	94.7	0	.0	
COLBY COLLEGE															
ME TOTAL	1	.1	12	.7	14	.9	14	.9	41	2.5	1,549	96.2	21	1.3	1,6
ME FEMALE	1	.1	6	.8	6	.8	6	.8	19	2.5	727	96.9	4	.5	7
ME MALE	0	.0	6	.7	8	.9	8	.9	22	2.6	822	95.5	17	2.0	8
COLLEGE OF THE ATLANTIC															
ME TOTAL	0	.0	0	.0	1	.8	0	.0	1	.8	124	99.2	0	.0	1
ME FEMALE	0	.0	0	.0	1	1.3	0	.0	1	1.3	74	98.7	0	.0	
ME MALE	0	.0	0	.0	0	.0	0	.0	0	.0	50	100.0	0	.0	
EASTERN VOC-TECH INST															
ME TOTAL	3	.6	0	.0	1	.2	0	.0	4	.8	511	99.2	0	.0	5
ME FEMALE	0	.0	0	.0	1	.7	0	.0	1	.7	150	99.3	0	.0	1
ME MALE	3	.8	0	.0	0	.0	0	.0	3	.8	361	99.2	0	.0	
GLEN COVE BIBLE COLLEGE															
ME TOTAL	0	.0	0	.0	0	.0	0	.0	0	.0	40	100.0	0	.0	
ME FEMALE	0	.0	0	.0	0	.0	0	.0	0	.0	17	100.0	0	.0	
ME MALE	0	.0	0	.0	0	.0	0	.0	0	.0	23	100.0	0	.0	
HUSSON COLLEGE															
ME TOTAL	10	.9	15	1.4	9	.8	7	.7	41	3.8	1,035	96.2	0	.0	1,
ME FEMALE	5	1.1	4	.9	1	.2	1	.2	11	2.4	451	97.6	0	.0	
ME MALE	5	.8	11	1.8	8	1.3	6	1.0	30	4.9	584	95.1	0	.0	
MAINE MARITIME ACADEMY															
ME TOTAL	1	.2	0	.0	2	.3	5	.8	8	1.2	633	98.4	2	.3	6
ME FEMALE	0	.0	0	.0	0	.0	0	.0	0	.0	7	100.0	0	.0	
ME MALE	1	.2	0	.0	2	.3	5	.8	8	1.3	626	98.4	2	.3	6
NASSON COLLEGE															
ME TOTAL	0	.0	3	.5	0	.0	0	.0	3	.5	636	98.1	9	1.4	6
ME FEMALE	0	.0	1	.4	0	.0	0	.0	1	.4	258	97.4	6	2.3	2
ME MALE	0	.0	2	.5	0	.0	0	.0	2	.5	370	98.7	3	.8	3
PORTLAND SCHOOL OF ART															
ME TOTAL	0	.0	0	.0	0	.0	1	.5	1	.5	198	99.0	1	.5	2
ME FEMALE	0	.0	0	.0	0	.0	0	.0	0	.0	127	100.0	0	.0	1
ME MALE	0	.0	0	.0	0	.0	1	1.4	1	1.4	71	97.3	1	1.4	
SAINT JOSEPH'S COLLEGE															
ME TOTAL	0	.0	6	1.5	3	.8	2	.5	11	2.8	389	97.3	0	.0	4
ME FEMALE	0	.0	3	1.0	2	.7	1	.3	6	2.1	282	97.9	0	.0	2
ME MALE	0	.0	3	2.7	1	.9	1	.9	5	4.5	107	95.5	0	.0	1
SOUTHERN ME VOC TECH INST															
ME TOTAL	2	.2	9	1.1	1	.1	0	.0	12	1.5	807	98.5	0	.0	8
ME FEMALE	0	.0	2	1.2	0	.0	0	.0	2	1.2	170	98.8	0	.0	1
ME MALE	2	.3	7	1.1	1	.2	0	.0	10	1.5	637	98.5	0	.0	6
THOMAS COLLEGE															
ME TOTAL	0	.0	0	.0	0	.0	0	.0	0	.0	446	98.2	8	1.8	4
ME FEMALE	0	.0	0	.0	0	.0	0	.0	0	.0	227	100.0	0	.0	2
ME MALE	0	.0	0	.0	0	.0	0	.0	0	.0	219	96.5	8	3.5	2
UNITY COLLEGE															
ME TOTAL	0	.0	2	.5	0	.0	5	1.2	7	1.6	421	98.4	0	.0	4
ME FEMALE	0	.0	1	1.2	0	.0	3	3.5	4	4.7	82	95.3	0	.0	
ME MALE	0	.0	1	.3	0	.0	2	.6	3	.9	339	99.1	0	.0	3
U OF MAINE AT AUGUSTA															
ME TOTAL	11	.7	4	.3	3	.2	3	.2	21	1.4	1,530	98.6	0	.0	1,5
ME FEMALE	7	.9	1	.1	3	.4	1	.1	12	1.5	807	98.5	0	.0	8
ME MALE	4	.5	3	.4	0	.0	2	.3	9	1.2	723	98.8	0	.0	7
U OF MAINE AT FARMINGTON															
ME TOTAL	3	.2	1	.1	0	.0	0	.0	4	.2	1,594	99.4	6	.4	1,6
ME FEMALE	3	.3	1	.1	0	.0	0	.0	4	.3	1,148	99.6	1	.1	1,1
ME MALE	0	.0	0	.0	0	.0	0	.0	0	.0	446	98.9	5	1.1	4
U OF MAINE AT FORT KENT															
ME TOTAL	3	.8	4	1.1	0	.0	0	.0	7	1.9	360	96.8	5	1.3	3
ME FEMALE	2	1.3	2	1.3	0	.0	0	.0	4	2.6	151	96.8	1	.6	1
ME MALE	1	.5	2	.9	0	.0	0	.0	3	1.4	209	96.8	4	1.9	2
U OF MAINE AT MACHIAS															
ME TOTAL	5	1.0	2	.4	0	.0	0	.0	7	1.3	511	97.9	4	.8	5
ME FEMALE	2	.7	0	.0	0	.0	0	.0	2	.7	281	97.9	4	1.4	2
ME MALE	3	1.3	2	.9	0	.0	0	.0	5	2.1	230	97.9	0	.0	2
U OF MAINE AT ORONO															
ME TOTAL	69	.8	14	.2	26	.3	10	.1	119	1.4	8,584	98.4	21	.2	8,7
ME FEMALE	37	1.0	6	.2	7	.2	3	.1	53	1.4	3,707	98.4	7	.2	3,7
ME MALE	32	.6	8	.2	19	.4	7	.1	66	1.3	4,877	98.4	14	.3	4,9

BLACK NON-HISPANIC		ASIAN OR PACIFIC ISLANDER		HISPANIC		TOTAL MINORITY		WHITE NON-HISPANIC		NON-RESIDENT ALIEN		TOTAL
NUMBER	%	NUMBER	%	NUMBER	%	NUMBER	%	NUMBER	%	NUMBER	%	NUMBER

'ED

3	.3	3	.3	5	.5	17	1.7	987	96.0	24	2.3	1,028
1	.2	1	.2	3	.6	8	1.5	504	96.6	10	1.9	522
2	.4	2	.4	2	.4	9	1.8	483	95.5	14	2.8	506
11	.2	11	.2	6	.1	45	1.0	4,478	98.7	14	.3	4,537
2	.1	4	.2	3	.1	17	.7	2,475	99.2	2	.1	2,494
9	.4	7	.3	3	.1	28	1.4	2,003	98.0	12	.6	2,043
1	.3	0	.0	0	.0	1	.3	392	99.0	3	.8	396
0	.0	0	.0	0	.0	0	.0	134	100.0	0	.0	134
1	.4	0	.0	0	.0	1	.4	258	98.5	3	1.1	262
2	.3	0	.0	0	.0	2	.3	797	99.7		.0	799
0	.0	0	.0	0	.0	0	.0	536	100.0	0	.0	536
2	.8	0	.0	0	.0	2	.8	261	99.2	0	.0	263

27 INSTITUTIONS)

157	.5	93	.3	71	.2	458	1.5	29,584	98.0	157	.5	30,199
61	.4	38	.3	25	.2	197	1.4	14,062	98.3	45	.3	14,304
96	.6	55	.3	46	.3	261	1.6	15,522	97.7	112	.7	15,895

26	1.6	1	.1	1	.1	29	1.8	1,577	98.1	1	.1	1,607
12	1.1	0	.0	1	.1	14	1.3	1,039	98.7	0	.0	1,053
14	2.5	1	.2	0	.0	15	2.7	538	97.1	1	.2	554
444	6.8	73	1.1	67	1.0	622	9.6	5,872	90.3	8	.1	6,502
230	6.4	32	.9	33	.9	311	8.7	3,254	91.2	3	.1	3,568
214	7.3	41	1.4	34	1.2	311	10.6	2,618	89.2	5	.2	2,934
0	.0	0	.0	0	.0	0	.0	41	97.6	1	2.4	42
0	.0	0	.0	0	.0	0	.0	29	96.7	1	3.3	30
0	.0	0	.0	0	.0	0	.0	12	100.0	0	.0	12
1,195	78.7	2	.1	4	.3	1,204	79.3	233	15.3	82	5.4	1,519
606	80.7	0	.0	2	.3	610	81.2	117	15.6	24	3.2	751
589	76.7	2	.3	2	.3	594	77.3	116	15.1	58	7.6	768
67	13.1	21	4.1	17	3.3	106	20.7	287	56.1	119	23.2	512
3	11.5	0	.0	0	.0	4	15.4	21	80.8	1	3.8	26
64	13.2	21	4.3	17	3.5	102	21.0	266	54.7	118	24.3	486
1,576	14.3	92	.8	41	.4	1,724	15.7	9,281	84.3	7	.1	11,012
927	15.9	38	.7	15	.3	988	16.9	4,857	83.1	1	.0	5,846
649	12.6	54	1.0	26	.5	736	14.2	4,424	85.6	6	.1	5,166
47	3.9	2	.2	4	.3	84	6.9	1,122	92.8	3	.2	1,209
22	3.7	1	.2	2	.3	41	6.9	554	93.1	0	.0	595
25	4.1	1	.2	2	.3	43	7.0	568	92.5	3	.5	614
350	10.1	37	1.1	59	1.7	450	13.0	3,007	86.9	5	.1	3,462
168	10.5	15	.9	7	.4	191	12.0	1,402	88.0	1	.1	1,594
182	9.7	22	1.2	52	2.8	259	13.9	1,605	85.9	4	.2	1,868
121	11.9	2	.2	3	.3	127	12.5	889	87.5	0	.0	1,016
74	12.3	0	.0	2	.3	77	12.8	526	87.2	0	.0	603
47	11.4	2	.5	1	.2	50	12.1	363	87.9	0	.0	413
60	9.5	7	1.1	31	4.	99	15.7	521	82.7	10	1.6	630
58	9.4	7	1.1	31	5.	97	15.6	513	82.7	10	1.6	620
2	20.0	0	.0	0	.0	2	20.0	8	80.0	0	.0	10
170	24.8	26	3.8	31	4.5	228	33.2	436	63.6	22	3.2	686
117	29.3	11	2.8	23	5.8	152	38.0	230	57.5	18	4.5	400
53	18.5	15	5.2	8	2.8	76	26.6	206	72.0	4	1.4	286
6,436	78.0	27	.3	19	.2	6,498	78.7	1,519	18.4	236	2.9	8,253
4,359	80.1	13	.2	12	.2	4,392	80.7	935	17.2	113	2.1	5,440
2,077	73.8	14	.5	7	.2	2,106	74.9	584	20.8	123	4.4	2,813
2,132	94.1	3	.1	2	.1	2,144	94.6	77	3.4	45	2.0	2,266
1,655	95.4	3	.2	2	.1	1,665	96.0	53	3.1	16	.9	1,734
477	89.7	0	.0	0	.0	479	90.0	24	4.5	29	5.5	532
169	8.3	15	.7		.4	201	.	1,832	90.1		.0	2,033
90	7.9	7	.6	8	.4	106	9.3	1,034	90.7	0	.0	1,140
79	8.8	8	.9	4	.4	95	10.6	798	89.4	0	.0	893
448	4.7	49	.5	3	.4	556	.9	8,878	94.0	12	.1	9,446
250	4.5	27	.5	2	.5	315	.7	5,199	94.1	12	.2	5,526
198	5.1	22	.6	8	.2	241	8.1	3,679	93.9	0	.0	3,920
64	3.7	11	.6	5	.3	84	4.	1,647	95.1	0	.0	1,731
37	3.6	4	.4	3	.3	46	4.	975	95.5	0	.0	1,021
27	3.8	7	1.0	2	.3	38	5.8	672	94.6	0	.0	710
190	6.5	1	.0	1	.6	213	7.3	2,704	92.2	15	.5	2,932
83	5.5	1	.1	8	.6	94	6.2	1,411	93.0	12	.8	1,517
107	7.6	0	.0	9	.6	119	8.4	1,293	91.4	3	.2	1,415

	AMERICAN INDIAN ALASKAN NATIVE		BLACK NON-HISPANIC		ASIAN OR PACIFIC ISLANDER		HISPANIC		TOTAL MINORITY		WHITE NON-HISPANIC		NON-RESIDENT ALIEN	
	NUMBER	%	NUMBER	%	NUMBER	%	NUMBER	%	NUMBER	%	NUMBER	%	NUMBER	%
MARYLAND CONTINUED														
GARRETT COMMUNITY COLLEGE														
MD TOTAL	0	.0	7	1.3	0	.0	0	.0	7	1.3	542	98.7	0	.0
MD FEMALE	0	.0	1	.4	0	.0	0	.0	1	.4	233	99.6	0	.0
MD MALE	0	.0	6	1.9	0	.0	0	.0	6	1.9	309	98.1	0	.0
GOUCHER COLLEGE														
MD TOTAL	2	.2	59	6.5	24	2.7	14	1.5	99	10.9	795	87.8	11	1.2
MD FEMALE	2	.2	59	6.5	24	2.7	14	1.5	99	10.9	795	87.8	11	1.2
MD MALE	0	.0	0	.0	0	.0	0	.0	0	.0	0	.0	0	.0
HAGERSTOWN JUNIOR COLLEGE														
MD TOTAL	5	.2	113	5.0	7	.3	5	.2	130	5.8	2,114	94.2	0	.0
MD FEMALE	2	.2	29	2.4	1	.1	1	.1	33	2.7	1,179	97.3	0	.0
MD MALE	3	.3	84	8.1	6	.6	4	.4	97	9.4	935	90.6	0	.0
HARFORD COMMUNITY COLLEGE														
MD TOTAL	9	.2	269	7.3	34	.9	33	.9	345	9.4	3,319	90.3	10	.3
MD FEMALE	4	.2	127	6.1	12	.6	12	.6	155	7.4	1,928	92.2	7	.3
MD MALE	5	.3	142	9.0	22	1.4	21	1.3	190	12.0	1,391	87.8	3	.2
HOOD COLLEGE														
MD TOTAL	0	.0	29	2.8	7	.7	4	.4	40	3.8	1,005	95.5	7	.7
MD FEMALE	0	.0	27	2.7	6	.6	4	.4	37	3.7	964	95.9	4	.4
MD MALE	0	.0	2	4.3	1	2.1	0	.0	3	6.4	41	87.2	3	6.4
HOWARD COMMUNITY COLLEGE														
MD TOTAL	6	.3	283	11.9	44	1.8	21	.9	354	14.8	2,023	84.8	10	.4
MD FEMALE	1	.1	200	12.4	30	1.9	19	1.2	250	15.5	1,359	84.2	5	.3
MD MALE	5	.6	83	10.7	14	1.8	2	.3	104	13.5	664	85.9	5	.6
JOHNS HOPKINS UNIVERSITY														
MD TOTAL	3	.1	117	5.0	101	4.4	28	1.2	249	10.7	2,035	87.8	33	1.4
MD FEMALE	1	.1	64	8.7	32	4.4	4	.5	101	13.8	626	85.4	6	.8
MD MALE	2	.1	53	3.3	69	4.4	24	1.5	148	9.3	1,409	89.0	27	1.7
LOYOLA COLLEGE														
MD TOTAL	15	.7	102	4.4	19	.8	13	.6	149	6.5	2,116	91.8	41	1.8
MD FEMALE	4	.4	66	6.8	7	.7	7	.7	84	8.6	876	90.1	12	1.2
MD MALE	11	.8	36	2.7	12	.9	6	.4	65	4.9	1,240	93.0	29	2.2
MARYLAND C ART AND DESIGN														
MD TOTAL	0	.0	12	20.7	0	.0	0	.0	12	20.7	39	67.2	7	12.1
MD FEMALE	0	.0	7	19.4	0	.0	0	.0	7	19.4	25	69.4	4	11.1
MD MALE	0	.0	5	22.7	0	.0	0	.0	5	22.7	14	63.6	3	13.6
MD INST COLLEGE OF ART														
MD TOTAL	0	.0	79	9.9	10	1.2	4	.5	93	11.6	703	87.7	6	.7
MD FEMALE	0	.0	54	10.9	6	1.2	3	.6	63	12.7	432	87.1	1	.2
MD MALE	0	.0	25	8.2	4	1.3	1	.3	30	9.8	271	88.6	5	1.6
MONTGOMERY C GERMANTOWN														
MD TOTAL	6	.5	52	4.1	20	1.6	18	1.4	96	7.7	1,145	91.3	13	1.0
MD FEMALE	2	.3	34	4.3	14	1.8	9	1.1	59	7.5	726	91.9	5	.6
MD MALE	4	.9	18	3.9	6	1.3	9	1.9	37	8.0	419	90.3	8	1.7
MONTGOMERY C ROCKVILLE														
MD TOTAL	25	.2	615	5.5	404	3.6	344	3.1	1,388	12.4	9,280	82.8	540	4.8
MD FEMALE	12	.2	312	5.3	229	3.9	185	3.2	738	12.6	4,952	84.6	161	2.8
MD MALE	13	.2	303	5.7	175	3.3	159	3.0	650	12.1	4,328	80.8	379	7.1
MONTGOMERY C TAKOMA PARK														
MD TOTAL	10	.3	680	23.2	191	5.2	140	4.8	981	33.5	1,634	55.8	312	10.7
MD FEMALE	8	.4	438	23.1	83	4.4	88	4.6	617	32.5	1,179	62.2	100	5.3
MD MALE	2	.2	242	23.5	68	6.6	52	5.0	364	35.3	455	44.1	212	20.6
MORGAN STATE UNIVERSITY														
MD TOTAL	6	.1	3,756	92.5	11	.3	2	.0	3,775	93.0	126	3.1	158	3.9
MD FEMALE	2	.1	2,207	94.4	5	.2	1	.0	2,215	94.7	70	3.0	54	2.3
MD MALE	4	.2	1,549	90.1	6	.3	1	.1	1,560	90.7	56	3.3	104	6.0
MOUNT SNT MARY'S COLLEGE														
MD TOTAL	1	.1	212	16.6	4	.3	1	.1	218	17.1	833	65.2	226	17.7
MD FEMALE	0	.0	72	13.8	0	.0	0	.0	72	13.8	334	64.0	116	22.2
MD MALE	1	.1	140	18.5	4	.5	1	.1	146	19.3	499	66.1	110	14.6
NER ISRAEL RAB COLLEGE														
MD TOTAL	0	.0	0	.0	0	.0	0	.0	0	.0	119	74.4	41	25.6
MD FEMALE	0	.0	0	.0	0	.0	0	.0	0	.0	0	.0	0	.0
MD MALE	0	.0	0	.0	0	.0	0	.0	0	.0	119	74.4	41	25.6
PEABODY INST OF JHU														
MD TOTAL	0	.0	12	5.2	13	5.6	6	2.6	31	13.4	193	83.2	8	3.4
MD FEMALE	0	.0	5	4.6	7	6.4	1	.9	13	11.9	90	82.6	6	5.5
MD MALE	0	.0	7	5.7	6	4.9	5	4.1	18	14.6	103	83.7	2	1.6
PRINCE GEORGES CC														
MD TOTAL	45	.3	4,707	34.0	273	2.0	165	1.2	5,190	37.5	8,525	61.7	113	.8
MD FEMALE	26	.3	2,749	35.0	138	1.8	97	1.2	3,010	38.4	4,792	61.1	46	.6
MD MALE	19	.3	1,958	32.7	135	2.3	68	1.1	2,180	36.5	3,733	62.4	67	1.1
SAINT JOHN'S C MAIN CAM														
MD TOTAL	0	.0	2	.5	2	.5	1	.3	5	1.3	361	97.3	5	1.3
MD FEMALE	0	.0	1	.6	0	.0	1	.6	2	1.2	163	97.0	3	1.8
MD MALE	0	.0	1	.5	2	1.0	0	.0	3	1.5	198	97.5	2	1.0
SNT JOHN'S C SANTA FE NM														
MD TOTAL	1	.4	1	.4	5	1.8	1	.4	8	2.9	269	96.1	3	1.1
MD FEMALE	0	.0	0	.0	5	3.8	0	.0	5	3.8	127	96.2	0	.0
MD MALE	1	.7	1	.7	0	.0	1	.7	3	2.0	142	95.9	3	2.0
SNT MARY'S COLLEGE OF MD														
MD TOTAL	0	.0	76	6.5	7	.6	9	.8	92	7.9	1,062	91.5	7	.6
MD FEMALE	0	.0	37	6.0	2	.3	4	.7	43	7.0	568	92.4	4	.7
MD MALE	0	.0	39	7.1	5	.9	5	.9	49	9.0	494	90.5	3	.5
SAINT MARY'S SEMINARY & U														
MD TOTAL	0	.0	3	15.8	0	.0	1	5.3	4	21.1	15	78.9	0	.0
MD FEMALE	0	.0	0	.0	0	.0	0	.0	0	.0	0	.0	0	.0
MD MALE	0	.0	3	15.8	0	.0	1	5.3	4	21.1	15	78.9	0	.0
SALISBURY STATE COLLEGE														
MD TOTAL	8	.3	233	7.4	11	.3	13	.4	265	8.4	2,873	91.0	18	.6
MD FEMALE	5	.3	134	7.7	7	.4	6	.3	152	8.8	1,570	90.6	11	.6
MD MALE	3	.2	99	7.0	4	.3	7	.5	113	7.9	1,303	91.6	7	.5

JATE ENROLLMENT IN INSTITUTIONS OF HIGHER EDUCATION BY RACE, ETHNICITY AND SEX!
TE AND NATION, 1978

	BLACK NON-HISPANIC		ASIAN OR PACIFIC ISLANDER		HISPANIC		TOTAL MINORITY		WHITE NON-HISPANIC		NON-RESIDENT ALIEN		TOTAL
	NUMBER	%	NUMBER	%	NUMBER	%	NUMBER	%	NUMBER	%	NUMBER	%	NUMBER
NUED													
	1,182	11.3	54	.5	39	.4	1,286	12.3	9,091	86.8	92	.9	10,469
	781	13.2	35	.6	20	.3	843	14.3	5,011	84.9	49	.8	5,903
	401	8.8	19	.4	19	.4	443	9.7	4,080	89.4	43	.9	4,566
	526	21.0	20	.8	8	.3	559	22.4	1,851	74.0	90	3.6	2,500
	235	28.6	6	.7	2	.2	244	29.7	557	67.8	20	2.4	821
	291	17.3	14	.8	6	.4	315	18.8	1,294	77.1	70	4.2	1,679
	2,179	7.8	429	1.5	300	1.1	3,012	10.8	23,532	84.4	1,327	4.8	27,871
	1,302	10.0	181	1.4	146	1.1	1,674	12.8	10,838	83.0	545	4.2	13,057
	877	5.9	248	1.7	154	1.0	1,338	9.0	12,694	85.7	782	5.3	14,814
	902	19.4	45	1.0	31	.7	992	21.4	3,470	74.8	179	3.9	4,641
	611	24.6	24	1.0	13	.5	656	26.4	1,735	69.9	91	3.7	2,482
	291	13.5	21	1.0	18	.8	336	15.6	1,735	80.4	88	4.1	2,159
	149	11.3	38	2.9	9	.7	196	14.9	1,112	84.6	6	.5	1,314
	126	11.8	27	2.5	5	.5	158	14.7	910	84.9	4	.4	1,072
	23	9.5	11	4.5	4	1.7	38	15.7	202	83.5	2	.8	242
	1,040	16.0	106	1.6	87	1.3	1,269	19.6	5,083	78.3	138	2.1	6,490
	585	19.1	47	1.5	38	1.2	684	22.3	2,297	75.0	80	2.6	3,061
	455	19.3	59	1.7	49	1.4	585	17.1	2,786	81.2	58	1.7	3,429
	784	85.9	7	.8	3	.3	797	87.3	111	12.2	5	.5	913
	353	87.8	2	.5	0	.0	357	88.8	43	10.7	2	.5	402
	431	84.3	5	1.0	3	.6	440	86.1	68	13.3	3	.6	511
	58	15.3	1	.3	0	.0	59	15.5	321	84.5	0	.0	380
	54	14.6	1	.3	0	.0	55	14.9	315	85.1	0	.0	370
	4	40.0	0	.0	0	.0	4	40.0	6	60.0	0	.0	10
	74	15.3	9	1.9	2	.4	85	17.5	377	77.7	23	4.7	485
	17	9.2	3	1.6	1	.5	21	11.4	155	83.8	9	4.9	185
	57	19.0	6	2.0	1	.3	64	21.3	222	74.0	14	4.7	300
	3	.4	0	.0	2	.3	6	.8	710	98.1	8	1.1	724
	1	.3	0	.0	1	.3	3	.9	337	98.0	4	1.2	344
	2	.5	0	.0	1	.3	3	.8	373	98.2	4	1.1	380
	35	2.7	6	.5	8	.6	49	3.7	1,261	95.8	6	.5	1,316
	14	2.0	3	.4	1	.1	18	2.6	664	97.2	1	.1	683
	21	3.3	3	.5	7	1.1	31	4.9	597	94.3	5	.8	633
	116	25.1	0	.0	0	.0	116	25.1	346	74.9	0	.0	462
	63	22.8	0	.0	0	.0	63	22.8	213	77.2	0	.0	276
	53	28.5	0	.0	0	.0	53	28.5	133	71.5	0	.0	186
(52 INSTITUTIONS)													
	31,962	19.0	2,231	1.3	1,657	1.0	36,326	21.5	128,314	76.1	4,009	2.4	168,649
	19,456	21.3	1,096	1.2	855	.9	21,635	23.7	68,212	74.6	1,573	1.7	91,420
	12,506	16.2	1,135	1.5	802	1.0	14,691	19.0	60,102	77.8	2,436	3.2	77,229
	108	7.4	2	.1	16	1.1	127	8.7	1,293	88.8	36	2.5	1,456
	51	8.1	1	.2	10	1.6	63	10.0	559	89.0	6	1.0	628
	57	6.9	1	.1	6	.7	64	7.7	734	88.6	30	3.6	828
	116	8.0	47	3.2	29	2.0	192	13.2	1,237	85.3	21	1.4	1,450
	40	9.0	22	4.9	6	1.3	68	15.2	373	83.6	5	1.1	446
	76	7.6	25	2.5	23	2.3	124	12.4	864	86.1	16	1.6	1,004
	4	2.5	1	.6	2	1.3	7	4.4	152	95.6	0	.0	159
	3	2.5	1	.8	2	1.6	6	4.9	116	95.1	0	.0	122
	1	2.7	0	.0	0	.0	1	2.7	36	97.3	0	.0	37
	2	.4	2	.4	6	1.2	15	3.0	474	95.2	9	1.8	498
	2	.4	2	.4	6	1.3	15	3.4	428	95.7	4	.9	447
	0	.0	0	.0	0	.0	0	.0	46	90.2	5	9.8	51
	2	.5	0	.0	0	.0	2	.5	402	99.5	0	.0	404
	2	.5	0	.0	0	.0	2	.5	402	99.5	0	.0	404
	0	.0	0	.0	0	.0	0	.0	0	.0	0	.0	0
	1	.3	0	.0	0	.0	296	100.0	0	.0	0	.0	296
	1	.3	0	.0	0	.0	296	100.0	0	.0	0	.0	296
	0	.0	0	.0	0	.0	0	.0	0	.0	0	.0	0
	8	.6	1	.1	10	.7	24	1.7	1,383	98.1	3	.2	1,410
	6	.8	0	.0	6	.8	14	2.0	699	97.9	1	.1	714
	2	.3	1	.1	4	.6	10	1.4	684	98.3	2	.3	696
	133	23.6	4	.7	58	10.3	197	34.9	319	56.6	48	8.5	564
	89	27.6	3	.9	30	9.3	122	37.9	180	55.9	20	6.2	322
	44	18.2	1	.4	28	11.6	75	31.0	139	57.4	28	11.6	242
	24	1.8	3	.2	2	.2	29	2.2	1,226	92.6	69	5.2	1,324
	12	3.5	0	.0	0	.0	12	3.5	323	93.9	9	2.6	344
	12	1.2	3	.3	2	.2	17	1.7	903	92.1	60	6.1	980

49

	AMERICAN INDIAN ALASKAN NATIVE		BLACK NON-HISPANIC		ASIAN OR PACIFIC ISLANDER		HISPANIC		TOTAL MINORITY		WHITE NON-HISPANIC		NON-RESIDENT ALIEN	
	NUMBER	%	NUMBER	%	NUMBER	%	NUMBER	%	NUMBER	%	NUMBER	%	NUMBER	%
MASSACHUSETTS CONTINUED														
BAY PATH JUNIOR COLLEGE														
MA TOTAL	0	.0	8	1.3	1	.2	2	.3	11	1.7	624	98.0	2	.3
MA FEMALE	0	.0	8	1.3	1	.2	2	.3	11	1.7	624	98.0	2	.3
MA MALE	0	.0	0	.0	0	.0	0	.0	0	.0	0	.0	0	.0
BAY STATE JC OF BUS														
MA TOTAL	0	.0	128	17.6	13	1.8	39	5.4	180	24.8	531	73.1	15	2.1
MA FEMALE	0	.0	128	17.6	13	1.8	39	5.4	180	24.8	531	73.1	15	2.1
MA MALE	0	.0	0	.0	0	.0	0	.0	0	.0	0	.0	0	.0
BECKER JC-LEICESTER														
MA TOTAL	0	.0	9	1.8	0	.0	1	.2	10	2.0	497	98.0	0	.0
MA FEMALE	0	.0	4	1.0	0	.0	0	.0	4	1.0	385	99.0	0	.0
MA MALE	0	.0	5	4.2	0	.0	1	.8	6	5.1	112	94.9	0	.0
BECKER JC-WORCESTER														
MA TOTAL	0	.0	7	1.4	0	.0	4	.8	11	2.1	502	97.3	3	.6
MA FEMALE	0	.0	6	1.2	0	.0	3	.6	9	1.8	485	97.8	2	.4
MA MALE	0	.0	1	5.0	0	.0	1	5.0	2	10.0	17	85.0	1	5.0
BENTLEY COLLEGE														
MA TOTAL	4	.1	50	.9	47	.9	21	.4	122	2.2	5,330	97.0	41	.7
MA FEMALE	2	.1	.17	.8	20	1.0	6	.3	45	2.2	1,981	97.3	11	.5
MA MALE	2	.1	33	1.0	27	.8	15	.4	77	2.2	3,349	96.9	30	.9
BERKLEE COLLEGE OF MUSIC														
MA TOTAL	12	.5	213	8.2	36	1.4	37	1.4	298	11.4	2,011	77.0	302	11.6
MA FEMALE	0	.0	18	5.0	9	2.5	3	.8	30	8.4	285	79.8	42	11.8
MA MALE	12	.5	195	8.7	27	1.2	34	1.5	268	11.9	1,726	76.6	260	11.5
BERKSHIRE CHRISTIAN C														
MA TOTAL	0	.0	3	2.6	0	.0	0	.0	3	2.6	109	94.8	3	2.6
MA FEMALE	0	.0	0	.0	0	.0	0	.0	0	.0	46	97.9	1	2.1
MA MALE	0	.0	3	4.4	0	.0	0	.0	3	4.4	63	92.6	2	2.9
BLUE HILLS REG TECH INST														
MA TOTAL	0	.0	1	.2	0	.0	2	.4	3	.6	467	99.4	0	.0
MA FEMALE	0	.0	0	.0	0	.0	1	.6	1	.6	173	99.4	0	.0
MA MALE	0	.0	1	.3	0	.0	1	.3	2	.7	294	99.3	0	.0
BOSTON COLLEGE														
MA TOTAL	13	.1	315	3.6	151	1.7	149	1.7	628	7.2	8,056	92.4	37	.4
MA FEMALE	7	.2	173	3.7	77	1.7	77	1.7	334	7.2	4,306	92.5	13	.3
MA MALE	6	.1	142	3.5	74	1.8	72	1.8	294	7.2	3,750	92.2	24	.6
BOSTON CONSV OF MUSIC														
MA TOTAL	1	.2	13	3.1	3	.7	1	.2	18	4.3	395	93.4	10	2.4
MA FEMALE	0	.0	11	4.0	3	1.1	0	.0	14	5.1	256	92.4	7	2.5
MA MALE	1	.7	2	1.4	0	.0	1	.7	4	2.7	139	95.2	3	2.1
BOSTON UNIVERSITY														
MA TOTAL	19	.1	602	4.6	141	1.1	189	1.5	951	7.3	11,489	88.5	549	4.2
MA FEMALE	8	.1	353	5.0	73	1.0	81	1.2	515	7.3	6,315	89.9	198	2.8
MA MALE	11	.2	249	4.2	68	1.1	108	1.8	436	7.3	5,174	86.8	351	5.9
BRADFORD COLLEGE														
MA TOTAL	1	.4	4	1.4	0	.0	9	3.2	14	5.0	244	87.1	22	7.9
MA FEMALE	1	.5	2	1.0	0	.0	6	3.1	9	4.7	171	89.5	11	5.8
MA MALE	0	.0	2	2.2	0	.0	3	3.4	5	5.6	73	82.0	11	12.4
BRANDEIS UNIVERSITY														
MA TOTAL	1	.0	126	4.5	52	1.9	44	1.6	223	7.9	2,482	88.5	101	3.6
MA FEMALE	0	.0	75	5.5	21	1.6	25	1.8	121	8.9	1,184	87.5	48	3.5
MA MALE	1	.1	51	3.5	31	2.1	19	1.3	102	7.0	1,298	89.3	53	3.6
CEN NEW ENG COLLEGE TECHN														
MA TOTAL	2	.9	2	.9	3	1.3	0	.0	7	3.1	211	92.1	11	4.8
MA FEMALE	1	7.7	0	.0	0	.0	0	.0	1	7.7	12	92.3	0	.0
MA MALE	1	.5	2	.9	3	1.4	0	.0	6	2.8	199	92.1	11	5.1
CHAMBERLAYNE JR COLLEGE														
MA TOTAL	0	.0	114	14.6	29	3.7	123	15.8	266	34.1	444	57.0	69	8.9
MA FEMALE	0	.0	68	14.3	22	4.6	72	15.2	162	34.1	260	54.7	53	11.2
MA MALE	0	.0	46	15.1	7	2.3	51	16.8	104	34.2	184	60.5	16	5.3
CLARK UNIVERSITY														
MA TOTAL	2	.1	56	2.6	11	.5	25	1.1	94	4.3	2,051	93.7	44	2.0
MA FEMALE	2	.2	41	3.8	4	.4	11	1.0	58	5.4	993	92.5	23	2.1
MA MALE	0	.0	15	1.3	7	.6	14	1.3	36	3.2	1,058	94.9	21	1.9
COLLEGE OF THE HOLY CROSS														
MA TOTAL	0	.0	95	3.7	12	.5	21	.8	128	5.0	2,436	94.8	5	.2
MA FEMALE	0	.0	37	3.4	5	.5	7	.6	49	4.5	1,040	95.4	1	.1
MA MALE	0	.0	58	3.9	7	.5	14	.9	79	5.3	1,396	94.4	4	.3
COLLEGE OUR LADY OF ELMS														
MA TOTAL	0	.0	7	1.8	3	.8	6	1.6	16	4.2	364	95.8	0	.0
MA FEMALE	0	.0	7	1.8	3	.8	6	1.6	16	4.2	364	95.8	0	.0
MA MALE	0	.0	0	.0	0	.0	0	.0	0	.0	0	.0	0	.0
CURRY COLLEGE														
MA TOTAL	0	.0	23	2.9	0	.0	0	.0	23	2.9	734	94.1	23	2.9
MA FEMALE	0	.0	13	3.6	0	.0	0	.0	13	3.6	349	95.4	4	1.1
MA MALE	0	.0	10	2.4	0	.0	0	.0	10	2.4	385	93.0	19	4.6
DEAN JUNIOR COLLEGE														
MA TOTAL	0	.0	35	3.0	3	.3	11	.9	49	4.2	1,128	95.8	0	.0
MA FEMALE	0	.0	5	.8	1	.2	4	.6	10	1.6	613	98.4	0	.0
MA MALE	0	.0	30	5.4	2	.4	7	1.3	39	7.0	515	93.0	0	.0
EASTERN NAZARENE COLLEGE														
MA TOTAL	0	.0	25	3.5	4	.6	6	.8	35	4.9	662	93.0	15	2.1
MA FEMALE	0	.0	14	3.4	1	.2	3	.7	18	4.3	390	94.2	6	1.4
MA MALE	0	.0	11	3.7	3	1.0	3	1.0	17	5.7	272	91.3	9	3.0
EMERSON COLLEGE														
MA TOTAL	1	.1	110	8.4	4	.3	22	1.7	137	10.4	1,141	86.7	38	2.9
MA FEMALE	0	.0	73	10.4	2	.3	10	1.4	85	12.1	599	85.1	20	2.8
MA MALE	1	.2	37	6.0	2	.3	12	2.0	52	8.5	542	88.6	18	2.9
EMMANUEL COLLEGE														
MA TOTAL	0	.0	21	4.0	0	.0	15	2.9	36	6.9	476	91.2	10	1.9
MA FEMALE	0	.0	21	4.0	0	.0	15	2.9	36	6.9	476	91.2	10	1.9
MA MALE	0	.0	0	.0	0	.0	0	.0	0	.0	0	.0	0	.0

	BLACK NON-HISPANIC		ASIAN OR PACIFIC ISLANDER		HISPANIC		TOTAL MINORITY		WHITE NON-HISPANIC		NON-RESIDENT ALIEN		TOTAL
N E	NUMBER	%	NUMBER	%	NUMBER	%	NUMBER	%	NUMBER	%	NUMBER	%	NUMBER
INUED													
	2	.2	0	.0	0	.0	2	.2	861	98.5	11	1.3	874
	2	.2	0	.0	0	.0	2	.2	861	98.5	11	1.3	874
	0	.0	0	.0	0	.0	0	.0	0	.0	0	.0	0
	0	.0	1	.1	23	3.2	27	3.8	681	96.2	0	.0	708
	0	.0	1	.2	10	2.3	12	2.7	430	97.3	0	.0	442
	0	.0	0	.0	13	4.9	15	5.6	251	94.4	0	.0	266
	181	8.1	14	.6	28	1.2	229	10.2	1,999	89.1	15	.7	2,243
	100	7.8	6	.5	16	1.2	125	9.7	1,149	89.3	13	1.0	1,287
	81	8.5	8	.8	12	1.3	104	10.9	850	88.9	2	.2	956
	4	2.0	6	3.0	0	.0	10	5.0	190	94.5	1	.5	201
	4	2.0	9	4.5	0	.0	9	4.5	190	95.0	1	.5	200
	0	.0	1	100.0	0	.0	1	100.0	0	.0	0	.0	1
	36	5.6	10	1.6	13	2.0	62	9.7	555	86.6	24	3.7	641
	3	8.8	2	5.9	0	.0	6	17.6	26	76.5	2	5.9	34
	33	5.4	8	1.3	13	2.1	56	9.2	529	87.1	22	3.6	607
	15	1.7	6	.7	9	1.0	31	3.4	855	94.1	23	2.5	909
	8	1.6	4	.8	3	.6	15	3.0	478	94.5	13	2.6	506
	7	1.7	2	.5	6	1.5	16	4.0	377	93.5	10	2.5	403
	81	21.3	0	.0	5	1.3	86	22.6	284	74.5	11	2.9	381
	29	30.2	0	.0	2	2.1	31	32.3	63	65.6	2	2.1	96
	52	18.2	0	.0	3	1.1	55	19.3	221	77.5	9	3.2	285
	31	2.5	7	.6	14	1.1	52	4.2	1,180	94.8	13	1.0	1,245
	19	2.8	1	.1	7	1.0	27	4.0	648	95.2	6	.9	681
	12	2.1	6	1.1	7	1.2	25	4.4	532	94.3	7	1.2	564
	243	5.7	141	3.3	112	2.6	506	11.8	3,569	83.0	225	5.2	4,300
	0	.0	0	.0	0	.0	0	.0	0	.0	0	.0	0
	243	5.7	141	3.3	112	2.6	506	11.8	3,569	83.0	225	5.2	4,300
	0	.0	0	.0	0	.0	0	.0	111	95.7	5	4.3	116
	0	.0	0	.0	0	.0	0	.0	76	95.0	4	5.0	80
	0	.0	0	.0	0	.0	0	.0	35	97.2	1	2.8	36
	0	.0	0	.0	0	.0	0	.0	65	85.5	11	14.5	76
	0	.0	0	.0	0	.0	0	.0	17	85.0	3	15.0	20
	0	.0	0	.0	0	.0	0	.0	48	85.7	8	14.3	56
	2	.5	0	.0	0	.0	2	.5	383	99.5	0	.0	385
	1	.3	0	.0	0	.0	1	.3	332	99.7	0	.0	333
	1	1.9	0	.0	0	.0	1	1.9	51	98.1	0	.0	52
	4	.9	2	.4	6	1.3	17	3.7	430	93.3	14	3.0	461
	4	.9	2	.4	6	1.3	17	3.7	430	93.3	14	3.0	461
	0	.0	0	.0	0	.0	0	.0	0	.0	0	.0	0
	15	3.7	1	.2	2	.5	18	4.4	388	95.6	0	.0	406
	15	4.1	0	.0	1	.3	16	4.3	354	95.7	0	.0	370
	0	.0	1	2.8	1	2.8	2	5.6	34	94.4	0	.0	36
	6	.9	3	.5	0	.0	9	1.4	630	96.6	13	2.0	652
	6	.9	3	.5	0	.0	9	1.4	630	96.6	13	2.0	652
	0	.0	0	.0	0	.0	0	.0	0	.0	0	.0	0
	52	6.3	5	.6	11	1.3	70	8.4	756	91.1	4	.5	830
	52	6.3	5	.6	11	1.3	70	8.5	754	91.1	4	.5	828
	0	.0	0	.0	0	.0	0	.0	2	100.0	0	.0	2
	59	2.9	9	.4	14	.7	82	4.0	1,976	95.7	6	.3	2,064
	30	2.9	1	.1	9	.9	40	3.8	1,010	96.0	2	.2	1,052
	29	2.9	8	.8	5	.5	42	4.2	966	95.5	4	.4	1,012
	25	.6	6	.2	9	.2	46	1.2	3,896	98.1	30	.8	3,972
	13	.6	5	.2	4	.2	27	1.3	2,100	98.5	4	.2	2,131
	12	.7	1	.1	5	.3	19	1.0	1,796	97.6	26	1.4	1,841
	65	2.7	16	.7	22	.9	112	4.6	2,316	95.2	6	.2	2,434
	41	2.9	13	.9	11	.8	69	4.9	1,335	94.9	3	.2	1,407
	24	2.3	3	.3	11	1.1	43	4.2	981	95.5	3	.3	1,027
	9	.5	7	.4	31	1.8	59	3.4	1,651	96.5	1	.1	1,711
	1	.1	6	.6	16	1.6	30	3.0	986	97.0	0	.0	1,016
	8	1.2	1	.1	15	2.2	29	4.2	665	95.7	1	.1	695
	7	.5	3	.2	3	.2	16	1.1	1,420	98.9	0	.0	1,436
	4	.5	3	.3	0	.0	8	.9	854	99.1	0	.0	862
	3	.5	0	.0	3	.5	8	1.4	566	98.6	0	.0	574
	75	1.6	23	.5	39	.8	267	5.7	4,418	94.3	2	.0	4,687
	43	1.6	16	.6	23	.8	164	5.9	2,599	94.0	2	.1	2,765
	32	1.7	7	.4	16	.8	103	5.4	1,819	94.6	0	.0	1,922
	25	1.3	9	.5	12	.6	46	2.4	1,842	97.6	0	.0	1,888
	16	1.4	9	.8	6	.5	31	2.6	1,141	97.4	0	.0	1,172
	9	1.3	0	.0	6	.8	15	2.1	701	97.9	0	.0	716

TABLE 1 - TOTAL UNDERGRADUATE ENROLLMENT IN INSTITUTIONS OF HIGHER EDUCATION BY RACE, ETHNICITY AND SEX:
INSTITUTION, STATE AND NATION, 1978

	AMERICAN INDIAN ALASKAN NATIVE		BLACK NON-HISPANIC		ASIAN OR PACIFIC ISLANDER		HISPANIC		TOTAL MINORITY		WHITE NON-HISPANIC		NON-RESIDENT ALIEN	
	NUMBER	%	NUMBER	%	NUMBER	%	NUMBER	%	NUMBER	%	NUMBER	%	NUMBER	%
MASSACHUSETTS CONTINUED														
MASSASOIT CMTY COLLEGE														
MA TOTAL	6	.3	43	2.0	8	.4	8	.4	65	3.0	2,111	97.0	0	.0
MA FEMALE	1	.1	29	2.5	6	.5	3	.3	39	3.3	1,137	96.7	0	.0
MA MALE	5	.5	14	1.4	2	.2	5	.5	26	2.6	974	97.4	0	.0
MIDDLESEX CMTY COLLEGE														
MA TOTAL	1	.0	11	.2	2	.0	4	.1	18	.3	6,065	99.7	1	.0
MA FEMALE	1	.0	9	.2	1	.0	2	.0	13	.3	4,187	99.7	0	.0
MA MALE	0	.0	2	.1	1	.1	2	.1	5	.3	1,878	99.7	1	.1
MT WACHUSETT CMTY COLLEGE														
MA TOTAL	8	.4	31	1.4	4	.2	5	.2	48	2.2	2,104	97.7	2	.1
MA FEMALE	6	.6	13	1.3	1	.1	2	.2	22	2.3	951	97.7	0	.0
MA MALE	2	.2	18	1.5	3	.3	3	.3	26	2.2	1,153	97.6	2	.2
NTHN ESSEX CMTY COLLEGE														
MA TOTAL	46	1.2	26	.7	30	.8	96	2.5	198	5.1	3,631	93.4	60	1.5
MA FEMALE	17	.8	6	.3	15	.7	36	1.6	74	3.3	2,145	96.2	10	.4
MA MALE	29	1.7	20	1.2	15	.9	60	3.6	124	7.5	1,486	89.5	50	3.0
NORTH SHORE CMTY COLLEGE														
MA TOTAL	2	.1	43	2.0	3	.1	30	1.4	78	3.6	2,093	95.9	11	.5
MA FEMALE	2	.2	27	2.1	3	.2	19	1.5	51	3.9	1,250	95.5	8	.6
MA MALE	0	.0	16	1.8	0	.0	11	1.3	27	3.1	843	96.6	3	.3
QUINSIGAMOND CMTY COLLEGE														
MA TOTAL	2	.1	36	1.9	2	.1	18	.9	58	3.0	1,803	94.2	53	2.8
MA FEMALE	1	.1	24	2.2	2	.2	12	1.1	39	3.5	1,055	95.5	11	1.0
MA MALE	1	.1	12	1.5	0	.0	6	.7	19	2.3	748	92.5	42	5.2
ROXBURY COMMUNITY COLLEGE														
MA TOTAL	3	.6	308	59.0	0	.0	156	29.9	467	89.5	7	1.3	48	9.2
MA FEMALE	3	.9	185	54.6	0	.0	119	35.1	307	90.6	5	1.5	27	8.0
MA MALE	0	.0	123	67.2	0	.0	37	20.2	160	87.4	2	1.1	21	11.5
SPRINGFIELD TECHNICAL CC														
MA TOTAL	2	.1	277	8.2	3	.1	108	3.2	390	11.6	2,918	86.7	56	1.7
MA FEMALE	0	.0	174	10.1	1	.1	80	4.7	255	14.8	1,441	83.8	24	1.4
MA MALE	2	.1	103	6.3	2	.1	28	1.7	135	8.2	1,477	89.8	32	1.9
MASS COLLEGE OF PHARMACY														
MA TOTAL	4	.3	24	1.8	35	2.6	8	.6	71	5.2	1,235	90.5	59	4.3
MA FEMALE	3	.6	14	2.9	15	3.1	6	1.2	38	7.9	426	88.0	20	4.1
MA MALE	1	.1	10	1.1	20	2.3	2	.2	33	3.7	809	91.8	39	4.4
MASS INST OF TECHNOLOGY														
MA TOTAL	8	.2	212	4.7	184	4.1	94	2.1	498	11.0	3,673	80.9	367	8.1
MA FEMALE	0	.0	67	8.6	44	5.7	6	.8	117	15.1	613	79.0	46	5.9
MA MALE	8	.2	145	3.9	140	3.7	88	2.3	381	10.1	3,060	81.3	321	8.5
BOSTON STATE COLLEGE														
MA TOTAL	30	.5	721	12.9	43	.8	79	1.4	873	15.7	4,469	80.2	231	4.1
MA FEMALE	16	.6	438	17.1	21	.8	49	1.9	524	20.5	1,931	75.6	100	3.9
MA MALE	14	.5	283	9.4	22	.7	30	1.0	349	11.6	2,538	84.1	131	4.3
BRIDGEWATER STATE COLLEGE														
MA TOTAL	13	.3	40	.9	42	.9	11	.2	106	2.3	4,417	96.8	42	.9
MA FEMALE	9	.3	23	.8	25	.8	5	.2	62	2.1	2,885	96.9	31	1.0
MA MALE	4	.3	17	1.1	17	1.1	6	.4	44	2.8	1,532	96.5	11	.7
FITCHBURG STATE COLLEGE														
MA TOTAL	6	.1	127	2.6	12	.2	52	1.1	197	4.1	4,648	95.8	6	.1
MA FEMALE	2	.1	50	2.0	6	.2	29	1.1	87	3.4	2,461	96.5	2	.1
MA MALE	4	.2	77	3.3	6	.3	23	1.0	110	4.8	2,187	95.0	4	.2
FRAMINGHAM STATE COLLEGE														
MA TOTAL	3	.1	19	.6	11	.3	52	1.6	85	2.6	3,097	96.5	28	.9
MA FEMALE	2	.1	9	.4	7	.3	33	1.5	51	2.3	2,120	96.8	18	.8
MA MALE	1	.1	10	1.0	4	.4	19	1.9	34	3.3	977	95.7	10	1.0
MASS COLLEGE OF ART														
MA TOTAL	0	.0	60	5.5	16	1.5	11	1.0	87	8.0	982	90.8	13	1.2
MA FEMALE	0	.0	30	4.3	13	1.9	4	.6	47	6.8	637	91.9	9	1.3
MA MALE	0	.0	30	7.7	3	.8	7	1.8	40	10.3	345	88.7	4	1.0
MASS MARITIME ACADEMY														
MA TOTAL	3	.3	8	.9	1	.1	0	.0	12	1.4	861	97.2	13	1.5
MA FEMALE	0	.0	0	.0	0	.0	0	.0	0	.0	11	100.0	0	.0
MA MALE	3	.3	8	.9	1	.1	0	.0	12	1.4	850	97.1	13	1.5
NORTH ADAMS STATE COLLEGE														
MA TOTAL	8	.4	26	1.2	19	.8	14	.6	67	3.0	2,172	96.3	17	.8
MA FEMALE	6	.5	14	1.2	8	.7	8	.7	36	3.1	1,121	96.1	9	.8
MA MALE	2	.2	12	1.1	11	1.0	6	.6	31	2.8	1,051	96.4	8	.7
SALEM STATE COLLEGE														
MA TOTAL	6	.1	104	1.9	12	.2	34	.6	156	2.9	5,193	96.8	15	.3
MA FEMALE	6	.2	60	1.9	7	.2	19	.6	92	2.9	3,117	97.0	5	.2
MA MALE	0	.0	44	2.0	5	.2	15	.7	64	3.0	2,076	96.6	10	.5
WESTFIELD STATE COLLEGE														
MA TOTAL	4	.1	64	2.3	3	.1	13	.5	84	3.0	2,682	96.9	2	.1
MA FEMALE	0	.0	35	2.1	1	.1	9	.5	45	2.6	1,660	97.4	0	.0
MA MALE	4	.4	29	2.7	2	.2	4	.4	39	3.7	1,022	96.1	2	.2
WORCESTER STATE COLLEGE														
MA TOTAL	2	.1	43	1.4	3	.1	22	.7	70	2.3	2,932	96.0	53	1.7
MA FEMALE	1	.1	21	1.2	1	.1	8	.4	31	1.7	1,738	97.1	20	1.1
MA MALE	1	.1	22	1.7	2	.2	14	1.1	39	3.1	1,194	94.3	33	2.6
MERRIMACK COLLEGE														
MA TOTAL	0	.0	15	.4	7	.2	14	.4	36	1.1	3,345	98.7	7	.2
MA FEMALE	0	.0	8	.6	3	.2	4	.3	15	1.2	1,267	98.8	0	.0
MA MALE	0	.0	7	.3	4	.2	10	.5	21	1.0	2,078	98.7	7	.3
MOUNT HOLYOKE COLLEGE														
MA TOTAL	0	.0	86	4.5	44	2.3	40	2.1	170	8.9	1,690	88.3	54	2.8
MA FEMALE	0	.0	86	4.5	44	2.3	40	2.1	170	8.9	1,689	88.3	54	2.8
MA MALE	0	.0	0	.0	0	.0	0	.0	0	.0	1	100.0	0	.0
MOUNT IDA JUNIOR COLLEGE														
MA TOTAL	0	.0	74	10.9	3	.4	9	1.3	86	12.6	570	83.6	26	3.8
MA FEMALE	0	.0	73	10.9	3	.4	9	1.3	85	12.7	566	84.7	17	2.5
MA MALE	0	.0	1	7.1	0	.0	0	.0	1	7.1	4	28.6	9	64.3

N E	BLACK NON-HISPANIC		ASIAN OR PACIFIC ISLANDER		HISPANIC		TOTAL MINORITY		WHITE NON-HISPANIC		NON-RESIDENT ALIEN		TOTAL
	NUMBER	%	NUMBER	%	NUMBER	%	NUMBER	%	NUMBER	%	NUMBER	%	NUMBER
INUED													
	381	23.1	3	.2	111	6.7	495	30.0	1,088	66.0	65	3.9	1,648
	230	23.2	3	.3	79	8.0	312	31.5	641	64.6	39	3.9	992
	151	23.0	0	.0	32	4.9	183	27.9	447	68.1	26	4.0	656
	22	4.3	11	2.2	13	2.6	46	9.1	445	87.6	17	3.3	508
	3	1.6	5	2.7	1	.5	9	4.8	172	91.5	7	3.7	188
	19	5.9	6	1.9	12	3.8	37	11.6	273	85.3	10	3.1	320
	9	6.2	0	.0	0	.0	9	6.2	136	93.2	1	.7	146
	3	25.0	0	.0	0	.0	3	25.0	9	75.0	0	.0	12
	6	4.5	0	.0	0	.0	6	4.5	127	94.8	1	.7	134
	3	.4	1	.1	2	.3	6	.8	695	98.0	8	1.1	709
	0	.0	0	.0	0	.0	0	.0	114	100.0	0	.0	114
	3	.5	1	.2	2	.3	6	1.0	581	97.6	8	1.3	595
	1,702	5.6	1,963	6.4	380	1.2	4,355	14.2	25,980	84.9	269	.9	30,604
	870	6.8	803	6.3	140	1.1	1,940	15.2	10,734	84.0	101	.8	12,775
	832	4.7	1,160	6.5	240	1.3	2,415	13.5	15,246	85.5	168	.9	17,829
	8	1.3	11	1.8	57	9.3	76	12.4	514	83.6	25	4.1	615
	8	1.4	11	1.9	57	10.1	76	13.5	464	82.1	25	4.4	565
	0	.0	0	.0	0	.0	0	.0	50	100.0	0	.0	50
	12	1.2	22	2.3	14	1.4	70	7.2	904	92.8	0	.0	974
	4	.6	10	1.6	6	1.0	30	4.8	592	95.2	0	.0	622
	8	2.3	12	3.4	8	2.3	40	11.4	312	88.6	0	.0	352
	219	10.0	98	4.5	65	3.0	393	17.9	1,720	78.3	85	3.9	2,198
	219	10.0	98	4.5	65	3.0	393	17.9	1,720	78.3	85	3.9	2,198
	0	.0	0	.0	0	.0	0	.0	0	.0	0	.0	0
	14	1.9	9	1.2	31	4.1	54	7.2	701	92.8	0	.0	755
	14	1.9	9	1.2	31	4.1	54	7.2	701	92.8	0	.0	755
	0	.0	0	.0	0	.0	0	.0	0	.0	0	.0	0
	1	2.3	0	.0	0	.0	1	2.3	40	93.0	2	4.7	43
	0	.0	0	.0	0	.0	0	.0	0	.0	0	.0	0
	1	2.3	0	.0	0	.0	1	2.3	40	93.0	2	4.7	43
	2	2.7	0	.0	3	4.1	5	6.8	68	93.2	0	.0	73
	0	.0	0	.0	0	.0	0	.0	0	.0	0	.0	0
	2	2.7	0	.0	3	4.1	5	6.8	68	93.2	0	.0	73
	8	1.4	7	1.2	1	.2	17	2.9	552	93.9	19	3.2	588
	4	1.0	3	.8	1	.3	9	2.3	372	93.7	16	4.0	397
	4	2.1	4	2.1	0	.0	8	4.2	180	94.2	3	1.6	191
	0	.0	0	.0	0	.0	0	.0	116	100.0	0	.0	116
	0	.0	0	.0	0	.0	0	.0	73	100.0	0	.0	73
	0	.0	0	.0	0	.0	0	.0	43	100.0	0	.0	43
	135	8.6	36	2.3	21	1.3	192	12.2	1,321	84.0	59	3.8	1,572
	135	8.6	36	2.3	21	1.3	192	12.2	1,321	84.0	59	3.8	1,572
	0	.0	0	.0	0	.0	0	.0	0	.0	0	.0	0
	14	6.4	3	1.4	0	.0	17	7.8	199	90.9	3	1.4	219
	8	5.4	3	2.0	0	.0	11	7.4	137	91.9	1	.7	149
	6	8.6	0	.0	0	.0	6	8.6	62	88.6	2	2.9	70
	142	5.6	79	3.1	25	1.0	250	9.8	2,242	87.9	58	2.3	2,550
	142	5.6	79	3.1	25	1.0	250	9.8	2,231	87.9	58	2.3	2,539
	0	.0	0	.0	0	.0	0	.0	11	100.0	0	.0	11
	130	2.7	29	.6	25	.5	198	4.1	4,536	94.0	91	1.9	4,825
	65	3.6	13	.7	14	.8	96	5.3	1,683	93.7	18	1.0	1,797
	65	2.1	16	.5	11	.4	102	3.4	2,853	94.2	73	2.4	3,028
	93	4.3	6	.3	28	1.3	130	6.0	2,021	93.3	16	.7	2,167
	43	4.1	3	.3	7	.7	56	5.3	998	94.2	6	.6	1,060
	50	4.5	3	.3	21	1.9	74	6.7	1,023	92.4	10	.9	1,107
	15	.9	2	.1	5	.2	25	1.2	2,053	98.7	2	.1	2,080
	10	1.1	0	.0	1	.1	11	1.2	932	98.8	0	.0	943
	8	.7	2	.2	4	.4	14	1.2	1,121	98.6	2	.2	1,137
	121	4.0	23	.8	5	.2	154	5.0	2,815	92.1	89	2.9	3,058
	70	5.2	7	.5	2	.1	79	5.9	1,238	92.3	25	1.9	1,342
	51	3.0	16	.9	3	.2	75	4.4	1,577	91.9	64	3.7	1,716
	8	4.1	0	.0	16	8.3	26	13.5	165	85.5	2	1.0	193
	6	5.7	0	.0	11	10.5	18	17.1	87	82.9	0	.0	105
	2	2.3	0	.0	5	5.7	8	9.1	78	88.6	2	2.3	88
	268	6.0	133	3.0	74	1.7	478	10.7	3,936	88.3	43	1.0	4,457
	147	6.7	60	2.7	35	1.6	242	11.1	1,924	88.1	17	.8	2,183
	121	5.3	73	3.2	39	1.7	236	10.4	2,012	88.5	26	1.1	2,274
	86	1.0	61	.7	46	.5	193	2.1	8,625	95.5	218	2.4	9,036
	29	1.0	10	.3	23	.8	62	2.1	2,904	96.9	31	1.0	2,997
	57	.9	51	.8	23	.4	131	2.2	5,721	94.7	187	3.1	6,039

TABLE 1 - TOTAL UNDERGRADUATE ENROLLMENT IN INSTITUTIONS OF HIGHER EDUCATION BY RACE, ETHNICITY AND SEX: INSTITUTION, STATE AND NATION, 1978

	AMERICAN INDIAN ALASKAN NATIVE		BLACK NON-HISPANIC		ASIAN OR PACIFIC ISLANDER		HISPANIC		TOTAL MINORITY		WHITE NON-HISPANIC		NON-RESIDENT ALIEN		
	NUMBER	%	NUMBER	%	NUMBER	%	NUMBER	%	NUMBER	%	NUMBER	%	NUMBER	%	
MASSACHUSETTS CONTINUED															
U OF MASS AMHERST CAMPUS															
MA TOTAL	44	.2	709	3.8	238	1.3	305	1.6	1,296	6.9	17,281	91.7	265	1.4	
MA FEMALE	23	.3	332	3.9	97	1.1	120	1.4	572	6.8	7,791	92.2	89	1.1	
MA MALE	21	.2	377	3.6	141	1.4	185	1.8	724	7.0	9,490	91.3	176	1.7	
U OF MASS BOSTON CAMPUS															
MA TOTAL	14	.2	542	7.9	81	1.2	193	2.8	830	12.1	5,884	86.1	123	1.8	
MA FEMALE	8	.2	337	9.6	39	1.1	84	2.4	468	13.4	2,974	85.0	57	1.6	
MA MALE	6	.2	205	6.1	42	1.3	109	3.3	362	10.8	2,910	87.2	66	2.0	
WELLESLEY COLLEGE															
MA TOTAL	2	.1	152	7.8	85	4.4	39	2.0	278	14.3	1,567	80.8	94	4.8	
MA FEMALE	2	.1	152	7.8	85	4.4	39	2.0	278	14.3	1,567	80.8	94	4.8	
MA MALE	0	.0	0	.0	0	.0	0	.0	0	.0	0	.0	0	.0	
WENTWORTH INST OF TECH															
MA TOTAL	15	.7	69	3.2	41	1.9	31	1.4	156	7.3	1,814	84.7	172	8.0	
MA FEMALE	2	2.3	6	6.9	2	2.3	0	.0	10	11.5	63	72.4	14	16.1	
MA MALE	13	.6	63	3.1	39	1.9	31	1.5	146	7.1	1,751	85.2	158	7.7	
WESTERN NEW ENG COLLEGE															
MA TOTAL	1	.0	101	3.8	9	.3	12	.5	123	4.6	2,513	94.6	20	.8	
MA FEMALE	1	.1	42	5.9	3	.4	6	.8	52	7.3	652	92.0	5	.7	
MA MALE	0	.0	59	3.0	6	.3	6	.3	71	3.6	1,861	95.6	15	.8	
WHEATON COLLEGE															
MA TOTAL	3	.2	24	1.8	16	1.2	14	1.0	57	4.3	1,267	94.8	12	.9	
MA FEMALE	3	.2	24	1.8	16	1.2	14	1.0	57	4.3	1,267	94.8	12	.9	
MA MALE	0	.0	0	.0	0	.0	0	.0	0	.0	0	.0	0	.0	
WHEELOCK COLLEGE															
MA TOTAL	0	.0	42	6.7	7	1.1	4	.6	53	8.5	563	90.2	8	1.3	
MA FEMALE	0	.0	40	6.6	7	1.1	3	.5	50	8.2	552	90.5	8	1.3	
MA MALE	0	.0	2	14.3	0	.0	1	7.1	3	21.4	11	78.6	0	.0	
WILLIAMS COLLEGE															
MA TOTAL	0	.0	116	6.0	33	1.7	20	1.0	169	8.7	1,720	88.6	52	2.7	
MA FEMALE	0	.0	54	6.5	16	1.9	9	1.1	79	9.5	736	88.2	19	2.3	
MA MALE	0	.0	62	5.6	17	1.5	11	1.0	90	8.1	984	88.9	33	3.0	
WORCESTER JUNIOR COLLEGE															
MA TOTAL	4	.5	28	3.3	12	1.4	10	1.2	54	6.3	672	78.6	129	15.1	
MA FEMALE	2	1.5	7	5.2	2	1.5	2	1.5	13	9.7	116	86.6	5	3.7	
MA MALE	2	.3	21	2.9	10	1.4	8	1.1	41	5.7	556	77.1	124	17.2	
WORCESTER POLY INSTITUTE															
MA TOTAL	6	.2	13	.5	21	.9	11	.5	51	2.1	2,260	92.7	128	5.2	
MA FEMALE	0	.0	1	.3	1	.3	2	.7	4	1.4	280	95.2	10	3.4	
MA MALE	6	.3	12	.6	20	.9	9	.4	47	2.2	1,980	92.3	118	5.5	
MASSACHUSETTS TOTAL (111 INSTITUTIONS)															
MA TOTAL	1,175	.4	10,892	4.1	4,369	1.7	3,642	1.4	20,078	7.6	238,437	90.6	5,140	1.9	2
MA FEMALE	713	.5	6,071	4.6	2,014	1.5	1,856	1.4	10,654	8.0	120,839	90.6	1,821	1.4	1
MA MALE	462	.4	4,821	3.7	2,355	1.8	1,786	1.4	9,424	7.2	117,598	90.2	3,319	2.5	1
MICHIGAN															
ADRIAN COLLEGE															
MI TOTAL	0	.0	14	1.8	1	.1	0	.0	15	2.0	738	97.5	4	.5	
MI FEMALE	0	.0	8	2.1	0	.0	0	.0	8	2.1	373	97.1	3	.8	
MI MALE	0	.0	6	1.6	1	.3	0	.0	7	1.9	365	97.9	1	.3	
ALBION COLLEGE															
MI TOTAL	0	.0	33	1.9	0	.0	14	.8	47	2.7	1,706	96.4	16	.9	
MI FEMALE	0	.0	17	2.1	0	.0	5	.6	22	2.7	776	96.6	5	.6	
MI MALE	0	.0	16	1.7	0	.0	9	.9	25	2.6	930	96.3	11	1.1	
ALMA COLLEGE															
MI TOTAL	3	.3	13	1.1	2	.2	7	.6	25	2.2	1,116	96.6	14	1.2	
MI FEMALE	1	.2	7	1.2	1	.2	3	.5	12	2.1	565	97.4	3	.5	
MI MALE	2	.3	6	1.0	1	.2	4	.7	13	2.3	551	95.8	11	1.9	
ALPENA COMMUNITY COLLEGE															
MI TOTAL	10	.6	47	2.7	20	1.1	2	.1	79	4.5	1,665	95.0	8	.5	
MI FEMALE	3	.4	18	2.4	6	.8	0	.0	27	3.6	716	96.4	0	.0	
MI MALE	7	.7	29	2.9	14	1.4	2	.2	52	5.2	949	94.1	8	.8	
ANDREWS UNIVERSITY															
MI TOTAL	6	.3	213	10.7	55	2.8	81	4.1	355	17.8	1,401	70.4	233	11.7	
MI FEMALE	3	.3	135	13.0	32	3.1	48	4.6	218	20.9	696	66.9	127	12.2	
MI MALE	3	.3	78	8.2	23	2.4	33	3.5	137	14.5	705	74.4	106	11.2	
AQUINAS COLLEGE															
MI TOTAL	3	.2	45	3.0	5	.3	9	.6	62	4.2	1,379	93.4	35	2.4	
MI FEMALE	3	.4	36	4.5	2	.2	3	.4	44	5.5	748	92.8	14	1.7	
MI MALE	0	.0	9	1.3	3	.4	6	.9	18	2.7	631	94.2	21	3.1	
BAKER JUNIOR COLLEGE BUS															
MI TOTAL	5	.4	355	27.1	2	.2	4	.3	366	27.9	946	72.1	0	.0	
MI FEMALE	5	.5	294	27.0	2	.2	4	.4	305	28.0	785	72.0	0	.0	
MI MALE	0	.0	61	27.5	0	.0	0	.0	61	27.5	161	72.5	0	.0	
BAY DE NOC CMTY COLLEGE															
MI TOTAL	20	1.7	0	.0	0	.0	0	.0	20	1.7	1,169	98.2	2	.2	
MI FEMALE	13	2.2	0	.0	0	.0	0	.0	13	2.2	585	97.5	2	.3	
MI MALE	7	1.2	0	.0	0	.0	0	.0	7	1.2	584	98.8	0	.0	
CALVIN COLLEGE															
MI TOTAL	5	.1	30	.8	33	.8	5	.1	73	1.9	3,494	90.0	316	8.1	
MI FEMALE	2	.1	15	.7	11	.5	2	.1	30	1.5	1,790	89.0	191	9.5	
MI MALE	3	.2	15	.8	22	1.2	3	.2	43	2.3	1,704	91.0	125	6.7	
CTR FOR CREATIVE STUDIES															
MI TOTAL	0	.0	91	9.1	11	1.1	11	1.1	113	11.3	881	88.4	3	.3	
MI FEMALE	0	.0	44	8.9	4	.8	2	.4	50	10.1	444	89.9	0	.0	
MI MALE	0	.0	47	9.3	7	1.4	9	1.8	63	12.5	437	86.9	3	.6	
CENTRAL MICH UNIVERSITY															
MI TOTAL	28	.2	276	1.9	25	.2	99	.7	428	3.0	13,785	96.6	58	.4	
MI FEMALE	14	.2	133	1.7	16	.2	54	.7	217	2.7	7,765	97.1	13	.2	
MI MALE	14	.2	143	2.3	9	.1	45	.7	211	3.4	6,020	95.9	45	.7	

54

INUED

BLACK NON-HISPANIC NUMBER	%	ASIAN OR PACIFIC ISLANDER NUMBER	%	HISPANIC NUMBER	%	TOTAL MINORITY NUMBER	%	WHITE NON-HISPANIC NUMBER	%	NON-RESIDENT ALIEN NUMBER	%	TOTAL NUMBER
1,878	20.8	67	.7	114	1.3	2,164	23.9	6,871	76.0	11	.1	9,046
1,137	23.4	40	.8	58	1.2	1,295	26.7	3,548	73.2	6	.1	4,849
741	17.7	27	.6	56	1.3	869	20.7	3,323	79.2	5	.1	4,197
106	23.1	2	.4	3	.7	111	24.2	337	73.4	11	2.4	459
81	23.8	2	.6	3	.9	86	25.2	248	72.7	7	2.1	341
25	21.2	0	.0	0	.0	25	21.2	89	75.4	4	3.4	118
3	.5	1	.2	0	.0	4	.7	510	92.7	36	6.5	550
1	.4	1	.4	0	.0	2	.9	213	93.8	12	5.3	227
2	.6	0	.0	0	.0	2	.6	297	92.0	24	7.4	323
0	.0	0	.0	0	.0	0	.0	4	80.0	1	20.0	5
0	.0	0	.0	0	.0	0	.0	2	100.0	0	.0	2
0	.0	0	.0	0	.0	0	.0	2	66.7	1	33.3	3
151	6.7	10	.4	19	.8	186	8.3	2,047	91.3	10	.4	2,243
85	6.0	6	.4	9	.6	103	7.3	1,312	92.7	1	.1	1,416
66	8.0	4	.5	10	1.2	83	10.0	735	88.9	9	1.1	827
797	8.6	44	.5	261	2.8	1,121	12.1	7,857	85.1	256	2.8	9,234
459	9.5	19	.4	120	2.5	608	12.6	4,175	86.8	25	.5	4,808
338	7.6	25	.6	141	3.2	513	11.6	3,682	83.2	231	5.2	4,426
42	16.7	2	.8	0	.0	45	17.9	203	80.6	4	1.6	252
11	12.9	0	.0	0	.0	11	12.9	73	85.9	1	1.2	85
31	18.6	2	1.2	0	.0	34	20.4	130	77.8	3	1.8	167
857	46.9	8	.4	29	1.6	922	50.5	902	49.4	3	.2	1,827
595	55.2	5	.5	20	1.9	632	58.7	445	41.3	0	.0	1,077
262	34.9	3	.4	9	1.2	290	38.7	457	60.9	3	.4	750
330	41.7	10	1.3	4	.5	347	43.8	125	15.8	320	40.4	792
166	75.8	2	.9	1	.5	170	77.6	20	9.1	29	13.2	219
164	28.6	8	1.4	3	.5	177	30.9	105	18.3	291	50.8	573
0	.0	0	.0	3	8.3	3	8.3	33	91.7	0	.0	36
0	.0	0	.0	0	.0	0	.0	0	.0	0	.0	0
0	.0	0	.0	3	8.3	3	8.3	33	91.7	0	.0	36
1,191	9.2	49	.4	102	.8	1,365	10.5	11,148	86.0	446	3.4	12,959
694	9.6	27	.4	57	.8	789	10.9	6,280	86.7	175	2.4	7,244
497	8.7	22	.4	45	.8	576	10.1	4,868	85.2	271	4.7	5,715
381	3.8	29	.3	14	.1	444	4.4	9,601	95.0	64	.6	10,109
173	4.4	13	.3	8	.2	202	5.1	3,742	94.7	7	.2	3,951
208	3.4	16	.3	6	.1	242	3.9	5,859	95.1	57	.9	6,158
211	9.7	106	4.9	39	1.8	368	16.9	1,678	77.0	133	6.1	2,179
61	9.2	27	4.1	9	1.4	101	15.3	541	81.8	19	2.9	661
150	9.9	79	5.2	30	2.0	267	17.6	1,137	74.9	114	7.5	1,518
20	1.8	0	.0	0	.0	20	1.8	1,069	97.9	3	.3	1,092
11	2.0	0	.0	0	.0	11	2.0	550	98.0	0	.0	561
9	1.7	0	.0	0	.0	9	1.7	519	97.7	3	.6	531
135	13.6	1	.1	0	.0	145	14.6	849	85.4	0	.0	994
1	.3	0	.0	0	.0	6	1.5	394	98.5	0	.0	400
134	22.6	1	.2	0	.0	139	23.4	455	76.6	0	.0	594
2	1.2	0	.0	4	2.5	6	3.7	154	94.5	3	1.9	163
0	.0	0	.0	1	1.4	1	1.4	70	95.9	2	2.7	73
2	2.2	0	.0	3	3.3	5	5.6	84	93.3	1	1.1	90
8	.9	2	.2	3	.3	13	1.5	849	98.3	2	.2	864
3	.6	1	.2	2	.4	6	1.3	461	98.5	1	.2	468
5	1.3	1	.3	1	.3	7	1.8	388	98.0	1	.3	396
441	6.2	50	.7	56	.8	567	8.0	6,388	90.0	139	2.0	7,094
192	5.3	15	.4	27	.7	242	6.7	3,381	93.0	14	.4	3,637
249	7.2	35	1.0	29	.8	325	9.4	3,007	87.0	125	3.6	3,457
5	.8	1	.2	0	.0	6	1.0	585	95.7	20	3.3	611
0	.0	0	.0	0	.0	0	.0	282	96.2	11	3.8	293
5	1.6	1	.3	0	.0	6	1.9	303	95.3	9	2.8	318
279	4.5	36	.6	58	.9	403	6.5	5,773	93.1	23	.4	6,199
133	4.3	16	.5	27	.9	194	6.3	2,853	93.4	7	.2	3,064
146	4.7	20	.6	31	1.0	209	6.7	2,910	92.8	16	.5	3,135
2	.9	1	.5	0	.0	4	1.8	213	98.2	0	.0	217
0	.0	1	1.2	0	.0	1	1.2	85	98.8	0	.0	86
2	1.5	0	.0	0	.0	3	2.3	128	97.7	0	.0	131
1,691	9.8	156	.9	292	1.7	2,347	13.6	14,881	86.4	0	.0	17,228
661	9.9	60	.9	113	1.7	915	13.6	5,795	86.4	0	.0	6,710
1,030	9.8	96	.9	179	1.7	1,432	13.6	9,086	86.4	0	.0	10,518
2,100	94.1	9	.4	2	.1	2,122	95.1	96	4.3	14	.6	2,232
1,371	94.2	6	.4	1	.1	1,386	95.3	63	4.3	6	.4	1,455
729	93.8	3	.4	1	.1	736	94.7	33	4.2	8	1.0	777

	AMERICAN INDIAN ALASKAN NATIVE		BLACK NON-HISPANIC		ASIAN OR PACIFIC ISLANDER		HISPANIC		TOTAL MINORITY		WHITE NON-HISPANIC		NON-RESIDENT ALIEN	
	NUMBER	%	NUMBER	%	NUMBER	%	NUMBER	%	NUMBER	%	NUMBER	%	NUMBER	%
MICHIGAN CONTINUED														
HILLSDALE COLLEGE														
MI TOTAL	0	.0	32	3.1	3	.3	2	.2	37	3.6	980	95.7	7	.7
MI FEMALE	0	.0	9	2.0	0	.0	0	.0	9	2.0	437	97.8	1	.2
MI MALE	0	.0	23	4.0	3	.5	2	.3	28	4.9	543	94.1	6	1.0
HOPE COLLEGE														
MI TOTAL	1	.0	31	1.5	13	.6	24	1.2	69	3.3	1,967	94.3	49	2.4
MI FEMALE	0	.0	12	1.2	6	.6	8	.8	26	2.6	934	95.1	22	2.2
MI MALE	1	.1	19	1.7	7	.6	16	1.5	43	3.9	1,033	93.7	27	2.4
JACKSON COMMUNITY COLLEGE														
MI TOTAL	12	.3	462	12.1	14	.4	43	1.1	531	13.9	3,283	86.0	2	.1
MI FEMALE	4	.3	67	4.4	5	.3	9	.6	85	5.5	1,454	94.5	0	.0
MI MALE	8	.4	395	17.3	9	.4	34	1.5	446	19.6	1,829	80.3	2	.1
JOHN WESLEY COLLEGE														
MI TOTAL	0	.0	60	27.1	3	1.4	2	.9	65	29.4	156	70.6	0	.0
MI FEMALE	0	.0	5	7.1	0	.0	0	.0	5	7.1	65	92.9	0	.0
MI MALE	0	.0	55	36.4	3	2.0	2	1.3	60	39.7	91	60.3	0	.0
JORDAN COLLEGE														
MI TOTAL	0	.0	4	1.4	3	1.1	3	1.1	10	3.6	270	96.1	1	.4
MI FEMALE	0	.0	0	.0	1	1.0	0	.0	1	1.0	97	98.0	1	1.0
MI MALE	0	.0	4	2.2	2	1.1	3	1.6	9	4.9	173	95.1	0	.0
KALAMAZOO COLLEGE														
MI TOTAL	1	.1	22	1.6	13	.9	10	.7	46	3.3	1,336	95.4	18	1.3
MI FEMALE	0	.0	14	2.1	5	.7	5	.7	24	3.6	638	95.7	5	.7
MI MALE	1	.1	8	1.1	8	1.1	5	.7	22	3.0	698	95.2	13	1.8
KALAMAZOO VALLEY CC														
MI TOTAL	43	.7	371	5.6	48	.7	34	.5	496	7.5	5,964	90.5	129	2.0
MI FEMALE	22	.6	202	5.5	21	.6	17	.5	262	7.1	3,405	92.3	23	.6
MI MALE	21	.7	169	5.8	27	.9	17	.6	234	8.1	2,559	88.3	106	3.7
KELLOGG COMMUNITY COLLEGE														
MI TOTAL	30	.7	310	7.2	12	.3	33	.8	385	8.9	3,886	90.3	33	.8
MI FEMALE	15	.6	194	7.4	8	.3	17	.7	234	9.0	2,366	90.7	9	.3
MI MALE	15	.9	116	6.8	4	.2	16	.9	151	8.9	1,520	89.7	24	1.4
KIRTLAND CMTY COLLEGE														
MI TOTAL	3	.3	50	4.5	0	.0	3	.3	56	5.0	1,062	95.0	0	.0
MI FEMALE	0	.0	0	.0	0	.0	0	.0	0	.0	513	100.0	0	.0
MI MALE	3	.5	50	8.3	0	.0	3	.5	56	9.3	549	90.7	0	.0
LAKE MICHIGAN COLLEGE														
MI TOTAL	3	.2	278	16.2	10	.6	23	1.3	314	18.3	1,395	81.5	3	.2
MI FEMALE	1	.1	185	20.1	3	.3	8	.9	197	21.4	723	78.5	1	.1
MI MALE	2	.3	93	11.8	7	.9	15	1.9	117	14.8	672	85.0	2	.3
LAKE SUPERIOR ST COLLEGE														
MI TOTAL	15	.6	6	.3	0	.0	0	.0	21	.9	2,109	88.9	242	10.2
MI FEMALE	11	1.1	3	.3	0	.0	0	.0	14	1.4	960	92.8	61	5.9
MI MALE	4	.3	3	.2	0	.0	0	.0	7	.5	1,149	85.9	181	13.5
LANSING COMMUNITY COLLEGE														
MI TOTAL	92	.5	874	5.0	105	.6	295	1.7	1,366	7.8	15,807	90.5	292	1.7
MI FEMALE	58	.6	444	4.7	60	.6	147	1.5	709	7.5	8,697	91.7	81	.9
MI MALE	34	.4	430	5.4	45	.6	148	1.9	657	8.2	7,110	89.1	211	2.6
LAWRENCE INST TECHNOLOGY														
MI TOTAL	42	.9	318	6.5	65	1.3	58	1.2	483	9.9	4,219	86.8	159	3.3
MI FEMALE	7	1.1	74	12.1	14	2.3	13	2.1	108	17.6	501	81.9	3	.5
MI MALE	35	.8	244	5.7	51	1.2	45	1.1	375	8.8	3,718	87.5	156	3.7
LEHIS C BUS-LEHIS BUS C														
MI TOTAL	13	2.5	450	87.9	0	.0	16	3.1	479	93.6	33	6.4	0	.0
MI FEMALE	8	2.1	346	89.2	0	.0	10	2.6	364	93.8	24	6.2	0	.0
MI MALE	5	4.0	104	83.9	0	.0	6	4.8	115	92.7	9	7.3	0	.0
MACOMB CO CC-CENTER CAM														
MI TOTAL	98	1.7	96	1.6	16	.3	26	.4	236	4.0	5,678	96.0	0	.0
MI FEMALE	62	1.7	61	1.6	10	.3	16	.4	149	4.3	3,583	96.0	0	.0
MI MALE	36	1.6	35	1.6	6	.3	10	.5	87	4.0	2,095	96.0	0	.0
MACOMB CO CC-SOUTH CAMPUS														
MI TOTAL	165	1.4	472	2.5	122	.6	164	.9	923	4.8	18,195	95.2	0	.0
MI FEMALE	70	.9	202	2.5	52	.6	70	.9	394	4.8	7,767	95.2	0	.0
MI MALE	95	.9	270	2.5	70	.6	94	.9	529	4.8	10,428	95.2	0	.0
MADONNA COLLEGE														
MI TOTAL	5	.2	284	11.2	9	.4	8	.3	306	12.1	2,222	87.9	0	.0
MI FEMALE	3	.2	210	11.6	7	.4	4	.2	224	12.4	1,582	87.6	0	.0
MI MALE	2	.3	74	10.2	2	.3	4	.6	82	11.4	640	88.6	0	.0
MARYGROVE COLLEGE														
MI TOTAL	0	.0	383	54.1	4	.6	5	.7	392	55.4	310	43.8	6	.8
MI FEMALE	0	.0	329	56.8	3	.5	4	.7	336	58.0	237	40.9	6	1.0
MI MALE	0	.0	54	41.9	1	.8	1	.8	56	43.4	73	56.6	0	.0
MERCY COLLEGE OF DETROIT														
MI TOTAL	2	.1	644	32.1	22	1.1	18	.9	686	34.2	1,319	65.7	3	.1
MI FEMALE	2	.1	508	33.1	20	1.3	13	.8	543	35.4	989	64.5	2	.1
MI MALE	0	.0	136	28.7	2	.4	5	1.1	143	30.2	330	69.6	1	.2
MERRILL-PALMER INSTITUTE														
MI TOTAL	0	.0	2	7.4	0	.0	0	.0	2	7.4	25	92.6	0	.0
MI FEMALE	0	.0	1	4.2	0	.0	0	.0	1	4.2	23	95.8	0	.0
MI MALE	0	.0	1	33.3	0	.0	0	.0	1	33.3	2	66.7	0	.0
MICH CHRISTIAN JR COLLEGE														
MI TOTAL	0	.0	29	9.7	0	.0	0	.0	29	9.7	265	88.6	5	1.7
MI FEMALE	0	.0	15	8.6	0	.0	0	.0	15	8.6	157	89.7	3	1.7
MI MALE	0	.0	14	11.3	0	.0	0	.0	14	11.3	108	87.1	2	1.6
MICHIGAN STATE UNIVERSITY														
MI TOTAL	86	.2	1,879	5.2	205	.6	217	.6	2,387	6.7	33,206	92.6	279	.8
MI FEMALE	49	.3	1,181	6.6	104	.6	98	.6	1,432	8.1	16,260	91.4	96	.5
MI MALE	37	.2	698	3.9	101	.6	119	.7	955	5.3	16,946	93.7	183	1.0
MICHIGAN TECHNOLOGICAL U														
MI TOTAL	24	.4	29	.4	24	.4	18	.3	95	1.4	6,463	96.7	129	1.9
MI FEMALE	4	.3	10	.7	3	.2	4	.3	21	1.4	1,440	97.8	12	.8
MI MALE	20	.4	19	.4	21	.4	14	.3	74	1.4	5,023	96.3	117	2.2

	AMERICAN INDIAN ALASKAN NATIVE		BLACK NON-HISPANIC		ASIAN OR PACIFIC ISLANDER		HISPANIC		TOTAL MINORITY		WHITE NON-HISPANIC		NON-RESIDENT ALIEN		TOTAL
	NUMBER	%	NUMBER	%	NUMBER	%	NUMBER	%	NUMBER	%	NUMBER	%	NUMBER	%	NUMBER
MICHIGAN CONTINUED															
MID MICHIGAN CMTY COLLEGE															
MI TOTAL	15	1.3	2	.2	2	.2	4	.4	23	2.0	1,111	97.7	3	.3	1,137
MI FEMALE	5	.8	2	.3	1	.2	1	.2	9	1.4	632	98.6	0	.0	641
MI MALE	10	2.0	0	.0	1	.2	3	.6	14	2.8	479	96.6	3	.6	496
MONROE CO CMTY COLLEGE															
MI TOTAL	5	.2	2	.1	0	.0	4	.2	11	.5	2,008	99.5	0	.0	2,019
MI FEMALE	3	.3	1	.1	0	.0	1	.1	5	.5	1,052	99.5	0	.0	1,057
MI MALE	2	.2	1	.1	0	.0	3	.3	6	.6	956	99.4	0	.0	962
MONTCALM CMTY COLLEGE															
MI TOTAL	6	.5	265	19.9	0	.0	11	.8	282	21.2	1,050	78.8	1	.1	1,333
MI FEMALE	4	.9	0	.0	0	.0	0	.0	4	.9	461	98.9	1	.2	466
MI MALE	2	.2	265	30.6	0	.0	11	1.3	278	32.1	589	67.9	0	.3	867
MUSKEGON BUSINESS COLLEGE															
MI TOTAL	0	.0	147	14.5	2	.2	15	1.5	164	16.1	853	83.9	0	.0	1,017
MI FEMALE	0	.0	114	16.5	0	.0	7	1.0	121	17.5	570	82.5	0	.0	691
MI MALE	0	.0	33	10.1	2	.6	8	2.5	43	13.2	283	86.8	0	.0	326
MUSKEGON CMTY COLLEGE															
MI TOTAL	26	.5	435	8.7	16	.3	46	.9	523	10.4	4,488	89.6	0	.0	5,011
MI FEMALE	12	.5	206	8.5	5	.2	19	.8	242	6.9	2,193	90.1	0	.0	2,435
MI MALE	14	.5	229	8.9	11	.4	27	1.0	281	10.9	2,295	89.1	0	.0	2,576
NAZARETH COLLEGE															
MI TOTAL	1	.2	21	4.9	1	.2	6	1.4	29	6.8	396	92.3	4	.9	429
MI FEMALE	1	.3	17	4.6	0	.0	5	1.3	23	6.2	349	93.8	0	.0	372
MI MALE	0	.0	4	7.0	1	1.8	1	1.8	6	10.5	47	82.5	4	7.0	57
NORTH CEN MICH COLLEGE															
MI TOTAL	10	.7	0	.0	0	.0	0	.0	10	.7	1,509	99.3	0	.0	1,519
MI FEMALE	4	.5	0	.0	0	.0	0	.0	4	.5	849	99.5	0	.0	853
MI MALE	6	.9	0	.0	0	.0	0	.0	6	.9	660	99.1	0	.0	666
NORTHERN MICH UNIVERSITY															
MI TOTAL	73	.9	218	2.7	28	.3	36	.4	355	4.4	7,671	95.3	27	.3	8,053
MI FEMALE	33	.9	58	1.5	10	.3	11	.3	112	3.0	3,659	96.7	11	.3	3,782
MI MALE	40	.9	160	3.7	18	.4	25	.6	243	5.7	4,012	93.9	16	.4	4,271
NORTHWESTERN MICH COLLEGE															
MI TOTAL	14	.5	6	.2	6	.2	12	.4	38	1.4	2,676	98.0	17	.6	2,731
MI FEMALE	4	.3	0	.0	3	.2	7	.5	14	1.0	1,375	98.7	4	.3	1,393
MI MALE	10	.7	6	.4	3	.2	5	.4	24	1.8	1,301	97.2	13	1.0	1,338
NORTHWOOD INST MAIN CAM															
MI TOTAL	0	.0	57	3.4	3	.2	4	.2	64	3.9	1,535	92.9	54	3.3	1,653
MI FEMALE	0	.0	15	3.1	1	.2	0	.0	16	3.3	470	95.9	4	.8	490
MI MALE	0	.0	42	3.6	2	.2	4	.3	48	4.1	1,065	91.6	50	4.3	1,163
NORTHWOOD INST INDIANA BR															
MI TOTAL	0	.0	7	5.3	0	.0	0	.0	7	5.3	121	92.4	3	2.3	131
MI FEMALE	0	.0	3	5.2	0	.0	0	.0	3	5.2	55	94.8	0	.0	58
MI MALE	0	.0	4	5.5	0	.0	0	.0	4	5.5	66	90.4	3	4.1	73
OAKLAND COMMUNITY COLLEGE															
MI TOTAL	122	.6	771	3.9	127	.6	1,710	8.7	2,730	13.9	16,812	85.9	37	.2	19,579
MI FEMALE	63	.6	474	4.1	65	.6	945	8.3	1,547	13.5	9,877	86.4	7	.1	11,431
MI MALE	59	.7	297	3.6	62	.8	765	9.4	1,183	14.5	6,935	85.1	30	.4	8,148
OAKLAND UNIVERSITY															
MI TOTAL	21	.2	593	7.0	47	.6	63	.7	724	8.6	7,667	90.8	53	.6	8,444
MI FEMALE	17	.4	357	7.4	27	.6	33	.7	434	9.1	4,338	90.5	23	.5	4,795
MI MALE	4	.1	236	6.5	20	.5	30	.8	290	7.9	3,329	91.2	30	.8	3,649
OLIVET COLLEGE															
MI TOTAL	0	.0	39	6.1	0	.0	0	.0	39	6.1	600	93.2	5	.8	644
MI FEMALE	0	.0	10	4.0	0	.0	0	.0	10	4.0	239	95.2	2	.8	251
MI MALE	0	.0	29	7.4	0	.0	0	.0	29	7.4	361	91.9	3	.8	393
REFORMED BIBLE COLLEGE															
MI TOTAL	3	1.6	5	2.6	10	5.2	11	5.8	29	15.2	123	64.4	39	20.4	191
MI FEMALE	2	2.1	0	.0	1	1.0	6	6.3	9	9.4	61	63.5	26	27.1	96
MI MALE	1	1.1	5	5.3	9	9.5	5	5.3	20	21.1	62	65.3	13	13.7	95
SACRED HEART SEMINARY C															
MI TOTAL	0	.0	0	.0	0	.0	0	.0	0	.0	45	100.0	0	.0	45
MI FEMALE	0	.0	0	.0	0	.0	0	.0	0	.0	0	.0	0	.0	0
MI MALE	0	.0	0	.0	0	.0	0	.0	0	.0	45	100.0	0	.0	45
SAGINAW VLY STATE COLLEGE															
MI TOTAL	11	.4	261	9.2	4	.1	119	4.2	395	13.8	2,440	85.6	17	.6	2,852
MI FEMALE	5	.3	160	10.7	3	.2	67	4.5	235	15.8	1,257	84.2	0	.0	1,492
MI MALE	6	.4	101	7.4	1	.1	52	3.8	160	11.8	1,183	87.0	17	1.3	1,360
SNT CLAIR CO CMTY COLLEGE															
MI TOTAL	3	.1	73	2.3	3	.1	16	.5	95	3.0	3,056	96.6	14	.4	3,165
MI FEMALE	3	.2	40	2.2	3	.2	10	.6	56	3.1	1,743	96.9	0	.0	1,799
MI MALE	0	.0	33	2.4	0	.0	6	.4	39	2.9	1,313	96.1	14	1.0	1,366
SAINT MARY'S COLLEGE															
MI TOTAL	1	.7	9	6.4	3	2.1	2	1.4	15	10.6	123	87.2	3	2.1	141
MI FEMALE	0	.0	2	3.2	1	1.6	2	3.2	5	7.9	58	92.1	0	.0	63
MI MALE	1	1.3	7	9.0	2	2.6	0	.0	10	12.8	65	83.3	3	3.8	78
SCHOOLCRAFT COLLEGE															
MI TOTAL	37	.5	75	1.0	37	.5	66	.8	215	2.7	7,659	97.0	20	.3	7,894
MI FEMALE	12	.3	32	.8	18	.5	34	.9	96	2.4	3,889	97.4	7	.2	3,992
MI MALE	25	.6	43	1.1	19	.5	32	.8	119	3.0	3,770	96.6	13	.3	3,902
SHAW COLLEGE AT DETROIT															
MI TOTAL	0	.0	793	99.5	0	.0	0	.0	793	99.5	3	.4	1	.1	797
MI FEMALE	0	.0	439	99.8	0	.0	0	.0	439	99.8	1	.2	0	.0	440
MI MALE	0	.0	354	99.2	0	.0	0	.0	354	99.2	2	.6	1	.3	357
SIENA HEIGHTS COLLEGE															
MI TOTAL	2	.2	91	9.2	5	.5	24	2.4	122	12.3	848	85.8	18	1.8	988
MI FEMALE	1	.2	47	7.8	5	.8	15	2.5	68	11.2	528	87.3	9	1.5	605
MI MALE	1	.3	44	11.5	0	.0	9	2.3	54	14.1	320	83.6	9	2.3	383
SOUTHWESTERN MICH COLLEGE															
MI TOTAL	9	.5	142	7.7	6	.3	9	.5	166	9.0	1,661	90.1	17	.9	1,844
MI FEMALE	5	.5	79	7.6	3	.3	4	.4	91	8.5	947	91.1	2	.2	1,040
MI MALE	4	.5	63	7.8	3	.4	5	.6	75	9.3	714	88.8	15	1.9	804

TABLE 1 - TOTAL UNDERGRADUATE ENROLLMENT IN INSTITUTIONS OF HIGHER EDUCATION BY RACE, ETHNICITY AND SEX:
INSTITUTION, STATE AND NATION, 1978

	AMERICAN INDIAN ALASKAN NATIVE		BLACK NON-HISPANIC		ASIAN OR PACIFIC ISLANDER		HISPANIC		TOTAL MINORITY		WHITE NON-HISPANIC		NON-RESIDENT ALIEN		TO
	NUMBER	%	NUMBER	%	NUMBER	%	NUMBER	%	NUMBER	%	NUMBER	%	NUMBER	%	NU
MICHIGAN	CONTINUED														
SPRING ARBOR COLLEGE															
MI TOTAL	1	.1	26	3 2	1	.1	2	.2	30	3.7	760	93.3	25	3.1	
MI FEMALE	1	.2	12	2 7	1	.2	0	.0	14	3.2	416	93.9	13	2.9	
MI MALE	0	.0	14	318	0	.0	2	.5	16	4.3	344	92.5	12	3.2	
SUOMI COLLEGE															
MI TOTAL	2	.4	38	7 1	1	.2	1	.2	42	7.9	439	82.1	54	1 1	
MI FEMALE	1	.4	11	3 9	1	.4	0	.0	13	4.6	250	89.3	17	8 1	
MI MALE	1	.4	27	1016	0	.0	1	.4	29	11.4	189	74.1	37	1615	
UNIVERSITY OF DETROIT															
MI TOTAL	0	.0	639	21.2	21	.7	55	1	715	23.8	2,206	73.3	87	2.9	3
MI FEMALE	0	.0	412	32.2	1	.1	13	1 8	426	33.3	839	65.5	15	1.2	
MI MALE	0	.0	227	13.1	20	1.2	42	218	289	16.7	1,367	79.1	72	4.2	1
U MICHIGAN-ANN ARBOR															
MI TOTAL	86	.4	1,382	.2	374	1.7	253	1.1	2,095	9.4	19,424	87.3	805	3.	22
MI FEMALE	41	.4	827	4.3	157	1.6	128	1.3	1,153	11.6	8,591	86.3	212	2.1	9
MI MALE	45	.4	555	8.3	217	1.8	125	1.0	942	7.6	10,833	87.6	593	4.8	12
U OF MICHIGAN-DEARBORN															
MI TOTAL	32	.7	260	5.5	32	.7	29	6	353	7.5	4,253	90.3	102	2.2	4
MI FEMALE	15	.8	171	8.6	15	.8	10	5	211	10 6	1,750	88.1	25	1.3	1
MI MALE	17	.6	89	3.3	17	.6	19	17	142	512	2,503	92.0	77	2.8	2
U OF MICHIGAN-FLINT															
MI TOTAL	8	.2	402	1' 9	15	.4	43	1.3	468	13 9	2,896	85.8	10	.3	
MI FEMALE	2	.1	252	1 3	9	.5	24	1.4	287	16 3	1,475	83.6	2	.1	2
MI MALE	6	.4	150	413	6	.4	19	1.2	181	1112	1,421	88.3	8	.5	1
WALSH C ACCTY & BUS ADMIN															
MI TOTAL	0	.0	20	1 9		.4	3	.3	27	2.	1,000	97.0		.4	1
MI FEMALE	0	.0	6	117		.0	0	.0	6	1.	354	98.1	1	.3	
MI MALE	0	.0	14	2.1	8	.6	3	.4	21	3.6	646	96.4	3	.4	
WASHTENAW CMTY COLLEGE															
MI TOTAL	7	.1	822	12.2	75	1.1	30	.4	934	13.9	5,781	86.1		.0	6
MI FEMALE	1	.0	395	11.7	41	1.2	12	.4	449	13.3	2,932	86.7	8	.0	3
MI MALE	6	.2	427	12.8	34	1.0	18	.5	485	14.5	2,849	85.5	0	.0	3
WAYNE COUNTY CMTY COLLEGE															
MI TOTAL	265	2.3	7,850	68.3	182	1.6	91	.8	8,308	73.0	2,951	25.7	149	1.3	11
MI FEMALE	179	2.3	5,579	71.1	52	.7	66	.8	5,876	74.9	1,951	24.9	17	.2	7
MI MALE	86	2.4	2,271	62.3	130	3.6	25	.7	2,512	68.9	1,000	27.4	132	3.6	3
WAYNE STATE UNIVERSITY															
MI TOTAL	230	1.0	5,587	25.4	258	1.2	389	1.8	6,464	29.3	15,492	70.3	82	.4	22
MI FEMALE	91	.9	3,422	32.7	117	1.1	190	1.8	3,820	36.5	6,615	63.2	28	.3	10
MI MALE	139	1.2	2,165	18.7	141	1.2	199	1.7	2,644	22.8	8,877	76.7	54	.5	11
WESTERN MICH UNIVERSITY															
MI TOTAL	56	.3	1,036	6.1	38	.2	102	.6	1,232	7.3	15,108	89.6	524	3.1	16
MI FEMALE	33	.4	548	6.7	23	.3	45	.5	649	7.9	7,427	90.7	111	1.4	8
MI MALE	23	.3	488	5.6	15	.2	57	.7	583	6.7	7,681	88.5	413	4.3	8
WEST SHORE CMTY COLLEGE															
MI TOTAL	2	.3	16	2.2	2	.3	1	.1	21	2.9	705	97.1	0	.0	
MI FEMALE	1	.3	5	1.4	0	.0	1	.3	7	2.0	349	98.0	0	.0	
MI MALE	1	.3	11	3.0	2	.5	0	.0	14	3.8	356	96.2	0	.0	
MICHIGAN	TOTAL (		92 INSTITUTIONS)												
MI TOTAL	2,259	.6	40,923	10.2	2,732	.7	5,394	1.3	51,308	12.7	346,073	85.9	5,720	1.4	403
MI FEMALE	1,128	.6	24,310	12.1	1,200	.6	2,676	1.3	29,314	14.6	170,190	84.7	1,544	.8	201
MI MALE	1,131	.6	16,613	8.2	1,532	.8	2,718	1.3	21,994	10.9	175,883	87.0	4,176	2.1	202
MINNESOTA															
AUGSBURG COLLEGE															
MN TOTAL	10	.7	60	4.1	16	1.1		.0	86	.8	1,377	93.3	13	.9	1
MN FEMALE	6	.7	31	3.8	7	.9	8	.0	44	.4	762	93.6	8	1.0	
MN MALE	4	.6	29	4.4	9	1.4	0	.0	42	6.3	615	92.9	5	.8	
BETHANY LUTHERAN COLLEGE															
MN TOTAL	2	.9		1.7	2	.9		.0	8	.	223	95.3	3	1.3	
MN FEMALE	1	.8		.0	0	.0	8	.0	1	3.	126	98.4	1	.8	
MN MALE	1	.9	6	3.8	2	1.9	0	.0	7	6.8	97	91.5	2	1.9	
BETHEL COLLEGE															
MN TOTAL	7	.4	13	.7	8	.4	5	.3	33	1.8	1,776	97.4	1	.8	1
MN FEMALE	4	.4	2	.2	4	.4	3	.3	13	1.3	971	97.8		.9	
MN MALE	3	.4	11	1.3	4	.5	2	.2	20	2.4	805	96.9	8	.7	
CARLETON COLLEGE															
MN TOTAL	5	.3	61	3.4	41	2.3	2	1.4	133	7	1,673	92.6	1	.1	1
MN FEMALE	2	.2	34	3.9	17	2.0	16	1.3	64	7 4	807	92.5		.0	
MN MALE	3	.3	27	2.9	24	2.6	15	1.6	69	718	866	92.5	•	.1	
COLLEGE OF SAINT BENEDICT															
MN TOTAL	3	.2	5	.3	5	.3	4	.2	17	1.1	1,573	97.7	20	1.2	1
MN FEMALE	3	.2	5	.3	5	.3	4	.2	17	1.1	1,573	97.7	20	1.2	1
MN MALE	0	.0	0	.0	0	.0	0	.0	0	.0	0	.0	0	.0	
COLLEGE OF SNT CATHERINE															
MN TOTAL	14	.7	1	.5	15	.8	16	.8	55	2.	1,903	96.2	21	1.1	1
MN FEMALE	14	.7	10	.5	15	.8	16	.8	55	2	1,903	96.2	21	1.1	1
MN MALE	0	.0	8	.0	0	.0	0	.0	0	18	0	.0	0	.0	
COLLEGE SAINT SCHOLASTICA															
MN TOTAL	30	2.7	7	.6	0	.0	0	.0	37	3 3	1,069	95.4	15	1.3	1
MN FEMALE	23	2.5	6	.7	0	.0	0	.0	29	3 2	879	96.7	1	.1	
MN MALE	7	3.3	1	.5	0	.0	0	.0	8	318	190	89.6	14	6.6	
COLLEGE OF SAINT TERESA															
MN TOTAL	2	.2		.6	2	.2	23	2.7	32	3	784	93.6	22	2.6	
MN FEMALE	2	.2		.6	2	.2	23	2.8	32	3	767	93.4	22	2.7	
MN MALE	0	.0	8	.0	0	.0	0	.0	0	18	17	100.0	0	.0	
COLLEGE OF SAINT THOMAS															
MN TOTAL	7	.3	12	.4	15	.5	18	.6	52	1.	2,701	97.1	29	1	2
MN FEMALE	1	.2	2	.3	1	.2	5	.9	9	1.0	575	98.5	0	18	
MN MALE	6	.3	10	.5	14	.6	13	.6	43	2.0	2,126	96.7	29	1.3	2

TABLE 1 - TOTAL UNDERGRADUATE ENROLLMENT IN INSTITUTIONS OF HIGHER EDUCATION BY RACE, ETHNICITY AND SEX: INSTITUTION, STATE AND NATION, 1978

	AMERICAN INDIAN ALASKAN NATIVE		BLACK NON-HISPANIC		ASIAN OR PACIFIC ISLANDER		HISPANIC		TOTAL MINORITY		WHITE NON-HISPANIC		NON-RESIDENT ALIEN		TOTAL
	NUMBER	%	NUMBER	%	NUMBER	%	NUMBER	%	NUMBER	%	NUMBER	%	NUMBER	%	NUMBER
MINNESOTA	**CONTINUED**														
CONCORDIA C AT MOORHEAD															
MN TOTAL	3	.1	20	.8	0	.0	1	.0	24	.9	2,558	97.2	50	1.9	2,632
MN FEMALE	0	.0	7	.5	0	.0	0	.0	7	.5	1,452	98.4	16	1.1	1,475
MN MALE	3	.3	13	1.1	0	.0	1	.1	17	1.5	1,106	95.6	34	2.9	1,157
CONCORDIA C-SAINT PAUL															
MN TOTAL	2	.3	62	10.0	2	.3	0	.0	66	10.6	545	87.8	10	1.6	621
MN FEMALE	1	.3	32	9.8	0	.0	0	.0	33	10.2	289	88.9	3	.9	325
MN MALE	1	.3	30	10.1	2	.7	0	.0	33	11.1	256	86.5	7	2.4	296
CROSIER SEMINARY															
MN TOTAL	0	.0	0	.0	0	.0	0	.0	0	.0	18	100.0		.0	18
MN FEMALE	0	.0	0	.0	0	.0	0	.0	0	.0	1	100.0	0	.0	1
MN MALE	0	.0	0	.0	0	.0	0	.0	0	.0	17	100.0	0	.0	17
DR MARTIN LUTHER COLLEGE															
MN TOTAL	1	.1	1	.1	0	.0	0	.0	2	.2	815	99.4	3	.4	820
MN FEMALE	1	.2	1	.2	0	.0	0	.0	2	.3	580	99.3	2	.3	584
MN MALE	0	.0	0	.0	0	.0	0	.0	0	.0	235	99.6	1	.4	236
GOLDEN VLY LUTH COLLEGE															
MN TOTAL	5	.9	23	4.0	0	.0	1	.2	29	5.0	543	93.9	6	1.0	578
MN FEMALE	1	.3	5	1.7	0	.0	0	.0	6	2.1	283	97.3	2	.7	291
MN MALE	4	1.4	18	6.3	0	.0	1	.3	23	8.0	260	90.6	4	1.4	287
GUSTAVUS ADOLPHUS COLLEGE															
MN TOTAL	0	.0	20	.9	0	.0	0	.0	20	.9	2,167	98.5	12	.5	2,199
MN FEMALE	0	.0	9	.7	0	.0	0	.0	9	.7	1,246	99.0	4	.3	1,259
MN MALE	0	.0	11	1.2	0	.0	0	.0	11	1.2	921	98.0	8	.9	940
HAMLINE UNIVERSITY															
MN TOTAL	1	.1	34	2.9	9	.8	2	.2	46	3.9	1,098	94.2	22	19	1,166
MN FEMALE	0	.0	14	2.6	6	1.1	1	.2	21	3.9	512	95.0	6	11	539
MN MALE	1	.2	20	3.2	3	.5	1	.2	25	4.0	586	93.5	16	216	627
MACALESTER COLLEGE															
MN TOTAL	23	1.3	66	3.9	15	.9	33	1.9	137	8.0	1,423	83.5	145	8	1,705
MN FEMALE	13	1.5	37	4.3	8	.9	16	1.9	74	8.6	747	87.0	38	4	859
MN MALE	10	1.2	29	3.4	7	.8	17	2.0	63	7.4	676	79.9	107	121	846
MINNEAPOLIS C-ART DESIGN															
MN TOTAL	14	2.1	24	3.5	3	.4	4	.6	45	6.6	626	92.1	9	1	680
MN FEMALE	6	1.7	11	3.0	1	.3	2	.6	20	5.5	340	93.7	3		363
MN MALE	8	2.5	13	4.1	2	.6	2	.6	25	7.9	286	90.2	6	11	317
MINNESOTA BIBLE COLLEGE															
MN TOTAL	0	.0	0	.0	0	.0	0	.0	0	.0	121	100.0		.0	121
MN FEMALE	0	.0	0	.0	0	.0	0	.0	0	.0	57	100.0	0	.0	57
MN MALE	0	.0	0	.0	0	.0	0	.0	0	.0	64	100.0	0	.0	64
ANOKA-RAMSEY CMTY COLLEGE															
MN TOTAL	5	.2	21	.7	10	.3	9	.3	45	1.5	2,882	98.5		.0	2,927
MN FEMALE	3	.2	1	.1	4	.2	5	.3	13	.7	1,747	99.3	0	.0	1,760
MN MALE	2	.2	20	1.7	6	.5	4	.3	32	2.7	1,135	97.3	0	.0	1,167
AUSTIN COMMUNITY COLLEGE															
MN TOTAL	1	.1	3	.4	1	.1	8	1.0	13	1.6	921	98.1	3	.4	837
MN FEMALE	1	.2	0	.0	0	.0	2	.4	3	.6	503	99.4	0	.0	506
MN MALE	0	.0	3	.9	1	.3	6	1.8	10	3.0	318	96.1	3	.9	331
BRAINERD CMTY COLLEGE															
MN TOTAL	0	.0	0	.0	0	.0	0	.0	0	.0	593	99.8	1	.2	594
MN FEMALE	0	.0	0	.0	0	.0	0	.0	0	.0	308	100.0	0	.0	308
MN MALE	0	.0	0	.0	0	.0	0	.0	0	.0	285	99.7	1	.3	286
FERGUS FALLS CMTY COLLEGE															
MN TOTAL	2	.4	7	1.3	0	.0	0	.0	9	1.6	526	95.8	14	2.6	549
MN FEMALE	1	.3	1	.3	0	.0	0	.0	2	.7	299	97.7	5	1.6	306
MN MALE	1	.4	6	2.5	0	.0	0	.0	7	2.9	227	93.4	9	3.7	243
HIBBING COMMUNITY COLLEGE															
MN TOTAL	4	.7	0	.0	0	.0	1	.2	5	.9	573	99.1		.0	578
MN FEMALE	3	.9	0	.0	0	.0	1	.3	4	1.1	347	98.9	0	.0	351
MN MALE	1	.4	0	.0	0	.0	0	.0	1	.4	226	99.6	0	.0	227
INVER HILLS CMTY COLLEGE															
MN TOTAL	8	.2	8	.2	5	.1	17	.5	38	1.1	3,325	98.8		.1	3,387
MN FEMALE	2	.1	2	.1	3	.1	7	.3	14	.7	2,020	99.1		.2	2,038
MN MALE	6	.5	6	.5	2	.2	10	.8	24	1.8	1,305	98.2	1	.0	1,329
ITASCA COMMUNITY COLLEGE															
MN TOTAL	12	1.9	0	.0	1	.2	1	.2	14	2.2	626	97.8		.0	640
MN FEMALE	7	1.7	0	.0	1	.2	0	.0	8	2.0	396	98.0	0	.0	404
MN MALE	5	2.1	0	.0	0	.0	1	.4	6	2.5	230	97.5	0	.0	236
LAKEWOOD CMTY COLLEGE															
MN TOTAL	2	.1	9	.3	2	.1	3	.1	16	.5	3,070	99.2	1	.3	3,096
MN FEMALE	1	.1	1	.1	1	.1	1	.1	4	.2	1,614	99.5	0	.2	1,622
MN MALE	1	.1	8	.5	1	.1	2	.1	12	.8	1,456	98.8	1	.4	1,474
MESABI COMMUNITY COLLEGE															
MN TOTAL	1	.1	0	.0	0	.0	1	.1	2	.3	704	98.3	10	1.4	716
MN FEMALE	0	.0	0	.0	0	.0	1	.3	1	.3	368	99.7	0	.0	369
MN MALE	1	.3	0	.0	0	.0	0	.0	1	.3	336	96.8	10	2.9	347
METROPOLITAN CMTY COLLEGE															
MN TOTAL	59	2.5	159	6.6	0	.0	0	.0	218	9.1	2,122	88.7	52	2.2	2,392
MN FEMALE	41	2.5	92	5.6	0	.0	0	.0	133	8.1	1,497	90.9	16	1.0	1,646
MN MALE	18	2.4	67	9.0	0	.0	0	.0	85	11.4	625	83.8	36	4.5	746
NORMANDALE CHTY COLLEGE															
MN TOTAL	9	.2	50	1.1	19	.4	10	.2	88	1.9	4,480	97.6	24	.5	4,592
MN FEMALE	4	.2	18	.8	10	.4	2	.1	34	1.4	2,350	98.2	9	.4	2,393
MN MALE	5	.2	32	1.5	9	.4	8	.4	54	2.5	2,130	96.9	15	.7	2,199
N HENNEPIN CMTY COLLEGE															
MN TOTAL	5	.1	17	.4	5	.1	3	.1	30	.8	3,899	98.4	3	.9	3,963
MN FEMALE	1	.0	4	.2	3	.1	0	.0	8	.4	2,194	99.5		.2	2,206
MN MALE	4	.2	13	.7	2	.1	3	.2	22	1.3	1,705	97.0	30	1.7	1,757
NORTHLAND CMTY COLLEGE															
MN TOTAL	9	1.8	4	.8	0	.0	0	.0	13	2.7	475	96.9	2	.4	490
MN FEMALE	2	.9	0	.0	0	.0	0	.0	2	.9	225	99.1	0	.0	227
MN MALE	7	2.7	4	1.5	0	.0	0	.0	11	4.2	250	95.1	2	.8	263

59

TABLE 1 - TOTAL UNDERGRADUATE ENROLLMENT IN INSTITUTIONS OF HIGHER EDUCATION BY RACE, ETHNICITY AND SEX:
INSTITUTION, STATE AND NATION, 1978

	AMERICAN INDIAN ALASKAN NATIVE		BLACK NON-HISPANIC		ASIAN OR PACIFIC ISLANDER		HISPANIC		TOTAL MINORITY		WHITE NON-HISPANIC		NON-RESIDENT ALIEN	
	NUMBER	%	NUMBER	%	NUMBER	%	NUMBER	%	NUMBER	%	NUMBER	%	NUMBER	%
MINNESOTA CONTINUED														
RAINY RIVER CMTY COLLEGE														
MN TOTAL	50	12.9	0	.0	0	.0	1	.3	51	13.1	308	79.4	29	7.5
MN FEMALE	27	12.2	0	.0	0	.0	1	.5	28	12.7	173	78.3	20	9.0
MN MALE	23	13.8	0	.0	0	.0	0	.0	23	13.9	135	80.8	9	5.4
ROCHESTER CMTY COLLEGE														
MN TOTAL	20	.7	33	1.2	26	.9	13	.5	92	3.3	2,644	95.3	39	1.4
MN FEMALE	13	.7	9	.5	17	1.0	10	.6	49	2.8	1,679	95.4	32	1.8
MN MALE	7	.7	24	2.4	9	.9	3	.3	43	4.2	965	95.1	7	.7
VERMILION CMTY COLLEGE														
MN TOTAL	2	.5	2	.5	0	.0	0	.0	4	.9	431	99.1	0	.0
MN FEMALE	0	.0	0	.0	0	.0	0	.0	0	.0	171	100.0	0	.0
MN MALE	2	.8	2	.8	0	.0	0	.0	4	1.5	260	98.5	0	.0
WILLMAR CMTY COLLEGE														
MN TOTAL	0	.0	8	1.1	3	.4	1	.1	12	1.7	690	95.8	18	2.5
MN FEMALE	0	.0	0	.0	2	.6	0	.0	2	.6	347	98.6	3	.9
MN MALE	0	.0	8	2.2	1	.3	1	.3	10	2.7	343	93.2	15	4.1
WORTHINGTON CMTY COLLEGE														
MN TOTAL	3	.6	2	.4	0	.0	0	.0	5	.9	521	98.3		.8
MN FEMALE	3	1.1	0	.0	0	.0	0	.0	3	1.1	281	98.9		
MN MALE	0	.0	2	.8	0	.0	0	.0	2	.8	240	97.6	4	1.6
NORTH CEN BIBLE COLLEGE														
MN TOTAL	4	.7	18	3.0	0	.0	7	1.2	29	4.8	576	94.9	2	.3
MN FEMALE	3	1.1	7	2.5	0	.0	5	1.8	15	5.3	268	94.0	2	.7
MN MALE	1	.3	11	3.4	0	.0	2	.6	14	4.3	308	95.7	0	.0
NORTHWESTERN COLLEGE														
MN TOTAL	0	.0	8	1.1	3	.4	5	.7	16	2.3	681	97.3	3	.4
MN FEMALE	0	.0	1	.3	1	.3	0	.0	2	.6	352	99.4	0	.0
MN MALE	0	.0	7	2.0	2	.6	5	1.4	14	4.0	329	95.1	3	.9
SAINT JOHN'S UNIVERSITY														
MN TOTAL	1	.1	4	.2	3	.2	2	.1	10	.6	1,736	98.1	2	1.4
MN FEMALE	0	.0	0	.0	0	.0	0	.0	0	.0	0	.0		.0
MN MALE	1	.1	4	.2	3	.2	2	.1	10	.6	1,736	98.1	2	1.4
SAINT MARY'S COLLEGE														
MN TOTAL	1	.1	15	1.2	3	.2	5	.4	24	2.0	1,171	97.5		.5
MN FEMALE	1	.2	4	.8	2	.4	3	.6	10	1.9	516	98.1		.0
MN MALE	0	.0	11	1.6	1	.1	2	.3	14	2.1	655	97.0	8	.9
SAINT MARY'S JR COLLEGE														
MN TOTAL	3	.4	12	1.6	5	.7	5	.7	25	3.4	715	96.6		.0
MN FEMALE	2	.3	10	1.5	5	.7	5	.7	22	3.2	659	96.8		.0
MN MALE	1	1.7	2	3.4	0	.0	0	.0	3	5.1	56	94.9	0	.0
SAINT OLAF COLLEGE														
MN TOTAL	4	.1	24	.8	15	.5	2	.1	45	1.6	2,813	97.8	18	.6
MN FEMALE	4	.3	14	1.0	8	.5	0	.0	26	1.8	1,429	97.4	12	.8
MN MALE	0	.0	10	.7	7	.5	2	.1	19	1.3	1,384	98.2	6	.4
SAINT PAUL BIBLE COLLEGE														
MN TOTAL	0	.0	0	.0	2	.3	5	.8	7	1.2	592	98.7	1	.2
MN FEMALE	0	.0	0	.0	2	.7	1	.3	3	1.0	299	98.7	1	.3
MN MALE	0	.0	0	.0	0	.0	4	1.3	4	1.3	293	98.7	0	.0
BEMIDJI STATE U														
MN TOTAL	153	3.7	31	.7	13	.3		.2	205	4.9	3,882	93.2	78	1.9
MN FEMALE	88	4.4	3	.2	6	.3		.2	101	5.1	1,862	93.7	24	1.2
MN MALE	65	3.0	28	1.3	7	.3	4	.2	104	4.8	2,020	92.7	54	2.5
MANKATO STATE UNIVERSITY														
MN TOTAL	18	.2	74	.9	26	.3	22	.3	140	1.7	8,074	96.1	191	2.3
MN FEMALE	7	.2	37	.9	13	.3	12	.3	69	1.6	4,216	97.5	37	.9
MN MALE	11	.3	37	.9	13	.3	10	.2	71	1.7	3,858	94.5	154	3.8
MOORHEAD STATE UNIVERSITY														
MN TOTAL	5	.1	20	.4	17	.3	12	.2	54	1.0	5,220	97.0	107	2.0
MN FEMALE	1	.0	4	.1	11	.4	7	.2	23	.8	2,810	98.3	27	.9
MN MALE	4	.2	16	.6	6	.2	5	.2	31	1.2	2,410	95.6	80	3.2
SAINT CLOUD ST UNIVERSITY														
MN TOTAL	16	.2	38	.4	22	.2	15	.2	91	1.0	8,950	97.7	118	1.3
MN FEMALE	7	.2	19	.4	7	.1	11	.2	44	.9	4,612	98.5	27	.6
MN MALE	9	.2	19	.4	15	.3	4	.1	47	1.1	4,338	96.9	91	2.0
STHWST STATE UNIVERSITY														
MN TOTAL	6	.3	13	.7	15	.9	7	.4	41	2.3	1,718	97.7	0	.0
MN FEMALE	3	.4	2	.3	6	.8	3	.4	14	1.8	750	98.2	0	.0
MN MALE	3	.3	11	1.1	9	.9	4	.4	27	2.7	968	97.3	0	.0
WINONA STATE UNIVERSITY														
MN TOTAL	5	.1	20	.5	2	.1	6	.2	33	.9	3,728	97.5	64	1.7
MN FEMALE	3	.1	3	.1	2	.1	5	.2	13	.6	2,146	98.7	16	.7
MN MALE	2	.1	17	1.0	0	.0	1	.1	20	1.2	1,582	95.9	48	2.9
U OF MINNESOTA DULUTH														
MN TOTAL	63	.8	50	.6	71	.9	26	.3	210	2.7	7,494	96.0	100	1.4
MN FEMALE	35	1.0	20	.6	31	.9	4	.1	90	2.5	3,460	96.6	32	.9
MN MALE	28	.7	30	.7	40	.9	22	.5	120	2.8	4,035	95.4	74	1.8
U OF MINN MHPLS SNT PAUL														
MN TOTAL	209	.5	776	1.7	696	1.6	267	.6	1,948	4.4	41,914	94.0	720	1.6
MN FEMALE	107	.5	372	1.7	290	1.3	126	.6	895	4.1	20,732	94.8	236	1.1
MN MALE	102	.4	404	1.8	406	1.8	141	.6	1,053	4.6	21,182	93.2	484	2.1
U OF MINNESOTA MORRIS														
MN TOTAL	54	3.4	55	3.5	5	.3	2	.1	116	7.3	1,434	90.8	30	1.9
MN FEMALE	28	3.8	22	3.0	1	.1	1	.1	52	7.0	684	92.1	7	.9
MN MALE	26	3.1	33	3.9	4	.5	1	.1	64	7.6	750	89.6	23	2.7
U MINN TECH COL CROOKSTON														
MN TOTAL	6	.7	2	.2	2	.2		.9	18	2.1	844	97.6	3	.3
MN FEMALE	5	1.3	0	.0	2	.5		1.1	11	3.0	360	97.0	0	.0
MN MALE	1	.2	2	.4	0	.0	4	.8	7	1.4	484	98.0	3	.6
U OF MINN TECH C-WASECA														
MN TOTAL	1	.1	0	.0	1	.1		.0	2	.2	824	98.0	15	1.8
MN FEMALE	0	.0	0	.0	1	.3		.0	1	.3	380	99.2	2	.5
MN MALE	1	.2	0	.0	0	.0	8	.0	1	.2	444	96.9	13	2.8

TABLE 4 - TOTAL UNDERGRADUATE ENROLLMENT IN INSTITUTIONS OF HIGHER EDUCATION BY RACE, ETHNICITY AND SEX: INSTITUTION, STATE AND NATION, 1978

	AMERICAN INDIAN ALASKAN NATIVE		BLACK NON-HISPANIC		ASIAN OR PACIFIC ISLANDER		HISPANIC		TOTAL MINORITY		WHITE NON-HISPANIC		NON-RESIDENT ALIEN		TOTAL
	NUMBER	%	NUMBER	%	NUMBER	%	NUMBER	%	NUMBER	%	NUMBER	%	NUMBER	%	NUMBER
MINNESOTA															
MINNESOTA		TOTAL (	55 INSTITUTIONS)												
MN TOTAL	869	.6	1,911	1.3	1,106	.7	605	.4	4,491	3 0	144,049	95.6	2,126	1.4	150,666
MN FEMALE	481	.6	857	1.1	495	.6	302	.4	2,135	2 7	75,924	96.4	676	.9	78,735
MN MALE	388	.5	1,054	1.5	611	.8	303	.4	2,356	3:3	68,125	94.7	1,450	2.0	71,931
MISSISSIPPI															
ALCORN STATE UNIVERSITY															
MS TOTAL	0	.0	2,018	96.2	5	.2	0	.0	2,023	96.5	74	3.5	0	.0	2,097
MS FEMALE	0	.0	1,173	94.4	2	.2	0	.0	1,175	94.5	68	5.5	0	.0	1,243
MS MALE	0	.0	845	98.9	3	.4	0	.0	848	99.3	6	.7	0	.0	854
BELHAVEN COLLEGE															
MS TOTAL	0	.0	13	2.9	0	.0	0	.0	13	2.9	433	95.6	7	1.5	453
MS FEMALE	0	.0	9	3.5	0	.0	0	.0	9	3.5	247	96.1	1	.4	257
MS MALE	0	.0	4	2.0	0	.0	0	.0	4	2.0	186	94.9	6	3.1	196
BLUE MOUNTAIN COLLEGE															
MS TOTAL	0	.0	7	2.5	0	.0	2	.7	9	3.2	270	96.4	1	.4	280
MS FEMALE	0	.0	6	2.8	0	.0	2	.9	8	3.8	204	95.8	1	.5	213
MS MALE	0	.0	1	1.5	0	.0	0	.0	1	1.5	66	98.5	0	.0	67
CLARKE COLLEGE															
MS TOTAL	1	.5	5	2.6	0	.0	0	.0	6	3.2	180	95.2	3	1.6	189
MS FEMALE	1	1.1	0	.0	0	.0	0	.0	1	1.1	89	97.8	1	1.1	91
MS MALE	0	.0	5	5.1	0	.0	0	.0	5	5.1	91	92.9	2	2.0	98
COAHOMA JUNIOR COLLEGE															
MS TOTAL	0	.0	1,384	97.1		.0	0	.0	1,384	97.1	41	2.9	0	.0	1,425
MS FEMALE	0	.0	833	99.5	0	.0	0	.0	833	99.5	4	.5	0	.0	837
MS MALE	0	.0	551	93.7	0	.0	0	.0	551	93.7	37	6.3	0	.0	588
COPIAH-LINCOLN JR COLLEGE															
MS TOTAL	0	.0	377	25.4		.0	0	.0	377	25.4	1,103	74.2	7	.5	1,487
MS FEMALE	0	.0	206	26.2	0	.0	0	.0	206	26.2	581	73.8	0	.0	787
MS MALE	0	.0	171	24.4	0	.0	0	.0	171	24.4	522	74.6	7	1.0	700
DELTA STATE UNIVERSITY															
MS TOTAL	2	.1	286	14.6	7	.4	1	.1	296	15.1	1,664	84.9	1	.1	1,961
MS FEMALE	2	.2	175	16.2	4	.4	1	.1	182	16.9	898	83.1	0	.0	1,080
MS MALE	0	.0	111	12.6	3	.3	0	.0	114	12.9	766	86.9	1	.1	881
EAST CENTRAL JR COLLEGE															
MS TOTAL	30	4.9	96	15.7	1	.2	0	.0	127	20.7	486	79.3	0	.0	613
MS FEMALE	18	5.1	64	18.2	1	.3	0	.0	83	23.6	268	76.4	0	.0	351
MS MALE	12	4.6	32	12.2	0	.0	0	.0	44	16.8	218	83.2	0	.0	262
EAST MISS JUNIOR COLLEGE															
MS TOTAL	1	.1	271	30.5	6	.7	1	.1	279	31.4	601	67.7	8	.9	888
MS FEMALE	0	.0	87	31.2	1	.4	0	.0	88	31.5	191	68.5	0	.0	279
MS MALE	1	.2	184	30.2		.8	1	.2	191	31.4	410	67.3	8	1.3	609
HINDS JUNIOR COLLEGE															
MS TOTAL	4	.1	864	16.9	10	.2		.1	881	17.2	4,227	82.7	4	.1	5,112
MS FEMALE	2	.1	626	20.7	5	.2		.0	636	21.0	2,385	78.9	1	.0	3,022
MS MALE	2	.1	238	11.4	5	.2	8	.0	245	11.7	1,842	88.1	3	.1	2,090
HOLMES JUNIOR COLLEGE															
MS TOTAL	0	.0	261	29.6	0	.0		.0	261	29.6	622	70.4	0	.0	883
MS FEMALE	0	.0	120	28.7	0	.0	0	.0	120	28.7	298	71.3	0	.0	418
MS MALE	0	.0	141	30.3	0	.0	0	.0	141	30.3	324	69.7	0	.0	465
ITAWAMBA JUNIOR COLLEGE															
MS TOTAL	0	.0	158	12.0	0	.0		.0	158	12.0	1,154	88.0		.0	1,312
MS FEMALE	0	.0	59	9.2	0	.0	0	.0	59	9.2	581	90.8	0	.0	640
MS MALE	0	.0	99	14.7	0	.0	0	.0	99	14.7	573	85.3		.0	672
JACKSON STATE UNIVERSITY															
MS TOTAL	14	.2	6,088	94.9	6	.1	3	.0	6,111	95.2	203	3.2	102	1.6	6,416
MS FEMALE	6	.2	3,447	97.2	4	.1	0	.0	3,457	97.5	71	2.0	18	.5	3,546
MS MALE	8	.3	2,641	92.0	2	.1	3	.1	2,654	92.5	132	4.6	84	2.9	2,870
JONES CO JUNIOR COLLEGE															
MS TOTAL	1	.0	475	21.3	1	.0	1	.0	478	21.4	1,753	78.4	4	.2	2,235
MS FEMALE	0	.0	274	22.7	1	.1	0	.0	275	22.7	933	77.2	1	.1	1,209
MS MALE	1	.1	201	19.6	0	.0	1	.1	203	19.8	820	79.9	3	.3	1,026
MARY HOLMES COLLEGE															
MS TOTAL	0	.0	642	98.6	5	.8	0	.0	647	99.4	4	.6	0	.0	651
MS FEMALE	0	.0	324	98.5	3	.9	0	.0	327	99.4	2	.6	0	.0	329
MS MALE	0	.0	318	98.8	2	.6	0	.0	320	99.4	2	.6	0	.0	322
MERIDIAN JUNIOR COLLEGE															
MS TOTAL	49	1.8	589	21.4	20	.7	7	.3	665	24.2	2,084	75.8	0	.0	2,749
MS FEMALE	35	2.2	395	24.4	7	.4	2	.1	439	27.1	1,181	72.9	0	.0	1,620
MS MALE	14	1.2	194	17.2	13	1.2	5	.4	226	20.0	903	80.0	0	.0	1,129
MILLSAPS COLLEGE															
MS TOTAL	0	.0	42	4.9	3	.4	1	.1	46	5.4	803	94.1	4	.5	853
MS FEMALE	0	.0	18	4.7	1	.3	1	.3	20	5.3	358	94.5	1	.3	379
MS MALE	0	.0	24	5.1	2	.4	0	.0	26	5.5	445	93.9	3	.6	474
MINISTERIAL INST AND C															
MS TOTAL	0	.0	400	100.0		.0		.0	400	100	0	.0	0	.0	400
MS FEMALE	0	.0	310	100.0	0	.0	0	.0	310	100	0	.0	0	.0	310
MS MALE	0	.0	90	100.0	0	.0	0	.0	90	100.0	0	.0	0	.0	90
MISSISSIPPI COLLEGE															
MS TOTAL	11	.7	110	6.6	1	.6	2	.1	133	7	1,529	91.4	11	.7	1,673
MS FEMALE	10	1.2	64	7.7	0	.0	1	.1	75	9	758	90.9	1	.1	834
MS MALE	1	.1	46	5.5	10	1.2	1	.1	58	6!0	771	91.9	10	1.2	839
MISS DELTA JUNIOR COLLEGE															
MS TOTAL	0	.0	492	32.7		.2	4	.3	499	33.2	1,006	66.8		.0	1,505
MS FEMALE	0	.0	254	31.7		.4	4	.0	261	32.6	540	67.4		.0	801
MS MALE	0	.0	238	33.8	8	.0	0	.0	238	33.8	466	66.2	0	.0	704
MISS GULF CST JC JACKSON															
MS TOTAL	4	.2	280	13.7	14	.7	4	.2	302	14.8	1,739	85.2	1	.0	2,042
MS FEMALE	2	.2	163	15.6	7	.7	1	.1	173	16.5	874	83.5	0	.0	1,047
MS MALE	2	.2	117	11.8	7	.7	3	.3	129	13.0	865	86.9	1	.1	995

61

TABLE 1 - TOTAL UNDERGRADUATE ENROLLMENT IN INSTITUTIONS OF HIGHER EDUCATION BY RACE, ETHNICITY AND SEX: INSTITUTION, STATE AND NATION, 1978

MISSISSIPPI   CONTINUED

	AMERICAN INDIAN ALASKAN NATIVE		BLACK NON-HISPANIC		ASIAN OR PACIFIC ISLANDER		HISPANIC		TOTAL MINORITY		WHITE NON-HISPANIC		NON-RESIDENT ALIEN		TOTAL
	NUMBER	%	NUMBER	%	NUMBER	%	NUMBER	%	NUMBER	%	NUMBER	%	NUMBER	%	NUMBER
MISS GULF CST JEFF DAVIS															
MS TOTAL	19	.5	377	10.9	57	1.6	14	.4	467	13.5	2,993	86.5	0	.0	3,460
MS FEMALE	9	.6	220	13.5	23	1.4	4	.2	256	15.7	1,373	84.3	0	.0	1,629
MS MALE	10	.5	157	8.6	34	1.9	10	.5	211	11.5	1,620	88.5	0	.0	1,831
MISS GULF CST JC PERKNSTN															
MS TOTAL	4	.5	128	17.2	4	.5		.0	136	18.3	608	81.7	0	.0	744
MS FEMALE	0	.0	58	16.7	0	.0	0	.0	58	16.7	290	83.3	0	.0	348
MS MALE	4	1.0	70	17.7	4	1.0	0	.0	78	19.7	318	80.3	0	.0	396
MISS INDUSTRIAL COLLEGE															
MS TOTAL	0	.0	270	100.0	0	.0	0	.0	270	100.0	0	.0	0	.0	270
MS FEMALE	0	.0	150	100.0	0	.0	0	.0	150	100.0	0	.0	0	.0	150
MS MALE	0	.0	120	100.0	0	.0	0	.0	120	100.0	0	.0	0	.0	120
MISSISSIPPI ST UNIVERSITY															
MS TOTAL	48	.5	750	7.6	23	.2	11	.1	832	8.4	8,991	90.7	86	.9	9,909
MS FEMALE	34	.9	397	10.4	9	.2	3	.1	443	11.6	3,373	88.0	18	.5	3,834
MS MALE	14	.2	353	5.8	14	.2	8	.1	389	6.4	5,618	92.5	68	1.1	6,075
MISS UNIVERSITY FOR WOMEN															
MS TOTAL	8	.4	446	19.7	9	.4	2	.1	465	20.6	1,761	77.9	34	1.5	2,260
MS FEMALE	8	.4	446	19.7	9	.4	2	.1	465	20.6	1,761	77.9	34	1.5	2,260
MS MALE	0	.0	0	.0	0	.0	0	.0	0	.0	0	.0	0	.0	0
MISS VLY ST UNIVERSITY															
MS TOTAL	0	.0	2,798	99.2	1	.0	.	.0	2,800	99.3	20	.7	1	.0	2,821
MS FEMALE	0	.0	1,559	99.8	0	.0	0	.0	1,559	99.8	3	.2	0	.0	1,562
MS MALE	0	.0	1,239	98.4	1	.1	1	.1	1,241	98.6	17	1.4	1	.1	1,259
NATCHEZ JUNIOR COLLEGE															
MS TOTAL	0	.0	62	100.0	0	.0		.0	62	100.0	0	.0	0	.0	62
MS FEMALE	0	.0	56	100.0	0	.0	0	.0	56	100.0	0	.0	0	.0	56
MS MALE	0	.0	6	100.0	0	.0	0	.0	6	100.0	0	.0	0	.0	6
NORTHEAST MISS JR COLLEGE															
MS TOTAL	0	.0	131	9.9	6	.5	0	.0	137	10.4	1,167	88.6	13	1.0	1,317
MS FEMALE	0	.0	82	11.1	0	.0	0	.0	82	11.1	656	88.5	3	.4	741
MS MALE	0	.0	49	8.5	6	1.0	0	.0	55	9.5	511	88.7	10	1.7	576
NORTHWEST MISS JR COLLEGE															
MS TOTAL	0	.0	702	30.4	0	.0	0	.0	702	30.4	1,588	68.7	20	.9	2,310
MS FEMALE	0	.0	427	32.5	0	.0	0	.0	427	32.5	883	67.3	3	.2	1,313
MS MALE	0	.0	275	27.6	0	.0	0	.0	275	27.6	705	70.7	17	1.7	997
PEARL RIVER JR COLLEGE															
MS TOTAL	0	.0	270	18.9	1	.1	0	.0	271	19.0	1,155	80.8	3	.2	1,429
MS FEMALE	0	.0	157	19.4	0	.0	0	.0	157	19.4	654	80.6	0	.0	811
MS MALE	0	.0	113	18.3	1	.2	0	.0	114	18.4	501	81.1	3	.5	618
PHILLIPS COLLEGE															
MS TOTAL	0	.0	187	34.4	2	.4	1	.2	190	35.0	353	65.0	0	.0	543
MS FEMALE	0	.0	102	40.8	1	.4	0	.0	103	41.2	147	58.8	0	.0	250
MS MALE	0	.0	85	29.0	1	.3	1	.3	87	29.7	206	70.3	0	.0	293
PRENTISS NORM-INDUS INST															
MS TOTAL	0	.0	81	100.0	0	.0	0	.0	81	100.0	0	.0	0	.0	81
MS FEMALE	0	.0	50	100.0	0	.0	0	.0	50	100.0	0	.0	0	.0	50
MS MALE	0	.0	31	100.0	0	.0	0	.0	31	100.0	0	.0	0	.0	31
RUST COLLEGE															
MS TOTAL	0	.0	609	97.9	0	.0	0	.0	609	97.9	13	2.1	0	.0	622
MS FEMALE	0	.0	415	97.2	0	.0	0	.0	415	97.2	12	2.8	0	.0	427
MS MALE	0	.0	194	99.5	0	.0	0	.0	194	99.5	1	.5	0	.0	195
SOUTHEASTERN BAPT COLLEGE															
MS TOTAL	0	.0	0	.0	0	.0	0	.0	0	.0	0	.0	0	.0	0
MS FEMALE	0	.0	0	.0	0	.0	0	.0	0	.0	0	.0	0	.0	0
MS MALE	0	.0	0	.0	0	.0	0	.0	0	.0	0	.0	0	.0	0
SOUTHWEST MISS JR COLLEGE															
MS TOTAL	0	.0	273	22.1	0	.0	0	.0	273	22.1	961	77.9	0	.0	1,234
MS FEMALE	0	.0	136	21.0	0	.0	0	.0	136	21.0	513	79.0	0	.0	649
MS MALE	0	.0	137	23.4	0	.0	0	.0	137	23.4	448	76.6	0	.0	585
TOUGALOO COLLEGE															
MS TOTAL	1	.1	820	98.2	0	.0	7	.8	828	99.2	1	.1	6	.7	835
MS FEMALE	0	.0	512	100.0	0	.0	0	.0	512	100.0	0	.0	0	.0	512
MS MALE	1	.3	308	95.4	0	.0	7	2.2	316	97.8	1	.3	6	1.9	323
U OF MISSISSIPPI MAIN CAM															
MS TOTAL	9	.1	541	7.1	32	.4	10	.1	592	7.7	6,817	88.9	262	3.4	7,671
MS FEMALE	2	.1	304	8.7	17	.5	4	.1	327	9.4	3,127	89.9	24	.7	3,478
MS MALE	7	.2	237	5.7	15	.4	6	.1	265	6.3	3,690	88.0	238	5.7	4,193
U OF MISSISSIPPI MEDL CTR															
MS TOTAL	1	.3	33	9.1	1	.3	1	.3	36	10.0	325	90.0	0	.0	361
MS FEMALE	1	.3	31	10.3	0	.0	1	.3	33	11.0	268	89.0	0	.0	301
MS MALE	0	.0	2	3.3	1	1.7	0	.0	3	5.0	57	95.0	0	.0	60
U OF SOUTHERN MISSISSIPPI															
MS TOTAL	33	.4	996	10.9	32	.4	33	.4	1,094	12.0	8,046	88.0		.0	9,140
MS FEMALE	14	.3	623	12.7	15	.3	15	.3	667	13.6	4,240	86.4	0	.0	4,907
MS MALE	19	.4	373	6.8	17	.4	18	.4	427	10.1	3,806	89.9	0	.0	4,233
UTICA JUNIOR COLLEGE															
MS TOTAL	0	.0	832	99.8	0	.0	0	.0	832	99.8	2	.2	0	.0	834
MS FEMALE	0	.0	491	99.8	0	.0	0	.0	491	99.8	1	.2	0	.0	492
MS MALE	0	.0	341	99.7	0	.0	0	.0	341	99.7	1	.3	0	.0	342
WESLEY COLLEGE															
MS TOTAL	0	.0	3	3.5	0	.0	0	.0	3	3.5	83	96.5	0	.0	86
MS FEMALE	0	.0	0	.0	0	.0	0	.0	0	.0	48	100.0	0	.0	48
MS MALE	0	.0	3	7.9	0	.0	0	.0	3	7.9	35	92.1	0	.0	38
WHITWORTH BIBLE COLLEGE															
MS TOTAL	0	.0	8	24.2	0	.0	0	.0	8	24.2	24	72.7	1	3.0	33
MS FEMALE	0	.0	7	28.0	0	.0	0	.0	7	28.0	18	72.0	0	.0	25
MS MALE	0	.0	1	12.5	0	.0	0	.0	1	12.5	6	75.0	1	12.5	8
WILLIAM CAREY COLLEGE															
MS TOTAL	2	.1	265	19.8	0	.0	3	.2	270	20.1	1,035	77.2	35	2.6	1,340
MS FEMALE	0	.0	186	21.7	0	.0	1	.1	187	21.8	660	76.8	12	1.4	859
MS MALE	2	.4	79	16.4	0	.0	2	.4	83	17.3	375	78.0	23	4.8	481

MISSISSIPPI   CONTINUED

TABLE 1 - TOTAL UNDERGRADUATE ENROLLMENT IN INSTITUTIONS OF HIGHER EDUCATION BY RACE, ETHNICITY AND SEX: INSTITUTION, STATE AND NATION, 1978

	AMERICAN INDIAN ALASKAN NATIVE		BLACK NON-HISPANIC		ASIAN OR PACIFIC ISLANDER		HISPANIC		TOTAL MINORITY		WHITE NON-HISPANIC		NON-RESIDENT ALIEN		TOTAL
	NUMBER	%	NUMBER	%	NUMBER	%	NUMBER	%	NUMBER	%	NUMBER	%	NUMBER	%	NUMBER
MISSISSIPPI															
WOOD JUNIOR COLLEGE															
MS TOTAL	0	.0	33	13.1	0	.0	0	.0	33	13.1	195	77.4	24	9.5	252
MS FEMALE	0	.0	17	12.6	0	.0	0	.0	17	12.6	113	83.7	5	3.7	135
MS MALE	0	.0	16	13.7	0	.0	0	.0	16	13.7	82	70.1	19	16.2	117
MISSISSIPPI TOTAL (45 INSTITUTIONS)															
MS TOTAL	242	.3	25,473	30.8	259	.3	112	.1	26,086	31.5	56,114	67.7	638	.8	82,838
MS FEMALE	144	.3	15,033	34.1	113	.3	45	.1	15,335	34.7	28,671	65.0	124	.3	44,130
MS MALE	98	.3	10,440	27.0	146	.4	67	.2	10,751	27.8	27,443	70.9	514	1.3	38,708
MISSOURI															
AVILA COLLEGE															
MO TOTAL	3	.2	169	10.3	10	.6	29	1.8	211	12.9	1,421	86.6		.5	1,641
MO FEMALE	3	.3	121	10.4	7	.6	23	2.0	154	13.3	1,003	86.3		.4	1,162
MO MALE	0	.0	48	10.0	3	.6	6	1.3	57	11.9	418	87.3		.8	479
BAPTIST BIBLE COLLEGE															
MO TOTAL	5	.2	7	.3	2	.1	16	.7	30	1.4	2,121	97.5	25	1.1	2,176
MO FEMALE	1	.1	1	.1	2	.2	6	.6	10	1.0	941	98.0	9	.9	960
MO MALE	4	.3	6	.5	0	.0	10	.8	20	1.6	1,180	97.0	16	1.3	1,216
CALVARY BIBLE COLLEGE															
MO TOTAL	0	.0	16	4.1	0	.0	1	.3	17	4.3	373	94.4	5	1.3	395
MO FEMALE	0	.0	7	3.7	0	.0	1	.5	8	4.2	178	94.2	3	1.6	189
MO MALE	0	.0	9	4.4	0	.0	0	.0	9	4.4	195	94.7	2	1.0	206
CARDINAL GLENNON COLLEGE															
MO TOTAL	0	.0	1	1.1	0	.0	1	1.1	2	2.2	88	97.8	0	.0	90
MO FEMALE	0	.0	0	.0	0	.0	0	.0	0	.0	0	.0	0	.0	0
MO MALE	0	.0	1	1.1	0	.0	1	1.1	2	2.2	88	97.8	0	.0	90
CARDINAL NEWMAN COLLEGE															
MO TOTAL	0	.0	1	1.8	0	.0	2	3.6	3	5.5	50	90.9	2	3.6	55
MO FEMALE	0	.0	1	2.9	0	.0	2	5.9	3	8.8	31	91.2	0	.0	34
MO MALE	0	.0	0	.0	0	.0	0	.0	0	.0	19	90.5	2	9.5	21
CENTRAL BIBLE COLLEGE															
MO TOTAL	12	1.1	8	.7	15	1.4	22	2.0	57	5.2	1,006	91.7	34	3.1	1,097
MO FEMALE	5	1.2	4	1.0	9	2.2	6	1.4	24	5.8	385	92.3	8	1.9	417
MO MALE	7	1.0	4	.6	6	.9	16	2.4	33	4.9	621	91.3	26	3.3	680
CENTRAL METHODIST COLLEGE															
MO TOTAL	0	.0	18	2.9	5	.8	0	.0	23	3.7	594	96.3	0	.0	617
MO FEMALE	0	.0	6	1.9	3	.9	0	.0	9	2.8	308	97.2	0	.0	317
MO MALE	0	.0	12	4.0	2	.7	0	.0	14	4.7	286	95.3	0	.0	300
CENTRAL MO ST UNIVERSITY															
MO TOTAL	2	.0	535	6.7	9	.1	18	.2	564	7.0	7,382	92.2	58	.7	8,004
MO FEMALE	1	.0	291	7.0	4	.1	11	.3	307	7.4	3,796	92.0	25	.6	4,128
MO MALE	1	.0	244	6.3	5	.1	7	.2	257	6.6	3,586	92.5	33	.9	3,876
COLUMBIA COLLEGE															
MO TOTAL	10	.3	418	13.9	12	.4	100	3.3	540	18.0	2,415	80.6	42	1.4	2,997
MO FEMALE	2	.2	125	14.2	3	.3	6	.7	136	15.4	731	82.8	16	1.9	883
MO MALE	8	.4	293	13.9	9	.4	94	4.4	404	19.1	1,684	79.7	26	1.2	2,114
CONCEPTION SEM COLLEGE															
MO TOTAL	0	.0	2	2.5	12	15.2	3	3.8	17	21.5	62	78.5	0	.0	79
MO FEMALE	0	.0	0	.0	0	.0	0	.0	0	.0	0	.0	0	.0	0
MO MALE	0	.0	2	2.5	12	15.2	3	3.8	17	21.5	62	78.5	0	.0	79
COTTEY COLLEGE															
MO TOTAL	4	1.2	0	.0	2	.6	4	1.2	10	2.9	318	93.8	11	3.2	339
MO FEMALE	4	1.2	0	.0	2	.6	4	1.2	10	2.9	318	93.8	11	3.2	339
MO MALE	0	.0	0	.0	0	.0	0	.0	0	.0	0	.0	0	.0	0
CROWDER COLLEGE															
MO TOTAL	5	.5	11	1.1	2	.2	7	.7	25	2.5	950	95.9	16	1.6	991
MO FEMALE	1	.2	1	.2	0	.0	2	.5	4	.9	429	98.8	1	.2	434
MO MALE	4	.7	10	1.8	2	.4	5	.9	21	3.8	521	93.5	15	2.7	557
CULVER-STOCKTON COLLEGE															
MO TOTAL	0	.0	43	10.7	0	.0	3	.7	46	11.5	352	87.8	3	.7	401
MO FEMALE	0	.0	18	9.3	0	.0	0	.0	18	9.3	175	90.7	0	.0	193
MO MALE	0	.0	25	12.0	0	.0	3	1.4	28	13.5	177	85.1	3	1.4	208
DRURY COLLEGE															
MO TOTAL	3	.2	68	4.3	16	1.0	9	.6	96	6.1	1,457	92.2	28	1.8	1,581
MO FEMALE	3	.5	26	4.2	7	1.1	3	.5	39	6.2	573	91.5	14	2.2	626
MO MALE	0	.0	42	4.4	9	.9	6	.6	57	6.0	884	92.6	14	1.5	955
EAST CENTRAL MO DIST JC															
MO TOTAL	6	.4	5	.3	2	.1	2	.1	15	1.0	1,508	99.0		.0	1,523
MO FEMALE	3	.4	0	.0	0	.0	1	.1	4	.5	767	99.5		.0	771
MO MALE	3	.4	5	.7	2	.3	1	.1	11	1.5	741	98.5		.0	752
EVANGEL COLLEGE															
MO TOTAL	4	.3	17	1.2	6	.4	21	1.5	48	3.5	1,320	95.1	20	1.4	1,388
MO FEMALE	1	.1	4	.5	2	.3	13	1.6	20	2.5	769	96.1	11	1.4	800
MO MALE	3	.5	13	2.2	4	.7	8	1.4	28	4.8	551	93.7	9	1.5	588
FONTBONNE COLLEGE															
MO TOTAL	1	.2	68	10.6	18	2.8	10	1.6	97	15.1	526	82.1	18	2.8	641
MO FEMALE	0	.0	62	10.8	11	1.9	9	1.6	82	14.3	484	84.5	7	1.2	573
MO MALE	1	1.5	6	8.8	7	10.3	1	1.5	15	22.1	42	61.8	11	16.2	68
HANNIBAL-LAGRANGE COLLEGE															
MO TOTAL	1	.3	17	5.3	1	.3	0	.0	19	6.0	292	91.5	8	2.5	319
MO FEMALE	0	.0	8	5.0	1	.6	0	.0	9	5.7	149	93.7	1	.6	159
MO MALE	1	.6	9	5.6	0	.0	0	.0	10	6.3	143	89.4	7	4.4	160
HARRIS STOWE COLLEGE															
MO TOTAL	3	.4	648	79.2	0	.0	1	.1	652	79.7	158	19.3	8	1.	818
MO FEMALE	2	.3	491	82.1	0	.0	0	.0	493	82.4	99	16.6	6	1.0	598
MO MALE	1	.5	157	71.4	0	.0	1	.5	159	72.3	59	26.8	2	.8	220
JEFFERSON COLLEGE															
MO TOTAL	4	.2	8	.4	0	.0	5	.3	17	.9	1,793	99.1		.0	1,810
MO FEMALE	2	.2	8	.6	0	.0	5	.6	12	1.3	878	98.7		.0	890
MO MALE	2	.2	3	.3	0	.0	0	.0	5	.5	915	99.5		.0	920

	AMERICAN INDIAN ALASKAN NATIVE		BLACK NON-HISPANIC		ASIAN OR PACIFIC ISLANDER		HISPANIC		TOTAL MINORITY		WHITE NON-HISPANIC		NON-RESIDENT ALIEN		TOTAL
	NUMBER	%	NUMBER	%	NUMBER	%	NUMBER	%	NUMBER	%	NUMBER	%	NUMBER	%	NUMBER
MISSOURI CONTINUED															
KANSAS CITY ART INSTITUTE															
MO TOTAL	7	1.2	28	4.8	5	.9	8	1.4	48	8.2	538	91.5	2	.3	588
MO FEMALE	1	.4	6	2.2	3	1.1	2	.7	12	4.4	259	95.2	1	.4	272
MO MALE	6	1.9	22	7.0	2	.6	6	1.9	36	11.4	279	88.3	1	.3	316
KEMPER MILITARY SCH AND C															
MO TOTAL	0	.0	8	13.1	19	31.1	0	.0	27	44.3	29	47.5	5	8.2	61
MO FEMALE	0	.0	0	.0	2	66.7	0	.0	2	66.7	1	33.3	0	.0	3
MO MALE	0	.0	8	13.8	17	29.3	0	.0	25	43.1	28	48.3	5	8.6	58
LINCOLN UNIVERSITY															
MO TOTAL	7	.3	807	38.7	19	.9	34	1.6	867	41.6	1,044	50.1	174	8.3	2,085
MO FEMALE	2	.2	341	36.7	4	.4	10	1.1	357	38.5	537	57.9	34	3.7	928
MO MALE	5	.4	466	40.3	15	1.3	24	2.1	510	44.1	507	43.8	140	12.1	1,157
THE LINDENWOOD COLLEGES															
MO TOTAL	2	.2	41	3.2	7	.5	8	.6	58	4.5	1,236	95.5	0	.0	1,294
MO FEMALE	0	.0	28	3.5	6	.7	5	.6	39	4.9	764	95.1	0	.0	803
MO MALE	2	.4	13	2.6	1	.2	3	.6	19	3.9	472	96.1	0	.0	491
MARYVILLE C-SAINT LOUIS															
MO TOTAL	1	.1	143	12.7	4	.4	5	.4	153	13.6	963	85.6	9	.8	1,125
MO FEMALE	0	.0	107	12.5	4	.5	2	.2	113	13.2	734	85.9	7	.8	854
MO MALE	1	.4	36	13.3	0	.0	3	1.1	40	14.8	229	84.5	2	.7	271
LONGVIEW CMTY COLLEGE															
MO TOTAL	13	.2	363	6.8	14	.3	157	2.9	547	10.2	4,786	89.5	14	.3	5,347
MO FEMALE	1	.0	187	6.6	9	.3	54	1.9	251	8.8	2,594	91.1	3	.1	2,848
MO MALE	12	.5	176	7.0	5	.2	103	4.1	296	11.8	2,192	87.7	11	.4	2,499
MAPLE WOODS CMTY COLLEGE															
MO TOTAL	6	.3	19	.9	7	.3	29	1.3	61	2.8	2,117	96.9	7	.3	2,185
MO FEMALE	4	.3	11	.9	3	.3	9	.8	27	2.3	1,148	97.2	6	.5	1,181
MO MALE	2	.2	8	.8	4	.4	20	2.0	34	3.4	969	96.5	1	.1	1,004
PENN VALLEY CHTY COLLEGE															
MO TOTAL	46	.9	1,871	36.1	51	1.0	166	3.2	2,134	41.2	2,763	53.4	279	5.4	5,176
MO FEMALE	34	1.2	1,214	41.8	25	.9	78	2.7	1,351	46.5	1,484	51.1	69	2.4	2,904
MO MALE	12	.5	657	28.9	26	1.1	88	3.9	783	34.5	1,279	56.3	210	9.2	2,272
PIONEER COMMUNITY COLLEGE															
MO TOTAL	5	.7	464	66.0	1	.1	13	1.8	483	68.7	219	31.2	1	.1	703
MO FEMALE	4	.8	321	63.1	0	.0	9	1.8	334	65.6	174	34.2	1	.2	509
MO MALE	1	.5	143	73.7	1	.5	4	2.1	149	76.8	45	23.2	0	.0	194
MINERAL AREA COLLEGE															
MO TOTAL	0	.0	3	.3	1	.1	0	.0	4	.4	1,102	99.6	0	.0	1,106
MO FEMALE	0	.0	1	.2	0	.0	0	.0	1	.2	650	99.8	0	.0	651
MO MALE	0	.0	2	.4	1	.2	0	.0	3	.7	452	99.3	0	.0	455
MISSOURI BAPTIST COLLEGE															
MO TOTAL	0	.0	25	6.3	0	.0	0	.0	25	6.3	371	93.7	0	.0	396
MO FEMALE	0	.0	9	3.5	0	.0	0	.0	9	3.5	245	96.5	0	.0	254
MO MALE	0	.0	16	11.3	0	.0	0	.0	16	11.3	126	88.7	0	.0	142
MISSOURI INST TECHNOLOGY															
MO TOTAL	14	1.8	107	14.0	3	.4	7	.9	131	17.2	632	82.8	0	.0	763
MO FEMALE	0	.0	12	50.0	0	.0	1	4.2	13	54.2	11	45.8	0	.0	24
MO MALE	14	1.9	95	12.9	3	.4	6	.8	118	16.0	621	84.0	0	.0	739
MISSOURI STHN ST COLLEGE															
MO TOTAL	47	1.2	70	1.8	19	.5	17	.4	153	3.9	3,741	95.9	6	.2	3,900
MO FEMALE	12	.6	24	1.3	7	.4	8	.4	51	2.7	1,852	97.3	1	.1	1,904
MO MALE	35	1.8	46	2.3	12	.6	9	.5	102	5.1	1,889	94.6	5	.3	1,996
MISSOURI VALLEY COLLEGE															
MO TOTAL	0	.0	44	12.5	6	1.7	0	.0	50	14.2	297	84.4	5	1.4	352
MO FEMALE	0	.0	11	8.0	1	.7	0	.0	12	8.8	124	90.5	1	.7	137
MO MALE	0	.0	33	15.3	5	2.3	0	.0	38	17.7	173	80.5	4	1.9	215
MISSOURI WSTN ST COLLEGE															
MO TOTAL	4	.1	111	3.3	9	.3	23	.7	147	4.4	3,197	95.4	8	.2	3,352
MO FEMALE	4	.3	38	2.4	4	.3	11	.7	57	3.6	1,528	96.4	0	.0	1,585
MO MALE	0	.0	73	4.1	5	.3	12	.7	90	5.1	1,669	94.5	8	.5	1,767
MOBERLY JUNIOR COLLEGE															
MO TOTAL	3	.4	87	11.0	0	.0	1	.1	91	11.5	684	86.4	17	2.1	792
MO FEMALE	2	.7	14	4.7	0	.0	0	.0	16	5.4	280	94.3	1	.3	297
MO MALE	1	.2	73	14.7	0	.0	1	.2	75	15.2	404	81.6	16	3.2	495
NTHEST MO ST UNIVERSITY															
MO TOTAL	7	.1	285	5.6	24	.5	23	.5	339	6.7	4,596	90.6	139	2.7	5,074
MO FEMALE	3	.1	144	5.0	9	.3	6	.2	162	5.7	2,643	92.7	47	1.6	2,852
MO MALE	4	.2	141	6.3	15	.7	17	.8	177	8.0	1,953	87.9	92	4.1	2,222
NTHWST MO ST UNIVERSITY															
MO TOTAL	47	1.4	42	1.2	7	.2	18	.5	114	3.3	3,318	95.9	29	.8	3,461
MO FEMALE	24	1.4	19	1.1	3	.2	7	.4	53	3.1	1,671	96.5	8	.5	1,732
MO MALE	23	1.3	23	1.3	4	.2	11	.6	61	3.5	1,647	95.3	21	1.2	1,729
PARK COLLEGE															
MO TOTAL	7	.8	204	22.1	29	3.1	10	1.1	250	27.1	661	71.5	13	1.4	924
MO FEMALE	4	1.0	96	23.4	7	1.7	6	1.5	113	27.5	296	72.0	2	.5	411
MO MALE	3	.6	108	21.1	22	4.3	4	.8	137	26.7	365	71.2	11	2.1	513
ROCKHURST COLLEGE															
MO TOTAL	0	.0	128	10.7	5	.4	25	2.1	158	13.2	1,026	85.7	13	1.1	1,197
MO FEMALE	0	.0	70	14.5	1	.2	10	2.1	81	16.8	398	82.6	3	.6	482
MO MALE	0	.0	58	8.1	4	.6	15	2.1	77	10.8	628	87.8	10	1.4	715
SNT LOUIS CHRISTIAN C															
MO TOTAL	0	.0	11	7.7	0	.0	0	.0	11	7.7	132	92.3	0	.0	143
MO FEMALE	0	.0	3	4.9	0	.0	0	.0	3	4.9	58	95.1	0	.0	61
MO MALE	0	.0	8	9.8	0	.0	0	.0	8	9.8	74	90.2	0	.0	82
SNT LOUIS COLLEGE OF PHAR															
MO TOTAL	0	.0	16	2.2	12	1.7	3	.4	31	4.3	690	95.4	2	.3	723
MO FEMALE	0	.0	11	4.0	5	1.8	1	.4	17	6.2	256	93.1	2	.7	275
MO MALE	0	.0	5	1.1	7	1.6	2	.4	14	3.1	434	96.9	0	.0	448
SNT LU CC-FLORISSANT VLY															
MO TOTAL	10	.2	1,355	22.6	42	.7	25	.4	1,432	23.9	4,547	75.8	23	.4	6,002
MO FEMALE	5	.2	727	25.3	25	.9	12	.4	769	26.7	2,105	73.1	5	.2	2,879
MO MALE	5	.2	628	20.1	17	.5	13	.4	663	21.2	2,442	78.2	18	.6	3,123

	BLACK NON-HISPANIC		ASIAN OR PACIFIC ISLANDER		HISPANIC		TOTAL MINORITY		WHITE NON-HISPANIC		NON-RESIDENT ALIEN		TOTAL
N / E	NUMBER	%	NUMBER	%	NUMBER	%	NUMBER	%	NUMBER	%	NUMBER	%	NUMBER
'INUED													
	2,152	55.2	23	.6	15	.4	2,197	56.3	1,696	43.5	9	.2	3,902
	1,350	57.2	8	.3	10	.4	1,372	58.1	986	41.8	2	.1	2,360
	802	52.0	15	1.0	5	.3	825	53.5	710	46.0	7	.5	1,542
	224	3.9	25	.4	37	.6	295	5.1	5,441	94.8	3	.1	5,739
	111	4.0	17	.6	19	.7	150	5.4	2,645	94.6	0	.0	2,795
	113	3.8	8	.3	18	.6	145	4.9	2,796	95.0	3	.1	2,944
	1	1.9	0	.0	0	.0	1	1.9	53	98.1		.0	54
	0	.0	0	.0	0	.0	0	.0	24	100.0	0	.0	24
	1	3.3	0	.0	0	.0	1	3.3	29	96.7		.0	30
	0	.0	0	.0	0	.0	0	.0	38	100.0		.0	38
	0	.0	0	.0	0	.0	0	.0	0	.0	0	.0	0
	0	.0	0	.0	0	.0	0	.0	38	100.0		.0	38
	588	11.2	63	1.2	26	.5	680	13.0	4,475	85.5	80	1.5	5,235
	397	13.9	18	.6	8	.3	423	14.8	2,412	84.3	25	.9	2,860
	191	8.0	45	1.9	18	.8	257	10.8	2,063	86.9	55	2.3	2,375
	37	4.5	1	.1	5	.6	43	5.2	735	89.2	4	5.6	824
	1	1.8	0	.0	0	.0	1	1.8	56	98.2	0	.0	57
	36	4.7	1	.1	5	.7	42	5.5	679	88.5	48	6.0	767
	10	2.1	0	.0	0	.0	10	2.1	477	97.9		.0	487
	5	1.4	0	.0	0	.0	5	1.4	364	98.6	0	.0	369
	5	4.2	0	.0	0	.0	5	4.2	113	95.8		.0	118
	1	.9	0	.0	0	.0	1	.9	113	99.1		.0	114
	1	1.4	0	.0	0	.0	1	1.4	69	98.6	0	.0	70
	0	.0	0	.0	0	.0	0	.0	44	100.0		.0	44
	12	.9	1	.1	0	.0	13	1.0	1,332	97.4	23	1.7	1,368
	0	.0	0	.0	0	.0	0	.0	729	98.9	8	1.1	737
	12	1.9	1	.2	0	.0	13	2.1	603	95.6	15	2.4	631
	264	3.3	14	.2	11	.1	295	3.7	7,716	95.8	42	.5	8,053
	134	3.1	9	.2	7	.2	155	3.6	4,194	96.1	14	.3	4,363
	130	3.5	5	.1	4	.1	140	3.8	3,522	95.4	28	.8	3,690
	10	.7	1	.1	0	.0	16	1.2	1,340	97.6	17	1.2	1,373
	4	.5	1	.1	0	.0	6	.8	721	98.5	5	.7	732
	6	.9	0	.0	0	.0	10	1.6	619	96.6	12	1.9	641
	82	.7	84	.7	25	.2	199	1.8	11,048	97.7	62	.5	11,309
	29	.5	30	.5	15	.3	79	1.4	5,719	98.3	21	.4	5,819
	53	1.0	54	1.0	10	.2	120	2.2	5,329	97.1	41	.7	5,490
	28	2.7	3	.3	11	1.0	54	5.1	1,000	94.9	0	.0	1,054
	15	2.7	1	.2	5	.9	28	5.1	518	94.9	0	.0	546
	13	2.6	2	.4	6	1.2	26	5.1	482	94.9	0	.0	508
	73	4.5	4	.2	2	.1	80	4.9	1,536	94.2	14	.9	1,630
	72	4.5	4	.3	2	.1	79	5.0	1,499	94.2	14	.9	1,592
	1	2.6	0	.0	0	.0	1	2.6	37	97.4	0	.0	38
	90	14.4	5	.8	4	.6	99	15.8	521	83.4	5	.8	625
	35	16.4	2	.9	3	1.4	40	18.8	171	80.3	2	.9	213
	55	13.3	3	.7	1	.2	59	14.3	350	85.0	3	.7	412
	37	4.0	0	.0	1	.1	38	4.1	884	95.9		.0	922
	17	3.1	0	.0	1	.2	18	3.3	529	96.7	0	.0	547
	20	5.3	0	.0	0	.0	20	5.3	355	94.7		.0	375
	9	1.9	1	.2	0	.0	11	2.3	465	97.5	1	.2	477
	0	.0	0	.0	0	.0	0	.0	297	99.7	1	.3	298
	9	5.0	1	.6	0	.0	11	6.1	168	93.9	0	.0	179
	572	3.3	121	.7	55	.3	784	4.6	16,181	94.4	181	1.1	17,146
	336	4.2	47	.6	19	.2	416	5.2	7,604	94.4	32	.4	8,052
	236	2.6	74	.8	36	.4	368	4.0	8,577	94.3	149	1.6	9,094
	431	7.8	45	.8	60	1.1	572	10.4	4,832	87.6	109	2.0	5,513
	277	10.0	26	.9	26	.9	349	12.6	2,381	86.0	37	1.3	2,767
	154	5.6	19	.7	34	1.2	223	8.1	2,451	89.3	72	2.6	2,746
	184	3.8	36	.7	13	.3	247	5.1	4,340	89.3	273	5.6	4,860
	45	5.3	5	.6	3	.4	55	6.5	752	88.4	44	5.2	851
	139	3.5	31	.8	10	.2	192	4.8	3,588	89.5	229	5.7	4,009
	1,174	12.4	65	.7	64	.7	1,347	14.2	8,103	85.5	24	.3	9,474
	715	17.2	35	.8	34	.8	799	19.2	3,358	80.6	11	.3	4,168
	459	8.7	30	.6	30	.6	548	10.3	4,745	89.4	13	.2	5,306
	447	6.7	182	2.7	76	1.1	713	10.7	5,833	87.6	115	1.7	6,661
	257	9.5	70	2.6	27	1.0	355	13.2	2,310	85.7	31	1.1	2,696
	190	4.8	112	2.8	49	1.2	358	9.0	3,523	88.9	84	2.1	3,965
	193	20.0	3	.3	7	.7	207	21.5	753	78.0	5	.5	965
	121	20.0	2	.3	6	1.0	132	21.9	472	78.1	0	.0	604
	72	19.9	1	.3	1	.3	75	20.8	281	77.8	5	1.4	361

	AMERICAN INDIAN ALASKAN NATIVE		BLACK NON-HISPANIC		ASIAN OR PACIFIC ISLANDER		HISPANIC		TOTAL MINORITY		WHITE NON-HISPANIC		NON-RESIDENT ALIEN		TOTAL
	NUMBER	%	NUMBER	%	NUMBER	%	NUMBER	%	NUMBER	%	NUMBER	%	NUMBER	%	NUMBER
MISSOURI CONTINUED															
WENTWORTH MILITARY ACAD															
MO TOTAL	0	.0	11	5.9	0	.0	2	1.1	13	7.0	164	88.2	9	4.8	186
MO FEMALE	0	.0	0	.0	0	.0	0	.0	0	.0	27	100.0	0	.0	27
MO MALE	0	.0	11	6.9	0	.0	2	1.3	13	8.2	137	86.2	9	5.7	159
WESTMINSTER COLLEGE															
MO TOTAL	1	.2	12	1.9	2	.3	7	1.1	22	3.4	610	95.0	10	1.6	642
MO FEMALE	0	.0	0	.0	0	.0	0	.0	0	.0	0	.0	0	.0	0
MO MALE	1	.2	12	1.9	2	.3	7	1.1	22	3.4	610	95.0	10	1.6	642
WILLIAM JEWELL COLLEGE															
MO TOTAL	3	.2	30	1.8	4	.2	8	.5	45	2.7	1,587	96.9	5	.3	1,637
MO FEMALE	2	.2	12	1.4	3	.3	3	.3	20	2.3	849	97.4	3	.3	872
MO MALE	1	.1	18	2.4	1	.1	5	.7	25	3.3	738	96.5	2	.3	765
WILLIAM WOODS COLLEGE															
MO TOTAL	1	.1	28	3.1	3	.3	3	.3	35	3.9	855	95.2	8	.9	898
MO FEMALE	1	.1	28	3.1	3	.3	3	.3	35	3.9	855	95.2	8	.9	898
MO MALE	0	.0	0	.0	0	.0	0	.0	0	.0	0	.0	0	.0	0
MISSOURI TOTAL (70 INSTITUTIONS)															
MO TOTAL	488	.3	14,992	9.1	1,082	.7	1,258	.8	17,820	10.8	145,003	87.9	2,074	1.3	164,897
MO FEMALE	212	.3	8,527	10.4	450	.6	514	.6	9,703	11.9	71,367	87.4	566	.7	81,636
MO MALE	276	.3	6,465	7.8	632	.8	744	.9	8,117	9.7	73,636	88.4	1,508	1.8	83,261
MONTANA															
CARROLL COLLEGE															
MT TOTAL	17	1.5	4	.4	16	1.4	6	.5	43	3.8	1,077	95.6	7	.6	1,127
MT FEMALE	9	1.4	1	.2	2	.3	3	.5	15	2.4	611	97.1	3	.5	629
MT MALE	8	1.6	3	.6	14	2.8	3	.6	28	5.6	466	93.6	4	.8	498
COLLEGE OF GREAT FALLS															
MT TOTAL	41	4.5	30	3.3	14	1.5	15	1.7	100	11.0	801	88.2	7	.8	908
MT FEMALE	30	6.2	16	3.3	4	.8	6	1.2	56	11.6	423	87.9	2	.4	481
MT MALE	11	2.6	14	3.3	10	2.3	9	2.1	44	10.3	378	88.5	5	1.2	427
DAWSON COMMUNITY COLLEGE															
MT TOTAL	14	5.4	0	.0	0	.0	0	.0	14	5.4	244	94.6	0	.0	258
MT FEMALE	10	8.2	0	.0	0	.0	0	.0	10	8.2	112	91.8	0	.0	122
MT MALE	4	2.9	0	.0	0	.0	0	.0	4	2.9	132	97.1	0	.0	136
FLATHEAD VLY CMTY COLLEGE															
MT TOTAL	75	14.1	2	.4	0	.0	7	1.3	84	15.8	442	83.2	5	.9	531
MT FEMALE	46	14.9	0	.0	0	.0	6	1.9	52	16.8	253	81.9	4	1.3	309
MT MALE	29	13.1	2	.9	0	.0	1	.5	32	14.4	189	85.1	1	.5	222
MILES COMMUNITY COLLEGE															
MT TOTAL	11	3.4	1	.3	0	.0	3	.9	15	4.6	312	95.1	1	.3	328
MT FEMALE	9	4.1	1	.5	0	.0	1	.5	11	5.1	206	94.9	0	.0	217
MT MALE	2	1.8	0	.0	0	.0	2	1.8	4	3.6	106	95.5	1	.9	111
MONTANA INST OF THE BIBLE															
MT TOTAL	0	.0	0	.0	2	.9	1	.5	3	1.4	209	97.2	3	1.4	215
MT FEMALE	0	.0	0	.0	0	.0	1	1.0	1	1.0	99	97.1	2	2.0	102
MT MALE	0	.0	0	.0	2	1.8	0	.0	2	1.8	110	97.3	1	.9	113
EASTERN MONTANA COLLEGE															
MT TOTAL	55	1.8	3	.1	3	.1	6	.2	67	2.2	2,976	97.7	4	.1	3,047
MT FEMALE	31	1.7	1	.1	0	.0	1	.1	33	1.8	1,801	98.2	0	.0	1,834
MT MALE	24	2.0	2	.2	3	.2	5	.4	34	2.8	1,175	96.9	4	.3	1,213
MONTANA C MINRL SCI-TECHN															
MT TOTAL	5	.4	4	.3	3	.3	12	1.0	24	2.0	1,128	94.2	46	3.8	1,198
MT FEMALE	2	.5	2	.5	1	.2	4	.9	9	2.1	408	96.7	5	1.2	422
MT MALE	3	.4	2	.3	2	.3	8	1.0	15	1.9	720	92.8	41	5.3	776
MONTANA STATE UNIVERSITY															
MT TOTAL	74	.8	7	.1	16	.2	10	.1	107	1.2	8,936	98.4	41	.5	9,084
MT FEMALE	39	1.0	4	.1	3	.1	5	.1	51	1.3	3,977	98.4	12	.3	4,040
MT MALE	35	.7	3	.1	13	.3	5	.1	56	1.1	4,959	98.3	29	.6	5,044
NORTHERN MONTANA COLLEGE															
MT TOTAL	96	9.2	9	.9	3	.3	7	.7	115	11.0	926	88.6	4	.4	1,045
MT FEMALE	62	13.7	0	.0	1	.2	0	.0	63	13.9	390	86.1	0	.0	453
MT MALE	34	5.7	9	1.5	2	.3	7	1.2	52	8.8	536	90.5	4	.7	592
UNIVERSITY OF MONTANA															
MT TOTAL	199	2.9	32	.5	32	.5	26	.4	289	4.2	6,472	94.7	74	1.1	6,835
MT FEMALE	114	3.6	11	.3	14	.4	13	.4	152	4.8	2,973	94.5	20	.6	3,145
MT MALE	85	2.3	21	.6	18	.5	13	.4	137	3.7	3,499	94.8	54	1.5	3,690
WESTERN MONTANA COLLEGE															
MT TOTAL	2	.3	1	.2	2	.3	1	.2	6	1.0	566	98.8	1	.2	573
MT FEMALE	0	.0	0	.0	0	.0	1	.3	1	.3	289	99.7	0	.0	290
MT MALE	2	.7	1	.4	2	.7	0	.0	5	1.8	277	97.9	1	.4	283
ROCKY MOUNTAIN COLLEGE															
MT TOTAL	21	4.2	5	1.0	0	.0	4	.8	30	6.0	451	90.2	19	3.8	500
MT FEMALE	14	5.4	2	.8	0	.0	3	1.1	19	7.3	239	91.6	3	1.1	261
MT MALE	7	2.9	3	1.3	0	.0	1	.4	11	4.6	212	88.7	16	6.7	239
MONTANA TOTAL (13 INSTITUTIONS)															
MT TOTAL	610	2.4	98	.4	91	.4	98	.4	897	3.5	24,540	95.7	212	.8	25,649
MT FEMALE	366	3.0	38	.3	25	.2	44	.4	473	3.8	11,781	95.7	51	.4	12,305
MT MALE	244	1.8	60	.4	66	.5	54	.4	424	3.2	12,759	95.6	161	1.2	13,344
NEBRASKA															
BELLEVUE COLLEGE															
NE TOTAL	7	.4	348	17.4	22	1.1	34	1.7	411	20.6	1,588	79.4	0	.0	1,999
NE FEMALE	1	.1	137	16.3	15	1.8	17	2.0	170	20.2	670	79.8	0	.0	840
NE MALE	6	.5	211	18.2	7	.6	17	1.5	241	20.8	918	79.2	0	.0	1,159
CENTRAL COMMUNITY COLLEGE															
NE TOTAL	3	.2	3	.2	5	.3	11	.6	22	1.3	1,729	98.7	0	.0	1,751
NE FEMALE	1	.2	1	.2	3	.5	5	.8	10	1.6	634	98.4	0	.0	644
NE MALE	2	.2	2	.2	2	.2	6	.5	12	1.1	1,095	98.9	0	.0	1,107

IN TE	BLACK NON-HISPANIC		ASIAN OR PACIFIC ISLANDER		HISPANIC		TOTAL MINORITY		WHITE NON-HISPANIC		NON-RESIDENT ALIEN		TOTAL
	NUMBER	%	NUMBER	%	NUMBER	%	NUMBER	%	NUMBER	%	NUMBER	%	NUMBER
TINUED													
	1	.1	1	.1	3	.3	7	.7	981	99.3	0	.0	988
	0	.0	1	.2	1	.2	3	.5	549	99.5	0	.0	552
	1	.2	0	.0	2	.5	4	.9	432	99.1	0	.0	436
	16	1.1	15	1.0	9	.6	53	3.6	1,423	95.4	15	1.0	1,491
	4	.5	6	.7	6	.7	23	2.7	836	96.9	4	.5	863
	12	1.9	9	1.4	3	.5	30	4.8	587	93.5	11	1.8	628
	32	6.2	2	.4	7	1.4	43	8.3	464	90.1	8	1.6	515
	32	6.6	2	.4	7	1.4	43	8.9	433	89.6	7	1.4	483
	0	.0	0	.0	0	.0	0	.0	31	96.9	1	3.1	32
	31	2.9	2	.2	1	.1	44	4.1	975	91.8	43	4.0	1,062
	5	.9	2	.3	1	.2	12	2.1	554	95.2	16	2.7	582
	26	5.4	0	.0	0	.0	32	6.7	421	87.7	27	5.6	480
	111	3.4	94	2.9	33	1.0	244	7.6	2,953	91.5	29	.9	3,226
	64	4.3	36	2.4	14	.9	117	7.9	1,355	91.5	9	.6	1,481
	47	2.7	58	3.3	19	1.1	127	7.3	1,598	91.6	20	1.1	1,745
	8	1.8	1	.2	1	.2	10	2.3	426	96.6	5	1.1	441
	2	.9	0	.0	1	.4	3	1.3	221	98.2	1	.4	225
	6	2.8	1	.5	0	.0	7	3.2	205	94.9	4	1.9	216
	44	6.8	0	.0	1	.2	48	7.4	598	92.4	1	.2	647
	8	2.5	0	.0	0	.0	9	2.8	310	97.2	0	.0	319
	36	11.0	0	.0	1	.3	39	11.9	288	87.8	1	.3	328
	5	1.1	0	.0	1	.2	8	1.8	419	95.9	10	2.3	437
	0	.0	0	.0	1	.5	2	1.0	194	98.5	1	.5	197
	5	2.1	0	.0	0	.0	6	2.5	225	93.8	9	3.8	240
	1	.1	2	.3	1	.1	4	.6	695	97.9	11	1.5	710
	1	.3	2	.5	1	.3	4	1.0	373	97.6	5	1.3	382
	0	.0	0	.0	0	.0	0	.0	322	98.2	6	1.8	328
	11	.2	11	.2	33	.6	61	1.1	5,291	98.2	35	.6	5,387
	2	.1	7	.2	16	.5	30	1.0	3,011	98.8	7	.2	3,048
	9	.4	4	.2	17	.7	31	1.3	2,280	97.5	28	1.2	2,339
	337	6.7	15	.3	55	1.1	419	8.4	4,559	91.3	15	.3	4,993
	174	7.1	6	.2	38	1.5	226	9.2	2,236	90.7	3	.1	2,465
	163	6.4	9	.4	17	.7	193	7.6	2,323	91.9	12	.5	2,528
	18	2.4	0	.0	0	.0	19	2.5	729	96.3	9	1.2	757
	5	1.1	0	.0	0	.0	5	1.1	443	98.7	1	.2	449
	13	4.2	0	.0	0	.0	14	4.5	286	92.9	8	2.6	308
	1	.4	1	.4	3	1.1	5	1.9	259	97.7	1	.4	265
	0	.0	1	.7	0	.0	1	.7	136	98.6	1	.7	138
	1	.8	0	.0	3	2.4	4	3.1	123	96.9	0	.0	127
	6	.4	8	.5	46	2.7	73	4.3	1,637	95.7	0	.0	1,710
	4	.5	3	.4	28	3.5	42	5.2	768	94.8	0	.0	810
	2	.2	5	.6	18	2.0	31	3.4	859	96.6	0	.0	900
	1	.7	0	.0	0	.0	1	.7	146	98.6	1	.7	148
	0	.0	0	.0	0	.0	0	.0	81	98.8	1	1.2	82
	1	1.5	0	.0	0	.0	1	1.5	65	98.5	0	.0	66
	23	2.2	12	1.2	4	.4	42	4.0	957	91.8	44	4.2	1,043
	12	2.3	5	1.0	3	.6	21	4.0	494	94.3	9	1.7	524
	11	2.1	7	1.3	1	.2	21	4.0	463	89.2	35	6.7	519
	9	1.0	11	1.3	66	7.7	89	10.3	772	89.6	1	.1	862
	1	.2	5	1.0	36	7.2	44	8.8	455	91.2	0	.0	499
	8	2.2	6	1.7	30	8.3	45	12.4	317	87.3	1	.3	363
	1	.1	0	.0	0	.0	3	.2	1,438	99.2	9	.6	1,450
	0	.0	0	.0	0	.0	1	.2	593	99.5	2	.3	596
	1	.1	0	.0	0	.0	2	.2	845	98.9	7	.8	854
	53	8.8	0	.0	3	.5	57	9.5	541	90.2	2	.3	600
	21	6.6	0	.0	1	.3	22	6.9	297	92.8	1	.3	320
	32	11.4	0	.0	2	.7	35	12.5	244	87.1	1	.4	280
	1	2.2	0	.0	1	2.2	2	4.3	43	93.5	1	2.2	46
	0	.0	0	.0	0	.0	0	.0	25	100.0	0	.0	25
	1	4.8	0	.0	1	4.8	2	9.5	18	85.7	1	4.8	21
	15	3.5	0	.0	0	.0	15	3.5	350	82.5	59	13.9	424
	1	.5	0	.0	0	.0	1	.5	198	96.1	7	3.4	206
	14	6.4	0	.0	0	.0	14	6.4	152	69.7	52	23.9	218
	154	9.4	13	.8	26	1.6	224	13.7	1,397	85.4	15	.9	1,636
	14	1.8	3	.4	11	1.4	31	4.0	734	94.6	11	1.4	776
	140	16.3	10	1.2	15	1.7	193	22.4	653	77.1	4	.5	860
	3	.3	0	.0	7	.8	10	1.1	896	98.7	2	.2	908
	0	.0	0	.0	0	.0	0	.0	52	100.0	0	.0	52
	3	.4	0	.0	7	.9	10	1.2	944	98.6	2	.2	856

	AMERICAN INDIAN ALASKAN NATIVE		BLACK NON-HISPANIC		ASIAN OR PACIFIC ISLANDER		HISPANIC		TOTAL MINORITY		WHITE NON-HISPANIC		NON-RESIDENT ALIEN		TOTAL
	NUMBER	%	NUMBER	%	NUMBER	%	NUMBER	%	NUMBER	%	NUMBER	%	NUMBER	%	NUMBER
NEBRASKA											CONTINUED				
UNION COLLEGE															
NE TOTAL	5	.6	34	4.1	6	.7	11	1.3	56	6.7	738	88.2	43	5.1	837
NE FEMALE	3	.7	13	3.0	3	.7	6	1.4	25	5.8	384	89.1	22	5.1	431
NE MALE	2	.5	21	5.2	3	.7	5	1.2	31	7.6	354	87.2	21	5.2	406
U OF NEBRASKA-LINCOLN															
NE TOTAL	65	.4	220	1.2	95	.3	118	.7	458	2.6	16,785	95.1	414	2	17,657
NE FEMALE	31	.4	98	1.3	20	.3	46	.6	195	2.5	7,508	96.5	80	1	7,783
NE MALE	34	.3	122	1.2	35	.4	72	.7	263	2*7	9,277	94.0	334	31#	9,874
U NEBRASKA MEDICAL CTR															
NE TOTAL	1	.2	8	1.4	6	1.0	2	.3	17	2.9	567	95.8	8	1.4	592
NE FEMALE	0	.0	6	1.2	5	1.0	2	.4	13	2.6	486	96.2	6	1.2	505
NE MALE	1	1.1	2	2.3	1	1.1	0	.0	4	4.6	81	93.1	2	2.3	87
U OF NEBRASKA AT OMAHA															
NE TOTAL	33	.3	713	6.2	65	.6	167	1.5	978	8.5	10,348	90.1	153	1.3	11,479
NE FEMALE	19	.4	386	7.3	28	.5	83	1.6	516	9.8	4,749	89.8	23	.4	5,288
NE MALE	14	.2	327	5.3	37	.6	84	1.4	462	7.5	5,599	90.4	130	2.1	6,191
WAYNE STATE COLLEGE															
NE TOTAL	22	1.0	25	1.2	0	.0	4	.2	51	2.	2,055	96.9	15	.7	2,121
NE FEMALE	11	.9	10	.8	0	.0	2	.2	23	1.#	1,154	97.8	3	.3	1,180
NE MALE	11	1.2	15	1.6	0	.0	2	.2	28	3.#	901	95.7	12	1.3	941
YORK COLLEGE															
NE TOTAL	0	.0	12	4.0	0	.0	6	2.0	18	6.#	271	91.2	8	2.7	297
NE FEMALE	0	.0	1	.6	0	.0	3	1.9	4	2.#	151	95.6	3	1.9	158
NE MALE	0	.0	11	7.9	0	.0	3	2.2	14	10.1	120	86.3	5	3.6	139
NEBRASKA			TOTAL (31 INSTITUTIONS)												
NE TOTAL	246	.4	2,245	3.4	347	.5	654	1.0	3,492	5.3	62,030	93.3	957	1.4	66,479
NE FEMALE	112	.4	1,002	3.1	153	.5	329	1.0	1,596	5.0	30,084	94.3	223	.7	31,903
NE MALE	134	.4	1,243	3.6	194	.6	325	.9	1,896	5.5	31,946	92.4	734	2.1	34,576
NEVADA															
SIERRA NEVADA COLLEGE															
NV TOTAL	1	.4	2	.8	1	.4	0	.0	4	1.6	237	95.2	8	3 2	249
NV FEMALE	1	.8	0	.0	0	.0	0	.0	1	.8	124	98.4	1	8	126
NV MALE	0	.0	2	1.6	1	.8	0	.0	3	2.4	113	91.9	7	517	123
U OF NEVADA LAS VEGAS															
NV TOTAL	27	.4	341	5.6	122	2.0	182	3.0	672	11.1	5,285	87.1	110	1 8	6,067
NV FEMALE	17	.6	170	6.1	49	1.8	78	2.8	314	11.3	2,433	87.3	41	1 5	2,788
NV MALE	10	.3	171	5.2	73	2.2	104	3.2	358	10.9	2,852	87.0	69	211	3,279
U OF NEVADA RENO															
NV TOTAL	62	1.1	89	1.6	89	1.6	84	1.5	324	5.9	4,943	90.8	179	3.3	5,446
NV FEMALE	38	1.5	29	1.1	38	1.5	38	1.5	143	5.7	2,347	93.0	35	*.4	2,525
NV MALE	24	.8	60	2.1	51	1.7	46	1.6	181	6.2	2,596	88.9	144	4.9	2,921
CLARK CO CMTY COLLEGE															
NV TOTAL	52	1.4	496	13.6	60	1.7	154	4.2	762	21.0	2,873	79.0	0	.0	3,635
NV FEMALE	23	1.4	217	13.2	21	1.3	57	3.5	318	19.4	1,323	80.6	0	.0	1,641
NV MALE	29	1.5	279	14.0	39	2.0	97	4.9	444	22.3	1,550	77.7	0	.0	1,994
NORTHERN NEV CMTY COLLEGE															
NV TOTAL	61	8.0	5	.7	14	1.	58	7.6	138	18.1	623	81.9	0	.0	761
NV FEMALE	45	10.0	2	.4	11	2.#	23	5.1	81	18.0	370	82.0	0	.0	451
NV MALE	16	5.2	3	1.0	3	1.#	35	11.3	57	18.4	253	81.6	0	.0	310
WESTERN NEV CMTY COLLEGE															
NV TOTAL	77	1.0	44	.6	41	.5	46	.6	208	2.6	7,661	97.0	25	.3	7,894
NV FEMALE	35	.9	18	.5	20	.5	26	.7	99	2.6	3,670	97.1	10	.3	3,779
NV MALE	42	1.0	26	.6	21	.5	20	.5	109	2.6	3,991	97.0	15	.4	4,115
NEVADA			TOTAL (6 INSTITUTIONS)												
NV TOTAL	280	1.2	977	4.1	327	1.4	524	2.2	2,108	8.8	21,622	89.9	322	1.3	24,052
NV FEMALE	159	1.4	436	3.9	139	1.2	222	2.0	956	8.5	10,267	90.8	87	.8	11,310
NV MALE	121	.9	541	4.2	188	1.5	302	2.4	1,152	9.0	11,355	89.1	235	1.8	12,742
NEW HAMPSHIRE															
CASTLE JUNIOR COLLEGE															
NH TOTAL	0	.0	0	.0	0	.0	0	.0		.0	96	98.0	2	2	98
NH FEMALE	0	.0	0	.0	0	.0	0	.0		.0	96	98.0	2	2 #	98
NH MALE	0	.0	0	.0	0	.0	0	.0	0	.0	0	.0	0	10	0
COLBY-SAWYER COLLEGE															
NH TOTAL	0	.0	0	.0	1	.1	3	.4		.6	675	98.7	5	.7	684
NH FEMALE	0	.0	0	.0	1	.1	3	.4		.6	672	98.7	5	.7	681
NH MALE	0	.0	0	.0	0	.0	0	.0		.0	3	100.0	0	.0	3
DANIEL WEBSTER COLLEGE															
NH TOTAL	0	.0	27	6.1	3	.7	8	1.8	38	8.6	391	88.7	12	2.7	441
NH FEMALE	0	.0	3	3.3	0	.0	1	1.1	4	4.4	85	93.4	2	2.2	91
NH MALE	0	.0	24	6.9	3	.9	7	2.0	34	9.7	306	87.4	10	2.9	350
DARTMOUTH COLLEGE															
NH TOTAL	32	.9	259	7.5	37	1.1	18	.5	346	10.1	2,997	87.2	92	2.7	3,435
NH FEMALE	18	1.9	88	9.1	13	1.3	6	.6	125	12.9	830	85.4	17	1.7	972
NH MALE	14	.6	171	6.9	24	1.0	12	.5	221	9.0	2,167	88.0	75	3.0	2,463
FRANKLIN PIERCE COLLEGE															
NH TOTAL	0	.0	33	3.1	13	1.2	9	.8	55	5.1	1,024	94.9	0	.0	1,079
NH FEMALE	0	.0	13	3.1	3	.7	5	1.2	21	4.9	405	95.1	0	.0	426
NH MALE	0	.0	20	3.1	10	1.5	4	.6	34	5.2	619	94.8	0	.0	653
MCINTOSH COLLEGE															
NH TOTAL	0	.0	0	.0	0	.0	0	.0	0	.0	106	100.0	0	.0	106
NH FEMALE	0	.0	0	.0	0	.0	0	.0	0	.0	94	100.0	0	.0	94
NH MALE	0	.0	0	.0	0	.0	0	.0	0	.0	12	100.0	0	.0	12
NATHANIEL HAWTHORNE C															
NH TOTAL	0	.0	24	1.7	4	.3	2	.1	30	2.2	1,242	90.1	107	7.8	1,379
NH FEMALE	0	.0	5	1.6	0	.0	1	.3	6	1.9	290	92.9	16	5.1	312
NH MALE	0	.0	19	1.8	4	.4	1	.1	24	2.2	952	89.2	91	8.5	1,067

	BLACK NON-HISPANIC		ASIAN OR PACIFIC ISLANDER		HISPANIC		TOTAL MINORITY		WHITE NON-HISPANIC		NON-RESIDENT ALIEN		TOTAL
E	NUMBER	%	NUMBER	%	NUMBER	%	NUMBER	%	NUMBER	%	NUMBER	%	NUMBER
INUED													
	14	.9	0	.0	2	.1	18	1.1	1,452	88.7	167	10.2	1,637
	4	.5	0	.0	2	.3	8	1.1	667	91.4	55	7.5	730
	10	1.1	0	.0	0	.0	10	1.1	785	86.5	112	12.3	907
	159	4.4	0	.0	136	3.7	297	8.2	3,319	91.5	11	.3	3,627
	72	6.4	0	.0	11	1.0	84	7.5	1,034	92.3	2	.2	1,120
	87	3.5	0	.0	125	5.0	213	8.5	2,285	91.1	9	.4	2,507
	7	.5	3	.2	0	.0	14	.9	1,473	99.1		.0	1,487
	2	.2	3	.3	0	.0	8	.9	882	99.1	8	.0	890
	5	.8	0	.0	0	.0	6	1.0	591	99.0	0	.0	597
	0	.0	0	.0	2	.5	2	.5	362	99.5		.0	364
	0	.0	0	.0	1	.7	1	.7	152	99.3	8	.0	153
	0	.0	0	.0	1	.5	1	.5	210	99.5	0	.0	211
	3	1.0	1	.3	1	.3	5	1.6	305	98.1	1	.3	311
	1	.5	1	.5	0	.0	2	1.0	206	99.0	0	.0	208
	2	1.9	0	.0	1	1.0	3	2.9	99	96.1	1	1.0	103
	0	.0	2	.9	2	.9	4	1.8	219	98.2		.0	223
	0	.0	0	.0	0	.0	0	.0	61	100.0	8	.0	61
	0	.0	2	1.2	2	1.2	4	2.5	158	97.5	0	.0	162
	0	.0	0	.0	0	.0	0	.0	304	100.0		.0	304
	0	.0	0	.0	0	.0	0	.0	6	100.0	8	.0	6
	0	.0	0	.0	0	.0	0	.0	298	100.0	0	.0	298
	9	1.0	5	.5	10	1.1	25	2.7	912	97.2	1	.1	938
	2	.6	1	.3	2	.6	6	1.9	314	97.8	1	.3	321
	7	1.1	4	.6	8	1.3	19	3.1	598	96.9	0	.0	617
	13	1.6	2	.2	0	.0	15	1.9	785	98.0	1	.1	801
	3	1.1	0	.0	0	.0	3	1.1	267	98.9	0	.0	270
	10	1.9	2	.4	0	.0	12	2.3	518	97.6	1	.2	531
	5	.9	0	.0	3	.6	10	1.9	517	97.9	1	.2	528
	5	1.0	0	.0	3	.6	10	2.1	474	97.7	1	.2	485
	0	.0	0	.0	0	.0	0	.0	43	100.0	0	.0	43
	1	.1	4	.4	1	.1	6	.7	885	99.1	2	.2	893
	1	.1	1	.1	1	.1	3	.4	752	99.3	2	.3	757
	0	.0	3	2.2	0	.0	3	2.2	133	97.8	0	.0	136
	6	.3	0	.0	5	.3	11	.6	1,916	99.2	5	.3	1,932
	1	.1	0	.0	0	.0	1	.1	792	99.5	3	.4	796
	5	.4	0	.0	5	.4	10	.9	1,124	98.9	2	.2	1,136
	25	.3	27	.3	28	.3	101	1.1	9,341	98.1	77	.8	9,519
	5	.1	11	.2	12	.2	35	.7	4,846	98.9	17	.3	4,898
	20	.4	16	.3	16	.3	66	1.4	4,495	97.3	60	1.3	4,621
	3	.1	1	.0	3	.1	9	.3	2,585	99.7		.0	2,594
	0	.0	1	.1	2	.1	3	.2	1,607	99.8	8	.0	1,610
	3	.3	0	.0	1	.1	6	.6	978	99.4	0	.0	984
	1	.0	3	.1	6	.2	19	.7	2,609	98.9		.3	2,637
	0	.0	3	.2	0	.0	4	.3	1,282	99.5	2	.2	1,289
	1	.1	0	.0	6	.4	15	1.1	1,327	98.4	8	.4	1,348
	0	.0	0	.0	0	.0	0	.0	71	97.3	2	2.7	73
	0	.0	0	.0	0	.0	0	.0	55	98.2	1	1.8	56
	0	.0	0	.0	0	.0	0	.0	16	94.1	1	5.9	17
I 23 INSTITUTIONS)													
	589	1.7	106	.3	239	.7	1,009	2.9	33,586	95.7	495	1.4	35,090
	205	1.3	50	.3	50	.3	328	2.0	15,869	97.2	127	.8	16,324
	384	2.0	68	.4	189	1.0	681	3.6	17,717	94.4	368	2.0	18,766
	0	.0	4	19.0	0	.0	4	19.0	17	81.0	0	.0	21
	0	.0	4	19.0	0	.0	4	19.0	17	81.0	0	.0	21
	0	.0	0	.0	0	.0	0	.0	0	.0	0	.0	0
	526	19.4	7	.3	79	2.9	616	22.7	2,102	77.3	0	.0	2,718
	368	23.2	5	.3	52	3.3	428	27.0	1,159	73.0	0	.0	1,587
	158	14.0	2	.2	27	2.4	188	16.6	943	83.4	0	.0	1,131
	147	2.4	59	1.0	153	2.5	402	6.6	5,627	91.7	106	1.7	6,135
	93	2.7	31	.9	89	2.6	235	6.9	3,143	92.1	35	1.0	3,413
	54	2.0	28	1.0	64	2.4	167	6.1	2,484	91.3	71	2.6	2,722
	25	5.7	0	.0	10	2.3	35	8.0	401	91.6	2	.5	438
	25	5.7	0	.0	10	2.3	35	8.0	401	91.6	2	.5	438
	0	.0	0	.0	0	.0	0	.0	0	.0	0	.0	0
	0	.0	0	.0	3	1.1	3	1.1	223	84.8	37	14.1	263
	0	.0	0	.0	0	.0	0	.0	0	.0	0	.0	0
	0	.0	0	.0	3	1.1	3	1.1	223	84.8	37	14.1	263

TABLE 1 - TOTAL UNDERGRADUATE ENROLLMENT IN INSTITUTIONS OF HIGHER EDUCATION BY RACE, ETHNICITY AND SEX:
INSTITUTION, STATE AND NATION, 1978

	AMERICAN INDIAN ALASKAN NATIVE		BLACK NON-HISPANIC		ASIAN OR PACIFIC ISLANDER		HISPANIC		TOTAL MINORITY		WHITE NON-HISPANIC		NON-RESIDENT ALIEN		TOT
	NUMBER	%	NUMBER	%	NUMBER	%	NUMBER	%	NUMBER	%	NUMBER	%	NUMBER	%	NUM
NEW JERSEY CONTINUED															
BLOOMFIELD COLLEGE															
NJ TOTAL	0	.0	708	35.5	10	.5	19	1.0	737	37.0	1,255	63.0	0	.0	1,
NJ FEMALE	0	.0	344	35.1	7	.7	10	1.0	361	36.9	618	63.1	0	.0	
NJ MALE	0	.0	364	35.9	3	.3	9	.9	376	37.1	637	62.9	0	.0	1,
BROOKDALE CMTY COLLEGE															
NJ TOTAL	10	.1	589	7.4	77	1.0	124	1.6	800	10.1	7,138	89.9	0	.0	7,
NJ FEMALE	9	.2	302	7.2	44	1.0	65	1.5	420	10.0	3,774	90.0	0	.0	4,
NJ MALE	1	.0	287	7.7	33	.9	59	1.6	380	10.1	3,364	89.9	0	.0	3,
BURLINGTON COUNTY COLLEGE															
NJ TOTAL	21	.3	756	12.3	67	1.1	119	1.9	963	15.7	5,188	84.3	0	.0	6,
NJ FEMALE	12	.4	410	12.1	37	1.1	65	1.9	524	15.5	2,865	84.5	0	.0	3,
NJ MALE	9	.3	346	12.5	30	1.1	54	2.0	439	15.9	2,323	84.1	0	.0	2,
CALDWELL COLLEGE															
NJ TOTAL	0	.0	67	12.9	6	1.2	30	5.8	103	19.8	394	75.6	24	4.6	
NJ FEMALE	0	.0	67	12.9	6	1.2	30	5.8	103	19.8	394	75.6	24	4.6	
NJ MALE	0	.0	0	.0	0	.0	0	.0	0	.0	0	.0	0	.0	
CAMDEN COUNTY COLLEGE															
NJ TOTAL	7	.1	1,141	15.3	59	.8	205	2.7	1,412	18.9	6,054	81.1	0	.0	7,
NJ FEMALE	5	.1	795	18.4	35	.8	127	2.9	962	22.3	3,360	77.7	0	.0	4,
NJ MALE	2	.1	346	11.0	24	.8	78	2.5	450	14.3	2,694	85.7	0	.0	3,
CENTENARY COLLEGE															
NJ TOTAL	0	.0	26	3.7	0	.0	0	.0	26	3.7	671	95.4	6	.9	
NJ FEMALE	0	.0	26	3.7	0	.0	0	.0	26	3.7	668	95.4	6	.9	
NJ MALE	0	.0	0	.0	0	.0	0	.0	0	.0	3	100.0	0	.0	
C MED & DENT OF NJ NEWARK															
NJ TOTAL	0	.0	55	24.9	7	3.2	8	3.6	70	31.7	150	67.9	1	.5	
NJ FEMALE	0	.0	48	28.6	3	1.8	7	4.2	58	34.5	110	65.5	0	.0	
NJ MALE	0	.0	7	13.2	4	7.5	1	1.9	12	22.6	40	75.5	1	1.9	
COLLEGE OF SNT ELIZABETH															
NJ TOTAL	0	.0	47	8.9	6	1.1	18	3.4	71	13.4	448	84.4	12	2.3	
NJ FEMALE	0	.0	47	8.9	6	1.1	17	3.2	70	13.3	445	84.4	12	2.3	
NJ MALE	0	.0	0	.0	0	.0	1	25.0	1	25.0	3	75.0	0	.0	
COUNTY COLLEGE OF MORRIS															
NJ TOTAL	29	.3	199	1.9	157	1.5	133	1.3	518	5.0	9,850	95.0	0	.0	10,
NJ FEMALE	13	.2	117	2.0	92	1.6	75	1.3	297	5.1	5,478	94.9	0	.0	5,
NJ MALE	16	.3	82	1.8	65	1.4	58	1.3	221	4.8	4,372	95.2	0	.0	4,
CUMBERLAND COUNTY COLLEGE															
NJ TOTAL	20	1.0	275	14.1	17	.9	145	7.4	457	23.4	1,499	76.6	0	.0	1,
NJ FEMALE	13	1.1	186	15.8	9	.8	83	7.0	291	24.7	888	75.3	0	.0	1,
NJ MALE	7	.9	89	11.5	8	1.0	62	8.0	166	21.4	611	78.6	0	.0	
DON BOSCO COLLEGE															
NJ TOTAL	0	.0	2	2.5	5	6.3	6	7.5	13	16.3	64	80.0	3	3.8	
NJ FEMALE	0	.0	0	.0	0	.0	0	.0	0	.0	0	.0	0	.0	
NJ MALE	0	.0	2	2.5	5	6.3	6	7.5	13	16.3	64	80.0	3	3.8	
DREW UNIVERSITY															
NJ TOTAL	0	.0	40	2.8	5	.3	27	1.9	72	5.0	1,331	92.0	43	3.0	1,
NJ FEMALE	0	.0	29	3.7	3	.4	10	1.3	42	5.3	734	92.6	17	2.1	
NJ MALE	0	.0	11	1.7	2	.3	17	2.6	30	4.6	597	91.4	26	4.0	
ESSEX COUNTY COLLEGE															
NJ TOTAL	12	.2	4,426	70.2	35	.6	641	10.2	5,114	81.1	805	12.8	388	6.2	6,
NJ FEMALE	7	.2	2,702	70.2	22	.6	387	10.1	3,118	81.0	490	12.7	241	6.3	3,
NJ MALE	5	.2	1,724	70.1	13	.5	254	10.3	1,996	81.2	315	12.8	147	6.0	2,
FARLGH DCKSN U EDH WMS C															
NJ TOTAL	0	.0	77	9.9	3	.4	27	3.5	107	13.7	668	85.8	4	.5	
NJ FEMALE	0	.0	42	10.0	2	.5	12	2.9	56	13.4	360	86.1	2	.5	
NJ MALE	0	.0	35	9.7	1	.3	15	4.2	51	14.1	308	85.3	2	.6	
FARLGH DCKSN MADISON CAM															
NJ TOTAL	9	.3	88	2.9	26	.9	47	1.6	170	5.6	2,800	93.0	41	1.4	3,
NJ FEMALE	7	.5	56	3.7	19	1.3	20	1.3	102	6.8	1,382	91.6	24	1.6	1,
NJ MALE	2	.1	32	2.1	7	.5	27	1.8	68	4.5	1,418	94.3	17	1.1	1,
FARLGH DCKSN U RUTHERFD															
NJ TOTAL	0	.0	169	6.6	8	.3	139	5.5	316	12.4	2,172	85.4	55	2.2	2,
NJ FEMALE	0	.0	121	9.4	4	.3	78	6.0	203	15.7	1,065	82.5	23	1.8	1,
NJ MALE	0	.0	48	3.8	4	.3	61	4.9	113	9.0	1,107	88.4	32	2.6	1,
FARLGH DCKSN TEANECK CAM															
NJ TOTAL	10	.2	190	4.2	28	.6	156	3.5	384	8.5	3,931	87.5	178	4.0	4,
NJ FEMALE	2	.1	113	6.6	9	.5	70	4.1	194	11.3	1,473	85.8	50	2.9	1,
NJ MALE	8	.3	77	2.8	19	.7	86	3.1	190	6.8	2,458	88.5	128	4.6	2,
FELICIAN COLLEGE															
NJ TOTAL	1	.2	20	3.5	3	.5	11	1.9	35	6.1	540	93.6	2	.3	
NJ FEMALE	1	.2	20	3.5	3	.5	11	1.9	35	6.1	539	93.6	2	.3	
NJ MALE	0	.0	0	.0	0	.0	0	.0	0	.0	1	100.0	0	.0	
GEORGIAN COURT COLLEGE															
NJ TOTAL	4	.7	37	6.6	7	1.2	17	3.0	65	11.6	489	87.0	8	1.4	
NJ FEMALE	4	.7	37	6.6	7	1.2	17	3.0	65	11.6	489	87.0	8	1.4	
NJ MALE	0	.0	0	.0	0	.0	0	.0	0	.0	0	.0	0	.0	
GLASSBORO STATE COLLEGE															
NJ TOTAL	107	1.2	1,188	13.2	30	.3	664	7.4	1,989	22.1	7,006	77.8	12	.1	9,
NJ FEMALE	77	1.5	820	15.6	20	.4	391	7.4	1,308	24.8	3,954	75.0	8	.2	5,
NJ MALE	30	.8	368	9.8	10	.3	273	7.3	681	18.2	3,052	81.7	4	.1	3,
GLOUCESTER COUNTY COLLEGE															
NJ TOTAL	1	.0	240	9.1	11	.4	10	.4	262	9.9	2,386	90.1	0	.0	2,
NJ FEMALE	1	.1	147	9.7	6	.4	4	.3	158	10.4	1,364	89.6	0	.0	1,
NJ MALE	0	.0	93	8.3	5	.4	6	.5	104	9.2	1,022	90.8	0	.0	1,
HUDSON CO CC COMMISSION															
NJ TOTAL	0	.0	153	24.8	19	3.1	190	30.8	362	58.8	251	40.7	3	.5	
NJ FEMALE	0	.0	93	25.1	14	3.8	128	34.6	235	63.5	134	36.2	1	.3	
NJ MALE	0	.0	60	24.1	5	2.0	62	25.2	127	51.6	117	47.6	2	.8	
JERSEY CITY STATE COLLEGE															
NJ TOTAL	35	.5	1,496	19.6	111	1.5	829	10.8	2,471	32.3	4,918	64.3	259	3.4	7,
NJ FEMALE	17	.4	1,008	23.4	60	1.4	468	10.9	1,553	36.1	2,716	63.2	31	.7	4,
NJ MALE	18	.5	488	14.6	51	1.5	361	10.8	918	27.4	2,202	65.8	228	6.8	3,

N E	BLACK NON-HISPANIC		ASIAN OR PACIFIC ISLANDER		HISPANIC		TOTAL MINORITY		WHITE NON-HISPANIC		NON-RESIDENT ALIEN		TOTAL
	NUMBER	%	NUMBER	%	NUMBER	%	NUMBER	%	NUMBER	%	NUMBER	%	NUMBER
INUED													
	19	4.2	1	.2	4	.9	24	5.3	430	94.7	0	.0	454
	19	4.2	1	.2	4	.9	24	5.3	430	94.7	0	.0	454
	0	.0	0	.0	0	.0	0	.0	0	.0	0	.0	0
	1,144	12.6	54	.6	647	7.1	1,870	20.6	7,079	77.8	146	1.6	9,095
	733	14.2	23	.4	366	7.1	1,131	21.8	4,000	77.2	49	.9	5,180
	411	10.5	31	.8	281	7.2	739	18.9	3,079	78.6	97	2.5	3,915
	723	16.2	35	.8	117	2.6	878	19.6	3,565	79.7	29	.6	4,472
	353	17.2	17	.8	53	2.6	423	20.6	1,619	78.8	13	.6	2,055
	370	15.3	18	.7	64	2.6	455	18.8	1,946	80.5	16	.7	2,417
	298	5.0	65	1.1	198	3.3	569	9.5	5,391	90.0	33	.6	5,993
	186	5.6	33	1.0	117	3.5	338	10.2	2,962	89.5	10	.3	3,310
	112	4.2	32	1.2	81	3.0	231	8.6	2,429	90.5	23	.9	2,683
	86	3.1	8	.3	32	1.2	126	4.6	2,608	95.4	1	.0	2,735
	47	3.5	2	.1	15	1.1	64	4.8	1,283	95.2	0	.0	1,347
	39	2.8	6	.4	17	1.2	62	4.5	1,325	95.5	1	.1	1,388
	555	4.7	69	.6	764	6.5	1,388	11.9	10,087	86.3	220	1.9	11,695
	359	5.1	43	.6	443	6.3	845	12.0	6,073	86.2	129	1.8	7,047
	196	4.2	26	.6	321	6.9	543	11.7	4,014	86.4	91	2.0	4,648
	216	5.4	104	2.6	182	4.6	502	12.7	3,358	84.6	108	2.7	3,968
	61	19.9	9	2.9	19	6.2	89	29.1	208	68.0	9	2.9	306
	155	4.2	95	2.6	163	4.5	413	11.3	3,150	86.0	99	2.7	3,662
	15	4.6	2	.6	5	1.5	22	6.8	293	90.7	8	2.5	323
	5	3.8	1	.8	1	.8	7	5.3	121	91.0	5	3.8	133
	10	5.3	1	.5	4	2.1	15	7.9	172	90.5	3	1.6	190
	74	2.2	13	.4	46	1.3	138	4.0	3,287	96.0	0	.0	3,425
	41	2.5	8	.5	21	1.3	73	4.5	1,542	95.5	0	.0	1,615
	33	1.8	5	.3	25	1.4	65	3.6	1,745	96.4	0	.0	1,810
	693	41.1	19	1.1	518	30.7	1,234	73.2	449	26.6	2	.1	1,685
	507	47.5	6	.6	323	30.2	838	78.5	230	21.5	0	.0	1,068
	186	30.1	13	2.1	195	31.6	396	64.2	219	35.5	2	.3	617
	322	7.3	135	3.1	176	4.0	647	14.6	3,565	80.6	210	4.7	4,422
	165	10.8	53	3.5	59	3.9	281	18.4	1,181	77.2	68	4.4	1,530
	157	5.4	82	2.8	117	4.0	366	12.7	2,384	82.4	142	4.9	2,892
	0	.0	0	.0	0	.0	0	.0	168	74.7	57	25.3	225
	0	.0	0	.0	0	.0	0	.0	0	.0	0	.0	0
	0	.0	0	.0	0	.0	0	.0	168	74.7	57	25.3	225
	176	4.4	7	.2	73	1.8	258	6.	3,733	92.9	27	.7	4,018
	89	4.7	4	.2	40	2.1	133	7.1	1,739	92.5	7	.4	1,879
	87	4.1	3	.1	33	1.5	125	5.8	1,994	93.2	20	.9	2,139
	218	6.0	22	.6	34	.9	276	7.6	3,347	91.7	28	.8	3,651
	145	9.2	11	.7	13	.8	169	10.7	1,395	88.2	17	1.1	1,581
	73	3.5	11	.5	21	1.0	107	5.2	1,952	94.3	11	.5	2,070
	325	11.8	18	.7	63	2.3	410	14.	2,322	84.6	13	.5	2,745
	202	15.1	8	.6	33	2.5	247	18.0	1,082	81.0	6	.4	1,335
	123	8.7	10	.7	30	2.1	163	11.6	1,240	87.9	7	.5	1,410
	522	13.7	49	1.3	315	8.3	889	23.4	2,886	75.8	31	.8	3,806
	354	20.1	31	1.8	187	10.6	574	32.6	1,180	67.1	5	.3	1,759
	168	8.2	18	.9	128	6.3	315	15.4	1,706	83.3	26	1.3	2,047
	1,874	9.0	364	1.8	617	3.0	2,878	13.9	17,716	85.5	124	.6	20,718
	1,090	10.6	195	1.9	315	3.1	1,614	15.7	8,632	84.0	31	.3	10,277
	784	7.9	169	1.6	302	2.9	1,264	12.1	9,084	87.0	93	.9	10,441
	327	9.7	61	1.8	435	12.9	835	24.7	2,530	75.0	10	.3	3,375
	213	13.9	20	1.3	267	17.5	504	33.0	1,019	66.7	4	.3	1,527
	114	6.2	41	2.2	168	9.1	331	17.9	1,511	81.8	6	.3	1,848
	242	22.7	6	.6	18	1.7	268	25.1	800	74.9	0	.0	1,068
	153	25.8	3	.5	7	1.2	164	27.7	429	72.3	0	.0	593
	89	18.7	3	.6	11	2.3	104	21.9	371	78.1	0	.0	475
	544	9.4	28	.5	104	1.8	682	11.7	5,071	87.2	62	1.1	5,815
	373	13.1	18	.6	66	2.3	460	16.1	2,373	83.2	18	.6	2,851
	171	5.8	10	.3	38	1.3	222	7.5	2,698	91.0	44	1.5	2,964
	151	6.4	38	1.6	44	1.9	243	10.3	2,111	89.7	0	.0	2,354
	94	7.5	24	1.9	25	2.0	147	11.7	1,105	88.3	0	.0	1,252
	57	5.2	14	1.3	19	1.7	96	8.7	1,006	91.3	0	.0	1,102
	40	2.8	54	3.8	73	5.2	167	11.9	1,183	84.0	58	4.1	1,408
	14	8.2	6	3.5	13	7.6	33	19.4	137	80.6	0	.0	170
	26	2.1	48	3.9	60	4.8	134	10.8	1,046	84.5	58	4.7	1,238
	273	6.1	21	.5	51	1.1	355	8.0	4,087	91.9	5	.1	4,447
	142	7.5	5	.3	24	1.3	174	9.2	1,722	90.7	3	.2	1,899
	131	5.1	16	.6	27	1.1	181	7.1	2,365	92.8	2	.1	2,548

TABLE 1 - TOTAL UNDERGRADUATE ENROLLMENT IN INSTITUTIONS OF HIGHER EDUCATION BY RACE, ETHNICITY AND SEX: INSTITUTION, STATE AND NATION, 1978

	AMERICAN INDIAN ALASKAN NATIVE		BLACK NON-HISPANIC		ASIAN OR PACIFIC ISLANDER		HISPANIC		TOTAL MINORITY		WHITE NON-HISPANIC		NON-RESIDENT ALIEN		TOTAL
	NUMBER	%	NUMBER	%	NUMBER	%	NUMBER	%	NUMBER	%	NUMBER	%	NUMBER	%	NUMBER
NEW JERSEY CONTINUED															
TALMUD INST OF CEN JERSEY															
NJ TOTAL	0	.0	0	.0	0	.0	0	.0	0	.0	48	100.0	0	.0	48
NJ FEMALE	0	.0	0	.0	0	.0	0	.0	0	.0	0	.0	0	.0	0
NJ MALE	0	.0	0	.0	0	.0	0	.0	0	.0	48	100.0	0	.0	48
TRENTON STATE COLLEGE															
NJ TOTAL	13	.1	619	7.1	44	.5	73	.8	749	8.6	7,946	91.4	0	.0	8,695
NJ FEMALE	7	.1	375	7.3	23	.4	34	.7	439	8.5	4,697	91.5	0	.0	5,136
NJ MALE	6	.2	244	6.9	21	.6	39	1.1	310	8.7	3,249	91.3	0	.0	3,559
UNION COLLEGE															
NJ TOTAL	8	.3	299	11.4	20	.8	133	5.1	460	17.5	2,160	82.0	13	.5	2,633
NJ FEMALE	7	.5	183	13.5	9	.7	67	4.9	266	19.6	1,085	80.1	4	.3	1,355
NJ MALE	1	.1	116	9.1	11	.9	66	5.2	194	15.2	1,075	84.1	9	.7	1,278
UNION CO TECHNICAL INST															
NJ TOTAL	3	.2	174	11.6	8	.5	82	5.5	267	17.8	1,235	82.2	1	.1	1,503
NJ FEMALE	3	.4	83	11.4	4	.5	42	5.7	132	18.1	599	81.9	0	.0	731
NJ MALE	0	.0	91	11.8	4	.5	40	5.2	135	17.5	636	82.4	1	.1	772
UPSALA COLLEGE															
NJ TOTAL	3	.3	198	17.2	11	1.0	36	3.1	248	21.6	890	77.5	11	1.0	1,149
NJ FEMALE	1	.2	103	20.6	6	1.2	12	2.4	122	24.4	373	74.6	5	1.0	500
NJ MALE	2	.3	95	14.6	5	.8	24	3.7	126	19.4	517	79.7	6	.9	649
WESTMINSTER CHOIR COLLEGE															
NJ TOTAL	0	.0	33	8.8	0	.0	3	.8	36	9.6	330	87.8	10	2.7	376
NJ FEMALE	0	.0	15	7.1	0	.0	2	1.0	17	8.1	186	88.6	7	3.3	210
NJ MALE	0	.0	18	10.8	0	.0	1	.6	19	11.4	144	86.7	3	1.8	166
WILLIAM PATERSON COLLEGE															
NJ TOTAL	13	.1	509	5.6	36	.4	184	2.0	742	8.1	8,376	91.9	0	.0	9,118
NJ FEMALE	6	.1	300	6.3	18	.4	98	2.0	422	8.8	4,375	91.2	0	.0	4,797
NJ MALE	7	.2	209	4.8	18	.4	86	2.0	320	7.4	4,001	92.6	0	.0	4,321
NEW JERSEY TOTAL (58 INSTITUTIONS)															
NJ TOTAL	486	.2	23,356	11.0	2,059	1.0	8,837	4.2	34,738	16.3	175,429	82.5	2,391	1.1	212,558
NJ FEMALE	272	.2	14,420	13.0	1,029	.9	4,892	4.4	20,613	18.5	89,797	80.7	876	.8	111,286
NJ MALE	214	.2	8,936	8.8	1,030	1.0	3,945	3.9	14,125	13.9	85,632	84.6	1,515	1.5	101,272
NEW MEXICO															
COLLEGE OF SANTA FE															
NM TOTAL	87	8.3	20	1.9	20	1.9	402	38.4	529	50.5	516	49.2	3	.3	1,048
NM FEMALE	65	11.2	6	1.0	5	.9	210	36.3	286	49.4	292	50.4	1	.2	579
NM MALE	22	4.7	14	3.0	15	3.2	192	40.9	243	51.8	224	47.8	2	.4	469
COLLEGE OF THE SOUTHWEST															
NM TOTAL	0	.0	4	3.5	0	.0	11	9.6	15	13.2	99	86.8	0	.0	114
NM FEMALE	0	.0	1	1.5	0	.0	7	10.3	8	11.8	60	88.2	0	.0	68
NM MALE	0	.0	3	6.5	0	.0	4	8.7	7	15.2	39	84.8	0	.0	46
EASTERN NM U MAIN CAMPUS															
NM TOTAL	92	2.9	191	6.1	23	.7	408	13.0	714	22.8	2,400	76.7	17	.5	3,131
NM FEMALE	61	3.7	75	4.6	11	.7	216	13.2	363	22.2	1,261	77.3	8	.5	1,632
NM MALE	31	2.1	116	7.7	12	.8	192	12.8	351	23.4	1,139	76.0	9	.6	1,499
EASTERN NM U ROSWELL CAM															
NM TOTAL	12	1.1	24	2.2	10	.9	230	21.5	276	25.7	774	72.2	22	2.1	1,072
NM FEMALE	7	1.3	15	2.8	6	1.1	118	22.3	146	27.7	370	70.1	12	2.3	528
NM MALE	5	.9	9	1.7	4	.7	112	20.6	130	23.9	404	74.3	10	1.8	544
INST AMERICAN INDIAN ARTS															
NM TOTAL	163	100.0	0	.0	0	.0	0	.0	163	100.0	0	.0	0	.0	163
NM FEMALE	70	100.0	0	.0	0	.0	0	.0	70	100.0	0	.0	0	.0	70
NM MALE	93	100.0	0	.0	0	.0	0	.0	93	100.0	0	.0	0	.0	93
NEW MEXICO HIGHLANDS U															
NM TOTAL	45	2.8	36	2.3	6	.4	1,152	72.2	1,239	77.7	330	20.7	26	1.6	1,595
NM FEMALE	28	3.4	4	.5	2	.2	622	75.5	656	79.6	164	19.9	4	.5	824
NM MALE	17	2.2	32	4.2	4	.5	530	68.7	583	75.6	166	21.5	22	2.9	771
NM INST OF MINING & TECHN															
NM TOTAL	11	1.4	6	.7	15	1.8	80	9.8	112	13.8	671	82.4	31	3.8	814
NM FEMALE	3	1.5	2	1.0	3	1.5	25	12.1	33	16.0	168	81.6	5	2.4	206
NM MALE	8	1.3	4	.7	12	2.0	55	9.0	79	13.0	503	82.7	26	4.3	608
NEW MEXICO JUNIOR COLLEGE															
NM TOTAL	6	.5	52	4.4	2	.2	111	9.4	171	14.5	964	82.0	41	3.5	1,176
NM FEMALE	4	.6	21	3.2	2	.3	62	9.6	89	13.7	553	85.2	7	1.1	649
NM MALE	2	.4	31	5.9	0	.0	49	9.3	82	15.6	411	78.0	34	6.5	527
NEW MEXICO MILITARY INST															
NM TOTAL	4	.9	48	10.2	10	2.1	53	11.3	115	24.5	323	68.7	32	6.8	470
NM FEMALE	1	2.3	6	14.0	0	.0	6	14.0	13	30.2	26	60.5	4	9.3	43
NM MALE	3	.7	42	9.8	10	2.3	47	11.0	102	23.9	297	69.6	28	6.6	427
NM STATE U MAIN CAMPUS															
NM TOTAL	185	1.9	162	1.7	35	.4	2,570	26.6	2,952	30.6	6,471	67.0	236	2.4	9,659
NM FEMALE	87	2.0	63	1.5	13	.3	1,201	28.0	1,364	31.8	2,910	67.8	19	.4	4,293
NM MALE	98	1.8	99	1.8	22	.4	1,369	25.5	1,588	29.6	3,561	66.4	217	4.0	5,366
NM STATE U ALAMOGORDO															
NM TOTAL	12	1.7	25	3.6	5	.7	121	17.6	163	23.7	525	76.3	0	.0	688
NM FEMALE	6	1.6	13	3.5	2	.5	62	16.6	83	22.3	290	77.7	0	.0	373
NM MALE	6	1.9	12	3.8	3	1.0	59	18.7	80	25.4	235	74.6	0	.0	315
NM STATE U CARLSBAD															
NM TOTAL	5	1.6	0	.0	0	.0	80	25.6	85	27.2	228	72.8	0	.0	313
NM FEMALE	2	1.0	0	.0	0	.0	51	26.7	53	27.7	138	72.3	0	.0	191
NM MALE	3	2.5	0	.0	0	.0	29	23.8	32	26.2	90	73.8	0	.0	122
NM STATE U GRANTS BRANCH															
NM TOTAL	27	16.3	2	1.2	1	.6	61	36.7	91	54.8	75	45.2	0	.0	166
NM FEMALE	18	17.5	1	1.0	0	.0	37	35.9	56	54.4	47	45.6	0	.0	103
NM MALE	9	14.3	1	1.6	1	1.6	24	38.1	35	55.6	28	44.4	0	.0	63
NM STATE U SAN JUAN															
NM TOTAL	115	19.6	0	.0	2	.3	51	8.7	168	28.7	418	71.3	0	.0	586
NM FEMALE	80	22.3	0	.0	1	.3	30	8.4	111	31.0	247	69.0	0	.0	358
NM MALE	35	15.4	0	.0	1	.4	21	9.2	57	25.0	171	75.0	0	.0	228

BLACK NON-HISPANIC		ASIAN OR PACIFIC ISLANDER		HISPANIC		TOTAL MINORITY		WHITE NON-HISPANIC		NON-RESIDENT ALIEN		TOTAL
NUMBER	%	NUMBER	%	NUMBER	%	NUMBER	%	NUMBER	%	NUMBER	%	NUMBER
NUED												
1	.1	0	.0	536	53.9	577	58.0	417	41.9	1	.1	995
0	.0	0	.0	291	56.3	315	60.9	202	39.1	0	.0	517
1	.2	0	.0	245	51.3	262	54.8	215	45.0	1	.2	478
98	4.1	31	1.3	568	23.8	817	34.3	1,540	64.6	26	1.1	2,383
37	3.8	16	1.7	243	25.1	373	38.5	584	60.3	12	1.2	969
61	4.3	15	1.1	325	23.0	444	31.4	956	67.6	14	1.0	1,414
256	1.8	124	.9	3,557	24.6	4,411	30.5	9,924	68.5	143	1.0	14,478
119	1.7	53	.7	1,810	25.4	2,259	31.7	4,832	67.8	33	.5	7,124
137	1.9	71	1.0	1,747	23.8	2,152	29.3	5,092	69.2	110	1.5	7,354
2	.8	1	.4	42	16.3	204	79.1	54	20.9	0	.0	258
1	.5	1	.5	26	14.1	145	78.8	39	21.2	0	.0	184
1	1.4	0	.0	16	21.6	59	79.7	15	20.3	0	.0	74
44	3.8	6	.5	468	40.0	561	48.0	608	52.0	0	.0	1,169
11	1.8	3	.5	233	38.8	271	45.2	329	54.8	0	.0	600
33	5.8	3	.5	235	41.3	290	51.0	279	49.0	0	.0	569
(19 INSTITUTIONS)												
971	2.4	291	.7	10,501	26.1	13,363	33.2	26,337	65.4	578	1.4	40,278
375	1.9	118	.6	5,250	27.2	6,694	34.7	12,512	64.8	105	.5	19,311
596	2.8	173	.8	5,291	25.0	6,669	31.8	13,825	65.9	473	2.3	20,967
244	16.1	50	3.3	303	20.0	597	39.4	887	58.5	32	2.1	1,516
1	25.0	0	.0	2	50.0	3	75.0	1	25.0	0	.0	4
243	16.1	50	3.3	301	19.9	594	39.3	886	58.6	32	2.1	1,512
654	11.2	22	.4	213	3.7	897	15.4	4,923	84.6	0	.0	5,820
472	12.3	12	.3	143	3.7	629	16.4	3,200	83.6	0	.0	3,829
182	9.1	10	.5	70	3.5	268	13.5	1,723	86.5	0	.0	1,991
160	24.9	2	.3	1	.2	165	25.7	472	73.5	5	.8	642
117	26.7	2	.5	0	.0	120	27.4	318	72.6	0	.0	438
43	21.1	0	.0	1	.5	45	22.1	154	75.5	5	2.5	204
1	.2	0	.0	1	.2	2	.3	608	99.3	2	.3	612
1	.3	0	.0	1	.3	2	.6	311	98.7	2	.6	315
0	.0	0	.0	0	.0	0	.0	297	100.0	0	.0	297
7	.4	2	.1	5	.3	16	.9	1,788	98.6	10	.6	1,814
3	.3	1	.1	2	.2	6	.7	870	99.0	3	.3	879
4	.4	1	.1	3	.3	10	1.1	918	98.2	7	.7	935
1	.2	0	.0	1	.2	2	.3	615	96.9	5	.8	622
0	.0	0	.0	1	.4	1	.4	242	99.2	1	.4	244
1	.3	0	.0	0	.0	1	.3	373	98.7	4	1.1	378
30	7.4	0	.0	14	3.5	44	10.9	352	86.9	9	2.2	405
17	8.9	0	.0	6	3.2	23	12.1	165	86.8	2	1.1	190
13	6.0	0	.0	8	3.7	21	9.8	187	87.0	7	3.3	215
0	.0	5	2.9	4	2.3	9	5.3	148	86.5	14	8.2	171
0	.0	5	2.9	4	2.3	9	5.3	148	86.5	14	8.2	171
0	.0	0	.0	0	.0	0	.0	0	.0	0	.0	0
51	7.5	2	.3	20	3.0	74	10.9	599	88.6	3	.4	676
31	8.3	0	.0	10	2.7	42	11.2	332	88.8	0	.0	374
20	6.6	2	.7	10	3.3	32	10.6	267	88.4	3	1.0	302
0	.0	0	.0	0	.0	0	.0	260	100.0	0	.0	260
0	.0	0	.0	0	.0	0	.0	0	.0	0	.0	0
0	.0	0	.0	0	.0	0	.0	260	100.0	0	.0	260
0	.0	0	.0	0	.0	0	.0	192	100.0	0	.0	192
0	.0	0	.0	0	.0	0	.0	0	.0	0	.0	0
0	.0	0	.0	0	.0	0	.0	192	100.0	0	.0	192
17	6.1	0	.0	3	1.1	20	7.2	258	92.5	1	.4	279
17	6.1	0	.0	3	1.1	20	7.2	258	92.5	1	.4	279
0	.0	0	.0	0	.0	0	.0	0	.0	0	.0	0
85	14.3	0	.0	144	24.2	229	38.6	365	61.4	0	.0	594
61	10.8	0	.0	139	24.6	200	35.5	364	64.5	0	.0	564
24	80.0	0	.0	5	16.7	29	96.7	1	3.3	0	.0	30
67	9.2	1	.1	18	2.5	86	11.8	641	88.2	0	.0	727
67	9.2	1	.1	18	2.5	86	11.8	641	88.2	0	.0	727
0	.0	0	.0	0	.0	0	.0	0	.0	0	.0	0
0	.0	0	.0	0	.0	0	.0	218	100.0	0	.0	218
0	.0	0	.0	0	.0	0	.0	0	.0	0	.0	0
0	.0	0	.0	0	.0	0	.0	218	100.0	0	.0	218
0	.0	0	.0	0	.0	0	.0	53	100.0	0	.0	53
0	.0	0	.0	0	.0	0	.0	0	.0	0	.0	0
0	.0	0	.0	0	.0	0	.0	53	100.0	0	.0	53

	AMERICAN INDIAN ALASKAN NATIVE		BLACK NON-HISPANIC		ASIAN OR PACIFIC ISLANDER		HISPANIC		TOTAL MINORITY		WHITE NON-HISPANIC		NON-RESIDENT ALIEN	
	NUMBER	%	NUMBER	%	NUMBER	%	NUMBER	%	NUMBER	%	NUMBER	%	NUMBER	%
NEW YORK CONTINUED														
BETH JACOB HEBREW TCHRS C														
NY TOTAL	0	.0	0	.0	0	.0	0	.0	0	.0	329	100.0		.0
NY FEMALE	0	.0	0	.0	0	.0	0	.0	0	.0	314	100.0	8	.0
NY MALE	0	.0	0	.0	0	.0	0	.0	0	.0	15	100.0		.0
BETH JOSEPH RAB SEMINARY														
NY TOTAL	0	.0	0	.0	0	.0	0	.0	0	.0	32	100.0		.0
NY FEMALE	0	.0	0	.0	0	.0	0	.0	0	.0	0	.0	8	.0
NY MALE	0	.0	0	.0	0	.0	0	.0	0	.0	32	100.0		.0
BETH MEDRASH EMEK HALACHA														
NY TOTAL	0	.0	0	.0	0	.0	0	.0	0	.0	54	100.0		.0
NY FEMALE	0	.0	0	.0	0	.0	0	.0	0	.0	0	.0	8	.0
NY MALE	0	.0	0	.0	0	.0	0	.0	0	.0	54	100.0		.0
BOBOVER YESH BNEI ZION														
NY TOTAL	0	.0	0	.0	0	.0	0	.0	0	.0	346	100.0		.0
NY FEMALE	0	.0	0	.0	0	.0	0	.0	0	.0	0	.0	8	.0
NY MALE	0	.0	0	.0	0	.0	0	.0	0	.0	346	100.0		.0
BORICUA COLLEGE														
NY TOTAL	0	.0	23	5.1	0	.0	432	94.9	455	100.0	0	.0		.0
NY FEMALE	0	.0	12	4.9	0	.0	234	95.1	246	100.0	0	.0	8	.0
NY MALE	0	.0	11	5.3	0	.0	198	94.7	209	100.0	0	.0		.0
BRYANT-STRATTON BUS INST														
NY TOTAL	0	.0	105	19.6	0	.0	11	2.0	116	21.6	421	78.4		.0
NY FEMALE	0	.0	64	15.1	0	.0	9	2.1	73	17.2	351	82.8	8	.0
NY MALE	0	.0	41	36.3	0	.0	2	1.8	43	38.1	70	61.9		.0
BRYANT-STRATTON BUS INST														
NY TOTAL	27	.7	594	16.0	3	.1	40	1.1	664	17.9	3,048	82.0	4	.1
NY FEMALE	20	.9	337	14.9	2	.1	23	1.0	382	16.9	1,875	83.0	1	.0
NY MALE	7	.5	257	17.6	1	.1	17	1.2	282	19.3	1,173	80.5	3	.2
CANISIUS COLLEGE														
NY TOTAL	10	.4	195	8.0	4	.2	1	.0	210	8.6	2,223	91.1	8	.3
NY FEMALE	1	.1	83	9.7	3	.4	0	.0	87	10.2	765	89.7	1	.1
NY MALE	9	.6	112	7.1	1	.1	1	.1	123	7.7	1,458	91.8	7	.4
CTHOL C IMMAC CONCEPTION														
NY TOTAL	0	.0	4	2.4	0	.0	11	6.6	15	9.0	152	91.0		.0
NY FEMALE	0	.0	0	.0	0	.0	0	.0	0	.0	0	.0	8	.0
NY MALE	0	.0	4	2.4	0	.0	11	6.6	15	9.0	152	91.0		.0
CAZENOVIA COLLEGE														
NY TOTAL	2	.4	25	5.2	0	.0	3	.6	30	6.2	448	92.9		.8
NY FEMALE	2	.4	25	5.2	0	.0	3	.6	30	6.2	448	92.9	4	.8
NY MALE	0	.0	0	.0	0	.0	0	.0	0	.0	0	.0		.0
CEN CITY BUSINESS INST														
NY TOTAL	0	.0	163	19.4	0	.0	0	.0	163	19.4	679	80.6		.0
NY FEMALE	0	.0	114	18.4	0	.0	0	.0	114	18.4	506	81.6	8	.0
NY MALE	0	.0	49	22.1	0	.0	0	.0	49	22.1	173	77.9		.0
CEN YESH TOM THIMIM LUBVZ														
NY TOTAL	0	.0	0	.0	0	.0	0	.0	0	.0	333	100.0		.0
NY FEMALE	0	.0	0	.0	0	.0	0	.0	0	.0	0	.0	8	.0
NY MALE	0	.0	0	.0	0	.0	0	.0	0	.0	333	100.0		.0
CUNY BERNARD BARUCH C														
NY TOTAL	60	.5	2,839	25.4	1,004	9.0	1,441	12.9	5,344	47.8	5,644	50.5	192	1.7
NY FEMALE	25	.5	1,771	32.1	549	10.0	776	14.1	3,121	56.6	2,302	41.7	91	1.7
NY MALE	35	.6	1,068	18.8	455	8.0	665	11.7	2,223	39.2	3,342	59.0	101	1.8
CUNY BORO OF MANHATTAN CC														
NY TOTAL	56	.6	4,623	52.5	332	3.8	2,054	23.3	7,065	80.2	1,714	19.5	31	.4
NY FEMALE	13	.2	3,414	57.2	156	2.6	1,318	22.1	4,901	82.1	1,071	17.9	0	.0
NY MALE	43	1.5	1,209	42.6	176	6.2	736	25.9	2,164	76.3	643	22.7	31	1.1
CUNY BRONX CMTY COLLEGE														
NY TOTAL	100	1.4	3,786	51.9	195	2.7	2,456	33.7	6,537	89.6	665	9.1	96	1.3
NY FEMALE	41	.9	2,565	57.5	88	2.0	1,410	31.6	4,104	92.0	314	7.0	42	.9
NY MALE	59	2.1	1,221	43.0	107	3.8	1,046	36.9	2,433	85.7	351	12.4	54	1.9
CUNY BROOKLYN COLLEGE														
NY TOTAL	103	1.2	2,975	20.0	610	4.1	1,228	8.2	4,996	33.5	9,761	65.5	135	.9
NY FEMALE	122	1.5	1,813	22.2	277	3.4	599	7.3	2,811	34.5	5,290	64.9	51	.6
NY MALE	61	.9	1,162	17.2	333	4.9	629	9.3	2,185	32.4	4,471	66.3	84	1.2
CUNY CITY COLLEGE														
NY TOTAL	134	1.1	4,339	36.8	849	7.2	2,572	21.8	7,894	66.9	3,540	30.0	364	3.1
NY FEMALE	33	.7	2,228	45.8	234	4.8	1,084	22.3	3,579	73.6	1,226	25.2	61	1.3
NY MALE	101	1.5	2,111	30.5	615	8.9	1,488	21.5	4,315	62.2	2,314	33.4	303	4.4
CUNY C OF STATEN ISLAND														
NY TOTAL	77	.8	1,567	17.1	346	3.8	729	7.9	2,719	29.6	6,365	69.3	103	1.1
NY FEMALE	54	1.2	872	19.5	92	2.1	375	8.4	1,393	31.2	3,028	67.8	45	1.0
NY MALE	23	.5	695	14.7	254	5.4	354	7.5	1,326	28.1	3,337	70.7	58	1.2
CUNY HOSTOS CMTY COLLEGE														
NY TOTAL	15	.6	507	19.2	12	.5	1,996	75.8	2,530	96.1	99	3.8	5	.2
NY FEMALE	10	.6	350	20.6	8	.5	1,268	74.5	1,636	96.2	65	3.8	0	.0
NY MALE	5	.5	157	16.8	4	.4	728	78.0	894	95.8	34	3.6	5	.5
CUNY HUNTER COLLEGE														
NY TOTAL	111	.9	3,594	29.7	549	4.5	1,828	15.1	6,082	50.2	5,872	48.4	167	1.4
NY FEMALE	58	.6	2,955	31.9	388	4.2	1,363	14.7	4,764	51.5	4,382	47.4	108	1.2
NY MALE	53	1.8	639	22.3	161	5.6	465	16.2	1,318	46.0	1,490	52.0	59	2.1
CUNY JOHN JAY C CRIM JUST														
NY TOTAL	56	1.0	1,805	33.8	90	1.7	969	18.1	2,920	54.6	2,400	44.9	25	.5
NY FEMALE	22	1.1	909	45.7	31	1.6	419	21.1	1,381	69.4	606	30.5	3	.2
NY MALE	34	1.0	896	26.7	59	1.8	550	16.4	1,539	45.9	1,794	53.5	22	.7
CUNY KINGSBOROUGH CC														
NY TOTAL	99	1.2	1,576	19.8	135	1.7	575	7.2	2,385	30.0	5,523	69.6	33	.4
NY FEMALE	58	1.2	1,104	23.8	58	1.2	349	7.5	1,569	33.8	3,053	65.8	20	.4
NY MALE	41	1.2	472	14.3	77	2.3	226	6.9	816	24.7	2,470	74.9	13	.4
CUNY LA GUARDIA CC														
NY TOTAL	97	1.6	2,153	36.0	190	3.2	1,889	31.6	4,329	72.4	1,626	27.2	25	.4
NY FEMALE	36	.9	1,536	37.9	105	2.6	1,374	33.9	3,051	75.2	996	24.5	11	.3
NY MALE	61	3.2	617	32.1	85	4.4	515	26.8	1,278	66.5	630	32.8	14	.7

74

N E	BLACK NON-HISPANIC		ASIAN OR PACIFIC ISLANDER		HISPANIC		TOTAL MINORITY		WHITE NON-HISPANIC		NON-RESIDENT ALIEN		TOTAL
	NUMBER	%	NUMBER	%	NUMBER	%	NUMBER	%	NUMBER	%	NUMBER	%	NUMBER
INUED													
	2,409	30.7	246	3.1	2,032	25.9	4,767	60.8	2,978	38.0	93	1.2	7,838
	1,634	32.5	150	3.0	1,327	26.4	3,145	62.5	1,844	36.6	43	.9	5,032
	775	27.6	96	3.4	705	25.1	1,622	57.8	1,134	40.4	50	1.8	2,806
	2,313	87.4	23	.9	232	8.8	2,582	97.5	31	1.2	34	1.3	2,647
	1,687	90.1	7	.4	139	7.4	1,837	98.1	26	1.4	9	.5	1,872
	626	80.8	16	2.1	93	12.0	745	96.1	5	.6	25	3.2	775
	5,841	47.7	634	5.2	2,180	17.8	8,828	72.1	3,284	26.8	129	1.1	12,241
	3,432	58.3	223	3.8	1,018	17.3	4,726	80.3	1,102	18.7	61	1.0	5,889
	2,409	37.9	411	6.5	1,162	18.3	4,102	64.6	2,182	34.4	68	1.1	6,352
	2,029	20.2	287	2.9	1,002	10.0	3,486	34.7	6,491	64.5	80	8	10,057
	1,228	24.8	86	1.7	401	8.1	1,739	35.1	3,202	64.6	13	.13	4,954
	801	15.7	201	3.9	601	11.8	1,747	34.2	3,289	64.5	67	1.3	5,103
	2,140	14.2	660	4.4	1,252	8.3	4,223	28.1	10,580	70.4	233	1.5	15,036
	1,420	16.7	388	4.6	722	8.5	2,623	30.8	5,800	68.2	85	1.0	8,508
	720	11.0	272	4.2	530	8.1	1,600	24.5	4,780	73.2	148	2.3	6,528
	2,003	55.7	126	3.5	471	13.1	2,643	73.5	910	25.3	41	1.1	3,594
	1,393	61.3	70	3.1	277	12.2	1,762	77.5	496	21.8	15	.7	2,273
	610	46.2	56	4.2	194	14.7	881	66.7	414	31.3	26	2.0	1,321
	5	.2	7	.2	11	.4	32	1.0	3,039	97.0	61	1	3,132
	1	.2	0	.0	2	.4	4	.8	495	98.2	5	.1 9	504
	4	.2	7	.3	9	.3	28	1.1	2,544	96.8	56	21.8	2,628
	96	4.1	44	1.9	51	2.2	192	8.3	2,082	89.9	43	1 9	2,317
	48	5.1	12	1.3	24	2.5	84	8.9	855	90.7	4	14	943
	48	3.5	32	2.3	27	2.0	108	7.9	1,227	89.3	39	2.8	1,374
	84	64.6	4	3.1	31	23.8	119	91.5	11	8.5	0	.0	130
	45	71.4	0	.0	12	19.0	57	90.5	6	9.5	0	.0	63
	39	58.2	4	6.0	19	28.4	.62	92.5	5	7.5	0	.0	67
	52	8.1	24	3.7	36	5.6	112	17.4	509	79.2	22	3.4	643
	16	8.2	10	5.1	9	4.6	35	17.9	159	81.5	1	.5	195
	36	8.0	14	3.1	27	6.0	77	17.2	350	78.1	21	4.7	448
	33	3.7	7	.8	45	5.1	85	9.6	782	88.6	16	1.9	883
	27	3.2	6	.7	40	4.8	73	8.9	743	89.3	16	1.9	832
	6	11.8	1	2.0	5	9.8	12	23.5	39	76.5	0	.0	51
	1,330	41.4	38	1.2	371	11.5	1,739	54.1	1,448	45.1	26	.8	3,213
	1,066	39.4	37	1.4	276	10.2	1,379	51.0	1,301	48.1	25	.9	2,705
	264	52.0	1	.2	95	18.7	360	70.9	147	28.9	1	.2	508
	47	3.1	2	.1	8	.5	57	3.8	1,436	96.1	2	.1	1,495
	33	3.0	1	.1	5	.5	39	3.6	1,054	96.3	1	.1	1,094
	14	3.5	1	.2	3	.7	18	4.5	382	95.3	1	.2	401
	317	5.8	374	6.9	260	4.8	960	17.7	4,239	78.0	236	4.3	5,435
	98	8.2	63	5.3	43	3.6	208	17.4	948	79.1	42	3.5	1,198
	219	5.2	311	7.3	217	5.1	752	17.7	3,291	77.7	194	4.6	4,237
	105	4.6	163	7.2	86	3.8	354	15.6	1,839	81.2	72	3 2	2,265
	105	4.6	163	7.2	86	3.8	354	15.6	1,839	81.2	72	312	2,265
	0	.0	0	.0	0	.0	0	.0	0	.0	0	.0	0
	30	7.2	2	.5	5	1.2	37	8.9	370	88.9	9	2.2	416
	15	6.4	1	.4	3	1.3	19	8.2	213	91.4	1	.4	233
	15	8.2	1	.5	2	1.1	18	9.8	157	85.8	8	4.4	183
	13	1.5	65	7.4	30	3.4	108	12.3	761	86.4	12	1 4	881
	1	.4	14	6.0	6	2.6	21	9.0	209	89.7	3	1 3	233
	12	1.9	51	7.9	24	3.7	87	13.4	552	85.2	9	114	649
	381	5.3	381	5.3	172	2.4	954	13.3	5,948	83.1	258	3.6	7,160
	172	7.1	139	5.8	68	2.8	382	15.8	1,982	82.1	50	2.1	2,414
	209	4.4	242	5.1	104	2.2	572	12.1	3,966	83.6	208	4.4	4,746
	1	1.0	6	5.8	0	.0	7	6.7	97	93.3	0	.0	104
	1	1.1	6	6.3	0	.0	7	7.4	88	92.6	0	.0	95
	0	.0	0	.0	0	.0	0	.0	9	100.0	0	.0	9
	474	8.1	127	2.2	138	2.3	759	12.9	5,078	86.2	51	.9	5,888
	299	9.3	86	2.7	66	2.0	460	14.3	2,750	85.2	16	.5	3,226
	175	6.6	41	1.5	72	2.7	299	11.2	2,328	87.5	35	1.3	2,662
	30	1.9	4	.3	8	.5	43	2.7	1,519	95.8	23	1.5	1,585
	7	2.5	1	.4	1	.4	9	3.2	268	95.0	5	1.8	282
	23	1.8	3	.2	7	.5	34	2.6	1,251	96.0	18	1.4	1,303
	221	17.6	5	.4	29	2.3	267	21.3	985	78.5	3	.2	1,255
	107	13.1	4	.5	14	1.7	132	16.1	686	83.9	0	.0	818
	114	26.1	1	.2	15	3.4	135	30.9	299	68.4	3	.7	437
	0	.0	0	.0	0	.0	0	.0	139	100.0	0	.0	139
	0	.0	0	.0	0	.0	0	.0	0	.0	0	.0	0
	0	.0	0	.0	0	.0	0	.0	139	100.0	0	.0	139

	AMERICAN INDIAN ALASKAN NATIVE		BLACK NON-HISPANIC		ASIAN OR PACIFIC ISLANDER		HISPANIC		TOTAL MINORITY		WHITE NON-HISPANIC		NON-RESIDENT ALIEN		T
	NUMBER	%	NUMBER	%	NUMBER	%	NUMBER	%	NUMBER	%	NUMBER	%	NUMBER	%	N
NEW YORK		CONTINUED													
DOMINICAN C OF BLAUVELT															
NY TOTAL	0	.0	26	2.8	6	.6	22	2.3	54	5.7	886	94.2	1	.1	
NY FEMALE	0	.0	23	3.4	2	.3	14	2.1	39	5.7	643	94.3	0	.0	
NY MALE	0	.0	3	1.2	4	1.5	8	3.1	15	5.8	243	93.8	1	.4	
DOWLING COLLEGE															
NY TOTAL	2	.1	76	3.9	0	.0	44	2.3	122	6.3	1,809	92.8	19	1.0	
NY FEMALE	1	.1	33	4.0	0	.0	17	2.0	51	6.1	773	92.9	8	1.0	
NY MALE	1	.1	43	3.8	0	.0	27	2.4	71	6.4	1,036	92.7	11	1.0	
D'YOUVILLE COLLEGE															
NY TOTAL	12	.8	134	9.3	21	1.5	36	2.5	203	14.1	1,240	85.9	0	.0	
NY FEMALE	12	.9	126	9.8	17	1.3	34	2.6	189	14.7	1,101	85.3	0	.0	
NY MALE	0	.0	8	5.2	4	2.6	2	1.3	14	9.2	139	90.8	0	.0	
EDUC INST OHOLEI TORAH															
NY TOTAL	0	.0	0	.0	0	.0	0	.0	0	.0	88	100.0	0	.0	
NY FEMALE	0	.0	0	.0	0	.0	0	.0	0	.0	0	.0	0	.0	
NY MALE	0	.0	0	.0	0	.0	0	.0	0	.0	88	100.0	0	.0	
EISENHOWER COLLEGE															
NY TOTAL	0	.0	30	6.3	0	.0	7	1.5	37	7.8	432	90.9	6	1.3	
NY FEMALE	0	.0	10	4.8	0	.0	2	1.0	12	5.8	193	93.2	2	1.0	
NY MALE	0	.0	20	7.5	0	.0	5	1.9	25	9.3	239	89.2	4	1.5	
ELIZABETH SETON COLLEGE															
NY TOTAL	3	.3	200	17.1	1	.1	100	8.5	304	25.9	861	73.5	7	.6	
NY FEMALE	2	.2	143	16.9	1	.1	69	8.1	215	25.4	632	74.5	1	.1	
NY MALE	1	.3	57	17.6	0	.0	31	9.6	89	27.5	229	70.7	6	1.9	
ELMIRA COLLEGE															
NY TOTAL	5	.3	51	2.7	15	.8	11	.6	82	4.3	1,784	93.1	50	2.6	
NY FEMALE	2	.2	26	2.5	9	.8	6	.6	43	4.1	991	93.4	27	2.5	
NY MALE	3	.4	25	2.9	6	.7	5	.6	39	4.6	793	92.7	23	2.7	
FIVE TOWNS COLLEGE															
NY TOTAL	0	.0	37	11.3	1	.3	1	.3	39	11.9	286	87.5	2	.6	
NY FEMALE	0	.0	10	10.5	0	.0	0	.0	10	10.5	84	88.4	1	1.1	
NY MALE	0	.0	27	11.6	1	.4	1	.4	29	12.5	202	87.1	1	.4	
FORDHAM UNIVERSITY															
NY TOTAL	18	.2	939	12.1	83	1.1	681	8.7	1,721	22.1	5,943	76.3	127	1.6	
NY FEMALE	8	.2	602	15.8	47	1.2	395	10.4	1,052	27.7	2,675	70.4	72	1.9	
NY MALE	10	.3	337	8.4	36	.9	286	7.2	669	16.8	3,268	81.9	55	1.4	
FRIENDS WORLD COLLEGE															
NY TOTAL	0	.0	21	12.7	4	2.4	5	3.0	30	18.2	118	71.5	17	10.3	
NY FEMALE	0	.0	12	11.8	4	3.9	2	2.0	18	17.6	75	73.5	9	8.8	
NY MALE	0	.0	9	14.3	0	.0	3	4.8	12	19.0	43	68.3	8	12.7	
HADAR HATORAH RAB SEM															
NY TOTAL	0	.0	0	.0	0	.0	0	.0	0	.0	279	100.0	0	.0	
NY FEMALE	0	.0	0	.0	0	.0	0	.0	0	.0	94	100.0	0	.0	
NY MALE	0	.0	0	.0	0	.0	0	.0	0	.0	185	100.0	0	.0	
HAMILTON COLLEGE															
NY TOTAL	1	.1	36	2.3	15	1.0	13	.8	65	4.1	1,477	94.0	29	1.8	
NY FEMALE	1	.2	17	3.0	5	.9	5	.9	28	5.0	521	93.0	11	2.0	
NY MALE	0	.0	19	1.9	10	1.0	8	.8	37	3.7	956	94.6	18	1.8	
HARRIMAN COLLEGE															
NY TOTAL	12	3.2	71	19.0	6	1.6	54	14.5	143	38.3	230	61.7	0	.0	
NY FEMALE	6	3.1	40	20.9	3	1.6	32	16.8	81	42.4	110	57.6	0	.0	
NY MALE	6	3.3	31	17.0	3	1.6	22	12.1	62	34.1	120	65.9	0	.0	
HARTWICK COLLEGE															
NY TOTAL	2	.1	21	1.5	8	.6	4	.3	35	2.5	1,357	97.5	0	.0	
NY FEMALE	2	.3	8	1.0	1	.1	1	.1	12	1.5	772	98.5	0	.0	
NY MALE	0	.0	13	2.1	7	1.2	3	.5	23	3.8	585	96.2	0	.0	
HILBERT COLLEGE															
NY TOTAL	2	.3	25	4.3	0	.0	12	2.1	39	6.7	542	93.3	0	.0	
NY FEMALE	1	.3	18	4.5	0	.0	7	1.8	26	6.5	372	93.5	0	.0	
NY MALE	1	.5	7	3.8	0	.0	5	2.7	13	7.1	170	92.9	0	.0	
HOBART-WM SMITH COLLEGES															
NY TOTAL	0	.0	61	3.4	1	.1	21	1.2	83	4.6	1,704	94.9	8	.4	
NY FEMALE	0	.0	24	3.4	1	.1	5	.7	30	4.3	666	95.3	3	.4	
NY MALE	0	.0	37	3.4	0	.0	16	1.5	53	4.8	1,038	94.7	5	.5	
HOFSTRA UNIVERSITY															
NY TOTAL	10	.2	407	6.2	48	.7	140	2.1	605	9.3	5,857	89.6	78	1.2	
NY FEMALE	4	.1	235	8.2	22	.8	70	2.4	331	11.5	2,493	87.0	42	1.5	
NY MALE	6	.2	172	4.7	26	.7	70	1.9	274	7.5	3,364	91.6	36	1.0	
HOLY TRIVITY ORTHODOX SEM															
NY TOTAL	0	.0	0	.0	2	5.7	0	.0	2	5.7	24	68.6	9	25.7	
NY FEMALE	0	.0	0	.0	0	.0	0	.0	0	.0	0	.0	0	.0	
NY MALE	0	.0	0	.0	2	5.7	0	.0	2	5.7	24	68.6	9	25.7	
HOUGHTON COLLEGE															
NY TOTAL	4	.3	15	1.3	4	.3	3	.3	26	2.2	1,095	94.3	40	3.4	
NY FEMALE	1	.2	6	.9	1	.2	1	.2	9	1.4	615	96.4	14	2.2	
NY MALE	3	.6	9	1.7	3	.6	2	.4	17	3.3	480	91.8	26	5.0	
INST OF DESIGN AND CONSTR															
NY TOTAL	0	.0	35	22.4	3	1.9	28	17.9	66	42.3	84	53.8	6	3.8	
NY FEMALE	0	.0	3	21.4	1	7.1	4	28.6	8	57.1	6	42.9	0	.0	
NY MALE	0	.0	32	22.5	2	1.4	24	16.9	58	40.8	78	54.9	6	4.2	
INTERBORO INSTITUTE															
NY TOTAL	3	.8	198	50.8	5	1.3	89	22.8	295	75.6	91	23.3	4	1.0	
NY FEMALE	1	.4	156	61.9	3	1.2	66	26.2	226	89.7	25	9.9	1	.4	
NY MALE	2	1.4	42	30.4	2	1.4	23	16.7	69	50.0	66	47.8	3	2.2	
IONA COLLEGE															
NY TOTAL	0	.0	198	4.8	19	.5	167	4.0	384	9.3	3,726	90.3	15	.4	
NY FEMALE	0	.0	98	6.3	7	.4	57	3.6	162	10.3	1,401	89.5	3	.2	
NY MALE	0	.0	100	3.9	12	.5	110	4.3	222	8.7	2,325	90.9	12	.5	
ITHACA COLLEGE															
NY TOTAL	1	.0	84	1.8	1	.0	10	.2	96	2.1	4,490	97.4	26	.6	
NY FEMALE	0	.0	46	1.8	1	.0	6	.2	53	2.1	2,430	97.2	16	.6	
NY MALE	1	.0	38	1.8	0	.0	4	.2	43	2.0	2,060	97.5	10	.5	

BLACK NON-HISPANIC		ASIAN OR PACIFIC ISLANDER		HISPANIC		TOTAL MINORITY		WHITE NON-HISPANIC		NON-RESIDENT ALIEN		TOTAL
NUMBER	%	NUMBER	%	NUMBER	%	NUMBER	%	NUMBER	%	NUMBER	%	NUMBER
1	.4	0	.0	1	.4	3	1.1	268	98.9	0	.0	271
1	.4	0	.0	1	.4	3	1.2	255	98.8	0	.0	258
0	.0	0	.0	0	.0	0	.0	13	100.0	0	.0	13
0	.0	0	.0	0	.0	0	.0	107	100.0	0	.0	107
0	.0	0	.0	0	.0	0	.0	32	100.0	0	.0	32
0	.0	0	.0	0	.0	0	.0	75	100.0	0	.0	75
40	5.8	61	8.9	19	2.8	120	17.4	499	72.5	69	10.0	688
18	5.7	46	14.6	11	3.5	75	23.8	214	67.9	26	8.3	315
22	5.9	15	4.0	8	2.1	45	12.1	285	76.4	43	11.5	373
28	3.8	8	1.1	31	4.2	67	9.1	664	90.2	5	.7	736
28	3.8	8	1.1	31	4.2	67	9.1	664	90.2	5	.7	736
0	.0	0	.0	0	.0	0	.0	0	.0	0	.0	0
0	.0	0	.0	0	.0	0	.0	228	100.0	0	.0	228
0	.0	0	.0	0	.0	0	.0	0	.0	0	.0	0
0	.0	0	.0	0	.0	0	.0	228	100.0	0	.0	228
19	3.6	3	.6	12	2.3	36	6.9	485	93.1	0	.0	521
19	3.7	3	.6	12	2.3	36	7.0	481	93.0	0	.0	517
0	.0	0	.0	0	.0	0	.0	4	100.0	0	.0	4
55	6.6	8	1.0	28	3.3	91	10.8	747	89.0	1	.1	839
31	6.4	4	.8	18	3.7	53	11.0	431	89.0	0	.0	484
24	6.8	4	1.1	10	2.8	38	10.7	316	89.0	1	.3	355
22	9.0	1	.4	3	1.2	26	10.6	219	89.4	0	.0	245
17	7.2	1	.4	2	.9	20	8.5	215	91.5	0	.0	235
5	50.0	0	.0	1	10.0	6	60.0	4	40.0	0	.0	10
28	7.6	1	.3	38	10.3	67	18.2	301	81.8	0	.0	368
28	7.8	1	.3	38	10.6	67	18.8	290	81.2	0	.0	357
0	.0	0	.0	0	.0	0	.0	11	100.0	0	.0	11
26	1.4	6	.3	13	.7	47	2.6	1,769	97.2	4	.2	1,820
12	1.6	1	.1	2	.3	16	2.1	755	97.2	2	.3	773
14	1.3	5	.5	11	1.1	31	3.0	1,014	96.8	2	.2	1,047
7	7.4	0	.0	1	1.1	8	8.5	86	91.5	0	.0	94
7	8.0	0	.0	1	1.1	8	9.2	79	90.8	0	.0	87
0	.0	0	.0	0	.0	0	.0	7	100.0	0	.0	7
0	.0	0	.0	0	.0	0	.0	141	100.0	0	.0	141
0	.0	0	.0	0	.0	0	.0	141	100.0	0	.0	141
0	.0	0	.0	0	.0	0	.0	0	.0	0	.0	0
59	5.9	77	7.7	45	4.5	181	18.2	799	80.1	17	1.7	997
30	11.2	35	13.1	24	9.0	89	33.3	173	64.8	5	1.9	267
29	4.0	42	5.8	21	2.9	92	12.6	626	85.8	12	1.6	730
1,389	33.7	168	4.1	412	10.0	1,969	47.8	1,823	44.2	329	8.0	4,121
820	31.7	106	4.1	261	10.1	1,187	45.8	1,199	46.3	204	7.9	2,590
569	37.2	62	4.0	151	9.9	782	51.1	624	40.8	125	8.2	1,531
380	5.3	76	1.1	146	2.0	606	8.4	6,526	90.1	105	1.5	7,237
165	4.5	34	.9	61	1.7	261	7.1	3,359	91.7	44	1.2	3,664
215	6.0	42	1.2	85	2.4	345	9.7	3,167	88.6	61	1.7	3,573
96	6.7	9	.6	41	2.9	155	10.9	1,272	89.1	0	.0	1,427
40	6.1	0	.0	16	2.4	59	9.0	598	91.0	0	.0	657
56	7.3	9	1.2	25	3.2	96	12.5	674	87.5	0	.0	770
0	.0	0	.0	0	.0	0	.0	203	100.0	0	.0	203
0	.0	0	.0	0	.0	0	.0	0	.0	0	.0	0
0	.0	0	.0	0	.0	0	.0	203	100.0	0	.0	203
170	4.4	56	1.4	214	5.5	440	11.4	3,368	86.9	66	1.7	3,874
55	5.8	12	1.3	57	6.0	124	13.1	816	85.9	10	1.1	950
115	3.9	44	1.5	157	5.4	316	10.8	2,552	87.3	56	1.9	2,924
17	4.1	10	2.4	14	3.4	41	9.9	349	84.3	24	5.8	414
7	3.6	8	4.1	4	2.0	19	9.7	164	83.7	13	6.6	196
10	4.6	2	.9	10	4.6	22	10.1	185	84.9	11	5.0	218
44	5.0	8	.9	37	4.2	89	10.2	762	87.0	25	2.9	876
28	4.2	6	.9	27	4.0	61	9.1	584	87.3	24	3.6	669
16	7.7	2	1.0	10	4.8	28	13.5	178	86.0	1	.5	207
4	2.0	3	1.5	1	.5	8	4.1	161	82.1	27	13.8	196
2	2.2	2	2.2	1	1.1	5	5.4	72	78.3	15	16.3	92
2	1.9	1	1.0	0	.0	3	2.9	89	85.6	12	11.5	104
15	2.8	2	.4	1	.2	18	3.4	509	96.6	0	.0	527
14	2.9	2	.4	1	.2	17	3.5	474	96.5	0	.0	491
1	2.8	0	.0	0	.0	1	2.8	35	97.2	0	.0	36
15	3.8	5	1.3	0	.0	20	5.0	376	94.2	3	.8	399
8	2.3	2	.6	0	.0	10	2.9	329	96.2	3	.9	342
7	12.3	3	5.3	0	.0	10	17.5	47	82.5	0	.0	57

TABLE 1 - TOTAL UNDERGRADUATE ENROLLMENT IN INSTITUTIONS OF HIGHER EDUCATION BY RACE, ETHNICITY AND SEX:
         INSTITUTION, STATE AND NATION, 1978

	AMERICAN INDIAN ALASKAN NATIVE		BLACK NON-HISPANIC		ASIAN OR PACIFIC ISLANDER		HISPANIC		TOTAL MINORITY		WHITE NON-HISPANIC		NON-RESIDENT ALIEN	
	NUMBER	%	NUMBER	%	NUMBER	%	NUMBER	%	NUMBER	%	NUMBER	%	NUMBER	%
NEW YORK	CONTINUED													
MARIST COLLEGE														
NY TOTAL	2	.1	50	2.6	8	.4	37	1.9	97	5.0	1,844	95.0	0	.0
NY FEMALE	1	.1	21	2.6	4	.5	15	1.8	41	5.0	776	95.0	0	.0
NY MALE	1	.1	29	2.6	4	.4	22	2.0	56	5.0	1,068	95.0	0	.0
MARYMOUNT COLLEGE														
NY TOTAL	0	.0	74	6.9	7	.7	63	5.9	144	13.4	890	82.8	41	3.8
NY FEMALE	0	.0	70	6.9	5	.5	59	5.8	134	13.1	846	82.9	41	4.0
NY MALE	0	.0	4	7.4	2	3.7	4	7.4	10	18.5	44	81.5	0	.0
MARYMOUNT MANHATTAN C														
NY TOTAL	0	.0	334	17.1	59	3.0	230	11.7	623	31.8	1,335	68.2	0	.0
NY FEMALE	0	.0	320	17.0	51	2.7	227	12.1	598	31.9	1,279	68.1	0	.0
NY MALE	0	.0	14	17.3	8	9.9	3	3.7	25	30.9	56	69.1	0	.0
MATER DEI COLLEGE														
NY TOTAL	66	29.6	1	.4	0	.0	1	.4	68	30.5	155	69.5	0	.0
NY FEMALE	53	32.9	1	.6	0	.0	1	.6	55	34.2	106	65.8	0	.0
NY MALE	13	21.0	0	.0	0	.0	0	.0	13	21.0	49	79.0	0	.0
MEDAILLE COLLEGE														
NY TOTAL	10	1.7	199	33.7	0	.0	9	1.5	218	36.9	371	62.9	1	.2
NY FEMALE	7	1.8	132	34.5	0	.0	7	1.8	146	38.1	237	61.9	0	.0
NY MALE	3	1.4	67	32.4	0	.0	2	1.0	72	34.8	134	64.7	1	.5
MERCY COLLEGE														
NY TOTAL	51	1.2	652	15.3	55	1.3	640	15.0	1,398	32.7	2,871	67.3	0	.0
NY FEMALE	34	1.4	360	15.2	28	1.2	321	13.6	743	31.5	1,618	68.5	0	.0
NY MALE	17	.9	292	15.3	27	1.4	319	16.7	655	34.3	1,253	65.7	0	.0
MESIVTA ESTN PKWY RAB SEM														
NY TOTAL	0	.0	0	.0	0	.0	0	.0	0	.0	0	.0	0	.0
NY FEMALE	0	.0	0	.0	0	.0	0	.0	0	.0	0	.0	0	.0
NY MALE	0	.0	0	.0	0	.0	0	.0	0	.0	0	.0	0	.0
MES TORAH VODAATH SEM														
NY TOTAL	0	.0	0	.0	0	.0	0	.0	0	.0	489	100.0	0	.0
NY FEMALE	0	.0	0	.0	0	.0	0	.0	0	.0	0	.0	0	.0
NY MALE	0	.0	0	.0	0	.0	0	.0	0	.0	489	100.0	0	.0
MIRRER YESHIVA CEN INST														
NY TOTAL	0	.0	0	.0	0	.0	0	.0	0	.0	310	100.0	0	.0
NY FEMALE	0	.0	0	.0	0	.0	0	.0	0	.0	0	.0	0	.0
NY MALE	0	.0	0	.0	0	.0	0	.0	0	.0	310	100.0	0	.0
MOLLOY COLLEGE														
NY TOTAL	4	.3	63	4.6	1	.1	32	2.3	100	7.3	1,274	92.6	2	.1
NY FEMALE	4	.3	62	4.6	1	.1	30	2.2	97	7.2	1,255	92.7	2	.1
NY MALE	1	4.5	1	4.5	0	.0	2	9.1	3	13.6	19	86.4	0	.0
MONROE BUSINESS INSTITUTE														
NY TOTAL	0	.0	404	40.8	0	.0	396	40.0	800	80.8	178	18.0	12	1.2
NY FEMALE	0	.0	221	40.6	0	.0	218	40.0	439	80.6	98	18.0	8	1.5
NY MALE	0	.0	183	41.1	0	.0	178	40.0	361	81.1	80	18.0	4	.9
MOUNT SAINT MARY COLLEGE														
NY TOTAL	0	.0	76	8.5	0	.0	28	3.1	104	11.6	793	88.3	1	.1
NY FEMALE	0	.0	66	8.2	0	.0	22	2.7	88	11.0	713	88.9	1	.1
NY MALE	0	.0	10	10.4	0	.0	6	6.3	16	16.7	80	83.3	0	.0
NAZARETH C OF ROCHESTER														
NY TOTAL	5	.4	70	5.0	3	.2	14	1.0	92	6.6	1,291	92.9	6	.4
NY FEMALE	4	.3	49	4.2	3	.3	14	1.2	70	6.0	1,098	93.6	5	.4
NY MALE	1	.5	21	9.7	0	.0	0	.0	22	10.2	193	89.4	1	.5
NEW SCH FOR SOC RESEARCH														
NY TOTAL	0	.0	21	6.3	2	.6	4	1.2	27	8.1	305	91.9	0	.0
NY FEMALE	0	.0	9	5.5	0	.0	3	1.8	12	7.3	153	92.7	0	.0
NY MALE	0	.0	12	7.2	2	1.2	1	.6	15	9.0	152	91.0	0	.0
NY INST TECHN MAIN CAMPUS														
NY TOTAL	9	.1	312	3.7	39	.5	106	1.3	466	5.6	7,662	92.0	202	2.
NY FEMALE	3	.1	114	5.0	8	.3	30	1.3	155	6.7	2,114	91.8	34	1.
NY MALE	6	.1	198	3.3	31	.5	76	1.3	311	5.2	5,548	92.1	168	2.8
NY INST TECHN NY CTY CAM														
NY TOTAL	0	.0	212	8.8	62	2.6	100	4.1	374	15.5	1,482	61.4	558	23.1
NY FEMALE	0	.0	63	11.6	11	2.0	22	4.0	96	17.6	367	67.3	82	15.0
NY MALE	0	.0	149	8.0	51	2.7	78	4.2	278	14.9	1,115	59.7	476	25.5
NY SCH OF INTERIOR DESIGN														
NY TOTAL	0	.0	4	3.3	5	4.2	3	2.5	12	10.0	98	81.7	10	8.3
NY FEMALE	0	.0	3	3.2	5	5.3	2	2.1	10	10.5	79	83.2	6	6.3
NY MALE	0	.0	1	4.0	0	.0	1	4.0	2	8.0	19	76.0	4	16.0
NEW YORK UNIVERSITY														
NY TOTAL	24	.3	799	8.9	496	5.5	481	5.3	1,800	20.0	6,869	76.3	331	3.7
NY FEMALE	12	.2	512	10.5	260	5.3	301	6.2	1,085	22.3	3,661	75.2	122	2.5
NY MALE	12	.3	287	6.9	236	5.7	180	4.4	715	17.3	3,208	77.6	209	5.1
NIAGARA UNIVERSITY														
NY TOTAL	17	.5	147	4.6	8	.2	24	.7	196	6.1	3,008	93.9	0	.0
NY FEMALE	9	.5	71	4.3	5	.3	8	.5	93	5.6	1,555	94.4	0	.0
NY MALE	8	.5	76	4.9	3	.2	16	1.0	103	6.6	1,453	93.4	0	.0
NYACK COLLEGE														
NY TOTAL	1	.2	28	4.6	12	2.0	19	3.1	60	9.8	543	88.9	8	1.3
NY FEMALE	1	.3	12	3.7	5	1.5	11	3.4	29	9.0	290	89.8	4	1.2
NY MALE	0	.0	16	5.6	7	2.4	8	2.8	31	10.8	253	87.8	4	1.4
OHR HAMEIP THEOL SEM														
NY TOTAL	0	.0	0	.0	0	.0	0	.0	0	.0	45	100.0	0	.0
NY FEMALE	0	.0	0	.0	0	.0	0	.0	0	.0	0	.0	0	.0
NY MALE	0	.0	0	.0	0	.0	0	.0	0	.0	45	100.0	0	.0
OLEAN BUSINESS INSTITUTE														
NY TOTAL	1	.5	1	.5	0	.0	0	.0	2	1.1	180	98.4	1	.5
NY FEMALE	0	.0	1	.6	0	.0	0	.0	1	.6	158	98.8	1	.6
NY MALE	1	4.3	0	.0	0	.0	0	.0	1	4.3	22	95.7	0	.0
PACE U C OF WHITE PLAINS														
NY TOTAL	5	.9	73	12.5	13	2.2	27	4.6	118	20.3	464	79.7	0	.0
NY FEMALE	4	1.1	59	15.8	6	1.6	20	5.3	89	23.8	285	76.2	0	.0
NY MALE	1	.5	14	6.7	7	3.4	7	3.4	29	13.9	179	86.1	0	.0

	BLACK NON-HISPANIC		ASIAN OR PACIFIC ISLANDER		HISPANIC		TOTAL MINORITY		WHITE NON-HISPANIC		NON-RESIDENT ALIEN		TOTAL
	NUMBER	%	NUMBER	%	NUMBER	%	NUMBER	%	NUMBER	%	NUMBER	%	NUMBER
INUED													
	1,010	19.5	247	4.8	467	9 0	1,741	33.7	3,318	64.1	114	2.2	5,173
	665	25.0	124	4.7	273	10 2	1,072	40.2	1,549	58.1	43	1.6	2,664
	345	13.8	123	4.9	194	7?7	669	26.7	1,769	70.5	71	2.8	2,509
	151	4.8	24	.8	52	1 7	239	7.6	2,881	91.7	23	.7	3,143
	116	6.4	12	.7	29	1 6	164	9.1	1,628	90.4	8	.4	1,800
	35	2.6	12	.9	23	117	75	5.6	1,253	93.3	15	1.1	1,343
	96	5.6	71	4.2	65	3 8	233	13.6	1,426	83.4	50	2	1,709
	48	4.2	53	4.7	23	2 0	125	11.0	977	86.1	33	2 0	1,135
	48	8.4	18	3.1	42	7?3	108	18.8	449	78.2	17	3?0	574
	1	.1	0	.0	1	.1	2	.2	1,024	98.0	19	1	1,045
	0	.0	0	.0	0	.0	0	.0	204	98.1	4	1 0	208
	1	.1	0	.0	1	.1	2	.2	820	98.0	15	11?	837
	213	8.9	428	17.9	166	7.0	817	34.2	1,477	61.9	93	3	2,387
	11	5.6	48	24.2	8	4.0	70	35.4	120	60.6	8	4 0	198
	202	9.2	380	17.4	158	7.2	747	34.1	1,357	62.0	85	3?0	2,189
	18	4.2	0	.0	0	.0	20	4.7	405	95.1	1	2	426
	12	3.3	0	.0	0	.0	13	3.6	351	96.2	1	3	365
	6	9.8	0	.0	0	.0	7	11.5	54	88.5	0	?0	61
	562	17.8	134	4.2	192	1	888	28.2	2,087	66.2	178		3,153
	300	23.7	60	4.7	61	6 8	421	33.2	773	61.0	74		1,268
	262	13.9	74	3.9	131	?19	467	24.8	1,314	69.7	104	51?	1,885
	0	.0	0	.0		.0	0	.0	60	98.4	1	1	61
	0	.0	0	.0		.0	0	.0	0	.0	0	?	0
	0	.0	0	.0	0	.0	0	.0	60	98.4	1	11?	61
	0	.0	0	.0		.0	0	.0	159	100.0		?0	159
	0	.0	0	.0		.0	0	.0	0	.0	0	?0	0
	0	.0	0	.0	0	.0	0	.0	159	100.0	0	.0	159
	0	.0	0	.0		.0	0	.0	39	100.0		.0	39
	0	.0	0	.0		.0	0	.0	0	.0	0	.0	0
	0	.0	0	.0	0	.0	0	.0	39	100.0	0	.0	39
	0	.0	0	.0		.0	0	.0	89	100.0		.0	89
	0	.0	0	.0		.0	0	.0	0	.0	0	.0	0
	0	.0	0	.0	0	.0	0	.0	89	100.0	0	.0	89
	0	.0	0	.0		.0	0	.0	57	100.0		.0	57
	0	.0	0	.0		.0	0	.0	0	.0	0	.0	0
	0	.0	0	.0	0	.0	0	.0	57	100.0	0	.0	57
	0	.0	0	.0		.0	0	.0	81	100.0		.0	81
	0	.0	0	.0		.0	0	.0	0	.0	0	.0	0
	0	.0	0	.0	0	.0	0	.0	81	100.0	0	.0	81
	0	.0	0	.0		.0	0	.0	160	100.0		.0	160
	0	.0	0	.0		.0	0	.0	0	.0	0	.0	0
	0	.0	0	.0	0	.0	0	.0	160	100.0	0	.0	160
	0	.0	0	.0		.0	0	.0	111	100.0		.0	111
	0	.0	0	.0		.0	0	.0	0	.0	0	.0	0
	0	.0	0	.0	0	.0	0	.0	111	100.0	0	.0	111
	0	.0	0	.0		.0	0	.0	134	100.0		.0	134
	0	.0	0	.0		.0	0	.0	0	.0	0	.0	0
	0	.0	0	.0	0	.0	0	.0	134	100.0	0	.0	134
	0	.0	0	.0		.0	0	.0	65	100.0		.0	65
	0	.0	0	.0		.0	0	.0	0	.0	0	.0	0
	0	.0	0	.0	0	.0	0	.3	65	100.0	0	.0	65
	0	.0	0	.0		.0	0	.0	77	100.0		.0	77
	0	.0	0	.0		.0	0	.0	0	.0	0	.0	0
	0	.0	0	.0	0	.0	0	.0	77	100.0	0	.0	77
	0	.0	0	.0		.0	0	.0	414	100.0		.0	414
	0	.0	0	.0		.0	0	.0	0	.0	0	?0	0
	0	.0	0	.0	0	.0	0	.0	414	100.0	0	.0	414
	99	2.4	89	2.1	4	1.0	231	5.6	3,802	91.5	122	2.9	4,155
	30	5.5	17	3.1		.7	51	9.3	492	89.8	5	.9	548
	69	1.9	72	2.0	3?	1.1	180	5.0	3,310	91.8	117	3.2	3,607
	0	.0	0	.0		.0	0	.0	170	96.6	6	3.4	176
	0	.0	0	.0		.0	0	.0	170	96.6	6	3.4	176
	0	.0	0	.0	0	.0	0	.0	0	.0	0	.0	0
	10	1.7	1	.2	15	2.5	32	5.3	555	91.9	17	2.8	604
	7	1.7	1	.2	10	2.4	24	5.7	394	92.9	6	1.4	424
	3	1.7	1	.2	5	2.8	8	4.4	161	89.4	11	6.1	180
	13	10.3	1	.8		.0	15	11.9	111	88.1	0	.0	126
	13	11.1	1	.9		.0	15	12.8	102	87.2	0	.0	117
	0	.0	0	.0	0	.0	0	.0	9	100.0	0	.0	9

TABLE 1 - TOTAL UNDERGRADUATE ENROLLMENT IN INSTITUTIONS OF HIGHER EDUCATION BY RACE, ETHNICITY AND SEX: INSTITUTION, STATE AND NATION, 1978

	AMERICAN INDIAN ALASKAN NATIVE		BLACK NON-HISPANIC		ASIAN OR PACIFIC ISLANDER		HISPANIC		TOTAL MINORITY		WHITE NON-HISPANIC		NON-RESIDENT ALIEN	
	NUMBER	%	NUMBER	%	NUMBER	%	NUMBER	%	NUMBER	%	NUMBER	%	NUMBER	%
NEW YORK CONTINUED														
ROCHESTER INST TECHNOLOGY														
NY TOTAL	27	.2	424	3.8	89	.8	73	.7	613	5.5	10,328	93.0	162	1.5
NY FEMALE	7	.2	153	4.6	23	.7	15	.4	198	5.9	3,095	92.8	42	1.3
NY MALE	20	.3	271	3.5	66	.8	58	.7	415	5.3	7,233	93.1	120	1.5
RUSSELL SAGE C MAIN CAM														
NY TOTAL	1	.1	36	2.0	2	.1	23	1.3	62	3.4	1,748	96.1	8	.4
NY FEMALE	1	.1	33	2.0	2	.1	23	1.4	59	3.5	1,602	96.0	8	.5
NY MALE	0	.0	3	2.0	0	.0	0	.0	3	2.0	146	98.0	0	.0
RUSSELL SAGE JC OF ALBANY														
NY TOTAL	2	.2	90	9.1	1	.1	10	1.0	103	10.4	865	87.6	19	1.9
NY FEMALE	0	.0	43	6.7	0	.0	3	.5	46	7.2	590	91.8	7	1.1
NY MALE	2	.6	47	13.7	1	.3	7	2.0	57	16.6	275	79.9	12	3.5
SAINT BONAVENTURE U														
NY TOTAL	4	.2	6	.3	2	.1	2	.1	14	.7	2,122	99.2	3	.1
NY FEMALE	2	.2	1	.1	0	.0	0	.0	3	.3	995	99.4	3	.3
NY MALE	2	.2	5	.4	2	.2	2	.2	11	1.0	1,127	99.0	0	.0
SAINT FRANCIS COLLEGE														
NY TOTAL	13	.4	481	14.4	108	3.2	152	4.5	754	22.6	2,530	75.7	57	1.7
NY FEMALE	3	.2	304	18.6	87	5.3	71	4.4	465	28.5	1,146	70.3	20	1.2
NY, MALE	10	.6	177	10.4	21	1.2	81	4.7	289	16.9	1,384	80.9	37	2.2
SAINT JOHN FISHER COLLEGE														
NY TOTAL	2	.1	31	1.9	2	.1	11	.7	46	2.8	1,602	96.9	5	.3
NY FEMALE	0	.0	19	2.9	1	.2	9	1.4	29	4.4	625	95.6	0	.0
NY MALE	2	.2	12	1.2	1	.1	2	.2	17	1.7	977	97.8	5	.5
SAINT JOHN'S UNIVERSITY														
NY TOTAL	34	.3	410	3.8	116	1.1	222	2.1	782	7.3	9,318	87.3	569	5.3
NY FEMALE	11	.3	211	4.9	54	1.3	106	2.5	382	8.9	3,657	84.9	268	6.2
NY MALE	23	.4	199	3.1	62	1.0	116	1.8	400	6.3	5,661	89.0	301	4.7
SNT JOSEPH'S C MAIN CAM														
NY TOTAL	0	.0	795	52.1	33	2.2	33	2.2	861	56.4	655	42.9	11	.7
NY FEMALE	0	.0	721	52.2	32	2.3	28	2.0	781	56.6	598	43.3	2	.1
NY MALE	0	.0	74	50.7	1	.7	5	3.4	80	54.8	57	39.0	9	6.2
SNT JOSEPHS C SUFFOLK CAM														
NY TOTAL	0	.0	9	2.4	0	.0	8	2.1	17	4.5	356	95.2	1	.3
NY FEMALE	0	.0	5	1.7	0	.0	5	1.7	10	3.4	287	96.3	1	.3
NY MALE	0	.0	4	5.3	0	.0	3	3.9	7	9.2	69	90.8	0	.0
SAINT LAWRENCE UNIVERSITY														
NY TOTAL	0	.0	45	2.0	0	.0	0	.0	45	2.0	2,207	96.5	36	1.6
NY FEMALE	0	.0	18	1.7	0	.0	0	.0	18	1.7	1,052	97.2	12	1.1
NY MALE	0	.0	27	2.2	0	.0	0	.0	27	2.2	1,155	95.8	24	2.0
SAINT THOMAS AQUINAS C														
NY TOTAL	1	.1	44	4.6	1	.1	90	9.4	136	14.2	824	85.7	1	.1
NY FEMALE	1	.2	19	3.3	1	.2	69	12.0	90	15.6	487	84.4	0	.0
NY MALE	0	.0	25	6.5	0	.0	21	5.5	46	12.0	337	87.8	1	.3
SARAH LAWRENCE COLLEGE														
NY TOTAL	0	.0	23	2.7	9	1.1	6	.7	38	4.5	793	93.1	21	2.5
NY FEMALE	0	.0	19	2.8	8	1.2	4	.6	31	4.6	625	92.6	19	2.8
NY MALE	0	.0	4	2.3	1	.6	2	1.1	7	4.0	168	94.9	2	1.1
SARA SCHENIRER TCHRS SEM														
NY TOTAL	0	.0	0	.0	0	.0	0	.0	0	.0	124	100.0	0	.0
NY FEMALE	0	.0	0	.0	0	.0	0	.0	0	.0	124	100.0	0	.0
NY MALE	0	.0	0	.0	0	.0	0	.0	0	.0	0	.0	0	.0
SCHOOL OF VISUAL ARTS														
NY TOTAL	0	.0	170	8.3	39	1.9	86	4.2	295	14.3	1,729	84.0	35	1.7
NY FEMALE	0	.0	49	5.1	19	2.0	38	4.0	106	11.1	838	87.6	13	1.4
NY MALE	0	.0	121	11.0	20	1.8	48	4.4	189	17.2	891	80.9	22	2.0
SH'OR YOSHUV RAB COLLEGE														
NY TOTAL	0	.0	0	.0	0	.0	0	.0	0	.0	70	100.0	0	.0
NY FEMALE	0	.0	0	.0	0	.0	0	.0	0	.0	0	.0	0	.0
NY MALE	0	.0	0	.0	0	.0	0	.0	0	.0	70	100.0	0	.0
SIENA COLLEGE														
NY TOTAL	0	.0	55	2.2	14	.6	26	1.0	95	3.7	2,437	96.2	2	.1
NY FEMALE	0	.0	20	2.0	8	.8	10	1.0	38	3.9	939	96.1	0	.0
NY MALE	0	.0	35	2.2	6	.4	16	1.0	57	3.7	1,498	96.2	2	.1
SKIDMORE COLLEGE														
NY TOTAL	0	.0	119	5.2	6	.3	18	.8	143	6.3	2,141	93.7	0	.0
NY FEMALE	0	.0	57	3.2	2	.1	9	.5	68	3.8	1,740	96.2	0	.0
NY MALE	0	.0	62	13.0	4	.8	9	1.9	75	15.8	401	84.2	0	.0
SUNY AT ALBANY														
NY TOTAL	47	.5	367	3.8	126	1.3	221	2.3	761	7.9	8,862	91.7	46	.5
NY FEMALE	12	.3	197	4.3	63	1.4	103	2.2	375	8.1	4,231	91.5	20	.4
NY MALE	35	.7	170	3.4	63	1.2	118	2.3	386	7.7	4,631	91.8	26	.5
SUNY AT BINGHAMTON														
NY TOTAL	12	.2	240	3.3	53	.7	126	1.7	431	5.9	6,821	93.2	66	.9
NY FEMALE	9	.2	140	3.7	20	.5	73	1.9	242	6.3	3,563	93.0	27	.7
NY MALE	3	.1	100	2.9	33	.9	53	1.5	189	5.4	3,258	93.5	39	1.1
SUNY AT BUFFALO MAIN CAM														
NY TOTAL	48	.3	1,041	7.2	246	1.7	157	1.1	1,492	10.4	12,516	86.9	398	2.8
NY FEMALE	24	.4	550	9.8	74	1.3	64	1.1	712	12.6	4,817	85.4	111	2.0
NY MALE	24	.3	491	5.6	172	2.0	93	1.1	780	8.9	7,699	87.8	287	3.3
SUNY HEALTH SCI CTR BFLO														
NY TOTAL	0	.0	37	3.3	15	1.3	8	.7	60	5.4	1,033	92.6	23	2.1
NY FEMALE	0	.0	29	3.8	8	1.0	5	.7	42	5.5	715	93.1	11	1.4
NY MALE	0	.0	8	2.3	7	2.0	3	.9	18	5.2	318	91.4	12	3.4
SUNY AT STONY BK MAIN CAM														
NY TOTAL	28	.3	472	4.8	525	5.4	260	2.7	1,285	13.2	8,282	85.0	178	1.8
NY FEMALE	13	.3	290	6.8	215	5.0	125	2.9	643	15.0	3,598	84.1	37	.9
NY MALE	15	.3	182	3.3	310	5.7	135	2.5	642	11.7	4,684	85.7	141	2.6
SUNY HLTH SCI CTR STNY BK														
NY TOTAL	0	.0	37	7.3	3	.6	17	3.4	57	11.3	444	87.9	4	.8
NY FEMALE	0	.0	33	8.7	3	.8	14	3.7	50	13.1	328	86.1	3	.8
NY MALE	0	.0	4	3.2	0	.0	3	2.4	7	5.6	116	93.5	1	.8

UATE ENROLLMENT IN INSTITUTIONS OF HIGHER EDUCATION BY RACE, ETHNICITY AND SEX:
ATE AND NATION, 1978

N E	BLACK NON-HISPANIC		ASIAN OR PACIFIC ISLANDER		HISPANIC		TOTAL MINORITY		WHITE NON-HISPANIC		NON-RESIDENT ALIEN		TOTAL
	NUMBER	%	NUMBER	%	NUMBER	%	NUMBER	%	NUMBER	%	NUMBER	%	NUMBER
INUED													
	22	5.0	14	3.2	14	3.2	51	11.5	390	88.0	2	.5	443
	17	4.6	10	2.7	13	3.5	41	11.0	330	88.5	2	.5	373
	5	7.1	4	5.7	1	1.4	10	14.3	60	85.7	0	.0	70
	3	1.2	2	.8	4	1.6	11	4.3	245	95.3	1	.4	257
	2	1.1	1	.6	3	1.7	7	3.9	171	96.1	0	.0	178
	1	1.3	1	1.3	1	1.3	4	5.1	74	93.7	1	1.3	79
	510	6.8	53	.7	87	1.2	688	9.1	6,795	90.2	54	.7	7,537
	279	7.3	22	.6	42	1.1	354	9.2	3,481	90.5	12	.3	3,847
	231	6.3	31	.8	45	1.2	334	9.1	3,314	89.8	42	1.1	3,690
	824	9.5	29	.3	93	1.1	984	11.3	7,636	87.6	95	1.1	8,715
	546	11.4	9	.2	49	1.0	632	13.2	4,122	86.3	21	.4	4,775
	278	7.1	20	.5	44	1.1	352	8.9	3,514	89.2	74	1.9	3,940
	90	1.8	28	.6	40	.8	165	3.2	4,897	96.5	15	.3	5,077
	51	1.7	14	.5	19	.6	90	2.9	2,965	96.8	7	.2	3,062
	39	1.9	14	.7	21	1.0	75	3.7	1,932	95.9	8	.4	2,015
	134	3.2	47	1.1	53	1.3	255	6.0	3,957	93.6	15	.4	4,227
	63	2.9	18	.8	15	.7	107	5.0	2,040	94.8	6	.3	2,153
	71	3.4	29	1.4	38	1.8	148	7.1	1,917	92.4	9	.4	2,074
	54	1.2	7	.2	29	.6	91	2.0	4,462	97.7	12	.3	4,565
	32	1.1	3	.1	17	.6	53	1.8	2,928	98.2	2	.1	2,983
	22	1.4	4	.3	12	.8	38	2.4	1,534	97.0	10	.6	1,582
	368	9.1	91	2.2	120	3.0	763	18.8	3,021	74.6	264	6.5	4,048
	217	9.5	52	2.3	64	2.8	431	19.0	1,721	75.7	122	5.4	2,274
	151	8.5	39	2.2	56	3.2	332	18.7	1,300	73.3	142	8.0	1,774
	851	37.7	16	.7	268	11.9	1,139	50.4	1,097	48.6	23	1.0	2,259
	516	37.3	3	.2	162	11.7	684	49.5	690	49.9	9	.7	1,383
	335	38.2	13	1.5	106	12.1	455	51.9	407	46.5	14	1.6	876
	260	4.7	9	.2	54	1.0	327	5.9	5,186	93.6	28	.5	5,541
	128	3.8	3	.1	26	.8	159	4.8	3,159	95.0	8	.2	3,326
	132	6.0	6	.3	28	1.3	168	7.6	2,027	91.5	20	.9	2,215
	157	2.3	30	.4	48	.7	241	3.6	6,393	95.6	50	.7	6,684
	80	2.6	9	.3	14	.5	108	3.5	2,917	96.0	12	.4	3,037
	77	2.1	21	.6	34	.9	133	3.6	3,476	95.3	38	1.0	3,647
	75	1.4	22	.4	42	.8	176	3.4	4,935	95.2	72	1.4	5,183
	32	1.1	12	.4	24	.8	90	3.0	2,847	96.3	18	.6	2,955
	43	1.9	10	.4	18	.8	86	3.9	2,088	93.7	54	2.4	2,228
	39	1.1	11	.3	9	.2	74	2.0	3,583	97.8	5	.1	3,662
	4	.2	5	.3	1	.1	18	.9	1,950	98.9	3	.2	1,971
	35	2.1	6	.4	8	.5	56	3.3	1,633	96.6	2	.1	1,691
	183	9.9	1	.1	22	1.2	206	11.2	1,606	87.0	35	1.9	1,847
	123	11.4	1	.1	12	1.1	136	12.6	930	86.0	16	1.5	1,082
	60	7.8	0	.0	10	1.3	70	9.2	676	88.4	19	2.5	765
	32	1.7	2	.1	8	.4	43	2.2	1,869	97.8	0	.0	1,912
	14	1.3	1	.1	5	.5	20	1.8	1,066	98.2	0	.0	1,086
	18	2.2	1	.1	3	.4	23	2.8	803	97.2	0	.0	826
	193	7.0	12	.4	43	1.6	254	9.3	2,474	90.3	11	.4	2,739
	110	7.0	8	.5	25	1.6	145	9.2	1,426	90.5	4	.3	1,575
	83	7.1	4	.3	18	1.5	109	9.4	1,048	90.0	7	.6	1,164
	6	.4	13	1.0	5	.4	25	1.8	1,320	96.6	22	1.6	1,367
	0	.0	4	1.2	2	.6	6	1.8	320	97.9	1	.3	327
	6	.6	9	.9	3	.3	19	1.8	1,000	96.2	21	2.0	1,040
	11	1.1	1	.1	12	1.2	24	2.5	842	86.9	103	10.6	969
	1	2.7	0	.0	1	2.7	2	5.4	34	91.9	1	2.7	37
	10	1.1	1	.1	11	1.2	22	2.4	808	86.7	102	10.9	932
	14	.4	3	.1	7	.2	74	1.9	3,897	97.9	9	.2	3,980
	7	.4	1	.1	4	.2	39	2.3	1,657	97.6	1	.1	1,697
	7	.3	2	.1	3	.1	35	1.5	2,240	98.1	8	.4	2,283
	38	1.6	4	.2	15	.6	73	3.1	2,253	96.4	10	.4	2,336
	11	1.1	0	.0	3	.3	26	2.7	939	97.0	3	.3	968
	27	2.0	4	.3	12	.9	47	3.4	1,314	96.1	7	.5	1,368
	40	1.6	3	.1	11	.4	55	2.2	2,479	97.8	0	.0	2,534
	28	2.0	2	.1	6	.4	36	2.6	1,373	97.4	0	.0	1,409
	12	1.1	1	.1	5	.4	19	1.7	1,106	98.3	0	.0	1,125
	43	1.7	4	.2	19	.8	72	2.9	2,384	96.5	15	.6	2,471
	16	1.5	2	.2	4	.4	23	2.2	1,023	97.3	5	.5	1,051
	27	1.9	2	.1	15	1.1	49	3.5	1,361	95.8	10	.7	1,420
	141	1.9	19	.3	72	1.0	237	3.2	7,245	96.8	0	.0	7,482
	66	1.9	7	.2	29	.8	103	3.0	3,388	97.0	0	.0	3,491
	75	1.9	12	.3	43	1.1	134	3.4	3,857	96.6	0	.0	3,991

TABLE 1 - TOTAL UNDERGRADUATE ENROLLMENT IN INSTITUTIONS OF HIGHER EDUCATION BY RACE, ETHNICITY AND SEX: INSTITUTION, STATE AND NATION, 1978

	AMERICAN INDIAN ALASKAN NATIVE		BLACK NON-HISPANIC		ASIAN OR PACIFIC ISLANDER		HISPANIC		TOTAL MINORITY		WHITE NON-HISPANIC		NON-RESIDENT ALIEN	
	NUMBER	%	NUMBER	%	NUMBER	%	NUMBER	%	NUMBER	%	NUMBER	%	NUMBER	%
NEW YORK	CONTINUED													
SUNY AGRL TECH C MORRISVL														
NY TOTAL	18	.7	26	1.0	1	.0	19	.7	64	2.5	2,492	97.4	3	.1
NY FEMALE	7	.6	9	.8	1	.1	6	.6	23	2.1	1,059	97.8	1	.1
NY MALE	11	.7	17	1.2	0	.0	13	.9	41	2.8	1,433	97.1	2	.1
ADIRONDACK CMTY COLLEGE														
NY TOTAL	2	.1	22	1.0	4	.2	7	.3	35	1.6	2,174	98.3	3	.1
NY FEMALE	0	.0	7	.6	2	.2	4	.3	13	1.0	1,242	98.8	2	.2
NY MALE	2	.2	15	1.6	2	.2	3	.3	22	2.3	932	97.6	1	.1
BROOME COMMUNITY COLLEGE														
NY TOTAL	13	.3	78	1.8	18	.4	8	.2	117	2.7	4,240	97.0	16	.4
NY FEMALE	7	.3	42	1.9	11	.5	5	.2	65	3.0	2,098	96.9	3	.1
NY MALE	6	.3	36	1.6	7	.3	3	.1	52	2.4	2,142	97.1	13	.6
CAYUGA CO CMTY COLLEGE														
NY TOTAL	1	.0	48	2.2	0	.0	4	.2	53	2.5	2,091	97.0	12	.6
NY FEMALE	0	.0	16	1.5	0	.0	1	.1	17	1.6	1,038	98.3	1	.1
NY MALE	1	.1	32	2.9	0	.0	3	.3	36	3.3	1,053	95.7	11	1.0
CLINTON COMMUNITY COLLEGE														
NY TOTAL	8	.7	74	6.3	2	.2	39	3.3	123	10.5	1,035	88.8	8	.7
NY FEMALE	5	1.1	16	3.5	0	.0	5	1.1	26	5.7	422	93.2	5	1.1
NY MALE	3	.4	58	8.1	2	.3	34	4.8	97	13.6	613	86.0	3	.4
COLUMBIA-GREENE CC														
NY TOTAL	1	.1	17	2.4	1	.1	2	.3	21	2.9	693	97.1	0	.0
NY FEMALE	0	.0	9	2.5	1	.3	1	.3	11	3.0	351	97.0	0	.0
NY MALE	1	.3	8	2.3	0	.0	1	.3	10	2.8	342	97.2	0	.0
CMTY COLLEGE FINGER LAKES														
NY TOTAL	1	.1	23	1.4	5	.3	7	.4	36	2.2	1,637	97.8	0	.0
NY FEMALE	1	.1	15	1.6	3	.3	2	.2	21	2.3	905	97.7	0	.0
NY MALE	0	.0	8	1.1	2	.3	5	.7	15	2.0	732	98.0	0	.0
CORNING COMMUNITY COLLEGE														
NY TOTAL	7	.3	101	.8	4	.2	23	1.1	135	.4	1,970	93.4	5	.2
NY FEMALE	2	.2	30	4.9	4	.4	2	.2	38	4.7	977	96.0	3	.3
NY MALE	5	.5	71	8.5	0	.0	21	1.9	97	8.9	993	90.9	2	.2
DUTCHESS CMTY COLLEGE														
NY TOTAL	8	.2	383	9.8	19	.5	109	2.	519	13.2	3,367	85.9	32	.8
NY FEMALE	3	.2	117	5.9	11	.6	33	1.6	164	8.3	1,811	91.1	12	.6
NY MALE	5	.3	266	13.8	8	.4	76	3.9	355	18.4	1,556	80.6	20	1.0
ERIE COMMUNITY COLLEGE														
NY TOTAL	21	.2	813	.1	44	.5	41	.5	919	10.3	7,975	89.1	60	.7
NY FEMALE	13	.4	457	12.9	17	.5	27	.8	514	14.5	3,015	85.0	20	.6
NY MALE	8	.1	356	8.6	27	.5	14	.3	405	7.5	4,960	91.8	40	.7
FASHION INST TECHNOLOGY														
NY TOTAL	6	.1	1,208	17.0	411	5.8	525	7.4	2,150	30.3	4,852	68.4	87	1.2
NY FEMALE	5	.1	904	16.1	320	5.7	385	6.9	1,614	28.8	3,947	70.3	50	.9
NY MALE	1	.1	304	20.6	91	6.2	140	9.5	536	36.3	905	61.2	37	2.5
FULTON-MONTGOMERY CC														
NY TOTAL	15	1.0	56	3.7	2	.1	6	.4	79	5.2	1,446	94.8	0	.0
NY FEMALE	7	.8	14	1.7	1	.1	4	.5	26	3.2	798	96.8	0	.0
NY MALE	8	1.1	42	6.0	1	.1	2	.3	53	7.6	648	92.4	0	.0
GENESEE COMMUNITY COLLEGE														
NY TOTAL	0	.0	69	3.7	4	.2	9	.5	82	4.4	1,800	95.6	0	.0
NY FEMALE	0	.0	15	1.4	3	.3	2	.2	20	1.8	1,070	98.2	0	.0
NY MALE	0	.0	54	6.8	1	.1	7	.9	62	7.8	730	92.2	0	.0
HERKIMER CO CMTY COLLEGE														
NY TOTAL	0	.0	41	2.7	0	.0	4	.3	45	2.9	1,480	97.0	1	.1
NY FEMALE	0	.0	19	2.5	0	.0	3	.4	22	2.9	725	97.1	0	.0
NY MALE	0	.0	22	2.8	0	.0	1	.1	23	3.0	755	96.9	1	.1
HUDSON VLY CMTY COLLEGE														
NY TOTAL	0	.0	110	2.2	17	.3	32	.6	159	3.1	4,880	96.6	11	.2
NY FEMALE	0	.0	37	2.0	5	.3	10	.6	52	2.9	1,755	97.1	1	.1
NY MALE	0	.0	73	2.3	12	.4	22	.7	107	3.3	3,125	96.4	10	.3
JAMESTOWN CMTY COLLEGE														
NY TOTAL	38	1.4	65	2.5		.2	12	.5	121	4.6	2,526	95.2	6	.2
NY FEMALE	27	1.9	28	2.0		.1	8	.6	65	4.7	1,331	95.3	1	.1
NY MALE	11	.9	37	2.9	8	.3	4	.3	56	4.5	1,195	95.1	5	.4
JEFFERSON CMTY COLLEGE														
NY TOTAL	3	.3	4	.4	2	.2	6	.5	15	1.4	1,089	98.5	2	.2
NY FEMALE	2	.3	3	.5	1	.2	1	.2	7	1.1	604	98.7	1	.2
NY MALE	1	.2	1	.2	1	.2	5	1.0	8	1.6	485	98.2	1	.2
MOHAWK VLY CMTY COLLEGE														
NY TOTAL	0	.0	117	2.9	11	.3	34	.8	162	.0	3,913	95.8	9	.2
NY FEMALE	0	.0	34	2.0	6	.4	10	.6	50	4.19	1,655	97.0	2	.1
NY MALE	0	.0	83	3.5	5	.2	24	1.0	112	4.7	2,258	95.0	7	.3
MONROE COMMUNITY COLLEGE														
NY TOTAL	35	.4	597	6.8	41	.5	99	1.1	772	8.	8,006	91.1	13	.1
NY FEMALE	19	.4	371	7.8	14	.3	47	1.0	451	91.8	4,322	90.5	2	.0
NY MALE	16	.4	226	5.6	27	.7	52	1.3	321	8.8	3,684	91.7	11	.3
NASSAU COMMUNITY COLLEGE														
NY TOTAL	169	1.2	656	4.5	93	.6	294	2.0	1,212	8.3	13,398	91.6	12	.1
NY FEMALE	89	1.2	445	5.9	44	.6	151	2.0	729	9.7	6,750	90.2	3	.0
NY MALE	80	1.1	211	3.0	49	.7	143	2.0	483	6.8	6,648	93.1	9	.1
NIAGARA CO CMTY COLLEGE														
NY TOTAL	27	.9	74	2.5	2	.1	14	.5	117	3.9	2,861	96.0	1	.0
NY FEMALE	13	.9	36	2.4	0	.0	5	.3	54	3.7	1,415	96.3	1	.1
NY MALE	14	.9	38	2.5	2	.1	9	.6	63	4.2	1,446	95.8	0	.0
N COUNTRY CMTY COLLEGE														
NY TOTAL	9	1.1	11	1.4	1	.1	3	.4	24	3.1	761	96.9	0	.0
NY FEMALE	9	2.0	2	.5	1	.2	1	.2	13	2.9	428	97.1	0	.0
NY MALE	0	.0	9	2.6	0	.0	2	.6	11	3.2	333	96.8	0	.0
ONONDAGA CMTY COLLEGE														
NY TOTAL	15	.4	121	3.1	1	.3	11	.3	160	4.1	3,730	95.9	0	.0
NY FEMALE	9	.5	79	4.3		.2	2	.1	94	5.1	1,748	94.9	0	.0
NY MALE	6	.3	42	2.1	1	.4	9	.4	66	3.2	1,982	96.8	0	.0

N E	BLACK NON-HISPANIC		ASIAN OR PACIFIC ISLANDER		HISPANIC		TOTAL MINORITY		WHITE NON-HISPANIC		NON-RESIDENT ALIEN		TOTAL
	NUMBER	%	NUMBER	%	NUMBER	%	NUMBER	%	NUMBER	%	NUMBER	%	NUMBER
INUED													
	139	2.8	20	.4	68	1.4	236	4.8	4,670	94.9	14	.3	4,920
	94	3.4	13	.5	32	1.2	145	5.3	2,579	94.5	5	.2	2,729
	45	2.1	7	.3	36	1.6	91	4.2	2,091	95.4	9	.4	2,191
	493	6.0	71	.9	148	1.8	784	9.5	7,353	88.8	143	1.7	8,280
	331	6.5	43	.8	91	1.8	506	9.9	4,564	89.7	20	.4	5,090
	162	5.1	28	.9	57	1.8	278	8.7	2,789	87.4	123	3.9	3,190
	59	4.5	6	.5	13	1.0	83	6.4	1,211	93.2	5	.4	1,299
	34	5.6	4	.7	8	1.3	48	7.9	555	91.4	4	.7	607
	25	3.6	2	.3	5	.7	35	5.1	656	94.8	1	.1	692
	296	2.3	56	.4	413	3.2	854	6.7	11,882	93.3	0	.0	12,736
	147	2.4	27	.4	200	3.2	417	6.7	5,819	93.3	0	.0	6,236
	149	2.3	29	.4	213	3.3	437	6.7	6,063	93.3	0	.0	6,500
	212	12.6	7	.4	38	2.3	257	15.2	1,430	84.8	0	.0	1,687
	67	8.2	1	.1	10	1.2	78	9.5	739	90.5	0	.0	817
	145	16.7	6	.7	28	3.2	179	20.6	691	79.4	0	.0	870
	55	3.6	18	1.2	13	.9	91	6.0	1,414	92.5	23	1.5	1,528
	30	3.6	15	1.8	6	.7	53	6.4	769	92.8	7	.8	829
	25	3.6	3	.4	7	1.0	38	5.4	645	92.3	16	2.3	699
	127	6.3	10	.5	54	2.7	194	9.7	1,802	90.0	7	.3	2,003
	23	2.3	4	.4	20	2.0	49	4.9	951	95.0	1	.1	1,001
	104	10.4	6	.6	34	3.4	145	14.5	851	84.9	6	.6	1,002
	565	10.4	147	2.7	102	1.9	844	15.6	4,484	82.7	94	1.7	5,422
	230	10.6	69	3.2	39	1.8	348	16.0	1,818	83.5	12	.6	2,178
	335	10.3	78	2.4	63	1.9	496	15.3	2,666	82.2	82	2.5	3,244
	784	6.6	94	.8	137	1.1	1,052	8.8	10,369	86.9	510	4.3	11,931
	415	7.6	44	.8	49	.9	529	9.7	4,807	88.3	107	2.0	5,443
	369	5.7	50	.8	88	1.4	523	8.1	5,562	85.7	403	6.2	6,488
	111	7.1	5	.3	23	1.5	143	9.1	1,416	90.6	4	.3	1,563
	62	7.6	3	.4	15	1.8	83	10.2	732	89.7	1	.1	816
	49	6.6	2	.3	8	1.1	60	8.0	684	91.6	3	.4	747
	703	51.0	25	1.8	359	26.0	1,087	78.8	287	20.8	5	.4	1,379
	457	51.3	15	1.7	233	26.2	705	79.1	185	20.8	1	.1	891
	246	50.4	10	2.0	126	25.8	382	78.3	102	20.9	4	.8	488
	94	10.0	61	6.5	24	2.5	179	19.0	648	68.7	116	12.3	943
	7	33.3	0	.0	2	9.5	9	42.9	12	57.1	0	.0	21
	87	9.4	61	6.6	22	2.4	170	18.4	636	69.0	116	12.6	922
	13	7.6	1	.6	6	3.5	20	11.8	145	85.3	5	2.9	170
	11	6.9	1	.6	5	3.1	17	10.6	138	86.3	5	3.1	160
	2	20.0	0	.0	1	10.0	3	30.0	7	70.0	0	.0	10
	502	36.0	35	2.5	134	9.6	675	48.4	685	49.1	36	2.6	1,396
	368	41.3	11	1.2	108	12.1	490	54.9	383	42.9	19	2.1	892
	134	26.6	24	4.8	26	5.2	185	36.7	302	59.9	17	3.4	504
	12	1.8	2	.3	2	.3	18	2.8	632	97.2	0	.0	650
	11	1.9	2	.3	2	.3	16	2.7	578	97.3	0	.0	594
	1	1.8	0	.0	0	.0	2	3.6	54	96.4	0	.0	56
	49	2.1	20	.9	23	1.0	95	4.1	2,212	94.7	29	1.2	2,336
	14	2.1	6	.9	7	1.0	27	4.0	639	95.2	5	.7	671
	35	2.1	14	.8	16	1.0	68	4.1	1,573	94.5	24	1.4	1,665
	0	.0	0	.0	0	.0	0	.0	634	100.0	0	.0	634
	0	.0	0	.0	0	.0	0	.0	0	.0	0	.0	0
	0	.0	0	.0	0	.0	0	.0	634	100.0	0	.0	634
	135	3.1	112	2.6	29	.7	285	6.5	4,028	92.0	67	1.5	4,380
	76	4.2	55	3.1	15	.8	148	8.2	1,631	90.5	23	1.3	1,802
	59	2.3	57	2.2	14	.5	137	5.3	2,397	93.0	44	1.7	2,578
	19	8.0	2	.8	5	2.1	26	11.0	210	88.6	1	.4	237
	15	7.3	1	.5	4	2.0	20	9.8	184	89.8	1	.5	205
	4	12.5	1	3.1	1	3.1	6	18.8	26	81.3	0	.0	32
	143	6.2	58	2.5	30	1.3	235	10.2	2,003	86.7	72	3.1	2,310
	118	8.3	43	3.0	19	1.3	183	12.9	1,189	83.9	46	3.2	1,418
	25	2.8	15	1.7	11	1.2	52	5.8	814	91.3	26	2.9	892
	47	10.3	0	.0	1	.2	48	10.5	408	89.5	0	.0	456
	20	6.1	0	.0	1	.3	21	6.4	306	93.6	0	.0	327
	27	20.9	0	.0	0	.0	27	20.9	102	79.1	0	.0	129
	66	88.0	0	.0	1	1.3	67	89.3	8	10.7	0	.0	75
	0	.0	0	.0	0	.0	0	.0	0	.0	0	.0	0
	66	88.0	0	.0	1	1.3	67	89.3	8	10.7	0	.0	75
	140	6.6	4	.2	47	2.2	192	9.1	1,791	84.9	126	6.0	2,109
	75	6.2	1	.1	21	1.7	97	8.1	1,031	85.8	73	6.1	1,201
	65	7.2	3	.3	26	2.9	95	10.5	760	83.7	53	5.8	908

TABLE 1 -   TOTAL UNDERGRADUATE ENROLLMENT IN INSTITUTIONS OF HIGHER EDUCATION BY RACE, ETHNICITY AND SEX:
INSTITUTION, STATE AND NATION, 1978

	AMERICAN INDIAN ALASKAN NATIVE		BLACK NON-HISPANIC		ASIAN OR PACIFIC ISLANDER		HISPANIC		TOTAL MINORITY		WHITE NON-HISPANIC		NON-RESIDENT ALIEN	
	NUMBER	%	NUMBER	%	NUMBER	%	NUMBER	%	NUMBER	%	NUMBER	%	NUMBER	%
NEW YORK CONTINUED														
HEBB INST OF NAVAL ARCH														
NY TOTAL	0	.0	1	1.3	1	1.3		.0	2	2.5	78	97.5		.0
NY FEMALE	0	.0	0	.0	0	.0		.0	0	.0	5	100.0		.0
NY MALE	0	.0	1	1.3	1	1.3		.0	2	2.7	73	97.3		.0
HELLS COLLEGE														
NY TOTAL	2	.4	18	3.6	3	.6	8	1.6	31	6.3	457	92.5		1.2
NY FEMALE	2	.4	18	3.6	3	.6	8	1.6	31	6.3	457	92.5		1.2
NY MALE	0	.0	0	.0	0	.0	0	.0	0	.0	0	.0	6	.0
THE WOOD SCHOOL														
NY TOTAL	0	.0	15	3.0	2	.4	47	9.4	64	12.8	434	86.8	2	.4
NY FEMALE	0	.0	15	3.0	2	.4	47	9.4	64	12.8	434	86.8	2	.4
NY MALE	0	.0	0	.0	0	.0	0	.0	0	.0	0	.0	0	.0
YESH BETH HILLEL KRASNA														
NY TOTAL	0	.0	0	.0	0	.0		.0	0	.0	49	100.0		.0
NY FEMALE	0	.0	0	.0	0	.0		.0	0	.0	0	.0		.0
NY MALE	0	.0	0	.0	0	.0		.0	0	.0	49	100.0		.0
YESH BETH SHEARM RAB INST														
NY TOTAL	0	.0	0	.0	0	.0		.0	0	.0	82	100.0		.0
NY FEMALE	0	.0	0	.0	0	.0		.0	0	.0	0	.0		.0
NY MALE	0	.0	0	.0	0	.0		.0	0	.0	82	100.0		.0
YESH CHOFETZ CHAIM RADUN														
NY TOTAL	0	.0	0	.0	0	.0		.0	0	.0	36	100.0		.0
NY FEMALE	0	.0	0	.0	0	.0		.0	0	.0	0	.0		.0
NY MALE	0	.0	0	.0	0	.0		.0	0	.0	36	100.0		.0
YESH KARLIN STOLIN INST														
NY TOTAL	0	.0	0	.0	0	.0		.0	0	.0	54	93.1		6.9
NY FEMALE	0	.0	0	.0	0	.0		.0	0	.0	0	.0		.0
NY MALE	0	.0	0	.0	0	.0		.0	0	.0	54	93.1		6.9
YESHIVA KIBBUTZ TASHBAR														
NY TOTAL	0	.0	0	.0	0	.0		.0	0	.0	27	100.0		.0
NY FEMALE	0	.0	0	.0	0	.0		.0	0	.0	0	.0		.0
NY MALE	0	.0	0	.0	0	.0		.0	0	.0	27	100.0		.0
YESHIVA NACHLAS HALEVIYIM														
NY TOTAL	0	.0	0	.0	0	.0		.0	0	.0	44	100.0		.0
NY FEMALE	0	.0	0	.0	0	.0		.0	0	.0	0	.0		.0
NY MALE	0	.0	0	.0	0	.0		.0	0	.0	44	100.0		.0
YESH OF NITRA RAB COLLEGE														
NY TOTAL	0	.0	0	.0	0	.0		.0	0	.0	147	100.0		.0
NY FEMALE	0	.0	0	.0	0	.0		.0	0	.0	0	.0		.0
NY MALE	0	.0	0	.0	0	.0		.0	0	.0	147	100.0		.0
YESHIVA UNIVERSITY														
NY TOTAL	0	.0	1	.1	4	.3		.0	5	.4	1,323	95.7	55	4.0
NY FEMALE	0	.0	0	.0	2	.3		.0	2	.3	623	95.8	25	3.8
NY MALE	0	.0	1	.1	2	.3		.0	3	.4	700	95.5	30	4.1
YESHIVATH VIZHITZ														
NY TOTAL	0	.0	0	.0	0	.0		.0	0	.0	0	.0		.0
NY FEMALE	0	.0	0	.0	0	.0		.0	0	.0	0	.0		.0
NY MALE	0	.0	0	.0	0	.0		.0	0	.0	0	.0		.0
YESHIVATH ZICHRON MOSHE														
NY TOTAL	0	.0	0	.0	0	.0		.0	0	.0	0	.0		.0
NY FEMALE	0	.0	0	.0	0	.0		.0	0	.0	0	.0		.0
NY MALE	0	.0	0	.0	0	.0		.0	0	.0	0	.0		.0
NEW YORK TOTAL (259 INSTITUTIONS)														
NY TOTAL	3,437	.5	81,450	12.2	13,418	2.0	38,789	5.8	137,094	20.5	523,075	78.1	9,724	1.5
NY FEMALE	1,645	.5	50,685	14.8	6,206	1.8	21,523	6.3	80,059	23.4	258,676	75.6	3,311	1.0
NY MALE	1,792	.5	30,765	9.4	7,212	2.2	17,266	5.3	57,035	17.4	264,399	80.6	6,413	2.0
NORTH CAROLINA														
ANSON TECHNICAL INSTITUTE														
NC TOTAL	0	.0	194	40.1	1	.2	5	1.0	200	41.3	284	58.7	0	.0
NC FEMALE	0	.0	93	42.9	0	.0	3	.9	95	43.8	122	56.2	0	.0
NC MALE	0	.0	101	37.8	1	.4	4	1.1	105	39.3	162	60.7	0	.0
ASHEBORO COLLEGE														
NC TOTAL	0	.0	50	28.6	0	.0	0	.0	50	28.6	119	68.0	6	3.4
NC FEMALE	0	.0	48	32.2	0	.0	0	.0	48	32.2	100	67.1	1	.7
NC MALE	0	.0	2	7.7	0	.0	0	.0	2	7.7	19	73.1	5	19.2
ASHEVL &UNCOMBE TECH INST														
NC TOTAL	7	.4	110	6.6	2	.1	1	.1	120	7.2	1,548	92.6	3	.2
NC FEMALE	3	.4	64	8.9	0	.0	0	.0	67	9.3	654	90.6	1	.1
NC MALE	4	.4	46	4.8	2	.2	1	.1	53	5.6	894	94.2	2	.2
ATLANTIC CHRISTIAN C														
NC TOTAL	4	.3	137	8.8	3	.2	4	.3	148	9.5	1,406	89.9	1	.6
NC FEMALE	4	.4	90	9.3	1	.1	3	.3	98	10.1	868	89.5	0	.0
NC MALE	0	.0	47	7.9	2	.3	1	.2	50	8.4	538	90.6	1	1.0
BARBER-SCOTIA COLLEGE														
NC TOTAL	0	.0	391	97.5	0	.0		.0	391	97.5	0	.0	1	2.5
NC FEMALE	0	.0	247	100.0	0	.0		.0	247	100.0	0	.0	0	.0
NC MALE	0	.0	144	93.5	0	.0		.0	144	93.5	0	.0	10	6.5
BEAUFORT CO TECH INST														
NC TOTAL	0	.0	271	27.0	1	.1		.0	272	27.1	731	72.9		.0
NC FEMALE	0	.0	110	24.0	1	.2		.0	111	24.2	348	75.8		.0
NC MALE	0	.0	161	29.6	0	.0		.0	161	29.6	383	70.4		.0
BELMONT ABBEY COLLEGE														
NC TOTAL	0	.0	27	4.0	3	.4		.7	35	5.2	627	92.3	17	2.5
NC FEMALE	0	.0	9	3.7	3	1.2		.4	13	5.4	226	93.4	3	1.2
NC MALE	0	.0	18	4.1	0	.0		.9	22	5.0	401	91.8	14	3.2
BENNETT COLLEGE														
NC TOTAL	0	.0	606	99.7	1	.2	*	.2	608	100.0	0	.0		.0
NC FEMALE	0	.0	606	99.7	1	.2		.2	608	100.0	0	.0		.0
NC MALE	0	.0	0	.0	0	.0		.0	0	.0	0	.0		.0

M E	BLACK NON-HISPANIC		ASIAN OR PACIFIC ISLANDER		HISPANIC		TOTAL MINORITY		WHITE NON-HISPANIC		NON-RESIDENT ALIEN		TOTAL
	NUMBER	%	NUMBER	%	NUMBER	%	NUMBER	%	NUMBER	%	NUMBER	%	NUMBER
INUED													
	157	43.3	0	.0	0	.0	160	44.1	203	55.9	0	.0	363
	85	45.9	0	.0	0	.0	86	46.5	99	53.5	0	.0	185
	72	40.4	0	.0	0	.0	74	41.6	104	58.4	0	.0	178
	56	28.7	1	.5	0	.0	58	29.7	137	70.3	0	.0	195
	28	29.2	0	.0	0	.0	28	29.2	68	70.8	0	.0	96
	28	28.3	1	1.0	0	.0	30	30.3	69	69.7	0	.0	99
	36	4.5	1	.1	2	.2	40	5.0	762	95.0	0	.0	802
	16	3.8	1	.2	2	.5	19	4.6	397	95.4	0	.0	416
	20	5.2	0	.0	0	.0	21	5.4	365	94.6	0	.0	386
	24	3.8	0	.0	0	.0	24	3.8	596	93.4	18	2.8	638
	7	2.3	0	.0	0	.0	7	2.3	295	96.1	5	1.6	307
	17	5.1	0	.0	0	.0	17	5.1	301	90.9	13	3.9	331
	91	7.5	1	.1	0	.0	94	7.7	1,118	91.6	9	.7	1,221
	40	6.6	0	.0	0	.0	41	6.8	564	93.2	0	.0	605
	51	8.3	1	.2	0	.0	53	8.6	554	89.9	9	1.5	616
	114	6.4	15	.8	1	.1	146	8.1	1,619	90.3	27	1.5	1,792
	42	5.1	2	.2	0	.0	53	6.5	755	92.0	13	1.6	821
	72	7.4	13	1.3	1	.1	93	9.6	864	89.0	14	1.4	971
	310	20.0	4	.3	0	.0	318	20.5	1,231	79.4	1	.1	1,550
	111	19.4	2	.4	0	.0	114	20.0	457	80.0	0	.0	571
	199	20.3	2	.2	0	.0	204	20.8	774	79.1	1	.1	979
	59	6.0	2	.2	6	.6	69	7.1	907	92.9	0	.0	976
	26	5.8	2	.4	3	.7	33	7.3	416	92.7	0	.0	449
	33	6.3	0	.0	3	.6	36	6.8	491	93.2	0	.0	527
	75	8.2	2	.2	8	.9	89	9.7	825	90.0	3	.3	917
	31	7.8	0	.0	5	1.3	38	9.5	359	90.2	1	.3	398
	44	8.5	2	.4	3	.6	51	9.8	466	89.8	2	.4	519
	129	7.5	5	.3	1	.1	136	7.9	1,584	92.1	0	.0	1,720
	42	6.8	1	.2	0	.0	43	7.0	572	93.0	0	.0	615
	87	7.9	4	.4	1	.1	93	8.4	1,012	91.6	0	.0	1,105
	55	19.9	1	.4	0	.0	56	20.2	221	79.8	0	.0	277
	29	18.5	0	.0	0	.0	29	18.5	128	81.5	0	.0	157
	26	21.7	1	.8	0	.0	27	22.5	93	77.5	0	.0	120
	362	19.2	3	.2	5	.3	383	20.3	1,500	79.6	1	.1	1,884
	156	18.0	1	.1	2	.2	163	18.8	704	81.1	1	.1	868
	206	20.3	2	.2	3	.3	220	21.7	796	78.3	0	.0	1,016
	2,750	18.8	136	.9	57	.4	2,971	20.3	11,543	79.0	101	.7	14,615
	1,524	19.2	54	.7	29	.4	1,620	20.4	6,267	78.9	58	.7	7,945
	1,226	18.4	82	1.2	28	.4	1,351	20.3	5,276	79.1	43	.6	6,670
	238	22.2	14	1.3	10	.9	265	24.7	748	69.8	59	5.5	1,072
	79	23.6	5	1.5	0	.0	85	25.4	236	70.4	14	4.2	335
	159	21.6	9	1.2	10	1.4	180	24.4	512	69.5	45	6.1	737
	261	26.0	3	.3	2	.2	267	26.6	731	72.9	5	.5	1,003
	133	32.4	2	.3	1	.2	137	33.3	274	66.7	0	.0	411
	128	21.6	1	.2	1	.2	130	22.0	457	77.2	5	.8	592
	340	16.0	18	.8	38	1.8	412	19.4	1,697	79.9	14	.7	2,123
	161	17.7	7	.8	10	1.1	182	20.0	722	79.3	6	.7	910
	179	14.8	11	.9	28	2.3	230	19.0	975	80.4	8	.7	1,213
	217	23.4	6	.6	0	.0	223	24.1	703	75.9	0	.0	926
	129	23.5	3	.5	0	.0	132	24.0	417	76.0	0	.0	549
	88	23.3	3	.8	0	.0	91	24.1	286	75.9	0	.0	377
	345	28.1	14	1.1	6	.5	366	29.8	862	70.2	0	.0	1,228
	207	32.9	10	1.6	4	.6	222	35.3	407	64.7	0	.0	629
	138	23.0	4	.7	2	.3	144	24.0	455	76.0	0	.0	599
	40	3.0	7	.5	2	.1	51	3.8	1,290	96.1	1	.1	1,342
	11	2.6	4	.9	0	.0	15	3.6	406	96.2	1	.2	422
	29	3.2	3	.3	2	.2	36	3.9	884	96.1	0	.0	920
	205	10.0	0	.0	0	.0	205	10.0	1,843	89.8	4	.2	2,052
	94	10.0	0	.0	0	.0	94	10.0	848	89.8	2	.2	944
	111	10.0	0	.0	0	.0	111	10.0	995	89.8	2	.2	1,108
	285	4.8	71	1.2	36	.6	397	6.8	5,355	91.1	127	2.2	5,879
	162	5.9	18	.7	10	.4	191	7.0	2,493	91.3	48	1.8	2,732
	123	3.9	53	1.7	26	.8	206	6.5	2,862	90.9	79	2.5	3,147
	169	100.0	0	.0	0	.0	169	100.0	0	.0	0	.0	169
	99	100.0	0	.0	0	.0	99	100.0	0	.0	0	.0	99
	70	100.0	0	.0	0	.0	70	100.0	0	.0	0	.0	70
	1,156	51.1	16	.7	8	.4	1,207	53.4	1,054	46.6	0	.0	2,261
	608	57.4	7	.7	6	.6	638	60.2	422	39.8	0	.0	1,060
	548	45.6	9	.7	2	.2	569	47.4	632	52.6	0	.0	1,201

TABLE 1 - TOTAL UNDERGRADUATE ENROLLMENT IN INSTITUTIONS OF HIGHER EDUCATION BY RACE, ETHNICITY AND SEX: INSTITUTION, STATE AND NATION, 1978

	AMERICAN INDIAN ALASKAN NATIVE		BLACK NON-HISPANIC		ASIAN OR PACIFIC ISLANDER		HISPANIC		TOTAL MINORITY		WHITE NON-HISPANIC		NON-RESIDENT ALIEN	
	NUMBER	%	NUMBER	%	NUMBER	%	NUMBER	%	NUMBER	%	NUMBER	%	NUMBER	%
NORTH CAROLINA CONTINUED														
EDGECOMBE TECH INST														
NC TOTAL	4	.6	395	55.3	1	.1	0	.0	400	56.0	314	44.0	0	.0
NC FEMALE	0	.0	198	61.1	0	.0	0	.0	198	61.1	126	38.9	0	.0
NC MALE	4	1.0	197	50.5	1	.3	0	.0	202	51.8	188	48.2	0	.0
ELON COLLEGE														
NC TOTAL	0	.0	167	7.7	3	.1	1	.0	171	7.8	2,001	91.7	11	.5
NC FEMALE	0	.0	60	6.7	1	.1	0	.0	61	6.8	832	92.9	3	.3
NC MALE	0	.0	107	8.3	2	.2	1	.1	110	8.5	1,169	90.8	8	.6
FAYETTEVILLE TECH INST														
NC TOTAL	47	1.0	1,317	27.1	36	.7	154	3.2	1,554	32.0	3,288	67.7	18	.4
NC FEMALE	25	1.0	714	28.8	25	1.0	68	2.7	832	33.6	1,639	66.2	5	.2
NC MALE	22	.9	603	25.3	11	.5	86	3.6	722	30.3	1,649	69.2	13	.5
FORSYTH TECHNICAL INST														
NC TOTAL	1	.0	667	27.3	6	.2	2	.1	676	27.7	1,764	72.3	0	.0
NC FEMALE	1	.1	353	28.0	2	.2	0	.0	356	28.2	905	71.8	0	.0
NC MALE	0	.0	314	26.6	4	.3	2	.2	320	27.1	859	72.9	0	.0
GARDNER-WEBB COLLEGE														
NC TOTAL	2	.2	125	9.6	4	.3	3	.2	134	10.3	1,153	88.4	17	1.3
NC FEMALE	0	.0	57	9.0	4	.6	1	.2	62	9.8	565	89.7	3	.5
NC MALE	2	.3	68	10.1	0	.0	2	.3	72	10.7	588	87.2	14	2.1
GASTON COLLEGE														
NC TOTAL	1	.0	311	11.3	0	.0	1	.0	313	11.4	2,402	87.2	41	1.5
NC FEMALE	1	.1	161	11.8	0	.0	0	.0	162	11.9	1,198	88.0	1	.1
NC MALE	0	.0	150	10.8	0	.0	1	.1	151	10.8	1,204	86.3	40	2.9
GREENSBORO COLLEGE														
NC TOTAL	2	.3	128	19.5	1	.2	2	.3	133	20.2	522	79.3	3	.5
NC FEMALE	1	.2	89	21.2	1	.2	2	.5	93	22.2	324	77.3	2	.5
NC MALE	1	.4	39	16.3	0	.0	0	.0	40	16.7	198	82.8	1	.4
GUILFORD COLLEGE														
NC TOTAL	1	.1	115	6.9	3	.2	8	.5	127	7.6	1,513	90.4	34	2.0
NC FEMALE	1	.1	51	7.4	0	.0	4	.6	56	8.1	620	89.5	1	.2
NC MALE	0	.0	64	6.5	3	.3	4	.4	71	7.2	893	91.0	19	1.7
GUILFORD TECHNICAL INST														
NC TOTAL	10	.4	699	24.7	14	.5	7	.2	730	25.8	2,101	74.2		.0
NC FEMALE	3	.3	296	25.4	5	.4	1	.1	305	26.2	861	73.8		.0
NC MALE	7		403	24.2	9	.5	6	.4	425	25.5	1,240	74.5	8	.0
HALIFAX CMTY COLLEGE														
NC TOTAL	18	1.9	477	49.2	4	.4	0	.0	499	51.4	471	48.6		.0
NC FEMALE	15	2.5	313	52.9	1	.2	0	.0	329	55.6	263	44.4		.0
NC MALE	3	.8	164	43.4	3	.8	0	.0	170	45.0	208	55.0	8	.0
HAMILTON COLLEGE														
NC TOTAL	0	.0	322	67.5	0	.0	0	.0	322	67.5	155	32.5		.0
NC FEMALE	0	.0	164	66.4	0	.0	0	.0	164	66.4	83	33.6		.0
NC MALE	0	.0	158	68.7	0	.0	0	.0	158	68.7	72	31.3	8	.0
HARDBARGER JC BUSINESS														
NC TOTAL	0	.0	255	28.6	0	.0	2	.2	257	28.8	631	70.7	5	.6
NC FEMALE	0	.0	179	29.3	0	.0	0	.0	179	29.3	430	70.5	1	.2
NC MALE	0	.0	76	26.9	0	.0	2	.7	78	27.6	201	71.0	4	1.4
MAYWOOD TECHNICAL INST														
NC TOTAL	6	.8	12	1.7	1	.1	3	.4	22	3.1	692	96.9		.0
NC FEMALE	1	.5	3	1.4	1	.5	3	1.4	8	3.7	209	96.3		.0
NC MALE	5	1.0	9	1.8	0	.0	0	.0	14	2.8	483	97.2	8	.0
HIGH POINT COLLEGE														
NC TOTAL	0	.0	63	6.1	0	.0	8	.8	71	6.9	941	91.4	18	1.7
NC FEMALE	0	.0	39	7.9	0	.0	3	.6	42	8.5	451	91.3	1	.2
NC MALE	0	.0	24	4.5	0	.0	5	.9	29	5.4	490	91.4	17	3.2
ISOTHERMAL CMTY COLLEGE														
NC TOTAL	0	.0	153	16.5	0	.0	1	.1	154	16.6	774	83.4		.0
NC FEMALE	0	.0	81	18.1	0	.0	1	.2	82	18.3	365	81.7		.0
NC MALE	0	.0	72	15.0	0	.0	0	.0	72	15.0	409	85.0	8	.0
JAMES SPRUNT INSTITUTE														
NC TOTAL	0	.0	296	39.9	1	.1	3	.4	300	40.5	441	59.5		.0
NC FEMALE	0	.0	157	42.7	1	.3	0	.0	158	42.9	210	57.1		.0
NC MALE	0	.0	139	37.3	0	.0	3	.8	142	38.1	231	61.9	8	.0
JEFFERSON COLLEGE														
NC TOTAL	0	.0	263	60.5	0	.0	0	.0	263	60.5	172	39.5		.0
NC FEMALE	0	.0	58	58.6	0	.0	0	.0	58	58.6	41	41.4		.0
NC MALE	0	.0	205	61.0	0	.0	0	.0	205	61.0	131	39.0	8	.0
JOHNSN C SMITH UNIVERSITY														
NC TOTAL	0	.0	1,434	98.6	0	.0	0	.0	1,434	98.6	2	.1	18	1.2
NC FEMALE	0	.0	752	99.3	0	.0	0	.0	752	99.3	0	.0	5	.7
NC MALE	0	.0	682	97.8	0	.0	0	.0	682	97.8	2	.3	13	1.9
JOHNSTON TECHNICAL INST														
NC TOTAL	9	.8	278	23.7	0	.0	2	.2	289	24.6	885	75.4		.0
NC FEMALE	3	.6	120	25.9	0	.0	0	.0	123	26.6	340	73.4		.0
NC MALE	6	.8	158	22.2	0	.0	2	.3	166	23.3	545	76.7	8	.0
JOHN WESLEY COLLEGE														
NC TOTAL	0	.0	4	5.8	0	.0	0	.0	4	5.8	65	94.2		.0
NC FEMALE	0	.0	1	8.3	0	.0	0	.0	1	8.3	11	91.7		.0
NC MALE	0	.0	3	5.3	0	.0	0	.0	3	5.3	54	94.7	8	.0
KING'S C-CHARLOTTE														
NC TOTAL	1	.3	77	21.2	0	.0	0	.0	78	21.5	289	78.5		.0
NC FEMALE	1	.4	48	17.0	0	.0	0	.0	49	17.3	234	82.7		.0
NC MALE	0	.0	29	36.3	0	.0	0	.0	29	36.3	51	63.8	8	.0
KING'S COLLEGE-RALEIGH														
NC TOTAL	0	.0	387	52.6	1	.1	10	1.4	398	54.1	332	45.1	6	.8
NC FEMALE	0	.0	111	51.4	0	.0	5	2.3	116	53.7	97	44.9	3	1.4
NC MALE	0	.0	276	53.1	1	.2	5	1.0	282	54.2	235	45.2	3	.6
LAFAYETTE COLLEGE														
NC TOTAL	3	.4	415	59.3	1	.1	4	.6	423	60.4	277	39.6		.0
NC FEMALE	2	.7	202	72.7	0	.0	1	.4	205	73.7	73	26.3		.0
NC MALE	1	.2	213	50.5	1	.2	3	.7	218	51.7	204	48.3	8	.0

ASIAN OR PACIFIC ISLANDER		HISPANIC		TOTAL MINORITY		WHITE NON-HISPANIC		NON-RESIDENT ALIEN		TOTAL
NUMBER	%	NUMBER	%	NUMBER	%	NUMBER	%	NUMBER	%	NUMBER
0	.0	1	.1	34	4.7	691	95.2	1	.1	726
0	.0	1	.6	4	1.5	257	98.5	0	.0	261
0	.0	0	.0	30	6.5	434	93.3	1	.2	465
8	.4	4	.2	640	35.0	1,189	65.0		.0	1,829
1	.1	3	.4	305	36.7	527	63.3	8	.0	832
7	.7	1	.1	335	33.6	662	66.4		.0	997
1	.1	1	.1	60	4.8	1,179	94.4	1	.8	1,249
1	.1	1	.1	23	3.2	698	96.3	8	.6	725
0	.0	0	.0	37	7.1	481	91.8		1.1	524
	.0		.0	783	98.0	3	.4	1	1.6	799
8	.0	8	.0	345	98.9	0	.0		1.1	349
	.0		.0	438	97.3	3	.7	4	2.0	450
5	.7	1	.1	83	12.3	589	87.3	3	.4	675
3	1.0	1	.3	40	13.6	254	86.4	0	.0	294
2	.5	0	.0	43	11.3	335	87.9	3	.8	381
2	.1	3	.2	109	6.4	1,602	93.6	1	.1	1,712
1	.1	1	.1	47	4.6	965	95.3	1	.1	1,013
1	.1	2	.3	62	8.9	637	91.1	0	.0	699
	.0		.0	295	43.8	378	56.2		.0	673
8	.0	8	.0	151	47.3	168	52.7	8	.0	319
	.0		.0	144	40.7	210	59.3		.0	354
	.0		.0	11	2.1	511	97.9		.0	522
8	.0	8	.0	1	.4	228	99.6	8	.0	229
	.0		.0	10	3.4	283	96.6		.0	293
	.0		.0	30	6.1	461	93.9		.0	491
8	.0	8	.0	12	6.9	163	93.1	8	.0	175
	.0		.0	18	5.7	298	94.3		.0	316
	.6		.6	35	2.5	1,382	97.2	5	.4	1,422
8	.6	8	.6	35	2.5	1,382	97.2	5	.4	1,422
	.0		.0	0	.0	0	.0	0	.0	0
19	1.9	22	2.3	192	20.3	717	75.9	3	3.8	945
7	1.6	11	2.5	91	20.4	346	77.8		1.8	445
11	2.2	11	2.2	101	20.2	371	74.2	28	5.6	500
2	.2	4	.4	189	20.2	747	79.8		.0	936
1	.2	1	.2	108	21.3	399	78.7	8	.0	507
1	.2	3	.7	81	18.9	348	81.1		.0	429
	.0	2	.6	97	26.9	262	72.8	1	.3	360
8	.0	0	.0	37	29.8	87	70.2	0	.0	124
	.0	2	.8	60	25.4	175	74.2	1	.4	236
	.0	3	.7	26	6.2	388	93.0	3	.7	417
8	.0	0	.0	7	3.4	199	95.7	2	1.0	208
	.0	3	1.4	19	9.1	189	90.4	1	.5	209
1	.2	3	.6	90	17.5	424	82.5		.0	514
0	.0	0	.0	38	16.3	195	83.7	8	.0	233
1	.4	3	1.1	52	18.5	229	81.5		.0	291
4	.4		.0	313	28.5	786	71.5	1	.1	1,100
2	.4	8	.0	145	26.0	413	74.0	0	.0	558
	.4		.0	168	31.0	373	68.8	1	.2	542
12	2.2		.0	157	28.9	387	71.1		.0	544
3	1.2	8	.0	87	34.5	165	65.5		.0	252
9	3.1		.0	70	24.0	222	76.0		.0	292
0	.0		.0	53	32.3	111	67.7		.0	164
0	.0	8	.0	35	36.8	60	63.2	8	.0	95
0	.0		.0	18	26.1	51	73.9		.0	69
2	.4	3	.6	8	1.6	497	98.2	1	.2	506
2	.4	3	.6	8	1.6	497	98.2	1	.2	506
0	.0	0	.0	0	.0	0	.0	0	.0	0
4	.4	6	.7	67	7.3	830	91.0	15	1.6	912
3	.7	4	.9	30	7.0	399	92.8	1	.2	430
1	.2	2	.4	37	7.7	431	89.4	14	2.9	482
	.0		.0	0	.0	426	98.2		1.8	434
8	.0	8	.0	0	.0	144	98.6	2	1.4	146
	.0		.0	0	.0	282	97.9	6	2.1	288
	.0		.0	347	49.6	351	50.2	1	.1	699
8	.0	8	.0	122	57.0	92	43.0	0	.0	214
	.0		.0	225	46.4	259	53.4	1	.2	485
3	.2	1	.1	406	29.5	970	70.5		.0	1,376
1	.1	1	.1	210	30.0	491	70.0	8	.0	701
2	.3	0	.0	196	29.0	479	71.0		.0	675

NORTH CAROLINA   CONTINUED

	AMERICAN INDIAN ALASKAN NATIVE		BLACK NON-HISPANIC		ASIAN OR PACIFIC ISLANDER		HISPANIC		TOTAL MINORITY		WHITE NON-HISPANIC		NON-RESIDENT ALIEN	
	NUMBER	%	NUMBER	%	NUMBER	%	NUMBER	%	NUMBER	%	NUMBER	%	NUMBER	%
QUEENS COLLEGE														
NC TOTAL	1	.2	20	4.2	2	.4	1	.2	24	5.0	453	94.8	1	.2
NC FEMALE	1	.2	20	4.2	2	.4	1	.2	24	5.1	446	94.7	1	.2
NC MALE	0	.0	0	.0	0	.0	0	.0	0	.0	7	100.0	0	.0
RANDOLPH TECHNICAL INST														
NC TOTAL	2	.2	40	4.3	1	.1	3	.3	46	5.0	876	95.0	0	.0
NC FEMALE	2	.5	19	4.4	0	.0	1	.2	22	5.1	409	94.9	0	.0
NC MALE	0	.0	21	4.3	1	.2	2	.4	24	4.9	467	95.1	0	.0
RICHMOND TECHNICAL INST														
NC TOTAL	29	3.0	336	34.7	2	.2	1	.1	368	38.1	597	61.7	2	.2
NC FEMALE	12	2.9	163	40.0	0	.0	0	.0	175	43.0	232	57.0	0	.0
NC MALE	17	3.0	173	30.9	2	.4	1	.2	193	34.5	365	65.2	2	.4
ROANOKE BIBLE COLLEGE														
NC TOTAL	0	.0	0	.0	0	.0	0	.0	0	.0	0	.0	0	.0
NC FEMALE	0	.0	0	.0	0	.0	0	.0	0	.0	0	.0	0	.0
NC MALE	0	.0	0	.0	0	.0	0	.0	0	.0	0	.0	0	.0
ROANOKE-CHOWAN TECH INST														
NC TOTAL	1	.1	430	61.0	0	.0	0	.0	431	61.1	274	38.9	0	.0
NC FEMALE	0	.0	276	66.8	0	.0	0	.0	276	66.8	137	33.2	0	.0
NC MALE	1	.3	154	52.7	0	.0	0	.0	155	53.1	137	46.9	0	.0
ROBESON TECHNICAL INST														
NC TOTAL	356	29.3	335	27.6	2	.2	6	.5	699	57.6	514	42.4	0	.0
NC FEMALE	201	32.6	172	27.9	0	.0	2	.3	375	60.8	242	39.2	0	.0
NC MALE	155	26.0	163	27.3	2	.3	4	.7	324	54.4	272	45.6	0	.0
ROCKINGHAM CMTY COLLEGE														
NC TOTAL	3	.3	227	19.6	1	.1	0	.0	231	19.9	925	79.9	2	.2
NC FEMALE	0	.0	114	18.5	0	.0	0	.0	114	18.5	503	81.5	0	.0
NC MALE	3	.6	113	20.9	1	.2	0	.0	117	21.6	422	78.0	2	.4
ROWAN TECHNICAL INSTITUTE														
NC TOTAL	0	.0	169	10.7	5	.3	0	.0	174	11.0	1,402	88.5	0	.6
NC FEMALE	0	.0	79	12.9	2	.3	0	.0	81	13.2	531	86.6	1	.2
NC MALE	0	.0	90	9.3	3	.3	0	.0	93	9.6	871	89.6	8	.8
SACRED HEART COLLEGE														
NC TOTAL	0	.0	18	7.2	9	3.6	8	3.2	35	13.9	203	80.9	13	5.2
NC FEMALE	0	.0	17	7.5	8	3.5	8	3.5	33	14.5	187	82.0	8	3.5
NC MALE	0	.0	1	4.3	1	4.3	0	.0	2	8.7	16	69.6	5	21.7
SNT ANDREWS PRESB COLLEGE														
NC TOTAL	2	.3	32	5.5	3	.5	3	.5	40	6.9	522	90.0	18	3.1
NC FEMALE	2	.8	15	6.0	2	.8	2	.8	21	8.5	223	89.9	4	1.6
NC MALE	0	.0	17	5.1	1	.3	1	.3	19	5.7	299	90.1	14	4.2
SAINT AUGUSTINES COLLEGE														
NC TOTAL	1	.1	1,672	95.8	0	.0	1	.1	1,674	95.9	6	.3	66	3.8
NC FEMALE	1	.1	981	98.2	0	.0	0	.0	982	98.3	2	.2	15	1.5
NC MALE	0	.0	691	92.5	0	.0	1	.1	692	92.6	4	.5	51	6.8
SAINT MARY'S COLLEGE														
NC TOTAL	0	.0	1	.3	0	.0	0	.0	1	.3	298	98.3	4	1.3
NC FEMALE	0	.0	1	.3	0	.0	0	.0	1	.3	298	98.3	4	1.3
NC MALE	0	.0	0	.0	0	.0	0	.0	0	.0	0	.0	0	.0
SALEM COLLEGE														
NC TOTAL	0	.0	5	.9	0	.0	0	.7	9	1.6	554	97.7	0	.7
NC FEMALE	0	.0	5	.9	0	.0	4	.7	9	1.6	553	97.7	4	.7
NC MALE	0	.0	0	.0	0	.0	0	.0	0	.0	1	100.0	0	.0
SAMPSON TECHNICAL INST														
NC TOTAL	16	1.9	301	35.9	0	.0	0	.0	317	37.8	521	62.2		.0
NC FEMALE	9	2.0	164	36.0	0	.0	0	.0	173	37.9	283	62.1		.0
NC MALE	7	1.8	137	35.9	0	.0	0	.0	144	37.7	238	62.3	8	.0
SANDHILLS CMTY COLLEGE														
NC TOTAL	22	1.4	212	13.3	0	.0	8	.5	242	15.2	1,349	84.8		.0
NC FEMALE	16	1.8	154	16.8	0	.0	0	.0	170	18.6	744	81.4		.0
NC MALE	6	.9	58	8.6	8	.0	1	1.2	72	10.6	605	89.4	8	.0
SHAW UNIVERSITY														
NC TOTAL	1	.1	1,104	93.6	0	.0	2	.2	1,107	93.8	16	1.4	57	4.8
NC FEMALE	0	.0	509	97.7	0	.0	1	.2	510	97.9	6	1.2	5	1.0
NC MALE	1	.2	595	90.3	8	.0	1	.2	597	90.6	10	1.5	52	7.9
SOUTHEASTERN CMTY COLLEGE														
NC TOTAL	56	3.0	536	28.9	0	.0	0	.0	592	31.9	1,258	67.9	3	.2
NC FEMALE	29	3.0	279	29.0	0	.0	0	.0	308	32.0	654	68.0	0	.0
NC MALE	27	3.0	257	28.8	8	.0	0	.0	284	31.9	604	67.8	3	.3
SOUTHWESTERN TECH INST														
NC TOTAL	94	14.2	14	2.1	0	.0	0	.0	108	16.3	550	83.0	5	.8
NC FEMALE	61	20.3	8	2.7	0	.0	0	.0	69	22.9	230	76.4	2	.7
NC MALE	33	9.1	6	1.7	0	.0	0	.0	39	10.8	320	88.4	3	.8
STANLY TECHNICAL INST														
NC TOTAL	2	.3	68	11.1	1	.2	1	.2	72	11.8	537	88.0	1	.2
NC FEMALE	1	.3	34	11.0	0	.0	0	.0	35	11.3	274	88.7	0	.0
NC MALE	1	.3	34	11.3	1	.3	1	.3	37	12.3	263	87.4	1	.3
SURRY COMMUNITY COLLEGE														
NC TOTAL	1	.1	123	8.1	3	.2	2	.1	129	8.5	1,381	91.5	0	.0
NC FEMALE	1	.1	35	4.8	2	.3	1	.1	39	5.4	689	94.6	0	.0
NC MALE	0	.0	88	11.3	1	.1	1	.1	90	11.5	692	88.5	0	.0
TECH INST OF ALAMANCE														
NC TOTAL	3	.2	235	19.5	0	.2	1	.1	242	20.1	963	79.9	1	.1
NC FEMALE	0	.0	115	20.0	0	.5	0	.0	118	20.5	457	79.5	0	.0
NC MALE	3	.5	120	19.0	8	.0	1	.2	124	19.7	506	80.2	1	.2
TRI-COUNTY COMMUNITY C														
NC TOTAL	6	1.1	8	1.4	1	.2	0	.9	20	3.6	534	96.4		.0
NC FEMALE	4	1.5	2	.8	1	.4	4	1.9	12	4.6	249	95.4		.0
NC MALE	2	.7	6	2.0	0	.0	8	.0	8	2.7	285	97.3	8	.0
APPALACHIAN ST UNIVERSITY														
NC TOTAL	11	.1	195	2.4	12	.1	1	.0	232	2.9	7,844	96.9	1	.2
NC FEMALE	6	.1	77	1.8	5	.1	4	.1	94	2.2	4,142	97.7	8	.1
NC MALE	5	.1	118	3.1	7	.2	8	.2	138	3.6	3,702	96.1	14	.4

TABLE 1 - TOTAL UNDERGRADUATE ENROLLMENT IN INSTITUTIONS OF HIGHER EDUCATION BY RACE, ETHNICITY AND SEX:
INSTITUTION, STATE AND NATION, 1978

	AMERICAN INDIAN ALASKAN NATIVE		BLACK NON-HISPANIC		ASIAN-OR PACIFIC ISLANDER		HISPANIC		TOTAL MINORITY		WHITE NON-HISPANIC		NON-RESIDENT ALIEN		TOTAL
	NUMBER	%	NUMBER	%	NUMBER	%	NUMBER	%	NUMBER	%	NUMBER	%	NUMBER	%	NUMBER
NORTH CAROLINA CONTINUED															
EAST CAROLINA UNIVERSITY															
NC TOTAL	28	.3	864	8.3	21	.2	8	.1	921	8.9	9,430	90.9	19	.2	10,370
NC FEMALE	20	.3	534	9.3	10	.2	6	.1	570	9.9	5,164	89.9	10	.2	5,744
NC MALE	.8	.2	330	7.1	11	.2	2	.0	351	7.6	4,266	92.2	9	.2	4,626
ELIZABETH CITY STATE U															
NC TOTAL	1	.1	1,425	91.8	0	.0	0	.0	1,426	91.9	114	7 3	12	.8	1,552
NC FEMALE	1	.1	833	93.9	0	.0	0	.0	834	94.0	49	5 5	4	.5	887
NC MALE	0	.0	592	89.0	0	.0	0	.0	592	89.0	65	918	8	1.2	665
FAYETTEVL ST UNIVERSITY															
NC TOTAL	3	.1	1,833	91.1	4	.2	7	.3	1,847	91.8	153	7.6	12	.6	2,012
NC FEMALE	3	.2	1,118	93.1	2	.2	4	.3	1,127	93.8	68	5.7	6	.5	1,201
NC MALE	0	.0	715	88.2	2	.2	3	.4	720	88.8	85	10.5	6	.7	811
NC AGRL & TECH STATE U															
NC TOTAL	0	.0	4,247	92.8	2	.0	4	.1	4,253	92.9	142	3.1	182	4.0	4,577
NC FEMALE	0	.0	2,040	96.6	1	.0	1	.0	2,042	96.7	43	2.0	26	1.2	2,111
NC MALE	0	.0	2,207	89.5	1	.0	3	.1	2,211	89.7	99	4.0	156	6.3	2,466
NC CENTRAL UNIVERSITY															
NC TOTAL	3	.1	3,326	95.2	0	.0	3	.1	3,332	95.3	121	3 5	42	1.2	3,495
NC FEMALE	3	.1	2,055	95.4	0	.0	3	.1	2,061	95.7	80	3 7	13	.6	2,154
NC MALE	0	.0	1,271	94.8	0	.0	0	.0	1,271	94.8	41	11	29	2.2	1,341
NC SCHOOL OF THE ARTS															
NC TOTAL	1	.2	42	9.8	3	.7	2	.5	48	11.2	374	87.2	7	1.6	429
NC FEMALE	0	.0	12	6.2	2	1.0	1	.5	15	7.7	176	90.3	4	2.1	195
NC MALE	1	.4	30	12.8	1	.4	1	.4	33	14.1	198	84.6	3	1.3	234
NC STATE U RALEIGH															
NC TOTAL	26	.2	761	5.7	87	.7	6	.4	930	7.0	12,045	90.9	276	2.1	13,251
NC FEMALE	8	.2	354	9.2	19	.5	16	.4	397	10.4	3,394	88.6	41	1.1	3,832
NC MALE	18	.2	407	4.3	68	.7	40	.4	533	5.7	8,651	91.8	235	2.5	9,419
PEMBROKE STATE UNIVERSITY															
NC TOTAL	456	22.9	224	11.2	7	.4	5	.3	692	34.7	1,302	65.3	0	.0	1,994
NC FEMALE	299	26.0	138	12.0	3	.3	2	.2	442	38.4	708	61.6	0	.0	1,150
NC MALE	157	18.6	86	10.2	4	.5	3	.4	250	29.6	594	70.4	0	.0	844
U OF NC AT ASHEVILLE															
NC TOTAL	2	.1	63	.7	7	.5	6	.4	78	5.8	1,260	93.7	7	.5	1,345
NC FEMALE	2	.3	35	4.9	2	.3	2	.3	41	5.8	668	93.7	4	.6	713
NC MALE	0	.0	28	4.4	5	.8	4	.6	37	5.9	592	93.7	3	.5	632
U OF NC AT CHAPEL HILL															
NC TOTAL	50	.4	911	6.8	60	.5	70	.5	1,091	8.2	12,188	91.6	32	.2	13,311
NC FEMALE	18	.3	557	7.8	29	.4	38	.5	642	9.0	6,448	90.8	10	.1	7,100
NC MALE	32	.5	354	5.7	31	.5	32	.5	449	7.2	5,740	92.4	22	.4	6,211
U OF NC AT CHARLOTTE															
NC TOTAL	8	.1	472	6.8	26	.4	39	.6	545	7.9	6,246	90.1	143	2.1	6,934
NC FEMALE	4	.1	277	9.0	12	.4	11	.4	304	9.9	2,750	89.7	13	.4	3,067
NC MALE	4	.1	195	5.0	14	.4	28	.7	241	6.2	3,496	90.4	130	3.4	3,867
U OF NC AT GREENSBORO															
NC TOTAL	9	.1	640	9.8	17	.3	10	.2	676	10.3	5,865	89.4	22	.3	6,563
NC FEMALE	8	.2	530	11.1	14	.3	7	.1	559	11.7	4,218	88.1	11	.2	4,788
NC MALE	1	.1	110	6.2	3	.2	3	.2	117	6.6	1,647	92.8	11	.6	1,775
U OF NC AT WILMINGTON															
NC TOTAL	5	.1	182	5.3	11	.3	12	.3	210	6.1	3,208	93.5	13	.4	3,431
NC FEMALE	1	.1	109	6.5	8	.5	5	.3	123	7.3	1,553	92.4	5	.3	1,681
NC MALE	4	.2	73	4.2	3	.2	7	.4	87	5.0	1,655	94.6	8	.5	1,750
WSTN CAROLINA UNIVERSITY															
NC TOTAL	43	.8	234	.3	15	.3	14	.3	306	5.7	5,062	93.7	35	.6	5,403
NC FEMALE	30	1.2	108	4.2	6	.2	12	.5	156	6.1	2,381	93.2	19	.7	2,556
NC MALE	13	.5	126	4.4	9	.3	2	.1	150	5.3	2,681	94.2	16	.6	2,847
WINSTON-SALEM STATE U															
NC TOTAL	0	.0	1,872	90.6	0	.0	0	.0	1,872	90.6	190	9.2	5	.2	2,067
NC FEMALE	0	.0	1,122	90.3	0	.0	0	.0	1,122	90.3	116	9.3	4	.3	1,242
NC MALE	0	.0	750	90.9	0	.0	0	.0	750	90.9	74	9.0	1	.1	825
VANCE-GRANVL CMTY COLLEGE															
NC TOTAL	0	.0	588	50.4	0	.0	0	.0	588	5 .	579	49.6	0	.0	1,167
NC FEMALE	0	.0	350	54.4	0	.0	0	.0	350	5.4	293	45.6	0	.0	643
NC MALE	0	.0	238	45.4	0	.0	0	.0	238	45.4	286	54.6	0	.0	524
WAKE FOREST UNIVERSITY															
NC TOTAL	4	.1	135	4.4	13	.4	15	.5	167	.5	2,880	94.3	8	.3	3,055
NC FEMALE	1	.1	47	4.1	7	.6	5	.4	60	.3	1,075	94.7	0	.0	1,135
NC MALE	3	.2	88	4.6	6	.3	10	.5	107	5.6	1,805	94.0	8	.4	1,920
WAKE TECHNICAL INSTITUTE															
NC TOTAL	3	.2	238	16.7	15	1.0	2	.1	258	18.1	1,171	81.9	0	.0	1,429
NC FEMALE	3	.5	116	18.7	7	1.1	1	.2	127	20.5	493	79.5	0	.0	620
NC MALE	0	.0	122	15.1	8	1.0	1	.1	131	16.2	678	83.8	0	.0	809
WARREN WILSON COLLEGE															
NC TOTAL	1	.2	12	2.3	13	2.5	6	1.1	32	6.1	445	85.1	46	8.8	523
NC FEMALE	1	.4	5	1.8	6	2.1	1	.4	13	4.6	258	91.2	12	4.2	283
NC MALE	0	.0	7	2.9	7	2.9	5	2.1	19	7.9	187	77.9	34	14.2	240
WAYNE COMMUNITY COLLEGE															
NC TOTAL	5	.2	544	25.9	7	.3	11	.5	567	27.0	1,528	72.7	6	.3	2,101
NC FEMALE	1	.1	279	30.8	4	.4	3	.3	287	31.7	618	68.2	1	.1	906
NC MALE	4	.3	265	22.2	3	.3	8	.7	280	23.4	910	76.2	5	.4	1,195
WESTERN PIEDMONT CC															
NC TOTAL	5	.4	88	7.6	1	.1	4	.3	98	8.	1,060	91.5	1	.1	1,159
NC FEMALE	0	.0	39	6.8	0	.0	1	.2	40	7.	531	93.0	0	.0	571
NC MALE	5	.9	49	8.3	1	.2	3	.5	58	9.8	529	90.0	1	.2	588
WILKES COMMUNITY COLLEGE															
NC TOTAL	2	.1	96	6 3	2	.1	1	.1	101	6.7	1,396	92.1	18	1.2	1,515
NC FEMALE	2	.3	52	6 9	1	.1	0	.0	55	7.3	695	91.8	7	.9	757
NC MALE	0	.0	44	518	1	.1	1	.1	46	6.1	701	92.5	11	1.5	758
WILSON CO TECHNICAL INST															
NC TOTAL	2	.2	349	37 6	1	.1	3	.3	355	38.3	573	61.7	0	.0	928
NC FEMALE	1	.2	180	43 4	1	.2	1	.2	183	44.1	232	55.9	0	.0	415
NC MALE	1	.2	169	3219	0	.0	2	.4	172	33.5	341	66.5	0	.0	513

	AMERICAN INDIAN ALASKAN NATIVE		BLACK NON-HISPANIC		ASIAN OR PACIFIC ISLANDER		HISPANIC		TOTAL MINORITY		WHITE NON-HISPANIC		NON-RESIDENT ALIEN	
	NUMBER	%	NUMBER	%	NUMBER	%	NUMBER	%	NUMBER	%	NUMBER	%	NUMBER	%
NORTH CAROLINA	CONTINUED													
WINGATE COLLEGE														
NC TOTAL	4	.3	119	8.6	2	.1	3	.2	128	9.2	1,243	89.4	19	1.4
NC FEMALE	1	.1	49	7.3	2	.3	1	.1	53	7.9	614	91.2	6	.9
NC MALE	3	.4	70	9.8	0	.0	2	.3	75	10.5	629	87.7	13	1.8
WINSALM COLLEGE														
NC TOTAL	0	.0	109	32.8	0	.0	2	.6	111	33.4	219	66.0	2	.6
NC FEMALE	0	.0	65	27.4	0	.0	1	.4	66	27.8	169	71.3	2	.8
NC MALE	0	.0	44	46.3	0	.0	1	1.1	45	47.4	50	52.6	0	.0
NORTH CAROLINA	TOTAL (	125	INSTITUTIONS)											
NC TOTAL	1,587	.7	46,893	21.4	837	.4	815	.4	50,132	22.8	167,677	76.4	1,797	.8
NC FEMALE	907	.8	25,313	23.2	361	.3	357	.3	26,938	24.6	81,915	74.9	473	.4
NC MALE	680	.6	21,580	19.6	476	.4	458	.4	23,194	21.0	85,762	77.8	1,324	1.2
NORTH DAKOTA														
BISMARCK JUNIOR COLLEGE														
ND TOTAL	147	9.2	5	.3	0	.0	0	.0	152	9.5	1,445	90.4	1	.1
ND FEMALE	93	11.9	1	.1	0	.0	0	.0	94	12.0	688	88.0	0	.0
ND MALE	54	6.6	4	.5	0	.0	0	.0	58	7.1	757	92.8	1	.1
DICKINSON STATE COLLEGE														
ND TOTAL	20	1.9	3	.3	2	.2	0	.0	25	2.3	1,023	95.6	22	2.1
ND FEMALE	10	1.6	0	.0	2	.3	0	.0	12	2.0	593	96.4	10	1.6
ND MALE	10	2.2	3	.7	0	.0	0	.0	13	2.9	430	94.5	12	2.6
JAMESTOWN COLLEGE														
ND TOTAL	1	.2	20	4.2	2	.4	2	.4	25	5.3	448	94.3	2	.4
ND FEMALE	0	.0	3	1.2	2	.8	1	.4	6	2.4	245	96.8	2	.8
ND MALE	1	.5	17	7.7	0	.0	1	.5	19	8.6	203	91.4	0	.0
LAKE REGION JR COLLEGE														
ND TOTAL	87	14.7	5	.8	1	.2	1	.2	94	15.9	495	83.9	1	.2
ND FEMALE	46	18.0	4	1.6	0	.0	0	.0	50	19.6	205	80.4	0	.0
ND MALE	41	12.2	1	.3	1	.3	1	.3	44	13.1	290	86.6	1	.3
MARY COLLEGE														
ND TOTAL	85	10.7	1	.1	1	.1	2	.3	89	11.2	698	87.5	11	1.4
ND FEMALE	49	9.0	1	.2	1	.2	0	.0	51	9.3	493	90.1	3	.5
ND MALE	36	14.3	0	.0	0.	.0	2	.8	38	15.1	205	81.7	8	3.2
MAYVILLE STATE COLLEGE														
ND TOTAL	93	12.0	6	.8	0	.0	1	.1	100	12.9	677	87.1		.0
ND FEMALE	65	13.4	2	.4	0	.0	1	.2	68	14.0	418	86.0	0	.0
ND MALE	28	9.6	4	1.4	0	.0	0	.0	32	11.0	259	89.0	0	.0
MINOT STATE COLLEGE														
ND TOTAL	40	1.7	37	1.6	8	.3	5	.2	90	3.8	2,251	94.5	40	1.7
ND FEMALE	22	1.4	13	.9	5	.3	4	.3	44	2.9	1,451	95.3	27	1.8
ND MALE	18	2.1	24	2.8	3	.3	1	.1	46	5.4	800	93.1	13	1.5
ND STATE SCHOOL SCIENCE														
ND TOTAL	60	1.8	6	.2	5	.2	2	.1	73	2.2	3,247	97.8	0	.0
ND FEMALE	12	1.1	0	.0	1	.1	0	.0	13	1.2	1,053	98.8	0	.0
ND MALE	48	2.1	6	.3	4	.2	2	.1	60	2.7	2,194	97.3	0	.0
ND STATE U MAIN CAMPUS														
ND TOTAL	34	.5	23	.4	25	.4	9	.1	91	1.4	6,333	98.2	27	.4
ND FEMALE	13	.5	3	.1	7	.3	2	.1	25	.9	2,608	98.7	9	.3
ND MALE	21	.6	20	.5	18	.5	7	.2	66	1.7	3,725	97.8	18	.5
ND STATE U BOTTINEAU BR														
ND TOTAL	139	28.5	0	.0	0	.0	0	.0	139	28.5	339	69.6	9	1.8
ND FEMALE	99	38.4	0	.0	0	.0	0	.0	99	38.4	156	60.5	3	1.2
ND MALE	40	17.5	0	.0	0	.0	0	.0	40	17.5	183	79.9	6	2.6
NORTHWEST BIBLE COLLEGE														
ND TOTAL	1	.7	0	.0	0	.0	2	1.3	3	2.0	143	96.0	3	2.0
ND FEMALE	1	1.7	0	.0	0	.0	1	1.7	2	3.3	57	95.0	1	1.7
ND MALE	0	.0	0	.0	0	.0	1	1.1	1	1.1	86	96.6	2	2.2
STANDING ROCK CC														
ND TOTAL	116	76.8	0	.0	0	.0	0	.0	116	76.8	35	23.2	0	.0
ND FEMALE	75	79.8	0	.0	0	.0	0	.0	75	79.8	19	20.2	0	.0
ND MALE	41	71.9	0	.0	0	.0	0	.0	41	71.9	16	28.1	0	.0
TRINITY BIBLE INSTITUTE														
ND TOTAL	3	.8	2	.5	0	.0	4	1.0	9	2.3	389	97.3	2	.5
ND FEMALE	2	1.1	0	.0	0	.0	1	.6	3	1.7	171	97.7	1	.6
ND MALE	1	.4	2	.9	0	.0	4	1.3	6	2.7	218	96.9	1	.4
U OF ND MAIN CAMPUS														
ND TOTAL	145	1.9	36	.5	32	.4	17	.2	230	3.0	7,263	96.2	59	.8
ND FEMALE	94	2.6	17	.5	11	.3	12	.3	134	3.7	3,511	95.9	16	.4
ND MALE	51	1.3	19	.5	21	.5	5	.1	96	2.5	3,752	96.4	43	1.1
U OF ND WILLISTON BRANCH														
ND TOTAL	14	2.4	0	.0	1	.2	0	.0	15	2.6	556	97.0	2	.3
ND FEMALE	3	1.0	0	.0	1	.3	0	.0	4	1.3	302	98.4	1	.3
ND MALE	11	4.1	0	.0	0	.0	0	.0	11	4.1	254	95.5	1	.4
VALLEY CITY STATE COLLEGE														
ND TOTAL	7	.7	9	1.0	1	.1	3	.3	20	2.1	919	97.5		.4
ND FEMALE	3	.6	0	.0	1	.2	2	.4	6	1.2	509	98.8		.0
ND MALE	4	.9	9	2.1	0	.0	1	.2	14	3.3	410	95.8	4	.9
NORTH DAKOTA	TOTAL (	16	INSTITUTIONS)											
ND TOTAL	992	3.6	153	.6	78	.3	48	.2	1,271	4.6	26,261	94.8	183	.7
ND FEMALE	587	4.4	44	.3	31	.2	24	.2	686	5.2	12,479	94.3	73	.6
ND MALE	405	2.8	109	.8	47	.3	24	.2	585	4.0	13,782	95.2	110	.8
OHIO														
ANTIOCH UNIVERSITY														
OH TOTAL	59	2.6	641	28.1	21	.9	147	6.4	868	38.0	1,384	60.6	30	1.3
OH FEMALE	36	2.7	418	30.9	15	1.1	97	7.2	566	41.8	778	57.5	10	.7
OH MALE	23	2.5	223	24.0	6	.6	50	5.4	302	32.5	606	65.3	20	2.2

BLACK NON-HISPANIC		ASIAN OR PACIFIC ISLANDER		HISPANIC		TOTAL MINORITY		WHITE NON-HISPANIC		NON-RESIDENT ALIEN		TOTAL
NUMBER	%	NUMBER	%	NUMBER	%	NUMBER	%	NUMBER	%	NUMBER	%	NUMBER

INUED

6	3.9	0	.0	1	.6	7	.5	148	95.5	0	.0	155
2	2.2	0	.0	1	1.1	3	3.3	88	96.7	0	.0	91
4	6.3	0	.0	0	.0	4	8.3	60	93.8	0	.0	64
165	10.5	0	.0	10	.6	176	11.2	1,365	86.7	33	2.1	1,574
37	5.3	0	.0	5	.7	42	6.1	639	92.3	11	1.6	692
128	14.5	0	.0	5	.6	134	15.2	726	82.3	22	2.5	882
0	.0	0	.0	0	.0	0	.	56	100.0	0	.0	56
0	.0	0	.0	0	.0	0	.0	0	.0	0	.0	0
0	.0	0	.0	0	.0	0	.0	56	100.0	0	.0	56
180	7.5	11	.5	31	1.3	225	4	2,157	90.3	7	.3	2,389
99	8.6	4	.3	17	1.5	120	1.5	1,022	89.1	5	.4	1,147
81	6.5	7	.6	14	1.1	105	815	1,135	91.4	2	.2	1,242
8	.9	0	.0		.0	8	.	890	98.7	4	.4	902
3	1.1	0	.0	8		3	1.	271	97.8	3	1.1	277
5	.8	0	.0		.0	5	.8	619	99.0	1	.2	625
26	4.2	0	.0	3	.5	29	4.7	567	92.3	18	2.9	614
11	3.3	0	.0	1	.3	12	3.6	314	93.5	10	3.0	336
15	5.4	0	.0	2	.7	17	6.1	253	91.0	8	2.9	278
0	.0	0	.0		.0	0		79	100.0	0	.0	79
0	.0	0	.0	0		0	.0	0	.0	0	.0	0
0	.0	0	.0		.0	0	10	79	100.0	0	.0	79
701	5.1	23	.2	2	.7	819	0	12,731	93.3	96	.7	13,646
453	5.7	13	.2	7	.7	523	6 6	7,351	92.9	35	.4	7,909
248	4.3	10	.2	5	.6	296	812	5,380	93.8	61	1.1	5,737
13	2.0	0	.0	2	.3	16	2 5	627	97.5	0	.0	643
11	3.0	0	.0	1	.3	12	3 3	356	96.7	0	.0	368
2	.7	0	.0	1	.4	4	115	271	98.5	0	.0	275
201	12.5	8	.5	5	.3	217	13 5	1,384	86.1	7	.4	1,608
133	14.0	5	.5	2	.2	141	14 9	802	84.7	4	.4	947
68	10.3	3	.5	3	.5	76	1115	582	88.0	3	.5	661
63	2.3	29	1.1	11	.4	106	3 9	2,468	90.7	147	5.4	2,721
41	5.1	11	1.4	3	.4	57	7 1	712	88.6	35	4.4	804
22	1.1	18	.9	8	.4	49	216	1,756	91.6	112	5.8	1,917
15	1.3	1	.1	2	.2	18	1.6	1,115	97.8	7	.6	1,140
5	.8	1	.2	1	.2	7	1.2	581	98.3	3	.5	591
10	1.8	0	.0	1	.2	11	2.0	534	97.3	4	.7	549
11	1.1	6	.6	2	.2	20	1.9	1,012	98.1	0	.0	1,032
8	1.5	4	.7	2	.4	15	2.7	536	97.3	0	.0	551
3	.6	2	.4	0	.0	5	1.0	476	99.0	0	.0	481
1,883	85.2	2	.1	3	.1	1,888	85.4	221	10.0	102	4.6	2,211
850	81.2	1	.1	0	.0	851	81.3	175	16.7	21	2.0	1,047
1,033	88.7	1	.1	3	.3	1,037	89.1	46	4.0	81	7.0	1,164
1	2.6	0	.0	0	.0	1	2.	37	97.4	0	.0	38
1	3.4	0	.0	0	.0	1	3.4	28	96.6	0	.0	29
0	.0	0	.0	0	.0	0	.0	9	100.0	0	.0	9
5	1.3	0	.0	0	.0	5	1.3	385	98.2	2	.5	392
1	.6	0	.0	0	.0	1	.6	168	99.4	0	.0	169
4	1.8	0	.0	0	.0	4	1.8	217	97.3	2	.9	223
282	15.6	17	.9	4	.2	306	16.9	1,494	82.6	8	.4	1,808
140	20.4	3	.4	3	.4	147	21.4	537	78.3	2	.3	686
142	12.7	14	1.2	1	.1	159	14.2	957	85.3	6	.5	1,122
0	.0	0	.0	1	.5	6	3.0	193	96.5	1	.5	200
0	.0	0	.0	0	.0	4	4.5	83	94.3	1	1.1	88
0	.0	0	.0	1	.9	2	1.8	110	98.2	0	.0	112
218	10.5	8	.4		.0	226	10.9	1,846	88.7	10	.5	2,082
147	11.4	4	.3	8	.0	151	11.7	1,143	88.3	0	.0	1,294
71	9.0	4	.5		.0	75	9.5	703	89.2	10	1.3	788
1	1.0	0	.0		.0	1	1.	102	97.1	2	1.9	105
0	.0	0	.0		.0	0	.0	86	97.7	2	2.3	88
1	5.9	0	.0	0	.0	1	5.8	16	94.1	0	.0	17
31	5.8	4	.8	6	1.1	41	7.7	488	91.7	3	.6	532
8	2.6	3	1.0	2	.7	13	4 3	288	95.0	2	.7	303
23	10.0	1	.4	4	1.7	28	1212	200	87.3	1	.4	229
4	2.3	2	1.1	1	.6	7	4.0	160	90.4	10	5.6	177
3	3.0	1	1.0	1	1.0	5	5.1	90	90.9	4	4.0	99
1	1.3	1	1.3	0	.0	2	2.6	70	89.7	6	7.7	78
1,371	11.5	20	.2	76	.6	1,476	12.	10,392	86.9	89	.7	11,957
853	16.8	8	.2	34	.7	901	17.	4,141	81.6	34	.7	5,076
518	7.5	12	.2	42	.6	575	8.8	6,251	90.8	55	.8	6,881

	AMERICAN INDIAN ALASKAN NATIVE		BLACK NON-HISPANIC		ASIAN OR PACIFIC ISLANDER		HISPANIC		TOTAL MINORITY		WHITE NON-HISPANIC		NON-RESIDENT ALIEN	
	NUMBER	%	NUMBER	%	NUMBER	%	NUMBER	%	NUMBER	%	NUMBER	%	NUMBER	%
OHIO CONTINUED														
C MT SNT JOS-ON-THE-OHIO														
OH TOTAL	1	.1	42	3.9	2	.2	7	.6	52	4.8	1,019	94.4	9	.8
OH FEMALE	1	.1	38	3.8	2	.2	7	.7	48	4.8	945	94.4	8	.8
OH MALE	0	.0	4	5.1	0	.0	0	.0	4	5.1	74	93.7	1	1.3
COLLEGE OF STEUBENVILLE														
OH TOTAL	3	.4	30	4.3	3	.4	6	.9	42	6.0	649	92.7	9	1.3
OH FEMALE	0	.0	17	4.5	1	.3	3	.8	21	5.6	353	93.9	2	.5
OH MALE	3	.9	13	4.0	2	.6	3	.9	21	6.5	296	91.4	7	2.2
COLLEGE OF WOOSTER														
OH TOTAL	0	.0	86	4.7	10	.5	6	.3	102	5.6	1,722	94.4	0	.0
OH FEMALE	0	.0	37	4.3	6	.7	4	.5	47	5.4	821	94.6	0	.0
OH MALE	0	.0	49	5.1	4	.4	2	.2	55	5.8	901	94.2	0	.0
COLUMBUS C ART AND DESIGN														
OH TOTAL	2	.3	49	6.1	8	1.0	5	.6	64	8.0	721	90.5	12	1.5
OH FEMALE	1	.2	23	5.6	6	1.5	2	.5	32	7.8	377	91.5	3	.7
OH MALE	1	.3	26	6.8	2	.5	3	.8	32	8.3	344	89.4	9	2.3
COLUMBUS TECHNICAL INST														
OH TOTAL	17	.3	733	13.4	21	.4	5	.1	776	14.2	4,666	85.2	32	.6
OH FEMALE	8	.3	411	14.0	15	.5	1	.2	435	14.8	2,497	85.0	6	.2
OH MALE	9	.4	322	12.7	6	.2	4	.2	341	13.4	2,169	85.5	26	1.0
CUYAHOGA CC EASTERN CAM														
OH TOTAL	15	.4	1,581	38.7	19	.5	15	.4	1,630	39.9	2,445	59.8	15	.4
OH FEMALE	11	.4	1,106	40.7	15	.6	8	.3	1,140	42.0	1,567	57.7	8	.3
OH MALE	4	.3	475	34.5	4	.3	7	.5	490	35.6	878	63.9	7	.5
CUYAHOGA CC METRO CAM														
OH TOTAL	38	.4	5,449	60.1	97	1.1	176	1.9	5,760	63.5	3,180	35.1	129	1.4
OH FEMALE	22	.4	3,475	66.5	42	.8	99	1.9	3,638	69.6	1,569	30.0	22	.4
OH MALE	16	.4	1,974	51.4	55	1.4	77	2.0	2,122	55.3	1,611	42.0	107	2.8
CUYAHOGA CC WESTERN CAM														
OH TOTAL	26	.2	195	1.7	69	.6	112	1.0	402	3.5	11,112	96.0	62	.5
OH FEMALE	14	.2	105	1.6	49	.8	59	.9	227	3.5	6,229	96.3	13	.2
OH MALE	12	.2	90	1.8	20	.4	53	1.0	175	3.4	4,883	95.6	49	1.0
DAVIS JUNIOR COLLEGE														
OH TOTAL	0	.0	147	26.2	0	.0	12	2.1	159	28.3	403	71.7	0	.0
OH FEMALE	0	.0	108	30.6	0	.0	10	2.8	118	33.4	235	66.6	0	.0
OH MALE	0	.0	39	18.7	0	.0	2	1.0	41	19.6	168	80.4	0	.0
DEFIANCE COLLEGE														
OH TOTAL	0	.0	37	4.8	0	.0	18	2.3	55	7.2	694	90.5	18	2.3
OH FEMALE	0	.0	16	4.3	0	.0	4	1.1	20	5.4	346	94.0	2	.5
OH MALE	0	.0	21	5.3	0	.0	14	3.5	35	8.8	348	87.2	16	4.0
DENISON UNIVERSITY														
OH TOTAL	0	.0	66	3.2	6	.3	3	.1	75	3.7	1,937	95.2	23	1.1
OH FEMALE	0	.0	32	3.3	4	.4	2	.2	38	3.9	937	95.3	8	.8
OH MALE	0	.0	34	3.2	2	.2	1	.1	37	3.5	1,000	95.1	15	1.4
DYKE COLLEGE														
OH TOTAL	1	.1	566	52.6	4	.4	10	.9	581	53.9	487	45.2	9	.8
OH FEMALE	1	.1	430	63.0	2	.3	6	.9	439	64.4	238	34.9	5	.7
OH MALE	0	.0	136	34.4	2	.5	4	1.0	142	35.9	249	63.0	4	1.0
EDGECLIFF COLLEGE														
OH TOTAL	5	.8	76	11.8	1	.2	6	.9	88	13.6	549	85.0	9	1.4
OH FEMALE	4	.8	69	13.2	1	.2	3	.6	77	14.7	445	84.9	2	.4
OH MALE	1	.8	7	5.7	0	.0	3	2.5	11	9.0	104	85.2	7	5.7
EDISON STATE CMTY COLLEGE														
OH TOTAL	9	.5	14	.9	4	.2	2	.1	29	1.7	1,693	98.3	0	.0
OH FEMALE	6	.6	11	1.2	1	.1	2	.2	20	2.1	928	97.9	0	.0
OH MALE	3	.4	3	.4	3	.4	0	.0	9	1.2	765	98.8	0	.0
FINDLAY COLLEGE														
OH TOTAL	0	.0	64	7.2	0	.0	2	.2	66	7.4	801	90.0	23	2.6
OH FEMALE	0	.0	23	4.4	0	.0	1	.2	24	5.1	438	92.6	11	2.3
OH MALE	0	.0	41	9.8	0	.0	1	.2	42	10.1	363	87.1	12	2.9
FRANKLIN UNIVERSITY														
OH TOTAL	15	.4	714	17.9	34	.9	10	.3	773	19.4	3,219	80.6	0	.0
OH FEMALE	11	.6	384	21.8	14	.8	3	.2	412	23.4	1,352	76.6	0	.0
OH MALE	4	.2	330	14.8	20	.9	7	.3	361	16.2	1,867	83.8	0	.0
HEBREW UNION C NY BRANCH														
OH TOTAL	0	.0	0	.0	0	.0	0	.0	0	.0	42	100.0	0	.0
OH FEMALE	0	.0	0	.0	0	.0	0	.0	0	.0	19	100.0	0	.0
OH MALE	0	.0	0	.0	0	.0	0	.0	0	.0	23	100.0	0	.0
HEIDELBERG COLLEGE														
OH TOTAL	0	.0	49	5.7	2	.2	2	.2	53	6.2	804	93.8	0	.0
OH FEMALE	0	.0	17	4.1	2	.5	1	.2	20	4.9	390	95.1	0	.0
OH MALE	0	.0	32	7.2	0	.0	1	.2	33	7.4	414	92.6	0	.0
HIRAM COLLEGE														
OH TOTAL	0	.0	103	9.1	7	.6	5	.4	115	10.1	1,018	89.8	1	.1
OH FEMALE	0	.0	65	12.2	3	.6	1	.2	69	13.0	462	87.0	0	.0
OH MALE	0	.0	38	6.3	4	.7	4	.7	46	7.6	556	92.2	1	.2
HOCKING TECHNICAL COLLEGE														
OH TOTAL	2	.1	17	.7	0	.0	0	.0	19	.8	2,275	97.6	36	1.5
OH FEMALE	1	.1	4	.4	0	.0	0	.0	5	.5	1,047	98.6	10	.9
OH MALE	1	.1	13	1.0	0	.0	0	.0	14	1.1	1,228	96.8	26	2.1
JEFFERSON TECHNICAL C														
OH TOTAL	0	.0	65	4.2	6	.4	0	.0	71	4.5	1,490	95.4	1	.1
OH FEMALE	0	.0	32	4.3	5	.7	0	.0	37	5.0	705	95.0	0	.0
OH MALE	0	.0	33	4.0	1	.1	0	.0	34	4.1	785	95.7	1	.1
JOHN CARROLL UNIVERSITY														
OH TOTAL	0	.0	126	4.3	21	.7	11	.4	158	5.4	2,746	94.2	11	.4
OH FEMALE	0	.0	35	3.0	11	.9	5	.4	51	4.4	1,107	95.1	6	.5
OH MALE	0	.0	91	5.2	10	.6	6	.3	107	6.1	1,639	93.6	5	.3
KENT STATE U MAIN CAMPUS														
OH TOTAL	18	.1	1,124	8.1	41	.3	42	.3	1,225	8.9	12,500	90.3	116	.8
OH FEMALE	10	.1	624	8.9	23	.3	18	.3	675	9.7	6,291	90.0	22	.3
OH MALE	8	.1	500	7.3	18	.3	24	.4	550	8.0	6,209	90.6	94	1.4

	AMERICAN INDIAN ALASKAN NATIVE		BLACK NON-HISPANIC		ASIAN OR PACIFIC ISLANDER		HISPANIC		TOTAL MINORITY		WHITE NON-HISPANIC		NON-RESIDENT ALIEN		TOTAL
	NUMBER	%	NUMBER	%	NUMBER	%	NUMBER	%	NUMBER	%	NUMBER	%	NUMBER	%	NUMBER

OHIO, CONTINUED

KENT ST ASHTABULA REG CAM
OH TOTAL	2	.2	17	1.8	5	.5	0	.0	24	2.6	895	97.4		.0	919
OH FEMALE	2	.4	9	1.7	3	.6	0	.0	14	2.6	523	97.4	0	.0	537
OH MALE	0	.0	8	2.1	2	.5	0	.0	10	2.6	372	97.4	0	.0	382

KENT ST E LIVERPL REG CAM
OH TOTAL	0	.0	20	3.9	0	.0	2	.4	22	4.3	495	95.7	0	.0	517
OH FEMALE	0	.0	12	3.6	0	.0	0	.0	12	3.6	326	96.4	0	.0	338
OH MALE	0	.0	8	4.5	0	.0	2	1.1	10	5.6	169	94.4	0	.0	179

KENT ST U SALEM REG CAM
OH TOTAL	0	.0	6	1.2	0	.0	0	.0	6	1.2	497	98.8		.0	503
OH FEMALE	0	.0	2	.9	0	.0	0	.0	2	.9	226	99.1	0	.0	228
OH MALE	0	.0	4	1.5	0	.0	0	.0	4	1.5	271	98.5	0	.0	275

KENT ST STARK CO REG CAM
OH TOTAL	2	.1	98	5.4	2	.1	7	.4	109	6.0	1,706	94.0		.0	1,815
OH FEMALE	2	.2	60	5.6	0	.0	5	.5	67	6.3	1,005	93.8	0	.0	1,072
OH MALE	0	.0	38	5.1	2	.3	2	.3	42	5.7	701	94.3	0	.0	743

KENT ST TRUMBULL REG CAM
OH TOTAL	3	.2	125	7.7	1	.1	1	.1	130	8.0	1,491	91.9	1	.1	1,622
OH FEMALE	2	.2	74	8.1	1	.1	1	.1	78	8.5	836	91.5	0	.0	914
OH MALE	1	.1	51	7.2	0	.0	0	.0	52	7.3	655	92.5	1	.1	708

KENT ST TUSCARAWS REG CAM
OH TOTAL	0	.0	5	.6	1	.1	0	.0	6	.7	811	99.3	0	.0	817
OH FEMALE	0	.0	2	.4	1	.2	0	.0	3	.6	459	99.4	0	.0	462
OH MALE	0	.0	3	.8	0	.0	0	.0	3	.8	352	99.2	0	.0	355

KENYON COLLEGE
OH TOTAL	0	.0	13	.9	10	.7	4	.3	27	1.8	1,418	97.1	16	1.1	1,461
OH FEMALE	0	.0	6	1.0	4	.7	1	.2	11	1.8	598	97.7	3	.5	612
OH MALE	0	.0	7	.8	6	.7	3	.4	16	1.9	820	96.6	13	1.5	849

KETTERING C MEDICAL ARTS
OH TOTAL	0	.0	7	1.8	8	2.0	3	.8	18	4.5	379	95.5	0	.0	397
OH FEMALE	0	.0	5	1.7	5	1.7	0	.0	10	3.4	285	96.6	0	.0	295
OH MALE	0	.0	2	2.0	3	2.9	3	2.9	8	7.8	94	92.2	0	.0	102

LAKE ERIE COLLEGE
OH TOTAL	0	.0	16	1.7	6	.6	3	.3	25	2.7	893	95.8	14	1.5	932
OH FEMALE	0	.0	7	1.1	1	.2	3	.5	11	1.8	606	97.0	8	1.3	625
OH MALE	0	.0	9	2.9	5	1.6	0	.0	14	4.6	287	93.5	6	2.0	307

LAKELAND CMTY COLLEGE
OH TOTAL	6	.1	90	1.3	25	.4	8	.1	129	1.9	6,700	97.7	30	.4	6,859
OH FEMALE	2	.1	52	1.4	15	.4	3	.1	72	1.9	3,770	97.9	9	.2	3,851
OH MALE	4	.1	38	1.3	10	.3	5	.2	57	1.9	2,930	97.4	21	.7	3,008

LIMA TECHNICAL COLLEGE
OH TOTAL	11	.9	67	5.2	7	.5	11	.9	96	7.5	1,179	92.3	2	.2	1,277
OH FEMALE	8	1.0	46	5.8	3	.4	7	.9	64	8.1	726	91.8	1	.1	791
OH MALE	3	.6	21	4.3	4	.8	4	.8	32	6.6	453	93.2	1	.2	486

LORAIN CO CMTY COLLEGE
OH TOTAL	7	.1	369	6.5	13	.2	215	3.8	604	10.7	4,981	88.4	49	.9	5,634
OH FEMALE	4	.1	254	7.5	8	.2	135	4.0	401	11.8	2,987	87.8	15	.4	3,403
OH MALE	3	.1	115	5.2	5	.2	80	3.6	203	9.1	1,994	89.4	34	1.5	2,231

LOURDES COLLEGE
OH TOTAL	0	.0	6	1.3	0	.0	0	.0	6	1.3	468	98.1	3	.6	477
OH FEMALE	0	.0	4	.9	0	.0	0	.0	4	.9	450	98.9	1	.2	455
OH MALE	0	.0	2	9.1	0	.0	0	.0	2	9.1	18	81.8	2	9.1	22

MALONE COLLEGE
OH TOTAL	0	.0	50	6.8	0	.0	2	.3	52	7.0	677	91.6	10	1.4	739
OH FEMALE	0	.0	22	5.6	0	.0	0	.0	22	5.6	363	93.1	5	1.3	390
OH MALE	0	.0	28	8.0	0	.0	2	.6	30	8.6	314	90.0	5	1.4	349

MARIETTA COLLEGE
OH TOTAL	0	.0	21	1.5	2	.1	3	.2	26	1.9	1,355	97.1	14	1.0	1,395
OH FEMALE	0	.0	9	1.8	0	.0	1	.2	10	2.0	499	97.5	3	.6	512
OH MALE	0	.0	12	1.4	2	.2	2	.2	16	1.8	856	96.9	11	1.2	883

MARION TECHNICAL COLLEGE
OH TOTAL	4	.5	60	6.8	8	.9	4	.5	76	8.7	796	90.8	5	.6	877
OH FEMALE	1	.2	3	.6	3	.6	1	.2	8	1.7	453	97.6	3	.6	464
OH MALE	3	.7	57	13.8	5	1.2	3	.7	68	16.5	343	83.1	2	.5	413

MIAMI-JACOBS JC BUSINESS
OH TOTAL	0	.0	256	39.9	0	.0	5	.8	261	40.7	375	58.4	6	.9	642
OH FEMALE	0	.0	27	10.7	0	.0	2	.8	29	11.5	221	87.7	2	.8	252
OH MALE	0	.0	229	58.7	0	.0	3	.8	232	59.5	154	39.5	4	1.0	390

MIAMI UNIVERSITY MATN CAM
OH TOTAL	7	.1	270	2.0	34	.3	22	.2	333	2.5	13,070	97.5		.0	13,403
OH FEMALE	2	.0	136	2.0	14	.2	13	.2	165	2.4	6,722	97.6	0	.0	6,887
OH MALE	5	.1	134	2.1	20	.3	9	.1	168	2.6	6,348	97.4	0	.0	6,516

MIAMI U HAMILTON BRANCH
OH TOTAL	2	.2	62	4.9	2	.2	2	.2	68	5.4	1,188	94.6		.0	1,256
OH FEMALE	1	.1	52	7.1	2	.3	1	.1	56	7.6	680	92.4	0	.0	736
OH MALE	1	.2	10	1.9	0	.0	1	.2	12	2.3	508	97.7	0	.0	520

MIAMI U MIDDLETOWN BRANCH
OH TOTAL	2	.2	35	2.8	2	.2	1	.1	40	3.2	1,201	96.8		.0	1,241
OH FEMALE	0	.0	27	3.5	1	.1	1	.1	29	3.8	743	96.2	0	.0	772
OH MALE	2	.4	8	1.7	1	.2	0	.0	11	2.3	458	97.7	0	.0	469

MICHAEL J OWENS TECH C
OH TOTAL	18	.6	298	9.3	17	.5	62	1.9	395	12.3	2,793	86.7	32	1.0	3,220
OH FEMALE	9	.5	177	10.6	7	.4	29	1.7	222	13.3	1,452	86.7	1	.1	1,675
OH MALE	9	.6	121	7.8	10	.6	33	2.1	173	11.2	1,341	86.8	31	2.0	1,545

MOUNT UNION COLLEGE
OH TOTAL	0	.0	41	3.4	0	.0	0	.0	41	3.4	1,150	95.9	8	.7	1,199
OH FEMALE	0	.0	18	3.4	0	.0	0	.0	18	3.4	501	96.0	3	.6	522
OH MALE	0	.0	23	3.4	0	.0	0	.0	23	3.4	649	95.9	5	.7	677

MOUNT VERNON NAZARENE C
OH TOTAL	1	.1	5	.6	0	.0	5	.6	11	1.3	846	98.3	4	.5	861
OH FEMALE	1	.2	1	.2	0	.0	2	.4	4	.9	460	98.7	2	.4	466
OH MALE	0	.0	4	1.0	0	.0	3	.8	7	1.8	386	97.7	2	.5	395

OHIO	AMERICAN INDIAN ALASKAN NATIVE NUMBER	%	BLACK NON-HISPANIC NUMBER	%	ASIAN OR PACIFIC ISLANDER NUMBER	%	HISPANIC NUMBER	%	TOTAL MINORITY NUMBER	%	WHITE NON-HISPANIC NUMBER	%	NON-RESIDENT ALIEN NUMBER	%
CONTINUED														
MUSKINGUM AREA TECH C														
OH TOTAL	0	.0	36	3.0	3	.2	2	.2	41	3.4	1,164	96.5	1	.1
OH FEMALE	0	.0	24	3.8	1	.2	0	.0	25	3.9	609	95.9	1	.2
OH MALE	0	.0	12	2.1	2	.4	2	.4	16	2.8	555	97.2	0	.0
MUSKINGUM COLLEGE														
OH TOTAL	0	.0	20	2.2	0	.0	3	.3	23	2.	872	95.5	18	2.0
OH FEMALE	0	.0	4	1.0	0	.0	2	.5	6	1.	409	97.8	3	.7
OH MALE	0	.0	16	3.2	0	.0	1	.2	17	3.4	463	93.5	15	3.0
NORTH CEN TECH COLLEGE														
OH TOTAL	0	.0	40	2.9	4	.3	5	.4	49	3.5	1,340	96.5	0	.0
OH FEMALE	0	.0	25	3.5	1	.1	1	.1	28	3.7	721	96.3	0	.0
OH MALE	0	.0	14	2.2	3	.5	4	.6	21	3.3	619	96.7	0	.0
NORTHWEST TECH COLLEGE														
OH TOTAL	4	.7	1	.2	1	.2	14	2.4	20	3.5	554	96.5	0	.0
OH FEMALE	2	.8	0	.0	1	.4	7	2.6	10	3.8	255	96.2	0	.0
OH MALE	2	.6	1	.3	0	.0	7	2.3	10	3.2	299	96.8	0	.0
NOTRE DAME COLLEGE														
OH TOTAL	0	.0	31	7.5	1	.2	1	.2	33	8.0	369	88.9	13	3.1
OH FEMALE	0	.0	29	7.2	1	.2	1	.2	31	7.7	360	89.1	13	.2
OH MALE	0	.0	2	18.2	0	.0	0	.0	2	18.2	9	81.8	0	.0
OBERLIN CCLLEGE														
OH TOTAL	4	.1	271	9.9	68	2.5	31	1.1	374	13.7	2,309	84.7	42	1.5
OH FEMALE	2	.1	138	10.0	44	3.2	15	1.1	199	14.5	1,161	84.4	16	1.2
OH MALE	2	.1	133	9.9	24	1.8	16	1.2	175	13.0	1,148	85.1	26	1.9
OHIO DOMINICAN COLLEGE														
OH TOTAL	1	.1	130	19.0	5	.7	8	1.2	144	21.0	495	72.3	46	6.7
OH FEMALE	1	.2	95	21.7	4	.9	4	.9	104	23.8	316	72.3	17	3.9
OH MALE	0	.0	35	14.1	1	.4	4	1.6	40	16.1	179	72.2	29	11.7
OHIO INST OF TECHNOLOGY														
OH TOTAL	0	.0	372	16.2	10	.4	4	.2	386	16.8	1,907	82.9	7	.3
OH FEMALE	0	.0	58	36.7	0	.0	0	.0	58	36.7	100	63.3	0	.0
OH MALE	0	.0	314	14.7	10	.5	4	.2	328	15.3	1,807	84.4	7	.3
OHIO NORTHERN UNIVERSITY														
OH TOTAL	5	.2	37	1.8	9	.4	2	.1	53	2.5	1,991	95.4	43	2.1
OH FEMALE	2	.2	13	1.5	3	.4	0	.0	18	2.1	820	97.5	3	.4
OH MALE	3	.2	24	1.9	6	.5	2	.2	35	2.8	1,171	94.0	40	3.2
OHIO STATE U MAIN CAMPUS														
OH TOTAL	38	.1	2,061	5.7	226	.6	151	.4	2,476	6.	33,706	92.5	273	.7
OH FEMALE	23	.1	1,214	7.3	106	.6	59	.4	1,402	8.8	15,216	91.2	59	.4
OH MALE	15	.1	847	4.3	120	.6	92	.5	1,074	5.4	18,490	93.5	214	1.1
OHIO ST U AGRL TECH INST														
OH TOTAL	1	.1	3	.4	0	.0	3	.4	7	.9	738	98.7	3	.4
OH FEMALE	0	.0	0	.0	0	.0	0	.0	0	.0	259	100.0	0	.0
OH MALE	1	.2	3	.6	0	.0	3	.6	7	1.4	479	98.0	3	.6
OHIO STATE U LIMA BR														
OH TOTAL	1	.2	16	2.4	2	.3	2	.3	21	3.2	632	96.6	1	.2
OH FEMALE	1	.3	12	3.8	1	.3	0	.0	14	4.4	301	95.3	1	.3
OH MALE	0	.0	4	1.2	1	.3	2	.6	7	2.1	331	97.9	0	.0
OHIO STATE U MANSFIELD BR														
OH TOTAL	1	.1	19	2.3	1	.1	2	.2	23	2.8	787	97.2	0	.0
OH FEMALE	0	.0	10	2.3	0	.0	1	.2	11	2.5	424	97.5	0	.0
OH MALE	1	.3	9	2.4	1	.3	1	.3	12	3.2	363	96.8	0	.0
OHIO STATE U MARION BR														
OH TOTAL	0	.0	2	.4	0	.0	1	.2	3	.6	537	99.4	0	.0
OH FEMALE	0	.0	1	.3	0	.0	1	.3	2	.7	286	99.3	0	.0
OH MALE	0	.0	1	.4	0	.0	0	.0	1	.4	251	99.6	0	.0
OHIO STATE U NEWARK BR														
OH TOTAL	0	.0	4	.6	3	.4	4	.6	11	1.6	682	98.4	0	.0
OH FEMALE	0	.0	2	.6	1	.3	1	.3	4	1.2	331	98.8	0	.0
OH MALE	0	.0	2	.6	2	.6	3	.8	7	2.0	351	98.0	0	.0
OHIO U MAIN CAMPUS														
OH TOTAL	33	.3	699	6.0	24	.2	21	.2	777	6.7	10,380	89.5	435	3.8
OH FEMALE	15	.3	387	7.2	14	.3	9	.2	425	7.9	4,867	90.3	397	1.8
OH MALE	18	.3	312	5.0	10	.2	12	.2	352	5.7	5,513	88.9	38	5.4
OHIO U BELMONT CO BRANCH														
OH TOTAL	0	.0	1	.1	0	.0	0	.0	1	.1	835	99.5	3	.4
OH FEMALE	0	.0	1	.2	0	.0	0	.0	1	.2	494	99.4	2	.4
OH MALE	0	.0	0	.0	0	.0	0	.0	0	.0	341	99.7	1	.3
OHIO U CHILLICOTHE BR														
OH TOTAL	6	.6	30	3.0	3	.3	2	.2	41	4.1	966	95.7	2	.2
OH FEMALE	6	1.1	17	3.1	2	.4	2	.4	27	4.9	521	96.3	1	.2
OH MALE	0	.0	13	2.8	1	.2	0	.0	14	3.0	445	96.7	1	.2
OHIO U IRONTON BRANCH														
OH TOTAL	5	.6	6	.7	1	.1	0	.0	12	1.4	831	98.3	2	.2
OH FEMALE	3	.6	6	1.1	0	.0	0	.0	9	1.7	531	98.2	1	.2
OH MALE	2	.7	0	.0	1	.3	0	.0	3	1.0	300	98.7	1	.3
OHIO U LANCASTER BRANCH														
OH TOTAL	5	.4	3	.2	2	.2	0	.0	10	.	1,227	98.6	7	.6
OH FEMALE	3	.4	2	.3	2	.3	0	.0	7	.6	695	98.3	1	.1
OH MALE	2	.4	1	.2	0	.0	0	.0	3	.8	532	98.3	6	1.1
OHIO U ZANESVILLE BRANCH														
OH TOTAL	8	.9	17	2.0	1	.1	4	.5	30	3.5	832	96.5	0	.0
OH FEMALE	8	1.4	13	2.3	1	.2	2	.4	24	4.3	531	95.7	0	.0
OH MALE	0	.0	4	1.3	0	.0	2	.7	6	2.0	301	98.0	0	.0
OHIO WESLEYAN UNIVERSITY														
OH TOTAL	0	.0	112	4.9	5	.2	10	.4	127	5.	2,058	90.0	101	4.4
OH FEMALE	0	.0	53	4.7	3	.3	3	.3	59	5.8	1,037	92.4	26	2.3
OH MALE	0	.0	59	5.1	2	.2	7	.6	68	5.8	1,021	87.7	75	6.4
OTTERBEIN COLLEGE														
OH TOTAL	1	.1	30	2.4	2	.2	1	.1	34	2.7	1,211	96.6	9	.7
OH FEMALE	1	.1	14	2.0	2	.3	0	.0	17	2.4	686	96.9	5	.7
OH MALE	0	.0	16	2.9	0	.0	1	.2	17	3.1	525	96.2	4	.7

TABLE 1 - TOTAL UNDERGRADUATE ENROLLMENT IN INSTITUTIONS OF HIGHER EDUCATION BY RACE, ETHNICITY AND SEX: INSTITUTION, STATE AND NATION, 1978

	AMERICAN INDIAN ALASKAN NATIVE		BLACK NON-HISPANIC		ASIAN OR PACIFIC ISLANDER		HISPANIC		TOTAL MINORITY		WHITE NON-HISPANIC		NON-RESIDENT ALIEN		TOTAL
	NUMBER	%	NUMBER	%	NUMBER	%	NUMBER	%	NUMBER	%	NUMBER	%	NUMBER	%	NUMBER
OHIO **CONTINUED**															
PAYNE THEOLOGICAL SEM															
OH TOTAL	0	.0	3	100.0	0	.0	0	.0	3	100.0		.0		.0	3
OH FEMALE	0	.0	1	100.0	0	.0	0	.0	1	100.0	0	.0	0	.0	1
OH MALE	0	.0	2	100.0	0	.0	0	.0	2	100.0	0	.0	0	.0	2
PONTIFICAL C JOSEPHINUM															
OH TOTAL	0	.0	1	1.1	3	3.4	7	8.0	11	12.5	77	87.5	0	.0	88
OH FEMALE	0	.0	0	.0	0	.0	0	.0	0	.0	0	.0	0	.0	0
OH MALE	0	.0	1	1.1	3	3.4	7	8.0	11	12.5	77	87.5	0	.0	88
RABBINICAL COLLEGE TELSHE															
OH TOTAL	0	.0	0	.0	0	.0	0	.0	0	.0	225	100.0	0	.0	225
OH FEMALE	0	.0	0	.0	0	.0	0	.0	0	.0	0	.0	0	.0	0
OH MALE	0	.0	0	.0	0	.0	0	.0	0	.0	225	100.0	0	.0	225
RIO GRANDE COLLEGE															
OH TOTAL	2	.2	13	1.5	1	.1	2	.2	18	2.0	848	94.9	28	3.1	894
OH FEMALE	0	.0	4	.9	0	.0	2	.5	6	1.4	417	98.6	0	.0	423
OH MALE	2	.4	9	1.9	1	.2	0	.0	12	2.5	431	91.5	28	5.9	471
SHAWNEE ST CMTY COLLEGE															
OH TOTAL	5	.3	80	4.7	8	.5	1	.1	94	5.6	1,588	94.1	5	.3	1,687
OH FEMALE	4	.4	19	1.9	4	.4	1	.1	28	2.8	972	96.9	3	.3	1,003
OH MALE	1	.1	61	8.9	4	.6	0	.0	66	9.6	616	90.1	2	.3	684
SINCLAIR CMTY COLLEGE															
OH TOTAL	40	.3	2,475	17.7	82	.6	64	.5	2,661	19.1	10,800	77.4	497	3.6	13,958
OH FEMALE	19	.2	1,649	19.6	49	.6	38	.5	1,755	20.9	6,320	75.3	317	3.8	8,392
OH MALE	21	.4	826	14.8	33	.6	26	.5	906	16.3	4,480	80.5	180	3.2	5,566
SOUTHERN OHIO COLLEGE															
OH TOTAL	0	.0	588	33.2	2	.1	5	.3	595	33.6	1,174	66.2	4	.2	1,773
OH FEMALE	0	.0	232	33.4	2	.3	1	.1	235	33.8	459	66.0	1	.1	695
OH MALE	0	.0	356	33.0	0	.0	4	.4	360	33.4	715	66.3	3	.3	1,078
STHN ST GEN-TECH COLLEGE															
OH TOTAL	3	.3	27	2.4	2	.2	0	.0	32	2.9	1,089	97.1	0	.0	1,121
OH FEMALE	1	.2	13	2.1	2	.3	0	.0	16	2.6	610	97.4	0	.0	626
OH MALE	2	.4	14	2.8	0	.0	0	.0	16	3.2	479	96.8	0	.0	495
STARK TECHNICAL COLLEGE															
OH TOTAL	4	.2	93	4.9	3	.2	3	.2	103	5.4	1,792	94.5	1	.1	1,896
OH FEMALE	2	.2	48	5.5	1	.1	1	.1	52	6.0	813	94.0	0	.0	865
OH MALE	2	.2	45	4.4	2	.2	2	.2	51	4.9	979	95.0	1	.1	1,031
TERRA TECHNICAL COLLEGE															
OH TOTAL	0	.0	25	1.3	0	.0	22	1.1	47	2.4	1,899	96.7	17	.9	1,963
OH FEMALE	0	.0	7	1.0	0	.0	9	1.3	16	2.3	695	97.7	0	.0	711
OH MALE	0	.0	18	1.4	0	.0	13	1.0	31	2.5	1,204	96.2	17	1.4	1,252
TIFFIN UNIVERSITY															
OH TOTAL	0	.0	12	2.8	0	.0	9	2.1	21	4.9	405	94.6	2	.5	428
OH FEMALE	0	.0	9	6.3	0	.0	3	2.1	12	8.5	130	91.5	0	.0	142
OH MALE	0	.0	3	1.0	0	.0	6	2.1	9	3.1	275	96.2	2	.7	286
UNION EXPERIMENTING C & U															
OH TOTAL	285	39.3	199	27.4	0	.0	36	5.0	520	71.7	202	27.9	3	.4	725
OH FEMALE	245	48.0	107	21.0	0	.0	26	5.1	378	74.1	131	25.7	1	.2	510
OH MALE	40	18.6	92	42.8	0	.0	10	4.7	142	66.0	71	33.0	2	.9	215
U OF AKRON MAIN CAMPUS															
OH TOTAL	71	.4	1,641	9.1	78	.4	55	.3	1,845	10.2	16,055	89.0	139	.8	18,039
OH FEMALE	31	.3	1,067	11.9	29	.3	34	.4	1,161	13.0	7,768	86.6	36	.4	8,965
OH MALE	40	.4	574	6.3	49	.5	21	.2	684	7.5	8,287	91.3	103	1.1	9,074
U AKRON WAYNE GEN-TECH C															
OH TOTAL	3	.5	10	1.8	0	.0	1	.2	14	2.5	548	97.5	0	.0	562
OH FEMALE	2	.7	6	2.0	0	.0	1	.3	9	3.0	292	97.0	0	.0	301
OH MALE	1	.4	4	1.5	0	.0	0	.0	5	1.9	256	98.1	0	.0	261
U OF CINCINNATI MATV CAM															
OH TOTAL	26	.1	2,459	12.4	91	.5	52	.3	2,628	13.2	17,202	86.4	80	.4	19,910
OH FEMALE	10	.1	1,523	18.2	45	.5	20	.2	1,598	19.1	6,732	80.6	25	.3	8,355
OH MALE	16	.1	936	8.1	46	.4	32	.3	1,030	8.9	10,470	90.6	55	.5	11,555
U CINCIN CLERMNT GEN-TECH															
OH TOTAL	1	.3	0	.0	1	.3	1	.3	3	.8	389	99.2	0	.0	392
OH FEMALE	1	.5	0	.0	1	.5	1	.5	3	1.4	205	98.6	0	.0	208
OH MALE	0	.0	0	.0	0	.0	0	.0	0	.0	184	100.0	0	.0	184
U CINCIN RAYMND WALTERS C															
OH TOTAL	7	.4	149	8.1	9	.5	2	.1	167	9.1	1,655	90.2	12	.7	1,834
OH FEMALE	4	.3	111	8.9	8	.6	2	.2	125	10.1	1,112	89.6	4	.3	1,241
OH MALE	3	.5	38	6.4	1	.2	0	.0	42	7.1	543	91.6	8	1.3	593
UNIVERSITY OF DAYTON															
OH TOTAL	6	.1	337	5.1	25	.4	61	.9	429	6.5	6,023	90.8	179	2.7	6,631
OH FEMALE	2	.1	182	6.9	9	.3	17	.6	210	8.0	2,411	91.4	17	.6	2,638
OH MALE	4	.1	155	3.9	16	.4	44	1.1	219	5.5	3,612	90.5	162	4.1	3,993
UNIVERSITY OF TOLEDO															
OH TOTAL	49	.4	1,401	10.3	125	.9	135	1.0	1,710	12.5	11,598	85.0	341	2.5	13,649
OH FEMALE	15	.2	896	13.4	61	.9	69	1.0	1,041	15.6	5,514	82.8	107	1.6	6,662
OH MALE	34	.5	505	7.2	64	.9	66	.9	669	9.6	6,084	87.1	234	3.3	6,987
URBANA COLLEGE															
OH TOTAL	8	1.1	153	21.5	0	.0	0	.0	161	22.7	549	77.3	0	.0	710
OH FEMALE	5	2.0	39	15.1	0	.0	0	.0	43	17.1	209	82.9	0	.0	252
OH MALE	3	.7	115	25.1	0	.0	0	.0	118	25.8	340	74.2	0	.0	458
URSULINE COLLEGE															
OH TOTAL	4	1.1	44	11.7	7	1.9	6	1.6	61	16.2	313	83.0	3	.8	377
OH FEMALE	4	1.1	44	11.9	6	1.6	6	1.6	60	16.2	308	83.0	3	.8	371
OH MALE	0	.0	0	.0	1	16.7	0	.0	1	16.7	5	83.3	0	.0	6
WALSH COLLEGE															
OH TOTAL	0	.0	7	1.3	5	.9	3	.5	15	2.7	511	93.4	21	3.8	547
OH FEMALE	0	.0	1	.3	0	.0	1	.3	2	.7	292	98.0	4	1.3	298
OH MALE	0	.0	6	2.4	5	2.0	2	.8	13	5.2	219	88.0	17	6.8	249
WASHINGTON TECH COLLEGE															
OH TOTAL	0	.0	2	.5	0	.0	0	.0	2	.5	432	99.5	0	.0	434
OH FEMALE	0	.0	1	.6	0	.0	0	.0	1	.6	156	99.4	0	.0	157
OH MALE	0	.0	1	.4	0	.0	0	.0	1	.4	276	99.6	0	.0	277

TABLE 1 - TOTAL UNDERGRADUATE ENROLLMENT IN INSTITUTIONS OF HIGHER EDUCATION BY RACE, ETHNICITY AND SEX:
INSTITUTION, STATE AND NATION, 1978

	AMERICAN INDIAN ALASKAN NATIVE		BLACK NON-HISPANIC		ASIAN OR PACIFIC ISLANDER		HISPANIC		TOTAL MINORITY		WHITE NON-HISPANIC		NON-RESIDENT ALIEN	
	NUMBER	%	NUMBER	%	NUMBER	%	NUMBER	%	NUMBER	%	NUMBER	%	NUMBER	%
OHIO CONTINUED														
WILBERFORCE UNIVERSITY														
OH TOTAL	0	.0	979	95.4	0	.0		.0	979	95.4	1	.1	46	4.5
OH FEMALE	0	.0	467	98.7	0	.0	0	.0	467	98.7	1	.2	5	1.1
OH MALE	0	.0	512	92.6	0	.0	0	.0	512	92.6	0	.0	41	7.4
WILMINGTON COLLEGE														
OH TOTAL	0	.0	156	18.9	1	.1	10	1.2	167	20.2	623	75.5	35	4.2
OH FEMALE	0	.0	19	8.4	0	.0	7	3.1	26	11.5	194	85.5	7	3.1
OH MALE	0	.0	137	22.9	1	.2	3	.5	141	23.6	429	71.7	28	4.7
WITTENBERG UNIVERSITY														
OH TOTAL	0	.0	119	5.3	4	.2	2	.1	125	5.5	2,109	93.6	19	.8
OH FEMALE	0	.0	58	5.0	2	.2	1	.1	61	5.2	1,101	94.2	7	.6
OH MALE	0	.0	61	5.6	2	.2	1	.1	64	5.9	1,008	93.0	12	1.1
WOOSTER BUSINESS COLLEGE														
OH TOTAL	0	.0	3	3.3	0	.0	0	.0	3	3.3	88	96.7	0	.0
OH FEMALE	0	.0	2	4.4	0	.0	0	.0	2	4.4	43	95.6	0	.0
OH MALE	0	.0	1	2.2	0	.0	0	.0	1	2.2	45	97.8	0	.0
WRIGHT ST U MAIN CAMPUS														
OH TOTAL	13	.1	655	6.8	66	.7	87	.9	821	8.5	8,742	90.6	82	.9
OH FEMALE	8	.2	374	7.8	37	.8	40	.8	459	9.6	4,311	90.0	19	.4
OH MALE	5	.1	281	5.8	29	.6	47	1.0	362	7.5	4,431	91.2	63	1.3
WRIGHT ST U WSTN OHIO BR														
OH TOTAL	1	.2	1	.2	1	.2	3	.5	6	.9	626	99.1	0	.0
OH FEMALE	1	.3	1	.3	1	.3	3	.8	6	1.6	359	98.4	0	.0
OH MALE	0	.0	0	.0	0	.0	0	.0	0	.0	267	100.0	0	.0
XAVIER UNIVERSITY														
OH TOTAL	0	.0	221	8.1	15	.5	32	1.2	268	9.8	2,419	88.6	43	1.6
OH FEMALE	0	.0	134	11.3	8	.7	9	.8	151	12.7	1,023	86.1	14	1.2
OH MALE	0	.0	87	5.6	7	.5	23	1.5	117	7.6	1,396	90.5	29	1.9
YOUNGSTOWN ST UNIVERSITY														
OH TOTAL	12	.1	1,218	9.0	17	.1	62	.5	1,309	9.7	11,959	88.6	233	1.7
OH FEMALE	8	.1	758	12.2	10	.2	38	.6	814	13.1	5,374	86.2	46	.7
OH MALE	4	.1	460	6.3	7	.1	24	.3	495	6.8	6,585	90.6	187	2.6
OHIO TOTAL (124 INSTITUTIONS)														
OH TOTAL	961	.3	36,108	10.1	1,567	.4	2,144	.6	40,780	11.5	311,201	87.4	4,081	1.1
OH FEMALE	604	.3	21,181	11.9	805	.5	1,109	.6	23,699	13.3	153,260	86.0	1,228	.7
OH MALE	357	.2	14,927	8.4	762	.4	1,035	.6	17,081	9.6	157,941	88.8	2,853	1.6
OKLAHOMA														
BACONE COLLEGE														
OK TOTAL	195	41.0	49	10.3	34	7.1	0	.0	278	58.4	197	41.4	.	.2
OK FEMALE	142	44.7	30	9.4	10	3.1	0	.0	182	57.2	136	42.8	1	.0
OK MALE	53	33.5	19	12.0	24	15.2	0	.0	96	60.8	61	38.6	8	.6
BARTLESVILLE WESLEYAN C														
OK TOTAL	3	.6	7	1.3	3	.6	0	.0	13	2.4	525	96.9	4	.7
OK FEMALE	3	1.0	2	.7	2	.7	0	.0	7	2.3	297	97.4	1	.3
OK MALE	0	.0	5	2.1	1	.4	0	.0	6	2.5	228	96.2	3	1.3
BETHANY NAZARENE COLLEGE														
OK TOTAL	21	1.7	8	.6	6	.5	11	.9	46	3.7	1,182	94.3	25	2.0
OK FEMALE	8	1.2	4	.6	4	.6	7	1.0	23	3.5	634	95.3	8	1.2
OK MALE	13	2.2	4	.7	2	.3	4	.7	23	3.9	548	93.2	17	2.9
CAMERON UNIVERSITY														
OK TOTAL	196	4.1	670	13.9	61	1.3	119	2.5	1,046	21.6	3,757	77.7	31	.6
OK FEMALE	109	4.7	314	13.6	27	1.2	46	2.0	496	21.5	1,802	78.0	11	.5
OK MALE	87	3.4	356	14.1	34	1.3	73	2.9	550	21.8	1,955	77.4	20	.8
CARL ALBERT JR COLLEGE														
OK TOTAL	44	5.2	47	5.5	2	.2	3	.4	96	11.3	669	78.6	86	10.1
OK FEMALE	21	5.1	29	7.0	1	.2	2	.2	51	12.3	360	87.2	2	.5
OK MALE	23	5.3	18	4.1	1	.2	3	.7	45	10.3	309	70.5	84	19.2
CENTRAL STATE UNIVERSITY														
OK TOTAL	153	1.7	929	10.3	68	.8	6	.0	1,218	13.5	7,549	83.6	258	2.9
OK FEMALE	78	1.6	502	10.6	32	.7	38	.0	650	13.7	4,041	85.3	45	1.0
OK MALE	75	1.7	427	10.0	36	.8	38	.7	568	13.2	3,508	81.8	213	5.0
CLAREMORE JUNIOR COLLEGE														
OK TOTAL	130	7.9	117	7.1	11	.7	6	.4	264	16.1	1,163	71.0	210	12.8
OK FEMALE	82	10.9	66	8.8	1	.1	0	.0	149	19.8	584	77.6	20	2.7
OK MALE	48	5.4	51	5.8	10	1.1	6	.7	115	13.0	579	65.5	190	21.5
CONNORS STATE COLLEGE														
OK TOTAL	109	9.0	153	12.6	2	.2	2	.2	266	21.9	947	78.1	0	.0
OK FEMALE	75	10.5	92	12.9	2	.3	2	.3	171	24.0	542	76.0	0	.0
OK MALE	34	6.8	61	12.2	0	.0	0	.0	95	19.0	405	81.0	0	.0
EAST CENTRAL OKLA STATE U														
OK TOTAL	207	6.8	139	4.5	13	.4	8	.3	367	12.0	2,676	87.5	15	.5
OK FEMALE	108	6.7	76	4.7	1	.1	3	.2	188	11.6	1,432	88.2	3	.2
OK MALE	99	6.9	63	4.4	12	.8	5	.3	179	12.5	1,244	86.7	12	.8
EASTERN OKLA ST COLLEGE														
OK TOTAL	122	6.4	94	4.9	2	.1	7	.4	225	11.7	1,657	86.5	33	1.7
OK FEMALE	68	7.9	37	4.3	1	.1	5	.6	111	12.8	750	86.8	3	.3
OK MALE	54	5.1	57	5.4	1	.1	2	.2	114	10.8	907	86.3	30	2.9
EL RENO JUNIOR COLLEGE														
OK TOTAL	33	4.0	89	10.7	2	.2	27	3.2	151	18.1	568	68.3	113	13.6
OK FEMALE	16	4.5	28	7.9	1	.3	10	2.8	55	15.6	285	80.7	13	3.7
OK MALE	17	3.5	61	12.7	1	.2	17	3.5	96	20.0	283	59.1	100	20.9
HILLSDL FREE WILL BAPT C														
OK TOTAL	1	.6	1	.6	0	.0	0	.0	2	1.2	163	97.0	3	1.8
OK FEMALE	1	1.3	0	.0	0	.0	0	.0	1	1.3	77	96.3	2	2.5
OK MALE	0	.0	1	1.1	0	.0	0	.0	1	1.1	86	97.7	1	1.1
LANGSTON UNIVERSITY														
OK TOTAL	0	.0	770	81.9	0	.0	1	.1	771	82.0	6	.6	163	17.3
OK FEMALE	0	.0	365	93.4	0	.0	1	.3	366	93.6	4	1.0	21	5.4
OK MALE	0	.0	405	73.8	0	.0	0	.0	405	73.8	2	.4	142	25.9

'INUED

	BLACK NON-HISPANIC		ASIAN OR PACIFIC ISLANDER		HISPANIC		TOTAL MINORITY		WHITE NON-HISPANIC		NON-RESIDENT ALIEN		TOTAL
	NUMBER	%	NUMBER	%	NUMBER	%	NUMBER	%	NUMBER	%	NUMBER	%	NUMBER
	1	1.0	0	.0	0	.0	1	1.0	101	97.1	2	1	104
	1	1.9	0	.0	0	.0	1	1.9	52	96.3	1	1.9	54
	0	.0	0	.0	0	.0	0	.0	49	98.0	1	2.0	50
	87	7.7	0	.0	3	.3	196	17.3	917	80.9	21	1.9	1,134
	62	10.0	0	.0	1	.2	127	20.6	491	79.4	0	.0	618
	25	4.8	0	.0	2	.4	69	13.4	426	82.6	21	4.1	516
	118	5.0	6	.3	8	.3	238	10.0	1,985	83.5	153	6.4	2,376
	38	3.7	3	.3	2	.2	96	9.4	911	89.0	17	1.7	1,024
	80	5.9	3	.2	6	.4	142	10.5	1,074	79.4	136	10.1	1,352
	277	6.8	10	.2	15	.4	980	24.0	3,056	74.8	47	1.2	4,083
	153	7.0	6	.3	7	.3	553	25.3	1,623	74.2	10	5	2,186
	124	6.5	4	.2	8	.4	427	22.5	1,433	75.5	37	210	1,897
	30	2.4	0	.0	5	.4	129	10.2	1,066	84.5	66	5.2	1,261
	13	2.0	0	.0	4	.6	76	11.6	569	86.7	11	1.7	656
	17	2.8	0	.0	1	.2	53	8.9	497	82.1	55	9.1	605
	60	3.8	9	.6	18	1.1	105	6.6	1,427	89.8	57	3.6	1,589
	16	1.9	6	.7	8	1.0	39	4.8	771	93.9	11	1.3	821
	44	5.7	3	.4	10	1.3	66	8.6	656	85.4	46	6.0	768
	23	1.5	3	.2	9	.6	66	4.3	1,437	94.2	22	1	1,525
	14	1.7	1	.1	7	.9	36	4.4	762	94.0	13		811
	9	1.3	2	.3	2	.3	30	4.2	675	94.5	9	1.8	714
	90	6.3	9	.6	3	.2	108	7.6	1,293	90.7	25	1.8	1,426
	52	6.7	5	.6	2	.3	60	7.8	701	90.7	12	1.6	773
	38	5.8	4	.6	1	.2	48	7.4	592	90.7	13	2.0	653
	41	5.5	7	.9	10	1.3	67	9.0	309	41.6	367	49.4	743
	21	8.8	2	.8	4	1.7	33	13.8	178	74.5	28	11.7	239
	20	4.0	5	1.0	6	1.2	34	6.7	131	26.0	339	67.3	504
	91	8.1	0	.0	19	1.7	133	11.9	899	80.3	87	7.8	1,119
	55	10.3	0	.0	7	1.3	74	13.9	432	80.9	28	5.2	534
	36	6.2	0	.0	12	2.1	59	10.1	467	79.8	59	10.1	585
	24	2.9	5	.6	18	2.2	56	6.8	750	91.2	16	1.9	822
	5	1.5	1	.3	3	.9	10	2.9	334	97.1	0	.0	344
	19	4.0	4	.8	15	3.1	46	9.6	416	87.0	16	3.3	478
	36	22.9	5	3.2	0	.0	43	27.4	99	63.1	15	9.6	157
	33	28.9	5	4.4	0	.0	39	34.2	67	58.8	8	7.0	114
	3	7.0	0	.0	0	.0	4	9.3	32	74.4	7	16.3	43
	955	3.0	134	.7	100	.5	1,098	5.9	16,608	89.6	831	4.5	18,537
	274	3.5	41	.5	42	.5	488	6.2	7,228	92.3	116	1.5	7,832
	281	2.6	93	.9	58	.5	610	5.7	9,380	87.6	715	6.7	10,705
	126	5.5	42	1.8	28	1.2	232	10.1	2,061	89.9	0	.0	2,293
	51	5.7	7	.8	13	1.5	90	10.0	806	90.0	0	.0	896
	75	5.4	35	2.5	15	1.1	142	10.2	1,255	89.8	0	.0	1,397
	132	3.8	28	.8	23	.7	193	5.5	3,162	90.3	148	4.2	3,503
	69	4.1	15	.9	5	.3	94	5.6	1,523	91.0	56	3.3	1,673
	63	3.4	13	.7	18	1.0	99	5.4	1,639	89.6	92	5.0	1,830
	1,226	16.1	126	1.7	124	1.6	1,776	23.3	5,163	67.7	687	9.0	7,626
	685	18.3	53	1.4	43	1.1	955	25.5	2,674	71.4	117	3.1	3,746
	541	13.9	73	1.9	81	2.1	821	21.2	2,489	64.1	570	14.7	3,880
	37	3.8	6	.6	7	.7	60	6.1	852	86.9	68	6.9	980
	23	4.5	4	.8	0	.0	32	6.3	438	86.4	37	7.3	507
	14	3.0	2	.4	7	1.5	28	5.9	414	87.5	31	6.6	473
	9	3.5	0	.0	4	1.5	28	10.8	189	73.0	42	16.2	259
	3	2.6	0	.0	3	2.6	14	12.0	95	81.2	8	6.8	117
	6	4.2	0	.0	1	.7	14	9.9	94	66.2	34	23.9	142
	3	1.0	1	.3	2	.6	8	2.5	305	96.8	2	.5	315
	3	1.3	1	.4	2	.8	7	3.0	230	97.0	0	.0	237
	0	.0	0	.0	0	.0	1	1.3	75	96.2	2	2.6	78
	81	6.3	0	.0	4	.3	195	15.1	936	72.4	162	12.5	1,293
	47	7.2	0	.0	3	.5	121	18.5	513	78.4	20	3.1	654
	34	5.3	0	.0	1	.2	74	11.6	423	66.2	142	22.2	639
	158	4.0	14	.4	15	.4	433	10.9	3,155	79.6	375	9.5	3,963
	69	3.8	6	.3	7	.4	224	12.2	1,549	84.7	36	3.1	1,829
	89	4.2	8	.4	8	.4	209	9.8	1,606	75.3	319	14.9	2,134
	250	4.7	32	.6	73	1.4	538	10.0	4,547	84.7	284	5	5,369
	147	4.8	15	.5	40	1.3	308	10.0	2,650	85.9	128	4.1	3,086
	103	4.5	17	.7	33	1.4	230	10.1	1,897	83.1	156	6.8	2,283
	125	3.1	31	.8	24	.6	309	7.8	3,627	91.2	39	1	3,975
	55	2.6	10	.5	11	.5	150	7.2	1,920	92.4	9	.0	2,079
	70	3.7	21	1.1	13	.7	159	8.4	1,707	90.0	30	1.8	1,896

	AMERICAN INDIAN ALASKAN NATIVE		BLACK NON-HISPANIC		ASIAN OR PACIFIC ISLANDER		HISPANIC		TOTAL MINORITY		WHITE NON-HISPANIC		NON-RESIDENT ALIEN	
	NUMBER	%	NUMBER	%	NUMBER	%	NUMBER	%	NUMBER	%	NUMBER	%	NUMBER	%
OKLAHOMA CONTINUED														
TULSA JUNIOR COLLEGE														
OK TOTAL	284	3.2	670	7.6	107	1.2	80	.9	1,141	13.0	7,649	87.0	0	.0
OK FEMALE	154	3.2	391	8.2	47	1.0	39	.8	631	13.3	4,127	86.7	0	.0
OK MALE	130	3.2	279	6.9	60	1.5	41	1.0	510	12.6	3,522	87.4	0	.0
U OF OKLA HEALTH SCI CTR														
OK TOTAL	19	2.1	25	2.7	11	1.2	3	.3	58	6.3	917	89.0	43	4.7
OK FEMALE	11	1.8	17	2.8	5	.8	2	.3	35	5.7	563	92.1	13	2.1
OK MALE	8	2.6	8	2.6	6	2.0	1	.3	23	7.5	254	82.7	30	9.8
U OF OKLAHOMA NORMAN CAM														
OK TOTAL	446	2.9	522	3.4	103	.7	96	.6	1,167	7.7	13,322	87.6	716	4.7
OK FEMALE	212	3.4	255	4.0	38	.6	43	.7	548	8.7	5,617	89.2	134	2.1
OK MALE	234	2.6	267	3.0	65	.7	53	.6	619	7.0	7,705	86.5	582	6.5
U OF SCI & ARTS OF OKLA														
OK TOTAL	107	11.6	77	8.4	14	1.5	8	.9	206	22.4	630	68.5	84	9.1
OK FEMALE	64	12.4	35	6.8	6	1.2	4	.8	109	21.2	386	75.0	20	3.9
OK MALE	43	10.6	42	10.4	8	2.0	4	1.0	97	24.0	244	60.2	64	15.8
UNIVERSITY OF TULSA														
OK TOTAL	64	1.5	131	3.1	14	.3	18	.4	227	5.4	3,625	86.2	354	8.4
OK FEMALE	31	1.6	47	2.4	8	.4	7	.4	93	4.7	1,806	91.9	67	3.4
OK MALE	33	1.5	84	3.8	6	.3	11	.5	134	6.0	1,819	81.2	287	12.8
WESTERN OKLAHOMA STATE C														
OK TOTAL	20	1.2	127	7.3	18	1.0	65	3.7	230	13.2	1,501	86.4	7	.4
OK FEMALE	10	1.1	54	6.1	9	1.0	27	3.1	100	11.3	781	88.3	3	.3
OK MALE	10	1.2	73	8.5	9	1.1	38	4.4	130	15.2	720	84.3	4	.5
OKLAHOMA TOTAL (42 INSTITUTIONS)														
OK TOTAL	4,586	3.7	8,205	6.7	939	.8	1,034	.8	14,764	12.0	102,547	83.4	5,662	4.6
OK FEMALE	2,536	4.3	4,233	7.1	376	.6	448	.8	7,593	12.8	50,741	85.4	1,052	1.8
OK MALE	2,050	3.2	3,972	6.2	563	.9	586	.9	7,171	11.3	51,806	81.5	4,610	7.2
OREGON														
BLUE MTN CMTY COLLEGE														
OR TOTAL	34	3.6	3	.3	11	1.2	4	.4	52	5.5	898	94.5	0	.0
OR FEMALE	25	5.3	0	.0	1	.2	1	.2	27	5.7	446	94.3	0	.0
OR MALE	9	1.9	3	.6	10	2.1	3	.6	25	5.2	452	94.8	0	.0
CENTRAL OREG CMTY COLLEGE														
OR TOTAL	27	1.6	5	.3	4	.2	12	.7	48	2.8	1,648	97.0	3	.2
OR FEMALE	23	2.5	1	.1	4	.4	4	.4	32	3.4	904	96.5	1	.1
OR MALE	4	.5	4	.5	0	.0	8	1.0	16	2.1	744	97.6	2	.3
CHEMEKETA CMTY COLLEGE														
OR TOTAL	23	.7	21	.6	32	.9	34	1.0	110	3.2	3,244	94.8	67	2.0
OR FEMALE	13	.8	5	.3	13	.8	14	.8	45	2.7	1,598	96.4	14	.8
OR MALE	10	.6	16	.9	19	1.1	20	1.1	65	3.7	1,646	93.3	53	3.0
CLACKAMAS CMTY COLLEGE														
OR TOTAL	7	.2	9	.2	14	.3	7	.2	37	.8	4,529	98.6	28	.6
OR FEMALE	3	.1	4	.2	6	.3	4	.2	17	.7	2,284	98.9	9	.4
OR MALE	4	.2	5	.2	8	.4	3	.1	20	.9	2,245	98.3	19	.8
CLATSOP COMMUNITY COLLEGE														
OR TOTAL	6	1.4	11	2.6	4	.9	5	1.2	26	6.1	397	93.4	2	.5
OR FEMALE	2	1.0	7	3.4	0	.0	1	.5	10	4.8	197	95.2	0	.0
OR MALE	4	1.8	4	1.8	4	1.8	4	1.8	16	7.3	200	91.7	2	.9
COLEGIO CESAR CHAVEZ														
OR TOTAL	0	.0	0	.0	0	.0	20	80.0	20	80.0	5	20.0	0	.0
OR FEMALE	0	.0	0	.0	0	.0	10	76.9	10	76.9	3	23.1	0	.0
OR MALE	0	.0	0	.0	0	.0	10	83.3	10	83.3	2	16.7	0	.0
COLUMBIA CHRISTIAN C														
OR TOTAL	5	1.7	8	2.7	3	1.0	5	1.7	21	7.2	268	92.1	2	.7
OR FEMALE	2	1.3	2	1.3	3	2.0	2	1.3	9	6.0	140	93.3	1	.7
OR MALE	3	2.1	6	4.3	0	.0	3	2.1	12	8.5	128	90.8	1	.7
CONCORDIA COLLEGE														
OR TOTAL	3	1.0	9	3.0	8	2.7	4	1.3	24	8.1	266	89.6	7	2.4
OR FEMALE	1	.6	2	1.3	6	3.8	2	1.3	11	7.1	142	91.0	3	1.9
OR MALE	2	1.4	7	5.0	2	1.4	2	1.4	13	9.2	124	87.9	4	2.8
GEORGE FOX COLLEGE														
OR TOTAL	3	.5	17	2.6	1	.2	3	.5	24	3.6	631	95.6	5	.8
OR FEMALE	2	.5	8	2.2	1	.3	1	.3	12	3.3	350	96.2	2	.5
OR MALE	1	.3	9	3.0	0	.0	2	.7	12	4.1	281	94.9	3	1.0
JUDSON BAPTIST COLLEGE														
OR TOTAL	2	.8	2	.8	0	.0	1	.4	5	2.1	235	97.9	0	.0
OR FEMALE	2	1.5	0	.0	0	.0	1	.8	3	2.3	127	97.7	0	.0
OR MALE	0	.0	2	1.8	0	.0	0	.0	2	1.8	108	98.2	0	.0
LANE COMMUNITY COLLEGE														
OR TOTAL	103	1.5	59	.8	60	.9	77	1.1	299	4.3	6,605	94.6	80	1.1
OR FEMALE	47	1.3	27	.7	31	.9	43	1.2	148	4.1	3,462	95.3	23	.6
OR MALE	56	1.7	32	1.0	29	.9	34	1.0	151	4.5	3,143	93.8	57	1.7
LEWIS AND CLARK COLLEGE														
OR TOTAL	15	.8	15	.8	74	4.2	17	1.0	121	6.8	1,589	89.4	68	3.8
OR FEMALE	10	1.0	8	.8	42	4.3	9	.9	69	7.0	883	89.4	36	3.6
OR MALE	5	.6	7	.9	32	4.1	8	1.0	52	6.6	706	89.4	32	4.1
LINFIELD COLLEGE														
OR TOTAL	9	.9	30	2.9	57	5.4	10	1.0	106	10.1	926	88.3	17	1.6
OR FEMALE	3	.6	6	1.2	24	4.7	5	1.0	38	7.5	465	91.2	7	1.4
OR MALE	6	1.1	24	4.5	33	6.1	5	.9	68	12.6	461	85.5	10	1.9
LINN-BENTON CMTY COLLEGE														
OR TOTAL	13	.6	9	.4	33	1.5	19	.9	74	3.4	2,112	96.0	13	.6
OR FEMALE	7	.7	4	.4	14	1.4	8	.8	33	3.4	941	96.1	5	.5
OR MALE	6	.5	5	.4	19	1.6	11	.9	41	3.4	1,171	96.0	8	.7
MARYLHURST ED CENTER														
OR TOTAL	6	2.8	13	6.0	2	.9	0	.0	21	9.7	193	89.4	2	.9
OR FEMALE	1	.7	4	2.9	1	.7	0	.0	6	4.4	129	94.2	2	1.5
OR MALE	5	6.3	9	11.4	1	1.3	0	.0	15	19.0	64	81.0	0	.0

BLACK NON-HISPANIC		ASIAN OR PACIFIC ISLANDER		HISPANIC		TOTAL MINORITY		WHITE NON-HISPANIC		NON-RESIDENT ALIEN		TOTAL
NUMBER	%	NUMBER	%	NUMBER	%	NUMBER	%	NUMBER	%	NUMBER	%	NUMBER
0	.0	4	10.0	0	.0	4	10.0	33	82.5	3	7.5	40
0	.0	0	.0	0	.0	0	.0	0	.0	0	.0	0
0	.0	4	10.0	0	.0	4	10.0	33	82.5	3	7.5	40
124	1.7	265	3.5	95	1.3	596	8	6,823	91.2	64	.9	7,483
37	1.0	125	3.3	44	1.2	272	7 2	3,465	92.0	29	.8	3,766
87	2.3	140	3.8	51	1.4	324	8:7	3,358	90.3	35	.9	3,717
2	.3	3	.5	4	.7	12	2.'	552	96.3	9	1.6	573
0	.0	2	.9	0	.0	3	1.	226	97.4	3	1.3	232
2	.6	1	.3	4	1.2	9	2.4	326	95.6	6	1.9	341
1	.5	6	3.2	0	.0	7	3 7	180	95.2	2	1	189
1	.8	6	4.9	0	.0	7	5 7	113	92.6	2	1	122
0	.0	0	.0	0	.0	0	10	67	100.0	0	1?	67
2	.8	3	1.2	4	1.6		3 6	228	91.6	12	4	249
0	.0	2	1.8	1	.9		2 7	104	93.7	4	3	111
2	1.4	1	.7	3	2.2	8	4:3	124	89.9	8	5?	138
23	1.6	20	1.4	27	1.9	91	.	1,218	86.3	102	7.2	1,411
3	.4	5	.7	14	2.1	30	.	608	90.2	36	5.3	674
20	2.7	15	2.0	13	1.8	61	8.3	610	82.8	66	9.0	737
32	1.4	46	2.0	6	.3	106	4 6	2,172	94.8	12	.5	2,290
7	.5	19	1.4	0	.0	39	2 8	1,342	97.2	0	.0	1,381
25	2.8	27	3.0	6	.7	67	71?	830	91.3	12	1.3	909
23	1.1	35	1.6	17	.8	102	4.8	1,975	93.1	45	2.1	2,122
5	.7	8	1.1	5	.7	28	4.0	669	95.2	6	.9	703
18	1.3	27	1.9	12	.8	74	5.2	1,306	92.0	39	2.7	1,419
91	.7	398	2.9	78	.6	809	.9	12,644	92.4	238	1.7	13,691
23	.4	166	2.9	30	.5	312	.5	5,285	93.7	45	.8	5,642
68	.8	232	2.9	48	.6	497	8.2	7,359	91.4	193	2.4	8,049
253	2.6	390	4.1	104	1.1	845	.	8,316	87.1	391	4.1	9,552
133	3.0	175	3.9	57	1.3	409	.	4,020	89.4	67	1.5	4,496
120	2.4	215	4.3	47	.9	436	8.6	4,296	85.0	324	6.4	5,056
11	.3	26	.7	29	.8	106	2 9	3,509	95.4	63	1 7	3,678
6	.3	14	.8	13	.7	55	3 0	1,787	95.9	21	1 1	1,863
5	.3	12	.7	16	.9	51	2?8	1,722	94.9	42	2?3	1,815
135	1.2	340	3.0	105	.9	680	.	10,495	91.4	313	2.7	11,488
47	.9	171	3.1	38	.7	303	.	5,110	92.5	112	2.0	5,525
88	1.5	169	2.8	67	1.1	377	8.2	5,385	90.3	201	3.4	5,963
3	.6	11	2.2	4	.8	20	4 0	473	95.7	1	.2	494
3	.7	9	2.0	4	.9	17	3 8	435	96.2	0	.0	452
0	.0	2	4.8	0	.0	3	7?1	38	90.5	1	2.4	42
29	4.3	97	14.5	10	1.5	152	22.8	510	76.5	5	.7	667
6	2.0	50	16.6	4	1.3	68	22.5	234	77.5	0	.0	302
23	6.3	47	12.9	6	1.6	84	23.0	276	75.6	5	1.4	365
380	2.2	483	2.8	345	2.0	1,433	8.3	15,194	88.0	639	3.7	17,266
190	2.2	242	2.8	173	2.0	718	8.3	7,614	88.0	320	3.7	8,652
190	2.2	241	2.8	172	2.0	715	8.3	7,580	88.0	319	3.7	8,614
9	.8	35	3.1	15	1.3	61	.5	1,030	92.0	28	2.5	1,119
3	.7	14	3.1	8	1.8	26	.7	423	92.6	8	1.8	457
6	.9	21	3.2	7	1.1	35	5.3	607	91.7	20	3.0	662
0	.0	3	.2	20	1.2	38	2 3	1,625	97.7	1	.1	1,664
0	.0	2	.2	10	1.1	22	2 4	876	97.4	1	.1	899
0	.0	1	.1	10	1.3	16	2?1	749	97.9	0	.0	765
3	.1	13	.4	23	.7	98	3 1	3,021	96.7	5	.2	3,124
0	.0	12	.7	12	.7	54	3 1	1,662	96.9	0	.0	1,716
3	.2	1	.1	11	.8	44	3?1	1,359	96.5	5	.4	1,408
8	.4	60	3.0	110	5.5	198	9	1,767	88.7	28	1.4	1,993
0	.0	33	2.9	67	5.8	111	.7	1,033	89.8	6	.5	1,150
8	.9	27	3.2	43	5.1	87	18?3	734	87.1	22	2.6	843
1	.1	6	.4	23	1.5	31	2 0	1,494	97.8	2	.1	1,527
0	.0	4	.5	13	1.6	17	2 1	781	97.9	0	.0	798
1	.1	2	.3	10	1.4	14	1?9	713	97.8	2	.3	729
70	3.3	59	2.8	17	.8	158	5	1,573	74.9	368	1 .	2,099
35	3.6	30	3.1	10	1.0	83	7 5	806	82.1	93	7?	982
35	3.1	29	2.6	7	.6	75	8?7	767	68.7	275	24.8	1,117
6	1.5	5	1.3	3	.8	17	4.3	337	86.2	37	9.5	391
4	2.1	1	.5	0	.0	6	3.1	176	90.3	13	6.7	195
2	1.0	4	2.0	3	1.5	11	5.6	161	82.1	24	12.2	196
0	.0	3	.7	0	.0	3	7	409	98.6	3	.7	415
0	.0	1	.5	0	.0	1	5	195	99.0	1	.5	197
0	.0	2	.9	0	.0	2	9	214	98.2	2	.9	218

TABLE 1 - TOTAL UNDERGRADUATE ENROLLMENT IN INSTITUTIONS OF HIGHER EDUCATION BY RACE, ETHNICITY AND SEX:
INSTITUTION, STATE AND NATION, 1978

	AMERICAN INDIAN ALASKAN NATIVE		BLACK NON-HISPANIC		ASIAN OR PACIFIC ISLANDER		HISPANIC		TOTAL MINORITY		WHITE NON-HISPANIC		NON-RESIDENT ALIEN		TOTAL
	NUMBER	%	NUMBER	%	NUMBER	%	NUMBER	%	NUMBER	%	NUMBER	%	NUMBER	%	NUMBER
OREGON	CONTINUED														
WILLAMETTE UNIVERSITY															
OR TOTAL	7	.6	28	2.2	58	4.6	1	1 3	109	8.6	1,146	90.1	17	1	1,272
OR FEMALE	4	.7	14	2.4	24	4.1	9	1 2	49	8.4	527	90.5	6	1	582
OR MALE	3	.4	14	2.0	34	4.9	9	1:3	60	8.7	619	89.7	11	1:8	690
OREGON	TOTAL (39 INSTITUTIONS)														
OR TOTAL	1,283	1.2	1,445	1.3	2,672	2.4	1,273	1 2	6,673	6.1	100,270	91.5	2,682	2.4	109,625
OR FEMALE	632	1.2	595	1.1	1,261	2.4	615	1 1	3,103	5.8	49,562	92.6	876	1.6	53,541
OR MALE	651	1.2	850	1.5	1,411	2.5	658	1:2	3,570	6.4	50,708	90.4	1,806	3.2	56,084
PENNSYLVANIA															
ACADEMY OF THE NEW CHURCH															
PA TOTAL	0	.0	0	.0	0	.0		.0	0	.0	111	83.5	22	16.5	.133
PA FEMALE	0	.0	0	.0	0	.0	0	.0	0	.0	54	78.3	15	21.7	69
PA MALE	0	.0	0	.0	0	.0	0	.0	0	.0	57	89.1	7	10.9	64
ALBRIGHT COLLEGE															
PA TOTAL	0	.0	11	.9	15	1.2	2	.2	28	2.2	1,225	96.7	14	1.1	1,267
PA FEMALE	0	.0	4	.6	5	.8	0	.0	9	1.4	644	98.3	2	.3	655
PA MALE	0	.0	7	1.1	10	1.6	2	.3	19	3.1	581	94.9	12	2.0	612
ALLEGHENY COLLEGE															
PA TOTAL	3	.2	55	3.0	7	.4	6	.3	71	3.8	1,781	96.1	2	.1	1,854
PA FEMALE	2	.2	30	3.4	2	.2	2	.2	36	4.1	833	95.7	1	.1	870
PA MALE	1	.1	25	2.5	5	.5	4	.4	35	3.6	948	96.3	1	.1	984
ALLNTWN C SNT FRAN DESALS															
PA TOTAL	5	.9	13	2.2	2	.3		1.0	26	4.4	550	93.5	12	2.0	588
PA FEMALE	3	1.0	7	2.2	0	.0		1.0	13	4.1	297	94.6	4	1.3	314
PA MALE	2	.7	6	2.2	2	.7	4	1.1	13	4.7	253	92.3	8	2.9	274
ALLIANCE COLLEGE															
PA TOTAL	0	.0	7	3.4	0	.0		.0	7	3.4	195	96.1	1	.5	203
PA FEMALE	0	.0	2	2.7	0	.0	0	.0	2	2.7	72	97.3	0	.0	74
PA MALE	0	.0	5	3.9	0	.0	0	.0	5	3.9	123	95.3	1	.8	129
ALVERNIA COLLEGE															
PA TOTAL	1	.3	10	2.6	3	.8	3	.8	17	4.4	365	94.1		1.5	388
PA FEMALE	0	.0	5	2.7	1	.5	0	.0	6	3.2	173	93.5		3.2	185
PA MALE	1	.5	5	2.5	2	1.0	3	1.5	11	5.4	192	94.6	6	.0	203
BAPT BIBLE COLLEGE OF PA															
PA TOTAL	0	.0	4	.6	1	.1	2	.3	7	1.0	709	99.0		.0	716
PA FEMALE	0	.0	1	.3	1	.3	2	.6	4	1.2	338	98.8	0	.0	342
PA MALE	0	.0	3	.8	0	.0	0	.0	3	.8	371	99.2	0	.0	374
BEAVER COLLEGE															
PA TOTAL	0	.0	96	15.1	3	.5	1	.2	100	15.7	521	82.0	14	2.2	635
PA FEMALE	0	.0	86	16.1	2	.4	0	.0	88	16.5	437	81.8	9	1.7	534
PA MALE	0	.0	10	9.9	1	1.0	1	1.0	12	11.9	84	83.2	5	5.0	101
BLOOMSBURG STATE COLLEGE															
PA TOTAL	3	.1	103	2.1	15	.3	12	.2	133	2.7	4,798	97.0	13	.3	4,944
PA FEMALE	1	.0	45	1.6	9	.3	5	.2	60	2.1	2,792	97.8	3	.1	2,855
PA MALE	2	.1	58	2.8	6	.3	7	.3	73	3.5	2,006	96.0	10	.5	2,089
BRYN MAWR COLLEGE															
PA TOTAL	0	.0	39	4.1	21	2.2	1	1.7	76	7.9	829	86.6	52	5.	957
PA FEMALE	0	.0	39	4.1	21	2.2	16	1.7	76	7.9	829	86.6	52	5.	957
PA MALE	0	.0	0	.0	0	.0	0	.0	0	.0	0	.0	0	.0	0
BUCKNELL UNIVERSITY															
PA TOTAL	0	.0	101	3.3	18	.6		.3	128	4.2	2,862	94.5	40	1 3	3,030
PA FEMALE	0	.0	34	2.4	7	.5	2	.2	44	3.2	1,329	95.7	16	1 2	1,389
PA MALE	0	.0	67	4.1	11	.7	2	.4	84	5.1	1,533	93.4	24	1:5	1,641
BUCKS COUNTY CMTY COLLEGE															
PA TOTAL	7	.1	41	.5	8	.1	1	.2	75	.9	8,102	99.1		.0	8,177
PA FEMALE	3	.1	23	.5	2	.0	10	.2	38	.8	4,496	99.2		.0	4,534
PA MALE	4	.1	18	.5	6	.2		.2	37	1.0	3,606	99.0	0	.0	3,643
BUTLER CO CMTY COLLEGE															
PA TOTAL	0	.0	2	.1	0	.0		.0	2	.1	1,764	99.9		.0	1,766
PA FEMALE	0	.0	0	.0	0	.0	0	.0	0	.0	1,003	100.0	0	.0	1,003
PA MALE	0	.0	2	.3	0	.0	0	.0	2	.3	761	99.7	0	.0	763
CABRINI COLLEGE															
PA TOTAL	0	.0	26	6.6	1	.3	5	1.3	32	8.2	354	90.3	6	1.5	392
PA FEMALE	0	.0	21	6.8	1	.3	5	1.6	27	8.7	281	90.4	3	1.0	311
PA MALE	0	.0	5	6.2	0	.0	0	.0	5	6.2	73	90.1	3	3.7	81
CALIFORNIA STATE COLLEGE															
PA TOTAL	6	.2	335	8.5	16	.4	9	.2	366	9.3	3,582	90.5	8	.2	3,956
PA FEMALE	2	.1	154	8.3	8	.4	5	.3	169	9.1	1,681	90.7	3	.2	1,853
PA MALE	4	.2	181	8.6	8	.4	4	.2	197	9.4	1,901	90.4	5	.2	2,103
CARLOW COLLEGE															
PA TOTAL	2	.3	95	12.0	10	1.3		.8	113	14.3	679	85.7		.0	792
PA FEMALE	2	.3	93	12.1	10	1.3		.8	111	14.4	659	85.6		.0	770
PA MALE	0	.0	2	9.1	0	.0	6		2	9.1	20	90.9	0	.0	22
CARNEGIE-MELLON U															
PA TOTAL	12	.3	198	5.0	56	1.4	17	.4	283	7.1	3,644	91.4	60	1.5	3,987
PA FEMALE	4	.3	81	6.5	22	1.8	3	.2	110	8.8	1,119	89.8	17	1.4	1,246
PA MALE	8	.3	117	4.3	34	1.2	14	.5	173	6.3	2,525	92.1	43	1.6	2,741
CEDAR CREST COLLEGE															
PA TOTAL	1	.1	20	2.5	3	.4		1.1	33	4.1	759	95.2	5	.6	797
PA FEMALE	1	.1	20	2.5	3	.4	9	1.1	33	4.2	747	95.2	5	.6	785
PA MALE	0	.0	0	.0	0	.0	0	.0	0	.0	12	100.0	0	.0	12
CHATHAM COLLEGE															
PA TOTAL	0	.0	80	15.1	1	.2		.0	81	15.3	443	83.7	5	.9	529
PA FEMALE	0	.0	80	15.1	1	.2	0	.0	81	15.3	443	83.7	5	.9	529
PA MALE	0	.0	0	.0	0	.0	0	.0	0	.0	0	.0	0	.0	0
CHESTNUT HILL COLLEGE															
PA TOTAL	0	.0	39	5.3	0	.0	42	5.8	81	11.1	637	87.4	11	1.5	729
PA FEMALE	0	.0	39	5.4	0	.0	42	5.8	81	11.2	631	87.3	11	1.5	723
PA MALE	0	.0	0	.0	0	.0	0	.0	0	.0	6	100.0	0	.0	6

100

	BLACK NON-HISPANIC		ASIAN OR PACIFIC ISLANDER		HISPANIC		TOTAL MINORITY		WHITE NON-HISPANIC		NON-RESIDENT ALIEN		TOTAL
	NUMBER	%	NUMBER	%	NUMBER	%	NUMBER	%	NUMBER	%	NUMBER	%	NUMBER
'INUED													
	2,267	95.3	6	.3		.4	2,301	96.8	77	3.2		.0	2,378
	1,177	96.5	2	.2	9	.3	1,193	97.8	27	2.2	8	.0	1,220
	1,090	94.1	4	.3	4	.4	1,108	95.7	50	4.3		.0	1,158
	199	4.6	4	.1	10	.2	217	5.1	4,047	94.2	33	.8	4,297
	110	4.9	2	.1	5	.2	120	5.3	2,133	94.4	7	.3	2,260
	89	4.4	2	.1	5	.2	97	4.8	1,914	94.0	26	1.3	2,037
	0	.0	0	.0		.0	1	.2	411	99.5	1	.2	413
	0	.0	0	.0	0	.0	0	.0	269	100.0	0	.0	269
	0	.0	0	.0	0	.0	1	.7	142	98.6	1	.7	144
	0	.0	0	.0		.0	0	.0	886	99.2	7	.8	893
	0	.0	0	.0	0	.0	0	.0	782	99.1	7	.9	789
	0	.0	0	.0	0	.0	0	.0	104	100.0	0	.0	104
	43	46.7	0	.0	2	2.2	45	48.9	45	48.9	2	2.2	92
	10	35.7	0	.0	2	7.1	12	42.9	16	57.1	0	.0	28
	33	51.6	0	.0	0	.0	33	51.6	29	45.3	2	3.1	64
	1,394	21.5	37	.6	19	.3	1,461	22.5	4,992	76.8	45	.7	6,498
	890	24.8	17	.5	10	.3	922	25.6	2,657	73.9	16	.4	3,595
	504	17.4	20	.7	9	.3	539	18.6	2,335	80.4	29	1.0	2,903
	195	5.3	11	.3	15	.4	233	6.4	3,429	93.6	2	.1	3,664
	91	5.0	8	.4	7	.4	113	6.1	1,724	93.8	1	.1	1,838
	104	5.7	3	.2	8	.4	120	6.6	1,705	93.4	1	.1	1,826
	58	2.6	6	.3	2	.1	71	3.2	2,160	96.8		.0	2,231
	19	2.1	3	.3	1	.1	26	2.9	870	97.1	8	.0	896
	39	2.9	3	.2	1	.1	45	3.4	1,290	96.6		.0	1,335
	138	4.3	7	.2	7	.2	156	.9	3,047	95.1		.0	3,205
	91	4.7	5	.3	2	.1	101	.2	1,833	94.8	8	.0	1,934
	47	3.7	2	.2	5	.4	57	4.5	1,214	95.5		.0	1,271
	109	5.5	0	.0	4	.2	113	.7	1,880	94.3		.0	1,993
	56	5.4	0	.0	2	.2	58	.6	982	94.4	8	.0	1,040
	53	5.6	0	.0	2	.2	55	5.8	898	94.2		.0	953
	288	4.7	14	.2	19	.3	332	5	5,743	94.5		.0	6,075
	175	5.5	9	.3	13	.4	203	3	2,994	93.7	8	.0	3,197
	113	3.9	5	.4	6	.2	129	4.5	2,749	95.5		.0	2,878
	7,710	61.6	226	1.8	626	5.0	8,624	.8	3,872	30.9	30	.2	12,526
	4,997	61.7	146	1.8	406	5.0	5,589	6.0	2,511	31.0	4	.0	8,104
	2,713	61.4	80	1.8	220	5.0	3,035	68.6	1,361	30.8	26	.6	4,422
	3	2.3	3	2.3	0	.0	6	7	96	75.0	26	20.3	128
	1	1.6	2	3.2	0	.0	3	8	48	76.2	12	19.0	63
	2	3.1	1	1.5	0	.0	3	4.6	48	73.8	14	21.5	65
	29	2.1	0	.0	0	.0	29	2.	1,339	97.9	0	.0	1,368
	7	1.6	0	.0	0	.0	7	1.	433	98.4	0	.0	440
	22	2.4	0	.0	0	.0	22	2.6	906	97.6	0	.0	928
	31	1.9	7	.4	18	1.1	57	3	1,597	96.2	6	.4	1,660
	18	2.1	2	.2	12	1.4	33	3	812	95.8	3	.4	848
	13	1.6	5	.6	6	.7	24	3.0	785	96.7	3	.4	812
	642	8.6	148	2.0	44	.6	836	11.2	6,516	87.2	118	1.6	7,470
	279	14.8	24	1.3	19	1.0	322	17.1	1,536	81.6	24	1.3	1,882
	363	6.5	124	2.2	25	.4	514	9.2	4,980	89.1	94	1.7	5,588
	201	4.2	0	.0	16	.3	217	4.5	4,566	95.5	0	.	4,783
	139	5.8	0	.0	5	.2	144	.	2,258	94.0	0	.0	2,402
	62	2.6	0	.0	11	.5	73	6.0	2,308	96.9	0	.0	2,381
	82	13.0	3	.5	10	1.6	97	15.4	517	82.2	15	2.	629
	49	12.3	3	.8	7	1.8	61	15.3	330	82.7	8	2.	399
	33	14.3	0	.0	3	1.3	36	15.7	187	81.3	7	3.0	230
	128	3.8	9	.3	29	.9	168	.0	3,203	94.7	12	.4	3,383
	55	2.9	7	.4	15	.8	78	.1	1,842	95.7	5	.3	1,925
	73	5.0	2	.1	14	1.0	90	6.2	1,361	93.3	7	.5	1,458
	152	3.2	17	.4	4	.1	177	3.7	4,361	91.3	236	4.9	4,774
	70	2.7	10	.4	2	.1	83	3.2	2,387	93.1	93	3.6	2,563
	82	3.7	7	.3	2	.1	94	4.3	1,974	89.3	143	6.5	2,211
	25	1.5	15	.9	5	.3	46	2.7	1,638	97.3	0	.0	1,684
	8	.8	5	.5	1	.1	15	1.6	945	98.4	0	.0	960
	17	2.3	10	1.4	4	.6	31	4.3	693	95.7	0	.0	724
	56	2.6	33	1.6	11	.5	100	.7	2,008	94.7	12	.6	2,120
	22	2.7	11	1.3	7	.9	40	4.9	779	95.0	1	.1	820
	34	2.6	22	1.7	4	.3	60	4.6	1,229	94.5	11	.8	1,300
	93	3.6	11	.4	11	.4	134	.2	2,402	93.6	31	1.2	2,567
	47	4.6	2	.2	0	.0	60	.9	950	93.6	5	.5	1,015
	46	3.0	9	.6	11	.7	74	4.8	1,452	93.6	26	1.7	1,552

TABLE 1 - TOTAL UNDERGRADUATE ENROLLMENT IN INSTITUTIONS OF HIGHER EDUCATION BY RACE, ETHNICITY AND SEX:
INSTITUTION, STATE AND NATION, 1978

	AMERICAN INDIAN ALASKAN NATIVE		BLACK NON-HISPANIC		ASIAN OR PACIFIC ISLANDER		HISPANIC		TOTAL MINORITY		WHITE NON-HISPANIC		NON-RESIDENT ALIEN	
	NUMBER	%	NUMBER	%	NUMBER	%	NUMBER	%	NUMBER	%	NUMBER	%	NUMBER	%
PENNSYLVANIA	CONTINUED													
GENEVA COLLEGE														
PA TOTAL	1	.1	47	4.0	13	1.1	5	.4	66		1,102	94.0	4	.3
PA FEMALE	0	.0	17	3.5	3	.6	2	.4	22		466	95.3	4	.2
PA MALE	1	.1	30	4.4	10	1.5	3	.4	44	6.4	636	93.1	4	.4
GETTYSBURG COLLEGE														
PA TOTAL	1	.1	17	.9	3	.2	8	.4	29	1	1,924	98.5	1	.1
PA FEMALE	1	.1	7	.7	1	.1	6	.6	15	1	932	98.3	1	.1
PA MALE	0	.0	10	1.0	2	.2	2	.2	14	11	992	98.6	0	.0
GRATZ COLLEGE														
PA TOTAL	0	.0	0	.0	0	.0		.0	0	.0	103	84.4	19	15.6
PA FEMALE	0	.0	0	.0	0	.0	0	.0	0	.0	66	84.6	12	15.4
PA MALE	0	.0	0	.0	0	.0	0	.0	0	.0	37	84.1	7	15.9
GROVE CITY COLLEGE														
PA TOTAL	0	.0	5	.2	4	.2	2	.1	11	.5	2,219	99.4	3	.1
PA FEMALE	0	.0	3	.3	2	.2	1	.1	6	.6	1,021	99.3	1	.1
PA MALE	0	.0	2	.2	2	.2	1	.1	5	.4	1,198	99.4	2	.2
GWYNEDD-MERCY COLLEGE														
PA TOTAL	1	.1	28	2.3	6	.5	5	.4	40	3.3	1,145	95.5	14	1 2
PA FEMALE	1	.1	21	1.9	5	.5	5	.5	32	3.0	1,037	95.8	13	1 2
PA MALE	0	.0	7	6.0	1	.9	0	.0	8	6.8	108	92.3	1	.19
HAHNEMANN MEDL C AND HOSP														
PA TOTAL	0	.0	146	20.1	6	.8	3	.4	155	21.3	562	77.4		1.2
PA FEMALE	0	.0	118	20.2	5	.9	1	.2	124	21.3	455	78.0	2	.7
PA MALE	0	.0	28	19.6	1	.7	2	1.4	31	21.7	107	74.8	5	3.5
MARCUM JUNIOR COLLEGE														
PA TOTAL	2	.2	68	8.3	0	.0	4	.5	74	9.0	741	89.9		1.1
PA FEMALE	2	.2	68	8.3	0	.0	4	.5	74	9.0	741	89.9		1.1
PA MALE	0	.0	0	.0	0	.0	0	.0	0	.0	0	.0	0	.0
HARRISBURG AREA CC														
PA TOTAL	9	.3	208	6.3	54	1.6	18	.5	289	8.7	3,032	91.2	4	.1
PA FEMALE	5	.3	124	7.5	20	1.2	6	.4	155	9.3	1,502	90.5	2	.1
PA MALE	4	.2	84	5.0	34	2.0	12	.7	134	8.0	1,530	91.8	2	.1
HAVERFORD COLLEGE														
PA TOTAL	0	.0	20	2.1	11	1.2	25	2.6	56	5.9	879	92.1	19	2.0
PA FEMALE	0	.0	0	.0	0	.0	0	.0	0	.0	30	100.0	0	.0
PA MALE	0	.0	20	2.2	11	1.2	25	2.7	56	6.1	849	91.9	19	2.1
HOLY FAMILY COLLEGE														
PA TOTAL	0	.0	12	1.1		.0	11	1.0	23	2.1	1,061	97.7	2	.2
PA FEMALE	0	.0	11	1.2		.0	9	1.0	20	2.1	912	97.6	2	.2
PA MALE	0	.0	1	.7	0	.0	2	1.3	3	2.0	149	98.0	0	.0
IMMACULATA COLLEGE														
PA TOTAL	0	.0	22	2.8	2	.3		.8	30	3.	764	96.2	0	.0
PA FEMALE	0	.0	20	2.8	2	.3		.8	28	3.4	693	96.1	0	.0
PA MALE	0	.0	2	2.7	0	.0	0	.0	2	2.7	71	97.3	0	.0
INDIANA U OF PENNSYLVANIA														
PA TOTAL	3	.0	403	3.9	9	.1	9	.1	424	4.1	9,934	95.0	97	.9
PA FEMALE	2	.0	246	4.1	6	.1	5	.1	259	4.3	5,778	95.2	34	.6
PA MALE	1	.0	157	3.6	3	.1	4	.1	165	3.8	4,156	94.8	63	1.4
JUNIATA COLLEGE														
PA TOTAL	0	.0	10	.	11	1.0	9	.8	30	2.7	1,081	96.8	6	.5
PA FEMALE	0	.0	0	.	5	1.1	3	.6	8	1.7	465	97.9	2	.4
PA MALE	0	.0	10	1.8	6	.9	6	.9	22	3.4	616	96.0	4	.6
KEYSTONE JUNIOR COLLEGE														
PA TOTAL	0	.0	23	2.7	0	.0	3	.4	26	3.	807	94.7	19	2.2
PA FEMALE	0	.0	7	1.5	0	.0	0	.0	7	1.5	471	97.7	4	.8
PA MALE	0	.0	16	4.3	0	.0	3	.8	19	5.1	336	90.8	15	4.1
KING'S COLLEGE														
PA TOTAL	0	.0	8	.4	11	.6	9	.5	28	1.	1,778	98.1	7	.4
PA FEMALE	0	.0	4	.6	3	.4	3	.4	10	1.	687	98.6	0	.0
PA MALE	0	.0	4	.4	8	.7	6	.5	18	1.8	1,091	97.8	7	.6
KUTZTOWN STATE COLLEGE														
PA TOTAL	5	.1	158	3.8	5	.1	28	.7	196	7	3,989	94.7	28	.7
PA FEMALE	2	.1	76	3.1	2	.1	17	.7	97	9	2,378	95.8	7	.3
PA MALE	3	.2	82	4.7	3	.2	11	.6	99	17	1,611	93.1	21	1.2
LACKAWANNA JUNIOR COLLEGE														
PA TOTAL	2	.2	12	.9	2	.2	0	.0	16	1.2	1,278	98.8	0	.0
PA FEMALE	0	.0	4	.7	2	.4	0	.0	6	1.1	561	98.9	0	.0
PA MALE	2	.3	8	1.1	0	.0	0	.0	10	1.4	717	98.6	0	.0
LAFAYETTE COLLEGE														
PA TOTAL	0	.0	55	2.5	2	.1	15	.7	72	3.2	2,133	95.7	24	1.1
PA FEMALE	0	.0	14	1.8	1	.1	5	.7	20	2.6	738	97.0	3	.4
PA MALE	0	.0	41	2.8	1	.1	10	.7	52	3.5	1,395	95.0	21	1.4
LANCASTER BIBLE COLLEGE														
PA TOTAL	0	.0	3	.	1	.3		.0	4	1	382	98.5	2	.5
PA FEMALE	0	.0	1	.	0	.0		.0	1	.0	176	99.4	0	.0
PA MALE	0	.0	2	.8	1	.5	0	.0	3	1.1	206	97.6	2	.9
LA ROCHE COLLEGE														
PA TOTAL	0	.0	44	4.2	6	.6		.0	50	4.	990	94.1	12	1.1
PA FEMALE	0	.0	13	2.0	3	.5	0	.0	16	2.4	637	97.3	2	.3
PA MALE	0	.0	31	7.8	3	.8	0	.0	34	8.6	353	88.9	10	2.5
LA SALLE COLLEGE														
PA TOTAL	2	.0	283	5	13	.3	7	.1	305	5	4,887	94.1		.0
PA FEMALE	1	.1	136	.9	8	.4	2	.1	147	7	1,813	92.5	0	.0
PA MALE	1	.0	147	15	5	.2	5	.2	158	6.2	3,074	95.1	0	.0
LEBANON VALLEY COLLEGE														
PA TOTAL	0	.0	10	.9	1	1.7		.0	29	2.7	1,054	96.6	8	.7
PA FEMALE	0	.0	7	1.3		.9	0	.0	12	2.2	538	97.5	2	.4
PA MALE	0	.0	3	.6	16	2.6	0	.0	17	3.2	516	95.7	6	1.1
LEHIGH CO CNTY COLLEGE														
PA TOTAL	0	.0	21	.8	30	1.1	41	1.5	92	3 3	2,672	96.6	2	.1
PA FEMALE	0	.0	11	.8	8	.5	21	1.4	40	2 7	1,420	97.3	0	.0
PA MALE	0	.0	10	.8	22	1.7	20	1.5	52	4.0	1,252	95.9	2	.2

102

BLACK NON-HISPANIC		ASIAN OR PACIFIC ISLANDER		HISPANIC		TOTAL MINORITY		WHITE NON-HISPANIC		NON-RESIDENT ALIEN		TOTAL
NUMBER	%	NUMBER	%	NUMBER	%	NUMBER	%	NUMBER	%	NUMBER	%	NUMBER
'INUED												
77	1.8	2	.0	16	.4	96	2.2	4,211	95.9	82	1.9	4,389
22	2.1	1	.1	3	.3	26	2.5	1,008	96.1	15	1.4	1,049
55	1.6	1	.0	13	.4	70	2.1	3,203	95.9	67	2.0	3,340
932	93.9	4	.4	0	.0	936	94.3	22	2.2	35	3.5	993
449	98.2	0	.0	0	.0	449	98.2	5	1.1	3	.7	457
483	90.1	4	.7	0	.0	487	90.9	17	3.2	32	6.0	536
91	4.1	4	.2	4	.2	101	4.5	2,056	92.2	74	3.3	2,231
31	2.7	2	.2	1	.1	36	3.1	1,099	94.0	34	2.9	1,169
60	5.6	2	.2	3	.3	65	6.1	957	90.1	40	3.8	1,062
47	1.5	0	.0	0	.0	47	1.5	3,176	98.5	0	.0	3,223
10	.6	0	.0	0	.0	10	.6	1,743	99.4	0	.0	1,753
37	2.5	0	.0	0	.0	37	2.5	1,433	97.5	0	.0	1,470
13	1.2	3	.3	4	.4	20	1.9	1,051	97.9	3	.3	1,074
7	1.7	2	.5	1	.2	10	2.4	400	97.1	2	.5	412
6	.9	1	.2	3	.5	10	1.5	651	98.3	1	.2	662
8	2.4	1	.3	1	.3	10	3.0	317	96.6	1	.3	328
8	2.6	1	.3	1	.3	10	3.2	301	96.5	1	.3	312
0	.0	0	.0	0	.0	0	.0	16	100.0	0	.0	16
77	3.5	1	.0	1	.0	79	3.6	2,093	96.4		.0	2,172
39	3.1	1	.1	0	.0	40	3.2	1,210	96.8	0	.0	1,250
38	4.1	0	.0	1	.1	39	4.2	983	95.8	0	.0	922
11	.7	0	.0	0	.0	11	.7	1,527	98.5	13	.8	1,551
10	.7	0	.0	0	.0	10	.7	1,358	99.0	4	.3	1,372
1	.6	0	.0	0	.0	1	.6	169	94.4	9	5.0	179
2	3.6	0	.0	0	.0	2	3.6	54	96.4		.0	56
2	4.2	0	.0	0	.0	2	4.2	46	95.8	0	.0	48
0	.0	0	.0	0	.0	0	.0	8	100.0	0	.0	8
65	5.4	0	.0	0	.0	65	5.4	1,130	94.3	3	.3	1,198
38	5.3	0	.0	0	.0	38	5.3	683	94.7	0	.0	721
27	5.7	0	.0	0	.0	27	5.7	447	93.7	3	.6	477
14	1.3	2	.2	4	.4	20	1.9	1,006	96.6	15	1.4	1,041
8	1.3	2	.0	2	.3	10	1.6	604	97.9	3	.5	617
6	1.4	2	.5	2	.5	10	2.4	402	94.8	12	2.8	424
270	5.5	74	1.5	56	1.1	406	8.3	4,464	91.1	30	.6	4,900
140	5.0	29	1.0	29	1.0	201	7.2	2,585	92.6	7	.3	2,793
130	6.2	45	2.1	27	1.3	205	9.7	1,879	89.2	23	1.1	2,107
173	2.5	51	.7	24	.3	259	3.7	6,659	95.3	66	.9	6,984
95	2.3	29	.7	15	.4	142	3.5	3,896	95.8	27	.7	4,065
78	2.7	22	.8	9	.3	117	4.0	2,763	94.7	39	1.3	2,919
38	6.5	5	.9	6	1.0	49	8.3	535	91.1	3	.5	587
38	6.5	5	.9	6	1.0	49	8.3	535	91.1	3	.5	587
0	.0	0	.0	0	.0	0	.0	0	.0	0	.0	0
13	1.0	10	.8	9	.7	32	2.4	1,288	97.6	0	.0	1,320
9	1.5	1	.2	7	1.1	17	2.8	592	97.2	0	.0	609
4	.6	9	1.3	2	.3	15	2.1	696	97.9	0	.0	711
14	2.8	0	.0	0	.0	14	2.8	475	96.5	3	.5	492
7	1.8	0	.0	0	.0	7	1.8	385	98.0	1	.3	393
7	7.1	0	.0	0	.0	7	7.1	90	90.9	2	2.0	99
4	.3	12	.8	6	.4	22	1.4	1,491	98.0	8	.5	1,521
1	.2	3	.5	4	.6	8	1.2	648	98.5	2	.3	658
3	.3	9	1.0	2	.2	14	1.6	843	97.7	6	.7	863
5	6.0	0	.0	0	.0	5	6.0	72	86.7	6	7.2	83
1	2.0	0	.0	0	.0	1	2.0	43	87.8	5	10.2	49
4	11.8	0	.0	0	.0	4	11.8	29	85.3	1	2.9	34
65	1.5	19	.5	76	1.8	162	3.9	4,029	96.0	8	.2	4,199
44	1.6	9	.3	49	1.8	102	3.8	2,576	96.0	6	.2	2,684
21	1.4	10	.7	27	1.8	60	4.0	1,453	95.9	2	.1	1,515
74	37.0	0	.0	2	1.0	76	38.0	120	60.0	4	2.0	200
49	39.5	0	.0	1	.8	50	40.3	72	58.1	2	1.6	124
25	32.9	0	.0	1	1.3	26	34.2	48	63.2	2	2.6	76
25	4.0	2	.3	0	.0	27	4.3	598	95.7	0	.0	625
23	4.5	2	.4	0	.0	25	4.9	489	95.1	0	.0	514
2	1.8	0	.0	0	.0	2	1.8	109	98.2	0	.0	111
538	34.8	6	.4	24	1.6	568	36.8	956	61.9	20	1.3	1,544
424	38.1	4	.4	12	1.1	440	39.5	661	59.3	13	1.2	1,114
114	26.5	2	.5	12	2.8	128	29.3	295	68.6	7	1.6	430
627	2.4	143	.5	111	.4	918	3.5	25,562	96.3	59	.2	26,539
349	3.1	53	.5	37	.3	453	4.0	10,818	95.9	10	.1	11,281
278	1.8	90	.6	74	.5	465	3.0	14,744	96.6	49	.3	15,256

	AMERICAN INDIAN ALASKAN NATIVE		BLACK NON-HISPANIC		ASIAN OR PACIFIC ISLANDER		HISPANIC		TOTAL MINORITY		WHITE NON-HISPANIC		NON-RESIDENT ALIEN			
	NUMBER	%	NUMBER	%	NUMBER	%	NUMBER	%	NUMBER	%	NUMBER	%	NUMBER	%	N	
PENNSYLVANIA CONTINUED																
PA STATE U ALLENTOWN CAM																
PA TOTAL	0	.0	3	1.0	2	.7	2	.7	7	2.3	294	97.7	0	.0		
PA FEMALE	0	.0	1	1.3	2	2.7	1	1.3	4	5.3	71	94.7	0	.0		
PA MALE	0	.0	2	.9	0	.0	1	.4	3	1.3	223	98.7	0	.0		
PA STATE U ALTOONA CAM																
PA TOTAL	5	.4	31	2.2	7	.5	4	.3	47	3.4	1,341	96.5	1	.1		
PA FEMALE	5	.9	17	3.1	4	.7	1	.2	27	5.0	517	95.0	0	.0		
PA MALE	0	.0	14	1.7	3	.4	3	.4	20	2.4	824	97.5	1	.1		
PA STATE U BEAVER CAMPUS																
PA TOTAL	0	.0	28	3.4	3	.4	2	.2	33	4.0	789	95.8	2	.2		
PA FEMALE	0	.0	13	4.7	0	.0	1	.4	14	5.0	264	95.0	0	.0		
PA MALE	0	.0	15	2.7	3	.5	1	.2	19	3.5	525	96.2	2	.4		
PA ST U BEHREND COLLEGE																
PA TOTAL	1	.1	35	2.7	3	.2	4	.3	43	3.3	1,249	96.7	0	.0		
PA FEMALE	0	.0	18	3.6	3	.6	1	.2	22	4.4	482	95.6	0	.0		
PA MALE	1	.1	17	2.2	0	.0	3	.4	21	2.7	767	97.3	0	.0		
PA STATE U BERKS CAMPUS																
PA TOTAL	0	.0	3	.4	9	1.3	3	.4	15	2.2	655	97.8	0	.0		
PA FEMALE	0	.0	1	.6	4	2.3	0	.0	5	2.9	167	97.1	0	.0		
PA MALE	0	.0	2	.4	5	1.0	3	.6	10	2.0	488	98.0	0	.0		
PA STATE U CAPITOL CAMPUS																
PA TOTAL	1	.1	64	4.0	18	1.1	6	.4	89	5.6	1,504	93.9	8	.5		
PA FEMALE	0	.0	41	8.6	4	.8	1	.2	46	9.7	428	90.1	1	.2		
PA MALE	1	.1	23	2.0	14	1.2	5	.4	43	3.8	1,076	95.6	7	.6		
PA STATE U DELAWARE CAM																
PA TOTAL	0	.0	20	2.1	3	.3	3	.3	26	2.7	939	97.3	0	.0		
PA FEMALE	0	.0	12	4.2	2	.7	0	.0	14	4.8	275	95.2	0	.0		
PA MALE	0	.0	8	1.2	1	.1	3	.4	12	1.8	664	98.2	0	.0		
PA STATE U DU BOIS CAMPUS																
PA TOTAL	0	.0	0	.0	0	.0	0	.0	0	.0	437	100.0	0	.0		
PA FEMALE	0	.0	0	.0	0	.0	0	.0	0	.0	118	100.0	0	.0		
PA MALE	0	.0	0	.0	0	.0	0	.0	0	.0	319	100.0	0	.0		
PA STATE U FAYETTE CAMPUS																
PA TOTAL	0	.0	9	1.8	2	.4	0	.0	11	2.2	495	97.8	0	.0		
PA FEMALE	0	.0	6	4.3	1	.7	0	.0	7	5.0	133	95.0	0	.0		
PA MALE	0	.0	3	.8	1	.3	0	.0	4	1.1	362	98.9	0	.0		
PA STATE U HAZLETON CAM																
PA TOTAL	0	.0	4	.5	1	.1	7	.9	12	1.5	808	98.5	0	.0		
PA FEMALE	0	.0	3	1.0	1	.3	4	1.3	8	2.7	289	97.3	0	.0		
PA MALE	0	.0	1	.2	0	.0	3	.6	4	.8	519	99.2	0	.0		
PA STATE U MCKEESPORT CAM																
PA TOTAL	1	.1	26	2.8	5	.5	2	.2	34	3.7	885	96.2	1	.1		
PA FEMALE	1	.4	14	5.8	1	.4	1	.4	17	7.1	223	92.9	1	.4		
PA MALE	0	.0	12	1.8	4	.6	1	.1	17	2.5	662	97.4	1	.1		
PA STATE U MONT ALTO CAM																
PA TOTAL	0	.0	4	.6	3	.4	3	.4	10	1.4	709	98.6	0	.0		
PA FEMALE	0	.0	4	2.0	2	1.0	0	.0	6	3.0	194	97.0	0	.0		
PA MALE	0	.0	0	.0	1	.2	3	.6	4	.8	515	99.2	0	.0		
PA ST U NEW KENSINGTN CAM																
PA TOTAL	0	.0	2	.3	0	.0	0	.0	2	.3	688	99.4	2	.3		
PA FEMALE	0	.0	0	.0	0	.0	0	.0	0	.0	223	100.0	0	.0		
PA MALE	0	.0	2	.4	0	.0	0	.0	2	.4	465	99.1	2	.4		
PA STATE U OGONTZ CAMPUS																
PA TOTAL	4	.2	87	5.1	17	1.0	9	.5	117	6.9	1,572	93.0	2	.1		
PA FEMALE	2	.3	49	7.3	8	1.2	3	.4	62	9.3	606	90.7	0	.0		
PA MALE	2	.2	38	3.7	9	.9	6	.6	55	5.4	966	94.4	2	.2		
PA STATE U SCHUYLKILL CAM																
PA TOTAL	0	.0	5	1.1	3	.7	0	.0	8	1.8	447	98.2	0	.0		
PA FEMALE	0	.0	4	2.0	2	1.0	0	.0	6	3.0	192	97.0	0	.0		
PA MALE	0	.0	1	.4	1	.4	0	.0	2	.8	255	99.2	0	.0		
PA ST U SHENANGO VLY CAM																
PA TOTAL	0	.0	11	2.8	0	.0	0	.0	11	2.8	388	97.2	0	.0		
PA FEMALE	0	.0	6	4.0	0	.0	0	.0	6	4.0	145	96.0	0	.0		
PA MALE	0	.0	5	2.0	0	.0	0	.0	5	2.0	243	98.0	0	.0		
PA ST U WILKES-BARRE CAM																
PA TOTAL	0	.0	3	.7	2	.5	3	.7	8	1.9	416	97.9	1	.2		
PA FEMALE	0	.0	1	1.3	0	.0	0	.0	1	1.3	78	98.7	0	.0		
PA MALE	0	.0	2	.6	2	.6	3	.9	7	2.0	338	97.7	1	.3		
PA ST U WRTHGTN SCRTN CAM																
PA TOTAL	1	.2	3	.5	1	.2	3	.5	8	1.3	605	98.5	1	.2		
PA FEMALE	0	.0	1	.6	0	.0	0	.0	1	.6	171	99.4	0	.0		
PA MALE	1	.2	2	.5	1	.2	3	.7	7	1.6	434	98.2	1	.2		
PA STATE U YORK CAMPUS																
PA TOTAL	1	.2	4	.7	6	1.0	2	.3	13	2.2	588	97.8	0	.0		
PA FEMALE	0	.0	3	1.9	1	.6	0	.0	4	2.6	150	97.4	0	.0		
PA MALE	1	.2	1	.2	5	1.1	2	.4	9	2.0	438	98.0	0	.0		
PHILA COLLEGE OF ART																
PA TOTAL	3	.3	122	11.4	8	.7	11	1.0	144	13.4	905	84.3	25	2.3		
PA FEMALE	3	.5	56	8.9	7	1.1	7	1.1	73	11.6	540	86.1	14	2.2		
PA MALE	0	.0	66	14.8	1	.2	4	.9	71	15.9	365	81.7	11	2.5		
PHILA COLLEGE OF BIBLE																
PA TOTAL	6	1.2	52	10.4	1	.2	5	1.0	64	12.9	423	84.9	11	2.2		
PA FEMALE	3	1.3	26	11.7	1	.4	4	1.8	34	15.2	184	82.5	5	2.2		
PA MALE	3	1.1	26	9.5	0	.0	1	.4	30	10.9	239	86.9	6	2.2		
PHILA C PERFORMING ARTS																
PA TOTAL	0	.0	31	10.4	4	1.3	3	1.0	38	12.8	251	84.5	8	2.7		
PA FEMALE	0	.0	11	9.0	3	2.5	0	.0	14	11.5	105	86.1	3	2.5		
PA MALE	0	.0	20	11.4	1	.6	3	1.7	24	13.7	146	83.4	5	2.9		
PHILA COLLEGE PHAR & SCI																
PA TOTAL	0	.0	16	1.6	17	1.7	6	.6	39	3.8	975	95.6	6	.6		
PA FEMALE	0	.0	11	2.6	8	1.9	3	.7	22	5.2	404	94.6	1	.2		
PA MALE	0	.0	5	.8	9	1.5	3	.5	17	2.9	571	96.3	5	.8		

	BLACK NON-HISPANIC		ASIAN OR PACIFIC ISLANDER		HISPANIC		TOTAL MINORITY		WHITE NON-HISPANIC		NON-RESIDENT ALIEN		TOTAL
	NUMBER	%	NUMBER	%	NUMBER	%	NUMBER	%	NUMBER	%	NUMBER	%	NUMBER
INUED													
	284	11.3	14	.6	5	.2	303	12.0	2,030	80.5	188	7.5	2,521
	167	13.7	7	.6	3	.2	177	14.5	1,005	82.4	37	3.0	1,219
	117	9.0	7	.5	2	.2	126	9.7	1,025	78.7	151	11.6	1,302
	6	7.5	0	.0	0	.0	6	7.5	71	88.8	3	3.8	80
	4	8.9	0	.0	0	.0	4	8.9	38	84.4	3	6.7	45
	2	5.7	0	.0	0	.0	2	5.7	33	94.3	0	.0	35
	255	12.7	8	.4	8	.4	272	13.5	1,491	74.1	248	12.3	2,011
	123	13.2	1	.1	4	.4	128	13.8	781	84.1	20	2.2	929
	132	12.2	7	.6	4	.4	144	13.3	710	65.6	228	21.1	1,082
	65	5.2	5	.4	31	2.5	101	8.1	1,151	91.9	0	.0	1,252
	47	6.1	3	.4	23	3.0	73	9.4	700	90.6	0	.0	773
	18	3.8	2	.4	8	1.7	28	5.8	451	94.2	0	.0	479
	257	6.5	5	.1	5	.1	270	6.9	3,658	92.9	10	.3	3,938
	156	8.0	4	.2	2	.1	165	8.4	1,788	91.5	2	.1	1,955
	101	5.1	1	.1	3	.2	105	5.3	1,870	94.3	8	.4	1,983
	14	2.9	7	1.4	13	2.7	34	7.0	453	93.0	0	.0	487
	14	2.9	7	1.4	13	2.7	34	7.0	453	93.0	0	.0	487
	0	.0	0	.0	0	.0	0	.0	0	.0	0	.0	0
	0	.0	0	.0	0	.0	0	.0	75	100.0	0	.0	75
	0	.0	0	.0	0	.0	0	.0	0	.0	0	.0	0
	0	.0	0	.0	0	.0	0	.0	75	100.0	0	.0	75
	0	.0	0	.0	0	.0	0	.0	26	100.0	0	.0	26
	0	.0	0	.0	0	.0	0	.0	0	.0	0	.0	0
	0	.0	0	.0	0	.0	0	.0	26	100.0	0	.0	26
	11	1.0	3	.3	10	.9	24	2.1	1,098	97.4	5	.4	1,127
	3	.6	1	.2	1	.2	5	1.0	471	98.7	1	.2	477
	8	1.2	2	.3	9	1.4	19	2.9	627	96.5	4	.6	650
	314	7.1	17	.4	34	.8	372	8.4	3,971	90.0	67	1.5	4,410
	186	9.9	10	.5	14	.7	214	11.4	1,647	87.4	24	1.3	1,885
	128	5.1	7	.3	20	.8	158	6.3	2,324	92.0	43	1.7	2,525
	24	2.9	3	.4	1	.1	28	3.3	794	94.7	16	1.9	838
	0	.0	0	.0	0	.0	0	.0	0	.0	0	.0	0
	24	2.9	3	.4	1	.1	28	3.3	794	94.7	16	1.9	838
	34	4.5	4	.5	16	2.1	54	7.2	694	92.8	0	.0	748
	34	4.5	4	.5	16	2.1	54	7.2	694	92.8	0	.0	748
	0	.0	0	.0	0	.0	0	.0	0	.0	0	.0	0
	197	4.3	16	.4	10	.2	225	5.0	4,309	94.9	6	.1	4,540
	109	4.7	9	.4	2	.1	120	5.2	2,204	94.8	1	.0	2,325
	88	4.0	7	.3	8	.4	105	4.7	2,105	95.0	5	.2	2,215
	212	4.2	4	.1	8	.2	229	4.6	4,783	95.3	9	.2	5,021
	80	3.0	3	.1	1	.0	85	3.2	2,586	96.7	3	.1	2,674
	132	5.6	1	.0	7	.3	144	6.1	2,197	93.6	6	.3	2,347
	63	6.1	5	.5	12	1.2	80	7.7	898	86.3	62	6.0	1,040
	24	12.2	3	1.5	2	1.0	29	14.8	146	74.5	21	10.7	196
	39	4.6	2	.2	10	1.2	51	6.0	752	89.1	41	4.9	844
	14	1.0	1	.1	7	.5	22	1.5	1,398	98.0	7	.5	1,427
	5	.8	1	.2	3	.5	9	1.5	606	98.4	1	.2	616
	9	1.1	0	.0	4	.5	13	1.6	792	97.7	6	.7	811
	80	6.5	22	1.8	12	1.0	115	9.3	1,072	87.1	44	3.6	1,231
	43	7.7	13	2.3	8	1.4	65	11.6	481	85.7	15	2.7	561
	37	5.5	9	1.3	4	.6	50	7.5	591	88.2	29	4.3	670
	0	.0	0	.0	0	.0	0	.0	85	89.5	10	10.5	95
	0	.0	0	.0	0	.0	0	.0	0	.0	0	.0	0
	0	.0	0	.0	0	.0	0	.0	85	89.5	10	10.5	95
	3,125	17.9	198	1.1	447	2.6	3,870	22.2	13,544	77.6	29	.2	17,443
	2,007	23.8	89	1.1	248	2.9	2,400	28.5	6,017	71.4	14	.2	8,431
	1,118	12.4	109	1.2	199	2.2	1,470	16.3	7,527	83.5	15	.2	9,012
	28	2.6	1	.1	0	.0	30	2.8	1,034	97.0	2	.2	1,066
	8	1.7	0	.0	0	.0	9	1.9	460	98.1	0	.0	469
	20	3.4	1	.2	0	.0	21	3.5	574	96.1	2	.3	597
	23	3.9	6	1.0	0	.0	31	5.3	553	93.7	6	1.0	590
	19	3.5	6	1.1	0	.0	27	5.0	510	94.6	2	.4	539
	4	7.8	0	.0	0	.0	4	7.8	43	84.3	4	7.8	51
	4	1.9	1	.5	0	.0	6	2.9	197	94.3	6	2.9	209
	3	4.0	1	1.3	0	.0	5	6.7	70	93.3	0	.0	75
	1	.7	0	.0	0	.0	1	.7	127	94.8	6	4.5	134
	494	5.7	276	3.2	120	1.4	900	10.5	7,462	86.7	242	2.8	8,604
	281	8.2	115	3.4	51	1.5	448	13.1	2,913	84.9	71	2.1	3,432
	213	4.1	161	3.1	69	1.3	452	8.7	4,549	88.0	171	3.3	5,172

TABLE 1 - TOTAL UNDERGRADUATE ENROLLMENT IN INSTITUTIONS OF HIGHER EDUCATION BY RACE, ETHNICITY AND SEX:
          INSTITUTION, STATE AND NATION, 1978

	AMERICAN INDIAN ALASKAN NATIVE		BLACK NON-HISPANIC		ASIAN OR PACIFIC ISLANDER		HISPANIC		TOTAL MINORITY		WHITE NON-HISPANIC		NON-RESIDENT ALIEN	
	NUMBER	%	NUMBER	%	NUMBER	%	NUMBER	%	NUMBER	%	NUMBER	%	NUMBER	%
PENNSYLVANIA	CONTINUED													
U OF PITTSBG MAIN CAMPUS														
PA TOTAL	23	.1	1,625	10.3	147	.9	72	.5	1,867	11.9	13,695	87.0	173	1.1
PA FEMALE	12	.2	940	12.7	50	.7	27	.4	1,029	13.9	6,369	85.7	30	.4
PA MALE	11	.1	685	8.2	97	1.2	45	.5	838	10.1	7,326	88.2	143	1.7
U OF PITTSBG BRADFORD CAM														
PA TOTAL	0	.0	13	1.6	1	.1		.0	14	1.8	783	98.2		.0
PA FEMALE	0	.0	5	1.5	0	.0		.0	5	1.5	328	98.5		.0
PA MALE	0	.0	8	1.7	1	.2	0	.0	9	1.9	455	98.1	0	.0
U OF PITTSBG GREENSBG CAM														
PA TOTAL	0	.0	10	.9	0	.0		.0	10	.9	1,062	99.0	1	.1
PA FEMALE	0	.0	6	1.3	0	.0		.0	6	1.3	449	98.7	0	.0
PA MALE	0	.0	4	.6	0	.0	0	.0	4	.6	613	99.2	1	.2
U OF PITTSBG JOHNSTWN CAM														
PA TOTAL	0	.0	53	1.7	3	.1		.0	56	1.8	3,013	98.1	3	.1
PA FEMALE	0	.0	28	2.1	2	.1		.0	30	2.2	1,334	97.7	1	.1
PA MALE	0	.0	25	1.5	1	.1	0	.0	26	1.5	1,679	98.4	2	.1
U OF PITTSBG TITUSVL CAM														
PA TOTAL	0	.0	6	1.1	5	.9	1	.2	12	2.2	539	97.8		.0
PA FEMALE	0	.0	4	1.6	2	.8	0	.0	6	2.4	241	97.6		.0
PA MALE	0	.0	2	.7	3	1.0	1	.3	6	2.0	298	98.0	0	.0
UNIVERSITY OF SCRANTON														
PA TOTAL	0	.0	15	.6	5	.2	1	.0	21	.8	2,651	99.2		.0
PA FEMALE	0	.0	7	.7	3	.3	0	.0	10	1.0	997	99.0		.0
PA MALE	0	.0	8	.5	2	.1	1	.1	11	.7	1,654	99.3	0	.0
URSINUS COLLEGE														
PA TOTAL	3	.2	23	1.3	25	1.5	55	3.2	106	.2	1,609	93.4	8	.5
PA FEMALE	1	.1	8	1.0	13	1.6	26	3.3	48	6.1	742	93.7	2	.3
PA MALE	2	.2	15	1.6	12	1.3	29	3.1	58	6.2	867	93.1	6	.6
VALLEY FORGE CHRISTIAN C														
PA TOTAL	3	.5	20	3.6	2	.4	11	2.0	36	6.4	518	92.7	5	.9
PA FEMALE	2	.9	5	2.3	0	.0	5	2.3	12	5.5	205	93.2	3	1.4
PA MALE	1	.3	15	4.4	2	.6	6	1.8	24	7.1	313	92.3	2	.6
VALLEY FORGE MILITARY JC														
PA TOTAL	1	.8	9	7.6	0	.0	2	1.7	12	10.1	76	63.9	1	26.1
PA FEMALE	0	.0	0	.0	0	.0	0	.0	0	.0	3	100.0		.0
PA MALE	1	.9	9	7.8	0	.0	2	1.7	12	10.3	73	62.9	40	26.7
VILLA MARIA COLLEGE														
PA TOTAL	0	.0	11	2.1	5	1.0	2	.4	18	3.5	494	96.5	0	.0
PA FEMALE	0	.0	11	2.2	5	1.0	2	.4	18	3.5	492	96.5	0	.0
PA MALE	0	.0	0	.0	0	.0	0	.0	0	.0	2	100.0	0	.0
VILLANOVA UNIVERSITY														
PA TOTAL	5	.1	98	1.6	22	.4	17	.3	142	2	5,940	96.5	75	1.2
PA FEMALE	3	.1	50	2.0	11	.4	6	.2	70	2	2,374	96.5	16	.7
PA MALE	2	.1	48	1.3	11	.3	11	.3	72	1.8	3,566	96.5	59	1.6
WASHINGTON JEFF COLLEGE														
PA TOTAL	0	.0	12	1.2	9	.9	4	.4	25	2	952	96.9	5	.5
PA FEMALE	0	.0	7	2.4	4	1.4	1	.3	12	4.5	278	95.2	2	.7
PA MALE	0	.0	5	.7	5	.7	3	.4	13	1.8	674	97.7	3	.4
WAYNESBURG COLLEGE														
PA TOTAL	0	.0	57	7.3	6	.8	0	.0	63	8.1	714	91.4	4	.5
PA FEMALE	0	.0	21	6.9	3	1.0	0	.0	24	7.8	278	90.8	4	1.3
PA MALE	0	.0	36	7.6	3	.6	0	.0	39	8.2	436	91.8	0	.0
WEST CHESTER ST COLLEGE														
PA TOTAL	3	.0	466	7.3	20	.3	38	.6	527	8.2	5,879	91.6	11	.2
PA FEMALE	1	.0	301	8.0	11	.3	23	.6	336	9.0	3,413	91.0	1	.0
PA MALE	2	.1	165	6.2	9	.3	15	.6	191	7.2	2,466	92.5	10	.4
WESTMINSTER COLLEGE														
PA TOTAL	0	.0	38	2.5	3	.2	3	.2	44	2.	1,483	97.1		.0
PA FEMALE	0	.0	11	1.4	0	.0	0	.0	11	1.0	758	98.6		.0
PA MALE	0	.0	27	3.6	3	.4	3	.4	33	4.4	725	95.6	0	.0
WESTMORELAND COUNTY CC														
PA TOTAL	0	.0	37	1.6	2	.1	2	.1	41	1	2,222	98.2		.0
PA FEMALE	0	.0	19	1.5	2	.2	2	.2	23	1	1,203	98.1		.0
PA MALE	0	.0	18	1.7	0	.0	0	.0	18	1.9	1,019	98.3	0	.0
WIDENER COLLEGE														
PA TOTAL	3	.1	266	8.5	14	.4		.3	292	9.3	2,834	90.7		.0
PA FEMALE	1	.1	165	12.0	5	.4		.2	174	12.7	1,197	87.3		.0
PA MALE	2	.1	101	5.8	9	.5	8	.3	118	6.7	1,637	93.3	0	.0
WILKES COLLEGE														
PA TOTAL	1	.0	17	.7	10	.4		.2	32	1.3	2,345	97.6	25	1.0
PA FEMALE	0	.0	6	.5	3	.3		.0	9	.8	1,088	98.5	8	.7
PA MALE	1	.1	11	.8	7	.5	4	.3	23	1.8	1,257	96.9	17	1.3
WILLIAMSPORT AREA CC														
PA TOTAL	5	.2	83	3.0	8	.3	1	.0	97	3.5	2,678	96.5		.0
PA FEMALE	0	.0	13	1.9	1	.1	0	.0	14	2.1	662	97.9		.0
PA MALE	5	.2	70	3.3	7	.3	1	.0	83	4.0	2,016	96.0	0	.0
HILSON COLLEGE														
PA TOTAL	0	.0	7	3.6	16	8.2	3	1.5	26	13.4	163	84.0	5	2.6
PA FEMALE	0	.0	7	3.6	16	8.2	3	1.5	26	13.4	163	84.0	5	2.6
PA MALE	0	.0	0	.0	0	.0	0	.0	0	.0	0	.0	0	.0
YESHIVATH BETH MOSHE														
PA TOTAL	0	.0	0	.0	0	.0		.0	0	.0	59	100.0	0	.0
PA FEMALE	0	.0	0	.0	0	.0		.0	0	.0	3	100.0	0	.0
PA MALE	0	.0	0	.0	0	.0	0	.0	0	.0	56	100.0	0	.0
YORK COLLEGE PENNSYLVANIA														
PA TOTAL	0	.0	49	2.4	0	.0	5	.2	54	2.7	1,941	96.0	26	1.3
PA FEMALE	0	.0	32	3.0	0	.0	2	.2	34	3.1	1,048	96.7	2	.2
PA MALE	0	.0	17	1.8	0	.0	3	.3	20	2.1	893	95.3	24	2.6
PENNSYLVANIA	TOTAL (	157 INSTITUTIONS)												
PA TOTAL	490	.1	28,886	8.1	2,298	.6	2,624	.7	34,298	9.6	320,011	89.6	2,969	.8
PA FEMALE	252	.1	17,044	9.6	1,038	.6	1,413	.8	19,747	11.2	156,404	88.3	888	.5
PA MALE	238	.1	11,842	6.6	1,260	.7	1,211	.7	14,551	8.1	163,607	90.8	2,081	1.2

.061

UATE ENROLLMENT IN INSTITUTIONS OF HIGHER EDUCATION BY RACE, ETHNICITY AND SEX:
ATE AND NATION, 1978

N E	BLACK NON-HISPANIC		ASIAN OR PACIFIC ISLANDER		HISPANIC		TOTAL MINORITY		WHITE NON-HISPANIC		NON-RESIDENT ALIEN		TOTAL
	NUMBER	%	NUMBER	%	NUMBER	%	NUMBER	%	NUMBER	%	NUMBER	%	NUMBER
	30	6.3	1	.2	6	1.3	37	7.8	425	89.3	14	2.9	476
	13	4.9	1	.4	4	1.5	18	6.8	241	91.6	4	1.5	263
	17	8.0	0	.0	2	.9	19	8.9	184	86.4	10	4.7	213
	330	6.2	161	3.0	63	1.2	555	10.5	4,633	87.3	119	2.2	5,307
	172	7.0	83	3.4	22	.9	277	11.3	2,137	87.5	27	1.1	2,441
	158	5.5	78	2.7	41	1.4	278	9.7	2,496	87.1	92	3.2	2,866
	11	.3	9	.2	10	.3	30	.8	3,721	98.8	14	.4	3,765
	2	.1	3	.2	5	.3	10	.7	1,448	99.0	4	.3	1,462
	9	.4	6	.3	5	.2	20	.9	2,273	98.7	10	.4	2,303
	469	10.6	8	.2	13	.3	490	11.1	3,898	88.0	42	.9	4,430
	180	13.5	1	.1	3	.2	184	13.8	1,136	85.3	12	.9	1,332
	289	9.3	7	.2	10	.3	306	9.9	2,762	89.2	30	1.0	3,098
	28	4.5	3	.5	2	.3	34	5.5	569	91.8	17	2.7	620
	1	16.7	0	.0	0	.0	1	16.7	5	83.3	0	.0	6
	27	4.4	3	.5	2	.3	33	5.4	564	91.9	17	2.8	614
	35	1.0	6	.2	12	.3	54	1.6	3,410	98.4	0	.0	3,464
	17	1.1	4	.3	4	.3	25	1.5	1,510	98.4	0	.0	1,535
	18	.9	2	.1	8	.4	29	1.5	1,900	98.5	0	.0	1,929
	149	3.5	22	.5	57	1.3	248	5.8	3,959	91.9	103	2.4	4,310
	97	3.3	15	.5	32	1.1	157	5.4	2,718	92.7	56	1.9	2,931
	52	3.8	7	.5	25	1.8	91	6.6	1,241	90.0	47	3.4	1,379
	164	2.5	27	.4	33	.5	244	3.7	6,288	96.3	0	.0	6,532
	102	2.9	15	.4	19	.5	150	4.2	3,420	95.8	0	.0	3,570
	62	2.1	12	.4	14	.5	94	3.2	2,868	96.8	0	.0	2,962
	23	1.7	24	1.8	12	.9	64	4.8	1,191	89.5	76	5.7	1,331
	8	1.0	12	1.5	8	1.0	31	4.0	708	91.4	36	4.6	775
	15	2.7	12	2.2	4	.7	33	5.9	483	86.9	40	7.2	556
	110	5.5	5	.2	14	.7	129	6.4	1,835	91.1	50	2.5	2,014
	35	5.6	0	.0	5	.8	40	6.5	574	92.6	6	1.0	620
	75	5.4	5	.4	9	.6	89	6.4	1,261	90.5	44	3.2	1,394
	33	2.2	2	.1	7	.5	42	2.8	1,440	97.2			1,482
	10	3.3	0	.0	3	1.0	13	4.3	288	95.7	0	.0	301
	23	1.9	2	.2	4	.3	29	2.5	1,152	97.5	0	.0	1,181
	20	1.6	1	.1	13	1.0	38	3.0	1,219	97.0		.0	1,257
	9	.9	1	.1	9	.9	20	2.0	964	98.0	0	.0	984
	11	4.0	0	.0	4	1.5	18	6.6	255	93.4	0	.0	273
	131	1.4	43	.4	30	.3	233	2.4	9,221	96.0	151	1.6	9,605
	50	1.1	17	.4	9	.2	92	2.0	4,580	97.3	37	.8	4,709
	81	1.7	26	.5	21	.4	141	2.9	4,641	94.8	114	2.3	4,896
(13 INSTITUTIONS)													
	1,533	3.4	312	.7	272	.6	2,198	4.9	41,809	93.8	586	1.3	44,593
	696	3.3	152	.7	123	.6	1,018	4.9	19,729	94.3	182	.9	20,929
	837	3.5	160	.7	149	.6	1,180	5.0	22,080	93.3	404	1.7	23,664
	247	27.0	9	1.0	0	.0	259	28.3	657	71.7		.0	916
	90	31.5	3	1.0	0	.0	95	33.2	191	66.8	0	.0	286
	157	24.9	6	1.0	0	.0	164	26.0	466	74.0	0	.0	630
	401	97.1	0	.0	0	.0	401	97.1	0	.0	12	2.9	413
	207	98.6	0	.0	0	.0	207	98.6	0	.0	3	1.4	210
	194	95.6	0	.0	0	.0	194	95.6	0	.0	9	4.4	203
	90	7.8	1	.1	0	.0	91	7.9	1,067	92.1		.0	1,158
	58	9.2	1	.2	0	.0	59	9.4	572	90.6	0	.0	631
	32	6.1	0	.0	0	.0	32	6.1	495	93.9	0	.0	527
	670	28.1	9	.4	0	.0	679	28.5	1,677	70.3	30	1.3	2,386
	393	32.4	4	.3	0	.0	397	32.7	810	66.8	6	.5	1,213
	277	23.6	5	.4	0	.0	282	24.0	867	73.9	24	2.0	1,173
	462	54.6	0	.0	1	.1	466	55.1	374	44.2	6	.7	846
	154	59.0	0	.0	0	.0	155	59.4	104	39.8	2	.8	261
	308	52.6	0	.0	1	.2	311	53.2	270	46.2	4	.7	585
	1,761	100.0	0	.0	0	.0	1,761	100.0	0	.0		.0	1,761
	1,152	100.0	0	.0	0	.0	1,152	100.0	0	.0	0	.0	1,152
	609	100.0	0	.0	0	.0	609	100.0	0	.0	0	.0	609
	0	.0	0	.0	0	.0	0	.0	0	.0		.0	0
	0	.0	0	.0	0	.0	0	.0	0	.0	0	.0	0
	0	.0	0	.0	0	.0	0	.0	0	.0	0	.0	0
	43	12.0	2	.6	4	1.1	49	13.6	304	84.7	6	1.7	359
	13	7.4	0	.0	0	.0	13	7.4	160	91.4	2	1.1	175
	30	16.3	2	1.1	4	2.2	36	19.6	144	78.3	4	2.2	184

TABLE 1 - TOTAL UNDERGRADUATE ENROLLMENT IN INSTITUTIONS OF HIGHER EDUCATION BY RACE, ETHNICITY AND SEX: INSTITUTION, STATE AND NATION, 1978

	AMERICAN INDIAN ALASKAN NATIVE		BLACK NON-HISPANIC		ASIAN OR PACIFIC ISLANDER		HISPANIC		TOTAL MINORITY		WHITE NON-HISPANIC		NON-RESIDENT ALIEN		T
	NUMBER	%	NUMBER	%	NUMBER	%	NUMBER	%	NUMBER	%	NUMBER	%	NUMBER	%	N
SOUTH CAROLINA CONTINUED															
CHESTERFLD-MARLBORO TECH															
SC TOTAL	1	.2	179	35.7	0	.0	2	.4	182	36.3	320	63.7	0	.0	
SC FEMALE	0	.0	81	42.4	0	.0	1	.5	82	42.9	109	57.1	0	.0	
SC MALE	1	.3	98	31.5	0	.0	1	.3	100	32.2	211	67.8	0	.0	
CITADEL MILITARY C OF SC															
SC TOTAL	0	.0	71	3.0	9	.4	13	.5	93	3.9	2,222	93.5	62	2.6	
SC FEMALE	0	.0	9	7.3	0	.0	0	.0	9	7.3	115	92.7	0	.0	
SC MALE	0	.0	62	2.8	9	.4	13	.6	84	3.7	2,107	93.5	62	2.8	
CLAFLIN COLLEGE															
SC TOTAL	0	.0	845	99.2	0	.0		.0	845	9.2	3	.4	4	.5	
SC FEMALE	0	.0	559	99.8	0	.0	0	.0	559	99.8	1	.2	0	.0	
SC MALE	0	.0	286	97.9	0	.0	0	.0	286	97.9	2	.7	4	1.4	
CLEMSON UNIVERSITY															
SC TOTAL	4	.0	149	1.7	24	.3	12	.1	189	2 1	8,677	97.2	60	.7	
SC FEMALE	0	.0	63	1.9	8	.2	5	.1	76	2 3	3,259	97.5	7	.2	
SC MALE	4	.1	86	1.5	16	.3	7	.1	113	210	5,418	97.0	53	.9	
CLINTON JUNIOR COLLEGE															
SC TOTAL	0	.0	122	100.0	0	.0		.0	122	100.0	0	.0	0	.0	
SC FEMALE	0	.0	34	100.0	0	.0		.0	34	100.0	0	.0	0	.0	
SC MALE	0	.0	88	100.0	0	.0	0	.0	88	100.0	0	.0	0	.0	
COKER COLLEGE															
SC TOTAL	2	.7	52	17.2	0	.0		.0	54	17.9	248	82.1	0	.0	
SC FEMALE	2	1.0	31	15.7	0	.0		.0	33	16.8	164	83.2	0	.0	
SC MALE	0	.0	21	20.0	0	.0	0	.0	21	20.0	84	80.0	0	.0	
COLLEGE OF CHARLESTON															
SC TOTAL	3	.1	181	4.6	8	.2	7	.2	199	5 1	3,666	94.0	34	.9	
SC FEMALE	2	.1	130	5.7	2	.1	4	.2	138	610	2,127	93.0	22	1.0	
SC MALE	1	.1	51	3.2	6	.4	3	.2	61	3.8	1,539	95.5	12	.7	
COLUMBIA BIBLE COLLEGE															
SC TOTAL	0	.0	8	1.5	3	.6	7	1.3	18	.4	496	93.4	17	3.2	
SC FEMALE	0	.0	0	.0	0	.0	3	1.3	3	1.3	219	96.1	6	2.6	
SC MALE	0	.0	8	2.6	3	1.0	4	1.3	15	5.0	277	91.4	11	3.6	
COLUMBIA COLLEGE															
SC TOTAL	3	.3	181	19.3	0	.0	1	.1	185	1g.	751	80.2	0	.0	
SC FEMALE	3	.3	181	19.4	0	.0	1	.1	185	19.g	747	80.2	0	.0	
SC MALE	0	.0	0	.0	0	.0	0	.0	0	.8	4	100.0	0	.0	
COLUMBIA COMMERCIAL C															
SC TOTAL	0	.0	722	65.5	0	.0	13	1.2	735	.7	365	33.1	2	.2	
SC FEMALE	0	.0	331	95.4	0	.0	1	.3	332	65.7	15	4.3	0	.0	
SC MALE	0	.0	391	51.8	0	.0	12	1.6	403	53.4	350	46.4	2	.3	
CONVERSE COLLEGE															
SC TOTAL	0	.0	19	2.6	3	.4		.0	22	3.0	704	97.0	0	.0	
SC FEMALE	0	.0	19	2.6	3	.4		.0	22	3.0	704	97.0	0	.0	
SC MALE	0	.0	0	.0	0	.0	0	.0	0	.0	0	.0	0	.0	
DENMARK TECH ED CENTER															
SC TOTAL	1	.2	521	95.6	0	.0		.0	522	95.8	22	4.0	1	.2	
SC FEMALE	0	.0	235	99.2	0	.0		.0	235	99.2	1	.4	1	.4	
SC MALE	1	.3	286	92.9	0	.0	0	.0	287	93.2	21	6.8	0	.0	
ERSKINE C AND SEMINARY															
SC TOTAL	0	.0	45	6.9	2	.3	2	.3	49	7.5	593	90.5	13	2.0	
SC FEMALE	0	.0	23	7.0	0	.0	0	.0	23	7.0	301	91.5	5	1.5	
SC MALE	0	.0	22	6.7	2	.6	2	.6	26	8.0	292	89.6	8	2.5	
FLORENCE DARLINGTON TECH															
SC TOTAL	4	.2	791	37.3	5	.2		.0	800	37.7	1,315	62.0	6	.3	
SC FEMALE	1	.1	371	39.2	2	.2		.0	374	39.5	571	60.4	1	.1	
SC MALE	3	.3	420	35.7	3	.3	0	.0	426	36.3	744	63.3	5	.4	
FRANCIS MARION COLLEGE															
SC TOTAL	0	.0	265	12.3	1	.0		.0	266	12.4	1,879	87.4	4	.2	
SC FEMALE	0	.0	158	15.1	0	.0		.0	158	15.1	887	84.8	1	.1	
SC MALE	0	.0	107	9.7	1	.1	0	.0	108	9.8	992	89.9	3	.3	
FRIENDSHIP COLLEGE															
SC TOTAL	0	.0	157	94.6	0	.0		.0	157	94.6	2	1.2	7	4.2	
SC FEMALE	0	.0	46	100.0	0	.0		.0	46	100.0	0	.0	0	.0	
SC MALE	0	.0	111	92.5	0	.0	0	.0	111	92.5	2	1.7	7	5.8	
FURMAN UNIVERSITY															
SC TOTAL	0	.0	75	3.1	12	.5		.3	93	3.9	2,289	96.1	0	.0	
SC FEMALE	0	.0	33	3.0	6	.5		.0	39	3.6	1,052	96.4	0	.0	
SC MALE	0	.0	42	3.3	6	.5	6	.5	54	4.2	1,237	95.8	0	.0	
GREENVILLE TECH COLLEGE															
SC TOTAL	3	.1	1,019	17.7	13	.2	9	.2	1,044	18.1	4,648	80.7	70	1.2	
SC FEMALE	0	.0	487	18.4	5	.2	4	.2	496	18.7	2,138	80.6	18	.7	
SC MALE	3	.1	532	17.1	8	.3	5	.2	548	17.6	2,510	80.7	52	1.7	
HORRY-GEORGETOWN TECH C															
SC TOTAL	5	.4	331	27.4	3	.2	5	.4	344	28.5	862	71.3	3	.2	
SC FEMALE	0	.0	110	30.2	0	.0	2	.5	112	30.8	250	68.7	2	.5	
SC MALE	5	.6	221	26.2	3	.4	3	.4	232	27.5	612	72.4	1	.1	
LANDER COLLEGE															
SC TOTAL	5	.3	283	16.5	8	.5		.2	297	17.5	1,382	81.6	15	.9	
SC FEMALE	4	.4	184	17.8	3	.3		.4	195	18.8	836	80.7	5	.5	
SC MALE	1	.2	96	14.6	5	.8		.0	102	15.5	546	83.0	10	1.5	
LIMESTONE COLLEGE															
SC TOTAL	0	.0	180	16.8	2	.2		.0	182	16.9	891	83.0	1	.1	
SC FEMALE	0	.0	86	21.0	2	.5		.0	88	21.5	321	78.5	0	.0	
SC MALE	0	.0	94	14.1	0	.0	0	.0	94	14.1	570	85.7	1	.2	
MEDICAL UNIVERSITY OF SC															
SC TOTAL	0	.0	70	6.3	1	.1	4	.4	75	6.8	1,029	92.8	5	.5	
SC FEMALE	0	.0	56	6.5	0	.0	1	.1	57	6.6	805	93.0	4	.5	
SC MALE	0	.0	14	5.8	1	.4	3	1.2	18	7.4	224	92.2	1	.4	
MIDLANDS TECH COLLEGE															
SC TOTAL	12	.2	1,906	35.0	36	.7	33	.6	1,987	36.5	3,410	62.6	51	.9	
SC FEMALE	5	.2	932	39.8	19	.8	12	.5	968	41.4	1,359	58.1	13	.6	
SC MALE	7	.2	974	31.3	17	.5	21	.7	1,019	32.8	2,051	66.0	38	1.2	

108

N E	BLACK NON-HISPANIC		ASIAN OR PACIFIC ISLANDER		HISPANIC		TOTAL MINORITY		WHITE NON-HISPANIC		NON-RESIDENT ALIEN		TOTAL
	NUMBER	%	NUMBER	%	NUMBER	%	NUMBER	%	NUMBER	%	NUMBER	%	NUMBER
INUED													
	637	100.0	0	.0	0	.0	637	100.0	0	.0	0	.0	637
	386	100.0	0	.0	0	.0	386	100.0	0	.0	0	.0	386
	251	100.0	0	.0	0	.0	251	100.0	0	.0	0	.0	251
	85	10.6	2	.2	2	.2	89	11.1	710	88.6	2	.2	801
	35	11.1	1	.3	0	.0	36	11.4	280	88.6	0	.0	316
	50	10.3	1	.2	2	.4	53	10.9	430	88.7	2	.4	485
	117	20.8	0	.0	0	.0	117	20.8	384	68.3	61	10.9	562
	61	30.0	0	.0	0	.0	61	30.0	141	69.5	1	.5	203
	56	15.6	0	.0	0	.0	56	15.6	243	67.7	60	16.7	359
	692	48.6	5	.4	0	.0	697	48.9	725	50.9	3	.2	1,425
	318	52.4	2	.3	0	.0	320	52.7	284	46.8	3	.5	607
	374	45.7	3	.4	0	.0	377	46.1	441	53.9	0	.0	818
	657	38.1	4	.2	0	.0	665	38.6	1,060	61.4	0	.0	1,725
	257	41.3	2	.3	0	.0	262	42.1	360	57.9	0	.0	622
	400	36.3	2	.2	0	.0	403	36.5	700	63.5	0	.0	1,103
	33	3.8	0	.0	0	.0	33	3.8	822	94.6	14	1.6	869
	10	2.6	0	.0	0	.0	10	2.6	376	96.4	4	1.0	390
	23	4.8	0	.0	0	.0	23	4.8	446	93.1	10	2.1	479
	127	59.3	2	.9	1	.5	130	60.7	84	39.3	0	.0	214
	97	63.8	1	.7	1	.7	99	65.1	53	34.9	0	.0	152
	30	48.4	1	1.6	0	.0	31	50.0	31	50.0	0	.0	62
	292	39.7	0	.0	1	.1	293	39.8	441	59.9	2	.3	736
	117	55.2	0	.0	0	.0	117	55.2	94	44.3	1	.5	212
	175	33.4	0	.0	1	.2	176	33.6	347	66.2	1	.2	524
	0	.0	0	.0	0	.0	0	.0	12	92.3	1	7.7	13
	0	.0	0	.0	0	.0	0	.0	12	92.3	1	7.7	13
	0	.0	0	.0	0	.0	0	.0	0	.0	0	.0	0
	2,872	99.1	0	.0	0	.0	2,872	99.1	22	.8	4	.1	2,898
	1,640	99.4	0	.0	0	.0	1,640	99.4	8	.5	2	.1	1,650
	1,232	98.7	0	.0	0	.0	1,232	98.7	14	1.1	2	.2	1,248
	253	22.7	2	.2	1	.1	256	22.9	857	76.8	3	.3	1,116
	159	29.2	0	.0	0	.0	159	29.2	384	70.6	1	.2	544
	94	16.4	2	.3	1	.2	97	17.0	473	82.7	2	.3	572
	269	16.1	8	.5	2	.1	282	16.8	1,386	82.7	8	.5	1,676
	122	19.9	3	.5	0	.0	127	20.7	484	78.8	3	.5	614
	147	13.8	5	.5	2	.2	155	14.6	902	84.9	5	.5	1,062
	500	43.0	4	.3	3	.3	510	43.9	648	55.7	5	.4	1,163
	135	50.6	1	.4	0	.0	136	50.9	130	48.7	1	.4	267
	365	40.7	3	.3	3	.3	374	41.7	518	57.8	4	.4	896
	313	14.1	7	.3	3	.1	334	15.0	1,877	84.3	15	.7	2,226
	101	15.1	3	.4	1	.1	106	15.8	558	83.4	5	.7	669
	212	13.6	4	.3	2	.1	228	14.6	1,319	84.7	10	.6	1,557
	1,389	24.7	54	1.0	26	.5	1,475	26.3	4,126	73.5	1	.2	5,615
	741	29.6	17	.7	8	.3	766	30.6	1,732	69.2	4	.2	2,502
	648	20.8	37	1.2	18	.6	709	22.8	2,394	76.9	10	.3	3,113
	225	14.5	2	.1	5	.3	235	15.2	1,312	84.8	0	.0	1,547
	156	18.1	1	.1	2	.2	162	18.8	699	81.2	0	.0	861
	69	10.1	1	.1	3	.4	73	10.6	613	89.4	0	.0	686
	72	19.8	2	.5	0	.0	75	20.6	289	79.4	0	.0	364
	56	29.6	1	.5	0	.0	58	30.7	131	69.3	0	.0	189
	16	9.1	1	.6	0	.0	17	9.7	158	90.3	0	.0	175
	127	7.5	6	.4	2	.1	136	8.0	1,546	91.4	10	.6	1,692
	75	10.4	2	.3	1	.1	78	10.9	638	88.9	2	.3	718
	52	5.3	4	.4	1	.1	58	6.0	908	93.2	8	.8	974
	2,205	13.0	114	.7	85	.5	2,426	14.4	14,420	85.3	59	.3	16,905
	1,361	16.7	58	.7	33	.4	1,461	17.9	6,693	82.0	10	.1	8,164
	844	9.7	56	.6	52	.6	965	11.0	7,727	88.4	49	.6	8,741
	95	14.3	2	.3	0	.0	98	14.7	567	85.3	0	.0	665
	58	15.7	1	.3	0	.0	60	16.3	309	83.7	0	.0	369
	37	12.5	1	.3	0	.0	38	12.8	258	87.2	0	.0	296
	66	23.9	0	.0	0	.0	66	23.9	210	76.1	0	.0	276
	52	32.1	0	.0	0	.0	52	32.1	110	67.9	0	.0	162
	14	12.3	0	.0	0	.0	14	12.3	100	87.7	0	.0	114
	107	5.1	71	3.4	7	.3	190	9.1	1,898	90.9	1	.0	2,089
	64	5.6	43	3.7	4	.3	113	9.8	1,040	90.2	0	.0	1,153
	43	4.6	28	3.0	3	.3	77	8.2	858	91.7	1	.1	936
	127	18.3	3	.4	0	.0	134	19.3	560	80.7	0	.0	694
	77	22.3	2	.6	0	.0	80	23.2	265	76.8	0	.0	345
	50	14.3	1	.3	0	.0	54	15.5	295	84.5	0	.0	349

TABLE 1 - TOTAL UNDERGRADUATE ENROLLMENT IN INSTITUTIONS OF HIGHER EDUCATION BY RACE, ETHNICITY AND SEX: INSTITUTION, STATE AND NATION, 1978

	AMERICAN INDIAN ALASKAN NATIVE		BLACK NON-HISPANIC		ASIAN OR PACIFIC ISLANDER		HISPANIC		TOTAL MINORITY		WHITE NON-HISPANIC		NON-RESIDENT ALIEN	
	NUMBER	%	NUMBER	%	NUMBER	%	NUMBER	%	NUMBER	%	NUMBER	%	NUMBER	%
SOUTH CAROLINA CONTINUED														
U OF SC AT UNION														
SC TOTAL	0	.0	52	22.3	1	.4	0	.0	53	22.7	180	77.3	0	.0
SC FEMALE	0	.0	32	30.2	1	.9	0	.0	33	31.1	73	68.9	0	.0
SC MALE	0	.0	20	15.7	0	.0	0	.0	20	15.7	107	84.3	0	.0
VOORHEES COLLEGE														
SC TOTAL	0	.0	775	99.2	2	.3	0	.0	777	99.5	1	.1	3	.4
SC FEMALE	0	.0	474	99.2	2	.4	0	.0	476	99.6	1	.2	1	.2
SC MALE	0	.0	301	99.3	0	.0	0	.0	301	99.3	0	.0	2	.7
WILLIAMSBURG TECH ED CTR														
SC TOTAL	0	.0	322	63.3	0	.0	0	.0	322	63.3	187	36.7	0	.0
SC FEMALE	0	.0	89	65.0	0	.0	0	.0	89	65.0	48	35.0	0	.0
SC MALE	0	.0	233	62.6	0	.0	0	.0	233	62.6	139	37.4	0	.0
WINTHROP COLLEGE														
SC TOTAL	2	.1	527	15.2	2	.1	0	.1	535	15.4	2,885	83.2	48	1.4
SC FEMALE	0	.0	405	16.3	2	.1	0	.1	410	16.5	2,063	83.1	8	.4
SC MALE	2	.2	122	12.4	0	.0	1	.1	125	12.7	822	83.4	39	4.0
WOFFORD COLLEGE														
SC TOTAL	1	.1	91	9.4	3	.3	8	.8	103	10.6	859	88.3	11	1.1
SC FEMALE	0	.0	32	18.6	1	.6	1	.6	34	19.8	137	79.7	1	.6
SC MALE	1	.1	59	7.4	2	.2	7	.9	69	8.6	722	90.1	10	1.2
YORK TECHNICAL COLLEGE														
SC TOTAL	6	.4	379	27.0	0	.0	0	.0	385	27.4	1,016	72.3	4	.3
SC FEMALE	0	.0	189	33.8	0	.0	0	.0	189	33.8	369	66.0	1	.2
SC MALE	6	.7	190	22.5	0	.0	0	.0	196	23.2	647	76.5	3	.4
SOUTH CAROLINA TOTAL (60 INSTITUTIONS)														
SC TOTAL	122	.1	25,249	23.9	447	.4	273	.3	26,091	24.7	78,937	74.7	677	.6
SC FEMALE	43	.1	13,525	27.4	202	.4	92	.2	13,862	28.1	35,290	71.6	148	.3
SC MALE	79	.1	11,724	20.8	245	.4	181	.3	12,229	21.7	43,647	77.4	529	.9
SOUTH DAKOTA														
AUGUSTANA COLLEGE														
SD TOTAL	14	.7	8	.4	4	.2	1	.0	27	1.3	2,104	98.0	1	.7
SD FEMALE	6	.5	5	.4	2	.2	0	.0	13	1.0	1,285	98.3	1	.7
SD MALE	8	1.0	3	.4	2	.2	1	.1	14	1.7	819	97.6	8	.7
BLACK HILLS STATE COLLEGE														
SD TOTAL	95	3.6	14	.5	0	.0	0	.0	109	4.2	2,500	95.4	12	.5
SD FEMALE	50	3.7	4	.3	0	.0	0	.0	54	4.0	1,280	95.8	2	.1
SD MALE	45	3.5	10	.8	0	.0	0	.0	55	4.3	1,220	94.9	10	.8
DAKOTA STATE COLLEGE														
SD TOTAL	11	1.3	5	.6	7	.8	0	.0	23	2.8	801	97.2	0	.0
SD FEMALE	6	1.4	0	.0	0	.0	0	.0	6	1.4	434	98.6	0	.0
SD MALE	5	1.3	5	1.3	7	1.8	0	.0	17	4.4	367	95.6	0	.0
DAKOTA WESLEYAN U														
SD TOTAL	18	3.8	8	1.7	1	.2	1	.2	28	5.8	435	90.6	1	3.5
SD FEMALE	5	1.8	1	.4	0	.0	0	.0	6	2.1	272	96.5	1	1.4
SD MALE	13	6.6	7	3.5	1	.5	1	.5	22	11.1	163	82.3	1	6.6
FREEMAN JUNIOR COLLEGE														
SD TOTAL	1	2.3	0	.0	0	.0	0	.0	1	2.3	42	95.5	1	2.3
SD FEMALE	0	.0	0	.0	0	.0	0	.0	0	.0	32	97.0	1	3.0
SD MALE	1	9.1	0	.0	0	.0	0	.0	1	9.1	10	90.9	0	.0
HURON COLLEGE														
SD TOTAL	21	6.9	40	13.1	2	.7	0	.0	63	20.7	241	79.0	1	.3
SD FEMALE	9	6.2	15	10.3	1	.7	0	.0	25	17.1	121	82.9	0	.0
SD MALE	12	7.5	25	15.7	1	.6	0	.0	38	23.9	120	75.5	1	.6
MOUNT MARTY COLLEGE														
SD TOTAL	10	1.9	5	.9	13	2.4	3	.6	31	5.8	486	91.5	14	2.6
SD FEMALE	8	2.3	5	.0	7	2.0	1	.3	16	4.5	330	93.2	8	2.3
SD MALE	2	1.1	5	2.8	6	3.4	2	1.1	15	8.5	156	88.1	6	3.4
NATL COLLEGE OF BUSINESS														
SD TOTAL	113	4.3	153	5.8	13	.5	249	9.5	528	20.0	2,088	79.3	18	.7
SD FEMALE	55	7.9	13	1.9	5	.7	25	3.6	98	14.2	591	85.4	3	.4
SD MALE	58	3.0	140	7.2	8	.4	224	11.5	430	22.1	1,497	77.1	15	.8
NORTHERN STATE COLLEGE														
SD TOTAL	34	1.6	3	.1	3	.1	0	.0	40	1.9	2,069	98.1	0	.0
SD FEMALE	17	1.4	0	.0	0	.0	0	.0	17	1.4	1,160	98.6	0	.0
SD MALE	17	1.8	3	.3	3	.3	0	.0	23	2.5	909	97.5	0	.0
PRESENTATION COLLEGE														
SD TOTAL	10	3.4	1	.3	3	1.0	0	.0	14	4.8	277	95.2	0	.0
SD FEMALE	8	3.0	1	.4	3	1.1	0	.0	12	4.5	257	95.5	0	.0
SD MALE	2	9.1	0	.0	0	.0	0	.0	2	9.1	20	90.9	0	.0
SINTE GLESKA COLLEGE														
SD TOTAL	237	77.2	1	.3	0	.0	0	.0	238	77.5	69	22.5	0	.0
SD FEMALE	162	73.6	0	.0	0	.0	0	.0	162	73.6	58	26.4	0	.0
SD MALE	75	86.2	1	1.1	0	.0	0	.0	76	87.4	11	12.6	0	.0
SIOUX FALLS COLLEGE														
SD TOTAL	4	.7	4	.7	0	.0	0	.0	8	1.4	548	97.2		1.4
SD FEMALE	3	1.0	0	.0	0	.0	0	.0	3	1.0	304	97.7		1.
SD MALE	1	.4	4	1.6	0	.0	0	.0	5	2.0	244	96.4		1.8
SD SCH MINES & TECHNOLOGY														
SD TOTAL	14	1.0	2	.1	10	.7	5	.3	31	2.1	1,322	91.4	94	6.
SD FEMALE	4	1.2	0	.0	1	.3	1	.3	5	1.5	323	97.0	5	1.
SD MALE	10	.9	2	.2	9	.8	0	.3	26	2.3	999	89.7	89	8.8
SD STATE UNIVERSITY														
SD TOTAL	32	.5	25	.4	25	.4	3	.1	85	1.5	5,651	96.7	110	1.
SD FEMALE	10	.4	12	.5	17	.6	1	.0	40	1.5	2,565	97.8	17	.8
SD MALE	22	.7	13	.4	8	.2	2	.1	45	1.4	3,086	95.7	93	2.8
U OF SD MAIN CAMPUS														
SD TOTAL	116	2.7	16	.4	13	.3	1	.3	159	3.7	4,098	96.1	7	.2
SD FEMALE	66	3.2	1	.0	6	.3	4	.4	81	3.9	2,005	96.1	1	.0
SD MALE	50	2.3	15	.7	7	.3	8	.3	78	3.6	2,093	96.1	6	.3

ACK ISPANIC	ASIAN OR PACIFIC ISLANDER		HISPANIC		TOTAL MINORITY		WHITE NON-HISPANIC		NON-RESIDENT ALIEN		TOTAL
%	NUMBER	%	NUMBER	%	NUMBER	%	NUMBER	%	NUMBER	%	NUMBER
.5	9	1.1	0	.0	33	4.0	792	96.0	0	.0	825
.0	1	.4	0	.0	5	2.0	239	98.0	0	.0	244
.7	8	1.4	0	.0	28	4.8	553	95.2	0	.0	581
11.6	1	.4	7	2.6	39	14.6	228	85.1	1	.4	268
8.7	0	.0	1	.9	11	9.6	103	89.6	1	.9	115
13.7	1	.7	6	3.9	28	18.3	125	81.7	0	.0	153
INSTITUTIONS)											
1.3	104	.4	283	1.1	1,457	5.7	23,751	93.1	298	1.2	25,506
.5	43	.4	36	.3	554	4.6	11,359	94.9	65	.5	11,968
1.9	61	.5	247	1.8	903	6.7	12,392	91.5	243	1.8	13,538
83.9	0	.0	0	.0	99	83.9	1	.8	18	15.3	118
72.7	0	.0	0	.0	8	72.7	0	.0	3	27.3	11
85.0	0	.0	0	.0	91	85.0	1	.9	15	14.0	107
11.8	0	.0	5	1.6	42	13.4	269	85.9	2	.6	313
9.4	0	.0	1	.8	13	10.2	113	89.0	1	.8	127
13.4	0	.0	4	2.2	29	15.6	156	83.9	1	.5	186
5.1	0	.0	0	.0	63	5.1	1,107	90.4	55	4.5	1,225
4.9	0	.0	0	.0	30	4.9	565	92.0	19	3.1	614
5.4	0	.0	0	.0	33	5.4	542	88.7	36	5.9	611
10.1	0	.0	0	.0	35	10.1	299	86.7	11	3.2	345
11.3	0	.0	0	.0	19	11.3	149	88.7	0	.0	168
9.0	0	.0	0	.0	16	9.0	150	84.7	11	6.2	177
7.4	1	.5	0	.0	17	7.8	198	91.2	2	.9	217
7.5	1	1.5	0	.0	6	9.0	60	89.6	1	1.5	67
7.3	0	.0	0	.0	11	7.3	138	92.0	1	.7	150
1.7	0	.0	0	.0	9	1.7	505	95.6	14	2.7	528
1.5	0	.0	0	.0	4	1.5	254	95.5	8	3.0	266
1.9	0	.0	0	.0	5	1.9	251	95.8	6	2.3	262
3.8	1	.1	1	.1	63	4.0	1,501	96.0	0	.0	1,564
1.4	1	.1	1	.1	14	1.8	758	98.2	0	.0	772
6.2	0	.0	0	.0	49	6.2	743	93.8	0	.0	792
10.7	9	.8	4	.3	139	11.9	967	82.9	61	5.2	1,167
21.6	4	1.1	2	.5	89	23.5	284	74.9	6	1.6	379
5.5	5	.6	2	.3	50	6.3	683	86.7	55	7.0	788
11.1	0	.0	0	.0	40	11.1	308	85.6	12	3.3	360
7.2	0	.0	0	.0	14	7.2	177	90.8	4	2.1	195
15.8	0	.0	0	.0	26	15.8	131	79.4	8	4.8	165
3.9	3	.1	4	.2	93	4.2	2,097	95.8	0	.0	2,190
4.3	1	.1	2	.2	51	4.6	1,069	95.4	0	.0	1,120
3.6	2	.2	2	.2	42	3.9	1,028	96.1	0	.0	1,070
54.5	1	.1	10	1.1	500	55.9	393	43.9	2	.2	895
52.4	0	.0	6	1.3	257	53.9	219	45.9	1	.2	477
56.9	1	.2	4	1.0	243	58.1	174	41.6	1	.2	418
14.3	0	.0	2	.3	86	14.7	501	85.3	0	.0	587
17.6	0	.0	1	.3	69	17.8	318	82.2	0	.0	387
8.0	0	.0	1	.5	17	8.5	183	91.5	0	.0	200
60.2	3	.7	2	.5	250	61.4	146	35.9	11	2.7	407
66.7	1	.4	1	.4	156	67.5	73	31.6	2	.9	231
51.7	2	1.1	1	.6	94	53.4	73	41.5	9	5.1	176
39.5	0	.0	0	.0	160	39.5	245	60.5	0	.0	405
39.7	0	.0	0	.0	114	39.7	173	60.3	0	.0	287
39.0	0	.0	0	.0	46	39.0	72	61.0	0	.0	118
97.3	0	.0	0	.0	1,074	97.3	0	.0	30	2.7	1,104
98.3	0	.0	0	.0	681	98.3	0	.0	12	1.7	693
95.6	0	.0	0	.0	393	95.6	0	.0	18	4.4	411
3.1	3	.2	2	.1	51	3.7	1,310	94.4	27	1.9	1,388
2.9	1	.1	1	.1	25	3.4	701	95.2	10	1.4	736
3.4	2	.3	1	.2	26	4.0	609	93.4	17	2.6	652
.0	0	.0	0	.0	0	.0	515	99.8	1	.2	516
.0	0	.0	0	.0	0	.0	212	100.0	0	.0	212
.0	0	.0	0	.0	0	.0	303	99.7	1	.3	304
10.9	3	.5	6	.9	80	12.3	558	86.0	11	1.7	649
7.7	3	.6	4	.9	43	9.2	418	89.3	7	1.5	468
19.3	0	.0	2	1.1	37	20.4	140	77.3	4	2.2	181
4.0	1	.2	0	.0	24	4.1	485	83.8	70	12.1	579
2.5	0	.0	0	.0	8	2.6	294	93.9	11	3.5	313
5.6	1	.4	0	.0	16	6.0	191	71.8	59	22.2	266

	AMERICAN INDIAN ALASKAN NATIVE		BLACK NON-HISPANIC		ASIAN OR PACIFIC ISLANDER		HISPANIC		TOTAL MINORITY		WHITE NON-HISPANIC		NON-RESIDENT ALIEN	
	NUMBER	%	NUMBER	%	NUMBER	%	NUMBER	%	NUMBER	%	NUMBER	%	NUMBER	%
TENNESSEE CONTINUED														
JOHN A GUPTON COLLEGE														
TN TOTAL	0	.0	20	32.8	0	.0	0	.0	20	32.8	41	67.2	0	.0
TN FEMALE	0	.0	6	46.2	0	.0	0	.0	6	46.2	7	53.8	0	.0
TN MALE	0	.0	14	29.2	0	.0	0	.0	14	29.2	34	70.8	0	.0
JOHNSON BIBLE COLLEGE														
TN TOTAL	2	.5	3	.8	0	.0	3	.8	8	2.1	370	96.4	6	1.6
TN FEMALE	1	.6	2	1.2	0	.0	2	1.2	5	2.9	162	95.3	3	1.8
TN MALE	1	.5	1	.5	0	.0	1	.5	3	1.4	208	97.2	3	1.4
KING COLLEGE														
TN TOTAL	0	.0	6	2.1	4	1.4	1	.3	11	3.8	269	94.1	6	2.1
TN FEMALE	0	.0	1	.8	0	.0	0	.0	1	.8	116	98.3	1	.8
TN MALE	0	.0	5	3.0	4	2.4	1	.6	10	6.0	153	91.1	5	3.0
KNOXVILLE BUSINESS C														
TN TOTAL	0	.0	103	21.5	0	.0	0	.0	103	21.5	373	77.7	4	.8
TN FEMALE	0	.0	62	36.5	0	.0	0	.0	62	36.5	107	62.9	1	.6
TN MALE	0	.0	41	13.2	0	.0	0	.0	41	13.2	266	85.8	3	1.0
KNOXVILLE COLLEGE														
TN TOTAL	0	.0	621	95.1	0	.0	0	.0	621	95.1	0	.0	32	4.9
TN FEMALE	0	.0	279	97.2	0	.0	0	.0	279	97.2	0	.0	8	2.8
TN MALE	0	.0	342	93.4	0	.0	0	.0	342	93.4	0	.0	24	6.6
LAMBUTH COLLEGE														
TN TOTAL	0	.0	106	15.3	0	.0	0	.0	106	15.3	579	83.7	7	1.0
TN FEMALE	0	.0	78	18.2	0	.0	0	.0	78	18.2	349	81.4	2	.5
TN MALE	0	.0	28	10.6	0	.0	0	.0	28	10.6	230	87.5	5	1.9
LANE COLLEGE														
TN TOTAL	0	.0	669	100.0	0	.0	0	.0	669	100.0	0	.0	0	.0
TN FEMALE	0	.0	343	100.0	0	.0	0	.0	343	100.0	0	.0	0	.0
TN MALE	0	.0	326	100.0	0	.0	0	.0	326	100.0	0	.0	0	.0
LEE COLLEGE														
TN TOTAL	0	.0	31	2.5	1	.1	18	1.4	50	4.0	1,197	95.3	9	.7
TN FEMALE	0	.0	12	2.1	0	.0	4	.7	16	2.8	550	96.7	3	.5
TN MALE	0	.0	19	2.8	1	.1	14	2.0	34	4.9	647	94.2	6	.9
LE MOYNE-OWEN COLLEGE														
TN TOTAL	0	.0	969	99.1	4	.4	0	.0	973	99.5	2	.2	3	.3
TN FEMALE	0	.0	628	99.8	0	.0	0	.0	628	99.8	1	.2	0	.0
TN MALE	0	.0	341	97.7	4	1.1	0	.0	345	98.9	1	.3	3	.9
LINCOLN MEM UNIVERSITY														
TN TOTAL	3	.3	56	5.8	1	.1	2	.2	62	6.4	894	92.3	10	1.0
TN FEMALE	3	.6	22	4.2	0	.0	1	.2	26	4.9	497	94.5	3	.6
TN MALE	0	.0	34	7.7	1	.2	1	.2	36	8.2	397	90.2	7	1.6
MARTIN COLLEGE														
TN TOTAL	0	.0	38	17.8	1	.5	0	.0	39	18.3	167	78.4	7	3.3
TN FEMALE	0	.0	20	18.9	0	.0	0	.0	20	18.9	84	79.2	2	1.9
TN MALE	0	.0	18	16.8	1	.9	0	.0	19	17.8	83	77.6	5	4.7
MARYVILLE COLLEGE														
TN TOTAL	0	.0	34	5.5	1	.2	2	.3	37	6.0	550	89.4	28	4.6
TN FEMALE	0	.0	12	4.2	1	.4	0	.0	13	4.6	261	91.6	11	3.9
TN MALE	0	.0	22	6.7	0	.0	2	.6	24	7.3	289	87.6	17	5.2
MCKENZIE COLLEGE														
TN TOTAL	0	.0	219	43.8	0	.0	0	.0	219	43.8	281	56.2	0	.0
TN FEMALE	0	.0	127	74.3	0	.0	0	.0	127	74.3	44	25.7	0	.0
TN MALE	0	.0	92	28.0	0	.0	0	.0	92	28.0	237	72.0	0	.0
MEHARRY MEDICAL COLLEGE														
TN TOTAL	0	.0	127	74.7	0	.0	0	.0	127	74.7	37	21.8	6	3.5
TN FEMALE	0	.0	104	71.2	0	.0	0	.0	104	71.2	36	24.7	6	4.1
TN MALE	0	.0	23	95.8	0	.0	0	.0	23	95.8	1	4.2	0	.0
MEMPHIS ACADEMY OF ARTS														
TN TOTAL	0	.0	23	11.9	1	.5	0	.0	24	12.4	162	83.9	7	3.6
TN FEMALE	0	.0	6	5.8	1	1.0	0	.0	7	6.8	93	90.3	3	2.9
TN MALE	0	.0	17	18.9	0	.0	0	.0	17	18.9	69	76.7	4	4.4
MID-SOUTH BIBLE COLLEGE														
TN TOTAL	0	.0	6	7.5	0	.0	0	.0	6	7.5	73	91.3	1	1.3
TN FEMALE	0	.0	1	5.9	0	.0	0	.0	1	5.9	15	88.2	1	5.9
TN MALE	0	.0	5	7.9	0	.0	0	.0	5	7.9	58	92.1	0	.0
MILLIGAN COLLEGE														
TN TOTAL	0	.0	11	1.6	0	.0	0	.0	11	1.6	688	97.7	5	.7
TN FEMALE	0	.0	4	1.0	0	.0	0	.0	4	1.0	392	98.5	2	.5
TN MALE	0	.0	7	2.3	0	.0	0	.0	7	2.3	296	96.7	3	1.0
MORRISTOWN COLLEGE														
TN TOTAL	0	.0	149	100.0	0	.0	0	.0	149	100.0	0	.0	0	.0
TN FEMALE	0	.0	68	100.0	0	.0	0	.0	68	100.0	0	.0	0	.0
TN MALE	0	.0	81	100.0	0	.0	0	.0	81	100.0	0	.0	0	.0
NASHVILLE STATE TECH INST														
TN TOTAL	6	.2	633	16.9	10	.3	17	.5	666	17.7	3,023	80.5	65	1.7
TN FEMALE	3	.2	359	20.0	2	.1	5	.3	369	20.6	1,410	78.7	12	.7
TN MALE	3	.2	274	14.0	8	.4	12	.6	297	15.1	1,613	82.2	53	2.7
SCARRITT COLLEGE														
TN TOTAL	1	3.0	2	6.1	0	.0	0	.0	3	9.1	27	81.8	3	9.1
TN FEMALE	1	5.3	2	10.5	0	.0	0	.0	3	15.8	16	84.2	0	.0
TN MALE	0	.0	0	.0	0	.0	0	.0	0	.0	11	78.6	3	21.4
STHN COLLEGE OF OPTOMETRY														
TN TOTAL	0	.0	1	6.3	0	.0	0	.0	1	6.3	15	93.8	0	.0
TN FEMALE	0	.0	1	7.7	0	.0	0	.0	1	7.7	12	92.3	0	.0
TN MALE	0	.0	0	.0	0	.0	0	.0	0	.0	3	100.0	0	.0
STHN MISSIONARY COLLEGE														
TN TOTAL	2	.1	50	2.9	12	.7	87	5.0	151	8.7	1,526	87.4	68	3.9
TN FEMALE	2	.2	35	3.6	5	.5	55	5.7	97	10.1	826	85.9	39	4.1
TN MALE	0	.0	15	1.9	7	.9	32	4.1	54	6.9	700	89.4	29	3.7
SOUTHWESTERN AT MEMPHIS														
TN TOTAL	0	.0	19	1.9	3	.3	7	.7	29	2.9	967	95.9	12	1.2
TN FEMALE	0	.0	15	3.0	2	.4	3	.6	20	4.0	471	95.0	5	1.0
TN MALE	0	.0	4	.8	1	.2	4	.8	9	1.8	496	96.9	7	1.4

	BLACK NON-HISPANIC		ASIAN OR PACIFIC ISLANDER		HISPANIC		TOTAL MINORITY		WHITE NON-HISPANIC		NON-RESIDENT ALIEN		TOTAL
	NUMBER	%	NUMBER	%	NUMBER	%	NUMBER	%	NUMBER	%	NUMBER	%	NUMBER
TINUED													
	150	9.4	9	.6	3	.2	166	10.4	1,367	85.5	66	4.1	1,599
	61	11.3	3	.6	0	.0	64	11.9	447	82.9	28	5.2	539
	89	8.4	6	.6	3	.3	102	9.6	920	86.8	38	3.6	1,060
	1,660	29.9	11	.2	52	.9	1,729	31.1	3,800	68.3	32	.6	5,561
	572	30.6	6	.3	9	.5	587	31.4	1,281	68.5	1	.1	1,869
	1,088	29.5	5	.1	43	1.2	1,142	30.9	2,519	68.2	31	.8	3,692
	733	19.0	39	1.0	61	1.6	842	21.9	3,008	78.1	0	.0	3,850
	448	21.7	18	.9	26	1.3	494	23.9	1,574	76.1	0	.0	2,068
	285	16.0	21	1.2	35	2.0	348	19.5	1,434	80.5	0	.0	1,782
	253	3.1	27	.3	17	.2	324	3.9	7,921	95.7	28	.3	8,273
	131	3.0	10	.2	10	.2	162	3.7	4,182	96.0	10	.2	4,354
	122	3.1	17	.4	7	.2	162	4.1	3,739	95.4	18	.5	3,919
	3,049	20.4	56	.4	6	.0	3,131	21.0	11,579	77.6	205	1.4	14,915
	1,959	25.4	22	.3	3	.0	1,993	25.9	5,647	73.3	59	.8	7,699
	1,090	15.1	34	.5	3	.0	1,138	15.8	5,932	82.2	146	2.0	7,216
	775	9.0	14	.2	17	.2	818	9.5	7,704	89.1	128	1.5	8,650
	455	10.5	8	.2	6	.1	472	10.9	3,825	88.5	25	.6	4,322
	320	7.4	6	.1	11	.3	346	8.0	3,879	89.6	103	2.4	4,328
	3,732	91.7	29	.7	0	.0	3,764	92.5	128	3.1	179	4.4	4,071
	1,909	95.9	5	.3	0	.0	1,916	96.3	71	3.6	3	.2	1,990
	1,823	87.6	24	1.2	0	.0	1,848	88.8	57	2.7	176	8.5	2,081
	147	2.4	11	.2	12	.2	182	2.9	5,771	92.3	298	4.8	6,251
	57	2.2	4	.2	0	.0	66	2.5	2,479	95.7	46	1.8	2,591
	90	2.5	7	.2	12	.3	116	3.2	3,292	89.9	252	6.9	3,660
	687	16.3	23	.5	12	.3	736	17.5	3,428	81.4	46	1.1	4,210
	409	18.0	11	.5	10	.4	438	19.3	1,809	79.8	20	.9	2,267
	278	14.3	12	.6	2	.1	298	15.3	1,619	83.3	26	1.3	1,943
	126	4.3	17	.6	21	.7	173	6.0	2,704	93.1	28	1.0	2,905
	72	4.6	8	.5	9	.6	96	6.1	1,462	93.4	8	.5	1,566
	54	4.0	9	.7	12	.9	77	5.8	1,242	92.8	20	1.5	1,339
	165	8.5	2	.1	3	.2	170	8.7	1,774	91.2	2	.1	1,946
	101	7.9	2	.2	1	.1	104	8.1	1,177	91.8	1	.1	1,282
	64	9.6	0	.0	2	.3	66	9.9	597	89.9	1	.2	664
	116	11.5	0	.0	0	.0	116	11.5	883	87.6	9	.9	1,008
	44	7.9	0	.0	0	.0	44	7.9	513	91.9	1	.2	558
	72	16.0	0	.0	0	.0	72	16.0	370	82.2	8	1.8	450
	362	14.3	0	.0	0	.0	362	14.3	2,168	85.7	0	.0	2,530
	196	13.4	0	.0	0	.0	196	13.4	1,270	86.6	0	.0	1,466
	166	15.6	0	.0	0	.0	166	15.6	898	84.4	0	.0	1,064
	73	6.5	0	.0	0	.0	73	6.5	1,050	92.8	8	.7	1,131
	40	6.1	0	.0	0	.0	40	6.1	610	93.4	3	.5	653
	33	6.9	0	.0	0	.0	33	6.9	440	92.1	5	1.0	478
	93	3.2	7	.2	9	.3	112	3.9	2,772	96.1	1	.0	2,885
	35	2.3	3	.2	3	.2	44	2.9	1,464	97.0	1	.1	1,509
	58	4.2	4	.3	6	.4	68	4.9	1,308	95.1	0	.0	1,376
	2,748	70.0	6	.2	6	.2	2,765	70.4	1,160	29.5	1	.0	3,926
	1,904	74.6	5	.2	3	.1	1,915	75.1	636	24.9	0	.0	2,551
	844	61.4	1	.1	5	.2	850	61.8	524	38.1	1	.1	1,375
	134	5.0	4	.1	11	.4	150	5.9	2,523	94.1	0	.0	2,682
	75	4.8	3	.2	3	.2	88	5.6	1,470	94.4	0	.0	1,558
	59	5.2	1	.1	8	.7	71	6.3	1,053	93.7	0	.0	1,124
	95	2.8	6	.2	2	.1	104	3.0	3,302	96.8	4	.1	3,410
	57	3.0	4	.2	0	.0	62	3.3	1,818	96.5	4	.2	1,884
	38	2.5	2	.1	2	.1	42	2.8	1,484	97.2	0	.0	1,526
	24	3.3	0	.0	0	.0	24	3.3	704	96.0	5	.7	733
	16	5.7	0	.0	0	.0	16	5.7	266	94.3	0	.0	282
	8	1.8	0	.0	0	.0	8	1.8	438	97.1	5	1.1	451
	7	.3	9	.4	9	.4	29	1.2	2,310	97.7	25	1.1	2,364
	3	.3	6	.5	6	.5	18	1.5	1,169	97.5	12	1.0	1,199
	4	.3	3	.3	3	.3	11	.9	1,141	97.9	13	1.1	1,165
	42	9.9	1	.2	0	.0	45	10.6	367	86.8	11	2.6	423
	12	6.7	0	.0	0	.0	14	7.8	164	91.6	1	.6	179
	30	12.3	1	.4	0	.0	31	12.7	203	83.2	10	4.1	244
	25	9.2	0	.0	4	1.5	30	11.0	217	79.5	26	9.5	273
	19	13.4	0	.0	1	.7	20	14.1	110	77.5	12	8.5	142
	6	4.6	0	.0	3	2.3	10	7.6	107	81.7	14	10.7	131
	368	27.4	0	.0	1	.1	370	27.5	962	71.6	12	.9	1,344
	174	28.5	0	.0	1	.2	176	28.8	428	70.0	7	1.1	611
	194	26.5	0	.0	0	.0	194	26.5	534	72.9	5	.7	733

TABLE 1 - TOTAL UNDERGRADUATE ENROLLMENT IN INSTITUTIONS OF HIGHER EDUCATION BY RACE, ETHNICITY AND SEX: INSTITUTION, STATE AND NATION, 1978

	AMERICAN INDIAN ALASKAN NATIVE		BLACK NON-HISPANIC		ASIAN OR PACIFIC ISLANDER		HISPANIC		TOTAL MINORITY		WHITE NON-HISPANIC		NON-RESIDENT ALIEN	
	NUMBER	%	NUMBER	%	NUMBER	%	NUMBER	%	NUMBER	%	NUMBER	%	NUMBER	%
TENNESSEE CONTINUED														
TUSCULUM COLLEGE														
TN TOTAL	0	.0	32	7.4	0	.0	1	.2	33	7.6	392	90.5	8	1.8
TN FEMALE	0	.0	14	7.0	0	.0	0	.0	14	7.0	185	92.5	1	.5
TN MALE	0	.0	18	7.7	0	.0	1	.4	19	8.2	207	88.8	7	3.0
UNION UNIVERSITY														
TN TOTAL	0	.0	71	6.2	0	.0	0	.0	71	6.2	1,058	92.7	12	1.1
TN FEMALE	0	.0	46	6.5	0	.0	0	.0	46	6.5	660	93.1	3	.4
TN MALE	0	.0	25	5.8	0	.0	0	.0	25	5.8	398	92.1	9	2.1
UNIVERSITY OF THE SOUTH														
TN TOTAL	0	.0	4	.4	0	.0	0	.0	4	.4	987	99.6	0	.0
TN FEMALE	0	.0	2	.5	0	.0	0	.0	2	.5	407	99.5	0	.0
TN MALE	0	.0	2	.3	0	.0	0	.0	2	.3	580	99.7	0	.0
U OF TENN CTR HEALTH SCI														
TN TOTAL	0	.0	30	4.4	8	1.2	1	.1	39	5.8	636	94.2	0	.0
TN FEMALE	0	.0	28	5.5	6	1.2	1	.2	35	6.9	473	93.1	0	.0
TN MALE	0	.0	2	1.2	2	1.2	0	.0	4	2.4	163	97.6	0	.0
U OF TENN AT CHATTANOOGA														
TN TOTAL	10	.2	598	11.4	30	.6	29	.6	667	12.7	4,553	86.5	44	.8
TN FEMALE	8	.3	362	14.1	10	.4	12	.5	392	15.2	2,170	84.3	12	.5
TN MALE	2	.1	236	8.8	20	.7	17	.6	275	10.2	2,383	88.6	32	1.2
U OF TENNESSEE KNOXVILLE														
TN TOTAL	44	.2	1,228	5.5	92	.4	73	.3	1,437	6.4	20,293	91.1	555	2.5
TN FEMALE	22	.2	692	6.0	39	.4	28	.3	781	7.6	9,297	91.1	132	1.3
TN MALE	22	.2	536	4.4	53	.4	45	.4	656	5.4	10,996	91.1	423	3.5
U OF TENNESSEE AT MARTIN														
TN TOTAL	5	.1	696	16.0	21	.5	9	.2	731	16.8	3,486	80.3	122	2.8
TN FEMALE	4	.2	431	20.0	10	.5	6	.3	451	21.0	1,682	78.2	17	.8
TN MALE	1	.0	265	12.1	11	.5	3	.1	280	12.8	1,804	82.4	105	4.8
U OF TENNESSEE NASHVILLE														
TN TOTAL	5	.1	573	16.6	8	.2	16	.5	602	17.4	2,812	81.5	36	1.0
TN FEMALE	4	.2	389	20.0	3	.2	9	.5	405	20.8	1,520	78.2	18	.9
TN MALE	1	.1	184	12.2	5	.3	7	.5	197	13.1	1,292	85.7	18	1.2
VANDERBILT UNIVERSITY														
TN TOTAL	0	.0	95	1.9	19	.4	5	.1	119	2.4	4,767	96.6	47	1.0
TN FEMALE	0	.0	55	2.4	10	.4	2	.1	67	2.9	2,234	96.6	11	.5
TN MALE	0	.0	40	1.5	9	.3	3	.1	52	2.0	2,533	96.6	36	1.4
TENNESSEE TOTAL (74 INSTITUTIONS)														
TN TOTAL	227	.1	25,545	16.1	512	.3	553	.3	26,837	16.9	129,232	81.5	2,544	1.6
TN FEMALE	120	.2	14,520	18.3	219	.3	238	.3	15,097	19.0	63,786	80.2	623	.8
TN MALE	107	.1	11,025	13.9	293	.4	315	.4	11,740	14.8	65,446	82.7	1,921	2.4
TEXAS														
ABILENE CHRSTN UNIVERSITY														
TX TOTAL	9	.2	142	3.4	10	.2	53	1.3	214	5.1	3,917	94.1	30	.7
TX FEMALE	1	.1	56	2.8	6	.3	20	1.0	83	4.2	1,878	95.5	5	.3
TX MALE	8	.4	86	3.9	4	.2	33	1.5	131	6.0	2,039	92.9	25	1.1
ALVIN COMMUNITY COLLEGE														
TX TOTAL	16	.7	220	9.6	6	.3	200	8.7	442	19.3	1,815	79.1	38	1.7
TX FEMALE	11	.9	73	6.2	5	.4	78	6.6	167	14.2	995	84.3	18	1.5
TX MALE	5	.4	147	13.2	1	.1	122	10.9	275	24.7	820	73.5	20	1.8
AMARILLO COLLEGE														
TX TOTAL	30	.7	168	4.0	29	.7	238	5.6	465	11.0	3,714	88.0	43	1.0
TX FEMALE	13	.6	102	4.5	12	.5	111	4.9	238	10.5	2,006	88.9	12	.5
TX MALE	17	.9	66	3.4	17	.9	127	6.5	227	11.5	1,708	86.9	31	1.6
AMERICAN TECHNOLOGICAL U														
TX TOTAL	1	.3	45	11.7	5	1.3	23	6.0	74	19.2	308	79.8	4	1.0
TX FEMALE	1	1.6	11	17.5	3	4.8	1	1.6	16	25.4	47	74.6	0	.0
TX MALE	0	.0	34	10.5	2	.6	22	6.8	58	18.0	261	80.8	4	1.2
ANGELINA COLLEGE														
TX TOTAL	1	.0	368	17.3	0	.0	27	1.3	396	18.6	1,737	81.4	0	.0
TX FEMALE	1	.1	255	18.9	0	.0	12	.9	268	19.8	1,084	80.2	0	.0
TX MALE	0	.0	113	14.5	0	.0	15	1.9	128	16.4	653	83.6	0	.0
ANGELO STATE UNIVERSITY														
TX TOTAL	3	.1	227	4.5	11	.2	547	10.8	788	15.6	4,243	84.1	15	.3
TX FEMALE	1	.0	95	3.7	7	.3	265	10.4	368	14.5	2,167	85.2	7	.3
TX MALE	2	.1	132	5.3	4	.2	282	11.3	420	16.8	2,076	82.9	7	.3
AUSTIN COLLEGE														
TX TOTAL	3	.3	55	5.2	7	.7	53	5.0	118	11.1	931	87.3	17	1.6
TX FEMALE	1	.2	21	4.7	3	.7	17	3.8	42	9.3	407	90.2	2	.4
TX MALE	2	.3	34	5.5	4	.7	36	5.9	76	12.4	524	85.2	15	2.4
AUSTIN COMMUNITY COLLEGE														
TX TOTAL	49	.5	1,251	13.7	37	.4	1,221	13.4	2,554	28.0	6,316	69.2	254	2.8
TX FEMALE	21	.5	589	13.7	18	.4	575	13.4	1,203	28.0	2,973	69.2	120	2.8
TX MALE	24	.5	662	13.7	19	.4	646	13.4	1,351	28.0	3,343	69.2	134	2.8
BAYLOR COLLEGE DENTISTRY														
TX TOTAL	0	.0	0	.0	1	1.4	0	.0	1	1.4	72	98.6	0	.0
TX FEMALE	0	.0	0	.0	1	1.4	0	.0	1	1.4	72	98.6	0	.0
TX MALE	0	.0	0	.0	0	.0	0	.0	0	.0	0	.0	0	.0
BAYLOR UNIVERSITY														
TX TOTAL	36	.4	132	1.6	34	.4	126	1.5	328	4.0	7,828	95.8	19	.2
TX FEMALE	17	.4	44	1.0	16	.4	54	1.2	131	3.0	4,187	96.9	3	.1
TX MALE	19	.5	88	2.3	18	.5	72	1.9	197	5.1	3,641	94.5	16	.4
BEE COUNTY COLLEGE														
TX TOTAL	0	.0	33	1.7	15	.8	770	39.7	818	42.2	1,007	52.0	113	5.8
TX FEMALE	0	.0	16	1.8	3	.3	358	40.5	377	42.6	499	56.4	8	.9
TX MALE	0	.0	17	1.6	12	1.1	412	39.1	441	41.8	508	48.2	105	10.0
BISHOP COLLEGE														
TX TOTAL	0	.0	1,122	96.6	0	.0	2	.2	1,124	96.8	37	3.2	0	.0
TX FEMALE	0	.0	465	98.5	0	.0	0	.0	465	98.5	7	1.5	0	.0
TX MALE	0	.0	657	95.4	0	.0	2	.3	659	95.6	30	4.4	0	.0

	BLACK NON-HISPANIC		ASIAN OR PACIFIC ISLANDER		HISPANIC		TOTAL MINORITY		WHITE NON-HISPANIC		NON-RESIDENT ALIEN		TOTAL
	NUMBER	%	NUMBER	%	NUMBER	%	NUMBER	%	NUMBER	%	NUMBER	%	NUMBER
INUED													
	178	7.9	54	2.4	44	2.0	276	12.3	1,554	69.4	410	18.3	2,240
	77	9.0	25	2.9	25	2.9	127	14.9	672	78.8	54	6.3	853
	101	7.3	29	2.1	19	1.4	149	10.7	882	63.6	356	25.7	1,387
	323	9.6	21	.6	293	8.7	669	19.9	2,680	79.7	12	.4	3,361
	120	8.9	8	.6	84	6.2	228	16.9	1,120	83.0	2	.1	1,350
	203	10.1	13	.6	209	10.4	441	21.9	1,560	77.6	10	.5	2,011
	766	16.5	114	2.5	386	8.3	1,295	27.8	3,311	71.2	47	1.0	4,653
	316	16.7	42	2.2	121	6.4	490	25.9	1,390	73.4	15	.8	1,895
	450	16.3	72	2.6	265	9.6	805	29.2	1,921	69.7	32	1.2	2,758
	117	7.3	0	.0	74	4.6	193	12.1	1,395	87.2	12	.8	1,600
	31	4.5	0	.0	30	4.3	63	9.1	626	90.3	4	.6	693
	86	9.5	0	.0	44	4.9	130	14.3	769	84.9	8	.9	907
	38	7.1	1	.2	14	2.6	54	10.1	482	89.9	0	.0	536
	18	5.6	1	.3	9	2.8	29	9.0	294	91.0	0	.0	323
	20	9.4	0	.0	5	2.3	25	11.7	188	88.3	0	.0	213
	383	17.8	6	.3	160	7.4	563	26.1	1,561	72.4	31	1.4	2,155
	253	20.0	4	.3	79	6.2	342	27.0	912	71.9	14	1.1	1,268
	130	14.7	2	.2	81	9.1	221	24.9	649	73.2	17	1.9	887
	9	3.7	0	.0	18	7.5	30	12.4	196	81.3	15	6.2	241
	4	4.0	0	.0	7	6.9	13	12.9	83	82.2	5	5.0	101
	5	3.6	0	.0	11	7.9	17	12.1	113	80.7	10	7.1	140
	42	3.2	0	.0	11	.8	59	4.5	1,059	81.3	185	14.2	1,303
	16	2.5	0	.0	3	.5	22	3.5	580	91.3	33	5.2	635
	26	3.9	0	.0	8	1.2	37	5.5	479	71.7	152	22.9	668
	120	12.7	1	.1	49	5.2	172	18.2	748	79.2	25	2.6	945
	66	14.8	0	.0	17	3.8	83	18.6	354	79.4	9	2.0	446
	54	10.8	1	.2	32	6.4	89	17.8	394	79.0	16	3.2	499
	14	5.8	0	.0	5	2.1	23	9.5	213	88.4	5	2.1	241
	1	1.3	0	.0	1	1.3	3	3.8	75	96.2	0	.0	78
	13	8.0	0	.0	4	2.5	20	12.3	138	84.7	5	3.1	163
	0	.0	0	.0	3	2.3	3	2.3	125	95.4	3	2.3	131
	0	.0	0	.0	1	1.8	1	1.8	52	94.5	2	3.6	55
	0	.0	0	.0	2	2.6	2	2.6	73	96.1	1	1.3	76
	683	45.8	2	.1	37	2.5	728	48.8	759	50.9	4	.3	1,491
	364	46.7	2	.3	22	2.8	392	50.3	398	49.7	0	.0	780
	319	44.9	0	.0	15	2.1	336	47.3	371	52.2	4	.6	711
	514	7.2	49	.7	332	4.7	929	13.0	6,191	86.8		.1	7,129
	296	8.1	20	.5	160	4.4	496	13.6	3,147	86.3		.1	3,648
	218	6.3	29	.8	172	4.9	433	12.4	3,044	87.4		.1	3,481
	2,374	43.9	69	1.3	452	8.4	2,917	53.9	2,433	45.0	59	1.1	5,409
	1,600	45.5	35	1.0	267	7.6	1,918	54.5	1,574	44.7	26	.7	3,518
	774	40.9	34	1.8	185	9.8	999	52.8	859	45.4	33	1.7	1,891
	1,185	25.1	29	.6	395	8.4	1,638	34.7	3,073	65.1	12	.3	4,723
	555	25.4	10	.5	159	7.3	736	33.6	1,448	66.1	5	.2	2,189
	630	24.9	19	.7	236	9.3	902	35.6	1,625	64.1	7	.3	2,534
	84	2.3	17	.5	119	3.3	239	6.7	3,292	92.1	44	1.2	3,575
	19	1.1	7	.4	47	2.7	82	4.7	1,665	94.8	10	.6	1,757
	65	3.6	10	.6	72	4.0	157	8.6	1,627	89.5	34	1.9	1,818
	267	2.6	93	.9	177	1.7	570	5.5	9,667	93.7	79	.8	10,316
	143	2.5	45	.8	82	1.5	280	5.1	5,341	94.5	25	.4	5,654
	124	2.7	48	1.0	95	2.0	282	6.0	4,326	92.3	54	1.2	4,662
	263	3.7	26	.4	3,178	44.7	3,494	49.1	3,597	50.6	18	.3	7,109
	174	4.7	12	.3	1,479	40.0	1,677	45.3	2,013	54.4	10	.3	3,700
	89	2.6	14	.4	1,699	49.8	1,817	53.3	1,584	46.5	8	.2	3,409
	182	24.2	15	2.0	72	9.6	274	36.5	455	60.6	22	2.9	751
	17	47.2	0	.0	6	16.7	23	63.9	13	36.1	0	.0	36
	165	23.1	15	2.1	66	9.2	251	35.1	442	61.8	22	3.1	715
	37	4.5	1	.1	11	1.3	51	6.3	748	91.8	16	2.0	815
	14	3.4	0	.0	6	1.5	22	5.4	379	93.3	5	1.2	406
	23	5.6	1	.2	5	1.2	29	7.1	369	90.2	11	2.7	409
	921	16.4	15	.3	101	1.8	1,060	18.8	4,373	77.6	200	3.6	5,633
	389	13.8	10	.4	56	2.0	469	16.6	2,218	78.4	141	5.0	2,828
	532	19.0	5	.2	45	1.6	591	21.1	2,155	76.8	59	2.1	2,805
	531	5.5	89	.9	5,912	61.6	6,621	69.0	2,800	29.2	174	1.8	9,595
	223	4.8	42	.9	3,016	64.3	3,326	70.9	1,327	28.3	38	.8	4,691
	308	6.3	47	1.0	2,896	59.1	3,295	67.2	1,473	30.0	136	2.8	4,904
	15	2.1	1	.1	10	1.4	28	3.9	688	96.1	0	.0	716
	5	1.2	1	.2	7	1.6	14	3.2	420	96.8	0	.0	434
	10	3.5	0	.0	3	1.1	14	5.0	268	95.0	0	.0	282

TABLE 1 - TOTAL UNDERGRADUATE ENROLLMENT IN INSTITUTIONS OF HIGHER EDUCATION BY RACE, ETHNICITY AND SEX: INSTITUTION, STATE AND NATION, 1978

	AMERICAN INDIAN ALASKAN NATIVE		BLACK NON-HISPANIC		ASIAN OR PACIFIC ISLANDER		HISPANIC		TOTAL MINORITY		WHITE NON-HISPANIC		NON-RESIDENT ALIEN	
	NUMBER	%	NUMBER	%	NUMBER	%	NUMBER	%	NUMBER	%	NUMBER	%	NUMBER	%
TEXAS	CONTINUED													
GALVESTON COLLEGE														
TX TOTAL	2	.1	278	17.6	19	1.2	168	10.6	467	29.5	900	56.9	215	13.6
TX FEMALE	1	.1	191	20.8	12	1.3	106	11.6	310	33.8	590	64.3	17	1.9
TX MALE	1	.2	87	13.1	7	1.1	62	9.3	157	23.6	310	46.6	198	29.8
GRAYSON CC JUNIOR COLLEGE														
TX TOTAL	5	.2	179	5.4	4	.1	41	1.2	229	6.9	3,066	93.1	0	.0
TX FEMALE	3	.2	94	4.9	4	.2	18	.9	119	6.3	1,781	93.7	0	.0
TX MALE	2	.1	85	6.1	0	.0	23	1.6	110	7.9	1,285	92.1	0	.0
GULF COAST BIBLE COLLEGE														
TX TOTAL	1	.3	9	2.8	1	.3	5	1.5	16	4.9	303	93.2	6	1.8
TX FEMALE	0	.0	3	2.1	0	.0	1	.7	4	2.8	136	96.5	1	.7
TX MALE	1	.5	6	3.3	1	.5	4	2.2	12	6.5	167	90.8	5	2.7
HARDIN-SIMMONS UNIVERSITY														
TX TOTAL	1	.1	40	2.6	6	.4	71	4.6	118	7.7	1,423	92.3	0	.0
TX FEMALE	0	.0	10	1.3	5	.6	36	4.7	51	6.6	722	93.4	0	.0
TX MALE	1	.1	30	3.9	1	.1	35	4.6	67	8.7	701	91.3	0	.0
HENDERSON CO JR COLLEGE														
TX TOTAL	2	.1	468	19.9	0	.0	100	4.3	570	24.3	1,718	73.1	61	2.6
TX FEMALE	0	.0	135	14.2	0	.0	9	.9	144	15.2	794	83.8	10	1.1
TX MALE	2	.1	333	23.8	0	.0	91	6.5	426	30.4	924	66.0	51	3.6
HILL JUNIOR COLLEGE														
TX TOTAL	1	.1	59	7.7	1	.1	29	3.8	90	11.7	675	87.9	3	.4
TX FEMALE	0	.0	23	5.7	1	.2	3	.7	27	6.7	376	93.3	0	.0
TX MALE	1	.3	36	9.9	0	.0	26	7.1	63	17.3	299	81.9	3	.8
HOUSTON BAPT UNIVERSITY														
TX TOTAL	5	.3	69	4.4	24	1.5	73	4.6	171	10.9	1,275	81.2	125	8.0
TX FEMALE	1	.1	40	4.3	13	1.4	43	4.6	97	10.4	781	83.4	59	6.3
TX MALE	4	.6	29	4.6	11	1.7	30	4.7	74	11.7	494	77.9	66	10.4
HOUSTON COMMUNITY COLLEGE														
TX TOTAL	31	.2	3,446	26.5	680	5.2	1,148	8.8	5,305	40.8	7,692	59.2	0	.0
TX FEMALE	16	.2	1,873	25.2	403	5.4	641	8.6	2,933	39.5	4,490	60.5	0	.0
TX MALE	19	.3	1,573	28.2	277	5.0	507	9.1	2,372	42.6	3,202	57.4	0	.0
HOWARD C AT BIG SPRING														
TX TOTAL	11	1.1	42	4.4	6	.6	122	12.7	181	18.8	768	79.8	13	1.4
TX FEMALE	6	1.2	18	3.6	6	1.2	66	13.0	96	18.9	407	80.3	4	.8
TX MALE	5	1.1	24	5.3	0	.0	56	12.3	85	18.7	361	79.3	9	2.0
HOWARD PAYNE UNIVERSITY														
TX TOTAL	1	.1	62	5.2	0	.0	86	7.2	149	12.6	1,031	86.9	7	.6
TX FEMALE	1	.2	16	2.7	0	.0	30	5.1	47	8.0	540	91.4	4	.7
TX MALE	0	.0	46	7.7	0	.0	56	9.4	102	17.1	491	82.4	3	.5
HUSTON-TILLOTSON COLLEGE														
TX TOTAL	0	.0	411	68.5	2	.3	21	3.5	434	72.3	6	1.0	160	26.7
TX FEMALE	0	.0	220	84.0	0	.0	9	3.4	229	87.4	2	.8	31	11.8
TX MALE	0	.0	191	56.5	2	.6	12	3.6	205	60.7	4	1.2	129	38.2
INCARNATE WORD COLLEGE														
TX TOTAL	1	.1	118	10.3	0	.0	420	36.7	539	47.1	543	47.4	63	5.5
TX FEMALE	1	.1	94	10.2	0	.0	359	38.9	454	49.1	441	47.7	29	3.1
TX MALE	0	.0	24	10.9	0	.0	61	27.6	85	38.5	102	46.2	34	15.4
JACKSONVILLE COLLEGE														
TX TOTAL	0	.0	19	6.2	0	.0	0	.0	19	6.2	217	70.5	72	23.4
TX FEMALE	0	.0	3	2.7	0	.0	0	.0	3	2.7	105	94.6	3	2.7
TX MALE	0	.0	16	8.1	0	.0	0	.0	16	8.1	112	56.9	69	35.0
JARVIS CHRISTIAN COLLEGE														
TX TOTAL	0	.0	466	97.5	3	.6	3	.6	472	98.7	1	.2	5	1.0
TX FEMALE	0	.0	228	97.0	0	.0	3	1.3	231	98.3	1	.4	3	1.3
TX MALE	0	.0	238	97.9	3	1.2	0	.0	241	99.2	0	.0	2	.8
KILGORE COLLEGE														
TX TOTAL	0	.0	387	11.5	2	.1	58	1.7	447	13.3	2,890	86.0	23	.7
TX FEMALE	0	.0	216	12.1	2	.1	31	1.7	249	13.9	1,537	86.0	11	.6
TX MALE	0	.0	171	10.9	0	.0	27	1.7	198	12.6	1,353	86.0	12	1.4
LAMAR UNIVERSITY														
TX TOTAL	74	.7	1,736	17.3	18	.2	410	4.1	2,238	22.3	7,349	73.1	470	4.7
TX FEMALE	36	.7	981	20.4	11	.2	186	3.9	1,214	25.3	3,536	73.6	53	1.1
TX MALE	38	.7	755	14.4	7	.1	224	4.3	1,024	19.5	3,813	72.6	417	7.9
LAREDO JUNIOR COLLEGE														
TX TOTAL	1	.0	7	.3	5	.2	2,336	87.3	2,349	87.8	270	10.1	56	2.1
TX FEMALE	1	.1	1	.1	1	.1	1,339	88.2	1,345	88.5	146	9.6	28	1.8
TX MALE	0	.0	6	.5	1	.1	997	86.2	1,004	86.9	124	10.7	28	2.4
LEE COLLEGE														
TX TOTAL	19	.4	878	19.1	23	.5	383	8.3	1,303	28.4	3,226	70.3	58	1.3
TX FEMALE	8	.4	174	12.9	9	.7	67	5.0	258	19.1	1,090	80.7	3	.2
TX MALE	11	.3	704	21.8	14	.4	316	9.8	1,045	32.3	2,136	66.0	55	1.7
LETOURNEAU COLLEGE														
TX TOTAL	1	.1	8	.9	5	.6	2	.2	16	1.8	848	93.6	42	4.6
TX FEMALE	0	.0	1	1.2	1	1.2	0	.0	2	2.4	79	94.0	3	3.6
TX MALE	1	.1	7	.9	4	.5	2	.2	14	1.7	769	93.6	39	4.7
LON MORRIS COLLEGE														
TX TOTAL	2	.6	46	14.3	1	.3	4	1.2	53	16.5	229	71.3	39	12.1
TX FEMALE	1	.6	18	11.7	0	.0	2	1.3	21	13.6	129	83.8	4	2.6
TX MALE	1	.6	28	16.8	1	.6	2	1.2	32	19.2	100	59.9	35	21.0
LUBBOCK CHRISTIAN COLLEGE														
TX TOTAL	1	.1	45	4.1	4	.4	39	3.5	89	8.0	999	90.1	21	1.9
TX FEMALE	0	.0	19	3.3	3	.5	22	3.9	44	7.7	521	91.2	6	1.1
TX MALE	1	.2	26	4.8	1	.2	17	3.2	45	8.4	478	88.8	15	2.8
MARY HARDIN-BAYLOR C														
TX TOTAL	2	.2	74	8.0	0	.0	50	5.4	126	13.6	726	78.6	72	7.8
TX FEMALE	2	.3	58	9.2	0	.0	30	4.8	90	14.3	512	81.5	26	4.1
TX MALE	0	.0	16	5.4	0	.0	20	6.8	36	12.2	214	72.3	46	15.5
MCLENNAN CMTY COLLEGE														
TX TOTAL	6	.2	366	11.8	8	.3	168	5.4	548	17.7	2,520	81.6	22	.7
TX FEMALE	3	.2	242	12.7	5	.3	96	5.0	346	18.2	1,550	81.5	6	.3
TX MALE	3	.3	124	10.4	3	.3	72	6.1	202	17.0	970	81.6	16	1.3

UATE ENROLLMENT IN INSTITUTIONS OF HIGHER EDUCATION BY RACE, ETHNICITY AND SEX:
ATE AND NATION, 1978

N/E	BLACK NON-HISPANIC		ASIAN OR PACIFIC ISLANDER		HISPANIC		TOTAL MINORITY		WHITE NON-HISPANIC		NON-RESIDENT ALIEN		TOTAL
	NUMBER	%	NUMBER	%	NUMBER	%	NUMBER	%	NUMBER	%	NUMBER	%	NUMBER
INUED													
	122	9.1	7	.5	73	5.4	209	15.5	1,118	83.0	20	1.5	1,347
	24	4.1	1	.2	23	3.9	50	8.5	533	90.2	8	1.4	591
	98	13.0	6	.8	50	6.6	159	21.0	585	77.4	12	1.6	756
	141	7.7	3	.2	105	5.7	257	14.0	1,550	84.5	27	1.5	1,834
	57	6.4	0	.0	46	5.1	108	12.1	780	87.2	7	.8	895
	84	8.9	3	.3	59	6.3	149	15.9	770	82.0	20	2.1	939
	180	4.4	22	.5	102	2.5	313	7.7	3,715	91.5	30	.7	4,058
	110	5.3	7	.3	39	1.9	160	7.7	1,904	91.8	10	.5	2,074
	70	3.5	15	.8	63	3.2	153	7.7	1,811	91.3	20	1.0	1,984
	211	13.9	3	.2	20	1.3	238	15.7	1,181	77.7	101	6.6	1,520
	110	15.5	1	.1	5	.7	118	16.7	581	82.1	9	1.3	708
	101	12.4	2	.2	15	1.8	120	14.8	600	73.9	92	11.3	812
	192	4.2	35	.8	251	5.5	551	12.2	3,962	87.4	18	.4	4,531
	91	3.7	12	.5	110	4.5	245	9.9	2,217	89.9	4	.2	2,466
	101	4.9	23	1.1	141	6.8	306	14.8	1,745	84.5	14	.7	2,065
	1,223	10.0	32	.3	345	2.8	1,631	13.3	10,022	81.9	577	4.7	12,230
	709	11.7	19	.3	169	2.8	911	15.0	4,994	82.4	158	2.6	6,063
	514	8.3	13	.2	176	2.9	720	11.7	5,028	81.5	419	6.8	6,167
	154	4.0	10	.3	463	12.2	637	16.7	3,125	82.1	45	1.2	3,807
	85	4.7	1	.1	193	10.8	285	15.9	1,498	83.6	8	.4	1,791
	69	3.4	9	.4	270	13.4	352	17.5	1,627	80.7	37	1.8	2,016
	100	9.1	4	.4	647	58.7	766	69.5	317	28.8	19	1.7	1,102
	70	9.2	2	.3	491	64.4	571	74.9	185	24.3	6	.8	762
	30	8.8	2	.6	156	45.9	195	57.4	132	38.8	13	18	340
	29	.4	60	.8	5,955	78.0	6,059	79.3	1,471	19.3	108	1	7,638
	7	.2	33	.8	3,259	79.2	3,307	80.3	771	18.7	38		4,116
	22	.8	27	.8	2,696	76.5	2,752	78.1	700	19.9	70	2.0	3,522
	168	17.7	0	.0	0	.0	168	17.7	716	75.4	65	5.8	949
	80	16.9	0	.0	0	.0	80	16.9	386	81.8	6	1.3	472
	88	18.4	0	.0	0	.0	88	18.4	330	69.2	59	12.4	477
	176	10.7	6	.4	7	.4	204	12.4	1,390	84.6	49	3.0	1,643
	86	10.2	4	.5	4	.5	100	11.8	741	87.5	6	.9	847
	90	11.3	2	.3	3	.4	104	13.1	649	81.5	43	5.4	796
	396	94.1	0	.0	3	.7	400	95.0	1	.2	20	.8	421
	186	95.4	0	.0	0	.0	187	95.9	0	.0	8	4.1	195
	210	92.9	0	.0	3	1.3	213	94.2	1	.4	12	5.3	226
	115	15.9	0	.0	54	7.5	172	23.8	520	72.0	30	4.2	722
	11	5.4	0	.0	4	2.0	15	7.3	187	91.2	3	1.5	205
	104	20.1	0	.0	50	9.7	157	30.4	333	64.4	27	5.2	517
	91	3.5	31	1.2	100	3.9	227	8.8	2,333	90.2	26	1.0	2,586
	36	4.0	14	1.6	40	4.5	91	10.2	790	88.7	10	1.1	891
	55	3.2	17	1.0	60	3.5	136	8.0	1,543	91.0	16	.9	1,695
	132	8.3	4	.3	449	28.2	587	36.8	852	53.4	156	9.8	1,595
	71	10.1	4	.6	210	30.0	286	40.9	371	53.0	43	6.1	700
	61	6.8	0	.0	239	26.7	301	33.6	481	53.7	113	12.6	895
	101	5.2	21	1.1	853	43.9	980	50.4	957	49.2	8	.4	1,945
	44	5.6	11	1.4	382	48.8	440	56.2	342	43.7	1	.1	783
	57	4.9	10	.9	471	40.5	540	46.5	615	52.9	7	.6	1,162
	655	7.0	52	.6	270	2.9	992	10.6	8,223	88.2	107	1.1	9,322
	384	8.2	15	.3	113	2.4	520	11.1	4,130	88.2	35	.7	4,685
	271	5.8	37	.8	157	3.4	472	10.2	4,093	88.3	72	1.6	4,637
	1,340	24.8	21	.4	2,045	37.9	3,436	63.6	1,889	35.0	75	1.4	5,400
	743	38.5	7	.4	567	29.4	1,331	68.9	580	30.0	20	1.0	1,931
	597	17.2	14	.4	1,478	42.6	2,105	60.7	1,309	37.7	55	1.6	3,469
	988	5.9	173	1.0	6,783	40.4	8,037	47.8	8,149	48.5	623	3.7	16,809
	559	6.3	93	1.0	3,659	41.2	4,358	49.1	4,337	48.8	184	2.1	8,879
	429	5.4	80	1.0	3,124	39.4	3,679	46.4	3,812	48.1	439	5.5	7,930
	237	2.9	67	.8	553	6.7	894	10.9	6,678	81.3	647	7.9	8,219
	94	2.4	30	.8	216	5.6	353	9.2	3,398	88.5	89	2.3	3,840
	143	3.3	37	.8	337	7.7	541	12.4	3,280	74.9	558	12.7	4,379
	163	6.8	23	1.0	163	6.8	352	14.6	2,045	84.9	11	.5	2,408
	77	6.4	11	.9	56	4.7	145	12.1	1,048	87.4	6	.5	1,199
	86	7.1	12	1.0	107	8.9	207	17.1	997	82.5	6	.4	1,209
	17	4.0	2	.5	37	8.6	58	13.6	323	75.5	47	11.0	428
	10	5.1	1	.5	17	8.7	30	15.3	161	82.1	5	2.6	196
	7	3.0	1	.4	20	8.6	28	12.1	162	69.8	42	18.1	232
	11	10.0	0	.0	6	5.5	17	15.5	92	83.6	1	.9	110
	0	.0	0	.0	2	4.8	2	4.8	40	95.2	0	.0	42
	11	16.2	0	.0	4	5.9	15	22.1	52	76.5	1	1.5	68

TABLE 1 - TOTAL UNDERGRADUATE ENROLLMENT IN INSTITUTIONS OF HIGHER EDUCATION BY RACE, ETHNICITY AND SEX:
INSTITUTION, STATE AND NATION, 1978

	AMERICAN INDIAN ALASKAN NATIVE		BLACK NON-HISPANIC		ASIAN OR PACIFIC ISLANDER		HISPANIC		TOTAL MINORITY		WHITE NON-HISPANIC		NON-RESIDENT ALIEN	
	NUMBER	%	NUMBER	%	NUMBER	%	NUMBER	%	NUMBER	%	NUMBER	%	NUMBER	%
TEXAS CONTINUED														
SOUTHERN METH UNIVERSITY														
TX TOTAL	6	.1	175	3.2	23	.4	154	2.8	358	6.6	4,964	91.6	99	1.8
TX FEMALE	2	.1	76	2.8	15	.6	65	2.4	158	5.9	2,487	93.2	23	.9
TX MALE	4	.1	99	3.6	8	.3	89	3.2	200	7.3	2,477	90.0	76	2.8
SOUTH PLAINS COLLEGE														
TX TOTAL	12	.5	146	5.8	14	.6	470	1.	642	25.4	1,852	73.2	37	1 5
TX FEMALE	4	.3	67	5.4	3	.2	207	1o.6	281	22.8	943	76.4	10	8
TX MALE	8	.6	79	6.1	11	.8	263	28.8	361	27.8	909	70.1	27	211
STHWSTN ADVENTIST COLLEGE														
TX TOTAL	6	.9	47	6.9	5	.7	75	11 0	133	19.5	522	76.4	28	4.1
TX FEMALE	5	1.4	31	8.9	2	.6	42	1201	80	23.0	255	73.3	13	3.7
TX MALE	1	.3	16	4.8	3	.9	33	9.9	53	15.8	267	79.7	15	4.5
SOUTHWESTERN ASSEMB GOD C														
TX TOTAL	6	.7	5	.6	2	.2	30	3 7	43	5.3	760	93.9	6	.7
TX FEMALE	5	1.3	3	.8	1	.3	18	4 8	27	7.2	343	92.0	3	.8
TX MALE	1	.2	2	.5	1	.2	12	218	16	3.7	417	95.6	3	.7
STHWSTN CHRISTIAN COLLEGE														
TX TOTAL	0	.0	280	59.6	0	.0	0	.0	280	59.6	0	.0	190	40.4
TX FEMALE	0	.0	130	94.2	0	.0	0	.0	130	94.2	0	.0	8	5.8
TX MALE	0	.0	150	45.2	0	.0	0	.0	150	45.2	0	.0	182	54.8
SOUTHWESTERN UNIVERSITY														
TX TOTAL	1	.1	22	2.3	5	.5	24	2 5	52	5.5	893	93.7	8	.8
TX FEMALE	1	.2	11	2.1	3	.6	12	2 3	27	5.2	492	94.6	1	.2
TX MALE	0	.0	11	2.5	2	.5	12	218	25	5.8	401	92.6	7	1.6
SOUTHWEST TEX JR COLLEGE														
TX TOTAL	3	.1	42	2.1	7	.3	1,024	51.1	1,076	53.7	897	44.7	32	1.6
TX FEMALE	0	.0	21	2.1	0	.0	519	51.8	540	53.9	460	45.9	2	.2
TX MALE	3	.3	21	2.1	7	.7	505	50.3	536	53.4	437	43.6	30	3.0
STHWST TEX ST UNIVERSITY														
TX TOTAL	45	.3	418	3.1	29	.2	1,152	8.5	1,644	12.2	11,791	87.3	74	.5
TX FEMALE	19	.3	187	2.7	10	.1	516	7.5	732	10.7	6,112	89.0	23	.3
TX MALE	26	.4	231	3.5	19	.3	636	9.6	912	13.7	5,679	85.5	51	.8
STEPHEN F AUSTIN STATE U														
TX TOTAL	18	.2	290	3.3	24	.3	140	1.6	472	5.4	8,263	94.0	53	.6
TX FEMALE	11	.2	149	3.2	7	.2	66	1.4	233	5.1	4,355	94.7	13	.3
TX MALE	7	.2	141	3.4	17	.4	74	1.8	239	5.7	3,908	93.3	40	1.0
SUL ROSS STATE UNIVERSITY														
TX TOTAL	2	.1	27	1.6	0	.0	584	35.1	613	36.8	1,027	61.6	26	1.
TX FEMALE	1	.1	6	.8	0	.0	254	33.7	261	34.7	479	63.6	13	1.4
TX MALE	1	.1	21	2.3	0	.0	330	36.1	352	38.6	548	60.0	13	1.4
TARRANT CO JUNIOR COLLEGE														
TX TOTAL	65	.4	1,697	10.4	159	1.0	730	4 5	2,651	16.2	13,719	83.8	0	.0
TX FEMALE	22	.3	942	11.1	73	.9	359	4 2	1,396	16.5	7,057	83.5	0	.0
TX MALE	43	.5	755	9.5	86	1.1	371	417	1,255	15.9	6,662	84.1	0	.0
TEMPLE JUNIOR COLLEGE														
TX TOTAL	7	.3	241	10.7	7	.3	111	4 9	366	16.2	1,868	82.7	26	1.2
TX FEMALE	4	.3	130	10.9	3	.3	55	4 6	192	16.0	1,002	83.6	4	.3
TX MALE	3	.3	111	10.5	4	.4	56	513	174	16.4	866	81.5	22	2.1
TEXARKANA CMTY COLLEGE														
TX TOTAL	7	.2	531	17.5	7	.2	62	2.0	607	20.0	2,417	79.5	17	.6
TX FEMALE	4	.3	279	17.9	7	.4	34	2.2	324	20.8	1,232	79.0	4	.3
TX MALE	3	.2	252	17.0	0	.0	28	1.9	283	19.1	1,185	80.0	13	.9
PRAIRIE VIEW A&M U														
TX TOTAL	12	.3	3,672	95.8	137	3.6	12	3	3,833	100.0	0	.0		.0
TX FEMALE	6	.3	1,859	96.1	65	3.4	5	3	1,935	100.0	0	.0		.0
TX MALE	6	.3	1,813	95.5	72	3.8	7	I4	1,898	100.0	0	.0	8	.0
TARLETON STATE UNIVERSITY														
TX TOTAL	10	.4	37	1.4	7	.3	30	1.1	84	3.2	2,538	96.5	8	.3
TX FEMALE	4	.3	10	.9	4	.3	8	.7	26	2.2	1,139	97.6	2	.2
TX MALE	6	.4	27	1.8	3	.2	22	1.5	58	4.0	1,399	95.6	6	.4
TEXAS A&M U MAIN CAMPUS														
TX TOTAL	127	.5	175	.7	99	.4	576	2.3	977	3.9	23,580	94.3	438	1.8
TX FEMALE	46	.5	51	.6	33	.4	138	1.6	268	3.0	8,524	96.3	56	.6
TX MALE	81	.5	124	.8	66	.4	438	2.7	709	4.4	15,056	93.2	382	2.4
TEX A&M U MOODY COLLEGE														
TX TOTAL	8	1.3	1	.2	0	.0	17	2.8	26	4.2	586	95.1	4	.6
TX FEMALE	1	.8	0	.0	0	.0	4	3 0	5	3.8	127	96.2	0	.0
TX MALE	7	1.4	1	.2	0	.0	13	217	21	4.3	459	94.8	4	.8
TEXAS CHRISTIAN U														
TX TOTAL	15	.3	222	5.0	19	.4	96	2.2	352	7.9	4,103	92.1		.0
TX FEMALE	7	.3	120	4.7	16	.6	48	1.9	191	7.5	2,372	92.5		.0
TX MALE	8	.4	102	5.4	3	.2	48	2.5	161	8.5	1,731	91.5	8	.0
TEXAS COLLEGE														
TX TOTAL	0	.0	462	100.0	0	.0	0	.0	462	100.0	0	.0		.0
TX FEMALE	0	.0	239	100.0	0	.0	0	.0	239	100.0	0	.0		.0
TX MALE	0	.0	223	100.0	0	.0	0	.0	223	100.0	0	.0	8	.0
TEXAS EASTERN UNIVERSITY														
TX TOTAL	0	.0	104	8.4	4	.3	6	.5	114	9.2	1,113	89.6	15	1.2
TX FEMALE	0	.0	59	9.3	1	.2	3	.5	63	10.0	566	89.4	4	.6
TX MALE	0	.0	45	7.4	3	.5	3	- .5	51	8.4	547	89.8	11	1.8
TEXAS LUTHERAN COLLEGE														
TX TOTAL	1	.1	74	7.7	1	.1	69	7.2	145	15.1	801	83.5	13	1.4
TX FEMALE	1	.2	21	4.5	1	.2	33	7.1	56	12.1	404	87.1	4	.9
TX MALE	0	.0	53	10.7	0	.0	36	7.3	89	18.0	397	80.2	9	1.8
TEXAS SOUTHERN UNIVERSITY														
TX TOTAL	2	.0	5,709	76.4	43	.6	98	1.3	5,852	78.4	64	.9	1,553	20.8
TX FEMALE	1	.0	3,257	90.8	5	.1	61	1.7	3,324	92.7	36	1.0	226	6.3
TX MALE	1	.0	2,452	63.1	38	1.0	37	1.0	2,528	65.1	28	.7	1,327	34.2
TEXAS SOUTHMOST COLLEGE														
TX TOTAL	2	.1	8	.2	2	.1	2,574	71.8	2,586	72.1	600	16.7	401	11.2
TX FEMALE	2	.1	4	.2	2	.1	1,469	70.5	1,477	70.9	363	17.4	244	11.7
TX MALE	0	.0	4	.3	0	.0	1,105	73.5	1,109	73.8	237	15.8	157	10.4

118

N E	BLACK NON-HISPANIC		ASIAN OR PACIFIC ISLANDER		HISPANIC		TOTAL MINORITY		WHITE NON-HISPANIC		NON-RESIDENT ALIEN		TOTAL
	NUMBER	%	NUMBER	%	NUMBER	%	NUMBER	%	NUMBER	%	NUMBER	%	NUMBER
INUED													
	13	2.1	13	2.1	46	7.6	78	12.9	520	85.8	8	1.3	606
	7	4.2	1	.6	7	4.2	18	10.9	146	88.5	1	.6	165
	6	1.4	12	2.7	39	8.8	60	13.6	374	84.8	7	1.6	441
	3	.3	0	.0	990	85.4	993	85.7	148	12.8	18	1.6	1,159
	2	.6	0	.0	262	84.2	264	84.9	45	14.5	2	.6	311
	1	.1	0	.0	728	85.8	729	86.0	103	12.1	16	1.9	848
	292	8.4	18	.5	263	7.6	578	16.7	2,753	79.6	127	3.7	3,458
	56	10.5	3	.6	33	6.2	93	17.5	427	80.3	12	2.3	532
	236	8.1	15	.5	230	7.9	485	16.6	2,326	79.5	115	3.9	2,926
	348	1.8	84	.4	530	2.7	1,003	5.2	18,124	93.8	194	1.0	19,321
	159	1.9	32	.4	208	2.4	409	4.8	8,125	94.8	41	.5	8,575
	189	1.8	52	.5	322	3.0	594	5.5	9,999	93.0	153	1.4	10,746
	201	13.7	11	.8	66	5	283	19.4	1,149	78.6	30	2.1	1,462
	122	17.1	3	.4	29	4.1	157	22.0	545	76.4	11	1.5	713
	79	10.5	8	1.1	37	4.9	126	16.8	604	80.6	19	2.5	749
	852	17.9	101	2.1	414	8.7	1,385	29.2	3,311	69.7	53	1.1	4,749
	843	18.4	97	2.1	406	8.8	1,364	29.7	3,176	69.2	52	1.1	4,592
	9	5.7	4	2.5	8	5.1	21	13.4	135	86.0	1	.6	157
	61	2.2	16	.6	273	10.1	355	13.1	2,293	84.5	67	2.5	2,715
	37	2.6	6	.4	119	8.5	165	11.8	1,218	87.0	17	1.2	1,400
	24	1.8	10	.8	154	11.7	190	14.4	1,075	81.7	50	3.8	1,315
	891	16.1	8	.1	59	1.1	971	17.5	4,516	81.6	50	.9	5,537
	512	16.5	5	.2	23	.7	547	17.7	2,535	81.8	17	.5	3,099
	379	15.5	3	.1	36	1.5	424	17.4	1,981	81.3	33	1.4	2,438
	26	2.8	4	.4	52	5.6	83	8.9	796	85.7	50	5.4	929
	13	3.2	2	.5	21	5.1	37	9.0	354	86.6	18	4.4	409
	13	2.5	2	.4	31	6.0	46	8.8	442	85.0	32	6.2	520
	2,331	10.3	301	1.3	1,587	7.0	4,304	18.9	17,366	76.4	1,064	4.7	22,734
	1,361	13.4	142	1.4	683	6.7	2,221	21.8	7,697	75.5	274	2.7	10,192
	970	7.7	159	1.3	904	7.2	2,083	16.6	9,669	77.1	790	6.3	12,542
	102	5.2	39	2.0	76	.9	228	11.7	1,694	86.8	30	1.5	1,952
	55	5.1	14	1.3	36	.3	109	10.1	958	89.1	8	.7	1,075
	47	5.4	25	2.9	40	4.6	119	13.6	736	83.9	22	2.5	877
	1,206	26.4	52	1.1	702	15.4	1,979	43.4	2,042	44.7	544	11.9	4,565
	771	37.4	24	1.2	309	15.0	1,115	54.1	811	39.3	135	6.6	2,061
	435	17.4	28	111	393	15.7	864	34.5	1,231	49.2	409	16.3	2,504
	8	2.6	0	.0	40	12.	51	16.5	257	82.9	2	.6	310
	5	2.5	0	.0	19	9.8	26	12.7	177	86.8	1	.5	204
	3	2.8	0	.0	21	19.8	25	23.6	80	75.5	1	.9	106
	118	8.0	25	1.7	200	13.	350	23.7	978	66.2	149	10.1	1,477
	91	9.5	14	1.5	120	12.8	230	24.1	652	68.2	74	7.7	956
	27	5.2	11	2.1	80	15.4	120	23.0	326	62.6	75	14.4	521
	27	1.9	3	.2	500	35.9	538	38.6	853	61.2	3	.2	1,394
	12	1.6	1	.1	231	30.7	250	33.2	500	66.5	2	.3	752
	15	2.3	2	.3	269	41.9	288	44.9	353	55.0	1	.2	642
	1	.2	0	.0	416	85.2	420	86.1	63	12.9	5	1.0	488
	0	.0	0	.0	235	83.3	236	83.7	42	14.9	4	1.4	282
	1	.5	0	.0	181	87.9	184	89.3	21	10.2	1	.5	206
	248	4.8	73	1.4	2,616	50.7	2,950	57.2	1,864	36.1	343	6.7	5,157
	109	4.6	19	.8	1,401	58.7	1,534	64.3	812	34.0	40	1.7	2,386
	139	5.0	54	1.9	1,215	43.8	1,416	51.1	1,052	38.0	303	10.9	2,771
	872	2.6	298	.9	2,581	7.7	3,798	11.3	28,959	86.0	912	2.7	33,669
	500	3.2	136	.9	1,119	7.2	1,772	11.4	13,530	87.1	240	1.5	15,542
	372	2.1	162	.9	1,462	8.1	2,026	11.2	15,429	85.1	672	3.7	18,127
	1,061	7.0	149	1.0	481	3.2	1,762	11.6	12,526	82.3	929	6.1	15,217
	510	8.7	47	.8	169	2.9	757	13.0	4,944	84.8	130	2.2	5,831
	551	5.9	102	1.1	312	3.3	1,005	10.7	7,582	80.8	799	8.5	9,386
	96	3.3	13	.5	80	2.8	198	6.9	2,557	88.8	124	4.	2,879
	50	3.4	7	.5	37	2.5	98	6.8	1,315	90.6	38	2.	1,451
	46	3.2	6	.4	43	3.0	100	7.0	1,242	87.0	86	6.8	1,428
	318	2.3	116	.8	5,419	39.1	5,915	42.6	7,042	50.8	916	6	13,873
	122	1.9	47	.7	2,473	39.2	2,676	42.4	3,356	53.2	281	5	6,313
	196	2.6	69	.9	2,946	39.0	3,239	42.8	3,686	48.8	635	8.14	7,560
	10	4.0	2	.8	12	4.	25	10.1	222	89.5	1	.4	248
	5	2.8	2	1.1	8	4.8	15	8.4	163	91.1	1	.6	179
	5	7.2	0	.0	4	5.8	10	14.5	59	85.5	0	.0	69
	39	7.1	3	.5	24	4	67	12.3	475	87.0		.7	546
	35	6.9	3	.6	23	4.4	62	12.2	441	87.0		.8	507
	4	10.3	0	.0	1	210	5	12.8	34	87.2		.0	39

TABLE 1 - TOTAL UNDERGRADUATE ENROLLMENT IN INSTITUTIONS OF HIGHER EDUCATION BY RACE, ETHNICITY AND SEX:
INSTITUTION, STATE AND NATION, 1978

	AMERICAN INDIAN ALASKAN NATIVE		BLACK NON-HISPANIC		ASIAN OR PACIFIC ISLANDER		HISPANIC		TOTAL MINORITY		WHITE NON-HISPANIC		NON-RESIDENT ALIEN		TOTAL
	NUMBER	%	NUMBER	%	NUMBER	%	NUMBER	%	NUMBER	%	NUMBER	%	NUMBER	%	NUMBER
TEXAS CONTINUED															
U TEX HLTH SCI SN ANTO															
TX TOTAL	0	.0	5	1.4	4	1.1	56	15.8	65	18.3	289	81.4	1	.3	355
TX FEMALE	0	.0	4	1.3	2	.6	47	15.2	53	17.1	257	82.9	0	.0	310
TX MALE	0	.0	1	2.2	2	4.4	9	20.0	12	26.7	32	71.1	1	2.2	45
U TEX HEOL BR GALVESTON															
TX TOTAL	3	.6	28	5.3	11	2.1	39	7.4	81	15.4	441	84.0	3	.6	525
TX FEMALE	3	.7	23	5.2	8	1.8	25	5.6	59	13.3	381	86.0	3	.7	443
TX MALE	0	.0	5	6.1	3	.17	14	17.1	22	26.8	60	73.2	0	.0	82
U OF TEXAS PERMIAN BASIN															
TX TOTAL	0	.0	35	3.9	6	.7	53	6.0	94	10.6	778	87.7	15	1.7	887
TX FEMALE	0	.0	15	3.2	*	.2	27	5.7	43	9.1	428	90.5	2	.4	473
TX MALE	0	.0	20	4.18	5	1.12	26	6.3	51	12.3	350	84.5	13	3.1	414
U OF TEXAS SAN ANTONIO															
TX TOTAL	13	.2	124	1.8	82	1.2	1,690	24.1	1,909	27.2	5,077	72.3	34	.5	7,020
TX FEMALE	4	.1	62	1.8	39	1.1	716	21.0	821	24.0	2,589	75.8	6	.2	3,416
TX MALE	9	.2	62	1.7	43	1.2	974	27.0	1,088	30.2	2,488	69.0	28	.8	3,604
VERNON-REG JUNIOR COLLEGE															
TX TOTAL	6	.5	116	10.3	12	1.1	54	4.8	188	16.7	940	83.3		.0	1,128
TX FEMALE	1	.2	64	11.4	5	.9	25	4.5	95	17.0	464	83.0	0	.0	559
TX MALE	5	.9	52	9.1	7	1.2	29	5.1	93	16.3	476	83.7	0	.0	569
VICTORIA COLLEGE															
TX TOTAL	7	.4	85	.5	1	.1	303	16.0	396	20.9	1,494	78.8	6	.3	1,896
TX FEMALE	3	.3	60	.2	1	.1	176	15.4	240	21.0	902	78.8	2	.2	1,144
TX MALE	4	.5	25	.3	0	.0	127	16.9	156	20.7	592	78.7	4	.5	752
WAYLAND BAPTIST COLLEGE															
TX TOTAL	11	.9	54	4.3	8	.6	87	7.0	160	12.8	1,081	86.7	6	.5	1,247
TX FEMALE	4	.9	10	2.3	5	1.2	33	7.7	52	12.1	378	87.7	1	.2	431
TX MALE	7	.9	44	5.4	3	.4	54	6.6	108	13.2	703	86.2	5	.6	816
WEATHERFORD COLLEGE															
TX TOTAL	4	.3	39	2.9	7	.5	19	1.4	69	5.1	1,135	84.6	138	10.3	1,342
TX FEMALE	3	.4	24	3.5	4	.6	13	1.9	44	6.4	623	90.8	19	2.8	686
TX MALE	1	.2	15	2.3	3	.5	6	.9	25	3.8	512	78.0	119	18.1	656
WESTERN TEXAS COLLEGE															
TX TOTAL	0	.0	49	4.5	1	.1	89	8.2	139	12.9	939	87.0	1	.1	1,079
TX FEMALE	0	.0	24	3.9	1	.2	44	7.1	69	11.2	548	88.7	1	.2	618
TX MALE	0	.0	25	5.4	0	.0	45	9.8	70	15.2	391	84.8	0	.0	461
WEST TEXAS ST UNIVERSITY															
TX TOTAL	16	.3	202	3.8	18	.3	267	5.0	503	9.4	4,820	89.7	51	.9	5,374
TX FEMALE	6	.2	76	2.8	10	.4	140	5.1	232	8.4	2,501	90.9	17	.6	2,750
TX MALE	10	.4	126	4.8	8	.3	127	4.8	271	10.3	2,319	88.4	34	1.3	2,624
WHARTON CO JR COLLEGE															
TX TOTAL	11	.6	239	13.1	5	.3	199	10.9	454	24.9	1,284	70.4	86	4.7	1,824
TX FEMALE	4	.4	136	15.0	3	.3	96	10.6	239	26.4	665	73.5	1	.1	905
TX MALE	7	.8	103	11.2	2	.2	103	11.2	215	23.4	619	67.4	85	9.2	919
WILEY COLLEGE															
TX TOTAL	0	.0	572	94.7		.0	0	.0	572	94.7	0	.0	32	5.3	604
TX FEMALE	0	.0	309	94.4	0	.0	0	.0	309	94.4	0	.0	2	.6	311
TX MALE	0	.0	263	89.8	0	.0	0	.0	263	89.8	0	.0	30	10.2	293
TEXAS TOTAL (139 INSTITUTIONS)															
TX TOTAL	1,938	.4	54,021	10.0	4,224	.8	68,451	12.7	128,634	23.9	393,773	73.2	15,282	2.9	537,689
TX FEMALE	896	.3	28,566	10.9	2,018	.8	33,106	12.7	64,586	24.7	193,106	73.9	3,643	1.4	261,335
TX MALE	1,042	.4	25,455	9.2	2,206	.8	35,345	12.8	64,048	23.2	200,667	72.6	11,639	4.2	276,354
UTAH															
BRIGHAM YOUNG U MAIN CAM															
UT TOTAL	366	1.4	11	.0	128	.5	60	.2	565	2.2	23,921	94.2	915	3.6	25,401
UT FEMALE	234	1.8	3	.0	62	.5	29	.2	328	2.5	12,313	93.6	508	3.9	13,149
UT MALE	132	1.1	8	.1	66	.5	31	.3	237	1.9	11,608	94.7	407	3.3	12,252
BRIGHAM YOUNG U-HAWA CAM															
UT TOTAL	2	.1	4	.2	469	26.4	9	.5	484	27.3	404	22.8	887	50.0	1,775
UT FEMALE	2	.2	1	.1	290	27.3	4	.4	297	28.0	232	21.8	533	50.2	1,062
UT MALE	0	.0	3	.4	179	25.1	5	.7	187	26.2	172	24.1	354	49.6	713
STEVENS HENAGER COLLEGE															
UT TOTAL	11	2.3	5	1.0	0	.0	25	5.2	41	8.5	437	90.7	4	.8	482
UT FEMALE	7	2.5	5	1.8	0	.0	16	5.7	28	9.9	253	89.7	1	.4	282
UT MALE	4	2.0	0	.0	0	.0	9	4.5	13	6.5	184	92.0	3	1.5	200
UNIVERSITY OF UTAH															
UT TOTAL	124	.7	88	.5	264	1.6	261	1.5	737	4	15,705	93.2	403	2.4	16,845
UT FEMALE	46	.7	30	.4	126	1.8	116	1.7	318	4.6	6,480	93.8	113	1.6	6,911
UT MALE	78	.8	58	.6	138	1.4	145	1.5	419	4.12	9,225	92.9	290	2.19	9,934
UTAH STATE UNIVERSITY															
UT TOTAL	39	.5	74	1.0	59	.8	58	.8	230	3.0	6,964	90.1	535	6.9	7,729
UT FEMALE	18	.5	16	.5	30	.9	32	1.0	96	2.19	3,147	93.6	120	3.6	3,363
UT MALE	21	.5	58	1.3	29	.7	26	.6	134	3.1	3,817	87.4	415	9.15	4,366
SOUTHERN UTAH ST COLLEGE															
UT TOTAL	50	2.8	17	.9	6	.3	23	1.3	96	5.3	1,672	93.0	30	*.7	1,798
UT FEMALE	32	3.8	1	.1	3	.4	7	.8	43	5.1	802	94.4	5	.6	850
UT MALE	18	1.9	16	1.7	3	.3	16	1.7	53	5.6	870	91.8	25	216	948
WEBER STATE COLLEGE															
UT TOTAL	59	.7	164	1.9	170	1.9	259	2.9	652	7.4	7,934	89.8	252	2.	8,838
UT FEMALE	32	.9	73	2.0	70	1.9	103	2.8	278	7.6	3,333	91.0	52	1.9	3,663
UT MALE	27	.5	91	1.8	100	1.9	156	3.0	374	7.2	4,601	88.9	200	3.9	5,175
COLLEGE OF EASTERN UTAH															
UT TOTAL	8	.8	4	.4	6	.6	72	7.4	90	9.3	864	89.3	14	1.4	968
UT FEMALE	4	1.2	2	.6	3	.9	16	4.7	25	7.3	314	92.1	2	.6	341
UT MALE	4	.6	2	.3	3	.5	56	8.9	65	10.4	550	87.7	12	1.9	627
DIXIE COLLEGE															
UT TCTAL	11	.7	12	.8	1	.1	15	1.0	39	2.6	1,375	93.3	60	4.1	1,474
UT FEMALE	8	1.1	4	.6	1	.1	5	.7	18	2.5	680	95.1	17	2.4	715
UT MALE	3	.4	8	1.1	0	.0	10	1.3	21	2.8	695	91.6	43	5.7	759

ENROLLMENT IN INSTITUTIONS OF HIGHER EDUCATION BY RACE, ETHNICITY AND SEX:
NO NATION, 1978

BLACK NON-HISPANIC		ASIAN OR PACIFIC ISLANDER		HISPANIC		TOTAL MINORITY		WHITE NON-HISPANIC		NON-RESIDENT ALIEN		TOTAL
NUMBER	%	NUMBER	%	NUMBER	%	NUMBER	%	NUMBER	%	NUMBER	%	NUMBER
2	.2	8	.8	6	.6	27	2.7	958	97.3		.0	985
0	.0	1	.2	1	.2	9	1.8	480	98.2	8	.0	489
2	.4	7	1.4	5	1.0	18	3.6	478	96.4		.0	496
1	.0	64	1.6	35	.9	175	4.4	3,743	93.8	72	1.8	3,990
0	.0	25	1.6	13	.9	64	4.2	1,459	95.4	6	.4	1,529
1	.0	39	1.6	22	.9	111	4.5	2,284	92.8	66	2.7	2,461
34	.5	77	1.2	187	2.9	398	6.1	6,080	93.7	9	.1	6,487
11	.6	22	1.2	48	2.6	98	5.3	1,740	94.5	3	.2	1,841
23	.5	55	1.2	139	3.0	300	6.5	4,340	93.4	6	.1	4,646
28	2.3	31	2.6	37	3.0	106	8.7	1,093	90.0	16	1.3	1,215
14	2.2	10	1.6	25	3.9	54	8.4	584	91.3	2	.3	640
14	2.4	21	3.7	12	2.1	52	9.0	509	88.5	14	2.4	575
13 INSTITUTIONS)												
444	.6	1,283	1.6	1,047	1.3	3,640	4.7	71,150	91.2	3,197	4.1	77,987
160	.5	643	1.8	415	1.2	1,656	4.8	31,817	91.3	1,362	3.9	34,835
284	.7	640	1.5	632	1.5	1,984	4.6	39,333	91.1	1,835	4.3	43,152
14	2.2	16	2.5	9	1.4	39	6.0	576	88.5	36	5.5	651
11	2.4	9	2.0	6	1.3	26	5.7	405	89.4	22	4.9	453
3	1.5	7	3.5	3	1.5	13	6.6	171	86.4	14	7.1	198
4	.3	4	.3	5	.3	23	1.6	1,442	98.2	3	.2	1,468
3	.4	2	.2	4	.5	14	1.7	793	98.1	1	.1	808
1	.2	2	.3	1	.2	9	1.4	649	98.3	2	.3	660
9	.7	2	.2	2	.2	13	1.0	1,226	98.3	8	.6	1,247
3	.4	1	.1	2	.3	6	.8	764	98.6	5	.6	775
6	1.3	1	.2	0	.0	7	1.5	462	97.9	3	.6	472
4	2.1	0	.0	0	.0	4	2.1	183	97.9		.0	187
1	.7	0	.0	0	.0	1	.7	145	99.3	8	.0	146
3	7.3	0	.0	0	.0	3	7.3	38	92.7	0	.0	41
0	.0	0	.0	0	.0	0	.0	1,694	100.0	0	.0	1,694
0	.0	0	.0	0	.0	0	.0	1,268	100.0	0	.0	1,268
0	.0	0	.0	0	.0	0	.0	426	100.0	0	.0	426
83	8.2	1	.1	35	3.5	119	11.8	879	86.9	14	1.4	1,012
59	8.9	0	.0	27	4.1	86	12.9	570	85.6	10	1.5	666
24	6.9	1	.3	8	2.3	33	9.5	309	89.3	4	1.2	346
5	1.2	0	.0	0	.0	5	1.2	417	98.6	1	.2	423
5	1.3	0	.0	0	.0	5	1.3	369	98.4	1	.3	375
0	.0	0	.0	0	.0	0	.0	48	100.0	0	.0	48
8	.8	1	.1	2	.2	18	1.9	927	98.0	1	.1	946
4	.8	1	.2	1	.2	8	1.6	504	98.4	0	.0	512
4	.9	0	.0	1	.2	10	2.3	423	97.5	1	.2	434
6	.6	1	.1	2	.2	10	1.0	1,000	98.5	5	.5	1,015
0	.0	1	.2	1	.2	2	.4	457	99.3	1	.2	460
6	1.1	0	.0	1	.2	8	1.4	543	97.8	4	.7	555
2	.9	0	.0	1	.5	3	1.4	212	96.8	4	1.8	219
1	.8	0	.0	0	.0	1	.8	117	97.5	2	1.7	120
1	1.0	0	.0	1	1.0	2	2.0	95	96.0	2	2.0	99
62	3.2	4	.2	8	.4	74	3.9	1,808	94.6	30	1.6	1,912
32	3.5	1	.1	3	.3	36	3.9	866	94.6	13	1.4	915
30	3.0	3	.3	5	.5	38	3.9	942	94.5	17	1.7	997
22	1.5	5	.3	15	1.0	49	3.3	1,265	86.3	151	10.3	1,465
4	2.2	2	1.1	1	.5	7	3.8	148	80.9	28	15.3	183
18	1.4	3	.2	14	1.1	42	3.3	1,117	87.1	123	9.6	1,282
5	1.2	2	.5	2	.5	16	3.9	388	95.6	2	.5	406
4	1.1	2	.6	2	.6	15	4.3	336	95.5	1	.3	352
1	1.9	0	.0	0	.0	1	1.9	52	96.3	1	1.9	54
1	.1	0	.0	9	.6	10	.6	1,524	96.9	8	2.4	1,572
0	.0	0	.0	2	.3	2	.3	597	98.8	5	.8	604
1	.1	0	.0	7	.7	8	.8	927	95.8	33	3.4	968
8	5.8	0	.0	3	2.2	11	8.0	126	91.3	1	.7	138
7	6.9	0	.0	2	2.0	9	8.9	91	90.1	1	1.0	101
1	2.7	0	.0	1	2.7	2	5.4	35	94.6	0	.0	37
9	2.7	0	.0	4	1.2	13	3.8	309	91.4	16	4.7	338
4	2.2	0	.0	3	1.7	7	3.9	163	91.6	8	4.5	178
5	3.1	0	.0	1	.6	6	3.8	146	91.3	8	5.0	160
0	.0	0	.0	3	1.1	5	1.8	272	98.2		.0	277
0	.0	0	.0	3	1.1	5	1.8	272	98.2	8	.0	277
0	.0	0	.0	0	.0	0	.0	0	.0		.0	0

	AMERICAN INDIAN ALASKAN NATIVE		BLACK NON-HISPANIC		ASIAN OR PACIFIC ISLANDER		HISPANIC		TOTAL MINORITY		WHITE NON-HISPANIC		NON-RESIDENT ALIEN	
	NUMBER	%	NUMBER	%	NUMBER	%	NUMBER	%	NUMBER	%	NUMBER	%	NUMBER	%
VERMONT		CONTINUED												
U VT & STATE AGRL COLLEGE														
VT TOTAL	9	.1	39	.5	13	.2	25	.3	86	1.1	7,557	98.5	28	.4
VT FEMALE	3	.1	21	.5	6	.1	11	.3	41	1.0	4,259	99.0	4	.1
VT MALE	6	.2	18	.5	7	.2	14	.4	45	1.3	3,298	98.0	24	.7
VT INST CMTY INVOLVEMENT														
VT TOTAL	0	.0	2	2.5	0	.0		.0	2	2.5	77	95.1	2	2.5
VT FEMALE	0	.0	2	3.8	0	.0	0	.0	2	3.8	50	96.2	0	.0
VT MALE	0	.0	0	.0	0	.0	0	.0	0	.0	27	93.1	2	6.9
VERMONT TECHNICAL COLLEGE														
VT TOTAL	0	.0	0	.0	1	.2		.0	1	.2	581	99.8	0	.0
VT FEMALE	0	.0	0	.0	1	1.0	0	.0	1	1.0	103	99.0	0	.0
VT MALE	0	.0	0	.0	0	.0	0	.0	0	.0	478	100.0	0	.0
VERMONT		TOTAL (	20 INSTITUTIONS)											
VT TOTAL	43	.2	283	1.2	50	.2	125	.5	501	2.1	22,463	96.4	340	1.5
VT FEMALE	19	.2	161	1.3	26	.2	68	.5	274	2.2	12,277	97.0	102	.8
VT MALE	24	.2	122	1.1	24	.2	57	.5	227	2.1	10,186	95.6	238	2.2
VIRGINIA														
AVERETT COLLEGE														
VA TOTAL	0	.0	99	15.3	0	.0	2	.3	101	15.6	543	83.9	3	.5
VA FEMALE	0	.0	68	15.4	0	.0	2	.5	70	15.8	371	83.9	1	.2
VA MALE	0	.0	31	15.1	0	.0	0	.0	31	15.1	172	83.9	2	1.0
BLUEFIELD COLLEGE														
VA TOTAL	0	.0	10	3.7	0	.0	0	.0	10	3.7	241	88.9	20	7.4
VA FEMALE	0	.0	3	3.0	0	.0	0	.0	3	3.0	95	94.1	3	3.0
VA MALE	0	.0	7	4.1	0	.0	0	.0	7	4.1	146	85.9	17	10.0
BRIDGEWATER COLLEGE														
VA TOTAL	1	.1	22	2.5	0	.0	2	.2	25	2.8	848	96.4	7	.8
VA FEMALE	0	.0	6	1.4	0	.0	1	.2	7	1.6	427	97.5	4	.9
VA MALE	1	.2	16	3.6	0	.0	1	.2	18	4.1	421	95.2	3	.7
C OF WILLIAM AND MARY														
VA TOTAL	10	.2	115	2.6	56	1.2	26	.6	207	4.6	4,202	93.5	85	1.9
VA FEMALE	3	.1	53	2.1	34	1.4	14	.6	104	4.2	2,365	94.5	33	1.3
VA MALE	7	.4	62	3.1	22	1.1	12	.6	103	5.2	1,837	92.2	52	2.6
CHRISTOPHER NEWPORT C														
VA TOTAL	7	.3	228	9.4	21	.9	13	.5	269	11.1	2,122	87.7	29	1.2
VA FEMALE	2	.2	123	9.6	12	.9	7	.5	144	11.2	1,127	87.8	13	1.0
VA MALE	5	.4	105	9.2	9	.8	6	.5	125	11.0	995	87.6	16	1.4
RICHARD BLAND C WM & MARY														
VA TOTAL	4	.4	124	11.1	19	1.7	11	1.0	158	14.1	961	85.7	2	.2
VA FEMALE	2	.3	86	11.5	7	.9	7	.9	102	13.6	646	86.2	1	.1
VA MALE	2	.5	38	10.2	12	3.2	4	1.1	56	15.1	315	84.7	1	.3
EASTERN MENNONITE COLLEGE														
VA TOTAL	2	.2	15	1.4	4	.4	6	.6	27	2.	967	93.4	41	4.0
VA FEMALE	1	.2	10	1.5	4	.6	4	.6	19	2.	613	94.3	18	2.8
VA MALE	1	.3	5	1.3	0	.0	2	.5	8	21?	354	91.9	23	6.0
EMORY AND HENRY COLLEGE														
VA TOTAL	0	.0	19	2.3	2	.2	2	.2	23	2.	802	96.7	4	.5
VA FEMALE	0	.0	5	1.3	1	.3	2	.5	8	2	391	98.0	0	.0
VA MALE	0	.0	14	3.3	1	.2	0	.0	15	318	411	95.6	4	.9
FERRUM COLLEGE														
VA TOTAL	3	.2	152	10.3	14	1.0	4	.3	173	11.8	1,291	87.9	5	.3
VA FEMALE	2	.4	76	13.7	5	.9	1	.2	84	15.1	471	84.9	0	.0
VA MALE	1	.1	76	8.3	9	1.0	3	.3	89	9.7	820	89.7	5	.5
GEORGE MASON UNIVERSITY														
VA TOTAL	28	.4	178	2.4	153	2.1	112	1.5	471	.4	6,757	91.8	137	1.9
VA FEMALE	18	.4	103	2.5	102	2.4	4	1.5	287	6.9	3,826	91.7	61	1.5
VA MALE	10	.3	75	2.3	51	1.6	48	1.5	184	8.7	2,941	91.9	76	2.4
HAMPDEN-SYDNEY COLLEGE														
VA TOTAL	0	.0	9	1.2	0	.0	2	.3	11	1 5	718	98.0	4	.5
VA FEMALE	0	.0	0	.0	0	.0	0	.0	0	0	0	.0	0	.0
VA MALE	0	.0	9	1.2	0	.0	2	.3	11	115	718	98.0	4	.5
HAMPTON INSTITUTE														
VA TOTAL	0	.0	2,438	96.6	3	.1	2	.1	2,443	6.8	46	1.8	35	1.4
VA FEMALE	0	.0	1,489	97.3	0	.0	1	.1	1,490	97.4	30	2.0	10	.7
VA MALE	0	.0	949	95.5	3	.3	1	.1	953	95.9	16	1.6	25	2.5
HOLLINS COLLEGE														
VA TOTAL	0	.0	13	1.4	2	.2	7	.8	22	2.4	880	95.8	17	1.8
VA FEMALE	0	.0	13	1.4	2	.2	7	.8	22	2.4	880	95.8	17	1.8
VA MALE	0	.0	0	.0	0	.0	0	.0	0	.0	0	.0	0	.0
JAMES MADISON UNIVERSITY														
VA TOTAL	3	.0	199	2.9	6	.1	16	.2	224	3.2	6,694	96.7	6	.1
VA FEMALE	1	.0	89	2.4	2	.1	8	.2	100	2 7	3,601	97.3	0	.0
VA MALE	2	.1	110	3.4	4	.1	8	.2	124	348	3,093	96.0	6	.2
LIBERTY BAPTIST COLLEGE														
VA TOTAL	25	1.1	47	2.1	10	.4	15	.7	97	.4	2,091	94.0	36	1.6
VA FEMALE	12	1.2	17	1.7	7	.7	5	.5	41	4.0	970	95.0	10	1.0
VA MALE	13	1.1	30	2.5	3	.2	10	.8	56	417	1,121	93.2	26	2.2
LONGWOOD COLLEGE														
VA TOTAL	0	.0	75	3.3	11	.5		.2	90	.	2,174	95.9	3	.1
VA FEMALE	0	.0	48	2.6	8	.4	4	.2	60	4.0	1,772	96.6	2	.1
VA MALE	0	.0	27	6.2	3	.7		.0	30	8.9	402	92.8	1	.2
LYNCHBURG COLLEGE														
VA TOTAL	0	.0	40	2.4	6	.4	6	.4	52	3 1	1,586	95.0	32	1.9
VA FEMALE	0	.0	24	2.6	3	.3	2	.2	29	3 2	868	95.6	11	1.2
VA MALE	0	.0	16	2.1	3	.4	4	.5	23	310	718	94.2	21	2.8
MARY BALDWIN COLLEGE														
VA TOTAL	0	.0	15	2.1	1	.1	7	1.0	23	3.	675	96.4	2	.3
VA FEMALE	0	.0	15	2.1	1	.1	7	1.0	23	3.	674	96.4	2	.3
VA MALE	0	.0	0	.0	0	.0	0	.0	0	.8	1	100.0	0	.0

IN /E	BLACK NON-HISPANIC		ASIAN OR PACIFIC ISLANDER		HISPANIC		TOTAL MINORITY		WHITE NON-HISPANIC		NON-RESIDENT ALIEN		TOTAL
	NUMBER	%	NUMBER	%	NUMBER	%	NUMBER	%	NUMBER	%	NUMBER	%	NUMBER
'INUED													
	59	6.9	13	1.5	17	2.0	90	10.6	653	76.6	109	12.8	852
	58	6.8	13	1.5	17	2.0	89	10.5	649	76.6	109	12.9	847
	1	20.0	0	.0	0	.0	1	20.0	4	80.0	0	.0	5
	27	1.3	28	1.3	16	.8	72	3.4	2,035	96.4		.2	2,111
	21	1.2	26	1.4	15	.8	63	3.5	1,754	96.3		.2	1,821
	6	2.1	2	.7	1	.3	9	3.1	281	96.9	0	.0	290
	133	16.1	0	.0	0	.0	133	16.1	687	83.0		1.0	828
	97	20.1	0	.0	0	.0	97	20.1	386	79.9		.0	483
	36	10.4	0	.0	0	.0	36	10.4	301	87.2		2.3	345
	6,132	97.0	15	.2	4	.1	6,156	97.4	129	2.0	34	.5	6,319
	3,484	97.8	8	.2	1	.0	3,494	98.0	60	1.7	10	.3	3,564
	2,648	96.1	7	.3	3	.1	2,662	96.5	69	2.5	24	.9	2,755
	588	6.6	96	1.1	65	.7	780	8.7	8,136	91.2	5	.1	8,921
	371	8.5	42	1.0	25	.6	455	10.4	3,905	89.5	1	.0	4,361
	217	4.8	54	1.2	40	.9	325	7.1	4,231	92.8	4	.1	4,560
	144	3.1	9	.2	22	.5	195	4.3	4,392	95.7	0	.0	4,587
	99	3.0	5	.2	16	.5	134	4.1	3,141	95.9	0	.0	3,275
	45	3.4	4	.3	6	.5	61	4.6	1,251	95.4	0	.0	1,312
	11	1.2	9	1.0	6	.6	29	3.1	892	96.1	7	.8	928
	2	.5	4	1.1	2	.5	8	2.2	359	97.6	1	.3	368
	9	1.6	5	.9	4	.7	21	3.8	533	95.2	6	1.1	560
	18	2.6	0	.0	3	.4	21	3.1	642	94.4	17	2.5	680
	18	2.7	0	.0	3	.4	21	3.1	640	94.4	17	2.5	678
	0	.0	0	.0	0	.0	0	.0	2	100.0	0	.0	2
	10	.9	4	.3	2	.2	16	1.4	1,137	98.6	0	.0	1,153
	5	.9	1	.2	1	.2	7	1.3	546	98.7	0	.0	553
	5	.8	3	.5	1	.2	9	1.5	591	98.5	0	.0	600
	605	99.2	0	.0	0	.0	605	99.2	1	.2	4	.7	610
	307	99.4	0	.0	0	.0	307	99.4	0	.0	2	.6	309
	298	99.0	0	.0	0	.0	298	99.0	1	.3	2	.7	301
	49	6.0	5	.6	1	.1	58	7.1	754	92.7	1	.1	813
	25	4.9	0	.0	1	.2	29	5.7	483	94.3	0	.0	512
	24	8.0	5	1.7	0	.0	29	9.6	271	90.0	1	.3	301
	4	1.7	0	.0	0	.0	4	1.7	226	95.4	7	3.0	237
	4	1.7	0	.0	0	.0	4	1.7	226	95.4	7	3.0	237
	0	.0	0	.0	0	.0	0	.0	0	.0	0	.0	0
	6	.9	2	.3	2	.3	10	1.5	624	95.0	23	3.5	657
	6	.9	2	.3	2	.3	10	1.5	624	95.0	23	3.5	657
	0	.0	0	.0	0	.0	0	.0	0	.0	0	.0	0
	43	1.7	3	.1	6	.2	53	2.1	2,484	96.9	26	1.0	2,563
	7	.7	0	.0	4	.4	12	1.1	1,028	98.3	6	.6	1,046
	36	2.4	3	.2	2	.1	41	2.7	1,456	96.0	20	1.3	1,517
	559	5.3	81	.8	7	.1	650	6.2	9,810	93.0	89	.8	10,549
	303	6.2	45	.9	2	.0	351	7.2	4,486	92.1	33	.7	4,870
	256	4.5	36	.6	5	.1	299	5.3	5,324	93.7	56	1.0	5,679
	27	2.6	7	.7	1	.1	35	3.4	991	96.6	0	.0	1,026
	13	2.1	2	.3	0	.0	15	2.4	617	97.6	0	.0	632
	14	3.6	5	1.3	1	.3	20	5.1	374	94.9	0	.0	394
	242	96.4	1	.4	0	.0	243	96.8	8	3.2	0	.0	251
	85	96.6	0	.0	0	.0	85	96.6	3	3.4	0	.0	88
	157	96.3	1	.6	0	.0	158	96.9	5	3.1	0	.0	163
	1,870	19.0	106	1.1	46	.5	2,053	20.8	7,787	79.0	20	.2	9,860
	1,324	22.2	61	1.0	21	.4	1,421	23.8	4,540	76.1	8	.1	5,969
	546	14.0	45	1.2	25	.6	632	16.2	3,247	83.4	12	.3	3,891
	49	7.3	0	.0	12	1.8	62	9.3	590	88.3	16	2.4	668
	38	6.8	0	.0	11	2.0	50	9.0	492	88.3	15	2.7	557
	11	9.9	0	.0	1	.9	12	10.8	98	88.3	1	.9	111
	48	3.6	12	.9	12	.9	72	5.5	1,204	91.4	41	3.1	1,317
	0	.0	0	.0	0	.0	0	.0	0	.0	0	.0	0
	48	3.6	12	.9	12	.9	72	5.5	1,204	91.4	41	3.1	1,317
	309	1.8	120	.7	37	.2	482	2.8	16,714	96.0	220	1.3	17,416
	111	1.7	46	.7	19	.3	185	2.9	6,210	96.4	48	.7	6,443
	198	1.8	74	.7	18	.2	297	2.7	10,504	95.7	172	1.6	10,973
	3,512	94.0	27	.7	23	.6	3,565	95.4	170	4.6		.0	3,735
	1,972	95.1	10	.5	10	.5	1,994	96.1	80	3.9		.0	2,074
	1,540	92.7	17	1.0	13	.8	1,571	94.6	90	5.4		.0	1,661
	40	3.9	6	.6	2	.2	48	4.7	971	95.3		.0	1,019
	22	4.8	1	.2	0	.0	23	5.0	437	95.0		.0	460
	18	3.2	5	.9	2	.4	25	4.5	534	95.5		.0	559

TABLE 1 - TOTAL UNDERGRADUATE ENROLLMENT IN INSTITUTIONS OF HIGHER EDUCATION BY RACE, ETHNICITY AND SEX: INSTITUTION, STATE AND NATION, 1978

	AMERICAN INDIAN ALASKAN NATIVE		BLACK NON-HISPANIC		ASIAN OR PACIFIC ISLANDER		HISPANIC		TOTAL MINORITY		WHITE NON-HISPANIC		NON-RESIDENT ALIEN	
	NUMBER	%	NUMBER	%	NUMBER	%	NUMBER	%	NUMBER	%	NUMBER	%	NUMBER	%
VIRGINIA CONTINUED														
CENTRAL VA CMTY COLLEGE														
VA TOTAL	3	.2	222	12.3	7	.4	4	.2	236	13.1	1,559	86.7	3	.2
VA FEMALE	3	.4	105	12.9	4	.5	0	.0	112	13.8	701	86.1	1	.1
VA MALE	0	.0	117	11.9	3	.3	4	.4	124	12.6	858	87.2	2	.2
DABNEY S LANCASTER CC														
VA TOTAL	0	.0	21	4.5	0	.0	0	.0	21	4.5	449	95.3	1	.2
VA FEMALE	0	.0	12	5.0	0	.0	0	.0	12	5.0	225	94.5	1	.4
VA MALE	0	.0	9	3.9	0	.0	0	.0	9	3.9	224	96.1	0	.0
DANVILLE CMTY COLLEGE														
VA TOTAL	3	.3	243	20.6	3	.3	0	.0	249	21.1	930	78.8	1	.1
VA FEMALE	1	.2	138	28.0	0	.0	0	.0	139	28.3	353	71.7	0	.0
VA MALE	2	.3	105	15.3	3	.4	0	.0	110	16.0	577	83.9	1	.1
ESTN SHORE CMTY COLLEGE														
VA TOTAL	1	.8	34	28.1	0	.0	0	.0	35	28.9	86	71.1	0	.0
VA FEMALE	1	1.6	16	25.4	0	.0	0	.0	17	27.0	46	73.0	0	.0
VA MALE	0	.0	18	31.0	0	.0	0	.0	18	31.0	40	69.0	0	.0
GERMANNA CMTY COLLEGE														
VA TOTAL	2	.5	50	12.3	0	.0	2	.5	54	13.2	354	86.8	0	.0
VA FEMALE	2	1.0	19	9.4	0	.0	1	.5	22	10.9	180	89.1	0	.0
VA MALE	5	.4	31	15.0	0	.0	1	.5	32	15.5	174	84.5	0	.0
J SARGEANT REYNOLDS CC														
VA TOTAL	16	.5	1,097	34.7	25	.8	8	.3	1,146	36.2	2,013	63.6	5	.2
VA FEMALE	11	.6	676	37.9	8	.4	2	.1	697	39.1	1,085	60.8	2	.1
VA MALE	5	.4	421	30.5	17	1.2	6	.4	449	32.5	928	67.2	3	.2
JOHN TYLER CMTY COLLEGE														
VA TOTAL	2	.2	252	23.3	4	.4	6	.6	264	24.4	818	75.6	0	.0
VA FEMALE	2	.4	134	25.6	1	.2	1	.2	138	26.3	386	73.7	0	.0
VA MALE	0	.0	118	21.1	3	.5	5	.9	126	22.6	432	77.4	0	.0
LORD FAIRFAX CMTY COLLEGE														
VA TOTAL	0	.0	36	3.6	3	.3	3	.3	42	4.2	966	95.6	2	.2
VA FEMALE	0	.0	21	4.0	1	.2	3	.6	25	4.8	493	95.0	1	.2
VA MALE	0	.0	15	3.1	2	.4	0	.0	17	3.5	473	96.3	1	.2
MTN EMPIRE CMTY COLLEGE														
VA TOTAL	0	.0	14	2.7	0	.0	1	.2	15	2.9	500	97.1	0	.0
VA FEMALE	0	.0	10	4.8	0	.0	0	.0	10	4.8	198	95.2	0	.0
VA MALE	0	.0	4	1.3	0	.0	1	.3	5	1.6	302	98.4	0	.0
NEW RIVER CMTY COLLEGE														
VA TOTAL	1	.1	79	5.1	2	.1	1	.1	83	5.3	1,454	93.4	19	1.2
VA FEMALE	1	.1	39	5.6	0	.0	0	.0	40	5.7	654	93.7	4	.6
VA MALE	0	.0	40	4.7	2	.2	1	.1	43	5.0	800	93.2	15	1.7
NORTHERN VA CMTY COLLEGE														
VA TOTAL	17	.2	615	7.4	277	3.3	129	1.5	1,038	12.4	7,094	85.0	212	2.5
VA FEMALE	11	.3	300	7.1	135	3.2	58	1.4	504	11.9	3,662	86.3	77	1.8
VA MALE	6	.1	315	7.7	142	3.5	71	1.7	534	13.0	3,432	83.7	135	3.3
PATRICK HENRY CC														
VA TOTAL	0	.0	100	14.3	2	.3	1	.1	103	14.8	594	85.2	0	.0
VA FEMALE	0	.0	57	13.8	1	.2	1	.2	59	14.3	355	85.7	0	.0
VA MALE	0	.0	43	15.2	1	.4	0	.0	44	15.5	239	84.5	0	.0
PAUL D CAMP CMTY COLLEGE														
VA TOTAL	5	.6	456	56.8	1	.1	1	.1	463	57.7	340	42.3	0	.0
VA FEMALE	2	.5	269	66.3	0	.0	0	.0	271	66.7	135	33.3	0	.0
VA MALE	3	.8	187	47.1	1	.3	1	.3	192	48.4	205	51.6	0	.0
PIEDMONT VA CMTY COLLEGE														
VA TOTAL	1	.1	103	10.7	2	.2	0	.0	106	11.0	845	87.9	10	1.0
VA FEMALE	0	.0	62	11.2	0	.0	0	.0	62	11.2	488	88.1	4	.7
VA MALE	1	.2	41	10.1	2	.5	0	.0	44	10.8	357	87.7	6	1.5
RAPPAHANNOCK CMTY COLLEGE														
VA TOTAL	2	.3	184	30.3	0	.0	0	.0	186	30.6	422	69.4	0	.0
VA FEMALE	2	.6	109	31.6	0	.0	0	.0	111	32.2	234	67.8	0	.0
VA MALE	0	.0	75	28.5	0	.0	0	.0	75	28.5	188	71.5	0	.0
SOUTHSIDE VA CMTY COLLEGE														
VA TOTAL	1	.1	324	40.6	1	.1	4	.5	330	41.4	468	58.6	0	.0
VA FEMALE	0	.0	151	47.9	0	.0	1	.3	152	48.3	163	51.7	0	.0
VA MALE	1	.2	173	35.8	1	.2	3	.6	178	36.9	305	63.1	0	.0
SOUTHWEST VA CMTY COLLEGE														
VA TOTAL	1	.1	32	1.7	2	.1	0	.0	35	1.9	1,854	98.1	0	.0
VA FEMALE	1	.1	24	2.6	1	.1	0	.0	26	2.8	891	97.2	0	.0
VA MALE	0	.0	8	.8	1	.1	0	.0	9	.9	963	99.1	0	.0
THOMAS NELSN CMTY COLLEGE														
VA TOTAL	8	.2	1,166	31.7	41	1.1	19	.5	1,234	33.6	2,435	66.3	4	.1
VA FEMALE	5	.3	617	36.8	16	1.0	4	.2	642	38.3	1,033	61.6	2	.1
VA MALE	3	.2	549	27.5	25	1.3	15	.8	592	29.7	1,402	70.2	2	.1
TIDEWATER CMTY COLLEGE														
VA TOTAL	34	.4	1,894	20.7	118	1.3	47	.5	2,093	22.9	7,010	76.8	27	.3
VA FEMALE	19	.4	999	23.4	30	.7	15	.4	1,063	24.9	3,202	75.0	4	.1
VA MALE	15	.3	895	18.4	88	1.8	32	.7	1,030	21.2	3,808	78.3	23	.5
VA HIGHLANDS CMTY COLLEGE														
VA TOTAL	2	.2	21	2.2	1	.1	0	.0	24	2.5	941	97.3	2	.2
VA FEMALE	2	.4	10	2.2	1	.2	0	.0	13	2.8	447	97.0	1	.2
VA MALE	0	.0	11	2.2	0	.0	0	.0	11	2.2	494	97.6	1	.2
VA WESTERN CMTY COLLEGE														
VA TOTAL	3	.1	192	6.7	14	.5	3	.1	212	7.3	2,638	91.4	35	1.2
VA FEMALE	0	.0	110	7.9	4	.3	2	.1	116	8.3	1,273	91.4	4	.3
VA MALE	3	.2	82	5.5	10	.7	1	.1	96	6.4	1,365	91.5	31	2.1
WYTHEVILLE CMTY COLLEGE														
VA TOTAL	0	.0	39	4.7	1	.1	2	.2	42	5.0	786	94.5	4	.5
VA FEMALE	0	.0	16	3.7	0	.0	0	.0	16	3.7	420	96.3	0	.0
VA MALE	0	.0	23	5.8	1	.3	2	.5	26	6.6	366	92.4	4	1.0
VIRGINIA UNION UNIVERSITY														
VA TOTAL	0	.0	1,042	95.1	0	.0	1	.1	1,043	95.2	5	.5	48	4.4
VA FEMALE	0	.0	597	98.4	0	.0	0	.0	597	98.4	0	.0	10	1.6
VA MALE	0	.0	445	91.0	0	.0	1	.2	446	91.2	5	1.0	38	7.8

	BLACK NON-HISPANIC		ASIAN OR PACIFIC ISLANDER		HISPANIC		TOTAL MINORITY		WHITE NON-HISPANIC		NON-RESIDENT ALIEN		TOTAL
N /E	NUMBER	%	NUMBER	%	NUMBER	%	NUMBER	%	NUMBER	%	NUMBER	%	NUMBER
TINUED													
	95	12.5	4	.5	7	.9	110	14.5	628	82.6	22	2.9	760
	46	13.0	3	.8	2	.6	55	15.5	296	83.6	3	.8	354
	49	12.1	1	.2	5	1.2	55	13.5	332	81.8	19	4.7	406
	15	1.1	2	.1	3	.2	20	1.5	1,347	98.2	4	.3	1,371
	0	.0	0	.0	0	.0	0	.0	0	.0	0	.0	0
	15	1.1	2	.1	3	.2	20	1.5	1,347	98.2	4	.3	1,371
. (86 INSTITUTIONS)													
	26,609	16.5	1,362	.8	763	.5	29,042	18.0	131,181	81.1	1,498	.9	161,721
	15,137	18.1	659	.8	376	.4	16,346	19.5	66,713	79.8	584	.7	83,643
	11,472	14.7	703	.9	387	.5	12,696	16.3	64,468	82.6	914	1.2	78,078
	84	2.5	58	1.7	27	.8	188	5.6	2,957	88.5	195	5.8	3,340
	42	2.3	29	1.6	18	1.0	101	5.4	1,677	90.0	85	4.6	1,863
	42	2.8	29	2.0	9	.6	87	5.9	1,280	86.7	110	7.4	1,477
	16	3.1	4	.8	32	6.1	56	10.7	383	73.2	84	16.1	523
	0	.0	1	.6	18	11.1	19	11.7	129	79.6	14	8.6	162
	16	4.4	3	.8	14	3.9	37	10.2	254	70.4	70	19.4	361
	3	.2	4	.3	5	.4	18	1.4	1,255	97.2	18	1.4	1,291
	0	.0	2	.3	2	.3	9	1.6	564	97.4	6	1.0	579
	3	.4	2	.3	3	.4	9	1.3	691	97.1	12	1.7	712
	71	1.3	88	1.6	94	1.7	361	6.6	5,069	92.5	49	.9	5,479
	40	1.4	43	1.5	57	2.0	176	6.2	2,675	93.5	9	.3	2,860
	31	1.2	45	1.7	37	1.4	185	7.1	2,394	91.4	40	1.5	2,619
	87	6.8	17	1.3	17	1.3	138	10.8	1,134	88.4	11	.9	1,283
	20	6.9	2	.7	5	1.7	36	12.5	245	84.8	8	2.8	289
	67	6.7	15	1.5	12	1.2	102	10.3	889	89.4	3	.3	994
	14	.6	16	.7	15	.7	65	2.9	2,137	94.5	59	2.6	2,261
	4	.4	4	.4	6	.5	25	2.3	1,058	95.6	24	2.2	1,107
	10	.9	12	1.0	9	.8	40	3.5	1,079	93.5	35	3.0	1,154
	39	1.5	30	1.	72	2.8	155	6.0	2,389	92.3	43	1.7	2,587
	21	1.6	20	1.	36	2.8	88	6.7	1,201	92.1	15	1.2	1,304
	18	1.4	10	1.	36	2.8	67	5.2	1,188	92.6	28	2.2	1,283
	26	7.6	9	2.6	4	1.2	41	11.9	292	84.9	11	3.2	344
	11	5.6	5	2.6	2	1.0	20	10.2	171	87.2	5	2.6	196
	15	10.1	4	2.7	2	1.4	21	14.2	121	81.8	6	4.1	148
	69	1.2	40	.7	31	.6	245	4.4	5,230	93.4	122	2.2	5,597
	24	.8	17	.6	16	.5	130	4.4	2,809	94.8	23	.8	2,962
	45	1.7	23	.9	15	.6	115	4.4	2,421	91.9	99	3.8	2,635
	72	3.1	32	1.4	30	1.3	209	9.0	2,102	90.6	8	.3	2,319
	31	2.6	15	1.3	14	1.2	102	8.7	1,070	91.1	3	.3	1,175
	41	3.6	17	1.5	16	1.4	107	9.4	1,032	90.2	5	.4	1,144
	474	12.3	137	3.5	136	3 5	786	20.3	3,048	78.9	31	.8	3,865
	137	8.9	61	3.9	27	1 7	240	15.5	1,297	83.8	10	.6	1,547
	337	14.5	76	3.3	109	4 7	546	23.6	1,751	75.5	21	.9	2,318
	9	3.4	11	4 2	11	.2	61	23.0	185	69.8	19	7.2	265
	3	3.2	4	2 12	5	2.7	42	22.6	141	75.8	3	1.6	186
	3	3.8	7	8.9	6	7.6	19	24.1	44	55.7	16	20.3	79
	9	.5	32	1.9	9	.5	65	3.8	1,594	92.8	59	3.4	1,718
	4	.5	19	2.3	5	.6	38	4.6	769	93.3	17	2.1	824
	5	.6	13	1.5	4	.4	27	3.0	825	92.3	42	4.7	894
	6	.5	11	.8	15	1.1	67	5.1	1,239	94.1	10	.8	1,316
	0	.0	4	.8	8	1.2	27	4.0	647	95.6	3	.4	677
	6	.9	7	1.1	7	1.1	40	6.3	592	92.6	7	1.1	639
	42	1.4	39	1.3	47	1 5	165	5.4	2,816	92.6	61	2.0	3,042
	19	1.4	14	1.1	12	9	64	4.8	1,248	94.0	16	1.2	1,328
	23	1.3	25	1.5	35	2 0	101	5.9	1,568	91.5	45	2.6	1,714
	73	2.0	110	3 0	39	1.1	269	7.4	3,260	89.2	125	3.4	3,654
	43	2.0	62	3 0	22	1.0	157	7.5	1,881	89.5	63	3.0	2,101
	30	1.9	48	3 1	17	1.1	112	7.2	1,379	88.8	62	4.0	1,553
	7	.4	8		13	.8	60	3.7	1,498	92.9	54	3.3	1,612
	3	.4	3		7	.9	31	4.1	715	94.0	15	2.0	761
	4	.5	5	1 8	6	.7	29	3.4	783	92.0	39	4.5	851
	1	.6	5	2.	1	.6	8	4.4	169	93.9	3	1.7	180
	0	.0	3	2.8		.0	4	3.7	103	94.5	2	1.8	109
	1	1.4	2	2.8	4	1.4		5.6	66	93.0	1	1.4	71
	6	.8	2	.3	6	.8	21	2.9	686	95.4	12	1.7	719
	1	.3	0	.0	2	.6	7	2.2	311	96.3	5	1.5	323
	5	1.3	2	.5	4	1.0	14	3.5	375	94.7	7	1.8	396

	AMERICAN INDIAN ALASKAN NATIVE		BLACK NON-HISPANIC		ASIAN OR PACIFIC ISLANDER		HISPANIC		TOTAL MINORITY		WHITE NON-HISPANIC		NON-RESIDENT ALIEN	
	NUMBER	%	NUMBER	%	NUMBER	%	NUMBER	%	NUMBER	%	NUMBER	%	NUMBER	%
WASHINGTON	CONTINUED													
OLYMPIA TECH CMTY COLLEGE														
HA TOTAL	14	1.5	8	.9	14	1.5	19	2.1	55	6 1	818	90.3	33	3.6
WA FEMALE	9	2.0	1	.2	9	2.0	7	1.6	26	5 8	408	91.7	11	2.5
WA MALE	5	1.1	7	1.5	5	1.1	12	2.6	29	613	410	88.9	22	4.8
OLYMPIC COLLEGE														
WA TOTAL	35	2.0	75	4.2	66	3.7	32	1.8	208	11.7	1,549	87.4	16	.9
WA FEMALE	19	2.5	14	1.9	22	2.9	11	1.5	66	8.7	683	90.5	6	.8
WA MALE	16	1.6	61	6.0	44	4.3	21	2.1	142	13.9	866	85.1	10	1.0
PACIFIC LUTH UNIVERSITY														
HA TOTAL	12	.4	67	2.5	51	1.9	15	.6	145	5 4	2,497	92.7	51	1.9
WA FEMALE	6	.4	31	2.0	32	2.0	9	.6	78	4 9	1,475	93.2	30	1.9
WA MALE	6	.5	36	3.2	19	1.7	6	.5	67	610	1,022	92.1	21	1.9
PENINSULA COLLEGE														
WA TOTAL	30	3.6	1	.1	3	.4	3	.4	37	4.4	786	93.8	15	1.8
WA FEMALE	18	4.1	0	.0	2	.5	2	.5	22	5.0	404	92.7	10	2.3
WA MALE	12	3.0	1	.2	1	.2	1	.2	15	3.7	382	95.0	5	1.2
PROMETHEUS COLLEGE														
WA TOTAL	3	11.5	3	11.5	1	3.8	0	.0	7	26	19	73.1	0	.0
WA FEMALE	3	15.8	2	10.5	1	5.3	0	.0	6	31	13	68.4	0	.0
WA MALE	0	.0	1	14.3	0	.0	0	.0	1	14	6	85.7	0	.0
PUGET SOUND C OF BIBLE														
HA TOTAL	0	.0	0	.0	0	.0	2	1.3	2	1.3	154	98.1	1	.6
HA FEMALE	0	.0	0	.0	0	.0	0	.0	0	.0	64	98.5	1	1.5
HA MALE	0	.0	0	.0	0	.0	2	2.2	2	2.2	90	97.8	0	.0
SAINT MARTIN'S COLLEGE														
WA TOTAL	8	1.8	11	2.4	32	7.0	18	4.0	69	15.2	377	82.9	9	2.0
WA FEMALE	3	1.5	4	2.0	10	5.0	12	5.9	29	14.4	170	84.2	3	1.5
WA MALE	5	2.0	7	2.8	22	8.7	6	2.4	40	15.8	207	81.8	6	2.4
NORTH SEATTLE CC														
HA TOTAL	43	1.5	57	2.0	66	2.	26	.9	192	6.7	2,481	86.2	206	7.2
WA FEMALE	26	1.7	26	1.7	27	1.	11	.7	90	6.0	1,339	88.9	78	5.2
WA MALE	17	1.2	31	2.3	39	2.8	15	1.1	102	7.4	1,142	83.2	128	9.3
SEATTLE CC CENTRAL CAMPUS														
WA TOTAL	122	3.1	544	13.7	180	4 5	58	1.5	904	22.8	2,543	64.0	525	13.2
WA FEMALE	70	3.4	277	13.5	97	4 7	27	1.3	471	22.9	1,358	66.1	225	11.0
WA MALE	52	2.7	267	13.9	83	413	31	1.6	433	22.6	1,185	61.8	300	15.6
SEATTLE CC SOUTH CAMPUS														
WA TOTAL	39	1.6	90	3.8	85	3.6	31	1.3	245	10.3	2,034	85.8	92	3.9
WA FEMALE	17	1.8	37	4.0	22	2.4	11	1.2	87	9.3	816	87.2	33	3.5
WA MALE	22	1.5	53	3.7	63	4.4	20	1.4	158	11.0	1,218	84.9	59	4.1
SEATTLE PACIFIC U														
HA TOTAL	19	.9	22	1.1	49	2.4	8	.4	98	4.8	1,895	92.8	48	2.4
WA FEMALE	10	.8	16	1.2	29	2.2	5	.4	60	4.6	1,216	93.4	26	2.0
WA MALE	9	1.2	6	.8	20	2.7	3	.4	38	5.1	679	91.9	22	3.0
SEATTLE UNIVERSITY														
WA TOTAL	29	1.2	140	5.7	164	.7	28	1.1	361	14.8	1,840	75.3	244	10.0
WA FEMALE	19	1.5	86	6.6	94	6.2	16	1.2	215	16.6	1,019	78.1	71	5.4
WA MALE	10	.9	54	4.7	70	6.1	12	1.1	146	12.8	821	72.0	173	15.2
SHORELINE CMTY COLLEGE														
WA TOTAL	20	.5	80	1.9	63	1 5	22	.5	185	4.4	3,651	87.1	354	8.4
WA FEMALE	12	.6	41	1.9	34	1 6	11	.5	98	4.5	1,922	88.3	157	7.2
WA MALE	8	.4	39	1.9	29	114	11	.5	87	4.3	1,729	85.9	197	9.8
SKAGIT VALLEY COLLEGE														
WA TOTAL	37	2.1	21	1.2	20	1.1	28	1.6	106	6.0	1,608	90.8	56	3.2
WA FEMALE	19	2.4	3	.4	6	.8	14	1.8	42	5.4	722	92.3	18	2.3
WA MALE	18	1.8	18	1.8	14	1.4	14	1.4	64	6.5	886	89.7	38	3.8
TACOMA COMMUNITY COLLEGE														
HA TOTAL	59	2.0	353	11.7	88	2.9	70	2.3	570	1 .9	2,249	74.5	199	6.6
HA FEMALE	34	2.4	150	10.5	49	3.4	24	1.7	257	1 .0	1,127	78.6	46	3.2
HA MALE	25	1.6	203	12.8	39	2.5	46	2.9	313	18.7	1,122	70.7	153	9.6
UNIVERSITY OF PUGET SOUND														
HA TOTAL	13	.5	73	2.8	125	4.7	7	.3	218	.3	2,361	89.4	62	2.
HA FEMALE	7	.5	40	2.8	79	5.5	6	.4	132	.3	1,279	89.8	14	1.
HA MALE	6	.5	33	2.7	46	3.8	1	.1	86	8.1	1,082	89.0	48	3.8
UNIVERSITY OF WASHINGTON														
WA TOTAL	203	.8	864	3.5	2,242	1.1	372	1.5	3,681	14.9	20,157	81.6	850	3.
HA FEMALE	113	1.0	432	3.8	1,081	9.5	165	1.5	1,791	15.8	9,333	82.4	198	1.4
WA MALE	90	.7	432	3.2	1,161	8.7	207	1.5	1,890	14.1	10,824	81.0	652	4.9
WALLA WALLA COLLEGE														
WA TOTAL	8	.5	25	1.5	32	1.9	18	1 0	83	4.8	1,434	83.5	201	11.7
WA FEMALE	6	.7	9	1.1	13	1.6	9	1 1	37	4.5	682	83.1	102	12.4
WA MALE	2	.2	16	1.8	19	2.1	9	110	46	5.1	752	83.8	99	11.0
WALLA WALLA CMTY COLLEGE														
HA TOTAL	18	1.6	71	6.3	13	1.1	38	3.4	140	12.4	963	85.0	30	2.6
WA FEMALE	4	.9	5	1.1	4	.9	9	1.9	22	4.8	428	92.4	13	2.8
WA MALE	14	2.1	66	9.9	9	1.3	29	4.3	118	17.6	535	79.9	17	2.5
EDMONDS COMMUNITY COLLEGE														
HA TOTAL	28	1.6	43	2.5	28	1.6	19	1.1	118	6.9	1,516	89.2	66	3.9
WA FEMALE	14	1.5	4	.4	9	1.0	13	1.4	40	4.3	859	92.8	27	2.9
WA MALE	14	1.8	39	5.0	19	2.5	6	.8	76	10.1	657	84.9	39	5.0
EVERETT CMTY COLLEGE														
WA TOTAL	55	1.9	34	1.2	17	.6	23	.8	129	4.5	2,648	92.5	87	3.
WA FEMALE	31	2.0	6	.4	8	.5	13	.8	58	3.8	1,452	94.0	35	2.
WA MALE	24	1.8	28	2.1	9	.7	10	.8	71	5.4	1,196	90.7	52	3.9
SPOKANE COMMUNITY COLLEGE														
WA TOTAL	83	2.0	38	.9	44	1.1	38	.9	203	5.0	3,837	94.3	31	.
WA FEMALE	35	2.0	12	.7	15	.9	14	.8	76	4.4	1,621	94.9	12	.8
WA MALE	48	2.0	26	1.1	29	1.2	24	1.0	127	5.4	2,216	93.8	19	.8
SPOKANE FLS CMTY COLLEGE														
HA TOTAL	102	2.1	87	1.8	54	1.1	48	1.0	291	6.0	4,468	92.8	55	1.1
WA FEMALE	51	2.0	30	1.2	28	1.1	25	1.0	134	5.3	2,379	93.5	32	1.3
WA MALE	51	2.2	57	2.5	26	1.1	23	1.0	157	6.9	2,089	92.1	23	1.0

TABLE 1 - TOTAL UNDERGRADUATE ENROLLMENT IN INSTITUTIONS OF HIGHER EDUCATION BY RACE, ETHNICITY AND SEX: INSTITUTION, STATE AND NATION, 1978

	AMERICAN INDIAN ALASKAN NATIVE		BLACK NON-HISPANIC		ASIAN OR PACIFIC ISLANDER		HISPANIC		TOTAL MINORITY		WHITE NON-HISPANIC		NON-RESIDENT ALIEN		TOTAL
	NUMBER	%	NUMBER	%	NUMBER	%	NUMBER	%	NUMBER	%	NUMBER	%	NUMBER	%	NUMBER
WASHINGTON CONTINUED															
WASHINGTON ST UNIVERSITY															
WA TOTAL	114	.8	241	1	224	1.6	129	.9	708	5 2	12,603	92.1	366	2.7	13,677
WA FEMALE	61	1.0	95	1 8	96	1.6	52	.9	304	5 0	5,701	93.3	108	1.8	6,113
WA MALE	53	.7	146	11?	128	1.7	77	1.0	404	513	6,902	91.2	258	3.4	7,564
WENATCHEE VALLEY COLLEGE															
WA TOTAL	31	2.6	11	.9	5	.4	9	.7	56	.7	1,136	94.4	12	1.0	1,204
WA FEMALE	16	2.9	1	.2	3	.5	3	.5	23	.2	520	95.2	3	.5	546
WA MALE	15	2.3	10	1.5	2	.3	6	.9	33	?.0	616	93.6	9	1.4	658
WESTERN WASH UNIVERSITY															
WA TOTAL	70	.8	94	1 1	111	1.3	49	.6	324	3.	7,933	95.3	70	.8	8,327
WA FEMALE	39	.9	52	1?2	63	1.5	19	.4	173	4.?	4,127	95.5	21	.5	4,321
WA MALE	31	.8	42	1.0	48	1.2	30	.7	151	3.8	3,806	95.0	49	1.2	4,006
WHATCOM CMTY COLLEGE															
WA TOTAL	24	4.5	7	1.3	3	.6	3	.6	37	9	440	82.6	56	10.5	533
WA FEMALE	18	6.8	2	.8	2	.8	2	.8	24	1	222	84.1	18	6.8	264
WA MALE	6	2.2	5	1.9	1	.4	1	.4	13	?8	218	81.0	38	14.1	269
WHITMAN COLLEGE															
WA TOTAL	6	.5	8	.7	41	3.5	8	.7	63	5.5	1,077	93.2	15	1.3	1,155
WA FEMALE	1	.2	2		27	4.9	2	.4	32	5.8	516	93.8	2	.4	550
WA MALE	5	.8	6	1.0	14	2.3	6	1.0	31	5*1	561	92.7	13	2.1	605
WHITWORTH COLLEGE															
WA TOTAL	8	.6	27	2	37	2.7	14	1.0	86	.	1,244	91.2	34	2.5	1,364
WA FEMALE	6	.8	11	1 0	22	2.8	8	1.0	47	?	733	93.5	4	.5	784
WA MALE	2	.3	16	2?8	15	2.6	6	1.0	39	?.?	511	88.1	30	5.2	580
YAKIMA VALLEY CC															
WA TOTAL	47	3.0	24	1.6	20	1.3	74	4.8	165	10 7	1,270	82.0	113	7.3	1,548
WA FEMALE	25	3.1	9	1.1	8	1.	32	4.0	74	9 3	712	89.6	9	1.1	795
WA MALE	22	2.9	15	2.0	12	1.8	42	5.6	91	12?1	558	74.1	104	13.8	753
WASHINGTON TOTAL (49 INSTITUTIONS)															
WA TOTAL	1,893	1.3	4,227	3.0	4,531	3.2	1,813	1.3	12,464	.8	125,031	87.8	4,871	3 4	142,366
WA FEMALE	1,032	1.5	1,804	2.6	2,200	3.2	794	1.1	5,830	?.?	62,011	89.3	1,639	2 4	69,480
WA MALE	861	1.2	2,423	3.3	2,331	3.2	1,019	1.4	6,634	?.1	63,020	86.5	3,232	4?4	72,886
WEST VIRGINIA															
ALDERSON BROADDUS COLLEGE															
WV TOTAL	3	.3	27	3 0	7	.8	5	.6	42	.7	854	95.3		.0	896
WV FEMALE	1	.2	17	3 0	2	.4	3	.5	23	?.	547	96.0	0	.0	570
WV MALE	2	.6	10	?1	5	1.5	2	.6	19	?.8	307	94.2	0	.0	326
APPALACHIAN BIBLE COLLEGE															
WV TOTAL	0	.0	1	.4	2	.9		.0	3	1.3	226	98.7	0	.0	229
WV FEMALE	0	.0	1	1.1	0	.0	0	.0	1	1.1	89	98.9	0	.0	90
WV MALE	0	.0	0	.0	2	1.4	0	.0	2	1.4	137	98.6	0	.0	139
BECKLEY COLLEGE															
WV TOTAL	2	.2	154	12.4	2	.2	1	.1	159	12.	1,078	86.9	3	.2	1,240
WV FEMALE	1	.1	96	14.3	1	.1	0	.0	98	14.?	573	85.1	2	.3	673
WV MALE	1	.2	58	10?2	1	.2	1	.2	61	10?8	505	89.1	1	.2	567
BETHANY COLLEGE															
WV TOTAL	0	.0	10	1.1	1	.1	9	1.0	20	2.2	887	95.6	21	2.3	928
WV FEMALE	0	.0	5	1.3	0	.0	2	.5	7	1.8	375	97.2	4	1.0	386
WV MALE	0	.0	5	.9	1	.2	7	1.3	13	2.4	512	94.5	17	3.1	542
BLUEFIELD STATE COLLEGE															
WV TOTAL	8	.5	330	18.7	2	.1		.0	340	19.3	1,417	80.3	7	.4	1,764
WV FEMALE	7	.8	189	22.1	2	.2	0	.0	198	23.2	657	76.8	0	.0	855
WV MALE	1	.1	141	15.5	0	.0	0	.0	142	15.6	760	83.6	7	.8	909
CONCORD COLLEGE															
WV TOTAL	14	.7	123	6.5	2	.1		.2	143	7 5	1,761	92.5	0	.0	1,904
WV FEMALE	6	.5	48	4.4	2	.2	0	.0	56	5?1	1,039	94.9	0	.0	1,095
WV MALE	8	1.0	75	9.3	0	.0	?	.5	87	10.8	722	89.2	0	.0	809
DAVIS AND ELKINS COLLEGE															
WV TOTAL	0	.0	38	4.	0	.0		.0	38	4.	807	92.5	27	3.1	872
WV FEMALE	0	.0	21	5.4	0	.0	0	.0	21	5.4	394	93.6	6	1.4	421
WV MALE	0	.0	17	3.8	0	.0	0	.0	17	3.8	413	91.6	21	4.7	451
FAIRMONT STATE COLLEGE															
WV TOTAL	13	.3	102	2.4	19	.4	8	.2	142	3.3	4,108	96.5	6	.1	4,256
WV FEMALE	6	.3	38	1.7	7	.3	2	.1	53	2.4	2,171	97.5	2	.1	2,226
WV MALE	7	.3	64	3.2	12	.6	6	.3	89	4.4	1,937	95.4	4	.2	2,030
GLENVILLE STATE COLLEGE															
WV TOTAL	10	.8	39	.	3	.2	1	.1	53	4.0	1,237	93.8	29	2.2	1,319
WV FEMALE	6	.9	9	1??	1	.2	1	.2	17	2.6	643	96.5	6	.9	666
WV MALE	4	.6	30	?.?	2	.3	0	.0	36	5.5	594	91.0	23	3.5	653
MARSHALL UNIVERSITY															
WV TOTAL	62	.8	383	4.7	43	.5	2	.3	512	.2	7,627	92.9	68	.8	8,207
WV FEMALE	41	.9	205	4.6	16	.4	14	.4	278	6?3	4,135	93.3	20	.5	4,433
WV MALE	21	.6	178	4.7	27	.7	?	.2	234	6?2	3,492	92.5	48	1.3	3,774
MORRIS HARVEY COLLEGE															
WV TOTAL	3	.2	55	3.5		.0	6	.4	64	4.1	1,484	95.1	12	.8	1,560
WV FEMALE	2	.2	30	3.1	0	.0	3	.3	35	3.6	930	96.3	1	.1	966
WV MALE	1	.2	25	4.2	0	.0	3	.5	29	4.9	554	93.3	11	1.9	594
OHIO VALLEY COLLEGE															
WV TOTAL	0	.0	13	5.4		.0		.0	13	5.4	226	93.8	2	.9	241
WV FEMALE	0	.0	1	.7	0	.0	0	.0	1	.7	133	98.5	1	.7	135
WV MALE	0	.0	12	11.3	0	.0	0	.0	12	11.3	93	87.7	1	.9	106
PARKERSBURG CMTY COLLEGE															
WV TOTAL	7	.4	11	.6	7	.4	5	.3	30	1 5	1,934	98.5		.0	1,964
WV FEMALE	5	.5	7	.7	3	.3	3	.3	18	1 7	1,015	98.3	0	.0	1,033
WV MALE	2	.2	4	.4	4	.4	2	.2	12	113	919	98.7	0	.0	931
POTOMAC STATE COLLEGE															
WV TOTAL	1	.1	54	5.6	2	.2		.0	57	5.	902	94.0	1	.1	960
WV FEMALE	0	.0	15	3.8	2	.5		.0	17	4.?	381	95.7	0	.0	398
WV MALE	1	.2	39	6.9	0	.0	0	.0	40	7.?	521	92.7	1	.2	562

127

	AMERICAN INDIAN ALASKAN NATIVE		BLACK NON-HISPANIC		ASIAN OR PACIFIC ISLANDER		HISPANIC		TOTAL MINORITY		WHITE NON-HISPANIC		NON-RESIDENT ALIEN	
	NUMBER	%	NUMBER	%	NUMBER	%	NUMBER	%	NUMBER	%	NUMBER	%	NUMBER	%

WEST VIRGINIA   CONTINUED

SALEM COLLEGE MAIN CAMPUS

WV TOTAL	1	.1	67	7.5	2	.2	11	1.2	81	.1	798	89.7	11	1.2
WV FEMALE	0	.0	10	2.3	2	.5	5	1.1	17	.9	420	95.9	1	.2
WV MALE	1	.2	57	12.6	0	.0	6	1.3	64	14.2	378	83.6	10	2.2

SALEM COLLEGE CLARKSBURG

WV TOTAL	0	.0	0	.0		.0	0	.0	0	.0	9	100.0		.0
WV FEMALE	0	.0	0	.0	0	.0	0	.0	0	.0	2	100.0	8	.0
WV MALE	0	.0	0	.0	0	.0	0	.0	0	.0	7	100.0		.0

SHEPHERD COLLEGE

WV TOTAL	8	.3	57	2.1	3	.1	0	.0	68	2.5	2,672	97.5		.0
WV FEMALE	7	.4	31	2.0	3	.2	0	.0	41	26	1,541	97.4	8	.0
WV MALE	1	.1	26	2.2	0	.0	0	.0	27	2ʃ3	1,131	97.7		.0

STHN W VA CC-LOGAN CAM

WV TOTAL	12	1.0	28	2.2		.3	1	.1	45	3.6	1,212	96.4		.0
WV FEMALE	6	1.0	16	2.6	4	.2	1	.2	24	3.9	597	96.1	8	.0
WV MALE	6	.9	12	1.9	3	.5	0	.0	21	3.3	615	96.7		.0

STHN W VA CC-WILLIAMSON

WV TOTAL	2	.3	32	4.9	5	.8	1	.2	40	6.2	608	93.8		.0
WV FEMALE	1	.3	23	5.9	3	.8	0	.0	27	6.9	363	93.1	8	.0
WV MALE	1	.4	9	3.5	2	.8	1	.4	13	5.0	245	95.0		.0

WEST LIBERTY ST COLLEGE

WV TOTAL	0	.0	42	1.7	5	.2	4	.2	51	2.0	2,411	95.7	58	2.3
WV FEMALE	0	.0	19	1.4	2	.1	3	.2	24	1.7	1,348	97.0	18	1.3
WV MALE	0	.0	23	2.0	3	.3	1	.1	27	2.4	1,063	94.1	40	3.5

WEST VA INST TECHNOLOGY

WV TOTAL	6	.2	206	6.5	20	.6	3	.1	235	4	2,779	87.1	175	5.5
WV FEMALE	2	.2	95	9.0	9	.9	0	.0	106	1ŋ.1	936	89.1	8	.8
WV MALE	4	.2	111	5ʃ2	11	.5	3	.1	129	8ʃ0	1,843	86.2	167	7.8

WEST VIRGINIA NORTHERN CC

WV TOTAL	11	.6	70	4.0	1	.1	21	1.2	103	.9	1,652	94.1		.0
WV FEMALE	5	.5	31	3.1	1	.1	4	.4	41	ʃ.1	970	95.9	8	.0
WV MALE	6	.8	39	5.2	0	.0	17	2.3	62	8.3	682	91.7		.0

W VA STATE COLLEGE

WV TOTAL	0	.0	697	22.3	52	1.7	1	.0	750	24.0	2,377	76.0		.0
WV FEMALE	0	.0	315	20.1	13	.8	1	.1	329	21.0	1,236	79.0	8	.0
WV MALE	0	.0	382	24.5	39	2.5	0	.0	421	27.0	1,141	73.0		.0

WEST VIRGINIA UNIVERSITY

WV TOTAL	7	.0	174	12	16	.1	14	.1	211	1.5	13,836	96.4	309	2.2
WV FEMALE	1	.0	72	12	5	.1	5	.1	83	1.3	6,027	97.8	52	.8
WV MALE	6	.1	102	1ʃ2	11	.1	9	.1	128	1.6	7,809	95.3	257	3.1

WEST VA WESLEYAN COLLEGE

WV TOTAL	3	.2	54	3.1	5	.3	1	.1	63	3.6	1,682	95.5	17	1.0
WV FEMALE	2	.2	18	1.8	1	.1	1	.1	22	2.2	994	97.5	3	.3
WV MALE	1	.1	36	4.8	4	.5	0	.0	41	5.5	688	92.6	14	1.9

WHEELING COLLEGE

WV TOTAL	0	.0	23	3.0	5	.6	3	.4	31	4.ŋ	740	95.2	6	.8
WV FEMALE	0	.0	5	1.3	2	.5	1	.3	8	2.ʃ	371	97.6	1	.3
WV MALE	0	.0	18	4.5	3	.8	2	.5	23	5.8	369	92.9	5	1.3

WEST VIRGINIA   TOTAL (26 INSTITUTIONS)

WV TOTAL	173	.3	2,790	4.7	208	.4	123	.2	3,294	5.5	55,324	93.2	752	1.3
WV FEMALE	99	.3	1,317	4.5	78	.3	51	.2	1,545	5.2	27,887	94.3	125	.4
WV MALE	74	.2	1,473	4.9	130	.4	72	.2	1,749	5.9	27,437	92.0	627	2.1

WISCONSIN

ALVERNO COLLEGE

WI TOTAL	3	.3	70	6.4	7	.6	6	.5	86	7	1,003	91.8	3	.3
WI FEMALE	3	.3	70	6.4	7	.6	6	.5	86	7 ŋ	1,003	91.8	3	.3
WI MALE	0	.0	0	.0	0	.0	0	.0	0	1ʃ0	0	.0	0	.0

BELOIT COLLEGE

WI TOTAL	1	.1	33	34	17	1.7	12	1.2	63	64	909	92.8	8	.8
WI FEMALE	0	.0	24	5ʃ0	9	1.9	5	1.0	38	7 ŋ	437	91.4	3	.6
WI MALE	1	.2	9	1.8	8	1.6	7	1.4	25	5ʃ0	472	94.0	5	1.0

BLACKHAWK TECHNICAL INST

WI TOTAL	4	.2	50	2.8	8	.4	1	.8	76	4.3	1,696	95.0	1	.8
WI FEMALE	2	.2	22	2 7	4	.5	4	.7	34	4.2	764	95.0		.7
WI MALE	2	.2	28	2ʃ9	4	.4	8	.8	42	4.3	932	94.9	8	.8

CARDINAL STRITCH COLLEGE

WI TOTAL	4	.7	27	45	2	.3	0	.0	33	5.5	564	93.7	5	.8
WI FEMALE	3	.6	15	3 1	2	.4	0	.0	20	4.1	462	95.1	4	.8
WI MALE	1	.9	12	10ʃ3	0	.0	0	.0	13	11.2	102	87.9	1	.9

CARROLL COLLEGE

WI TOTAL	0	.0	52	4.3	5	.8	50	4.2	108	9.0	1,089	90.7	4	.3
WI FEMALE	0	.0	34	5.5	5	.8	26	4.2	65	10.4	557	89.4	'	.2
WI MALE	0	.0	18	3.1	1	.2	24	4.2	43	7.4	532	92.0	3	.5

CARTHAGE COLLEGE

WI TOTAL	0	.0	47	3.	3	.3	3	.3	53	44	1,140	95.2	4	.3
WI FEMALE	0	.0	20	3.	2	.3	0	.0	22	3 8	559	95.7	3	.5
WI MALE	0	.0	27	4.ʃ	1	.2	3	.5	31	5ʃ0	582	94.8	1	.2

CONCORDIA COLLEGE

WI TOTAL	2	.6	39	12.1		.0	0	.0	41	12.7	279	86.4	3	.9
WI FEMALE	1	.5	24	13 ;	8	.0	0	.0	25	13.	157	85.8	1	.5
WI MALE	1	.7	15	10ʃ9		.0	0	.0	16	11.9	122	87.1	2	1.4

DISTRICT ONE TECH INST

WI TOTAL	7	.3	1	.0	5	.2	2	.1	15	6	2,526	99.0	11	.4
WI FEMALE	1	.1	0	.0	'	.1	0	.0	2	.2	939	99.7	1	.1
WI MALE	6	.4	1	.1	4	.2	2	.1	13	1ʃ8	1,587	98.6	10	.6

EDGEWOOD COLLEGE

WI TOTAL	1	.3	17	4.3	2	.5		.0	20	5 1	355	90.3	18	4.6
WI FEMALE	1	.3	10	3.5	2	.7	8	.0	13	45	264	91.7	11	3.8
WI MALE	0	.0	7	6.7	0	.0		.0	7	6ʃ7	91	86.7	7	6.7

AM VE		BLACK NON-HISPANIC		ASIAN OR PACIFIC ISLANDER		HISPANIC		TOTAL MINORITY		WHITE NON-HISPANIC		NON-RESIDENT ALIEN		TOTAL
NUMBER	%	NUMBER	%	NUMBER	%	NUMBER	%	NUMBER	%	NUMBER	%	NUMBER	%	NUMBER

TINUED

		8	.2	34	.8	58	1.3	192	4.5	4,117	95.5		.0	4,309
		3	.2	14	.7	33	1.7	96	4.9	1,846	95.1		.0	1,942
		5	.2	20	.8	25	1.1	96	4.1	2,271	95.9	8	.0	2,367
		52	2.7	9	.5	22	1.1	87	4.5	1,867	95.5		.0	1,954
		33	2.9	5	.4	7	.6	48	4.3	1,080	95.7		.0	1,128
		19	2.3	4	.5	15	1.8	39	4.7	787	95.3	8	.0	826
		83	8.1	8	.8	18	1.8	110	10.8	910	89.0	3	.3	1,023
		33	8.0	5	1.2	6	1.5	44	10.7	366	89.1	1	.2	411
		50	8.2	3	.5	12	2.0	66	10.8	544	88.9	2	.3	612
		1	2.6	0	.0	3	7.7	5	12.8	34	87.2		.0	39
		0	.0	0	.0	0	.0	0	.0	0	.0		.0	0
		1	2.6	0	.0	3	7.7	5	12.8	34	87.2	8	.0	39
		46	8.7	4	.8	2	.4	60	11.4	459	87.1	8	1.5	527
		12	5.5	0	.0	2	.9	21	9.6	197	90.0		.5	219
		34	11.0	4	1.3	0	.0	39	12.7	262	85.1	4	2.3	308
		3	.1	10	.4	2	.1	16	.6	2,516	99.4	0	.0	2,532
		0	.0	7	.5	1	.1	8	.6	1,269	99.4	0	.0	1,277
		3	.2	3	.2	1	.1	8	.6	1,247	99.4	0	.0	1,255
		13	1.1	5	.4	3	.3	24	2.1	1,101	96.0	22	1.9	1,147
		6	1.1	1	.2	1	.2	10	1.8	557	97.5	4	.7	571
		7	1.2	4	.7	2	.3	14	2.4	544	94.4	18	3.1	576
		121	1.6	68	.9	54	.7	259	3.4	7,298	95.7	71	.9	7,628
		51	1.2	43	1.0	21	.5	127	2.9	4,165	96.6	20	.5	4,312
		70	2.1	25	.8	33	1.0	132	4.0	3,133	94.5	51	1.5	3,316
		17	5.1	0	.0	1	.3	18	5.4	297	89.5	17	5.1	332
		13	6.0	0	.0	0	.0	13	6.0	189	87.9	13	6.0	215
		4	3.4	0	.0	1	.9	5	4.3	108	92.3	4	3.4	117
		0	.0	4	.9	1	.2	9	2.0	450	98.0	0	.0	459
		0	.0	0	.0	0	.0	4	1.0	407	99.0	0	.0	411
		0	.0	4	8.3	1	2.1	5	10.4	43	89.6	0	.0	48
		434	5.4	84	1.0	140	1.7	680	8.4	7,344	90.8	64	.8	8,088
		240	6.8	32	.9	63	1.8	344	9.7	3,184	90.0	11	.3	3,539
		194	4.3	52	1.1	77	1.7	336	7.4	4,160	91.4	53	1.2	4,549
		0	.0	17	1.4	15	1.2	42	3.4	1,189	96.4	3	.2	1,234
		0	.0	13	2.1	10	1.6	28	4.4	601	95.1	3	.5	632
		0	.0	4	.7	5	.8	14	2.3	588	97.7	0	.0	602
		34	4.5	13	1.7	3	.4	50	6.6	705	93.4		.0	755
		7	2.0	5	1.4	2	.6	14	4.0	334	96.0		.0	348
		27	6.6	8	2.0	1	.2	36	8.8	371	91.2	8	.0	407
		2,244	16.1	107	.8	251	1.8	2,708	19.5	11,205	80.5		.0	13,913
		1,350	18.7	61	.8	113	1.6	1,586	21.9	5,644	78.1		.0	7,230
		894	13.4	46	.7	138	2.1	1,122	16.8	5,561	83.2	8	.0	6,683
		2	1.2	0	.0	4	2.4	8	4.7	160	94.7	1	.6	169
		0	.0	0	.0	2	2.2	3	3.3	88	95.7	1	1.1	92
		2	2.6	0	.0	2	2.6	5	6.5	72	93.5	0	.0	77
		94	4.5	7	.3	7	.3	108	5.2	1,925	91.8	64	3.1	2,097
		20	20.6	0	.0	0	.0	20	20.6	75	77.3	2	2.1	97
		74	3.7	7	.4	7	.4	88	4.4	1,850	92.5	62	3.1	2,000
		172	36.9	0	.0	10	2.1	185	39.7	281	60.3		.0	466
		71	38.8	0	.0	1	.5	74	40.4	109	59.6		.0	183
		101	35.7	0	.0	9	3.2	111	39.2	172	60.8	0	.0	283
		43	1.1	11	.3	13	.3	100	2.5	3,885	97.5		.0	3,985
		30	1.8	7	.4	9	.5	67	4.0	1,608	96.0		.0	1,675
		13	.6	4	.2	4	.2	33	1.4	2,277	98.6	8	.0	2,310
		47	4.3	0	.0	4	.4	56	5.2	1,008	92.7	23	2.1	1,087
		47	4.3	0	.0	4	.4	56	5.2	1,008	92.7	23	2.1	1,087
		0	.0	0	.0	0	.0	0	.0	0	.0	0	.0	0
		18	5.4	0	.0	6	1.8	82	24.6	237	71.0	15	.5	334
		5	3.1	0	.0	3	1.9	47	29.2	107	66.5	7	.3	161
		13	7.5	0	.0	3	1.7	35	20.2	130	75.1	8	4.6	173
		0	.0	0	.0	0	.0	46	7.6	558	92.2	1	.2	605
		0	.0	0	.0	0	.0	19	7.1	248	92.5	1	.4	268
		0	.0	0	.0	0	.0	27	8.0	310	92.0	0	.0	337
		3	.0	4	.2	2	.1	27	1.3	2,105	98.7		.0	2,132
		0	.0	0	.0	1	.1	18	2.6	682	97.4		.0	700
		0	.0	4	.3	1	.1	9	.6	1,423	99.4	8	.0	1,432
		11	.4	7	.2	11	.4	91	3.1	2,823	96.8		.1	2,917
		3	.2	3	.2	4	.2	33	2.1	1,568	97.8		.2	1,604
		8	.6	4	.3	7	.5	58	4.4	1,255	95.6	8	.0	1,313

TABLE 1 - TOTAL UNDERGRADUATE ENROLLMENT IN INSTITUTIONS OF HIGHER EDUCATION BY RACE, ETHNICITY AND SEX: INSTITUTION, STATE AND NATION, 1978

	AMERICAN INDIAN ALASKAN NATIVE		BLACK NON-HISPANIC		ASIAN OR PACIFIC ISLANDER		HISPANIC		TOTAL MINORITY		WHITE NON-HISPANIC		NON-RESIDENT ALIEN	
	NUMBER	%	NUMBER	%	NUMBER	%	NUMBER	%	NUMBER	%	NUMBER	%	NUMBER	%
WISCONSIN	CONTINUED													
NORTHLAND COLLEGE														
WI TOTAL	32	5.2	14	2.3	8	1.3	5	.8	59	9.6	545	88.9		1.5
WI FEMALE	16	6.2	3	1.2	3	1.2	4	1.5	26	10.0	229	88.4	9	1.5
WI MALE	16	4.5	11	3.1	5	1.4	1	.3	33	9.3	316	89.3		1.4
NORTHWESTERN COLLEGE														
HI TOTAL	0	.0	2	.8	0	.0	0	.0	2	.8	235	98.7	1	.4
WI FEMALE	0	.0	0	.0	0	.0	0	.0	0	.0	0	.0	0	.0
WI MALE	0	.0	2	.8	0	.0	0	.0	2	.8	235	98.7	1	.4
RIPON COLLEGE														
WI TOTAL	1	.1	19	2.1	5	.5	7	.8	32	3.5	884	95.5	10	1.1
WI FEMALE	0	.0	10	2.4	5	1.2	4	1.0	19	4.5	397	95.0	2	.5
WI MALE	1	.2	9	1.8	0	.0	3	.6	13	2.6	487	95.9	8	1.6
SNT FRANCIS DE SALES C														
WI TOTAL	0	.0	0	.0	0	.0	1	1.3	1	1.3	77	98.7		.0
WI FEMALE	0	.0	0	.0	0	.0	0	.0	0	.0	1	100.0		.0
WI MALE	0	.0	0	.0	0	.0	1	1.3	1	1.3	76	98.7	0	.0
SAINT NORBERT COLLEGE														
NI TOTAL	3	.2	5	.3	2	.1	1	.1	11	.7	1,497	98.6	1	.7
WI FEMALE	1	.1	2	.3	2	.3	0	.0	5	.7	703	98.7		.6
WI MALE	2	.2	3	.4	0	.0	1	.1	6	.7	794	98.5		.7
SILVER LAKE COLLEGE														
WI TOTAL	0	.0	1	.4	1	.4	1	.4	3	1.2	237	97.9	2	.8
WI FEMALE	0	.0	1	.5	1	.5	1	.5	3	1.5	192	97.5	2	1.0
HI MALE	0	.0	0	.0	0	.0	0	.0	0	.0	45	100.0	0	.0
STHWST WIS VOC TECH INST														
HI TOTAL	4	.5	0	.0	3	.4	1	.1	8	1.0	816	99.0		.0
HI FEMALE	1	.2	0	.0	2	.5	0	.0	3	.7	414	99.3		.0
HI MALE	3	.7	0	.0	1	.2	1	.2	5	1.2	402	98.8	8	.3
U OF WISCONSIN EAU CLAIRE														
HI TOTAL	40	.4	72	.8	22	.2	14	.1	148	1.6	9,226	97.6	7	.8
HI FEMALE	24	.5	27	.5	12	.2	6	.1	69	1.3	5,155	98.1	29	.6
WI MALE	16	.4	45	1.1	10	.2	8	.2	79	1.9	4,071	97.0	47	1.1
U OF WISCONSIN GREEN BAY														
WI TOTAL	53	2.0	24	.9	14	.5	8	.3	99	3.7	2,510	94.2	56	2.1
WI FEMALE	39	2.8	13	.9	6	.4	4	.3	62	4.5	1,305	94.4	15	1.1
WI MALE	14	1.1	11	.9	8	.6	4	.3	37	2.9	1,205	93.9	41	3.2
U OF WISCONSIN LA CROSSE														
WI TOTAL	16	.2	47	.6	21	.3	23	.3	107	1.4	7,451	98.1	3	.5
WI FEMALE	8	.2	14	.3	14	.3	13	.3	49	1.2	4,173	98.6	9	.2
WI MALE	8	.2	33	1.0	7	.2	10	.3	58	1.7	3,278	97.4	30	.9
U OF WISCONSIN MADISON														
HI TOTAL	56	.2	583	2.3	229	.9	216	.8	1,084	4.2	24,401	94.2	426	1.6
HI FEMALE	27	.2	321	2.7	99	.8	79	.7	526	4.3	11,476	94.9	93	.8
WI MALE	29	.2	262	1.9	130	.9	137	1.0	558	4.0	12,925	93.6	333	2.4
U OF WISCONSIN MILWAUKEE														
WI TOTAL	98	.5	1,308	7.1	170	.9	350	1.9	1,926	10.5	16,165	88.2	234	1.3
WI FEMALE	60	.7	837	9.3	75	.8	175	1.9	1,147	12.7	7,849	86.9	37	.4
WI MALE	38	.4	471	5.1	95	1.0	175	1.9	779	8.4	8,317	89.5	197	2.1
U OF WISCONSIN OSHKOSH														
WI TOTAL	29	.4	183	2.4	18	.2	23	.3	253	3.4	7,205	96.1	37	.5
WI FEMALE	17	.4	89	2.3	10	.3	8	.2	124	3.2	3,759	96.5	11	.3
HI MALE	12	.3	94	2.6	8	.2	15	.4	129	3.6	3,446	95.7	26	.7
U OF WISCONSIN PARKSIDE														
HI TOTAL	10	.2	182	4.4	19	.5	42	1.0	253	6.2	3,799	92.5	54	1.3
WI FEMALE	2	.1	106	5.7	9	.5	14	.8	131	7.1	1,695	91.5	26	1.4
WI MALE	8	.4	76	3.4	10	.4	28	1.2	122	5.4	2,104	93.3	28	1.2
U OF WISCONSIN PLATTEVL														
HI TOTAL	5	.1	71	1.7	6	.1	10	.2	92	2.2	4,066	96.9	39	.9
HI FEMALE	0	.0	31	2.3	4	.3	3	.2	38	2.9	1,282	96.9	3	.2
WI MALE	5	.2	40	1.4	2	.1	7	.2	54	1.9	2,784	96.9	36	1.3
U OF WISCONSIN RIVER FLS														
HI TOTAL	12	.3	63	1.4	7	.2	3	.1	85	1.9	4,259	96.5	69	1.6
WI FEMALE	6	.3	11	.5	4	.2	0	.0	21	1.0	1,971	98.4	12	.6
WI MALE	6	.2	52	2.2	3	.1	3	.1	64	2.7	2,288	95.0	57	2.4
U OF WISCONSIN STEVNS PNT														
HI TOTAL	63	.8	25	.3	21	.3	11	.1	120	1.5	7,702	97.3	96	1.2
HI FEMALE	32	.8	12	.3	7	.2	4	.1	55	1.4	3,720	97.8	27	.7
WI MALE	31	.8	13	.3	14	.3	7	.2	65	1.6	3,982	96.7	69	1.7
U OF WISCONSIN STOUT														
HI TOTAL	23	.4	61	1.0	6	.1	11	.2	101	1.7	5,865	96.6	107	1.8
WI FEMALE	9	.3	24	.8	4	.1	4	.1	41	1.4	2,910	97.6	32	1.1
WI MALE	14	.5	37	1.2	2	.1	7	.2	60	1.9	2,955	95.6	75	2.4
U OF WISCONSIN SUPERIOR														
WI TOTAL	27	1.6	43	2.5	3	.2	5	.3	78	4.5	1,587	91.2	76	4.4
HI FEMALE	12	1.6	6	.8	2	.3	0	.0	20	2.7	712	95.4	14	1.9
WI MALE	15	1.5	37	3.7	1	.1	5	.5	58	5.8	875	87.9	62	6.2
U OF WISCONSIN WHITEWATER														
HI TOTAL	13	.2	199	2.8	12	.2	75	1.0	299	4.2	6,766	94.5	92	1.3
WI FEMALE	6	.2	110	3.1	5	.1	31	.9	152	4.3	3,371	95.1	21	.6
WI MALE	7	.2	89	2.5	7	.2	44	1.2	147	4.1	3,395	94.0	71	2.0
U OF WISCONSIN CTR SYS														
HI TOTAL	22	.3	63	1.0	22	.3	30	.5	137	2.1	6,400	97.6	18	.3
WI FEMALE	13	.4	10	.3	10	.3	12	.4	45	1.4	3,232	98.6	1	.0
WI MALE	9	.3	53	1.6	12	.4	18	.5	92	2.8	3,168	96.7	17	.5
VITERBO COLLEGE														
WI TOTAL	1	.1	17	1.8	6	.6	4	.4	28	3.0	895	94.8	21	2.2
WI FEMALE	0	.0	16	2.1	3	.4	3	.4	22	2.8	740	95.7	11	1.4
HI MALE	1	.6	1	.5	3	1.8	1	.6	6	3.5	155	90.6	10	5.8
WAUKESHA COUNTY TECH INST														
HI TOTAL	1	.0	1	.0	4	.1	4	.1	10	.2	4,146	99.8	0	.0
HI FEMALE	1	.0	0	.0	0	.0	0	.0	2	.1	2,114	99.9	0	.0
HI MALE	0	.0	1	.0	3	.1	4	.2	8	.4	2,032	99.6	0	.0

# OR ISLANDER	HISPANIC		TOTAL MINORITY		WHITE NON-HISPANIC		NON-RESIDENT ALIEN		TOTAL
%	NUMBER	%	NUMBER	%	NUMBER	%	NUMBER	%	NUMBER
.1	5	.1	16	.4	3,898	99.6		.0	3,914
.1	1	.1	7	.4	1,736	99.6	0	.0	1,743
.1	4	.2	9	.4	2,162	99.6	8	.0	2,171
.0	3	3.1	27	27.6	70	71.4	1	1.0	98
.0	0	.0	9	27.3	24	72.7	0	.0	33
.0	3	4.6	18	27.7	46	70.8	1	1.5	65
.5	1,570	.8	10,437	5.4	182,737	93.7	1,838	.9	195,012
.5	692	.7	5,561	5.8	89,632	93.7	476	.5	95,669
.5	878	.9	4,876	4.9	93,105	93.7	1,362	1.4	99,343
.1	24	1.7	43	3.0	1,369	95.9	16	1.1	1,428
.0	13	1.7	18	2.4	719	96.6	7	.9	744
.3	11	1.6	25	3.7	650	95.0	9	1.3	684
1.7	9	2.2	81	19.5	330	79.3	5	1.2	416
.8	4	1.6	46	18.8	197	80.4	2	.8	245
2.9	5	2.9	35	20.5	133	77.8	3	1.8	171
.3	14	3.7	22	5.8	357	94.2	0	.0	379
.0	6	2.6	9	3.9	224	96.1	0	.0	233
.7	8	5.5	13	8.9	133	91.1	0	.0	146
.6	84	3.7	181	7.9	2,093	91.8	5	.2	2,279
.6	49	3.8	105	8.1	1,191	91.8	2	.2	1,298
.5	35	3.6	76	7.7	902	91.9	3	.3	981
.0	20	1.7	26	2.2	1,132	96.8	12	1.0	1,170
.0	14	1.9	15	2.0	719	97.7	2	.3	736
.0	6	1.4	11	2.5	413	95.2	10	2.3	434
.4	3	.3	25	2.6	908	95.1	22	2.3	955
.4	0	.0	10	1.8	554	97.7	3	.5	567
.5	3	.8	15	3.9	354	91.2	19	4.9	388
.6	105	1.5	279	3.9	6,641	92.8	240	3.4	7,160
.8	51	1.7	124	4.0	2,917	95.1	27	.9	3,068
.4	54	1.3	155	3.8	3,724	91.0	213	5.2	4,092
1.2	38	4.1	77	8.3	819	89.7	27	2.9	923
.6	13	2.7	24	4.9	460	94.1	5	1.2	489
1.8	25	5.8	53	12.2	359	82.7	22	5.1	434
.6	297	2.0	734	5.0	13,649	92.8	327	2.2	14,710
.6	150	2.0	351	4.8	6,981	94.6	48	.7	7,380
.6	147	2.0	383	5.2	6,668	91.0	279	3.8	7,330
2.1	344,958	4.0	1,471,708	17.2	6,938,999	81.0	154,869	1.8	8,565,576
1.9	171,135	4.0	792,524	18.4	3,468,053	80.5	46,634	1.1	4,307,211
2.2	173,823	4.1	679,184	15.9	3,470,946	81.5	108,235	2.5	4,258,365
94.0	0	.0	782	94.1	49	5.9		.0	831
93.3	0	.0	418	93.5	29	6.5	0	.0	447
94.8	0	.0	364	94.8	20	5.2	0	.0	384
94.0	0	.0	782	94.1	49	5 9		.0	831
93.3	0	.0	418	93.5	29	6 5	0	.0	447
94.8	0	.0	364	94.8	20	5 12	0	.0	384
.0	132	31.4	176	41.9	244	58.1		.0	420
.0	70	29.5	95	40.1	142	59.9	0	.0	237
.0	62	33.9	81	44.3	102	55.7	0	.0	183
.0	132	31.4	176	41.9	244	58.1		.0	420
.0	70	29.5	95	40.1	142	59.9	0	.0	237
.0	62	33.9	81	44.3	102	55.7	0	.0	183
72.3	58	2.0	2,239	75.6	510	17.2	212	7 2	2,961
76.4	21	1.4	1,187	79.1	239	15.9	74	4 9	1,500
68.2	37	2.5	1,052	72.0	271	18.5	138	9,4	1,461
72.3	58	2.0	2,239	75.6	510	17.2	212	7.2	2,961
76.4	21	1.4	1,187	79.1	239	15.9	74	4.9	1,500
68.2	37	2.5	1,052	72.0	271	18.5	138	9.4	1,461

TABLE 1 - TOTAL UNDERGRADUATE ENROLLMENT IN INSTITUTIONS OF HIGHER EDUCATION BY RACE, ETHNICITY AND SEX:
INSTITUTION, STATE AND NATION, 1978

	AMERICAN INDIAN ALASKAN NATIVE		BLACK NON-HISPANIC		ASIAN OR PACIFIC ISLANDER		HISPANIC		TOTAL MINORITY		WHITE NON-HISPANIC		NON-RESIDENT ALIEN	
	NUMBER	%	NUMBER	%	NUMBER	%	NUMBER	%	NUMBER	%	NUMBER	%	NUMBER	%
PUERTO RICO														
AMERICAN C PUERTO RICO														
PR TOTAL	0	.0	0	.0	0	.0	1,141	100.0	1,141	100.0	0	.0	0	.0
PR FEMALE	0	.0	0	.0	0	.0	660	100.0	660	100.0	0	.0	0	.0
PR MALE	0	.0	0	.0	0	.0	481	100.0	481	100.0	0	.0	0	.0
ANTILLIAN COLLEGE														
PR TOTAL	0	.0	0	.0	0	.0	686	99.9	686	99.9	1	.1	0	.0
PR FEMALE	0	.0	0	.0	0	.0	389	99.7	389	99.7	1	.3	0	.0
PR MALE	0	.0	0	.0	0	.0	297	100.0	297	100.0	0	.0	0	.0
BAYAMON CEN UNIVERSITY														
PR TOTAL	0	.0	0	.0	0	.0	2,865	100.0	2,865	100.0	0	.0	0	.0
PR FEMALE	0	.0	0	.0	0	.0	1,419	100.0	1,419	100.0	0	.0	0	.0
PR MALE	0	.0	0	.0	0	.0	1,446	100.0	1,446	100.0	0	.0	0	.0
CAGUAS CITY COLLEGE														
PR TOTAL	0	.0	0	.0	0	.0	651	100.0	651	100.0	0	.0	0	.0
PR FEMALE	0	.0	0	.0	0	.0	431	100.0	431	100.0	0	.0	0	.0
PR MALE	0	.0	0	.0	0	.0	220	100.0	220	100.0	0	.0	0	.0
CARIBBEAN U COLLEGE														
PR TOTAL	0	.0	0	.0	0	.0	1,204	100.0	1,204	100.0	0	.0	0	.0
PR FEMALE	0	.0	0	.0	0	.0	781	100.0	781	100.0	0	.0	0	.0
PR MALE	0	.0	0	.0	0	.0	423	100.0	423	100.0	0	.0	0	.0
CATHOLIC U PUERTO RICO														
PR TOTAL	0	.0	0	.0	0	.0	10,675	100.0	10,675	100.0	0	.0	0	.0
PR FEMALE	0	.0	0	.0	0	.0	6,934	100.0	6,934	100.0	0	.0	0	.0
PR MALE	0	.0	0	.0	0	.0	3,741	100.0	3,741	100.0	0	.0	0	.0
CONSERVATORY OF MUSIC PR														
PR TOTAL	10	3.8	0	.0	0	.0	249	95.0	259	98.9	0	.0	3	1.1
PR FEMALE	2	3.1	0	.0	0	.0	63	96.9	65	100.0	0	.0	0	.0
PR MALE	8	4.1	0	.0	0	.0	186	94.4	194	98.5	0	.0	3	1.5
EDP C OF PUERTO RICO														
PR TOTAL	0	.0	0	.0	0	.0	1,226	100.0	1,226	100.0	0	.0	0	.0
PR FEMALE	0	.0	0	.0	0	.0	267	100.0	267	100.0	0	.0	0	.0
PR MALE	0	.0	0	.0	0	.0	959	100.0	959	100.0	0	.0	0	.0
COLEGIO U DEL TURABO														
PR TOTAL	0	.0	0	.0	0	.0	5,135	100.0	5,135	100.0	0	.0	0	.0
PR FEMALE	0	.0	0	.0	0	.0	2,731	100.0	2,731	100.0	0	.0	0	.0
PR MALE	0	.0	0	.0	0	.0	2,404	100.0	2,404	100.0	0	.0	0	.0
PUERTO RICO JR COLLEGE														
PR TOTAL	0	.0	0	.0	0	.0	6,710	100.0	6,710	100.0	0	.0	0	.0
PR FEMALE	0	.0	0	.0	0	.0	4,392	100.0	4,392	100.0	0	.0	0	.0
PR MALE	0	.0	0	.0	0	.0	2,318	100.0	2,318	100.0	0	.0	0	.0
INST COMERCIAL DE PR JC														
PR TOTAL	0	.0	0	.0	0	.0	1,800	100.0	1,800	100.0	0	.0	0	.0
PR FEMALE	0	.0	0	.0	0	.0	1,010	100.0	1,010	100.0	0	.0	0	.0
PR MALE	0	.0	0	.0	0	.0	790	100.0	790	100.0	0	.0	0	.0
INST TECNICO COMERCIAL JC														
PR TOTAL	0	.0	0	.0	0	.0	1,256	98.4	1,256	98.4	0	.0	21	1.6
PR FEMALE	0	.0	0	.0	0	.0	822	98.6	822	98.6	0	.0	12	1.4
PR MALE	0	.0	0	.0	0	.0	434	98.0	434	98.0	0	.0	9	2.0
INTER AMER U HATO REY CAM														
PR TOTAL	0	.0	0	.0	0	.0	7,665	99.0	7,665	99.0	79	1.0		.0
PR FEMALE	0	.0	0	.0	0	.0	4,506	99.0	4,506	99.0	47	1.0	0	.0
PR MALE	0	.0	0	.0	0	.0	3,159	99.0	3,159	99.0	32	1.0		.0
INTER AMER U ARECIBO BR														
PR TOTAL	0	.0	0	.0	0	.0	2,347	99.0	2,347	99.0	23	1.0		.0
PR FEMALE	0	.0	0	.0	0	.0	1,330	99.1	1,330	99.1	12	.9	0	.0
PR MALE	0	.0	0	.0	0	.0	1,017	98.9	1,017	98.9	11	1.1		.0
INTER AMER U BARRANQUITS BR														
PR TOTAL	0	.0	0	.0	0	.0	1,003	99.1	1,003	99.1	9	.9		.0
PR FEMALE	0	.0	0	.0	0	.0	568	99.1	568	99.1	5	.9	0	.0
PR MALE	0	.0	0	.0	0	.0	435	99.1	435	99.1	4	.9		.0
INTER AMER U BAYAMON BR														
PR TOTAL	0	.0	0	.0	0	.0	2,979	99.0	2,979	99.0	30	1.0		.0
PR FEMALE	0	.0	0	.0	0	.0	1,749	99.0	1,749	99.0	18	1.0	0	.0
PR MALE	0	.0	0	.0	0	.0	1,230	99.0	1,230	99.0	12	1.0		.0
INTER AMER SAN GERMAN CAM														
PR TOTAL	0	.0	0	.0	0	.0	6,041	98.0	6,041	98.0	122	2.0		.0
PR FEMALE	0	.0	0	.0	0	.0	3,087	98.0	3,087	98.0	62	2.0	0	.0
PR MALE	0	.0	0	.0	0	.0	2,954	98.0	2,954	98.0	60	2.0		.0
INTER AMER U AGUADILLA BR														
PR TOTAL	0	.0	0	.0	0	.0	2,185	99.0	2,185	99.0	22	1.0		.0
PR FEMALE	0	.0	0	.0	0	.0	1,219	99.0	1,219	99.0	12	1.0	0	.0
PR MALE	0	.0	0	.0	0	.0	966	99.0	966	99.0	10	1.0		.0
INTER AMER U FAJARDO BR														
PR TOTAL	0	.0	0	.0	0	.0	1,556	99.0	1,556	99.0	16	1.0		.0
PR FEMALE	0	.0	0	.0	0	.0	844	99.1	844	99.1	8	.9	0	.0
PR MALE	0	.0	0	.0	0	.0	712	98.9	712	98.9	8	1.1		.0
INTER AMER U GUAYAMA BR														
PR TOTAL	0	.0	0	.0	0	.0	964	99.0	964	99.0	10	1.0		.0
PR FEMALE	0	.0	0	.0	0	.0	643	98.9	643	98.9	7	1.1	0	.0
PR MALE	0	.0	0	.0	0	.0	321	99.1	321	99.1	3	.9		.0
INTER AMER U PONCE BR														
PR TOTAL	0	.0	0	.0	0	.0	1,772	99.0	1,772	99.0	18	1.0		.0
PR FEMALE	0	.0	0	.0	0	.0	1,010	99.0	1,010	99.0	10	1.0	0	.0
PR MALE	0	.0	0	.0	0	.0	762	99.0	762	99.0	8	1.0		.0
RAMIREZ C BUS AND TECHN														
PR TOTAL	0	.0	0	.0	0	.0	609	100.0	609	100.0	0	.0		.0
PR FEMALE	0	.0	0	.0	0	.0	430	100.0	430	100.0	0	.0	0	.0
PR MALE	0	.0	0	.0	0	.0	179	100.0	179	100.0	0	.0		.0
SAN JUAN TECHNOLOGICAL CC														
PR TOTAL	0	.0	0	.0	0	.0	903	100.0	903	100.0	0	.0		.0
PR FEMALE	0	.0	0	.0	0	.0	284	100.0	284	100.0	0	.0	0	.0
PR MALE	0	.0	0	.0	0	.0	619	100.0	619	100.0	0	.0		.0

TABLE 1 - TOTAL UNDERGRADUATE ENROLLMENT IN INSTITUTIONS OF HIGHER EDUCATION BY RACE, ETHNICITY AND SEX: INSTITUTION, STATE AND NATION, 1978

	AMERICAN INDIAN ALASKAN NATIVE		BLACK NON-HISPANIC		ASIAN OR PACIFIC ISLANDER		HISPANIC		TOTAL MINORITY		WHITE NON-HISPANIC		NON-RESIDENT ALIEN		TOTAL
	NUMBER	%	NUMBER	%	NUMBER	%	NUMBER	%	NUMBER	%	NUMBER	%	NUMBER	%	NUMBER
PUERTO RICO CONTINUED															
UNIV POLITECNICA DE PR															
PR TOTAL	0	.0	0	.0	0	.0	143	98.6	143	98.6	2	1.4	0	.0	145
PR FEMALE	0	.0	0	.0	0	.0	5	100.0	5	100.0	0	.0	0	.0	5
PR MALE	0	.0	0	.0	0	.0	138	98.6	138	98.6	2	1.4	0	.0	140
UNIVERSIDAD DE PONCE															
PR TOTAL	0	.0	0	.0	0	.0	347	100.0	347	100.0	0	.0	0	.0	347
PR FEMALE	0	.0	0	.0	0	.0	116	100.0	116	100.0	0	.0	0	.0	116
PR MALE	0	.0	0	.0	0	.0	231	100.0	231	100.0	0	.0	0	.0	231
U OF PR RIO PIEDRAS															
PR TOTAL	0	.0	0	.0	0	.0	19,613	100.0	19,613	100.0	0	.0	0	.0	19,613
PR FEMALE	0	.0	0	.0	0	.0	12,047	100.0	12,047	100.0	0	.0	0	.0	12,047
PR MALE	0	.0	0	.0	0	.0	7,566	100.0	7,566	100.0	0	.0	0	.0	7,566
U OF PR MAYAGUEZ															
PR TOTAL	0	.0	0	.0	0	.0	8,435	100.0	8,435	100.0	0	.0	0	.0	8,435
PR FEMALE	0	.0	0	.0	0	.0	3,259	100.0	3,259	100.0	0	.0	0	.0	3,259
PR MALE	0	.0	0	.0	0	.0	5,176	100.0	5,176	100.0	0	.0	0	.0	5,176
U OF PR MEDICAL SCIENCES															
PR TOTAL	0	.0	0	.0	0	.0	1,108	100.0	1,108	100.0	0	.0	0	.0	1,108
PR FEMALE	0	.0	0	.0	0	.0	948	100.0	948	100.0	0	.0	0	.0	948
PR MALE	0	.0	0	.0	0	.0	160	100.0	160	100.0	0	.0	0	.0	160
U PR CAYEY UNIVERSITY C															
PR TOTAL	0	.0	0	.0	0	.0	2,512	100.0	2,512	100.0	0	.0	0	.0	2,512
PR FEMALE	0	.0	0	.0	0	.0	1,523	100.0	1,523	100.0	0	.0	0	.0	1,523
PR MALE	0	.0	0	.0	0	.0	989	100.0	989	100.0	0	.0	0	.0	989
U PR HUMACAO U COLLEGE															
PR TOTAL	0	.0	0	.0	0	.0	3,282	100.0	3,282	100.0	0	.0	0	.0	3,282
PR FEMALE	0	.0	0	.0	0	.0	2,053	100.0	2,053	100.0	0	.0	0	.0	2,053
PR MALE	0	.0	0	.0	0	.0	1,229	100.0	1,229	100.0	0	.0	0	.0	1,229
U PR REG COLLEGES ADMIN															
PR TOTAL	0	.0	0	.0	1	.0	7,015	100.0	7,016	100.0	0	.0	0	.0	7,016
PR FEMALE	0	.0	0	.0	1	.0	4,124	100.0	4,125	100.0	0	.0	0	.0	4,125
PR MALE	0	.0	0	.0	0	.0	2,891	100.0	2,891	100.0	0	.0	0	.0	2,891
U OF THE SACRED HEART															
PR TOTAL	0	.0	0	.0	0	.0	5,929	100.0	5,929	100.0	0	.0	0	.0	5,929
PR FEMALE	0	.0	0	.0	0	.0	3,722	100.0	3,722	100.0	0	.0	0	.0	3,722
PR MALE	0	.0	0	.0	0	.0	2,207	100.0	2,207	100.0	0	.0	0	.0	2,207
WORLD UNIVERSITY															
PR TOTAL	0	.0	0	.0	0	.0	4,072	99.0	4,072	99.0	0	.0	41	1.0	4,113
PR FEMALE	0	.0	0	.0	0	.0	2,040	99.0	2,040	99.0	0	.0	21	1.0	2,061
PR MALE	0	.0	0	.0	0	.0	2,032	99.0	2,032	99.0	0	.0	20	1.0	2,052
PUERTO RICO TOTAL (33 INSTITUTIONS)															
PR TOTAL	0	.0	10	.0	1	.0	114,078	99.6	114,089	99.7	332	.3	65	.1	114,486
PR FEMALE	0	.0	2	.0			65,406	99.7	65,409	99.7	182	.3	33	.1	65,624
PR MALE	0	.0	8	.0			48,672	99.6	48,680	99.6	150	.3	32	.1	48,862
TRUST TERRITORY															
CMTY COLLEGE MICRONESIA															
TQ TOTAL	0	.0	0	.0	251	100.0	0	.0	251	100.0	0	.0	0	.0	251
TQ FEMALE	0	.0	0	.0	88	100.0	0	.0	88	100.0	0	.0	0	.0	88
TQ MALE	0	.0	0	.0	163	100.0	0	.0	163	100.0	0	.0	0	.0	163
TRUST TERRITORY TOTAL (1 INSTITUTIONS)															
TQ TOTAL	0	.0	0	.0	251	100.0	0	.0	251	100.0	0	.0	0	.0	251
TQ FEMALE	0	.0	0	.0	88	100.0	0	.0	88	100.0	0	.0	0	.0	88
TQ MALE	0	.0	0	.0	163	100.0	0	.0	163	100.0	0	.0	0	.0	163
VIRGIN ISLANDS															
COLLEGE OF VIRGIN ISLANDS															
VI TOTAL	0	.0	311	60.4	1	.2	27	5.2	339	65.8	51	9.9	125	24.3	515
VI FEMALE	0	.0	237	64.2	1	.3	18	4.9	256	69.4	22	6.0	91	24.7	369
VI MALE	0	.0	74	50.7	0	.0	9	6.2	83	56.8	29	19.9	34	23.3	146
VIRGIN ISLANDS TOTAL (1 INSTITUTIONS)															
VI TOTAL	0	.0	311	60.4	1	.2	27	5.2	339	65.8	51	9.9	125	24.3	515
VI FEMALE	0	.0	237	64.2	1	.3	18	4.9	256	69.4	22	6.0	91	24.7	369
VI MALE	0	.0	74	50.7	0	.0	9	6.2	83	56.8	29	19.9	34	23.3	146
OUTLYING AREAS (38 INSTITUTIONS)															
VI TOTAL	11	.0	394	.3	3,176	2.7	114,295	95.7	117,876	98.7	1,186	1.0	402	.3	119,464
VI FEMALE	4	.0	281	.4	1,653	2.4	65,515	96.0	67,453	98.8	614	.9	198	.3	68,265
VI MALE	7	.0	113	.2	1,523	3.0	48,780	95.3	50,423	98.5	572	1.1	204	.4	51,199
NATION TOTAL (2,941 INSTITUTIONS)															
TOTAL	61,418	.7	887,899	10.2	181,014	2.1	459,253	5.3	1,589,584	18.3	6,940,185	79.9	155,271	1.8	8,685,040
FEMALE	32,385	.7	505,607	11.6	85,335	2.0	236,650	5.4	859,977	19.7	3,468,667	79.3	46,832	1.1	4,375,476
MALE	29,033	.7	382,292	8.9	95,679	2.2	222,603	5.2	729,607	16.9	3,471,518	80.6	108,439	2.5	4,309,564

133

TABLE 2 - TOTAL GRADUATE ENROLLMENT IN INSTITUTIONS OF HIGHER EDUCATION BY RACE, ETHNICITY AND SEX:
INSTITUTION, STATE AND NATION, 1978

	AMERICAN INDIAN ALASKAN NATIVE		BLACK NON-HISPANIC		ASIAN OR PACIFIC ISLANDER		HISPANIC		TOTAL MINORITY		WHITE NON-HISPANIC		NON-RESIDENT ALIEN	
	NUMBER	%	NUMBER	%	NUMBER	%	NUMBER	%	NUMBER	%	NUMBER	%	NUMBER	%
ALABAMA														
ALABAMA A & M UNIVERSITY														
AL TOTAL	0	.0	321	32.0		.0		.0	321	32.0	579	57.8	102	10.2
AL FEMALE	0	.0	206	37.5	0	.0	0	.0	206	37.5	332	60.5	11	2.0
AL MALE	0	.0	115	25.4	0	.0	0	.0	115	25.4	247	54.5	91	20.1
ALABAMA STATE UNIVERSITY														
AL TOTAL	0	.0	243	98.8	0	.0		.0	243	98.8	2	.8	1	.4
AL FEMALE	0	.0	147	99.3	0	.0	0	.0	147	99.3	1	.7	0	.0
AL MALE	0	.0	96	98.0 .	0	.0	0	.0	96	98.0	1	1.0	1	1.0
AUBURN U MAIN CAMPUS														
AL TOTAL	0	.0	80	4.4	7	.4	1	.1	88	4.9	1,532	84.9	185	10.2
AL FEMALE	0	.0	47	6.0	1	.1	0	.0	48	6.1	684	87.6	49	6.3
AL MALE	0	.0	33	3.2	6	.6	1	.1	40	3.9	848	82.8	136	13.3
AUBURN U AT MONTGOMERY														
AL TOTAL	0	.0	102	11.4		.0		.0	102	11.4	790	88.6		.0
AL FEMALE	0	.0	57	14.4	0	.0	0	.0	57	14.4	339	85.6	0	.0
AL MALE	0	.0	45	9.1	0	.0	0	.0	45	9.1	451	90.9	0	.0
JACKSONVL ST UNIVERSITY														
AL TOTAL	5	.6	81	9.3	5	.6	12	1.4	103	11.8	772	88.2		.0
AL FEMALE	2	.5	45	10.2	1	.2	3	.7	51	11.6	389	88.4	0	.0
AL MALE	3	.7	36	8.3	4	.9	9	2.1	52	12.0	383	88.0	0	.0
LIVINGSTON UNIVERSITY														
AL TOTAL	0	.0	57	30.3	0	.0	0	.0	57	30.3	129	68.6	2	1.1
AL FEMALE	0	.0	41	28.9	0	.0	0	.0	41	28.9	101	71.1	0	.0
AL MALE	0	.0	16	34.8	0	.0	0	.0	16	34.8	28	60.9	2	4.3
SAMFORD UNIVERSITY														
AL TOTAL	0	.0	26	10.9	1	.4	5	2.1	32	13.4	200	84.0		2.5
AL FEMALE	0	.0	10	10.2	1	1.0	2	2.0	13	13.3	84	85.7	1	1.0
AL MALE	0	.0	16	11.4	0	.0	3	2.1	19	13.6	116	82.9	5	3.6
STHESTN BIBLE COLLEGE														
AL TOTAL	0	.0	1	14.3		.0	0	.0	1	14.3	6	85.7		.0
AL FEMALE	0	.0	0	.0	0	.0	0	.0	0	.0	1	100.0	0	.0
AL MALE	0	.0	1	16.7	0	.0	0	.0	1	16.7	5	83.3	0	.0
TROY STATE U MAIN CAMPUS														
AL TOTAL	6	.7	117	13.4	7	.8	10	1.1	140	16.1	727	83.6	3	.3
AL FEMALE	0	.0	65	21.5	1	.3	2	.7	68	22.5	233	77.2	1	.3
AL MALE	6	1.1	52	9.2	6	1.1	8	1.4	72	12.7	494	87.0	2	.4
TROY ST U DOTHN-FT RUCKER														
AL TOTAL	1	.1	76	10.1	4	.5	2	.3	83	11.0	670	89.0		.0
AL FEMALE	1	.3	42	11.4	2	.5	0	.0	45	12.3	322	87.7	0	.0
AL MALE	0	.0	34	8.8	2	.5	2	.5	38	9.8	348	90.2	0	.0
TROY STATE U MONTGOMERY														
AL TOTAL	1	.1	170	22.8	2	.3	2	.3	175	23.4	571	76.4	1	.1
AL FEMALE	0	.0	93	32.3	1	.3	0	.0	94	32.6	194	67.4	0	.0
AL MALE	1	.2	77	16.8	1	.2	2	.4	81	17.6	377	82.1	1	.2
TUSKEGEE INSTITUTE														
AL TOTAL	0	.0	78	50.0	6	23.1	5	3.2	119	76.3	0	.0	37	23.7
AL FEMALE	0	.0	54	87.	6	9.0	0	.0	60	9.6	0	.0	7	10.4
AL MALE	0	.0	24	20.8	30	33.7	5	5.6	59	86.3	0	.0	30	33.7
UNIVERSITY OF ALABAMA														
AL TOTAL	1	.0	212	.6	2	.1	8	.2	223		2,876	89.2	126	3.9
AL FEMALE	1	.1	144	1	1	.1	4	.2	150		1,615	90.3	23	1.3
AL MALE	0	.0	68	17	1	.1	4	.3	73	815	1,261	87.8	103	7.2
U ALABAMA IN BIRMINGHAM														
AL TOTAL	1	.0	313	12.4	20	.8	2	.1	336	13.3	2,140	84.7	52	2.1
AL FEMALE	1	.1	240	15.9	3	.2	1	.1	245	16.2	1,256	83.0	12	.8
AL MALE	0	.0	73	7.2	17	1.7	1	.1	91	9.0	884	87.1	40	3.9
U ALABAMA IN HUNTSVILLE														
AL TOTAL	2	.4	18	3.3	11	2.0	8	1.4	39	7.1	501	90.8	12	2.2
AL FEMALE	0	.0	8	4.9	3	1.8	0	.0	11	6.7	151	92.6	1	.6
AL MALE	2	.5	10	2.6	8	2.1	8	2.1	28	7.2	350	90.0	11	2.8
UNIVERSITY OF MONTEVALLO														
AL TOTAL	0	.0	55	12.	0	.0	0	.0	55	12.	372	86.3	4	.9
AL FEMALE	0	.0	36	12.0	0	.0	0	.0	36	12.0	239	86.0	3	1.1
AL MALE	0	.0	19	12.6	0	.0	0	.0	19	12.6	133	86.9	1	.7
U OF NORTH ALABAMA														
AL TOTAL	1	.1	42	5.8	2	.3	3	.4	48	6.6	674	93.4		.0
AL FEMALE	1	.2	29	6.1	2	.4	3	.6	35	7.4	439	92.6	0	.0
AL MALE	0	.0	13	5.2	0	.0	0	.0	13	5.2	235	94.8	0	.0
U OF SOUTH ALABAMA														
AL TOTAL	0	.0	70	9.3	2	.3	1	.1	73	9.7	673	89.9	3	.4
AL FEMALE	0	.0	56	12.8	1	.2	0	.0	57	12.1	416	87.9	0	.0
AL MALE	0	.0	14	5.1	1	.4	1	.4	16	5.8	257	93.1	3	1.1
ALABAMA TOTAL I 18 INSTITUTIONS)														
AL TOTAL	18	.1	2,062	12.9	99	.6	59	.4	2,238	14.0	13,214	82.7	534	3.3
AL FEMALE	6	.1	1,320	16.0	23	.3	15	.2	1,364	16.5	6,796	82.2	108	1.3
AL MALE	12	.2	742	9.6	76	1.0	44	.6	874	11.3	6,418	83.2	426	5.5
ALASKA														
ALASKA PACIFIC UNIVERSITY														
AK TOTAL	1	9.1	3	27.3	1	9.1		.0	5	45.5	6	54.5	0	.0
AK FEMALE	1	16.7	1	16.7	1	16.7	0	.0	3	50.0	3	50.0	0	.0
AK MALE	0	.0	2	40.0	0	.0	0	.0	2	40.0	3	60.0	0	.0
U ALASKA FAIRBANKS CAMPUS														
AK TOTAL	3	.9	4	1.2	4	1.2	1	.3	12	3.6	301	89.3	24	7.1
AK FEMALE	3	2.5	2	1.7	2	1.7	1	.8	8	6.8	105	89.0	5	4.2
AK MALE	0	.0	2	.9	2	.9	0	.0	4	1.8	196	89.5	19	8.7
U ALAS ANCHORAGE CAMPUS														
AK TOTAL	10	2.0	21	4.3	6	1.2	1	2.0	47	9.6	442	90.2	1	.2
AK FEMALE	6	2.2	11	4.0	2	.7	0	2.2	25	9.1	250	90.6	1	.4
AK MALE	4	1.9	10	4.7	4	1.9	8	1.9	22	10.3	192	89.7	0	.0

134

BLACK NON-HISPANIC		ASIAN OR PACIFIC ISLANDER		HISPANIC		TOTAL MINORITY		WHITE NON-HISPANIC		NON-RESIDENT ALIEN		TOTAL
NUMBER	%	NUMBER	%	NUMBER	%	NUMBER	%	NUMBER	%	NUMBER	%	NUMBER
5	10.9	1	2.2	1	2.2	9	19.6	37	80.4	0	.0	46
1	4.0	1	4.0	1	4.0	4	16.0	21	84.0	0	.0	25
4	19.0	0	.0	0	.0	5	23.8	16	76.2	0	.0	21
0	.0	1	11.1	0	.0	1	11.1	8	88.9	0	.0	9
0	.0	1	16.7	0	.0	1	16.7	5	83.3	0	.0	6
0	.0	0	.0	0	.0	0	.0	3	100.0	0	.0	3
0	.0	1	3.7	0	.0	1	3.7	26	96.3	0	.0	27
0	.0	1	5.6	0	.0	1	5.6	17	94.4	0	.0	18
0	.0	0	.0	0	.0	0	.0	9	100.0	0	.0	9
5	2.2	5	2.2	1	.4	34	15.0	192	85.0	0	.0	226
2	1.6	3	2.4	1	.8	19	15.4	104	84.6	0	.0	123
3	2.9	2	1.9	0	.0	15	14.6	88	85.4	0	.0	103
(7 INSTITUTIONS)												
38	3.3	19	1.7	13	1.1	109	9.5	1,012	88.3	25	2.2	1,146
17	3.0	11	1.9	9	1.6	61	10.7	505	88.3	6	1.0	572
21	3.7	8	1.4	4	.7	48	8.4	507	88.3	19	3.3	574
7	.8	7	.8	9	1.0	23	2.5	688	74.9	207	22.5	918
3	4.5	4	6.1	3	4.5	10	15.2	46	69.7	10	15.2	66
4	.5	3	.4	6	.7	13	1.5	642	75.4	197	23.1	852
58	1.1	47	.9	136	2.7	276	5.5	4,581	90.7	194	3.8	5,051
23	1.0	15	.6	58	2.4	118	4.9	2,237	93.4	40	1.7	2,395
35	1.3	32	1.2	78	2.9	158	5.9	2,344	88.3	154	5.8	2,656
4	.2	4	.2	14	.8	41	2.3	1,695	97.1	9	.5	1,745
1	.1	3	.4	3	.4	20	2.6	756	96.9	4	.5	780
3	.3	1	.1	11	1.1	21	2.2	939	97.3	5	.5	965
47	.7	56	.9	187	2.9	327	5.2	5,491	86.6	523	8.2	6,341
28	1.0	21	.8	94	3.4	163	5.9	2,494	91.0	83	3.0	2,740
19	.5	35	1.0	93	2.6	164	4.6	2,997	83.2	440	12.2	3,601
(4 INSTITUTIONS)												
116	.8	114	.8	346	2.5	667	4.7	12,455	88.6	933	6.6	14,055
55	.9	43	.7	158	2.6	311	5.2	5,533	92.5	137	2.3	5,981
61	.8	71	.9	188	2.3	356	4.4	6,922	85.7	796	9.9	8,074
60	9.1	2	.3	3	.5	69	10.5	589	89.2	2	.3	660
40	11.7	2	.6	2	.6	44	12.9	296	86.8	1	.3	341
20	6.3	0	.0	1	.3	25	7.8	293	91.8	1	.3	319
7	5.0	1	.7	0	.0	9	6.4	131	92.9	1	.7	141
3	3.0	1	1.0	0	.0	5	5.1	94	94.9	0	.0	99
4	9.5	0	.0	0	.0	4	9.5	37	88.1	1	2.4	42
0	.0	0	.0	0	.0	0	.0	29	100.0	0	.0	29
0	.0	0	.0	0	.0	0	.0	14	100.0	0	.0	14
0	.0	0	.0	0	.0	0	.0	15	100.0	0	.0	15
1	.8	0	.0	0	.0	1	.8	116	98.3	1	.8	118
0	.0	0	.0	0	.0	0	.0	3	100.0	0	.0	3
1	.9	0	.0	0	.0	1	.9	113	98.3	1	.9	115
17	7.1	1	.4	0	.0	18	7.5	222	92.5	0	.0	240
12	7.8	0	.0	0	.0	12	7.8	142	92.2	0	.0	154
5	5.8	1	1.2	0	.0	6	7.0	80	93.0	0	.0	86
46	42.6	0	.0	1	.9	47	43.5	61	56.5	0	.0	108
31	43.7	0	.0	0	.0	31	43.7	40	56.3	0	.0	71
15	40.5	0	.0	1	2.7	16	43.2	21	56.8	0	.0	37
15	13.9	1	.9	0	.0	16	14.8	92	85.2	0	.0	108
9	12.5	1	1.4	0	.0	10	13.9	62	86.1	0	.0	72
6	16.7	0	.0	0	.0	6	16.7	30	83.3	0	.0	36
213	7.1	30	1.0	14	.5	284	9.5	2,508	84.0	194	6.5	2,986
126	9.5	12	.9	4	.3	156	11.7	1,146	86.3	26	2.0	1,328
87	5.2	18	1.1	10	.6	128	7.7	1,362	82.1	168	10.1	1,658
48	8.5	1	.2	0	.0	55	9.7	509	90.1	1	.2	565
29	9.0	0	.0	0	.0	33	10.3	288	89.7	0	.0	321
19	7.8	1	.4	0	.0	22	9.0	221	90.6	1	.4	244
9	4.8	2	1.1	2	1.1	13	7.0	169	90.9	4	2.2	186
9	7.3	2	1.6	1	.8	12	9.7	111	89.5	1	.8	124
0	.0	0	.0	1	1.6	1	1.6	58	93.5	3	4.8	62
48	6.9	0	.0	0	.0	48	6.9	640	92.5	4	.6	692
33	6.9	0	.0	0	.0	33	6.9	441	92.6	2	.4	476
15	6.9	0	.0	0	.0	15	6.9	199	92.1	2	.9	216

TABLE 2 - TOTAL GRADUATE ENROLLMENT IN INSTITUTIONS OF HIGHER EDUCATION BY RACE, ETHNICITY AND SEX: INSTITUTION, STATE AND NATION, 1978

	AMERICAN INDIAN ALASKAN NATIVE		BLACK NON-HISPANIC		ASIAN OR PACIFIC ISLANDER		HISPANIC		TOTAL MINORITY		WHITE NON-HISPANIC		NON-RESIDENT ALIEN		TO
	NUMBER	%	NUMBER	%	NUMBER	%	NUMBER	%	NUMBER	%	NUMBER	%	NUMBER	%	NU
ARKANSAS															
ARKANSAS TOTAL (	11 INSTITUTIONS)														
AR TOTAL	38	.7	464	8.0	38	.7	20	.3	560	9.6	5,066	86.9	207	3.5	5
AR FEMALE	19	.6	292	9.7	18	.6	7	.2	336	11.2	2,637	87.8	30	1.0	3
AR MALE	19	.7	172	6.1	20	.7	13	.5	224	7.9	2,429	85.8	177	6.3	2
CALIFORNIA															
AMER BAPT SEM OF WEST															
CA TOTAL	0	.0	1	3.4	0	.0	2	6.9	3	10.3	25	86.2	1	3.4	
CA FEMALE	0	.0	0	.0	0	.0	0	.0	0	.0	5	83.3	1	16.7	
CA MALE	0	.0	1	4.3	0	.0	2	8.7	3	13.0	20	87.0	0	.0	
AMERICAN CONSV THEATRE															
CA TOTAL	0	.0	4	8.5	1	2.1	0	.0	5	10.6	42	89.4			
CA FEMALE	0	.0	1	5.9	1	5.9	0	.0	2	11.8	15	88.2	0	.0	
CA MALE	0	.0	3	10.0	0	.0	0	.0	3	10.0	27	90.0	0	.0	
ARMSTRONG COLLEGE															
CA TOTAL	0	.0	5	3.5	2	1.4	0	.0	7	4.9	14	9.9	121	85.2	
CA FEMALE	0	.0	1	2.9	1	2.9	0	.0	2	5.9	6	17.6	26	76.5	
CA MALE	0	.0	4	3.7	1	.9	0	.0	5	4.6	8	7.4	95	88.0	
ART CTR COLLEGE OF DESIGN															
CA TOTAL	0	.0		.		.0	0	.0	0	.0	2	100.0	0	.0	
CA FEMALE	0	.0				.0	0	.0	0	.0	1	100.0	0	.0	
CA MALE	0	.0	0	.0	0	.0	0	.0	0	.0	1	100.0	0	.0	
AZUSA PACIFIC COLLEGE															
CA TOTAL	3	.4	39	.7	18	2.2	24	2.9		10.0	723	86.4	30	3 6	
CA FEMALE	1	.2	22	4.9	7	1.6	10	2.2	4	8.9	401	89.7	6	1 3	
CA MALE	2	.5	17	4.4	11	2.8	14	3.6	48	11.3	322	82.6	24	642	
BIOLA COLLEGE															
CA TOTAL	1	.1	9	1 1	30	3.6	7	.8	47	5.6	746	89.2	43	5.	
CA FEMALE	0	.0	1	8	9	7.4	0	.0	10	8.3	104	86.0	7	5.	
CA MALE	1	.1	8	111	21	2.9	7	1.0	37	5.2	642	89.8	36	5.8	
BROOKS INSTITUTE															
CA TOTAL	0	.0	0	.0	0	.0	0	.0	0	.0	0	.0		.0	
CA FEMALE	0	.0	0	.0	0	.0	0	.0	0	.0	0	.0		.0	
CA MALE	0	.0	0	.0	0	.0	0	.0	0	.0	0	.0	0	.0	
CAL COLLEGE ARTS & CRAFTS															
CA TOTAL	1	1.5	1	1.5	5	7.7	2	3.1		13.8	48	73.8		12.3	
CA FEMALE	0	.0	1	3.6	3	10.7	0	.0	4	14.3	20	71.4	4	14.3	
CA MALE	1	2.7	0	.0	2	5.4	2	5.4	4	13.5	28	75.7		10.8	
CAL COLLEGE PODIATRIC MED															
CA TOTAL	0			.0		.0	0	.0		.0	2	100.0		.0	
CA FEMALE	0	.0	0	.0		.0	0	.0		.0	0	.0		.0	
CA MALE	0	.0	0	.0	0	.0	0	.0	0	.0	2	100.0	0	.0	
CALIFORNIA INST OF ARTS															
CA TOTAL	0	.0	5	2.9	4	2.3	3	1.7	12	7.0	141	82.0	19	11.0	
CA FEMALE	0	.0	1	1.3	4	5.3	2	2.7	7	9.3	64	85.3	4	5.3	
CA MALE	0	.0	4	4.1	0	.0	1	1.0	5	5.2	77	79.4	15	15.5	
CAL INST OF ASIAN STUDIES															
CA TOTAL	0	.0	2	1.4	0	.0	3	2.1	5	3.6	132	94.3	3	2.1	
CA FEMALE	0	.0	1	1.7	0	.0	0	.0	1	1.7	57	95.0	2	3.3	
CA MALE	0	.0	1	1.3	0	.0	3	3.8	4	5.0	75	93.8	1	1.3	
CAL INST OF TECHNOLOGY															
CA TOTAL	1	.1	2	.2	25	2.9	6	.7	34	4.0	607	71.3	210	24.7	
CA FEMALE	0	.0	1	1.0	6	6.1	1	1.0	8	8.1	77	77.8	14	14.1	
CA MALE	1	.1	1	.1	19	2.5	5	.7	26	3.5	530	70.5	196	26.1	
CAL LUTHERAN COLLEGE															
CA TOTAL	4	.3	62	5.2	40	3.3	40	3.3	146	12.1	1,051	87.4	5	.4	1
CA FEMALE	2	.3	51	7.4	20	2.9	13	1.9	86	12.5	598	87.2	2	.3	
CA MALE	2	.4	11	2.1	20	3.9	27	5.2	60	11.6	453	87.8	3	.6	
CAL SCH PSYC BERKELEY															
CA TOTAL	0	.0	4	1 5	10	3	7	2.7	21	8.1	226	87.3	12	4.6	
CA FEMALE	0	.0	2	1 5	5	3	4	3.1	11	8.4	114	87.0	6	4.6	
CA MALE	0	.0	2	16	5	318	3	2.3	10	7.8	112	87.5	6	4.7	
CAL SCH PROF PSYC FRESNO															
CA TOTAL	1	.7	2		1	.7	2	1.4	8	5.6	136	94.4		.0	
CA FEMALE	0	.0	2		0	.0	2	4.7	3	7.0	40	93.0	0	.0	
CA MALE	1	1.0	3	318	1	1.0	0	.0	5	5.0	96	95.0	0	.0	
CAL SCH PROF PSYC LOS ANG															
CA TOTAL	0	.0	8	2	8	2.8	7	2.5	23	8 2	257	91.5	1	.4	
CA FEMALE	0	.0	7	4	3	1.9	2	1.2	12	7 4	149	92.0	1	.6	
CA MALE	0	.0	1	18	5	4.2	5	4.2	11	912	108	90.8	0	.0	
CAL SCH PROF PSYC SN DIEGO															
CA TOTAL	1	1 3	2	.9	5	2.1	11	4 7	222	94.5	2	.9			
CA FEMALE	1	1.1	0	0	2	2.2	1	1.1	4	424	85	94.4	1	1.1	
CA MALE	0	.0	3	211	0	.0	4	2.8	7	4.8	137	94.5	1	.7	
CAL ST COLLEGE-BAKERSFLD															
CA TOTAL	12	2.1	24	4 3	43	2.3	43	7.7	92	1 .	451	80.7	16	2.	
CA FEMALE	6	2.1	14	4 9	7	2.5	20	7.0	47	14.	232	81.7	5	1.8	
CA MALE	6	2.2	10	316	6	2.2	23	8.4	45	16.8	219	79.6	11	4.8	
CAL STATE C-SN BERNARDINO															
CA TOTAL	9	1.3	75	11.2	5	.7	67	10.0	156	2 3	497	74.2	17	2.5	
CA FEMALE	9	2.6	40	11.4	2	.6	34	9.7	85	24.3	257	73.4	8	2.3	
CA MALE			35	10.9	3	.9	33	10.3	71	22.2	240	75.0	9	2.8	
CAL ST COLLEGE-STANISLAUS															
CA TOTAL	4	1.1	11	2.9		2.4	18	4.7	42	11.1	313	82.4	25	6	
CA FEMALE	1	.6	8	4.7		1.8	6	3.6	18	10.7	141	83.4	10	5.	
CA MALE	3	1.4	3	1.8	9	2.8	12	5.7	24	11.4	172	81.5	15	714	
CAL POLY ST U-SN LUIS OB															
CA TOTAL	8	1.6	5	1.0	12	2.3	23	4.5	48	9.4	443	86.4	22	4.3	
CA FEMALE	4	1.8	3	1.3	6	2.7	9	4.0	22	9.8	200	88.9	3	1.3	
CA MALE	4	1.4	2	.7	6	2.1	14	4.9	26	9.0	243	84.4	19	6.6	

136

	BLACK NON-HISPANIC		ASIAN OR PACIFIC ISLANDER		HISPANIC		TOTAL MINORITY		WHITE NON-HISPANIC		NON-RESIDENT ALIEN		TOTAL
	NUMBER	%	NUMBER	%	NUMBER	%	NUMBER	%	NUMBER	%	NUMBER	%	NUMBER
'INUED													
	6	1.1	29	5.3	22	4.0	59	10.8	385	70.8	100	18 4	544
	5	2.9	5	2.9	8	4.6	18	10.4	139	80.3	16	912	173
	1	.3	24	6.5	14	3.8	41	11.1	246	66.3	84	22.6	371
	12	1.6	13	1.7	20	2.6	56	7.2	664	85.8	54	7	774
	5	1.5	5	1.5	11	3.2	25	7.4	297	87.6	17	5	339
	7	1.6	8	1.8	9	2.1	31	7.1	367	84.4	37	818	435
	206	22.2	53	5.7	46	5.0	325	35.0	584	62.9	20	2 2	929
	126	26.8	19	4.0	19	4.0	174	36.9	294	62.4	3	3 6	471
	80	17.5	34	7.4	27	5.9	151	33.0	290	63.3	17	17	458
	51	2.8	71	4.0	95	5.3	238	13.3	1,321	73.7	234	13.1	1,793
	31	3.5	36	4.1	51	5.8	126	14.3	680	77.3	74	8.4	880
	20	2.2	35	3.8	44	4.8	112	12.3	641	70.2	160	17.5	913
	51	1.8	131	4.5	165	5.7	369	12.7	2,436	84.0	95	3.3	2,900
	29	1.9	49	3.2	101	6.6	188	12.2	1,326	86.1	26	1.7	1,540
	22	1.6	82	6.0	64	4.7	181	13.3	1,110	81.6	69	5.1	1,360
	115	8.7	79	6.0	53	4.0	255	19.3	987	74.5	82	6.2	1,324
	73	10.5	31	4.5	25	3.6	134	19.4	521	75.3	37	5 3	692
	42	6.6	48	7.6	28	4.4	121	19.1	466	73.7	45	711	632
	141	3.7	309	8.0	155	4.0	629	16.4	3,043	79.1	174	4 5	3,846
	57	3.3	104	6.0	60	3.5	229	13.2	1,458	84.0	48	2 8	1,735
	84	4.0	205	9.7	95	4.5	400	18.9	1,585	75.1	126	610	2,111
	523	12.5	573	13.7	403	9.6	1,535	36.6	2,511	59.9	145	3 5	4,191
	360	15.6	263	11.4	175	7.6	813	35.3	1,442	62.7	46	2 3	2,301
	163	8.6	310	16.4	228	12.1	722	38.2	1,069	56.6	99	512	1,890
	79	2.3	234	6.7	196	5.6	593	16.9	2,846	81.3	63	1.8	3,502
	49	2.3	124	5.9	107	5.1	317	15.0	1,780	84.2	17	.9	2,114
	30	2.2	110	7.9	89	6.4	276	19.9	1,066	76.8	46	3.3	1,388
	84	3.9	143	6.6	90	4.2	346	16.0	1,726	79.8	91	4 2	2,163
	44	4.1	55	5.1	45	4.2	157	14.6	893	83.0	26	2 4	1,076
	40	3.7	88	8.1	45	4.1	189	17.4	833	76.6	65	610	1,087
	2	.4	7	1.4	2	.4	21	4.2	450	90.5	26	5 2	497
	1	.5	1	.5	1	.5	11	5.2	197	92.5	5	2 3	213
	1	.4	6	2.1	1	.4	10	3.5	253	89.1	21	714	284
	84	2.0	138	3.4	264	6.4	532	12.9	3,429	83.3	156	3 8	4,117
	54	2.6	72	3.4	132	6.3	274	13.1	1,789	85.4	32	1 5	2,095
	30	1.5	66	3.3	132	6.5	258	12.8	1,640	81.1	124	611	2,022
	285	5.9	522	10.9	166	3.5	995	20.7	3,589	74.8	214	4.5	4,798
	171	6.1	285	10.2	85	3.0	551	19.7	2,158	77.0	93	3.3	2,802
	114	5.7	237	11.9	81	4.1	444	22.2	1,431	71.7	121	6.1	1,996
	95	2.9	311	9.4	197	5.9	626	18.9	2,416	72.8	276	8	3,318
	60	3.6	111	6.8	88	5.4	269	16.4	1,298	79.0	77	4	1,644
	35	2.1	200	11.9	109	6.5	357	21.3	1,118	66.8	199	1119	1,674
	5	1.4	13	3.5	15	4.1	36	9.7	329	88.9	5	1.4	370
	1	.6	8	4.6	7	4.0	18	10.3	155	89.1	1	.6	174
	4	2.0	5	2.6	8	4.1	18	9.2	174	88.8	4	2.0	196
	2	9.1	1	4.5	1	4.5	4	18.2	18	81.8		.0	22
	2	10.0	1	5.0	0	.0	3	15.0	17	85.0	0	.0	20
	0	.0	0	.0	1	50.0	1	50.0	1	50.0		.0	2
	11	1.5	17	2.4	12	1.7	50	7.0	604	85.1	56	7.9	710
	4	1.3	5	1.7	4	1.3	17	5.7	273	91.3	9	3.0	299
	7	1.7	12	2.9	8	1.9	33	8.0	331	80.5	47	11.4	411
	0	.0	0	.0	1	6.7	1	6.7	10	66.7		26.7	1
	0	.0	0	.0	1	16.7	1	16.7	5	83.3		.0	
	0	.0	0	.0	0	.0	0	.0	5	55.6		44.4	
	71	4.6	31	2.0	82	5.3	190	12.4	1,102	71.8	243	15.8	1,535
	39	7.5	19	3.6	25	4.8	83	15.9	393	75.1	47	9.0	523
	32	3.2	12	1.2	57	5.6	107	10.6	709	70.1	196	19.4	1,012
	0	.0	0	.0	0	.0	0	.0	2	100.0	0	.0	2
	0	.0	0	.0	0	.0	0	.0	0	.0	0	.0	0
	0	.0	0	.0	0	.0	0	.0	2	100.0	0	.0	2
	4	1.5	6	2.2	9	3.3	19	7.0	193	71.0	60	22.1	272
	2	1.4	3	2.1	7	5.0	12	8.5	115	81.6	14	9.9	141
	2	1.5	3	2.3	2	1.5	7	5.3	78	59.5	46	35.1	131
	1	.9	2	1.8	2	1.8	5	4.5	106	95.5		.0	111
	1	1.2	1	1.2	2	2.3	4	4.7	82	95.3		.0	86
	0	.0	1	4.0	0	.0	1	4.0	24	96.0		.0	25
	0	.0	0	.0	0	.0	0	.0	15	100.0		.0	15
	0	.0	0	.0	0	.0	0	.0	4	100.0		.0	4
	0	.0	0	.0	0	.0	0	.0	11	100.0		.0	11

	AMERICAN INDIAN ALASKAN NATIVE		BLACK NON-HISPANIC		ASIAN OR PACIFIC ISLANDER		HISPANIC		TOTAL MINORITY		WHITE NON-HISPANIC		NON-RESIDENT ALIEN		
	NUMBER	%	NUMBER	%	NUMBER	%	NUMBER	%	NUMBER	%	NUMBER	%	NUMBER	%	
CALIFORNIA	CONTINUED														
FIELDING INSTITUTE															
CA TOTAL	0	.0	7	2.4	0	.0	0	.0	7	2.4	290	97.6	0	.0	
CA FEMALE	0	.0	5	3.0	0	.0	0	.0	5	3.0	159	97.0	0	.0	
CA MALE	0	.0	2	1.5	0	.0	0	.0	2	1.5	131	98.5	0	.0	
FRANCISCAN SCH THEOLOGY															
CA TOTAL	0	.0	0	.0	0	.0	3	4.9	3	4.9	52	85.2	6	9.8	
CA FEMALE	0	.0	0	.0	0	.0	1	3.4	1	3.4	27	93.1	1	3.4	
CA MALE	0	.0	0	.0	0	.0	2	6.3	2	6.3	25	78.1	5	15.6	
FRESNO PACIFIC COLLEGE															
CA TOTAL	3	1.3	5	2.2	2	.9	9	4.0	19	8.4	207	91.6	0	.0	
CA FEMALE	0	.0	2	1.3	2	1.3	2	1.3	6	3.9	146	96.1	0	.0	
CA MALE	3	4.1	3	4.1	0	.0	7	9.5	13	17.6	61	82.4	0	.0	
FULLER THEOLOGICAL SEM															
CA TOTAL	2	.9	7	3.0	18	7.8	3	1.3	30	12.9	173	74.6	29	12.5	
CA FEMALE	0	.0	0	.0	2	5.3	0	.0	2	5.3	34	89.5	2	5.3	
CA MALE	2	1.0	7	3.6	16	8.2	3	1.5	28	14.4	139	71.6	27	13.9	
GOLDEN GATE BAPT SEMINARY															
CA TOTAL	0	.0	0	.0	0	.0	0	.0	0	.0	0	.0		.0	
CA FEMALE	0	.0	0	.0	0	.0	0	.0	0	.0	0	.0		.0	
CA MALE	0	.0	0	.0	0	.0	0	.0	0	.0	0	.0	8	.0	
GOLDEN GATE UNIVERSITY															
CA TOTAL	2	.0	162	2.9	240	4.3	50	.9	454	8.2	4,990	90.1	95	1.7	
CA FEMALE	0	.0	8	.6	62	4.8	9	.7	79	6.1	1,195	92.9	13	1.0	
CA MALE	2	.0	154	3.6	178	4.2	41	1.0	375	8.8	3,795	89.3	82	1.9	
GRADUATE THEOL UNION															
CA TOTAL	2	.6	9	2.8	4	1.3	10	3.2	25	7.9	268	84.8	23	7.3	
CA FEMALE	1	1.0	3	3.1	1	1.0	1	1.0	6	6.1	87	88.8	5	5.1	
CA MALE	1	.5	6	2.8	3	1.4	9	4.1	19	8.7	181	83.0	18	8.3	
HOLY NAMES COLLEGE															
CA TOTAL	0	.0	14	7.3	8	4.2	9	4.7	31	16.2	145	75.9	15	7.9	
CA FEMALE	0	.0	13	7.8	8	4.8	9	5.4	30	18.0	127	76.0	10	6.0	
CA MALE	0	.0	1	4.2	0	.0	0	.0	1	4.2	18	75.0	5	20.8	
IMMACULATE HEART COLLEGE															
CA TOTAL	0	.0	0	.0	4	3.7	4	3.7	8	7.3	99	90.8	2	1.8	
CA FEMALE	0	.0	0	.0	3	3.0	4	4.0	7	7.1	90	90.9	2	2.0	
CA MALE	0	.0	0	.0	1	10.0	0	.0	1	10.0	9	90.0	0	.0	
INTERNATIONAL COLLEGE															
CA TOTAL	1	.5	4	1.9	0	.0	0	.0	5	2.4	183	88.4	19	9.2	
CA FEMALE	0	.0	2	1.7	0	.0	0	.0	2	1.7	113	97.4	1	.9	
CA MALE	1	1.1	2	2.2	0	.0	0	.0	3	3.3	70	76.9	18	19.8	
JESUIT SCHOOL OF THEOLOGY															
CA TOTAL	0	.0	3	1.7	4	2.2	6	3.3	13	7.2	156	86.2	12	6.6	
CA FEMALE	0	.0	0	.0	0	.0	3	7.3	3	7.3	38	92.7	0	.0	
CA MALE	0	.0	3	2.1	4	2.9	3	2.1	10	7.1	118	84.3	12	8.6	
JOHN F KENNEDY UNIVERSITY															
CA TOTAL	0	.0	14	2.3	8	1.3	6	1.0	28	4.6	569	93.0	15	2.5	
CA FEMALE	0	.0	7	1.8	7	1.8	2	.5	16	4.2	361	93.8	8	2.1	
CA MALE	0	.0	7	3.1	1	.4	4	1.8	12	5.3	208	91.6	7	3.1	
LINCOLN UNIVERSITY															
CA TOTAL	0	.0	0	.0	5	14.7	0	.0	5	14.7	1	2.9	28	82.4	
CA FEMALE	0	.0	0	.0	3	23.1	0	.0	3	23.1	0	.0	10	76.9	
CA MALE	0	.0	0	.0	2	9.5	0	.0	2	9.5	1	4.8	18	85.7	
LOMA LINDA UNIVERSITY															
CA TOTAL	2	.2	52	6.2	41	4.9	37	4.4	132	15.8	606	72.6	97	11.6	
CA FEMALE	1	.2	34	8.2	20	4.8	20	4.8	75	18.1	306	73.9	33	8.0	
CA MALE	1	.2	18	4.3	21	5.0	17	4.0	57	13.5	300	71.3	64	15.2	
LOS ANGELES BAPT COLLEGE															
CA TOTAL	0	.0	0	.0	0	.0	0	.0	0	.0	11	100.0	0	.0	
CA FEMALE	0	.0	0	.0	0	.0	0	.0	0	.0	8	100.0	0	.0	
CA MALE	0	.0	0	.0	0	.0	0	.0	0	.0	3	100.0	0	.0	
LOYOLA MARYMOUNT U															
CA TOTAL	3	.3	46	4.5	14	1.4	47	4.6	110	10.8	782	76.4	131	12.8	
CA FEMALE	3	.6	29	5.8	7	1.4	17	3.4	56	11.1	404	80.3	43	8.5	
CA MALE	0	.0	17	3.3	7	1.3	30	5.8	54	10.4	378	72.7	88	16.9	
MELODYLAND SCH THEOLOGY															
CA TOTAL	0	.0	5	2.3	5	2.3	7	3.2	17	7.8	192	88.5	8	3.7	
CA FEMALE	0	.0	1	2.3	2	4.5	2	4.5	5	11.4	37	84.1	2	4.5	
CA MALE	0	.0	4	2.3	3	1.7	5	2.9	12	6.9	155	89.6	6	3.5	
MENNONITE BRTHREN BIB SEM															
CA TOTAL	0	.0	2	3.4	0	.0	2	3.4	4	6.9	44	75.9	10	17.2	
CA FEMALE	0	.0	0	.0	0	.0	0	.0	0	.0	2	66.7	1	33.3	
CA MALE	0	.0	2	3.6	0	.0	2	3.6	4	7.3	42	76.4	9	16.4	
MILLS COLLEGE															
CA TOTAL	0	.0	6	4.5	5	3.7	1	.7	12	9.0	114	85.1	8	6.0	
CA FEMALE	0	.0	5	4.7	4	3.8	1	.9	10	9.4	89	84.0	7	6.6	
CA MALE	0	.0	1	3.6	1	3.6	0	.0	2	7.1	25	89.3	1	3.6	
MNTREY INST FORGN STUDIES															
CA TOTAL	0	.0	6	2.5	6	2.5	14	5.9	26	10.9	183	76.9	29	12.2	
CA FEMALE	0	.0	1	.7	6	4.3	7	5.0	14	9.9	109	77.3	18	12.8	
CA MALE	0	.0	5	5.2	0	.0	7	7.2	12	12.4	74	76.3	11	11.3	
MOUNT SNT MARY'S COLLEGE															
CA TOTAL	0	.0	7	11.1	4	6.3	13	20.6	24	38.1	39	61.9	0	.0	
CA FEMALE	0	.0	6	11.8	3	5.9	11	21.6	20	39.2	31	60.8	0	.0	
CA MALE	0	.0	1	8.3	1	8.3	2	16.7	4	33.3	8	66.7	0	.0	
NATIONAL UNIVERSITY															
CA TOTAL	11	.8	99	7.4	91	6.8	45	3.3	246	18.3	1,031	76.7	67	5.0	
CA FEMALE	2	.8	20	7.9	18	7.1	9	3.6	49	19.4	193	76.6	10	4.0	
CA MALE	9	.8	79	7.2	73	6.7	36	3.3	197	18.0	838	76.7	57	5.2	
NORTHROP UNIVERSITY															
CA TOTAL	0	.0	0	.0	0	.0	0	.0	0	.0	117	50.0	117	50.0	
CA FEMALE	0	.0	0	.0	0	.0	0	.0	0	.0	11	42.3	15	57.7	
CA MALE	0	.0	0	.0	0	.0	0	.0	0	.0	106	51.0	102	49.0	

ENROLLMENT IN INSTITUTIONS OF HIGHER EDUCATION BY RACE, ETHNICITY AND SEX:
ATE AND NATION, 1978

BLACK NON-HISPANIC		ASIAN OR PACIFIC ISLANDER		HISPANIC		TOTAL MINORITY		WHITE NON-HISPANIC		NON-RESIDENT ALIEN		TOTAL
NUMBER	%	NUMBER	%	NUMBER	%	NUMBER	%	NUMBER	%	NUMBER	%	NUMBER
INUED												
0	.0	1	7.7	0	.0	1	7.7	11	84.6	1	7.7	13
0	.0	0	.0	0	.0	0	.0	0	.0	0	.0	0
0	.0	1	7.7	0	.0	1	7.7	11	84.6	1	7.7	13
1	3.4	1	3.4	0	.0	2	6.9	21	72.4	6	20.7	29
0	.0	1	9.1	0	.0	1	9.1	8	72.7	2	18.2	11
1	5.6	0	.0	0	.0	1	5.6	13	72.2	4	22.2	18
5	5.8	5	5.8	3	3.5	13	15.1	67	77.9	6	7.0	86
0	.0	2	3.9	0	.0	2	3.9	47	92.2	2	3.9	51
5	14.3	3	8.6	3	8.6	11	31.4	20	57.1	4	11.4	35
0	.0	1	5.3	1	5.3	2	10.5	17	89.5	0	.0	19
0	.0	0	.0	1	16.7	1	16.7	5	83.3	0	.0	6
0	.0	1	7.7	0	.0	1	7.7	12	92.3	0	.0	13
2	2.9	0	.0	0	.0	3	4.3	66	94.3	1	1.4	70
0	.0	0	.0	0	.0	0	.0	4	100.0	0	.0	4
2	3.0	0	.0	0	.0	3	4.5	62	93.9	1	1.5	66
8	5.4	3	2.0	3	2.0	15	10.2	126	85.7	6	4.1	147
6	4.5	2	1.5	1	6.7	11	8.3	115	87.1	6	4.5	132
2	13.3	1	6.7	1	6.7	4	26.7	11	73.3	0	.0	15
3	3.8	3	3.8	1	1.3	8	10.3	68	87.2	2	2.6	78
0	.0	1	2.6	1	2.6	2	5.3	36	94.7	0	.0	38
3	7.5	2	5.0	0	.0	6	15.0	32	80.0	2	5.0	40
1	3.6	0	.0	1	3.6	2	7.1	24	85.7	2	7.1	28
1	5.9	0	.0	1	5.9	2	11.8	13	76.5	2	11.8	17
0	.0	0	.0	0	.0	0	.0	11	100.0	0	.0	11
436	11.7	134	3.6	113	3.0	704	18.9	2,775	74.6	241	6.5	3,720
232	21.8	43	4.0	43	4.0	323	30.3	688	64.6	54	5.1	1,065
204	7.7	91	3.4	70	2.6	381	14.4	2,087	78.6	187	7.0	2,655
6	3.8	6	3.8	8	5.0	21	13.2	138	86.8	0	.0	159
4	4.9	3	3.7	4	4.9	11	13.4	71	86.6	0	.0	82
2	2.6	3	3.9	4	5.2	10	13.0	67	87.0	0	.0	77
0	.0	4	9.5	3	7.1	7	16.7	32	76.2	3	7.1	42
0	.0	2	22.2	0	.0	2	22.2	7	77.8	0	.0	9
0	.0	2	6.1	3	9.1	5	15.2	25	75.9	3	9.1	33
4	4.1	1	1.0	17	17.5	22	22.7	70	72.2	5	5.2	97
0	.0	0	.0	0	.0	0	.0	0	.0	0	.0	0
4	4.1	1	1.0	17	17.5	22	22.7	70	72.2	5	5.2	97
7	1.3	3	.5	12	2.2	23	4.2	511	93.4	13	2.4	547
4	1.4	1	.3	9	3.1	15	5.2	269	93.7	3	1.0	287
3	1.2	2	.8	3	1.2	8	3.1	242	93.1	10	3.8	260
0	.0	2	2.6	5	6.4	7	9.0	71	91.0	0	.0	78
0	.0	0	.0	0	.0	0	.0	0	.0	0	.0	0
0	.0	2	2.6	5	6.4	7	9.0	71	91.0	0	.0	78
4	3.3	5	4.2	6	5.0	17	14.2	93	77.5	10	8.3	120
0	.0	3	5.6	3	5.6	7	13.0	44	81.5	3	5.6	54
4	6.1	2	3.0	3	4.5	10	15.2	49	74.2	7	10.6	66
0	.0	0	.0	1	3.0	1	3.0	30	90.9	2	6.1	33
0	.0	0	.0	0	.0	0	.0	12	92.3	1	7.7	13
0	.0	0	.0	1	5.0	1	5.0	18	90.0	1	5.0	20
26	3.3	14	1.8	3	.4	43	5.5	720	91.7	22	2.8	785
4	4.5	1	1.1	0	.0	5	5.7	82	93.2	1	1.1	88
22	3.2	13	1.9	3	.4	38	5.5	638	91.5	21	3.0	697
3	4.2	3	4.2	1	1.4	7	9.7	60	83.3	5	6.9	72
1	5.0	0	.0	0	.0	1	5.0	17	85.0	2	10.0	20
2	3.8	3	5.8	1	1.9	6	11.5	43	82.7	3	5.8	52
0	.0	0	.0	1	5.9	1	5.9	16	94.1	0	.0	17
0	.0	0	.0	0	.0	0	.0	5	100.0	0	.0	5
0	.0	0	.0	1	8.3	1	8.3	11	91.7	0	.0	12
1	1.3	5	6.3	2	2.5	8	10.1	58	73.4	13	16.5	79
0	.0	1	4.2	0	.0	1	4.2	20	83.3	3	12.5	24
1	1.8	4	7.3	2	3.6	7	12.7	38	69.1	10	18.2	55
138	2.8	167	3.4	115	2.3	434	8.8	3,282	66.2	1,238	25.0	4,954
59	4.9	53	4.4	42	3.5	160	13.3	858	71.3	186	15.4	1,204
79	2.1	114	3.0	73	1.9	274	7.3	2,424	64.6	1,052	28.1	3,750
40	3.0	26	1.9	80	5.9	150	11.1	925	68.7	271	20.1	1,346
19	3.4	9	1.6	33	5.9	63	11.4	449	80.9	43	7.7	555
21	2.7	17	2.1	47	5.9	87	11.0	476	60.2	228	28.8	791
244	3.0	517	6.3	238	2.9	1,046	12.8	5,911	72.1	1,243	15.2	8,200
121	4.3	174	6.2	85	3.0	406	14.5	2,190	78.4	199	7.1	2,795
123	2.3	343	6.3	153	2.8	640	11.8	3,721	68.9	1,044	19.3	5,405

	AMERICAN INDIAN ALASKAN NATIVE		BLACK NON-HISPANIC		ASIAN OR PACIFIC ISLANDER		HISPANIC		TOTAL MINORITY		WHITE NON-HISPANIC		NON-RESIDENT ALIEN	
	NUMBER	%	NUMBER	%	NUMBER	%	NUMBER	%	NUMBER	%	NUMBER	%	NUMBER	%
CALIFORNIA	CONTINUED													
U OF CAL-DAVIS														
CA TOTAL	8	.3	18	.6	119	4.1	54	1.9	199	6.9	2,134	73.7	563	19.4
CA FEMALE	2	.2	8	.8	39	4.1	21	2.2	70	7.4	777	82.5	95	10.1
CA MALE	6	.3	10	.5	80	4.1	33	1.7	129	6.6	1,357	69.4	468	24.0
U OF CAL-IRVINE														
CA TOTAL	0	.0	21	1.5	81	6.0	106	7.8	208	15.3	1,060	77.9	93	.8
CA FEMALE	0	.0	10	1.8	25	4.0	47	8.6	82	15.0	442	81.0	22	.0
CA MALE	0	.0	11	1.3	56	6.8	59	7.2	126	15.5	618	75.8	71	8.7
U OF CAL-LOS ANGELES														
CA TOTAL	41	.5	293	3.7	494	2.0	377	4.7	1,205	15.1	5,651	70.9	1,119	1.0
CA FEMALE	21	.6	160	4.7	228	6.7	156	4.6	565	16.6	2,546	74.9	290	.5
CA MALE	20	.4	133	2.9	266	8.8	221	4.8	640	14.0	3,105	67.9	829	18.1
U OF CAL-RIVERSIDE														
CA TOTAL	3	.2	27	2.1	37	2.	62	4.8	129	9.9	959	73.9	210	1.2
CA FEMALE	1	.2	14	2.9	14	2.	29	6.1	58	12.2	370	77.9	47	4.9
CA MALE	2	.2	13	1.6	23	2.0	33	4.0	71	8.6	589	71.6	163	19.8
U OF CAL-SAN DIEGO														
CA TOTAL	6	.4	18	1.2	42	2.9	45	3.1	111	7.6	1,150	78.7	200	13.7
CA FEMALE	0	.0	7	1.6	20	4.6	18	4.1	45	10.3	337	77.1	55	12.6
CA MALE	6	.6	11	1.1	22	2.1	27	2.6	66	6.4	813	79.4	145	14.2
U OF CAL-SAN FRANCISCO														
CA TOTAL	2	.3	26	3.7	39	5.5	13	1.8	80	11.3	598	84.2	32	4.5
CA FEMALE	2	.4	19	3.8	23	4.6	11	2.2	55	10.9	431	85.7	17	3.4
CA MALE	0	.0	7	3.4	16	7.7	2	1.0	25	12.1	167	80.7	15	7.2
U OF CAL-SANTA BARBARA														
CA TOTAL	4	.2	36	1.9	58	3.1	124	6.7	222	11.9	1,353	72.7	287	15.4
CA FEMALE	1	.1	15	2.2	18	2.7	51	7.5	85	12.6	524	77.5	67	9.9
CA MALE	3	.3	21	1.8	40	3.4	73	6.2	137	11.6	929	69.9	220	18.5
U OF CAL-SANTA CRUZ														
CA TOTAL	3	.9	8	2.3	9	2.6	11	3.2	31	9.0	280	80.9	35	10.1
CA FEMALE	2	1.9	3	2.9	3	2.9	5	4.8	13	12.4	86	81.9	6	5.7
CA MALE	1	.4	5	2.1	6	2.5	6	2.5	18	7.5	194	80.5	29	12.0
UNIVERSITY OF JUDAISM														
CA TOTAL	0	.0	0	.0	0	.0	0	.0	0	.0	97	100.0	0	.0
CA FEMALE	0	.0	0	.0	0	.0	0	.0	0	.0	61	100.0	0	.0
CA MALE	0	.0	0	.0	0	.0	0	.0	0	.0	36	100.0	0	.0
UNIVERSITY OF LA VERNE														
CA TOTAL	4	.3	75	6.4	9	.8	88	7.6	176	15.1	877	75.4	110	9.5
CA FEMALE	2	.5	27	6.1	2	.5	37	8.4	68	15.4	355	80.5	18	4.1
CA MALE	2	.3	48	6.6	7	1.0	51	7.1	108	15.0	522	72.5	92	12.7
UNIVERSITY OF THE PACIFIC														
CA TOTAL	1	.3	8	2.0	47	11.8	42	10.6	98	24.6	271	68.1	29	7.3
CA FEMALE	1	.4	5	2.0	31	12.7	23	9.4	60	24.6	173	70.9	11	4.5
CA MALE	0	.0	3	1.9	16	10.4	19	12.3	38	24.7	98	63.6	18	11.7
UNIVERSITY OF REDLANDS														
CA TOTAL	2	.4	113	9.6	44	.	28	2.4	187	16.0	984	84.0	1	.1
CA FEMALE	0	.0	57	8.5	25	.0	17	2.5	99	14.7	572	85.1	1	.1
CA MALE	2	.4	56	11.2	19	3.8	11	2.2	88	17.6	412	82.4	0	.0
UNIVERSITY OF SAN DIEGO														
CA TOTAL	0	.0	17	3.7	9	2.0	33	7.3	59	13.0	383	84.4	12	2.6
CA FEMALE	0	.0	13	4.9	6	2.2	19	7.1	38	14.2	223	83.5	6	2.2
CA MALE	0	.0	4	2.1	3	1.6	14	7.5	21	11.2	160	85.6	6	3.2
U OF SAN FRANCISCO														
CA TOTAL	7	.5	147	10.4	211	14.9	130	9.2	495	35.0	732	51.7	188	13.3
CA FEMALE	7	.9	107	14.5	120	16.2	67	9.1	301	40.7	394	53.2	45	6.1
CA MALE	0	.0	40	5.9	91	13.5	63	9.3	194	28.7	338	50.1	143	21.2
UNIVERSITY OF SANTA CLARA														
CA TOTAL	1	.0	28	1.1	204	7.	32	1.2	265	10.3	2,007	78.2	296	11.5
CA FEMALE	1	.1	6	.7	34	4.0	9	1.1	50	5.9	744	87.1	60	7.0
CA MALE	0	.0	22	1.3	170	9.8	23	1.3	215	12.5	1,263	73.7	236	13.8
U OF SOUTHERN CALIFORNIA														
CA TOTAL	70	.7	366	3.8	511	5.3	345	3.6	1,292	13.4	6,771	70.1	1,598	16.5
CA FEMALE	21	.7	191	6.4	183	6.1	141	4.7	536	17.9	2,119	70.9	333	11.1
CA MALE	49	.7	175	2.6	328	4.9	204	3.1	756	11.3	4,652	69.7	1,265	19.0
WEST COAST U MAIN CAMPUS														
CA TOTAL	0	.0	16	3.2	31	6.1	13	2.6	60	11.9	288	56.9	158	31.2
CA FEMALE	0	.0	1	1.5	4	5.9	0	.0	5	7.4	29	42.6	34	50.0
CA MALE	0	.0	15	3.4	27	6.2	13	3.0	55	12.6	259	59.1	124	28.3
W COAST U ORANGE CO CTR														
CA TOTAL	0	.0	1	.6	7	3.	2	1.1	10	5.6	134	74.9	35	19.6
CA FEMALE	0	.0	0	.0	0	.0	0	.0	0	.0	13	61.9	8	38.1
CA MALE	0	.0	1	.6	7	4.8	2	1.3	10	6.3	121	76.6	27	17.1
WHITTIER COLLEGE														
CA TOTAL	0	.0	1	1.5	4	6.1	7	10.6	12	18.2	53	80.3	1	1.5
CA FEMALE	0	.0	0	.0	2	5.0	2	5.0	4	10.0	35	87.5	1	2.5
CA MALE	0	.0	1	3.8	2	7.7	5	19.2	8	30.8	18	69.2	0	.0
WOODBURY UNIVERSITY														
CA TOTAL	1	1.4	5	7.0	7	9.9	6	8.5	19	26.8	22	31.0	30	42.3
CA FEMALE	0	.0	0	.0	1	5.3	2	10.5	3	15.8	3	15.8	13	68.4
CA MALE	1	1.9	5	9.6	6	11.5	4	7.7	16	30.8	19	36.5	17	32.7
THE WRIGHT INSTITUTE														
CA TOTAL	0	.0	7	8.0	2	2.	6	6.8	15	17.0	72	81.8	1	1.1
CA FEMALE	0	.0	6	10.0	1	1.	2	3.3	9	15.0	51	85.0	0	.0
CA MALE	0	.0	1	3.6	1	3.8	4	14.3	6	21.4	21	75.0	1	3.6
CALIFORNIA		TOTAL (	111 INSTITUTIONS)											
CA TOTAL	694	.6	4,700	4.1	6,193	5.	4,659	4.1	16,246	14.3	86,064	75.7	11,432	10.1
CA FEMALE	293	.6	2,505	5.4	2,499	5.	2,037	4.4	7,334	15.8	36,674	78.8	2,505	5.4
CA MALE	401	.6	2,195	3.3	3,694	5.8	2,622	3.9	8,912	13.3	49,390	73.5	8,927	13.3

N E	BLACK NON-HISPANIC		ASIAN OR PACIFIC ISLANDER		HISPANIC		TOTAL MINORITY		WHITE NON-HISPANIC		NON-RESIDENT ALIEN		TOTAL
	NUMBER	%	NUMBER	%	NUMBER	%	NUMBER	%	NUMBER	%	NUMBER	%	NUMBER
	5	.9	0	.0	154	27.9	159	28.8	386	69.9	7	1.3	552
	2	.7	0	.0	81	28.1	83	28.8	203	70.5	2	.7	288
	3	1.1	0	.0	73	27.7	76	28.8	183	69.3	5	1.9	264
	0	.0	0	.0	0	.0	0	.0	12	100.0	0	.0	12
	0	.0	0	.0	0	.0	0	.0	8	100.0	0	.0	8
	0	.0	0	.0	0	.0	0	.0	4	100.0	0	.0	4
	0	.0	1	.2	3	.6	7	1.5	329	68.4	145	30.1	481
	0	.0	0	.0	0	.0	0	.0	39	84.8	7	15.2	46
	0	.0	1	.2	3	.7	7	1.6	290	66.7	138	31.7	435
	31	1.3	18	.7	19	.8	76	3.1	1,952	80.8	388	16.1	2,416
	11	1.5	10	1.4	6	.8	30	4.1	637	88.1	56	7.7	723
	20	1.2	8	.5	13	.8	46	2.7	1,315	77.7	332	19.6	1,693
	2	1.9	2	1.9	1	1.0	5	4.8	97	93.3	2	1.9	104
	0	.0	2	6.9	0	.0	2	6.9	27	93.1	0	.0	29
	2	2.7	0	.0	1	1.3	3	4.0	70	93.3	2	2.7	75
	1	1.4	0	.0	0	.0	1	1.4	68	94.4	3	4.2	72
	0	.0	0	.0	0	.0	0	.0	7	100.0	0	.0	7
	1	1.5	0	.0	0	.0	1	1.5	61	93.8	3	4.6	65
	0	.0	0	.0	0	.0	0	.0	7	100.0	0	.0	7
	0	.0	0	.0	0	.0	0	.0	1	100.0	0	.0	1
	0	.0	0	.0	0	.0	0	.0	6	100.0	0	.0	6
	46	1.4	37	1.1	85	2.5	172	5.1	2,928	86.9	269	8.0	3,369
	19	1.4	13	1.0	30	2.2	63	4.7	1,240	91.9	47	3.5	1,350
	27	1.3	24	1.2	55	2.7	109	5.4	1,688	83.6	222	11.0	2,019
	14	2.8	2	.4	18	3.6	34	6.9	461	93.1	0	.0	495
	2	.9	0	.0	8	3.6	10	4.5	212	95.5	0	.0	222
	12	4.4	2	.7	10	3.7	24	8.8	249	91.2	0	.0	273
	39	2.1	26	1.4	59	3.2	127	6.9	1,674	90.7	44	2.4	1,845
	22	2.6	12	1.4	23	2.7	59	7.0	767	91.5	12	1.4	838
	17	1.7	14	1.4	36	3.6	68	6.8	907	90.1	32	3.2	1,007
	10	2.5	16	4.0	12	3.0	40	10.0	360	90.0	0	.0	400
	9	3.2	7	2.5	8	2.9	26	9.3	253	90.7	0	.0	279
	1	.8	9	7.4	4	3.3	14	11.6	107	88.4	0	.0	121
	42	1.9	28	1.2	40	1.8	132	5.9	1,979	87.7	145	6.4	2,256
	19	1.5	15	1.2	22	1.8	70	5.7	1,111	90.4	48	3.9	1,229
	23	2.2	13	1.3	18	1.8	62	6.0	868	84.5	97	9.4	1,027
	32	2.7	14	1.2	40	3.4	90	7.6	998	84.5	93	7.9	1,181
	15	2.4	5	.8	21	3.4	43	7.0	554	89.9	19	3.1	616
	17	3.0	9	1.6	19	3.4	47	8.3	444	78.6	74	13.1	565
	0	.0	0	.0	0	.0	0	.0	8	100.0	0	.0	8
	0	.0	0	.0	0	.0	0	.0	3	100.0	0	.0	3
	0	.0	0	.0	0	.0	0	.0	5	100.0	0	.0	5
	1	.6	1	.6	0	.0	3	1.8	160	97.6	1	.6	164
	1	1.3	0	.0	0	.0	1	1.3	75	98.7	0	.0	76
	0	.0	1	1.1	0	.0	2	2.3	85	96.6	1	1.1	88
	0	.0	0	.0	0	.0	0	.0	3	100.0	0	.0	3
	0	.0	0	.0	0	.0	0	.0	0	.0	0	.0	0
	0	.0	0	.0	0	.0	0	.0	3	100.0	0	.0	3
(16 INSTITUTIONS)	223	1.7	145	1.1	431	3.2	846	6.3	11,422	85.5	1,097	8.2	13,365
	100	1.7	64	1.1	199	3.5	387	6.8	5,137	89.9	191	3.3	5,715
	123	1.6	81	1.1	232	3.0	459	6.0	6,285	82.2	906	11.8	7,650
	0	.0	0	.0	0	.0	0	.0	12	100.0	0	.0	12
	0	.0	0	.0	0	.0	0	.0	0	.0	0	.0	0
	0	.0	0	.0	0	.0	0	.0	12	100.0	0	.0	12
	31	1.5	10	.5	13	.6	57	2.7	2,039	97.3	0	.0	2,096
	22	1.6	5	.4	9	.7	37	2.7	1,342	97.3	0	.0	1,379
	9	1.3	5	.7	4	.6	20	2.8	697	97.2	0	.0	717
	0	.0	1	1.7	0	.0	1	1.7	56	96.6	1	1.7	58
	0	.0	0	.0	0	.0	0	.0	38	97.4	1	2.6	39
	0	.0	1	5.3	0	.0	1	5.3	18	94.7	0	.0	19
	10	3.1	1	.3	0	.0	15	4.6	310	95.4	0	.0	325
	9	3.8	1	.4	0	.0	13	5.5	224	94.5	0	.0	237
	1	1.1	0	.0	0	.0	2	2.3	86	97.7	0	.0	88
	17	1.6	2	.2	11	1.0	30	2.8	1,030	95.7	16	1.5	1,076
	8	1.1	1	.1	7	.9	16	2.1	732	97.2	5	.7	753
	9	2.8	1	.3	4	1.2	14	4.3	298	92.3	11	3.4	323

TABLE 2 - TOTAL GRADUATE ENROLLMENT IN INSTITUTIONS OF HIGHER EDUCATION BY RACE, ETHNICITY AND SEX: INSTITUTION, STATE AND NATION, 1978

	AMERICAN INDIAN ALASKAN NATIVE		BLACK NON-HISPANIC		ASIAN OR PACIFIC ISLANDER		HISPANIC		TOTAL MINORITY		WHITE NON-HISPANIC		NON-RESIDENT ALIEN		
	NUMBER	%	NUMBER	%	NUMBER	%	NUMBER	%	NUMBER	%	NUMBER	%	NUMBER	%	
CONNECTICUT	CONTINUED														
HARTFORD GRADUATE CENTER															
CT TOTAL	0	.0	9	1.1	15	1.9	6	.7	30	3.7	773	95.8	4	.5	
CT FEMALE	0	.0	1	.6	9	5.8	0	.0	10	6.4	145	92.9	1	.6	
CT MALE	0	.0	8	1.2	6	.9	6	.9	20	3.1	628	96.5	3	.5	
HARTFORD SEM FOUNDATION															
CT TOTAL	0	.0	4	7.7	2	3.8	0	.0	6	11.5	46	88.5	0	.0	
CT FEMALE	0	.0	0	.0	0	.0	0	.0	0	.0	7	100.0	0	.0	
CT MALE	0	.0	4	8.9	2	4.4	0	.0	6	13.3	39	86.7	0	.0	
HOLY APOSTLES COLLEGE															
CT TOTAL	0	.0	0	.0	0	.0	0	.0	0	.0	6	100.0	0	.0	
CT FEMALE	0	.0	0	.0	0	.0	0	.0	0	.0	0	.0	0	.0	
CT MALE	0	.0	0	.0	0	.0	0	.0	0	.0	6	100.0	0	.0	
QUINNIPIAC COLLEGE															
CT TOTAL	0	.0	1	.4	0	.0	2	.8	3	1.2	243	98.8	0	.0	
CT FEMALE	0	.0	1	.8	0	.0	1	.8	2	1.7	116	98.3	0	.0	
CT MALE	0	.0	0	.0	0	.0	1	.8	1	.8	127	99.2	0	.0	
SACRED HEART UNIVERSITY															
CT TOTAL	0	.0	5	2.2	1	.4	2	.9	8	3.6	213	94.7	4	1.8	
CT FEMALE	0	.0	2	3.1	0	.0	1	1.6	3	4.7	61	95.3	0	.0	
CT MALE	0	.0	3	1.9	1	.6	1	.6	5	3.1	152	94.4	4	2.5	
SAINT JOSEPH COLLEGE															
CT TOTAL	0	.0	3	.7	0	.0	3	.7	6	1.5	394	98.3	1	.2	
CT FEMALE	0	.0	3	.9	0	.0	1	.3	4	1.2	328	98.5	1	.3	
CT MALE	0	.0	0	.0	0	.0	2	2.9	2	2.9	66	97.1	0	.0	
SOUTHERN CONN ST COLLEGE															
CT TOTAL	0	.0	25	1.3	3	.2	10	.5	38	2.0	1,840	97.8	4	.2	
CT FEMALE	0	.0	13	1.0	3	.2	6	.5	22	1.7	1,208	98.1	3	.2	
CT MALE	0	.0	12	2.1	0	.0	4	.7	16	2.8	552	97.0	1	.2	
TRINITY COLLEGE															
CT TOTAL	0	.0	3	1.0	0	.0	0	.0	3	1.0	287	98.6	1	.3	
CT FEMALE	0	.0	2	1.6	0	.0	0	.0	2	1.6	126	98.4	0	.0	
CT MALE	0	.0	1	.6	0	.0	0	.0	1	.6	161	98.8	1	.6	
UNIVERSITY OF BRIDGEPORT															
CT TOTAL	0	.0	16	.8	3	.2	0	.0	19	1.0	1,840	92.8	124	6.3	
CT FEMALE	0	.0	8	.8	1	.1	0	.0	9	.9	947	96.9	21	2.1	
CT MALE	0	.0	8	.8	2	.2	0	.0	10	1.0	893	88.8	103	10.2	
UNIVERSITY OF CONNECTICUT															
CT TOTAL	4	.1	75	1.8	26	.6	51	1.2	156	3.8	3,858	93.7	103	2.5	
CT FEMALE	1	.1	47	2.6	9	.5	23	1.3	80	4.5	1,679	93.7	33	1.8	
CT MALE	3	.1	28	1.2	17	.7	28	1.2	76	3.3	2,179	93.7	70	3.0	
UNIVERSITY OF HARTFORD															
CT TOTAL	1	.0	83	2.9	23	.8	33	1.2	140	4.9	2,703	95.1	0	.0	
CT FEMALE	1	.1	46	4.0	7	.6	15	1.3	69	6.0	1,083	94.0	0	.0	
CT MALE	0	.0	37	2.2	16	.9	18	1.1	71	4.2	1,620	95.8	0	.0	
UNIVERSITY OF NEW HAVEN															
CT TOTAL	0	.0	187	9.2	11	.5	55	2.7	253	12.5	1,713	84.4	63	3.1	
CT FEMALE	0	.0	40	7.6	6	1.2	15	2.9	61	11.7	448	85.7	14	2.7	
CT MALE	0	.0	147	9.8	5	.3	40	2.7	192	12.7	1,265	84.0	49	3.3	
WESLEYAN UNIVERSITY															
CT TOTAL	0	.0	8	2.9	11	4.0	1	.4	20	7.4	245	90.1	7	2.6	
CT FEMALE	0	.0	5	3.4	3	2.1	0	.0	8	5.5	134	92.4	3	2.1	
CT MALE	0	.0	3	2.4	8	6.3	1	.8	12	9.4	111	87.4	4	3.1	
WESTERN CONN ST COLLEGE															
CT TOTAL	4	.3	17	1.4	1	.1	0	.0	22	1.8	1,174	97.3	10	.8	
CT FEMALE	3	.4	9	1.2	1	.1	0	.0	13	1.8	716	97.5	5	.7	
CT MALE	1	.2	8	1.7	0	.0	0	.0	9	1.9	458	97.0	5	1.1	
YALE UNIVERSITY															
CT TOTAL	7	.2	83	2.7	41	1.3	138	4.5	269	8.8	2,372	77.7	411	13.5	
CT FEMALE	4	.3	42	3.6	19	1.6	45	3.8	110	9.3	980	83.0	91	7.7	
CT MALE	3	.2	41	2.2	22	1.2	93	5.0	159	8.5	1,392	74.4	320	17.1	
CONNECTICUT	TOTAL (	20 INSTITUTIONS)													
CT TOTAL	23	.1	577	2.5	151	.7	325	1.4	1,076	4.7	21,154	92.1	749	3.3	
CT FEMALE	13	.1	258	2.3	65	.6	123	1.1	459	4.2	10,394	94.2	178	1.6	
CT MALE	10	.1	319	2.7	86	.7	202	1.7	617	5.2	10,760	90.1	571	4.8	
DELAWARE															
UNIVERSITY OF DELAWARE															
DE TOTAL	2	.1	27	1.9	4	.3	4	.3	37	2.7	1,268	91.2	85	6.1	
DE FEMALE	0	.0	15	2.3	1	.2	3	.5	19	2.9	615	94.3	18	2.8	
DE MALE	2	.3	12	1.6	3	.4	1	.1	18	2.4	653	88.5	67	9.1	
WILMINGTON COLLEGE															
DE TOTAL	0	.0	30	33.0	4	4.4	0	.0	34	37.4	55	60.4	2	2.2	
DE FEMALE	0	.0	4	50.0	0	.0	0	.0	4	50.0	4	50.0	0	.0	
DE MALE	0	.0	26	31.3	4	4.8	0	.0	30	36.1	51	61.4	2	2.4	
DELAWARE	TOTAL (	2 INSTITUTIONS)													
DE TOTAL	2	.1	57	3.8	8	.5	4	.3	71	4.8	1,323	89.3	87	5.9	
DE FEMALE	0	.0	19	2.9	1	.2	3	.5	23	3.5	619	93.8	18	2.7	
DE MALE	2	.2	38	4.6	7	.9	1	.1	48	5.8	704	85.7	69	8.4	
DISTRICT OF COLUMBIA															
AMERICAN UNIVERSITY															
DC TOTAL	6	.2	219	6.9	58	1.8	41	1.3	324	10.2	2,403	75.7	447	14.1	
DC FEMALE	1	.1	112	8.7	25	1.9	17	1.3	155	12.1	997	77.5	134	10.4	
DC MALE	5	.3	107	5.7	33	1.7	24	1.3	169	9.0	1,406	74.5	313	16.6	
CAMPUS-FREE COLLEGE															
DC TOTAL	0	.0	5	6.4	0	.0	0	.0	5	6.4	73	93.6	0	.0	
DC FEMALE	0	.0	1	2.1	0	.0	0	.0	1	2.1	47	97.9	0	.0	
DC MALE	0	.0	4	13.3	0	.0	0	.0	4	13.3	26	86.7	0	.0	

142

N E	BLACK NON-HISPANIC		ASIAN OR PACIFIC ISLANDER		HISPANIC		TOTAL MINORITY		WHITE NON-HISPANIC		NON-RESIDENT ALIEN		TOTAL
	NUMBER	%	NUMBER	%	NUMBER	%	NUMBER	%	NUMBER	%	NUMBER	%	NUMBER
INUED													
	200	5.3	84	2.2	49	1.3	336	8.8	3,148	82.8	320	8.4	3,804
	129	7.3	38	2.1	23	1.3	190	10.7	1,447	81.6	137	7.7	1,774
	71	3.5	46	2.3	26	1.3	146	7.2	1,701	83.8	183	9.0	2,030
	0	.0	0	.0	0	.0	0	0	7	100.0		.0	7
	0	.0	0	.0	0	.0	0	0	1	100.0	0	.0	1
	0	.0	0	.0	0	.0	0	10	6	100.0	0	.0	6
	8	4.0	0	.0	3	1.5	11	5 5	171	85.1	19	9.5	201
	7	4.7	0	.0	3	2.0	10	6 7	128	85.9	11	7.4	149
	1	1.9	0	.0	0	.0	1	119	43	82.7	8	15.4	52
	56	2.6	28	1.3	36	1.7	124	5.8	1,706	79.1	326	15.1	2,156
	28	3.7	13	1.7	16	2.1	58	7.7	577	76.9	115	15.3	750
	28	2.0	15	1.1	20	1.4	66	4.7	1,129	80.3	211	15.0	1,406
	634	7.9	214	2.7	130	1.6	1,001	12.5	6,274	78.4	728	9.1	8,003
	356	12.0	40	1.3	47	1.6	446	15.0	2,347	78.9	180	6.1	2,973
	278	5.5	174	3.5	83	1.7	555	11.0	3,927	78.1	548	10.9	5,030
	1,222	62.5	27	1.4	5	.3	1,255	64.2	80	4.1	619	31.7	1,954
	720	77.8	9	1.0	1	.1	731	79.0	33	3.6	161	17.4	925
	502	48.8	18	1.7	4	.4	524	50.9	47	4.6	458	44.5	1,029
	167	29.7	27	4.8	9	1.6	208	37.0	164	29.2	190	33.8	562
	61	53.0	3	2.6	1	.9	67	58.3	30	26.1	18	15.7	115
	106	23.7	24	5.4	8	1.8	141	31.5	134	30.0	172	38.5	447
	217	78.1	6	2.2	4	1.4	227	81.7	51	18.3	0	.0	278
	197	79.1	3	1.2	4	1.6	204	81.9	45	18.1	0	.0	249
	20	69.0	3	10.3	0	.0	23	79.3	6	20.7	0	.0	29
	290	86.1	11	3.3	2	.6	307	91.1	12	3.6	18	5.3	337
	183	90.6	2	1.0	2	1.0	187	92.6	4	2.0	11	5.4	202
	107	79.3	9	6.7	0	.0	120	88.9	8	5.9	7	5.2	135
	2	3.5	0	.0	0	.0	2	3.5	53	93.0	2	3.5	57
	1	4.2	0	.0	0	.0	1	4.2	23	95.8	0	.0	24
	1	3.0	0	.0	0	.0	1	3.0	30	90.9	2	6.1	33
(12 INSTITUTIONS)													
	3,020	14.7	455	2.2	279	1.4	3,800	18.4	14,142	68.6	2,669	12.9	20,611
	1,795	21.1	133	1.6	114	1.3	2,050	24.1	5,679	66.8	767	9.0	8,496
	1,225	10.1	322	2.7	165	1.4	1,750	14.4	8,463	69.9	1,902	15.7	12,115
	39	7.0	2	.4	72	13.0	115	20.7	432	77.8	8	1.4	555
	27	6.4	0	.0	60	14.2	89	21.0	333	78.7	1	.2	423
	12	9.1	2	1.5	12	9.1	26	19.7	99	75.0	7	5.3	132
	69	25.7	0	.0	51	19.0	120	44.8	146	54.5	2	.7	268
	37	32.2	0	.0	33	28.7	70	60.9	45	39.1	0	.0	115
	32	20.9	0	.0	18	11.8	50	32.7	101	66.0	2	1.3	153
	29	16.1	7	3.9	2	1.1	38	21.1	142	78.9		.0	180
	0	.0	0	.0	0	.0	0	.0	0	.0	0	.0	0
	29	16.1	7	3.9	2	1.1	38	21.1	142	78.9	0	.0	180
	74	4.7	8	.5	22	1.4	109	6.9	1,325	83.4	155	9.8	1,589
	21	8.4	1	.4	3	1.2	25	10.0	205	81.7	21	8.4	251
	53	4.0	7	.5	19	1.4	84	6.3	1,120	83.7	134	10.0	1,338
	15	11.9	2	1.6	1	.8	18	14.3	106	84.1	2	1.6	126
	7	12.5	0	.0	0	.0	7	12.5	48	85.7	1	1.8	56
	8	11.4	2	2.9	1	1.4	11	15.7	58	82.9	1	1.4	70
	4	3.6	2	1.8	4	3.6	10	9.1	98	89.1	2	1.8	110
	3	4.8	1	1.6	3	4.8	7	11.1	55	87.3	1	1.6	63
	1	2.1	1	2.1	1	2.1	3	6.4	43	91.5	1	2.1	47
	5	9.4	0	.0	2	3.8	7	13.2	46	86.8	0	.0	53
	2	50.0	0	.0	0	.0	2	50.0	2	50.0	0	.0	4
	3	6.1	0	.0	2	4.1	5	10.2	44	89.8	0	.0	49
	946	22.5	47	1.1	115	2.7	1,120	26.6	3,008	71.5	79	1.9	4,207
	565	30.0	17	.9	49	2.6	633	33.6	1,243	66.0	7	.4	1,883
	381	16.4	30	1.3	66	2.8	487	21.0	1,765	75.9	72	3.1	2,324
	105	7.8	8	.6	22	1.6	135	10.0	1,211	89.4	8	.5	1,354
	59	10.8	3	.6	10	1.8	72	13.2	472	86.6	1	.2	545
	46	5.7	5	.6	12	1.5	63	7.8	739	91.3	7	.9	809
	1	1.4	0	.0	17	24.6	18	26.1	50	72.5	1	1.4	69
	0	.0	0	.0	0	.0	0	.0	0	.0	0	.0	0
	1	1.4	0	.0	17	24.6	18	26.1	50	72.5	1	1.4	69
	438	66.6	2	.3	1	.2	441	67.0	210	31.9	7	1.1	658
	311	77.0	1	.2	0	.0	312	77.2	90	22.3	2	.5	404
	127	50.0	1	.4	1	.4	129	50.8	120	47.2	5	2.0	254

143

TABLE 2 - TOTAL GRADUATE ENROLLMENT IN INSTITUTIONS OF HIGHER EDUCATION BY RACE, ETHNICITY AND SEX:
INSTITUTION, STATE AND NATION, 1978

	AMERICAN INDIAN ALASKAN NATIVE		BLACK NON-HISPANIC		ASIAN OR PACIFIC ISLANDER		HISPANIC		TOTAL MINORITY		WHITE NON-HISPANIC		NON-RESIDENT ALIEN	
	NUMBER	%	NUMBER	%	NUMBER	%	NUMBER	%	NUMBER	%	NUMBER	%	NUMBER	%
FLORIDA		CONTINUED												
FLA ATLANTIC UNIVERSITY														
FL TOTAL	1	.1	41	4.3	6	.6	25	2.6	73	7.7	862	90.8	14	1.5
FL FEMALE	1	.2	26	5.1	3	.6	12	2.3	42	8.2	466	91.2	3	.6
FL MALE	0	.0	15	3.4	3	.7	13	3.0	31	7.1	396	90.4	11	2.5
FLORIDA INTERNATIONAL U														
FL TOTAL	2	.2	77	7.1	21	1.9	181	16.7	281	25.9	773	71.2	31	2.
FL FEMALE	1	.2	49	8.7	7	1.2	90	16.0	147	26.2	399	71.0	16	2.
FL MALE	1	.2	28	5.4	14	2.7	91	17.4	134	25.6	374	71.5	15	2.8
FLORIDA STATE UNIVERSITY														
FL TOTAL	8	.2	198	5.7	10	.3	54	1.6	270	7.8	2,969	85.5	235	6.
FL FEMALE	2	.1	118	7.1	5	.3	30	1.8	155	9.3	1,448	87.2	57	3.
FL MALE	6	.3	80	4.4	5	.3	24	1.3	115	6.3	1,521	83.8	178	9.8
FLORIDA TECHNOLOGICAL U														
FL TOTAL	1	.1	40	4.5	10	1.1	23	2.6	74	8.3	818	91.4	3	.3
FL FEMALE	1	.2	26	5.2	2	.4	7	1.4	36	7.2	480	92.6	1	.2
FL MALE	0	.0	14	3.5	8	2.0	16	4.0	38	9.5	358	89.9	2	.5
UNIVERSITY OF FLORIDA														
FL TOTAL	5	.1	135	3.3	35	.8	118	2.8	293	7.1	3,351	80.9	499	12.0
FL FEMALE	2	.1	78	5.1	12	.8	52	3.4	144	9.4	1,296	84.7	90	5.9
FL MALE	3	.1	57	2.2	23	.9	66	2.5	149	5.7	2,055	78.6	409	15.7
U OF NORTH FLORIDA														
FL TOTAL	1	.1	51	5.8	1	.1	7	.8	60	6.8	817	92.3	8	.9
FL FEMALE	1	.2	35	7.6	0	.0	2	.4	38	8.2	423	91.4	2	.4
FL MALE	0	.0	16	3.8	1	.2	5	1.2	22	5.2	394	93.4	6	1.4
U OF SOUTH FLORIDA														
FL TOTAL	3	.1	56	2.4	4	.2	29	1.2	92	3.9	2,237	95.4	15	.6
FL FEMALE	1	.1	30	2.4	3	.2	13	1.0	47	3.8	1,196	95.9	4	.3
FL MALE	2	.2	26	2.4	1	.1	16	1.5	45	4.1	1,041	94.9	11	1.0
U OF WEST FLORIDA														
FL TOTAL	3	.4	43	5.0	22	2.6	6	.7	74	8.6	781	91.1	2	.2
FL FEMALE	1	.3	25	7.1	8	2.3	2	.6	36	10.2	315	89.2	2	.6
FL MALE	2	.4	18	3.6	14	2.8	4	.8	38	7.5	466	92.5	0	.0
STETSON UNIVERSITY														
FL TOTAL	0	.0	6	3.4	0	.0	0	.0	6	3.4	169	94.9	3	1.7
FL FEMALE	0	.0	4	3.8	0	.0	0	.0	4	3.8	100	95.2	1	1.0
FL MALE	0	.0	2	2.7	0	.0	0	.0	2	2.7	69	94.5	2	2.7
TALMUDIC C OF FLORIDA														
FL TOTAL	0	.0	0	.0	0	.0	0	.0	0	.0	2	100.0	0	.0
FL FEMALE	0	.0	0	.0	0	.0	0	.0	0	.0	0	.0	0	.0
FL MALE	0	.0	0	.0	0	.0	0	.0	0	.0	2	100.0	0	.0
UNIVERSITY OF MIAMI														
FL TOTAL	8	.4	112	5.4	56	2.7	193	9.2	369	17.6	1,714	82.0	8	.4
FL FEMALE	4	.5	54	6.5	11	1.3	96	11.6	165	20.0	659	79.9	1	.1
FL MALE	4	.3	58	4.6	45	3.6	97	7.7	204	16.1	1,055	83.3	7	.6
UNIVERSITY OF SARASOTA														
FL TOTAL	1	.7	46	32.4	1	.7	3	2.1	51	35.9	84	59.2	7	4.9
FL FEMALE	0	.0	21	39.6	1	1.9	1	1.9	23	43.4	30	56.6	0	.0
FL MALE	1	1.1	25	28.1	0	.0	2	2.2	28	31.5	54	60.7	7	7.9
UNIVERSITY OF TAMPA														
FL TOTAL	1	.2	78	13.5	3	.5	41	7.1	123	21.4	446	77.4	7	1.2
FL FEMALE	0	.0	63	18.5	2	.6	29	8.5	94	27.6	246	72.1	1	.3
FL MALE	1	.4	15	6.4	1	.4	12	5.1	29	12.3	200	85.1	6	2.6
FLORIDA		TOTAL (	24	INSTITUTIONS)										
FL TOTAL	53	.2	2,608	9.7	247	.9	989	3.7	3,897	14.5	21,797	81.4	1,096	4.1
FL FEMALE	18	.2	1,561	13.1	77	.6	492	4.1	2,148	18.1	9,531	80.2	212	1.8
FL MALE	35	.2	1,047	7.0	170	1.1	497	3.3	1,749	11.7	12,266	82.3	884	5.9
GEORGIA														
ARMSTRONG STATE COLLEGE														
GA TOTAL	0	.0	47	28.7	1	.6	1	.6	49	29.9	112	68.3	3	1.8
GA FEMALE	0	.0	37	30.6	1	.8	0	.0	38	31.4	82	67.8	1	.8
GA MALE	0	.0	10	23.3	0	.0	1	2.3	11	25.6	30	69.8	2	4.7
ATLANTA UNIVERSITY														
GA TOTAL	0	.0	979	79.8	0	.0	0	.0	979	79.8	45	3.7	203	16.5
GA FEMALE	0	.0	619	94.1	0	.0	0	.0	619	94.1	20	3.0	19	2.9
GA MALE	0	.0	360	63.3	0	.0	0	.0	360	63.3	25	4.4	184	32.3
AUGUSTA COLLEGE														
GA TOTAL	1	.4	18	7.0	1	.4	3	1.2	23	8.9	234	90.7	1	.4
GA FEMALE	1	.7	13	8.9	1	.7	1	.7	16	11.0	129	88.4	1	.7
GA MALE	0	.0	5	4.5	0	.0	2	1.8	7	6.3	105	93.8	0	.0
BERRY COLLEGE														
GA TOTAL	0	.0	11	6.2	0	.0	1	.6	12	6.8	164	92.7	1	.6
GA FEMALE	0	.0	10	7.0	0	.0	1	.7	11	7.7	130	91.5	1	.7
GA MALE	0	.0	1	2.9	0	.0	0	.0	1	2.9	34	97.1	0	.0
BRENAU COLLEGE														
GA TOTAL	0	.0	2	1.6	0	.0	0	.0	2	1.6	126	97.7	1	.8
GA FEMALE	0	.0	1	1.2	0	.0	0	.0	1	1.2	81	98.8	0	.0
GA MALE	0	.0	1	2.1	0	.0	0	.0	1	2.1	45	95.7	1	2.1
COLUMBIA THEOLOGICAL SEM														
GA TOTAL	0	.0	0	.0	0	.0	0	.0	0	.0	132	99.2	1	.8
GA FEMALE	0	.0	0	.0	0	.0	0	.0	0	.0	12	100.0	0	.0
GA MALE	0	.0	0	.0	0	.0	0	.0	0	.0	120	99.2	1	.8
COLUMBUS COLLEGE														
GA TOTAL	0	.0	74	18.4	3	.7	2	.5	79	19.7	322	80.1	1	.2
GA FEMALE	0	.0	59	23.3	2	.8	1	.4	62	24.5	191	75.5	0	.0
GA MALE	0	.0	15	10.1	1	.7	1	.7	17	11.4	131	87.9	1	.7
EMORY UNIVERSITY														
GA TOTAL	3	.2	57	4.7	5	.4	5	.4	70	5.8	1,079	88.7	67	5.5
GA FEMALE	2	.3	42	6.5	1	.2	3	.5	48	7.4	574	89.0	23	3.6
GA MALE	1	.2	15	2.6	4	.7	2	.4	22	3.9	505	88.4	44	7.7

144

ENROLLMENT IN INSTITUTIONS OF HIGHER EDUCATION BY RACE, ETHNICITY AND SEX:
ATE AND NATION, 1978

N E	BLACK NON-HISPANIC		ASIAN OR PACIFIC ISLANDER		HISPANIC		TOTAL MINORITY		WHITE NON-HISPANIC		NON-RESIDENT ALIEN		TOTAL
	NUMBER	%	NUMBER	%	NUMBER	%	NUMBER	%	NUMBER	%	NUMBER	%	NUMBER

INUED

84 85.7	0 .0	0 .0	84 85.7	14 14.3	0 .0	98
57 83.8	0 .0	0 .0	57 83.8	11 16.2	0 .0	68
27 90.0	0 .0	0 .0	27 90.0	3 10.0	0 .0	30
124 16.4	1 .1	1 .1	126 16.7	628 83.3	0 .0	754
83 21.0	1 .3	1 .3	85 21.5	311 78.5	0 .0	396
41 11.5	0 .0	0 .0	41 11.5	317 88.5	0 .0	358
49 3.1	15 .9	19 1.2	83 5.2	1,131 71.2	374 23.6	1,588
10 4.8	2 1.0	2 1.0	14 6.8	167 80.7	26 12.6	207
39 2.8	13 .9	17 1.2	69 5.0	964 69.8	348 25.2	1,381
113 10.3	4 .4	2 .2	119 10.8	901 82.1	77 7.0	1,097
92 11.9	2 .3	2 .3	96 12.5	627 81.4	47 6.1	770
21 6.4	2 .6	0 .0	23 7.0	274 83.8	30 9.2	327
82 14.1	1 .2	1 .2	85 14.6	498 85.4	0 .0	583
67 14.2	1 .2	0 .0	68 14.4	403 85.6	0 .0	471
15 13.4	0 .0	1 .9	17 15.2	95 84.8	0 .0	112
944 13.6	62 .9	7 .1	1,024 14.8	5,802 83.8	97 1.4	6,923
694 17.7	27 .7	2 .1	727 18.5	3,157 80.4	41 1.0	3,925
250 8.3	35 1.2	5 .2	297 9.9	2,645 88.2	56 1.9	2,998
7 87.5	0 .0	0 .0	7 87.5	1 12.5	0 .0	8
1 50.0	0 .0	0 .0	1 50.0	1 50.0	0 .0	2
6 100.0	0 .0	0 .0	6 100.0	0 .0	0 .0	6
4 15.4	0 .0	0 .0	4 15.4	22 84.6	0 .0	26
4 18.2	0 .0	0 .0	4 18.2	18 81.8	0 .0	22
0 .0	0 .0	0 .0	0 .0	4 100.0	0 .0	4
16 6.7	2 .8	2 .8	20 8.4	214 89.5	5 2.1	239
15 8.9	1 .6	1 .6	17 10.1	152 89.9	0 .0	169
1 1.4	1 1.4	1 1.4	3 4.3	62 88.6	5 7.1	70
2 10.0	0 .0	0 .0	2 10.0	18 90.0	0 .0	20
2 11.8	0 .0	0 .0	2 11.8	15 88.2	0 .0	17
0 .0	0 .0	0 .0	0 .0	3 100.0	0 .0	3
1 1.2	0 .0	0 .0	1 1.2	82 98.8	0 .0	83
1 1.2	0 .0	0 .0	1 1.2	82 98.8	0 .0	83
0 .0	0 .0	0 .0	0 .0	0 .0	0 .0	0
0 .0	0 .0	0 .0	0 .0	7 100.0	0 .0	7
0 .0	0 .0	0 .0	0 .0	2 100.0	0 .0	2
0 .0	0 .0	0 .0	0 .0	5 100.0	0 .0	5
1 .3	0 .0	1 .3	2 .7	302 99.3	0 .0	304
1 .4	0 .0	1 .4	2 .8	238 99.2	0 .0	240
0 .0	0 .0	0 .0	0 .0	64 100.0	0 .0	64
0 .0	0 .0	0 .0	0 .0	31 100.0	0 .0	31
0 .0	0 .0	0 .0	0 .0	31 100.0	0 .0	31
0 .0	0 .0	0 .0	0 .0	0 .0	0 .0	0
48 29.4	2 1.2	0 .0	50 30.7	112 68.7	1 .6	163
37 30.3	2 1.6	0 .0	39 32.0	83 68.0	0 .0	122
11 26.8	0 .0	0 .0	11 26.8	29 70.7	1 2.4	41
152 4.0	19 .5	11 .3	195 5.1	3,397 88.6	243 6.3	3,835
89 5.1	10 .6	3 .2	108 6.2	1,557 89.4	77 4.4	1,742
63 3.0	9 .4	8 .4	87 4.2	1,840 87.9	166 7.9	2,093
176 16.3	0 .0	0 .0	176 16.3	892 82.6	12 1.1	1,080
126 18.0	0 .0	0 .0	126 18.0	572 81.7	2 .3	700
50 13.2	0 .0	0 .0	50 13.2	320 84.2	10 2.6	380
125 9.0	0 .0	3 .2	128 9.2	1,250 90.1	9 .6	1,387
106 10.9	0 .0	1 .1	107 11.0	867 88.8	2 .2	976
19 4.6	0 .0	2 .5	21 5.1	383 93.2	7 1.7	411
(26 INSTITUTIONS)						
3,116 14.2	116 .5	59 .3	3,320 15.1	17,516 79.9	1,096 5.0	21,932
2,166 18.0	51 .4	19 .2	2,249 18.7	9,513 79.3	240 2.0	12,002
950 9.6	65 .7	40 .4	1,071 10.8	8,003 80.6	856 8.6	9,930
1 1.0	37 35.9	0 .0	38 36.9	65 63.1	0 .0	103
0 .0	13 52.0	0 .0	13 52.0	12 48.0	0 .0	25
1 1.3	24 30.8	0 .0	25 32.1	53 67.9	0 .0	78
24 .6	1,486 40.0	55 1.5	1,569 42.3	1,893 51.0	251 6.8	3,713
8 .5	710 42.2	23 1.4	744 44.2	863 51.3	76 4.5	1,683
16 .8	776 38.2	32 1.6	825 40.6	1,030 50.7	175 8.6	2,030
(2 INSTITUTIONS)						
25 .7	1,523 39.9	55 1.4	1,607 42.1	1,958 51.3	251 6.6	3,816
8 .5	723 42.3	23 1.3	757 44.3	875 51.2	76 4.4	1,708
17 .8	800 38.0	32 1.5	850 40.3	1,083 51.4	175 8.3	2,108

145

TABLE 2 - TOTAL GRADUATE ENROLLMENT IN INSTITUTIONS OF HIGHER EDUCATION BY RACE, ETHNICITY AND SEX: INSTITUTION, STATE AND NATION, 1978

	AMERICAN INDIAN ALASKAN NATIVE		BLACK NON-HISPANIC		ASIAN OR PACIFIC ISLANDER		HISPANIC		TOTAL MINORITY		WHITE NON-HISPANIC		NON-RESIDENT ALIEN		T
	NUMBER	%	NUMBER	%	NUMBER	%	NUMBER	%	NUMBER	%	NUMBER	%	NUMBER	%	N
IDAHO															
BOISE STATE UNIVERSITY															
ID TOTAL	7	.6	3	.3	16	1.5	1	1.	41	3.8	1,050	96.1	2	.2	
ID FEMALE	4	.6	2	.3	9	1.3		1.	24	3.4	671	96.3	2	.3	
ID MALE	3	.8	1	.3	7	1.8	8	1.8	17	4.3	379	95.7	0	.0	
COLLEGE OF IDAHO															
ID TOTAL	0	.0	0	.0	0	.0	4	5.5	4	5.5	69	94.5	0	.0	
ID FEMALE	0	.0	0	.0	0	.0	2	5.4	2	5.4	35	94.6	0	.0	
ID MALE	0	.0	0	.0	0	.0	2	5.6	2	5.6	34	94.4	0	.0	
IDAHO STATE UNIVERSITY															
ID TOTAL	4	.5	5	.7	13	1.8		.5	26	3.5	715	96.5	0	.0	
ID FEMALE	2	.6	1	.3	3	1.0		.0	6	1.9	303	98.1	0	.0	
ID MALE	2	.5	4	.9	10	2.3	8	.9	20	4.6	412	95.4	0	.0	
NTHWST NAZARENE COLLEGE															
ID TOTAL	0	.0	0	.0	0	.0		.0	0	.0	16	100.0	0	.0	
ID FEMALE	0	.0	0	.0	0	.0		.0	0	.0	14	100.0	0	.0	
ID MALE	0	.0	0	.0	0	.0	8	.0	0	.0	2	100.0	0	.0	
UNIVERSITY OF IDAHO															
ID TOTAL	6	.5	9	.8	9	.8	4	.3	28	2.3	1,083	90.7	83	7.0	
ID FEMALE	2	.6	2	.6	1	.3	2	.6	7	2.1	310	93.7	14	4.2	
ID MALE	4	.5	7	.8	8	.9	2	.2	21	2.4	773	89.6	69	8.0	
IDAHO	TOTAL (		5 INSTITUTIONS)												
ID TOTAL	17	.5	17	.5	38	1.2	27	.9	99	3.2	2,933	94.1	85	2.7	
ID FEMALE	8	.6	5	.4	13	.9	13	.9	39	2.8	1,333	96.0	16	1.2	
ID MALE	9	.5	12	.7	25	1.4	14	.8	60	3.5	1,600	92.5	69	4.0	
ILLINOIS															
ALFRED ADLER INST CHICAGO															
IL TOTAL	0	.0	4	3.8	0	.0	0	.0	4	3.8	99	94.3	2	1.9	
IL FEMALE	0	.0	2	3.4	0	.0	0	.0	2	3.4	55	94.8	1	1.7	
IL MALE	0	.0	2	4.3	0	.0	0	.0	2	4.3	44	93.6	1	2.1	
AMERICAN CONSV OF MUSIC															
IL TOTAL	0	.0	2	2.9	0	.0		.0	2	2.9	58	84.1	9	13.0	
IL FEMALE	0	.0	1	2.1	0	.0		.0	1	2.1	40	83.3	7	14.6	
IL MALE	0	.0	1	4.8	0	.0	8	.0	1	4.8	18	85.7	2	9.5	
AUGUSTANA COLLEGE															
IL TOTAL	0	.0	0	.0	0	.0		.0	0	.0	18	100.0	0	.0	
IL FEMALE	0	.0	0	.0	0	.0		.0	0	.0	9	100.0	0	.0	
IL MALE	0	.0	0	.0	0	.0	8	.0	0	.0	9	100.0	0	.0	
BETHANY THEOLOGICAL SEM															
IL TOTAL	0	.0	0	.0	0	.0		.0	0	.0	26	96.3	1	3.7	
IL FEMALE	0	.0	0	.0	0	.0		.0	0	.0	1	100.0	0	.0	
IL MALE	0	.0	0	.0	0	.0	8	.0	0	.0	25	96.2	1	3.8	
BRADLEY UNIVERSITY															
IL TOTAL	1	.4	21	8.0	1	.4		.0	23	8.7	228	86.4	13	4.9	
IL FEMALE	0	.0	11	9.6	0	.0		.0	11	9.6	101	88.6	2	1.8	
IL MALE	1	.7	10	6.7	1	.7	8	.0	12	8.0	127	84.7	11	7.3	
BRISK RABBINICAL COLLEGE															
IL TOTAL	0	.0	0	.0	0	.0		.0	0	.0	9	100.0	0	.0	
IL FEMALE	0	.0	0	.0	0	.0		.0	0	.0	0	.0	0	.0	
IL MALE	0	.0	0	.0	0	.0	8	.0	0	.0	9	100.0	0	.0	
CATHOLIC THEOL UNION															
IL TOTAL	0	.0	0	.0	1	2.2		.0	1	2.2	36	80.0	8	17.8	
IL FEMALE	0	.0	0	.0	0	.0		.0	0	.0	20	100.0	0	.0	
IL MALE	0	.0	0	.0	1	4.0	8	.0	1	4.0	16	64.0	8	32.0	
CHGO CONSERVATORY COLLEGE															
IL TOTAL	0	.0	0	.0	0	.0		.0	0	.0	2	100.0	0	.0	
IL FEMALE	0	.0	0	.0	0	.0		.0	0	.0	1	100.0	0	.0	
IL MALE	0	.0	0	.0	0	.0	8	.0	0	.0	1	100.0	0	.0	
CHICAGO STATE UNIVERSITY															
IL TOTAL	1	.1	369	49.5	8	1.1	2	2.7	398	53.4	345	46.3	2	.3	
IL FEMALE	0	.0	282	55.6	6	1.2	10	2.8	302	59.6	205	40.4	0	.0	
IL MALE	1	.4	87	36.6	2	.8	6	2.5	96	40.3	140	58.8	2	.8	
CHICAGO THEOLOGICAL SEM															
IL TOTAL	0	.0	3	11.1	0	.0		.0	3	11.1	17	63.0	7	25.9	
IL FEMALE	0	.0	0	.0	0	.0		.0	0	.0	0	.0	1	100.0	
IL MALE	0	.0	3	11.5	0	.0	8	.0	3	11.5	17	65.4	6	23.1	
CONCORDIA TCHRS COLLEGE															
IL TOTAL	0	.0	20	9.2	0	.0		.0	20	9.2	197	90.8	0	.0	
IL FEMALE	0	.0	16	10.7	0	.0		.0	16	10.7	133	89.3	0	.0	
IL MALE	0	.0	4	5.9	0	.0	8	.0	4	5.9	64	94.1	0	.0	
DEPAUL UNIVERSITY															
IL TOTAL	5	.2	145	4.7	73	2.3	26	.8	249	8.0	2,829	90.9	34	1.1	
IL FEMALE	2	.2	115	10.7	31	2.9	10	.9	158	14.6	911	84.4	10	.9	
IL MALE	3	.1	30	1.5	42	2.1	16	.8	91	4.5	1,918	94.3	24	1.2	
EASTERN ILL UNIVERSITY															
IL TOTAL	6	.5	36	2.8	4	.3	3	.2	49	3.9	1,167	92.0	53	4.2	
IL FEMALE	3	.4	20	2.9	0	.0	0	.0	23	3.3	655	94.4	16	2.3	
IL MALE	3	.5	16	2.8	4	.7	3	.5	26	4.5	512	89.0	37	6.4	
EUREKA COLLEGE															
IL TOTAL	0	.0	0	.0	0	.0		.0	0	.0	0	.0	0	.0	
IL FEMALE	0	.0	0	.0	0	.0		.0	0	.0	0	.0	0	.0	
IL MALE	0	.0	0	.0	0	.0	8	.0	0	.0	0	.0	0	.0	
GARRETT-EVANGELCL THEOL															
IL TOTAL	0	.0	12	12.2	0	.0		.0	12	12.2	82	83.7	4	4.1	
IL FEMALE	0	.0	3	12.5	0	.0		.0	3	12.5	20	83.3	1	4.2	
IL MALE	0	.0	9	12.2	0	.0	8	.0	9	12.2	62	83.8	3	4.1	
GEORGE WILLIAMS COLLEGE															
IL TOTAL	1	.2	24	4.3	2	.4	6	1.1	33	5.9	511	91.7	13	2.3	
IL FEMALE	0	.0	13	3.9	0	.0	4	1.2	17	5.2	305	92.4	8	2.4	
IL MALE	1	.4	11	4.8	2	.9	2	.9	16	7.0	206	90.7	5	2.2	

146

ENROLLMENT IN INSTITUTIONS OF HIGHER EDUCATION BY RACE, ETHNICITY AND SEX:
STATE AND NATION, 1978

IN
/E

(TINUED)

BLACK NON-HISPANIC		ASIAN OR PACIFIC ISLANDER		HISPANIC		TOTAL MINORITY		WHITE NON-HISPANIC		NON-RESIDENT ALIEN		TOTAL
NUMBER	%	NUMBER	%	NUMBER	%	NUMBER	%	NUMBER	%	NUMBER	%	NUMBER
552	31.6	28	1.6	68	3.9	651	37.3	1,055	60.4	40	2.3	1,746
360	37.3	10	1.0	36	3.7	407	42.2	549	57.0	8	.8	964
192	24.6	18	2.3	32	4.1	244	31.2	506	64.7	32	4.1	782
0	.0	0	.0	0	.0	0	.0	31	96.9	1	3.1	32
0	.0	0	.0	0	.0	0	.0	8	100.0	0	.0	8
0	.0	0	.0	0	.0	0	.0	23	95.8	1	4.2	24
2	.9	1	.4	2	.9	5	2.2	225	97.0	2	.9	232
2	4.2	0	.0	0	.0	2	4.2	46	95.8	0	.0	48
0	.0	1	.5	2	1.1	3	1.6	179	97.3	2	1.1	184
113	5.9	184	9.7	18	.9	316	16.6	1,257	66.0	331	17.4	1,904
38	11.0	19	5.5	5	1.4	62	17.9	261	75.4	23	6.6	346
75	4.8	165	10.6	13	.8	254	16.3	996	63.9	308	19.8	1,558
42	2.2	11	.6	7	.4	64	3.4	1,725	91.6	95	5.0	1,884
20	2.1	6	.6	4	.4	31	3.2	892	93.5	31	3.2	954
22	2.4	5	.5	3	.3	33	3.5	833	89.6	64	6.9	930
5	3.2	3	1.9	0	.0	8	5.2	145	94.2	1	.6	154
1	4.0	0	.0	0	.0	1	4.0	24	96.0	0	.0	25
4	3.1	3	2.3	0	.0	7	5.4	121	93.8	1	.8	129
123	16.0	2	.3	0	.0	125	16.3	639	83.3	3	.4	767
26	16.4	1	.6	0	.0	27	17.0	132	83.0	0	.0	159
97	16.0	1	.2	0	.0	98	16.1	507	83.4	3	.5	608
1	3.7	0	.0	1	3.7	2	7.4	25	92.6	0	.0	27
0	.0	0	.0	1	4.8	1	4.8	20	95.2	0	.0	21
1	16.7	0	.0	0	.0	1	16.7	5	83.3	0	.0	6
8	2.4	2	.6	2	.6	12	3.7	313	95.4	3	.9	328
3	4.0	1	1.3	1	1.3	5	6.7	70	93.3	0	.0	75
5	2.0	1	.4	1	.4	7	2.8	243	96.0	3	1.2	253
1	1.3	5	6.6	1	1.3	7	9.2	64	84.2	5	6.6	76
0	.0	1	5.6	0	.0	1	5.6	16	88.9	1	5.6	18
1	1.7	4	6.9	1	1.7	6	10.3	48	82.8	4	6.9	58
129	4.7	56	2.1	63	2.3	250	9.2	2,370	87.2	99	3.6	2,719
93	6.7	31	2.2	40	2.9	165	11.9	1,187	85.5	37	2.7	1,389
36	2.7	25	1.9	23	1.7	85	6.4	1,183	88.9	62	4.7	1,330
2	3.2	5	8.1	2	3.2	9	14.5	53	85.5	0	.0	62
0	.0	0	.0	0	.0	0	.0	0	.0	0	.0	0
2	3.2	5	8.1	2	3.2	9	14.5	53	85.5	0	.0	62
25	5.0	12	2.4	7	1.4	44	8.7	459	90.9	2	.4	505
1	9.1	0	.0	0	.0	1	9.1	10	90.9	0	.0	11
24	4.9	12	2.4	7	1.4	43	8.7	449	90.9	2	.4	494
0	.0	0	.0	0	.0	0	.0	34	97.1	1	2.9	35
0	.0	0	.0	0	.0	0	.0	14	100.0	0	.0	14
0	.0	0	.0	0	.0	0	.0	20	95.2	1	4.8	21
0	.0	1	3.4	0	.0	1	3.4	28	96.6	0	.0	29
0	.0	0	.0	0	.0	0	.0	1	100.0	0	.0	1
0	.0	1	3.6	0	.0	1	3.6	27	96.4	0	.0	28
1	1.5	0	.0	0	.0	2	3.1	62	95.4	1	1.5	65
1	2.0	0	.0	0	.0	1	2.0	48	98.0	0	.0	49
0	.0	0	.0	0	.0	1	6.3	14	87.5	1	6.3	16
97	11.5	10	1.2	14	1.7	121	14.4	720	85.5	1	.1	842
79	10.9	8	1.1	8	1.1	95	13.0	632	86.8	1	.1	728
18	15.8	2	1.8	6	5.3	26	22.8	88	77.2	0	.0	114
88	8.8	17	1.7	32	3.2	140	14.0	846	84.5	15	1.5	1,001
55	8.1	7	1.0	16	2.4	81	11.9	596	87.6	3	.4	680
33	10.3	10	3.1	16	5.0	59	16.4	250	77.9	12	3.7	321
1	4.5	1	4.5	1	4.5	3	13.6	19	86.4	0	.0	22
0	.0	0	.0	0	.0	0	.0	0	.0	0	.0	0
1	4.5	1	4.5	1	4.5	3	13.6	19	86.4	0	.0	22
121	2.4	29	.6	23	.5	184	3.7	4,605	91.8	230	4.6	5,019
61	2.5	14	.6	9	.4	89	3.6	2,277	93.2	78	3.2	2,444
60	2.3	15	.6	14	.5	95	3.7	2,328	90.4	152	5.9	2,575
132	3.1	79	1.8	34	.8	251	5.8	3,493	80.9	575	13.3	4,319
66	4.1	28	1.7	9	.6	105	6.5	1,428	88.5	81	5.0	1,614
66	2.4	51	1.9	25	.9	146	5.4	2,065	76.3	494	18.3	2,705
1	1.6	0	.0	0	.0	1	1.6	61	96.8	1	1.6	63
1	9.1	0	.0	0	.0	1	9.1	9	81.8	1	9.1	11
0	.0	0	.0	0	.0	0	.0	52	100.0	0	.0	52
3	7.5	0	.0	0	.0	3	7.5	37	92.5	0	.0	40
1	9.1	0	.0	0	.0	1	9.1	10	90.9	0	.0	11
2	6.9	0	.0	0	.0	2	6.9	27	93.1	0	.0	29

TABLE 2 - TOTAL GRADUATE ENROLLMENT IN INSTITUTIONS OF HIGHER EDUCATION BY RACE, ETHNICITY AND SEX:
INSTITUTION, STATE AND NATION, 1978

	AMERICAN INDIAN ALASKAN NATIVE		BLACK NON-HISPANIC		ASIAN OR PACIFIC ISLANDER		HISPANIC		TOTAL MINORITY		WHITE NON-HISPANIC		NON-RESIDENT ALIEN	
	NUMBER	%	NUMBER	%	NUMBER	%	NUMBER	%	NUMBER	%	NUMBER	%	NUMBER	%
ILLINOIS CONTINUED														
ROOSEVELT UNIVERSITY														
IL TOTAL	13	.5	578	21.3	130	4.8	41	1.5	762	28.0	1,680	61.8	278	10.2
IL FEMALE	7	.6	337	31.2	51	4.7	13	1.2	408	37.8	572	53.0	99	9.2
IL MALE	6	.4	241	14.7	79	4.8	28	1.7	354	21.6	1,108	67.5	179	10.9
ROSARY COLLEGE														
IL TOTAL	1	.2	15	2.5	12	2.0	7	1.1	35	5.7	574	94.1	1	.2
IL FEMALE	0	.0	10	2.5	7	1.7	3	.7	20	4.9	385	95.1	0	.0
IL MALE	1	.5	5	2.4	5	2.4	4	2.0	15	7.3	189	92.2	1	.5
RUSH UNIVERSITY														
IL TOTAL	0	.0	7	4.9	8	5.6	0	.0	15	10.5	126	88.1	2	1.4
IL FEMALE	0	.0	7	5.8	6	5.0	0	.0	13	10.8	106	88.3	1	.8
IL MALE	0	.0	0	.0	2	8.7	0	.0	2	8.7	20	87.0	1	4.3
SNT MARY OF THE LAKE SEM														
IL TOTAL	0	.0	0	.0	0	.0	1	1.8	1	1.8	56	98.2		.0
IL FEMALE	0	.0	0	.0	0	.0	1	25.0	1	25.0	3	75.0	0	.0
IL MALE	0	.0	0	.0	0	.0	0	.0	0	.0	53	100.0	0	.0
SAINT XAVIER COLLEGE														
IL TOTAL	0	.0	5	5.3	2	2.1	1	1.1	8	8.4	87	91.6		.0
IL FEMALE	0	.0	5	6.3	2	2.5	1	1.3	8	10.1	71	89.9	0	.0
IL MALE	0	.0	0	.0	0	.0	0	.0	0	.0	16	100.0	0	.0
SANGAMON STATE UNIVERSITY														
IL TOTAL	0	.0	87	5.9	19	1.3	8	.5	114	7.7	1,337	90.7	23	1.6
IL FEMALE	0	.0	40	6.6	4	.7	1	.2	45	7.4	558	91.6	6	1.0
IL MALE	0	.0	47	5.4	15	1.7	7	.8	69	8.0	779	90.1	17	2.0
SCH ART INSTITUTE CHICAGO														
IL TOTAL	0	.0	2	1.0	6	2.9	6	2.9	14	6.7	189	90.0	7	3.3
IL FEMALE	0	.0	0	.0	3	2.8	2	1.9	5	4.6	99	91.7	4	3.7
IL MALE	0	.0	2	2.0	3	2.9	4	3.9	9	8.8	90	88.2	3	2.9
SEABURY-WESTERN THEOL SEM														
IL TOTAL	0	.0	0	.0	0	.0	0	.0	0	.0	3	100.0		.0
IL FEMALE	0	.0	0	.0	0	.0	0	.0	0	.0	0	.0	0	.0
IL MALE	0	.0	0	.0	0	.0	0	.0	0	.0	3	100.0	0	.0
STHN ILLINOIS U CARBONDL														
IL TOTAL	11	.3	173	5.3	16	.5	7	.2	207	6.3	2,733	83.3	342	10.4
IL FEMALE	5	.3	89	6.2	6	.4	4	.3	104	7.2	1,213	83.8	130	9.0
IL MALE	6	.3	84	4.6	10	.5	3	.2	103	5.6	1,520	82.8	212	11.6
STHN ILLINOIS U EDWARDSVL														
IL TOTAL	1	.1	195	9.8	8	.4	7	.4	211	10.6	1,746	87.4	40	2.0
IL FEMALE	0	.0	121	14.9	2	.2	2	.2	125	15.4	677	83.5	9	1.1
IL MALE	1	.1	74	6.2	6	.5	5	.4	86	7.3	1,069	90.1	31	2.6
SPERTUS COLLEGE JUDAICA														
IL TOTAL	0	.0	0	.0	0	.0	0	.0	0	.0	7	87.5	1	12.5
IL FEMALE	0	.0	0	.0	0	.0	0	.0	0	.0	4	80.0	1	20.0
IL MALE	0	.0	0	.0	0	.0	0	.0	0	.0	3	100.0	0	.0
TELSHE YESHIVA-CHICAGO														
IL TOTAL	0	.0	0	.0	0	.0	0	.0	0	.0	11	100.0	0	.0
IL FEMALE	0	.0	0	.0	0	.0	0	.0	0	.0	0	.0	0	.0
IL MALE	0	.0	0	.0	0	.0	0	.0	0	.0	11	100.0	0	.0
TRINITY EVANGELCL DIV SCH														
IL TOTAL	0	.0	3	.9	1	.3	1	.3	5	1.5	305	93.8	15	6
IL FEMALE	0	.0	1	1.7	0	.0	0	.0	1	1.7	53	91.4	4	9
IL MALE	0	.0	2	.7	1	.4	1	.4	4	1.5	252	94.4	11	4.1
UNIVERSITY OF CHICAGO														
IL TOTAL	4	.1	222	4.0	158	2.9	92	1.7	476	8.7	4,547	82.7	473	6
IL FEMALE	1	.1	97	5.9	52	3.2	32	1.9	182	11.1	1,381	84.1	79	8
IL MALE	3	.1	125	3.2	106	2.8	60	1.6	294	7.6	3,166	82.1	394	1?2
U HLTH SCI-CHGO MEDL SCH														
IL TOTAL	1	.9	7	6.1	11	9.6	1	.9	20	17.5	93	81.6	1	
IL FEMALE	0	.0	5	9.8	4	7.8	0	.0	9	17.6	41	80.4	1	2
IL MALE	1	1.6	2	3.2	7	11.1	1	1.6	11	17.5	52	82.5	0	
U OF ILL CHICAGO CIRCLE														
IL TOTAL	10	.3	327	10.8	115	3.8	63	2.1	515	17.1	2,276	75.5	224	7.4
IL FEMALE	4	.3	204	14.2	33	2.3	33	2.3	274	19.1	1,113	77.5	50	3.5
IL MALE	6	.4	123	7.8	82	5.2	30	1.9	241	15.3	1,163	73.7	174	11.0
U OF ILL MEDL CTR CHGO														
IL TOTAL	0	.0	23	3.2	26	3.6	6	.8	55	7.7	627	87.3	36	5.0
IL FEMALE	0	.0	18	4.1	14	3.2	3	.7	35	7.9	392	88.5	16	3.6
IL MALE	0	.0	5	1.8	12	4.4	3	1.1	20	7.3	235	85.5	20	7.3
U OF ILL URBANA CAMPUS														
IL TOTAL	21	.3	161	2.3	191	2.7	97	1.4	470	6.6	5,539	77.9	1,098	15.4
IL FEMALE	10	.4	80	3.4	55	2.3	43	1.8	188	8.0	1,911	81.3	253	10.5
IL MALE	11	.2	81	1.7	136	2.9	54	1.1	282	5.9	3,628	76.3	845	17.8
VANDERCOOK C OF MUSIC														
IL TOTAL	0	.0	9	47.4	0	.0	0	.0	9	47.4	10	52.6	0	
IL FEMALE	0	.0	1	20.0	0	.0	0	.0	1	20.0	4	80.0	0	
IL MALE	0	.0	8	57.1	0	.0	0	.0	8	57.1	6	42.9	0	0
WESTERN ILL UNIVERSITY														
IL TOTAL	3	.2	45	2.4	3	.2	17	.9	68	3.7	1,662	90.4	109	5.9
IL FEMALE	2	.2	20	2.0	2	.2	13	1.3	37	3.8	923	93.6	26	2.6
IL MALE	1	.1	25	2.9	1	.1	4	.5	31	3.6	739	86.6	83	9.7
WHEATON COLLEGE														
IL TOTAL	0	.0	5	1.6	4	1.3	4	1.3	13	4.2	267	85.3	33	10.5
IL FEMALE	0	.0	2	1.8	0	.0	0	.0	2	1.8	99	87.6	12	10.6
IL MALE	0	.0	3	1.5	4	2.0	4	2.0	9	5.5	168	84.0	21	10.5
ILLINOIS TOTAL (60 INSTITUTIONS)														
IL TOTAL	110	.2	3,947	6.8	1,245	2.1	689	1.2	5,991	10.3	47,765	82.4	4,235	7.3
IL FEMALE	47	.2	2,308	9.5	404	1.7	308	1.3	3,067	12.6	20,291	83.3	1,001	4.1
IL MALE	63	.2	1,639	6.9	841	2.5	381	1.1	2,924	8.7	27,474	81.7	3,234	9.6

N E	BLACK NON-HISPANIC		ASIAN OR PACIFIC ISLANDER		HISPANIC		TOTAL MINORITY		WHITE NON-HISPANIC		NON-RESIDENT ALIEN		TOTAL
	NUMBER	%	NUMBER	%	NUMBER	%	NUMBER	%	NUMBER	%	NUMBER	%	NUMBER
	97	3.9	11	.4	10	.4	123	5.0	2,335	94.3	17	.7	2,475
	47	3.8	5	.4	4	.3	59	4.7	1,182	94.9	5	.4	1,246
	50	4.1	6	.5	6	.5	64	5.2	1,153	93.8	12	1.0	1,229
	0	.0	0	.0	0	.0	0	.0	5	100.0	0	.0	5
	0	.0	0	.0	0	.0	0	.0	1	100.0	0	.0	1
	0	.0	0	.0	0	.0	0	.0	4	100.0	0	.0	4
	72	5.1	21	1.5	6	.4	100	7.1	1,298	92.5	5	.4	1,403
	45	5.5	9	1.1	1	.1	55	6.7	768	93.2	1	.1	824
	27	4.7	12	2.1	5	.9	45	7.8	530	91.5	4	.7	579
	3	3.6	0	.0	1	1.2	4	4.8	75	89.3	5	6.0	84
	1	4.3	0	.0	0	.0	1	4.3	21	91.3	1	4.3	23
	2	3.3	0	.0	1	1.6	3	4.9	54	88.5	4	6.6	61
	0	.0	1	3.1	0	.0	1	3.1	31	96.9	0	.0	32
	0	.0	0	.0	0	.0	0	.0	0	.0	0	.0	0
	0	.0	1	3.1	0	.0	1	3.1	31	96.9	0	.0	32
	0	.0	0	.0	0	.0	0	.0	70	100.0	0	.0	70
	0	.0	0	.0	0	.0	0	.0	51	100.0	0	.0	51
	0	.0	0	.0	0	.0	0	.0	19	100.0	0	.0	19
	0	.0	0	.0	1	1.6	1	1.6	56	91.8	4	6.6	61
	0	.0	0	.0	0	.0	0	.0	25	100.0	0	.0	25
	0	.0	0	.0	1	2.8	1	2.8	31	86.1	4	11.1	36
	0	.0	0	.0	0	.0	0	.0	5	83.3	1	16.7	6
	0	.0	0	.0	0	.0	0	.0	5	100.0	0	.0	5
	0	.0	0	.0	0	.0	0	.0	0	.0	1	100.0	1
	0	.0	0	.0	0	.0	0	.0	23	85.2	4	14.8	27
	0	.0	0	.0	0	.0	0	.0	2	100.0	0	.0	2
	0	.0	0	.0	0	.0	0	.0	21	84.0	4	16.0	25
	0	.0	0	.0	0	.0	0	.0	37	100.0	0	.0	37
	0	.0	0	.0	0	.0	0	.0	1	100.0	0	.0	1
	0	.0	0	.0	0	.0	0	.0	36	100.0	0	.0	36
	10	5.1	5	2.5	1	.5	17	8.6	177	89.8	3	1.5	197
	1	1.6	2	3.1	1	1.6	4	6.3	59	92.2	1	1.6	64
	9	6.8	3	2.3	0	.0	13	9.8	118	88.7	2	1.5	133
	12	32.4	0	.0	0	.0	12	32.4	25	67.6	0	.0	37
	3	100.0	0	.0	0	.0	3	100.0	0	.0	0	.0	3
	9	26.5	0	.0	0	.0	9	26.5	25	73.5	0	.0	34
	36	1.9	8	.4	2	.1	47	2.5	1,788	94.3	62	3.3	1,897
	19	2.0	2	.2	0	.0	22	2.3	935	96.2	15	1.5	972
	17	1.8	6	.6	2	.2	25	2.7	853	92.2	47	5.1	925
	176	2.6	44	.7	64	1.0	316	4.7	5,437	80.8	980	14.6	6,733
	86	3.0	19	.7	23	.8	147	5.2	2,397	84.1	307	10.8	2,851
	90	2.3	25	.6	41	1.1	169	4.4	3,040	78.3	673	17.3	3,882
	1	2.9	0	.0	0	.0	1	2.9	34	97.1	0	.0	35
	1	5.0	0	.0	0	.0	1	5.0	19	95.0	0	.0	20
	0	.0	0	.0	0	.0	0	.0	15	100.0	0	.0	15
	2	.8	0	.0	0	.0	2	.8	261	99.2	0	.0	263
	1	.5	0	.0	0	.0	1	.5	199	99.5	0	.0	200
	1	1.6	0	.0	0	.0	1	1.6	62	98.4	0	.0	63
	59	8.8	0	.0	20	3.0	80	11.9	584	87.0	7	1.0	671
	41	11.7	0	.0	16	4.6	58	16.6	290	82.9	2	.6	350
	18	5.6	0	.0	4	1.2	22	6.9	294	91.6	5	1.6	321
	248	6.3	23	.6	10	.3	291	7.4	3,581	91.4	47	1.2	3,919
	171	7.3	13	.6	6	.3	198	8.4	2,135	90.9	16	.7	2,349
	77	4.9	10	.6	4	.3	93	5.9	1,446	92.1	31	2.0	1,570
	44	3.0	9	.6	6	.4	61	4.1	1,408	95.3	8	.5	1,477
	30	3.7	4	.5	3	.4	39	4.8	772	94.8	3	.4	814
	14	2.1	5	.8	3	.5	22	3.3	636	95.9	5	.8	663
	10	1.6	2	.3	1	.2	14	2.3	595	97.7	0	.0	609
	7	1.7	2	.5	1	.2	11	2.7	404	97.3	0	.0	415
	3	1.5	0	.0	0	.0	3	1.5	191	98.5	0	.0	194
	23	2.2	2	.2	3	.3	29	2.7	1,021	96.7	6	.6	1,056
	14	2.2	1	.2	1	.2	17	2.7	606	96.7	4	.6	627
	9	2.1	1	.2	2	.5	12	2.8	415	96.7	2	.5	429
	0	.0	0	.0	0	.0	0	.0	21	100.0	0	.0	21
	0	.0	0	.0	0	.0	0	.0	13	100.0	0	.0	13
	0	.0	0	.0	0	.0	0	.0	8	100.0	0	.0	8
	0	.0	0	.0	0	.0	0	.0	0	.0	3	100.0	3
	0	.0	0	.0	0	.0	0	.0	0	.0	0	.0	0
	0	.0	0	.0	0	.0	0	.0	0	.0	3	100.0	3

TABLE 2 - TOTAL GRADUATE ENROLLMENT IN INSTITUTIONS OF HIGHER EDUCATION BY RACE, ETHNICITY AND SEX: INSTITUTION, STATE AND NATION, 1978

	AMERICAN INDIAN ALASKAN NATIVE		BLACK NON-HISPANIC		ASIAN OR PACIFIC ISLANDER		HISPANIC		TOTAL MINORITY		WHITE NON-HISPANIC		NON-RESIDENT ALIEN	
	NUMBER	%	NUMBER	%	NUMBER	%	NUMBER	%	NUMBER	%	NUMBER	%	NUMBER	%
INDIANA CONTINUED														
PURDUE U MAIN CAMPUS														
IN TOTAL	6	.1	53	1.2	35	.8	22	.5	116	2.6	3,647	81.6	707	15.8
IN FEMALE	2	.1	25	1.8	10	.7	8	.6	45	3.3	1,199	88.2	116	8.5
IN MALE	4	.1	28	.9	25	.8	14	.5	71	2.3	2,448	78.7	591	19.0
PURDUE U CALUMET CAMPUS														
IN TOTAL	0	.0	31	7.0	0	.0	5	1.1	36	8.1	409	91.9	0	.0
IN FEMALE	0	.0	26	8.3	0	.0	4	1.3	30	9.6	284	90.4	0	.0
IN MALE	0	.0	5	3.8	0	.0	1	.8	6	4.6	125	95.4	0	.0
PURDUE U NORTH CEN CAMPUS														
IN TOTAL	0	.0	0	.0	0	.0	0	.0	0	.0	63	100.0	0	.0
IN FEMALE	0	.0	0	.0	0	.0	0	.0	0	.0	16	100.0	0	.0
IN MALE	0	.0	0	.0	0	.0	0	.0	0	.0	47	100.0	0	.0
ROSE-MULMAN INST OF TECHN														
IN TOTAL	0	.0	0	.0	0	.0	0	.0	0	.0	4	100.0	0	.0
IN FEMALE	0	.0	0	.0	0	.0	0	.0	0	.0	0	.0	0	.0
IN MALE	0	.0	0	.0	0	.0	0	.0	0	.0	4	100.0	0	.0
SAINT FRANCIS COLLEGE														
IN TOTAL	0	.0	20	4.0	5	1.0	3	.6	28	5.5	473	93.7	4	.8
IN FEMALE	0	.0	12	4.7	2	.0	0	.0	14	5.5	240	94.5	0	.0
IN MALE	0	.0	8	3.2	3	1.2	3	1.2	14	5.6	233	92.8	4	1.6
UNIVERSITY OF EVANSVILLE														
IN TOTAL	1	.2	13	2.1	2	.3	0	.0	16	2.6	584	95.6	11	1.8
IN FEMALE	0	.3	10	2.6	0	.0	0	.0	11	2.9	367	96.6	2	.5
IN MALE	0	.0	3	1.3	2	.9	0	.0	5	2.2	217	93.9	9	3.9
UNIVERSITY OF NOTRE DAME														
IN TOTAL	1	.1	16	1.3	10	.8	34	2.8	61	5.1	977	81.7	158	13.2
IN FEMALE	0	.0	6	1.7	5	1.4	6	1.7	17	4.8	308	87.0	29	8.2
IN MALE	1	.1	10	1.2	5	.6	28	3.3	44	5.2	669	79.5	129	15.3
VALPARAISO UNIVERSITY														
IN TOTAL	0	.0	8	3.6	1	.5	1	.5	10	4.5	211	95.5	0	.0
IN FEMALE	0	.0	6	3.6	1	.6	1	.6	8	4.8	159	95.2	0	.0
IN MALE	0	.0	2	3.7	0	.0	0	.0	2	3.7	52	96.3	0	.0
INDIANA TOTAL (31 INSTITUTIONS)														
IN TOTAL	63	.2	934	3.3	179	.6	190	.7	1,366	2.6	25,235	88.1	2,032	7.1
IN FEMALE	39	.3	552	4.0	75	.5	75	.5	741	5.4	12,458	90.9	502	3.7
IN MALE	24	.2	382	2.6	104	.7	115	.8	625	4.2	12,777	85.6	1,530	10.2
IOWA														
AQUINAS INST OF THEOLOGY														
IA TOTAL	0	.0	0	.0	0	.0	0	.0	0	.0	53	86.9	8	13.1
IA FEMALE	0	.0	0	.0	0	.0	0	.0	0	.0	25	92.6	2	7.4
IA MALE	0	.0	0	.0	0	.0	0	.0	0	.0	28	82.4	6	17.6
CLARKE COLLEGE														
IA TOTAL	0	.0	0	.0	0	.0	0	.0	0	.0	62	100.0	0	.0
IA FEMALE	0	.0	0	.0	0	.0	0	.0	0	.0	50	100.0	0	.0
IA MALE	0	.0	0	.0	0	.0	0	.0	0	.0	12	100.0	0	.0
DRAKE UNIVERSITY														
IA TOTAL	1	.1	35	2.8	3	.2	3	.2	42	3.4	1,192	95.7	12	1.0
IA FEMALE	1	.2	17	2.8	1	.2	1	.2	20	3.3	575	96.0	4	.7
IA MALE	0	.0	18	2.8	2	.3	2	.3	22	3.4	617	95.4	8	1.2
IOWA STATE U SCI & TECHN														
IA TOTAL	3	.1	80	2.2	36	1.0	6	.2	125	3.	2,854	77.9	684	18.7
IA FEMALE	0	.0	41	3.6	12	1.1	2	.2	55	4.	952	84.3	122	10.8
IA MALE	3	.1	39	1.5	24	.9	4	.2	70	2.8	1,902	75.1	562	22.2
LORAS COLLEGE														
IA TOTAL	0	.0	0	.0	0	.0	0	.0	0	.	62	100.0	0	.0
IA FEMALE	0	.0	0	.0	0	.0	0	.0	0	.0	37	100.0	0	.0
IA MALE	0	.0	0	.0	0	.0	0	.0	0	.0	25	100.0	0	.0
MAHARISHI INTRNATL U														
IA TOTAL	0	.0	2	1.4	0	.0	4	2.9	6	4.3	130	92.9	4	2.9
IA FEMALE	0	.0	2	3.5	0	.0	3	5.3	5	8.8	50	87.7	2	3.5
IA MALE	0	.0	0	.0	0	.0	1	1.2	1	1.2	80	96.4	2	2.4
MARYCREST COLLEGE														
IA TOTAL	0	.0	1	.4	1	.4	0	.0	2	.8	244	99.2	0	.0
IA FEMALE	0	.0	1	.5	1	.5	0	.0	2	.9	209	99.1	0	.0
IA MALE	0	.0	0	.0	0	.0	0	.0	0	.0	35	100.0	0	.0
MORNINGSIDE COLLEGE														
IA TOTAL	0	.0	0	.0	0	.0	0	.0	0	.0	51	100.0	0	.0
IA FEMALE	0	.0	0	.0	0	.0	0	.0	0	.0	46	100.0	0	.0
IA MALE	0	.0	0	.0	0	.0	0	.0	0	.0	5	100.0	0	.0
SAINT AMBROSE COLLEGE														
IA TOTAL	0	.0	2	1.8	0	.0	0	.0	2	1.8	111	98.2	0	.0
IA FEMALE	0	.0	1	2.3	0	.0	0	.0	1	2.3	42	97.7	0	.0
IA MALE	0	.0	1	1.4	0	.0	0	.0	1	1.4	69	98.6	0	.0
UNIVERSITY OF IOWA														
IA TOTAL	19	.3	127	2.0	66	1.0	33	.5	245	3.8	5,674	87.4	576	8.9
IA FEMALE	11	.4	67	2.2	26	.9	12	.4	116	3.8	2,759	90.5	172	5.6
IA MALE	8	.2	60	1.7	40	1.2	21	.6	129	3.7	2,915	84.5	404	11.7
U OF NORTHERN IOWA														
IA TOTAL	2	.1	47	2.5	8	.4	10	.5	67	3.	1,764	95.6	15	.8
IA FEMALE	1	.1	28	2.5	3	.3	7	.6	39	3.	1,075	96.1	5	.4
IA MALE	1	.1	19	2.6	5	.7	3	.4	28	3.0	689	94.8	10	1.4
WARTBURG THEOLOGICAL SEM														
IA TOTAL	0	.0	0	.0	0	.0	0	.0	0	.0	15	83.3	3	16.7
IA FEMALE	0	.0	0	.0	0	.0	0	.0	0	.0	2	100.0	0	.0
IA MALE	0	.0	0	.0	0	.0	0	.0	0	.0	13	81.3	3	18.7
IOWA TOTAL (12 INSTITUTIONS)														
IA TOTAL	25	.2	294	2.1	114	.8	56	.4	489	3.5	12,212	87.2	1,302	9.3
IA FEMALE	13	.2	157	2.5	43	.7	25	.4	238	3.7	5,822	91.4	307	4.8
IA MALE	12	.2	137	1.8	71	.9	31	.4	251	3.3	6,390	83.7	995	13.0

N E	BLACK NON-HISPANIC		ASIAN OR PACIFIC ISLANDER		HISPANIC		TOTAL MINORITY		WHITE NON-HISPANIC		NON-RESIDENT ALIEN		TOTAL
	NUMBER	%	NUMBER	%	NUMBER	%	NUMBER	%	NUMBER	%	NUMBER	%	NUMBER
	8	7.1	0	.0		.0	8	7.1	104	92.9		.0	112
	4	6.2	0	.0		.0	4	6.2	61	93.8		.0	65
	4	8.5	0	.0		.0	4	8.5	43	91.5		.0	47
	13	17.6	0	.0		.0	14	18.9	60	81.1		.0	74
	0	.0	0	.0		.0	1	7.1	13	92.9		.0	14
	13	21.7	0	.0		.0	13	21.7	47	78.3		.0	60
	24	2.7	11	1.3		.9	45	5.1	805	91.7	28	3.2	878
	13	2.5	7	1.4		.6	24	4.6	487	94.0	7	1.4	518
	11	3.1	4	1.1		1.4	21	5.8	318	88.3	21	5.8	360
	2	.2	3	.2		.3	10	.8	1,303	98.0	17	1.3	1,330
	1	.1	1	.1		.1	3	.3	874	99.2	4	.5	881
	1	.2	2	.4		.7	7	1.6	429	95.5	13	2.9	449
	72	2.1	8	.2	17	.5	110	3.2	2,914	84.0	446	12.9	3,470
	37	2.4	3	.2	12	.8	56	3.6	1,370	88.4	124	8.0	1,550
	35	1.9	5	.3	5	.3	54	2.8	1,544	80.4	322	16.8	1,920
	9	.6	7	.5	10	.7	39	2.7	1,359	94.2	44	3.1	1,442
	6	.8	1	.1	4	.5	15	1.9	772	96.6	12	1.5	799
	3	.5	6	.9	6	.9	24	3.7	587	91.3	32	5.0	643
	133	2.4	29	.5	52	.9	236	4.3	4,648	84.4	622	11.3	5,506
	73	2.7	14	.5	21	.8	118	4.3	2,433	89.6	165	6.1	2,716
	60	2.2	15	.5	31	1.1	118	4.2	2,215	79.4	457	16.4	2,790
	7	1.9	5	1.4	3	.8	17	4.7	331	91.2	15	4.1	363
	7	2.4	2	.7	2	.7	17	4.2	270	94.4	4	1.4	286
	0	.0	3	3.9	7	1.3	5	6.5	61	79.2	11	14.3	77
	4	4.4	1	1.1	2	2.2	7	7.7	84	92.3	0	.0	91
	2	3.0	1	1.5	1	1.5	4	6.1	62	93.9	0	.0	66
	2	8.0	0	.0	1	4.0	3	12.0	22	88.0	0	.0	25
	152	4.2	33	.9	54	1.5	252	6.9	3,318	91.0	76	2.1	3,646
	97	4.7	13	.6	25	1.2	143	6.9	1,908	92.4	14	.7	2,065
	55	3.5	20	1.3	29	1.8	109	6.9	1,410	89.2	62	3.9	1,581
(10 INSTITUTIONS)													
	424	2.5	97	.6	150	.9	738	4.4	14,926	88.3	1,248	7.4	16,912
	240	2.7	42	.5	69	.8	380	4.2	8,250	92.1	330	3.7	8,960
	184	2.3	55	.7	81	1.0	358	4.5	6,676	84.0	918	11.5	7,952
	0	.0	0	.0	0	.0	1	1.0	91	87.5	12	11.5	104
	0	.0	0	.0	0	.0	0	.0	41	91.1	4	8.9	45
	0	.0	0	.0	0	.0	1	1.7	50	84.7	8	13.6	59
	9	3.8	2	.8	2	.8	13	5.4	221	92.1	6	2.5	240
	1	2.0	1	2.0	0	.0	2	4.1	45	91.8	2	4.1	49
	8	4.2	1	.5	2	1.0	11	5.8	176	92.1	4	2.1	191
	49	2.1	1	.0	1	.0	53	2.3	2,265	96.9	19	.8	2,337
	35	2.3	1	.1	0	.0	37	2.4	1,511	97.2	6	.4	1,554
	14	1.8	0	.0	1	.1	16	2.0	754	96.3	13	1.7	783
	4	2.5	1	.6		.0	5	3.2	153	96.8		.0	158
	3	2.3	0	.0		.0	3	2.3	128	97.7		.0	131
	1	3.7	1	3.7		.0	2	7.4	25	92.6		.0	27
	37	22.2	2	1.2		.0	39	23.4	91	54.5	37	22.2	167
	21	36.8	1	1.8		.0	22	38.6	30	52.6	5	8.8	57
	16	14.5	1	.9		.0	17	15.5	61	55.5	32	29.1	110
	1	2.3	1	2.3		.0	2	4.7	41	95.3		.0	43
	0	.0	0	.0		.0	0	.0	4	100.0		.0	4
	1	2.6	1	2.6		.0	2	5.1	37	94.9		.0	39
	0	.0	0	.0		.0	0	.0	13	100.0	0	.0	13
	0	.0	0	.0		.0	0	.0	0	.0	0	.0	0
	0	.0	0	.0		.0	0	.0	13	100.0	0	.0	13
	14	.5	18	.7	7	1.5	39	1.5	2,529	97.6	23	.9	2,591
	4	.2	5	.3	4	.2	13	.8	1,620	98.9	5	.3	1,638
	10	1.0	13	1.4	3	2.7	26	2.7	909	95.4	18	1.9	953
	71	4.1	3	.2	6	.3	85	4.9	1,643	93.9	22	1.3	1,750
	35	3.1	0	.0	1	.1	40	3.5	1,098	96.5	0	.0	1,138
	36	5.9	3	.5	5	.8	45	7.4	545	89.1	22	3.6	612
	0	.0	0	.0		.0	0	.0	388	100.0		.0	388
	0	.0	0	.0		.0	0	.0	312	100.0		.0	312
	0	.0	0	.0		.0	0	.0	76	100.0		.0	76
	0	.0	0	.0		.0	0	.0	0	.0		.0	0
	0	.0	0	.0		.0	0	.0	0	.0		.0	0
	0	.0	0	.0		.0	0	.0	0	.0		.0	0

TABLE 2 - TOTAL GRADUATE ENROLLMENT IN INSTITUTIONS OF HIGHER EDUCATION BY RACE, ETHNICITY AND SEX: INSTITUTION, STATE AND NATION, 1978

	AMERICAN INDIAN ALASKAN NATIVE		BLACK NON-HISPANIC		ASIAN OR PACIFIC ISLANDER		HISPANIC		TOTAL MINORITY		WHITE NON-HISPANIC		NON-RESIDENT ALIEN	
	NUMBER	%	NUMBER	%	NUMBER	%	NUMBER	%	NUMBER	%	NUMBER	%	NUMBER	%
KENTUCKY CONTINUED														
SPALDING COLLEGE														
KY TOTAL	1	.4	16	6.2	0	.0	1	.4	18	6.9	239	92.3	2	.8
KY FEMALE	1	.5	15	7.4	0	.0	0	.0	16	7.9	184	91.1	2	1.0
KY MALE	0	.0	1	1.8	0	.0	1	1.8	2	3.5	55	96.5	0	.0
UNION COLLEGE														
KY TOTAL	7	1.0	3	.4	0	.0	0	.0	10	1.4	714	97.5	8	1.1
KY FEMALE	3	.6	3	.6	0	.0	0	.0	6	1.3	473	98.5	1	.2
KY MALE	4	1.6	0	.0	0	.0	0	.0	4	1.6	241	95.6	7	2.8
UNIVERSITY OF KENTUCKY														
KY TOTAL	88	3.1	53	1.8	14	.5	20	.7	175	6.1	2,451	85.0	259	9.0
KY FEMALE	53	3.8	29	2.1	4	.3	11	.8	97	7.0	1,234	89.4	50	3.6
KY MALE	35	2.3	24	1.6	10	.7	9	.6	78	5.2	1,217	80.9	209	13.9
UNIVERSITY OF LOUISVILLE														
KY TOTAL	5	.2	148	5.7	50	1.9	16	.6	219	8.5	2,297	89.1	62	2.4
KY FEMALE	1	.1	105	7.0	17	1.1	6	.4	129	8.5	1,370	90.7	11	.7
KY MALE	4	.4	43	4.0	33	3.1	10	.9	90	8.4	927	86.8	51	4.8
HESTERN KY UNIVERSITY														
KY TOTAL	1	.0	126	4.2	1	.0	4	.1	132	4.4	2,812	93.7	57	1.9
KY FEMALE	0	.0	72	3.7	1	.1	1	.1	74	3.8	1,847	95.3	18	.9
KY MALE	1	.1	54	5.1	0	.0	3	.3	58	5.5	965	90.9	39	3.7
KENTUCKY TOTAL (16 INSTITUTIONS)														
KY TOTAL	110	.6	531	3.1	93	.5	57	.3	791	4.6	15,948	92.5	507	2.9
KY FEMALE	63	.6	323	3.1	30	.3	23	.2	439	4.2	9,897	94.8	104	1.0
KY MALE	47	.7	208	3.1	63	.9	34	.5	352	5.2	6,051	88.9	403	5.9
LOUISIANA														
CENTENARY C OF LOUISIANA														
LA TOTAL	0	.0	8	9.0	1	1.1	0	.0	9	10.1	79	88.8	1	1.1
LA FEMALE	0	.0	5	15.2	1	3.0	0	.0	6	18.2	27	81.8	0	.0
LA MALE	0	.0	3	5.4	0	.0	0	.0	3	5.4	52	92.9	1	1.8
GRAMBLING STATE U														
LA TOTAL	0	.0	192	97.5	0	.0	0	.0	192	97.5	2	1.0	3	1.5
LA FEMALE	0	.0	140	99.3	0	.0	0	.0	140	99.3	0	.0	1	.7
LA MALE	0	.0	52	92.9	0	.0	0	.0	52	92.9	2	3.6	2	3.6
LA STATE U AND AGM C														
LA TOTAL	8	.2	190	4.7	4	.1	35	.9	237	5.9	3,344	83.1	442	11.0
LA FEMALE	4	.2	138	6.8	2	.1	18	.9	162	8.0	1,761	86.8	105	5.2
LA MALE	4	.2	52	2.6	2	.1	17	.9	75	3.8	1,583	79.3	337	16.9
LA ST U MEDICAL CENTER														
LA TOTAL	0	.0	12	5.4	9	4.1	6	2.7	27	12.2	191	86.4	3	1.4
LA FEMALE	0	.0	12	9.9	2	1.7	3	2.5	17	14.0	104	86.0	0	.0
LA MALE	0	.0	0	.0	7	7.0	3	3.0	10	10.0	87	87.0	3	3.0
LA STATE U SHREVEPORT														
LA TOTAL	0	.0	13	28.9	0	.0	0	.0	13	28.9	32	71.1	0	.0
LA FEMALE	0	.0	9	23.1	0	.0	0	.0	9	23.1	30	76.9	0	.0
LA MALE	0	.0	4	66.7	0	.0	0	.0	4	66.7	2	33.3	0	.0
UNIVERSITY OF NEW ORLEANS														
LA TOTAL	3	.2	279	14.9	12	.6	37	2.0	331	17.6	1,493	79.6	52	2.8
LA FEMALE	0	.0	206	19.2	4	.4	19	1.8	229	21.4	831	77.6	11	1.0
LA MALE	3	.4	73	9.1	8	1.0	18	2.2	102	12.7	662	82.2	41	5.1
LOUISIANA TECH UNIVERSITY														
LA TOTAL	3	.4	97	12.9	1	.1	0	.0	101	13.4	631	83.8	21	2.8
LA FEMALE	1	.3	81	20.8	0	.0	0	.0	82	21.0	306	78.5	2	5
LA MALE	2	.6	16	4.4	1	.3	0	.0	19	5.2	325	89.5	19	5.2
LOYOLA U IN NEW ORLEANS														
LA TOTAL	1	.3	33	9.8	4	1.2	9	2.7	47	13.9	290	86.1	0	.0
LA FEMALE	0	.0	18	11.5	1	.6	3	1.9	22	14.0	135	86.0	0	.0
LA MALE	1	.6	15	8.3	3	1.7	6	3.3	25	13.9	155	86.1	0	.0
MCNEESE STATE UNIVERSITY														
LA TOTAL	1	.2	92	15.0	2	.3	5	.8	100	16.3	505	82.5	7	1.1
LA FEMALE	1	.3	72	18.0	1	.3	2	.5	76	19.0	323	81.0	0	.0
LA MALE	0	.0	20	9.4	1	.5	3	1.4	24	11.3	182	85.4	7	3.3
NEW ORLS BAPT THEOL SEM														
LA TOTAL	0	.0	0	.0	0	.0	0	.0	0	.0	0	.0	0	.0
LA FEMALE	0	.0	0	.0	0	.0	0	.0	0	.0	0	.0	0	.0
LA MALE	0	.0	0	.0	0	.0	0	.0	0	.0	0	.0	0	.0
NICHOLLS STATE UNIVERSITY														
LA TOTAL	1	.1	111	14.1	1	.1	3	.4	116	14.8	664	84.6	5	.6
LA FEMALE	1	.2	89	15.6	0	.0	2	.4	92	16.1	477	83.5	2	.4
LA MALE	0	.0	22	10.3	1	.5	1	.5	24	11.2	187	87.4	3	1.4
NORTHEAST LOUISIANA U														
LA TOTAL	1	.1	268	21.6	0	.0	0	.0	269	21.7	948	76.3	25	2.0
LA FEMALE	1	.1	209	25.0	0	.0	0	.0	210	25.1	621	74.3	5	.6
LA MALE	0	.0	59	14.5	0	.0	0	.0	59	14.5	327	80.5	20	4.9
NTHWSTN ST U OF LA														
LA TOTAL	3	.2	172	13.9	0	.0	55	4.4	230	18.5	1,000	80.6	10	.8
LA FEMALE	3	.3	139	15.4	0	.0	36	4.0	178	19.8	719	79.8	4	.4
LA MALE	0	.0	33	9.7	0	.0	19	5.6	52	15.3	281	82.9	6	1.8
NOTRE DAME SEM SCH THEO														
LA TOTAL	0	.0	1	14.3	0	.0	0	.0	1	14.3	6	85.7	0	.0
LA FEMALE	0	.0	0	.0	0	.0	0	.0	0	.0	1	100.0	0	.0
LA MALE	0	.0	1	16.7	0	.0	0	.0	1	16.7	5	83.3	0	.0
STHESTN LA UNIVERSITY														
LA TOTAL	1	.1	193	22.6	1	.1	2	.2	197	23.1	636	74.5	21	2.5
LA FEMALE	0	.0	159	26.3	0	.0	2	.3	161	26.6	439	72.6	5	.8
LA MALE	1	.4	34	13.7	1	.4	0	.0	36	14.5	197	79.1	16	6.4
SOUTHERN U AGM C MATN CAM														
LA TOTAL	1	.1	665	92.6	0	.0	0	.0	666	92.8	35	4.9	17	2.4
LA FEMALE	1	.2	487	94.4	0	.0	0	.0	488	94.6	24	4.7	4	.8
LA MALE	0	.0	178	88.1	0	.0	0	.0	178	88.1	11	5.4	13	6.4

	BLACK NON-HISPANIC		ASIAN OR PACIFIC ISLANDER		HISPANIC		TOTAL MINORITY		WHITE NON-HISPANIC		NON-RESIDENT ALIEN		TOTAL
	NUMBER	%	NUMBER	%	NUMBER	%	NUMBER	%	NUMBER	%	NUMBER	%	NUMBER
NUEO													
	97	4.1	34	1.4	78	3.3	223	9.4	1,995	83.8	164	6.9	2,382
	64	6.7	5	.5	35	3.6	108	11.3	825	86.0	26	2.7	959
	33	2.3	29	2.0	43	3.0	115	8.1	1,170	82.2	138	9.7	1,423
	71	7.5	1	.1	4	.4	76	8.0	788	83.2	83	8.8	947
	45	9.6	0	.0	3	.6	48	10.3	407	87.0	13	2.8	468
	26	5.4	1	.2	1	.2	28	5.8	381	79.5	70	14.6	479
	86	80.4	0	.0	1	.9	87	81.3	20	18.7	0	.0	107
	65	81.3	0	.0	1	1.3	66	82.5	14	17.5	0	.0	80
	21	77.8	0	.0	0	.0	21	77.8	6	22.2	0	.0	27
(19 INSTITUTIONS)													
	2,580	15.7	70	.4	235	1.4	2,922	17.8	12,659	77.0	854	5.2	16,435
	1,938	20.8	16	.2	124	1.3	2,094	22.5	7,044	75.6	178	1.9	9,316
	642	9.0	54	.8	111	1.6	828	11.6	5,615	78.9	676	9.5	7,119
	0	.0	0	.0	0	.0	0	.0	34	100.0		.0	34
	0	.0	0	.0	0	.0	0	.0	10	100.0		.0	10
	0	.0	0	.0	0	.0	0	.0	24	100.0		.0	24
	0	.0	0	.0	0	.0	0	.0	33	100.0		.0	33
	0	.0	0	.0	0	.0	0	.0	3	100.0		.0	3
	0	.0	0	.0	0	.0	0	.0	30	100.0		.0	30
	3	.3	2	.2	4	.4	10	1.0	947	96.9	2	2.0	977
	0	.0	1	.3	2	.5	4	1.0	373	97.4	0	1.6	383
	3	.5	1	.2	2	.3	6	1.0	574	96.6	18	2.4	594
	0	.0	0	.0	2	.3	3	.4	674	99.1	3	.4	680
	0	.0	0	.0	0	.0	0	.0	365	99.2	3	.8	368
	0	.0	0	.0	2	.6	3	1.0	309	99.0	0	.0	312
(4 INSTITUTIONS)													
	3	.2	2	.1	6	.3	13	.8	1,688	97.9	23	1.3	1,724
	0	.0	1	.1	2	.3	4	.5	751	98.3	9	1.2	764
	3	.3	1	.1	4	.4	9	.9	937	97.6	14	1.5	960
	1	.9	0	.0	0	.0	1	.9	101	94.4	5	4.7	107
	0	.0	0	.0	0	.0	0	.0	78	97.5	2	2.5	80
	1	3.7	0	.0	0	.0	1	3.7	23	85.2	3	11.1	27
	264	38.5	3	.4	7	1.0	277	40.4	403	58.8	5	.7	685
	185	40.1	2	.4	1	.2	191	41.4	268	58.1	2	.4	461
	79	35.3	1	.4	6	2.7	86	38.4	135	60.3	3	1.3	224
	135	79.4	1	.6	0	.0	138	81.2	25	14.7	7	4.1	170
	90	85.7	0	.0	0	.0	91	86.7	13	12.4	1	1.0	105
	45	69.2	1	1.5	0	.0	47	72.3	12	18.5	6	9.2	65
	0	.0	0	.0	0	.0	0	.0	10	100.0	0	.0	10
	0	.0	0	.0	0	.0	0	.0	1	100.0	0	.0	1
	0	.0	0	.0	0	.0	0	.0	9	100.0	0	.0	9
	6	1.5	1	.2	2	.5	9	2.2	394	96.3	6	1.5	409
	2	1.4	0	.0	0	.0	2	1.4	137	97.9	1	.7	140
	4	1.5	1	.4	2	.7	7	2.6	257	95.5	5	1.9	269
	0	.0	0	.0	1	20.0	1	20.0	4	80.0	0	.0	5
	0	.0	0	.0	1	20.0	1	20.0	4	80.0	0	.0	5
	0	.0	0	.0	0	.0	0	.0	0	.0	0	.0	0
	8	1.3	2	.3	2	.3	12	2.0	579	97.6	2	.3	593
	6	1.5	2	.5	2	.5	10	2.4	403	97.6	0	.0	413
	2	1.1	0	.0	0	.0	2	1.1	176	97.8	2	1.1	180
	274	6.1	82	1.8	37	.8	408	9.1	3,781	84.7	274	6.1	4,463
	193	8.9	40	1.8	22	1.0	264	12.2	1,837	84.8	64	3.0	2,165
	81	3.5	42	1.8	15	.7	144	6.3	1,944	84.6	210	9.1	2,298
	66	4.5	7	.5	5	.3	84	5.8	1,347	92.6	23	1.6	1,454
	48	6.9	1	.1	2	.3	55	7.9	634	91.2	6	.9	695
	18	2.4	6	.8	3	.4	29	3.8	713	93.9	17	2.2	759
	4	4.2	1	1.0	2	2.1	7	7.3	83	86.5	6	6.3	96
	2	3.8	1	1.9	0	.0	3	5.7	50	94.3	0	.0	53
	2	4.7	0	.0	2	4.7	4	9.3	33	76.7	6	14.0	43
	395	66.8	4	.7	1	.2	404	68.4	129	21.8	58	9.8	591
	199	84.7	0	.0	0	.0	201	85.5	28	11.9	6	2.6	235
	196	55.1	4	1.1	1	.3	203	57.0	101	28.4	52	14.6	356
	0	.0	1	.6	0	.0	1	.6	106	62.4	63	37.1	170
	0	.0	0	.0	0	.0	0	.0	22	91.7	2	8.3	24
	0	.0	1	.7	0	.0	1	.7	84	57.5	61	41.8	146

TABLE 2 - TOTAL GRADUATE ENROLLMENT IN INSTITUTIONS OF HIGHER EDUCATION BY RACE, ETHNICITY AND SEX:
INSTITUTION, STATE AND NATION, 1978

	AMERICAN INDIAN ALASKAN NATIVE		BLACK NON-HISPANIC		ASIAN OR PACIFIC ISLANDER		HISPANIC		TOTAL MINORITY		WHITE NON-HISPANIC		NON-RESIDENT ALIEN		TO
	NUMBER	%	NUMBER	%	NUMBER	%	NUMBER	%	NUMBER	%	NUMBER	%	NUMBER	%	NU
MARYLAND		**CONTINUED**													
NER ISRAEL RAB COLLEGE															
MD TOTAL	0	.0	0	.0		.0	0	.0	0	.0	82	93.2	6	6.8	
MD FEMALE	0	.0	0	.0		.0	0	.0	0	.0	0	.0	0	.0	
MD MALE	0	.0	0	.0	8	.0	0	.0	0	.0	82	93.2	6	6.8	
PEABODY INST OF JHU															
MD TOTAL	0	.0	3	2.8	7	6.6	2	1.9	12	11.3	87	82.1	7	6.6	
MD FEMALE	0	.0	1	2.1	4	8.5	1	2.1	6	12.8	36	76.6	5	10.6	
MD MALE	1	.0	2	3.4	3	5.1	1	1.7	6	10.2	51	86.4	2	3.4	
SNT JOHN'S C SANTA FE NM															
MD TOTAL	0	.0	0	.0		.0	1	6.3	1	6.3	14	87.5	1	6.3	
MD FEMALE	0	.0	0	.0		.0	0	.0	0	.0	6	100.0	0	.0	
MD MALE	0	.0	0	.0	8	.0	1	10.0	1	10.0	8	80.0	1	10.0	
SAINT MARY'S SEMINARY & U															
MD TOTAL	0	.0	2	1.6	1	.8	0	.0	3	2.4	114	90.5	9	7.1	
MD FEMALE	0	.0	0	.0	0	.0	0	.0	0	.0	4	66.7	2	33.3	
MD MALE	0	.0	2	1.7	1	.8	0	.0	3	2.5	110	91.7	7	5.8	
SALISBURY STATE COLLEGE															
MD TOTAL	2	.4	61	12.7		.0		.6	66	13.7	415	86.3	0	.0	
MD FEMALE	2	.6	51	15.1		.0		.9	56	16.6	281	83.4	0	.0	
MD MALE	0	.0	10	6.9	8	.0	8	.0	10	6.9	134	93.1	0	.0	
TOWSON STATE UNIVERSITY															
MD TOTAL	3	.2	120	8.6	4	.3	4	.3	131	9.4	1,250	89.9	9	.6	1
MD FEMALE	2	.2	102	10.0	2	.2	4	.4	110	10.8	901	88.8	4	.4	1
MD MALE	1	.3	18	4.8	2	.5	0	.0	21	516	349	93.1	5	1.3	
UNIVERSITY OF BALTIMORE															
MD TOTAL	4	.4	150	15.9	11	1.2	2	.2	167	17.7	723	76.8	51	5.4	
MD FEMALE	1	.5	73	35.14	1	.5	0	.0	75	36.4	121	58.7	10	4.9	
MD MALE	3	.4	77	10.5	10	1.4	2	.3	92	12.15	602	81.9	41	5.6	
U OF MD COLLEGE PARK CAM															
MD TOTAL	19	.3	384	5.8	77	1.2	7	1.0	550	8.2	5,541	83.0	584	8.7	6
MD FEMALE	11	.3	245	7.6	43	1.3	40	1.4	343	10.6	2,712	83.7	184	5.7	3
MD MALE	8	.2	139	4.0	34	1.0	24	.8	207	6.0	2,829	82.3	400	11.6	3
U OF MD BALTIMORE CO CAM															
MD TOTAL	0	.0	31	9.2	2	.6	5	1.5	38	11.3	278	82.5	21	6.2	
MD FEMALE	0	.0	23	13.6	2	1.2	3	.0	25	14.8	135	79.9	9	5.3	
MD MALE	0	.0	8	4.8	0	.0	0	3.0	13	7.7	143	85.1	12	7.1	
U OF MD BALT PROF SCHOOLS															
MD TOTAL	3	.2	107	.4	15	1.2	8	.6	133	10.4	1,120	87.7	24	1.9	1
MD FEMALE	3	.3	92	8.5	11	1.1	5	.5	111	11.5	849	87.7	8	.8	
MD MALE	0	.0	15	4.19	4	1.13	3	1.0	22	7.1	271	87.7	16	512	
U MD UNIVERSITY COLLEGE															
MD TOTAL	0	.0	37	10.1	9	2.5	5	1.4	51	14.0	311	85.2	3	.8	
MD FEMALE	0	.0	15	8.0	9	4.8	0	.0	24	12.8	163	87.2	0	.0	
MD MALE	0	.0	22	12.4	0	.0	5	2.8	27	15.2	148	83.1	3	1.7	
WASHINGTON BIBLE COLLEGE															
MD TOTAL	0	.0	6	7	2	2.2	1	1.1	9	10.0	75	83.3	6	6.7	
MD FEMALE	0	.0	1	2.0	0	0	0	.0	1	25.0	2	50.0	1	25.0	
MD MALE	0	.0	5	9.18	2	2.13	1	1.2	8	9.3	73	84.9	5	5.8	
WASHINGTON COLLEGE															
MD TOTAL	1	1.2	6	7.1	1	1.2	1	1.2		10.6	76	89.4	0	.0	
MD FEMALE	1	1.7	3	5.0	1	1.7	1	1.7		10.0	54	90.0	0	.0	
MD MALE	0	.0	3	12.0	0	10	0	.0	8	12.0	22	88.0	0	.0	
WASHINGTON THEOL UNION															
MD TOTAL	0	.0	0	.0	0	.0	0	.0	0	.0	0	.0	0	.0	
MD FEMALE	0	.0	0	.0	0	.0	0	.0	0	.0	0	.0	0	.0	
MD MALE	0	.0	0	.0	0	.0	0	.0	8	.0	0	.0	0	.0	
WESTERN MARYLAND COLLEGE															
MD TOTAL	0	.0	3	.8	0	.0	2	.5	5	1.4	361	98.6	0	.0	
MD FEMALE	0	.0	3	1.3	0	.0	1	.4	4	1.7	231	98.3	0	.0	
MD MALE	0	.0	0	.0	0	.0	1	.8	1	.8	130	99.2	0	.0	
MARYLAND															
MD TOTAL	62	.3	2,063	9.8	231	1.1	161	.8	2,517	11.9	17,409	82.5	1,170	5.5	2
MD FEMALE	39	.4	1,334	12.3	119	1.1	87	.8	1,579	14.5	8,970	82.6	307	2.8	1
MD MALE	23	.2	729	7.1	112	1.1	74	.7	938	9.2	8,439	82.4	863	8.4	1
(27 INSTITUTIONS)															
MASSACHUSETTS															
AMERICAN INTRNATL COLLEGE															
MA TOTAL	0	.0	16	2.7	5	.9	7	1.2	28	.	945	93.2	12	2.1	
MA FEMALE	0	.0	11	4.0	2	.7	3	1.1	16		259	93.5	2	.7	
MA MALE	0	.0	5	1.6	3	1.0	4	1.3	12	3.19	286	92.9	10	3.2	
ANDOVER NEWTON THEOL SCH															
MA TOTAL	2	1.3	7	4.6	2	1.3	2	1.3	13	8.6	136	90.1	2	1.3	
MA FEMALE	0	.0	2	10.0	0	.0	0	.0	2	10.0	18	90.0	0	.0	
MA MALE	2	1.5	5	3.8	2	1.5	2	1.5	11	8.4	118	90.1	2	1.5	
ANNA MARIA COLLEGE															
MA TOTAL	0	.0	1	.4	1	.4	2	.8	4	1.	250	97.7	2	.8	
MA FEMALE	0	.0	0	.0	1	.9	1	.9	2	.0	103	97.2	1	.9	
MA MALE	0	.0	1	.7	0	.0	1	.7	2	1.8	147	98.0	1	.7	
ADL MGMT ED INSTITUTE															
MA TOTAL	0	.0	5	7.2	0	.0	0	.0	5	7.2	3	4.3	61	88.4	
MA FEMALE	0	.0	1	25.0	0	.0	0	.0	1	25.0	1	25.0	2	50.0	
MA MALE	0	.0	4	6.2	0	.0	0	.0	4	6.2	2	3.1	59	90.8	
ASSUMPTION COLLEGE															
MA TOTAL	0	.0	2	.5	1	.3	10	2.7	13	3.5	354	95.4	4	1.1	
MA FEMALE	0	.0	1	.4	1	.4	4	1.8	6	2.7	217	96.4	2	.9	
MA MALE	0	.0	1	.7	0	.0	6	4.1	7	4.8	137	93.8	2	1.4	
BABSON COLLEGE															
MA TOTAL	0	.0	9	.6	8	.5	1	.1	18	1.2	1,484	96.9	30	2.0	
MA FEMALE	0	.0	3	.7	0	.0	0	.0	3	.7	429	98.8	2	.5	
MA MALE	0	.0	6	.5	8	.7	1	.1	15	1.4	1,055	96.1	28	2.6	

N E	BLACK NON-HISPANIC		ASIAN OR PACIFIC ISLANDER		HISPANIC		TOTAL MINORITY		WHITE NON-HISPANIC		NON-RESIDENT ALIEN		TOTAL
	NUMBER	%	NUMBER	%	NUMBER	%	NUMBER	%	NUMBER	%	NUMBER	%	NUMBER
INUED													
	2	.3	2	.3	0	.0	4	.7	584	98.6	4	.7	592
	0	.0	0	.0	0	.0	0	.0	88	98.9	1	1.1	89
	2	.4	2	.4	0	.0	4	.8	496	98.6	3	.6	503
	68	2.3	36	1.2	25	.8	131	4.4	2,828	95.2	12	.4	2,971
	43	2.5	27	1.6	11	.6	82	4.8	1,636	95.0	4	.2	1,722
	25	2.0	9	.7	14	1.1	49	3.9	1,192	95.4	8	.6	1,249
	3	6.4	0	.0	1	2.1	4	8.5	42	89.4	1	2.1	47
	2	6.1	0	.0	1	3.0	3	9.1	30	90.9	0	.0	33
	1	7.1	0	.0	0	.0	1	7.1	12	85.7	1	7.1	14
	150	2.3	73	1.1	72	1.1	301	4.5	5,705	87.2	536	8.2	6,542
	84	2.4	39	1.1	33	.9	159	4.5	3,198	89.7	210	5.4	3,567
	66	2.2	34	1.1	39	1.3	142	4.8	2,507	84.3	326	11.0	2,975
	17	2.5	5	.7	11	1.6	34	5.1	550	82.3	8	12.6	668
	11	3.5	2	.6	4	1.3	17	5.4	272	86.9	24	7.7	313
	4	1.7	3	.8	7	2.0	17	4.8	278	78.3	60	16.9	355
	7	1.3	2	.4	8	1.5	17	3.2	447	83.4	72	13.4	536
	3	1.4	0	.0	1	.5	4	1.9	182	87.5	22	10.6	208
	4	1.2	2	.6	7	2.1	13	4.0	265	80.8	50	15.2	328
	0	.0	0	.0	0	.0	0	.0	3	100.0	0	.0	3
	0	.0	0	.0	0	.0	0	.0	1	100.0	0	.0	1
	0	.0	0	.0	0	.0	0	.0	2	100.0	0	.0	2
	0	.5	0	.0	0	.0	0	.0	4	100.0	0	.0	4
	0	.0	0	.0	0	.0	0	.0	1	100.0	0	.0	1
	0	.0	0	.0	0	.0	0	.0	3	100.0	0	.0	3
	6	5.6	1	.8	3	2.5	11	9.1	101	83.5	9	7.4	121
	3	3.4	0	.0	2	2.3	6	6.9	76	87.4	5	5.7	87
	3	8.8	1	2.9	1	2.9	5	14.7	25	73.5	4	11.8	34
	0	.0	0	.0	0	.0	0	.0	62	100.0	0	.0	62
	0	.0	0	.0	0	.0	0	.0	57	100.0	0	.0	57
	0	.0	0	.0	0	.0	0	.0	5	100.0	0	.0	5
	0	.0	0	.0	0	.0	0	.0	7	100.0	0	.0	7
	0	.0	0	.0	0	.0	0	.0	4	100.0	0	.0	4
	0	.0	0	.0	0	.0	0	.0	3	100.0	0	.0	3
	9	6.1	1	.7	1	.7	11	7.5	127	86.4	9	6.1	147
	3	4.6	1	1.5	0	.0	4	6.2	56	86.2	5	7.7	65
	6	7.3	0	.0	1	1.2	7	8.5	71	86.6	4	4.9	82
	250	3.8	139	2.1	151	2.3	564	8.5	5,299	80.3	734	11.1	6,597
	104	4.6	49	2.2	57	2.5	221	9.8	1,831	81.4	197	8.8	2,249
	146	3.4	90	2.1	94	2.2	343	7.9	3,468	79.8	537	12.4	4,348
	0	.0	0	.0	0	.0	0	.0	21	100.0	0	.0	21
	0	.0	0	.0	0	.0	0	.0	13	100.0	0	.0	13
	0	.0	0	.0	0	.0	0	.0	8	100.0	0	.0	8
	0	.0	0	.0	0	.0	0	.0	70	90.9	7	9.1	77
	0	.0	0	.0	0	.0	0	.0	4	100.0	0	.0	4
	0	.0	0	.0	0	.0	0	.0	66	90.4	7	9.6	73
	20	2.9	4	.6	4	.6	28	4.1	638	94.1	12	1.8	678
	18	3.0	4	.7	3	.5	25	4.1	572	94.2	10	1.6	607
	2	2.8	0	.0	1	1.4	3	4.2	66	93.0	2	2.8	71
	0	.0	2	2.0	0	.0	2	2.0	83	83.5	14	14.1	99
	0	.0	1	4.2	0	.0	1	4.2	19	79.2	4	16.7	24
	0	.0	1	1.3	0	.0	1	1.3	64	85.3	10	13.3	75
	102	2.6	50	1.3	26	.7	183	4.6	2,600	65.9	1,161	29.4	3,944
	36	5.9	7	1.1	6	1.0	50	8.2	468	76.7	92	15.1	610
	66	2.0	43	1.3	20	.6	133	4.0	2,132	63.9	1,069	32.1	3,334
	17	4.2	2	.5	2	.5	26	6.4	376	92.2	6	1.5	409
	9	4.5	0	.0	0	.0	9	4.5	186	93.5	4	2.0	199
	8	3.8	2	1.0	2	1.0	17	8.1	190	90.9	2	1.0	209
	1	.1	4	.5	1	.1	7	.8	846	98.9	2	.2	855
	0	.0	2	.4	0	.0	2	.4	509	99.4	1	.2	512
	1	.3	2	.6	1	.3	5	1.5	337	98.3	1	.3	343
	12	1.2	0	.0	3	.3	15	1.5	958	98.5	0	.0	973
	3	.5	0	.0	1	.2	4	.7	561	99.3	0	.0	565
	9	2.2	0	.0	2	.5	11	2.7	397	97.3	0	.0	408
	2	.6	3	1.0	2	.6	7	2.3	302	97.1	2	.6	311
	1	.4	2	.9	1	.4	4	1.8	220	97.3	2	.9	226
	1	1.2	1	1.2	1	1.2	3	3.5	82	96.5	0	.0	85
	0	.0	0	.0	0	.0	0	.0	72	96.0	3	4.0	75
	0	.0	0	.0	0	.0	0	.0	54	96.4	2	3.6	56
	0	.0	0	.0	0	.0	0	.0	18	94.7	1	5.3	19

	AMERICAN INDIAN ALASKAN NATIVE		BLACK NON-HISPANIC		ASIAN OR PACIFIC ISLANDER		HISPANIC		TOTAL MINORITY		WHITE NON-HISPANIC		NON-RESIDENT ALIEN		T
	NUMBER	%	NUMBER	%	NUMBER	%	NUMBER	%	NUMBER	%	NUMBER	%	NUMBER	%	N
MASSACHUSETTS CONTINUED															
NORTH ADAMS STATE COLLEGE															
MA TOTAL	0	.0	0	.0	0	.0	0	.0	0	.0	278	100.0	0	.0	
MA FEMALE	0	.0	0	.0	0	.0	0	.0	0	.0	144	100.0	0	.0	
MA MALE	0	.0	0	.0	0	.0	0	.0	0	.0	134	100.0	0	.0	
SALEM STATE COLLEGE															
MA TOTAL	1	.1	3	.3	2	.2	5	.5	11	1.1	949	98.9	0	.0	
MA FEMALE	0	.0	3	.5	1	.2	3	.5	7	1.1	623	98.9	0	.0	
MA MALE	1	.3	0	.0	1	.3	2	.6	4	1.2	326	98.8	0	.0	
WORCESTER STATE COLLEGE															
MA TOTAL	0	.0	8	2.0	2	.5	1	.3	11	2.8	369	94.1	12	3.1	
MA FEMALE	0	.0	5	2.1	1	.4	0	.0	6	2.6	220	94.4	7	3.0	
MA MALE	0	.0	3	1.9	1	.6	1	.6	5	3.1	149	93.7	5	3.1	
MOUNT HOLYOKE COLLEGE															
MA TOTAL	0	.0	0	.0	0	.0	0	.0	0	.0	15	78.9	4	21.1	
MA FEMALE	0	.0	0	.0	0	.0	0	.0	0	.0	11	73.3	4	26.7	
MA MALE	0	.0	0	.0	0	.0	0	.0	0	.0	4	100.0	0	.0	
NEW ENG CONSV OF MUSIC															
MA TOTAL	0	.0	6	2.4	4	1.6	6	2.4	16	6.3	222	87.1	17	6.7	
MA FEMALE	0	.0	3	2.1	2	1.4	4	2.8	9	6.4	118	83.7	14	9.9	
MA MALE	0	.0	3	2.6	2	1.8	2	1.8	7	6.1	104	91.2	3	2.6	
NICHOLS COLLEGE															
MA TOTAL	0	.0	0	.0	0	.0	0	.0	0	.0	96	98.0	2	2.0	
MA FEMALE	0	.0	0	.0	0	.0	0	.0	0	.0	15	100.0	0	.0	
MA MALE	0	.0	0	.0	0	.0	0	.0	0	.0	81	97.6	2	2.4	
NORTHEASTERN UNIVERSITY															
MA TOTAL	14	.3	155	3.2	252	5.3	65	1.4	486	10.2	4,200	87.9	91	1.9	
MA FEMALE	3	.2	45	2.7	70	4.2	21	1.3	139	8.3	1,512	90.5	20	1.2	
MA MALE	11	.4	110	3.5	182	5.9	44	1.4	347	11.2	2,688	86.5	71	2.3	
REGIS COLLEGE															
MA TOTAL	0	.0	7	4.0	3	1.7	4	2.3	14	7.9	163	92.1	0	.0	
MA FEMALE	0	.0	5	3.1	3	1.8	3	1.8	11	6.7	152	93.3	0	.0	
MA MALE	0	.0	2	14.3	0	.0	1	7.1	3	21.4	11	78.6	0	.0	
SCH OF MUSEUM FINE ARTS															
MA TOTAL	0	.0	0	.0	0	.0	0	.0	0	.0	24	100.0	0	.0	
MA FEMALE	0	.0	0	.0	0	.0	0	.0	0	.0	15	100.0	0	.0	
MA MALE	0	.0	0	.0	0	.0	0	.0	0	.0	9	100.0	0	.0	
SIMMONS COLLEGE															
MA TOTAL	0	.0	38	3.7	12	1.2	9	.9	59	5.8	942	92.2	21	2.1	
MA FEMALE	0	.0	33	3.7	11	1.2	8	.9	52	5.8	819	91.9	20	2.2	
MA MALE	0	.0	5	3.8	1	.8	1	.8	7	5.3	123	93.9	1	.8	
SMITH COLLEGE															
MA TOTAL	0	.0	1	1.1	0	.0	0	.0	1	1.1	76	87.4	10	11.5	
MA FEMALE	0	.0	0	.0	0	.0	0	.0	0	.0	68	90.7	7	9.3	
MA MALE	0	.0	1	8.3	0	.0	0	.0	1	8.3	8	66.7	3	25.0	
STHESTN MASS UNIVERSITY															
MA TOTAL	0	.0	0	.0	0	.0	0	.0	0	.0	134	97.8	3	2 2	
MA FEMALE	0	.0	0	.0	0	.0	0	.0	0	.0	32	100.0	0	0	
MA MALE	0	.0	0	.0	0	.0	0	.0	0	.0	102	97.1	3	219	
SPRINGFIELD COLLEGE															
MA TOTAL	0	.0	23	6.6	7	2.0	9	2.6	39	11.1	287	81.8	25	7	
MA FEMALE	0	.0	10	5.5	3	1.7	5	2.8	18	9.9	156	86.2	7	3	
MA MALE	0	.0	13	7.6	4	2.4	4	2.4	21	12.4	131	77.1	18	101	
SUFFOLK UNIVERSITY															
MA TOTAL	0	.0	46	4.1	6	.5	4	.4	56	5.0	1,034	92.5	28	2 5	
MA FEMALE	0	.0	21	5.4	3	.8	2	.5	26	6.7	351	90.9	9	2 3	
MA MALE	0	.C	25	3.4	3	.4	2	.3	30	4.1	683	93.3	19	216	
TUFTS UNIVERSITY															
MA TOTAL	0	.0	9	1.4	4	.6	3	.5	16	2.6	587	94.2	20	3 2	
MA FEMALE	0	.0	4	1.1	1	.3	0	.0	5	1.4	340	95.5	11	3 1	
MA MALE	0	.0	5	1.9	3	1.1	3	1.1	11	4.1	247	92.5	9	314	
UNIVERSITY OF LOWELL															
MA TOTAL	0	.0	27	2.3	22	1.9	12	1.0	61	5.2	984	83.8	129	11.0	
MA FEMALE	0	.0	9	2.2	6	1.5	4	1.0	19	4.7	369	92.0	13	3.2	
MA MALE	0	.0	18	2.3	16	2.1	8	1.0	42	5.4	615	79.6	116	15.0	
U OF MASS AMHERST CAMPUS															
MA TOTAL	13	.3	257	6.1	82	1.9	113	2.7	465	11.0	3,326	79.0	421	10.0	
MA FEMALE	6	.4	103	6.1	27	1.6	48	2.8	184	10.9	1,365	80.9	139	8.2	
MA MALE	7	.3	154	6.1	55	2.2	65	2.6	281	11.1	1,961	77.7	282	11.2	
U OF MASS BOSTON CAMPUS															
MA TOTAL	0	.0	7	7.0	2	2.0	2	2.0	11	11.0	89	89.0	0	.0	
MA FEMALE	0	.0	3	6.3	1	2.1	1	2.1	5	10.4	43	89.6	0	.0	
MA MALE	0	.0	4	7.7	1	1.9	1	1.9	6	11.5	46	88.5	0	.0	
WESTERN NEW ENG COLLEGE															
MA TOTAL	2	.2	47	4.4	10	.9	3	.3	62	5.8	1,004	94.1	1	.1	
MA FEMALE	0	.0	15	7.2	2	1.0	1	.5	18	8.7	189	91.3	0	.0	
MA MALE	2	.2	32	3.7	8	.9	2	.2	44	5.1	815	94.8	1	.1	
WHEELOCK COLLEGE															
MA TOTAL	0	.0	3	2.8	0	.0	0	.0	3	2.8	101	93.5	4	3.7	
MA FEMALE	0	.0	3	3.0	0	.0	0	.0	3	3.0	93	93.0	4	4.0	
MA MALE	0	.0	0	.0	0	.0	0	.0	0	.0	8	100.0	0	.0	
WILLIAMS COLLEGE															
MA TOTAL	0	.0	0	.0	0	.0	0	.0	0	.0	20	50.0	20	50.0	
MA FEMALE	0	.0	0	.0	0	.0	0	.0	0	.0	15	71.4	6	28.6	
MA MALE	0	.0	0	.0	0	.0	0	.0	0	.0	5	26.3	14	73.7	
WORCESTER POLY INSTITUTE															
MA TOTAL	0	.0	5	.6	10	1.2	1	.1	16	1.9	709	85.3	106	12.8	
MA FEMALE	0	.0	0	.0	0	.0	0	.0	0	.0	101	96.2	4	3.8	
MA MALE	0	.0	5	.7	10	1.4	1	.1	16	2.2	608	83.7	102	14.0	
MASSACHUSETTS TOTAL (51 INSTITUTIONS)															
MA TOTAL	77	.2	1,348	2.9	759	1.6	569	1.2	2,753	5.9	40,106	86.2	3,693	7.9	
MA FEMALE	26	.1	600	3.0	269	1.4	228	1.2	1,123	5.7	17,816	90.0	857	4.3	
MA MALE	51	.2	748	2.8	490	1.8	341	1.3	1,630	6.1	22,290	83.3	2,836	10.6	

ENROLLMENT IN INSTITUTIONS OF HIGHER EDUCATION BY RACE, ETHNICITY AND SEX:
TATE AND NATION, 1978

IN /E	BLACK NON-HISPANIC		ASIAN OR PACIFIC ISLANDER		HISPANIC		TOTAL MINORITY		WHITE NON-HISPANIC		NON-RESIDENT ALIEN		TOTAL
	NUMBER	%	NUMBER	%	NUMBER	%	NUMBER	%	NUMBER	%	NUMBER	%	NUMBER
	0	.0	0	.0	0	.0	0	.0	21	100.0	0	.0	21
	0	.0	0	.0	0	.0	0	.0	11	100.0	0	.0	11
	0	.0	0	.0	0	.0	0	.0	10	100.0	0	.0	10
	37	7.2	13	2.5	29	5.7	80	15.6	279	54.4	154	30.0	513
	18	8.7	4	1.9	14	6.8	37	17.9	129	62.3	41	19.8	207
	19	6.2	9	2.9	15	4.9	43	14.1	150	49.0	113	36.9	306
	3	1.8	0	.0	1	.6	4	2.4	163	95.9	3	1.8	170
	2	3.5	0	.0	0	.0	2	3.5	55	96.5	0	.0	57
	1	.9	0	.0	1	.9	2	1.8	108	95.6	3	2.7	113
	0	.0	0	.0	0	.0	0	.0	15	88.2	2	11.8	17
	0	.0	0	.0	0	.0	0	.0	9	90.0	1	10.0	10
	0	.0	0	.0	0	.0	0	.0	6	85.7	1	14.3	7
	0	.0	0	.0	0	.0	0	.0	22	84.6	4	15.4	26
	0	.0	0	.0	0	.0	0	.0	0	.0	0	.0	0
	0	.0	0	.0	0	.0	0	.0	22	84.6	4	15.4	26
	26	.8	8	.2	14	.4	50	1.5	3,218	96.3	75	2.2	3,343
	15	.9	3	.2	11	.6	31	1.8	1,695	97.5	13	.7	1,739
	11	.7	5	.3	3	.2	19	1.2	1,523	95.0	62	3.9	1,604
	2	1.5	3	2.2	2	1.5	7	5.1	124	90.5	6	4.4	137
	1	1.8	2	3.6	0	.0	3	5.5	51	92.7	1	1.8	55
	1	1.2	1	1.2	2	2.4	4	4.9	73	89.0	5	6.1	82
	340	6.1	46	.8	24	.4	417	7.4	4,982	89.0	201	3.6	5,600
	212	6.3	22	.7	9	.3	249	7.5	3,008	90.1	83	2.5	3,340
	128	5.7	24	1.1	15	.7	168	7.4	1,974	87.3	118	5.2	2,260
	4	8.0	0	.0	0	.0	4	8.0	46	92.0	0	.0	50
	0	.0	0	.0	0	.0	0	.0	7	100.0	0	.0	7
	4	9.3	0	.0	0	.0	4	9.3	39	90.7	0	.0	43
	22	2.5	6	.7	11	1.3	44	5.1	822	94.9	0	.0	866
	13	3.4	1	.3	6	1.6	20	5.2	362	94.8	0	.0	382
	9	1.9	5	1.0	5	1.0	24	5.0	460	95.0	0	.0	484
	0	.0	0	.0	0	.0	0	.0	19	65.5	10	34.5	29
	0	.0	0	.0	0	.0	0	.0	8	57.1	6	42.9	14
	0	.0	0	.0	0	.0	0	.0	11	73.3	4	26.7	15
	42	35.3	0	.0	0	.0	42	35.3	76	63.9	1	.8	119
	40	38.8	0	.0	0	.0	40	38.8	63	61.2	0	.0	103
	2	12.5	0	.0	0	.0	2	12.5	13	81.3	1	6.3	16
	9	10.2	2	2.3	2	2.3	13	14.8	73	83.0	2	2.3	88
	6	10.5	2	3.5	1	1.8	9	15.8	47	82.5	1	1.8	57
	3	9.7	0	.0	1	3.2	4	12.9	26	83.9	1	3.2	31
	406	4.2	86	.9	91	.9	605	6.3	7,933	82.6	1,063	11.1	9,601
	229	5.2	34	.8	43	1.0	312	7.1	3,871	87.6	237	5.4	4,420
	177	3.4	52	1.0	48	.9	293	5.7	4,062	78.4	826	15.9	5,181
	1	.4	2	.8	1	.4	5	2.0	211	86.1	29	11.8	245
	0	.0	0	.0	0	.0	0	.0	19	86.4	3	13.6	22
	1	.4	2	.9	1	.4	5	2.2	192	86.1	26	11.7	223
	1	.1	3	.4	4	.5	12	1.4	807	95.1	30	3.5	849
	1	.2	2	.4	1	.2	7	1.5	460	96.2	11	2.3	478
	0	.0	1	.3	3	.8	5	1.3	347	93.5	19	5.1	371
	90	4.0	4	.2	9	.4	106	4.8	2,111	94.7	11	.5	2,228
	78	4.5	1	.1	7	.4	89	5.2	1,636	94.7	3	.2	1,728
	12	2.4	3	.6	2	.4	17	3.4	475	95.0	8	1.6	500
	0	.0	0	.0	0	.0	0	.0	1	100.0	0	.0	1
	0	.0	0	.0	0	.0	0	.0	0	.0	0	.0	0
	0	.0	0	.0	0	.0	0	.0	1	100.0	0	.0	1
	20	3.3	1	.2	9	1.5	34	5.6	566	94.0	2	.3	602
	11	2.9	1	.3	3	.8	17	4.5	360	95.5	0	.0	377
	9	4.0	0	.0	6	2.7	17	7.6	206	91.6	2	.9	225
	2	2.2	0	.0	2	2.2	4	4.3	88	94.6	1	1.1	93
	0	.0	0	.0	2	3.0	2	3.0	64	97.0	0	.0	66
	2	7.4	0	.0	0	.0	2	7.4	24	88.9	1	3.7	27
	216	9.7	23	1.0	8	.4	247	11.1	1,832	82.4	143	6.4	2,222
	133	18.8	7	1.0	1	.1	141	20.0	546	77.3	19	2.7	706
	83	5.5	16	1.1	7	.5	106	7.0	1,286	84.8	124	8.2	1,516
	773	7.1	200	1.8	144	1.3	1,150	10.5	8,440	77.3	1,329	12.2	10,919
	471	9.8	75	1.6	53	1.1	623	13.0	3,848	80.3	320	6.7	4,791
	302	4.9	125	2.0	91	1.5	527	8.6	4,592	74.9	1,009	16.5	6,128
	27	6.2	9	2.1	2	.5	39	8.9	383	87.6	15	3.4	437
	18	11.3	2	1.3	0	.0	21	13.1	136	85.0	3	1.9	160
	9	3.2	7	2.5	2	.7	18	6.5	247	89.2	12	4.3	277

TABLE 2 - TOTAL GRADUATE ENROLLMENT IN INSTITUTIONS OF HIGHER EDUCATION BY RACE, ETHNICITY AND SEX:
INSTITUTION, STATE AND NATION, 1978

	AMERICAN INDIAN ALASKAN NATIVE		BLACK NON-HISPANIC		ASIAN OR PACIFIC ISLANDER		HISPANIC		TOTAL MINORITY		WHITE NON-HISPANIC		NON-RESIDENT ALIEN	
	NUMBER	%	NUMBER	%	NUMBER	%	NUMBER	%	NUMBER	%	NUMBER	%	NUMBER	%
MICHIGAN	**CONTINUED**													
U OF MICHIGAN-FLINT														
MI TOTAL	0	.0	5	13.5	0	.0	1	2.7	6	16.2	31	83.8	0	.0
MI FEMALE	0	.0	1	4.5	0	.0	1	4.5	2	9.1	20	90.9	0	.0
MI MALE	0	.0	4	26.7	0	.0	0	.0	4	26.7	11	73.3	0	.0
WALSH C ACCTY & BUS ADMIN														
MI TOTAL	0	.0	3	1.3	4	1.7	0	.0	7	3.0	226	97.0	0	.0
MI FEMALE	0	.0	0	.0	1	4.0	0	.0	1	4.0	24	96.0	0	.0
MI MALE	0	.0	3	1.4	3	1.4	0	.0	6	2.9	202	97.1	0	.0
WAYNE STATE UNIVERSITY														
MI TOTAL	57	.9	1,013	15.2	159	2.4	58	.9	1,287	19.3	5,229	78.4	150	2.3
MI FEMALE	24	.7	731	20.5	37	1.0	35	1.0	827	23.2	2,700	75.8	35	1.0
MI MALE	33	1.1	262	9.1	122	3.9	23	.7	460	14.8	2,529	81.5	115	3.7
WESTERN MICH UNIVERSITY														
MI TOTAL	6	.2	113	3.1	18	.5	38	1.0	175	4.8	3,240	88.1	264	7.2
MI FEMALE	4	.2	69	3.5	11	.6	22	1.1	106	5.4	1,783	91.2	66	3.4
MI MALE	2	.1	44	2.6	7	.4	16	.9	69	4.0	1,457	84.5	198	11.5
WESTERN THEOLOGICAL SEM														
MI TOTAL	0	.0	0	.0	0	.0	0	.0	0	.0	10	71.4	4	28.6
MI FEMALE	0	.0	0	.0	0	.0	0	.0	0	.0	0	.0	0	.0
MI MALE	0	.0	0	.0	0	.0	0	.0	0	.0	10	71.4	4	28.6
MICHIGAN	**TOTAL (28 INSTITUTIONS)**													
MI TOTAL	146	.3	3,155	6.5	587	1.2	450	.9	4,338	8.9	40,968	83.9	3,499	7.2
MI FEMALE	76	.3	2,049	8.4	205	.8	209	.9	2,539	10.5	20,912	86.1	843	3.5
MI MALE	70	.3	1,106	4.5	382	1.6	241	1.0	1,799	7.3	20,056	81.8	2,656	10.8
MINNESOTA														
BETHEL THEOL SEMINARY														
MN TOTAL	0	.0	0	.0	0	.0	0	.0	0	.0	56	94.9	3	5.1
MN FEMALE	0	.0	0	.0	0	.0	0	.0	0	.0	0	.0	0	.0
MN MALE	0	.0	0	.0	0	.0	0	.0	0	.0	56	94.9	3	5.1
COLLEGE OF SAINT THOMAS														
MN TOTAL	2	.2	15	1.1	10	.8	2	.2	29	2.2	1,279	97.3	7	.5
MN FEMALE	0	.0	7	1.3	1	.2	1	.2	9	1.6	540	98.0	2	.4
MN MALE	2	.3	8	1.0	9	1.2	1	.1	20	2.6	739	96.7	5	.7
LUTHER THEOLOGICAL SEM														
MN TOTAL	0	.0	0	.0	0	.0	0	.0	0	.0	79	95.2	4	4.8
MN FEMALE	0	.0	0	.0	0	.0	0	.0	0	.0	1	100.0	0	.0
MN MALE	0	.0	0	.0	0	.0	0	.0	0	.0	78	95.1	4	4.9
NTHWSTN LUTH THEOL SEM														
MN TOTAL	0	.0	0	.0	0	.0	0	.0	0	.0	16	100.0	0	.0
MN FEMALE	0	.0	0	.0	0	.0	0	.0	0	.0	2	100.0	0	.0
MN MALE	0	.0	0	.0	0	.0	0	.0	0	.0	14	100.0	0	.0
SAINT JOHN'S UNIVERSITY														
MN TOTAL	0	.0	0	.0	0	.0	1	.7	1	.7	128	95.5	5	3.7
MN FEMALE	0	.0	0	.0	0	.0	0	.0	0	.0	20	95.2	1	4.8
MN MALE	0	.0	0	.0	0	.0	1	.9	1	.9	108	95.6	4	3.5
SAINT MARY'S COLLEGE														
MN TOTAL	0	.0	0	.0	0	.0	0	.0	0	.0	39	100.0	0	.0
MN FEMALE	0	.0	0	.0	0	.0	0	.0	0	.0	20	100.0	0	.0
MN MALE	0	.0	0	.0	0	.0	0	.0	0	.0	19	100.0	0	.0
SAINT PAUL SEMINARY														
MN TOTAL	0	.0	0	.0	0	.0	0	.0	0	.0	21	100.0	0	.0
MN FEMALE	0	.0	0	.0	0	.0	0	.0	0	.0	0	.0	0	.0
MN MALE	0	.0	0	.0	0	.0	0	.0	0	.0	21	100.0	0	.0
BEMIDJI STATE U														
MN TOTAL	4	.9	2	.4	14	3.1	0	.0	20	4.5	403	89.8	26	5.8
MN FEMALE	2	1.0	1	.5	7	3.4	0	.0	10	4.9	192	93.2	4	1.9
MN MALE	2	.8	1	.4	7	2.9	0	.0	10	4.1	211	86.8	22	9.1
MANKATO STATE UNIVERSITY														
MN TOTAL	2	.1	5	.2	1	.0	0	.0	8	.3	2,248	93.9	139	5.8
MN FEMALE	0	.0	2	.2	1	.1	0	.0	3	.3	1,122	97.6	25	2.2
MN MALE	2	.2	3	.2	0	.0	0	.0	5	.4	1,126	90.4	114	9.2
MOORHEAD STATE UNIVERSITY														
MN TOTAL	0	.0	1	1.1	0	.0	0	.0	1	1.1	88	92.6	6	6.3
MN FEMALE	0	.0	0	.0	0	.0	0	.0	0	.0	47	92.2	4	7.8
MN MALE	0	.0	1	2.3	0	.0	0	.0	1	2.3	41	93.2	2	4.5
SAINT CLOUD ST UNIVERSITY														
MN TOTAL	0	.0	0	.0	0	.0	0	.0	0	.0	466	99.1	4	.9
MN FEMALE	0	.0	0	.0	0	.0	0	.0	0	.0	223	100.0	0	.0
MN MALE	0	.0	0	.0	0	.0	0	.0	0	.0	243	98.4	4	1.6
WINONA STATE UNIVERSITY														
MN TOTAL	0	.0	0	.0	0	.0	0	.0	0	.0	463	100.0	0	.0
MN FEMALE	0	.0	0	.0	0	.0	0	.0	0	.0	265	100.0	0	.0
MN MALE	0	.0	0	.0	0	.0	0	.0	0	.0	198	100.0	0	.0
UNITED THEOLOGICAL SEM														
MN TOTAL	0	.0	0	.0	0	.0	0	.0	0	.0	69	98.6	1	1.4
MN FEMALE	0	.0	0	.0	0	.0	0	.0	0	.0	19	100.0	0	.0
MN MALE	0	.0	0	.0	0	.0	0	.0	0	.0	50	98.0	1	2.0
U OF MINNESOTA DULUTH														
MN TOTAL	1	.2	1	.2	2	.5	1	.2	5	1.1	421	96.1	12	2.7
MN FEMALE	1	.5	0	.0	1	.5	1	.5	3	1.5	192	96.0	5	2.5
MN MALE	0	.0	1	.4	1	.4	0	.0	2	.8	229	96.2	7	2.9
U MINN MAYO GRAD SCH MED														
MN TOTAL	1	.2	8	1.8	8	1.8	7	1.6	24	5.5	397	91.7	12	2.8
MN FEMALE	0	.0	1	2.5	0	.0	0	.0	1	2.5	37	92.5	2	5.0
MN MALE	1	.3	7	1.8	8	2.0	7	1.8	23	5.9	360	91.6	10	2.5
U OF MINN MNPLS SNT PAUL														
MN TOTAL	29	.3	119	1.2	136	1.3	86	.8	370	3.6	8,906	87.4	912	9.0
MN FEMALE	11	.2	59	1.2	47	1.0	39	.8	156	3.3	4,376	92.4	206	4.3
MN MALE	18	.3	60	1.1	89	1.6	47	.9	214	3.9	4,530	83.1	706	13.0

158

BLACK NON-HISPANIC		ASIAN OR PACIFIC ISLANDER		HISPANIC		TOTAL MINORITY		WHITE NON-HISPANIC		NON-RESIDENT ALIEN		TOTAL
NUMBER	%	NUMBER	%	NUMBER	%	NUMBER	%	NUMBER	%	NUMBER	%	NUMBER

INUED

1	3.2	0	.0	0	.0	7	22.6	24	77.4	0	.0	31
1	3.6	0	.0	0	.0	6	21.4	22	78.6	0	.0	28
0	.0	0	.0	1	33.3	1	33.3	2	66.7	0	.0	3

(17 INSTITUTIONS)

152	.9	171	1.0	97	.6	465	2.8	15,103	90.4	1,131	6.8	16,699
71	.9	57	.8	41	.5	188	2.5	7,078	94.2	249	3.3	7,515
81	.9	114	1.2	56	.6	277	3.0	8,025	87.4	882	9.6	9,184
198	99.5	0	.0	0	.0	198	99.5	1	.5	0	.0	199
121	99.2	0	.0	0	.0	121	99.2	1	.8	0	.0	122
77	100.0	0	.0	0	.0	77	100.0	0	.0	0	.0	77
124	34.5	3	.8	0	.0	127	35.4	232	64.6	0	.0	359
89	38.0	1	.4	0	.0	90	38.5	144	61.5	0	.0	234
35	28.0	2	1.6	0	.0	37	29.6	88	70.4	0	.0	125
1,042	84.8	10	.8	2	.2	1,055	85.8	120	9.8	54	4.4	1,229
671	92.2	4	.5	0	.0	675	92.7	47	6.5	6	.8	728
371	74.1	6	1.2	2	.4	380	75.8	73	14.6	48	9.5	501
29	5.6	20	3.8	0	.0	59	11.3	453	86.8	10	1.9	522
21	10.0	3	1.4	0	.0	34	16.1	174	82.5	3	1.4	211
8	2.6	17	5.5	0	.0	25	8.0	279	89.7	7	2.3	311
149	8.5	3	.2	1	.1	159	9 1	1,414	81.1	171	9.8	1,744
100	13.4	1	.1	1	.1	105	14 1	615	82.3	27	3.6	747
49	4.9	2	.2	0	.0	54	514	799	80.1	144	14.4	997
66	22.8	0	.0	0	.0	66	22.8	216	74.5	8	2.8	290
66	22.8	0	.0	0	.0	66	22.8	216	74.5	8	2.8	290
0	.0	0	.0	0	.0	0	.0	0	.0	0	.0	0
77	98.7	1	1.3	0	.0	78	100.0	0	.0	0	.0	78
66	98.5	1	1.5	0	.0	67	100.0	0	.0	0	.0	67
11	100.0	0	.0	0	.0	11	100.0	0	.0	0	.0	11
7	2.4	5	1.7	1	.3	13	5	267	91.8	11	3.8	291
0	.0	1	4.5	0	.0	1	4.5	19	86.4	2	9.1	22
7	2.6	4	1.5	1	.4	12	4 15	248	92.2	9	3.3	269
38	5.2	5	.7	3	.4	46	6 3	612	84.1	70	9.6	728
24	7.1	3	.9	3	.9	30	8 8	296	87.3	13	3.8	339
14	3.6	2	.5	0	.0	16	411	316	81.2	57	14.7	389
8	7.8	0	.0	0	.0	8	7 8	90	88.2	4	3.9	102
6	9.7	0	.0	0	.0	6	9 7	54	87.1	2	3.2	62
2	5.0	0	.0	0	.0	2	510	36	90.0	2	5.0	40
256	9.7	21	.8	3	.1	282	10 6	2,370	89.4	0	.0	2,652
160	11.3	6	.4	1	.1	168	11 9	1,244	88.1	0	.0	1,412
96	7.7	15	1.2	2	.2	114	912	1,126	90.8	0	.0	1,240
106	26.0	0	.0	1	.2	107	26 2	301	73.8	0	.0	408
83	25.9	0	.0	0	.0	83	25 9	238	74.1	0	.0	321
23	26.4	0	.0	1	1.1	24	2716	63	72.4	0	.0	87

(12 INSTITUTIONS)

2,100	24.4	68	.8	11	.1	2,198	25.6	6,076	70.6	328	3.8	8,602
1,407	30.9	20	.4	5	.1	1,446	31.7	3,048	66.9	61	1.3	4,555
693	17.1	48	1.2	6	.1	752	18.6	3,028	74.8	267	6.6	4,047
0	.0	0	.0	0	.0		.0	176	94.6	10	5.4	186
0	.0	0	.0	0	.0	0	.0	27	100.0	0	.0	27
0	.0	0	.0	0	.0	0	.0	149	93.7	10	6.3	159
1	1.6	3	4.7	2	3.1	6	9.4	58	90.6	0	.0	64
1	3.2	1	3.2	0	.0	2	6.5	29	93.5	0	.0	31
0	.0	2	6.1	2	6.1	4	12.1	29	87.9	0	.0	33
3	8.1	0	.0	0	.0	3	8.1	32	86.5	2	5.4	37
1	33.3	0	.0	0	.0	1	33.3	2	66.7	0	.0	3
2	5.9	0	.0	0	.0	2	5.9	30	88.2	2	5.9	34
60	4.3	1	.1	2	.1	63	4.5	1,190	84.9	148	10.6	1,401
34	5.3	0	.0	1	.2	35	5.4	562	86.9	50	7.7	647
26	3.4	1	.1	1	.1	28	3.7	628	83.3	98	13.0	754
0	.0	0	.0	0	.0	0	.0	29	96.7	1	3.3	30
0	.0	0	.0	0	.0	0	.0	7	100.0	0	.0	7
0	.0	0	.0	0	.0	0	.0	22	95.7	1	4.3	23
0	.0	0	.0	0	.0	0	.0	49	76.6	15	23.4	64
0	.0	0	.0	0	.0	0	.0	0	.0	1	100.0	1
0	.0	0	.0	0	.0	0	.0	49	77.8	14	22.2	63

TABLE 2 - TOTAL GRADUATE ENROLLMENT IN INSTITUTIONS OF HIGHER EDUCATION BY RACE, ETHNICITY AND SEX:
INSTITUTION, STATE AND NATION, 1978

	AMERICAN INDIAN ALASKAN NATIVE		BLACK NON-HISPANIC		ASIAN OR PACIFIC ISLANDER		HISPANIC		TOTAL MINORITY		WHITE NON-HISPANIC		NON-RESIDENT ALIEN		T(
	NUMBER	%	NUMBER	%	NUMBER	%	NUMBER	%	NUMBER	%	NUMBER	%	NUMBER	%	NU
MISSOURI	CONTINUED														
COVENANT THEOLOGICAL SEM															
MO TOTAL	0	.0	1	2.2	1	2.2	0	.0	2	4.4	37	82.2	6	13.3	
MO FEMALE	0	.0	0	.0	0	.0	0	.0	0	.0	20	90.9	2	9.1	
MO MALE	0	.0	1	4.3	1	4.3	0	.0	2	8.7	17	73.9	4	17.4	
DRURY COLLEGE															
MO TOTAL	0	.0	1	.4	5	2.0	0	.0	6	2.4	243	96.0		1.6	
MO FEMALE	0	.0	0	.0	1	.7	0	.0	1	.7	146	99.3		.0	
MO MALE	0	.0	1	.9	4	3.8	0	.0	5	4.7	97	91.5	4	3.8	
EDEN THEOLOGICAL SEMINARY															
MO TOTAL	0	.0	1	1.4	0	.0	1	1.4	2	2.8	67	94.4	2	2.8	
MO FEMALE	0	.0	0	.0	0	.0	0	.0	0	.0	4	100.0	0	.0	
MO MALE	0	.0	1	1.5	0	.0	1	1.5	2	3.0	63	94.0	2	3.0	
FONTBONNE COLLEGE															
MO TOTAL	0	.0	3	9.7	1	3.2	0	.0	4	12.9	27	87.1	0	.0	
MO FEMALE	0	.0	2	7.7	1	3.8	0	.0	3	11.5	23	88.5	0	.0	
MO MALE	0	.0	1	20.0	0	.0	0	.0	1	20.0	4	80.0	0	.0	
KENRICK SEMINARY															
MO TOTAL	0	.0	0	.0	1	7.7	0	.0	1	7.7	11	84.6	1	7 7	
MO FEMALE	0	.0	0	.0	0	.0	0	.0	0	.0	0	.0	0		
MO MALE	0	.0	0	.0	1	7.7	0	.0	1	7.7	11	84.6	1	718	
LINCOLN UNIVERSITY															
MO TOTAL	2	.8	41	16.6	5	2.0	3	1.2	51	20.6	174	70.4	22	8	
MO FEMALE	1	.8	19	16.0	0	.0	1	.8	21	17.6	95	79.8	3	2 9	
MO MALE	1	.8	22	17.2	5	3.9	2	1.6	30	23.4	79	61.7	19	1418	
THE LINDENWOOD COLLEGES															
MO TOTAL	1	.2	10	2.3	0	.0	0	.0	11	2.5	422	97.5	0	.0	
MO FEMALE	0	.0	6	3.0	0	.0	0	.0	6	3.0	197	97.0	0	.0	
MO MALE	1	.4	4	1.7	0	.0	0	.0	5	2.2	225	97.8	0	.0	
MARYVILLE C-SAINT LOUIS															
MO TOTAL	0	.0	0	.0	0	.0	0	.0	0	.0	36	100.0	0	.0	
MO FEMALE	0	.0	0	.0	0	.0	0	.0	0	.0	36	100.0	0	.0	
MO MALE	0	.0	0	.0	0	.0	0	.0	0	.0	0	.0	0	.0	
MIDWESTERN BAPT THEOL SEM															
MO TOTAL	0	.0	1	.9	2	1.7	1	.9	4	3.4	110	94.8	2	1.7	
MO FEMALE	0	.0	1	7.1	0	.0	0	.0	1	7.1	13	92.9	0	.0	
MO MALE	0	.0	0	.0	2	2.0	1	1.0	3	2.9	97	95.1	2	2.0	
NAZARENE THEOLOGICAL SEM															
MO TOTAL	0	.0	1	1.1	1	1.1	2	2.1	4	4.3	82	87.2	8	9.5	
MO FEMALE	0	.0	0	.0	0	.0	0	.0	0	.0	25	96.2	1	3.8	
MO MALE	0	.0	1	1.5	1	1.5	2	2.9	4	5.9	57	83.8	7	10.3	
NTHEST MO ST UNIVERSITY															
MO TOTAL	2	.3	4	.5	15	1.9	2	.3	23	3.0	690	89.1	61	7.9	
MO FEMALE	2	.5	0	.0	3	.8	2	.5	7	1.8	375	94.0	17	4.3	
MO MALE	0	.0	4	1.1	12	3.2	0	.0	16	4.3	315	84.0	44	11.7	
NTHWST MO ST UNIVERSITY															
MO TOTAL	2	.3	1	.1	1	.1	0	.0	4	.6	646	96.9	17	2 5	
MO FEMALE	1	.3	0	.0	1	.3	0	.0	2	.6	349	97.2	8	2 2	
MO MALE	1	.3	1	.3	0	.0	0	.0	2	.6	297	96.4	9	2½9	
ROCKHURST COLLEGE															
MO TOTAL	2	.4	17	3.6	2	.4	3	.6	24	5.1	438	93.4	7	1.5	
MO FEMALE	0	.0	8	7.2	0	.0	1	.9	9	8.1	102	91.9	0	.0	
MO MALE	2	.6	9	2.5	2	.6	2	.6	15	4.2	336	93.9	7	2.3	
SNT LOUIS CHRISTIAN C															
MO TOTAL	0	.0	0	.0	0	.0	0	.0	0	.0	3	100.0	0	.0	
MO FEMALE	0	.0	0	.0	0	.0	0	.0	0	.0	0	.0	0	.0	
MO MALE	0	.0	0	.0	0	.0	0	.0	0	.0	3	100.0	0	.0	
SAINT LOUIS U MAIN CAMPUS															
MO TOTAL	3	.2	160	8.2	33	1.7	10	.5	206	10.6	1,686	86.9	49	2.5	
MO FEMALE	0	.0	104	10.4	12	1.2	5	.5	121	12.1	873	87.0	10	1.0	
MO MALE	3	.3	56	6.0	21	2.2	5	.5	85	9.1	813	86.8	39	4.2	
SNT PAUL SCH OF THEOLOGY															
MO TOTAL	0	.0	0	.0	0	.0	0	.0	0	.0	9	100.0	0	.0	
MO FEMALE	0	.0	0	.0	0	.0	0	.0	0	.0	0	.0	0	.0	
MO MALE	0	.0	0	.0	0	.0	0	.0	0	.0	9	100.0	0	.0	
STHEST MO ST UNIVERSITY															
MO TOTAL	1	.1	25	2.4	4	.4	3	.3	33	3.2	991	95.5	14	1.3	
MO FEMALE	0	.0	12	2.0	0	.0	2	.3	14	2.3	588	96.6	7	1.1	
MO MALE	1	.2	13	3.0	4	.9	1	.2	19	4.4	403	93.9	7	1.6	
STHWST MO ST UNIVERSITY															
MO TOTAL	1	.1	6	.6	4	.4	3	.3	14	1.5	942	98.2	3	.3	
MO FEMALE	0	.0	2	.4	1	.2	1	.2	4	.7	554	98.9	2	.4	
MO MALE	1	.2	4	1.0	3	.8	2	.5	10	2.5	388	97.2	1	.3	
U OF MISSOURI-COLUMBIA															
MO TOTAL	8	.2	90	2.1	143	3.3	36	.8	277	6.4	3,645	84.4	398	9.2	
MO FEMALE	2	.1	46	3.0	42	2.7	10	.6	100	6.5	1,344	87.2	97	6.3	
MO MALE	6	.2	44	1.6	101	3.6	26	.9	177	6.4	2,301	82.8	301	10.8	
U OF MISSOURI-KANSAS CITY															
MO TOTAL	11	.4	194	7.8	11	.4	23	.9	239	9.6	2,168	87.1	82	3.3	
MO FEMALE	5	.4	119	9.3	5	.4	13	1.0	142	11.0	1,120	87.1	24	1.9	
MO MALE	6	.5	75	6.2	6	.5	10	.8	97	8.1	1,048	87.1	58	4.8	
U OF MISSOURI-ROLLA															
MO TOTAL	1	.1	6	.8	13	1.8	5	.7	25	3.4	588	79.7	125	16.9	
MO FEMALE	1	1.7	0	.0	2	3.4	0	.0	3	5.2	40	69.0	15	25.9	
MO MALE	0	.0	6	.9	11	1.6	5	.7	22	3.2	548	80.6	110	16.2	
U OF MISSOURI-SAINT LOUIS															
MO TOTAL	7	.4	135	8.1	32	1.9	15	.9	189	11.4	1,461	88.0	11	.7	
MO FEMALE	4	.4	109	11.6	15	1.6	7	.7	135	14.4	797	85.1	5	.5	
MO MALE	3	.4	26	3.6	17	2.3	8	1.1	54	7.5	664	91.7	6	.8	
WASHINGTON UNIVERSITY															
MO TOTAL	2	.1	177	6.5	277	10.2	25	.9	481	17.7	2,033	74.9	201	7.4	
MO FEMALE	0	.0	101	9.5	23	2.2	7	.7	131	12.3	884	83.1	49	4.6	
MO MALE	2	.1	76	4.6	254	15.4	18	1.1	350	21.2	1,149	69.6	152	9.2	

TABLE 2 - TOTAL GRADUATE ENROLLMENT IN INSTITUTIONS OF HIGHER EDUCATION BY RACE, ETHNICITY AND SEX:
INSTITUTION, STATE AND NATION, 1978

	AMERICAN INDIAN ALASKAN NATIVE		BLACK NON-HISPANIC		ASIAN OR PACIFIC ISLANDER		HISPANIC		TOTAL MINORITY		WHITE NON-HISPANIC		NON-RESIDENT ALIEN		TOTAL
MISSOURI	NUMBER	%	NUMBER	%	NUMBER	%	NUMBER	%	NUMBER	%	NUMBER	%	NUMBER	%	NUMBER
MISSOURI	CONTINUED														
WEBSTER COLLEGE															
MO TOTAL	3	.1	356	12.1	13	.4	19	.6	391	13.3	2,552	86.6	4	.1	2,947
MO FEMALE	2	.2	144	16.9	3	.4	2	.2	151	17.7	701	82.2	1	.1	853
MO MALE	1	.0	212	10.1	10	.5	17	.8	240	11.5	1,851	88.4	3	.1	2,094
MISSOURI		TOTAL (	30 INSTITUTIONS)												
MO TOTAL	46	.2	1,294	5.4	568	2.4	155	.6	2,063	8.6	20,595	86.3	1,193	5.0	23,851
MO FEMALE	18	.2	709	7.0	110	1.1	52	.5	889	8.8	8,913	88.3	292	2.9	10,094
MO MALE	28	.2	585	4.3	458	3.3	103	.7	1,174	8.5	11,682	84.9	901	6.5	13,757
MONTANA															
COLLEGE OF GREAT FALLS															
MT TOTAL	0	.0	0	.0	0	.0	0	.0	0	.0	58	100.0	0	.0	58
MT FEMALE	0	.0	0	.0	0	.0	0	.0	0	.0	22	100.0	0	.0	22
MT MALE	0	.0	0	.0	0	.0	0	.0	0	.0	36	100.0	0	.0	36
EASTERN MONTANA COLLEGE															
MT TOTAL	5	1.2	1	.2	0	.0	0	.0	6	1.5	398	98.5	0	.0	404
MT FEMALE	5	2.0	0	.0	0	.0	0	.0	5	2.0	250	98.0	0	.0	255
MT MALE	0	.0	1	.7	0	.0	0	.0	1	.7	148	99.3	0	.0	149
MONTANA C MINRL SCI-TECHN															
MT TOTAL	0	.0	0	.0	1	5.3	0	.0	1	5.3	13	68.4	5	26.3	19
MT FEMALE	0	.0	0	.0	1	100.0	0	.0	1	100.0	0	.0	0	.0	1
MT MALE	0	.0	0	.0	0	.0	0	.0	0	.0	13	72.2	5	27.8	18
MONTANA STATE UNIVERSITY															
MT TOTAL	12	2.4	1	.2	2	.4	0	.0	15	2.9	484	94.9	11	2.2	510
MT FEMALE	6	3.7	0	.0	1	.6	0	.0	7	4.3	154	93.9	3	1.8	164
MT MALE	6	1.7	1	.3	1	.3	0	.0	8	2.3	330	95.4	8	2.3	346
NORTHERN MONTANA COLLEGE															
MT TOTAL	5	3.3	2	1.3	0	.0	1	.7	8	5.3	142	94.7	0	.0	150
MT FEMALE	3	4.4	0	.0	0	.0	0	.0		4.4	65	95.6	0	.0	68
MT MALE	2	2.4	2	2.4	0	.0	1	1.2	8	6.1	77	93.9	0	.0	82
UNIVERSITY OF MONTANA															
MT TOTAL	8	1.0	1	.1	5	.7	4	.5	18	2.4	728	95.4	17	2.2	763
MT FEMALE	4	1.3	0	.0	2	.7	1	.3	7	2.4	280	94.3	10	3.4	297
MT MALE	4	.9	1	.2	3	.6	3	.6	11	2.4	448	96.1	7	1.5	466
WESTERN MONTANA COLLEGE															
MT TOTAL	0	.0	0	.0	0	.0	0	.0	0	.0	197	100.0		.0	197
MT FEMALE	0	.0	0	.0	0	.0	0	.0	0	.0	122	100.0	0	.0	122
MT MALE	0	.0	0	.0	0	.0	0	.0	0	.0	75	100.0	0	.0	75
MONTANA		TOTAL (	7 INSTITUTIONS)												
MT TOTAL	30	1.4	5	.2		.4	5	.2	48	2.3	2,020	96.1	33	1.6	2,101
MT FEMALE	18	1.9	0	.0		.4	1	.1	23	2.5	893	96.1	13	1.4	929
MT MALE	12	1.0	5	.4	8	.3	4	.3	25	2.1	1,127	96.2	20	1.7	1,172
NEBRASKA															
CHADRON STATE COLLEGE															
NE TOTAL	3	1.2	1	.4	2	.8	1	.4	7	2.8	240	96.4	2	.8	249
NE FEMALE	1	.6	0	.0	1	.6	1	.6	3	1.9	153	98.1	0	.0	156
NE MALE	2	2.2	1	1.1	1	1.1	0	.0	4	4.3	87	93.5	2	2.2	93
CONCORDIA TCHRS COLLEGE															
NE TOTAL	0	.0	0	.0	0	.0	0	.0	0	.0	46	100.0		.0	46
NE FEMALE	0	.0	0	.0	0	.0	0	.0	0	.0	37	100.0	0	.0	37
NE MALE	0	.0	0	.0	0	.0	0	.0	0	.0	9	100.0	0	.0	9
CREIGHTON UNIVERSITY															
NE TOTAL	1	.4	4	1.6	5	2.0	4	1.6	14	5.7	227	92.7	4	1.6	245
NE FEMALE	0	.0	0	.0	1	1.3	1	1.3	2	2.6	75	96.2	1	1.3	78
NE MALE	1	.6	4	2.4	4	2.4	3	1.8	12	7.2	152	91.0	3	1.8	167
KEARNEY STATE COLLEGE															
NE TOTAL	1	.2	1	.2	0	.0	3	.6	5	.9	526	98.9	1	.2	532
NE FEMALE	0	.0	0	.0	0	.0	1	.3	1	.3	292	99.7	0	.0	293
NE MALE	1	.4	1	.4	0	.0	2	.8	4	1.7	234	97.9	1	.4	239
U OF NEBRASKA-LINCOLN															
NE TOTAL	8	.2	41	1.1	29	.8	29	.8	107	3.0	3,259	91.3	205	5 7	3,571
NE FEMALE	3	.2	11	.8	13	.9	7	.5	34	2.3	1,390	96.0	24	1 7	1,448
NE MALE	5	.2	30	1.4	16	.8	22	1.0	73	3.4	1,869	88.0	181	815	2,123
U NEBRASKA MEDICAL CTR															
NE TOTAL	0	.0	9	3.2	8	2.9	1	.4	18	6.5	242	87.4	17	6 1	277
NE FEMALE	0	.0	5	3.0	3	1.8	1	.6	9	5.5	151	92.1	4	2 4	164
NE MALE	0	.0	4	3.5	5	4.4	0	.0	9	8.0	91	80.5	13	11 15	113
U OF NEBRASKA AT OMAHA															
NE TOTAL	1	.0	88	4.1	12	.6	16	.7	117	5.4	1,981	92.1	53	2 5	2,151
NE FEMALE	1	.1	57	4.5	9	.7	5	.4	72	5.7	1,176	93.1	15	1 2	1,263
NE MALE	0	.0	31	3.5	3	.3	11	1.2	45	5.1	805	90.7	38	413	888
WAYNE STATE COLLEGE															
NE TOTAL	0	.0	0	.0	0	.0	0	.0	0	.0	119	99.2	1	.	120
NE FEMALE	0	.0	0	.0	0	.0	0	.0	0	.0	58	100.0	0	.	58
NE MALE	0	.0	0	.0	0	.0	0	.0	0	.0	61	98.4	1	1.8	62
NEBRASKA		TOTAL (	8 INSTITUTIONS)												
NE TOTAL	14	.2	144	2.0	56	.8	54	.8	268	3.7	6,640	92.3	283	3 9	7,191
NE FEMALE	5	.1	73	2.1	27	.8	16	.5	121	3.5	3,332	95.3	44	1 3	3,497
NE MALE	9	.2	71	1.9	29	.8	38	1.0	147	4.0	3,308	89.6	239	615	3,694
NEVADA															
U OF NEVADA LAS VEGAS															
NV TOTAL	7	1.0	39	5.8	6	.9	17	2.5	69	10.3	597	89.1	4	.6	670
NV FEMALE	2	.5	24	6.4	1	.3	6	1.6	33	8.8	339	90.4	3	.8	375
NV MALE	5	1.7	15	5.1	5	1.7	11	3.7	36	12.2	258	87.5	1	.3	295

TABLE 2 - TOTAL GRADUATE ENROLLMENT IN INSTITUTIONS OF HIGHER EDUCATION BY RACE, ETHNICITY AND SEX: INSTITUTION, STATE AND NATION, 1978

	AMERICAN INDIAN ALASKAN NATIVE		BLACK NON-HISPANIC		ASIAN OR PACIFIC ISLANDER		HISPANIC		TOTAL MINORITY		WHITE NON-HISPANIC		NON-RESIDENT ALIEN		
	NUMBER	%	NUMBER	%	NUMBER	%	NUMBER	%	NUMBER	%	NUMBER	%	NUMBER	%	
NEVADA	CONTINUED														
U OF NEVADA RENO															
NV TOTAL	4	.5	6	.7	15	1.7	10	1.1	35	4.0	791	89.5	58	5	
NV FEMALE	1	.2	3	.7	6	1.5	7	1.7	17	4.1	383	92.7	13	11	
NV MALE	3	.6	3	.6	9	1.9	3	.6	18	3.8	408	86.6	45	9.6	
NEVADA	TOTAL (	2 INSTITUTIONS)													
NV TOTAL	11	.7	45	2.9	21	1.4	27	1.7	104	6.7	1,388	89.3	62	4.0	
NV FEMALE	3	.4	27	3.4	7	.9	13	1.6	50	6.3	722	91.6	16	2.0	
NV MALE	8	1.0	18	2.3	14	1.8	14	1.8	54	7.0	666	86.9	46	6.0	
NEW HAMPSHIRE															
DARTMOUTH COLLEGE															
NH TOTAL	1	.2	11	2.3	15	3.1	2	.4	29	5.9	459	94.1	0	.0	
NH FEMALE	0	.0	3	3.1	5	5.2	0	.0	8	8.3	88	91.7	0	.0	
NH MALE	1	.3	8	2.0	10	2.6	2	.5	21	5.4	371	94.6	0	.0	
NEW HAMPSHIRE COLLEGE															
NH TOTAL	0	.0	8	2.1	5	1.3	0	.0	13	3.5	363	96.5	0	.0	
NH FEMALE	0	.0	1	3.2	2	6.5	0	.0	3	9.7	28	90.3	0	.0	
NH MALE	0	.0	7	2.0	3	.9	0	.0	10	2.9	335	97.1	0	.0	
NOTRE DAME COLLEGE															
NH TOTAL	0	.0	0	.0	0	.0	0	.0	0	.0	140	100.0	0	.0	
NH FEMALE	0	.0	0	.0	0	.0	0	.0	0	.0	129	100.0	0	.0	
NH MALE	0	.0	0	.0	0	.0	0	.0	0	.0	11	100.0	0	.0	
RIVIER COLLEGE															
NH TOTAL	0	.0	7	1.1	3	.5	0	.0	10	1.6	628	97.7	5	.8	
NH FEMALE	0	.0	3	1.2	2	.8	0	.0	5	2.0	241	97.6	1	.4	
NH MALE	0	.0	4	1.0	1	.3	0	.0	5	1.3	387	97.7	4	1.0	
U OF NEW HAMPSHIRE															
NH TOTAL	2	.2	4	.4	3	.3	7	.8	16	1.8	871	96.9	12	1.3	
NH FEMALE	1	.3	1	.3	2	.5	5	1.3	9	2.4	367	97.1	2	.5	
NH MALE	1	.2	3	.6	1	.2	2	.4	7	1.3	504	96.7	10	1.9	
U OF NH KEENE ST COLLEGE															
NH TOTAL	0	.0	0	.0	0	.0	0	.0	0	.0	64	100.0	0	.0	
NH FEMALE	0	.0	0	.0	0	.0	0	.0	0	.0	56	100.0	0	.0	
NH MALE	0	.0	0	.0	0	.0	0	.0	0	.0	8	100.0	0	.0	
U NH PLYMOUTH ST COLLEGE															
NH TOTAL	0	.0	0	.0	0	.0	1	.8	1	.8	117	95.9	4	3.3	
NH FEMALE	0	.0	0	.0	0	.0	0	.0	0	.0	59	96.7	2	3.3	
NH MALE	0	.0	0	.0	0	.0	1	1.6	1	1.6	58	95.1	2	3.3	
NEW HAMPSHIRE	TOTAL (	7 INSTITUTIONS)													
NH TOTAL	3	.1	30	1.1	26	1.0	10	.4	69	2.5	2,642	96.7	21	.8	
NH FEMALE	1	.1	8	.8	11	1.1	5	.5	25	2.5	968	97.0	5	.5	
NH MALE	2	.1	22	1.3	15	.9	5	.3	44	2.5	1,674	96.5	16	.9	
NEW JERSEY															
BETH MEDRASH GOVOHA															
NJ TOTAL	0	.0	0	.0	0	.0	5	2.0	5	2.0	249	97.6	1	.4	
NJ FEMALE	0	.0	0	.0	0	.0	0	.0	0	.0	0	.0	0	.0	
NJ MALE	0	.0	0	.0	0	.0	5	2.0	5	2.0	249	97.6	1	.4	
C MED C DENT OF NJ NEWARK															
NJ TOTAL	0	.0	6	4.5	5	3.7	7	5.2	18	13.4	114	85.1	2	1.5	
NJ FEMALE	0	.0	3	4.5	3	4.5	3	4.5	9	13.4	57	85.1	1	1.5	
NJ MALE	0	.0	3	4.5	2	3.0	4	6.0	9	13.4	57	85.1	1	1.5	
DREW UNIVERSITY															
NJ TOTAL	0	.0	18	3.7	8	1.7	9	1.9	35	7.3	408	84.6	39	8.1	
NJ FEMALE	0	.0	1	.9	1	.9	2	1.9	4	3.7	98	91.6	35	4.7	
NJ MALE	0	.0	17	4.5	7	1.9	7	1.9	31	8.3	310	82.7	4	9.1	
FARLGH DCKSN MADISON CAM															
NJ TOTAL	0	.0	30	3.2	14	1.5	5	.5	49	5.3	845	91.2	33	3 6	
NJ FEMALE	0	.0	11	4.1	3	1.1	0	.0	14	5.2	251	93.0	5	1 9	
NJ MALE	0	.0	19	2.9	11	1.7	5	.8	35	5.3	594	90.4	28	413	
FARLGH DCKSN U RUTHERFD															
NJ TOTAL	1	.1	40	3.5	12	1.1	16	1.4	69	6.1	1,021	90.3	41	3 6	
NJ FEMALE	0	.0	10	2.8	1	.3	8	2.2	19	5.3	321	90.2	16	4 5	
NJ MALE	1	.1	30	3.9	11	1.4	8	1.0	50	6.5	700	90.3	25	312	
FARLGH DCKSN TEANECK CAM															
NJ TOTAL	2	.1	32	2.3	21	1.5	25	1.8	80	5.8	1,217	87.9	87	6.3	
NJ FEMALE	1	.2	6	1.4	6	1.4	9	2.1	22	5.1	393	90.8	18	4.2	
NJ MALE	1	.1	26	2.7	15	1.6	16	1.7	58	6.1	824	86.6	69	7.3	
GEORGIAN COURT COLLEGE															
NJ TOTAL	0	.0	6	1.8	0	.0	4	1.2	10	3.0	328	97.0	0	.0	
NJ FEMALE	0	.0	5	2.1	0	.0	2	.8	7	2.9	236	97.1	0	.0	
NJ MALE	0	.0	1	1.1	0	.0	2	2.1	3	3.2	92	96.8	0	.0	
GLASSBORO STATE COLLEGE															
NJ TOTAL	8	.7	84	7.2	6	.5	72	6.2	170	14.6	988	85.0	4	.3	
NJ FEMALE	5	.7	52	7.7	4	.6	36	5.3	97	14.4	576	85.3	2	.3	
NJ MALE	3	.6	32	6.6	2	.4	36	7.4	73	15.0	412	84.6	2	.4	
IMMACULATE CONCEPTION SEM															
NJ TOTAL	0	.0	0	.0	0	.0	2	5.7	2	5.7	33	94.3	0	.0	
NJ FEMALE	0	.0	0	.0	0	.0	0	.0	0	.0	13	100.0	0	.0	
NJ MALE	0	.0	0	.0	0	.0	2	9.1	2	9.1	20	90.9	0	.0	
JERSEY CITY STATE COLLEGE															
NJ TOTAL	0	.0	86	8.4	15	1.5	95	9.3	196	19.3	822	80.7	0	.0	
NJ FEMALE	0	.0	69	10.0	11	1.6	71	10.3	151	22.0	536	78.0	0	.0	
NJ MALE	0	.0	17	5.1	4	1.2	24	7.3	45	13.6	286	86.4	0	.0	
KEAN C OF NEW JERSEY															
NJ TOTAL	2	.1	126	8.5	4	.3	21	1.4	153	10.3	1,318	88.9	11	.7	
NJ FEMALE	1	.1	98	9.4	4	.4	12	1.2	115	11.1	919	88.5	5	.5	
NJ MALE	1	.2	28	6.3	0	.0	9	2.0	38	8.6	399	90.1	6	1.4	

N 'E	BLACK NON-HISPANIC		ASIAN OR PACIFIC ISLANDER		HISPANIC		TOTAL MINORITY		WHITE NON-HISPANIC		NON-RESIDENT ALIEN		TOTAL
	NUMBER	%	NUMBER	%	NUMBER	%	NUMBER	%	NUMBER	%	NUMBER	%	NUMBER
'TINUED													
	9	1.3	8	1.2	1	.1	18	2.6	668	96.8	4	.6	690
	5	1.8	1	.4	0	.0	6	2.1	275	97.9	0	.0	281
	4	1.0	7	1.7	1	.2	12	2.9	393	96.1	4	1.0	409
	26	1.8	8	.6	27	1.9	61	4.2	1,350	93.4	35	2.4	1,446
	18	1.9	6	.6	15	1.5	39	4.0	911	93.8	21	2.2	971
	8	1.7	2	.4	12	2.5	22	4.6	439	92.4	14	2.9	475
	0	.0	0	.0	1	7.1	1	7.1	13	92.9	0	.0	14
	0	.0	0	.0	0	.0	0	.0	7	100.0	0	.0	7
	0	.0	0	.0	1	14.3	1	14.3	6	85.7	0	.0	7
	30	3.8	50	6.3	17	2.1	97	12.2	667	84.2	28	3.5	792
	13	16.3	6	7.5	2	2.5	21	26.3	58	72.5	1	1.3	80
	17	2.4	44	6.2	15	2.1	76	10.7	609	85.5	27	3.8	712
	8	2.4	1	.3	3	.9	12	3.6	276	82.6	46	13.5	334
	1	1.9	0	.0	1	1.9	2	3.7	48	88.9	4	7.4	54
	7	2.5	1	.4	2	.7	10	3.6	228	81.4	42	15.0	280
	27	1.9	24	1.7	16	1.1	71	5.0	1,064	74.9	286	20.1	1,421
	7	1.6	8	1.9	5	1.2	21	4.9	347	80.9	61	14.2	429
	20	2.0	16	1.6	11	1.1	50	5.0	717	72.3	225	22.7	992
	18	1.7	11	1.0	4	.4	33	3.1	1,023	96.1	8	.8	1,064
	4	1.0	5	1.2	2	.5	11	2.7	401	97.1	1	.2	413
	14	2.2	6	.9	2	.3	22	3.4	622	95.5	7	1.1	651
	0	.0	0	.0	0	.0	0	.0	14	100.0	0	.0	14
	0	.0	0	.0	0	.0	0	.0	4	100.0	0	.0	4
	0	.0	0	.0	0	.0	0	.0	10	100.0	0	.0	10
	107	7.3	40	2.7	20	1.4	168	11.5	1,244	85.0	51	3.5	1,463
	53	12.7	13	3.1	3	.7	69	16.6	338	81.3	9	2.2	416
	54	5.2	27	2.6	17	1.6	99	9.5	906	86.5	42	4.0	1,047
	574	6.3	188	2.1	167	1.8	940	10.3	7,677	84.0	525	5.7	9,142
	357	7.7	70	1.5	94	2.0	528	11.3	4,001	85.9	130	2.8	4,659
	217	4.8	118	2.6	73	1.6	412	9.2	3,676	82.0	395	8.8	4,483
	121	5.3	51	2.2	47	2.0	220	9.6	2,042	88.8	38	1.7	2,300
	76	6.7	26	2.3	39	3.4	142	12.5	972	85.7	20	1.8	1,134
	45	3.9	25	2.1	8	.7	78	6.7	1,070	91.8	18	1.5	1,166
	18	1.9	42	4.4	21	2.2	82	8.5	746	77.7	132	13.8	960
	8	5.2	5	3.3	3	2.0	16	10.5	131	85.6	6	3.9	153
	10	1.2	37	4.6	18	2.2	66	8.2	615	76.2	126	15.6	807
	140	6.5	7	.3	13	.6	162	7.5	1,989	92.5	0	.0	2,151
	94	6.6	3	.2	7	.5	105	7.3	1,330	92.7	0	.0	1,435
	46	6.4	4	.6	6	.8	57	8.0	659	92.0	0	.0	716
	17	41.5	0	.0	0	.0	17	41.5	24	58.5	0	.0	41
	15	46.9	0	.0	0	.0	15	46.9	17	53.1	0	.0	32
	2	22.2	0	.0	0	.0	2	22.2	7	77.8	0	.0	9
	2	3.6	0	.0	0	.0	2	3.6	52	94.5	1	1.8	55
	1	3.6	0	.0	0	.0	1	3.6	27	96.4	0	.0	28
	1	3.7	0	.0	0	.0	1	3.7	25	92.6	1	3.7	27
	43	3.1	3	.2	25	1.8	71	5.2	1,305	94.8	0	.0	1,376
	25	2.7	2	.2	18	2.0	45	4.9	876	95.1	0	.0	921
	18	4.0	1	.2	7	1.5	26	5.7	429	94.3	0	.0	455
(27 INSTITUTIONS)													
	1,568	5.0	518	1.6	623	2.0	2,742	8.7	27,497	87.0	1,372	4.3	31,611
	932	6.3	178	1.2	332	2.2	1,459	9.8	13,143	88.2	305	2.0	14,907
	636	3.8	340	2.0	291	1.7	1,283	7.7	14,354	85.9	1,067	6.4	16,704
	21	2.8	3	.4	39	5.1	76	10.0	591	77.8	93	12.2	760
	10	2.9	1	.3	21	6.2	38	11.1	292	85.6	11	3.2	341
	11	2.6	2	.5	18	4.3	38	9.1	299	71.4	82	19.6	419
	1	.5	2	.9	145	67.4	151	70.2	58	27.0	6	2.8	215
	0	.0	0	.0	64	62.7	67	65.7	35	34.3	0	.0	102
	1	.9	2	1.8	81	71.7	84	74.3	23	20.4	6	5.3	113
	1	.6	4	2.6	8	5.2	13	8.4	124	80.5	17	11.0	154
	0	.0	0	.0	1	3.2	1	3.2	30	96.8	0	.0	31
	1	.8	4	3.3	7	5.7	12	9.8	94	76.4	17	13.8	123
	9	.7	7	.5	169	12.9	197	15.0	976	74.3	140	10.7	1,313
	4	.8	1	.2	74	14.4	85	16.6	417	81.3	11	2.1	513
	5	.6	6	.8	95	11.9	112	14.0	559	69.9	129	16.1	800
	57	1.6	35	1.0	541	15.2	716	20.1	2,692	75.6	153	4.3	3,561
	26	1.5	21	1.2	255	15.1	346	20.4	1,309	77.4	37	2.2	1,692
	31	1.7	14	.7	286	15.3	370	19.8	1,383	74.0	116	6.2	1,869

	AMERICAN INDIAN ALASKAN NATIVE		BLACK NON-HISPANIC		ASIAN OR PACIFIC ISLANDER		HISPANIC		TOTAL MINORITY		WHITE NON-HISPANIC		NON-RESIDENT ALIEN	
	NUMBER	%	NUMBER	%	NUMBER	%	NUMBER	%	NUMBER	%	NUMBER	%	NUMBER	%
NEW MEXICO	CONTINUED													
U OF NM GALLUP BRANCH														
NM TOTAL	2	100.0	0	.0	0	.0	0	.0	2	100.0	0	.0	0	.0
NM FEMALE	1	100.0	0	.0	0	.0	0	.0	1	100.0	0	.0	0	.0
NM MALE	1	100.0	0	.0	0	.0	0	.0	1	100.0	0	.0	0	.0
HESTERN NM UNIVERSITY														
NM TOTAL	3	2.3	0	.0	1	.8	37	28.7	41	31.8	88	68.2	0	.0
NM FEMALE	2	3.2	0	.0	0	.0	12	19.4	14	22.6	48	77.4	0	.0
NM MALE	1	1.5	0	.0	1	1.5	25	37.3	27	40.3	40	59.7	0	.0
NEW MEXICO	TOTAL (		7 INSTITUTIONS)											
NM TOTAL	116	1.9	89	1.5	52	.8	939	15.3	1,196	19.5	4,529	73.8	409	6.7
NM FEMALE	62	2.3	40	1.5	23	.8	427	15.6	552	20.1	2,131	77.7	59	2.2
NM MALE	54	1.6	49	1.4	29	.9	512	15.1	644	19.0	2,398	70.7	350	10.3
NEW YORK														
ADELPHI UNIVERSITY														
NY TOTAL	6	.2	256	9.3	29	1.1	47	1.7	338	12.3	2,410	87.7	0	.0
NY FEMALE	2	.1	206	11.8	8	.5	23	1.3	239	13.7	1,504	86.3	0	.0
NY MALE	4	.4	50	5.0	21	2.1	24	2.4	99	9.9	906	90.1	0	.0
ALBANY MEDICAL COLLEGE														
NY TOTAL	0	.0	0	.0	0	.0		.0	0	.0	51	100.0	0	.0
NY FEMALE	0	.0	0	.0	0	.0	0	.0	0	.0	17	100.0	0	.0
NY MALE	0	.0	0	.0	0	.0	0	.0	0	.0	34	100.0	0	.0
ALFRED UNIVERSITY														
NY TOTAL	1	.5	0	.0	0	.0		.0	1	.5	202	96.7	6	2.9
NY FEMALE	0	.0	0	.0	0	.0	0	.0	0	.0	101	98.1	2	1.9
NY MALE	1	.9	0	.0	0	.0	0	.0	1	.9	101	95.3	4	3.8
NY ST C CERAMICS ALFRED U														
NY TOTAL	0	.0	0	.0	1	2.1		.0	1	2.1	42	89.4	4	8.5
NY FEMALE	0	.0	0	.0	1	16.7	0	.0	1	16.7	4	66.7	1	16.7
NY MALE	0	.0	0	.0	0	.0	0	.0	0	.0	38	92.7	3	7.3
BANK STREET COLLEGE OF ED														
NY TOTAL	3	.3	196	19.9	22	2 2	45	4.6	266	27.0	700	71.0	20	2.0
NY FEMALE	3	.4	155	18.5	13	1 6	28	3.3	199	23.7	619	73.9	20	2.4
NY MALE	0	.0	41	27.7	9	611	17	11.5	67	45.3	81	54.7	0	.0
BELZER YESH-MACHZIKEI SEM														
NY TOTAL	0	.0	0	.0	0	.0	0	.0	0	.0.	3	100.0	0	.0
NY FEMALE	0	.0	0	.0	0	.0	0	.0	0	.0	0	.0	0	.0
NY MALE	0	.0	0	.0	0	.0	0	.0	0	.0	3	100.0	0	.0
BETH HMDRSH SHAAREI YOSH														
NY TOTAL	0	.0	0	.0	0	.0	0	.0	0	.0	17	100.0	0	.0
NY FEMALE	0	.0	0	.0	0	.0	0	.0	0	.0	0	.0	0	.0
NY MALE	0	.0	0	.0	0	.0	0	.0	0	.0	17	100.0	0	.0
BETH HATALMUD RAB C														
NY TOTAL	0	.0	0	.0	0	.0	0	.0	0	.0	42	100.0	0	.0
NY FEMALE	0	.0	0	.0	0	.0	0	.0	0	.0	0	.0	0	.0
NY MALE	0	.0	0	.0	0	.0	0	.0	0	.0	42	100.0	0	.0
BETH JOSEPH RAB SEMINARY														
NY TOTAL	0	.0	0	.0	0	.0		.0	0	.0	13	100.0	0	.0
NY FEMALE	0	.0	0	.0	0	.0	0	.0	0	.0	0	.0	0	.0
NY MALE	0	.0	0	.0	0	.0	0	.0	0	.0	13	100.0	0	.0
BETH MEDRASH EMEK HALACHA														
NY TOTAL	0	.0	0	.0	0	.0		.0	0	.0	17	100.0	0	.0
NY FEMALE	0	.0	0	.0	0	.0	0	.0	0	.0	0	.0	0	.0
NY MALE	0	.0	0	.0	0	.0	0	.0	0	.0	17	100.0	0	.0
CANISIUS COLLEGE														
NY TOTAL	22	2.7	30	3.7	10	1.2		.5	66	8.2	719	89.1	22	2.7
NY FEMALE	4	1.0	16	4.1	3	.8	3	1.0	27	7.0	349	90.2	11	2.8
NY MALE	18	4.3	14	3.3	7	1.7	4	.0	39	9.3	370	88.1	11	2.6
CEN YESH TOM THIMIM LUBYZ														
NY TOTAL	0	.0	0	.0	0	.0	0	.0	0	.0	61	100.0	0	.0
NY FEMALE	0	.0	0	.0	0	.0	0	.0	0	.0	0	.0	0	.0
NY MALE	0	.0	0	.0	0	.0	0	.0	0	.0	61	100.0	0	.0
CHRIST THE KING SEMINARY														
NY TOTAL	0	.0	0	.0	0	.0	0	.0	0	.0	47	100.0	0	.0
NY FEMALE	0	.0	0	.0	0	.0	0	.0	0	.0	9	100.0	0	.0
NY MALE	0	.0	0	.0	0	.0	0	.0	0	.0	38	100.0	0	.0
CUNY BERNARD BARUCH C														
NY TOTAL	20	.9	155	6.7	121	.2	75	3.2	371	16.0	1,886	81.2	66	2 9
NY FEMALE	8	1.0	62	7.8	36	.5	38	4.0	138	17.3	647	80.9	15	1 9
NY MALE	12	.8	93	6.1	85	4.5	4	2.8	233	15.3	1,239	81.4	51	313
CUNY BROOKLYN COLLEGE														
NY TOTAL	10	.9	158	13.7	32	2 8	91	7.	291	25.2	842	72.9	22	1.9
NY FEMALE	4	.5	112	14.3	20	2 5	66	8.4	202	25.7	573	73.0	10	1.3
NY MALE	6	1.6	46	12.4	12	312	25	6.8	89	24.1	269	72.7	12	3.2
CUNY CITY COLLEGE														
NY TOTAL	11	.8	147	11.1	60	4.5	77	5.8	295	22.2	979	73.8	52	3.9
NY FEMALE	5	.7	84	12.4	19	2.8	48	7.1	156	23.0	513	75.7	9	1.3
NY MALE	6	.9	63	9.7	41	6.3	29	4.5	139	21.5	466	71.9	43	6.6
CUNY C OF STATEN ISLAND														
NY TOTAL	3	.8	50	12.6	13	.	29	7.3	95	23.9	297	74.8	5	1.3
NY FEMALE	1	.4	33	13.5	8	3.3	20	8.2	62	25.4	179	73.4	3	1.2
NY MALE	2	1.3	17	11.1	5		9	5.9	33	21.6	118	77.1	2	1.3
CUNY GRAD SCH & U CENTER														
NY TOTAL	27	1.1	113	4.4	106	4.1	104	4.0	350	13.6	1,977	77.0	242	9 4
NY FEMALE	6	.5	57	4.8	26	2.2	41	3.4	130	10.9	1,016	84.8	52	413
NY MALE	21	1.5	56	4.1	80	5.8	63	4.6	220	16.0	961	70.1	190	13.9
CUNY HUNTER COLLEGE														
NY TOTAL	20	.8	326	13.6	59	2 5	179	7.5	584	24.4	1,758	73.6	48	2.0
NY FEMALE	9	.5	250	13.9	40	2 2	139	7.8	438	24.4	1,329	74.1	26	1.5
NY MALE	11	1.8	76	12.7	19	312	40	6.7	146	24.5	429	71.9	22	3.7

	AMERICAN INDIAN ALASKAN NATIVE		BLACK NON-HISPANIC		ASIAN OR PACIFIC ISLANDER		HISPANIC		TOTAL MINORITY		WHITE NON-HISPANIC		NON-RESIDENT ALIEN		TOTAL
	NUMBER	%	NUMBER	%	NUMBER	%	NUMBER	%	NUMBER	%	NUMBER	%	NUMBER	%	NUMBER
NEW YORK	CONTINUED														
CUNY JOHN JAY C CRIM JUST															
NY TOTAL	9	1.2	75	9.8	29	3.8	40	5.2	153	20.0	591	77.3	21	2.7	765
NY FEMALE	2	1.2	21	12.4	5	3.0	11	6.5	39	23.1	128	75.7	2	1.2	169
NY MALE	7	1.2	54	9.1	24	4.0	29	4.9	114	19.1	463	77.7	19	3.2	596
CUNY LEHMAN COLLEGE															
NY TOTAL	3	.7	65	14.4	11	2.4	38	8.4	117	25.9	327	72.5	7	1.6	451
NY FEMALE	1	.3	52	14.7	9	2.5	31	8.8	93	26.3	256	72.5	4	1.1	353
NY MALE	2	2.0	13	13.3	2	2.0	7	7.1	24	24.5	71	72.4	3	3.1	98
CUNY QUEENS COLLEGE															
NY TOTAL	11	.8	187	13.6	38	2.8	109	7.9	345	25.0	1,008	73.0	27	2.0	1,380
NY FEMALE	4	.4	136	14.1	24	2.5	81	8.4	245	25.4	707	73.3	12	1.2	964
NY MALE	7	1.7	51	12.3	14	3.4	28	6.7	100	24.0	301	72.4	15	3.6	416
CLARKSON COLLEGE OF TECHN															
NY TOTAL	0	.0	0	.0	0	.0	0	.0	0	.0	188	72.0	73	28.0	261
NY FEMALE	0	.0	0	.0	0	.0	0	.0	0	.0	27	79.4	7	20.6	34
NY MALE	0	.0	0	.0	0	.0	0	.0	0	.0	161	70.9	66	29.1	227
COLG ROCH-BEXLEY-CROZER															
NY TOTAL	0	.0	2	4.5	1	2.3	0	.0	3	6.8	40	90.9	1	2.3	44
NY FEMALE	0	.0	0	.0	0	.0	0	.0	0	.0	9	100.0	0	.0	9
NY MALE	0	.0	2	5.7	1	2.9	0	.0	3	8.6	31	88.6	1	2.9	35
COLGATE UNIVERSITY															
NY TOTAL	0	.0	4	8.0	0	.0	0	.0	4	8.0	46	92.0	0	.0	50
NY FEMALE	0	.0	1	4.8	0	.0	0	.0	1	4.8	20	95.2	0	.0	21
NY MALE	0	.0	3	10.3	0	.0	0	.0	3	10.3	26	89.7	0	.0	29
COLLEGE OF INSURANCE															
NY TOTAL	0	.0	10	10.4	3	3.1	3	3.1	16	16.7	76	79.2	4	4.2	96
NY FEMALE	0	.0	4	16.7	0	.0	0	.0	4	16.7	19	79.2	1	4.2	24
NY MALE	0	.0	6	8.3	3	4.2	3	4.2	12	16.7	57	79.2	3	4.2	72
COLLEGE OF NEW ROCHELLE															
NY TOTAL	0	.0	39	5.2	1	.1	11	1.5	51	6.8	694	93.2	0	.0	745
NY FEMALE	0	.0	37	5.5	1	.1	11	1.6	49	7.3	623	92.7	0	.0	672
NY MALE	0	.0	2	2.7	0	.0	0	.0	2	2.7	71	97.3	0	.0	73
COLLEGE OF SAINT ROSE															
NY TOTAL	0	.0	4	.9	0	.0	1	.2	5	1.1	460	98.5	2	.4	467
NY FEMALE	0	.0	4	1.1	0	.0	0	.0	4	1.1	357	98.3	2	.6	363
NY MALE	0	.0	0	.0	0	.0	1	1.0	1	1.0	103	99.0	0	.0	104
COLUMBIA U MAIN DIVISION															
NY TOTAL	12	.1	348	4.3	276	3.4	153	1.9	789	9.7	6,522	80.0	842	10.3	8,153
NY FEMALE	5	.1	198	5.4	101	2.7	69	1.9	373	10.1	3,133	85.0	180	4.9	3,686
NY MALE	7	.2	150	3.4	175	3.9	84	1.9	416	9.3	3,389	75.9	662	14.8	4,467
COLUMBIA U TCHRS COLLEGE															
NY TOTAL	14	.3	584	13.1	181	4.1	199	4.5	978	21.9	3,196	71.6	289	6.5	4,463
NY FEMALE	10	.3	458	14.9	140	4.6	122	4.0	730	23.8	2,166	70.6	170	5.5	3,066
NY MALE	4	.3	126	9.0	41	2.9	77	5.5	248	17.8	1,030	73.7	119	8.5	1,397
COOPER UNION															
NY TOTAL	0	.0	1	12.5	2	25.0	0	.0	3	37.5	5	62.5	0	.0	8
NY FEMALE	0	.0	1	50.0	0	.0	0	.0	1	50.0	1	50.0	0	.0	2
NY MALE	0	.0	0	.0	2	33.3	0	.0	2	33.3	4	66.7	0	.0	6
CORNEL U ENDOWED COLLEGES															
NY TOTAL	7	.3	56	2.4	61	2.6	41	1.7	165	7.0	1,705	71.8	503	21.2	2,373
NY FEMALE	1	.2	18	3.1	11	1.9	9	1.6	39	6.8	451	78.7	83	14.5	573
NY MALE	6	.3	38	2.1	50	2.8	32	1.8	126	7.0	1,254	69.7	420	23.3	1,800
CORNELL U MEDICAL CENTER															
NY TOTAL	0	.0	1	.8	10	7.9	1	.8	12	9.5	108	85.7	6	4.8	126
NY FEMALE	0	.0	0	.0	4	6.6	0	.0	4	6.6	52	85.2	5	8.2	61
NY MALE	0	.0	1	1.5	6	9.2	1	1.5	8	12.3	56	86.2	1	1.5	65
CORNELL U STATUTORY C															
NY TOTAL	5	.4	61	4.4	57	4.1	49	3.5	172	12.4	949	68.6	262	18.9	1,383
NY FEMALE	0	.0	26	4.6	23	4.1	11	2.0	60	10.7	436	77.7	65	11.6	561
NY MALE	5	.6	35	4.3	34	4.1	38	4.6	112	13.6	513	62.4	197	24.0	822
DERECH AYSON RAB SEMINARY															
NY TOTAL	0	.0	0	.0	0	.0	0	.0	0	.0	10	100.0	0	.0	10
NY FEMALE	0	.0	0	.0	0	.0	0	.0	0	.0	0	.0	0	.0	0
NY MALE	0	.0	0	.0	0	.0	0	.0	0	.0	10	100.0	0	.0	10
DOWLING COLLEGE															
NY TOTAL	0	.0	3	1.2	1	.4	0	.0	4	1.7	238	98.3	0	.0	242
NY FEMALE	0	.0	1	1.0	1	1.0	0	.0	2	2.0	97	98.0	0	.0	99
NY MALE	0	.0	2	1.4	0	.0	0	.0	2	1.4	141	98.6	0	.0	143
ELMIRA COLLEGE															
NY TOTAL	1	.2	4	.9	1	.2	0	.0	6	1.3	443	97.8	4	.9	453
NY FEMALE	1	.3	4	1.3	1	.3	0	.0	6	1.9	306	96.8	4	1.3	316
NY MALE	0	.0	0	.0	0	.0	0	.0	0	.0	137	100.0	0	.0	137
FORDHAM UNIVERSITY															
NY TOTAL	30	.7	357	7.7	97	2.1	394	8.5	878	19.0	3,630	78.7	105	2.3	4,613
NY FEMALE	14	.6	219	9.0	45	1.8	261	10.7	539	22.1	1,857	76.2	42	1.7	2,438
NY MALE	16	.7	138	6.3	52	2.4	133	6.1	339	15.6	1,773	81.5	63	2.9	2,175
GENERAL THEOLOGICAL SEM															
NY TOTAL	0	.0	0	.0	0	.0	0	.0	0	.0	37	90.2	4	9.8	41
NY FEMALE	0	.0	0	.0	0	.0	0	.0	0	.0	6	100.0	0	.0	6
NY MALE	0	.0	0	.0	0	.0	0	.0	0	.0	31	88.6	4	11.4	35
HOFSTRA UNIVERSITY															
NY TOTAL	0	.0	114	3.4	23	.7	82	2.4	219	6.5	3,101	92.4	35	1.0	3,355
NY FEMALE	0	.0	76	4.4	7	.4	53	3.1	136	7.8	1,584	91.2	17	1.0	1,737
NY MALE	0	.0	38	2.3	16	1.0	29	1.8	83	5.1	1,517	93.8	18	1.1	1,618
IONA COLLEGE															
NY TOTAL	0	.0	23	2.3	11	1.1	6	.6	40	4.0	964	95.7	3	.3	1,007
NY FEMALE	0	.0	8	2.4	1	.3	4	1.2	13	4.0	314	96.0	0	.0	327
NY MALE	0	.0	15	2.2	10	1.5	2	.3	27	4.0	650	95.5	3	.4	680
ITHACA COLLEGE															
NY TOTAL	1	.7	2	1.5	0	.0	0	.0	3	2.2	126	93.3	6	4.4	135
NY FEMALE	1	1.1	1	1.1	0	.0	0	.0	2	2.2	88	95.7	2	2.2	92
NY MALE	0	.0	1	2.3	0	.0	0	.0	1	2.3	38	88.4	4	9.3	43

TABLE 2 - TOTAL GRADUATE ENROLLMENT IN INSTITUTIONS OF HIGHER EDUCATION BY RACE, ETHNICITY AND SEX: INSTITUTION, STATE AND NATION, 1978

	AMERICAN INDIAN ALASKAN NATIVE		BLACK NON-HISPANIC		ASIAN OR PACIFIC ISLANDER		HISPANIC		TOTAL MINORITY		WHITE NON-HISPANIC		NON-RESIDENT ALIEN	
	NUMBER	%	NUMBER	%	NUMBER	%	NUMBER	%	NUMBER	%	NUMBER	%	NUMBER	%
NEW YORK				CONTINUED										
JEWISH THEOL SEM AMERICA														
NY TOTAL	0	.0	0	.0	0	.0	0	.0	0	.0	162	100.0	0	.0
NY FEMALE	0	.0	0	.0	0	.0	0	.0	0	.0	74	100.0	0	.0
NY MALE	0	.0	0	.0	0	.0	0	.0	0	.0	88	100.0	0	.0
THE JUILLIARD SCHOOL														
NY TOTAL	0	.0	2	1.1	13	7.0	3	1.6	18	9.7	161	86.6	7	3.8
NY FEMALE	0	.0	0	.0	7	11.1	2	3.2	9	14.3	51	81.0	3	4.8
NY MALE	0	.0	2	1.6	6	4.9	1	.8	9	7.3	110	89.4	4	3.3
LONG IS U SCHWARTZ C PHAR														
NY TOTAL	0	.0	7	3.9	42	23.3	1	.6	50	27.8	112	62.2	18	10.0
NY FEMALE	0	.0	4	8.9	5	11.1	0	.0	9	20.0	29	64.4	7	15.6
NY MALE	0	.0	3	2.2	37	27.4	1	.7	41	30.4	83	61.5	11	8.1
LONG IS U BROOKLYN CENTER														
NY TOTAL	0	.0	958	36.3	134	5.1	288	10.9	1,380	52.3	996	37.7	263	10.0
NY FEMALE	0	.0	366	34.7	59	5.6	126	11.9	551	52.2	412	39.0	93	8.8
NY MALE	0	.0	592	37.4	75	4.7	162	10.2	829	52.4	584	36.9	170	10.7
LONG IS U C H POST CENTER														
NY TOTAL	3	.1	117	2.1	71	1.3	83	1.5	274	4.9	5,266	94.2	50	.9
NY FEMALE	2	.1	59	1.8	35	1.1	45	1.4	141	4.4	3,028	94.9	21	.7
NY MALE	1	.0	58	2.4	36	1.5	38	1.6	133	5.5	2,238	93.3	29	1.2
MANHATTAN COLLEGE														
NY TOTAL	0	.0	28	4.6	13	2.1	18	2.9	59	9.6	552	89.8	4	.7
NY FEMALE	0	.0	10	5.7	1	.6	2	1.1	13	7.4	163	92.6	0	.0
NY MALE	0	.0	18	4.1	12	2.7	16	3.6	46	10.5	389	88.6	4	.9
MANHATTAN SCHOOL OF MUSIC														
NY TOTAL	0	.0	8	3.4	10	4.3	2	.9	20	8.5	194	82.9	20	8.5
NY FEMALE	0	.0	4	3.1	8	6.3	1	.8	13	10.2	102	80.3	12	9.4
NY MALE	0	.0	4	3.7	2	1.9	1	.9	7	6.5	92	86.0	8	7.5
MANHATTANVILLE COLLEGE														
NY TOTAL	0	.0	1	.6	0	.0	0	.0	1	.6	170	99.4	0	.0
NY FEMALE	0	.0	1	.6	0	.0	0	.0	1	.6	156	99.4	0	.0
NY MALE	0	.0	0	.0	0	.0	0	.0	0	.0	14	100.0	0	.0
MARIST COLLEGE														
NY TOTAL	1	.3	3	.8	0	.0	2	.6	6	1.7	355	98.3	0	.0
NY FEMALE	1	.9	0	.0	0	.0	0	.0	1	.9	115	99.1	0	.0
NY MALE	0	.0	3	1.2	0	.0	2	.8	5	2.0	240	98.0	0	.0
MARYKNOLL SEMINARY														
NY TOTAL	0	.0	1	4.0	1	4.0	2	8.0	4	16.0	14	56.0	7	28.0
NY FEMALE	0	.0	0	.0	0	.0	0	.0	0	.0	14	100.0	0	.0
NY MALE	0	.0	1	9.1	1	9.1	2	18.2	4	36.4	0	.0	7	63.6
MES TORAH VODAATH SEM														
NY TOTAL	0	.0	0	.0	0	.0	0	.0	0	.0	55	100.0	0	.0
NY FEMALE	0	.0	0	.0	0	.0	0	.0	0	.0	0	.0	0	.0
NY MALE	0	.0	0	.0	0	.0	0	.0	0	.0	55	100.0	0	.0
MESIVTHA TIFERETH JER AMR														
NY TOTAL	0	.0	0	.0	0	.0	0	.0	0	.0	28	100.0	0	.0
NY FEMALE	0	.0	0	.0	0	.0	0	.0	0	.0	0	.0	0	.0
NY MALE	0	.0	0	.0	0	.0	0	.0	0	.0	28	100.0	0	.0
MIRRER YESHIVA CEN INST														
NY TOTAL	0	.0	0	.0	0	.0	0	.0	0	.0	44	100.0	0	.0
NY FEMALE	0	.0	0	.0	0	.0	0	.0	0	.0	0	.0	0	.0
NY MALE	0	.0	0	.0	0	.0	0	.0	0	.0	44	100.0	0	.0
MOUNT SAINT ALPHONSUS SEM														
NY TOTAL	0	.0	2	4.5	0	.0	2	4.5	4	9.1	38	86.4	2	4.5
NY FEMALE	0	.0	0	.0	0	.0	0	.0	0	.0	0	.0	0	.0
NY MALE	0	.0	2	4.5	0	.0	2	4.5	4	9.1	38	86.4	2	4.5
NAZARETH C OF ROCHESTER														
NY TOTAL	0	.0	15	2.4	1	.2	6	1.0	22	3.6	593	96.4	0	.0
NY FEMALE	0	.0	14	2.6	1	.2	6	1.1	21	3.9	516	96.1	0	.0
NY MALE	0	.0	1	1.3	0	.0	0	.0	1	1.3	77	98.7	0	.0
NEW SCH FOR SOC RESEARCH														
NY TOTAL	15	.7	279	12.2	51	2.2	108	4.7	453	19.8	1,742	76.2	91	4.0
NY FEMALE	8	.7	154	13.6	23	2.0	52	4.6	237	21.0	869	76.9	24	2.1
NY MALE	7	.7	125	10.8	28	2.4	56	4.8	216	18.7	873	75.5	67	5.8
NY INST TECHN MAIN CAMPUS														
NY TOTAL	0	.0	14	2.3	7	1.2	5	.8	26	4.3	570	94.1	10	1.7
NY FEMALE	0	.0	6	2.9	0	.0	1	.5	7	3.4	199	96.1	1	.5
NY MALE	0	.0	8	2.0	7	1.8	4	1.0	19	4.8	371	93.0	9	2.3
NY INST TECHN NY CTY CAM														
NY TOTAL	0	.0	11	3.9	11	3.9	6	2.1	28	9.9	238	83.8	18	6.3
NY FEMALE	0	.0	2	2.1	3	3.2	2	2.1	7	7.4	85	89.5	3	3.2
NY MALE	0	.0	9	4.8	8	4.2	4	2.1	21	11.1	153	81.0	15	7.9
NEW YORK MEDICAL COLLEGE														
NY TOTAL	0	.0	5	4.7	0	.0	1	.8	7	5.4	116	89.9	6	4.7
NY FEMALE	0	.0	3	4.8	0	.0	0	.0	3	4.8	58	92.1	2	3.2
NY MALE	0	.0	3	4.5	0	.0	1	1.5	4	6.1	58	87.9	4	6.1
NEW YORK THEOL SEMINARY														
NY TOTAL	0	.0	11	12.4	11	12.4	4	4.5	26	29.2	62	69.7	1	1.1
NY FEMALE	0	.0	0	.0	0	.0	0	.0	0	.0	5	100.0	0	.0
NY MALE	0	.0	11	13.1	11	13.1	4	4.8	26	31.0	57	67.9	1	1.2
NEW YORK UNIVERSITY														
NY TOTAL	49	.3	789	5.0	554	3.5	447	2.8	1,839	11.7	13,095	83.2	808	5.1
NY FEMALE	26	.3	508	6.1	295	3.5	245	2.9	1,074	12.9	6,917	83.0	338	4.1
NY MALE	23	.3	281	3.8	259	3.5	202	2.7	765	10.3	6,178	83.3	470	6.3
NIAGARA UNIVERSITY														
NY TOTAL	11	.9	39	3.2	20	1.6	6	.5	76	6.2	1,159	93.8	0	.0
NY FEMALE	7	1.2	17	2.9	6	1.0	3	.5	33	5.6	558	94.4	0	.0
NY MALE	4	.6	22	3.4	14	2.2	3	.5	43	6.7	601	93.3	0	.0
NYACK COLLEGE														
NY TOTAL	0	.0	0	.0	1	.9	1	.9	2	1.8	110	96.5	2	1.8
NY FEMALE	0	.0	0	.0	0	.0	1	3.3	1	3.3	28	93.3	1	3.3
NY MALE	0	.0	0	.0	1	1.2	0	.0	1	1.2	82	97.6	1	1.2

ENROLLMENT IN INSTITUTIONS OF HIGHER EDUCATION BY RACE, ETHNICITY AND SEX:
TATE AND NATION, 1978

AN VE	BLACK NON-HISPANIC		ASIAN OR PACIFIC ISLANDER		HISPANIC		TOTAL MINORITY		WHITE NON-HISPANIC		NON-RESIDENT ALIEN		TOTAL
	NUMBER	%	NUMBER	%	NUMBER	%	NUMBER	%	NUMBER	%	NUMBER	%	NUMBER

TINUED

	NUMBER	%	NUMBER	%	NUMBER	%	NUMBER	%	NUMBER	%	NUMBER	%	NUMBER
	0	.0	0	.0	0	.0	0	.0	3	100.0		.0	3
	0	.0	0	.0	0	.0	0	.0	0	.0	0	.0	0
	0	.0	0	.0	0	.0	0	.0	3	100.0	8	.0	3
	9	2.8	8	2.5	7	2.2	26	8.0	297	91.7	1	.3	324
	8	5.2	4	2.6	5	3.3	17	11.1	136	88.9	0	.0	153
	1	.6	4	2.3	2	1.2	9	5.3	161	94.2	1	.6	171
	178	6.4	119	4.3	69	2.5	378	13.6	2,326	83.6	77	2.8	2,781
	75	9.1	48	5.8	21	2.5	148	17.9	651	78.7	28	3.4	827
	103	5.3	71	3.6	48	2.5	230	11.8	1,675	85.7	49	2.5	1,954
	6	.7	7	.9	10	1.2	30	3.7	782	96.1	2	.2	814
	2	.6	1	.3	3	.9	10	3.1	313	96.9	0	.0	323
	4	.8	6	1.2	7	1.4	20	4.1	469	95.5	2	.4	491
	1	4.2	0	.0	1	4.2	2	8.3	20	83.3	2	8.3	24
	0	.0	0	.0	1	7.7	1	7.7	11	84.6	1	7 7	13
	1	9.1	0	.0	0	.0	1	9.1	9	81.8	1	9:1	11
	78	4.2	350	18.9	52	2.8	485	26.2	1,192	64.3	177	9.5	1,854
	6	3.3	30	16.4	12	6.6	48	26.2	125	68.3	10	5.5	183
	72	4.3	320	19.2	40	2.4	437	26.2	1,067	63.9	167	10.0	1,671
	79	8.5	54	5.8	19	2.0	152	16.3	700	75.0	81	9.7	933
	44	8.0	27	4.9	7	1.3	78	14.3	442	80.8	27	4.9	547
	35	9.1	27	7.0	12	3.1	74	19.2	258	66.8	54	14.0	386
	0	.0	0	.0	0	.0	0	.0	35	100.0		.0	35
	0	.0	0	.0	0	.0	0	.0	0	.0	0	.0	0
	0	.0	0	.0	0	.0	0	.0	35	100.0	8	.0	35
	0	.0	0	.0	0	.0	0	.0	8	100.0		.0	8
	0	.0	0	.0	0	.0	0	.0	0	.0	0	.0	0
	0	.0	0	.0	0	.0	0	.0	8	100.0	8	.0	8
	0	.0	0	.0	0	.0	0	.0	4	100.0		.0	4
	0	.0	0	.0	0	.0	0	.0	0	.0	0	.0	0
	0	.0	0	.0	0	.0	0	.0	4	100.0	8	.0	4
	0	.0	0	.0	0	.0	0	.0	3	100.0		.0	3
	0	.0	0	.0	0	.0	0	.0	0	.0	0	.0	0
	0	.0	0	.0	0	.0	0	.0	3	100.0	8	.0	3
	0	.0	0	.0	0	.0	0	.0	16	100.0		.0	1
	0	.0	0	.0	0	.0	0	.0	0	.0	0	.0	0
	0	.0	0	.0	0	.0	0	.0	16	100.0	8	.0	16
	0	.0	0	.0	0	.0	0	.0	18	100.0		.0	18
	0	.0	0	.0	0	.0	0	.0	0	.0	0	.0	0
	0	.0	0	.0	0	.0	0	.0	18	100.0	8	.0	18
	0	.0	0	.0	0	.0	0	.0	60	100.0		.0	60
	0	.0	0	.0	0	.0	0	.0	0	.0	0	.0	0
	0	.0	0	.0	0	.0	0	.0	60	100.0	8	.0	60
	0	.0	0	.0	0	.0	0	.0	41	100.0		.0	4'
	0	.0	0	.0	0	.0	0	.0	0	.0	0	.0	0
	0	.0	0	.0	0	.0	0	.0	41	100.0	8	.0	46
	0	.0	0	.0	0	.0	0	.0	26	100.0		.0	2
	0	.0	0	.0	0	.0	0	.0	0	.0	0	.0	0
	0	.0	0	.0	0	.0	0	.0	26	100.0	8	.0	26
	14	.8	12	.7	8	.5	34	2.0	1,357	80.5	294	17.4	1,685
	5	1.9	0	.0	5	1.9	5	1.9	235	87.7	28	10.4	268
	9	.6	12	.8	8	.6	29	2.0	1,122	79.2	266	18.9	1,417
	34	2.5	22	1.6	11	.8	71	5.3	1,244	93.2	20	1.5	1,335
	7	2.1	7	2.1	0	.0	16	4.7	319	93.8	5	1.5	340
	27	2.7	15	1.5	11	1.1	55	5.5	925	93.0	15	1.5	995
	0	.0	1	1.0	0	.0	1	1.0	81	82.7	16	16.3	98
	0	.0	1	3.8	0	.0	1	3.8	22	84.6	3	11.5	26
	0	.0	0	.0	0	.0	0	.0	59	81.9	13	18.1	72
	4	.9	1	.2	0	.0	6	1.3	462	98.7		.0	468
	2	.6	1	.3	0	.0	4	1.2	323	98.8	0	.0	327
	7	1.4	0	.0	0	.0	2	1.4	139	98.6	8	.0	141
	0	.0	0	.0	0	.0	0	.0	19	100.0		.0	19
	0	.0	0	.0	0	.0	0	.0	6	100.0	0	.0	6
	0	.0	0	.0	0	.0	0	.0	13	100.0	8	.0	13
	1	.3	0	.0	0	.0	2	.5	375	97.4	8	2.1	385
	1	.7	0	.0	0	.0	2	1.4	141	97.2	2	1.4	145
	0	.0	0	.0	0	.0	0	.0	234	97.5	6	2.5	240
	95	2.7	65	1.8	41	1.1	201	5.6	2,947	82.3	434	12.1	3,582
	51	4.0	20	1.6	12	.9	83	6.4	1,052	81.7	152	11.8	1,287
	44	1.9	45	2.0	29	1.3	118	5.1	1,895	82.6	282	12.3	2,295

	AMERICAN INDIAN ALASKAN NATIVE		BLACK NON-HISPANIC		ASIAN OR PACIFIC ISLANDER		HISPANIC		TOTAL MINORITY		WHITE NON-HISPANIC		NON-RESIDENT ALIEN	
	NUMBER	%	NUMBER	%	NUMBER	%	NUMBER	%	NUMBER	%	NUMBER	%	NUMBER	%

NEW YORK — CONTINUED

	NUMBER	%	NUMBER	%	NUMBER	%	NUMBER	%	NUMBER	%	NUMBER	%	NUMBER	%
SAINT LAWRENCE UNIVERSITY														
NY TOTAL	0	.0	1	1.1	0	.0	0	.0	1	1.1	93	98.9	0	.0
NY FEMALE	0	.0	1	2.1	0	.0	0	.0	1	2.1	47	97.9	0	.0
NY MALE	0	.0	0	.0	0	.0	0	.0	0	.0	46	100.0	0	.0
SNT VLADMR ORTH THEOL SEM														
NY TOTAL	0	.0	0	.0	0	.0	0	.0	0	.0	3	50.0	3	50.0
NY FEMALE	0	.0	0	.0	0	.0	0	.0	0	.0	0	.0	1	100.0
NY MALE	0	.0	0	.0	0	.0	0	.0	0	.0	3	60.0	2	40.0
SARAH LAWRENCE COLLEGE														
NY TOTAL	0	.0	2	1.7	0	.0	1	.8	3	2.5	114	96.6	1	.8
NY FEMALE	0	.0	2	1.9	0	.0	1	.9	3	2.8	103	96.3	1	.9
NY MALE	0	.0	0	.0	0	.0	0	.0	0	.0	11	100.0	0	.0
SEM IMMAC CONCEPTION														
NY TOTAL	0	.0	0	.0	0	.0	1	.7	1	.7	135	99.3	0	.0
NY FEMALE	0	.0	0	.0	0	.0	1	.9	1	.9	110	99.1	0	.0
NY MALE	0	.0	0	.0	0	.0	0	.0	0	.0	25	100.0	0	.0
SH*OR YOSHUV RAB COLLEGE														
NY TOTAL	0	.0	0	.0	0	.0	0	.0	0	.0	23	100.0	0	.0
NY FEMALE	0	.0	0	.0	0	.0	0	.0	0	.0	0	.0	0	.0
NY MALE	0	.0	0	.0	0	.0	0	.0	0	.0	23	100.0	0	.0
SUNY AT ALBANY														
NY TOTAL	10	.3	87	2.7	39	1.2	83	2.5	219	6.7	2,870	88.1	167	5.1
NY FEMALE	2	.1	44	2.7	19	1.2	52	3.2	117	7.1	1,471	89.4	57	3.5
NY MALE	8	.5	43	2.7	20	1.2	31	1.9	102	6.3	1,399	86.8	110	6.8
SUNY AT BINGHAMTON														
NY TOTAL	4	.2	31	1.7	30	1.7	27	1.5	92	5.1	1,549	86.5	149	8.3
NY FEMALE	1	.1	11	1.6	10	1.4	13	1.9	35	5.0	619	89.1	41	5.9
NY MALE	3	.3	20	1.8	20	1.8	14	1.3	57	5.2	930	84.9	108	9.9
SUNY AT BUFFALO MAIN CAM														
NY TOTAL	16	.4	189	4.3	60	1.4	38	.9	303	6.9	3,394	77.2	701	15.9
NY FEMALE	3	.2	112	6.2	14	.8	20	1.1	149	8.3	1,493	83.1	154	8.6
NY MALE	13	.5	77	3.0	46	1.8	18	.7	154	5.9	1,901	73.1	547	21.0
SUNY HEALTH SCI CTR BELO														
NY TOTAL	1	.1	18	2.2	10	1.2	2	.2	31	3.8	718	88.5	62	7.6
NY FEMALE	1	.7	10	2.4	8	1.9	1	.2	20	4.7	384	90.8	19	4.5
NY MALE	0	.0	8	2.1	2	.5	1	.3	11	2.8	334	86.1	43	11.1
SUNY AT STONY BK MAIN CAM														
NY TOTAL	13	.4	68	2.1	40	1.2	45	1.4	166	5.1	2,687	82.9	387	11.9
NY FEMALE	5	.3	34	2.3	16	1.1	20	1.4	75	5.1	1,311	89.1	86	5.8
NY MALE	8	.5	34	1.9	24	1.4	25	1.4	91	5.1	1,376	77.8	301	17.0
SUNY HLTH SCI CTR STNY BK														
NY TOTAL	1	.2	60	14.0	6	1.4	28	6.5	95	22.1	324	75.3	11	2.6
NY FEMALE	0	.0	32	11.1	4	1.4	16	5.5	52	18.0	231	79.9	6	2.1
NY MALE	1	.7	28	19.9	2	1.4	12	8.5	43	30.5	93	66.0	5	3.5
SUNY DOWNSTATE MEDL CTR														
NY TOTAL	0	.0	3	2.5	5	4.1	2	1.6	10	8.2	99	81.1	13	10.7
NY FEMALE	0	.0	0	.0	1	3.8	1	3.8	2	7.7	20	76.9	4	15.4
NY MALE	0	.0	3	3.1	4	4.2	1	1.0	8	8.3	79	82.3	9	9.4
SUNY UPSTATE MEDICAL CTR														
NY TOTAL	0	.0	0	.0	0	.0	0	.0	0	.0	58	100.0	0	.0
NY FEMALE	0	.0	0	.0	0	.0	0	.0	0	.0	26	100.0	0	.0
NY MALE	0	.0	0	.0	0	.0	0	.0	0	.0	32	100.0	0	.0
SUNY COLLEGE AT BROCKPORT														
NY TOTAL	2	.3	50	8.5	2	.3	5	.8	59	10.0	524	88.7	8	1.4
NY FEMALE	0	.0	27	8.7	2	.6	4	1.3	33	10.6	278	89.1	1	.3
NY MALE	2	.7	23	8.2	0	.0	1	.4	26	9.3	246	88.2	7	2.5
SUNY COLLEGE AT BUFFALO														
NY TOTAL	2	.2	29	2.8	2	.2	3	.3	36	3.4	1,003	95.3	14	1.3
NY FEMALE	1	.1	24	3.0	2	.3	3	.4	30	3.8	762	95.8	3	.4
NY MALE	1	.4	5	1.9	0	.0	0	.0	6	2.3	241	93.4	11	4.3
SUNY COLLEGE AT CORTLAND														
NY TOTAL	1	.3	4	1.1	2	.6	1	.3	8	2.2	348	96.7	4	1.1
NY FEMALE	0	.0	4	1.8	0	.0	1	.4	5	2.2	218	97.3	1	.4
NY MALE	1	.7	0	.0	2	1.5	0	.0	3	2.2	130	95.6	3	2.2
SUNY COLLEGE AT FREDONIA														
NY TOTAL	3	1.0	4	1.3	0	.0	3	1.0	10	3.2	300	95.8	3	1.0
NY FEMALE	0	.0	4	?.9	0	.0	3	1.4	7	3.3	208	96.7	0	.0
NY MALE	3	3.1	0	.0	0	.0	0	.0	3	3.1	92	93.9	3	3.1
SUNY COLLEGE AT GENESEO														
NY TOTAL	0	.0	1	.2	0	.0	0	.0	1	.2	395	97.8	8	2.0
NY FEMALE	0	.0	1	.3	0	.0	0	.0	1	.3	307	98.4	4	1.3
NY MALE	0	.0	0	.0	0	.0	0	.0	0	.0	88	95.7	4	4.3
SUNY COLLEGE AT NEW PALTZ														
NY TOTAL	4	.4	21	1.9	2	.2	16	1.5	43	4.0	1,028	94.7	14	1.3
NY FEMALE	2	.3	12	1.6	0	.0	12	1.6	26	3.5	720	95.7	6	.8
NY MALE	2	.6	9	2.7	2	.6	4	1.2	17	5.1	308	92.5	8	2.4
SUNY COLLEGE AT ONEONTA														
NY TOTAL	0	.0	1	.4	0	.0	0	.0	1	.4	222	99.6	0	.0
NY FEMALE	0	.0	1	.7	0	.0	0	.0	1	.7	148	99.3	0	.0
NY MALE	0	.0	0	.0	0	.0	0	.0	0	.0	74	100.0	0	.0
SUNY COLLEGE AT OSWEGO														
NY TOTAL	1	.3	1	.3	1	.3	1	.3	4	1.2	332	98.8	0	.0
NY FEMALE	1	.6	0	.0	0	.0	0	.0	1	.6	172	99.4	0	.0
NY MALE	0	.0	1	.6	1	.6	1	.6	3	1.8	160	98.2	0	.0
SUNY COLLEGE PLATTSBURGH														
NY TOTAL	4	2.3	4	2.3	2	1.2	0	.0	10	5.8	154	89.5	8	4.7
NY FEMALE	4	3.9	3	2.9	1	1.0	0	.0	8	7.8	90	88.2	4	3.9
NY MALE	0	.0	1	1.4	1	1.4	0	.0	2	2.9	64	91.4	4	5.7
SUNY COLLEGE AT POTSDAM														
NY TOTAL	0	.0	0	.0	0	.0	0	.0	0	.0	140	100.0	0	.0
NY FEMALE	0	.0	0	.0	0	.0	0	.0	0	.0	104	100.0	0	.0
NY MALE	0	.0	0	.0	0	.0	0	.0	0	.0	36	100.0	0	.0

	BLACK NON-HISPANIC		ASIAN OR PACIFIC ISLANDER		HISPANIC		TOTAL MINORITY		WHITE NON-HISPANIC		NON-RESIDENT ALIEN		TOTAL
	NUMBER	%	NUMBER	%	NUMBER	%	NUMBER	%	NUMBER	%	NUMBER	%	NUMBER
:NUED													
	0	.0	0	.0	1	.3	1	.3	287	99.7	0	.0	288
	0	.0	0	.0	1	.5	1	.5	202	99.5	0	.0	203
	0	.0	0	.0	0	.0	0	.0	85	100.0	0	.0	85
	1	.3	3	.9	1	.3	5	1.5	266	81.6	55	16.9	326
	0	.0	0	.0	0	.0	0	.0	52	85.2	9	14.8	61
	1	.4	3	1.1	1	.4	5	1.9	214	80.8	46	17.4	265
	5	3.7	22	16.4	11	8.2	38	28.4	85	63.4	11	8.2	134
	0	.0	1	16.7	1	16.7	2	33.3	2	33.3	2	33.3	6
	5	3.9	21	16.4	10	7.8	36	28.1	83	64.8	9	7.0	128
	0	.0	0	.0	0	.0	0	.0	2	100.0		.0	2
	0	.0	0	.0	0	.0	0	.0	0	.0	0	.0	0
	0	.0	0	.0	0	.0	0	.0	2	100.0	0	.0	2
	62	1.7	35	1.0	22	.6	122	3.3	3,033	82.9	502	13.7	3,657
	26	1.7	14	.9	12	.8	52	3.4	1,383	89.5	111	7.2	1,546
	36	1.7	21	1.0	10	.5	70	3.3	1,650	78.2	391	19.5	2,111
	13	1.7	18	2.3	10	1.3	44	5.6	725	92.8	12	1.5	781
	6	3.1	9	4.7	4	2.1	19	9.9	171	89.1	2	1.0	192
	7	1.2	9	1.5	6	1.0	25	4.2	554	94.1	10	1.7	589
	13	16.7	1	1.3	1	1.3	15	19.2	41	52.6	22	28.2	78
	1	12.5	0	.0	0	.0	1	12.5	5	62.5	2	25.0	8
	12	17.1	1	1.4	1	1.4	14	20.0	36	51.4	20	28.6	70
	0	.0	0	.0	0	.0	0	.0	35	100.0	0	.0	35
	0	.0	0	.0	0	.0	0	.0	0	.0	0	.0	0
	0	.0	0	.0	0	.0	0	.0	35	100.0	0	.0	35
	32	1.6	29	1.5	3	.2	70	3.5	1,687	84.4	243	12.2	2,000
	15	2.1	11	1.5	1	.1	29	4.0	653	90.2	42	5.8	724
	17	1.3	18	1.4	2	.2	41	3.2	1,034	81.0	201	15.8	1,276
	0	.0	0	.0	0	.0	0	.0	3	100.0		.0	3
	0	.0	0	.0	0	.0	0	.0	1	100.0	0	.0	1
	0	.0	0	.0	0	.0	0	.0	2	100.0	0	.0	2
	4	1.3	2	.6	1	.3	7	2.2	273	86.7	3	11.1	315
	2	1.2	0	.0	0	.0	2	1.2	155	93.4	9	5.4	166
	2	1.3	2	1.3	1	.7	5	3.4	118	79.2	26	17.4	149
	0	.0	0	.0	0	.0	0	.0	8	100.0		.0	8
	0	.0	0	.0	0	.0	0	.0	0	.0	0	.0	0
	0	.0	0	.0	0	.0	0	.0	8	100.0	0	.0	8
	0	.0	0	.0	0	.0	0	.0	9	100.0		.0	9
	0	.0	0	.0	0	.0	0	.0	0	.0	0	.0	0
	0	.0	0	.0	0	.0	0	.0	9	100.0	0	.0	9
	0	.0	0	.0	0	.0	0	.0	11	100.0		.0	11
	0	.0	0	.0	0	.0	0	.0	0	.0	0	.0	0
	0	.0	0	.0	0	.0	0	.0	11	100.0	0	.0	11
	0	.0	0	.0	0	.0	0	.0	14	100.0		.0	14
	0	.0	0	.0	0	.0	0	.0	0	.0	0	.0	0
	0	.0	0	.0	0	.0	0	.0	14	100.0	0	.0	14
	0	.0	0	.0	0	.0	0	.0	48	100.0		.0	48
	0	.0	0	.0	0	.0	0	.0	0	.0	0	.0	0
	0	.0	0	.0	0	.0	0	.0	48	100.0	0	.0	48
	2	.2	3	.3	0	.0	5	.4	1,126	96.3	38	3.3	1,169
	1	.2	3	.5	0	.0	4	.6	633	97.4	13	2.0	650
	1	.2	0	.0	0	.0	1	.2	493	95.0	25	4.8	519
(128 INSTITUTIONS)													
	6,867	5.7	3,149	2.6	3,287	2.7	13,704	11.4	98,541	82.2	7,571	6.3	119,816
	3,962	6.8	1,244	2.1	1,778	3.1	7,143	12.3	48,731	84.1	2,084	3.6	57,958
	2,905	4.7	1,905	3.1	1,509	2.4	6,561	10.6	49,810	80.5	5,487	8.9	61,858
	8	3.3	1	.4	0	.0	12	5.0	227	94.6	1	.4	240
	5	3.2	0	.0	0	.0	6	3.9	149	96.1	0	.0	155
	3	3.5	1	1.2	0	.0	6	7.1	78	91.8	1	1.2	85
	51	2.4	10	.5	8	.4	72	3.4	1,900	91.0	117	5.6	2,089
	25	3.3	4	.5	5	.7	36	4.7	696	91.1	32	4.2	764
	26	2.0	6	.5	3	.2	36	2.7	1,204	90.9	85	6.4	1,325
	0	.0	0	.0		.0	0	.0	0	.0	0	.0	0
	0	.0	0	.0	0	.0	0	.0	0	.0	0	.0	0
	0	.0	0	.0	0	.0	0	.0	0	.0	0	.0	0
	62	4.7	3	.2		.3	72	5.5	1,234	93.8	10	.8	1,316
	28	3.7	0	.0	4	.4	32	4.2	723	95.5	2	.3	757
	34	6.1	3	.5	1	.2	40	7.2	511	91.4	8	1.4	559

TABLE 2 - TOTAL GRADUATE ENROLLMENT IN INSTITUTIONS OF HIGHER EDUCATION BY RACE, ETHNICITY AND SEX: INSTITUTION, STATE AND NATION, 1978

	AMERICAN INDIAN ALASKAN NATIVE		BLACK NON-HISPANIC		ASIAN OR PACIFIC ISLANDER		HISPANIC		TOTAL MINORITY		WHITE NON-HISPANIC		NON-RESIDENT ALIEN	
	NUMBER	%	NUMBER	%	NUMBER	%	NUMBER	%	NUMBER	%	NUMBER	%	NUMBER	%
NORTH CAROLINA CONTINUED														
EAST CAROLINA UNIVERSITY														
NC TOTAL	7	.4	273	13.8	4	.2	1	.1	285	14.4	1,687	85.2	9	.5
NC FEMALE	3	.2	201	15.2	1	.1	1	.1	206	15.5	1,117	84.2	3	.2
NC MALE	4	.6	72	11.0	3	.5	0	.0	79	12.1	570	87.0	6	.9
NC AGRL & TECH STATE U														
NC TOTAL	1	.1	523	75.3	1	.1	0	.0	525	75.5	143	20.6	27	3.9
NC FEMALE	1	.3	331	83.6	1	.3	0	.0	333	84.1	55	13.9	8	2.0
NC MALE	0	.0	192	64.2	0	.0	0	.0	192	64.2	88	29.4	19	6.4
NC CENTRAL UNIVERSITY														
NC TOTAL	0	.0	531	77.4	0	.0	0	.0	531	77.4	137	20.0	18	2.6
NC FEMALE	0	.0	350	80.1	0	.0	0	.0	350	80.1	84	19.2	3	.7
NC MALE	0	.0	181	72.7	0	.0	0	.0	181	72.7	53	21.3	15	6.0
NC STATE U RALEIGH														
NC TOTAL	9	.3	97	3.7	33	1.3	15	.6	154	5.9	1,975	75.4	492	18.8
NC FEMALE	1	.1	36	4.7	10	1.3	4	.5	51	6.7	649	85.6	58	7.7
NC MALE	8	.4	61	3.3	23	1.2	11	.6	103	5.5	1,326	71.2	434	23.3
PEMBROKE STATE UNIVERSITY														
NC TOTAL	12	9.9	8	6.6	0	.0	0	.0	20	16.5	101	83.5	0	.0
NC FEMALE	8	8.5	4	4.3	0	.0	0	.0	12	12.8	82	87.2	0	.0
NC MALE	4	14.8	4	14.8	0	.0	0	.0	8	29.6	19	70.4	0	.0
U OF NC AT CHAPEL HILL														
NC TOTAL	15	.4	253	6.3	40	1.0	35	.9	343	8.6	3,497	87.5	155	3.9
NC FEMALE	8	.4	156	8.2	16	.8	19	1.0	199	10.4	1,648	86.5	59	3.1
NC MALE	7	.3	97	4.6	24	1.1	16	.8	144	6.9	1,849	88.5	96	4.6
U OF NC AT CHARLOTTE														
NC TOTAL	2	.2	126	13.1	0	.0	1	.1	129	13.4	932	86.3	3	.3
NC FEMALE	1	.2	100	17.9	0	.0	1	.2	102	18.2	457	81.8	0	.0
NC MALE	1	.2	26	6.4	0	.0	0	.0	27	6.7	375	92.6	3	.7
U OF NC AT GREENSBORO														
NC TOTAL	2	.1	127	6.6	6	.3	5	.3	140	7.3	1,769	91.8	18	.9
NC FEMALE	1	.1	86	7.1	4	.3	5	.4	96	8.0	1,103	91.4	8	.7
NC MALE	1	.1	41	5.7	2	.3	0	.0	44	6.1	666	92.5	10	1.4
U OF NC AT WILMINGTON														
NC TOTAL	1	1.1	9	9.9	0	.0	0	.0	10	11.0	81	89.0	0	.0
NC FEMALE	1	1.6	8	13.1	0	.0	0	.0	9	14.8	52	85.2	0	.0
NC MALE	0	.0	1	3.3	0	.0	0	.0	1	3.3	29	96.7	0	.0
WSTN CAROLINA UNIVERSITY														
NC TOTAL			33	4.2	3	.4	0	.0	39	5.0	715	92.0	23	3.0
NC FEMALE			22	4.7	2	.4	0	.0	27	5.7	425	89.9	21	4.4
NC MALE			11	3.6	1	.3	0	.0	12	3.9	290	95.4	2	.7
WAKE FOREST UNIVERSITY														
NC TOTAL	0	.0	13	2.6	2	.4	5	1.0	20	4.1	455	92.5	17	3.5
NC FEMALE	0	.0	5	2.9	1	.6	3	1.7	9	5.2	157	90.2	8	4.6
NC MALE	0	.0	8	2.5	1	.3	2	.6	11	3.5	298	93.7	9	2.8
NORTH CAROLINA TOTAL (15 INSTITUTIONS)														
NC TOTAL	61	.3	2,114	11.7	103	.6	74	.4	2,352	13.1	14,753	82.0	890	4.9
NC FEMALE	31	.3	1,357	15.0	39	.4	41	.5	1,468	16.2	7,397	81.6	202	2.2
NC MALE	30	.3	757	8.5	64	.7	33	.4	884	9.9	7,356	82.4	688	7.7
NORTH DAKOTA														
MINOT STATE COLLEGE														
ND TOTAL	0	.0	0	.0	0	.0	0	.0	0	.0	0	.0	9	100.0
ND FEMALE	0	.0	0	.0	0	.0	0	.0	0	.0	0	.0	8	100.0
ND MALE	0	.0	0	.0	0	.0	0	.0	0	.0	0	.0	1	100.0
ND STATE U MAIN CAMPUS														
ND TOTAL	2	.3	4	.5	6	.8	2	.3	14	1.8	648	83.8	111	14.4
ND FEMALE	2	.9	0	.0	1	.5	1	.5	4	1.8	201	91.4	15	6.8
ND MALE	0	.0	4	.7	5	.9	1	.2	10	1.8	447	80.8	96	17.4
U OF ND MAIN CAMPUS														
ND TOTAL	9	1.2	6	.8	11	1.4	2	.3	28	3.7	712	93.4	22	2.9
ND FEMALE	6	2.1	3	1.0	4	1.4	0	.0	13	4.5	269	93.1	7	2.4
ND MALE	3	.6	3	.6	7	1.5	2	.4	15	3.2	443	93.7	15	3.2
NORTH DAKOTA TOTAL (3 INSTITUTIONS)														
ND TOTAL	11	.7	10	.6	17	1.1	4	.3	42	2.7	1,360	88.1	142	9.2
ND FEMALE	8	1.5	3	.6	5	1.0	1	.2	17	3.3	470	90.9	30	5.8
ND MALE	3	.3	7	.7	12	1.2	3	.3	25	2.4	890	86.7	112	10.9
OHIO														
ANTIOCH UNIVERSITY														
OH TOTAL	16	.8	372	19.6	12	.6	54	2.8	454	23.9	1,394	73.4	51	2.7
OH FEMALE	8	.7	233	19.0	6	.5	26	2.1	273	22.3	920	75.2	31	2.5
OH MALE	8	1.2	139	20.6	6	.9	28	4.1	181	26.8	474	70.2	20	3.0
ASHLAND COLLEGE														
OH TOTAL	0	.0	100	21.8	3	.7	3	.7	106	23.1	346	75.5	6	1.3
OH FEMALE	0	.0	13	12.4	1	1.0	0	.0	14	13.3	91	86.7	0	.0
OH MALE	0	.0	87	24.6	2	.6	3	.8	92	26.1	255	72.2	6	1.7
ATHENAEUM OF OHIO														
OH TOTAL	0	.0	7	6.9	0	.0	0	.0	7	6.9	95	93.1	0	.0
OH FEMALE	0	.0	6	13.6	0	.0	0	.0	6	13.6	38	86.4	0	.0
OH MALE	0	.0	1	1.7	0	.0	0	.0	1	1.7	57	98.3	0	.0
BALDWIN-WALLACE COLLEGE														
OH TOTAL	0	.0	52	8.8	8	1.4	5	.9	65	11.1	523	88.9	0	.0
OH FEMALE	0	.0	17	9.4	0	.0	3	1.7	20	11.1	160	88.9	0	.0
OH MALE	0	.0	35	8.6	8	2.0	2	.5	45	11.0	363	89.0	0	.0
BOWLING GRN ST U MAIN CAM														
OH TOTAL	2	.1	105	3.6	34	1.2	21	.7	162	5.5	2,720	92.8	48	1.6
OH FEMALE	1	.1	60	3.8	11	.7	9	.6	81	5.1	1,501	94.0	15	.9
OH MALE	1	.1	45	3.4	23	1.7	12	.9	81	6.1	1,219	91.4	33	2.5

ENROLLMENT IN INSTITUTIONS OF HIGHER EDUCATION BY RACE, ETHNICITY AND SEX:
STATE AND NATION, 1978

TINUED

	BLACK NON-HISPANIC		ASIAN OR PACIFIC ISLANDER		HISPANIC		TOTAL MINORITY		WHITE NON-HISPANIC		NON-RESIDENT ALIEN		TOTAL
	NUMBER	%	NUMBER	%	NUMBER	%	NUMBER	%	NUMBER	%	NUMBER	%	NUMBER
	3	3.2	0	.0	0	.0	3	3.2	91	96.8	0	.0	94
	1	1.9	0	.0	0	.0	1	1.9	52	98.1	0	.0	53
	2	4.9	0	.0	0	.0	2	4.9	39	95.1	0	.0	41
	14	6.9	2	1.0	1	.5	18	8.8	184	90.2	2	1.0	204
	5	13.2	0	.0	0	.0	5	13.2	33	86.8	0	.0	38
	9	5.4	2	1.2	1	.6	13	7.8	151	91.0	2	1.2	166
	73	2.3	18	.6	8	.2	102	3.1	2,736	84.4	405	12.5	3,243
	50	3.2	10	.6	5	.3	68	4.3	1,414	90.4	82	5.2	1,564
	23	1.4	8	.5	3	.2	34	2.0	1,322	78.7	323	19.2	1,679
	0	.0	0	.0	0	.0	0	.0	71	100.0	0	.0	71
	0	.0	0	.0	0	.0	0	.0	5	100.0	0	.0	5
	0	.0	0	.0	0	.0	0	.0	66	100.0	0	.0	66
	0	.0	0	.0	0	.0	0	.0	12	92.3	1	7.7	13
	0	.0	0	.0	0	.0	0	.0	9	90.0	1	10.0	10
	0	.0	0	.0	0	.0	0	.0	3	100.0	0	.0	3
	2	3.1	2	3.1	0	.0	4	6.2	57	87.7	4	6.2	65
	1	3.1	1	3.1	0	.0	2	6.3	27	84.4	3	9.4	32
	1	3.0	1	3.0	0	.0	2	6.1	30	90.9	1	3.0	33
	299	9.9	39	1.3	10	.3	350	11.6	2,647	87.6	26	.9	3,023
	212	13.8	13	.8	5	.3	231	15.1	1,291	84.3	9	.6	1,531
	87	5.8	26	1.7	5	.3	119	8.0	1,356	90.9	17	1.1	1,492
	0	.0	0	.0	0	.0	0	.0	98	97.0	3	3.0	101
	0	.0	0	.0	0	.0	0	.0	19	100.0	0	.0	19
	0	.0	0	.0	0	.0	0	.0	79	96.3	3	3.7	82
	0	.0	0	.0	0	.0	0	.0	51	100.0	0	.0	51
	0	.0	0	.0	0	.0	0	.0	25	100.0	0	.0	25
	0	.0	0	.0	0	.0	0	.0	26	100.0	0	.0	26
	0	.0	0	.0	0	.0	0	.0	49	100.0	0	.0	49
	0	.0	0	.0	0	.0	0	.0	29	100.0	0	.0	29
	0	.0	0	.0	0	.0	0	.0	20	100.0	0	.0	20
	56	7.9	0	.0	0	.0	56	7.9	653	92.0	1	.1	710
	43	10.9	0	.0	0	.0	43	10.9	353	89.1	0	.0	396
	13	4.1	0	.0	0	.0	13	4.1	300	95.5	1	.3	314
	127	3.9	8	.2	7	.2	147	4.5	3,003	92.6	3	2.9	3,243
	70	4.1	6	.4	2	.1	80	4.7	1,583	93.6	9	1.7	1,692
	57	3.7	2	.1	5	.3	67	4.3	1,420	91.6	84	4.1	1,551
	0	.0	0	.0	0	.0	0	.0	1	100.0	0	.0	1
	0	.0	0	.0	0	.0	0	.0		.0	0	.0	0
	0	.0	0	.0	0	.0	0	.0	1	100.0	0	.0	1
	0	.0	0	.0	0	.0	0	.0	1	100.0	0	.0	1
	0	.0	0	.0	0	.0	0	.0	1	100.0	0	.0	1
	0	.0	0	.0	0	.0	0	.0	0	.0	0	.0	0
	0	.0	0	.0	0	.0	0	.0	1	100.0	0	.0	1
	0	.0	0	.0	0	.0	0	.0	1	100.0	0	.0	1
	0	.0	0	.0	0	.0	0	.0	0	.0	0	.0	0
	0	.0	0	.0	0	.0	0	.0	17	100.0	0	.0	17
	0	.0	0	.0	0	.0	0	.0	11	100.0	0	.0	11
	0	.0	0	.0	0	.0	0	.0	6	100.0	0	.0	6
	0	.0	1	11.1	0	.0	1	11.1	8	88.9	0	.0	9
	0	.0	0	.0	0	.0	0	.0	4	100.0	0	.0	4
	0	.0	1	20.0	0	.0	1	20.0	4	80.0	0	.0	5
	0	.0	0	.0	0	.0	0	.0	10	100.0	0	.0	10
	0	.0	0	.0	0	.0	0	.0	6	100.0	0	.0	6
	0	.0	0	.0	0	.0	0	.0	4	100.0	0	.0	4
	1	1.6	0	.0	0	.0	1	1.6	60	98.4		.0	61
	1	1.8	0	.0	0	.0	1	1.8	55	98.2	0	.0	56
	0	.0	0	.0	0	.0	0	.0	5	100.0	0	.0	5
	0	.0	0	.0	0	.0	0	.0	12	100.0	0	.0	12
	0	.0	0	.0	0	.0	0	.0	10	100.0	0	.0	10
	0	.0	0	.0	0	.0	0	.0	2	100.0	0	.0	2
	0	.0	1	4.0	0	.0	1	4.0	23	92.0	1	4.0	25
	0	.0	0	.0	0	.0	0	.0	10	100.0	0	.0	10
	0	.0	1	6.7	0	.0	1	6.7	13	86.7	1	6.7	15
	2	9.5	0	.0	0	.0	2	9.5	19	90.5	0	.0	21
	0	.0	0	.0	0	.0	0	.0	1	100.0	0	.0	1
	2	10.0	0	.0	0	.0	2	10.0	18	90.0	0	.0	20
	44	3.7	4	.3	9	.8	57	4.8	1,136	95.2	0	.0	1,193
	24	4.6	1	.2	5	1.0	30	5.8	487	94.2	0	.0	517
	20	3.0	3	.4	4	.6	27	4.0	649	96.0	0	.0	676

171

	AMERICAN INDIAN ALASKAN NATIVE		BLACK NON-HISPANIC		ASIAN OR PACIFIC ISLANDER		HISPANIC		TOTAL MINORITY		WHITE NON-HISPANIC		NON-RESIDENT ALIEN		
	NUMBER	%	NUMBER	%	NUMBER	%	NUMBER	%	NUMBER	%	NUMBER	%	NUMBER	%	
OHIO	CONTINUED														
MIAMI U HAMILTON BRANCH															
OH TOTAL	0	.0	3	2.3		.0		.0	3	2.3	129	97.7		.0	
OH FEMALE	0	.0	3	3.5		.0		.0	3	3.5	83	96.5		.0	
OH MALE	0	.0	0	.0	0	.0	0	.0	0	.0	46	100.0	0	.0	
MIAMI U MIDDLETOWN BRANCH															
OH TOTAL	0	.0	6	5.		.0		.0		5.4	105	94.6		.0	
OH FEMALE	0	.0	6	7.4		.0		.0		7.6	73	92.4		.0	
OH MALE	0	.0	0	.0	0	.0	0	.0	0	.0	32	100.0	0	.0	
OBERLIN COLLEGE															
OH TOTAL	0	.0		.		.0	0	.0		.0	6	85.7	1	14.3	
OH FEMALE	0	.0				.0	0	.0		.0	3	75.0	1	25.0	
OH MALE	0	.0	0	.0	0	.0	0	.0	0	.0	3	100.0	0	.0	
OHIO STATE U MAIN CAMPUS															
OH TOTAL	16	.2	467	4.9	64	.7	50	.5	5 7	6.3	7,938	83.3	999	10.5	
OH FEMALE	7	.2	290	6 7	28	.6	20	.5	3,5	8.0	3,779	87.4	199	4.6	
OH MALE	9	.2	177	314	36	.7	30	.6	2$2	4.8	4,159	79.8	800	15.4	
OHIO STATE U LIMA BR															
OH TOTAL	0	.0	1	1.		.0	1	1.6	2	3.2	61	96.8		.0	
OH FEMALE	0	.0	1	1.		.0	1	1.9	2	3.8	51	96.2		.0	
OH MALE	0	.0	0	.8	0	.0	0	.0	0	.0	10	100.0	0	.0	
OHIO STATE U MANSFIELD BR															
OH TOTAL	0	.0	1	1.6		.0	0	.0	1	1.6	60	98.4		.0	
OH FEMALE	0	.0	1	1.9		.0	0	.0	1	1.9	53	98.1		.0	
OH MALE	0	.0	0	.0	0	.0	0	.0	0	.0	7	100.0	0	.0	
OHIO STATE U MARION BR															
OH TOTAL	0	.0		.0		.0	0	.0		.0	35	100.0		.0	
OH FEMALE	0	.0		.0		.0	0	.0		.0	31	100.0		.0	
OH MALE	0	.0	0	.0	0	.0	0	.0	0	.0	4	100.0	0	.0	
OHIO STATE U NEWARK BR															
OH TOTAL	0	.0		.0		.0	0	.0		.0	50	100.0		.0	
OH FEMALE	0	.0		.0		.0	0	.0		.0	43	100.0		.0	
OH MALE	0	.0	0	.0	0	.0	0	.0	0	.0	7	100.0	0	.0	
OHIO U MAIN CAMPUS															
OH TOTAL	5	.3	53	2.9	1	.1	4	.2	6	3.4	1,438	77.7	3 9	18.9	
OH FEMALE	1	.1	3	.4	1	.1	1	.1		.7	747	89.6	41	9.7	
OH MALE	4	.4	50	4.4	0	.0	3	.3	5$	5.6	691	68.0	288	26.4	
OHIO U BELMONT CO BRANCH															
OH TOTAL	0	.0		.0		.0	0	.0		.0	61	98.4	1	1.6	
OH FEMALE	0	.0		.0		.0	0	.0		.0	48	100.0	0	.0	
OH MALE	0	.0	0	.0	0	.0	0	.0	0	.0	13	92.9	1	7.1	
OHIO U CHILLICOTHE BR															
OH TOTAL	0	.0		.0		.0	0	.0		.0	36	100.0		.0	
OH FEMALE	0	.0		.0		.0	0	.0		.0	19	100.0		.0	
OH MALE	0	.0	0	.0	0	.0	0	.0	0	.0	17	100.0	0	.0	
OHIO U IRONTON BRANCH															
OH TOTAL	0	.0		.0		.0	0	.0		.0	65	100.0		.0	
OH FEMALE	0	.0		.0		.0	0	.0		.0	38	100.0		.0	
OH MALE	0	.0	0	.0	0	.0	0	.0	0	.0	27	100.0	0	.0	
OHIO U LANCASTER BRANCH															
OH TOTAL	0	.0	1	.8		.0	0	.0	1	.8	119	97.5	2	1.6	
OH FEMALE	0	.0	0	.0		.0	0	.0	0	.0	45	100.0	0	.0	
OH MALE	0	.0	1	1.3	0	.0	0	.0	1	1.3	74	96.1	2	2.6	
OHIO U ZANESVILLE BRANCH															
OH TOTAL	0	.0		.0		.0	0	.0		.0	81	100.0	0	.0	
OH FEMALE	0	.0		.0		.0	0	.0		.0	50	100.0	0	.0	
OH MALE	0	.0	0	.0	0	.0	0	.0	0	.0	31	100.0	0	.0	
PONTIFICAL C JOSEPHINUM															
OH TOTAL	0	.0	3	3.4		.0	0	.0	3	3.4	85	95.5	1	1.1	
OH FEMALE	0	.0	0	.0		.0	0	.0	0	.0	1	100.0	0	.0	
OH MALE	0	.0	3	3.4	0	.0	0	.0	3	3.4	84	95.5	1	1.1	
RABBINICAL COLLEGE TELSHE															
OH TOTAL	0	.0		.0		.0	0	.0	0	.0	70	100.0		.0	
OH FEMALE	0	.0		.0		.0	0	.0	0	.0	0	.0		.0	
OH MALE	0	.0	0	.0	0	.0	0	.0	0	.0	70	100.0	0	.0	
TRINITY LUTHERAN SEMINARY															
OH TOTAL	18	72.0	2	8.0		.0	0	.0	20	80.0	0	.0	5	20.0	
OH FEMALE	0	.0	1	100.0		.0	0	.0	1	100.0	0	.0	0	.0	
OH MALE	18	75.0	1	4.2	0	.0	0	.0	19	79.2	0	.0	5	20.8	
UNION EXPERIMENTING C C U															
OH TOTAL	9	1.3	177	25.8	7	1.0	42	6.1	235	34.3	451	65.7		.0	
OH FEMALE	6	1.6	99	26.8	2	.5	23	6.2	130	35.2	239	64.8		.0	
OH MALE	3	.9	78	24.6	5	1.6	19	6.0	105	33.1	212	66.9		.0	
UNITED THEOLOGICAL SEM															
OH TOTAL	0	.0		8.5		.0	0	.0	4	8.5	43	91.5	0	.0	
OH FEMALE	0	.0		.0		.0	0	.0	0	.0	1	100.0	0	.0	
OH MALE	0	.0		8.7	0	.0	0	.0	4	8.7	42	91.3	0	.0	
U OF AKRON MAIN CAMPUS															
OH TOTAL	4	.0	108	4.0	14	.5	11	.4	137	5.1	2,419	90.0	132	4.9	
OH FEMALE	0	.0	66	5.2	4	.3	2	.2	72	5 7	1,164	92.2	26	2.1	
OH MALE	4	.3	42	2.9	10	.7	9	.6	65	416	1,255	88.0	106	7.4	
U AKRON WAYNE GEN-TECH C															
OH TOTAL	0	.0	0	.0	0	.0	0	.0	0	.0	11	100.0	0	.0	
OH FEMALE	0	.0	0	.0	0	.0	0	.0	0	.0	8	100.0	0	.0	
OH MALE	0	.0	0	.0	0	.0	0	.0	0	.0	3	100.0	0	.0	
U OF CINCINNATI MAIN CAM															
OH TOTAL	5	.1	242	.2	37	.9	29	.7	313	8.0	3,154	80.7	442	11.3	
OH FEMALE	3	.2	133	6.1	8	.5	16	1.0	160	9.8	1,373	83.9	104	6.4	
OH MALE	2	.1	109	8.8	29	1.3	13	.6	153	6.7	1,781	78.4	338	14.9	
UNIVERSITY OF DAYTON															
OH TOTAL	4	.2	90	5.2	24	1.4	24	1.4	142	8.2	1,548	89.9	32	1.9	
OH FEMALE	1	.2	48	7.8	10	1.6	10	1.6	69	11.2	539	87.8	6	1.0	
OH MALE	3	.3	42	3.8	14	1.3	14	1.3	73	6.6	1,009	91.1	26	2.3	

172

BLACK NON-HISPANIC		ASIAN OR PACIFIC ISLANDER		HISPANIC		TOTAL MINORITY		WHITE NON-HISPANIC		NON-RESIDENT ALIEN		TOTAL
UMBER	%	NUMBER	%	NUMBER	%	NUMBER	%	NUMBER	%	NUMBER	%	NUMBER
126	5.6	28	1.2	12	.5	174	7.7	1,967	86.7	127	5	2,268
80	6.9	11	.9	4	.3	103	8.9	1,025	88.2	34	2↓	1,162
46	4.2	17	1.5	8	.7	71	6.4	942	85.2	93	8.↓	1,106
0	.0	0	.0	0	.0	0	.0	9	100.0	0	.0	9
0	.0	0	.0	0	.0	0	.0	6	100.0	0	.0	6
0	.0	0	.0	0	.0	0	.0	3	100.0	0	.0	3
100	5.0	25	1.3	6	.3	133	6.7	1,825	91.5	36	1.8	1,994
73	7.1	10	1.0	3	.3	88	8.5	936	90.4	11	1.1	1,035
27	2.8	15	1.6	3	.3	45	4.7	889	92.7	25	2.6	959
0	.0	0	.0	0	.0	0	.0	14	100.0	0	.0	14
0	.0	0	.0	0	.0	0	.0	12	100.0	0	.0	12
0	.0	0	.0	0	.0	0	.0	2	100.0	0	.0	2
451	12.7	0	.0	0	.0	452	12.7	3,084	86.6	24	.7	3,560
233	17.6	0	.0	0	.0	234	17.6	1,090	82.2	2	.2	1,326
218	9.8	0	.0	0	.0	218	9.8	1,994	89.3	22	1.0	2,234
60	2.8	4	.2	9	.4	76	3.5	2,013	93.6	62	2.9	2,151
36	2.9	2	.2	5	.4	45	3.7	1,164	95.3	13	1.1	1,222
24	2.6	2	.2	4	.4	31	3.3	849	91.4	49	5.3	929
57 INSTITUTIONS)												
3,152	6.3	336	.7	306	.6	3,898	7.9	42,895	86.4	2,854	5.7	49,647
1,809	7.7	125	.5	140	.6	2,120	9.0	20,757	88.2	647	2.8	23,524
1,343	5.1	211	.8	166	.6	1,778	6.8	22,138	84.7	2,207	8.4	26,123
1	1.4	0	.0	0	.0	1	1.4	68	93.2		5.5	73
0	.0	0	.0	0	.0	0	.0	38	100.0		.0	38
1	2.9	0	.0	0	.0	1	2.9	30	85.7	4	11.4	35
140	6.7	6	.3	10	.5	179	8.6	1,742	83.3	169	8.1	2,090
85	7.7	1	.1	3	.3	98	8.9	965	87.5	40	3.6	1,103
55	5.6	5	.5	7	.7	81	8.2	777	78.7	129	13.1	987
6	1.8	0	.0	1	.3	27	8.2	301	91.8		.0	328
2	.9	0	.0	1	.5	11	5.0	211	95.0	0	.0	222
4	3.8	0	.0	0	.0	16	15.1	90	84.9	0	.0	106
68	6.9	3	.3	2	.2	201	20.3	784	79.0	7	.7	992
47	8.0	3	.5	1	.2	130	22.0	460	78.0	0	.0	590
21	5.2	0	.0	1	.2	71	17.7	324	80.6	7	1.7	402
0	.0	0	.0	1	.3	3	1.0	287	97.6	4	1.4	294
0	.0	0	.0	0	.0	0	.0	163	98.2	3	1.8	166
0	.0	0	.0	1	.8	3	2.3	124	96.9	1	.8	128
16	2.2	0	.0	1	.1	19	2.6	500	67.7	220	29.8	739
8	3.8	0	.0	0	.0	9	4.3	166	78.7	36	17.1	211
8	1.5	0	.0	1	.2	10	1.9	334	63.3	184	34.8	528
61	2.4	22	.9	17	.7	128	5.0	1,904	74.1	536	20.9	2,568
35	4.0	6	.7	4	.5	54	6.1	715	81.3	110	12.5	879
26	1.5	16	.9	13	.8	74	4.4	1,189	70.4	426	25.2	1,689
11	4.0	0	.0	1	.4	12	4.4	241	88.0	21	7.7	274
5	17.9	0	.0	0	.0	5	17.9	22	78.6	1	3.6	28
6	2.4	0	.0	1	.4	7	2.8	219	89.0	20	8.1	246
13	6.4	6	3.0	3	1.5	25	12.4	165	81.7	12	5.9	202
5	6.0	3	3.6	2	2.4	12	14.3	71	84.5	1	1.2	84
8	6.8	3	2.5	1	.8	13	11.0	94	79.7	11	9.3	118
7	1.3	1	..	1	.2	39	7.5	410	78.4	74	14.1	523
3	1.0	0	.0	0	.0	25	8.7	242	84.3	20	7.0	287
4	1.7	1	.4	1	.4	14	5.9	168	71.2	54	22.9	236
20	3.5	3	.5	3	.5	41	7.2	519	91.4	8	1.4	568
7	2.0	1	.3	1	.3	16	4.6	331	94.8	2	.6	349
13	5.9	2	.9	2	.9	25	11.4	188	85.8	6	2.7	219
22	4.2	8	1.5	4	.8	46	8.8	447	85.6	29	5.6	522
13	4.2	5	1.6	3	1.0	28	9.2	271	88.6	7	2.3	306
9	4.2	3	1.4	1	.5	18	8.3	176	81.5	22	10.2	216
122	9.5	26	.7	23	.7	236	6.7	2,700	76.9	576	16.4	3,512
62	4.6	10	.7	8	.6	113	8.5	1,133	84.9	89	5.7	1,335
60	2.8	16	.7	15	.7	123	5.6	1,567	72.0	487	22.4	2,177
18	1.9	3	.3	2	.2	29	3.0	848	87.8	89	9.2	966
7	1.7	1	.2	2	.5	14	3.4	386	93.7	12	2.9	412
11	2.0	2	.4	0	.0	15	2.7	462	83.4	77	13.9	554
14 INSTITUTIONS)												
505	3.7	78	.6	69	.5	986	7.2	10,916	80.0	1,749	12.8	13,651
279	4.6	30	.5	25	.4	515	8.5	5,174	86.1	321	5.3	6,010
226	3.0	48	.6	44	.6	471	6.2	5,742	75.1	1,428	18.7	7,641

	AMERICAN INDIAN ALASKAN NATIVE		BLACK NON-HISPANIC		ASIAN OR PACIFIC ISLANDER		HISPANIC		TOTAL MINORITY		WHITE NON-HISPANIC		NON-RESIDENT ALIEN		T
	NUMBER	%	NUMBER	%	NUMBER	%	NUMBER	%	NUMBER	%	NUMBER	%	NUMBER	%	N
OREGON															
LEWIS AND CLARK COLLEGE															
OR TOTAL	3	.7	4	.9	4	.9	4	.9	15	3.5	418	96.5	0	.0	
OR FEMALE	2	.7	2	.7	2	.7	4	1.4	10	3.6	267	96.4	0	.0	
OR MALE	1	.6	2	1.3	2	1.3	0	.0	5	3.2	151	96.8	0	.0	
LINFIELD COLLEGE															
OR TOTAL	0	.0	0	.0	1	3.7	0	.0	1	3.7	25	92.6	1	3.7	
OR FEMALE	0	.0	0	.0	0	.0	0	.0	0	.0	19	100.0	0	.0	
OR MALE	0	.0	0	.0	1	12.5	0	.0	1	12.5	6	75.0	1	12.5	
MOUNT ANGEL SEMINARY															
OR TOTAL	0	.0	0	.0	0	.0	2	3.7	2	3.7	52	96.3	0	.0	
OR FEMALE	0	.0	0	.0	0	.0	0	.0	0	.0	1	100.0	0	.0	
OR MALE	0	.0	0	.0	0	.0	2	3.8	2	3.8	51	96.2	0	.0	
MULTNOMAH SCHOOL OF BIBLE															
OR TOTAL	0	.0	0	.0	3	2.6	1	.9	4	3.4	109	94.0	3	2.6	
OR FEMALE	0	.0	0	.0	2	3.8	1	1.9	3	5.8	47	90.4	2	3.8	
OR MALE	0	.0	0	.0	1	1.6	0	.0	1	1.6	62	96.9	1	1.6	
OREGON GRADUATE CENTER															
OR TOTAL	0	.0	0	.0	0	.0	0	.0	0	.0	26	65.0	14	35.0	
OR FEMALE	0	.0	0	.0	0	.0	0	.0	0	.0	2	66.7	1	33.3	
OR MALE	0	.0	0	.0	0	.0	0	.0	0	.0	24	64.9	13	35.1	
EASTERN OREGON ST COLLEGE															
OR TOTAL	0	.0	0	.0	5	10.6	0	.0	5	10.6	34	72.3	8	17.0	
OR FEMALE	0	.0	0	.0	3	10.0	0	.0	3	10.0	22	73.3	5	16.7	
OR MALE	0	.0	0	.0	2	11.8	0	.0	2	11.8	12	70.6	3	17.6	
OREGON COLLEGE OF ED															
OR TOTAL	2	1.5	0	.0	3	2.2	0	.0	5	3.6	131	95.6	1	.7	
OR FEMALE	2	2.4	0	.0	1	1.2	0	.0	3	3.7	79	96.3	0	.0	
OR MALE	0	.0	0	.0	2	3.6	0	.0	2	3.6	52	94.5	1	1.8	
OREGON STATE UNIVERSITY															
OR TOTAL	26	1.2	18	.8	29	1.4	11	.5	84	3.9	1,607	75.4	440	20.6	
OR FEMALE	8	1.3	4	.7	13	2.2	2	.3	27	4.5	498	83.3	73	12.2	
OR MALE	18	1.2	14	.9	16	1.0	9	.6	57	3.7	1,109	72.3	367	23.9	
PORTLAND STATE UNIVERSITY															
OR TOTAL	12	.6	37	1.9	62	3.1	10	.5	121	6.1	1,744	88.2	113	5.7	
OR FEMALE	9	.8	13	1.2	26	2.4	3	.3	51	4.6	1,010	91.7	41	3.7	
OR MALE	3	.3	24	2.7	36	4.1	7	.8	70	8.0	734	83.8	72	8.2	
STHN OREGON ST COLLEGE															
OR TOTAL	0	.0	0	.0	1	.7	0	.0	1	.7	139	93.3	9	6.0	
OR FEMALE	0	.0	0	.0	1	1.4	0	.0	1	1.4	71	95.9	2	2.7	
OR MALE	0	.0	0	.0	0	.0	0	.0	0	.0	68	90.7	7	9.3	
U OF OREGON MAIN CAMPUS															
OR TOTAL	14	.5	25	.8	43	1.4	32	1.0	114	3.7	2,465	80.6	481	15.7	
OR FEMALE	4	.3	13	1.0	18	1.4	14	1.1	49	3.7	1,121	85.6	140	10.7	
OR MALE	10	.6	12	.7	25	1.4	18	1.0	65	3.7	1,344	76.8	341	19.5	
U OF OREGON HLTH SCI CTR															
OR TOTAL	0	.0	2	.8	8	3.1	1	.4	11	4.3	239	93.4	6	2.3	
OR FEMALE	0	.0	1	.6	5	2.9	0	.0	6	3.5	164	95.3	2	1.2	
OR MALE	0	.0	1	1.2	3	3.6	1	1.2	5	6.0	75	89.3	4	4.8	
PACIFIC UNIVERSITY															
OR TOTAL	0	.0	0	.0	0	.0	0	.0	0	.0	40	100.0	0	.0	
OR FEMALE	0	.0	0	.0	0	.0	0	.0	0	.0	34	100.0	0	.0	
OR MALE	0	.0	0	.0	0	.0	0	.0	0	.0	6	100.0	0	.0	
REED COLLEGE															
OR TOTAL	0	.0	0	.0	0	.0	0	.0	0	.0	17	100.0	0	.0	
OR FEMALE	0	.0	0	.0	0	.0	0	.0	0	.0	12	100.0	0	.0	
OR MALE	0	.0	0	.0	0	.0	0	.0	0	.0	5	100.0	0	.0	
UNIVERSITY OF PORTLAND															
OR TOTAL	0	.0	5	1.1	5	1.1	0	.0	10	2.2	395	87.8	45	10.0	
OR FEMALE	0	.0	1	.8	2	1.5	0	.0	3	2.3	124	93.9	5	3.8	
OR MALE	0	.0	4	1.3	3	.9	0	.0	7	2.2	271	85.2	40	12.6	
WARNER PACIFIC COLLEGE															
OR TOTAL	0	.0	0	.0	0	.0	0	.0	0	.0	9	64.3	5	35.7	
OR FEMALE	0	.0	0	.0	0	.0	0	.0	0	.0	3	100.0	0	.0	
OR MALE	0	.0	0	.0	0	.0	0	.0	0	.0	6	54.5	5	45.5	
WESTERN BAPTIST COLLEGE															
OR TOTAL	0	.0	0	.0	0	.0	0	.0	0	.0	1	50.0	1	50.0	
CR FEMALE	0	.0	0	.0	0	.0	0	.0	0	.0	0	.0	0	.0	
OR MALE	0	.0	0	.0	0	.0	0	.0	0	.0	1	50.0	1	50.0	
WESTERN CONS BAPTIST SEM															
OR TOTAL	0	.0	0	.0	1	.8	2	1.5	3	2.3	123	94.6	4	3.1	
OR FEMALE	0	.0	0	.0	0	.0	0	.0	0	.0	15	100.0	0	.0	
OR MALE	0	.0	0	.0	1	.9	2	1.7	3	2.6	108	93.9	4	3.5	
WSTN EVANGELICAL SEM															
OR TOTAL	0	.0	1	2.6	1	2.6	0	.0	2	5.3	35	92.1	1	2.6	
OR FEMALE	0	.0	0	.0	1	10.0	0	.0	1	10.0	9	90.0	0	.0	
OR MALE	0	.0	1	3.6	0	.0	0	.0	1	3.6	26	92.9	1	3.6	
WILLAMETTE UNIVERSITY															
OR TOTAL	0	.0	3	2.2	1	.7	3	2.2	7	5.0	131	94.2	1	.7	
OR FEMALE	0	.0	1	2.6	0	.0	1	2.6	2	5.1	37	94.9	0	.0	
OR MALE	0	.0	2	2.0	1	1.0	2	2.0	5	5.0	94	94.0	1	1.0	
OREGON TOTAL (	20 INSTITUTIONS)														
OR TOTAL	57	.6	95	1.0	167	1.8	66	.7	385	4.2	7,740	83.6	1,133	12.2	
OR FEMALE	25	.6	35	.9	74	1.9	25	.6	159	4.0	3,535	89.2	271	6.8	
OR MALE	32	.6	60	1.1	93	1.8	41	.8	226	4.3	4,205	79.4	862	16.3	
PENNSYLVANIA															
ALLEGHENY COLLEGE															
PA TOTAL	0	.0	1	5.6	0	.0	0	.0	1	5.6	17	94.4	0	.0	
PA FEMALE	0	.0	1	7.7	0	.0	0	.0	1	7.7	12	92.3	0	.0	
PA MALE	0	.0	0	.0	0	.0	0	.0	0	.0	5	100.0	0	.0	

ENROLLMENT IN INSTITUTIONS OF HIGHER EDUCATION BY RACE, ETHNICITY AND SEX:
ATE AND NATION, 1978

N E	BLACK NON-HISPANIC		ASIAN OR PACIFIC ISLANDER		HISPANIC		TOTAL MINORITY		WHITE NON-HISPANIC		NON-RESIDENT ALIEN		TOTAL
	NUMBER	%	NUMBER	%	NUMBER	%	NUMBER	%	NUMBER	%	NUMBER	%	NUMBER
INUED													
	0	.0	0	.0	0	.0	0	.0	0	.0	0	.0	0
	0	.0	0	.0	0	.0	0	.0	0	.0	0	.0	0
	0	.0	0	.0	0	.0	0	.0	0	.0	0	.0	0
	105	13.1	2	.3	4	.5	111	13.9	688	86.1	0	.0	799
	87	12.8	2	.3	4	.6	93	13.7	586	86.3	0	.0	679
	18	15.0	0	.0	0	.0	18	15.0	102	85.0	0	.0	120
	0	.0	0	.0	0	.0	0	.0	649	99.8	1	.2	650
	0	.0	0	.0	0	.0	0	.0	409	100.0	0	.0	409
	0	.0	0	.0	0	.0	0	.0	240	99.6	1	.4	241
	39	6.1	3	.5	6	.9	50	7.9	553	87.1	32	5.0	635
	31	6.6	3	.6	3	.6	37	7.9	406	86.4	27	5.7	470
	8	4.8	0	.0	3	1.8	13	7.9	147	89.1	5	3.3	165
	1	1.1	1	1.1	0	.0	2	2.1	93	97.9	0	.0	95
	0	.0	0	.0	0	.0	0	.0	35	100.0	0	.0	35
	1	1.7	1	1.7	0	.0	2	3.3	58	96.7	0	.0	60
	27	4.1	6	.9	1	.2	34	5.2	617	94.6	1	.2	652
	19	4.7	5	1.2	1	.2	25	6.1	381	93.6	1	.2	407
	8	3.3	1	.4	0	.0	9	3.7	236	96.3	0	.0	245
	39	2.9	46	3.4	11	.8	104	7.8	1,024	76.5	210	15.7	1,338
	12	3.9	9	2.9	1	.3	22	7.1	262	84.8	25	8.1	309
	27	2.6	37	3.6	10	1.0	82	8.0	762	74.1	185	18.0	1,029
	156	64.7	2	.8	0	.0	160	66.4	81	33.6	0	.0	241
	90	81.1	1	.9	0	.0	93	83.8	18	16.2	0	.0	111
	66	50.8	1	.8	0	.0	67	51.5	63	48.5	0	.0	130
	4	1.2	0	.0	0	.0	4	1.2	316	95.2	12	3.6	332
	1	.5	0	.0	0	.0	1	.5	193	97.0	5	2.5	199
	3	2.3	0	.0	0	.0	3	2.3	123	92.5	7	5.3	133
	1	14.3	1	14.3	0	.0	2	28.6	5	71.4	0	.0	7
	0	.0	1	100.0	0	.0	1	100.0	0	.0	0	.0	1
	1	16.7	0	.0	0	.0	1	16.7	5	83.3	0	.0	6
	0	.0	0	.0	0	.0	0	.0	0	.0	2	100.0	2
	0	.0	0	.0	0	.0	0	.0	0	.0	0	.0	0
	0	.0	0	.0	0	.0	0	.0	0	.0	2	100.0	2
	103	5.7	49	2.7	8	.4	167	9.3	1,551	86.3	79	4.4	1,797
	48	8.5	11	1.9	2	.4	63	11.1	493	87.1	10	1.8	566
	55	4.5	38	3.1	6	.5	104	8.4	1,058	85.9	69	5.5	1,231
	3	4.4	3	4.4	0	.0	6	8.8	58	85.3	4	5.9	68
	0	.0	0	.0	0	.0	0	.0	14	100.0	0	.0	14
	3	5.6	3	5.6	0	.0	6	11.1	44	81.5	4	7.4	54
	49	2.9	0	.0	9	.5	58	3.5	1,612	96.5	0	.0	1,670
	27	3.4	0	.0	6	.8	33	4.1	766	95.9	0	.0	799
	22	2.5	0	.0	3	.3	25	2.9	846	97.1	0	.0	871
	1	1.4	0	.0	1	1.4	2	2.9	62	89.9	5	7.2	69
	1	20.0	0	.0	1	20.0	2	40.0	2	40.0	1	20.0	5
	0	.0	0	.0	0	.0	0	.0	60	93.8	4	6.3	64
	1	.4	1	.4	2	.9	4	1.7	226	97.8	1	.4	231
	1	.8	1	.8	1	.8	3	2.5	115	97.5	0	.0	118
	0	.0	0	.0	1	.9	1	.9	111	98.2	1	.9	113
	8	1.2	2	.3	2	.3	13	1.9	658	96.6	10	1.5	681
	6	1.3	1	.2	2	.4	10	2.2	448	97.2	3	.7	461
	2	.9	1	.5	0	.0	3	1.4	210	95.5	7	3.2	220
	0	.0	3	23.1	0	.0	3	23.1	3	23.1	7	53.8	13
	0	.0	0	.0	0	.0	0	.0	0	.0	0	.0	0
	0	.0	3	23.1	0	.0	3	23.1	3	23.1	7	53.8	13
	8	1.3	2	.3	3	.5	13	2.1	566	91.7	38	6.2	617
	0	.0	0	.0	1	.6	1	.6	168	97.1	4	2.3	173
	8	1.8	2	.5	2	.5	12	2.7	398	89.6	34	7.7	444
	0	.0	0	.0	0	.0	0	.0	15	83.3	3	16.7	18
	0	.0	0	.0	0	.0	0	.0	7	77.8	2	22.2	9
	0	.0	0	.0	0	.0	0	.0	8	88.9	1	11.1	9
	12	4.9	0	.0	1	.4	13	5.3	231	93.9	2	.8	246
	7	4.5	0	.0	1	.6	8	5.1	149	94.9	0	.0	157
	5	5.6	0	.0	0	.0	5	5.6	82	92.1	2	2.2	89
	7	.6	0	.0	0	.0	7	.6	1,147	96.4	36	3.0	1,190
	4	.6	0	.0	0	.0	4	.6	684	97.0	17	2.4	705
	3	.6	0	.0	0	.0	3	.6	463	95.5	19	3.9	485
	8	1.3	3	.5	4	.7	16	2.7	582	96.7	4	.7	602
	5	1.2	3	.7	2	.5	10	2.5	390	97.0	2	.5	402
	3	1.5	0	.0	2	1.0	6	3.0	192	96.0	2	1.0	200

	AMERICAN INDIAN ALASKAN NATIVE		BLACK NON-HISPANIC		ASIAN OR PACIFIC ISLANDER		HISPANIC		TOTAL MINORITY		WHITE NON-HISPANIC		NON-RESIDENT ALIEN	
	NUMBER	%	NUMBER	%	NUMBER	%	NUMBER	%	NUMBER	%	NUMBER	%	NUMBER	%
PENNSYLVANIA CONTINUED														
LANCASTER THEOLOGICAL SEM														
PA TOTAL	0	.0	2	1.7	1	.9	0	.0	3	2.6	113	97.4	0	.0
PA FEMALE	0	.0	0	.0	1	11.1	0	.0	1	11.1	8	88.9	0	.0
PA MALE	0	.0	2	1.9	0	.0	0	.0	2	1.9	105	98.1	0	.0
LA SALLE COLLEGE														
PA TOTAL	0	.0	44	6.2	11	1.6	2	.3	57	8.1	650	91.9	0	.0
PA FEMALE	0	.0	15	11.8	2	1.6	1	.8	18	14.2	109	85.8	0	.0
PA MALE	0	.0	29	5.0	9	1.6	1	.2	39	6.7	541	93.3	0	.0
LEHIGH UNIVERSITY														
PA TOTAL	1	.1	12	.7	3	.2	20	1.1	36	2.0	1,673	92.3	104	5.7
PA FEMALE	0	.0	1	.2	2	.4	9	1.6	12	2.2	532	96.0	10	1.8
PA MALE	1	.1	11	.9	1	.1	11	.9	24	1.9	1,141	90.6	94	7.5
LINCOLN UNIVERSITY														
PA TOTAL	0	.0	29	42.0	1	1.4	1	1.4	31	44.9	38	55.1	0	.0
PA FEMALE	0	.0	15	42.9	0	.0	0	.0	15	42.9	20	57.1	0	.0
PA MALE	0	.0	14	41.2	1	2.9	1	2.9	16	47.1	18	52.9	0	.0
LUTH THEOL SEM GETTYSBURG														
PA TOTAL	0	.0	0	.0	0	.0	0	.0	0	.0	52	98.1	1	1.9
PA FEMALE	0	.0	0	.0	0	.0	0	.0	0	.0	17	100.0	0	.0
PA MALE	0	.0	0	.0	0	.0	0	.0	0	.0	35	97.2	1	2.8
LUTHERAN THEOL SEM PHILA														
PA TOTAL	0	.0	2	3.1	1	1.6	1	1.6	4	6.3	60	93.8	0	.0
PA FEMALE	0	.0	0	.0	0	.0	0	.0	0	.0	10	100.0	0	.0
PA MALE	0	.0	2	3.7	1	1.9	1	1.9	4	7.4	50	92.6	0	.0
MANSFIELD STATE COLLEGE														
PA TOTAL	0	.0	0	.0	0	.0	0	.0	0	.0	187	100.0	0	.0
PA FEMALE	0	.0	0	.0	0	.0	0	.0	0	.0	118	100.0	0	.0
PA MALE	0	.0	0	.0	0	.0	0	.0	0	.0	69	100.0	0	.0
MARY IMMACULATE SEMINARY														
PA TOTAL	0	.0	0	.0	0	.0	0	.0	0	.0	16	100.0	0	.0
PA FEMALE	0	.0	0	.0	0	.0	0	.0	0	.0	0	.0	0	.0
PA MALE	0	.0	0	.0	0	.0	0	.0	0	.0	16	100.0	0	.0
MARYWOOD COLLEGE														
PA TOTAL	0	.0	1	.1	0	.0	0	.0	1	.1	962	97.4	25	2.5
PA FEMALE	0	.0	0	.0	0	.0	0	.0	0	.0	625	99.7	2	.3
PA MALE	0	.0	1	.3	0	.0	0	.0	1	.3	337	93.4	23	6.4
THE MED COLLEGE OF PA														
PA TOTAL	0	.0	0	.0	0	.0	0	.0	0	.0	78	98.7	1	1.3
PA FEMALE	0	.0	0	.0	0	.0	0	.0	0	.0	45	97.8	1	2.2
PA MALE	0	.0	0	.0	0	.0	0	.0	0	.0	33	100.0	0	.0
MERCYHURST COLLEGE														
PA TOTAL	0	.0	2	7.4	0	.0	0	.0	2	7.4	25	92.6	0	.0
PA FEMALE	0	.0	0	.0	0	.0	0	.0	0	.0	4	100.0	0	.0
PA MALE	0	.0	2	8.7	0	.0	0	.0	2	8.7	21	91.3	0	.0
MILLERSVILLE ST COLLEGE														
PA TOTAL	1	.1	5	.6	0	.0	0	.0	6	.7	804	98.9	3	.4
PA FEMALE	0	.0	2	.4	0	.0	0	.0	2	.4	528	99.4	1	.2
PA MALE	1	.4	3	1.1	0	.0	0	.0	4	1.4	276	97.9	2	.7
OUR LADY ANGELS COLLEGE														
PA TOTAL	0	.0	0	.0	0	.0	0	.0	0	.0	3	100.0	0	.0
PA FEMALE	0	.0	0	.0	0	.0	0	.0	0	.0	3	100.0	0	.0
PA MALE	0	.0	0	.0	0	.0	0	.0	0	.0	0	.0	0	.0
PA STATE U MAIN CAMPUS														
PA TOTAL	22	.5	106	2.4	52	1.2	54	1.2	234	5.2	3,585	80.0	665	14.8
PA FEMALE	7	.5	54	3.7	21	1.5	23	1.6	105	7.3	1,217	84.1	125	8.6
PA MALE	15	.5	52	1.7	31	1.0	31	1.0	129	4.2	2,368	78.0	540	17.8
PA STATE U ALTOONA CAM														
PA TOTAL	0	.0	0	.0	0	.0	0	.0	0	.0	11	100.0	0	.0
PA FEMALE	0	.0	0	.0	0	.0	0	.0	0	.0	8	100.0	0	.0
PA MALE	0	.0	0	.0	0	.0	0	.0	0	.0	3	100.0	0	.0
PA STATE U BEAVER CAMPUS														
PA TOTAL	0	.0	0	.0	0	.0	0	.0	0	.0	1	100.0	0	.0
PA FEMALE	0	.0	0	.0	0	.0	0	.0	0	.0	1	100.0	0	.0
PA MALE	0	.0	0	.0	0	.0	0	.0	0	.0	0	.0	0	.0
PA ST U BEHREND COLLEGE														
PA TOTAL	0	.0	0	.0	0	.0	0	.0	0	.0	12	100.0	0	.0
PA FEMALE	0	.0	0	.0	0	.0	0	.0	0	.0	2	100.0	0	.0
PA MALE	0	.0	0	.0	0	.0	0	.0	0	.0	10	100.0	0	.0
PA STATE U BERKS CAMPUS														
PA TOTAL	0	.0	0	.0	0	.0	0	.0	0	.0	3	100.0	0	.0
PA FEMALE	0	.0	0	.0	0	.0	0	.0	0	.0	1	100.0	0	.0
PA MALE	0	.0	0	.0	0	.0	0	.0	0	.0	2	100.0	0	.0
PA STATE U CAPITOL CAMPUS														
PA TOTAL	0	.0	17	2.9	2	.3	5	.9	24	4.1	546	94.1	10	1.7
PA FEMALE	0	.0	9	4.2	2	.9	2	.9	11	5.2	198	93.4	3	1.4
PA MALE	0	.0	8	2.2	2	.5	3	.8	13	3.5	348	94.6	7	1.9
PA STATE U DELAWARE CAM														
PA TOTAL	0	.0	0	.0	0	.0	0	.0	0	.0	1	100.0	0	.0
PA FEMALE	0	.0	0	.0	0	.0	0	.0	0	.0	1	100.0	0	.0
PA MALE	0	.0	0	.0	0	.0	0	.0	0	.0	0	.0	0	.0
PA STATE U DU BOIS CAMPUS														
PA TOTAL	0	.0	0	.0	0	.0	0	.0	0	.0	2	100.0	0	.0
PA FEMALE	0	.0	0	.0	0	.0	0	.0	0	.0	2	100.0	0	.0
PA MALE	0	.0	0	.0	0	.0	0	.0	0	.0	0	.0	0	.0
PA ST U HERSHEY MEDL CTR														
PA TOTAL	1	1.1	2	2.2	2	2.2	2	2.2	7	7.8	73	81.1	10	11.1
PA FEMALE	0	.0	2	6.5	2	6.5	2	6.5	6	19.4	23	74.2	2	6.5
PA MALE	1	1.7	0	.0	0	.0	0	.0	1	1.7	50	84.7	8	13.6
PA STATE U OGONTZ CAMPUS														
PA TOTAL	0	.0	0	.0	0	.0	0	.0	0	.0	2	100.0	0	.0
PA FEMALE	0	.0	0	.0	0	.0	0	.0	0	.0	1	100.0	0	.0
PA MALE	0	.0	0	.0	0	.0	0	.0	0	.0	1	100.0	0	.0

N E	BLACK NON-HISPANIC		ASIAN OR PACIFIC ISLANDER		HISPANIC		TOTAL MINORITY		WHITE NON-HISPANIC		NON-RESIDENT ALIEN		TOTAL
	NUMBER	%	NUMBER	%	NUMBER	%	NUMBER	%	NUMBER	%	NUMBER	%	NUMBER

INUED

10	5.3	6	3.2	1	.5	17	9.0	171	90.5	1	.5	189
3	6.8	1	2.3	1	2.3	5	11.4	39	88.6	0	.0	44
7	4.8	5	3.4	0	.0	12	8.3	132	91.0	1	.7	145
0	.0	0	.0	0	.0	0	.0	4	100.0	0	.0	4
0	.0	0	.0	0	.0	0	.0	1	100.0	0	.0	1
0	.0	0	.0	0	.0	0	.0	3	100.0	0	.0	3
0	.0	0	.0	0	.0	0	.0	5	100.0	0	.0	5
0	.0	0	.0	0	.0	0	.0	2	100.0	0	.0	2
0	.0	0	.0	0	.0	0	.0	3	100.0	0	.0	3
1	4.5	0	.0	0	.0	1	4.5	21	95.5	0	.0	22
0	.0	0	.0	0	.0	0	.0	15	100.0	0	.0	15
1	14.3	0	.0	0	.0	1	14.3	6	85.7	0	.0	7
1	10.0	0	.0	0	.0	1	10.0	9	90.0	0	.0	10
1	25.0	0	.0	0	.0	1	25.0	3	75.0	0	.0	4
0	.0	0	.0	0	.0	0	.0	6	100.0	0	.0	6
0	.0	1	2.5	0	.0	1	2.5	26	65.0	13	32.5	40
0	.0	0	.0	0	.0	0	.0	8	80.0	2	20.0	10
0	.0	1	3.3	0	.0	1	3.3	18	60.0	11	36.7	30
10	7.0	2	1.4	0	.0	12	8.5	115	81.0	15	10.6	142
5	17.9	1	3.6	0	.0	6	21.4	17	60.7	5	17.9	28
5	4.4	1	.9	0	.0	6	5.3	98	86.0	10	8.8	114
9	5.8	3	1.9	0	.0	12	7.7	144	92.3	0	.0	156
2	8.7	1	4.3	0	.0	3	13.0	20	87.0	0	.0	23
7	5.3	2	1.5	0	.0	9	6.8	124	93.2	0	.0	133
0	.0	0	.0	0	.0	0	.0	70	100.0	0	.0	70
0	.0	0	.0	0	.0	0	.0	10	100.0	0	.0	10
0	.0	0	.0	0	.0	0	.0	60	100.0	0	.0	60
1	1.2	0	.0	0	.0	1	1.2	82	98.8	0	.0	83
0	.0	0	.0	0	.0	0	.0	42	100.0	0	.0	42
1	2.4	0	.0	0	.0	1	2.4	40	97.6	0	.0	41
4	1.4	1	.3	0	.0	5	1.7	280	97.6	2	.7	287
2	2.3	1	1.1	0	.0	3	3.4	84	96.6	0	.0	87
2	1.0	0	.0	0	.0	2	1.0	196	98.0	2	1.0	200
15	2.5	1	.2	2	.3	21	3.5	561	94.4	12	2.0	594
10	6.1	0	.0	2	1.2	12	7.4	150	92.0	1	.6	163
5	1.2	1	.2	2	.5	9	2.1	411	95.4	11	2.6	431
0	.0	0	.0	0	.0	0	.0	12	100.0	0	.0	12
0	.0	0	.0	0	.0	0	.0	1	100.0	0	.0	1
0	.0	0	.0	0	.0	0	.0	11	100.0	0	.0	11
4	.3	23	2.0	5	.4	44	3.8	1,104	96.1	1	.1	1,149
2	.3	11	1.8	1	.2	21	3.5	582	96.5	0	.0	603
2	.4	12	2.2	4	.7	23	4.2	522	95.6	1	.2	546
4	.7	0	.0	0	.0	4	.7	538	98.5	4	.7	546
2	.5	0	.0	0	.0	2	.5	368	98.9	2	.5	372
2	1.1	0	.0	0	.0	2	1.1	170	97.7	2	1.1	174
0	.0	0	.0	0	.0	0	.0	3	100.0	0	.0	3
0	.0	0	.0	0	.0	0	.0	1	100.0	0	.0	1
0	.0	0	.0	0	.0	0	.0	2	100.0	0	.0	2
0	.0	0	.0	0	.0	0	.0	2	100.0	0	.0	2
0	.0	0	.0	0	.0	0	.0	0	.0	0	.0	0-
0	.0	0	.0	0	.0	0	.0	2	100.0	0	.0	2
381	7.0	89	1.6	55	1.0	549	10.0	4,928	90.0	0	.0	5,477
255	9.9	40	1.5	37	1.4	341	13.2	2,243	86.8	0	.0	2,584
126	4.4	49	1.7	18	.6	208	7.2	2,685	92.8	0	.0	2,893
1	1.1	2	2.3	0	.0	3	3.4	80	90.9	5	5.7	88
0	.0	1	2.9	0	.0	1	2.9	30	88.2	3	8.8	34
1	1.9	1	1.9	0	.0	2	3.7	50	92.6	2	3.7	54
99	1.7	65	1.1	72	1.2	243	4.1	4,930	82.6	794	13.3	5,967
65	2.7	27	1.1	24	1.0	121	4.9	2,170	88.5	160	6.5	2,451
34	1.0	38	1.1	48	1.4	122	3.5	2,760	78.5	634	18.0	3,516
355	7.7	113	2.4	49	1.1	522	11.3	3,356	72.4	755	16.3	4,633
199	9.0	44	2.0	28	1.3	272	12.3	1,819	82.2	122	5.5	2,213
156	6.4	69	2.9	21	.9	250	10.3	1,537	63.5	633	26.2	2,420
10	1.1	0	.0	0	.0	10	1.1	849	94.0	44	4.9	903
0	.0	0	.0	0	.0	0	.0	353	98.6	5	1.4	358
10	1.8	0	.0	0	.0	10	1.8	496	91.0	39	7.2	545
36	2.3	32	2.0	9	.6	79	5.0	1,484	94.3	11	.7	1,574
21	2.8	13	1.7	2	.3	37	4.9	714	94.8	2	.3	753
15	1.8	19	2.3	7	.9	42	5.1	770	93.8	9	1.1	821

	AMERICAN INDIAN ALASKAN NATIVE		BLACK NON-HISPANIC		ASIAN OR PACIFIC ISLANDER		HISPANIC		TOTAL MINORITY		WHITE NON-HISPANIC		NON-RESIDENT ALIEN	
	NUMBER	%	NUMBER	%	NUMBER	%	NUMBER	%	NUMBER	%	NUMBER	%	NUMBER	%
PENNSYLVANIA CONTINUED														
WEST CHESTER ST COLLEGE														
PA TOTAL	0	.0	60	4.4	3	.2	5	.4	68	5.0	1,290	95.0	0	.0
PA FEMALE	0	.0	40	4.9	2	.2	2	.2	44	5.4	776	94.6	0	.0
PA MALE	0	.0	20	3.7	1	.2	3	.6	24	4.5	514	95.5	0	.0
WESTMINSTER COLLEGE														
PA TOTAL	0	.0	8	3.4	0	.0		.0	8	3.4	225	96.6	0	.0
PA FEMALE	0	.0	6	4.3	0	.0	0	.0	6	4.3	132	95.7	0	.0
PA MALE	0	.0	2	2.1	0	.0		.0	2	2.1	93	97.9	0	.0
WESTMINSTER THEOL SEM														
PA TOTAL	0	.0	4	1.4	5	1.8	2	.7	11	4.0	234	84.8	31	11.2
PA FEMALE	0	.0	0	.0	0	.0	0	.0	0	.0	14	100.0	0	.0
PA MALE	0	.0	4	1.5	5	1.9	2	.8	11	4.2	220	84.0	31	11.8
WIDENER COLLEGE														
PA TOTAL	0	.0	25	3.7	0	.0		.0	25	3.7	656	96.3	0	.0
PA FEMALE	0	.0	6	8.6	0	.0	0	.0	6	8.6	64	91.4	0	.0
PA MALE	0	.0	19	3.1	0	.0		.0	19	3.1	592	96.9	0	.0
WILKES COLLEGE														
PA TOTAL	0	.0	1	.5	0	.0		.0	1	.5	181	99.5	0	.0
PA FEMALE	0	.0	0	.0	0	.0	0	.0	0	.0	59	100.0	0	.0
PA MALE	0	.0	1	.8	0	.0		.0	1	.8	122	99.2	0	.0
YESHIVATH BETH MOSHE														
PA TOTAL	0	.0	0	.0	0	.0		.0	0	.0	9	100.0	0	.0
PA FEMALE	0	.0	0	.0	0	.0	0	.0	0	.0	0	.0	0	.0
PA MALE	0	.0	0	.0	0	.0		.0	0	.0	9	100.0	0	.0
YORK COLLEGE PENNSYLVANIA														
PA TOTAL	0	.0	1	1.1	0	.0	0	.0	1	1.1	87	98.9	0	.0
PA FEMALE	0	.0	0	.0	0	.0	0	.0	0	.0	12	100.0	0	.0
PA MALE	0	.0	1	1.3	0	.0	0	.0	1	1.3	75	98.7	0	.0
PENNSYLVANIA TOTAL (77 INSTITUTIONS)														
PA TOTAL	99	.2	1,835	3.9	543	1.2	337	.7	2,814	6.0	41,107	87.7	2,954	6.3
PA FEMALE	37	.2	1,057	5.1	207	1.0	157	.8	1,458	7.0	18,740	90.4	543	2.6
PA MALE	62	.2	778	3.0	336	1.3	180	.7	1,356	5.2	22,367	85.6	2,411	9.2
RHODE ISLAND														
BROWN UNIVERSITY														
RI TOTAL	5	.4	25	2.2	16	1.4	9	.8	55	4.9	886	78.9	182	16.2
RI FEMALE	3	.7	12	2.9	4	1.0	3	.7	22	5.3	359	85.9	37	8.9
RI MALE	2	.3	13	1.8	12	1.7	6	.9	33	4.7	527	74.8	145	20.6
BRYANT C BUSINESS ADMIN														
RI TOTAL	2	.2	15	1.7	18	2.0	6	.7	41	4.6	832	92.5	26	2.9
RI FEMALE	1	.5	3	1.6	1	.5	2	1.1	7	3.8	173	94.5	3	1.6
RI MALE	1	.1	12	1.7	17	2.4	4	.6	34	4.7	659	92.0	23	3.2
PROVIDENCE COLLEGE														
RI TOTAL	0	.0	7	1.0	0	.0	2	.3	9	1.3	692	98.7	0	.0
RI FEMALE	0	.0	3	.9	0	.0	1	.3	4	1.2	320	98.8	0	.0
RI MALE	0	.0	4	1.1	0	.0	1	.3	5	1.3	372	98.7	0	.0
RHODE ISLAND COLLEGE														
RI TOTAL	1	.1	10	1.0	1	.1	5	.5	17	1.8	906	93.9	42	4.4
RI FEMALE	1	.2	8	1.2	0	.0	2	.3	11	1.7	620	94.5	25	3.8
RI MALE	0	.0	2	.6	1	.3	3	1.0	6	1.9	286	92.6	17	5.5
RI SCHOOL OF DESIGN														
RI TOTAL	1	.9	2	1.9	0	.0		.0	3	2.8	98	91.6	6	5.6
RI FEMALE	1	1.9	1	1.9	0	.0	0	.0	2	3.8	48	92.3	2	3.8
RI MALE	0	.0	1	1.8	0	.0		.0	1	1.8	50	90.9	4	7.3
SALVE REGINA-NEWPORT C														
RI TOTAL	1	.7	2	1.5	1	.7	2	1.5	6	4.5	128	95.5	0	.0
RI FEMALE	0	.0	1	1.4	1	1.4	1	1.4	3	4.3	67	95.7	0	.0
RI MALE	1	1.6	1	1.6	0	.0	1	1.6	3	4.7	61	95.3	0	.0
U OF RHODE ISLAND														
RI TOTAL	5	.2	22	1.0	28	1.3	7	.3	62	2.9	1,908	90.3	142	6.7
RI FEMALE	2	.2	10	1.1	9	1.0	5	.6	26	3.0	823	93.8	28	3.2
RI MALE	3	.2	12	1.0	19	1.5	2	.2	36	2.9	1,085	87.9	114	9.2
RHODE ISLAND TOTAL (7 INSTITUTIONS)														
RI TOTAL	15	.2	83	1.4	64	1.1	31	.5	193	3.2	5,450	90.2	398	6.6
RI FEMALE	8	.3	38	1.5	15	.6	14	.5	75	2.9	2,410	93.4	95	3.7
RI MALE	7	.2	45	1.3	49	1.4	17	.5	118	3.4	3,040	87.8	303	8.8
SOUTH CAROLINA														
BOB JONES UNIVERSITY														
SC TOTAL	0	.0	0	.0	0	.0		.0	0	.0	0	.0	0	.0
SC FEMALE	0	.0	0	.0	0	.0	0	.0	0	.0	0	.0	0	.0
SC MALE	0	.0	0	.0	0	.0		.0	0	.0	0	.0	0	.0
CITADEL MILITARY C OF SC														
SC TOTAL	0	.0	186	19.1	0	.0		.0	186	19.1	790	80.9	0	.0
SC FEMALE	0	.0	147	23.0	0	.0	0	.0	147	23.0	492	77.0	0	.0
SC MALE	0	.0	39	11.6	0	.0		.0	39	11.6	298	88.4	0	.0
CLEMSON UNIVERSITY														
SC TOTAL	0	.0	41	1.8	2	.1	5	.2	48	2.1	2,152	94.6	75	3.3
SC FEMALE	0	.0	14	1.1	0	.0	1	.1	15	1.2	1,206	97.3	19	1.5
SC MALE	0	.0	27	2.6	2	.2	4	.4	33	3.2	946	91.4	56	5.4
COLLEGE OF CHARLESTON														
SC TOTAL	0	.0	24	10.5	2	.9		.0	26	11.4	203	88.6	0	.0
SC FEMALE	0	.0	15	8.2	2	1.1	0	.0	17	9.3	165	90.7	0	.0
SC MALE	0	.0	9	19.1	0	.0		.0	9	19.1	38	80.9	0	.0
COLUMBIA BIBLE COLLEGE														
SC TOTAL	0	.0	2	2.0	0	.0	1	1.0	3	2.9	97	95.1	2	2.0
SC FEMALE	0	.0	0	.0	0	.0	0	.0	0	.0	48	98.0	1	2.0
SC MALE	0	.0	2	3.8	0	.0	1	1.9	3	5.7	49	92.5	1	1.9

ENROLLMENT IN INSTITUTIONS OF HIGHER EDUCATION BY RACE, ETHNICITY AND SEX:
ATE AND NATION, 1978

	BLACK NON-HISPANIC		ASIAN OR PACIFIC ISLANDER		HISPANIC		TOTAL MINORITY		WHITE NON-HISPANIC		NON-RESIDENT ALIEN		TOTAL
	NUMBER	%	NUMBER	%	NUMBER	%	NUMBER	%	NUMBER	%	NUMBER	%	NUMBER
INUED													
	1	50.0	0	.0	0	.0	1	50.0	1	50.0	0	.0	2
	1	50.0	0	.0	0	.0	1	50.0	1	50.0	0	.0	2
	0	.0	0	.0	0	.0	0	.0	0	.0	0	.0	0
	7	3.2	0	.0	1	.5	8	3.6	211	95.5	2	.9	221
	7	3.7	0	.0	1	.5	8	4.2	182	95.3	1	.5	191
	0	.0	0	.0	0	.0	0	.0	29	96.7	1	3.3	30
	140	29.2	0	.0	0	.0	140	29.2	340	70.8	0	.0	480
	115	28.3	0	.0	0	.0	115	28.3	292	71.7	0	.0	407
	25	34.2	0	.0	0	.0	25	34.2	48	65.8	0	.0	73
	24	6.9	4	1.1	1	.3	29	8.3	319	91.7	0	.0	348
	16	8.8	2	1.1	1	.6	19	10.5	162	89.5	0	.0	181
	8	4.8	2	1.2	0	.0	10	6.0	157	94.0	0	.0	167
	2	5.0	0	.0	0	.0	2	5.0	38	95.0	0	.0	40
	0	.0	0	.0	0	.0	0	.0	6	100.0	0	.0	6
	2	5.9	0	.0	0	.0	2	5.9	32	94.1	0	.0	34
	1	.9	2	1.8	0	.0	3	2.7	100	89.3	9	8.0	112
	1	2.4	1	2.4	0	.0	2	4.8	38	90.5	2	4.8	42
	0	.0	1	1.4	0	.0	1	1.4	62	88.6	7	10.0	70
	301	83.8	0	.0	0	.0	301	83.8	57	15.9	1	.3	359
	208	84.6	0	.0	0	.0	208	84.6	37	15.0	1	.4	246
	93	82.3	0	.0	0	.0	93	82.3	20	17.7	0	.0	113
	543	8.6	25	.4	28	.4	607	9.6	5,563	88.0	153	2.4	6,323
	371	11.3	6	.2	13	.4	395	12.1	2,842	86.9	32	1.0	3,269
	172	5.6	19	.6	15	.5	212	6.9	2,721	89.1	121	4.0	3,054
	43	8.4	0	.0	1	.2	45	8.8	463	90.6	3	.6	511
	32	8.5	0	.0	1	.3	34	9.2	336	90.6	1	.3	371
	11	7.9	0	.0	0	.0	11	7.9	127	90.7	2	1.4	140
(14 INSTITUTIONS)													
	1,315	11.0	35	.3	37	.3	1,399	11.7	10,334	86.3	245	2.0	11,978
	927	13.6	11	.2	17	.2	961	14.1	5,807	85.1	57	.8	6,825
	388	7.5	24	.5	20	.4	438	8.5	4,527	87.9	188	3.6	5,153
	0	.0	0	.0	0	.0	0	.0	46	100.0	0	.0	46
	0	.0	0	.0	0	.0	0	.0	23	100.0	0	.0	23
	0	.0	0	.0	0	.0	0	.0	23	100.0	0	.0	23
	0	.0	0	.0	0	.0	0	.0	23	95.8	1	4.2	24
	0	.0	0	.0	0	.0	0	.0	2	100.0	0	.0	2
	0	.0	0	.0	0	.0	0	.0	21	95.5	1	4.5	22
	1	.9	1	.9	0	.0	4	3.6	108	96.4	0	.0	112
	1	1.7	0	.0	0	.0	3	5.0	57	95.0	0	.0	60
	0	.0	1	1.9	0	.0	1	1.9	51	98.1	0	.0	52
	0	.0	0	.0	1	.6	1	.6	90	55.6	71	43.8	162
	0	.0	0	.0	0	.0	0	.0	14	73.7	5	26.3	19
	0	.0	0	.0	1	.7	1	.7	76	53.1	66	45.2	143
	1	.1	0	.0	0	.0	2	.3	762	96.0	30	3.8	794
	0	.0	0	.0	0	.0	1	.3	375	98.9	3	.8	379
	1	.2	0	.0	0	.0	1	.2	387	93.3	27	6.5	415
	1	.1	1	.1	1	.1	26	3.4	717	94.8	13	1.7	756
	0	.0	0	.0	0	.0	7	2.7	252	95.8	4	1.5	263
	1	.2	1	.2	1	.2	19	3.9	465	94.3	9	1.8	493
(6 INSTITUTIONS)													
	3	.2	2	.1	2	.1	33	1.7	1,746	92.2	115	6.1	1,894
	1	.1	0	.0	0	.0	11	1.5	723	96.9	12	1.6	746
	2	.2	2	.2	2	.2	22	1.9	1,023	89.1	103	9.0	1,148
	0	.0	2	8.3	0	.0	2	8.3	22	91.7	0	.0	24
	0	.0	0	.0	0	.0	0	.0	3	100.0	0	.0	3
	0	.0	2	9.5	0	.0	2	9.5	19	90.5	0	.0	21
	37	90.2	0	.0	0	.0	37	90.2	2	4.9	2	4.9	41
	26	100.0	0	.0	0	.0	26	100.0	0	.0	0	.0	26
	11	73.3	0	.0	0	.0	11	73.3	2	13.3	2	13.3	15
	148	12.0	9	.7	4	.3	165	13.4	955	77.5	112	9.1	1,232
	98	13.6	4	.6	2	.3	106	14.7	564	78.1	52	7.2	722
	50	9.8	5	1.0	2	.4	59	11.6	391	76.7	60	11.8	510
	55	85.9	0	.0	0	.0	55	85.9	0	.0	9	14.1	64
	38	92.7	0	.0	0	.0	38	92.7	0	.0	3	7.3	41
	17	73.9	0	.0	0	.0	17	73.9	0	.0	6	26.1	23

179

TABLE 2 - TOTAL GRADUATE ENROLLMENT IN INSTITUTIONS OF HIGHER EDUCATION BY RACE, ETHNICITY AND SEX: INSTITUTION, STATE AND NATION, 1978

	AMERICAN INDIAN ALASKAN NATIVE		BLACK NON-HISPANIC		ASIAN OR PACIFIC ISLANDER		HISPANIC		TOTAL MINORITY		WHITE NON-HISPANIC		NON-RESIDENT ALIEN	
	NUMBER	%	NUMBER	%	NUMBER	%	NUMBER	%	NUMBER	%	NUMBER	%	NUMBER	%
TENNESSEE	CONTINUED													
MEMPHIS THEOLOGICAL SEM														
TN TOTAL	0	.0	27	17.8	1	.7	0	.0	28	18.4	124	81.6	0	.0
TN FEMALE	0	.0	2	9.5	1	4.8	0	.0	3	14.3	18	85.7	0	.0
TN MALE	0	.0	25	19.1	0	.0	0	.0	25	19.1	106	80.9	0	.0
SCARRITT COLLEGE														
TN TOTAL	2	2.0	1	1.0	0	.0	0	.0	3	3.0	94	94.0	3	3.0
TN FEMALE	2	3.2	0	.0	0	.0	0	.0	2	3.2	58	93.5	2	3.2
TN MALE	0	.0	1	2.6	0	.0	0	.0	1	2.6	36	94.7	1	2.6
AUSTIN PEAY ST UNIVERSITY														
TN TOTAL	0	.0	41	7.5	1	.2	2	.4	44	8.1	502	91.9	0	.0
TN FEMALE	0	.0	29	8.0	1	.3	1	.3	31	8.5	332	91.5	0	.0
TN MALE	0	.0	12	6.6	0	.0	1	.5	13	7.1	170	92.9	0	.0
EAST TENN ST UNIVERSITY														
TN TOTAL	1	.1	21	2.4	17	2.0	5	.6	44	5.1	805	93.1	16	1.8
TN FEMALE	1	.2	9	2.0	9	2.0	2	.5	21	4.7	419	94.6	3	.7
TN MALE	0	.0	12	2.8	8	1.9	3	.7	23	5.5	386	91.5	13	3.1
MEMPHIS STATE UNIVERSITY														
TN TOTAL	1	.0	402	13.9	5	.2	3	.1	411	14.2	2,405	83.3	71	2.5
TN FEMALE	0	.0	273	17.0	2	.1	2	.1	277	17.2	1,313	81.6	19	1.2
TN MALE	1	.1	129	10.1	3	.2	1	.1	134	10.5	1,092	85.4	52	4.1
MIDDLE TENN ST UNIVERSITY														
TN TOTAL	1	.1	69	7.2	1	.1	1	.1	72	7.5	774	81.0	110	11.5
TN FEMALE	0	.0	40	8.1	1	.2	1	.2	42	8.6	422	85.9	27	5.5
TN MALE	1	.2	29	6.2	0	.0	0	.0	30	6.5	352	75.7	83	17.8
TENNESSEE TECHNOLOGICAL U														
TN TOTAL	0	.0	5	.7	2	.3	2	.3	9	1.3	626	87.1	84	11.7
TN FEMALE	0	.0	2	.6	0	.0	0	.0	2	.6	347	96.1	12	3.3
TN MALE	0	.0	3	.8	2	.6	2	.6	7	2.0	279	77.9	72	20.1
TENNESSEE TEMPLE COLLEGE														
TN TOTAL	0	.0	0	.0	0	.0	0	.0	0	.0	12	100.0	0	.0
TN FEMALE	0	.0	0	.0	0	.0	0	.0	0	.0	6	100.0	0	.0
TN MALE	0	.0	0	.0	0	.0	0	.0	0	.0	6	100.0	0	.0
U OF TENN CTR HEALTH SCI														
TN TOTAL	0	.0	3	2.1	7	4.8	0	.0	10	6.9	120	82.8	15	10.3
TN FEMALE	0	.0	2	2.8	2	2.8	0	.0	4	5.6	63	88.7	4	5.6
TN MALE	0	.0	1	1.4	5	6.8	0	.0	6	8.1	57	77.0	11	14.9
U OF TENN AT CHATTANOOGA														
TN TOTAL	5	.8	31	4.7	1	.2	2	.3	39	5.9	613	93.4	4	.6
TN FEMALE	4	1.1	21	5.8	0	.0	0	.0	25	6.8	340	93.2	0	.0
TN MALE	1	.3	10	3.4	1	.3	2	.7	14	4.8	273	93.8	4	1.4
U OF TENNESSEE KNOXVILLE														
TN TOTAL	13	.2	239	4.3	58	1.0	29	.5	339	6.1	4,797	86.3	420	7.6
TN FEMALE	6	.3	151	6.5	15	.6	15	.6	187	8.0	2,059	88.3	85	3.6
TN MALE	7	.2	88	2.7	43	1.3	14	.4	152	4.7	2,738	84.9	335	10.4
U OF TENNESSEE AT MARTIN														
TN TOTAL	0	.0	19	6.6	0	.0	0	.0	19	6.6	267	92.7	2	.7
TN FEMALE	0	.0	15	7.5	0	.0	0	.0	15	7.5	183	91.5	2	1.0
TN MALE	0	.0	4	4.5	0	.0	0	.0	4	4.5	84	95.5	0	.0
U OF TENNESSEE NASHVILLE														
TN TOTAL	2	.4	61	11.0	0	.0	1	.2	64	11.5	472	84.9	20	3.6
TN FEMALE	1	.8	27	22.3	0	.0	0	.0	28	23.1	90	74.4	3	2.5
TN MALE	1	.2	34	7.8	0	.0	1	.2	36	8.3	382	87.0	17	3.9
VANDERBILT UNIVERSITY														
TN TOTAL	0	.0	16	1.5	4	.4	0	.0	20	1.9	861	81.6	174	16.5
TN FEMALE	0	.0	6	1.6	2	.5	0	.0	8	2.2	340	91.6	23	6.2
TN MALE	0	.0	10	1.5	2	.3	0	.0	12	1.8	521	76.2	151	22.1
TENNESSEE TOTAL (18 INSTITUTIONS)														
TN TOTAL	29	.2	1,175	7.4	108	.7	49	.3	1,361	8.6	13,451	84.8	1,042	6.6
TN FEMALE	16	.2	739	9.7	37	.5	23	.3	815	10.7	6,557	86.2	235	3.1
TN MALE	13	.2	436	5.3	71	.9	26	.3	546	6.6	6,894	83.6	807	9.8
TEXAS														
ABILENE CHRSTN UNIVERSITY														
TX TOTAL	3	.5	57	9.5	3	.5	10	1.7	73	12.2	522	87.0	5	.8
TX FEMALE	1	.6	15	9.3	1	.6	1	.6	18	11.2	140	87.0	3	1.9
TX MALE	2	.5	42	9.6	2	.5	9	2.1	55	12.5	382	87.0	2	.5
AMERICAN TECHNOLOGICAL U														
TX TOTAL	1	.2	39	9.6	8	2.0	19	4.7	67	16.4	330	80.9	11	2.7
TX FEMALE	0	.0	9	9.3	0	.0	3	3.1	12	12.4	82	84.5	3	3.1
TX MALE	1	.3	30	9.6	8	2.6	16	5.1	55	17.7	248	79.7	8	2.6
ANGELO STATE UNIVERSITY														
TX TOTAL	0	.0	15	4.3	1	.3	16	4.6	32	9.2	314	90.5	1	.3
TX FEMALE	0	.0	7	4.4	1	.6	4	2.5	12	7.6	146	92.4	0	.0
TX MALE	0	.0	8	4.2	0	.0	12	6.3	20	10.6	168	88.9	1	.5
AUSTIN COLLEGE														
TX TOTAL	0	.0	3	6.8	0	.0	1	2.3	4	9.1	40	90.9	0	.0
TX FEMALE	0	.0	1	3.3	0	.0	0	.0	1	3.3	29	96.7	0	.0
TX MALE	0	.0	2	14.3	0	.0	1	7.1	3	21.4	11	78.6	0	.0
AUSTIN PRESB THEOL SEM														
TX TOTAL	0	.0	0	.0	0	.0	4	6.6	4	6.6	57	93.4	0	.0
TX FEMALE	0	.0	0	.0	0	.0	0	.0	0	.0	1	100.0	0	.0
TX MALE	0	.0	0	.0	0	.0	4	6.7	4	6.7	56	93.3	0	.0
BAYLOR COLLEGE DENTISTRY														
TX TOTAL	0	.0	0	.0	1	2.2	1	2.2	2	4.3	43	93.5	1	2.2
TX FEMALE	0	.0	0	.0	0	.0	0	.0	0	.0	4	100.0	0	.0
TX MALE	0	.0	0	.0	1	2.4	1	2.4	2	4.8	39	92.9	1	2.4
BAYLOR COLLEGE MEDICINE														
TX TOTAL	0	.0	0	.0	1	.8	5	4.1	6	5.0	105	86.8	10	8.3
TX FEMALE	0	.0	0	.0	1	2.7	1	2.7	2	5.4	33	89.2	2	5.4
TX MALE	0	.0	0	.0	0	.0	4	4.8	4	4.8	72	85.7	8	9.5

ENROLLMENT IN INSTITUTIONS OF HIGHER EDUCATION BY RACE, ETHNICITY AND SEX:
ATE AND NATION, 1978

	BLACK NON-HISPANIC		ASIAN OR PACIFIC ISLANDER		HISPANIC		TOTAL MINORITY		WHITE NON-HISPANIC		NON-RESIDENT ALIEN		TOTAL
	NUMBER	%	NUMBER	%	NUMBER	%	NUMBER	%	NUMBER	%	NUMBER	%	NUMBER
INUED													
	10	1.2	11	1.3	5	.6	29	3.5	757	92.3	34	4.1	820
	8	2.4	2	.6	2	.6	12	3.5	321	94.4	7	2.1	340
	2	.4	9	1.9	3	.6	17	3.5	436	90.8	27	5.8	480
	14	1.5	6	.7	3	.3	23	2.5	841	91.5	55	6.0	919
	0	.0	1	6.3	0	.0	1	6.3	15	93.8	0	.0	16
	14	1.6	5	.6	3	.3	22	2.4	826	91.5	55	6.1	903
	323	8.8	7	.2	129	3.5	484	13.2	2,982	81.4	197	5.4	3,663
	123	7.6	4	.2	51	3.1	187	11.5	1,315	80.7	127	7.8	1,629
	200	9.8	3	.1	78	3.8	297	14.6	1,667	82.0	70	3.4	2,034
	0	.0	0	.0	1	16.7	1	16.7	5	83.3		.0	6
	0	.0	0	.0	0	.0	0	.0	3	100.0	0	.0	3
	0	.0	0	.0	1	33.3	1	33.3	2	66.7	0	.0	3
	6	3.2	0	.0	7	3.7	14	7.4	175	92.6		.0	189
	4	3.6	0	.0	2	1.8	6	5.5	104	94.5	0	.0	110
	2	2.5	0	.0	5	6.3	8	10.1	71	89.9	0	.0	79
	2	2.1	2	2.1	2	2.1	6	6.3	86	89.6		4.2	96
	0	.0	1	4.0	1	4.0	2	8.0	23	92.0		.0	25
	2	2.8	1	1.4	1	1.4	4	5.6	63	88.7	4	5.6	71
	16	10.8	0	.0	21	14.2	38	25.7	106	71.6	4	2.7	148
	14	12.7	0	.0	16	14.5	31	28.2	78	70.9	1	.9	110
	2	5.3	0	.0	5	13.2	7	18.4	28	73.7	3	7.9	38
	23	4.0	7	1.2	16	2.8	46	8.1	427	75.0	96	16.9	569
	16	6.2	3	1.2	7	2.7	27	10.4	227	87.3	6	2.3	260
	7	2.3	1	.3	9	2.9	19	6.1	200	64.7	90	29.1	309
	2	.8	1	.4	4	1.7	7	2.9	229	94.6	6	2.5	242
	1	.8	1	.8	1	.8	3	2.5	118	96.7	1	.8	122
	1	.8	0	.0	3	2.5	4	3.3	111	92.5	5	4.2	120
	250	4.9	19	.4	96	1.9	386	7.6	4,163	82.1	523	10.3	5,072
	148	6.1	6	.2	44	1.8	207	8.5	2,119	86.8	114	4.7	2,440
	102	3.9	13	.5	52	2.0	179	6.8	2,044	77.7	409	15.5	2,632
	0	.0	0	.0	2	11.1	2	11.1	15	83.3	1	5.6	18
	0	.0	0	.0	1	7.1	1	7.1	13	92.9	0	.0	14
	0	.0	0	.0	1	25.0	1	25.0	2	50.0	1	25.0	4
	35	7.1	1	.2	187	37.9	224	45.3	270	54.7		.0	494
	25	7.6	0	.0	131	39.9	157	47.9	171	52.1		.0	328
	10	6.0	1	.6	56	33.7	67	40.4	99	59.6	0	.0	166
	9	.8	14	1.2	683	58.7	712	61.2	436	37.5	16	1.4	1,164
	6	.9	9	1.4	354	55.7	372	58.6	258	40.6	5	.8	635
	3	.6	5	.9	329	62.2	340	64.3	178	33.6	11	2.1	529
	11	1.2	64	6.8	14	1.5	89	9.5	802	85.3	49	5.2	940
	2	.7	13	4.5	4	1.4	19	6.6	259	90.2	9	3.1	287
	9	1.4	51	7.8	10	1.5	70	10.7	543	83.2	40	6.1	653
	13	4.0	1	.3	17	5.3	34	10.5	226	70.0	63	.5	323
	2	3.9	0	.0	3	5.9	7	13.7	37	72.5	7	1.7	51
	11	4.0	1	.4	14	5.1	27	9.9	189	69.5	56	20.6	272
	18	3.6	40	7.9	130	25.7	191	37.7	314	62.1	1	.2	506
	9	4.8	6	3.2	44	23.5	60	32.1	126	67.4	1	.5	187
	9	2.8	34	10.7	86	27.0	131	41.1	188	58.9	0	.0	319
	55	4.5	45	3.7	31	2.5	134	10.9	1,039	84.9	51	4.2	1,224
	29	4.1	8	1.1	16	2.3	54	7.7	640	91.0	9	1.3	703
	26	5.0	37	7.1	15	2.9	80	15.4	399	76.6	42	8.1	521
	38	2.1	23	1.3	45	2.5	110	6.1	1,513	83.8	182	1.1	1,805
	16	2.5	8	1.3	27	4.3	51	8.1	556	88.4	22	.5	629
	22	1.9	15	1.3	18	1.5	59	5.0	957	81.4	160	13.6	1,176
	33	2.5	10	.7	79	5.9	141	10.5	1,174	87.8	22	1.6	1,337
	16	2.4	4	.6	35	5.2	61	9.0	609	90.0	7	110	677
	17	2.6	6	.9	44	6.7	80	12.1	565	85.6	15	2.3	660
	47	5.3	7	.8	21	2.4	77	8.7	797	89.7	15	1.7	889
	30	6.3	2	.4	8	1.7	41	8.7	429	90.7	3	.6	473
	17	4.1	5	1.2	13	3.1	36	8.7	368	88.5	12	2.9	416
	3	.6	0	.0	130	23.9	133	24.4	306	56.3	105	19.3	544
	1	.5	0	.0	51	26.4	52	26.9	122	63.2	19	9.8	193
	2	.6	0	.0	79	22.5	81	23.1	184	52.4	86	24.5	351
	911	71.8	39	3.1	6	.5	968	76.3	300	23.7	0	.0	1,268
	542	74.0	11	1.5	2	.3	558	76.2	174	23.8	0	.0	732
	369	68.8	28	5.2	4	.7	410	76.5	126	23.5	0	.0	536
	13	1.9	21	3.0	15	2.2	50	7.2	606	87.6	36	5.2	692
	5	1.8	4	1.4	3	1.1	12	4.3	265	94.0	5	1.8	282
	8	2.0	17	4.1	12	2.9	38	9.3	341	83.2	31	7.6	410

TABLE 2 - TOTAL GRADUATE ENROLLMENT IN INSTITUTIONS OF HIGHER EDUCATION BY RACE, ETHNICITY AND SEX:
INSTITUTION, STATE AND NATION, 1978

	AMERICAN INDIAN ALASKAN NATIVE		BLACK NON-HISPANIC		ASIAN OR PACIFIC ISLANDER		HISPANIC		TOTAL MINORITY		WHITE NON-HISPANIC		NON-RESIDENT ALIEN	
	NUMBER	%	NUMBER	%	NUMBER	%	NUMBER	%	NUMBER	%	NUMBER	%	NUMBER	%
TEXAS CONTINUED														
TEXAS A&M U MAIN CAMPUS														
TX TOTAL	17	.4	17	.4	24	.6	40	1.0	98	2.4	3,531	87.0	428	10.5
TX FEMALE	3	.3	2	.2	7	.7	5	.5	17	1.6	959	92.5	61	5.9
TX MALE	14	.5	15	.5	17	.6	35	1.2	81	2.7	2,572	85.2	367	12.2
TEXAS CHRISTIAN U														
TX TOTAL	4	.5	18	2.2	6	.7	14	1.7	42	5.2	772	94.8		.0
TX FEMALE	1	.3	6	1.8	0	.0	5	1.5	12	3.6	322	96.4	0	.0
TX MALE	3	.6	12	2.5	6	1.3	9	1.9	30	6.3	450	93.8	0	.0
TEXAS EASTERN UNIVERSITY														
TX TOTAL	0	.0	35	9.2	0	.0	1	.3	36	9.5	338	89.2	5	1.3
TX FEMALE	0	.0	25	10.2	0	.0	1	.4	26	10.6	217	88.6	2	.8
TX MALE	0	.0	10	7.5	0	.0	0	.0	10	7.5	121	90.3	3	2.2
TEXAS SOUTHERN UNIVERSITY														
TX TOTAL	0	.0	684	68.3	4	.4	39	3.9	727	72.6	72	7.2	202	20.2
TX FEMALE	0	.0	466	83.4	2	.4	15	2.7	483	86.4	48	8.6	28	5.0
TX MALE	0	.0	218	49.3	2	.5	24	5.4	244	55.2	24	5.4	174	39.4
TEXAS TECH UNIVERSITY														
TX TOTAL	11	.7	7	.4	53	3.2	30	1.8	101	6.1	1,420	85.5	140	4
TX FEMALE	5	.8	2	.3	20	3.3	9	1.5	36	6.0	540	89.7	26	8 3
TX M/LE	6	.6	5	.5	33	3.1	21	2.0	65	6.1	880	83.1	114	10.8
TEXAS WOMAN'S UNIVERSITY														
TX TOTAL	11	.3	300	9.2	99	3.0	125	3.8	535	16.3	2,694	82.3	45	1.4
TX FEMALE	9	.3	279	9.5	78	2.6	105	3.6	471	16.0	2,435	82.5	44	1.5
TX MALE	2	.6	21	6.5	21	6.5	20	6.2	64	19.8	259	79.9	1	.3
TRINITY UNIVERSITY														
TX TOTAL	1	.1	25	3.4	6	.8	156	21.1	188	25.4	543	73.3	10	1.3
TX FEMALE	0	.0	11	3.2	2	.6	63	18.1	76	21.8	271	77.7	2	.6
TX MALE	1	.3	14	3.6	4	1.0	93	23.7	112	28.6	272	69.4	8	2.0
UNIVERSITY OF DALLAS														
TX TOTAL	3	.3	26	2.6	5	.5	17	1.7	51	5.1	716	71.6	233	23.3
TX FEMALE	0	.0	13	5.9	1	.5	3	1.4	17	7.7	178	80.5	26	11.8
TX MALE	3	.4	13	1.7	4	.5	14	1.8	34	4.4	538	69.1	207	26.6
U OF HOUSTON CEN CAMPUS														
TX TOTAL	18	.3	239	4.4	53	1.0	201	3.7	511	9.5	4,098	75.9	789	14.6
TX FEMALE	8	.3	171	7.1	21	.9	112	4.7	312	13.0	1,934	80.3	161	6.7
TX MALE	10	.3	68	2.3	32	1.1	89	3.0	199	6.7	2,164	72.4	628	21.0
U HOUSTON CLEAR LAKE CITY														
TX TOTAL	16	.5	179	5.1	69	2.0	150	4.3	414	11.8	3,054	86.8	50	1.4
TX FEMALE	7	.4	97	5.0	29	1.5	71	3.6	204	10.5	1,731	88.8	14	.7
TX MALE	9	.6	82	5.2	40	2.5	79	5.0	210	13.4	1,323	84.3	36	2.3
U HOUSTON VICTORIA CAMPUS														
TX TOTAL	0	.0	4	2.9	0	.0	4	2.9	8	5.7	132	94.3	0	.0
TX FEMALE	0	.0	1	1.1	0	.0	2	2.2	3	3.3	87	96.7	0	.0
TX MALE	0	.0	3	6.0	0	.0	2	4.0	5	10.0	45	90.0	0	.0
UNIVERSITY OF SNT THOMAS														
TX TOTAL	0	.0	1	1.9	0	.0	5	9.6	6	11.5	46	88.5	0	.0
TX FEMALE	0	.0	1	2.2	0	.0	4	8.9	5	11.1	40	88.9	0	.0
TX MALE	0	.0	0	.0	0	.0	1	14.3	1	14.3	6	85.7	0	.0
CORPUS CHRISTI STATE U														
TX TOTAL	4	.4	19	1.7	8	.7	274	24.9	305	27.8	775	70.5	19	1.7
TX FEMALE	3	.5	9	1.5	4	.7	121	20.5	137	23.2	449	76.1	4	.7
TX MALE	1	.2	10	2.0	4	.8	193	30.1	168	33.0	326	64.0	15	2.9
LAREDO STATE UNIVERSITY														
TX TOTAL	0	.0	0	.0	2	.6	259	77.1	261	77.7	61	18.2	14	4.2
TX FEMALE	0	.0	0	.0	2	1.0	162	78.6	164	79.6	40	19.4	2	1.0
TX MALE	0	.0	0	.0	0	.0	97	74.6	97	74.6	21	16.2	12	9.2
TEXAS A&I UNIVERSITY														
TX TOTAL	1	.1	22	2.0	57	5.1	554	49.8	634	57.0	381	34.3	97	8.7
TX FEMALE	0	.0	15	2.5	16	2.7	328	55.5	359	60.7	218	36.9	14	2.4
TX MALE	2	.3	7	1.3	41	7.9	226	43.4	275	52.8	163	31.3	83	15.9
U OF TEXAS AT AUSTIN														
TX TOTAL	17	.2	124	1.6	80	1.0	359	4.6	580	7.4	6,207	79.4	1,032	13.2
TX FEMALE	5	.2	62	2.0	20	.7	148	4.8	235	7.7	2,573	84.1	253	8 3
TX MALE	12	.3	62	1.3	60	1.3	211	4.4	345	7.3	3,634	76.4	779	16.4
U OF TEXAS AT ARLINGTON														
TX TOTAL	9	.3	151	5.4	77	2.8	57	2.0	294	10.5	2,082	74.5	419	15.
TX FEMALE	3	.3	59	6.1	26	2.7	26	2.7	114	11.7	786	80.9	72	7.0
TX MALE	6	.3	92	5.0	51	2.8	31	1.7	180	9.9	1,296	71.1	347	19.8
U OF TEXAS AT DALLAS														
TX TOTAL	5	.3	34	2.0	7	.4	30	1.8	76	4.5	1,369	81.4	237	14.1
TX FEMALE	1	.1	19	2.7	2	.3	12	1.7	34	4.9	610	88.3	47	6.8
TX MALE	4	.4	15	1.5	5	.5	18	1.8	42	4.2	759	76.6	190	19.2
U OF TEXAS AT EL PASO														
TX TOTAL	1	.1	13	1.5	5	.6	228	26.7	247	28.9	524	61.3	84	9.8
TX FEMALE	0	.0	4	1.1	2	.6	94	27.0	100	28.7	230	66.1	18	5.2
TX MALE	1	.2	9	1.8	3	.6	134	26.4	147	29.0	294	58.0	66	13.0
U TEX MLTH SCI CTR DALLAS														
TX TOTAL	0	.0	1	.4	4	1.7	2	.9	7	3.0	215	91.5	13	5 5
TX FEMALE	0	.0	1	1.0	2	2.0	0	.0	3	3.1	93	94.9	2	2 0
TX MALE	0	.0	0	.0	2	1.5	2	1.5	4	2.9	122	89.1	11	810
U TEX MLTH SCI CTR HOUSTN														
TX TOTAL	3	.4	42	5.1	9	1.1	29	3.5	83	10.1	670	81.2	72	.
TX FEMALE	3	.7	29	6.8	4	.9	16	3.8	52	12.2	345	81.0	29	.7
TX MALE	0	.0	13	3.3	5	1.3	13	3.3	31	7.8	325	81.5	43	10.8
U TEX MEDL SCI SN ANTO														
TX TOTAL	1	.3	6	2.1	2	.7	10	3.5	19	6.6	262	91.3	6	2.
TX FEMALE	1	.5	4	1.9	2	1.0	8	3.9	15	7.3	189	91.7	2	1.
TX MALE	0	.0	2	2.5	0	.0	2	2.5	4	4.9	73	90.1	4	4.8
U TEX MEDL BR GALVESTON														
TX TOTAL	0	.0	1	.6	7	3.9	6	3.4	14	7.8	163	91.1	2	1.1
TX FEMALE	0	.0	1	1.3	2	2.5	4	5.1	7	8.9	72	91.1	0	.0
TX MALE	0	.0	0	.0	5	5.0	2	2.0	7	7.0	91	91.0	2	2.0

NROLLMENT IN INSTITUTIONS OF HIGHER EDUCATION BY RACE, ETHNICITY AND SEX:
TE AND NATION, 1978

BLACK NON-HISPANIC		ASIAN OR PACIFIC ISLANDER		HISPANIC		TOTAL MINORITY		WHITE NON-HISPANIC		NON-RESIDENT ALIEN		TOTAL
NUMBER	%	NUMBER	%	NUMBER	%	NUMBER	%	NUMBER	%	NUMBER	%	NUMBER

NUED

15	3.1	1	.2	25	5.1	41	8.4	436	89.3	11	2.3	488
9	4.0	1	.4	11	4.9	21	9.3	202	89.8	2	.9	225
6	2.3	0	.0	14	5.3	20	7.6	234	89.0	9	3.4	263
39	3.3	9	.8	183	15.5	233	19.7	925	78.1	26	2.2	1,184
25	4.0	5	.8	104	16.7	134	21.5	480	76.9	10	1.6	624
14	2.5	4	.7	79	14.1	99	17.7	445	79.5	16	2.9	560
14	1.1	35	2.9	23	1.9	81	6.6	1,125	91.8	20	1.6	1,226
7	1.1	15	2.4	10	1.6	36	5.8	578	93.8	2	.3	616
7	1.1	20	3.3	13	2.1	45	7.4	547	89.7	18	3.0	610

(56 INSTITUTIONS)

3,962	5.9	951	1.4	4,521	6.8	9,679	14.5	51,591	77.3	5,442	8.2	66,712
2,347	7.8	349	1.2	2,251	7.4	5,039	16.7	24,044	79.5	1,172	3.9	30,255
1,615	4.4	602	1.7	2,270	6.2	4,640	12.7	27,547	75.6	4,270	11.7	36,457
0	.0	22	.8	8	.3	42	1.5	2,483	89.9	238	8.6	2,763
0	.0	7	.9	5	.7	16	2.1	656	87.4	79	10.5	751
0	.0	15	.7	3	.1	26	1.3	1,827	90.8	159	7.9	2,012
28	.7	73	1.9	56	1.5	193	5.1	3,332	87.4	288	7.6	3,813
10	.7	32	2.1	23	1.5	83	5.5	1,376	90.6	60	3.9	1,519
18	.8	41	1.8	33	1.4	110	4.8	1,956	85.3	228	9.9	2,294
5	.5	8	.7	3	.3	16	1.4	831	75.3	257	23.3	1,104
4	1.4	3	1.0	2	.7	9	3.1	233	79.0	53	18.0	295
1	.1	5	.6	1	.1	7	.9	598	73.9	204	25.2	809
0	.0	0	.0	1	1.5	1	1.5	66	98.5	0	.0	67
0	.0	0	.0	1	2.6	1	2.6	37	97.4	0	.0	38
0	.0	0	.0	0	.0	0	.0	29	100.0	0	.0	29

(4 INSTITUTIONS)

33	.4	103	1.3	68	.9	252	3.3	6,712	86.6	783	13.1	7,747
14	.5	42	1.6	31	1.2	109	4.2	2,302	88.4	192	7.4	2,603
19	.4	61	1.2	37	.7	143	2.8	4,410	85.7	591	11.5	5,144
0	.0	0	.0	0	.0	0	.0	4	100.0	0	.0	4
0	.0	0	.0	0	.0	0	.0	2	100.0	0	.0	2
0	.0	0	.0	0	.0	0	.0	2	100.0	0	.0	2
0	.0	0	.0	0	.0	0	.0	408	100.0	0	.0	408
0	.0	0	.0	0	.0	0	.0	276	100.0	0	.0	276
0	.0	0	.0	0	.0	0	.0	132	100.0	0	.0	132
1	3.4	0	.0	0	.0	1	3.4	28	96.6	0	.0	29
1	4.2	0	.0	0	.0	1	4.2	23	95.8	0	.0	24
0	.0	0	.0	0	.0	0	.0	5	100.0	0	.0	5
31	5.7	7	1.3	15	2.8	53	9.8	467	86.3	21	3.9	541
14	4.0	5	1.4	6	1.7	25	7.1	318	89.8	11	3.1	354
17	9.1	2	1.1	9	4.8	28	15.0	149	79.7	10	5.3	187
0	.0	0	.0	0	.0	0	.0	72	100.0	0	.0	72
0	.0	0	.0	0	.0	0	.0	48	100.0	0	.0	48
0	.0	0	.0	0	.0	0	.0	24	100.0	0	.0	24
0	.0	0	.0	0	.0	0	.0	57	98.3	1	1.7	58
0	.3	0	.0	0	.0	0	.0	38	97.4	1	2.6	39
0	.0	0	.0	0	.0	0	.0	19	100.0	0	.0	19
0	.0	0	.0	0	.0	0	.0	1	100.0	0	.0	1
0	.0	0	.0	0	.0	0	.0	0	.0	0	.0	0
0	.0	0	.0	0	.0	0	.0	1	100.0	0	.0	1
0	.0	0	.0	0	.0	0	.0	24	100.0	0	.0	24
0	.0	0	.0	0	.0	0	.0	7	100.0	0	.0	7
0	.0	0	.0	0	.0	0	.0	17	100.0	0	.0	17
0	.0	0	.0	0	.0	0	.0	76	70.4	32	29.6	108
0	.0	0	.0	0	.0	0	.0	49	83.1	10	16.9	59
0	.0	0	.0	0	.0	0	.0	27	55.1	22	44.9	49
11	3.4	1	.3	4	1.3	17	5.3	268	84.0	34	10.7	319
8	4.7	1	.6	0	.0	9	5.2	146	84.9	17	9.9	172
3	2.0	0	.0	4	2.7	8	5.4	122	83.0	17	11.6	147
2	.2	0	.0	0	.0	4	.5	805	97.0	21	2.5	830
0	.0	0	.0	0	.0	0	.0	365	99.5	2	.5	367
2	.4	0	.0	0	.0	4	.9	440	95.0	19	4.1	463

11 INSTITUTIONS)

45	1.9	8	.3	19	.8	75	3.1	2,210	92.3	109	4.6	2,394
23	1.7	6	.4	6	.4	35	2.6	1,272	94.4	41	3.0	1,348
22	2.1	2	.2	13	1.2	40	3.9	938	89.7	68	6.5	1,046

TABLE 2 - TOTAL GRADUATE ENROLLMENT IN INSTITUTIONS OF HIGHER EDUCATION BY RACE, ETHNICITY AND SEX: INSTITUTION, STATE AND NATION, 1978

	AMERICAN INDIAN ALASKAN NATIVE		BLACK NON-HISPANIC		ASIAN OR PACIFIC ISLANDER		HISPANIC		TOTAL MINORITY		WHITE NON-HISPANIC		NON-RESIDENT ALIEN	
	NUMBER	%	NUMBER	%	NUMBER	%	NUMBER	%	NUMBER	%	NUMBER	%	NUMBER	%
VIRGINIA														
AVERETT COLLEGE														
VA TOTAL	0	.0	0	.0	0	.0	0	.0	0	.0	28	100.0	0	.0
VA FEMALE	0	.0	0	.0	0	.0	0	.0	0	.0	27	100.0	0	.0
VA MALE	0	.0	0	.0	0	.0	0	.0	0	.0	1	100.0	0	.0
C OF WILLIAM AND MARY														
VA TOTAL	0	.0	33	3.3	13	1.3	5	.5	51	5.2	913	92.4	24	2.4
VA FEMALE	0	.0	19	4.9	3	.8	1	.3	23	6.0	356	92.2	7	1.8
VA MALE	0	.0	14	2.3	10	1.7	4	.7	28	4.7	557	92.5	17	2.8
GEORGE MASON UNIVERSITY														
VA TOTAL	10	.7	51	3.6	12	.9	29	2.1	102	7.3	1,286	91.8	13	.9
VA FEMALE	2	.2	35	4.3	1	.1	21	2.6	59	7.2	745	91.5	10	1.2
VA MALE	8	1.4	16	2.7	11	1.9	8	1.4	43	7.3	541	92.2	3	.5
HAMPTON INSTITUTE														
VA TOTAL	0	.0	166	80.6	5	2.4	2	1.0	173	84.0	30	14.6	3	1.5
VA FEMALE	0	.0	129	83.2	5	3.2	2	1.3	136	87.7	19	12.3	0	.0
VA MALE	0	.0	37	72.5	0	.0	0	.0	37	72.5	11	21.6	3	5.9
HOLLINS COLLEGE														
VA TOTAL	0	.0	0	.0	0	.0	0	.0	0	.0	63	98.4	1	1.6
VA FEMALE	0	.0	0	.0	0	.0	0	.0	0	.0	46	100.0	0	.0
VA MALE	0	.0	0	.0	0	.0	0	.0	0	.0	17	94.4	1	5.6
INST TEXTILE TECHNOLOGY														
VA TOTAL	0	.0	1	6.3	0	.0	0	.0	1	6.3	15	93.8	0	.0
VA FEMALE	0	.0	0	.0	0	.0	0	.0	0	.0	2	100.0	0	.0
VA MALE	0	.0	1	7.1	0	.0	0	.0	1	7.1	13	92.9	0	.0
JAMES MADISON UNIVERSITY														
VA TOTAL	2	.2	31	2.8	0	.0	3	.3	36	3.2	1,074	96.2	7	.6
VA FEMALE	1	.1	23	3.4	0	.0	2	.3	26	3.8	653	95.9	2	.3
VA MALE	1	.2	8	1.8	0	.0	1	.2	10	2.3	421	96.6	5	1.1
LONGWOOD COLLEGE														
VA TOTAL	0	.0	3	4.2	0	.0	0	.0	3	4.2	68	95.8	0	.0
VA FEMALE	0	.0	2	4.3	0	.0	0	.0	2	4.3	44	95.7	0	.0
VA MALE	0	.0	1	4.0	0	.0	0	.0	1	4.0	24	96.0	0	.0
LYNCHBURG COLLEGE														
VA TOTAL	0	.0	47	10.9	0	.0	0	.0	47	10.9	368	85.0	18	4.2
VA FEMALE	0	.0	23	12.0	0	.0	0	.0	23	12.0	164	85.4	5	2.6
VA MALE	0	.0	24	10.0	0	.0	0	.0	24	10.0	204	84.6	13	5.4
NORFOLK STATE COLLEGE														
VA TOTAL	1	.2	414	75.7	0	.0	0	.0	415	75.9	129	23.6	3	.5
VA FEMALE	1	.3	256	72.5	0	.0	0	.0	257	72.8	93	26.3	3	.8
VA MALE	0	.0	158	81.4	0	.0	0	.0	158	81.4	36	18.6	0	.0
OLD DOMINION UNIVERSITY														
VA TOTAL	0	.0	146	7.7	37	1.9	9	.5	192	10.1	1,713	89.8	3	.2
VA FEMALE	0	.0	95	10.1	7	.7	4	.4	106	11.3	831	88.7	0	.0
VA MALE	0	.0	51	5.3	30	3.1	5	.5	86	8.9	882	90.8	3	.3
PRESB SCH OF CHRISTIAN ED														
VA TOTAL	0	.0	5	4.8	1	1.0	2	1.9	8	7.6	88	83.8	9	8.6
VA FEMALE	0	.0	4	5.3	1	1.3	1	1.3	6	7.9	66	86.8	4	5.3
VA MALE	0	.0	1	3.4	0	.0	1	3.4	2	6.9	22	75.9	5	17.2
PROT EPIS THEOL SEM IN VA														
VA TOTAL	0	.0	1	2.0	0	.0	0	.0	1	2.0	46	90.2	4	7.8
VA FEMALE	0	.0	0	.0	0	.0	0	.0	0	.0	11	100.0	0	.0
VA MALE	0	.0	1	2.5	0	.0	0	.0	1	2.5	35	87.5	4	10.0
RADFORD COLLEGE														
VA TOTAL	1	.1	12	1.4	0	.0	0	.0	13	1.5	858	98.5	0	.0
VA FEMALE	1	.2	7	1.2	0	.0	0	.0	8	1.4	583	98.6	0	.0
VA MALE	0	.0	5	1.8	0	.0	0	.0	5	1.8	275	98.2	0	.0
UNION THEOL SEM IN VA														
VA TOTAL	0	.0	3	1.3	0	.0	1	.4	4	1.7	223	94.9	8	3.4
VA FEMALE	0	.0	0	.0	0	.0	0	.0	0	.0	41	100.0	0	.0
VA MALE	0	.0	3	1.5	0	.0	1	.5	4	2.1	182	93.8	8	4.1
UNIVERSITY OF RICHMOND														
VA TOTAL	0	.0	19	5.3	0	.0	1	.3	20	5.6	327	91.3	11	3.1
VA FEMALE	0	.0	9	7.0	0	.0	1	.8	10	7.8	115	89.1	4	3.1
VA MALE	0	.0	10	4.4	0	.0	0	.0	10	4.4	212	92.6	7	3.1
U OF VIRGINIA MAIN CAMPUS														
VA TOTAL	3	.1	75	2.0	15	.4	3	.1	96	2.6	3,383	92.2	189	5.2
VA FEMALE	2	.1	34	2.3	8	.5	0	.0	44	2.9	1,394	92.9	63	4.2
VA MALE	1	.0	41	1.9	7	.3	3	.1	52	2.4	1,989	91.8	126	5.8
VIRGINIA COMMONWEALTH U														
VA TOTAL	5	.2	346	11.5	20	.7	10	.3	381	12.7	2,585	85.9	42	1.4
VA FEMALE	1	.1	248	14.6	8	.5	4	.2	261	15.3	1,432	84.0	11	.6
VA MALE	4	.3	98	7.5	12	.9	6	.5	120	9.2	1,153	88.4	31	2.4
VA POLY INST AND STATE U														
VA TOTAL	3	.1	109	2.5	56	1.3	3	.1	171	4.0	3,877	90.1	253	5.9
VA FEMALE	1	.1	59	3.6	10	.6	1	.1	71	4.3	1,536	94.1	26	1.6
VA MALE	2	.1	50	1.9	46	1.7	2	.1	100	3.7	2,341	87.7	227	8.5
VIRGINIA STATE COLLEGE														
VA TOTAL	1	.2	388	74.2	16	3.1	3	.6	408	78.0	115	22.0	0	.0
VA FEMALE	1	.3	263	81.7	5	1.6	1	.3	270	83.9	52	16.1	0	.0
VA MALE	0	.0	125	62.2	11	5.5	2	1.0	138	68.7	63	31.3	0	.0
VIRGINIA UNION UNIVERSITY														
VA TOTAL	0	.0	76	92.7	0	.0	0	.0	76	92.7	5	6.1	1	1.2
VA FEMALE	0	.0	10	90.9	0	.0	0	.0	10	90.9	1	9.1	0	.0
VA MALE	0	.0	66	93.0	0	.0	0	.0	66	93.0	4	5.6	1	1.4
VIRGINIA TOTAL (21 INSTITUTIONS)														
VA TOTAL	26	.1	1,926	9.6	175	.9	71	.4	2,198	11.0	17,194	86.1	589	2.9
VA FEMALE	10	.1	1,216	12.6	48	.5	38	.4	1,312	13.6	8,211	85.0	135	1.4
VA MALE	16	.2	710	6.9	127	1.2	33	.3	886	8.6	8,983	87.0	454	4.4

N E	BLACK NON-HISPANIC		ASIAN OR PACIFIC ISLANDER		HISPANIC		TOTAL MINORITY		WHITE NON-HISPANIC		NON-RESIDENT ALIEN		TOTAL
	NUMBER	%	NUMBER	%	NUMBER	%	NUMBER	%	NUMBER	%	NUMBER	%	NUMBER
	2	.8	3	1.2	2	.8	8	3.1	246	94.6	6	2.3	260
	1	.7	1	.7	2	1.5	5	3.6	128	93.4	4	2.9	137
	1	.8	2	1.6	0	.0	3	2.4	118	95.9	2	1.6	123
	33	6.2	11	2.1	3	.6	50	9.3	481	89.7	5	.9	536
	4	4.0	0	.0	0	.0	4	4.0	96	96.0	0	.0	100
	29	6.7	11	2.5	3	.7	46	10.6	385	88.3	5	1.1	436
	10	1.7	4	.7	10	1.7	30	5.1	546	92.2	16	2.7	592
	5	1.7	3	1.0	3	1.0	13	4.3	282	94.3	4	1.3	299
	5	1.7	1	.3	7	2.4	17	5.8	264	90.1	12	4.1	293
	1	3.4	1	3.4	3	10.3	9	31.0	19	65.5	1	3.4	29
	0	.0	1	5.6	2	11.1	6	33.3	11	61.1	1	5.6	18
	1	9.1	0	.0	1	9.1	3	27.3	8	72.7	0	.0	11
	6	1.4	3	.7	4	.9	16	3.7	285	65.7	133	30.6	434
	0	.0	0	.0	0	.0	1	.9	72	66.7	35	32.4	108
	6	1.8	3	.9	4	1.2	15	4.6	213	65.3	98	30.1	326
	12	4.2	6	2.1	1	.4	21	7.4	261	91.6	3	1.1	285
	3	2.8	2	1.9	0	.0	6	5.7	98	92.5	2	1.9	106
	9	5.0	.4	2.2	1	.6	15	8.4	163	91.1	1	.6	179
	0	.0	0	.0	0	.0	2	10.0	18	90.0	0	.0	20
	0	.0	0	.0	0	.0	0	.0	10	100.0	0	.0	10
	0	.0	0	.0	0	.0	2	20.0	8	80.0	0	.0	10
	0	.0	0	.0	0	.0	0	.0	17	100.0	0	.0	17
	0	.0	0	.0	0	.0	0	.0	1	100.0	0	.0	1
	0	.0	0	.0	0	.0	0	.0	16	100.0	0	.0	16
	2	2.7	7	9.3	2	2.7	12	16.0	58	77.3	5	6.7	75
	2	3.8	4	7.7	2	3.8	9	17.3	39	75.0	4	7.7	52
	0	.0	3	13.0	0	.0	3	13.0	19	82.6	1	4.3	23
	33	3.7	30	3.3	10	1.1	75	8.4	789	87.9	34	3.8	898
	19	4.9	12	3.1	3	.8	35	9.0	347	89.4	6	1.5	388
	14	2.7	18	3.5	7	1.4	40	7.8	442	86.7	28	5.5	510
	0	.0	1	1.6	0	.0	2	3.2	54	87.1	6	9.7	62
	0	.0	1	2.8	0	.0	1	2.8	34	94.4	1	2.8	36
	0	.0	0	.0	0	.0	1	3.8	20	76.9	5	19.2	26
	153	2.0	290	3.8	69	.9	559	7.4	6,190	81.8	817	10.8	7,566
	78	2.5	120	3.8	21	.7	239	7.5	2,772	87.2	168	5.3	3,179
	75	1.7	170	3.9	48	1.1	320	7.3	3,418	77.9	649	14.8	4,387
	1	4.0	0	.0	1	4.0	2	8.0	18	72.0	5	20.0	25
	0	.0	0	.0	0	.0	0	.0	5	62.5	3	37.5	8
	1	5.9	0	.0	1	5.9	2	11.8	13	76.5	2	11.8	17
	37	1.8	32	1.6	30	1.5	117	5.7	1,568	76.6	363	17.7	2,048
	13	2.0	10	1.5	7	1.1	40	6.1	539	82.8	72	11.1	651
	24	1.7	22	1.6	23	1.6	77	5.5	1,029	73.7	291	20.8	1,397
	5	.8	7	1.1	3	.5	18	2.7	503	76.3	138	20.9	659
	3	1.0	4	1.4	2	.7	12	4.1	248	84.1	35	11.9	295
	2	.5	3	.8	1	.3	6	1.6	255	70.1	103	28.3	364
	0	.0	0	.0	0	.0	0	.0	164	97.6	4	2.4	168
	0	.0	0	.0	0	.0	0	.0	94	97.9	2	2.1	96
	0	.0	0	.0	0	.0	0	.0	70	97.2	2	2.8	72
(16 INSTITUTIONS)													
	295	2.2	395	2.9	138	1.0	921	6.7	11,217	82.0	1,536	11.2	13,674
	128	2.3	158	2.9	42	.8	371	6.8	4,776	87.1	337	6.1	5,484
	167	2.0	237	2.9	96	1.2	550	6.7	6,441	78.6	1,199	14.6	8,190
	57	2.2	51	2.0	5	.2	138	5.4	2,373	93.2	36	1.4	2,547
	26	1.8	15	1.1	2	.1	57	4.0	1,360	95.3	10	.7	1,427
	31	2.8	36	3.2	3	.3	81	7.2	1,013	90.4	26	2.3	1,120
	154	5.1	25	.8	11	.4	196	6.5	2,805	93.3	5	.2	3,006
	102	5.5	8	.4	4	.2	117	6.3	1,745	93.7	1	.1	1,863
	52	4.5	17	1.5	7	.6	79	6.9	1,060	92.7	4	.3	1,143
	57	1.0	7	.1	6	.1	82	1.4	5,426	93.0	325	5.6	5,833
	30	.9	4	.1	4	.1	44	1.4	3,129	96.7	64	2.0	3,237
	27	1.0	3	.1	2	.1	38	1.5	2,297	88.5	261	10.1	2,596
	0	.0	0	.0	0	.0	0	.0	14	100.0	0	.0	14
	0	.0	0	.0	0	.0	0	.0	10	100.0	0	.0	10
	0	.0	0	.0	0	.0	0	.0	4	100.0	0	.0	4
	0	.0	0	.0	0	.0	0	.0	52	100.0	0	.0	52
	0	.0	0	.0	0	.0	0	.0	12	100.0	0	.0	12
	0	.0	0	.0	0	.0	0	.0	40	100.0	0	.0	40

	AMERICAN INDIAN ALASKAN NATIVE		BLACK NON-HISPANIC		ASIAN OR PACIFIC ISLANDER		HISPANIC		TOTAL MINORITY		WHITE NON-HISPANIC		NON-RESIDENT ALIEN	
	NUMBER	%	NUMBER	%	NUMBER	%	NUMBER	%	NUMBER	%	NUMBER	%	NUMBER	%
WEST VIRGINIA														
WEST VIRGINIA	TOTAL (	5 INSTITUTIONS)												
WV TOTAL	43	.4	268	2.3	83	.7	22	.2	416	3.6	10,670	93.2	366	3.2
WV FEMALE	23	.4	158	2.4	27	.4	10	.2	218	3.3	6,256	95.5	75	1.1
WV MALE	20	.4	110	2.2	56	1.1	12	.2	198	4.0	4,414	90.0	291	5.9
WISCONSIN														
BELOIT COLLEGE														
WI TOTAL	0	.0		.0		.0		.0		.0	7	100.0	0	.0
WI FEMALE	0	.0	0	.0	0	.0	0	.0	0	.0	4	100.0	0	.0
WI MALE	0	.0	0	.0	0	.0	0	.0	0	.0	3	100.0	0	.0
CARDINAL STRITCH COLLEGE														
WI TOTAL	1	.4	23	9.2		1.2		.0	27	10.8	221	88.8	1	.4
WI FEMALE	1	.5	22	10.1		1.4	0	.0	26	11.9	191	87.6	1	.5
HI MALE	0	.0	1	3.2	3	.0	0	.0	1	3.2	30	96.8	0	.0
CARTHAGE COLLEGE														
WI TOTAL	0	.0		.0		.0		.0		.0	43	100.0		.0
WI FEMALE	0	.0	0	.0	0	.0	0	.0	0	.0	33	100.0	0	.0
HI MALE	0	.0	0	.0	0	.0	0	.0	0	.0	10	100.0	0	.0
INSTITUTE PAPER CHEMISTRY														
WI TOTAL	0	.0		.0		4.2		.0		4.2	88	92.6		3.2
WI FEMALE	0	.0	0	.0	1	16.7	0	.0	1	16.7	5	83.3		.0
WI MALE	0	.0	0	.0	3	3.4	0	.0	4	3.4	83	93.3	3	3.4
MARQUETTE UNIVERSITY														
WI TOTAL	2	.2	15	1.4	5	.5	4	.4	26	2.4	965	88.2	103	9.4
WI FEMALE	2	.5	8	1.9	2	.5	3	.7	15	3.5	392	90.7	25	5.8
WI MALE	0	.0	7	1.1	3	.5	1	.2	11	1.7	573	86.6	78	11.8
MEDICAL COLLEGE OF WIS														
WI TOTAL	1	1.1		.0	4	4.3	3	3.2	8	8.6	82	88.2	3	3.2
WI FEMALE	1	3.1	0	.0	2	6.3	1	3.1	4	12.5	27	84.4	1	3.1
WI MALE	0	.0	0	.0	2	3.3	2	3.3	4	6.6	55	90.2	2	3.3
MILWAUKEE SCH ENGINEERING														
WI TOTAL	0	.0		.0		.0	1	1.1	1	1.1	89	94.7	4	4.3
WI FEMALE	0	.0	0	.0	0	.0	1	25.0	1	25.0	3	75.0	0	.0
WI MALE	0	.0	0	.0	0	.0	0	.0	0	.0	86	95.6	4	4.4
NASHOTAH HOUSE														
WI TOTAL	0	.0		.0		.0		.0	0	.0	1	100.0		.0
WI FEMALE	0	.0	0	.0	0	.0	0	.0	0	.0	0	.0	0	.0
HI MALE	0	.0	0	.0	0	.0	0	.0	0	.0	1	100.0	0	.0
U OF WISCONSIN EAU CLAIRE														
WI TOTAL	1	.3	4	1.3	2	.7		.0	7	2.3	293	96.4	4	1.3
WI FEMALE	1	.5	0	.0	0	.0	0	.0	1	.5	205	98.6	2	1.0
WI MALE	0	.0	4	4.2	2	2.1	0	.0	6	6.3	88	91.7	2	2.1
U OF WISCONSIN GREEN BAY														
WI TOTAL	3	2.6	2	1.7	0	.0		.0	5	4.3	109	94.0	2	1.7
WI FEMALE	1	2.2	0	.0	0	.0	0	.0	1	2.2	44	95.7	1	2.2
WI MALE	2	2.9	2	2.9	0	.0	0	.0	4	5.7	65	92.9	1	1.4
U OF WISCONSIN LA CROSSE														
WI TOTAL	0	.0	4	1.1		.0	1	.3	5	1.3	369	97.6	4	1.1
WI FEMALE	0	.0	1	.5	0	.0	0	.0	1	.5	209	99.1	1	.5
HI MALE	0	.0	3	1.8	0	.0	1	.6	4	2.4	160	95.8	3	1.8
U OF WISCONSIN MADISON														
WI TOTAL	19	.2	175	2.0	191	2 1	99	1.1	484	5.4	7,209	80.4	1,276	14.2
WI FEMALE	9	.3	87	2.5	72	2 1	41	1.2	209	6.1	2,934	85.9	273	8.0
WI MALE	10	.2	88	1.6	119	2 1	58	1.0	275	5.0	4,275	77.0	1,003	18.1
U OF WISCONSIN MILWAUKEE														
WI TOTAL	18	.5	172	4 8	54	1.5	66	1.8	310	.6	3,121	86.7	167	4.5
WI FEMALE	11	.6	106	519	11	.6	37	2.1	165	8.2	1,595	88.6	40	2.2
WI MALE	7	.4	66	3.7	43	2.4	29	1.6	145	8.1	1,526	84.9	127	7.1
U OF WISCONSIN OSHKOSH														
WI TOTAL	4	.3	15	1.1	3	.2	5	.4	27	2.1	1,277	97.1	11	.8
WI FEMALE	1	.2	6	1.1	0	.0	2	.4	9	1.6	547	97.9	3	.5
WI MALE	3	.4	9	1.2	3	.4	3	.4	18	2.4	730	96.6	8	1.1
U OF WISCONSIN PARKSIDE														
WI TOTAL	1	.9	0	.0	0	.0		.0	1	.9	114	99.1		.0
WI FEMALE	0	.0	0	.0	0	.0	0	.0	0	.0	31	100.0	0	.0
WI MALE	0	.0	1	1.2	0	.0	0	.0	1	1.2	93	98.3	0	.0
U OF WISCONSIN PLATTEVL														
WI TOTAL	0	.0	7	4.0	4	2.3	1	.6	12	6.8	165	93.2		.0
WI FEMALE	0	.0	2	2.1	3	3.2	0	.0	5	5.3	89	94.7		.0
WI MALE	0	.0	5	6.0	1	1.2	1	1.2	7	8.4	76	91.6	0	.0
U OF WISCONSIN RIVER FLS														
WI TOTAL	6	1.	1	.3	2	.5	9	2 4	339	90.9	2	6 7		
WI FEMALE	0	.0	0	.6	1	.4	1	.4	2	8	225	95.3	3	8
WI MALE	0	.0	6	4.8	0	.0	1	.7	7	511	114	83.2	16	11.7
U OF WISCONSIN STEVNS PNT														
WI TOTAL	3	1.0	2	.7	2	.7		.0	7	2 4	282	94.9	8	2 7
WI FEMALE	1	.5	1	.5	2	1.1	0	.0	4	2 2	176	95.1	5	2 7
WI MALE	1	.9	1	.9	0	.0	0	.0	3	217	106	94.6	3	217
U OF WISCONSIN STOUT														
WI TOTAL	2	.4	7	1 5	1	.2	3	.6	13	2.	404	86.3	51	10 9
WI FEMALE	1	.4	2	.9	0	.0	1	.4	4	1.8	209	92.1	14	6 2
WI MALE	1	.4	5	211	1	.4	2	.8	9	3.8	195	80.9	37	1514
U OF WISCONSIN SUPERIOR														
WI TOTAL	3	1.2	5	2.0		.0		.0		3	227	92.7	10	4.1
WI FEMALE	2	1.6	2	1.6	0	.0	0	.0	4	3 3	118	95.9	1	.8
WI MALE	1	.8	3	2.5	0	.0	0	.0	4	13	109	89.3	9	7.4
U OF WISCONSIN WHITEWATER														
WI TOTAL	1	.1	17	1.5	5	.4	11	.9	34	2.9	1,106	95.5	18	1.6
WI FEMALE	1	.2	11	1.9	3	.5	4	.7	19	3.2	563	95.9	5	.9
WI MALE	0	.0	6	1.1	2	.4	7	1.2	15	2.6	543	95.1	13	2.3

	AMERICAN INDIAN ALASKAN NATIVE		BLACK NON-HISPANIC		ASIAN OR PACIFIC ISLANDER		HISPANIC		TOTAL MINORITY		WHITE NON-HISPANIC		NON-RESIDENT ALIEN		TOTAL
	NUMBER	%	NUMBER	%	NUMBER	%	NUMBER	%	NUMBER	%	NUMBER	%	NUMBER	%	NUMBER
CONSIN	CONTINUED														
CONSIN CONSV OF MUSIC															
TOTAL	0	.0	0	.0	0	.0	0	.0	0	.0	16	100.0		.0	16
FEMALE	0	.0	0	.0	0	.0	0	.0	0	.0	5	100.0	0	.0	5
MALE	0	.0	0	.0	0	.0	0	.0	0	.0	11	100.0	0	.0	11
CONSIN	TOTAL (		22 INSTITUTIONS)												
TOTAL	58	.3	455	2.4	279	1.5	196	1.0	988	5.1	16,527	86.1	1,690	8.8	19,205
FEMALE	32	.4	248	2.9	100	1.2	91	1.1	471	5.6	7,605	89.9	381	4.5	8,457
MALE	26	.2	207	1.9	179	1.7	105	1.0	517	4.8	8,922	83.0	1,309	12.2	10,748
MING															
VERSITY OF WYOMING															
TOTAL	3	.3	4	.4	5	.5	8	.8	20	1.9	925	88.2	104	9 9	1,049
FEMALE	1	.2	3	.7	3	.7	2	.5	9	2.1	408	94.0	17	3 9	434
MALE	2	.3	1	.2	2	.3	6	1.0	11	1.8	517	84.1	87	1411	615
MING	TOTAL (		1 INSTITUTIONS)												
TOTAL	3	.3	4	.4	5	.5	8	.8	20	1.9	925	88.2	104	9 9	1,049
FEMALE	1	.2	3	.7	3	.7	2	.5	9	2.1	408	94.0	17	3 9	434
MALE	2	.3	1	.2	2	.3	6	1.0	11	1.8	517	84.1	87	1411	615
STATES AND D.C. (	1,128 INSTITUTIONS)														
TOTAL	3,785	.4	61,871	5.8	20,612	1.9	21,055	2.0	107,323	10.0	890,801	83.1	73,368	6.8	1,071,492
FEMALE	1,740	.4	37,213	7.5	7,882	1.6	9,946	2.0	56,781	11.4	422,840	85.2	16,813	3.4	496,434
MALE	2,045	.4	24,658	4.3	12,730	2.2	11,109	1.9	50,542	8.8	467,961	81.4	56,555	9.8	575,058
M															
VERSITY OF GUAM															
TOTAL	0	.0	0	.0	118	47.8	11	4.5	129	52.2	118	47.8		.0	247
FEMALE	0	.0	0	.0	94	58.0	11	6.8	105	64.8	57	35.2	0	.0	162
MALE	0	.0	0	.0	24	28.2	0	.0	24	28.2	61	71.8	0	.0	85
M	TOTAL (		1 INSTITUTIONS)												
TOTAL	0	.0	0	.0	118	47.8	11	4.5	129	52.2	118	47.8		.0	247
FEMALE	0	.0	0	.0	94	58.0	11	6.8	105	64.8	57	35.2	0	.0	162
MALE	0	.0	0	.0	24	28.2	0	.0	24	28.2	61	71.8	0	.0	85
RTO RICO															
IBBEAN CTR ADV STUDIES															
TOTAL	0	.0	0	.0	0	.0	0	.0	0	.0	210	97.2	6	2.8	216
FEMALE	0	.0	0	.0	0	.0	0	.0	0	.0	129	97.0	4	3.0	133
MALE	0	.0	0	.0	0	.0	0	.0	0	.0	81	97.6	2	2.4	83
HOLIC U PUERTO RICO															
TOTAL	0	.0	0	.0	0	.0	279	100.0	279	100.0	0	.0		.0	279
FEMALE	0	.0	0	.0	0	.0	152	100.0	152	100.0	0	.0	0	.0	152
MALE	0	.0	0	.0	0	.0	127	100.0	127	100.0	0	.0	0	.0	127
ER AMER U HATO REY CAM															
TOTAL	0	.0	0	.0	0	.0	346	99.4	346	99.4	2	.6		.0	348
FEMALE	0	.0	0	.0	0	.0	155	99.4	155	99.4	1	.6	0	.0	156
MALE	0	.0	0	.0	0	.0	191	99.5	191	99.5	1	.5	0	.0	192
ER AMER U BAYAMON BR															
TOTAL	0	.0	0	.0	0	.0	123	99.2	123	99.2	1	.8		.0	124
FEMALE	0	.0	0	.0	0	.0	54	100.0	54	100.0	0	.0	0	.0	54
MALE	0	.0	0	.0	0	.0	69	98.6	69	98.6	1	1.4	0	.0	70
ER AMER SAN GERMAN CAM															
TOTAL	0	.0	0	.0	0	.0	277	98.2	277	98.2	5	1.8		.0	282
FEMALE	0	.0	0	.0	0	.0	159	98.1	159	98.1	3	1.9	0	.0	162
MALE	0	.0	0	.0	0	.0	118	98.3	118	98.3	2	1.7	0	.0	120
F PR RIO PIEDRAS															
TOTAL	0	.0	0	.0	0	.0	2,247	100.0	2,247	100.0	0	.0		.0	2,247
FEMALE	0	.0	0	.0	0	.0	1,420	100.0	1,420	100.0	0	.0	0	.0	1,420
MALE	0	.0	0	.0	0	.0	827	100.0	827	100.0	0	.0	0	.0	827
F PR MAYAGUEZ															
TOTAL	0	.0	0	.0	0	.0	267	100.0	267	100.0	0	.0		.0	267
FEMALE	0	.0	0	.0	0	.0	84	100.0	84	100.0	0	.0	0	.0	84
MALE	0	.0	0	.0	0	.0	183	100.0	183	100.0	0	.0	0	.0	183
F PR MEDICAL SCIENCES															
TOTAL	0	.0	0	.0	0	.0	319	100.0	319	100.0	0	.0		.0	319
FEMALE	0	.0	0	.0	0	.0	243	100.0	243	100.0	0	.0	0	.0	243
MALE	0	.0	0	.0	0	.0	76	100.0	76	100.0	0	.0	0	.0	76
LD UNIVERSITY															
TOTAL	0	.0	0	.0	0	.0	252	98.1	252	98.1	0	.0	5	1.9	257
FEMALE	0	.0	0	.0	0	.0	57	100.0	57	100.0	0	.0	0	.0	57
MALE	0	.0	0	.0	0	.0	195	97.5	195	97.5	0	.0	5	2.5	200
RTO RICO	TOTAL (		9 INSTITUTIONS)												
TOTAL	0	.0	0	.0	0	.0	4,110	94.7	4,110	94.7	218	5.0	11	.3	4,339
FEMALE	0	.0	0	.0	0	.0	2,324	94.4	2,324	94.4	133	5.4	4	.2	2,461
MALE	0	.0	0	.0	0	.0	1,786	95.1	1,786	95.1	85	4.5	7	.4	1,878
GIN ISLANDS															
LEGE OF VIRGIN ISLANDS															
TOTAL	0	.0	47	65.3	1	1.4	2	2.8	50	69.4	20	27.8	2	2.8	72
FEMALE	0	.0	29	65.9	0	.0	1	2.3	30	68.2	14	31.8	0	.0	44
MALE	0	.0	18	64.3	1	3.6	1	3.6	20	71.4	6	21.4	2	7.1	28
GIN ISLANDS	TOTAL (		1 INSTITUTIONS)												
TOTAL	0	.0	47	65.3	1	1.4	2	2.8	50	69.4	20	27.8	2	2.8	72
FEMALE	0	.0	29	65.9	0	.0	1	2.3	30	68.2	14	31.8	0	.0	44
MALE	0	.0	18	64.3	1	3.6	1	3.6	20	71.4	6	21.4	2	7.1	28

TABLE 2 - TOTAL GRADUATE ENROLLMENT IN INSTITUTIONS OF HIGHER EDUCATION BY RACE, ETHNICITY AND SEX: INSTITUTION, STATE AND NATION, 1978

	AMERICAN INDIAN ALASKAN NATIVE		BLACK NON-HISPANIC		ASIAN OR PACIFIC ISLANDER		HISPANIC		TOTAL MINORITY		WHITE NON-HISPANIC		NON-RESIDENT ALIEN		TOTAL
	NUMBER	%	NUMBER	%	NUMBER	%	NUMBER	%	NUMBER	%	NUMBER	%	NUMBER	%	NUMBER
OUTLYING AREAS (11 INSTITUTIONS)															
VI TOTAL	0	.0	47	1.0	119	2.6	4,123	88.5	4,289	92.1	356	7.6	13	.3	4,658
VI FEMALE	0	.0	29	1.1	94	3.5	2,336	87.6	2,459	92.2	204	7.6	4	.1	2,667
VI MALE	0	.0	18	.9	25	1.3	1,787	89.8	1,830	91.9	152	7.6	9	.5	1,991
NATION TOTAL (1,139 INSTITUTIONS)															
TOTAL	3,785	.4	61,918	5.8	20,731	1.9	25,178	2.3	111,612	10.4	891,157	82.8	73,381	6.	1,076,150
FEMALE	1,740	.3	37,242	7.5	7,976	1.6	12,282	2.5	59,240	11.9	423,044	84.8	16,817	3.	499,101
MALE	2,045	.4	24,676	4.3	12,755	2.2	12,896	2.2	52,372	9.1	468,113	81.1	56,564	9.8	577,049

TABLE 3 - TOTAL FIRST PROFESSIONAL ENROLLMENT OF INSTITUTIONS OF HIGHER EDUCATION BY RACE, ETHNICITY AND SEX:
INSTITUTION, STATE AND NATION, 1978

	AMERICAN INDIAN ALASKAN NATIVE		BLACK NON-HISPANIC		ASIAN OR PACIFIC ISLANDER		HISPANIC		TOTAL MINORITY		WHITE NON-HISPANIC		NON-RESIDENT ALIEN		TOTAL
	NUMBER	%	NUMBER	%	NUMBER	%	NUMBER	%	NUMBER	%	NUMBER	%	NUMBER	%	NUMBER
ALABAMA															
AUBURN U MAIN CAMPUS															
AL TOTAL	0	.0	0	.0	0	.0	1	.2	1	.2	458	99.8	0	.0	459
AL FEMALE	0	.0	0	.0	0	.0	0	.0	0	.0	114	100.0	0	.0	114
AL MALE	0	.0	0	.0	0	.0	1	.3	1	.3	344	99.7	0	.0	345
SAMFORD UNIVERSITY															
AL TOTAL	0	.0	13	1.7	0	.0	3	.4	16	2.0	769	97.8	1	.1	786
AL FEMALE	0	.0	5	4.0	0	.0	1	.8	6	4.8	119	95.2	0	.0	125
AL MALE	0	.0	8	1.2	0	.0	2	.3	10	1.5	650	98.3	1	.2	661
TUSKEGEE INSTITUTE															
AL TOTAL	0	.0	103	52.8	8	4.1	0	.0	111	56.9	67	34.4	17	8.7	195
AL FEMALE	0	.0	50	61.7	2	2.5	0	.0	52	64.2	28	34.6	1	1.2	81
AL MALE	0	.0	53	46.5	6	5.3	0	.0	59	51.8	39	34.2	16	14.0	114
UNIVERSITY OF ALABAMA															
AL TOTAL	0	.0	15	2.6	0	.0	0	.0	15	2.6	562	97.1	2	.3	579
AL FEMALE	0	.0	5	4.0	0	.0	0	.0	5	4.0	119	94.4	2	1.6	126
AL MALE	0	.0	10	2.2	0	.0	0	.0	10	2.2	443	97.8	0	.0	453
U ALABAMA IN BIRMINGHAM															
AL TOTAL	1	.1	56	5.2	8	.7	0	.0	65	6.1	1,006	93.9	0	.0	1,071
AL FEMALE	0	.0	21	10.5	4	2.0	0	.0	25	12.5	175	87.5	0	.0	200
AL MALE	1	.1	35	4.0	4	.5	0	.0	40	4.6	831	95.4	0	.0	871
U ALABAMA IN HUNTSVILLE															
AL TOTAL	0	.0	3	4.7	0	.0	0	.0	3	4.7	61	95.3	0	.0	64
AL FEMALE	0	.0	2	20.0	0	.0	0	.0	2	20.0	8	80.0	0	.0	10
AL MALE	0	.0	1	1.9	0	.0	0	.0	1	1.9	53	98.1	0	.0	54
U OF SOUTH ALABAMA															
AL TOTAL	0	.0	6	2.3	6	2.3	2	.8	14	5.4	241	93.8	2	.8	257
AL FEMALE	0	.0	2	4.5	2	4.5	1	2.3	5	11.4	38	86.4	1	2.3	44
AL MALE	0	.0	4	1.9	4	1.9	1	.5	9	4.2	203	95.3	1	.5	213
ALABAMA TOTAL (7 INSTITUTIONS)															
AL TOTAL	1	.0	196	5.7	22	.6	6	.2	225	6.6	3,164	92.8	22	.6	3,411
AL FEMALE	0	.0	85	12.1	8	1.1	2	.3	95	13.6	601	85.9	4	.6	700
AL MALE	1	.0	111	4.1	14	.5	4	.1	130	4.8	2,563	94.5	18	.7	2,711
ARIZONA															
ARIZONA STATE UNIVERSITY															
AZ TOTAL	2	.5	1	.2	1	.2	7	1.7	11	2.6	407	97.1	1	.2	419
AZ FEMALE	0	.0	0	.0	1	.6	3	1.9	4	2.5	154	97.5	0	.0	158
AZ MALE	2	.8	1	.4	0	.0	4	1.5	7	2.7	253	96.9	1	.4	261
UNIVERSITY OF ARIZONA															
AZ TOTAL	2	.3	0	.0	3	.4	18	2.3	23	3.0	744	96.6	3	.4	770
AZ FEMALE	1	.5	0	.0	1	.5	5	2.4	7	3.3	204	96.2	1	.5	212
AZ MALE	1	.2	0	.0	2	.4	13	2.3	16	2.9	540	96.8	2	.4	558
ARIZONA TOTAL (2 INSTITUTIONS)															
AZ TOTAL	4	.3	1	.1	4	.3	25	2.1	34	2.9	1,151	96.8	4	.3	1,189
AZ FEMALE	1	.3	0	.0	2	.5	8	2.2	11	3.0	358	96.8	1	.3	370
AZ MALE	3	.4	1	.1	2	.2	17	2.1	23	2.8	793	96.8	3	.4	819
ARKANSAS															
HARDING GRAD SCH RELIGION															
AR TOTAL	0	.0	4	3.0	0	.0	0	.0	4	3.0	127	94.1	4	3.0	135
AR FEMALE	0	.0	0	.0	0	.0	0	.0	0	.0	0	.0	0	.0	0
AR MALE	0	.0	4	3.0	0	.0	0	.0	4	3.0	127	94.1	4	3.0	135
U OF ARKANSAS MAIN CAMPUS															
AR TOTAL	4	.7	12	2.2	1	.2	2	.4	19	3.5	523	96.5	0	.0	542
AR FEMALE	0	.0	2	2.1	0	.0	1	1.1	3	3.2	92	96.8	0	.0	95
AR MALE	4	.9	10	2.2	1	.2	1	.2	16	3.6	431	96.4	0	.0	447
U OF ARK AT LITTLE ROCK															
AR TOTAL	0	.0	22	6.8	2	.6	2	.6	26	8.0	298	92.0	0	.0	324
AR FEMALE	0	.0	8	7.5	1	.9	0	.0	9	8.4	98	91.6	0	.0	107
AR MALE	0	.0	14	6.5	1	.5	2	.9	17	7.8	200	92.2	0	.0	217
U OF ARK MEDL SCI CAMPUS															
AR TOTAL	2	.4	29	5.6	11	2.1	1	.2	43	8.2	479	91.8	0	.0	522
AR FEMALE	1	.9	10	9.4	2	1.9	1	.9	14	13.7	92	86.8	0	.0	106
AR MALE	1	.2	19	4.6	9	2.2	0	.0	29	7.0	387	93.0	0	.0	416
ARKANSAS TOTAL (4 INSTITUTIONS)															
AR TOTAL	6	.4	67	4.4	14	.9	5	.3	92	6.0	1,427	93.7		.3	1,523
AR FEMALE	1	.3	20	6.5	3	1.0	2	.6	26	8.4	282	91.6	0	.0	308
AR MALE	5	.4	47	3.9	11	.9	3	.2	66	5.4	1,145	94.2	4	.3	1,215
CALIFORNIA															
AMER BAPT SEM OF WEST															
CA TOTAL	0	.0	3	7.0	2	4.7	0	.0	5	11.6	37	86.0	1	2.3	43
CA FEMALE	0	.0	1	7.1	2	14.3	0	.0	3	21.4	11	78.6	0	.0	14
CA MALE	0	.0	2	6.9	0	.0	0	.0	2	6.9	26	89.7	1	3.4	29
ARMSTRONG COLLEGE															
CA TOTAL	0	.0	12	16.9	3	4.2	1	1.4	16	22.5	55	77.5	0	.0	71
CA FEMALE	0	.0	5	23.8	2	9.5	0	.0	7	33.3	14	66.7	0	.0	21
CA MALE	0	.0	7	14.0	1	2.0	1	2.0	9	18.0	41	82.0	0	.0	50
CAL COLLEGE PODIATRIC MED															
CA TOTAL	2	.5	4	1.1	28	7.5	5	1.3	39	10.4	329	87.7	7	1.9	375
CA FEMALE	0	.0	1	2.4	6	14.3	0	.0	7	16.7	35	83.3	0	.0	42
CA MALE	2	.6	3	.9	22	6.6	5	1.5	32	9.6	294	88.3	7	2.1	333
CAL WESTERN SCHOOL OF LAW															
CA TOTAL	0	.0	11	1.6	20	2.9	16	2.3	47	6.9	635	92.7	3	.4	685
CA FEMALE	0	.0	4	2.5	8	5.1	8	5.1	20	12.7	138	87.3	0	.0	158
CA MALE	0	.0	7	1.3	12	2.3	8	1.5	27	5.1	497	94.3	3	.6	527

TABLE 3 - TOTAL FIRST PROFESSIONAL ENROLLMENT OF INSTITUTIONS OF HIGHER EDUCATION BY RACE, ETHNICITY AND SEX:
           INSTITUTION, STATE AND NATION, 1978

	AMERICAN INDIAN ALASKAN NATIVE		BLACK NON-HISPANIC		ASIAN OR PACIFIC ISLANDER		HISPANIC		TOTAL MINORITY		WHITE NON-HISPANIC		NON-RESIDENT ALIEN	
	NUMBER	%	NUMBER	%	NUMBER	%	NUMBER	%	NUMBER	%	NUMBER	%	NUMBER	%
CALIFORNIA CONTINUED														
CHURCH DIV SCH OF PACIFIC														
CA TOTAL	1	1.3	1	1.3	0	.0			3	4.0	70	93.3	2	2.7
CA FEMALE	0	.0	1	3.2	0	.0	0	.0	1	3.2	29	93.5	1	3.2
CA MALE	1	2.3	0	.0	1	2.3	0	.0	2	4.5	41	93.2	1	2.3
COLLEGE OSTEO MED PACIFIC														
CA TOTAL	0	.0	0	.0	2	5.6	0	.0	2	5.6	34	94.4	0	.0
CA FEMALE	0	.0	0	.0	0	.0	0	.0	0	.0	4	100.0	0	.0
CA MALE	0	.0	0	.0	2	6.3	0	.0	2	6.3	30	93.8	0	.0
DOMINICAN SCH PHIL & THEO														
CA TOTAL	0	.0	1	2.6	0	.0	2	5.1	3	7.7	35	89.7	1	2.6
CA FEMALE	0	.0	0	.0	0	.0	0	.0	0	.0	4	100.0	0	.0
CA MALE	0	.0	1	2.9	0	.0	2	5.7	3	8.6	31	88.6	1	2.9
FRANCISCAN SCH THEOLOGY														
CA TOTAL	0	.0	0	.0	1	2.4	7	17.1	8	19.5	32	78.0	1	2.4
CA FEMALE	0	.0	0	.0	0	.0	0	.0	0	.0	0	.0	0	.0
CA MALE	0	.0	0	.0	1	2.4	7	17.1	8	19.5	32	78.0	1	2.4
FULLER THEOLOGICAL SEM														
CA TOTAL	2	.2	57	4.8	50	4.2	39	3.3	148	12.4	1,006	84.3	39	3.3
CA FEMALE	0	.0	7	3.2	10	4.5	3	1.4	20	9.1	199	90.5	1	.5
CA MALE	2	.2	50	5.1	40	4.1	36	3.7	128	13.2	807	82.9	38	3.9
GOLDEN GATE UNIVERSITY														
CA TOTAL	1	.1	29	3.2	29	3.2	15	1.7	74	8.2	797	88.5	30	3.3
CA FEMALE	0	.0	8	2.2	13	3.5	8	2.2	29	7.8	334	89.8	9	2.4
CA MALE	1	.2	21	4.0	16	3.0	7	1.3	45	8.5	463	87.5	21	4.0
GRADUATE THEOL UNION														
CA TOTAL	0	.0	0	.0	3	3.7	0	.0	3	3.7	64	79.0	14	17.3
CA FEMALE	0	.0	0	.0	2	6.3	0	.0	2	6.3	27	84.4	3	9.4
CA MALE	0	.0	0	.0	1	2.0	0	.0	1	2.0	37	75.5	11	22.4
HUMPHREYS COLLEGE														
CA TOTAL	2	1.6	2	1.6	3	2.5	7	5.7	14	11.5	108	88.5	0	.0
CA FEMALE	1	3.6	0	.0	2	7.1	1	3.6	4	14.3	24	85.7	0	.0
CA MALE	1	1.1	2	2.1	1	1.1	6	6.4	10	10.6	84	89.4	0	.0
JESUIT SCHOOL OF THEOLOGY														
CA TOTAL	0	.0	2	1.9	1	.9	4	3.7	7	6.5	99	92.5	1	.9
CA FEMALE	0	.0	0	.0	0	.0	0	.0	0	.0	14	100.0	0	.0
CA MALE	0	.0	2	2.2	1	1.1	4	4.3	7	7.5	85	91.4	1	1.1
JOHN F KENNEDY UNIVERSITY														
CA TOTAL	1	.6	5	3.0	3	1.8	0	.0	9	5.3	160	94.7	0	.0
CA FEMALE	0	.0	1	1.6	1	1.6	0	.0	2	3.2	60	96.8	0	.0
CA MALE	1	.9	4	3.7	2	1.9	0	.0	7	6.5	100	93.5	0	.0
LINCOLN UNIVERSITY														
CA TOTAL	0	.0	17	4.6	7	1.9	5	1.4	29	7.9	332	90.0	8	2.2
CA FEMALE	0	.0	6	5.3	1	.9	4	3.5	11	9.7	101	89.4	1	.9
CA MALE	0	.0	11	4.3	6	2.3	1	.4	18	7.0	231	90.2	7	2.7
LOMA LINDA UNIVERSITY														
CA TOTAL	1	.1	28	3.1	81	9.0	16	1.8	126	14.0	701	73.1	70	7.8
CA FEMALE	1	.6	10	6.1	23	13.9	2	1.2	36	21.8	113	68.5	16	9.7
CA MALE	0	.0	18	2.5	58	7.9	14	1.9	90	12.3	588	80.3	54	7.4
LOS ANG C OF CHIROPRACTIC														
CA TOTAL	12	1.7	11	1.6	25	3.6	17	2.5	65	9.4	612	88.8	12	1.7
CA FEMALE	5	4.8	3	2.9	7	6.7	4	3.8	19	18.1	82	78.1	4	3.8
CA MALE	7	1.2	8	1.4	18	3.1	13	2.2	46	7.9	530	90.8	8	1.4
LOYOLA MARYMOUNT U														
CA TOTAL	10	.8	32	2.6	32	2.6	38	3.1	112	9.1	1,115	90.9	0	.0
CA FEMALE	3	.6	19	4.0	11	2.3	13	2.8	46	9.8	424	90.2	0	.0
CA MALE	7	.9	13	1.7	21	2.8	25	3.3	66	8.7	691	91.3	0	.0
MENNONITE BRTHREN BIB SEM														
CA TOTAL	0	.0	0	.0	1	2.2	2	4.4	3	6.7	34	75.6	8	17.8
CA FEMALE	0	.0	0	.0	0	.0	0	.0	0	.0	0	.0	0	.0
CA MALE	0	.0	0	.0	1	2.2	2	4.4	3	6.7	34	75.6	8	17.8
NEW COLLEGE OF CALIFORNIA														
CA TOTAL	1	.6	16	8.8	5	2.8	8	4.4	30	16.6	151	83.4	0	.0
CA FEMALE	0	.0	5	6.4	2	2.6	3	3.8	10	12.8	68	87.2	0	.0
CA MALE	1	1.0	11	10.7	3	2.9	5	4.9	20	19.4	83	80.6	0	.0
NORTHROP UNIVERSITY														
CA TOTAL	0	.0	0	.0	0	.0	0	.0	0	.0	169	100.0	0	.0
CA FEMALE	0	.0	0	.0	0	.0	0	.0	0	.0	5	100.0	0	.0
CA MALE	0	.0	0	.0	0	.0	0	.0	0	.0	164	100.0	0	.0
PACIFIC LUTH THEOL SEM														
CA TOTAL	0	.0	3	2.4	1	.8	1	.8	5	4.0	117	94.4	2	1.6
CA FEMALE	0	.0	2	5.4	0	.0	0	.0	2	5.4	35	94.6	0	.0
CA MALE	0	.0	1	1.1	1	1.1	1	1.1	3	3.4	82	94.3	2	2.3
PACIFIC SCH OF RELIGION														
CA TOTAL	3	2.4	6	4.9	7	5.7	0	.0	16	13.0	104	84.6	3	2.4
CA FEMALE	2	3.8	0	.0	3	5.8	0	.0	5	9.6	45	86.5	2	3.8
CA MALE	1	1.4	6	8.5	4	5.6	0	.0	11	15.5	59	83.1	1	1.4
PASADENA COLLEGE CHIRO														
CA TOTAL	0	.0	2	1.0	6	3.1	6	3.1	14	7.3	177	91.7	2	1.0
CA FEMALE	0	.0	0	.0	3	7.0	0	.0	3	7.0	40	93.0	0	.0
CA MALE	0	.0	2	1.3	3	2.0	6	4.0	11	7.3	137	91.3	2	1.3
PEPPERDINE UNIVERSITY														
CA TOTAL	0	.0	3	.5	3	.5	1	.2	7	1.3	550	98.2	3	.5
CA FEMALE	0	.0	2	2.1	2	2.1	0	.0	4	4.2	90	93.8	2	2.1
CA MALE	0	.0	1	.2	1	.2	1	.2	3	.6	460	99.1	1	.2
SAN FERNANDO VALLEY C LAW														
CA TOTAL	1	.2	7	1.6	5	1.1	7	1.6	20	4.5	424	95.1	2	.4
CA FEMALE	0	.0	1	.9	1	.9	4	3.5	6	5.2	109	94.8	0	.0
CA MALE	1	.3	6	1.8	4	1.2	3	.9	14	4.2	315	95.2	2	.6
SAN FRANCISCO THEOL SEM														
CA TOTAL	3	1.8	8	4.8	2	2.4	2	1.2	17	10.2	145	87.3	4	2.4
CA FEMALE	1	1.3	3	3.9	3	3.9	0	.0	7	9.2	65	85.5	4	5.3
CA MALE	2	2.2	5	5.6	1	1.1	2	2.2	10	11.1	80	88.9	0	.0

TOTAL FIRST PROFESSIONAL ENROLLMENT OF INSTITUTIONS OF HIGHER EDUCATION BY RACE, ETHNICITY AND SEX: INSTITUTION, STATE AND NATION, 1978

	AMERICAN INDIAN ALASKAN NATIVE		BLACK NON-HISPANIC		ASIAN OR PACIFIC ISLANDER		HISPANIC		TOTAL MINORITY		WHITE NON-HISPANIC		NON-RESIDENT ALIEN		TOTAL
	NUMBER	%	NUMBER	%	NUMBER	%	NUMBER	%	NUMBER	%	NUMBER	%	NUMBER	%	NUMBER
ALIFORNIA CONTINUED															
CH OF THEO AT CLAREMONT															
A TOTAL	0	.0	7	3.6	18	9.2	4	2.0	29	14.8	146	74.5	21	10.7	196
A FEMALE	0	.0	2	3.8	0	.0	0	.0	2	3.8	47	90.4	3	5.8	52
A MALE	0	.0	5	3.5	18	12.5	4	2.8	27	18.8	99	68.8	18	12.5	144
THN CAL C OF OPTOMETRY															
A TOTAL	2	.5	2	.5	33	8.5	13	3.4	50	12.9	336	86.8	1	.3	387
A FEMALE	0	.0	0	.0	11	17.7	1	1.6	12	19.4	50	80.6	0	.0	62
A MALE	2	.6	2	.6	22	6.8	12	3.7	38	11.7	286	88.0	1	.3	325
THWSTN U SCHOOL OF LAW															
A TOTAL	3	.2	29	1.6	35	2.0	47	2.7	114	6.5	1,641	93.2	5	.3	1,760
A FEMALE	1	.2	13	2.5	10	1.9	19	3.7	43	8.3	475	91.3	2	.4	520
A MALE	2	.2	16	1.3	25	2.0	28	2.3	71	5.7	1,166	94.0	3	.2	1,240
TANFORD UNIVERSITY															
A TOTAL	13	1.2	48	4.3	34	3.0	59	5.2	154	13.7	860	76.5	110	9.8	1,124
A FEMALE	4	1.4	23	8.0	13	4.5	17	5.9	57	19.9	203	71.0	26	9.1	286
A MALE	9	1.1	25	3.0	21	2.5	42	5.0	97	11.6	657	78.4	84	10.0	838
TARR KNG SCH FOR MINSTRY															
A TOTAL	0	.0	0	.0	0	.0	0	.0	0	.0	41	97.6	1	2.4	42
A FEMALE	0	.0	0	.0	0	.0	0	.0	0	.0	19	100.0	0	.0	19
A MALE	0	.0	0	.0	0	.0	0	.0	0	.0	22	95.7	1	4.3	23
OF CAL-BERKELEY															
A TOTAL	3	.4	78	9.3	45	5.3	77	9.1	203	24.1	627	74.5	12	1.4	842
A FEMALE	1	.3	41	13.2	24	7.7	27	8.7	93	29.9	214	68.8	4	1.3	311
A MALE	2	.4	37	7.0	21	4.0	50	9.4	110	20.7	413	77.8	8	1.5	531
OF CAL-DAVIS															
A TOTAL	4	.3	43	3.3	101	7.7	47	3.6	195	14.8	1,102	83.5	23	1.7	1,320
A FEMALE	1	.2	20	3.9	34	6.6	11	2.1	66	12.8	440	85.6	8	1.6	514
A MALE	3	.4	23	2.9	67	8.3	36	4.5	129	16.0	662	82.1	15	1.9	806
OF CAL HASTINGS C LAW															
A TOTAL	14	.9	82	5.5	125	8.4	96	6.4	317	21.3	1,168	78.4	5	.3	1,490
A FEMALE	7	1.3	42	7.9	45	8.4	35	6.5	129	24.1	404	75.5	2	.4	535
A MALE	7	.7	40	4.2	80	8.4	61	6.4	188	19.7	764	80.0	3	.3	955
OF CAL-IRVINE															
A TOTAL	0	.0	39	12.5	11	3.5	48	15.4	98	31.4	202	64.7	12	3.8	312
A FEMALE	0	.0	17	26.2	3	4.6	7	10.8	27	41.5	36	55.4	2	3.1	65
A MALE	0	.0	22	8.9	8	3.2	41	16.6	71	28.7	166	67.2	10	4.0	247
OF CAL-LOS ANGELES															
A TOTAL	8	.4	161	8.3	162	8.4	198	10.3	529	27.4	1,370	71.0	30	1.6	1,929
A FEMALE	3	.5	75	12.1	48	7.7	53	8.5	179	28.8	433	69.6	10	1.6	622
A MALE	5	.4	86	6.6	114	8.7	145	11.1	350	26.8	937	71.7	20	1.5	1,307
OF CAL-RIVERSIDE															
A TOTAL	0	.0	0	.0	8	22.9	0	.0	8	22.9	27	77.1	0	.0	35
A FEMALE	0	.0	0	.0	3	37.5	0	.0	3	37.5	5	62.5	0	.0	8
A MALE	0	.0	0	.0	5	18.5	0	.0	5	18.5	22	81.5	0	.0	27
OF CAL-SAN DIEGO															
A TOTAL	2	.5	11	2.6	56	13.3	29	6.9	98	23.3	316	75.2	6	1.4	420
A FEMALE	1	1.1	3	3.4	12	13.8	4	4.6	20	23.0	67	77.0	0	.0	87
A MALE	1	.3	8	2.4	44	13.2	25	7.5	78	23.4	249	74.8	6	1.8	333
OF CAL-SAN FRANCISCO															
A TOTAL	5	.3	103	7.0	291	19.8	151	10.3	550	37.4	907	61.7	13	.9	1,470
A FEMALE	0	.0	50	10.0	97	19.3	32	6.4	179	35.7	318	63.3	5	1.0	502
A MALE	5	.5	53	5.5	194	20.0	119	12.3	371	38.3	589	60.8	8	.8	968
NIVERSITY OF JUDAISM															
A TOTAL	0	.0	0	.0	0	.0	0	.0	0	.0	10	100.0	0	.0	10
A FEMALE	0	.0	0	.0	0	.0	0	.0	0	.0	1	100.0	0	.0	1
A MALE	0	.0	0	.0	0	.0	0	.0	0	.0	9	100.0	0	.0	9
NIVERSITY OF LA VERNE															
A TOTAL	0	.0	7	3.7	0	.0	8	4.2	15	7.9	176	92.1	0	.0	191
A FEMALE	0	.0	2	3.6	0	.0	3	5.5	5	9.1	50	90.9	0	.0	55
A MALE	0	.0	5	3.7	0	.0	5	3.7	10	7.4	126	92.6	0	.0	136
NIVERSITY OF THE PACIFIC															
A TOTAL	6	.3	31	1.7	99	5.6	35	2.0	171	9.6	1,601	90.0	6	.3	1,778
A FEMALE	1	.3	10	2.6	17	4.4	6	1.5	34	8.8	353	91.0	1	.3	388
A MALE	5	.4	21	1.5	82	5.9	29	2.1	137	9.9	1,248	89.8	5	.4	1,390
NIVERSITY OF SAN DIEGO															
A TOTAL	2	.2	11	1.1	16	1.6	24	2.4	53	5.3	926	93.3	13	1.3	992
A FEMALE	0	.0	4	1.4	5	1.7	6	2.0	15	5.1	274	93.5	4	1.4	293
A MALE	2	.3	7	1.0	11	1.6	18	2.6	38	5.4	652	93.3	9	1.3	699
OF SAN FRANCISCO															
A TOTAL	5	.7	30	4.0	48	6.4	45	6.0	128	17.0	622	82.8	1	.1	751
A FEMALE	2	.7	16	5.4	18	6.1	18	6.1	54	18.2	243	81.8	0	.0	297
A MALE	3	.7	14	3.1	30	6.6	27	5.9	74	16.3	379	83.5	1	.2	454
NIVERSITY OF SANTA CLARA															
A TOTAL	0	.0	24	2.6	76	8.3	45	4.9	145	15.7	767	83.3	9	1.0	921
A FEMALE	0	.0	6	1.8	27	8.0	15	4.5	48	14.2	289	85.8	0	.0	337
A MALE	0	.0	18	3.1	49	8.4	30	5.1	97	16.6	478	81.8	9	1.5	584
OF SOUTHERN CALIFORNIA															
A TOTAL	14	.6	54	2.5	366	16.6	145	6.6	579	26.3	1,579	71.8	41	1.9	2,199
A FEMALE	4	.7	28	5.0	117	20.9	25	4.5	174	31.0	372	66.3	15	2.7	561
A MALE	10	.6	26	1.6	249	15.2	120	7.3	405	24.7	1,207	73.7	26	1.6	1,638
OF WEST LOS ANGELES															
A TOTAL	11	1.6	115	17.1	21	3.1	42	6.2	189	28.1	483	71.8	1	.1	673
A FEMALE	6	2.4	51	20.2	5	2.0	17	6.7	79	31.3	173	68.7	0	.0	252
A MALE	5	1.2	64	15.2	16	3.8	25	5.9	110	26.1	310	73.6	1	.2	421
STN ST U C LAW ORANGE CO															
A TOTAL	21	1.3	63	4.0	41	2.6	85	5.4	210	13.2	1,369	86.4	6	.4	1,585
A FEMALE	4	1.1	15	4.0	6	1.6	15	4.0	40	10.7	332	89.0	1	.3	373
A MALE	17	1.4	48	4.0	35	2.9	70	5.8	170	14.0	1,037	85.6	5	.4	1,212
STN ST U C LAW SAN DIEGO															
A TOTAL	14	1.6	40	4.6	9	1.0	53	6.0	116	13.2	759	86.5	2	.2	877
A FEMALE	5	2.1	16	6.6	4	1.7	4	1.7	29	12.0	211	87.6	1	.4	241
A MALE	9	1.4	24	3.8	5	.8	49	7.7	87	13.7	548	86.2	1	.2	636

TABLE 3 - TOTAL FIRST PROFESSIONAL ENROLLMENT OF INSTITUTIONS OF HIGHER EDUCATION BY RACE, ETHNICITY AND SEX: INSTITUTION, STATE AND NATION, 1978

	AMERICAN INDIAN ALASKAN NATIVE		BLACK NON-HISPANIC		ASIAN OR PACIFIC ISLANDER		HISPANIC		TOTAL MINORITY		WHITE NON-HISPANIC		NON-RESIDENT ALIEN		T
	NUMBER	%	NUMBER	%	NUMBER	%	NUMBER	%	NUMBER	%	NUMBER	%	NUMBER	%	N
CALIFORNIA CONTINUED															
WHITTIER COLLEGE															
CA TOTAL	0	.0	12	2.7	7	1.6	8	1.8	27	6.1	408	91.9	9	2.0	
CA FEMALE	0	.0	8	5.0	4	2.5	2	1.3	14	8.8	141	88.7	4	2.5	
CA MALE	0	.0	4	1.4	3	1.1	6	2.1	13	4.6	267	93.7	5	1.8	
CALIFORNIA TOTAL (51 INSTITUTIONS)															
CA TOTAL	167	.5	1,250	4.0	1,925	6.2	1,458	4.7	4,800	15.5	25,535	82.7	540	1.7	3
CA FEMALE	53	.6	521	5.9	605	6.8	367	4.1	1,546	17.4	7,220	81.2	131	1.5	(
CA MALE	114	.5	729	3.3	1,320	6.0	1,091	5.0	3,254	14.8	18,315	83.3	409	1.9	2.
COLORADO															
COLORADO STATE UNIVERSITY															
CO TOTAL	1	.2	3	.7	9	2.0	2	.4	15	3.3	444	96.5	1	.2	
CO FEMALE	0	.0	3	2.0	3	2.0	1	.7	7	4.6	144	95.4	0	.0	
CO MALE	1	.3	0	.0	6	1.9	1	.3	8	2.6	300	97.1	1	.3	
CONS BAPTIST THEOL SEM															
CO TOTAL	0	.0	2	.8	0	.0	2	.8	4	1.6	249	96.9	4	1.6	
CO FEMALE	0	.0	0	.0	0	.0	0	.0	0	.0	5	100.0	0	.0	
CO MALE	0	.0	2	.8	0	.0	2	.8	4	1.6	244	96.8	4	1.6	
ILIFF SCHOOL OF THEOLOGY															
CO TOTAL	0	.0	5	2.4	2	1.0	0	.0	7	3.4	199	96.1	1	.5	
CO FEMALE	0	.0	2	2.6	0	.0	0	.0	2	2.6	76	97.4	0	.0	
CO MALE	0	.0	3	2.3	2	1.6	0	.0	5	3.9	123	95.3	1	.8	
SAINT THOMAS SEMINARY															
CO TOTAL	0	.0	1	1.5	1	1.5	5	7.6	7	10.6	57	86.4	2	3.0	
CO FEMALE	0	.0	0	.0	0	.0	0	.0	0	.0	0	.0	0	.0	
CO MALE	0	.0	1	1.5	1	1.5	5	7.6	7	10.6	57	86.4	2	3.0	
U OF COLORADO AT BOULDER															
CO TOTAL	1	.2	10	2.2	1	.2	31	6.9	43	9.5	408	90.5	0	.0	
CO FEMALE	0	.0	4	2.5	0	.0	7	4.5	11	7.0	146	93.0	0	.0	
CO MALE	1	.3	6	2.0	1	.3	24	8.2	32	10.9	262	89.1	0	.0	
U OF COLO AT DENVER															
CO TOTAL	0	.0	0	.0	0	.0	0	.0	0	.0	3	100.0	0	.0	
CO FEMALE	0	.0	0	.0	0	.0	0	.0	0	.0	1	100.0	0	.0	
CO MALE	0	.0	0	.0	0	.0	0	.0	0	.0	2	100.0	0	.0	
U OF COLO MEDICAL CENTER															
CO TOTAL	10	1.6	21	3.4	23	3.7	57	9.1	111	17.7	515	82.3	0	.0	
CO FEMALE	4	2.7	7	4.7	6	4.0	17	11.3	34	22.7	116	77.3	0	.0	
CO MALE	6	1.3	14	2.9	17	3.6	40	8.4	77	16.2	399	83.8	0	.0	
UNIVERSITY OF DENVER															
CO TOTAL	14	1.6	21	2.4	3	.3	23	2.6	61	6.9	817	92.7	3	.3	
CO FEMALE	4	1.2	5	1.5	2	.6	7	2.0	18	5.3	323	94.4	1	.3	
CO MALE	10	1.9	16	3.0	1	.2	16	3.0	43	8.0	494	91.7	2	.4	
YESH TORAS CHAIM TALMUD															
CO TOTAL	0	.0	0	.0	0	.0	0	.0	0	.0	3	100.0	0	.0	
CO FEMALE	0	.0	0	.0	0	.0	0	.0	0	.0	0	.0	0	.0	
CO MALE	0	.0	0	.0	0	.0	0	.0	0	.0	3	100.0	0	.0	
COLORADO TOTAL (9 INSTITUTIONS)															
CO TOTAL	26	.9	63	2.1	39	1.3	120	4.1	248	8.4	2,695	91.2	11	.4	
CO FEMALE	8	.9	21	2.4	11	1.2	32	3.6	72	8.1	811	91.7	1	.1	
CO MALE	18	.9	42	2.0	28	1.4	88	4.3	176	8.5	1,884	91.0	10	.5	
CONNECTICUT															
HOLY APOSTLES COLLEGE															
CT TOTAL	0	.0	0	.0	0	.0	0	.0	0	.0	2	100.0	0	.0	
CT FEMALE	0	.0	0	.0	0	.0	0	.0	0	.0	0	.0	0	.0	
CT MALE	0	.0	0	.0	0	.0	0	.0	0	.0	2	100.0	0	.0	
UNIVERSITY OF BRIDGEPORT															
CT TOTAL	0	.0	1	.2	0	.0	4	.9	5	1.1	430	98.9	0	.0	
CT FEMALE	0	.0	0	.0	0	.0	1	1.3	1	1.3	76	98.7	0	.0	
CT MALE	0	.0	1	.3	0	.0	3	.8	4	1.1	354	98.9	0	.0	
UNIVERSITY OF CONNECTICUT															
CT TOTAL	1	.2	22	3.4	3	.5	11	1.7	37	5.8	605	94.1	1	.2	
CT FEMALE	1	.4	9	3.5	1	.4	3	1.2	14	5.4	244	94.2	1	.4	
CT MALE	0	.0	13	3.4	2	.5	8	2.1	23	6.0	361	94.0	0	.0	
U OF CONN HEALTH CENTER															
CT TOTAL	0	.0	13	2.5	6	1.1	5	.9	24	4.6	502	95.3	1	.2	
CT FEMALE	0	.0	5	4.0	0	.0	2	1.6	7	5.6	117	94.4	0	.0	
CT MALE	0	.0	8	2.0	6	1.5	3	.7	17	4.2	385	95.5	1	.2	
YALE UNIVERSITY															
CT TOTAL	3	.2	95	7.2	23	1.7	69	5.2	190	14.3	1,098	82.7	40	3.0	
CT FEMALE	2	.5	36	8.5	10	2.3	22	5.2	70	16.4	351	82.4	5	1.2	
CT MALE	1	.1	59	6.5	13	1.4	47	5.2	120	13.3	747	82.8	35	3.9	
CONNECTICUT TOTAL (5 INSTITUTIONS)															
CT TOTAL	4	.1	131	4.5	32	1.1	89	3.0	256	8.7	2,637	89.8	42	1.4	
CT FEMALE	3	.3	50	5.6	11	1.2	28	3.2	92	10.4	788	88.9	6	.7	
CT MALE	1	.0	81	4.0	21	1.0	61	3.0	164	8.0	1,849	90.2	36	1.8	
DISTRICT OF COLUMBIA															
AMERICAN UNIVERSITY															
DC TOTAL	0	.0	37	4.8	0	.0	6	.8	43	5.5	730	94.2	2	.3	
DC FEMALE	0	.0	20	5.9	0	.0	1	.3	21	6.2	316	93.5	1	.3	
DC MALE	0	.0	17	3.9	0	.0	5	1.1	22	5.0	414	94.7	1	.2	
CATHOLIC U OF AMERICA															
DC TOTAL	1	.1	55	7.1	3	.4	24	3.1	83	10.6	686	87.9	11	1.4	
DC FEMALE	0	.0	34	9.4	0	.0	10	2.8	44	12.2	312	86.2	6	1.7	
DC MALE	1	.2	21	5.0	3	.7	14	3.3	39	9.3	374	89.5	5	1.2	

	AMERICAN INDIAN ALASKAN NATIVE		BLACK NON-HISPANIC		ASIAN OR PACIFIC ISLANDER		HISPANIC		TOTAL MINORITY		WHITE NON-HISPANIC		NON-RESIDENT ALIEN		TOTAL
	NUMBER	%	NUMBER	%	NUMBER	%	NUMBER	%	NUMBER	%	NUMBER	%	NUMBER	%	NUMBER

RICT OF COLUMBIA CONTINUED

NICAN HOUSE STUDIES
TOTAL	0	.0	2	5.6	0	.0	0	.0	2	5.6	34	94.4	0	.0	36
EMALE	0	.0	0	.0	0	.0	0	.0	0	.0	0	.0	0	.0	0
MALE	0	.0	2	5.6	0	.0	0	.0	2	5.6	34	94.4	0	.0	36

GETOWN UNIVERSITY
TOTAL	6	.2	238	6.9	105	.0	117	3.4	466	13.5	2,948	85.3	41	1.2	3,455
EMALE	2	.2	138	13.9	48	.8	40	4.0	228	23.0	750	75.6	14	1.4	992
MALE	4	.2	100	4.1	57	2.3	77	3.1	238	9.7	2,198	89.2	27	1.1	2,463

GE WASH UNIVERSITY
TOTAL	7	.4	108	5.5	27	1.4	44	2.3	186	9.6	1,757	90.3	3	.2	1,946
EMALE	0	.0	64	9.6	8	1.2	11	1.6	83	12.4	587	87.6	0	.0	670
MALE	7	.5	44	3.4	19	1.5	33	2.6	103	8.1	1,170	91.7	3	.2	1,276

RD UNIVERSITY
TOTAL	3	.2	1,113	75.4	16	1 1	14	.9	1,146	77.6	204	13.8	127	.6	1,477
EMALE	1	.2	406	84.6	6	1	4	.8	417	86.9	31	6.5	32	.7	480
MALE	2	.2	707	70.9	10	11.0	10	1.0	729	73.1	173	17.4	95	9.5	997

TE COLLEGE
TOTAL	0	.0	0	.0	0	.0	0	.0	0	.0	32	100.0	0	.0	32
EMALE	0	.0	0	.0	0	.0	0	.0	0	.0	0	.0	0	.0	0
MALE	0	.0	0	.0	0	.0	0	.0	0	.0	32	100.0	0	.0	32

EY THEOLOGICAL SEM
TOTAL	0	.0	21	8.1	1	.4	0	.0	22	8.5	234	90.3	3	1.2	259
EMALE	0	.0	2	2.3	1	1.2	0	.0	3	3.5	82	95.3	1	1.2	86
MALE	0	.0	19	11.0	0	.0	0	.0	19	11.0	152	87.9	2	1.2	173

RICT OF COLUMBIA TOTAL (8 INSTITUTIONS)
TOTAL	17	.2	1,574	18.0	152	1.7	205	2.3	1,948	22.2	6,625	75.6	187	2.1	8,760
EMALE	3	.1	664	22.7	63	2.2	66	2.3	796	27.2	2,078	71.0	54	1.8	2,928
MALE	14	.2	910	15.6	89	1.5	139	2.4	1,152	19.8	4,547	78.0	133	2.3	5,832

IDA

UNIVERSITY
TOTAL	0	.0	13	2.3	2	.4	35	6.3	50	9.0	495	88.9	12	2.2	557
EMALE	0	.0	2	1.1	0	.0	4	2.2	6	3.3	172	94.5	4	2.2	182
MALE	0	.0	11	2.9	2	.5	31	8.3	44	11.7	323	86.1	8	2.1	375

IDA STATE UNIVERSITY
TOTAL	1	.2	20	.7	1	.2	15	2.	37	6.9	498	92.9	1	.2	536
EMALE	0	.0	7	.5	0	.0	5	3.9	12	.7	143	92.3	0	.0	155
MALE	1	.3	13	9.4	1	.3	10	2.8	25	8.6	355	93.2	1	.3	381

ERSITY OF FLORIDA
TOTAL	4	.2	110	6.0	8	.4	68	.7	190	10.4	1,630	89.5	1	.1	1,821
EMALE	0	.0	27	5.8	2	.4	19	.1	48	10.3	419	89.5	1	.2	468
MALE	4	.3	83	6.1	6	.4	49	9.6	142	10.5	1,211	89.5	0	.0	1,353

SOUTH FLORIDA
TOTAL	1	.3	4	1.4	0	.0	21	7.	26	9.0	262	91.0	0	.0	288
EMALE	0	.0	1	1.9	0	.0	1	1.	2	3.8	51	96.2	0	.0	53
MALE	1	.4	3	1.3	0	.0	20	8.9	24	10.2	211	89.8	0	.0	235

SON UNIVERSITY
TOTAL	8	.8	6	.	6	.6	30	3.	50	5.1	938	94.9	0	.0	988
EMALE	2	.7	2	.6	0	.0	6	2	10	3.7	258	96.3	0	.0	268
MALE	6	.8	4	.8	6	.8	24	31.0	40	5.6	680	94.4	0	.0	720

ERSITY OF MIAMI
TOTAL	1	.1	39	2.2	9	.5	136	7.5	185	10.2	1,627	89.8	0	.0	1,812
EMALE	0	.0	11	2.4	2	.4	34	7.4	47	10.2	414	89.8	0	.0	461
MALE	1	.1	28	2.1	7	.5	102	7.5	138	10.2	1,213	89.8	0	.0	1,351

IDA   TOTAL (6 INSTITUTIONS)
TOTAL	15	.2	192	3.2	26	.4	305	5.1	538	9.	5,450	90.8	14	.2	6,002
EMALE	2	.1	50	3.2	4	.3	69	4.3	125	7.	1,457	91.8	5	.3	1,587
MALE	13	.3	142	3.2	22	.5	236	5.3	413	9.0	3,993	90.4	9	.2	4,415

GIA

MBIA THEOLOGICAL SEM
TOTAL	0	.0	1	.6	0	.0	1	.6	2	1.3	155	98.7	0	.0	157
EMALE	0	.0	0	0	0	.0	0	.0	0	.0	23	100.0	0	.0	23
MALE	0	.0	1	.7	0	.0	1	.7	2	1.5	132	98.5	0	.0	134

Y UNIVERSITY
TOTAL	1	.0	62	2.9	12	.6	20	.9	95	4.4	2,037	95.0	12	.6	2,144
EMALE	1	.2	33	6.8	1	.2	4	.8	39	8.0	449	92.0	0	.0	488
MALE	0	.0	29	1.8	11	.7	16	1.0	56	3.4	1,588	95.9	12	.7	1,656

DENOMINATL THEOL CTR
TOTAL	0	.0	272	97.1		.0	0	.0	272	97.1	8	2.9	0	.0	280
EMALE	0	.0	36	92.3	0	.0	0	.0	36	92.3	3	7.7	0	.0	39
MALE	0	.0	236	97.9	0	.0	0	.0	236	97.9	5	2.1	0	.0	241

CHIROPRACTIC COLLEGE
TOTAL	0	.0	9	1.0	0	.0	2	.2	11	1.3	843	96.2	22	2.5	876
EMALE	0	.0	2	1.4	0	.0	0	.0	2	1.4	137	96.5	3	2.1	142
MALE	0	.0	7	1.0	0	.0	2	.3	9	1.2	706	96.2	19	2.6	734

CAL COLLEGE OF GA
TOTAL	2	.2	35	.	4	.4	7	.8	48	5.2	868	94.8	0	.0	916
EMALE	0	.0	10	.	1	.7	1	.7	12	7.9	140	92.1	0	.0	152
MALE	2	.3	25	9.8	3	.4	6	.8	36	9.17	728	95.3	0	.0	764

ER U MAIN CAMPUS
TOTAL	0	.0	12	.	0	.0	3	.8	15	.2	346	95.8	0	.0	361
EMALE	0	.0	4	.	0	.0	1	1.1	5	.4	87	94.6	0	.0	92
MALE	0	.0	8	9.8	0	.0	2	.7	10	5.7	259	96.3	0	.0	269

ERSITY OF GEORGIA
TOTAL	4	.4	37	3.9	3	.3	4	.4	48	5.0	905	94.8	2	.2	955
EMALE	2	.7	18	6.5	2	.7	0	.0	22	7.9	253	91.3	2	.7	277
MALE	2	.3	19	2.8	1	.1	4	.6	26	3.8	652	96.2	0	.0	678

TABLE 3 - TOTAL FIRST PROFESSIONAL ENROLLMENT OF INSTITUTIONS OF HIGHER EDUCATION BY RACE, ETHNICITY AND SEX:
INSTITUTION, STATE AND NATION, 1978

	AMERICAN INDIAN ALASKAN NATIVE		BLACK NON-HISPANIC		ASIAN OR PACIFIC ISLANDER		HISPANIC		TOTAL MINORITY		WHITE NON-HISPANIC		NON-RESIDENT ALIEN	
	NUMBER	%	NUMBER	%	NUMBER	%	NUMBER	%	NUMBER	%	NUMBER	%	NUMBER	%
GEORGIA														
GEORGIA														
GA TOTAL — TOTAL (7 INSTITUTIONS)	7	.1	428	7.5	19	.3	37	.7	491	8.	5,162	90.7	36	.6
GA FEMALE	3	.2	103	8.5	4	.3	6	.5	116	9.	1,092	90.0	5	.4
GA MALE	4	.1	325	7.3	15	.3	31	.7	375	8.8	4,070	90.9	31	.7
HAWAII														
U OF HAWAII AT MANOA														
HI TOTAL	0	.0	0	.0	360	73.5	3	.6	363	74.1	116	23.7	11	2.2
HI FEMALE	0	.0	0	.0	108	66.7	2	1.2	110	67.9	50	30.9	2	1.2
HI MALE	0	.0	0	.0	252	76.8	1	.3	253	77.1	66	20.1	9	2.7
HAWAII														
HI TOTAL — TOTAL (1 INSTITUTIONS)	0	.0	0	.0	360	73.5	3	.6	363	74.1	116	23.7	11	2.2
HI FEMALE	0	.0	0	.0	108	66.7	2	1.2	110	67.9	50	30.9	2	1.2
HI MALE	0	.0	0	.0	252	76.8	1	.3	253	77.1	66	20.1	9	2.7
IDAHO														
UNIVERSITY OF IDAHO														
ID TOTAL	0	.0	1	.4	2	.7		.0	3	1.1	267	98.9	0	.0
ID FEMALE	0	.0	1	2.0	1	2.0	8	.0	2	4.0	48	96.0	0	.0
ID MALE	0	.0	0	.0	1	.5	0	.0	1	.5	219	99.5	0	.0
IDAHO														
ID TOTAL — TOTAL (1 INSTITUTIONS)	0	.0	1	.4	2	.7		.0	3	1.1	267	98.9	0	.0
ID FEMALE	0	.0	1	2.0	1	2.0	8	.0	2	4.0	48	96.0	0	.0
ID MALE	0	.0	0	.0	1	.5	0	.0	1	.5	219	99.5	0	.0
ILLINOIS														
BETHANY THEOLOGICAL SEM														
IL TOTAL	0	.0	2	2.2	0	.0	2	2.2	4	4.5	85	95.5	0	.0
IL FEMALE	0	.0	1	3.6	0	.0	0	.0	1	3.6	27	96.4	0	.0
IL MALE	0	.0	1	1.6	0	.0	2	3.3	3	4.9	58	95.1	0	.0
CATHOLIC THEOL UNION														
IL TOTAL	0	.0	0	.0	1	.7	3	2.0	4	2.6	130	85.5	18	11.8
IL FEMALE	0	.0	0	.0	0	.0	0	.0	0	.0	5	100.0	0	.0
IL MALE	0	.0	0	.0	1	.7	3	2.0	4	2.7	125	85.0	18	12.2
CHGO C OSTEOPATHIC MED														
IL TOTAL	0	.0	5	1.3	0	.0	1	.3	6	1.	373	97.4	4	1.0
IL FEMALE	0	.0	1	1.9	0	.0	0	.0	1	1.	51	98.1	0	.0
IL MALE	0	.0	4	1.2	0	.0	1	.3	5	1.8	322	97.3	4	1.2
CHICAGO THEOLOGICAL SEM														
IL TOTAL	0	.0	11	13.6	0	.0	0	.0	11	13.6	65	80.2	5	6.2
IL FEMALE	0	.0	1	2.8	0	.0	0	.0	1	2.8	33	91.7	2	5.6
IL MALE	0	.0	10	22.2	0	.0	0	.0	10	22.2	32	71.1	3	6.7
DEPAUL UNIVERSITY														
IL TOTAL	2	.2	52	4.3	20	1.6	23	1.9	97	8.0	1,121	92.0	0	.0
IL FEMALE	0	.0	24	6.1	6	1.5	8	2.0	38	9.6	357	90.4	0	.0
IL MALE	2	.2	28	3.4	14	1.7	15	1.8	59	7.2	764	92.8	0	.0
GARRETT-EVANGELCL THEOL														
IL TOTAL	0	.0	28	14.7	2	1.0		.0	30	15.7	160	83.8	1	.5
IL FEMALE	0	.0	5	7.1	0	.0	8	.0	5	7.1	65	92.9	0	.0
IL MALE	0	.0	23	19.0	2	1.7		.0	25	20.7	95	78.5	1	.8
HEBREW THEOL COLLEGE														
IL TOTAL	0	.0	0	.0	0	.0		.0	0		36	100.0	0	.0
IL FEMALE	0	.0	0	.0	0	.0	0	.0	0	.0	18	100.0	0	.0
IL MALE	0	.0	0	.0	0	.0	0	.0	0	10	18	100.0	0	.0
ILL COLLEGE OF OPTOMETRY														
IL TOTAL	0	.0	5	.8	22	3.7	2	.3	29	4.9	562	94.9	1	.2
IL FEMALE	0	.0	4	5.3	6	7.9	0	.0	10	13.2	66	86.8	0	.0
IL MALE	0	.0	1	.2	16	3.1	2	.4	19	3.17	496	96.1	1	.2
ILL COLLEGE PODIATRIC MED														
IL TOTAL	2	.3	23	3.6	4	.6	7	1.1	36	5.7	596	94.3	0	.0
IL FEMALE	0	.0	3	4.9	0	.0	1	1.6	4	6.6	57	93.4	0	.0
IL MALE	2	.4	20	3.5	4	.7	6	1.1	32	5.16	539	94.4	0	.0
ILLINOIS INST TECHNOLOGY														
IL TOTAL	4	.5	26	2.9	6	.7		.7	42	7	836	94.3	9	1.0
IL FEMALE	3	1.0	11	3.5	2	.6		1.0	19	4.11	288	92.9	3	1.0
IL MALE	1	.2	15	2.6	4	.7		.5	23	6.10	548	95.0	6	1.0
JOHN MARSHALL LAW SCHOOL														
IL TOTAL	0	.0	35	2.4	11	.7		.5	53	3.6	1,429	96.4	0	.0
IL FEMALE	0	.0	16	5.4	1	.3		1.3	21	7.0	277	93.0	0	.0
IL MALE	0	.0	19	1.6	10	.8		.3	32	2.17	1,152	97.3	0	.0
LEWIS UNIVERSITY														
IL TOTAL	4	.8	8	1.5	8	1.5	5	1.0	25		489	94.4	4	.8
IL FEMALE	1	.8	1	.8	3	2.4	0	.0	5	.8	118	94.4	2	1.6
IL MALE	3	.8	7	1.8	5	1.3	5	1.3	20	4.8	371	94.4	2	.5
LINCOLN CHRISTIAN COLLEGE														
IL TOTAL	0	.0	0	.0	0	.0	0	.0	0		108	100.0	0	.0
IL FEMALE	0	.0	0	.0	0	.0	0	.0	0		4	100.0	0	.0
IL MALE	0	.0	0	.0	0	.0	0	.0	0	10	104	100.0	0	.0
LOYOLA U OF CHICAGO														
IL TOTAL	4	.2	31	1.8	24	1.4	18	1.1	77		1,601	94.7	13	.8
IL FEMALE	1	.2	17	3.7	6	1.3	5	1.1	29	4.	434	93.5	1	.2
IL MALE	3	.2	14	1.1	18	1.5	13	1.1	48	81.6	1,167	95.1	12	1.0
LUTH SCH THEOLOGY CHICAGO														
IL TOTAL	0	.0	4	2.1	3	1.6	0	.0	7	3.7	180	96.3	0	.0
IL FEMALE	0	.0	2	4.3	1	2.1	0	.0	3	6.4	44	93.6	0	.0
IL MALE	0	.0	2	1.4	2	1.4	0	.0	4	2.9	136	97.1	0	.0

194

ESSIONAL ENROLLMENT OF INSTITUTIONS OF HIGHER EDUCATION BY RACE, ETHNICITY AND SEX:
TE AND NATION, 1978

	BLACK NON-HISPANIC		ASIAN OR PACIFIC ISLANDER		HISPANIC		TOTAL MINORITY		WHITE NON-HISPANIC		NON-RESIDENT ALIEN		TOTAL
	NUMBER	%	NUMBER	%	NUMBER	%	NUMBER	%	NUMBER	%	NUMBER	%	NUMBER
NUED													
	7	5.0	2	1.4	6	4.3	15	10.8	124	89.2	0	.0	139
	2	3.6	0	.0	1	1.8	3	5.5	52	94.5	0	.0	55
	5	6.0	2	2.4	5	6.0	12	14.3	72	85.7	0	.0	84
	11	1.3	6	.7	2	.2	21	2.4	818	93.2	39	4.4	878
	5	4.5	1	.9	0	.0	6	5.4	100	89.3	6	5.4	112
	6	.8	5	.7	2	.3	15	2.0	718	93.7	33	4.3	766
	9	7.3	2	1.6	1	.8	12	9.7	107	86.3	5	4.0	124
	1	4.2	0	.0	0	.0	1	4.2	23	95.8	0	.0	24
	8	8.0	2	2.0	1	1.0	11	11.0	84	84.0	5	5.0	100
	6	4.0	2	1.3	0	.0	8	5.3	136	90.7	6	4.0	150
	2	9.5	0	.0	0	.0	2	9.5	17	81.0	2	9.5	21
	4	3.1	2	1.6	0	.0	6	4.7	119	92.2	4	3.1	129
	81	4.9	54	3.3	15	.9	152	9.2	1,485	90.1	11	.7	1,648
	38	8.7	13	3.0	1	.2	52	12.0	380	87.4	3	.7	435
	43	3.5	41	3.4	14	1.2	100	8.2	1,105	91.1	8	.7	1,213
	35	7.0	15	3.0	16	3.2	67	13.5	430	86.5	0	.0	497
	15	9.2	9	5.5	2	1.2	26	16.0	137	84.0	0	.0	163
	20	6.0	6	1.8	14	4.2	41	12.3	293	87.7	0	.0	334
	1	1.2	0	.0	1	1.2	2	2.4	81	97.6	0	.0	83
	0	.0	0	.0	0	.0	0	.0	0	.0	0	.0	0
	1	1.2	0	.0	1	1.2	2	2.4	81	97.6	0	.0	83
	2	2.8	0	.0	0	.0	2	2.8	69	97.2	0	.0	71
	1	8.3	0	.0	0	.0	1	8.3	11	91.7	0	.0	12
	1	1.7	0	.0	0	.0	1	1.7	58	98.3	0	.0	59
	25	5.3	2	.4	2	.4	29	6.1	436	92.2	8	1.7	473
	7	6.3	0	.0	1	.9	8	7.2	101	91.0	2	1.8	111
	18	5.0	2	.6	1	.3	21	5.8	335	92.5	6	1.7	362
	2	1.4	0	.0	0	.0	2	1.4	146	98.6	0	.0	148
	0	.0	0	.0	0	.0	0	.0	19	100.0	0	.0	19
	2	1.6	0	.0	0	.0	2	1.6	127	98.4	0	.0	129
	0	.0	0	.0	0	.0	0	.0	19	100.0	0	.0	19
	0	.0	0	.0	0	.0	0	.0	0	.0	0	.0	0
	0	.0	0	.0	0	.0	0	.0	19	100.0	0	.0	19
	3	.7	6	1.3	1	.2	10	2.2	421	92.3	25	5.5	456
	0	.0	0	.0	0	.0	0	.0	19	90.5	2	9.5	21
	3	.7	6	1.4	1	.2	10	2.3	402	92.4	23	5.3	435
	28	3.0	22	2.3	15	1.6	65	6.9	867	91.5	16	1.7	948
	12	5.6	6	2.8	2	.9	20	9.3	192	89.3	3	1.4	215
	16	2.2	16	2.2	13	1.8	45	6.1	675	92.1	13	1.8	733
	21	4.9	13	3.1	1	.2	37	8.7	385	90.4	4	.9	426
	11	10.8	2	2.0	1	1.0	15	14.7	85	83.3	2	2.0	102
	10	3.1	11	3.4	0	.0	22	6.8	300	92.6	2	.6	324
	130	6.6	53	2.7	55	2.8	241	12.2	1,723	87.5	6	.3	1,970
	57	15.0	9	2.4	14	3.7	80	21.0	301	79.0	0	.0	381
	73	4.6	44	2.8	41	2.6	161	10.1	1,422	89.5	6	.4	1,589
	28	2.9	2	.2	14	1.4	48	5.0	918	95.0	0	.0	966
	9	3.1	1	.3	1	.3	15	5.2	271	94.8	0	.0	286
	19	2.8	1	.1	13	1.9	33	4.9	647	95.1	0	.0	680
(	31 INSTITUTIONS)												
	619	3.6	280	1.6	203	1.2	1,132	6.6	15,936	92.4	175	1.0	17,243
	246	6.2	66	1.7	44	1.1	366	9.3	3,552	90.0	28	.7	3,946
	373	2.8	214	1.6	159	1.2	766	5.8	12,384	93.1	147	1.1	13,297
	2	1.1	0	.0	0	.0	2	1.1	163	91.6	13	7.3	178
	1	3.7	0	.0	0	.0	1	3.7	24	88.9	2	7.4	27
	1	.7	0	.0	0	.0	1	.7	139	92.1	11	7.3	151
	4	2.7	0	.0	2	1.4	6	4.1	138	94.5	2	1.4	146
	0	.0	0	.0	1	2.0	1	2.0	48	96.0	1	2.0	50
	4	4.2	0	.0	1	1.0	5	5.2	90	93.8	1	1.0	96
	7	1.5	1	.2	4	.9	12	2.6	450	97.4	0	.0	462
	0	.0	0	.0	0	.0	0	.0	0	.0	0	.0	0
	7	1.5	1	.2	4	.9	12	2.6	450	97.4	0	.0	462
	1	1.6	0	.0	0	.0	1	1.6	51	81.0	11	17.5	63
	1	7.1	0	.0	0	.0	1	7.1	12	85.7	1	7.1	14
	0	.0	0	.0	0	.0	0	.0	39	79.6	10	20.4	49
	4	1.2	3	.9	3	.9	11	2.3	318	94.9	6	1.8	335
	0	.0	0	.0	0	.0	0	.0	3	100.0	0	.0	3
	4	1.2	3	.9	3	.9	11	3.3	315	94.9	6	1.8	332

195

TABLE 3 - TOTAL FIRST PROFESSIONAL ENROLLMENT OF INSTITUTIONS OF HIGHER EDUCATION BY RACE, ETHNICITY AND SEX:
INSTITUTION, STATE AND NATION, 1978

	AMERICAN INDIAN ALASKAN NATIVE		BLACK NON-HISPANIC		ASIAN OR PACIFIC ISLANDER		HISPANIC		TOTAL MINORITY		WHITE NON-HISPANIC		NON-RESIDENT ALIEN	
	NUMBER	%	NUMBER	%	NUMBER	%	NUMBER	%	NUMBER	%	NUMBER	%	NUMBER	%
INDIANA CONTINUED														
INDIANA STATE U MAIN CAM														
IN TOTAL	0	.0	0	.0	0	.0	0	.0	0	.0	20	100.0	0	.0
IN FEMALE	0	.0	0	.0	0	.0	0	.0	0	.0	5	100.0	0	.0
IN MALE	0	.0	0	.0	0	.0	0	.0	0	.0	15	100.0	0	.0
INDIANA U BLOOMINGTON														
IN TOTAL	4	.4	48	5.1	8	.8	24	2.5	84	8.9	832	88.1	28	3.0
IN FEMALE	2	.7	24	8.8	2	.7	7	2.6	35	12.8	230	84.2	8	2.9
IN MALE	2	.3	24	3.6	6	.9	17	2.5	49	7.3	602	89.7	20	3.0
IND-PURDUE U INDIANAPOLIS														
IN TOTAL	8	.3	46	1.8	21	.8	7	.3	82	3.2	2,477	95.5	34	1.3
IN FEMALE	2	.4	20	3.6	4	.7	2	.4	28	5.0	519	93.5	8	1.4
IN MALE	6	.3	26	1.3	17	.8	5	.2	54	2.6	1,958	96.1	26	1.3
MENNONITE BIBLICAL SEM														
IN TOTAL	0	.0	0	.0	0	.0	0	.0	0	.0	26	76.5		23.5
IN FEMALE	0	.0	0	.0	0	.0	0	.0	0	.0	6	100.0		.0
IN MALE	0	.0	0	.0	0	.0	0	.0	0	.0	20	71.4	8	28.6
PURDUE U MAIN CAMPUS														
IN TOTAL	0	.0	5	1.7	0	.0	2	.7	7	2.3	296	97.7		.0
IN FEMALE	0	.0	5	5.2	0	.0	1	1.0	6	6.3	90	93.8	0	.0
IN MALE	0	.0	0	.0	0	.0	1	.5	1	.5	206	99.5	0	.0
SNT MEINRAD SCH THEOLOGY														
IN TOTAL	0	.0	0	.0	2	1.3	12	7.5	14	8.8	145	90.6	1	.6
IN FEMALE	0	.0	0	.0	0	.0	0	.0	0	.0	0	.0	0	.0
IN MALE	0	.0	0	.0	2	1.3	12	7.5	14	8.8	145	90.6	1	.6
UNIVERSITY OF NOTRE DAME														
IN TOTAL	4	.7	19	3.4	5	.9	15	2.7	43	7.8	509	92.2		.0
IN FEMALE	0	.0	6	3.9	1	.6	4	2.6	11	7.1	144	92.9	0	.0
IN MALE	4	1.0	13	3.3	4	1.0	11	2.8	32	8.1	365	91.9	0	.0
VALPARAISO UNIVERSITY														
IN TOTAL	2	.7	40	13.6	1	.3	4	1.4	47	15.9	247	83.7	1	.3
IN FEMALE	0	.0	15	20.8	0	.0	0	.0	15	20.8	57	79.2	0	.0
IN MALE	2	.9	25	11.2	1	.4	4	1.8	32	14.3	190	85.2	1	.4
INDIANA TOTAL (13 INSTITUTIONS)														
IN TOTAL	19	.3	176	2.9	41	.7	73	1.2	309	5.1	5,672	93.2	104	1.7
IN FEMALE	4	.3	72	5.7	7	.6	15	1.2	98	7.8	1,138	90.6	20	1.6
IN MALE	15	.3	104	2.2	34	.7	58	1.2	211	4.4	4,534	93.9	84	1.7
IOWA														
AQUINAS INST OF THEOLOGY														
IA TOTAL	0	.0	1	4.3	0	.0	1	4.3	2	8.7	21	91.3		.0
IA FEMALE	0	.0	0	.0	0	.0	0	.0	0	.0	2	100.0	0	.0
IA MALE	0	.0	1	4.8	0	.0	1	4.8	2	9.5	19	90.5	0	.0
COLLEGE OSTEO MED-SURGERY														
IA TOTAL	7	1.3	3	.6	5	.9	5	.9	20	3.8	505	95.5	4	.8
IA FEMALE	0	.0	1	1.7	1	1.2	0	.0	2	2.4	83	97.6	0	.0
IA MALE	7	1.6	2	.5	4	.9	5	1.1	18	4.1	422	95.0	4	.9
DRAKE UNIVERSITY														
IA TOTAL	1	.2	12	2.1	0	.0	6	1.1	19	3.4	539	96.4	1	.2
IA FEMALE	0	.0	2	1.8	0	.0	0	.0	2	1.8	107	98.2	0	.0
IA MALE	1	.2	10	2.2	0	.0	6	1.3	17	3.9	432	96.0	1	.2
IOWA STATE U SCI & TECHN														
IA TOTAL	1	.2	0	.0	4	.9	1	.2	6	1.3	449	98.7	0	.0
IA FEMALE	0	.0	0	.0	2	1.7	0	.0	2	1.7	119	98.3	0	.0
IA MALE	1	.3	0	.0	2	.6	1	.3	4	1.2	330	98.8	0	.0
PALMER C OF CHIROPRACTIC														
IA TOTAL	3	.2	5	.3	9	.5	18	1.0	35	1.9	1,571	86.2	217	11.9
IA FEMALE	1	.4	0	.0	2	.8	3	1.3	6	2.5	216	90.8	16	6.7
IA MALE	2	.1	5	.3	7	.4	15	.9	29	1.8	1,355	85.5	201	12.7
UNIVERSITY OF IOWA														
IA TOTAL	14	.6	45	2.0	16	.7	16	.7	91	4.1	2,061	93.4	54	2.4
IA FEMALE	3	.7	13	2.9	6	1.3	3	.7	25	5.5	413	90.6	18	3.9
IA MALE	11	.6	32	1.8	10	.6	13	.7	66	3.8	1,648	94.2	36	2.1
WARTBURG THEOLOGICAL SEM														
IA TOTAL	1	.4	0	.0	0	.0	1	.4	2	.8	235	97.5		1.7
IA FEMALE	0	.0	0	.0	0	.0	1	2.9	1	2.9	34	97.1	0	.0
IA MALE	1	.5	0	.0	0	.0	0	.0	1	.5	201	97.6		1.9
IOWA TOTAL (7 INSTITUTIONS)														
IA TOTAL	27	.5	66	1.1	34	.6	48	.8	175	3.0	5,381	92.2	280	4.8
IA FEMALE	4	.4	16	1.5	11	1.1	7	.7	38	3.6	974	93.1	34	3.3
IA MALE	23	.5	50	1.0	23	.5	41	.9	137	2.9	4,407	92.0	246	5.1
KANSAS														
KANSAS ST U AGR & APP SCI														
KS TOTAL	2	.5	4	1.0	3	.7	8	2.0	17	4.2	387	95.8		.0
KS FEMALE	0	.0	1	1.2	0	.0	2	2.4	3	3.5	82	96.5	0	.0
KS MALE	2	.6	3	.9	3	.9	6	1.9	14	4.4	305	95.6	0	.0
U OF KANSAS MAIN CAMPUS														
KS TOTAL	1	.2	12	2.4	1	.2	7	1.4	21	4.1	489	95.9		.0
KS FEMALE	0	.0	6	4.1	1	.7	1	.7	8	5.5	137	94.5	0	.0
KS MALE	1	.3	6	1.6	0	.0	6	1.6	13	3.6	352	96.4	0	.0
U OF KANS MEDICAL CENTER														
KS TOTAL	3	.4	18	2.4	8	1.1	9	1.2	38	5.2	697	94.8		.0
KS FEMALE	0	.0	6	4.3	2	1.4	5	3.6	13	9.4	125	90.6	0	.0
KS MALE	3	.5	12	2.0	6	1.0	4	.7	25	4.2	572	95.8	0	.0
WASHBURN U OF TOPEKA														
KS TOTAL	1	.2	10	1.6	3	.5	11	1.8	25	4.1	583	95.9		.0
KS FEMALE	0	.0	2	1.6	1	.8	3	2.4	6	4.8	118	95.2	0	.0
KS MALE	1	.2	8	1.7	2	.4	8	1.7	19	3.9	465	96.1	0	.0

ᶠESSIONAL ENROLLMENT OF INSTITUTIONS OF HIGHER EDUCATION BY RACE, ETHNICITY AND SEX:
ᴬTE AND NATION, 1978

BLACK NON-HISPANIC		ASIAN OR PACIFIC ISLANDER		HISPANIC		TOTAL MINORITY		WHITE NON-HISPANIC		NON-RESIDENT ALIEN		TOTAL
NUMBER	%	NUMBER	%	NUMBER	%	NUMBER	%	NUMBER	%	NUMBER	%	NUMBER
(4 INSTITUTIONS)												
44	1.9	15	.7	35	1.6	101	4.5	2,156	95.5		.0	2,257
15	3.0	4	.8	11	2.2	30	6.1	462	93.9		.0	492
29	1.6	11	.6	24	1.4	71	4.0	1,694	96.0	8	.0	1,765
4	.7	0	.0	2	.3	7	1.2	588	96.7	13	2.1	608
0	.0	0	.0	0	.0	0	.0	27	96.4	1	3.6	28
4	.7	0	.0	2	.3	7	1.2	561	96.7	12	2.1	580
5	5.6	0	.0	1	1.1	6	6.7	83	93.3		.0	89
3	17.6	0	.0	1	5.9	4	23.5	13	76.5		.0	17
2	2.8	0	.0	0	.0	2	2.8	70	97.2	8	.0	72
9	5.5	0	.0		.0	10	6.1	153	93.9		.0	163
1	2.5	0	.0		.0	1	2.5	39	97.5		.0	40
8	6.5	0	.0	8	.0	9	7.3	114	92.7	8	.0	123
12	2.3	2	.4	1	.2	15	2.9	500	96.9	1	.2	516
1	1.1	0	.0	0	.0	1	1.1	88	98.9	0	.0	89
11	2.6	2	.5	1	.2	14	3.3	412	96.5	1	.2	427
0	.0	0	.0	0	.0	0	.0	0	.0		.0	0
0	.0	0	.0	0	.0	0	.0	0	.0		.0	0
0	.0	0	.0	0	.0	0	.0	0	.0	8	.0	0
31	2.6	6	.5	5	.4	47	3.9	1,157	96.1		.0	1,204
12	3.9	1	.3	1	.3	16	5.2	293	94.8		.0	309
19	2.1	5	.6	4	.4	31	3.5	864	96.5	8	.0	895
37	2.0	69	3.7	10	.5	121	6.5	1,734	93.2	6	.3	1,861
11	2.6	18	4.3	2	.5	31	7.5	382	91.8	3	.7	416
26	1.8	51	3.5	8	.6	90	6.2	1,352	93.6	3	.2	1,445
(7 INSTITUTIONS)												
98	2.2	77	1.7	19	.4	206	4.6	4,215	94.9	20	.5	4,441
28	3.1	19	2.1	4	.4	53	5.9	842	93.7	4	.4	899
70	2.0	58	1.6	15	.4	153	4.3	3,373	95.2	16	.5	3,542
4	1.4	1	.3	1	.3	6	2.0	289	97.6	1	.3	296
0	.0	1	1.2	1	1.2	2	2.5	79	97.5	0	.0	81
4	1.9	0	.0	0	.0	4	1.9	210	97.7	1	.5	215
31	2.1	4	.3	4	.3	40	2.7	1,416	96.8	7	.5	1,463
12	5.0	2	.8	2	.8	16	6.6	224	92.9	1	.4	241
19	1.6	2	.2	2	.2	24	2.0	1,192	97.5	6	.5	1,222
36	4.6	4	.5	1	1.	56	7.2	725	92.8		.0	781
13	5.9	1	.5		2.9	21	9.5	201	90.5		.0	222
23	4.1	3	.5		1.8	35	6.3	524	93.7	8	.0	559
2	5.7	2	5.7	2	5.7	6	17.1	29	82.9		.0	35
0	.0	0	.0	0	.0	0	.0	0	.0		.0	0
2	5.7	2	5.7	2	5.7	6	17.1	29	82.9	8	.0	35
141	71.2	1	.5	0	.0	142	71.7	55	27.8	1	.5	198
35	85.4	0	.0	0	.0	35	85.4	6	14.6	0	.0	41
106	67.5	1	.6	0	.0	107	68.2	49	31.2	1	.6	157
48	3.9	16	1.3	3	25	100	8.2	1,108	91.1	8	.7	1,216
18	5.7	2	.6		119	28	8.9	287	90.8	1	.3	316
30	3.3	14	1.6	26	2.7	72	8.0	821	91.2	7	.8	900
(6 INSTITUTIONS)												
262	6.6	28	.7	52	1.3	350	8.8	3,622	90.8	17	.4	3,989
78	8.7	6	.7	15	1.7	102	11.3	797	88.5	2	.2	901
184	6.0	22	.7	37	1.2	248	8.0	2,825	91.5	15	.5	3,088
1	1.1	0	.0	1	1.1	2	2.3	85	97.7	0	.0	87
0	.0	0	.0	0	.0	0	.0	21	100.0	0	.0	21
1	1.5	0	.0	1	1.5	2	3.0	64	97.0	0	.0	66
0	.0	0	.0		.0	0	.0	245	100.0		.0	245
0	.0	0	.0		.0	0	.0	94	100.0		.0	94
0	.0	0	.0	8	.0	0	.0	151	100.0	8	.0	151
(2 INSTITUTIONS)												
1	.3	0	.0	1	.3	2	.6	330	99.4		.0	332
0	.0	0	.0	0	.0	0	.0	115	100.0		.0	115
1	.5	0	.0	1	.5	2	.9	215	99.1	8	.0	217

TABLE 3 - TOTAL FIRST PROFESSIONAL ENROLLMENT OF INSTITUTIONS OF HIGHER EDUCATION BY RACE, ETHNICITY AND SEX: INSTITUTION, STATE AND NATION, 1978

	AMERICAN INDIAN ALASKAN NATIVE		BLACK NON-HISPANIC		ASIAN OR PACIFIC ISLANDER		HISPANIC		TOTAL MINORITY		WHITE NON-HISPANIC		NON-RESIDENT ALIEN	
	NUMBER	%	NUMBER	%	NUMBER	%	NUMBER	%	NUMBER	%	NUMBER	%	NUMBER	%
MARYLAND														
JOHNS HOPKINS UNIVERSITY														
MD TOTAL	0	.0	13	2.6	30	6.0	3	.6	46	9.2	445	89.0	9	1.8
MD FEMALE	0	.0	3	3.3	8	8.9	0	.0	11	12.1	79	86.8	1	1.1
MD MALE	0	.0	10	2.4	22	5.4	3	.7	35	8.6	366	89.5	8	2.0
UNIVERSITY OF BALTIMORE														
MD TOTAL	1	.1	36	3.7	1	.1	7	.7	45	4.6	932	94.9	5	.5
MD FEMALE	0	.0	15	6.1	0	.0	5	2.0	20	8.1	225	91.1	2	.8
MD MALE	1	.1	21	2.9	1	.1	2	.3	25	3.4	707	96.2	3	.4
U OF MD BALT PROF SCHOOLS														
MD TOTAL	1	.0	175	8.5	45	2.2	17	.8	238	11.5	1,824	88.3	3	.1
MD FEMALE	0	.0	68	11.9	12	2.1	2	.4	82	14.4	488	85.6	0	.0
MD MALE	1	.1	107	7.2	33	2.2	15	1.0	156	10.4	1,336	89.4	3	.2
MARYLAND TOTAL (3 INSTITUTIONS)														
MD TOTAL	2	.1	224	6.3	76	2.1	27	.8	329	9.3	3,201	90.2	17	.5
MD FEMALE	0	.0	86	9.5	20	2.2	7	.8	113	12.4	792	87.2	3	.3
MD MALE	2	.1	138	5.2	56	2.1	20	.8	216	8.2	2,409	91.3	14	.5
MASSACHUSETTS														
ANDOVER NENTON THEOL SCH														
MA TOTAL	0	.0	7	2.8	0	.0	1	.4	8	3.2	244	96.4	1	.4
MA FEMALE	0	.0	1	.7	0	.0	0	.0	1	.7	135	99.3	0	.0
MA MALE	0	.0	6	5.1	0	.0	1	.9	7	6.0	109	93.2	1	.9
BOSTON COLLEGE														
MA TOTAL	3	.4	44	5.5	22	2.8	22	2.8	91	11.4	697	87.6	8	1.0
MA FEMALE	2	.8	18	7.2	9	3.6	9	3.6	38	15.1	211	84.1	2	.8
MA MALE	1	.2	26	4.8	13	2.4	13	2.4	53	9.7	486	89.2	6	1.1
BOSTON UNIVERSITY														
MA TOTAL	1	.1	37	2.1	28	1.6	24	1.4	90	5.2	1,633	93.7	20	1.1
MA FEMALE	1	.2	20	3.2	11	1.8	10	1.6	42	6.8	572	92.1	7	1.1
MA MALE	0	.0	17	1.5	17	1.5	14	1.2	48	4.3	1,061	94.6	13	1.2
EPISCOPAL DIVINITY SCHOOL														
MA TOTAL	0	.0	2	1.8	0	.0	0	.0	2	1.8	104	95.4	3	2.8
MA FEMALE	0	.0	0	.0	0	.0	0	.0	0	.0	54	100.0	0	.0
MA MALE	0	.0	2	3.6	0	.0	0	.0	2	3.6	50	90.9	3	5.5
GORDON-CONWELL THEOL SEM														
MA TOTAL	2	.4	8	1.7	1	.2	2	.4	13	2.8	442	94.0	15	3.2
MA FEMALE	0	.0	0	.0	0	.0	0	.0	0	.0	23	100.0	0	.0
MA MALE	2	.4	8	1.8	1	.2	2	.4	13	2.9	419	93.7	15	3.4
HARVARD UNIVERSITY														
MA TOTAL	9	.4	185	8.5	42	1.9	74	3.4	310	14.3	1,716	79.3	139	6.4
MA FEMALE	2	.3	71	11.5	16	2.6	16	2.6	105	17.0	483	78.4	28	4.5
MA MALE	7	.5	114	7.4	26	1.7	58	3.7	205	13.2	1,233	79.6	111	7.2
MASS INST OF TECHNOLOGY														
MA TOTAL	0	.0	1	1.9	0	.0	0	.0	1	1.9	44	84.6	7	13.5
MA FEMALE	0	.0	0	.0	0	.0	0	.0	0	.0	8	100.0	0	.0
MA MALE	0	.0	1	2.3	0	.0	0	.0	1	2.3	36	81.8	7	15.9
NEW ENGLAND C OPTOMETRY														
MA TOTAL	0	.0	4	1.1	6	1.7	2	.6	12	3.4	333	94.9	6	1.7
MA FEMALE	0	.0	0	.0	4	4.7	0	.0	4	4.7	78	91.8	3	3.5
MA MALE	0	.0	4	1.5	2	.8	2	.8	8	3.0	255	95.9	3	1.1
NEW ENG CONSV OF MUSIC														
MA TOTAL	0	.0	0	.0	1	11.1	0	.0	1	11.1	5	55.6	3	33.3
MA FEMALE	0	.0	0	.0	0	.0	0	.0	0	.0	1	50.0	1	50.0
MA MALE	0	.0	0	.0	1	14.3	0	.0	1	14.3	4	57.1	2	28.6
NEW ENGLAND SCHOOL OF LAW														
MA TOTAL	0	.0	4	.4	2	.2	5	.6	11	1.2	878	98.8	0	.0
MA FEMALE	0	.0	2	.8	0	.0	3	1.2	5	1.9	255	98.1	0	.0
MA MALE	0	.0	2	.3	2	.3	2	.3	6	1.0	623	99.0	0	.0
NORTHEASTERN UNIVERSITY														
MA TOTAL	0	.0	31	7.5	1	.2	15	3.6	47	11.3	369	88.7	0	.0
MA FEMALE	0	.0	13	5.8	0	.0	7	3.1	20	8.9	205	91.1	0	.0
MA MALE	0	.0	18	9.4	1	.5	8	4.2	27	14.1	164	85.9	0	.0
POPE JOHN XXIII NATL SEM														
MA TOTAL	0	.0	2	3.3	0	.0	0	.0	2	3.3	59	96.7	0	.0
MA FEMALE	0	.0	0	.0	0	.0	0	.0	0	.0	0	.0	0	.0
MA MALE	0	.0	2	3.3	0	.0	0	.0	2	3.3	59	96.7	0	.0
SAINT JOHN'S SEMINARY														
MA TOTAL	0	.0	0	.0	0	.0	4	3.6	4	3.6	108	96.4	0	.0
MA FEMALE	0	.0	0	.0	0	.0	0	.0	0	.0	0	.0	0	.0
MA MALE	0	.0	0	.0	0	.0	4	3.6	4	3.6	108	96.4	0	.0
SMITH COLLEGE														
MA TOTAL	0	.0	10	5.4	2	1.1	2	1.1	14	7.6	169	91.4	2	1.1
MA FEMALE	0	.0	9	6.3	2	1.4	1	.7	12	8.4	130	90.9	1	.7
MA MALE	0	.0	1	2.4	0	.0	1	2.4	2	4.8	39	92.9	1	2.4
SUFFOLK UNIVERSITY														
MA TOTAL	5	.3	33	2.0	8	.5	11	.7	57	3.5	1,592	96.5	0	.0
MA FEMALE	3	.5	14	2.4	4	.7	5	.9	26	4.5	553	95.5	0	.0
MA MALE	2	.2	19	1.8	4	.4	6	.6	31	2.9	1,039	97.1	0	.0
TUFTS UNIVERSITY														
MA TOTAL	3	.4	32	4.4	30	4.2	16	2.2	81	11.2	628	87.0	13	1.8
MA FEMALE	0	.0	16	8.5	12	6.3	5	2.6	33	17.5	154	81.5	2	1.1
MA MALE	3	.6	16	3.0	18	3.4	11	2.1	48	9.0	474	88.9	11	2.1
U MASS MEDL SCH-WORCESTER														
MA TOTAL	0	.0	16	3.9	13	3.1	4	1.0	33	8.0	380	92.0	0	.0
MA FEMALE	0	.0	4	3.4	4	3.4	1	.9	9	7.8	107	92.2	0	.0
MA MALE	0	.0	12	4.0	9	3.0	3	1.0	24	8.1	273	91.9	0	.0
WESTERN NEW ENG COLLEGE														
MA TOTAL	2	.2	5	.6	2	.2	1	.1	10	1.2	841	98.6	2	.2
MA FEMALE	1	.4	2	.8	2	.8	0	.0	5	2.1	238	97.9	0	.0
MA MALE	1	.2	3	.5	0	.0	1	.2	5	.8	603	98.9	2	.3

BLE 3 - TOTAL FIRST PROFESSIONAL ENROLLMENT OF INSTITUTIONS OF HIGHER EDUCATION BY RACE, ETHNICITY AND SEX:
INSTITUTION, STATE AND NATION, 1978

	AMERICAN INDIAN ALASKAN NATIVE		BLACK NON-HISPANIC		ASIAN OR PACIFIC ISLANDER		HISPANIC		TOTAL MINORITY		WHITE NON-HISPANIC		NON-RESIDENT ALIEN		TOTAL
	NUMBER	%	NUMBER	%	NUMBER	%	NUMBER	%	NUMBER	%	NUMBER	%	NUMBER	%	NUMBER
SSACHUSETTS															
SSACHUSETTS TOTAL (18 INSTITUTIONS)															
TOTAL	25	.2	421	3.7	158	1.4	103	1.6	787	7.0	10,242	91.1	219	1.9	11,248
FEMALE	9	.3	170	4.8	64	1.8	57	1.6	300	8.4	3,207	90.3	44	1.2	3,551
MALE	16	.2	251	3.3	94	1.2	126	1.6	487	6.3	7,035	91.4	175	2.3	7,697
CHIGAN															
DREWS UNIVERSITY															
TOTAL	0	.0	48	12.5	10	2	23	6.0	81	21.0	241	62.6	63	16.4	385
FEMALE	0	.0	0	.0	0	.0	0	.0	0	.0	5	71.4	2	29.6	7
MALE	0	.0	48	12.7	10	2.8	23	6.1	81	21.4	236	62.4	61	15.1	378
LVIN THEOLOGICAL SEM															
TOTAL	0	.0	0	.0	5	2.9	0	.0	5	2.9	134	78.8	31	18.2	170
FEMALE	0	.0	0	.0	2	22.2	0	.0	2	22.2	5	55.6	2	22.2	9
MALE	0	.0	0	.0	3	1.9	0	.0	3	1.9	129	80.1	29	18.0	161
TROIT COLLEGE OF LAW															
TOTAL	0	.0	21	2.5	0	.0	0	.0	21	2.5	824	97.5	0	.0	845
FEMALE	0	.0	7	3.7	0	.0	0	.0	7	3.7	184	96.3	0	.0	191
MALE	0	.0	14	2.1	0	.0	0	.0	14	2.1	640	97.9	0	.0	654
RRIS STATE COLLEGE															
TOTAL	0	.0	1	1.0	1	1.0	0	.0	2	2.0	97	98.0	0	.0	99
FEMALE	0	.0	0	.0	0	.0	0	.0	0	.0	12	100.0	0	.0	12
MALE	0	.0	1	1.1	1	1.1	0	.0	2	2.3	85	97.7	0	.0	87
AND RAPIDS BAPT C & SEM															
TOTAL	0	.0	0	.0	0	.0	1	1.0	1	1.0	93	96.9	2	2.1	96
FEMALE	0	.0	0	.0	0	.0	0	.0	0	.0	0	.0	0	.0	0
MALE	0	.0	0	.0	0	.0	1	1.0	1	1.0	93	96.9	2	2.1	96
CHIGAN STATE UNIVERSITY															
TOTAL	9	.8	91	8.3	16	1.5	37	3.4	153	14.0	937	85.6	4	.4	1,094
FEMALE	4	1.0	46	11.0	4	1.0	9	2.2	63	15.1	353	84.4	2	.5	418
MALE	5	.7	45	6.7	12	1.8	28	4.1	90	13.3	584	86.4	2	.3	676
OMAS M COOLEY LAW SCH															
TOTAL	4	.4	21	2.0	12	1.1	15	1.4	52	5.0	994	95.0	0	.0	1,046
FEMALE	1	.4	6	2.7	2	.9	3	1.3	12	5.3	213	94.7	0	.0	225
MALE	3	.4	15	1.8	10	1.2	12	1.5	40	4.9	781	95.1	0	.0	821
IVERSITY OF DETROIT															
TOTAL	0	.0	32	3.0	3	.3	6	.6	41	3.9	1,023	96.1	0	.0	1,064
FEMALE	0	.0	8	3.5	1	.4	2	.9	11	4.8	219	95.2	0	.0	230
MALE	0	.0	24	2.9	2	.2	4	.5	30	3.6	804	96.4	0	.0	834
MICHIGAN-ANN ARBOR															
TOTAL	11	.3	185	5.5	51	1.5	57	1.7	304	9.1	2,756	82.7	274	9.2	3,334
FEMALE	4	.5	71	9.1	17	2.2	20	2.6	112	14.3	621	79.3	50	6.4	783
MALE	7	.3	114	4.5	34	1.3	37	1.5	192	7.5	2,135	83.7	224	918	2,551
YNE STATE UNIVERSITY															
TOTAL	5	.2	188	9.0	27	1.3	30	1.4	250	12.0	1,826	87.8	3	.1	2,079
FEMALE	0	.0	93	15.8	8	1.4	8	1.4	109	18.5	480	81.4	1	.2	590
MALE	5	.3	95	6.4	19	1.3	22	1.5	141	9.5	1,346	90.4	2	.1	1,489
STERN THEOLOGICAL SEM															
TOTAL	0	.0	1	.9	0	.0	1	.9	2	1.8	107	98.2	0	.0	109
FEMALE	0	.0	0	.0	0	.0	0	.0	0	.0	9	100.0	0	.0	9
MALE	0	.0	1	1.0	0	.0	1	1.0	2	2.0	98	98.0	0	.0	100
CHIGAN TOTAL (11 INSTITUTIONS)															
TOTAL	29	.3	588	5.7	125	1.2	170	1.6	912	8.8	9,032	87.5	377	3.7	10,321
FEMALE	9	.4	231	9.3	34	1.4	42	1.7	316	12.8	2,101	84.9	57	2.3	2,474
MALE	20	.3	357	4.5	91	1.2	128	1.6	596	7.6	6,931	88.3	320	4.1	7,847
NNESOTA															
THEL THEOL SEMINARY															
TOTAL	0	.0	0	.0	0	.0	0	.0	0	.0	358	96.8	12	3.2	370
FEMALE	0	.0	0	.0	0	.0	0	.0	0	.0	38	100.0	0	.0	38
MALE	0	.0	0	.0	0	.0	0	.0	0	.0	320	96.4	12	3.6	332
MLINE UNIVERSITY															
TOTAL	1	.2	3	.6	1	.2	3	.6	8	1.7	471	98.3	0	.0	479
FEMALE	0	.0	1	.8	1	.8	3	2.4	5	4.1	118	95.9	0	.0	123
MALE	1	.3	2	.6	0	.0	0	.0	3	.8	353	99.2	0	.0	356
THER THEOLOGICAL SEM															
TOTAL	0	.0	2	.4	1	.2	0	.0	3	.5	551	98.4	6	1.1	560
FEMALE	0	.0	1	1.0	0	.0	0	.0	1	1.0	97	98.0	1	1.0	99
MALE	0	.0	1	.2	1	.2	0	.0	2	.4	454	98.5	5	1.1	461
YO MEDICAL SCHOOL															
TOTAL	1	.6	6	3.7	2	1.2	2	1.2	11	6.8	151	93.2	0	.0	162
FEMALE	0	.0	3	7.7	0	.0	0	.0	3	7.7	36	92.3	0	.0	39
MALE	1	.8	3	2.4	2	1.6	2	1.6	8	6.5	115	93.5	0	.0	123
HWSTN C CHIROPRACTIC															
TOTAL	0	.0	1	.3	3	.8	0	.0	4	1.0	372	96.6	9	2.3	385
FEMALE	0	.0	0	.0	0	.0	0	.0	0	.0	34	97.1	1	2.9	35
MALE	0	.0	1	.3	3	.9	0	.0	4	1.1	338	96.6	8	2.3	350
HWSTN LUTH THEOL SEM															
TOTAL	1	.6	0	.0	1	.6	0	.0	2	1.1	176	97.2	3	1.7	181
FEMALE	0	.0	0	.0	0	.0	0	.0	0	.0	34	97.1	1	2.9	35
MALE	1	.7	0	.0	1	.7	0	.0	2	1.4	142	97.3	2	1.4	146
INT PAUL SEMINARY															
TOTAL	0	.0	0	.0	0	.0	1	.9	1	.9	111	99.1	0	.0	112
FEMALE	0	.0	0	.0	0	.0	0	.0	0	.0	2	100.0	0	.0	2
MALE	0	.0	0	.0	0	.0	1	.9	1	.9	109	99.1	0	.0	110
ITED THEOLOGICAL SEM															
TOTAL	0	.0	0	.0	0	.0	0	.0	0	.0	109	100.0	0	.0	109
FEMALE	0	.0	0	.0	0	.0	0	.0	0	.0	57	100.0	0	.0	57
MALE	0	.0	0	.0	0	.0	0	.0	0	.0	52	100.0	0	.0	52

TABLE 3 - TOTAL FIRST PROFESSIONAL ENROLLMENT OF INSTITUTIONS OF HIGHER EDUCATION BY RACE, ETHNICITY AND SEX: INSTITUTION, STATE AND NATION, 1978

	AMERICAN INDIAN ALASKAN NATIVE		BLACK NON-HISPANIC		ASIAN OR PACIFIC ISLANDER		HISPANIC		TOTAL MINORITY		WHITE NON-HISPANIC		NON-RESIDENT ALIEN	
	NUMBER	%	NUMBER	%	NUMBER	%	NUMBER	%	NUMBER	%	NUMBER	%	NUMBER	%
MINNESOTA		**CONTINUED**												
U OF MINNESOTA DULUTH														
MN TOTAL	3	3.2	0	.0	1	1.1	0	.0	4	4.3	90	95.7	0	.0
MN FEMALE	1	4.5	0	.0	0	.0	0	.0	1	4.5	21	95.5	0	.0
MN MALE	2	2.8	0	.0	1	1.4	0	.0	3	4.2	69	95.8	0	.0
U OF MINN MNPLS SNT PAUL														
MN TOTAL	25	.9	56	2.1	19	.7	63	2.3	163	6.0	2,531	93.3	18	.7
MN FEMALE	8	1.1	22	3.2	6	.9	14	2.0	50	7.2	640	92.0	6	.9
MN MALE	17	.8	34	1.7	13	.6	49	2.4	113	5.6	1,891	93.8	12	.6
WM MITCHELL COLLEGE LAW														
MN TOTAL	1	.1	13	1.1	5	.4	1	.1	20	1.7	1,140	98.3		.0
MN FEMALE	1	.3	7	1.9	3	.8	0	.0	11	3.0	358	97.0	0	.0
MN MALE	0	.0	6	.8	2	.3	1	.1	9	1.1	782	98.9	0	.0
MINNESOTA		**TOTAL (**	**11 INSTITUTIONS)**											
MN TOTAL	32	.5	81	1.3	33	.5	70	1.1	216	3.4	6,060	95.8	48	.8
MN FEMALE	10	.7	34	2.2	10	.7	17	1.1	71	4.7	1,435	94.7	9	.6
MN MALE	22	.5	47	1.0	23	.5	53	1.1	145	3.0	4,625	96.2	39	.8
MISSISSIPPI														
MISSISSIPPI COLLEGE														
MS TOTAL	1	.3	5	1.5	1	.3	0	.0	7	2.1	324	95.9	7	2.1
MS FEMALE	1	1.4	2	2.8	0	.0	0	.0	3	4.2	61	85.9	7	9.9
MS MALE	0	.0	3	1.1	1	.4	0	.0	4	1.5	263	98.5	0	.0
MISSISSIPPI ST UNIVERSITY														
MS TOTAL	0	.0	2	3.6	0	.0	0	.0	2	3.6	53	96.4	0	.0
MS FEMALE	0	.0	2	10.5	0	.0	0	.0	2	10.5	17	89.5	0	.0
MS MALE	0	.0	0	.0	0	.0	0	.0	0	.0	36	100.0	0	.0
RUST COLLEGE														
MS TOTAL	0	.0	4	100.0	0	.0	0	.0	4	100.0	0	.0		.0
MS FEMALE	0	.0	4	100.0	0	.0	0	.0	4	100.0	0	.0	0	.0
MS MALE	0	.0	0	.0	0	.0	0	.0	0	.0	0	.0	0	.0
U OF MISSISSIPPI MAIN CAM														
MS TOTAL	0	.0	24	4.0	1	.2	3	.5	28	4.6	576	95.4		.0
MS FEMALE	0	.0	9	6.8	0	.0	1	.8	10	7.6	122	92.4	0	.0
MS MALE	0	.0	15	3.2	1	.2	2	.4	18	3.8	454	96.2	0	.0
U OF MISSISSIPPI MEDL CTR														
MS TOTAL	2	.3	45	6.1	9	1.2	1	.1	57	7.8	678	92.2	0	.0
MS FEMALE	1	.7	12	8.6	3	2.2	0	.0	16	11.5	123	88.5	0	.0
MS MALE	1	.2	33	5.5	6	1.0	1	.2	41	6.9	555	93.1	0	.0
MISSISSIPPI		**TOTAL (**	**5 INSTITUTIONS)**											
MS TOTAL	3	.2	80	4.6	11	.6	4	.2	98	5.6	1,631	94.0	7	.4
MS FEMALE	2	.5	29	7.9	3	.8	1	.3	35	9.6	323	88.5	7	1.9
MS MALE	1	.1	51	3.7	8	.6	3	.2	63	4.6	1,308	95.4	0	.0
MISSOURI														
CHRIST SEMINARY-SEMINEX														
MO TOTAL	0	.0	2	1.0	0	.0	0	.0	2	1.0	195	98.5	1	.5
MO FEMALE	0	.0	0	.0	0	.0	0	.0	0	.0	19	100.0	0	.0
MO MALE	0	.0	2	1.1	0	.0	0	.0	2	1.1	176	98.3	1	.6
CLEVELAND CHIROPRACTIC C														
MO TOTAL	3	1.3	1	.4	0	.0	0	.0	4	1.7	215	93.1	12	5.2
MO FEMALE	0	.0	0	.0	0	.0	0	.0	0	.0	43	93.5	3	6.5
MO MALE	3	1.6	1	.5	0	.0	0	.0	4	2.2	172	93.0	9	4.9
CONCORDIA SEMINARY														
MO TOTAL	0	.0	2	.4	0	.0	1	.2	3	.7	449	98.9	2	.4
MO FEMALE	0	.0	0	.0	0	.0	0	.0	0	.0	0	.0	0	.0
MO MALE	0	.0	2	.4	0	.0	1	.2	3	.7	449	98.9	2	.4
COVENANT THEOLOGICAL SEM														
MO TOTAL	1	.8	0	.0	1	.8	0	.0	2	1.5	121	91.7		6.8
MO FEMALE	0	.0	0	.0	0	.0	0	.0	0	.0	3	100.0	0	.0
MO MALE	1	.8	0	.0	1	.8	0	.0	2	1.6	118	91.5	9	7.0
EDEN THEOLOGICAL SEMINARY														
MO TOTAL	0	.0	10	8.3	0	.0	0	.0	10	8.3	110	91.7		.0
MO FEMALE	0	.0	1	3.1	0	.0	0	.0	1	3.1	31	96.9	0	.0
MO MALE	0	.0	9	10.2	0	.0	0	.0	9	10.2	79	89.8	0	.0
KANSAS CITY C OSTEO MED														
MO TOTAL	2	.3	0	.0	3	.5	3	.5	8	1.3	605	98.2	3	.5
MO FEMALE	1	1.3	0	.0	0	.0	2	2.6	3	3.9	73	96.1	0	.0
MO MALE	1	.2	0	.0	3	.6	1	.2	5	.9	532	98.5	3	.6
KENRICK SEMINARY														
MO TOTAL	0	.0	2	1.6	11	8.7	1	.8	14	11.0	110	86.6	3	2.4
MO FEMALE	0	.0	0	.0	0	.0	0	.0	0	.0	0	.0	0	.0
MO MALE	0	.0	2	1.6	11	8.7	1	.8	14	11.0	110	86.6	3	2.4
KIRKSVL COLLEGE OSTEO MED														
MO TOTAL	6	1.2	5	1.0	10	2.0	5	1.0	26	5.2	471	94.4	2	.4
MO FEMALE	2	2.9	0	.0	2	2.9	1	1.5	5	7.4	63	92.6	0	.0
MO MALE	4	.9	5	1.2	8	1.9	4	.9	21	4.9	408	94.7	2	.5
LOGAN C OF CHIROPRACTIC														
MO TOTAL	0	.0	2	.4	5	.9	0	.0	7	1.2	542	96.4	13	2.3
MO FEMALE	0	.0	0	.0	1	1.4	0	.0	1	1.4	72	97.3	1	1%
MO MALE	0	.0	2	.4	4	.8	0	.0	6	1.2	470	96.3	12	2.5
MIDWESTERN BAPT THEOL SEM														
MO TOTAL	1	.3	3	1.0	5	1.6	1	.3	10	3.3	294	96.1	2	.7
MO FEMALE	0	.0	0	.0	0	.0	0	.0	0	.0	15	100.0	0	.0
MO MALE	1	.3	3	1.0	5	1.7	1	.3	10	3.4	279	95.9	2	.7
NAZARENE THEOLOGICAL SEM														
MO TOTAL	3	.8	1	.3	3	.8	0	.0	8	2.1	349	91.8	23	6 1
MO FEMALE	0	.0	1	6.3	0	.0	0	.0	1	6.3	14	87.5	1	6 3
MO MALE	1	.3	2	.5	1	.3	3	.8	7	1.9	335	92.0	22	610

200

	BLACK NON-HISPANIC		ASIAN OR PACIFIC ISLANDER		HISPANIC		TOTAL MINORITY		WHITE NON-HISPANIC		NON-RESIDENT ALIEN		TOTAL
	NUMBER	%	NUMBER	%	NUMBER	%	NUMBER	%	NUMBER	%	NUMBER	%	NUMBER
INUED													
	83	4.7	37	2.1	6	.3	126	7.2	1,607	91.7	19	1.1	1,752
	44	9.2	10	2.1	1	.2	55	11.5	419	87.3	6	1.3	480
	39	3.1	27	2.1	5	.4	71	5.6	1,188	93.4	13	1.0	1,272
	0	.0	0	.0	0	.0	0	.0	0	.0	0	.0	0
	0	.0	0	.0	0	.0	0	.0	0	.0	0	.0	0
	0	.0	0	.0	0	.0	0	.0	0	.0	0	.0	0
	4	2.4	0	.0	0	.0	5	3.0	160	97.0	0	.0	165
	0	.0	0	.0	0	.0	0	.0	36	100.0	0	.0	36
	4	3.1	0	.0	0	.0	5	3.9	124	96.1	0	.0	129
	22	1.9	10	.9	3	.3	41	3.5	1,124	96.2	4	.3	1,169
	10	3.7	1	.4	0	.0	13	4.8	257	95.2	0	.0	270
	12	1.3	9	1.0	3	.3	28	3.1	867	96.4	4	.4	899
	35	2.5	22	1.6	13	.9	77	5.5	1,319	94.1	5	.4	1,401
	16	5.2	6	1.9	1	.3	26	8.4	281	90.9	2	.6	309
	19	1.7	16	1.5	12	1.1	51	4.7	1,038	95.1	3	.3	1,092
	87	5.8	49	3.2	12	.8	153	10.1	1,346	89.1	11	.7	1,510
	36	9.3	18	4.6	2	.5	57	14.7	329	84.8	2	.5	388
	51	4.5	31	2.8	10	.9	96	8.6	1,017	90.6	9	.8	1,122
(17 INSTITUTIONS)													
	262	2.7	153	1.6	49	.5	496	5.2	9,017	93.7	109	1.1	9,622
	108	5.9	38	2.1	7	.4	162	8.8	1,655	90.3	15	.8	1,832
	154	2.0	115	1.5	42	.5	334	4.3	7,362	94.5	94	1.2	7,790
	0	.0	0	.0	0	.0	0	.0	222	99.6	1	.4	223
	0	.0	0	.0	0	.0	0	.0	67	100.0	0	.0	67
	0	.0	0	.0	0	.0	0	.0	155	99.4	1	.6	156
(1 INSTITUTIONS)													
	0	.0	0	.0	0	.0	0	.0	222	99.6	1	.4	223
	0	.0	0	.0	0	.0	0	.0	67	100.0	0	.0	67
	0	.0	0	.0	0	.0	0	.0	155	99.4	1	.6	156
	36	2.8	22	1.7	35	2.7	97	7.5	1,196	92.3	3	.2	1,296
	11	5.3	2	1.0	2	1.0	16	7.8	190	92.2	0	.0	206
	25	2.3	20	1.8	33	3.0	81	7.4	1,006	92.3	3	.3	1,090
	0	.0	0	.0	0	.0	0	.0	9	100.0	0	.0	9
	0	.0	0	.0	0	.0	0	.0	1	100.0	0	.0	1
	0	.0	0	.0	0	.0	0	.0	8	100.0	0	.0	8
	5	.7	3	.4	1	.1	10	1.3	754	98.6	1	.1	765
	2	1.0	2	1.0	0	.0	4	2.0	196	98.0	0	.0	200
	3	.5	1	.2	1	.2	6	1.1	558	98.8	1	.2	565
	8	1.1	14	1.9	2	.3	26	3.5	714	95.5	8	1.1	748
	2	.9	4	1.9	1	.5	8	3.8	204	95.8	1	.5	213
	6	1.1	10	1.9	1	.2	18	3.4	510	95.3	7	1.3	535
(4 INSTITUTIONS)													
	49	1.7	39	1.4	38	1.3	133	4.7	2,673	94.9	12	.4	2,818
	15	2.4	8	1.3	3	.5	28	4.5	591	95.3	1	.2	620
	34	1.5	31	1.4	35	1.6	105	4.8	2,082	94.7	11	.5	2,198
	9	4.8	8	4.3	6	3.2	26	14.0	160	86.0	0	.0	186
	3	5.5	5	9.1	3	5.5	12	21.8	43	78.2	0	.0	55
	6	4.6	3	2.3	3	2.3	14	10.7	117	89.3	0	.0	131
	0	.0	3	1.2	5	2.0	11	4.4	240	95.6	0	.0	251
	0	.0	2	13.3	1	6.7	5	33.3	10	66.7	0	.0	15
	0	.0	1	.4	4	1.7	6	2.5	230	97.5	0	.0	236
(2 INSTITUTIONS)													
	9	2.1	11	2.5	11	2.5	37	8.5	400	91.5	0	.0	437
	3	4.3	7	10.0	4	5.7	17	24.3	53	75.7	0	.0	70
	6	1.6	4	1.1	7	1.9	20	5.4	347	94.6	0	.0	367
	0	.0	0	.0	0	.0	0	.0	223	93.3	16	6.7	239
	0	.0	0	.0	0	.0	0	.0	0	.0	0	.0	0
	0	.0	0	.0	0	.0	0	.0	223	93.3	16	6.7	239
	167	13.7	16	1.3	51	4.2	236	19.3	985	80.7	0	.0	1,221
	67	22.9	8	2.7	15	5.1	91	31.1	202	68.9	0	.0	293
	100	10.8	8	.9	36	3.9	145	15.6	783	84.4	0	.0	928

	AMERICAN INDIAN ALASKAN NATIVE		BLACK NON-HISPANIC		ASIAN OR PACIFIC ISLANDER		HISPANIC		TOTAL MINORITY		WHITE NON-HISPANIC		NON-RESIDENT ALIEN		T
	NUMBER	%	NUMBER	%	NUMBER	%	NUMBER	%	NUMBER	%	NUMBER	%	NUMBER	%	N
NEW JERSEY		CONTINUED													
DREW UNIVERSITY															
NJ TOTAL	0	.0	16	10.5	2	1.3	2	1.3	20	13.1	126	82.4	7	4.6	
NJ FEMALE	0	.0	2	5.9	1	2.9	0	.0	3	8.8	31	91.2	0	.0	
NJ MALE	0	.0	14	11.8	1	.8	2	1.7	17	14.3	95	79.8	7	5.9	
FARLGH DCKSN TEANECK CAM															
NJ TOTAL	0	.0	4	1.2	3	.9	2	.6	9	2.8	318	97.2	0	.0	
NJ FEMALE	0	.0	1	3.1	0	.0	1	3.1	2	6.3	30	93.8	0	.0	
NJ MALE	0	.0	3	1.0	3	1.0	1	.3	7	2.4	288	97.6	0	.0	
IMMACULATE CONCEPTION SEM															
NJ TOTAL	0	.0	2	1.5	0	.0	4	3.0	6	4.5	126	95.5	0	.0	
NJ FEMALE	0	.0	0	.0	0	.0	0	.0	0	.0	42	100.0	0	.0	
NJ MALE	0	.0	2	2.2	0	.0	4	4.4	6	6.7	84	93.3	0	.0	
NEW BRUNSWICK THEOL SEM															
NJ TOTAL	1	1.3	13	17.3	3	4.0	3	4.0	20	26.7	55	73.3	0	.0	
NJ FEMALE	0	.0	0	.0	0	.0	0	.0	0	.0	7	100.0	0	.0	
NJ MALE	1	1.5	13	19.1	3	4.4	3	4.4	20	29.4	48	70.6	0	.0	
PRINCETON THEOLOGICAL SEM															
NJ TOTAL	1	.2	23	4.6	4	.8	0	.0	28	5.6	457	92.0	12	2.4	
NJ FEMALE	0	.0	9	6.5	2	1.4	0	.0	11	7.9	126	90.6	2	1.4	
NJ MALE	1	.3	14	3.9	2	.6	0	.0	17	4.7	331	92.5	10	2.8	
RUTGERS U CAMDEN CAMPUS															
NJ TOTAL	1	.1	44	5.9	8	1.1	13	1.7	66	8.8	686	91.2	0	.0	
NJ FEMALE	0	.0	20	8.1	5	2.0	6	2.4	31	12.6	215	87.4	0	.0	
NJ MALE	1	.2	24	4.7	3	.6	7	1.4	35	6.9	471	93.1	0	.0	
RUTGERS U NEWARK CAMPUS															
NJ TOTAL	3	.4	103	13.7	18	2.4	43	5.7	167	22.2	585	77.8	0	.0	
NJ FEMALE	2	.6	52	14.7	9	2.5	23	6.5	86	24.3	268	75.7	0	.0	
NJ MALE	1	.3	51	12.8	9	2.3	20	5.0	81	20.4	317	79.6	0	.0	
SNT MICHAELS PASIONST MON															
NJ TOTAL	0	.0	0	.0	0	.0	0	.0	0	.0	0	.0	0	.0	
NJ FEMALE	0	.0	0	.0	0	.0	0	.0	0	.0	0	.0	0	.0	
NJ MALE	0	.0	0	.0	0	.0	0	.0	0	.0	0	.0	0	.0	
SETON HALL UNIVERSITY															
NJ TOTAL	0	.0	55	4.7	6	.5	47	4.0	108	9.2	1,070	90.8	0	.0	
NJ FEMALE	0	.0	26	7.6	3	.9	16	4.7	45	13.1	298	86.9	0	.0	
NJ MALE	0	.0	29	3.5	3	.4	31	3.7	63	7.5	772	92.5	0	.0	
NEW JERSEY		TOTAL (	11 INSTITUTIONS)												
NJ TOTAL	8	.2	427	8.0	60	1.1	165	3.1	660	12.4	4,631	87.0	35	.7	
NJ FEMALE	3	.2	177	11.9	28	1.9	61	4.1	269	18.1	1,219	81.8	2	.1	
NJ MALE	5	.1	250	6.5	32	.8	104	2.7	391	10.2	3,412	88.9	33	.9	
NEW MEXICO															
U OF NM MAIN CAMPUS															
NM TOTAL	22	3.5	7	1.1	11	1.8	149	23.9	189	30.3	435	69.7	0	.0	
NM FEMALE	7	3.2	3	1.4	6	2.7	47	21.5	63	28.8	156	71.2	0	.0	
NM MALE	15	3.7	4	1.0	5	1.2	102	25.2	126	31.1	279	68.9	0	.0	
NEW MEXICO		TOTAL (	1 INSTITUTIONS)												
NM TOTAL	22	3.5	7	1.1	11	1.8	149	23.9	189	30.3	435	69.7	0	.0	
NM FEMALE	7	3.2	3	1.4	6	2.7	47	21.5	63	28.8	156	71.2	0	.0	
NM MALE	15	3.7	4	1.0	5	1.2	102	25.2	126	31.1	279	68.9	0	.0	
NEW YORK															
ALBANY LAW SCHOOL															
NY TOTAL	1	.1	7	1.0	3	.4	6	.9	17	2.4	687	97.6	0	.0	
NY FEMALE	0	.0	4	1.9	2	.9	0	.0	6	2.8	208	97.2	0	.0	
NY MALE	1	.2	3	.6	1	.2	6	1.2	11	2.2	479	97.8	0	.0	
ALBANY MEDICAL COLLEGE															
NY TOTAL	0	.0	8	1.6	10	2.0	5	1.0	23	4.5	488	95.3	1	.2	
NY FEMALE	0	.0	2	1.6	3	2.5	1	.8	6	4.9	116	95.1	0	.0	
NY MALE	0	.0	6	1.5	7	1.8	4	1.0	17	4.4	372	95.4	1	.3	
BROOKLYN LAW SCHOOL															
NY TOTAL	0	.0	22	2.0	6	.6	17	1.6	45	4.1	1,042	95.9	0	.0	
NY FEMALE	0	.0	17	4.2	1	.2	5	1.2	23	5.6	386	94.4	0	.0	
NY MALE	0	.0	5	.7	5	.7	12	1.8	22	3.2	656	96.8	0	.0	
CHRIST THE KING SEMINARY															
NY TOTAL	0	.0	0	.0	0	.0	0	.0	0	.0	106	100.0	0	.0	
NY FEMALE	0	.0	0	.0	0	.0	0	.0	0	.0	0	.0	0	.0	
NY MALE	0	.0	0	.0	0	.0	0	.0	0	.0	106	100.0	0	.0	
COLG ROCH-BEXLEY-CROZER															
NY TOTAL	0	.0	21	17.9	0	.0	0	.0	21	17.9	96	82.1	0	.0	
NY FEMALE	0	.0	6	12.2	0	.0	0	.0	6	12.2	43	87.8	0	.0	
NY MALE	0	.0	15	22.1	0	.0	0	.0	15	22.1	53	77.9	0	.0	
COLUMBIA U MAIN DIVISION															
NY TOTAL	1	.1	98	5.8	38	2.3	66	3.9	203	12.0	1,475	87.5	7	.4	
NY FEMALE	0	.0	49	9.3	16	3.0	23	4.3	88	16.6	440	83.2	1	.2	
NY MALE	1	.1	49	4.2	22	1.9	43	3.7	115	9.9	1,035	89.5	6	.5	
CORNEL U ENDOWED COLLEGES															
NY TOTAL	4	.8	17	3.4	4	.8	6	1.2	31	6.2	463	93.0	4	.8	
NY FEMALE	0	.0	8	7.0	0	.0	3	2.6	11	9.6	102	89.5	1	.9	
NY MALE	4	1.0	9	2.3	4	1.0	3	.8	20	5.2	361	94.0	3	.8	
CORNELL U MEDICAL CENTER															
NY TOTAL	3	.7	32	7.9	18	4.4	14	3.4	67	16.5	332	81.6	8	2.0	
NY FEMALE	2	1.7	9	7.4	9	7.4	3	2.5	23	19.0	95	78.5	3	2.5	
NY MALE	1	.3	23	8.0	9	3.1	11	3.8	44	15.4	237	82.9	5	1.7	
CORNELL U STATUTORY C															
NY TOTAL	2	.6	3	1.0	3	1.0	1	.3	9	2.9	299	97.1	0	.0	
NY FEMALE	0	.0	3	2.1	2	1.4	0	.0	5	3.5	136	96.5	0	.0	
NY MALE	2	1.2	0	.0	1	.6	1	.6	4	2.4	163	97.6	0	.0	

202

IN /E	BLACK NON-HISPANIC		ASIAN OR PACIFIC ISLANDER		HISPANIC		TOTAL MINORITY		WHITE NON-HISPANIC		NON-RESIDENT ALIEN		TOTAL
	NUMBER	%	NUMBER	%	NUMBER	%	NUMBER	%	NUMBER	%	NUMBER	%	NUMBER
TINUED													
	5	.4	2	.2	7	.6	14	1.3	1,101	98.7	0	.0	1,115
	1	.3	0	.0	0	.0	1	.3	356	99.7	0	.0	357
	4	.5	2	.3	7	.9	13	1.7	745	98.3	0	.0	758
	4	4.3	0	.0	1	1.1	5	5.4	85	91.4	3	3.2	93
	1	3.8	0	.0	0	.0	1	3.8	25	96.2	0	.0	26
	3	4.5	0	.0	1	1.5	4	6.0	60	89.6	3	4.5	67
	60	8.3	4	.6	19	2.6	88	12.1	633	87.2	5	.7	726
	36	11.5	0	.0	5	1.6	46	14.6	268	85.4	0	.0	314
	24	5.8	4	1.0	14	3.4	42	10.2	365	88.6	5	1.2	412
	0	.0	0	.0	0	.0	0	.0	91	100.0	0	.0	91
	0	.0	0	.0	0	.0	0	.0	0	.0	0	.0	0
	0	.0	0	.0	0	.0	0	.0	91	100.0	0	.0	91
	0	.0	0	.0	0	.0	0	.0	51	100.0	0	.0	51
	0	.0	0	.0	0	.0	0	.0	2	100.0	0	.0	2
	0	.0	0	.0	0	.0	0	.0	49	100.0	0	.0	49
	0	.0	0	.0	6	18.2	6	18.2	27	81.8	0	.0	33
	0	.0	0	.0	0	.0	0	.0	1	100.0	0	.0	1
	0	.0	0	.0	6	18.8	6	18.8	26	81.3	0	.0	32
	25	5.7	10	2.3	18	4.1	53	12.0	387	87.6	2	.5	442
	16	12.1	5	3.8	6	4.5	27	20.5	105	79.5	0	.0	132
	9	2.9	5	1.6	12	3.9	26	8.4	282	91.0	2	.6	310
	5	.8	0	.0	0	.0	5	.8	641	98.8	3	.5	649
	2	1.7	0	.0	0	.0	2	1.7	117	98.3	0	.0	119
	3	.6	0	.0	0	.0	3	.6	524	98.9	3	.6	530
	12	2.7	7	1.6	7	1.6	26	5.9	411	93.6	2	.5	439
	4	10.8	3	8.1	2	5.4	9	24.3	28	75.7	0	.0	37
	8	2.0	4	1.0	5	1.2	17	4.2	383	95.3	2	.5	402
	0	.0	2	2.2	0	.0	2	2.2	89	97.8	0	.0	91
	0	.0	2	9.5	0	.0	2	9.5	19	90.5	0	.0	21
	0	.0	0	.0	0	.0	0	.0	70	100.0	0	.0	70
	52	4.1	15	1.2	35	2.8	103	8.1	1,165	91.7	3	.2	1,271
	29	8.0	5	1.4	8	2.2	43	11.8	320	88.2	0	.0	363
	23	2.5	10	1.1	27	3.0	60	6.6	845	93.1	3	.3	908
	23	3.0	7	.9	19	2.5	49	6.5	705	93.3	2	.3	756
	12	6.2	0	.0	7	3.6	19	9.7	176	90.3	0	.0	195
	11	2.0	7	1.2	12	2.1	30	5.3	529	94.3	2	.4	561
	24	49.0	3	6.1	3	6.1	30	61.2	19	38.8	0	.0	49
	3	20.0	0	.0	1	6.7	4	26.7	11	73.3	0	.0	15
	21	61.8	3	8.8	2	5.9	26	76.5	8	23.5	0	.0	34
	89	3.4	70	2.7	66	2.5	227	8.7	2,364	90.2	30	1.1	2,621
	55	7.1	26	3.4	29	3.8	110	14.2	656	85.0	6	.8	772
	34	1.8	44	2.4	37	2.0	117	6.3	1,708	92.4	24	1.3	1,849
	4	.6	2	.3	8	1.2	17	2.5	664	97.5	0	.0	681
	2	.8	0	.0	7	2.7	11	4.3	244	95.7	0	.0	255
	2	.5	2	.5	1	.2	6	1.4	420	98.6	0	.0	426
	0	.0	0	.0	0	.0	0	.0	137	92.6	11	7.4	148
	0	.0	0	.0	0	.0	0	.0	0	.0	0	.0	0
	0	.0	0	.0	0	.0	0	.0	137	92.6	11	7.4	148
	0	.0	0	.0	1	1.5	1	1.5	60	90.9	5	7.6	66
	0	.0	0	.0	1	25.0	1	25.0	3	75.0	0	.0	4
	0	.0	0	.0	0	.0	0	.0	57	91.9	5	8.1	62
	20	1.8	4	.4	20	1.8	44	4.0	1,068	96.0	0	.0	1,112
	7	2.1	2	.6	13	3.9	22	6.6	311	93.4	0	.0	333
	13	1.7	2	.3	7	.9	22	2.8	757	97.2	0	.0	779
	1	2.3	1	2.3	2	4.7	4	9.3	39	90.7	0	.0	43
	0	.0	0	.0	0	.0	0	.0	0	.0	0	.0	0
	1	2.3	1	2.3	2	4.7	4	9.3	39	90.7	0	.0	43
	0	.0	0	.0	0	.0	0	.0	57	91.9	5	8.1	62
	0	.0	0	.0	0	.0	0	.0	5	100.0	0	.0	5
	0	.0	0	.0	0	.0	0	.0	52	91.2	5	8.8	57
	2	2.2	0	.0	1	1.1	3	3.3	87	95.6	1	1.1	91
	0	.0	0	.0	0	.0	0	.0	0	.0	0	.0	0
	2	2.2	0	.0	1	1.1	3	3.3	87	95.6	1	1.1	91
	29	3.8	3	.4	10	1.3	44	5.8	711	94.2	0	.0	755
	10	3.8	0	.0	1	.4	12	4.6	248	95.4	0	.0	260
	19	3.8	3	.6	9	1.8	32	6.5	463	93.5	0	.0	495
	53	5.6	15	1.6	18	1.9	88	9.3	852	90.3	4	.4	944
	28	12.6	5	2.2	8	3.6	42	18.8	178	79.8	3	1.3	223
	25	3.5	10	1.4	10	1.4	46	6.4	674	93.5	1	.1	721

	AMERICAN INDIAN ALASKAN NATIVE		BLACK NON-HISPANIC		ASIAN OR PACIFIC ISLANDER		HISPANIC		TOTAL MINORITY		WHITE NON-HISPANIC		NON-RESIDENT ALIEN	
	NUMBER	%	NUMBER	%	NUMBER	%	NUMBER	%	NUMBER	%	NUMBER	%	NUMBER	%
NEW YORK	**CONTINUED**													
SUNY HLTH SCI CTR STNY BK														
NY TOTAL	0	.0	20	6.4	10	3.2	20	6.4	50	15.9	264	84.1	0	.0
NY FEMALE	0	.0	7	6.5	3	2.8	12	11.2	22	20.6	85	79.4	0	.0
NY MALE	0	.0	13	6.3	7	3.4	8	3.9	28	13.5	179	86.5	0	.0
SUNY DOWNSTATE MEDL CTR														
NY TOTAL	1	.1	47	5.3	17	1.9	18	2.0	83	9.3	806	90.6	1	.1
NY FEMALE	1	.5	19	8.8	6	2.8	5	2.3	31	14.4	183	85.1	1	.5
NY MALE	0	.0	28	4.1	11	1.6	13	1.9	52	.7.7	623	92.3	0	.0
SUNY UPSTATE MEDICAL CTR														
NY TOTAL	1	.2	22	4.1	10	1.9	3	.6	36	6.8	496	93.2	0	.0
NY FEMALE	1	.8	9	6.8	6	4.5	1	.8	17	12.8	116	87.2	0	.0
NY MALE	0	.0	13	3.3	4	1.0	2	.5	19	4.8	380	95.2	0	.0
SUNY STATE C OF OPTOMETRY														
NY TOTAL	1	.5	2	.9	6	2.7	2	.9	11	5.0	206	93.6	3	1.4
NY FEMALE	0	.0	2	3.6	4	7.1	1	1.8	7	12.5	48	85.7	1	1.8
NY MALE	1	.6	0	.0	2	1.2	1	.6	4	2.4	158	96.3	2	1.2
SYRACUSE U MAIN CAMPUS														
NY TOTAL	7	1.0	33	4.9	2	.3	9	1.3	51	7.6	623	92.3	1	.1
NY FEMALE	5	2.4	12	5.7	1	.5	2	.9	20	9.5	191	90.5	0	.0
NY MALE	2	.4	21	4.5	1	.2	7	1.5	31	6.7	432	93.1	1	.2
UNION THEOLOGICAL SEM														
NY TOTAL	0	.0	25	11.1	1	.4	10	4.4	36	16.0	189	84.0	0	.0
NY FEMALE	0	.0	8	6.3	0	.0	3	2.4	11	8.7	115	91.3	0	.0
NY MALE	0	.0	17	17.2	1	1.0	7	7.1	25	25.3	74	74.7	0	.0
UNIVERSITY OF ROCHESTER														
NY TOTAL	0	.0	6	1.5	4	1.0	4	1.0	14	3.5	381	95.3	5	1.3
NY FEMALE	0	.0	1	.9	0	.0	1	.9	2	1.8	109	98.2	0	.0
NY MALE	0	.0	5	1.7	4	1.4	3	1.0	12	4.2	272	94.1	5	1.7
YESHIVA UNIVERSITY														
NY TOTAL	1	.1	20	1.3	28	1.8	19	1.2	68	4.3	1,481	93.1	42	2.6
NY FEMALE	0	.0	13	1.9	9	1.3	5	.7	27	4.0	637	95.1	6	.9
NY MALE	1	.1	7	.8	19	2.1	14	1.5	41	4.5	844	91.6	36	3.9
YESHIVATH ZICHRON MOSHE														
NY TOTAL	0	.0	0	.0	0	.0	0	.0	0	.0	0	.0	0	.0
NY FEMALE	0	.0	0	.0	0	.0	0	.0	0	.0	0	.0	0	.0
NY MALE	0	.0	0	.0	0	.0	0	.0	0	.0	0	.0	0	.0
NEW YORK	**TOTAL (**		**41 INSTITUTIONS)**											
NY TOTAL	37	.2	791	3.5	305	1.3	441	2.0	1,574	7.0	20,878	92.4	148	.7
NY FEMALE	19	.3	375	5.5	110	1.6	153	2.3	657	9.7	6,083	90.0	22	.3
NY MALE	18	.1	416	2.6	195	1.2	288	1.8	917	5.8	14,795	93.4	126	.9
NORTH CAROLINA														
CAMPBELL COLLEGE														
NC TOTAL	0	.0	5	1.8	1	.4	0	.0	6	2.2	265	97.8	0	.0
NC FEMALE	0	.0	0	.0	0	.0	0	.0	0	.0	38	100.0	0	.0
NC MALE	0	.0	5	2.1	1	.4	0	.0	6	2.6	227	97.4	0	.0
DUKE UNIVERSITY														
NC TOTAL	1	.1	89	6.2	9	.6	4	.3	103	7.2	1,313	91.8	15	1.0
NC FEMALE	0	.0	29	7.1	1	.2	2	.5	32	7.8	374	91.0	5	1.2
NC MALE	1	.1	60	5.9	8	.8	2	.2	71	7.0	939	92.1	10	1.0
STHESTH BAPTIST THEOL SEM														
NC TOTAL	0	.0	0	.0	0	.0	0	.0	0	.0	0	.0	0	.0
NC FEMALE	0	.0	0	.0	0	.0	0	.0	0	.0	0	.0	0	.0
NC MALE	0	.0	0	.0	0	.0	0	.0	0	.0	0	.0	0	.0
EAST CAROLINA UNIVERSITY														
NC TOTAL	0	.0	5	7.7	2	3.1	0	.0	7	10.8	58	89.2	0	.0
NC FEMALE	0	.0	1	8.3	0	.0	0	.0	1	8.3	11	91.7	0	.0
NC MALE	0	.0	4	7.5	2	3.8	0	.0	6	11.3	47	88.7	0	.0
NC CENTRAL UNIVERSITY														
NC TOTAL	0	.0	115	56.9	0	.0	1	.5	116	57.4	85	42.1	1	.5
NC FEMLE	0	.0	30	61.2	0	.0	0	.0	30	61.2	19	38.8	0	.0
NC MALE	0	.0	85	55.6	0	.0	1	.7	86	56.2	66	43.1	1	.7
U OF NC AT CHAPEL HILL														
NC TOTAL	15	.9	138	8.5	9	.6	6	.4	168	10.4	1,452	89.5	2	.1
NC FEMALE	3	.7	52	12.4	4	1.0	2	.5	61	14.5	360	85.5	0	.0
NC MALE	12	1.0	86	7.2	5	.4	4	.3	107	8.9	1,092	90.9	2	.2
HAKE FOREST UNIVERSITY														
NC TOTAL	8	.9	20	2.2	3	.3	5	.6	36	4.0	847	94.8	10	1.1
NC FEMALE	2	1.1	5	2.8	2	1.1	0	.0	9	5.0	168	93.3	3	1.7
NC MALE	6	.8	15	2.1	1	.1	5	.7	27	3.8	679	95.2	7	1.0
NORTH CAROLINA	**TOTAL (**		**7 INSTITUTIONS)**											
NC TOTAL	24	.5	372	8.3	24	.5	16	.4	436	9.7	4,020	89.7	28	.6
NC FEMALE	5	.5	117	10.5	7	.6	4	.4	133	12.0	970	87.3	8	.7
NC MALE	19	.6	255	7.6	17	.5	12	.4	303	9.0	3,050	90.4	20	.6
NORTH DAKOTA														
U OF ND MAIN CAMPUS														
ND TOTAL	10	2.1	0	.0	2	.4	0	.0	12	2.5	473	97.5	0	.0
ND FEMALE	1	1.1	0	.0	0	.0	0	.0	1	1.1	93	98.9	0	.0
ND MALE	9	2.3	0	.0	2	.5	0	.0	11	2.8	380	97.2	0	.0
NORTH DAKOTA	**TOTAL (**		**1 INSTITUTIONS)**											
ND TOTAL	10	2.1	0	.0	2	.4	0	.0	12	2.5	473	97.5	0	.0
ND FEMALE	1	1.1	0	.0	0	.0	0	.0	1	1.1	93	98.9	0	.0
ND MALE	9	2.3	0	.0	2	.5	0	.0	11	2.8	380	97.2	0	.0

FESSIONAL ENROLLMENT OF INSTITUTIONS OF HIGHER EDUCATION BY RACE, ETHNICITY AND SEX:
TATE AND NATION, 1978

	BLACK NON-HISPANIC		ASIAN OR PACIFIC ISLANDER		HISPANIC		TOTAL MINORITY		WHITE NON-HISPANIC		NON-RESIDENT ALIEN		TOTAL
	NUMBER	%	NUMBER	%	NUMBER	%	NUMBER	%	NUMBER	%	NUMBER	%	NUMBER
	89	21.8	19	4.6	20	4.9	133	32.5	260	63.6	16	3.9	409
	42	23.7	6	3.4	6	3.4	57	32.2	115	65.0	5	2.8	177
	47	20.3	13	5.6	14	6.0	76	32.8	145	62.5	11	4.7	232
	0	.0	0	.0	0	.0	0	.0	63	98.4	1	1.6	64
	0	.0	0	.0	0	.0	0	.0	0	.0	0	.0	0
	0	.0	0	.0	0	.0	0	.0	63	98.4	1	1.6	64
	21	3.3	0	.0	2	.3	24	3.8	608	96.2	0	.0	632
	6	3.7	0	.0	0	.0	6	3.7	157	96.3	0	.0	163
	15	3.2	0	.0	2	.4	18	3.8	451	96.2	0	.0	469
	57	3.3	12	.7	6	.4	78	4.6	1,596	93.8	28	1.6	1,702
	30	5.9	4	.8	1	.2	38	7.5	466	91.6	5	1.0	509
	27	2.3	8	.7	5	.4	40	3.4	1,130	94.7	23	1.9	1,193
	0	.0	0	.0	0	.0	0	.0	42	97.7	1	2.3	43
	0	.0	0	.0	0	.0	0	.0	2	100.0	0	.0	2
	0	.0	0	.0	0	.0	0	.0	40	97.6	1	2.4	41
	96	8.2	5	.4	4	.3	107	9.2	1,057	90.7	1	.1	1,165
	35	10.4	0	.0	0	.0	36	10.7	301	89.3	0	.0	337
	61	7.4	5	.6	4	.5	71	8.6	756	91.3	1	.1	828
	0	.0	0	.0	0	.0	0	.0	29	96.7	1	3.3	30
	0	.0	0	.0	0	.0	0	.0	5	100.0	0	.0	5
	0	.0	0	.0	0	.0	0	.0	24	96.0	1	4.0	25
	0	.0	0	.0	0	.0	0	.0	22	100.0	0	.0	22
	0	.0	0	.0	0	.0	0	.0	4	100.0	0	.0	4
	0	.0	0	.0	0	.0	0	.0	18	100.0	0	.0	18
	0	.0	0	.0	0	.0	0	.0	37	100.0	0	.0	37
	0	.0	0	.0	0	.0	0	.0	15	100.0	0	.0	15
	0	.0	0	.0	0	.0	0	.0	22	100.0	0	.0	22
	25	6.8	5	1.4	4	1.1	34	9.2	335	90.8	0	.0	369
	6	5.9	2	2.0	0	.0	8	7.9	93	92.1	0	.0	101
	19	7.1	3	1.1	4	1.5	26	9.7	242	90.3	0	.0	268
	15	6.8	3	1.4	0	.0	18	8.1	202	91.0	2	.9	222
	3	4.8	1	1.6	0	.0	4	6.5	58	93.5	0	.0	62
	12	7.5	2	1.3	0	.0	14	8.8	144	90.0	2	1.3	160
	2	2.1	0	.0	0	.0	2	2.1	93	97.9	0	.0	95
	2	6.1	0	.0	0	.0	2	6.1	31	93.9	0	.0	33
	0	.0	0	.0	0	.0	0	.0	62	100.0	0	.0	62
	27	4.8	3	.5	4	.7	34	6.1	516	92.0	11	2.0	561
	9	18.4	2	4.1	1	2.0	12	24.5	36	73.5	1	2.0	49
	18	3.5	1	.2	3	.6	22	4.3	480	93.8	10	2.0	512
	3	.6	1	.2	1	.2	5	.9	529	99.1	0	.0	534
	1	1.1	0	.0	1	1.1	2	2.2	87	97.8	0	.0	89
	2	.4	1	.2	0	.0	3	.7	442	99.3	0	.0	445
	82	2.9	15	.5	17	.6	114	4.1	2,668	95.9	0	.0	2,782
	32	4.9	3	.5	6	.9	41	6.3	611	93.7	0	.0	652
	50	2.3	12	.6	11	.5	73	3.4	2,057	96.6	0	.0	2,130
	0	.0	0	.0	0	.0	0	.0	105	100.0	0	.0	105
	0	.0	0	.0	0	.0	0	.0	26	100.0	0	.0	26
	0	.0	0	.0	0	.0	0	.0	79	100.0	0	.0	79
	17	85.0	0	.0	0	.0	17	85.0	1	5.0	2	10.0	20
	2	100.0	0	.0	0	.0	2	100.0	0	.0	0	.0	2
	15	83.3	0	.0	0	.0	15	83.3	1	5.6	2	11.1	18
	1	1.4	0	.0	0	.0	1	1.4	69	98.6	0	.0	70
	0	.0	0	.0	0	.0	0	.0	1	100.0	0	.0	1
	1	1.4	0	.0	0	.0	1	1.4	68	98.6	0	.0	69
	7	2.7	0	.0	0	.0	253	99.2	0	.0	2	.8	255
	2	6.3	0	.0	0	.0	31	96.9	0	.0	1	3.1	32
	5	2.2	0	.0	0	.0	222	99.6	0	.0	1	.4	223
	18	6.7	0	.0	0	.0	18	6.7	250	92.6	2	.7	270
	4	6.6	0	.0	0	.0	4	6.6	57	93.4	0	.0	61
	14	6.7	0	.0	0	.0	14	6.7	193	92.3	2	1.0	209
	16	2.9	0	.0	3	.5	20	3.6	539	96.3	1	.2	560
	9	5.4	0	.0	1	.6	11	6.6	156	93.4	0	.0	167
	7	1.8	0	.0	2	.5	9	2.3	383	97.5	1	.3	393
	80	6.9	12	1.0	11	1.0	103	8.9	1,051	90.8	3	.3	1,157
	40	11.9	3	.9	3	.6	45	13.4	289	86.0	2	.6	336
	40	4.9	9	1.1	9	1.1	58	7.1	762	92.8	1	.1	821
	16	3.6	0	.0	2	.5	19	4.3	422	95.7	0	.0	441
	5	4.5	0	.0	0	.0	6	5.4	105	94.6	0	.0	111
	11	3.3	0	.0	2	.6	13	3.9	317	96.1	0	.0	330

	AMERICAN INDIAN ALASKAN NATIVE		BLACK NON-HISPANIC		ASIAN OR PACIFIC ISLANDER		HISPANIC		TOTAL MINORITY		WHITE NON-HISPANIC		NON-RESIDENT ALIEN	
	NUMBER	%	NUMBER	%	NUMBER	%	NUMBER	%	NUMBER	%	NUMBER	%	NUMBER	%
OHIO CONTINUED														
UNIVERSITY OF TOLEDO														
OH TOTAL	3	.4	41	5.0	2	.2	3	.4	49	6.0	749	91.5	21	2.6
OH FEMALE	0	.0	18	9.8	2	1.1	2	1.1	22	12.0	155	84.7	6	3.3
OH MALE	3	.5	23	3.6	0	.0	1	.2	27	4.2	594	93.4	15	2.4
WRIGHT ST U MAIN CAMPUS														
OH TOTAL	0	.0	16	10.2	4	2.5	0	.0	20	12.7	137	87.3	0	.0
OH FEMALE	0	.0	7	17.5	1	2.5	0	.0	8	20.0	32	80.0	0	.0
OH MALE	0	.0	9	7.7	3	2.6	0	.0	12	10.3	105	89.7	0	.0
OHIO TOTAL (25 INSTITUTIONS)														
OH TOTAL	262	2.1	629	5.0	81	.6	77	.6	1,049	8.4	11,380	90.9	92	.7
OH FEMALE	38	1.2	253	8.0	24	.8	20	.6	335	10.6	2,802	88.8	20	.6
OH MALE	224	2.4	376	4.0	57	.6	57	.6	714	7.6	8,578	91.6	72	.8
OKLAHOMA														
OKLAHOMA CITY UNIVERSITY														
OK TOTAL	7	1.6	12	2.7	2	.4	4	.9	25	5.6	423	94.4	0	.0
OK FEMALE	1	1.0	5	5.0	0	.0	0	.0	6	5.9	95	94.1	0	.0
OK MALE	6	1.7	7	2.0	2	.6	4	1.2	19	5.5	328	94.5	0	.0
OKLA C OSTEO MED AND SURG														
OK TOTAL	5	2.1	4	1.7	2	.8	1	.4	12	5.1	225	94.9	0	.0
OK FEMALE	0	.0	2	5.7	1	2.9	0	.0	3	8.6	32	91.4	0	.0
OK MALE	5	2.5	2	1.0	1	.5	1	.5	9	4.5	193	95.5	0	.0
OKLA STATE U MAIN CAMPUS														
OK TOTAL	4	1.6	1	.4	3	1.2	1	.4	9	3.5	247	96.5	0	.0
OK FEMALE	0	.0	0	.0	1	1.7	0	.0	1	1.7	58	98.3	0	.0
OK MALE	4	2.0	1	.5	2	1.0	1	.5	8	4.1	189	95.9	0	.0
PHILLIPS UNIVERSITY														
OK TOTAL	0	.0	0	.0	0	.0	0	.0	0	.0	140	100.0	0	.0
OK FEMALE	0	.0	0	.0	0	.0	0	.0	0	.0	27	100.0	0	.0
OK MALE	0	.0	0	.0	0	.0	0	.0	0	.0	113	100.0	0	.0
STHWSTN OKLA STATE U														
OK TOTAL	0	.0	0	.0	0	.0	0	.0	0	.0	3	100.0	0	.0
OK FEMALE	0	.0	0	.0	0	.0	0	.0	0	.0	2	100.0	0	.0
OK MALE	0	.0	0	.0	0	.0	0	.0	0	.0	1	100.0	0	.0
U OF OKLA HEALTH SCI CTR														
OK TOTAL	24	2.5	12	1.3	13	1.4	11	1.2	60	6.3	887	93.4	3	.3
OK FEMALE	6	3.9	3	2.0	4	2.6	2	1.3	15	9.8	138	90.2	0	.0
OK MALE	18	2.3	9	1.1	9	1.1	9	1.1	45	5.6	749	94.0	3	.4
U OF OKLAHOMA NORMAN CAM														
OK TOTAL	18	2.9	14	2.2	4	.6	7	1.1	43	6.9	580	92.9	1	.2
OK FEMALE	4	2.2	7	3.8	2	1.1	3	1.6	16	8.6	169	91.4	0	.0
OK MALE	14	3.2	7	1.6	2	.5	4	.9	27	6.2	411	93.6	1	.2
UNIVERSITY OF TULSA														
OK TOTAL	20	2.9	8	1.2	3	.4	1	.1	32	4.7	635	93.7	11	1.6
OK FEMALE	6	3.6	1	.6	1	.6	0	.0	8	4.8	157	93.5	3	1.8
OK MALE	14	2.7	7	1.4	2	.4	1	.2	24	4.7	478	93.7	8	1.6
OKLAHOMA TOTAL (8 INSTITUTIONS)														
OK TOTAL	78	2.3	51	1.5	27	.8	25	.7	181	5.4	3,140	94.1	15	.4
OK FEMALE	17	2.3	18	2.5	9	1.2	5	.7	49	6.7	678	92.9	3	.4
OK MALE	61	2.3	33	1.3	18	.7	20	.8	132	5.1	2,462	94.5	12	.5
OREGON														
LEWIS AND CLARK COLLEGE														
OR TOTAL	1	.1	12	1.6	13	1.8	7	1.0	33	4.5	698	95.5	0	.0
OR FEMALE	1	.5	4	1.9	3	1.4	2	.9	10	4.7	203	95.3	0	.0
OR MALE	0	.0	8	1.5	10	1.9	5	1.0	23	4.4	495	95.6	0	.0
U OF OREGON MAIN CAMPUS														
OR TOTAL	7	1.4	7	1.4	16	3.2	7	1.4	37	7.3	469	92.7	0	.0
OR FEMALE	3	1.7	2	1.2	8	4.7	1	.6	14	8.1	158	91.9	0	.0
OR MALE	4	1.2	5	1.5	8	2.4	6	1.8	23	6.9	311	93.1	0	.0
U OF OREGON HLTH SCI CTR														
OR TOTAL	3	.4	7	.9	23	2.9	8	1.0	41	5.2	748	94.8	0	.0
OR FEMALE	2	1.4	3	2.1	4	2.8	1	.7	10	7.1	131	92.9	0	.0
OR MALE	1	.2	4	.6	19	2.9	7	1.1	31	4.8	617	95.2	0	.0
PACIFIC UNIVERSITY														
OR TOTAL	1	.3	1	.3	29	8.8	1	.3	32	9.7	294	89.1	4	1.2
OR FEMALE	0	.0	0	.0	11	19.3	0	.0	11	19.3	46	80.7	0	.0
OR MALE	1	.4	1	.4	18	6.6	1	.4	21	7.7	248	90.8	4	1.5
WARNER PACIFIC COLLEGE														
OR TOTAL	0	.0	0	.0	0	.0	0	.0	0	.0	1	100.0	0	.0
OR FEMALE	0	.0	0	.0	0	.0	0	.0	0	.0	0	.0	0	.0
OR MALE	0	.0	0	.0	0	.0	0	.0	0	.0	1	100.0	0	.0
WESTERN CONS BAPTIST SEM														
OR TOTAL	1	.3	2	.6	5	1.4	1	.3	9	2.6	333	96.0	5	1.4
OR FEMALE	0	.0	0	.0	1	14.3	0	.0	1	14.3	6	85.7	0	.0
OR MALE	1	.3	2	.6	4	1.2	1	.3	8	2.4	327	96.2	5	1.5
WSTN EVANGELICAL SEM														
OR TOTAL	0	.0	1	.8	11	8.3	0	.0	12	9.1	110	83.3	10	7.6
OR FEMALE	0	.0	0	.0	3	25.0	0	.0	3	25.0	8	66.7	1	8.3
OR MALE	0	.0	1	.8	8	6.7	0	.0	9	7.5	102	85.0	9	7.5
WSTN STATES CHIRPRCTC C														
OR TOTAL	0	.0	3	.6	1	.2	3	.6	7	1.4	494	96.7	10	2.0
OR FEMALE	0	.0	0	.0	0	.0	0	.0	0	.0	85	97.7	2	2.3
OR MALE	0	.0	3	.7	1	.2	3	.7	7	1.7	409	96.5	8	1.9
WILLAMETTE UNIVERSITY														
OR TOTAL	2	.5	6	1.4	16	3.9	5	1.2	29	7.0	384	92.5	2	.5
OR FEMALE	1	.9	2	1.8	3	2.8	1	.9	7	6.4	102	93.6	0	.0
OR MALE	1	.3	4	1.3	13	4.2	4	1.3	22	7.2	282	92.2	2	.7

)FESSIONAL ENROLLMENT OF INSTITUTIONS OF HIGHER EDUCATION BY RACE, ETHNICITY AND SEX:
'ATE AND NATION, 1978

	BLACK NON-HISPANIC		ASIAN OR PACIFIC ISLANDER		HISPANIC		TOTAL MINORITY		WHITE NON-HISPANIC		NON-RESIDENT ALIEN		TOTAL
	NUMBER	%	NUMBER	%	NUMBER	%	NUMBER	%	NUMBER	%	NUMBER	%	NUMBER
(9 INSTITUTIONS)													
	39	1.0	114	3.0	32	.9	200	5.3	3,531	93.9	31	.8	3,762
	11	1.4	33	4.1	5	.6	56	7.0	739	92.6	3	.4	798
	28	.9	81	2.7	27	.9	144	4.9	2,792	94.2	28	.9	2,964
	0	.0	0	.0	0	.0	0	.0	15	100.0	0	.0	15
	0	.0	0	.0	0	.0	0	.0	0	.0	0	.0	0
	0	.0	0	.0	0	.0	0	.0	15	100.0	0	.0	15
	1	1.8	0	.0	0	.0	1	1.8	55	98.2	0	.0	56
	0	.0	0	.0	0	.0	0	.0	0	.0	0	.0	0
	1	1.8	0	.0	0	.0	1	1.8	55	98.2	0	.0	56
	5	1.1	2	.4	6	1.3	14	3.0	455	97.0	0	.0	469
	1	.7	0	.0	1	.7	2	1.4	137	98.6	0	.0	139
	4	1.2	2	.6	5	1.5	12	3.6	318	96.4	0	.0	330
	0	.0	0	.0	0	.0	0	.0	727	100.0		.0	727
	0	.0	0	.0	0	.0	0	.0	122	100.0		.0	122
	0	.0	0	.0	0	.0	0	.0	605	100.0	0	.0	605
	23	12.2	0	.0	1	.5	24	12.8	159	84.6	5	2.7	188
	4	9.5	0	.0	0	.0	4	9.5	37	88.1	1	2.4	42
	19	13.0	0	.0	1	.7	20	13.7	122	83.6	4	2.7	146
	0	.0	4	11.4	0	.0	4	11.4	15	42.9	16	45.7	35
	0	.0	1	20.0	0	.0	1	20.0	0	.0	4	80.0	5
	0	.0	3	10.0	0	.0	3	10.0	15	50.0	12	40.0	30
	64	8.1	4	.5	10	1.3	79	10.0	709	89.7	2	.3	790
	29	15.8	2	1.1	2	1.1	33	18.0	150	82.0	0	.0	183
	35	5.8	2	.3	8	1.3	46	7.6	559	92.1	2	.3	607
	4	3.0	0	.0	3	2.2	7	5.2	126	93.3	2	1.5	135
	0	.0	0	.0	3	8.8	3	8.8	29	85.3	2	5.9	34
	4	4.0	0	.0	0	.0	4	4.0	97	96.0	0	.0	101
	1	.4	1	.4	0	.0	2	.9	220	98.7	1	.4	223
	1	2.4	0	.0	0	.0	1	2.4	40	97.6	0	.0	41
	0	.0	1	.5	0	.0	1	.5	180	98.9	1	.5	182
	6	3.7	2	1.2	1	.6	9	5.6	153	94.4	0	.0	162
	0	.0	1	2.0	0	.0	1	2.0	48	98.0	0	.0	49
	6	5.3	1	.9	1	.9	8	7.1	105	92.9	0	.0	113
	0	.0	0	.0	0	.0	0	.0	38	92.7	3	7.3	41
	0	.0	0	.0	0	.0	0	.0	0	.0	0	.0	0
	0	.0	0	.0	0	.0	0	.0	38	92.7	3	7.3	41
	12	2.6	6	1.3	3	.7	22	4.8	433	94.5	3	.7	458
	9	3.4	6	2.3	3	1.1	19	7.2	242	92.0	2	.8	263
	3	1.5	0	.0	0	.0	3	1.5	191	97.9	1	.5	195
	5	.9	6	1.0	7	1.2	18	3.1	552	96.5	2	.3	572
	5	7.5	5	7.5	4	6.0	14	20.9	53	79.1	0	.0	67
	0	.0	1	.2	3	.6	4	.8	499	98.8	2	.4	505
	9	1.9	6	1.3	3	.6	21	4.5	433	93.5	9	1.9	463
	3	3.9	1	1.3	1	1.3	6	7.8	69	89.6	2	2.6	77
	6	1.6	5	1.3	2	.5	15	3.9	364	94.3	7	1.8	386
	15	3.9	3	.8	8	2.1	27	7.0	357	92.7	1	.3	385
	4	4.3	0	.0	1	1.1	5	5.4	88	94.6	0	.0	93
	11	3.8	3	1.0	7	2.4	22	7.5	269	92.1	1	.3	292
	16	2.0	3	.4	0	.0	19	2.3	796	97.3	3	.4	818
	3	2.2	1	.7	0	.0	4	3.0	131	97.0	0	.0	135
	13	1.9	2	.3	0	.0	15	2.2	665	97.4	3	.4	683
	1	3.6	2	7.1	0	.0	3	10.7	24	85.7	1	3.6	28
	1	9.1	1	9.1	0	.0	2	18.2	8	72.7	1	9.1	11
	0	.0	1	5.9	0	.0	1	5.9	16	94.1	0	.0	17
	16	11.0	3	2.1	0	.0	19	13.1	126	86.9	0	.0	145
	5	10.9	1	2.2	0	.0	6	13.0	40	87.0	0	.0	46
	11	11.1	2	2.0	0	.0	13	13.1	86	86.9	0	.0	99
	0	.0	0	.0	0	.0	0	.0	35	100.0	0	.0	35
	0	.0	0	.0	0	.0	0	.0	0	.0	0	.0	0
	0	.0	0	.0	0	.0	0	.0	35	100.0	0	.0	35
	2	1.9	0	.0	0	.0	2	1.9	104	98.1	0	.0	106
	0	.0	0	.0	0	.0	0	.0	0	.0	0	.0	0
	2	1.9	0	.0	0	.0	2	1.9	104	99.1	0	.0	106
	0	.0	0	.0	1	2.3	1	2.3	42	97.7	0	.0	43
	0	.0	0	.0	0	.0	0	.0	0	.0	0	.0	0
	0	.0	0	.0	1	2.3	1	2.3	42	97.7	0	.0	43

TABLE 3 - TOTAL FIRST PROFESSIONAL ENROLLMENT OF INSTITUTIONS OF HIGHER EDUCATION BY RACE, ETHNICITY AND SEX:
INSTITUTION, STATE AND NATION, 1978

	AMERICAN INDIAN ALASKAN NATIVE		BLACK NON-HISPANIC		ASIAN OR PACIFIC ISLANDER		HISPANIC		TOTAL MINORITY		WHITE NON-HISPANIC		NON-RESIDENT ALIEN	
	NUMBER	%	NUMBER	%	NUMBER	%	NUMBER	%	NUMBER	%	NUMBER	%	NUMBER	%
PENNSYLVANIA CONTINUED														
SAINT VINCENT SEMINARY														
PA TOTAL	0	.0	1	1.7	0	.0	2	3.4	3	5.2	55	94.8	0	.0
PA FEMALE	0	.0	0	.0	0	.0	0	.0	0	.0	3	100.0	0	.0
PA MALE	0	.0	1	1.8	0	.0	2	3.6	3	5.5	52	94.5	0	.0
TEMPLE UNIVERSITY														
PA TOTAL	4	.2	188	7.7	30	1.2	40	1.6	262	10.7	2,178	88.8	14	.6
PA FEMALE	2	.3	84	12.4	12	1.8	14	2.1	112	16.5	559	82.3	8	1.2
PA MALE	2	.1	104	5.9	18	1.0	26	1.5	150	8.5	1,619	91.2	6	.3
THEOL SEM REFORMO EPIS CH														
PA TOTAL	0	.0	5	6.7	1	1.3	0	.0	6	8.0	69	92.0	0	.0
PA FEMALE	0	.0	0	.0	0	.0	0	.0	0	.0	4	100.0	0	.0
PA MALE	0	.0	5	7.0	1	1.4	0	.0	6	8.5	65	91.5	0	.0
THOMAS JEFF UNIVERSITY														
PA TOTAL	4	.4	40	4.4	26	2.9	9	1.0	79	8.8	822	91.2	0	.0
PA FEMALE	1	.6	15	8.7	8	4.6	2	1.2	26	15.0	147	85.0	0	.0
PA MALE	3	.4	25	3.4	18	2.5	7	1.0	53	7.3	675	92.7	0	.0
U OF PENNSYLVANIA														
PA TOTAL	6	.2	87	3.6	32	1.3	31	1.3	156	6.4	2,241	91.7	47	1.9
PA FEMALE	2	.3	51	6.8	8	1.1	11	1.5	72	9.5	669	88.7	13	1.7
PA MALE	4	.2	36	2.1	24	1.4	20	1.2	84	5.0	1,572	93.0	34	2.0
U OF PITTSBG MAIN CAMPUS														
PA TOTAL	1	.1	61	3.5	17	1.0	8	.5	87	5.0	1,658	95.0	0	.0
PA FEMALE	0	.0	28	6.9	5	1.2	3	.7	36	8.9	367	91.1	0	.0
PA MALE	1	.1	33	2.5	12	.9	5	.4	51	3.8	1,291	96.2	0	.0
VILLANOVA UNIVERSITY														
PA TOTAL	0	.0	0	.0	0	.0	0	.0	0	.0	631	100.0	0	.0
PA FEMALE	0	.0	0	.0	0	.0	0	.0	0	.0	218	100.0	0	.0
PA MALE	0	.0	0	.0	0	.0	0	.0	0	.0	413	100.0	0	.0
WESTMINSTER THEOL SEM														
PA TOTAL	0	.0	0	.0	4	4.0	2	2.0	6	5.9	88	87.1	7	6.9
PA FEMALE	0	.0	0	.0	0	.0	0	.0	0	.0	0	.0	0	.0
PA MALE	0	.0	0	.0	4	4.0	2	2.0	6	5.9	88	87.1	7	6.9
PENNSYLVANIA TOTAL (29 INSTITUTIONS)														
PA TOTAL	22	.2	562	3.9	152	1.1	135	.9	871	6.1	13,316	93.1	116	.8
PA FEMALE	7	.2	243	6.9	52	1.5	45	1.3	347	9.8	3,161	89.3	33	.9
PA MALE	15	.1	319	3.0	100	.9	90	.8	524	4.9	10,155	94.4	83	.8
RHODE ISLAND														
BROWN UNIVERSITY														
RI TOTAL	0	.0	14	5.5	11	4.3	5	2.0	30	11.9	219	86.6	4	1.6
RI FEMALE	0	.0	5	5.9	9	10.6	0	.0	14	16.5	70	82.4	1	1.2
RI MALE	0	.0	9	5.4	2	1.2	5	3.0	16	9.5	149	88.7	3	1.8
RHODE ISLAND TOTAL (1 INSTITUTIONS)														
RI TOTAL	0	.0	14	5.5	11	4.3	5	2.0	30	11.9	219	86.6	4	1.6
RI FEMALE	0	.0	5	5.9	9	10.6	0	.0	14	16.5	70	82.4	1	1.2
RI MALE	0	.0	9	5.4	2	1.2	5	3.0	16	9.5	149	88.7	3	1.8
SOUTH CAROLINA														
BOB JONES UNIVERSITY														
SC TOTAL	0	.0	0	.0	0	.0	0	.0	0	.0	0	.0	0	.0
SC FEMALE	0	.0	0	.0	0	.0	0	.0	0	.0	0	.0	0	.0
SC MALE	0	.0	0	.0	0	.0	0	.0	0	.0	0	.0	0	.0
COLUMBIA BIBLE COLLEGE														
SC TOTAL	0	.0	0	.0	1	1.6	0	.0	1	1.6	57	90.5	5	7.9
SC FEMALE	0	.0	0	.0	0	.0	0	.0	0	.0	1	100.0	0	.0
SC MALE	0	.0	0	.0	1	1.6	0	.0	1	1.6	56	90.3	5	8.1
ERSKINE C AND SEMINARY														
SC TOTAL	0	.0	1	2.6	0	.0	0	.0	1	2.6	36	94.7	1	2.6
SC FEMALE	0	.0	0	.0	0	.0	0	.0	0	.0	3	100.0	0	.0
SC MALE	0	.0	1	2.9	0	.0	0	.0	1	2.9	33	94.3	1	2.9
LUTHERAN THEOL STHN SEM														
SC TOTAL	0	.0	2	1.8	0	.0	1	.9	3	2.6	110	96.5	1	.9
SC FEMALE	0	.0	0	.0	0	.0	0	.0	0	.0	12	100.0	0	.0
SC MALE	0	.0	2	2.0	0	.0	1	1.0	3	2.9	98	96.1	1	1.0
MEDICAL UNIVERSITY OF SC														
SC TOTAL	1	.1	36	4.1	3	.3	1	.1	41	4.7	828	95.1	2	.2
SC FEMALE	1	.6	10	6.3	0	.0	0	.0	11	7.0	147	93.0	0	.0
SC MALE	0	.0	26	3.6	3	.4	1	.1	30	4.2	681	95.5	2	.3
SHERMAN C OF CHIROPRACTIC														
SC TOTAL	1	.2	0	.0	0	.0	2	.5	3	.7	355	87.9	46	11.4
SC FEMALE	1	1.2	0	.0	0	.0	1	1.2	2	2.4	68	81.0	14	16.7
SC MALE	0	.0	0	.0	0	.0	1	.3	1	.3	287	89.7	32	10.0
U OF SC AT COLUMBIA														
SC TOTAL	0	.0	52	7.1	0	.0	0	.0	52	7.1	681	92.9	0	.0
SC FEMALE	0	.0	14	7.8	0	.0	0	.0	14	7.8	165	92.2	0	.0
SC MALE	0	.0	38	6.9	0	.0	0	.0	38	6.9	516	93.1	0	.0
SOUTH CAROLINA TOTAL (7 INSTITUTIONS)														
SC TOTAL	2	.1	91	4.1	4	.2	4	.2	101	4.5	2,067	93.0	55	2.5
SC FEMALE	2	.5	24	5.5	0	.0	1	.2	27	6.2	396	90.6	14	3.2
SC MALE	0	.0	67	3.8	4	.2	3	.2	74	4.1	1,671	93.6	41	2.3
SOUTH DAKOTA														
NORTH AMERICAN BAPT SEM														
SD TOTAL	0	.0	1	1.1	0	.0	1	1.1	2	2.2	72	79.1	17	18.7
SD FEMALE	0	.0	0	.0	0	.0	0	.0	0	.0	9	75.0	3	25.0
SD MALE	0	.0	1	1.3	0	.0	1	1.3	2	2.5	63	79.7	14	17.7

208

BLACK NON-HISPANIC		ASIAN OR PACIFIC ISLANDER		HISPANIC		TOTAL MINORITY		WHITE NON-HISPANIC		NON-RESIDENT ALIEN		TOTAL
NUMBER	%	NUMBER	%	NUMBER	%	NUMBER	%	NUMBER	%	NUMBER	%	NUMBER
NUE D												
0	.0	1	.2	0	.0	2	.5	414	99.5	0	.0	416
0	.0	0	.0	0	.0	0	.0	85	100.0	0	.0	85
0	.0	1	.3	0	.0	2	.6	329	99.4	0	.0	331
(2 INSTITUTIONS)												
1	.2	1	.2	1	.2	4	.8	486	95.9	17	3.4	507
0	.0	0	.0	0	.0	0	.0	94	96.9	3	3.1	97
1	.2	1	.2	1	.2	4	1.0	392	95.6	14	3.4	410
0	.0	0	.0	0	.0	0	.0	101	100.0	0	.0	101
0	.0	0	.0	0	.0	0	.0	0	.0	0	.0	0
0	.0	0	.0	0	.0	0	.0	101	100.0	0	.0	101
575	84.1	6	.9	20	2.9	609	89.0	55	8.0	20	2.9	684
177	88.9	1	.5	3	1.5	182	91.5	12	6.0	5	2.5	199
398	82.1	5	1.0	17	3.5	427	88.0	43	8.9	15	3.1	485
4	.7	5	.8	0	.0	9	1.5	584	98.5	0	.0	593
1	2.4	1	2.4	0	.0	2	4.9	39	95.1	0	.0	41
3	.5	4	.7	0	.0	7	1.3	545	98.7	0	.0	552
0	.0	0	.0	0	.0	0	.0	24	100.0	0	.0	24
0	.0	0	.0	0	.0	0	.0	6	100.0	0	.0	6
0	.0	0	.0	0	.0	0	.0	18	100.0	0	.0	18
21	3.9	1	.2	0	.0	23	4.2	522	95.8	0	.0	545
14	9.5	0	.0	0	.0	14	9.5	134	90.5	0	.0	148
7	1.8	1	.3	0	.0	9	2.3	388	97.7	0	.0	397
2	2.6	0	.0	0	.0	2	2.6	71	91.0	5	6.4	78
1	7.7	0	.0	0	.0	1	7.7	12	92.3	0	.0	13
1	1.5	0	.0	0	.0	1	1.5	59	90.8	5	7.7	65
19	1.5	10	.8	3	.2	33	2.5	1,267	97.4	1	.1	1,301
11	6.3	2	1.1	0	.0	13	7.4	162	92.0	1	.6	176
8	.7	8	.7	3	.3	20	1.8	1,105	98.2	0	.0	1,125
15	1.9	1	.1	3	.4	19	2.4	767	97.3	2	.3	788
7	3.0	0	.0	1	.4	8	3.4	227	96.2	1	.4	236
8	1.4	1	.2	2	.4	11	2.0	540	97.8	1	.2	552
73	5.3	0	.0	0	.0	73	5.3	1,309	94.2	7	.5	1,389
22	6.1	0	.0	0	.0	22	6.1	336	93.3	2	.6	360
51	5.0	0	.0	0	.0	51	5.0	973	94.6	5	.5	1,029
(9 INSTITUTIONS)												
709	12.9	23	.4	26	.5	768	14.0	4,700	85.4	35	.6	5,503
233	19.8	4	.3	4	.3	242	20.5	928	78.7	9	.8	1,179
476	11.0	19	.4	22	.5	526	12.2	3,772	87.2	26	.6	4,324
1	1.9	0	.0	0	.0	1	1.9	49	94.2	2	3.8	52
0	.0	0	.0	0	.0	0	.0	0	.0	0	.0	0
1	1.9	0	.0	0	.0	1	1.9	49	94.2	2	3.8	52
3	2.8	0	.0	5	4.6	8	7.4	99	91.7	1	.9	108
1	3.8	0	.0	2	7.7	3	11.5	23	88.5	0	.0	26
2	2.4	0	.0	3	3.7	5	6.1	76	92.7	1	1.2	82
3	.8	5	1.3	3	.8	13	3.3	384	96.5	1	.3	398
1	2.4	1	2.4	1	2.4	3	7.3	38	92.7	0	.0	41
2	.6	4	1.1	2	.6	10	2.8	346	96.9	1	.3	357
32	5.1	15	2.4	55	8.8	105	16.7	516	82.2	7	1.1	628
12	8.4	9	6.3	9	6.3	30	21.0	110	76.9	3	2.1	143
20	4.1	6	1.2	46	9.5	75	15.5	406	83.7	4	.8	485
0	.0	0	.0	2	.5	2	.5	381	99.2	1	.3	384
0	.0	0	.0	1	1.2	1	1.2	85	98.8	0	.0	86
0	.0	0	.0	1	.3	1	.3	296	99.3	1	.3	298
0	.0	0	.0	1	2.0	1	2.0	48	96.0	1	2.0	50
0	.0	0	.0	1	16.7	1	16.7	5	83.3	0	.0	6
0	.0	0	.0	0	.0	0	.0	43	97.7	1	2.3	44
0	.0	1	2.8	15	41.7	16	44.4	20	55.6	0	.0	36
0	.0	0	.0	0	.0	0	.0	0	.0	0	.0	0
0	.0	1	2.8	15	41.7	16	44.4	20	55.6	0	.0	36
2	.3	6	.9	61	8.9	72	10.5	614	89.5	0	.0	686
1	.5	2	1.1	11	6.0	15	8.2	169	91.8	0	.0	184
1	.2	4	.8	50	10.0	57	11.4	445	88.6	0	.0	502
28	2.4	10	.8	22	1.9	63	5.3	1,076	90.9	45	3.8	1,184
4	1.4	3	1.0	5	1.7	12	4.2	271	94.1	5	1.7	288
24	2.7	7	.8	17	1.9	51	5.7	805	89.8	40	4.5	896

TABLE 3 - TOTAL FIRST PROFESSIONAL ENROLLMENT OF INSTITUTIONS OF HIGHER EDUCATION BY RACE, ETHNICITY AND SEX:
INSTITUTION, STATE AND NATION, 1978

	AMERICAN INDIAN ALASKAN NATIVE		BLACK NON-HISPANIC		ASIAN OR PACIFIC ISLANDER		HISPANIC		TOTAL MINORITY		WHITE NON-HISPANIC		NON-RESIDENT ALIEN		
	NUMBER	%	NUMBER	%	NUMBER	%	NUMBER	%	NUMBER	%	NUMBER	%	NUMBER	%	A
TEXAS CONTINUED															
SOUTH TEXAS COLLEGE LAW															
TX TOTAL	0	.0	13	1.1	5	.4	50	4.3	68	5.9	1,087	94.1		.0	
TX FEMALE	0	.0	2	.7	1	.3	7	2.4	10	3.5	278	96.5	8	.0	
TX MALE	0	.0	11	1.3	4	.5	43	5.0	58	6.7	809	93.3		.0	
TEXAS A&M U MAIN CAMPUS															
TX TOTAL	8	1.7	1	.2	1	.2	4	.8	14	2.9	468	97.1	0	.0	
TX FEMALE	1	.6	0	.0	1	.6	0	.0	2	1.2	159	98.8	0	.0	
TX MALE	7	2.2	1	.3	0	.0	4	1.2	12	3.7	309	96.3	0	.0	
TEXAS CHIROPRACTIC C															
TX TOTAL	0	.0	3	1.0	2	.6	9	2.9	14	4.5	283	91.0	14	4.5	
TX FEMALE	0	.0	0	.0	0	.0	0	.0	0	.0	38	92.7	3	7.3	
TX MALE	0	.0	3	1.1	2	.7	9	3.3	14	5.2	245	90.7	11	4.1	
TEXAS CHRISTIAN U															
TX TOTAL	1	.4	18	7.9	0	.0	4	1.8	23	10.1	205	89.9		.0	
TX FEMALE	0	.0	3	7.3	0	.0	2	4.9	5	12.2	36	87.8	8	.0	
TX MALE	1	.5	15	8.0	0	.0	2	1.1	18	9.6	169	90.4		.0	
TEXAS COLLEGE OSTEO MED															
TX TOTAL	0	.0	4	1.3	4	1.3	7	2.3	15	5.0	284	95.0		.0	
TX FEMALE	0	.0	1	2.3	1	2.3	2	4.5	4	9.1	40	90.9	8	.0	
TX MALE	0	.0	3	1.2	3	1.2	5	2.0	11	4.3	244	95.7		.0	
TEXAS SOUTHERN UNIVERSITY															
TX TOTAL	2	.6	215	64.8	0	.0	91	27.4	308	92.8	13	3.9	11	3.3	
TX FEMALE	0	.0	95	81.9	0	.0	13	11.2	108	93.1	6	5.2	2	1.7	
TX MALE	2	.9	120	55.6	0	.0	78	36.1	200	92.6	7	3.2	9	4.2	
TEXAS TECH UNIVERSITY															
TX TOTAL	3	.6	1	.2	2	.4	20	3.8	26	4.9	500	95.1		.0	
TX FEMALE	1	.8	1	.8	1	.8	6	4.9	9	7.3	114	92.7	8	.0	
TX MALE	2	.5	0	.0	1	.2	14	3.5	17	4.2	386	95.8		.0	
UNIVERSITY OF DALLAS															
TX TOTAL	0	.0	1	2.9	1	2.9	2	5.7	4	11.4	30	85.7	1	2.9	
TX FEMALE	0	.0	0	.0	0	.0	0	.0	0	.0	0	.0	0	.0	
TX MALE	0	.0	1	2.9	1	2.9	2	5.7	4	11.4	30	85.7	1	2.9	
U OF HOUSTON CEN CAMPUS															
TX TOTAL	12	.8	57	3.7	11	.7	120	7.8	200	13.0	1,290	84.1	43	2.8	
TX FEMALE	4	.8	24	5.0	7	1.5	33	6.4	68	14.2	403	84.3	7	1.5	
TX MALE	8	.8	33	3.1	4	.4	87	7.2	132	12.5	887	84.1	36	3.4	
UNIVERSITY OF SNT THOMAS															
TX TOTAL	0	.0	2	3.1	2	3.1	5	7.7	9	13.8	56	86.2	0	.0	
TX FEMALE	0	.0	1	3.0	0	.0	2	6.1	3	9.1	30	90.9	0	.0	
TX MALE	0	.0	1	3.1	2	6.3	3	9.4	6	18.8	26	81.3	0	.0	
U OF TEXAS AT AUSTIN															
TX TOTAL	2	.1	55	3.5	2	.1	140	8.9	199	12.7	1,361	86.8	8	.5	
TX FEMALE	0	.0	28	5.7	0	.0	45	9.2	73	14.9	414	84.5	3	.6	
TX MALE	2	.2	27	2.5	2	.2	95	8.8	126	11.7	947	87.8	5	.5	
U TEX HLTH SCI CTR DALLAS															
TX TOTAL	1	.1	24	2.9	10	1.2	57	6.9	92	11.2	730	88.8	0	.0	
TX FEMALE	0	.0	7	5.2	2	1.5	9	6.7	18	13.3	117	86.7	0	.0	
TX MALE	1	.1	17	2.5	8	1.2	48	7.0	74	10.8	613	89.2	0	.0	
U TEX HLTH SCI CTR HOUSTN															
TX TOTAL	2	.2	23	2.6	18	2.1	44	5.1	87	10.0	782	89.8	2	.2	
TX FEMALE	1	.7	12	8.1	6	4.1	9	6.1	28	18.9	120	81.1	0	.0	
TX MALE	1	.1	11	1.5	12	1.7	35	4.8	59	8.2	662	91.6	2	.3	
U TEX HLTH SCI SN ANTO															
TX TOTAL	2	.2	21	1.8	22	1.9	119	10.0	164	13.8	1,010	85.2	12	1.0	
TX FEMALE	0	.0	8	3.4	7	3.0	28	12.1	43	18.5	187	80.6	2	.9	
TX MALE	2	.2	13	1.4	15	1.6	91	9.5	121	12.7	823	86.3	10	1.0	
U TEX HEOL BR GALVESTON															
TX TOTAL	0	.0	15	1.9	21	2.6	38	4.8	74	9.3	720	90.3	3	.4	
TX FEMALE	0	.0	5	2.7	5	2.7	12	6.4	22	11.8	164	87.7	1	.5	
TX MALE	0	.0	10	1.6	16	2.6	26	4.3	52	8.5	556	91.1	2	.3	
TEXAS TOTAL (24 INSTITUTIONS)															
TX TOTAL	44	.3	522	3.8	138	1.0	874	6.4	1,578	11.5	12,006	87.4	152	1.1	
TX FEMALE	8	.2	205	6.3	46	1.4	198	6.0	458	13.9	2,807	85.3	26	.8	
TX MALE	36	.3	316	3.0	92	.9	676	6.5	1,120	10.7	9,199	88.1	126	1.2	
UTAH															
BRIGHAM YOUNG U MAIN CAM															
UT TOTAL	1	.2	0	.0	5	1.1	1	.2	7	1.5	440	96.5		2.0	
UT FEMALE	0	.0	0	.0	0	.0	0	.0	0	.0	53	93.0	8	7.0	
UT MALE	1	.3	0	.0	5	1.3	1	.3	7	1.8	387	97.0		1.3	
UNIVERSITY OF UTAH															
UT TOTAL	4	.5	10	1.3	9	1.1	24	3.1	47	6.0	735	93.5	4	.5	
UT FEMALE	0	.0	4	2.6	2	1.3	4	2.6	10	6.6	141	92.8	1	.7	
UT MALE	4	.6	6	.9	7	1.1	20	3.2	37	5.8	594	93.7	3	.5	
UTAH TOTAL (2 INSTITUTIONS)															
UT TOTAL	5	.4	10	.8	14	1.1	25	2.0	54	4.3	1,175	94.6	13	1.0	
UT FEMALE	0	.0	4	1.9	2	1.0	4	1.9	10	4.8	194	92.8	5	2.4	
UT MALE	5	.5	6	.6	12	1.2	21	2.0	44	4.3	981	95.0	8	.8	
VERMONT															
U VT & STATE AGRL COLLEGE															
VT TOTAL	0	.0	0	.0	2	.6	0	.0	2	.6	318	98.8	2	.6	
VT FEMALE	0	.0	0	.0	0	.0	0	.0	0	.0	68	100.0	0	.0	
VT MALE	0	.0	0	.0	2	.8	0	.0	2	.8	250	98.4	2	.8	
VERMONT LAW SCHOOL															
VT TOTAL	0	.0	0	.0	1	.3	0	.0	1	.3	322	99.4	1	.3	
VT FEMALE	0	.0	0	.0	1	1.1	0	.0	1	1.1	86	97.7	1	1.1	
VT MALE	0	.0	0	.0	0	.0	0	.0	0	.0	236	100.0	0	.0	

N E	BLACK NON-HISPANIC NUMBER	%	ASIAN OR PACIFIC ISLANDER NUMBER	%	HISPANIC NUMBER	%	TOTAL MINORITY NUMBER	%	WHITE NON-HISPANIC NUMBER	%	NON-RESIDENT ALIEN NUMBER	%	TOTAL NUMBER
(2 INSTITUTIONS)													
	0	.0	3	.5	0	.0	3	.5	640	99.1	3	.5	646
	0	.0	1	.6	0	.0	1	.6	154	98.7	1	.6	156
	0	.C	2	.4	0	.0	2	.4	486	99.2	2	.4	490
	15	3.5	3	.7	1	.2	20	4.6	410	95.1	1	.2	431
	9	6.8	0	.0	0	.0	10	7.5	122	91.7	1	.8	133
	6	2.0	3	1.0	1	.3	10	3.4	288	96.6	0	.0	298
	0	.0	0	.0	0	.0	0	.0	74	98.7	1	1.3	75
	0	.0	0	.0	0	.0	0	.0	8	100.0	0	.0	8
	0	.0	0	.0	0	.0	0	.0	66	98.5	1	1.5	67
	14	6.5	6	2.8	1	.5	22	10.2	193	89.8	0	.0	215
	5	8.8	0	.0	0	.0	5	8.8	52	91.2	0	.0	57
	9	5.7	6	3.8	1	.6	17	10.8	141	89.2	0	.0	158
	2	1.7	0	.0	0	.0	2	1.7	115	98.3	0	.0	117
	0	.0	0	.0	0	.0	0	.0	20	100.0	0	.0	20
	2	2.1	0	.0	0	.0	2	2.1	95	97.9	0	.0	97
	0	.0	0	.0	0	.0	0	.0	25	100.0	0	.0	25
	0	.0	0	.0	0	.0	0	.0	10	100.0	0	.0	10
	0	.0	0	.0	0	.0	0	.0	15	100.0	0	.0	15
	18	4.2	0	.0	1	.2	19	4.4	407	94.9	3	.7	429
	12	10.2	0	.0	1	.8	13	11.0	103	87.3	2	1.7	118
	6	1.9	0	.0	0	.0	6	1.9	304	97.7	1	.3	311
	60	3.7	9	.6	3	.2	72	4.5	1,528	94.7	13	.8	1,613
	26	6.4	4	1.0	0	.0	30	7.4	374	91.7	4	1.0	408
	34	2.8	5	.4	3	.2	42	3.5	1,154	95.8	9	.7	1,205
	47	4.3	17	1.5	6	.5	70	6.3	1,033	93.7	0	.0	1,103
	18	7.6	6	2.5	1	.4	25	10.5	213	89.5	0	.0	238
	29	3.4	11	1.3	5	.6	45	5.2	820	94.8	0	.0	865
	10	2.9	0	.0	1	.3	11	3.2	334	96.8	0	.0	345
	3	3.8	0	.0	0	.0	3	3.8	77	96.3	0	.0	80
	7	2.6	0	.0	1	.4	8	3.0	257	97.0	0	.0	265
(9 INSTITUTIONS)													
	166	3.8	35	.8	13	.3	216	5.0	4,119	94.6	18	.4	4,353
	73	6.8	10	.9	2	.2	86	8.0	979	91.3	7	.7	1,072
	93	2.8	25	.8	11	.3	130	4.0	3,140	95.7	11	.3	3,281
	1	.1	13	1.5	11	1.3	32	3.7	838	96.1	2	.2	872
	0	.0	3	1.6	3	1.6	10	5.4	174	94.6	0	.0	184
	1	.1	10	1.5	8	1.2	22	3.2	664	96.5	2	.3	688
	13	1.5	15	1.7	8	.9	39	4.5	821	95.5	0	.0	860
	7	2.9	3	1.2	5	2.1	16	6.6	225	93.4	0	.0	241
	6	1.0	12	1.9	3	.5	23	3.7	596	96.3	0	.0	619
	22	1.4	54	3.6	32	2.1	120	7.9	1,395	91.8	4	.3	1,519
	7	1.8	18	4.7	8	2.1	36	9.3	350	90.4	1	.3	387
	15	1.3	36	3.2	24	2.1	84	7.4	1,045	92.3	3	.3	1,132
	1	.3	5	1.6	1	.3	7	2.2	311	97.8	0	.0	318
	1	1.0	2	1.9	1	1.0	3	3.8	101	96.2	0	.0	105
	0	.0	3	1.4	0	1.0	3	1.4	210	98.6	0	.0	213
(4 INSTITUTIONS)													
	37	1.0	87	2.4	52	1.5	198	5.5	3,365	94.3	6	.2	3,569
	15	1.6	26	2.8	17	1.9	66	7.2	850	92.7	1	.1	917
	22	.8	61	2.3	35	1.3	132	5.0	2,515	94.8	5	.2	2,652
	0	.0	0	.0	0	.0	0	.0	47	100.0	0	.0	47
	0	.0	0	.0	0	.0	0	.0	10	100.0	0	.0	10
	0	.0	0	.0	0	.0	0	.0	37	100.0	0	.0	37
	4	2.0	1	.5	1	.5	6	3.0	195	96.1	2	1.0	203
	1	3.4	0	.0	1	3.4	2	6.9	27	93.1	0	.0	29
	3	1.7	1	.6	0	.0	4	2.3	168	96.6	2	1.1	174
	9	.9	1	.1	2	.2	15	1.5	999	98.4	1	.1	1,015
	5	2.7	0	.0	1	.5	7	3.7	180	95.7	1	.5	188
	4	.5	1	.1	1	.1	8	1.0	819	99.0	0	.0	827
(3 INSTITUTIONS)													
	13	1.0	2	.2	3	.2	21	1.7	1,241	98.1	3	.2	1,265
	6	2.6	0	.0	2	.9	9	4.0	217	95.6	1	.4	227
	7	.7	2	.2	1	.1	12	1.2	1,024	98.7	2	.2	1,038

	AMERICAN INDIAN ALASKAN NATIVE		BLACK NON-HISPANIC		ASIAN OR PACIFIC ISLANDER		HISPANIC		TOTAL MINORITY		WHITE NON-HISPANIC		NON-RESIDENT ALIEN	
	NUMBER	%	NUMBER	%	NUMBER	%	NUMBER	%	NUMBER	%	NUMBER	%	NUMBER	%
WISCONSIN														
MARQUETTE UNIVERSITY														
HI TOTAL	3	.3	9	.9	5	.5	7	.7	24	2.5	998	97.7	0	.0
HI FEMALE	1	.6	3	1.8	2	1.2	3	1.8	9	5.3	161	94.7	0	.0
WI MALE	2	.2	6	.7	3	.4	4	.5	15	1.8	837	98.2	0	.0
MEDICAL COLLEGE OF WIS														
HI TOTAL	2	.3	34	5.6	8	1.3	26	4.3	70	11.5	533	87.8	4	.7
WI FEMALE	0	.0	15	11.7	2	1.6	3	2.3	20	15.6	106	82.8	2	1.6
WI MALE	2	.4	19	4.0	6	1.3	23	4.8	50	10.4	427	89.1	2	.4
NASHOTAH HOUSE														
HI TOTAL	0	.0	1	1.2	0	.0	0	.0	1	1.2	83	96.5	2	2.3
HI FEMALE	0	.0	0	.0	0	.0	0	.0	0	.0	6	100.0	0	.0
WI MALE	0	.0	1	1.3	0	.0	0	.0	1	1.3	77	96.3	2	2.5
SACRED HEART SCH THEOLOGY														
HI TOTAL	0	.0	1	.9	0	.0	8	7.1	9	8.0	103	92.0	0	.0
WI FEMALE	0	.0	0	.0	0	.0	0	.0	0	.0	0	.0	0	.0
WI MALE	0	.0	1	.9	0	.0	8	7.1	9	8.0	103	92.0	0	.0
SNT FRAN SEM PSTL MINSTRY														
HI TOTAL	0	.0	0	.0	0	.0	0	.0	0	.0	94	98.9	1	1.1
WI FEMALE	0	.0	0	.0	0	.0	0	.0	0	.0	16	100.0	0	.0
HI MALE	0	.0	0	.0	0	.0	0	.0	0	.0	78	98.7	1	1.3
U OF WISCONSIN MADISON														
HI TOTAL	14	.9	55	3.5	16	1.0	31	2.0	116	7.4	1,443	92.0	9	.6
HI FEMALE	3	.6	22	4.4	8	1.6	9	1.8	42	8.4	455	91.0	3	.6
WI MALE	11	1.0	33	3.1	8	.7	22	2.1	74	6.9	988	92.5	6	.6
WISCONSIN			TOTAL (		6 INSTITUTIONS)									
HI TOTAL	19	.5	100	2.9	29	.8	72	2.1	220	6.3	3,254	93.2	16	.5
HI FEMALE	4	.5	40	4.9	12	1.5	15	1.8	71	8.7	744	90.7	5	.6
HI MALE	15	.6	60	2.2	17	.6	57	2.1	149	5.6	2,510	94.0	11	.4
WYOMING														
UNIVERSITY OF WYOMING														
WY TOTAL	0	.0	0	.0	1	.5	2	.9	3	1.4	211	98.6	0	.0
WY FEMALE	0	.0	0	.0	1	1.9	1	1.9	2	3.7	52	96.3	0	.0
WY MALE	0	.0	0	.0	0	.0	1	.6	1	.6	159	99.4	0	.0
WYOMING			TOTAL (		1 INSTITUTIONS)									
HY TOTAL	0	.0	0	.0	1	.5	2	.9	3	1.4	211	98.6	0	.0
WY FEMALE	0	.0	0	.0	1	1.9	1	1.9	2	3.7	52	96.3	0	.0
WY MALE	0	.0	0	.0	0	.0	1	.6	1	.6	159	99.4	0	.0
THE STATES AND D.C.	(		445 INSTITUTIONS)											
PR TOTAL	1,072	.4	11,424	4.5	4,800	1.9	5,353	2.1	22,649	8.9	229,306	89.9	3,044	1.2
PR FEMALE	270	.4	4,449	6.9	1,497	2.3	1,400	2.2	7,616	11.8	56,275	87.3	597	.9
PR MALE	802	.4	6,975	3.7	3,303	1.7	3,953	2.1	15,033	7.9	173,031	90.8	2,447	1.3
PUERTO RICO														
CATHOLIC U PUERTO RICO														
PR TOTAL	0	.0	0	.0	0	.0	285	100.0	285	100.0	0	.0	0	.0
PR FEMALE	0	.0	0	.0	0	.0	67	100.0	67	100.0	0	.0	0	.0
PR MALE	0	.0	0	.0	0	.0	218	100.0	218	100.0	0	.0	0	.0
INTER AMER U BAYAMON BR														
PR TOTAL	0	.0	0	.0	0	.0	9	100.0	9	100.0	0	.0	0	.0
PR FEMALE	0	.0	0	.0	0	.0	6	100.0	6	100.0	0	.0	0	.0
PR MALE	0	.0	0	.0	0	.0	3	100.0	3	100.0	0	.0	0	.0
U OF PR RIO PIEDRAS														
PR TOTAL	0	.0	0	.0	0	.0	466	100.0	466	100.0	0	.0	0	.0
PR FEMALE	0	.0	0	.0	0	.0	173	100.0	173	100.0	0	.0	0	.0
PR MALE	0	.0	0	.0	0	.0	293	100.0	293	100.0	0	.0	0	.0
U OF PR MEDICAL SCIENCES														
PR TOTAL	0	.0	0	.0	0	.0	832	100.0	832	100.0	0	.0	0	.0
PR FEMALE	0	.0	0	.0	0	.0	287	100.0	287	100.0	0	.0	0	.0
PR MALE	0	.0	0	.0	0	.0	545	100.0	545	100.0	0	.0	0	.0
PUERTO RICO			TOTAL (		4 INSTITUTIONS)									
PR TOTAL	0	.0	0	.0	0	.0	1,592	100.0	1,592	100.0	0	.0	0	.0
PR FEMALE	0	.0	0	.0	0	.0	533	100.0	533	100.0	0	.0	0	.0
PR MALE	0	.0	0	.0	0	.0	1,059	100.0	1,059	100.0	0	.0	0	.0
OUTLYING AREAS	(		4 INSTITUTIONS)											
PR TOTAL	0	.0	0	.0	0	.0	1,592	100.0	1,592	100.0	0	.0	0	.0
PR FEMALE	0	.0	0	.0	0	.0	533	100.0	533	100.0	0	.0	0	.0
PR MALE	0	.0	0	.0	0	.0	1,059	100.0	1,059	100.0	0	.0	0	.0
NATION TOTAL (		449 INSTITUTIONS)												
TOTAL	1,072	.4	11,424	4.5	4,800	1.9	6,945	2.7	24,241	9.4	229,306	89.4	3,044	1.2
FEMALE	270	.4	4,449	6.8	1,497	2.3	1,933	3.0	8,149	12.5	56,275	86.5	597	.9
MALE	802	.4	6,975	3.6	3,303	1.7	5,012	2.6	16,092	8.4	173,031	90.3	2,447	1.3

TOTAL UNDERGRADUATE ENROLLMENT IN INSTITUTIONS OF HIGHER EDUCATION BY RACE, ETHNICITY AND SEX: STATE AND NATION, 1978

AMERICAN INDIAN ALASKAN NATIVE		BLACK NON-HISPANIC		ASIAN OR PACIFIC ISLANDER		HISPANIC		TOTAL MINORITY		WHITE NON-HISPANIC		NON-RESIDENT ALIEN		TOTAL
NUMBER	%	NUMBER	%	NUMBER	%	NUMBER	%	NUMBER	%	NUMBER	%	NUMBER	%	NUMBER
(58 INSTITUTIONS)														
171	.1	32,086	23.6	394	.3	448	.3	33,099	24.3	101,281	74.4	1,813	1.3	136,193
63	.1	18,995	27.8	150	.2	176	.3	19,404	28.4	48,679	71.2	304	.4	68,387
88	.1	13,091	19.3	244	.4	272	.4	13,695	20.2	52,602	77.6	1,509	2.2	67,806
(14 INSTITUTIONS)														
1,513	.1	602	3.6	321	1.9	217	1.3	2,653	15.9	13,947	83.7	56	.3	16,656
925	.7	290	3.0	165	1.7	119	1.2	1,499	15.7	8,028	84.0	26	.3	9,553
588	4.3	312	4.4	156	2.2	98	1.4	1,154	16.2	5,919	83.3	30	.4	7,103
(22 INSTITUTIONS)														
4,680	3.3	4,256	3.0	1,398	1.0	13,811	9.6	24,145	16.8	117,055	81.6	2,206	1.5	143,406
2,654	3.8	1,724	2.5	755	1.1	7,196	10.4	12,329	17.7	56,488	81.3	647	.9	69,464
2,026	2.7	2,532	3.4	643	.9	6,615	8.9	11,816	16.0	60,567	81.9	1,559	2.1	73,942
(34 INSTITUTIONS)														
384	.6	9,891	16.2	382	.6	227	.4	10,884	17.8	49,693	81.4	502	.8	61,079
172	.6	5,621	18.0	131	.4	106	.3	6,030	19.3	25,101	80.4	97	.3	31,228
212	.7	4,270	14.3	251	.8	121	.4	4,854	16.3	24,592	82.4	405	1.4	29,851
(226 INSTITUTIONS)														
17,638	1.4	116,371	9.2	82,558	6.6	123,430	8	339,997	27.0	890,490	70.7	28,598	2.3	1,259,085
9,014	1.4	62,099	9.5	39,449	6.1	60,144	9.2	170,706	26.2	471,342	72.4	9,223	1.4	651,271
8,624	1.4	54,272	8.9	43,109	7.1	63,286	10.4	169,291	27.9	419,148	69.0	19,375	3.2	607,814
(39 INSTITUTIONS)														
976	.9	3,680	3.2	1,540	1.3	6,455	5.7	12,651	11.1	99,195	86.9	2,256	2.0	114,102
506	.9	1,669	3.1	729	1.3	2,962	5.4	5,866	10.8	48,055	88.3	511	.9	54,432
470	.8	2,011	3.4	811	1.4	3,493	5.9	6,785	11.4	51,140	85.7	1,745	2.9	59,670
(44 INSTITUTIONS)														
233	.2	6,307	5.6	867	.8	2,013	1.8	9,420	8.3	102,655	90.7	1,058	.9	113,133
128	.2	3,484	6.0	398	.7	1,017	1.8	5,027	8.7	52,601	90.7	355	.6	57,983
105	.2	2,823	5.1	469	.9	996	1.8	4,393	8.0	50,054	90.8	703	1.3	55,150
(10 INSTITUTIONS)														
33	.1	3,064	12.5	94	.4	147	.6	3,338	13.6	20,871	85.3	257	1.1	24,466
15	.1	1,745	13.3	49	.4	84	.6	1,893	14.4	11,160	84.8	104	.8	13,157
18	.2	1,319	11.7	45	.4	63	.6	1,445	12.8	9,711	85.9	153	1.4	11,309
COLUMBIA (13 INSTITUTIONS)														
292	.7	20,266	45.7	948	2.1	698	1.6	22,204	50.1	18,080	40.8	4,052	9.1	44,336
77	.3	11,970	50.1	283	1.2	366	1.5	12,696	53.2	9,543	40.0	1,641	6.9	23,880
215	1.1	8,295	40.6	665	3.3	332	1.6	9,508	46.5	8,537	41.7	2,411	11.8	20,456
(74 INSTITUTIONS)														
916	.3	35,529	11.8	2,208	.7	22,641	7.5	61,294	20.4	232,041	77.3	6,721	2.2	300,056
470	.3	21,448	14.4	877	.6	11,421	7.7	34,216	23.0	112,721	75.7	2,034	1.4	148,971
446	.3	14,081	9.3	1,331	.9	11,220	7.4	27,078	17.9	119,320	79.0	4,687	3.1	151,085
(68 INSTITUTIONS)														
220	.2	27,223	19.8	555	.4	738	.5	28,736	20.9	106,418	77.5	2,228	1.6	137,382
95	.1	15,583	22.9	243	.4	263	.4	16,184	23.7	51,407	75.4	561	.8	68,152
125	.2	11,640	16.8	312	.5	475	.7	12,552	18.1	55,011	79.5	1,667	2.4	69,230
(12 INSTITUTIONS)														
78	.2	602	1.5	25,708	66.2	1,237	3.2	27,625	71.1	9,572	24.6	1,663	4.3	38,860
33	.2	170	.9	12,211	67.5	541	3.0	12,955	71.6	4,412	24.4	728	4.0	18,095
45	.2	432	2.1	13,497	65.0	696	3.4	14,670	70.6	5,160	24.8	935	4.5	20,765
(9 INSTITUTIONS)														
207	.6	174	.5	334	1.0	282	.9	997	3.1	30,826	95.4	486	1.5	32,309
126	.8	41	.3	140	.9	145	.9	452	2.8	15,371	95.7	235	1.5	16,058
81	.5	133	.8	194	1.2	137	.8	545	3.4	15,455	95.1	251	1.5	16,251
(135 INSTITUTIONS)														
1,667	.4	65,881	14.2	6,389	1.4	11,147	2.4	85,084	18.4	369,835	80.0	7,440	1.6	462,359
861	.4	39,704	16.5	2,989	1.2	5,427	2.3	48,977	20.4	189,258	78.6	2,434	1.0	240,669
806	.4	26,177	11.8	3,404	1.5	5,720	2.6	36,107	16.3	180,577	81.5	5,006	2.3	221,690
(60 INSTITUTIONS)														
359	.2	10,441	6.0	883	.5	1,664	1.0	13,347	7	158,830	91.1	2,217	1.3	174,394
147	.2	5,777	6.9	419	.5	742	.9	7,085	8	75,963	90.7	669	.8	83,717
212	.2	4,664	5.1	464	.5	922	1.0	6,262	6.9	82,867	91.4	1,548	1.7	90,677
(58 INSTITUTIONS)														
346	.3	2,407	2.3	580	.6	536	.5	3,869	3.7	99,207	94.5	1,851	1.8	104,927
184	.4	1,017	2.0	251	.5	231	.4	1,683	3.2	49,700	95.6	599	1.2	51,982
162	.3	1,390	2.6	329	.6	305	.6	2,186	4.1	49,507	93.5	1,252	2.4	52,945
(52 INSTITUTIONS)														
1,425	1.5	4,753	4.9	484	.5	1,425	1.5	8,087	8.3	87,620	89.6	2,092	2.1	97,799
711	1.5	2,096	4.3	198	.4	628	1.3	3,633	7.5	44,419	91.6	421	.9	48,473
714	1.4	2,657	5.4	286	.6	797	1.6	4,454	9.0	43,201	87.6	1,671	3.4	49,326
(39 INSTITUTIONS)														
185	.2	7,890	7.7	510	.5	279	.3	8,864		91,813	90.0	1,350	1.3	102,027
95	.2	4,294	8.1	215	.4	121	.2	4,725	8.7	47,980	90.5	297	.6	53,002
90	.2	3,596	7.3	295	.6	158	.3	4,139	8.4	43,833	89.4	1,053	2.1	49,025
(30 INSTITUTIONS)														
234	.2	30,367	24.3	624	.5	1,674	1.3	32,899	26.3	88,373	70.6	3,896	3.1	125,168
114	.2	17,896	28.5	260	.4	756	1.2	19,026	30.3	42,625	68.0	1,042	1.7	62,693
120	.2	12,471	20.0	364	.6	918	1.5	13,873	22.2	45,748	73.2	2,854	4.6	62,475

213

TABLE 4 - TOTAL UNDERGRADUATE ENROLLMENT IN INSTITUTIONS OF HIGHER EDUCATION BY RACE, ETHNICITY AND SEX: STATE AND NATION, 1978

	AMERICAN INDIAN ALASKAN NATIVE		BLACK NON-HISPANIC		ASIAN OR PACIFIC ISLANDER		HISPANIC		TOTAL MINORITY		WHITE NON-HISPANIC		NON-RESIDENT ALIEN	
	NUMBER	%	NUMBER	%	NUMBER	%	NUMBER	%	NUMBER	%	NUMBER	%	NUMBER	%
MAINE	(		27 INSTITUTIONS)											
TOTAL	137	.5	157	.5	93	.3	71	.2	458	1.5	29,584	98.0	157	.5
FEMALE	73	.5	61	.4	38	.3	25	.2	197	1.4	14,062	98.3	45	.3
MALE	64	.4	96	.6	55	.3	46	.3	261	1.6	15,522	97.7	112	.7
MARYLAND	(		52 INSTITUTIONS)											
TOTAL	476	.3	31,962	19.0	2,231	1.3	1,657	1.0	36,326	21.5	128,314	76.1	4,009	2.4
FEMALE	228	.2	19,456	21.3	1,096	1.2	855	.9	21,635	23.7	68,212	74.6	1,573	1.7
MALE	248	.3	12,506	16.2	1,135	1.5	802	1.0	14,691	19.0	60,102	77.8	2,436	3.2
MASSACHUSETTS	(		111 INSTITUTIONS)											
TOTAL	1,175	.4	10,892	4.1	4,369	1.7	3,642	1.4	20,078	7.6	238,437	90.4	5,140	1.9
FEMALE	713	.5	6,071	4.6	2,014	1.5	1,856	1.4	10,654	8.0	120,839	90.6	1,821	1.4
MALE	462	.4	4,821	3.7	2,355	1.8	1,786	1.4	9,424	7.2	117,598	90.2	3,319	2.5
MICHIGAN	(		92 INSTITUTIONS)											
TOTAL	2,259	.6	40,923	10.2	2,732	.7	5,394	1.3	51,308	12.7	346,073	85.9	5,720	1.4
FEMALE	1,128	.6	24,310	12.1	1,200	.6	2,676	1.3	29,314	14.6	170,190	84.7	1,544	.8
MALE	1,131	.6	16,613	8.2	1,532	.8	2,718	1.3	21,994	10.9	175,883	87.0	4,176	2.1
MINNESOTA	(		55 INSTITUTIONS)											
TOTAL	869	.6	1,911	1.3	1,106	.7	605	.4	4,491	3.0	144,049	95.6	2,126	1.4
FEMALE	481	.6	857	1.1	495	.6	302	.4	2,135	2.7	75,924	96.4	676	.9
MALE	388	.5	1,054	1.5	611	.8	303	.4	2,356	3.3	68,125	94.7	1,450	2.0
MISSISSIPPI	(		45 INSTITUTIONS)											
TOTAL	242	.3	25,473	30.8	259	.3	112	.1	26,086	31.5	56,114	67.7	638	.8
FEMALE	144	.3	15,033	34.1	113	.3	45	.1	15,335	34.7	28,671	65.0	124	.3
MALE	98	.3	10,440	27.0	146	.4	67	.2	10,751	27.8	27,443	70.9	514	1.3
MISSOURI	(		70 INSTITUTIONS)											
TOTAL	488	.3	14,992	9.1	1,082	.7	1,258	.8	17,820	10.8	145,003	87.9	2,074	1.3
FEMALE	212	.3	8,527	10.4	450	.6	514	.6	9,703	11.9	71,367	87.4	566	.7
MALE	276	.3	6,465	7.8	632	.8	744	.9	8,117	9.7	73,636	88.4	1,508	1.8
MONTANA	(		13 INSTITUTIONS)											
TOTAL	610	2.4	98	.4	91	.4	98	.4	897	3.5	24,540	95.7	212	.8
FEMALE	366	3.0	38	.3	25	.2	44	.4	473	3.8	11,781	95.7	51	.4
MALE	244	1.8	60	.4	66	.5	54	.4	424	3.2	12,759	95.6	161	1.2
NEBRASKA	(		31 INSTITUTIONS)											
TOTAL	246	.4	2,245	3.4	347	.5	654	1.0	3,492	5.3	62,030	93.3	957	1.4
FEMALE	112	.4	1,002	3.1	153	.5	329	1.0	1,596	5.0	30,084	94.3	223	.7
MALE	134	.4	1,243	3.6	194	.6	325	.9	1,896	5.3	31,946	92.4	734	2.1
NEVADA	(		6 INSTITUTIONS)											
TOTAL	280	1.2	977	4.1	327	1.4	524	2.2	2,108	8.8	21,622	89.9	322	1.3
FEMALE	159	1.4	436	3.9	139	1.2	222	2.0	956	8.5	10,267	90.8	87	.8
MALE	121	.9	541	4.2	188	1.5	302	2.4	1,152	9.0	11,355	89.1	235	1.8
NEW HAMPSHIRE	(		23 INSTITUTIONS)											
TOTAL	75	.2	589	1.7	106	.3	239	.7	1,009	2.9	33,586	95.7	495	1.4
FEMALE	35	.2	205	1.3	38	.2	50	.3	328	2.0	15,869	97.2	127	.8
MALE	40	.2	384	2.0	68	.4	189	1.0	681	3.6	17,717	94.4	368	2.0
NEW JERSEY	(		58 INSTITUTIONS)											
TOTAL	486	.2	23,356	11.0	2,059	1.0	8,837	4.2	34,738	16.3	175,429	82.5	2,391	1.1
FEMALE	272	.2	14,420	13.0	1,029	.9	4,892	4.4	20,613	18.5	89,797	80.7	876	.8
MALE	214	.2	8,936	8.8	1,030	1.0	3,945	3.9	14,125	13.9	85,632	84.6	1,515	1.5
NEW MEXICO	(		19 INSTITUTIONS)											
TOTAL	1,600	4.0	971	2.4	291	.7	10,501	26.1	13,363	33.2	26,337	65.4	578	1.4
FEMALE	951	4.9	375	1.9	118	.6	5,250	27.2	6,694	34.7	12,512	64.8	105	.5
MALE	649	3.1	596	2.8	173	.8	5,251	25.0	6,669	31.8	13,825	65.9	473	2.3
NEW YORK	(		259 INSTITUTIONS)											
TOTAL	3,437	.5	81,450	12.2	13,418	2.0	38,789	5.8	137,094	20.5	523,075	78.1	9,724	1.5
FEMALE	1,645	.5	50,685	14.8	6,206	1.8	21,523	6.3	80,059	23.4	258,676	75.6	3,311	1.0
MALE	1,792	.5	30,765	9.4	7,212	2.2	17,266	5.3	57,035	17.4	264,399	80.6	6,413	2.0
NORTH CAROLINA	(		125 INSTITUTIONS)											
TOTAL	1,587	.7	46,893	21.4	837	.4	815	.4	50,132	22.8	167,677	76.4	1,797	.8
FEMALE	907	.8	25,313	23.2	361	.3	357	.3	26,938	24.6	81,915	74.9	473	.4
MALE	680	.6	21,580	19.6	476	.4	458	.4	23,194	21.0	85,762	77.8	1,324	1.2
NORTH DAKOTA	(		16 INSTITUTIONS)											
TOTAL	992	3.6	153	.6	78	.3	48	.2	1,271	4.6	26,261	94.8	183	.7
FEMALE	587	4.4	44	.3	31	.2	24	.2	686	5.2	12,479	94.3	73	.6
MALE	405	2.8	109	.8	47	.3	24	.2	585	4.0	13,782	95.2	110	.8
OHIO	(		124 INSTITUTIONS)											
TOTAL	961	.3	36,108	10.1	1,567	.4	2,144	.6	40,780	11.5	311,201	87.4	4,081	1.1
FEMALE	604	.3	21,181	11.9	805	.5	1,109	.6	23,699	13.3	153,260	86.0	1,228	.7
MALE	357	.2	14,927	8.4	762	.4	1,035	.6	17,081	9.6	157,941	88.8	2,853	1.6
OKLAHOMA	(		42 INSTITUTIONS)											
TOTAL	4,586	3.7	8,205	6.7	939	.8	1,034	.8	14,764	12.0	102,547	83.4	5,662	4.6
FEMALE	2,536	4.3	4,233	7.1	376	.6	448	.8	7,593	12.8	50,741	85.4	1,052	1.8
MALE	2,050	3.2	3,972	6.2	563	.9	586	.9	7,171	11.3	51,806	81.5	4,610	7.2
OREGON	(		39 INSTITUTIONS)											
TOTAL	1,283	1.2	1,445	1.3	2,672	2.4	1,273	1.2	6,673	6.1	100,270	91.5	2,682	2.4
FEMALE	632	1.2	595	1.1	1,261	2.4	615	1.1	3,103	5.8	49,562	92.6	876	1.6
MALE	651	1.2	850	1.5	1,411	2.5	658	1.2	3,570	6.4	50,708	90.4	1,806	3.2

	AMERICAN INDIAN ALASKAN NATIVE		BLACK NON-HISPANIC		ASIAN OR PACIFIC ISLANDER		HISPANIC		TOTAL MINORITY		WHITE NON-HISPANIC		NON-RESIDENT ALIEN		TOTAL
	NUMBER	%	NUMBER	%	NUMBER	%	NUMBER	%	NUMBER	%	NUMBER	%	NUMBER	%	NUMBER
PENNSYLVANIA	(	157	INSTITUTIONS)												
TOTAL	490	.1	28,886	8.1	2,298	.6	2,624	.7	34,298	9.6	320,011	89.6	2,969	.8	357,278
FEMALE	252	.1	17,044	9.6	1,038	.6	1,413	.8	19,747	11.2	156,404	88.3	888	.5	177,039
MALE	238	.1	11,842	6.6	1,260	.7	1,211	.7	14,551	8.1	163,607	90.8	2,081	1.2	180,239
RHODE ISLAND	(	13	INSTITUTIONS)												
TOTAL	81	.2	1,533	3.4	312	.7	272	.6	2,198	4.9	41,809	93.8	586	1.3	44,593
FEMALE	47	.2	696	3.3	152	.7	123	.6	1,018	4.9	19,729	94.3	182	.9	20,929
MALE	34	.1	837	3.5	160	.7	149	.6	1,180	5.0	22,080	93.3	404	1.7	23,664
SOUTH CAROLINA	(	60	INSTITUTIONS)												
TOTAL	122	.1	25,249	23.9	447	.4	273	.3	26,091	24.7	78,937	74.7	677	.6	105,705
FEMALE	43	.1	13,525	27.4	202	.4	92	.2	13,862	28.1	35,290	71.6	148	.3	49,300
MALE	79	.1	11,724	20.8	245	.4	181	.3	12,229	21.7	43,647	77.4	529	.9	56,405
SOUTH DAKOTA	(	17	INSTITUTIONS)												
TOTAL	750	2.9	320	1.3	104	.4	283	1.1	1,457	5.7	23,751	93.1	298	1.2	25,506
FEMALE	413	3.5	62	.5	43	.4	36	.3	554	4.6	11,359	94.9	55	.5	11,968
MALE	337	2.5	258	1.9	61	.5	247	1.8	903	6.7	12,392	91.5	243	1.8	13,538
TENNESSEE	(	74	INSTITUTIONS)												
TOTAL	227	.1	25,545	16.1	512	.3	553	.3	26,837	16.9	129,232	81.5	2,544	1.6	158,613
FEMALE	120	.2	14,520	18.3	219	.3	238	.3	15,097	19.0	63,786	80.2	623	.8	79,506
MALE	107	.1	11,025	13.9	293	.4	315	.4	11,740	14.8	65,446	82.7	1,921	2.4	79,107
TEXAS	(	139	INSTITUTIONS)												
TOTAL	1,938	.4	54,021	10.0	4,224	.8	68,451	12.7	128,634	23.9	393,773	73.2	15,282	2.8	537,689
FEMALE	896	.3	28,566	10.9	2,018	.8	33,106	12.7	64,586	24.7	193,106	73.9	3,643	1.4	261,335
MALE	1,042	.4	25,455	9.2	2,206	.8	35,345	12.8	64,048	23.2	200,667	72.6	11,639	4.2	276,354
UTAH	(	13	INSTITUTIONS)												
TOTAL	866	1.1	444	.6	1,283	1.6	1,047	1.3	3,640	4.7	71,150	91.2	3,197	.1	77,987
FEMALE	438	1.3	160	.5	643	1.8	415	1.2	1,656	4.8	31,817	91.3	1,362	.9	34,835
MALE	428	1.0	284	.7	640	1.5	632	1.5	1,984	4.6	39,333	91.1	1,835	4.3	43,152
VERMONT	(	20	INSTITUTIONS)												
TOTAL	43	.2	283	1.2	50	.2	125	.5	501	2.1	22,463	96.4	340	1.5	23,304
FEMALE	19	.2	161	1.3	26	.2	68	.5	274	2.2	12,277	97.0	102	.8	12,653
MALE	24	.2	122	1.1	24	.2	57	.5	227	2.1	10,186	95.6	238	2.2	10,651
VIRGINIA	(	66	INSTITUTIONS)												
TOTAL	308	.2	26,609	16.5	1,362	.8	763	.5	29,042	18.0	131,181	81.1	1,498	.9	161,721
FEMALE	174	.2	15,137	18.1	659	.8	376	.4	16,346	19.5	66,713	79.8	584	.7	83,643
MALE	134	.2	11,472	14.7	703	.9	387	.5	12,696	16.3	64,468	82.6	914	1.2	78,078
WASHINGTON	(	49	INSTITUTIONS)												
TOTAL	1,893	1.3	4,227	3.0	4,531	3.2	1,813	1.3	12,464	8.8	125,031	87.8	4,871	3.4	142,366
FEMALE	1,032	1.5	1,804	2.6	2,200	3.2	794	1.1	5,830	8.4	62,011	89.3	1,639	2.4	69,480
MALE	861	1.2	2,423	3.3	2,331	3.2	1,019	1.4	6,634	9.1	63,020	86.5	3,232	4.4	72,886
WEST VIRGINIA	(	26	INSTITUTIONS)												
TOTAL	173	.3	2,790	4.7	208	.4	123	.2	3,294	5.5	55,324	93.2	752	1.3	59,370
FEMALE	99	.3	1,317	4.5	78	.3	51	.2	1,545	5.2	27,887	94.3	125	.4	29,557
MALE	74	.2	1,473	4.9	130	.4	72	.2	1,749	5.9	27,437	92.0	627	2.1	29,813
WISCONSIN	(	57	INSTITUTIONS)												
TOTAL	1,035	.5	6,788	3.5	1,044	.5	1,570	.8	10,437	5.4	182,737	93.7	1,838	.9	195,012
FEMALE	566	.6	3,796	4.0	507	.5	692	.7	5,561	5.8	89,632	93.7	476	.5	95,669
MALE	469	.5	2,992	3.0	537	.5	878	.9	4,876	4.9	93,105	93.7	1,362	1.4	99,343
WYOMING	(	8	INSTITUTIONS)												
TOTAL	135	.9	220	1.5	82	.6	297	2.0	734	5.0	13,649	92.8	327	2.2	14,710
FEMALE	87	1.2	73	1.0	41	.6	150	2.0	351	4.8	6,981	94.6	48	.7	7,380
MALE	48	.7	147	2.0	41	.6	147	2.0	383	5.2	6,668	91.0	279	3.8	7,330
THE STATES AND D.C.	(	2,903	INSTITUTIONS)												
TOTAL	61,407	.7	887,505	10.4	177,838	2.1	344,958	4.0	1,471,708	17.2	6,938,999	81.0	154,869	1.8	8,565,576
FEMALE	32,381	.8	505,326	11.7	83,682	1.9	171,135	4.0	792,524	18.4	3,465,053	80.5	46,634	1.1	4,307,211
MALE	29,026	.7	392,179	9.0	94,156	2.2	173,823	4.1	679,184	15.9	3,470,946	81.5	108,235	2.5	4,258,365
AMERICAN SAMOA	(	1	INSTITUTIONS)												
TOTAL	0	.0	1	.1	781	94.0	0	.0	782	94.1	49	5.9		.0	831
FEMALE	0	.0	1	.2	417	93.3	0	.0	418	93.5	29	6.5	0	.0	447
MALE	0	.0	0	.0	364	94.8	0	.0	364	94.8	20	5.2		.0	384
CANAL ZONE	(	1	INSTITUTIONS)												
TOTAL	0	.0	44	10.5	0	.0	132	31.4	176	41.9	244	58.1		.0	420
FEMALE	0	.0	25	10.5	0	.0	70	29.5	95	40.1	142	59.9	0	.0	237
MALE	0	.0	19	10.4	0	.0	62	33.9	81	44.3	102	55.7		.0	183
GUAM	(	1	INSTITUTIONS)												
TOTAL	11	.4	28	.9	2,142	72.3	58	2.0	2,239	75.6	510	17.2	212	7.2	2,961
FEMALE	4	.3	16	1.1	1,146	76.4	21	1.4	1,187	79.1	239	15.9	74	4.9	1,500
MALE	7	.5	12	.8	996	68.2	37	2.5	1,052	72.0	271	18.5	138	9.4	1,461
PUERTO RICO	(	33	INSTITUTIONS)												
TOTAL	0	.0	10	.0	1	.0	114,078	99.6	114,089	99.7	332	.3	65	.1	114,486
FEMALE	0	.0	2	.0	1	.0	65,406	99.7	65,409	99.7	182	.3	33	.1	65,624
MALE	0	.0	8	.0	0	.0	48,672	99.6	48,680	99.6	150	.3	32	.1	48,862
TRUST TERRITORY	(	1	INSTITUTIONS)												
TOTAL	0	.0	0	.0	251	100.0	0	.0	251	100.0	0	.0		.0	251
FEMALE	0	.0	0	.0	88	100.0	0	.0	88	100.0	0	.0	0	.0	88
MALE	0	.0	0	.0	163	100.0	0	.0	163	100.0	0	.0		.0	163

215

TABLE 4 - TOTAL UNDERGRADUATE ENROLLMENT IN INSTITUTIONS OF HIGHER EDUCATION BY RACE, ETHNICITY AND SEX: STATE AND NATION, 1978

	AMERICAN INDIAN ALASKAN NATIVE		BLACK NON-HISPANIC		ASIAN OR PACIFIC ISLANDER		HISPANIC		TOTAL MINORITY		WHITE NON-HISPANIC		NON-RESIDENT ALIEN	
	NUMBER	%	NUMBER	%	NUMBER	%	NUMBER	%	NUMBER	%	NUMBER	%	NUMBER	%
VIRGIN ISLANDS	(1 INSTITUTIONS)													
TOTAL	0	.0	311	60.4	1	.2	27	5.2	339	65.8	51	9.9	125	24.3
FEMALE	0	.0	237	64.2	1	.3	18	4.9	256	69.4	22	6.0	91	24.7
MALE	0	.0	74	50.7	0	.0	9	6.2	83	56.8	29	19.9	34	23.3
OUTLYING AREAS	(38 INSTITUTIONS)													
TOTAL	11	.0	394	.3	3,176	2.7	114,295	95.7	117,876	98.7	1,186	1.0	402	.3
FEMALE	4	.0	281	.4	1,653	2.4	65,515	96.0	67,453	98.8	614	.9	198	.3
MALE	7	.0	113	.2	1,523	3.0	48,780	95.3	50,423	98.5	572	1.1	204	.4
NATION TOTAL	(2,941 INSTITUTIONS)													
TOTAL	61,418	.7	887,899	10.2	181,014	2.1	459,293	5.3	1,589,584	18.3	6,940,185	79.9	155,271	1.8
FEMALE	32,385	.7	505,607	11.6	85,335	2.0	236,650	5.4	859,977	19.7	3,468,667	79.3	46,832	1.1
MALE	29,033	.7	382,292	8.9	95,679	2.2	222,603	5.2	729,607	16.9	3,471,518	80.6	108,439	2.5

TOTAL GRADUATE ENROLLMENT IN INSTITUTIONS OF HIGHER EDUCATION BY RACE, ETHNICITY AND SEX:
STATE AND NATION, 1978

| AMERICAN INDIAN ALASKAN NATIVE | | BLACK NON-HISPANIC | | ASIAN OR PACIFIC ISLANDER | | HISPANIC | | TOTAL MINORITY | | WHITE NON-HISPANIC | | NON-RESIDENT ALIEN | | TOTAL |
NUMBER	%	NUMBER	%	NUMBER	%	NUMBER	%	NUMBER	%	NUMBER	%	NUMBER	%	NUMBER
(18 INSTITUTIONS)														
18	.1	2,062	12.9	99	.6	59	.4	2,238	14.0	13,214	82.7	534	3.3	15,986
6	.1	1,320	16.0	23	.3	15	.2	1,364	16.5	6,796	82.2	108	1.3	8,268
12	.2	742	9.6	76	1.0	44	.6	874	11.3	6,418	83.2	426	5.5	7,718
(7 INSTITUTIONS)														
39	3.4	38	3.3	19	1.7	13	1.1	109	9.5	1,012	88.3	25	2.2	1,146
24	4.2	17	3.0	11	1.9	9	1.6	61	10.7	505	88.3	6	1.0	572
15	2.6	21	3.7	8	1.4	4	.7	48	8.4	507	88.3	19	3.3	574
(4 INSTITUTIONS)														
91	.6	116	.8	114	.8	346	2.5	667	4.7	12,455	88.6	933	6.6	14,055
55	.9	55	.9	43	.7	158	2.6	311	5.2	5,533	92.5	137	2.3	5,981
36	.4	61	.8	71	.9	188	2.3	356	4.4	6,922	85.7	796	9.9	8,074
(11 INSTITUTIONS)														
38	.7	464	8.0	38	.7	20	.3	560	9.6	5,066	86.9	207	3.5	5,833
19	.6	292	9.7	18	.6	7	.2	336	11.2	2,637	87.8	30	1.0	3,003
19	.7	172	6.1	20	.7	13	.5	224	7.9	2,429	85.8	177	6.3	2,830
(111 INSTITUTIONS)														
694	.6	4,700	4.1	6,193	5.4	4,659	4.1	16,246	14.3	86,064	75.7	11,432	10.1	113,742
293	.6	2,505	5.4	2,499	5.4	2,037	4.4	7,334	15.8	36,674	78.3	2,505	5.4	46,513
401	.6	2,195	3.3	3,694	5.5	2,622	3.9	8,912	13.3	49,390	73.5	8,927	13.3	67,229
(16 INSTITUTIONS)														
47	.4	223	1.7	145	1.1	431	3.2	846	6.3	11,422	85.5	1,097	8.2	13,365
24	.4	100	1.7	64	1.1	199	3.5	387	6.8	5,137	89.9	191	3.3	5,715
23	.3	123	1.6	81	1.1	232	3.0	459	6.0	6,285	82.2	906	11.8	7,650
(20 INSTITUTIONS)														
23	.1	577	2.5	151	.7	325	1.4	1,076	4.7	21,154	92.1	749	3.3	22,979
13	.1	258	2.3	65	.6	123	1.1	459	4.2	10,394	94.2	178	1.6	11,031
10	.1	319	2.7	86	.7	202	1.7	617	5.2	10,760	90.1	571	4.8	11,948
(2 INSTITUTIONS)														
2	.1	57	3.8	8	.5	4	.3	71	4.8	1,323	89.3	87	5.9	1,481
0	.0	19	2.9	1	.2	3	.5	23	3.5	619	93.8	18	2.7	660
2	.2	38	4.6	7	.9	1	.1	48	5.8	704	85.7	69	8.4	821
F COLUMBIA (12 INSTITUTIONS)														
46	.2	3,020	14.7	455	2.2	279	1.4	3,800	18.4	14,142	68.6	2,669	12.9	20,611
8	.1	1,795	21.1	133	1.6	114	1.3	2,050	24.1	5,679	66.8	767	9.0	8,496
38	.3	1,225	10.1	322	2.7	165	1.4	1,750	14.4	8,463	69.9	1,902	15.7	12,115
(24 INSTITUTIONS)														
53	.2	2,608	9.7	247	.9	989	3.7	3,897	14.5	21,797	81.4	1,096	4.1	26,790
18	.2	1,561	13.1	77	.6	492	4.1	2,148	18.1	9,531	80.2	212	1.8	11,891
35	.2	1,047	7.0	170	1.1	497	3.3	1,749	11.7	12,266	82.3	884	5.9	14,899
(26 INSTITUTIONS)														
29	.1	3,116	14.2	116	.5	59	.3	3,320	15.1	17,516	79.9	1,096	5.0	21,932
13	.1	2,166	18.0	51	.4	19	.2	2,249	18.7	9,513	79.3	240	2.0	12,002
16	.2	950	9.6	65	.7	40	.4	1,071	10.8	8,003	80.6	856	8.6	9,930
(2 INSTITUTIONS)														
4	.1	25	.7	1,523	39.9	55	1.4	1,607	42.1	1,958	51.3	251	6.6	3,816
3	.2	8	.5	723	42.3	23	1.3	757	44.3	875	51.2	76	4.4	1,708
1	.0	17	.8	800	38.0	32	1.5	850	40.3	1,083	51.4	175	8.3	2,108
(5 INSTITUTIONS)														
17	.5	17	.5	38	1.2	27	.9	99	3.2	2,933	94.1	85	2.7	3,117
8	.6	5	.4	13	.9	13	.9	39	2.8	1,333	96.0	16	1.2	1,388
9	.5	12	.7	25	1.4	14	.8	60	3.5	1,600	92.5	69	4.0	1,729
(60 INSTITUTIONS)														
110	.2	3,947	6.8	1,245	2.1	689	1.2	5,991	10.3	47,765	82.4	4,235	7.3	57,991
47	.2	2,309	9.5	404	1.7	308	1.3	3,067	12.6	20,291	83.3	1,001	4.1	24,359
63	.2	1,639	4.9	841	2.5	381	1.1	2,924	8.7	27,474	81.7	3,234	9.6	33,632
(31 INSTITUTIONS)														
63	.2	934	3.3	179	.6	190	.7	1,366	4.8	25,235	88.1	2,032	7.1	28,633
39	.3	552	4.0	75	.5	75	.5	741	5.4	12,458	90.9	502	3.7	13,701
24	.2	382	2.6	104	.7	115	.8	625	4.2	12,777	85.6	1,530	10.2	14,932
(12 INSTITUTIONS)														
25	.2	294	2.1	114	.8	56	.4	489	3.5	12,212	87.2	1,302	9.3	14,003
13	.2	157	2.5	43	.7	25	.4	238	3.7	5,822	91.4	307	4.8	6,367
12	.2	137	1.8	71	.9	31	.4	251	3.3	6,390	83.7	995	13.0	7,636
(10 INSTITUTIONS)														
67	.4	424	2.5	97	.6	150	.9	738	4.4	14,926	88.3	1,248	7.4	16,912
29	.3	240	2.7	42	.5	69	.8	380	4.2	8,250	92.1	330	3.7	8,960
38	.5	184	2.3	55	.7	81	1.0	358	4.5	6,676	84.0	918	11.5	7,952
(16 INSTITUTIONS)														
110	.6	531	3.1	93	.5	57	.3	791	4.6	15,948	92.5	507	2.9	17,246
63	.6	323	3.1	30	.3	23	.2	439	4.2	9,897	94.6	104	1.0	10,440
47	.7	208	3.1	63	.9	34	.5	352	5.2	6,051	88.9	403	5.9	6,806
(19 INSTITUTIONS)														
37	.2	2,580	15.7	70	.4	235	1.4	2,922	17.8	12,659	77.0	854	5.2	16,435
16	.2	1,938	20.8	16	.2	124	1.3	2,094	22.5	7,044	75.6	178	1.9	9,316
21	.3	642	9.0	54	.8	111	1.6	828	11.6	5,615	78.9	676	9.5	7,119

	AMERICAN INDIAN ALASKAN NATIVE		BLACK NON-HISPANIC		ASIAN OR PACIFIC ISLANDER		HISPANIC		TOTAL MINORITY		WHITE NON-HISPANIC		NON-RESIDENT ALIEN	
	NUMBER	%	NUMBER	%	NUMBER	%	NUMBER	%	NUMBER	%	NUMBER	%	NUMBER	%
MAINE (4 INSTITUTIONS)														
TOTAL	2	.1	3	.2	2	.1	6	.3	13	.8	1,688	97.9	23	1.3
FEMALE	1	.1	0	.0	1	.1	2	.3	4	.5	751	98.3	9	1.2
MALE	1	.1	3	.3	1	.1	4	.4	9	.9	937	97.6	14	1.5
MARYLAND (27 INSTITUTIONS)														
TOTAL	62	.3	2,063	9.8	231	1.1	161	.8	2,517	11.9	17,409	82.5	1,170	5.5
FEMALE	39	.4	1,334	12.3	119	1.1	87	.8	1,579	14.5	8,970	82.6	307	2.8
MALE	23	.2	729	7.1	112	1.1	74	.7	938	9.2	8,439	82.4	863	8.4
MASSACHUSETTS (51 INSTITUTIONS)														
TOTAL	77	.2	1,348	2.9	759	1.6	569	1.2	2,753	5.9	40,106	86.2	3,693	7.9
FEMALE	26	.1	600	3.0	269	1.4	228	1.2	1,123	5.7	17,816	90.0	857	4.3
MALE	51	.2	748	2.8	490	1.8	341	1.3	1,630	6.1	22,290	83.3	2,836	10.6
MICHIGAN (28 INSTITUTIONS)														
TOTAL	146	.3	3,155	6.5	587	1.2	450	.9	4,338	8.9	40,968	83.9	3,499	7.2
FEMALE	76	.3	2,049	8.4	205	.8	209	.9	2,539	10.5	20,912	86.1	843	3.5
MALE	70	.3	1,106	4.5	382	1.6	241	1.0	1,799	7.3	20,056	81.8	2,656	10.8
MINNESOTA (17 INSTITUTIONS)														
TOTAL	45	.3	152	.9	171	1.0	97	.6	465	2.8	15,103	90.4	1,131	6.8
FEMALE	19	.3	71	.9	57	.8	41	.5	188	2.5	7,078	94.2	249	3.3
MALE	26	.3	81	.9	114	1.2	56	.6	277	3.0	8,025	87.4	882	9.6
MISSISSIPPI (12 INSTITUTIONS)														
TOTAL	19	.2	2,100	24.4	68	.8	11	.1	2,198	25.6	6,076	70.6	328	3.8
FEMALE	14	.3	1,407	30.9	20	.4	5	.1	1,446	31.7	3,048	66.9	61	1.3
MALE	5	.1	693	17.1	48	1.2	6	.1	752	18.6	3,028	74.8	267	6.6
MISSOURI (30 INSTITUTIONS)														
TOTAL	46	.2	1,294	5.4	568	2.4	155	.6	2,063	8.6	20,595	86.3	1,193	5.0
FEMALE	18	.2	709	7.0	110	1.1	52	.5	889	8.8	8,913	88.3	292	2.9
MALE	28	.2	585	4.3	458	3.3	103	.7	1,174	8.5	11,682	84.9	901	6.5
MONTANA (7 INSTITUTIONS)														
TOTAL	30	1.4	5	.2	8	.4	5	.2	48	2.3	2,020	96.1	33	1.6
FEMALE	18	1.9	0	.0	4	.4	1	.1	23	2.5	893	96.1	13	1.4
MALE	12	1.0	5	.4	4	.3	4	.3	25	2.1	1,127	96.2	20	1.7
NEBRASKA (8 INSTITUTIONS)														
TOTAL	14	.2	144	2.0	56	.8	54	.8	268	3.7	6,640	92.3	283	3.9
FEMALE	5	.1	73	2.1	27	.8	16	.5	121	3.5	3,332	95.3	44	1.3
MALE	9	.2	71	1.9	29	.8	38	1.0	147	4.0	3,308	89.6	239	6.5
NEVADA (2 INSTITUTIONS)														
TOTAL	11	.7	45	2.9	21	1.4	27	1.7	104	6.7	1,388	89.3	62	4.0
FEMALE	3	.4	27	3.4	7	.9	13	1.6	50	6.3	722	91.6	16	2.0
MALE	8	1.0	18	2.3	14	1.8	14	1.8	54	7.0	666	86.9	46	5.0
NEW HAMPSHIRE (7 INSTITUTIONS)														
TOTAL	3	.1	30	1.1	26	1.0	10	.4	69	2.5	2,642	96.7	21	.8
FEMALE	1	.1	8	.8	11	1.1	5	.5	25	2.5	968	97.0	5	.5
MALE	2	.1	22	1.3	15	.9	5	.3	44	2.5	1,674	96.5	16	.9
NEW JERSEY (27 INSTITUTIONS)														
TOTAL	33	.1	1,568	5.0	518	1.6	623	2.0	2,742	8.7	27,497	87.0	1,372	4.3
FEMALE	17	.1	932	6.3	178	1.2	332	2.2	1,459	9.8	13,143	88.2	305	2.0
MALE	16	.1	636	3.8	340	2.0	291	1.7	1,283	7.7	14,354	85.9	1,067	6.4
NEW MEXICO (7 INSTITUTIONS)														
TOTAL	116	1.9	89	1.5	52	.8	939	15.3	1,196	19.5	4,529	73.8	409	6.7
FEMALE	62	2.3	40	1.5	23	.8	427	15.6	552	20.1	2,131	77.7	59	2.2
MALE	54	1.6	49	1.4	29	.9	512	15.1	644	19.0	2,398	70.7	350	10.3
NEW YORK (128 INSTITUTIONS)														
TOTAL	401	.3	6,867	5.7	3,149	2.6	3,287	2.7	13,704	11.4	98,541	82.2	7,571	6.3
FEMALE	159	.3	3,962	6.8	1,244	2.1	1,778	3.1	7,143	12.3	48,731	84.1	2,084	3.6
MALE	242	.4	2,905	4.7	1,905	3.1	1,509	2.4	6,561	10.6	49,810	80.5	5,487	8.9
NORTH CAROLINA (15 INSTITUTIONS)														
TOTAL	61	.3	2,114	11.7	103	.6	74	.4	2,352	13.1	14,753	82.0	890	4.9
FEMALE	31	.3	1,357	15.0	39	.4	41	.5	1,468	16.2	7,397	81.6	202	2.2
MALE	30	.3	757	8.5	64	.7	33	.4	884	9.9	7,356	82.4	688	7.7
NORTH DAKOTA (3 INSTITUTIONS)														
TOTAL	11	.7	10	.6	17	1.1	4	.3	42	2.7	1,360	88.1	142	9.2
FEMALE	8	1.5	3	.6	5	1.0	1	.2	17	3.3	470	90.9	30	5.8
MALE	3	.3	7	.7	12	1.2	3	.3	25	2.4	890	86.7	112	10.9
OHIO (57 INSTITUTIONS)														
TOTAL	104	.2	3,152	6.3	336	.7	306	.6	3,898	7.9	42,895	86.4	2,854	5.7
FEMALE	46	.2	1,809	7.7	125	.5	140	.6	2,120	9.0	20,757	88.2	647	2.8
MALE	58	.2	1,343	5.1	211	.8	166	.6	1,778	6.8	22,138	84.7	2,207	8.4
OKLAHOMA (14 INSTITUTIONS)														
TOTAL	334	2.4	505	3.7	78	.6	69	.5	986	7.2	10,916	80.0	1,749	12.8
FEMALE	181	3.0	279	4.6	30	.5	25	.4	515	8.6	5,174	86.1	321	5.3
MALE	153	2.0	226	3.0	48	.6	44	.6	471	6.2	5,742	75.1	1,428	18.7
OREGON (20 INSTITUTIONS)														
TOTAL	57	.6	95	1.0	167	1.8	66	.7	385	4.2	7,740	83.6	1,133	12.2
FEMALE	25	.6	35	.9	74	1.9	25	.6	159	4.0	3,535	89.2	271	6.8
MALE	32	.6	60	1.1	93	1.8	41	.8	226	4.3	4,205	79.4	862	15.3

:RICAN INDIAN :ASKAN NATIVE		BLACK NON-HISPANIC		ASIAN OR PACIFIC ISLANDER		HISPANIC		TOTAL MINORITY		WHITE NON-HISPANIC		NON-RESIDENT ALIEN		TOTAL
IMBER	%	NUMBER	%	NUMBER	%	NUMBER	%	NUMBER	%	NUMBER	%	NUMBER	%	NUMBER
(77 INSTITUTIONS)														
99	.2	1,835	3.9	543	1.2	337	.7	2,814	6.0	41,107	87.7	2,954	6.3	46,875
37	.2	1,057	5.1	207	1.0	157	.8	1,458	7.0	18,740	90.4	543	2.6	20,741
62	.2	778	3.0	336	1.3	180	.7	1,356	5.2	22,367	85.6	2,411	9.2	26,134
(7 INSTITUTIONS)														
15	.2	83	1.4	64	1.1	31	.5	193	3.2	5,450	90.2	398	6.6	6,041
8	.3	38	1.5	15	.6	14	.5	75	2.9	2,410	93.4	95	3.7	2,580
7	.2	45	1.3	49	1.4	17	.5	118	3.4	3,040	87.8	303	9.8	3,461
(14 INSTITUTIONS)														
12	.1	1,315	11.0	35	.3	37	.3	1,399	11.7	10,334	86.3	245	2.0	11,978
6	.1	927	13.6	11	.2	17	.2	961	14.1	5,807	85.1	57	.8	6,825
6	.1	388	7.5	24	.5	20	.4	438	8.5	4,527	87.9	188	3.6	5,153
(6 INSTITUTIONS)														
26	1.4	3	.2	2	.1	2	.1	33	1.7	1,746	92.2	115	6.1	1,894
10	1.3	1	.1	0	.0	0	.0	11	1.5	723	96.9	12	1.6	746
16	1.4	2	.2	2	.2	2	.2	22	1.9	1,023	89.1	103	9.0	1,148
(18 INSTITUTIONS)														
29	.2	1,175	7.4	108	.7	49	.3	1,361	8.6	13,451	84.8	1,042	6.6	15,854
16	.2	739	9.7	37	.5	23	.3	815	10.7	6,557	86.2	235	3.1	7,607
13	.2	436	5.3	71	.9	26	.3	546	6.6	6,894	83.6	807	9.8	8,247
(56 INSTITUTIONS)														
245	.4	3,962	5.9	951	1.4	4,521	6.8	9,679	14.5	51,591	77.3	5,442	8.2	66,712
92	.3	2,347	7.8	349	1.2	2,251	7.4	5,039	16.7	24,044	79.5	1,172	3.9	30,255
153	.4	1,615	4.4	602	1.7	2,270	6.2	4,640	12.7	27,547	75.6	4,270	11.7	36,457
(4 INSTITUTIONS)														
48	.6	33	.4	103	1.3	68	.9	252	3.3	6,712	86.6	783	10.1	7,747
22	.8	14	.5	42	1.6	31	1.2	109	4.2	2,302	88.4	192	7.4	2,603
26	.5	19	.4	61	1.2	37	.7	143	2.8	4,410	85.7	591	11.5	5,144
(11 INSTITUTIONS)														
3	.1	45	1.9	8	.3	19	.8	75	3.1	2,210	92.3	109	4.6	2,394
0	.0	23	1.7	6	.4	6	.4	35	2.6	1,272	94.4	41	3.0	1,348
3	.3	22	2.1	2	.2	13	1.2	40	3.8	938	89.7	68	6.5	1,046
(21 INSTITUTIONS)														
26	.1	1,926	9.6	175	.9	71	.4	2,198	11.0	17,194	86.1	589	2.9	19,981
10	.1	1,216	12.6	48	.5	38	.4	1,312	13.6	8,211	85.0	135	1.4	9,658
16	.2	710	6.9	127	1.2	33	.3	886	8.6	8,983	87.0	454	4.4	10,323
(16 INSTITUTIONS)														
93	.7	295	2.2	395	2.9	138	1.0	921	6.7	11,217	82.0	1,536	11.2	13,674
43	.8	128	2.3	158	2.9	42	.8	371	6.8	4,776	87.1	337	6.1	5,484
50	.6	167	2.0	237	2.9	96	1.2	550	6.7	6,441	78.6	1,199	14.6	8,190
(5 INSTITUTIONS)														
43	.4	268	2.3	83	.7	22	.2	416	3.6	10,670	93.2	366	3.2	11,452
23	.4	158	2.4	27	.4	10	.2	218	3.3	6,256	95.5	75	1.1	6,549
20	.4	110	2.2	56	1.1	12	.2	198	4.0	4,414	90.0	291	5.9	4,903
(22 INSTITUTIONS)														
58	.3	455	2.4	279	1.5	196	1.0	988	5.1	16,527	86.1	1,690	8.8	19,205
32	.4	248	2.9	100	1.2	91	1.1	471	5.6	7,605	89.9	381	4.5	8,457
26	.2	207	1.9	179	1.7	105	1.0	517	4.8	8,922	83.0	1,309	12.2	10,748
(1 INSTITUTIONS)														
3	.3	4	.4	5	.5	8	.8	20	1.9	925	88.2	104	9.9	1,049
1	.2	3	.7	3	.7	2	.5	9	2.1	408	94.0	17	3.9	434
2	.3	1	.2	2	.3	6	1.0	11	1.8	517	84.1	87	14.1	615
O.C. (1,128 INSTITUTIONS)														
,785	.4	61,871	5.8	20,612	1.9	21,055	2.0	107,323	10.0	890,801	83.1	73,368	6.8	1,071,492
,740	.4	37,213	7.5	7,882	1.6	9,946	2.0	56,781	11.4	422,840	85.2	16,813	3.4	496,434
,045	.4	24,658	4.3	12,730	2.2	11,109	1.9	50,542	8.8	467,961	81.4	56,555	9.8	575,058
(1 INSTITUTIONS)														
0	.0	0	.0	118	47.8	11	4.5	129	52.2	118	47.8	0	.0	247
0	.0	0	.0	94	58.0	11	6.8	105	64.8	57	35.2	0	.0	162
0	.0	0	.0	24	28.2	0	.0	24	28.2	61	71.8	0	.0	85
(9 INSTITUTIONS)														
0	.0	0	.0	0	.0	4,110	94.7	4,110	94.7	218	5.0	11	.3	4,339
0	.0	0	.0	0	.0	2,324	94.4	2,324	94.4	133	5.4	4	.2	2,461
0	.0	0	.0	0	.0	1,786	95.1	1,786	95.1	85	4.5	7	.4	1,878
(1 INSTITUTIONS)														
0	.0	47	65.3	1	1.4	2	2.8	50	69.4	20	27.8	2	2.8	72
0	.0	29	65.9	0	.0	1	2.3	30	68.2	14	31.8	0	.0	44
0	.0	18	64.3	1	3.6	1	3.6	20	71.4	6	21.4	2	7.1	28
(11 INSTITUTIONS)														
0	.0	47	1.0	119	2.6	4,123	88.5	4,289	92.1	356	7.6	13	.3	4,658
0	.0	29	1.1	94	3.5	2,336	87.6	2,459	92.2	204	7.6	4	.1	2,667
0	.0	18	.9	25	1.3	1,787	89.8	1,830	91.9	152	7.6	9	.5	1,991
(1,139 INSTITUTIONS)														
,785	.4	61,918	5.8	20,731	1.9	25,178	2.3	111,612	10.4	891,157	82.8	73,381	6.8	1,076,150
,740	.3	37,242	7.5	7,976	1.6	12,282	2.5	59,240	11.9	423,044	84.8	16,817	3.4	499,101
,045	.4	24,676	4.3	12,755	2.2	12,896	2.2	52,372	9.1	468,113	81.1	56,564	9.8	577,049

	AMERICAN INDIAN ALASKAN NATIVE		BLACK NON-HISPANIC		ASIAN OR PACIFIC ISLANDER		HISPANIC		TOTAL MINORITY		WHITE NON-HISPANIC		NON-RESIDENT ALIEN	
	NUMBER	%	NUMBER	%	NUMBER	%	NUMBER	%	NUMBER	%	NUMBER	%	NUMBER	%
ALABAMA (7 INSTITUTIONS)														
TOTAL	1	.0	196	5.7	22	.6	6	.2	225		3,164	92.8	22	.6
FEMALE	0	.0	85	12.1	8	1.1	2	.3	95		601	85.9	4	.6
MALE	1	.0	111	4.1	14	.5	4	.1	130		2,563	94.5	18	.7
ARIZONA (2 INSTITUTIONS)														
TOTAL	4	.3	1	.1	4	.3	25	2.1	34	2.9	1,151	96.8		
FEMALE	1	.3	0	.0	2	.5	8	2.2	11	3.0	358	96.8	1	.3
MALE	3	.4	1	.1	2	.2	17	2.1	23	2.8	793	96.8	3	.4
ARKANSAS (4 INSTITUTIONS)														
TOTAL	6	.4	67	4.4	14	.9	5	.3	92	6.0	1,427	93.7		.3
FEMALE	1	.3	20	6.5	3	1.0	2	.6	26	8.4	282	91.6		.0
MALE	5	.4	47	3.9	11	.9	3	.2	66	5.4	1,145	94.2		.3
CALIFORNIA (51 INSTITUTIONS)														
TOTAL	167	.5	1,250	4.0	1,925	.2	1,458	4.7	4,800	15.5	25,535	82.7	540	1.7
FEMALE	53	.6	521	5.9	605	.8	367	4.1	1,546	17.4	7,220	81.2	131	1.5
MALE	114	.5	729	3.3	1,320	8.0	1,091	5.0	3,254	14.8	18,315	83.3	409	1.9
COLORADO (9 INSTITUTIONS)														
TOTAL	26	.9	63	2.1	39	1.3	120	4.1	248	8.4	2,695	91.2	11	.4
FEMALE	8	.9	21	2.4	11	1.2	32	3.	72	8.1	811	91.7	1	.1
MALE	18	.9	42	2.0	28	1.4	88	4.4	176	8.5	1,884	91.0	10	.5
CONNECTICUT (5 INSTITUTIONS)														
TOTAL	4	.1	131	4.5	32	1.1	89	3.0	256	8.7	2,637	89.8	42	1.4
FEMALE	3	.3	50	5.6	11	1.2	28	3.2	92	10.4	788	88.9	6	.7
MALE	1	.0	81	4.0	21	1.0	61	3.0	164	8.0	1,849	90.2	36	1.8
DISTRICT OF COLUMBIA (8 INSTITUTIONS)														
TOTAL	17	.2	1,574	18.0	152	1.7	205	2.3	1,948	22.2	6,625	75.6	187	2.1
FEMALE	3	.1	664	22.7	63	2.2	66	2.3	796	27.2	2,078	71.0	54	1.8
MALE	14	.2	910	15.6	89	1.5	139	2.4	1,152	19.8	4,547	78.0	133	2.3
FLORIDA (6 INSTITUTIONS)														
TOTAL	15	.2	192	3.2	26	.4	305	5.1	538	9.0	5,450	90.8	14	.2
FEMALE	2	.1	50	3.2	4	.3	69	4.3	125	7.9	1,457	91.8	5	.3
MALE	13	.3	142	3.2	22	.5	236	5.3	413	9.4	3,993	90.4	9	.2
GEORGIA (7 INSTITUTIONS)														
TOTAL	7	.1	428	7.5	19	.3	37	.7	491	8.6	5,162	90.7	36	.6
FEMALE	3	.2	103	8.5	4	.3	6	.5	116	9.6	1,092	90.0	5	.4
MALE	4	.1	325	7.3	15	.3	31	.7	375	8.4	4,070	90.9	31	.7
HAWAII (1 INSTITUTIONS)														
TOTAL	0	.0	0	.0	360	73.5	3	.6	363	74.1	116	23.7	11	2.2
FEMALE	0	.0	0	.0	108	66.7	2	1.2	110	67.9	50	30.9	2	1.2
MALE	0	.0	0	.0	252	76.8	1	.3	253	77.1	66	20.1	9	2.7
IDAHO (1 INSTITUTIONS)														
TOTAL	0	.0	1	.4	2	.7	0	.0	3	1.1	267	98.9		.0
FEMALE	0	.0	1	2.0	1	2.0	0	.0	2	4.0	48	96.0		.0
MALE	0	.0	0	.0	1	.5	0	.0	1	.5	219	99.5		.0
ILLINOIS (31 INSTITUTIONS)														
TOTAL	30	.2	619	3.6	280	1.6	203	1.2	1,132	6	15,936	92.4	175	1.0
FEMALE	10	.3	246	6.2	66	1.7	44	1.1	366	3	3,552	90.0	28	.7
MALE	20	.2	373	2.8	214	1.6	159	1.2	766		12,384	93.1	147	1.1
INDIANA (13 INSTITUTIONS)														
TOTAL	19	.3	176	2.9	41	.7	73	1.2	309	5.	5,672	93.2	104	1.7
FEMALE	4	.3	72	5.7	7	.6	15	1.2	98	7.	1,138	90.6	20	1.6
MALE	15	.3	104	2.2	34	.7	58	1.2	211	4.	4,534	93.9	84	1.7
IOWA (7 INSTITUTIONS)														
TOTAL	27	.5	66	1.1	34	.6	48	.8	175	3	5,381	92.2	280	8
FEMALE	4	.4	16	1.5	11	1.1	7	.7	38	3	974	93.1	34	3
MALE	23	.5	50	1.0	23	.5	41	.9	137		4,407	92.0	246	11
KANSAS (4 INSTITUTIONS)														
TOTAL	7	.3	44	1.9	15	.7	35	1.6	101		2,156	95.5		.0
FEMALE	0	.0	15	3.0	4	.8	11	2.2	30		462	93.9		.5
MALE	7	.4	29	1.6	11	.6	24	1.4	71		1,694	96.0		.0
KENTUCKY (7 INSTITUTIONS)														
TOTAL	12	.3	98	2.2	77	1.7	19	.4	206		4,215	94.9	20	.5
FEMALE	2	.2	28	3.1	19	2.1	4	.4	53		842	93.7	4	.4
MALE	10	.3	70	2.0	58	1.6	15	.4	153		3,373	95.2	16	.5
LOUISIANA (6 INSTITUTIONS)														
TOTAL	8	.2	262	6.6	29	.7	52	1.3	350	8.	3,622	90.8	17	.4
FEMALE	3	.3	78	8.7	6	.7	15	1.7	102	11.	797	88.5	2	.2
MALE	5	.2	184	6.0	22	.7	37	1.2	248	8.0	2,825	91.5	15	.5
MAINE (2 INSTITUTIONS)														
TOTAL	0	.0	1	.3	0	.0	1	.3	2	.6	330	99.4	0	.0
FEMALE	0	.0	0	.0	0	.0	0	.0	0	.0	115	100.0	0	.0
MALE	0	.0	1	.5	0	.0	1	.5	2	.9	215	99.1	0	.0
MARYLAND (3 INSTITUTIONS)														
TOTAL	2	.1	224	6.3	76	2.1	27	.8	329	9.3	3,201	90.2	17	.5
FEMALE	0	.0	86	9.5	20	2.2	7	.8	113	12.4	792	87.2	3	.3
MALE	2	.1	138	5.2	56	2.1	20	.8	216	8.2	2,409	91.3	14	.5

AL FIRST PROFESSIONAL ENROLLMENT IN INSTITUTIONS OF HIGHER EDUCATION BY RACE, ETHNICITY AND SEX:
TE AND NATION, 1978

ERICAN INDIAN/LASKAN NATIVE		BLACK NON-HISPANIC		ASIAN OR PACIFIC ISLANDER		HISPANIC		TOTAL MINORITY		WHITE NON-HISPANIC		NON-RESIDENT ALIEN		TOTAL
UMBER	%	NUMBER	%	NUMBER	%	NUMBER	%	NUMBER	%	NUMBER	%	NUMBER	%	NUMBER
(18 INSTITUTIONS)														
25	.2	421	3.7	158	1.4	183	1.6	787	7.0	10,242	91.1	219	1.9	11,248
9	.3	170	4.8	64	1.8	57	1.6	300	8.4	3,207	90.3	44	1.2	3,551
16	.2	251	3.3	94	1.2	126	1.6	487	6.3	7,035	91.4	175	2.3	7,697
(11 INSTITUTIONS)														
29	.3	588	5.7	125	1.2	170	1.6	912	8.8	9,032	87.5	377	3.7	10,321
9	.4	231	9.3	34	1.4	42	1.7	316	12.8	2,101	84.9	57	2.3	2,474
20	.3	357	4.5	91	1.2	128	1.6	596	7.6	6,931	88.3	320	4.1	7,847
(11 INSTITUTIONS)														
32	.5	81	1.3	33	.5	70	1.1	216	3.4	6,060	95.8	48	.8	6,324
10	.7	34	2.2	10	.7	17	1.1	71	4.7	1,435	94.7	9	.6	1,515
22	.5	47	1.0	23	.5	53	1.1	145	3.0	4,625	96.2	39	.8	4,809
(5 INSTITUTIONS)														
3	.2	80	4.6	11	.6	4	.2	98	5.6	1,631	94.0	7	.4	1,736
2	.5	29	7.9	3	.8	1	.3	35	9.6	323	88.5	7	1.9	365
1	.1	51	3.7	8	.6	3	.2	63	4.6	1,308	95.4	0	.0	1,371
(17 INSTITUTIONS)														
32	.3	262	2.7	153	1.6	49	.5	496	5.2	9,017	93.7	109	1.1	9,622
9	.5	108	5.9	38	2.1	7	.4	162	8.8	1,655	90.3	15	.8	1,832
23	.3	154	2.0	115	1.5	42	.5	334	4.3	7,362	94.5	94	1.2	7,790
(1 INSTITUTIONS)														
0	.0	0	.0	0	.0	0	.0	0	.0	222	99.6	1	.4	223
0	.0	0	.0	0	.0	0	.0	0	.0	67	100.0	0	.0	67
0	.0	0	.0	0	.0	0	.0	0	.0	155	99.4	1	.6	156
(4 INSTITUTIONS)														
7	.2	49	1.7	39	1.4	38	1.3	133	4.7	2,673	94.9	12	.4	2,818
2	.3	15	2.4	8	1.3	3	.5	28	4.5	591	95.3	1	.2	620
5	.2	34	1.5	31	1.4	35	1.6	105	4.8	2,082	94.7	11	.5	2,198
(2 INSTITUTIONS)														
6	1.4	9	2.1	11	2.5	11	2.5	37	8.5	400	91.5	0	.0	437
3	4.3	3	4.3	7	10.0	4	5.7	17	24.3	53	75.7	0	.0	70
3	.8	6	1.6	4	1.1	7	1.9	20	5.4	347	94.6	0	.0	367
(11 INSTITUTIONS)														
8	.2	427	8.0	60	1.1	165	3.1	660	12.4	4,631	87.0	35	.7	5,326
3	.2	177	11.9	28	1.9	61	4.1	269	18.1	1,219	81.8	2	.1	1,490
5	.1	250	6.5	32	.8	104	2.7	391	10.2	3,412	88.9	33	.9	3,836
(1 INSTITUTIONS)														
22	3.5	7	1.1	11	1.8	149	23.9	189	30.3	435	69.7	0	.0	624
7	3.2	3	1.4	6	2.7	47	21.5	63	28.8	156	71.2	0	.0	219
15	3.7	4	1.0	5	1.2	102	25.2	126	31.1	279	68.9	0	.0	405
(41 INSTITUTIONS)														
37	.2	791	3.5	305	1.3	441	2.0	1,574	7.0	20,878	92.4	148	.7	22,600
19	.3	375	5.5	110	1.6	153	2.3	657	9.7	6,083	90.0	22	.3	6,762
18	.1	416	2.6	195	1.2	288	1.8	917	5.8	14,795	93.4	126	.8	15,838
(7 INSTITUTIONS)														
24	.5	372	8.3	24	.5	16	.4	436	9.7	4,020	89.7	28	.6	4,484
5	.5	117	10.5	7	.6	4	.4	133	12.0	970	87.3	8	.7	1,111
19	.6	255	7.6	17	.5	12	.4	303	9.0	3,050	90.4	20	.6	3,373
(1 INSTITUTIONS)														
10	2.1	0	.0	2	.4	0	.0	12	2.5	473	97.5	0	.0	485
1	1.1	0	.0	0	.0	0	.0	1	1.1	93	98.9	0	.0	94
9	2.3	0	.0	2	.5	0	.0	11	2.8	380	97.2	0	.0	391
(25 INSTITUTIONS)														
262	2.1	629	5.0	81	.6	77	.6	1,049	8.4	11,380	90.9	92	.7	12,521
38	1.2	253	8.0	24	.8	20	.6	335	10.6	2,802	88.8	20	.6	3,157
224	2.4	376	4.0	57	.6	57	.6	714	7.6	8,578	91.6	72	.8	9,364
(8 INSTITUTIONS)														
78	2.3	51	1.5	27	.8	25	.7	181	5.4	3,140	94.1	15	.4	3,336
17	2.3	18	2.5	9	1.2	5	.7	49	6.7	678	92.9	3	.4	730
61	2.3	33	1.3	18	.7	20	.8	132	5.1	2,462	94.5	12	.5	2,606
(9 INSTITUTIONS)														
15	.4	39	1.0	114	3.0	32	.9	200	5.3	3,531	93.9	31	.8	3,762
7	.9	11	1.4	33	4.1	5	.6	56	7.0	739	92.6	3	.4	798
8	.3	28	.9	81	2.7	27	.9	144	4.9	2,792	94.2	28	.9	2,964
(29 INSTITUTIONS)														
22	.2	562	3.9	152	1.1	135	.9	871	6.1	13,316	93.1	116	.8	14,303
7	.2	243	6.9	52	1.5	45	1.3	347	9.8	3,161	89.3	33	.9	3,541
15	.1	319	3.0	100	.9	90	.8	524	4.9	10,155	94.4	83	.8	10,762
(1 INSTITUTIONS)														
0	.0	14	5.5	11	4.3	5	2.0	30	11.9	219	86.6	4	1.6	253
0	.0	5	5.9	9	10.6			14	16.5	70	82.4	1	1.2	85
0	.0	9	5.4	2	1.2	5	3.0	16	9.5	149	88.7	3	1.8	168
(7 INSTITUTIONS)														
2	.1	91	4.1	4	.2	4	.2	101	4.5	2,067	93.0	55	2.5	2,223
2	.5	24	5.5	0	.0	1	.2	27	6.2	396	90.6	14	3.2	437
0	.0	67	3.8	4	.2	3	.2	74	4.1	1,671	93.6	41	2.3	1,786

TABLE 6 - TOTAL FIRST PROFESSIONAL ENROLLMENT IN INSTITUTIONS OF HIGHER EDUCATION BY RACE, ETHNICITY AND SEX:
STATE AND NATION, 1978

	AMERICAN INDIAN ALASKAN NATIVE		BLACK NON-HISPANIC		ASIAN OR PACIFIC ISLANDER		HISPANIC		TOTAL MINORITY		WHITE NON-HISPANIC		NON-RESIDENT ALIEN	
	NUMBER	%	NUMBER	%	NUMBER	%	NUMBER	%	NUMBER	%	NUMBER	%	NUMBER	%
SOUTH DAKOTA (2 INSTITUTIONS)														
TOTAL	1	.2	1	.2	1	.2	1	.2	4	.8	486	95.9	17	3.4
FEMALE	0	.0	0	.0	0	.0	0	.0	0	.0	94	96.9	3	3.1
MALE	1	.2	1	.2	1	.2	1	.2	4	1.0	392	95.6	14	3.4
TENNESSEE (9 INSTITUTIONS)														
TOTAL	10	.2	709	12.9	23	.4	26	.5	768	14.0	4,700	85.4	35	.6
FEMALE	1	.1	233	19.8	4	.3	4	.3	242	20.5	928	78.7	9	.8
MALE	9	.2	476	11.0	19	.4	22	.5	526	12.2	3,772	87.2	26	.6
TEXAS (24 INSTITUTIONS)														
TOTAL	44	.3	522	3.8	138	1.0	874	6.4	1,578	11.5	12,006	87.4	152	1.1
FEMALE	8	.2	206	6.3	46	1.4	198	6.0	458	13.9	2,807	85.3	26	.8
MALE	36	.3	316	3.0	92	.9	676	6.5	1,120	10.7	9,199	88.1	126	1.2
UTAH (2 INSTITUTIONS)														
TOTAL	5	.4	10	.8	14	1.1	25	2.0	54	4.3	1,175	94.6	13	1.0
FEMALE	0	.0	4	1.9	2	1.0	4	1.9	10	4.8	194	92.8	5	2.4
MALE	5	.5	6	.6	12	1.2	21	2.0	44	4.3	981	95.0	8	.8
VERMONT (2 INSTITUTIONS)														
TOTAL	0	.0	0	.0	3	.5	0	.0	3	.5	640	99.1	3	.5
FEMALE	0	.0	0	.0	1	.6	0	.0	1	.6	154	98.7	1	.6
MALE	0	.0	0	.0	2	.4	0	.0	2	.4	486	99.2	2	.4
VIRGINIA (9 INSTITUTIONS)														
TOTAL	2	.0	166	3.8	35	.8	13	.3	216	5.0	4,119	94.6	18	.4
FEMALE	1	.1	73	6.8	10	.9	2	.2	86	8.0	979	91.3	7	.7
MALE	1	.0	93	2.8	25	.8	11	.3	130	4.0	3,140	95.7	11	.3
WASHINGTON (4 INSTITUTIONS)														
TOTAL	22	.6	37	1.0	87	2.4	52	1.5	198	5.5	3,365	94.3	6	.2
FEMALE	8	.9	15	1.6	26	2.8	17	1.9	66	7.2	850	92.7	1	.1
MALE	14	.5	22	.8	61	2.3	35	1.3	132	5.0	2,515	94.8	5	.2
WEST VIRGINIA (3 INSTITUTIONS)														
TOTAL	3	.2	13	1.0	2	.2	3	.2	21	1.7	1,241	98.1	3	.2
FEMALE	1	.4	6	2.6	0	.0	2	.9	9	4.0	217	95.6	1	.4
MALE	2	.2	7	.7	2	.2	1	.1	12	1.2	1,024	98.7	2	.2
WISCONSIN (6 INSTITUTIONS)														
TOTAL	19	.5	100	2.9	29	.8	72	2.1	220	6.3	3,254	93.2	16	.5
FEMALE	4	.5	40	4.9	12	1.5	15	1.8	71	8.7	744	90.7	5	.6
MALE	15	.6	60	2.2	17	.6	57	2.1	149	5.6	2,510	94.0	11	.4
WYOMING (1 INSTITUTIONS)														
TOTAL	0	.0	0	.0	1	.5	2	.9	3	1.4	211	98.6	0	.0
FEMALE	0	.0	0	.0	1	1.9	1	1.9	2	3.7	52	96.3	0	.0
MALE	0	.0	0	.0	0	.0	1	.6	1	.6	159	99.4	0	.0
THE STATES AND D.C. (445 INSTITUTIONS)														
TOTAL	1,072	.4	11,424	4.5	4,800	1.9	5,353	2.1	22,649	8.9	229,306	89.9	3,044	1.2
FEMALE	270	.4	4,449	6.9	1,497	2.3	1,400	2.2	7,616	11.8	56,275	87.3	597	.9
MALE	802	.4	6,975	3.7	3,303	1.7	3,953	2.1	15,033	7.9	173,031	90.8	2,447	1.3
PUERTO RICO (4 INSTITUTIONS)														
TOTAL	0	.0	0	.0	0	.0	1,592	100.0	1,592	100.0	0	.0	0	.0
FEMALE	0	.0	0	.0	0	.0	533	100.0	533	100.0	0	.0	0	.0
MALE	0	.0	0	.0	0	.0	1,059	100.0	1,059	100.0	0	.0	0	.0
OUTLYING AREAS (4 INSTITUTIONS)														
TOTAL	0	.0	0	.0	0	.0	1,592	100.0	1,592	100.0	0	.0	0	.0
FEMALE	0	.0	0	.0	0	.0	533	100.0	533	100.0	0	.0	0	.0
MALE	0	.0	0	.0	0	.0	1,059	100.0	1,059	100.0	0	.0	0	.0
NATION TOTAL (449 INSTITUTIONS)														
TOTAL	1,072	.4	11,424	4.5	4,800	1.9	6,945	2.7	24,241	9.4	229,306	89.4	3,044	1.2
FEMALE	270	.4	4,449	6.8	1,497	2.3	1,933	3.0	8,149	12.5	56,275	86.5	597	.9
MALE	802	.4	6,975	3.6	3,303	1.7	5,012	2.6	16,092	8.4	173,031	90.3	2,447	1.3

TABLE 7 - TOTAL ENROLLMENT IN TWO YEAR INSTITUTIONS OF HIGHER EDUCATION BY RACE, ETHNICITY AND SEX: STATE AND NATION, 1978

	AMERICAN INDIAN ALASKAN NATIVE		BLACK NON-HISPANIC		ASIAN OR PACIFIC ISLANDER		HISPANIC		TOTAL MINORITY		WHITE NON-HISPANIC		NON-RESIDENT ALIEN		TOTAL
	NUMBER	%	NUMBER	%	NUMBER	%	NUMBER	%	NUMBER	%	NUMBER	%	NUMBER	%	NUMBER
ALABAMA (28 INSTITUTIONS)															
TOTAL	68	.2	10,931	25.1	66	.2	73	.2	11,138	25.6	31,818	73.2	535	1.2	43,491
FEMALE	29	.1	6,656	29.5	29	.1	27	.1	6,741	29.9	15,725	69.7	98	.4	22,564
MALE	39	.2	4,275	20.4	37	.2	46	.2	4,397	21.0	16,093	76.9	437	2.1	20,927
ALASKA (9 INSTITUTIONS)															
TOTAL	1,675	9.6	624	3.6	329	1.9	233	1.3	2,861	16.4	14,558	83.4	32	.2	17,451
FEMALE	1,020	9.9	301	2.9	185	1.8	125	1.2	1,631	15.9	8,640	84.0	18	.2	10,289
MALE	655	9.1	323	4.5	144	2.0	108	1.5	1,230	17.2	5,918	82.6	14	.2	7,162
ARIZONA (15 INSTITUTIONS)															
TOTAL	4,502	4.7	3,308	3.5	900	.9	12,220	12.8	20,930	22.0	73,123	76.7	1,222	1.3	95,275
FEMALE	2,607	5.2	1,327	2.7	536	1.1	6,665	13.4	11,135	22.4	38,123	76.7	452	.9	49,710
MALE	1,895	4.2	1,981	4.3	364	.8	5,555	12.2	9,795	21.5	35,000	76.8	770	1.7	45,565
ARKANSAS (14 INSTITUTIONS)															
TOTAL	141	1.2	1,994	16.4	118	1.0	49	.4	2,302	18.9	9,786	80.5	67	.6	12,155
FEMALE	72	1.1	1,166	17.9	35	.5	29	.4	1,302	20.0	5,197	79.9	9	.1	6,508
MALE	69	1.2	828	14.7	83	1.5	20	.4	1,000	17.7	4,589	81.3	58	1.0	5,647
CALIFORNIA (114 INSTITUTIONS)															
TOTAL	15,751	1.5	99,977	9.8	58,143	5.7	105,975	10.4	279,846	27.4	728,503	71.3	12,791	1.3	1,021,140
FEMALE	8,117	1.5	52,731	9.7	27,653	5.1	51,965	9.6	140,466	25.8	398,429	73.3	4,789	.9	543,684
MALE	7,634	1.6	47,246	9.9	30,490	6.4	54,010	11.3	139,380	29.2	330,074	69.1	8,002	1.7	477,456
COLORADO (15 INSTITUTIONS)															
TOTAL	556	1.3	1,579	3.8	437	1.1	3,601	8.7	6,173	15.0	34,041	82.6	974	2.4	41,188
FEMALE	269	1.3	674	3.2	224	1.1	1,446	6.9	2,613	12.4	18,149	86.4	245	1.2	21,007
MALE	287	1.4	905	4.5	213	1.1	2,155	10.7	3,560	17.6	15,892	78.7	729	3.6	20,181
CONNECTICUT (20 INSTITUTIONS)															
TOTAL	118	.3	3,540	8.7	258	.6	1,061	2.6	4,977	12.2	35,674	87.3	193	.5	40,844
FEMALE	67	.3	2,093	9.3	115	.5	589	2.6	2,864	12.8	19,472	87.0	53	.2	22,389
MALE	51	.3	1,447	7.8	143	.8	472	2.6	2,113	11.4	16,202	87.3	140	.8	18,455
DELAWARE (6 INSTITUTIONS)															
TOTAL	15	.2	1,237	15.3	41	.5	80	1.0	1,373	16.9	6,724	82.9	11	.1	8,108
FEMALE	9	.2	784	17.0	17	.4	47	1.0	857	18.6	3,736	81.2	6	.1	4,599
MALE	6	.2	453	12.9	24	.7	33	.9	516	14.7	2,988	85.2	5	.1	3,509
FLORIDA (33 INSTITUTIONS)															
TOTAL	813	.4	22,636	11.8	1,313	.7	16,132	8.4	40,894	21.3	147,367	76.6	4,097	2.1	192,358
FEMALE	460	.4	14,599	13.8	625	.6	8,689	8.2	24,373	23.0	80,326	75.8	1,317	1.2	106,016
MALE	353	.4	8,037	9.3	688	.8	7,443	8.6	16,521	19.1	67,041	77.6	2,780	3.2	86,342
GEORGIA (28 INSTITUTIONS)															
TOTAL	122	.3	7,736	17.4	143	.3	271	.6	8,272	18.6	35,571	79.8	729	1.6	44,572
FEMALE	62	.3	4,199	18.6	70	.3	96	.4	4,427	19.6	18,010	79.8	137	.6	22,574
MALE	60	.3	3,537	16.1	73	.3	175	.8	3,845	17.5	17,561	79.8	592	2.7	21,998
HAWAII (6 INSTITUTIONS)															
TOTAL	41	.2	238	1.2	13,268	69.4	835	4.4	14,382	75.2	4,078	21.3	660	3.5	19,120
FEMALE	14	.2	103	1.1	6,086	66.7	389	4.3	6,592	72.2	2,230	24.4	302	3.3	9,124
MALE	27	.3	135	1.4	7,182	71.8	446	4.5	7,790	77.9	1,848	18.5	358	3.6	9,996
IDAHO (3 INSTITUTIONS)															
TOTAL	38	.3	20	.2	51	.5	99	.9	208	1.9	10,627	95.1	345	3.1	11,180
FEMALE	17	.3	0	.0	16	.3	54	.9	87	1.4	6,061	95.4	203	3.2	6,351
MALE	21	.4	20	.4	35	.7	45	.9	121	2.5	4,566	94.6	142	2.9	4,829
ILLINOIS (59 INSTITUTIONS)															
TOTAL	1,274	.4	42,666	14.8	3,373	1.2	7,192	2.5	54,505	18.9	228,752	79.5	4,453	1.5	287,710
FEMALE	699	.4	25,520	16.0	1,789	1.1	3,480	2.2	31,488	19.7	126,462	79.2	1,675	1.0	159,625
MALE	575	.4	17,146	13.4	1,584	1.2	3,712	2.9	23,017	18.0	102,290	79.9	2,778	2.2	128,085
INDIANA (17 INSTITUTIONS)															
TOTAL	122	.5	2,333	10.5	120	.5	149	.7	2,724	12.2	19,333	86.9	201	.9	22,258
FEMALE	42	.4	1,066	11.3	43	.5	51	.5	1,202	12.8	8,179	86.9	33	.4	9,414
MALE	80	.6	1,267	9.9	77	.6	98	.8	1,522	11.8	11,154	86.8	168	1.3	12,844
IOWA (25 INSTITUTIONS)															
TOTAL	214	.6	639	1.9	175	.5	222	.7	1,250	3.8	31,638	95.2	348	1.0	33,236
FEMALE	116	.7	207	1.2	63	.4	100	.6	486	2.8	16,572	96.7	85	.5	17,143
MALE	98	.6	432	2.7	112	.7	122	.8	764	4.7	15,066	93.6	263	1.6	16,093
KANSAS (25 INSTITUTIONS)															
TOTAL	1,084	3.3	2,009	6.0	110	.3	547	1.6	3,750	11.3	29,007	87.2	515	1.5	33,272
FEMALE	535	3.0	818	4.6	46	.3	250	1.4	1,649	9.3	15,934	90.3	57	.3	17,640
MALE	549	3.5	1,191	7.6	64	.4	297	1.9	2,101	13.4	13,073	83.6	458	2.9	15,632
KENTUCKY (13 INSTITUTIONS)															
TOTAL	48	.2	2,450	11.5	56	.3	44	.2	2,598	12.2	18,416	86.6	262	1.2	21,276
FEMALE	35	.3	1,506	12.1	30	.2	26	.2	1,597	12.8	10,798	86.6	79	.6	12,474
MALE	13	.1	944	10.7	26	.3	18	.2	1,001	11.4	7,618	86.5	183	2.1	8,802
LOUISIANA (7 INSTITUTIONS)															
TOTAL	50	.3	4,600	30.2	117	.8	312	2.0	5,079	33.3	9,815	64.4	337	2.2	15,231
FEMALE	30	.4	2,359	32.2	54	.7	139	1.9	2,582	35.2	4,634	63.2	119	1.6	7,335
MALE	20	.3	2,241	28.4	63	.8	173	2.2	2,497	31.6	5,181	65.6	218	2.8	7,896
MAINE (6 INSTITUTIONS)															
TOTAL	23	.3	17	.3	8	.1	8	.1	56	.8	6,719	99.1	4	.1	6,779
FEMALE	13	.4	3	.1	6	.2	4	.1	26	.8	3,377	99.2	1	.0	3,404
MALE	10	.3	14	.4	2	.1	4	.1	30	.9	3,342	99.0	3	.1	3,375

	AMERICAN INDIAN ALASKAN NATIVE		BLACK NON-HISPANIC		ASIAN OR PACIFIC ISLANDER		HISPANIC		TOTAL MINORITY		WHITE NON-HISPANIC		NON-RESIDENT ALIEN	
	NUMBER	%	NUMBER	%	NUMBER	%	NUMBER	%	NUMBER	%	NUMBER	%	NUMBER	%
MARYLAND	(		21 INSTITUTIONS)											
TOTAL	253	.3	16,634	19.2	1,248	1.4	974	1.1	19,109	22.1	66,233	76.5	1,277	1.5
FEMALE	126	.3	10,211	20.6	648	1.3	521	1.1	11,506	23.2	37,554	75.8	458	.9
MALE	127	.3	6,423	17.3	600	1.6	453	1.2	7,603	20.5	28,679	77.3	819	2.2
MASSACHUSETTS	(		41 INSTITUTIONS)											
TOTAL	684	.9	2,652	3.3	402	.5	1,187	1.5	4,925	6.2	74,146	92.8	860	1.1
FEMALE	511	1.1	1,576	3.4	235	.5	710	1.5	3,032	6.5	43,244	92.8	338	.7
MALE	173	.5	1,076	3.2	167	.5	477	1.4	1,893	5.7	30,902	92.8	522	1.6
MICHIGAN	(		38 INSTITUTIONS)											
TOTAL	1,518	.8	24,557	12.7	1,215	.6	3,507	1.8	30,797	16.0	160,791	83.4	1,262	.7
FEMALE	814	.8	14,651	14.3	537	.5	1,802	1.8	17,804	17.4	84,085	82.3	239	.2
MALE	704	.8	9,906	10.9	678	.7	1,705	1.9	12,993	14.3	76,706	84.6	1,023	1.1
MINNESOTA	(		24 INSTITUTIONS)											
TOTAL	211	.6	368	1.1	87	.3	86	.2	752	2.2	33,548	97.0	279	.8
FEMALE	121	.6	145	.7	53	.3	43	.2	362	1.8	19,303	97.6	106	.5
MALE	90	.6	223	1.5	34	.2	43	.3	390	2.6	14,245	96.2	173	1.2
MISSISSIPPI	(		25 INSTITUTIONS)											
TOTAL	116	.3	9,859	28.0	131	.4	35	.1	10,141	28.8	25,014	71.0	87	.2
FEMALE	69	.4	5,609	30.0	52	.3	14	.1	5,744	30.8	12,915	69.2	14	.1
MALE	47	.3	4,250	25.7	79	.5	21	.1	4,397	26.5	12,099	73.0	73	.4
MISSOURI	(		20 INSTITUTIONS)											
TOTAL	175	.4	8,787	17.7	253	.5	517	1.0	9,732	19.6	39,454	79.6	405	.8
FEMALE	101	.4	5,411	19.7	132	.5	231	.8	5,875	21.4	21,432	78.2	103	.4
MALE	74	.4	3,376	15.2	121	.5	286	1.3	3,857	17.4	18,022	81.2	302	1.4
MONTANA	(		3 INSTITUTIONS)											
TOTAL	316	11.9	7	.3	0	.0	33	1.2	356	13.4	2,294	86.1	15	.6
FEMALE	223	13.3	1	.1	0	.0	29	1.7	253	15.1	1,412	84.3	10	.6
MALE	93	9.4	6	.6	0	.0	4	.4	103	10.4	882	89.1	5	.5
NEBRASKA	(		11 INSTITUTIONS)											
TOTAL	71	.4	542	3.2	56	.3	236	1.4	905	5.4	15,831	94.0	111	.7
FEMALE	27	.3	196	2.5	22	.3	132	1.7	377	4.8	7,531	94.9	27	.3
MALE	44	.5	346	3.9	34	.4	104	1.2	528	5.9	8,300	93.1	84	.9
NEVADA	(		3 INSTITUTIONS)											
TOTAL	262	1.6	1,081	6.4	182	1.1	485	2.9	2,010	12.0	14,771	87.9	25	.1
FEMALE	135	1.7	490	6.1	77	1.0	188	2.4	890	11.1	7,099	88.7	10	.1
MALE	127	1.4	591	6.7	105	1.2	297	3.4	1,120	12.7	7,673	87.1	15	.2
NEW HAMPSHIRE	(		10 INSTITUTIONS)											
TOTAL	5	.1	33	.7	15	.3	15	.3	68	1.4	4,914	98.5	7	.1
FEMALE	4	.2	8	.3	7	.3	3	.1	22	.9	2,308	98.9	4	.2
MALE	1	.0	25	.9	8	.3	12	.5	46	1.7	2,606	98.2	3	.1
NEW JERSEY	(		22 INSTITUTIONS)											
TOTAL	232	.2	13,225	13.2	1,008	1.0	3,717	3.7	18,182	18.1	81,603	81.2	653	.7
FEMALE	130	.2	8,040	14.2	581	1.0	2,186	3.9	10,937	19.3	45,435	80.1	351	.6
MALE	102	.2	5,185	11.9	427	1.0	1,531	3.5	7,245	16.6	36,168	82.7	302	.3
NEW MEXICO	(		10 INSTITUTIONS)											
TOTAL	939	10.7	186	2.1	43	.5	1,657	19.0	2,825	32.3	5,822	66.6	96	1.1
FEMALE	600	12.5	71	1.5	18	.4	906	18.9	1,595	33.2	3,186	66.3	23	.5
MALE	339	8.6	115	2.9	25	.6	751	19.1	1,230	31.2	2,636	66.9	73	1.9
NEW YORK	(		81 INSTITUTIONS)											
TOTAL	1,704	.6	31,839	12.1	2,890	1.1	16,783	6.4	53,216	20.3	208,282	79.3	1,264	.5
FEMALE	811	.6	19,749	14.1	1,231	.9	9,466	6.8	31,257	22.4	108,208	77.4	332	.2
MALE	893	.7	12,090	9.8	1,659	1.3	7,317	6.0	21,959	17.9	100,074	81.4	932	.8
NORTH CAROLINA	(		76 INSTITUTIONS)											
TOTAL	944	.9	22,437	21.8	383	.4	416	.4	24,180	23.5	78,402	76.2	358	.3
FEMALE	523	1.0	11,597	22.5	171	.3	174	.3	12,465	24.2	38,878	75.5	118	.2
MALE	421	.8	10,840	21.1	212	.4	242	.5	11,715	22.8	39,524	76.8	240	.5
NORTH DAKOTA	(		6 INSTITUTIONS)											
TOTAL	607	8.2	16	.2	7	.1	3	.0	633	8.	6,742	91.3	13	.2
FEMALE	351	11.4	5	.2	2	.1	0	.0	358	11.6	2,705	88.2	4	.1
MALE	256	5.9	11	.3	5	.1	3	.1	275	6.8	4,037	93.4	9	.2
OHIO	(		55 INSTITUTIONS)											
TOTAL	306	.3	14,171	12.1	494	.4	805	.7	15,776	13.5	99,979	85.6	985	.8
FEMALE	180	.3	8,750	13.3	282	.4	449	.7	9,661	14.7	55,466	84.6	429	.7
MALE	126	.3	5,421	10.6	212	.4	356	.7	6,115	11.9	44,513	87.0	556	1.1
OKLAHOMA	(		19 INSTITUTIONS)											
TOTAL	2,082	4.7	3,472	7.9	417	1.0	471	1.1	6,442	14.7	35,143	80.1	2,281	5.2
FEMALE	1,251	5.5	1,892	8.4	166	.7	212	.9	3,521	15.5	18,739	82.7	388	1.7
MALE	831	3.9	1,580	7.4	251	1.2	259	1.2	2,921	13.8	16,404	77.3	1,893	8.9
OREGON	(		14 INSTITUTIONS)											
TOTAL	789	1.2	706	1.0	1,151	1.7	919	1.4	3,565	5.	63,249	93.3	977	1.4
FEMALE	425	1 2	306	.9	566	1.6	465	1.3	1,762	4.	33,500	93.9	420	1.2
MALE	364	1|1	400	1.2	585	1.8	454	1.4	1,803	5.8	29,749	92.7	557	1.7
PENNSYLVANIA	(		47 INSTITUTIONS)											
TOTAL	192	.2	12,040	11.7	620	.6	1,031	1.0	13,883	13.5	88,892	86.3	274	.3
FEMALE	95	.2	7,630	14.1	319	.6	618	1.1	8,662	16.0	45,379	83.8	96	.2
MALE	97	.2	4,410	9.0	301	.6	413	.8	5,221	10.7	43,513	89.0	178	.4

ABLE 7 - TOTAL ENROLLMENT IN TWO YEAR INSTITUTIONS OF HIGHER EDUCATION BY RACE, ETHNICITY AND SEX: STATE AND NATION, 1978

	AMERICAN INDIAN ALASKAN NATIVE		BLACK NON-HISPANIC		ASIAN OR PACIFIC ISLANDER		HISPANIC		TOTAL MINORITY		WHITE NON-HISPANIC		NON-RESIDENT ALIEN		TOTAL
	NUMBER	%	NUMBER	%	NUMBER	%	NUMBER	%	NUMBER	%	NUMBER	%	NUMBER	%	NUMBER
RHODE ISLAND (2 INSTITUTIONS)															
TOTAL	26	.2	275	2.5	41	.4	46	.4	388	3.5	10,555	96.3	17	.2	10,960
FEMALE	15	.2	147	2.4	21	.3	22	.4	205	3.4	5,810	96.6	0	.0	6,015
MALE	11	.2	128	2.6	20	.4	24	.5	183	3.7	4,745	96.0	17	.3	4,945
SOUTH CAROLINA (29 INSTITUTIONS)															
TOTAL	76	.2	12,728	30.0	167	.4	108	.3	13,079	30.8	29,040	68.5	281	.7	42,400
FEMALE	23	.1	5,874	33.2	65	.4	33	.2	5,995	33.8	11,654	65.8	67	.4	17,716
MALE	53	.2	6,854	27.8	102	.4	75	.3	7,084	28.7	17,386	70.4	214	.9	24,684
SOUTH DAKOTA (2 INSTITUTIONS)															
TOTAL	11	2.5	1	.2	3	.7	0	.0	15	3.4	427	96.4	1	.2	443
FEMALE	8	2.0	1	.2	3	.7	0	.0	12	3.0	389	96.8	1	.2	402
MALE	3	7.3	0	.0	0	.0	0	.0	3	7.3	38	92.7	0	.0	41
TENNESSEE (27 INSTITUTIONS)															
TOTAL	68	.1	9,193	20.0	113	.2	167	.4	9,541	20.7	36,063	78.4	408	.9	46,012
FEMALE	39	.2	5,221	21.7	58	.2	58	.2	5,376	22.3	18,589	77.2	118	.5	24,083
MALE	29	.1	3,972	18.1	55	.3	109	.5	4,165	19.0	17,474	79.7	290	1.3	21,929
TEXAS (62 INSTITUTIONS)															
TOTAL	1,076	.4	26,998	11.1	2,276	.9	40,154	16.5	70,504	29.0	167,343	68.8	5,367	2.2	243,214
FEMALE	498	.4	13,818	11.5	1,148	1.0	18,738	15.6	34,202	28.4	84,759	70.5	1,273	1.1	120,234
MALE	578	.5	13,180	10.7	1,128	.9	21,416	17.4	36,302	29.5	82,584	67.2	4,094	3.3	122,980
UTAH (7 INSTITUTIONS)															
TOTAL	235	1.5	64	.4	176	1.1	365	2.4	840	5.5	14,376	93.5	159	1.0	15,375
FEMALE	88	1.6	27	.5	67	1.2	109	1.9	291	5.1	5,353	94.4	29	.5	5,673
MALE	147	1.5	37	.4	109	1.1	256	2.6	549	5.7	9,023	93.0	130	1.3	9,702
VERMONT (3 INSTITUTIONS)															
TOTAL	0	.0	9	.2	3	.1	3	.1	15	.4	3,620	99.4	8	.2	3,643
FEMALE	0	.0	3	.1	2	.1	2	.1	7	.3	2,146	99.4	5	.2	2,158
MALE	0	.0	6	.4	1	.1	1	.1	8	.5	1,474	99.3	3	.2	1,485
VIRGINIA (27 INSTITUTIONS)															
TOTAL	254	.2	14,310	14.0	1,489	1.5	728	.7	16,781	16.4	84,407	82.6	970	.9	102,158
FEMALE	167	.3	8,152	14.6	721	1.3	353	.6	9,393	16.8	46,094	82.5	398	.7	55,885
MALE	87	.2	6,158	13.3	768	1.7	375	.8	7,388	16.0	38,313	82.8	572	1.2	46,273
WASHINGTON (27 INSTITUTIONS)															
TOTAL	2,413	1.4	3,853	2.3	2,864	1.7	2,503	1.5	11,633	6.8	152,747	89.9	5,575	3.3	169,955
FEMALE	1,405	1.5	1,606	1.7	1,590	1.7	1,219	1.3	5,820	6.2	85,200	90.8	2,771	3.0	93,791
MALE	1,008	1.3	2,247	3.0	1,274	1.7	1,284	1.7	5,813	7.6	67,547	88.7	2,804	3.7	76,164
WEST VIRGINIA (8 INSTITUTIONS)															
TOTAL	44	.4	414	3.5	27	.2	42	.4	527	4.5	11,256	95.5	6	.1	11,789
FEMALE	23	.4	212	3.3	13	.2	14	.2	262	4.1	6,076	95.8	3	.0	6,341
MALE	21	.4	202	3.7	14	.3	28	.5	265	4.9	5,180	95.1	3	.1	5,448
WISCONSIN (20 INSTITUTIONS)															
TOTAL	501	.7	3,496	4.9	392	.6	595	.8	4,984	7.0	65,879	92.8	151	.2	71,014
FEMALE	263	.8	1,894	5.5	205	.6	264	.8	2,626	7.6	32,006	92.3	53	.2	34,685
MALE	238	.7	1,602	4.4	187	.5	331	.9	2,358	6.5	33,873	93.2	98	.3	36,329
WYOMING (7 INSTITUTIONS)															
TOTAL	116	1.1	129	1.2	44	.4	227	2.1	516	4.7	10,417	94.5	90	.8	11,023
FEMALE	82	1.3	46	.7	16	.3	122	1.9	266	4.2	6,106	95.5	23	.4	6,395
MALE	34	.7	83	1.8	28	.6	105	2.3	250	5.4	4,311	93.2	67	1.4	4,628
THE STATES AND D.C. (1,190 INSTITUTIONS)															
TOTAL	42,881	1.1	442,616	11.0	97,223	2.4	226,918	5.6	809,638	20.1	3,166,790	78.6	52,038	1.3	4,028,466
FEMALE	23,321	1.1	249,451	11.6	46,630	2.2	113,254	5.3	432,656	20.2	1,692,614	79.0	17,889	.8	2,143,159
MALE	19,560	1.0	193,165	10.2	50,593	2.7	113,664	6.0	376,982	20.0	1,474,176	78.2	34,149	1.8	1,885,307
AMERICAN SAMOA (1 INSTITUTIONS)															
TOTAL	0	.0	1	.1	781	94.0	0	.0	782	94.1	49	5.9	0	.0	831
FEMALE	0	.0	1	.2	417	93.3	0	.0	418	93.5	29	6.5	0	.0	447
MALE	0	.0	0	.0	364	94.8	0	.0	364	94.8	20	5.2	0	.0	384
PUERTO RICO (16 INSTITUTIONS)															
TOTAL	0	.0	0	.0	1	.0	35,342	99.6	35,343	99.6	130	.4	21	.1	35,494
FEMALE	0	.0	0	.0	1	.0	20,457	99.6	20,458	99.6	73	.4	12	.1	20,543
MALE	0	.0	0	.0	0	.0	14,885	99.6	14,885	99.6	57	.4	9	.1	14,951
TRUST TERRITORY (1 INSTITUTIONS)															
TOTAL	0	.0	0	.0	366	100.0	0	.0	366	100.0	0	.0	0	.0	366
FEMALE	0	.0	0	.0	120	100.0	0	.0	120	100.0	0	.0	0	.0	120
MALE	0	.0	0	.0	246	100.0	0	.0	246	100.0	0	.0	0	.0	246
OUTLYING AREAS (18 INSTITUTIONS)															
TOTAL	0	.0	1	.0	1,148	3.1	35,342	96.3	36,491	99.5	179	.5	21	.1	36,691
FEMALE	0	.0	1	.0	538	2.5	20,457	96.9	20,996	99.5	102	.5	12	.1	21,110
MALE	0	.0	0	.0	610	3.9	14,885	95.5	15,495	99.4	77	.5	9	.1	15,581
NATION TOTAL (1,208 INSTITUTIONS)															
TOTAL	42,881	1.1	442,617	10.9	98,371	2.4	262,260	6.5	846,129	20.8	3,166,969	77.9	52,059	1.3	4,065,157
FEMALE	23,321	1.1	249,452	11.5	47,168	2.2	133,711	6.2	453,652	21.0	1,692,716	78.2	17,901	.8	2,164,269
MALE	19,560	1.0	193,165	10.2	51,203	2.7	128,549	6.8	392,477	20.6	1,474,253	77.6	34,158	1.8	1,900,888

	AMERICAN INDIAN ALASKAN NATIVE		BLACK NON-HISPANIC		ASIAN OR PACIFIC ISLANDER		HISPANIC		TOTAL MINORITY		WHITE NON-HISPANIC		NON-RESIDENT ALIEN	
	NUMBER	%	NUMBER	%	NUMBER	%	NUMBER	%	NUMBER	%	NUMBER	%	NUMBER	%
ALABAMA	(30 INSTITUTIONS)													
TOTAL	128	.1	24,729	20.9	468	.4	452	.4	25,777	21.8	90,392	76.5	1,919	1.6
FEMALE	66	.1	14,611	25.2	163	.3	170	.3	15,010	25.9	42,647	73.5	337	.6
MALE	62	.1	10,118	16.8	305	.5	282	.5	10,767	17.9	47,745	79.5	1,582	2.6
ALASKA	(7 INSTITUTIONS)													
TOTAL	788	8.9	281	3.2	144	1.6	104	1.2	1,317	14.8	7,522	84.5	61	.7
FEMALE	498	10.5	120	2.5	69	1.5	49	1.0	736	15.5	3,990	84.1	21	.4
MALE	290	7.0	161	3.9	75	1.8	55	1.3	581	14.0	3,532	85.0	40	1.0
ARIZONA	(8 INSTITUTIONS)													
TOTAL	1,008	1.2	1,332	1.6	714	.9	3,245	4.0	6,299	7.7	73,006	89.8	2,032	2.5
FEMALE	554	1.5	565	1.5	299	.8	1,357	3.7	2,775	7.6	33,345	91.3	390	1.1
MALE	454	1.0	767	1.7	415	.9	1,888	4.2	3,524	7.9	39,661	88.5	1,642	3.7
ARKANSAS	(20 INSTITUTIONS)													
TOTAL	307	.5	8,746	14.5	374	.6	218	.4	9,645	16.0	49,847	82.9	671	1.1
FEMALE	132	.4	4,957	16.4	138	.5	96	.3	5,323	17.6	24,851	82.0	132	.4
MALE	175	.6	3,789	12.7	236	.8	122	.4	4,322	14.5	24,996	83.7	539	1.8
CALIFORNIA	(147 INSTITUTIONS)													
TOTAL	5,808	.9	37,260	5.9	48,922	7.8	41,655	6.6	133,645	21.3	462,366	73.7	31,699	5
FEMALE	2,769	1.0	20,247	7.0	22,738	7.8	19,021	6.5	64,775	22.3	217,476	74.8	8,502	2.9
MALE	3,039	.9	17,013	5.0	26,184	7.8	22,634	6.7	68,870	20.4	244,890	72.7	23,197	6.9
COLORADO	(26 INSTITUTIONS)													
TOTAL	760	.7	3,171	2.9	1,488	1.3	5,380	4.8	10,799	9.7	97,779	88.0	2,593	2.3
FEMALE	413	.8	1,547	3.0	690	1.3	2,519	4.8	5,169	9.9	46,284	89.0	527	1.0
MALE	347	.6	1,624	2.7	798	1.3	2,861	4.8	5,630	9.5	51,495	87.0	2,066	3.5
CONNECTICUT	(27 INSTITUTIONS)													
TOTAL	189	.2	3,931	3.5	879	.8	1,579	1.4	6,578	5.9	103,269	92.5	1,740	1.6
FEMALE	101	.2	2,001	3.6	410	.7	692	1.2	3,204	5.7	52,111	93.3	932	1.0
MALE	88	.2	1,930	3.5	469	.8	887	1.6	3,374	6.1	51,158	91.8	1,208	2.2
DELAWARE	(4 INSTITUTIONS)													
TOTAL	31	.1	2,249	9.9	84	.4	101	.4	2,465	10.8	19,866	87.1	479	2.1
FEMALE	13	.1	1,164	9.8	43	.4	56	.5	1,276	10.8	10,385	87.8	168	1.4
MALE	18	.2	1,085	9.9	41	.4	45	.4	1,189	10.8	9,481	86.3	311	2.8
DISTRICT OF COLUMBIA	(16 INSTITUTIONS)													
TOTAL	386	.5	26,200	32.0	1,769	2.2	1,329	1.6	29,684	36.3	44,168	54.0	7,955	9.7
FEMALE	104	.3	15,215	38.6	575	1.5	640	1.6	16,534	42.0	19,957	50.7	2,900	7.4
MALE	282	.7	10,985	25.9	1,194	2.8	689	1.6	13,150	31.0	24,211	57.1	5,055	11.9
FLORIDA	(44 INSTITUTIONS)													
TOTAL	309	.2	19,806	10.7	1,475	.8	10,883	5.9	32,473	17.6	148,106	80.2	4,163	2.3
FEMALE	109	.1	11,058	13.5	474	.6	5,078	6.2	16,719	20.4	63,981	78.2	1,078	1.3
MALE	200	.2	8,748	8.5	1,001	1.0	5,805	5.6	15,754	15.3	84,125	81.7	3,085	3.0
GEORGIA	(44 INSTITUTIONS)													
TOTAL	160	.1	24,753	19.0	601	.5	635	.5	26,149	20.1	101,255	77.7	2,891	2.2
FEMALE	64	.1	14,683	22.9	256	.4	220	.3	15,223	23.8	48,108	75.1	757	1.2
MALE	96	.1	10,070	15.2	345	.5	415	.6	10,926	16.5	53,147	80.3	2,134	3.2
HAWAII	(6 INSTITUTIONS)													
TOTAL	52	.2	482	1.7	16,728	58.9	601	2.1	17,863	62.9	9,199	32.4	1,353	4.8
FEMALE	25	.2	101	.8	8,303	62.5	241	1.8	8,670	65.3	4,067	30.6	547	4.1
MALE	27	.2	381	2.5	8,425	55.7	360	2.4	9,193	60.8	5,132	33.9	806	5.3
IDAHO	(6 INSTITUTIONS)													
TOTAL	216	.8	181	.6	373	1.3	242	.9	1,012	3.6	26,833	95.6	230	.8
FEMALE	131	1.0	49	.4	162	1.3	117	.9	459	3.5	12,423	96.1	51	.4
MALE	85	.6	132	.9	211	1.4	125	.8	553	3.7	14,410	95.2	179	1.2
ILLINOIS	(95 INSTITUTIONS)													
TOTAL	778	.2	34,170	10.6	6,018	1.9	6,717	2.1	47,683	14.7	267,207	82.5	8,812	2.7
FEMALE	358	.2	20,589	13.5	2,464	1.6	3,268	2.1	26,679	17.4	123,893	81.0	2,427	1.6
MALE	420	.2	13,581	8.0	3,554	2.1	3,449	2.0	21,004	12.3	143,314	84.0	6,385	3.7
INDIANA	(49 INSTITUTIONS)													
TOTAL	362	.2	10,044	5.0	1,085	.5	1,912	1.0	13,403	6.7	182,704	91.1	4,426	2.2
FEMALE	177	.2	5,870	6.0	502	.5	849	.9	7,398	7.6	88,638	91.1	1,279	1.3
MALE	185	.2	4,174	4.0	583	.6	1,063	1.0	6,005	5.8	94,066	91.1	3,147	3.0
IOWA	(37 INSTITUTIONS)													
TOTAL	201	.2	2,194	2.3	564	.6	428	.4	3,387	3.5	89,368	93.1	3,190	3.3
FEMALE	95	.2	1,018	2.3	249	.6	171	.4	1,533	3.4	42,588	94.6	900	2.0
MALE	106	.2	1,176	2.3	315	.6	257	.5	1,854	3.6	46,780	91.9	2,290	4.5
KANSAS	(27 INSTITUTIONS)													
TOTAL	505	.5	3,684	3.9	594	.6	1,171	1.2	5,954	6.3	84,971	90.3	3,126	3.3
FEMALE	259	.6	1,767	3.8	253	.5	518	1.1	2,797	6.1	42,524	92.2	796	1.7
MALE	246	.5	1,917	4.0	341	.7	653	1.4	3,157	6.6	42,447	88.6	2,330	4.9
KENTUCKY	(29 INSTITUTIONS)													
TOTAL	288	.3	6,470	5.9	658	.6	347	.3	7,763	7.1	99,936	91.4	1,684	1.5
FEMALE	146	.3	3,365	6.0	257	.5	148	.3	3,916	7.0	51,686	92.4	358	.6
MALE	142	.3	3,105	5.8	401	.8	199	.4	3,847	7.2	48,250	90.3	1,326	2.5
LOUISIANA	(25 INSTITUTIONS)													
TOTAL	240	.2	29,407	21.6	627	.5	1,726	1.3	32,000	23.5	99,371	73.1	4,511	3.3
FEMALE	110	.2	18,110	26.3	237	.3	795	1.2	19,252	27.9	48,500	70.4	1,147	1.7
MALE	130	.2	11,297	16.9	390	.6	931	1.4	12,748	19.0	50,871	75.9	3,364	5.0

AM. INDIAN/NATIVE	BLACK NON-HISPANIC		ASIAN OR PACIFIC ISLANDER		HISPANIC		TOTAL MINORITY		WHITE NON-HISPANIC		NON-RESIDENT ALIEN		TOTAL
%	NUMBER	%	NUMBER	%	NUMBER	%	NUMBER	%	NUMBER	%	NUMBER	%	NUMBER
(21 INSTITUTIONS)													
.4	166	.5	101	.3	74	.2	474	1.4	33,999	98.0	208	.6	34,681
.4	63	.4	39	.2	26	.2	195	1.1	16,823	98.4	72	.4	17,090
.4	103	.6	62	.4	48	.3	279	1.6	17,176	97.6	136	.8	17,591
(33 INSTITUTIONS)													
.3	20,816	16.3	1,620	1.3	1,046	.8	23,848	18.7	99,245	77.6	4,743	3.7	127,836
.3	12,623	19.4	748	1.1	508	.8	14,067	21.6	49,286	75.7	1,737	2.7	65,090
.3	8,193	13.1	872	1.4	538	.9	9,781	15.6	49,959	79.6	3,006	4.5	62,746
(78 INSTITUTIONS)													
.2	11,445	3.8	5,406	1.8	3,845	1.3	21,447	7.0	273,678	89.9	9,444	3.1	304,569
.2	6,099	4.2	2,413	1.7	1,799	1.2	10,636	7.3	131,900	90.7	2,917	2.0	145,453
.3	5,346	3.4	2,993	1.9	2,046	1.3	10,811	6.8	141,778	89.1	6,527	4.1	159,116
(58 INSTITUTIONS)													
.4	24,404	8.3	2,548	.9	2,714	.9	30,760	10.5	253,028	86.5	8,654	3.0	292,442
.4	14,553	10.5	1,002	.7	1,247	.9	17,312	12.5	119,223	85.9	2,275	1.6	138,810
.4	9,851	6.4	1,546	1.0	1,467	1.0	13,448	8.8	133,805	87.1	6,379	4.2	153,632
(41 INSTITUTIONS)													
.5	1,973	1.3	1,293	.8	748	.5	4,844	3.1	146,286	94.7	3,378	2.2	154,508
.6	905	1.2	552	.7	341	.4	2,238	2.9	73,381	95.8	999	1.3	76,618
.5	1,068	1.4	741	1.0	407	.5	2,606	3.3	72,905	93.6	2,379	3.1	77,890
(21 INSTITUTIONS)													
.3	18,728	30.1	242	.4	96	.2	19,259	30.9	42,020	67.5	970	1.6	62,249
.3	11,270	34.8	89	.3	38	.1	11,510	35.6	20,638	63.8	196	.6	32,344
.3	7,458	24.9	153	.5	58	.2	7,749	25.9	21,382	71.5	774	2.6	29,905
(64 INSTITUTIONS)													
.3	11,565	6.7	1,742	1.0	1,147	.7	14,960	8.7	154,345	89.5	3,073	1.8	172,378
.2	6,137	7.7	559	.7	426	.5	7,316	9.2	71,146	89.7	814	1.0	79,276
.3	5,428	5.8	1,183	1.3	721	.8	7,644	8.2	83,199	89.4	2,259	2.4	93,102
(10 INSTITUTIONS)													
2.0	153	.5	107	.4	100	.4	916	3.2	27,263	95.9	259	.9	28,438
2.5	56	.4	34	.3	41	.3	463	3.4	12,968	96.1	68	.5	13,499
1.5	97	.6	73	.5	59	.4	453	3.0	14,295	95.7	191	1.3	14,939
(20 INSTITUTIONS)													
.3	1,963	3.0	423	.7	539	.8	3,140	4.8	60,525	93.3	1,179	1.8	64,844
.3	927	3.0	181	.6	232	.7	1,446	4.6	29,719	94.6	254	.8	31,419
.3	1,036	3.1	242	.7	307	.9	1,694	5.1	30,806	92.2	925	2.8	33,425
(3 INSTITUTIONS)													
.7	516	3.1	277	1.7	336	2.0	1,244	7.4	15,129	90.4	360	2.2	16,733
.8	240	2.9	116	1.4	147	1.8	569	7.0	7,480	91.9	94	1.2	8,143
.6	276	3.2	161	1.9	189	2.2	675	7.9	7,649	89.0	266	3.1	8,590
(14 INSTITUTIONS)													
.2	602	1.6	140	.4	254	.7	1,084	3.0	34,964	95.6	512	1.4	36,560
.2	209	1.2	56	.3	62	.4	369	2.2	16,652	97.1	128	.7	17,149
.2	393	2.0	84	.4	192	1.0	715	3.7	18,312	94.3	384	2.0	19,411
(41 INSTITUTIONS)													
.2	17,554	8.4	2,283	1.1	7,600	3.7	27,864	13.4	176,392	84.9	3,588	1.7	207,844
.2	10,758	10.5	993	1.0	4,028	3.9	15,990	15.6	85,634	83.4	1,016	1.0	102,640
.2	6,796	6.5	1,290	1.2	3,572	3.4	11,874	11.3	90,758	86.3	2,572	2.4	105,204
(9 INSTITUTIONS)													
2.8	1,043	2.2	368	.8	11,620	24.7	14,337	30.5	31,676	67.4	961	2.0	46,974
3.4	422	1.9	158	.7	5,812	25.7	7,151	31.6	15,316	67.7	165	.7	22,632
2.2	621	2.6	210	.9	5,808	23.9	7,186	29.5	16,360	67.2	796	3.3	24,342
(205 INSTITUTIONS)													
.4	67,543	10.0	16,112	2.4	30,142	4.5	116,540	17.2	542,206	80.2	17,562	2.6	676,308
.4	41,728	12.3	7,361	2.2	16,470	4.8	66,931	19.7	267,033	78.6	5,762	1.7	339,726
.4	25,815	7.7	8,751	2.6	13,672	4.1	49,609	14.7	275,173	81.8	11,800	3.5	336,582
(50 INSTITUTIONS)													
.6	29,599	18.6	689	.4	606	.4	31,828	20.0	124,519	78.4	2,496	1.6	159,843
.7	16,926	21.0	293	.4	285	.4	18,071	22.4	61,872	76.8	618	.8	80,561
.5	12,673	16.2	396	.5	321	.4	13,757	17.6	62,647	80.0	1,878	2.4	78,282
(10 INSTITUTIONS)													
1.9	153	.6	98	.4	51	.2	776	3.1	23,837	95.6	324	1.3	24,937
2.3	45	.4	36	.3	26	.2	386	3.2	11,639	95.9	107	.9	12,132
1.5	108	.8	62	.5	25	.2	390	3.0	12,198	95.3	217	1.7	12,805
(78 INSTITUTIONS)													
.3	27,925	8.4	1,701	.5	1,834	.6	32,589	9.8	294,985	88.3	6,319	1.9	333,893
.4	15,840	10.0	776	.5	879	.6	18,066	11.4	138,245	87.6	1,569	1.0	157,879
.3	12,085	6.9	925	.5	955	.5	14,523	8.3	156,740	89.0	4,751	2.7	176,014
(24 INSTITUTIONS)													
3.1	5,618	5.3	669	.6	714	.7	10,270	9.7	89,842	85.1	5,419	5.1	105,531
3.5	2,807	5.8	267	.5	298	.6	5,083	10.4	42,593	87.4	1,073	2.2	48,749
2.7	2,811	5.0	402	.7	416	.7	5,187	9.1	47,249	83.2	4,346	7.7	56,782
(29 INSTITUTIONS)													
1.0	1,022	1.3	2,152	2.7	670	.9	4,621	5.9	70,727	90.0	3,210	4.1	78,558
1.0	403	1.1	978	2.7	288	.8	2,021	5.6	33,551	92.2	826	2.3	36,398
1.0	619	1.5	1,179	2.8	382	.9	2,600	6.2	37,176	88.2	2,384	5.7	42,160

TABLE 8 - TOTAL ENROLLMENT IN FOUR YEAR INSTITUTIONS OF HIGHER EDUCATION BY RACE, ETHNICITY AND SEX:
STATE AND NATION, 1978

	AMERICAN INDIAN ALASKAN NATIVE		BLACK NON-HISPANIC		ASIAN OR PACIFIC ISLANDER		HISPANIC		TOTAL MINORITY		WHITE NON-HISPANIC		NON-RESIDENT ALIEN	
	NUMBER	%	NUMBER	%	NUMBER	%	NUMBER	%	NUMBER	%	NUMBER	%	NUMBER	%
PENNSYLVANIA (130 INSTITUTIONS)														
TOTAL	540	.1	22,547	6.1	2,952	.8	2,444	.7	28,483	7.7	333,996	90.6	6,153	1.7
FEMALE	251	.1	12,660	7.2	1,188	.7	1,196	.7	15,295	8.7	159,430	90.5	1,534	.9
MALE	289	.2	9,887	5.1	1,764	.9	1,248	.6	13,188	6.9	174,566	90.7	4,619	2.4
RHODE ISLAND (11 INSTITUTIONS)														
TOTAL	95	.2	1,712	3.3	408	.8	305	.6	2,520	4.8	49,037	93.2	1,036	2.0
FEMALE	51	.2	780	3.1	187	.7	142	.6	1,160	4.6	23,900	94.2	308	1.2
MALE	44	.2	932	3.4	221	.8	163	.6	1,360	5.0	25,137	92.3	728	2.7
SOUTH CAROLINA (32 INSTITUTIONS)														
TOTAL	74	.1	14,897	17.9	352	.4	224	.3	15,547	18.7	66,871	80.4	777	.9
FEMALE	37	.1	9,179	21.8	161	.4	84	.2	9,461	22.4	32,503	77.1	202	.5
MALE	37	.4	5,718	13.9	191	.5	140	.3	6,086	14.8	34,368	83.8	575	1.4
SOUTH DAKOTA (16 INSTITUTIONS)														
TOTAL	923	3.0	329	1.1	106	.3	293	1.0	1,651	5.4	28,394	93.1	443	1.5
FEMALE	530	3.7	66	.5	41	.3	37	.3	674	4.7	13,472	94.7	76	.5
MALE	393	2.4	263	1.6	65	.4	256	1.6	977	6.0	14,922	91.7	367	2.3
TENNESSEE (49 INSTITUTIONS)														
TOTAL	252	.2	20,663	13.9	606	.4	496	.3	22,017	14.8	123,012	82.7	3,626	2.4
FEMALE	114	.2	11,775	16.2	242	.3	224	.3	12,355	17.0	59,423	81.7	963	1.3
MALE	138	.2	8,888	11.7	364	.5	272	.4	9,662	12.7	63,589	83.8	2,663	3.5
TEXAS (85 INSTITUTIONS)														
TOTAL	1,351	.3	35,085	8.5	3,402	.8	38,600	4	78,633	19.0	317,986	77.0	16,171	3.
FEMALE	577	.2	19,134	9.9	1,458	.8	18,772	9.7	39,941	20.7	149,098	77.3	3,792	2.0
MALE	774	.4	15,946	7.2	1,944	.9	20,028	911	38,692	17.6	168,888	76.8	12,379	5.8
UTAH (7 INSTITUTIONS)														
TOTAL	705	1.0	432	.6	1,258	1.7	804	1 1	3,199	4.3	66,453	90.3	3,962	
FEMALE	393	1.2	157	.5	643	1.9	351	1|1	1,544	4.7	29,880	90.6	1,570	
MALE	312	.8	275	.7	615	1.5	453	1.1	1,655	4.1	36,573	90.0	2,392	
VERMONT (18 INSTITUTIONS)														
TOTAL	48	.2	324	1.2	60	.2	144	.6	576	2.2	24,729	95.4	629	2.4
FEMALE	20	.1	183	1.3	33	.2	73	.5	309	2.2	13,277	96.4	187	1.4
MALE	28	.2	141	1.2	27	.2	71	.6	267	2.2	11,452	94.2	442	3.6
VIRGINIA (44 INSTITUTIONS)														
TOTAL	291	.2	23,007	14.7	1,181	.8	713	.5	25,192	16.1	129,072	82.6	1,946	1.2
FEMALE	159	.2	13,443	16.6	579	.7	374	.5	14,555	18.0	65,721	81.2	694	.9
MALE	132	.2	9,564	12.7	602	.8	339	.5	10,637	14.1	63,351	84.2	1,252	1.7
WASHINGTON (22 INSTITUTIONS)														
TOTAL	1,025	1.0	2,417	2.3	4,023	3.8	1,138	1.1	8,603	8.2	92,536	87.8	4,205	4.0
FEMALE	563	1.1	1,151	2.3	1,963	3.9	511	1.0	4,188	8.3	44,909	89.4	1,142	2.3
MALE	462	.8	1,266	2.3	2,060	3.7	627	1.1	4,415	8.0	47,627	86.4	3,063	5.6
WEST VIRGINIA (20 INSTITUTIONS)														
TOTAL	189	.3	2,853	4.2	294	.4	125	.2	3,461	5.1	62,620	93.2	1,137	1.7
FEMALE	108	.3	1,367	4.0	102	.3	57	.2	1,634	4.8	32,116	94.6	207	.6
MALE	81	.2	1,486	4.5	192	.6	68	.2	1,827	5.5	30,504	91.7	930	2.8
WISCONSIN (42 INSTITUTIONS)														
TOTAL	986	.6	4,825	2.8	1,167	.7	1,434	.8	8,412	4.9	158,365	93.0	3,593	2 1
FEMALE	567	.7	2,648	3.2	510	.6	634	.8	4,359	5.3	77,516	93.6	902	1|1
MALE	419	.5	2,177	2.5	657	.8	800	.9	4,053	4.6	80,849	92.3	2,691	3.1
WYOMING (1 INSTITUTIONS)														
TOTAL	40	.4	100	1.1	54	.6	122	1.4	316	3.5	8,238	92.5	356	4.0
FEMALE	18	.5	33	.9	31	.8	58	1.5	140	3.7	3,633	95.0	51	1.3
MALE	22	.4	67	1.3	23	.5	64	1.3	176	3.5	4,605	90.5	305	6.0
THE STATES AND D.C. (1,933 INSTITUTIONS)														
TOTAL	34,941	.5	611,064	8.5	137,399	1.9	189,903	2.6	973,307	13.5	6,013,140	83.7	200,228	2.8
FEMALE	17,717	.5	351,624	10.1	62,071	1.8	91,471	2.6	522,883	15.1	2,887,431	83.3	55,166	1.6
MALE	17,224	.5	259,440	7.0	75,328	2.0	98,432	2.6	450,424	12.1	3,125,709	84.0	145,062	3.9
CANAL ZONE (1 INSTITUTIONS)														
TOTAL	0	.0	169	10.3		.0	504	30.8	673	41.1	965	58.9		.0
FEMALE	0	.0	95	10.3	8	.0	281	30.6	376	40.9	543	59.1	8	.0
MALE	0	.0	74	10.3	8	.0	223	31.0	297	41.3	422	58.7		.0
GUAM (1 INSTITUTIONS)														
TOTAL	11	.3	28	.9	2,260	70.4	69	.2	2,368	73.8	628	19.6	212	6.6
FEMALE	4	.2	16	1.0	1,240	74.6	32	1.9	1,292	77.7	296	17.8	74	4.5
MALE	7	.5	12	.8	1,020	66.0	37	2.4	1,076	69.6	332	21.5	138	8.9
PUERTO RICO (18 INSTITUTIONS)														
TOTAL	0	.0	10	.0		.0	87,987	99.5	87,997	99.5	421	.5	55	.1
FEMALE	0	.0	2	.0	8	.0	49,795	99.5	49,797	99.5	243	.5	25	.0
MALE	0	.0	8	.0	8	.0	38,192	99.4	38,200	99.5	178	.5	30	.1
VIRGIN ISLANDS (1 INSTITUTIONS)														
TOTAL	0	.0	1,385	74.9	12	.6	96	5.2	1,493	80.8	199	10.8	156	8.4
FEMALE	0	.0	969	76.5	5	.4	62	4.9	1,036	81.8	120	9.5	110	8.7
MALE	0	.0	416	71.5	7	1.2	34	5.8	457	78.5	79	13.6	46	7.9
OUTLYING AREAS (21 INSTITUTIONS)														
TOTAL	11	.0	1,592	1.7	2,272	2.4	88,656	93.2	92,531	97.2	2,213	2.3	423	.4
FEMALE	4	.0	1,082	2.0	1,245	2.3	50,170	93.1	52,501	97.4	1,202	2.2	209	.4
MALE	7	.0	510	1.2	1,027	2.5	38,486	93.3	40,030	97.0	1,011	2.5	214	.5

BLE B - TOTAL ENROLLMENT IN FOUR YEAR INSTITUTIONS OF HIGHER EDUCATION BY RACE, ETHNICITY AND SEX:
STATE AND NATION, 1978

	AMERICAN INDIAN ALASKAN NATIVE		BLACK NON-HISPANIC		ASIAN OR PACIFIC ISLANDER		HISPANIC		TOTAL MINORITY		WHITE NON-HISPANIC		NON-RESIDENT ALIEN		TOTAL
	NUMBER	%	NUMBER	%	NUMBER	%	NUMBER	%	NUMBER	%	NUMBER	%	NUMBER	%	NUMBER
TION TOTAL	(1,954 INSTITUTIONS)														
TOTAL	34,952	.5	612,656	8.4	139,671	1.9	278,559	3.8	1,065,838	14.6	6,015,353	82.6	200,651	2.8	7,281,842
FEMALE	17,721	.5	352,706	10.0	63,316	1.8	141,641	4.0	575,384	16.3	2,888,633	82.1	55,375	1.6	3,519,392
MALE	17,231	.5	259,950	6.9	76,355	2.0	136,918	3.6	490,454	13.0	3,126,720	83.1	145,276	3.9	3,762,450

	AMERICAN INDIAN ALASKAN NATIVE		BLACK NON-HISPANIC		ASIAN OR PACIFIC ISLANDER		HISPANIC		TOTAL MINORITY		WHITE NON-HISPANIC	
	NUMBER	%	NUMBER	%	NUMBER	%	NUMBER	%	NUMBER	%	NUMBER	%
ALABAMA												
1974 (52 INSTITUTIONS)	147	.2	21,376	24.3	391	.4	277	.3	22,191	25.3	65,672	74.7
1976 (56 INSTITUTIONS)	106	.1	25,120	25.2	160	.2	214	.2	25,600	25.7	73,984	74.3
% CHANGE 1974 TO 1976	- 27.9		17.5		- 59.1		- 22.7		15.4		12.7	
1978 (58 INSTITUTIONS)	104	.1	27,076	26.6	297	.3	344	.3	27,821	27.4	73,884	72.6
% CHANGE 1976 TO 1978	- 1.9		7.8		85.6		60.7		8.7		- .1	
ALASKA.												
1974 (0 INSTITUTIONS)	0	.0	0	.0	0	.0	0	.0	0	.0	0	.0
1976 (5 INSTITUTIONS)	274	14.1	71	3.6	136	7.0	27	1.4	508	26.1	1,442	73.9
% CHANGE 1974 TO 1976	100.0		100.0		100.0		100.0		100.0		100.0	
1978 (14 INSTITUTIONS)	729	14.0	197	3.8	105	2.0	49	.9	1,080	20.7	4,142	79.3
% CHANGE 1976 TO 1978	166.1		177.5		- 22.8		81.5		112.6		187.2	
ARIZONA												
1974 (19 INSTITUTIONS)	1,509	2.3	1,686	2.6	536	.8	5,272	8.0	9,003	13.7	56,675	86.3
1976 (21 INSTITUTIONS)	2,050	2.7	2,110	2.8	587	.8	5,912	7.9	10,659	14.2	64,594	85.8
% CHANGE 1974 TO 1976	35.9		25.1		9.5		12.1		18.4		14.0	
1978 (22 INSTITUTIONS)	2,111	2.9	2,183	3.0	723	1.0	5,692	7.7	10,709	14.5	63,096	85.5
% CHANGE 1976 TO 1978	3.0		3.5		23.2		- 3.7		.5		- 2.3	
ARKANSAS.												
1974 (24 INSTITUTIONS)	249	.6	5,542	14.2	41	.1	59	.2	5,891	15.0	33,267	85.0
1976 (28 INSTITUTIONS)	152	.3	8,324	18.1	195	.4	75	.2	8,746	19.0	37,299	81.0
% CHANGE 1974 TO 1976	- 39.0		50.2		375.6		27.1		48.5		12.1	
1978 (33 INSTITUTIONS)	265	.6	8,332	17.4	278	.6	173	.4	9,048	18.9	38,927	81.1
% CHANGE 1976 TO 1978	74.3		.1		42.6		130.7		3.5		4.4	
CALIFORNIA.												
1974 (208 INSTITUTIONS)	6,618	.9	50,784	7.2	32,195	4.6	52,297	7.5	141,894	20.2	559,665	79.8
1976 (221 INSTITUTIONS)	8,592	1.4	54,188	8.7	40,192	6.4	58,199	9.3	161,171	25.8	464,664	74.2
% CHANGE 1974 TO 1976	29.8		6.7		24.8		11.3		13.6		- 17.0	
1978 (226 INSTITUTIONS)	6,959	1.2	52,425	9.2	46,182	8.1	53,951	9.5	159,517	28.0	411,029	72.0
% CHANGE 1976 TO 1978	- 19.0		- 3.3		14.9		- 7.3		- 1.0		- 11.5	
COLORADO.												
1974 (37 INSTITUTIONS)	662	.8	2,498	3.0	886	1.1	4,823	5.8	8,869	10.6	74,866	89.4
1976 (37 INSTITUTIONS)	695	.8	2,894	3.3	1,037	1.2	5,626	6.5	10,252	11.8	76,941	88.2
% CHANGE 1974 TO 1976	5.0		15.9		17.0		16.6		15.6		2.8	
1978 (39 INSTITUTIONS)	710	.9	2,524	3.1	1,222	1.5	4,741	5.8	9,197	11.2	72,625	88.8
% CHANGE 1976 TO 1978	2.2		- 12.8		17.8		- 15.7		- 10.3		- 5.6	
CONNECTICUT												
1974 (48 INSTITUTIONS)	67	.1	3,674	4.9	399	.5	984	1.3	5,124	6.8	70,522	93.2
1976 (42 INSTITUTIONS)	104	.1	3,780	5.0	411	.5	1,120	1.5	5,415	7.2	70,223	92.8
% CHANGE 1974 TO 1976	55.2		2.9		3.0		13.8		5.7		- .4	
1978 (43 INSTITUTIONS)	136	.2	3,658	5.0	674	.9	1,178	1.6	5,646	7.8	67,128	92.2
% CHANGE 1976 TO 1978	30.8		- 3.2		64.0		5.2		4.3		- 4.4	
DELAWARE.												
1974 (9 INSTITUTIONS)	14	.1	2,149	12.4	32	.2	76	.4	2,271	13.1	15,071	86.9
1976 (10 INSTITUTIONS)	14	.1	2,501	12.6	103	.5	113	.6	2,731	13.7	17,162	86.3
% CHANGE 1974 TO 1976	.0		16.4		221.9		48.7		20.3		13.9	
1978 (10 INSTITUTIONS)	23	.1	2,327	12.3	64	.3	80	.4	2,494	13.1	16,475	86.9
% CHANGE 1976 TO 1978	64.3		- 7.0		- 37.9		- 29.2		- 8.7		- 4.0	
DISTRICT OF COLUMBIA. . . .												
1974 (14 INSTITUTIONS)	53	.2	12,838	40.0	210	.7	402	1.3	13,503	42.0	18,630	58.0
1976 (17 INSTITUTIONS)	103	.4	11,804	41.8	441	1.6	580	2.1	12,928	45.7	15,337	54.3
% CHANGE 1974 TO 1976	94.3		- 8.1		110.0		44.3		- 4.3		- 17.7	
1978 (13 INSTITUTIONS)	121	.4	10,915	39.9	486	1.8	510	1.9	12,032	44.0	15,308	56.0
% CHANGE 1976 TO 1978	17.5		- 7.5		10.2		- 12.1		- 6.9		- .2	

FULL-TIME UNDERGRADUATE ENROLLMENT IN INSTITUTIONS OF HIGHER EDUCATION BY RACE AND ETHNICITY: , 1974, 1976, 1978

AMERICAN INDIAN/ALASKAN NATIVE		BLACK NON-HISPANIC		ASIAN OR PACIFIC ISLANDER		HISPANIC		TOTAL MINORITY		WHITE NON-HISPANIC		TOTAL
NUMBER	%	NUMBER	%	NUMBER	%	NUMBER	%	NUMBER	%	NUMBER	%	NUMBER
278	.2	18,081	10.6	562	.3	3,987	2.3	22,908	13.5	147,230	86.5	170,138
466	.3	24,412	13.8	1,420	.8	9,372	5.3	35,670	20.2	141,115	79.8	176,785
67.6		35.0		152.7		135.1		55.7		- 4.2		3.9
559	.3	23,876	13.6	1,306	.7	11,979	6.8	37,720	21.5	138,123	78.5	175,843
20.0		- 2.2		- 8.0		27.8		5.7		- 2.1		- .5
201	.2	15,687	17.5	285	.3	285	.3	16,458	18.4	73,033	81.6	89,491
262	.3	21,197	21.3	433	.4	410	.4	22,302	22.5	76,990	77.5	99,292
30.3		35.1		51.9		43.9		35.5		5.4		11.0
141	.1	22,352	22.2	397	.4	523	.5	23,413	23.3	77,140	76.7	100,553
46.2		5.4		- 8.3		27.6		5.0		.2		1.3
0	.0	0	.0	0	.0	0	.0	0	.0	0	.0	0
47	.2	226	.8	20,377	75.3	710	2.6	21,360	78.9	5,716	21.1	27,076
100.0		100.0		100.0		100.0		100.0		100.0		100.0
59	.2	233	1.0	17,840	73.6	717	3.0	18,849	77.8	5,388	22.2	24,237
25.5		3.1		- 12.5		1.0		- 11.8		- 5.7		- 10.5
184	.7	360	1.4	289	1.2	469	1.9	1,302	5.2	23,697	94.8	24,999
219	.9	160	.6	341	1.4	286	1.2	1,006	4.1	23,730	95.9	24,736
19.0		- 55.6		18.0		- 39.0		- 22.7		.1		- 1.1
161	.7	139	.6	280	1.2	204	.8	784	3.2	23,409	96.8	24,193
26.5		- 13.1		- 17.9		- 28.7		- 22.1		- 1.4		- 2.2
586	.2	33,792	12.8	2,135	.8	3,639	1.4	40,152	15.3	222,838	84.7	262,990
620	.2	38,926	14.3	2,982	1.1	5,674	2.1	48,202	17.7	223,413	82.3	271,615
5.8		15.2		39.7		55.9		20.0		.3		3.3
754	.3	39,619	14.8	4,058	1.5	6,349	2.4	50,780	18.9	217,513	81.1	268,293
21.6		1.8		36.1		11.9		5.3		- 2.6		- 1.2
207	.2	5,405	4.5	416	.3	1,031	.8	7,059	5.8	114,332	94.2	121,391
232	.2	7,231	5.5	540	.4	1,011	.8	9,014	6.9	122,514	93.1	131,528
12.1		33.8		29.8		- 1.9		27.7		7.2		8.4
216	.2	6,996	5.4	688	.5	1,197	.9	9,097	7.0	120,004	93.0	129,101
6.9		- 3.2		27.4		18.4		.9		- 2.0		- 1.8
154	.2	2,141	2.5	238	.3	270	.3	2,803	3.3	82,635	96.7	85,438
242	.3	2,017	2.4	407	.5	379	.5	3,045	3.6	80,678	96.4	83,723
57.1		- 5.8		71.0		40.4		8.6		- 2.4		- 2.0
267	.3	2,098	2.4	482	.6	440	.5	3,287	3.8	83,901	96.2	87,188
10.3		4.0		18.4		16.1		7.9		4.0		4.1
1,411	2.0	2,718	3.0	210	.3	888	1.	5,227	7.4	65,056	92.6	70,283
1,431	2.0	3,523	5.0	367	.5	991	1.4	6,312	9.0	63,561	91.0	69,873
1.4		29.6		74.8		11.6		20.8		- 2.3		- .6
1,197	1.7	3,437	5.0	360	.5	1,002	1.5	5,996	8.7	62,926	91.3	68,922
16.4		- 2.4		- 1.9		1.1		- 5.0		- 1.0		- 1.4
174	.2	4,691	6.7	213	.3	126	.2	5,204	7.5	64,463	92.5	69,667
240	.3	6,985	8.9	180	.2	188	.2	7,553	9.7	70,862	90.3	78,455
37.9		48.9		- 15.5		49.2		45.9		9.9		12.6
142	.2	6,310	8.2	427	.6	197	.3	7,076	9.2	70,186	90.8	77,262
40.8		- 9.7		137.2		4.8		- 6.8		- 1.0		- 1.5

	AMERICAN INDIAN ALASKAN NATIVE		BLACK NON-HISPANIC		ASIAN OR PACIFIC ISLANDER		HISPANI(
	NUMBER	%	NUMBER	%	NUMBER	%	NUMBER
LOUISIANA							
1974 (28 INSTITUTIONS)	150	.2	22,170	22.8	221	.2	614
1976 (30 INSTITUTIONS)	147	.1	25,950	26.4	498	.5	1,136
% CHANGE 1974 TO 1976	- 2.0		17.1		125.3		85.0
1978 (30 INSTITUTIONS)	164	.2	25,408	26.6	447	.5	1,188
% CHANGE 1976 TO 1978	11.6		- 2.1		- 10.2		4.6
MAINE							
1974 (24 INSTITUTIONS)	73	.3	227	.9	65	.3	88
1976 (25 INSTITUTIONS)	97	.4	222	.8	73	.3	60
% CHANGE 1974 TO 1976	32.9		2.2		12.3		- 31.8
1978 (27 INSTITUTIONS)	108	.4	141	.5	85	.3	65
% CHANGE 1976 TO 1978	11.3		- 36.5		16.4		8.3
MARYLAND							
1974 (48 INSTITUTIONS)	371	.4	15,098	17.2	886	1.0	607
1976 (50 INSTITUTIONS)	360	.4	19,445	20.8	897	1.0	593
% CHANGE 1974 TO 1976	- 3.0		28.8		1.2		2.3
1978 (52 INSTITUTIONS)	227	.2	18,357	20.1	1,180	1.3	880
% CHANGE 1976 TO 1978	- 36.9		5.6		31.5		48.4
MASSACHUSETTS							
1974 (112 INSTITUTIONS)	455	.2	8,630	4.0	1,673	.8	1,986
1976 (112 INSTITUTIONS)	939	.5	8,719	4.3	1,885	.9	2,698
% CHANGE 1974 TO 1976	106.4		1.0		12.7		35.9
1978 (111 INSTITUTIONS)	962	.5	9,381	4.5	2,959	1.4	3,140
% CHANGE 1976 TO 1978	2.4		7.6		57.0		16.4
MICHIGAN							
1974 (91 INSTITUTIONS)	922	.4	20,830	8.7	1,122	.5	1,796
1976 (90 INSTITUTIONS)	1,289	.5	28,537	11.8	1,481	.6	2,034
% CHANGE 1974 TO 1976	39.8		37.0		32.0		13.3
1978 (92 INSTITUTIONS)	1,108	.5	23,459	10.1	1,706	.7	2,477
% CHANGE 1976 TO 1978	- 14.0		- 17.8		15.2		21.8
MINNESOTA							
1974 (56 INSTITUTIONS)	755	.7	1,801	1.7	843	.8	375
1976 (55 INSTITUTIONS)	844	.8	1,754	1.6	837	.8	943
% CHANGE 1974 TO 1976	11.8		2.6		.7		151.5
1978 (55 INSTITUTIONS)	714	.6	1,548	1.4	804	.7	479
% CHANGE 1976 TO 1978	- 15.4		- 11.7		3.9		- 49.2
MISSISSIPPI							
1974 (43 INSTITUTIONS)	94	.2	18,558	30.9	160	.3	66
1976 (43 INSTITUTIONS)	140	.2	21,878	33.0	168	.3	61
% CHANGE 1974 TO 1976	48.9		17.9		5.0		7.6
1978 (45 INSTITUTIONS)	108	.2	22,526	33.8	180	.3	82
% CHANGE 1976 TO 1978	- 22.9		3.0		7.1		34.4
MISSOURI							
1974 (68 INSTITUTIONS)	340	.3	8,633	7.2	377	.3	647
1976 (71 INSTITUTIONS)	375	.3	10,119	8.3	556	.5	659
% CHANGE 1974 TO 1976	10.3		17.2		47.5		1.9
1978 (70 INSTITUTIONS)	336	.3	9,197	7.9	778	.7	767
% CHANGE 1976 TO 1978	- 10.4		9.1		39.9		16.4
MONTANA							
1974 (12 INSTITUTIONS)	775	3.6	158	.7	101	.5	95
1976 (12 INSTITUTIONS)	864	3.9	135	.6	94	.4	98
% CHANGE 1974 TO 1976	11.5		- 14.6		6.9		3.2
1978 (13 INSTITUTIONS)	510	2.3	80	.4	78	.3	74
% CHANGE 1976 TO 1978	- 41.0		- 40.7		- 17.0		- 24.5

FULL-TIME UNDERGRADUATE ENROLLMENT IN INSTITUTIONS OF HIGHER EDUCATION BY RACE AND ETHNICITY: 1974, 1976, 1978

AMERICAN INDIAN/ALASKAN NATIVE		BLACK NON-HISPANIC		ASIAN OR PACIFIC ISLANDER		HISPANIC		TOTAL MINORITY		WHITE NON-HISPANIC		TOTAL
NUMBER	%	NUMBER	%	NUMBER	%	NUMBER	%	NUMBER	%	NUMBER	%	NUMBER
185	.4	1,085	2.4	159	.4	404	.9	1,833	4.1	42,467	95.9	44,300
154	.3	1,493	3.1	242	.5	367	.8	2,256	4.7	45,812	95.3	48,068
16.8		37.6		52.2		- 9.2		23.1		7.9		8.5
166	.4	1,355	2.9	253	.5	415	.9	2,189	4.8	43,818	95.2	46,007
7.8		- 9.2		4.5		13.1		- 3.0		- 4.4		- 4.3
372	1.8	911	4.4	239	1.2	779	3.8	2,301	11.2	18,186	88.8	20,487
94	1.1	433	4.9	100	1.1	148	1.7	775	8.8	8,026	91.2	8,801
74.7		- 52.5		- 58.2		- 81.0		- 66.3		- 55.9		- 57.0
116	1.3	464	5.1	159	1.7	233	2.6	972	10.7	8,116	89.3	9,088
23.4		7.2		59.0		57.4		25.4		1.1		3.3
117	.4	479	1.7	76	.3	149	.5	821	2.9	27,812	97.1	28,633
71	.2	511	1.8	81	.3	300	1.0	963	3.4	27,667	96.6	28,630
39.3		6.7		6.6		101.3		17.3		- .5		.0
73	.3	556	1.9	94	.3	214	.7	937	3.2	28,037	96.8	28,974
2.8		8.8		16.0		- 28.7		- 2.7		1.3		1.2
320	.2	14,215	10.2	1,001	.7	4,765	3.4	20,301	14.6	119,168	85.4	139,469
381	.3	16,096	11.2	1,272	.9	5,483	3.8	23,232	16.1	120,723	83.9	143,955
19.1		13.2		27.1		15.1		14.4		1.3		3.2
334		16,434	11.5	1,402	1.0	6,734	4.7	24,904	17.5	117,699	82.5	142,603
12.3		2.1		10.2		22.8		7.2		- 2.5		- .9
948	3.1	739	2.4	206	.7	6,761	21.9	8,654	28.0	22,210	72.0	30,864
1,078	3.5	819	2.6	186	.6	8,138	26.3	10,221	33.0	20,707	67.0	30,928
13.7		10.8		- 9.7		20.4		18.1		- 6.8		.2
1,205	4.0	787	2.6	232	.8	7,984	26.5	10,208	33.9	19,899	66.1	30,107
11.8		- 3.9		24.7		- 1.9		- .1		- 3.9		- 2.7
1,260	.2	48,881	9.7	6,935	1.4	21,813	4.3	78,889	15.6	427,588	84.4	506,477
2,501	.5	52,940	10.3	8,848	1.7	26,210	5.1	90,499	17.7	421,845	82.3	512,344
98.5		8.3		27.6		20.2		14.7		- 1.3		1.2
2,613	.5	61,479	11.8	10,931	2.1	30,921	5.9	105,944	20.3	415,226	79.7	521,170
4.5		16.1		23.5		18.0		17.1		- 1.6		1.7
920	.6	31,499	20.3	247	.2	394	.3	33,060	21.3	122,151	78.7	155,211
1,194	.7	35,739	21.7	336	.2	470	.3	37,739	22.9	126,923	77.1	164,662
29.8		13.5		36.0		19.3		14.2		3.9		6.1
1,192	.7	38,450	22.6	667	.4	617	.4	40,926	24.0	129,491	76.0	170,417
.2		7.6		98.5		31.3		8.4		2.0		3.5
610	2.7	95	.4	30	.1	18	.1	753	3.3	21,782	96.7	22,535
564	2.4	116	.5	48	.2	51	.2	779	3:3	22,641	96.7	23,420
7.5		22.1		60.0		183.3		3.5		3.9		3.9
794	3.1	145	.6	73	.3	43	.2	1,055	4.1	24,697	95.9	25,752
40.8		25.0		52.1		- 15.7		35.4		9.1		10.0
397	.2	21,101	9.0	775	.3	933	.4	23,206	9.9	210,799	90.1	234,005
420	.2	26,904	10.6	1,104	.4	1,310	.5	29,738	11.7	224,900	88.3	254,638
5.8		27.5		42.5		40.4		28.1		6.7		8.8
724	.3	24,295	10.0	1,063	.4	1,469	.6	27,551	11.3	216,323	88.7	243,874
72.4		- 9.7		- 3.7		12.1		- 7.4		- 3.8		- 4.2

233

	AMERICAN INDIAN ALASKAN NATIVE		BLACK NON-HISPANIC		ASIAN OR PACIFIC ISLANDER		HISPANIC		TOTAL MINORITY		WHITE NON-HISPANIC	
	NUMBER	%	NUMBER	%	NUMBER	%	NUMBER	%	NUMBER	%	NUMBER	%
OKLAHOMA.												
1974 (42 INSTITUTIONS)	3,391	4.2	4,817	5.9	283	.3	417	.5	8,908	10.9	72,654	89.1
1976 (43 INSTITUTIONS)	3,962	4.6	6,181	7.2	761	.9	561	.7	11,465	13.4	74,240	86.6
% CHANGE 1974 TO 1976	16.8		28.3		168.9		34.5		28.7		2.2	
1978 (42 INSTITUTIONS)	3,406	4.2	5,628	6.9	656	.8	640	.8	10,330	12.6	71,577	87.4
% CHANGE 1976 TO 1978	- 14.0		- 8.9		- 13.8		14.1		- 9.9		- 3.6	
OREGON.												
1974 (39 INSTITUTIONS)	959	1 2	1,070	1.4	1,383	1.8	549	.7	3,961	5.0	74,478	95.0
1976 (39 INSTITUTIONS)	756	110	1,138	1.5	1,430	1.9	794	1.1	4,118	5.5	70,317	94.5
% CHANGE 1974 TO 1976	- 21.2	.	6.4		3.4		44.6		4.0		- 5.6	
1978 (39 INSTITUTIONS)	890	1.3	1,022	1.4	1,897	2.7	792	1.1	4,601	6.5	66,144	93.5
% CHANGE 1976 TO 1978	17.7		- 10.2		32.7		- .3		11.7		- 5.9	
PENNSYLVANIA.												
1974 (157 INSTITUTIONS)	330	.1	15,619	5.8	761	.3	1,349	.5	18,059	6.7	252,961	93.3
1976 (158 INSTITUTIONS)	356	.1	18,872	6.8	2,118	.8	3,647	1.3	24,993	9.0	253,387	91.0
% CHANGE 1974 TO 1976	7.9		20.8		178.3		170.3		38.4		.2	
1978 (157 INSTITUTIONS)	343	.1	19,952	7.2	1,859	.7	1,842	.7	23,996	8.7	253,080	91.3
% CHANGE 1976 TO 1978	- 3.7		5.7		- 12.2		- 49.5		- 4.0		- .1	
RHODE ISLAND.												
1974 (12 INSTITUTIONS)	62	.2	1,139	3.3	165	.5	220	.6	1,586	4.6	33,199	95.4
1976 (12 INSTITUTIONS)	87	.2	1,264	3.6	217	.6	240	.7	1,808	5.1	33,776	94.9
% CHANGE 1974 TO 1976	40.3		11.0		31.5		9.1		14.0		1.7	
1978 (12 INSTITUTIONS)	62	.2	1,383	3.8	290	.8	233	.6	1,968	5.4	34,506	94.6
% CHANGE 1976 TO 1978	- 28.7		9.4		33.6		- 2.9		8.8		2.2	
SOUTH CAROLINA.												
1974 (52 INSTITUTIONS)	54	.1	14,360	20.4	79	.1	114	.2	14,607	20.8	55,677	79.2
1976 (55 INSTITUTIONS)	113	.1	19,127	24.6	125	.2	124	.2	19,489	25.0	58,329	75.0
% CHANGE 1974 TO 1976	109.3		33.2		58.2		8.8		33.4		4.8	
1978 (60 INSTITUTIONS)	78	.1	19,403	24.1	335	.4	199	.2	20,015	24.9	60,446	75.1
% CHANGE 1976 TO 1978	- 31.0		1.4		168.0		60.5		2.7		3.6	
SOUTH DAKOTA.												
1974 (16 INSTITUTIONS)	437	2.2	131	.6	24	.1	26	.1	618	0	19,682	97.0
1976 (16 INSTITUTIONS)	542	2.4	120	.5	61	.3	41	.2	764	a13	22,090	96.7
% CHANGE 1974 TO 1976	24.0		- 8.4		154.2		57.7		23.6		12.2	
1978 (17 INSTITUTIONS)	607	2.6	311	1.3	83	.4	280	1.2	1,281	5.5	22,167	94.5
% CHANGE 1976 TO 1978	12.0		159.2		36.1		582.9		67.7		.3	
TENNESSEE												
1974 (64 INSTITUTIONS)	118	.1	13,848	13.4	196	.2	221	.2	14,383	13.9	88,967	86.1
1976 (65 INSTITUTIONS)	139	.1	18,864	16.7	325	.3	232	.2	19,560	17.3	93,685	82.7
% CHANGE 1974 TO 1976	17.8		36.2		65.8		5.0		36.0		5.3	
1978 (74 INSTITUTIONS)	150	.1	21,020	18.3	398	.3	399	.3	21,967	19.1	92,877	80.9
% CHANGE 1976 TO 1978	7.9		11.4		22.5		72.0		12.3		- .9	
TEXAS												
1974 (129 INSTITUTIONS)	1,466	.5	28,150	9.0	1,524	.5	33,489	10.7	64,629	20.7	247,204	79.3
1976 (137 INSTITUTIONS)	1,459	.4	39,267	11.5	1,862	.5	39,850	11.7	82,438	24.2	258,000	75.8
% CHANGE 1974 TO 1976	- .5		39.5		22.2		19.0		27.6		4.4	
1978 (139 INSTITUTIONS)	1,015	.3	32,276	9.9	2,433	.7	40,831	12.5	76,555	23.4	250,754	76.6
% CHANGE 1976 TO 1978	- 30.4		- 17.8		30.7		2.5		- 7.1		- 2.8	
UTAH.												
1974 (11 INSTITUTIONS)	682	1.2	314	.6	494	.9	703	1 2	2,193	3.9	54,207	96.1
1976 (13 INSTITUTIONS)	717	1.3	342	.6	935	1.7	705	1‡3	2,699	4.9	52,746	95.1
% CHANGE 1974 TO 1976	5.1		8.9		89.3		.3		23.1		- 2.7	
1978 (13 INSTITUTIONS)	719	1.3	349	.6	1,069	2.0	642	1.2	2,779	5.1	51,343	94.9
% CHANGE 1976 TO 1978	.3		2.0		14.3		- 8.9		3.0		2.7	

JLL-TIME UNDERGRADUATE ENROLLMENT IN INSTITUTIONS OF HIGHER EDUCATION BY RACE AND ETHNICITY:
1974, 1976, 1978

ICAN INDIAN SKAN NATIVE		BLACK NON-HISPANIC		ASIAN OR PACIFIC ISLANDER		HISPANIC		TOTAL MINORITY		WHITE NON-HISPANIC		TOTAL
NUMBER	%	NUMBER	%	NUMBER	%	NUMBER	%	NUMBER	%	NUMBER	%	NUMBER
71	.3	295	1.5	116	.6	106	.5	588	2.9	19,716	97.1	20,304
66	.3	336	1.7	22	.1	137	.7	561	2.8	19,742	97.2	20,303
7.0		13.9		- 81.0		29.2		- 4.6		.1		.0
40	.2	278	1.4	50	.3	122	.6	490	2.5	19,471	97.5	19,961
39.4		- 17.3		127.3		- 10.9		- 12.7		- 1.4		- 1.7
186	.2	16,418	15.7	338	.3	351	.3	17,293	16.6	87,102	83.4	104,395
138	.1	20,301	17.1	506	.4	400	.3	21,345	18.0	97,554	82.0	118,899
25.8		23.7		49.7		14.0		23.4		12.0		13.9
219	.2	20,474	16.5	1,001	.8	541	.4	22,235	18.0	101,477	82.0	123,712
58.7		.9		97.8		35.3		4.2		4.0		4.0
2,001	1 6	4,715	3.7	3,556	2.8	1,639	1.3	11,911	9.4	115,145	90.6	127,056
1,442	1±3	3,648	3.3	3,285	3.0	1,299	1.2	9,674	8.7	101,674	91.3	111,348
27.9		- 22.6		- 7.6		- 20.7		- 18.8		- 11.7		- 12.4
1,535	1.4	3,397	3.0	3,776	3.4	1,439	1.3	10,147	9.1	101,363	90.9	111,510
6.4		- 6.9		14.9		10.8		4.9		- .3		·
120	.3	1,993	4.6	92	.2	105	.2	2,310	5.3	40,904	94.7	43,214
96	.2	2,432	5.5	259	.6	123	.3	2,910	6.6	41,506	93.4	44,416
20.0		22.0		181.5		17.1		26.0		1.5		2.8
93	.2	2,195	5.0	154	.4	98	.2	2,540	5.8	41,156	94.2	43,696
3.1		- 9.7		- 40.5		- 20.3		- 12.7		- .8		- 1.6
781	.6	4,050	3.0	421	.3	852	.6	6,104	4.	130,020	95.5	136,124
986	.7	5,373	3.7	594	.4	1,053	.7	8,006	5±8	139,018	94.6	147,024
26.2		32.7		41.1		23.6		31.2		6.9		8.0
806	.6	4,296	3.0	766	.5	1,110	.8	6,978	4.9	136,453	95.1	143,431
18.3		- 20.0		29.0		5.4		- 12.8		- 1.8		- 2.4
121	1.3	150	1.6	195	2.0	256	2.7	722	7.5	8,927	92.5	9,649
101	1.0	161	1.5	64	.6	213	2.0	539	5.2	9,854	94.8	10,393
16.5		7.3		- 67.2		- 16.8		- 25.3		10.4		7.7
121	1.2	161	1.6	63	.6	176	1.7	521	5.0	9,807	95.0	10,328
19.8		.0		- 1.6		- 17.4		- 3.3		- .5		- .6
2,357	.6	505,601	9.0	63,781	1.1	157,572	2.	759,311	13.5	4,858,306	86.5	5,617,617
8,321	.7	604,705	10.5	101,579	1.8	191,065	3.4	935,670	16.3	4,819,468	83.7	5,755,138
18.4		19.6		59.3		21.3		23.2		- .8		2.4
6,192	.6	600,904	10.6	113,790	2.0	196,452	3.5	947,338	16.7	4,716,593	83.3	5,663,931
5.6		- .6		12.0		12.0		1.2		- 2.1		- 1.6
0	.0	0	.0	0	.0	0	.0	0	.0	0	.0	0
0	.0	0	.0	337	98.3	0	.0	337	98.3	6	1.7	343
.0		.0		100.0		.0		100.0		100.0		100.0
0	.0	0	.0	367	97.6	0	.0	367	97.6	9	2.4	376
.0		.0		8.9		.0		8.9		50.0		9.6
0	.0	0	.0	0	.0	0	.0	0	.0	0	.0	0
0	.0	44	10.2	0	.0	109	25.2	153	35.3	280	64.7	433
.0		100.0		.0		100.0		100.0		100.0		100.0
0	.0	44	.10.5	0	.0	132	31.4	176	41.9	244	58.1	420
.0		.0		.0		21.1		15.0		- 12.9		- 3.0

TABLE 9 - COMPARISIONS OF FULL-TIME UNDERGRADUATE ENROLLMENT IN INSTITUTIONS OF HIGHER EDUCATION BY RACE AND ETHNICITY: STATE AND NATION, 1974, 1976, 1978

	AMERICAN INDIAN ALASKAN NATIVE		BLACK NON-HISPANIC		ASIAN OR PACIFIC ISLANDER		HISPANIC		TOTAL MINORITY		WHITE NON-HISPANIC	
	NUMBER	%	NUMBER	%	NUMBER	%	NUMBER	%	NUMBER	%	NUMBER	%
GUAM.............												
1974 (0 INSTITUTIONS)	0	.0	0	.0	0	.0	0	.0	0	.0	0	..0
1976 (1 INSTITUTIONS)	19	1.2	0	.0	1,169	74.5	21	1.3	1,209	77.1	360	22.9
% CHANGE 1974 TO 1976	100.0		.0		100.0		100.0		100.0		100.0	
1978 (1 INSTITUTIONS)	7	.5	12	.8	1,153	81.1	36	2.5	1,208	85.0	213	15.0
% CHANGE 1976 TO 1978	- 63.2		100.0		- 1.4		71.4		- .1		- 40.8	
PUERTO RICO												
1974 (0 INSTITUTIONS)	0	.0	0	.0	0	.0	0	.0	0	.0	0	.0
1976 (23 INSTITUTIONS)	80	.1	1	.0	0	.0	72,768	99.1	72,849	99.2	551	.8
% CHANGE 1974 TO 1976	100.0		100.0		.0		100.0		100.0		100.0	
1978 (33 INSTITUTIONS)	0	.0	10	.0	1	.0	94,550	99.7	94,561	99.7	272	.3
% CHANGE 1976 TO 1978	- 100.0		900.0		100.0		29.9		29.8		- 50.6	
TRUST TERRITORY												
1974 (0 INSTITUTIONS)	0	.0	0	.0	0	.0	0	.0	0	.0	0	.0
1976 (1 INSTITUTIONS)	0	.0	0	.0	161	100.0	0	.0	161	100.0	0	.0
% CHANGE 1974 TO 1976	.0		.0		100.0		.0		100.0		.0	
1978 (1 INSTITUTIONS)	0	.0	0	.0	248	100.0	0	.0	248	100.0	0	.0
% CHANGE 1976 TO 1978	.0		.0		54.0		.0		54.0		.0	
VIRGIN ISLANDS........												
1974 (0 INSTITUTIONS)	0	.0	0	.0	0	.0	0	.0	0	.0	0	.0
1976 (1 INSTITUTIONS)	0	.0	366	83.8	1	.2	19	4.3	386	88.3	51	11.7
% CHANGE 1974 TO 1976	.0		100.0		100.0		100.0		100.0		100.0	
1978 (1 INSTITUTIONS)	0	.0	311	79.7	1	.3	27	6.9	339	86.9	51	13.1
% CHANGE 1976 TO 1978	.0		- 15.0		.0		42.1		- 12.2		.0	
OUTLYING AREAS........												
1974 (0 INSTITUTIONS)	0	.0	0	.0	0	.0	0	.0	0	.0	0	.0
1976 (28 INSTITUTIONS)	99	.1	411	.5	1,668	2.2	72,917	95.5	75,095	98.4	1,248	1.6
% CHANGE 1974 TO 1976	100.0		100.0		100.0		100.0		100.0		100.0	
1978 (38 INSTITUTIONS)	7	.0	377	.4	1,770	1.8	94,745	97.0	96,899	99.2	789	.8
% CHANGE 1976 TO 1978	- 92.9		- 8.3		6.1		6.1		29.0		- 36.8	
NATION, TOTAL												
1974 (2734 INSTITUTIONS)	32,357	.6	505,601	9.0	63,781	1.1	157,572	2.8	759,311	13.5	4,858,306	86.5
1976 (2849 INSTITUTIONS)	38,420	.7	605,116	10.4	103,247	1.8	263,982	4.5	1,010,765	17.3	4,820,716	82.7
% CHANGE 1974 TO 1976	18.7		19.7		61.9		67.5		33.1		- .8	
1978 (2935 INSTITUTIONS)	36,199	.6	601,281	10.4	115,560	2.0	291,197	5.1	1,044,237	18.1	4,717,382	81.9
% CHANGE 1976 TO 1978	- 5.8		- .6		11.9		11.9		3.3		2.1	

236

E GRADUATE ENROLLMENT IN INSTITUTIONS OF HIGHER EDUCATION BY RACE AND ETHNICITY: 1976, 1978

DIAN TIVE %	BLACK NON-HISPANIC		ASIAN OR PACIFIC ISLANDER		HISPANIC		TOTAL MINORITY		WHITE NON-HISPANIC		TOTAL
	NUMBER	%	NUMBER	%	NUMBER	%	NUMBER	%	NUMBER	%	NUMBER
.2	1,031	23.7	25	.6	19	.4	1,083	24.9	3,273	75.1	4,356
.1	730	15.4	43	.9	12	.3	790	16.7	3,941	83.3	4,731
-	29.2		72.0		- 36.8		- 27.1		20.4		8.6
.2	613	12.5	51	1.0	29	.6	705	14.4	4,188	85.6	4,893
..	16.0		18.6		141.7		- 10.8		6.3		3.4
.0	0	.0	0	.0	0	.0	0	.0	0	.0	0
7.0	8	4.3	3	1.6	4	2.2	28	15.1	158	84.9	186
	100.0		100.0		100.0		100.0		100.0		100.0
2.2	8	3.4	3	1.3	4	1.7	20	8.6	212	91.4	232
	.0		.0		.0		- 28.6		34.2		24.7
.7	55	1.0	34	.6	315	5 6	444	7.8	5,218	92.2	5,662
.8	41	.8	39	.7	335	6:3	459	8.6	4,851	91.4	5,310
-	25.5		14.7		6.3		3.4		- 7.0		- 6.2
.7	50	.9	52	1.0	115	2.2	256	4.8	5,081	95.2	5,337
	22.0		33.3		- 65.7		- 44.2		4.7		.5
1.8	93	6.6	5	.4	20	1.4	144	10.2	1,271	89.8	1,415
.4	180	8.5	26	1.2	7	.3	222	10.5	1,891	89.5	2,113
	93.5		420.0		- 65.0		54.2		48.8		49.3
1.0	142	7.1	17	.8	15	.7	195	9.7	1,807	90.3	2,002
	- 21.1		- 34.6		114.3		- 12.2		- 4.4		- 5.3
.4	1,766	4.5	1,729	4.4	1,173	3.0	4,837	12.4	34,027	87.6	38,864
.7	2,155	4.7	2,599	5.6	2,016	4:4	7,072	15.3	39,017	84.7	46,089
.	22.0		50.3		71.9		46.2		14.7		18.6
.5	1,960	4.3	2,624	5.8	2,059	4.5	6,890	15.2	38,426	84.8	45,316
	9.0		1.0		2.1		- 2.6		- 1.5		- 1.7
.4	179	2.1	93	1.1	210	2.5	514	6.0	7,995	94.0	8,509
.2	116	1.5	65	.8	182	2.3	380	4.8	7,597	95.2	7,977
-	35.2		- 30.1		- 13.3		- 26.1		- 5.0		- 6.3
.3	149	2.1	87	1.2	221	3.1	482	6.7	6,742	93.3	7,224
	28.4		33.8		21.4		26.8		- 11.3		- 9.4
.1	266	3.7	115	1.6	76	1.0	462	6.	6,823	93.7	7,285
.1	191	3.2	58	1.0	60	1.0	316	5.2	5,695	94.7	6,011
-	28.2		- 49.6		- 21.1		- 31.6		- 16.5		- 17.5
.2	169	2.9	64	1.1	168	2.9	410	7.0	5,459	93.0	5,869
-	11.5		10.3		180.0		29.7		- 4.1		- 2.4
.1	18	2.1	3	.3	7	.8	29	3.3	841	96.7	870
.6	10	2.0	3	.6	2	.4	18	3.6	484	96.4	502
-	44.4		.0		- 71.4		- 37.9		- 42.4		- 42.3
.3	16	5.3	2	.7	0	.0	19	6.3	283	93.7	302
	60.0		- 33.3		- 100.0		5.6		- 41.5		- 39.8
.2	1,443	21.8	113	1.7	80	1.2	1,647	24.9	4,973	75.1	6,620
.5	933	15.8	171	2.9	96	1.6	1,228	20.7	4,694	79.3	5,922
-	35.3		51.3		20.0		- 25.4		- 5.6		- 10.5
.1	1,122	20.2	111	2.0	96	1.7	1,336	24.1	4,218	75.9	5,554
	20.3		- 35.1		.0		8.8		- 10.1		- 6.2

237

TABLE 10 - COMPARISIONS OF FULL-TIME GRADUATE ENROLLMENT IN INSTITUTIONS OF HIGHER EDUCATION BY RACE AND ETHNICITY: STATE AND NATION, 1974, 1976, 1978

	AMERICAN INDIAN ALASKAN NATIVE		BLACK NON-HISPANIC		ASIAN OR PACIFIC ISLANDER		HISPANIC		TOTAL MINORITY		WHITE NON-HISPANIC		TOTAL
	NUMBER	%	NUMBER	%	NUMBER	%	NUMBER	%	NUMBER	%	NUMBER	%	NUMBER
FLORIDA													
1974 (19 INSTITUTIONS)	17	.2	594	5.7	193	1.9	273	2.6	1,077	10.4	9,269	89.6	10,346
1976 (24 INSTITUTIONS)	23	.2	1,364	10.4	78	.6	603	4.6	2,068	15.8	11,044	84.2	13,112
% CHANGE 1974 TO 1976	35.3		129.6		- 59.6		120.9		92.0		19.1		26.7
1978 (24 INSTITUTIONS)	27	.2	1,394	10.6	155	1.2	520	4.0	2,096	16.0	10,994	84.0	13,090
% CHANGE 1976 TO 1978	17.4		2.2		98.7		- 13.8		1.4		.5		- .2
GEORGIA													
1974 (23 INSTITUTIONS)	18	.2	1,670	16.9	106	1.1	31	.3	1,825	18.4	8,079	81.6	9,904
1976 (21 INSTITUTIONS)	24	.3	1,413	15.8	38	.4	28	.3	1,503	16.8	7,435	83.2	8,938
% CHANGE 1974 TO 1976	33.3		- 15.4		- 64.2		- 9.7		- 17.6		- 8.0		- 9.8
1978 (23 INSTITUTIONS)	9	.1	1,400	16.7	55	.7	35	.4	1,499	17.9	6,868	82.1	8,367
% CHANGE 1976 TO 1978	- 62.5		- .9		44.7		25.0		- .3		- 7.6		- 6.4
HAWAII													
1974 (0 INSTITUTIONS)	0	.0	0	.0	0	.0	0	.0	0	.0	0	.0	0
1976 (2 INSTITUTIONS)	4	.2	21	1.1	793	40.6	26	1.3	844	43.2	1,109	56.8	1,953
% CHANGE 1974 TO 1976	100.0		100.0		100.0		100.0		100.0		100.0		100.0
1978 (2 INSTITUTIONS)	0	.0	16	.9	763	41.2	35	1.9	814	43.9	1,040	56.1	1,854
% CHANGE 1976 TO 1978	- 100.0		- 23.8		- 3.8		34.6		- 3.6		- 6.2		- 5.1
IDAHO													
1974 (4 INSTITUTIONS)	4	.5	10	1.2	10	1.2	10	1.2	34	4.1	800	95.9	834
1976 (3 INSTITUTIONS)	5	.4	16	1.4	21	1.9	12	1.1	54	4.8	1,067	95.2	1,121
% CHANGE 1974 TO 1976	25.0		60.0		110.0		20.0		58.8		33.4		34.4
1978 (4 INSTITUTIONS)	5	.6	9	1.0	17	1.9	8	.9	39	4.3	862	95.7	901
% CHANGE 1976 TO 1978	.0		- 43.8		- 19.0		- 33.3		- 27.8		- 19.2		- 19.6
ILLINOIS													
1974 (46 INSTITUTIONS)	37	.1	1,646	6.2	341	1.3	212	.8	2,236	8.4	24,420	91.6	26,656
1976 (49 INSTITUTIONS)	32	.2	1,255	6.3	401	2.0	250	1.3	1,938	9.7	18,001	90.3	19,939
% CHANGE 1974 TO 1976	- 13.5		- 23.8		17.6		17.9		- 13.3		- 26.3		- 25.2
1978 (53 INSTITUTIONS)	34	.2	1,032	5.5	507	2.7	311	1.7	1,884	10.1	16,802	89.9	18,686
% CHANGE 1976 TO 1978	6.3		- 17.8		26.4		24.4		- 2.8		- 6.7		- 6.3
INDIANA													
1974 (26 INSTITUTIONS)	33	.3	380	3.2	255	2.2	138	1.2	806	6.9	10,945	93.1	11,751
1976 (29 INSTITUTIONS)	37	.4	329	3.2	100	1.0	74	.7	540	5.3	9,593	94.7	10,133
% CHANGE 1974 TO 1976	12.1		- 13.4		- 60.8		- 46.4		- 33.0		- 12.4		- 13.8
1978 (27 INSTITUTIONS)	34	.4	290	3.2	88	1.0	120	1.3	532	5.8	8,582	94.2	9,114
% CHANGE 1976 TO 1978	- 8.1		- 11.9		- 12.0		62.2		- 1.5		- 10.5		- 10.1
IOWA													
1974 (8 INSTITUTIONS)	5	.1	141	2.2	71	1.1	34	.5	251	3.9	6,178	96.1	6,429
1976 (7 INSTITUTIONS)	15	.3	152	3.2	61	1.3	29	.6	257	5.4	4,519	94.6	4,776
% CHANGE 1974 TO 1976	200.0		7.8		- 14.1		- 14.7		2.4		- 26.9		- 25.7
1978 (8 INSTITUTIONS)	9	.2	149	3.2	63	1.4	36	.8	257	5.5	4,381	94.5	4,638
% CHANGE 1976 TO 1978	- 40.0		- 2.0		3.3		24.1		.0		- 3.1		- 2.9
KANSAS													
1974 (6 INSTITUTIONS)	22	.4	139	2.4	159	2.8	77	1.4	397	7.0	5,280	93.0	5,677
1976 (7 INSTITUTIONS)	35	.9	134	3.4	30	.8	53	1.14	252	6.4	3,671	93.6	3,923
% CHANGE 1974 TO 1976	59.1		- 3.6		- 81.1		- 31.2		- 36.5		- 30.5		- 30.9
1978 (10 INSTITUTIONS)	26	.7	139	3.5	36	.9	60	1.5	261	6.7	3,658	93.3	3,919
% CHANGE 1976 TO 1978	- 25.7		3.7		20.0		13.2		3.6		- .4		- .1
KENTUCKY													
1974 (11 INSTITUTIONS)	10	.2	163	4.0	54	1.3	13	.3	240	5.9	3,827	94.1	4,067
1976 (15 INSTITUTIONS)	5	.1	179	4.4	13	.3	19	.5	216	5.3	3,878	94.7	4,094
% CHANGE 1974 TO 1976	- 50.0		9.8		- 75.9		46.2		- 10.0		1.3		.7
1978 (16 INSTITUTIONS)	64	1.7	102	2.8	48	1.3	29	.8	243	6.6	3,458	93.4	3,701
% CHANGE 1976 TO 1978	1180.0		- 43.0		269.2		52.6		12.5		- 10.8		- 9.6

E GRADUATE ENROLLMENT IN INSTITUTIONS OF HIGHER EDUCATION BY RACE AND ETHNICITY:
1976, 1978

DIAN TIVE	BLACK NON-HISPANIC		ASIAN OR PACIFIC ISLANDER		HISPANIC		TOTAL MINORITY		WHITE NON-HISPANIC		TOTAL
%	NUMBER	%	NUMBER	%	NUMBER	%	NUMBER	%	NUMBER	%	NUMBER
.3	630	11.2	38	.7	44	.8	727	13.0	4,875	87.0	5,602
.2	501	9.2	37	.7	119	2.2	667	12.3	4,756	87.7	5,423
-	20.5		-	2.6	170.5		-	8.3	-	2.4	- 3.2
.4	389	8.4	31	.7	85	1.8	523	11.3	4,085	88.7	4,608
-	22.4		-	16.2	-	28.6	-	21.6	-	14.1	- 15.0
.2	3	.5	1	.2	1	.2	6	1.0	601	99.0	607
.0	0	.0	2	.2	0	.0	2	.2	924	99.8	926
-	100.0		100.0		-	100.0	-	66.7	53.7		52.6
.1	2	.2	2	.2	4	.4	9	1.0	885	99.0	894
	100.0		.0		100.0		350.0		-	4.2	- 3.5
.4	605	9.1	173	2.6	82	1.2	888	13.4	5,749	86.6	6,637
.4	494	8.3	56	.9	61	1.0	633	10.6	5,337	89.4	5,970
-	18.3		-	67.6	-	25.6	-	28.7	-	7.2	- 10.0
.3	452	7.8	95	1.6	64	1.1	628	10.8	5,201	89.2	5,829
	8.5		69.6		4.9		-	.8	-	2.5	- 2.4
.1	754	3.9	221	1.1	178	.9	1,181	6.0	18,355	94.0	19,536
.2	697	3.8	298	1.6	251	1.4	1,279	7.0	17,059	93.0	18,338
	7.6		34.8		41.0		8.3		-	7.1	- 6.1
.2	731	3.8	439	2.3	337	1.8	1,542	8.1	17,491	91.9	19,033
	4.9		47.3		34.3		20.6		2.5		3.8
.3	1,552	8.2	213	1.1	210	1.1	2,031	10.7	16,897	89.3	18,928
.5	1,475	9.0	340	2.1	269	1.6	2,159	13.2	14,216	86.8	16,375
	5.0		59.6		28.1		6.3		-	15.9	- 13.5
.4	1,197	7.7	311	2.0	234	1.5	1,800	11.6	13,654	88.4	15,454
-	18.8		-	8.5	-	13.0	-	16.6	-	4.0	- 5.6
.6	218	2.4	89	1.0	47	.5	411	4.5	8,674	95.5	9,085
.5	186	2.1	134	1.5	63	.7	431	4.8	8,553	95.2	8,984
-	14.7		50.6		34.0		4.9		-	1.4	- 1.1
.4	133	1.6	134	1.6	84	1.0	384	4.6	7,933	95.4	8,317
-	28.5		.0		33.3		-	10.9	-	7.2	- 7.4
.1	395	15.3	37	1.4	3	.1	438	17.0	2,140	83.0	2,578
.0	515	19.5	23	.9	4	.2	543	20.6	2,092	79.4	2,635
	30.4		-	37.8		33.3		24.0		-	2.2	2.2
.1	514	19.6	23	.9	5	.2	544	20.7	2,082	79.3	2,626
	.2		.0		25.0		.2		-	.5	- .3
.3	379	4.6	53	.6	36	.4	495	6.0	7,696	94.0	8,191
.4	471	5.8	125	1.5	66	.8	694	8.6	7,374	91.4	8,068
	24.3		135.8		83.3		40.2		-	4.2	- 1.5
.2	503	6.7	200	2.7	60	.8	779	10.4	6,696	89.6	7,475
	6.8		60.0		-	9.1		12.2		-	9.2	- 7.4
1.3	4	.4	2	.2	1	.1	20	2.0	965	98.0	985
2.1	2	.3	9	1.2	1	.1	27	3.7	703	96.3	730
-	50.0		350.0		.0		35.0		-	27.2	- 25.9
2.3	3	.4	2	.3	1	.1	24	3.1	748	96.9	772
	50.0		-	77.8		.0		-	11.1		6.4	5.8

TABLE 10 - COMPARISIONS OF FULL-TIME GRADUATE ENROLLMENT IN INSTITUTIONS OF HIGHER EDUCATION BY RACE
STATE AND NATION, 1974, 1976, 1978

	AMERICAN INDIAN ALASKAN NATIVE		BLACK NON-HISPANIC		ASIAN OR PACIFIC ISLANDER		HISPANIC		TOTAL MINORITY
	NUMBER	%	NUMBER	%	NUMBER	%	NUMBER	%	NUMBER
NEBRASKA.									
1974 (8 INSTITUTIONS)	2	.3	33	4.5	8	1.1	13	1.8	56
1976 (7 INSTITUTIONS)	7	.4	29	1.5	11	.6	18	.9	65
% CHANGE 1974 TO 1976	250.0		- 12.1		37.5		38.5		16.1
1978 (8 INSTITUTIONS)	7	.4	37	2.1	26	1.5	20	1.1	90
% CHANGE 1976 TO 1978	.0		27.6		136.4		11.1		38.5
NEVADA.									
1974 (2 INSTITUTIONS)	2	.4	9	2 0	10	2.2	5	1.1	26
1976 (2 INSTITUTIONS)	1	.2	6	1.4	10	2.3	6	1.4	23
% CHANGE 1974 TO 1976	- 50.0		- 33.3		.0		20.0		- 11.5
1978 (2 INSTITUTIONS)	2	.5	7	1.8	7	1.8	4	1.0	20
% CHANGE 1976 TO 1978	100.0		16.7		- 30.0		- 33.3		- 13.0
NEW HAMPSHIRE									
1974 (6 INSTITUTIONS)	12	1.0	16	1.4	3	.3	7	.6	38
1976 (7 INSTITUTIONS)	6	.5	10	.9	13	1.1	4	.3	33
% CHANGE 1974 TO 1976	- 50.0		- 37.5		333.3		- 42.9		- 13.2
1978 (7 INSTITUTIONS)	3	.3	18	1.6	21	1.9	4	.4	46
% CHANGE 1976 TO 1978	- 50.0		80.0		61.5		.0		39.4
NEW JERSEY.									
1974 (23 INSTITUTIONS)		.1	489	6.4	197	2	138	1.8	830
1976 (26 INSTITUTIONS)	5	.1	339	5.4	116	1.6	113	1.8	573
% CHANGE 1974 TO 1976	- 16.7		- 30.7		- 41.1		- 18.1		- 31.0
1978 (27 INSTITUTIONS)	10	.2	309	5.3	142	2.4	106	1.8	567
% CHANGE 1976 TO 1978	100.0		- 8.8		22.4		- 6.2		- 1.0
NEW MEXICO.									
1974 (7 INSTITUTIONS)	31	1 3	32	1.3	31	1.3	253	10.3	347
1976 (6 INSTITUTIONS)	30	1.3	49	2.2	18	.8	313	13.9	410
% CHANGE 1974 TO 1976	- 3.2		53.1		- 41.9		23.7		18.2
1978 (6 INSTITUTIONS)	51	2.3	28	1.3	28	1.3	331	15.0	438
% CHANGE 1976 TO 1978	70.0		- 42.9		55.6		5.8		6.8
NEW YORK.									
1974 (102 INSTITUTIONS)	74	.2	2,147	5.1	1,225	2.9	872	2.1	4,318
1976 (107 INSTITUTIONS)	138	.4	2,166	5.7	1,011	2.7	1,105	2.6	4,420
% CHANGE 1974 TO 1976	86.5		.9		- 17.5		26.7		2.4
1978 (124 INSTITUTIONS)	138	.3	2,258	5.7	1,096	2.7	1,146	2.9	4,638
% CHANGE 1976 TO 1978	.0		4.2		8.4		3.7		4.9
NORTH CAROLINA.									
1974 (11 INSTITUTIONS)	16	.3	491	7.8	26	.4	41	.7	574
1976 (12 INSTITUTIONS)	15	.2	613	8.2	34	.5	41	.5	703
% CHANGE 1974 TO 1976	- 6.3		24.8		30.8		.0		22.5
1978 (14 INSTITUTIONS)	20	.3	547	7.3	50	.7	44	.6	661
% CHANGE 1976 TO 1978	33.3		- 10.8		47.1		7.3		- 6.0
NORTH DAKOTA.									
1974 (3 INSTITUTIONS)	4	.8	1	.2	2	.4	1	.2	8
1976 (3 INSTITUTIONS)	2	.4	3	.6	3	.6	5	1.0	13
% CHANGE 1974 TO 1976	- 50.0		200.0		50.0		400.0		62.5
1978 (3 INSTITUTIONS)	1	.2	5	1.0	9	1.8	0	.0	15
% CHANGE 1976 TO 1978	- 50.0		66.7		200.0		- 100.0		15.4
OHIO.									
1974 (42 INSTITUTIONS)	28	.2	1,226	6.7	186	1.0	181	1.0	1,621
1976 (40 INSTITUTIONS)	34	.2	1,647	8.7	341	1.8	243	1.3	2,265
% CHANGE 1974 TO 1976	21.4		34.3		83.3		34.3		39.7
1978 (42 INSTITUTIONS)	60	.3	1,385	7.6	168	.9	198	1.1	1,811
% CHANGE 1976 TO 1978	76.5		- 15.9		- 50.7		- 18.5		- 20.0

DIAN TIVE	BLACK NON-HISPANIC		ASIAN OR PACIFIC ISLANDER		HISPANIC		TOTAL MINORITY		WHITE NON-HISPANIC		TOTAL
%	NUMBER	%	NUMBER	%	NUMBER	%	NUMBER	%	NUMBER	%	NUMBER
2.6	168	3.4	31	.6	27	.6	352	7.2	4,543	92.8	4,895
2.6	188	4.7	53	1.3	36	.9	381	9.6	3,590	90.4	3,971
	11.9		71.0		33.3		8.2		- 21.0		- 18.9
2.9	153	4.2	36	1.0	29	.8	323	8.9	3,294	91.1	3,617
-	18.6		- 32.1		- 19.4		- 15.2		- 8.2		8.9
1.1	71	1.2	74	1.3	44	.8	252	4.4	5,503	95.6	5,755
1.4	49	1.1	66	1.5	40	.9	216	5.0	4,110	95.0	4,326
-	31.0		- 10.8		- 9.1		- 14.3		- 25.3		- 24.8
.9	62	1.3	95	2.0	38	.8	237	5.0	4,515	95.0	4,752
	26.5		43.9		- 5.0		9.7		9.9		9.8
.1	749	4.0	205	1.1	124	.7	1,104	5.9	17,600	94.1	18,704
.3	630	3.7	221	1.3	164	1.0	1,063	6.2	16,182	93.8	17,245
	15.9		7.8		32.3		- 3.7		- 8.1		- 7.8
.3	653	4.4	269	1.8	204	1.4	1,175	7.9	13,611	92.1	14,786
	3.7		21.7		24.4		10.5		- 15.9		- 14.3
.1	44	1.5	57	2.0	15	.5	119	4 1	2,801	95.9	2,920
.0	57	2.8	27	1.3	15	.7	100	419	1,944	95.1	2,044
	29.5		- 52.6		.0		- 16.0		- 30.6		- 30.0
.3	41	2.0	34	1.7	14	.7	96	4.8	1,921	95.2	2,017
-	28.1		25.9		- 6.7		- 4.0		- 1.2		- 1.3
.1	265	8.5	8	.3	6	.2	283	9.0	2,845	91.0	3,128
.2	292	9.3	9	.3	12	.4	319	10.2	2,806	89.8	3,125
	10.2		12.5		100.0		12.7		- 1.4		- .1
.1	179	6.7	14	.5	15	.6	212	7.9	2,458	92.1	2,670
-	38.7		55.6		25.0		- 33.5		- 12.4		- 14.6
7.0	8	1.2	5	.7		.7	66	9.6	623	90.4	689
4.7	3	.5	1	.2	8	.0	33	5.4	580	94.6	613
-	62.5		- 80.0		- 100.0		- 50.0		- 6.9		- 11.0
4.4	1	.2	1	.2	2	.4	27	5.1	500	94.9	527
-	66.7		.0		100.0		- 18.2		- 13.8		- 14.0
1.0	511	7.3	17	.2	33	.5	634	9.1	6,367	90.9	7,001
.6	451	8.8	17	.3	14	.3	515	10.0	4,627	90.0	5,142
	11.7		.0		- 57.6		- 18.8		- 27.3		- 26.6
.3	400	7.8	62	1.2	26	.5	505	9.8	4,625	90.2	5,130
	11.3		264.7		85.7		- 1.9		.0		- .2
.4	718	3.5	334	1.6	834	4.0	1,978	9.5	18,787	90.5	20,765
.4	889	4.0	356	1.6	970	4.3	2,306	10.3	20,075	89.7	22,381
	23.8		6.6		16.3		16.6		6.9		7.8
.4	1,057	4.5	612	2.6	1,093	4.6	2,847	12.1	20,674	87.9	23,521
	18.9		71.9		12.7		23.5		3.0		5.1
.7	31	.8	58	1.5	30	.8	146	3.8	3,651	96.2	3,797
.7	25	.9	44	1.5	41	1.4	131	4.5	2,773	95.5	2,904
-	19.4		- 24.1		36.7		- 10.3		- 24.0		- 23.5
1.0	18	.5	49	1.3	37	1.0	141	3.9	3,504	96.1	3,645
-	28.0		11.4		- 9.8		7.6		26.4		25.5

TABLE 10 - COMPARISIONS OF FULL-TIME GRADUATE ENROLLMENT IN INSTITUTIONS OF HIGHER EDUCATION BY RACI
STATE AND NATION, 1974, 1976, 1978

	AMERICAN INDIAN ALASKAN NATIVE		BLACK NON-HISPANIC		ASIAN OR PACIFIC ISLANDER		HISPANIC		TOTAL MINORIT'
	NUMBER	%	NUMBER	%	NUMBER	%.	NUMBER	%	NUMBER
VERMONT									
1974 (5 INSTITUTIONS)	0	.0	12	1.3	3	.3	5	.5	20
1976 (8 INSTITUTIONS)	3	.3	53	4.8	14	1.3	11	1.0	81
% CHANGE 1974 TO 1976	100.0		341.7		366.7		120.0		305.0
1978 (8 INSTITUTIONS)	2	.2	34	3.2	7	.7	17	1.6	60
% CHANGE 1976 TO 1978	- 33.3		- 35.8		- 50.0		54.5		- 25.9
VIRGINIA									
1974 (19 INSTITUTIONS)	6	.1	326	4.7	92	1.3	9	.1	433
1976 (19 INSTITUTIONS)	7	.1	503	6.6	73	1.0	27	.4	610
% CHANGE 1974 TO 1976	16.7		54.3		- 20.7		200.0		40.9
1978 (19 INSTITUTIONS)	7	.1	635	8.2	90	1.2	28	.4	760
% CHANGE 1976 TO 1978	.0		26.2		23.3		3.7		24.6
WASHINGTON									
1974 (13 INSTITUTIONS)	52	.7	214	2 9	230	3.1	68	.9	564
1976 (13 INSTITUTIONS)	58	.8	181	2t5	242	3.4	108	1.5	589
% CHANGE 1974 TO 1976	11.5		- 15.4		5.2		58.8		4.4
1978 (15 INSTITUTIONS)	54	.8	172	2.4	246	3.4	94	1.3	566
% CHANGE 1976 TO 1978	- 6.9		- 5.0		1.7		- 13.0		- 3.9
WEST VIRGINIA									
1974 (3 INSTITUTIONS)	3	.1	68	2.7	6	.2	12	.5	89
1976 (4 INSTITUTIONS)	2	.1	67	2.9	91	4.0	14	.6	174
% CHANGE 1974 TO 1976	- 33.3		- 1.5		1416.7		16.7		95.5
1978 (5 INSTITUTIONS)	7	.4	29	1.5	31	1.6	7	.4	74
% CHANGE 1976 TO 1978	250.0		- 56.7		- 65.9		- 50.0		- 57.5
WISCONSIN									
1974 (20 INSTITUTIONS)	32	.3	319	3 0	86	.8	89	.8	526
1976 (19 INSTITUTIONS)	18	.2	233	2t6	123	1.4	93	1.0	467
% CHANGE 1974 TO 1976	- 43.8		- 27.0		43.0		4.5		- 11.2
1978 (20 INSTITUTIONS)	37	.4	270	3.2	193	2.3	129	1.5	629
% CHANGE 1976 TO 1978	105.6		15.9		56.9		38.7		34.7
WYOMING									
1974 (1 INSTITUTIONS)	1	.1	4	.6	2	.3	8	1.2	15
1976 (1 INSTITUTIONS)	3	.4	7	1.0	5	.7	10	1.5	25
% CHANGE 1974 TO 1976	200.0		75.0		150.0		25.0		66.7
1978 (1 INSTITUTIONS)	0	.0	3	.5	1	.2	4	.7	8
% CHANGE 1976 TO 1978	- 100.0		- 57.1		- 80.0		- 60.0		- 68.0
THE STATES AND D.C.									
1974 (905 INSTITUTIONS)	1,397	.4	22,086	5.5	7,029	1.8	6,110	1.5	36,622
1976 (965 INSTITUTIONS)	1,567	.4	22,058	5.8	8,465	2.2	8,045	2.1	40,135
% CHANGE 1974 TO 1976	12.2		- .1		20.4		31.7		9.6
1978 (1047 INSTITUTIONS)	1,540	.4	20,985	5.7	9,267	2.5	8,325	2.2	40,117
% CHANGE 1976 TO 1978	- 1.7		- 4.9		9.5		9.5		.0
GUAM									
1974 (0 INSTITUTIONS)	0	.0	0	.0	0	.0	0	.0	0
1976 (1 INSTITUTIONS)	2	2.5	0	.0	29	35.8	2	2.5	33
% CHANGE 1974 TO 1976	100.0		.0		100.0		100.0		100.0
1978 (1 INSTITUTIONS)	0	.0	0	.0	10	76.9	0	.0	10
% CHANGE 1976 TO 1978	- 100.0		.0		- 65.5		- 100.0		- 69.7
PUERTO RICO									
1974 (0 INSTITUTIONS)	0	.0	0	.0	0	.0	0	.0	0
1976 (7 INSTITUTIONS)	22	1.6	0	.0	0	.0	1,375	98.3	1,397
% CHANGE 1974 TO 1976	100.0		.0		.0		100.0		100.0
1978 (9 INSTITUTIONS)	0	.0	0	.0	0	.0	1,508	91.0	1,508
% CHANGE 1976 TO 1978	- 100.0		.0		.0		9.7		7.9

242

E GRADUATE ENROLLMENT IN INSTITUTIONS OF HIGHER EDUCATION BY RACE AND ETHNICITY:
1976, 1978

DIAN TIVE	BLACK NON-HISPANIC		ASIAN OR PACIFIC ISLANDER		HISPANIC		TOTAL MINORITY		WHITE NON-HISPANIC		TOTAL
%	NUMBER	%	NUMBER	%	NUMBER	%	NUMBER	%	NUMBER	%	NUMBER
.0	0	.0	0	.0	0	.0	0	.0	0	.0	0
1.6	0	.0	29	2.0	1,377	93.0	1,430	96.6	50	3.4	1,480
	.0		100.0		100.0		100.0		100.0		100.0
.0	0	.0	10	.6	1,508	90.3	1,518	90.9	152	9.1	1,670
	.0		- 65.5		- 65.5		6.2		204.0		12.8
.4	22,086	5.5	7,029	1.8	6,110	1.5	36,622	9.2	361,423	90.8	398,045
.4	22,058	5.8	8,494	2.2	9,422	2.5	41,565	10.9	340,926	89.1	382,491
	.1		20.8		54.2		13.5		- 5.7		- 3.9
.4	20,985	5.6	9,277	2.5	9,833	2.6	41,635	11.2	331,158	88.8	372,793
	- 4.9		9.2		9.2		.2		- 2.9		- 2.5

TABLE 11 - COMPARISIONS OF FULL-TIME FIRST PROFESSIONAL ENROLLMENT IN INSTITUTIONS OF HIGHER EDUCATI
STATE AND NATION, 1974, 1976, 1978

	AMERICAN INDIAN ALASKAN NATIVE		BLACK NON-HISPANIC		ASIAN OR PACIFIC ISLANDER		HISPANIC		TOTAL MINORIT
	NUMBER	%	NUMBER	%	NUMBER	%	NUMBER	%	NUMBER
ALABAMA									
1974 (8 INSTITUTIONS)	1	.0	84	3.5	4	.2	9	.4	98
1976 (8 INSTITUTIONS)	2	.1	219	7.6	12	.4	8	.3	241
% CHANGE 1974 TO 1976	100.0		160.7		200.0		- 11.1		145.9
1978 (7 INSTITUTIONS)	1	.0	195	5.8	22	.7	6	.2	224
% CHANGE 1976 TO 1978	- 50.0		- 11.0		83.3		- 25.0		- 7.1
ARIZONA									
1974 (3 INSTITUTIONS)	2	.2	5	.5	16	1.5	54	5.1	77
1976 (2 INSTITUTIONS)	1	.1	4	.4	8	.8	31	3.0	44
% CHANGE 1974 TO 1976	- 50.0		- 20.0		- 50.0		- 42.6		- 42.9
1978 (2 INSTITUTIONS)	4	.4	1	.1	3	.3	24	2.1	32
% CHANGE 1976 TO 1978	300.0		- 75.0		- 62.5		- 22.6		- 27.3
ARKANSAS									
1974 (3 INSTITUTIONS)	25	2.6	17	1.7	6	.6	3	.3	51
1976 (4 INSTITUTIONS)	5	.4	41	3.6	10	.9	3	.3	59
% CHANGE 1974 TO 1976	- 80.0		141.2		66.7		.0		15.7
1978 (4 INSTITUTIONS)	6	.5	56	4.3	13	1.0	4	.3	79
% CHANGE 1976 TO 1978	20.0		36.6		30.0		33.3		33.9
CALIFORNIA									
1974 (41 INSTITUTIONS)	90	.4	955	4.4	1,122	5.1	962	4.4	3,129
1976 (47 INSTITUTIONS)	161	.7	939	4.2	1,571	7.0	1,161	5.1	3,832
% CHANGE 1974 TO 1976	78.9		- 1.7		40.0		20.7		22.5
1978 (50 INSTITUTIONS)	129	.5	951	3.9	1,771	7.2	1,234	5.0	4,085
% CHANGE 1976 TO 1978	- 19.9		1.3		12.7		6.3		6.6
COLORADO									
1974 (6 INSTITUTIONS)	15	.9	43	2.7	25	1.6	70	4.4	153
1976 (8 INSTITUTIONS)	12	.5	49	2.0	34	1.4	101	4.1	196
% CHANGE 1974 TO 1976	- 20.0		14.0		36.0		44.3		28.1
1978 (9 INSTITUTIONS)	21	.9	44	1.8	38	1.6	108	4.4	211
% CHANGE 1976 TO 1978	75.0		- 10.2		11.8		6.9		7.7
CONNECTICUT									
1974 (5 INSTITUTIONS)	3	.1	143	6.8	21	1.0	27	1.3	194
1976 (3 INSTITUTIONS)	4	.2	135	6.4	28	1.3	33	1.6	200
% CHANGE 1974 TO 1976	33.3		- 5.6		33.3		22.2		3.1
1978 (5 INSTITUTIONS)	4	.2	120	4.9	31	1.3	85	3.5	240
% CHANGE 1976 TO 1978	.0		- 11.1		10.7		157.6		20.0
DELAWARE									
1974 (0 INSTITUTIONS)	0	.0	0	.0	0	.0	0	.0	0
1976 (0 INSTITUTIONS)	0	.0	0	.0	0	.0	0	.0	0
% CHANGE 1974 TO 1976	.0		.0		.0		.0		.0
1978 (0 INSTITUTIONS)	0	.0	0	.0	0	.0	0	.0	0
% CHANGE 1976 TO 1978	.0		.0		.0		.0		.0
DISTRICT OF COLUMBIA									
1974 (5 INSTITUTIONS)	11	.2	1,216	18.4	64	1.0	109	1.7	1,400
1976 (6 INSTITUTIONS)	8	.1	1,136	17.4	107	1.6	125	1.9	1,376
% CHANGE 1974 TO 1976	- 27.3		- 6.6		67.2		14.7		- 1.7
1978 (8 INSTITUTIONS)	13	.2	1,407	19.9	139	2.0	169	2.4	1,728
% CHANGE 1976 TO 1978	62.5		23.9		29.9		35.2		25.6
FLORIDA									
1974 (6 INSTITUTIONS)	4	.1	116	3.3	2	.1	64	1.8	186
1976 (6 INSTITUTIONS)	10	.2	163	3.3	15	.3	196	4.0	384
% CHANGE 1974 TO 1976	150.0		40.5		650.0		206.3		106.5
1978 (6 INSTITUTIONS)	11	.2	187	3.4	23	.4	286	5.2	507
% CHANGE 1976 TO 1978	10.0		14.7		53.3		45.9		32.0

DIAN TIVE %	BLACK NON-HISPANIC NUMBER	%	ASIAN OR PACIFIC ISLANDER NUMBER	%	HISPANIC NUMBER	%	TOTAL MINORITY NUMBER	%	WHITE NON-HISPANIC NUMBER	%	TOTAL NUMBER
.3	137	3.4	21	.5	19	.5	189	4.7	3,806	95.3	3,995
.1	321	7.5	18	.4	23	.5	368	8.6	3,908	91.4	4,276
	134.3		- 14.3		21.1		94.7		2.7		7.0
.1	407	7.5	19	.3	37	.7	470	8.7	4,959	91.3	5,429
	26.8		5.6		60.9		27.7		26.9		27.0
.0	0	.0	0	.0	0	.0	0	.0	0	.0	0
.2	0	.0	321	71.7	1	.2	323	72.1	125	27.9	448
	.0		100.0		100.0		100.0		100.0		100.0
.0	0	.0	348	75.8	3	.7	351	76.5	108	23.5	459
	.0		8.4		200.0		8.7		- 13.6		2.5
.3	0	.0	5	1.6	1	.3	7	2.2	305	97.8	312
.4	0	.0	0	.0	1	.4	2	.8	251	99.2	253
	.0		- 100.0		.0		- 71.4		- 17.7		- 18.9
.0	1	.4	2	.8	0	.0	3	1.1	259	98.9	262
	100.0		100.0		- 100.0		50.0		3.2		3.6
.1	833	6.1	206	1.5	159	1.2	1,216	8.9	12,460	91.1	13,676
.2	589	4.0	232	1.6	174	1.2	1,025	6.9	13,800	93.1	14,825
	- 29.3		12.6		9.4		- 15.7		10.8		8.4
.2	544	3.5	258	1.7	187	1.2	1,018	6.6	14,366	93.4	15,384
	- 7.6		11.2		7.5		- .7		4.1		3.8
.1	80	2.2	10	.3	23	.6	117	3.2	3,555	96.8	3,672
8.4	168	3.4	22	.4	69	1.4	672	13.6	4,272	86.4	4,944
	110.0		120.0		200.0		474.4		20.2		34.6
.3	153	3.0	37	.7	68	1.3	274	5.4	4,775	94.6	5,049
	8.9		68.2		- 1.4		- 59.2		11.8		2.1
.1	32	1.1	12	.4	11	.4	58	1.9	2,941	98.1	2,999
.3	80	1.5	26	.5	43	.8	166	3.1	5,229	96.9	5,395
	150.0		116.7		290.9		186.2		77.8		79.9
.5	64	1.2	34	.6	47	.9	172	3.1	5,347	96.9	5,519
	- 20.0		30.8		9.3		3.6		2.3		2.3
.5	42	3.1	6	.4	17	1.3	72	5.3	1,276	94.7	1,348
1.9	58	2.9	14	.7	17	.9	127	6.4	1,868	93.6	1,995
	38.1		133.3		.0		76.4		46.4		48.0
.3	42	1.9	14	.6	33	1.5	96	4.4	2,108	95.6	2,204
	- 27.6		.0		94.1		- 24.4		12.8		10.5
.2	77	2.1	14	.4	5	.1	104	2.8	3,629	97.2	3,733
.2	89	2.3	11	.3	6	.2	115	3.0	3,768	97.0	3,883
	15.6		- 21.4		20.0		10.6		3.8		4.0
.2	87	2.1	76	1.8	17	.4	188	4.5	3,995	95.5	4,183
	2.2		590.9		183.3		63.5		6.0		7.7
.2	238	5.4	23	.5	32	.7	303	6.8	4,126	93.2	4,429
.3	220	4.8	15	.3	37	.8	285	6.2	4,287	93.8	4,572
	- 7.6		- 34.8		15.6		- 5.9		3.9		3.2
.2	235	6.4	27	.7	46	1.3	315	8.6	3,357	91.4	3,672
	6.8		80.0		24.3		10.5		- 21.7		- 19.7

TABLE 11 - COMPARISIONS OF FULL-TIME FIRST PROFESSIONAL ENROLLMENT IN INSTITUTIONS OF HIGHER EDUCATION BY RACE AND ETHNICITY STATE AND NATION, 1974, 1976, 1978

	AMERICAN INDIAN ALASKAN NATIVE		BLACK NON-HISPANIC		ASIAN OR PACIFIC ISLANDER		HISPANIC		TOTAL MINORITY		WHITE NON-HISPANIC	
	NUMBER	%	NUMBER	%	NUMBER	%	NUMBER	%	NUMBER	%	NUMBER	%
MAINE												
1974 (2 INSTITUTIONS)	0	.0	2	.7	1	.3	1	.3	4	1.4	290	98.6
1976 (2 INSTITUTIONS)	0	.0	0	.0	0	.0	0	.0	0	.0	338	100.0
% CHANGE 1974 TO 1976	.0		- 100.0		- 100.0		- 100.0		- 100.0		16.6	
1978 (2 INSTITUTIONS)	0	.0	1	.3	0	.0	1	.3	2	.6	318	99.4
% CHANGE 1976 TO 1978	.0		100.0		.0		100.0		100.0		- 5.9	
MARYLAND.												
1974 (5 INSTITUTIONS)	11	.3	198	5.6	32	.9	14	.4	255	7.2	3,302	92.8
1976 (5 INSTITUTIONS)	0	.0	228	6.5	41	1.2	10	.3	279	8.0	3,217	92.0
% CHANGE 1974 TO 1976	- 100.0		15.2		28.1		- 28.6		9.4		- 2.6	-
1978 (3 INSTITUTIONS)	2	.1	202	6.2	75	2.3	26	.8	305	9.3	2,963	90.7
% CHANGE 1976 TO 1978	100.0		- 11.4		82.9		160.0		9.3		- 7.9	-
MASSACHUSETTS												
1974 (18 INSTITUTIONS)	27	.2	559	4.8	227	2.0	108	.9	921	7.9	10,664	92.1
1976 (15 INSTITUTIONS)	37	.4	448	4.5	163	1.6	155	1.6	803	8.0	9,195	92.0
% CHANGE 1974 TO 1976	37.0		- 19.9		- 28.2		43.5		- 12.8		- 13.8	
1978 (17 INSTITUTIONS)	21	.2	399	4.2	153	1.6	176	1.9	749	7.9	8,722	92.1
% CHANGE 1976 TO 1978	- 43.2		- 10.9		- 6.1		13.5		- 6.7		- 5.1	-
MICHIGAN.												
1974 (8 INSTITUTIONS)	20	.2	715	7.0	62	.6	116	1.1	913	9.0	9,236	91.0
1976 (11 INSTITUTIONS)	31	.3	764	7.6	102	1.0	189	1.9	1,086	10.7	9,027	89.3
% CHANGE 1974 TO 1976	55.0		6.9		64.5		62.9		18.9		- 2.3	
1978 (11 INSTITUTIONS)	29	.3	540	5.8	121	1.3	163	1.8	853	9.2	8,400	90.8
% CHANGE 1976 TO 1978	- 6.5		- 29.3		18.6		- 13.8		- 21.5		- 6.9	
MINNESOTA												
1974 (10 INSTITUTIONS)	21	.4	69	1.4	23	.5	29	.6	142	2.9	4,807	97.1
1976 (12 INSTITUTIONS)	16	.3	84	1.4	23	.4	50	.8	173	2.9	5,716	97.1
% CHANGE 1974 TO 1976	- 23.8		21.7		.0		72.4		21.8		18.9	
1978 (11 INSTITUTIONS)	31	.5	80	1.3	33	.5	70	1.2	214	3.5	5,861	96.5
% CHANGE 1976 TO 1978	93.8		- 4.8		43.5		40.0		23.7		2.5	
MISSISSIPPI												
1974 (2 INSTITUTIONS)	0	.0	46	4.5	8	.8	1	.1	55	5.3	978	94.7
1976 (4 INSTITUTIONS)	4	.3	75	4.8	15	1.0	3	.2	97	6.2	1,459	93.8
% CHANGE 1974 TO 1976	100.0		63.0		87.5		200.0		76.4		49.2	
1978 (4 INSTITUTIONS)	2	.1	73	5.1	9	.6	4	.3	88	6.1	1,343	93.9
% CHANGE 1976 TO 1978	- 50.0		- 2.7		- 40.0		33.3		- 9.3		- 8.0	
MISSOURI.												
1974 (12 INSTITUTIONS)	16	.2	279	3.9	46	.6	34	.5	375	5.3	6,712	94.7
1976 (16 INSTITUTIONS)	21	.3	263	3.2	75	.9	31	.4	390	4.7	7,854	95.3
% CHANGE 1974 TO 1976	31.3		- 5.7		63.0		- 8.8		4.0		17.0	
1978 (17 INSTITUTIONS)	30	.3	250	2.7	145	1.6	44	.5	469	5.1	8,648	94.9
% CHANGE 1976 TO 1978	42.9		- 4.9		93.3		41.9		20.3		10.1	
MONTANA												
1974 (1 INSTITUTIONS)	0	.0	0	.0	0	.0	0	.0	0	.0	202	100.0
1976 (1 INSTITUTIONS)	2	.9	0	.0	0	.0	0	.0	2	.9	212	99.1
% CHANGE 1974 TO 1976	100.0		.0		.0		.0		100.0		5.0	
1978 (1 INSTITUTIONS)	0	.0	0	.0	0	.0	0	.0	0	.0	217	100.0
% CHANGE 1976 TO 1978	- 100.0		.0		.0		.0		- 100.0		2.4	
NEBRASKA.												
1974 (4 INSTITUTIONS)	6	.3	44	2.5	27	1.5	12	.7	89	5.0	1,691	95.0
1976 (4 INSTITUTIONS)	10	.4	50	2.0	28	1.1	26	1.0	114	4.5	2,434	95.5
% CHANGE 1974 TO 1976	66.7		13.6		3.7		116.7		28.1		43.9	
1978 (4 INSTITUTIONS)	7	.3	48	1.7	39	1.4	38	1.4	132	4.7	2,656	95.3
% CHANGE 1976 TO 1978	- 30.0		- 4.0		39.3		46.2		15.8		9.1	

E FIRST PROFESSIONAL ENROLLMENT IN INSTITUTIONS OF HIGHER EDUCATION BY RACE AND ETHNICITY:
1976, 1978

DIAN TIVE %	BLACK NON-HISPANIC NUMBER	%	ASIAN OR PACIFIC ISLANDER NUMBER	%	HISPANIC NUMBER	%	TOTAL MINORITY NUMBER	%	WHITE NON-HISPANIC NUMBER	%	TOTAL NUMBER
.0	0	.0	0	.0	0	.0	0	.0	0	.0	0
.0	0	.0	0	.0	0	.0	0	.0	0	.0	0
.0		.0		.0		.0		.0		.0	.0
.0	0	.0	0	.0	0	.0	0	.0	0	.0	0
.0		.0		.0		.0		.0		.0	.0
.0	1	2.8	0	.0	0	.0	1	2.8	35	97.2	36
2.1	13	6.7	3	1.5	6	3.1	26	13.3	169	86.7	195
	1200.0		100.0		100.0		2500.0		382.9		441.7
1.4	9	2.1	11	2.5	11	2.5	37	8.5	400	91.5	437
-	30.8		266.7		83.3		42.3		136.7		124.1
.2	296	9.3	16	.5	78	2.5	395	12.4	2,787	87.6	3,182
.3	306	7.8	44	1.1	120	3.1	480	12.3	3,429	87.7	3,909
	3.4		175.0		53.8		21.5		23.0		22.8
.1	347	8.1	49	1.1	129	3.0	530	12.4	3,738	87.6	4,268
	13.4		11.4		7.5		10.4		9.0		9.2
3.7	11	1.9	2	.3	101	17.1	136	23.1	453	76.9	589
3.4	9	1.5	5	.9	126	21.6	160	27.5	422	72.5	582
-	18.2		150.0		24.8		17.6	-	6.8	-	1.2
3.4	7	1.1	10	1.6	147	24.1	185	30.3	425	69.7	610
-	22.2		100.0		16.7		15.6		.7		4.8
.1	603	4.2	150	1.1	184	1.3	949	6.7	13,304	93.3	14,253
.1	786	4.1	285	1.5	314	1.6	1,408	7.4	17,684	92.6	19,092
	30.3		90.0		70.7		48.4		32.9		34.0
.2	716	3.5	293	1.4	403	2.0	1,448	7.0	19,095	93.0	20,545
	8.9		2.8		28.3		2.8		8.0		7.6
.3	330	8.5	11	.3	12	.3	365	9.4	3,501	90.6	3,866
.7	346	8.2	9	.2	19	.4	403	9.5	3,835	90.5	4,238
	4.8	-	18.2		58.3		10.4		9.5		9.6
.5	367	8.3	24	.5	16	.4	431	9.8	3,989	90.2	4,420
	6.1		166.7	-	15.8		6.9		4.0		4.3
1.4	0	.0	0	.0	0	.0	6	1.4	409	98.6	415
2.0	2	.4	0	.0	0	.0	11	2.4	439	97.6	450
	100.0		.0		.0		83.3		7.3		8.4
2.1	0	.0	2	.4	0	.0	12	2.5	469	97.5	481
-	100.0		100.0		.0		9.1		6.8		6.9
.1	342	4.1	42	.5	34	.4	427	5.1	8,001	94.9	8,428
.1	499	4.8	83	.8	64	.6	660	6.3	9,842	93.7	10,502
	45.9		97.6		88.2		54.6		23.0		24.6
2.3	540	4.9	78	.7	73	.7	945	8.5	10,116	91.5	11,061
	8.2	-	6.0		14.1		43.2		2.8		5.3
2.5	28	1.2	7	.3	21	.9	112	4.9	2,159	95.1	2,271
2.2	30	1.1	15	.5	13	.5	120	4.4	2,638	95.6	2,758
	7.1		114.3	-	38.1		7.1		22.2		21.4
2.4	45	1.5	27	.9	24	.8	168	5.5	2,879	94.5	3,047
	50.0		80.0		84.6		40.0		9.1		10.5

TABLE 11 - COMPARISIONS OF FULL-TIME FIRST PROFESSIONAL ENROLLMENT IN INSTITUTIONS OF HIGHER EDUCAT)
STATE AND NATION, 1974, 1976, 1978

	AMERICAN INDIAN ALASKAN NATIVE		BLACK NON-HISPANIC		ASIAN OR PACIFIC ISLANDER		HISPANIC		TOTAL MINORITY
	NUMBER	%	NUMBER	%	NUMBER	%	NUMBER	%	NUMBER
OREGON.									
1974 (8 INSTITUTIONS)	13	.6	24	1.1	56	2.6	13	.6	106
1976 (8 INSTITUTIONS)	17	.5	28	.8	82	2.4	18	.5	145
% CHANGE 1974 TO 1976	30.8		16.7		46.4		38.5		36.8
1978 (9 INSTITUTIONS)	14	.4	35	1.1	108	3.3	27	.8	184
% CHANGE 1976 TO 1978	- 17.6		25.0		31.7		50.0		26.9
PENNSYLVANIA.									
1974 (21 INSTITUTIONS)	7	.1	363	.1	50	.6	57	.6	477
1976 (29 INSTITUTIONS)	21	.2	498	9.8	139	1.0	145	1.1	803
% CHANGE 1974 TO 1976	200.0		37.2		178.0		154.4		68.3
1978 (29 INSTITUTIONS)	22	.2	539	3.9	147	1.1	131	.9	839
% CHANGE 1976 TO 1978	4.8		8.2		5.8		- 9.7		4.5
RHODE ISLAND.									
1974 (1 INSTITUTIONS)	0	.0	1	.5	2	1.0	0	.0	3
1976 (1 INSTITUTIONS)	0	.0	7	2.8	7	2.8	1	.4	15
% CHANGE 1974 TO 1976	.0		600.0		250.0		100.0		400.0
1978 (1 INSTITUTIONS)	0	.0	14	5.6	11	4.4	5	2.0	30
% CHANGE 1976 TO 1978	.0		100.0		57.1		400.0		100.0
SOUTH CAROLINA.									
1974 (4 INSTITUTIONS)	0	.0	59	3.1	1	.1	1	.1	61
1976 (6 INSTITUTIONS)	2	.1	80	4.4	2	.1	1	.1	85
% CHANGE 1974 TO 1976	100.0		35.6		100.0		.0		39.3
1978 (7 INSTITUTIONS)	2	.1	88	4.2	4	.2	4	.2	98
% CHANGE 1976 TO 1978	.0		10.0		100.0		300.0		15.3
SOUTH DAKOTA.									
1974 (2 INSTITUTIONS)	3	.7	0	.0	0	.0	1	.2	.4
1976 (2 INSTITUTIONS)	0	.0	0	.0	1	.2	1	.2	2
% CHANGE 1974 TO 1976	- 100.0		.0		100.0		.0		- 50.0
1978 (2 INSTITUTIONS)	1	.2	1	.2	1	.2	1	.2	4
% CHANGE 1976 TO 1978	100.0		100.0		.0		.0		100.0
TENNESSEE									
1974 (7 INSTITUTIONS)	3	.1	583	13.2	15	.3	9	.2	610
1976 (9 INSTITUTIONS)	10	.2	641	13.6	19	.4	25	.5	695
% CHANGE 1974 TO 1976	233.3		9.9		26.7		177.8		13.9
1978 (9 INSTITUTIONS)	9	.2	700	13.3	22	.4	25	.5	756
% CHANGE 1976 TO 1978	- 10.0		9.2		15.8		.0		8.8
TEXAS									
1974 (22 INSTITUTIONS)	33	.3	347	3.6	65	.7	418	.4	863
1976 (26 INSTITUTIONS)	47	.4	341	3.0	96	.8	635	5.8	1,119
% CHANGE 1974 TO 1976	42.4		- 1.7		47.7		51.9		29.7
1978 (24 INSTITUTIONS)	42	.3	447	3.6	132	1.1	809	6.6	1,430
% CHANGE 1976 TO 1978	- 10.6		31.1		37.5		27.4		27.8
UTAH.									
1974 (3 INSTITUTIONS)	8	.7	7	.6	13	1.2	33	3.0	61
1976 (2 INSTITUTIONS)	8	.7	6	.5	13	1.1	27	2.2	54
% CHANGE 1974 TO 1976	.0		- 14.3		.0		- 18.2		- 11.5
1978 (2 INSTITUTIONS)	5	.4	10	.8	14	1.2	24	2.0	53
% CHANGE 1976 TO 1978	- 37.5		66.7		7.7		- 11.1		- 1.9
VERMONT									
1974 (2 INSTITUTIONS)	0	.0	3	.9	2	.6	0	.0	8
1976 (2 INSTITUTIONS)	0	.0	2	.3	1	.2	3	.5	
% CHANGE 1974 TO 1976	.0		- 33.3		- 50.0		100.0		20.0
1978 (2 INSTITUTIONS)	0	.0	0	.0	3	.5	0	.0	3
% CHANGE 1976 TO 1978	.0		- 100.0		200.0		- 100.0		- 50.0

E FIRST PROFESSIONAL ENROLLMENT IN INSTITUTIONS OF HIGHER EDUCATION BY RACE AND ETHNICITY:
1976, 1978

DIAN TIVE	BLACK NON-HISPANIC		ASIAN OR PACIFIC ISLANDER		HISPANIC		TOTAL MINORITY		WHITE NON-HISPANIC		TOTAL
%	NUMBER	%	NUMBER	%	NUMBER	%	NUMBER	%	NUMBER	%	NUMBER
.0	119	3.2	6	.2	3	.1	128	3.4	3,636	96.6	3,764
.0	160	3.9	22	.5	9	.2	191	4.7	3,893	95.3	4,084
	34.5		266.7		200.0		49.2		7.1		8.5
.0	165	3.8	35	.8	13	.3	215	5.0	4,083	95.0	4,298
	3.1		59.1		44.4		12.6		4.9		5.2
.5	59	1.8	83	2.5	31	.9	188	5.7	3,134	94.3	3,322
.7	42	1.3	83	2.6	47	1.5	195	6.2	2,955	93.8	3,150
	28.8		.0		51.6		3.7	-	5.7	-	5.2
.6	34	1.0	83	2.6	50	1.5	186	5.7	3,054	94.3	3,240
	19.0		.0		6.4	-	4.6		3.4		2.9
.0	9	1.0	3	.3	2	.2	14	1.5	891	98.5	905
.0	18	1.7	6	.6	0	.0	24	2.2	1,047	97.8	1,071
	100.0		100.0	-	100.0		71.4		17.5		18.3
.2	13	1.0	2	.2	3	.2	21	1.7	1,218	98.3	1,239
-	27.8	-	66.7		100.0	-	12.5		16.3		15.7
.2	91	3.0	11	.4	28	.9	137	4.5	2,893	95.5	3,030
.4	91	2.9	21	.7	37	1.2	162	5.2	2,982	94.8	3,144
	.0		90.9		32.1		18.2		3.1		3.8
.5	96	2.9	28	.8	72	2.1	212	6.3	3,144	93.7	3,356
	5.5		33.3		94.6		30.9		5.4		6.7
.0	2	.7	3	1.0	0	.0	5	1.7	281	98.3	286
.5	1	.5	0	.0	0	.0	2	1.0	206	99.0	208
-	50.0	-	100.0		.0	-	60.0	-	26.7	-	27.3
.0	0	.0	1	.5	2	.9	3	1.4	210	98.6	213
-	100.0		100.0		100.0	.	50.0		1.9		2.4
.3	9,208	4.9	2,521	1.3	2,906	1.5	15,161	8.1	173,143	91.9	188,304
.5	10,029	4.6	3,827	1.8	4,104	1.9	19,125	8.8	198,063	91.2	217,188
	8.9		51.8		41.2		26.1		14.4		15.3
.4	10,260	4.5	4,515	2.0	4,845	2.1	20,595	9.0	207,912	91.0	228,507
	2.3		18.0		18.0		7.7		5.0		5.2
.0	0	.0	0	.0	0	.0	0	.0	0	.0	0
4.8	0	.0	0	.0	1,340	94.6	1,408	99.4	8	.6	1,416
	.0		.0		100.0		100.0		100.0		100.0
.0	0	.0	0	.0	1,430	100.0	1,430	100.0	0	.0	1,430
	.0		.0		6.7		1.6	-	100.0		1.0
.0	0	.0	0	.0	0	.0	0	.0	0	.0	0
4.8	0	.0	0	.0	1,340	94.6	1,408	99.4	8	.6	1,416
	.0		.0		100.0		100.0		100.0		100.0
.0	0	.0	0	.0	1,430	100.0	1,430	100.0	0	.0	1,430
	.0		.0		.0		1.6	-	100.0		1.0
.3	9,208	4.9	2,521	1.3	2,906	1.5	15,161	8.1	173,143	91.9	188,304
.6	10,029	4.6	3,827	1.8	5,444	2.5	20,533	9.4	198,071	90.6	218,604
	8.9		51.8		87.3		35.4		14.4		16.1
.4	10,260	4.5	4,515	2.0	6,275	2.7	22,025	9.6	207,912	90.4	229,937
	2.3		18.0		18.0		7.3		5.0		5.2

TABLE 12 - COMPARISIONS OF FULL-TIME ENROLLMENT IN PUBLICLY CONTROLLED INSTITUTIONS OF HIGHER EDUCATION BY RACE AND ETHNI
STATE AND NATION, 1974, 1976, 1978

	AMERICAN INDIAN ALASKAN NATIVE		BLACK NON-HISPANIC		ASIAN OR PACIFIC ISLANDER		HISPANIC		TOTAL MINORITY		WHITE NON-HISPANIC	
	NUMBER	%	NUMBER	%	NUMBER	%	NUMBER	%	NUMBER	%	NUMBER	%
ALABAMA												
1974 (33 INSTITUTIONS)	143	.2	16,276	19.9	407	.5	264	.3	17,090	20.9	64,542	79.1
1976 (36 INSTITUTIONS)	106	.1	17,517	19.0	202	.2	202	.2	18,027	19.5	74,223	80.5
% CHANGE 1974 TO 1976	- 25.9		7.6		- 50.4		- 23.5		5.5		15.0	
1978 (36 INSTITUTIONS)	109	.1	18,731	20.0	291	.3	298	.3	19,429	20.7	74,206	79.3
% CHANGE 1976 TO 1978	2.8		6.9		44.1		47.5		7.8		.0	
ALASKA												
1974 (0 INSTITUTIONS)	0	.0	0	.0	0	.0	0	.0	0	.0	0	.0
1976 (7 INSTITUTIONS)	287	7.1	179	4.4	58	1.4	74	1.8	598	14.8	3,445	85.2
% CHANGE 1974 TO 1976	100.0		100.0		100.0		100.0		100.0		100.0	
1978 (12 INSTITUTIONS)	772	12.8	237	3.9	120	2.0	60	1.0	1,189	19.6	4,863	80.4
% CHANGE 1976 TO 1978	169.0		32.4		106.9		- 18.9		98.8		41.2	
ARIZONA												
1974 (14 INSTITUTIONS)	1,277	1.9	1,574	2.3	530	.8	5,431	8.0	8,812	13.0	59,036	87.0
1976 (17 INSTITUTIONS)	1,997	2.5	2,142	2.7	614	.8	6,418	8.1	11,171	14.0	68,537	86.0
% CHANGE 1974 TO 1976	56.4		36.1		15.8		18.2		26.8		16.1	
1978 (17 INSTITUTIONS)	2,071	2.7	2,146	2.8	745	1.0	5,773	7.5	10,735	13.9	66,658	86.1
% CHANGE 1976 TO 1978	3.7		.2		21.3		- 10.0		- 3.9		- 2.7	
ARKANSAS												
1974 (13 INSTITUTIONS)	295	.9	4,157	12.4	45	.1	75	.2	4,572	13.6	28,992	86.4
1976 (16 INSTITUTIONS)	155	.4	7,235	17.4	211	.5	69	.2	7,670	18.5	33,858	81.5
% CHANGE 1974 TO 1976	- 47.5		74.0		368.9		- 8.0		67.8		16.8	
1978 (19 INSTITUTIONS)	270	.6	7,048	16.4	230	.5	170	.4	7,718	18.0	35,243	82.0
% CHANGE 1976 TO 1978	74.2		- 2.6		9.0		146.4		.6		4.1	
CALIFORNIA												
1974 (129 INSTITUTIONS)	6,326	1.0	48,016	7.3	30,086	4.6	49,551	7.5	133,979	20.4	523,216	79.6
1976 (133 INSTITUTIONS)	8,649	1.4	52,178	8.5	39,107	6.4	57,091	9.3	157,025	25.6	456,789	74.4
% CHANGE 1974 TO 1976	36.7		8.7		30.0		15.2		17.2		- 12.7	
1978 (136 INSTITUTIONS)	7,151	1.3	51,601	9.1	46,010	8.1	54,270	9.6	159,032	28.1	405,935	71.9
% CHANGE 1976 TO 1978	- 17.3		- 1.1		17.7		- 4.9		1.3		- 11.1	
COLORADO												
1974 (27 INSTITUTIONS)	646	.8	2,463	3.0	916	1.1	4,861	5.9	8,886	10.7	73,933	89.3
1976 (27 INSTITUTIONS)	695	.8	3,021	3.3	1,073	1.2	6,032	6.6	10,821	11.9	80,444	88.1
% CHANGE 1974 TO 1976	7.6		22.7		17.1		24.1		21.8		8.8	
1978 (27 INSTITUTIONS)	724	.8	2,709	3.1	1,269	1.5	5,280	6.1	9,982	11.6	76,133	88.4
% CHANGE 1976 TO 1978	4.2		- 10.3		18.3		- 12.5		- 7.8		- 5.4	
CONNECTICUT												
1974 (27 INSTITUTIONS)	38	.1	2,341	4.5	169	.3	609	1.2	3,157	6.1	48,600	93.9
1976 (22 INSTITUTIONS)	83	.2	2,492	4.9	181	.4	727	1.4	3,483	6.8	47,760	93.2
% CHANGE 1974 TO 1976	118.4		6.5		7.1		19.4		10.3		- 1.7	
1978 (22 INSTITUTIONS)	115	.2	2,356	4.9	292	.6	703	1.5	3,466	7.3	44,317	92.7
% CHANGE 1976 TO 1978	38.6		- 5.5		61.3		- 3.3		- .5		- 7.2	
DELAWARE												
1974 (5 INSTITUTIONS)	5	.0	1,985	12.6	27	.2	71	.5	2,088	13.2	13,675	86.8
1976 (6 INSTITUTIONS)	17	.1	2,204	12.4	102	.6	109	.6	2,432	13.7	15,299	86.3
% CHANGE 1974 TO 1976	240.0		11.0		277.8		53.5		16.5		11.9	
1978 (6 INSTITUTIONS)	22	.1	2,061	12.2	66	.4	73	.4	2,222	13.1	14,681	86.9
% CHANGE 1976 TO 1978	29.4		- 6.5		- 35.3		- 33.0		- 8.6		- 4.0	
DISTRICT OF COLUMBIA												
1974 (3 INSTITUTIONS)	7	.1	6,736	90.1	17	.2	66	.9	6,826	91.4	646	8.6
1976 (3 INSTITUTIONS)	27	.5	5,176	94.9	76	1.4	78	1.4	5,357	98.3	95	1.7
% CHANGE 1974 TO 1976	285.7		- 23.2		347.1		18.2		- 21.5		- 85.3	
1978 (1 INSTITUTIONS)	67	1.8	3,364	86.6	158	4.2	41	1.1	3,630	95.6	166	4.4
% CHANGE 1976 TO 1978	148.1		- 35.0		107.9		- 47.4		- 32.2		74.7	

ULL-TIME ENROLLMENT IN PUBLICLY CONTROLLED INSTITUTIONS OF HIGHER EDUCATION BY RACE AND ETHNICITY:
1974, 1976, 1978

ICAN INDIAN SKAN NATIVE		BLACK NON-HISPANIC		ASIAN OR PACIFIC ISLANDER		HISPANIC		TOTAL MINORITY		WHITE NON-HISPANIC		TOTAL
NUMBER	%	NUMBER	%	NUMBER	%	NUMBER	%	NUMBER	%	NUMBER	%	NUMBER
199	.1	15,219	10.3	574	.4	2,768	1.9	18,760	12.6	129,644	87.4	148,404
413	.3	21,141	13.6	1,395	.9	7,368	4.7	30,317	19.5	125,461	80.5	155,778
107.5		38.9		143.0		166.2		61.6		- 3.2		5.0
308	.2	20,259	13.2	1,155	.8	9,872	6.5	31,594	20.7	121,384	79.3	152,978
25.4		- 4.2		- 17.2		34.0		4.2		- 3.2		- 1.8
206	.3	10,261	13.0	322	.4	239	.3	11,028	13.9	68,112	86.1	79,140
280	.3	15,386	17.2	380	.4	379	.4	16,425	18.3	73,112	81.7	89,537
35.9		49.9		18.0		58.6		48.9		7.3		13.1
126	.1	15,052	17.3	367	.4	399	.5	15,944	18.3	70,963	81.7	86,907
55.0		- 2.2		- 3.4		5.3		- 2.9		- 2.9		- 2.9
0	.0	0	.0	0	.0	0	.0	0	.0	0	.0	0
47	.2	222	.8	21,402	73.6	733	2.5	22,404	77.0	6,681	23.0	29,085
100.0		100.0		100.0		100.0		100.0		100.0		100.0
58	.2	209	.8	19,031	72.2	745	2.8	20,043	76.0	6,319	24.0	26,362
23.4		- 5.9		- 11.1		1.6		- 10.5		- 5.4		- 9.4
156	.8	347	1.8	279	1.4	408	2.1	1,190	6.1	18,254	93.9	19,444
194	1.0	157	.8	282	1.4	251	1.3	884	4.5	18,736	95.5	19,620
24.4		- 54.8		1.1		- 38.5		- 25.7		2.6		.9
160	.8	145	.7	265	1.3	182	.9	752	3.8	19,076	96.2	19,828
17.5		- 7.6		- 6.0		- 27.5		- 14.9		1.8		1.1
504	.2	28,627	13.2	1,712	.8	2,744	1.3	33,587	15.5	183,105	84.5	216,692
573	.3	31,378	14.2	2,276	1.0	4,131	1.9	38,358	17.4	182,467	82.6	220,825
13.7		9.6		32.9		50.5		14.2		- .3		1.9
662	.3	31,371	14.6	3,331	1.5	4,767	2.2	40,131	18.7	174,902	81.3	215,033
15.5		.0		46.4		15.4		4.6		- 4.1		- 2.6
202	.2	4,634	4.8	544	.6	821	.8	6,201	6.4	50,756	93.6	96,957
234	.2	6,630	6.2	503	.5	754	.7	8,121	7.6	98,569	92.4	106,690
15.8		43.1		- 7.5		- 8.2		31.0		8.6		10.0
210		6,061	5.9	594	.6	886	.9	7,751	7.5	95,157	92.5	102,908
10.3		- 8.6		18.1		17.5		- 4.6		- 3.5		- 3.5
110	.2	1,375	2.1	224	.3	214	.3	1,923	3.0	62,622	97.0	64,545
203	.3	1,295	2.0	298	.5	305	.5	2,101	3.2	63,194	96.8	65,295
84.5		- 5.8		33.0		42.5		9.3		.9		1.2
211	.3	1,245	1.9	375	.6	340	.5	2,171	3.3	63,518	96.7	65,689
3.9		- 3.9		25.8		11.5		3.3		.5		.6
1,393	2.1	2,198	3.3	363	.5	830	1.2	4,784	7.2	61,936	92.8	66,720
1,446	2.2	2,881	4.4	317	.5	886	1.3	5,530	8.4	60,684	91.6	66,214
3.8		31.1		- 12.7		6.7		15.6		- 2.0		- .8
1,191	1.8	2,911	4.4	390	.6	921	1.4	5,413	8.2	60,415	91.8	65,828
17.6		1.0		23.0		4.0		- 2.1		.4		.6
188	.3	4,354	6.8	259	.4	119	.2	4,920	7.7	58,862	92.3	63,782
88	.1	6,344	8.9	183	.3	188	.3	6,803	9.5	64,802	90.5	71,605
53.2		45.7		- 29.3		58.0		38.3		10.1		12.3
210	.3	5,449	7.9	512	.7	209	.3	6,376	9.2	62,663	90.8	69,039
38.6		- 14.2		179.8		11.2		- 6.3		- 3.3		- 3.6

	AMERICAN INDIAN ALASKAN NATIVE		BLACK NON-HISPANIC		ASIAN OR PACIFIC ISLANDER		HISPANIC		TOTAL MINORITY		WHITE NON-HISPANIC	
	NUMBER	%	NUMBER	%	NUMBER	%	NUMBER	%	NUMBER	%	NUMBER	%
LOUISIANA												
1974 (19 INSTITUTIONS)	146	.2	19,746	21.2	195	.2	441	.5	20,528	22.1	72,420	77.9
1976 (20 INSTITUTIONS)	121	.1	23,519	25.2	290	.3	808	.9	24,738	26.6	68,421	73.4
% CHANGE 1974 TO 1976	- 17.1		19.1		48.7		83.2		20.5		- 5.5	
1978 (20 INSTITUTIONS)	145	.2	22,738	25.4	357	.4	749	.8	23,989	26.8	65,404	73.2
% CHANGE 1976 TO 1978	19.8		- 3.3		23.1		- 7.3		- 3.0		- 4.4	
MAINE												
1974 (10 INSTITUTIONS)	69	.4	38	.2	37	.2	19	.1	163	.9	17,276	99.1
1976 (10 INSTITUTIONS)	92	.5	52	.3	47	.2	26	.1	217	1.1	19,822	98.9
% CHANGE 1974 TO 1976	33.3		36.8		27.0		36.8		33.1		14.7	
1978 (10 INSTITUTIONS)	98	.5	43	.2	43	.2	28	.1	212	1.1	18,636	98.9
% CHANGE 1976 TO 1978	6.5		- 17.3		- 8.5		7.7		- 2.3		- 6.0	
MARYLAND												
1974 (29 INSTITUTIONS)	382	.5	14,268	17.7	933	1.2	537	.7	16,120	20.0	64,315	80.0
1976 (30 INSTITUTIONS)	375	.4	19,635	21.8	840	.9	554	.6	21,404	23.7	68,801	76.3
% CHANGE 1974 TO 1976	- 1.8		37.6		- 10.0		3.2		32.8		7.0	
1978 (32 INSTITUTIONS)	234	.3	18,733	21.5	1,068	1.2	822	.9	20,857	23.9	66,254	76.1
% CHANGE 1976 TO 1978	- 37.6		- 4.6		27.1		48.4		- 2.6		- 3.7	
MASSACHUSETTS												
1974 (35 INSTITUTIONS)	333	.3	2,989	2.7	609	.6	844	.8	4,775	4.3	105,546	95.7
1976 (33 INSTITUTIONS)	358	.4	3,152	3.2	537	.5	1,206	1.2	5,253	5.3	93,300	94.7
% CHANGE 1974 TO 1976	7.5		5.5		- 11.8		42.9		10.0		- 11.6	
1978 (33 INSTITUTIONS)	252	.3	3,552	3.4	710	.7	1,320	1.4	5,834	6.1	90,490	93.9
% CHANGE 1976 TO 1978	- 29.6		12.7		32.2		9.5		11.1		- 3.0	
MICHIGAN												
1974 (47 INSTITUTIONS)	889	.4	18,166	7.9	1,146	.5	1,807	.8	22,008	9.6	206,711	90.4
1976 (45 INSTITUTIONS)	1,287	.6	26,261	11.5	1,488	.7	2,104	.9	31,140	13.6	197,782	86.4
% CHANGE 1974 TO 1976	44.8		44.6		29.8		16.4		41.5		- 4.3	
1978 (45 INSTITUTIONS)	1,132	.5	21,321	9.8	1,920	.9	2,453	1.1	26,826	12.3	191,553	87.7
% CHANGE 1976 TO 1978	- 12.0		- 18.8		29.0		16.6		- 13.9		- 3.1	
MINNESOTA												
1974 (31 INSTITUTIONS)	686	.8	1,305	1.5	876	1.0	330	.4	3,197	3.7	83,329	96.3
1976 (29 INSTITUTIONS)	789	.9	1,403	1.5	879	1.0	383	.4	3,454	3.8	87,809	96.2
% CHANGE 1974 TO 1976	15.0		7.5		.3		16.1		8.0		5.4	
1978 (30 INSTITUTIONS)	653	.7	1,300	1.4	799	.9	477	.5	3,229	3.5	88,549	96.5
% CHANGE 1976 TO 1978	- 17.2		- 7.3		- 9.1		24.5		- 6.5		.8	
MISSISSIPPI												
1974 (27 INSTITUTIONS)	88	.2	16,534	29.2	198	.3	48	.1	16,868	29.7	39,832	70.3
1976 (27 INSTITUTIONS)	145	.2	20,216	31.0	199	.3	53	.1	20,613	31.6	44,698	68.4
% CHANGE 1974 TO 1976	64.8		22.3		.5		10.4		22.2		12.2	
1978 (27 INSTITUTIONS)	106	.2	20,209	31.0	205	.3	76	.1	20,596	31.6	44,514	68.4
% CHANGE 1976 TO 1978	- 26.9		.0		3.0		43.4		- .1		- .4	
MISSOURI												
1974 (27 INSTITUTIONS)	305	.3	6,843	7.1	248	.3	477	.5	7,873	8.2	87,955	91.8
1976 (28 INSTITUTIONS)	331	.3	8,920	9.2	413	.4	435	.5	10,099	10.5	86,343	89.5
% CHANGE 1974 TO 1976	8.5		30.4		66.5		- 8.8		28.3		- 1.8	
1978 (28 INSTITUTIONS)	284	.3	7,623	8.3	591	.6	493	.5	8,991	9.8	82,313	90.2
% CHANGE 1976 TO 1978	- 14.2		- 14.5		43.1		13.3		- 11.0		- 4.7	
MONTANA												
1974 (9 INSTITUTIONS)	678	3.3	89	.4	93	.4	59	.3	919	4.4	19,893	95.6
1976 (9 INSTITUTIONS)	761	3.5	87	.4	102	.5	87	.4	1,037	4.8	20,461	95.2
% CHANGE 1974 TO 1976	12.2		- 2.2		9.7		47.5		12.8		2.9	
1978 (9 INSTITUTIONS)	497	2.3	59	.3	56	.3	61	.3	673	3.1	21,001	96.9
% CHANGE 1976 TO 1978	- 34.7		- 32.2		- 45.1		- 29.9		- 35.1		2.6	

ICAN INDIAN SKAN NATIVE		BLACK NON-HISPANIC		ASIAN OR PACIFIC ISLANDER		HISPANIC		TOTAL MINORITY		WHITE NON-HISPANIC		TOTAL
NUMBER	%	NUMBER	%	NUMBER	%	NUMBER	%	NUMBER	%	NUMBER	%	NUMBER
156	.5	726	2.1	128	.4	304	.9	1,314	8	33,343	96.2	34,657
142	.3	1,133	2.7	154	.4	316	.8	1,745	3.12	40,059	95.8	41,804
9.0		56.1		20.3		3.9		32.8		20.1		20.6
149	.4	1,045	2.6	183	.5	359	.9	1,736	4.3	38,260	95.7	39,996
4.9		- 7.8		18.8		13.6		- .5		- 4.5		- 4.3
374	1.8	920	4.4	249	1.2	784	3.	2,327	11.1	18,608	88.9	20,935
108	1.1	554	5.4	122	1.2	174	1.7	958	9.4	9,210	90.6	10,168
71.1		- 39.8		- 51.0		- 77.8		- 58.8		- 50.5		- 51.4
129	1.3	579	5.7	181	1.8	279	2.7	1,168	11.5	9,003	88.5	10,171
19.4		4.5		48.4		60.3		21.9		- 2.2		.0
90	.6	63	.4	54	.3	29	.2	236	1.5	15,680	98.5	15,916
49	.3	54	.3	37	.2	52	.3	192	1.1	16,838	98.9	17,030
45.6		- 14.3		- 31.5		79.3		- 18.6		7.4		7.0
38	.2	38	.2	40	.2	46	.3	162	1.0	16,795	99.0	16,957
22.4		- 29.6		8.1		- 11.5		- 15.6		.3		- .4
251	.2	12,295	11.2	755	.7	3,939	3.6	17,240	15.7	92,856	84.3	110,096
358	.3	14,110	12.1	1,033	.9	4,431	3.8	19,932	17.1	96,898	82.9	116,830
42.6		14.8		36.8		12.5		15.6		4.4		6.1
297	.3	15,009	12.7	1,226	1.0	5,849	5.0	22,381	19.0	95,401	81.0	117,782
17.0		6.4		18.7		32.0		12.3		- 1.5		.8
866	2.7	686	2.2	218	.7	6,351	20.1	8,121	25.7	23,535	74.3	31,656
1,112	3.3	852	2.5	202	.6	8,308	24.7	10,474	31.2	23,138	68.8	33,612
28.4		24.2		- 7.3		30.8		29.0		- 1.7		6.2
1,219	3.7	825	2.5	255	.8	8,256	25.3	10,555	32.3	22,081	67.7	32,636
9.6		- 3.2		26.2		- .6		.8		- 4.6		- 2.9
1,006	.3	38,645	11.2	5,140	1.5	17,720	5.2	62,511	18.2	281,156	81.8	343,667
2,419	.7	41,966	12.4	6,730	2.0	22,245	6.6	73,360	21.7	264,505	78.3	337,865
140.5		8.6		30.9		25.5		17.4		- 5.9		- 1.7
2,338	.7	47,238	14.1	7,670	2.3	23,773	7.1	81,019	24.2	253,249	75.8	334,268
3.3		12.6		14.0		6.9		10.4		- 4.3		- 1.1
885	.7	23,623	19.5	198	.2	297	.2	25,003	20.7	95,950	79.3	120,953
1,166	.9	28,323	21.5	266	.2	381	.3	30,136	22.9	101,612	77.1	131,748
31.8		19.9		34.3		28.3		20.5		5.9		8.9
1,174	.9	29,430	22.0	510	.4	491	.4	31,605	23.6	102,345	76.4	133,950
.7		3.9		91.7		28.9		4.9		.7		1.7
538	2 4	87	.4	31	.1	16	.1	672	3.0	21,632	97.0	22,304
523	213	100	.4	44	.2	51	.2	718	3.1	22,160	96.9	22,878
2.8		14.9		41.9		218.8		6.8		2.4		2.6
668	2.6	131	.5	82	.3	33	.1	914	3.6	24,295	96.4	25,209
27.7		31.0		86.4		- 35.3		27.3		9.6		10.2
251	.1	15,763	8.3	628	.3	670	.4	17,312	9.2	171,814	90.8	189,126
342	.2	21,592	10.2	859	.4	973	.5	23,766	11.2	188,130	88.8	211,896
36.3		37.0		36.8		45.2		37.3		9.5		12.0
347	.2	18,979	9.3	929	.5	1,062	.5	21,317	10.4	182,687	89.6	204,004
1.5		- 12.1		8.1		9.1		- 10.3		- 2.9		- 3.7

TABLE 12 - COMPARISIONS OF FULL-TIME ENROLLMENT IN PUBLICLY CONTROLLED INSTITUTIONS OF HIGHER EDUCATION BY RACE AND ETHN
STATE AND NATION, 1974, 1976, 1978

	AMERICAN INDIAN ALASKAN NATIVE		BLACK NON-HISPANIC		ASIAN OR PACIFIC ISLANDER		HISPANIC		TOTAL MINORITY		WHITE NON-HISPANIC	
	NUMBER	%	NUMBER	%	NUMBER	%	NUMBER	%	NUMBER	%	NUMBER	%
OKLAHOMA												
1974 (28 INSTITUTIONS)	3,139	4.2	4,348	5.9	269	.4	362	.5	8,118	11.0	65,870	89.0
1976 (29 INSTITUTIONS)	3,656	4.6	5,847	7.4	760	1.0	498	.6	10,761	13.5	68,673	86.5
% CHANGE 1974 TO 1976	16.5		34.5		182.5		37.6		32.6		4.3	
1978 (29 INSTITUTIONS)	3,287	4.4	5,291	7.0	623	.8	614	.8	9,815	13.0	65,742	87.0
% CHANGE 1976 TO 1978	- 10.1		- 9.5		- 18.0		23.3		- 8.8		- 4.3	
OREGON												
1974 (22 INSTITUTIONS)	984	1.3	843	1.1	1,194	1.6	529	.7	3,550	4.7	71,657	95.3
1976 (21 INSTITUTIONS)	760	1.1	946	1.3	1,227	1.7	650	.9	3,583	5.0	67,814	95.0
% CHANGE 1974 TO 1976	- 22.8		12.2		2.8		22.9		.9		- 5.4	
1978 (21 INSTITUTIONS)	891	1.3	886	1.3	1,673	2.5	723	1.1	4,173	6.1	63,969	93.9
% CHANGE 1976 TO 1978	17.2		- 6.3		36.3		11.2		16.5		- 5.7	
PENNSYLVANIA												
1974 (63 INSTITUTIONS)	282	.2	11,998	6.9	432	.2	859	.5	13,571	7.8	159,343	92.2
1976 (62 INSTITUTIONS)	354	.2	15,140	8.2	1,671	.9	3,249	1.8	20,414	11.0	165,180	89.0
% CHANGE 1974 TO 1976	25.5		26.2		286.8		278.2		50.4		3.7	
1978 (61 INSTITUTIONS)	318	.2	16,096	9.0	1,326	.7	1,412	.8	19,152	10.7	159,156	89.3
% CHANGE 1976 TO 1978	- 10.2		6.3		- 20.6		- 56.5		- 6.2		- 3.6	
RHODE ISLAND												
1974 (3 INSTITUTIONS)	48	.3	230	1.4	105	.6	99	.6	482	2.9	16,337	97.1
1976 (3 INSTITUTIONS)	49	.3	391	2.2	80	.5	62	.4	582	3.3	16,919	96.7
% CHANGE 1974 TO 1976	2.1		70.0		- 23.8		- 37.4		20.7		3.6	
1978 (3 INSTITUTIONS)	56	.3	441	2.5	102	.6	106	.6	705	3.9	17,243	96.1
% CHANGE 1976 TO 1978	14.3		12.8		27.5		71.0		21.1		1.9	
SOUTH CAROLINA												
1974 (30 INSTITUTIONS)	45	.1	9,752	16.7	82	.1	96	.2	9,975	17.0	48,551	83.0
1976 (32 INSTITUTIONS)	117	.2	13,259	20.2	124	.2	111	.2	13,611	20.8	51,953	79.2
% CHANGE 1974 TO 1976	160.0		36.0		51.2		15.6		36.5		- 7.0	
1978 (33 INSTITUTIONS)	83	.1	12,925	19.4	329	.5	188	.3	13,525	20.3	53,251	79.7
% CHANGE 1976 TO 1978	- 29.1		- 2.5		165.3		69.4		- .6		2.5	
SOUTH DAKOTA												
1974 (7 INSTITUTIONS)	364	2.2	57	.3	20	.1	15	.1	456	2.8	15,882	97.2
1976 (7 INSTITUTIONS)	404	2.4	39	.2	34	.2	25	.1	502	3.0	16,450	97.0
% CHANGE 1974 TO 1976	11.0		- 31.6		70.0		66.7		10.1		3.6	
1978 (7 INSTITUTIONS)	346	1.9	64	.4	53	.3	23	.1	486	2.7	17,470	97.3
% CHANGE 1976 TO 1978	- 14.4		64.1		55.9		- 8.0		- 3.2		6.2	
TENNESSEE												
1974 (23 INSTITUTIONS)	163	.2	9,721	12.0	154	.2	153	.2	10,191	12.6	70,934	87.4
1976 (23 INSTITUTIONS)	148	.2	14,184	16.1	234	.3	148	.2	14,714	16.7	73,410	83.3
% CHANGE 1974 TO 1976	- 9.2		45.9		51.9		- 3.3		44.4		3.5	
1978 (24 INSTITUTIONS)	152	.2	15,424	17.7	418	.5	275	.3	16,269	18.6	71,023	81.4
% CHANGE 1976 TO 1978	2.7		8.7		78.6		85.8		10.6		- 3.3	
TEXAS												
1974 (86 INSTITUTIONS)	1,447	.5	23,453	8.1	1,661	.6	31,299	10.9	57,860	20.1	229,945	79.9
1976 (92 INSTITUTIONS)	1,455	.4	34,566	10.7	1,991	.6	39,176	12.1	77,188	23.8	246,704	76.2
% CHANGE 1974 TO 1976	.6		47.4		19.9		25.2		33.4		7.3	
1978 (94 INSTITUTIONS)	1,047	.3	28,867	9.3	2,822	.9	40,065	12.8	72,801	23.3	239,148	76.7
% CHANGE 1976 TO 1978	- 28.0		- 16.5		41.7		2.3		- 5.7		- 3.1	
UTAH												
1974 (9 INSTITUTIONS)	383	1.0	325	.8	463	1.2	708	1.8	1,879	4.8	37,137	95.2
1976 (9 INSTITUTIONS)	455	1.2	344	.9	559	1.5	753	2.0	2,111	5.6	35,369	94.4
% CHANGE 1974 TO 1976	18.8		5.8		20.7		6.4		12.3		- 4.8	
1978 (9 INSTITUTIONS)	421	1.2	339	1.0	533	1.5	607	1.7	1,900	5.4	33,576	94.6
% CHANGE 1976 TO 1978	- 7.5		- 1.5		- 4.7		- 19.4		- 10.0		- 5.1	

FULL-TIME ENROLLMENT IN PUBLICLY CONTROLLED INSTITUTIONS OF HIGHER EDUCATION BY RACE AND ETHNICITY: , 1974, 1976, 1978

American Indian / Alaskan Native		Black Non-Hispanic		Asian or Pacific Islander		Hispanic		Total Minority		White Non-Hispanic		Total
NUMBER	%	NUMBER	%	NUMBER	%	NUMBER	%	NUMBER	%	NUMBER	%	NUMBER
42	.3	128	1.1	13	.1	50	.4	233	1.9	11,799	98.1	12,032
42	.3	88	.7	7	.1	50	.4	187	1.5	12,125	98.5	12,312
.0		- 31.3		- 46.2		.0		- 19.7		2.8		2.3
25	.2	54	.5	23	.2	34	.3	136	1.1	11,770	98.9	11,906
40.5		- 38.6		228.6		- 32.0		- 27.3		- 2.9		- 3.3
164	.2	11,981	13.1	399	.4	280	.3	12,824	14.0	78,746	86.0	91,570
146	.1	18,055	15.4	783	.7	428	.4	19,412	16.6	97,485	83.4	116,897
11.0		50.7		96.2		52.9		51.4		23.8		27.7
224	.2	18,378	15.3	1,358	1.1	589	.5	20,549	17.1	99,415	82.9	119,964
53.4		1.8		73.4		37.6		5.9		2.0		2.6
1,943	1.6	4,535	3.8	2,919	2.4	1,629	1.4	11,026	9.2	108,879	90.8	119,905
1,729	1.4	4,234	3.5	3,349	2.8	1,778	1.5	11,090	9.2	109,211	90.8	120,301
11.0		- 6.6		14.7		9.1		.6		.3		.3
1,754	1.5	3,689	3.1	3,918	3.3	1,761	1.5	11,122	9.4	106,755	90.6	117,877
1.4		- 12.9		17.0		- 1.0		.3		- 2.2		- 2.0
97	.3	1,743	4.5	62	.2	89	.2	1,991	5.2	36,572	94.8	38,563
79	.2	2,175	5.4	326	.8	102	.3	2,682	6.7	37,635	93.3	40,317
18.6		24.8		425.8		14.6		34.7		2.9		4.5
94	.2	1,890	4.8	173	.4	78	.2	2,235	5.6	37,411	94.4	39,646
19.0		- 13.1		- 46.9		- 23.5		- 16.7		.6		- 1.7
708	.6	3,400	2.7	396	.3	768	.6	5,272	4.2	121,382	95.8	126,654
927	.7	4,750	3.4	610	.4	963	.7	7,250	5.3	130,588	94.7	137,838
30.9		39.7		54.0		25.4		37.5		7.6		8.8
764	.6	3,675	2.8	817	.6	1,037	.8	6,293	4.7	126,483	95.3	132,776
17.6		- 22.6		33.9		7.7		- 13.2		- 3.1		- 3.7
122	1.2	156	1.5	200	1.9	264	2.5	742	7.0	9,863	93.0	10,605
109	.9	170	1.5	70	.6	229	2.0	578	5.0	10,923	95.0	11,501
10.7		9.0		- 65.0		- 13.3		- 22.1		10.7		8.4
125	1.1	166	1.5	68	.6	186	1.6	545	4.8	10,757	95.2	11,302
14.7		- 2.4		- 2.9		- 18.8		- 5.7		- 1.5		- 1.7
29,619	.6	406,019	8.7	56,579	1.2	140,943	3.0	633,160	13.6	4,020,679	86.4	4,653,839
36,402	.7	503,695	10.3	94,727	1.9	176,604	3.6	811,428	16.6	4,064,582	83.4	4,876,010
22.9		24.1		67.4		25.3		28.2		1.1		4.8
33,784	.7	489,988	10.4	106,262	2.2	179,314	3.8	809,348	17.1	3,922,598	82.9	4,731,946
7.2		- 2.7		12.2		12.2		- .3		- 3.5		- 3.0
0	.0	0	.0	0	.0	0	.0	0	.0	0		0
0	.0	0	.0	0	.0	360	97.8	360	97.8	8	2.2	368
.0		.0				100.0		100.0		100.0		100.0
0	.0	0	.0	367	97.6	0	.0	367	97.6	9	2.4	376
.0		.0		1.9		.0		1.9		12.5		2.2
0	.0	44	10.2	0	.0	109	25.2	153	35.3	280	64.7	433
0	.0	44	10.2	0	.0	109	25.2	153	35.3	280	64.7	433
.0		100.0				100.0		100.0		100.0		100.0
0	.0	44	10.5	0	.0	132	31.4	176	41.9	244	58.1	420
.0		.0				21.1		15.0		- 12.9		- 3.0

TABLE 12 - COMPARISIONS OF FULL-TIME ENROLLMENT IN PUBLICLY CONTROLLED INSTITUTIONS OF HIGHER EDUCATION BY RACE AND ETHN STATE AND NATION, 1974, 1976, 1978

	AMERICAN INDIAN ALASKAN NATIVE		BLACK NON-HISPANIC		ASIAN OR PACIFIC ISLANDER		HISPANIC		TOTAL MINORITY		WHITE NON-HISPANIC	
	NUMBER	%	NUMBER	%	NUMBER	%	NUMBER	%	NUMBER	%	NUMBER	%
GUAM.												
1974 (0 INSTITUTIONS)	0	.0	0	.0	0	.0	0	.0	0	.0	0	.0
1976 (1 INSTITUTIONS)	21	1.3	0	.0	1,198	72.6	23	1.4	1,242	75.3	408	24.7
% CHANGE 1974 TO 1976	100.0		.0		100.0		100.0		100.0		100.0	
1978 (1 INSTITUTIONS)	7	.5	12	.8	1,163	81.1	36	2.5	1,218	84.9	216	15.1
% CHANGE 1976 TO 1978	- 66.7		100.0		- 2.9		56.5		- 1.9		- 47.1	
PUERTO RICO												
1974 (0 INSTITUTIONS)	0	.0	0	.0	0	.0	0	.0	0	.0	0	.0
1976 (7 INSTITUTIONS)	194	.5	0	.0	0	.0	41,310	99.5	41,504	100.0	14	.0
% CHANGE 1974 TO 1976	100.0		.0		.0		100.0		100.0		100.0	
1978 (9 INSTITUTIONS)	0	.0	10	.0	1	.0	39,268	100.0	39,279	100.0	0	.0
% CHANGE 1976 TO 1978	- 100.0		100.0		100.0		- 4.9		- 5.4		- 100.0	
TRUST TERRITORY												
1974 (0 INSTITUTIONS)	0	.0	0	.0	0	.0	0	.0	0	.0	0	.0
1976 (1 INSTITUTIONS)	0	.0	0	.0	259	100.0	0	.0	259	100.0	0	.0
% CHANGE 1974 TO 1976	.0		.0		100.0		.0		100.0		.0	
1978 (1 INSTITUTIONS)	0	.0	0	.0	248	100.0	0	.0	248	100.0	0	.0
% CHANGE 1976 TO 1978	.0		.0		4.2		.0		4.2		.0	
VIRGIN ISLANDS.												
1974 (0 INSTITUTIONS)	0	.0	0	.0	0	.0	0	.0	0	.0	0	.0
1976 (1 INSTITUTIONS)	0	.0	366	83.8	1	.2	19	4.3	386	88.3	51	11.7
% CHANGE 1974 TO 1976	.0		100.0		100.0		100.0		100.0		100.0	
1978 (1 INSTITUTIONS)	0	.0	311	79.7	1	.3	27	6.9	339	86.9	51	13.1
% CHANGE 1976 TO 1978	.0		- 15.0		.0		42.1		- 12.2		.0	
OUTLYING AREAS.												
1974 (0 INSTITUTIONS)	0	.0	0	.0	0	.0	0	.0	0	.0	0	.0
1976 (12 INSTITUTIONS)	215	.5	410	.9	1,818	4.1	41,461	92.8	43,904	98.3	761	1.7
% CHANGE 1974 TO 1976	100.0		100.0		100.0		100.0		100.0		100.0	
1978 (14 INSTITUTIONS)	7	.0	377	.9	1,780	4.2	39,463	93.6	41,627	98.8	520	1.2
% CHANGE 1976 TO 1978	- 96.7		- 8.0		- 2.1		- 2.1		- 5.2		- 31.7	
NATION, TOTAL												
1974 (1410 INSTITUTIONS)	29,619	.6	406,019	8.7	56,579	1.2	140,943	3.0	633,160	13.6	4,020,679	86.4
1976 (1454 INSTITUTIONS)	36,617	.7	504,105	10.2	96,545	2.0	218,065	4.4	855,332	17.4	4,065,343	82.6
% CHANGE 1974 TO 1976	23.6		24.2		70.6		54.7		35.1		1.1	
1978 (1476 INSTITUTIONS)	33,791	.7	490,365	10.3	108,042	2.3	218,777	4.6	850,975	17.8	3,923,118	82.2
% CHANGE 1976 TO 1978	- 7.7		- 2.7		11.9		11.9		- .5		- 3.5	

FULL-TIME ENROLLMENT IN PRIVATELY CONTROLLED INSTITUTIONS OF HIGHER EDUCATION BY RACE AND ETHNICITY:
, 1974, 1976, 1978

RICAN INDIAN ASKAN NATIVE		BLACK NON-HISPANIC		ASIAN OR PACIFIC ISLANDER		HISPANIC		TOTAL MINORITY		WHITE NON-HISPANIC		TOTAL
NUMBER	%	NUMBER	%	NUMBER	%	NUMBER	%	NUMBER	%	NUMBER	%	NUMBER
13	.1	6,215	47.8	13	.1	41	.3	6,282	48.3	6,732	51.7	13,014
8	.0	8,800	53.5	19	.1	34	.2	8,861	53.9	7,578	46.1	16,439
38.5		41.6		46.2	-	17.1		41.1		12.6	-	26.3
9	.1	9,572	53.7	89	.5	86	.5	9,756	54.8	8,060	45.2	17,816
12.5		8.8		368.4		152.9		10.1		6.4		8.4
0	.0	0	.0	0	.0	0	.0	0	.0	0	.0	0
158	48.2	1	.3	114	34.8	0	.0	273	83.2	55	16.8	328
100.0		100.0		100.0		.0		100.0		100.0		100.0
120	57.1	4	1.9	1	.5	0	.0	125	59.5	85	40.5	210
24.1		300.0	-	99.1		.0	-	54.2		54.5	-	36.0
274	6.0	172	3.8	56	1.2	210	4	712	15.6	3,846	84.4	4,558
163	4.0	103	2.5	36	.9	154	3i8	456	11.1	3,646	88.9	4,102
40.5	-	40.1	-	35.7	-	26.7	-	36.0	-	5.2	-	10.0
134	3.3	107	2.6	49	1.2	133	3.3	423	10.4	3,637	89.6	4,060
17.8		3.9		36.1	-	13.6	-	7.2		.2	-	1.0
5	.1	1,495	18.7	7	.1	7	.1	1,514	19.0	6,469	81.0	7,983
14	.2	1,411	16.8	30	.4	18	.2	1,473	17.5	6,936	82.5	8,409
180.0	-	5.6		328.6		157.1	-	2.7		7.2		5.3
26	.3	1,561	17.3	94	1.0	25	.3	1,706	18.9	7,334	81.1	9,040
85.7		10.6		213.3		38.9		15.8		5.7		7.5
551	.5	5,489	5.2	4,960	4.7	4,881	4.6	15,881	15.1	89,206	84.9	105,087
784	.7	6,373	5.9	6,564	6.1	6,317	5.9	20,038	18.7	87,126	81.3	107,164
42.3		16.1		32.3		29.4		26.2	-	-2.3		2.0
614	.5	6,529	5.7	7,355	6.5	6,921	6.1	21,419	18.8	92,536	81.2	113,955
21.7		2.4		12.1		9.6		6.9		6.2		6.3
63	.6	257	2.3	88	.8	242	2.2	650	5.9	10,368	94.1	11,018
59	.6	239	2.3	86	.8	261	2.6	645	6.3	9,555	93.7	10,200
6.3	-	7.0	-	2.3		7.9	-	.8	-	7.8	-	7.4
95	.9	306	3.0	144	1.4	300	2.9	845	8.3	9,336	91.7	10,181
61.0		28.0		67.4		14.9		31.0	-	2.3	-	.2
37	.1	1,742	5.2	366	1.1	478	1.4	2,623	7.9	30,647	92.1	33,270
34	.1	1,660	5.0	327	1.0	504	1.5	2,525	7.6	30,918	92.4	33,443
8.1	-	4.7	-	10.7		5.4	-	3.7		.9		.5
40	.1	1,656	4.9	488	1.4	769	2.3	2,953	8.7	30,982	91.3	33,935
17.6	-	.2		49.2		52.6		17.0		.2		1.5
10	.4	182	7.4	8	.3	12	.5	212	8.7	2,237	91.3	2,449
0	.0	332	11.0	6	.2	6	.2	344	11.4	2,676	88.6	3,020
100.0		82.4	-	25.0	-	50.0	-	62.3		19.6		23.3
3	.1	286	11.0	1	.0	7	.3	297	11.4	2,306	88.6	2,603
100.0	-	13.9	-	83.3	-	16.7	-	13.7	-	13.8	-	13.8
68	.2	8,761	23.1	370	1.0	525	1.4	9,724	25.7	28,148	74.3	37,872
119	.3	8,835	24.4	674	1.9	756	2.1	10,384	28.7	25,764	71.3	36,148
75.0		.8		82.2		44.0		6.8	-	8.5	-	4.6
79	.2	10,237	27.9	607	1.7	742	2.0	11,665	31.8	25,064	68.2	36,729
33.6		15.9	-	9.9	-	1.9	-	12.3	-	2.7		1.6

257

TABLE 13 - COMPARISIONS OF FULL-TIME ENROLLMENT IN PRIVATELY CONTROLLED INSTITUTIONS OF HIGHER EDUCATION BY RACE AND ETHN: STATE AND NATION, 1974, 1976, 1978

	AMERICAN INDIAN ALASKAN NATIVE		BLACK NON-HISPANIC		ASIAN OR PACIFIC ISLANDER		HISPANIC		TOTAL MINORITY		WHITE NON-HISPANIC	
	NUMBER	%	NUMBER	%	NUMBER	%	NUMBER	%	NUMBER	%	NUMBER	%
FLORIDA												
1974 (31 INSTITUTIONS)	100	.3	3,572	10.0	183	.5	1,556	4.4	5,411	15.2	30,161	84.8
1976 (36 INSTITUTIONS)	100	.2	5,430	12.3	161	.4	2,971	6.7	8,662	19.6	35,427	80.4
% CHANGE 1974 TO 1976	.0		52.0		- 12.0		90.9		60.1		17.5	
1978 (40 INSTITUTIONS)	311	.7	5,981	12.6	402	.8	3,536	7.4	10,230	21.5	37,289	78.5
% CHANGE 1976 TO 1978	211.0		10.1		149.7		19.0		18.1		5.3	
GEORGIA												
1974 (32 INSTITUTIONS)	25	.1	7,233	29.8	90	.4	96	.4	7,444	30.7	16,806	69.3
1976 (32 INSTITUTIONS)	21	.1	8,643	31.9	118	.4	104	.4	8,886	32.8	18,233	67.2
% CHANGE 1974 TO 1976	- 16.0		19.5		31.1		8.3		19.4		8.5	
1978 (38 INSTITUTIONS)	38	.1	9,937	32.3	116	.4	221	.7	10,312	33.5	20,495	66.5
% CHANGE 1976 TO 1978	81.0		15.0		- 1.7		112.5		16.0		12.4	
HAWAII.												
1974 (0 INSTITUTIONS)	0	.0	0	.0	0	.0	0	.0	0	.0	0	.0
1976 (3 INSTITUTIONS)	7	.6	30	2.8	436	40.0	12	1.1	485	44.5	605	55.5
% CHANGE 1974 TO 1976	100.0		100.0		100.0		100.0		100.0		100.0	
1978 (3 INSTITUTIONS)	11	.7	116	7.3	618	38.9	73	4.6	818	51.4	772	48.6
% CHANGE 1976 TO 1978	57.1		286.7		41.7		508.3		68.7		27.6	
IDAHO												
1974 (3 INSTITUTIONS)	33	.5	23	.3	25	.4	72	1.1	153	2.3	6,548	97.7
1976 (3 INSTITUTIONS)	33	.5	20	.3	82	1.2	49	.7	184	2.8	6,503	97.2
% CHANGE 1974 TO 1976	.0		- 13.0		228.0		- 31.9		20.3		- .7	
1978 (3 INSTITUTIONS)	26	.4	11	.2	55	.8	43	.6	135	1.9	6,791	98.1
% CHANGE 1976 TO 1978	- 21.2		- 45.0		- 32.9		- 12.2		- 26.6		4.4	
ILLINOIS.												
1974 (78 INSTITUTIONS)	137	.2	7,644	8.8	970	1.1	1,266	1.5	10,017	11.6	76,613	88.4
1976 (88 INSTITUTIONS)	131	.1	10,892	11.4	1,487	1.6	2,224	2.3	14,734	15.4	80,830	84.6
% CHANGE 1974 TO 1976	- 4.4		42.5		53.3		75.7		47.1		5.5	
1978 (90 INSTITUTIONS)	195	.2	10,898	11.5	1,690	1.8	2,319	2.5	15,102	16.0	79,425	84.0
% CHANGE 1976 TO 1978	48.9		.1		13.7		4.3		2.5		1.7	
INDIANA												
1974 (40 INSTITUTIONS)	42	.1	1,231	3.1	137	.3	371	.9	1,781	4.5	38,076	95.5
1976 (41 INSTITUTIONS)	453	1.1	1,288	3.1	176	.4	411	1.0	2,328	5.6	39,502	94.4
% CHANGE 1974 TO 1976	978.6		4.6		28.5		10.8		30.7		3.7	
1978 (42 INSTITUTIONS)	56	.1	1,482	3.6	240	.6	510	1.2	2,288	5.5	39,398	94.5
% CHANGE 1976 TO 1978	- 87.6		15.1		36.4		24.1		- 1.7		- .3	
IOWA.												
1974 (38 INSTITUTIONS)	52	.2	939	3.1	97	.3	101	.3	1,189	3.9	29,132	96.1
1976 (39 INSTITUTIONS)	73	.2	982	3.3	205	.7	148	.5	1,408	4.7	28,298	95.3
% CHANGE 1974 TO 1976	40.4		4.6		111.3		46.5		18.4		- 2.9	
1978 (40 INSTITUTIONS)	94	.3	1,079	3.3	204	.6	184	.6	1,561	4.8	30,702	95.2
% CHANGE 1976 TO 1978	28.8		9.9		- .5		24.3		10.9		8.5	
KANSAS.												
1974 (22 INSTITUTIONS)	47	.4	701	6.6	12	.1	152	1.4	912	8.6	9,676	91.4
1976 (23 INSTITUTIONS)	71	.6	919	8.1	104	.9	187	1.7	1,281	11.3	10,020	88.7
% CHANGE 1974 TO 1976	51.1		31.1		766.7		23.0		40.5		3.6	
1978 (23 INSTITUTIONS)	64	.6	840	7.5	63	.6	206	1.8	1,173	10.5	9,967	89.5
% CHANGE 1976 TO 1978	- 9.9		- 8.6		- 39.4		10.2		- 8.4		- .5	
KENTUCKY.												
1974 (26 INSTITUTIONS)	4	.0	577	4.2	22	.2	25	.2	628	4.6	13,057	95.4
1976 (29 INSTITUTIONS)	168	1.1	957	6.3	24	.2	28	.2	1,177	7.7	14,101	92.3
% CHANGE 1974 TO 1976	4100.0		65.9		9.1		12.0		87.4		8.0	
1978 (33 INSTITUTIONS)	14	.1	1,140	6.7	42	.2	44	.3	1,240	7.3	15,779	92.7
% CHANGE 1976 TO 1978	- 91.7		19.1		75.0		57.1		5.4		11.9	

ULL-TIME ENROLLMENT IN PRIVATELY CONTROLLED INSTITUTIONS OF HIGHER EDUCATION BY RACE AND ETHNICITY:
1974, 1976, 1978

:ICAN INDIAN :SKAN NATIVE		BLACK NON-HISPANIC		ASIAN OR PACIFIC ISLANDER		HISPANIC		TOTAL MINORITY		WHITE NON-HISPANIC		TOTAL
NUMBER	%	NUMBER	%	NUMBER	%	NUMBER	%	NUMBER	%	NUMBER	%	NUMBER
29	.2	3,292	23.2	87	.6	249	1.8	3,657	25.8	10,535	74.2	14,192
50	.3	3,309	20.5	266	1.7	492	3.1	4,117	25.5	12,002	74.5	16,119
72.4		.5		205.7		97.6		12.6		13.9		13.6
49	.3	3,447	22.4	153	1.0	605	3.9	4,254	27.6	11,134	72.4	15,388
2.0		4.2		- 42.5		23.0		3.3		- 7.2		- 4.5
5	.1	194	2.3	30	.4	71	.9	300	3.6	8,013	96.4	8,313
10	.1	171	1.9	30	.3	35	.4	246	2.7	8,725	97.3	8,971
100.0		- 11.9		.0		- 50.7		- 18.0		8.9		7.9
15	.2	105	1.2	45	.5	42	.5	207	2.3	8,850	97.7	9,057
50.0		- 38.6		50.0		20.0		- 15.9		1.4		1.0
16	.1	1,355	8.7	150	1.0	151	1.0	1,672	10.7	13,956	89.3	15,628
22	.1	1,612	9.6	199	1.2	146	.9	1,979	11.8	14,755	88.2	16,734
37.5		19.0		32.7		- 3.3		18.4		5.7		7.1
21	.1	981	6.2	314	2.0	178	1.1	1,494	9.5	14,232	90.5	15,726
4.5		- 39.1		57.8		21.9		- 24.5		- 3.5		- 6.0
177	.1	6,954	5.1	1,512	1.1	1,428	1.0	10,071	7.4	126,053	92.6	136,124
657	.5	6,835	5.1	1,819	1.4	1,938	1.4	11,249	8.4	123,211	91.6	134,460
271.2		- 1.7		20.3		35.7		11.7		- 2.3		- 1.2
767	.5	7,041	4.8	2,865	2.0	2,368	1.6	13,041	8.9	133,751	91.1	146,792
16.7		3.0		57.5		22.2		15.9		8.6		9.2
109	.3	4,931	12.7	251	.6	315	.8	5,606	14.4	33,315	85.6	38,921
146	.3	6,101	14.2	462	1.1	418	1.0	7,127	16.6	35,785	83.4	42,912
33.9		23.7		84.1		32.7		27.1		7.4		10.3
109	.3	5,309	12.5	406	1.0	482	1.1	6,306	14.9	36,078	85.1	42,384
25.3		- 13.0		- 12.1		15.3		- 11.5		.8		- 1.2
147	.5	783	2.5	79	.3	121	.4	1,130	3.6	30,004	96.4	31,134
155	.4	655	1.9	131	.4	681	2.0	1,622	4.7	32,880	95.3	34,502
5.4		- 16.3		65.8		462.8		43.5		9.6		10.8
146	.4	513	1.4	185	.5	175	.5	1,019	2.9	34,406	97.1	35,425
5.8		- 21.7		41.2		- 74.3		- 37.2		4.6		2.7
9	.1	2,465	35.2	7	.1	22	.3	2,503	35.8	4,495	64.2	6,998
8	.1	3,070	42.0	12	.2	18	.2	3,108	42.5	4,198	57.5	7,306
11.1		24.5		71.4		- 18.2		24.2		- 6.6		4.4
8	.1	3,391	45.6	17	.2	17	.2	3,433	46.1	4,008	53.9	7,441
.0		10.5		41.7		- 5.6		10.5		- 4.5		1.8
78	.2	2,448	6.1	228	.6	240	.6	2,994	7.5	37,084	92.5	40,078
104	.2	2,703	6.1	381	.9	332	.7	3,520	7.9	40,907	92.1	44,427
33.3		10.4		67.1		38.3		17.6		10.3		10.9
120	.3	3,248	7.1	590	1.3	427	.9	4,385	9.6	41,387	90.4	45,772
15.4		20.2		54.9		28.6		24.6		1.2		3.0
110	5.6	73	3.7	10	.5	37	1.9	230	11.8	1,720	88.2	1,950
135	6.4	60	2.9	5	.2	17	.8	217	10.4	1,879	89.6	2,096
22.7		- 17.8		- 50.0		- 54.1		- 5.7		9.2		7.5
64	2.7	27	1.2	25	1.1	20	.9	136	5.8	2,211	94.2	2,347
52.6		- 55.0		400.0		17.6		- 37.3		17.7		12.0

TABLE 13 - COMPARISIONS OF FULL-TIME ENROLLMENT IN PRIVATELY CONTROLLED INSTITUTIONS OF HIGHER EDUCATION BY RACE AND ETHN STATE AND NATION, 1974, 1976, 1978

	AMERICAN INDIAN ALASKAN NATIVE		BLACK NON-HISPANIC		ASIAN OR PACIFIC ISLANDER		HISPANIC		TOTAL MINORITY		WHITE NON-HISPANIC	
	NUMBER	%	NUMBER	%	NUMBER	%	NUMBER	%	NUMBER	%	NUMBER	%
NEBRASKA.												
1974 (14 INSTITUTIONS)	37	.3	436	3.6	66	.5	125	1.0	664	5.5	11,488	94.5
1976 (13 INSTITUTIONS)	30	.3	454	4.1	129	1.2	100	.9	713	6.4	10,375	93.6
% CHANGE 1974 TO 1976	- 18.9		4.1		95.5		- 20.0		7.4		- 9.7	
1978 (14 INSTITUTIONS)	38	.3	411	3.6	147	1.3	118	1.0	714	6.3	10,628	93.7
% CHANGE 1976 TO 1978	26.7		- 9.5		14.0		18.0		.1		2.4	
NEVADA.												
1974 (0 INSTITUTIONS)	0	.0	0	.0	0	.0	0	.0	0	.0	0	.0
1976 (1 INSTITUTIONS)	0	.0	1	.8	0	.0	1	.8	2	1.6	124	98.4
% CHANGE 1974 TO 1976	.0		100.0		.0		100.0		100.0		100.0	
1978 (1 INSTITUTIONS)	1	.8	1	.8	1	.8	0	.0	3	2.4	124	97.6
% CHANGE 1976 TO 1978	100.0		.0		100.0		- 100.0		50.0		.0	
NEW HAMPSHIRE												
1974 (14 INSTITUTIONS)	39	.3	433	3.1	25	.2	127	.9	624	4.5	13,273	95.5
1976 (14 INSTITUTIONS)	34	.3	482	3.6	60	.4	260	1.9	836	6.3	12,501	93.7
% CHANGE 1974 TO 1976	- 12.8		11.3		140.0		104.7		34.0		- 5.8	
1978 (14 INSTITUTIONS)	45	.3	547	3.9	88	.6	186	1.3	866	6.2	13,023	93.8
% CHANGE 1976 TO 1978	32.4		13.5		46.7		- 28.5		3.6		4.2	
NEW JERSEY.												
1974 (31 INSTITUTIONS)	80	.2	2,705	6.7	459	1.1	1,042	2.6	4,286	10.7	35,911	89.3
1976 (34 INSTITUTIONS)	49	.1	3,503	8.4	436	1.0	1,503	3.6	5,491	13.1	36,403	86.9
% CHANGE 1974 TO 1976	- 38.8		29.5		- 5.0		44.2		28.1		1.4	
1978 (32 INSTITUTIONS)	65	.2	3,260	7.8	449	1.1	1,506	3.6	5,280	12.6	36,556	87.4
% CHANGE 1976 TO 1978	32.7		- 6.9		3.0		.2		3.8		.4	
NEW MEXICO.												
1974 (3 INSTITUTIONS)	135	6.0	96	4.2	21	.9	764	33.7	1,016	44.9	1,249	55.1
1976 (3 INSTITUTIONS)	140	7.6	72	3.9	16	.9	668	36.3	896	48.7	944	51.3
% CHANGE 1974 TO 1976	3.7		- 25.0		- 23.8		- 12.6		- 11.8		- 24.4	
1978 (3 INSTITUTIONS)	150	8.6	58	3.3	27	1.5	550	31.5	785	45.0	959	55.0
% CHANGE 1976 TO 1978	7.1		- 19.4		68.8		- 17.7		- 12.4		1.6	
NEW YORK.												
1974 (184 INSTITUTIONS)	340	.2	12,986	5.9	3,170	1.4	5,149	2.3	21,645	9.9	197,893	90.1
1976 (202 INSTITUTIONS)	457	.2	17,196	6.9	3,865	1.5	6,630	2.7	28,148	11.3	221,673	88.7
% CHANGE 1974 TO 1976	34.4		32.4		21.9		28.8		30.0		12.0	
1978 (204 INSTITUTIONS)	537	.2	19,505	7.5	4,908	1.9	9,507	3.6	34,457	13.2	227,290	86.8
% CHANGE 1976 TO 1978	17.5		13.4		27.0		43.4		22.4		2.5	
NORTH CAROLINA.												
1974 (41 INSTITUTIONS)	63	.1	8,697	19.6	86	.2	150	.3	8,996	20.3	35,399	79.7
1976 (43 INSTITUTIONS)	101	.2	8,995	18.9	124	.3	156	.3	9,376	19.7	38,193	80.3
% CHANGE 1974 TO 1976	60.3		3.4		44.2		4.0		4.2		7.9	
1978 (53 INSTITUTIONS)	104	.2	10,515	20.7	246	.5	202	.4	11,067	21.8	39,674	78.2
% CHANGE 1976 TO 1978	3.0		16.9		98.4		29.5		18.0		3.9	
NORTH DAKOTA.												
1974 (2 INSTITUTIONS)	82	7.0	9	.8	1	.1	3	.3	95	8.1	1,076	91.9
1976 (4 INSTITUTIONS)	68	3.9	22	1.3	7	.4	7	.4	104	6.0	1,638	94.0
% CHANGE 1974 TO 1976	- 17.1		144.4		600.0		133.3		9.5		52.2	
1978 (5 INSTITUTIONS)	144	8.3	20	1.2	3	.2	10	.6	177	10.2	1,561	89.8
% CHANGE 1976 TO 1978	111.8		- 9.1		- 57.1		42.9		70.2		- 4.7	
OHIO.												
1974 (72 INSTITUTIONS)	183	.3	6,906	9.6	375	.5	478	.7	7,942	11.1	63,796	88.9
1976 (70 INSTITUTIONS)	238	.3	8,226	10.7	691	.9	756	1.0	9,911	12.9	66,831	87.1
% CHANGE 1974 TO 1976	30.1		19.1		84.3		58.2		24.8		4.8	
1978 (71 INSTITUTIONS)	702	1.0	7,749	10.5	410	.6	692	.9	9,553	12.9	64,310	87.1
% CHANGE 1976 TO 1978	195.0		- 5.8		- 40.7		- 8.5		- 3.6		- 3.8	

FULL-TIME ENROLLMENT IN PRIVATELY CONTROLLED INSTITUTIONS OF HIGHER EDUCATION BY RACE AND ETHNICITY: 1974, 1976, 1978

AMERICAN INDIAN/ALASKAN NATIVE		BLACK NON-HISPANIC		ASIAN OR PACIFIC ISLANDER		HISPANIC		TOTAL MINORITY		WHITE NON-HISPANIC		TOTAL
NUMBER	%	NUMBER	%	NUMBER	%	NUMBER	%	NUMBER	%	NUMBER	%	NUMBER
434	2.9	665	4.5	52	.4	103	.7	1,254	8.5	13,486	91.5	14,740
536	3.7	643	4.4	115	.8	129	.9	1,423	9.8	13,081	90.2	14,504
23.5		- 3.3		121.2		25.2		13.5		- 3.0		- 1.6
345	2.4	592	4.2	104	.7	90	.6	1,131	7.9	13,121	92.1	14,252
35.6		- 7.9		- 9.6		- 30.2		- 20.5		.3		- 1.7
51	.5	322	2.9	319	2.9	77	.7	769	6.9	10,376	93.1	11,145
88	.7	302	2.4	411	3.2	213	1.7	1,014	8.0	11,660	92.0	12,674
72.5		- 6.2		28.8		176.6		31.9		12.4		13.7
85	.7	252	2.0	487	3.8	152	1.2	976	7.7	11,738	92.3	12,714
3.4		- 16.6		18.5		- 28.6		- 3.7		.7		.3
81	.1	4,733	3.8	584	.5	671	.5	6,069	4.8	119,663	95.2	125,732
90	.1	5,467	4.2	858	.7	753	.6	7,168	5.5	123,502	94.5	130,670
11.1		15.5		46.9		12.2		18.1		3.2		3.9
121	.1	5,748	4.2	1,200	.9	882	.6	7,951	5.8	128,980	94.2	136,931
34.4		-5.1		39.9		17.1		10.9		4.4		4.8
17	.1	954	4.5	119	.6	136	.6	1,226	5.8	19,863	94.2	21,089
42	.2	1,088	5.0	178	.8	202	.9	1,510	7.0	20,119	93.0	21,629
147.1		14.0		49.6		48.5		23.2		1.3		2.6
15	.1	1,054	4.9	247	1.1	151	.7	1,467	6.8	20,162	93.2	21,629
64.3		- 3.1		38.8		- 25.2		- 2.8		.2		.0
13	.1	4,932	29.4	6	.0	25	.1	4,976	29.7	11,801	70.3	16,777
4	.0	6,575	36.0	12	.1	36	.2	6,627	36.2	11,662	63.8	18,289
69.2		33.3		100.0		44.0		33.2		- 1.2		9.0
6	.0	7,044	36.2	35	.2	32	.2	7,117	36.5	12,358	63.5	19,475
50.0		7.1		191.7		- 11.1		7.4		6.0		6.5
124	2.5	82	1.6	9	.2	17	.3	232	4.6	4,821	95.4	5,053
174	2.4	85	1.2	31	.4	18	.2	308	4.2	7,014	95.8	7,322
40.3		3.7		244.4		5.9		32.8		45.5		44.9
305	4.4	250	3.6	33	.5	261	3.8	849	12.2	6,082	87.8	6,931
75.3		194.1		6.5		1350.0		175.6		- 13.3		- 5.3
31	.1	5,221	15.5	74	.2	110	.3	5,436	16.2	28,219	83.8	33,655
42	.1	6,140	16.8	135	.4	127	.3	6,444	17.6	30,207	82.4	36,651
35.5		17.6		82.4		15.5		18.5		7.0		8.9
31	.1	7,331	18.3	96	.2	180	.4	7,638	19.1	32,409	80.9	40,047
26.2		19.4		- 28.9		41.7		18.5		7.3		9.3
144	.3	5,762	10.6	262	.5	3,442	6.3	9,610	17.7	44,817	82.3	54,427
188	.3	6,882	11.5	374	.6	3,824	6.4	11,268	18.8	48,619	81.2	59,887
30.6		19.4		42.7		11.1		17.3		8.5		10.0
155	.3	5,958	10.0	447	.7	4,161	7.0	10,721	17.9	49,055	82.1	59,776
17.6		- 13.4		19.5		8.8		- 4.9		.9		- .2
334	1.5	27	.1	102	.5	58	.3	521	2.3	21,761	97.7	22,282
307	1.3	36	.2	438	1.9	35	.2	816	3.5	22,399	96.5	23,215
8.1		33.3		329.4		- 39.7		56.6		2.9		4.2
350	1.5	42	.2	611	2.5	108	.4	1,111	4.6	23,021	95.4	24,132
14.0		16.7		39.5		208.6		36.2		2.8		4.0

TABLE 13 - COMPARISIONS OF FULL-TIME ENROLLMENT IN PRIVATELY CONTROLLED INSTITUTIONS OF HIGHER EDUCATION BY RACE AND ETHN STATE AND NATION, 1974, 1976, 1978

	AMERICAN INDIAN ALASKAN NATIVE		BLACK NON-HISPANIC		ASIAN OR PACIFIC ISLANDER		HISPANIC		TOTAL MINORITY		WHITE NON-HISPANIC	
	NUMBER	%	NUMBER	%	NUMBER	%	NUMBER	%	NUMBER	%	NUMBER	%
VERMONT												
1974 (15 INSTITUTIONS)	29	.3	182	1.9	108	1.1	61	.6	380	4.0	9,167	96.0
1976 (17 INSTITUTIONS)	28	.3	304	2.9	30	.3	102	1.0	464	4.5	9,846	95.5
% CHANGE 1974 TO 1976	- 3.4		67.0		- 72.2		67.2		22.1		7.4	
1978 (15 INSTITUTIONS)	17	.2	259	2.6	39	.4	108	1.1	423	4.2	9,634	95.8
% CHANGE 1976 TO 1978	- 39.3		- 14.8		30.0		5.9		- 8.8		- 2.2	
VIRGINIA												
1974 (33 INSTITUTIONS)	28	.1	4,882	20.8	37	.2	83	.4	5,030	21.4	18,449	78.6
1976 (33 INSTITUTIONS)	29	.1	5,330	20.7	42	.2	90	.3	5,491	21.3	20,274	78.7
% CHANGE 1974 TO 1976	3.6		9.2		13.5		8.4		9.2		9.9	
1978 (32 INSTITUTIONS)	46	.2	5,164	18.7	92	.3	116	.4	5,418	19.6	22,226	80.4
% CHANGE 1976 TO 1978	58.6		- 3.1		119.0		28.9		- 1.3		9.6	
WASHINGTON												
1974 (12 INSTITUTIONS)	125	.7	453	2.5	950	5.3	109	.6	1,637	9.2	16,172	90.8
1976 (15 INSTITUTIONS)	121	.7	396	2.2	577	3.2	124	.7	1,218	6.8	16,598	93.2
% CHANGE 1974 TO 1976	- 3.2		- 12.6		- 39.3		13.8		- 25.6		2.6	
1978 (16 INSTITUTIONS)	169	.9	485	2.6	598	3.2	177	.9	1,429	7.6	17,437	92.4
% CHANGE 1976 TO 1978	39.7		22.5		3.6		42.7		17.3		5.1	
WEST VIRGINIA												
1974 (11 INSTITUTIONS)	26	.3	327	4.1	39	.5	30	.4	422	5.2	7,644	94.8
1976 (11 INSTITUTIONS)	19	.2	372	4.6	36	.4	41	.5	468	5.8	7,582	94.2
% CHANGE 1974 TO 1976	- 26.9		13.8		- 7.7		36.7		10.9		- .8	
1978 (11 INSTITUTIONS)	9	.1	382	4.9	19	.2	33	.4	443	5.7	7,379	94.3
% CHANGE 1976 TO 1978	- 52.6		2.7		- 47.2		- 19.5		- 5.3		- 2.7	
WISCONSIN												
1974 (28 INSTITUTIONS)	112	.5	1,060	4.6	122	.5	201	.9	1,495	6.5	21,507	93.5
1976 (28 INSTITUTIONS)	131	.6	1,054	4.5	137	.6	239	1.0	1,561	6.6	22,046	93.4
% CHANGE 1974 TO 1976	17.0		- .6		12.3		18.9		4.4		2.5	
1978 (32 INSTITUTIONS)	137	.6	1,118	4.6	189	.8	294	1.2	1,738	7.1	22,660	92.9
% CHANGE 1976 TO 1978	4.6		6.1		38.0		23.0		11.3		2.8	
THE STATES AND D.C.												
1974 (1472 INSTITUTIONS)	4,649	.3	130,598	8.4	16,744	1.1	25,630	1.7	177,621	11.5	1,370,728	88.5
1976 (1583 INSTITUTIONS)	6,599	.4	155,056	9.4	22,656	1.4	34,275	2.1	218,586	13.2	1,435,406	86.8
% CHANGE 1974 TO 1976	41.9		18.7		35.3		33.7		23.1		4.7	
1978 (1653 INSTITUTIONS)	6,805	.4	163,549	9.5	27,334	1.6	39,949	2.3	237,637	13.9	1,476,402	86.1
% CHANGE 1976 TO 1978	3.1		5.5		20.6		20.6		8.7		2.9	
PUERTO RICO												
1974 (0 INSTITUTIONS)	0	.0	0	.0	0	.0	0	.0	0	.0	0	.0
1976 (16 INSTITUTIONS)	0	.0	1	.0	0	.0	36,229	98.4	36,230	98.4	586	1.6
% CHANGE 1974 TO 1976	.0		100.0		.0		100.0		100.0		100.0	
1978 (25 INSTITUTIONS)	0	.0	0	.0	0	.0	60,009	99.3	60,009	99.3	421	.7
% CHANGE 1976 TO 1978	.0		- 100.0		.0		65.6		65.6		- 28.2	
OUTLYING AREAS												
1974 (0 INSTITUTIONS)	0	.0	0	.0	0	.0	0	.0	0	.0	0	.0
1976 (16 INSTITUTIONS)	0	.0	1	.0	0	.0	36,229	98.4	36,230	98.4	586	1.6
% CHANGE 1974 TO 1976	.0		100.0		.0		100.0		100.0		100.0	
1978 (25 INSTITUTIONS)	0	.0	0	.0	0	.0	60,009	99.3	60,009	99.3	421	.7
% CHANGE 1976 TO 1978	.0		- 100.0		.0		65.6		65.6		- 28.2	
NATION, TOTAL												
1974 (1472 INSTITUTIONS)	4,649	.3	130,598	8.4	16,744	1.1	25,630	1.7	177,621	11.5	1,370,728	88.5
1976 (1599 INSTITUTIONS)	6,599	.4	155,057	9.2	16,504	1.3	70,504	4.2	254,816	15.1	1,435,992	84.9
% CHANGE 1974 TO 1976	41.9		18.7		35.3		175.1		43.5		4.8	
1978 (1678 INSTITUTIONS)	6,805	.4	163,549	9.2	27,334	1.5	99,958	5.6	297,646	16.8	1,476,823	83.2
% CHANGE 1976 TO 1978	3.1		5.5		20.6		20.6		16.8		2.8	

FULL- AND PART-TIME UNDERGRADUATE ENROLLMENT IN INSTITUTIONS OF HIGHER EDUCATION
TY AND SEX: STATE AND NATION, 1976, 1978

RICAN INDIAN ASKAN NATIVE		BLACK NON-HISPANIC		ASIAN OR PACIFIC ISLANDER		HISPANIC		TOTAL MINORITY		WHITE NON-HISPANIC		TOTAL
NUMBER	%	NUMBER	%	NUMBER	%	NUMBER	%	NUMBER	%	NUMBER	%	NUMBER
68	.1	16,009	26.7	78	.1	95	.2	16,250	27.1	43,692	72.9	59,942
83	.1	18,995	27.9	150	.2	176	.3	19,404	28.5	48,679	71.5	68,083
22.1		18.7		92.3		85.3		19.4		11.4		13.6
84	.1	13,181	18.9	134	.2	194	.3	13,593	19.5	56,202	80.5	69,795
88	.1	13,091	19.7	244	.4	272	.4	13,695	20.7	52,602	79.3	66,297
4.8		- .7		82.1		40.2		.8		- 6.4		- 5.0
243	10.0	103	4.2	158	6.5	39	1.6	543	22.3	1,891	77.7	2,434
925	9.7	290	3.0	165	1.7	119	1.2	1,499	15.7	8,028	84.3	9,527
280.7		181.6		4.4		205.1		176.1		324.5		291.4
203	9.7	83	4.0	111	5.3	29	1.4	426	20.5	1,657	79.5	2,083
588	8.3	312	4.4	156	2.2	98	1.4	1,154	16.3	5,919	83.7	7,073
189.7		275.9		40.5		237.9		170.9		257.2		239.6
2,346	3.7	1,701	2.7	454	.7	4,873	7.6	9,374	14.7	54,529	85.3	63,903
2,654	3.9	1,724	2.5	755	1.1	7,196	10.5	12,329	17.9	56,488	82.1	68,817
13.1		1.4		66.3		47.7		31.5		3.6		7.7
2,039	2.7	2,443	3.2	561	.7	7,176	9.5	12,219	16.2	63,439	83.8	75,658
2,026	2.8	2,532	3.5	643	.9	6,615	9.1	11,816	16.3	60,567	83.7	72,383
.6		3.6		14.6		- 7.8		- 3.3		- 4.5		- 4.3
70	.3	5,079	18.7	106	.4	48	.2	5,303	19.5	21,849	80.5	27,152
172	.6	5,621	18.1	131	.4	106	.3	6,030	19.4	25,101	80.6	31,131
145.7		10.7		23.6		120.8		13.7		14.9		14.7
139	.5	4,231	14.6	182	.6	70	.2	4,622	16.0	24,319	84.0	28,941
212	.7	4,270	14.5	251	.9	121	.4	4,854	16.5	24,592	83.5	29,446
52.5		.9		37.9		72.9		5.0		1.1		1.7
9,382	1.5	58,945	9.2	32,706	5.1	55,296	8.6	156,329	24.3	487,274	75.7	643,603
9,014	1.4	62,099	9.7	39,449	6.1	60,144	9.4	170,706	26.6	471,342	73.4	642,048
3.9		5.4		20.6		8.8		9.2		- 3.3		- .2
10,092	1.5	58,668	8.7	37,322	5.5	69,235	10.2	175,317	25.9	501,135	74.1	676,452
8,624	1.5	54,272	9.2	43,109	7.3	63,286	10.8	169,291	28.8	419,148	71.2	588,439
14.5		- 7.5		15.5		- 8.6		- 3.4		16.4		- 13.0
446	.8	1,748	3.3	579	1.1	3,109	5.9	5,882	11.2	46,711	88.8	52,593
506	.9	1,669	3.1	729	1.4	2,962	5.5	5,866	10.9	48,055	89.1	53,921
13.5		- 4.5		25.9		- 4.7		- .3		2.9		2.5
420	.7	2,247	3.5	699	1.1	4,521	7.1	7,887	12.4	55,706	87.6	63,593
470	.8	2,011	3.5	811	1.4	3,493	6.0	6,785	11.7	51,140	88.3	57,925
11.9		- 10.5		16.0		- 22.7		- 14.0		- 8.2		- 8.9
119	.2	2,970	5.7	258	.5	812	1.5	4,159	7.9	48,368	92.1	52,527
128	.2	3,484	6.0	398	.7	1,017	1.8	5,027	8.7	52,601	91.3	57,628
7.6		17.3		54.3		25.2		20.9		8.8		9.7
111	.2	2,808	5.0	284	.5	850	1.5	4,053	7.2	51,968	92.8	56,021
105	.2	2,823	5.2	469	.9	996	1.8	4,393	8.1	50,054	91.9	54,447
5.4		.5		65.1		17.2		8.4		- 3.7		- 2.8

TABLE 14 - COMPARISIONS OF FULL- AND PART-TIME UNDERGRADUATE ENROLLMENT IN INSTITUTIONS OF HIGHER EDUCATION BY RACE, ETHNICITY AND SEX: STATE AND NATION, 1976, 1978

	AMERICAN INDIAN ALASKAN NATIVE		BLACK NON-HISPANIC		ASIAN OR PACIFIC ISLANDER		HISPANIC		TOTAL MINORITY		WHITE NON-HISPANIC	
	NUMBER	%	NUMBER	%	NUMBER	%	NUMBER	%	NUMBER	%	NUMBER	%
DELAWARE.												
FEMALE												
1976 (10 INSTITUTIONS)	10	.1	1,607	13.2	68	.6	105	.9	1,790	14.7	10,384	85.3
1978 (10 INSTITUTIONS)	15	.1	1,745	13.4	49	.4	84	.6	1,893	14.5	11,160	85.5
% CHANGE 1976 TO 1978	50.0		8.6		- 27.9		- 20.0		5.8		7.5	
MALE												
1976 (10 INSTITUTIONS)	9	.1	1,633	13.2	74	.6	75	.6	1,791	14.5	10,591	85.5
1978 (10 INSTITUTIONS)	18	.2	1,319	11.8	45	.4	63	.6	1,445	13.0	9,711	87.0
% CHANGE 1976 TO 1978	100.0		- 19.2		- 39.2		- 16.0		- 19.3		- 8.3	
DISTRICT OF COLUMBIA. . . .												
FEMALE												
1976 (17 INSTITUTIONS)	108	.5	10,741	52.5	266	1.3	416	2.0	11,531	56.3	8,943	43.7
1978 (13 INSTITUTIONS)	77	.3	11,970	53.8	283	1.3	366	1.6	12,696	57.1	9,543	42.9
% CHANGE 1976 TO 1978	- 28.7		11.4		6.4		- 12.0		10.1		6.7	
MALE												
1976 (17 INSTITUTIONS)	60	.3	8,447	46.4	326	1.8	373	2.1	9,206	50.6	8,983	49.4
1978 (13 INSTITUTIONS)	215	1.2	8,296	46.0	665	3.7	332	1.8	9,508	52.7	8,537	47.3
% CHANGE 1976 TO 1978	258.3		- 1.8		104.0		- 11.0		3.3		5.0	
FLORIDA												
FEMALE												
1976 (71 INSTITUTIONS)	357	.3	19,482	14.9	1,060	.8	8,494	6.5	29,393	22.5	101,215	77.5
1978 (74 INSTITUTIONS)	470	.3	21,448	14.6	877	.6	11,421	7.8	34,216	23.3	112,721	76.7
% CHANGE 1976 TO 1978	31.7		10.1		- 17.3		34.5		16.4		11.4	
MALE												
1976 (71 INSTITUTIONS)	451	.3	15,183	10.1	1,272	.9	8,976	6.0	25,882	17.3	123,727	82.7
1978 (74 INSTITUTIONS)	446	.3	14,081	9.6	1,331	.9	11,220	7.7	27,078	18.5	119,320	81.5
% CHANGE 1976 TO 1978	- 1.1		- 7.3		4.6		25.0		4.6		- 3.6	
GEORGIA												
FEMALE												
1976 (64 INSTITUTIONS)	209	.3	14,077	22.9	221	.4	198	.3	14,705	23.9	46,858	76.1
1978 (68 INSTITUTIONS)	95	.1	15,583	23.1	243	.4	263	.4	16,184	23.9	51,407	76.1
% CHANGE 1976 TO 1978	- 54.5		10.7		10.0		32.8		10.1		9.7	
MALE												
1976 (64 INSTITUTIONS)	243	.3	11,453	16.4	351	.5	315	.5	12,362	17.7	57,469	82.3
1978 (68 INSTITUTIONS)	125	.2	11,640	17.2	312	.5	475	.7	12,552	18.6	55,011	81.4
% CHANGE 1976 TO 1978	- 48.6		1.6		- 11.1		50.8		1.5		4.3	
HAWAII.												
FEMALE												
1976 (11 INSTITUTIONS)	27	.2	129	.7	12,455	71.7	450	2.6	13,061	75.2	4,303	24.8
1978 (12 INSTITUTIONS)	33	.2	170	1.0	12,211	70.3	541	3.1	12,955	74.6	4,412	25.4
% CHANGE 1976 TO 1978	22.2		31.8		- 2.0		20.2		- .8		2.5	
MALE												
1976 (11 INSTITUTIONS)	60	.3	255	1.2	14,676	71.9	645	3.2	15,636	76.6	4,765	23.4
1978 (12 INSTITUTIONS)	45	.2	432	2.2	13,497	68.1	696	3.5	14,670	74.0	5,160	26.0
% CHANGE 1976 TO 1978	- 25.0		69.4		- 8.0		7.9		6.2		8.3	
IDAHO												
FEMALE												
1976 (9 INSTITUTIONS)	173	1.1	40	.3	165	1.1	164	1.1	542	3.5	15,007	96.5
1978 (9 INSTITUTIONS)	126	.8	41	.3	140	.9	145	.9	452	2.9	15,371	97.1
% CHANGE 1976 TO 1978	- 27.2		2.5		- 15.2		- 11.6		- 16.6		2.4	
MALE												
1976 (9 INSTITUTIONS)	137	.8	183	1.1	237	1.4	198	1.2	755	4.6	15,664	95.4
1978 (9 INSTITUTIONS)	81	.5	133	.8	194	1.2	137	.9	545	3.4	15,455	96.6
% CHANGE 1976 TO 1978	- 40.9		- 27.3		- 18.1		- 30.8		- 27.8		- 1.3	
ILLINOIS.												
FEMALE												
1976 (132 INSTITUTIONS)	586	.3	36,916	16.1	2,360	1.0	4,858	2.1	44,720	19.4	185,214	80.6
1978 (135 INSTITUTIONS)	861	.4	39,704	16.7	2,985	1.3	5,427	2.3	48,977	20.6	189,258	79.4
% CHANGE 1976 TO 1978	46.9		7.6		26.5		11.7		9.5		2.2	
MALE												
1976 (132 INSTITUTIONS)	608	.3	26,502	11.7	2,654	1.2	5,300	2.3	35,064	15.5	191,470	84.5
1978 (135 INSTITUTIONS)	806	.4	26,177	12.1	3,404	1.6	5,720	2.6	36,107	16.7	180,577	83.3
% CHANGE 1976 TO 1978	32.6		- 1.2		28.3		7.9		3.0		- 5.7	

264

ICAN INDIAN SKAN NATIVE		BLACK NON-HISPANIC		ASIAN OR PACIFIC ISLANDER		HISPANIC		TOTAL MINORITY		WHITE NON-HISPANIC		TOTAL
NUMBER	%	NUMBER	%	NUMBER	%	NUMBER	%	NUMBER	%	NUMBER	%	NUMBER
134	.2	5,199	6.8	317	.4	567	.7	6,217	8.1	70,182	91.9	76,399
147	.2	5,777	7.0	419	.5	742	.9	7,085	8.5	75,963	91.5	83,048
9.7		11.1		32.2		30.9		14.0		8.2		8.7
207	.2	4,781	5.3	375	.4	835	.9	6,198	6.8	84,867	93.2	91,065
212	.2	4,664	5.2	464	.5	922	1.0	6,262	7.0	82,867	93.0	89,129
2.4		- 2.4		23.7		10.4		1.0		- 2.4		- 2.1
115	.3	975	2.1	152	.3	201	.4	1,443	3.2	44,025	96.8	45,468
184	.4	1,017	2.0	251	.5	231	.4	1,683	3.3	49,700	96.7	51,383
60.0		4.3		65.1		14.9		16.6		12.9		13.0
162	.3	1,276	2.5	294	.6	238	.5	1,970	3.9	48,923	96.1	50,893
162	.3	1,390	2.7	329	.6	305	.6	2,186	4.2	49,507	95.8	51,693
.0		8.9		11.9		28.2		11.0		1.2		1.6
797	1.8	2,128	4.9	188	.4	601	1.4	3,714	8.5	39,796	91.5	43,510
711	1.5	2,096	4.4	198	.4	628	1.3	3,633	7.6	44,419	92.4	48,052
10.8		- 1.5		5.3		4.5		- 2.2		11.6		10.4
932	1.9	2,597	5.	302	.6	823	1.7	4,654	9.6	43,659	90.4	48,313
714	1.5	2,657	5.8	286	.6	797	1.7	4,454	9.3	43,201	90.7	47,655
23.4		2.3		- 5.3		- 3.2		- 4.3		- 1.0		- 1.4
134	.3	4,438	8.8	117	.2	100	.2	4,789	9.5	45,361	90.5	50,150
95	.2	4,294	8.1	215	.4	121	.2	4,725	9.0	47,980	91.0	52,705
29.1		- 3.2		83.8		21.0		- 1.3		5.8		5.1
152	.3	4,272	8.1	149	.3	171	.3	4,744	9.0	47,773	91.0	52,517
90	.2	3,596	7.5	295	.6	158	.3	4,139	8.6	43,833	91.4	47,972
40.8		- 15.8		98.0		- 7.6		- 12.8		- 8.2		- 8.7
93	.2	18,069	29.6	276	.5	655	1 1	19,093	31.3	41,895	68.7	60,988
114	.2	17,896	29.0	260	.4	756	112	19,026	30.9	42,625	69.1	61,651
22.6		- 1.0		- 5.8		15.4		- .4		1.7		1.1
98	.2	14,098	22.1	425	.7	855	1 3	15,476	24.2	48,414	75.8	63,890
120	.2	12,471	20.9	364	.6	918	115	13,873	23.3	45,748	76.7	59,621
22.4		- 11.5		- 14.4		7.4		- 10.4		- 5.5		- 6.7
52	.4	85	.7	27	.2	18	.1	182	1 4	12,616	98.6	12,798
73	.5	61	.4	38	.3	25	.2	197	114	14,062	98.6	14,259
40.4		- 28.2		40.7		38.9		8.2		11.5		11.4
59	.4	143	.9	47	.3	44	.3	293	1.8	16,270	98.2	16,563
64	.4	96	.6	55	.3	46	.3	261	1.7	15,522	98.3	15,783
8.5		- 32.9		17.0		4.5		- 10.9		- 4.6		- 4.7
286	.3	18,574	22.6	766	.9	525	.6	20,151	24.5	62,133	75.5	82,284
228	.3	19,456	21.7	1,096	1.2	855	1.0	21,635	24.1	68,212	75.9	89,847
20.3		4.7		43.1		62.9		7.4		9.8		9.2
279	.4	12,755	16.8	772	1.0	570	.8	14,376	18.9	61,528	81.1	75,904
248	.3	12,506	16.7	1,135	1.5	802	1.1	14,691	19.6	60,102	80.4	74,793
11.1		- 2.0		47.0		40.7		2.2		- 2.3		- 1.5

TABLE 14 - COMPARISIONS OF FULL- AND PART-TIME UNDERGRADUATE ENROLLMENT IN INSTITUTIONS OF HIGHER EDUCATION
BY RACE, ETHNICITY AND SEX: STATE AND NATION, 1976, 1978

	AMERICAN INDIAN ALASKAN NATIVE		BLACK NON-HISPANIC		ASIAN OR PACIFIC ISLANDER		HISPANIC		TOTAL MINORITY		WHITE NON-HISPANIC	
	NUMBER	%	NUMBER	%	NUMBER	%	NUMBER	%	NUMBER	%	NUMBER	%
MASSACHUSETTS												
FEMALE												
1976 (112 INSTITUTIONS)	656	.6	5,431	4.6	972	.8	1,445	1.2	8,504	7.2	109,110	92.8
1978 (111 INSTITUTIONS)	713	.5	6,071	4.6	2,014	1.5	1,856	1.4	10,654	8.1	120,839	91.9
% CHANGE 1976 TO 1978	8.7		11.8		107.2		28.4		25.3		10.7	
MALE												
1976 (112 INSTITUTIONS)	372	.3	4,526	3.7	1,195	1.0	1,637	1.3	7,730	6.3	114,538	93.7
1978 (111 INSTITUTIONS)	462	.4	4,821	3.8	2,355	1.9	1,786	1.4	9,424	7.4	117,598	92.6
% CHANGE 1976 TO 1978	24.2		6.5		97.1		9.1		21.9		2.7	
MICHIGAN.												
FEMALE												
1976 (90 INSTITUTIONS)	1,004	.6	24,514	13.5	939	.5	1,479	.8	27,936	15.4	153,051	84.6
1978 (92 INSTITUTIONS)	1,128	.6	24,310	12.2	1,200	.6	2,676	1.3	29,314	14.7	170,190	85.3
% CHANGE 1976 TO 1978	12.4		- .8		27.8		80.9		4.9		11.2	
MALE												
1976 (90 INSTITUTIONS)	1,239	.6	19,338	9.6	1,289	.6	1,951	1.0	23,817	11.8	178,433	88.2
1978 (92 INSTITUTIONS)	1,131	.6	16,613	8.4	1,532	.8	2,718	1.4	21,994	11.1	175,883	88.9
% CHANGE 1976 TO 1978	- 8.7		- 14.1		18.9		39.3		- 7.7		- 1.4	
MINNESOTA												
FEMALE												
1976 (56 INSTITUTIONS)	551	.8	1,159	1.6	432	.6	551	.8	2,693	3.7	69,707	96.3
1978 (55 INSTITUTIONS)	481	.6	857	1.1	495	.6	302	.4	2,135	2.7	75,924	97.3
% CHANGE 1976 TO 1978	- 12.7		- 26.1		14.6		- 45.2		- 20.7		8.9	
MALE												
1976 (56 INSTITUTIONS)	467	.6	1,323	1.8	639	.9	651	.9	3,080	4.2	70,134	95.8
1978 (55 INSTITUTIONS)	388	.6	1,054	1.5	611	.9	303	.4	2,356	3.3	68,125	96.7
% CHANGE 1976 TO 1978	- 16.9		- 20.3		- 4.4		- 53.5		- 23.5		- 2.9	
MISSISSIPPI												
FEMALE												
1976 (43 INSTITUTIONS)	124	.3	13,762	35.5	79	.2	37	.1	14,002	36.1	24,807	63.9
1978 (45 INSTITUTIONS)	144	.3	15,033	34.2	113	.3	45	.1	15,335	34.8	28,671	65.2
% CHANGE 1976 TO 1978	16.1		9.2		43.0		21.6		9.5		15.6	
MALE												
1976 (43 INSTITUTIONS)	100	.3	11,483	29.3	130	.3	47	.1	11,760	30.0	27,478	70.0
1978 (45 INSTITUTIONS)	98	.3	10,440	27.3	146	.4	67	.2	10,751	28.1	27,443	71.9
% CHANGE 1976 TO 1978	- 2.0		- 9.1		12.3		42.6		- 8.6		- .1	
MISSOURI.												
FEMALE												
1976 (71 INSTITUTIONS)	247	.3	8,466	10.5	336	.4	370	.5	9,419	11.7	70,890	88.3
1978 (70 INSTITUTIONS)	212	.3	8,527	10.5	450	.6	514	.6	9,703	12.0	71,367	88.0
% CHANGE 1976 TO 1978	- 14.2		.7		33.9		38.9		3.0		.7	
MALE												
1976 (71 INSTITUTIONS)	328	.4	6,885	7.7	470	.5	542	.6	8,225	9.2	80,751	90.8
1978 (70 INSTITUTIONS)	276	.3	6,465	7.9	632	.8	744	.9	8,117	9.9	73,636	90.1
% CHANGE 1976 TO 1978	- 15.9		- 6.1		34.5		37.3		- 1.3		- 8.8	
MONTANA												
FEMALE												
1976 (12 INSTITUTIONS)	544	4.6	34	.3	41	.3	40	.3	659	5.6	11,193	94.4
1978 (13 INSTITUTIONS)	366	3.0	38	.3	25	.2	44	.4	473	3.9	11,781	96.1
% CHANGE 1976 TO 1978	- 32.7		11.8		- 39.0		10.0		- 28.2		5.3	
MALE												
1976 (12 INSTITUTIONS)	419	3.1	121	.9	68	.5	68	.5	676	5.0	12,954	95.0
1978 (13 INSTITUTIONS)	244	1.9	60	.5	66	.5	54	.4	424	3.2	12,759	96.8
% CHANGE 1976 TO 1978	- 41.8		- 50.4		- 2.9		- 20.6		- 37.3		- 1.5	
NEBRASKA.												
FEMALE												
1976 (29 INSTITUTIONS)	85	.3	1,139	3.9	122	.4	218	.7	1,564	5.3	27,753	94.7
1978 (31 INSTITUTIONS)	112	.4	1,002	3.2	153	.5	329	1.0	1,596	5.0	30,084	95.0
% CHANGE 1976 TO 1978	31.8		- 12.0		25.4		50.9		2.0		8.4	
MALE												
1976 (29 INSTITUTIONS)	104	.3	1,284	3.7	170	.5	312	.9	1,870	5.3	33,148	94.7
1978 (31 INSTITUTIONS)	134	.4	1,243	3.7	194	.6	325	1.0	1,896	5.6	31,946	94.4
% CHANGE 1976 TO 1978	28.8		- 3.2		14.1		4.2		1.4		3.6	

ICAN INDIAN SKAN NATIVE		BLACK NON-HISPANIC		ASIAN OR PACIFIC ISLANDER		HISPANIC		TOTAL MINORITY		WHITE NON-HISPANIC		TOTAL
NUMBER	%	NUMBER	%	NUMBER	%	NUMBER	%	NUMBER	%	NUMBER	%	NUMBER
112	1.3	409	4.9	111	1.3	159	1.9	791	9.5	7,556	90.5	8,347
159	1.4	436	3.9	139	1.2	222	2.0	956	8.5	10,267	91.5	11,223
42.0		6.6		25.2		39.6		20.9		35.9		34.5
110	1.1	433	4.2	136	1.3	211	2.0	890	8.6	9,413	91.4	10,303
121	1.0	541	4.3	188	1.5	302	2.4	1,152	9.2	11,355	90.8	12,507
10.0		24.9		38.2		43.1		29.4		20.6		21.4
33	.2	186	1.3	34	.2	59	.4	312	2.2	13,671	97.8	13,983
35	.2	205	1.3	38	.2	50	.3	328	2.0	15,869	98.0	16,197
6.1		10.2		11.8		- 15.3		5.1		16.1		15.8
38	.2	345	1.9	49	.3	258	1.4	690	3.8	17,627	96.2	18,317
40	.2	384	2.1	68	.4	189	1.0	681	3.7	17,717	96.3	18,398
5.3		11.3		. 38.8		- 26.7		- 1.3		.5		.4
291	.3	13,614	12.7	741	.7	4,131	3 9	18,777	17.6	88,135	82.4	106,912
272	.2	14,420	13.1	1,029	.9	4,892	414	20,613	18.7	89,797	81.3	110,410
6.5		5.9		38.9		18.4		9.8		1.9		3.3
249	.2	9,399	9.1	1,024	1 0	3,767	3.	14,439	13.9	89,385	86.1	103,824
214	.2	8,936	9.0	1,030	110	3,945	4.0	14,125	14.2	85,632	85.8	99,757
14.1		- 4.9		.6		4.7		- 2.2		- 4.2		- 3.9
977	5 4	367	2.0	81	.4	4,761	26.3	6,186	34.2	11,912	65.8	18,098
951	510	375	2.0	118	.6	5,250	27.3	6,694	34.9	12,512	65.1	19,206
2.7		2.2		45.7		10.3		8.2		5.0		6.1
575	2.7	630	2.9	152	.7	5,561	25.8	6,918	32.0	14,674	68.0	21,592
649	3.2	596	2.9	173	.8	5,251	25.6	6,669	32.5	13,825	67.5	20,494
12.9		- 5.4		13.8		- 5.6		- 3.6		- 5.8		- 5.1
1,682	.5	44,317	13.9	5,244	1.6	18,087	5.7	69,330	21.8	248,721	78.2	318,051
1,645	.5	50,685	15.0	6,206	1.8	21,523	6.4	80,059	23.6	258,676	76.4	338,735
2.2		14.4		18.3		19.0		15.5		4.0		6.5
1,667	.5	30,150	9.2	5,901	1 8	16,344	5.0	54,062	16.5	273,595	83.5	327,657
1,792	.6	30,765	9.6	7,212	2±2	17,266	5.4	57,035	17.7	264,399	82.3	321,434
7.5		2.0		22.2		5.6		5.5		- 3.4		- 1.9
731	.8	21,557	23.4	167	.2	217	.2	22,672	24.6	69,609	75.4	92,281
907	.8	25,313	23.3	361	.3	357	.3	26,938	24.7	81,915	75.3	108,853
24.1		17.4		116.2		64.5		18.8		17.7		18.0
793	.7	20,942	18.9	253	.2	389	.4	22,377	20.2	88,316	79.8	110,693
680	.6	21,580	19.8	476	.4	458	.4	23,194	21.3	85,762	78.7	108,956
14.2		3.0		88.1		17.7		3.7		- 2.9		- 1.6
432	3.7	24	.2	24	.2	20	.2	500	4.2	11,267	95.8	11,767
587	4.5	44	.3	31	.2	24	.2	686	5.2	12,479	94.8	13,165
35.9		83.3		29.2		20.0		37.2		10.8		11.9
324	2.	111	.8	28	.2	38	.3	501	4.2	13,377	96.4	13,878
405	2.8	109	.8	47	.3	24	.2	585	4.1	13,782	95.9	14,367
25.0		- 1.8		67.9		- 36.8		16.8		3.0		3.5

TABLE 14 - COMPARISIONS OF FULL- AND PART-TIME UNDERGRADUATE ENROLLMENT IN INSTITUTIONS OF HIGHER EDUCATION
BY RACE, ETHNICITY AND SEX: STATE AND NATION, 1976, 1978

	AMERICAN INDIAN ALASKAN NATIVE		BLACK NON-HISPANIC		ASIAN OR PACIFIC ISLANDER		HISPANIC		TOTAL MINORITY		WHITE NON-HISPANIC	
	NUMBER	%	NUMBER	%	NUMBER	%	NUMBER	%	NUMBER	%	NUMBER	%
OHIO.												
FEMALE												
1976 (121 INSTITUTIONS)	292	.2	22,088	13.3	685	.4	936	.6	24,001	14.4	142,098	85.6
1978 (124 INSTITUTIONS)	604	.3	21,181	12.0	805	.5	1,109	.6	23,699	13.4	153,260	86.6
% CHANGE 1976 TO 1978	106.8		- 4.1		17.5		18.5		- 1.3		7.9	
MALE												
1976 (121 INSTITUTIONS)	320	.2	17,368	9 3	868	.5	996	.5	19,552	10.4	168,060	89.6
1978 (124 INSTITUTIONS)	357	.2	14,927	8 5	762	.4	1,035	.6	17,081	9.8	157,941	90.2
% CHANGE 1976 TO 1978	11.6		- 14.1		- 12.2		3.9		- 12.6		- 6.0	
OKLAHOMA.												
FEMALE												
1976 (43 INSTITUTIONS)	2,617	4.0	4,040	7.5	321	.6	332	.6	7,310	13.6	46,341	86.4
1978 (42 INSTITUTIONS)	2,536	4.3	4,233	7.3	376	.6	448	.8	7,593	13.0	50,741	87.0
% CHANGE 1976 TO 1978	- 3.1		4.8		17.1		34.9		3.9		9.5	
MALE												
1976 (43 INSTITUTIONS)	2,319	3.7	4,372	7.0	602	1.0	528	.8	7,821	12.5	54,820	87.5
1978 (42 INSTITUTIONS)	2,050	3.5	3,972	6.7	563	1.0	586	1.0	7,171	12.2	51,806	87.8
% CHANGE 1976 TO 1978	- 11.6		- 9.1		- 6.5		11.0		- 8.3		- 5.5	
OREGON.												
FEMALE												
1976 (39 INSTITUTIONS)	480	1.0	601	1.2	789	1.6	440	.9	2,310	.7	46,443	95.3
1978 (39 INSTITUTIONS)	632	1.2	595	1.1	1,261	2.4	615	1.2	3,103	5.9	49,562	94.1
% CHANGE 1976 TO 1978	31.7		- 1.0		59.8		39.8		34.3		6.7	
MALE												
1976 (39 INSTITUTIONS)	556	1.0	876	1.6	979	1.8	583	1.1	2,994	5.	52,130	94.6
1978 (39 INSTITUTIONS)	651	1.2	850	1.6	1,411	2.6	658	1.2	3,570	6.8	50,708	93.4
% CHANGE 1976 TO 1978	17.1		- 3.0		44.1		12.9		19.2		- 2.7	
PENNSYLVANIA.												
FEMALE												
1976 (158 INSTITUTIONS)	211	.1	14,007	8.7	1,062	.7	2,239	1.4	17,519	10.9	143,465	89.1
1978 (157 INSTITUTIONS)	252	.1	17,044	9.7	1,038	.6	1,413	.8	19,747	11.2	156,404	88.8
% CHANGE 1976 TO 1978	19.4		21.7		- 2.3		- 36.9		12.7		9.0	
MALE												
1976 (158 INSTITUTIONS)	267	.1	11,314	6.3	1,425	.8	2,155	1.2	15,161	8.4	165,292	91.6
1978 (157 INSTITUTIONS)	238	.1	11,842	6.6	1,260	.7	1,211	.7	14,551	8.2	163,607	91.8
% CHANGE 1976 TO 1978	- 10.9		4.7		- 11.6		- 43.8		- 4.0		- 1.0	
RHODE ISLAND.												
FEMALE												
1976 (12 INSTITUTIONS)	27	.1	591	3.2	98	.5	121	.7	837	4.6	17,375	95.4
1978 (13 INSTITUTIONS)	47	.2	696	3.4	152	.7	123	.6	1,018	4.9	19,729	95.1
% CHANGE 1976 TO 1978	74.1		17.8		55.1		1.7		21.6		13.5	
MALE												
1976 (12 INSTITUTIONS)	74	.3	833	3	130	.6	158	.7	1,195	5 1	22,276	94.9
1978 (13 INSTITUTIONS)	34	.1	837	3.8	160	.7	149	.6	1,180	5 1	22,080	94.9
% CHANGE 1976 TO 1978	- 54.1		.5		23.1		- 5.7		- 1.3		- .9	
SOUTH CAROLINA.												
FEMALE												
1976 (55 INSTITUTIONS)	50	.1	11,619	26.9	73	.2	57	.1	11,799	27.3	31,469	72.7
1978 (60 INSTITUTIONS)	43	.1	13,525	27.5	202	.4	92	.2	13,862	28.2	35,290	71.8
% CHANGE 1976 TO 1978	- 14.0		16.4		176.7		61.4		17.5		12.1	
MALE												
1976 (55 INSTITUTIONS)	85	.2	11,301	20.7	102	.2	91	.2	11,579	21.2	43,015	78.8
1978 (60 INSTITUTIONS)	79	.1	11,724	21.0	245	.4	181	.3	12,229	21.9	43,647	78.1
% CHANGE 1976 TO 1978	- 7.1		3.7		140.2		98.9		5.6		1.5	
SOUTH DAKOTA.												
FEMALE												
1976 (16 INSTITUTIONS)	291	2.7	26	.2	30	.3	22	.2	369	3.5	10,234	96.5
1978 (17 INSTITUTIONS)	413	3.5	62	.5	43	.4	36	.3	554	4.7	11,359	95.3
% CHANGE 1976 TO 1978	41.9		138.5		43.3		63.6		50.1		11.0	
MALE												
1976 (16 INSTITUTIONS)	273	2.0	98	.7	39	.3	26	.2	436	3.2	13,326	96.8
1978 (17 INSTITUTIONS)	337	2.5	258	1.9	61	.5	247	1.9	903	6.8	12,392	93.2
% CHANGE 1976 TO 1978	23.4		163.3		56.4		850.0		107.1		- 7.0	

268

ULL- AND PART-TIME UNDERGRADUATE ENROLLMENT IN INSTITUTIONS OF HIGHER EDUCATION
Y AND SEX: STATE AND NATION, 1976, 1978

ICAN INDIAN SKAN NATIVE		BLACK NON-HISPANIC		ASIAN OR PACIFIC ISLANDER		HISPANIC		TOTAL - MINORITY		WHITE NON-HISPANIC		TOTAL
NUMBER	%	NUMBER	%	NUMBER	%	NUMBER	%	NUMBER	%	NUMBER	%	NUMBER
86	.1	12,363	18.1	183	.3	122	.2	12,754	18.7	55,615	81.3	68,369
120	.2	14,520	18.4	219	.3	238	.3	15,097	19.1	63,786	80.9	78,883
39.5		17.4		19.7		95.1		18.4		14.7		15.4
106	.1	10,352	13.5	239	.3	213	.3	10,910	14.3	65,634	85.7	76,544
107	.1	11,025	14.3	293	.4	315	.4	11,740	15.2	65,446	84.8	77,186
.9		6.5		22.6		47.9		7.6		-	.3	.8
986	.4	27,411	11.9	1,268	.6	27,835	12.1	57,500	25.0	172,717	75.0	230,217
896	.3	26,566	11.1	2,018	.8	33,106	12.8	64,586	25.1	193,106	74.9	257,692
9.1		4.2		59.1		18.9		12.3		11.8		11.9
1,307	.5	26,682	10.0	1,622	.6	34,771	13.0	64,382	24.1	202,230	75.9	266,612
1,042	.4	25,455	9.6	2,206	.8	35,345	13.4	64,048	24.2	200,667	75.8	264,715
20.3		- 4.6		36.0		1.7		- .5		- .8		- .7
412	1 3	135	.4	494	1.5	399	1 2	1,440	4.5	30,704	95.5	32,144
438	1:3	160	.5	643	1.9	415	1:2	1,656	4.9	31,817	95.1	33,473
6.3		18.5		30.2		4.0		15.0		3.6		4.1
405	1.0	317	.8	599	1.4	635	1 5	1,956	4.7	39,699	95.3	41,655
428	1.0	284	.7	640	1.5	632	1:5	1,984	4.8	39,333	95.2	41,317
5.7		- 10.4		6.8		- .5		1.4		- .9		- .8
36	.3	172	1.4	18	.1	67	.5	293	2.4	11,922	97.6	12,215
19	.2	161	1.3	26	.2	68	.5	274	2.2	12,277	97.8	12,551
47.2		- 6.4		44.4		1.5		- 6.5		3.0		2.8
41	.4	170	1 5	10	.1	77	.7	298	2.7	10,706	97.3	11,004
24	.2	122	1:2	24	.2	57	.5	227	2.2	10,186	97.8	10,413
41.5		- 28.2		140.0		- 26.0		- 23.8		- 4.9		- 5.4
102	.1	14,412	19.2	340	.5	278	.4	15,132	20.1	60,104	79.9	75,236
174	.2	15,137	18.2	659	.8	376	.5	16,346	19.7	66,713	80.3	83,059
70.6		5.0		93.8		35.3		8.0		11.0		10.4
120	.2	11,422	15.2	349	.5	282	.4	12,173	16.2	63,197	83.8	75,370
134	.2	11,472	14.9	703	.9	387	.4	12,696	16.5	64,468	83.5	77,164
11.7		.4		101.4		37.2		4.3		2.0		2.4
929	1 4	2,359	3.5	1,994	2.9	882	1.3	6,164	9.1	61,857	90.9	68,021
1,032	1:5	1,804	2.7	2,200	3.2	794	1.2	5,830	8.6	62,011	91.4	67,841
11.1		- 23.5		10.3		- 10.0		- 5.4		.2		- .3
880	1.3	2,024	3 1	1,856	2.8	779	1.2	5,539	8.4	60,381	91.6	65,920
861	1.2	2,423	3:5	2,331	3.3	1,019	1.5	6,634	8.5	63,020	90.5	69,654
2.2		19.7		25.6		30.8		19.8		4.4		5.7
70	.3	1,420	5.1	102	.4	76	.3	1,668	6.0	25,914	94.0	27,582
99	.3	1,317	4.5	78	.3	51	.2	1,545	5.2	27,887	94.8	29,432
41.4		- 7.3		- 23.5		- 32.9		- 7.4		7.6		6.7
64	.2	1,605	5.4	201	.7	77	.3	1,947	6.5	27,976	93.5	29,923
74	.3	1,473	5.0	130	.4	72	.2	1,749	6.0	27,437	94.0	29,186
15.6		- 8.2		- 35.3		- 6.5		- 10.2		- 1.9		- 2.5

	AMERICAN INDIAN ALASKAN NATIVE		BLACK NON-HISPANIC		ASIAN OR PACIFIC ISLANDER		HISPANIC		TOTAL MINORITY		WHITE NON-HISPANIC	
	NUMBER	%	NUMBER	%	NUMBER	%	NUMBER	%	NUMBER	%	NUMBER	%
WISCONSIN												
FEMALE												
1976 (54 INSTITUTIONS)	618	.7	3,913	4.4	380	.4	558	.6	5,469	6.2	83,274	93.8
1978 (57 INSTITUTIONS)	566	.6	3,796	4.0	507	.5	692	.7	5,561	5.8	89,632	94.2
% CHANGE 1976 TU 1978	- 8.4		- 3.0		33.4		24.0		1.7		7.6	
MALE												
1976 (54 INSTITUTIONS)	591	.6	3,542	3.5	446	.4	865	.9	5,444	5.4	95,438	94.6
1978 (57 INSTITUTIONS)	469	.5	2,992	3.1	537	.5	878	.9	4,876	5.0	93,105	95.0
% CHANGE 1976 TO 1978	- 20.6		- 15.5		20.4		1.5		- 10.4		- 2.4	
WYOMING												
FEMALE												
1976 (8 INSTITUTIONS)	60	.9	77	1.1	51	.7	174	2.5	362	5.3	6,525	94.7
1978 (8 INSTITUTIONS)	87	1.2	73	1.0	41	.6	150	2.0	351	4.8	6,981	95.2
% CHANGE 1976 TO 1978	45.0		- 5.2		- 19.6		- 13.8		- 3.0		7.0	
MALE												
1976 (8 INSTITUTIONS)	64	.9	142	1.9	31	.4	204	2.8	441	6.0	6,940	94.0
1978 (8 INSTITUTIONS)	48	.7	147	2.1	41	.6	147	2.1	383	5.4	6,668	94.6
% CHANGE 1976 TO 1978	- 25.0		3.5		32.3		- 27.9		- 13.2		- 3.9	
THE STATES AND D.C.												
FEMALE												
1976 (2824 INSTITUTIONS)	30,491	.8	469,228	11.8	69,988	1.8	147,736	3.7	717,443	18.1	3,255,685	81.9
1978 (2903 INSTITUTIONS)	32,381	.8	505,326	11.9	83,682	2.0	171,135	4.0	792,524	18.6	3,468,053	81.4
% CHANGE 1976 TO 1978	6.2		7.7		19.6		15.8		10.5		6.5	
MALE												
1976 (2824 INSTITUTIONS)	30,802	.7	396,627	9.2	82,249	1.9	175,709	4.1	685,387	15.9	3,633,472	84.1
1978 (2903 INSTITUTIONS)	29,026	.7	382,179	9.2	94,156	2.3	173,823	4.2	679,184	16.4	3,470,946	83.6
% CHANGE 1976 TO 1978	- 5.8		- 3.6		14.5		14.5		- .9		- 4.5	
AMERICAN SAMOA.												
FEMALE												
1976 (1 INSTITUTIONS)	0	.0	0	.0	360	98.6	0	.0	360	98.6	5	1.4
1978 (1 INSTITUTIONS)	0	.0	1	.2	417	93.3	0	.0	418	93.5	29	6.5
% CHANGE 1976 TO 1978	.0		100.0		15.8		.0		16.1		480.0	
MALE												
1976 (1 INSTITUTIONS)	0	.0	0	.0	310	98.4	0	.0	310	98.4	5	1.6
1978 (1 INSTITUTIONS)	0	.0	0	.0	364	94.8	0	.0	364	94.8	20	5.2
% CHANGE 1976 TO 1978	.0		.0		17.4		.0		17.4		300.0	
CANAL ZONE.												
FEMALE												
1976 (1 INSTITUTIONS)	0	.0	21	9.3	0	.0	55	24.3	76	33.6	150	66.4
1978 (1 INSTITUTIONS)	0	.0	25	10.5	0	.0	70	29.5	95	40.1	142	59.9
% CHANGE 1976 TO 1978	.0		19.0		.0		27.3		25.0		- 5.3	
MALE												
1976 (1 INSTITUTIONS)	0	.0	23	11.1	0	.0	54	26.1	77	37.2	130	62.8
1978 (1 INSTITUTIONS)	0	.0	19	10.4	0	.0	62	33.9	81	44.3	102	55.7
% CHANGE 1976 TO 1978	.0		- 17.4		.0		14.8		5.2		- 21.5	
GUAM.												
FEMALE												
1976 (1 INSTITUTIONS)	26	1.8	19	1.3	1,005	68.4	20	1.4	1,070	72.8	400	27.2
1978 (1 INSTITUTIONS)	4	.3	16	1.1	1,146	80.4	21	1.5	1,187	83.2	239	16.8
% CHANGE 1976 TO 1978	- 84.6		- 15.8		14.0		5.0		10.9		- 40.3	
MALE												
1976 (1 INSTITUTIONS)	15	1.0	30	2.0	872	58.7	29	2.0	946	63.7	540	36.3
1978 (1 INSTITUTIONS)	7	.5	12	.9	996	75.3	37	2.8	1,052	79.5	271	20.5
% CHANGE 1976 TO 1978	- 53.3		- 60.0		14.2		27.6		11.2		- 49.8	
PUERTO RICO												
FEMALE												
1976 (23 INSTITUTIONS)	77	.2	1	.0	0	.0	48,314	99.1	48,392	99.3	339	.7
1978 (33 INSTITUTIONS)	0	.0	2	.0	1	.0	65,406	99.7	65,409	99.7	182	.3
% CHANGE 1976 TO 1978	- 100.0		100.0		100.0		35.4		35.2		- 46.3	
MALE												
1976 (23 INSTITUTIONS)	5	.0	0	.0	0	.0	37,728	99.2	37,733	99.2	316	.8
1978 (33 INSTITUTIONS)	0	.0	8	.0	0	.0	48,672	99.7	48,680	99.7	150	.
% CHANGE 1976 TO 1978	- 100.0		100.0		.0		29.0		29.0		- 52.5	

RICAN INDIAN ASKAN NATIVE		BLACK NON-HISPANIC		ASIAN OR PACIFIC ISLANDER		HISPANIC		TOTAL MINORITY		WHITE NON-HISPANIC		TOTAL
NUMBER	%	NUMBER	%	NUMBER	%	NUMBER	%	NUMBER	%	NUMBER	%	NUMBER
0	.0	0	.0	61	100.0	0	.0	61	100.0	0	.0	61
0	.0	0	.0	88	100.0	0	.0	88	100.0	0	.0	88
.0		.0		44.3		.0		44.3		.0		44.3
0	.0	0	.0	101	100.0	0	.0	101	100.0	0	.0	101
0	.0	0	.0	163	100.0	0	.0	163	100.0	0	.0	163
.0		.0		61.4		.0		61.4		.0		61.4
0	.0	242	87.1	0	.0	13	4.7	255	91.7	23	8.	278
0	.0	237	85.3	1	.4	18	6.5	256	92.1	22	7.9	278
.0		- 2.1		100.0		38.5		.4		- 4.3		.0
0	.0	124	78.0	1	.6	6	3.8	131	82.4	28	17.6	159
0	.0	74	66.1	0	.0	9	8.0	83	74.1	29	25.9	112
.0		- 40.3		- 100.0		50.0		- 36.6		3.6		- 29.6
103	.2	283	.6	1,426	2.8	48,402	94.7	50,214	98.2	917	1.8	51,131
4	.0	281	.4	1,653	2.4	65,515	96.3	67,453	99.1	614	.9	68,067
96.1		- .7		15.9		35.4		34.3		- 33.0		33.1
20	.0	177	.4	1,284	3.2	37,817	93.8	39,298	97.5	1,019	2 5	40,317
7	.0	113	.2	1,523	3.0	48,780	95.7	50,423	98.9	572	1:1	50,995
65.0		- 36.2		18.6		18.6		28.3		- 43.9		26.5
30,594	.8	469,511	11.7	71,414	1.8	196,138	4.	767,657	19.1	3,256,602	80.9	4,024,259
32,385	.7	505,607	11.7	85,335	2.0	236,650	5.2	859,977	19.9	3,468,667	80.1	4,328,644
5.9		7.7		19.5		20.7		12.0		6.5		7.6
30,822	.7	396,804	9.1	83,533	1.9	213,526	4 9	724,685	16.6	3,634,491	83.4	4,359,176
29,033	.7	382,292	9.1	95,679	2.3	222,603	5:3	729,607	17.4	3,471,518	82.6	4,201,125
5.8		- 3.7		14.5		14.5		.7		- 4.5		- 3.6

TABLE 15 - COMPARISIONS OF FULL- AND PART-TIME GRADUATE ENROLLMENT IN INSTITUTIONS OF HIGHER EDUCATION BY RACE, ETHNICITY AND SEX: STATE AND NATION, 1976, 1978

	AMERICAN INDIAN ALASKAN NATIVE		BLACK NON-HISPANIC		ASIAN OR PACIFIC ISLANDER		HISPANIC		TOTAL MINORITY		WHITE NON-HISPANIC	
	NUMBER	%	NUMBER	%	NUMBER	%	NUMBER	%	NUMBER	%	NUMBER	%
ALABAMA												
FEMALE												
1976 (18 INSTITUTIONS)	4	.0	1,824	22.4	18	.2	7	.1	1,853	22.8	6,278	77.2
1978 (18 INSTITUTIONS)	6	.1	1,320	16.2	23	.3	15	.2	1,364	16.7	6,796	83.3
% CHANGE 1976 TO 1978	50.0		- 27.6		27.8		114.3		- 26.4		8.3	
MALE												
1976 (18 INSTITUTIONS)	11	.1	948	12.6	50	.7	22	.3	1,031	13.7	6,499	86.3
1978 (18 INSTITUTIONS)	12	.2	742	10.2	76	1.0	44	.6	874	12.0	6,418	88.0
% CHANGE 1976 TO 1978	9.1		- 21.7		52.0		100.0		- 15.2		- 1.2	
ALASKA												
FEMALE												
1976 (3 INSTITUTIONS)	24	7 3	15	4.5	5	1.5	6	1.	50	15.1	281	84.9
1978 (7 INSTITUTIONS)	24	412	17	3.0	11	1.9	9	1.8	61	10.8	505	89.2
% CHANGE 1976 TO 1978	.0		13.3		120.0		50.0		22.0		79.7	
MALE												
1976 (3 INSTITUTIONS)	31	7.	19	4.		1.	9	2.1	65	14.9	371	85.1
1978 (7 INSTITUTIONS)	15	2.4	21	3.6	8	1.4	4	.7	48	8.6	507	91.4
% CHANGE 1976 TO 1978	- 51.6		10.5		33.3		- 55.6		- 26.2		36.7	
ARIZONA												
FEMALE												
1976 (4 INSTITUTIONS)	47	.8	55	1.0	24	.4	214	3.8	340	6.1	5,266	93.9
1978 (4 INSTITUTIONS)	55	.9	55	.9	43	.7	158	2.7	311	5.3	5,533	94.7
% CHANGE 1976 TO 1978	17.0		.0		79.2		- 26.2		- 8.5		5.1	
MALE												
1976 (4 INSTITUTIONS)	50	.7	71	1.0	47	.6	415	5.7	583	8.1	6,654	91.9
1978 (4 INSTITUTIONS)	36	.5	61	.8	71	1.0	188	2.6	356	4.9	6,922	95.1
% CHANGE 1976 TO 1978	- 28.0		- 14.1		51.1		- 54.7		- 38.9		4.0	
ARKANSAS												
FEMALE												
1976 (11 INSTITUTIONS)	8	.3	283	10.5	23	.9	6	.2	320	11.9	2,367	88.1
1978 (11 INSTITUTIONS)	19	.6	292	9.8	18	.6	7	.2	336	11.3	2,637	88.7
% CHANGE 1976 TO 1978	137.5		3.2		- 21.7		16.7		5.0		11.4	
MALE												
1976 (11 INSTITUTIONS)	14	.5	188	7.2	20	.8	8	.3	230	8.8	2,374	91.2
1978 (11 INSTITUTIONS)	19	.7	172	6.5	20	.8	13	.5	224	8.4	2,429	91.6
% CHANGE 1976 TO 1978	35.7		- 8.5		.0		62.5		- 2.6		2.3	
CALIFORNIA												
FEMALE												
1976 (102 INSTITUTIONS)	360	.8	2,797	6.3	2,450	5.5	1,774	4.0	7,381	16.6	37,095	83.4
1978 (111 INSTITUTIONS)	293	.7	2,505	5.7	2,499	5.7	2,037	4.6	7,334	16.7	36,674	83.3
% CHANGE 1976 TO 1978	- 18.6		- 10.4		2.0		14.8		- .6		- 1.1	
MALE												
1976 (102 INSTITUTIONS)	487	.8	2,603	4.1	3,937	6.2	2,885	4.6	9,912	15.7	53,113	84.3
1978 (111 INSTITUTIONS)	401	.7	2,195	3.8	3,694	6.3	2,622	4.5	8,912	15.3	49,390	84.7
% CHANGE 1976 TO 1978	- 17.7		- 15.7		- 6.2		- 9.1		- 10.1		- 7.0	
COLORADO												
FEMALE												
1976 (15 INSTITUTIONS)	6	.1	67	1.3	39	.7	100	1 9	212	4.0	5,063	96.0
1978 (16 INSTITUTIONS)	24	.4	100	1.8	64	1.2	199	3 6	387	7.0	5,137	93.0
% CHANGE 1976 TO 1978	300.0		49.3		64.1		99.0		82.5		1.5	
MALE												
1976 (15 INSTITUTIONS)	19	.3	111	1.5	67	.9	183	2 5	380	5.2	6,967	94.8
1978 (16 INSTITUTIONS)	23	.3	123	1.8	81	1.2	232	3 4	459	6.8	6,285	93.2
% CHANGE 1976 TO 1978	21.1		10.8		20.9		26.8		20.8		- 9.8	
CONNECTICUT												
FEMALE												
1976 (17 INSTITUTIONS)	19	.2	245	2.1	50	.4	73	.6	387	3.3	11,234	96.7
1978 (20 INSTITUTIONS)	13	.1	258	2.4	65	.6	123	1.1	459	4.2	10,394	95.8
% CHANGE 1976 TO 1978	- 31.6		5.3		30.0		68.5		18.6		- 7.5	
MALE												
1976 (17 INSTITUTIONS)	15	.1	266	2.2	72	.6	85	.7	438	3.	11,577	96.4
1978 (20 INSTITUTIONS)	10	.1	319	2.8	86	.8	202	1.8	617	5.4	10,760	94.6
% CHANGE 1976 TO 1978	- 33.3		19.9		19.4		137.6		40.9		- 7.1	

PART-TIME GRADUATE ENROLLMENT IN INSTITUTIONS OF HIGHER EDUCATION
X: STATE AND NATION, 1976, 1978

IAN IVE %	BLACK NON-HISPANIC NUMBER	%	ASIAN OR PACIFIC ISLANDER NUMBER	%	HISPANIC NUMBER	%	TOTAL MINORITY NUMBER	%	WHITE NON-HISPANIC NUMBER	%	TOTAL NUMBER
.2	9	1.6	2	.4	'	.2	13	2.3	552	97.7	565
.0	19	3.0	1	.2	4	.5	23	3.6	619	96.4	642
111.1			- 50.0		200.0		76.9		12.1		13.6
.4	17	2.2	2	.3	5	.7	27	3.5	739	96.5	766
.3	38	5.1	7	.9	1	.1	48	6.4	704	93.6	752
123.5			250.0		- 80.0		77.8		- 4.7		- 1.8
.4	1,906	25.3	123	1.6	90	1 2	2,146	28.5	5,373	71.5	7,519
.1	1,795	23.2	133	1.7	114	1:5	2,050	26.5	5,679	73.5	7,729
5.8			8.1		26.7		- 4.5		5.7		2.8
.4	1,334	12.5	429	4.0	189	1.8	1,997	18.7	8,681	81.3	10,678
.4	1,225	12.0	322	3.2	165	1.6	1,750	17.1	8,463	82.9	10,213
- 8.2			- 24.9		- 12.7		- 12.4		- 2.5		- 4.4
.2	1,219	11.8	52	.5	588	5.7	1,875	18.1	8,487	81.9	10,362
.2	1,561	13.4	77	.7	492	4.2	2,148	18.4	9,531	81.6	11,679
28.1			48.1		- 16.3		14.6		12.3		12.7
.2	832	6.2	92	.7	480	3.6	1,431	10.7	11,897	89.3	13,328
.2	1,047	7.5	170	1.2	497	3.5	1,749	12.5	12,266	87.5	14,015
25.8			84.8		3.5		22.2		3.1		5.2
.3	2,143	19.4	27	.2	22	.2	2,220	20.1	8,824	79.9	11,044
.1	2,166	18.4	51	.4	19	.2	2,249	19.1	9,513	80.9	11,762
1.1			88.9		- 13.6		1.3		7.8		6.5
.3	954	10.1	62	.7	29	.3	1,072	11.4	8,349	88.6	9,421
.2	950	10.5	65	.7	40	.4	1,071	11.8	8,003	88.2	9,074
.4			4.8		37.9		- .1		- 4.1		- 3.7
.2	12	.8	684	43.9	20	1.3	719	46.1	839	53.9	1,558
.2	8	.5	723	44.3	23	1.4	757	46.4	875	53.6	1,632
- 33.3			5.7		15.0		5.3		4.3		4.7
.1	17	.8	872	43.0	25	1.2	916	45.1	1,113	54.9	2,029
.1	17	.9	800	41.4	32	1.7	850	44.0	1,083	56.0	1,933
.0			- 8.3		28.0		- 7.2		- 2.7		- 4.7
.0	7	.3	25	1.2	27	1.3	60	2.9	2,009	97.1	2,069
.6	5	.4	13	.9	13	.9	39	2.8	1,333	97.2	1,372
- 28.6			- 48.0		- 51.9		- 35.0		- 33.6		- 33.7
.2	30	1.1	44	1.6	33	1.2	113	4.0	2,678	96.0	2,791
.5	12	.7	25	1.5	14	.8	60	3.8	1,600	96.4	1,660
- 60.0			- 43.2		- 57.6		- 46.9		- 40.3		- 40.5
.2	2,543	10.6	301	1.3	236	1.0	3,131	13.1	20,788	86.9	23,919
.2	2,308	9.9	404	1.7	308	1.3	3,067	13.1	20,291	86.9	23,358
9.2			34.2		30.5		- 2.0		- 2.4		- 2.3
.2	1,654	5.5	558	1.8	348	1.1	2,610	8.6	27,679	91.4	30,289
.2	1,639	5.4	841	2.8	381	1.3	2,924	9.6	27,474	90.4	30,398
.9			50.7		9.5		12.0		- .7		.4

	AMERICAN INDIAN ALASKAN NATIVE		BLACK NON-HISPANIC		ASIAN OR PACIFIC ISLANDER		HISPANIC		TOTAL MINORITY		WHITE NON-HISPANIC	
	NUMBER	%	NUMBER	%	NUMBER	%	NUMBER	%	NUMBER	%	NUMBER	%
INDIANA												
FEMALE												
1976 (30 INSTITUTIONS)	42	.3	598	4.4	82	.6	56	.4	778	5.7	12,935	94.3
1978 (31 INSTITUTIONS)	39	.3	552	4.2	75	.6	75	.6	741	5.6	12,458	94.4
% CHANGE 1976 TO 1978	- 7.1		- 7.7		- 8.5		33.9		- 4.8		- 3.7	
MALE												
1976 (30 INSTITUTIONS)	53	.3	403	2.7	118	.8	110	.7	684	4.5	14,514	95.5
1978 (31 INSTITUTIONS)	24	.2	382	2.9	104	.8	115	.9	625	4.7	12,777	95.3
% CHANGE 1976 TO 1978	- 54.7		- 5.2		- 11.9		4.5		- 8.6		- 12.0	
IOWA												
FEMALE												
1976 (10 INSTITUTIONS)	10	.2	126	3.0	39	.9	12	.3	187	4.	4,075	95.6
1978 (12 INSTITUTIONS)	13	.3	157	2.6	43	.7	25	.4	238	3.9	5,822	96.1
% CHANGE 1976 TO 1978	30.0		24.6		10.3		108.3		27.3		42.9	
MALE												
1976 (10 INSTITUTIONS)	19	.3	141	2.5	61	1.1	28	.5	249	4.4	5,418	95.6
1978 (12 INSTITUTIONS)	12	.2	137	2.1	71	1.1	31	.5	251	3.8	6,390	96.2
% CHANGE 1976 TO 1978	- 36.8		- 2.8		16.4		10.7		.8		17.9	
KANSAS												
FEMALE												
1976 (9 INSTITUTIONS)	33	.4	187	2.5	33	.4	59	.8	312	4.1	7,242	95.9
1978 (10 INSTITUTIONS)	29	.3	240	2.8	42	.5	69	.8	380	4.4	8,250	95.6
% CHANGE 1976 TO 1978	- 12.1		28.3		27.3		16.9		21.8		13.9	
MALE												
1976 (9 INSTITUTIONS)	64	.9	188	2.7	52	.8	94	1.4	398	5.8	6,489	94.2
1978 (10 INSTITUTIONS)	38	.5	184	2.6	55	.8	81	1.2	358	5.1	6,676	94.9
% CHANGE 1976 TO 1978	- 40.6		- 2.1		5.8		- 13.8		- 10.1		2.9	
KENTUCKY.												
FEMALE												
1976 (15 INSTITUTIONS)	4	.0	384	.4	8	.1	24	.3	420	4.9	8,221	95.1
1978 (16 INSTITUTIONS)	63	.6	323	3.1	30	.3	23	.2	439	4.2	9,897	95.8
% CHANGE 1976 TO 1978	1475.0		- 15.9		275.0		- 4.2		4.5		20.4	
MALE												
1976 (15 INSTITUTIONS)	7	.1	249	3.5	25	.4	14	.2	295	4.2	6,806	95.8
1978 (16 INSTITUTIONS)	47	.7	208	3.2	63	1.0	34	.5	352	5.5	6,051	94.5
% CHANGE 1976 TO 1978	571.4		- 16.5		152.0		142.9		19.3		- 11.1	
LOUISIANA												
FEMALE												
1976 (18 INSTITUTIONS)	8	.1	1,930	22.9	32	.4	124	1.5	2,094	24.8	6,351	75.2
1978 (19 INSTITUTIONS)	16	.2	1,938	21.2	16	.2	124	1.4	2,094	22.9	7,044	77.1
% CHANGE 1976 TO 1978	100.0		.4		- 50.0		.0		.0		10.9	
MALE												
1976 (18 INSTITUTIONS)	17	.2	832	11.1	44	.6	154	2.0	1,047	13.9	6,481	86.1
1978 (19 INSTITUTIONS)	21	.3	642	10.0	54	.8	111	1.7	828	12.9	5,615	87.1
% CHANGE 1976 TO 1978	23.5		- 22.8		22.7		- 27.9		- 20.9		- 13.4	
MAINE												
FEMALE												
1976 (4 INSTITUTIONS)	0	.0	0	.0	1	.1	1	.1	2	.3	716	99.7
1978 (4 INSTITUTIONS)	1	.1	0	.0	1	.1	2	.3	4	.5	751	99.5
% CHANGE 1976 TO 1978	100.0		.0		.0		100.0		100.0		4.9	
MALE												
1976 (4 INSTITUTIONS)	0	.0	1	.1	2	.2	0	.0	3	.3	944	99.7
1978 (4 INSTITUTIONS)	1	.1	3	.3	1	.1	4	.4	9	1.0	937	99.0
% CHANGE 1976 TO 1978	100.0		200.0		- 50.0		100.0		200.0		- .7	
MARYLAND												
FEMALE												
1976 (23 INSTITUTIONS)	18	.2	1,495	14.1	61	.6	71	.7	1,645	15.5	8,941	84.5
1978 (27 INSTITUTIONS)	39	.4	1,334	12.6	119	1.1	87	.8	1,579	15.0	8,970	85.0
% CHANGE 1976 TO 1978	116.7		- 10.8		95.1		22.5		- 4.0		.3	
MALE												
1976 (23 INSTITUTIONS)	36	.4	854	8.9	71	.7	65	.7	1,026	10.7	8,577	89.3
1978 (27 INSTITUTIONS)	23	.2	729	7.8	112	1.2	74	.8	938	10.0	8,439	90.0
% CHANGE 1976 TO 1978	- 36.1		- 14.6		57.7		13.8		- 8.6		- 1.6	

ULL- AND PART-TIME GRADUATE ENROLLMENT IN INSTITUTIONS OF HIGHER EDUCATION
Y AND SEX: STATE AND NATION, 1976, 1978

ICAN INDIAN SKAN NATIVE		BLACK NON-HISPANIC		ASIAN OR PACIFIC ISLANDER		HISPANIC		TOTAL MINORITY		WHITE NON-HISPANIC		TOTAL
NUMBER	%	NUMBER	%	NUMBER	%	NUMBER	%	NUMBER	%	NUMBER	%	NUMBER
31	.2	584	3.1	102	1.0	167	.9	964	5.1	17,980	94.9	18,944
26	.1	600	3.2	269	1.4	228	1.2	1,123	5.9	17,816	94.1	18,939
16.1		2.7		47.8		36.5		16.5		- .9		.0
43	.2	699	2.8	379	1.5	240	1.0	1,361	5	23,583	94.5	24,944
51	.2	748	3.1	490	2.0	341	1.4	1,630	8｡8	22,290	93.2	23,920
18.6		7.0		29.3		42.1		19.8		- 5.5		- 4.1
75	.3	2,134	9.3	184	.8	244	1.1	2,637	11.5	20,336	88.5	22,973
76	.3	2,049	8.7	205	.9	209	.9	2,539	10.8	20,912	89.2	23,451
1.3		- 4.0		11.4		- 14.3		- 3.7		2.8		2.1
89	.4	1,403	6.0	370	1.6	280	1.2	2,142	9.2	21,073	90.8	23,215
70	.3	1,106	5.1	382	1.7	241	1.1	1,799	8.2	20,056	91.8	21,855
21.3		- 21.2		3.2		- 13.9		- 16.0		- 4.8		- 5.9
27	.3	134	1.7	60	.8	30	.4	251	3.2	7,656	96.8	7,907
19	.3	71	1.0	57	.8	41	.6	188	2.6	7,078	97.4	7,266
29.6		- 47.0		- 5.0		36.7		- 25.1		- 7.5		- 8.1
37	.4	170	1.7	96	1.0	49	.5	352	3.5	9,590	96.5	9,942
26	.3	81	1.0	114	1.4	56	.7	277	3.3	8,025	96.7	8,302
29.7		- 52.4		18.8		14.3		- 21.3		- 16.3		- 16.5
2	.0	1,398	32.0	13	.3	3	.1	1,417	32.5	2,948	67.5	4,365
14	.3	1,407	31.3	20	.4	3	.1	1,446	32.2	3,048	67.8	4,494
600.0		.6		53.8		25.0		2.0		3.4		3.0
5	.1	828	20.3	27	.7	2	.0	862	21.1	3,215	78.9	4,077
5	.1	693	18.3	48	1.3	6	.2	752	19.9	3,028	80.1	3,780
.0		- 16.3		77.8		200.0		- 12.8		- 5.8		- 7.3
31	.3	626	6.3	70	.7	41	.4	768	7.8	9,100	92.2	9,868
18	.2	709	7.2	110	1.1	52	.5	889	9.1	8,913	90.9	9,802
41.9		13.3		57.1		26.8		15.8		- 2.1		- .7
54	.4	549	4.1	172	1.3	89	.7	864	6.4	12,642	93.6	13,506
28	.2	585	4.6	458	3.6	103	.8	1,174	9.1	11,682	90.9	12,856
48.1.		6.6		166.3		15.7		35.9		- 7.6		- 4.8
12	1.7	1	.1	3	.4	1	.1	17	2.4	686	97.6	703
18	2.0	0	.0	4	.4	1	.1	23	2.5	893	97.5	916
50.0		- 100.0		33.3		.0		35.3		30.2		30.3
18	1.5	6	.5	9	.7	1	.1	34	2.8	1,189	97.2	1,223
12	1.0	5	.4	4	.3	4	.3	25	2.2	1,127	97.8	1,152
33.3		- 16.7		- 55.6		300.0		- 26.5		- 5.2		- 5.8
5	.1	85	2.4	9	.3	19	.5	118	3.4	3,382	96.6	3,500
5	.1	73	2.1	27	.8	16	.5	121	3.5	3,332	96.5	3,453
.0		- 14.1		200.0		- 15.8		2.5		- 1.5		- 1.3
11	.3	102	2.6	19	.5	31	.8	163	4.1	3,809	95.9	3,972
9	.3	71	2.1	29	.8	38	1.1	147	4.3	3,308	95.7	3,455
18.2		- 30.4		52.6		22.6		- 9.8		- 13.2		- 13.0

TABLE 15 — COMPARISIONS OF FULL- AND PART-TIME GRADUATE ENROLLMENT IN INSTITUTIONS OF HIGHER EDUCATION
BY RACE, ETHNICITY AND SEX: STATE AND NATION, 1976, 1978

	AMERICAN INDIAN ALASKAN NATIVE		BLACK NON-HISPANIC		ASIAN OR PACIFIC ISLANDER		HISPANIC		TOTAL MINORITY		WHITE NON-HISPANIC	
	NUMBER	%	NUMBER	%	NUMBER	%	NUMBER	%	NUMBER	%	NUMBER	%
NEVADA												
FEMALE												
1976 (2 INSTITUTIONS)	2	.3	43	6.2	8	1.1	9	1.3	62	8.9	634	91.1
1978 (2 INSTITUTIONS)	3	.4	27	3.5	7	.9	13	1.7	50	6.5	722	93.5
% CHANGE 1976 TO 1978	50.0		- 37.2		- 12.5		44.4		- 19.4		13.9	
MALE												
1976 (2 INSTITUTIONS)	3	.4	14	1.8	20	2.6	13	1.7	50	6.5	714	93.5
1978 (2 INSTITUTIONS)	8	1.1	18	2.5	14	1.9	14	1.9	54	7.5	666	92.5
% CHANGE 1976 TO 1978	166.7		28.6		- 30.0		7.7		8.0		6.7	
NEW HAMPSHIRE												
FEMALE												
1976 (7 INSTITUTIONS)	2	.2	0	.0	3	.3	2	.2	7	.8	884	99.2
1978 (7 INSTITUTIONS)	1	.1	8	.8	11	1.1	5	.5	25	2.5	968	97.5
% CHANGE 1976 TO 1978	- 50.0		100.0		266.7		150.0		257.1		9.5	
MALE												
1976 (7 INSTITUTIONS)	4	.2	12	.7	13	.8	4	.2	33	2.0	1,626	98.0
1978 (7 INSTITUTIONS)	2	.1	22	1.3	15	.9	5	.3	44	2.6	1,674	97.4
% CHANGE 1976 TO 1978	- 50.0		83.3		15.4		25.0		33.3		3.0	
NEW JERSEY												
FEMALE												
1976 (27 INSTITUTIONS)	21	.1	1,086	6.8	195	1.2	343	2.1	1,645	10.3	14,315	89.7
1978 (27 INSTITUTIONS)	17	.1	932	6.4	178	1.2	332	2.3	1,459	10.0	13,143	90.0
% CHANGE 1976 TO 1978	- 19.0		- 14.2		- 8.7		- 3.2		- 11.3		- 8.2	
MALE												
1976 (27 INSTITUTIONS)	8	.0	746	4.1	314	1.7	311	1.7	1,379	7.5	16,912	92.5
1978 (27 INSTITUTIONS)	16	.1	636	4.1	340	2.2	291	1.9	1,283	8.2	14,354	91.8
% CHANGE 1976 TO 1978	100.0		- 14.7		8.3		- 6.4		- 7.0		- 15.1	
NEW MEXICO												
FEMALE												
1976 (6 INSTITUTIONS)	43	1.7	37	1.4	14	.5	380	14.8	474	18.5	2,087	81.5
1978 (7 INSTITUTIONS)	62	2.3	40	1.5	23	.9	427	15.9	552	20.6	2,131	79.4
% CHANGE 1976 TO 1978	44.2		8.1		64.3		12.4		16.5		2.1	
MALE												
1976 (6 INSTITUTIONS)	40	1.3	52	1.7	25	.8	490	15.7	607	19.4	2,518	80.6
1978 (7 INSTITUTIONS)	54	1.8	49	1.6	29	1.0	512	16.8	644	21.2	2,398	78.8
% CHANGE 1976 TO 1978	35.0		- 5.8		16.0		4.5		6.1		- 4.8	
NEW YORK												
FEMALE												
1976 (110 INSTITUTIONS)	157	.3	3,802	7.1	1,075	2.0	1,529	2.9	6,563	12.3	46,808	87.7
1978 (128 INSTITUTIONS)	159	.3	3,962	7.1	1,244	2.2	1,778	3.2	7,143	12.8	48,731	87.2
% CHANGE 1976 TO 1978	1.3		4.2		15.7		16.3		8.8		4.1	
MALE												
1976 (110 INSTITUTIONS)	197	.3	3,192	5.5	1,678	2.9	1,677	2.9	6,744	11.7	50,942	88.3
1978 (128 INSTITUTIONS)	242	.4	2,905	5.2	1,905	3.4	1,509	2.7	6,561	11.6	49,810	88.4
% CHANGE 1976 TO 1978	22.8		- 9.0		13.5		- 10.0		- 2.7		- 2.2	
NORTH CAROLINA												
FEMALE												
1976 (12 INSTITUTIONS)	33	.4	1,353	14.9	28	.3	32	.4	1,446	15.9	7,651	84.1
1978 (15 INSTITUTIONS)	31	.3	1,357	15.3	39	.4	41	.5	1,468	16.6	7,397	83.4
% CHANGE 1976 TO 1978	- 6.1		.3		39.3		28.1		1.5		3.3	
MALE												
1976 (12 INSTITUTIONS)	43	.5	833	8.9	55	.6	47	.5	978	10.5	8,337	89.5
1978 (15 INSTITUTIONS)	30	.4	757	9.2	64	.8	33	.4	884	10.7	7,356	89.3
% CHANGE 1976 TO 1978	- 30.2		- 9.1		16.4		- 29.8		- 9.6		- 11.8	
NORTH DAKOTA												
FEMALE												
1976 (3 INSTITUTIONS)	2	.4	0	.0	3	.7	4	.9	9	2.0	438	98.0
1978 (3 INSTITUTIONS)	8	1.6	3	.6	5	1.0	1	.2	17	3.5	470	96.5
% CHANGE 1976 TO 1978	300.0		100.0		66.7		- 75.0		88.9		7.3	
MALE												
1976 (3 INSTITUTIONS)	7	.6	6	.5	6	.5	8	.7	27	2.2	1,198	97.8
1978 (3 INSTITUTIONS)	3	.3	7	.8	12	1.3	3	.3	25	2.7	890	97.3
% CHANGE 1976 TO 1978	- 57.1		16.7		100.0		- 62.5		- 7.4		- 25.7	

PART-TIME GRADUATE ENROLLMENT IN INSTITUTIONS OF HIGHER EDUCATION
X: STATE AND NATION, 1976, 1978

IAN IVE	BLACK NON-HISPANIC		ASIAN OR PACIFIC ISLANDER		HISPANIC		TOTAL MINORITY		WHITE NON-HISPANIC		TOTAL
%	NUMBER	%	NUMBER	%	NUMBER	%	NUMBER	%	NUMBER	%	NUMBER
.2	1,785	9.1	169	.9	109	.6	2,096	10.7	17,544	89.3	19,640
.2	1,809	7.9	125	.5	140	.6	2,120	9.3	20,757	90.7	22,877
	1.3		- 26.0		28.4		1.1		18.3		16.5
.1	1,498	6.1	372	1.5	196	.8	2,095	8.5	22,525	91.5	24,620
.2	1,343	5.6	211	.9	166	.7	1,778	7.4	22,138	92.6	23,916
	- 10.3		- 43.3		- 15.3		- 15.1		- 1.7		- 2.9
2.6	384	6.2	43	.7	22	.4	611	9.9	5,562	90.1	6,173
3.2	279	4.9	30	.5	25	.4	515	9.1	5,174	90.9	5,689
	- 27.3		- 30.2		13.6		- 15.7		- 7.0		- 7.8
2 3	306	4.3	69	1.0	60	.8	599	8.5	6,473	91.5	7,072
2:5	226	3.6	48	.8	44	.7	471	7.6	5,742	92.4	6,213
	- 26.1		- 30.4		- 26.7		- 21.4		- 11.3		- 12.1
.9	35	.9	55	1.4	20	.5	145	3.8	3,681	96.2	3,826
.7	35	.9	74	2.0	25	.7	159	4.3	3,535	95.7	3,694
	.0		34.5		25.0		9.7		- 4.0		- 3.5
1.1	56	1.2	60	1.2	58	1.2	227	4.7	4,587	95.3	4,814
.7	60	1.4	93	2.1	41	.9	226	5.1	4,205	94.9	4,431
	7.1		55.0		- 29.3		- .4		- 8.3		- 8.0
.2	1,049	4.6	132	.6	157	.7	1,373	6.1	21,203	93.9	22,576
.2	1,057	5.2	207	1.0	157	.8	1,458	7.2	18,740	92.8	20,198
	.8		56.8		.0		6.2		- 11.6		- 10.5
.2	867	3.1	278	1.0	164	.6	1,372	4.	26,947	95.2	28,319
.3	778	3.3	336	1.4	180	.6	1,356	5.7	22,367	94.3	23,723
	· 10.3		20.9		9.8		- 1.2		- 17.0		- 16.2
.0	53	2.4	13	.6	17	.8	84	3.8	2,106	96.2	2,190
.3	38	1.5	15	.6	14	.6	75	3.0	2,410	97.0	2,485
	·· 28.3		15.4		- 17.6		- 10.7		14.4		13.5
.1	54	1.7	30	1.0	16	.5	103	3.3	3,051	96.7	3,154
.2	45	1.4	49	1.6	17	.5	118	3.7	3,040	96.3	3,158
	· 16.7		63.3		6.3		14.6		- .4		· 1
.1	1,066	16.2	13	.2	13	.2	1,098	16.6	5,498	83.4	6,596
.1	927	13.7	11	.2	17	.3	961	14.2	5,807	85.8	6,768
	- 13.0		- 15.4		30.8		- 12.5		5.6		2.6
.1	526	9.6	20	.4	11	.2	563	10.3	4,921	89.7	5,484
.1	388	7.8	24	.5	20	.4	438	8.8	4,527	91.2	4,965
	· 26.2		20.0		81.8		- 22.2		- 8.0		- 9.5
2.0	0	.0	0	.0	0	.0	12	2.0	583	98.0	595
1.4	1	.1	0	.0	0	.0	11	1.5	723	98.5	734
	100.0		.0		.0		- 8.3		24.0		23.4
2.0	9	.8	1	.1	1	.1	33	3.0	1,073	97.0	1,106
1.5	2	.2	2	.2	2	.2	22	2.1	1,023	97.9	1,045
	· 77.8		100.0		100.0		- 33.3		- 4.7		- 5.5

TABLE 15 - COMPARISIONS OF FULL- AND PART-TIME GRADUATE ENROLLMENT IN INSTITUTIONS OF HIGHER EDUCATION
BY RACE, ETHNICITY AND SEX: STATE AND NATION, 1976, 1978

	AMERICAN INDIAN ALASKAN NATIVE		BLACK NON-HISPANIC		ASIAN OR PACIFIC ISLANDER		HISPANIC		TOTAL MINORITY		WHITE NON-HISPANIC	
	NUMBER	%	NUMBER	%	NUMBER	%	NUMBER	%	NUMBER	%	NUMBER	%
TENNESSEE												
FEMALE												
1976 (19 INSTITUTIONS)	18	.3	855	12.2	13	.2	12	.2	898	12.8	6,122	87.2
1978 (18 INSTITUTIONS)	16	.2	739	10.0	37	.5	23	.3	815	11.1	6,557	88.9
% CHANGE 1976 TO 1978	- 11.1		- 13.6		184.6		91.7		- 9.2		7.1	
MALE												
1976 (19 INSTITUTIONS)	41	.5	595	7.8	25	.3	16	.2	677	8.9	6,958	91.1
1978 (18 INSTITUTIONS)	13	.2	436	5.9	71	1.0	26	.3	546	7.3	6,894	92.7
% CHANGE 1976 TO 1978	- 68.3		- 26.7		184.0		62.5		- 19.4		- .9	
TEXAS												
FEMALE												
1976 (55 INSTITUTIONS)	120	.4	2,414	8.6	217	.8	2,051	7.3	4,802	17.1	23,310	82.9
1978 (56 INSTITUTIONS)	92	.3	2,347	8.1	349	1.2	2,251	7.7	5,039	17.3	24,044	82.7
% CHANGE 1976 TO 1978	- 23.3		- 2.8		60.8		9.8		4.9		3.1	
MALE												
1976 (55 INSTITUTIONS)	161	.5	1,643	5.1	370	1.1	2,117	6.6	4,291	13.3	27,886	86.7
1978 (56 INSTITUTIONS)	153	.5	1,615	5.0	602	1.9	2,270	7.1	4,640	14.4	27,547	85.6
% CHANGE 1976 TO 1978	- 5.0		- 1.7		62.7		7.2		8.1		- 1.2	
UTAH.												
FEMALE												
1976 (4 INSTITUTIONS)	16	.9	19	1.1	35	2.0	32	1.8	102	5.8	1,666	94.2
1978 (4 INSTITUTIONS)	22	.9	14	.6	42	1.7	31	1.3	109	4.5	2,302	95.5
% CHANGE 1976 TO 1978	37.5		- 26.3		20.0		- 3.1		6.9		38.2	
MALE												
1976 (4 INSTITUTIONS)	16	.4	18	.5	45	1.2	39	1.1	118	3.2	3,554	96.8
1978 (4 INSTITUTIONS)	26	.6	19	.4	61	1.3	37	.8	143	3.1	4,410	96.9
% CHANGE 1976 TO 1978	62.5		5.6		35.6		- 5.1		21.2		24.1	
VERMONT												
FEMALE												
1976 (11 INSTITUTIONS)	1	.1	33	2.7	8	.6	11	.9	53	4.3	1,190	95.7
1978 (11 INSTITUTIONS)	0	.0	23	1.8	6	.5	6	.5	35	2.7	1,272	97.3
% CHANGE 1976 TO 1978	- 100.0		- 30.3		- 25.0		- 45.5		- 34.0		6.9	
MALE												
1976 (11 INSTITUTIONS)	5	.4	27	2.3	9	.8	5	.4	46	3.8	1,149	96.2
1978 (11 INSTITUTIONS)	3	.3	22	2.2	2	.2	13	1.3	40	4.1	938	95.9
% CHANGE 1976 TO 1978	- 40.0		- 18.5		- 77.8		160.0		- 13.0		- 18.4	
VIRGINIA.												
FEMALE												
1976 (20 INSTITUTIONS)	13	.2	983	11.9	24	.3	30	.4	1,050	12.7	7,215	87.3
1978 (21 INSTITUTIONS)	10	.1	1,216	12.8	48	.5	38	.4	1,312	13.8	8,211	86.2
% CHANGE 1976 TO 1978	- 23.1		23.7		100.0		26.7		25.0		13.8	
MALE												
1976 (20 INSTITUTIONS)	11	.1	589	6.0	98	1.0	22	.2	720	7.3	9,118	92.7
1978 (21 INSTITUTIONS)	16	.2	710	7.2	127	1.3	33	.3	886	9.0	8,983	91.0
% CHANGE 1976 TO 1978	45.5		20.5		29.6		50.0		23.1		- 1.5	
WASHINGTON.												
FEMALE												
1976 (14 INSTITUTIONS)	55	1.1	150	3.1	132	2.7	54	1.1	391	8.0	4,486	92.0
1978 (16 INSTITUTIONS)	43	.8	128	2.5	158	3.1	42	.8	371	7.2	4,776	92.8
% CHANGE 1976 TO 1978	- 21.8		- 14.7		19.7		- 22.2		- 5.1		6.5	
MALE												
1976 (14 INSTITUTIONS)	46	.7	145	2.1	212	3.0	89	1.3	492	7.0	6,523	93.0
1978 (16 INSTITUTIONS)	50	.7	167	2.4	237	3.4	96	1.4	550	7.9	6,441	92.1
% CHANGE 1976 TO 1978	8.7		15.2		11.8		7.9		11.8		- 1.3	
WEST VIRGINIA												
FEMALE												
1976 (4 INSTITUTIONS)	13	.2	135	2.3	38	.7	13	.2	199	3.4	5,628	96.6
1978 (5 INSTITUTIONS)	23	.4	158	2.4	27	.4	10	.2	218	3.4	6,256	96.6
% CHANGE 1976 TO 1978	76.9		17.0		- 28.9		- 23.1		9.5		11.2	
MALE												
1976 (4 INSTITUTIONS)	8	.2	117	2.5	80	1.7	14	.3	219	4.6	4,493	95.4
1978 (5 INSTITUTIONS)	20	.4	110	2.4	56	1.2	12	.3	198	4.3	4,414	95.7
% CHANGE 1976 TO 1978	150.0		- 6.0		- 30.0		- 14.3		- 9.6		- 1.8	

278

FULL- AND PART-TIME GRADUATE ENROLLMENT IN INSTITUTIONS OF HIGHER EDUCATION
BY AND SEX: STATE AND NATION, 1976, 1978

RICAN INDIAN ASKAN NATIVE		BLACK NON-HISPANIC		ASIAN OR PACIFIC ISLANDER		HISPANIC		TOTAL MINORITY		WHITE NON-HISPANIC		TOTAL
NUMBER	%	NUMBER	%	NUMBER	%	NUMBER	%	NUMBER	%	NUMBER	%	NUMBER
19	.2	243	3.1	67	.8	55	.7	384	4.8	7,552	95.2	7,936
32	.4	248	3.1	100	1.2	91	1.1	471	5.8	7,605	94.2	8,076
68.4		2.1		49.3		65.5		22.7		.7		1.8
21	.2	210	2.0	111	1.1	89	.9	431	4.2	9,814	95.8	10,245
26	.3	207	2.2	179	1.9	105	1.1	517	5.5	8,922	94.5	9,439
23.8		- 1.4		61.3		18.0		20.0		- 9.1		- 7.9
2	.7	4	1.3	2	.7	3	1.0	11	3.6	292	96.4	303
1	.2	3	.7	3	.7	2	.5	9	2.2	408	97.8	417
50.0		- 25.0		50.0		- 33.3		- 18.2		39.7		37.6
2	.2	6	.7	4	.5	9	1.1	21	2.5	806	97.5	827
2	.4	1	.2	2	.4	6	1.1	11	2.1	517	97.9	528
.0		- 83.3		- 50.0		- 33.3		- 47.6		- 35.9		- 36.2
1,694	.4	38,336	8.2	6,887	1.5	8,915	1.9	55,832	11.9	411,480	88.1	467,312
1,740	.4	37,213	7.8	7,862	1.6	9,946	2.1	56,781	11.8	422,840	88.2	479,621
2.7		- 2.9		14.4		11.6		1.7		2.8		2.6
2,193	.4	26,990	4.9	11,598	2.1	11,329	2 1	52,110	9.5	495,146	90.5	547,256
2,045	.4	24,658	4.8	12,730	2.5	11,109	2.1	50,542	9.7	467,961	90.3	518,503
6.7		- 8.6		9.8		9.8		- 3.0		- 5.5		- 5.3
3	1.2	0	.0	148	59.4	3	1.2	154	61.8	95	38.2	249
0	.0	0	.0	94	58.0	11	6.8	105	64.8	57	35.2	162
100.0		.0		- 36.5		266.7		- 31.8		- 40.0		- 34.9
6	3.9	0	.0	57	37.3	9	5.9	72	47.1	81	52.9	153
0	.0	0	.0	24	28.2	0	.0	24	28.2	61	71.8	85
100.0		.0		- 57.9		- 100.0		- 66.7		- 24.7		- 44.4
19	.9	0	.0	0	.0	2,132	98.5	2,151	99.4	14	.6	2,165
0	.0	0	.0	0	.0	2,324	94.6	2,324	94.6	133	5.4	2,457
100.0		.0		.0		9.0		8.0		850.0		13.5
5	.3	0	.0	0	.0	1,809	98.6	1,814	98.9	20	1.1	1,834
0	.0	0	.0	0	.0	1,786	95.5	1,786	95.5	85	4.5	1,871
100.0		.0		.0		- 1.3		- 1.5		325.0		2.0
0	.0	16	45.7	0	.0	0	.0	16	45.7	19	54.3	35
0	.0	29	65.9	0	.0	1	2.3	30	68.2	14	31.8	44
.0		81.3		.0		100.0		87.5		- 26.3		25.7
0	.0	3	42.9	0	.0	0	.0	3	42.9	4	57.1	7
0	.0	18	69.2	1	3.8	1	3.8	20	76.9	6	23.1	26
.0		500.0		100.0		100.0		566.7		50.0		271.4
22	.9	16	.7	148	6.0	2,135	87.2	2,321	94.8	128	5.2	2,449
0	.0	29	1.1	94	3.5	2,336	87.7	2,459	92.3	204	7.7	2,663
100.0		81.3		- 36.5		9.4		5.9		59.4		8.7
11	.6	3	.2	57	2.9	1,818	91.2	1,889	94.7	105	.3	1,994
0	.0	18	.9	25	1.3	1,787	90.2	1,830	92.3	152	7.7	1,982
100.0		500.0		- 56.1		- 56.1		- 3.1		44.8		- .6

279

TABLE 15 - COMPARISIONS OF FULL- AND PART-TIME GRADUATE ENROLLMENT IN INSTITUTIONS OF HIGHER EDUCATION
BY RACE, ETHNICITY AND SEX: STATE AND NATION, 1976, 1978

	AMERICAN INDIAN ALASKAN NATIVE		BLACK NON-HISPANIC		ASIAN OR PACIFIC ISLANDER		HISPANIC		TOTAL MINORITY		WHITE NON-HISPANIC	
	NUMBER	%	NUMBER	%	NUMBER	%	NUMBER	%	NUMBER	%	NUMBER	%
NATION, TOTAL												
FEMALE												
1976 (1052 INSTITUTIONS)	1,716	.4	38,352	8.2	7,035	1.5	11,050	2.4	58,153	12.4	411,608	87.6
1978 (1139 INSTITUTIONS)	1,740	.4	37,242	7.7	7,976	1.7	12,282	2.5	59,240	12.3	423,044	87.7
% CHANGE 1976 TO 1978	1.4		- 2.9		13.4		11.1		1.9		2.8	
MALE												
1976 (1052 INSTITUTIONS)	2,204	.4	26,993	.9	11,655	2.1	13,147	2.4	53,999	9.8	495,251	90.2
1978 (1139 INSTITUTIONS)	2,045	.4	24,676	2.7	12,755	2.5	12,896	2.5	52,372	10.1	468,113	89.9
% CHANGE 1976 TO 1978	- 7.2		- 8.6		9.4		9.4		- 3.0		- 5.5	

FULL- AND PART-TIME FIRST PROFESSIONAL ENROLLMENT IN INSTITUTIONS OF HIGHER EDUCATION
TY AND SEX: STATE AND NATION, 1976, 1978

RICAN INDIAN ASKAN NATIVE		BLACK NON-HISPANIC		ASIAN OR PACIFIC ISLANDER		HISPANIC		TOTAL MINORITY		WHITE NON-HISPANIC		TOTAL
NUMBER	%	NUMBER	%	NUMBER	%	NUMBER	%	NUMBER	%	NUMBER	%	NUMBER
0	.0	70	14.4	1	.2	1	.2	72	14.8	414	85.2	486
0	.0	85	12.2	8	1.1	2	.3	95	13.6	601	86.4	696
.0		21.4		700.0		100.0		31.9		45.2		43.2
2	.1	154	6.4	11	.5	7	.3	174	7.2	2,242	92.8	2,416
1	.0	111	4.1	14	.5	4	.1	130	4.8	2,563	95.2	2,693
50.0		- 27.9		27.3		- 42.9		- 25.3		14.3		11.5
1	.3	1	.3	2	.6	10	2.9	14	4.0	335	96.0	349
1	.3	0	.0	2	.5	8	2.2	11	3.0	358	97.0	369
.0		- 100.0		.0		- 20.0		- 21.4		6.9		5.7
2	.3	3	.4	7	.9	22	3.0	34	4.6	704	95.4	738
3	.4	2	.1	2	.2	17	2.1	23	2.8	793	97.2	816
50.0		- 66.7		- 71.4		- 22.7		- 32.4		12.6		10.6
4	1.4	17	6.1	1	.4	1	.4	23	8.2	256	91.8	279
1	.3	20	6.5	3	1.0	2	.6	26	8.4	282	91.6	308
75.0		17.6		200.0		100.0		13.0		10.2		10.4
4	.3	47	4.0	9	.8	3	.3	63	5.3	1,117	94.7	1,180
5	.4	47	3.9	11	.9	3	.2	66	5.5	1,145	94.5	1,211
25.0		.0		22.2		.0		4.8		2.5		2.6
51	.7	460	6.0	516	6.7	304	3.9	1,331	17.3	6,371	82.7	7,702
53	.6	521	5.9	605	6.9	367	4.2	1,546	17.6	7,220	82.4	8,766
3.9		13.3		17.2		20.7		16.2		13.3		13.8
145	.7	753	3.5	1,188	5.5	1,048	4.9	3,134	14.6	18,395	85.4	21,529
114	.5	729	3.4	1,320	6.1	1,091	5.1	3,254	15.1	18,315	84.9	21,569
21.4		- 3.2		11.1		4.1		3.8		- .4		.2
3	.4	16	2.3	11	1.6	24	3.4	54	7.7	646	92.3	700
8	.9	21	2.4	11	1.2	32	3.6	72	8.2	811	91.8	883
166.7		31.3		.0		33.3		33.3		25.5		26.1
10	.5	36	1.8	23	1.2	81	4.1	150	7.6	1,824	92.4	1,974
18	.9	42	2.0	28	1.4	88	4.3	176	8.5	1,884	91.5	2,060
80.0		16.7		21.7		8.6		17.3		3.3		4.4
1	.1	43	6.1	9	1.3	9	1.3	62	8.8	639	91.2	701
3	.3	50	5.7	11	1.3	28	3.2	92	10.5	788	89.5	880
200.0		16.3		22.2		211.1		48.4		23.3		25.5
3	.2	96	5.8	21	1.3	27	1.6	147	8.8	1,517	91.2	1,664
1	.0	81	4.0	21	1.0	61	3.0	164	8.1	1,849	91.9	2,013
66.7		- 15.6		.0		125.9		11.6		21.9		21.0
4	.2	510	21.4	43	1.8	37	1.6	594	24.9	1,793	75.1	2,387
3	.1	664	23.1	63	2.2	66	2.3	796	27.7	2,078	72.3	2,874
25.0		30.2		46.5		78.4		34.0		15.9		20.4
10	.2	763	13.6	75	1.3	116	2.1	964	17.1	4,657	82.9	5,621
14	.2	910	16.0	89	1.6	139	2.4	1,152	20.2	4,547	79.8	5,699
40.0		19.3		18.7		19.8		19.5		- 2.4		1.4

	AMERICAN INDIAN ALASKAN NATIVE		BLACK NON-HISPANIC		ASIAN OR PACIFIC ISLANDER		HISPANIC		TOTAL MINORITY		WHITE NON-HISPANIC	
	NUMBER	%	NUMBER	%	NUMBER	%	NUMBER	%	NUMBER	%	NUMBER	%
FLORIDA												
FEMALE												
1976 (6 INSTITUTIONS)	0	.0	43	4.0	2	.2	37	3.4	82	7.6	1,004	92.4
1978 (6 INSTITUTIONS)	2	.1	50	3.2	4	.3	69	4.4	125	7.9	1,457	92.1
% CHANGE 1976 TO 1978	100.0		16.3		100.0		86.5		52.4		45.1	
MALE												
1976 (6 INSTITUTIONS)	10	.3	124	3.2	13	.3	162	4.2	309	7.9	3,584	92.1
1978 (6 INSTITUTIONS)	13	.3	142	3.2	22	.5	236	5.4	413	9.4	3,993	90.6
% CHANGE 1976 TO 1978	30.0		14.5		69.2		45.7		33.7		11.4	
GEORGIA												
FEMALE												
1976 (6 INSTITUTIONS)	2	.2	79	9.3	2	.2	8	.9	91	10.8	754	89.2
1978 (7 INSTITUTIONS)	3	.2	103	8.5	4	.3	6	.5	116	9.6	1,092	90.4
% CHANGE 1976 TO 1978	50.0		30.4		100.0		- 25.0		27.5		44.8	
MALE												
1976 (6 INSTITUTIONS)	4	1	254	7.1	16	.4	15	.4	289	8.1	3,301	91.9
1978 (7 INSTITUTIONS)	4	#1	325	7.3	15	.3	31	.7	375	8.4	4,070	91.6
% CHANGE 1976 TO 1978	.0		28.0		- 6.3		106.7		29.8		23.3	
HAWAII												
FEMALE												
1976 (1 INSTITUTIONS)	0	.0	0	.0	89	64.0	1	.7	90	64.7	49	35.3
1978 (1 INSTITUTIONS)	0	.0	0	.0	108	67.5	2	1.3	110	68.8	50	31.3
% CHANGE 1976 TO 1978	.0		.0		21.3		100.0		22.2		2.0	
MALE												
1976 (1 INSTITUTIONS)	1	.3	0	.0	249	73.9	0	.0	250	74.2	87	25.8
1978 (1 INSTITUTIONS)	0	.0	0	.0	252	79.0	1	.3	253	79.3	66	20.7
% CHANGE 1976 TO 1978	- 100.0		.0		1.2		100.0		1.2		- 24.1	
IDAHO												
FEMALE												
1976 (1 INSTITUTIONS)	0	.0	0	.0	0	.0	0	.0	0	.0	49	100.0
1978 (1 INSTITUTIONS)	0	.0	1	2.0	1	2.0	0	.0	2	4.0	48	96.0
% CHANGE 1976 TO 1978	.0		100.0		100.0		.0		100.0		- 2.0	
MALE												
1976 (1 INSTITUTIONS)	1	.5	0	.0	0	.0	1	.5	2	1.0	208	99.0
1978 (1 INSTITUTIONS)	0	.0	0	.0	1	.5	0	.0	1	.5	219	99.5
% CHANGE 1976 TO 1978	- 100.0		.0		100.0		- 100.0		- 50.0		5.3	
ILLINOIS												
FEMALE												
1976 (30 INSTITUTIONS)	6	.2	237	7.1	50	1.5	42	1 3	335	10.0	3,025	90.0
1978 (31 INSTITUTIONS)	10	.3	246	6.3	60	1.7	44	111	366	9.3	3,552	90.7
% CHANGE 1976 TO 1978	66.7		3.8		32.0		4.8		9.3		17.4	
MALE												
1976 (30 INSTITUTIONS)	29	.2	413	3.2	192	1.5	165	1.3	799	6.1	12,298	93.9
1978 (31 INSTITUTIONS)	20	.2	373	2.8	214	1.6	159	1.2	766	5.8	12,384	94.2
% CHANGE 1976 TO 1978	- 31.0		- 9.7		11.5		- 3.6		- 4.1		.7	
INDIANA												
FEMALE												
1976 (15 INSTITUTIONS)	3	.3	69	6.1	4	.4	14	1.2	90	8.0	1,035	92.0
1978 (13 INSTITUTIONS)	4	.3	72	5.8	7	.6	15	1.2	98	7.9	1,138	92.1
% CHANGE 1976 TO 1978	33.3		4.3		75.0		7.1		8.9		10.0	
MALE												
1976 (15 INSTITUTIONS)	412	8.6	133	2.8	18	.4	60	1.3	623	13.0	4,168	87.0
1978 (13 INSTITUTIONS)	15	.3	104	2.2	34	.7	58	1.2	211	4.4	4,534	95.6
% CHANGE 1976 TO 1978	- 96.4		- 21.8		88.9		- 3.3		- 66.1		8.8	
IOWA												
FEMALE												
1976 (7 INSTITUTIONS)	3	.4	22	2.7	6	.7	5	.6	36	4.3	793	95.7
1978 (7 INSTITUTIONS)	4	.4	16	1.6	11	1.1	7	.7	38	3.8	974	96.2
% CHANGE 1976 TO 1978	33.3		- 27.3		83.3		40.0		5.6		22.8	
MALE												
1976 (7 INSTITUTIONS)	14	.3	59	1.3	20	.4	39	.8	132	2.9	4,462	97.1
1978 (7 INSTITUTIONS)	23	.5	50	1.1	23	.5	41	.9	137	3.0	4,407	97.0
% CHANGE 1976 TO 1978	64.3		- 15.3		15.0		5.1		3.8		- 1.2	

FULL- AND PART-TIME FIRST PROFESSIONAL ENROLLMENT IN INSTITUTIONS OF HIGHER EDUCATION
TY AND SEX: STATE AND NATION, 1976, 1978

..ICAN INDIAN ..SKAN NATIVE		BLACK NON-HISPANIC		ASIAN OR PACIFIC ISLANDER		HISPANIC		TOTAL MINORITY		WHITE NON-HISPANIC		TOTAL
NUMBER	%	NUMBER	%	NUMBER	%	NUMBER	%	NUMBER	%	NUMBER	%	NUMBER
4	1.0	15	3.6	2	.5	1	.2	22	5.3	393	94.7	415
0	.0	15	3.0	4	.8	11	2.2	30	6.1	462	93.9	492
100.0		.0		100.0		1000.0		36.4		17.6		18.6
37	2.2	45	2.7	12	.7	16	1.0	110	6.5	1,572	93.5	1,682
7	.4	29	1.6	11	.6	24	1.4	71	4.0	1,694	96.0	1,765
81.1 -		35.6 -		8.3 -		50.0 -		35.5 -		7.8		4.9
3	.4	24	3.2	2	.3	1	.1	30	4.0	723	96.0	753
2	.2	28	3.1	19	2.1	4	.4	53	5.9	842	94.1	895
33.3		16.7		850.0		300.0		76.7		16.5		18.9
6	.2	66	2.0	10	.3	5	.2	87	2.6	3,197	97.4	3,284
10	.3	70	2.0	58	1.6	15	.4	153	4.3	3,373	95.7	3,526
66.7		6.1		480.0		200.0		75.9		5.5		7.4
7	.8	67	7.2	9	1.0	7	.8	90	9.7	838	90.3	928
3	.3	78	8.7	6	.7	15	1.7	102	11.3	797	88.7	899
57.1		16.4		33.3 -		114.3		13.3		4.9 -		3.1 -
6	.1	186	4.4	10	.2	33	.8	235	5.6	3,948	94.4	4,183
5	.2	184	6.0	22	.7	37	1.2	248	8.1	2,825	91.9	3,073
16.7		1.1 -		120.0		12.1		5.5		28.4 -		26.5 -
0	.0	0	.0	0	.0	0	.0	0	.0	88	100.0	88
0	.0	0	.0	0	.0	0	.0	0	.0	115	100.0	115
.0		.0		.0		.0		.0		30.7		30.7
0	.0	0	.0	0	.0	0	.0	0	.0	262	100.0	262
0	.0	1	.5	0	.0	1	.5	2	.9	215	99.1	217
.0		100.0		.0		100.0		100.0		17.9 -		17.2 -
0	.0	86	11.0	15	1.9	3	.4	104	13.3	679	86.7	783
0	.0	86	9.5	20	2.2	7	.8	113	12.5	792	87.5	905
.0		.0		33.3		133.3		8.7		16.6		15.6
0	.0	154	5.3	27	.9	7	.2	188	6.4	2,740	93.6	2,928
2	.1	138	5.3	56	2.1	20	.8	216	8.2	2,409	91.8	2,625
100.0 -		10.4		107.4		185.7		14.9 -		12.1 -		10.3 -
17	.5	169	5.4	57	1.8	47	1.5	290	9.3	2,820	90.7	3,110
9	.3	170	4.8	64	1.8	57	1.6	300	8.6	3,207	91.4	3,507
47.1		.6		12.3		21.3		3.4		13.7		12.8
26	.3	304	3.6	113	1.3	114	1.3	557	6.6	7,931	93.4	8,488
16	.2	251	3.3	94	1.2	126	1.7	487	6.5	7,035	93.5	7,522
38.5 -		17.4 -		16.8 -		10.5		12.6 -		11.3 -		11.4 -
7	.2	326	11.5	28	1.0	63	2.2	424	15.0	2,405	85.0	2,829
9	.4	231	9.6	34	1.4	42	1.7	316	13.1	2,101	86.9	2,417
28.6 -		29.1 -		21.4		33.3 -		25.5 -		12.6 -		14.6 -
25	.3	491	6.1	79	1.0	132	1.6	727	9.1	7,278	90.9	8,005
20	.3	357	4.7	91	1.2	128	1.7	596	7.9	6,931	92.1	7,527
20.0 -		27.3 -		15.2		3.0 -		18.0 -		4.8 -		6.0 -

TABLE 16 - COMPARISIONS OF FULL- AND PART-TIME FIRST PROFESSIONAL ENROLLMENT IN INSTITUTIONS OF HIGHER EDUCATION BY RACE, ETHNICITY AND SEX: STATE AND NATION, 1976, 1978

	AMERICAN INDIAN ALASKAN NATIVE		BLACK NON-HISPANIC		ASIAN OR PACIFIC ISLANDER		HISPANIC		TOTAL MINORITY		WHITE NON-HISPANIC	
	NUMBER	%	NUMBER	%	NUMBER	%	NUMBER	%	NUMBER	%	NUMBER	%
MINNESOTA												
FEMALE												
1976 (12 INSTITUTIONS)	2	.2	26	2.2	6	.5	8	.7	42	3.5	1,158	96.5
1978 (11 INSTITUTIONS)	10	.7	34	2.3	10	.7	17	1.1	71	4.7	1,435	95.3
% CHANGE 1976 TO 1978	400.0		30.8		66.7		112.5		69.0		23.9	
MALE												
1976 (12 INSTITUTIONS)	14	.3	58	1.2	17	.4	42	.9	131	2.7	4,661	97.3
1978 (11 INSTITUTIONS)	22	.5	47	1.0	23	.5	53	1.1	145	3.0	4,625	97.0
% CHANGE 1976 TO 1978	57.1		- 19.0		35.3		26.2		10.7		- .8	
MISSISSIPPI												
FEMALE												
1976 (4 INSTITUTIONS)	4	1.3	30	9.8	2	.7	2	.7	38	12.4	268	87.6
1978 (5 INSTITUTIONS)	2	.6	29	8.1	3	.8	1	.3	35	9.8	323	90.2
% CHANGE 1976 TO 1978	- 50.0		- 3.3		50.0		- 50.0		- 7.9		20.5	
MALE												
1976 (4 INSTITUTIONS)	3	.2	62	3.6	14	.8	1	.1	80	4.7	1,635	95.3
1978 (5 INSTITUTIONS)	1	.1	51	3.7	8	.6	3	.2	63	4.6	1,308	95.4
% CHANGE 1976 TO 1978	- 66.7		- 17.7		- 42.9		200.0		- 21.3		- 20.0	
MISSOURI												
FEMALE												
1976 (16 INSTITUTIONS)	6	.4	106	6.9	19	1.2	6	.4	137	8.9	1,398	91.1
1978 (17 INSTITUTIONS)	9	.5	108	5.9	38	2.1	7	.4	162	8.9	1,655	91.1
% CHANGE 1976 TO 1978	50.0		1.9		100.0		16.7		18.2		18.4	
MALE												
1976 (16 INSTITUTIONS)	15	.2	198	2.6	62	.8	28	.4	303	4.0	7,244	96.0
1978 (17 INSTITUTIONS)	23	.3	154	2.0	115	1.5	42	.5	334	4.3	7,362	95.7
% CHANGE 1976 TO 1978	53.3		- 22.2		85.5		50.0		10.2		1.6	
MONTANA												
FEMALE												
1976 (1 INSTITUTIONS)	0	.0	0	.0	0	.0	0	.0	0	.0	46	100.0
1978 (1 INSTITUTIONS)	0	.0	0	.0	0	.0	0	.0	0	.0	67	100.0
% CHANGE 1976 TO 1978	.0		.0		.0		.0		.0		45.7	
MALE												
1976 (1 INSTITUTIONS)	2	1.2	0	.0	0	.0	0	.0	2	1.2	168	98.8
1978 (1 INSTITUTIONS)	0	.0	0	.0	0	.0	0	.0	0	.0	155	100.0
% CHANGE 1976 TO 1978	- 100.0		.0		.0		.0		- 100.0		- 7.7	
NEBRASKA												
FEMALE												
1976 (4 INSTITUTIONS)	0	.0	12	2.7	4	.9	1	.2	17	3.8	428	96.2
1978 (4 INSTITUTIONS)	2	.3	15	2.4	8	1.3	3	.5	28	4.5	591	95.5
% CHANGE 1976 TO 1978	100.0		25.0		100.0		200.0		64.7		38.1	
MALE												
1976 (4 INSTITUTIONS)	10	.5	38	1.8	24	1.1	25	1.2	97	4.6	2,030	95.4
1978 (4 INSTITUTIONS)	5	.2	34	1.6	31	1.4	35	1.6	105	4.8	2,082	95.2
% CHANGE 1976 TO 1978	- 50.0		- 10.5		29.2		40.0		8.2		2.6	
NEW HAMPSHIRE												
FEMALE												
1976 (1 INSTITUTIONS)	1	2.0	3	5.9	1	2.0	2	3.9	7	13.7	44	86.3
1978 (2 INSTITUTIONS)	3	4.3	3	4.3	7	10.0	4	5.7	17	24.3	53	75.7
% CHANGE 1976 TO 1978	200.0		.0		600.0		100.0		142.9		20.5	
MALE												
1976 (1 INSTITUTIONS)	3	2.1	10	6.9	2	1.4	4	2.8	19	13.2	125	86.8
1978 (2 INSTITUTIONS)	3	.8	6	1.6	4	1.1	7	1.9	20	5.4	347	94.6
% CHANGE 1976 TO 1978	.0		- 40.0		100.0		75.0		5.3		177.6	
NEW JERSEY												
FEMALE												
1976 (12 INSTITUTIONS)	4	.3	142	11.9	17	1.4	37	3.1	200	16.7	997	83.3
1978 (11 INSTITUTIONS)	3	.2	177	11.9	28	1.9	61	4.1	269	18.1	1,219	81.9
% CHANGE 1976 TO 1978	- 25.0		24.6		64.7		64.9		34.5		22.3	
MALE												
1976 (12 INSTITUTIONS)	8	.2	230	6.5	29	.8	109	3.1	376	10.7	3,144	89.3
1978 (11 INSTITUTIONS)	5	.1	250	6.6	32	.8	104	2.7	391	10.3	3,412	89.7
% CHANGE 1976 TO 1978	- 37.5		8.7		10.3		- 4.6		4.0		8.5	

284

COMPARISIONS OF FULL- AND PART-TIME FIRST PROFESSIONAL ENROLLMENT IN INSTITUTIONS OF HIGHER EDUCATION
BY RACE, ETHNICITY AND SEX: STATE AND NATION, 1976, 1978

	AMERICAN INDIAN ALASKAN NATIVE		BLACK NON-HISPANIC		ASIAN OR PACIFIC ISLANDER		HISPANIC		TOTAL MINORITY		WHITE NON-HISPANIC		TOTAL
	NUMBER	%	NUMBER	%	NUMBER	%	NUMBER	%	NUMBER	%	NUMBER	%	NUMBER
INSTITUTIONS)	8	4.0	4	2.0	3	1.5	27	13.6	42	21.2	156	78.8	198
INSTITUTIONS)	7	3.2	3	1.4	6	2.7	47	21.5	63	28.8	156	71.2	219
976 TO 1978	- 12.5		- 25.0		100.0		74.1		50.0		.0		10.6
INSTITUTIONS)	12	2.8	7	1.6	3	.7	106	24.8	128	30.0	299	70.0	427
INSTITUTIONS)	15	3.7	4	1.0	5	1.2	102	25.2	126	31.1	279	68.9	405
976 TO 1978	25.0		- 42.9		66.7		- 3.8		- 1.6		- 6.7		- 5.2
INSTITUTIONS)	10	.2	359	6.7	83	1.5	109	2.0	561	10.4	4,827	89.6	5,388
INSTITUTIONS)	19	.3	375	5.6	110	1.6	153	2.3	657	9.7	6,083	90.3	6,740
976 TO 1978	90.0		4.5		32.5		40.4		17.1		26.0		25.1
INSTITUTIONS)	14	.1	500	3.2	223	1.4	250	1.6	987	6.4	14,481	93.6	15,468
INSTITUTIONS)	18	.1	416	2.6	195	1.2	288	1.8	917	5.8	14,795	94.2	15,712
976 TO 1978	28.6		- 16.8		- 12.6		15.2		- 7.1		2.2		1.6
NA.													
INSTITUTIONS)	7	.8	114	12.5	3	.3	6	.7	130	14.3	780	85.7	910
INSTITUTIONS)	5	.5	117	10.6	7	.6	4	.4	133	12.1	970	87.9	1,103
976 TO 1978	- 28.6		2.6		133.3		- 33.3		2.3		24.4		21.2
INSTITUTIONS)	22	.6	236	6.7	6	.2	13	.4	277	7.9	3,235	92.1	3,512
INSTITUTIONS)	19	.6	255	7.6	17	.5	12	.4	303	9.0	3,050	91.0	3,353
976 TO 1978	- 13.6		8.1		183.3		- 7.7		9.4		- 5.7		- 4.5
INSTITUTIONS)	2	2.3	1	1.2	0	.0	0	.0	3	3.5	83	96.5	86
INSTITUTIONS)	1	1.1	0	.0	0	.0	0	.0	1	1.1	93	98.9	94
976 TO 1978	- 50.0		- 100.0		.0		.0		- 66.7		12.0		9.3
INSTITUTIONS)	7	1.9	1	.3	0	.0	0	.0	8	2.2	358	97.8	366
INSTITUTIONS)	9	2.3	0	.0	2	.5	0	.0	11	2.8	380	97.2	391
976 TO 1978	28.6		- 100.0		100.0		.0		37.5		6.1		6.8
INSTITUTIONS)	6	.2	194	7.7	22	.9	17	.7	239	9.5	2,277	90.5	2,516
INSTITUTIONS)	38	1.2	253	8.1	24	.8	20	.6	335	10.7	2,802	89.3	3,137
976 TO 1978	533.3		30.4		9.1		17.6		40.2		23.1		24.7
INSTITUTIONS)	11	.1	390	4.3	64	.7	54	.6	519	5.7	8,657	94.3	9,176
INSTITUTIONS)	224	2.4	376	4.0	57	.6	57	.6	714	7.7	8,578	92.3	9,292
976 TO 1978	1936.4		- 3.6		- 10.9		5.6		37.6		- .9		1.3
INSTITUTIONS)	21	3.7	13	2.3	5	.9	5	.9	44	7.7	526	92.3	570
INSTITUTIONS)	17	2.3	18	2.5	9	1.2	5	.7	49	6.7	678	93.3	727
976 TO 1978	- 19.0		38.5		80.0		.0		11.4		28.9		27.5
INSTITUTIONS)	47	1.9	25	1.0	13	.5	10	.4	95	3.8	2,424	96.2	2,519
INSTITUTIONS)	61	2.4	33	1.3	18	.7	20	.8	132	5.1	2,462	94.9	2,594
976 TO 1978	29.8		32.0		38.5		100.0		38.9		1.6		3.0
INSTITUTIONS)	7	1.2	8	1.3	14	2.4	2	.3	31	5.2	563	94.8	594
INSTITUTIONS)	7	.9	11	1.4	33	4.2	5	.6	56	7.0	739	93.0	795
976 TO 1978	.0		37.5		135.7		150.0		80.6		31.3		33.8
INSTITUTIONS)	11	.4	21	.7	69	2.4	17	.6	118	4.0	2,801	96.0	2,919
INSTITUTIONS)	8	.3	28	1.0	81	2.8	27	.9	144	4.9	2,792	95.1	2,936
976 TO 1978	- 27.3		33.3		17.4		58.8		22.0		- .3		.6

TABLE 16 - COMPARISIONS OF FULL- AND PART-TIME FIRST PROFESSIONAL ENROLLMENT IN INSTITUTIONS OF HIGHER EDUCATION BY RACE, ETHNICITY AND SEX: STATE AND NATION, 1976, 1978

	AMERICAN INDIAN ALASKAN NATIVE		BLACK NON-HISPANIC		ASIAN OR PACIFIC ISLANDER		HISPANIC		TOTAL MINORITY		WHITE NON-HISPANIC	
	NUMBER	%	NUMBER	%	NUMBER	%	NUMBER	%	NUMBER	%	NUMBER	%
PENNSYLVANIA.												
FEMALE												
1976 (29 INSTITUTIONS)	6	.2	208	6.5	32	1.0	41	1.3	287	9.0	2,892	91.0
1978 (29 INSTITUTIONS)	7	.2	243	6.9	52	1.5	45	1.3	347	9.9	3,161	90.1
% CHANGE 1976 TO 1978	16.7		16.8		62.5		9.8		20.9		9.3	
MALE												
1976 (29 INSTITUTIONS)	15	.1	336	3.2	110	1.0	107	1.0	568	5.4	10,031	94.6
1978 (29 INSTITUTIONS)	15	.1	319	3.0	100	.9	90	.8	524	4.9	10,155	95.1
% CHANGE 1976 TO 1978	.0		- 5.1		- 9.1		- 15.9		- 7.7		1.2	
RHODE ISLAND.												
FEMALE												
1976 (1 INSTITUTIONS)	0	.0	1	1.4	5	6.8	0	.0	6	8.2	67	91.8
1978 (1 INSTITUTIONS)	0	.0	5	6.0	9	10.7	0	.0	14	16.7	70	83.3
% CHANGE 1976 TO 1978	.0		400.0		80.0		.0		133.3		4.5	
MALE												
1976 (1 INSTITUTIONS)	0	.0	6	3.4	2	1.1	1	.6	9	5.1	166	94.9
1978 (1 INSTITUTIONS)	0	.0	9	5.5	2	1.2	5	3.0	16	9.7	149	90.3
% CHANGE 1976 TO 1978	.0		50.0		.0		400.0		77.8		- 10.2	
SOUTH CAROLINA.												
FEMALE												
1976 (6 INSTITUTIONS)	1	.4	19	6.8	0	.0	0	.0	20	7.2	258	92.8
1978 (7 INSTITUTIONS)	2	.5	24	5.7	0	.0	1	.2	27	6.4	396	93.6
% CHANGE 1976 TO 1978	100.0		26.3		.0		100.0		35.0		53.5	
MALE												
1976 (6 INSTITUTIONS)	1	.1	64	4.1	2	.1	1	.1	68	4.4	1,486	95.6
1978 (7 INSTITUTIONS)	0	.0	67	3.8	4	.2	3	.2	74	4.2	1,671	95.8
% CHANGE 1976 TO 1978	- 100.0		4.7		100.0		200.0		8.8		12.4	
SOUTH DAKOTA.												
FEMALE												
1976 (2 INSTITUTIONS)	0	.0	0	.0	0	.0	1	1.0	1	1.0	103	99.0
1978 (2 INSTITUTIONS)	0	.0	0	.0	0	.0	0	.0	0	.0	94	100.0
% CHANGE 1976 TO 1978	.0		.0		.0		- 100.0		- 100.0		- 8.7	
MALE												
1976 (2 INSTITUTIONS)	0	.0	0	.0	1	.2	0	.0	1	.2	401	99.8
1978 (2 INSTITUTIONS)	1	.3	1	.3	1	.3	1	.3	4	1.0	392	99.0
% CHANGE 1976 TO 1978	100.0		100.0		.0		100.0		300.0		- 2.2	
TENNESSEE												
FEMALE												
1976 (9 INSTITUTIONS)	3	.3	200	22.1	6	.7	4	.4	213	23.5	692	76.5
1978 (9 INSTITUTIONS)	1	.1	233	19.9	4	.3	4	.3	242	20.7	928	79.3
% CHANGE 1976 TO 1978	- 66.7		16.5		- 33.3		.0		13.6		34.1	
MALE												
1976 (9 INSTITUTIONS)	7	.2	443	11.0	14	.3	21	.5	485	12.0	3,558	88.0
1978 (9 INSTITUTIONS)	9	.2	476	11.1	19	.4	22	.5	526	12.2	3,772	87.8
% CHANGE 1976 TO 1978	28.6		7.4		35.7		4.8		8.5		6.0	
TEXAS												
FEMALE												
1976 (26 INSTITUTIONS)	10	.4	153	5.7	32	1.2	143	5.3	338	12.6	2,350	87.4
1978 (24 INSTITUTIONS)	8	.2	206	6.3	46	1.4	198	6.1	458	14.0	2,807	86.0
% CHANGE 1976 TO 1978	- 20.0		34.6		43.8		38.5		35.5		19.4	
MALE												
1976 (26 INSTITUTIONS)	44	.4	299	2.9	67	.7	550	5.4	960	9.4	9,219	90.6
1978 (24 INSTITUTIONS)	36	.3	316	3.1	92	.9	676	6.6	1,120	10.9	9,199	89.1
% CHANGE 1976 TO 1978	- 18.2		5.7		37.3		22.9		16.7		- .2	
UTAH.												
FEMALE												
1976 (2 INSTITUTIONS)	0	.0	2	1.2	2	1.2		1.8	7	4.2	160	95.8
1978 (2 INSTITUTIONS)	0	.0	4	2.0	2	1.0	4	2.0	10	4.9	194	95.1
% CHANGE 1976 TO 1978	.0		100.0		.0		33.3		42.9		21.3	
MALE												
1976 (2 INSTITUTIONS)	8	.7	4	.4	11	1.0	25	2.3	48	4.5	1,029	95.5
1978 (2 INSTITUTIONS)	5	.5	6	.6	12	1.2	21	2.0	44	4.3	981	95.7
% CHANGE 1976 TO 1978	- 37.5		50.0		9.1		- 16.0		- 8.3		- 4.7	

16 - COMPARISIONS·OF FULL- AND PART-TIME FIRST PROFESSIONAL ENROLLMENT IN INSTITUTIONS OF HIGHER EDUCATION
BY RACE, ETHNICITY AND SEX: STATE AND NATION, 1976, 1978

	AMERICAN INDIAN ALASKAN NATIVE		BLACK NON-HISPANIC		ASIAN OR PACIFIC ISLANDER		HISPANIC		TOTAL MINORITY		WHITE NON-HISPANIC		TOTAL
	NUMBER	%	NUMBER	%	NUMBER	%	NUMBER	%	NUMBER	%	NUMBER	%	NUMBER
NT													
LE													
6 (2 INSTITUTIONS)	0	.0	0	.0	0	.0	2	1.6	2	1.6	120	98.4	122
8 (2 INSTITUTIONS)	0	.0	0	.0	1	.6	0	.0	1	.6	154	99.4	155
HANGE 1976 TO 1978	.0		.0		100.0		- 100.0		- 50.0		28.3		27.0
6 (2 INSTITUTIONS)	0	.0	2	.4	1	.2	1	.2	4	.7	532	99.3	536
8 (2 INSTITUTIONS)	0	.0	0	.0	2	.4	0	.0	2	.4	486	99.6	488
HANGE 1976 TO 1978	.0		- 100.0		100.0		- 100.0		- 50.0		- 8.6		- 9.0
NIA.													
LE													
6 (9 INSTITUTIONS)	0	.0	56	7.1	5	.6	2	.3	63	8.0	729	92.0	792
8 (9 INSTITUTIONS)	1	.1	73	6.9	10	.9	2	.2	86	8.1	979	91.9	1,065
HANGE 1976 TO 1978	100.0		30.4		100.0		.0		36.5		34.3		34.5
6 (9 INSTITUTIONS)	0	.0	105	3.2	17	.5	7	.2	129	3.9	3,195	96.1	3,324
8 (9 INSTITUTIONS)	1	.0	93	2.8	25	.8	11	.3	130	4.0	3,140	96.0	3,270
HANGE 1976 TO 1978	100.0		- 11.4		47.1		57.1		.8		- 1.7		- 1.6
NGTON.													
LE													
6 (6 INSTITUTIONS)	5	.7	11	1.5	23	3.1	11	1.5	50	6.6	702	93.4	752
8 (4 INSTITUTIONS)	8	.9	15	1.6	26	2.8	17	1.9	66	7.2	850	92.8	916
HANGE 1976 TO 1978	60.0		36.4		13.0		54.5		32.0		21.1		21.8
6 (6 INSTITUTIONS)	19	.7	34	1.2	71	2.5	38	1.4	162	5.8	2,643	94.2	2,805
8 (4 INSTITUTIONS)	14	.5	22	.8	61	2.3	35	1.3	132	5.0	2,515	95.0	2,647
HANGE 1976 TO 1978	- 26.3		- 35.3		- 14.1		- 7.9		- 18.5		- 4.8		- 5.6
VIRGINIA													
LE													
6 (2 INSTITUTIONS)	0	.0	4	2.4	2	1.2	0	.0	6	3.6	161	96.4	167
8 (3 INSTITUTIONS)	1	.4	6	2.7	0	.0	2	.9	9	4.0	217	96.0	226
HANGE 1976 TO 1978	100.0		50.0		- 100.0		100.0		50.0		34.8		35.3
6 (2 INSTITUTIONS)	0	.0	14	1.5	4	.4	0	.0	18	2.0	895	98.0	913
8 (3 INSTITUTIONS)	2	.2	7	.7	2	.2	1	.1	12	1.2	1,024	98.8	1,036
HANGE 1976 TO 1978	100.0		- 50.0		- 50.0		100.0		- 33.3		14.4		13.5
NSIN													
LE													
6 (5 INSTITUTIONS)	2	.3	27	4.0	7	1.0	5	.7	41	6.0	638	94.0	679
8 (6 INSTITUTIONS)	4	.5	40	4.9	12	1.5	15	1.8	71	8.7	744	91.3	815
HANGE 1976 TO 1978	100.0		48.1		71.4		200.0		73.2		16.6		20.0
6 (5 INSTITUTIONS)	11	.4	69	2.7	14	.6	35	1.4	129	5.1	2,402	94.9	2,531
8 (6 INSTITUTIONS)	15	.6	60	2.3	17	.6	57	2.1	149	5.6	2,510	94.4	2,659
HANGE 1976 TO 1978	36.4		- 13.0		21.4		62.9		15.5		4.5		5.1
NG													
LE													
6 (1 INSTITUTIONS)	0	.0	0	.0	0	.0	0	.0	0	.0	49	100.0	49
8 (1 INSTITUTIONS)	0	.0	0	.0	1	1.9	1	1.9	2	3.7	52	96.3	54
HANGE 1976 TO 1978	.0		.0		100.0		100.0		100.0		6.1		10.2
6 (1 INSTITUTIONS)	1	.6	1	.6	0	.0	0	.0	2	1.2	159	98.8	161
8 (1 INSTITUTIONS)	0	.0	0	.0	0	.0	1	.6	1	.6	159	99.4	160
HANGE 1976 TO 1978	- 100.0		- 100.0		.0		100.0		- 50.0		.0		.6
TATES AND D.C.													
LE													
6 (459 INSTITUTIONS)	221	.4	3,947	7.3	1,142	2.1	1,049	1.9	6,359	11.8	47,581	88.2	53,940
8 (445 INSTITUTIONS)	270	.4	4,449	7.0	1,497	2.3	1,400	2.2	7,616	11.9	56,275	88.1	63,891
HANGE 1976 TO 1978	22.2		12.7		31.1		33.5		19.8		18.3		18.4
6 (459 INSTITUTIONS)	1,032	.6	7,234	3.9	2,933	1.6	3,498	1.9	14,697	7.9	172,470	92.1	187,167
8 (445 INSTITUTIONS)	802	.4	6,975	3.7	3,303	1.8	3,953	2.1	15,033	8.0	173,031	92.0	188,064
HANGE 1976 TO 1978	- 22.3		- 3.6		12.6		12.6		2.3		.3		.5

TABLE 16 - COMPARISIONS OF FULL- AND PART-TIME FIRST PROFESSIONAL ENROLLMENT IN INSTITUTIONS OF HIGHER EDUCATION
BY RACE, ETHNICITY AND SEX: STATE AND NATION, 1976, 1978

	AMERICAN INDIAN ALASKAN NATIVE		BLACK NON-HISPANIC		ASIAN OR PACIFIC ISLANDER		HISPANIC		TOTAL MINORITY		WHITE NON-HISPANIC	
	NUMBER	%	NUMBER	%	NUMBER	%	NUMBER	%	NUMBER	%	NUMBER	%
PUERTO RICO												
FEMALE												
1976 (3 INSTITUTIONS)	23	4.9	0	.0	0	.0	443	94.9	466	99.8	1	.2
1978 (4 INSTITUTIONS)	0	.0	0	.0	0	.0	533	100.0	533	100.0	0	.0
% CHANGE 1976 TO 1978	- 100.0		.0		.0		20.3		14.4		- 100.0	
MALE												
1976 (3 INSTITUTIONS)	45	3.9	0	.0	0	.0	1,102	95.5	1,147	99.4	7	.6
1978 (4 INSTITUTIONS)	0	.0	0	.0	0	.0	1,059	100.0	1,059	100.0	0	.0
% CHANGE 1976 TO 1978	- 100.0		.0		.0		- 3.9		- 7.7		- 100.0	
OUTLYING AREAS.												
FEMALE												
1976 (3 INSTITUTIONS)	23	4.9	0	.0	0	.0	443	94.9	466	99.8	1	.2
1978 (4 INSTITUTIONS)	0	.0	0	.0	0	.0	533	100.0	533	100.0	0	.0
% CHANGE 1976 TO 1978	- 100.0		.0		.0		20.3		14.4		- 100.0	
MALE												
1976 (3 INSTITUTIONS)	45	3.9	0	.0	0	.0	1,102	95.5	1,147	99.4	7	.6
1978 (4 INSTITUTIONS)	0	.0	0	.0	0	.0	1,059	100.0	1,059	100.0	0	.0
% CHANGE 1976 TO 1978	- 100.0		.0		.0		.0		- 7.7		- 100.0	
NATION, TOTAL												
FEMALE												
1976 (462 INSTITUTIONS)	244	.4	3,947	7.3	1,142	2.1	1,492	2.7	6,825	12.5	47,582	87.5
1978 (449 INSTITUTIONS)	270	.4	4,449	6.9	1,497	2.3	1,933	3.0	8,149	12.6	56,275	87.4
% CHANGE 1976 TO 1978	10.7		12.7		31.1		29.6		19.4		18.3	
MALE												
1976 (462 INSTITUTIONS)	1,077	.6	7,234	3.8	2,933	1.6	4,600	2.4	15,844	8.4	172,477	91.6
1978 (449 INSTITUTIONS)	802	.4	6,975	3.7	3,303	1.7	5,012	2.7	16,092	8.5	173,031	91.5
% CHANGE 1976 TO 1978	- 25.5		- 3.6		12.6		12.6		1.6		.3	

ENROLLMENT IN INSTITUTIONS OF HIGHER EDUCATION FOR SELECTED MAJOR FIELDS OF STUDY AND LEVEL OF ENROLLMENT E, ETHNICITY, AND SEX: STATE, 1978

- AGRICULTURE AND NATURAL RESOURCES

AN INDIAN N NATIVE		BLACK NON-HISPANIC		ASIAN/OR PACIFIC ISLANDER		HISPANIC		TOTAL MINORITY		WHITE NON-HISPANIC		NON-RESIDENT ALIEN		TOTAL
R	%	NUMBER	%	NUMBER	%	NUMBER	%	NUMBER	%	NUMBER	%	NUMBER	%	NUMBER
(22 INSTITUTIONS)														
0	.0	347	20.6	9	.5	7	.4	363	21.5	1,223	72.6	99	5.9	1,685
0	.0	131	36.2	3	.8	1	.3	135	37.3	219	60.5	8	2.2	362
0	.0	216	16.3	6	.5	6	.5	228	17.2	1,004	75.9	91	6.9	1,323
0	.0	7	4.0	0	.0	0	.0	7	4.0	170	96.0	0	.0	177
0	.0	3	7.5	0	.0	0	.0	3	7.5	37	92.5	0	.0	40
0	.0	4	2.9	0	.0	0	.0	4	2.9	133	97.1	0	.0	137
0	.0	354	19.0	9	.5	7	.4	370	19.9	1,393	74.8	99	5.3	1,862
0	.0	134	33.3	3	.7	1	.2	138	34.3	256	63.7	8	2.0	402
0	.0	220	15.1	6	.4	6	.4	232	15.9	1,137	77.9	91	6.2	1,460
0	.0	5	4.0	6	4.8	1	.8	12	9.6	76	60.8	37	29.6	125
0	.0	1	5.3	0	.0	0	.0	1	5.3	8	42.1	10	52.6	19
0	.0	4	3.8	6	5.7	1	.9	11	10.4	68	64.2	27	25.5	106
0	.0	4	2.6	0	.0	0	.0	4	2.6	110	70.5	42	26.9	156
0	.0	1	3.7	0	.0	0	.0	1	3.7	19	70.4	7	25.9	27
0	.0	3	2.3	0	.0	0	.0	3	2.3	91	70.5	35	27.1	129
0	.0	9	3.2	6	2.1	1	.4	16	5.7	186	66.2	79	28.1	281
0	.0	2	4.3	0	.0	0	.0	2	4.3	27	58.7	17	37.0	46
0	.0	7	3.0	6	2.6	1	.4	14	6.0	159	67.7	62	26.4	235
0	.0	0	.0	0	.0	0	.0	0	.0	0	.0	0	.0	0
0	.0	0	.0	0	.0	0	.0	0	.0	0	.0	0	.0	0
0	.0	0	.0	0	.0	0	.0	0	.0	0	.0	0	.0	0
0	.0	0	.0	0	.0	0	.0	0	.0	0	.0	0	.0	0
0	.0	0	.0	0	.0	0	.0	0	.0	0	.0	0	.0	0
0	.0	0	.0	0	.0	0	.0	0	.0	0	.0	0	.0	0
0	.0	0	.0	0	.0	0	.0	0	.0	0	.0	0	.0	0
0	.0	0	.0	0	.0	0	.0	0	.0	0	.0	0	.0	0
0	.0	0	.0	0	.0	0	.0	0	.0	0	.0	0	.0	0
0	.0	352	19.4	15	.8	8	.4	375	20.7	1,299	71.8	136	7.5	1,810
0	.0	132	34.6	3	.8	1	.3	136	35.7	227	59.6	18	4.7	381
0	.0	220	15.4	12	.8	7	.5	239	16.7	1,072	75.0	118	8.3	1,429
0	.0	11	3.3	0	.0	0	.0	11	3.3	280	84.1	42	12.6	333
0	.0	4	6.0	0	.0	0	.0	4	6.0	56	83.6	7	10.4	67
0	.0	7	2.6	0	.0	0	.0	7	2.6	224	84.2	35	13.2	266
0	.0	363	16.9	15	.7	8	.4	386	18.0	1,579	73.7	178	8.3	2,143
0	.0	136	30.4	3	.7	1	.2	140	31.3	283	63.2	25	5.6	448
0	.0	227	13.4	12	.7	7	.4	246	14.5	1,296	76.5	153	9.0	1,695
0	.0	3	8.8	0	.0	0	.0	3	8.8	24	70.6	7	20.6	34
0	.0	1	25.0	0	.0	0	.0	1	25.0	2	50.0	1	25.0	4
0	.0	2	6.7	0	.0	0	.0	2	6.7	22	73.3	6	20.0	30
0	.0	366	16.8	15	.7	8	.4	389	17.9	1,603	73.6	185	8.5	2,177
0	.0	137	30.3	3	.7	1	.2	141	31.2	285	63.1	26	5.8	452
0	.0	229	13.3	12	.7	7	.4	248	14.4	1,318	76.4	159	9.2	1,725
(1 INSTITUTIONS)														
4	2.7	1	.7	1	.7	0	.0	6	4.1	140	95.2	1	.7	147
0	.0	0	.0	0	.0	0	.0	0	.0	25	100.0	0	.0	25
4	3.3	1	.8	1	.8	0	.0	6	4.9	115	94.3	1	.8	122
1	3.2	0	.0	0	.0	0	.0	1	3.2	29	93.5	1	3.2	31
0	.0	0	.0	0	.0	0	.0	0	.0	3	75.0	1	25.0	4
1	3.7	0	.0	0	.0	0	.0	1	3.7	26	96.3	0	.0	27
5	2.8	1	.6	1	.6	0	.0	7	3.9	169	94.9	2	1.1	178
0	.0	0	.0	0	.0	0	.0	0	.0	28	96.6	1	3.4	29
5	3.4	1	.7	1	.7	0	.0	7	4.7	141	94.6	1	.7	149
0	.0	0	.0	0	.0	0	.0	0	.0	17	89.5	2	10.5	19
0	.0	0	.0	0	.0	0	.0	0	.0	8	100.0	0	.0	8
0	.0	0	.0	0	.0	0	.0	0	.0	9	81.8	2	18.2	11
0	.0	0	.0	2	6.9	0	.0	2	6.9	26	89.7	1	3.4	29
0	.0	0	.0	1	14.3	0	.0	1	14.3	6	85.7	0	.0	7
0	.0	0	.0	1	4.5	0	.0	1	4.5	20	90.9	1	4.5	22
0	.0	0	.0	2	4.2	0	.0	2	4.2	43	89.6	3	6.3	48
0	.0	0	.0	1	6.7	0	.0	1	6.7	14	93.3	0	.0	15
0	.0	0	.0	1	3.0	0	.0	1	3.0	29	87.9	3	9.1	33
0	.0	0	.0	0	.0	0	.0	0	.0	0	.0	0	.0	0
0	.0	0	.0	0	.0	0	.0	0	.0	0	.0	0	.0	0

TABLE 17 - TOTAL ENROLLMENT IN INSTITUTIONS OF HIGHER EDUCATION FOR SELECTED MAJOR FIELDS OF STUDY AND LEVEL OF ENROLLMENT BY RACE, ETHNICITY, AND SEX: STATE, 1978

MAJOR FIELD 0100 - AGRICULTURE AND NATURAL RESOURCES

	AMERICAN INDIAN ALASKAN NATIVE		BLACK NON-HISPANIC		ASIAN OR PACIFIC ISLANDER		HISPANIC		TOTAL MINORITY		WHITE NON-HISPANIC		NON-RESIDENT ALIEN	
	NUMBER	%	NUMBER	%	NUMBER	%	NUMBER	%	NUMBER	%	NUMBER	%	NUMBER	%
ALASKA	CONTINUED													
PROFESSIONAL:														
PART-TIME	0	.0	0	.0	0	.0	0	.0	0	.0	0	.0	0	.0
FEMALE	0	.0	0	.0	0	.0	0	.0	0	.0	0	.0	0	.0
MALE	0	.0	0	.0	0	.0	0	.0	0	.0	0	.0	0	.0
TOTAL	0	.0	0	.0	0	.0	0	.0	0	.0	0	.0	0	.0
FEMALE	0	.0	0	.0	0	.0	0	.0	0	.0	0	.0	0	.0
MALE	0	.0	0	.0	0	.0	0	.0	0	.0	0	.0	0	.0
UND+GRAD+PROF:														
FULL-TIME	4	2.4	1	.6	1	.6	0	.0	6	3.6	157	94.6	3	1.8
FEMALE	0	.0	0	.0	0	.0	0	.0	0	.0	33	100.0	0	.0
MALE	4	3.0	1	.8	1	.8	0	.0	6	4.5	124	93.2	3	2.3
PART-TIME	1	1.7	0	.0	2	3.3	0	.0	3	5.0	55	91.7	2	3.3
FEMALE	0	.0	0	.0	1	9.1	0	.0	1	9.1	9	81.8	1	9.1
MALE	1	2.0	0	.0	1	2.0	0	.0	2	4.1	46	93.9	1	2.0
TOTAL	5	2.2	1	.4	3	1.3	0	.0	9	4.0	212	93.8	5	2.2
FEMALE	0	.0	0	.0	1	2.3	0	.0	1	2.3	42	95.5	1	2.3
MALE	5	2.7	1	.5	2	1.1	0	.0	8	4.4	170	93.4	4	2.2
UNCLASSIFIED:														
TOTAL	0	.0	0	.0	0	.0	0	.0	0	.0	5	100.0	0	.0
FEMALE	0	.0	0	.0	0	.0	0	.0	0	.0	4	100.0	0	.0
MALE	0	.0	0	.0	0	.0	0	.0	0	.0	1	100.0	0	.0
TOTAL ENROLLMENT:														
TOTAL	5	2.2	1	.4	3	1.3	0	.0	9	3.9	217	93.9	5	2.2
FEMALE	0	.0	0	.0	1	2.1	0	.0	1	2.1	46	95.8	1	2.1
MALE	5	2.7	1	.5	2	1.1	0	.0	8	4.4	171	93.4	4	2.2
ARIZONA (11 INSTITUTIONS)														
UNDERGRADUATES:														
FULL-TIME	25	1.2	9	.4	8	.3	62	2.7	108	4.6	2,164	93.1	52	2.2
FEMALE	10	1.2	2	.2	4	.5	21	2.4	37	4.3	820	95.0	6	.7
MALE	19	1.3	7	.5	4	.3	41	2.8	71	4.9	1,344	92.0	46	3.1
PART-TIME	2	.5	2	.5	2	.5	17	4.3	23	5.8	370	93.9	1	.3
FEMALE	0	.0	1	.7	0	.0	4	2.9	5	3.6	134	96.4	0	.0
MALE	2	.8	1	.4	2	.8	13	5.1	18	7.1	236	92.5	1	.4
TOTAL	31	1.1	11	.4	10	.4	79	2.9	131	4.8	2,534	93.2	53	1.9
FEMALE	10	1.0	3	.3	4	.4	25	2.5	42	4.2	954	95.2	6	.6
MALE	21	1.2	8	.5	6	.3	54	3.1	89	5.2	1,580	92.1	47	2.7
GRADUATE:														
FULL-TIME	1	.4	0	.0	0	.0	2	.9	3	1.3	175	75.4	54	23.3
FEMALE	0	.0	0	.0	0	.0	0	.0	0	.0	64	94.1	4	5.9
MALE	1	.6	0	.0	0	.0	2	1.2	3	1.8	111	67.7	50	30.5
PART-TIME	2	1.0	0	.0	1	.5	1	.5	4	1.9	161	78.2	41	19.9
FEMALE	1	2.0	0	.0	0	.0	1	2.0	2	3.9	44	86.3	5	9.8
MALE	1	.6	0	.0	1	.6	0	.0	2	1.3	117	75.5	36	23.2
TOTAL	3	.7	0	.0	1	.2	3	.7	7	1.6	336	76.7	95	21.7
FEMALE	1	.8	0	.0	0	.0	1	.8	2	1.7	108	90.8	9	7.6
MALE	2	.6	0	.0	1	.3	2	.6	5	1.6	228	71.5	86	27.0
PROFESSIONAL:														
FULL-TIME	0	.0	0	.0	0	.0	0	.0	0	.0	0	.0	0	.0
FEMALE	0	.0	0	.0	0	.0	0	.0	0	.0	0	.0	0	.0
MALE	0	.0	0	.0	0	.0	0	.0	0	.0	0	.0	0	.0
PART-TIME	0	.0	0	.0	0	.0	0	.0	0	.0	0	.0	0	.0
FEMALE	0	.0	0	.0	0	.0	0	.0	0	.0	0	.0	0	.0
MALE	0	.0	0	.0	0	.0	0	.0	0	.0	0	.0	0	.0
TOTAL	0	.0	0	.0	0	.0	0	.0	0	.0	0	.0	0	.0
FEMALE	0	.0	0	.0	0	.0	0	.0	0	.0	0	.0	0	.0
MALE	0	.0	0	.0	0	.0	0	.0	0	.0	0	.0	0	.0
UND+GRAD+PROF:														
FULL-TIME	30	1.2	9	.4	8	.3	64	2.5	111	4.3	2,339	91.5	106	4.1
FEMALE	10	1.1	2	.2	4	.4	21	2.3	37	4.0	884	95.0	10	1.1
MALE	20	1.2	7	.4	4	.2	43	2.6	74	4.6	1,455	89.5	96	5.9
PART-TIME	4	.7	2	.3	3	.5	18	3.0	27	4.5	531	88.5	42	7.0
FEMALE	1	.5	1	.5	0	.0	5	2.6	7	3.7	178	93.7	5	2.6
MALE	3	.7	1	.2	3	.7	13	3.2	20	4.9	353	86.1	37	9.0
TOTAL	34	1.1	11	.3	11	.3	82	2.6	138	4.4	2,870	90.9	148	4.7
FEMALE	11	1.0	3	.3	4	.4	26	2.3	44	3.9	1,062	94.7	15	1.3
MALE	23	1.1	8	.4	7	.3	56	2.8	94	4.6	1,808	88.8	133	6.5
UNCLASSIFIED:														
TOTAL	0	.0	0	.0	0	.0	2	5.7	2	5.7	26	74.3	7	20.0
FEMALE	0	.0	0	.0	0	.0	0	.0	0	.0	10	90.9	1	9.1
MALE	0	.0	0	.0	0	.0	2	8.3	2	8.3	16	66.7	6	25.0
TOTAL ENROLLMENT:														
TOTAL	34	1.1	11	.3	11	.3	84	2.6	140	4.4	2,896	90.8	155	4.9
FEMALE	11	1.0	3	.3	4	.4	26	2.3	44	3.9	1,072	94.7	16	1.4
MALE	23	1.1	8	.4	7	.3	58	2.8	96	4.7	1,824	88.6	139	6.8

17 - TOTAL ENROLLMENT IN INSTITUTIONS OF HIGHER EDUCATION FOR SELECTED MAJOR FIELDS OF STUDY AND LEVEL OF ENROLLMENT
BY RACE, ETHNICITY, AND SEX: STATE, 1978

FIELD 0100 - AGRICULTURE AND NATURAL RESOURCES

	AMERICAN INDIAN ALASKAN NATIVE		BLACK NON-HISPANIC		ASIAN OR PACIFIC ISLANDER		HISPANIC		TOTAL MINORITY		WHITE NON-HISPANIC		NON-RESIDENT ALIEN		TOTAL
	NUMBER	%	NUMBER	%	NUMBER	%	NUMBER	%	NUMBER	%	NUMBER	%	NUMBER	%	NUMBER
SAS (8 INSTITUTIONS)															
GRADUATES:															
TIME	11	.7	68	4.3	4	.3	5	.3	88	5.5	1,485	93.4	17	1.1	1,590
MALE	0	.0	14	5.4	0	.0	0	.0	14	5.4	247	94.6	0	.0	261
MALE	11	.8	54	4.1	4	.3	5	.4	74	5.6	1,238	93.2	17	1.3	1,329
TIME	1	1.2	2	2.4	0	.0	0	.0	3	3.6	81	96.4	0	.0	84
MALE	0	.0	0	.0	0	.0	0	.0	0	.0	14	100.0	0	.0	14
MALE	1	1.4	2	2.9	0	.0	0	.0	3	4.3	67	95.7	0	.0	70
	12	.7	70	4.2	4	.2	5	.3	91	5.4	1,566	93.5	17	1.0	1,674
MALE	0	.0	14	5.1	0	.0	0	.0	14	5.1	261	94.9	0	.0	275
MALE	12	.9	56	4.0	4	.3	5	.4	77	5.5	1,305	93.3	17	1.2	1,399
ATE:															
TIME	1	.7	6	4.3	0	.0	1	.7	8	5.7	102	72.9	30	21.4	140
MALE	0	.0	1	3.3	0	.0	0	.0	1	3.3	26	86.7	3	10.0	30
MALE	1	.9	5	4.5	0	.0	1	.9	7	6.4	76	69.1	27	24.5	110
TIME	1	1.7	2	3.4	0	.0	0	.0	3	5.1	50	84.7	6	10.2	59
MALE	0	.0	1	10.0	0	.0	0	.0	1	10.0	9	90.0	0	.0	10
MALE	1	2.0	1	2.0	0	.0	0	.0	2	4.1	41	83.7	6	12.2	49
	2	1.0	8	4.0	0	.0	1	.5	11	5.5	152	76.4	36	18.1	199
MALE	0	.0	2	5.0	0	.0	0	.0	2	5.0	35	87.5	3	7.5	40
MALE	2	1.3	6	3.8	0	.0	1	.6	9	5.7	117	73.6	33	20.8	159
SSIONAL:															
TIME	0	.0	0	.0	0	.0	0	.0	0	.0	0	.0	0	.0	0
MALE	0	.0	0	.0	0	.0	0	.0	0	.0	0	.0	0	.0	0
MALE	0	.0	0	.0	0	.0	0	.0	0	.0	0	.0	0	.0	0
TIME	0	.0	0	.0	0	.0	0	.0	0	.0	0	.0	0	.0	0
MALE	0	.0	0	.0	0	.0	0	.0	0	.0	0	.0	0	.0	0
MALE	0	.0	0	.0	0	.0	0	.0	0	.0	0	.0	0	.0	0
MALE	0	.0	0	.0	0	.0	0	.0	0	.0	0	.0	0	.0	0
MALE	0	.0	0	.0	0	.0	0	.0	0	.0	0	.0	0	.0	0
RAD+PROF:															
TIME	12	.7	74	4.3	4	.2	6	.3	96	5.5	1,587	91.7	47	2.7	1,730
MALE	0	.0	15	5.2	0	.0	0	.0	15	5.2	273	93.8	3	1.0	291
MALE	12	.8	59	4.1	4	.3	6	.4	81	5.6	1,314	91.3	44	3.1	1,439
TIME	2	1.4	4	2.8	0	.0	0	.0	6	4.2	131	91.6	6	4.2	143
MALE	0	.0	1	4.2	0	.0	0	.0	1	4.2	23	95.8	0	.0	24
MALE	2	1.7	3	2.5	0	.0	0	.0	5	4.2	108	90.8	6	5.0	119
	14	.7	78	4.2	4	.2	6	.3	102	5.4	1,718	91.7	53	2.8	1,873
MALE	0	.0	16	5.1	0	.0	0	.0	16	5.1	296	94.0	3	1.0	315
MALE	14	.9	62	4.0	4	.3	6	.4	86	5.5	1,422	91.3	50	3.2	1,558
SSIFIED:															
	0	.0	0	.0	0	.0	0	.0	0	.0	40	95.2	2	4.8	42
MALE	0	.0	0	.0	0	.0	0	.0	0	.0	6	100.0	0	.0	6
MALE	0	.0	0	.0	0	.0	0	.0	0	.0	34	94.4	2	5.6	36
ENROLLMENT:															
	14	.7	78	4.1	4	.2	6	.3	102	5.3	1,758	91.8	55	2.9	1,915
MALE	0	.0	16	5.0	0	.0	0	.0	16	5.0	302	94.1	3	.9	321
MALE	14	.9	62	3.9	4	.3	6	.4	86	5.4	1,456	91.3	52	3.3	1,594
ORNIA (79 INSTITUTIONS)															
GRADUATES:															
TIME	180	1.5	170	1.4	516	4.3	591	4.9	1,457	12.2	10,303	86.0	214	1.8	11,974
MALE	57	1.3	53	1.2	226	5.2	134	3.1	470	10.9	3,834	88.6	24	.6	4,328
MALE	123	1.6	117	1.5	290	3.8	457	6.0	987	12.9	6,469	84.6	190	2.5	7,646
TIME	108	2.5	78	1.8	142	3.2	262	6.0	590	13.5	3,755	85.7	39	.9	4,384
MALE	44	2.8	23	1.5	37	2.4	64	4.1	168	10.9	1,373	88.9	3	.2	1,544
MALE	64	2.3	55	1.9	105	3.7	198	7.0	422	14.9	2,382	83.9	36	1.3	2,840
	288	1.6	248	1.5	658	4.0	853	5.2	2,047	12.5	14,058	85.9	253	1.5	16,358
MALE	101	1.7	76	1.3	263	4.5	198	3.4	638	10.9	5,207	88.7	27	.5	5,872
MALE	187	1.8	172	1.6	395	3.8	655	6.2	1,409	13.4	8,851	84.4	226	2.2	10,486
ATE:															
TIME	1	.1	4	.5	21	2.8	14	1.9	40	5.4	488	66.2	209	28.4	737
MALE	0	.0	1	.6	9	5.1	2	1.1	12	6.8	144	81.8	20	11.4	176
MALE	1	.2	3	.5	12	2.1	12	2.1	28	5.0	344	61.3	189	33.7	561
TIME	2	.8	1	.4	12	4.6	6	2.3	21	8.1	169	65.3	69	26.6	259
MALE	0	.0	1	2.1	1	2.1	2	4.3	4	8.5	36	76.6	7	14.9	47
MALE	2	.9	0	.0	11	5.2	4	1.9	17	8.0	133	62.7	62	29.2	212
	3	.3	5	.5	33	3.3	20	2.0	61	6.1	657	66.0	278	27.9	996
MALE	0	.0	2	.9	10	4.5	4	1.8	16	7.2	180	80.7	27	12.1	223
MALE	3	.4	3	.4	23	3.0	16	2.1	45	5.8	477	61.7	251	32.5	773
SSIONAL:															
TIME	0	.0	0	.0	0	.0	0	.0	0	.0	0	.0	0	.0	0
MALE	0	.0	0	.0	0	.0	0	.0	0	.0	0	.0	0	.0	0
MALE	0	.0	0	.0	0	.0	0	.0	0	.0	0	.0	0	.0	0

TABLE 17 - TOTAL ENROLLMENT IN INSTITUTIONS OF HIGHER EDUCATION FOR SELECTED MAJOR FIELDS OF STUDY AND LEVEL OF ENROLLMENT BY RACE, ETHNICITY, AND SEX: STATE, 1978

MAJOR FIELD 0100 - AGRICULTURE AND NATURAL RESOURCES

	AMERICAN INDIAN ALASKAN NATIVE		BLACK NON-HISPANIC		ASIAN OR PACIFIC ISLANDER		HISPANIC		TOTAL MINORITY		WHITE NON-HISPANIC		NON-RESIDENT ALIEN	
	NUMBER	%	NUMBER	%	NUMBER	%	NUMBER	%	NUMBER	%	NUMBER	%	NUMBER	%
CALIFORNIA CONTINUED														
PROFESSIONAL:														
PART-TIME														
FEMALE	0	.0	0	.0	0	.0	0	.0	0	.0	0	.0	0	.0
MALE	0	.0	0	.0	0	.0	0	.0	0	.0	0	.0	0	.0
TOTAL														
FEMALE	0	.0	0	.0	0	.0	0	.0	0	.0	0	.0	0	.0
MALE	0	.0	0	.0	0	.0	0	.0	0	.0	0	.0	0	.0
UNG+GRAD+PROF:														
FULL-TIME	181	1.4	174	1.4	537	4.2	605	4.8	1,497	11.8	10,791	84.9	423	3.3
FEMALE	57	1.3	54	1.2	235	5.2	136	3.0	482	10.7	3,978	88.3	44	1.0
MALE	124	1.5	120	1.5	302	3.7	469	5.7	1,015	12.4	6,813	83.0	379	4.6
PART-TIME	110	2.4	79	1.7	154	3.3	268	5.8	611	13.2	3,924	84.5	108	2.3
FEMALE	44	2.8	24	1.5	38	2.4	66	4.1	172	10.8	1,409	88.6	10	.6
MALE	66	2.2	55	1.8	116	3.8	202	6.6	439	14.4	2,515	82.4	98	3.2
TOTAL	291	1.7	253	1.5	691	4.0	873	5.0	2,108	12.1	14,715	84.8	531	3.1
FEMALE	101	1.7	78	1.3	273	4.5	202	3.3	654	10.7	5,387	88.4	54	.9
MALE	190	1.7	175	1.6	418	3.7	671	6.0	1,454	12.9	9,328	82.8	477	4.2
UNCLASSIFIED:														
TOTAL	20	2.0	15	1.5	39	3.9	46	4.5	120	11.9	883	87.3	9	.9
FEMALE	7	2.1	8	2.5	12	3.7	7	2.1	34	10.4	291	89.3	1	.3
MALE	13	1.9	7	1.0	27	3.9	39	5.7	86	12.5	592	86.3	8	1.2
TOTAL ENROLLMENT:														
TOTAL	311	1.7	268	1.5	730	4.0	919	5.0	2,228	12.1	15,598	84.9	540	2.9
FEMALE	108	1.7	86	1.3	285	4.4	209	3.3	688	10.7	5,678	88.4	55	.9
MALE	203	1.7	182	1.5	445	3.7	710	5.9	1,540	12.9	9,920	83.0	485	4.1
COLORADO (6 INSTITUTIONS)														
UNDERGRADUATES:														
FULL-TIME	8	.3	4	.1	18	.6	48	1.7	78	2.8	2,728	96.8	13	.5
FEMALE	3	.4	1	.1	4	.5	8	.9	16	1.9	840	98.0	1	.1
MALE	5	.3	3	.2	14	.7	40	2.0	62	3.2	1,888	96.2	12	.6
PART-TIME	0	.0	0	.0	2	1.3	2	1.3	4	2.6	151	97.4	0	.0
FEMALE	0	.0	0	.0	1	1.9	1	1.9	2	3.8	51	96.2	0	.0
MALE	0	.0	0	.0	1	1.0	1	1.0	2	2.0	100	98.0	0	.0
TOTAL	8	.3	4	.1	20	.7	50	1.7	82	2.8	2,879	96.8	13	.4
FEMALE	3	.3	1	.1	5	.5	9	1.0	18	2.0	891	97.9	1	.1
MALE	5	.2	3	.1	15	.7	41	2.0	64	3.1	1,988	96.3	12	.6
GRADUATE:														
FULL-TIME	0	.0	2	.6	1	.3	1	.3	4	1.3	266	85.0	43	13.7
FEMALE	0	.0	0	.0	0	.0	0	.0	0	.0	53	89.8	6	10.2
MALE	0	.0	2	.8	1	.4	1	.4	4	1.6	213	83.9	37	14.6
PART-TIME	0	.0	0	.0	1	1.2	0	.0	1	1.2	62	76.5	18	22.2
FEMALE	0	.0	0	.0	1	5.6	0	.0	1	5.6	16	88.9	1	5.6
MALE	0	.0	0	.0	0	.0	0	.0	0	.0	46	73.0	17	27.0
TOTAL	0	.0	2	.5	2	.5	1	.3	5	1.3	328	83.2	61	15.5
FEMALE	0	.0	0	.0	1	1.3	0	.0	1	1.3	69	89.6	7	9.1
MALE	0	.0	2	.6	1	.3	1	.3	4	1.3	259	81.7	54	17.0
PROFESSIONAL:														
FULL-TIME	0	.0	0	.0	0	.0	0	.0	0	.0	0	.0	0	.0
FEMALE	0	.0	0	.0	0	.0	0	.0	0	.0	0	.0	0	.0
MALE	0	.0	0	.0	0	.0	0	.0	0	.0	0	.0	0	.0
PART-TIME	0	.0	0	.0	0	.0	0	.0	0	.0	0	.0	0	.0
FEMALE	0	.0	0	.0	0	.0	0	.0	0	.0	0	.0	0	.0
MALE	0	.0	0	.0	0	.0	0	.0	0	.0	0	.0	0	.0
TOTAL	0	.0	0	.0	0	.0	0	.0	0	.0	0	.0	0	.0
FEMALE	0	.0	0	.0	0	.0	0	.0	0	.0	0	.0	0	.0
MALE	0	.0	0	.0	0	.0	0	.0	0	.0	0	.0	0	.0
UNG+GRAD+PROF:														
FULL-TIME	8	.3	6	.2	19	.6	49	1.6	82	2.6	2,994	95.6	56	1.8
FEMALE	3	.3	1	.1	4	.4	8	.9	16	1.7	893	97.5	7	.8
MALE	5	.2	5	.2	15	.7	41	1.9	66	3.0	2,101	94.8	49	2.2
PART-TIME	0	.0	0	.0	3	1.3	2	.8	5	2.1	213	90.3	18	7.6
FEMALE	0	.0	0	.0	2	2.8	1	1.4	3	4.2	67	94.4	1	1.4
MALE	0	.0	0	.0	1	.6	1	.6	2	1.2	146	88.5	17	10.3
TOTAL	8	.2	6	.2	22	.7	51	1.5	87	2.6	3,207	95.2	74	2.2
FEMALE	3	.3	1	.1	6	.6	9	.9	19	1.9	960	97.3	8	.8
MALE	5	.2	5	.2	16	.7	42	1.8	68	2.9	2,247	94.4	66	2.8
UNCLASSIFIED:														
TOTAL	0	.0	0	.0	0	.0	0	.0	0	.0	2	100.0	0	.0
FEMALE	0	.0	0	.0	0	.0	0	.0	0	.0	2	100.0	0	.0
MALE	0	.0	0	.0	0	.0	0	.0	0	.0	0	.0	0	.0
TOTAL ENROLLMENT:														
TOTAL	8	.2	6	.2	22	.7	51	1.5	87	2.6	3,209	95.2	74	2.2
FEMALE	3	.3	1	.1	6	.6	9	.9	19	1.9	962	97.3	8	.8
MALE	5	.2	5	.2	16	.7	42	1.8	68	2.9	2,247	94.4	66	2.8

LU 0100 - AGRICULTURE AND NATURAL RESOURCES

	AMERICAN INDIAN ALASKAN NATIVE		BLACK NON-HISPANIC		ASIAN OR PACIFIC ISLANDER		HISPANIC		TOTAL MINORITY		WHITE NON-HISPANIC		NON-RESIDENT ALIEN		TOTAL
	NUMBER	%	NUMBER	%	NUMBER	%	NUMBER	%	NUMBER	%	NUMBER	%	NUMBER	%	NUMBER

UT   (3 INSTITUTIONS)

UATES:

	2	.2	6	.6	7	.6	8	.7	23	2.1	1,066	97.9	0	.0	1,089
	0	.0	2	.4	5	.9	2	.4	9	1.6	538	98.4	0	.0	547
	2	.4	4	.7	2	.4	6	1.1	14	2.6	528	97.4	0	.0	542
	0	.0	0	.0	0	.0	0	.0	0	.0	57	100.0	0	.0	57
	0	.0	0	.0	0	.0	0	.0	0	.0	26	100.0	0	.0	26
	0	.0	0	.0	0	.0	0	.0	0	.0	31	100.0	0	.0	31
	2	.2	6	.5	7	.6	8	.7	23	2.0	1,123	98.0	0	.0	1,146
	0	.0	2	.3	5	.9	2	.3	9	1.6	564	98.4	0	.0	573
	2	.3	4	.7	2	.3	6	1.0	14	2.4	559	97.6	0	.0	573
	0	.0	2	1.0	4	2.1	3	1.6	9	4.7	168	87.0	16	8.3	193
	0	.0	0	.0	3	4.8	0	.0	3	4.8	58	92.1	2	3.2	63
	0	.0	2	1.5	1	.8	3	2.3	6	4.6	110	84.6	14	10.8	130
	1	4.0	0	.0	0	.0	0	.0	1	4.0	23	92.0	1	4.0	25
	0	.0	0	.0	0	.0	0	.0	0	.0	10	100.0	0	.0	10
	1	6.7	0	.0	0	.0	0	.0	1	6.7	13	86.7	1	6.7	15
	1	.5	2	.9	4	1.8	3	1.4	10	4.6	191	87.6	17	7.8	218
	0	.0	0	.0	3	4.1	0	.0	3	4.1	68	93.2	2	2.7	73
	1	.7	2	1.4	1	.7	3	2.1	7	4.8	123	84.8	15	10.3	145

NAL:

	0	.0	0	.0	0	.0	0	.0	0	.0	0	.0	0	.0	0
	0	.0	0	.0	0	.0	0	.0	0	.0	0	.0	0	.0	0
	0	.0	0	.0	0	.0	0	.0	0	.0	0	.0	0	.0	0
	0	.0	0	.0	0	.0	0	.0	0	.0	0	.0	0	.0	0
	0	.0	0	.0	0	.0	0	.0	0	.0	0	.0	0	.0	0
	0	.0	0	.0	0	.0	0	.0	0	.0	0	.0	0	.0	0
	0	.0	0	.0	0	.0	0	.0	0	.0	0	.0	0	.0	0
	0	.0	0	.0	0	.0	0	.0	0	.0	0	.0	0	.0	0
	0	.0	0	.0	0	.0	0	.0	0	.0	0	.0	0	.0	0

PROF:

	2	.2	8	.6	11	.9	11	.9	32	2.5	1,234	96.3	16	1.2	1,282
	0	.0	2	.3	8	1.3	2	.3	12	2.0	596	97.7	2	.3	610
	2	.3	6	.9	3	.4	9	1.3	20	3.0	638	94.9	14	2.1	672
	1	1.2	0	.0	0	.0	0	.0	1	1.2	80	97.6	1	1.2	82
	0	.0	0	.0	0	.0	0	.0	0	.0	36	100.0	0	.0	36
	1	2.2	0	.0	0	.0	0	.0	1	2.2	44	95.7	1	2.2	46
	3	.2	8	.6	11	.8	11	.8	33	2.4	1,314	96.3	17	1.2	1,364
	0	.0	2	.3	8	1.2	2	.3	12	1.9	632	97.8	2	.3	646
	3	.4	6	.8	3	.4	9	1.3	21	2.9	682	95.0	15	2.1	718

IED:

	0	.0	0	.0	0	.0	0	.0	0	.0	2	100.0	0	.0	2
	0	.0	0	.0	0	.0	0	.0	0	.0	0	.0	0	.0	0
	0	.0	0	.0	0	.0	0	.0	0	.0	2	100.0	0	.0	2

OLLMENT:

	3	.2	8	.6	11	.8	11	.8	33	2.4	1,316	96.3	17	1.2	1,366
	0	.0	2	.3	8	1.2	2	.3	12	1.9	632	97.8	2	.3	646
	3	.4	6	.8	3	.4	9	1.3	21	2.9	684	95.0	15	2.1	720

        (5 INSTITUTIONS)

UATES:

	1	.2	38	6.0	1	.2	0	.0	40	6.4	583	92.7	6	1.0	629
	0	.0	6	2.4	0	.0	0	.0	6	2.4	237	96.3	3	1.2	246
	1	.3	32	8.4	1	.3	0	.0	34	8.9	346	90.3	3	.8	383
	0	.0	5	8.2	0	.0	0	.0	5	8.2	56	91.8	0	.0	61
	0	.0	2	13.3	0	.0	0	.0	2	13.3	13	86.7	0	.0	15
	0	.0	3	6.5	0	.0	0	.0	3	6.5	43	93.5	0	.0	46
	1	.1	43	6.2	1	.1	0	.0	45	6.5	639	92.6	6	.9	690
	0	.0	8	3.1	0	.0	0	.0	8	3.1	250	95.8	3	1.1	261
	1	.2	35	8.2	1	.2	0	.0	37	8.6	389	90.7	3	.7	429
	0	.0	0	.0	0	.0	0	.0	0	.0	10	100.0	0	.0	10
	0	.0	0	.0	0	.0	0	.0	0	.0	6	100.0	0	.0	6
	0	.0	0	.0	0	.0	0	.0	0	.0	4	100.0	0	.0	4
	0	.0	0	.0	0	.0	0	.0	0	.0	26	100.0	0	.0	26
	0	.0	0	.0	0	.0	0	.0	0	.0	12	100.0	0	.0	12
	0	.0	0	.0	0	.0	0	.0	0	.0	14	100.0	0	.0	14
	0	.0	0	.0	0	.0	0	.0	0	.0	36	100.0	0	.0	36
	0	.0	0	.0	0	.0	0	.0	0	.0	18	100.0	0	.0	18
	0	.0	0	.0	0	.0	0	.0	0	.0	18	100.0	0	.0	18

NAL:

	0	.0	0	.0	0	.0	0	.0	0	.0	0	.0	0	.0	0
	0	.0	0	.0	0	.0	0	.0	0	.0	0	.0	0	.0	0
	0	.0	0	.0	0	.0	0	.0	0	.0	0	.0	0	.0	0

TABLE 17 - TOTAL ENROLLMENT IN INSTITUTIONS OF HIGHER EDUCATION FOR SELECTED MAJOR FIELDS OF STUDY AND LEVEL OF ENROLLMENT
BY RACE, ETHNICITY, AND SEX: STATE, 1978

MAJOR FIELD 0100 - AGRICULTURE AND NATURAL RESOURCES

	AMERICAN INDIAN ALASKAN NATIVE		BLACK NON-HISPANIC		ASIAN OR PACIFIC ISLANDER		HISPANIC		TOTAL MINORITY		WHITE NON-HISPANIC		NON-RESIDENT ALIEN		TOT
	NUMBER	%	NUMBER	%	NUMBER	%	NUMBER	%	NUMBER	%	NUMBER	%	NUMBER	%	NUM
DELAWARE	CONTINUED														
PROFESSIONAL:															
PART-TIME	0	.0	0	.0	0	.0	0	.0	0	.0	0	.0	0	.0	
FEMALE	0	.0	0	.0	0	.0	0	.0	0	.0	0	.0	0	.0	
MALE	0	.0	0	.0	0	.0	0	.0	0	.0	0	.0	0	.0	
TOTAL	0	.0	0	.0	0	.0	0	.0	0	.0	0	.0	0	.0	
FEMALE	0	.0	0	.0	0	.0	0	.0	0	.0	0	.0	0	.0	
MALE	0	.0	0	.0	0	.0	0	.0	0	.0	0	.0	0	.0	
UNG+GRAD+PROF:															
FULL-TIME	1	.2	38	5.9	1	.2	0	.0	40	6.3	543	92.8	6	.9	
FEMALE	0	.0	6	2.4	0	.0	0	.0	6	2.4	243	96.4	3	1.2	
MALE	1	.3	32	8.3	1	.3	0	.0	34	8.8	350	90.4	3	.8	
PART-TIME	0	.0	5	5.7	0	.0	0	.0	5	5.7	82	94.3	0	.0	
FEMALE	0	.0	2	7.4	0	.0	0	.0	2	7.4	25	92.6	0	.0	
MALE	0	.0	3	5.0	0	.0	0	.0	3	5.0	57	95.0	0	.0	
TOTAL	1	.1	43	5.9	1	.1	0	.0	45	6.2	675	93.0	6	.8	
FEMALE	0	.0	8	2.9	0	.0	0	.0	8	2.9	268	96.1	3	1.1	
MALE	1	.2	35	7.8	1	.2	0	.0	37	8.3	407	91.1	3	.7	
UNCLASSIFIED:															
TOTAL	0	.0	0	.0	0	.0	0	.0	0	.0	75	98.7	1	1.3	
FEMALE	0	.0	0	.0	0	.0	0	.0	0	.0	21	100.0	0	.0	
MALE	0	.0	0	.0	0	.0	0	.0	0	.0	54	98.2	1	1.8	
TOTAL ENROLLMENT:															
TOTAL	1	.1	43	5.4	1	.1	0	.0	45	5.6	750	93.5	7	.9	
FEMALE	0	.0	8	2.7	0	.0	0	.0	8	2.7	289	96.3	3	1.0	
MALE	1	.2	35	7.0	1	.2	0	.0	37	7.4	461	91.8	4	.8	
DISTRICT OF COLUMBIA (	2 INSTITUTIONS)														
UNDERGRADUATES:															
FULL-TIME	1	1.5	56	84.8	4	6.1	0	.0	61	92.4	3	4.5	2	3.0	
FEMALE	0	.0	24	96.0	0	.0	0	.0	24	96.0	0	.0	1	4.0	
MALE	1	2.4	32	78.0	4	9.8	0	.0	37	90.2	3	7.3	1	2.4	
PART-TIME	2	1.7	97	80.8	6	5.0	0	.0	105	87.5	9	7.5	6	5.0	
FEMALE	0	.0	41	85.4	0	.0	0	.0	41	85.4	4	8.3	3	6.3	
MALE	2	2.8	56	77.8	6	8.3	0	.0	64	88.9	5	6.9	3	4.2	
TOTAL	3	1.6	153	82.3	10	5.4	0	.0	166	89.2	12	6.5	8	4.3	
FEMALE	0	.0	65	89.0	0	.0	0	.0	65	89.0	4	5.5	4	5.5	
MALE	3	2.7	88	77.9	10	8.8	0	.0	101	89.4	8	7.1	4	3.5	
GRADUATE:															
FULL-TIME	0	.0	0	.0	0	.0	0	.0	0	.0	0	.0	0	.0	
FEMALE	0	.0	0	.0	0	.0	0	.0	0	.0	0	.0	0	.0	
MALE	0	.0	0	.0	0	.0	0	.0	0	.0	0	.0	0	.0	
PART-TIME	0	.0	0	.0	0	.0	0	.0	0	.0	1	100.0	0	.0	
FEMALE	0	.0	0	.0	0	.0	0	.0	0	.0	1	100.0	0	.0	
MALE	0	.0	0	.0	0	.0	0	.0	0	.0	0	.0	0	.0	
TOTAL	0	.0	0	.0	0	.0	0	.0	0	.0	1	100.0	0	.0	
FEMALE	0	.0	0	.0	0	.0	0	.0	0	.0	1	100.0	0	.0	
MALE	0	.0	0	.0	0	.0	0	.0	0	.0	0	.0	0	.0	
PROFESSIONAL:															
FULL-TIME	0	.0	0	.0	0	.0	0	.0	0	.0	0	.0	0	.0	
FEMALE	0	.0	0	.0	0	.0	0	.0	0	.0	0	.0	0	.0	
MALE	0	.0	0	.0	0	.0	0	.0	0	.0	0	.0	0	.0	
PART-TIME	0	.0	0	.0	0	.0	0	.0	0	.0	0	.0	0	.0	
FEMALE	0	.0	0	.0	0	.0	0	.0	0	.0	0	.0	0	.0	
MALE	0	.0	0	.0	0	.0	0	.0	0	.0	0	.0	0	.0	
TOTAL	0	.0	0	.0	0	.0	0	.0	0	.0	0	.0	0	.0	
FEMALE	0	.0	0	.0	0	.0	0	.0	0	.0	0	.0	0	.0	
MALE	0	.0	0	.0	0	.0	0	.0	0	.0	0	.0	0	.0	
UNG+GRAD+PROF:															
FULL-TIME	1	1.5	56	84.8	4	6.1	0	.0	61	92.4	3	4.5	2	3.0	
FEMALE	0	.0	24	96.0	0	.0	0	.0	24	96.0	0	.0	1	4.0	
MALE	1	2.4	32	78.0	4	9.8	0	.0	37	90.2	3	7.3	1	2.4	
PART-TIME	2	1.7	97	80.2	6	5.0	0	.0	105	86.8	10	8.3	6	5.0	
FEMALE	0	.0	41	83.7	0	.0	0	.0	41	83.7	5	10.2	3	6.1	
MALE	2	2.8	56	77.8	6	8.3	0	.0	64	88.9	5	6.9	3	4.2	
TOTAL	3	1.6	153	81.8	10	5.3	0	.0	166	88.8	13	7.0			4 3
FEMALE	0	.0	65	87.8	0	.0	0	.0	65	87.8	5	6.8			5 14
MALE	3	2.7	88	77.9	10	8.8	0	.0	101	89.4	8	7.1	9	3.5	
UNCLASSIFIED:															
TOTAL	0	.0	0	.0	0	.0	0	.0	0	.0	0	.0	0	.0	
FEMALE	0	.0	0	.0	0	.0	0	.0	0	.0	0	.0			.0
MALE	0	.0	0	.0	0	.0	0	.0	0	.0	0	.0	0	.0	
TOTAL ENROLLMENT:															
TOTAL	3	1.6	153	81.8	10	5.3	0	.0	166	88.8	13	7.0	8	4.3	
FEMALE	0	.0	65	87.8	0	.0	0	.0	65	87.8	5	6.8	4	5.4	
MALE	3	2.7	88	77.9	10	8.8	0	.0	101	89.4	8	7.1	4	3.5	

294

100 - AGRICULTURE AND NATURAL RESOURCES

AMERICAN INDIAN ALASKAN NATIVE		BLACK NON-HISPANIC		ASIAN OR PACIFIC ISLANDER		HISPANIC		TOTAL MINORITY		WHITE NON-HISPANIC		NON-RESIDENT ALIEN		TOTAL
NUMBER	%	NUMBER	%	NUMBER	%	NUMBER	%	NUMBER	%	NUMBER	%	NUMBER	%	NUMBER
(4 INSTITUTIONS)														
2	.1	62	4.6	4	.3	33	2.4	101	7.5	1,196	88.3	58	4.3	1,355
1	.2	14	2.9	0	.0	7	1.4	22	4.5	457	93.8	8	1.6	487
1	.1	48	5.5	4	.5	26	3.0	79	9.1	738	85.1	50	5.8	868
0	.0	7	5.9	0	.0	6	5.0	13	10.9	104	87.4	2	1.7	119
0	.0	0	.0	0	.0	0	.0	0	.0	40	100.0	0	.0	40
0	.0	7	8.9	0	.0	6	7.6	13	16.5	64	81.0	2	2.5	79
2	.1	69	4.7	4	.3	39	2.6	114	7.7	1,300	88.2	60	4.1	1,474
1	.2	14	2.7	0	.0	7	1.3	22	4.2	497	94.3	8	1.5	527
1	.1	55	5.8	4	.4	32	3.4	92	9.7	803	84.8	52	5.5	947
0	.0	4	1.1	4	1.1	4	1.1	12	3.4	206	59.2	130	37.4	348
0	.0	0	.0	3	4.1	0	.0	3	4.1	57	77.0	14	18.9	74
0	.0	4	1.5	1	.4	4	1.5	9	3.3	149	54.4	116	42.3	274
0	.0	1	1.4	2	2.7	1	1.4	4	5.4	53	71.6	17	23.0	74
0	.0	0	.0	1	6.7	0	.0	1	6.7	13	86.7	1	6.7	15
0	.0	1	1.7	1	1.7	1	1.7	3	5.1	40	67.8	16	27.1	59
0	.0	5	1.2	6	1.4	5	1.2	16	3.8	259	61.4	147	34.8	422
0	.0	0	.0	4	4.5	0	.0	4	4.5	70	78.7	15	16.9	89
0	.0	5	1.5	2	.6	5	1.5	12	3.6	189	56.8	132	39.6	333
0	.0	0	.0	0	.0	0	.0	0	.0	0	.0	0	.0	0
0	.0	0	.0	0	.0	0	.0	0	.0	0	.0	0	.0	0
0	.0	0	.0	0	.0	0	.0	0	.0	0	.0	0	.0	0
0	.0	0	.0	0	.0	0	.0	0	.0	0	.0	0	.0	0
0	.0	0	.0	0	.0	0	.0	0	.0	0	.0	0	.0	0
0	.0	0	.0	0	.0	0	.0	0	.0	0	.0	0	.0	0
0	.0	0	.0	0	.0	0	.0	0	.0	0	.0	0	.0	0
0	.0	0	.0	0	.0	0	.0	0	.0	0	.0	0	.0	0
0	.0	0	.0	0	.0	0	.0	0	.0	0	.0	0	.0	0
2	.1	66	3.9	8	.5	37	2.2	113	6.6	1,402	82.3	188	11.0	1,703
1	.2	14	2.5	3	.5	7	1.2	25	4.5	514	91.6	22	3.9	561
1	.1	52	4.6	5	.4	30	2.6	88	7.7	888	77.8	166	14.5	1,142
0	.0	8	4.1	2	1.0	7	3.6	17	8.8	157	81.3	19	9.8	193
0	.0	0	.0	1	1.8	0	.0	1	1.8	53	96.4	1	1.8	55
0	.0	8	5.8	1	.7	7	5.1	16	11.6	104	75.4	18	13.0	138
2	.1	74	3.9	10	.5	44	2.3	130	6.9	1,559	82.2	207	10.9	1,896
1	.2	14	2.3	4	.6	7	1.1	26	4.2	567	92.0	23	3.7	616
1	.1	60	4.7	6	.5	37	2.9	104	8.1	992	77.5	184	14.4	1,280
1	.8	4	3.2	2	1.6	3	2.4	10	7.9	105	83.3	11	8.7	126
0	.0	2	3.6	1	1.8	1	1.8	4	7.3	47	85.5	4	7.3	55
1	1.4	2	2.8	1	1.4	2	2.8	6	8.5	58	81.7	7	9.9	71
NTI														
3	.1	78	3.9	12	.6	47	2.3	140	6.9	1,664	82.3	218	10.8	2,022
1	.1	16	2.4	5	.7	8	1.2	30	4.5	614	91.5	27	4.0	671
2	.1	62	4.6	7	.5	39	2.9	110	8.1	1,050	77.7	191	14.1	1,351
(22 INSTITUTIONS)														
2	.1	74	4.0	2	.1	13	.7	91	4.9	1,719	93.2	34	1.8	1,844
0	.0	17	4.2	1	.2	2	.5	20	5.0	380	94.3	3	.7	403
2	.1	57	4.0	1	.1	11	.8	71	4.9	1,339	92.9	31	2.2	1,441
0	.0	2	.8	0	.0	1	.4	3	1.1	258	97.4	4	1.5	265
0	.0	0	.0	0	.0	0	.0	0	.0	61	100.0	0	.0	61
0	.0	2	1.0	0	.0	1	.5	3	1.5	197	96.6	4	2.0	204
2	.1	76	3.6	2	.1	14	.7	94	4.5	1,977	93.7	38	1.8	2,109
0	.0	17	3.7	1	.2	2	.4	20	4.3	441	95.0	3	.6	464
2	.1	59	3.6	1	.1	12	.7	74	4.5	1,536	93.4	35	2.1	1,645
0	.0	0	.0	0	.9	0	.0	1	.9	98	87.5	13	11.6	112
0	.0	0	.0	0	.0	0	.0	0	.0	16	72.7	6	27.3	22
0	.0	0	.0	1	1.1	0	.0	1	1.1	82	91.1	7	7.8	90
0	.7	0	.0	4	2.9	0	.0	5	3.6	120	86.3	14	10.1	139
0	.0	0	.0	2	6.7	0	.0	2	6.7	25	83.3	3	10.0	30
1	.9	0	.0	2	1.8	0	.0	3	2.8	95	87.2	11	10.1	109
1	.4	0	.0	5	2.0	0	.0	6	2.4	218	86.9	27	10.8	251
0	.0	0	.0	2	3.8	0	.0	2	3.8	41	78.8	9	17.3	52
1	.5	0	.0	3	1.5	0	.0	4	2.0	177	88.9	18	9.0	199
0	.0	0	.0	0	.0	0	.0	0	.0	0	.0	0	.0	0
0	.0	0	.0	0	.0	0	.0	0	.0	0	.0	0	.0	0
0	.0	0	.0	0	.0	0	.0	0	.0	0	.0	0	.0	0

TABLE 17 - TOTAL ENROLLMENT IN INSTITUTIONS OF HIGHER EDUCATION FOR SELECTED MAJOR FIELDS OF STUDY AND LEVEL OF ENROLLMENT
BY RACE, ETHNICITY, AND SEX: STATE, 1978

MAJOR FIELD 0100 - AGRICULTURE AND NATURAL RESOURCES

	AMERICAN INDIAN ALASKAN NATIVE		BLACK NON-HISPANIC		ASIAN OR PACIFIC ISLANDER		HISPANIC		TOTAL MINORITY		WHITE NON-HISPANIC		NON-RESIDENT ALIEN	
	NUMBER	%	NUMBER	%	NUMBER	%	NUMBER	%	NUMBER	%	NUMBER	%	NUMBER	%
GEORGIA	CONTINUED													
PROFESSIONAL:														
PART-TIME	0	.0	0	.0	0	.0	0	.0	0	.0	0	.0	0	.0
FEMALE	0	.0	0	.0	0	.0	0	.0	0	.0	0	.0	0	.0
MALE	0	.0	0	.0	0	.0	0	.0	0	.0	0	.0	0	.0
TOTAL	0	.0	0	.0	0	.0	0	.0	0	.0	0	.0	0	.0
FEMALE	0	.0	0	.0	0	.0	0	.0	0	.0	0	.0	0	.0
MALE	0	.0	0	.0	0	.0	0	.0	0	.0	0	.0	0	.0
UND+GRAD+PROF:														
FULL-TIME	2	.1	74	3.8	3	.2	13	.7	92	4.7	1,817	92.9	47	2.4
FEMALE	0	.0	17	4.0	1	.2	2	.5	20	4.7	396	93.2	9	2.1
MALE	2	.1	57	3.7	2	.1	11	.7	72	4.7	1,421	92.8	38	2.5
PART-TIME	1	.2	2	.5	4	1.0	1	.2	8	2.0	378	93.6	18	4.5
FEMALE	0	.0	0	.0	2	2.2	0	.0	2	2.2	86	94.5	3	3.3
MALE	1	.3	2	.6	2	.6	1	.3	6	1.9	292	93.3	15	4.8
TOTAL	3	.1	76	3.2	7	.3	14	.6	100	4.2	2,195	93.0	65	2.8
FEMALE	0	.0	17	3.3	3	.6	2	.4	22	4.3	482	93.4	12	2.3
MALE	3	.2	59	3.2	4	.2	12	.7	78	4.2	1,713	92.9	53	2.9
UNCLASSIFIED:														
TOTAL	0	.0	1	1.2	0	.0	1	1.2	2	2.4	66	78.6	16	19.0
FEMALE	0	.0	0	.0	0	.0	0	.0	0	.0	16	84.2	3	15.8
MALE	0	.0	1	1.5	0	.0	1	1.5	2	3.1	50	76.9	13	20.0
TOTAL ENROLLMENT:														
TOTAL	3	.1	77	3.2	7	.3	15	.6	102	4.2	2,261	92.5	81	3.3
FEMALE	0	.0	17	3.2	3	.6	2	.4	22	4.1	498	93.1	15	2.8
MALE	3	.2	60	3.1	4	.2	13	.7	80	4.2	1,763	92.4	66	3.5
HAWAII	(	2 INSTITUTIONS)												
UNDERGRADUATES:														
FULL-TIME	0	.0	2	.4	289	62.7	4	.9	295	64.0	151	32.8	15	3.3
FEMALE	0	.0	2	1.3	91	59.5	2	1.3	95	62.1	55	35.9	3	2.0
MALE	0	.0	0	.0	198	64.3	2	.6	200	64.9	96	31.2	12	3.9
PART-TIME	0	.0	0	.0	60	69.0	1	1.1	61	70.1	25	28.7	1	1.1
FEMALE	0	.0	0	.0	13	52.0	0	.0	13	52.0	12	48.0	0	.0
MALE	0	.0	0	.0	47	75.8	1	1.6	48	77.4	13	21.0	1	1.6
TOTAL	0	.0	2	.4	349	63.7	5	.9	356	65.0	176	32.1	16	2.9
FEMALE	0	.0	2	1.1	104	58.4	2	1.1	108	60.7	67	37.6	3	1.7
MALE	0	.0	0	.0	245	66.2	3	.8	248	67.0	109	29.5	13	3.5
GRADUATE:														
FULL-TIME	0	.0	3	2.5	48	40.7	6	5.1	57	48.3	38	32.2	23	19.5
FEMALE	0	.0	0	.0	21	75.0	0	.0	21	75.0	3	10.7	4	14.3
MALE	0	.0	3	3.3	27	30.0	6	6.7	36	40.0	35	38.9	19	21.1
PART-TIME	0	.0	0	.0	40	51.3	0	.0	40	51.3	31	39.7	7	9.0
FEMALE	0	.0	0	.0	9	81.8	0	.0	9	81.8	1	9.1	1	9.1
MALE	0	.0	0	.0	31	46.3	0	.0	31	46.3	30	44.8	6	9.0
TOTAL	0	.0	3	1.5	88	44.9	6	3.1	97	49.5	69	35.2	30	15.3
FEMALE	0	.0	0	.0	30	76.9	0	.0	30	76.9	4	10.3	5	12.8
MALE	0	.0	3	1.9	58	36.9	6	3.8	67	42.7	65	41.4	25	15.9
PROFESSIONAL:														
FULL-TIME	0	.0	0	.0	0	.0	0	.0	0	.0	0	.0	0	.0
FEMALE	0	.0	0	.0	0	.0	0	.0	0	.0	0	.0	0	.0
MALE	0	.0	0	.0	0	.0	0	.0	0	.0	0	.0	0	.0
PART-TIME	0	.0	0	.0	0	.0	0	.0	0	.0	0	.0	0	.0
FEMALE	0	.0	0	.0	0	.0	0	.0	0	.0	0	.0	0	.0
MALE	0	.0	0	.0	0	.0	0	.0	0	.0	0	.0	0	.0
TOTAL	0	.0	0	.0	0	.0	0	.0	0	.0	0	.0	0	.0
FEMALE	0	.0	0	.0	0	.0	0	.0	0	.0	0	.0	0	.0
MALE	0	.0	0	.0	0	.0	0	.0	0	.0	0	.0	0	.0
UND+GRAD+PROF:														
FULL-TIME	0	.0	5	.9	337	58.2	10	1.7	352	60.8	189	32.6	38	6.6
FEMALE	0	.0	2	1.1	112	61.9	2	1.1	116	64.1	58	32.0	7	3.9
MALE	0	.0	3	.8	225	56.5	8	2.0	236	59.3	131	32.9	31	7.8
PART-TIME	0	.0	0	.0	100	60.6	1	.6	101	61.2	56	33.9	8	4.8
FEMALE	0	.0	0	.0	22	61.1	0	.0	22	61.1	13	36.1	1	2.8
MALE	0	.0	0	.0	78	60.5	1	.8	79	61.2	43	33.3	7	5.4
TOTAL	0	.0	5	.7	437	58.7	11	1.5	453	60.9	245	32.9	46	6.2
FEMALE	0	.0	2	.9	134	61.8	2	.9	138	63.6	71	32.7	8	3.7
MALE	0	.0	3	.6	303	57.5	9	1.7	315	59.8	174	33.0	38	7.2
UNCLASSIFIED:														
TOTAL	0	.0	0	.0	0	.0	0	.0	0	.0	0	.0	0	.0
FEMALE	0	.0	0	.0	0	.0	0	.0	0	.0	0	.0	0	.0
MALE	0	.0	0	.0	0	.0	0	.0	0	.0	0	.0	0	.0
TOTAL ENROLLMENT:														
TOTAL	0	.0	5	.7	437	58.7	11	1.5	453	60.9	245	32.9	46	6.2
FEMALE	0	.0	2	.9	134	61.8	2	.9	138	63.6	71	32.7	8	3.7
MALE	0	.0	3	.6	303	57.5	9	1.7	315	59.8	174	33.0	38	7.2

296

AL ENROLLMENT IN INSTITUTIONS OF HIGHER EDUCATION FOR SELECTED MAJOR FIELDS OF STUDY AND LEVEL OF ENROLLMENT
RACE, ETHNICITY, AND SEX: STATE, 1978

00 - AGRICULTURE AND NATURAL RESOURCES

RICAN INDIAN SKAN NATIVE		BLACK NON-HISPANIC		ASIAN OR PACIFIC ISLANDER		HISPANIC		TOTAL MINORITY		WHITE NON-HISPANIC		NON-RESIDENT ALIEN		TOTAL
MBER	%	NUMBER	%	NUMBER	%	NUMBER	%	NUMBER	%	NUMBER	%	NUMBER	%	NUMBER
(6 INSTITUTIONS)														
5	.4	1	.1	7	.6	1	.1	14	1.2	1,119	97.7	12	1.0	1,145
0	.0	0	.0	3	1.1	1	.4	4	1.4	269	97.5	3	1.1	276
5	.6	1	.1	4	.5	0	.0	10	1.2	850	97.8	9	1.0	869
0	.0	0	.0	1	1.0	0	.0	1	1.0	100	99.0	0	.0	101
0	.0	0	.0	1	2.7	0	.0	1	2.7	36	97.3	0	.0	37
0	.0	0	.0	0	.0	0	.0	0	.0	64	100.0	0	.0	64
5	.4	1	.1	8	.6	1	.1	15	1.2	1,219	97.8	12	1.0	1,246
0	.0	0	.0	4	1.3	1	.3	5	1.6	305	97.4	3	1.0	313
5	.5	1	.1	4	.4	0	.0	10	1.1	914	98.0	9	1.0	933
1	.7	0	.0	0	.0	1	.7	2	1.4	127	87.0	17	11.6	146
1	4.3	0	.0	0	.0	0	.0	1	4.3	18	78.3	4	17.4	23
0	.0	0	.0	0	.0	1	.8	1	.8	109	88.6	13	10.6	123
0	.0	0	.0	0	.0	0	.0	0	.0	60	93.8	4	6.3	64
0	.0	0	.0	0	.0	0	.0	0	.0	12	100.0	0	.0	12
0	.0	0	.0	0	.0	0	.0	0	.0	48	92.3	4	7.7	52
1	.5	0	.0	0	.0	1	.5	2	1.0	187	89.0	21	10.0	210
1	2.9	0	.0	0	.0	0	.0	1	2.9	30	85.7	4	11.4	35
0	.0	0	.0	0	.0	1	.6	1	.6	157	89.7	17	9.7	175
0	.0	0	.0	0	.0	0	.0	0	.0	0	.0	0	.0	0
0	.0	0	.0	0	.0	0	.0	0	.0	0	.0	0	.0	0
0	.0	0	.0	0	.0	0	.0	0	.0	0	.0	0	.0	0
0	.0	0	.0	0	.0	0	.0	0	.0	0	.0	0	.0	0
0	.0	0	.0	0	.0	0	.0	0	.0	0	.0	0	.0	0
0	.0	0	.0	0	.0	0	.0	0	.0	0	.0	0	.0	0
0	.0	0	.0	0	.0	0	.0	0	.0	0	.0	0	.0	0
0	.0	0	.0	0	.0	0	.0	0	.0	0	.0	0	.0	0
6	.5	1	.1	7	.5	2	.2	16	1.2	1,246	96.5	29	2.2	1,291
1	.3	0	.0	3	1.0	1	.3	5	1.7	287	96.0	7	2.3	259
5	.5	1	.1	4	.4	1	.1	11	1.1	959	96.7	22	2.2	992
0	.0	0	.0	1	.6	0	.0	1	.6	160	97.0	4	2.4	165
0	.0	0	.0	1	2.0	0	.0	1	2.0	48	98.0	0	.0	49
0	.0	0	.0	0	.0	0	.0	0	.0	112	96.6	4	3.4	116
6	.4	1	.1	8	.5	2	.1	17	1.2	1,406	96.6	33	2.3	1,456
1	.3	0	.0	4	1.1	1	.3	6	1.7	335	96.3	7	2.0	348
5	.5	1	.1	4	.4	1	.1	11	1.0	1,071	96.7	26	2.3	1,108
0	.0	0	.0	0	.0	0	.0	0	.0	2	100.0	0	.0	2
0	.0	0	.0	0	.0	0	.0	0	.0	1	100.0	0	.0	1
0	.0	0	.0	0	.0	0	.0	0	.0	1	100.0	0	.0	1
Tl														
6	.4	1	.1	8	.5	2	.1	17	1.2	1,408	96.6	33	2.3	1,458
1	.3	0	.0	4	1.1	1	.3	6	1.7	336	96.3	7	2.0	349
5	.5	1	.1	4	.4	1	.1	11	1.0	1,072	96.7	26	2.3	1,109
(23 INSTITUTIONS)														
18	.5	22	.6	23	.6	15	.4	78	2.0	3,742	95.5	97	2.5	3,917
5	.5	8	.8	11	1.1	2	.2	26	2.5	987	96.3	12	1.2	1,025
13	.4	14	.5	12	.4	13	.4	52	1.8	2,755	95.3	85	2.9	2,892
6	2.2	3	1.1	1	.4	4	1.4	14	5.0	258	92.8	6	2.2	278
1	1.5	1	1.5	1	1.5	1	1.5	4	6.1	62	93.9	0	.0	66
5	2.4	2	.9	0	.0	3	1.4	10	4.7	196	92.5	6	2.8	212
24	.6	25	.6	24	.6	19	.5	92	2.2	4,000	95.4	103	2.5	4,195
6	.5	9	.8	12	1.1	3	.3	30	2.7	1,049	96.2	12	1.1	1,091
18	.6	16	.5	12	.4	16	.5	62	2.0	2,951	95.1	91	2.9	3,104
0	.0	6	2.2	5	1.8	1	.4	12	4.3	196	70.3	71	25.4	279
0	.0	2	3.3	1	1.6	1	1.6	4	6.6	48	78.7	9	14.8	61
0	.0	4	1.8	4	1.8	0	.0	8	3.7	148	67.9	62	28.4	218
0	.0	3	1.4	3	1.4	0	.0	6	2.8	168	79.2	38	17.9	212
0	.0	0	.0	1	2.3	0	.0	1	2.3	37	86.0	5	11.6	43
0	.0	3	1.8	2	1.2	0	.0	5	3.0	131	77.5	33	19.5	169
0	.0	9	1.8	8	1.6	1	.2	18	3.7	364	74.1	109	22.2	491
0	.0	2	1.9	2	1.9	1	1.0	5	4.8	85	81.7	14	13.5	104
0	.0	7	1.8	6	1.6	0	.0	13	3.4	279	72.1	95	24.5	387
0	.0	0	.0	0	.0	0	.0	0	.0	0	.0	0	.0	0
0	.0	0	.0	0	.0	0	.0	0	.0	0	.0	0	.0	0
0	.0	0	.0	0	.0	0	.0	0	.0	0	.0	0	.0	0

MAJOR FIELD 0100 - AGRICULTURE AND NATURAL RESOURCES

	AMERICAN INDIAN ALASKAN NATIVE		BLACK NON-HISPANIC		ASIAN GR PACIFIC ISLANDER		HISPANIC		TOTAL MINORITY		WHITE NON-HISPANIC		NON-RESIDENT ALIEN	
	NUMBER	%	NUMBER	%	NUMBER	%	NUMBER	%	NUMBER	%	NUMBER	%	NUMBER	%
ILLINOIS	CONTINUED													
PROFESSIONAL:														
PART-TIME	0	.0	0	.0	0	.0	0	.0	0	.0	0	.0	0	.0
FEMALE	0	.0	0	.0	0	.0	0	.0	0	.0	0	.0	0	.0
MALE	0	.0	0	.0	0	.0	0	.0	0	.0	0	.0	0	.0
TOTAL	0	.0	0	.0	0	.0	0	.0	0	.0	0	.0	0	.0
FEMALE	0	.0	0	.0	0	.0	0	.0	0	.0	0	.0	0	.0
MALE	0	.0	0	.0	0	.0	0	.0	0	.0	0	.0	0	.0
UND+GRAD+PROF:														
FULL-TIME	18	.4	28	.7	28	.7	16	.4	90	2.1	3,938	93.9	168	4.0
FEMALE	5	.5	10	.9	12	1.1	3	.3	30	2.8	1,035	95.3	21	1.9
MALE	13	.4	18	.6	16	.5	13	.4	60	1.9	2,903	93.3	147	4.7
PART-TIME	6	1.2	6	1.2	4	.8	4	.8	20	4.1	426	86.9	44	9.0
FEMALE	1	.9	1	.9	2	1.8	1	.9	5	4.6	99	90.8	5	4.6
MALE	5	1.3	5	1.3	2	.5	3	.8	15	3.9	327	85.8	39	10.2
TOTAL	24	.5	34	.7	32	.7	20	.4	110	2.3	4,364	93.1	212	4.5
FEMALE	6	.5	11	.9	14	1.2	4	.3	35	2.9	1,134	94.9	26	2.2
MALE	18	.5	23	.7	18	.5	16	.5	75	2.1	3,230	92.5	186	5.3
UNCLASSIFIED:														
TOTAL	0	.0	0	.0	0	.0	0	.0	0	.0	53	91.4	5	8.6
FEMALE	0	.0	0	.0	0	.0	0	.0	0	.0	17	94.4	1	5.6
MALE	0	.0	0	.0	0	.0	0	.0	0	.0	36	90.0	4	10.0
TOTAL ENROLLMENT:														
TOTAL	24	.5	34	.7	32	.7	20	.4	110	2.3	4,417	93.1	217	4.6
FEMALE	6	.5	11	.9	14	1.2	4	.3	35	2.9	1,151	94.9	27	2.2
MALE	18	.5	23	.7	18	.5	16	.5	75	2.1	3,266	92.5	190	5.4
INDIANA	(9 INSTITUTIONS)													
UNDERGRADUATES:														
FULL-TIME	0	.0	7	.2	3	.1	7	.2	17	.6	2,789	99.0	11	.4
FEMALE	0	.0	4	.5	1	.1	2	.2	7	.8	831	99.0	1	.1
MALE	0	.0	3	.2	2	.1	5	.3	10	.5	1,958	99.0	10	.5
PART-TIME	0	.0	1	.6	0	.0	0	.0	1	.6	174	98.9	1	.6
FEMALE	0	.0	1	1.6	0	.0	0	.0	1	1.6	62	98.4	0	.0
MALE	0	.0	0	.0	0	.0	0	.0	0	.0	112	99.1	1	.9
TOTAL	0	.0	8	.3	3	.1	7	.2	18	.6	2,963	99.0	12	.4
FEMALE	0	.0	5	.6	1	.1	2	.2	8	.9	893	99.0	1	.1
MALE	0	.0	3	.1	2	.1	5	.2	10	.5	2,070	99.0	11	.5
GRADUATE:														
FULL-TIME	0	.0	0	.0	3	1.0	0	.0	3	1.0	212	74.1	71	24.8
FEMALE	0	.0	0	.0	2	3.6	0	.0	2	3.6	45	81.8	8	14.5
MALE	0	.0	0	.0	1	.4	0	.0	1	.4	167	72.3	63	27.3
PART-TIME	0	.0	0	.0	1	.9	0	.0	1	.9	93	86.1	14	13.0
FEMALE	0	.0	0	.0	1	4.5	0	.0	1	4.5	18	81.8	3	13.6
MALE	0	.0	0	.0	0	.0	0	.0	0	.0	75	87.2	11	12.8
TOTAL	0	.0	0	.0	4	1.0	0	.0	4	1.0	305	77.4	85	21.6
FEMALE	0	.0	0	.0	3	3.9	0	.0	3	3.9	63	81.8	11	14.3
MALE	0	.0	0	.0	1	.3	0	.0	1	.3	242	76.3	74	23.3
PROFESSIONAL:														
FULL-TIME	0	.0	0	.0	0	.0	0	.0	0	.0	0	.0	0	.0
FEMALE	0	.0	0	.0	0	.0	0	.0	0	.0	0	.0	0	.0
MALE	0	.0	0	.0	0	.0	0	.0	0	.0	0	.0	0	.0
PART-TIME	0	.0	0	.0	0	.0	0	.0	0	.0	0	.0	0	.0
FEMALE	0	.0	0	.0	0	.0	0	.0	0	.0	0	.0	0	.0
MALE	0	.0	0	.0	0	.0	0	.0	0	.0	0	.0	0	.0
TOTAL	0	.0	0	.0	0	.0	0	.0	0	.0	0	.0	0	.0
FEMALE	0	.0	0	.0	0	.0	0	.0	0	.0	0	.0	0	.0
MALE	0	.0	0	.0	0	.0	0	.0	0	.0	0	.0	0	.0
UND+GRAD+PROF:														
FULL-TIME	0	.0	7	.2	6	.2	7	.2	20	.6	3,001	96.7	82	2.6
FEMALE	0	.0	4	.4	3	.3	2	.2	9	1.0	876	98.0	9	1.0
MALE	0	.0	3	.1	3	.1	5	.2	11	.5	2,125	96.2	73	3.3
PART-TIME	0	.0	1	.4	1	.4	0	.0	2	.7	267	94.0	15	5.3
FEMALE	0	.0	1	1.2	1	1.2	0	.0	2	2.4	80	94.1	3	3.5
MALE	0	.0	0	.0	0	.0	0	.0	0	.0	187	94.0	12	6.0
TOTAL	0	.0	8	.2	7	.2	7	.2	22	.6	3,268	96.5	97	2.9
FEMALE	0	.0	5	.5	4	.4	2	.2	11	1.1	956	97.7	12	1.2
MALE	0	.0	3	.1	3	.1	5	.2	11	.5	2,312	96.0	85	3.5
UNCLASSIFIED:														
TOTAL	0	.0	0	.0	0	.0	0	.0	0	.0	23	79.3	6	20.7
FEMALE	0	.0	0	.0	0	.0	0	.0	0	.0	6	85.7	1	14.3
MALE	0	.0	0	.0	0	.0	0	.0	0	.0	17	77.3	5	22.7
TOTAL ENROLLMENT:														
TOTAL	0	.0	8	.2	7	.2	7	.2	22	.6	3,291	96.3	103	3.0
FEMALE	0	.0	5	.5	4	.4	2	.2	11	1.1	962	97.6	13	1.3
MALE	0	.0	3	.1	3	.1	5	.2	11	.5	2,329	95.8	90	3.7

ROLLMENT IN INSTITUTIONS OF HIGHER EDUCATION FOR SELECTED MAJOR FIELDS OF STUDY AND LEVEL OF ENROLLMENT
ETHNICITY, AND SEX: STATE, 1978

AGRICULTURE AND NATURAL RESOURCES

INDIAN NATIVE	BLACK NON-HISPANIC		ASIAN OR PACIFIC ISLANDER		HISPANIC		TOTAL MINORITY		WHITE NON-HISPANIC		NON-RESIDENT ALIEN		TOTAL
%	NUMBER	%	NUMBER	%	NUMBER	%	NUMBER	%	NUMBER	%	NUMBER	%	NUMBER

(10 INSTITUTIONS)

%	NUMBER	%	NUMBER	%	NUMBER	%	NUMBER	%	NUMBER	%	NUMBER	%	NUMBER
.0	9	.3	8	.2	4	.1	22	.7	3,289	97.5	64	1.9	3,375
.0	3	.5	1	.2	1	.2	5	.8	570	96.6	15	2.5	590
.0	6	.2	7	.3	3	.1	17	.6	2,719	97.6	49	1.8	2,785
.0	0	.0	0	.0	0	.0	0	.0	119	99.2	1	.8	120
.0	0	.0	0	.0	0	.0	0	.0	32	97.0	1	3.0	33
.0	0	.0	0	.0	0	.0	0	.0	87	100.0	0	.0	87
.0	9	.3	8	.2	4	.1	22	.6	3,408	97.5	65	1.9	3,495
.0	3	.5	1	.2	1	.2	5	.8	602	96.6	16	2.6	623
.0	6	.2	7	.2	3	.1	17	.6	2,806	97.7	49	1.7	2,872
.0	5	1.7	4	1.3	0	.0	9	3.0	200	66.7	91	30.3	300
.0	1	1.4	1	1.4	0	.0	2	2.9	55	79.7	12	17.4	69
.0	4	1.7	3	1.3	0	.0	7	3.0	145	62.8	79	34.2	231
.0	2	1.1	1	.5	1	.5	4	2.2	113	61.7	66	36.1	183
.0	0	.0	0	.0	0	.0	0	.0	15	68.2	7	31.8	22
.0	2	1.2	1	.6	1	.6	4	2.5	98	60.9	59	36.6	161
.0	7	1.4	5	1.0	1	.2	13	2.7	313	64.8	157	32.5	483
.0	1	1.1	1	1.1	0	.0	2	2.2	70	76.9	19	20.9	91
.0	6	1.5	4	1.0	1	.3	11	2.8	243	62.0	138	35.2	392
.0	0	.0	0	.0	0	.0	0	.0	0	.0	0	.0	0
.0	0	.0	0	.0	0	.0	0	.0	0	.0	0	.0	0
.0	0	.0	0	.0	0	.0	0	.0	0	.0	0	.0	0
.0	0	.0	0	.0	0	.0	0	.0	0	.0	0	.0	0
.0	0	.0	0	.0	0	.0	0	.0	0	.0	0	.0	0
.0	0	.0	0	.0	0	.0	0	.0	0	.0	0	.0	0
.0	0	.0	0	.0	0	.0	0	.0	0	.0	0	.0	0
.0	0	.0	0	.0	0	.0	0	.0	0	.0	0	.0	0
.0	0	.0	0	.0	0	.0	0	.0	0	.0	0	.0	0
.0	14	.4	12	.3	4	.1	31	.8	3,489	94.9	155	4.2	3,675
.0	4	.6	2	.3	1	.2	7	1.1	625	94.8	27	4.1	659
.0	10	.3	10	.3	3	.1	24	.8	2,864	95.0	128	4.2	3,016
.0	2	.7	1	.3	1	.3	4	1.3	232	76.6	67	22.1	303
.0	0	.0	0	.0	0	.0	0	.0	47	85.5	8	14.5	55
.0	2	.8	1	.4	1	.4	4	1.6	185	74.6	59	23.8	248
.0	16	.4	13	.3	5	.1	35	.9	3,721	93.5	222	5.6	3,978
.0	4	.6	2	.3	1	.1	7	1.0	672	94.1	35	4.9	714
.0	12	.4	11	.3	4	.1	28	.9	3,049	93.4	187	5.7	3,264
.0	0	.0	0	.0	0	.0	0	.0	20	95.2	1	4.8	21
.0	0	.0	0	.0	0	.0	0	.0	3	75.0	1	25.0	4
.0	0	.0	0	.0	0	.0	0	.0	17	100.0	0	.0	17
.0	16	.4	13	.3	5	.1	35	.9	3,741	93.5	223	5.6	3,999
.0	4	.6	2	.3	1	.1	7	1.0	675	94.0	36	5.0	718
.0	12	.4	11	.3	4	.1	28	.9	3,066	93.4	187	5.7	3,281

(20 INSTITUTIONS)

%	NUMBER	%	NUMBER	%	NUMBER	%	NUMBER	%	NUMBER	%	NUMBER	%	NUMBER
.6	10	.4	3	.1	27	1.0	56	2.0	2,651	94.4	100	3.6	2,807
.6	3	.6	1	.2	8	1.5	15	2.8	514	96.4	4	.8	533
.6	7	.3	2	.1	19	.8	41	1.8	2,137	94.0	96	4.2	2,274
3.0	0	.0	0	.0	2	3.0	4	6.1	59	89.4	3	4.5	66
.0	0	.0	0	.0	0	.0	0	.0	15	100.0	0	.0	15
3.9	0	.0	0	.0	2	3.9	4	7.8	44	86.3	3	5.9	51
.6	10	.3	3	.1	29	1.0	60	2.1	2,710	94.3	103	3.6	2,873
.5	3	.5	1	.2	8	1.5	15	2.7	529	96.5	4	.7	548
.6	7	.3	2	.1	21	.9	45	1.9	2,181	93.8	99	4.3	2,325
.0	0	.0	1	.5	1	.5	2	1.0	126	62.1	75	36.9	203
.0	0	.0	0	.0	1	2.7	1	2.7	21	56.8	15	40.5	37
.0	0	.0	1	.6	1	.6	1	.6	105	63.3	60	36.1	166
.0	0	.0	0	.0	0	.0	0	.0	70	63.1	41	36.9	111
.0	0	.0	0	.0	0	.0	0	.0	9	40.9	13	59.1	22
.0	0	.0	0	.0	0	.0	0	.0	61	68.5	28	31.5	89
.0	0	.0	1	.3	1	.3	2	.6	196	62.4	116	36.9	314
.0	0	.0	0	.0	1	1.7	1	1.7	30	50.8	28	47.5	59
.0	0	.0	1	.4	0	.0	1	.4	166	65.1	88	34.5	255
.0	0	.0	0	.0	0	.0	0	.0	0	.0	0	.0	0
.0	0	.0	0	.0	0	.0	0	.0	0	.0	0	.0	0

TABLE 17 - TOTAL ENROLLMENT IN INSTITUTIONS OF HIGHER EDUCATION FOR SELECTED MAJOR FIELDS OF STUDY AND LEVEL OF ENROLLMENT
BY RACE, ETHNICITY, AND SEX: STATE, 1978

MAJOR FIELD 0100 - AGRICULTURE AND NATURAL RESOURCES

	AMERICAN INDIAN ALASKAN NATIVE		BLACK NON-HISPANIC		ASIAN OR PACIFIC ISLANDER		HISPANIC		TOTAL MINORITY		WHITE NON-HISPANIC		NON-RESIDENT ALIEN	
	NUMBER	%	NUMBER	%	NUMBER	%	NUMBER	%	NUMBER	%	NUMBER	%	NUMBER	%
KANSAS	CONTINUED													
PROFESSIONAL:														
PART-TIME	0	.0	0	.0	0	.0	0	.0	0	.0	0	.0	0	.0
FEMALE	0	.0	0	.0	0	.0	0	.0	0	.0	0	.0	0	.0
MALE	0	.0	0	.0	0	.0	0	.0	0	.0	0	.0	0	.0
TOTAL	0	.0	0	.0	0	.0	0	.0	0	.0	0	.0	0	.0
FEMALE	0	.0	0	.0	0	.0	0	.0	0	.0	0	.0	0	.0
MALE	0	.0	0	.0	0	.0	0	.0	0	.0	0	.0	0	.0
UND+GRAD+PROF:														
FULL-TIME	16	.5	10	.3	4	.1	28	.9	58	1.9	2,777	92.3	175	5.8
FEMALE	3	.5	3	.5	1	.2	9	1.6	16	2.8	535	93.9	19	3.3
MALE	13	.5	7	.3	3	.1	19	.8	42	1.7	2,242	91.9	156	6.4
PART-TIME	2	1.1	0	.0	0	.0	2	1.1	4	2.3	129	72.9	44	24.9
FEMALE	0	.0	0	.0	0	.0	0	.0	0	.0	24	64.9	13	35.1
MALE	2	1.4	0	.0	0	.0	2	1.4	4	2.9	105	75.0	31	22.1
TOTAL	18	.6	10	.3	4	.1	30	.9	62	1.9	2,906	91.2	219	6.9
FEMALE	3	.5	3	.5	1	.2	9	1.5	16	2.6	559	92.1	32	5.3
MALE	15	.6	7	.3	3	.1	21	.8	46	1.8	2,347	91.0	187	7.2
UNCLASSIFIED:														
TOTAL	0	.0	0	.0	0	.0	2	2.3	2	2.3	79	90.8	6	6.9
FEMALE	0	.0	0	.0	0	.0	2	7.4	2	7.4	22	81.5	3	11.1
MALE	0	.0	0	.0	0	.0	0	.0	0	.0	57	95.0	3	5.0
TOTAL ENROLLMENT:														
TOTAL	18	.5	10	.3	4	.1	32	1.0	64	2.0	2,985	91.2	225	6.9
FEMALE	3	.5	3	.5	1	.2	11	1.7	18	2.8	581	91.6	35	5.5
MALE	15	.6	7	.3	3	.1	21	.8	46	1.7	2,404	91.1	190	7.2
KENTUCKY	(	9 INSTITUTIONS)												
UNDERGRADUATES:														
FULL-TIME	5	.2	17	.8	18	.9	5	.2	45	2.2	1,960	96.5	26	1.3
FEMALE	4	.5	3	.5	4	.6	2	.3	13	2.1	614	97.5	3	.5
MALE	1	.1	14	1.0	14	1.0	3	.2	32	2.3	1,346	96.1	23	1.6
PART-TIME	2	1.4	1	.7	1	.7	0	.0	4	2.7	142	96.6	1	.7
FEMALE	1	1.9	1	1.9	1	1.9	0	.0	3	5.6	51	94.4	0	.0
MALE	1	1.1	0	.0	0	.0	0	.0	1	1.1	91	97.8	1	1.1
TOTAL	7	.3	18	.8	19	.9	5	.2	49	2.2	2,102	96.5	27	1.2
FEMALE	5	.7	4	.6	5	.7	2	.3	16	2.3	665	97.2	3	.4
MALE	2	.1	14	.9	14	.9	3	.2	33	2.2	1,437	96.2	24	1.6
GRADUATE:														
FULL-TIME	4	2.5	0	.0	0	.0	1	.6	5	3.1	120	74.5	36	22.4
FEMALE	2	6.5	0	.0	0	.0	0	.0	2	6.5	24	77.4	5	16.1
MALE	2	1.5	0	.0	0	.0	1	.8	3	2.3	96	73.8	31	23.8
PART-TIME	0	.0	1	1.1	1	1.1	0	.0	2	2.2	83	90.2	7	7.6
FEMALE	0	.0	0	.0	1	9.1	0	.0	1	9.1	10	90.9	0	.0
MALE	0	.0	1	1.2	0	.0	0	.0	1	1.2	73	90.1	7	8.6
TOTAL	4	1.6	1	.4	1	.4	1	.4	7	2.8	203	80.2	43	17.0
FEMALE	2	4.8	0	.0	1	2.4	0	.0	3	7.1	34	81.0	5	11.9
MALE	2	.9	1	.5	0	.0	1	.5	4	1.9	169	80.1	38	18.0
PROFESSIONAL:														
FULL-TIME	0	.0	0	.0	0	.0	0	.0	0	.0	0	.0	0	.0
FEMALE	0	.0	0	.0	0	.0	0	.0	0	.0	0	.0	0	.0
MALE	0	.0	0	.0	0	.0	0	.0	0	.0	0	.0	0	.0
PART-TIME	0	.0	0	.0	0	.0	0	.0	0	.0	0	.0	0	.0
FEMALE	0	.0	0	.0	0	.0	0	.0	0	.0	0	.0	0	.0
MALE	0	.0	0	.0	0	.0	0	.0	0	.0	0	.0	0	.0
TOTAL	0	.0	0	.0	0	.0	0	.0	0	.0	0	.0	0	.0
FEMALE	0	.0	0	.0	0	.0	0	.0	0	.0	0	.0	0	.0
MALE	0	.0	0	.0	0	.0	0	.0	0	.0	0	.0	0	.0
UND+GRAD+PROF:														
FULL-TIME	9	.4	17	.8	18	.8	6	.3	50	2.3	2,080	94.9	62	2.8
FEMALE	6	.9	3	.5	4	.6	2	.3	15	2.3	638	96.5	8	1.2
MALE	3	.2	14	.9	14	.9	4	.3	35	2.3	1,442	94.2	54	3.5
PART-TIME	2	.8	2	.8	2	.8	0	.0	6	2.5	225	94.1	8	3.3
FEMALE	1	1.5	1	1.5	2	3.1	0	.0	4	6.2	61	93.8	0	.0
MALE	1	.6	1	.6	0	.0	0	.0	2	1.1	164	94.3	8	4.6
TOTAL	11	.5	19	.8	20	.8	6	.2	56	2.3	2,305	94.8	70	2.9
FEMALE	7	1.0	4	.6	6	.8	2	.3	19	2.6	699	96.3	8	1.1
MALE	4	.2	15	.9	14	.8	4	.2	37	2.2	1,606	94.2	62	3.6
UNCLASSIFIED:														
TOTAL	0	.0	0	.0	0	.0	0	.0	0	.0	5	100.0	0	.0
FEMALE	0	.0	0	.0	0	.0	0	.0	0	.0	2	100.0	0	.0
MALE	0	.0	0	.0	0	.0	0	.0	0	.0	3	100.0	0	.0
TOTAL ENROLLMENT:														
TOTAL	11	.5	19	.8	20	.8	6	.2	56	2.3	2,310	94.8	70	2.9
FEMALE	7	1.0	4	.5	6	.8	2	.3	19	2.6	701	96.3	8	1.1
MALE	4	.2	15	.9	14	.8	4	.2	37	2.2	1,609	94.2	62	3.6

ROLLMENT IN INSTITUTIONS OF HIGHER EDUCATION FOR SELECTED MAJOR FIELDS OF STUDY AND LEVEL OF ENROLLMENT
ETHNICITY, AND SEX: STATE, 1978

AGRICULTURE AND NATURAL RESOURCES

INDIAN NATIVE	BLACK NON-HISPANIC		ASIAN OR PACIFIC ISLANDER		HISPANIC		TOTAL MINORITY		WHITE NON-HISPANIC		NON-RESIDENT ALIEN		TOTAL
%	NUMBER	%	NUMBER	%	NUMBER	%	NUMBER	%	NUMBER	%	NUMBER	%	NUMBER

(12 INSTITUTIONS)

INDIAN NATIVE %	BLACK NUMBER	%	ASIAN NUMBER	%	HISPANIC NUMBER	%	TOTAL MINORITY NUMBER	%	WHITE NUMBER	%	NON-RES NUMBER	%	TOTAL NUMBER
.1	131	5.2	6	.2	18	.7	157	6.2	2,125	83.6	261	10.3	2,543
.3	28	4.3	1	.2	5	.8	36	5.5	573	87.3	47	7.2	656
.0	103	5.5	5	.3	13	.7	121	6.4	1,552	82.2	214	11.3	1,887
.6	12	6.7	0	.0	1	.6	14	7.8	160	89.4	5	2.8	179
.0	1	2.3	0	.0	0	.0	1	2.3	41	93.2	2	4.5	44
.7	11	8.1	0	.0	1	.7	13	9.6	119	88.1	3	2.2	135
.1	143	5.3	6	.2	19	.7	171	6.3	2,285	83.9	266	9.8	2,722
.3	29	4.1	1	.1	5	.7	37	5.3	614	87.7	49	7.0	700
.0	114	5.6	5	.2	14	.7	134	6.6	1,671	82.6	217	10.7	2,022
.0	3	1.4	0	.0	0	.0	3	1.4	131	63.0	74	35.6	208
.0	0	.0	0	.0	0	.0	0	.0	25	58.1	18	41.9	43
.0	3	1.8	0	.0	0	.0	3	1.8	106	64.2	56	33.9	165
.0	2	2.6	0	.0	1	1.3	3	3.8	61	78.2	14	17.9	78
.0	1	7.1	0	.0	0	.0	1	7.1	11	78.6	2	14.3	14
.0	1	1.6	0	.0	1	1.6	2	3.1	50	78.1	12	18.8	64
.0	5	1.7	0	.0	1	.3	6	2.1	192	67.1	88	30.8	286
.0	1	1.8	0	.0	0	.0	1	1.8	36	63.2	20	35.1	57
.0	4	1.7	0	.0	1	.4	5	2.2	156	68.1	68	29.7	229
.0	0	.0	0	.0	0	.0	0	.0	0	.0	0	.0	0
.0	0	.0	0	.0	0	.0	0	.0	0	.0	0	.0	0
.0	0	.0	0	.0	0	.0	0	.0	0	.0	0	.0	0
.0	0	.0	0	.0	0	.0	0	.0	0	.0	0	.0	0
.0	0	.0	0	.0	0	.0	0	.0	0	.0	0	.0	0
.0	0	.0	0	.0	0	.0	0	.0	0	.0	0	.0	0
.0	0	.0	0	.0	0	.0	0	.0	0	.0	0	.0	0
.0	0	.0	0	.0	0	.0	0	.0	0	.0	0	.0	0
.0	0	.0	0	.0	0	.0	0	.0	0	.0	0	.0	0
.1	134	4.9	6	.2	18	.7	160	5.8	2,256	82.0	335	12.2	2,751
.3	28	4.0	1	.1	5	.7	36	5.2	598	85.6	65	9.3	699
.0	106	5.2	5	.2	13	.6	124	6.0	1,658	80.8	270	13.2	2,052
.0	14	5.4	0	.0	2	.8	17	6.6	221	86.0	19	7.4	257
.0	2	3.4	0	.0	0	.0	2	3.4	52	89.7	4	6.9	58
.5	12	6.0	0	.0	2	1.0	15	7.5	169	84.9	15	7.5	199
.1	148	4.9	6	.2	20	.7	177	5.9	2,477	82.3	354	11.8	3,008
.3	30	4.0	1	.1	5	.7	38	5.0	650	85.9	69	9.1	757
.0	118	5.2	5	.2	15	.7	139	6.2	1,827	81.2	285	12.7	2,251
.0	2	8.7	0	.0	0	.0	2	8.7	21	91.3	0	.0	23
.0	1	10.0	0	.0	0	.0	1	10.0	9	90.0	0	.0	10
.0	1	7.7	0	.0	0	.0	1	7.7	12	92.3	0	.0	13
.1	150	4.9	6	.2	20	.7	179	5.9	2,498	82.4	354	11.7	3,031
.3	31	4.0	1	.1	5	.7	39	5.1	659	85.9	69	9.0	767
.0	119	5.3	5	.2	15	.7	140	6.2	1,839	81.2	285	12.6	2,264

(3 INSTITUTIONS)

INDIAN NATIVE %	BLACK NUMBER	%	ASIAN NUMBER	%	HISPANIC NUMBER	%	TOTAL MINORITY NUMBER	%	WHITE NUMBER	%	NON-RES NUMBER	%	TOTAL NUMBER
.2	2	.2	2	.2	4	.2	11	.8	1,292	98.9	3	.2	1,306
.3	0	.0	1	.3	3	.8	5	1.3	392	98.5	1	.3	398
.2	2	.2	1	.1	1	.1	6	.7	900	99.1	2	.2	908
1.8	0	.0	0	.0	0	.0	1	1.8	56	98.2	0	.0	57
.0	0	.0	0	.0	0	.0	0	.0	20	100.0	0	.0	20
2.7	0	.0	0	.0	0	.0	1	2.7	36	97.3	0	.0	37
.2	2	.1	2	.1	4	.3	12	.9	1,348	98.9	3	.2	1,363
.2	0	.0	1	.2	3	.7	5	1.2	412	98.6	1	.2	418
.3	2	.2	1	.1	1	.1	7	.7	936	99.0	2	.2	945
.0	0	.0	0	.0	2	2.6	2	2.6	74	96.1	1	1.3	77
.0	0	.0	0	.0	0	.0	0	.0	15	100.0	0	.0	15
.0	0	.0	0	.0	2	3.2	2	3.2	59	95.2	1	1.6	62
.0	0	.0	0	.0	0	.0	0	.0	28	100.0	0	.0	28
.0	0	.0	0	.0	0	.0	0	.0	9	100.0	0	.0	H
.0	0	.0	0	.0	0	.0	0	.0	19	100.0	0	.0	19
.0	0	.0	0	.0	2	1.9	2	1.9	102	97.1	1	1.0	105
.0	0	.0	0	.0	0	.0	0	.0	24	100.0	0	.0	24
.0	0	.0	0	.0	2	2.5	2	2.5	78	96.3	1	1.2	81
.0	0	.0	0	.0	0	.0	0	.0	0	.0	0	.0	0
.0	0	.0	0	.0	0	.0	0	.0	0	.0	0	.0	0
.0	0	.0	0	.0	0	.0	0	.0	0	.0	0	.0	0

MAJOR FIELD 0100 - AGRICULTURE AND NATURAL RESOURCES

	AMERICAN INDIAN ALASKAN NATIVE		BLACK NON-HISPANIC		ASIAN OR PACIFIC ISLANDER		HISPANIC		TOTAL MINORITY		WHITE NON-HISPANIC		NON-RESIDENT ALIEN	
	NUMBER	%	NUMBER	%	NUMBER	%	NUMBER	%	NUMBER	%	NUMBER	%	NUMBER	%
MAINE	CONTINUED													
PROFESSIONAL:														
PART-TIME														
FEMALE	0	.0	0	.0	0	.0	0	.0	0	.0	0	.0	0	.0
MALE	0	.0	0	.0	0	.0	0	.0	0	.0	0	.0	0	.0
TOTAL														
FEMALE	0	.0	0	.0	0	.0	0	.0	0	.0	0	.0	0	.0
MALE	0	.0	0	.0	0	.0	0	.0	0	.0	0	.0	0	.0
UNC+GRAD+PROF:														
FULL-TIME	3	.2	2	.1	2	.1	6	.4	13	.9	1,366	98.8	4	.3
FEMALE	1	.2	0	.0	1	.2	3	.7	5	1.2	407	98.5	1	.2
MALE	2	.2	2	.2	1	.1	3	.3	8	.8	959	98.9	3	.3
PART-TIME	1	1.2	0	.0	0	.0	0	.0	1	1.2	84	98.8	0	.0
FEMALE	0	.0	0	.0	0	.0	0	.0	0	.0	29	100.0	0	.0
MALE	1	1.8	0	.0	0	.0	0	.0	1	1.8	55	98.2	0	.0
TOTAL	4	.3	2	.1	2	.1	6	.4	14	1.0	1,450	98.8	4	.3
FEMALE	1	.2	0	.0	1	.2	3	.7	5	1.1	436	98.6	1	.2
MALE	3	.3	2	.2	1	.1	3	.3	9	.9	1,014	98.8	3	.3
UNCLASSIFIED:														
TOTAL	0	.0	1	1.9	0	.0	0	.0	1	1.9	53	98.1	0	.0
FEMALE	0	.0	1	3.2	0	.0	0	.0	1	3.2	30	96.8	0	.0
MALE	0	.0	0	.0	0	.0	0	.0	0	.0	23	100.0	0	.0
TOTAL ENROLLMENT:														
TOTAL	4	.3	3	.2	2	.1	6	.4	15	1.0	1,503	98.8	4	.3
FEMALE	1	.2	1	.2	1	.2	3	.6	6	1.3	466	98.5	1	.2
MALE	3	.3	2	.2	1	.1	3	.3	9	.9	1,037	98.9	3	.3
MARYLAND	(	4 INSTITUTIONS)												
UNDERGRADUATES:														
FULL-TIME	3	.3	25	2.5	11	1.1	6	.6	45	4.5	928	93.2	23	2.3
FEMALE	0	.0	7	1.6	4	.9	4	.9	15	3.4	415	94.5	9	2.1
MALE	3	.5	18	3.2	7	1.3	2	.4	30	5.4	513	92.1	14	2.5
PART-TIME	0	.0	3	1.6	2	1.1	0	.0	5	2.7	175	93.1	8	4.3
FEMALE	0	.0	2	2.5	1	1.3	0	.0	3	3.8	73	92.4	3	3.8
MALE	0	.0	1	.9	1	.9	0	.0	2	1.8	102	93.6	5	4.6
TOTAL	3	.3	28	2.4	13	1.1	6	.5	50	4.2	1,103	93.2	31	2.6
FEMALE	0	.0	9	1.7	5	1.0	4	.8	18	3.5	488	94.2	12	2.3
MALE	3	.5	19	2.9	8	1.2	2	.4	32	4.8	615	92.3	19	2.9
GRADUATE:														
FULL-TIME	0	.0	4	2.9	1	.7	2	1.4	7	5.0	101	72.1	32	22.9
FEMALE	0	.0	1	2.4	1	2.4	1	2.4	3	7.1	33	78.6	6	14.3
MALE	0	.0	3	3.1	0	.0	1	1.0	4	4.1	68	69.4	26	26.5
PART-TIME	0	.0	5	3.6	1	.7	1	.7	7	5.1	107	78.1	23	16.8
FEMALE	0	.0	3	6.7	1	2.2	0	.0	4	8.9	38	84.4	3	6.7
MALE	0	.0	2	2.2	0	.0	1	1.1	3	3.3	69	75.0	20	21.7
TOTAL	0	.0	9	3.2	2	.7	3	1.1	14	5.1	208	75.1	55	19.9
FEMALE	0	.0	4	4.6	2	2.3	1	1.1	7	8.0	71	81.6	9	10.3
MALE	0	.0	5	2.6	0	.0	2	1.1	7	3.7	137	72.1	46	24.2
PROFESSIONAL:														
FULL-TIME	0	.0	0	.0	0	.0	0	.0	0	.0	0	.0	0	.0
FEMALE	0	.0	0	.0	0	.0	0	.0	0	.0	0	.0	0	.0
MALE	0	.0	0	.0	0	.0	0	.0	0	.0	0	.0	0	.0
PART-TIME	0	.0	0	.0	0	.0	0	.0	0	.0	0	.0	0	.0
FEMALE	0	.0	0	.0	0	.0	0	.0	0	.0	0	.0	0	.0
MALE	0	.0	0	.0	0	.0	0	.0	0	.0	0	.0	0	.0
TOTAL	0	.0	0	.0	0	.0	0	.0	0	.0	0	.0	0	.0
FEMALE	0	.0	0	.0	0	.0	0	.0	0	.0	0	.0	0	.0
MALE	0	.0	0	.0	0	.0	0	.0	0	.0	0	.0	0	.0
UND+GRAD+PROF:														
FULL-TIME	3	.3	29	2.6	12	1.1	8	.7	52	4.6	1,029	90.6	55	4.8
FEMALE	0	.0	8	1.7	5	1.0	5	1.0	18	3.7	448	93.1	15	3.1
MALE	3	.5	21	3.2	7	1.1	3	.5	34	5.2	581	88.7	40	6.1
PART-TIME	0	.0	8	2.5	3	.9	1	.3	12	3.7	282	86.8	31	9.5
FEMALE	0	.0	5	4.0	2	1.6	0	.0	7	5.6	111	89.5	6	4.8
MALE	0	.0	3	1.5	1	.5	1	.5	5	2.5	171	85.1	25	12.4
TOTAL	3	.2	37	2.5	15	1.0	9	.6	64	4.4	1,311	89.7	86	5.9
FEMALE	0	.0	13	2.1	7	1.2	5	.8	25	4.1	559	92.4	21	3.5
MALE	3	.4	24	2.8	8	.9	4	.5	39	4.6	752	87.9	65	7.6
UNCLASSIFIED:														
TOTAL	0	.0	3	3.0	0	.0	0	.0	3	3.0	89	89.9	7	7.1
FEMALE	0	.0	1	2.6	0	.0	0	.0	1	2.6	33	86.8	4	10.5
MALE	0	.0	2	3.3	0	.0	0	.0	2	3.3	56	91.8	3	4.9
TOTAL ENROLLMENT:														
TOTAL	3	.2	40	2.6	15	1.0	9	.6	67	4.3	1,400	89.7	93	6.0
FEMALE	0	.0	14	2.2	7	1.1	5	.8	26	4.0	592	92.1	25	3.9
MALE	3	.3	26	2.8	8	.9	4	.4	41	4.5	808	88.1	68	7.4

ROLLMENT IN INSTITUTIONS OF HIGHER EDUCATION FOR SELECTED MAJOR FIELDS OF STUDY AND LEVEL OF ENROLLMENT ETHNICITY, AND SEX: STATE, 1978

AGRICULTURE AND NATURAL RESOURCES

INDIAN NATIVE	BLACK NON-HISPANIC		ASIAN OR PACIFIC ISLANDER		HISPANIC		TOTAL MINORITY		WHITE NON-HISPANIC		NON-RESIDENT ALIEN		TOTAL
%	NUMBER	%	NUMBER	%	NUMBER	%	NUMBER	%	NUMBER	%	NUMBER	%	NUMBER

(3 INSTITUTIONS)

%	NUMBER	%	NUMBER	%	NUMBER	%	NUMBER	%	NUMBER	%	NUMBER	%	NUMBER
.3	44	1.4	36	1.1	26	.8	115	3.6	3,076	95.7	22	.7	3,213
.2	21	1.3	18	1.1	11	.7	54	3.3	1,555	96.2	8	.5	1,617
.3	23	1.4	18	1.1	15	.9	61	3.8	1,521	95.3	14	.9	1,596
.0	0	.0	0	.0	0	.0	0	.0	10	100.0	0	.0	10
.0	0	.0	0	.0	0	.0	0	.0	3	100.0	0	.0	3
.0	0	.0	0	.0	0	.0	0	.0	7	100.0	0	.0	7
.3	44	1.4	36	1.1	26	.8	115	3.6	3,086	95.7	22	.7	3,223
.2	21	1.3	18	1.1	11	.7	54	3.3	1,558	96.2	8	.5	1,620
.3	23	1.4	18	1.1	15	.9	61	3.8	1,528	95.3	14	.9	1,603
.6	1	.6	5	2.8	2	1.1	9	5.1	143	81.3	24	13.6	176
.0	0	.0	1	1.8	1	1.8	2	3.6	46	82.1	8	14.3	56
.8	1	.8	4	3.3	1	.8	7	5.8	97	80.8	16	13.3	120
.0	0	.0	3	2.2	0	.0	3	2.2	116	83.5	20	14.4	139
.0	0	.0	1	2.0	0	.0	1	2.0	41	83.7	7	14.3	49
.0	0	.0	2	2.2	0	.0	2	2.2	75	83.3	13	14.4	90
.3	1	.3	8	2.5	2	.6	12	3.8	259	82.2	44	14.0	315
.0	0	.0	2	1.9	1	1.0	3	2.9	87	82.9	15	14.3	105
.5	1	.5	6	2.9	1	.5	9	4.3	172	81.9	29	13.8	210
.0	0	.0	0	.0	0	.0	0	.0	0	.0	0	.0	0
.0	0	.0	0	.0	0	.0	0	.0	0	.0	0	.0	0
.0	0	.0	0	.0	0	.0	0	.0	0	.0	0	.0	0
.0	0	.0	0	.0	0	.0	0	.0	0	.0	0	.0	0
.0	0	.0	0	.0	0	.0	0	.0	0	.0	0	.0	0
.0	0	.0	0	.0	0	.0	0	.0	0	.0	0	.0	0
.0	0	.0	0	.0	0	.0	0	.0	0	.0	0	.0	0
.0	0	.0	0	.0	0	.0	0	.0	0	.0	0	.0	0
.0	0	.0	0	.0	0	.0	0	.0	0	.0	0	.0	0
.3	45	1.3	41	1.2	28	.8	124	3.7	3,219	95.0	46	1.4	3,389
.2	21	1.3	19	1.1	12	.7	56	3.3	1,601	95.7	16	1.0	1,673
.3	24	1.4	22	1.3	16	.9	68	4.0	1,618	94.3	30	1.7	1,716
.0	0	.0	3	2.0	0	.0	3	2.0	126	84.6	20	13.4	149
.0	0	.0	1	1.9	0	.0	1	1.9	44	84.6	7	13.5	52
.0	0	.0	2	2.1	0	.0	2	2.1	82	84.5	13	13.4	97
.3	45	1.3	44	1.2	28	.8	127	3.6	3,345	94.5	66	1.9	3,538
.2	21	1.2	20	1.2	12	.7	57	3.3	1,645	95.4	23	1.3	1,725
.3	24	1.3	24	1.3	16	.9	70	3.9	1,700	93.8	43	2.4	1,813
.0	0	.0	0	.0	0	.0	0	.0	0	.0	0	.0	0
.0	0	.0	0	.0	0	.0	0	.0	0	.0	0	.0	0
.0	0	.0	0	.0	0	.0	0	.0	0	.0	0	.0	0
.3	45	1.3	44	1.2	28	.8	127	3.6	3,345	94.5	66	1.9	3,538
.2	21	1.2	20	1.2	12	.7	57	3.3	1,645	95.4	23	1.3	1,725
.3	24	1.3	24	1.3	16	.9	70	3.9	1,700	93.8	43	2.4	1,813

(21 INSTITUTIONS)

%	NUMBER	%	NUMBER	%	NUMBER	%	NUMBER	%	NUMBER	%	NUMBER	%	NUMBER
.2	63	1.5	17	.4	17	.4	107	2.5	4,115	96.7	35	.8	4,257
.2	28	2.0	9	.6	3	.2	43	3.0	1,371	96.3	9	.6	1,423
.2	35	1.2	8	.3	14	.5	64	2.3	2,744	96.8	26	.9	2,834
.7	13	2.4	4	.7	1	.2	22	4.1	509	94.6	7	1.3	538
1.0	6	3.1	1	.5	0	.0	9	4.6	185	94.9	1	.5	195
.6	7	2.0	3	.9	1	.3	13	3.8	324	94.5	6	1.7	343
.3	76	1.6	21	.4	18	.4	129	2.7	4,624	96.4	42	.9	4,795
.3	34	2.1	10	.6	3	.2	52	3.2	1,556	96.2	10	.6	1,618
.3	42	1.3	11	.3	15	.5	77	2.4	3,068	96.6	32	1.0	3,177
.0	10	1.7	6	1.0	3	.5	19	3.3	380	65.9	178	30.8	577
.0	2	1.9	1	1.0	0	.0	3	2.9	84	80.0	18	17.1	105
.0	8	1.7	5	1.1	3	.6	16	3.4	296	62.7	163	33.9	472
.0	2	.5	2	.5	0	.0	4	1.1	277	74.7	90	24.3	371
.0	0	.0	0	.0	0	.0	0	.0	70	84.3	13	15.7	83
.0	2	.7	2	.7	0	.0	4	1.4	207	71.9	77	26.7	288
.0	12	1.3	8	.8	3	.3	23	2.4	657	69.3	268	28.3	948
.0	2	1.1	1	.5	0	.0	3	1.6	154	81.9	31	16.5	188
.0	10	1.3	7	.9	3	.4	20	2.6	503	66.2	237	31.2	760
.0	0	.0	0	.0	0	.0	0	.0	0	.0	0	.0	0
.0	0	.0	0	.0	0	.0	0	.0	0	.0	0	.0	0
.0	0	.0	0	.0	0	.0	0	.0	0	.0	0	.0	0

TABLE 17 - TOTAL ENROLLMENT IN INSTITUTIONS OF HIGHER EDUCATION FOR SELECTED MAJOR FIELDS OF STUDY AND LEVEL OF ENROLLMENT BY RACE, ETHNICITY, AND SEX: STATE, 1978

MAJOR FIELD 0100 - AGRICULTURE AND NATURAL RESOURCES

	AMERICAN INDIAN ALASKAN NATIVE		BLACK NON-HISPANIC		ASIAN OR PACIFIC ISLANDER		HISPANIC		TOTAL MINORITY		WHITE NON-HISPANIC		NON-RESIDENT ALIEN	
	NUMBER	%	NUMBER	%	NUMBER	%	NUMBER	%	NUMBER	%	NUMBER	%	NUMBER	%
MICHIGAN CONTINUED														
PROFESSIONAL:														
PART-TIME														
FEMALE	0	.0	0	.0	0	.0	0	.0	0	.0	0	.0	0	.0
MALE	0	.0	0	.0	0	.0	0	.0	0	.0	0	.0	0	.0
TOTAL														
FEMALE	0	.0	0	.0	0	.0	0	.0	0	.0	0	.0	0	.0
MALE	0	.0	0	.0	0	.0	0	.0	0	.0	0	.0	0	.0
UND+GRAD+PROF:														
FULL-TIME	10	.2	73	1.5	23	.5	20	.4	126	2.6	4,495	93.0	213	4.4
FEMALE	3	.2	30	2.0	10	.7	3	.2	46	3.0	1,455	95.2	27	1.8
MALE	7	.2	43	1.3	13	.4	17	.5	80	2.4	3,040	92.0	186	5.6
PART-TIME	4	.4	15	1.7	6	.7	1	.1	26	2.9	784	86.5	97	10.7
FEMALE	2	.7	6	2.2	1	.4	0	.0	9	3.2	256	91.7	14	5.0
MALE	2	.3	9	1.4	5	.8	1	.2	17	2.7	531	84.2	83	13.2
TOTAL	14	.2	88	1.5	29	.5	21	.4	152	2.6	5,281	92.0	310	5.4
FEMALE	5	.3	36	2.0	11	.6	3	.2	55	3.0	1,710	94.7	41	2.3
MALE	9	.2	52	1.3	18	.5	18	.5	97	2.5	3,571	90.7	269	6.8
UNCLASSIFIED:														
TOTAL	0	.0	0	.0	0	.0	0	.0	0	.0	1	100.0	0	.0
FEMALE	0	.0	0	.0	0	.0	0	.0	0	.0	1	100.0	0	.0
MALE	0	.0	0	.0	0	.0	0	.0	0	.0	0	.0	0	.0
TOTAL ENROLLMENT:														
TOTAL	14	.2	88	1.5	29	.5	21	.4	152	2.6	5,282	92.0	310	5.4
FEMALE	5	.3	36	2.0	11	.6	3	.2	55	3.0	1,711	94.7	41	2.3
MALE	9	.2	52	1.3	18	.5	18	.5	97	2.5	3,571	90.7	269	6.8
MINNESOTA (25 INSTITUTIONS)														
UNDERGRADUATES:														
FULL-TIME	9	.4	6	.3	12	.5	7	.3	34	1.6	2,114	96.6	40	1.8
FEMALE	2	.3	3	.5	4	.7	3	.5	12	2.1	566	96.8	7	1.2
MALE	7	.4	3	.2	8	.5	4	.2	22	1.4	1,548	96.6	33	2.1
PART-TIME	0	.0	0	.0	4	1.5	1	.4	5	1.9	257	98.1	0	.0
FEMALE	0	.0	0	.0	1	1.3	0	.0	1	1.3	77	98.7	0	.0
MALE	0	.0	0	.0	3	1.6	1	.5	4	2.2	180	97.8	0	.0
TOTAL	9	.4	6	.2	16	.7	8	.3	39	1.6	2,371	96.8	40	1.6
FEMALE	2	.3	3	.5	5	.8	3	.5	13	2.0	643	97.0	7	1.1
MALE	7	.4	3	.2	11	.6	5	.3	26	1.5	1,728	96.7	33	1.8
GRADUATE:														
FULL-TIME	3	.6	4	.8	5	1.0	2	.4	14	2.9	370	77.6	93	19.5
FEMALE	1	.9	0	.0	0	.0	0	.0	1	.9	93	84.5	16	14.5
MALE	2	.5	4	1.1	5	1.4	2	.5	13	3.5	277	75.5	77	21.0
PART-TIME	0	.0	0	.0	0	.0	0	.0	0	.0	0	.0	0	.0
FEMALE	0	.0	0	.0	0	.0	0	.0	0	.0	0	.0	0	.0
MALE	0	.0	0	.0	0	.0	0	.0	0	.0	0	.0	0	.0
TOTAL	3	.6	4	.8	5	1.0	2	.4	14	2.9	370	77.6	93	19.5
FEMALE	1	.9	0	.0	0	.0	0	.0	1	.9	93	84.5	16	14.5
MALE	2	.5	4	1.1	5	1.4	2	.5	13	3.5	277	75.5	77	21.0
PROFESSIONAL:														
FULL-TIME	0	.0	0	.0	0	.0	0	.0	0	.0	0	.0	0	.0
FEMALE	0	.0	0	.0	0	.0	0	.0	0	.0	0	.0	0	.0
MALE	0	.0	0	.0	0	.0	0	.0	0	.0	0	.0	0	.0
PART-TIME	0	.0	0	.0	0	.0	0	.0	0	.0	0	.0	0	.0
FEMALE	0	.0	0	.0	0	.0	0	.0	0	.0	0	.0	0	.0
MALE	0	.0	0	.0	0	.0	0	.0	0	.0	0	.0	0	.0
TOTAL	0	.0	0	.0	0	.0	0	.0	0	.0	0	.0	0	.0
FEMALE	0	.0	0	.0	0	.0	0	.0	0	.0	0	.0	0	.0
MALE	0	.0	0	.0	0	.0	0	.0	0	.0	0	.0	0	.0
UND+GRAD+PROF:														
FULL-TIME	12	.5	10	.4	17	.6	9	.3	48	1.8	2,484	93.2	133	5.0
FEMALE	3	.4	3	.4	4	.6	3	.4	13	1.9	659	94.8	23	3.3
MALE	9	.5	7	.4	13	.7	6	.3	35	1.8	1,825	92.6	110	5.6
PART-TIME	0	.0	0	.0	4	1.5	1	.4	5	1.9	257	98.1	0	.0
FEMALE	0	.0	0	.0	1	1.3	0	.0	1	1.3	77	98.7	0	.0
MALE	0	.0	0	.0	3	1.6	1	.5	4	2.2	180	97.8	0	.0
TOTAL	12	.4	10	.3	21	.7	10	.3	53	1.8	2,741	93.6	133	4.5
FEMALE	3	.4	3	.4	5	.6	3	.4	14	1.8	736	95.2	23	3.0
MALE	9	.4	7	.3	16	.7	7	.3	39	1.8	2,005	93.1	110	5.1
UNCLASSIFIED:														
TOTAL	0	.0	0	.0	1	1.1	0	.0	1	1.1	75	80.6	17	18.3
FEMALE	0	.0	0	.0	0	.0	0	.0	0	.0	29	96.7	1	3.3
MALE	0	.0	0	.0	1	1.6	0	.0	1	1.6	46	73.0	16	25.4
TOTAL ENROLLMENT:														
TOTAL	12	.4	10	.3	22	.7	10	.3	54	1.8	2,816	93.2	150	5.0
FEMALE	3	.4	3	.4	5	.6	3	.4	14	1.7	765	95.3	24	3.0
MALE	9	.4	7	.3	17	.8	7	.3	40	1.8	2,051	92.5	126	5.7

ROLLMENT IN INSTITUTIONS OF HIGHER EDUCATION FOR SELECTED MAJOR FIELDS OF STUDY AND LEVEL OF ENROLLMENT ETHNICITY, AND SEX: STATE, 1978

AGRICULTURE AND NATURAL RESOURCES

INDIAN NATIVE	BLACK NON-HISPANIC		ASIAN OR PACIFIC ISLANDER		HISPANIC		TOTAL MINORITY		WHITE NON-HISPANIC		NON-RESIDENT ALIEN		TOTAL
%	NUMBER	%	NUMBER	%	NUMBER	%	NUMBER	%	NUMBER	%	NUMBER	%	NUMBER

(19 INSTITUTIONS)

%	NUMBER	%	NUMBER	%	NUMBER	%	NUMBER	%	NUMBER	%	NUMBER	%	NUMBER
.1	349	22.1	3	.2	1	.1	354	22.4	1,219	77.1	9	.6	1,582
.3	87	29.6	2	.7	0	.0	90	30.6	203	69.0	1	.3	294
.0	262	20.3	1	.1	1	.1	264	20.5	1,016	78.9	8	.6	1,288
.0	30	21.3	0	.0	0	.0	30	21.3	109	77.3	2	1.4	141
.0	11	33.3	0	.0	0	.0	11	33.3	22	66.7	0	.0	33
.0	19	17.6	0	.0	0	.0	19	17.6	87	80.6	2	1.9	108
.1	379	22.0	3	.2	1	.1	384	22.3	1,328	77.1	11	.6	1,723
.3	98	30.0	2	.6	0	.0	101	30.9	225	68.8	1	.3	327
.0	281	20.1	1	.1	1	.1	283	20.3	1,103	79.0	10	.7	1,396
.0	2	1.3	3	1.9	0	.0	5	3.2	99	63.1	53	33.8	157
.0	1	3.7	0	.0	0	.0	1	3.7	19	70.4	7	25.9	27
.0	1	.8	3	2.3	0	.0	4	3.1	80	61.5	46	35.4	130
.0	0	.0	0	.0	0	.0	0	.0	60	81.1	14	18.9	74
.0	0	.0	0	.0	0	.0	0	.0	5	55.6	4	44.4	9
.0	0	.0	0	.0	0	.0	0	.0	55	84.6	10	15.4	65
.0	2	.9	3	1.3	0	.0	5	2.2	159	68.8	67	29.0	231
.0	1	2.8	0	.0	0	.0	1	2.8	24	66.7	11	30.6	36
.0	1	.5	3	1.5	0	.0	4	2.1	135	69.2	56	28.7	195
.0	0	.0	0	.0	0	.0	0	.0	0	.0	0	.0	0
.0	0	.0	0	.0	0	.0	0	.0	0	.0	0	.0	0
.0	0	.0	0	.0	0	.0	0	.0	0	.0	0	.0	0
.0	0	.0	0	.0	0	.0	0	.0	0	.0	0	.0	0
.0	0	.0	0	.0	0	.0	0	.0	0	.0	0	.0	0
.0	0	.0	0	.0	0	.0	0	.0	0	.0	0	.0	0
.0	0	.0	0	.0	0	.0	0	.0	0	.0	0	.0	0
.0	0	.0	0	.0	0	.0	0	.0	0	.0	0	.0	0
.0	0	.0	0	.0	0	.0	0	.0	0	.0	0	.0	0
.1	351	20.2	6	.3	1	.1	359	20.6	1,318	75.8	62	3.6	1,739
.3	88	27.4	2	.6	0	.0	91	28.3	222	69.2	8	2.5	321
.0	263	18.5	4	.3	1	.1	268	18.9	1,096	77.3	54	3.8	1,418
.0	30	14.0	0	.0	0	.0	30	14.0	169	78.6	16	7.4	215
.0	11	26.2	0	.0	0	.0	11	26.2	27	64.3	4	9.5	42
.0	19	11.0	0	.0	0	.0	19	11.0	142	82.1	12	6.9	173
.1	381	19.5	6	.3	1	.1	389	19.9	1,487	76.1	78	4.0	1,954
.3	99	27.3	2	.6	0	.0	102	28.1	249	68.6	12	3.3	363
.0	282	17.7	4	.3	1	.1	287	18.0	1,238	77.8	66	4.1	1,591
.0	0	.0	0	.0	0	.0	0	.0	2	100.0	0	.0	2
.0	0	.0	0	.0	0	.0	0	.0	1	100.0	0	.0	1
.0	0	.0	0	.0	0	.0	0	.0	1	100.0	0	.0	1
.1	381	19.5	6	.3	1	.1	389	19.9	1,489	76.1	78	4.0	1,956
.3	99	27.2	2	.5	0	.0	102	28.0	250	68.7	12	3.3	364
.0	282	17.7	4	.3	1	.1	287	18.0	1,239	77.8	66	4.1	1,592

(11 INSTITUTIONS)

%	NUMBER	%	NUMBER	%	NUMBER	%	NUMBER	%	NUMBER	%	NUMBER	%	NUMBER
.2	56	1.7	3	.1	9	.3	76	2.3	3,211	96.4	44	1.3	3,331
.0	23	3.1	1	.1	1	.1	25	3.4	709	96.1	4	.5	738
.3	33	1.3	2	.1	8	.3	51	2.0	2,502	96.5	40	1.5	2,593
.0	6	2.6	1	.4	0	.0	7	3.0	220	95.7	3	1.3	230
.0	0	.0	0	.0	0	.0	0	.0	65	100.0	0	.0	65
.0	6	3.6	1	.6	0	.0	7	4.2	155	93.9	3	1.8	165
.2	62	1.7	4	.1	9	.3	83	2.3	3,431	96.3	47	1.3	3,561
.0	23	2.9	1	.1	1	.1	25	3.1	774	96.4	4	.5	803
.3	39	1.4	3	.1	8	.3	58	2.1	2,657	96.3	43	1.6	2,758
.5	3	1.4	12	5.8	3	1.4	19	9.1	151	72.6	38	18.3	208
.0	0	.0	2	4.3	0	.0	2	4.3	34	73.9	10	21.7	46
.6	3	1.9	10	6.2	3	1.9	17	10.5	117	72.2	28	17.3	162
.0	1	.6	3	1.9	1	.6	5	3.2	135	87.1	15	9.7	155
.0	1	3.4	2	6.9	0	.0	3	10.3	23	79.3	3	10.3	29
.0	0	.0	1	.8	1	.8	2	1.6	112	88.9	12	9.5	126
.3	4	1.1	15	4.1	4	1.1	24	6.6	286	78.8	53	14.6	363
.0	1	1.3	4	5.3	0	.0	5	6.7	57	76.0	13	17.3	75
.3	3	1.0	11	3.8	4	1.4	19	6.6	229	79.5	40	13.9	288
.0	8	.0	8	.0	8	.0	8	.0	0	.0	8	.0	8
.0	8	.0	8	.0	8	.0	8	.0	0	.0	8	.0	8
.0	8	.0	8	.0	8	.0	8	.0	0	.0	8	.0	8

TABLE 17 - TOTAL ENROLLMENT IN INSTITUTIONS OF HIGHER EDUCATION FOR SELECTED MAJOR FIELDS OF STUDY AND LEVEL OF ENROLLMENT
BY RACE, ETHNICITY, AND SEX: STATE, 1978

MAJOR FIELD 0100 - AGRICULTURE AND NATURAL RESOURCES

	AMERICAN INDIAN ALASKAN NATIVE		BLACK NON-HISPANIC		ASIAN OR PACIFIC ISLANDER		HISPANIC		TOTAL MINORITY		WHITE NON-HISPANIC		NON-RESIDENT ALIEN	
	NUMBER	%	NUMBER	%	NUMBER	%	NUMBER	%	NUMBER	%	NUMBER	%	NUMBER	%
MISSOURI	CONTINUED													
PROFESSIONAL:														
PART-TIME	0	.0	0	.0	0	.0	0	.0	0	.0	0	.0	0	.0
FEMALE	0	.0	0	.0	0	.0	0	.0	0	.0	0	.0	0	.0
MALE	0	.0	0	.0	0	.0	0	.0	0	.0	0	.0	0	.0
TOTAL	0	.0	0	.0	0	.0	0	.0	0	.0	0	.0	0	.0
FEMALE	0	.0	0	.0	0	.0	0	.0	0	.0	0	.0	0	.0
MALE	0	.0	0	.0	0	.0	0	.0	0	.0	0	.0	0	.0
UND+GRAD+PROF:														
FULL-TIME	9	.3	59	1.7	15	.4	12	.3	95	2.7	3,362	95.0	82	2.3
FEMALE	0	.0	23	2.9	3	.4	1	.1	27	3.4	743	94.8	14	1.8
MALE	9	.3	36	1.3	12	.4	11	.4	68	2.5	2,619	95.1	68	2.5
PART-TIME	0	.0	7	1.8	4	1.0	1	.3	12	3.1	355	92.2	18	4.7
FEMALE	0	.0	1	1.1	2	2.1	0	.0	3	3.2	88	93.6	3	3.2
MALE	0	.0	6	2.1	2	.7	1	.3	9	3.1	267	91.8	15	5.2
TOTAL	9	.2	66	1.7	19	.5	13	.3	107	2.7	3,717	94.7	100	2.5
FEMALE	0	.0	24	2.7	5	.6	1	.1	30	3.4	831	94.6	17	1.9
MALE	9	.3	42	1.4	14	.5	12	.4	77	2.5	2,886	94.7	83	2.7
UNCLASSIFIED:														
TOTAL	0	.0	0	.0	0	.0	0	.0	0	.0	0	.0	0	.0
FEMALE	0	.0	0	.0	0	.0	0	.0	0	.0	0	.0	0	.0
MALE	0	.0	0	.0	0	.0	0	.0	0	.0	0	.0	0	.0
TOTAL ENROLLMENT:														
TOTAL	9	.2	66	1.7	19	.5	13	.3	107	2.7	3,717	94.7	100	2.5
FEMALE	0	.0	24	2.7	5	.6	1	.1	30	3.4	831	94.6	17	1.9
MALE	9	.3	42	1.4	14	.5	12	.4	77	2.5	2,886	94.7	83	2.7
MONTANA	(	3 INSTITUTIONS)												
UNDERGRADUATES:														
FULL-TIME	15	.9	1	.1	2	.1	6	.4	24	1.4	1,632	97.7	15	.9
FEMALE	0	.0	0	.0	0	.0	3	.7	3	.7	454	99.1	1	.2
MALE	15	1.2	1	.1	2	.2	3	.2	21	1.7	1,178	97.1	14	1.2
PART-TIME	2	1.8	0	.0	0	.0	0	.0	2	1.8	107	96.4	2	1.8
FEMALE	0	.0	0	.0	0	.0	0	.0	0	.0	27	100.0	0	.0
MALE	2	2.4	0	.0	0	.0	0	.0	2	2.4	80	95.2	2	2.4
TOTAL	17	1.0	1	.1	2	.1	6	.3	26	1.5	1,739	97.6	17	1.0
FEMALE	0	.0	0	.0	0	.0	3	.6	3	.6	481	99.2	1	.2
MALE	17	1.3	1	.1	2	.2	3	.2	23	1.8	1,258	97.0	16	1.2
GRADUATE:														
FULL-TIME	0	.0	0	.0	0	.0	0	.0	0	.0	54	98.2	1	1.8
FEMALE	0	.0	0	.0	0	.0	0	.0	0	.0	8	100.0	0	.0
MALE	0	.0	0	.0	0	.0	0	.0	0	.0	46	97.9	1	2.1
PART-TIME	0	.0	0	.0	0	.0	0	.0	0	.0	80	100.0	0	.0
FEMALE	0	.0	0	.0	0	.0	0	.0	0	.0	15	100.0	0	.0
MALE	0	.0	0	.0	0	.0	0	.0	0	.0	65	100.0	0	.0
TOTAL	0	.0	0	.0	0	.0	0	.0	0	.0	134	99.3	1	.7
FEMALE	0	.0	0	.0	0	.0	0	.0	0	.0	23	100.0	0	.0
MALE	0	.0	0	.0	0	.0	0	.0	0	.0	111	99.1	1	.9
PROFESSIONAL:														
FULL-TIME	0	.0	0	.0	0	.0	0	.0	0	.0	0	.0	0	.0
FEMALE	0	.0	0	.0	0	.0	0	.0	0	.0	0	.0	0	.0
MALE	0	.0	0	.0	0	.0	0	.0	0	.0	0	.0	0	.0
PART-TIME	0	.0	0	.0	0	.0	0	.0	0	.0	0	.0	0	.0
FEMALE	0	.0	0	.0	0	.0	0	.0	0	.0	0	.0	0	.0
MALE	0	.0	0	.0	0	.0	0	.0	0	.0	0	.0	0	.0
TOTAL	0	.0	0	.0	0	.0	0	.0	0	.0	0	.0	0	.0
FEMALE	0	.0	0	.0	0	.0	0	.0	0	.0	0	.0	0	.0
MALE	0	.0	0	.0	0	.0	0	.0	0	.0	0	.0	0	.0
UND+GRAD+PROF:														
FULL-TIME	15	.9	1	.1	2	.1	6	.3	24	1.4	1,686	97.7	16	.9
FEMALE	0	.0	0	.0	0	.0	3	.6	3	.6	462	99.1	1	.2
MALE	15	1.2	1	.1	2	.2	3	.2	21	1.7	1,224	97.1	15	1.2
PART-TIME	2	1.0	0	.0	0	.0	0	.0	2	1.0	187	97.9	2	1.0
FEMALE	0	.0	0	.0	0	.0	0	.0	0	.0	42	100.0	0	.0
MALE	2	1.3	0	.0	0	.0	0	.0	2	1.3	145	97.3	2	1.3
TOTAL	17	.9	1	.1	2	.1	6	.3	26	1.4	1,873	97.7	18	.9
FEMALE	0	.0	0	.0	0	.0	3	.6	3	.6	504	99.2	1	.2
MALE	17	1.2	1	.1	2	.1	3	.2	23	1.6	1,369	97.2	17	1.2
UNCLASSIFIED:														
TOTAL	0	.0	0	.0	0	.0	0	.0	0	.0	0	.0	0	.0
FEMALE	0	.0	0	.0	0	.0	0	.0	0	.0	0	.0	0	.0
MALE	0	.0	0	.0	0	.0	0	.0	0	.0	0	.0	0	.0
TOTAL ENROLLMENT:														
TOTAL	17	.9	1	.1	2	.1	6	.3	26	1.4	1,873	97.7	18	.9
FEMALE	0	.0	0	.0	0	.0	3	.6	3	.6	504	99.2	1	.2
MALE	17	1.2	1	.1	2	.1	3	.2	23	1.6	1,369	97.2	17	1.2

306

AGRICULTURE AND NATURAL RESOURCES

	INDIAN NATIVE	BLACK NON-HISPANIC		ASIAN OR PACIFIC ISLANDER		HISPANIC		TOTAL MINORITY		WHITE NON-HISPANIC		NON-RESIDENT ALIEN		TOTAL
%	NUMBER	%	NUMBER	%	NUMBER	%	NUMBER	%	NUMBER	%	NUMBER	%	NUMBER
(8 INSTITUTIONS)														
.2	3	.2	2	.1	9	.5	18	1.0	1,728	97.2	31	1.7	1,777
.0	1	.3	0	.0	0	.0	1	.3	312	98.1	5	1.6	318
.3	2	.1	2	.1	9	.6	17	1.2	1,416	97.1	26	1.8	1,459
.0	0	.0	0	.0	0	.0	0	.0	112	98.2	2	1.8	114
.0	0	.0	0	.0	0	.0	0	.0	30	100.0	0	.0	30
.0	0	.0	0	.0	0	.0	0	.0	82	97.6	2	2.4	84
.2	3	.2	2	.1	9	.5	18	1.0	1,840	97.3	33	1.7	1,891
.0	1	.3	0	.0	0	.0	1	.3	342	98.3	5	1.4	348
.3	2	.1	2	.1	9	.6	17	1.1	1,498	97.1	28	1.8	1,543
.0	3	1.8	1	.6	1	.6	5	3.0	124	75.2	36	21.8	165
.0	1	4.0	0	.0	0	.0	1	4.0	20	80.0	4	16.0	25
.0	2	1.4	1	.7	1	.7	4	2.9	104	74.3	32	22.9	140
.0	0	.0	2	1.9	0	.0	2	1.9	90	84.9	14	13.2	106
.0	0	.0	0	.0	0	.0	0	.0	11	84.6	2	15.4	13
.0	0	.0	2	2.2	0	.0	2	2.2	79	84.9	12	12.9	93
.0	3	1.1	3	1.1	1	.4	7	2.6	214	79.0	50	18.5	271
.0	1	2.6	0	.0	0	.0	1	2.6	31	81.6	6	15.8	38
.0	2	.9	3	1.3	1	.4	6	2.6	183	78.5	44	18.9	233
.0	0	.0	0	.0	0	.0	0	.0	0	.0	0	.0	0
.0	0	.0	0	.0	0	.0	0	.0	0	.0	0	.0	0
.0	0	.0	0	.0	0	.0	0	.0	0	.0	0	.0	0
.0	0	.0	0	.0	0	.0	0	.0	0	.0	0	.0	0
.0	0	.0	0	.0	0	.0	0	.0	0	.0	0	.0	0
.0	0	.0	0	.0	0	.0	0	.0	0	.0	0	.0	0
.0	0	.0	0	.0	0	.0	0	.0	0	.0	0	.0	0
.0	0	.0	0	.0	0	.0	0	.0	0	.0	0	.0	0
.0	0	.0	0	.0	0	.0	0	.0	0	.0	0	.0	0
.2	6	.3	3	.2	10	.5	23	1.2	1,852	95.4	67	3.5	1,942
.0	2	.6	0	.0	0	.0	2	.6	332	96.8	9	2.6	343
.3	4	.3	3	.2	10	.6	21	1.3	1,520	95.1	58	3.6	1,599
.0	0	.0	2	.9	0	.0	2	.9	202	91.8	16	7.3	220
.0	0	.0	0	.0	0	.0	0	.0	41	95.3	2	4.7	43
.0	0	.0	2	1.1	0	.0	2	1.1	161	91.0	14	7.9	177
.2	6	.3	5	.2	10	.5	25	1.2	2,054	95.0	83	3.8	2,162
.0	2	.5	0	.0	0	.0	2	.5	373	96.6	11	2.8	386
.2	4	.2	5	.3	10	.6	23	1.3	1,681	94.7	72	4.1	1,776
.0	0	.0	0	.0	0	.0	0	.0	24	100.0	0	.0	24
.0	0	.0	0	.0	0	.0	0	.0	0	.0	0	.0	0
.0	0	.0	0	.0	0	.0	0	.0	24	100.0	0	.0	24
.2	6	.3	5	.2	10	.5	25	1.1	2,078	95.1	83	3.8	2,186
.0	2	.5	0	.0	0	.0	2	.5	373	96.6	11	2.8	386
.2	4	.2	5	.3	10	.6	23	1.3	1,705	94.7	72	4.0	1,800
(2 INSTITUTIONS)														
1.6	4	1.3	3	1.0	1	.3	13	4.2	290	93.5	7	2.3	310
.0	0	.0	1	.9	1	.9	2	1.8	109	96.5	2	1.8	113
2.5	4	2.0	2	1.0	0	.0	11	5.6	181	91.9	5	2.5	197
.0	1	.8	2	1.7	3	2.5	6	5.1	109	92.4	3	2.5	118
.0	0	.0	0	.0	2	4.4	2	4.4	42	93.3	1	2.2	45
.0	1	1.4	2	2.7	1	1.4	4	5.5	67	91.8	2	2.7	73
1.2	5	1.2	5	.2	4	.9	19	4.4	399	93.2	10	2.3	428
.0	0	.0	1	.6	3	1.9	4	2.5	151	95.6	3	1.9	158
1.9	5	1.9	4	1.5	1	.4	15	5.6	248	91.9	7	2.6	270
.0	1	3.6	0	.0	0	.0	1	3.6	25	89.3	2	7.1	28
.0	0	.0	0	.0	0	.0	0	.0	4	100.0	0	.0	4
.0	1	4.2	0	.0	0	.0	1	4.2	21	87.5	2	8.3	24
.0	0	.0	0	.0	0	.0	0	.0	26	86.7	4	13.3	30
.0	0	.0	0	.0	0	.0	0	.0	8	80.0	2	20.0	10
.0	0	.0	0	.0	0	.0	0	.0	18	90.0	2	10.0	20
.0	1	1.7	0	.0	0	.0	1	1.7	51	87.9	6	10.3	58
.0	0	.0	0	.0	0	.0	0	.0	12	85.7	2	14.3	14
.0	1	2.3	0	.0	0	.0	1	2.3	39	88.6	4	9.1	44
.0	0	.0	0	.0	0	.0	0	.0	0	.0	0	.0	0
.0	0	.0	0	.0	0	.0	0	.0	0	.0	0	.0	0
.0	0	.0	0	.0	0	.0	0	.0	0	.0	0	.0	0

MAJOR FIELD 0100 - AGRICULTURE AND NATURAL RESOURCES

	AMERICAN INDIAN ALASKAN NATIVE		BLACK NON-HISPANIC		ASIAN OR PACIFIC ISLANDER		HISPANIC		TOTAL MINORITY		WHITE NON-HISPANIC		NON-RESIDENT ALIEN		T
	NUMBER	%	NUMBER	%	NUMBER	%	NUMBER	%	NUMBER	%	NUMBER	%	NUMBER	%	N
NEVADA		CONTINUED													
PROFESSIONAL:															
PART-TIME	0	.0	0	.0	0	.0	0	.0	0	.0	0	.0	0	.0	
FEMALE	0	.0	0	.0	0	.0	0	.0	0	.0	0	.0	0	.0	
MALE	0	.0	0	.0	0	.0	0	.0	0	.0	0	.0	0	.0	
TOTAL	0	.0	0	.0	0	.0	0	.0	0	.0	0	.0	0	.0	
FEMALE	0	.0	0	.0	0	.0	0	.0	0	.0	0	.0	0	.0	
MALE	0	.0	0	.0	0	.0	0	.0	0	.0	0	.0	0	.0	
UNDG+GRAD+PROF:															
FULL-TIME	5	1.5	5	1.5	3	.9	1	.3	14	4.1	315	93.2	9	2.7	
FEMALE	0	.0	0	.0	1	.9	1	.9	2	1.7	113	96.6	2	1.7	
MALE	5	2.3	5	2.3	2	.9	0	.0	12	5.4	202	91.4	7	3.2	
PART-TIME	0	.0	1	.7	2	1.4	3	2.0	6	4.1	135	91.2	7	4.7	
FEMALE	0	.0	0	.0	0	.0	2	3.6	2	3.6	50	90.9	3	5.5	
MALE	0	.0	1	1.1	2	2.2	1	1.1	4	4.3	85	91.4	4	4.3	
TOTAL	5	1.0	6	1.2	5	1.0	4	.8	20	4.1	450	92.6	16	3.3	
FEMALE	0	.0	0	.0	1	.6	3	1.7	4	2.3	163	94.8	5	2.9	
MALE	5	1.6	6	1.9	4	1.3	1	.3	16	5.1	287	91.4	11	3.5	
UNCLASSIFIED:															
TOTAL	0	.0	0	.0	0	.0	2	2.9	2	2.9	67	97.1	0	.0	
FEMALE	0	.0	0	.0	0	.0	0	.0	0	.0	38	100.0	0	.0	
MALE	0	.0	0	.0	0	.0	2	6.5	2	6.5	29	93.5	0	.0	
TOTAL ENROLLMENT:															
TOTAL	5	.9	6	1.1	5	.9	6	1.1	22	4.0	517	93.2	16	2.9	
FEMALE	0	.0	0	.0	1	.5	3	1.4	4	1.9	201	95.7	5	2.4	
MALE	5	1.4	6	1.7	4	1.2	3	.9	18	5.2	316	91.6	11	3.2	
NEW HAMPSHIRE	(	2 INSTITUTIONS)													
UNDERGRADUATES:															
FULL-TIME	1	.1	0	.0	1	.1	2	.2	4	.5	798	99.1	3	.4	
FEMALE	0	.0	0	.0	0	.0	1	.3	1	.3	398	99.5	1	.3	
MALE	1	.2	0	.0	1	.2	1	.2	3	.7	400	98.8	2	.5	
PART-TIME	0	.0	0	.0	0	.0	0	.0	0	.0	33	100.0	0	.0	
FEMALE	0	.0	0	.0	0	.0	0	.0	0	.0	12	100.0	0	.0	
MALE	0	.0	0	.0	0	.0	0	.0	0	.0	21	100.0	0	.0	
TOTAL	1	.1	0	.0	1	.1	2	.2	4	.5	831	99.2	3	.4	
FEMALE	0	.0	0	.0	0	.0	1	.2	1	.2	410	99.5	1	.2	
MALE	1	.2	0	.0	1	.2	1	.2	3	.7	421	98.8	2	.5	
GRADUATE:															
FULL-TIME	0	.0	0	.0	0	.0	0	.0	0	.0	31	100.0	0	.0	
FEMALE	0	.0	0	.0	0	.0	0	.0	0	.0	4	100.0	0	.0	
MALE	0	.0	0	.0	0	.0	0	.0	0	.0	27	100.0	0	.0	
PART-TIME	0	.0	0	.0	0	.0	0	.0	0	.0	14	100.0	0	.0	
FEMALE	0	.0	0	.0	0	.0	0	.0	0	.0	3	100.0	0	.0	
MALE	0	.0	0	.0	0	.0	0	.0	0	.0	11	100.0	0	.0	
TOTAL	0	.0	0	.0	0	.0	0	.0	0	.0	45	100.0	0	.0	
FEMALE	0	.0	0	.0	0	.0	0	.0	0	.0	7	100.0	0	.0	
MALE	0	.0	0	.0	0	.0	0	.0	0	.0	38	100.0	0	.0	
PROFESSIONAL:															
FULL-TIME	0	.0	0	.0	0	.0	0	.0	0	.0	0	.0	0	.0	
FEMALE	0	.0	0	.0	0	.0	0	.0	0	.0	0	.0	0	.0	
MALE	0	.0	0	.0	0	.0	0	.0	0	.0	0	.0	0	.0	
PART-TIME	0	.0	0	.0	0	.0	0	.0	0	.0	0	.0	0	.0	
FEMALE	0	.0	0	.0	0	.0	0	.0	0	.0	0	.0	0	.0	
MALE	0	.0	0	.0	0	.0	0	.0	0	.0	0	.0	0	.0	
TOTAL	0	.0	0	.0	0	.0	0	.0	0	.0	0	.0	0	.0	
FEMALE	0	.0	0	.0	0	.0	0	.0	0	.0	0	.0	0	.0	
MALE	0	.0	0	.0	0	.0	0	.0	0	.0	0	.0	0	.0	
UNDG+GRAD+PROF:															
FULL-TIME	1	.1	0	.0	1	.1	2	.2	4	.5	829	99.2	3	.4	
FEMALE	0	.0	0	.0	0	.0	1	.2	1	.2	402	99.5	1	.2	
MALE	1	.2	0	.0	1	.2	1	.2	3	.7	427	98.8	2	.5	
PART-TIME	0	.0	0	.0	0	.0	0	.0	0	.0	47	100.0	0	.0	
FEMALE	0	.0	0	.0	0	.0	0	.0	0	.0	15	100.0	0	.0	
MALE	0	.0	0	.0	0	.0	0	.0	0	.0	32	100.0	0	.0	
TOTAL	1	.1	0	.0	1	.1	2	.2	4	.5	876	99.2	3	.3	
FEMALE	0	.0	0	.0	0	.0	1	.2	1	.2	417	99.5	1	.2	
MALE	1	.2	0	.0	1	.2	1	.2	3	.6	459	98.9	2	.4	
UNCLASSIFIED:															
TOTAL	0	.0	0	.0	0	.0	0	.0	0	.0	0	.0	0	.0	
FEMALE	0	.0	0	.0	0	.0	0	.0	0	.0	0	.0	0	.0	
MALE	0	.0	0	.0	0	.0	0	.0	0	.0	0	.0	0	.0	
TOTAL ENROLLMENT:															
TOTAL	1	.1	0	.0	1	.1	2	.2	4	.5	876	99.2	3	.3	
FEMALE	0	.0	0	.0	0	.0	1	.2	1	.2	417	99.5	1	.2	
MALE	1	.2	0	.0	1	.2	1	.2	3	.6	459	98.9	2	.4	

IO - AGRICULTURE AND NATURAL RESOURCES

:ICAN INDIAN / KAN NATIVE		BLACK NON-HISPANIC		ASIAN OR PACIFIC ISLANDER		HISPANIC		TOTAL MINORITY		WHITE NON-HISPANIC		NON-RESIDENT ALIEN		TOTAL
IdER	%	NUMBER	%	NUMBER	%	NUMBER	%	NUMBER	%	NUMBER	%	NUMBER	%	NUMBER
(4 INSTITUTIONS)														
1	.1	16	1.7	6	.6	10	1.0	33	3.4	936	96.6	0	.0	969
0	.0	6	1.3	1	.2	5	1.1	12	2.6	451	97.4	0	.0	463
1	.2	10	2.0	5	1.0	5	1.0	21	4.2	485	95.8	0	.0	506
0	.0	3	4.3	0	.0	1	1.4	4	5.7	66	94.3	0	.0	70
0	.0	2	6.3	0	.0	0	.0	2	6.3	30	93.8	0	.0	32
0	.0	1	2.6	0	.0	1	2.6	2	5.3	36	94.7	0	.0	38
1	.1	19	1.8	6	.6	11	1.1	37	3.6	1,002	96.4	0	.0	1,039
0	.0	8	1.6	1	.2	5	1.0	14	2.8	481	97.2	0	.0	495
1	.2	11	2.0	5	.9	6	1.1	23	4.2	521	95.8	0	.0	544
0	.0	1	1.3	3	3.8	1	1.3	5	6.4	73	93.6	0	.0	78
0	.0	1	4.8	0	.0	0	.0	1	4.8	20	95.2	0	.0	21
0	.0	0	.0	3	5.3	1	1.8	4	7.0	53	93.0	0	.0	57
0	.0	1	.9	7	6.3	1	.9	9	8.0	103	92.0	0	.0	112
0	.0	0	.0	4	11.1	0	.0	4	11.1	32	88.9	0	.0	36
0	.0	1	1.3	3	3.9	1	1.3	5	6.6	71	93.4	0	.0	76
0	.0	2	1.1	10	5.3	2	1.1	14	7.4	176	92.6	0	.0	190
0	.0	1	1.8	4	7.0	0	.0	5	8.8	52	91.2	0	.0	57
0	.0	1	.8	6	4.5	2	1.5	9	6.8	124	93.2	0	.0	133
0	.0	0	.0	0	.0	0	.0	0	.0	0	.0	0	.0	0
0	.0	0	.0	0	.0	0	.0	0	.0	0	.0	0	.0	0
0	.0	0	.0	0	.0	0	.0	0	.0	0	.0	0	.0	0
0	.0	0	.0	0	.0	0	.0	0	.0	0	.0	0	.0	0
0	.0	0	.0	0	.0	0	.0	0	.0	0	.0	0	.0	0
0	.0	0	.0	0	.0	0	.0	0	.0	0	.0	0	.0	0
0	.0	0	.0	0	.0	0	.0	0	.0	0	.0	0	.0	0
0	.0	0	.0	0	.0	0	.0	0	.0	0	.0	0	.0	0
0	.0	0	.0	0	.0	0	.0	0	.0	0	.0	0	.0	0
1	.1	17	1.6	9	.9	11	1.1	38	3.6	1,009	96.4	0	.0	1,047
0	.0	7	1.4	1	.2	5	1.0	13	2.7	471	97.3	0	.0	484
1	.2	10	1.8	8	1.4	6	1.1	25	4.4	538	95.6	0	.0	563
0	.0	4	2.2	7	3.8	2	1.1	13	7.1	169	92.9	0	.0	182
0	.0	2	2.9	4	5.9	0	.0	6	8.8	62	91.2	0	.0	68
0	.0	2	1.8	3	2.6	2	1.8	7	6.1	107	93.9	0	.0	114
1	.1	21	1.7	16	1.3	13	1.1	51	4.1	1,178	95.9	0	.0	1,229
0	.0	9	1.6	5	.9	5	.9	19	3.4	533	96.6	0	.0	552
1	.1	12	1.8	11	1.6	8	1.2	32	4.7	645	95.3	0	.0	677
0	.0	0	.0	0	.0	0	.0	0	.0	10	100.0	0	.0	10
0	.0	0	.0	0	.0	0	.0	0	.0	0	.0	0	.0	0
0	.0	0	.0	0	.0	0	.0	0	.0	10	100.0	0	.0	10
1	.1	21	1.7	16	1.3	13	1.0	51	4.1	1,188	95.9	0	.0	1,239
0	.0	9	1.6	5	.9	5	.9	19	3.4	533	96.6	0	.0	552
1	.1	12	1.7	11	1.6	8	1.2	32	4.7	655	95.3	0	.0	687
(8 INSTITUTIONS)														
34	2.8	2	.2	3	.2	196	16.3	235	19.5	867	71.9	104	8.6	1,206
10	3.2	0	.0	1	.3	36	11.7	47	15.3	256	83.1	5	1.6	308
24	2.7	2	.2	2	.2	160	17.8	188	20.9	611	68.0	99	11.0	898
0	.0	0	.0	0	.0	14	22.2	14	22.2	46	73.0	3	4.8	63
0	.0	0	.0	0	.0	5	18.5	5	18.5	22	81.5	0	.0	27
0	.0	0	.0	0	.0	9	25.0	9	25.0	24	66.7	3	8.3	36
34	2.7	2	.2	3	.2	210	16.5	249	19.6	913	71.9	107	8.4	1,269
10	3.0	0	.0	1	.3	41	12.2	52	15.5	278	83.0	5	1.5	335
24	2.6	2	.2	2	.2	169	18.1	197	21.1	635	68.0	102	10.9	934
0	.0	0	.0	0	.0	6	3.8	6	3.8	96	61.5	54	34.6	156
0	.0	0	.0	0	.0	1	5.9	1	5.9	14	82.4	2	11.8	17
0	.0	0	.0	0	.0	5	3.6	5	3.6	82	59.0	52	37.4	139
0	.0	1	1.9	0	.0	6	11.5	6	11.5	37	71.2	9	17.3	52
0	.0	0	.0	0	.0	0	.0	0	.0	10	100.0	0	.0	10
0	.0	1	2.4	0	.0	5	11.9	6	14.3	27	64.3	9	21.4	42
0	.0	1	.5	0	.0	11	5.3	12	5.8	133	63.9	63	30.3	208
0	.0	0	.0	0	.0	1	3.7	1	3.7	24	88.9	2	7.4	27
0	.0	1	.6	0	.0	10	5.5	11	6.1	109	60.2	61	33.7	181
0	.0	0	.0	0	.0	0	.0	0	.0	0	.0	0	.0	0
0	.0	0	.0	0	.0	0	.0	0	.0	0	.0	0	.0	0
0	.0	0	.0	0	.0	0	.0	0	.0	0	.0	0	.0	0

TABLE 17 - TOTAL ENROLLMENT IN INSTITUTIONS OF HIGHER EDUCATION FOR SELECTED MAJOR FIELDS OF STUDY AND LEVEL OF ENROLLMENT BY RACE, ETHNICITY, AND SEX: STATE, 1978

MAJOR FIELD 0100 - AGRICULTURE AND NATURAL RESOURCES

	AMERICAN INDIAN ALASKAN NATIVE		BLACK NON-HISPANIC		ASIAN OR PACIFIC ISLANDER		HISPANIC		TOTAL MINORITY		WHITE NON-HISPANIC		NON-RESIDENT ALIEN	
	NUMBER	%	NUMBER	%	NUMBER	%	NUMBER	%	NUMBER	%	NUMBER	%	NUMBER	%
NEW MEXICO CONTINUED														
PROFESSIONAL:														
PART-TIME FEMALE	0	.0	0	.0	0	.0	0	.0	0	.0	0	.0	0	.0
MALE	0	.0	0	.0	0	.0	0	.0	0	.0	0	.0	0	.0
TOTAL FEMALE	0	.0	0	.0	0	.0	0	.0	0	.0	0	.0	0	.0
MALE	0	.0	0	.0	0	.0	0	.0	0	.0	0	.0	0	.0
UND+GRAD+PROF:														
FULL-TIME	34	2.5	2	.1	3	.2	202	14.8	241	17.7	963	70.7	158	11.6
FEMALE	10	3.1	1	.3	1	.3	37	11.4	48	14.8	270	83.1	7	2.2
MALE	24	2.3	2	.2	2	.2	165	15.9	193	18.6	693	66.8	151	14.6
PART-TIME	0	.0	1	.9	0	.0	19	16.5	20	17.4	83	72.2	12	10.4
FEMALE	0	.0	0	.0	0	.0	5	13.5	5	13.5	32	86.5	0	.0
MALE	0	.0	1	1.3	0	.0	14	17.9	15	19.2	51	65.4	12	15.4
TOTAL	34	2.3	3	.2	3	.2	221	15.0	261	17.7	1,046	70.8	170	11.5
FEMALE	10	2.8	0	.0	1	.3	42	11.6	53	14.6	302	83.4	7	1.9
MALE	24	2.2	3	.3	2	.2	179	16.1	208	18.7	744	66.7	163	14.6
UNCLASSIFIED:														
TOTAL	0	.0	0	.0	1	2.5	9	22.5	10	25.0	30	75.0	0	.0
FEMALE	0	.0	0	.0	0	.0	2	22.2	2	22.2	7	77.8	0	.0
MALE	0	.0	0	.0	1	3.2	7	22.6	8	25.8	23	74.2	0	.0
TOTAL ENROLLMENT:														
TOTAL	34	2.2	3	.2	4	.3	230	15.2	271	17.9	1,076	70.9	170	11.2
FEMALE	10	2.7	0	.0	1	.3	44	11.9	55	14.8	309	83.3	7	1.9
MALE	24	2.1	3	.3	3	.3	186	16.2	216	18.8	767	66.9	163	14.2
NEW YORK (5 INSTITUTIONS)														
UNDERGRADUATES:														
FULL-TIME	9	.4	56	2.2	39	1.5	28	1.1	132	5.2	2,378	93.2	41	1.6
FEMALE	5	.6	22	2.6	22	2.6	12	1.4	61	7.1	791	92.2	6	.7
MALE	4	.2	34	2.0	17	1.0	16	.9	71	4.2	1,587	93.7	35	2.1
PART-TIME	0	.0	0	.0	0	.0	0	.0	0	.0	10	100.0	0	.0
FEMALE	0	.0	0	.0	0	.0	0	.0	0	.0	1	100.0	0	.0
MALE	0	.0	0	.0	0	.0	0	.0	0	.0	9	100.0	0	.0
TOTAL	9	.4	56	2.2	39	1.5	28	1.1	132	5.2	2,388	93.2	41	1.6
FEMALE	5	.6	22	2.6	22	2.6	12	1.4	61	7.1	792	92.2	6	.7
MALE	4	.2	34	2.0	17	1.0	16	.9	71	4.2	1,596	93.8	35	2.1
GRADUATE:														
FULL-TIME	2	.4	20	4.0	35	7.0	27	5.4	84	16.8	275	55.0	141	28.2
FEMALE	0	.0	3	2.3	9	6.9	2	1.5	14	10.8	96	73.8	20	15.4
MALE	2	.5	17	4.6	26	7.0	25	6.8	70	18.9	179	48.4	121	32.7
PART-TIME	0	.0	0	.0	0	.0	0	.0	0	.0	34	97.1	1	2.9
FEMALE	0	.0	0	.0	0	.0	0	.0	0	.0	4	100.0	0	.0
MALE	0	.0	0	.0	0	.0	0	.0	0	.0	30	96.8	1	3.2
TOTAL	2	.4	20	3.7	35	6.5	27	5.0	84	15.7	309	57.8	142	26.5
FEMALE	0	.0	3	2.2	9	6.7	2	1.5	14	10.4	100	74.6	20	14.9
MALE	2	.5	17	4.2	26	6.5	25	6.2	70	17.5	209	52.1	122	30.4
PROFESSIONAL:														
FULL-TIME	0	.0	0	.0	0	.0	0	.0	0	.0	0	.0	0	.0
FEMALE	0	.0	0	.0	0	.0	0	.0	0	.0	0	.0	0	.0
MALE	0	.0	0	.0	0	.0	0	.0	0	.0	0	.0	0	.0
PART-TIME	0	.0	0	.0	0	.0	0	.0	0	.0	0	.0	0	.0
FEMALE	0	.0	0	.0	0	.0	0	.0	0	.0	0	.0	0	.0
MALE	0	.0	0	.0	0	.0	0	.0	0	.0	0	.0	0	.0
TOTAL	0	.0	0	.0	0	.0	0	.0	0	.0	0	.0	0	.0
FEMALE	0	.0	0	.0	0	.0	0	.0	0	.0	0	.0	0	.0
MALE	0	.0	0	.0	0	.0	0	.0	0	.0	0	.0	0	.0
UND+GRAD+PROF:														
FULL-TIME	11	.4	76	2.5	74	2.4	55	1.8	216	7.1	2,653	87.0	182	6.0
FEMALE	5	.5	25	2.5	31	3.1	14	1.4	75	7.6	887	89.8	26	2.6
MALE	6	.3	51	2.5	43	2.1	41	2.0	141	6.8	1,766	85.6	156	7.6
PART-TIME	0	.0	0	.0	0	.0	0	.0	0	.0	44	97.8	1	2.2
FEMALE	0	.0	0	.0	0	.0	0	.0	0	.0	5	100.0	0	.0
MALE	0	.0	0	.0	0	.0	0	.0	0	.0	39	97.5	1	2.5
TOTAL	11	.4	76	2.5	74	2.4	55	1.8	216	7.0	2,697	87.1	183	5.9
FEMALE	5	.5	25	2.5	31	3.1	14	1.4	75	7.6	892	89.8	26	2.6
MALE	6	.3	51	2.4	43	2.0	41	1.9	141	6.7	1,805	85.8	157	7.5
UNCLASSIFIED:														
TOTAL	0	.0	0	.0	0	.0	0	.0	0	.0	0	.0	0	.0
FEMALE	0	.0	0	.0	0	.0	0	.0	0	.0	0	.0	0	.0
MALE	0	.0	0	.0	0	.0	0	.0	0	.0	0	.0	0	.0
TOTAL ENROLLMENT:														
TOTAL	11	.4	76	2.5	74	2.4	55	1.8	216	7.0	2,697	87.1	183	5.9
FEMALE	5	.5	25	2.5	31	3.1	14	1.4	75	7.6	892	89.8	26	2.6
MALE	6	.3	51	2.4	43	2.0	41	1.9	141	6.7	1,805	85.8	157	7.5

AGRICULTURE AND NATURAL RESOURCES

(INDIAN NATIVE	BLACK NON-HISPANIC		ASIAN OR PACIFIC ISLANDER		HISPANIC		TOTAL MINORITY		WHITE NON-HISPANIC		NON-RESIDENT ALIEN		TOTAL
%	NUMBER	%	NUMBER	%	NUMBER	%	NUMBER	%	NUMBER	%	NUMBER	%	NUMBER
(5 INSTITUTIONS)													
.1	150	9.5	3	.2	4	.3	158	10.0	1,380	87.4	41	2.6	1,579
.0	38	8.3	0	.0	2	.4	40	8.8	409	89.5	8	1.8	457
.1	112	10.0	3	.3	2	.2	118	10.5	971	86.5	33	2.9	1,122
.0	9	10.2	0	.0	1	1.1	10	11.4	74	84.1	4	4.5	88
.0	1	4.3	0	.0	0	.0	1	4.3	20	87.0	2	8.7	23
.0	8	12.3	0	.0	1	1.5	9	13.8	54	83.1	2	3.1	65
.1	159	9.5	3	.2	5	.3	168	10.1	1,454	87.2	45	2.7	1,667
.0	39	8.1	0	.0	2	.4	41	8.5	429	89.4	10	2.1	480
.1	120	10.1	3	.3	3	.3	127	10.7	1,025	86.4	35	2.9	1,187
.4	8	3.0	1	.4	5	1.9	15	5.7	200	75.8	49	18.6	264
1.6	0	.0	0	.0	1	1.6	2	3.2	54	85.7	7	11.1	63
.0	8	4.0	1	.5	4	2.0	13	6.5	146	72.6	42	20.9	201
.4	11	4.3	4	1.6	0	.0	16	6.2	177	68.6	65	25.2	258
.0	2	3.4	1	1.7	0	.0	3	5.1	50	84.7	6	10.2	59
.5	9	4.5	3	1.5	0	.0	13	6.5	127	63.8	59	29.6	199
.4	19	3.6	5	1.0	5	1.0	31	5.9	377	72.2	114	21.8	522
.8	2	1.6	1	.8	1	.8	5	4.1	104	85.2	13	10.7	122
.3	17	4.3	4	1.0	4	1.0	26	6.5	273	68.3	101	25.3	400
.0	0	.0	0	.0	0	.0	0	.0	0	.0	0	.0	0
.0	0	.0	0	.0	0	.0	0	.0	0	.0	0	.0	0
.0	0	.0	0	.0	0	.0	0	.0	0	.0	0	.0	0
.0	0	.0	0	.0	0	.0	0	.0	0	.0	0	.0	0
.0	0	.0	0	.0	0	.0	0	.0	0	.0	0	.0	0
.0	0	.0	0	.0	0	.0	0	.0	0	.0	0	.0	0
.0	0	.0	0	.0	0	.0	0	.0	0	.0	0	.0	0
.0	0	.0	0	.0	0	.0	0	.0	0	.0	0	.0	0
.0	0	.0	0	.0	0	.0	0	.0	0	.0	0	.0	0
.1	158	8.6	4	.2	9	.5	173	9.4	1,580	85.7	90	4.9	1,843
.2	38	7.3	0	.0	3	.6	42	8.1	463	89.0	15	2.9	520
.1	120	9.1	4	.3	6	.5	131	9.9	1,117	84.4	75	5.7	1,323
.3	20	5.8	4	1.2	1	.3	26	7.5	251	72.5	69	19.9	346
.0	3	3.7	1	1.2	0	.0	4	4.9	70	85.4	8	9.8	82
.4	17	6.4	3	1.1	1	.4	22	8.3	181	68.6	61	23.1	264
.1	178	8.1	8	.4	10	.5	199	9.1	1,831	83.6	159	7.3	2,189
.2	41	6.8	1	.2	3	.5	46	7.6	533	88.5	23	3.8	602
.1	137	8.6	7	.4	7	.4	153	9.6	1,298	81.8	136	8.6	1,587
.0	0	.0	0	.0	0	.0	0	.0	0	.0	0	.0	0
.0	0	.0	0	.0	0	.0	0	.0	0	.0	0	.0	0
.0	0	.0	0	.0	0	.0	0	.0	0	.0	0	.0	0
.1	178	8.1	8	.4	10	.5	199	9.1	1,831	83.6	159	7.3	2,189
.2	41	6.8	1	.2	3	.5	46	7.6	533	88.5	23	3.8	602
.1	137	8.6	7	.4	7	.4	153	9.6	1,298	81.8	136	8.6	1,587
(6 INSTITUTIONS)													
.6	0	.0	0	.0	0	.0	8	.6	1,358	98.8	8	.6	1,374
.8	0	.0	0	.0	0	.0	2	.8	235	98.7	1	.4	238
.5	0	.0	0	.0	0	.0	6	.5	1,123	98.9	7	.6	1,136
.0	0	.0	0	.0	0	.0	0	.0	6	100.0	0	.0	6
.0	0	.0	0	.0	0	.0	0	.0	1	100.0	0	.0	1
.0	0	.0	0	.0	0	.0	0	.0	5	100.0	0	.0	5
.6	0	.0	0	.0	0	.0	8	.6	1,364	98.8	8	.6	1,380
.8	0	.0	0	.0	0	.0	2	.8	236	98.7	1	.4	239
.5	0	.0	0	.0	0	.0	6	.5	1,128	98.9	7	.6	1,141
.0	0	.0	0	.0	0	.0	0	.0	51	67.1	25	32.9	76
.0	0	.0	0	.0	0	.0	0	.0	10	90.9	1	9.1	11
.0	0	.0	0	.0	0	.0	0	.0	41	63.1	24	36.9	65
.0	1	2.0	1	2.0	0	.0	2	4.1	35	71.4	12	24.5	49
.0	0	.0	0	.0	0	.0	0	.0	2	66.7	1	33.3	3
.0	1	2.2	1	2.2	0	.0	2	4.3	33	71.7	11	23.9	46
.0	1	.8	1	.8	0	.0	2	1.6	86	68.8	37	29.6	125
.0	0	.0	0	.0	0	.0	0	.0	12	85.7	2	14.3	14
.0	1	.9	1	.9	0	.0	2	1.8	74	66.7	35	31.5	111
.0	0	.0	0	.0	0	.0	0	.0	0	.0	0	.0	0
.0	0	.0	0	.0	0	.0	0	.0	0	.0	0	.0	0
.0	0	.0	0	.0	0	.0	0	.0	0	.0	0	.0	0

MAJOR FIELD 0100 - AGRICULTURE AND NATURAL RESOURCES

	AMERICAN INDIAN ALASKAN NATIVE		BLACK NON-HISPANIC		ASIAN OR PACIFIC ISLANDER		HISPANIC		TOTAL MINORITY		WHITE NON-HISPANIC		NON-RESIDENT ALIEN	
	NUMBER	%	NUMBER	%	NUMBER	%	NUMBER	%	NUMBER	%	NUMBER	%	NUMBER	%
NORTH DAKOTA	CONTINUED													
PROFESSIONAL:														
PART-TIME	0	.0	0	.0	0	.0	0	.0	0	.0	0	.0	0	.0
FEMALE	0	.0	0	.0	0	.0	0	.0	0	.0	0	.0	0	.0
MALE	0	.0	0	.0	0	.0	0	.0	0	.0	0	.0	0	.0
TOTAL	0	.0	0	.0	0	.0	0	.0	0	.0	0	.0	0	.0
FEMALE	0	.0	0	.0	0	.0	0	.0	0	.0	0	.0	0	.0
MALE	0	.0	0	.0	0	.0	0	.0	0	.0	0	.0	0	.0
UND+GRAD+PROF:														
FULL-TIME	8	.6	0	.0	0	.0	0	.0	8	.6	1,409	97.2	33	2.3
FEMALE	2	.8	0	.0	0	.0	0	.0	2	.8	245	98.4	2	.8
MALE	6	.5	0	.0	0	.0	0	.0	6	.5	1,164	96.9	31	2.6
PART-TIME	0	.0	1	1.8	1	1.8	0	.0	2	3.6	41	74.5	12	21.8
FEMALE	0	.0	0	.0	0	.0	0	.0	0	.0	3	75.0	1	25.0
MALE	0	.0	1	2.0	1	2.0	0	.0	2	3.9	38	74.5	11	21.6
TOTAL	8	.5	1	.1	1	.1	0	.0	10	.7	1,450	96.3	45	3.0
FEMALE	2	.8	0	.0	0	.0	0	.0	2	.8	248	98.0	3	1.2
MALE	6	.5	1	.1	1	.1	0	.0	8	.6	1,202	96.0	42	3.4
UNCLASSIFIED:														
TOTAL	0	.0	1	3.1	0	.0	0	.0	1	3.1	31	96.9	0	.0
FEMALE	0	.0	0	.0	0	.0	0	.0	0	.0	4	100.0	0	.0
MALE	0	.0	1	3.6	0	.0	0	.0	1	3.6	27	96.4	0	.0
TOTAL ENROLLMENT:														
TOTAL	8	.5	2	.1	1	.1	0	.0	11	.7	1,481	96.4	45	2.9
FEMALE	2	.8	0	.0	0	.0	0	.0	2	.8	252	98.1	3	1.2
MALE	6	.5	2	.2	1	.1	0	.0	9	.7	1,229	96.0	42	3.3
OHIO	(18 INSTITUTIONS)													
UNDERGRADUATES:														
FULL-TIME	4	.1	17	.6	5	.2	8	.3	34	1.2	2,879	98.2	19	.6
FEMALE	1	.1	6	.6	0	.0	2	.2	9	1.0	926	98.8	2	.2
MALE	3	.2	11	.6	5	.3	6	.3	25	1.3	1,953	97.9	17	.9
PART-TIME	1	.6	0	.0	1	.6	0	.0	2	1.2	169	98.3	1	.6
FEMALE	1	1.3	0	.0	1	1.3	0	.0	2	2.6	74	97.4	0	.0
MALE	0	.0	0	.0	0	.0	0	.0	0	.0	95	99.0	1	1.0
TOTAL	5	.2	17	.5	6	.2	8	.3	36	1.2	3,048	98.2	20	.6
FEMALE	2	.2	6	.6	1	.1	2	.2	11	1.1	1,000	98.7	2	.2
MALE	3	.1	11	.6	5	.2	6	.3	25	1.2	2,048	97.9	18	.9
GRADUATE:														
FULL-TIME	3	.8	8	2.2	3	.8	5	1.4	19	5.3	249	69.4	91	25.3
FEMALE	1	1.3	2	2.5	1	1.3	2	2.5	6	7.5	64	80.0	10	12.5
MALE	2	.7	6	2.2	2	.7	3	1.1	13	4.7	185	66.3	81	29.0
PART-TIME	1	.7	3	2.1	0	.0	0	.0	4	2.7	124	84.9	18	12.3
FEMALE	0	.0	1	2.4	0	.0	0	.0	1	2.4	40	95.2	1	2.4
MALE	1	1.0	2	1.9	0	.0	0	.0	3	2.9	84	80.8	17	16.3
TOTAL	4	.8	11	2.2	3	.6	5	1.0	23	4.6	373	73.9	109	21.6
FEMALE	1	.8	3	2.5	1	.8	2	1.6	7	5.7	104	85.2	11	9.0
MALE	3	.8	8	2.1	2	.5	3	.8	16	4.2	269	70.2	98	25.6
PROFESSIONAL:														
FULL-TIME	0	.0	0	.0	0	.0	0	.0	0	.0	0	.0	0	.0
FEMALE	0	.0	0	.0	0	.0	0	.0	0	.0	0	.0	0	.0
MALE	0	.0	0	.0	0	.0	0	.0	0	.0	0	.0	0	.0
PART-TIME	0	.0	0	.0	0	.0	0	.0	0	.0	0	.0	0	.0
FEMALE	0	.0	0	.0	0	.0	0	.0	0	.0	0	.0	0	.0
MALE	0	.0	0	.0	0	.0	0	.0	0	.0	0	.0	0	.0
TOTAL	0	.0	0	.0	0	.0	0	.0	0	.0	0	.0	0	.0
FEMALE	0	.0	0	.0	0	.0	0	.0	0	.0	0	.0	0	.0
MALE	0	.0	0	.0	0	.0	0	.0	0	.0	0	.0	0	.0
UND+GRAD+PROF:														
FULL-TIME	7	.2	25	.8	8	.2	13	.4	53	1.6	3,128	95.0	110	3.3
FEMALE	2	.2	8	.8	1	.1	4	.4	15	1.5	990	97.3	12	1.2
MALE	5	.2	17	.7	7	.3	9	.4	38	1.7	2,138	94.0	98	4.3
PART-TIME	2	.6	3	.9	1	.3	0	.0	6	1.9	293	92.1	19	6.0
FEMALE	1	.8	1	.8	1	.8	0	.0	3	2.5	114	96.6	1	.8
MALE	1	.5	2	1.0	0	.0	0	.0	3	1.5	179	89.5	18	9.0
TOTAL	9	.2	28	.8	9	.2	13	.4	59	1.6	3,421	94.8	129	3.6
FEMALE	3	.3	9	.8	2	.2	4	.4	18	1.6	1,104	97.3	13	1.1
MALE	6	.2	19	.8	7	.3	9	.4	41	1.7	2,317	93.7	116	4.7
UNCLASSIFIED:														
TOTAL	0	.0	0	.0	0	.0	0	.0	0	.0	50	100.0	0	.0
FEMALE	0	.0	0	.0	0	.0	0	.0	0	.0	16	100.0	0	.0
MALE	0	.0	0	.0	0	.0	0	.0	0	.0	34	100.0	0	.0
TOTAL ENROLLMENT:														
TOTAL	9	.2	28	.8	9	.2	13	.4	59	1.6	3,471	94.9	129	3.5
FEMALE	3	.3	9	.8	2	.2	4	.3	18	1.6	1,120	97.3	13	1.1
MALE	6	.2	19	.8	7	.3	9	.4	41	1.6	2,351	93.7	116	4.6

0 = AGRICULTURE AND NATURAL RESOURCES

ICAN INDIAN KAN NATIVE		BLACK NON-HISPANIC		ASIAN OR PACIFIC ISLANDER		HISPANIC		TOTAL MINORITY		WHITE NON-HISPANIC		NON-RESIDENT ALIEN		TOTAL
BER	%	NUMBER	%	NUMBER	%	NUMBER	%	NUMBER	%	NUMBER	%	NUMBER	%	NUMBER

(13 INSTITUTIONS)

BER	%	NUMBER	%	NUMBER	%	NUMBER	%	NUMBER	%	NUMBER	%	NUMBER	%	NUMBER
51	1.9	28	1.1	10	.4	12	.5	101	3.8	2,412	91.6	120	4.6	2,633
14	2.6	8	1.5	2	.4	4	.7	28	5.1	508	92.5	13	2.4	549
37	1.8	20	1.0	8	.4	8	.4	73	3.5	1,904	91.4	107	5.1	2,084
4	3.1	5	3.8	0	.0	1	.8	10	7.7	115	88.5	5	3.8	130
1	2.5	1	2.5	0	.0	0	.0	2	5.0	38	95.0	0	.0	40
3	3.3	4	4.4	0	.0	1	1.1	8	8.9	77	85.6	5	5.6	90
55	2.0	33	1.2	10	.4	13	.5	111	4.0	2,527	91.5	125	4.5	2,763
15	2.5	9	1.5	2	.3	4	.7	30	5.1	546	92.7	13	2.2	589
40	1.8	24	1.1	8	.4	9	.4	81	3.7	1,981	91.1	112	5.2	2,174
0	.0	0	.0	2	1.2	1	.6	3	1.8	112	66.7	53	31.5	168
0	.0	0	.0	1	4.3	0	.0	1	4.3	16	69.6	6	26.1	23
0	.0	0	.0	1	.7	1	.7	2	1.4	96	66.2	47	32.4	145
1	1.6	1	1.6	1	1.6	1	1.6	4	6.3	40	62.5	20	31.3	64
0	.0	0	.0	0	.0	0	.0	0	.0	5	71.4	2	28.6	7
1	1.8	1	1.8	1	1.8	1	1.8	4	7.0	35	61.4	18	31.6	57
1	.4	1	.4	3	1.3	2	.9	7	3.0	152	65.5	73	31.5	232
0	.0	0	.0	1	3.3	0	.0	1	3.3	21	70.0	8	26.7	30
1	.5	1	.5	2	1.0	2	1.0	6	3.0	131	64.9	65	32.2	202
0	.0	0	.0	0	.0	0	.0	0	.0	0	.0	0	.0	0
0	.0	0	.0	0	.0	0	.0	0	.0	0	.0	0	.0	0
0	.0	0	.0	0	.0	0	.0	0	.0	0	.0	0	.0	0
0	.0	0	.0	0	.0	0	.0	0	.0	0	.0	0	.0	0
0	.0	0	.0	0	.0	0	.0	0	.0	0	.0	0	.0	0
0	.0	0	.0	0	.0	0	.0	0	.0	0	.0	0	.0	0
0	.0	0	.0	0	.0	0	.0	0	.0	0	.0	0	.0	0
0	.0	0	.0	0	.0	0	.0	0	.0	0	.0	0	.0	0
0	.0	0	.0	0	.0	0	.0	0	.0	0	.0	0	.0	0
51	1.8	28	1.0	12	.4	13	.5	104	3.7	2,524	90.1	173	6.2	2,801
14	2.4	8	1.4	3	.5	4	.7	29	5.1	524	91.6	19	3.3	572
37	1.7	20	.9	9	.4	9	.4	75	3.4	2,000	89.7	154	6.9	2,229
5	2.6	6	3.1	1	.5	2	1.0	14	7.2	155	79.9	25	12.9	194
1	2.1	1	2.1	0	.0	0	.0	2	4.3	43	91.5	2	4.3	47
4	2.7	5	3.4	1	.7	2	1.4	12	8.2	112	76.2	23	15.6	147
56	1.9	34	1.1	13	.4	15	.5	118	3.9	2,679	89.4	198	6.6	2,995
15	2.4	9	1.5	3	.5	4	.6	31	5.0	567	91.6	21	3.4	619
41	1.7	25	1.1	10	.4	11	.5	87	3.7	2,112	88.9	177	7.4	2,376
1	1.9	0	.0	1	1.9	1	1.9	3	5.7	48	90.6	2	3.8	53
0	.0	0	.0	0	.0	0	.0	0	.0	8	100.0	0	.0	8
1	2.2	0	.0	1	2.2	1	2.2	3	6.7	40	88.9	2	4.4	45
57	1.9	34	1.1	14	.5	16	.5	121	4.0	2,727	89.5	200	6.6	3,048
15	2.4	9	1.4	3	.5	4	.6	31	4.9	575	91.7	21	3.3	627
42	1.7	25	1.0	11	.5	12	.5	90	3.7	2,152	88.9	179	7.4	2,421

(12 INSTITUTIONS)

BER	%	NUMBER	%	NUMBER	%	NUMBER	%	NUMBER	%	NUMBER	%	NUMBER	%	NUMBER
28	1.3	5	.2	28	1.3	6	.3	67	3.2	1,989	95.9	19	.9	2,075
7	1.1	1	.2	7	1.1	1	.2	16	2.6	600	96.6	5	.8	621
21	1.4	4	.3	21	1.4	5	.3	51	3.5	1,389	95.5	14	1.0	1,454
3	1.7	1	.6	1	.6	1	.6	6	3.5	165	95.9	1	.6	172
0	.0	0	.0	0	.0	0	.0	0	.0	65	100.0	0	.0	65
3	2.8	1	.9	1	.9	1	.9	6	5.6	100	93.5	1	.9	107
31	1.4	6	.3	29	1.3	7	.3	73	3.2	2,154	95.9	20	.9	2,247
7	1.0	1	.1	7	1.0	1	.1	16	2.3	665	96.9	5	.7	686
24	1.5	5	.3	22	1.4	6	.4	57	3.7	1,489	95.4	15	1.0	1,561
8	1.9	6	1.4	3	.7	2	.5	19	4.4	311	72.3	100	23.3	430
2	2.1	0	.0	0	.0	0	.0	2	2.1	79	81.4	16	16.5	97
6	1.8	6	1.8	3	.9	2	.6	17	5.1	232	69.7	84	25.2	333
0	.0	0	.0	2	2.2	0	.0	2	2.2	77	86.5	10	11.2	89
0	.0	0	.0	1	5.9	0	.0	1	5.9	14	82.4	2	11.8	17
0	.0	0	.0	1	1.4	0	.0	1	1.4	63	87.5	8	11.1	72
8	1.5	6	1.2	5	1.0	2	.4	21	4.0	388	74.8	110	21.2	519
2	1.8	0	.0	1	.9	0	.0	3	2.6	93	81.6	18	15.8	114
6	1.5	6	1.5	4	1.0	2	.5	18	4.4	295	72.8	92	22.7	405
0	.0	0	.0	0	.0	0	.0	0	.0	0	.0	0	.0	0
0	.0	0	.0	0	.0	0	.0	0	.0	0	.0	0	.0	0
0	.0	0	.0	0	.0	0	.0	0	.0	0	.0	0	.0	0

TABLE 17 - TOTAL ENROLLMENT IN INSTITUTIONS OF HIGHER EDUCATION FOR SELECTED MAJOR FIELDS OF STUDY AND LEVEL OF ENROLLMENT BY RACE, ETHNICITY, AND SEX: STATE, 1978

MAJOR FIELD 0100 - AGRICULTURE AND NATURAL RESOURCES

	AMERICAN INDIAN ALASKAN NATIVE		BLACK NON-HISPANIC		ASIAN OR PACIFIC ISLANDER		HISPANIC		TOTAL MINORITY		WHITE NON-HISPANIC		NON-RESIDENT ALIEN	
	NUMBER	%	NUMBER	%	NUMBER	%	NUMBER	%	NUMBER	%	NUMBER	%	NUMBER	%
OREGON		CONTINUED												
PROFESSIONAL:														
PART-TIME	0	.0	0	.0	0	.0	0	.0	0	.0	0	.0	0	.0
FEMALE	0	.0	0	.0	0	.0	0	.0	0	.0	0	.0	0	.0
MALE	0	.0	0	.0	0	.0	0	.0	0	.0	0	.0	0	.0
TOTAL	0	.0	0	.0	0	.0	0	.0	0	.0	0	.0	0	.0
FEMALE	0	.0	0	.0	0	.0	0	.0	0	.0	0	.0	0	.0
MALE	0	.0	0	.0	0	.0	0	.0	0	.0	0	.0	0	.0
UND+GRAD+PROF:														
FULL-TIME	36	1.4	11	.4	31	1.2	8	.3	86	3.4	2,300	91.8	119	4.8
FEMALE	9	1.3	1	.1	7	1.0	1	.1	18	2.5	679	94.6	21	2.9
MALE	27	1.5	10	.6	24	1.3	7	.4	68	3.8	1,621	90.7	98	5.5
PART-TIME	3	1.1	1	.4	3	1.1	1	.4	8	3.1	242	92.7	11	4.2
FEMALE	0	.0	0	.0	1	1.2	0	.0	1	1.2	79	96.3	2	2.4
MALE	3	1.7	1	.6	2	1.1	1	.6	7	3.9	163	91.1	9	5.0
TOTAL	39	1.4	12	.4	34	1.2	9	.3	94	3.4	2,542	91.9	130	4.7
FEMALE	9	1.1	1	.1	8	1.0	1	.1	19	2.4	758	94.8	23	2.9
MALE	30	1.5	11	.6	26	1.3	8	.4	75	3.8	1,784	90.7	107	5.4
UNCLASSIFIED:														
TOTAL	1	.7	0	.0	1	.7	0	.0	2	1.4	135	97.1	2	1.4
FEMALE	1	1.8	0	.0	1	1.8	0	.0	2	3.6	53	94.6	1	1.8
MALE	0	.0	0	.0	0	.0	0	.0	0	.0	82	98.8	1	1.2
TOTAL ENROLLMENT:														
TOTAL	40	1.4	12	.4	35	1.2	9	.3	96	3.3	2,677	92.2	132	4.5
FEMALE	10	1.2	1	.1	9	1.1	1	.1	21	2.5	811	94.7	24	2.8
MALE	30	1.5	11	.5	26	1.3	8	.4	75	3.7	1,866	91.1	108	5.3
PENNSYLVANIA	(	26 INSTITUTIONS)												
UNDERGRADUATES:														
FULL-TIME	11	.2	101	1.6	23	.4	14	.2	149	2.4	6,138	97.3	23	.4
FEMALE	4	.2	38	1.6	20	.8	3	.1	65	2.7	2,320	96.7	13	.5
MALE	7	.2	63	1.6	3	.1	11	.3	84	2.1	3,818	97.6	10	.3
PART-TIME	0	.0	6	3.9	1	.6	0	.0	7	4.5	148	95.5	0	.0
FEMALE	0	.0	0	.0	1	1.9	0	.0	1	1.9	52	98.1	0	.0
MALE	0	.0	6	5.9	0	.0	0	.0	6	5.9	96	94.1	0	.0
TOTAL	11	.2	107	1.7	24	.4	14	.2	156	2.4	6,286	97.2	23	.4
FEMALE	4	.2	38	1.6	21	.9	3	.1	66	2.7	2,372	96.8	13	.5
MALE	7	.2	69	1.7	3	.1	11	.3	90	2.2	3,914	97.5	10	.2
GRADUATE:														
FULL-TIME	0	.0	21	4.4	6	1.3	2	.4	29	6.1	399	83.3	51	10.6
FEMALE	0	.0	9	7.0	2	1.6	1	.8	12	9.3	105	81.4	12	9.3
MALE	0	.0	12	3.4	4	1.1	1	.3	17	4.9	294	84.0	39	11.1
PART-TIME	0	.0	4	1.3	4	1.3	1	.3	9	3.0	285	96.0	3	1.0
FEMALE	0	.0	2	1.9	1	.9	0	.0	3	2.8	103	96.3	1	.9
MALE	0	.0	2	1.1	3	1.6	1	.5	6	3.2	182	95.8	2	1.1
TOTAL	0	.0	25	3.2	10	1.3	3	.4	38	4.9	684	88.1	54	7.0
FEMALE	0	.0	11	4.7	3	1.3	1	.4	15	6.4	208	88.1	13	5.5
MALE	0	.0	14	2.6	7	1.3	2	.4	23	4.3	476	88.1	41	7.6
PROFESSIONAL:														
FULL-TIME	0	.0	0	.0	0	.0	0	.0	0	.0	0	.0	0	.0
FEMALE	0	.0	0	.0	0	.0	0	.0	0	.0	0	.0	0	.0
MALE	0	.0	0	.0	0	.0	0	.0	0	.0	0	.0	0	.0
PART-TIME	0	.0	0	.0	0	.0	0	.0	0	.0	0	.0	0	.0
FEMALE	0	.0	0	.0	0	.0	0	.0	0	.0	0	.0	0	.0
MALE	0	.0	0	.0	0	.0	0	.0	0	.0	0	.0	0	.0
TOTAL	0	.0	0	.0	0	.0	0	.0	0	.0	0	.0	0	.0
FEMALE	0	.0	0	.0	0	.0	0	.0	0	.0	0	.0	0	.0
MALE	0	.0	0	.0	0	.0	0	.0	0	.0	0	.0	0	.0
UND+GRAD+PROF:														
FULL-TIME	11	.2	122	1.8	29	.4	16	.2	178	2.6	6,537	96.3	74	1.1
FEMALE	4	.2	47	1.9	22	.9	4	.2	77	3.0	2,425	96.0	25	1.0
MALE	7	.2	75	1.8	7	.2	12	.3	101	2.4	4,112	96.5	49	1.1
PART-TIME	0	.0	10	2.2	5	1.1	1	.2	16	3.5	433	95.8	3	.7
FEMALE	0	.0	2	1.3	2	1.3	0	.0	4	2.5	155	96.9	1	.6
MALE	0	.0	8	2.7	3	1.0	1	.3	12	4.1	278	95.2	2	.7
TOTAL	11	.2	132	1.8	34	.5	17	.2	194	2.7	6,970	96.3	77	1.1
FEMALE	4	.1	49	1.8	24	.9	4	.1	81	3.0	2,580	96.0	26	1.0
MALE	7	.2	83	1.8	10	.2	13	.3	113	2.5	4,390	96.4	51	1.1
UNCLASSIFIED:														
TOTAL	1	.8	2	1.5	3	2.3	0	.0	6	4.5	126	94.7	1	.8
FEMALE	0	.0	1	1.8	2	3.5	0	.0	3	5.3	54	94.7	0	.0
MALE	1	1.3	1	1.3	1	1.3	0	.0	3	3.9	72	94.7	1	1.3
TOTAL ENROLLMENT:														
TOTAL	12	.2	134	1.8	37	.5	17	.2	200	2.7	7,096	96.2	78	1.1
FEMALE	4	.1	50	1.8	26	.9	4	.1	84	3.1	2,634	96.0	26	.9
MALE	8	.2	84	1.8	11	.2	13	.3	116	2.5	4,462	96.4	52	1.1

314

ENROLLMENT IN INSTITUTIONS OF HIGHER EDUCATION FOR SELECTED MAJOR FIELDS OF STUDY AND LEVEL OF ENROLLMENT
:E, ETHNICITY, AND SEX: STATE, 1978

- AGRICULTURE AND NATURAL RESOURCES

:AN INDIAN :N NATIVE		BLACK NON-HISPANIC		ASIAN OR PACIFIC ISLANDER		HISPANIC		TOTAL MINORITY		WHITE NON-HISPANIC		NON-RESIDENT ALIEN		TOTAL
:R	%	NUMBER	%	NUMBER	%	NUMBER	%	NUMBER	%	NUMBER	%	NUMBER	%	NUMBER

(I INSTITUTIONS)

3	.4	1	.1	3	.4	0	.0	7	.9	764	98.1	8	1.0	759
2	.6	0	.0	1	.3	0	.0	3	.9	316	98.8	1	.3	320
1	.2	1	.2	2	.4	0	.0	4	.8	468	97.7	7	1.5	479
0	.0	0	.0	0	.0	2	2.6	2	2.6	74	96.1	1	1.3	77
0	.0	0	.0	0	.0	1	2.9	1	2.9	33	97.1	0	.0	34
0	.0	c	.0	0	.0	1	2.3	1	2.3	41	95.3	1	2.3	43
3	.3	1	.1	3	.3	2	.2	9	1.0	858	97.9	9	1.0	876
2	.6	0	.0	1	.3	1	.3	4	1.1	349	98.6	1	.3	354
1	.2	1	.2	2	.4	1	.2	5	1.0	509	97.5	8	1.5	522
0	.0	0	.0	0	.0	0	.0	0	.0	56	90.3	6	9.7	62
0	.0	0	.0	0	.0	0	.0	0	.0	14	93.3	1	6.7	15
0	.0	0	.0	0	.0	0	.0	0	.0	42	89.4	5	10.6	47
0	.0	0	.0	0	.0	0	.0	0	.0	33	94.3	2	5.7	35
0	.0	0	.0	0	.0	0	.0	0	.0	12	100.0	0	.0	12
0	.0	0	.0	0	.0	0	.0	0	.0	21	91.3	2	8.7	23
0	.0	0	.0	0	.0	0	.0	0	.0	89	91.8	8	8.2	97
0	.0	0	.0	0	.0	0	.0	0	.0	26	96.3	1	3.7	27
0	.0	0	.0	0	.0	0	.0	0	.0	63	90.0	7	10.0	70
0	.0	0	.0	0	.0	0	.0	0	.0	0	.0	0	.0	0
0	.0	0	.0	0	.0	0	.0	0	.0	0	.0	0	.0	0
0	.0	0	.0	0	.0	0	.0	0	.0	0	.0	0	.0	0
0	.0	0	.0	0	.0	0	.0	0	.0	0	.0	0	.0	0
0	.0	0	.0	0	.0	0	.0	0	.0	0	.0	0	.0	0
0	.0	0	.0	0	.0	0	.0	0	.0	0	.0	0	.0	0
0	.0	0	.0	0	.0	0	.0	0	.0	0	.0	0	.0	0
0	.0	0	.0	0	.0	0	.0	0	.0	0	.0	0	.0	0
0	.0	0	.0	0	.0	0	.0	0	.0	0	.0	0	.0	0
3	.3	1	.1	3	.3	0	.0	7	.8	840	97.6	14	1.6	861
2	.6	0	.0	1	.3	0	.0	3	.9	330	98.5	2	.6	335
1	.2	1	.2	2	.4	0	.0	4	.8	510	97.0	12	2.3	526
0	.0	0	.0	0	.0	2	1.8	2	1.8	107	95.5	3	2.7	112
0	.0	0	.0	0	.0	1	2.2	1	2.2	45	97.8	0	.0	46
0	.0	0	.0	0	.0	1	1.5	1	1.5	62	93.9	3	4.5	66
3	.3	1	.1	3	.3	2	.2	9	.9	947	97.3	17	1.7	973
2	.5	0	.0	1	.3	1	.3	4	1.0	375	98.4	2	.5	381
1	.2	1	.2	2	.3	1	.2	5	.8	572	96.6	15	2.5	592
0	.0	0	.0	0	.0	0	.0	0	.0	0	.0	0	.0	0
0	.0	0	.0	0	.0	0	.0	0	.0	0	.0	0	.0	0
0	.0	0	.0	0	.0	0	.0	0	.0	0	.0	0	.0	0
3	.3	1	.1	3	.3	2	.2	9	.9	947	97.3	17	1.7	973
2	.5	0	.0	1	.3	1	.3	4	1.0	375	98.4	2	.5	381
1	.2	1	.2	2	.3	1	.2	5	.8	572	96.6	15	2.5	592

(2 INSTITUTIONS)

1	.1	3	.4	1	.1	0	.0	5	.7	720	98.9	3	.4	728
0	.0	1	.4	1	.4	0	.0	2	.9	229	99.1	0	.0	231
1	.2	2	.4	0	.0	0	.0	3	.6	491	98.8	3	.6	497
0	.0	0	.0	0	.0	0	.0	0	.0	17	100.0	0	.0	17
0	.0	0	.0	0	.0	0	.0	0	.0	6	100.0	0	.0	6
0	.0	0	.0	0	.0	0	.0	0	.0	11	100.0	0	.0	11
1	.1	3	.4	1	.1	0	.0	5	.7	737	98.9	3	.4	745
0	.0	1	.4	1	.4	0	.0	2	.8	235	99.2	0	.0	237
1	.2	2	.4	0	.0	0	.0	3	.6	502	98.8	3	.6	508
0	.0	1	1.3	0	.0	0	.0	1	1.3	72	93.5	4	5.2	77
0	.0	0	.0	0	.0	0	.0	0	.0	20	90.9	2	9.1	22
0	.0	1	1.8	0	.0	0	.0	1	1.8	52	94.5	2	3.6	55
0	.0	0	.0	0	.0	1	2.0	1	2.0	50	98.0	0	.0	51
0	.0	0	.0	0	.0	0	.0	0	.0	23	100.0	0	.0	23
0	.0	0	.0	0	.0	1	3.6	1	3.6	27	96.4	0	.0	28
0	.0	1	.8	0	.0	1	.8	2	1.6	122	95.3	4	3.1	128
0	.0	0	.0	0	.0	0	.0	0	.0	43	95.6	2	4.4	45
0	.0	1	1.2	0	.0	1	1.2	2	2.4	79	95.2	2	2.4	83
0	.0	0	.0	0	.0	0	.0	0	.0	0	.0	0	.0	0
0	.0	0	.0	0	.0	0	.0	0	.0	0	.0	0	.0	0
0	.0	0	.0	0	.0	0	.0	0	.0	0	.0	0	.0	0

TABLE 17 - TOTAL ENROLLMENT IN INSTITUTIONS OF HIGHER EDUCATION FOR SELECTED MAJOR FIELDS OF STUDY AND LEVEL OF ENROLLMENT
BY RACE, ETHNICITY, AND SEX: STATE, 1978

MAJOR FIELD 0100 - AGRICULTURE AND NATURAL RESOURCES

	AMERICAN INDIAN ALASKAN NATIVE		BLACK NON-HISPANIC		ASIAN OR PACIFIC ISLANDER		HISPANIC		TOTAL MINORITY		WHITE NON-HISPANIC		NON-RESIDENT ALIEN		TO NU
	NUMBER	%	NUMBER	%	NUMBER	%	NUMBER	%	NUMBER	%	NUMBER	%	NUMBER	%	
SOUTH CAROLINA CONTINUED															
PROFESSIONAL:															
PART-TIME	0	.0	0	.0	0	.0	0	.0	0	.0	0	.0	0	.0	
FEMALE	0	.0	0	.0	0	.0	0	.0	0	.0	0	.0	0	.0	
MALE	0	.0	0	.0	0	.0	0	.0	0	.0	0	.0	0	.0	
TOTAL	0	.0	0	.0	0	.0	0	.0	0	.0	0	.0	0	.0	
FEMALE	0	.0	0	.0	0	.0	0	.0	0	.0	0	.0	0	.0	
MALE	0	.0	0	.0	0	.0	0	.0	0	.0	0	.0	0	.0	
UNG+GRAD+PROF:															
FULL-TIME	1	.1	4	.5	1	.1	0	.0	6	.7	792	98.4	7	.9	
FEMALE	0	.0	1	.4	1	.4	0	.0	2	.8	249	98.4	2	.8	
MALE	1	.2	3	.5	0	.0	0	.0	4	.7	543	98.4	5	.9	
PART-TIME	0	.0	0	.0	0	.0	1	1.5	1	1.5	67	98.5	0	.0	
FEMALE	0	.0	0	.0	0	.0	0	.0	0	.0	29	100.0	0	.0	
MALE	0	.0	0	.0	0	.0	1	2.6	1	2.6	38	97.4	0	.0	
TOTAL	1	.1	4	.5	1	.1	1	.1	7	.8	859	98.4	7	.8	
FEMALE	0	.0	1	.4	1	.4	0	.0	2	.7	278	98.6	2	.7	
MALE	1	.2	3	.5	0	.0	1	.2	5	.8	581	98.3	5	.8	
UNCLASSIFIED:															
TOTAL	0	.0	0	.0	0	.0	0	.0	0	.0	6	100.0	0	.0	
FEMALE	0	.0	0	.0	0	.0	0	.0	0	.0	0	.0	0	.0	
MALE	0	.0	0	.0	0	.0	0	.0	0	.0	6	100.0	0	.0	
TOTAL ENROLLMENT:															
TOTAL	1	.1	4	.5	1	.1	1	.1	7	.8	865	98.4	7	.8	
FEMALE	0	.0	1	.4	1	.4	0	.0	2	.7	278	98.6	2	.7	
MALE	1	.2	3	.5	0	.0	1	.2	5	.8	587	98.3	5	.8	
SOUTH DAKOTA (3 INSTITUTIONS)															
UNDERGRADUATES:															
FULL-TIME	2	.2	0	.0	0	.0	0	.0	2	.2	908	99.0	7	.8	
FEMALE	0	.0	0	.0	0	.0	0	.0	0	.0	119	100.0	0	.0	
MALE	2	.3	0	.0	0	.0	0	.0	2	.3	789	98.9	7	.9	
PART-TIME	0	.0	0	.0	0	.0	0	.0	0	.0	36	94.7	2	5.3	
FEMALE	0	.0	0	.0	0	.0	0	.0	0	.0	5	100.0	0	.0	
MALE	0	.0	0	.0	0	.0	0	.0	0	.0	31	93.9	2	6.1	
TOTAL	2	.2	0	.0	0	.0	0	.0	2	.2	944	98.8	9	.9	
FEMALE	0	.0	0	.0	0	.0	0	.0	0	.0	124	100.0	0	.0	
MALE	2	.2	0	.0	0	.0	0	.0	2	.2	820	98.7	9	1.1	
GRADUATE:															
FULL-TIME	0	.0	0	.0	0	.0	0	.0	0	.0	21	67.7	10	32.3	
FEMALE	0	.0	0	.0	0	.0	0	.0	0	.0	2	100.0	0	.0	
MALE	0	.0	0	.0	0	.0	0	.0	0	.0	19	65.5	10	34.5	
PART-TIME	0	.0	0	.0	0	.0	0	.0	0	.0	36	94.7	2	5.3	
FEMALE	0	.0	0	.0	0	.0	0	.0	0	.0	4	100.0	0	.0	
MALE	0	.0	0	.0	0	.0	0	.0	0	.0	32	94.1	2	5.9	
TOTAL	0	.0	0	.0	0	.0	0	.0	0	.0	57	82.6	12	17.4	
FEMALE	0	.0	0	.0	0	.0	0	.0	0	.0	6	100.0	0	.0	
MALE	0	.0	0	.0	0	.0	0	.0	0	.0	51	81.0	12	19.0	
PROFESSIONAL:															
FULL-TIME	0	.0	0	.0	0	.0	0	.0	0	.0	0	.0	0	.0	
FEMALE	0	.0	0	.0	0	.0	0	.0	0	.0	0	.0	0	.0	
MALE	0	.0	0	.0	0	.0	0	.0	0	.0	0	.0	0	.0	
PART-TIME	0	.0	0	.0	0	.0	0	.0	0	.0	0	.0	0	.0	
FEMALE	0	.0	0	.0	0	.0	0	.0	0	.0	0	.0	0	.0	
MALE	0	.0	0	.0	0	.0	0	.0	0	.0	0	.0	0	.0	
TOTAL	0	.0	0	.0	0	.0	0	.0	0	.0	0	.0	0	.0	
FEMALE	0	.0	0	.0	0	.0	0	.0	0	.0	0	.0	0	.0	
MALE	0	.0	0	.0	0	.0	0	.0	0	.0	0	.0	0	.0	
UNG+GRAD+PROF:															
FULL-TIME	2	.2	0	.0	0	.0	0	.0	2	.2	929	98.0	17	1.8	
FEMALE	0	.0	0	.0	0	.0	0	.0	0	.0	121	100.0	0	.0	
MALE	2	.2	0	.0	0	.0	0	.0	2	.2	808	97.7	17	2.1	
PART-TIME	0	.0	0	.0	0	.0	0	.0	0	.0	72	94.7	4	5.3	
FEMALE	0	.0	0	.0	0	.0	0	.0	0	.0	9	100.0	0	.0	
MALE	0	.0	0	.0	0	.0	0	.0	0	.0	63	94.0	4	6.0	
TOTAL	2	.2	0	.0	0	.0	0	.0	2	.2	1,001	97.8	21	2.1	
FEMALE	0	.0	0	.0	0	.0	0	.0	0	.0	130	100.0	0	.0	
MALE	2	.2	0	.0	0	.0	0	.0	2	.2	871	97.4	21	2.3	
UNCLASSIFIED:															
TOTAL	0	.0	0	.0	0	.0	0	.0	0	.0	11	100.0	0	.0	
FEMALE	0	.0	0	.0	0	.0	0	.0	0	.0	2	100.0	0	.0	
MALE	0	.0	0	.0	0	.0	0	.0	0	.0	9	100.0	0	.0	
TOTAL ENROLLMENT:															
TOTAL	2	.2	0	.0	0	.0	0	.0	2	.2	1,012	97.8	21	2.0	
FEMALE	0	.0	0	.0	0	.0	0	.0	0	.0	132	100.0	0	.0	
MALE	2	.2	0	.0	0	.0	0	.0	2	.2	880	97.5	21	2.3	

316

ENROLLMENT IN INSTITUTIONS OF HIGHER EDUCATION FOR SELECTED MAJOR FIELDS OF STUDY AND LEVEL OF ENROLLMENT, ETHNICITY, AND SEX: STATE, 1978

AGRICULTURE AND NATURAL RESOURCES

AMER INDIAN/NATIVE %	BLACK NON-HISPANIC NUMBER	%	ASIAN OR PACIFIC ISLANDER NUMBER	%	HISPANIC NUMBER	%	TOTAL MINORITY NUMBER	%	WHITE NON-HISPANIC NUMBER	%	NON-RESIDENT ALIEN NUMBER	%	TOTAL NUMBER
(13 INSTITUTIONS)													
.1	146	6.2	4	.2	1	.0	153	6.5	2,126	89.9	86	3.6	2,365
.2	23	4.1	2	.4	0	.0	26	4.7	520	93.5	10	1.8	556
.1	123	6.8	2	.1	1	.1	127	7.0	1,606	88.8	76	4.2	1,809
.0	2	1.0	0	.0	2	1.0	4	1.9	202	97.6	1	.5	207
.0	0	.0	0	.0	1	2.0	1	2.0	49	98.0	0	.0	50
.0	2	1.3	0	.0	1	.6	3	1.9	153	97.5	1	.6	157
.1	148	5.8	4	.2	3	.1	157	6.1	2,328	90.5	87	3.4	2,572
.2	23	3.8	2	.3	1	.2	27	4.5	569	93.9	10	1.7	606
.1	125	6.4	2	.1	2	.1	130	6.6	1,759	89.5	77	3.9	1,966
.6	4	2.5	3	1.9	0	.0	8	5.1	101	64.3	48	30.6	157
.0	1	3.4	0	.0	0	.0	1	3.4	22	75.9	6	20.7	29
.0	3	2.3	3	2.3	0	.0	7	5.5	79	61.7	42	32.8	128
.0	2	1.6	6	4.8	0	.0	8	6.4	104	83.2	13	10.4	125
.0	0	.0	3	9.4	0	.0	3	9.4	26	81.3	3	9.4	32
.0	2	2.2	3	3.2	0	.0	5	5.4	78	83.9	10	10.8	93
.4	6	2.1	9	3.2	0	.0	16	5.7	205	72.7	61	21.6	282
.0	1	1.6	3	4.9	0	.0	4	6.6	48	78.7	9	14.8	61
.5	5	2.3	6	2.7	0	.0	12	5.4	157	71.0	52	23.5	221
.0	0	.0	0	.0	0	.0	0	.0	0	.0	0	.0	0
.0	0	.0	0	.0	0	.0	0	.0	0	.0	0	.0	0
.0	0	.0	0	.0	0	.0	0	.0	0	.0	0	.0	0
.0	0	.0	0	.0	0	.0	0	.0	0	.0	0	.0	0
.0	0	.0	0	.0	0	.0	0	.0	0	.0	0	.0	0
.0	0	.0	0	.0	0	.0	0	.0	0	.0	0	.0	0
.0	0	.0	0	.0	0	.0	0	.0	0	.0	0	.0	0
.0	0	.0	0	.0	0	.0	0	.0	0	.0	0	.0	0
.0	0	.0	0	.0	0	.0	0	.0	0	.0	0	.0	0
.1	150	5.9	7	.3	1	.0	161	6.4	2,227	88.3	134	5.3	2,522
.2	24	4.1	2	.3	0	.0	27	4.6	542	92.6	16	2.7	585
.1	126	6.5	5	.3	1	.1	134	6.9	1,685	87.0	118	6.1	1,937
.0	4	1.2	6	1.8	2	.6	12	3.6	306	92.2	14	4.2	332
.0	0	.0	3	3.7	1	1.2	4	4.9	75	91.5	3	3.7	82
.0	4	1.6	3	1.2	1	.4	8	3.2	231	92.4	11	4.4	250
.1	154	5.4	13	.5	3	.1	173	6.1	2,533	88.8	148	5.2	2,854
.1	24	3.6	5	.7	1	.1	31	4.6	617	92.5	19	2.8	667
.1	130	5.9	8	.4	2	.1	142	6.5	1,916	87.6	129	5.9	2,187
.0	7	46.7	0	.0	0	.0	7	46.7	5	33.3	3	20.0	15
.0	0	.0	0	.0	0	.0	0	.0	1	50.0	1	50.0	2
.0	7	53.8	0	.0	0	.0	7	53.8	4	30.8	2	15.4	13
.1	161	5.6	13	.5	3	.1	180	6.3	2,538	88.5	151	5.3	2,869
.1	24	3.6	5	.7	1	.1	31	4.6	618	92.4	20	3.0	669
.1	137	6.2	8	.4	2	.1	149	6.8	1,920	87.3	131	6.0	2,200
(56 INSTITUTIONS)													
.3	158	1.9	21	.3	272	3.2	479	5.7	7,695	91.7	221	2.6	8,395
.4	22	1.0	4	.2	41	1.9	75	3.6	2,009	95.4	22	1.0	2,106
.3	136	2.2	17	.3	231	3.7	404	6.4	5,686	90.4	199	3.2	6,289
.2	15	1.8	1	.1	40	4.9	58	7.1	747	91.1	15	1.8	820
.0	1	.4	0	.0	6	2.6	7	3.1	218	95.6	3	1.3	228
.3	14	2.4	1	.2	34	5.7	51	8.6	529	89.4	12	2.0	592
.3	173	1.9	22	.2	312	3.4	537	5.8	8,442	91.6	236	2.6	9,215
.3	23	1.0	4	.2	47	2.0	82	3.5	2,227	95.4	25	1.1	2,334
.3	150	2.2	18	.3	265	3.9	455	6.6	6,215	90.3	211	3.1	6,881
.3	24	2.8	23	2.7	20	2.3	70	8.1	651	75.7	139	16.2	860
.3	5	3.5	3	2.1	4	2.8	12	8.4	119	83.2	12	8.4	143
.4	19	2.6	20	2.8	16	2.2	58	8.1	532	74.2	127	17.7	717
1.6	7	1.8	2	.5	6	1.6	21	5.5	330	87.1	28	7.4	379
1.9	2	3.8	0	.0	0	.0	3	5.8	47	90.4	2	3.8	52
1.5	5	1.5	2	.6	6	1.8	18	5.5	283	86.5	26	8.0	327
.7	31	2.5	25	2.0	26	2.1	91	7.3	981	79.2	167	13.5	1,239
.5	7	3.6	3	1.5	4	2.1	15	7.7	166	85.1	14	7.2	195
.8	24	2.3	22	2.1	22	2.1	76	7.3	815	78.1	153	14.7	1,044
.0	0	.0	0	.0	0	.0	0	.0	0	.0	0	.0	0
.0	0	.0	0	.0	0	.0	0	.0	0	.0	0	.0	0
.0	0	.0	0	.0	0	.0	0	.0	0	.0	0	.0	0

TABLE 17 - TOTAL ENROLLMENT IN INSTITUTIONS OF HIGHER EDUCATION FOR SELECTED MAJOR FIELDS OF STUDY AND LEVEL OF ENROLLMENT
BY RACE, ETHNICITY, AND SEX: STATE, 1978

MAJOR FIELD 0100 - AGRICULTURE AND NATURAL RESOURCES

	AMERICAN INDIAN ALASKAN NATIVE		BLACK NON-HISPANIC		ASIAN OR PACIFIC ISLANDER		HISPANIC		TOTAL MINORITY		WHITE NON-HISPANIC		NON-RESIDENT ALIEN	
	NUMBER	%	NUMBER	%	NUMBER	%	NUMBER	%	NUMBER	%	NUMBER	%	NUMBER	%
TEXAS	CONTINUED													
PROFESSIONAL:														
PART-TIME	0	.0	0	.0	0	.0	0	.0	0	.0	0	.0	0	.0
FEMALE	0	.0	0	.0	0	.0	0	.0	0	.0	0	.0	0	.0
MALE	0	.0	0	.0	0	.0	0	.0	0	.0	0	.0	0	.0
TOTAL	0	.0	0	.0	0	.0	0	.0	0	.0	0	.0	0	.0
FEMALE	0	.0	0	.0	0	.0	0	.0	0	.0	0	.0	0	.0
MALE	0	.0	0	.0	0	.0	0	.0	0	.0	0	.0	0	.0
UNC+GRAD+PROF:														
FULL-TIME	31	.3	182	2.0	44	.5	292	3.2	549	5.9	8,346	90.2	360	3.9
FEMALE	8	.4	27	1.2	7	.3	45	2.0	87	3.9	2,128	94.6	34	1.5
MALE	23	.3	155	2.2	37	.5	247	3.5	462	6.6	6,218	88.8	326	4.7
PART-TIME	8	.7	22	1.8	3	.3	46	3.8	79	6.6	1,077	89.8	43	3.6
FEMALE	1	.4	3	1.1	0	.0	6	2.1	10	3.6	265	94.6	5	1.8
MALE	7	.8	19	2.1	3	.3	40	4.4	69	7.5	812	88.4	38	4.1
TOTAL	39	.4	204	2.0	47	.5	338	3.2	628	6.0	9,423	90.1	403	3.9
FEMALE	9	.4	30	1.2	7	.3	51	2.0	97	3.8	2,393	94.6	39	1.5
MALE	30	.4	174	2.2	40	.5	287	3.6	531	6.7	7,030	88.7	364	4.6
UNCLASSIFIED:														
TOTAL	0	.0	6	1.8	0	.0	1	.3	7	2.1	313	95.4	8	2.4
FEMALE	0	.0	0	.0	0	.0	0	.0	0	.0	64	97.0	2	3.0
MALE	0	.0	6	2.3	0	.0	1	.4	7	2.7	249	95.0	6	2.3
TOTAL ENROLLMENT:														
TOTAL	39	.4	210	1.9	47	.4	339	3.1	635	5.9	9,736	90.3	411	3.8
FEMALE	9	.3	30	1.2	7	.3	51	2.0	97	3.7	2,457	94.7	41	1.6
MALE	30	.4	180	2.2	40	.5	288	3.5	538	6.6	7,279	88.9	370	4.5
UTAH	(	4 INSTITUTIONS)												
UNDERGRADUATES:														
FULL-TIME	6	.4	6	.4	12	.8	9	.6	33	2.3	1,321	92.8	70	4.9
FEMALE	4	1.1	2	.6	4	1.1	1	.3	11	3.2	326	93.4	12	3.4
MALE	2	.2	4	.4	8	.7	8	.7	22	2.0	995	92.6	58	5.4
PART-TIME	0	.0	0	.0	0	.0	1	1.1	1	1.1	83	93.3	5	5.6
FEMALE	0	.0	0	.0	0	.0	0	.0	0	.0	26	96.3	1	3.7
MALE	0	.0	0	.0	0	.0	1	1.6	1	1.6	57	91.9	4	6.5
TOTAL	6	.4	6	.4	12	.8	10	.7	34	2.2	1,404	92.8	75	5.0
FEMALE	4	1.1	2	.5	4	1.1	1	.3	11	2.9	352	93.6	13	3.5
MALE	2	.2	4	.4	8	.7	9	.8	23	2.0	1,052	92.5	62	5.5
GRADUATE:														
FULL-TIME	0	.0	0	.0	0	.0	0	.0	0	.0	126	81.3	29	18.7
FEMALE	0	.0	0	.0	0	.0	0	.0	0	.0	27	100.0	0	.0
MALE	0	.0	0	.0	0	.0	0	.0	0	.0	99	77.3	29	22.7
PART-TIME	0	.0	0	.0	1	.8	0	.0	1	.8	100	76.9	29	22.3
FEMALE	0	.0	0	.0	0	.0	0	.0	0	.0	18	64.3	10	35.7
MALE	0	.0	0	.0	1	1.0	0	.0	1	1.0	82	80.4	19	18.6
TOTAL	0	.0	0	.0	1	.4	0	.0	1	.4	226	79.3	58	20.4
FEMALE	0	.0	0	.0	0	.0	0	.0	0	.0	45	81.8	10	18.2
MALE	0	.0	0	.0	1	.4	0	.0	1	.4	181	78.7	48	20.9
PROFESSIONAL:														
FULL-TIME	0	.0	0	.0	0	.0	0	.0	0	.0	0	.0	0	.0
FEMALE	0	.0	0	.0	0	.0	0	.0	0	.0	0	.0	0	.0
MALE	0	.0	0	.0	0	.0	0	.0	0	.0	0	.0	0	.0
PART-TIME	0	.0	0	.0	0	.0	0	.0	0	.0	0	.0	0	.0
FEMALE	0	.0	0	.0	0	.0	0	.0	0	.0	0	.0	0	.0
MALE	0	.0	0	.0	0	.0	0	.0	0	.0	0	.0	0	.0
TOTAL	0	.0	0	.0	0	.0	0	.0	0	.0	0	.0	0	.0
FEMALE	0	.0	0	.0	0	.0	0	.0	0	.0	0	.0	0	.0
MALE	0	.0	0	.0	0	.0	0	.0	0	.0	0	.0	0	.0
UND+GRAD+PROF:														
FULL-TIME	6	.4	6	.4	12	.8	9	.6	33	2.1	1,447	91.6	99	6.3
FEMALE	4	1.1	2	.5	4	1.1	1	.3	11	2.9	353	93.9	12	3.2
MALE	2	.2	4	.3	8	.7	8	.7	22	1.8	1,094	90.9	87	7.2
PART-TIME	0	.0	0	.0	1	.5	1	.5	2	.9	183	83.6	34	15.5
FEMALE	0	.0	0	.0	0	.0	0	.0	0	.0	44	80.0	11	20.0
MALE	0	.0	0	.0	1	.6	1	.6	2	1.2	139	84.8	23	14.0
TOTAL	6	.3	6	.3	13	.7	10	.6	35	1.9	1,630	90.7	133	7.4
FEMALE	4	.9	2	.5	4	.9	1	.2	11	2.6	397	92.1	23	5.3
MALE	2	.1	4	.3	9	.7	9	.7	24	1.8	1,233	90.2	110	8.0
UNCLASSIFIED:														
TOTAL	0	.0	0	.0	0	.0	0	.0	0	.0	1	50.0	1	50.0
FEMALE	0	.0	0	.0	0	.0	0	.0	0	.0	1	100.0	0	.0
MALE	0	.0	0	.0	0	.0	0	.0	0	.0	0	.0	1	100.0
TOTAL ENROLLMENT:														
TOTAL	6	.3	6	.3	13	.7	10	.6	35	1.9	1,631	90.6	134	7.4
FEMALE	4	.9	2	.5	4	.9	1	.2	11	2.5	398	92.1	23	5.3
MALE	2	.1	4	.3	9	.7	9	.7	24	1.8	1,233	90.1	111	8.1

17 - TOTAL ENROLLMENT IN INSTITUTIONS OF HIGHER EDUCATION FOR SELECTED MAJOR FIELDS OF STUDY AND LEVEL OF ENROLLMENT BY RACE, ETHNICITY, AND SEX: STATE, 1978

FIELD 0100 - AGRICULTURE AND NATURAL RESOURCES

	AMERICAN INDIAN ALASKAN NATIVE		BLACK NON-HISPANIC		ASIAN OR PACIFIC ISLANDER		HISPANIC		TOTAL MINORITY		WHITE NON-HISPANIC		NON-RESIDENT ALIEN		TOTAL
	NUMBER	%	NUMBER	%	NUMBER	%	NUMBER	%	NUMBER	%	NUMBER	%	NUMBER	%	NUMBER

HT   (4 INSTITUTIONS)

GRADUATES:

TIME	0	.0	2	.2	0	.0	0	.0	2	.2	1,007	99.6	2	.2	1,011
MALE	0	.0	2	.5	0	.0	0	.0	2	.5	413	99.5	0	.0	415
MALE	0	.0	0	.0	0	.0	0	.0	0	.0	594	99.7	2	.3	596
TIME	0	.0	0	.0	0	.0	0	.0	0	.0	45	100.0	0	.0	45
MALE	0	.0	0	.0	0	.0	0	.0	0	.0	20	100.0	0	.0	20
MALE	0	.0	0	.0	0	.0	0	.0	0	.0	25	100.0	0	.0	25
	0	.0	2	.2	0	.0	0	.0	2	.2	1,052	99.6	2	.2	1,056
MALE	0	.0	2	.5	0	.0	0	.0	2	.5	433	99.5	0	.0	435
MALE	0	.0	0	.0	0	.0	0	.0	0	.0	619	99.7	2	.3	621

ATE:

TIME	0	.0	0	.0	0	.0	0	.0	0	.0	31	93.9	2	6.1	33
MALE	0	.0	0	.0	0	.0	0	.0	0	.0	11	100.0	0	.0	11
MALE	0	.0	0	.0	0	.0	0	.0	0	.0	20	90.9	2	9.1	22
TIME	0	.0	0	.0	0	.0	0	.0	0	.0	24	100.0	0	.0	24
MALE	0	.0	0	.0	0	.0	0	.0	0	.0	6	100.0	0	.0	6
MALE	0	.0	0	.0	0	.0	0	.0	0	.0	18	100.0	0	.0	18
	0	.0	0	.0	0	.0	0	.0	0	.0	55	96.5	2	3.5	57
MALE	0	.0	0	.0	0	.0	0	.0	0	.0	17	100.0	0	.0	17
MALE	0	.0	0	.0	0	.0	0	.0	0	.0	38	95.0	2	5.0	40

SSIONAL:

TIME	0	.0	0	.0	0	.0	0	.0	0	.0	0	.0	0	.0	0
MALE	0	.0	0	.0	0	.0	0	.0	0	.0	0	.0	0	.0	0
MALE	0	.0	0	.0	0	.0	0	.0	0	.0	0	.0	0	.0	0
TIME	0	.0	0	.0	0	.0	0	.0	0	.0	0	.0	0	.0	0
MALE	0	.0	0	.0	0	.0	0	.0	0	.0	0	.0	0	.0	0
MALE	0	.0	0	.0	0	.0	0	.0	0	.0	0	.0	0	.0	0
	0	.0	0	.0	0	.0	0	.0	0	.0	0	.0	0	.0	0
MALE	0	.0	0	.0	0	.0	0	.0	0	.0	0	.0	0	.0	0
MALE	0	.0	0	.0	0	.0	0	.0	0	.0	0	.0	0	.0	0

RAD+PROF:

TIME	0	.0	2	.2	0	.0	0	.0	2	.2	1,038	99.4	4	.4	1,044
MALE	0	.0	2	.5	0	.0	0	.0	2	.5	424	99.5	0	.0	426
MALE	0	.0	0	.0	0	.0	0	.0	0	.0	614	99.4	4	.6	618
TIME	0	.0	0	.0	0	.0	0	.0	0	.0	69	100.0	0	.0	69
MALE	0	.0	0	.0	0	.0	0	.0	0	.0	26	100.0	0	.0	26
MALE	0	.0	0	.0	0	.0	0	.0	0	.0	43	100.0	0	.0	43
	0	.0	2	.2	0	.0	0	.0	2	.2	1,107	99.5	4	.4	1,113
MALE	0	.0	2	.4	0	.0	0	.0	2	.4	450	99.6	0	.0	452
MALE	0	.0	0	.0	0	.0	0	.0	0	.0	657	99.4	4	.6	661

SSIFIED:

	0	.0	0	.0	0	.0	0	.0	0	.0	0	.0	0	.0	0
MALE	0	.0	0	.0	0	.0	0	.0	0	.0	0	.0	0	.0	0
MALE	0	.0	0	.0	0	.0	0	.0	0	.0	0	.0	0	.0	0

ENROLLMENT:

	0	.0	2	.2	0	.0	0	.0	2	.2	1,107	99.5	4	.4	1,113
MALE	0	.0	2	.4	0	.0	0	.0	2	.4	450	99.6	0	.0	452
MALE	0	.0	0	.0	0	.0	0	.0	0	.0	657	99.4	4	.6	661

NIA   (6 INSTITUTIONS)

GRADUATES:

TIME	2	.1	36	1.6	4	.2	3	.1	45	2.0	2,162	97.3	16	.7	2,223
MALE	2	.2	11	1.2	2	.2	3	.3	18	2.0	899	97.5	5	.5	922
MALE	0	.0	25	1.9	2	.2	0	.0	27	2.1	1,263	97.1	11	.8	1,301
TIME	0	.0	5	3.8	0	.0	0	.0	5	3.8	128	96.2	0	.0	133
MALE	0	.0	1	1.8	0	.0	0	.0	1	1.8	56	98.2	0	.0	57
MALE	0	.0	4	5.3	0	.0	0	.0	4	5.3	72	94.7	0	.0	76
	2	.1	41	1.7	4	.2	3	.1	50	2.1	2,290	97.2	16	.7	2,356
MALE	2	.2	12	1.2	2	.2	3	.3	19	1.9	955	97.5	5	.5	979
MALE	0	.0	29	2.1	2	.1	0	.0	31	2.3	1,335	96.9	11	.8	1,377

ATE:

TIME	0	.0	1	.4	5	2.0	0	.0	6	2.4	230	91.6	15	6.0	251
MALE	0	.0	0	.0	1	2.3	0	.0	1	2.3	42	95.5	1	2.3	44
MALE	0	.0	1	.5	4	1.9	0	.0	5	2.4	188	90.8	14	6.8	207
TIME	0	.0	1	1.4	1	1.4	0	.0	2	2.7	71	95.9	1	1.4	74
MALE	0	.0	0	.0	0	.0	0	.0	0	.0	8	100.0	0	.0	8
MALE	0	.0	1	1.5	1	1.5	0	.0	2	3.0	63	95.5	1	1.5	66
	0	.0	2	.6	6	1.8	0	.0	8	2.5	301	92.6	16	4.9	325
MALE	0	.0	0	.0	1	1.9	0	.0	1	1.9	50	96.2	1	1.9	52
MALE	0	.0	2	.7	5	1.8	0	.0	7	2.6	251	91.9	15	5.5	273

SSIONAL:

TIME	0	.0	0	.0	0	.0	0	.0	0	.0	0	.0	0	.0	0
MALE	0	.0	0	.0	0	.0	0	.0	0	.0	0	.0	0	.0	0
MALE	0	.0	0	.0	0	.0	0	.0	0	.0	0	.0	0	.0	0

MAJOR FIELD 0100 - AGRICULTURE AND NATURAL RESOURCES

	AMERICAN INDIAN ALASKAN NATIVE		BLACK NON-HISPANIC		ASIAN OR PACIFIC ISLANDER		HISPANIC		TOTAL MINORITY		WHITE NON-HISPANIC		NON-RESIDENT ALIEN	
	NUMBER	%	NUMBER	%	NUMBER	%	NUMBER	%	NUMBER	%	NUMBER	%	NUMBER	%
VIRGINIA	CONTINUED													
PROFESSIONAL:														
PART-TIME	0	.0	0	.0	0	.0	0	.0	0	.0	0	.0	0	.0
FEMALE	0	.0	0	.0	0	.0	0	.0	0	.0	0	.0	0	.0
MALE	0	.0	0	.0	0	.0	0	.0	0	.0	0	.0	0	.0
TOTAL	0	.0	0	.0	0	.0	0	.0	0	.0	0	.0	0	.0
FEMALE	0	.0	0	.0	0	.0	0	.0	0	.0	0	.0	0	.0
MALE	0	.0	0	.0	0	.0	0	.0	0	.0	0	.0	0	.0
UND+GRAD+PROF:														
FULL-TIME	2	.1	37	1.5	9	.4	3	.1	51	2.1	2,392	96.7	31	1.3
FEMALE	2	.2	11	1.1	3	.3	3	.3	19	2.0	941	97.4	6	.6
MALE	0	.0	26	1.7	6	.4	0	.0	32	2.1	1,451	96.2	25	1.7
PART-TIME	0	.0	6	2.9	1	.5	0	.0	7	3.4	199	96.1	1	.5
FEMALE	0	.0	1	1.5	0	.0	0	.0	1	1.5	64	98.5	0	.0
MALE	0	.0	5	3.5	1	.7	0	.0	6	4.2	135	95.1	1	.7
TOTAL	2	.1	43	1.6	10	.4	3	.1	58	2.2	2,591	96.6	32	1.2
FEMALE	2	.2	12	1.2	3	.3	3	.3	20	1.9	1,005	97.5	6	.6
MALE	0	.0	31	1.9	7	.4	0	.0	38	2.3	1,586	96.1	26	1.6
UNCLASSIFIED:														
TOTAL	0	.0	0	.0	0	.0	0	.0	0	.0	25	86.2	4	13.8
FEMALE	0	.0	0	.0	0	.0	0	.0	0	.0	11	91.7	1	8.3
MALE	0	.0	0	.0	0	.0	0	.0	0	.0	14	82.4	3	17.6
TOTAL ENROLLMENT:														
TOTAL	2	.1	43	1.6	10	.4	3	.1	58	2.1	2,616	96.5	36	1.3
FEMALE	2	.2	12	1.2	3	.3	3	.3	20	1.9	1,016	97.4	7	.7
MALE	0	.0	31	1.9	7	.4	0	.0	38	2.3	1,600	96.0	29	1.7
WASHINGTON	(	4 INSTITUTIONS)												
UNDERGRADUATES:														
FULL-TIME	11	.7	7	.4	32	2.0	8	.5	58	3.7	1,484	93.9	38	2.4
FEMALE	2	.5	1	.2	7	1.7	2	.5	12	2.9	399	95.5	7	1.7
MALE	9	.8	6	.5	25	2.2	6	.5	46	4.0	1,085	93.4	31	2.7
PART-TIME	2	1.9	1	1.0	4	3.8	1	1.0	8	7.7	92	88.5	4	3.8
FEMALE	1	4.2	0	.0	0	.0	1	4.2	2	8.3	22	91.7	0	.0
MALE	1	1.3	1	1.3	4	5.0	0	.0	6	7.5	70	87.5	4	5.0
TOTAL	13	.8	8	.5	36	2.1	9	.5	66	3.9	1,576	93.6	42	2.5
FEMALE	3	.7	1	.2	7	1.6	3	.7	14	3.2	421	95.2	7	1.6
MALE	10	.8	7	.6	29	2.3	6	.5	52	4.2	1,155	93.0	35	2.8
GRADUATE:														
FULL-TIME	4	.6	2	.3	6	.9	3	.5	15	2.3	476	73.9	153	23.8
FEMALE	1	.8	1	.8	2	1.7	1	.8	5	4.2	99	83.9	14	11.9
MALE	3	.6	1	.2	4	.8	2	.4	10	1.9	377	71.7	139	26.4
PART-TIME	0	.0	0	.0	2	.8	0	.0	2	.8	218	90.1	22	9.1
FEMALE	0	.0	0	.0	2	3.4	0	.0	2	3.4	53	91.4	3	5.2
MALE	0	.0	0	.0	0	.0	0	.0	0	.0	165	89.7	19	10.3
TOTAL	4	.5	2	.2	8	.9	3	.3	17	1.9	694	78.3	175	19.8
FEMALE	1	.6	1	.6	4	2.3	1	.6	7	4.0	152	86.4	17	9.7
MALE	3	.4	1	.1	4	.6	2	.3	10	1.4	542	76.3	158	22.3
PROFESSIONAL:														
FULL-TIME	0	.0	0	.0	0	.0	0	.0	0	.0	0	.0	0	.0
FEMALE	0	.0	0	.0	0	.0	0	.0	0	.0	0	.0	0	.0
MALE	0	.0	0	.0	0	.0	0	.0	0	.0	0	.0	0	.0
PART-TIME	0	.0	0	.0	0	.0	0	.0	0	.0	0	.0	0	.0
FEMALE	0	.0	0	.0	0	.0	0	.0	0	.0	0	.0	0	.0
MALE	0	.0	0	.0	0	.0	0	.0	0	.0	0	.0	0	.0
TOTAL	0	.0	0	.0	0	.0	0	.0	0	.0	0	.0	0	.0
FEMALE	0	.0	0	.0	0	.0	0	.0	0	.0	0	.0	0	.0
MALE	0	.0	0	.0	0	.0	0	.0	0	.0	0	.0	0	.0
UND+GRAD+PROF:														
FULL-TIME	15	.7	9	.4	38	1.7	11	.5	73	3.3	1,960	88.1	191	8.6
FEMALE	3	.6	2	.4	9	1.7	3	.6	17	3.2	498	92.9	21	3.9
MALE	12	.7	7	.4	29	1.7	8	.5	56	3.3	1,462	86.6	170	10.1
PART-TIME	2	.6	1	.3	6	1.7	1	.3	10	2.9	310	89.6	26	7.5
FEMALE	1	1.2	0	.0	2	2.4	1	1.2	4	4.9	75	91.5	3	3.7
MALE	1	.4	1	.4	4	1.5	0	.0	6	2.3	235	89.0	23	8.7
TOTAL	17	.7	10	.4	44	1.7	12	.5	83	3.2	2,270	88.3	217	8.4
FEMALE	4	.6	2	.3	11	1.8	4	.6	21	3.4	573	92.7	24	3.9
MALE	13	.7	8	.4	33	1.7	8	.4	62	3.2	1,697	86.9	193	9.9
UNCLASSIFIED:														
TOTAL	0	.0	0	.0	2	3.0	0	.0	2	3.0	56	84.8	8	12.1
FEMALE	0	.0	0	.0	0	.0	0	.0	0	.0	15	88.2	2	11.8
MALE	0	.0	0	.0	2	4.1	0	.0	2	4.1	41	83.7	6	12.2
TOTAL ENROLLMENT:														
TOTAL	17	.6	10	.4	46	1.7	12	.5	85	3.2	2,326	88.2	225	8.5
FEMALE	4	.6	2	.3	11	1.7	4	.6	21	3.3	588	92.6	26	4.1
MALE	13	.6	8	.4	35	1.7	8	.4	64	3.2	1,738	86.9	199	9.9

00 - AGRICULTURE AND NATURAL RESOURCES

RICAN INDIAN SKAN NATIVE		BLACK NON-HISPANIC		ASIAN OR PACIFIC ISLANDER		HISPANIC		TOTAL MINORITY		WHITE NON-HISPANIC		NON-RESIDENT ALIEN		TOTAL
MBER	%	NUMBER	%	NUMBER	%	NUMBER	%	NUMBER	%	NUMBER	%	NUMBER	%	NUMBER
	(3 INSTITUTIONS)													
6	.4	8	.6	2	.1	17	1.2	33	2.3	1,384	96.7	14	1.0	1,431
0	.0	1	.3	2	.5	1	.3	4	1.0	374	98.2	3	.8	381
6	.6	7	.7	0	.0	16	1.5	29	2.8	1,010	96.2	11	1.0	1,050
1	.7	9	6.0	0	.0	1	.7	11	7.3	137	91.3	2	1.3	150
0	.0	1	2.7	0	.0	0	.0	1	2.7	35	94.6	1	2.7	37
1	.9	8	7.1	0	.0	1	.9	10	8.8	102	90.3	1	.9	113
7	.4	17	1.1	2	.1	18	1.1	44	2.8	1,521	96.2	16	1.0	1,581
0	.0	2	.5	2	.5	1	.2	5	1.2	409	97.8	4	1.0	418
7	.6	15	1.3	0	.0	17	1.5	39	3.4	1,112	95.6	12	1.0	1,163
1	1.1	1	1.1	0	.0	0	.0	2	2.3	68	77.3	18	20.5	88
0	.0	1	4.8	0	.0	0	.0	1	4.8	19	90.5	1	4.8	21
1	1.5	0	.0	0	.0	0	.0	1	1.5	49	73.1	17	25.4	67
0	.0	0	.0	0	.0	0	.0	0	.0	23	76.7	7	23.3	30
0	.0	0	.0	0	.0	0	.0	0	.0	5	83.3	1	16.7	6
0	.0	0	.0	0	.0	0	.0	0	.0	18	75.0	6	25.0	24
1	.8	1	.8	0	.0	0	.0	2	1.7	91	77.1	25	21.2	118
0	.0	1	3.7	0	.0	0	.0	1	3.7	24	88.9	2	7.4	27
1	1.1	0	.0	0	.0	0	.0	1	1.1	67	73.6	23	25.3	91
0	.0	0	.0	0	.0	0	.0	0	.0	0	.0	0	.0	0
0	.0	0	.0	0	.0	0	.0	0	.0	0	.0	0	.0	0
0	.0	0	.0	0	.0	0	.0	0	.0	0	.0	0	.0	0
0	.0	0	.0	0	.0	0	.0	0	.0	0	.0	0	.0	0
0	.0	0	.0	0	.0	0	.0	0	.0	0	.0	0	.0	0
0	.0	0	.0	0	.0	0	.0	0	.0	0	.0	0	.0	0
0	.0	0	.0	0	.0	0	.0	0	.0	0	.0	0	.0	0
0	.0	0	.0	0	.0	0	.0	0	.0	0	.0	0	.0	0
0	.0	0	.0	0	.0	0	.0	0	.0	0	.0	0	.0	0
7	.5	9	.6	2	.1	17	1.1	35	2.3	1,452	95.6	32	2.1	1,519
0	.0	2	.5	2	.5	1	.2	5	1.2	393	97.8	4	1.0	402
7	.6	7	.6	0	.0	16	1.4	30	2.7	1,059	94.8	28	2.5	1,117
1	.6	9	5.0	0	.0	1	.6	11	6.1	160	88.9	9	5.0	180
0	.0	1	2.3	0	.0	0	.0	1	2.3	40	93.0	2	4.7	43
1	.7	8	5.8	0	.0	1	.7	10	7.3	120	87.6	7	5.1	137
8	.5	18	1.1	2	.1	18	1.1	46	2.7	1,612	94.9	41	2.4	1,699
0	.0	3	.7	2	.4	1	.2	6	1.3	433	97.3	6	1.3	445
8	.6	15	1.2	0	.0	17	1.4	40	3.2	1,179	94.0	35	2.8	1,254
1	3.1	0	.0	0	.0	3	9.4	4	12.5	28	87.5	0	.0	32
0	.0	0	.0	0	.0	0	.0	0	.0	4	100.0	0	.0	4
1	3.6	0	.0	0	.0	3	10.7	4	14.3	24	85.7	0	.0	28
T1														
9	.5	18	1.0	2	.1	21	1.2	50	2.9	1,640	94.7	41	2.4	1,731
0	.0	3	.7	2	.4	1	.2	6	1.3	437	97.3	6	1.3	449
9	.7	15	1.2	0	.0	20	1.6	44	3.4	1,203	93.8	35	2.7	1,282
	(13 INSTITUTIONS)													
33	.7	7	.2	5	.1	13	.3	58	1.3	4,313	97.6	49	1.1	4,420
8	.6	1	.1	0	.0	1	.1	10	.8	1,219	98.5	9	.7	1,238
25	.8	6	.2	5	.2	12	.4	48	1.5	3,094	97.2	40	1.3	3,182
1	.1	1	.1	0	.0	1	.1	3	.3	918	99.7	0	.0	921
0	.0	0	.0	0	.0	0	.0	0	.0	126	100.0	0	.0	126
1	.1	1	.1	0	.0	1	.1	3	.4	792	99.6	0	.0	795
34	.6	8	.1	5	.1	14	.3	61	1.1	5,231	97.9	49	.9	5,341
8	.6	1	.1	0	.0	1	.1	10	.7	1,345	98.6	9	.7	1,364
26	.7	7	.2	5	.1	13	.3	51	1.3	3,886	97.7	40	1.0	3,977
0	.0	6	1.3	6	1.3	3	.7	15	3.3	324	70.4	121	26.3	460
0	.0	2	2.5	0	.0	2	2.5	4	5.0	63	77.8	16	19.8	81
0	.0	6	1.6	6	1.6	1	.3	13	3.4	261	68.9	105	27.7	379
2	2.1	2	2.1	1	1.1	0	.0	5	5.3	78	83.0	11	11.7	94
0	.0	0	.0	0	.0	0	.0	0	.0	22	91.7	2	8.3	24
2	2.9	2	2.9	1	1.4	0	.0	5	7.1	56	80.0	9	12.9	70
2	.4	8	1.4	7	1.3	3	.5	20	3.6	402	72.6	132	23.8	554
0	.0	0	.0	0	.0	2	1.9	2	1.9	85	81.0	18	17.1	105
2	.4	8	1.8	7	1.6	1	.2	18	4.0	317	70.6	114	25.4	449
0	.0	0	.0	0	.0	0	.0	0	.0	0	.0	0	.0	0
0	.0	0	.0	0	.0	0	.0	0	.0	0	.0	0	.0	0
0	.0	0	.0	0	.0	0	.0	0	.0	0	.0	0	.0	0

TABLE 17 - TOTAL ENROLLMENT IN INSTITUTIONS OF HIGHER EDUCATION FOR SELECTED MAJOR FIELDS OF STUDY AND LEVEL OF ENROLLMENT BY RACE, ETHNICITY, AND SEX: STATE, 1978

MAJOR FIELD 0100 - AGRICULTURE AND NATURAL RESOURCES

	AMERICAN INDIAN ALASKAN NATIVE		BLACK NON-HISPANIC		ASIAN OR PACIFIC ISLANDER		HISPANIC		TOTAL MINORITY		WHITE NON-HISPANIC		NON-RESIDENT ALIEN	
	NUMBER	%	NUMBER	%	NUMBER	%	NUMBER	%	NUMBER	%	NUMBER	%	NUMBER	%
WISCONSIN CONTINUED														
PROFESSIONAL:														
PART-TIME	0	.0	0	.0	0	.0	0	.0	0	.0	0	.0	0	.0
FEMALE	0	.0	0	.0	0	.0	0	.0	0	.0	0	.0	0	.0
MALE	0	.0	0	.0	0	.0	0	.0	0	.0	0	.0	0	.0
TOTAL	0	.0	0	.0	0	.0	0	.0	0	.0	0	.0	0	.0
FEMALE	0	.0	0	.0	0	.0	0	.0	0	.0	0	.0	0	.0
MALE	0	.0	0	.0	0	.0	0	.0	0	.0	0	.0	0	.0
UND+GRAD+PROF:														
FULL-TIME	33	.7	13	.3	11	.2	16	.3	73	1.5	4,637	95.0	170	3.5
FEMALE	8	.6	1	.1	0	.0	3	.2	12	.9	1,282	97.2	25	1.9
MALE	25	.7	12	.3	11	.3	13	.4	61	1.7	3,355	94.2	145	4.1
PART-TIME	3	.3	3	.3	1	.1	1	.1	8	.8	996	98.1	11	1.1
FEMALE	0	.0	0	.0	0	.0	0	.0	0	.0	148	98.7	2	1.3
MALE	3	.3	3	.3	1	.1	1	.1	8	.9	848	98.0	9	1.0
TOTAL	36	.6	16	.3	12	.2	17	.3	81	1.4	5,633	95.6	181	3.1
FEMALE	8	.5	1	.1	0	.0	3	.2	12	.8	1,430	97.3	27	1.8
MALE	28	.6	15	.3	12	.3	14	.3	69	1.6	4,203	95.0	154	3.5
UNCLASSIFIED:														
TOTAL	1	2.7	0	.0	0	.0	0	.0	1	2.7	34	91.9	2	5.4
FEMALE	0	.0	0	.0	0	.0	0	.0	0	.0	9	100.0	0	.0
MALE	1	3.6	0	.0	0	.0	0	.0	1	3.6	25	89.3	2	7.1
TOTAL ENROLLMENT:														
TOTAL	37	.6	16	.3	12	.2	17	.3	82	1.4	5,667	95.5	183	3.1
FEMALE	8	.5	1	.1	0	.0	3	.2	12	.8	1,439	97.4	27	1.8
MALE	29	.7	15	.3	12	.3	14	.3	70	1.6	4,228	94.9	156	3.5
WYOMING (5 INSTITUTIONS)														
UNDERGRADUATES:														
FULL-TIME	3	.5	0	.0	2	.3	2	.3	7	1.1	630	96.3	17	2.6
FEMALE	2	1.2	0	.0	0	.0	1	.6	3	1.8	162	96.4	3	1.8
MALE	1	.2	0	.0	2	.4	1	.2	4	.8	468	96.3	14	2.9
PART-TIME	0	.0	0	.0	0	.0	0	.0	0	.0	56	100.0	0	.0
FEMALE	0	.0	0	.0	0	.0	0	.0	0	.0	16	100.0	0	.0
MALE	0	.0	0	.0	0	.0	0	.0	0	.0	40	100.0	0	.0
TOTAL	3	.4	0	.0	2	.3	2	.3	7	1.0	686	96.6	17	2.4
FEMALE	2	1.1	0	.0	0	.0	1	.5	3	1.6	178	96.7	3	1.6
MALE	1	.2	0	.0	2	.4	1	.2	4	.8	508	96.6	14	2.7
GRADUATE:														
FULL-TIME	0	.0	0	.0	0	.0	0	.0	0	.0	30	93.8	2	6.3
FEMALE	0	.0	0	.0	0	.0	0	.0	0	.0	4	80.0	1	20.0
MALE	0	.0	0	.0	0	.0	0	.0	0	.0	26	96.3	1	3.7
PART-TIME	0	.0	0	.0	0	.0	1	2.9	1	2.9	25	73.5	8	23.5
FEMALE	0	.0	0	.0	0	.0	0	.0	0	.0	4	80.0	1	20.0
MALE	0	.0	0	.0	0	.0	1	3.4	1	3.4	21	72.4	7	24.1
TOTAL	0	.0	0	.0	0	.0	1	1.5	1	1.5	55	83.3	10	15.2
FEMALE	0	.0	0	.0	0	.0	0	.0	0	.0	8	80.0	2	20.0
MALE	0	.0	0	.0	0	.0	1	1.8	1	1.8	47	83.9	8	14.3
PROFESSIONAL:														
FULL-TIME	0	.0	0	.0	0	.0	0	.0	0	.0	0	.0	0	.0
FEMALE	0	.0	0	.0	0	.0	0	.0	0	.0	0	.0	0	.0
MALE	0	.0	0	.0	0	.0	0	.0	0	.0	0	.0	0	.0
PART-TIME	0	.0	0	.0	0	.0	0	.0	0	.0	0	.0	0	.0
FEMALE	0	.0	0	.0	0	.0	0	.0	0	.0	0	.0	0	.0
MALE	0	.0	0	.0	0	.0	0	.0	0	.0	0	.0	0	.0
TOTAL	0	.0	0	.0	0	.0	0	.0	0	.0	0	.0	0	.0
FEMALE	0	.0	0	.0	0	.0	0	.0	0	.0	0	.0	0	.0
MALE	0	.0	0	.0	0	.0	0	.0	0	.0	0	.0	0	.0
UND+GRAD+PROF:														
FULL-TIME	3	.4	0	.0	2	.3	2	.3	7	1.0	660	96.2	19	2.8
FEMALE	2	1.2	0	.0	0	.0	1	.6	3	1.7	166	96.0	4	2.3
MALE	1	.2	0	.0	2	.4	1	.2	4	.8	494	96.3	15	2.9
PART-TIME	0	.0	0	.0	0	.0	1	1.1	1	1.1	81	90.0	8	8.9
FEMALE	0	.0	0	.0	0	.0	0	.0	0	.0	20	95.2	1	4.8
MALE	0	.0	0	.0	0	.0	1	1.4	1	1.4	61	88.4	7	10.1
TOTAL	3	.4	0	.0	2	.3	3	.4	8	1.0	741	95.5	27	3.5
FEMALE	2	1.0	0	.0	0	.0	1	.5	3	1.5	186	95.9	5	2.6
MALE	1	.2	0	.0	2	.3	2	.3	5	.9	555	95.4	22	3.8
UNCLASSIFIED:														
TOTAL	0	.0	0	.0	0	.0	0	.0	0	.0	7	87.5	1	12.5
FEMALE	0	.0	0	.0	0	.0	0	.0	0	.0	1	100.0	0	.0
MALE	0	.0	0	.0	0	.0	0	.0	0	.0	6	85.7	1	14.3
TOTAL ENROLLMENT:														
TOTAL	3	.4	0	.0	2	.3	3	.4	8	1.0	748	95.4	28	3.6
FEMALE	2	1.0	0	.0	0	.0	1	.5	3	1.5	187	95.9	5	2.6
MALE	1	.2	0	.0	2	.3	2	.3	5	.8	561	95.2	23	3.9

AGRICULTURE AND NATURAL RESOURCES

N INDIAN NATIVE	BLACK NON-HISPANIC		ASIAN OR PACIFIC ISLANDER		HISPANIC		TOTAL MINORITY		WHITE NON-HISPANIC		NON-RESIDENT ALIEN		TOTAL
%	NUMBER	%	NUMBER	%	NUMBER	%	NUMBER	%	NUMBER	%	NUMBER	%	NUMBER
(566 INSTITUTIONS)													
.5	2,336	2.1	1,226	1.1	1,539	1.4	5,700	5.0	105,710	93.0	2,220	2.0	113,630
.5	668	2.0	472	1.4	343	1.0	1,651	4.9	31,975	94.2	315	.9	33,941
.5	1,668	2.1	754	.9	1,196	1.5	4,049	5.1	73,735	92.5	1,905	2.4	79,689
1.2	327	2.7	236	1.9	367	3.0	1,076	8.7	11,108	90.1	142	1.2	12,326
1.3	100	2.6	59	1.5	86	2.2	296	7.7	3,538	91.8	22	.6	3,856
1.1	227	2.7	177	2.1	281	3.3	780	9.2	7,570	89.4	120	1.4	8,470
.6	2,663	2.1	1,462	1.2	1,906	1.5	6,776	5.4	116,818	92.7	2,362	1.9	125,956
.6	768	2.0	531	1.4	429	1.1	1,947	5.2	35,513	94.0	337	.9	37,797
.6	1,895	2.1	931	1.1	1,477	1.7	4,829	5.5	81,305	92.2	2,025	2.3	88,159
.3	171	1.5	227	2.0	126	1.1	560	4.9	8,260	72.6	2,561	22.5	11,381
.3	34	1.4	64	2.7	20	.8	127	5.3	1,939	80.7	337	14.0	2,403
.3	137	1.5	163	1.8	106	1.2	433	4.8	6,321	70.4	2,224	24.8	8,978
.3	58	1.1	111	2.0	28	.5	215	3.9	4,417	80.7	841	15.4	5,473
.2	15	1.3	34	2.8	3	.3	54	4.5	1,015	85.1	124	10.4	1,193
.4	43	1.0	77	1.8	25	.6	161	3.8	3,402	79.5	717	16.8	4,280
.3	229	1.4	338	2.0	154	.9	775	4.6	12,677	75.2	3,402	20.2	16,854
.3	49	1.4	98	2.7	23	.6	181	5.0	2,954	82.1	461	12.8	3,596
.3	180	1.4	240	1.8	131	1.0	594	4.5	9,723	73.3	2,941	22.2	13,258
.0	0	.0	0	.0	0	.0	0	.0	0	.0	0	.0	0
.0	0	.0	0	.0	0	.0	0	.0	0	.0	0	.0	0
.0	0	.0	0	.0	0	.0	0	.0	0	.0	0	.0	0
.0	0	.0	0	.0	0	.0	0	.0	0	.0	0	.0	0
.0	0	.0	0	.0	0	.0	0	.0	0	.0	0	.0	0
.0	0	.0	0	.0	0	.0	0	.0	0	.0	0	.0	0
.0	0	.0	0	.0	0	.0	0	.0	0	.0	0	.0	0
.0	0	.0	0	.0	0	.0	0	.0	0	.0	0	.0	0
.0	0	.0	0	.0	0	.0	0	.0	0	.0	0	.0	0
.5	2,507	2.0	1,453	1.2	1,665	1.3	6,260	5.0	113,970	91.2	4,781	3.8	125,011
.5	702	1.9	536	1.5	363	1.0	1,778	4.9	33,914	93.3	652	1.8	36,344
.5	1,805	2.0	917	1.0	1,302	1.5	4,482	5.1	80,056	90.3	4,129	4.7	88,667
.9	385	2.2	347	1.9	395	2.2	1,291	7.3	15,325	87.2	983	5.5	17,199
1.0	115	2.3	93	1.8	89	1.8	350	6.9	4,553	90.2	146	2.9	5,049
.9	270	2.1	254	2.0	306	2.4	941	7.4	10,972	86.1	837	6.6	12,750
.6	2,892	2.0	1,800	1.3	2,060	1.4	7,551	5.3	129,495	90.7	5,764	4.0	142,610
.6	817	2.0	629	1.5	452	1.1	2,128	5.1	34,467	92.9	798	1.9	41,393
.6	2,075	2.0	1,171	1.2	1,608	1.6	5,423	5.3	91,028	89.8	4,966	4.9	101,417
.9	45	1.5	50	1.7	70	2.4	191	6.4	2,658	89.3	127	4.3	2,976
.9	15	1.6	16	1.7	12	1.3	51	5.5	841	91.4	28	3.0	920
.9	30	1.5	34	1.7	58	2.8	140	6.8	1,817	88.4	99	4.8	2,056
.6	2,937	2.0	1,850	1.3	2,130	1.5	7,742	5.3	132,153	90.6	5,891	4.0	145,786
.6	832	2.0	645	1.5	464	1.1	2,179	5.2	39,308	92.9	826	2.0	42,313
.6	2,105	2.0	1,205	1.2	1,666	1.6	5,563	5.4	92,845	89.7	5,065	4.9	103,473
(1 INSTITUTIONS)													
.0	0	.0	6	37.5	0	.0	6	37.5	1	6.3	9	56.3	16
.0	0	.0	0	.0	0	.0	0	.0	0	.0	0	.0	0
.0	0	.0	6	37.5	0	.0	6	37.5	1	6.3	9	56.3	16
.0	0	.0	2	100.0	0	.0	2	100.0	0	.0	0	.0	2
.0	0	.0	0	.0	0	.0	0	.0	0	.0	0	.0	0
.0	0	.0	2	100.0	0	.0	2	100.0	0	.0	0	.0	2
.0	0	.0	8	44.4	0	.0	8	44.4	1	5.6	9	50.0	18
.0	0	.0	0	.0	0	.0	0	.0	0	.0	0	.0	0
.0	0	.0	8	44.4	0	.0	8	44.4	1	5.6	9	50.0	18
.0	0	.0	0	.0	0	.0	0	.0	0	.0	0	.0	0
.0	0	.0	0	.0	0	.0	0	.0	0	.0	0	.0	0
.0	0	.0	0	.0	0	.0	0	.0	0	.0	0	.0	0
.0	0	.0	0	.0	0	.0	0	.0	0	.0	0	.0	0
.0	0	.0	0	.0	0	.0	0	.0	0	.0	0	.0	0
.0	0	.0	0	.0	0	.0	0	.0	0	.0	0	.0	0
.0	0	.0	0	.0	0	.0	0	.0	0	.0	0	.0	0
.0	0	.0	0	.0	0	.0	0	.0	0	.0	0	.0	0
.0	0	.0	0	.0	0	.0	0	.0	0	.0	0	.0	0

TABLE 17 - TOTAL ENROLLMENT IN INSTITUTIONS OF HIGHER EDUCATION FOR SELECTED MAJOR FIELDS OF STUDY AND LEVEL OF ENROLLMENT
BY RACE, ETHNICITY, AND SEX: STATE, 1978

MAJOR FIELD 0100 - AGRICULTURE AND NATURAL RESOURCES

	AMERICAN INDIAN ALASKAN NATIVE		BLACK NON-HISPANIC		ASIAN OR PACIFIC ISLANDER		HISPANIC		TOTAL MINORITY		WHITE NON-HISPANIC		NON-RESIDENT ALIEN		TOT
	NUMBER	%	NUMBER	%	NUMBER	%	NUMBER	%	NUMBER	%	NUMBER	%	NUMBER	%	NUM
GUAM	CONTINUED														
PROFESSIONAL:															
PART-TIME		.0		.0		.0		.0		.0		.0		.0	
FEMALE		.0		.0		.0		.0		.0		.0		.0	
MALE	0	.0	0	.0	0	.0	0	.0	0	.0	0	.0	0	.0	
TOTAL		.0		.0		.0		.0		.0		.0		.0	
FEMALE		.0		.0		.0		.0		.0		.0		.0	
MALE	0	.0	0	.0	0	.0	0	.0	0	.0	0	.0	0	.0	
UND+GRAD+PROF:															
FULL-TIME		.0		.0	6	37.5		.0	6	37.5	1	6.3		56.3	
FEMALE		.0		.0	0	.0		.0	0	.0	0	.0		.0	
MALE	0	.0		.0	6	37.5		.0	6	37.5	1	6.3		56.3	
PART-TIME	0	.0		.0	2	100.0		.0	2	100.0	0	.0		.0	
FEMALE		.0		.0	0	.0		.0	0	.0	0	.0		.0	
MALE	0	.0	0	.0	2	100.0	0	.0	2	100.0	0	.0	0	.0	
TOTAL	0	.0		.0		44.4		.0		44.4	1	5.6		50.0	
FEMALE	0	.0		.0	0	.0		.0	0	.0	0	.0		.0	
MALE	0	.0	0	.0	8	44.4	0	.0	8	44.4	1	5.6	0	50.0	
UNCLASSIFIED:															
TOTAL	0	.0		.0		.0		.0		.0	0	.0		.0	
FEMALE	0	.0		.0		.0		.0		.0	0	.0		.0	
MALE	0	.0	0	.0	0	.0	0	.0	0	.0	0	.0	0	.0	
TOTAL ENROLLMENT:															
TOTAL		.0	0	.0	8	44.4		.0		44.4	1	5.6		50.0	
FEMALE		.0	0	.0	0	.0		.0		.0	0	.0		.0	
MALE	0	.0	0	.0	8	44.4	0	.0	8	44.4	1	5.6	0	50.0	
PUERTO RICO	(	1 INSTITUTIONS)													
UNDERGRADUATES:															
FULL-TIME		.0		.0		.0	811	100.0	811	100.0		.0		.0	
FEMALE		.0		.0		.0	204	100.0	204	100.0		.0		.0	
MALE		.0		.0		.0	607	100.0	607	100.0		.0		.0	
PART-TIME		.0		.0		.0	85	100.0	85	100.0		.0		.0	
FEMALE		.0		.0		.0	24	100.0	24	100.0		.0		.0	
MALE	0	.0	0	.0	0	.0	61	100.0	61	100.0	0	.0	0	.0	
TOTAL		.0		.0		.0	896	100.0	896	100.0		.0		.0	
FEMALE		.0		.0		.0	228	100.0	228	100.0		.0		.0	
MALE	0	.0	0	.0	0	.0	668	100.0	668	100.0	0	.0	0	.0	
GRADUATE:															
FULL-TIME		.0		.0		.0	11	100.0	11	100.0		.0		.0	
FEMALE		.0		.0		.0	1	100.0	1	100.0		.0		.0	
MALE		.0		.0		.0	10	100.0	10	100.0		.0		.0	
PART-TIME		.0		.0		.0	58	100.0	58	100.0		.0		.0	
FEMALE		.0		.0		.0	16	100.0	16	100.0		.0		.0	
MALE	0	.0	0	.0	0	.0	42	100.0	42	100.0	0	.0	0	.0	
TOTAL		.0		.0		.0	69	100.0	69	100.0	0	.0		.0	
FEMALE		.0		.0		.0	17	100.0	17	100.0	0	.0		.0	
MALE	0	.0	0	.0	0	.0	52	100.0	52	100.0	0	.0	0	.0	
PROFESSIONAL:															
FULL-TIME		.0		.0		.0		.0		.0		.0		.0	
FEMALE		.0		.0		.0		.0		.0		.0		.0	
MALE		.0		.0		.0		.0		.0		.0		.0	
PART-TIME		.0		.0		.0		.0		.0		.0		.0	
FEMALE		.0		.0		.0		.0		.0		.0		.0	
MALE	0	.0	0	.0	0	.0	0	.0	0	.0	0	.0	0	.0	
TOTAL		.0		.0		.0		.0		.0		.0		.0	
FEMALE		.0		.0		.0		.0		.0		.0		.0	
MALE	0	.0	0	.0	0	.0	0	.0	0	.0	0	.0	0	.0	
UND+GRAD+PROF:															
FULL-TIME	0	.0		.0		.0	822	100.0	822	100.0		.0		.0	
FEMALE	0	.0		.0		.0	205	100.0	205	100.0		.0		.0	
MALE	0	.0		.0		.0	617	100.0	617	100.0		.0		.0	
PART-TIME	0	.0		.0		.0	143	100.0	143	100.0		.0		.0	
FEMALE	0	.0		.0		.0	40	100.0	40	100.0		.0		.0	
MALE	0	.0	0	.0	0	.0	103	100.0	103	100.0	0	.0	0	.0	
TOTAL		.0		.0		.0	965	100.0	965	100.0		.0		.0	
FEMALE		.0		.0		.0	245	100.0	245	100.0		.0		.0	
MALE	0	.0	0	.0	0	.0	720	100.0	720	100.0	0	.0	0	.0	
UNCLASSIFIED:															
TOTAL		.0		.0		.0	1	100.0	1	100.0		.0		.0	
FEMALE		.0		.0		.0	0	.0	0	.0		.0		.0	
MALE	0	.0	0	.0	0	.0	1	100.0	1	100.0	0	.0	0	.0	
TOTAL ENROLLMENT:															
TOTAL		.0		.0		.0	966	100.0	966	100.0		.0		.0	
FEMALE		.0		.0		.0	245	100.0	245	100.0		.0		.0	
MALE	0	.0	0	.0	0	.0	721	100.0	721	100.0	0	.0	0	.0	

) - AGRICULTURE AND NATURAL RESOURCES

ICAN INDIAN / AN NATIVE		BLACK NON-HISPANIC		ASIAN OR PACIFIC ISLANDER		HISPANIC		TOTAL MINORITY		WHITE NON-HISPANIC		NON-RESIDENT ALIEN		TOTAL
)ER	%	NUMBER	%	NUMBER	%	NUMBER	%	NUMBER	%	NUMBER	%	NUMBER	%	NUMBER
(1 INSTITUTIONS)														
	.0	1	50.0		.0	0	.0	1	50.0	1	50.0		.0	2
	.0	1	50.0		.0	0	.0	1	50.0	1	50.0		.0	2
	.0	0	.0		.0	0	.0	0	.0	0	.0		.0	0
	.0	0	.0		.0	0	.0	0	.0	0	.0		.0	0
8	.0	0	.0	8	.0	0	.0	0	.0	0	.0	8	.0	0
	.0	1	50.0		.0	0	.0	1	50.0	1	50.0		.0	2
8	.0	0	.0	8	.0	0	.0	0	.0	0	.0	8	.0	0
	.0		.0		.0	0	.0	0	.0		.0		.0	
	.0		.0		.0	0	.0	0	.0		.0		.0	
	.0		.0		.0	0	.0	0	.0		.0		.0	
	.0		.0		.0	0	.0	0	.0		.0		.0	
8	.0	8	.0	8	.0	0	.0	0	.0	8	.0	8	.0	8
8	.0	8	.0	8	.0	0	.0	0	.0	8	.0	8	.0	8
	.0		.0		.0	0	.0	0	.0		.0		.0	
	.0		.0		.0	0	.0	0	.0		.0		.0	
	.0		.0		.0	0	.0	0	.0		.0		.0	
	.0		.0		.0	0	.0	0	.0		.0		.0	
8	.0	8	.0	8	.0	0	.0	0	.0	8	.0	8	.0	8
8	.0	8	.0	8	.0	0	.0	0	.0	8	.0	8	.0	8
	.0	1	50.0		.0	0	.0	1	50.0	1	50.0		.0	2
	.0	1	50.0		.0	0	.0	1	50.0	1	50.0		.0	2
	.0	0	.0		.0	0	.0	0	.0	0	.0		.0	0
	.0	0	.0		.0	0	.0	0	.0	0	.0		.0	0
8	.0	0	.0	8	.0	0	.0	0	.0	0	.0	8	.0	0
	.0	1	50.0		.0	0	.0	1	50.0	1	50.0		.0	2
8	.0	1	50.0	8	.0	0	.0	1	50.0	1	50.0	8	.0	2
	.0	0	.0		.0	0	.0	0	.0	0	.0		.0	0
8	.0	8	.0	8	.0	0	.0	0	.0	8	.0	8	.0	8
	.0	1	50.0		.0	0	.0	1	50.0	1	50.0		.0	2
8	.0	0	.0	8	.0	0	.0	1	50.0	8	50.0	8	.0	2
	.0		.0		.0	0	.0	0	.0		.0		.0	0
(3 INSTITUTIONS)														
	.0	1	.1	6	.7	811	97.8	818	98.7	2	.2		1.1	829
	.0	1	.5	0	.0	204	99.0	205	99.5	1	.5		.0	206
	.0	0	.0	6	1.0	607	97.4	613	98.4	1	.2		1.4	623
	.0	0	.0	2	2.3	85	97.7	87	100.0	0	.0		.0	87
	.0	0	.0	0	.0	24	100.0	24	100.0	0	.0		.0	24
8	.0	0	.0	2	3.2	61	96.8	63	100.0	0	.0	8	.0	63
	.0	1	.1		.9	896	97.8	905	98.8	2	.2		1.0	916
	.0	1	.4		.0	228	99.1	229	99.6	1	.4		.0	230
8	.0	0	.0	8	1.2	668	97.4	676	98.5	1	.1	8	1.3	686
	.0		.0		.0	11	100.0	11	100.0		.0		.0	11
	.0		.0		.0	1	100.0	1	100.0		.0		.0	1
	.0		.0		.0	10	100.0	10	100.0		.0		.0	10
	.0		.0		.0	58	100.0	58	100.0		.0		.0	58
	.0		.0		.0	16	100.0	16	100.0		.0		.0	16
8	.0	8	.0	8	.0	42	100.0	42	100.0	8	.0	8	.0	42
	.0		.0		.0	69	100.0	69	100.0		.0		.0	69
	.0		.0		.0	17	100.0	17	100.0		.0		.0	17
8	.0	8	.0	8	.0	52	100.0	52	100.0	8	.0	8	.0	52
8	.0	8	.0	8	.0	0	.0	0	.0	8	.0	8	.0	8

TABLE 17 - TOTAL ENROLLMENT IN INSTITUTIONS OF HIGHER EDUCATION FOR SELECTED MAJOR FIELDS OF STUDY AND LEVEL OF ENROLLMENT
BY RACE, ETHNICITY, AND SEX: STATE, 1978

MAJOR FIELD 0100 - AGRICULTURE AND NATURAL RESOURCES

	AMERICAN INDIAN ALASKAN NATIVE		BLACK NON-HISPANIC		ASIAN OR PACIFIC ISLANDER		HISPANIC		TOTAL MINORITY		WHITE NON-HISPANIC		NON-RESIDENT ALIEN	
	NUMBER	%	NUMBER	%	NUMBER	%	NUMBER	%	NUMBER	%	NUMBER	%	NUMBER	%
OUTLYING AREAS	CONTINUED													
PROFESSIONAL														
PART-TIME	0	.0	0	.0	0	.0	0	.0	0	.0	0	.0	0	.0
FEMALE	0	.0	0	.0	0	.0	0	.0	0	.0	0	.0	0	.0
MALE	0	.0	0	.0	0	.0	0	.0	0	.0	0	.0	0	.0
TOTAL	0	.0	0	.0	0	.0	0	.0	0	.0	0	.0	0	.0
FEMALE	0	.0	0	.0	0	.0	0	.0	0	.0	0	.0	0	.0
MALE	0	.0	0	.0	0	.0	0	.0	0	.0	0	.0	0	.0
UND+GRAD+PROF:														
FULL-TIME	0	.0	1	.1	6	.7	822	97.9	829	98.7	2	.2	9	1.1
FEMALE	0	.0	1	.5	0	.0	205	99.0	206	99.5	1	.5	0	.0
MALE	0	.0	0	.0	6	.9	617	97.5	623	98.4	1	.2	9	1.4
PART-TIME	0	.0	0	.0	2	1.4	143	98.6	145	100.0	0	.0	0	.0
FEMALE	0	.0	0	.0	0	.0	40	100.0	40	100.0	0	.0	0	.0
MALE	0	.0	0	.0	2	1.9	103	98.1	105	100.0	0	.0	0	.0
TOTAL	0	.0	1	.1	8	.8	965	98.0	974	98.9	2	.2	9	.9
FEMALE	0	.0	1	.4	0	.0	245	99.2	246	99.6	1	.4	0	.0
MALE	0	.0	0	.0	8	1.1	720	97.6	728	98.6	1	.1	9	1.2
UNCLASSIFIED:														
TOTAL	0	.0	0	.0	0	.0	1	100.0	1	100.0	0	.0	0	.0
FEMALE	0	.0	0	.0	0	.0	0	.0	0	.0	0	.0	0	.0
MALE	0	.0	0	.0	0	.0	1	100.0	1	100.0	0	.0	0	.0
TOTAL ENROLLMENT:														
TOTAL	0	.0	1	.1	8	.8	966	98.0	975	98.9	2	.2	9	.9
FEMALE	0	.0	1	.4	0	.0	245	99.2	246	99.6	1	.4	0	.0
MALE	0	.0	0	.0	8	1.1	721	97.6	729	98.6	1	.1	9	1.2

MAJOR FIELD AGGREGATE 0100 (569 INSTITUTIONS)

	AMERICAN INDIAN ALASKAN NATIVE		BLACK NON-HISPANIC		ASIAN OR PACIFIC ISLANDER		HISPANIC		TOTAL MINORITY		WHITE NON-HISPANIC		NON-RESIDENT ALIEN	
	NUMBER	%	NUMBER	%	NUMBER	%	NUMBER	%	NUMBER	%	NUMBER	%	NUMBER	%
UNDERGRADUATES:														
FULL-TIME	599	.5	2,337	2.0	1,232	1.1	2,350	2.1	6,518	5.7	105,712	92.4	2,229	1.9
FEMALE	168	.5	669	2.0	472	1.4	547	1.6	1,856	5.4	31,976	93.6	315	.9
MALE	431	.5	1,668	2.1	760	.9	1,803	2.2	4,662	5.8	73,736	91.8	1,914	2.4
PART-TIME	146	1.2	327	2.6	238	1.9	452	3.6	1,163	9.4	11,108	89.5	142	1.1
FEMALE	51	1.3	100	2.6	59	1.5	110	2.8	320	8.2	3,538	91.2	22	.6
MALE	95	1.1	227	2.7	179	2.1	342	4.0	843	9.9	7,570	88.7	120	1.4
TOTAL	745	.6	2,664	2.1	1,470	1.2	2,802	2.2	7,681	6.1	116,820	92.1	2,371	1.9
FEMALE	219	.6	769	2.0	531	1.4	657	1.7	2,176	5.7	35,514	93.4	337	.9
MALE	526	.6	1,895	2.1	939	1.1	2,145	2.4	5,505	6.2	81,306	91.5	2,034	2.3
GRADUATE:														
FULL-TIME	36	.3	171	1.5	227	2.0	137	1.2	571	5.0	8,260	72.5	2,561	22.5
FEMALE	9	.4	34	1.4	64	2.7	21	.9	128	5.3	1,939	80.7	337	14.0
MALE	27	.3	137	1.5	163	1.8	116	1.3	443	4.9	6,321	70.3	2,224	24.7
PART-TIME	18	.3	56	1.0	111	2.0	86	1.6	273	4.9	4,417	79.9	841	15.2
FEMALE	2	.2	15	1.2	34	2.8	19	1.6	70	5.8	1,015	84.0	124	10.3
MALE	16	.4	43	1.0	77	1.8	67	1.6	203	4.7	3,402	78.7	717	16.6
TOTAL	54	.3	229	1.4	338	2.0	223	1.3	844	5.0	12,677	74.9	3,402	20.1
FEMALE	11	.3	49	1.4	98	2.7	40	1.1	198	5.5	2,954	81.8	461	12.8
MALE	43	.3	180	1.4	240	1.8	183	1.4	646	4.9	9,723	73.1	2,941	22.1
PROFESSIONAL:														
FULL-TIME	0	.0	0	.0	0	.0	0	.0	0	.0	0	.0	0	.0
FEMALE	0	.0	0	.0	0	.0	0	.0	0	.0	0	.0	0	.0
MALE	0	.0	0	.0	0	.0	0	.0	0	.0	0	.0	0	.0
PART-TIME	0	.0	0	.0	0	.0	0	.0	0	.0	0	.0	0	.0
FEMALE	0	.0	0	.0	0	.0	0	.0	0	.0	0	.0	0	.0
MALE	0	.0	0	.0	0	.0	0	.0	0	.0	0	.0	0	.0
TOTAL	0	.0	0	.0	0	.0	0	.0	0	.0	0	.0	0	.0
FEMALE	0	.0	0	.0	0	.0	0	.0	0	.0	0	.0	0	.0
MALE	0	.0	0	.0	0	.0	0	.0	0	.0	0	.0	0	.0
UND+GRAD+PROF:														
FULL-TIME	635	.5	2,508	2.0	1,459	1.2	2,487	2.0	7,089	5.6	113,972	90.6	4,790	3.8
FEMALE	177	.5	703	1.9	536	1.5	568	1.6	1,984	5.4	33,915	92.8	652	1.8
MALE	458	.5	1,805	2.0	923	1.0	1,919	2.1	5,105	5.7	80,057	89.6	4,138	4.6
PART-TIME	164	.9	385	2.1	349	1.9	538	3.0	1,436	8.0	15,525	86.5	983	5.5
FEMALE	53	1.0	115	2.3	93	1.8	129	2.5	390	7.7	4,553	89.5	146	2.9
MALE	111	.9	270	2.1	256	2.0	409	3.2	1,046	8.1	10,972	85.4	837	6.5
TOTAL	799	.6	2,893	2.0	1,808	1.3	3,025	2.1	8,525	5.9	129,497	90.1	5,773	4.0
FEMALE	230	.6	818	2.0	629	1.5	697	1.7	2,374	5.7	38,468	92.4	798	1.9
MALE	569	.6	2,075	2.0	1,179	1.2	2,328	2.3	6,151	6.0	91,029	89.1	4,975	4.9
UNCLASSIFIED:														
TOTAL	26	.9	45	1.5	50	1.7	71	2.4	192	6.4	2,658	89.3	127	4.3
FEMALE	8	.9	15	1.6	16	1.7	12	1.3	51	5.5	841	91.4	28	3.0
MALE	18	.9	30	1.5	34	1.7	59	2.9	141	6.9	1,817	88.3	99	4.8
TOTAL ENROLLMENT:														
TOTAL	825	.6	2,938	2.0	1,858	1.3	3,096	2.1	8,717	5.9	132,155	90.0	5,900	4.0
FEMALE	238	.6	833	2.0	645	1.5	709	1.7	2,425	5.7	39,309	92.4	826	1.9
MALE	587	.6	2,105	2.0	1,213	1.2	2,387	2.3	6,292	6.0	92,846	89.1	5,074	4.9

ARCHITECTURE AND ENVIRONMENTAL DESIGN

N INDIAN NATIVE	BLACK NON-HISPANIC		ASIAN OR PACIFIC ISLANDER		HISPANIC		TOTAL MINORITY		WHITE NON-HISPANIC		NON-RESIDENT ALIEN		TOTAL
%	NUMBER	%	NUMBER	%	NUMBER	%	NUMBER	%	NUMBER	%	NUMBER	%	NUMBER

(13 INSTITUTIONS)

.1	137	12.7	5	.5	2	.2	145	13.4	917	85.0	17	1.6	1,079
.0	20	10.0	2	1.0	1	.5	23	11.4	177	88.1	1	.5	201
.1	117	13.3	3	.3	1	.1	122	13.9	740	84.3	16	1.8	878
.0	4	3.5	0	.0	0	.0	4	3.5	109	95.6	1	.9	114
.0	0	.0	0	.0	0	.0	0	.0	14	100.0	0	.0	14
.0	4	4.0	0	.0	0	.0	4	4.0	95	95.0	1	1.0	100
.1	141	11.8	5	.4	2	.2	149	12.5	1,026	86.0	18	1.5	1,193
.0	20	9.3	2	.9	1	.5	23	10.7	191	88.8	1	.5	215
.1	121	12.4	3	.3	1	.1	126	12.9	835	85.4	17	1.7	978
.0	0	.0	0	.0	0	.0	0	.0	1	100.0	0	.0	1
.0	0	.0	0	.0	0	.0	0	.0	0	.0	0	.0	0
.0	0	.0	0	.0	0	.0	0	.0	1	100.0	0	.0	1
.0	0	.0	0	.0	0	.0	0	.0	1	100.0	0	.0	1
.0	0	.0	0	.0	0	.0	0	.0	0	.0	0	.0	0
.0	0	.0	0	.0	0	.0	0	.0	1	100.0	0	.0	1
.0	0	.0	0	.0	0	.0	0	.0	2	100.0	0	.0	2
.0	0	.0	0	.0	0	.0	0	.0	0	.0	0	.0	0
.0	0	.0	0	.0	0	.0	0	.0	2	100.0	0	.0	2
.0	0	.0	0	.0	0	.0	0	.0	0	.0	0	.0	0
.0	0	.0	0	.0	0	.0	0	.0	0	.0	0	.0	0
.0	0	.0	0	.0	0	.0	0	.0	0	.0	0	.0	0
.0	0	.0	0	.0	0	.0	0	.0	0	.0	0	.0	0
.0	0	.0	0	.0	0	.0	0	.0	0	.0	0	.0	0
.0	0	.0	0	.0	0	.0	0	.0	0	.0	0	.0	0
.0	0	.0	0	.0	0	.0	0	.0	0	.0	0	.0	0
.0	0	.0	0	.0	0	.0	0	.0	0	.0	0	.0	0
.0	0	.0	0	.0	0	.0	0	.0	0	.0	0	.0	0
.1	137	12.7	5	.5	2	.2	145	13.4	918	85.0	17	1.6	1,080
.0	20	10.0	2	1.0	1	.5	23	11.4	177	88.1	1	.5	201
.1	117	13.3	3	.3	1	.1	122	13.9	741	84.3	16	1.8	879
.0	4	3.5	0	.0	0	.0	4	3.5	110	95.7	1	.9	115
.0	0	.0	0	.0	0	.0	0	.0	14	100.0	0	.0	14
.0	4	4.0	0	.0	0	.0	4	4.0	96	95.0	1	1.0	101
.1	141	11.8	5	.4	2	.2	149	12.5	1,028	86.0	18	1.5	1,195
.0	20	9.3	2	.9	1	.5	23	10.7	191	88.8	1	.5	215
.1	121	12.3	3	.3	1	.1	126	12.9	837	85.4	17	1.7	980
.0	0	.0	0	.0	0	.0	0	.0	6	100.0	0	.0	6
.0	0	.0	0	.0	0	.0	0	.0	1	100.0	0	.0	1
.0	0	.0	0	.0	0	.0	0	.0	5	100.0	0	.0	5
.1	141	11.7	5	.4	2	.2	149	12.4	1,034	86.1	18	1.5	1,201
.0	20	9.3	2	.9	1	.5	23	10.6	192	88.9	1	.5	216
.1	121	12.3	3	.3	1	.1	126	12.8	842	85.5	17	1.7	985

(6 INSTITUTIONS)

.8	11	.9	16	1.3	53	4.4	90	7.5	1,090	90.2	28	2.3	1,208
.6	1	.3	4	1.2	12	3.6	19	5.7	311	92.8	5	1.5	335
.9	10	1.1	12	1.4	41	4.7	71	8.1	779	89.2	23	2.6	873
.6	0	.0	4	2.5	7	4.4	12	7.5	146	91.3	2	1.3	160
.0	0	.0	0	.0	1	2.2	1	2.2	45	97.8	0	.0	46
.9	0	.0	4	3.5	6	5.3	11	9.6	101	88.6	2	1.8	114
.8	11	.8	20	1.5	60	4.4	102	7.5	1,236	90.4	30	2.2	1,368
.5	1	.3	4	1.0	13	3.4	20	5.2	356	93.4	5	1.3	381
.9	10	1.0	16	1.6	47	4.8	82	8.3	880	89.2	25	2.5	987
.0	0	.0	0	.0	0	.0	0	.0	19	76.0	6	24.0	25
.0	0	.0	0	.0	0	.0	0	.0	3	60.0	2	40.0	5
.0	0	.0	0	.0	0	.0	0	.0	16	80.0	4	20.0	20
.0	0	.0	0	.0	0	.0	0	.0	9	81.8	2	18.2	11
.0	0	.0	0	.0	0	.0	0	.0	1	100.0	0	.0	1
.0	0	.0	0	.0	0	.0	0	.0	8	80.0	2	20.0	10
.0	0	.0	0	.0	0	.0	0	.0	28	77.8	8	22.2	36
.0	0	.0	0	.0	0	.0	0	.0	4	66.7	2	33.3	6
.0	0	.0	0	.0	0	.0	0	.0	24	80.0	6	20.0	30
.0	0	.0	0	.0	0	.0	0	.0	0	.0	0	.0	0
.0	0	.0	0	.0	0	.0	0	.0	0	.0	0	.0	0
.0	0	.0	0	.0	0	.0	0	.0	0	.0	0	.0	0

TABLE 17 - TOTAL ENROLLMENT IN INSTITUTIONS OF HIGHER EDUCATION FOR SELECTED MAJOR FIELDS OF STUDY AND LEVEL OF ENROLLMENT
BY RACE, ETHNICITY, AND SEX: STATE, 1978 .

MAJOR FIELD 0200 - ARCHITECTURE AND ENVIRONMENTAL DESIGN

	AMERICAN INDIAN ALASKAN NATIVE		BLACK NON-HISPANIC		ASIAN OR PACIFIC ISLANDER		HISPANIC		TOTAL MINORITY		WHITE NON-HISPANIC		NON-RESIDENT ALIEN	
	NUMBER	%	NUMBER	%	NUMBER	%	NUMBER	%	NUMBER	%	NUMBER	%	NUMBER	%
ARIZONA		CONTINUED												
PROFESSIONAL														
PART-TIME	0	.0	0	.0	0	.0	0	.0	0	.0	0	.0	0	.0
FEMALE	0	.0	0	.0	0	.0	0	.0	0	.0	0	.0	0	.0
MALE	0	.0	0	.0	0	.0	0	.0	0	.0	0	.0	0	.0
TOTAL	0	.0	0	.0	0	.0	0	.0	0	.0	0	.0	0	.0
FEMALE	0	.0	0	.0	0	.0	0	.0	0	.0	0	.0	0	.0
MALE	0	.0	0	.0	0	.0	0	.0	0	.0	0	.0	0	.0
UNG+GRAD+PROF:														
FULL-TIME	10	.8	11	.9	16	1.3	53	4.3	90	7.3	1,109	89.9	34	2.8
FEMALE	2	.6	1	.3	4	1.2	12	3.5	19	5.6	314	92.4	7	2.1
MALE	8	.9	10	1.1	12	1.3	41	4.6	71	8.0	795	89.0	27	3.0
PART-TIME	1	.6	0	.0	4	2.3	7	4.1	12	7.0	155	90.6	4	2.3
FEMALE	0	.0	0	.0	0	.0	1	2.1	1	2.1	46	97.9	0	.0
MALE	1	.8	0	.0	4	3.2	6	4.8	11	8.9	'109	87.9	4	3.2
TOTAL	11	.8	11	.8	20	1.4	60	4.3	102	7.3	1,264	90.0	38	2.7
FEMALE	2	.5	1	.3	4	1.0	13	3.4	20	5.2	360	93.0	7	1.8
MALE	9	.9	10	1.0	16	1.6	47	4.6	82	8.1	904	88.9	31	3.0
UNCLASSIFIED:														
TOTAL	0	.0	0	.0	0	.0	0	.0	0	.0	2	66.7	1	33.3
FEMALE	0	.0	0	.0	0	.0	0	.0	0	.0	2	100.0	0	.0
MALE	0	.0	0	.0	0	.0	0	.0	0	.0	0	.0	1	100.0
TOTAL ENROLLMENT:														
TOTAL	11	.8	11	.8	20	1.4	60	4.3	102	7.2	1,266	90.0	39	2.8
FEMALE	2	.5	1	.3	4	1.0	13	3.3	20	5.1	362	93.1	7	1.8
MALE	9	.9	10	1.0	16	1.6	47	4.6	82	8.1	904	88.8	32	3.1
ARKANSAS	(	4 INSTITUTIONS)												
UNDERGRADUATES:														
FULL-TIME	1	.2	14	3.4	5	1.2	0	.0	20	4.8	372	89.9	22	5.3
FEMALE	0	.0	1	2.2	2	4.4	0	.0	3	6.7	38	84.4	4	8.9
MALE	1	.3	13	3.5	3	.8	0	.0	17	4.6	334	90.5	18	4.9
PART-TIME	2	6.3	0	.0	0	.0	0	.0	2	6.3	30	93.8	0	.0
FEMALE	0	.0	0	.0	0	.0	0	.0	0	.0	6	100.0	0	.0
MALE	2	7.7	0	.0	0	.0	0	.0	2	7.7	24	92.3	0	.0
TOTAL	3	.7	14	3.1	5	1.1	0	.0	22	4.9	402	90.1	22	4.9
FEMALE	0	.0	1	2.0	2	3.9	0	.0	3	5.9	44	86.3	4	7.8
MALE	3	.8	13	3.3	3	.8	0	.0	19	4.8	358	90.6	18	4.6
GRADUATE:														
FULL-TIME	0	.0	0	.0	0	.0	0	.0	0	.0	0	.0	0	.0
FEMALE	0	.0	0	.0	0	.0	0	.0	0	.0	0	.0	0	.0
MALE	0	.0	0	.0	0	.0	0	.0	0	.0	0	.0	0	.0
PART-TIME	0	.0	0	.0	0	.0	0	.0	0	.0	0	.0	0	.0
FEMALE	0	.0	0	.0	0	.0	0	.0	0	.0	0	.0	0	.0
MALE	0	.0	0	.0	0	.0	0	.0	0	.0	0	.0	0	.0
TOTAL	0	.0	0	.0	0	.0	0	.0	0	.0	0	.0	0	.0
FEMALE	0	.0	0	.0	0	.0	0	.0	0	.0	0	.0	0	.0
MALE	0	.0	0	.0	0	.0	0	.0	0	.0	0	.0	0	.0
PROFESSIONAL:														
FULL-TIME	0	.0	0	.0	0	.0	0	.0	0	.0	0	.0	0	.0
FEMALE	0	.0	0	.0	0	.0	0	.0	0	.0	0	.0	0	.0
MALE	0	.0	0	.0	0	.0	0	.0	0	.0	0	.0	0	.0
PART-TIME	0	.0	0	.0	0	.0	0	.0	0	.0	0	.0	0	.0
FEMALE	0	.0	0	.0	0	.0	0	.0	0	.0	0	.0	0	.0
MALE	0	.0	0	.0	0	.0	0	.0	0	.0	0	.0	0	.0
TOTAL	0	.0	0	.0	0	.0	0	.0	0	.0	0	.0	0	.0
FEMALE	0	.0	0	.0	0	.0	0	.0	0	.0	0	.0	0	.0
MALE	0	.0	0	.0	0	.0	0	.0	0	.0	0	.0	0	.0
UNG+GRAD+PROF:														
FULL-TIME	1	.2	14	3.4	5	1.2	0	.0	20	4.8	372	89.9	22	5.3
FEMALE	0	.0	1	2.2	2	4.4	0	.0	3	6.7	38	84.4	4	8.9
MALE	1	.3	13	3.5	3	.8	0	.0	17	4.6	334	90.5	18	4.9
PART-TIME	2	6.3	0	.0	0	.0	0	.0	2	6.3	30	93.8	0	.0
FEMALE	0	.0	0	.0	0	.0	0	.0	0	.0	6	100.0	0	.0
MALE	2	7.7	0	.0	0	.0	0	.0	2	7.7	24	92.3	0	.0
TOTAL	3	.7	14	3.1	5	1.1	0	.0	22	4.9	402	90.1	22	4.9
FEMALE	0	.0	1	2.0	2	3.9	0	.0	3	5.9	44	86.3	4	7.8
MALE	3	.8	13	3.3	3	.8	0	.0	19	4.8	358	90.6	18	4.6
UNCLASSIFIED:														
TOTAL	0	.0	0	.0	1	25.0	1	25.0	2	50.0	1	25.0	1	25.0
FEMALE	0	.0	0	.0	0	.0	0	.0	0	.0	0	.0	0	.0
MALE	0	.0	0	.0	1	25.0	1	25.0	2	50.0	1	25.0	1	25.0
TOTAL ENROLLMENT:														
TOTAL	3	.7	14	3.1	6	1.3	1	.2	24	5.3	403	89.6	23	5.1
FEMALE	0	.0	1	2.0	2	3.9	0	.0	3	5.9	44	86.3	4	7.8
MALE	3	.8	13	3.3	4	1.0	1	.3	21	5.3	359	90.0	19	4.8

328

ARCHITECTURE AND ENVIRONMENTAL DESIGN

% INDIAN NATIVE	BLACK NON-HISPANIC NUMBER	%	ASIAN OR PACIFIC ISLANDER NUMBER	%	HISPANIC NUMBER	%	TOTAL MINORITY NUMBER	%	WHITE NON-HISPANIC NUMBER	%	NON-RESIDENT ALIEN NUMBER	%	TOTAL NUMBER
(71 INSTITUTIONS)													
.9	165	3.5	449	9.5	356	7.6	1,013	21.5	3,341	71.1	348	7.4	4,702
.8	28	2.5	121	1C.8	58	5.2	216	19.4	829	74.3	71	6.4	1,116
.9	137	3.8	328	9.1	298	8.3	797	22.2	2,512	70.1	277	7.7	3,586
1.6	130	5.7	145	6.4	252	11.0	564	24.7	1,646	72.1	73	3.2	2,283
2.2	23	4.2	31	5.6	39	7.1	105	19.0	426	77.0	22	4.0	553
1.4	107	6.2	114	6.6	213	12.3	459	26.5	1,220	70.5	51	2.9	1,730
1.1	295	4.2	594	8.5	608	8.7	1,577	22.6	4,987	71.4	421	6.0	6,985
1.3	51	3.1	152	9.1	97	5.8	321	19.2	1,255	75.2	93	5.6	1,669
1.1	244	4.6	442	8.3	511	9.6	1,256	23.6	3,732	70.2	328	6.2	5,316
.5	31	3.3	68	7.3	37	4.0	141	15.1	611	65.3	184	19.7	936
.0	12	3.4	28	7.9	10	2.8	50	14.2	255	72.2	48	13.6	353
.9	19	3.3	40	6.9	27	4.6	91	15.6	356	61.1	136	23.3	583
.0	5	2.0	20	8.0	13	5.2	38	15.2	177	70.8	35	14.0	250
.0	3	3.5	7	8.1	4	4.7	14	16.3	62	72.1	10	11.6	86
.0	2	1.2	13	7.9	9	5.5	24	14.6	115	70.1	25	15.2	164
.4	36	3.0	88	7.4	50	4.2	179	15.1	788	66.4	219	18.5	1,186
.0	15	3.4	35	8.0	14	3.2	64	14.6	317	72.2	58	13.2	439
.7	21	2.8	53	7.1	36	4.8	115	15.4	471	63.1	161	21.6	747
.0	0	.0	0	.0	0	.0	0	.0	0	.0		.0	0
.0	0	.0	0	.0	0	.0	0	.0	0	.0		.0	0
.0	0	.0	0	.0	0	.0	0	.0	0	.0		.0	0
.0	0	.0	0	.0	0	.0	0	.0	0	.0		.0	0
.0	0	.0	0	.0	0	.0	0	.0	0	.0	8	.0	0
.0	0	.0	0	.0	0	.0	0	.0	0	.0		.0	0
.0	0	.0	0	.0	0	.0	0	.0	0	.0		.0	0
.0	0	.0	0	.0	0	.0	0	.0	0	.0	8	.0	0
.0	0	.0	0	.0	0	.0	0	.0	0	.0		.0	0
.9	196	3.5	517	9.2	393	7.0	1,154	20.5	3,952	70.1	532	9.4	5,638
.6	40	2.7	149	10.1	68	4.6	266	18.1	1,084	73.8	119	8.1	1,469
.9	156	3.7	368	8.8	325	7.8	888	21.3	2,868	68.8	413	9.9	4,169
1.5	135	5.3	165	6.5	265	10.5	602	23.8	1,823	72.0	108	4.3	2,537
1.9	26	4.1	38	5.9	43	6.7	119	18.6	488	76.4	32	5.0	639
1.3	109	5.8	127	6.7	222	11.7	483	25.5	1,335	70.5	76	4.0	1,894
1.0	331	4.1	682	8.3	658	8.1	1,756	21.7	5,775	70.7	640	7.8	8,171
1.0	66	3.1	187	8.9	111	5.3	385	18.3	1,572	74.6	151	7.2	2,108
1.1	265	4.4	495	8.2	547	9.0	1,371	22.6	4,203	69.3	489	8.1	6,063
1.9	22	4.2	43	8.3	27	5.2	102	19.6	400	76.8	19	3.6	521
.0	10	5.5	9	5.0	4	2.2	23	12.7	157	86.7	1	.6	181
2.9	12	3.5	34	10.0	23	6.8	79	23.2	243	71.5	18	5.3	340
1.1	353	4.1	725	8.3	685	7.9	1,858	21.4	6,175	71.0	659	7.6	8,692
.9	76	3.3	196	8.6	115	5.0	408	17.8	1,729	75.5	152	6.6	2,289
1.2	277	4.3	529	8.3	570	8.9	1,450	22.6	4,446	69.4	507	7.9	6,403
(5 INSTITUTIONS)													
.2	8	1.7	10	2.2	8	1.7	27	5.9	430	93.5	3	.7	460
.0	5	4.1	1	.8	3	2.5	9	7.4	112	91.8	1	.8	122
.3	3	.9	9	2.7	5	1.5	18	5.3	318	94.1	2	.6	338
.0	0	.0	0	.0	0	.0	0	.0	18	100.0	0	.0	18
.0	0	.0	0	.0	0	.0	0	.0	5	100.0	0	.0	5
.0	0	.0	0	.0	0	.0	0	.0	13	100.0	0	.0	13
.2	8	1.7	10	2.1	8	1.7	27	5.6	448	93.7	3	.6	478
.0	5	3.9	1	.8	3	2.4	9	7.1	117	92.1	1	.8	127
.3	3	.9	9	2.6	5	1.4	18	5.1	331	94.3	2	.6	351
.0	3	1.1	4	1.4	3	1.1	10	3.5	257	90.2	18	6.3	285
.0	1	1.0	1	1.0	0	.0	2	2.0	94	92.2	6	5.9	102
.0	2	1.1	3	1.6	3	1.6	8	4.4	163	89.1	12	6.6	183
.0	0	.0	0	.0	1	2.8	1	2.8	35	97.2	0	.0	36
.0	0	.0	0	.0	0	.0	0	.0	16	100.0	0	.0	16
.0	0	.0	0	.0	1	5.0	1	5.0	19	95.0	0	.0	20
.0	3	.9	4	1.2	4	1.2	11	3.4	292	91.0	18	5.6	321
.0	1	.8	1	.8	0	.0	2	1.7	110	93.2	6	5.1	118
.0	2	1.0	3	1.5	4	2.0	9	4.4	182	89.7	12	5.9	203
.0	0	.0	0	.0	0	.0	0	.0	0	.0	0	.0	0
.0	0	.0	0	.0	0	.0	0	.0	0	.0	0	.0	0
.0	0	.0	0	.0	0	.0	0	.0	0	.0	0	.0	0

MAJOR FIELD 0200 - ARCHITECTURE AND ENVIRONMENTAL DESIGN

	AMERICAN INDIAN ALASKAN NATIVE		BLACK NON-HISPANIC		ASIAN OR PACIFIC ISLANDER		HISPANIC		TOTAL MINORITY		WHITE NON-HISPANIC		NON-RESIDENT ALIEN		TO NU
	NUMBER	%	NUMBER	%	NUMBER	%	NUMBER	%	NUMBER	%	NUMBER	%	NUMBER	%	
COLORADO		CONTINUED													
PROFESSIONAL:															
PART-TIME															
FEMALE	0	.0	0	.0	0	.0	0	.0	0	.0	0	.0	0	.0	
MALE	0	.0	0	.0	0	.0	0	.0	0	.0	0	.0	0	.0	
TOTAL															
FEMALE	0	.0	0	.0	0	.0	0	.0	0	.0	0	.0	0	.0	
MALE	0	.0	0	.0	0	.0	0	.0	0	.0	0	.0	0	.0	
UND+GRAD+PROF:															
FULL-TIME	1	.1	11	1.5	14	1.9	11	1.5	37	5.0	687	92.2	21	2.8	
FEMALE	0	.0	6	2.7	2	.9	3	1.3	11	4.9	206	92.0	7	3.1	
MALE	1	.2	5	1.0	12	2.3	8	1.5	26	5.0	481	92.3	14	2.7	
PART-TIME	0	.0	0	.0	0	.0	1	1.9	1	1.9	53	98.1	0	.0	
FEMALE	0	.0	0	.0	0	.0	0	.0	0	.0	21	100.0	0	.0	
MALE	0	.0	0	.0	0	.0	1	3.0	1	3.0	32	97.0	0	.0	
TOTAL	1	.1	11	1.4	14	1.8	12	1.5	38	4.8	740	92.6	21	2.6	
FEMALE	0	.0	6	2.4	2	.8	3	1.2	11	4.5	227	92.7	7	2.9	
MALE	1	.2	5	.9	12	2.2	9	1.6	27	4.9	513	92.6	14	2.5	
UNCLASSIFIED:															
TOTAL	0	.0	0	.0	0	.0	0	.0	0	.0	0	.0	0	.0	
FEMALE	0	.0	0	.0	0	.0	0	.0	0	.0	0	.0	0	.0	
MALE	0	.0	0	.0	0	.0	0	.0	0	.0	0	.0	0	.0	
TOTAL ENROLLMENT:															
TOTAL	1	.1	11	1.4	14	1.8	12	1.5	38	4.8	740	92.6	21	2.6	
FEMALE	0	.0	6	2.4	2	.8	3	1.2	11	4.5	227	92.7	7	2.9	
MALE	1	.2	5	.9	12	2.2	9	1.6	27	4.9	513	92.6	14	2.5	
CONNECTICUT	(	4 INSTITUTIONS)													
UNDERGRADUATES:															
FULL-TIME	1	.5	11	5.5	4	2.0	6	3.0	22	10.9	169	84.1	10	5.0	
FEMALE	1	1.8	3	5.4	1	1.8	1	1.8	6	10.7	48	85.7	2	3.6	
MALE	0	.0	8	5.5	3	2.1	5	3.4	16	11.0	121	83.4	8	5.5	
PART-TIME	0	.0	2	3.0	0	.0	5	7.5	7	10.4	60	89.6	0	.0	
FEMALE	0	.0	1	5.9	0	.0	1	5.9	2	11.8	15	88.2	0	.0	
MALE	0	.0	1	2.0	0	.0	4	8.0	5	10.0	45	90.0	0	.0	
TOTAL	1	.4	13	4.9	4	1.5	11	4.1	29	10.8	229	85.4	10	3.7	
FEMALE	1	1.4	4	5.5	1	1.4	2	2.7	8	11.0	63	86.3	2	2.7	
MALE	0	.0	9	4.6	3	1.5	9	4.6	21	10.8	166	85.1	8	4.1	
GRADUATE:															
FULL-TIME	1	.7	0	.0	4	2.7	3	2.1	8	5.5	121	82.9	17	11.6	
FEMALE	1	2.8	0	.0	1	2.8	1	2.8	3	8.3	30	83.3	3	8.3	
MALE	0	.0	0	.0	3	2.7	2	1.8	5	4.5	91	82.7	14	12.7	
PART-TIME	0	.0	0	.0	0	.0	0	.0	0	.0	3	100.0	0	.0	
FEMALE	0	.0	0	.0	0	.0	0	.0	0	.0	0	.0	0	.0	
MALE	0	.0	0	.0	0	.0	0	.0	0	.0	3	100.0	0	.0	
TOTAL	1	.7	0	.0	4	2.7	3	2.0	8	5.4	124	83.2	17	11.4	
FEMALE	1	2.8	0	.0	1	2.8	1	2.8	3	8.3	30	83.3	3	8.3	
MALE	0	.0	0	.0	3	2.7	2	1.8	5	4.4	94	83.2	14	12.4	
PROFESSIONAL:															
FULL-TIME	0	.0	0	.0	0	.0	0	.0	0	.0	0	.0	0	.0	
FEMALE	0	.0	0	.0	0	.0	0	.0	0	.0	0	.0	0	.0	
MALE	0	.0	0	.0	0	.0	0	.0	0	.0	0	.0	0	.0	
PART-TIME	0	.0	0	.0	0	.0	0	.0	0	.0	0	.0	0	.0	
FEMALE	0	.0	0	.0	0	.0	0	.0	0	.0	0	.0	0	.0	
MALE	0	.0	0	.0	0	.0	0	.0	0	.0	0	.0	0	.0	
TOTAL	0	.0	0	.0	0	.0	0	.0	0	.0	0	.0	0	.0	
FEMALE	0	.0	0	.0	0	.0	0	.0	0	.0	0	.0	0	.0	
MALE	0	.0	0	.0	0	.0	0	.0	0	.0	0	.0	0	.0	
UND+GRAD+PROF:															
FULL-TIME	2	.6	11	3.2	8	2.3	9	2.6	30	8.6	290	83.6	27	7.8	
FEMALE	2	2.2	3	3.3	2	2.2	2	2.2	9	9.8	78	84.8	5	5.4	
MALE	0	.0	8	3.1	6	2.4	7	2.7	21	8.2	212	83.1	22	8.6	
PART-TIME	0	.0	2	2.9	0	.0	5	7.1	7	10.0	63	90.0	0	.0	
FEMALE	0	.0	1	5.9	0	.0	1	5.9	2	11.8	15	88.2	0	.0	
MALE	0	.0	1	1.9	0	.0	4	7.5	5	9.4	48	90.6	0	.0	
TOTAL	2	.5	13	3.1	8	1.9	14	3.4	37	8.9	353	84.7	27	6.5	
FEMALE	2	1.8	4	3.7	2	1.8	3	2.8	11	10.1	93	85.3	5	4.6	
MALE	0	.0	9	2.9	6	1.9	11	3.6	26	8.4	260	84.4	22	7.1	
UNCLASSIFIED:															
TOTAL	0	.0	0	.0	0	.0	0	.0	0	.0	0	.0	0	.0	
FEMALE	0	.0	0	.0	0	.0	0	.0	0	.0	0	.0	0	.0	
MALE	0	.0	0	.0	0	.0	0	.0	0	.0	0	.0	0	.0	
TOTAL ENROLLMENT:															
TOTAL	2	.5	13	3.1	8	1.9	14	3.4	37	8.9	353	84.7	27	6.5	
FEMALE	2	1.8	4	3.7	2	1.8	3	2.8	11	10.1	93	85.3	5	4.6	
MALE	0	.0	9	2.9	6	1.9	11	3.6	26	8.4	260	84.4	22	7.1	

ARCHITECTURE AND ENVIRONMENTAL DESIGN

I INDIAN NATIVE	BLACK NON-HISPANIC		ASIAN OR PACIFIC ISLANDER		HISPANIC		TOTAL MINORITY		WHITE NON-HISPANIC		NON-RESIDENT ALIEN		TOTAL
%	NUMBER	%	NUMBER	%	NUMBER	%	NUMBER	%	NUMBER	%	NUMBER	%	NUMBER

(3 INSTITUTIONS)

I INDIAN NATIVE %	BLACK NUMBER	BLACK %	ASIAN NUMBER	ASIAN %	HISPANIC NUMBER	HISPANIC %	TOTAL MINORITY NUMBER	TOTAL MINORITY %	WHITE NUMBER	WHITE %	NON-RES NUMBER	NON-RES %	TOTAL NUMBER
.0	9	6.2	1	.7	1	.7	11	7.5	135	92.5	0	.0	146
.0	0	.0	1	3.8	0	.0	1	3.8	25	96.2	0	.0	26
.0	9	7.5	0	.0	1	.8	10	8.3	110	91.7	0	.0	120
1.1	8	9.0	1	1.1	1	1.1	11	12.4	78	87.6	0	.0	89
.0	2	22.2	0	.0	0	.0	2	22.2	7	77.8	0	.0	9
1.3	6	7.5	1	1.3	1	1.3	9	11.3	71	88.8	0	.0	80
.4	17	7.2	2	.9	2	.9	22	9.4	213	90.6	0	.0	235
.0	2	5.7	1	2.9	0	.0	3	8.6	32	91.4	0	.0	35
.5	15	7.5	1	.5	2	1.0	19	9.5	181	90.5	0	.0	200
.0	0	.0	0	.0	0	.0	0	.0	0	.0	0	.0	0
.0	0	.0	0	.0	0	.0	0	.0	0	.0	0	.0	0
.0	0	.0	0	.0	0	.0	0	.0	0	.0	0	.0	0
.0	0	.0	0	.0	0	.0	0	.0	0	.0	0	.0	0
.0	0	.0	0	.0	0	.0	0	.0	0	.0	0	.0	0
.0	0	.0	0	.0	0	.0	0	.0	0	.0	0	.0	0
.0	0	.0	0	.0	0	.0	0	.0	0	.0	0	.0	0
.0	0	.0	0	.0	0	.0	0	.0	0	.0	0	.0	0
.0	0	.0	0	.0	0	.0	0	.0	0	.0	0	.0	0
.0	0	.0	0	.0	0	.0	0	.0	0	.0	0	.0	0
.0	0	.0	0	.0	0	.0	0	.0	0	.0	0	.0	0
.0	0	.0	0	.0	0	.0	0	.0	0	.0	0	.0	0
.0	0	.0	0	.0	0	.0	0	.0	0	.0	0	.0	0
.0	0	.0	0	.0	0	.0	0	.0	0	.0	0	.0	0
.0	0	.0	0	.0	0	.0	0	.0	0	.0	0	.0	0
.0	9	6.2	1	.7	1	.7	11	7.5	135	92.5	0	.0	146
.0	0	.0	1	3.8	0	.0	1	3.8	25	96.2	0	.0	26
.0	9	7.5	0	.0	1	.8	10	8.3	110	91.7	0	.0	120
1.1	8	9.0	1	1.1	1	1.1	11	12.4	78	87.6	0	.0	89
.0	2	22.2	0	.0	0	.0	2	22.2	7	77.8	0	.0	9
1.3	6	7.5	1	1.3	1	1.3	9	11.3	71	88.8	0	.0	80
.4	17	7.2	2	.9	2	.9	22	9.4	213	90.6	0	.0	235
.0	2	5.7	1	2.9	0	.0	3	8.6	32	91.4	0	.0	35
.5	15	7.5	1	.5	2	1.0	19	9.5	181	90.5	0	.0	200
.0	0	.0	0	.0	0	.0	0	.0	0	.0	0	.0	0
.0	0	.0	0	.0	0	.0	0	.0	0	.0	0	.0	0
.0	0	.0	0	.0	0	.0	0	.0	0	.0	0	.0	0
.4	17	7.2	2	.9	2	.9	22	9.4	213	90.6	0	.0	235
.0	2	5.7	1	2.9	0	.0	3	8.6	32	91.4	0	.0	35
.5	15	7.5	1	.5	2	1.0	19	9.5	181	90.5	0	.0	200

(5 INSTITUTIONS)

I INDIAN NATIVE %	BLACK NUMBER	BLACK %	ASIAN NUMBER	ASIAN %	HISPANIC NUMBER	HISPANIC %	TOTAL MINORITY NUMBER	TOTAL MINORITY %	WHITE NUMBER	WHITE %	NON-RES NUMBER	NON-RES %	TOTAL NUMBER
.4	171	30.4	4	.7	13	2.3	190	33.7	248	44.0	125	22.2	563
.0	40	27.6	0	.0	5	3.4	45	31.0	84	57.9	16	11.0	145
.5	131	31.3	4	1.0	8	1.9	145	34.7	164	39.2	109	26.1	418
.0	34	54.0	2	3.2	0	.0	36	57.1	17	27.0	10	15.9	63
.0	8	42.1	0	.0	0	.0	8	42.1	10	52.6	1	5.3	19
.0	26	59.1	2	4.5	0	.0	28	63.6	7	15.9	9	20.5	44
.3	205	32.7	6	1.0	13	2.1	226	36.1	265	42.3	135	21.6	626
.0	48	29.3	0	.0	5	3.0	53	32.3	94	57.3	17	10.4	164
.4	157	34.0	6	1.3	8	1.7	173	37.4	171	37.0	118	25.5	462
.0	27	20.5	1	.8	3	2.3	31	23.5	50	37.9	51	38.6	132
.0	8	24.2	0	.0	0	.0	8	24.2	12	36.4	13	39.4	33
.0	19	19.2	1	1.0	3	3.0	23	23.2	38	38.4	38	38.4	99
.0	12	15.4	5	6.4	3	3.8	20	25.6	44	56.4	14	17.9	78
.0	3	15.0	2	10.0	1	5.0	6	30.0	12	60.0	2	10.0	20
.0	9	15.5	3	5.2	2	3.4	14	24.1	32	55.2	12	20.7	58
.0	39	18.4	6	2.9	6	2.9	51	24.3	94	44.8	65	31.0	210
.0	11	20.8	2	3.8	1	1.9	14	26.4	24	45.3	15	28.3	53
.0	28	17.8	4	2.5	5	3.2	37	23.6	70	44.6	50	31.8	157
.0	0	.0	0	.0	0	.0	0	.0	0	.0	0	.0	0
.0	0	.0	0	.0	0	.0	0	.0	0	.0	0	.0	0
.0	0	.0	0	.0	0	.0	0	.0	0	.0	0	.0	0

MAJOR FIELD 0200 - ARCHITECTURE AND ENVIRONMENTAL DESIGN

	AMERICAN INDIAN ALASKAN NATIVE		BLACK NON-HISPANIC		ASIAN OR PACIFIC ISLANDER		HISPANIC		TOTAL MINORITY		WHITE NON-HISPANIC		NON-RESIDENT ALIEN		T
	NUMBER	%	NUMBER	%	NUMBER	%	NUMBER	%	NUMBER	%	NUMBER	%	NUMBER	%	N

DISTRICT OF COLUMBIA CONTINUED

PROFESSIONAL:
PART-TIME	0	.0	0	.0	0	.0	0	.0	0	.0	0	.0	0	.0	
FEMALE	0	.0	0	.0	0	.0	0	.0	0	.0	0	.0	0	.0	
MALE	0	.0	0	.0	0	.0	0	.0	0	.0	0	.0	0	.0	

TOTAL	0	.0	0	.0	0	.0	0	.0	0	.0	0	.0	0	.0	
FEMALE	0	.0	0	.0	0	.0	0	.0	0	.0	0	.0	0	.0	
MALE	0	.0	0	.0	0	.0	0	.0	0	.0	0	.0	0	.0	

UND+GRAD+PROF:
FULL-TIME	2	.3	198	28.5	5	.7	16	2.3	221	31.8	298	42.9	176	25.3	
FEMALE	0	.0	48	27.0	0	.0	5	2.8	53	29.8	96	53.9	29	16.3	
MALE	2	.4	150	29.0	5	1.0	11	2.1	168	32.5	202	39.1	147	28.4	
PART-TIME	0	.0	46	32.6	7	5.0	3	2.1	56	39.7	61	43.3	24	17.0	
FEMALE	0	.0	11	28.2	2	5.1	1	2.6	14	35.9	22	56.4	3	7.7	
MALE	0	.0	35	34.3	5	4.9	2	2.0	42	41.2	39	38.2	21	20.6	

TOTAL	2	.2	244	29.2	12	1.4	19	2.3	277	33.1	359	42.9	200	23.9	
FEMALE	0	.0	59	27.2	2	.9	6	2.8	67	30.9	118	54.4	32	14.7	
MALE	2	.3	185	29.9	10	1.6	13	2.1	210	33.9	241	38.9	168	27.1	

UNCLASSIFIED:
TOTAL	0	.0	3	100.0	0	.0	0	.0	3	100.0	0	.0	0	.0	
FEMALE	0	.0	2	100.0	0	.0	0	.0	2	100.0	0	.0	0	.0	
MALE	0	.0	1	100.0	0	.0	0	.0	1	100.0	0	.0	0	.0	

TOTAL ENROLLMENT:
TOTAL	2	.2	247	29.4	12	1.4	19	2.3	280	33.4	359	42.8	200	23.8	
FEMALE	0	.0	61	27.9	2	.9	6	2.7	69	31.5	118	53.9	32	14.6	
MALE	2	.3	186	30.0	10	1.6	13	2.1	211	34.0	241	38.9	168	27.1	

FLORIDA   (6 INSTITUTIONS)

UNDERGRADUATES:
FULL-TIME	2	.1	90	5.0	34	1.9	190	10.5	316	17.4	1,463	80.5	39	2.1	
FEMALE	0	.0	23	4.4	4	.8	48	9.2	75	14.4	436	83.8	9	1.7	
MALE	2	.2	67	5.2	30	2.3	142	10.9	241	18.6	1,027	79.1	30	2.3	
PART-TIME	0	.0	9	2.9	3	1.0	67	21.3	79	25.1	229	72.7	7	2.2	
FEMALE	0	.0	0	.0	1	1.1	13	14.0	14	15.1	77	82.8	2	2.2	
MALE	0	.0	9	4.1	2	.9	54	24.3	65	29.3	152	68.5	5	2.3	

TOTAL	2	.1	99	4.6	37	1.7	257	12.0	395	18.5	1,692	79.3	46	2.2	
FEMALE	0	.0	23	3.8	5	.8	61	10.0	89	14.5	513	83.7	11	1.8	
MALE	2	.1	76	5.0	32	2.1	196	12.9	306	20.1	1,179	77.6	35	2.3	

GRADUATE:
FULL-TIME	0	.0	9	3.9	2	.9	11	4.8	22	9.6	194	84.3	14	6.1	
FEMALE	0	.0	4	7.5	0	.0	1	1.9	5	9.4	46	86.8	2	3.8	
MALE	0	.0	5	2.8	2	1.1	10	5.6	17	9.6	148	83.6	12	6.8	
PART-TIME	1	1.9	0	.0	0	.0	2	3.7	3	5.6	49	90.7	2	3.7	
FEMALE	0	.0	0	.0	0	.0	1	9.1	1	9.1	9	81.8	1	9.1	
MALE	1	2.3	0	.0	0	.0	1	2.3	2	4.7	40	93.0	1	2.3	

TOTAL	1	.4	9	3.2	2	.7	13	4.6	25	8.8	243	85.6	16	5.6	
FEMALE	0	.0	4	6.3	0	.0	2	3.1	6	9.4	55	85.9	3	4.7	
MALE	1	.5	5	2.3	2	.9	11	5.0	19	8.6	188	85.5	13	5.9	

PROFESSIONAL:
FULL-TIME	0	.0	0	.0	0	.0	0	.0	0	.0	0	.0	0	.0	
FEMALE	0	.0	0	.0	0	.0	0	.0	0	.0	0	.0	0	.0	
MALE	0	.0	0	.0	0	.0	0	.0	0	.0	0	.0	0	.0	
PART-TIME	0	.0	0	.0	0	.0	0	.0	0	.0	0	.0	0	.0	
FEMALE	0	.0	0	.0	0	.0	0	.0	0	.0	0	.0	0	.0	
MALE	0	.0	0	.0	0	.0	0	.0	0	.0	0	.0	0	.0	

TOTAL	0	.0	0	.0	0	.0	0	.0	0	.0	0	.0	0	.0	
FEMALE	0	.0	0	.0	0	.0	0	.0	0	.0	0	.0	0	.0	
MALE	0	.0	0	.0	0	.0	0	.0	0	.0	0	.0	0	.0	

UND+GRAD+PROF:
FULL-TIME	2	.1	99	4.8	36	1.8	201	9.8	338	16.5	1,657	80.9	53	2.6	
FEMALE	0	.0	27	4.7	4	.7	49	8.6	80	14.0	482	84.1	11	1.9	
MALE	2	.1	72	4.9	32	2.2	152	10.3	258	17.5	1,175	79.7	42	2.8	
PART-TIME	1	.3	9	2.4	3	.8	69	18.7	82	22.2	278	75.3	9	2.4	
FEMALE	0	.0	0	.0	1	1.0	14	13.5	15	14.4	86	82.7	3	2.9	
MALE	1	.4	9	3.4	2	.8	55	20.8	67	25.3	192	72.5	6	2.3	

TOTAL	3	.1	108	4.5	39	1.6	270	11.2	420	17.4	1,935	80.1	62	2.6	
FEMALE	0	.0	27	4.0	5	.7	63	9.3	95	14.0	568	83.9	14	2.1	
MALE	3	.2	81	4.7	34	2.0	207	11.9	325	18.7	1,367	78.6	48	2.8	

UNCLASSIFIED:
TOTAL	0	.0	1	1.9	0	.0	4	7.7	5	9.6	46	88.5	1	1.9	
FEMALE	0	.0	1	4.8	0	.0	1	4.8	2	9.5	19	90.5	0	.0	
MALE	0	.0	0	.0	0	.0	3	9.7	3	9.7	27	87.1	1	3.2	

TOTAL ENROLLMENT:
TOTAL	3	.1	109	4.4	39	1.6	274	11.1	425	17.2	1,981	80.2	63	2.6	
FEMALE	0	.0	28	4.0	5	.7	64	9.2	97	13.9	587	84.1	14	2.0	
MALE	3	.2	81	4.6	34	1.9	210	11.9	328	18.5	1,394	78.7	49	2.8	

332

ARCHITECTURE AND ENVIRONMENTAL DESIGN

INDIAN NATIVE	BLACK NON-HISPANIC		ASIAN OR PACIFIC ISLANDER		HISPANIC		TOTAL MINORITY		WHITE NON-HISPANIC		NON-RESIDENT ALIEN		TOTAL
%	NUMBER	%	NUMBER	%	NUMBER	%	NUMBER	%	NUMBER	%	NUMBER	%	NUMBER
(10 INSTITUTIONS)													
.1	33	3.7	5	.6	12	1.3	51	5.7	814	91.2	28	3.1	893
.5	6	2.9	4	1.9	4	1.9	15	7.1	185	88.1	10	4.8	210
.0	27	4.0	1	.1	8	1.2	36	5.3	629	92.1	18	2.6	683
.0	8	6.4	2	1.6	2	1.6	12	9.6	110	88.0	3	2.4	125
.0	3	13.0	0	.0	1	4.3	4	17.4	18	78.3	1	4.3	23
.0	5	4.9	2	2.0	1	1.0	8	7.8	92	90.2	2	2.0	102
.1	41	4.0	7	.7	14	1.4	63	6.2	924	90.8	31	3.0	1,018
.4	9	3.9	4	1.7	5	2.1	19	8.2	203	87.1	11	4.7	233
.0	32	4.1	3	.4	9	1.1	44	5.6	721	91.8	20	2.5	785
.0	8	5.9	1	.7	3	2.2	12	8.8	111	81.6	13	9.6	136
.0	3	13.6	0	.0	0	.0	3	13.6	16	72.7	3	13.6	22
.0	5	4.4	1	.9	3	2.6	9	7.9	95	83.3	10	8.8	114
.0	3	5.7	0	.0	1	1.9	4	7.5	45	84.9	1	7.5	53
.0	1	7.1	0	.0	0	.0	1	7.1	12	85.7	1	7.1	14
.0	2	5.1	0	.0	1	2.6	3	7.7	33	84.6	3	7.7	39
.0	11	5.8	1	.9	4	2.1	16	8.5	156	82.5	17	9.0	189
.0	4	11.1	0	.0	0	.0	4	11.1	28	77.8	4	11.1	36
.0	7	4.6	1	.7	4	2.6	12	7.8	128	83.7	13	8.5	153
.0	0	.0	0	.0	0	.0	0	.0	0	.0	0	.0	0
.0	0	.0	0	.0	0	.0	0	.0	0	.0	0	.0	0
.0	0	.0	0	.0	0	.0	0	.0	0	.0	0	.0	0
.0	0	.0	0	.0	0	.0	0	.0	0	.0	0	.0	0
.0	0	.0	0	.0	0	.0	0	.0	0	.0	0	.0	0
.0	0	.0	0	.0	0	.0	0	.0	0	.0	0	.0	0
.0	0	.0	0	.0	0	.0	0	.0	0	.0	0	.0	0
.0	0	.0	0	.0	0	.0	0	.0	0	.0	0	.0	0
.0	0	.0	0	.0	0	.0	0	.0	0	.0	0	.0	0
.1	41	4.0	6	.6	15	1.5	63	6.1	925	89.9	41	4.0	1,029
.4	9	3.9	4	1.7	4	1.7	18	7.8	201	86.6	13	5.6	232
.0	32	4.0	2	.3	11	1.4	45	5.6	724	90.8	28	3.5	797
.0	11	6.2	2	1.1	3	1.7	16	9.0	155	87.1	7	3.9	178
.0	4	10.8	0	.0	1	2.7	5	13.5	30	81.1	2	5.4	37
.0	7	5.0	2	1.4	2	1.4	11	7.8	125	88.7	5	3.5	141
.1	52	4.3	8	.7	18	1.5	79	6.5	1,080	89.5	48	4.0	1,207
.4	13	4.8	4	1.5	5	1.9	23	8.6	231	85.9	15	5.6	269
.0	39	4.2	4	.4	13	1.4	56	6.0	849	90.5	33	3.5	938
.0	3	7.3	0	.0	1	2.4	4	9.8	35	85.4	2	4.9	41
.0	0	.0	0	.0	0	.0	0	.0	12	100.0	0	.0	12
.0	3	10.3	0	.0	1	3.4	4	13.8	23	79.3	2	6.9	29
.1	55	4.4	8	.6	19	1.5	83	6.7	1,115	89.3	50	4.0	1,248
.4	13	4.6	4	1.4	5	1.8	23	8.2	243	86.5	15	5.3	281
.0	42	4.3	4	.4	14	1.4	60	6.2	872	90.2	35	3.6	967
(1 INSTITUTIONS)													
.0	0	.0	68	74.7	0	.0	68	74.7	20	22.0	3	3.3	91
.0	0	.0	20	69.0	0	.0	20	69.0	8	27.6	1	3.4	29
.0	0	.0	48	77.4	0	.0	48	77.4	12	19.4	2	3.2	62
.0	0	.0	11	84.6	1	7.7	12	92.3	1	7.7	0	.0	13
.0	0	.0	3	100.0	0	.0	3	100.0	0	.0	0	.0	3
.0	0	.0	8	80.0	1	10.0	9	90.0	1	10.0	0	.0	10
.0	0	.0	79	76.0	1	1.0	80	76.9	21	20.2	3	2.9	104
.0	0	.0	23	71.9	0	.0	23	71.9	8	25.0	1	3.1	32
.0	0	.0	56	77.8	1	1.4	57	79.2	13	18.1	2	2.8	72
.0	0	.0	21	43.8	0	.0	21	43.8	22	45.8	5	10.4	48
.0	0	.0	4	30.8	0	.0	4	30.8	8	61.5	1	7.7	13
.0	0	.0	17	48.6	0	.0	17	48.6	14	40.0	4	11.4	35
.0	0	.0	18	48.6	1	2.7	19	51.4	13	35.1	5	13.5	37
.0	0	.0	2	33.3	0	.0	2	33.3	4	66.7	0	.0	6
.0	0	.0	16	51.6	1	3.2	17	54.8	9	29.0	5	16.1	31
.0	0	.0	39	45.9	1	1.2	40	47.1	35	41.2	10	11.8	85
.0	0	.0	6	31.6	0	.0	6	31.6	12	63.2	1	5.3	19
.0	0	.0	33	50.0	1	1.5	34	51.5	23	34.8	9	13.6	66
.0	0	.0	0	.0	0	.0	0	.0	0	.0	0	.0	0
.0	0	.0	0	.0	0	.0	0	.0	0	.0	0	.0	0
.0	0	.0	0	.0	0	.0	0	.0	0	.0	0	.0	0

TABLE 17 — TOTAL ENROLLMENT IN INSTITUTIONS OF HIGHER EDUCATION FOR SELECTED MAJOR FIELDS OF STUDY AND LEVEL OF ENROLLMENT BY RACE, ETHNICITY, AND SEX: STATE, 1978

MAJOR FIELD 0200 — ARCHITECTURE AND ENVIRONMENTAL DESIGN

	AMERICAN INDIAN ALASKAN NATIVE		BLACK NON-HISPANIC		ASIAN OR PACIFIC ISLANDER		HISPANIC		TOTAL MINORITY		WHITE NON-HISPANIC		NON-RESIDENT ALIEN		T
	NUMBER	%	NUMBER	%	NUMBER	%	NUMBER	%	NUMBER	%	NUMBER	%	NUMBER	%	N
HAWAII	CONTINUED														
PROFESSIONAL:															
PART-TIME	0	.0	0	.0	0	.0	0	.0	0	.0	0	.0	0	.0	
FEMALE	0	.0	0	.0	0	.0	0	.0	0	.0	0	.0	0	.0	
MALE	0	.0	0	.0	0	.0	0	.0	0	.0	0	.0	0	.0	
TOTAL	0	.0	0	.0	0	.0	0	.0	0	.0	0	.0	0	.0	
FEMALE	0	.0	0	.0	0	.0	0	.0	0	.0	0	.0	0	.0	
MALE	0	.0	0	.0	0	.0	0	.0	0	.0	0	.0	0	.0	
UND+GRAD+PROF:															
FULL-TIME	0	.0	0	.0	89	64.0	0	.0	89	64.0	42	30.2	8	5.8	
FEMALE	0	.0	0	.0	24	57.1	0	.0	24	57.1	16	38.1	2	4.8	
MALE	0	.0	0	.0	65	67.0	0	.0	65	67.0	26	26.8	6	6.2	
PART-TIME	0	.0	0	.0	29	58.0	2	4.0	31	62.0	14	28.0	5	10.0	
FEMALE	0	.0	0	.0	5	55.6	0	.0	5	55.6	4	44.4	0	.0	
MALE	0	.0	0	.0	24	58.5	2	4.9	26	63.4	10	24.4	5	12.2	
TOTAL	0	.0	0	.0	118	62.4	2	1.1	120	63.5	56	29.6	13	6.9	
FEMALE	0	.0	0	.0	29	56.9	0	.0	29	56.9	20	39.2	2	3.9	
MALE	0	.0	0	.0	89	64.5	2	1.4	91	65.9	36	26.1	11	8.0	
UNCLASSIFIED:															
TOTAL	0	.0	0	.0	0	.0	0	.0	0	.0	0	.0	0	.0	
FEMALE	0	.0	0	.0	0	.0	0	.0	0	.0	0	.0	0	.0	
MALE	0	.0	0	.0	0	.0	0	.0	0	.0	0	.0	0	.0	
TOTAL ENROLLMENT:															
TOTAL	0	.0	0	.0	118	62.4	2	1.1	120	63.5	56	29.6	13	6.9	
FEMALE	0	.0	0	.0	29	56.9	0	.0	29	56.9	20	39.2	2	3.9	
MALE	0	.0	0	.0	89	64.5	2	1.4	91	65.9	36	26.1	11	8.0	
IDAHO	(3 INSTITUTIONS)														
UNDERGRADUATES:															
FULL-TIME	0	.0	2	.4	9	1.9	3	.6	14	2.9	445	91.8	26	5.4	
FEMALE	0	.0	0	.0	0	.0	1	1.2	1	1.2	84	97.7	1	1.2	
MALE	0	.0	2	.5	9	2.3	2	.5	13	3.3	361	90.5	25	6.3	
PART-TIME	0	.0	0	.0	1	3.6	0	.0	1	3.6	26	92.9	1	3.6	
FEMALE	0	.0	0	.0	0	.0	0	.0	0	.0	8	100.0	0	.0	
MALE	0	.0	0	.0	1	5.0	0	.0	1	5.0	18	90.0	1	5.0	
TOTAL	0	.0	2	.4	10	1.9	3	.6	15	2.9	471	91.8	27	5.3	
FEMALE	0	.0	0	.0	0	.0	1	1.1	1	1.1	92	97.9	1	1.1	
MALE	0	.0	2	.5	10	2.4	2	.5	14	3.3	379	90.5	26	6.2	
GRADUATE:															
FULL-TIME	0	.0	0	.0	0	.0	0	.0	0	.0	4	80.0	1	20.0	
FEMALE	0	.0	0	.0	0	.0	0	.0	0	.0	0	.0	0	.0	
MALE	0	.0	0	.0	0	.0	0	.0	0	.0	4	80.0	1	20.0	
PART-TIME	0	.0	0	.0	0	.0	0	.0	0	.0	0	.0	0	.0	
FEMALE	0	.0	0	.0	0	.0	0	.0	0	.0	0	.0	0	.0	
MALE	0	.0	0	.0	0	.0	0	.0	0	.0	0	.0	0	.0	
TOTAL	0	.0	0	.0	0	.0	0	.0	0	.0	4	80.0	1	20.0	
FEMALE	0	.0	0	.0	0	.0	0	.0	0	.0	0	.0	0	.0	
MALE	0	.0	0	.0	0	.0	0	.0	0	.0	4	80.0	1	20.0	
PROFESSIONAL:															
FULL-TIME	0	.0	0	.0	0	.0	0	.0	0	.0	0	.0	0	.0	
FEMALE	0	.0	0	.0	0	.0	0	.0	0	.0	0	.0	0	.0	
MALE	0	.0	0	.0	0	.0	0	.0	0	.0	0	.0	0	.0	
PART-TIME	0	.0	0	.0	0	.0	0	.0	0	.0	0	.0	0	.0	
FEMALE	0	.0	0	.0	0	.0	0	.0	0	.0	0	.0	0	.0	
MALE	0	.0	0	.0	0	.0	0	.0	0	.0	0	.0	0	.0	
TOTAL	0	.0	0	.0	0	.0	0	.0	0	.0	0	.0	0	.0	
FEMALE	0	.0	0	.0	0	.0	0	.0	0	.0	0	.0	0	.0	
MALE	0	.0	0	.0	0	.0	0	.0	0	.0	0	.0	0	.0	
UND+GRAD+PROF:															
FULL-TIME	0	.0	2	.4	9	1.8	3	.6	14	2.9	449	91.6	27	5.5	
FEMALE	0	.0	0	.0	0	.0	1	1.2	1	1.2	84	97.7	1	1.2	
MALE	0	.0	2	.5	9	2.2	2	.5	13	3.2	365	90.3	26	6.4	
PART-TIME	0	.0	0	.0	1	3.6	0	.0	1	3.6	26	92.9	1	3.6	
FEMALE	0	.0	0	.0	0	.0	0	.0	0	.0	8	100.0	0	.0	
MALE	0	.0	0	.0	1	5.0	0	.0	1	5.0	18	90.0	1	5.0	
TOTAL	0	.0	2	.4	10	1.9	3	.6	15	2.9	475	91.7	28	5.4	
FEMALE	0	.0	0	.0	0	.0	1	1.1	1	1.1	92	97.9	1	1.1	
MALE	0	.0	2	.5	10	2.4	2	.5	14	3.3	383	90.3	27	6.4	
UNCLASSIFIED:															
TOTAL	0	.0	0	.0	0	.0	0	.0	0	.0	0	.0	0	.0	
FEMALE	0	.0	0	.0	0	.0	0	.0	0	.0	0	.0	0	.0	
MALE	0	.0	0	.0	0	.0	0	.0	0	.0	0	.0	0	.0	
TOTAL ENROLLMENT:															
TOTAL	0	.0	2	.4	10	1.9	3	.6	15	2.9	475	91.7	28	5.4	
FEMALE	0	.0	0	.0	0	.0	1	1.1	1	1.1	92	97.9	1	1.1	
MALE	0	.0	2	.5	10	2.4	2	.5	14	3.3	383	90.3	27	6.4	

- ARCHITECTURE AND ENVIRONMENTAL DESIGN

:AN INDIAN IN NATIVE		BLACK NON-HISPANIC		ASIAN OR PACIFIC ISLANDER		HISPANIC		TOTAL MINORITY		WHITE NON-HISPANIC		NON-RESIDENT ALIEN		TOTAL
:R	%	NUMBER	%	NUMBER	%	NUMBER	%	NUMBER	%	NUMBER	%	NUMBER	%	NUMBER

(10 INSTITUTIONS)

6	.3	143	6.6	52	2.4	67	3.1	268	12.4	1,810	83.6	87	4.0	2,165
1	.2	32	5.4	15	2.5	10	1.7	58	9.8	519	87.5	16	2.7	593
5	.3	111	7.1	37	2.4	57	3.6	210	13.4	1,291	82.1	71	4.5	1,572
1	.3	45	15.3	6	2.0	14	4.8	66	22.4	224	76.2	4	1.4	294
0	.0	6	9.1	3	4.5	1	1.5	10	15.2	54	81.8	2	3.0	66
1	.4	39	17.1	3	1.3	13	5.7	56	24.6	170	74.6	2	.9	228
7	.3	188	7.6	58	2.4	81	3.3	334	13.6	2,034	82.7	91	3.7	2,459
1	.2	38	5.8	18	2.7	11	1.7	68	10.3	573	86.9	18	2.7	659
6	.3	150	8.3	40	2.2	70	3.9	266	14.8	1,461	81.2	73	4.1	1,800
0	.0	5	1.6	11	3.4	2	.6	18	5.6	265	82.6	38	11.8	321
0	.0	2	2.8	1	1.4	0	.0	3	4.2	62	87.3	6	8.5	71
0	.0	3	1.2	10	4.0	2	.8	15	6.0	203	81.2	32	12.8	250
1	.9	7	6.1	5	4.4	0	.0	13	11.4	83	72.8	18	15.8	114
0	.0	3	9.4	1	3.1	0	.0	4	12.5	27	84.4	1	3.1	32
1	1.2	4	4.9	4	4.9	0	.0	9	11.0	56	68.3	17	20.7	82
1	.2	12	2.8	16	3.7	2	.5	31	7.1	348	80.0	56	12.9	435
0	.0	5	4.9	2	1.9	0	.0	7	6.8	89	86.4	7	6.8	103
1	.3	7	2.1	14	4.2	2	.6	24	7.2	259	78.0	49	14.8	332
0	.0	0	.0	0	.0	0	.0	0	.0	0	.0	0	.0	0
0	.0	0	.0	0	.0	0	.0	0	.0	0	.0	0	.0	0
0	.0	0	.0	0	.0	0	.0	0	.0	0	.0	0	.0	0
0	.0	0	.0	0	.0	0	.0	0	.0	0	.0	0	.0	0
0	.0	0	.0	0	.0	0	.0	0	.0	0	.0	0	.0	0
0	.0	0	.0	0	.0	0	.0	0	.0	0	.0	0	.0	0
0	.0	0	.0	0	.0	0	.0	0	.0	0	.0	0	.0	0
0	.0	0	.0	0	.0	0	.0	0	.0	0	.0	0	.0	0
0	.0	0	.0	0	.0	0	.0	0	.0	0	.0	0	.0	0
6	.2	148	6.0	63	2.5	69	2.8	286	11.5	2,075	83.5	125	5.0	2,486
1	.2	34	5.1	16	2.4	10	1.5	61	9.2	581	87.5	22	3.3	664
5	.3	114	6.3	47	2.6	59	3.2	225	12.3	1,494	82.0	103	5.7	1,822
2	.5	52	12.7	11	2.7	14	3.4	79	19.4	307	75.2	22	5.4	408
0	.0	9	9.2	4	4.1	1	1.0	14	14.3	81	82.7	3	3.1	98
2	.6	43	13.9	7	2.3	13	4.2	65	21.0	226	72.9	19	6.1	310
8	.3	200	6.9	74	2.6	83	2.9	365	12.6	2,382	82.3	147	5.1	2,894
1	.1	43	5.6	20	2.6	11	1.4	75	9.8	662	86.9	25	3.3	762
7	.3	157	7.4	54	2.5	72	3.4	290	13.6	1,720	80.7	122	5.7	2,132
0	.0	4	4.5	4	4.5	1	1.1	9	10.1	77	86.5	3	3.4	89
0	.0	1	4.5	1	4.5	0	.0	2	9.1	19	86.4	1	4.5	22
0	.0	3	4.5	3	4.5	1	1.5	7	10.4	58	86.6	2	3.0	67
8	.3	204	6.8	78	2.6	84	2.8	374	12.5	2,459	82.4	150	5.0	2,983
1	.1	44	5.6	21	2.7	11	1.4	77	9.8	681	86.9	26	3.3	784
7	.3	160	7.3	57	2.6	73	3.3	297	13.5	1,778	80.9	124	5.6	2,199

(5 INSTITUTIONS)

0	.0	24	2.2	7	.6	16	1.5	47	4.3	1,037	95.1	6	.6	1,090
0	.0	5	1.5	2	.6	5	1.5	12	3.6	321	95.5	3	.9	336
0	.0	19	2.5	5	.7	11	1.5	35	4.6	716	95.0	3	.4	754
0	.0	2	4.8	2	4.8	0	.0	4	9.5	37	88.1	1	2.4	42
0	.0	0	.0	0	.0	0	.0	0	.0	9	100.0	0	.0	9
0	.0	2	6.1	2	6.1	0	.0	4	12.1	28	84.8	1	3.0	33
0	.0	26	2.3	9	.8	16	1.4	51	4.5	1,074	94.9	7	.6	1,132
0	.0	5	1.4	2	.6	5	1.4	12	3.5	330	95.7	3	.9	345
0	.0	21	2.7	7	.9	11	1.4	39	5.0	744	94.5	4	.5	787
0	.0	1	3.3	1	3.3	0	.0	2	6.7	23	76.7	5	16.7	30
0	.0	1	14.3	0	.0	0	.0	1	14.3	5	71.4	1	14.3	7
0	.0	0	.0	1	4.3	0	.0	1	4.3	18	78.3	4	17.4	23
0	.0	0	.0	0	.0	0	.0	0	.0	14	93.3	1	6.7	15
0	.0	0	.0	0	.0	0	.0	0	.0	1	100.0	0	.0	1
0	.0	0	.0	0	.0	0	.0	0	.0	13	92.9	1	7.1	14
0	.0	1	2.2	1	2.2	0	.0	2	4.4	37	82.2	6	13.3	45
0	.0	1	12.5	0	.0	0	.0	1	12.5	6	75.0	1	12.5	8
0	.0	0	.0	1	2.7	0	.0	1	2.7	31	83.8	5	13.5	37
0	.0	0	.0	0	.0	0	.0	0	.0	0	.0	0	.0	0
0	.0	0	.0	0	.0	0	.0	0	.0	0	.0	0	.0	0

MAJOR FIELD 0200 - ARCHITECTURE AND ENVIRONMENTAL DESIGN

	AMERICAN INDIAN ALASKAN NATIVE		BLACK NON-HISPANIC		ASIAN OR PACIFIC ISLANDER		HISPANIC		TOTAL MINORITY		WHITE NON-HISPANIC		NON-RESIDENT ALIEN	
	NUMBER	%	NUMBER	%	NUMBER	%	NUMBER	%	NUMBER	%	NUMBER	%	NUMBER	%
INDIANA	CONTINUED													
PROFESSIONAL:														
PART-TIME														
FEMALE	0	.0	0	.0	0	.0	0	.0	0	.0	0	.0	0	.0
MALE	0	.0	0	.0	0	.0	0	.0	0	.0	0	.0	0	.0
TOTAL	0	.0	0	.0	0	.0	0	.0	0	.0	0	.0	0	.0
FEMALE	0	.0	0	.0	0	.0	0	.0	0	.0	0	.0	0	.0
MALE	0	.0	0	.0	0	.0	0	.0	0	.0	0	.0	0	.0
UND+GRAD+PROF:														
FULL-TIME	0	.0	25	2.2	8	.7	16	1.4	49	4.4	1,060	94.6	11	1.0
FEMALE	0	.0	6	1.7	2	.6	5	1.5	13	3.8	326	95.0	4	1.2
MALE	0	.0	19	2.4	6	.8	11	1.4	36	4.6	734	94.5	7	.9
PART-TIME	0	.0	2	3.5	2	3.5	0	.0	4	7.0	51	89.5	2	3.5
FEMALE	0	.0	0	.0	0	.0	0	.0	0	.0	10	100.0	0	.0
MALE	0	.0	2	4.3	2	4.3	0	.0	4	8.5	41	87.2	2	4.3
TOTAL	0	.0	27	2.3	10	.8	16	1.4	53	4.5	1,111	94.4	13	1.1
FEMALE	0	.0	6	1.7	2	.6	5	1.4	13	3.7	336	95.2	4	1.1
MALE	0	.0	21	2.5	8	1.0	11	1.3	40	4.9	775	94.1	9	1.1
UNCLASSIFIED:														
TOTAL	0	.0	0	.0	0	.0	0	.0	0	.0	0	.0	2	100.0
FEMALE	0	.0	0	.0	0	.0	0	.0	0	.0	0	.0	1	100.0
MALE	0	.0	0	.0	0	.0	0	.0	0	.0	0	.0	1	100.0
TOTAL ENROLLMENT:														
TOTAL	0	.0	27	2.3	10	.8	16	1.4	53	4.5	1,111	94.2	15	1.3
FEMALE	0	.0	6	1.7	2	.6	5	1.4	13	3.7	336	94.9	5	1.4
MALE	0	.0	21	2.5	8	1.0	11	1.3	40	4.8	775	93.9	10	1.2
IOWA	(	6 INSTITUTIONS)												
UNDERGRADUATES:														
FULL-TIME	0	.0	19	1.5	4	.3	2	.2	25	2.0	1,218	95.4	34	2.7
FEMALE	0	.0	4	.8	1	.2	1	.2	6	1.3	461	97.1	8	1.7
MALE	0	.0	15	1.9	3	.4	1	.1	19	2.4	757	94.4	26	3.2
PART-TIME	0	.0	2	1.9	1	.9	0	.0	3	2.8	100	93.5	4	3.7
FEMALE	0	.0	0	.0	1	3.1	0	.0	1	3.1	30	93.8	1	3.1
MALE	0	.0	2	2.7	0	.0	0	.0	2	2.7	70	93.3	3	4.0
TOTAL	0	.0	21	1.5	5	.4	2	.1	28	2.0	1,318	95.2	38	2.7
FEMALE	0	.0	4	.8	2	.4	1	.2	7	1.4	491	96.8	9	1.8
MALE	0	.0	17	1.9	3	.3	1	.1	21	2.4	827	94.3	29	3.3
GRADUATE:														
FULL-TIME	0	.0	3	4.3	0	.0	0	.0	3	4.3	53	76.8	13	18.8
FEMALE	0	.0	2	15.4	0	.0	0	.0	2	15.4	7	53.8	4	30.8
MALE	0	.0	1	1.8	0	.0	0	.0	1	1.8	46	82.1	9	16.1
PART-TIME	1	5.3	1	5.3	0	.0	0	.0	2	10.5	14	73.7	3	15.8
FEMALE	1	25.0	0	.0	0	.0	0	.0	1	25.0	2	50.0	1	25.0
MALE	0	.0	1	6.7	0	.0	0	.0	1	6.7	12	80.0	2	13.3
TOTAL	1	1.1	4	4.5	0	.0	0	.0	5	5.7	67	76.1	16	18.2
FEMALE	1	5.9	2	11.8	0	.0	0	.0	3	17.6	9	52.9	5	29.4
MALE	0	.0	2	2.8	0	.0	0	.0	2	2.8	58	81.7	11	15.5
PROFESSIONAL:														
FULL-TIME	0	.0	0	.0	0	.0	0	.0	0	.0	0	.0	0	.0
FEMALE	0	.0	0	.0	0	.0	0	.0	0	.0	0	.0	0	.0
MALE	0	.0	0	.0	0	.0	0	.0	0	.0	0	.0	0	.0
PART-TIME	0	.0	0	.0	0	.0	0	.0	0	.0	0	.0	0	.0
FEMALE	0	.0	0	.0	0	.0	0	.0	0	.0	0	.0	0	.0
MALE	0	.0	0	.0	0	.0	0	.0	0	.0	0	.0	0	.0
TOTAL	0	.0	0	.0	0	.0	0	.0	0	.0	0	.0	0	.0
FEMALE	0	.0	0	.0	0	.0	0	.0	0	.0	0	.0	0	.0
MALE	0	.0	0	.0	0	.0	0	.0	0	.0	0	.0	0	.0
UND+GRAD+PROF:														
FULL-TIME	0	.0	22	1.6	4	.3	2	.1	28	2.1	1,271	94.4	47	3.5
FEMALE	0	.0	6	1.2	1	.2	1	.2	8	1.6	468	95.9	12	2.5
MALE	0	.0	16	1.9	3	.3	1	.1	20	2.3	803	93.6	35	4.1
PART-TIME	1	.8	3	2.4	1	.8	0	.0	5	4.0	114	90.5	7	5.6
FEMALE	1	2.8	0	.0	1	2.8	0	.0	2	5.6	32	88.9	2	5.6
MALE	0	.0	3	3.3	0	.0	0	.0	3	3.3	82	91.1	5	5.6
TOTAL	1	.1	25	1.7	5	.3	2	.1	33	2.2	1,385	94.1	54	3.7
FEMALE	1	.2	6	1.1	2	.4	1	.2	10	1.9	500	95.4	14	2.7
MALE	0	.0	19	2.0	3	.3	1	.1	23	2.4	885	93.4	40	4.2
UNCLASSIFIED:														
TOTAL	0	.0	0	.0	0	.0	0	.0	0	.0	10	90.9	1	9.1
FEMALE	0	.0	0	.0	0	.0	0	.0	0	.0	7	87.5	1	12.5
MALE	0	.0	0	.0	0	.0	0	.0	0	.0	3	100.0	0	.0
TOTAL ENROLLMENT:														
TOTAL	1	.1	25	1.7	5	.3	2	.1	33	2.2	1,395	94.1	55	3.7
FEMALE	1	.2	6	1.1	2	.4	1	.2	10	1.9	507	95.3	15	2.8
MALE	0	.0	19	2.0	3	.3	1	.1	23	2.4	888	93.4	40	4.2

0 - ARCHITECTURE AND ENVIRONMENTAL DESIGN

ICAN INDIAN KAN NATIVE		BLACK NON-HISPANIC		ASIAN OR PACIFIC ISLANDER		HISPANIC		TOTAL MINORITY		WHITE NON-HISPANIC		NON-RESIDENT ALIEN		TUTAL
8ER	%	NUMBER	%	NUMBER	%	NUMBER	%	NUMBER	%	NUMBER	%	NUMBER	%	NUMBER
(8 INSTITUTIONS)														
8	.6	38	2.7	9	.6	16	1.1	71	5.1	1,293	92.3	37	2.6	1,401
1	.4	5	1.9	2	.8	4	1.6	12	4.7	238	92.6	7	2.7	257
7	.6	33	2.9	7	.6	12	1.0	59	5.2	1,055	92.2	30	2.6	1,144
0	.0	3	5.2	0	.0	1	1.7	4	6.9	53	91.4	1	1.7	58
0	.0	1	6.3	0	.0	1	6.3	2	12.5	13	81.3	1	6.3	16
0	.0	2	4.8	0	.0	0	.0	2	4.8	40	95.2	0	.0	42
8	.5	41	2.8	9	.6	17	1.2	75	5.1	1,346	92.3	38	2.6	1,459
1	.4	6	2.2	2	.7	5	1.8	14	5.1	251	91.9	8	2.9	273
7	.6	35	3.0	7	.6	12	1.0	61	5.1	1,095	92.3	30	2.5	1,186
1	1.4	6	8.7	0	.0	2	2.9	9	13.0	40	58.0	20	29.0	69
0	.0	3	15.8	0	.0	0	.0	3	15.8	13	68.4	3	15.8	19
1	2.0	3	6.0	0	.0	2	4.0	6	12.0	27	54.0	17	34.0	50
1	1.7	1	1.7	0	.0	0	.0	2	3.4	50	86.2	6	10.3	58
0	.0	0	.0	0	.0	0	.0	0	.0	12	92.3	1	7.7	13
1	2.2	1	2.2	0	.0	0	.0	2	4.4	38	84.4	5	11.1	45
2	1.6	7	5.5	0	.0	2	1.6	11	8.7	90	70.9	26	20.5	127
0	.0	3	9.4	0	.0	0	.0	3	9.4	25	78.1	4	12.5	32
2	2.1	4	4.2	0	.0	2	2.1	8	8.4	65	68.4	22	23.2	95
0	.0	0	.0	0	.0	0	.0	0	.0	0	.0	0	.0	0
0	.0	0	.0	0	.0	0	.0	0	.0	0	.0	0	.0	0
0	.0	0	.0	0	.0	0	.0	0	.0	0	.0	0	.0	0
0	.0	0	.0	0	.0	0	.0	0	.0	0	.0	0	.0	0
0	.0	0	.0	0	.0	0	.0	0	.0	0	.0	0	.0	0
0	.0	0	.0	0	.0	0	.0	0	.0	0	.0	0	.0	0
0	.0	0	.0	0	.0	0	.0	0	.0	0	.0	0	.0	0
0	.0	0	.0	0	.0	0	.0	0	.0	0	.0	0	.0	0
0	.0	0	.0	0	.0	0	.0	0	.0	0	.0	0	.0	0
9	.6	44	3.0	9	.6	18	1.2	80	5.4	1,333	90.7	57	3.9	1,470
1	.4	6	2.9	2	.7	4	1.4	15	5.4	251	90.9	10	3.6	276
8	.7	36	3.0	7	.6	14	1.2	65	5.4	1,082	90.6	47	3.9	1,194
0	.0	3	3.4	0	.0	1	.9	6	5.2	103	88.8	7	6.0	116
0	.0	1	3.4	0	.0	1	3.4	2	6.9	25	86.2	2	6.9	29
1	1.1	3	3.4	0	.0	0	.0	4	4.6	78	89.7	5	5.7	87
10	.6	48	3.0	9	.6	19	1.2	86	5.4	1,436	90.5	64	4.0	1,586
1	.3	9	3.0	2	.7	5	1.6	17	5.6	276	90.5	12	3.9	305
9	.7	39	3.0	7	.5	14	1.1	69	5.4	1,160	90.6	52	4.1	1,281
0	.0	1	2.1	0	.0	2	4.3	3	6.4	42	89.4	2	4.3	47
0	.0	0	.0	0	.0	0	.0	0	.0	13	92.9	1	7.1	14
0	.0	1	3.0	0	.0	2	6.1	3	9.1	29	87.9	1	3.0	33
10	.6	49	3.0	9	.6	21	1.3	89	5.5	1,478	90.5	66	4.0	1,633
1	.3	9	2.8	2	.6	5	1.6	17	5.3	289	90.6	13	4.1	319
9	.7	40	3.0	7	.5	16	1.2	72	5.5	1,189	90.5	53	4.0	1,314
(6 INSTITUTIONS)														
2	.4	9	1.7	8	1.5	1	.2	20	3.7	507	94.1	12	2.2	539
1	.5	3	1.6	1	.5	0	.0	5	2.6	187	97.4	0	.0	192
1	.3	6	1.7	7	2.0	1	.3	15	4.3	320	92.2	12	3.5	347
0	.0	1	1.8	1	1.8	0	.0	2	3.5	52	91.2	3	5.3	57
0	.0	0	.0	0	.0	0	.0	0	.0	22	100.0	0	.0	22
0	.0	1	2.9	1	2.9	0	.0	2	5.7	30	85.7	3	8.6	35
2	.3	10	1.7	9	1.5	1	.2	22	3.7	559	93.8	15	2.5	596
1	.5	3	1.4	1	.5	0	.0	5	2.3	209	97.7	0	.0	214
1	.3	7	1.8	8	2.1	1	.3	17	4.5	350	91.6	15	3.9	382
0	.0	0	.0	0	.0	0	.0	0	.0	0	.0	0	.0	0
0	.0	0	.0	0	.0	0	.0	0	.0	0	.0	0	.0	0
0	.0	0	.0	0	.0	0	.0	0	.0	0	.0	0	.0	0
0	.0	0	.0	0	.0	0	.0	0	.0	0	.0	0	.0	0
0	.0	0	.0	0	.0	0	.0	0	.0	0	.0	0	.0	0
0	.0	0	.0	0	.0	0	.0	0	.0	0	.0	0	.0	0
0	.0	0	.0	0	.0	0	.0	0	.0	0	.0	0	.0	0
0	.0	0	.0	0	.0	0	.0	0	.0	0	.0	0	.0	0
0	.0	0	.0	0	.0	0	.0	0	.0	0	.0	0	.0	0
0	.0	0	.0	0	.0	0	.0	0	.0	0	.0	0	.0	0
0	.0	0	.0	0	.0	0	.0	0	.0	0	.0	0	.0	0
0	.0	0	.0	0	.0	0	.0	0	.0	0	.0	0	.0	0

MAJOR FIELD 0200 - ARCHITECTURE AND ENVIRONMENTAL DESIGN

	AMERICAN INDIAN ALASKAN NATIVE		BLACK NON-HISPANIC		ASIAN OR PACIFIC ISLANDER		HISPANIC		TOTAL MINORITY		WHITE NON-HISPANIC		NON-RESIDENT ALIEN		T
	NUMBER	%	NUMBER	%	NUMBER	%	NUMBER	%	NUMBER	%	NUMBER	%	NUMBER	%	N
KENTUCKY	**CONTINUED**														
PROFESSIONAL:															
PART-TIME	0	.0	0	.0	0	.0	0	.0	0	.0	0	.0	0	.0	
FEMALE	0	.0	0	.0	0	.0	0	.0	0	.0	0	.0	0	.0	
MALE	0	.0	0	.0	0	.0	0	.0	0	.0	0	.0	0	.0	
TOTAL	0	.0	0	.0	0	.0	0	.0	0	.0	0	.0	0	.0	
FEMALE	0	.0	0	.0	0	.0	0	.0	0	.0	0	.0	0	.0	
MALE	0	.0	0	.0	0	.0	0	.0	0	.0	0	.0	0	.0	
UNC+GRAD+PROF:															
FULL-TIME	2	.4	9	1.7	8	1.5	1	.2	20	3.7	507	94.1	12	2.2	
FEMALE	1	.5	3	1.6	1	.5	0	.0	5	2.6	187	97.4	0	.0	
MALE	1	.3	6	1.7	7	2.0	1	.3	15	4.3	320	92.2	12	3.5	
PART-TIME	0	.0	1	1.8	1	1.8	0	.0	2	3.5	52	91.2	3	5.3	
FEMALE	0	.0	0	.0	0	.0	0	.0	0	.0	22	100.0	0	.0	
MALE	0	.0	1	2.9	1	2.9	0	.0	2	5.7	30	85.7	3	8.6	
TOTAL	2	.3	10	1.7	9	1.5	1	.2	22	3.7	559	93.8	15	2.5	
FEMALE	1	.5	3	1.4	1	.5	0	.0	5	2.3	209	97.7	0	.0	
MALE	1	.3	7	1.8	8	2.1	1	.3	17	4.5	350	91.6	15	3.9	
UNCLASSIFIED:															
TOTAL	0	.0	0	.0	0	.0	0	.0	0	.0	0	.0	0	.0	
FEMALE	0	.0	0	.0	0	.0	0	.0	0	.0	0	.0	0	.0	
MALE	0	.0	0	.0	0	.0	0	.0	0	.0	0	.0	0	.0	
TOTAL ENROLLMENT:															
TOTAL	2	.3	10	1.7	9	1.5	1	.2	22	3.7	559	93.8	15	2.5	
FEMALE	1	.5	3	1.4	1	.5	0	.0	5	2.3	209	97.7	0	.0	
MALE	1	.3	7	1.8	8	2.1	1	.3	17	4.5	350	91.6	15	3.9	
LOUISIANA	**(9 INSTITUTIONS)**														
UNDERGRADUATES:															
FULL-TIME	7	.3	94	4.3	8	.4	48	2.2	157	7.1	1,839	83.7	201	9.1	
FEMALE	0	.0	28	4.5	0	.0	14	2.2	42	6.7	522	83.8	59	9.5	
MALE	7	.4	66	4.2	8	.5	34	2.2	115	7.3	1,317	83.7	142	9.0	
PART-TIME	1	.5	7	3.7	1	.5	2	1.1	11	5.8	170	89.5	9	4.7	
FEMALE	1	1.4	1	1.4	0	.0	1	1.4	3	4.3	63	90.0	4	5.7	
MALE	0	.0	6	5.0	1	.8	1	.8	8	6.7	107	89.2	5	4.2	
TOTAL	8	.3	101	4.2	9	.4	50	2.1	168	7.0	2,009	84.2	210	8.8	
FEMALE	1	.1	29	4.2	0	.0	15	2.2	45	6.5	585	84.4	63	9.1	
MALE	7	.4	72	4.3	9	.5	35	2.1	123	7.3	1,424	84.1	147	8.7	
GRADUATE:															
FULL-TIME	0	.0	0	.0	0	.0	0	.0	0	.0	43	97.7	1	2.3	
FEMALE	0	.0	0	.0	0	.0	0	.0	0	.0	13	100.0	0	.0	
MALE	0	.0	0	.0	0	.0	0	.0	0	.0	30	96.8	1	3.2	
PART-TIME	1	6.3	0	.0	0	.0	0	.0	1	6.3	15	93.8	0	.0	
FEMALE	0	.0	0	.0	0	.0	0	.0	0	.0	5	100.0	0	.0	
MALE	1	9.1	0	.0	0	.0	0	.0	1	9.1	10	90.9	0	.0	
TOTAL	1	1.7	0	.0	0	.0	0	.0	1	1.7	58	96.7	1	1.7	
FEMALE	0	.0	0	.0	0	.0	0	.0	0	.0	18	100.0	0	.0	
MALE	1	2.4	0	.0	0	.0	0	.0	1	2.4	40	95.2	1	2.4	
PROFESSIONAL:															
FULL-TIME	0	.0	0	.0	0	.0	0	.0	0	.0	0	.0	0	.0	
FEMALE	0	.0	0	.0	0	.0	0	.0	0	.0	0	.0	0	.0	
MALE	0	.0	0	.0	0	.0	0	.0	0	.0	0	.0	0	.0	
PART-TIME	0	.0	0	.0	0	.0	0	.0	0	.0	0	.0	0	.0	
FEMALE	0	.0	0	.0	0	.0	0	.0	0	.0	0	.0	0	.0	
MALE	0	.0	0	.0	0	.0	0	.0	0	.0	0	.0	0	.0	
TOTAL	0	.0	0	.0	0	.0	0	.0	0	.0	0	.0	0	.0	
FEMALE	0	.0	0	.0	0	.0	0	.0	0	.0	0	.0	0	.0	
MALE	0	.0	0	.0	0	.0	0	.0	0	.0	0	.0	0	.0	
UNC+GRAD+PROF:															
FULL-TIME	7	.3	94	4.2	8	.4	48	2.1	157	7.0	1,882	84.0	202	9.0	
FEMALE	0	.0	28	4.4	0	.0	14	2.2	42	6.6	535	84.1	59	9.3	
MALE	7	.4	66	4.1	8	.5	34	2.1	115	7.2	1,347	83.9	143	8.9	
PART-TIME	2	1.0	7	3.4	1	.5	2	1.0	12	5.8	185	89.8	9	4.4	
FEMALE	1	1.3	1	1.3	0	.0	1	1.3	3	4.0	68	90.7	4	5.3	
MALE	1	.8	6	4.6	1	.8	1	.8	9	6.9	117	89.3	5	3.8	
TOTAL	9	.4	101	4.1	9	.4	50	2.0	169	6.9	2,067	84.5	211	8.6	
FEMALE	1	.1	29	4.1	0	.0	15	2.1	45	6.3	603	84.8	63	8.9	
MALE	8	.5	72	4.1	9	.5	35	2.0	124	7.1	1,464	84.3	148	8.5	
UNCLASSIFIED:															
TOTAL	0	.0	1	100.0	0	.0	0	.0	1	100.0	0	.0	0	.0	
FEMALE	0	.0	0	.0	0	.0	0	.0	0	.0	0	.0	0	.0	
MALE	0	.0	1	100.0	0	.0	0	.0	1	100.0	0	.0	0	.0	
TOTAL ENROLLMENT:															
TOTAL	9	.4	102	4.2	9	.4	50	2.0	170	6.9	2,067	84.4	211	8.6	
FEMALE	1	.1	29	4.1	0	.0	15	2.1	45	6.3	603	84.8	63	8.9	
MALE	8	.5	73	4.2	9	.5	35	2.0	125	7.2	1,464	84.3	148	8.5	

AL ENROLLMENT IN INSTITUTIONS OF HIGHER EDUCATION FOR SELECTED MAJOR FIELDS OF STUDY AND LEVEL OF ENROLLMENT
RACE, ETHNICITY, AND SEX: STATE, 1978

:00 = ARCHITECTURE AND ENVIRONMENTAL DESIGN

RICAN INDIAN SKAN NATIVE		BLACK NON-HISPANIC		ASIAN OR PACIFIC ISLANDER		HISPANIC		TOTAL MINORITY		WHITE NON-HISPANIC		NON-RESIDENT ALIEN		TOTAL
IMBER	%	NUMBER	%	NUMBER	%	NUMBER	%	NUMBER	%	NUMBER	%	NUMBER	%	NUMBER
(3 INSTITUTIONS)														
0	.0	22	6.8	5	1.6	5	1.6	32	9.9	271	84.2	19	5.9	322
0	.0	13	9.9	3	2.3	0	.0	16	12.2	109	83.2	6	4.6	131
0	.0	9	4.7	2	1.0	5	2.6	16	8.4	162	84.8	13	6.8	191
0	.0	4	5.1	1	1.3	1	1.3	6	7.6	69	87.3	4	5.1	79
0	.0	3	5.5	1	1.8	0	.0	4	7.3	48	87.3	3	5.5	55
0	.0	1	4.2	0	.0	1	4.2	2	8.3	21	87.5	1	4.2	24
0	.0	26	6.5	6	1.5	6	1.5	38	9.5	340	84.8	23	5.7	401
0	.0	16	8.6	4	2.2	0	.0	20	10.8	157	84.4	9	4.8	186
0	.0	10	4.7	2	.9	6	2.8	18	8.4	183	85.1	14	6.5	215
0	.0	6	60.0	0	.0	1	10.0	7	70.0	1	10.0	2	20.0	10
0	.0	4	80.0	0	.0	0	.0	4	80.0	1	20.0	0	.0	5
0	.0	2	40.0	0	.0	1	20.0	3	60.0	0	.0	2	40.0	5
1	4.0	16	64.0	0	.0	0	.0	17	68.0	6	24.0	2	8.0	25
1	12.5	4	50.0	0	.0	0	.0	5	62.5	3	37.5	0	.0	8
0	.0	12	70.6	0	.0	0	.0	12	70.6	3	17.6	2	11.8	17
1	2.9	22	62.9	0	.0	1	2.9	24	68.6	7	20.0	4	11.4	35
1	7.7	8	61.5	0	.0	0	.0	9	69.2	4	30.8	0	.0	13
0	.0	14	63.6	0	.0	1	4.5	15	68.2	3	13.6	4	18.2	22
0	.0	0	.0	0	.0	0	.0	0	.0	0	.0	0	.0	0
0	.0	0	.0	0	.0	0	.0	0	.0	0	.0	0	.0	0
0	.0	0	.0	0	.0	0	.0	0	.0	0	.0	0	.0	0
0	.0	0	.0	0	.0	0	.0	0	.0	0	.0	0	.0	0
0	.0	0	.0	0	.0	0	.0	0	.0	0	.0	0	.0	0
0	.0	0	.0	0	.0	0	.0	0	.0	0	.0	0	.0	0
0	.0	0	.0	0	.0	0	.0	0	.0	0	.0	0	.0	0
0	.0	0	.0	0	.0	0	.0	0	.0	0	.0	0	.0	0
0	.0	0	.0	0	.0	0	.0	0	.0	0	.0	0	.0	0
0	.0	28	8.4	5	1.5	6	1.8	39	11.7	272	81.9	21	6.3	332
0	.0	17	12.5	3	2.2	0	.0	20	14.7	110	80.9	6	4.4	136
0	.0	11	5.6	2	1.0	6	3.1	19	9.7	162	82.7	15	7.7	196
1	1.0	20	19.2	1	1.0	1	1.0	23	22.1	75	72.1	6	5.8	104
1	1.6	7	11.1	1	1.6	0	.0	9	14.3	51	81.0	3	4.8	63
0	.0	13	31.7	0	.0	1	2.4	14	34.1	24	58.5	3	7.3	41
1	.2	48	11.0	6	1.4	7	1.6	62	14.2	347	79.6	27	6.2	436
1	.5	24	12.1	4	2.0	0	.0	29	14.6	161	80.9	9	4.5	199
0	.0	24	10.1	2	.8	7	3.0	33	13.9	186	78.5	18	7.6	237
0	.0	4	16.0	0	.0	0	.0	4	16.0	16	64.0	5	20.0	25
0	.0	2	33.3	0	.0	0	.0	2	33.3	3	50.0	1	16.7	6
0	.0	2	10.5	0	.0	0	.0	2	10.5	13	68.4	4	21.1	19
T:														
1	.2	52	11.3	6	1.3	7	1.5	66	14.3	363	78.7	32	6.9	461
1	.5	26	12.7	4	2.0	0	.0	31	15.1	164	80.0	10	4.9	205
0	.0	26	10.2	2	.8	7	2.7	35	13.7	199	77.7	22	8.6	256
(8 INSTITUTIONS)														
2	.3	12	1.9	8	1.3	2	.3	24	3.9	578	93.8	14	2.3	616
0	.0	6	2.2	3	1.1	1	.4	10	3.7	255	94.8	4	1.5	269
2	.6	6	1.7	5	1.4	1	.3	14	4.0	323	93.1	10	2.9	347
0	.0	0	.0	0	.0	1	14.3	1	14.3	5	71.4	1	14.3	7
0	.0	0	.0	0	.0	1	20.0	1	20.0	3	60.0	1	20.0	5
0	.0	0	.0	0	.0	0	.0	0	.0	2	100.0	0	.0	2
2	.3	12	1.9	8	1.3	3	.5	25	4.0	583	93.6	15	2.4	623
0	.0	6	2.2	3	1.1	2	.7	11	4.0	258	94.2	5	1.8	274
2	.6	6	1.7	5	1.4	1	.3	14	4.0	325	93.1	10	2.9	349
7	.7	56	5.5	41	4.0	25	2.4	129	12.6	749	73.1	146	14.3	1,024
2	.5	24	6.6	11	3.0	7	1.9	44	12.1	293	80.5	27	7.4	364
5	.8	32	4.8	30	4.5	18	2.7	85	12.9	456	69.1	119	18.0	660
0	.0	0	.0	0	.0	1	2.7	1	2.7	33	89.2	3	8.1	37
0	.0	0	.0	0	.0	0	.0	0	.0	18	94.7	1	5.3	19
0	.0	0	.0	0	.0	1	5.6	1	5.6	15	83.3	2	11.1	18
7	.7	56	5.3	41	3.9	26	2.5	130	12.3	782	73.7	149	14.0	1,061
2	.5	24	6.3	11	2.9	7	1.8	44	11.5	311	81.2	28	7.3	383
5	.7	32	4.7	30	4.4	19	2.8	86	12.7	471	69.5	121	17.8	678
0	.0	0	.0	0	.0	0	.0	0	.0	0	.0	0	.0	0
0	.0	0	.0	0	.0	0	.0	0	.0	0	.0	0	.0	0
0	.0	0	.0	0	.0	0	.0	0	.0	0	.0	0	.0	0

MAJOR FIELD 0200 - ARCHITECTURE AND ENVIRONMENTAL DESIGN

	AMERICAN INDIAN ALASKAN NATIVE		BLACK NON-HISPANIC		ASIAN OR PACIFIC ISLANDER		HISPANIC		TOTAL MINORITY		WHITE NON-HISPANIC		NON-RESIDENT ALIEN	
	NUMBER	%	NUMBER	%	NUMBER	%	NUMBER	%	NUMBER	%	NUMBER	%	NUMBER	%
MASSACHUSETTS CONTINUED														
PROFESSIONAL:														
PART-TIME	C	.0	0	.0	0	.0	0	.0	0	.0	0	.0	0	.0
FEMALE	0	.0	0	.0	0	.0	0	.0	0	.0	0	.0	0	.0
MALE	0	.0	0	.0	0	.0	0	.0	0	.0	0	.0	0	.0
TOTAL	0	.0	0	.0	0	.0	0	.0	0	.0	0	.0	0	.0
FEMALE	0	.0	0	.0	0	.0	0'	.0	0	.0	0	.0	0	.0
MALE	0	.0	0	.0	0	.0	0	.0	0	.0	0	.0	0	.0
UND+GRAD+PROF:														
FULL-TIME	9	.5	68	4.1	49	3.0	27	1.6	153	9.3	1,327	80.9	160	9.8
FEMALE	2	.3	30	4.7	14	2.2	8	1.3	54	8.5	548	86.6	31	4.9
MALE	7	.7	38	3.8	35	3.5	19	1.9	99	9.8	779	77.4	129	12.8
PART-TIME	0	.0	0	.0	0	.0	2	4.5	2	4.5	38	86.4	4	9.1
FEMALE	0	.0	0	.0	0	.0	1	4.2	1	4.2	21	87.5	2	8.3
MALE	0	.0	0	.0	0	.0	1	5.0	1	5.0	17	85.0	2	10.0
TOTAL	9	.5	68	4.0	49	2.9	29	1.7	155	9.2	1,365	81.1	164	9.7
FEMALE	2	.3	30	4.6	14	2.1	9	1.4	55	8.4	569	86.6	33	5.0
MALE	7	.7	38	3.7	35	3.4	20	1.9	100	9.7	796	77.5	131	12.8
UNCLASSIFIED:														
TOTAL	0	.0	0	.0	0	.0	0	.0	0	.0	21	55.3	17	44.7
FEMALE	0	.0	0	.0	0	.0	0	.0	0	.0	10	71.4	4	28.6
MALE	0	.0	0	.0	0	.0	0	.0	0	.0	11	45.8	13	54.2
TOTAL ENROLLMENT:														
TOTAL	9	.5	68	3.9	49	2.8	29	1.7	155	9.0	1,386	80.5	181	10.5
FEMALE	2	.3	30	4.5	14	2.1	9	1.3	55	8.2	579	86.3	37	5.5
MALE	7	.7	38	3.6	35	3.3	20	1.9	100	9.5	807	76.8	144	13.7
MICHIGAN (21 INSTITUTIONS)														
UNDERGRADUATES:														
FULL-TIME	3	.2	116	6.3	24	1.3	34	1.9	177	9.7	1,586	86.5	70	3.8
FEMALE	1	.3	27	7.9	7	2.1	7	2.1	42	12.3	292	85.6	7	2.1
MALE	2	.1	89	6.0	17	1.1	27	1.8	135	9.0	1,294	86.7	63	4.2
PART-TIME	5	.6	80	6.8	14	1.6	14	1.6	93	10.6	770	87.9	13	1.5
FEMALE	2	1.3	13	8.7	3	2.0	2	1.3	20	13.3	128	85.3	2	1.3
MALE	3	.4	47	6.5	11	1.5	12	1.7	73	10.1	642	88.4	11	1.5
TOTAL	8	.3	176	6.5	38	1.4	48	1.8	270	10.0	2,356	87.0	83	3.1
FEMALE	3	.6	40	8.1	10	2.0	9	1.8	62	12.6	420	85.5	9	1.8
MALE	5	.2	136	6.1	28	1.3	39	1.8	208	9.4	1,936	87.3	74	3.3
GRADUATE:														
FULL-TIME	0	.0	19	5.6	7	2.1	2	.6	28	8.3	276	81.7	34	10.1
FEMALE	0	.0	4	4.2	2	2.1	0	.0	6	6.3	83	87.4	6	6.3
MALE	0	.0	15	6.2	5	2.1	2	.8	22	9.1	193	79.4	28	11.5
PART-TIME	0	.0	10	12.7	2	2.5	1	1.3	13	16.5	58	73.4	8	10.1
FEMALE	0	.0	4	14.3	0	.0	1	3.6	5	17.9	21	75.0	2	7.1
MALE	0	.0	6	11.8	2	3.9	0	.0	8	15.7	37	72.5	6	11.8
TOTAL	0	.0	29	7.0	9	2.2	3	.7	41	9.8	334	80.1	42	10.1
FEMALE	0	.0	8	6.5	2	1.6	1	.8	11	8.9	104	84.6	8	6.5
MALE	0	.0	21	7.1	7	2.4	2	.7	30	10.2	230	78.2	34	11.6
PROFESSIONAL:														
FULL-TIME	0	.0	0	.0	0	.0	0	.0	0	.0	0	.0	0	.0
FEMALE	0	.0	0	.0	0	.0	0	.0	0	.0	0	.0	0	.0
MALE	0	.0	0	.0	0	.0	0	.0	0	.0	0	.0	0	.0
PART-TIME	0	.0	0	.0	0	.0	0	.0	0	.0	0	.0	0	.0
FEMALE	0	.0	0	.0	0	.0	0	.0	0	.0	0	.0	0	.0
MALE	0	.0	0	.0	0	.0	0	.0	0	.0	0	.0	0	.0
TOTAL	0	.0	0	.0	0	.0	0	.0	0	.0	0	.0	0	.0
FEMALE	0	.0	0	.0	0	.0	0	.0	0	.0	0	.0	0	.0
MALE	0	.0	0	.0	0	.0	0	.0	0	.0	0	.0	0	.0
UND+GRAD+PROF:														
FULL-TIME	3	.1	135	6.2	31	1.4	36	1.7	205	9.4	1,862	85.8	104	4.8
FEMALE	1	.1	31	7.1	9	2.1	7	1.6	48	11.0	375	86.0	13	3.0
MALE	2	.1	104	6.0	22	1.3	29	1.7	157	9.0	1,487	85.7	91	5.2
PART-TIME	5	.5	70	7.3	16	1.7	15	1.6	106	11.1	828	86.7	21	2.2
FEMALE	2	1.1	17	9.6	3	1.7	3	1.7	25	14.0	149	83.7	4	2.2
MALE	3	.4	53	6.8	13	1.7	12	1.5	81	10.4	679	87.4	17	2.2
TOTAL	8	.3	205	6.6	47	1.5	51	1.6	311	9.9	2,690	86.1	125	4.0
FEMALE	3	.5	48	7.8	12	2.0	10	1.6	73	11.9	524	85.3	17	2.8
MALE	5	.2	157	6.3	35	1.6	41	1.6	238	9.5	2,166	86.2	108	4.3
UNCLASSIFIED:														
TOTAL	C	.0	2	6.3	1	4.2	1	4.2	4	16.7	18	75.0	2	8.3
FEMALE	0	.0	1	10.0	0	.0	1	10.0	2	20.0	8	80.0	0	.0
MALE	0	.0	1	7.1	1	7.1	0	.0	2	14.3	10	71.4	2	14.3
TOTAL ENROLLMENT:														
TOTAL	8	.3	207	6.6	48	1.5	52	1.7	315	10.0	2,708	86.0	127	4.0
FEMALE	3	.5	49	7.9	12	1.9	11	1.8	75	12.0	532	85.3	17	2.7
MALE	5	.2	158	6.3	36	1.4	41	1.6	240	9.5	2,176	86.1	110	4.4

L ENROLLMENT IN INSTITUTIONS OF HIGHER EDUCATION FOR SELECTED MAJOR FIELDS OF STUDY AND LEVEL OF ENROLLMENT
IAGE, ETHNICITY, AND SEX: STATE, 1978

IO = ARCHITECTURE AND ENVIRONMENTAL DESIGN

ICAN INDIAN/KAN NATIVE		BLACK NON-HISPANIC		ASIAN OR PACIFIC ISLANDER		HISPANIC		TOTAL MINORITY		WHITE NON-HISPANIC		NON-RESIDENT ALIEN		TOTAL
IBER	%	NUMBER	%	NUMBER	%	NUMBER	%	NUMBER	%	NUMBER	%	NUMBER	%	NUMBER

(19 INSTITUTIONS)

3	.3	9	.9	21	2.0	4	.4	37	3.5	980	93.1	36	3.4	1,053
0	.0	1	.3	5	1.5	0	.0	6	1.8	312	96.0	7	2.2	325
3	.4	8	1.1	16	2.2	4	.5	31	4.3	668	91.8	29	4.0	728
0	.0	3	1.5	3	1.5	1	.5	7	3.6	188	96.4	0	.0	195
0	.0	1	1.2	1	1.2	0	.0	2	2.5	79	97.5	0	.0	81
0	.0	2	1.8	2	1.8	1	.9	5	4.4	109	95.6	0	.0	114
3	.2	12	1.0	24	1.9	5	.4	44	3.5	1,168	93.6	3	2.9	1,248
0	.0	2	.5	6	1.5	0	.0	8	2.0	391	96.3	7	1.7	406
3	.4	10	1.2	18	2.1	5	.6	36	4.3	777	92.3	29	3.4	842
1	.9	0	.0	3	2.7	0	.0	4	3.5	102	90.3	7	2	113
1	4.0	0	.0	0	.0	0	.0	1	4.0	23	92.0	1	0	25
0	.0	0	.0	3	3.4	0	.0	3	3.4	79	89.8	6	18	88
0	.0	0	.0	0	.0	0	.0	0	.0	0	.0	0	.0	0
0	.0	0	.0	0	.0	0	.0	0	.0	0	.0	0	.0	0
1	.9	0	.0	3	2.7	0	.0	4	3.5	102	90.3	7	2	113
1	4.0	0	.0	0	.0	0	.0	1	4.0	23	92.0	1	0	25
0	.0	0	.0	3	3.4	0	.0	3	3.4	79	89.8	6	18	88
0	.0	0	.0	0	.0	0	.0	0	.0	0	.0	0	.0	0
0	.0	0	.0	0	.0	0	.0	0	.0	0	.0	0	.0	0
0	.0	0	.0	0	.0	0	.0	0	.0	0	.0	0	.0	0
0	.0	0	.0	0	.0	0	.0	0	.0	0	.0	0	.0	0
0	.0	0	.0	0	.0	0	.0	0	.0	0	.0	0	.0	0
0	.0	0	.0	0	.0	0	.0	0	.0	0	.0	0	.0	0
0	.0	0	.0	0	.0	0	.0	0	.0	0	.0	0	.0	0
0	.0	0	.0	0	.0	0	.0	0	.0	0	.0	0	.0	0
4	.3	9	.8	24	2.1	4	.3	41	3.5	1,082	92.8	43	3.7	1,166
1	.3	5	1.4	5	1.4	0	.0	7	2.0	335	95.7	8	2.3	350
3	.4	8	1.0	19	2.3	4	.5	34	4.2	747	91.5	35	4.3	816
0	.0	3	1.5	3	1.5	1	.5	7	3.6	188	96.4	0	.0	195
0	.0	1	1.2	1	1.2	0	.0	2	2.5	79	97.5	0	.0	81
0	.0	2	1.8	2	1.8	1	.9	5	4.4	109	95.6	0	.0	114
4	.3	12	.9	27	2.0	5	.4	48	3.5	1,270	93.3	43	3.2	1,361
1	.2	2	.5	6	1.4	0	.0	9	2.1	414	96.1	8	1.9	431
3	.3	10	1.1	21	2.3	5	.5	39	4.2	856	92.0	35	3.8	930
0	.0	0	.0	0	.0	0	.0	0	.0	12	100.0	0		12
0	.0	0	.0	0	.0	0	.0	0	.0	4	100.0	0		4
0	.0	0	.0	0	.0	0	.0	0	.0	8	100.0	0		8
4	.3	12	.9	27	2.0	5	.4	48	3.5	1,282	93.4	43	3.1	1,373
1	.2	2	.5	6	1.4	0	.0	9	2.1	418	96.1	8	1.8	435
3	.3	10	1.1	21	2.2	5	.5	39	4.2	864	92.1	35	3.7	938

(16 INSTITUTIONS)

1	.1	27	3.9	3	.4	1	.1	32	4.6	656	94.8	4	.6	692
1	.5	5	2.3	1	.5	0	.0	7	3.3	205	96.2	1	.5	213
0	.0	22	4.6	2	.4	1	.2	25	5.2	451	94.2	3	.6	479
1	2.1	0	.0	0	.0	0	.0	1	2.1	46	97.9	0	.0	47
0	.0	0	.0	0	.0	0	.0	0	.0	12	100.0	0	.0	12
1	2.9	0	.0	0	.0	0	.0	1	2.9	34	97.1	0	.0	35
2	.3	27	3.7	3	.4	1	.1	33	4.5	702	95.0	4	.5	739
1	.4	5	2.2	1	.4	0	.0	7	3.1	217	96.4	1	.4	225
1	.2	22	4.3	2	.4	1	.2	26	5.1	485	94.4	3	.6	514
0	.0	2	11.1	0	.0	0	.0	2	11.1	13	72.2	3	16.7	18
0	.0	2	50.0	0	.0	0	.0	2	50.0	1	25.0	1	25.0	4
0	.0	0	.0	0	.0	0	.0	0	.0	12	85.7	2	14.3	14
0	.0	0	.0	0	.0	0	.0	0	.0	1	100.0	0	.0	1
0	.0	0	.0	0	.0	0	.0	0	.0	1	100.0	0	.0	1
0	.0	0	.0	0	.0	0	.0	0	.0	0	.0	0	.0	0
0	.0	2	10.5	0	.0	0	.0	2	10.5	14	73.7	3	15.8	19
0	.0	2	40.0	0	.0	0	.0	2	40.0	2	40.0	1	20.0	5
0	.0	0	.0	0	.0	0	.0	0	.0	12	85.7	2	14.3	14
0	.0	0	.0	0	.0	0	.0	0	.0	0	.0	0	.0	0
0	.0	0	.0	0	.0	0	.0	0	.0	0	.0	0	.0	0
0	.0	0	.0	0	.0	0	.0	0	.0	0	.0	8	.0	8

TABLE 17 - TOTAL ENROLLMENT IN INSTITUTIONS OF HIGHER EDUCATION FOR SELECTED MAJOR FIELDS OF STUDY AND LEVEL OF ENROLLMENT BY RACE, ETHNICITY, AND SEX: STATE, 1978

MAJOR FIELD 0200 - ARCHITECTURE AND ENVIRONMENTAL DESIGN

	AMERICAN INDIAN ALASKAN NATIVE		BLACK NON-HISPANIC		ASIAN OR PACIFIC ISLANDER		HISPANIC		TOTAL MINORITY		WHITE NON-HISPANIC		NON-RESIDENT ALIEN		TO
	NUMBER	%	NUMBER	%	NUMBER	%	NUMBER	%	NUMBER	%	NUMBER	%	NUMBER	%	NU
MISSISSIPPI	CONTINUED														
PROFESSIONAL:															
PART-TIME															
FEMALE	0	.0	0	.0	0	.0	0	.0	0	.0	0	.0	0	.0	
MALE	0	.0	0	.0	0	.0	0	.0	0	.0	0	.0	0	.0	
TOTAL	0	.0	0	.0	0	.0	0	.0	0	.0	0	.0	0	.0	
FEMALE	0	.0	0	.0	0	.0	0	.0	0	.0	0	.0	0	.0	
MALE	0	.0	0	.0	0	.0	0	.0	0	.0	0	.0	0	.0	
UND+GRAD+PROF:															
FULL-TIME	1	.1	29	4.1	3	.4	1	.1	34	4.8	669	94.2	7	1.0	
FEMALE	1	.5	7	3.2	1	.5	0	.0	9	4.1	206	94.9	2	.9	
MALE	0	.0	22	4.5	2	.4	1	.2	25	5.1	463	93.9	5	1.0	
PART-TIME	1	2.1	0	.0	0	.0	0	.0	1	2.1	47	97.9	0	.0	
FEMALE	0	.0	0	.0	0	.0	0	.0	0	.0	13	100.0	0	.0	
MALE	1	2.9	0	.0	0	.0	0	.0	1	2.9	34	97.1	0	.0	
TOTAL	2	.3	29	3.8	3	.4	1	.1	35	4.6	716	94.5	7	.9	
FEMALE	1	.4	7	3.0	1	.4	0	.0	9	3.9	219	95.2	2	.9	
MALE	1	.2	22	4.2	2	.4	1	.2	26	4.9	497	94.1	5	.9	
UNCLASSIFIED:															
TOTAL	0	.0	2	25.0	0	.0	0	.0	2	25.0	5	62.5	1	12.5	
FEMALE	0	.0	0	.0	0	.0	0	.0	0	.0	1	100.0	0	.0	
MALE	0	.0	2	28.6	0	.0	0	.0	2	28.6	4	57.1	1	14.3	
TOTAL ENROLLMENT:															
TOTAL	2	.3	31	4.0	3	.4	1	.1	37	4.8	721	94.1	8	1.0	
FEMALE	1	.4	7	3.0	1	.4	0	.0	9	3.9	220	95.2	2	.9	
MALE	1	.2	24	4.5	2	.4	1	.2	28	5.2	501	93.6	6	1.1	
MISSOURI	(	4 INSTITUTIONS)													
UNDERGRADUATES:															
FULL-TIME	1	.4	12	4.5	10	3.7	5	1.9	28	10.5	223	83.5	16	6.0	
FEMALE	0	.0	9	8.7	5	4.8	1	1.0	15	14.4	86	82.7	3	2.9	
MALE	1	.6	3	1.8	5	3.1	4	2.5	13	8.0	137	84.0	13	8.0	
PART-TIME	0	.0	0	.0	0	.0	1	4.8	1	4.8	18	85.7	2	9.5	
FEMALE	0	.0	0	.0	0	.0	1	6.7	1	6.7	13	86.7	1	6.7	
MALE	0	.0	0	.0	0	.0	0	.0	0	.0	5	83.3	1	16.7	
TOTAL	1	.3	12	4.2	10	3.5	6	2.1	29	10.1	241	83.7	18	6.3	
FEMALE	0	.0	9	7.6	5	4.2	2	1.7	16	13.4	99	83.2	4	3.4	
MALE	1	.6	3	1.8	5	3.0	4	2.4	13	7.7	142	84.0	14	8.3	
GRADUATE:															
FULL-TIME	0	.0	2	1.6	6	4.9	1	.8	9	7.4	104	85.2	9	7.4	
FEMALE	0	.0	0	.0	1	3.0	0	.0	1	3.0	30	90.9	2	6.1	
MALE	0	.0	2	2.2	5	5.6	1	1.1	8	9.0	74	83.1	7	7.9	
PART-TIME	0	.0	1	6.3	1	6.3	0	.0	2	12.5	13	81.3	1	6.3	
FEMALE	0	.0	0	.0	0	.0	0	.0	0	.0	2	100.0	0	.0	
MALE	0	.0	1	7.1	1	7.1	0	.0	2	14.3	11	78.6	1	7.1	
TOTAL	0	.0	3	2.2	7	5.1	1	.7	11	8.0	117	84.8	10	7.2	
FEMALE	0	.0	0	.0	1	2.9	0	.0	1	2.9	32	91.4	2	5.7	
MALE	0	.0	3	2.9	6	5.8	1	1.0	10	9.7	85	82.5	8	7.8	
PROFESSIONAL:															
FULL-TIME	0	.0	0	.0	0	.0	0	.0	0	.0	0	.0	0	.0	
FEMALE	0	.0	0	.0	0	.0	0	.0	0	.0	0	.0	0	.0	
MALE	0	.0	0	.0	0	.0	0	.0	0	.0	0	.0	0	.0	
PART-TIME	0	.0	0	.0	0	.0	0	.0	0	.0	0	.0	0	.0	
FEMALE	0	.0	0	.0	0	.0	0	.0	0	.0	0	.0	0	.0	
MALE	0	.0	0	.0	0	.0	0	.0	0	.0	0	.0	0	.0	
TOTAL	0	.0	0	.0	0	.0	0	.0	0	.0	0	.0	0	.0	
FEMALE	0	.0	0	.0	0	.0	0	.0	0	.0	0	.0	0	.0	
MALE	0	.0	0	.0	0	.0	0	.0	0	.0	0	.0	0	.0	
UND+GRAD+PROF:															
FULL-TIME	1	.3	14	3.6	16	4.1	6	1.5	37	9.5	327	84.1	25	6.4	
FEMALE	0	.0	9	6.6	6	4.4	1	.7	16	11.7	116	84.7	5	3.6	
MALE	1	.4	5	2.0	10	4.0	5	2.0	21	8.3	211	83.7	20	7.9	
PART-TIME	0	.0	1	2.7	1	2.7	1	2.7	3	8.1	31	83.8	3	8.1	
FEMALE	0	.0	0	.0	0	.0	1	5.9	1	5.9	15	88.2	1	5.9	
MALE	0	.0	1	5.0	1	5.0	0	.0	2	10.0	16	80.0	2	10.0	
TOTAL	1	.2	15	3.5	17	4.0	7	1.6	40	9.4	358	84.0	28	6.6	
FEMALE	0	.0	9	5.8	6	3.9	2	1.3	17	11.0	131	85.1	6	3.9	
MALE	1	.4	6	2.2	11	4.0	5	1.8	23	8.5	227	83.5	22	8.1	
UNCLASSIFIED:															
TOTAL	0	.0	0	.0	0	.0	0	.0	0	.0	0	.0	0	.0	
FEMALE	0	.0	0	.0	0	.0	0	.0	0	.0	0	.0	0	.0	
MALE	0	.0	0	.0	0	.0	0	.0	0	.0	0	.0	0	.0	
TOTAL ENROLLMENT:															
TOTAL	1	.2	15	3.5	17	4.0	7	1.6	40	9.4	358	84.0	28	6.6	
FEMALE	0	.0	9	5.8	6	3.9	2	1.3	17	11.0	131	85.1	6	3.9	
MALE	1	.4	6	2.2	11	4.0	5	1.8	23	8.5	227	83.5	22	8.1	

0 - ARCHITECTURE AND ENVIRONMENTAL DESIGN

ICAN INDIAN KAN NATIVE		BLACK NON-HISPANIC		ASIAN OR PACIFIC ISLANDER		HISPANIC		TOTAL MINORITY		WHITE NON-HISPANIC		NON-RESIDENT ALIEN		TOTAL
BER	%	NUMBER	%	NUMBER	%	NUMBER	%	NUMBER	%	NUMBER	%	NUMBER	%	NUMBER
(1 INSTITUTIONS)														
3	1.1	0	.0	0	.0	0	.0	3	1.1	264	95.3	10	3.6	277
1	2.3	0	.0	0	.0	0	.0	1	2.3	38	88.4	4	9.3	43
2	.9	0	.0	0	.0	0	.0	2	.9	226	96.6	6	2.6	234
0	.0	0	.0	0	.0	0	.0	0	.0	35	100.0	0	.0	35
0	.0	0	.0	0	.0	0	.0	0	.0	3	100.0	0	.0	3
0	.0	0	.0	0	.0	0	.0	0	.0	32	100.0	0	.0	32
3	1.0	0	.0	0	.0	0	.0	3	1.0	299	95.8	10	3.2	312
1	2.2	0	.0	0	.0	0	.0	1	2.2	41	89.1	4	8.7	46
2	.8	0	.0	0	.0	0	.0	2	.8	258	97.0	6	2.3	266
0	.0	0	.0	0	.0	0	.0	0	.0	0	.0	0	.0	0
0	.0	0	.0	0	.0	0	.0	0	.0	0	.0	0	.0	0
0	.0	0	.0	0	.0	0	.0	0	.0	0	.0	0	.0	0
0	.0	0	.0	0	.0	0	.0	0	.0	0	.0	0	.0	0
0	.0	0	.0	0	.0	0	.0	0	.0	0	.0	0	.0	0
0	.0	0	.0	0	.0	0	.0	0	.0	0	.0	0	.0	0
0	.0	0	.0	0	.0	0	.0	0	.0	0	.0	0	.0	0
0	.0	0	.0	0	.0	0	.0	0	.0	0	.0	0	.0	0
0	.0	0	.0	0	.0	0	.0	0	.0	0	.0	0	.0	0
0	.0	0	.0	0	.0	0	.0	0	.0	0	.0	0	.0	0
0	.0	0	.0	0	.0	0	.0	0	.0	0	.0	0	.0	0
0	.0	0	.0	0	.0	0	.0	0	.0	0	.0	0	.0	0
0	.0	0	.0	0	.0	0	.0	0	.0	0	.0	0	.0	0
0	.0	0	.0	0	.0	0	.0	0	.0	0	.0	0	.0	0
0	.0	0	.0	0	.0	0	.0	0	.0	0	.0	0	.0	0
3	1.1	0	.0	0	.0	0	.0	3	1.1	264	95.3	10	3.6	277
1	2.3	0	.0	0	.0	0	.0	1	2.3	38	88.4	4	9.3	43
2	.9	0	.0	0	.0	0	.0	2	.9	226	96.6	6	2.6	234
0	.0	0	.0	0	.0	0	.0	0	.0	35	100.0	0	.0	35
0	.0	0	.0	0	.0	0	.0	0	.0	3	100.0	0	.0	3
0	.0	0	.0	0	.0	0	.0	0	.0	32	100.0	0	.0	32
3	1.0	0	.0	0	.0	0	.0	3	1.0	299	95.8	10	3.2	312
1	2.2	0	.0	0	.0	0	.0	1	2.2	41	89.1	4	8.7	46
2	.8	0	.0	0	.0	0	.0	2	.8	258	97.0	6	2.3	266
0	.0	0	.0	0	.0	0	.0	0	.0	0	.0	0	.0	0
0	.0	0	.0	0	.0	0	.0	0	.0	0	.0	0	.0	0
0	.0	0	.0	0	.0	0	.0	0	.0	0	.0	0	.0	0
3	1.0	0	.0	0	.0	0	.0	3	1.0	299	95.8	10	3.2	312
1	2.2	0	.0	0	.0	0	.0	1	2.2	41	89.1	4	8.7	46
2	.8	0	.0	0	.0	0	.0	2	.8	258	97.0	6	2.3	266
(4 INSTITUTIONS)														
2	.4	4	.7	3	.6	5	.9	14	2.6	479	88.1	51	9.4	544
0	.0	0	.0	0	.0	0	.0	0	.0	63	91.3	6	8.7	69
2	.4	4	.8	3	.6	5	1.1	14	2.9	416	87.6	45	9.5	475
0	.0	3	4.5	0	.0	1	1.5	4	6.0	57	85.1	6	9.0	67
0	.0	0	.0	0	.0	0	.0	0	.0	8	88.9	1	11.1	9
0	.0	3	5.2	0	.0	1	1.7	4	6.9	49	84.5	5	8.6	58
2	.3	7	1.1	3	.5	6	1.0	18	2.9	536	87.7	57	9.3	611
0	.0	0	.0	0	.0	0	.0	0	.0	71	91.0	7	9.0	78
2	.4	7	1.3	3	.6	6	1.1	18	3.4	465	87.2	50	9.4	533
0	.0	2	5.4	1	2.7	0	.0	3	8.1	34	91.9	0	.0	37
0	.0	0	.0	0	.0	0	.0	0	.0	5	100.0	0	.0	5
0	.0	2	6.3	1	3.1	0	.0	3	9.4	29	90.6	0	.0	32
0	.0	0	.0	0	.0	0	.0	0	.0	14	87.5	2	12.5	16
0	.0	0	.0	0	.0	0	.0	0	.0	2	100.0	0	.0	2
0	.0	0	.0	0	.0	0	.0	0	.0	12	85.7	2	14.3	14
0	.0	2	3.8	1	1.9	0	.0	3	5.7	48	90.6	2	3.8	53
0	.0	0	.0	0	.0	0	.0	0	.0	7	100.0	0	.0	7
0	.0	2	4.3	1	2.2	0	.0	3	6.5	41	89.1	2	4.3	46
0	.0	0	.0	0	.0	0	.0	0	.0	8	100.0	0	.0	8
0	.0	0	.0	0	.0	0	.0	0	.0	1	100.0	0	.0	1
0	.0	0	.0	0	.0	0	.0	0	.0	7	100.0	0	.0	7

TABLE 17 - TOTAL ENROLLMENT IN INSTITUTIONS OF HIGHER EDUCATION FOR SELECTED MAJOR FIELDS OF STUDY AND LEVEL OF ENROLLMENT BY RACE, ETHNICITY, AND SEX: STATE, 1978

MAJOR FIELD 0200 - ARCHITECTURE AND ENVIRONMENTAL DESIGN

	AMERICAN INDIAN ALASKAN NATIVE		BLACK NON-HISPANIC		ASIAN OR PACIFIC ISLANDER		HISPANIC		TOTAL MINORITY		WHITE NON-HISPANIC		NON-RESIDENT ALIEN	
	NUMBER	%	NUMBER	%	NUMBER	%	NUMBER	%	NUMBER	%	NUMBER	%	NUMBER	%
NEBRASKA CONTINUED														
PROFESSIONAL:														
PART-TIME														
FEMALE	0	.0	0	.0	0	.0	0	.0	0	.0	1	100.0	0	.0
MALE	0	.0	0	.0	0	.0	0	.0	0	.0	1	100.0	0	.0
TOTAL	0	.0	0	.0	0	.0	0	.0		.0	9	100.0		.0
FEMALE	0	.0	0	.0	0	.0	0	.0	0	.0	1	100.0	0	.0
MALE	0	.0	0	.0	0	.0	0	.0	0	.0	8	100.0	0	.0
UND+GRAD+PROF:														
FULL-TIME	2	.3	6	1.0	4	.7	5	.8	17	2.9	521	88.5	51	8.7
FEMALE	0	.0	0	.0	0	.0	0	.0	0	.0	69	92.0	6	8.0
MALE	2	.4	6	1.2	4	.8	5	1.0	17	.13	452	87.9	45	8.8
PART-TIME	0	.0	3	3.6	0	.0	1	1.2	4	.8	72	85.7	8	9.5
FEMALE	0	.0	0	.0	0	.0		.0	0	.10	10	90.9	1	9.1
MALE	0	.0	3	4.1	0	.0	1	1.4	4	5.5	62	84.9	7	9.6
TOTAL	2	.3	9	1.3	4	.6	6	.9	21	3.1	593	88.1	59	8.8
FEMALE	0	.0	0	.0	0	.0	0	.0	0	.0	79	91.9	7	8.1
MALE	2	.3	9	1.5	4	.7	6	1.0	21	3.6	514	87.6	52	0.9
UNCLASSIFIED:														
TOTAL	0	.0	0	.0	0	.0	0	.0	0	.0	0	.0	0	.0
FEMALE	0	.0	0	.0	0	.0	0	.0	0	.0	0	.0	0	.0
MALE	0	.0	0	.0	0	.0	0	.0	0	.0	0	.0	0	.0
TOTAL ENROLLMENT:														
TOTAL	2	.3	9	1.3	4	.6	6	.9	21	3.1	593	88.1	59	8.8
FEMALE	0	.0	0	.0	0	.0	0	.0	0	.0	79	91.9	7	8.1
MALE	2	.3	9	1.5	4	.7	6	1.0	21	3.6	514	87.6	52	8.9
NEW HAMPSHIRE (3 INSTITUTIONS)														
UNDERGRADUATES:														
FULL-TIME	0	.0	0	.0	0	.0	1	1.7	1	1.7	57	98.3	0	.0
FEMALE	0	.0	0	.0	0	.0	0	.0	0	.0	20	100.0	0	.0
MALE	0	.0	0	.0	0	.0	1	2.6	1	2.6	37	97.4	0	.0
PART-TIME	0	.0	0	.0	0	.0	0	.0	0	.0	5	100.0	0	.0
FEMALE	0	.0	0	.0	0	.0	0	.0	0	.0	1	100.0	0	.0
MALE	0	.0	0	.0	0	.0	0	.0	0	.0	4	100.0	0	.0
TOTAL	0	.0	0	.0	0	.0	1	1.6	1	1.6	62	98.4	0	.0
FEMALE	0	.0	0	.0	0	.0	0	.0	0	.0	21	100.0	0	.0
MALE	0	.0	0	.0	0	.0	1	2.4	1	2.4	41	97.6	0	.0
GRADUATE:														
FULL-TIME	0	.0	0	.0	0	.0	0	.0	0	.0	2	100.0	0	.0
FEMALE	0	.0	0	.0	0	.0	0	.0	0	.0	2	100.0	0	.0
MALE	0	.0	0	.0	0	.0	0	.0	0	.0	0	.0	0	.0
PART-TIME	0	.0	0	.0	0	.0	0	.0	0	.0	0	.0	0	.0
FEMALE	0	.0	0	.0	0	.0	0	.0	0	.0	0	.0	0	.0
MALE	0	.0	0	.0	0	.0	0	.0	0	.0	0	.0	0	.0
TOTAL	0	.0	0	.0	0	.0	0	.0	0	.0	2	100.0	0	.0
FEMALE	0	.0	0	.0	0	.0	0	.0	0	.0	2	100.0	0	.0
MALE	0	.0	0	.0	0	.0	0	.0	0	.0	0	.0	0	.0
PROFESSIONAL:														
FULL-TIME	0	.0	0	.0	0	.0	0	.0	0	.0	0	.0	0	.0
FEMALE	0	.0	0	.0	0	.0	0	.0	0	.0	0	.0	0	.0
MALE	0	.0	0	.0	0	.0	0	.0	0	.0	0	.0	0	.0
PART-TIME	0	.0	0	.0	0	.0	0	.0	0	.0	0	.0	0	.0
FEMALE	0	.0	0	.0	0	.0	0	.0	0	.0	0	.0	0	.0
MALE	0	.0	0	.0	0	.0	0	.0	0	.0	0	.0	0	.0
TOTAL	0	.0	0	.0	0	.0	0	.0		.0	0	.0	0	.0
FEMALE	0	.0	0	.0	0	.0	0	.0	0	.0	0	.0	0	.0
MALE	0	.0	0	.0	0	.0	0	.0	0	.0	0	.0	0	.0
UND+GRAD+PROF:														
FULL-TIME	0	.0	0	.0	0	.0	1	1.7	1	1.7	59	98.3	0	.0
FEMALE	0	.0	0	.0	0	.0	0	.0	0	.0	22	100.0	0	.0
MALE	0	.0	0	.0	0	.0	1	2.6	1	2.6	37	97.4	0	.0
PART-TIME	0	.0	0	.0	0	.0	0	.0	0	.0	5	100.0	0	.0
FEMALE	0	.0	0	.0	0	.0	0	.0	0	.0	1	100.0	0	.0
MALE	0	.0	0	.0	0	.0	0	.0	0	.0	4	100.0	0	.0
TOTAL	0	.0	0	.0	0	.0	1	1.5	1	1.5	64	98.5	0	.0
FEMALE	0	.0	0	.0	0	.0	0	.0	0	.0	23	100.0	0	.0
MALE	0	.0	0	.0	0	.0	1	2.4	1	2.4	41	97.6	0	.0
UNCLASSIFIED:														
TOTAL	0	.0	0	.0	0	.0	0	.0	0	.0	0	.0		.0
FEMALE	0	.0	0	.0	0	.0	0	.0	0	.0	0	.0	0	.0
MALE	0	.0	0	.0	0	.0	0	.0	0	.0	0	.0	0	.0
TOTAL ENROLLMENT:														
TOTAL	C	.0	0	.0	0	.0	1	1.5	1	1.5	64	98.5		.0
FEMALE	0	.0	0	.0	0	.0	0	.0	0	.0	23	100.0	0	.0
MALE	0	.0	0	.0	0	.0	1	2.4	1	2.4	41	97.6	8	.0

O - ARCHITECTURE AND ENVIRONMENTAL DESIGN

ICAN INDIAN KAN NATIVE		BLACK NON-HISPANIC		ASIAN OR PACIFIC ISLANDER		HISPANIC		TOTAL MINORITY		WHITE NON-HISPANIC		NON-RESIDENT ALIEN		TOTAL
BER	%	NUMBER	%	NUMBER	%	NUMBER	%	NUMBER	%	NUMBER	%	NUMBER	%	NUMBER

(8 INSTITUTIONS)

3	.2	77	5.8	24	1.8	44	3.3	148	11.2	1,172	88.3	7	.5	1,327
1	.2	33	7.1	7	1.5	10	2.1	51	10.9	412	88.2	4	.9	467
2	.2	44	5.1	17	2.0	34	4.0	97	11.3	760	88.4	3	.3	860
0	.0	2	3.9	0	.0	2	3.9	4	7.8	47	92.2	0	.0	51
0	.0	0	.0	0	.0	0	.0	0	.0	11	100.0	0	.0	11
0	.0	2	5.0	0	.0	2	5.0	4	10.0	36	90.0	0	.0	40
3	.2	79	5.7	24	1.7	46	3.3	152	11.0	1,219	88.5	7	.5	1,378
1	.2	33	6.9	7	1.5	10	2.1	51	10.7	423	88.5	4	.8	478
2	.2	46	5.1	17	1.9	36	4.0	101	11.2	796	88.4	3	.3	900
0	.0	6	4.3	3	2.2	1	.7	10	7.2	116	84.1	12	8.7	138
0	.0	4	7.8	2	3.9	0	.0	6	11.8	41	80.4	4	7.8	51
0	.0	2	2.3	1	1.1	1	1.1	4	4.6	75	86.2	8	9.2	87
0	.0	1	1.3	0	.0	1	1.3	2	2.6	74	97.4	0	.0	76
0	.0	1	2.9	0	.0	0	.0	1	2.9	34	97.1	0	.0	35
0	.0	0	.0	0	.0	1	2.4	1	2.4	40	97.6	0	.0	41
0	.0	7	3.3	3	1.4	2	.9	12	5.6	190	88.8	12	5.6	214
0	.0	5	5.8	2	2.3	0	.0	7	8.1	75	87.2	4	4.7	86
0	.0	2	1.6	1	.8	2	1.6	5	3.9	115	89.8	8	6.3	128
0	.0	0	.0	0	.0	0	.0	0	.0	0	.0	0	.0	0
0	.0	0	.0	0	.0	0	.0	0	.0	0	.0	0	.0	0
0	.0	0	.0	0	.0	0	.0	0	.0	0	.0	0	.0	0
0	.0	0	.0	0	.0	0	.0	0	.0	0	.0	0	.0	0
0	.0	0	.0	0	.0	0	.0	0	.0	0	.0	0	.0	0
0	.0	0	.0	0	.0	0	.0	0	.0	0	.0	0	.0	0
0	.0	0	.0	0	.0	0	.0	0	.0	0	.0	0	.0	0
0	.0	0	.0	0	.0	0	.0	0	.0	0	.0	0	.0	0
0	.0	0	.0	0	.0	0	.0	0	.0	0	.0	0	.0	0
3	.2	83	5.7	27	1.8	45	3.1	158	10.8	1,288	87.9	19	1.3	1,465
1	.2	37	7.1	9	1.7	10	1.9	57	11.0	453	87.5	8	1.5	518
2	.2	46	4.9	18	1.9	35	3.7	101	10.7	835	88.2	11	1.2	947
0	.0	3	2.4	0	.0	3	2.4	6	4.7	121	95.3	0	.0	127
0	.0	1	2.2	0	.0	0	.0	1	2.2	45	97.8	0	.0	46
0	.0	2	2.5	0	.0	3	3.7	5	6.2	76	93.8	0	.0	81
3	.2	86	5.4	27	1.7	48	3.0	164	10.3	1,409	88.5	19	1 2	1,592
1	.2	38	6.7	9	1.6	10	1.8	58	10.3	498	88.3	8	1 4	564
2	.2	48	4.7	18	1.8	38	3.7	106	10.3	911	88.6	11	111	1,028
0	.0	19	55.9	0	.0	2	5.9	21	61.8	12	35.3	1	2.9	34
0	.0	16	61.5	0	.0	2	7.7	18	69.2	8	30.8	0	.0	26
0	.0	3	37.5	0	.0	0	.0	3	37.5	4	50.0	8	12.5	8
3	.2	105	6.5	27	1.7	50	3.1	185	11.4	1,421	87.4	20	1.2	1,626
1	.2	54	9.2	9	1.7	12	2.0	76	12.9	506	85.8	8	1.4	590
2	.2	51	4.9	18	1.7	38	3.7	109	10.5	915	88.3	12	1.2	1,036

(2 INSTITUTIONS)

4	1.7	2	.9	2	.9	54	23.6	62	27.1	163	71.2	4	1.7	229
1	2.5	2	5.0	0	.0	7	17.5	10	25.0	29	72.5	1	2.5	40
3	1.6	0	.0	2	1.1	47	24.9	52	27.5	134	70.9	3	1.6	189
0	.0	0	.0	0	.0	21	37.5	21	37.5	34	60.7	1	1.8	56
0	.0	0	.0	0	.0	5	62.5	5	62.5	3	37.5	0	.0	8
0	.0	0	.0	0	.0	16	33.3	16	33.3	31	64.6	1	2.1	48
4	1.4	2	.7	2	.7	75	26.3	83	29.1	197	69.1	5	1.8	285
1	2.1	2	4.2	0	.0	12	25.0	15	31.3	32	66.7	1	2.1	48
3	1.3	0	.0	2	.8	63	26.6	68	28.7	165	69.6	4	1.7	237
0	.0	1	2.1	0	.0	2	4.3	3	6.4	42	89.4	2	4.3	47
0	.0	0	.0	0	.0	0	.0	0	.0	10	100.0	0	.0	10
0	.0	1	2.7	0	.0	2	5.4	3	8.1	32	86.5	2	5.4	37
0	.0	1	2.3	0	.0	4	9.3	5	11.6	37	86.0	1	2.3	43
0	.0	0	.0	0	.0	2	20.0	2	20.0	8	80.0	0	.0	10
0	.0	1	3.0	0	.0	2	6.1	3	9.1	29	87.9	1	3.0	33
0	.0	2	2.2	0	.0	6	6.7	8	8.9	79	87.8		3.3	90
0	.0	0	.0	0	.0	2	10.0	2	10.0	18	90.0	0	.0	20
0	.0	2	2.9	0	.0	4	5.7	6	8.6	61	87.1	3	4.3	70
0	.0	0	.0	0	.0	0	.0	0	.0	0	.0	0	.0	0
0	.0	0	.0	0	.0	0	.0	0	.0	0	.0	0	.0	0

MAJOR FIELD 0200 - ARCHITECTURE AND ENVIRONMENTAL DESIGN

	AMERICAN INDIAN ALASKAN NATIVE		BLACK NON-HISPANIC		ASIAN OR PACIFIC ISLANDER		HISPANIC		TOTAL MINORITY		WHITE NON-HISPANIC		NON-RESIDENT ALIEN		
	NUMBER	%	NUMBER	%	NUMBER	%	NUMBER	%	NUMBER	%	NUMBER	%	NUMBER	%	N

NEW MEXICO   CONTINUED

PROFESSIONAL:															
PART-TIME	0	.0	0	.0	0	.0	0	.0	0	.0	0	.0	0	.0	
FEMALE	0	.0	0	.0	0	.0	0	.0	0	.0	0	.0	0	.0	
MALE	0	.0	0	.0	0	.0	0	.0	0	.0	0	.0	0	.0	
TOTAL	0	.0	0	.0	0	.0	0	.0	0	.0	0	.0	0	.0	
FEMALE	0	.0	0	.0	0	.0	0	.0	0	.0	0	.0	0	.0	
MALE	0	.0	0	.0	0	.0	0	.0	0	.0	0	.0	0	.0	
UND+GRAD+PROF:															
FULL-TIME	4	1.4	3	1.1	2	.7	56	20.3	65	23.6	205	74.3	6	2.2	
FEMALE	1	2.0	2	4.0	0	.0	7	14.0	10	20.0	39	78.0	1	2.0	
MALE	3	1.3	1	.4	2	.9	49	21.7	55	24.3	166	73.5	5	2.2	
PART-TIME	0	.0	1	1.0	0	.0	25	26.3	26	26.3	71	71.7	2	2.0	
FEMALE	0	.0	0	.0	0	.0	7	38.9	7	38.9	11	61.1	0	.0	
MALE	0	.0	1	1.2	0	.0	18	22.2	19	23.5	60	74.1	2	2.5	
TOTAL	4	1.1	4	1.1	2	.5	81	21.6	91	24.3	276	73.6	8	2.1	
FEMALE	1	1.5	2	2.9	0	.0	14	20.6	17	25.0	50	73.5	1	1.5	
MALE	3	1.0	2	.7	2	.7	67	21.8	74	24.1	226	73.6	7	2.3	
UNCLASSIFIED:															
TOTAL	0	.0	0	.0	0	.0	0	.0	0	.0	1	50.0	1	50.0	
FEMALE	0	.0	0	.0	0	.0	0	.0	0	.0	0	.0	0	.0	
MALE	0	.0	0	.0	0	.0	0	.0	0	.0	1	50.0	1	50.0	
TOTAL ENROLLMENT:															
TOTAL	4	1.1	4	1.1	2	.5	81	21.5	91	24.1	277	73.5	9	2.4	
FEMALE	1	1.5	2	2.9	0	.0	14	20.6	17	25.0	50	73.5	1	1.5	
MALE	3	1.0	2	.6	2	.6	67	21.7	74	23.9	227	73.5	8	2.6	

NEW YORK   (19 INSTITUTIONS)

UNDERGRADUATES:															
FULL-TIME	9	.2	213	5.3	139	3.5	173	4.3	534	13.3	3,204	79.6	288	7.2	
FEMALE	1	.1	45	4.0	59	5.3	39	3.5	144	12.9	908	81.6	61	5.5	
MALE	8	.3	168	5.8	80	2.7	134	4.6	390	13.4	2,296	78.8	227	7.8	
PART-TIME	8	1.4	41	7.0	11	1.9	49	8.3	109	18.6	463	78.9	15	2.6	
FEMALE	0	.0	5	5.6	2	2.2	14	15.7	21	23.6	67	75.3	1	1.1	
MALE	8	1.6	36	7.2	9	1.8	35	7.0	88	17.7	396	79.5	14	2.8	
TOTAL	17	.4	254	5.5	150	3.3	222	4.8	643	13.9	3,667	79.5	303	6.6	
FEMALE	1	.1	50	4.2	61	5.1	53	4.4	165	13.7	975	81.1	62	5.2	
MALE	16	.5	204	6.0	89	2.6	169	5.0	478	14.0	2,692	78.9	241	7.1	
GRADUATE:															
FULL-TIME	2	.3	58	7.5	24	3.1	14	1.8	98	12.7	551	71.2	125	16.1	
FEMALE	0	.0	31	9.6	9	2.8	1	.3	41	12.7	247	76.5	35	10.8	
MALE	2	.4	27	6.0	15	3.3	13	2.9	57	12.6	304	67.4	90	20.0	
PART-TIME	2	1.2	13	7.8	8	4.8	3	1.8	26	15.6	123	73.7	18	10.8	
FEMALE	1	1.4	5	7.2	6	8.7	1	1.4	13	18.8	49	71.0	7	10.1	
MALE	1	1.0	8	8.2	2	2.0	2	2.0	13	13.3	74	75.5	11	11.2	
TOTAL	4	.4	71	7.5	32	3.4	17	1.8	124	13.2	674	71.6	143	15.2	
FEMALE	1	.3	36	9.2	15	3.8	2	.5	54	13.8	296	75.5	42	10.7	
MALE	3	.5	35	6.4	17	3.1	15	2.7	70	12.8	378	68.9	101	18.4	
PROFESSIONAL:															
FULL-TIME	0	.0	0	.0	0	.0	0	.0	0	.0	0	.0	0	.0	
FEMALE	0	.0	0	.0	0	.0	0	.0	0	.0	0	.0	0	.0	
MALE	0	.0	0	.0	0	.0	0	.0	0	.0	0	.0	0	.0	
PART-TIME	0	.0	0	.0	0	.0	0	.0	0	.0	0	.0	0	.0	
FEMALE	0	.0	0	.0	0	.0	0	.0	0	.0	0	.0	0	.0	
MALE	0	.0	0	.0	0	.0	0	.0	0	.0	0	.0	0	.0	
TOTAL	0	.0	0	.0	0	.0	0	.0	0	.0	0	.0	0	.0	
FEMALE	0	.0	0	.0	0	.0	0	.0	0	.0	0	.0	0	.0	
MALE	0	.0	0	.0	0	.0	0	.0	0	.0	0	.0	0	.0	
UND+GRAD+PROF:															
FULL-TIME	11	.2	271	5.6	163	3.4	187	3.9	632	13.2	3,755	78.2	413	8.6	
FEMALE	1	.1	76	6.3	68	4.7	40	2.8	185	12.9	1,155	80.4	96	6.7	
MALE	10	.3	195	5.8	95	2.8	147	4.4	447	13.3	2,600	77.3	317	9.4	
PART-TIME	10	1.3	54	7.2	19	2.5	52	6.9	135	17.9	586	77.7	33	4.4	
FEMALE	1	.6	10	6.3	8	5.1	15	9.5	34	21.5	116	73.4	8	5.1	
MALE	9	1.5	44	7.4	11	1.8	37	6.2	101	16.9	470	78.9	25	4.2	
TOTAL	21	.4	325	5.9	182	3.3	239	4.3	767	13.8	4,341	78.2	446	8.0	
FEMALE	2	.1	86	5.4	76	4.8	55	3.5	219	13.7	1,271	79.7	104	6.5	
MALE	19	.5	239	6.0	106	2.7	184	4.6	548	13.8	3,070	77.5	342	8.6	
UNCLASSIFIED:															
TOTAL	0	.0	0	.0	0	.0	1	3.7	1	3.7	26	96.3	0	.0	
FEMALE	0	.0	0	.0	0	.0	0	.0	0	.0	13	100.0	0	.0	
MALE	0	.0	0	.0	0	.0	1	7.1	1	7.1	13	92.9	0	.0	
TOTAL ENROLLMENT:															
TOTAL	21	.4	325	5.8	182	3.3	240	4.3	768	13.8	4,367	78.2	446	8.0	
FEMALE	2	.1	86	5.4	76	4.7	55	3.4	219	13.6	1,284	79.9	104	6.5	
MALE	19	.5	239	6.0	106	2.7	185	4.7	549	13.8	3,083	77.6	342	8.6	

- ARCHITECTURE AND ENVIRONMENTAL DESIGN

CAN INDIAN AN NATIVE		BLACK NON-HISPANIC		ASIAN OR PACIFIC ISLANDER		HISPANIC		TOTAL MINORITY		WHITE NON-HISPANIC		NON-RESIDENT ALIEN		TOTAL
ER	%	NUMBER	%	NUMBER	%	NUMBER	%	NUMBER	%	NUMBER	%	NUMBER	%	NUMBER

(7 INSTITUTIONS)

0	.0	54	8.4	4	.6	6	.9	64	9.9	569	88.2	12	1.9	645
0	.0	14	7.8	1	.6	1	.6	16	8.9	159	88.8	4	2.2	179
0	.0	40	8.6	3	.6	5	1.1	48	10.3	410	88.0	8	1.7	466
0	.0	1	3.1	0	.0	0	.0	1	3.1	31	96.9	0	.0	32
0	.0	1	12.5	0	.0	0	.0	1	12.5	7	87.5	0	.0	8
0	.0	0	.0	0	.0	0	.0	0	.0	24	100.0	0	.0	24
0	.0	55	8.1	4	.6	6	.9	65	9.6	600	88.6	12	1.8	677
0	.0	15	8.0	1	.5	1	.5	17	9.1	166	88.8	4	2.1	187
0	.0	40	8.2	3	.6	5	1.0	48	9.8	434	88.6	8	1.6	490
0	.0	13	6.8	1	.5	1	.5	15	7.9	167	87.4	9	4.7	191
0	.0	7	8.8	1	1.3	1	1.3	9	11.3	69	86.3	2	2.5	80
0	.0	6	5.4	0	.0	0	.0	6	5.4	98	88.3	7	6.3	111
0	.0	1	2.6	0	.0	0	.0	1	2.6	36	94.7	1	2.6	38
0	.0	1	6.7	0	.0	0	.0	1	6.7	14	93.3	0	.0	15
0	.0	0	.0	0	.0 .	0	.0	0	.0	22	95.7	1	4.3	23
0	.0	14	6.1	1	.4	1	.4	16	7.0	203	88.6	10	4.4	229
0	.0	8	8.4	1	1.1	1	1.1	10	10.5	83	87.4	2	2.1	95
0	.0	6	4.5	0	.0	0	.0	6	4.5	120	89.6	8	6.0	134
0	.0	0	.0	0	.0	0	.0	0	.0	0	.0	0	.0	0
0	.0	0	.0	0	.0	0	.0	0	.0	0	.0	0	.0	0
0	.0	0	.0	0	.0	0	.0	0	.0	0	.0	0	.0	0
0	.0	0	.0	0	.0	0	.0	0	.0	0	.0	0	.0	0
0	.0	0	.0	0	.0	0	.0	0	.0	0	.0	0	.0	0
0	.0	0	.0	0	.0	0	.0	0	.0	0	.0	0	.0	0
0	.0	0	.0	0	.0	0	.0	0	.0	0	.0	0	.0	0
0	.0	0	.0	0	.0	0	.0	0	.0	0	.0	0	.0	0
0	.0	0	.0	0	.0	0	.0	0	.0	0	.0	0	.0	0
0	.0	67	8.0	5	.6	7	.8	79	9.4	736	88.0	21	2.5	836
0	.0	21	8.1	2	.8	2	.8	25	9.7	228	88.0	6	2.3	259
0	.0	46	8.0	3	.5	5	.9	54	9.4	508	88.0	15	2.6	577
0	.0	2	2.9	0	.0	0	.0	2	2.9	67	95.7	1	1.4	70
0	.0	2	8.7	0	.0	0	.0	2	8.7	21	91.3	0	.0	23
0	.0	0	.0	0	.0	0	.0	0	.0	46	97.9	1	2.1	47
0	.0	69	7.6	5	.6	7	.8	81	8.9	803	88.6	22	2.4	906
0	.0	23	8.2	2	.7	2	.7	27	9.6	249	88.3	6	2.1	282
0	.0	46	7.4	3	.5	5	.8	54	8.7	554	88.8	16	2.6	624
0	.0	0	.0	0	.0	0	.0	0	.0	0	.0	0	.0	0
0	.0	0	.0	0	.0	0	.0	0	.0	0	.0	0	.0	0
0	.0	0	.0	0	.0	0	.0	0	.0	0	.0	0	.0	0
0	.0	69	7.6	5	.6	7	.8	81	8.9	803	88.6	22	2.4	906
0	.0	23	8.2	2	.7	2	.7	27	9.6	249	88.3	6	2.1	282
0	.0	46	7.4	3	.5	5	.8	54	8.7	554	88.8	16	2.6	624

(2 INSTITUTIONS)

2	.6	2	.6	2	.6	3	.9	9	2.6	340	96.9	2	.6	351
0	.0	0	.0	0	.0	0	.0	0	.0	75	98.7	1	1.3	76
2	.7	2	.7	2	.7	3	1.1	9	3.3	265	96.4	1	.4	275
0	.0	0	.0	0	.0	0	.0	0	.0	0	.0	0	.0	0
0	.0	0	.0	0	.0	0	.0	0	.0	0	.0	0	.0	0
0	.0	0	.0	0	.0	0	.0	0	.0	0	.0	0	.0	0
2	.6	2	.6	2	.6	3	.9	9	2.6	340	96.9	2	.6	351
0	.0	0	.0	0	.0	0	.0	0	.0	75	98.7	1	1.3	76
2	.7	2	.7	2	.7	3	1.1	9	3.3	265	96.4	1	.4	275
0	.0	0	.0	0	.0	0	.0	0	.0	0	.0	0	.0	0
0	.0	0	.0	0	.0	0	.0	0	.0	0	.0	0	.0	0
0	.0	0	.0	0	.0	0	.0	0	.0	0	.0	0	.0	0
0	.0	0	.0	0	.0	0	.0	0	.0	0	.0	0	.0	0
0	.0	0	.0	0	.0	0	.0	0	.0	0	.0	0	.0	0
0	.0	0	.0	0	.0	0	.0	0	.0	0	.0	0	.0	0
0	.0	0	.0	0	.0	0	.0	0	.0	0	.0	0	.0	0
0	.0	0	.0	0	.0	0	.0	0	.0	0	.0	0	.0	0
0	.0	0	.0	0	.0	0	.0	0	.0	0	.0	0	.0	0

TABLE 17 - TOTAL ENROLLMENT IN INSTITUTIONS OF HIGHER EDUCATION FOR SELECTED MAJOR FIELDS OF STUDY AND LEVEL OF ENROLLMENT BY RACE, ETHNICITY, AND SEX: STATE, 1978

MAJOR FIELD 0200 - ARCHITECTURE AND ENVIRONMENTAL DESIGN

	AMERICAN INDIAN ALASKAN NATIVE		BLACK NON-HISPANIC		ASIAN OR PACIFIC ISLANDER		HISPANIC		TOTAL MINORITY		WHITE NON-HISPANIC		NON-RESIDENT ALIEN		T	
	NUMBER	%	NUMBER	%	NUMBER	%	NUMBER	%	NUMBER	%	NUMBER	%	NUMBER	%	N	
NORTH DAKOTA CONTINUED																
PROFESSIONAL:																
PART-TIME	0	.0	0	.0	0	.0	0	.0	0	.0	0	.0	0	.0		
FEMALE	0	.0	0	.0	0	.0	0	.0	0	.0	0	.0	0	.0		
MALE	0	.0	0	.0	0	.0	0	.0	0	.0	0	.0	0	.0		
TOTAL	0	.0	0	.0	0	.0	0	.0	0	.0	0	.0	0	.0		
FEMALE	0	.0	0	.0	0	.0	0	.0	0	.0	0	.0	0	.0		
MALE	0	.0	0	.0	0	.0	0	.0	0	.0	0	.0	0	.0		
UND+GRAD+PROF:																
FULL-TIME	2	.6	2	.6	2	.6	3	.9	9	2.6	340	96.9	2	.6		
FEMALE	0	.0	0	.0	0	.0	0	.0	0	.0	75	98.7	1	1.3		
MALE	2	.7	2	.7	2	.7	3	1.1	9	3.3	265	96.4	1	.4		
PART-TIME	0	.0	0	.0	0	.0	0	.0	0	.0	0	.0	0	.0		
FEMALE	0	.0	0	.0	0	.0	0	.0	0	.0	0	.0	0	.0		
MALE	0	.0	0	.0	0	.0	0	.0	0	.0	0	.0	0	.0		
TOTAL	2	.6	2	.6	2	.6	3	.9	9	2.6	340	96.9	2	.6		
FEMALE	0	.0	0	.0	0	.0	0	.0	0	.0	75	98.7	1	1.3		
MALE	2	.7	2	.7	2	.7	3	1.1	9	3.3	265	96.4	1	.4		
UNCLASSIFIED:																
TOTAL	0	.0	0	.0	0	.0	0	.0	0	.0	0	.0	0	.0		
FEMALE	0	.0	0	.0	0	.0	0	.0	0	.0	0	.0	0	.0		
MALE	0	.0	0	.0	0	.0	0	.0	0	.0	0	.0	0	.0		
TOTAL ENROLLMENT:																
TOTAL	2	.6	2	.6	2	.6	3	.9	9	2.6	340	96.9	2	.6		
FEMALE	0	.0	0	.0	0	.0	0	.0	0	.0	75	98.7	1	1.3		
MALE	2	.7	2	.7	2	.7	3	1.1	9	3.3	265	96.4	1	.4		
OHIO (18 INSTITUTIONS)																
UNDERGRADUATES:																
FULL-TIME	5	.2	67	3.2	10	.5	12	.6	94	4.5	1,974	93.9	35	1.7		
FEMALE	1	.2	18	3.8	2	.4	5	1.1	26	5.5	440	93.4	5	1.1		
MALE	4	.2	49	3.0	8	.5	7	.4	68	4.2	1,534	94.0	30	1.8		
PART-TIME	1	.3	11	2.9	3	.8	1	.3	16	4.2	368	95.8	0	.0		
FEMALE	1	1.0	2	2.1	1	1.0	1	1.0	5	5.2	92	94.8	0	.0		
MALE	0	.0	9	3.1	2	.7	0	.0	11	3.8	276	96.2	0	.0		
TOTAL	6	.2	78	3.1	13	.5	13	.5	110	4.4	2,342	94.2	35	1.4		
FEMALE	2	.4	20	3.5	3	.5	6	1.1	31	5.5	532	93.7	5	.9		
MALE	4	.2	58	3.0	10	.5	7	.4	79	4.1	1,810	94.3	30	1.6		
GRADUATE:																
FULL-TIME	2	.8	25	9.8	1	.4	3	1.2	31	12.2	193	75.7	31	12.2		
FEMALE	1	1.7	8	13.3	1	1.7	2	3.3	12	20.0	43	71.7	5	8.3		
MALE	1	.5	17	8.7	0	.0	1	.5	19	9.7	150	76.9	26	13.3		
PART-TIME	0	.0	4	10.5	0	.0	0	.0	4	10.5	33	86.8	1	2.6		
FEMALE	0	.0	2	16.7	0	.0	0	.0	2	16.7	10	83.3	0	.0		
MALE	0	.0	2	7.7	0	.0	0	.0	2	7.7	23	88.5	1	3.8		
TOTAL	2	.7	29	9.9	1	.3	3	1.0	35	11.9	226	77.1	32	10.9		
FEMALE	1	1.4	10	13.9	1	1.4	2	2.8	14	19.4	53	73.6	5	6.9		
MALE	1	.5	19	8.6	0	.0	1	.5	21	9.5	173	78.3	27	12.2		
PROFESSIONAL:																
FULL-TIME	0	.0	0	.0	0	.0	0	.0	0	.0	0	.0	0	.0		
FEMALE	0	.0	0	.0	0	.0	0	.0	0	.0	0	.0	0	.0		
MALE	0	.0	0	.0	0	.0	0	.0	0	.0	0	.0	0	.0		
PART-TIME	0	.0	0	.0	0	.0	0	.0	0	.0	0	.0	0	.0		
FEMALE	0	.0	0	.0	0	.0	0	.0	0	.0	0	.0	0	.0		
MALE	0	.0	0	.0	0	.0	0	.0	0	.0	0	.0	0	.0		
TOTAL	0	.0	0	.0	0	.0	0	.0	0	.0	0	.0	0	.0		
FEMALE	0	.0	0	.0	0	.0	0	.0	0	.0	0	.0	0	.0		
MALE	0	.0	0	.0	0	.0	0	.0	0	.0	0	.0	0	.0		
UND+GRAD+PROF:																
FULL-TIME	7	.3	92	3.9	11	.5	15	.6	125	5.3	2,167	91.9	66	2.8		
FEMALE	2	.4	26	4.9	3	.6	7	1.3	38	7.2	483	91.0	10	1.9		
MALE	5	.3	66	3.6	8	.4	8	.4	87	4.8	1,684	92.2	56	3.1		
PART-TIME	1	.2	15	3.6	3	.7	1	.2	20	4.7	401	95.0	1	.2		
FEMALE	1	.9	4	3.7	1	.9	1	.9	7	6.4	102	93.6	0	.0		
MALE	0	.0	11	3.5	2	.6	0	.0	13	4.2	299	95.5	1	.3		
TOTAL	8	.3	107	3.8	14	.5	16	.6	145	5.2	2,568	92.4	67	2.4		
FEMALE	3	.5	30	4.7	4	.6	8	1.3	45	7.0	585	91.4	10	1.6		
MALE	5	.2	77	3.6	10	.5	8	.4	100	4.7	1,983	92.7	57	2.7		
UNCLASSIFIED:																
TOTAL	0	.0	0	.0	1	2.1	0	.0	1	2.1	45	93.8	2	4.2		
FEMALE	0	.0	0	.0	0	.0	0	.0	0	.0	16	100.0	0	.0		
MALE	0	.0	0	.0	1	3.1	0	.0	1	3.1	29	90.6	2	6.3		
TOTAL ENROLLMENT:																
TOTAL	8	.3	107	3.8	15	.5	16	.6	146	5.2	2,613	92.4	69	2.4		
FEMALE	3	.5	30	4.6	4	.6	8	1.2	45	6.9	601	91.6	10	1.5		
MALE	5	.2	77	3.5	11	.5	8	.4	101	4.7	2,012	92.6	59	2.7		

) = ARCHITECTURE AND ENVIRONMENTAL DESIGN

[AMERI]CAN INDIAN/[ALAS]KAN NATIVE		BLACK NON-HISPANIC		ASIAN OR PACIFIC ISLANDER		HISPANIC		TOTAL MINORITY		WHITE NON-HISPANIC		NON-RESIDENT ALIEN		TOTAL
[NUMB]ER	%	NUMBER	%	NUMBER	%	NUMBER	%	NUMBER	%	NUMBER	%	NUMBER	%	NUMBER
		(2 INSTITUTIONS)												
12	1.7	11	1.6	13	1.9	4	.6	40	5.8	536	77.5	116	16.8	692
3	2.8	6	5.7	3	2.8	1	.9	13	12.3	77	72.6	16	15.1	106
9	1.5	5	.9	10	1.7	3	.5	27	4.6	459	78.3	100	17.1	586
4	4.9	2	2.4	0	.0	1	1.2	7	8.5	64	78.0	11	13.4	82
1	6.7	0	.0	0	.0	0	.0	1	6.7	9	60.0	5	33.3	15
3	4.5	2	3.0	0	.0	1	1.5	6	9.0	55	82.1	6	9.0	67
16	2.1	13	1.7	13	1.7	5	.6	47	6.1	600	77.5	127	16.4	774
4	3.3	6	5.0	3	2.5	1	.8	14	11.6	86	71.1	21	17.4	121
12	1.8	7	1.1	10	1.5	4	.6	33	5.1	514	78.7	106	16.2	653
0	.0	2	2.0	1	1.0		.0	3	3.0	76	76.0	21	21.0	100
0	.0	0	.0	0	.0		.0	0	.0	12	75.0	4	25.0	16
0	.0	2	2.4	1	1.2		.0	3	3.6	64	76.2	17	20.2	84
1	3.8	0	.0	0	.0		.0	1	3.8	22	84.6	3	11.5	26
0	.0	0	.0	0	.0	0	.0	0	.0	1	100.0	0	.0	1
1	4.0	0	.0	0	.0	0	.0	1	4.0	21	84.0	3	12.0	25
1	.8	2	1.6	1	.8		.0	4	3.2	98	77.8	24	19.0	126
0	.0	0	.0	0	.0		.0	0	.0	13	76.5	4	23.5	17
1	.9	2	1.8	1	.9		.0	4	3.7	85	78.0	20	18.3	109
	.0		.0	0	.0		.0	0	.0	0	.0		.0	
	.0		.0	0	.0		.0	0	.0	0	.0		.0	
	.0		.0	0	.0		.0	0	.0	0	.0		.0	
	.0		.0	0	.0		.0	0	.0	0	.0		.0	
0	.0	0	.0	0	.0	0	.0	0	.0	0	.0	0	.0	0
0	.0	0	.0	0	.0	0	.0	0	.0	0	.0	0	.0	0
	.0		.0	0	.0		.0	0	.0	0	.0		.0	
0	.0	0	.0	0	.0	0	.0	0	.0	0	.0	0	.0	0
12	1.5	13	1.6	14	1.8	4	.5	43	5.4	612	77.3	137	17.3	792
3	2.5	6	4.9	3	2.5	1	.8	13	10.7	89	73.0	20	16.4	122
9	1.3	7	1.0	11	1.6	3	.4	30	4.5	523	78.1	117	17.5	670
5	4.6	2	1.9	0	.0	1	.9	8	7.4	86	79.6	14	13.0	108
1	6.3	0	.0	0	.0	0	.0	1	6.3	10	62.5	5	31.3	16
4	4.3	2	2.2	0	.0	1	1.1	7	7.6	76	82.6	9	9.8	92
17	1.9	1	1.7	14	1.6	5	.6	51	5.7	698	77.6	151	16.8	900
4	2.9		4.3	3	2.2	1	.7	14	10.1	99	71.7	25	18.1	138
13	1.7	8	1.2	11	1.4	4	.5	37	4.9	599	78.6	126	16.5	762
	.0		.0	0	.0	0	.0	0	.0	5	83.3	1	16.7	
	.0		.0							0	.0	0	.0	
0	.0	0	.0	0	.0	0	.0	0	.0	5	83.3	1	16.7	
17	1.9	15	1.7	14	1.5	5	.6	51	5.6	703	77.6	152	16.8	906
4	2.9	6	4.3	3	2.2	1	.7	14	10.1	99	71.7	25	18.1	138
13	1.7	9	1.2	11	1.4	4	.5	37	4.8	604	78.6	127	16.5	768
		(9 INSTITUTIONS)												
12	1.4	5	.6	26	3.1	8	1.0	51	6.1	745	88.8	43	5.1	839
6	2.3	1	.4	7	2.7	0	.0	14	5.5	229	89.5	13	5.1	256
6	1.0	4	.7	19	3.3	8	1.4	37	6.3	516	88.5	30	5.1	583
2	2.0	0	.0	6	6.1	2	2.0	10	10.2	87	88.8	1	1.0	98
0	.0	0	.0	3	10.0	0	.0	3	10.0	27	90.0	0	.0	30
2	2.9	0	.0	3	4.4	2	2.9	7	10.3	60	88.2	1	1.5	68
14	1.5	5	.5	32	3.4	10	1.1	61	6.5	832	88.8	44	4.7	937
6	2.1	1	.3	10	3.5	0	.0	17	5.9	256	89.5	13	4.5	286
8	1.2	4	.6	22	3.4	10	1.5	44	6.8	576	88.5	31	4.8	651
1	.7		.0	2	1.4	0	.0	3	2.1	125	85.6	18	12.3	146
0	.0		.0	0	.0	0	.0	0	.0	42	89.4	5	10.6	47
1	1.0		.0	2	2.0	0	.0	3	3.0	83	83.8	13	13.1	99
0	.0		.0	0	.0	1	4.2	1	4.2	21	87.5	2	8.3	24
0	.0		.0	0	.0	0	.0	0	.0	9	90.0	1	10.0	10
0	.0	0	.0	0	.0	1	7.1	1	7.1	12	85.7	1	7.1	14
1	.6	0	.0	2	1.2	1	.6	4	2.4	146	85.9	20	11.8	170
0	.0	0	.0	0	.0	0	.0	0	.0	51	89.5	6	10.5	57
1	.9	0	.0	2	1.8	1	.9	4	3.5	95	84.1	14	12.4	113
0	.0		.0	0	.0		.0	0	.0	0	.0		.0	0
0	.0		.0	0	.0		.0	0	.0	0	.0		.0	0
0	.0	0	.0	0	.0	0	.0	0	.0	0	.0	0	.0	J

TABLE 17 - TOTAL ENROLLMENT IN INSTITUTIONS OF HIGHER EDUCATION FOR SELECTED MAJOR FIELDS OF STUDY AND LEVEL OF ENROLLMENT
BY RACE, ETHNICITY, AND SEX: STATE, 1978

MAJOR FIELD 0200 - ARCHITECTURE AND ENVIRONMENTAL DESIGN

	AMERICAN INDIAN ALASKAN NATIVE		BLACK NON-HISPANIC		ASIAN OR PACIFIC ISLANDER		HISPANIC		TOTAL MINORITY		WHITE NON-HISPANIC		NON-RESIDENT ALIEN	
	NUMBER	%	NUMBER	%	NUMBER	%	NUMBER	%	NUMBER	%	NUMBER	%	NUMBER	%
OREGON CONTINUED														
PROFESSIONAL														
PART-TIME	0	.0	0	.0	0	.0	0	.0	0	.0	0	.0	0	.0
FEMALE	0	.0	0	.0	0	.0	0	.0	0	.0	0	.0	0	.0
MALE	0	.0	0	.0	0	.0	0	.0	0	.0	0	.0	0	.0
TOTAL	0	.0	0	.0	0	.0	0	.0	0	.0	0	.0	0	.0
FEMALE	0	.0	0	.0	0	.0	0	.0	0	.0	0	.0	0	.0
MALE	0	.0	0	.0	0	.0	0	.0	0	.0	0	.0	0	.0
UNC+GRAD+PROF:														
FULL-TIME	13	1.3	5	.5	28	2.8	8	.8	54	5.5	870	88.3	61	6.2
FEMALE	6	2.0	1	.3	7	2.3	0	.0	14	4.6	271	89.4	18	5.9
MALE	7	1.0	4	.6	21	3.1	8	1.2	40	5.9	599	87.8	43	6.3
PART-TIME	2	1.6	0	.0	6	4.9	3	2.5	11	9.0	108	88.5	3	2.5
FEMALE	0	.0	0	.0	3	7.5	0	.0	3	7.5	36	90.0	1	2.5
MALE	2	2.4	0	.0	3	3.7	3	3.7	8	9.8	72	87.8	2	2.4
TOTAL	15	1.4	5	.5	34	3.1	11	1.0	65	5.9	978	88.3	64	5.8
FEMALE	6	1.7	1	.3	10	2.9	0	.0	17	5.0	307	89.5	19	5.5
MALE	9	1.2	4	.5	24	3.1	11	1.4	48	6.3	671	87.8	45	5.9
UNCLASSIFIED:														
TOTAL	0	.0	0	.0	0	.0	0	.0	0	.0	11	78.6	3	21.4
FEMALE	0	.0	0	.0	0	.0	0	.0	0	.0	6	85.7	1	14.3
MALE	0	.0	0	.0	0	.0	0	.0	0	.0	5	71.4	2	28.6
TOTAL ENROLLMENT:														
TOTAL	15	1.3	5	.4	34	3.0	11	1.0	65	5.8	989	88.2	67	6.0
FEMALE	6	1.7	1	.3	10	2.9	0	.0	17	4.9	313	89.4	20	5.7
MALE	9	1.2	4	.5	24	3.1	11	1.4	48	6.2	676	87.7	47	6.1
PENNSYLVANIA (13 INSTITUTIONS)														
UNDERGRADUATES:														
FULL-TIME	4	.3	97	6.4	16	1.1	9	.6	126	8.3	1,378	90.5	18	1.2
FEMALE	0	.0	19	6.0	7	2.2	3	.9	29	9.2	280	88.6	7	2.2
MALE	4	.3	78	6.5	9	.7	6	.5	97	8.0	1,098	91.0	11	.9
PART-TIME	0	.0	62	18.4	4	1.2	4	1.2	70	20.8	258	76.6	9	2.7
FEMALE	0	.0	10	20.8	1	2.1	1	2.1	12	25.0	34	70.8	2	4.2
MALE	0	.0	52	18.0	3	1.0	3	1.0	58	20.1	224	77.5	7	2.4
TOTAL	4	.2	159	8.6	20	1.1	13	.7	196	10.5	1,636	88.0	27	1.5
FEMALE	0	.0	29	6.0	8	2.2	4	1.1	41	11.3	314	86.3	9	2.5
MALE	4	.3	130	8.7	12	.8	9	.6	155	10.4	1,322	88.4	18	1.2
GRADUATE:														
FULL-TIME	0	.0	8	1.9	5	1.2	4	1.0	17	4.1	322	76.8	80	19.1
FEMALE	0	.0	2	1.7	1	.8	1	.8	4	3.3	106	88.3	10	8.3
MALE	0	.0	6	2.0	4	1.3	3	1.0	13	4.3	216	72.2	70	23.4
PART-TIME	1	.9	2	1.8	1	.9	1	.9	5	4.5	96	86.5	10	9.0
FEMALE	0	.0	0	.0	0	.0	0	.0	0	.0	33	89.2	4	10.8
MALE	1	1.4	2	2.7	1	1.4	1	1.4	5	6.8	63	85.1	6	8.1
TOTAL	1	.2	10	1.9	6	1.1	5	.9	22	4.2	418	78.9	90	17.0
FEMALE	0	.0	2	1.3	1	.6	1	.6	4	2.5	139	88.5	14	8.9
MALE	1	.3	8	2.1	5	1.3	4	1.1	18	4.8	279	74.8	76	20.4
PROFESSIONAL:														
FULL-TIME	0	.0	0	.0	0	.0	0	.0	0	.0	0	.0	0	.0
FEMALE	0	.0	0	.0	0	.0	0	.0	0	.0	0	.0	0	.0
MALE	0	.0	0	.0	0	.0	0	.0	0	.0	0	.0	0	.0
PART-TIME	0	.0	0	.0	0	.0	0	.0	0	.0	0	.0	0	.0
FEMALE	0	.0	0	.0	0	.0	0	.0	0	.0	0	.0	0	.0
MALE	0	.0	0	.0	0	.0	0	.0	0	.0	0	.0	0	.0
TOTAL	0	.0	0	.0	0	.0	0	.0	0	.0	0	.0	0	.0
FEMALE	0	.0	0	.0	0	.0	0	.0	0	.0	0	.0	0	.0
MALE	0	.0	0	.0	0	.0	0	.0	0	.0	0	.0	0	.0
UNC+GRAD+PROF:														
FULL-TIME	4	.2	105	5.4	21	1.1	13	.7	143	7.4	1,700	87.6	98	5.0
FEMALE	0	.0	21	4.8	8	1.8	4	.9	33	7.6	386	88.5	17	3.9
MALE	4	.3	84	5.6	13	.9	9	.6	110	7.3	1,314	87.3	81	5.4
PART-TIME	1	.2	64	14.3	5	1.1	5	1.1	75	16.7	354	79.0	19	4.2
FEMALE	0	.0	10	11.8	1	1.2	1	1.2	12	14.1	67	78.8	6	7.1
MALE	1	.3	54	14.9	4	1.1	4	1.1	63	17.4	287	79.1	13	3.6
TOTAL	5	.2	169	7.1	26	1.1	18	.8	218	9.1	2,054	86.0	117	4.9
FEMALE	0	.0	31	6.0	9	1.7	5	1.0	45	8.6	453	86.9	23	4.4
MALE	5	.3	138	7.4	17	.9	13	.7	173	9.3	1,601	85.7	94	5.0
UNCLASSIFIED:														
TOTAL	0	.0	0	.0	0	.0	0	.0	0	.0	2	66.7	1	33.3
FEMALE	0	.0	0	.0	0	.0	0	.0	0	.0	1	100.0	0	.0
MALE	0	.0	0	.0	0	.0	0	.0	0	.0	1	50.0	1	50.0
TOTAL ENROLLMENT:														
TOTAL	5	.2	169	7.1	26	1.1	18	.8	218	9.1	2,056	86.0	118	4.9
FEMALE	0	.0	31	5.9	9	1.7	5	1.0	45	8.6	454	87.0	23	4.4
MALE	5	.3	138	7.4	17	.9	13	.7	173	9.3	1,602	85.7	95	5.1

JOR FIELD 0200 - ARCHITECTURE AND ENVIRONMENTAL DESIGN

	American Indian Alaskan Native		Black Non-Hispanic		Asian or Pacific Islander		Hispanic		Total Minority		White Non-Hispanic		Non-Resident Alien		Total
	Number	%	Number	%	Number	%	Number	%	Number	%	Number	%	Number	%	Number
ODE ISLAND (5 INSTITUTIONS)															
UNDERGRADUATES:															
LL-TIME	1	.2	17	2.9	8	1.4	3	.5	29	5.0	538	92.9	12	2.1	579
FEMALE	0	.0	3	1.9	1	.6	1	.6	5	3.2	147	95.5	2	1.3	154
MALE	1	.2	14	3.3	7	1.6	2	.5	24	5.6	391	92.0	10	2.4	425
RT-TIME	0	.0	7	5.1	1	.7	0	.0	8	5.8	130	94.2	0	.0	138
FEMALE	0	.0	2	13.3	0	.0	0	.0	2	13.3	13	86.7	0	.0	15
MALE	0	.0	5	4.1	1	.8	0	.0	6	4.9	117	95.1	0	.0	123
TAL	1	.1	24	3.3	9	1.3	3	.4	37	5.2	668	93.2	12	1.7	717
FEMALE	0	.0	5	3.0	1	.6	1	.6	7	4.1	160	94.7	2	1.2	169
MALE	1	.2	19	3.5	8	1.5	2	.4	30	5.5	508	92.7	10	1.8	548
ADUATE:															
LL-TIME	0	.0	0	.0	1	1.9	0	.0	1	1.9	48	92.3	3	5.8	52
FEMALE	0	.0	0	.0	0	.0	0	.0	0	.0	11	91.7	1	8.3	12
MALE	0	.0	0	.0	1	2.5	0	.0	1	2.5	37	92.5	2	5.0	40
RT-TIME	0	.0	2	14.3	0	.0	0	.0	2	14.3	12	85.7	0	.0	14
FEMALE	0	.0	0	.0	0	.0	0	.0	0	.0	3	100.0	0	.0	3
MALE	0	.0	2	18.2	0	.0	0	.0	2	18.2	9	81.8	0	.0	11
TAL	0	.0	2	3.0	1	1.5	0	.0	3	4.5	60	90.9	3	4.5	66
FEMALE	0	.0	0	.0	0	.0	0	.0	0	.0	14	93.3	1	6.7	15
MALE	0	.0	2	3.9	1	2.0	0	.0	3	5.9	46	90.2	2	3.9	51
OFESSIONAL:															
LL-TIME	0	.0	0	.0	0	.0	0	.0	0	.0	0	.0	0	.0	0
FEMALE	0	.0	0	.0	0	.0	0	.0	0	.0	0	.0	0	.0	0
MALE	0	.0	0	.0	0	.0	0	.0	0	.0	0	.0	0	.0	0
RT-TIME	0	.0	0	.0	0	.0	0	.0	0	.0	0	.0	0	.0	0
FEMALE	0	.0	0	.0	0	.0	0	.0	0	.0	0	.0	0	.0	0
MALE	0	.0	0	.0	0	.0	0	.0	0	.0	0	.0	0	.0	0
TAL	0	.0	0	.0	0	.0	0	.0	0	.0	0	.0	0	.0	0
FEMALE	0	.0	0	.0	0	.0	0	.0	0	.0	0	.0	0	.0	0
MALE	0	.0	0	.0	0	.0	0	.0	0	.0	0	.0	0	.0	0
D+GRAD+PROF:															
LL-TIME	1	.2	17	2.7	9	1.4	3	.5	30	4.8	586	92.9	15	2.4	631
FEMALE	0	.0	3	1.8	1	.6	1	.6	5	3.0	158	95.2	3	1.8	166
MALE	1	.2	14	3.0	8	1.7	2	.4	25	5.4	428	92.0	12	2.6	465
RT-TIME	0	.0	9	5.9	1	.7	0	.0	10	6.6	142	93.4	0	.0	152
FEMALE	0	.0	2	11.1	0	.0	0	.0	2	11.1	16	88.9	0	.0	14
MALE	0	.0	7	5.2	1	.7	0	.0	8	6.0	126	94.0	0	.0	134
TAL	1	.1	26	3.3	10	1.3	3	.4	40	5.1	728	93.0	15	1.9	783
FEMALE	0	.0	5	2.7	1	.5	1	.5	7	3.8	174	94.6	3	1.6	184
MALE	1	.2	21	3.5	9	1.5	2	.3	33	5.5	554	92.5	12	2.0	599
CLASSIFIED:															
TAL	0	.0	0	.0	0	.0	0	.0	0	.0	0	.0	0	.0	0
FEMALE	0	.0	0	.0	0	.0	0	.0	0	.0	0	.0	0	.0	0
MALE	0	.0	0	.0	0	.0	0	.0	0	.0	0	.0	0	.0	0
TAL ENROLLMENT:															
TAL	1	.1	26	3.3	10	1.3	3	.4	40	5.1	728	93.0	15	1.9	783
FEMALE	0	.0	5	2.7	1	.5	1	.5	7	3.8	174	94.6	3	1.6	184
MALE	1	.2	21	3.5	9	1.5	2	.3	33	5.5	554	92.5	12	2.0	599
UTH CAROLINA (2 INSTITUTIONS)															
UNDERGRADUATES:															
LL-TIME	0	.0	5	1.2	1	.2	1	.2	7	1.7	393	97.5	3	.7	403
FEMALE	0	.0	3	2.4	0	.0	0	.0	3	2.4	120	97.6	0	.0	123
MALE	0	.0	2	.7	1	.4	1	.4	4	1.4	273	97.5	3	1.1	280
RT-TIME	0	.0	0	.0	0	.0	0	.0	0	.0	10	90.9	1	9.1	11
FEMALE	0	.0	0	.0	0	.0	0	.0	0	.0	3	75.0	1	25.0	4
MALE	0	.0	0	.0	0	.0	0	.0	0	.0	7	100.0	0	.0	7
TAL	0	.0	5	1.2	1	.2	1	.2	7	1.7	403	97.3	4	1.0	414
FEMALE	0	.0	3	2.4	0	.0	0	.0	3	2.4	123	96.9	1	.8	127
MALE	0	.0	2	.7	1	.4	1	.3	4	1.4	280	97.6	3	1.0	287
ADUATE:															
LL-TIME	0	.0	3	4.3	0	.0	1	1.4	4	5.7	65	92.9	1	1.4	70
FEMALE	0	.0	0	.0	0	.0	0	.0	0	.0	10	90.9	1	9.1	11
MALE	0	.0	3	5.1	0	.0	1	1.7	4	6.8	55	93.2	0	.0	59
RT-TIME	0	.0	0	.0	0	.0	1	10.0	1	10.0	9	90.0	0	.0	10
FEMALE	0	.0	0	.0	0	.0	0	.0	0	.0	2	100.0	0	.0	2
MALE	0	.0	0	.0	0	.0	1	12.5	1	12.5	7	87.5	0	.0	8
TAL	0	.0	3	3.8	0	.0	2	2.5	5	6.3	74	92.5	1	1.3	80
FEMALE	0	.0	0	.0	0	.0	0	.0	0	.0	12	92.3	1	7.7	13
MALE	0	.0	3	4.5	0	.0	2	3.0	5	7.5	62	92.5	0	.0	67
OFESSIONAL:															
LL-TIME	0	.0	0	.0	0	.0	0	.0	0	.0	0	.0	0	.0	0
FEMALE	0	.0	0	.0	0	.0	0	.0	0	.0	0	.0	0	.0	0
MALE	0	.0	0	.0	0	.0	0	.0	0	.0	0	.0	0	.0	0

MAJOR FIELD 0200 - ARCHITECTURE AND ENVIRONMENTAL DESIGN

	AMERICAN INDIAN ALASKAN NATIVE		BLACK NON-HISPANIC		ASIAN OR PACIFIC ISLANDER		HISPANIC		TOTAL MINORITY		WHITE NON-HISPANIC		NON-RESIDENT ALIEN		TOTAL
	NUMBER	%	NUMBER	%	NUMBER	%	NUMBER	%	NUMBER	%	NUMBER	%	NUMBER	%	NUMBER
SOUTH CAROLINA CONTINUED															
PROFESSIONAL:															
PART-TIME															
FEMALE	0	.0	0	.0	0	.0	0	.0	0	.0	0	.0	0	.0	0
MALE	0	.0	0	.0	0	.0	0	.0	0	.0	0	.0	0	.0	0
TOTAL	0	.0	0	.0	0	.0	0	.0	0	.0	0	.0	0	.0	0
FEMALE	0	.0	0	.0	0	.0	0	.0	0	.0	0	.0	0	.0	0
MALE	0	.0	0	.0	0	.0	0	.0	0	.0	0	.0	0	.0	0
UND+GRAD+PROF:															
FULL-TIME	0	.0	8	1.7	1	.2	2	.4	11	2.3	458	96.8	4	.8	473
FEMALE	0	.0	3	2.2	0	.0	0	.0	3	2.2	130	97.0	1	.7	134
MALE	0	.0	5	1.5	1	.3	2	.6	8	2.4	328	96.8	3	.9	339
PART-TIME	0	.0	0	.0	0	.0	1	4.8	1	4.8	19	90.5	1	4.8	21
FEMALE	0	.0	0	.0	0	.0	0	.0	0	.0	5	83.3	1	16.7	6
MALE	0	.0	0	.0	0	.0	1	6.7	1	6.7	14	93.3	0	.0	15
TOTAL	0	.0	8	1.6	1	.2	3	.6	12	2.4	477	96.6	5	1.0	494
FEMALE	0	.0	3	2.1	0	.0	0	.0	3	2.1	135	96.4	2	1.4	140
MALE	0	.0	5	1.4	1	.3	3	.8	9	2.5	342	96.6	3	.8	354
UNCLASSIFIED:															
TOTAL	0	.0	0	.0	0	.0	0	.0	0	.0	13	92.9	1	7.1	14
FEMALE	0	.0	0	.0	0	.0	0	.0	0	.0	1	100.0	0	.0	1
MALE	0	.0	0	.0	0	.0	0	.0	0	.0	12	92.3	1	7.7	13
TOTAL ENROLLMENT:															
TOTAL	0	.0	8	1.6	1	.2	3	.6	12	2.4	490	96.5	6	1.2	508
FEMALE	0	.0	3	2.1	0	.0	0	.0	3	2.1	136	96.5	2	1.4	141
MALE	0	.0	5	1.4	1	.3	3	.8	9	2.5	354	96.5	4	1.1	367
SOUTH DAKOTA (1 INSTITUTIONS)															
UNDERGRADUATES:															
FULL-TIME	0	.0	0	.0	0	.0	0	.0	0	.0	21	100.0	0	.0	21
FEMALE	0	.0	0	.0	0	.0	0	.0	0	.0	6	100.0	0	.0	6
MALE	0	.0	0	.0	0	.0	0	.0	0	.0	15	100.0	0	.0	15
PART-TIME	0	.0	0	.0	0	.0	0	.0	0	.0	3	100.0	0	.0	3
FEMALE	0	.0	0	.0	0	.0	0	.0	0	.0	1	100.0	0	.0	1
MALE	0	.0	0	.0	0	.0	0	.0	0	.0	2	100.0	0	.0	2
TOTAL	0	.0	0	.0	0	.0	0	.0	0	.0	24	100.0	0	.0	24
FEMALE	0	.0	0	.0	0	.0	0	.0	0	.0	7	100.0	0	.0	7
MALE	0	.0	0	.0	0	.0	0	.0	0	.0	17	100.0	0	.0	17
GRADUATE:															
FULL-TIME	0	.0	0	.0	0	.0	0	.0	0	.0	0	.0	0	.0	0
FEMALE	0	.0	0	.0	0	.0	0	.0	0	.0	0	.0	0	.0	0
MALE	0	.0	0	.0	0	.0	0	.0	0	.0	0	.0	0	.0	0
PART-TIME	0	.0	0	.0	0	.0	0	.0	0	.0	0	.0	0	.0	0
FEMALE	0	.0	0	.0	0	.0	0	.0	0	.0	0	.0	0	.0	0
MALE	0	.0	0	.0	0	.0	0	.0	0	.0	0	.0	0	.0	0
TOTAL	0	.0	0	.0	0	.0	0	.0	0	.0	0	.0	0	.0	0
FEMALE	0	.0	0	.0	0	.0	0	.0	0	.0	0	.0	0	.0	0
MALE	0	.0	0	.0	0	.0	0	.0	0	.0	0	.0	0	.0	0
PROFESSIONAL:															
FULL-TIME	0	.0	0	.0	0	.0	0	.0	0	.0	0	.0	0	.0	0
FEMALE	0	.0	0	.0	0	.0	0	.0	0	.0	0	.0	0	.0	0
MALE	0	.0	0	.0	0	.0	0	.0	0	.0	0	.0	0	.0	0
PART-TIME	0	.0	0	.0	0	.0	0	.0	0	.0	0	.0	0	.0	0
FEMALE	0	.0	0	.0	0	.0	0	.0	0	.0	0	.0	0	.0	0
MALE	0	.0	0	.0	0	.0	0	.0	0	.0	0	.0	0	.0	0
TOTAL	0	.0	0	.0	0	.0	0	.0	0	.0	0	.0	0	.0	0
FEMALE	0	.0	0	.0	0	.0	0	.0	0	.0	0	.0	0	.0	0
MALE	0	.0	0	.0	0	.0	0	.0	0	.0	0	.0	0	.0	0
UND+GRAD+PROF:															
FULL-TIME	0	.0	0	.0	0	.0	0	.0	0	.0	21	100.0	0	.0	21
FEMALE	0	.0	0	.0	0	.0	0	.0	0	.0	6	100.0	0	.0	6
MALE	0	.0	0	.0	0	.0	0	.0	0	.0	15	100.0	0	.0	15
PART-TIME	0	.0	0	.0	0	.0	0	.0	0	.0	3	100.0	0	.0	3
FEMALE	0	.0	0	.0	0	.0	0	.0	0	.0	1	100.0	0	.0	1
MALE	0	.0	0	.0	0	.0	0	.0	0	.0	2	100.0	0	.0	2
TOTAL	0	.0	0	.0	0	.0	0	.0	0	.0	24	100.0	0	.0	24
FEMALE	0	.0	0	.0	0	.0	0	.0	0	.0	7	100.0	0	.0	7
MALE	0	.0	0	.0	0	.0	0	.0	0	.0	17	100.0	0	.0	17
UNCLASSIFIED:															
TOTAL	0	.0	0	.0	0	.0	0	.0	0	.0	0	.0	0	.0	0
FEMALE	0	.0	0	.0	0	.0	0	.0	0	.0	0	.0	0	.0	0
MALE	0	.0	0	.0	0	.0	0	.0	0	.0	0	.0	0	.0	0
TOTAL ENROLLMENT:															
TOTAL	0	.0	0	.0	0	.0	0	.0	0	.0	24	100.0	0	.0	24
FEMALE	0	.0	0	.0	0	.0	0	.0	0	.0	7	100.0	0	.0	7
MALE	0	.0	0	.0	0	.0	0	.0	0	.0	17	100.0	0	.0	17

ARCHITECTURE AND ENVIRONMENTAL DESIGN

N INDIAN NATIVE	BLACK NON-HISPANIC		ASIAN OR PACIFIC ISLANDER		HISPANIC		TOTAL MINORITY		WHITE NON-HISPANIC		NON-RESIDENT ALIEN		TOTAL
%	NUMBER	%	NUMBER	%	NUMBER	%	NUMBER	%	NUMBER	%	NUMBER	%	NUMBER

(7 INSTITUTIONS).

.2	15	2.5	2	.3	4	.7	22	3.6	557	91.5	30	4.	609
.0	4	3.1	0	.0	0	.0	4	3.1	118	91.5	7	5.	125
.2	11	2.3	2	.4	4	.8	18	3.8	439	91.5	23	4.	480
.0	3	3.8	0	.0	0	.0	3	3.8	73	93.6	2	2.	78
.0	0	.0	0	.0	0	.0	0	.0	12	100.0	0	.0	12
.0	3	4.5	0	.0	0	.0	3	4.5	61	92.4	2	3.0	66
.1	18	2.6	2	.3	4	.6	25	3.6	630	91.7	32	4 7	687
.0	4	2.8	0	.0	0	.0	4	2.8	130	92.2	7	5 0	141
.2	14	2.6	2	.4	4	.7	21	3.8	500	91.6	25	416	546
.0	11	12.8	0	.0	3	3.5	14	16.3	69	80.2	3	3.5	86
.0	7	24.1	0	.0	0	.0	7	24.1	19	65.5	3	10.3	29
.0	4	7.0	0	.0	3	5.3	7	12.3	50	87.7	0	.0	57
.0	7	10.8	0	.0	0	.0	7	10.8	57	87.7	1	1 5	65
.0	3	18.8	0	.0	0	.0	3	18.8	12	75.0	1	6I3	16
.0	4	8.2	0	.0	0	.0	4	8.2	45	91.8	0	.0	49
.0	18	11.9	0	.0	3	2.0	21	13.9	126	83.4		2.	151
.0	10	22.2	0	.0	0	.0	10	22.2	31	68.9		8.	45
.0	8	7.5	0	.0	3	2.8	11	10.4	95	89.6	0	.0	106
.0	0	.0	0	.0	0	.0	0	.0	0	.0		.0	
.0	0	.0	0	.0	0	.0	0	.0	0	.0		.0	
.0	0	.0	0	.0	0	.0	0	.0	0	.0		.0	
.0	0	.0	0	.0	0	.0	0	.0	0	.0		.0	
.0	0	.0	0	.0	0	.0	0	.0	0	.0	0	.0	0
.0	0	.0	0	.0	0	.0	0	.0	0	.0	0	.0	0
.0	0	.0	0	.0	0	.0	0	.0	0	.0		.0	
.0	0	.0	0	.0	0	.0	0	.0	0	.0		.0	
.0	0	.0	0	.0	0	.0	0	.0	0	.0	0	.0	0
.1	26	3.7	2	.3	7	1.0	36	5.2	626	90.1	33	4.7	695
.0	11	7.0	0	.0	0	.0	11	7.0	137	86.7	10	6.3	158
.2	15	2.8	2	.4	7	1.3	25	4.7	489	91.1	23	4.3	537
.0	10	7.0	0	.0	0	.0	10	7.0	130	90.9	3	2.'	143
.0	3	10.7	0	.0	0	.0	3	10.7	24	85.7	1	3.	28
.0	7	6.1	0	.0	0	.0	7	6.1	106	92.2	2	1.8	115
.1	36	4.3	2	.2	7	.8	46	5.5	756	90.2	36	3	838
.0	14	7.5	0	.0	0	.0	14	7.5	161	86.6	11	9	186
.2	22	3.4	2	.3	7	1.1	32	4.9	595	91.3	25	318	652
.0	0	.0	0	.0	0	.0	0	.0	11	100.0		.0	11
.0	0	.0	0	.0	0	.0	0	.0	10	100.0		.0	10
.0	0	.0	0	.0	0	.0	0	.0	1	100.0	0	.0	1
.1	36	4.2	2	.2	7	.8	46	5.4	767	90.3	36	4 2	849
.0	14	7.1	0	.0	0	.0	14	7.1	171	87.2	11	5 6	196
.2	22	3.4	2	.3	7	1.1	32	4.9	596	91.3	25	318	653

(41 INSTITUTIONS)

.3	201	4.6	41	.9	358	8.1	613	13.9	3,553	80.5	248	5.	4,414
.4	41	4.9	6	.7	50	6.0	100	12.0	682	81.7	53	6.	835
.3	160	4.5	35	1.0	308	8.6	513	14.3	2,871	80.2	195	5.	3,579
.8	27	3.8	2	.3	73	10.2	108	15.0	584	81.2	27	3.	719
.0	1	.7	0	.0	10	7.0	11	7.7	125	87.4	7	4.0	143
1.0	26	4.5	2	.3	63	10.9	97	16.8	459	79.7	20	3.8	576
.4	228	4.4	43	.8	431	8.4	721	14.0	4,137	80.6	275	5.4	5,133
.3	42	4.3	6	.6	60	6.1	111	11.3	807	82.5	60	6.1	978
.4	186	4.5	37	.9	371	8.9	610	14.7	3,330	80.1	215	5.2	4,155
.0	7	1.4	7	1.4	14	2.7	28	5.5	422	82.3	63	12.3	513
.0	1	.8	2	1.6	3	2.3	6	4.7	111	86.0	12	9.3	129
.0	6	1.6	5	1.3	11	2.9	22	5.7	311	81.0	51	13.3	384
.8	5	3.8	0	.0	2	1.5	8	6.1	112	85.5	11	8.4	131
.0	1	2.4	0	.0	1	2.4	2	4.9	35	85.4	4	9.8	41
1.1	4	4.4	0	.0	1	1.1	6	6.7	77	85.6	7	7.8	90
.2	12	1.9	7	1.1	16	2.5	36	5.6	534	82.9	74	11.5	644
.0	2	1.2	2	1.2	4	2.4	8	4.7	146	85.9	16	9.4	170
.2	10	2.1	5	1.1	12	2.5	28	5.9	388	81.9	58	12.2	474
.0	0	.0	0	.0	0	.0	0	.0	0	.0	0	.0	
.0	0	.0	0	.0	0	.0	0	.0	0	.0	0	.0	0

MAJOR FIELD 0200 - ARCHITECTURE AND ENVIRONMENTAL DESIGN

	AMERICAN INDIAN ALASKAN NATIVE		BLACK NON-HISPANIC		ASIAN OR PACIFIC ISLANDER		HISPANIC		TOTAL MINORITY		WHITE NON-HISPANIC		NON-RESIDENT ALIEN	
	NUMBER	%	NUMBER	%	NUMBER	%	NUMBER	%	NUMBER	%	NUMBER	%	NUMBER	%
TEXAS	CONTINUED													
PROFESSIONAL:														
PART-TIME	0	.0	0	.0	0	.0	0	.0	0	.0	0	.0	0	.0
FEMALE	0	.0	0	.0	0	.0	0	.0	0	.0	0	.0	0	.0
MALE	0	.0	0	.0	0	.0	0	.0	0	.0	0	.0	0	.0
TOTAL	0	.0	0	.0	0	.0	0	.0	0	.0	0	.0	0	.0
FEMALE	0	.0	0	.0	0	.0	0	.0	0	.0	0	.0	0	.0
MALE	0	.0	0	.0	0	.0	0	.0	0	.0	0	.0	0	.0
UND+GRAD+PROF:														
FULL-TIME	13	.3	208	4.2	48	1.0	372	7.6	641	13.0	3,975	80.7	311	6.3
FEMALE	3	.3	42	4.4	8	.8	53	5.5	106	11.0	793	82.3	65	6.7
MALE	10	.3	166	4.2	40	1.0	319	8.0	535	13.5	3,182	80.3	246	6.2
PART-TIME	7	.8	32	3.8	2	.2	75	8.8	116	13.6	696	81.9	38	4.5
FEMALE	0	.0	2	1.1	0	.0	11	6.0	13	7.1	160	87.0	11	6.0
MALE	7	1.1	30	4.5	2	.3	64	9.6	103	15.5	536	80.5	27	4.1
TOTAL	20	.3	240	4.2	50	.9	447	7.7	757	13.1	4,671	80.9	349	6.0
FEMALE	3	.3	44	3.8	8	.7	64	5.6	119	10.4	953	83.0	76	6.6
MALE	17	.4	196	4.2	42	.9	383	8.3	638	13.8	3,718	80.3	273	5.9
UNCLASSIFIED:														
TOTAL	0	.0	4	4.5	1	1.1	25	28.4	30	34.1	53	60.2	5	5.7
FEMALE	0	.0	1	5.3	0	.0	1	5.3	2	10.5	14	73.7	3	15.8
MALE	0	.0	3	4.3	1	1.4	24	34.8	28	40.6	39	56.5	2	2.9
TOTAL ENROLLMENT:														
TOTAL	20	.3	244	4.2	51	.9	472	8.0	787	13.4	4,724	80.5	354	6.0
FEMALE	3	.3	45	3.9	8	.7	65	5.6	121	10.4	967	82.9	79	6.8
MALE	17	.4	199	4.2	43	.9	407	8.7	666	14.2	3,757	80.0	275	5.9
UTAH (4 INSTITUTIONS)														
UNDERGRADUATES:														
FULL-TIME	1	.5	1	.5	0	.0	2	1.1	4	2.1	167	88.4	18	9.5
FEMALE	0	.0	1	2.0	0	.0	2	4.0	3	6.0	39	78.0	8	16.0
MALE	1	.7	0	.0	0	.0	0	.0	1	.7	128	92.1	10	7.2
PART-TIME	0	.0	0	.0	0	.0	0	.0	0	.0	10	100.0	0	.0
FEMALE	0	.0	0	.0	0	.0	0	.0	0	.0	1	100.0	0	.0
MALE	0	.0	0	.0	0	.0	0	.0	0	.0	9	100.0	0	.0
TOTAL	1	.5	1	.5	0	.0	2	1.0	4	2.0	177	88.9	18	9.0
FEMALE	0	.0	1	2.0	0	.0	2	3.9	3	5.9	40	78.4	8	15.7
MALE	1	.7	0	.0	0	.0	0	.0	1	.7	137	92.6	10	6.8
GRADUATE:														
FULL-TIME	0	.0	0	.0	0	.0	0	.0	0	.0	67	91.8	6	8.2
FEMALE	0	.0	0	.0	0	.0	0	.0	0	.0	7	100.0	0	.0
MALE	0	.0	0	.0	0	.0	0	.0	0	.0	60	90.9	6	9.1
PART-TIME	0	.0	0	.0	1	10.0	0	.0	1	10.0	9	90.0	0	.0
FEMALE	0	.0	0	.0	0	.0	0	.0	0	.0	2	100.0	0	.0
MALE	0	.0	0	.0	1	12.5	0	.0	1	12.5	7	87.5	0	.0
TOTAL	0	.0	0	.0	1	1.2	0	.0	1	1.2	76	91.6	6	7.2
FEMALE	0	.0	0	.0	0	.0	0	.0	0	.0	9	100.0	0	.0
MALE	0	.0	0	.0	1	1.4	0	.0	1	1.4	67	90.5	6	8.1
PROFESSIONAL:														
FULL-TIME	0	.0	0	.0	0	.0	0	.0	0	.0	0	.0	0	.0
FEMALE	0	.0	0	.0	0	.0	0	.0	0	.0	0	.0	0	.0
MALE	0	.0	0	.0	0	.0	0	.0	0	.0	0	.0	0	.0
PART-TIME	0	.0	0	.0	0	.0	0	.0	0	.0	0	.0	0	.0
FEMALE	0	.0	0	.0	0	.0	0	.0	0	.0	0	.0	0	.0
MALE	0	.0	0	.0	0	.0	0	.0	0	.0	0	.0	0	.0
TOTAL	0	.0	0	.0	0	.0	0	.0	0	.0	0	.0	0	.0
FEMALE	0	.0	0	.0	0	.0	0	.0	0	.0	0	.0	0	.0
MALE	0	.0	0	.0	0	.0	0	.0	0	.0	0	.0	0	.0
UND+GRAD+PROF:														
FULL-TIME	1	.4	1	.4	0	.0	2	.8	4	1.5	234	89.3	24	9.2
FEMALE	0	.0	1	1.8	0	.0	2	3.5	3	5.3	46	80.7	8	14.0
MALE	1	.5	0	.0	0	.0	0	.0	1	.7	188	91.7	16	7.8
PART-TIME	0	.0	0	.0	1	5.0	0	.0	1	5.0	19	95.0	0	.0
FEMALE	0	.0	0	.0	0	.0	0	.0	0	.0	3	100.0	0	.0
MALE	0	.0	0	.0	1	5.9	0	.0	1	5.9	16	94.1	0	.0
TOTAL	1	.4	1	.4	1	.4	2	.7	5	1.8	253	89.7	24	8.5
FEMALE	0	.0	1	1.7	0	.0	2	3.3	3	5.0	49	81.7	8	13.3
MALE	1	.5	0	.0	1	.5	0	.0	2	.9	204	91.9	16	7.2
UNCLASSIFIED:														
TOTAL	0	.0	0	.0	0	.0	0	.0	0	.0	0	.0	0	.0
FEMALE	0	.0	0	.0	0	.0	0	.0	0	.0	0	.0	0	.0
MALE	0	.0	0	.0	0	.0	0	.0	0	.0	0	.0	0	.0
TOTAL ENROLLMENT:														
TOTAL	1	.4	1	.4	1	.4	2	.7	5	1.8	253	89.7	24	8.5
FEMALE	0	.0	1	1.7	0	.0	2	3.3	3	5.0	49	81.7	8	13.3
MALE	1	.5	0	.0	1	.5	0	.0	2	.9	204	91.9	16	7.2

- ARCHITECTURE AND ENVIRONMENTAL DESIGN

CAN INDIAN AN NATIVE		BLACK NON-HISPANIC		ASIAN OR PACIFIC ISLANDER		HISPANIC		TOTAL MINORITY		WHITE NON-HISPANIC		NON-RESIDENT ALIEN		TOTAL
ER	%	NUMBER	%	NUMBER	%	NUMBER	%	NUMBER	%	NUMBER	%	NUMBER	%	NUMBER

(2 INSTITUTIONS)

	.0		.0	1	.9	1	.9	2	1.8	109	98.2	0	.0	111
	.0		.0	1	4.8		.0	1	4.8	20	95.2	0	.0	21
	.0		.0	0	.0	1	1.1	1	1.1	89	98.9	0	.0	90
	.0		.0	0	.0	0	.0	0	.0	1	100.0	0	.0	1
0	.0	0	.0	0	.0	0	.0	0	.0	0	.0	0	.0	0
0	.0	0	.0	0	.0	0	.0	0	.0	1	100.0	0	.0	1
	.0		.0	1	.9	1	.9	2	1.8	110	98.2	0	.0	112
	.0		.0	1	4.8		.0	1	4.8	20	95.2	0	.0	21
0	.0	0	.0	0	.0	1	1.1	1	1.1	90	98.9	0	.0	91

	.0		.0		.0		.0		.0	4	100.0	0	.0	
	.0		.0		.0		.0		.0	0	.0	0	.0	
0	.0		.0		.0		.0		.0	4	100.0	0	.0	
0	.0		.0		.0		.0		.0	0	.0	0	.0	
0	.0	0	.0	0	.0	0	.0	0	.0	0	.0	0	.0	4
	.0		.0		.0		.0		.0	4	100.0	0	.0	
	.0		.0		.0		.0		.0	0	.0	0	.0	
0	.0	0	.0	0	.0	0	.0	0	.0	4	100.0	0	.0	4

0	.0		.0		.0		.0	0	.0	0	.0	0	.0	
	.0		.0		.0		.0	0	.0	0	.0	0	.0	
0	.0		.0		.0		.0	0	.0	0	.0	0	.0	
	.0		.0		.0		.0	0	.0	0	.0	0	.0	
0	.0	0	.0	0	.0	0	.0	0	.0	0	.0	0	.0	0
0	.0	0	.0	0	.0	0	.0	0	.0	0	.0	0	.0	0

	.0		.0	1	.9	1	.9	2	1.7	113	98.3	0	.0	115
	.0		.0	1	4.8	0	.0	1	4.8	20	95.2	0	.0	21
	.0		.0	0	.0	1	1.1	1	1.1	93	98.9	0	.0	94
	.0		.0	0	.0	0	.0	0	.0	1	100.0	0	.0	1
0	.0	0	.0	0	.0	0	.0	0	.0	0	.0	0	.0	0
0	.0	0	.0	0	.0	0	.0	0	.0	1	100.0	0	.0	1
	.0		.0	1	.9	1	.9	2	1.7	114	98.3	0	.0	116
	.0		.0	1	4.8	0	.0	1	4.8	20	95.2	0	.0	21
0	.0	0	.0	0	.0	1	1.1	1	1.1	94	98.9	0	.0	95

	.0		.0	0	.0	0	.0	0	.0	0	.0	0	.0	
0	.0	0	.0	0	.0	0	.0	0	.0	0	.0	0	.0	0
	.0	0	.0	1	.9	1	.9	2	1.7	114	98.3	0	.0	116
	.0	0	.0	1	4.8	0	.0	1	4.8	20	95.2	0	.0	21
0	.0	0	.0	0	.0	1	1.1	1	1.1	94	98.9	0	.0	95

(5 INSTITUTIONS)

	.0	131	10.6	8	.6	1	.1	140	11.3	1,073	86.9	22	1.8	1,235
	.0	31	8.9	4	1.2	0	.0	35	10.1	304	87.6	8	2.3	347
	.0	100	11.3		.5	1	.1	105	11.8	769	86.6	14	1.6	888
	.0	5	10.9		.0	0	.0	5	10.9	40	87.0	1	2.2	46
	.0	1	16.7		.0	0	.0	1	16.7	4	66.7	1	16.7	6
0	.0	4	10.0	0	.0	0	.0	4	10.0	36	90.0	0	.0	40
	.0	136	10.6		.6	1	.1	145	11.3	1,113	86.9	23	1.8	1,281
	.0	32	9.1	0	1.1	0	.0	36	10.2	308	87.3	9	2.5	353
0	.0	104	11.2	4	.4	1	.1	109	11.7	805	86.7	14	1.5	928

	.0	6	2.0	2	.7	0	.0	8	2.7	268	91.2	18	6.1	294
	.0	2	1.9	0	.0	0	.0	2	1.9	94	90.4	8	7.7	104
	.0	4	2.1	2	1.1	0	.0	6	3.2	174	91.6	10	5.3	190
	.0	2	3.2	1	1.6	2	3.2	5	8.1	53	85.5	4	6.5	62
	.0	1	5.9	0	.0	0	.0		5.	14	82.4	2	11.8	17
0	.0	1	2.2	1	2.2	2	4.4	4	8.9	39	86.7	2	4.4	45
	.0		2.2	3	.8	2	.6	13	3.7	321	90.2	22	6.2	356
	.0		2.5	0	.0	0	.0	3	2.5	108	89.3	10	8.3	121
0	.0	9	2.1	3	1.3	2	.9	10	4.3	213	90.6	12	5.1	235

	.0		.0		.0		.0	0	.0	0	.0	0	.0	
0	.0	0	.0	0	.0	0	.0	0	.0	0	.0	0	.0	0

MAJOR FIELD 0200 - ARCHITECTURE AND ENVIRONMENTAL DESIGN

	AMERICAN INDIAN ALASKAN NATIVE		BLACK NON-HISPANIC		ASIAN OR PACIFIC ISLANDER		HISPANIC		TOTAL MINORITY		WHITE NON-HISPANIC		NON-RESIDENT ALIEN	
	NUMBER	%	NUMBER	%	NUMBER	%	NUMBER	%	NUMBER	%	NUMBER	%	NUMBER	%
VIRGINIA	CONTINUED													
PROFESSIONAL:														
PART-TIME	0	.0	0	.0	0	.0	0	.0	0	.0	0	.0	0	.0
FEMALE	0	.0	0	.0	0	.0	0	.0	0	.0	0	.0	0	.0
MALE	0	.0	0	.0	0	.0	0	.0	0	.0	0	.0	0	.0
TOTAL	0	.0	0	.0	0	.0	0	.0	0	.0	0	.0	0	.0
FEMALE	0	.0	0	.0	0	.0	0	.0	0	.0	0	.0	0	.0
MALE	0	.0	0	.0	0	.0	0	.0	0	.0	0	.0	0	.0
UND+GRAD+PROF:														
FULL-TIME	0	.0	137	9.0	10	.7	1	.1	148	9.7	1,341	87.7	40	2.6
FEMALE	0	.0	33	7.3	4	.9	0	.0	37	8.2	398	88.2	16	3.5
MALE	0	.0	104	9.6	6	.6	1	.1	111	10.3	943	87.5	24	2.2
PART-TIME	0	.0	7	6.5	1	.9	2	1.9	10	9.3	93	86.1	5	4.6
FEMALE	0	.0	2	8.7	0	.0	0	.0	2	8.7	18	78.3	3	13.0
MALE	0	.0	5	5.9	1	1.2	2	2.4	8	9.4	75	88.2	2	2.4
TOTAL	0	.0	144	8.8	11	.7	3	.2	158	9.7	1,434	87.6	45	2.7
FEMALE	0	.0	35	7.4	4	.8	0	.0	39	8.2	416	87.8	19	4.0
MALE	0	.0	109	9.4	7	.6	3	.3	119	10.2	1,018	87.5	26	2.2
UNCLASSIFIED:														
TOTAL	0	.0	0	.0	0	.0	0	.0	0	.0	1	50.0	1	50.0
FEMALE	0	.0	0	.0	0	.0	0	.0	0	.0	0	.0	1	100.0
MALE	0	.0	0	.0	0	.0	0	.0	0	.0	1	100.0	0	.0
TOTAL ENROLLMENT:														
TOTAL	0	.0	144	8.8	11	.7	3	.2	158	9.6	1,435	87.6	46	2.8
FEMALE	0	.0	35	7.4	4	.8	0	.0	39	8.2	416	87.6	20	4.2
MALE	0	.0	109	9.4	7	.6	3	.3	119	10.2	1,019	87.5	26	2.2
WASHINGTON	(4 INSTITUTIONS)													
UNDERGRADUATES:														
FULL-TIME	2	.3	9	1.4	29	4.4	2	.3	42	6.4	533	81.7	77	11.8
FEMALE	2	1.5	3	2.2	5	3.7	0	.0	10	7.5	111	82.8	13	9.7
MALE	0	.0	6	1.2	24	4.6	2	.4	32	6.2	422	81.5	64	12.4
PART-TIME	0	.0	2	1.6	15	12.3	1	.8	18	14.8	93	76.2	11	9.0
FEMALE	0	.0	0	.0	3	11.5	0	.0	3	11.5	22	84.6	1	3.8
MALE	0	.0	2	2.1	12	12.5	1	1.0	15	15.6	71	74.0	10	10.4
TOTAL	2	.3	11	1.4	44	5.7	3	.4	60	7.8	626	80.9	88	11.4
FEMALE	2	1.3	3	1.9	8	5.0	0	.0	13	8.1	133	83.1	14	8.8
MALE	0	.0	8	1.3	36	5.9	3	.5	47	7.7	493	80.3	74	12.1
GRADUATE:														
FULL-TIME	0	.0	8	3.6	11	5.0	1	.5	20	9.0	177	80.1	24	10.9
FEMALE	0	.0	2	2.7	5	6.7	0	.0	7	9.3	66	88.0	2	2.7
MALE	0	.0	6	4.1	6	4.1	1	.7	13	8.9	111	76.0	22	15.1
PART-TIME	0	.0	1	1.4	4	5.5	0	.0	5	6.8	63	86.3	5	6.8
FEMALE	0	.0	0	.0	0	.0	0	.0	0	.0	21	95.5	1	4.5
MALE	0	.0	1	2.0	4	7.8	0	.0	5	9.8	42	82.4	4	7.8
TOTAL	0	.0	9	3.1	15	5.1	1	.3	25	8.5	240	81.6	29	9.9
FEMALE	0	.0	2	2.1	5	5.2	0	.0	7	7.2	87	89.7	3	3.1
MALE	0	.0	7	3.6	10	5.1	1	.5	18	9.1	153	77.7	26	13.2
PROFESSIONAL:														
FULL-TIME	0	.0	0	.0	0	.0	0	.0	0	.0	0	.0	0	.0
FEMALE	0	.0	0	.0	0	.0	0	.0	0	.0	0	.0	0	.0
MALE	0	.0	0	.0	0	.0	0	.0	0	.0	0	.0	0	.0
PART-TIME	0	.0	0	.0	0	.0	0	.0	0	.0	0	.0	0	.0
FEMALE	0	.0	0	.0	0	.0	0	.0	0	.0	0	.0	0	.0
MALE	0	.0	0	.0	0	.0	0	.0	0	.0	0	.0	0	.0
TOTAL	0	.0	0	.0	0	.0	0	.0	0	.0	0	.0	0	.0
FEMALE	0	.0	0	.0	0	.0	0	.0	0	.0	0	.0	0	.0
MALE	0	.0	0	.0	0	.0	0	.0	0	.0	0	.0	0	.0
UND+GRAD+PROF:														
FULL-TIME	2	.2	17	1.9	40	4.6	3	.3	62	7.1	710	81.3	101	11.6
FEMALE	2	1.0	5	2.4	10	4.8	0	.0	17	8.1	177	84.7	15	7.2
MALE	0	.0	12	1.8	30	4.5	3	.5	45	6.8	533	80.3	86	13.0
PART-TIME	0	.0	3	1.5	19	9.7	1	.5	23	11.8	156	80.0	16	8.2
FEMALE	0	.0	0	.0	3	6.3	0	.0	3	6.3	43	89.6	2	4.2
MALE	0	.0	3	2.0	16	10.9	1	.7	20	13.6	113	76.9	14	9.5
TOTAL	2	.2	20	1.9	59	5.5	4	.4	85	8.0	866	81.1	117	11.0
FEMALE	2	.8	5	1.9	13	5.1	0	.0	20	7.8	220	85.6	17	6.6
MALE	0	.0	15	1.8	46	5.7	4	.5	65	8.0	646	79.7	100	12.3
UNCLASSIFIED:														
TOTAL	1	3.1	0	.0	2	6.3	0	.0	3	9.4	23	71.9	6	18.8
FEMALE	0	.0	0	.0	1	14.3	0	.0	1	14.3	6	85.7	0	.0
MALE	1	4.0	0	.0	1	4.0	0	.0	2	8.0	17	68.0	6	24.0
TOTAL ENROLLMENT:														
TOTAL	3	.3	20	1.8	61	5.5	4	.4	88	8.0	889	80.8	123	11.2
FEMALE	2	.8	5	1.9	14	5.3	0	.0	21	8.0	226	85.6	17	6.4
MALE	1	.1	15	1.8	47	5.6	4	.5	67	8.0	663	79.3	106	12.7

- ARCHITECTURE AND ENVIRONMENTAL DESIGN

CAN INDIAN AN NATIVE		BLACK NON-HISPANIC		ASIAN OR PACIFIC ISLANDER		HISPANIC		TOTAL MINORITY		WHITE NON-HISPANIC		NON-RESIDENT ALIEN		TOTAL
ER	%	NUMBER	%	NUMBER	%	NUMBER	%	NUMBER	%	NUMBER	%	NUMBER	%	NUMBER
(2 INSTITUTIONS)														
0	.0	3	1.7	0	.0	0	.0	3	1.7	172	97.7	1	.6	176
0	.0	2	4.1	0	.0	0	.0	2	4.1	47	95.9	0	.0	49
0	.0	1	.8	0	.0	0	.0	1	.8	125	98.4	1	.8	127
0	.0	0	.0	1	2.1	0	.0	1	2.1	47	97.9	0	.0	48
0	.0	0	.0	0	.0	0	.0	0	.0	18	100.0	0	.0	18
0	.0	0	.0	1	3.3	0	.0	1	3.3	29	96.7	0	.0	30
0	.0	3	1.3	1	.4	0	.0	4	1.8	219	97.8	1	.4	224
0	.0	2	3.0	0	.0	0	.0	2	3.0	65	97.0	0	.0	67
0	.0	1	.6	1	.6	0	.0	2	1.3	154	98.1	1	.6	157
0	.0	0	.0	0	.0	0	.0	0	.0	0	.0	0	.0	0
0	.0	0	.0	0	.0	0	.0	0	.0	0	.0	0	.0	0
0	.0	0	.0	0	.0	0	.0	0	.0	0	.0	0	.0	0
0	.0	0	.0	0	.0	0	.0	0	.0	0	.0	0	.0	0
0	.0	0	.0	0	.0	0	.0	0	.0	0	.0	0	.0	0
0	.0	0	.0	0	.0	0	.0	0	.0	0	.0	0	.0	0
0	.0	0	.0	0	.0	0	.0	0	.0	0	.0	0	.0	0
0	.0	0	.0	0	.0	0	.0	0	.0	0	.0	0	.0	0
0	.0	0	.0	0	.0	0	.0	0	.0	0	.0	0	.0	0
0	.0	0	.0	0	.0	0	.0	0	.0	0	.0	0	.0	0
0	.0	0	.0	0	.0	0	.0	0	.0	0	.0	0	.0	0
0	.0	0	.0	0	.0	0	.0	0	.0	0	.0	0	.0	0
0	.0	0	.0	0	.0	0	.0	0	.0	0	.0	0	.0	0
0	.0	0	.0	0	.0	0	.0	0	.0	0	.0	0	.0	0
0	.0	0	.0	0	.0	0	.0	0	.0	0	.0	0	.0	0
0	.0	3	1.7	0	.0	0	.0	3	1.7	172	97.7	1	.6	176
0	.0	2	4.1	0	.0	0	.0	2	4.1	47	95.9	0	.0	49
0	.0	1	.8	0	.0	0	.0	1	.8	125	98.4	1	.8	127
0	.0	0	.0	1	2.1	0	.0	1	2.1	47	97.9	0	.0	48
0	.0	0	.0	0	.0	0	.0	0	.0	18	100.0	0	.0	18
0	.0	0	.0	1	3.3	0	.0	1	3.3	29	96.7	0	.0	30
0	.0	3	1.3	1	.4	0	.0	4	1.8	219	97.8	1	.4	224
0	.0	2	3.0	0	.0	0	.0	2	3.0	65	97.0	0	.0	67
0	.0	1	.6	1	.6	0	.0	2	1.3	154	98.1	1	.6	157
0	.0	0	.0	0	.0	0	.0	0	.0	9	100.0	0	.0	9
0	.0	0	.0	0	.0	0	.0	0	.0	2	100.0	0	.0	2
0	.0	0	.0	0	.0	0	.0	0	.0	7	100.0	0	.0	7
0	.0	3	1.3	1	.4	0	.0	4	1.7	228	97.9	1	.4	233
0	.0	2	2.9	0	.0	0	.0	2	2.9	67	97.1	0	.0	69
0	.0	1	.6	1	.6	0	.0	2	1.2	161	98.2	1	.6	164
(5 INSTITUTIONS)														
0	.0	5	1.0	2	.4	6	1.2	13	2.6	468	94.5	14	2.8	495
0	.0	3	1.2	0	.0	3	1.2	6	2.4	245	96.1	4	1.6	255
0	.0	2	.8	2	.8	3	1.3	7	2.9	223	92.9	10	4.2	240
1	.8	0	.0	0	.0	1	.8	2	1.7	119	98.3	0	.0	121
0	.0	0	.0	0	.0	0	.0	0	.0	67	100.0	0	.0	67
1	1.9	0	.0	0	.0	1	1.9	2	3.7	52	96.3	0	.0	54
1	.2	5	.8	2	.3	7	1.1	15	2.4	587	95.3	14	2.3	616
0	.0	3	.9	0	.0	3	.9	6	1.9	312	96.9	4	1.2	322
1	.3	2	.7	2	.7	4	1.4	9	3.1	275	93.5	10	3.4	294
3	1.4	8	3.8	3	1.4	1	.5	15	7.1	176	83.0	21	9.9	212
0	.0	0	.0	1	1.7	1	1.7	2	3.4	52	88.1	5	8.5	59
3	2.0	8	5.2	2	1.3	0	.0	13	8.5	124	81.0	16	10.5	153
0	.0	0	.0	1	1.8	3	5.4	4	7.1	49	87.5	3	5.4	56
0	.0	0	.0	1	7.1	0	.0	1	7.1	13	92.9	0	.0	14
0	.0	0	.0	0	.0	3	7.1	3	7.1	36	85.7	3	7.1	42
3	1.1	8	3.0	4	1.5	4	1.5	19	7.1	225	84.0	24	9.0	268
0	.0	0	.0	2	2.7	1	1.4	3	4.1	65	89.0	5	6.8	73
3	1.5	8	4.1	2	1.0	3	1.5	16	8.2	160	82.1	19	9.7	195
0	.0	0	.0	0	.0	0	.0	0	.0	0	.0	0	.0	0
0	.0	0	.0	0	.0	0	.0	0	.0	0	.0	0	.0	0

TABLE 17 - TOTAL ENROLLMENT IN INSTITUTIONS OF HIGHER EDUCATION FOR SELECTED MAJOR FIELDS OF STUDY AND LEVEL OF ENROLLMENT
BY RACE, ETHNICITY, AND SEX: STATE, 1978

MAJOR FIELD 0200 - ARCHITECTURE AND ENVIRONMENTAL DESIGN

	AMERICAN INDIAN ALASKAN NATIVE		BLACK NON-HISPANIC		ASIAN OR PACIFIC ISLANDER		HISPANIC		TOTAL MINORITY		WHITE NON-HISPANIC		NON-RESIDENT ALIEN		TOT
	NUMBER	%	NUMBER	%	NUMBER	%	NUMBER	%	NUMBER	%	NUMBER	%	NUMBER	%	NUM

WISCONSIN   CONTINUED

PROFESSIONAL:
PART-TIME	0	.0	0	.0	0	.0	0	.0	0	.0	0	.0	0	.0	
FEMALE	0	.0	0	.0	0	.0	0	.0	0	.0	0	.0	0	.0	
MALE	0	.0	0	.0	0	.0	0	.0	0	.0	0	.0	0	.0	
TOTAL	0	.0	0	.0	0	.0	0	.0	0	.0	0	.0	0	.0	
FEMALE	0	.0	0	.0	0	.0	0	.0	0	.0	0	.0	0	.0	
MALE	0	.0	0	.0	0	.0	0	.0	0	.0	0	.0	0	.0	

UNL+GRAD+PROF:
FULL-TIME	3	.4	13	1.8	5	.7	7	1.0	28	4.0	644	91.1	35	5.0	
FEMALE	0	.0	3	1.0	1	.3	4	1.3	8	2.5	297	94.6	9	2.9	
MALE	3	.8	10	2.5	4	1.0	3	.8	20	5.1	347	88.3	26	6.6	
PART-TIME	1	.6	0	.0	1	.6	4	2.3	6	3.4	168	94.9	3	1.7	
FEMALE	0	.0	0	.0	1	1.2	0	.0	1	1.2	80	98.8	0	.0	
MALE	1	1.0	0	.0	0	.0	4	4.2	5	5.2	88	91.7	3	3.1	
TOTAL	4	.5	13	1.5	6	.7	11	1.2	34	3.8	812	91.9	38	4.3	
FEMALE	0	.0	3	.8	2	.5	4	1.0	9	2.3	377	95.4	9	2.3	
MALE	4	.8	10	2.0	4	.8	7	1.4	25	5.1	435	89.0	29	5.9	

UNCLASSIFIED:
TOTAL	0	.0	0	.0	0	.0	0	.0	0	.0	0	.0	0	.0	
FEMALE	0	.0	0	.0	0	.0	0	.0	0	.0	0	.0	0	.0	
MALE	0	.0	0	.0	0	.0	0	.0	0	.0	0	.0	0	.0	

TOTAL ENROLLMENT:
TOTAL	4	.5	13	1.5	6	.7	11	1.2	34	3.8	812	91.9	38	4.3	
FEMALE	0	.0	3	.8	2	.5	4	1.0	9	2.3	377	95.4	9	2.3	
MALE	4	.8	10	2.0	4	.8	7	1.4	25	5.1	435	89.0	29	5.9	

WYOMING   (1 INSTITUTIONS)

UNDERGRADUATES:
FULL-TIME	0	.0	0	.0	0	.0	0	.0	0	.0	1	100.0		.0	
FEMALE	0	.0	0	.0	0	.0	0	.0	0	.0	0	.0		.0	
MALE	0	.0	0	.0	0	.0	0	.0	0	.0	1	100.0		.0	
PART-TIME	0	.0	0	.0	0	.0	0	.0	0	.0	0	.0		.0	
FEMALE	0	.0	0	.0	0	.0	0	.0	0	.0	0	.0	0	.0	
MALE	0	.0	0	.0	0	.0	0	.0	0	.0	0	.0	0	.0	
TOTAL	0	.0	0	.0	0	.0	0	.0	0	.0	1	100.0	0	.0	
FEMALE	0	.0	0	.0	0	.0	0	.0	0	.0	0	.0	0	.0	
MALE	0	.0	0	.0	0	.0	0	.0	0	.0	1	100.0	0	.0	

GRADUATE:
FULL-TIME	0	.0	0	.0	0	.0	0	.0	0	.0	0	.0		.0	
FEMALE	0	.0	0	.0	0	.0	0	.0	0	.0	0	.0		.0	
MALE	0	.0	0	.0	0	.0	0	.0	0	.0	0	.0		.0	
PART-TIME	0	.0	0	.0	0	.0	0	.0	0	.0	0	.0		.0	
FEMALE	0	.0	0	.0	0	.0	0	.0	0	.0	0	.0		.0	
MALE	0	.0	0	.0	0	.0	0	.0	0	.0	0	.0	0	.0	
TOTAL	0	.0	0	.0	0	.0	0	.0	0	.0	0	.0		.0	
FEMALE	0	.0	0	.0	0	.0	0	.0	0	.0	0	.0		.0	
MALE	0	.0	0	.0	0	.0	0	.0	0	.0	0	.0	0	.0	

PROFESSIONAL:
FULL-TIME	0	.0	0	.0	0	.0	0	.0	0	.0	0	.0		.0	
FEMALE	0	.0	0	.0	0	.0	0	.0	0	.0	0	.0		.0	
MALE	0	.0	0	.0	0	.0	0	.0	0	.0	0	.0		.0	
PART-TIME	0	.0	0	.0	0	.0	0	.0	0	.0	0	.0		.0	
FEMALE	0	.0	0	.0	0	.0	0	.0	0	.0	0	.0		.0	
MALE	0	.0	0	.0	0	.0	0	.0	0	.0	0	.0	0	.0	
TOTAL	0	.0	0	.0	0	.0	0	.0	0	.0	0	.0		.0	
FEMALE	0	.0	0	.0	0	.0	0	.0	0	.0	0	.0		.0	
MALE	0	.0	0	.0	0	.0	0	.0	0	.0	0	.0	0	.0	

UND+GRAD+PROF:
FULL-TIME	0	.0	0	.0	0	.0	0	.0	0	.0	1	100.0		.0	
FEMALE	0	.0	0	.0	0	.0	0	.0	0	.0	0	.0		.0	
MALE	0	.0	0	.0	0	.0	0	.0	0	.0	1	100.0		.0	
PART-TIME	0	.0	0	.0	0	.0	0	.0	0	.0	0	.0		.0	
FEMALE	0	.0	0	.0	0	.0	0	.0	0	.0	0	.0		.0	
MALE	0	.0	0	.0	0	.0	0	.0	0	.0	0	.0	0	.0	
TOTAL	0	.0	0	.0	0	.0	0	.0	0	.0	1	100.0		.0	
FEMALE	0	.0	0	.0	0	.0	0	.0	0	.0	0	.0		.0	
MALE	0	.0	0	.0	0	.0	0	.0	0	.0	1	100.0	0	.0	

UNCLASSIFIED:
TOTAL	0	.0	0	.0	0	.0	0	.0	0	.0	0	.0		.0	
FEMALE	0	.0	0	.0	0	.0	0	.0	0	.0	0	.0		.0	
MALE	0	.0	0	.0	0	.0	0	.0	0	.0	0	.0	0	.0	

TOTAL ENROLLMENT:
TOTAL	0	.0	0	.0	0	.0	0	.0	0	.0	1	100.0		.0	
FEMALE	0	.0	0	.0	0	.0	0	.0	0	.0	0	.0		.0	
MALE	0	.0	0	.0	0	.0	0	.0	0	.0	1	100.0	0	.0	

!00 - ARCHITECTURE AND ENVIRONMENTAL DESIGN

ERICAN INDIAN ISKAN NATIVE		BLACK NON-HISPANIC		ASIAN OR PACIFIC ISLANDER		HISPANIC		TOTAL MINORITY		WHITE NON-HISPANIC		NON-RESIDENT ALIEN		TOTAL
JMBER	%	NUMBER	%	NUMBER	%	NUMBER	%	NUMBER	%	NUMBER	%	NUMBER	%	NUMBER

D.C. (421 INSTITUTIONS)

169	.4	2,095	4.5	1,100	2.3	1,542	3.3	4,906	10.4	39,908	84.9	2,196	4.7	47,010
37	.3	494	4.1	308	2.6	298	2.5	1,137	9.5	10,413	86.7	459	3.8	12,009
132	.4	1,601	4.6	792	2.3	1,244	3.6	3,769	10.8	29,495	84.3	1,737	5.0	35,001
71	.9	468	5.9	241	2.9	526	6.3	1,326	16.0	6,761	81.4	224	2.7	8,311
17	.9	84	4.3	54	2.8	93	4.8	248	12.8	1,633	84.1	60	3.1	1,941
54	.8	404	6.3	187	2.9	433	6.8	1,078	16.9	5,128	80.5	164	2.6	6,370
240	.4	2,583	.7	1,341	2.4	2,068	3.7	6,232	11.3	46,669	84.4	2,420	4.4	55,321
54	.4	578	.1	362	2.6	391	2.8	1,385	9.9	12,046	86.4	519	3.7	13,950
186	.4	2,005	4.8	979	2.4	1,677	4.1	4,847	11.7	34,623	83.7	1,901	4.6	41,371
23	.3	336	4.3	232	3.0	138	1.8	729	9.4	5,983	77.3	1,024	13.2	7,736
5	.2	134	5.6	71	3.0	28	1.2	238	9.9	1,942	80.7	226	9.4	2,406
18	.3	202	3.8	161	3.0	110	2.1	491	9.2	4,041	75.8	798	15.0	5,330
11	.6	95	5.1	67	3.6	41	2.2	214	11.5	1,483	79.6	166	8.9	1,863
3	.5	32	5.6	19	3.3	11	1.9	65	11.3	470	81.7	40	7.0	575
8	.6	63	4.9	48	3.7	30	2.3	149	11.6	1,013	78.6	126	9.8	1,288
34	.4	431	4.5	299	3.1	179	1.9	943	9.8	7,466	77.8	1,190	12.4	9,599
8	.3	168	5.6	90	3.0	39	1.3	303	10.2	2,412	80.9	266	8.9	2,981
26	.4	265	4.0	209	3.2	140	2.1	640	9.7	5,054	76.4	924	14.0	6,618
	.0		.0	0	.0	0	.0	0	.0	8	100.0	0	.0	8
	.0		.0	0	.0	0	.0	0	.0	1	100.0	0	.0	
	.0		.0	0	.0	0	.0	0	.0	7	100.0	0	.0	
	.0		.0	0	.0	0	.0	0	.0	1	100.0	0	.0	
8	.0	8	.0	0	.0	0	.0	0	.0	0	.0	0	.0	
	.0		.0	0	.0	0	.0	0	.0	1	100.0	0	.0	8
8	.0	8	.0	0	.0	0	.0	0	.0	9	100.0	0	.0	9
	.0		.0	0	.0	0	.0	0	.0	1	100.0	0	.0	1
	.0		.0	0	.0	0	.0	0	.0	8	100.0	0	.0	8
192	.4	2,431	4.4	1,332	2.4	1,680	3.1	5,635	10.3	45,899	83.8	3,220	5.9	54,754
42	.3	628	4.4	379	2.6	326	2.3	1,375	9.5	12,356	85.7	685	4.8	14,416
150	.4	1,803	4.5	953	2.4	1,354	3.4	4,260	10.6	33,543	83.2	2,535	6.3	40,338
82	.8	583	5.7	308	3.0	567	5.6	1,540	15.1	8,245	81.0	390	3.8	10,175
20	.8	116	4.6	73	2.9	104	4.1	313	12.4	2,103	83.6	100	4.0	2,516
62	.8	467	6.1	235	3.1	463	6.0	1,227	16.0	6,142	80.2	290	3.8	7,659
274	.4	3,014	4.6	1,640	2.5	2,247	3.5	7,175	11.1	54,144	83.4	3,610	5.6	64,929
62	.4	744	4.4	452	2.7	430	2.5	1,688	10.0	14,459	85.4	785	4.6	16,932
212	.4	2,270	4.7	1,188	2.5	1,817	3.8	5,487	11.4	39,685	82.7	2,825	5.9	47,997
11	.9	66	5.6	53	4.5	65	5.5	195	16.6	903	76.7	79	6.7	1,177
0	.0	34	8.5	11	2.7	9	2.2	54	13.4	333	82.8	15	3.7	402
11	1.4	32	4.1	42	5.4	56	7.2	141	18.2	570	73.5	64	8.3	775
T:														
285	.4	3,080	4.7	1,693	2.6	2,312	3.5	7,370	11.1	55,047	83.3	3,689	5.6	66,106
62	.4	778	4.5	463	2.7	439	2.5	1,742	10.0	14,792	85.3	800	4.6	17,334
223	.5	2,302	4.7	1,230	2.5	1,873	3.8	5,628	11.5	40,255	82.5	2,889	5.9	48,772

(1 INSTITUTIONS)

	.0		.0	0	.0	229	100.0	229	100.0	0	.0	0	.0	229
	.0		.0	0	.0	56	100.0	56	100.0	0	.0	0	.0	56
	.0		.0	0	.0	173	100.0	173	100.0	0	.0	0	.0	173
	.0		.0	0	.0	32	100.0	32	100.0	0	.0	0	.0	32
8	.0	8	.0	0	.0	7	100.0	7	100.0	0	.0	0	.0	7
	.0		.0	0	.0	25	100.0	25	100.0	0	.0	0	.0	25
8	.0	0	.0	0	.0	261	100.0	261	100.0	0	.0	0	.0	261
8	.0	0	.0	0	.0	63	100.0	63	100.0	0	.0	0	.0	63
0	.0	0	.0	0	.0	198	100.0	198	100.0	0	.0	0	.0	198
0	.0	0	.0	0	.0	3	100.0	3	100.0	0	.0	0	.0	
0	.0	0	.0	0	.0	0	.0	0	.0	0	.0	0	.0	
0	.0	0	.0	0	.0	3	100.0	3	100.0	0	.0	0	.0	
0	.0	0	.0	0	.0	1	100.0	1	100.0	0	.0	0	.0	1
0	.0	8	.0	0	.0	1	100.0	1	100.0	0	.0	0	.0	1
	.0		.0	0	.0		.0	0	.0	0	.0	0	.0	0
	.0		.0	0	.0	4	100.0	4	100.0	0	.0	0	.0	4
	.0		.0	0	.0	1	100.0	1	100.0	0	.0	0	.0	1
8	.0	8	.0	0	.0	3	100.0	3	100.0	0	.0	0	.0	3
0	.0	0	.0	0	.0	0	.0	0	.0	0	.0	0	.0	0
0	.0	8	.0	0	.0	0	.0	0	.0	0	.0	0	.0	0
0	.0	0	.0	0	.0	0	.0	0	.0	0	.0	0	.0	0

TABLE 17 - TOTAL ENROLLMENT IN INSTITUTIONS OF HIGHER EDUCATION FOR SELECTED MAJOR FIELDS OF STUDY AND LEVEL OF ENROLLMENT
BY RACE, ETHNICITY, AND SEX: STATE, 1978

MAJOR FIELD 0200 - ARCHITECTURE AND ENVIRONMENTAL DESIGN

	AMERICAN INDIAN ALASKAN NATIVE		BLACK NON-HISPANIC		ASIAN OR PACIFIC ISLANDER		HISPANIC		TOTAL MINORITY		WHITE NON-HISPANIC		NON-RESIDENT ALIEN		TO
	NUMBER	%	NUMBER	%	NUMBER	%	NUMBER	%	NUMBER	%	NUMBER	%	NUMBER	%	NU
PUERTO RICO	CONTINUED														
PROFESSIONAL:															
PART-TIME	0	.0	0	.0	0	.0	0	.0	0	.0	0	.0	0	.0	
FEMALE	0	.0	0	.0	0	.0	0	.0	0	.0	0	.0	0	.0	
MALE	0	.0	0	.0	0	.0	0	.0	0	.0	0	.0	0	.0	
TOTAL	0	.0	0	.0	0	.0	0	.0	0	.0	0	.0	0	.0	
FEMALE	0	.0	0	.0	0	.0	0	.0	0	.0	0	.0	0	.0	
MALE	0	.0	0	.0	0	.0	0	.0	0	.0	0	.0	0	.0	
UND+GRAD+PROF:															
FULL-TIME	0	.0	0	.0	0	.0	232	100.0	232	100.0	0	.0	0	.0	
FEMALE	0	.0	0	.0	0	.0	56	100.0	56	100.0	0	.0	0	.0	
MALE	0	.0	0	.0	0	.0	176	100.0	176	100.0	0	.0	0	.0	
PART-TIME	0	.0	0	.0	0	.0	33	100.0	33	100.0	0	.0	0	.0	
FEMALE	0	.0	0	.0	0	.0	8	100.0	8	100.0	0	.0	0	.0	
MALE	0	.0	0	.0	0	.0	25	100.0	25	100.0	0	.0	0	.0	
TOTAL	0	.0	0	.0	0	.0	265	100.0	265	100.0	0	.0	0	.0	
FEMALE	0	.0	0	.0	0	.0	64	100.0	64	100.0	0	.0	0	.0	
MALE	0	.0	0	.0	0	.0	201	100.0	201	100.0	0	.0	0	.0	
UNCLASSIFIED:															
TOTAL	0	.0	0	.0	0	.0	0	.0	0	.0	0	.0	0	.0	
FEMALE	0	.0	0	.0	0	.0	0	.0	0	.0	0	.0	0	.0	
MALE	0	.0	0	.0	0	.0	0	.0	0	.0	0	.0	0	.0	
TOTAL ENROLLMENT:															
TOTAL	0	.0	0	.0	0	.0	265	100.0	265	100.0	0	.0	0	.0	
FEMALE	0	.0	0	.0	0	.0	64	100.0	64	100.0	0	.0	0	.0	
MALE	0	.0	0	.0	0	.0	201	100.0	201	100.0	0	.0	0	.0	
OUTLYING AREAS	(	1 INSTITUTIONS)													
UNDERGRADUATES:															
FULL-TIME	0	.0	0	.0	0	.0	229	100.0	229	100.0	0	.0	0	.0	
FEMALE	0	.0	0	.0	0	.0	56	100.0	56	100.0	0	.0	0	.0	
MALE	0	.0	0	.0	0	.0	173	100.0	173	100.0	0	.0	0	.0	
PART-TIME	0	.0	0	.0	0	.0	32	100.0	32	100.0	0	.0	0	.0	
FEMALE	0	.0	0	.0	0	.0	7	100.0	7	100.0	0	.0	0	.0	
MALE	0	.0	0	.0	0	.0	25	100.0	25	100.0	0	.0	0	.0	
TOTAL	0	.0	0	.0	0	.0	261	100.0	261	100.0	0	.0	0	.0	
FEMALE	0	.0	0	.0	0	.0	63	100.0	63	100.0	0	.0	0	.0	
MALE	0	.0	0	.0	0	.0	198	100.0	198	100.0	0	.0	0	.0	
GRADUATE:															
FULL-TIME	0	.0	0	.0	0	.0	3	100.0	3	100.0	0	.0	0	.0	
FEMALE	0	.0	0	.0	0	.0	0	.0	0	.0	0	.0	0	.0	
MALE	0	.0	0	.0	0	.0	3	100.0	3	100.0	0	.0	0	.0	
PART-TIME	0	.0	0	.0	0	.0	1	100.0	1	100.0	0	.0	0	.0	
FEMALE	0	.0	0	.0	0	.0	1	100.0	1	100.0	0	.0	0	.0	
MALE	0	.0	0	.0	0	.0	0	.0	0	.0	0	.0	0	.0	
TOTAL	0	.0	0	.0	0	.0	4	100.0	4	100.0	0	.0	0	.0	
FEMALE	0	.0	0	.0	0	.0	1	100.0	1	100.0	0	.0	0	.0	
MALE	0	.0	0	.0	0	.0	3	100.0	3	100.0	0	.0	0	.0	
PROFESSIONAL:															
FULL-TIME	0	.0	0	.0	0	.0	0	.0	0	.0	0	.0	0	.0	
FEMALE	0	.0	0	.0	0	.0	0	.0	0	.0	0	.0	0	.0	
MALE	0	.0	0	.0	0	.0	0	.0	0	.0	0	.0	0	.0	
PART-TIME	0	.0	0	.0	0	.0	0	.0	0	.0	0	.0	0	.0	
FEMALE	0	.0	0	.0	0	.0	0	.0	0	.0	0	.0	0	.0	
MALE	0	.0	0	.0	0	.0	0	.0	0	.0	0	.0	0	.0	
TOTAL	0	.0	0	.0	0	.0	0	.0	0	.0	0	.0	0	.0	
FEMALE	0	.0	0	.0	0	.0	0	.0	0	.0	0	.0	0	.0	
MALE	0	.0	0	.0	0	.0	0	.0	0	.0	0	.0	0	.0	
UND+GRAD+PROF:															
FULL-TIME	0	.0	0	.0	0	.0	232	100.0	232	100.0	0	.0	0	.0	
FEMALE	0	.0	0	.0	0	.0	56	100.0	56	100.0	0	.0	0	.0	
MALE	0	.0	0	.0	0	.0	176	100.0	176	100.0	0	.0	0	.0	
PART-TIME	0	.0	0	.0	0	.0	33	100.0	33	100.0	0	.0	0	.0	
FEMALE	0	.0	0	.0	0	.0	8	100.0	8	100.0	0	.0	0	.0	
MALE	0	.0	0	.0	0	.0	25	100.0	25	100.0	0	.0	0	.0	
TOTAL	0	.0	0	.0	0	.0	265	100.0	265	100.0	0	.0	0	.0	
FEMALE	0	.0	0	.0	0	.0	64	100.0	64	100.0	0	.0	0	.0	
MALE	0	.0	0	.0	0	.0	201	100.0	201	100.0	0	.0	0	.0	
UNCLASSIFIED:															
TOTAL	0	.0	0	.0	0	.0	0	.0	0	.0	0	.0	0	.0	
FEMALE	0	.0	0	.0	0	.0	0	.0	0	.0	0	.0	0	.0	
MALE	0	.0	0	.0	0	.0	0	.0	0	.0	0	.0	0	.0	
TOTAL ENROLLMENT:															
TOTAL	0	.0	0	.0	0	.0	265	100.0	265	100.0	0	.0	0	.0	
FEMALE	0	.0	0	.0	0	.0	64	100.0	64	100.0	0	.0	0	.0	
MALE	0	.0	0	.0	0	.0	201	100.0	201	100.0	0	.0	0	.0	

ENROLLMENT IN INSTITUTIONS OF HIGHER EDUCATION FOR SELECTED MAJOR FIELDS OF STUDY AND LEVEL OF ENROLLMENT ETHNICITY, AND SEX: STATE, 1978

ARCHITECTURE AND ENVIRONMENTAL DESIGN

E 0200 (422 INSTITUTIONS)

INDIAN NATIVE	BLACK NON-HISPANIC		ASIAN OR PACIFIC ISLANDER		HISPANIC		TOTAL MINORITY		WHITE NON-HISPANIC		NON-RESIDENT ALIEN		TOTAL
%	NUMBER	%	NUMBER	%	NUMBER	%	NUMBER	%	NUMBER	%	NUMBER	%	NUMBER
.4	2,095	4.4	1,100	2.3	1,771	3.7	5,135	10.9	39,908	84.5	2,196	4.6	47,239
.3	494	4.1	308	2.6	354	2.9	1,193	9.9	10,413	86.3	459	3.8	12,065
.4	1,601	4.6	792	2.3	1,417	4.0	3,942	11.2	29,495	83.9	1,737	4.9	35,174
.9	488	5.8	241	2.9	558	6.7	1,358	16.3	6,761	81.0	224	2.7	8,343
.9	84	4.3	54	2.8	100	5.1	255	13.1	1,633	83.8	60	3.1	1,948
.8	404	6.3	187	2.9	456	7.2	1,103	17.2	5,128	80.2	164	2.6	6,395
.4	2,583	4.6	1,341	2.4	2,329	4.2	6,493	11.7	46,669	84.0	2,420	4.4	55,582
.4	578	4.1	362	2.6	454	3.2	1,448	10.3	12,046	86.0	519	3.7	14,013
.4	2,005	4.8	979	2.4	1,875	4.5	5,045	12.1	34,623	83.3	1,901	4.6	41,569
.3	336	4.3	232	3.0	141	1.8	732	9.5	5,983	77.3	1,024	13.2	7,739
.2	134	5.6	71	3.0	28	1.2	238	9.9	1,942	80.7	226	9.4	2,406
.3	202	3.8	161	3.0	113	2.1	494	9.3	4,041	75.8	798	15.0	5,333
.6	95	5.1	67	3.6	42	2.3	215	11.5	1,483	79.6	166	8.9	1,864
.5	32	5.6	19	3.3	12	2.1	66	11.5	470	81.6	40	6.9	576
.6	63	4.9	48	3.7	30	2.3	149	11.6	1,013	76.6	120	9.8	1,288
.4	431	4.5	299	3.1	183	1.9	947	9.9	7,466	77.7	1,190	12.4	9,603
.3	166	5.6	90	3.0	40	1.3	304	10.2	2,412	80.9	266	8.9	2,982
.4	265	4.0	209	3.2	143	2.2	643	9.7	5,054	76.3	924	14.0	6,621
.0	0	.0	0	.0	0	.0	0	.0	8	100.0	0	.0	8
.0	0	.0	0	.0	0	.0	0	.0	1	100.0	0	.0	1
.0	0	.0	0	.0	0	.0	0	.0	7	100.0	0	.0	7
.0	0	.0	0	.0	0	.0	0	.0	1	100.0	0	.0	1
.0	0	.0	0	.0	0	.0	0	.0	0	.0	0	.0	0
.0	0	.0	0	.0	0	.0	0	.0	1	100.0	0	.0	1
.0	0	.0	0	.0	0	.0	0	.0	9	100.0	0	.0	9
.0	0	.0	0	.0	0	.0	0	.0	1	100.0	0	.0	1
.0	0	.0	0	.0	0	.0	0	.0	8	100.0	0	.0	8
.3	2,431	4.4	1,332	2.4	1,912	3.5	5,867	10.7	45,899	83.5	3,220	5.9	54,986
.3	628	4.3	379	2.6	382	2.6	1,431	9.9	12,356	85.4	685	4.7	14,472
.4	1,803	4.5	953	2.4	1,530	3.8	4,436	10.9	33,543	82.8	2,535	6.3	40,514
.8	583	5.7	308	3.0	600	5.9	1,573	15.4	8,245	80.8	390	3.8	10,208
.8	116	4.6	73	2.9	112	4.4	321	12.7	2,103	83.3	100	4.0	2,524
.8	467	6.1	235	3.1	488	6.4	1,252	16.3	6,142	79.9	290	3.8	7,684
.4	3,014	4.6	1,640	2.5	2,512	3.9	7,440	11.4	54,144	83.1	3,610	5.5	65,194
.4	744	4.4	452	2.7	494	2.9	1,752	10.3	14,459	85.1	785	4.6	16,996
.4	2,270	4.7	1,188	2.5	2,018	4.2	5,688	11.8	39,685	82.3	2,825	5.9	48,198
.9	66	5.6	53	4.5	65	5.5	195	16.6	903	76.7	79	6.7	1,177
.0	34	8.5	11	2.7	9	2.2	54	13.4	333	82.8	15	3.7	402
1.4	32	4.1	42	5.4	56	7.2	141	18.2	570	73.5	64	8.3	775
.4	3,080	4.6	1,693	2.6	2,577	3.9	7,635	11.5	55,047	82.9	3,689	5.6	66,371
.4	778	4.5	463	2.7	503	2.9	1,806	10.4	14,792	85.0	800	4.6	17,398
.5	2,302	4.7	1,230	2.5	2,074	4.2	5,829	11.9	40,255	82.2	2,889	5.9	48,973

MAJOR FIELD 0400 - BIOLOGICAL SCIENCES

	AMERICAN INDIAN ALASKAN NATIVE		BLACK NON-HISPANIC		ASIAN OR PACIFIC ISLANDER		HISPANIC		TOTAL MINORITY		WHITE NON-HISPANIC		NON-RESIDENT ALIEN	
	NUMBER	%	NUMBER	%	NUMBER	%	NUMBER	%	NUMBER	%	NUMBER	%	NUMBER	%
ALABAMA (44 INSTITUTIONS)														
UNDERGRADUATES														
FULL-TIME	3	.1	748	22.8	16	.5	27	.8	794	24.2	2,436	74.2	52	1.6
FEMALE	2	.1	417	28.9	12	.8	8	.6	439	30.5	992	68.8	10	.7
MALE	1	.1	331	18.0	4	.2	19	1.0	355	19.3	1,444	78.4	42	2.3
PART-TIME	0	.0	44	10.0	2	.5	1	.2	47	10.7	390	88.6	3	.7
FEMALE	0	.0	25	13.7	0	.0	0	.0	25	13.7	157	86.3	0	.0
MALE	0	.0	19	7.4	2	.8	1	.4	22	8.5	233	90.3	3	1.2
TOTAL	3	.1	792	21.3	18	.5	28	.8	841	22.6	2,826	75.9	55	1.5
FEMALE	2	.1	442	27.2	12	.7	8	.5	464	28.6	1,149	70.8	10	.6
MALE	1	.0	350	16.7	6	.3	20	1.0	377	18.0	1,677	79.9	45	2.1
GRADUATE:														
FULL-TIME	0	.0	22	7.2	8	2.6	0	.0	30	9.8	257	84.3	18	5.9
FEMALE	0	.0	12	13.2	3	3.3	0	.0	15	16.5	71	78.0	5	5.5
MALE	0	.0	10	4.7	5	2.3	0	.0	15	7.0	186	86.9	13	6.1
PART-TIME	0	.0	34	13.2	0	.0	1	.4	35	13.6	218	84.5	5	1.9
FEMALE	0	.0	17	17.7	0	.0	0	.0	17	17.7	76	79.2	3	3.1
MALE	0	.0	17	10.5	0	.0	1	.6	18	11.1	142	87.7	2	1.2
TOTAL	0	.0	56	9.9	8	1.4	1	.2	65	11.5	475	84.4	23	4.1
FEMALE	0	.0	29	15.5	3	1.6	0	.0	32	17.1	147	78.6	8	4.3
MALE	0	.0	27	7.2	5	1.3	1	.3	33	8.8	328	87.2	15	4.0
PROFESSIONAL:														
FULL-TIME	0	.0	0	.0	0	.0	0	.0	0	.0	0	.0	0	.0
FEMALE	0	.0	0	.0	0	.0	0	.0	0	.0	0	.0	0	.0
MALE	0	.0	0	.0	0	.0	0	.0	0	.0	0	.0	0	.0
PART-TIME	0	.0	0	.0	0	.0	0	.0	0	.0	0	.0	0	.0
FEMALE	0	.0	0	.0	0	.0	0	.0	0	.0	0	.0	0	.0
MALE	0	.0	0	.0	0	.0	0	.0	0	.0	0	.0	0	.0
TOTAL	0	.0	0	.0	0	.0	0	.0	0	.0	0	.0	0	.0
FEMALE	0	.0	0	.0	0	.0	0	.0	0	.0	0	.0	0	.0
MALE	0	.0	0	.0	0	.0	0	.0	0	.0	0	.0	0	.0
UND+GRAD+PROF:														
FULL-TIME	3	.1	770	21.5	24	.7	27	.8	824	23.0	2,693	75.1	70	2.0
FEMALE	2	.1	429	28.0	15	1.0	8	.5	454	29.6	1,063	69.4	15	1.0
MALE	1	.0	341	16.6	9	.4	19	.9	370	18.0	1,630	79.3	55	2.7
PART-TIME	0	.0	78	11.2	2	.3	2	.3	82	11.7	608	87.1	8	1.1
FEMALE	0	.0	42	15.1	0	.0	0	.0	42	15.1	233	83.8	3	1.1
MALE	0	.0	36	8.6	2	.5	2	.5	40	9.5	375	89.3	5	1.2
TOTAL	3	.1	848	19.8	26	.6	29	.7	906	21.1	3,301	77.0	78	1.8
FEMALE	2	.1	471	26.0	15	.8	8	.4	496	27.4	1,296	71.6	18	1.0
MALE	1	.0	377	15.2	11	.4	21	.8	410	16.6	2,005	81.0	60	2.4
UNCLASSIFIED:														
TOTAL	0	.0	23	18.1	0	.0	0	.0	23	18.1	104	81.9	0	.0
FEMALE	0	.0	13	28.3	0	.0	0	.0	13	28.3	33	71.7	0	.0
MALE	0	.0	10	12.3	0	.0	0	.0	10	12.3	71	87.7	0	.0
TOTAL ENROLLMENT:														
TOTAL	3	.1	871	19.7	26	.6	29	.7	929	21.1	3,405	77.2	78	1.8
FEMALE	2	.1	484	26.1	15	.8	8	.4	509	27.4	1,329	71.6	18	1.0
MALE	1	.0	387	15.1	11	.4	21	.8	420	16.4	2,076	81.2	60	2.3
ALASKA (7 INSTITUTIONS)														
UNDERGRADUATES:														
FULL-TIME	12	7.6	1	.6	0	.0	0	.0	13	8.2	142	89.9	3	1.9
FEMALE	7	9.0	0	.0	0	.0	0	.0	7	9.0	71	91.0	0	.0
MALE	5	6.3	1	1.3	0	.0	0	.0	6	7.5	71	88.8	3	3.8
PART-TIME	6	7.1	3	3.6	2	2.4	2	2.4	13	15.5	70	83.3	1	1.2
FEMALE	6	14.0	2	4.7	2	4.7	2	4.7	12	27.9	31	72.1	0	.0
MALE	0	.0	1	2.4	0	.0	0	.0	1	2.4	39	95.1	1	2.4
TOTAL	18	7.4	4	1.7	2	.8	2	.8	26	10.7	212	87.6	4	1.7
FEMALE	13	10.7	2	1.7	2	1.7	2	1.7	19	15.7	102	84.3	0	.0
MALE	5	4.1	2	1.7	0	.0	0	.0	7	5.8	110	90.9	4	3.3
GRADUATE:														
FULL-TIME	0	.0	0	.0	0	.0	0	.0	0	.0	15	100.0	0	.0
FEMALE	0	.0	0	.0	0	.0	0	.0	0	.0	5	100.0	0	.0
MALE	0	.0	0	.0	0	.0	0	.0	0	.0	10	100.0	0	.0
PART-TIME	0	.0	0	.0	0	.0	0	.0	0	.0	37	100.0	0	.0
FEMALE	0	.0	0	.0	0	.0	0	.0	0	.0	14	100.0	0	.0
MALE	0	.0	0	.0	0	.0	0	.0	0	.0	23	100.0	0	.0
TOTAL	0	.0	0	.0	0	.0	0	.0	0	.0	52	100.0	0	.0
FEMALE	0	.0	0	.0	0	.0	0	.0	0	.0	19	100.0	0	.0
MALE	0	.0	0	.0	0	.0	0	.0	0	.0	33	100.0	0	.0
PROFESSIONAL:														
FULL-TIME	0	.0	0	.0	0	.0	0	.0	0	.0	0	.0	0	.0
FEMALE	0	.0	0	.0	0	.0	0	.0	0	.0	0	.0	0	.0
MALE	0	.0	0	.0	0	.0	0	.0	0	.0	0	.0	0	.0

ASIAN OR PACIFIC ISLANDER		HISPANIC		TOTAL MINORITY		WHITE NON-HISPANIC		NON-RESIDENT ALIEN		TOTAL
NUMBER	X	NUMBER	X	NUMBER	X	NUMBER	X	NUMBER	X	NUMBER
0	.0	0	.0	0	.0	0	.0	0	.0	0
0	.0	0	.0	0	.0	0	.0	0	.0	0
0	.0	0	.0	0	.0	0	.0	0	.0	0
0	.0	0	.0	0	.0	0	.0	0	.0	0
0	.0	0	.0	0	.0	0	.0	0	.0	0
0	.0	0	.0	0	.0	0	.0	0	.0	0
0	.0	0	.0	13	7.5	157	90.8	3	1.7	173
0	.0	0	.0	7	8.4	76	91.6	0	.0	83
0	.0	0	.0	6	6.7	81	90.0	3	3.3	90
2	1.7	2	1.7	13	10.7	107	88.4	1	.8	121
2	3.5	2	3.5	12	21.1	45	78.9	0	.0	57
0	.0	0	.0	1	1.6	62	96.9	1	1.6	64
2	.7	2	.7	26	8.8	264	89.8	4	1.4	294
2	1.4	2	1.4	19	13.6	121	86.4	0	.0	140
0	.0	0	.0	7	4.5	143	92.9	4	2.6	154
1	3.2	0	.0	18	58.1	12	38.7	1	3.2	31
1	4.5	0	.0	16	72.7	6	27.3	0	.0	22
0	.0	0	.0	2	22.2	6	66.7	1	11.1	9
3	.9	2	.6	44	13.5	276	84.9	5	1.5	325
3	1.9	2	1.2	35	21.6	127	78.4	0	.0	162
0	.0	0	.0	9	5.5	149	91.4	5	3.1	163
11	.7	67	4.2	110	6.9	1,449	91.5	24	1.5	1,583
5	.8	26	4.3	43	7.1	554	91.1	11	1.8	608
6	.6	41	4.2	67	6.9	895	91.8	13	1.3	975
1	.3	19	5.3	30	8.3	329	91.1	2	.6	361
0	.0	7	4.0	14	8.0	159	91.4	1	.6	174
1	.5	12	6.4	16	8.6	170	90.9	1	.5	187
12	.6	86	4.4	140	7.2	1,778	91.5	26	1.3	1,944
5	.6	33	4.2	57	7.3	713	91.2	12	1.5	782
7	.6	53	4.6	83	7.1	1,065	91.7	14	1.2	1,162
1	.8	2	1.6	3	2.5	115	94.3	4	3.3	122
0	.0	1	2.5	1	2.5	38	95.0	1	2.5	40
1	1.2	1	1.2	2	2.4	77	93.9	3	3.7	82
1	.4	0	.0	3	1.3	225	97.0	4	1.7	232
0	.0	0	.0	0	.0	71	98.6	1	1.4	72
1	.6	0	.0	3	1.9	154	96.3	3	1.9	160
2	.6	2	.6	6	1.7	340	96.0	8	2.3	354
0	.0	1	.9	1	.9	109	97.3	2	1.8	112
2	.8	1	.4	5	2.1	231	95.5	6	2.5	242
0	.0	0	.0	0	.0	0	.0	0	.0	0
0	.0	0	.0	0	.0	0	.0	0	.0	0
0	.0	0	.0	0	.0	0	.0	0	.0	0
0	.0	0	.0	0	.0	0	.0	0	.0	0
0	.0	0	.0	0	.0	0	.0	0	.0	0
0	.0	0	.0	0	.0	0	.0	0	.0	0
0	.0	0	.0	0	.0	0	.0	0	.0	0
0	.0	0	.0	0	.0	0	.0	0	.0	0
0	.0	0	.0	0	.0	0	.0	0	.0	0
12	.7	69	4.0	113	6.6	1,564	91.7	28	1.6	1,705
5	.8	27	4.2	44	6.8	592	91.4	12	1.9	648
7	.7	42	4.0	69	6.5	972	92.0	16	1.5	1,057
2	.3	19	3.2	33	5.6	554	93.4	6	1.0	593
0	.0	7	2.8	14	5.7	230	93.5	2	.8	246
2	.6	12	3.5	19	5.5	324	93.4	4	1.2	347
14	.6	88	3.8	146	6.4	2,118	92.2	34	1.5	2,298
5	.6	34	3.8	58	6.5	822	91.9	14	1.6	894
9	.6	54	3.8	88	6.3	1,296	92.3	20	1.4	1,404
1	1.1	10	11.2	55	61.8	34	38.2	0	.0	89
1	1.6	9	14.8	36	59.0	25	41.0	0	.0	61
0	.0	1	3.6	19	67.9	9	32.1	0	.0	28
15	.6	98	4.1	201	8.4	2,152	90.2	34	1.4	2,387
6	.6	43	4.5	94	9.8	847	88.7	14	1.5	955
9	.6	55	3.8	107	7.5	1,305	91.1	20	1.4	1,432

TABLE 17 - TOTAL ENROLLMENT IN INSTITUTIONS OF HIGHER EDUCATION FOR SELECTED MAJOR FIELDS OF STUDY AND LEVEL OF ENROLLMENT
BY RACE, ETHNICITY, AND SEX: STATE, 1978

MAJOR FIELD 0400 - BIOLOGICAL SCIENCES

	AMERICAN INDIAN ALASKAN NATIVE		BLACK NON-HISPANIC		ASIAN OR PACIFIC ISLANDER		HISPANIC		TOTAL MINORITY		WHITE NON-HISPANIC		NON-RESIDENT ALIEN	
	NUMBER	%	NUMBER	%	NUMBER	%	NUMBER	%	NUMBER	%	NUMBER	%	NUMBER	%
ARKANSAS (22 INSTITUTIONS)														
UNDERGRADUATES:														
FULL-TIME	11	.7	168	12.4	16	1.1	8	.5	223	14.7	1,285	85.0	4	.3
FEMALE	5	.8	97	15.1	7	1.1	4	.6	113	17.6	526	82.1	2	.3
MALE	0	.7	91	10.4	9	1.0	4	.5	110	12.6	759	87.1	2	.2
PART-TIME	1	.6	17	9.8	2	1.1	1	.6	21	12.1	153	87.9	0	.0
FEMALE	1	1.1	3	3.4	1	1.1	1	1.1	6	6.9	81	93.1	0	.0
MALE	0	.0	14	16.1	1	1.1	0	.0	15	17.2	72	82.8	0	.0
TOTAL	12	.7	205	12.2	18	1.1	9	.5	244	14.5	1,438	85.3	4	.2
FEMALE	6	.8	100	13.7	8	1.1	5	.7	119	16.3	607	83.4	2	.3
MALE	6	.6	105	11.0	10	1.0	4	.4	125	13.0	831	86.7	2	.2
GRADUATE:														
FULL-TIME	1	.6	3	1.8	1	.6	2	1.2	7	4.2	145	87.3	14	8.4
FEMALE	0	.0	2	4.4	1	2.2	0	.0	3	6.7	41	91.1	1	2.2
MALE	1	.8	1	.8	0	.0	2	1.7	4	3.3	104	86.0	13	10.7
PART-TIME	2	2.6	4	5.1	0	.0	0	.0	6	7.7	69	88.5	3	3.8
FEMALE	1	2.9	3	8.6	0	.0	0	.0	4	11.4	29	82.9	2	5.7
MALE	1	2.3	1	2.3	0	.0	0	.0	2	4.7	40	93.0	1	2.3
TOTAL	3	1.2	7	2.9	1	.4	2	.8	13	5.3	214	87.7	17	7.0
FEMALE	1	1.3	5	6.3	1	1.3	0	.0	7	8.8	70	87.5	3	3.8
MALE	2	1.2	2	1.2	0	.0	2	1.2	6	3.7	144	87.8	14	8.5
PROFESSIONAL:														
FULL-TIME	0	.0	0	.0	0	.0	0	.0	0	.0	0	.0	0	.0
FEMALE	0	.0	0	.0	0	.0	0	.0	0	.0	0	.0	0	.0
MALE	0	.0	0	.0	0	.0	0	.0	0	.0	0	.0	0	.0
PART-TIME	0	.0	0	.0	0	.0	0	.0	0	.0	0	.0	0	.0
FEMALE	0	.0	0	.0	0	.0	0	.0	0	.0	0	.0	0	.0
MALE	0	.0	0	.0	0	.0	0	.0	0	.0	0	.0	0	.0
TOTAL	0	.0	0	.0	0	.0	0	.0	0	.0	0	.0	0	.0
FEMALE	0	.0	0	.0	0	.0	0	.0	0	.0	0	.0	0	.0
MALE	0	.0	0	.0	0	.0	0	.0	0	.0	0	.0	0	.0
UND+GRAD+PROF:														
FULL-TIME	12	.7	191	11.4	17	1.0	10	.6	230	13.7	1,430	85.2	18	1.1
FEMALE	5	.7	99	14.4	8	1.2	4	.6	116	16.9	567	82.7	3	.4
MALE	7	.7	92	9.3	9	.9	6	.6	114	11.5	863	87.0	15	1.5
PART-TIME	3	1.2	21	8.3	2	.8	1	.4	27	10.7	222	88.1	3	1.2
FEMALE	2	1.6	6	4.9	1	.8	1	.8	10	8.2	110	90.2	2	1.6
MALE	1	.8	15	11.5	1	.8	0	.0	17	13.1	112	86.2	1	.8
TOTAL	15	.8	212	11.0	19	1.0	11	.6	257	13.3	1,652	85.6	21	1.1
FEMALE	7	.9	105	13.0	9	1.1	5	.6	126	15.6	677	83.8	5	.6
MALE	8	.7	107	9.5	10	.9	6	.5	131	11.7	975	86.9	16	1.4
UNCLASSIFIED:														
TOTAL	0	.0	4	6.2	0	.0	1	1.5	5	7.7	60	92.3	0	.0
FEMALE	0	.0	1	3.3	0	.0	1	3.3	2	6.7	28	93.3	0	.0
MALE	0	.0	3	8.6	0	.0	0	.0	3	8.6	32	91.4	0	.0
TOTAL ENROLLMENT:														
TOTAL	15	.8	216	10.8	19	1.0	12	.6	262	13.1	1,712	85.8	21	1.1
FEMALE	7	.8	106	12.6	9	1.1	6	.7	128	15.3	705	84.1	5	.6
MALE	8	.7	110	9.5	10	.9	6	.5	134	11.6	1,007	87.0	16	1.4
CALIFORNIA (134 INSTITUTIONS)														
UNDERGRADUATES:														
FULL-TIME	214	.8	1,292	4.9	3,064	11.7	1,711	6.5	6,281	24.0	18,977	72.4	945	3.6
FEMALE	93	.8	688	5.7	1,387	11.5	691	5.7	2,859	23.7	8,809	73.1	378	3.1
MALE	121	.9	604	4.3	1,677	11.8	1,020	7.2	3,422	24.2	10,168	71.8	567	4.0
PART-TIME	125	1.5	515	6.0	686	8.0	613	7.2	1,939	22.6	6,465	75.4	167	1.9
FEMALE	68	1.5	277	6.1	324	7.2	262	5.8	931	20.6	3,523	77.8	73	1.6
MALE	57	1.4	238	5.9	362	9.0	351	8.7	1,008	24.9	2,942	72.7	94	2.3
TOTAL	339	1.0	1,807	5.2	3,750	10.8	2,324	6.7	8,220	23.6	25,442	73.2	1,112	3.2
FEMALE	161	1.0	965	5.8	1,711	10.3	953	5.8	3,790	22.9	12,332	74.4	451	2.7
MALE	178	1.0	842	4.6	2,039	11.2	1,371	7.5	4,430	24.3	13,110	72.0	661	3.6
GRADUATE:														
FULL-TIME	12	.3	30	.8	240	6.8	65	1.8	347	9.8	2,795	79.0	395	11.2
FEMALE	3	.3	14	1.2	76	6.5	24	2.1	117	10.0	941	80.7	108	9.3
MALE	9	.4	16	.7	164	6.9	41	1.7	230	9.7	1,854	78.2	287	12.1
PART-TIME	12	.8	20	1.3	135	8.5	39	2.5	206	13.0	1,300	82.0	80	5.0
FEMALE	7	1.1	10	1.6	56	9.1	16	2.6	89	14.5	490	79.8	35	5.7
MALE	5	.5	10	1.0	79	8.1	23	2.4	117	12.0	810	83.3	45	4.6
TOTAL	24	.5	50	1.0	375	7.3	104	2.0	553	10.8	4,095	79.9	475	9.3
FEMALE	10	.6	24	1.3	132	7.4	40	2.2	206	11.6	1,431	80.4	143	8.0
MALE	14	.4	26	.8	243	7.3	64	1.9	347	10.4	2,664	79.7	332	9.9
PROFESSIONAL:														
FULL-TIME	0	.0	0	.0	0	.0	0	.0	0	.0	0	.0	0	.0
FEMALE	0	.0	0	.0	0	.0	0	.0	0	.0	0	.0	0	.0
MALE	0	.0	0	.0	0	.0	0	.0	0	.0	0	.0	0	.0

ASIAN OR ACIFIC ISLANDER		HISPANIC		TOTAL MINORITY		WHITE NON-HISPANIC		NON-RESIDENT ALIEN		TOTAL
NUMBER	%	NUMBER	%	NUMBER	%	NUMBER	%	NUMBER	%	NUMBER
0	.0	0	.0	0	.0	0	.0	0	.0	0
0	.0	0	.0	0	.0	0	.0	0	.0	0
0	.0	0	.0	0	.0	0	.0	0	.0	0
0	.0	0	.0	0	.0	0	.0	0	.0	0
0	.0	0	.0	0	.0	0	.0	0	.0	0
0	.0	0	.0	0	.0	0	.0	0	.0	0
3,304	11.1	1,776	6.0	6,628	22.3	21,772	73.2	1,340	4.5	29,740
1,463	11.1	715	5.4	2,976	22.5	9,750	73.8	486	3.7	13,212
1,841	11.1	1,061	6.4	3,652	22.1	12,022	72.7	854	5.2	16,528
821	8.1	652	6.4	2,145	21.1	7,765	76.4	247	2.4	10,157
380	7.4	278	5.4	1,020	19.8	4,013	78.1	108	2.1	5,141
441	8.8	374	7.5	1,125	22.4	3,752	74.8	139	2.8	5,016
4,125	10.3	2,428	6.1	8,773	22.0	29,537	74.0	1,587	4.0	39,897
1,843	10.0	993	5.4	3,996	21.8	13,763	75.0	594	3.2	18,353
2,282	10.6	1,435	6.7	4,777	22.2	15,774	73.2	993	4.6	21,544
112	6.5	92	5.4	270	15.8	1,405	82.1	36	2.1	1,711
51	5.7	38	4.2	122	13.6	762	84.9	14	1.6	898
61	7.5	54	6.6	148	18.2	643	79.1	22	2.7	813
4,237	10.2	2,520	6.1	9,043	21.7	30,942	74.4	1,623	3.9	41,608
1,894	9.8	1,031	5.4	4,118	21.4	14,525	75.5	608	3.2	19,251
2,343	10.5	1,489	6.7	4,925	22.0	16,417	73.4	1,015	4.5	22,357
56	1.6	99	2.8	253	7.1	3,269	91.9	37	1.0	3,559
31	1.8	42	2.4	128	7.4	1,580	91.6	17	1.0	1,725
25	1.4	57	3.1	125	6.8	1,689	92.1	20	1.1	1,834
8	1.7	14	2.9	42	8.7	432	89.3	10	2.1	484
4	1.7	5	2.1	22	9.1	215	89.2	4	1.7	241
4	1.6	9	3.7	20	8.2	217	89.3	6	2.5	243
64	1.6	113	2.8	295	7.3	3,701	91.5	47	1.2	4,043
35	1.8	47	2.4	150	7.6	1,795	91.3	21	1.1	1,966
29	1.4	66	3.2	145	7.0	1,906	91.8	26	1.3	2,077
10	2.4	3	.7	22	5.4	359	87.3	30	7.3	411
2	1.4	1	.7	8	5.6	127	89.4	7	4.9	142
8	3.0	2	.7	14	5.2	232	86.2	23	8.6	269
4	2.5	0	.0	4	2.5	143	91.1	10	6.4	157
0	.0	0	.0	0	.0	50	94.3	3	5.7	53
4	3.8	0	.0	4	3.8	93	89.4	7	6.7	104
14	2.5	3	.5	26	4.6	502	88.4	40	7.0	568
2	1.0	1	.5	8	4.1	177	90.8	10	5.1	195
12	3.2	2	.5	18	4.8	325	87.1	30	8.0	373
0	.0	0	.0	0	.0	0	.0	0	.0	0
0	.0	0	.0	0	.0	0	.0	0	.0	0
0	.0	0	.0	0	.0	0	.0	0	.0	0
0	.0	0	.0	0	.0	0	.0	0	.0	0
0	.0	0	.0	0	.0	0	.0	0	.0	0
0	.0	0	.0	0	.0	0	.0	0	.0	0
0	.0	0	.0	0	.0	0	.0	0	.0	0
0	.0	0	.0	0	.0	0	.0	0	.0	0
0	.0	0	.0	0	.0	0	.0	0	.0	0
66	1.7	102	2.6	275	6.9	3,628	91.4	67	1.7	3,970
33	1.8	43	2.3	136	7.3	1,707	91.4	24	1.3	1,807
33	1.6	59	2.8	139	6.6	1,921	91.3	43	2.0	2,103
12	1.9	14	2.2	46	7.2	575	89.7	20	3.1	641
4	1.4	5	1.7	22	7.5	265	90.1	7	2.4	294
8	2.3	9	2.6	24	6.9	310	89.3	13	3.7	347
78	1.7	116	2.5	321	7.0	4,203	91.2	87	1.9	4,611
37	1.7	48	2.2	158	7.3	1,972	91.3	31	1.4	2,161
41	1.7	68	2.8	163	6.7	2,231	91.1	56	2.3	2,450
1	1.1	4	4.5	10	11.4	76	86.4	2	2.3	88
1	2.1	2	4.3	6	12.8	41	87.2	0	.0	47
0	.0	2	4.9	4	9.8	35	85.4	2	4.9	41
79	1.7	120	2.6	331	7.0	4,279	91.1	89	1.9	4,699
38	1.7	50	2.3	164	7.4	2,013	91.2	31	1.4	2,208
41	1.6	70	2.8	167	6.7	2,266	91.0	58	2.3	2,491

365

MAJOR FIELD 0400 - BIOLOGICAL SCIENCES

	AMERICAN INDIAN ALASKAN NATIVE		BLACK NON-HISPANIC		ASIAN OR PACIFIC ISLANDER		HISPANIC		TOTAL MINORITY		WHITE NON-HISPANIC		NON-RESIDENT ALIEN	
	NUMBER	%	NUMBER	%	NUMBER	%	NUMBER	%	NUMBER	%	NUMBER	%	NUMBER	%
CONNECTICUT (21 INSTITUTIONS)														
UNDERGRADUATES:														
FULL-TIME	3	.1	96	2.8	44	1.3	48	1.4	191	5.6	3,188	93.4	33	1.0
FEMALE	1	.1	50	3.3	19	1.2	13	.8	83	5.4	1,434	93.6	15	1.0
MALE	2	.1	46	2.4	25	1.3	35	1.9	108	5.7	1,754	93.3	18	1.0
PART-TIME	1	.4	9	3.8	0	.0	1	.4	11	4.6	223	94.1	3	1.3
FEMALE	1	.9	7	6.6	0	.0	1	.9	9	8.5	96	90.6	1	.9
MALE	0	.0	2	1.5	0	.0	0	.0	2	1.5	127	96.9	2	1.5
TOTAL	4	.1	105	2.9	44	1.2	49	1.3	202	5.5	3,411	93.5	36	1.0
FEMALE	2	.1	57	3.5	19	1.2	14	.9	92	5.6	1,530	93.4	16	1.0
MALE	2	.1	48	2.4	25	1.2	35	1.7	110	5.5	1,881	93.5	20	1.0
GRADUATE:														
FULL-TIME	0	.0	5	1.0	10	2.1	6	1.2	21	4.4	430	89.4	30	6.2
FEMALE	0	.0	2	1.0	6	3.1	2	1.0	10	5.2	173	90.1	9	4.7
MALE	0	.0	3	1.0	4	1.4	4	1.4	11	3.8	257	88.9	21	7.3
PART-TIME	0	.0	1	.3	1	.3	2	.6	4	1.2	326	96.2	9	2.7
FEMALE	0	.0	1	.6	0	.0	1	.6	2	1.3	154	98.1	1	.6
MALE	0	.0	0	.0	1	.5	1	.5	2	1.1	172	94.5	8	4.4
TOTAL	0	.0	6	.7	11	1.3	8	1.0	25	3.0	756	92.2	39	4.8
FEMALE	0	.0	3	.9	6	1.7	3	.9	12	3.4	327	93.7	10	2.9
MALE	0	.0	3	.6	5	1.1	5	1.1	13	2.8	429	91.1	29	6.2
PROFESSIONAL:														
FULL-TIME	0	.0	0	.0	0	.0	0	.0	0	.0	0	.0	0	.0
FEMALE	0	.0	0	.0	0	.0	0	.0	0	.0	0	.0	0	.0
MALE	0	.0	0	.0	0	.0	0	.0	0	.0	0	.0	0	.0
PART-TIME	0	.0	0	.0	0	.0	0	.0	0	.0	0	.0	0	.0
FEMALE	0	.0	0	.0	0	.0	0	.0	0	.0	0	.0	0	.0
MALE	0	.0	0	.0	0	.0	0	.0	0	.0	0	.0	0	.0
TOTAL	0	.0	0	.0	0	.0	0	.0	0	.0	0	.0	0	.0
FEMALE	0	.0	0	.0	0	.0	0	.0	0	.0	0	.0	0	.0
MALE	0	.0	0	.0	0	.0	0	.0	0	.0	0	.0	0	.0
UND+GRAD+PROF:														
FULL-TIME	3	.1	101	2.6	54	1.4	54	1.4	212	5.4	3,618	92.9	63	1.6
FEMALE	1	.1	52	3.0	25	1.5	15	.9	93	5.4	1,607	93.2	24	1.4
MALE	2	.1	49	2.3	29	1.3	39	1.8	119	5.5	2,011	92.7	39	1.8
PART-TIME	1	.2	10	1.7	1	.2	3	.5	15	2.6	549	95.3	12	2.1
FEMALE	1	.4	8	3.0	0	.0	2	.8	11	4.2	250	95.1	2	.8
MALE	0	.0	2	.6	1	.3	1	.3	4	1.3	299	95.5	10	3.2
TOTAL	4	.1	111	2.5	55	1.2	57	1.3	227	5.1	4,167	93.2	75	1.7
FEMALE	2	.1	60	3.0	25	1.3	17	.9	104	5.2	1,857	93.5	26	1.3
MALE	2	.1	51	2.1	30	1.2	40	1.6	123	5.0	2,310	93.1	49	2.0
UNCLASSIFIED:														
TOTAL	0	.0	0	.0	0	.0	0	.0	0	.0	2	100.0	0	.0
FEMALE	0	.0	0	.0	0	.0	0	.0	0	.0	1	100.0	0	.0
MALE	0	.0	0	.0	0	.0	0	.0	0	.0	1	100.0	0	.0
TOTAL ENROLLMENT:														
TOTAL	4	.1	111	2.5	55	1.2	57	1.3	227	5.1	4,169	93.2	75	1.7
FEMALE	2	.1	60	3.0	25	1.3	17	.9	104	5.2	1,858	93.5	26	1.3
MALE	2	.1	51	2.1	30	1.2	40	1.6	123	5.0	2,311	93.1	49	2.0
DELAWARE (3 INSTITUTIONS)														
UNDERGRADUATES:														
FULL-TIME	1	.1	40	4.6	4	.5	3	.3	48	5.5	798	92.3	19	2.2
FEMALE	0	.0	25	6.5	3	.8	0	.0	28	7.2	351	90.7	8	2.1
MALE	1	.2	15	3.1	1	.2	3	.6	20	4.2	447	93.5	11	2.3
PART-TIME	0	.0	1	1.6	1	1.6	0	.0	2	3.3	58	95.1	1	1.6
FEMALE	0	.0	0	.0	1	3.4	0	.0	1	3.4	27	93.1	1	3.4
MALE	0	.0	1	3.1	0	.0	0	.0	1	3.1	31	96.9	0	.0
TOTAL	1	.1	41	4.4	5	.5	3	.3	50	5.4	856	92.4	20	2.2
FEMALE	0	.0	25	6.0	4	1.0	0	.0	29	7.0	378	90.9	9	2.2
MALE	1	.2	16	3.1	1	.2	3	.6	21	4.1	478	93.7	11	2.2
GRADUATE:														
FULL-TIME	0	.0	0	.0	0	.0	0	.0	0	.0	33	89.2	4	10.8
FEMALE	0	.0	0	.0	0	.0	0	.0	0	.0	8	88.9	1	11.1
MALE	0	.0	0	.0	0	.0	0	.0	0	.0	25	89.3	3	10.7
PART-TIME	0	.0	0	.0	0	.0	0	.0	0	.0	69	94.5	4	5.5
FEMALE	0	.0	0	.0	0	.0	0	.0	0	.0	26	96.3	1	3.7
MALE	0	.0	0	.0	0	.0	0	.0	0	.0	43	93.5	3	6.5
TOTAL	0	.0	0	.0	0	.0	0	.0	0	.0	102	92.7	8	7.3
FEMALE	0	.0	0	.0	0	.0	0	.0	0	.0	34	94.4	2	5.6
MALE	0	.0	0	.0	0	.0	0	.0	0	.0	68	91.9	6	8.1
PROFESSIONAL:														
FULL-TIME	0	.0	0	.0	0	.0	0	.0	0	.0	0	.0	0	.0
FEMALE	0	.0	0	.0	0	.0	0	.0	0	.0	0	.0	0	.0
MALE	0	.0	0	.0	0	.0	0	.0	0	.0	0	.0	0	.0

ASIAN OR PACIFIC ISLANDER		HISPANIC		TOTAL MINORITY		WHITE NON-HISPANIC		NON-RESIDENT ALIEN		TOTAL
NUMBER	%	NUMBER	%	NUMBER	%	NUMBER	%	NUMBER	%	NUMBER
0	.0	0	.0	0	.0	0	.0	0	.0	J
0	.0	0	.0	0	.0	0	.0	0	.0	0
0	.0	0	.0	0	.0	0	.0	0	.0	0
0	.0	0	.0	0	.0	0	.0	0	.0	0
0	.0	0	.0	0	.0	0	.0	0	.0	0
0	.0	0	.0	0	.0	0	.0	0	.0	0
4	.4	3	.3	48	5.3	831	92.1	23	2.5	902
3	.8	0	.0	28	7.1	359	90.7	9	2.3	396
1	.2	3	.6	20	4.0	472	93.3	14	2.8	506
1	.7	0	.0	2	1.5	127	94.8	5	3.7	134
1	1.8	0	.0	1	1.8	53	94.6	2	3.6	56
0	.0	0	.0	1	1.3	74	94.9	3	3.8	78
5	.5	3	.3	50	4.8	958	92.5	28	2.7	1,036
4	.9	0	.0	29	6.4	412	91.2	11	2.4	452
1	.2	3	.5	21	3.6	546	93.5	17	2.9	584
3	1.5	1	.5	8	4.0	184	92.0	8	4.0	200
1	1.1	0	.0	3	3.4	80	90.9	5	5.7	88
2	1.8	1	.9	5	4.5	104	92.9	3	2.7	112
8	.6	4	.3	58	4.7	1,142	92.4	36	2.9	1,236
5	.9	0	.0	32	5.9	492	91.1	16	3.0	540
3	.4	4	.6	26	3.7	650	93.4	20	2.9	696
33	2.5	34	2.6	675	51.0	499	37.7	149	11.3	1,323
18	2.8	12	1.9	362	56.7	214	33.5	63	9.9	639
15	2.2	22	3.2	313	45.8	285	41.7	86	12.6	684
8	3.2	3	1.2	161	64.1	61	24.3	29	11.6	251
2	1.4	2	1.4	94	65.7	36	25.2	13	9.1	143
6	5.6	1	.9	67	62.0	25	23.1	16	14.8	108
41	2.6	37	2.4	836	53.1	560	35.6	178	11.3	1,574
20	2.6	14	1.8	456	58.3	250	32.0	76	9.7	782
21	2.7	23	2.9	380	48.0	310	39.1	102	12.9	792
8	1.8	9	2.1	99	22.9	238	55.0	96	22.2	433
4	2.2	5	2.8	56	30.9	94	51.9	31	17.1	181
4	1.6	4	1.6	43	17.1	144	57.1	65	25.8	252
13	4.3	3	1.0	51	17.0	188	62.7	61	20.3	300
5	3.6	1	.7	27	19.3	94	67.1	19	13.6	140
8	5.0	2	1.3	24	15.0	94	58.8	42	26.3	160
21	2.9	12	1.6	150	20.5	426	58.1	157	21.4	733
9	2.8	6	1.9	83	25.9	188	58.6	50	15.6	321
12	2.9	6	1.5	67	16.3	238	57.8	107	26.0	412
0	.0	0	.0	0	.0	0	.0	0	.0	0
0	.0	0	.0	0	.0	0	.0	0	.0	0
0	.0	0	.0	0	.0	0	.0	0	.0	0
0	.0	0	.0	0	.0	0	.0	0	.0	0
0	.0	0	.0	0	.0	0	.0	0	.0	0
0	.0	0	.0	0	.0	0	.0	0	.0	0
0	.0	0	.0	0	.0	0	.0	0	.0	0
0	.0	0	.0	0	.0	0	.0	0	.0	0
0	.0	0	.0	0	.0	0	.0	0	.0	0
41	2.3	43	2.4	774	44.1	737	42.0	245	14.0	1,756
22	2.7	17	2.1	418	51.0	308	37.6	94	11.5	820
19	2.0	26	2.8	356	38.0	429	45.8	151	16.1	936
21	3.8	6	1.1	212	38.5	249	45.2	90	16.3	551
7	2.5	3	1.1	121	42.8	130	45.9	32	11.3	283
14	5.2	3	1.1	91	34.0	119	44.4	58	21.6	268
62	2.7	49	2.1	986	42.7	986	42.7	335	14.5	2,307
29	2.6	20	1.8	539	48.9	438	39.7	126	11.4	1,103
33	2.7	29	2.4	447	37.1	548	45.5	209	17.4	1,204
0	.0	0	.0	9	23.7	25	65.8	4	10.5	38
0	.0	0	.0	3	18.8	12	75.0	1	6.3	16
0	.0	0	.0	6	27.3	13	59.1	3	13.6	22
62	2.6	49	2.1	995	42.4	1,011	43.1	339	14.5	2,345
29	2.6	20	1.8	542	48.4	450	40.2	127	11.3	1,119
33	2.7	29	2.4	453	36.9	561	45.8	212	17.3	1,226

TABLE 17 - TOTAL ENROLLMENT IN INSTITUTIONS OF HIGHER EDUCATION FOR SELECTED MAJOR FIELDS UF STUDY AND LEVEL OF ENROLLMENT BY RACE, ETHNICITY, AND SEX: STATE, 1978

MAJOR FIELD 0400 - BIOLOGICAL SCIENCES

	AMERICAN INDIAN ALASKAN NATIVE		BLACK NON-HISPANIC		ASIAN OR PACIFIC ISLANDER		HISPANIC		TOTAL MINORITY		WHITE NON-HISPANIC		NON-RESIDENT ALIEN	
	NUMBER	%	NUMBER	%	NUMBER	%	NUMBER	%	NUMBER	%	NUMBER	%	NUMBER	%
FLORIDA 25 INSTITUTIONS)														
UNDERGRADUATES:														
FULL-TIME	13	.2	405	6.9	51	.9	343	5.8	812	13.8	4,941	84.1	125	2.1
FEMALE	2	.1	202	9.7	21	1.0	123	5.9	348	16.8	1,677	80.8	50	2.4
MALE	11	.3	203	5.3	30	.8	220	5.8	464	12.2	3,264	85.8	75	2.0
PART-TIME	0	.0	49	5.3	5	.5	76	8.3	130	14.2	777	84.8	9	1.0
FEMALE	0	.0	26	7.4	2	.6	32	9.1	60	17.0	289	81.9	4	1.1
MALE	0	.0	23	4.1	3	.5	44	7.8	70	12.4	488	86.7	5	.9
TOTAL	13	.2	454	6.7	56	.8	419	6.2	942	13.9	5,718	84.2	134	2.0
FEMALE	2	.1	228	9.4	23	.9	155	6.4	408	16.8	1,966	81.0	54	2.2
MALE	11	.3	226	5.2	33	.8	264	6.0	534	12.2	3,752	85.9	80	1.8
GRADUATE:														
FULL-TIME	2	.4	6	1.1	4	.7	9	1.6	21	3.8	468	85.4	59	10.8
FEMALE	0	.0	2	1.4	2	1.4	1	.7	5	3.4	126	85.7	16	10.9
MALE	2	.5	4	1.0	2	.5	8	2.0	16	4.0	342	85.3	43	10.7
PART-TIME	1	.3	2	.5	7	1.8	8	2.0	18	4.6	356	90.8	18	4.6
FEMALE	1	.9	0	.0	2	1.7	3	2.6	6	5.1	105	89.7	6	5.1
MALE	0	.0	2	.7	5	1.8	5	1.8	12	4.4	251	91.3	12	4.4
TOTAL	3	.3	8	.9	11	1.2	17	1.8	39	4.1	824	87.7	77	8.2
FEMALE	1	.4	2	.8	4	1.5	4	1.5	11	4.2	231	87.5	22	8.3
MALE	2	.3	6	.9	7	1.0	13	1.9	28	4.1	593	87.7	55	8.1
PROFESSIONAL:														
FULL-TIME	0	.0	0	.0	0	.0	0	.0	0	.0	0	.0	0	.0
FEMALE	0	.0	0	.0	0	.0	0	.0	0	.0	0	.0	0	.0
MALE	0	.0	0	.0	0	.0	0	.0	0	.0	0	.0	0	.0
PART-TIME	0	.0	0	.0	0	.0	0	.0	0	.0	0	.0	0	.0
FEMALE	0	.0	0	.0	0	.0	0	.0	0	.0	0	.0	0	.0
MALE	0	.0	0	.0	0	.0	0	.0	0	.0	0	.0	0	.0
TOTAL	0	.0	0	.0	0	.0	0	.0	0	.0	0	.0	0	.0
FEMALE	0	.0	0	.0	0	.0	0	.0	0	.0	0	.0	0	.0
MALE	0	.0	0	.0	0	.0	0	.0	0	.0	0	.0	0	.0
UNC+GRAD+PROF:														
FULL-TIME	15	.2	411	6.4	55	.9	352	5.5	833	13.0	5,409	84.2	184	2.9
FEMALE	2	.1	204	9.2	23	1.0	124	5.6	353	15.9	1,803	81.1	66	3.0
MALE	13	.3	207	4.9	32	.8	228	5.4	480	11.4	3,606	85.8	118	2.8
PART-TIME	1	.2	51	3.9	12	.9	84	6.4	148	11.3	1,133	86.6	27	2.1
FEMALE	1	.2	26	5.5	4	.9	35	7.4	66	14.0	394	83.8	10	2.1
MALE	0	.0	25	3.0	8	1.0	49	5.8	82	9.8	739	88.2	17	2.0
TOTAL	16	.2	462	6.0	67	.9	436	5.6	981	12.7	6,542	84.6	211	2.7
FEMALE	3	.1	230	8.5	27	1.0	159	5.9	419	15.6	2,197	81.6	76	2.8
MALE	13	.3	232	4.6	40	.8	277	5.5	562	11.1	4,345	86.2	135	2.7
UNCLASSIFIED:														
TOTAL	0	.0	11	4.8	1	.4	9	3.9	21	9.2	204	89.1	4	1.7
FEMALE	0	.0	3	3.3	0	.0	3	3.3	6	6.7	84	93.3	0	.0
MALE	0	.0	8	5.8	1	.7	6	4.3	15	10.8	120	86.3	4	2.9
TOTAL ENROLLMENT:														
TOTAL	16	.2	473	5.9	68	.9	445	5.6	1,002	12.6	6,746	84.7	215	2.7
FEMALE	3	.1	233	8.4	27	1.0	162	5.8	425	15.3	2,281	82.0	76	2.7
MALE	13	.3	240	4.6	41	.8	283	5.5	577	11.1	4,465	86.2	139	2.7
GEORGIA 53 INSTITUTIONS)														
UNDERGRADUATES:														
FULL-TIME	5	.1	1,204	24.9	32	.6	28	.6	1,329	26.2	3,676	72.3	76	1.5
FEMALE	0	.0	675	30.6	14	.6	10	.5	699	31.7	1,484	67.3	21	1.0
MALE	5	.2	589	20.5	18	.6	18	.6	630	21.9	2,192	76.2	55	1.9
PART-TIME	1	.1	122	14.2	11	1.3	4	.5	138	16.1	716	83.4	5	.6
FEMALE	1	.3	65	16.6	4	1.0	2	.5	72	18.4	315	80.6	4	1.0
MALE	0	.0	57	12.2	7	1.5	2	.4	66	14.1	401	85.7	1	.2
TOTAL	6	.1	1,386	23.3	43	.7	32	.5	1,467	24.7	4,392	73.9	81	1.4
FEMALE	1	.0	740	28.5	18	.7	12	.5	771	29.7	1,799	69.3	25	1.0
MALE	5	.1	646	19.3	25	.7	20	.6	696	20.8	2,593	77.5	56	1.7
GRADUATE:														
FULL-TIME	0	.0	54	13.1	1	.2	3	.7	58	14.1	302	73.3	52	12.6
FEMALE	0	.0	31	20.3	0	.0	0	.0	31	20.3	111	72.5	11	7.2
MALE	0	.0	23	8.9	1	.4	3	1.2	27	10.4	191	73.7	41	15.8
PART-TIME	0	.0	44	12.5	4	1.1	0	.0	48	13.7	284	80.9	19	5.4
FEMALE	0	.0	15	10.9	3	2.2	0	.0	18	13.1	110	80.3	9	6.6
MALE	0	.0	29	13.6	1	.5	0	.0	30	14.0	174	81.3	10	4.7
TOTAL	0	.0	98	12.8	5	.7	3	.4	106	13.9	586	76.8	71	9.3
FEMALE	0	.0	46	15.9	3	1.0	0	.0	49	16.9	221	76.2	20	6.9
MALE	0	.0	52	11.0	2	.4	3	.6	57	12.1	365	77.2	51	10.8
PROFESSIONAL:														
FULL-TIME	0	.0	0	.0	0	.0	0	.0	0	.0	0	.0	0	.0
FEMALE	0	.0	0	.0	0	.0	0	.0	0	.0	0	.0	0	.0
MALE	0	.0	0	.0	0	.0	0	.0	0	.0	0	.0	0	.0

IOLOGICAL SCIENCES

INDIAN ATIVE		BLACK NON-HISPANIC		ASIAN OR PACIFIC ISLANDER		HISPANIC		TOTAL MINORITY		WHITE NON-HISPANIC		NON-RESIDENT ALIEN		TOTAL
%	NUMBER	%	NUMBER	%	NUMBER	%	NUMBER	%	NUMBER	%	NUMBER	%	NUMBER	%	NUMBER

CONTINUED

.0	0	.0	0	.0	0	.0	0	.0	0	.0	0	.0	0	.0	0
.0	0	.0	0	.0	0	.0	0	.0	0	.0	0	.0	0	.0	0
.0	0	.0	0	.0	0	.0	0	.0	0	.0	0	.0	0	.0	0
.0	0	.0	0	.0	0	.0	0	.0	0	.0	0	.0	0	.0	0
.0	0	.0	0	.0	0	.0	0	.0	0	.0	0	.0	0	.0	0
.0	0	.0	0	.0	0	.0	0	.0	0	.0	0	.0	0	.0	0
.1	1,318	24.0	33	.6	31	.6	1,387	25.3	3,978	72.4	124	2.3	5,493
.0	708	30.0	14	.6	10	.4	730	31.0	1,595	67.7	32	1.4	2,357
.1	612	19.5	19	.8	21	.7	657	21.0	2,383	76.0	96	3.1	3,136
.2	166	13.7	15	1.2	4	.3	186	15.4	1,000	82.6	24	2.0	1,210
.2	80	15.2	7	1.3	2	.4	90	17.0	425	80.5	13	2.5	528
.0	86	12.6	8	1.2	2	.3	96	14.1	575	84.3	11	1.6	682
.1	1,484	22.1	48	.7	35	.5	1,573	23.5	4,978	74.3	152	2.3	6,703
.0	786	27.2	21	.7	12	.4	820	28.4	2,020	70.0	45	1.6	2,885
.1	698	18.3	27	.7	23	.6	753	19.7	2,958	77.5	107	2.8	3,818
.0	19	15.6	1	.8	2	1.6	22	18.0	96	78.7	4	3.3	122
.0	13	21.7	0	.0	0	.0	13	21.7	45	75.0	2	3.3	60
.0	6	9.7	1	1.6	2	3.2	9	14.5	51	82.3	2	3.2	62
.1	1,503	22.0	49	.7	37	.5	1,595	23.4	5,074	74.3	156	2.3	6,825
.0	799	27.1	21	.7	12	.4	833	28.3	2,065	70.1	47	1.6	2,945
.1	704	18.1	28	.7	25	.6	762	19.6	3,009	77.6	109	2.8	3,880

(3 INSTITUTIONS)

.2	5	1.0	285	57.9	7	1.4	298	60.6	183	37.2	11	2.2	492
.5	4	2.0	114	55.6	2	1.0	121	59.0	77	37.6	7	3.4	205
.0	1	.3	171	59.6	5	1.7	177	61.7	106	36.9	4	1.4	287
.0	2	1.5	75	56.4	5	3.8	82	61.7	51	38.3	0	.0	133
.0	0	.0	11	25.0	2	4.5	13	29.5	31	70.5	0	.0	44
.0	2	2.2	64	71.9	3	3.4	69	77.5	20	22.5	0	.0	89
.2	7	1.1	360	57.6	12	1.9	380	60.8	234	37.4	11	1.8	625
.4	4	1.6	125	50.2	4	1.6	134	53.8	108	43.4	7	2.8	249
.0	3	.8	235	62.5	8	2.1	246	65.4	126	33.5	4	1.1	376
.0	0	.0	53	37.9	0	.0	53	37.9	79	56.4	8	5.7	140
.0	0	.0	17	34.0	0	.0	17	34.0	32	64.0	1	2.0	50
.0	0	.0	36	40.0	0	.0	36	40.0	47	52.2	7	7.8	90
.6	1	.6	52	31.5	3	1.8	57	34.5	98	59.4	10	6.1	165
1.9	0	.0	14	25.9	1	1.9	16	29.6	33	61.1	5	9.3	54
.0	1	.9	38	34.2	2	1.8	41	36.9	65	58.6	5	4.5	111
.3	1	.3	105	34.4	3	1.0	110	36.1	177	58.0	18	5.9	305
1.0	0	.0	31	29.8	1	1.0	33	31.7	65	62.5	6	5.8	104
.0	1	.5	74	36.8	2	1.0	77	38.3	112	55.7	12	6.0	201
.0	0	.0	0	.0	0	.0	0	.0	0	.0	0	.0	0
.0	0	.0	0	.0	0	.0	0	.0	0	.0	0	.0	0
.0	0	.0	0	.0	0	.0	0	.0	0	.0	0	.0	0
.0	0	.0	0	.0	0	.0	0	.0	0	.0	0	.0	0
.0	0	.0	0	.0	0	.0	0	.0	0	.0	0	.0	0
.0	0	.0	0	.0	0	.0	0	.0	0	.0	0	.0	0
.0	0	.0	0	.0	0	.0	0	.0	0	.0	0	.0	0
.0	0	.0	0	.0	0	.0	0	.0	0	.0	0	.0	0
.0	0	.0	0	.0	0	.0	0	.0	0	.0	0	.0	0
.2	5	.8	338	53.5	7	1.1	351	55.5	262	41.5	19	3.0	632
.4	4	1.6	131	51.4	2	.8	138	54.1	109	42.7	8	3.1	255
.0	1	.3	201	54.9	5	1.3	213	56.5	153	40.6	11	2.9	377
.3	3	1.0	127	42.6	8	2.7	139	46.6	149	50.0	10	3.4	298
1.0	0	.0	25	25.5	3	3.1	29	29.6	64	65.3	5	5.1	98
.0	3	1.5	102	51.0	5	2.5	110	55.0	85	42.5	5	2.5	200
.2	8	.9	465	50.0	15	1.6	490	52.7	411	44.2	29	3.1	930
.6	4	1.1	156	44.2	5	1.4	167	47.3	173	49.0	13	3.7	353
.0	4	.7	309	53.6	10	1.7	323	56.0	238	41.2	16	2.8	577
.0	0	.0	1	33.3	0	.0	1	33.3	2	66.7	0	.0	3
.0	0	.0	1	100.0	0	.0	1	100.0	0	.0	0	.0	1
.0	0	.0	0	.0	0	.0	0	.0	0	.0	2	100.0	2
.2	8	.9	466	49.9	15	1.6	491	52.6	413	44.3	29	3.1	933
.6	4	1.1	157	44.4	5	1.4	168	47.5	173	48.9	13	3.7	354
.0	4	.7	309	53.4	10	1.7	323	55.8	240	41.5	16	2.8	579

369

MAJOR FIELD 0400 - BIOLOGICAL SCIENCES

	AMERICAN INDIAN ALASKAN NATIVE		BLACK NON-HISPANIC		ASIAN OR PACIFIC ISLANDER		HISPANIC		TOTAL MINORITY		WHITE NON-HISPANIC		NON-RESIDENT ALIEN	
	NUMBER	%	NUMBER	%	NUMBER	%	NUMBER	%	NUMBER	%	NUMBER	%	NUMBER	%
IDAHO (7 INSTITUTIONS)														
UNDERGRADUATES:														
FULL-TIME	0	.0	1	.2	13	2.4	1	.2	15	2.8	508	95.3	10	1.9
FEMALE	0	.0	0	.0	5	2.3	0	.0	5	2.3	212	96.8	2	.9
MALE	0	.0	1	.3	8	2.5	1	.3	10	3.2	296	94.3	8	2.5
PART-TIME	0	.0	0	.0	2	3.1	0	.0	2	3.1	61	95.3	1	1.6
FEMALE	0	.0	0	.0	0	.0	0	.0	0	.0	29	96.7	1	3.3
MALE	0	.0	0	.0	2	5.9	0	.0	2	5.9	32	94.1	0	.0
TOTAL	0	.0	1	.2	15	2.5	1	.2	17	2.8	569	95.3	11	1.8
FEMALE	0	.0	0	.0	5	2.0	0	.0	5	2.0	241	96.8	3	1.2
MALE	0	.0	1	.3	10	2.9	1	.3	12	3.4	328	94.3	8	2.3
GRADUATE:														
FULL-TIME	0	.0	3	2.5	1	.8	0	.0	4	3.3	108	89.3	9	7.4
FEMALE	0	.0	0	.0	0	.0	0	.0	0	.0	18	100.0	0	.0
MALE	0	.0	3	2.9	1	1.0	0	.0	4	3.9	90	87.4	9	8.7
PART-TIME	1	2.3	0	.0	0	.0	0	.0	1	2.3	41	93.2	2	4.5
FEMALE	0	.0	0	.0	0	.0	0	.0	0	.0	9	90.0	1	10.0
MALE	1	2.9	0	.0	0	.0	0	.0	1	2.9	32	94.1	1	2.9
TOTAL	1	.6	3	1.8	1	.6	0	.0	5	3.0	149	90.3	11	6.7
FEMALE	0	.0	0	.0	0	.0	0	.0	0	.0	27	96.4	1	3.6
MALE	1	.7	3	2.2	1	.7	0	.0	5	3.6	122	89.1	10	7.3
PROFESSIONAL:														
FULL-TIME	0	.0	0	.0	0	.0	0	.0	0	.0	0	.0	0	.0
FEMALE	0	.0	0	.0	0	.0	0	.0	0	.0	0	.0	0	.0
MALE	0	.0	0	.0	0	.0	0	.0	0	.0	0	.0	0	.0
PART-TIME	0	.0	0	.0	0	.0	0	.0	0	.0	0	.0	0	.0
FEMALE	0	.0	0	.0	0	.0	0	.0	0	.0	0	.0	0	.0
MALE	0	.0	0	.0	0	.0	0	.0	0	.0	0	.0	0	.0
TOTAL	0	.0	0	.0	0	.0	0	.0	0	.0	0	.0	0	.0
FEMALE	0	.0	0	.0	0	.0	0	.0	0	.0	0	.0	0	.0
MALE	0	.0	0	.0	0	.0	0	.0	0	.0	0	.0	0	.0
UND+GRAD+PROF:														
FULL-TIME	0	.0	4	.6	14	2.1	1	.2	19	2.9	616	94.2	19	2.9
FEMALE	0	.0	0	.0	5	2.1	0	.0	5	2.1	230	97.0	2	.8
MALE	0	.0	4	1.0	9	2.2	1	.2	14	3.4	386	92.6	17	4.1
PART-TIME	1	.9	0	.0	2	1.9	0	.0	3	2.8	102	94.4	3	2.8
FEMALE	0	.0	0	.0	0	.0	0	.0	0	.0	38	95.0	2	5.0
MALE	1	1.5	0	.0	2	2.9	0	.0	3	4.4	64	94.1	1	1.5
TOTAL	1	.1	4	.5	16	2.1	1	.1	22	2.9	718	94.2	22	2.9
FEMALE	0	.0	0	.0	5	1.8	0	.0	5	1.8	268	96.8	4	1.4
MALE	1	.2	4	.8	11	2.3	1	.2	17	3.5	450	92.8	18	3.7
UNCLASSIFIED:														
TOTAL	0	.0	0	.0	1	6.7	0	.0	1	6.7	14	93.3	0	.0
FEMALE	0	.0	0	.0	1	11.1	0	.0	1	11.1	8	88.9	0	.0
MALE	0	.0	0	.0	0	.0	0	.0	0	.0	6	100.0	0	.0
TOTAL ENROLLMENT:														
TOTAL	1	.1	4	.5	17	2.2	1	.1	23	3.0	732	94.2	22	2.8
FEMALE	0	.0	0	.0	6	2.1	0	.0	6	2.1	276	96.5	4	1.4
MALE	1	.2	4	.8	11	2.2	1	.2	17	3.5	456	92.9	18	3.7
ILLINOIS (60 INSTITUTIONS)														
UNDERGRADUATES:														
FULL-TIME	21	.2	1,226	10.4	410	3.5	309	2.6	1,966	16.6	9,656	81.7	204	1.7
FEMALE	11	.2	814	14.6	215	3.9	154	2.8	1,194	21.4	4,309	77.2	80	1.4
MALE	10	.2	412	6.6	195	3.1	155	2.5	772	12.4	5,347	85.6	124	2.0
PART-TIME	6	.4	273	17.4	40	2.5	48	3.1	367	23.3	1,189	75.6	17	1.1
FEMALE	3	.3	179	19.2	19	2.0	20	2.1	221	23.7	705	75.7	5	.5
MALE	3	.5	94	14.6	21	3.3	28	4.4	146	22.7	484	75.4	12	1.9
TOTAL	27	.2	1,499	11.2	450	3.4	357	2.7	2,333	17.4	10,845	80.9	221	1.6
FEMALE	14	.2	993	15.2	234	3.6	174	2.7	1,415	21.7	5,014	77.0	85	1.3
MALE	13	.2	506	7.3	216	3.1	183	2.7	918	13.3	5,831	84.7	136	2.0
GRADUATE:														
FULL-TIME	4	.3	13	1.0	54	4.0	12	.9	83	6.1	1,149	84.7	124	9.1
FEMALE	1	.2	7	1.6	24	5.4	4	.9	36	8.2	356	80.7	49	11.1
MALE	3	.3	6	.7	30	3.3	8	.9	47	5.1	793	86.7	75	8.2
PART-TIME	3	.3	67	7.6	27	3.1	11	1.2	108	12.2	735	83.1	41	4.6
FEMALE	1	.3	38	12.9	17	5.8	6	2.0	62	21.1	219	74.5	13	4.4
MALE	2	.3	29	4.9	10	1.7	5	.8	46	7.8	516	87.5	28	4.7
TOTAL	7	.3	80	3.6	81	3.6	23	1.0	191	8.5	1,884	84.1	165	7.4
FEMALE	2	.3	45	6.1	41	5.6	10	1.4	98	13.3	575	78.2	62	8.4
MALE	5	.3	35	2.3	40	2.7	13	.9	93	6.2	1,309	87.0	103	6.8
PROFESSIONAL:														
FULL-TIME	0	.0	0	.0	0	.0	0	.0	0	.0	0	.0	0	.0
FEMALE	0	.0	0	.0	0	.0	0	.0	0	.0	0	.0	0	.0
MALE	0	.0	0	.0	0	.0	0	.0	0	.0	0	.0	0	.0

ASIAN OR PACIFIC ISLANDER		HISPANIC		TOTAL MINORITY		WHITE NON-HISPANIC		NON-RESIDENT ALIEN		TOTAL
NUMBER	%	NUMBER	%	NUMBER	%	NUMBER	%	NUMBER	%	NUMBER
0	.0	0	.0	0	.0	0	.0	0	.0	0
0	.0	0	.0	0	.0	0	.0	0	.0	0
0	.0	0	.0	0	.0	0	.0	0	.0	0
0	.0	0	.0	0	.0	0	.0	0	.0	0
0	.0	0	.0	0	.0	0	.0	0	.0	0
0	.0	0	.0	0	.0	0	.0	0	.0	0
464	3.5	321	2.4	2,049	15.5	10,805	82.0	328	2.5	13,182
239	4.0	158	2.6	1,230	20.4	4,665	77.4	129	2.1	6,024
225	3.1	163	2.3	819	11.4	6,140	85.8	199	2.8	7,158
67	2.7	59	2.4	475	19.3	1,924	78.3	58	2.4	2,457
36	2.9	26	2.1	283	23.1	924	75.4	18	1.5	1,225
31	2.5	33	2.7	192	15.6	1,000	81.2	40	3.2	1,232
531	3.4	380	2.4	2,524	16.1	12,729	81.4	386	2.5	15,639
275	3.8	184	2.5	1,513	20.9	5,589	77.1	147	2.0	7,249
256	3.1	196	2.3	1,011	12.1	7,140	85.1	239	2.8	8,390
15	2.9	13	2.5	59	11.5	445	87.1	7	1.4	511
8	2.5	5	1.6	26	8.1	292	90.7	4	1.2	322
7	3.7	8	4.2	33	17.5	153	81.0	3	1.6	189
546	3.4	393	2.4	2,583	16.0	13,174	81.6	393	2.4	16,150
283	3.7	189	2.5	1,539	20.3	5,881	77.7	151	2.0	7,571
263	3.1	204	2.4	1,044	12.2	7,293	85.0	242	2.8	8,579
58	1.3	47	1.1	277	6.4	3,990	91.9	73	1.7	4,340
35	1.8	21	1.1	147	7.6	1,763	90.9	29	1.5	1,939
23	1.0	26	1.1	130	5.4	2,227	92.8	44	1.8	2,401
5	.9	7	1.3	45	8.5	478	90.7	4	.8	527
3	1.4	4	1.8	26	11.8	192	87.3	2	.9	220
2	.7	3	1.0	19	6.2	286	93.2	2	.7	307
63	1.3	54	1.1	322	6.6	4,468	91.8	77	1.6	4,867
38	1.4	25	1.2	173	8.0	1,955	90.6	31	1.4	2,159
25	.9	29	1.1	149	5.5	2,513	92.8	46	1.7	2,708
11	1.7	3	.5	25	3.9	546	85.4	68	10.6	639
5	2.5	0	.0	10	5.0	173	85.6	19	9.4	202
6	1.4	3	.7	15	3.4	373	85.4	49	11.2	437
3	1.1	0	.0	8	2.9	254	91.0	17	6.1	279
3	2.7	0	.0	6	5.4	95	85.6	10	9.0	111
0	.0	0	.0	2	1.2	159	94.6	7	4.2	168
14	1.5	3	.3	33	3.6	800	87.1	85	9.3	918
8	2.6	0	.0	16	5.1	268	85.6	29	9.3	313
6	1.0	3	.5	17	2.8	532	87.9	56	9.3	605
0	.0	0	.0	0	.0	32	94.1	2	5.9	34
0	.0	0	.0	0	.0	6	85.7	1	14.3	7
0	.0	0	.0	0	.0	26	96.3	1	3.7	27
0	.0	0	.0	0	.0	0	.0	0	.0	0
0	.0	0	.0	0	.0	0	.0	0	.0	0
0	.0	0	.0	0	.0	0	.0	0	.0	0
0	.0	0	.0	0	.0	32	94.1	2	5.9	34
0	.0	0	.0	0	.0	6	85.7	1	14.3	7
0	.0	0	.0	0	.0	26	96.3	1	3.7	27
69	1.4	50	1.0	302	6.0	4,568	91.1	143	2.9	5,013
40	1.9	21	1.0	157	7.3	1,942	90.4	49	2.3	2,148
29	1.0	29	1.0	145	5.1	2,626	91.7	94	3.3	2,865
8	1.0	7	.9	53	6.6	732	90.8	21	2.6	806
6	1.8	4	1.2	32	9.7	287	86.7	12	3.6	331
2	.4	3	.6	21	4.4	445	93.7	9	1.9	475
77	1.3	57	1.0	355	6.1	5,300	91.1	164	2.8	5,819
46	1.9	25	1.0	189	7.6	2,229	89.9	61	2.5	2,479
31	.9	32	1.0	166	5.0	3,071	91.9	103	3.1	3,340
2	1.9	1	.9	12	11.1	91	84.3	5	4.6	108
0	.0	1	2.1	3	6.3	43	89.6	2	4.2	48
2	3.3	0	.0	9	15.0	48	80.0	3	5.0	60
79	1.3	58	1.0	367	6.2	5,391	91.0	169	2.9	5,927
46	1.8	26	1.0	192	7.6	2,272	89.9	63	2.5	2,527
33	1.0	32	.9	175	5.1	3,119	91.7	106	3.1	3,400

TABLE 17 - TOTAL ENROLLMENT IN INSTITUTIONS OF HIGHER EDUCATION FOR SELECTED MAJOR FIELDS OF STUDY AND LEVEL OF ENROLLMENT BY RACE, ETHNICITY, AND SEX: STATE, 1978

MAJOR FIELD 0400 - BIOLOGICAL SCIENCES

	AMERICAN INDIAN ALASKAN NATIVE		BLACK NON-HISPANIC		ASIAN OR PACIFIC ISLANDER		HISPANIC		TOTAL MINORITY		WHITE NON-HISPANIC		NON-RESIDENT ALIEN	
	NUMBER	%	NUMBER	%	NUMBER	%	NUMBER	%	NUMBER	%	NUMBER	%	NUMBER	%
IOWA (32 INSTITUTIONS)														
UNDERGRADUATES:														
FULL-TIME	9	.3	75	2.6	28	1.0	12	.4	124	4.3	2,701	93.1	76	2.6
FEMALE	6	.5	32	2.4	12	.9	6	.5	56	4.3	1,232	93.6	28	2.1
MALE	3	.2	43	2.7	16	1.0	6	.4	68	4.3	1,469	92.7	48	3.0
PART-TIME	3	1.1	2	.7	3	1.1	1	.4	9	3.3	263	95.6	3	1.1
FEMALE	1	.8	2	1.7	1	.8	1	.8	5	4.2	111	94.1	2	1.7
MALE	2	1.3	0	.0	2	1.3	0	.0	4	2.5	152	96.8	1	.6
TOTAL	12	.4	77	2.4	31	1.0	13	.4	133	4.2	2,964	93.3	79	2.5
FEMALE	7	.5	34	2.4	13	.9	7	.5	61	4.3	1,343	93.7	30	2.1
MALE	5	.3	43	2.5	18	1.0	6	.3	72	4.1	1,621	93.1	49	2.8
GRADUATE:														
FULL-TIME	0	.0	5	1.2	7	1.7	1	.2	13	3.2	362	90.0	27	6.7
FEMALE	0	.0	2	1.4	1	.7	1	.7	4	2.8	125	86.8	19	10.4
MALE	0	.0	3	1.2	6	2.3	0	.0	9	3.5	237	91.9	12	4.7
PART-TIME	0	.0	1	.6	1	.6	0	.0	2	1.2	142	87.1	19	11.7
FEMALE	0	.0	0	.0	1	.9	0	.0	1	1.9	46	86.8	6	11.3
MALE	0	.0	1	.9	0	.0	0	.0	1	.9	96	87.3	13	11.8
TOTAL	0	.0	6	1.1	8	1.4	1	.2	15	2.7	504	89.2	46	8.1
FEMALE	0	.0	2	1.0	2	1.0	1	.5	5	2.5	171	86.8	21	10.7
MALE	0	.0	4	1.1	6	1.6	0	.0	10	2.7	333	90.5	25	6.8
PROFESSIONAL:														
FULL-TIME	0	.0	0	.0	0	.0	0	.0	0	.0	0	.0	0	.0
FEMALE	0	.0	0	.0	0	.0	0	.0	0	.0	0	.0	0	.0
MALE	0	.0	0	.0	0	.0	0	.0	0	.0	0	.0	0	.0
PART-TIME	0	.0	0	.0	0	.0	0	.0	0	.0	0	.0	0	.0
FEMALE	0	.0	0	.0	0	.0	0	.0	0	.0	0	.0	0	.0
MALE	0	.0	0	.0	0	.0	0	.0	0	.0	0	.0	0	.0
TOTAL	0	.0	0	.0	0	.0	0	.0	0	.0	0	.0	0	.0
FEMALE	0	.0	0	.0	0	.0	0	.0	0	.0	0	.0	0	.0
MALE	0	.0	0	.0	0	.0	0	.0	0	.0	0	.0	0	.0
UND+GRAD+PROF:														
FULL-TIME	9	.3	80	2.4	35	1.1	13	.4	137	4.1	3,063	92.7	103	3.1
FEMALE	6	.4	34	2.3	13	.9	7	.5	60	4.1	1,357	92.9	43	2.9
MALE	3	.2	46	2.5	22	1.2	6	.3	77	4.2	1,706	92.6	60	3.3
PART-TIME	3	.7	3	.7	4	.9	1	.2	11	2.5	405	92.5	22	5.0
FEMALE	1	.6	2	1.2	2	1.2	1	.6	6	3.5	157	91.8	8	4.7
MALE	2	.7	1	.4	2	.7	0	.0	5	1.9	248	92.9	14	5.2
TOTAL	12	.3	83	2.2	39	1.0	14	.4	148	4.0	3,468	92.7	125	3.3
FEMALE	7	.4	36	2.2	15	.9	8	.5	66	4.0	1,514	92.8	51	3.1
MALE	5	.2	47	2.2	24	1.1	6	.3	82	3.9	1,954	92.6	74	3.5
UNCLASSIFIED:														
TOTAL	0	.0	0	.0	0	.0	0	.0	0	.0	7	100.0	0	.0
FEMALE	0	.0	0	.0	0	.0	0	.0	0	.0	5	100.0	0	.0
MALE	0	.0	0	.0	0	.0	0	.0	0	.0	2	100.0	0	.0
TOTAL ENROLLMENT:														
TOTAL	12	.3	83	2.2	39	1.0	14	.4	148	3.9	3,475	92.7	125	3.3
FEMALE	7	.4	36	2.2	15	.9	8	.5	66	4.0	1,519	92.8	51	3.1
MALE	5	.2	47	2.2	24	1.1	6	.3	82	3.9	1,956	92.6	74	3.5
KANSAS (38 INSTITUTIONS)														
UNDERGRADUATES:														
FULL-TIME	22	.8	106	4.0	22	.8	39	1.5	189	7.0	2,423	90.3	70	2.6
FEMALE	12	1.0	56	4.8	9	.8	17	1.4	94	8.0	1,059	90.0	24	2.0
MALE	10	.7	50	3.3	13	.9	22	1.5	95	6.3	1,364	90.6	46	3.1
PART-TIME	3	1.0	19	5.0	0	.0	9	2.4	31	8.2	336	89.1	10	2.7
FEMALE	2	1.0	5	2.6	0	.0	6	3.1	13	6.6	178	90.8	5	2.6
MALE	1	.6	14	7.7	0	.0	3	1.7	18	9.9	158	87.3	5	2.8
TOTAL	25	.8	125	4.1	22	.7	48	1.6	220	7.2	2,759	90.2	80	2.6
FEMALE	14	1.0	61	4.4	9	.7	23	1.7	107	7.8	1,237	90.1	29	2.1
MALE	11	.7	64	3.8	13	.8	25	1.5	113	6.7	1,522	90.3	51	3.0
GRADUATE:														
FULL-TIME	3	.9	4	1.2	2	.6	4	1.2	13	4.0	247	75.5	67	20.5
FEMALE	0	.0	1	1.1	0	.0	1	1.1	2	2.1	74	77.9	19	20.0
MALE	3	1.3	3	1.3	2	.9	3	1.3	11	4.7	173	74.6	48	20.7
PART-TIME	1	.3	4	1.0	6	1.6	4	1.0	15	3.9	331	86.2	38	9.9
FEMALE	0	.0	3	2.2	2	1.5	0	.0	5	3.7	121	89.0	10	7.4
MALE	1	.4	1	.4	4	1.6	4	1.6	10	4.0	210	84.7	28	11.3
TOTAL	4	.6	8	1.1	8	1.1	8	1.1	28	3.9	578	81.3	105	14.8
FEMALE	0	.0	4	1.7	2	.9	1	.4	7	3.0	195	84.4	29	12.6
MALE	4	.8	4	.8	6	1.3	7	1.5	21	4.4	383	79.8	76	15.8
PROFESSIONAL:														
FULL-TIME	0	.0	0	.0	0	.0	0	.0	0	.0	0	.0	0	.0
FEMALE	0	.0	0	.0	0	.0	0	.0	0	.0	0	.0	0	.0
MALE	0	.0	0	.0	0	.0	0	.0	0	.0	0	.0	0	.0

IOLOGICAL SCIENCES

INDIAN IATIVE		BLACK NON-HISPANIC		ASIAN OR PACIFIC ISLANDER		HISPANIC		TOTAL MINORITY		WHITE NON-HISPANIC		NON-RESIDENT ALIEN		TOTAL
%	NUMBER	%	NUMBER	%	NUMBER	%	NUMBER	%	NUMBER	%	NUMBER	%	NUMBER	%	NUMBER

CONTINUED

.0	0	.0	0	.0	0	.0	0	.0	0	.0	0	.0	0	.0	0
.0	0	.0	0	.0	0	.0	0	.0	0	.0	0	.0	0	.0	0
.0	0	.0	0	.0	0	.0	0	.0	0	.0	0	.0	0	.0	0
.0	0	.0	0	.0	0	.0	0	.0	0	.0	0	.0	0	.0	0
.0	0	.0	0	.0	0	.0	0	.0	0	.0	0	.0	0	.0	0
.0	0	.0	0	.0	0	.0	0	.0	0	.0	0	.0	0	.0	0
.8	110	3.7	24	.8	43	1.4	202	6.7	2,670	88.7	137	4.6	3,009
.9	57	4.5	9	.7	18	1.4	96	7.5	1,133	89.1	43	3.4	1,272
.7	53	3.1	15	.9	25	1.4	106	6.1	1,537	88.5	94	5.4	1,737
.5	23	3.0	6	.8	13	1.7	46	6.0	667	87.6	48	6.3	761
.6	8	2.4	2	.6	6	1.8	18	5.4	299	90.1	15	4.5	332
.5	15	3.5	4	.9	7	1.6	28	6.5	368	85.8	33	7.7	429
.8	133	3.5	30	.8	56	1.5	248	6.6	3,337	88.5	185	4.9	3,770
.9	65	4.1	11	.7	24	1.5	114	7.1	1,432	89.3	58	3.6	1,604
.7	68	3.1	19	.9	32	1.5	134	6.2	1,905	88.0	127	5.9	2,166
.0	4	3.7	3	2.8	1	.9	8	7.5	96	89.7	3	2.8	107
.0	1	2.0	2	4.0	0	.0	3	6.0	45	90.0	2	4.0	50
.0	3	5.3	1	1.8	1	1.8	5	8.8	51	89.5	1	1.8	57
.7	137	3.5	33	.9	57	1.5	256	6.6	3,433	88.5	188	4.8	3,877
.8	66	4.0	13	.8	24	1.5	117	7.1	1,477	89.3	60	3.6	1,654
.7	71	3.2	20	.9	33	1.5	139	6.3	1,956	88.0	128	5.8	2,223

(24 INSTITUTIONS)

.2	112	3.9	37	1.3	9	.3	163	5.6	2,685	93.0	40	1.4	2,888
.3	53	4.5	19	1.6	1	.1	77	6.5	1,099	92.4	13	1.1	1,189
.1	59	3.5	18	1.1	8	.5	86	5.1	1,586	93.3	27	1.6	1,699
.3	11	3.3	1	.3	1	.3	14	4.2	318	94.9	3	.9	335
.0	4	2.7	1	.7	0	.0	5	3.4	141	96.6	0	.0	146
.5	7	3.7	0	.0	1	.5	9	4.8	177	93.7	3	1.6	189
.2	123	3.8	38	1.2	10	.3	177	5.5	3,003	93.2	43	1.3	3,223
.3	57	4.3	20	1.5	1	.1	82	6.1	1,240	92.9	13	1.0	1,335
.1	66	3.5	18	1.0	9	.5	95	5.0	1,763	93.4	30	1.6	1,888
1.9	2	.6	7	2.2	4	1.3	19	6.0	271	85.8	26	8.2	316
2.5	0	.0	3	3.8	2	2.5	7	8.9	64	81.0	8	10.1	79
1.7	2	.8	4	1.7	2	.8	12	5.1	207	87.3	18	7.6	237
1.1	4	2.2	5	2.7	0	.0	11	5.9	195	83.8	19	10.3	185
1.3	3	3.9	1	1.3	0	.0	5	6.6	64	84.2	7	9.2	76
.9	1	.9	4	3.7	0	.0	6	5.5	91	83.5	12	11.0	109
1.6	6	1.2	12	2.4	4	.8	30	6.0	426	85.0	45	9.0	501
1.9	3	1.9	4	2.6	2	1.3	12	7.7	128	82.6	15	9.7	155
1.4	3	.9	8	2.3	2	.6	18	5.2	298	86.1	30	8.7	346
.0	0	.0	0	.0	0	.0	0	.0	0	.0	0	.0	0
.0	0	.0	0	.0	0	.0	0	.0	0	.0	0	.0	0
.0	0	.0	0	.0	0	.0	0	.0	0	.0	0	.0	0
.0	0	.0	0	.0	0	.0	0	.0	0	.0	0	.0	0
.0	0	.0	0	.0	0	.0	0	.0	0	.0	0	.0	0
.0	0	.0	0	.0	0	.0	0	.0	0	.0	0	.0	0
.0	0	.0	0	.0	0	.0	0	.0	0	.0	0	.0	0
.0	0	.0	0	.0	0	.0	0	.0	0	.0	0	.0	0
.0	0	.0	0	.0	0	.0	0	.0	0	.0	0	.0	0
.3	114	3.6	44	1.4	13	.4	182	5.7	2,956	92.3	66	2.1	3,204
.5	53	4.2	22	1.7	3	.2	84	6.6	1,163	91.7	21	1.7	1,268
.3	61	3.2	22	1.1	10	.5	98	5.1	1,793	92.6	45	2.3	1,936
.6	15	2.9	6	1.2	1	.2	25	4.8	473	91.0	22	4.2	520
.5	7	3.2	2	.9	0	.0	10	4.5	205	92.3	7	3.2	222
.7	8	2.7	4	1.3	1	.3	15	5.0	268	89.9	15	5.0	298
.4	129	3.5	50	1.3	14	.4	207	5.6	3,429	92.1	88	2.4	3,724
.5	60	4.0	24	1.6	3	.2	94	6.3	1,368	91.8	28	1.9	1,490
.3	69	3.1	26	1.2	11	.5	113	5.1	2,061	92.3	60	2.7	2,234
.0	2	4.3	0	.0	3	6.5	5	10.9	39	84.8	2	4.3	46
.0	0	.0	0	.0	2	15.4	2	15.4	10	76.9	1	7.7	13
.0	2	6.1	0	.0	1	3.0	3	9.1	29	87.9	1	3.0	33
.4	131	3.5	50	1.3	17	.5	212	5.6	3,468	92.0	90	2.4	3,770
.5	60	4.0	24	1.6	5	.3	96	6.4	1,378	91.7	29	1.9	1,503
.3	71	3.1	26	1.1	12	.5	116	5.1	2,090	92.2	61	2.7	2,267

TABLE 17 - TOTAL ENROLLMENT IN INSTITUTIONS OF HIGHER EDUCATION FOR SELECTED MAJOR FIELDS OF STUDY AND LEVEL OF ENROLLMENT BY RACE, ETHNICITY, AND SEX: STATE, 1978

MAJOR FIELD 0400 - BIOLOGICAL SCIENCES

	AMERICAN INDIAN ALASKAN NATIVE		BLACK NON-HISPANIC		ASIAN OR PACIFIC ISLANDER		HISPANIC		TOTAL MINORITY		WHITE NON-HISPANIC		NON-RESIDENT ALIEN	
	NUMBER	%	NUMBER	%	NUMBER	%	NUMBER	%	NUMBER	%	NUMBER	%	NUMBER	%
LOUISIANA (26 INSTITUTIONS)														
UNDERGRADUATES:														
FULL-TIME	7	.2	563	16.1	13	.4	67	1.9	650	18.6	2,770	79.1	83	2.4
FEMALE	3	.2	366	26.4	2	.1	25	1.8	396	28.6	965	69.6	26	1.9
MALE	4	.2	197	9.3	11	.5	42	2.0	254	12.0	1,805	85.3	57	2.7
PART-TIME	0	.0	82	16.6	5	1.0	11	2.2	98	19.9	392	79.5	3	.6
FEMALE	0	.0	50	17.1	4	1.4	10	3.4	64	21.9	227	77.7	1	.3
MALE	0	.0	32	15.9	1	.5	1	.5	34	16.9	165	82.1	2	1.0
TOTAL	7	.2	645	16.1	18	.5	78	2.0	748	18.7	3,162	79.1	86	2.2
FEMALE	3	.2	416	24.8	6	.4	35	2.1	460	27.4	1,192	71.0	27	1.6
MALE	4	.2	229	9.9	12	.5	43	1.9	288	12.4	1,970	85.0	59	2.5
GRADUATE														
FULL-TIME	1	.2	16	3.2	10	2.0	8	1.6	35	7.1	411	83.4	47	9.5
FEMALE	1	.7	9	5.9	2	1.3	4	2.6	16	10.5	125	81.7	12	7.8
MALE	0	.0	7	2.1	8	2.4	4	1.2	19	5.6	286	84.1	35	10.3
PART-TIME	0	.0	15	7.8	2	1.0	3	1.6	20	10.4	165	85.9	7	3.6
FEMALE	0	.0	10	13.2	1	1.3	2	2.6	13	17.1	61	80.3	2	2.6
MALE	0	.0	5	4.3	1	.9	1	.9	7	6.0	104	89.7	5	4.3
TOTAL	1	.1	31	4.5	12	1.8	11	1.6	55	8.0	576	84.1	54	7.9
FEMALE	1	.4	19	8.3	3	1.3	6	2.6	29	12.7	186	81.2	14	6.1
MALE	0	.0	12	2.6	9	2.0	5	1.1	26	5.7	390	85.5	40	8.8
PROFESSIONAL:														
FULL-TIME	0	.0	0	.0	0	.0	0	.0	0	.0	0	.0	0	.0
FEMALE	0	.0	0	.0	0	.0	0	.0	0	.0	0	.0	0	.0
MALE	0	.0	0	.0	0	.0	0	.0	0	.0	0	.0	0	.0
PART-TIME	0	.0	0	.0	0	.0	0	.0	0	.0	0	.0	0	.0
FEMALE	0	.0	0	.0	0	.0	0	.0	0	.0	0	.0	0	.0
MALE	0	.0	0	.0	0	.0	0	.0	0	.0	0	.0	0	.0
TOTAL	0	.0	0	.0	0	.0	0	.0	0	.0	0	.0	0	.0
FEMALE	0	.0	0	.0	0	.0	0	.0	0	.0	0	.0	0	.0
MALE	0	.0	0	.0	0	.0	0	.0	0	.0	0	.0	0	.0
UND+GRAD+PROF:														
FULL-TIME	8	.2	579	14.5	23	.6	75	1.9	685	17.1	3,181	79.6	130	3.3
FEMALE	4	.3	375	24.4	4	.3	29	1.9	412	26.8	1,090	70.8	38	2.5
MALE	4	.2	204	8.3	19	.8	46	1.9	273	11.1	2,091	85.1	92	3.7
PART-TIME	0	.0	97	14.2	7	1.0	14	2.0	118	17.2	557	81.3	10	1.5
FEMALE	0	.0	60	16.3	5	1.4	12	3.3	77	20.9	288	78.3	3	.8
MALE	0	.0	37	11.7	2	.6	2	.6	41	12.9	269	84.9	7	2.2
TOTAL	8	.2	676	14.4	30	.6	89	1.9	803	17.2	3,738	79.9	140	3.0
FEMALE	4	.2	435	22.8	9	.5	41	2.1	489	25.6	1,378	72.2	41	2.1
MALE	4	.1	241	8.7	21	.8	48	1.7	314	11.3	2,360	85.1	99	3.6
UNCLASSIFIED:														
TOTAL	0	.0	10	10.9	0	.0	0	.0	10	10.9	80	87.0	2	2.2
FEMALE	0	.0	3	6.8	0	.0	0	.0	3	6.8	41	93.2	0	.0
MALE	0	.0	7	14.6	0	.0	0	.0	7	14.6	39	81.3	2	4.2
TOTAL ENROLLMENT:														
TOTAL	8	.2	686	14.4	30	.6	89	1.9	813	17.0	3,818	80.0	142	3.0
FEMALE	4	.2	438	22.4	9	.5	41	2.1	492	25.2	1,419	72.7	41	2.1
MALE	4	.1	248	8.8	21	.7	48	1.7	321	11.4	2,399	85.0	101	3.6
MAINE (12 INSTITUTIONS)														
UNDERGRADUATES:														
FULL-TIME	1	.1	14	.9	12	.8	2	.1	29	1.9	1,480	97.2	14	.9
FEMALE	1	.2	7	1.1	1	.2	1	.2	10	1.6	615	97.3	7	1.1
MALE	0	.0	7	.8	11	1.2	1	.1	19	2.1	865	97.1	7	.8
PART-TIME	0	.0	0	.0	0	.0	0	.0	0	.0	75	100.0	0	.0
FEMALE	0	.0	0	.0	0	.0	0	.0	0	.0	32	100.0	0	.0
MALE	0	.0	0	.0	0	.0	0	.0	0	.0	43	100.0	0	.0
TOTAL	1	.1	14	.9	12	.8	2	.1	29	1.8	1,555	97.3	14	.9
FEMALE	1	.2	7	1.1	1	.2	1	.2	10	1.5	647	97.4	7	1.1
MALE	0	.0	7	.7	11	1.2	1	.1	19	2.0	908	97.2	7	.7
GRADUATE:														
FULL-TIME	0	.0	0	.0	0	.0	0	.0	0	.0	63	100.0	0	.0
FEMALE	0	.0	0	.0	0	.0	0	.0	0	.0	14	100.0	0	.0
MALE	0	.0	0	.0	0	.0	0	.0	0	.0	49	100.0	0	.0
PART-TIME	0	.0	1	5.9	0	.0	0	.0	1	5.9	15	88.2	1	5.9
FEMALE	0	.0	0	.0	0	.0	0	.0	0	.0	3	100.0	0	.0
MALE	0	.0	1	7.1	0	.0	0	.0	1	7.1	12	85.7	1	7.1
TOTAL	0	.0	1	1.3	0	.0	0	.0	1	1.3	78	97.5	1	1.3
FEMALE	0	.0	0	.0	0	.0	0	.0	0	.0	17	100.0	0	.0
MALE	0	.0	1	1.6	0	.0	0	.0	1	1.6	61	96.8	1	1.6
PROFESSIONAL:														
FULL-TIME	0	.0	0	.0	0	.0	0	.0	0	.0	0	.0	0	.0
FEMALE	0	.0	0	.0	0	.0	0	.0	0	.0	0	.0	0	.0
MALE	0	.0	0	.0	0	.0	0	.0	0	.0	0	.0	0	.0

BIOLOGICAL SCIENCES

INDIAN NATIVE	BLACK NON-HISPANIC		ASIAN OR PACIFIC ISLANDER		HISPANIC		TOTAL MINORITY		WHITE NON-HISPANIC		NON-RESIDENT ALIEN		TOTAL
%	NUMBER	%	NUMBER	%	NUMBER	%	NUMBER	%	NUMBER	%	NUMBER	%	NUMBER
CONTINUED													
.0	0	.0	0	.0	0	.0	0	.0	0	.0	0	.0	0
.0	0	.0	0	.0	0	.0	0	.0	0	.0	0	.0	0
.0	0	.0	0	.0	0	.0	0	.0	0	.0	0	.0	0
.0	0	.0	0	.0	0	.0	0	.0	0	.0	0	.0	0
.0	0	.0	0	.0	0	.0	0	.0	0	.0	0	.0	0
.0	0	.0	0	.0	0	.0	0	.0	0	.0	0	.0	0
.1	14	.9	12	.8	2	.1	29	1.8	1,543	97.3	14	.9	1,586
.2	7	1.1	1	.2	1	.2	10	1.5	629	97.4	7	1.1	646
.0	7	.7	11	1.2	1	.1	19	2.0	914	97.2	7	.7	940
.0	1	1.1	0	.0	0	.0	1	1.1	90	97.8	1	1.1	92
.0	0	.0	0	.0	0	.0	0	.0	35	100.0	0	.0	35
.0	1	1.8	0	.0	0	.0	1	1.8	55	96.5	1	1.8	57
.1	15	.9	12	.7	2	.1	30	1.8	1,633	97.3	15	.9	1,678
.1	7	1.0	1	.1	1	.1	10	1.5	664	97.5	7	1.0	681
.0	8	.8	11	1.1	1	.1	20	2.0	969	97.2	8	.8	997
.0	0	.0	0	.0	0	.0	0	.0	14	100.0	0	.0	14
.0	0	.0	0	.0	0	.0	0	.0	7	100.0	0	.0	7
.0	0	.0	0	.0	0	.0	0	.0	7	100.0	0	.0	7
.1	15	.9	12	.7	2	.1	30	1.8	1,647	97.3	15	.9	1,692
.1	7	1.0	1	.1	1	.1	10	1.5	671	97.5	7	1.0	688
.0	8	.8	11	1.1	1	.1	20	2.0	976	97.2	8	.8	1,004
(20 INSTITUTIONS)													
.3	475	12.3	101	2.6	48	1.2	635	16.5	3,014	78.2	206	5.3	3,855
.2	267	16.6	43	2.7	18	1.1	331	20.5	1,204	74.7	77	4.8	1,612
.4	208	9.3	58	2.6	30	1.3	304	13.6	1,810	80.7	129	5.8	2,243
1.2	50	12.1	10	2.4	7	1.7	72	17.4	317	76.8	24	5.8	413
.5	26	13.5	4	2.1	2	1.0	33	17.1	147	76.2	13	6.7	193
1.8	24	10.9	6	2.7	5	2.3	39	17.7	170	77.3	11	5.0	220
.4	525	12.3	111	2.6	55	1.3	707	16.6	3,331	78.0	230	5.4	4,268
.2	293	16.2	47	2.6	20	1.1	364	20.2	1,351	74.8	90	5.0	1,805
.5	232	9.4	64	2.6	35	1.4	343	13.9	1,980	80.4	140	5.7	2,463
.0	8	1.8	9	2.1	5	1.1	22	5.1	393	90.3	20	4.6	435
.0	4	2.4	4	2.4	1	.6	9	5.3	151	88.8	10	5.9	170
.0	4	1.5	5	1.9	4	1.5	13	4.9	242	91.3	10	3.8	265
.0	10	3.2	5	1.6	3	1.0	18	5.8	271	87.1	22	7.1	311
.0	6	4.3	2	1.4	1	.7	9	6.4	119	84.4	13	9.2	141
.0	4	2.4	3	1.8	2	1.2	9	5.3	152	89.4	9	5.3	170
.0	18	2.4	14	1.9	8	1.1	40	5.4	664	89.0	42	5.6	746
.0	10	3.2	6	1.9	2	.6	18	5.8	270	86.8	23	7.4	311
.0	8	1.8	8	1.8	6	1.4	22	5.1	394	90.6	19	4.4	435
.0	0	.0	0	.0	0	.0	0	.0	0	.0	0	.0	0
.0	0	.0	0	.0	0	.0	0	.0	0	.0	0	.0	0
.0	0	.0	0	.0	0	.0	0	.0	0	.0	0	.0	0
.0	0	.0	0	.0	0	.0	0	.0	0	.0	0	.0	0
.0	0	.0	0	.0	0	.0	0	.0	0	.0	0	.0	0
.0	0	.0	0	.0	0	.0	0	.0	0	.0	0	.0	0
.3	483	11.3	110	2.6	53	1.2	657	15.3	3,407	79.4	226	9.3	4,290
.2	271	15.2	47	2.6	19	1.1	340	19.1	1,355	76.0	87	4.9	1,782
.3	212	8.5	63	2.5	34	1.4	317	12.6	2,052	81.8	139	5.5	2,508
.7	60	8.3	15	2.1	10	1.4	90	12.4	588	81.2	46	6.4	724
.3	32	9.6	6	1.8	3	.9	42	12.6	266	79.6	26	7.8	334
1.0	28	7.2	9	2.3	7	1.8	48	12.3	322	82.6	20	5.1	390
.3	543	10.8	125	2.5	63	1.3	747	14.9	3,995	79.7	272	5.4	5,014
.2	303	14.3	53	2.5	22	1.0	382	18.1	1,621	76.6	113	5.3	2,116
.4	240	8.3	72	2.5	41	1.4	365	12.6	2,374	81.9	159	5.5	2,898
.0	25	13.0	4	2.1	5	2.6	34	17.6	146	75.6	13	6.7	193
.0	14	16.9	2	2.4	1	1.2	17	20.5	60	72.3	6	7.2	83
.0	11	10.0	2	1.8	4	3.6	17	15.5	86	78.2	7	6.4	110
.3	568	10.9	129	2.5	68	1.3	781	15.0	4,141	79.5	285	5.5	5,207
.2	317	14.4	55	2.5	23	1.0	399	18.1	1,681	76.4	119	5.4	2,199
.4	251	8.3	74	2.5	45	1.5	382	12.7	2,460	81.8	166	5.5	3,008

MAJOR FIELD 0400 - BIOLOGICAL SCIENCES

	AMERICAN INDIAN ALASKAN NATIVE		BLACK NON-HISPANIC		ASIAN OR PACIFIC ISLANDER		HISPANIC		TOTAL MINORITY		WHITE NON-HISPANIC		NON-RESIDENT ALIEN	
	NUMBER	%	NUMBER	%	NUMBER	%	NUMBER	%	NUMBER	%	NUMBER	%	NUMBER	%
MASSACHUSETTS (49 INSTITUTIONS)														
UNDERGRADUATES:														
FULL-TIME	18	.2	321	3.6	193	2.1	112	1.2	644	7.2	8,156	90.7	188	2.1
FEMALE	9	.2	175	4.1	89	2.1	46	1.1	319	7.5	3,844	90.5	83	2.0
MALE	9	.2	146	3.1	104	2.2	66	1.4	325	6.9	4,312	90.9	105	2.2
PART-TIME	0	.0	8	3.2	1	.4	4	1.6	13	5.2	234	93.6	3	1.2
FEMALE	0	.0	4	3.0	0	.0	1	.7	5	3.7	128	94.8	2	1.5
MALE	0	.0	4	3.5	1	.9	3	2.6	8	7.0	106	92.2	1	.9
TOTAL	18	.2	329	3.6	194	2.1	116	1.3	657	7.1	8,390	90.8	191	2.1
FEMALE	9	.2	179	4.1	89	2.0	47	1.1	324	7.4	3,972	90.7	85	1.9
MALE	9	.2	150	3.1	105	2.2	69	1.4	333	6.9	4,418	91.0	106	2.2
GRADUATE:														
FULL-TIME	0	.0	12	1.1	27	2.4	10	.9	49	4.3	919	81.3	163	14.4
FEMALE	0	.0	4	1.0	11	2.7	4	1.0	19	4.7	339	83.1	50	12.3
MALE	0	.0	8	1.1	16	2.2	6	.8	30	4.1	580	80.2	113	15.6
PART-TIME	0	.0	6	1.5	1	.3	1	.3	8	2.0	366	92.9	20	5.1
FEMALE	0	.0	2	1.0	0	.0	0	.0	2	1.0	192	95.5	7	3.5
MALE	0	.0	4	2.1	1	.5	1	.5	6	3.1	174	90.2	13	6.7
TOTAL	0	.0	18	1.2	28	1.8	11	.7	57	3.7	1,285	84.3	183	12.0
FEMALE	0	.0	6	1.0	11	1.8	4	.7	21	3.4	531	87.2	57	9.4
MALE	0	.0	12	1.3	17	1.9	7	.8	36	3.9	754	82.3	126	13.8
PROFESSIONAL:														
FULL-TIME	0	.0	0	.0	1	16.7	0	.0	1	16.7	5	83.3	0	.0
FEMALE	0	.0	0	.0	0	.0	0	.0	0	.0	1	100.0	0	.0
MALE	0	.0	0	.0	1	20.0	0	.0	1	20.0	4	80.0	0	.0
PART-TIME	0	.0	0	.0	0	.0	0	.0	0	.0	0	.0	0	.0
FEMALE	0	.0	0	.0	0	.0	0	.0	0	.0	0	.0	0	.0
MALE	0	.0	0	.0	0	.0	0	.0	0	.0	0	.0	0	.0
TOTAL	0	.0	0	.0	1	16.7	0	.0	1	16.7	5	83.3	0	.0
FEMALE	0	.0	0	.0	0	.0	0	.0	0	.0	1	100.0	0	.0
MALE	0	.0	0	.0	1	20.0	0	.0	1	20.0	4	80.0	0	.0
UNG+GRAD+PROF:														
FULL-TIME	18	.2	333	3.3	221	2.2	122	1.2	694	6.9	9,080	89.7	351	3.5
FEMALE	9	.2	179	3.8	100	2.1	50	1.1	338	7.3	4,184	89.9	133	2.9
MALE	9	.2	154	2.8	121	2.2	72	1.3	356	6.5	4,896	89.5	218	4.0
PART-TIME	0	.0	14	2.2	2	.3	5	.8	21	3.3	600	93.2	23	3.6
FEMALE	0	.0	6	1.8	0	.0	1	.3	7	2.1	320	95.2	9	2.7
MALE	0	.0	8	2.6	2	.6	4	1.3	14	4.5	280	90.9	14	4.5
TOTAL	18	.2	347	3.2	223	2.1	127	1.2	715	6.6	9,680	89.9	374	3.5
FEMALE	9	.2	185	3.7	100	2.0	51	1.0	345	6.9	4,504	90.2	142	2.8
MALE	9	.2	162	2.8	123	2.1	76	1.3	370	6.4	5,176	89.6	232	4.0
UNCLASSIFIED:														
TOTAL	0	.0	3	1.9	2	1.3	5	3.2	10	6.3	136	86.1	12	7.6
FEMALE	0	.0	3	3.5	1	1.2	2	2.3	6	7.0	75	87.2	5	5.8
MALE	0	.0	0	.0	1	1.4	3	4.2	4	5.6	61	84.7	7	9.7
TOTAL ENROLLMENT:														
TOTAL	18	.2	350	3.2	225	2.1	132	1.2	725	6.6	9,816	89.8	386	3.5
FEMALE	9	.2	188	3.7	101	2.0	53	1.0	351	6.9	4,579	90.2	147	2.9
MALE	9	.2	162	2.8	124	2.1	79	1.4	374	6.4	5,237	89.5	239	4.1
MICHIGAN (43 INSTITUTIONS)														
UNDERGRADUATES:														
FULL-TIME	29	.4	358	5.3	84	1.3	65	1.0	536	8.0	6,047	90.1	130	1.9
FEMALE	11	.4	207	7.5	33	1.2	32	1.2	283	10.3	2,429	88.1	44	1.6
MALE	18	.5	151	3.8	51	1.3	33	.8	253	6.4	3,618	91.4	86	2.2
PART-TIME	4	.3	73	5.9	10	.8	10	.8	97	7.8	1,125	90.9	15	1.2
FEMALE	3	.6	38	7.3	4	.8	3	.6	48	9.2	470	90.0	4	.8
MALE	1	.1	35	4.9	6	.8	7	1.0	49	6.9	655	91.6	11	1.5
TOTAL	33	.4	431	5.4	94	1.2	75	.9	633	8.0	7,172	90.2	145	1.8
FEMALE	14	.4	245	7.5	37	1.1	35	1.1	331	10.1	2,899	88.4	48	1.5
MALE	19	.4	186	4.0	57	1.2	40	.9	302	6.5	4,273	91.5	97	2.1
GRADUATE:														
FULL-TIME	2	.2	18	1.7	12	1.1	7	.6	39	3.6	959	88.1	91	8.4
FEMALE	1	.3	10	3.1	3	.9	5	1.5	19	5.9	280	86.4	25	7.7
MALE	1	.1	8	1.0	9	1.2	2	.3	20	2.6	679	88.8	66	8.6
PART-TIME	2	.4	10	1.9	7	1.3	3	.6	22	4.1	477	89.7	33	6.2
FEMALE	0	.0	5	2.7	4	2.2	2	1.1	11	6.0	156	84.8	17	9.2
MALE	2	.6	5	1.4	3	.9	1	.3	11	3.2	321	92.2	16	4.6
TOTAL	4	.2	28	1.7	19	1.2	10	.6	61	3.8	1,436	88.6	124	7.6
FEMALE	1	.2	15	3.0	7	1.4	7	1.4	30	5.9	436	85.8	42	8.3
MALE	3	.3	13	1.2	12	1.1	3	.3	31	2.8	1,000	89.6	82	7.4
PROFESSIONAL:														
FULL-TIME	0	.0	0	.0	0	.0	0	.0	0	.0	0	.0	0	.0
FEMALE	0	.0	0	.0	0	.0	0	.0	0	.0	0	.0	0	.0
MALE	0	.0	0	.0	0	.0	0	.0	0	.0	0	.0	0	.0

IOLOGICAL SCIENCES

INDIAN ATIVE	BLACK NON-HISPANIC		ASIAN OR PACIFIC ISLANDER		HISPANIC		TOTAL MINORITY		WHITE NON-HISPANIC		NON-RESIDENT ALIEN		TOTAL
%	NUMBER	%	NUMBER	%	NUMBER	%	NUMBER	%	NUMBER	%	NUMBER	%	NUMBER
CONTINUED													
.0	0	.0	0	.0	0	.0	0	.0	0	.0	0	.0	0
.0	0	.0	0	.0	0	.0	0	.0	0	.0	0	.0	0
.0	0	.0	0	.0	0	.0	0	.0	0	.0	0	.0	0
.0	0	.0	0	.0	0	.0	0	.0	0	.0	0	.0	0
.0	0	.0	0	.0	0	.0	0	.0	0	.0	0	.0	0
.4	376	4.8	96	1.2	72	.9	575	7.4	7,006	89.8	221	2.8	7,802
.4	217	7.0	36	1.2	37	1.2	302	9.8	2,709	88.0	69	2.2	3,080
.4	159	3.4	60	1.3	35	.7	273	5.8	4,297	91.0	152	3.2	4,722
.3	83	4.7	17	1.0	13	.7	119	6.7	1,602	90.6	48	2.7	1,769
.4	43	6.1	8	1.1	5	.7	59	8.4	626	88.7	21	3.0	706
.3	40	3.8	9	.8	8	.8	60	5.6	976	91.8	27	2.5	1,063
.4	459	4.8	113	1.2	85	.9	694	7.3	8,608	89.9	269	2.8	9,571
.4	260	6.9	44	1.2	42	1.1	361	9.5	3,335	88.1	90	2.4	3,786
.4	199	3.4	69	1.2	43	.7	333	5.8	5,273	91.1	179	3.1	5,785
.0	12	10.5	1	.9	0	.0	13	11.4	100	87.7	1	.9	114
.0	10	15.2	0	.0	0	.0	10	15.2	56	84.8	0	.0	66
.0	2	4.2	1	2.1	0	.0	3	6.3	44	91.7	1	2.1	48
.4	471	4.9	114	1.2	85	.9	707	7.3	8,708	89.9	270	2.8	9,685
.4	270	7.0	44	1.1	42	1.1	371	9.6	3,391	88.0	90	2.3	3,852
.4	201	3.4	70	1.2	43	.7	336	5.8	5,317	91.2	180	3.1	5,833
(45 INSTITUTIONS)													
.4	29	.6	41	.9	17	.4	104	2.2	4,627	96.4	68	1.4	4,799
.3	16	.8	22	1.1	7	.3	52	2.5	2,015	96.4	24	1.1	2,091
.4	13	.5	19	.7	10	.4	52	1.9	2,612	96.5	44	1.6	2,708
.3	2	.6	3	.9	2	.6	8	2.3	344	97.7	0	.0	352
.0	1	.7	2	1.3	1	.7	4	2.7	146	97.3	0	.0	150
.5	1	.5	1	.5	1	.5	4	2.0	198	98.0	0	.0	202
.3	31	.6	44	.9	19	.4	112	2.2	4,971	96.5	68	1.3	5,151
.3	17	.8	24	1.1	8	.4	56	2.5	2,161	96.4	24	1.1	2,241
.4	14	.5	20	.7	11	.4	56	1.9	2,810	96.6	44	1.5	2,910
.0	1	.1	15	1.8	3	.4	19	2.3	743	88.0	82	9.7	844
.0	0	.0	3	1.0	1	.3	4	1.3	279	90.0	27	8.7	310
.0	1	.2	12	2.2	2	.4	15	2.8	464	86.9	55	10.3	534
.0	0	.0	0	.0	0	.0	0	.0	37	94.9	2	5.1	39
.0	0	.0	0	.0	0	.0	0	.0	11	91.7	1	8.3	12
.0	0	.0	0	.0	0	.0	0	.0	26	96.3	1	3.7	27
.0	1	.1	15	1.7	3	.3	19	2.2	780	88.3	84	9.5	883
.0	0	.0	3	.9	1	1.2	4	1.2	290	90.1	28	8.7	322
.0	1	.2	12	2.1	2	.4	15	2.7	490	87.3	56	10.0	561
.0	0	.0	0	.0	0	.0	0	.0	0	.0	0	.0	0
.0	0	.0	0	.0	0	.0	0	.0	0	.0	0	.0	0
.0	0	.0	0	.0	0	.0	0	.0	0	.0	0	.0	0
.0	0	.0	0	.0	0	.0	0	.0	0	.0	0	.0	0
.0	0	.0	0	.0	0	.0	0	.0	0	.0	0	.0	0
.0	0	.0	0	.0	0	.0	0	.0	0	.0	0	.0	0
.0	0	.0	0	.0	0	.0	0	.0	0	.0	0	.0	0
.0	0	.0	0	.0	0	.0	0	.0	0	.0	0	.0	0
.0	0	.0	0	.0	0	.0	0	.0	0	.0	0	.0	0
.3	30	.5	56	1.0	20	.4	123	2.2	5,370	95.2	150	2.7	5,643
.3	16	.7	25	1.0	8	.3	56	2.3	2,294	95.5	51	2.1	2,401
.3	14	.4	31	1.0	12	.4	67	2.1	3,076	94.9	99	3.1	3,242
.3	2	.5	3	.8	2	.5	8	2.0	381	97.4	2	.5	391
.0	1	.6	2	1.2	1	.6	4	2.5	157	96.9	1	.6	162
.4	1	.4	1	.4	1	.4	4	1.7	224	97.8	1	.4	229
.3	32	.5	59	1.0	22	.4	131	2.2	5,751	95.3	152	2.5	6,034
.3	17	.7	27	1.1	9	.4	60	2.3	2,451	95.6	52	2.0	2,563
.3	15	.4	32	.9	13	.4	71	2.0	3,300	95.1	100	2.9	3,471
.0	1	.6	4	2.5	1	.6	6	3.7	148	90.8	9	5.5	163
.0	1	1.6	0	.0	0	.0	1	1.6	61	96.8	1	1.6	63
.0	0	.0	4	4.0	1	1.0	5	5.0	87	87.0	8	8.0	100
.3	33	.5	63	1.0	23	.4	137	2.2	5,899	95.2	161	2.6	6,197
.3	18	.7	27	1.0	9	.3	61	2.3	2,512	95.7	53	2.0	2,626
.3	15	.4	36	1.0	14	.4	76	2.1	3,387	94.8	108	3.0	3,571

MAJOR FIELD 0400 - BIOLOGICAL SCIENCES

	AMERICAN INDIAN ALASKAN NATIVE		BLACK NON-HISPANIC		ASIAN OR PACIFIC ISLANDER		HISPANIC		TOTAL MINORITY		WHITE NON-HISPANIC		NON-RESIDENT ALIEN	
	NUMBER	%	NUMBER	%	NUMBER	%	NUMBER	%	NUMBER	%	NUMBER	%	NUMBER	%
MISSISSIPPI (20 INSTITUTIONS)														
UNDERGRADUATES:														
FULL-TIME	4	.2	1,042	41.3	6	.2	4	.2	1,056	41.9	1,451	57.6	13	.5
FEMALE	2	.1	740	48.0	2	.1	0	.0	744	48.2	795	51.5	4	.3
MALE	2	.2	302	30.9	4	.4	4	.4	312	31.9	656	67.1	9	.9
PART-TIME	0	.0	71	28.6	2	.8	1	.4	74	29.8	173	69.8	1	.4
FEMALE	0	.0	51	30.9	0	.0	0	.0	51	30.9	113	68.5	1	.6
MALE	0	.0	20	24.1	2	2.4	1	1.2	23	27.7	60	72.3	0	.0
TOTAL	4	.1	1,113	40.2	8	.3	5	.2	1,130	40.8	1,624	58.7	14	.5
FEMALE	2	.1	791	46.3	2	.1	0	.0	795	46.5	908	53.2	5	.3
MALE	2	.2	322	30.4	6	.6	5	.5	335	31.6	716	67.5	9	.8
GRADUATE:														
FULL-TIME	0	.0	27	12.7	3	1.4	1	.5	31	14.6	167	78.4	15	7.0
FEMALE	0	.0	12	21.1	0	.0	1	1.8	13	22.8	39	68.4	5	8.8
MALE	0	.0	15	9.6	3	1.9	0	.0	18	11.5	128	82.1	10	6.4
PART-TIME	0	.0	30	20.4	1	.7	0	.0	31	21.1	107	72.8	9	6.1
FEMALE	0	.0	17	30.4	1	1.8	0	.0	18	42.1	36	64.3	2	3.6
MALE	0	.0	13	14.3	0	.0	0	.0	13	14.3	71	78.0	7	7.7
TOTAL	0	.0	57	15.8	4	1.1	1	.3	62	17.2	274	76.1	24	6.7
FEMALE	0	.0	29	25.7	1	.9	1	.9	31	27.4	75	66.4	7	6.2
MALE	0	.0	28	11.3	3	1.2	0	.0	31	12.6	199	80.6	17	6.9
PROFESSIONAL:														
FULL-TIME	0	.0	0	.0	0	.0	0	.0	0	.0	0	.0	0	.0
FEMALE	0	.0	0	.0	0	.0	0	.0	0	.0	0	.0	0	.0
MALE	0	.0	0	.0	0	.0	0	.0	0	.0	0	.0	0	.0
PART-TIME	0	.0	0	.0	0	.0	0	.0	0	.0	2	100.0	0	.0
FEMALE	0	.0	0	.0	0	.0	0	.0	0	.0	0	.0	0	.0
MALE	0	.0	0	.0	0	.0	0	.0	0	.0	2	100.0	0	.0
TOTAL	0	.0	0	.0	0	.0	0	.0	0	.0	2	100.0	0	.0
FEMALE	0	.0	0	.0	0	.0	0	.0	0	.0	0	.0	0	.0
MALE	0	.0	0	.0	0	.0	0	.0	0	.0	2	100.0	0	.0
UNG+GRAD+PROF:														
FULL-TIME	4	.1	1,069	39.1	9	.3	5	.2	1,087	39.8	1,618	59.2	28	1.0
FEMALE	2	.1	752	47.0	2	.1	1	.1	757	47.3	834	52.1	9	.6
MALE	2	.2	317	28.0	7	.6	4	.4	330	29.1	784	69.2	19	1.7
PART-TIME	0	.0	101	25.4	3	.8	1	.3	105	26.4	282	71.0	10	2.5
FEMALE	0	.0	68	30.8	1	.5	0	.0	69	31.2	149	67.4	3	1.4
MALE	0	.0	33	18.8	2	1.1	1	.6	36	20.5	133	75.6	7	4.0
TOTAL	4	.1	1,170	37.4	12	.4	6	.2	1,192	38.1	1,900	60.7	38	1.2
FEMALE	2	.1	820	45.0	3	.2	1	.1	826	45.4	983	54.0	12	.7
MALE	2	.2	350	26.7	9	.7	5	.4	366	28.0	917	70.1	26	2.0
UNCLASSIFIED:														
TOTAL	0	.0	3	7.5	0	.0	0	.0	3	7.5	36	90.0	1	2.5
FEMALE	0	.0	3	18.8	0	.0	0	.0	3	18.8	13	81.3	0	.0
MALE	0	.0	0	.0	0	.0	0	.0	0	.0	23	95.8	1	4.2
TOTAL ENROLLMENT:														
TOTAL	4	.1	1,173	37.0	12	.4	6	.2	1,195	37.7	1,936	61.1	39	1.2
FEMALE	2	.1	823	44.8	3	.2	1	.1	829	45.1	996	54.2	12	.7
MALE	2	.2	350	26.3	9	.7	5	.4	366	27.5	940	70.5	27	2.0
MISSOURI (35 INSTITUTIONS)														
UNDERGRADUATES:														
FULL-TIME	11	.4	118	4.3	25	.9	22	.8	176	6.4	2,526	92.0	45	1.6
FEMALE	3	.3	66	5.8	15	1.3	11	1.0	95	8.4	1,023	90.0	19	1.7
MALE	8	.5	52	3.2	10	.6	11	.7	81	5.0	1,503	93.4	26	1.6
PART-TIME	1	.2	34	6.6	6	1.2	2	.4	43	8.4	404	90.4	6	1.2
FEMALE	0	.0	21	7.3	0	.0	1	.3	22	7.7	262	91.3	3	1.0
MALE	1	.4	13	5.8	6	2.7	1	.4	21	9.3	202	89.4	3	1.3
TOTAL	12	.4	152	4.7	31	1.0	24	.7	219	6.7	2,990	91.7	51	1.6
FEMALE	3	.2	87	6.1	15	1.1	12	.8	117	8.2	1,285	90.2	22	1.5
MALE	9	.5	65	3.5	16	.9	12	.7	102	5.6	1,705	92.9	29	1.6
GRADUATE:														
FULL-TIME	0	.0	9	2.7	10	3.0	3	.9	22	6.5	289	85.8	26	7.7
FEMALE	0	.0	2	2.3	3	3.4	1	1.1	6	6.9	71	81.6	10	11.5
MALE	0	.0	7	2.8	7	2.8	2	.8	16	6.4	218	87.2	16	6.4
PART-TIME	0	.0	5	2.1	10	4.2	1	.4	16	6.8	206	86.9	15	6.3
FEMALE	0	.0	1	1.3	6	7.5	0	.0	7	8.8	66	82.5	7	8.8
MALE	0	.0	4	2.5	4	2.5	1	.6	9	5.7	140	89.2	8	5.1
TOTAL	0	.0	14	2.4	20	3.5	4	.7	38	6.6	495	86.2	41	7.1
FEMALE	0	.0	3	1.8	9	5.4	1	.6	13	7.8	137	82.0	17	10.2
MALE	0	.0	11	2.7	11	2.7	3	.7	25	6.1	358	88.0	24	5.9
PROFESSIONAL:														
FULL-TIME	0	.0	1	100.0	0	.0	0	.0	1	100.0	0	.0	0	.0
FEMALE	0	.0	1	100.0	0	.0	0	.0	1	100.0	0	.0	0	.0
MALE	0	.0	0	.0	0	.0	0	.0	0	.0	0	.0	0	.0

BIOLOGICAL SCIENCES

INDIAN NATIVE	BLACK NON-HISPANIC		ASIAN OR PACIFIC ISLANDER		HISPANIC		TOTAL MINORITY		WHITE NON-HISPANIC		NON-RESIDENT ALIEN		TOTAL
%	NUMBER	%	NUMBER	%	NUMBER	%	NUMBER	%	NUMBER	%	NUMBER	%	NUMBER

CONTINUED

.0	0	.0	0	.0	0	.0	0	.0	0	.0	0	.0	0
.0	0	.0	0	.0	0	.0	0	.0	0	.0	0	.0	0
.0	0	.0	0	.0	0	.0	0	.0	0	.0	0	.0	0
.0	1	100.0	0	.0	0	.0	1	100.0	0	.0	0	.0	1
.0	1	100.0	0	.0	0	.0	1	100.0	0	.0	0	.0	1
.0	0	.0	0	.0	0	.0	0	.0	0	.0	0	.0	0
.4	128	4.1	35	1.1	25	.8	199	6.5	2,815	91.2	71	2.3	3,085
.2	69	5.6	18	1.5	12	1.0	102	8.3	1,094	89.3	29	2.4	1,225
.4	59	3.2	17	.9	13	.7	97	5.2	1,721	92.5	42	2.3	1,860
.1	39	5.2	16	2.1	3	.4	59	7.9	670	89.3	21	2.8	750
.0	22	6.0	6	1.6	1	.3	29	7.9	328	89.4	10	2.7	367
.3	17	4.4	10	2.6	2	.5	30	7.8	342	89.3	11	2.9	383
.3	167	4.4	51	1.3	28	.7	258	6.7	2,485	90.9	92	2.4	3,035
.2	91	5.7	24	1.5	13	.8	131	8.2	1,422	89.3	39	2.4	1,592
.4	76	3.4	27	1.2	15	.7	127	5.7	2,063	92.0	53	2.4	2,243
.0	0	.0	1	3.3	1	3.3	2	6.7	28	93.3	0	.0	30
.0	0	.0	1	4.0	1	4.0	2	8.0	23	92.0	0	.0	25
.0	0	.0	0	.0	0	.0	0	.0	5	100.0	0	.0	5
.3	167	4.3	52	1.3	29	.8	260	6.7	3,513	90.9	92	2.4	3,865
.2	91	5.6	25	1.5	14	.9	133	8.2	1,445	89.4	39	2.4	1,617
.4	76	3.4	27	1.2	15	.7	127	5.6	2,068	92.0	53	2.4	2,248

(7 INSTITUTIONS)

.9	1	.1	4	.5	5	.6	18	2.0	859	97.2	7	.8	884
1.2	1	.2	2	.5	2	.5	10	2.3	420	97.2	2	.5	432
.7	0	.0	2	.4	3	.7	8	1.8	439	97.1	5	1.1	452
5.2	1	1.3	1	1.3	1	1.3	7	9.1	69	89.6	1	1.3	77
.0	1	3.7	0	.0	0	.0	1	3.7	26	96.3	0	.0	27
8.0	0	.0	1	2.0	1	2.0	6	12.0	43	86.0	1	2.0	50
1.2	2	.2	5	.5	6	.6	25	2.6	928	96.6	8	.8	961
1.1	2	.4	2	.4	2	.4	11	2.4	446	97.2	2	.4	459
1.4	0	.0	3	.6	4	.8	14	2.8	482	96.0	6	1.2	502
.0	0	.0	0	.0	0	.0	0	.0	43	95.6	2	4.4	45
.0	0	.0	0	.0	0	.0	0	.0	11	84.6	2	15.4	13
.0	0	.0	0	.0	0	.0	0	.0	32	100.0	0	.0	32
.0	0	.0	0	.0	0	.0	0	.0	70	98.6	1	1.4	71
.0	0	.0	0	.0	0	.0	0	.0	25	100.0	0	.0	25
.0	0	.0	0	.0	0	.0	0	.0	45	97.8	1	2.2	46
.0	0	.0	0	.0	0	.0	0	.0	113	97.4	3	2.6	116
.0	0	.0	0	.0	0	.0	0	.0	36	94.7	2	5.3	38
.0	0	.0	0	.0	0	.0	0	.0	77	98.7	1	1.3	78
.0	0	.0	0	.0	0	.0	0	.0	0	.0	0	.0	0
.0	0	.0	0	.0	0	.0	0	.0	0	.0	0	.0	0
.0	0	.0	0	.0	0	.0	0	.0	0	.0	0	.0	0
.0	0	.0	0	.0	0	.0	0	.0	0	.0	0	.0	0
.0	0	.0	0	.0	0	.0	0	.0	0	.0	0	.0	0
.0	0	.0	0	.0	0	.0	0	.0	0	.0	0	.0	0
.0	0	.0	0	.0	0	.0	0	.0	0	.0	0	.0	0
.0	0	.0	0	.0	0	.0	0	.0	0	.0	0	.0	0
.0	0	.0	0	.0	0	.0	0	.0	0	.0	0	.0	0
.9	1	.1	4	.4	5	.5	18	1.9	902	97.1	9	1.0	929
1.1	1	.2	2	.4	2	.4	10	2.2	431	96.9	4	.9	445
.6	0	.0	2	.4	3	.6	8	1.7	471	97.3	5	1.0	484
2.7	1	.7	1	.7	1	.7	7	4.7	139	93.9	2	1.4	148
.0	1	1.9	0	.0	0	.0	1	1.9	51	98.1	0	.0	52
4.2	0	.0	1	1.0	1	1.0	6	6.3	88	91.7	2	2.1	96
1.1	2	.2	5	.5	6	.6	25	2.3	1,041	96.7	11	1.0	1,077
1.0	2	.4	2	.4	2	.4	11	2.2	482	97.0	4	.8	497
1.2	0	.0	3	.5	4	.7	14	2.4	559	96.4	7	1.2	580
.0	0	.0	0	.0	0	.0	0	.0	3	100.0	0	.0	3
.0	0	.0	0	.0	0	.0	0	.0	0	.0	0	.0	0
.0	0	.0	0	.0	0	.0	0	.0	3	100.0	0	.0	3
1.1	2	.2	5	.5	6	.6	25	2.3	1,044	96.7	11	1.0	1,080
1.0	2	.4	2	.4	2	.4	11	2.2	482	97.0	4	.8	497
1.2	0	.0	3	.5	4	.7	14	2.4	562	96.4	7	1.2	583

TABLE 17 - TOTAL ENROLLMENT IN INSTITUTIONS OF HIGHER EDUCATION FOR SELECTED MAJOR FIELDS OF STUDY AND LEVEL OF ENROLLMENT
BY RACE, ETHNICITY, AND SEX: STATE, 1978

MAJOR FIELD 0400 - BIOLOGICAL SCIENCES

	AMERICAN INDIAN ALASKAN NATIVE		BLACK NON-HISPANIC		ASIAN OR PACIFIC ISLANDER		HISPANIC		TOTAL MINORITY		WHITE NON-HISPANIC		NON-RESIDENT ALIEN	
	NUMBER	%	NUMBER	%	NUMBER	%	NUMBER	%	NUMBER	%	NUMBER	%	NUMBER	%
NEBRASKA (20 INSTITUTIONS)														
UNDERGRADUATES:														
FULL-TIME	1	.1	34	2.3	30	2.0	13	.9	78	5.3	1,373	93.0	25	1.7
FEMALE	1	.2	14	2.6	8	1.5	4	.8	27	5.1	503	94.4	3	.6
MALE	0	.0	20	2.1	22	2.3	9	1.0	51	5.4	870	92.3	22	2.3
PART-TIME	2	.8	5	1.9	1	.4	3	1.1	11	4.2	249	95.0	2	.8
FEMALE	0	.0	1	.9	1	.9	1	.9	3	2.8	106	97.2	0	.0
MALE	2	1.3	4	2.6	0	.0	2	1.3	8	5.2	143	93.5	2	1.3
TOTAL	3	.2	39	2.2	31	1.8	16	.9	89	5.1	1,622	93.3	27	1.6
FEMALE	1	.2	15	2.3	9	1.4	5	.8	30	4.7	609	94.9	3	.5
MALE	2	.2	24	2.2	22	2.0	11	1.0	59	5.4	1,013	92.4	24	2.2
GRADUATE:														
FULL-TIME	0	.0	1	.7	4	2.7	1	.7	6	4.1	122	82.4	20	13.5
FEMALE	0	.0	0	.0	1	2.3	1	2.3	2	4.5	37	84.1	5	11.4
MALE	0	.0	1	1.0	3	2.9	0	.0	4	3.8	85	81.7	15	14.4
PART-TIME	0	.0	3	1.6	3	1.6	0	.0	6	3.3	166	90.7	11	6.0
FEMALE	0	.0	0	.0	1	2.1	0	.0	1	2.1	44	93.6	2	4.3
MALE	0	.0	3	2.2	2	1.5	0	.0	5	3.7	122	89.7	9	6.6
TOTAL	0	.0	4	1.2	7	2.1	1	.3	12	3.6	288	87.0	31	9.4
FEMALE	0	.0	0	.0	2	2.2	1	1.1	3	3.3	81	89.0	7	7.7
MALE	0	.0	4	1.7	5	2.1	0	.0	9	3.8	207	86.3	24	10.0
PROFESSIONAL:														
FULL-TIME	0	.0	0	.0	0	.0	0	.0	0	.0	0	.0	0	.0
FEMALE	0	.0	0	.0	0	.0	0	.0	0	.0	0	.0	0	.0
MALE	0	.0	0	.0	0	.0	0	.0	0	.0	0	.0	0	.0
PART-TIME	0	.0	0	.0	0	.0	0	.0	0	.0	0	.0	0	.0
FEMALE	0	.0	0	.0	0	.0	0	.0	0	.0	0	.0	0	.0
MALE	0	.0	0	.0	0	.0	0	.0	0	.0	0	.0	0	.0
TOTAL	0	.0	0	.0	0	.0	0	.0	0	.0	0	.0	0	.0
FEMALE	0	.0	0	.0	0	.0	0	.0	0	.0	0	.0	0	.0
MALE	0	.0	0	.0	0	.0	0	.0	0	.0	0	.0	0	.0
UNG+GRAD+PROF:														
FULL-TIME	1	.1	35	2.2	34	2.1	14	.9	84	5.2	1,495	92.1	45	2.8
FEMALE	1	.2	14	2.4	9	1.6	5	.9	29	5.0	540	93.6	8	1.4
MALE	0	.0	21	2.0	25	2.4	9	.9	55	5.3	955	91.2	37	3.5
PART-TIME	2	.4	8	1.8	4	.9	3	.7	17	3.8	415	93.3	13	2.9
FEMALE	0	.0	1	.6	2	1.3	1	.6	4	2.6	150	96.2	2	1.3
MALE	2	.7	7	2.4	2	.7	2	.7	13	4.5	265	91.7	11	3.8
TOTAL	3	.1	43	2.1	38	1.8	17	.8	101	4.9	1,910	92.3	58	2.8
FEMALE	1	.1	15	2.0	11	1.5	6	.8	33	4.5	690	94.1	10	1.4
MALE	2	.1	28	2.1	27	2.0	11	.8	68	5.1	1,220	91.3	48	3.6
UNCLASSIFIED:														
TOTAL	0	.0	0	.0	0	.0	0	.0	0	.0	5	100.0	0	.0
FEMALE	0	.0	0	.0	0	.0	0	.0	0	.0	1	100.0	0	.0
MALE	0	.0	0	.0	0	.0	0	.0	0	.0	4	100.0	0	.0
TOTAL ENROLLMENT:														
TOTAL	3	.1	43	2.1	38	1.8	17	.8	101	4.9	1,915	92.3	58	2.8
FEMALE	1	.1	15	2.0	11	1.5	6	.8	33	4.5	691	94.1	10	1.4
MALE	2	.1	28	2.1	27	2.0	11	.8	68	5.1	1,224	91.3	48	3.6
NEVADA (2 INSTITUTIONS)														
UNDERGRADUATES:														
FULL-TIME	1	.5	4	1.9	6	2.8	5	2.3	16	7.5	192	90.1	5	2.3
FEMALE	0	.0	2	2.2	5	5.4	1	1.1	8	8.7	79	85.9	5	5.4
MALE	1	.8	2	1.7	1	.8	4	3.3	8	6.6	113	93.4	0	.0
PART-TIME	0	.0	0	.0	0	.0	2	1.9	2	1.9	102	96.2	2	1.9
FEMALE	0	.0	0	.0	0	.0	1	2.2	1	2.2	43	95.6	2	2.2
MALE	0	.0	0	.0	0	.0	1	1.6	1	1.6	59	96.7	1	1.6
TOTAL	1	.3	4	1.3	6	1.9	7	2.2	18	5.6	294	92.2	7	2.2
FEMALE	0	.0	2	1.5	5	3.6	2	1.5	9	6.6	122	89.1	6	4.4
MALE	1	.5	2	1.1	1	.5	5	2.7	9	4.9	172	94.5	1	.5
GRADUATE:														
FULL-TIME	0	.0	0	.0	2	6.7	0	.0	2	6.7	23	76.7	5	16.7
FEMALE	0	.0	0	.0	1	10.0	0	.0	1	10.0	8	80.0	1	10.0
MALE	0	.0	0	.0	1	5.0	0	.0	1	5.0	15	75.0	4	20.0
PART-TIME	0	.0	0	.0	2	4.7	1	2.3	3	7.0	36	83.7	4	9.3
FEMALE	0	.0	0	.0	0	.0	0	.0	0	.0	5	71.4	2	28.6
MALE	0	.0	0	.0	2	5.6	1	2.8	3	8.3	31	86.1	2	5.6
TOTAL	0	.0	0	.0	4	5.5	1	1.4	5	6.8	59	80.8	9	12.3
FEMALE	0	.0	0	.0	1	5.9	0	.0	1	5.9	13	76.5	3	17.6
MALE	0	.0	0	.0	3	5.4	1	1.8	4	7.1	46	82.1	6	10.7
PROFESSIONAL:														
FULL-TIME	0	.0	0	.0	0	.0	0	.0	0	.0	0	.0	0	.0
FEMALE	0	.0	0	.0	0	.0	0	.0	0	.0	0	.0	0	.0
MALE	0	.0	0	.0	0	.0	0	.0	0	.0	0	.0	0	.0

BIOLOGICAL SCIENCES

INDIAN NATIVE	BLACK NON-HISPANIC		ASIAN OR PACIFIC ISLANDER		HISPANIC		TOTAL MINORITY		WHITE NON-HISPANIC		NON-RESIDENT ALIEN		TOTAL
%	NUMBER	%	NUMBER	%	NUMBER	%	NUMBER	%	NUMBER	%	NUMBER	%	NUMBER

CONTINUED

.0	0	.0	0	.0	0	.0	0	.0	0	.0	0	.0	0
.0	0	.0	0	.0	0	.0	0	.0	0	.0	0	.0	0
.0	0	.0	0	.0	0	.0	0	.0	0	.0	0	.0	0
.0	0	.0	0	.0	0	.0	0	.0	0	.0	0	.0	0
.0	0	.0	0	.0	0	.0	0	.0	0	.0	0	.0	0
.0	0	.0	0	.0	0	.0	0	.0	0	.0	0	.0	0
.4	4	1.6	8	3.3	5	2.1	18	7.4	215	88.5	10	4.1	243
.0	2	2.0	6	5.9	1	1.0	9	8.8	87	85.3	6	5.9	102
.7	2	1.4	2	1.4	4	2.8	9	6.4	128	90.8	4	2.8	141
.0	0	.0	2	1.3	3	2.0	5	3.4	138	92.6	6	4.0	149
.0	0	.0	0	.0	1	1.9	1	1.9	48	92.3	3	5.8	52
.0	0	.0	2	2.1	2	2.1	4	4.1	90	92.8	3	3.1	97
.3	4	1.0	10	2.6	8	2.0	23	5.9	353	90.1	16	4.1	392
.0	2	1.3	6	3.9	2	1.3	10	6.5	135	87.7	9	5.8	154
.4	2	.8	4	1.7	6	2.5	13	5.5	218	91.6	7	2.9	238
6.3	0	.0	1	6.3	0	.0	2	12.5	14	87.5	0	.0	16
8.3	0	.0	1	8.3	0	.0	2	16.7	10	83.3	0	.0	12
.0	0	.0	0	.0	0	.0	0	.0	4	100.0	0	.0	4
.5	4	1.0	11	2.7	8	2.0	25	6.1	367	90.0	16	3.9	408
.6	2	1.2	7	4.2	2	1.2	12	7.2	145	87.3	9	5.4	166
.4	2	.8	4	1.7	6	2.5	13	5.4	222	91.7	7	2.9	242

(11 INSTITUTIONS)

.2	15	1.2	4	.3	4	.3	25	2.0	1,184	97.0	12	1.0	1,221
.2	7	1.2	3	.5	3	.5	14	2.4	561	96.7	5	.9	580
.2	8	1.2	1	.2	1	.2	11	1.7	623	97.2	7	1.1	641
.0	0	.0	0	.0	0	.0	0	.0	72	98.6	1	1.4	73
.0	0	.0	0	.0	0	.0	0	.0	42	100.0	0	.0	42
.0	0	.0	0	.0	0	.0	0	.0	30	96.8	1	3.2	31
.2	15	1.2	4	.3	4	.3	25	1.9	1,256	97.1	13	1.0	1,294
.2	7	1.1	3	.5	3	.5	14	2.3	603	96.9	5	.8	622
.1	8	1.2	1	.1	1	.1	11	1.6	653	97.2	8	1.2	672
.0	1	.8	4	3.1	0	.0	5	3.8	125	96.2	0	.0	130
.0	0	.0	2	4.5	0	.0	2	4.5	42	95.5	0	.0	44
.0	1	1.2	2	2.3	0	.0	3	3.5	83	96.5	0	.0	86
.0	0	.0	0	.0	0	.0	0	.0	59	98.3	1	1.7	60
.0	0	.0	0	.0	0	.0	0	.0	31	96.9	1	3.1	32
.0	0	.0	0	.0	0	.0	0	.0	28	100.0	0	.0	28
.0	1	.5	4	2.1	0	.0	5	2.6	184	96.8	1	.5	190
.0	0	.0	2	2.6	0	.0	2	2.6	73	96.1	1	1.3	76
.0	1	.9	2	1.8	0	.0	3	2.6	111	97.4	0	.0	114
.0	0	.0	0	.0	0	.0	0	.0	0	.0	0	.0	0
.0	0	.0	0	.0	0	.0	0	.0	0	.0	0	.0	0
.0	0	.0	0	.0	0	.0	0	.0	0	.0	0	.0	0
.0	0	.0	0	.0	0	.0	0	.0	0	.0	0	.0	0
.0	0	.0	0	.0	0	.0	0	.0	0	.0	0	.0	0
.0	0	.0	0	.0	0	.0	0	.0	0	.0	0	.0	0
.0	0	.0	0	.0	0	.0	0	.0	0	.0	0	.0	0
.0	0	.0	0	.0	0	.0	0	.0	0	.0	0	.0	0
.0	0	.0	0	.0	0	.0	0	.0	0	.0	0	.0	0
.1	16	1.2	8	.6	4	.3	30	2.2	1,309	96.9	12	.9	1,351
.2	7	1.1	5	.8	3	.5	16	2.6	603	96.6	5	.8	624
.1	9	1.2	3	.4	1	.1	14	1.9	706	97.1	7	1.0	727
.0	0	.0	0	.0	0	.0	0	.0	131	98.5	2	1.5	133
.0	0	.0	0	.0	0	.0	0	.0	73	98.6	1	1.4	74
.0	0	.0	0	.0	0	.0	0	.0	58	98.3	1	1.7	59
.1	16	1.1	8	.5	4	.3	30	2.0	1,440	97.0	14	.9	1,484
.1	7	1.0	5	.7	3	.4	16	2.3	676	96.8	6	.9	698
.1	9	1.1	3	.4	1	.1	14	1.8	764	97.2	8	1.0	786
.0	0	.0	0	.0	0	.0	0	.0	0	.0	0	.0	0
.0	0	.0	0	.0	0	.0	0	.0	0	.0	0	.0	0
.0	0	.0	0	.0	0	.0	0	.0	0	.0	0	.0	0
.1	16	1.1	8	.5	4	.3	30	2.0	1,440	97.0	14	.9	1,484
.1	7	1.0	5	.7	3	.4	16	2.3	676	96.8	6	.9	698
.1	9	1.1	3	.4	1	.1	14	1.8	764	97.2	8	1.0	786

TABLE 17 - TOTAL ENROLLMENT IN INSTITUTIONS OF HIGHER EDUCATION FOR SELECTED MAJOR FIELDS OF STUDY AND LEVEL OF ENROLLMENT
          BY RACE, ETHNICITY, AND SEX: STATE, 1978

MAJOR FIELD 0400 - BIOLOGICAL SCIENCES

	AMERICAN INDIAN ALASKAN NATIVE		BLACK NON-HISPANIC		ASIAN OR PACIFIC ISLANDER		HISPANIC		TOTAL MINORITY		WHITE NON-HISPANIC		NON-RESIDENT ALIEN		TO
	NUMBER	%	NUMBER	%	NUMBER	%	NUMBER	%	NUMBER	%	NUMBER	%	NUMBER	%	NU
NEW JERSEY (33 INSTITUTIONS)															
UNDERGRADUATES:															
FULL-TIME	17	.3	398	6.7	81	1.4	212	3.6	708	11.9	5,197	86.8	76	1.3	5
FEMALE	6	.2	236	9.5	38	1.5	100	4.0	380	15.3	2,071	83.4	33	1.3	2
MALE	11	.3	162	4.7	43	1.2	112	3.2	328	9.5	3,086	89.3	43	1.2	3
PART-TIME	2	.2	79	6.8	6	.5	36	3.1	123	10.5	1,036	88.7	9	.8	1
FEMALE	1	.2	48	8.3	5	.9	17	2.9	71	12.2	507	87.4	2	.3	
MALE	1	.2	31	5.3	1	.2	19	3.2	52	8.8	529	90.0	7	1.2	
TOTAL	19	.3	477	6.7	87	1.2	248	3.5	831	11.7	6,193	87.1	85	1.2	7
FEMALE	7	.2	284	9.3	43	1.4	117	3.8	451	14.7	2,578	84.1	35	1.1	3
MALE	12	.3	193	4.8	44	1.1	131	3.2	380	9.4	3,615	89.4	50	1.2	
GRADUATE:															
FULL-TIME	1	.2	11	2.0	18	3.3	5	.9	35	6.4	499	91.7	10	1.8	
FEMALE	1	.5	3	1.4	6	2.8	2	.9	12	5.6	200	93.0	3	1.4	
MALE	0	.0	8	2.4	12	3.6	3	.9	23	7.0	299	90.9	7	2.1	
PART-TIME	0	.0	22	3.2	24	3.5	9	1.3	55	7.9	633	91.1	7	1.0	
FEMALE	0	.0	12	4.0	13	4.4	4	1.3	29	9.7	266	89.3	3	1.0	
MALE	0	.0	10	2.5	11	2.8	5	1.3	26	6.5	367	92.4	4	1.0	
TOTAL	1	.1	33	2.7	42	3.4	14	1.1	90	7.3	1,132	91.4	17	1.4	1
FEMALE	1	.2	15	2.9	19	3.7	6	1.2	41	8.0	466	90.8	6	1.2	
MALE	0	.0	18	2.5	23	3.2	8	1.1	49	6.7	666	91.7	11	1.5	
PROFESSIONAL:															
FULL-TIME	0	.0	0	.0	0	.0	0	.0	0	.0	0	.0	0	.0	
FEMALE	0	.0	0	.0	0	.0	0	.0	0	.0	0	.0	0	.0	
MALE	0	.0	0	.0	0	.0	0	.0	0	.0	0	.0	0	.0	
PART-TIME	0	.0	0	.0	0	.0	0	.0	0	.0	0	.0	0	.0	
FEMALE	0	.0	0	.0	0	.0	0	.0	0	.0	0	.0	0	.0	
MALE	0	.0	0	.0	0	.0	0	.0	0	.0	0	.0	0	.0	
TOTAL	0	.0	0	.0	0	.0	0	.0	0	.0	0	.0	0	.0	
FEMALE	0	.0	0	.0	0	.0	0	.0	0	.0	0	.0	0	.0	
MALE	0	.0	0	.0	0	.0	0	.0	0	.0	0	.0	0	.0	
UND+GRAD+PROF:															
FULL-TIME	18	.3	409	6.3	99	1.5	217	3.3	743	11.5	5,656	87.2	86	1.3	6
FEMALE	7	.2	239	6.9	44	1.6	102	3.8	392	14.5	2,271	84.1	36	1.3	2
MALE	11	.3	170	4.5	55	1.5	115	3.0	351	9.3	3,385	89.4	50	1.3	3
PART-TIME	2	.1	101	5.4	30	1.6	45	2.4	178	9.6	1,669	89.6	16	.9	1
FEMALE	1	.1	60	6.8	18	2.1	21	2.4	100	11.4	773	88.0	5	.6	
MALE	1	.1	41	4.2	12	1.2	24	2.4	78	7.9	896	91.0	11	1.1	
TOTAL	20	.2	510	6.1	129	1.5	262	3.1	921	11.0	7,325	87.7	102	1.2	8
FEMALE	8	.2	299	8.4	62	1.7	123	3.4	492	13.8	3,044	85.1	41	1.1	3
MALE	12	.3	211	4.4	67	1.4	139	2.9	429	9.0	4,281	89.7	61	1.3	4
UNCLASSIFIED:															
TOTAL	0	.0	19	8.2	7	3.0	8	3.4	34	14.6	199	85.4	0	.0	
FEMALE	0	.0	9	10.1	2	2.2	4	4.5	15	16.9	74	83.1	0	.0	
MALE	0	.0	10	6.9	5	3.5	4	2.8	19	13.2	125	86.8	0	.0	
TOTAL ENROLLMENT:															
TOTAL	20	.2	529	6.2	136	1.6	270	3.1	955	11.1	7,524	87.7	102	1.2	8
FEMALE	8	.2	308	8.4	64	1.7	127	3.5	507	13.8	3,118	85.1	41	1.1	3
MALE	12	.2	221	4.5	72	1.5	143	2.9	448	9.1	4,406	89.6	61	1.2	4
NEW MEXICO (15 INSTITUTIONS)															
UNDERGRADUATES:															
FULL-TIME	46	3.1	43	2.9	19	1.3	311	21.1	419	28.4	1,032	70.0	24	1.6	1
FEMALE	28	4.3	15	2.3	8	1.2	132	20.2	183	28.0	467	71.4	4	.6	
MALE	18	2.2	28	3.4	11	1.3	179	21.8	236	28.7	565	68.8	20	2.4	
PART-TIME	10	3.0	7	2.1	2	.6	67	20.0	86	25.7	249	74.3	0	.0	
FEMALE	9	5.4	4	2.4	1	.6	28	16.9	42	25.3	124	74.7	0	.0	
MALE	1	.6	3	1.8	1	.6	39	23.1	44	26.0	125	74.0	0	.0	
TOTAL	56	3.1	50	2.8	21	1.2	378	20.9	505	27.9	1,281	70.8	24	1.3	1
FEMALE	37	4.5	19	2.3	9	1.1	160	19.5	225	27.4	591	72.1	4	.5	
MALE	19	1.9	31	3.1	12	1.2	218	22.0	280	28.3	690	69.7	20	2.0	
GRADUATE:															
FULL-TIME	0	.0	0	.0	2	1.9	8	7.8	10	9.7	78	75.7	15	14.6	
FEMALE	0	.0	0	.0	0	.0	1	4.0	1	4.0	24	96.0	0	.0	
MALE	0	.0	0	.0	2	2.6	7	9.0	9	11.5	54	69.2	15	19.2	
PART-TIME	0	.0	0	.0	0	.0	5	5.3	5	5.3	86	90.5	4	4.2	
FEMALE	0	.0	0	.0	0	.0	1	3.3	1	3.3	28	93.3	1	3.3	
MALE	0	.0	0	.0	0	.0	4	6.2	4	6.2	58	89.2	3	4.6	
TOTAL	0	.0	0	.0	2	1.0	13	6.6	15	7.6	164	82.8	19	9.6	
FEMALE	0	.0	0	.0	0	.0	2	3.6	2	3.6	52	94.5	1	1.8	
MALE	0	.0	0	.0	2	1.4	11	7.7	13	9.1	112	78.3	18	12.6	
PROFESSIONAL:															
FULL-TIME	0	.0	0	.0	0	.0	0	.0	0	.0	0	.0	0	.0	
FEMALE	0	.0	0	.0	0	.0	0	.0	0	.0	0	.0	0	.0	
MALE	0	.0	0	.0	0	.0	0	.0	0	.0	0	.0	0	.0	

BIOLOGICAL SCIENCES

INDIAN NATIVE	BLACK NON-HISPANIC		ASIAN OR PACIFIC ISLANDER		HISPANIC		TOTAL MINORITY		WHITE NON-HISPANIC		NON-RESIDENT ALIEN		TOTAL
%	NUMBER	%	NUMBER	%	NUMBER	%	NUMBER	%	NUMBER	%	NUMBER	%	NUMBER

CONTINUED

%	NUMBER	%	NUMBER	%	NUMBER	%	NUMBER	%	NUMBER	%	NUMBER	%	NUMBER
.0	0	.0	0	.0	0	.0	0	.0	0	.0	0	.0	0
.0	0	.0	0	.0	0	.0	0	.0	0	.0	0	.0	0
.0	0	.0	0	.0	0	.0	0	.0	0	.0	0	.0	0
.0	0	.0	0	.0	0	.0	0	.0	0	.0	0	.0	0
.0	0	.0	0	.0	0	.0	0	.0	0	.0	0	.0	3
.0	0	.0	0	.0	0	.0	0	.0	0	.0	0	.0	0
2.9	43	2.7	21	1.3	319	20.2	429	27.2	1,110	70.3	39	2.5	1,578
4.1	15	2.2	8	1.2	133	19.6	184	27.1	491	72.3	4	.6	679
2.0	28	3.1	13	1.4	186	20.7	245	27.3	619	68.9	35	3.9	894
2.3	7	1.6	2	.5	72	16.7	91	21.2	335	77.9	4	.9	430
4.6	4	2.0	1	.5	29	14.8	43	21.9	152	77.6	1	.5	156
.4	3	1.3	1	.4	43	18.4	48	20.5	183	78.2	3	1.3	234
2.8	50	2.5	23	1.1	391	19.5	520	25.9	1,445	72.0	43	2.1	2,008
4.2	19	2.2	9	1.0	162	18.5	227	25.9	643	73.5	5	.6	875
1.7	31	2.7	14	1.2	229	20.2	293	25.9	802	70.8	38	3.4	1,133
.0	0	.0	0	.0	2	18.2	2	18.2	7	63.6	2	18.2	11
.0	0	.0	0	.0	1	50.0	1	50.0	1	50.0	0	.0	2
.0	0	.0	0	.0	1	11.1	1	11.1	6	66.7	2	22.2	9
2.8	50	2.5	23	1.1	393	19.5	522	25.9	1,452	71.9	45	2.2	2,019
4.2	19	2.2	9	1.0	163	18.6	228	26.0	644	73.4	5	.6	877
1.7	31	2.7	14	1.2	230	20.1	294	25.7	808	70.8	40	3.5	1,142

(107 INSTITUTIONS)

%	NUMBER	%	NUMBER	%	NUMBER	%	NUMBER	%	NUMBER	%	NUMBER	%	NUMBER
.3	1,186	7.1	422	2.5	599	3.6	2,252	13.5	14,010	84.3	360	2.2	16,622
.2	648	8.8	214	2.9	322	4.4	1,202	16.4	5,987	81.6	146	2.0	7,335
.3	538	5.8	208	2.2	277	3.0	1,050	11.3	8,023	86.4	214	2.3	9,287
.7	159	11.7	25	1.8	65	4.8	259	19.1	1,068	78.6	31	2.3	1,358
.7	97	12.9	15	2.0	33	4.4	150	20.0	589	78.4	12	1.6	751
.8	62	10.2	10	1.6	32	5.3	109	18.0	479	78.9	19	3.1	607
.3	1,345	7.5	447	2.5	664	3.7	2,511	14.0	15,078	83.9	391	2.2	17,980
.3	745	9.2	229	2.8	355	4.4	1,352	16.7	6,576	81.3	158	2.0	8,086
.3	600	6.1	218	2.2	309	3.1	1,159	11.7	8,502	85.9	233	2.4	9,894
.3	42	1.6	69	2.6	19	.7	138	5.3	2,263	86.6	212	8.1	2,613
.0	25	2.5	33	3.3	5	.5	63	6.4	855	86.3	73	7.4	991
.5	17	1.0	36	2.2	14	.9	75	4.6	1,408	86.8	139	8.6	1,622
.1	75	4.3	61	3.5	36	2.1	173	10.0	1,482	85.9	71	4.1	1,726
.0	38	5.3	29	4.1	20	2.8	87	12.2	595	83.2	33	4.6	715
.1	37	3.7	32	3.2	16	1.6	86	8.5	887	87.7	38	3.8	1,011
.2	117	2.7	130	3.0	55	1.3	311	7.2	3,745	86.3	283	6.5	4,339
.0	63	3.7	62	3.6	25	1.5	150	8.8	1,450	85.0	106	6.2	1,706
.3	54	2.1	68	2.6	30	1.1	161	6.1	2,295	87.2	177	6.7	2,633
.0	0	.0	0	.0	0	.0	0	.0	0	.0	0	.0	0
.0	0	.0	0	.0	0	.0	0	.0	0	.0	0	.0	0
.0	0	.0	0	.0	0	.0	0	.0	0	.0	0	.0	0
.0	0	.0	0	.0	0	.0	0	.0	0	.0	0	.0	0
.0	0	.0	0	.0	0	.0	0	.0	0	.0	0	.0	0
.0	0	.0	0	.0	0	.0	0	.0	0	.0	0	.0	0
.0	0	.0	0	.0	0	.0	0	.0	0	.0	0	.0	0
.0	0	.0	0	.0	0	.0	0	.0	0	.0	0	.0	0
.0	0	.0	0	.0	0	.0	0	.0	0	.0	0	.0	0
.3	1,228	6.4	491	2.6	618	3.2	2,390	12.4	16,273	84.6	572	3.0	19,235
.2	673	8.1	247	3.0	327	3.9	1,265	15.2	6,842	82.2	219	2.6	8,326
.3	555	5.1	244	2.2	291	2.7	1,125	10.3	9,431	86.5	353	3.2	10,909
.4	234	7.6	86	2.8	101	3.3	432	14.0	2,550	82.7	102	3.3	3,084
.3	135	9.2	44	3.0	53	3.6	237	16.2	1,184	80.8	45	3.1	1,466
.4	99	6.1	42	2.6	48	3.0	195	12.1	1,366	84.4	57	3.5	1,618
.3	1,462	6.6	577	2.6	719	3.2	2,822	12.6	18,823	84.3	674	3.0	22,319
.2	808	8.3	291	3.0	380	3.9	1,502	15.3	8,026	82.0	264	2.7	9,792
.3	654	5.2	286	2.3	339	2.7	1,320	10.5	10,797	86.2	410	3.3	12,527
.5	14	3.8	11	3.0	15	4.1	42	11.5	317	86.8	6	1.6	365
1.1	7	3.8	4	2.2	13	7.0	26	14.0	158	84.9	2	1.1	186
.0	7	3.9	7	3.9	2	1.1	16	8.9	159	88.8	4	2.2	179
.3	1,476	6.5	588	2.6	734	3.2	2,864	12.6	19,140	84.4	680	3.0	22,684
.3	815	8.2	295	3.0	393	3.9	1,528	15.3	8,184	82.0	266	2.7	9,978
.3	661	5.2	293	2.3	341	2.7	1,336	10.5	10,956	86.2	414	3.3	12,706

TABLE 17 - TOTAL ENROLLMENT IN INSTITUTIONS OF HIGHER EDUCATION FOR SELECTED MAJOR FIELDS OF STUDY AND LEVEL OF ENROLLMENT BY RACE, ETHNICITY, AND SEX: STATE, 1978

MAJOR FIELD 0400 - BIOLOGICAL SCIENCES

	AMERICAN INDIAN ALASKAN NATIVE		BLACK NON-HISPANIC		ASIAN OR PACIFIC ISLANDER		HISPANIC		TOTAL MINORITY		WHITE NON-HISPANIC		NON-RESIDENT ALIEN		TOTAL
	NUMBER	%	NUMBER	%	NUMBER	%	NUMBER	%	NUMBER	%	NUMBER	%	NUMBER	%	NUMBER
NORTH CAROLINA (46 INSTITUTIONS)															
UNDERGRADUATES:															
FULL-TIME	46	.8	1,151	19.4	40	.7	29	.5	1,268	21.3	4,600	77.3	79	1.3	5,947
FEMALE	26	.9	641	23.4	18	.7	20	.7	705	25.7	2,015	73.5	21	.8	2,741
MALE	22	.7	510	15.9	22	.7	9	.3	563	17.6	2,585	80.6	58	1.8	3,206
PART-TIME	3	.8	41	11.5	1	.3	1	.3	46	12.8	305	85.2	7	2.0	358
FEMALE	2	1.2	17	10.6	1	.6	1	.6	21	13.0	138	85.7	2	1.2	161
MALE	1	.5	24	12.2	0	.0	0	.0	25	12.7	167	84.8	5	2.5	197
TOTAL	51	.8	1,192	18.9	41	.7	30	.5	1,314	20.8	4,905	77.8	86	1.4	6,305
FEMALE	28	1.0	658	22.7	19	.7	21	.7	726	25.0	2,153	74.2	23	.8	2,902
MALE	23	.7	534	15.7	22	.6	9	.3	588	17.3	2,752	80.9	63	1.9	3,403
GRADUATE:															
FULL-TIME	1	.2	41	6.5	12	1.9	3	.5	57	9.1	536	85.4	35	5.6	628
FEMALE	1	.4	27	10.8	6	2.4	2	.8	36	14.3	201	80.1	14	5.6	251
MALE	0	.0	14	3.7	6	1.6	1	.3	21	5.6	335	88.9	21	5.6	377
PART-TIME	0	.0	31	5.0	9	1.5	5	.8	45	7.3	531	85.9	42	6.8	618
FEMALE	0	.0	16	7.6	4	1.9	2	1.0	22	10.5	182	86.7	6	2.9	210
MALE	0	.0	15	3.7	5	1.2	3	.7	23	5.6	349	85.5	36	8.8	408
TOTAL	1	.1	72	5.8	21	1.7	8	.6	102	8.2	1,067	85.6	77	6.2	1,246
FEMALE	1	.2	43	9.3	10	2.2	4	.9	58	12.6	383	83.1	20	4.3	461
MALE	0	.0	29	3.7	11	1.4	4	.5	44	5.6	684	87.1	57	7.3	785
PROFESSIONAL:															
FULL-TIME	0	.0	0	.0	0	.0	0	.0	0	.0	0	.0	0	.0	0
FEMALE	0	.0	0	.0	0	.0	0	.0	0	.0	0	.0	0	.0	0
MALE	0	.0	0	.0	0	.0	0	.0	0	.0	0	.0	0	.0	0
PART-TIME	0	.0	0	.0	0	.0	0	.0	0	.0	0	.0	0	.0	0
FEMALE	0	.0	0	.0	0	.0	0	.0	0	.0	0	.0	0	.0	0
MALE	0	.0	0	.0	0	.0	0	.0	0	.0	0	.0	0	.0	0
TOTAL	0	.0	0	.0	0	.0	0	.0	0	.0	0	.0	0	.0	0
FEMALE	0	.0	0	.0	0	.0	0	.0	0	.0	0	.0	0	.0	0
MALE	0	.0	0	.0	0	.0	0	.0	0	.0	0	.0	0	.0	0
UND+GRAD+PROF:															
FULL-TIME	49	.7	1,192	18.1	52	.8	32	.5	1,325	20.2	5,136	78.1	114	1.7	6,575
FEMALE	27	.9	668	22.3	24	.8	22	.7	741	24.8	2,216	74.1	35	1.2	2,992
MALE	22	.6	524	14.6	28	.8	10	.3	584	16.3	2,920	81.5	79	2.2	3,583
PART-TIME	3	.3	72	7.4	10	1.0	6	.6	91	9.3	836	85.7	49	5.0	976
FEMALE	2	.5	33	8.9	5	1.3	3	.8	43	11.6	320	86.3	8	2.2	371
MALE	1	.2	39	6.4	5	.8	3	.5	48	7.9	516	85.3	41	6.8	605
TOTAL	52	.7	1,264	16.7	62	.8	38	.5	1,416	18.8	5,972	79.1	163	2.2	7,551
FEMALE	29	.9	701	20.8	29	.9	25	.7	784	23.3	2,536	75.4	43	1.3	3,363
MALE	23	.5	563	13.4	33	.8	13	.3	632	15.1	3,436	82.0	120	2.9	4,188
UNCLASSIFIED:															
TOTAL	0	.0	5	29.4	0	.0	0	.0	5	29.4	11	64.7	1	5.9	17
FEMALE	0	.0	3	42.9	0	.0	0	.0	3	42.9	4	57.1	0	.0	7
MALE	0	.0	2	20.0	0	.0	0	.0	2	20.0	7	70.0	1	10.0	10
TOTAL ENROLLMENT:															
TOTAL	52	.7	1,269	16.8	62	.8	38	.5	1,421	18.8	5,983	79.1	164	2.2	7,568
FEMALE	29	.9	704	20.9	29	.9	25	.7	787	23.4	2,540	75.4	43	1.3	3,370
MALE	23	.5	565	13.5	33	.8	13	.3	634	15.1	3,443	82.0	121	2.9	4,198
NORTH DAKOTA (9 INSTITUTIONS)															
UNDERGRADUATES:															
FULL-TIME	10	1.9	7	1.4	5	1.0	0	.0	22	4.3	491	95.5	1	.2	514
FEMALE	6	3.5	4	2.3	0	.0	0	.0	10	5.8	163	94.2	0	.0	173
MALE	4	1.2	3	.9	5	1.5	0	.0	12	3.5	328	96.2	1	.3	341
PART-TIME	0	.0	0	.0	0	.0	0	.0	0	.0	17	100.0	0	.0	17
FEMALE	0	.0	0	.0	0	.0	0	.0	0	.0	7	100.0	0	.0	7
MALE	0	.0	0	.0	0	.0	0	.0	0	.0	10	100.0	0	.0	10
TOTAL	10	1.9	7	1.3	5	.9	0	.0	22	4.1	508	95.7	1	.2	531
FEMALE	6	3.3	4	2.2	0	.0	0	.0	10	5.6	170	94.4	0	.0	180
MALE	4	1.1	3	.9	5	1.4	0	.0	12	3.4	338	96.3	1	.3	351
GRADUATE:															
FULL-TIME	0	.0	1	1.1	2	2.1	0	.0	3	3.2	81	86.2	10	10.6	94
FEMALE	0	.0	0	.0	1	5.9	0	.0	1	5.9	13	76.5	3	17.6	17
MALE	0	.0	1	1.3	1	1.3	0	.0	2	2.6	68	88.3	7	9.1	77
PART-TIME	0	.0	0	.0	1	1.2	0	.0	1	1.2	77	93.9	4	4.9	82
FEMALE	0	.0	0	.0	0	.0	0	.0	0	.0	18	100.0	0	.0	18
MALE	0	.0	0	.0	1	1.6	0	.0	1	1.6	59	92.2	4	6.3	64
TOTAL	0	.0	1	.6	3	1.7	0	.0	4	2.3	158	89.8	14	8.0	176
FEMALE	0	.0	0	.0	1	2.9	0	.0	1	2.9	31	88.6	3	8.6	35
MALE	0	.0	1	.7	2	1.4	0	.0	3	2.1	127	90.1	11	7.8	141
PROFESSIONAL:															
FULL-TIME	0	.0	0	.0	0	.0	0	.0	0	.0	0	.0	0	.0	0
FEMALE	0	.0	0	.0	0	.0	0	.0	0	.0	0	.0	0	.0	0
MALE	0	.0	0	.0	0	.0	0	.0	0	.0	0	.0	0	.0	0

BIOLOGICAL SCIENCES

INDIAN NATIVE	BLACK NON-HISPANIC		ASIAN OR PACIFIC ISLANDER		HISPANIC		TOTAL MINORITY		WHITE NON-HISPANIC		NON-RESIDENT ALIEN		TOTAL
%	NUMBER	%	NUMBER	%	NUMBER	%	NUMBER	%	NUMBER	%	NUMBER	%	NUMBER

CONTINUED

.0	0	.0	0	.0	0	.0	0	.0	0	.0	0	.0	0
.0	0	.0	0	.0	0	.0	0	.0	0	.0	0	.0	0
.0	0	.0	0	.0	0	.0	0	.0	0	.0	0	.0	0
.0	0	.0	0	.0	0	.0	0	.0	0	.0	0	.0	0
.0	0	.0	0	.0	0	.0	0	.0	0	.0	0	.0	0
.0	0	.0	0	.0	0	.0	0	.0	0	.0	0	.0	0
1.6	8	1.3	7	1.2	0	.0	25	4.1	572	94.1	11	1.8	608
3.2	4	2.1	1	.5	0	.0	11	5.8	176	92.6	3	1.6	190
1.0	4	1.0	6	1.4	0	.0	14	3.3	396	94.7	8	1.9	418
.0	0	.0	1	1.0	0	.0	1	1.0	94	94.9	4	4.0	99
.0	0	.0	0	.0	0	.0	0	.0	25	100.0	0	.0	25
.0	0	.0	1	1.4	0	.0	1	1.4	69	93.2	4	5.4	74
1.4	8	1.1	8	1.1	0	.0	26	3.7	666	94.2	15	2.1	707
2.8	4	1.9	1	.5	0	.0	11	5.1	201	93.5	3	1.4	215
.8	4	.8	7	1.4	0	.0	15	3.0	465	94.5	12	2.4	492
16.7	0	.0	0	.0	0	.0	3	16.7	15	83.3	0	.0	18
20.0	0	.0	0	.0	0	.0	2	20.0	8	80.0	0	.0	10
12.5	0	.0	0	.0	0	.0	1	12.5	7	87.5	0	.0	8
1.8	8	1.1	8	1.1	0	.0	29	4.0	681	93.9	15	2.1	725
3.6	4	1.8	1	.4	0	.0	13	5.8	209	92.9	3	1.3	225
1.0	4	.8	7	1.4	0	.0	16	3.2	472	94.4	12	2.4	500

(71 INSTITUTIONS)

.1	458	6.4	52	.7	32	.4	551	7.7	6,480	90.5	130	1.8	7,161
.2	275	8.7	24	.8	16	.5	320	10.1	2,807	88.4	47	1.5	3,174
.1	183	4.6	28	.7	16	.4	231	5.8	3,673	92.1	83	2.1	3,987
.2	62	5.9	3	.3	7	.7	74	7.1	960	92.0	9	.9	1,043
.2	46	8.1	2	.4	5	.9	54	9.5	510	90.1	2	.4	566
.2	16	3.4	1	.2	2	.4	20	4.2	450	94.3	7	1.5	477
.1	520	6.3	55	.7	39	.5	625	7.6	7,440	90.7	139	1.7	8,204
.2	321	8.6	26	.7	21	.6	374	10.0	3,317	88.7	49	1.3	3,740
.1	199	4.5	29	.6	18	.4	251	5.6	4,123	92.4	90	2.0	4,464
.1	35	2.8	20	1.6	7	.6	63	5.1	1,104	89.2	71	5.7	1,238
.0	21	4.8	7	1.6	4	.9	32	7.3	382	86.6	27	6.1	441
.1	14	1.8	13	1.6	3	.4	31	3.9	722	90.6	44	5.5	797
.2	9	2.2	7	1.7	5	1.2	22	5.3	371	90.0	19	4.6	412
.6	6	3.5	5	2.9	3	1.7	15	8.7	152	87.9	6	3.5	173
.0	3	1.3	2	.8	2	.8	7	2.9	219	91.6	13	5.4	239
.1	44	2.7	27	1.6	12	.7	85	5.2	1,475	89.4	90	5.5	1,650
.2	27	4.4	12	2.0	7	1.1	47	7.7	534	87.0	33	5.4	614
.1	17	1.6	15	1.4	5	.5	38	3.7	941	90.8	57	5.5	1,036
.0	0	.0	0	.0	0	.0	0	.0	0	.0	0	.0	0
.0	0	.0	0	.0	0	.0	0	.0	0	.0	0	.0	0
.0	0	.0	0	.0	0	.0	0	.0	0	.0	0	.0	0
.0	0	.0	0	.0	0	.0	0	.0	0	.0	0	.0	0
.0	0	.0	0	.0	0	.0	0	.0	0	.0	0	.0	0
.0	0	.0	0	.0	0	.0	0	.0	0	.0	0	.0	0
.0	C	.0	0	.0	0	.0	0	.0	0	.0	0	.0	0
.0	0	.0	0	.0	0	.0	0	.0	0	.0	0	.0	0
.0	0	.0	0	.0	0	.0	0	.0	0	.0	0	.0	0
.1	493	5.9	72	.9	39	.5	614	7.3	7,584	90.3	201	2.4	8,399
.1	296	8.2	31	.9	20	.6	352	9.7	3,189	88.2	74	2.0	3,615
.1	197	4.1	41	.9	19	.4	262	5.5	4,395	91.9	127	2.7	4,784
.2	71	4.9	10	.7	12	.8	96	6.6	1,331	91.5	28	1.9	1,455
.3	52	7.0	7	.9	8	1.1	69	9.3	662	89.6	8	1.1	739
.1	19	2.7	3	.4	4	.6	27	3.8	669	93.4	20	2.8	716
.1	564	5.7	82	.8	51	.5	710	7.2	8,915	90.5	229	2.3	9,854
.2	348	8.0	38	.9	28	.6	421	9.7	3,851	88.4	82	1.9	4,354
.1	216	3.9	44	.8	23	.4	289	5.3	5,064	92.1	147	2.7	5,500
.0	12	8.7	2	1.4	0	.0	14	10.1	121	87.7	3	2.2	138
.0	7	10.0	1	1.4	0	.0	8	11.4	61	87.1	1	1.4	70
.0	5	7.4	1	1.5	0	.0	6	8.8	60	88.2	2	2.9	68
.1	576	5.8	84	.8	51	.5	724	7.2	9,036	90.4	232	2.3	9,992
.2	355	8.0	39	.9	28	.6	429	9.7	3,912	88.4	83	1.9	4,424
.1	221	4.0	45	.8	23	.4	295	5.3	5,124	92.0	149	2.7	5,568

385

MAJOR FIELD 0400 - BIOLOGICAL SCIENCES

	AMERICAN INDIAN ALASKAN NATIVE		BLACK NON-HISPANIC		ASIAN OR PACIFIC ISLANDER		HISPANIC		TOTAL MINORITY		WHITE NON-HISPANIC		NON-RESIDENT ALIEN	
	NUMBER	%	NUMBER	%	NUMBER	%	NUMBER	%	NUMBER	%	NUMBER	%	NUMBER	%
OKLAHOMA (35 INSTITUTIONS)														
UNDERGRADUATES:														
FULL-TIME	132	3.5	216	5.8	24	.6	51	1.4	423	11.4	3,171	85.2	130	3.5
FEMALE	71	4.5	124	7.9	11	.7	17	1.1	223	14.1	1,321	83.8	32	2.0
MALE	61	2.8	92	4.3	13	.6	34	1.6	200	9.3	1,850	86.1	98	4.6
PART-TIME	37	4.2	78	8.9	11	1.3	5	.6	131	15.0	732	83.8	11	1.3
FEMALE	25	4.7	54	10.1	3	.6	2	.4	84	15.6	451	84.0	2	.4
MALE	12	3.6	24	7.1	8	2.4	3	.9	47	13.9	281	83.4	9	2.7
TOTAL	169	3.7	294	6.4	35	.8	56	1.2	554	12.0	3,903	84.9	141	3.1
FEMALE	96	4.5	178	8.4	14	.7	19	.9	307	14.5	1,772	83.9	34	1.6
MALE	73	2.9	116	4.7	21	.8	37	1.5	247	9.9	2,131	85.8	107	4.3
GRADUATE:														
FULL-TIME	0	.0	2	.9	5	2.4	0	.0	7	3.3	170	80.6	34	16.1
FEMALE	0	.0	2	3.3	1	1.6	0	.0	3	4.9	48	78.7	10	16.4
MALE	0	.0	0	.0	4	2.7	0	.0	4	2.7	122	81.3	24	16.0
PART-TIME	0	.0	2	1.1	1	.6	0	.0	3	1.7	167	94.4	7	4.0
FEMALE	0	.0	0	.0	0	.0	0	.0	0	.0	53	93.0	4	7.0
MALE	0	.0	2	1.7	1	.8	0	.0	3	2.5	114	95.0	3	2.5
TOTAL	0	.0	4	1.0	6	1.5	0	.0	10	2.6	337	86.9	41	10.6
FEMALE	0	.0	2	1.7	1	.8	0	.0	3	2.5	101	85.6	14	11.9
MALE	0	.0	2	.7	5	1.9	0	.0	7	2.6	236	87.4	27	10.0
PROFESSIONAL:														
FULL-TIME	0	.0	0	.0	0	.0	0	.0	0	.0	0	.0	0	.0
FEMALE	0	.0	0	.0	0	.0	0	.0	0	.0	0	.0	0	.0
MALE	0	.0	0	.0	0	.0	0	.0	0	.0	0	.0	0	.0
PART-TIME	0	.0	0	.0	0	.0	0	.0	0	.0	0	.0	0	.0
FEMALE	0	.0	0	.0	0	.0	0	.0	0	.0	0	.0	0	.0
MALE	0	.0	0	.0	0	.0	0	.0	0	.0	0	.0	0	.0
TOTAL	0	.0	0	.0	0	.0	0	.0	0	.0	0	.0	0	.0
FEMALE	0	.0	0	.0	0	.0	0	.0	0	.0	0	.0	0	.0
MALE	0	.0	0	.0	0	.0	0	.0	0	.0	0	.0	0	.0
UNG+GRAD+PROF:														
FULL-TIME	132	3.4	218	5.5	29	.7	51	1.3	430	10.9	3,341	84.9	164	4.2
FEMALE	71	4.3	126	7.7	12	.7	17	1.0	226	13.8	1,369	83.6	42	2.6
MALE	61	2.7	92	4.0	17	.7	34	1.5	204	8.9	1,972	85.8	122	5.3
PART-TIME	37	3.5	80	7.6	12	1.1	5	.5	134	12.7	899	85.5	18	1.7
FEMALE	25	4.2	54	9.1	3	.5	2	.3	84	14.1	504	84.8	6	1.0
MALE	12	2.6	26	5.7	9	2.0	3	.7	50	10.9	395	86.4	12	2.6
TOTAL	169	3.4	298	6.0	41	.8	56	1.1	564	11.3	4,240	85.0	182	3.7
FEMALE	96	4.3	180	8.1	15	.7	19	.9	310	13.9	1,873	84.0	48	2.2
MALE	73	2.6	118	4.3	26	.9	37	1.3	254	9.2	2,367	85.9	134	4.9
UNCLASSIFIED:														
TOTAL	6	3.7	10	6.2	5	3.1	2	1.2	23	14.2	137	84.6	2	1.2
FEMALE	3	3.5	5	5.9	2	2.4	1	1.2	11	12.9	74	87.1	0	.0
MALE	3	3.9	5	6.5	3	3.9	1	1.3	12	15.6	63	81.8	2	2.6
TOTAL ENROLLMENT:														
TOTAL	175	3.4	308	6.0	46	.9	58	1.1	587	11.4	4,377	85.0	184	3.6
FEMALE	99	4.3	185	8.0	17	.7	20	.9	321	13.9	1,947	84.1	48	2.1
MALE	76	2.7	123	4.3	29	1.0	38	1.3	266	9.4	2,430	85.8	136	4.8
OREGON (23 INSTITUTIONS)														
UNDERGRADUATES:														
FULL-TIME	22	1.0	19	.9	65	3.0	16	.8	122	5.7	1,981	92.9	30	1.4
FEMALE	11	1.2	9	1.0	28	3.0	5	.5	53	5.7	873	93.3	10	1.1
MALE	11	.9	10	.8	37	3.1	11	.9	69	5.8	1,108	92.6	20	1.7
PART-TIME	2	1.2	3	.9	8	2.4	1	.3	14	4.2	316	94.9	3	.9
FEMALE	0	.0	0	.0	5	3.0	1	.6	6	3.6	158	95.8	1	.6
MALE	2	1.2	3	1.8	3	1.8	0	.0	8	4.8	158	94.0	2	1.2
TOTAL	24	1.0	22	.9	73	3.0	17	.7	136	5.5	2,297	93.1	33	1.3
FEMALE	11	1.0	9	.8	33	3.0	6	.5	59	5.4	1,031	93.6	11	1.0
MALE	13	1.0	13	1.0	40	3.1	11	.8	77	5.6	1,266	92.7	22	1.6
GRADUATE:														
FULL-TIME	0	.0	0	.0	7	2.2	3	.9	10	3.1	273	84.3	41	12.7
FEMALE	0	.0	0	.0	4	3.7	2	1.8	6	5.5	89	81.7	14	12.8
MALE	0	.0	0	.0	3	1.4	1	.5	4	1.9	184	85.6	27	12.6
PART-TIME	2	2.7	1	1.4	4	5.4	1	1.4	8	10.8	64	86.5	2	2.7
FEMALE	0	.0	1	3.8	1	3.8	0	.0	2	7.7	24	92.3	0	.0
MALE	2	4.2	0	.0	3	6.3	1	2.1	6	12.5	40	83.3	2	4.2
TOTAL	2	.5	1	.3	11	2.8	4	1.0	18	4.5	337	84.7	43	10.8
FEMALE	0	.0	1	.7	5	3.7	2	1.5	8	5.9	113	83.7	14	10.4
MALE	2	.8	0	.0	6	2.3	2	.8	10	3.8	224	85.2	29	11.0
PROFESSIONAL:														
FULL-TIME	0	.0	0	.0	0	.0	0	.0	0	.0	0	.0	0	.0
FEMALE	0	.0	0	.0	0	.0	0	.0	0	.0	0	.0	0	.0
MALE	0	.0	0	.0	0	.0	0	.0	0	.0	0	.0	0	.0

BIOLOGICAL SCIENCES

N INDIAN NATIVE %	BLACK NON-HISPANIC NUMBER	%	ASIAN OR PACIFIC ISLANDER NUMBER	%	HISPANIC NUMBER	%	TOTAL MINORITY NUMBER	%	WHITE NON-HISPANIC NUMBER	%	NON-RESIDENT ALIEN NUMBER	%	TOTAL NUMBER
CONTINUED													
.0	0	.0	0	.0	0	.0	0	.0	0	.0	0	.0	0
.0	0	.0	0	.0	0	.0	0	.0	0	.0	0	.0	0
.0	0	.0	0	.0	0	.0	0	.0	0	.0	0	.0	0
.0	0	.0	0	.0	0	.0	0	.0	0	.0	0	.0	0
.0	0	.0	0	.0	0	.0	0	.0	0	.0	0	.0	0
.0	0	.0	0	.0	0	.0	0	.0	0	.0	0	.0	0
.9	19	.8	72	2.9	19	.8	132	5.4	2,254	91.7	71	2.9	2,457
1.1	9	.9	32	3.1	7	.7	59	5.6	962	92.1	24	2.3	1,045
.8	10	.7	40	2.8	12	.8	73	5.2	1,292	91.5	47	3.3	1,412
1.0	4	1.0	12	2.9	2	.5	22	5.4	380	93.4	5	1.2	407
.0	1	.5	6	3.1	1	.5	8	4.2	182	95.3	1	.5	191
1.9	3	1.4	6	2.8	1	.5	14	6.5	198	91.7	4	1.9	216
.9	23	.8	84	2.9	21	.7	154	5.4	2,634	92.0	76	2.7	2,864
.9	10	.8	38	3.1	8	.6	67	5.4	1,144	92.6	25	2.0	1,236
.9	13	.8	46	2.8	13	.8	87	5.3	1,490	91.5	51	3.1	1,628
.6	0	.0	6	3.5	0	.0	7	4.1	160	93.0	5	2.9	172
.0	0	.0	2	2.9	0	.0	2	2.9	63	92.6	3	4.4	68
1.0	0	.0	4	3.8	0	.0	5	4.8	97	93.3	2	1.9	104
.9	23	.8	90	3.0	21	.7	161	5.3	2,794	92.0	81	2.7	3,036
.8	10	.8	40	3.1	8	.6	69	5.3	1,207	92.6	28	2.1	1,304
.8	13	.8	50	2.9	13	.8	92	5.3	1,587	91.6	53	3.1	1,732
(124 INSTITUTIONS)													
.1	579	4.3	149	1.1	84	.6	824	6.1	12,518	93.0	115	.9	13,457
.1	348	6.0	62	1.1	48	.8	462	7.9	5,333	91.4	41	.7	5,836
.1	231	3.0	87	1.1	36	.5	362	4.8	7,185	94.3	74	1.0	7,621
.4	76	6.8	8	.7	3	.3	91	8.1	1,018	90.9	11	1.0	1,120
.2	40	6.6	3	.5	0	.0	44	7.3	553	91.9	5	.8	602
.6	36	6.9	5	1.0	3	.6	47	9.1	465	89.8	6	1.2	518
.1	655	4.5	157	1.1	87	.6	915	6.3	13,536	92.9	126	.9	14,577
.1	388	6.0	65	1.0	48	.7	506	7.9	5,886	91.4	46	.7	6,438
.1	267	3.3	92	1.1	39	.5	409	5.0	7,650	94.0	80	1.0	8,139
.1	11	1.2	14	1.5	33	3.6	59	6.4	803	86.7	64	6.9	926
.3	8	2.5	6	1.9	16	5.0	31	9.8	264	83.3	22	6.9	317
.2	3	.5	8	1.3	17	2.8	28	4.6	539	88.5	42	6.9	609
.1	8	1.6	7	1.4	0	.0	16	3.1	485	94.4	13	2.5	514
.5	4	2.0	5	2.5	0	.0	10	5.1	180	91.4	7	3.6	197
.0	4	1.3	2	.6	0	.0	6	1.9	305	96.2	6	1.9	317
.1	19	1.3	21	1.5	33	2.3	75	5.2	1,288	89.4	77	5.3	1,440
.4	12	2.3	11	2.1	16	3.1	41	8.0	444	86.4	29	5.6	514
.0	7	.8	10	1.1	17	1.8	34	3.7	844	91.1	48	5.2	926
.0	0	.0	0	.0	0	.0	0	.0	0	.0	0	.0	0
.0	0	.0	0	.0	0	.0	0	.0	0	.0	0	.0	0
.0	0	.0	0	.0	0	.0	0	.0	0	.0	0	.0	0
.0	0	.0	0	.0	0	.0	0	.0	0	.0	0	.0	0
.0	0	.0	0	.0	0	.0	0	.0	0	.0	0	.0	0
.0	0	.0	0	.0	0	.0	0	.0	0	.0	0	.0	0
.1	590	4.1	163	1.1	117	.8	883	6.1	13,321	92.6	179	1.2	14,383
.1	356	5.8	68	1.1	64	1.0	493	8.0	5,597	91.0	63	1.0	6,153
.1	234	2.8	95	1.2	53	.6	390	4.7	7,724	93.9	116	1.4	8,230
.3	84	5.1	15	.9	3	.2	107	6.5	1,503	92.0	24	1.5	1,634
.3	44	5.5	8	1.0	0	.0	54	6.8	733	91.7	12	1.5	759
.4	40	4.8	7	.8	3	.4	53	6.3	770	92.2	12	1.4	835
.1	674	4.2	178	1.1	120	.7	990	6.2	14,824	92.6	203	1.3	16,017
.1	400	5.8	76	1.1	64	.9	547	7.9	6,330	91.1	75	1.1	6,952
.1	274	3.0	102	1.1	56	.6	443	4.9	8,494	93.7	128	1.4	9,065
.6	9	2.5	13	3.7	1	.3	25	7.1	326	92.4	2	.6	353
.6	3	1.9	6	3.9	1	.6	11	7.1	143	92.9	0	.0	154
.5	6	3.0	7	3.5	0	.0	14	7.0	183	92.0	2	1.0	199
.1	683	4.2	191	1.2	121	.7	1,015	6.2	15,150	92.5	205	1.3	16,370
.1	403	5.7	82	1.2	65	.9	558	7.9	6,473	91.1	75	1.1	7,106
.1	280	3.0	109	1.2	56	.6	457	4.9	8,677	93.7	130	1.4	9,264

MAJOR FIELD 0400 - BIOLOGICAL SCIENCES

	AMERICAN INDIAN ALASKAN NATIVE		BLACK NON-HISPANIC		ASIAN OR PACIFIC ISLANDER		HISPANIC		TOTAL MINORITY		WHITE NON-HISPANIC		NON-RESIDENT ALIEN		TOT
	NUMBER	%	NUMBER	%	NUMBER	%	NUMBER	%	NUMBER	%	NUMBER	%	NUMBER	%	NUM
RHODE ISLAND	(	6 INSTITUTIONS)													
UNDERGRADUATES:															
FULL-TIME	4	.3	76	5.1	35	2.4	11	.7	126	8.5	1,335	90.3	18	1.2	1
FEMALE		.0	35	5.5	18	2.8	4	.6	57	9.0	573	90.2	5	.8	
MALE	4	.5	41	4.9	17	2.0	7	.8	69	8.2	762	90.3	13	1.5	
PART-TIME		.0	0	.0	0	.0	1	1.3	1	1.3	74	97.4	1	1.3	
FEMALE		.0	0	.0	0	.0	0	.0	0	.0	27	100.0	0	.0	
MALE	0	.0	0	.0	0	.0	1	2.0	1	2.0	47	95.9	1	2.0	
TOTAL	4	.3	76	4.9	35	2.3	12	.8	127	8.2	1,409	90.6	19	1.2	1
FEMALE	0	.0	35	5.3	18	2.7	4	.6	57	8.6	600	90.6	5	.8	
MALE	4	.4	41	4.6	17	1.9	8	.9	70	7.8	809	90.6	14	1.6	
GRADUATE:															
FULL-TIME		.0	0	.0	3	2.2		.0	3	2.2	122	91.0	9	6.7	
FEMALE		.0	0	.0	1	1.9		.0	1	1.9	50	94.3	2	3.8	
MALE		.0	0	.0	2	2.5		.0	2	2.5	72	88.9	7	8.6	
PART-TIME		.0	0	.0	1	1.2		.0	1	1.2	83	96.5	2	2.3	
FEMALE		.0	0	.0	1	2.9		.0	1	2.9	32	94.1	1	2.9	
MALE	8	.0	0	.0	0	.0	8	.0	0	.0	51	98.1	1	1.9	
TOTAL		.0	0	.0	4	1.8		.0	4	1.8	205	93.2	11	5.0	
FEMALE		.0	0	.0	2	2.3		.0	2	2.3	82	94.3	3	3.4	
MALE	8	.0	0	.0	2	1.5	8	.0	2	1.5	123	92.5	8	6.0	
PROFESSIONAL:															
FULL-TIME		.0	0	.0	0	.0		.0	0	.0	0	.0	0	.0	
FEMALE		.0	0	.0	0	.0		.0	0	.0	0	.0	0	.0	
MALE		.0	0	.0	0	.0		.0	0	.0	0	.0	0	.0	
PART-TIME		.0	0	.0	0	.0		.0	0	.0	0	.0	0	.0	
FEMALE		.0	0	.0	0	.0		.0	0	.0	0	.0	0	.0	
MALE	0	.0	0	.0	0	.0	8	.0	0	.0	0	.0	0	.0	
TOTAL		.0	0	.0	0	.0		.0	0	.0	0	.0	0	.0	
FEMALE		.0	0	.0	0	.0		.0	0	.0	0	.0	0	.0	
MALE	8	.0	0	.0	0	.0	8	.0	0	.0	0	.0	0	.0	
UND+GRAD+PROF:															
FULL-TIME	4	.2	76	4.7	38	2.4	11	.7	129	8.0	1,457	90.3	27	1.7	1
FEMALE		.0	35	5.1	19	2.8	4	.6	58	8.4	623	90.6	7	1.0	
MALE	4	.4	41	4.4	19	2.1	7	.8	71	7.7	834	90.2	20	2.2	
PART-TIME		.0	0	.0	1	.6	1	.6	2	1.2	157	96.9	3	1.9	
FEMALE	0	.0	0	.0	1	1.6	0	.0	1	1.6	59	96.7	1	1.6	
MALE	0	.0	0	.0	0	.0	1	1.0	1	1.0	98	97.0	2	2.0	
TOTAL		.2	76	4.3	39	2.2	12	.7	131	7.4	1,614	90.9	30	1.7	1
FEMALE		.0	35	4.7	20	2.7	4	.5	59	7.9	682	91.1	8	1.1	
MALE	8	.4	41	4.0	19	1.9	8	.8	72	7.0	932	90.8	22	2.1	1
UNCLASSIFIED:															
TOTAL	0	.0	0	.0	1	20.0	0	.0	1	20.0	4	80.0	0	.0	
FEMALE	0	.0	0	.0	1	33.3	0	.0	1	33.3	2	66.7	0	.0	
MALE	0	.0	0	.0	0	.0	0	.0	0	.0	2	100.0	0	.0	
TOTAL ENROLLMENT:															
TOTAL		.2	76	4.3	40	2.2	12	.7	132	7.4	1,618	90.9	30	1.7	1
FEMALE		.0	35	4.7	21	2.8	4	.5	60	8.0	684	91.0	8	1.1	
MALE	8	.4	41	4.0	19	1.8	8	.8	72	7.0	934	90.9	22	2.1	1
SOUTH CAROLINA	(	33 INSTITUTIONS)													
UNDERGRADUATES:															
FULL-TIME	1	.0	550	18.6	17	.6	12	.4	580	19.6	2,363	79.8	19	.6	2
FEMALE	1	.1	337	27.2	7	.6	4	.3	349	28.2	885	71.4	5	.4	1
MALE	0	.0	213	12.4	10	.6	8	.5	231	13.4	1,478	85.8	14	.8	1
PART-TIME	0	.0	42	15.0	3	1.1	0	.0	45	16.1	234	83.6	1	.4	
FEMALE	0	.0	18	13.0	2	1.4	0	.0	20	14.5	117	84.8	1	.7	
MALE	0	.0	24	16.9	1	.7	0	.0	25	17.6	117	82.4	0	.0	
TOTAL	1	.0	592	18.3	20	.6	12	.4	625	19.3	2,597	80.1	20	.6	3
FEMALE	1	.1	355	25.8	9	.7	4	.3	369	26.8	1,002	72.8	6	.4	1
MALE	0	.0	237	12.7	11	.6	8	.4	256	13.7	1,595	85.5	14	.8	1
GRADUATE:															
FULL-TIME	0	.0	4	2.1	1	.5	0	.0	5	2.6	180	92.3	10	5.1	
FEMALE	0	.0	2	3.3	0	.0	0	.0	2	3.3	53	88.3	5	8.3	
MALE	0	.0	2	1.5	1	.7	0	.0	3	2.2	127	94.1	5	3.7	
PART-TIME	0	.0	5	3.0	1	.6	2	1.2	8	4.8	154	92.2	5	3.0	
FEMALE	0	.0	2	3.2	1	1.6	2	3.2	5	7.9	56	88.9	2	3.2	
MALE	0	.0	3	2.9	0	.0	0	.0	3	2.9	98	94.2	3	2.9	
TOTAL		.0	9	2.5	2	.6	2	.6	13	3.6	334	92.3	15	4.1	
FEMALE		.0	4	3.3	1	.8	2	1.6	7	5.7	109	88.6	7	5.7	
MALE	8	.0	5	2.1	1	.4	0	.0	6	2.5	225	94.1	8	3.3	
PROFESSIONAL:															
FULL-TIME		.0	0	.0	0	.0	0	.0	0	.0	0	.0	0	.0	
FEMALE		.0	0	.0	0	.0	0	.0	0	.0	0	.0	0	.0	
MALE	8	.0	0	.0	0	.0	0	.0	0	.0	0	.0	0	.0	

BIOLOGICAL SCIENCES

I INDIAN NATIVE	BLACK NON-HISPANIC		ASIAN OR PACIFIC ISLANDER		HISPANIC		TOTAL MINORITY		WHITE NON-HISPANIC		NON-RESIDENT ALIEN		TOTAL
X	NUMBER	X	NUMBER	X	NUMBER	X	NUMBER	X	NUMBER	X	NUMBER	X	NUMBER
CONTINUED													
.0	0	.0	0	.0	0	.0	0	.0	0	.0	0	.0	0
.0	0	.0	0	.0	0	.0	0	.0	0	.0	0	.0	0
.0	0	.0	0	.0	0	.0	0	.0	0	.0	0	.0	0
.0	0	.0	0	.0	0	.0	0	.0	0	.0	0	.0	0
.0	0	.0	0	.0	0	.0	0	.0	0	.0	0	.0	0
.0	0	.0	0	.0	0	.0	0	.0	0	.0	0	.0	0
.0	594	17.5	18	.6	12	.4	585	18.5	2,543	80.6	29	.9	3,157
.1	339	26.1	7	.5	4	.3	351	27.0	938	72.2	10	.8	1,299
.0	215	11.6	11	.6	8	.4	234	12.6	1,605	86.4	19	1.0	1,858
.0	47	10.5	4	.9	2	1.0	53	11.9	388	86.8	6	1.3	447
.0	20	10.0	3	1.5	2	1.0	25	12.4	173	86.1	3	1.5	201
.0	27	11.0	1	.4	0	.0	28	11.4	215	87.4	3	1.2	246
.0	601	16.7	22	.6	14	.4	638	17.7	2,931	81.3	35	1.0	3,604
.1	359	23.9	10	.7	6	.4	376	25.1	1,111	74.1	13	.9	1,500
.0	242	11.5	12	.6	8	.4	262	12.5	1,820	86.5	22	1.0	2,104
.0	6	11.3	0	.0	0	.0	6	11.3	46	86.8	1	1.9	53
.0	5	17.2	0	.0	0	.0	5	17.2	23	79.3	1	3.4	29
.0	1	4.2	0	.0	0	.0	1	4.2	23	95.8	0	.0	24
.0	607	16.6	22	.6	14	.4	644	17.6	2,977	81.4	36	1.0	3,657
.1	364	23.8	10	.7	6	.4	381	24.9	1,134	74.2	14	.9	1,529
.0	243	11.4	12	.6	8	.4	263	12.4	1,843	86.6	22	1.0	2,128
(12 INSTITUTIONS)													
1.0	4	.6	5	.7	1	.1	17	2.5	652	96.3	8	1.2	677
.8	1	.4	1	.4	0	.0	4	1.5	258	97.4	3	1.1	265
1.2	3	.7	4	1.0	1	.2	13	3.2	394	95.6	5	1.2	412
.0	0	.0	0	.0	0	.0	0	.0	32	100.0	0	.0	32
.0	0	.0	0	.0	0	.0	0	.0	14	100.0	0	.0	14
.0	0	.0	0	.0	0	.0	0	.0	18	100.0	0	.0	18
1.0	4	.6	5	.7	1	.1	17	2.4	684	96.5	8	1.1	709
.7	1	.4	1	.4	0	.0	4	1.4	272	97.5	3	1.1	279
1.2	3	.7	4	.9	1	.2	13	3.0	412	95.8	5	1.2	430
.0	0	.0	0	.0	0	.0	0	.0	26	96.3	1	3.7	27
.0	0	.0	0	.0	0	.0	0	.0	4	100.0	0	.0	4
.0	0	.0	0	.0	0	.0	0	.0	22	95.7	1	4.3	23
.0	0	.0	0	.0	0	.0	0	.0	56	96.6	2	3.4	58
.0	0	.0	0	.0	0	.0	0	.0	13	100.0	0	.0	13
.0	0	.0	0	.0	0	.0	0	.0	43	95.6	2	4.4	45
.0	0	.0	0	.0	0	.0	0	.0	82	96.5	3	3.5	85
.0	0	.0	0	.0	0	.0	0	.0	17	100.0	0	.0	17
.0	0	.0	0	.0	0	.0	0	.0	65	95.6	3	4.4	68
.0	0	.0	0	.0	0	.0	0	.0	0	.0	0	.0	0
.0	0	.0	0	.0	0	.0	0	.0	0	.0	0	.0	0
.0	0	.0	0	.0	0	.0	0	.0	0	.0	0	.0	0
.0	0	.0	0	.0	0	.0	0	.0	0	.0	0	.0	0
.0	0	.0	0	.0	0	.0	0	.0	0	.0	0	.0	0
.0	0	.0	0	.0	0	.0	0	.0	0	.0	0	.0	0
.0	0	.0	0	.0	0	.0	0	.0	0	.0	0	.0	0
.0	0	.0	0	.0	0	.0	0	.0	0	.0	0	.0	0
.0	0	.0	0	.0	0	.0	0	.0	0	.0	0	.0	0
1.0	4	.6	5	.7	1	.1	17	2.4	678	96.3	9	1.3	704
.7	1	.4	1	.4	0	.0	4	1.5	262	97.4	3	1.1	269
1.1	3	.7	4	.9	1	.2	13	3.0	416	95.6	6	1.4	435
.0	0	.0	0	.0	0	.0	0	.0	88	97.8	2	2.2	90
.0	0	.0	0	.0	0	.0	0	.0	27	100.0	0	.0	27
.0	0	.0	0	.0	0	.0	0	.0	61	96.8	2	3.2	63
.9	4	.5	5	.6	1	.1	17	2.4	766	96.5	11	1.4	794
.7	1	.3	1	.3	0	.0	4	1.4	289	97.6	3	1.0	296
1.0	3	.6	4	.8	1	.2	13	2.6	477	95.8	8	1.6	498
.0	0	.0	0	.0	0	.0	0	.0	13	100.0	0	.0	13
.0	0	.0	0	.0	0	.0	0	.0	7	100.0	0	.0	7
.0	0	.0	0	.0	0	.0	0	.0	6	100.0	0	.0	6
.9	4	.5	5	.6	1	.1	17	2.1	779	96.5	11	1.4	807
.7	1	.3	1	.3	0	.0	4	1.3	296	97.7	3	1.0	303
1.0	3	.6	4	.8	1	.2	13	2.6	483	95.8	8	1.6	504

TABLE 17 - TOTAL ENROLLMENT IN INSTITUTIONS OF HIGHER EDUCATION FOR SELECTED MAJOR FIELDS OF STUDY AND LEVEL OF ENROLLMENT BY RACE, ETHNICITY, AND SEX: STATE, 1978

MAJOR FIELD 0400 - BIOLOGICAL SCIENCES

	AMERICAN INDIAN ALASKAN NATIVE		BLACK NON-HISPANIC		ASIAN OR PACIFIC ISLANDER		HISPANIC		TOTAL MINORITY		WHITE NON-HISPANIC		NON-RESIDENT ALIEN		
	NUMBER	%	NUMBER	%	NUMBER	%	NUMBER	%	NUMBER	%	NUMBER	%	NUMBER	%	
TENNESSEE	(	40 INSTITUTIONS)													
UNDERGRADUATES:															
FULL-TIME	4	.1	751	22.7	20	.6	15	.5	790	23.9	2,470	74.7	48	1.5	
FEMALE	0	.0	455	30.2	7	.5	3	.2	465	30.9	1,025	68.1	15	1.0	
MALE	4	.2	296	16.4	13	.7	12	.7	325	18.0	1,445	80.1	33	1.8	
PART-TIME	2	.6	26	7.8	1	.3	1	.3	30	9.0	302	90.1	3	.9	
FEMALE	1	.8	13	9.8	1	.8	0	.0	15	11.3	118	88.7	0	.0	
MALE	1	.5	13	6.4	0	.0	1	.5	15	7.4	184	91.1	3	1.5	
TOTAL	6	.2	777	21.3	21	.6	16	.4	820	22.5	2,772	76.1	51	1.4	
FEMALE	1	.1	468	28.6	8	.5	3	.2	480	29.3	1,143	69.8	15	.9	
MALE	5	.2	309	15.4	13	.6	13	.6	340	17.0	1,629	81.2	36	1.8	
GRADUATE:															
FULL-TIME	1	.2	31	6.7	10	2.2	4	.9	46	10.0	373	80.9	42	9.1	
FEMALE	1	.6	18	11.5	4	2.6	1	.6	24	15.4	122	78.2	10	6.4	
MALE	0	.0	13	4.3	6	2.0	3	1.0	22	7.2	251	82.3	32	10.5	
PART-TIME	1	.4	8	2.9	1	.4	2	.7	12	4.3	248	88.6	20	7.1	
FEMALE	0	.0	4	4.8	0	.0	1	1.2	5	6.0	75	89.3	4	4.8	
MALE	1	.5	4	2.0	1	.5	1	.5	7	3.6	173	88.3	16	8.2	
TOTAL	2	.3	39	5.3	11	1.5	6	.8	58	7.8	621	83.8	62	8.4	
FEMALE	1	.4	22	9.2	4	1.7	2	.8	29	12.1	197	82.1	14	5.8	
MALE	1	.2	17	3.4	7	1.4	4	.8	29	5.8	424	84.6	48	9.6	
PROFESSIONAL:															
FULL-TIME	0	.0	0	.0	0	.0	0	.0	0	.0	0	.0	0	.0	
FEMALE	0	.0	0	.0	0	.0	0	.0	0	.0	0	.0	0	.0	
MALE	0	.0	0	.0	0	.0	0	.0	0	.0	0	.0	0	.0	
PART-TIME	0	.0	0	.0	0	.0	0	.0	0	.0	0	.0	0	.0	
FEMALE	0	.0	0	.0	0	.0	0	.0	0	.0	0	.0	0	.0	
MALE	0	.0	0	.0	0	.0	0	.0	0	.0	0	.0	0	.0	
TOTAL	0	.0	0	.0	0	.0	0	.0	0	.0	0	.0	0	.0	
FEMALE	0	.0	0	.0	0	.0	0	.0	0	.0	0	.0	0	.0	
MALE	0	.0	0	.0	0	.0	0	.0	0	.0	0	.0	0	.0	
UND+GRAD+PRUF:															
FULL-TIME	5	.1	782	20.7	30	.8	19	.5	836	22.2	2,843	75.4	90	2.4	
FEMALE	1	.1	473	28.5	11	.7	4	.2	489	29.4	1,147	69.1	25	1.5	
MALE	4	.2	309	14.7	19	.9	15	.7	347	16.5	1,696	80.5	65	3.1	
PART-TIME	3	.5	34	5.5	2	.3	3	.5	42	6.8	550	89.4	23	3.7	
FEMALE	1	.5	17	7.8	1	.5	1	.5	20	9.2	193	88.9	4	1.8	
MALE	2	.5	17	4.3	1	.3	2	.5	22	5.5	357	89.7	19	4.8	
TOTAL	8	.2	816	18.6	32	.7	22	.5	878	20.0	3,393	77.4	113	2.6	
FEMALE	2	.1	490	26.1	12	.6	5	.3	509	27.1	1,340	71.4	29	1.5	
MALE	6	.2	326	13.0	20	.8	17	.7	369	14.7	2,053	81.9	84	3.4	
UNCLASSIFIED:															
TOTAL	0	.0	43	60.6	1	1.4	0	.0	44	62.0	23	32.4	4	5.6	
FEMALE	0	.0	31	73.8	0	.0	0	.0	31	73.8	11	26.2	0	.0	
MALE	0	.0	12	41.4	1	3.4	0	.0	13	44.8	12	41.4	4	13.8	
TOTAL ENROLLMENT:															
TOTAL	8	.2	859	19.3	33	.7	22	.5	922	20.7	3,416	76.7	117	2.6	
FEMALE	2	.1	521	27.1	12	.6	5	.3	540	28.1	1,351	70.4	29	1.5	
MALE	6	.2	338	13.3	21	.8	17	.7	382	15.1	2,065	81.5	88	3.5	
TEXAS	(	110 INSTITUTIONS)													
UNDERGRADUATES:															
FULL-TIME	49	.3	1,162	8.1	167	1.2	1,518	10.6	2,896	20.2	10,917	76.3	495	3.5	
FEMALE	21	.3	724	10.7	69	1.0	626	9.3	1,440	21.4	5,130	76.2	166	2.5	
MALE	28	.4	438	5.8	98	1.3	892	11.8	1,456	19.2	5,787	76.4	329	4.3	
PART-TIME	24	.6	385	9.5	62	1.5	375	9.3	846	20.9	3,143	77.6	62	1.5	
FEMALE	12	.5	224	10.0	36	1.6	163	7.3	435	19.5	1,772	79.3	27	1.2	
MALE	12	.7	161	8.9	26	1.4	212	11.7	411	22.6	1,371	75.5	35	1.9	
TOTAL	73	.4	1,547	8.4	229	1.2	1,893	10.3	3,742	20.4	14,060	76.6	557	3.0	
FEMALE	33	.4	948	10.6	105	1.2	789	8.8	1,875	20.9	6,902	76.9	193	2.2	
MALE	40	.4	599	6.4	124	1.3	1,104	11.8	1,867	19.9	7,158	76.2	364	3.9	
GRADUATE:															
FULL-TIME	4	.2	21	1.2	41	2.3	43	2.4	109	6.1	1,531	85.7	146	8.2	
FEMALE	2	.3	9	1.4	20	3.1	14	2.2	45	7.0	552	86.4	42	6.6	
MALE	2	.2	12	1.0	21	1.8	29	2.5	64	5.6	979	85.4	104	9.1	
PART-TIME	3	.3	33	3.8	6	.7	55	6.3	97	11.2	739	85.0	33	3.8	
FEMALE	1	.3	22	5.5	2	.9	24	6.0	49	12.3	337	84.9	11	2.8	
MALE	2	.4	11	2.3	4	.8	31	6.6	48	10.2	402	85.2	22	4.7	
TOTAL	7	.3	54	2.0	47	1.8	98	3.7	206	7.8	2,270	85.5	179	6.7	
FEMALE	3	.3	31	3.0	22	2.1	38	3.7	94	9.1	889	85.8	53	5.1	
MALE	4	.2	23	1.4	25	1.5	60	3.7	112	6.9	1,381	85.3	126	7.8	
PROFESSIONAL:															
FULL-TIME	0	.0	0	.0	0	.0	0	.0	0	.0	0	.0	0	.0	
FEMALE	0	.0	0	.0	0	.0	0	.0	0	.0	0	.0	0	.0	
MALE	0	.0	0	.0	0	.0	0	.0	0	.0	0	.0	0	.0	

ENROLLMENT IN INSTITUTIONS OF HIGHER EDUCATION FOR SELECTED MAJOR FIELDS OF STUDY AND LEVEL OF ENROLLMENT
, ETHNICITY, AND SEX: STATE, 1978

BIOLOGICAL SCIENCES

AMERICAN INDIAN NATIVE		BLACK NON-HISPANIC		ASIAN OR PACIFIC ISLANDER		HISPANIC		TOTAL MINORITY		WHITE NON-HISPANIC		NON-RESIDENT ALIEN		TOTAL
%	NUMBER	%	NUMBER	%	NUMBER	%	NUMBER	%	NUMBER	%	NUMBER	%	NUMBER	%	NUMBER

CONTINUED

.0	0	.0	0	.0	0	.0	0	.0	0	.0	0	.0	0	.0	0
.0	0	.0	0	.0	0	.0	0	.0	0	.0	0	.0	0	.0	0
.0	0	.0	0	.0	0	.0	0	.0	0	.0	0	.0	0	.0	0

.0	0	.0	0	.0	0	.0	0	.0	0	.0	0	.0	0	.0	0
.0	0	.0	0	.0	0	.0	0	.0	0	.0	0	.0	0	.0	0
.0	0	.0	0	.0	0	.0	0	.0	0	.0	0	.0	0	.0	0

.3	1,183	7.4	208	1.3	1,561	9.7	3,005	18.7	12,448	77.3	641	4.0	16,094
.3	733	9.9	89	1.2	640	8.7	1,485	20.1	5,682	77.0	208	2.8	7,375
.3	450	5.2	119	1.4	921	10.6	1,520	17.4	6,766	77.6	433	5.0	8,719
.5	418	8.5	68	1.4	430	8.7	943	19.2	3,882	78.9	95	1.9	4,920
.5	246	9.4	38	1.4	187	7.1	484	18.4	2,109	80.2	38	1.4	2,631
.6	172	7.5	30	1.3	243	10.6	459	20.1	1,773	77.5	57	2.5	2,289

.4	1,601	7.6	276	1.3	1,991	9.5	3,948	18.8	16,330	77.7	736	3.5	21,014
.4	979	9.8	127	1.3	827	8.3	1,969	19.7	7,791	77.9	246	2.5	10,006
.4	622	5.7	149	1.4	1,164	10.6	1,979	18.0	8,539	77.6	490	4.5	11,008

.5	63	7.3	14	1.6	78	9.0	159	18.3	685	78.9	24	2.8	868
.0	31	9.3	4	1.2	21	6.3	56	16.8	270	80.8	8	2.4	334
.7	32	6.0	10	1.9	57	10.7	103	19.3	415	77.7	16	3.0	534

.4	1,664	7.6	290	1.3	2,069	9.5	4,107	18.8	17,015	77.8	760	3.5	21,882
.3	1,010	9.8	131	1.3	848	8.2	2,025	19.6	8,061	78.0	254	2.5	10,340
.4	654	5.7	159	1.4	1,221	10.6	2,082	18.0	8,954	77.6	506	4.4	11,542

(10 INSTITUTIONS)

.4	7	.4	47	2.4	17	.9	79	4.0	1,829	92.0	81	4.1	1,989
.2	2	.4	13	2.5	3	.6	19	3.7	470	91.8	23	4.5	512
.5	5	.3	34	2.3	14	.9	60	4.1	1,359	92.0	58	3.9	1,477
.2	2	.4	6	1.3	15	3.3	24	5.3	418	92.7	9	2.0	451
.2	1	1.0	1	1.0	4	4.1	6	6.1	88	89.8	4	4.1	98
.3	1	.3	5	1.4	11	3.1	18	5.1	330	93.5	5	1.4	353

.4	9	.4	53	2.2	32	1.3	103	4.2	2,247	92.1	90	3.7	2,440
.2	3	.5	14	2.3	7	1.1	25	4.1	558	91.5	27	4.4	610
.4	6	.3	39	2.1	25	1.4	78	4.3	1,689	92.3	63	3.4	1,830

.5	0	.0	1	.5	0	.0	2	.9	193	88.9	22	10.1	217
.0	0	.0	0	.0	0	.0	0	.0	40	88.9	5	11.1	45
.6	0	.0	1	.6	0	.0	2	1.2	153	89.0	17	9.9	172
.0	0	.0	1	.7	0	.0	1	.7	117	87.3	16	11.9	134
.0	0	.0	1	3.4	0	.0	1	3.4	24	82.8	4	13.8	29
.0	0	.0	0	.0	0	.0	0	.0	93	88.6	12	11.4	105

.3	0	.0	2	.6	0	.0	3	.9	310	88.3	38	10.8	351
.0	0	.0	1	1.4	0	.0	1	1.4	64	86.5	9	12.2	74
.4	0	.0	1	.4	0	.0	2	.7	246	88.8	29	10.5	277

.0	0	.0	0	.0	0	.0	0	.0	0	.0	0	.0	0
.0	0	.0	0	.0	0	.0	0	.0	0	.0	0	.0	0
.0	0	.0	0	.0	0	.0	0	.0	0	.0	0	.0	0
.0	0	.0	0	.0	0	.0	0	.0	0	.0	0	.0	0
.0	0	.0	0	.0	0	.0	0	.0	0	.0	0	.0	0
.0	0	.0	0	.0	0	.0	0	.0	0	.0	0	.0	0

.0	0	.0	0	.0	0	.0	0	.0	0	.0	0	.0	0
.0	0	.0	0	.0	0	.0	0	.0	0	.0	0	.0	0
.0	0	.0	0	.0	0	.0	0	.0	0	.0	0	.0	0

.4	7	.3	48	2.2	17	.8	81	3.7	2,022	91.7	103	4.7	2,206
.2	2	.4	13	2.3	3	.5	19	3.4	510	91.6	28	5.0	557
.5	5	.3	35	2.1	14	.8	62	3.8	1,512	91.7	75	4.5	1,649
.2	2	.3	7	1.2	15	2.6	25	4.3	535	91.5	25	4.3	585
.0	1	.8	2	1.6	4	3.1	7	5.5	112	88.2	8	6.3	127
.2	1	.2	5	1.1	11	2.4	18	3.9	423	92.4	17	3.7	458

.4	9	.3	55	2.0	32	1.1	106	3.8	2,557	91.6	128	4.6	2,791
.1	3	.4	15	2.2	7	1.0	26	3.8	622	90.9	36	5.3	684
.4	6	.3	40	1.9	25	1.2	80	3.8	1,935	91.8	92	4.4	2,107

.0	0	.0	0	.0	0	.0	0	.0	0	.0	0	.0	0
.0	0	.0	0	.0	0	.0	0	.0	0	.0	0	.0	0
.0	0	.0	0	.0	0	.0	0	.0	0	.0	0	.0	0

.4	9	.3	55	2.0	32	1.1	106	3.8	2,557	91.6	128	4.6	2,791
.1	3	.4	15	2.2	7	1.0	26	3.8	622	90.9	36	5.3	684
.4	6	.3	40	1.9	25	1.2	80	3.8	1,935	91.8	92	4.4	2,107

391

MAJOR FIELD 0400 - BIOLOGICAL SCIENCES

	AMERICAN INDIAN ALASKAN NATIVE		BLACK NON-HISPANIC		ASIAN OR PACIFIC ISLANDER		HISPANIC		TOTAL MINORITY		WHITE NON-HISPANIC		NON-RESIDENT ALIEN		TO
	NUMBER	%	NUMBER	%	NUMBER	%	NUMBER	%	NUMBER	%	NUMBER	%	NUMBER	%	NU
VERMONT	(	9 INSTITUTIONS)													
UNDERGRADUATES:															
FULL-TIME	1	.1	4	.4	9	.4	6	.6	15	1.4	1,068	98.3	4	.4	1
FEMALE	0	.0	2	.4		.2	3	.6	6	1.3	457	98.1	3	.6	
MALE	1	.2	2	.3	4	.5	3	.5	9	1.4	611	98.4	1	.2	
PART-TIME		.0	0	.0		.0	0	.0	0	.0	33	97.1	1	2.9	
FEMALE		.0	0	.0		.0	0	.0	0	.0	17	100.0	0	.0	
MALE	0	.0	0	.0	0	.0	0	.0	0	.0	16	94.1	1	5.9	
TOTAL	1	.1	4	.4	4	.4	6	.5	15	1.3	1,101	98.2	5	.4	1
FEMALE	0	.0	2	.4	1	.2	3	.6	6	1.2	474	98.1	3	.6	
MALE	1	.2	2	.3	3	.5	3	.5	9	1.4	627	98.3	2	.3	
GRADUATE															
FULL-TIME		.0	2	3.1		.0		.0	2	3.1	62	95.4	1	1.5	
FEMALE		.0	0	.0		.0		.0	0	.0	19	100.0	0	.0	
MALE		.0	2	4.3		.0		.0	2	4.3	43	93.5	1	2.2	
PART-TIME		.0	0	.0		.0		.0	0	.0	63	100.0	0	.0	
FEMALE		.0	0	.0		.0		.0	0	.0	17	100.0	0	.0	
MALE	0	.0	0	.0	0	.0	0	.0	0	.0	46	100.0	0	.0	
TOTAL		.0	2	1.6		.0		.0	2	1.6	125	97.7	1	.8	
FEMALE		.0	0	.0		.0		.0	0	.0	36	100.0	0	.0	
MALE	0	.0	2	2.2	0	.0	0	.0	2	2.2	89	96.7	1	1.1	
PROFESSIONAL:															
FULL-TIME		.0		.0		.0		.0	0	.0	0	.0		.0	
FEMALE		.0		.0		.0		.0	0	.0	0	.0		.0	
MALE		.0		.0		.0		.0	0	.0	0	.0		.0	
PART-TIME		.0		.0		.0		.0	0	.0	0	.0		.0	
FEMALE		.0		.0		.0		.0	0	.0	0	.0		.0	
MALE	0	.0	0	.0	0	.0	0	.0	0	.0	0	.0	0	.0	
TOTAL		.0		.0		.0		.0	0	.0	0	.0		.0	
FEMALE		.0		.0		.0		.0	0	.0	0	.0		.0	
MALE	0	.0	0	.0	0	.0	0	.0	0	.0	0	.0	0	.0	
UND+GRAD+PROF:															
FULL-TIME	1	.1	6	.5	4	.3		.5	17	1.5	1,130	98.1	5	.4	1
FEMALE	0	.0	2	.4	1	.2		.6	6	1.2	476	98.1	3	.6	
MALE	1	.1	4	.6	3	.4		.4	11	1.6	654	98.1	2	.3	
PART-TIME	0	.0	0	.0	0	.0		.0	0	.0	96	99.0	1	1.0	
FEMALE	0	.0	0	.0	0	.0		.0	0	.0	34	100.0	0	.0	
MALE	0	.0	0	.0	0	.0	0	.0	0	.0	62	98.4	1	1.6	
TOTAL	1	.1	6	.5	4	.3	6	.5	17	1.4	1,226	98.2	6	.5	1
FEMALE	0	.0	2	.4	1	.2	3	.6	6	1.2	510	98.3	3	.6	
MALE	1	.1	4	.5	3	.4	3	.4	11	1.5	716	98.1	3	.4	
UNCLASSIFIED:															
TOTAL		.0		.0		.0		.0	0	.0	3	100.0		.0	
FEMALE		.0		.0		.0		.0	0	.0	3	100.0		.0	
MALE	0	.0	0	.0	0	.0	0	.0	0	.0	0	.0	0	.0	
TOTAL ENROLLMENT:															
TOTAL	1	.1	6	.5	4	.3	6	.5	17	1.4	1,229	98.2	6	.5	1
FEMALE	0	.0	2	.4	1	.2	3	.6	6	1.1	513	98.3	3	.6	
MALE	1	.1	4	.5	3	.4	3	.4	11	1.5	716	98.1	3	.4	
VIRGINIA	(	35 INSTITUTIONS)													
UNDERGRADUATES:															
FULL-TIME	6	.1	561	11.5	56	1.	35	.7	658	13.4	4,184	85.5	52	1.1	4
FEMALE	2	.1	316	13.5	30	1.	14	.6	362	15.5	1,956	83.6	22	.9	2
MALE	4	.2	245	9.6	26	1.	21	.8	296	11.6	2,228	87.2	30	1.2	2
PART-TIME	3	.7	51	11.8	2	.	3	.7	59	13.6	371	85.5	4	.9	
FEMALE	2	1.0	27	13.1	2	1.	2	1.0	33	16.0	172	83.5	1	.5	
MALE	1	.4	24	10.5	0	.8	1	.4	26	11.4	199	87.3	3	1.3	
TOTAL	9	.2	612	11.5	58	1.1	38	.7	717	13.5	4,555	85.5	56	1.1	5
FEMALE	4	.2	343	13.5	32	1.3	16	.6	395	15.5	2,128	83.6	23	.9	2
MALE	5	.2	269	9.7	26	.9	22	.8	322	11.6	2,427	87.2	33	1.2	2
GRADUATE:															
FULL-TIME	1	.2	16	2.7	5	.8	2	.3	24	4.0	536	90.2	34	5.7	
FEMALE	0	.0	7	3.4	3	1.5	1	.5	11	5.4	184	90.6	8	3.9	
MALE	1	.3	9	2.3	2	.5	1	.3	13	3.3	352	90.0	26	6.6	
PART-TIME	0	.0	12	3.	6	1.5	1	.2	19	4.7	383	94.8	2	.5	
FEMALE	0	.0	6	4.8	2	1.6	0	.0	8	6.4	117	93.6	0	.0	
MALE	0	.0	6	2.8	4	1.4	1	.4	11	3.9	266	95.3	2	.7	
TOTAL	1	.1	28	2.8	11	1.1	3	.3	43	4.3	919	92.1	36	3.6	
FEMALE	0	.0	13	4.0	5	1.5	1	.3	19	5.8	301	91.8	8	2.4	
MALE	1	.1	15	2.2	6	.9	2	.3	24	3.6	618	92.2	28	4.2	
PROFESSIONAL:															
FULL-TIME		.0		.0		.0	0	.0	0	.0	0	.0	0	.0	
FEMALE		.0		.0		.0	0	.0	0	.0	0	.0	0	.0	
MALE	0	.0	0	10	0	.0	0	.0	0	.0	0	.0	0	.0	

BIOLOGICAL SCIENCES

INDIAN NATIVE	BLACK NON-HISPANIC		ASIAN OR PACIFIC ISLANDER		HISPANIC		TOTAL MINORITY		WHITE NON-HISPANIC		NON-RESIDENT ALIEN		TOTAL
%	NUMBER	%	NUMBER	%	NUMBER	%	NUMBER	%	NUMBER	%	NUMBER	%	NUMBER

CONTINUED

.0	0	.0	0	.0	0	.0	0	.0	0	.0	0	.0	0
.0	0	.0	0	.0	0	.0	0	.0	0	.0	0	.0	0
.0	0	.0	0	.0	0	.0	0	.0	0	.0	0	.0	0
.0	0	.0	0	.0	0	.0	0	.0	0	.0	0	.0	0
.0	0	.0	0	.0	0	.0	0	.0	0	.0	0	.0	0
.0	0	.0	0	.0	0	.0	0	.0	0	.0	0	.0	0
.1	577	10.5	61	1.1	37	.7	682	12.4	4,720	86.0	86	1.6	5,488
.1	323	12.7	33	1.3	15	.6	373	14.7	2,140	84.2	30	1.2	2,543
.2	254	8.6	28	1.0	22	.7	309	10.5	2,580	87.6	56	1.9	2,945
.4	63	7.5	8	1.0	4	.5	78	9.3	754	90.0	6	.7	838
.6	33	10.0	4	1.2	2	.6	41	12.4	289	87.3	1	.3	331
.2	30	5.9	4	.8	2	.4	37	7.3	465	91.7	5	1.0	507
.2	640	10.1	69	1.1	41	.6	760	12.0	5,474	86.5	92	1.5	6,326
.1	358	12.4	37	1.3	17	.6	414	14.4	2,429	84.5	31	1.1	2,874
.2	284	8.2	32	.9	24	.7	346	10.0	3,045	88.2	61	1.8	3,452
1.1	15	15.8	0	.0	1	1.1	17	17.9	77	81.1	1	1.1	95
.0	5	12.2	0	.0	0	.0	5	12.2	36	87.8	0	.0	41
1.9	10	18.5	0	.0	1	1.9	12	22.2	41	75.9	1	1.9	54
.2	655	10.2	69	1.1	42	.7	777	12.1	5,551	86.5	93	1.4	6,421
.1	361	12.4	37	1.3	17	.6	419	14.4	2,465	84.6	31	1.1	2,915
.2	294	8.4	32	.9	25	.7	358	10.2	3,086	88.0	62	1.8	3,506

(15 INSTITUTIONS)

.6	20	.7	104	3.9	21	.8	162	6.0	2,451	91.4	68	2.5	2,681
.5	9	.7	47	3.5	7	.5	70	5.1	1,269	93.2	23	1.7	1,362
.8	11	.8	57	4.3	14	1.1	92	7.0	1,182	89.6	45	3.4	1,319
.0	5	1.8	9	3.2	1	.4	15	5.3	264	92.6	6	2.1	285
.0	1	.8	3	2.3	0	.0	4	3.0	126	94.7	3	2.3	133
.0	4	2.6	6	3.9	1	.7	11	7.2	138	90.8	3	2.0	152
.6	25	.8	113	3.8	22	.7	177	6.0	2,715	91.5	74	2.5	2,966
.5	10	.7	50	3.3	7	.5	74	4.9	1,395	93.3	26	1.7	1,495
.7	15	1.0	63	4.3	15	1.0	103	7.0	1,320	89.7	48	3.3	1,471
.0	2	.3	19	3.3	2	.3	23	4.0	515	88.6	43	7.4	581
.0	1	.5	7	3.6	0	.0	8	4.1	173	89.2	13	6.7	194
.0	1	.3	12	3.1	2	.5	15	3.9	342	88.4	30	7.8	387
.9	2	1.8	4	3.6	1	.9	8	7.3	96	87.3	6	5.5	110
.0	1	3.1	1	3.1	0	.0	2	6.3	30	93.8	0	.0	32
1.3	1	1.3	3	3.8	1	1.3	6	7.7	66	84.6	6	7.7	76
.1	4	.6	23	3.3	3	.4	31	4.5	611	88.4	49	7.1	691
.0	2	.9	8	3.5	0	.0	10	4.4	203	89.8	13	5.8	226
.2	2	.4	15	3.2	3	.6	21	4.5	408	87.7	36	7.7	465
.0	0	.0	0	.0	0	.0	0	.0	0	.0	0	.0	0
.0	0	.0	0	.0	0	.0	0	.0	0	.0	0	.0	0
.0	0	.0	0	.0	0	.0	0	.0	0	.0	0	.0	0
.0	0	.0	0	.0	0	.0	0	.0	0	.0	0	.0	0
.0	0	.0	0	.0	0	.0	0	.0	0	.0	0	.0	0
.0	0	.0	0	.0	0	.0	0	.0	0	.0	0	.0	0
.0	0	.0	0	.0	0	.0	0	.0	0	.0	0	.0	0
.0	0	.0	0	.0	0	.0	0	.0	0	.0	0	.0	0
.0	0	.0	0	.0	0	.0	0	.0	0	.0	0	.0	0
.5	22	.7	123	3.8	23	.7	185	5.7	2,966	90.9	111	3.4	3,282
.4	10	.6	54	3.5	7	.4	78	5.0	1,442	92.7	36	2.3	1,556
.6	12	.7	69	4.0	16	.9	107	6.3	1,524	89.3	75	4.4	1,706
.3	7	1.8	13	3.3	2	.5	23	5.8	360	91.1	12	3.0	395
.0	2	1.2	4	2.4	0	.0	6	3.6	156	94.5	3	1.8	165
.4	5	2.2	9	3.9	2	.9	17	7.4	204	88.7	9	3.9	230
.5	29	.8	136	3.7	25	.7	208	5.7	3,326	90.9	123	3.4	3,657
.4	12	.7	58	3.4	7	.4	84	4.9	1,598	92.9	39	2.3	1,721
.6	17	.9	78	4.0	18	.9	124	6.4	1,728	89.3	84	4.3	1,936
.0	3	2.0	4	2.6	1	.7	8	5.2	142	92.8	3	2.0	153
.0	1	1.5	2	2.9	0	.0	3	4.4	63	92.6	2	2.9	68
.0	2	2.4	2	2.4	1	1.2	5	5.9	79	92.9	1	1.2	85
.5	32	.8	140	3.7	26	.7	216	5.7	3,468	91.0	126	3.3	3,810
.4	13	.7	60	3.4	7	.4	87	4.9	1,661	92.8	41	2.3	1,789
.5	19	.9	80	4.0	19	.9	129	6.4	1,807	89.4	85	4.2	2,021

TABLE 17 - TOTAL ENROLLMENT IN INSTITUTIONS OF HIGHER EDUCATION FOR SELECTED MAJOR FIELDS OF STUDY AND LEVEL OF ENROLLMENT
BY RACE, ETHNICITY, AND SEX: STATE, 1978

MAJOR FIELD 0400 - BIOLOGICAL SCIENCES

	AMERICAN INDIAN ALASKAN NATIVE		BLACK NON-HISPANIC		ASIAN OR PACIFIC ISLANDER		HISPANIC		TOTAL MINORITY		WHITE NON-HISPANIC		NON-RESIDENT ALIEN	
	NUMBER	%	NUMBER	%	NUMBER	%	NUMBER	%	NUMBER	%	NUMBER	%	NUMBER	%
WEST VIRGINIA (20 INSTITUTIONS)														
UNDERGRADUATES:														
FULL-TIME	4	.3	52	3.5	10	.7	4	.3	70	4.7	1,405	94.2	16	1.1
FEMALE	1	.2	20	3.8	2	.4	0	.0	23	4.4	496	95.0	3	.6
MALE	3	.3	32	3.3	8	.8	4	.4	47	4.9	909	93.8	13	1.3
PART-TIME	0	.0	3	1.6	0	.0	1	.5	4	2.2	177	97.3	1	.5
FEMALE	0	.0	2	2.3	0	.0	1	1.1	3	3.4	85	96.6	0	.0
MALE	0	.0	1	1.1	0	.0	0	.0	1	1.1	92	97.9	1	1.1
TOTAL	4	.2	55	3.3	10	.6	5	.3	74	4.4	1,582	94.6	17	1.0
FEMALE	1	.2	22	3.6	2	.3	1	.2	26	4.3	581	95.2	3	.5
MALE	3	.3	33	3.1	8	.8	4	.4	48	4.5	1,001	94.2	14	1.3
GRADUATE														
FULL-TIME	0	.0	0	.0	3	2.0	0	.0	3	2.0	132	89.2	13	8.8
FEMALE	0	.0	0	.0	2	4.3	0	.0	2	4.3	39	84.8	5	10.9
MALE	0	.0	0	.0	1	1.0	0	.0	1	1.0	93	91.2	8	7.8
PART-TIME	0	.0	2	2.3	1	1.1	0	.0	3	3.4	83	95.4	1	1.1
FEMALE	0	.0	1	3.7	0	.0	0	.0	1	3.7	26	96.3	0	.0
MALE	0	.0	1	1.7	1	1.7	0	.0	2	3.3	57	95.0	1	1.7
TOTAL	0	.0	2	.9	4	1.7	0	.0	6	2.6	215	91.5	14	6.0
FEMALE	0	.0	1	1.4	2	2.7	0	.0	3	4.1	65	89.0	5	6.8
MALE	0	.0	1	.6	2	1.2	0	.0	3	1.9	150	92.6	9	5.6
PROFESSIONAL:														
FULL-TIME	0	.0	0	.0	0	.0	0	.0	0	.0	0	.0	0	.0
FEMALE	0	.0	0	.0	0	.0	0	.0	0	.0	0	.0	0	.0
MALE	0	.0	0	.0	0	.0	0	.0	0	.0	0	.0	0	.0
PART-TIME	0	.0	0	.0	0	.0	0	.0	0	.0	0	.0	0	.0
FEMALE	0	.0	0	.0	0	.0	0	.0	0	.0	0	.0	0	.0
MALE	0	.0	0	.0	0	.0	0	.0	0	.0	0	.0	0	.0
TOTAL	0	.0	0	.0	0	.0	0	.0	0	.0	0	.0	0	.0
FEMALE	0	.0	0	.0	0	.0	0	.0	0	.0	0	.0	0	.0
MALE	0	.0	0	.0	0	.0	0	.0	0	.0	0	.0	0	.0
UND+GRAD+PROF:														
FULL-TIME	4	.2	52	3.2	13	.8	4	.2	73	4.5	1,537	93.8	29	1.8
FEMALE	1	.2	20	3.5	4	.7	0	.0	25	4.4	535	94.2	8	1.4
MALE	3	.3	32	3.0	9	.8	4	.4	48	4.6	1,002	93.6	21	2.0
PART-TIME	0	.0	5	1.9	1	.4	1	.4	7	2.6	260	96.7	2	.7
FEMALE	0	.0	3	2.6	0	.0	1	.9	4	3.5	111	96.5	0	.0
MALE	0	.0	2	1.3	1	.6	0	.0	3	1.9	149	96.8	2	1.3
TOTAL	4	.2	57	3.0	14	.7	5	.3	80	4.2	1,797	94.2	31	1.6
FEMALE	1	.1	23	3.4	4	.6	1	.1	29	4.2	646	94.6	8	1.2
MALE	3	.2	34	2.8	10	.8	4	.3	51	4.2	1,151	94.0	23	1.9
UNCLASSIFIED:														
TOTAL	0	.0	0	.0	0	.0	1	2.0	1	2.0	48	98.0	0	.0
FEMALE	0	.0	0	.0	0	.0	1	4.3	1	4.3	22	95.7	0	.0
MALE	0	.0	0	.0	0	.0	0	.0	0	.0	26	100.0	0	.0
TOTAL ENROLLMENT:														
TOTAL	4	.2	57	2.9	14	.7	6	.3	81	4.1	1,845	94.3	31	1.6
FEMALE	1	.1	23	3.3	4	.6	2	.3	30	4.2	668	94.6	8	1.1
MALE	3	.2	34	2.7	10	.8	4	.3	51	4.1	1,177	94.1	23	1.8
WISCONSIN (33 INSTITUTIONS)														
UNDERGRADUATES:														
FULL-TIME	13	.4	54	1.7	22	.7	26	.8	115	3.7	2,964	94.9	43	1.4
FEMALE	8	.6	31	2.3	9	.7	9	.7	57	4.2	1,284	94.7	15	1.1
MALE	5	.3	23	1.3	13	.7	17	1.0	58	3.3	1,680	95.1	28	1.6
PART-TIME	3	.6	8	1.6	6	1.2	3	.6	20	3.9	489	95.5	3	.6
FEMALE	2	.6	5	1.6	6	1.9	1	.3	14	4.5	294	95.5	0	.0
MALE	1	.5	3	1.5	0	.0	2	1.0	6	2.9	195	95.6	3	1.5
TOTAL	16	.4	62	1.7	28	.8	29	.8	135	3.7	3,453	95.0	46	1.3
FEMALE	10	.6	36	2.2	15	.9	10	.6	71	4.3	1,578	94.8	15	.9
MALE	6	.3	26	1.3	13	.7	19	1.0	64	3.2	1,875	95.2	31	1.6
GRADUATE:														
FULL-TIME	3	.3	1	.1	26	2.9	5	.6	35	3.9	748	83.1	117	13.0
FEMALE	2	.6	1	.3	10	3.2	2	.6	15	4.8	259	83.3	37	11.9
MALE	1	.2	0	.0	16	2.7	3	.5	20	3.4	489	83.0	80	13.6
PART-TIME	0	.0	1	.4	4	1.8	2	.9	7	3.1	208	93.3	8	3.6
FEMALE	0	.0	0	.0	3	3.4	1	1.1	4	4.6	81	93.1	2	2.3
MALE	0	.0	1	.7	1	.7	1	.7	3	2.2	127	93.4	6	4.4
TOTAL	3	.3	2	.2	30	2.7	7	.6	42	3.7	956	85.1	125	11.1
FEMALE	2	.5	1	.3	13	3.3	3	.8	19	4.8	340	85.4	39	9.8
MALE	1	.1	1	.1	17	2.3	4	.6	23	3.2	616	85.0	86	11.9
PROFESSIONAL:														
FULL-TIME	0	.0	0	.0	0	.0	0	.0	0	.0	0	.0	0	.0
FEMALE	0	.0	0	.0	0	.0	0	.0	0	.0	0	.0	0	.0
MALE	0	.0	0	.0	0	.0	0	.0	0	.0	0	.0	0	.0

CES

ACK ISPANIC	ASIAN OR PACIFIC ISLANDER		HISPANIC		TOTAL MINORITY		WHITE NON-HISPANIC		NON-RESIDENT ALIEN		TOTAL
%	NUMBER	%	NUMBER	%	NUMBER	%	NUMBER	%	NUMBER	%	NUMBER
.0	0	.0	0	.0	0	.0	0	.0	0	.0	0
.0	0	.0	0	.0	0	.0	0	.0	0	.0	0
.0	0	.0	0	.0	0	.0	0	.0	0	.0	0
.0	0	.0	0	.0	0	.0	0	.0	0	.0	0
.0	0	.0	0	.0	0	.0	0	.0	0	.0	0
.0	0	.0	0	.0	0	.0	0	.0	0	.0	0
1.4	48	1.2	31	.8	150	3.7	3,712	92.3	160	4.0	4,022
1.9	19	1.1	11	.7	72	4.3	1,543	92.6	52	3.1	1,667
1.0	29	1.2	20	.8	78	3.3	2,169	92.1	108	4.6	2,355
1.2	10	1.4	5	.7	27	3.7	697	94.8	11	1.5	735
1.3	9	2.3	2	.5	18	4.6	375	94.9	2	.5	395
1.2	1	.3	3	.9	9	2.6	322	94.7	9	2.6	340
1.3	58	1.2	36	.8	177	3.7	4,409	92.7	171	3.6	4,757
1.8	28	1.4	13	.6	90	4.4	1,918	93.0	54	2.6	2,062
1.0	30	1.1	23	.9	87	3.2	2,491	92.4	117	4.3	2,695
6.2	1	1.5	0	.0	5	7.7	60	92.3	0	.0	65
6.9	0	.0	0	.0	2	6.9	27	93.1	0	.0	29
5.6	1	2.8	0	.0	3	8.3	33	91.7	0	.0	36
1.4	59	1.2	36	.7	182	3.8	4,469	92.7	171	3.5	4,822
1.9	28	1.3	13	.6	92	4.4	1,945	93.0	54	2.6	2,091
1.1	31	1.1	23	.8	90	3.3	2,524	92.4	117	4.3	2,731

LTIONS)

%	NUMBER	%	NUMBER	%	NUMBER	%	NUMBER	%	NUMBER	%	NUMBER
.0	3	.9	2	.6	6	1.7	339	97.7	2	.6	347
.0	2	1.3	1	.6	4	2.5	154	96.9	1	.6	159
.0	1	.5	1	.5	2	1.1	185	98.4	1	.5	188
.0	0	.0	0	.0	0	.0	46	100.0	0	.0	46
.0	0	.0	0	.0	0	.0	39	100.0	0	.0	39
.0	0	.0	0	.0	0	.0	7	100.0	0	.0	7
.0	3	.8	2	.5	6	1.5	385	98.0	2	.5	393
.0	2	1.0	1	.5	4	2.0	193	97.5	1	.5	198
.0	1	.5	1	.5	2	1.0	192	98.5	1	.5	195
.0	0	.0	0	.0	0	.0	86	95.6	4	4.4	90
.0	0	.0	0	.0	0	.0	23	95.8	1	4.2	24
.0	0	.0	0	.0	0	.0	63	95.5	3	4.5	66
.0	0	.0	0	.0	1	3.8	23	88.5	2	7.7	26
.0	0	.0	0	.0	0	.0	7	100.0	0	.0	7
.0	0	.0	0	.0	1	5.3	16	84.2	2	10.5	19
.0	0	.0	0	.0	1	.9	109	94.0	6	5.2	116
.0	0	.0	0	.0	0	.0	30	96.8	1	3.2	31
.0	0	.0	0	.0	1	1.2	79	92.9	5	5.9	85
.0	0	.0	0	.0	0	.0	0	.0	0	.0	0
.0	0	.0	0	.0	0	.0	0	.0	0	.0	0
.0	0	.0	0	.0	0	.0	0	.0	0	.0	0
.0	0	.0	0	.0	0	.0	0	.0	0	.0	0
.0	0	.0	0	.0	0	.0	0	.0	0	.0	0
.0	0	.0	0	.0	0	.0	0	.0	0	.0	0
.0	0	.0	0	.0	0	.0	0	.0	0	.0	0
.0	0	.0	0	.0	0	.0	0	.0	0	.0	0
.0	0	.0	0	.0	0	.0	0	.0	0	.0	0
.0	3	.7	2	.5	6	1.4	425	97.3	6	1.4	437
.0	2	1.1	1	.5	4	2.2	177	96.7	2	1.1	183
.0	1	.4	1	.4	2	.8	248	97.6	4	1.6	254
.0	0	.0	0	.0	1	1.4	69	95.8	2	2.8	72
.0	0	.0	0	.0	0	.0	46	100.0	0	.0	46
.0	0	.0	0	.0	1	3.8	23	88.5	2	7.7	26
.0	3	.6	2	.4	7	1.4	494	97.1	8	1.6	509
.0	2	.9	1	.4	4	1.7	223	97.4	2	.9	229
.0	1	.4	1	.4	3	1.1	271	96.8	6	2.1	280
.0	0	.0	0	.0	1	25.0	3	75.0	0	.0	4
.0	0	.0	0	.0	0	.0	1	100.0	0	.0	1
.0	0	.0	0	.0	1	33.3	2	66.7	0	.0	3
.0	3	.6	2	.4	8	1.6	497	96.9	8	1.6	513
.0	2	.9	1	.4	4	1.7	224	97.4	2	.9	230
.0	1	.4	1	.4	4	1.4	273	96.5	6	2.1	283

MAJOR FIELD 0400 - BIOLOGICAL SCIENCES

	AMERICAN INDIAN ALASKAN NATIVE		BLACK NON-HISPANIC		ASIAN OR PACIFIC ISLANDER		HISPANIC		TOTAL MINORITY		WHITE NON-HISPANIC		NON-RESIDENT ALIEN	
	NUMBER	%	NUMBER	%	NUMBER	%	NUMBER	%	NUMBER	%	NUMBER	%	NUMBER	%
THE STATES AND D.C. (1,646 INSTITUTIONS)														
UNDERGRADUATES:														
FULL-TIME	935	.4	16,692	7.9	6,046	2.8	6,158	2.9	29,831	14.1	177,902	83.8	4,546	2.1
FEMALE	429	.5	9,663	10.3	2,760	2.9	2,614	2.8	15,486	16.5	76,890	81.8	1,675	1.8
MALE	506	.4	7,009	5.9	3,286	2.8	3,544	3.0	14,345	12.1	101,012	85.4	2,871	2.4
PART-TIME	278	.8	2,622	7.9	1,044	3.1	1,433	4.3	5,377	16.2	27,270	82.3	498	1.5
FEMALE	157	.9	1,505	8.9	476	2.8	625	3.7	2,763	16.3	13,964	82.5	203	1.2
MALE	121	.7	1,117	6.9	568	3.5	808	5.0	2,614	16.1	13,306	82.1	295	1.8
TOTAL	1,213	.5	19,314	7.9	7,090	2.9	7,591	3.1	35,208	14.3	205,172	83.6	5,044	2.1
FEMALE	586	.5	11,168	10.1	3,236	2.9	3,239	2.9	18,249	16.4	90,854	81.9	1,878	1.7
MALE	627	.5	8,126	6.0	3,854	2.9	4,352	3.2	16,959	12.6	114,318	85.0	3,166	2.4
GRADUATE:														
FULL-TIME	38	.2	557	2.1	772	2.9	295	1.1	1,682	6.3	22,487	84.5	2,436	9.2
FEMALE	18	.2	293	3.3	285	3.2	110	1.2	706	7.8	7,567	83.9	742	8.2
MALE	40	.2	264	1.5	487	2.8	185	1.1	976	5.5	14,920	84.8	1,694	9.6
PART-TIME	34	.3	512	3.4	429	2.9	207	1.4	1,187	7.9	13,095	87.1	751	5.0
FEMALE	16	.3	267	4.7	187	3.3	91	1.6	561	9.8	4,868	85.4	270	4.7
MALE	23	.2	245	2.6	242	2.6	116	1.2	626	6.7	8,227	88.1	481	5.2
TOTAL	97	.2	1,069	2.6	1,201	2.9	502	1.2	2,869	6.9	35,582	85.5	3,187	7.7
FEMALE	34	.2	560	3.8	472	3.2	201	1.4	1,267	8.6	12,435	84.5	1,012	6.9
MALE	63	.2	509	1.9	729	2.7	301	1.1	1,602	6.0	23,147	86.0	2,175	8.1
PROFESSIONAL:														
FULL-TIME	0	.0	1	2.4	1	2.4	0	.0	2	4.9	37	90.2	2	4.9
FEMALE	0	.0	1	11.1	0	.0	0	.0	1	11.1	7	77.8	1	11.1
MALE	0	.0	0	.0	1	3.1	0	.0	1	3.1	30	93.8	1	3.1
PART-TIME	0	.0	0	.0	0	.0	0	.0	0	.0	2	100.0	0	.0
FEMALE	0	.0	0	.0	0	.0	0	.0	0	.0	0	.0	0	.0
MALE	0	.0	0	.0	0	.0	0	.0	0	.0	2	100.0	0	.0
TOTAL	0	.0	1	2.3	1	2.3	0	.0	2	4.7	39	90.7	2	4.7
FEMALE	0	.0	1	11.1	0	.0	0	.0	1	11.1	7	77.8	1	11.1
MALE	0	.0	0	.0	1	2.9	0	.0	1	2.9	32	94.1	1	2.9
UND+GRAD+PROF:														
FULL-TIME	993	.4	17,250	7.2	6,819	2.9	6,453	2.7	31,515	13.2	200,426	83.9	6,984	2.9
FEMALE	447	.4	9,977	9.7	3,045	3.0	2,724	2.6	16,193	15.7	84,464	81.9	2,418	2.3
MALE	546	.4	7,273	5.4	3,774	2.8	3,729	2.7	15,322	11.3	115,962	85.4	4,566	3.4
PART-TIME	312	.7	3,134	6.5	1,473	3.1	1,640	3.4	6,564	13.6	40,367	83.8	1,249	2.6
FEMALE	173	.8	1,772	7.8	663	2.9	716	3.2	3,324	14.7	18,832	83.2	473	2.1
MALE	144	.6	1,362	5.3	810	3.2	924	3.6	3,240	12.7	21,535	84.3	776	3.0
TOTAL	1,310	.5	20,384	7.1	8,292	2.9	8,093	2.8	38,079	13.3	240,793	83.9	8,233	2.9
FEMALE	620	.5	11,749	9.3	3,708	2.9	3,440	2.7	19,517	15.5	103,296	82.2	2,891	2.3
MALE	690	.4	8,635	5.4	4,584	2.8	4,653	2.9	18,562	11.5	137,497	85.2	5,342	3.3
UNCLASSIFIED:														
TOTAL	100	1.4	426	5.9	220	3.1	258	3.6	1,004	14.0	6,003	83.7	168	2.3
FEMALE	56	1.6	224	6.5	96	2.8	107	3.1	483	14.0	2,918	84.3	60	1.7
MALE	44	1.2	202	5.4	124	3.3	151	4.1	521	14.0	3,085	83.1	108	2.9
TOTAL ENROLLMENT:														
TOTAL	1,410	.5	20,810	7.1	8,512	2.9	8,351	2.8	39,083	13.3	246,796	83.9	8,401	2.9
FEMALE	676	.5	11,973	9.3	3,804	2.9	3,547	2.7	20,000	15.5	106,214	82.2	2,951	2.3
MALE	734	.4	8,837	5.4	4,708	2.9	4,804	2.9	19,083	11.6	140,582	85.1	5,450	3.3
UTAH (1 INSTITUTIONS)														
UNDERGRADUATES:														
FULL-TIME	0	.0	1	2.5	17	42.5	1	2.5	19	47.5	18	45.0	3	7.5
FEMALE	0	.0	1	6.3	7	43.8	1	6.3	9	56.3	7	43.8	0	.0
MALE	0	.0	0	.0	10	41.7	0	.0	10	41.7	11	45.8	3	12.5
PART-TIME	0	.0	0	.0	5	45.5	1	9.1	6	54.5	5	45.5	0	.0
FEMALE	0	.0	0	.0	1	25.0	0	.0	1	25.0	3	75.0	0	.0
MALE	0	.0	0	.0	4	57.1	1	14.3	5	71.4	2	28.6	0	.0
TOTAL	0	.0	1	2.0	22	43.1	2	3.9	25	49.0	23	45.1	3	5.9
FEMALE	0	.0	1	5.0	8	40.0	1	5.0	10	50.0	10	50.0	0	.0
MALE	0	.0	0	.0	14	45.2	1	3.2	15	48.4	13	41.9	3	9.7
GRADUATE:														
FULL-TIME	0	.0	0	.0	0	.0	0	.0	0	.0	0	.0	0	.0
FEMALE	0	.0	0	.0	0	.0	0	.0	0	.0	0	.0	0	.0
MALE	0	.0	0	.0	0	.0	0	.0	0	.0	0	.0	0	.0
PART-TIME	0	.0	0	.0	0	.0	0	.0	0	.0	1	100.0	0	.0
FEMALE	0	.0	0	.0	0	.0	0	.0	0	.0	0	.0	0	.0
MALE	0	.0	0	.0	0	.0	0	.0	0	.0	1	100.0	0	.0
TOTAL	0	.0	0	.0	0	.0	0	.0	0	.0	1	100.0	0	.0
FEMALE	0	.0	0	.0	0	.0	0	.0	0	.0	0	.0	0	.0
MALE	0	.0	0	.0	0	.0	0	.0	0	.0	1	100.0	0	.0
PROFESSIONAL:														
FULL-TIME	0	.0	0	.0	0	.0	0	.0	0	.0	0	.0	0	.0
FEMALE	0	.0	0	.0	0	.0	0	.0	0	.0	0	.0	0	.0
MALE	0	.0	0	.0	0	.0	0	.0	0	.0	0	.0	0	.0

ENROLLMENT IN INSTITUTIONS OF HIGHER EDUCATION FOR SELECTED MAJOR FIELDS OF STUDY AND LEVEL OF ENROLLMENT ETHNICITY, AND SEX: STATE, 1978

BIOLOGICAL SCIENCES

INDIAN NATIVE	BLACK NON-HISPANIC		ASIAN OR PACIFIC ISLANDER		HISPANIC		TOTAL MINORITY		WHITE NON-HISPANIC		NON-RESIDENT ALIEN		TOTAL
%	NUMBER	%	NUMBER	%	NUMBER	%	NUMBER	%	NUMBER	%	NUMBER	%	NUMBER

CONTINUED

.0	0	.0	0	.0	0	.0	0	.0	0	.0	0	.0	
.0	0	.0	0	.0	0	.0	0	.0	0	.0	0	.0	8
.0	0	.0	0	.0	0	.0	0	.0	0	.0	0	.0	8
.0	0	.0	0	.0	0	.0	0	.0	0	.0		.0	
.0	0	.0	0	.0	0	.0	0	.0	0	.0	8	.0	8
.0	0	.0	0	.0	0	.0	0	.0	0	.0		.0	8
.0	1	2.5	17	42.5	1	2.5	19	47.5	18	45.0		7.5	40
.0	1	6.3	7	43.8	1	6.3	9	56.3	7	43.8		.0	16
.0	0	.0	10	41.7	0	.0	10	41.7	11	45.8		12.5	24
.0	0	.0	5	41.7	1	8.3	6	50.0	6	50.0		.0	12
.0	0	.0	1	25.0	0	.0	1	25.0	3	75.0		.0	4
.0	0	.0	4	50.0	1	12.5	5	62.5	3	37.5	8	.0	8
.0	1	1.9	22	42.3	2	3.8	25	48.1	24	46.2		5.8	52
.0	1	5.0	8	40.0	1	5.0	10	50.0	10	50.0		.0	20
.0	0	.0	14	43.8	1	3.1	15	46.9	14	43.8	8	9.4	32
.0	0	.0	0	.0	0	.0	0	.0	0	.0	0	.0	
.0	0	.0	0	.0	0	.0	0	.0	0	.0	0	.0	8
.0	0	.0	0	.0	0	.0	0	.0	0	.0	0	.0	8
.0	1	1.9	22	42.3	2	3.8	25	48.1	24	46.2	3	5.8	52
.0	1	5.0	8	40.0	1	5.0	10	50.0	10	50.0	0	.0	20
.0	0	.0	14	43.8	1	3.1	15	46.9	14	43.8	3	9.4	32

(17 INSTITUTIONS)

.0	0	.0	0	.0	6,290	99.5	6,290	99.5	30	.5		.0	6,320
.0	0	.0	0	.0	3,533	99.5	3,533	99.5	17	.5		.0	3,550
.0	0	.0	0	.0	2,757	99.5	2,757	99.5	13	.5		.0	2,770
.0	0	.0	0	.0	824	99.5	824	99.5	4	.5		.0	828
.0	0	.0	0	.0	450	99.6	450	99.6	2	.4		.0	452
.0	0	.0	0	.0	374	99.5	374	99.5	2	.5	0	.0	376
.0	0	.0	0	.0	7,114	99.5	7,114	99.5	34	.5	0	.0	7,148
.0	0	.0	0	.0	3,983	99.5	3,983	99.5	19	.5	0	.0	4,002
.0	0	.0	0	.0	3,131	99.5	3,131	99.5	15	.5	0	.0	3,146
.0	0	.0	0	.0	39	100.0	39	100.0	0	.0		.0	39
.0	0	.0	0	.0	19	100.0	19	100.0	0	.0		.0	19
.0	0	.0	0	.0	20	100.0	20	100.0	0	.0		.0	20
.0	0	.0	0	.0	107	100.0	107	100.0	0	.0		.0	107
.0	0	.0	0	.0	43	100.0	43	100.0	0	.0		.0	43
.0	0	.0	0	.0	64	100.0	64	100.0	0	.0	8	.0	64
.0	0	.0	0	.0	146	100.0	146	100.0	0	.0		.0	146
.0	0	.0	0	.0	62	100.0	62	100.0	0	.0		.0	62
.0	0	.0	0	.0	84	100.0	84	100.0	0	.0	8	.0	84
.0	0	.0	0	.0	0	.0	0	.0	0	.0		.0	
.0	0	.0	0	.0	0	.0	0	.0	0	.0		.0	
.0	0	.0	0	.0	0	.0	0	.0	0	.0		.0	
.0	0	.0	0	.0	0	.0	0	.0	0	.0		.0	
.0	0	.0	0	.0	0	.0	0	.0	0	.0		.0	
.0	0	.0	0	.0	0	.0	0	.0	0	.0	8	.0	0
.0	0	.0	0	.0	0	.0	0	.0	0	.0		.0	0
.0	0	.0	0	.0	0	.0	0	.0	0	.0		.0	0
.0	0	.0	0	.0	0	.0	0	.0	0	.0	8	.0	0
.0	0	.0	0	.0	6,329	99.5	6,329	99.5	30	.5		.0	6,359
.0	0	.0	0	.0	3,552	99.5	3,552	99.5	17	.5		.0	3,569
.0	0	.0	0	.0	2,777	99.5	2,777	99.5	13	.5		.0	2,790
.0	0	.0	0	.0	931	99.6	931	99.6	4	.4		.0	935
.0	0	.0	0	.0	493	99.6	493	99.6	2	.4		.0	495
.0	0	.0	0	.0	438	99.5	438	99.5	2	.5	8	.0	440
.0	0	.0	0	.0	7,260	99.5	7,260	99.5	34	.5	0	.0	7,294
.0	0	.0	0	.0	4,045	99.5	4,045	99.5	19	.5	0	.0	4,064
.0	0	.0	0	.0	3,215	99.5	3,215	99.5	15	.5	0	.0	3,230
.0	0	.0	0	.0	33	100.0	33	100.0	0	.0		.0	33
.0	0	.0	0	.0	19	100.0	19	100.0	0	.0		.0	19
.0	0	.0	0	.0	14	100.0	14	100.0	0	.0	8	.0	14
.0	0	.0	0	.0	7,293	99.5	7,293	99.5	34	.5		.0	7,327
.0	0	.0	0	.0	4,064	99.5	4,064	99.5	19	.5		.0	4,083
.0	0	.0	0	.0	3,229	99.5	3,229	99.5	15	.5	8	.0	3,244

MAJOR FIELD 0400 - BIOLOGICAL SCIENCES

	AMERICAN INDIAN ALASKAN NATIVE		BLACK NON-HISPANIC		ASIAN OR PACIFIC ISLANDER		HISPANIC		TOTAL MINORITY		WHITE NON-HISPANIC		NON-RESIDENT ALIEN		T
	NUMBER	%	NUMBER	%	NUMBER	%	NUMBER	%	NUMBER	%	NUMBER	%	NUMBER	%	N
VIRGIN ISLANDS (1 INSTITUTIONS)															
UNDERGRADUATES:															
FULL-TIME	0	.0	16	39.0	0	.0	2	4.9	18	43.9	14	34.1	9	22.0	
FEMALE	0	.0	12	60.0	0	.0	0	.0	12	60.0	6	30.0	2	10.0	
MALE	0	.0	4	19.0	0	.0	2	9.5	6	28.6	8	38.1	7	33.3	
PART-TIME	0	.0	0	.0	0	.0	0	.0	0	.0	0	.0	0	.0	
FEMALE	0	.0	0	.0	0	.0	0	.0	0	.0	0	.0	0	.0	
MALE	0	.0	0	.0	0	.0	0	.0	0	.0	0	.0	0	.0	
TOTAL	0	.0	16	39.0	0	.0	2	4.9	18	43.9	14	34.1	9	22.0	
FEMALE	0	.0	12	60.0	0	.0	0	.0	12	60.0	6	30.0	2	10.0	
MALE	0	.0	4	19.0	0	.0	2	9.5	6	28.6	8	38.1	7	33.3	
GRADUATE:															
FULL-TIME	0	.0	0	.0	0	.0	0	.0	0	.0	0	.0	0	.0	
FEMALE	0	.0	0	.0	0	.0	0	.0	0	.0	0	.0	0	.0	
MALE	0	.0	0	.0	0	.0	0	.0	0	.0	0	.0	0	.0	
PART-TIME	0	.0	0	.0	0	.0	0	.0	0	.0	0	.0	0	.0	
FEMALE	0	.0	0	.0	0	.0	0	.0	0	.0	0	.0	0	.0	
MALE	0	.0	0	.0	0	.0	0	.0	0	.0	0	.0	0	.0	
TOTAL	0	.0	0	.0	0	.0	0	.0	0	.0	0	.0	0	.0	
FEMALE	0	.0	0	.0	0	.0	0	.0	0	.0	0	.0	0	.0	
MALE	0	.0	0	.0	0	.0	0	.0	0	.0	0	.0	0	.0	
PROFESSIONAL:															
FULL-TIME	0	.0	0	.0	0	.0	0	.0	0	.0	0	.0	0	.0	
FEMALE	0	.0	0	.0	0	.0	0	.0	0	.0	0	.0	0	.0	
MALE	0	.0	0	.0	0	.0	0	.0	0	.0	0	.0	0	.0	
PART-TIME	0	.0	0	.0	0	.0	0	.0	0	.0	0	.0	0	.0	
FEMALE	0	.0	0	.0	0	.0	0	.0	0	.0	0	.0	0	.0	
MALE	0	.0	0	.0	0	.0	0	.0	0	.0	0	.0	0	.0	
TOTAL	0	.0	0	.0	0	.0	0	.0	0	.0	0	.0	0	.0	
FEMALE	0	.0	0	.0	0	.0	0	.0	0	.0	0	.0	0	.0	
MALE	0	.0	0	.0	0	.0	0	.0	0	.0	0	.0	0	.0	
UNG+GRAD+PROF:															
FULL-TIME	0	.0	16	39.0	0	.0	2	4.9	18	43.9	14	34.1	9	22.0	
FEMALE	0	.0	12	60.0	0	.0	0	.0	12	60.0	6	30.0	2	10.0	
MALE	0	.0	4	19.0	0	.0	2	9.5	6	28.6	8	38.1	7	33.3	
PART-TIME	0	.0	0	.0	0	.0	0	.0	0	.0	0	.0	0	.0	
FEMALE	0	.0	0	.0	0	.0	0	.0	0	.0	0	.0	0	.0	
MALE	0	.0	0	.0	0	.0	0	.0	0	.0	0	.0	0	.0	
TOTAL	0	.0	16	39.0	0	.0	2	4.9	18	43.9	14	34.1	9	22.0	
FEMALE	0	.0	12	60.0	0	.0	0	.0	12	60.0	6	30.0	2	10.0	
MALE	0	.0	4	19.0	0	.0	2	9.5	6	28.6	8	38.1	7	33.3	
UNCLASSIFIED:															
TOTAL	0	.0	0	.0	0	.0	0	.0	0	.0	0	.0	0	.0	
FEMALE	0	.0	0	.0	0	.0	0	.0	0	.0	0	.0	0	.0	
MALE	0	.0	0	.0	0	.0	0	.0	0	.0	0	.0	0	.0	
TOTAL ENROLLMENT:															
TOTAL	0	.0	16	39.0	0	.0	2	4.9	18	43.9	14	34.1	9	22.0	
FEMALE	0	.0	12	60.0	0	.0	0	.0	12	60.0	6	30.0	2	10.0	
MALE	0	.0	4	19.0	0	.0	2	9.5	6	28.6	8	38.1	7	33.3	
OUTLYING AREAS (19 INSTITUTIONS)															
UNDERGRADUATES:															
FULL-TIME	0	.0	17	.3	17	.3	6,293	98.3	6,327	98.8	62	1.0	12	.2	
FEMALE	0	.0	13	.4	7	.2	3,534	98.5	3,554	99.1	30	.8	2	.1	
MALE	0	.0	4	.1	10	.4	2,759	98.0	2,773	98.5	32	1.1	10	.4	
PART-TIME	0	.0	0	.0	5	.6	825	98.3	830	98.9	9	1.1	0	.0	
FEMALE	0	.0	0	.0	1	.2	450	98.7	451	98.9	5	1.1	0	.0	
MALE	0	.0	0	.0	4	1.0	375	97.9	379	99.0	4	1.0	0	.0	
TOTAL	0	.0	17	.2	22	.3	7,118	98.3	7,157	98.9	71	1.0	12	.2	
FEMALE	0	.0	13	.3	8	.2	3,984	98.6	4,005	99.1	35	.9	2	.0	
MALE	0	.0	4	.1	14	.4	3,134	98.0	3,152	98.6	36	1.1	10	.3	
GRADUATE:															
FULL-TIME	0	.0	0	.0	0	.0	39	100.0	39	100.0	0	.0	0	.0	
FEMALE	0	.0	0	.0	0	.0	19	100.0	19	100.0	0	.0	0	.0	
MALE	0	.0	0	.0	0	.0	20	100.0	20	100.0	0	.0	0	.0	
PART-TIME	0	.0	0	.0	0	.0	107	99.1	107	99.1	1	.9	0	.0	
FEMALE	0	.0	0	.0	0	.0	43	100.0	43	100.0	0	.0	0	.0	
MALE	0	.0	0	.0	0	.0	64	98.5	64	98.5	1	1.5	0	.0	
TOTAL	0	.0	0	.0	0	.0	146	99.3	146	99.3	1	.7	0	.0	
FEMALE	0	.0	0	.0	0	.0	62	100.0	62	100.0	0	.0	0	.0	
MALE	0	.0	0	.0	0	.0	84	98.8	84	98.8	1	1.2	0	.0	
PROFESSIONAL:															
FULL-TIME	0	.0	0	.0	0	.0	0	.0	0	.0	0	.0	0	.0	
FEMALE	0	.0	0	.0	0	.0	0	.0	0	.0	0	.0	0	.0	
MALE	0	.0	0	.0	0	.0	0	.0	0	.0	0	.0	0	.0	

ROLLMENT IN INSTITUTIONS OF HIGHER EDUCATION FOR SELECTED MAJOR FIELDS OF STUDY AND LEVEL OF ENROLLMENT
ETHNICITY, AND SEX: STATE, 1978

BIOLOGICAL SCIENCES

INDIAN NATIVE	BLACK NON-HISPANIC		ASIAN OR PACIFIC ISLANDER		HISPANIC		TOTAL MINORITY		WHITE NON-HISPANIC		NON-RESIDENT ALIEN		TOTAL
%	NUMBER	%	NUMBER	%	NUMBER	%	NUMBER	%	NUMBER	%	NUMBER	%	NUMBER

CONTINUED

.0	0	.0	0	.0	0	.0	0	.0	0	.0	0	.0	0
.0	0	.0	0	.0	0	.0	0	.0	0	.0	0	.0	0
.0	0	.0	0	.0	0	.0	0	.0	0	.0	0	.0	0
.0	0	.0	0	.0	0	.0	0	.0	0	.0	0	.0	0
.0	0	.0	0	.0	0	.0	0	.0	0	.0	0	.0	0
.0	0	.0	0	.0	0	.0	0	.0	0	.0	0	.0	0
.0	17	.3	17	.3	6,332	98.3	6,366	96.9	62	1.0	12	.2	6,440
.0	13	.4	7	.2	3,553	98.6	3,573	99.1	30	.8	2	.1	3,605
.0	4	.1	10	.4	2,779	98.0	2,793	98.5	32	1.1	10	.4	2,835
.0	0	.0	5	.5	932	98.4	937	98.9	10	1.1	0	.0	947
.0	0	.0	1	.2	493	98.8	494	99.0	5	1.0	0	.0	459
.0	0	.0	4	.9	439	98.0	443	98.9	5	1.1	0	.0	448
.0	17	.2	22	.3	7,264	98.3	7,303	98.9	72	1.0	12	.2	7,387
.0	13	.3	8	.2	4,046	98.6	4,067	99.1	35	.9	2	.0	4,104
.0	4	.1	14	.4	3,218	98.0	3,236	98.6	37	1.1	10	.3	3,283
.0	0	.0	0	.0	33	100.0	33	100.0	0	.0	0	.0	33
.0	0	.0	0	.0	19	100.0	19	100.0	0	.0	0	.0	19
.0	0	.0	0	.0	14	100.0	14	100.0	0	.0	0	.0	14
.0	17	.2	22	.3	7,297	98.3	7,336	98.9	72	1.0	12	.2	7,420
.0	13	.3	8	.2	4,065	98.6	4,086	99.1	35	.8	2	.0	4,123
.0	4	.1	14	.4	3,232	98.6	3,250	98.6	37	1.1	10	.3	3,297

E 0400 (1,665 INSTITUTIONS)

.4	16,709	7.6	6,063	2.8	12,451	5.7	36,158	16.5	177,964	81.4	4,558	2.1	218,680
.4	9,696	9.9	2,767	2.8	6,148	6.3	19,040	19.5	76,920	78.8	1,677	1.7	97,637
.4	7,013	5.8	3,296	2.7	6,303	5.2	17,118	14.1	101,044	83.5	2,881	2.4	121,043
.8	2,622	7.7	1,049	3.1	2,258	6.6	6,207	18.3	27,279	80.3	498	1.5	33,984
.9	1,505	8.7	477	2.7	1,075	6.2	3,214	18.5	13,969	80.3	203	1.2	17,386
.7	1,117	6.7	572	3.4	1,183	7.1	2,993	18.0	13,310	80.2	295	1.8	16,598
.5	19,331	7.7	7,112	2.8	14,709	5.8	42,365	16.8	205,243	81.2	5,056	2.0	252,664
.5	11,201	9.7	3,244	2.8	7,223	6.3	22,254	19.3	90,889	79.0	1,880	1.6	115,023
.5	8,130	5.9	3,868	2.8	7,486	5.4	20,111	14.6	114,354	83.1	3,176	2.3	137,641
.2	557	2.1	772	2.9	334	1.3	1,721	6.5	22,487	84.4	2,436	9.1	26,644
.2	293	3.2	285	3.2	129	1.4	725	8.0	7,567	83.8	742	8.2	9,034
.2	264	1.5	487	2.8	205	1.2	996	5.7	14,920	84.7	1,694	9.6	17,610
.3	512	3.4	429	2.8	314	2.1	1,294	8.5	13,096	86.5	751	5.0	15,141
.3	267	4.6	187	3.3	134	2.3	604	10.5	4,868	84.8	270	4.7	5,742
.2	245	2.6	242	2.6	180	1.9	690	7.3	8,228	87.5	481	5.1	9,399
.2	1,069	2.6	1,201	2.9	648	1.6	3,015	7.2	35,583	85.2	3,187	7.6	41,785
.2	560	3.8	472	3.2	263	1.8	1,329	9.0	12,435	84.2	1,012	6.8	14,776
.2	509	1.9	729	2.7	385	1.4	1,686	6.2	23,148	85.7	2,175	8.1	27,009
.0	1	2.4	1	2.4	0	.0	2	4.9	37	90.2	2	4.9	41
.0	1	11.1	0	.0	0	.0	1	11.1	7	77.8	1	11.1	9
.0	0	.0	1	3.1	0	.0	1	3.1	30	93.8	1	3.1	32
.0	0	.0	0	.0	0	.0	0	.0	2	100.0	0	.0	2
.0	0	.0	0	.0	0	.0	0	.0	0	.0	0	.0	0
.0	0	.0	0	.0	0	.0	0	.0	2	100.0	0	.0	2
.0	1	2.3	1	2.3	0	.0	2	4.7	39	90.7	2	4.7	43
.0	1	11.1	0	.0	0	.0	1	11.1	7	77.8	1	11.1	9
.0	0	.0	1	2.9	0	.0	1	2.9	32	94.1	1	2.9	34
.4	17,267	7.0	6,836	2.8	12,785	5.2	37,881	15.4	200,488	81.7	6,996	2.9	245,365
.4	9,990	9.4	3,052	2.9	6,277	5.9	19,766	18.5	84,494	79.2	2,420	2.3	106,680
.4	7,277	5.2	3,784	2.7	6,508	4.7	18,115	13.1	115,994	83.6	4,576	3.3	138,685
.6	3,134	6.4	1,478	3.0	2,572	5.2	7,501	15.3	40,377	82.2	1,249	2.5	49,127
.7	1,772	7.7	664	2.9	1,209	5.2	3,818	16.5	18,837	81.4	473	2.0	23,128
.6	1,362	5.2	814	3.1	1,363	5.2	3,683	14.2	21,540	82.8	776	3.0	25,999
.4	20,401	6.9	8,314	2.8	15,357	5.2	45,382	15.4	240,865	81.8	8,245	2.8	294,492
.5	11,762	9.1	3,716	2.9	7,486	5.8	23,584	18.2	103,331	79.6	2,893	2.2	129,808
.4	8,639	5.2	4,598	2.8	7,871	4.8	21,798	13.2	137,534	83.5	5,352	3.2	164,684
1.4	426	5.9	220	3.1	291	4.0	1,037	14.4	6,003	83.3	164	2.3	7,208
1.6	224	6.4	96	2.8	126	3.6	502	14.4	2,918	83.9	60	1.7	3,480
1.2	202	5.4	124	3.3	165	4.4	535	14.4	3,085	82.8	108	2.9	3,728
.5	20,827	6.9	8,534	2.8	15,648	5.2	46,419	15.4	246,868	81.8	8,413	2.8	301,700
.5	11,986	9.0	3,812	2.9	7,612	5.7	24,086	18.1	106,249	79.7	2,953	2.2	133,288
.4	8,841	5.2	4,722	2.8	8,036	4.8	22,333	13.3	140,619	83.5	5,460	3.2	168,412

MAJOR FIELD 0500 - BUSINESS AND MANAGEMENT

	AMERICAN INDIAN ALASKAN NATIVE		BLACK NON-HISPANIC		ASIAN OR PACIFIC ISLANDER		HISPANIC		TOTAL MINORITY		WHITE NON-HISPANIC		NON-RESIDENT ALIEN	
	NUMBER	%	NUMBER	%	NUMBER	%	NUMBER	%	NUMBER	%	NUMBER	%	NUMBER	%
ALABAMA			52 INSTITUTIONS)											
UNDERGRADUATES:														
FULL-TIME	11	.1	4,793	21.9	41	.2	44	.2	4,889	22.3	16,718	76.3	310	1.4
FEMALE	2	.0	2,550	30.2	20	.2	12	.1	2,584	30.6	5,826	68.9	41	.5
MALE	9	.1	2,243	16.7	21	.2	32	.2	2,305	17.1	10,892	80.9	269	2.0
PART-TIME	14	.2	971	12.3	21	.3	27	.3	1,033	13.1	6,828	86.6	25	.3
FEMALE	8	.3	487	15.6	6	.2	9	.3	510	16.3	2,601	83.4	9	.3
MALE	6	.1	484	10.2	15	.3	18	.4	523	11.0	4,227	88.7	16	.3
TOTAL	25	.1	5,764	19.3	62	.2	71	.2	5,922	19.9	23,546	79.0	335	1.1
FEMALE	10	.1	3,037	26.2	26	.2	21	.2	3,094	26.7	8,427	72.8	50	.4
MALE	15	.1	2,727	15.0	36	.2	50	.3	2,828	15.5	15,119	82.9	285	1.6
GRADUATE:														
FULL-TIME	2	.2	76	7.9	4	.4	3	.3	85	8.9	793	82.6	82	8.5
FEMALE	0	.0	26	15.6	2	1.2	0	.0	28	16.8	125	74.9	14	8.4
MALE	2	.3	50	6.3	2	.3	3	.4	57	7.2	668	84.2	68	8.6
PART-TIME	1	.1	159	12.0	3	.2	3	.2	166	12.5	1,133	85.6	24	1.8
FEMALE	0	.0	72	24.3	1	.3	0	.0	73	24.7	218	73.6	5	1.7
MALE	1	.1	87	8.5	2	.2	3	.3	93	9.1	915	89.1	19	1.9
TOTAL	3	.1	235	10.3	7	.3	6	.3	251	11.0	1,926	84.4	106	4.6
FEMALE	0	.0	98	21.2	3	.6	0	.0	101	21.8	343	74.1	19	4.1
MALE	3	.2	137	7.5	4	.2	6	.3	150	8.2	1,583	87.0	87	4.8
PROFESSIONAL:														
FULL-TIME	0	.0	0	.0	0	.0	0	.0	0	.0	0	.0	0	.0
FEMALE	0	.0	0	.0	0	.0	0	.0	0	.0	0	.0	0	.0
MALE	0	.0	0	.0	0	.0	0	.0	0	.0	0	.0	0	.0
PART-TIME	0	.0	0	.0	0	.0	0	.0	0	.0	0	.0	0	.0
FEMALE	0	.0	0	.0	0	.0	0	.0	0	.0	0	.0	0	.0
MALE	0	.0	0	.0	0	.0	0	.0	0	.0	0	.0	0	.0
TOTAL	0	.0	0	.0	0	.0	0	.0	0	.0	0	.0	0	.0
FEMALE	0	.0	0	.0	0	.0	0	.0	0	.0	0	.0	0	.0
MALE	0	.0	0	.0	0	.0	0	.0	0	.0	0	.0	0	.0
UND+GRAD+PROF:														
FULL-TIME	13	.1	4,869	21.3	45	.2	47	.2	4,974	21.7	17,511	76.5	392	1.7
FEMALE	2	.0	2,576	29.9	22	.3	12	.1	2,612	30.3	5,951	69.1	55	.6
MALE	11	.1	2,293	16.1	23	.2	35	.2	2,362	16.6	11,560	81.1	337	2.4
PART-TIME	15	.1	1,130	12.3	24	.3	30	.3	1,199	13.0	7,961	86.4	49	.5
FEMALE	8	.2	559	16.4	7	.2	9	.3	583	17.1	2,819	82.5	14	.4
MALE	7	.1	571	9.9	17	.3	21	.4	616	10.6	5,142	88.8	35	.6
TOTAL	28	.1	5,999	18.7	69	.2	77	.2	6,173	19.2	25,472	79.4	441	1.4
FEMALE	10	.1	3,135	26.1	29	.2	21	.2	3,195	26.5	8,770	72.9	69	.6
MALE	18	.1	2,864	14.3	40	.2	56	.3	2,978	14.9	16,702	83.3	372	1.9
UNCLASSIFIED:														
TOTAL	0	.0	114	15.2	0	.0	0	.0	114	15.2	632	84.4	3	.4
FEMALE	0	.0	65	21.5	0	.0	0	.0	65	21.5	237	78.5	0	.0
MALE	0	.0	49	11.0	0	.0	0	.0	49	11.0	395	88.4	3	.7
TOTAL ENROLLMENT:														
TOTAL	28	.1	6,113	18.6	69	.2	77	.2	6,287	19.1	26,104	79.5	444	1.4
FEMALE	10	.1	3,200	25.9	29	.2	21	.2	3,260	26.4	9,007	73.0	69	.6
MALE	18	.1	2,913	14.2	40	.2	56	.3	3,027	14.8	17,097	83.4	375	1.8
ALASKA			10 INSTITUTIONS)											
UNDERGRADUATES:														
FULL-TIME	50	14.7	12	3.5	11	3.2	4	1.2	77	22.6	260	76.2	4	1.2
FEMALE	30	18.3	4	2.4	6	3.7	2	1.2	42	25.6	122	74.4	0	.0
MALE	20	11.3	8	4.5	5	2.8	2	1.1	35	19.8	138	78.0	4	2.3
PART-TIME	17	5.3	13	4.1	6	1.9	3	.9	39	12.2	281	87.8	0	.0
FEMALE	10	5.0	8	4.0	2	1.0	0	.0	20	10.1	179	89.9	0	.0
MALE	7	5.8	5	4.1	4	3.3	3	2.5	19	15.7	102	84.3	0	.0
TOTAL	67	10.1	25	3.8	17	2.6	7	1.1	116	17.5	541	81.8	4	.6
FEMALE	40	11.0	12	3.3	8	2.2	2	.6	62	17.1	301	82.9	0	.0
MALE	27	9.1	13	4.4	9	3.0	5	1.7	54	18.1	240	80.5	4	1.3
GRADUATE:														
FULL-TIME	0	.0	0	.0	0	.0	0	.0	0	.0	16	88.9	2	11.1
FEMALE	0	.0	0	.0	0	.0	0	.0	0	.0	6	100.0	0	.0
MALE	0	.0	0	.0	0	.0	0	.0	0	.0	10	83.3	2	16.7
PART-TIME	3	3.3	4	4.3	0	.0	1	1.1	8	8.7	83	90.2	1	1.1
FEMALE	2	6.9	0	.0	0	.0	0	.0	2	6.9	27	93.1	0	.0
MALE	1	1.6	4	6.3	0	.0	1	1.6	6	9.5	56	88.9	1	1.6
TOTAL	3	2.7	4	3.6	0	.0	1	.9	8	7.3	99	90.0	3	2.7
FEMALE	2	5.7	0	.0	0	.0	0	.0	2	5.7	33	94.3	0	.0
MALE	1	1.3	4	5.3	0	.0	1	1.3	6	8.0	66	88.0	3	4.0
PROFESSIONAL:														
FULL-TIME	0	.0	0	.0	0	.0	0	.0	0	.0	0	.0	0	.0
FEMALE	0	.0	0	.0	0	.0	0	.0	0	.0	0	.0	0	.0
MALE	0	.0	0	.0	0	.0	0	.0	0	.0	0	.0	0	.0

BUSINESS AND MANAGEMENT

INDIAN NATIVE	BLACK NON-HISPANIC		ASIAN OR PACIFIC ISLANDER		HISPANIC		TOTAL MINORITY		WHITE NON-HISPANIC		NON-RESIDENT ALIEN		TOTAL
%	NUMBER	%	NUMBER	%	NUMBER	%	NUMBER	%	NUMBER	%	NUMBER	%	NUMBER
CONTINUED													
.0	0	.0	0	.0	0	.0	0	.0	0	.0	0	.0	0
.0	0	.0	0	.0	0	.0	0	.0	0	.0	0	.0	0
.0	0	.0	0	.0	0	.0	0	.0	0	.0	0	.0	0
.0	0	.0	0	.0	0	.0	0	.0	0	.0	0	.0	0
.0	0	.0	0	.0	0	.0	0	.0	0	.0	0	.0	0
.0	0	.0	0	.0	0	.0	0	.0	0	.0	0	.0	0
13.9	12	3.3	11	3.1	4	1.1	77	21.4	276	76.9	6	1.7	359
17.6	4	2.4	6	3.5	2	1.2	42	24.7	128	75.3	0	.0	170
10.6	8	4.2	5	2.6	2	1.1	35	18.5	148	78.3	6	3.2	189
4.9	17	4.1	6	1.5	4	1.0	47	11.4	364	88.3	1	.2	412
5.3	8	3.5	2	.9	0	.0	22	9.6	206	90.4	0	.0	228
4.3	9	4.9	4	2.2	4	2.2	25	13.6	158	85.9	1	.5	184
9.1	29	3.8	17	2.2	8	1.0	124	16.1	640	83.0	7	.9	771
10.6	12	3.0	8	2.0	2	.5	64	16.1	334	83.9	0	.0	398
7.5	17	4.6	9	2.4	6	1.6	60	16.1	306	82.0	7	1.9	373
21.0	5	2.0	8	3.2	1	.4	66	26.6	182	73.4	0	.0	248
21.9	1	.6	6	3.6	0	.0	44	26.0	125	74.0	0	.0	169
19.0	4	5.1	2	2.5	1	1.3	22	27.8	57	72.2	0	.0	79
12.0	34	3.3	25	2.5	9	.9	190	18.6	822	80.7	7	.7	1,019
13.9	13	2.3	14	2.5	2	.4	108	19.0	459	81.0	0	.0	567
9.5	21	4.6	11	2.4	7	1.5	82	18.1	363	80.3	7	1.5	452
(16 INSTITUTIONS)													
1.7	352	2.7	141	1.1	739	5.6	1,461	11.0	11,566	87.5	198	1.5	13,225
3.1	131	2.8	68	1.4	306	6.5	649	13.8	4,021	85.2	47	1.0	4,717
1.0	221	2.6	73	.9	433	5.1	812	9.5	7,545	88.7	151	1.8	8,508
1.7	305	3.9	116	1.5	728	9.3	1,278	16.4	6,473	82.9	57	.7	7,808
2.3	140	3.9	70	2.0	352	9.9	645	18.1	2,908	81.4	19	.5	3,572
1.1	165	3.9	46	1.1	376	8.9	633	14.9	3,565	84.2	38	.9	4,236
1.7	657	3.1	257	1.2	1,467	7.0	2,739	13.0	18,039	85.8	255	1.2	21,033
2.7	271	3.3	138	1.7	658	7.9	1,294	15.6	6,929	83.6	66	.8	8,289
1.0	386	3.0	119	.9	809	6.3	1,445	11.3	11,110	87.2	189	1.5	12,744
.3	9	.6	16	1.0	16	1.0	46	2.8	1,297	80.1	276	17.0	1,619
1.3	4	1.7	6	2.6	6	2.6	19	8.1	195	83.0	21	8.9	235
.1	5	.4	10	.7	10	.7	27	2.0	1,102	79.6	255	18.4	1,384
.3	3	.6	8	1.1	10	1.4	23	3.3	664	94.3	17	2.4	704
.6	0	.0	1	.6	2	1.1	4	2.3	167	96.0	3	1.7	174
.2	3	.6	7	1.3	8	1.5	19	3.6	497	93.8	14	2.6	530
.3	12	.5	24	1.0	26	1.1	69	3.0	1,961	84.4	293	12.6	2,323
1.0	4	1.0	7	1.7	8	2.0	23	5.6	362	88.5	24	5.9	409
.2	8	.4	17	.9	18	.9	46	2.4	1,599	83.5	269	14.1	1,914
.0	0	.0	0	.0	0	.0	0	.0	0	.0	0	.0	0
.0	0	.0	0	.0	0	.0	0	.0	0	.0	0	.0	0
.0	0	.0	0	.0	0	.0	0	.0	0	.0	0	.0	0
.0	0	.0	0	.0	0	.0	0	.0	0	.0	0	.0	0
.0	0	.0	0	.0	0	.0	0	.0	0	.0	0	.0	0
.0	0	.0	0	.0	0	.0	0	.0	0	.0	0	.0	0
.0	0	.0	0	.0	0	.0	0	.0	0	.0	0	.0	0
.0	0	.0	0	.0	0	.0	0	.0	0	.0	0	.0	0
1.6	361	2.4	157	1.1	755	5.1	1,507	10.2	12,863	86.7	474	3.2	14,844
3.0	135	2.7	74	1.5	312	6.3	668	13.5	4,216	85.1	68	1.4	4,952
.9	226	2.3	83	.8	443	4.5	839	8.5	8,647	87.4	406	4.1	9,692
1.5	308	3.6	124	1.5	738	8.7	1,301	15.3	7,137	83.8	74	.9	8,512
2.2	140	3.7	71	1.9	354	9.5	649	17.3	3,075	82.1	22	.6	3,746
1.0	168	3.5	53	1.1	384	8.1	652	13.7	4,062	85.2	52	1.1	4,766
1.6	669	2.9	281	1.2	1,493	6.4	2,808	12.0	20,000	85.6	548	2.3	23,356
2.7	275	3.2	145	1.7	666	7.7	1,317	15.1	7,291	83.8	90	1.0	8,698
.9	394	2.7	136	.9	827	5.6	1,491	10.2	12,709	86.7	458	3.1	14,658
3.8	9	3.8	1	.4	38	15.9	57	23.8	180	75.3	2	.8	239
6.1	3	2.3	0	.0	24	18.3	35	26.7	95	72.5	1	.8	131
.9	6	5.6	1	.9	14	13.0	22	20.4	85	78.7	1	.9	108
1.6	678	2.9	282	1.2	1,531	6.5	2,865	12.1	20,180	85.5	550	2.3	23,595
2.7	278	3.1	145	1.6	690	7.8	1,352	15.3	7,386	83.7	91	1.0	8,829
.9	400	2.7	137	.9	841	5.7	1,513	10.2	12,794	86.6	459	3.1	14,766

TABLE 17 - TOTAL ENROLLMENT IN INSTITUTIONS OF HIGHER EDUCATION FOR SELECTED MAJOR FIELDS OF STUDY AND LEVEL OF ENROLLMENT
BY RACE, ETHNICITY, AND SEX: STATE, 1978

MAJOR FIELD 0500 - BUSINESS AND MANAGEMENT

	AMERICAN INDIAN ALASKAN NATIVE		BLACK NON-HISPANIC		ASIAN OR PACIFIC ISLANDER		HISPANIC		TOTAL MINORITY		WHITE NON-HISPANIC		NON-RESIDENT ALIEN	
	NUMBER	%	NUMBER	%	NUMBER	%	NUMBER	%	NUMBER	%	NUMBER	%	NUMBER	%
ARKANSAS	(	24 INSTITUTIONS)												
UNDERGRADUATES:														
FULL-TIME	61	.6	1,732	17.5	45	.5	22	.2	1,860	18.8	7,976	80.4	83	.8
FEMALE	22	.5	901	22.2	14	.3	6	.1	943	23.2	3,111	76.6	9	.2
MALE	39	.7	831	14.2	31	.5	16	.3	917	15.7	4,865	83.1	74	1.3
PART-TIME	29	1.4	230	11.4	6	.3	8	.4	273	13.5	1,742	86.2	5	.2
FEMALE	20	2.0	135	13.7	4	.4	6	.6	165	16.7	822	83.3	5	.0
MALE	9	.9	95	9.2	2	.2	2	.2	108	10.5	920	89.1	5	.5
TOTAL	90	.8	1,962	16.4	51	.4	30	.3	2,133	17.9	9,718	81.4	88	.7
FEMALE	42	.8	1,036	20.5	18	.4	12	.2	1,108	21.9	3,933	77.9	9	.2
MALE	48	.7	926	13.4	33	.5	18	.3	1,025	14.9	5,785	84.0	79	1.1
GRADUATE:														
FULL-TIME	1	.4	10	4.2	4	1.7	1	.4	16	6.7	202	84.5	21	8.8
FEMALE	1	1.5	4	6.1	1	1.5	0	.0	6	9.1	55	83.3	5	7.6
MALE	0	.0	6	3.5	3	1.7	1	.6	10	5.8	147	85.0	16	9.2
PART-TIME	1	.3	23	7.7	1	.3	0	.0	25	8.3	271	90.3	4	1.3
FEMALE	0	.0	11	13.1	1	1.2	0	.0	12	14.3	72	85.7	0	.0
MALE	1	.5	12	5.6	0	.0	0	.0	13	6.0	199	92.1	4	1.9
TOTAL	2	.4	33	6.1	5	.9	1	.2	41	7.6	473	87.8	25	4.6
FEMALE	1	.7	15	10.0	2	1.3	0	.0	18	12.0	127	84.7	5	3.3
MALE	1	.3	18	4.6	3	.8	1	.3	23	5.9	346	88.9	20	5.1
PROFESSIONAL:														
FULL-TIME	0	.0	0	.0	0	.0	0	.0	0	.0	0	.0	0	.0
FEMALE	0	.0	0	.0	0	.0	0	.0	0	.0	0	.0	0	.0
MALE	0	.0	0	.0	0	.0	0	.0	0	.0	0	.0	0	.0
PART-TIME	0	.0	0	.0	0	.0	0	.0	0	.0	0	.0	0	.0
FEMALE	0	.0	0	.0	0	.0	0	.0	0	.0	0	.0	0	.0
MALE	0	.0	0	.0	0	.0	0	.0	0	.0	0	.0	0	.0
TOTAL	0	.0	0	.0	0	.0	0	.0	0	.0	0	.0	0	.0
FEMALE	0	.0	0	.0	0	.0	0	.0	0	.0	0	.0	0	.0
MALE	0	.0	0	.0	0	.0	0	.0	0	.0	0	.0	0	.0
UND+GRAD+PROF:														
FULL-TIME	62	.6	1,742	17.1	49	.5	23	.2	1,876	18.5	8,178	80.5	104	1.0
FEMALE	23	.6	905	21.9	15	.4	6	.1	949	23.0	3,166	76.7	14	.3
MALE	39	.6	837	13.9	34	.6	17	.3	927	15.4	5,012	83.1	90	1.5
PART-TIME	30	1.3	253	10.9	7	.3	8	.3	298	12.8	2,013	86.8	9	.4
FEMALE	20	1.9	146	13.6	5	.5	6	.6	177	16.5	894	83.5	0	.0
MALE	10	.8	107	8.6	2	.2	2	.2	121	9.7	1,119	89.6	9	.7
TOTAL	92	.7	1,995	16.0	56	.4	31	.2	2,174	17.4	10,191	81.7	113	.9
FEMALE	43	.8	1,051	20.2	20	.4	12	.2	1,126	21.7	4,060	78.1	14	.3
MALE	49	.7	944	13.0	36	.5	19	.3	1,048	14.4	6,131	84.2	99	1.4
UNCLASSIFIED:														
TOTAL	3	.5	38	6.7	4	.7	2	.4	47	8.3	515	91.5	1	.2
FEMALE	3	1.1	17	6.5	0	.0	0	.0	20	7.6	241	92.0	1	.4
MALE	0	.0	21	7.0	4	1.3	2	.7	27	9.0	274	91.0	0	.0
TOTAL ENROLLMENT:														
TOTAL	95	.7	2,033	15.6	60	.5	33	.2	2,221	17.0	10,706	82.1	114	.9
FEMALE	46	.8	1,068	19.6	20	.4	12	.2	1,146	21.0	4,301	78.7	15	.3
MALE	49	.7	965	12.7	40	.5	21	.3	1,075	14.2	6,405	84.5	99	1.3
CALIFORNIA	(	138 INSTITUTIONS)												
UNDERGRADUATES:														
FULL-TIME	750	1.1	6,538	9.7	5,865	8.7	5,018	7.5	18,171	27.0	45,394	67.6	3,629	5.4
FEMALE	346	1.3	3,325	12.1	2,846	10.4	2,309	8.4	8,826	32.1	17,391	63.2	1,280	4.7
MALE	404	1.0	3,213	8.1	3,019	7.6	2,709	6.8	9,345	23.5	28,003	70.5	2,349	5.9
PART-TIME	963	1.4	6,523	9.7	4,327	6.5	5,308	7.9	17,121	25.6	48,857	73.0	957	1.4
FEMALE	520	1.5	3,469	10.3	2,002	5.9	2,678	7.9	8,669	25.7	24,660	73.1	414	1.2
MALE	443	1.3	3,054	9.2	2,325	7.0	2,630	7.9	8,452	25.5	24,197	72.9	543	1.6
TOTAL	1,713	1.3	13,061	9.7	10,192	7.6	10,326	7.7	35,292	26.3	94,251	70.3	4,586	3.4
FEMALE	866	1.4	6,794	11.1	4,848	7.9	4,987	8.1	17,495	28.6	42,051	68.7	1,694	2.8
MALE	847	1.2	6,267	8.6	5,344	7.3	5,339	7.3	17,797	24.4	52,200	71.6	2,892	4.0
GRADUATE:														
FULL-TIME	29	.4	240	3.1	441	5.8	192	2.5	902	11.8	5,274	69.2	1,445	19.0
FEMALE	10	.5	75	4.0	136	7.3	46	2.5	267	14.4	1,364	73.4	228	12.3
MALE	19	.3	165	2.9	305	5.3	146	2.5	635	11.0	3,910	67.9	1,217	21.1
PART-TIME	47	.3	360	2.6	876	6.4	229	1.7	1,512	11.1	11,325	83.2	774	5.7
FEMALE	10	.3	72	2.1	236	6.9	42	1.2	360	10.6	2,864	84.2	178	5.2
MALE	37	.4	288	2.8	640	6.3	187	1.8	1,152	11.3	8,461	82.9	596	5.8
TOTAL	76	.4	600	2.8	1,317	6.2	421	2.0	2,414	11.4	16,599	78.2	2,219	10.5
FEMALE	20	.4	147	2.8	372	7.1	88	1.7	627	11.9	4,228	80.4	406	7.7
MALE	56	.4	453	2.8	945	5.9	333	2.1	1,787	11.2	12,371	77.5	1,813	11.4
PROFESSIONAL:														
FULL-TIME	0	.0	0	.0	0	.0	0	.0	0	.0	0	.0	0	.0
FEMALE	0	.0	0	.0	0	.0	0	.0	0	.0	0	.0	0	.0
MALE	0	.0	0	.0	0	.0	0	.0	0	.0	0	.0	0	.0

BUSINESS AND MANAGEMENT

INDIAN NATIVE	BLACK NON-HISPANIC		ASIAN OR PACIFIC ISLANDER		HISPANIC		TOTAL MINORITY		WHITE NON-HISPANIC		NON-RESIDENT ALIEN		TOTAL
%	NUMBER	%	NUMBER	%	NUMBER	%	NUMBER	%	NUMBER	%	NUMBER	%	NUMBER

CONTINUED

.0	0	.0	0	.0	0	.0	0	.0	0	.0	1	100.0	1
.0	0	.0	0	.0	0	.0	0	.0	0	.0	1	100.0	1
.0	0	.0	0	.0	0	.0	0	.0	0	.0	0	.0	0
.0	0	.0	0	.0	0	.0	0	.0	0	.0	1	100.0	1
.0	0	.0	0	.0	0	.0	0	.0	0	.0	1	100.0	1
.0	0	.0	0	.0	0	.0	0	.0	0	.0	0	.0	0
1.0	6,778	9.1	6,308	8.4	5,210	7.0	19,073	25.5	50,668	67.7	5,074	6.8	74,815
1.2	3,400	11.6	2,982	10.2	2,355	8.0	9,093	31.0	18,755	63.9	1,508	5.1	29,356
.9	3,378	7.4	3,324	7.3	2,855	6.3	9,980	22.0	31,913	70.2	3,566	7.8	45,459
1.3	6,883	8.5	5,203	6.5	5,537	6.9	18,633	23.1	60,182	74.7	1,732	2.2	80,547
1.4	3,541	9.5	2,238	6.0	2,720	7.3	9,029	24.3	27,524	74.1	593	1.6	37,146
1.1	3,342	7.7	2,965	6.8	2,817	6.5	9,604	22.1	32,658	75.2	1,139	2.6	43,401
1.2	13,661	8.8	11,509	7.4	10,747	6.9	37,706	24.3	110,850	71.3	6,806	4.4	155,362
1.3	6,941	10.4	5,220	7.8	5,075	7.6	18,122	27.3	46,279	69.6	2,101	3.2	66,502
1.0	6,720	7.6	6,289	7.1	5,672	6.4	19,584	22.0	64,571	72.7	4,705	5.3	88,860
1.1	941	6.2	1,006	6.7	961	6.4	3,068	20.3	11,328	75.0	704	4.7	15,100
1.1	435	6.6	442	6.7	413	6.3	1,364	20.8	4,957	75.6	233	3.6	6,554
1.0	506	5.9	564	6.6	548	6.4	1,704	19.9	6,371	74.5	471	5.5	8,546
1.1	14,602	8.6	12,515	7.3	11,708	6.9	40,774	23.9	122,178	71.7	7,510	4.4	170,462
1.3	7,376	10.1	5,662	7.8	5,488	7.5	19,486	26.7	51,236	70.1	2,334	3.2	73,056
1.0	7,226	7.4	6,853	7.0	6,220	6.4	21,288	21.9	70,942	72.8	5,176	5.3	97,406

(19 INSTITUTIONS)

.7	218	1.8	160	1.4	336	2.8	794	6.7	10,779	91.0	268	2.3	11,841
1.1	89	2.1	71	1.7	126	3.0	330	8.0	3,761	90.6	59	1.4	4,150
.5	129	1.7	89	1.2	210	2.7	464	6.0	7,018	91.2	209	2.7	7,691
.5	42	2.0	19	.9	86	4.1	153	7.5	1,920	91.4	23	1.1	2,101
.4	17	1.9	11	1.2	32	3.6	64	7.2	817	91.9	8	.9	889
.6	25	2.1	8	.7	54	4.5	94	7.8	1,103	91.0	15	1.2	1,212
.7	260	1.9	179	1.3	422	3.0	952	6.8	12,699	91.1	291	2.1	13,942
1.0	106	2.1	82	1.6	158	3.1	394	7.8	4,578	90.9	67	1.3	5,039
.5	154	1.7	97	1.1	264	3.0	558	6.3	8,121	91.2	224	2.5	8,903
.4	13	1.3	12	1.2	9	.9	38	3.9	884	89.8	62	6.3	984
.0	2	.8	5	1.9	1	.4	8	3.1	243	94.2	7	2.7	258
.6	11	1.5	7	1.0	8	1.1	30	4.1	641	88.3	55	7.6	726
.6	9	1.4	6	.9	7	1.1	26	4.0	598	91.6	29	4.4	653
.5	2	1.0	3	1.5	2	1.0	8	3.9	192	94.6	3	1.5	203
.7	7	1.6	3	.7	5	1.1	18	4.0	406	90.2	26	5.8	450
.5	22	1.3	18	1.1	16	1.0	64	3.9	1,482	90.5	91	5.6	1,637
.2	4	.9	8	1.7	3	.7	16	3.5	435	94.4	10	2.2	461
.6	18	1.5	10	.9	13	1.1	48	4.1	1,047	89.0	81	6.9	1,176
.0	0	.0	0	.0	0	.0	0	.0	0	.0	0	.0	0
.0	0	.0	0	.0	0	.0	0	.0	0	.0	0	.0	0
.0	0	.0	0	.0	0	.0	0	.0	0	.0	0	.0	0
.0	0	.0	0	.0	0	.0	0	.0	0	.0	0	.0	0
.0	0	.0	0	.0	0	.0	0	.0	0	.0	0	.0	0
.0	0	.0	0	.0	0	.0	0	.0	0	.0	0	.0	0
.7	231	1.8	172	1.3	345	2.7	832	6.5	11,663	90.9	330	2.6	12,825
1.0	91	2.1	76	1.7	127	2.9	338	7.7	4,004	90.8	66	1.5	4,408
.5	140	1.7	96	1.1	218	2.6	494	5.9	7,659	91.0	264	3.1	8,417
.5	51	1.9	25	.9	93	3.4	184	6.7	2,518	91.4	52	1.9	2,754
.5	19	1.7	14	1.3	34	3.1	72	6.6	1,009	92.4	11	1.0	1,092
.6	32	1.9	11	.7	59	3.5	112	6.7	1,509	90.8	41	2.5	1,662
.6	282	1.8	197	1.3	438	2.8	1,016	6.5	14,181	91.0	382	2.5	15,579
.9	110	2.0	90	1.6	161	2.9	410	7.5	5,013	91.1	77	1.4	5,500
.5	172	1.7	107	1.1	277	2.7	806	6.0	9,168	91.0	305	3.0	10,079
.5	24	4.0	4	.7	30	5.0	61	10.2	533	88.8	6	1.0	600
.7	7	2.5	0	.0	10	3.6	19	6.9	258	93.1	0	.0	277
.3	17	5.3	4	1.2	20	6.2	42	13.0	275	85.1	6	1.9	323
.6	306	1.9	201	1.2	468	2.9	1,077	6.7	14,714	90.9	388	2.4	16,179
.9	117	2.0	90	1.6	171	3.0	429	7.4	5,271	91.2	77	1.3	5,777
.5	189	1.8	111	1.1	297	2.9	648	6.2	9,443	90.8	311	3.0	10,402

TABLE 17 - TOTAL ENROLLMENT IN INSTITUTIONS OF HIGHER EDUCATION FOR SELECTED MAJOR FIELDS OF STUDY AND LEVEL OF ENROLLMENT BY RACE, ETHNICITY, AND SEX: STATE, 1978

MAJOR FIELD 0500 - BUSINESS AND MANAGEMENT

	AMERICAN INDIAN ALASKAN NATIVE		BLACK NON-HISPANIC		ASIAN OR PACIFIC ISLANDER		HISPANIC		TOTAL MINORITY		WHITE NON-HISPANIC		NON-RESIDENT ALIEN	
	NUMBER	%	NUMBER	%	NUMBER	%	NUMBER	%	NUMBER	%	NUMBER	%	NUMBER	%
CONNECTICUT (27 INSTITUTIONS)														
UNDERGRADUATES:														
FULL-TIME	21	.2	680	5.3	75	.6	217	1.7	993	7.7	11,800	91.1	157	1.2
FEMALE	7	.1	299	5.9	39	.8	98	1.9	443	8.7	4,590	90.4	42	.8
MALE	14	.2	381	4.8	36	.5	119	1.5	550	7.0	7,210	91.6	115	1.5
PART-TIME	17	.2	592	8.0	40	.5	140	1.9	789	10.7	6,593	89.1	17	.2
FEMALE	8	.2	325	8.5	24	.6	72	1.9	429	11.3	3,377	88.6	7	.2
MALE	9	.3	267	7.4	16	.4	68	1.9	360	10.0	3,216	89.7	10	.3
TOTAL	38	.2	1,272	6.3	115	.6	357	1.8	1,782	8.8	18,393	90.4	174	.9
FEMALE	15	.2	624	7.0	63	.7	170	1.9	872	9.8	7,967	89.6	49	.6
MALE	23	.2	648	5.7	52	.5	187	1.6	910	7.9	10,426	91.0	125	1.1
GRADUATE:														
FULL-TIME	2	.3	27	3.6	7	.9	11	1.5	47	6.2	640	84.8	68	9.0
FEMALE	2	.9	8	3.5	2	.9	3	1.3	15	6.6	203	89.0	10	4.4
MALE	0	.0	19	3.6	5	.9	8	1.5	32	6.1	437	82.9	58	11.0
PART-TIME	2	.0	140	2.8	33	.6	43	.8	218	4.3	4,821	94.8	48	.9
FEMALE	2	.1	35	2.6	14	1.0	8	.6	59	4.3	1,304	95.5	2	.1
MALE	0	.0	105	2.8	19	.5	35	.9	159	4.3	3,517	94.5	46	1.2
TOTAL	4	.1	167	2.9	40	.7	54	.9	265	4.5	5,461	93.5	116	2.0
FEMALE	4	.3	43	2.7	16	1.0	11	.7	74	4.6	1,507	94.6	12	.8
MALE	0	.0	124	2.9	24	.6	43	1.0	191	4.5	3,954	93.1	104	2.4
PROFESSIONAL:														
FULL-TIME	0	.0	0	.0	0	.0	0	.0	0	.0	0	.0	0	.0
FEMALE	0	.0	0	.0	0	.0	0	.0	0	.0	0	.0	0	.0
MALE	0	.0	0	.0	0	.0	0	.0	0	.0	0	.0	0	.0
PART-TIME	0	.0	0	.0	0	.0	0	.0	0	.0	0	.0	0	.0
FEMALE	0	.0	0	.0	0	.0	0	.0	0	.0	0	.0	0	.0
MALE	0	.0	0	.0	0	.0	0	.0	0	.0	0	.0	0	.0
TOTAL	0	.0	0	.0	0	.0	0	.0	0	.0	0	.0	0	.0
FEMALE	0	.0	0	.0	0	.0	0	.0	0	.0	0	.0	0	.0
MALE	0	.0	0	.0	0	.0	0	.0	0	.0	0	.0	0	.0
UNC+GRAD+PROF:														
FULL-TIME	23	.2	707	5.2	82	.6	228	1.7	1,040	7.6	12,440	90.8	225	1.6
FEMALE	9	.2	307	5.8	41	.8	101	1.9	458	8.6	4,793	90.4	52	1.0
MALE	14	.2	400	4.6	41	.5	127	1.5	582	6.9	7,647	91.0	173	2.1
PART-TIME	19	.2	732	5.9	73	.6	183	1.5	1,007	8.1	11,414	91.4	65	.5
FEMALE	10	.2	360	7.0	38	.7	80	1.5	488	9.4	4,681	90.4	9	.2
MALE	9	.1	372	5.1	35	.5	103	1.4	519	7.1	6,733	92.1	56	.8
TOTAL	42	.2	1,439	5.5	155	.6	411	1.6	2,047	7.8	23,854	91.1	290	1.1
FEMALE	19	.2	667	6.4	79	.8	181	1.7	946	9.0	9,474	90.4	61	.6
MALE	23	.1	772	4.9	76	.5	230	1.5	1,101	7.0	14,380	91.5	229	1.5
UNCLASSIFIED:														
TOTAL	3	.9	5	1.4	6	1.7	6	1.7	20	5.7	328	93.2	4	1.1
FEMALE	1	.8	3	2.5	1	.8	2	1.7	7	5.6	110	91.7	3	2.5
MALE	2	.9	2	.9	5	2.2	4	1.7	13	5.6	218	94.0	1	.4
TOTAL ENROLLMENT:														
TOTAL	45	.2	1,444	5.4	161	.6	417	1.6	2,067	7.8	24,182	91.1	294	1.1
FEMALE	20	.2	670	6.3	80	.8	183	1.7	953	9.0	9,584	90.4	64	.6
MALE	25	.2	774	4.9	81	.5	234	1.5	1,114	7.0	14,598	91.6	230	1.4
DELAWARE (10 INSTITUTIONS)														
UNDERGRADUATES:														
FULL-TIME	4	.1	802	17.7	11	.2	22	.5	839	18.5	3,668	80.7	36	.8
FEMALE	2	.1	448	19.4	6	.3	13	.6	469	20.3	1,830	79.2	12	.5
MALE	2	.1	354	15.9	5	.2	9	.4	370	16.6	1,830	82.3	24	1.1
PART-TIME	3	.2	246	14.7	9	.5	21	1.3	279	16.6	1,395	83.1	5	.3
FEMALE	1	.1	149	17.1	5	.6	12	1.4	167	19.2	701	80.5	3	.3
MALE	2	.2	97	12.0	4	.5	9	1.1	112	13.9	694	85.9	2	.2
TOTAL	7	.1	1,048	16.8	20	.3	43	.7	1,118	18.0	5,063	81.4	41	.7
FEMALE	3	.1	597	18.8	11	.3	25	.8	636	20.0	2,531	79.5	15	.5
MALE	4	.1	451	14.8	9	.3	18	.6	482	15.9	2,532	83.3	26	.9
GRADUATE:														
FULL-TIME	0	.0	10	16.4	0	.0	0	.0	10	16.4	47	77.0	4	6.6
FEMALE	0	.0	1	7.7	0	.0	0	.0	1	7.7	12	92.3	0	.0
MALE	0	.0	9	18.8	0	.0	0	.0	9	18.8	35	72.9	4	8.3
PART-TIME	0	.0	20	7.8	4	1.6	1	.4	25	9.8	226	88.6	4	1.6
FEMALE	0	.0	3	4.9	0	.0	0	.0	3	4.9	57	93.4	1	1.6
MALE	0	.0	17	8.8	4	2.1	1	.5	22	11.3	169	87.1	3	1.5
TOTAL	0	.0	30	9.5	4	1.3	1	.3	35	11.1	273	86.4	8	2.5
FEMALE	0	.0	4	5.4	0	.0	0	.0	4	5.4	69	93.2	1	1.4
MALE	0	.0	26	10.7	4	1.7	1	.4	31	12.8	204	84.3	7	2.9
PROFESSIONAL:														
FULL-TIME	0	.0	0	.0	0	.0	0	.0	0	.0	0	.0	0	.0
FEMALE	0	.0	0	.0	0	.0	0	.0	0	.0	0	.0	0	.0
MALE	0	.0	0	.0	0	.0	0	.0	0	.0	0	.0	0	.0

404

ASIAN OR PACIFIC ISLANDER		HISPANIC		TOTAL MINORITY		WHITE NON-HISPANIC		NON-RESIDENT ALIEN		TOTAL
NUMBER	%	NUMBER	%	NUMBER	%	NUMBER	%	NUMBER	%	NUMBER
0	.0	0	.0	0	.0	0	.0	0	.0	0
0	.0	0	.0	0	.0	0	.0	0	.0	0
0	.0	0	.0	0	.0	0	.0	0	.0	0
0	.0	0	.0	0	.0	0	.0	0	.0	0
0	.0	0	.0	0	.0	0	.0	0	.0	0
0	.0	0	.0	0	.0	0	.0	0	.0	0
11	.2	22	.5	849	18.4	3,715	80.7	40	.9	4,604
6	.3	13	.6	470	20.2	1,842	79.3	12	.5	2,324
5	.2	9	.4	379	16.6	1,873	82.1	28	1.2	2,280
13	.7	22	1.1	304	15.7	1,621	83.8	9	.5	1,934
5	.5	12	1.3	170	18.2	758	81.3	4	.4	932
8	.8	10	1.0	134	13.4	863	86.1	5	.5	1,002
24	.4	44	.7	1,153	17.6	5,336	81.6	49	.7	6,538
11	.3	25	.8	640	19.7	2,600	79.9	16	.5	3,256
13	.4	19	.6	513	15.6	2,736	83.4	33	1.0	3,282
7	.8	4	.5	42	4.8	813	93.8	12	1.4	867
5	1.0	1	.2	20	4.1	468	94.9	5	1.0	493
2	.5	3	.8	22	5.9	345	92.2	7	1.9	374
31	.4	48	.6	1,195	16.1	6,149	83.0	61	.8	7,405
16	.4	26	.7	660	17.6	3,068	81.8	21	.6	3,749
15	.4	22	.6	535	14.6	3,081	84.3	40	1.1	3,656
75	1.6	51	1.1	2,250	46.6	1,905	39.4	676	14.0	4,831
29	1.4	18	.8	1,203	56.8	668	31.5	248	11.7	2,119
46	1.7	33	1.2	1,047	38.6	1,237	45.6	428	15.8	2,712
103	3.3	42	1.3	2,354	75.1	549	17.5	231	7.4	3,134
20	1.1	22	1.2	1,420	80.1	245	13.8	108	6.1	1,773
83	6.1	20	1.5	934	68.6	304	22.3	123	9.0	1,361
178	2.2	93	1.2	4,604	57.8	2,454	30.8	907	11.4	7,965
49	1.3	40	1.0	2,623	67.4	913	23.5	356	9.1	3,892
129	3.2	53	1.3	1,981	48.6	1,541	37.8	551	13.5	4,073
20	2.2	14	1.6	171	19.0	495	54.9	236	26.2	902
8	2.9	3	1.1	64	22.9	172	61.6	43	15.4	279
12	1.9	11	1.8	107	17.2	323	51.8	193	31.0	623
64	2.2	35	1.2	417	14.6	2,285	80.1	150	5.3	2,852
11	1.4	6	.7	165	20.4	609	75.4	34	4.2	838
53	2.6	29	1.4	252	12.3	1,676	82.0	116	5.7	2,044
84	2.2	49	1.3	588	15.7	2,780	74.1	386	10.3	3,754
19	1.7	9	.8	229	21.1	781	71.8	77	7.1	1,087
65	2.4	40	1.5	359	13.5	1,999	75.0	309	11.6	2,667
0	.0	0	.0	0	.0	0	.0	0	.0	0
0	.0	0	.0	0	.0	0	.0	0	.0	0
0	.0	0	.0	0	.0	0	.0	0	.0	0
0	.0	0	.0	0	.0	0	.0	0	.0	0
0	.0	0	.0	0	.0	0	.0	0	.0	0
0	.0	0	.0	0	.0	0	.0	0	.0	0
0	.0	0	.0	0	.0	0	.0	0	.0	0
0	.0	0	.0	0	.0	0	.0	0	.0	0
0	.0	0	.0	0	.0	0	.0	0	.0	0
95	1.7	65	1.1	2,421	42.2	2,400	41.9	912	15.9	5,733
37	1.5	21	.9	1,267	52.8	840	35.0	291	12.1	2,398
58	1.7	44	1.3	1,154	34.6	1,560	46.8	621	18.6	3,335
167	2.8	77	1.3	2,771	46.3	2,834	47.3	381	6.4	5,986
31	1.2	28	1.1	1,585	61.4	854	33.1	142	5.5	2,581
136	4.0	49	1.4	1,186	34.8	1,980	58.1	239	7.0	3,405
262	2.2	142	1.2	5,192	44.3	5,234	44.7	1,293	11.0	11,719
68	1.4	49	1.0	2,852	57.3	1,694	34.0	433	8.7	4,979
194	2.9	93	1.4	2,340	34.7	3,540	52.5	860	12.8	6,740
4	1.9	3	1.5	77	37.4	117	56.8	12	5.8	206
2	2.2	1	1.1	48	52.2	42	45.7	2	2.2	92
2	1.8	2	1.8	29	25.4	75	65.8	10	8.8	114
266	2.2	145	1.2	5,269	44.2	5,351	44.9	1,305	10.9	11,925
70	1.4	50	1.0	2,900	57.2	1,736	34.2	435	8.6	5,071
196	2.9	95	1.4	2,369	34.6	3,615	52.7	870	12.7	6,854

MAJOR FIELD 0500 - BUSINESS AND MANAGEMENT

	AMERICAN INDIAN ALASKAN NATIVE		BLACK NON-HISPANIC		ASIAN OR PACIFIC ISLANDER		HISPANIC		TOTAL MINORITY		WHITE NON-HISPANIC		NON-RESIDENT ALIEN	
	NUMBER	%	NUMBER	%	NUMBER	%	NUMBER	%	NUMBER	%	NUMBER	%	NUMBER	%
FLORIDA (37 INSTITUTIONS)														
UNDERGRADUATES:														
FULL-TIME	150	.6	3,122	12.5	171	.7	1,373	5.5	4,816	19.3	19,542	78.4	568	2.3
FEMALE	20	.3	1,368	18.0	59	.8	522	6.9	1,969	25.8	5,541	72.7	108	1.4
MALE	130	.8	1,754	10.1	112	.6	851	4.9	2,847	16.4	14,001	80.9	460	2.7
PART-TIME	17	.2	452	6.1	64	.9	910	12.2	1,443	19.4	5,905	79.3	101	1.4
FEMALE	9	.3	193	7.3	22	.8	357	13.6	581	22.1	2,026	77.0	24	.9
MALE	8	.2	259	5.4	42	.9	553	11.5	862	17.9	3,879	80.5	77	1.6
TOTAL	167	.5	3,574	11.0	235	.7	2,283	7.1	6,259	19.3	25,447	78.6	669	2.1
FEMALE	29	.3	1,561	15.2	81	.8	679	8.6	2,550	24.9	7,567	73.8	132	1.3
MALE	138	.6	2,013	9.1	154	.7	1,404	6.3	3,709	16.8	17,880	80.8	537	2.4
GRADUATE:														
FULL-TIME	2	.1	100	5.4	39	2.1	103	5.6	244	13.2	1,476	80.0	126	6.8
FEMALE	0	.0	29	7.0	8	1.9	26	6.3	63	15.2	330	79.7	21	5.1
MALE	2	.1	71	5.0	31	2.2	77	5.4	181	12.6	1,146	80.0	105	7.3
PART-TIME	5	.2	166	5.7	20	.7	116	4.0	307	10.5	2,573	88.4	32	1.1
FEMALE	0	.0	57	9.3	5	.8	39	6.4	101	16.5	510	83.2	2	.3
MALE	5	.2	109	4.7	15	.7	77	3.3	206	9.0	2,063	89.7	30	1.3
TOTAL	7	.1	266	5.6	59	1.2	219	4.6	551	11.6	4,049	85.1	158	3.3
FEMALE	0	.0	86	8.4	13	1.3	65	6.3	164	16.0	840	81.8	23	2.2
MALE	7	.2	180	4.8	46	1.2	154	4.1	387	10.4	3,209	86.0	135	3.6
PROFESSIONAL:														
FULL-TIME	0	.0	0	.0	0	.0	0	.0	0	.0	0	.0	0	.0
FEMALE	0	.0	0	.0	0	.0	0	.0	0	.0	0	.0	0	.0
MALE	0	.0	0	.0	0	.0	0	.0	0	.0	0	.0	0	.0
PART-TIME	0	.0	0	.0	0	.0	0	.0	0	.0	0	.0	0	.0
FEMALE	0	.0	0	.0	0	.0	0	.0	0	.0	0	.0	0	.0
MALE	0	.0	0	.0	0	.0	0	.0	0	.0	0	.0	0	.0
TOTAL	0	.0	0	.0	0	.0	0	.0	0	.0	0	.0	0	.0
FEMALE	0	.0	0	.0	0	.0	0	.0	0	.0	0	.0	0	.0
MALE	0	.0	0	.0	0	.0	0	.0	0	.0	0	.0	0	.0
UND+GRAD+PROF:														
FULL-TIME	152	.6	3,222	12.0	210	.8	1,476	5.5	5,060	18.9	21,018	78.5	694	2.6
FEMALE	20	.2	1,397	17.4	67	.8	548	6.8	2,032	25.3	5,871	73.1	129	1.6
MALE	132	.7	1,825	9.7	143	.8	928	5.0	3,028	16.2	15,147	80.0	565	3.0
PART-TIME	22	.2	618	6.0	84	.8	1,026	9.9	1,750	16.9	8,478	81.8	133	1.3
FEMALE	9	.3	250	7.7	27	.8	396	12.2	682	21.0	2,536	78.2	26	.8
MALE	13	.2	368	5.2	57	.8	630	8.9	1,068	15.0	5,942	83.5	107	1.5
TOTAL	174	.5	3,840	10.3	294	.8	2,502	6.7	6,810	18.3	29,496	79.4	827	2.2
FEMALE	29	.3	1,647	14.6	94	.8	944	8.4	2,714	24.1	8,407	74.6	155	1.4
MALE	145	.6	2,193	8.5	200	.8	1,558	6.0	4,096	15.8	21,089	81.6	672	2.6
UNCLASSIFIED:														
TOTAL	0	.0	62	7.0	9	1.0	22	2.5	93	10.5	775	87.6	17	1.9
FEMALE	0	.0	30	10.5	4	1.4	8	2.8	42	14.7	242	84.6	2	.7
MALE	0	.0	32	5.3	5	.8	14	2.3	51	8.5	533	89.0	15	2.5
TOTAL ENROLLMENT:														
TOTAL	174	.5	3,902	10.3	303	.8	2,524	6.6	6,903	18.2	30,271	79.6	844	2.2
FEMALE	29	.3	1,677	14.5	98	.8	952	8.2	2,756	23.8	8,649	74.8	157	1.4
MALE	145	.5	2,225	8.4	205	.8	1,572	5.9	4,147	15.7	21,622	81.7	687	2.6
GEORGIA (57 INSTITUTIONS)														
UNDERGRADUATES:														
FULL-TIME	13	.1	3,959	21.8	59	.3	66	.4	4,097	22.5	13,851	76.1	249	1.4
FEMALE	4	.1	1,874	25.9	23	.3	17	.2	1,918	26.6	5,259	72.8	45	.6
MALE	9	.1	2,085	19.0	36	.3	49	.4	2,179	19.9	8,592	78.3	204	1.9
PART-TIME	11	.1	1,079	12.5	25	.3	41	.5	1,156	13.4	7,440	86.4	20	.2
FEMALE	6	.2	536	15.0	12	.3	11	.3	565	15.8	2,998	84.0	7	.2
MALE	5	.1	543	10.8	13	.3	30	.6	591	11.7	4,442	88.0	13	.3
TOTAL	24	.1	5,038	18.8	84	.3	107	.4	5,253	19.6	21,291	79.4	269	1.0
FEMALE	10	.1	2,410	22.3	35	.3	28	.3	2,483	23.0	8,257	76.5	52	.5
MALE	14	.1	2,628	16.4	49	.3	79	.5	2,770	17.3	13,034	81.4	217	1.4
GRADUATE														
FULL-TIME	3	.2	210	11.4	24	1.3	3	.2	240	13.0	1,440	78.1	163	8.8
FEMALE	1	.2	89	19.8	10	2.2	0	.0	100	22.3	326	72.6	23	5.1
MALE	2	.1	121	8.7	14	1.0	3	.2	140	10.0	1,114	79.9	140	10.0
PART-TIME	4	.3	96	6.7	4	.3	3	.2	107	7.4	1,313	91.2	20	1.4
FEMALE	0	.0	34	9.6	0	.0	1	.3	35	9.9	314	88.5	6	1.7
MALE	4	.4	62	5.7	4	.4	2	.2	72	6.6	999	92.1	14	1.3
TOTAL	7	.2	306	9.3	28	.9	6	.2	347	10.6	2,753	83.9	183	5.6
FEMALE	1	.1	123	15.3	10	1.2	1	.1	135	16.8	640	79.6	29	3.6
MALE	6	.2	183	7.4	18	.7	5	.2	212	8.6	2,113	85.2	154	6.2
PROFESSIONAL:														
FULL-TIME	0	.0	0	.0	0	.0	0	.0	0	.0	0	.0	0	.0
FEMALE	0	.0	0	.0	0	.0	0	.0	0	.0	0	.0	0	.0
MALE	0	.0	0	.0	0	.0	0	.0	0	.0	0	.0	0	.0

ROLLMENT IN INSTITUTIONS OF HIGHER EDUCATION FOR SELECTED MAJOR FIELDS OF STUDY AND LEVEL OF ENROLLMENT
ETHNICITY, AND SEX: STATE, 1978

BUSINESS AND MANAGEMENT

INDIAN NATIVE	BLACK NON-HISPANIC		ASIAN OR PACIFIC ISLANDER		HISPANIC		TOTAL MINORITY		WHITE NON-HISPANIC		NON-RESIDENT ALIEN		TOTAL
%	NUMBER	%	NUMBER	%	NUMBER	%	NUMBER	%	NUMBER	%	NUMBER	%	NUMBER

CONTINUED

%	NUMBER	%	NUMBER	%	NUMBER	%	NUMBER	%	NUMBER	%	NUMBER	%	NUMBER
.0	0	.0	0	.0	0	.0	0	.0	0	.0	0	.0	0
.0	0	.0	0	.0	0	.0	0	.0	0	.0	0	.0	0
.0	0	.0	0	.0	0	.0	0	.0	0	.0	0	.0	0
.0	0	.0	0	.0	0	.0	0	.0	0	.0	0	.0	0
.0	0	.0	0	.0	0	.0	0	.0	0	.0	0	.0	0
.0	0	.0	0	.0	0	.0	0	.0	0	.0	0	.0	0
.1	4,169	20.8	83	.4	69	.3	4,337	21.6	15,291	76.3	412	2.1	20,040
.1	1,963	25.6	33	.4	17	.2	2,018	26.3	5,585	72.8	68	.9	7,671
.1	2,206	17.8	50	.4	52	.4	2,319	18.7	9,706	78.5	344	2.8	12,369
.1	1,175	11.7	29	.3	44	.4	1,203	12.0	8,793	87.0	40	.4	10,056
.2	570	14.5	12	.3	12	.3	600	15.3	3,312	84.4	13	.3	3,925
.1	605	9.9	17	.3	32	.5	663	10.8	5,441	88.7	27	.4	6,131
.1	5,344	17.8	112	.4	113	.4	5,600	18.6	24,044	79.9	452	1.5	30,096
.1	2,533	21.8	45	.4	29	.3	2,618	22.6	8,897	76.7	81	.7	11,596
.1	2,811	15.2	67	.4	84	.5	2,982	16.1	15,147	81.9	371	2.0	18,500
.3	229	19.9	5	.4	4	.3	242	21.0	886	76.9	24	2.1	1,152
.2	127	26.0	1	.2	3	.6	132	27.0	350	71.6	7	1.4	489
.5	102	15.4	4	.6	1	.2	110	16.6	536	80.8	17	2.6	663
.1	5,573	17.8	117	.4	117	.4	5,842	18.7	24,930	79.8	476	1.5	31,248
.1	2,660	22.0	46	.4	32	.3	2,750	22.8	9,247	76.5	88	.7	12,085
.1	2,913	19.2	71	.4	85	.4	3,092	16.1	15,683	81.8	388	2.0	19,163

(5 INSTITUTIONS)

%	NUMBER	%	NUMBER	%	NUMBER	%	NUMBER	%	NUMBER	%	NUMBER	%	NUMBER
.1	19	1.0	1,311	67.3	31	1.6	1,362	70.0	363	18.6	222	11.4	1,947
.0	7	.8	638	73.2	14	1.6	659	75.6	126	14.4	87	10.0	872
.1	12	1.1	673	62.6	17	1.6	703	65.4	237	22.0	135	12.6	1,075
.1	193	11.2	409	23.8	52	3.0	656	38.2	1,051	61.2	9	.5	1,716
.7	4	1.3	151	49.8	3	1.0	160	52.8	137	45.2	6	2.0	303
.0	189	13.4	258	18.3	49	3.5	496	35.1	914	64.7	3	.2	1,413
.1	212	5.8	1,720	47.0	83	2.3	2,018	55.1	1,414	38.6	231	6.3	3,663
.2	11	.9	789	67.1	17	1.4	819	69.7	263	22.4	93	7.9	1,175
.0	201	8.1	931	37.4	66	2.7	1,199	48.2	1,151	46.3	138	5.5	2,488
.0	1	.7	53	36.8	0	.0	54	37.5	72	50.0	18	12.5	144
.0	0	.0	18	38.3	0	.0	18	38.3	23	48.9	6	12.8	47
.0	1	1.0	35	36.1	0	.0	36	37.1	49	50.5	12	12.4	97
.0	1	.4	138	58.5	2	.8	141	59.7	91	38.6	4	1.7	236
.0	0	.0	31	51.7	0	.0	31	51.7	29	48.3	0	.0	60
.0	1	.6	107	60.8	2	1.1	110	62.5	62	35.2	4	2.3	176
.0	2	.5	191	50.3	2	.5	195	51.3	163	42.9	22	5.8	380
.0	0	.0	49	45.8	0	.0	49	45.8	52	48.6	6	5.6	107
.0	2	.7	142	52.0	2	.7	146	53.5	111	40.7	16	5.9	273
.0	0	.0	0	.0	0	.0	0	.0	0	.0	0	.0	0
.0	0	.0	0	.0	0	.0	0	.0	0	.0	0	.0	0
.0	0	.0	0	.0	0	.0	0	.0	0	.0	0	.0	0
.0	0	.0	0	.0	0	.0	0	.0	0	.0	0	.0	0
.0	0	.0	0	.0	0	.0	0	.0	0	.0	0	.0	0
.0	0	.0	0	.0	0	.0	0	.0	0	.0	0	.0	0
.0	20	1.0	1,364	65.2	31	1.5	1,416	67.7	435	20.8	240	11.5	2,091
.0	7	.8	656	71.4	14	1.5	677	73.7	149	16.2	93	10.1	919
.0	13	1.1	708	60.4	17	1.5	739	63.1	286	24.4	147	12.5	1,172
.1	194	9.9	547	28.0	54	2.8	797	40.8	1,142	58.5	13	.7	1,952
.6	4	1.1	182	50.1	3	.8	191	52.6	166	45.7	6	1.7	363
.0	190	12.0	365	23.0	51	3.2	606	38.1	976	61.4	7	.4	1,589
.1	214	5.3	1,911	47.3	85	2.1	2,213	54.7	1,577	39.0	253	6.3	4,043
.2	11	.9	838	65.4	17	1.3	868	67.7	315	24.6	99	7.7	1,282
.0	203	7.4	1,073	38.9	68	2.5	1,345	48.7	1,262	45.7	154	5.6	2,761
.0	0	.0	35	34.7	2	2.0	37	36.6	64	63.4	0	.0	101
.0	0	.0	18	34.6	0	.0	18	34.6	34	65.4	0	.0	52
.0	0	.0	17	34.7	2	4.1	19	38.8	30	61.2	0	.0	49
.1	214	5.2	1,946	47.0	87	2.1	2,250	54.3	1,641	39.6	253	6.1	4,144
.1	11	.8	856	64.2	17	1.3	886	66.4	349	26.2	99	7.4	1,334
.0	203	7.2	1,090	38.8	70	2.5	1,364	48.5	1,292	46.0	154	5.5	2,810

MAJOR FIELD 0500 - BUSINESS AND MANAGEMENT

	AMERICAN INDIAN ALASKAN NATIVE		BLACK NON-HISPANIC		ASIAN OR PACIFIC ISLANDER		HISPANIC		TOTAL MINORITY		WHITE NON-HISPANIC		NON-RESIDENT ALIEN	
	NUMBER	%	NUMBER	%	NUMBER	%	NUMBER	%	NUMBER	%	NUMBER	%	NUMBER	%
IDAHO (9 INSTITUTIONS)														
UNDERGRADUATES:														
FULL-TIME	14	.4	17	.5	53	1.4	42	1.1	126	3.4	3,495	95.5	40	1.1
FEMALE	6	.5	3	.2	23	1.8	20	1.5	52	4.0	1,226	94.9	14	1.1
MALE	8	.3	14	.6	30	1.3	22	.9	74	3.1	2,269	95.8	26	1.1
PART-TIME	5	.5	2	.2	8	.8	14	1.4	29	2.9	962	96.8	3	.3
FEMALE	5	1.1	1	.2	3	.6	8	1.7	17	3.6	448	96.1	1	.2
MALE	0	.0	1	.2	5	.9	6	1.1	12	2.3	514	97.3	2	.4
TOTAL	19	.4	19	.4	61	1.3	56	1.2	155	3.3	4,457	95.7	43	.9
FEMALE	11	.6	4	.2	26	1.5	28	1.6	69	3.9	1,674	95.2	15	.9
MALE	8	.3	15	.5	35	1.2	28	1.0	86	3.0	2,783	96.1	28	1.0
GRADUATE:														
FULL-TIME	0	.0	0	.0	3	4.5	2	3.0	5	7.6	58	87.9	3	4.5
FEMALE	0	.0	0	.0	1	7.7	0	.0	1	7.7	10	76.9	2	15.4
MALE	0	.0	0	.0	2	3.8	2	3.8	4	7.5	48	90.6	1	1.9
PART-TIME	1	.6	0	.0	2	1.2	0	.0	3	1.9	158	98.1	0	.0
FEMALE	1	3.3	0	.0	0	.0	0	.0	1	3.3	29	96.7	0	.0
MALE	0	.0	0	.0	2	1.5	0	.0	2	1.5	129	98.5	0	.0
TOTAL	1	.4	0	.0	5	2.2	2	.9	8	3.5	216	95.2	3	1.3
FEMALE	1	2.3	0	.0	1	2.3	0	.0	2	4.7	39	90.7	2	4.7
MALE	0	.0	0	.0	4	2.2	2	1.1	6	3.3	177	96.2	1	.5
PROFESSIONAL:														
FULL-TIME	0	.0	0	.0	0	.0	0	.0	0	.0	0	.0	0	.0
FEMALE	0	.0	0	.0	0	.0	0	.0	0	.0	0	.0	0	.0
MALE	0	.0	0	.0	0	.0	0	.0	0	.0	0	.0	0	.0
PART-TIME	0	.0	0	.0	0	.0	0	.0	0	.0	0	.0	0	.0
FEMALE	0	.0	0	.0	0	.0	0	.0	0	.0	0	.0	0	.0
MALE	0	.0	0	.0	0	.0	0	.0	0	.0	0	.0	0	.0
TOTAL	0	.0	0	.0	0	.0	0	.0	0	.0	0	.0	0	.0
FEMALE	0	.0	0	.0	0	.0	0	.0	0	.0	0	.0	0	.0
MALE	0	.0	0	.0	0	.0	0	.0	0	.0	0	.0	0	.0
UND+GRAD+PROF:														
FULL-TIME	14	.4	17	.5	56	1.5	44	1.2	131	3.5	3,553	95.3	43	1.2
FEMALE	6	.5	3	.2	24	1.8	20	1.5	53	4.1	1,236	94.7	16	1.2
MALE	8	.3	14	.6	32	1.3	24	1.0	78	3.2	2,317	95.7	27	1.1
PART-TIME	6	.5	2	.2	10	.9	14	1.2	32	2.8	1,120	97.0	3	.3
FEMALE	6	1.2	1	.2	3	.6	8	1.6	18	3.6	477	96.2	1	.2
MALE	0	.0	1	.2	7	1.1	6	.9	14	2.1	643	97.6	2	.3
TOTAL	20	.4	19	.4	66	1.4	58	1.2	163	3.3	4,673	95.7	46	.9
FEMALE	12	.7	4	.2	27	1.5	28	1.6	71	3.9	1,713	95.1	17	.9
MALE	8	.3	15	.5	39	1.3	30	1.0	92	3.0	2,960	96.1	29	.9
UNCLASSIFIED:														
TOTAL	2	1.0	0	.0	1	.5	0	.0	3	1.6	190	98.4	0	.0
FEMALE	0	.0	0	.0	0	.0	0	.0	0	.0	68	100.0	0	.0
MALE	2	1.6	0	.0	1	.8	0	.0	3	2.4	122	97.6	0	.0
TOTAL ENROLLMENT:														
TOTAL	22	.4	19	.4	67	1.3	58	1.1	166	3.3	4,863	95.8	46	.9
FEMALE	12	.6	4	.2	27	1.4	28	1.5	71	3.8	1,781	95.3	17	.9
MALE	10	.3	15	.5	40	1.2	30	.9	95	3.0	3,082	96.1	29	.9
ILLINOIS (83 INSTITUTIONS)														
UNDERGRADUATES:														
FULL-TIME	94	.2	5,706	14.3	431	1.1	521	1.3	6,752	16.9	32,453	81.3	732	1.8
FEMALE	39	.3	3,540	23.0	175	1.1	247	1.6	4,001	26.0	11,175	72.7	202	1.3
MALE	55	.2	2,166	8.8	256	1.0	274	1.1	2,751	11.2	21,278	86.6	530	2.2
PART-TIME	49	.3	3,187	21.7	124	.8	280	1.9	3,640	24.8	10,914	74.5	105	.7
FEMALE	22	.3	1,993	28.5	45	.6	116	1.7	2,176	31.1	4,765	68.2	45	.6
MALE	27	.4	1,194	15.6	79	1.0	164	2.1	1,464	19.1	6,149	80.1	60	.8
TOTAL	143	.3	8,893	16.3	555	1.0	801	1.5	10,392	19.0	43,367	79.4	837	1.5
FEMALE	61	.3	5,533	24.7	220	1.0	363	1.6	6,177	27.6	15,940	71.3	247	1.1
MALE	82	.3	3,360	10.4	335	1.0	438	1.4	4,215	13.1	27,427	85.1	590	1.8
GRADUATE:														
FULL-TIME	3	.1	186	4.8	79	2.0	30	.8	298	7.7	2,945	76.2	624	16.1
FEMALE	0	.0	65	6.8	22	2.3	8	.8	95	9.9	761	79.5	101	10.6
MALE	3	.1	121	4.2	57	2.0	22	.8	203	7.0	2,184	75.1	523	18.0
PART-TIME	17	.2	587	6.4	227	2.5	67	.7	898	9.8	8,149	88.7	137	1.5
FEMALE	7	.3	237	9.2	61	2.4	19	.7	324	12.5	2,231	86.4	28	1.1
MALE	10	.2	350	5.3	166	2.5	48	.7	574	8.7	5,918	89.7	109	1.7
TOTAL	20	.2	773	5.9	306	2.3	97	.7	1,196	9.2	11,094	85.0	761	5.8
FEMALE	7	.2	302	8.5	83	2.3	27	.8	419	11.8	2,992	84.5	129	3.6
MALE	13	.1	471	5.0	223	2.3	70	.7	777	8.2	8,102	85.2	632	6.6
PROFESSIONAL:														
FULL-TIME	0	.0	0	.0	0	.0	0	.0	0	.0	0	.0	0	.0
FEMALE	0	.0	0	.0	0	.0	0	.0	0	.0	0	.0	0	.0
MALE	0	.0	0	.0	0	.0	0	.0	0	.0	0	.0	0	.0

ROLLMENT IN INSTITUTIONS OF HIGHER EDUCATION FOR SELECTED MAJOR FIELDS OF STUDY AND LEVEL OF ENROLLMENT
ETHNICITY, AND SEX: STATE, 1978

BUSINESS AND MANAGEMENT

INDIAN NATIVE %	BLACK NON-HISPANIC NUMBER	%	ASIAN OR PACIFIC ISLANDER NUMBER	%	HISPANIC NUMBER	%	TOTAL MINORITY NUMBER	%	WHITE NON-HISPANIC NUMBER	%	NON-RESIDENT ALIEN NUMBER	%	TOTAL NUMBER
CONTINUED													
.0	0	.0	0	.0	0	.0	0	.0	0	.0	0	.0	0
.0	0	.0	0	.0	0	.0	0	.0	0	.0	0	.0	0
.0	0	.0	0	.0	0	.0	0	.0	0	.0	0	.0	0
.0	0	.0	0	.0	0	.0	0	.0	0	.0	0	.0	0
.0	0	.0	0	.0	0	.0	0	.0	0	.0	0	.0	0
.0	0	.0	0	.0	0	.0	0	.0	0	.0	0	.0	0
.2	5,892	13.5	510	1.2	551	1.3	7,050	16.1	35,398	80.8	1,356	3.1	43,804
.2	3,605	22.1	197	1.2	255	1.6	4,096	25.1	11,936	73.1	303	1.9	16,335
.2	2,287	8.3	313	1.1	296	1.1	2,954	10.8	23,462	85.4	1,053	3.8	27,469
.3	3,774	15.8	351	1.5	347	1.5	4,538	19.0	19,063	80.0	242	1.0	23,843
.3	2,230	23.3	106	1.1	135	1.4	2,500	26.1	6,996	73.1	73	.8	9,569
.3	1,544	10.8	245	1.7	212	1.5	2,038	14.3	12,067	84.5	169	1.2	14,274
.2	9,666	14.3	861	1.3	898	1.3	11,588	17.1	54,461	80.5	1,598	2.4	67,647
.3	5,835	22.5	303	1.2	390	1.5	6,596	25.5	18,932	73.1	376	1.5	25,904
.2	3,831	9.2	558	1.3	508	1.2	4,992	12.0	35,529	85.1	1,222	2.9	41,743
.5	164	6.4	61	2.4	80	3.1	318	12.4	2,165	84.7	74	2.9	2,557
.4	89	6.8	19	1.5	30	2.3	143	10.9	1,146	87.5	21	1.6	1,310
.6	75	6.0	42	3.4	50	4.0	175	14.0	1,019	81.7	53	4.3	1,247
.3	9,830	14.0	922	1.3	978	1.4	11,906	17.0	56,626	80.7	1,672	2.4	70,204
.3	5,924	21.8	322	1.2	420	1.5	6,739	24.8	20,078	73.8	397	1.5	27,214
.2	3,906	9.1	600	1.4	558	1.3	5,167	12.0	36,548	85.0	1,275	3.0	42,990
(44 INSTITUTIONS)													
.1	1,461	6.6	76	.3	176	.8	1,740	7.8	20,167	90.8	313	1.4	22,220
.1	728	9.1	36	.5	74	.9	843	10.6	7,052	88.5	77	1.0	7,972
.2	733	5.1	40	.3	102	.7	897	6.3	13,115	92.0	236	1.7	14,248
.3	529	8.3	19	.3	76	1.2	640	10.0	5,718	89.4	36	.6	6,394
.2	279	10.9	14	.5	37	1.4	336	13.1	2,217	86.3	17	.7	2,570
.3	250	6.5	5	.1	39	1.0	304	7.9	3,501	91.6	19	.5	3,824
.2	1,990	7.0	95	.3	252	.9	2,380	8.3	25,885	90.5	349	1.2	28,614
.1	1,007	9.6	50	.5	111	1.1	1,179	11.2	9,269	87.9	94	.9	10,542
.2	983	5.4	45	.2	141	.8	1,201	6.6	16,616	91.9	255	1.4	18,072
.7	47	3.8	16	1.3	16	1.3	87	7.1	1,002	81.9	135	11.0	1,224
2.1	16	5.7	6	2.1	4	1.4	32	11.3	231	81.6	20	7.1	283
.2	31	3.3	10	1.1	12	1.3	55	5.8	771	81.9	115	12.2	941
.2	61	2.6	18	.8	11	.5	94	4.0	2,197	94.4	37	1.6	2,328
.4	12	2.2	2	.4	2	.4	18	3.2	529	95.5	7	1.3	554
.1	49	2.8	16	.9	9	.5	76	4.3	1,668	94.0	30	1.7	1,774
.3	108	3.0	34	1.0	27	.8	181	5.1	3,199	90.1	172	4.8	3,552
1.0	28	3.3	8	1.0	6	.7	50	6.0	760	90.8	27	3.2	837
.1	80	2.9	26	1.0	21	.8	131	4.8	2,439	89.8	145	5.3	2,715
.0	0	.0	1	11.1	0	.0	1	11.1	8	88.9	0	.0	9
.0	0	.0	1	50.0	0	.0	1	50.0	1	50.0	0	.0	2
.0	0	.0	0	.0	0	.0	0	.0	7	100.0	0	.0	7
.0	0	.0	0	.0	0	.0	0	.0	0	.0	0	.0	0
.0	0	.0	0	.0	0	.0	0	.0	0	.0	0	.0	0
.0	0	.0	0	.0	0	.0	0	.0	0	.0	0	.0	0
.0	0	.0	1	11.1	0	.0	1	11.1	8	88.9	0	.0	9
.0	0	.0	1	50.0	0	.0	1	50.0	1	50.0	0	.0	2
.0	0	.0	0	.0	0	.0	0	.0	7	100.0	0	.0	7
.1	1,508	6.4	93	.4	192	.8	1,828	7.8	21,177	90.3	448	1.9	23,453
.1	744	9.0	43	.5	78	.9	876	10.6	7,284	88.2	97	1.2	8,257
.2	764	5.0	50	.3	114	.8	952	6.3	13,893	91.4	351	2.3	15,196
.2	590	6.8	37	.4	87	1.0	734	8.4	7,915	90.7	73	.8	8,722
.3	291	9.3	16	.5	39	1.2	354	11.3	2,746	87.9	24	.8	3,124
.2	299	5.3	21	.4	48	.9	380	6.8	5,169	92.3	49	.9	5,598
.2	2,098	6.5	130	.4	279	.9	2,562	8.0	29,092	90.4	521	1.6	32,175
.2	1,035	9.1	59	.5	117	1.0	1,230	10.8	10,030	88.1	121	1.1	11,381
.2	1,063	5.1	71	.3	162	.8	1,332	6.4	19,062	91.7	400	1.9	20,794
.6	78	7.8	12	1.2	7	.7	103	10.3	887	88.3	14	1.4	1,004
.6	52	10.1	3	.6	2	.4	60	11.6	450	87.0	7	1.4	517
.6	26	5.3	9	1.8	5	1.0	43	8.8	437	89.7	7	1.4	487
.2	2,176	6.6	142	.4	286	.9	2,665	8.0	29,979	90.4	535	1.6	33,179
.2	1,087	9.1	62	.5	119	1.0	1,290	10.8	10,480	88.1	128	1.1	11,898
.2	1,089	5.1	80	.4	167	.8	1,375	6.5	19,499	91.6	407	1.9	21,261

TABLE 17 - TOTAL ENROLLMENT IN INSTITUTIONS OF HIGHER EDUCATION FOR SELECTED MAJOR FIELDS OF STUDY AND LEVEL OF ENROLLMENT BY RACE, ETHNICITY, AND SEX: STATE, 1978

MAJOR FIELD 0500 - BUSINESS AND MANAGEMENT

	AMERICAN INDIAN ALASKAN NATIVE		BLACK NON-HISPANIC		ASIAN OR PACIFIC ISLANDER		HISPANIC		TOTAL MINORITY		WHITE NON-HISPANIC		NON-RESIDENT ALIEN	
	NUMBER	%	NUMBER	%	NUMBER	%	NUMBER	%	NUMBER	%	NUMBER	%	NUMBER	%
IOWA (36 INSTITUTIONS)														
UNDERGRADUATES:														
FULL-TIME	23	.2	288	2.4	45	.4	39	.3	395	3.2	11,734	95.8	119	1.0
FEMALE	11	.2	115	2.4	23	.5	10	.2	159	3.3	4,568	95.9	38	.8
MALE	12	.2	173	2.3	22	.3	29	.4	236	3.2	7,166	95.8	81	1.1
PART-TIME	11	.6	52	2.9	17	.9	6	.3	86	4.8	1,710	94.6	12	.7
FEMALE	7	1.0	18	2.5	5	.7	2	.3	32	4.5	671	94.8	5	.7
MALE	4	.4	34	3.1	12	1.1	4	.4	54	4.9	1,039	94.5	7	.6
TOTAL	34	.2	340	2.4	62	.4	45	.3	481	3.4	13,444	95.6	131	.9
FEMALE	18	.3	133	2.4	28	.5	12	.2	191	3.5	5,239	95.7	43	.8
MALE	16	.2	207	2.4	34	.4	33	.4	290	3.4	8,205	95.6	88	1.0
GRADUATE:														
FULL-TIME	0	.0	3	1.1	3	1.1	1	.4	7	2.5	250	88.3	26	9.2
FEMALE	0	.0	2	2.3	2	2.3	1	1.2	5	5.8	79	91.9	2	2.3
MALE	0	.0	1	.5	1	.5	0	.0	2	1.0	171	86.8	24	12.2
PART-TIME	1	.2	3	.5	2	.3	1	.2	7	1.2	567	95.9	17	2.9
FEMALE	0	.0	1	.7	1	.7	1	.7	3	2.1	139	95.9	3	2.1
MALE	1	.2	2	.4	1	.2	0	.0	4	.9	428	96.0	14	3.1
TOTAL	1	.1	6	.7	5	.6	2	.2	14	1.6	817	93.5	43	4.9
FEMALE	0	.0	3	1.3	3	1.3	2	.9	8	3.5	218	94.4	5	2.2
MALE	1	.2	3	.5	2	.3	0	.0	6	.9	599	93.2	38	5.9
PROFESSIONAL:														
FULL-TIME	0	.0	0	.0	0	.0	0	.0	0	.0	0	.0	0	.0
FEMALE	0	.0	0	.0	0	.0	0	.0	0	.0	0	.0	0	.0
MALE	0	.0	0	.0	0	.0	0	.0	0	.0	0	.0	0	.0
PART-TIME	0	.0	0	.0	0	.0	0	.0	0	.0	0	.0	0	.0
FEMALE	0	.0	0	.0	0	.0	0	.0	0	.0	0	.0	0	.0
MALE	0	.0	0	.0	0	.0	0	.0	0	.0	0	.0	0	.0
TOTAL	0	.0	0	.0	0	.0	0	.0	0	.0	0	.0	0	.0
FEMALE	0	.0	0	.0	0	.0	0	.0	0	.0	0	.0	0	.0
MALE	0	.0	0	.0	0	.0	0	.0	0	.0	0	.0	0	.0
UND+GRAD+PROF:														
FULL-TIME	23	.2	291	2.3	48	.4	40	.3	402	3.2	11,984	95.6	145	1.2
FEMALE	11	.2	117	2.4	25	.5	11	.2	164	3.4	4,647	95.8	40	.8
MALE	12	.2	174	2.3	23	.3	29	.4	238	3.1	7,337	95.5	105	1.4
PART-TIME	12	.5	55	2.3	19	.8	7	.3	93	3.9	2,277	94.9	29	1.2
FEMALE	7	.8	19	2.2	6	.7	3	.3	35	4.1	810	95.0	8	.9
MALE	5	.3	36	2.3	13	.8	4	.3	58	3.8	1,467	94.9	21	1.4
TOTAL	35	.2	346	2.3	67	.4	47	.3	495	3.3	14,261	95.5	174	1.2
FEMALE	18	.3	136	2.4	31	.5	14	.2	199	3.5	5,457	95.7	48	.8
MALE	17	.2	210	2.3	36	.4	33	.4	296	3.2	8,804	95.4	126	1.4
UNCLASSIFIED:														
TOTAL	0	.0	4	1.3	1	.3	0	.0	5	1.6	302	97.4	3	1.0
FEMALE	0	.0	1	.6	0	.0	0	.0	1	.6	162	98.2	2	1.2
MALE	0	.0	3	2.1	1	.7	0	.0	4	2.8	140	96.6	1	.7
TOTAL ENROLLMENT:														
TOTAL	35	.2	350	2.3	68	.4	47	.3	500	3.3	14,563	95.6	177	1.2
FEMALE	18	.3	137	2.3	31	.5	14	.2	200	3.4	5,619	95.7	50	.9
MALE	17	.2	213	2.3	37	.4	33	.4	300	3.2	8,944	95.4	127	1.4
KANSAS (41 INSTITUTIONS)														
UNDERGRADUATES:														
FULL-TIME	49	.4	609	5.2	55	.5	159	1.4	872	7.4	10,663	90.6	234	2.0
FEMALE	24	.4	224	5.0	23	.5	47	1.0	318	7.1	4,117	91.7	56	1.2
MALE	25	.3	385	5.3	32	.4	112	1.5	554	7.6	6,546	89.9	178	2.4
PART-TIME	30	.8	270	7.4	15	.4	98	2.7	413	11.2	3,244	88.3	15	.4
FEMALE	9	.5	138	7.9	10	.6	48	2.8	205	11.8	1,523	87.7	8	.5
MALE	21	1.1	132	6.8	5	.3	50	2.6	208	10.7	1,721	88.9	7	.4
TOTAL	79	.5	879	5.7	70	.5	257	1.7	1,285	8.3	13,907	90.1	249	1.6
FEMALE	33	.5	362	5.8	33	.5	95	1.5	523	8.4	5,640	90.6	64	1.0
MALE	46	.5	517	5.6	37	.4	162	1.8	762	8.3	8,267	89.7	185	2.0
GRADUATE:														
FULL-TIME	2	.5	7	1.7	4	.9	2	.5	15	3.6	347	82.2	60	14.2
FEMALE	0	.0	3	2.7	3	2.7	0	.0	6	5.4	93	83.0	13	11.6
MALE	2	.6	4	1.3	1	.3	2	.6	9	2.9	254	81.9	47	15.2
PART-TIME	2	.3	7	1.1	8	1.3	8	1.3	25	4.0	583	93.7	14	2.3
FEMALE	0	.0	2	1.2	2	1.2	2	1.2	6	3.6	158	95.2	2	1.2
MALE	2	.4	5	1.1	6	1.3	6	1.3	19	4.2	425	93.2	12	2.6
TOTAL	4	.4	14	1.3	12	1.1	10	1.0	40	3.8	930	89.1	74	7.1
FEMALE	0	.0	5	1.8	5	1.8	2	.7	12	4.3	251	90.3	15	5.4
MALE	4	.5	9	1.2	7	.9	8	1.0	28	3.7	679	88.6	59	7.7
PROFESSIONAL:														
FULL-TIME	0	.0	0	.0	0	.0	0	.0	0	.0	0	.0	0	.0
FEMALE	0	.0	0	.0	0	.0	0	.0	0	.0	0	.0	0	.0
MALE	0	.0	0	.0	0	.0	0	.0	0	.0	0	.0	0	.0

BUSINESS AND MANAGEMENT

INDIAN NATIVE	BLACK NON-HISPANIC		ASIAN OR PACIFIC ISLANDER		HISPANIC		TOTAL MINORITY		WHITE NON-HISPANIC		NON-RESIDENT ALIEN		TOTAL
%	NUMBER	%	NUMBER	%	NUMBER	%	NUMBER	%	NUMBER	%	NUMBER	%	NUMBER
CONTINUED													
.0	0	.0	0	.0	0	.0	0	.0	0	.0	0	.0	0
.0	0	.0	0	.0	0	.0	0	.0	0	.0	0	.0	0
.0	0	.0	0	.0	0	.0	0	.0	0	.0	0	.0	0
.0	0	.0	0	.0	0	.0	0	.0	0	.0	0	.0	0
.0	0	.0	0	.0	0	.0	0	.0	0	.0	0	.0	0
.0	0	.0	0	.0	0	.0	0	.0	0	.0	0	.0	0
.4	616	5.1	59	.5	161	1.3	887	7.3	11,010	90.3	294	2.4	12,191
.5	227	4.9	26	.6	47	1.0	324	7.0	4,210	91.5	69	1.5	4,603
.4	389	5.1	33	.4	114	1.5	563	7.4	6,800	89.6	225	3.0	7,588
.7	277	6.5	23	.5	106	2.5	438	10.2	3,827	89.1	29	.7	4,294
.5	140	7.4	12	.6	50	2.6	211	11.1	1,681	88.4	10	.5	1,902
1.0	137	5.7	11	.5	56	2.3	227	9.5	2,146	89.7	19	.8	2,392
.5	893	5.4	82	.5	267	1.6	1,325	8.0	14,837	90.0	323	2.0	16,485
.5	367	5.6	38	.6	97	1.5	535	8.2	5,891	90.6	79	1.2	6,505
.5	526	5.3	44	.4	170	1.7	790	7.9	8,946	89.6	244	2.4	9,980
.4	38	7.5	8	1.6	3	.6	51	10.1	448	88.7	6	1.2	505
.0	14	6.8	2	1.0	0	.0	16	7.7	188	90.8	3	1.4	207
.7	24	8.1	6	2.0	3	1.0	35	11.7	260	87.2	3	1.0	298
.5	931	5.5	90	.5	270	1.6	1,376	8.1	15,285	90.0	329	1.9	16,990
.5	381	5.7	40	.6	97	1.4	551	8.2	6,079	90.6	82	1.2	6,712
.5	550	5.4	50	.5	173	1.7	825	8.0	9,206	89.6	247	2.4	10,278
(31 INSTITUTIONS)													
.1	1,368	9.6	65	.5	42	.3	1,490	10.4	12,597	88.3	180	1.3	14,267
.1	657	12.5	24	.5	15	.3	702	13.4	4,505	85.9	38	.7	5,245
.1	711	7.9	41	.5	27	.3	788	8.7	8,092	89.7	142	1.6	9,022
.1	331	7.7	12	.3	18	.4	366	8.5	3,914	91.3	5	.1	4,285
.1	187	9.3	4	.2	10	.5	203	10.1	1,799	89.8	1	.0	2,003
.1	144	6.3	8	.4	8	.4	163	7.1	2,115	92.7	4	.2	2,282
.1	1,699	9.2	77	.4	60	.3	1,856	10.0	16,511	89.0	185	1.0	18,552
.1	844	11.6	28	.4	25	.3	905	12.5	6,304	87.0	39	.5	7,248
.1	855	7.6	49	.4	35	.3	951	8.4	10,207	90.3	146	1.3	11,304
.7	2	.7	13	4.6	0	.0	17	6.0	225	78.9	43	15.1	285
1.5	1	1.5	3	4.5	0	.0	5	7.5	56	83.6	6	9.0	67
.5	1	.5	10	4.6	0	.0	12	5.5	169	77.5	37	17.0	218
.6	22	2.7	10	1.2	6	.7	43	5.2	765	92.5	19	2.3	827
.6	7	4.0	3	1.7	1	.6	12	6.8	162	92.0	2	1.1	176
.6	15	2.3	7	1.1	5	.8	31	4.8	603	92.6	17	2.6	651
.6	24	2.2	23	2.1	6	.5	60	5.4	990	89.0	62	5.6	1,112
.8	8	3.3	6	2.5	1	.4	17	7.0	218	89.7	8	3.3	243
.6	16	1.8	17	2.0	5	.6	43	4.9	772	88.8	54	6.2	869
.0	0	.0	0	.0	0	.0	0	.0	0	.0	0	.0	0
.0	0	.0	0	.0	0	.0	0	.0	0	.0	0	.0	0
.0	0	.0	0	.0	0	.0	0	.0	0	.0	0	.0	0
.0	0	.0	0	.0	0	.0	0	.0	0	.0	0	.0	0
.0	0	.0	0	.0	0	.0	0	.0	0	.0	0	.0	0
.0	0	.0	0	.0	0	.0	0	.0	0	.0	0	.0	0
.1	1,310	9.4	78	.5	42	.3	1,507	10.4	12,822	88.1	223	1.5	14,552
.1	658	12.4	27	.5	15	.3	707	13.3	4,561	85.9	44	.8	5,312
.1	712	7.7	51	.6	27	.3	800	8.7	8,261	89.4	179	1.9	9,240
.2	353	6.9	22	.4	24	.5	409	8.0	4,679	91.5	24	.5	5,112
.1	194	8.9	7	.3	11	.5	215	9.9	1,961	90.0	3	.1	2,179
.2	159	5.4	15	.5	13	.4	194	6.6	2,718	92.7	21	.7	2,933
.1	1,723	8.8	100	.5	66	.3	1,916	9.7	17,501	89.0	247	1.3	19,664
.1	852	11.4	34	.5	26	.3	922	12.3	6,522	87.1	47	.6	7,491
.1	871	7.2	66	.5	40	.3	994	8.2	10,979	90.2	200	1.6	12,173
.0	19	4.5	1	.3	4	1.0	22	5.8	359	94.0	1	.3	382
.0	5	3.0	1	.6	1	.6	7	4.2	158	95.8	0	.0	165
.0	12	5.5	0	.0	3	1.4	15	6.9	201	92.6	1	.5	217
.1	1,740	8.7	101	.5	70	.3	1,938	9.7	17,860	89.1	248	1.2	20,046
.1	857	11.2	35	.5	27	.4	929	12.1	6,680	87.3	47	.6	7,656
.1	883	7.1	66	.5	43	.3	1,009	8.1	11,180	90.2	201	1.6	12,390

TABLE 17 - TOTAL ENROLLMENT IN INSTITUTIONS OF HIGHER EDUCATION FOR SELECTED MAJOR FIELDS OF STUDY AND LEVEL OF ENROLLMENT
BY RACE, ETHNICITY, AND SEX: STATE, 1978

MAJOR FIELD 0500 - BUSINESS AND MANAGEMENT

	AMERICAN INDIAN ALASKAN NATIVE		BLACK NON-HISPANIC		ASIAN OR PACIFIC ISLANDER		HISPANIC		TOTAL MINORITY		WHITE NON-HISPANIC		NON-RESIDENT ALIEN	
	NUMBER	%	NUMBER	%	NUMBER	%	NUMBER	%	NUMBER	%	NUMBER	%	NUMBER	%
LOUISIANA	(	27 INSTITUTIONS)												
UNDERGRADUATES:														
FULL-TIME	18	.1	4,191	23.1	70	.4	215	1.2	4,494	24.8	13,257	73.0	401	2.2
FEMALE	8	.1	2,305	29.7	39	.5	103	1.3	2,455	31.6	5,174	66.7	133	1.7
MALE	10	.1	1,886	18.2	31	.3	112	1.1	2,039	19.6	8,083	77.8	268	2.6
PART-TIME	19	.4	937	18.5	29	.6	91	1.8	1,076	21.2	3,959	78.0	38	.7
FEMALE	14	.6	489	19.5	14	.6	43	1.7	560	22.3	1,933	77.1	14	.6
MALE	5	.2	448	17.5	15	.6	48	1.9	516	20.1	2,026	79.0	24	.9
TOTAL	37	.2	5,128	22.1	99	.4	306	1.3	5,570	24.0	17,216	74.1	439	1.9
FEMALE	22	.2	2,794	27.2	53	.5	146	1.4	3,015	29.4	7,107	69.2	147	1.4
MALE	15	.1	2,334	18.0	46	.4	160	1.2	2,555	19.7	10,109	78.0	292	2.3
GRADUATE:														
FULL-TIME	4	.6	22	3.1	4	.6	16	2.3	46	6.5	550	78.1	108	15.3
FEMALE	0	.0	11	5.6	0	.0	5	2.6	16	8.2	162	83.1	17	8.7
MALE	4	.8	11	2.2	4	.8	11	2.2	30	5.9	388	76.2	91	17.9
PART-TIME	0	.0	52	5.0	4	.4	7	.7	63	6.1	932	90.1	39	3.8
FEMALE	0	.0	19	8.1	1	.4	4	1.7	24	10.2	208	88.5	3	1.3
MALE	0	.0	33	4.1	3	.4	3	.4	39	4.9	724	90.6	36	4.5
TOTAL	4	.2	74	4.3	8	.5	23	1.3	109	6.3	1,482	85.3	147	8.5
FEMALE	0	.0	30	7.0	1	.2	9	2.1	40	9.3	370	86.0	20	4.7
MALE	4	.3	44	3.4	7	.5	14	1.1	69	5.3	1,112	85.0	127	9.7
PROFESSIONAL:														
FULL-TIME	0	.0	0	.0	0	.0	0	.0	0	.0	0	.0	0	.0
FEMALE	0	.0	0	.0	0	.0	0	.0	0	.0	0	.0	0	.0
MALE	0	.0	0	.0	0	.0	0	.0	0	.0	0	.0	0	.0
PART-TIME	0	.0	0	.0	0	.0	0	.0	0	.0	0	.0	0	.0
FEMALE	0	.0	0	.0	0	.0	0	.0	0	.0	0	.0	0	.0
MALE	0	.0	0	.0	0	.0	0	.0	0	.0	0	.0	0	.0
TOTAL	0	.0	0	.0	0	.0	0	.0	0	.0	0	.0	0	.0
FEMALE	0	.0	0	.0	0	.0	0	.0	0	.0	0	.0	0	.0
MALE	0	.0	0	.0	0	.0	0	.0	0	.0	0	.0	0	.0
UNG+GRAD+PROF:														
FULL-TIME	22	.1	4,213	22.3	74	.4	231	1.2	4,540	24.1	13,807	73.2	509	2.7
FEMALE	8	.1	2,316	29.1	39	.5	108	1.4	2,471	31.1	5,336	67.1	150	1.9
MALE	14	.1	1,897	17.4	35	.3	123	1.1	2,069	19.0	8,471	77.7	359	3.3
PART-TIME	19	.3	989	16.2	33	.5	98	1.6	1,139	18.7	4,891	80.1	77	1.3
FEMALE	14	.5	508	18.5	15	.5	47	1.7	584	21.3	2,141	78.1	17	.6
MALE	5	.1	481	14.3	18	.5	51	1.5	555	16.5	2,750	81.7	60	1.8
TOTAL	41	.2	5,202	20.8	107	.4	329	1.3	5,679	22.7	18,698	74.9	586	2.3
FEMALE	22	.2	2,824	26.4	54	.5	155	1.4	3,055	28.6	7,477	69.9	167	1.6
MALE	19	.1	2,378	16.7	53	.4	174	1.2	2,624	18.4	11,221	78.7	419	2.9
UNCLASSIFIED:														
TOTAL	0	.0	24	8.8	3	1.1	2	.7	29	10.6	241	88.3	3	1.1
FEMALE	0	.0	14	12.2	1	.9	1	.9	16	13.9	97	84.3	2	1.7
MALE	0	.0	10	6.3	2	1.3	1	.6	13	8.2	144	91.1	1	.6
TOTAL ENROLLMENT:														
TOTAL	41	.2	5,226	20.7	110	.4	331	1.3	5,708	22.6	18,939	75.0	589	2.3
FEMALE	22	.2	2,838	26.2	55	.5	156	1.4	3,071	28.4	7,574	70.0	169	1.6
MALE	19	.1	2,388	16.6	55	.4	175	1.2	2,637	18.3	11,365	78.8	420	2.9
MAINE	(	15 INSTITUTIONS)												
UNDERGRADUATES:														
FULL-TIME	25	.7	13	.3	15	.4	14	.4	67	1.8	3,733	97.7	19	.5
FEMALE	12	.8	4	.3	3	.2	3	.2	22	1.5	1,455	98.2	4	.3
MALE	13	.6	9	.4	12	.5	11	.5	45	1.9	2,278	97.4	15	.6
PART-TIME	4	.4	6	.6	2	.2	4	.4	16	1.5	1,041	98.5	0	.0
FEMALE	2	.6	2	.6	1	.3	2	.6	7	2.1	324	97.9	0	.0
MALE	2	.3	4	.6	1	.1	2	.3	9	1.2	717	98.8	0	.0
TOTAL	29	.6	19	.4	17	.3	18	.4	83	1.7	4,774	97.9	19	.4
FEMALE	14	.8	6	.3	4	.2	5	.3	29	1.6	1,779	98.2	4	.2
MALE	15	.5	13	.4	13	.4	13	.4	54	1.8	2,995	97.7	15	.5
GRADUATE:														
FULL-TIME	0	.0	0	.0	0	.0	0	.0	0	.0	105	97.2	3	2.8
FEMALE	0	.0	0	.0	0	.0	0	.0	0	.0	22	100.0	0	.0
MALE	0	.0	0	.0	0	.0	0	.0	0	.0	83	96.5	3	3.5
PART-TIME	0	.0	0	.0	0	.0	0	.0	0	.0	133	100.0	0	.0
FEMALE	0	.0	0	.0	0	.0	0	.0	0	.0	25	100.0	0	.0
MALE	0	.0	0	.0	0	.0	0	.0	0	.0	108	100.0	0	.0
TOTAL	0	.0	0	.0	0	.0	0	.0	0	.0	238	98.8	3	1.2
FEMALE	0	.0	0	.0	0	.0	0	.0	0	.0	47	100.0	0	.0
MALE	0	.0	0	.0	0	.0	0	.0	0	.0	191	98.5	3	1.5
PROFESSIONAL:														
FULL-TIME	0	.0	0	.0	0	.0	0	.0	0	.0	0	.0	0	.0
FEMALE	0	.0	0	.0	0	.0	0	.0	0	.0	0	.0	0	.0
MALE	0	.0	0	.0	0	.0	0	.0	0	.0	0	.0	0	.0

BUSINESS AND MANAGEMENT

INDIAN NATIVE	BLACK NON-HISPANIC		ASIAN OR PACIFIC ISLANDER		HISPANIC		TOTAL MINORITY		WHITE NON-HISPANIC		NON-RESIDENT ALIEN		TOTAL
%	NUMBER	%	NUMBER	%	NUMBER	%	NUMBER	%	NUMBER	%	NUMBER	%	NUMBER
CONTINUED													
.0	0	.0	0	.0	0	.0	0	.0	0	.0	0	.0	0
.0	0	.0	0	.0	0	.0	0	.0	0	.0	0	.0	0
.0	0	.0	0	.0	0	.0	0	.0	0	.0	0	.0	0
.0	0	.0	0	.0	0	.0	0	.0	0	.0	0	.0	0
.0	0	.0	0	.0	0	.0	0	.0	0	.0	0	.0	0
.0	0	.0	0	.0	0	.0	0	.0	0	.0	0	.0	0
.6	13	.3	15	.4	14	.4	67	1.7	3,838	97.7	22	.6	3,927
.8	4	.3	3	.2	3	.2	22	1.5	1,477	98.3	4	.3	1,503
.5	9	.4	12	.5	11	.5	45	1.9	2,361	97.4	18	.7	2,424
.3	6	.5	2	.2	4	.3	16	1.3	1,174	98.7	0	.0	1,190
.6	2	.6	1	.3	2	.6	7	2.0	349	98.0	0	.0	356
.2	4	.5	1	.1	2	.2	9	1.1	825	98.9	0	.0	834
.6	19	.4	17	.3	18	.4	83	1.6	5,012	97.9	22	.4	5,117
.8	6	.3	4	.2	5	.3	29	1.6	1,826	98.2	4	.2	1,859
.5	13	.4	13	.4	13	.4	54	1.7	3,186	97.8	18	.6	3,258
.2	6	.6	6	.6	0	.0	14	1.5	911	98.5	0	.0	925
.4	0	.0	1	.2	0	.0	3	.6	489	99.4	0	.0	492
.0	6	1.4	5	1.2	0	.0	11	2.5	422	97.5	0	.0	433
.5	25	.4	23	.4	18	.3	97	1.6	5,923	98.0	22	.4	6,042
.7	6	.3	5	.2	5	.2	32	1.4	2,315	98.5	4	.2	2,351
.4	19	.5	18	.5	13	.4	65	1.8	3,608	97.8	18	.5	3,691
(33 INSTITUTIONS)													
.2	2,650	20.3	135	1.0	107	.8	2,921	22.4	9,728	74.4	419	3.2	13,068
.2	1,354	28.9	58	1.2	38	.8	1,459	31.1	3,070	65.5	156	3.3	4,685
.2	1,296	15.5	77	.9	69	.8	1,462	17.4	6,658	79.4	263	3.1	8,383
.3	1,296	20.2	70	1.1	49	.8	1,433	22.3	4,910	76.4	80	1.2	6,423
.3	706	24.2	30	1.0	18	.6	764	26.1	2,130	72.9	28	1.0	2,922
.2	590	16.9	40	1.1	31	.9	669	19.1	2,780	79.4	52	1.5	3,501
.2	3,946	20.2	205	1.1	156	.8	4,354	22.3	14,638	75.1	499	2.6	19,491
.2	2,060	27.1	88	1.2	56	.7	2,223	29.2	5,200	68.4	184	2.4	7,607
.2	1,886	15.9	117	1.0	100	.8	2,131	17.9	9,438	79.4	315	2.7	11,884
.5	75	17.6	6	1.4	2	.5	85	20.0	282	66.4	58	13.6	425
.0	30	23.3	1	.8	1	.8	32	24.8	90	69.8	7	5.4	129
.7	45	15.2	5	1.7	1	.3	53	17.9	192	64.9	51	17.2	296
.2	235	10.7	22	1.0	7	.3	268	12.2	1,867	85.1	60	2.7	2,195
.0	104	17.9	6	1.0	2	.3	112	19.3	462	79.5	7	1.2	581
.2	131	8.1	16	1.0	5	.3	156	9.7	1,405	87.1	53	3.3	1,614
.2	310	11.8	28	1.1	9	.3	353	13.5	2,149	82.0	118	4.5	2,620
.0	134	18.9	7	1.0	3	.4	144	20.3	552	77.7	14	2.0	710
.3	176	9.2	21	1.1	6	.3	209	10.9	1,597	83.6	104	5.4	1,910
.0	0	.0	0	.0	0	.0	0	.0	0	.0	0	.0	0
.0	0	.0	0	.0	0	.0	0	.0	0	.0	0	.0	0
.0	0	.0	0	.0	0	.0	0	.0	0	.0	0	.0	0
.0	0	.0	0	.0	0	.0	0	.0	0	.0	0	.0	0
.0	0	.0	0	.0	0	.0	0	.0	0	.0	0	.0	0
.0	0	.0	0	.0	0	.0	0	.0	0	.0	0	.0	0
.2	2,725	20.2	141	1.0	109	.8	3,006	22.3	10,010	74.2	477	3.5	13,493
.2	1,384	28.7	59	1.2	39	.8	1,491	31.0	3,160	65.6	163	3.4	4,814
.3	1,341	15.5	82	.9	70	.8	1,515	17.5	6,850	78.9	314	3.6	8,679
.3	1,531	17.8	92	1.1	56	.6	1,701	19.7	6,777	78.6	140	1.6	8,618
.3	810	23.1	36	1.0	20	.6	876	25.0	2,592	74.0	35	1.0	3,503
.2	721	14.1	56	1.1	36	.7	825	16.1	4,185	81.8	105	2.1	5,115
.2	4,256	19.2	233	1.1	165	.7	4,707	21.3	16,787	75.9	617	2.8	22,111
.2	2,194	26.4	95	1.1	59	.7	2,367	28.5	5,752	69.2	198	2.4	8,317
.2	2,062	14.9	138	1.0	106	.8	2,340	17.0	11,035	80.0	419	3.0	13,794
.5	252	17.3	14	1.0	7	.5	280	19.2	1,115	76.6	61	4.2	1,456
.4	129	23.7	7	1.3	5	.9	143	26.3	383	70.4	18	3.3	544
.5	123	13.5	7	.8	2	.2	137	15.0	732	80.3	43	4.7	912
.3	4,508	19.1	247	1.0	172	.7	4,987	21.2	17,902	76.0	678	2.9	23,567
.2	2,323	26.2	102	1.2	64	.7	2,510	28.3	6,135	69.2	216	2.4	8,861
.3	2,185	14.9	145	1.0	108	.7	2,477	16.8	11,767	80.0	462	3.1	14,706

TABLE 17 - TOTAL ENROLLMENT IN INSTITUTIONS OF HIGHER EDUCATION FOR SELECTED MAJOR FIELDS OF STUDY AND LEVEL OF ENROLLMENT BY RACE, ETHNICITY, AND SEX: STATE, 1978

MAJOR FIELD 0500 - BUSINESS AND MANAGEMENT

	AMERICAN INDIAN ALASKAN NATIVE		BLACK NON-HISPANIC		ASIAN OR PACIFIC ISLANDER		HISPANIC		TOTAL MINORITY		WHITE NON-HISPANIC		NON-RESIDENT ALIEN	
	NUMBER	%	NUMBER	%	NUMBER	%	NUMBER	%	NUMBER	%	NUMBER	%	NUMBER	%
MASSACHUSETTS (58 INSTITUTIONS)														
UNDERGRADUATES:														
FULL-TIME	82	.2	1,356	3.9	340	1.0	413	1.2	2,191	6.4	31,481	91.7	667	1.9
FEMALE	22	.2	722	5.5	181	1.4	238	1.8	1,163	8.9	11,677	89.3	238	1.8
MALE	60	.3	634	3.0	159	.7	175	.8	1,028	4.8	19,804	93.1	429	2.0
PART-TIME	39	.2	558	3.3	51	.3	174	1.0	822	4.9	15,971	94.7	66	.4
FEMALE	21	.3	296	3.8	19	.2	86	1.1	422	5.5	7,285	94.2	25	.3
MALE	18	.2	262	2.9	32	.4	88	1.0	400	4.4	8,686	95.2	41	.4
TOTAL	121	.2	1,914	3.7	391	.8	587	1.1	3,013	5.9	47,452	92.7	733	1.4
FEMALE	43	.2	1,018	4.9	200	1.0	324	1.6	1,585	7.6	18,962	91.1	263	1.3
MALE	78	.3	896	2.9	191	.6	263	.9	1,428	4.7	28,490	93.8	470	1.5
GRADUATE:														
FULL-TIME	1	.0	104	2.8	51	1.4	38	1.0	194	5.3	3,133	85.8	323	8.8
FEMALE	1	.1	28	3.1	15	1.6	11	1.2	55	6.0	828	90.9	28	3.1
MALE	0	.0	76	2.8	36	1.3	27	1.0	139	5.1	2,305	84.2	295	10.8
PART-TIME	7	.1	85	1.5	58	1.0	25	.4	175	3.0	5,558	96.2	46	.8
FEMALE	2	.1	29	1.8	20	1.2	6	.4	57	3.6	1,532	95.7	12	.7
MALE	5	.1	56	1.3	38	.9	19	.5	118	2.8	4,026	96.4	34	.8
TOTAL	8	.1	189	2.0	109	1.2	63	.7	369	3.9	8,691	92.2	369	3.9
FEMALE	3	.1	57	2.3	35	1.4	17	.7	112	4.5	2,360	93.9	40	1.6
MALE	5	.1	132	1.9	74	1.1	46	.7	257	3.7	6,331	91.5	329	4.8
PROFESSIONAL:														
FULL-TIME	0	.0	0	.0	0	.0	0	.0	0	.0	136	100.0		.0
FEMALE	0	.0	0	.0	0	.0	0	.0	0	.0	80	100.0		.0
MALE	0	.0	0	.0	0	.0	0	.0	0	.0	56	100.0		.0
PART-TIME	0	.0	0	.0	0	.0	0	.0	0	.0	0	.0		.0
FEMALE	0	.0	0	.0	0	.0	0	.0	0	.0	0	.0		.0
MALE	0	.0	0	.0	0	.0	0	.0	0	.0	0	.0	0	.0
TOTAL	0	.0	0	.0	0	.0	0	.0	0	.0	136	100.0		.0
FEMALE	0	.0	0	.0	0	.0	0	.0	0	.0	80	100.0		.0
MALE	0	.0	0	.0	0	.0	0	.0	0	.0	56	100.0	0	.0
UND+GRAD+PROF:														
FULL-TIME	83	.2	1,460	3.8	391	1.0	451	1.2	2,385	6.3	34,750	91.1	990	2
FEMALE	23	.2	750	5.3	196	1.4	249	1.8	1,218	8.7	12,585	89.5	266	1
MALE	60	.2	710	3.0	195	.8	202	.8	1,167	4.9	22,165	92.1	724	3
PART-TIME	46	.2	643	2.8	109	.5	199	.9	997	4.4	21,529	95.1	112	.
FEMALE	23	.2	325	3.5	39	.4	92	1.0	479	5.1	8,817	94.5	37	.
MALE	23	.2	318	2.4	70	.5	107	.8	518	3.9	12,712	95.5	75	.8
TOTAL	129	.2	2,103	3.5	500	.8	650	1.1	3,382	5.6	56,279	92.6	1,102	18
FEMALE	46	.2	1,075	4.8	235	1.0	341	1.5	1,697	7.3	21,402	91.5	303	13
MALE	83	.2	1,028	2.8	265	.7	309	.8	1,685	4.5	34,877	93.4	799	211
UNCLASSIFIED:														
TOTAL	3	.1	67	2.4	31	1.1	21	.8	122	4.5	2,502	91.4	114	4.2
FEMALE	0	.0	29	2.8	13	1.2	10	1.0	52	4.9	974	92.7	25	2.4
MALE	3	.2	38	2.3	18	1.1	11	.7	70	4.1	1,528	90.6	89	513
TOTAL ENROLLMENT:														
TOTAL	132	.2	2,170	3.4	531	.8	671	1.1	3,504	5.5	58,781	92.6	1,216	1
FEMALE	46	.2	1,104	4.5	248	1.0	351	1.4	1,749	7.2	22,376	91.5	328	1
MALE	86	.2	1,066	2.7	283	.7	320	.8	1,755	4.5	36,405	93.2	888	212
MICHIGAN (65 INSTITUTIONS)														
UNDERGRADUATES:														
FULL-TIME	136	.4	3,887	10.3	154	.4	347	.9	4,524	12.0	32,561	86.4	617	1.6
FEMALE	62	.4	2,406	14.9	67	.4	164	1.0	2,699	16.7	13,367	82.5	134	.8
MALE	74	.3	1,481	6.9	87	.4	183	.9	1,825	8.5	19,194	89.3	483	2.2
PART-TIME	87	.4	1,933	9.0	98	.5	426	2.0	2,544	11.9	18,755	87.7	81	.4
FEMALE	42	.4	1,161	10.0	51	.4	273	2.4	1,527	13.2	10,035	86.6	31	.3
MALE	45	.5	772	7.9	47	.5	153	1.6	1,017	10.4	8,720	89.1	50	.5
TOTAL	223	.4	5,820	9.9	252	.4	773	1.3	7,068	12.0	51,316	86.9	698	1.2
FEMALE	104	.4	3,567	12.8	118	.4	437	1.6	4,226	15.2	23,402	84.2	165	.6
MALE	119	.4	2,253	7.2	134	.4	336	1.1	2,842	9.1	27,914	89.2	533	1.7
GRADUATE:														
FULL-TIME	10	.5	49	2.6	25	1.3	16	.8	100	5.2	1,592	83.2	222	11.6
FEMALE	2	.5	23	5.3	10	2.3	0	.0	35	8.1	369	85.2	29	6.7
MALE	8	.5	26	1.8	15	1.0	16	1.1	65	4.4	1,223	82.6	193	13.0
PART-TIME	3	.1	195	4.6	47	1.1	18	.4	263	6.1	3,929	91.8	89	2.1
FEMALE	0	.0	82	8.4	15	1.6	0	.0	97	10.5	816	87.9	15	1.6
MALE	3	.1	113	3.4	32	1.0	18	.5	166	5.0	3,113	92.8	74	2.2
TOTAL	13	.2	244	3.9	72	1.2	34	.5	363	5.9	5,521	89.1	311	5.0
FEMALE	2	.1	105	7.7	25	1.8	0	.0	132	9.7	1,185	87.1	44	3.2
MALE	11	.2	139	2.9	47	1.0	34	.7	231	4.8	4,336	89.7	267	5.5
PROFESSIONAL:														
FULL-TIME	0	.0	0	.0	0	.0	0	.0	0	.0	0	.0		.0
FEMALE	0	.0	0	.0	0	.0	0	.0	0	.0	0	.0		.0
MALE	0	.0	0	.0	0	.0	0	.0	0	.0	0	.0		.0

BUSINESS AND MANAGEMENT

% INDIAN NATIVE %	BLACK NON-HISPANIC NUMBER	%	ASIAN OR PACIFIC ISLANDER NUMBER	%	HISPANIC NUMBER	%	TOTAL MINORITY NUMBER	%	WHITE NON-HISPANIC NUMBER	%	NON-RESIDENT ALIEN NUMBER	%	TOTAL NUMBER
CONTINUED													
.0	0	.0	0	.0	0	.0	0	.0	0	.0	0	.0	0
.0	0	.0	0	.0	0	.0	0	.0	0	.0	0	.0	0
.0	0	.0	0	.0	0	.0	0	.0	0	.0	0	.0	0
.0	0	.0	0	.0	0	.0	0	.0	0	.0	0	.0	0
.0	0	.0	0	.0	0	.0	0	.0	0	.0	0	.0	0
.0	0	.0	0	.0	0	.0	0	.0	0	.0	0	.0	0
.4	3,936	9.9	179	.5	363	.9	4,624	11.7	34,153	86.2	839	2.1	39,616
.4	2,429	14.6	77	.5	164	1.0	2,734	16.4	13,736	82.6	163	1.0	16,633
.4	1,507	6.6	102	.4	199	.9	1,890	8.2	20,417	88.8	676	2.9	22,983
.4	2,128	8.3	145	.6	444	1.7	2,807	10.9	22,684	88.4	170	.7	25,661
.3	1,243	9.9	66	.5	273	2.2	1,624	13.0	10,851	86.7	46	.4	12,521
.2	885	6.7	79	.6	171	1.3	1,183	9.0	11,833	90.1	124	.9	13,140
.4	6,064	9.3	324	.5	807	1.2	7,431	11.4	56,837	87.1	1,009	1.5	65,277
.4	3,672	12.6	143	.5	437	1.5	4,358	14.9	24,587	84.3	209	.7	29,154
.4	2,392	6.6	181	.5	370	1.0	3,073	8.5	32,250	89.3	800	2.2	36,123
.6	402	21.6	21	1.1	14	.8	448	24.1	1,394	74.9	19	1.0	1,861
.5	247	29.6	6	.7	6	.7	263	31.5	569	68.1	3	.4	835
.7	155	15.1	15	1.5	8	.8	185	18.0	825	80.4	16	1.6	1,026
.4	6,466	9.6	345	.5	821	1.2	7,879	11.7	58,231	86.7	1,028	1.5	67,138
.4	3,919	13.1	149	.5	443	1.5	4,621	15.4	25,156	83.9	212	.7	29,989
.4	2,547	6.9	196	.5	378	1.0	3,258	8.8	33,075	89.0	816	2.2	37,149
(41 INSTITUTIONS)													
.3	187	1.2	91	.6	46	.3	379	2.4	15,491	96.1	254	1.6	16,124
.2	62	1.2	46	.9	20	.4	148	2.9	4,935	95.9	65	1.3	5,148
.3	125	1.1	45	.4	26	.2	231	2.1	10,556	96.2	189	1.7	10,976
.2	23	1.0	19	.8	7	.3	53	2.3	2,206	97.3	8	.4	2,287
.2	6	.6	10	1.0	1	.1	19	1.9	986	98.0	1	.1	1,006
.2	17	1.3	9	.7	6	.5	34	2.7	1,220	96.7	7	.6	1,261
.3	210	1.1	110	.6	53	.3	432	2.3	17,697	96.2	262	1.4	18,391
.4	68	1.1	56	.9	21	.3	167	2.7	5,921	96.2	64	1.1	6,154
.3	142	1.2	54	.4	32	.3	265	2.2	11,776	96.2	196	1.6	12,237
.3	6	1.0	5	.8	2	.3	15	2.4	527	84.1	85	13.6	627
.0	2	1.1	4	2.2	1	.6	7	3.9	156	86.7	17	9.4	180
.4	4	.9	1	.2	1	.2	8	1.8	371	83.0	68	15.2	447
.2	3	.3	9	1.0	1	.1	15	1.6	914	96.9	14	1.5	943
.0	0	.0	0	.0	0	.0	0	.0	187	98.9	2	1.1	189
.3	3	.4	9	1.2	1	.1	15	2.0	727	96.4	12	1.6	754
.3	9	.6	14	.9	3	.2	30	1.9	1,441	91.8	99	6.3	1,570
.0	2	.5	4	1.1	1	.3	7	1.9	343	93.0	19	5.1	369
.3	7	.6	10	.8	2	.2	23	1.9	1,098	91.4	80	6.7	1,201
.0	0	.0	0	.0	0	.0	0	.0	0	.0	0	.0	0
.0	0	.0	0	.0	0	.0	0	.0	0	.0	0	.0	0
.0	0	.0	0	.0	0	.0	0	.0	0	.0	0	.0	0
.0	0	.0	0	.0	0	.0	0	.0	0	.0	0	.0	0
.0	0	.0	0	.0	0	.0	0	.0	0	.0	0	.0	0
.0	0	.0	0	.0	0	.0	0	.0	0	.0	0	.0	0
.0	0	.0	0	.0	0	.0	0	.0	0	.0	0	.0	0
.0	0	.0	0	.0	0	.0	0	.0	0	.0	0	.0	0
.0	0	.0	0	.0	0	.0	0	.0	0	.0	0	.0	0
.3	193	1.2	96	.6	48	.3	394	2.4	16,018	95.6	339	2.0	16,751
.4	64	1.2	50	.9	21	.4	155	2.9	5,091	95.6	82	1.5	5,328
.3	129	1.1	46	.4	27	.2	239	2.1	10,927	95.7	257	2.2	11,423
.2	26	.8	28	.9	8	.2	68	2.1	3,120	97.2	22	.7	3,210
.2	6	.5	10	.8	1	.1	19	1.6	1,173	98.2	3	.3	1,195
.2	20	1.0	18	.9	7	.3	49	2.4	1,947	96.6	19	.9	2,015
.3	219	1.1	124	.6	56	.3	462	2.3	19,138	95.9	361	1.8	19,961
.3	70	1.1	60	.9	22	.3	174	2.7	6,264	96.0	85	1.3	6,523
.3	149	1.1	64	.5	34	.3	288	2.1	12,874	95.8	276	2.1	13,438
1.0	3	1.0	3	1.0	0	.0	9	3.1	280	94.9	6	2.0	295
.8	1	.8	3	2.4	0	.0	5	4.1	118	95.9	0	.0	123
1.2	2	1.2	0	.0	0	.0	4	2.3	162	94.2	6	3.5	172
.3	222	1.1	127	.6	56	.3	471	2.3	19,418	95.9	367	1.8	20,256
.3	71	1.1	63	.9	22	.3	179	2.7	6,382	96.0	85	1.3	6,646
.3	151	1.1	64	.5	34	.2	292	2.1	13,036	95.8	282	2.1	13,610

MAJOR FIELD 0500 - BUSINESS AND MANAGEMENT

	AMERICAN INDIAN ALASKAN NATIVE		BLACK NON-HISPANIC		ASIAN OR PACIFIC ISLANDER		HISPANIC		TOTAL MINORITY		WHITE NON-HISPANIC		NON-RESIDENT ALIEN	
	NUMBER	%	NUMBER	%	NUMBER	%	NUMBER	%	NUMBER	%	NUMBER	%	NUMBER	%
MISSISSIPPI (36 INSTITUTIONS)														
UNDERGRADUATES:														
FULL-TIME	15	.1	3,852	30.6	32	.3	11	.1	3,910	31.1	8,560	68.1	98	.8
FEMALE	8	.1	2,332	41.1	19	.3	1	.0	2,360	41.6	3,299	58.1	17	.3
MALE	7	.1	1,520	22.1	13	.2	10	.1	1,550	22.5	5,261	76.3	81	1.2
PART-TIME	8	.3	354	14.5	10	.4	6	.2	378	15.5	2,054	84.4	3	.1
FEMALE	6	.5	194	17.5	2	.2	4	.4	206	18.6	901	81.3	1	.1
MALE	2	.2	160	12.1	8	.6	2	.2	172	13.0	1,153	86.9	2	.2
TOTAL	23	.2	4,206	28.0	42	.3	17	.1	4,288	28.6	10,614	70.7	101	.7
FEMALE	14	.2	2,526	37.2	21	.3	5	.1	2,566	37.8	4,200	61.9	18	.3
MALE	9	.1	1,680	20.4	21	.3	12	.1	1,722	21.0	6,414	78.0	83	1.0
GRADUATE:														
FULL-TIME	0	.0	50	17.5	4	1.4	0	.0	54	18.9	198	69.2	34	11.9
FEMALE	0	.0	20	23.8	0	.0	0	.0	20	23.8	55	65.5	9	10.7
MALE	0	.0	30	14.9	4	2.0	0	.0	34	16.8	143	70.8	25	12.4
PART-TIME	2	.3	81	13.6	9	1.5	3	.5	95	16.0	479	80.5	21	3.5
FEMALE	2	1.4	34	24.1	2	1.4	0	.0	38	27.0	100	70.9	3	2.1
MALE	0	.0	47	10.4	7	1.5	3	.7	57	12.6	379	83.5	18	4.0
TOTAL	2	.2	131	14.9	13	1.5	3	.3	149	16.9	677	76.8	55	6.2
FEMALE	2	.9	54	24.0	2	.9	0	.0	58	25.8	155	68.9	12	5.3
MALE	0	.0	77	11.7	11	1.7	3	.5	91	13.9	522	79.6	43	6.6
PROFESSIONAL:														
FULL-TIME	0	.0	0	.0	0	.0	0	.0	0	.0	0	.0	0	.0
FEMALE	0	.0	0	.0	0	.0	0	.0	0	.0	0	.0	0	.0
MALE	0	.0	0	.0	0	.0	0	.0	0	.0	0	.0	0	.0
PART-TIME	0	.0	0	.0	0	.0	0	.0	0	.0	1	100.0	0	.0
FEMALE	0	.0	0	.0	0	.0	0	.0	0	.0	0	.0	0	.0
MALE	0	.0	0	.0	0	.0	0	.0	0	.0	1	100.0	0	.0
TOTAL	0	.0	0	.0	0	.0	0	.0	0	.0	1	100.0	0	.0
FEMALE	0	.0	0	.0	0	.0	0	.0	0	.0	0	.0	0	.0
MALE	0	.0	0	.0	0	.0	0	.0	0	.0	1	100.0	0	.0
UND+GRAD+PROF:														
FULL-TIME	15	.1	3,902	30.4	36	.3	11	.1	3,964	30.8	8,758	68.1	132	1.0
FEMALE	8	.1	2,352	40.8	19	.3	1	.0	2,380	41.3	3,354	58.2	26	.5
MALE	7	.1	1,550	21.8	17	.2	10	.1	1,584	22.3	5,404	76.2	106	1.5
PART-TIME	10	.3	435	14.4	19	.6	9	.3	473	15.6	2,534	83.6	24	.8
FEMALE	8	.6	228	18.3	4	.3	4	.3	244	19.5	1,001	80.1	4	.3
MALE	2	.1	207	11.6	15	.8	5	.3	229	12.9	1,533	86.0	20	1.1
TOTAL	25	.2	4,337	27.3	55	.3	20	.1	4,437	27.9	11,292	71.1	156	1.0
FEMALE	16	.2	2,580	36.8	23	.3	5	.1	2,624	37.4	4,355	62.1	30	.4
MALE	9	.1	1,757	19.8	32	.4	15	.2	1,813	20.4	6,937	78.2	126	1.4
UNCLASSIFIED:														
TOTAL	0	.0	23	10.5	2	.9	0	.0	25	11.4	191	86.8	4	1.8
FEMALE	0	.0	23	17.6	1	.8	0	.0	24	18.3	107	81.7	0	.0
MALE	0	.0	0	.0	1	1.1	0	.0	1	1.1	84	94.4	4	4.5
TOTAL ENROLLMENT:														
TOTAL	25	.2	4,360	27.1	57	.4	20	.1	4,462	27.7	11,483	71.3	160	1.0
FEMALE	16	.2	2,603	36.5	24	.3	5	.1	2,648	37.1	4,462	62.5	30	.4
MALE	9	.1	1,757	19.6	33	.4	15	.2	1,814	20.2	7,021	78.3	130	1.5
MISSOURI (35 INSTITUTIONS)														
UNDERGRADUATES:														
FULL-TIME	46	.3	1,222	7.0	87	.5	101	.6	1,456	8.3	15,882	90.7	179	1.0
FEMALE	16	.2	598	9.3	37	.6	34	.5	685	10.7	5,671	88.5	54	.8
MALE	30	.3	624	5.6	50	.5	67	.6	771	6.9	10,211	91.9	125	1.1
PART-TIME	19	.4	424	8.9	23	.5	48	1.0	514	10.8	4,227	88.7	26	.5
FEMALE	10	.6	192	10.7	14	.8	13	.7	229	12.8	1,555	86.7	9	.5
MALE	9	.3	232	7.8	9	.3	35	1.2	285	9.6	2,672	89.9	15	.5
TOTAL	65	.3	1,646	7.4	110	.5	149	.7	1,970	8.8	20,109	90.2	203	.9
FEMALE	26	.3	790	9.6	51	.6	47	.6	914	11.1	7,226	88.1	63	.8
MALE	39	.3	856	6.1	59	.4	102	.7	1,056	7.5	12,883	91.5	140	1.0
GRADUATE:														
FULL-TIME	3	.2	92	6.4	31	2.1	9	.6	135	9.3	1,206	83.3	107	7.4
FEMALE	1	.3	26	8.3	7	2.2	1	.3	35	11.2	243	77.9	34	10.9
MALE	2	.2	66	5.8	24	2.1	8	.7	100	8.8	963	84.8	73	6.4
PART-TIME	7	.2	133	4.2	26	.8	15	.5	181	5.7	2,952	93.1	38	1.2
FEMALE	1	.1	38	4.9	6	.8	3	.4	48	6.2	715	92.7	8	1.0
MALE	6	.3	95	4.0	20	.8	12	.5	133	5.5	2,237	93.2	30	1.3
TOTAL	10	.2	225	4.9	57	1.2	24	.5	316	6.8	4,158	90.0	145	3.1
FEMALE	2	.2	64	5.9	13	1.2	4	.4	83	7.7	958	88.5	42	3.9
MALE	8	.2	161	4.6	44	1.2	20	.6	233	6.6	3,200	90.5	103	2.9
PROFESSIONAL:														
FULL-TIME	0	.0	0	.0	0	.0	0	.0	0	.0	2	100.0	0	.0
FEMALE	0	.0	0	.0	0	.0	0	.0	0	.0	0	.0	0	.0
MALE	0	.0	0	.0	0	.0	0	.0	0	.0	2	100.0	0	.0

BUSINESS AND MANAGEMENT

INDIAN NATIVE %	BLACK NON-HISPANIC NUMBER	%	ASIAN OR PACIFIC ISLANDER NUMBER	%	HISPANIC NUMBER	%	TOTAL MINORITY NUMBER	%	WHITE NON-HISPANIC NUMBER	%	NON-RESIDENT ALIEN NUMBER	%	TOTAL NUMBER

CONTINUED

INDIAN NATIVE %	BLACK NUMBER	%	ASIAN NUMBER	%	HISPANIC NUMBER	%	MINORITY NUMBER	%	WHITE NUMBER	%	NON-RES NUMBER	%	TOTAL
.0	0	.0	0	.0	0	.0	0	.0	1	100.0	0	.0	1
.0	0	.0	0	.0	0	.0	0	.0	0	.0	0	.0	0
.0	0	.0	0	.0	0	.0	0	.0	1	100.0	0	.0	1
.0	0	.0	0	.0	0	.0	0	.0	3	100.0	0	.0	3
.0	0	.0	0	.0	0	.0	0	.0	0	.0	0	.0	0
.0	0	.0	0	.0	0	.0	0	.0	3	100.0	0	.0	3
.3	1,314	6.9	118	.6	110	.6	1,591	8.4	17,090	90.1	286	1.5	18,967
.3	624	9.3	44	.7	35	.5	720	10.7	5,914	88.0	88	1.3	6,722
.3	690	5.6	74	.6	75	.6	871	7.1	11,176	91.3	198	1.6	12,245
.3	557	7.0	49	.6	63	.8	695	8.8	7,180	90.5	62	.8	7,937
.4	230	9.0	20	.8	16	.6	277	10.8	2,270	88.5	17	.7	2,564
.3	327	6.1	29	.5	47	.9	418	7.8	4,910	91.4	45	.8	5,373
.3	1,871	7.0	167	.6	173	.6	2,286	8.5	24,270	90.2	348	1.3	26,904
.3	854	9.2	64	.7	51	.5	997	10.7	8,184	88.1	105	1.1	9,286
.3	1,017	5.8	103	.6	122	.7	1,289	7.3	16,086	91.3	243	1.4	17,618
.0	16	7.6	4	1.9	2	1.0	22	10.5	186	88.6	2	1.0	210
.0	9	9.7	2	2.2	1	1.1	12	12.9	80	86.0	1	1.1	93
.0	7	6.0	2	1.7	1	.9	10	8.5	106	90.6	1	.9	117
.3	1,887	7.0	171	.6	175	.6	2,308	8.5	24,456	90.2	350	1.3	27,114
.3	863	9.2	66	.7	52	.6	1,009	10.8	8,264	88.1	106	1.1	9,379
.3	1,024	5.8	105	.6	123	.7	1,299	7.3	16,192	91.3	244	1.4	17,735

(9 INSTITLTIONS)

INDIAN NATIVE %	BLACK NUMBER	%	ASIAN NUMBER	%	HISPANIC NUMBER	%	MINORITY NUMBER	%	WHITE NUMBER	%	NON-RES NUMBER	%	TOTAL
.9	13	.4	13	.4	9	.3	65	1.9	3,424	97.7	14	.4	3,503
1.2	3	.2	3	.2	5	.3	28	1.9	1,423	98.1	0	.0	1,451
.6	10	.5	10	.5	4	.2	37	1.8	2,001	97.5	14	.7	2,052
2.1	1	.2	3	.7	2	.5	15	3.5	405	95.5	4	.9	424
2.2	1	.6	1	.6	1	.6	7	3.9	172	95.6	1	.6	180
2.0	0	.0	2	.8	1	.4	8	3.3	233	95.5	3	1.2	244
1.0	14	.4	16	.4	11	.3	80	2.0	3,829	97.5	18	.5	3,927
1.3	4	.2	4	.2	6	.4	35	2.1	1,595	97.8	1	.1	1,631
.8	10	.4	12	.5	5	.2	45	2.0	2,234	97.3	17	.7	2,296
1.8	0	.0	0	.0	1	1.8	2	3.5	54	94.7	1	1.8	57
9.1	0	.0	0	.0	0	.0	1	9.1	10	90.9	0	.0	11
.0	0	.0	0	.0	1	2.2	1	2.2	44	95.7	1	2.2	46
1.0	0	.0	0	.0	0	.0	1	1.0	99	98.0	1	1.0	101
7.7	0	.0	0	.0	0	.0	1	7.7	12	92.3	0	.0	13
.0	0	.0	0	.0	0	.0	0	.0	87	98.9	1	1.1	88
1.3	0	.0	0	.0	1	.6	3	1.9	153	96.8	2	1.3	158
8.3	0	.0	0	.0	0	.0	2	8.3	22	91.7	0	.0	24
.0	0	.0	0	.0	1	.7	1	.7	131	97.8	2	1.5	134
.0	0	.0	0	.0	0	.0	0	.0	0	.0	0	.0	0
.0	0	.0	0	.0	0	.0	0	.0	0	.0	0	.0	0
.0	0	.0	0	.0	0	.0	0	.0	0	.0	0	.0	0
.0	0	.0	0	.0	0	.0	0	.0	0	.0	0	.0	0
.0	0	.0	0	.0	0	.0	0	.0	0	.0	0	.0	0
.0	0	.0	0	.0	0	.0	0	.0	0	.0	0	.0	0
.0	0	.0	0	.0	0	.0	0	.0	0	.0	0	.0	0
.0	0	.0	0	.0	0	.0	0	.0	0	.0	0	.0	0
.0	0	.0	0	.0	0	.0	0	.0	0	.0	0	.0	0
.9	13	.4	13	.4	10	.3	67	1.9	3,478	97.7	15	.4	3,560
1.2	3	.2	3	.2	5	.3	29	2.0	1,433	98.0	0	.0	1,462
.6	10	.5	10	.5	5	.2	38	1.8	2,045	97.5	15	.7	2,098
1.9	1	.2	3	.6	2	.4	16	3.0	504	96.0	5	1.0	525
2.6	1	.5	1	.5	1	.5	8	4.1	184	95.3	1	.5	193
1.5	0	.0	2	.6	1	.3	8	2.4	320	96.4	4	1.2	332
1.0	14	.3	16	.4	12	.3	83	2.0	3,982	97.5	20	.5	4,085
1.4	4	.2	4	.2	6	.4	37	2.2	1,617	97.7	1	.1	1,655
.7	10	.4	12	.5	6	.2	46	1.9	2,365	97.3	19	.8	2,430
.0	0	.0	0	.0	0	.0	0	.0	59	100.0	0	.0	59
.0	0	.0	0	.0	0	.0	0	.0	23	100.0	0	.0	23
.0	0	.0	0	.0	0	.0	0	.0	36	100.0	0	.0	36
1.0	14	.3	16	.4	12	.3	83	2.0	4,041	97.5	20	.5	4,144
1.4	4	.2	4	.2	6	.4	37	2.2	1,640	97.7	1	.1	1,678
.7	10	.4	12	.5	6	.2	46	1.9	2,401	97.4	19	.8	2,460

TABLE 17 - TOTAL ENROLLMENT IN INSTITUTIONS OF HIGHER EDUCATION FOR SELECTED MAJOR FIELDS OF STUDY AND LEVEL OF ENROLLMENT
BY RACE, ETHNICITY, AND SEX: STATE, 1978

MAJOR FIELD 0500 - BUSINESS AND MANAGEMENT

	AMERICAN INDIAN ALASKAN NATIVE		BLACK NON-HISPANIC		ASIAN OR PACIFIC ISLANDER		HISPANIC		TOTAL MINORITY		WHITE NON-HISPANIC		NON-RESIDENT ALIEN	
	NUMBER	%	NUMBER	%	NUMBER	%	NUMBER	%	NUMBER	%	NUMBER	%	NUMBER	%
NEBRASKA (20 INSTITUTIONS)														
UNDERGRADUATES:														
FULL-TIME	18	.3	196	3.0	31	.5	48	.7	293	4.5	6,080	93.9	105	1.6
FEMALE	8	.4	82	3.9	8	.4	17	.8	115	5.4	1,986	93.6	21	1.0
MALE	10	.2	114	2.6	23	.5	31	.7	178	4.1	4,094	94.0	84	1.9
PART-TIME	3	.2	83	4.8	9	.5	19	1.1	114	6.5	1,620	92.9	9	.5
FEMALE	1	.2	40	6.9	3	.5	4	.7	48	8.2	529	90.9	5	.9
MALE	2	.2	43	3.7	6	.5	15	1.3	66	5.7	1,091	94.0	4	.3
TOTAL	21	.3	279	3.4	40	.5	67	.8	407	5.0	7,700	93.7	114	1.4
FEMALE	9	.3	122	4.5	11	.4	21	.8	163	6.0	2,515	93.0	26	1.0
MALE	12	.2	157	2.8	29	.5	46	.8	244	4.4	5,185	94.0	88	1.6
GRADUATE:														
FULL-TIME	0	.0	1	.8	2	1.6	1	.8	4	3.2	102	82.3	18	14.5
FEMALE	0	.0	0	.0	0	.0	0	.0	0	.0	23	92.0	2	8.0
MALE	0	.0	1	1.0	2	2.0	1	1.0	4	4.0	79	79.8	16	16.2
PART-TIME	1	.2	6	1.3	5	1.1	5	1.1	17	3.7	430	92.7	17	3.7
FEMALE	0	.0	1	1.0	3	3.0	0	.0	4	4.0	93	92.1	4	4.0
MALE	1	.3	5	1.4	2	.6	5	1.4	13	3.6	337	92.8	13	3.6
TOTAL	1	.2	7	1.2	7	1.2	6	1.0	21	3.6	532	90.5	35	6.0
FEMALE	0	.0	1	.8	3	2.4	0	.0	4	3.2	116	92.1	6	4.8
MALE	1	.2	6	1.3	4	.9	6	1.3	17	3.7	416	90.0	29	6.3
PROFESSIONAL:														
FULL-TIME	0	.0	0	.0	0	.0	0	.0	0	.0	0	.0	0	.0
FEMALE	0	.0	0	.0	0	.0	0	.0	0	.0	0	.0	0	.0
MALE	0	.0	0	.0	0	.0	0	.0	0	.0	0	.0	0	.0
PART-TIME	0	.0	0	.0	0	.0	0	.0	0	.0	0	.0	0	.0
FEMALE	0	.0	0	.0	0	.0	0	.0	0	.0	0	.0	0	.0
MALE	0	.0	0	.0	0	.0	0	.0	0	.0	0	.0	0	.0
TOTAL	0	.0	0	.0	0	.0	0	.0	0	.0	0	.0	0	.0
FEMALE	0	.0	0	.0	0	.0	0	.0	0	.0	0	.0	0	.0
MALE	0	.0	0	.0	0	.0	0	.0	0	.0	0	.0	0	.0
UND+GRAD+PROF:														
FULL-TIME	18	.3	197	3.0	33	.5	49	.7	297	4.5	6,182	93.6	123	1.9
FEMALE	8	.4	82	3.8	8	.4	17	.8	115	5.4	2,009	93.6	23	1.1
MALE	10	.2	115	2.6	25	.6	32	.7	182	4.1	4,173	93.7	100	2.2
PART-TIME	4	.2	89	4.0	14	.6	24	1.1	131	5.9	2,050	92.9	26	1.2
FEMALE	1	.1	41	6.0	6	.9	4	.6	52	7.6	622	91.1	9	1.3
MALE	3	.2	48	3.1	8	.5	20	1.3	79	5.2	1,428	93.7	17	1.1
TOTAL	22	.2	286	3.2	47	.5	73	.8	428	4.9	8,232	93.4	149	1.7
FEMALE	9	.3	123	4.3	14	.5	21	.7	167	5.9	2,631	93.0	32	1.1
MALE	13	.2	163	2.7	33	.6	52	.9	261	4.4	5,601	93.7	117	2.0
UNCLASSIFIED:														
TOTAL	0	.0	8	6.6	1	.8	4	3.3	13	10.7	109	89.3	0	.0
FEMALE	0	.0	3	5.9	0	.0	2	3.9	5	9.8	46	90.2	0	.0
MALE	0	.0	5	7.0	1	1.4	2	2.8	8	11.3	63	88.7	0	.0
TOTAL ENROLLMENT:														
TOTAL	22	.2	294	3.3	48	.5	77	.9	441	4.9	8,341	93.4	149	1.7
FEMALE	9	.3	126	4.4	14	.5	23	.8	172	6.0	2,677	92.9	32	1.1
MALE	13	.2	168	2.8	34	.6	54	.9	269	4.4	5,664	93.6	117	1.9
NEVADA (4 INSTITUTIONS)														
UNDERGRADUATES:														
FULL-TIME	23	1.6	66	4.5	28	1.9	36	2.5	153	10.5	1,262	86.7	41	2.8
FEMALE	14	3.2	22	5.0	13	3.0	11	2.5	60	13.7	362	82.6	16	3.7
MALE	9	.9	44	4.3	15	1.5	25	2.5	93	9.1	900	88.4	25	2.5
PART-TIME	38	2.7	21	1.5	26	1.8	41	2.9	126	8.8	1,283	89.7	21	1.5
FEMALE	27	4.1	7	1.1	11	1.7	20	3.1	65	9.9	581	88.8	8	1.2
MALE	11	1.4	14	1.8	15	1.9	21	2.7	61	7.9	702	90.5	13	1.7
TOTAL	61	2.1	87	3.0	54	1.9	77	2.7	279	9.7	2,545	86.2	62	2.1
FEMALE	41	3.8	29	2.7	24	2.2	31	2.8	125	11.4	943	86.4	24	2.2
MALE	20	1.1	58	3.2	30	1.7	46	2.6	154	8.6	1,602	89.3	38	2.1
GRADUATE:														
FULL-TIME	0	.0	0	.0	1	1.9	0	.0	1	1.9	43	82.7	8	15.4
FEMALE	0	.0	0	.0	1	6.7	0	.0	1	6.7	10	66.7	4	26.7
MALE	0	.0	0	.0	0	.0	0	.0	0	.0	33	89.2	4	10.8
PART-TIME	1	.9	1	.9	2	1.8	1	.9	5	4.5	105	93.8	1	.9
FEMALE	0	.0	0	.0	0	.0	0	.0	0	.0	21	95.5	1	4.5
MALE	1	1.1	1	1.1	2	2.2	1	1.1	5	5.6	84	93.3	1	1.1
TOTAL	1	.6	1	.6	3	1.8	1	.6	6	3.7	148	90.2	10	6.1
FEMALE	0	.0	0	.0	1	2.7	0	.0	1	2.7	31	83.8	5	13.5
MALE	1	.8	1	.8	2	1.6	1	.8	5	3.9	117	92.1	5	3.9
PROFESSIONAL:														
FULL-TIME	0	.0	0	.0	0	.0	0	.0	0	.0	0	.0	0	.0
FEMALE	0	.0	0	.0	0	.0	0	.0	0	.0	0	.0	0	.0
MALE	0	.0	0	.0	0	.0	0	.0	0	.0	0	.0	0	.0

BUSINESS AND MANAGEMENT

INDIAN NATIVE	BLACK NON-HISPANIC		ASIAN OR PACIFIC ISLANDER		HISPANIC		TOTAL MINORITY		WHITE NON-HISPANIC		NON-RESIDENT ALIEN		TOTAL
%	NUMBER	%	NUMBER	%	NUMBER	%	NUMBER	%	NUMBER	%	NUMBER	%	NUMBER
CONTINUED													
.0	0	.0	0	.0	0	.0	0	.0	0	.0	0	.0	0
.0	0	.0	0	.0	0	.0	0	.0	0	.0	0	.0	0
.0	0	.0	0	.0	0	.0	0	.0	0	.0	0	.0	0
.0	0	.0	0	.0	0	.0	0	.0	0	.0	0	.0	0
.0	0	.0	0	.0	0	.0	0	.0	0	.0	0	.0	0
.0	0	.0	0	.0	0	.0	0	.0	0	.0	0	.0	0
1.5	66	4.4	29	1.9	36	2.4	154	10.2	1,305	86.5	49	3.2	1,508
3.1	22	4.9	14	3.1	11	2.4	61	13.5	372	82.1	20	4.4	453
.9	44	4.2	15	1.4	25	2.4	93	8.8	933	88.4	29	2.7	1,055
2.5	22	1.4	28	1.8	42	2.7	131	8.5	1,388	90.0	23	1.5	1,542
4.0	7	1.0	11	1.6	20	3.0	65	9.6	602	89.1	9	1.3	676
1.4	15	1.7	17	2.0	22	2.5	66	7.6	786	90.8	14	1.6	866
2.0	88	2.9	57	1.9	78	2.6	285	9.3	2,693	88.3	72	2.4	3,050
3.6	29	2.6	25	2.2	31	2.7	126	11.2	974	86.3	29	2.6	1,129
1.1	59	3.1	32	1.7	47	2.4	159	8.3	1,719	89.5	43	2.2	1,921
.5	2	1.0	6	3.1	4	2.0	13	6.6	183	93.4	0	.0	196
.0	0	.0	0	.0	0	.0	0	.0	91	100.0	0	.0	91
1.0	2	1.9	6	5.7	4	3.8	13	12.4	92	87.6	0	.0	105
1.9	90	2.8	63	1.9	82	2.5	298	9.2	2,876	88.6	72	2.2	3,246
3.4	29	2.4	25	2.0	31	2.5	126	10.3	1,065	87.3	29	2.4	1,220
1.1	61	3.0	38	1.9	51	2.5	172	8.5	1,811	89.4	43	2.1	2,026
(1d INSTITUTIONS)													
.2	83	1.3	12	.2	134	2.1	240	3.8	6,033	94.3	127	2.0	6,400
.1	13	.6	4	.2	11	.5	30	1.4	2,052	96.8	38	1.8	2,120
.2	70	1.6	8	.2	123	2.9	210	4.9	3,981	93.0	89	2.1	4,280
.0	14	.6	3	.1	17	.7	34	1.4	2,419	98.5	3	.1	2,456
.0	4	.5	0	.0	3	.4	7	.8	821	99.2	0	.0	828
.0	10	.6	3	.2	14	.9	27	1.7	1,598	98.2	3	.2	1,628
.1	97	1.1	15	.2	151	1.7	274	3.1	8,452	95.4	130	1.5	8,856
.1	17	.6	4	.1	14	.5	37	1.3	2,873	97.5	38	1.3	2,948
.2	80	1.4	11	.2	137	2.3	237	4.0	5,579	94.4	92	1.6	5,908
.0	14	3.4	4	1.0	3	.7	21	5.0	390	93.5	6	1.4	417
.0	5	4.9	3	2.9	0	.0	8	7.8	92	90.2	2	2.0	102
.0	9	2.9	1	.3	3	1.0	13	4.1	298	94.6	4	1.3	315
.0	10	1.3	5	.6	0	.0	15	1.9	782	98.0	1	.1	798
.0	2	1.8	1	.9	0	.0	3	2.7	109	97.3	0	.0	112
.0	8	1.2	4	.6	0	.0	12	1.7	673	98.1	1	.1	686
.0	24	2.0	9	.7	3	.2	36	3.0	1,172	96.5	7	.6	1,215
.0	7	3.3	4	1.9	0	.0	11	5.1	201	93.9	2	.9	214
.0	17	1.7	5	.5	3	.3	25	2.5	971	97.0	5	.5	1,001
.0	0	.0	0	.0	0	.0	0	.0	0	.0	0	.0	0
.0	0	.0	0	.0	0	.0	0	.0	0	.0	0	.0	0
.0	0	.0	0	.0	0	.0	0	.0	0	.0	0	.0	0
.0	0	.0	0	.0	0	.0	0	.0	0	.0	0	.0	0
.0	0	.0	0	.0	0	.0	0	.0	0	.0	0	.0	0
.0	0	.0	0	.0	0	.0	0	.0	0	.0	0	.0	0
.0	0	.0	0	.0	0	.0	0	.0	0	.0	0	.0	0
.0	0	.0	0	.0	0	.0	0	.0	0	.0	0	.0	0
.0	0	.0	0	.0	0	.0	0	.0	0	.0	0	.0	0
.2	97	1.4	16	.2	137	2.0	261	3.8	6,423	94.2	133	2.0	6,817
.1	18	.8	7	.3	11	.5	38	1.7	2,144	96.5	40	1.8	2,222
.2	79	1.7	9	.2	126	2.7	223	4.9	4,279	93.1	93	2.0	4,595
.0	24	.7	8	.2	17	.5	49	1.5	3,201	98.4	4	.1	3,254
.0	6	.6	1	.1	3	.3	10	1.1	930	98.9	0	.0	940
.0	18	.8	7	.3	14	.6	39	1.7	2,271	98.1	4	.2	2,314
.1	121	1.2	24	.2	154	1.5	310	3.1	9,624	95.6	137	1.4	10,071
.1	24	.8	8	.3	14	.4	48	1.5	3,074	97.2	40	1.3	3,162
.1	97	1.4	16	.2	140	2.0	262	3.8	6,550	94.8	97	1.4	6,909
.0	0	.0	1	.6	0	.0	1	.6	178	99.4	0	.0	179
.0	0	.0	1	1.1	0	.0	1	1.1	87	98.9	0	.0	88
.0	0	.0	0	.0	0	.0	0	.0	91	100.0	0	.0	91
.1	121	1.2	25	.2	154	1.5	311	3.0	9,802	95.6	137	1.3	10,250
.1	24	.7	9	.3	14	.4	49	1.5	3,161	97.3	40	1.2	3,250
.1	97	1.4	16	.2	140	2.0	262	3.7	6,641	94.9	97	1.4	7,000

TABLE 17 - TOTAL ENROLLMENT IN INSTITUTIONS OF HIGHER EDUCATION FOR SELECTED MAJOR FIELDS OF STUDY AND LEVEL OF ENROLLMENT BY RACE, ETHNICITY, AND SEX: STATE, 1978

MAJOR FIELD 0500 - BUSINESS AND MANAGEMENT

	AMERICAN INDIAN ALASKAN NATIVE		BLACK NON-HISPANIC		ASIAN OR PACIFIC ISLANDER		HISPANIC		TOTAL MINORITY		WHITE NON-HISPANIC		NON-RESIDENT ALIEN	
	NUMBER	%	NUMBER	%	NUMBER	%	NUMBER	%	NUMBER	%	NUMBER	%	NUMBER	%
NEW JERSEY (40 INSTITUTIONS)														
UNDERGRADUATES:														
FULL-TIME	42	.2	1,826	8.6	139	.7	643	3.0	2,650	12.5	18,369	86.6	183	.9
FEMALE	21	.3	912	12.3	49	.7	281	3.8	1,263	17.0	6,084	82.0	70	.9
MALE	21	.2	914	6.6	90	.7	362	2.6	1,387	10.1	12,285	89.1	113	.8
PART-TIME	16	.1	982	9.2	102	1.0	298	2.8	1,398	13.0	9,295	86.3	69	.6
FEMALE	7	.1	547	10.9	50	1.0	120	2.4	724	14.4	4,281	85.0	31	.6
MALE	9	.2	435	7.7	52	.9	178	3.1	674	11.9	4,974	87.5	38	.7
TOTAL	58	.2	2,808	8.8	241	.8	941	2.9	4,048	12.7	27,624	86.5	252	.8
FEMALE	28	.2	1,459	11.7	99	.8	401	3.2	1,987	16.0	10,365	83.2	101	.8
MALE	30	.2	1,349	6.9	142	.7	540	2.8	2,061	10.6	17,259	88.6	151	.8
GRADUATE:														
FULL-TIME	0	.0	28	3.8	9	1.2	5	.7	42	5.8	641	87.8	47	6.4
FEMALE	0	.0	4	2.3	4	2.3	0	.0	8	4.5	153	86.9	15	8.5
MALE	0	.0	24	4.3	5	.9	5	.9	34	6.1	488	88.1	32	5.8
PART-TIME	3	.1	171	3.8	75	1.7	40	.9	289	6.4	4,140	91.8	82	1.8
FEMALE	0	.0	60	5.4	16	1.4	10	.9	86	7.7	1,014	91.4	10	.9
MALE	3	.1	111	3.3	59	1.7	30	.9	203	6.0	3,126	91.9	72	2.1
TOTAL	3	.1	199	3.8	84	1.6	45	.9	331	6.3	4,781	91.2	129	2.5
FEMALE	0	.0	64	5.0	20	1.6	10	.8	94	7.3	1,167	90.7	25	1.9
MALE	3	.1	135	3.4	64	1.6	35	.9	237	6.0	3,614	91.4	104	2.6
PROFESSIONAL:														
FULL-TIME	0	.0	0	.0	0	.0	0	.0	0	.0	0	.0	0	.0
FEMALE	0	.0	0	.0	0	.0	0	.0	0	.0	0	.0	0	.0
MALE	0	.0	0	.0	0	.0	0	.0	0	.0	0	.0	0	.0
PART-TIME	0	.0	0	.0	0	.0	0	.0	0	.0	0	.0	0	.0
FEMALE	0	.0	0	.0	0	.0	0	.0	0	.0	0	.0	0	.0
MALE	0	.0	0	.0	0	.0	0	.0	0	.0	0	.0	0	.0
TOTAL	0	.0	0	.0	0	.0	0	.0	0	.0	0	.0	0	.0
FEMALE	0	.0	0	.0	0	.0	0	.0	0	.0	0	.0	0	.0
MALE	0	.0	0	.0	0	.0	0	.0	0	.0	0	.0	0	.0
UND+GRAD+PROF:														
FULL-TIME	42	.2	1,854	8.5	148	.7	648	3.0	2,692	12.3	19,010	86.7	230	1.0
FEMALE	21	.3	916	12.1	53	.7	281	3.7	1,271	16.7	6,237	82.1	85	1.1
MALE	21	.1	938	6.5	95	.7	367	2.6	1,421	9.9	12,773	89.1	145	1.0
PART-TIME	19	.1	1,153	7.6	177	1.2	338	2.2	1,687	11.1	13,395	87.9	151	1.0
FEMALE	7	.1	607	9.9	66	1.1	130	2.1	810	13.2	5,295	86.2	41	.7
MALE	12	.1	546	6.0	111	1.2	208	2.3	877	9.7	8,100	89.1	110	1.2
TOTAL	61	.2	3,007	8.1	325	.9	986	2.7	4,379	11.8	32,405	87.2	381	1.0
FEMALE	28	.2	1,523	16.1	119	.9	411	3.0	2,081	15.1	11,532	83.9	126	.9
MALE	33	.1	1,484	6.3	206	.9	575	2.5	2,298	9.8	20,873	89.1	255	1.1
UNCLASSIFIED:														
TOTAL	11	.3	756	18.6	35	.9	79	1.9	881	21.6	3,193	78.4	0	.0
FEMALE	7	.5	463	30.1	14	.9	27	1.8	511	33.2	1,028	66.8	0	.0
MALE	4	.2	293	11.6	21	.8	52	2.1	370	14.6	2,165	85.4	0	.0
TOTAL ENROLLMENT:														
TOTAL	72	.2	3,763	9.1	360	.9	1,065	2.6	5,260	12.8	35,598	86.3	381	.9
FEMALE	35	.2	1,986	13.0	133	.9	438	2.9	2,592	17.0	12,560	82.2	126	.8
MALE	37	.1	1,777	6.8	227	.9	627	2.4	2,668	10.3	23,038	88.7	255	1.0
NEW MEXICO (15 INSTITUTIONS)														
UNDERGRADUATES:														
FULL-TIME	131	3.1	123	2.9	34	.8	1,187	28.4	1,475	35.3	2,646	63.4	54	1.3
FEMALE	83	5.0	24	1.5	12	.7	488	29.5	607	36.7	1,036	62.7	9	.5
MALE	48	1.9	99	3.9	22	.9	699	27.7	868	34.4	1,610	63.8	45	1.8
PART-TIME	33	2.5	34	2.6	10	.8	440	34.0	517	39.9	772	59.6	6	.5
FEMALE	19	3.1	12	2.0	6	1.0	205	33.8	242	39.9	362	59.6	3	.5
MALE	14	2.0	22	3.2	4	.6	235	34.2	275	40.0	410	59.6	3	.4
TOTAL	164	3.0	157	2.9	44	.8	1,627	29.7	1,992	36.4	3,418	62.5	60	1.1
FEMALE	102	4.5	36	1.6	18	.8	693	30.7	849	37.6	1,398	61.9	12	.5
MALE	62	1.9	121	3.8	26	.8	934	29.1	1,143	35.6	2,020	62.9	48	1.5
GRADUATE:														
FULL-TIME	6	2.7	2	.9	3	1.4	13	5.9	24	10.9	174	78.7	23	10.4
FEMALE	1	1.6	0	.0	3	4.9	2	3.3	6	9.8	54	88.5	1	1.6
MALE	5	3.1	2	1.3	0	.0	11	6.9	18	11.3	120	75.0	22	13.8
PART-TIME	2	.6	3	.9	5	1.6	16	5.0	26	8.2	277	86.8	16	5.0
FEMALE	0	.0	1	1.1	2	2.2	4	4.3	7	7.6	82	89.1	3	3.3
MALE	2	.9	2	.9	3	1.3	12	5.3	19	8.4	195	85.9	13	5.7
TOTAL	8	1.5	5	.9	8	1.5	29	5.4	50	9.3	451	83.5	39	7.2
FEMALE	1	.7	1	.7	5	3.3	6	3.9	13	8.5	136	88.9	4	2.6
MALE	7	1.8	4	1.0	3	.8	23	5.9	37	9.6	315	81.4	35	9.0
PROFESSIONAL:														
FULL-TIME	0	.0	0	.0	0	.0	0	.0	0	.0	0	.0	0	.0
FEMALE	0	.0	0	.0	0	.0	0	.0	0	.0	0	.0	0	.0
MALE	0	.0	0	.0	0	.0	0	.0	0	.0	0	.0	0	.0

ROLLMENT IN INSTITUTIONS OF HIGHER EDUCATION FOR SELECTED MAJOR FIELDS OF STUDY AND LEVEL OF ENROLLMENT
ETHNICITY, AND SEX: STATE, 1978

BUSINESS AND MANAGEMENT

I INDIAN NATIVE %	BLACK NON-HISPANIC NUMBER	%	ASIAN OR PACIFIC ISLANDER NUMBER	%	HISPANIC NUMBER	%	TOTAL MINORITY NUMBER	%	WHITE NON-HISPANIC NUMBER	%	NON-RESIDENT ALIEN NUMBER	%	TOTAL NUMBER
CONTINUED													
.0	0	.0	0	.0	0	.0	0	.0	0	.0	0	.0	0
.0	0	.0	0	.0	0	.0	0	.0	0	.0	0	.0	0
.0	0	.0	0	.0	0	.0	0	.0	0	.0	0	.0	0
.0	0	.0	0	.0	0	.0	0	.0	0	.0	0	.0	0
.0	0	.0	0	.0	0	.0	0	.0	0	.0	0	.0	0
.0	0	.0	0	.0	0	.0	0	.0	0	.0	0	.0	0
3.1	125	2.8	37	.8	1,200	27.3	1,499	34.1	2,820	64.1	77	1.8	4,396
4.9	24	1.4	15	.9	490	28.6	613	35.8	1,090	63.6	10	.6	1,713
2.0	101	3.8	22	.8	710	26.5	886	33.0	1,730	64.5	67	2.5	2,683
2.2	37	2.3	15	.9	456	28.3	543	33.6	1,049	65.0	22	1.4	1,614
2.7	13	1.9	8	1.1	209	29.9	249	35.6	444	63.5	6	.9	699
1.7	24	2.6	7	.8	247	27.0	294	32.1	605	66.1	16	1.7	915
2.9	162	2.7	52	.9	1,656	27.6	2,042	34.0	3,869	64.4	99	1.6	6,010
4.3	37	1.5	23	1.0	699	29.0	862	35.7	1,534	63.6	16	.7	2,412
1.9	125	3.5	29	.8	957	26.6	1,180	32.8	2,335	64.9	83	2.3	3,598
2.7	4	2.7	0	.0	46	31.1	54	36.5	90	60.8	4	2.7	148
6.0	1	1.5	0	.0	13	19.4	18	26.9	47	70.1	2	3.0	67
.0	3	3.7	0	.0	33	40.7	36	44.4	43	53.1	2	2.5	81
2.9	166	2.7	52	.8	1,702	27.6	2,096	34.0	3,959	64.3	103	1.7	6,150
4.3	38	1.5	23	.9	712	28.7	880	35.5	1,581	63.8	18	.7	2,479
1.9	128	3.5	29	.8	990	26.9	1,216	33.1	2,378	64.6	85	2.3	3,679
(121 INSTITUTIONS)													
.2	4,497	7.7	949	1.6	1,971	3.4	7,553	13.0	49,540	85.3	982	1.7	58,075
.2	2,443	10.3	426	1.8	995	4.2	3,921	16.5	19,513	82.3	263	1.1	23,697
.2	2,054	6.0	523	1.5	976	2.8	3,632	10.6	30,027	87.3	719	2.1	34,378
.3	2,382	12.4	339	1.8	913	4.7	3,693	19.2	15,397	79.8	193	1.0	19,283
.4	1,179	14.4	165	2.0	365	4.4	1,740	21.2	6,409	78.1	59	.7	8,208
.3	1,203	10.9	174	1.6	548	4.9	1,953	17.6	8,988	81.2	134	1.2	11,075
.3	6,879	8.9	1,288	1.7	2,884	3.7	11,246	14.5	64,937	83.9	1,175	1.5	77,358
.3	3,622	11.4	591	1.6	1,360	4.3	5,661	17.7	25,922	81.2	322	1.0	31,905
.2	3,257	7.2	697	1.5	1,524	3.4	5,505	12.3	39,015	85.8	853	1.9	45,453
.2	264	4.4	189	3.1	73	1.2	540	8.9	4,735	78.1	788	13.0	6,063
.2	103	5.7	52	2.9	18	1.0	176	9.7	1,482	81.9	151	8.3	1,809
.3	161	3.8	137	3.2	55	1.3	364	8.6	3,253	76.5	637	15.0	4,254
.3	797	4.6	506	2.9	329	1.9	1,683	9.8	15,020	87.3	498	2.9	17,201
.4	217	4.4	158	3.2	90	1.8	484	9.9	4,302	87.7	119	2.4	4,905
.3	580	4.7	348	2.8	239	1.9	1,199	9.8	10,718	87.2	379	3.1	12,296
.3	1,061	4.6	695	3.0	402	1.7	2,223	9.6	19,755	84.9	1,286	5.5	23,264
.3	320	4.8	210	3.1	108	1.6	660	9.8	5,784	86.1	270	4.0	6,714
.3	741	4.5	485	2.9	294	1.8	1,563	9.4	13,971	84.4	1,016	6.1	16,550
.0	0	.0	0	.0	0	.0	0	.0	0	.0	0	.0	0
.0	0	.0	0	.0	0	.0	0	.0	0	.0	0	.0	0
.0	0	.0	0	.0	0	.0	0	.0	0	.0	0	.0	0
.0	0	.0	0	.0	0	.0	0	.0	0	.0	0	.0	0
.0	0	.0	0	.0	0	.0	0	.0	0	.0	0	.0	0
.0	0	.0	0	.0	0	.0	0	.0	0	.0	0	.0	0
.0	0	.0	0	.0	0	.0	0	.0	0	.0	0	.0	0
.0	0	.0	0	.0	0	.0	0	.0	0	.0	0	.0	0
.0	0	.0	0	.0	0	.0	0	.0	0	.0	0	.0	0
.2	4,761	7.4	1,138	1.8	2,044	3.2	8,093	12.6	54,275	84.6	1,770	2.8	64,138
.2	2,546	10.0	478	1.9	1,013	4.0	4,097	16.1	20,995	82.3	414	1.6	25,506
.2	2,215	5.7	660	1.7	1,031	2.7	3,996	10.3	33,280	86.1	1,356	3.5	38,632
.3	3,179	8.7	845	2.3	1,242	3.4	5,376	14.7	30,617	83.4	691	1.9	36,484
.4	1,396	10.6	323	2.5	455	3.5	2,224	17.0	10,711	81.7	178	1.4	13,113
.3	1,783	7.6	522	2.2	787	3.4	3,152	13.5	19,706	84.3	513	2.2	23,371
.3	7,940	7.9	1,983	2.0	3,286	3.3	13,469	13.4	84,692	84.2	2,461	2.4	100,622
.3	3,942	10.2	801	2.1	1,468	3.8	6,321	16.4	31,706	82.1	592	1.5	38,619
.2	3,998	6.4	1,182	1.9	1,818	2.9	7,140	11.5	52,986	85.5	1,869	3.0	62,003
.1	225	6.9	89	2.7	94	2.9	410	12.7	2,776	85.7	54	1.7	3,240
.0	113	8.7	34	2.6	42	3.2	189	14.5	1,099	84.4	14	1.1	1,302
.1	112	5.8	55	2.8	52	2.7	221	11.4	1,677	86.5	40	2.1	1,938
.3	8,165	7.9	2,072	2.0	3,380	3.3	13,879	13.4	87,468	84.2	2,515	2.4	103,862
.3	4,055	10.2	835	2.1	1,510	3.8	6,510	16.3	32,805	82.2	606	1.5	39,921
.2	4,110	6.4	1,237	1.9	1,870	2.9	7,369	11.5	54,663	85.5	1,909	3.0	63,941

TABLE 17 - TOTAL ENROLLMENT IN INSTITUTIONS OF HIGHER EDUCATION FOR SELECTED MAJOR FIELDS OF STUDY AND LEVEL OF ENROLLMENT BY RACE, ETHNICITY, AND SEX: STATE, 1978

MAJOR FIELD 0500 - BUSINESS AND MANAGEMENT

	AMERICAN INDIAN ALASKAN NATIVE		BLACK NON-HISPANIC		ASIAN OR PACIFIC ISLANDER		HISPANIC		TOTAL MINORITY		WHITE NON-HISPANIC		NON-RESIDENT ALIEN	
	NUMBER	%	NUMBER	%	NUMBER	%	NUMBER	%	NUMBER	%	NUMBER	%	NUMBER	%
NORTH CAROLINA (57 INSTITUTIONS)														
UNDERGRADUATES:														
FULL-TIME	80	.3	7,372	31.2	58	.2	64	.3	7,574	32.1	15,773	66.8	270	1.1
FEMALE	46	.5	3,595	38.9	22	.2	21	.2	3,684	39.9	5,495	59.5	63	.7
MALE	34	.2	3,777	26.3	36	.3	43	.3	3,890	27.1	10,278	71.5	207	1.4
PART-TIME	21	.8	520	19.7	7	.3	13	.5	561	21.3	2,055	77.9	21	.8
FEMALE	6	.5	302	25.2	3	.3	7	.6	318	26.5	875	72.9	7	.6
MALE	15	1.0	218	15.2	4	.3	6	.4	243	16.9	1,180	82.1	14	1.0
TOTAL	101	.4	7,892	30.1	65	.2	77	.3	8,135	31.0	17,828	67.9	291	1.1
FEMALE	52	.5	3,897	37.3	25	.2	28	.3	4,002	38.3	6,370	61.0	70	.7
MALE	49	.3	3,995	25.3	40	.3	49	.3	4,133	26.1	11,458	72.5	221	1.4
GRADUATE:														
FULL-TIME	2	.2	72	6.7	4	.4	4	.4	82	7.7	937	87.5	52	4.9
FEMALE	1	.4	35	13.0	1	.4	2	.7	39	14.5	221	82.2	9	3.3
MALE	1	.1	37	4.6	3	.4	2	.2	43	5.4	716	89.3	43	5.4
PART-TIME	3	.4	74	10.0	8	1.1	1	.1	86	11.7	631	85.5	21	2.8
FEMALE	1	.5	39	19.3	4	2.0	1	.5	45	22.3	155	76.7	2	1.0
MALE	2	.4	35	6.5	4	.7	0	.0	41	7.6	476	88.8	19	3.5
TOTAL	5	.3	146	8.1	12	.7	5	.3	168	9.3	1,568	86.7	73	4.0
FEMALE	2	.4	74	15.7	5	1.1	3	.6	84	17.8	376	79.8	11	2.3
MALE	3	.2	72	5.4	7	.5	2	.1	84	6.3	1,192	89.1	62	4.6
PROFESSIONAL:														
FULL-TIME	0	.0	0	.0	0	.0	0	.0	0	.0	0	.0	0	.0
FEMALE	0	.0	0	.0	0	.0	0	.0	0	.0	0	.0	0	.0
MALE	0	.0	0	.0	0	.0	0	.0	0	.0	0	.0	0	.0
PART-TIME	0	.0	0	.0	0	.0	0	.0	0	.0	0	.0	0	.0
FEMALE	0	.0	0	.0	0	.0	0	.0	0	.0	0	.0	0	.0
MALE	0	.0	0	.0	0	.0	0	.0	0	.0	0	.0	0	.0
TOTAL	0	.0	0	.0	0	.0	0	.0	0	.0	0	.0	0	.0
FEMALE	0	.0	0	.0	0	.0	0	.0	0	.0	0	.0	0	.0
MALE	0	.0	0	.0	0	.0	0	.0	0	.0	0	.0	0	.0
UND+GRAD+PROF:														
FULL-TIME	82	.3	7,444	30.2	62	.3	68	.3	7,656	31.0	16,710	67.7	322	1.3
FEMALE	47	.5	3,630	38.2	23	.2	23	.2	3,723	39.1	5,716	60.1	72	.8
MALE	35	.2	3,814	25.1	39	.3	45	.3	3,933	25.9	10,994	72.4	250	1.6
PART-TIME	24	.7	594	17.6	15	.4	14	.4	647	19.2	2,686	79.6	42	1.2
FEMALE	7	.5	341	24.3	7	.5	8	.6	363	25.9	1,030	73.5	9	.6
MALE	17	.9	253	12.8	8	.4	6	.3	284	14.4	1,656	83.9	33	1.7
TOTAL	106	.4	8,038	28.6	77	.3	82	.3	8,303	29.6	19,396	69.1	364	1.3
FEMALE	54	.5	3,971	36.4	30	.3	31	.3	4,086	37.4	6,746	61.8	81	.7
MALE	52	.3	4,067	23.7	47	.3	51	.3	4,217	24.6	12,650	73.8	283	1.7
UNCLASSIFIED:														
TOTAL	0	.0	16	14.5	1	.9	3	2.7	20	18.2	87	79.1	3	2.7
FEMALE	0	.0	5	13.2	0	.0	1	2.6	6	15.8	31	81.6	1	2.6
MALE	0	.0	11	15.3	1	1.4	2	2.8	14	19.4	56	77.8	2	2.8
TOTAL ENROLLMENT:														
TOTAL	106	.4	8,054	28.6	78	.3	85	.3	8,323	29.5	19,483	69.2	347	1.3
FEMALE	54	.5	3,976	36.3	30	.3	32	.3	4,092	37.4	6,777	61.9	82	.7
MALE	52	.3	4,078	23.7	48	.3	53	.3	4,231	24.6	12,706	73.8	285	1.7
NORTH DAKOTA (13 INSTITUTIONS)														
UNDERGRADUATES:														
FULL-TIME	117	3.2	29	.8	9	.2	7	.2	162	4.5	3,433	95.1	13	.4
FEMALE	75	6.0	10	.8	4	.3	5	.4	94	7.6	1,146	92.2	3	.2
MALE	42	1.8	19	.8	5	.2	2	.1	68	2.9	2,287	96.7	10	.4
PART-TIME	10	5.0	1	.5	0	.0	0	.0	11	5.5	189	94.5	0	.0
FEMALE	8	9.1	0	.0	0	.0	0	.0	8	9.1	80	90.9	0	.0
MALE	2	1.8	1	.9	0	.0	0	.0	3	2.7	109	97.3	0	.0
TOTAL	127	3.3	30	.8	9	.2	7	.2	173	4.5	3,622	95.1	13	.3
FEMALE	83	6.2	10	.8	4	.3	5	.4	102	7.7	1,226	92.1	3	.2
MALE	44	1.8	20	.8	5	.2	2	.1	71	2.9	2,396	96.7	10	.4
GRADUATE:														
FULL-TIME	0	.0	0	.0	0	.0	0	.0	0	.0	32	88.9	4	11.1
FEMALE	0	.0	0	.0	0	.0	0	.0	0	.0	8	100.0	0	.0
MALE	0	.0	0	.0	0	.0	0	.0	0	.0	24	85.7	4	14.3
PART-TIME	0	.0	0	.0	2	4.3	0	.0	2	4.3	40	87.0	4	8.7
FEMALE	0	.0	0	.0	1	16.7	0	.0	1	16.7	5	83.3	0	.0
MALE	0	.0	0	.0	1	2.5	0	.0	1	2.5	35	87.5	4	10.0
TOTAL	0	.0	0	.0	2	2.4	0	.0	2	2.4	72	87.8	8	9.8
FEMALE	0	.0	0	.0	1	7.1	0	.0	1	7.1	13	92.9	0	.0
MALE	0	.0	0	.0	1	1.5	0	.0	1	1.5	59	86.8	8	11.8
PROFESSIONAL:														
FULL-TIME	0	.0	0	.0	0	.0	0	.0	0	.0	0	.0	0	.0
FEMALE	0	.0	0	.0	0	.0	0	.0	0	.0	0	.0	0	.0
MALE	0	.0	0	.0	0	.0	0	.0	0	.0	0	.0	0	.0

BUSINESS AND MANAGEMENT

INDIAN NATIVE	BLACK NON-HISPANIC		ASIAN OR PACIFIC ISLANDER		HISPANIC		TOTAL MINORITY		WHITE NON-HISPANIC		NON-RESIDENT ALIEN		TOTAL
%	NUMBER	%	NUMBER	%	NUMBER	%	NUMBER	%	NUMBER	%	NUMBER	%	NUMBER
CONTINUED													
.0	0	.0	0	.0	0	.0	0	.0	0	.0	0	.0	0
.0	0	.0	0	.0	0	.0	0	.0	0	.0	0	.0	0
.0	0	.0	0	.0	0	.0	0	.0	0	.0	0	.0	0
.0	0	.0	0	.0	0	.0	0	.0	0	.0	0	.0	0
.0	0	.0	0	.0	0	.0	0	.0	0	.0	0	.0	0
.0	0	.0	0	.0	0	.0	0	.0	0	.0	0	.0	0
3.2	29	.8	9	.2	7	.2	162	4.4	3,465	95.1	17	.5	3,684
8.0	10	.8	4	.3	5	.4	94	7.5	1,154	92.2	3	.2	1,251
1.8	19	.8	5	.2	2	.1	68	2.8	2,311	96.6	14	.6	2,393
4.1	1	.4	2	.8	0	.0	13	5.3	229	93.1	4	1.6	246
8.5	0	.0	1	1.1	0	.0	9	9.6	85	90.4	0	.0	94
1.3	1	.7	1	.7	0	.0	4	2.6	144	94.7	4	2.6	152
3.3	30	.8	11	.3	7	.2	175	4.5	3,694	95.0	21	.5	3,890
6.2	10	.7	5	.4	5	.4	103	7.7	1,239	92.1	3	.2	1,345
1.7	20	.8	6	.2	2	.1	72	2.8	2,455	96.5	18	.7	2,545
.3	0	.0	0	.0	0	.0	1	.3	397	99.7	0	.0	398
1.6	0	.0	0	.0	0	.0	1	1.6	60	98.4	0	.0	61
.0	0	.0	0	.0	0	.0	0	.0	337	100.0	0	.0	337
3.0	30	.7	11	.3	7	.2	176	4.1	4,091	95.4	21	.5	4,288
6.0	10	.7	5	.4	5	.4	104	7.4	1,299	92.4	3	.2	1,406
1.5	20	.7	6	.2	2	.1	72	2.5	2,792	96.9	18	.6	2,882
(95 INSTITUTIONS)													
.2	5,530	12.7	145	.3	212	.5	5,966	13.7	37,173	85.2	486	1.1	43,625
.2	2,794	17.1	74	.5	83	.5	2,990	18.2	13,268	81.0	126	.8	16,384
.1	2,736	10.0	71	.3	129	.5	2,976	10.9	23,905	87.8	360	1.3	27,241
.2	3,154	11.5	119	.4	131	.5	3,459	12.6	23,763	86.7	192	.7	27,414
.2	1,907	13.7	71	.5	80	.6	2,089	15.0	11,716	84.2	102	.7	13,907
.2	1,247	9.2	48	.4	51	.4	1,370	10.1	12,047	89.2	90	.7	13,507
.2	8,684	12.2	264	.4	343	.5	9,425	13.3	60,936	85.8	678	1.0	71,039
.2	4,701	15.5	145	.5	163	.5	5,079	16.8	24,984	82.5	228	.8	30,291
.2	3,983	9.8	119	.3	180	.4	4,346	10.7	35,952	88.2	450	1.1	40,748
.1	190	9.0	22	1.0	13	.6	228	10.8	1,675	79.1	214	10.1	2,117
.0	77	14.0	5	.9	5	.9	87	15.8	430	78.2	33	6.0	550
.2	113	7.2	17	1.1	8	.5	141	9.0	1,245	79.5	181	11.6	1,567
.0	167	2.7	44	.7	15	.2	227	3.7	5,784	95.1	69	1.1	6,080
.0	40	3.1	9	.7	3	.2	52	4.0	1,241	94.9	15	1.1	1,308
.0	127	2.7	35	.7	12	.3	175	3.7	4,543	95.2	54	1.1	4,772
.0	357	4.4	66	.8	28	.3	455	5.6	7,459	91.0	283	3.5	8,197
.0	117	6.3	14	.8	8	.4	139	7.5	1,671	89.9	48	2.6	1,858
.1	240	3.8	52	.8	20	.3	316	5.0	5,788	91.3	235	3.7	6,339
.0	0	.0	0	.0	0	.0	0	.0	0	.0	0	.0	0
.0	0	.0	0	.0	0	.0	0	.0	0	.0	0	.0	0
.0	0	.0	0	.0	0	.0	0	.0	0	.0	0	.0	0
.0	0	.0	0	.0	0	.0	0	.0	0	.0	0	.0	0
.0	0	.0	0	.0	0	.0	0	.0	0	.0	0	.0	0
.0	0	.0	0	.0	0	.0	0	.0	0	.0	0	.0	0
.0	0	.0	0	.0	0	.0	0	.0	0	.0	0	.0	0
.2	5,720	12.5	167	.4	225	.5	6,194	13.5	38,848	84.9	700	1.5	45,742
.2	2,871	17.0	79	.5	88	.5	3,077	18.2	13,698	80.9	159	.9	16,934
.1	2,849	9.9	88	.3	137	.5	3,117	10.8	25,150	87.3	541	1.9	28,808
.2	3,321	9.9	103	.4	146	.4	3,686	11.0	29,547	88.2	261	.8	33,494
.2	1,947	12.8	80	.5	83	.5	2,141	14.1	12,957	85.2	117	.8	15,215
.1	1,374	7.5	83	.5	63	.3	1,545	8.5	16,590	90.8	144	.8	18,279
.2	9,041	11.4	330	.5	371	.5	9,880	12.5	68,395	86.3	961	1.2	79,236
.2	4,818	15.0	159	.5	171	.5	5,218	16.2	26,655	82.9	276	.9	32,149
.1	4,223	9.0	171	.4	200	.4	4,662	9.9	41,740	88.6	685	1.5	47,087
.0	238	9.7	10	.4	13	.5	261	10.6	2,179	88.6	20	.8	2,460
.0	136	11.5	6	.5	5	.4	147	12.5	1,032	87.5	1	.1	1,180
.0	102	8.0	4	.3	8	.4	114	8.9	1,147	89.6	19	1.5	1,280
.2	9,279	11.4	340	.5	384	.5	10,141	12.4	70,574	86.4	981	1.2	81,696
.2	4,954	14.9	165	.5	176	.5	5,365	16.1	27,687	83.1	277	.8	33,329
.1	4,325	8.9	175	.4	208	.4	4,776	9.9	42,887	88.7	704	1.5	48,367

TABLE 17 - TOTAL ENROLLMENT IN INSTITUTIONS OF HIGHER EDUCATION FOR SELECTED MAJOR FIELDS OF STUDY AND LEVEL OF ENROLLMENT BY RACE, ETHNICITY, AND SEX: STATE, 1978

MAJOR FIELD 0500 - BUSINESS AND MANAGEMENT

	AMERICAN INDIAN ALASKAN NATIVE		BLACK NON-HISPANIC		ASIAN OR PACIFIC ISLANDER		HISPANIC		TOTAL MINORITY		WHITE NON-HISPANIC		NON-RESIDENT ALIEN	
	NUMBER	%	NUMBER	%	NUMBER	%	NUMBER	%	NUMBER	%	NUMBER	%	NUMBER	%
OKLAHOMA (39 INSTITUTIONS)														
UNDERGRADUATES:														
FULL-TIME	518	3.5	1,062	7.1	110	.7	98	.7	1,788	12.0	12,611	84.3	563	3.8
FEMALE	246	4.3	501	8.7	50	.9	46	.8	843	14.6	4,791	82.9	143	2.5
MALE	272	3.0	561	6.1	60	.7	52	.6	945	10.3	7,820	85.1	420	4.6
PART-TIME	194	3.0	417	6.4	40	.6	68	1.0	719	11.0	5,708	87.6	92	1.4
FEMALE	113	3.6	208	6.5	14	.4	30	.9	365	11.5	2,780	87.4	35	1.1
MALE	81	2.4	209	6.3	26	.8	38	1.1	354	10.6	2,928	87.7	57	1.7
TOTAL	712	3.3	1,479	6.9	150	.7	166	.8	2,507	11.7	18,319	85.3	655	3.0
FEMALE	359	4.0	709	7.9	64	.7	76	.8	1,208	13.5	7,571	84.5	178	2.0
MALE	353	2.8	770	6.1	86	.7	90	.7	1,299	10.4	10,748	85.8	477	3.8
GRADUATE:														
FULL-TIME	12	1.3	13	1.4	6	.7	3	.3	34	3.8	462	51.2	406	45.0
FEMALE	4	2.3	7	4.0	1	.6	0	.0	12	6.8	100	56.5	65	36.7
MALE	8	1.1	6	.8	5	.7	3	.4	22	3.0	362	49.9	341	47.0
PART-TIME	18	1.5	49	4.1	8	.7	5	.4	80	6.7	1,033	85.9	90	7.5
FEMALE	4	1.7	20	8.5	2	.9	0	.0	26	11.1	198	84.6	10	4.3
MALE	14	1.4	29	3.0	6	.6	5	.5	54	5.6	835	86.2	80	8.3
TOTAL	30	1.4	62	2.9	14	.7	8	.4	114	5.4	1,495	71.0	496	23.6
FEMALE	8	1.9	27	6.6	3	.7	0	.0	38	9.2	298	72.5	75	18.2
MALE	22	1.3	35	2.1	11	.6	8	.5	76	4.5	1,197	70.7	421	24.9
PROFESSIONAL:														
FULL-TIME	0	.0	0	.0	0	.0	0	.0	0	.0	0	.0	0	.0
FEMALE	0	.0	0	.0	0	.0	0	.0	0	.0	0	.0	0	.0
MALE	0	.0	0	.0	0	.0	0	.0	0	.0	0	.0	0	.0
PART-TIME	0	.0	0	.0	0	.0	0	.0	0	.0	0	.0	0	.0
FEMALE	0	.0	0	.0	0	.0	0	.0	0	.0	0	.0	0	.0
MALE	0	.0	0	.0	0	.0	0	.0	0	.0	0	.0	0	.0
TOTAL	0	.0	0	.0	0	.0	0	.0	0	.0	0	.0	0	.0
FEMALE	0	.0	0	.0	0	.0	0	.0	0	.0	0	.0	0	.0
MALE	0	.0	0	.0	0	.0	0	.0	0	.0	0	.0	0	.0
UND+GRAD+PROF:														
FULL-TIME	530	3.3	1,075	6.8	116	.7	101	.6	1,822	11.5	13,073	82.4	969	6.1
FEMALE	250	4.2	508	8.5	51	.9	46	.8	855	14.4	4,891	82.1	208	3.5
MALE	280	2.8	567	5.7	65	.7	55	.6	967	9.8	8,182	82.6	761	7.7
PART-TIME	212	2.7	466	6.0	48	.6	73	.9	799	10.3	6,741	87.3	182	2.4
FEMALE	117	3.4	228	6.7	16	.5	30	.9	391	11.5	2,978	87.2	45	1.3
MALE	95	2.2	238	5.5	32	.7	43	1.0	408	9.5	3,763	87.3	137	3.2
TOTAL	742	3.1	1,541	6.5	164	.7	174	.7	2,621	11.1	19,814	84.0	1,151	4.9
FEMALE	367	3.9	736	7.9	67	.7	76	.8	1,246	13.3	7,869	84.0	253	2.7
MALE	375	2.6	805	5.7	97	.7	98	.7	1,375	9.7	11,945	84.0	898	6.3
UNCLASSIFIED:														
TOTAL	20	2.2	42	4.6	5	.5	5	.5	72	7.8	827	89.8	22	2.4
FEMALE	10	2.7	19	5.1	3	.8	3	.8	35	9.4	333	89.0	6	1.6
MALE	10	1.8	23	4.2	2	.4	2	.4	37	6.8	494	90.3	16	2.9
TOTAL ENROLLMENT:														
TOTAL	762	3.1	1,583	6.5	169	.7	179	.7	2,693	11.0	20,641	84.2	1,173	4.8
FEMALE	377	3.9	755	7.7	70	.7	79	.8	1,281	13.1	8,202	84.2	259	2.7
MALE	385	2.6	828	5.6	99	.7	100	.7	1,412	9.6	12,439	84.2	914	6.2
OREGON (27 INSTITUTIONS)														
UNDERGRADUATES:														
FULL-TIME	112	1.2	158	1.7	295	3.1	75	.8	640	6.7	8,559	89.7	339	3.6
FEMALE	47	1.3	61	1.7	138	3.9	27	.8	273	7.7	3,179	90.0	80	2.3
MALE	65	1.1	97	1.6	157	2.6	48	.8	367	6.1	5,380	89.6	259	4.3
PART-TIME	14	.9	29	1.2	51	2.2	17	.7	111	4.7	2,227	94.1	28	1.2
FEMALE	9	.9	13	1.2	23	2.2	7	.7	52	4.9	1,000	94.7	4	.4
MALE	5	.4	16	1.2	28	2.1	10	.8	59	4.5	1,227	93.7	24	1.8
TOTAL	126	1.1	187	1.6	346	2.9	92	.8	751	6.3	10,786	90.6	367	3.1
FEMALE	56	1.2	74	1.6	161	3.5	34	.7	325	7.1	4,179	91.1	84	1.8
MALE	70	1.0	113	1.5	185	2.5	58	.8	426	5.8	6,607	90.3	283	3.9
GRADUATE:														
FULL-TIME	2	.4	7	1.3	12	2.2	3	.6	24	4.4	448	83.0	68	12.6
FEMALE	0	.0	1	.8	4	3.3	1	.8	6	4.9	103	84.4	13	10.7
MALE	2	.5	6	1.4	8	1.9	2	.5	18	4.3	345	82.5	55	13.2
PART-TIME	2	.4	2	.4	21	3.7	1	.2	26	4.6	522	91.9	20	3.5
FEMALE	0	.0	1	.6	5	3.2	0	.0	6	3.8	150	95.5	1	.6
MALE	2	.5	1	.2	16	3.9	1	.2	20	4.9	372	90.5	19	4.6
TOTAL	4	.4	9	.8	33	3.0	4	.4	50	4.5	970	87.5	88	7.9
FEMALE	0	.0	2	.7	9	3.2	1	.4	12	4.3	253	90.7	14	5.0
MALE	4	.5	7	.8	24	2.9	3	.4	38	4.6	717	86.5	74	8.9
PROFESSIONAL:														
FULL-TIME	0	.0	0	.0	0	.0	0	.0	0	.0	0	.0	0	.0
FEMALE	0	.0	0	.0	0	.0	0	.0	0	.0	0	.0	0	.0
MALE	0	.0	0	.0	0	.0	0	.0	0	.0	0	.0	0	.0

BUSINESS AND MANAGEMENT

INDIAN NATIVE	BLACK NON-HISPANIC		ASIAN OR PACIFIC ISLANDER		HISPANIC		TOTAL MINORITY		WHITE NON-HISPANIC		NON-RESIDENT ALIEN		TOTAL
%	NUMBER	%	NUMBER	%	NUMBER	%	NUMBER	%	NUMBER	%	NUMBER	%	NUMBER
CONTINUED													
.0	0	.0	0	.0	0	.0	0	.0	0	.0	0	.0	0
.0	0	.0	0	.0	0	.0	0	.0	0	.0	0	.0	0
.0	0	.0	0	.0	0	.3	0	.0	0	.0	0	.0	0
.0	0	.0	0	.0	0	.0	0	.0	0	.0	0	.0	0
.0	0	.0	0	.0	0	.0	0	.0	0	.0	0	.0	0
.0	0	.0	0	.0	0	.0	0	.0	0	.0	0	.0	0
1.1	165	1.6	307	3.0	78	.8	664	6.6	9,007	89.4	407	4.0	10,078
1.3	62	1.7	142	3.9	28	.8	279	7.6	3,282	89.8	93	2.5	3,654
1.0	103	1.6	165	2.6	50	.8	385	6.0	5,725	89.1	314	4.9	6,424
.5	31	1.1	72	2.5	18	.6	137	4.7	2,749	93.7	48	1.6	2,934
.7	14	1.2	28	2.3	7	.6	58	4.8	1,150	94.8	5	.4	1,213
.4	17	1.0	44	2.6	11	.6	79	4.6	1,599	92.9	43	2.5	1,721
1.0	196	1.5	379	2.9	96	.7	801	6.2	11,756	90.3	455	3.5	13,012
1.2	76	1.6	170	3.5	35	.7	337	6.9	4,432	91.1	98	2.0	4,867
.9	120	1.5	209	2.6	61	.7	464	5.7	7,324	89.9	357	4.4	8,145
.3	6	.7	27	3.1	8	.9	44	5.0	769	88.2	59	6.8	872
.5	4	1.1	10	2.7	3	.8	19	5.1	341	91.7	12	3.2	372
.2	2	.4	17	3.4	5	1.0	25	5.0	428	85.6	47	9.4	500
1.0	202	1.5	406	2.9	104	.7	845	6.1	12,525	90.2	514	3.7	13,884
1.1	80	1.5	180	3.4	38	.7	356	6.8	4,773	91.1	110	2.1	5,239
.9	122	1.4	226	2.6	66	.8	489	5.7	7,752	89.7	404	4.7	8,645
(121 INSTITUTIONS)													
.1	3,307	6.4	241	.5	211	.4	3,807	7.4	47,127	91.8	408	.8	51,342
.1	1,612	9.2	111	.6	77	.4	1,822	10.4	15,553	89.1	76	.4	17,451
.1	1,695	5.0	130	.4	134	.4	1,985	5.9	31,574	93.2	332	1.0	33,891
.2	1,956	10.1	66	.3	168	.9	2,223	11.5	17,023	88.2	56	.3	19,302
.2	1,059	11.2	37	.4	75	.8	1,186	12.5	8,251	87.2	26	.3	9,463
.2	897	9.1	29	.3	93	.9	1,037	10.5	8,772	89.2	30	.3	9,839
.1	5,263	7.5	307	.4	379	.5	6,030	8.5	64,150	90.8	464	.7	70,644
.1	2,671	9.9	148	.5	152	.6	3,008	11.2	23,804	88.4	102	.4	26,914
.1	2,592	5.9	159	.4	227	.5	3,022	6.9	40,346	92.3	362	.8	43,730
.3	79	2.5	65	2.1	20	.6	174	5.5	2,629	83.8	336	10.7	3,139
.8	29	3.9	11	1.5	4	.5	50	6.7	669	89.1	32	4.3	751
.2	50	2.1	54	2.3	16	.7	124	5.2	1,960	82.1	304	12.7	2,388
.3	123	2.4	41	.8	14	.3	193	3.7	4,925	94.1	114	2.2	5,232
.4	33	3.5	9	.9	2	.2	48	5.1	889	93.7	12	1.3	949
.3	90	2.1	32	.7	12	.3	145	3.4	4,036	94.2	102	2.4	4,283
.3	202	2.4	106	1.3	34	.4	367	4.4	7,554	90.2	450	5.4	8,371
.6	62	3.6	20	1.2	6	.4	98	5.8	1,558	91.6	44	2.6	1,700
.2	140	2.1	86	1.3	28	.4	269	4.0	5,996	89.9	406	6.1	6,671
.0	0	.0	0	.0	0	.0	0	.0	0	.0	0	.0	0
.0	0	.0	0	.0	0	.0	0	.0	0	.0	0	.0	0
.0	0	.0	0	.0	0	.0	0	.0	0	.0	0	.0	0
.0	0	.0	0	.0	0	.0	0	.0	0	.0	0	.0	0
.0	0	.0	0	.0	0	.0	0	.0	0	.0	0	.0	0
.0	0	.0	0	.0	0	.0	0	.0	0	.0	0	.0	0
.1	3,386	6.2	306	.6	231	.4	3,981	7.3	49,756	91.3	744	1.4	54,481
.2	1,641	9.0	122	.7	81	.4	1,872	10.3	16,222	89.1	108	.6	18,202
.1	1,745	4.8	184	.5	150	.4	2,109	5.8	33,534	92.4	636	1.8	36,279
.2	2,079	8.5	107	.4	182	.7	2,416	9.8	21,948	89.5	170	.7	24,534
.2	1,092	10.5	46	.4	77	.7	1,234	11.9	9,140	87.8	38	.4	10,412
.2	987	7.0	61	.4	105	.7	1,182	8.4	12,808	90.7	132	.9	14,122
.1	5,465	6.9	413	.5	413	.5	6,397	8.1	71,704	90.7	914	1.2	79,015
.2	2,733	9.6	168	.6	158	.6	3,106	10.9	25,362	88.6	146	.5	28,614
.1	2,732	5.4	245	.5	255	.5	3,291	6.5	46,342	91.9	768	1.5	50,401
.1	139	7.2	6	.3	3	.2	150	7.8	1,761	91.6	12	.6	1,923
.1	77	10.3	4	.5	0	.0	82	10.9	661	88.3	6	.8	749
.1	62	5.3	2	.2	3	.3	68	5.8	1,100	93.7	6	.5	1,174
.1	5,604	6.9	419	.5	416	.5	6,547	8.1	73,465	90.8	926	1.1	80,938
.2	2,810	9.6	172	.6	158	.5	3,188	10.9	26,023	88.6	152	.5	29,363
.1	2,794	5.4	247	.5	258	.5	3,359	6.5	47,442	92.0	774	1.5	51,575

TABLE 17 — TOTAL ENROLLMENT IN INSTITUTIONS OF HIGHER EDUCATION FOR SELECTED MAJOR FIELDS OF STUDY AND LEVEL OF ENROLLMENT BY RACE, ETHNICITY, AND SEX: STATE, 1978

MAJOR FIELD 0500 — BUSINESS AND MANAGEMENT

	AMERICAN INDIAN ALASKAN NATIVE		BLACK NON-HISPANIC		ASIAN OR PACIFIC ISLANDER		HISPANIC		TOTAL MINORITY		WHITE NON-HISPANIC		NON-RESIDENT ALIEN	
	NUMBER	%	NUMBER	%	NUMBER	%	NUMBER	%	NUMBER	%	NUMBER	%	NUMBER	%
RHODE ISLAND (9 INSTITUTIONS)														
UNDERGRADUATES:														
FULL-TIME	3	.0	530	5.8	16	.2	33	.4	582	6.3	8,522	92.7	88	1.0
FEMALE	0	.0	196	7.2	2	.1	8	.3	206	7.6	2,497	91.8	18	.7
MALE	3	.0	334	5.2	14	.2	25	.4	376	5.8	6,025	93.1	70	1.1
PART-TIME	1	.1	31	2.0	5	.3	10	.7	47	3.1	1,480	96.8	2	.1
FEMALE	1	.2	13	2.1	1	.2	2	.3	17	2.7	612	97.1	1	.2
MALE	0	.0	18	2.0	4	.4	8	.9	30	3.3	868	96.6	1	.1
TOTAL	4	.0	561	5.2	21	.2	43	.4	629	5.9	10,002	93.3	90	.8
FEMALE	1	.0	209	6.2	3	.1	10	.3	223	6.7	3,109	92.8	19	.6
MALE	3	.0	352	4.8	18	.2	33	.4	406	5.5	6,893	93.5	71	1.0
GRADUATE:														
FULL-TIME	0	.0	8	5.2	5	3.2	0	.0	13	8.4	116	74.8	26	16.8
FEMALE	0	.0	2	4.7	0	.0	0	.0	2	4.7	36	83.7	5	11.6
MALE	0	.0	6	5.4	5	4.5	0	.0	11	9.8	80	71.4	21	18.8
PART-TIME	1	.1	14	1.1	15	1.2	7	.6	37	3.0	1,180	96.4	7	.6
FEMALE	0	.0	4	1.5	2	.7	2	.7	8	2.9	263	96.7	1	.4
MALE	1	.1	10	1.1	13	1.4	5	.5	29	3.0	917	96.3	6	.6
TOTAL	1	.1	22	1.6	20	1.5	7	.5	50	3.6	1,296	94.0	33	2.4
FEMALE	0	.0	6	1.9	2	.6	2	.6	10	3.2	299	94.9	6	1.9
MALE	1	.1	16	1.5	18	1.7	5	.5	40	3.8	997	93.7	27	2.5
PROFESSIONAL:														
FULL-TIME	0	.0	0	.0	0	.0	0	.0	0	.0	0	.0	0	.0
FEMALE	0	.0	0	.0	0	.0	0	.0	0	.0	0	.0	0	.0
MALE	0	.0	0	.0	0	.0	0	.0	0	.0	0	.0	0	.0
PART-TIME	0	.0	0	.0	0	.0	0	.0	0	.0	0	.0	0	.0
FEMALE	0	.0	0	.0	0	.0	0	.0	0	.0	0	.0	0	.0
MALE	0	.0	0	.0	0	.0	0	.0	0	.0	0	.0	0	.0
TOTAL	0	.0	0	.0	0	.0	0	.0	0	.0	0	.0	0	.0
FEMALE	0	.0	0	.0	0	.0	0	.0	0	.0	0	.0	0	.0
MALE	0	.0	0	.0	0	.0	0	.0	0	.0	0	.0	0	.0
UND+GRAD+PROF:														
FULL-TIME	3	.0	538	5.8	21	.2	33	.4	595	6.4	8,638	92.4	114	1.2
FEMALE	0	.0	198	7.2	2	.1	8	.3	208	7.5	2,533	91.6	23	.8
MALE	3	.0	340	5.2	19	.3	25	.4	387	5.9	6,105	92.7	91	1.4
PART-TIME	2	.1	45	1.6	20	.7	17	.6	84	3.1	2,660	96.6	9	.3
FEMALE	1	.1	17	1.9	3	.3	4	.4	25	2.8	875	97.0	2	.2
MALE	1	.1	28	1.5	17	.9	13	.7	59	3.2	1,785	96.4	7	.4
TOTAL	5	.0	583	4.8	41	.3	50	.4	679	5.6	11,298	93.4	123	1.0
FEMALE	1	.0	215	5.9	5	.1	12	.3	233	6.4	3,408	93.0	25	.7
MALE	4	.0	368	4.4	36	.4	38	.5	446	5.3	7,890	93.5	98	1.2
UNCLASSIFIED:														
TOTAL	0	.0	62	12.4	0	.0	0	.0	62	12.4	439	87.6	0	.0
FEMALE	0	.0	24	14.0	0	.0	0	.0	24	14.0	147	86.0	0	.0
MALE	0	.0	38	11.5	0	.0	0	.0	38	11.5	292	88.5	0	.0
TOTAL ENROLLMENT:														
TOTAL	5	.0	645	5.1	41	.3	50	.4	741	5.9	11,737	93.1	123	1.0
FEMALE	1	.0	239	6.2	5	.1	12	.3	257	6.7	3,555	92.7	25	.7
MALE	4	.0	406	4.4	36	.4	38	.4	484	5.5	8,182	93.4	98	1.1
SOUTH CAROLINA (36 INSTITUTIONS)														
UNDERGRADUATES:														
FULL-TIME	8	.1	3,110	27.4	36	.3	22	.2	3,176	28.0	8,076	71.1	105	.9
FEMALE	3	.1	1,744	42.3	23	.6	4	.1	1,774	43.0	2,339	56.7	9	.2
MALE	5	.1	1,366	18.9	13	.2	18	.2	1,402	19.4	5,737	79.3	96	1.3
PART-TIME	2	.1	604	23.1	8	.3	15	.6	629	24.0	1,990	76.0	1	.0
FEMALE	0	.0	166	20.8	3	.4	2	.3	171	21.4	629	78.6	0	.0
MALE	2	.1	438	24.1	5	.3	13	.7	458	25.2	1,361	74.8	1	.1
TOTAL	10	.1	3,714	26.6	44	.3	37	.3	3,805	27.2	10,066	72.0	106	.8
FEMALE	3	.1	1,910	38.8	26	.5	6	.1	1,945	39.5	2,968	60.3	9	.2
MALE	7	.1	1,804	19.9	18	.2	31	.3	1,860	20.5	7,098	78.4	97	1.1
GRADUATE:														
FULL-TIME	0	.0	7	2.0	1	.3	3	.9	11	3.1	313	88.9	28	8.0
FEMALE	0	.0	2	2.1	0	.0	0	.0	2	2.1	90	94.7	3	3.2
MALE	0	.0	5	1.9	1	.4	3	1.2	9	3.5	223	86.8	25	9.7
PART-TIME	1	.1	25	2.7	9	1.0	3	.3	38	4.1	871	94.3	15	1.6
FEMALE	0	.0	10	5.4	2	1.1	0	.0	12	6.5	169	91.8	3	1.6
MALE	1	.1	15	2.0	7	.9	3	.4	26	3.5	702	94.9	12	1.6
TOTAL	1	.1	32	2.5	10	.8	6	.5	49	3.8	1,184	92.8	43	3.4
FEMALE	0	.0	12	4.3	2	.7	0	.0	14	5.0	259	92.8	6	2.2
MALE	1	.1	20	2.0	8	.8	6	.6	35	3.5	925	92.8	37	3.7
PROFESSIONAL:														
FULL-TIME	0	.0	0	.0	0	.0	0	.0	0	.0	0	.0	0	.0
FEMALE	0	.0	0	.0	0	.0	0	.0	0	.0	0	.0	0	.0
MALE	0	.0	0	.0	0	.0	0	.0	0	.0	0	.0	0	.0

426

S AND MANAGEMENT

BLACK NON-HISPANIC		ASIAN OR PACIFIC ISLANDER		HISPANIC		TOTAL MINORITY		WHITE NON-HISPANIC		NON-RESIDENT ALIEN		TOTAL
NUMBER	%	NUMBER	%	NUMBER	%	NUMBER	%	NUMBER	%	NUMBER	%	NUMBER

NUED

0	.0	0	.0	0	.0	0	.0	0	.0	0	.0	0
0	.0	0	.0	0	.0	0	.0	0	.0	0	.0	0
0	.0	0	.0	0	.0	0	.0	0	.0	0	.0	0
0	.0	0	.0	0	.0	0	.0	0	.0	0	.0	0
0	.0	0	.0	0	.0	0	.0	0	.0	0	.0	0
0	.0	0	.0	0	.0	0	.0	0	.0	0	.0	0
3,117	26.6	37	.3	25	.2	3,187	27.2	8,309	71.6	133	1.1	11,709
1,746	41.4	23	.5	4	.1	1,776	42.1	2,429	57.6	12	.3	4,217
1,371	18.3	14	.2	21	.3	1,411	18.8	5,960	79.6	121	1.6	7,492
629	17.7	17	.5	18	.5	667	18.8	2,861	80.7	16	.5	3,544
176	17.9	5	.5	2	.2	183	18.6	798	81.1	3	.3	984
453	17.7	12	.5	16	.6	484	18.9	2,063	80.6	13	.5	2,560
3,746	24.6	54	.4	43	.3	3,854	25.3	11,250	73.8	149	1.0	15,253
1,922	37.0	28	.5	6	.1	1,959	37.7	3,227	62.0	15	.3	5,201
1,824	18.1	26	.3	37	.4	1,895	18.9	8,023	79.8	134	1.3	10,052
45	13.6	5	1.5	0	.0	50	15.2	270	81.8	10	3.0	330
19	14.8	1	.8	0	.0	20	15.6	107	83.6	1	.8	128
26	12.9	4	2.0	0	.0	30	14.9	163	80.7	9	4.5	202
3,791	24.3	59	.4	43	.3	3,904	25.1	11,520	73.9	159	1.0	15,583
1,941	36.4	29	.5	6	.1	1,979	37.1	3,334	62.6	16	.3	5,329
1,850	18.0	30	.3	37	.4	1,925	18.8	8,186	79.8	143	1.4	10,254

(5 INSTITUTIONS)

176	3.5	16	.3	253	5.0	621	12.2	4,437	87.1	36	.7	5,094
16	1.0	7	.4	25	1.6	147	9.2	1,449	90.4	6	.4	1,602
160	4.6	9	.3	228	6.5	474	13.6	2,988	85.6	30	.9	3,492
1	.5	0	.0	1	.5	20	10.2	177	89.8	0	.0	197
0	.0	0	.0	0	.0	14	16.9	69	83.1	0	.0	83
1	.9	0	.0	1	.9	6	5.3	108	94.7	0	.0	114
177	3.3	16	.3	254	4.8	641	12.1	4,614	87.2	36	.7	5,291
16	.9	7	.4	25	1.5	161	9.6	1,518	90.1	6	.4	1,685
161	4.5	9	.2	229	6.4	480	13.3	3,096	85.9	30	.8	3,606
0	.0	0	.0	0	.0	0	.0	41	95.3	2	4.7	43
0	.0	0	.0	0	.0	0	.0	13	100.0	0	.0	13
0	.0	0	.0	0	.0	0	.0	28	93.3	2	6.7	30
0	.0	0	.0	0	.0	1	.4	267	99.6	0	.0	268
0	.0	0	.0	0	.0	0	.0	44	100.0	0	.0	44
0	.0	0	.0	0	.0	1	.4	223	99.6	0	.0	224
0	.0	0	.0	0	.0	1	.3	308	99.0	2	.6	311
0	.0	0	.0	0	.0	0	.0	57	100.0	0	.0	57
0	.0	0	.0	0	.0	1	.4	251	98.8	2	.8	254
0	.0	0	.0	0	.0	0	.0	0	.0	0	.0	0
0	.0	0	.0	0	.0	0	.0	0	.0	0	.0	0
0	.0	0	.0	0	.0	0	.0	0	.0	0	.0	0
0	.0	0	.0	0	.0	0	.0	0	.0	0	.0	0
0	.0	0	.0	0	.0	0	.0	0	.0	0	.0	0
0	.0	0	.0	0	.0	0	.0	0	.0	0	.0	0
0	.0	0	.0	0	.0	0	.0	0	.0	0	.0	0
0	.0	0	.0	0	.0	0	.0	0	.0	0	.0	0
0	.0	0	.0	0	.0	0	.0	0	.0	0	.0	0
176	3.4	16	.3	253	4.9	621	12.1	4,478	87.2	38	.7	5,137
16	1.0	7	.4	25	1.5	147	9.1	1,462	90.5	6	.4	1,615
160	4.5	9	.3	228	6.5	474	13.5	3,016	85.6	32	.9	3,522
1	.2	0	.0	1	.2	21	4.5	444	95.5	0	.0	469
0	.0	0	.0	0	.0	14	11.0	113	89.0	0	.0	127
1	.3	0	.0	1	.3	7	2.1	331	97.9	0	.0	338
177	3.2	16	.3	254	4.5	642	11.5	4,922	87.9	38	.7	5,602
16	.9	7	.4	25	1.4	161	9.2	1,575	90.4	6	.3	1,742
161	4.2	9	.2	229	5.9	481	12.5	3,347	86.7	32	.8	3,860
3	2.2	0	.0	1	.7	4	2.9	135	97.1	0	.0	139
2	2.8	0	.0	0	.0	2	2.8	69	97.2	0	.0	71
1	1.5	0	.0	1	1.5	2	2.9	66	97.1	0	.0	68
180	3.1	16	.3	255	4.4	646	11.3	5,057	88.1	38	.7	5,741
18	1.0	7	.4	25	1.4	163	9.0	1,644	90.7	6	.3	1,813
162	4.1	9	.2	230	5.9	483	12.3	3,413	86.9	32	.8	3,928

TABLE 17 - TOTAL ENROLLMENT IN INSTITUTIONS OF HIGHER EDUCATION FOR SELECTED MAJOR FIELDS OF STUDY AND LEVEL OF ENROLLMENT BY RACE, ETHNICITY, AND SEX: STATE, 1978

MAJOR FIELD 0500 - BUSINESS AND MANAGEMENT

	AMERICAN INDIAN ALASKAN NATIVE		BLACK NON-HISPANIC		ASIAN OR PACIFIC ISLANDER		HISPANIC		TOTAL MINORITY		WHITE NON-HISPANIC		NON-RESIDENT ALIEN	
	NUMBER	%	NUMBER	%	NUMBER	%	NUMBER	%	NUMBER	%	NUMBER	%	NUMBER	%
TENNESSEE (54 INSTITUTIONS)														
UNDERGRADUATES:														
FULL-TIME	24	.1	4,914	22.5	63	.3	64	.3	5,065	23.1	16,481	75.3	339	1.5
FEMALE	14	.2	2,626	29.4	21	.2	16	.2	2,677	30.0	6,156	69.0	84	.9
MALE	10	.1	2,288	17.6	42	.3	48	.4	2,388	18.4	10,325	79.6	255	2.0
PART-TIME	10	.1	796	11.8	18	.3	22	.3	846	12.6	5,866	87.1	21	.3
FEMALE	4	.1	434	13.4	10	.3	12	.4	460	14.2	2,769	85.5	10	.3
MALE	6	.2	362	10.4	8	.2	10	.3	386	11.0	3,097	88.6	11	.3
TOTAL	34	.1	5,710	20.0	81	.3	86	.3	5,911	20.7	22,347	78.1	360	1.3
FEMALE	18	.1	3,060	25.2	31	.3	28	.2	3,137	25.8	8,925	73.4	94	.8
MALE	16	.1	2,650	16.1	50	.3	58	.4	2,774	16.9	13,422	81.5	266	1.6
GRADUATE:														
FULL-TIME	1	.2	10	2.3	4	.9	2	.5	17	3.8	367	82.7	60	13.5
FEMALE	0	.0	3	2.6	3	2.6	0	.0	6	5.1	98	83.8	13	11.1
MALE	1	.3	7	2.1	1	.3	2	.6	11	3.4	269	82.3	47	14.4
PART-TIME	2	.1	71	4.9	7	.5	3	.2	83	5.7	1,311	90.5	54	3.7
FEMALE	1	.3	34	10.1	1	.3	2	.6	38	11.3	285	85.1	12	3.6
MALE	1	.1	37	3.3	6	.5	1	.1	45	4.0	1,026	92.2	42	3.8
TOTAL	3	.2	81	4.3	11	.6	5	.3	100	5.3	1,678	88.7	114	6.0
FEMALE	1	.2	37	8.2	4	.9	2	.4	44	9.7	383	84.7	25	5.5
MALE	2	.1	44	3.1	7	.5	3	.2	56	3.9	1,295	89.9	89	6.2
PROFESSIONAL:														
FULL-TIME	0	.0	0	.0	0	.0	0	.0	0	.0	187	98.4	3	1.6
FEMALE	0	.0	0	.0	0	.0	0	.0	0	.0	43	100.0	0	.0
MALE	0	.0	0	.0	0	.0	0	.0	0	.0	144	98.0	3	2.0
PART-TIME	0	.0	0	.0	0	.0	0	.0	0	.0	0	.0	0	.0
FEMALE	0	.0	0	.0	0	.0	0	.0	0	.0	0	.0	0	.0
MALE	0	.0	0	.0	0	.0	0	.0	0	.0	0	.0	0	.0
TOTAL	0	.0	0	.0	0	.0	0	.0	0	.0	187	98.4	3	1.6
FEMALE	0	.0	0	.0	0	.0	0	.0	0	.0	43	100.0	0	.0
MALE	0	.0	0	.0	0	.0	0	.0	0	.0	144	98.0	3	2.0
UND+GRAD+PROF:														
FULL-TIME	25	.1	4,924	21.9	67	.3	66	.3	5,082	22.6	17,035	75.6	402	1.8
FEMALE	14	.2	2,629	29.0	24	.3	16	.2	2,683	29.6	6,297	69.4	97	1.1
MALE	11	.1	2,295	17.1	43	.3	50	.4	2,399	17.8	10,738	79.9	305	2.3
PART-TIME	12	.1	867	10.6	25	.3	25	.3	929	11.4	7,177	87.7	75	.9
FEMALE	5	.1	468	13.1	11	.3	14	.4	498	13.9	3,054	85.5	22	.6
MALE	7	.2	399	8.7	14	.3	11	.2	431	9.4	4,123	89.5	53	1.2
TOTAL	37	.1	5,791	18.9	92	.3	91	.3	6,011	19.6	24,212	78.9	477	1.6
FEMALE	19	.2	3,097	24.5	35	.3	30	.2	3,181	25.1	9,351	73.9	119	.9
MALE	18	.1	2,694	14.9	57	.3	61	.3	2,830	15.7	14,861	82.3	358	2.0
UNCLASSIFIED:														
TOTAL	0	.0	48	32.2	0	.0	0	.0	48	32.2	101	67.8	0	.0
FEMALE	0	.0	22	31.9	0	.0	0	.0	22	31.9	47	68.1	0	.0
MALE	0	.0	26	32.5	0	.0	0	.0	26	32.5	54	67.5	0	.0
TOTAL ENROLLMENT:														
TOTAL	37	.1	5,839	18.9	92	.3	91	.3	6,059	19.6	24,313	78.8	477	1.5
FEMALE	19	.1	3,119	24.5	35	.3	30	.2	3,203	25.2	9,398	73.9	119	.9
MALE	18	.1	2,720	15.0	57	.3	61	.3	2,856	15.8	14,915	82.3	358	2.0
TEXAS (118 INSTITUTIONS)														
UNDERGRADUATES:														
FULL-TIME	143	.2	5,941	9.4	450	.7	5,880	9.3	12,414	19.7	48,653	77.2	1,939	3.1
FEMALE	67	.3	3,185	12.6	241	1.0	2,427	9.6	5,920	23.5	18,769	74.5	519	2.1
MALE	76	.2	2,756	7.3	209	.6	3,453	9.1	6,494	17.2	29,884	79.1	1,420	3.8
PART-TIME	136	.4	3,970	10.7	370	1.0	4,179	11.3	8,655	23.3	28,109	75.8	337	.9
FEMALE	64	.4	2,399	12.4	241	1.2	2,040	10.5	4,744	24.4	14,545	75.0	114	.6
MALE	72	.4	1,571	8.9	129	.7	2,139	12.1	3,911	22.1	13,564	76.6	223	1.3
TOTAL	279	.3	9,911	9.9	820	.8	10,059	10.0	21,069	21.0	76,762	76.7	2,276	2.3
FEMALE	131	.3	5,584	12.5	482	1.1	4,467	10.0	10,664	23.9	33,314	74.7	633	1.4
MALE	148	.3	4,327	7.8	338	.6	5,592	10.1	10,405	18.7	43,448	78.3	1,643	3.0
GRADUATE:														
FULL-TIME	7	.2	115	2.7	111	2.6	103	2.4	336	8.0	2,928	69.6	945	22.5
FEMALE	1	.1	36	3.2	35	3.1	27	2.4	99	8.9	838	75.1	179	16.0
MALE	6	.2	79	2.6	76	2.5	76	2.5	237	7.7	2,090	67.6	766	24.8
PART-TIME	22	.3	276	4.0	72	1.0	343	5.0	713	10.4	5,753	83.9	393	5.7
FEMALE	6	.3	115	5.9	23	1.2	73	3.7	217	11.1	1,665	85.1	74	3.8
MALE	16	.3	161	3.3	49	1.0	270	5.5	496	10.1	4,088	83.4	319	6.5
TOTAL	29	.3	391	3.5	183	1.7	446	4.0	1,049	9.5	8,681	78.4	1,338	12.1
FEMALE	7	.2	151	4.9	58	1.9	100	3.3	316	10.3	2,503	81.5	253	8.2
MALE	22	.3	240	3.0	125	1.6	346	4.3	733	9.2	6,178	77.3	1,085	13.6
PROFESSIONAL:														
FULL-TIME	0	.0	0	.0	0	.0	0	.0	0	.0	0	.0	0	.0
FEMALE	0	.0	0	.0	0	.0	0	.0	0	.0	0	.0	0	.0
MALE	0	.0	0	.0	0	.0	0	.0	0	.0	0	.0	0	.0

BUSINESS AND MANAGEMENT

INDIAN NATIVE		BLACK NON-HISPANIC		ASIAN OR PACIFIC ISLANDER		HISPANIC		TOTAL MINORITY		WHITE NON-HISPANIC		NON-RESIDENT ALIEN		TOTAL
%	NUMBER	%	NUMBER	%	NUMBER	%	NUMBER	%	NUMBER	%	NUMBER	%	NUMBER	%	NUMBER

CONTINUED

.0	0	.0	0	.0	0	.0	0	.0	0	.0	0	.0	0
.0	0	.0	0	.0	0	.0	0	.0	0	.0	0	.0	0
.0	0	.0	0	.0	0	.0	0	.0	0	.0	0	.0	0
.0	0	.0	0	.0	0	.0	0	.0	0	.0	0	.0	0
.0	0	.0	0	.0	0	.0	0	.0	0	.0	0	.0	0
.0	0	.0	0	.0	0	.0	0	.0	0	.0	0	.0	0
.2	6,056	9.0	561	.8	5,983	8.9	12,750	19.0	51,581	76.7	2,884	4.3	67,215
.3	3,221	12.2	276	1.0	2,454	9.3	6,019	22.9	19,607	74.5	698	2.7	26,324
.2	2,835	6.9	285	.7	3,529	8.6	6,731	16.5	31,974	78.2	2,186	5.3	40,891
.4	4,246	9.7	442	1.0	4,522	10.3	9,368	21.3	33,862	77.0	730	1.7	43,960
.3	2,514	11.8	264	1.2	2,113	9.9	4,961	23.2	16,210	75.9	188	.9	21,359
.4	1,732	7.7	178	.8	2,409	10.7	4,407	19.5	17,652	78.1	542	2.4	22,601
.3	10,302	9.3	1,003	.9	10,505	9.4	22,118	19.9	85,443	76.9	3,614	3.3	111,175
.3	5,735	12.0	540	1.1	4,567	9.6	10,980	23.0	35,817	75.1	886	1.9	47,683
.3	4,567	7.2	463	.7	5,938	9.4	11,138	17.5	49,626	78.2	2,728	4.3	63,492
.5	639	13.2	85	1.8	651	13.5	1,398	28.9	3,384	69.9	57	1.2	4,839
.4	364	16.6	57	2.6	236	10.8	666	30.4	1,506	68.8	18	.8	2,190
.5	275	10.4	28	1.1	415	15.7	732	27.6	1,878	70.9	39	1.5	2,649
.3	10,941	9.4	1,088	.9	11,156	9.6	23,516	20.3	88,827	76.6	3,671	3.2	116,014
.3	6,099	12.2	597	1.2	4,803	9.6	11,646	23.4	37,323	74.8	904	1.8	49,873
.3	4,842	7.3	491	.7	6,353	9.6	11,870	17.9	51,504	77.9	2,767	4.2	66,141

(14 INSTITUTIONS)

.6	42	.6	142	2.1	88	1.3	314	4.6	6,262	91.2	293	4.3	6,869
1.3	13	.6	60	3.0	35	1.7	135	6.7	1,782	88.5	96	4.8	2,013
.3	29	.6	82	1.7	53	1.1	179	3.7	4,480	92.3	197	4.1	4,856
.7	21	.6	29	.8	79	2.2	154	4.2	3,447	95.0	26	.7	3,627
1.0	10	1.3	5	.7	16	2.1	39	5.1	718	93.7	9	1.2	766
.6	11	.4	24	.8	63	2.2	115	4.0	2,729	95.4	17	.6	2,861
.6	63	.6	171	1.6	167	1.6	468	4.5	9,709	92.5	319	3.0	10,496
1.3	23	.8	65	2.3	51	1.8	174	6.3	2,500	90.0	105	3.8	2,779
.4	40	.5	106	1.4	116	1.5	294	3.8	7,209	93.4	214	2.8	7,717
.2	0	.0	6	.9	2	.3	9	1.4	599	91.0	50	7.6	658
.0	0	.0	0	.0	0	.0	0	.0	75	91.5	7	8.5	82
.2	0	.0	6	1.0	2	.3	9	1.6	524	91.0	43	7.5	576
.0	1	.4	0	.0	5	2.0	6	2.4	222	88.4	23	9.2	251
.0	0	.0	0	.0	2	3.5	2	3.5	45	78.9	10	17.5	57
.0	1	.5	0	.0	3	1.5	4	2.1	177	91.2	13	6.7	194
.1	1	.1	6	.7	7	.8	15	1.7	821	90.3	73	8.0	909
.0	0	.0	0	.0	2	1.4	2	1.4	120	86.3	17	12.2	139
.1	1	.1	6	.8	5	.6	13	1.7	701	91.0	56	7.3	770
.0	0	.0	0	.0	0	.0	0	.0	0	.0	0	.0	0
.0	0	.0	0	.0	0	.0	0	.0	0	.0	0	.0	0
.0	0	.0	0	.0	0	.0	0	.0	0	.0	0	.0	0
.0	0	.0	0	.0	0	.0	0	.0	0	.0	0	.0	0
.0	0	.0	0	.0	0	.0	0	.0	0	.0	0	.0	0
.0	0	.0	0	.0	0	.0	0	.0	0	.0	0	.0	0
.0	0	.0	0	.0	0	.0	0	.0	0	.0	0	.0	0
.0	0	.0	0	.0	0	.0	0	.0	0	.0	0	.0	0
.0	0	.0	0	.0	0	.0	0	.0	0	.0	0	.0	0
.6	42	.6	148	2.0	90	1.2	323	4.3	6,861	91.2	343	4.6	7,527
1.3	13	.6	60	2.9	35	1.7	135	6.4	1,857	88.6	103	4.9	2,095
.3	29	.5	88	1.6	55	1.0	188	3.5	5,004	92.1	240	4.4	5,432
.6	22	.6	29	.7	84	2.2	160	4.1	3,669	94.6	49	1.3	3,878
1.0	10	1.2	5	.6	18	2.2	41	5.0	763	92.7	19	2.3	823
.6	12	.4	24	.8	66	2.2	119	3.9	2,906	95.1	30	1.0	3,055
.6	64	.6	177	1.6	174	1.5	483	4.2	10,530	92.3	392	3.4	11,405
1.2	23	.8	65	2.2	53	1.8	176	6.0	2,620	89.8	122	4.2	2,918
.4	41	.5	112	1.3	121	1.4	307	3.6	7,910	93.2	270	3.2	8,487
1.9	6	.6	21	2.1	25	2.5	71	7.0	943	92.9	1	.1	1,015
3.9	5	1.0	15	3.1	10	2.0	49	10.0	439	90.0	0	.0	488
.0	1	.2	6	1.1	15	2.8	22	4.2	504	95.6	1	.2	527
.7	70	.6	198	1.6	199	1.6	554	4.5	11,473	92.4	393	3.2	12,420
1.6	28	.8	80	2.3	63	1.8	225	6.6	3,059	89.8	122	3.6	3,406
.4	42	.5	118	1.3	136	1.5	329	3.6	8,414	93.3	271	3.0	9,014

TABLE 17 - TOTAL ENROLLMENT IN INSTITUTIONS OF HIGHER EDUCATION FOR SELECTED MAJOR FIELDS OF STUDY AND LEVEL OF ENROLLMENT BY RACE, ETHNICITY, AND SEX: STATE, 1978

MAJOR FIELD 0500 - BUSINESS AND MANAGEMENT

	AMERICAN INDIAN ALASKAN NATIVE		BLACK NON-HISPANIC		ASIAN OR PACIFIC ISLANDER		HISPANIC		TOTAL MINORITY		WHITE NON-HISPANIC		NON-RESIDENT ALIEN	
	NUMBER	%	NUMBER	%	NUMBER	%	NUMBER	%	NUMBER	%	NUMBER	%	NUMBER	%
VERMONT	**(13 INSTITUTIONS)**													
UNDERGRADUATES:														
FULL-TIME	4	.2	21	.9	3	.1	16	.7	44	1.8	2,305	94.4	93	3.8
FEMALE	1	.1	6	.7	1	.1	6	.7	14	1.7	799	96.6	14	1.7
MALE	3	.2	15	.9	2	.1	10	.6	30	1.9	1,506	93.3	79	4.9
PART-TIME	1	.3	1	.3	0	.0	1	.3	3	1.0	304	99.0	0	.0
FEMALE	0	.0	0	.0	0	.0	0	.0	0	.0	132	100.0	0	.0
MALE	1	.6	1	.6	0	.0	1	.6	3	1.7	172	98.3	0	.0
TOTAL	5	.2	22	.8	3	.1	17	.6	47	1.7	2,609	94.9	93	3.4
FEMALE	1	.1	6	.6	1	.1	6	.6	14	1.5	931	97.1	14	1.5
MALE	4	.2	16	.9	2	.1	11	.6	33	1.8	1,678	93.7	79	4.4
GRADUATE:														
FULL-TIME	1	1.1	3	3.3	0	.0	2	2.2	6	6.7	70	77.8	14	15.6
FEMALE	0	.0	3	8.3	0	.0	0	.0	3	8.3	26	72.2	7	19.4
MALE	1	1.9	0	.0	0	.0	2	3.7	3	5.6	44	81.5	7	13.0
PART-TIME	0	.0	7	4.6	1	.7	2	1.3	10	6.6	135	88.8	7	4.6
FEMALE	0	.0	4	5.6	1	1.4	0	.0	5	7.0	64	90.1	2	2.8
MALE	0	.0	3	3.7	0	.0	2	2.5	5	6.2	71	87.7	5	6.2
TOTAL	1	.4	10	4.1	1	.4	4	1.7	16	6.6	205	84.7	21	8.7
FEMALE	0	.0	7	6.5	1	.9	0	.0	8	7.5	90	84.1	9	8.4
MALE	1	.7	3	2.2	0	.0	4	3.0	8	3.9	115	85.2	12	8.9
PROFESSIONAL:														
FULL-TIME	0	.0	0	.0	0	.0	0	.0	0	.0	0	.0	0	.0
FEMALE	0	.0	0	.0	0	.0	0	.0	0	.0	0	.0	0	.0
MALE	0	.0	0	.0	0	.0	0	.0	0	.0	0	.0	0	.0
PART-TIME	0	.0	0	.0	0	.0	0	.0	0	.0	0	.0	0	.0
FEMALE	0	.0	0	.0	0	.0	0	.0	0	.0	0	.0	0	.0
MALE	0	.0	0	.0	0	.0	0	.0	0	.0	0	.0	0	.0
TOTAL	0	.0	0	.0	0	.0	0	.0	0	.0	0	.0	0	.0
FEMALE	0	.0	0	.0	0	.0	0	.0	0	.0	0	.0	0	.0
MALE	0	.0	0	.0	0	.0	0	.0	0	.0	0	.0	0	.0
UND+GRAD+PROF:														
FULL-TIME	5	.2	24	.9	3	.1	18	.7	50	2.0	2,375	93.8	107	4.2
FEMALE	1	.1	9	1.0	1	.1	6	.7	17	2.0	825	95.6	21	2.4
MALE	4	.2	15	.9	2	.1	12	.7	33	2.0	1,550	92.9	86	5.2
PART-TIME	1	.2	8	1.7	1	.2	3	.7	13	2.8	439	95.6	7	1.5
FEMALE	0	.0	4	2.0	1	.5	0	.0	5	2.5	196	96.6	2	1.0
MALE	1	.4	4	1.6	0	.0	3	1.2	8	3.1	243	94.9	5	2.0
TOTAL	6	.2	32	1.1	4	.1	21	.7	63	2.1	2,814	94.1	114	3.8
FEMALE	1	.1	13	1.2	2	.2	6	.6	22	2.1	1,021	95.8	23	2.2
MALE	5	.3	19	1.0	2	.1	15	.8	41	2.1	1,793	93.1	91	4.7
UNCLASSIFIED:														
TOTAL	0	.0	0	.0	1	.8	0	.0	1	.8	122	99.2	0	.0
FEMALE	0	.0	0	.0	1	1.6	0	.0	1	1.6	63	98.4	0	.0
MALE	0	.0	0	.0	0	.0	0	.0	0	.0	59	100.0	0	.0
TOTAL ENROLLMENT:														
TOTAL	6	.2	32	1.0	5	.2	21	.7	64	2.1	2,936	94.3	114	3.7
FEMALE	1	.1	13	1.2	3	.3	6	.5	23	2.0	1,084	95.9	23	2.0
MALE	5	.3	19	1.0	2	.1	15	.8	41	2.1	1,852	93.3	91	4.6
VIRGINIA	**(57 INSTITUTIONS)**													
UNDERGRADUATES:														
FULL-TIME	26	.1	4,057	21.5	143	.8	82	.4	4,308	22.9	14,343	76.1	192	1.0
FEMALE	12	.2	2,101	28.4	73	.9	34	.4	2,220	27.9	5,667	71.3	63	.8
MALE	14	.1	1,956	18.0	70	.6	48	.4	2,088	19.2	8,676	79.6	129	1.2
PART-TIME	9	.2	776	16.0	47	1.0	37	.8	869	18.0	3,942	81.4	30	.6
FEMALE	5	.3	327	16.7	23	1.2	13	.7	368	18.8	1,577	80.6	11	.6
MALE	4	.1	449	15.6	24	.8	24	.8	501	17.4	2,365	82.0	19	.7
TOTAL	35	.1	4,833	20.4	190	.8	119	.5	5,177	21.9	18,285	77.2	222	.9
FEMALE	17	.2	2,428	24.5	96	1.0	47	.5	2,588	26.1	7,244	73.1	74	.7
MALE	18	.1	2,405	17.5	94	.7	72	.5	2,589	18.8	11,041	80.1	148	1.1
GRADUATE:														
FULL-TIME	0	.0	41	3.9	13	1.2	3	.3	57	5.4	954	90.2	47	4.4
FEMALE	0	.0	11	4.1	3	1.1	0	.0	14	5.2	251	92.6	6	2.2
MALE	0	.0	30	3.8	10	1.3	3	.4	43	5.5	703	89.3	41	5.2
PART-TIME	4	.2	90	4.8	18	1.0	8	.4	120	6.5	1,727	93.0	9	.5
FEMALE	0	.0	32	8.4	4	1.1	2	.5	38	10.0	341	90.0	0	.0
MALE	4	.3	58	3.4	14	.9	6	.4	82	5.6	1,386	93.8	9	.6
TOTAL	4	.1	131	4.5	31	1.1	11	.4	177	6.1	2,681	92.0	56	1.9
FEMALE	0	.0	43	6.6	7	1.1	2	.3	52	8.0	592	91.1	0	.9
MALE	4	.2	88	3.9	24	1.1	9	.4	125	5.5	2,089	92.3	50	2.2
PROFESSIONAL:														
FULL-TIME	0	.0	0	.0	0	.0	0	.0	0	.0	0	.0	0	.0
FEMALE	0	.0	0	.0	0	.0	0	.0	0	.0	0	.0	0	.0
MALE	0	.0	0	.0	0	.0	0	.0	0	.0	0	.0	0	.0

BUSINESS AND MANAGEMENT

INDIAN NATIVE %	BLACK NON-HISPANIC NUMBER	%	ASIAN OR PACIFIC ISLANDER NUMBER	%	HISPANIC NUMBER	%	TOTAL MINORITY NUMBER	%	WHITE NON-HISPANIC NUMBER	%	NON-RESIDENT ALIEN NUMBER	%	TOTAL NUMBER
CONTINUED													
.0	0	.0	0	.0	0	.0	0	.0	0	.0	0	.0	0
.0	0	.0	0	.0	0	.0	0	.0	0	.0	0	.0	0
.0	0	.0	0	.0	0	.0	0	.0	0	.0	0	.0	U
.0	0	.0	0	.0	0	.0	0	.0	0	.0	0	.0	0
.0	0	.0	0	.0	0	.0	0	.0	0	.0	0	.0	0
.0	0	.0	0	.0	0	.0	0	.0	0	.0	0	.0	0
.1	4,098	20.6	156	.8	85	.4	4,365	21.9	15,297	76.9	239	1.2	19,901
.1	2,112	25.7	76	.9	34	.4	2,234	27.2	5,918	72.0	69	.8	8,221
.1	1,986	17.0	80	.7	51	.4	2,131	18.2	9,379	80.3	170	1.5	11,680
.2	866	12.9	65	1.0	45	.7	989	14.8	5,669	84.6	39	.6	6,697
.2	359	15.4	27	1.2	15	.6	406	17.4	1,918	82.1	11	.5	2,335
.2	503	11.6	38	.9	30	.7	583	13.4	3,751	86.0	28	.6	4,362
.1	4,964	18.7	221	.8	130	.5	5,354	20.1	20,966	78.8	278	1.0	26,598
.2	2,471	23.4	103	1.0	49	.5	2,640	25.0	7,836	74.2	80	.8	10,556
.1	2,493	15.5	118	.7	81	.5	2,714	16.9	13,130	81.8	198	1.2	16,042
.5	81	21.8	1	.3	3	.8	87	23.5	278	74.9	6	1.6	371
1.2	33	20.1	0	.0	1	.6	36	22.0	125	76.2	3	1.8	164
.0	48	23.2	1	.5	2	1.0	51	24.6	153	73.9	3	1.4	207
.2	5,045	18.7	222	.8	133	.5	5,441	20.2	21,244	78.8	284	1.1	26,969
.2	2,504	23.4	103	1.0	50	.5	2,676	25.0	7,961	74.3	83	.8	10,720
.1	2,541	15.6	119	.7	83	.5	2,765	17.0	13,283	81.7	201	1.2	16,249
(16 INSTITUTIONS)													
.6	150	2.3	254	3.9	42	.6	486	7.5	5,729	88.6	250	3.9	6,465
.6	62	2.8	107	4.9	16	.7	199	9.1	1,910	87.8	67	3.1	2,176
.6	88	2.1	147	3.4	26	.6	287	6.7	3,819	89.0	183	4.3	4,289
1.0	53	3.9	60	4.4	6	.4	132	9.7	1,207	88.5	25	1.8	1,364
1.1	14	3.2	29	6.7	2	.5	50	11.5	377	86.5	9	2.1	436
.9	39	4.2	31	3.3	4	.4	82	8.8	830	89.4	16	1.7	928
.7	203	2.6	314	4.0	48	.6	618	7.9	6,936	88.6	275	3.5	7,829
.7	76	2.9	136	5.2	18	.7	249	9.5	2,287	87.6	76	2.9	2,612
.7	127	2.4	178	3.4	30	.6	369	7.1	4,649	89.1	199	3.8	5,217
.6	28	2.8	32	3.2	13	1.3	79	7.9	821	82.0	101	10.1	1,001
.0	8	3.5	14	6.1	1	.4	23	10.0	189	81.8	19	8.2	231
.8	20	2.6	18	2.3	12	1.6	56	7.3	632	82.1	82	10.6	770
.3	21	2.3	31	3.4	4	.4	59	6.5	830	91.0	23	2.5	912
.0	2	1.0	2	1.0	2	1.0	6	3.0	191	96.5	1	.5	198
.4	19	2.7	29	4.1	2	.3	53	7.4	639	89.5	22	3.1	714
.5	49	2.6	63	3.3	17	.9	138	7.2	1,651	86.3	124	6.5	1,913
.0	10	2.3	16	3.7	3	.7	29	6.8	380	88.6	20	4.7	429
.6	39	2.6	47	3.2	14	.9	109	7.3	1,271	85.6	104	7.0	1,484
.0	0	.0	0	.0	0	.0	0	.0	0	.0	0	.0	0
.0	0	.0	0	.0	0	.0	0	.0	0	.0	0	.0	0
.0	0	.0	0	.0	0	.0	0	.0	0	.0	0	.0	0
.0	0	.0	0	.0	0	.0	0	.0	0	.0	0	.0	0
.0	0	.0	0	.0	0	.0	0	.0	0	.0	0	.0	0
.0	0	.0	0	.0	0	.0	0	.0	0	.0	0	.0	0
.0	0	.0	0	.0	0	.0	0	.0	0	.0	0	.0	0
.0	0	.0	0	.0	0	.0	0	.0	0	.0	0	.0	0
.0	0	.0	0	.0	0	.0	0	.0	0	.0	0	.0	0
.6	178	2.4	286	3.8	55	.7	565	7.6	6,550	87.7	351	4.7	7,466
.6	70	2.9	121	5.0	17	.7	222	9.2	2,099	87.2	86	3.6	2,407
.6	108	2.1	165	3.3	38	.8	343	6.8	4,451	88.0	265	5.2	5,059
.7	74	3.3	91	4.0	10	.4	191	8.4	2,037	89.5	48	2.1	2,276
.8	16	2.5	31	4.9	4	.6	56	8.8	568	89.6	10	1.6	634
.7	58	3.5	60	3.7	6	.4	135	8.2	1,469	89.5	38	2.3	1,642
.6	252	2.6	377	3.9	65	.7	756	7.8	8,587	88.1	399	4.1	9,742
.6	86	2.8	152	5.0	21	.7	278	9.1	2,667	87.7	96	3.2	3,041
.6	166	2.5	225	3.4	44	.7	478	7.1	5,920	88.3	303	4.5	6,701
.3	6	1.7	9	2.6	0	.0	16	4.6	309	88.3	25	7.1	350
.0	1	.8	6	4.8	0	.0	7	5.6	112	90.3	5	4.0	124
.4	5	2.2	3	1.3	0	.0	9	4.0	197	87.2	20	8.8	226
.6	258	2.6	386	3.8	65	.6	772	7.6	8,896	88.1	424	4.2	10,092
.6	87	2.7	198	5.0	21	.7	285	9.0	2,779	87.8	101	3.2	3,165
.6	171	2.5	228	3.3	44	.6	487	7.0	6,117	88.3	323	4.7	6,927

MAJOR FIELD 0500 - BUSINESS AND MANAGEMENT

	AMERICAN INDIAN ALASKAN NATIVE		BLACK NON-HISPANIC		ASIAN OR PACIFIC ISLANDER		HISPANIC		TOTAL MINORITY		WHITE NON-HISPANIC		NON-RESIDENT ALIEN	
	NUMBER	%	NUMBER	%	NUMBER	%	NUMBER	%	NUMBER	%	NUMBER	%	NUMBER	%
WEST VIRGINIA (22 INSTITUTIONS)														
UNDERGRADUATES:														
FULL-TIME	14	.2	404	5.1	33	.4	11	.1	462	5.9	7,323	92.9	100	1.3
FEMALE	3	.1	147	5.7	8	.3	4	.2	162	6.2	2,406	92.8	26	1.0
MALE	11	.2	257	4.9	25	.5	7	.1	300	5.7	4,917	92.9	74	1.4
PART-TIME	4	.2	143	7.0	5	.2	0	.0	152	7.5	1,874	92.1	9	.4
FEMALE	2	.2	68	7.3	2	.2	0	.0	72	7.8	855	92.0	2	.2
MALE	2	.2	75	6.8	3	.3	0	.0	80	7.2	1,019	92.1	7	.6
TOTAL	18	.2	547	5.5	38	.4	11	.1	614	6.2	9,197	92.7	109	1.1
FEMALE	5	.1	215	6.1	10	.3	4	.1	234	6.6	3,261	92.6	28	.8
MALE	13	.2	332	5.2	28	.4	7	.1	380	5.9	5,936	92.8	81	1.3
GRADUATE:														
FULL-TIME	0	.0	1	.5	7	3.2	2	.9	10	4.6	176	80.7	32	14.7
FEMALE	0	.0	0	.0	1	2.0	1	2.0	2	3.9	44	86.3	5	9.8
MALE	0	.0	1	.6	6	3.6	1	.6	8	4.8	132	79.0	27	16.2
PART-TIME	3	.3	25	2.9	13	1.5	2	.2	43	4.9	816	93.6	13	1.5
FEMALE	1	.4	11	4.5	4	1.6	0	.0	16	6.5	229	92.7	2	.8
MALE	2	.3	14	2.2	9	1.4	2	.3	27	4.3	587	93.9	11	1.8
TOTAL	3	.3	26	2.4	20	1.8	4	.4	53	4.9	992	91.0	45	4.1
FEMALE	1	.3	11	3.7	5	1.7	1	.3	18	6.0	273	91.6	7	2.3
MALE	2	.3	15	1.9	15	1.9	3	.4	35	4.4	719	90.8	38	4.8
PROFESSIONAL:														
FULL-TIME	0	.0	0	.0	0	.0	0	.0	0	.0	0	.0	0	.0
FEMALE	0	.0	0	.0	0	.0	0	.0	0	.0	0	.0	0	.0
MALE	0	.0	0	.0	0	.0	0	.0	0	.0	0	.0	0	.0
PART-TIME	0	.0	0	.0	0	.0	0	.0	0	.0	0	.0	0	.0
FEMALE	0	.0	0	.0	0	.0	0	.0	0	.0	0	.0	0	.0
MALE	0	.0	0	.0	0	.0	0	.0	0	.0	0	.0	0	.0
TOTAL	0	.0	0	.0	0	.0	0	.0	0	.0	0	.0	0	.0
FEMALE	0	.0	0	.0	0	.0	0	.0	0	.0	0	.0	0	.0
MALE	0	.0	0	.0	0	.0	0	.0	0	.0	0	.0	0	.0
UND+GRAD+PROF:														
FULL-TIME	14	.2	405	5.0	40	.5	13	.2	472	5.8	7,499	92.5	132	1.6
FEMALE	3	.1	147	5.6	9	.3	5	.2	164	6.2	2,450	92.6	31	1.2
MALE	11	.2	258	4.7	31	.6	8	.1	308	5.6	5,049	92.5	101	1.9
PART-TIME	7	.2	168	5.8	18	.6	2	.1	195	6.7	2,690	92.5	22	.8
FEMALE	3	.3	79	6.7	6	.5	0	.0	88	7.5	1,084	92.2	4	.3
MALE	4	.2	89	5.1	12	.7	2	.1	107	6.2	1,606	92.8	18	1.0
TOTAL	21	.2	573	5.2	58	.5	15	.1	667	6.1	10,189	92.5	154	1.4
FEMALE	6	.2	226	5.9	15	.4	5	.1	252	6.6	3,534	92.5	35	.9
MALE	15	.2	347	4.8	43	.6	10	.1	415	5.8	6,655	92.6	119	1.7
UNCLASSIFIED:														
TOTAL	2	.2	31	3.0	1	.1	1	.1	35	3.3	1,010	96.7	0	.0
FEMALE	0	.0	16	4.2	0	.0	0	.0	16	4.2	366	95.8	0	.0
MALE	2	.3	15	2.3	1	.2	1	.2	19	2.9	644	97.1	0	.0
TOTAL ENROLLMENT:														
TOTAL	23	.2	604	5.0	59	.5	16	.1	702	5.8	11,199	92.9	154	1.3
FEMALE	6	.1	242	5.8	15	.4	5	.1	268	6.4	3,900	92.8	35	.8
MALE	17	.2	362	4.6	44	.6	11	.1	434	5.5	7,299	93.0	119	1.5
WISCONSIN (39 INSTITUTIONS)														
UNDERGRADUATES:														
FULL-TIME	60	.3	574	2.9	73	.4	102	.5	809	4.0	18,927	94.7	253	1.3
FEMALE	34	.5	282	3.9	33	.5	31	.4	380	5.2	6,802	93.7	78	1.1
MALE	26	.2	292	2.3	40	.3	71	.6	429	3.4	12,125	95.3	175	1.4
PART-TIME	10	.2	195	4.0	18	.4	36	.7	259	5.4	4,548	94.3	16	.3
FEMALE	3	.2	75	3.9	8	.4	12	.6	98	5.1	1,813	94.7	4	.2
MALE	7	.2	120	4.1	10	.3	24	.8	161	5.5	2,735	94.1	12	.4
TOTAL	70	.3	769	3.1	91	.4	138	.6	1,068	4.3	23,475	94.6	269	1.1
FEMALE	37	.4	357	3.9	41	.4	43	.5	478	5.2	8,615	93.9	82	.9
MALE	33	.2	412	2.6	50	.3	95	.6	590	3.8	14,860	95.0	187	1.2
GRADUATE:														
FULL-TIME	2	.3	37	4.7	9	1.1	9	1.1	57	7.2	606	77.0	124	15.8
FEMALE	1	.5	21	10.3	2	1.0	1	.5	25	12.3	158	77.8	20	9.9
MALE	1	.2	16	2.7	7	1.2	8	1.4	32	5.5	448	76.7	104	17.8
PART-TIME	0	.0	20	1.1	20	1.1	11	.6	51	2.8	1,752	96.0	22	1.2
FEMALE	0	.0	5	1.4	2	.6	1	.3	8	2.3	337	96.0	6	1.7
MALE	0	.0	15	1.0	18	1.2	10	.7	43	2.9	1,415	96.0	16	1.1
TOTAL	2	.1	57	2.2	29	1.1	20	.8	108	4.1	2,358	90.3	146	5.6
FEMALE	1	.2	26	4.7	4	.7	2	.4	33	6.0	495	89.4	26	4.7
MALE	1	.0	31	1.5	25	1.2	18	.9	75	3.6	1,863	90.5	120	5.8
PROFESSIONAL:														
FULL-TIME	0	.0	0	.0	0	.0	0	.0	0	.0	0	.0	0	.0
FEMALE	0	.0	0	.0	0	.0	0	.0	0	.0	0	.0	0	.0
MALE	0	.0	0	.0	0	.0	0	.0	0	.0	0	.0	0	.0

ROLLMENT IN INSTITUTIONS OF HIGHER EDUCATION FOR SELECTED MAJOR FIELDS OF STUDY AND LEVEL OF ENROLLMENT ETHNICITY, AND SEX: STATE, 1978

BUSINESS AND MANAGEMENT

INDIAN NATIVE	BLACK NON-HISPANIC		ASIAN OR PACIFIC ISLANDER		HISPANIC		TOTAL MINORITY		WHITE NON-HISPANIC		NON-RESIDENT ALIEN		TOTAL
%	NUMBER	%	NUMBER	%	NUMBER	%	NUMBER	%	NUMBER	%	NUMBER	%	NUMBER
CONTINUED													
.0	0	.0	0	.0	0	.0	0	.0	0	.0	0	.0	0
.0	0	.0	0	.0	0	.0	0	.0	0	.0	0	.0	0
.0	0	.0	0	.0	0	.0	0	.0	0	.0	0	.0	0
.0	0	.0	0	.0	0	.0	0	.0	0	.0	0	.0	0
.0	0	.0	0	.0	0	.0	0	.0	0	.0	0	.0	0
.0	0	.0	0	.0	0	.0	0	.0	0	.0	0	.0	0
.3	611	2.9	82	.4	111	.5	866	4.2	19,533	94.0	377	1.8	20,776
.5	303	4.1	35	.5	32	.4	405	5.4	6,960	93.3	98	1.3	7,463
.2	308	2.3	47	.4	79	.6	461	3.5	12,573	94.4	279	2.1	13,313
.2	215	3.2	38	.6	47	.7	310	4.7	6,300	94.8	38	.6	6,648
.1	80	3.5	10	.4	13	.6	106	4.7	2,150	94.9	10	.4	2,266
.2	135	3.1	28	.6	34	.8	204	4.7	4,150	94.7	28	.6	4,382
.3	826	3.0	120	.4	158	.6	1,176	4.3	25,833	94.2	415	1.5	27,424
.4	383	3.9	45	.5	45	.5	511	5.3	9,110	93.6	108	1.1	9,729
.2	443	2.5	75	.4	113	.6	665	3.8	16,723	94.5	307	1.7	17,695
.5	39	5.3	4	.5	5	.7	52	7.1	663	90.8	15	2.1	730
.7	23	8.3	2	.7	2	.7	29	10.5	244	88.4	3	1.1	276
.4	16	3.5	2	.4	3	.7	23	5.1	419	92.3	12	2.6	454
.3	865	3.1	124	.4	163	.6	1,228	4.4	26,496	94.1	430	1.5	28,154
.4	406	4.1	47	.5	47	.5	540	5.4	9,354	93.5	111	1.1	10,005
.2	459	2.5	77	.4	116	.6	688	3.8	17,142	94.5	319	1.8	18,149
(6 INSTITUTIONS)													
.4	24	1.7	11	.8	33	2.4	74	5.4	1,259	91.8	39	2.8	1,372
1.1	4	.8	8	1.5	15	2.8	33	6.2	493	92.7	6	1.1	532
.0	20	2.4	3	.4	18	2.1	41	4.9	766	91.2	33	3.9	840
.0	3	1.0	0	.0	13	4.3	16	5.3	283	94.0	2	.7	301
.0	1	.5	0	.0	10	5.0	11	5.4	191	94.6	0	.0	202
.0	2	2.0	0	.0	3	3.0	5	5.1	92	92.9	2	2.0	99
.4	21	1.6	11	.7	46	2.7	90	5.4	1,542	92.2	41	2.5	1,673
.8	5	.7	8	1.1	25	3.4	44	6.0	684	93.2	6	.8	734
.0	22	2.3	3	.3	21	2.2	46	4.9	858	91.4	35	3.7	939
.0	0	.0	0	.0	0	.0	0	.0	51	81.0	12	19.0	63
.0	0	.0	0	.0	0	.0	0	.0	15	93.8	1	6.3	16
.0	0	.0	0	.0	0	.0	0	.0	36	76.6	11	23.4	47
.0	0	.0	0	.0	0	.0	0	.0	35	94.6	2	5.4	37
.0	0	.0	0	.0	0	.0	0	.0	5	83.3	1	16.7	6
.0	0	.0	0	.0	0	.0	0	.0	30	96.8	1	3.2	31
.0	0	.0	0	.0	0	.0	0	.0	86	86.0	14	14.0	100
.0	0	.0	0	.0	0	.0	0	.0	20	90.9	2	9.1	22
.0	0	.0	0	.0	0	.0	0	.0	66	84.6	12	15.4	78
.0	0	.0	0	.0	0	.0	0	.0	0	.0	0	.0	0
.0	0	.0	0	.0	0	.0	0	.0	0	.0	0	.0	0
.0	0	.0	0	.0	0	.0	0	.0	0	.0	0	.0	0
.0	0	.0	0	.0	0	.0	0	.0	0	.0	0	.0	0
.0	0	.0	0	.0	0	.0	0	.0	0	.0	0	.0	0
.0	0	.0	0	.0	0	.0	0	.0	0	.0	0	.0	0
.0	0	.0	0	.0	0	.0	0	.0	0	.0	0	.0	0
.0	0	.0	0	.0	0	.0	0	.0	0	.0	0	.0	0
.0	0	.0	0	.0	0	.0	0	.0	0	.0	0	.0	0
.4	24	1.7	11	.8	33	2.3	74	5.2	1,310	91.3	51	3.6	1,435
1.1	4	.7	8	1.5	15	2.7	33	6.0	508	92.7	7	1.3	548
.0	20	2.3	3	.3	18	2.0	41	4.6	802	90.4	44	5.0	887
.0	3	.9	0	.0	13	3.8	16	4.7	318	94.1	4	1.2	338
.0	1	.5	0	.0	10	4.8	11	5.3	196	94.2	1	.5	208
.0	2	1.5	0	.0	3	2.3	5	3.8	122	93.8	3	2.3	130
.3	27	1.5	11	.6	46	2.6	90	5.1	1,628	91.8	55	3.1	1,773
.8	5	.7	8	1.1	25	3.3	44	5.8	704	93.1	8	1.1	756
.0	22	2.2	3	.3	21	2.1	46	4.5	924	90.9	47	4.6	1,017
.0	0	.0	0	.0	0	.0	0	.0	14	93.3	1	6.7	15
.0	0	.0	0	.0	0	.0	0	.0	6	100.0	0	.0	6
.0	0	.0	0	.0	0	.0	0	.0	8	88.9	1	11.1	9
.3	27	1.5	11	.6	46	2.6	90	5.0	1,642	91.8	56	3.1	1,788
.8	5	.7	8	1.0	25	3.3	44	5.8	710	93.2	8	1.0	762
.0	22	2.1	3	.3	21	2.0	46	4.5	932	90.8	48	4.7	1,026

TABLE 17 - TOTAL ENROLLMENT IN INSTITUTIONS OF HIGHER EDUCATION FOR SELECTED MAJOR FIELDS OF STUDY AND LEVEL OF ENROLLMENT BY RACE, ETHNICITY, AND SEX: STATE, 1978

MAJOR FIELD 0500 - BUSINESS AND MANAGEMENT

	AMERICAN INDIAN ALASKAN NATIVE		BLACK NON-HISPANIC		ASIAN OR PACIFIC ISLANDER		HISPANIC		TOTAL MINORITY		WHITE NON-HISPANIC		NON-RESIDENT ALIEN	
	NUMBER	%	NUMBER	%	NUMBER	%	NUMBER	%	NUMBER	%	NUMBER	%	NUMBER	%
THE STATES AND D.C. (1,941 INSTITUTIONS)														
UNDERGRADUATES:														
FULL-TIME	3,909	.4	95,343	10.9	12,918	1.5	21,477	2.5	133,647	15.3	719,971	82.6	17,984	2.1
FEMALE	1,832	.6	49,650	14.9	6,071	1.8	9,145	2.8	66,698	20.1	260,494	78.4	5,098	1.5
MALE	2,377	.4	45,693	8.5	6,847	1.3	12,332	2.3	66,949	12.4	459,477	85.2	12,886	2.4
PART-TIME	2,278	.6	38,908	10.5	6,977	1.9	15,189	4.1	63,352	17.1	303,962	82.1	3,089	.8
FEMALE	1,213	.7	21,282	12.2	3,257	1.9	7,241	4.2	32,993	18.9	140,187	80.4	1,232	.7
MALE	1,065	.5	17,626	9.0	3,720	1.9	7,948	4.1	30,359	15.5	163,775	83.6	1,857	.9
TOTAL	6,187	.5	134,251	10.8	19,895	1.6	36,666	3.0	196,999	15.9	1,023,933	82.4	21,073	1.7
FEMALE	3,045	.6	70,932	14.0	9,328	1.8	16,386	3.2	99,691	19.7	400,681	79.1	6,330	1.2
MALE	3,142	.4	63,319	8.6	10,567	1.4	20,280	2.8	97,308	13.2	623,252	84.8	14,743	2.0
GRADUATE:														
FULL-TIME	153	.3	2,396	4.2	1,369	2.4	764	1.3	4,682	8.2	44,420	78.1	7,746	13.6
FEMALE	46	.3	865	6.1	413	2.9	179	1.3	1,503	10.6	11,397	80.5	1,255	8.9
MALE	107	.3	1,531	3.6	956	2.2	585	1.4	3,179	7.4	33,023	77.3	6,491	15.2
PART-TIME	272	.2	4,703	4.1	2,507	2.2	1,434	1.2	8,916	7.7	103,253	89.5	3,141	2.7
FEMALE	72	.2	1,627	5.6	673	2.3	334	1.2	2,706	9.4	25,565	88.5	615	2.1
MALE	200	.2	3,076	3.6	1,834	2.1	1,100	1.3	6,210	7.2	77,688	89.9	2,526	2.9
TOTAL	425	.2	7,099	4.1	3,876	2.3	2,198	1.3	13,598	7.9	147,673	85.8	10,887	6.3
FEMALE	118	.3	2,492	5.8	1,086	2.5	513	1.2	4,209	9.8	36,962	85.9	1,870	4.3
MALE	307	.2	4,607	3.6	2,790	2.2	1,685	1.3	9,389	7.3	110,711	85.7	9,017	7.0
PROFESSIONAL:														
FULL-TIME	0	.0	0	.0	1	.3	0	.0	1	.3	333	98.8	3	.9
FEMALE	0	.0	0	.0	1	.8	0	.0	1	.8	124	99.2	0	.0
MALE	0	.0	0	.0	0	.0	0	.0	0	.0	209	98.6	3	1.4
PART-TIME	0	.0	0	.0	0	.0	0	.0	0	.0	2	66.7	1	33.3
FEMALE	0	.0	0	.0	0	.0	0	.0	0	.0	0	.0	1	100.0
MALE	0	.0	0	.0	0	.0	0	.0	0	.0	2	100.0	0	.0
TOTAL	0	.0	0	.0	1	.3	0	.0	1	.3	335	98.5	4	1.2
FEMALE	0	.0	0	.0	1	.8	0	.0	1	.8	124	98.4	1	.8
MALE	0	.0	0	.0	0	.0	0	.0	0	.0	211	98.6	3	1.4
UNG+GRAD+PROF:														
FULL-TIME	4,062	.4	97,739	10.5	14,288	1.5	22,241	2.4	138,330	14.9	764,724	82.3	25,733	2.8
FEMALE	1,878	.5	50,515	14.6	6,485	1.9	9,324	2.7	68,202	19.7	272,015	78.5	6,353	1.8
MALE	2,184	.4	47,224	8.1	7,803	1.3	12,917	2.2	70,128	12.0	492,709	84.6	19,380	3.3
PART-TIME	2,550	.5	43,611	9.0	9,484	2.0	16,623	3.4	72,268	14.9	407,217	83.6	6,231	1.3
FEMALE	1,285	.6	22,909	11.3	3,930	1.9	7,575	3.7	35,699	17.6	165,752	81.5	1,848	.9
MALE	1,265	.4	20,702	7.3	5,554	2.0	9,048	3.2	36,569	12.9	241,465	85.5	4,383	1.6
TOTAL	6,612	.5	141,350	10.0	23,772	1.7	38,864	2.7	210,598	14.9	1,171,941	82.9	31,964	2.3
FEMALE	3,163	.6	73,424	13.4	10,415	1.9	16,899	3.1	103,901	18.9	437,767	79.6	8,201	1.5
MALE	3,449	.4	67,926	7.9	13,357	1.5	21,965	2.5	106,697	12.3	734,174	84.9	23,763	2.7
UNCLASSIFIED:														
TOTAL	383	.7	5,013	8.6	1,565	2.7	2,158	3.7	9,119	15.6	47,800	82.0	1,381	2.4
FEMALE	203	.8	2,687	10.7	692	2.8	863	3.4	4,445	17.7	20,258	80.7	408	1.6
MALE	180	.5	2,326	7.0	873	2.6	1,295	3.9	4,674	14.1	27,542	83.0	973	2.9
TOTAL ENROLLMENT:														
TOTAL	6,995	.5	146,363	9.9	25,337	1.7	41,022	2.8	219,717	14.9	1,219,741	82.8	33,345	2.3
FEMALE	3,366	.6	76,111	13.2	11,107	1.9	17,762	3.1	108,346	18.8	458,025	79.7	8,609	1.5
MALE	3,629	.4	70,252	7.8	14,230	1.6	23,260	2.6	111,371	12.4	761,716	84.8	24,736	2.8
AMERICAN SAMOA (1 INSTITUTIONS)														
UNDERGRADUATES:														
FULL-TIME	0	.0	0	.0	81	97.6	0	.0	81	97.6	2	2.4	0	.0
FEMALE	0	.0	0	.0	47	95.9	0	.0	47	95.9	2	4.1	0	.0
MALE	0	.0	0	.0	34	100.0	0	.0	34	100.0	0	.0	0	.0
PART-TIME	0	.0	1	.9	111	96.5	0	.0	112	97.4	3	2.6	0	.0
FEMALE	0	.0	1	1.2	78	96.3	0	.0	79	97.5	2	2.5	0	.0
MALE	0	.0	0	.0	33	97.1	0	.0	33	97.1	1	2.9	0	.0
TOTAL	0	.0	1	.5	192	97.0	0	.0	193	97.5	5	2.5	0	.0
FEMALE	0	.0	1	.8	125	96.2	0	.0	126	96.9	4	3.1	0	.0
MALE	0	.0	0	.0	67	98.5	0	.0	67	98.5	1	1.5	0	.0
GRADUATE:														
FULL-TIME	0	.0	0	.0	0	.0	0	.0	0	.0	0	.0	0	.0
FEMALE	0	.0	0	.0	0	.0	0	.0	0	.0	0	.0	0	.0
MALE	0	.0	0	.0	0	.0	0	.0	0	.0	0	.0	0	.0
PART-TIME	0	.0	0	.0	0	.0	0	.0	0	.0	0	.0	0	.0
FEMALE	0	.0	0	.0	0	.0	0	.0	0	.0	0	.0	0	.0
MALE	0	.0	0	.0	0	.0	0	.0	0	.0	0	.0	0	.0
TOTAL	0	.0	0	.0	0	.0	0	.0	0	.0	0	.0	0	.0
FEMALE	0	.0	0	.0	0	.0	0	.0	0	.0	0	.0	0	.0
MALE	0	.0	0	.0	0	.0	0	.0	0	.0	0	.0	0	.0
PROFESSIONAL:														
FULL-TIME	0	.0	0	.0	0	.0	0	.0	0	.0	0	.0	0	.0
FEMALE	0	.0	0	.0	0	.0	0	.0	0	.0	0	.0	0	.0
MALE	0	.0	0	.0	0	.0	0	.0	0	.0	0	.0	0	.0

BUSINESS AND MANAGEMENT

INDIAN NATIVE	BLACK NON-HISPANIC		ASIAN OR PACIFIC ISLANDER		HISPANIC		TOTAL MINORITY		WHITE NON-HISPANIC		NON-RESIDENT ALIEN		TOTAL
%	NUMBER	%	NUMBER	%	NUMBER	%	NUMBER	%	NUMBER	%	NUMBER	%	NUMBER
CONTINUED													
.0	0	.0	0	.0	0	.0	0	.0	0	.0	0	.0	0
.0	0	.0	0	.0	0	.0	0	.0	0	.0	0	.0	0
.0	0	.0	0	.0	0	.0	0	.0	0	.0	0	.0	0
.0	0	.0	0	.0	0	.0	0	.0	0	.0	0	.0	0
.0	0	.0	0	.0	0	.0	0	.0	0	.0	0	.0	0
.0	0	.0	0	.0	0	.0	0	.0	0	.0	0	.0	0
.0	0	.0	81	97.6	0	.0	81	97.6	2	2.4	0	.0	83
.0	0	.0	47	95.9	0	.0	47	95.9	2	4.1	0	.0	49
.0	0	.0	34	100.0	0	.0	34	100.0	0	.0	0	.0	34
.0	1	.9	111	96.5	0	.0	112	97.4	3	2.6	0	.0	115
.0	1	1.2	78	96.3	0	.0	79	97.5	2	2.5	0	.0	81
.0	0	.0	33	97.1	0	.0	33	97.1	1	2.9	0	.0	34
.0	1	.5	192	97.0	0	.0	193	97.5	5	2.5	0	.0	198
.0	1	.8	125	96.2	0	.0	126	96.9	4	3.1	0	.0	130
.0	0	.0	67	98.5	0	.0	67	98.5	1	1.5	0	.0	68
.0	0	.0	0	.0	0	.0	0	.0	0	.0	0	.0	0
.0	0	.0	0	.0	0	.0	0	.0	0	.0	0	.0	0
.0	0	.0	0	.0	0	.0	0	.0	0	.0	0	.0	0
.0	1	.5	192	97.0	0	.0	193	97.5	5	2.5	0	.0	198
.0	1	.8	125	96.2	0	.0	126	96.9	4	3.1	0	.0	130
.0	0	.0	67	98.5	0	.0	67	98.5	1	1.5	0	.0	68
(1 INSTITUTIONS)													
.0	0	.0	202	67.6	7	2.3	209	69.9	31	10.4	59	19.7	299
.0	0	.0	125	78.1	2	1.3	127	79.4	11	6.9	22	13.8	160
.0	0	.0	77	55.4	5	3.6	82	59.0	20	14.4	37	26.6	139
.9	2	1.8	84	74.3	2	1.8	89	78.8	21	18.6	3	2.7	113
1.8	1	2.3	34	79.1	1	2.3	36	83.7	6	14.0	1	2.3	43
1.4	1	1.4	50	71.4	1	1.4	53	75.7	15	21.4	2	2.9	70
.2	2	.5	286	69.4	9	2.2	298	72.3	52	12.6	62	15.0	412
.0	1	.5	159	78.3	3	1.5	163	80.3	17	8.4	23	11.3	203
.5	1	.5	127	60.8	6	2.9	135	64.6	35	16.7	39	18.7	209
.0	0	.0	1	100.0	0	.0	1	100.0	0	.0	0	.0	1
.0	0	.0	0	.0	0	.0	0	.0	0	.0	0	.0	0
.0	0	.0	1	100.0	0	.0	1	100.0	0	.0	0	.0	1
.0	0	.0	2	40.0	1	20.0	3	60.0	2	40.0	0	.0	5
.0	0	.0	0	.0	1	100.0	1	100.0	0	.0	0	.0	1
.0	0	.0	2	50.0	0	.0	2	50.0	2	50.0	0	.0	4
.0	0	.0	3	50.0	1	16.7	4	66.7	2	33.3	0	.0	6
.0	0	.0	0	.0	1	100.0	1	100.0	0	.0	0	.0	1
.0	0	.0	3	60.0	0	.0	3	60.0	2	40.0	0	.0	5
.0	0	.0	0	.0	0	.0	0	.0	0	.0	0	.0	0
.0	0	.0	0	.0	0	.0	0	.0	0	.0	0	.0	0
.0	0	.0	0	.0	0	.0	0	.0	0	.0	0	.0	0
.0	0	.0	0	.0	0	.0	0	.0	0	.0	0	.0	0
.0	0	.0	0	.0	0	.0	0	.0	0	.0	0	.0	0
.0	0	.0	0	.0	0	.0	0	.0	0	.0	0	.0	0
.0	0	.0	0	.0	0	.0	0	.0	0	.0	0	.0	0
.0	0	.0	0	.0	0	.0	0	.0	0	.0	0	.0	0
.0	0	.0	0	.0	0	.0	0	.0	0	.0	0	.0	0
.0	0	.0	203	67.7	7	2.3	210	70.0	31	10.3	59	19.7	300
.0	0	.0	125	78.1	2	1.3	127	79.4	11	6.9	22	13.8	160
.0	0	.0	78	55.7	5	3.6	83	59.3	20	14.3	37	26.4	140
.8	2	1.7	86	72.9	3	2.5	92	78.0	23	19.5	3	2.5	118
.0	1	2.3	34	77.3	2	4.5	37	84.1	6	13.6	1	2.3	44
1.4	1	1.4	52	70.3	1	1.4	55	74.3	17	23.0	2	2.7	74
.2	2	.5	289	69.1	10	2.4	302	72.2	54	12.9	62	14.8	418
.0	1	.5	159	77.9	4	2.0	164	80.4	17	8.3	23	11.3	204
.5	1	.5	130	60.7	6	2.8	138	64.5	37	17.3	39	18.2	214
.0	0	.0	0	.0	0	.0	0	.0	0	.0	0	.0	0
.0	0	.0	0	.0	0	.0	0	.0	0	.0	0	.0	0
.0	0	.0	0	.0	0	.0	0	.0	0	.0	0	.0	0
.2	2	.5	289	69.1	10	2.4	302	72.2	54	12.9	62	14.8	418
.0	1	.5	159	77.9	4	2.0	164	80.4	17	8.3	23	11.3	204
.5	1	.5	130	60.7	6	2.8	138	64.5	37	17.3	39	18.2	214

TABLE 17 - TOTAL ENROLLMENT IN INSTITUTIONS OF HIGHER EDUCATION FOR SELECTED MAJOR FIELDS OF STUDY AND LEVEL OF ENROLLMENT BY RACE, ETHNICITY, AND SEX: STATE, 1978

MAJOR FIELD 0500 - BUSINESS AND MANAGEMENT

	AMERICAN INDIAN ALASKAN NATIVE		BLACK NON-HISPANIC		ASIAN OR PACIFIC ISLANDER		HISPANIC		TOTAL MINORITY		WHITE NON-HISPANIC		NON-RESIDENT ALIEN	
	NUMBER	%	NUMBER	%	NUMBER	%	NUMBER	%	NUMBER	%	NUMBER	%	NUMBER	%
PUERTO RICO	(28 INSTITUTIONS)													
UNDERGRADUATES:														
FULL-TIME	0	.0	0	.0	1	.0	25,866	99.6	25,867	99.6	75	.3	21	.1
FEMALE	0	.0	0	.0	1	.0	12,071	99.7	12,072	99.7	32	.2	12	.1
MALE	0	.0	0	.0	0	.0	12,995	99.6	12,995	99.6	43	.3	9	.1
PART-TIME	0	.0	0	.0	0	.0	4,789	99.6	4,789	99.6	19	.4	0	.0
FEMALE	0	.0	0	.0	0	.0	2,079	99.6	2,079	99.6	8	.4	0	.0
MALE	0	.0	0	.0	0	.0	2,710	99.6	2,710	99.6	11	.4	0	.0
TOTAL	0	.0	0	.0	1	.0	30,655	99.6	30,656	99.6	94	.3	21	.1
FEMALE	0	.0	0	.0	1	.0	14,950	99.6	14,951	99.7	40	.3	12	.1
MALE	0	.0	0	.0	0	.0	15,705	99.6	15,705	99.6	54	.3	9	.1
GRADUATE:														
FULL-TIME	0	.0	0	.0	0	.0	124	97.6	124	97.6	0	.0	3	2.4
FEMALE	0	.0	0	.0	0	.0	45	100.0	45	100.0	0	.0	0	.0
MALE	0	.0	0	.0	0	.0	79	96.3	79	96.3	0	.0	3	3.7
PART-TIME	0	.0	0	.0	0	.0	488	99.4	488	99.4	1	.2	2	.4
FEMALE	0	.0	0	.0	0	.0	139	100.0	139	100.0	0	.0	0	.0
MALE	0	.0	0	.0	0	.0	349	99.1	349	99.1	1	.3	2	.6
TOTAL	0	.0	0	.0	0	.0	612	99.0	612	99.0	1	.2	5	.8
FEMALE	0	.0	0	.0	0	.0	184	100.0	184	100.0	0	.0	0	.0
MALE	0	.0	0	.0	0	.0	428	98.6	428	98.6	1	.2	5	1.2
PROFESSIONAL:														
FULL-TIME	0	.0	0	.0	0	.0	0	.0	0	.0	0	.0	0	.0
FEMALE	0	.0	0	.0	0	.0	0	.0	0	.0	0	.0	0	.0
MALE	0	.0	0	.0	0	.0	0	.0	0	.0	0	.0	0	.0
PART-TIME	0	.0	0	.0	0	.0	0	.0	0	.0	0	.0	0	.0
FEMALE	0	.0	0	.0	0	.0	0	.0	0	.0	0	.0	0	.0
MALE	0	.0	0	.0	0	.0	0	.0	0	.0	0	.0	0	.0
TOTAL	0	.0	0	.0	0	.0	0	.0	0	.0	0	.0	0	.0
FEMALE	0	.0	0	.0	0	.0	0	.0	0	.0	0	.0	0	.0
MALE	0	.0	0	.0	0	.0	0	.0	0	.0	0	.0	0	.0
UND+GRAD+PROF:														
FULL-TIME	0	.0	0	.0	1	.0	25,990	99.6	25,991	99.6	75	.3	24	.1
FEMALE	0	.0	0	.0	1	.0	12,916	99.7	12,917	99.7	32	.2	12	.1
MALE	0	.0	0	.0	0	.0	13,074	99.6	13,074	99.6	43	.3	12	.1
PART-TIME	0	.0	0	.0	0	.0	5,277	99.6	5,277	99.6	20	.4	2	.0
FEMALE	0	.0	0	.0	0	.0	2,218	99.6	2,218	99.6	8	.4	0	.0
MALE	0	.0	0	.0	0	.0	3,059	99.5	3,059	99.5	12	.4	2	.1
TOTAL	0	.0	0	.0	1	.0	31,267	99.6	31,268	99.6	95	.3	26	.1
FEMALE	0	.0	0	.0	1	.0	15,134	99.7	15,135	99.7	40	.3	12	.1
MALE	0	.0	0	.0	0	.0	16,133	99.6	16,133	99.6	55	.3	14	.1
UNCLASSIFIED:														
TOTAL	0	.0	0	.0	0	.0	319	100.0	319	100.0	0	.0	0	.0
FEMALE	0	.0	0	.0	0	.0	142	100.0	142	100.0	0	.0	0	.0
MALE	0	.0	0	.0	0	.0	177	100.0	177	100.0	0	.0	0	.0
TOTAL ENROLLMENT:														
TOTAL	0	.0	0	.0	1	.0	31,586	99.6	31,587	99.6	95	.3	26	.1
FEMALE	0	.0	0	.0	1	.0	15,276	99.7	15,277	99.7	40	.3	12	.1
MALE	0	.0	0	.0	0	.0	16,310	99.6	16,310	99.6	55	.3	14	.1
TRUST TERRITORY	(1 INSTITUTIONS)													
UNDERGRADUATES:														
FULL-TIME	0	.0	0	.0	27	100.0	0	.0	27	100.0	0	.0	0	.0
FEMALE	0	.0	0	.0	10	100.0	0	.0	10	100.0	0	.0	0	.0
MALE	0	.0	0	.0	17	100.0	0	.0	17	100.0	0	.0	0	.0
PART-TIME	0	.0	0	.0	0	.0	0	.0	0	.0	0	.0	0	.0
FEMALE	0	.0	0	.0	0	.0	0	.0	0	.0	0	.0	0	.0
MALE	0	.0	0	.0	0	.0	0	.0	0	.0	0	.0	0	.0
TOTAL	0	.0	0	.0	27	100.0	0	.0	27	100.0	0	.0	0	.0
FEMALE	0	.0	0	.0	10	100.0	0	.0	10	100.0	0	.0	0	.0
MALE	0	.0	0	.0	17	100.0	0	.0	17	100.0	0	.0	0	.0
GRADUATE:														
FULL-TIME	0	.0	0	.0	0	.0	0	.0	0	.0	0	.0	0	.0
FEMALE	0	.0	0	.0	0	.0	0	.0	0	.0	0	.0	0	.0
MALE	0	.0	0	.0	0	.0	0	.0	0	.0	0	.0	0	.0
PART-TIME	0	.0	0	.0	0	.0	0	.0	0	.0	0	.0	0	.0
FEMALE	0	.0	0	.0	0	.0	0	.0	0	.0	0	.0	0	.0
MALE	0	.0	0	.0	0	.0	0	.0	0	.0	0	.0	0	.0
TOTAL	0	.0	0	.0	0	.0	0	.0	0	.0	0	.0	0	.0
FEMALE	0	.0	0	.0	0	.0	0	.0	0	.0	0	.0	0	.0
MALE	0	.0	0	.0	0	.0	0	.0	0	.0	0	.0	0	.0
PROFESSIONAL:														
FULL-TIME	0	.0	0	.0	0	.0	0	.0	0	.0	0	.0	0	.0
FEMALE	0	.0	0	.0	0	.0	0	.0	0	.0	0	.0	0	.0
MALE	0	.0	0	.0	0	.0	0	.0	0	.0	0	.0	0	.0

ROLLMENT IN INSTITUTIONS OF HIGHER EDUCATION FOR SELECTED MAJOR FIELDS OF STUDY AND LEVEL OF ENROLLMENT
ETHNICITY, AND SEX: STATE, 1978

BUSINESS AND MANAGEMENT

INDIAN NATIVE	BLACK NON-HISPANIC		ASIAN OR PACIFIC ISLANDER		HISPANIC		TOTAL MINORITY		WHITE NON-HISPANIC		NON-RESIDENT ALIEN		TOTAL
%	NUMBER	%	NUMBER	%	NUMBER	%	NUMBER	%	NUMBER	%	NUMBER	%	NUMBER

CONTINUED

.0	0	.0	0	.0	0	.0	0	.0	0	.0	0	.0	0
.0	0	.0	0	.0	0	.0	0	.0	0	.0	0	.0	0
.0	0	.0	0	.0	0	.0	0	.0	0	.0	0	.0	0
.0	0	.0	0	.0	0	.0	0	.0	0	.0	0	.0	0
.0	0	.0	0	.0	0	.0	0	.0	0	.0	0	.0	0
.0	0	.0	0	.0	0	.0	0	.0	0	.0	0	.0	0
.0	0	.0	27	100.0	0	.0	27	100.0	0	.0	0	.0	27
.0	0	.0	10	100.0	0	.0	10	100.0	0	.0	0	.0	10
.0	0	.0	17	100.0	0	.0	17	100.0	0	.0	0	.0	17
.0	0	.0	0	.0	0	.0	0	.0	0	.0	0	.0	0
.0	0	.0	0	.0	0	.0	0	.0	0	.0	0	.0	0
.0	0	.0	0	.0	0	.0	0	.0	0	.0	0	.0	0
.0	0	.0	27	100.0	0	.0	27	100.0	0	.0	0	.0	27
.0	0	.0	10	100.0	0	.0	10	100.0	0	.0	0	.0	10
.0	0	.0	17	100.0	0	.0	17	100.0	0	.0	0	.0	17
.0	0	.0	0	.0	0	.0	0	.0	0	.0	0	.0	0
.0	0	.0	0	.0	0	.0	0	.0	0	.0	0	.0	0
.0	0	.0	0	.0	0	.0	0	.0	0	.0	0	.0	0
.0	0	.0	27	100.0	0	.0	27	100.0	0	.0	0	.0	27
.0	0	.0	10	100.0	0	.0	10	100.0	0	.0	0	.0	10
.0	0	.0	17	100.0	0	.0	17	100.0	0	.0	0	.0	17

(1 INSTITUTIONS)

.0	87	60.8	0	.0	10	7.0	97	67.8	14	9.8	32	22.4	143
.0	63	63.6	0	.0	6	6.1	69	69.7	3	3.0	27	27.3	99
.0	24	54.5	0	.0	4	9.1	28	63.6	11	25.0	5	11.4	44
.0	0	.0	0	.0	0	.0	0	.0	0	.0	0	.0	0
.0	0	.0	0	.0	0	.0	0	.0	0	.0	0	.0	0
.0	0	.0	0	.0	0	.0	0	.0	0	.0	0	.0	0
.0	87	60.8	0	.0	10	7.0	97	67.8	14	9.8	32	22.4	143
.0	63	63.6	0	.0	6	6.1	69	69.7	3	3.0	27	27.3	99
.0	24	54.5	0	.0	4	9.1	28	63.6	11	25.0	5	11.4	44
.0	0	.0	0	.0	0	.0	0	.0	0	.0	0	.0	0
.0	0	.0	0	.0	0	.0	0	.0	0	.0	0	.0	0
.0	0	.0	0	.0	0	.0	0	.0	0	.0	0	.0	0
.0	19	65.5	1	3.4	1	3.4	21	72.4	6	20.7	2	6.9	29
.0	10	90.9	0	.0	0	.0	10	90.9	1	9.1	0	.0	11
.0	9	50.0	1	5.6	1	5.6	11	61.1	5	27.8	2	11.1	18
.0	19	65.5	1	3.4	1	3.4	21	72.4	6	20.7	2	6.9	29
.0	10	90.9	0	.0	0	.0	10	90.9	1	9.1	0	.0	11
.0	9	50.0	1	5.6	1	5.6	11	61.1	5	27.8	2	11.1	18
.0	0	.0	0	.0	0	.0	0	.0	0	.0	0	.0	0
.0	0	.0	0	.0	0	.0	0	.0	0	.0	0	.0	0
.0	0	.0	0	.0	0	.0	0	.0	0	.0	0	.0	0
.0	0	.0	0	.0	0	.0	0	.0	0	.0	0	.0	0
.0	0	.0	0	.0	0	.0	0	.0	0	.0	0	.0	0
.0	0	.0	0	.0	0	.0	0	.0	0	.0	0	.0	0
.0	0	.0	0	.0	0	.0	0	.0	0	.0	0	.0	0
.0	0	.0	0	.0	0	.0	0	.0	0	.0	0	.0	0
.0	0	.0	0	.0	0	.0	0	.0	0	.0	0	.0	0
.0	87	60.8	0	.0	10	7.0	97	67.8	14	9.8	32	22.4	143
.0	63	63.6	0	.0	6	6.1	69	69.7	3	3.0	27	27.3	99
.0	24	54.5	0	.0	4	9.1	28	63.6	11	25.0	5	11.4	44
.0	19	65.5	1	3.4	1	3.4	21	72.4	6	20.7	2	6.9	29
.0	10	90.9	0	.0	0	.0	10	90.9	1	9.1	0	.0	11
.0	9	50.0	1	5.6	1	5.6	11	61.1	5	27.8	2	11.1	18
.0	106	61.6	1	.6	11	6.4	118	68.6	20	11.6	34	19.8	172
.0	73	66.4	0	.0	6	5.5	79	71.8	4	3.6	27	24.5	110
.0	33	53.2	1	1.6	5	8.1	39	62.9	16	25.8	7	11.3	62
.0	0	.0	0	.0	0	.0	0	.0	0	.0	0	.0	0
.0	0	.0	0	.0	0	.0	0	.0	0	.0	0	.0	0
.0	0	.0	0	.0	0	.0	0	.0	0	.0	0	.0	0
.0	106	61.6	1	.6	11	6.4	118	68.6	20	11.6	34	19.8	172
.0	73	66.4	0	.0	6	5.5	79	71.8	4	3.6	27	24.5	110
.0	33	53.2	1	1.6	5	8.1	39	62.9	16	25.8	7	11.3	62

437

TABLE 17 - TOTAL ENROLLMENT IN INSTITUTIONS OF HIGHER EDUCATION FOR SELECTED MAJOR FIELDS OF STUDY AND LEVEL OF ENROLLMENT BY RACE, ETHNICITY, AND SEX: STATE, 1978

MAJOR FIELD 0500 - BUSINESS AND MANAGEMENT

	AMERICAN INDIAN ALASKAN NATIVE		BLACK NON-HISPANIC		ASIAN OR PACIFIC ISLANDER		HISPANIC		TOTAL MINORITY		WHITE NON-HISPANIC		NON-RESIDENT ALIEN	
	NUMBER	%	NUMBER	%	NUMBER	%	NUMBER	%	NUMBER	%	NUMBER	%	NUMBER	%
OUTLYING AREAS (32 INSTITUTIONS)														
UNDERGRADUATES:														
FULL-TIME	0	.0	87	.3	311	1.2	25,883	97.6	26,281	99.1	122	.5	112	.4
FEMALE	0	.0	63	.5	183	1.4	12,879	97.3	13,125	99.2	48	.4	61	.5
MALE	0	.0	24	.2	128	1.0	13,004	97.9	13,156	99.1	74	.6	51	.4
PART-TIME	1	.0	3	.1	195	3.9	4,791	95.1	4,990	99.1	43	.9	3	.1
FEMALE	0	.0	2	.1	112	5.1	2,080	94.1	2,194	99.2	16	.7	1	.0
MALE	1	.0	1	.0	83	2.9	2,711	96.0	2,796	99.0	27	1.0	2	.1
TOTAL	1	.0	9C	.3	506	1.6	30,674	97.2	31,271	99.1	165	.5	115	.4
FEMALE	0	.0	65	.4	295	1.9	14,959	96.9	15,319	99.2	64	.4	62	.4
MALE	1	.0	25	.2	211	1.3	15,715	97.6	15,952	99.0	101	.6	53	.3
GRADUATE:														
FULL-TIME	0	.0	0	.0	1	.8	124	96.9	125	97.7	0	.0	3	2.3
FEMALE	0	.0	0	.0	0	.0	45	100.0	45	100.0	0	.0	0	.0
MALE	0	.0	0	.0	1	1.2	79	95.2	80	96.4	0	.0	3	3.6
PART-TIME	0	.0	19	3.6	3	.6	490	93.3	512	97.5	9	1.7	4	.8
FEMALE	0	.0	10	6.6	0	.0	140	92.7	150	99.3	1	.7	0	.0
MALE	0	.0	9	2.4	3	.8	350	93.6	362	96.8	8	2.1	4	1.1
TOTAL	0	.0	19	2.9	4	.6	614	94.0	637	97.5	9	1.4	7	1.1
FEMALE	0	.0	10	5.1	0	.0	185	94.4	195	99.5	1	.5	0	.0
MALE	0	.0	9	2.0	4	.9	429	93.9	442	96.7	8	1.8	7	1.5
PROFESSIONAL:														
FULL-TIME	0	.0	0	.0	0	.0	0	.0	0	.0	0	.0	0	.0
FEMALE	0	.0	0	.0	0	.0	0	.0	0	.0	0	.0	0	.0
MALE	0	.0	0	.0	0	.0	0	.0	0	.0	0	.0	0	.0
PART-TIME	0	.0	0	.0	0	.0	0	.0	0	.0	0	.0	0	.0
FEMALE	0	.0	0	.0	0	.0	0	.0	0	.0	0	.0	0	.0
MALE	0	.0	0	.0	0	.0	0	.0	0	.0	0	.0	0	.0
TOTAL	0	.0	0	.0	0	.0	0	.0	0	.0	0	.0	0	.0
FEMALE	0	.0	0	.0	0	.0	0	.0	0	.0	0	.0	0	.0
MALE	0	.0	0	.0	0	.0	0	.0	0	.0	0	.0	0	.0
UND+GRAD+PROF:														
FULL-TIME	0	.0	87	.3	312	1.2	26,007	97.6	26,406	99.1	122	.5	115	.4
FEMALE	0	.0	63	.5	183	1.4	12,924	97.3	13,170	99.2	48	.4	61	.5
MALE	0	.0	24	.2	129	1.0	13,083	97.9	13,236	99.0	74	.6	54	.4
PART-TIME	1	.0	22	.4	198	3.6	5,281	95.0	5,502	98.9	52	.9	7	.1
FEMALE	0	.0	12	.4	112	4.7	2,220	94.0	2,344	99.2	17	.7	1	.0
MALE	1	.0	10	.3	86	2.7	3,061	95.7	3,158	98.7	35	1.1	6	.2
TOTAL	1	.0	109	.3	510	1.6	31,288	97.2	31,908	99.1	174	.5	122	.4
FEMALE	0	.0	75	.5	295	1.9	15,144	96.8	15,514	99.2	65	.4	62	.4
MALE	1	.0	34	.2	215	1.3	16,144	97.5	16,394	99.0	109	.7	60	.4
UNCLASSIFIED:														
TOTAL	0	.0	0	.0	0	.0	319	100.0	319	100.0	0	.0	0	.0
FEMALE	0	.0	0	.0	0	.0	142	100.0	142	100.0	0	.0	0	.0
MALE	0	.0	0	.0	0	.0	177	100.0	177	100.0	0	.0	0	.0
TOTAL ENROLLMENT:														
TOTAL	1	.0	109	.3	510	1.6	31,607	97.2	32,227	99.1	174	.5	122	.4
FEMALE	0	.0	75	.5	295	1.9	15,286	96.9	15,656	99.2	65	.4	62	.4
MALE	1	.0	34	.2	215	1.3	16,321	97.5	16,571	99.0	109	.7	60	.4

MAJOR FIELD AGGREGATE 0500 (1,973 INSTITUTIONS)

	AMERICAN INDIAN ALASKAN NATIVE		BLACK NON-HISPANIC		ASIAN OR PACIFIC ISLANDER		HISPANIC		TOTAL MINORITY		WHITE NON-HISPANIC		NON-RESIDENT ALIEN	
UNDERGRADUATES:														
FULL-TIME	3,909	.4	95,430	10.6	13,229	1.5	47,360	5.3	159,928	17.8	720,093	80.2	18,096	2.0
FEMALE	1,832	.5	49,713	14.4	6,254	1.8	22,024	6.4	79,823	23.1	260,542	75.4	5,159	1.5
MALE	2,077	.4	45,717	8.3	6,975	1.3	25,336	4.6	80,105	14.5	459,551	83.2	12,937	2.3
PART-TIME	2,279	.6	38,911	10.4	7,172	1.9	19,980	5.3	68,342	18.2	304,005	81.0	3,092	.8
FEMALE	1,213	.7	21,284	12.1	3,369	1.9	9,321	5.3	35,187	19.9	140,203	79.4	1,233	.7
MALE	1,066	.5	17,627	8.9	3,803	1.9	10,659	5.4	33,155	16.7	163,802	82.4	1,859	.9
TOTAL	6,188	.5	134,341	10.5	20,401	1.6	67,340	5.3	228,270	17.9	1,024,098	80.4	21,188	1.7 1
FEMALE	3,045	.6	70,997	13.6	9,623	1.8	31,345	6.0	115,010	22.0	400,745	76.7	6,392	1.2
MALE	3,143	.4	63,344	8.4	10,778	1.4	35,995	4.8	113,260	15.1	623,353	83.0	14,796	2.0
GRADUATE:														
FULL-TIME	153	.3	2,396	4.2	1,370	2.4	888	1.6	4,807	8.4	44,420	78.0	7,749	13.6
FEMALE	46	.3	865	6.1	413	2.9	224	1.6	1,548	10.9	11,397	80.3	1,255	8.8
MALE	107	.3	1,531	3.6	957	2.2	664	1.6	3,259	7.6	33,023	77.2	6,494	15.2
PART-TIME	272	.2	4,722	4.1	2,510	2.2	1,924	1.7	9,428	8.1	103,262	89.1	3,145	2.7
FEMALE	72	.2	1,637	5.6	673	2.3	474	1.6	2,856	9.8	25,566	88.0	615	2.1
MALE	200	.2	3,085	3.6	1,837	2.1	1,450	1.7	6,572	7.6	77,696	89.5	2,530	2.9
TOTAL	425	.2	7,118	4.1	3,880	2.2	2,812	1.6	14,235	8.2	147,682	85.5	10,894	6.3
FEMALE	118	.3	2,502	5.8	1,086	2.5	698	1.6	4,404	10.2	36,963	85.5	1,870	4.3
MALE	307	.2	4,616	3.6	2,794	2.2	2,114	1.6	9,831	7.6	110,719	85.4	9,024	7.0
PROFESSIONAL:														
FULL-TIME	0	.0	0	.0	1	.3	0	.0	1	.3	333	98.8	3	.9
FEMALE	0	.0	0	.0	1	.8	0	.0	1	.8	124	99.2	0	.0
MALE	0	.0	0	.0	0	.0	0	.0	0	.0	209	98.6	3	1.4

ROLLMENT IN INSTITUTIONS OF HIGHER EDUCATION FOR SELECTED MAJOR FIELDS OF STUDY AND LEVEL OF ENROLLMENT ETHNICITY, AND SEX: STATE: 1978

BUSINESS AND MANAGEMENT

INDIAN NATIVE	BLACK NON-HISPANIC		ASIAN OR PACIFIC ISLANDER		HISPANIC		TOTAL MINORITY		WHITE NON-HISPANIC		NON-RESIDENT ALIEN		TOTAL
%	NUMBER	%	NUMBER	%	NUMBER	%	NUMBER	%	NUMBER	%	NUMBER	%	NUMBER
E 0500 CONTINUED													
.0	0	.0	0	.0	0	.0	0	.0	2	66.7	1	33.3	3
.0	0	.0	0	.0	0	.0	0	.0	0	.0	1	100.0	1
.0	0	.0	0	.0	0	.0	0	.0	2	100.0	0	.0	2
.0	0	.0	1	.3	0	.0	1	.3	335	98.5	4	1.2	340
.0	0	.0	1	.8	0	.0	1	.8	124	98.4	1	.8	126
.0	0	.0	0	.0	0	.0	0	.0	211	98.6	3	1.4	214
.4	97,826	10.2	14,600	1.5	48,248	5.0	164,736	17.2	764,846	80.1	25,848	2.7	955,430
.5	50,578	14.1	6,668	1.9	22,248	6.2	81,372	22.6	272,063	75.6	6,414	1.8	359,849
.4	47,248	7.9	7,932	1.3	26,000	4.4	83,364	14.0	492,783	82.7	19,434	3.3	595,581
.5	43,633	8.9	9,682	2.0	21,904	4.5	77,770	15.8	407,269	82.9	6,230	1.3	491,277
.6	22,521	11.1	4,042	2.0	9,795	4.8	38,043	18.5	165,769	80.6	1,849	.9	205,661
.4	20,712	7.3	5,640	2.0	12,109	4.2	39,727	13.9	241,500	84.6	4,389	1.5	285,616
.5	141,459	9.8	24,282	1.7	70,152	4.8	242,506	16.8	1,172,115	81.0	32,086	2.2	1,446,707
.6	73,499	13.0	10,710	1.9	32,043	5.7	119,415	21.1	437,832	77.4	8,263	1.5	565,510
.4	67,960	7.7	13,572	1.5	38,109	4.3	123,091	14.0	734,283	83.3	23,823	2.7	881,197
.7	5,013	8.6	1,565	2.7	2,477	4.2	9,438	16.1	47,800	81.5	1,381	2.4	58,619
.8	2,687	10.6	692	2.7	1,005	4.0	4,587	18.2	20,258	80.2	408	1.6	25,253
.5	2,326	7.0	873	2.6	1,472	4.4	4,851	14.5	27,542	82.5	973	2.9	33,306
.5	146,472	9.7	25,847	1.7	72,629	4.8	251,944	16.7	1,219,915	81.0	33,467	2.2	1,505,326
.6	76,186	12.9	11,402	1.9	33,048	5.6	124,002	21.0	458,090	77.5	8,671	1.5	590,763
.4	70,286	7.7	14,445	1.6	39,581	4.3	127,942	14.0	761,825	83.3	24,796	2.7	914,563

TABLE 17 - TOTAL ENROLLMENT IN INSTITUTIONS OF HIGHER EDUCATION FOR SELECTED MAJOR FIELDS OF STUDY AND LEVEL OF ENROLLMENT BY RACE, ETHNICITY, AND SEX: STATE, 1978

MAJOR FIELD 0900 - ENGINEERING

	AMERICAN INDIAN ALASKAN NATIVE		BLACK NON-HISPANIC		ASIAN OR PACIFIC ISLANDER		HISPANIC		TOTAL MINORITY		WHITE NON-HISPANIC		NON-RESIDENT ALIEN	
	NUMBER	%	NUMBER	%	NUMBER	%	NUMBER	%	NUMBER	%	NUMBER	%	NUMBER	%
ALABAMA	30 INSTITUTIONS)													
UNDERGRADUATES:														
FULL-TIME	8	.1	919	13.4	62	.9	42	.6	1,031	15.0	5,276	76.9	555	8.1
FEMALE	2	.3	186	24.7	5	.7	3	.4	196	26.1	533	70.9	23	3.1
MALE	6	.1	733	12.0	57	.9	39	.6	835	13.7	4,743	77.6	532	8.7
PART-TIME	3	.2	78	5.4	17	1.2	5	.3	103	7.1	1,327	91.5	21	1.4
FEMALE	0	.0	14	10.5	7	5.3	1	.8	22	16.5	111	83.5	0	.0
MALE	3	.2	64	4.9	10	.8	4	.3	81	6.1	1,216	92.3	21	1.6
TOTAL	11	.1	997	12.0	79	1.0	47	.6	1,134	13.6	6,603	79.4	576	6.9
FEMALE	2	.2	200	22.6	12	1.4	4	.5	218	24.6	644	72.8	23	2.6
MALE	9	.1	797	10.7	67	.9	43	.6	916	12.3	5,959	80.2	553	7.4
GRADUATE:														
FULL-TIME	1	.5	3	1.4	11	5.3	1	.5	16	7.7	127	61.1	65	31.3
FEMALE	0	.0	0	.0	0	.0	0	.0	0	.0	10	90.9	1	9.1
MALE	1	.5	3	1.5	11	5.6	1	.5	16	8.1	117	59.4	64	32.5
PART-TIME	0	.0	4	1.5	13	4.8	2	.7	19	7.0	207	75.8	47	17.2
FEMALE	0	.0	0	.0	0	.0	0	.0	0	.0	17	85.0	3	15.0
MALE	0	.0	4	1.6	13	5.1	2	.8	19	7.5	190	75.1	44	17.4
TOTAL	1	.2	7	1.5	24	5.0	3	.6	35	7.3	334	69.4	112	23.3
FEMALE	0	.0	0	.0	0	.0	0	.0	0	.0	27	87.1	4	12.9
MALE	1	.2	7	1.6	24	5.3	3	.7	35	7.8	307	68.2	108	24.0
PROFESSIONAL:														
FULL-TIME	0	.0	0	.0	0	.0	0	.0	0	.0	0	.0	0	.0
FEMALE	0	.0	0	.0	0	.0	0	.0	0	.0	0	.0	0	.0
MALE	0	.0	0	.0	0	.0	0	.0	0	.0	0	.0	0	.0
PART-TIME	0	.0	0	.0	0	.0	0	.0	0	.0	0	.0	0	.0
FEMALE	0	.0	0	.0	0	.0	0	.0	0	.0	0	.0	0	.0
MALE	0	.0	0	.0	0	.0	0	.0	0	.0	0	.0	0	.0
TOTAL	0	.0	0	.0	0	.0	0	.0	0	.0	0	.0	0	.0
FEMALE	0	.0	0	.0	0	.0	0	.0	0	.0	0	.0	0	.0
MALE	0	.0	0	.0	0	.0	0	.0	0	.0	0	.0	0	.0
UND+GRAD+PROF:														
FULL-TIME	9	.1	922	13.0	73	1.0	43	.6	1,047	14.8	5,403	76.4	620	8.8
FEMALE	2	.3	186	24.4	5	.7	3	.4	196	25.7	543	71.2	24	3.1
MALE	7	.1	736	11.7	68	1.1	40	.6	851	13.5	4,860	77.1	596	9.4
PART-TIME	3	.2	82	4.8	30	1.7	7	.4	122	7.1	1,534	89.0	68	3.9
FEMALE	0	.0	14	9.2	7	4.6	1	.7	22	14.4	128	83.7	3	2.0
MALE	3	.2	68	4.3	23	1.5	6	.4	100	6.4	1,406	89.5	65	4.1
TOTAL	12	.1	1,004	11.4	103	1.2	50	.6	1,169	13.3	6,937	78.9	688	7.8
FEMALE	2	.2	200	21.8	12	1.3	4	.4	218	23.8	671	73.3	27	2.9
MALE	10	.1	804	10.2	91	1.2	46	.6	951	12.1	6,266	79.5	661	8.4
UNCLASSIFIED:														
TOTAL	0	.0	10	9.4	2	1.9	0	.0	12	11.3	89	84.0	5	4.7
FEMALE	0	.0	2	12.5	1	6.3	0	.0	3	18.8	13	81.3	0	.0
MALE	0	.0	8	8.9	1	1.1	0	.0	9	10.0	76	84.4	5	5.6
TOTAL ENROLLMENT:														
TOTAL	12	.1	1,014	11.4	105	1.2	50	.6	1,181	13.3	7,026	78.9	693	7.8
FEMALE	2	.2	202	21.7	13	1.4	4	.4	221	23.7	684	73.4	27	2.9
MALE	10	.1	812	10.2	92	1.2	46	.6	960	12.0	6,342	79.6	666	8.4
ALASKA	2 INSTITUTIONS)													
UNDERGRADUATES:														
FULL-TIME	9	4.1	3	1.4	10	4.5	1	.5	23	10.4	197	88.7	2	.9
FEMALE	0	.0	0	.0	0	.0	0	.0	0	.0	14	100.0	0	.0
MALE	9	4.3	3	1.4	10	4.8	1	.5	23	11.1	183	88.0	2	1.0
PART-TIME	1	1.5	3	4.4	3	4.4	0	.0	7	10.3	61	89.7	0	.0
FEMALE	0	.0	1	9.1	0	.0	0	.0	1	9.1	10	90.9	0	.0
MALE	1	1.8	2	3.5	3	5.3	0	.0	6	10.5	51	89.5	0	.0
TOTAL	10	3.4	6	2.1	13	4.5	1	.3	30	10.3	258	89.0	2	.7
FEMALE	0	.0	1	4.0	0	.0	0	.0	1	4.0	24	96.0	0	.0
MALE	10	3.8	5	1.9	13	4.9	1	.4	29	10.9	234	88.3	2	.8
GRADUATE:														
FULL-TIME	0	.0	1	6.7	1	6.7	0	.0	2	13.3	9	60.0	4	26.7
FEMALE	0	.0	0	.0	0	.0	0	.0	0	.0	1	100.0	0	.0
MALE	0	.0	1	7.1	1	7.1	0	.0	2	14.3	8	57.1	4	28.6
PART-TIME	0	.0	0	.0	1	2.6	0	.0	1	2.6	37	94.9	1	2.6
FEMALE	0	.0	0	.0	0	.0	0	.0	0	.0	1	100.0	0	.0
MALE	0	.0	0	.0	1	2.6	0	.0	1	2.6	36	94.7	1	2.6
TOTAL	0	.0	1	1.9	2	3.7	0	.0	3	5.6	46	85.2	5	9.3
FEMALE	0	.0	0	.0	0	.0	0	.0	0	.0	2	100.0	0	.0
MALE	0	.0	1	1.9	2	3.8	0	.0	3	5.8	44	84.6	5	9.6
PROFESSIONAL:														
FULL-TIME	0	.0	0	.0	0	.0	0	.0	0	.0	0	.0	0	.0
FEMALE	0	.0	0	.0	0	.0	0	.0	0	.0	0	.0	0	.0
MALE	0	.0	0	.0	0	.0	0	.0	0	.0	0	.0	0	.0

ENGINEERING

INDIAN NATIVE	BLACK NON-HISPANIC		ASIAN OR PACIFIC ISLANDER		HISPANIC		TOTAL MINORITY		WHITE NON-HISPANIC		NON-RESIDENT ALIEN		TOTAL
%	NUMBER	%	NUMBER	%	NUMBER	%	NUMBER	%	NUMBER	%	NUMBER	%	NUMBER

CONTINUED

INDIAN NATIVE	BLACK NON-HISPANIC		ASIAN OR PACIFIC ISLANDER		HISPANIC		TOTAL MINORITY		WHITE NON-HISPANIC		NON-RESIDENT ALIEN		TOTAL
.0	0	.0	0	.0	0	.0	0	.0	0	.0	0	.0	0
.0	0	.0	0	.0	0	.0	0	.0	0	.0	0	.0	0
.0	0	.0	0	.0	0	.0	0	.0	0	.0	0	.0	0
.0	0	.0	0	.0	0	.0	0	.0	0	.0	0	.0	0
.0	0	.0	0	.0	0	.0	0	.0	0	.0	0	.0	0
.0	0	.0	0	.0	0	.0	0	.0	0	.0	0	.0	0
3.8	4	1.7	11	4.6	1	.4	25	10.5	206	86.9	6	2.5	237
.0	0	.0	0	.0	0	.0	0	.0	15	100.0	0	.0	15
4.1	4	1.8	11	5.0	1	.5	25	11.3	191	86.0	6	2.7	222
.9	3	2.8	4	3.7	0	.0	8	7.5	98	91.6	1	.9	107
.0	1	8.3	0	.0	0	.0	1	8.3	11	91.7	0	.0	12
1.1	2	2.1	4	4.2	0	.0	7	7.4	87	91.6	1	1.1	95
2.9	7	2.0	15	4.4	1	.3	33	9.6	304	88.4	7	2.0	344
.0	1	3.7	0	.0	0	.0	1	3.7	26	96.3	0	.0	27
3.2	6	1.9	15	4.7	1	.3	32	10.1	278	87.7	7	2.2	317
2.3	1	2.3	2	4.7	0	.0	4	9.3	39	90.7	0	.0	43
.0	0	.0	0	.0	0	.0	0	.0	9	100.0	0	.0	9
2.9	1	2.9	2	5.9	0	.0	4	11.8	30	88.2	0	.0	34
2.8	8	2.1	17	4.4	1	.3	37	9.6	343	88.6	7	1.8	387
.0	1	2.8	0	.0	0	.0	1	2.8	35	97.2	0	.0	36
3.1	7	2.0	17	4.8	1	.3	36	10.3	308	87.7	7	2.0	351

(12 INSTITUTIONS)

INDIAN NATIVE	BLACK NON-HISPANIC		ASIAN OR PACIFIC ISLANDER		HISPANIC		TOTAL MINORITY		WHITE NON-HISPANIC		NON-RESIDENT ALIEN		TOTAL
1.4	70	1.3	103	2.0	276	5.3	523	10.0	4,182	80.1	514	9.8	5,219
1.0	12	2.5	17	3.6	27	5.7	61	12.8	398	83.4	18	3.8	477
1.5	58	1.2	86	1.8	249	5.3	462	9.7	3,784	79.8	496	10.5	4,742
.8	41	2.2	30	1.6	127	6.7	214	11.3	1,573	83.3	102	5.4	1,889
1.8	1	.6	3	1.8	9	5.3	16	9.4	148	86.5	7	4.1	171
.8	40	2.3	27	1.6	118	6.9	198	11.5	1,425	82.9	95	5.5	1,716
1.3	111	1.6	133	1.9	403	5.7	737	10.4	5,755	81.0	616	8.7	7,108
1.2	13	2.0	20	3.1	36	5.6	77	11.9	546	84.3	25	3.9	648
1.3	98	1.5	113	1.7	367	5.7	660	10.2	5,209	80.6	591	9.1	6,460
.0	0	.0	4	1.2	2	.6	6	1.8	236	69.6	97	28.6	339
.0	0	.0	1	3.3	1	3.3	2	6.7	24	80.0	4	13.3	30
.0	0	.0	3	1.0	1	.3	4	1.3	212	68.6	93	30.1	309
.6	6	1.2	20	3.9	10	1.9	39	7.6	408	79.2	68	13.2	515
.0	2	5.7	0	.0	0	.0	2	5.7	30	85.7	3	8.6	35
.6	4	.8	20	4.2	10	2.1	37	7.7	378	78.8	65	13.5	480
.4	6	.7	24	2.8	12	1.4	45	5.3	644	75.4	165	19.3	854
.0	2	3.1	1	1.5	1	1.5	4	6.2	54	83.1	7	10.8	65
.4	4	.5	23	2.9	11	1.4	41	5.2	590	74.8	158	20.0	789
.0	0	.0	0	.0	0	.0	0	.0	0	.0	0	.0	0
.0	0	.0	0	.0	0	.0	0	.0	0	.0	0	.0	0
.0	0	.0	0	.0	0	.0	0	.0	0	.0	0	.0	0
.0	0	.0	0	.0	0	.0	0	.0	0	.0	0	.0	0
.0	0	.0	0	.0	0	.0	0	.0	0	.0	0	.0	0
.0	0	.0	0	.0	0	.0	0	.0	0	.0	0	.0	0
.0	0	.0	0	.0	0	.0	0	.0	0	.0	0	.0	0
.0	0	.0	0	.0	0	.0	0	.0	0	.0	0	.0	0
.0	0	.0	0	.0	0	.0	0	.0	0	.0	0	.0	0
1.3	70	1.3	107	1.9	278	5.0	529	9.5	4,418	79.5	611	11.0	5,558
1.0	12	2.4	18	3.6	28	5.5	63	12.4	422	83.2	22	4.3	507
1.4	58	1.1	89	1.8	250	4.9	466	9.2	3,996	79.1	589	11.7	5,051
.8	47	2.0	50	2.1	137	5.7	253	10.5	1,981	82.4	170	7.1	2,404
1.5	3	1.5	3	1.5	9	4.4	18	8.7	178	86.4	10	4.9	206
.7	44	2.0	47	2.1	128	5.8	235	10.7	1,803	82.0	160	7.3	2,198
1.2	117	1.5	157	2.0	415	5.2	782	9.8	6,399	80.4	781	9.8	7,962
1.1	15	2.1	21	2.9	37	5.2	81	11.4	600	84.2	32	4.5	713
1.2	102	1.4	136	1.9	378	5.2	701	9.7	5,799	80.0	749	10.3	7,249
.0	0	.0	0	.0	1	2.6	1	2.6	32	82.1	6	15.4	39
.0	0	.0	0	.0	0	.0	0	.0	5	100.0	0	.0	5
.0	0	.0	0	.0	1	2.9	1	2.9	27	79.4	6	17.6	34
1.2	117	1.5	157	2.0	416	5.2	783	9.8	6,431	80.4	787	9.8	8,001
1.1	15	2.1	21	2.9	37	5.2	81	11.3	605	84.3	32	4.5	718
1.2	102	1.4	136	1.9	379	5.2	702	9.6	5,826	80.0	755	10.4	7,283

MAJOR FIELD 0900 - ENGINEERING

	AMERICAN INDIAN ALASKAN NATIVE		BLACK NON-HISPANIC		ASIAN OR PACIFIC ISLANDER		HISPANIC		TOTAL MINORITY		WHITE NON-HISPANIC		NON-RESIDENT ALIEN	
	NUMBER	%	NUMBER	%	NUMBER	%	NUMBER	%	NUMBER	%	NUMBER	%	NUMBER	%
ARKANSAS (13 INSTITUTIONS)														
UNDERGRADUATES:														
FULL-TIME	10	.5	111	6.1	37	2.0	10	.5	168	9.2	1,487	81.3	174	9.5
FEMALE	0	.0	16	11.5	1	.7	0	.0	17	12.2	116	83.5	6	4.3
MALE	10	.6	95	5.6	36	2.1	10	.6	151	8.9	1,371	81.1	168	9.9
PART-TIME	1	.6	11	6.7	4	2.4	0	.0	16	9.8	145	88.4	3	1.8
FEMALE	0	.0	0	.0	0	7.0	0	.0	0	.0	11	100.0	0	.0
MALE	1	.7	11	7.2	4	2.6	0	.0	16	10.5	134	87.6	3	2.0
TOTAL	11	.6	122	6.1	41	2.1	10	.5	184	9.2	1,632	81.9	177	8.9
FEMALE	0	.0	16	10.7	1	.7	0	.0	17	11.3	127	84.7	6	4.0
MALE	11	.6	106	5.8	40	2.2	10	.5	167	9.1	1,505	81.7	171	9.3
GRADUATE:														
FULL-TIME	3	2.7	1	.9	2	1.8	0	.0	6	5.5	63	57.3	41	37.3
FEMALE	0	.0	0	.0	0	.0	0	.0	0	.0	7	87.5	1	12.5
MALE	3	2.9	1	1.0	2	2.0	0	.0	6	5.9	56	54.9	40	39.2
PART-TIME	0	.0	0	.0	2	3.4	0	.0	2	3.4	53	89.8	4	6.8
FEMALE	0	.0	0	.0	0	.0	0	.0	0	.0	4	100.0	0	.0
MALE	0	.0	0	.0	2	3.6	0	.0	2	3.6	49	89.1	4	7.3
TOTAL	3	1.8	1	.6	4	2.4	0	.0	8	4.7	116	68.6	45	26.6
FEMALE	0	.0	0	.0	0	.0	0	.0	0	.0	11	91.7	1	8.3
MALE	3	1.9	1	.6	4	2.5	0	.0	8	5.1	105	66.9	44	28.0
PROFESSIONAL:														
FULL-TIME	0	.0	0	.0	0	.0	0	.0	0	.0	0	.0	0	.0
FEMALE	0	.0	0	.0	0	.0	0	.0	0	.0	0	.0	0	.0
MALE	0	.0	0	.0	0	.0	0	.0	0	.0	0	.0	0	.0
PART-TIME	0	.0	0	.0	0	.0	0	.0	0	.0	0	.0	0	.0
FEMALE	0	.0	0	.0	0	.0	0	.0	0	.0	0	.0	0	.0
MALE	0	.0	0	.0	0	.0	0	.0	0	.0	0	.0	0	.0
TOTAL	0	.0	0	.0	0	.0	0	.0	0	.0	0	.0	0	.0
FEMALE	0	.0	0	.0	0	.0	0	.0	0	.0	0	.0	0	.0
MALE	0	.0	0	.0	0	.0	0	.0	0	.0	0	.0	0	.0
UNG+GRAD+PROF:														
FULL-TIME	13	.7	112	5.8	39	2.0	10	.5	174	9.0	1,550	79.9	215	11.1
FEMALE	0	.0	16	10.9	1	.7	0	.0	17	11.6	123	83.7	7	4.8
MALE	13	.7	96	5.4	38	2.1	10	.6	157	8.8	1,427	79.6	208	11.6
PART-TIME	1	.4	11	4.9	6	2.7	0	.0	18	8.1	198	88.8	7	3.1
FEMALE	0	.0	0	.0	0	.0	0	.0	0	.0	15	100.0	0	.0
MALE	1	.5	11	5.3	6	2.9	0	.0	18	8.7	183	86.0	7	3.4
TOTAL	14	.6	123	5.7	45	2.1	10	.5	192	8.9	1,748	80.9	222	10.3
FEMALE	0	.0	16	9.9	1	.6	0	.0	17	10.5	138	85.2	7	4.3
MALE	14	.7	107	5.4	44	2.2	10	.5	175	8.8	1,610	80.5	215	10.8
UNCLASSIFIED:														
TOTAL	0	.0	3	6.5	7	15.2	1	2.2	11	23.9	32	69.6	3	6.5
FEMALE	0	.0	0	.0	0	.0	0	.0	0	.0	5	100.0	0	.0
MALE	0	.0	3	7.3	7	17.1	1	2.4	11	26.8	27	65.9	3	7.3
TOTAL ENROLLMENT:														
TOTAL	14	.6	126	5.7	52	2.4	11	.5	203	9.2	1,780	80.6	225	10.2
FEMALE	0	.0	16	9.6	1	.6	0	.0	17	10.2	143	85.6	7	4.2
MALE	14	.7	110	5.4	51	2.5	11	.5	186	9.1	1,637	80.2	218	10.7
CALIFORNIA (109 INSTITUTIONS)														
UNDERGRADUATES:														
FULL-TIME	264	.8	1,661	4.9	4,038	11.9	2,089	6.2	8,052	23.8	20,669	61.2	5,074	15.0
FEMALE	28	.8	247	7.3	526	15.5	207	6.1	1,008	29.6	2,100	61.8	292	8.6
MALE	236	.8	1,414	4.7	3,512	11.6	1,882	6.2	7,044	23.2	18,569	61.1	4,782	15.7
PART-TIME	229	1.3	1,367	7.7	1,525	8.4	1,619	9.0	4,760	26.3	12,238	67.7	1,070	5.9
FEMALE	24	1.5	165	10.5	119	7.5	102	6.5	410	26.0	1,121	71.1	46	2.9
MALE	205	1.2	1,222	7.4	1,406	8.5	1,517	9.2	4,350	26.4	11,117	67.4	1,024	6.2
TOTAL	493	1.0	3,048	5.9	5,563	10.7	3,708	7.1	12,812	24.7	32,907	63.4	6,144	11.8
FEMALE	52	1.0	412	8.3	645	13.0	309	6.2	1,418	28.5	3,221	64.7	338	6.8
MALE	441	.9	2,636	5.6	4,918	10.5	3,399	7.2	11,394	24.3	29,686	63.3	5,806	12.4
GRADUATE:														
FULL-TIME	6	.1	30	.7	336	7.4	56	1.2	428	9.4	2,260	50.0	1,851	40.6
FEMALE	1	.3	4	1.3	21	6.6	1	.3	27	8.4	200	62.5	93	29.1
MALE	5	.1	26	.6	315	7.4	55	1.3	401	9.5	2,080	49.1	1,758	41.5
PART-TIME	10	.3	65	1.7	562	15.1	100	2.7	737	19.8	2,073	55.6	919	24.6
FEMALE	1	.5	4	1.8	24	10.8	2	.9	31	14.0	151	68.0	40	18.0
MALE	9	.3	61	1.7	538	15.3	98	2.8	706	20.1	1,922	54.8	879	25.1
TOTAL	16	.2	95	1.1	898	10.8	156	1.9	1,165	14.1	4,353	52.5	2,770	33.4
FEMALE	2	.4	8	1.5	45	8.3	3	.6	58	10.7	351	64.8	133	24.5
MALE	14	.2	87	1.1	853	11.0	153	2.0	1,107	14.3	4,002	51.7	2,637	34.0
PROFESSIONAL:														
FULL-TIME	0	.0	0	.0	0	.0	0	.0	0	.0	0	.0	0	.0
FEMALE	0	.0	0	.0	0	.0	0	.0	0	.0	0	.0	0	.0
MALE	0	.0	0	.0	0	.0	0	.0	0	.0	0	.0	0	.0

ENGINEERING

INDIAN NATIVE %	BLACK NON-HISPANIC NUMBER	%	ASIAN OR PACIFIC ISLANDER NUMBER	%	HISPANIC NUMBER	%	TOTAL MINORITY NUMBER	%	WHITE NON-HISPANIC NUMBER	%	NON-RESIDENT ALIEN NUMBER	%	TOTAL NUMBER
CONTINUED													
.0	0	.0	0	.0	0	.0	0	.0	0	.0	0	.0	0
.0	0	.0	0	.0	0	.0	0	.0	0	.0	0	.0	0
.0	0	.0	0	.0	0	.0	0	.0	0	.0	0	.0	0
.0	0	.0	0	.0	0	.0	0	.0	0	.0	0	.0	0
.0	0	.0	0	.0	0	.0	0	.0	0	.0	0	.0	0
.0	0	.0	0	.0	0	.0	0	.0	0	.0	0	.0	0
.7	1,691	4.4	4,374	11.4	2,145	5.6	8,480	22.1	22,949	59.8	6,925	18.1	38,354
.8	251	6.7	547	14.7	208	5.6	1,035	27.8	2,300	61.8	385	10.3	3,720
.7	1,440	4.2	3,827	11.0	1,937	5.6	7,445	21.5	20,649	59.6	6,540	18.9	34,634
1.1	1,452	6.7	2,087	9.6	1,719	7.9	5,497	25.2	14,311	65.7	1,989	9.1	21,797
1.4	169	9.4	143	7.9	104	5.8	441	24.5	1,272	70.7	86	4.8	1,799
1.1	1,283	6.4	1,944	9.7	1,615	8.1	5,056	25.3	13,039	65.2	1,903	9.5	19,998
.8	3,143	5.2	6,461	10.7	3,864	6.4	13,977	23.2	37,260	61.9	8,914	14.8	60,151
1.0	420	7.6	690	12.5	312	5.7	1,476	26.7	3,572	64.7	471	8.5	5,519
.8	2,723	5.0	5,771	10.6	3,552	6.5	12,501	22.9	33,688	61.7	8,443	15.5	54,632
1.5	201	4.7	395	9.2	295	6.9	956	22.3	3,031	70.7	301	7.0	4,288
.9	31	6.7	32	6.9	21	4.5	88	19.0	360	77.6	16	3.4	464
1.6	170	4.4	363	9.5	274	7.2	868	22.7	2,671	69.8	285	7.5	3,824
.9	3,344	5.2	6,856	10.6	4,159	6.5	14,933	23.2	40,291	62.5	9,215	14.3	64,439
1.0	451	7.5	722	12.1	333	5.6	1,564	26.1	3,932	65.7	487	8.1	5,983
.9	2,893	4.9	6,134	10.5	3,826	6.5	13,369	22.9	36,359	62.2	8,728	14.9	58,456
(12 INSTITUTIONS)													
.3	48	.7	160	2.2	184	2.5	415	5.7	6,396	87.6	492	6.7	7,303
.2	6	.7	18	2.1	20	2.3	46	5.3	804	91.9	25	2.9	875
.3	42	.7	142	2.2	164	2.6	369	5.7	5,592	87.0	467	7.3	6,428
.8	23	2.2	17	1.6	44	4.2	92	8.8	928	88.6	27	2.6	1,047
2.2	2	2.2	4	4.4	0	.0	8	8.9	79	87.8	3	3.3	90
.6	21	2.2	13	1.4	44	4.6	84	8.8	849	88.7	24	2.5	957
.4	71	.9	177	2.1	228	2.7	507	6.1	7,324	87.7	519	6.2	8,350
.4	8	.8	22	2.3	20	2.1	54	5.6	883	91.5	28	2.9	965
.4	63	.9	155	2.1	208	2.8	453	6.1	6,441	87.2	491	6.6	7,385
.1	7	.8	8	1.0	5	.6	21	2.5	525	62.4	296	35.2	842
.0	1	2.0	0	.0	0	.0	1	2.0	38	77.6	10	20.4	49
.1	6	.8	8	1.0	5	.6	20	2.5	487	61.4	286	36.1	793
.3	0	.0	4	1.4	3	1.0	8	2.7	230	78.5	55	18.8	293
.0	0	.0	0	.0	0	.0	0	.0	26	96.3	1	3.7	27
.4	0	.0	4	1.5	3	1.1	8	3.0	204	76.7	54	20.3	266
.2	7	.6	12	1.1	8	.7	29	2.6	755	66.5	351	30.9	1,135
.0	1	1.3	0	.0	0	.0	1	1.3	64	84.2	11	14.5	76
.2	6	.6	12	1.1	8	.8	28	2.6	691	65.3	340	32.1	1,059
.0	0	.0	0	.0	0	.0	0	.0	0	.0	0	.0	0
.0	0	.0	0	.0	0	.0	0	.0	0	.0	0	.0	0
.0	0	.0	0	.0	0	.0	0	.0	0	.0	0	.0	0
.0	0	.0	0	.0	0	.0	0	.0	0	.0	0	.0	0
.0	0	.0	0	.0	0	.0	0	.0	0	.0	0	.0	0
.0	0	.0	0	.0	0	.0	0	.0	0	.0	0	.0	0
.0	0	.0	0	.0	0	.0	0	.0	0	.0	0	.0	0
.0	0	.0	0	.0	0	.0	0	.0	0	.0	0	.0	0
.0	0	.0	0	.0	0	.0	0	.0	0	.0	0	.0	0
.3	55	.7	168	2.1	189	2.3	436	5.4	6,921	85.0	788	9.7	8,145
.2	7	.8	18	1.9	20	2.2	47	5.1	842	91.1	35	3.8	924
.3	48	.7	150	2.1	169	2.3	389	5.4	6,079	84.2	753	10.4	7,221
.7	23	1.7	21	1.6	47	3.5	100	7.5	1,158	86.4	82	6.1	1,340
1.7	2	1.7	4	3.4	0	.0	8	6.8	105	89.7	4	3.4	117
.6	21	1.7	17	1.4	47	3.8	92	7.5	1,053	86.1	78	6.4	1,223
.3	78	.8	189	2.0	236	2.5	536	5.7	8,079	85.2	870	9.2	9,485
.3	9	.9	22	2.1	20	1.9	55	5.3	947	91.0	39	3.7	1,041
.3	69	.8	167	2.0	216	2.6	481	5.7	7,132	84.5	831	9.8	8,444
.7	8	2.9	3	1.1	22	8.1	35	12.9	233	85.7	4	1.5	272
.0	1	2.5	0	.0	2	5.0	3	7.5	35	87.5	2	5.0	40
.9	7	3.0	3	1.3	20	8.6	32	13.8	198	85.3	2	.9	232
.4	86	.9	192	2.0	258	2.6	571	5.9	8,312	85.2	874	9.0	9,757
.4	10	.9	22	2.0			58	5.4	982	90.8	41	3.8	1,081
.4	76	.9	170	2.0	236	2.7	513	5.9	7,330	84.5	833	9.6	8,670

TABLE 17 - TOTAL ENROLLMENT IN INSTITUTIONS OF HIGHER EDUCATION FOR SELECTED MAJOR FIELDS OF STUDY AND LEVEL OF ENROLLMENT BY RACE, ETHNICITY, AND SEX: STATE, 1978

MAJOR FIELD 0900 - ENGINEERING

	AMERICAN INDIAN ALASKAN NATIVE		BLACK NON-HISPANIC		ASIAN OR PACIFIC ISLANDER		HISPANIC		TOTAL MINORITY		WHITE NON-HISPANIC		NON-RESIDENT ALIEN	
	NUMBER	%	NUMBER	%	NUMBER	%	NUMBER	%	NUMBER	%	NUMBER	%	NUMBER	%
CONNECTICUT (15 INSTITUTIONS)														
UNDERGRADUATES:														
FULL-TIME	3	.1	144	3.7	63	1.6	49	1.3	259	6.7	3,421	88.7	176	4.6
FEMALE	0	.0	17	5.5	6	1.9	5	1.6	28	9.1	277	89.6	4	1.3
MALE	3	.1	127	3.6	57	1.6	44	1.2	231	6.5	3,144	88.6	172	4.8
PART-TIME	0	.0	93	4.3	14	.6	39	1.8	146	6.8	1,999	92.6	14	.6
FEMALE	0	.0	14	10.7	0	.0	3	2.3	17	13.0	114	87.0	0	.0
MALE	0	.0	79	3.9	14	.7	36	1.8	129	6.4	1,885	92.9	14	.7
TOTAL	3	.0	237	3.9	77	1.3	88	1.5	405	6.7	5,420	90.1	190	3.2
FEMALE	0	.0	31	7.0	6	1.4	8	1.8	45	10.2	391	88.9	4	.9
MALE	3	.1	206	3.7	71	1.3	80	1.4	360	6.5	5,029	90.2	186	3.3
GRADUATE:														
FULL-TIME	0	.0	2	.9	5	2.3	0	.0	7	3.2	143	65.9	67	30.9
FEMALE	0	.0	1	6.7	1	6.7	0	.0	2	13.3	12	80.0	1	6.7
MALE	0	.0	1	.5	4	2.0	0	.0	5	2.5	131	64.9	66	32.7
PART-TIME	0	.0	11	2.2	7	1.4	5	1.0	23	4.6	463	93.3	10	2.0
FEMALE	0	.0	0	.0	2	6.7	0	.0	2	6.7	28	93.3	0	.0
MALE	0	.0	11	2.4	5	1.1	5	1.1	21	4.5	435	93.3	10	2.1
TOTAL	0	.0	13	1.8	12	1.7	5	.7	30	4.2	606	85.0	77	10.8
FEMALE	0	.0	1	2.2	3	6.7	0	.0	4	8.9	40	88.9	1	2.2
MALE	0	.0	12	1.8	9	1.3	5	.7	26	3.9	566	84.7	76	11.4
PROFESSIONAL:														
FULL-TIME	0	.0	0	.0	0	.0	0	.0	0	.0	0	.0	0	.0
FEMALE	0	.0	0	.0	0	.0	0	.0	0	.0	0	.0	0	.0
MALE	0	.0	0	.0	0	.0	0	.0	0	.0	0	.0	0	.0
PART-TIME	0	.0	0	.0	0	.0	0	.0	0	.0	0	.0	0	.0
FEMALE	0	.0	0	.0	0	.0	0	.0	0	.0	0	.0	0	.0
MALE	0	.0	0	.0	0	.0	0	.0	0	.0	0	.0	0	.0
TOTAL	0	.0	0	.0	0	.0	0	.0	0	.0	0	.0	0	.0
FEMALE	0	.0	0	.0	0	.0	0	.0	0	.0	0	.0	0	.0
MALE	0	.0	0	.0	0	.0	0	.0	0	.0	0	.0	0	.0
UND+GRAD+PROF:														
FULL-TIME	3	.1	146	3.6	68	1.7	49	1.2	266	6.5	3,564	87.5	243	6.0
FEMALE	0	.0	18	5.6	7	2.2	5	1.5	30	9.3	289	89.2	5	1.5
MALE	3	.1	128	3.4	61	1.6	44	1.2	236	6.3	3,275	87.4	238	6.3
PART-TIME	0	.0	104	3.9	21	.8	44	1.7	169	6.4	2,462	92.7	24	.9
FEMALE	0	.0	14	8.7	2	1.2	3	1.9	19	11.8	142	88.2	0	.0
MALE	0	.0	90	3.6	19	.8	41	1.6	150	6.0	2,320	93.0	24	1.0
TOTAL	3	.0	250	3.7	89	1.3	93	1.4	435	6.5	6,026	89.6	267	4.0
FEMALE	0	.0	32	6.6	9	1.9	8	1.6	49	10.1	431	88.9	5	1.0
MALE	3	.0	218	3.5	80	1.3	85	1.4	386	6.2	5,595	89.6	262	4.2
UNCLASSIFIED:														
TOTAL	0	.0	2	2.2	8	8.8	0	.0	10	11.0	81	89.0	0	.0
FEMALE	0	.0	0	.0	0	.0	0	.0	0	.0	8	100.0	0	.0
MALE	0	.0	2	2.4	8	9.6	0	.0	10	12.0	73	88.0	0	.0
TOTAL ENROLLMENT:														
TOTAL	3	.0	252	3.7	97	1.4	93	1.4	445	6.5	6,107	89.6	267	3.9
FEMALE	0	.0	32	6.5	9	1.8	8	1.6	49	9.9	439	89.0	5	1.0
MALE	3	.0	220	3.5	88	1.4	85	1.3	396	6.3	5,668	89.6	262	4.1
DELAWARE (6 INSTITUTIONS)														
UNDERGRADUATES:														
FULL-TIME	0	.0	99	5.7	8	.5	6	.3	113	6.4	1,579	90.1	60	3.4
FEMALE	0	.0	25	10.9	2	.9	0	.0	27	11.8	192	83.8	10	4.4
MALE	0	.0	74	4.9	6	.4	6	.4	86	5.6	1,387	91.1	50	3.3
PART-TIME	1	.2	32	6.2	5	1.0	2	.4	40	7.7	474	91.2	6	1.2
FEMALE	0	.0	2	3.7	0	.0	0	.0	2	3.7	51	94.4	1	1.9
MALE	1	.2	30	6.4	5	1.1	2	.4	38	8.2	423	90.8	5	1.1
TOTAL	1	.0	131	5.8	13	.6	8	.4	153	6.7	2,053	90.4	66	2.9
FEMALE	0	.0	27	9.5	2	.7	0	.0	29	10.2	243	85.9	11	3.9
MALE	1	.1	104	5.2	11	.6	8	.4	124	6.2	1,810	91.0	55	2.8
GRADUATE:														
FULL-TIME	0	.0	1	3.8	0	.0	0	.0	1	3.8	15	57.7	10	38.5
FEMALE	0	.0	1	33.3	0	.0	0	.0	1	33.3	1	33.3	1	33.3
MALE	0	.0	0	.0	0	.0	0	.0	0	.0	14	60.9	9	39.1
PART-TIME	0	.0	3	2.9	1	1.0	1	1.0	5	4.8	78	74.3	22	21.0
FEMALE	0	.0	0	.0	0	.0	1	10.0	1	10.0	7	70.0	2	20.0
MALE	0	.0	3	3.2	1	1.1	0	.0	4	4.2	71	74.7	20	21.1
TOTAL	0	.0	4	3.1	1	.8	1	.8	6	4.6	93	71.0	32	24.4
FEMALE	0	.0	1	7.7	0	.0	1	7.7	2	15.4	8	61.5	3	23.1
MALE	0	.0	3	2.5	1	.8	0	.0	4	3.4	85	72.0	29	24.6
PROFESSIONAL:														
FULL-TIME	0	.0	0	.0	0	.0	0	.0	0	.0	0	.0	0	.0
FEMALE	0	.0	0	.0	0	.0	0	.0	0	.0	0	.0	0	.0
MALE	0	.0	0	.0	0	.0	0	.0	0	.0	0	.0	0	.0

444

ERING

N	BLACK NON-HISPANIC		ASIAN OR PACIFIC ISLANDER		HISPANIC		TOTAL MINORITY		WHITE NON-HISPANIC		NON-RESIDENT ALIEN		TOTAL
	NUMBER	%	NUMBER	%	NUMBER	%	NUMBER	%	NUMBER	%	NUMBER	%	NUMBER
INUED													
	0	.0	0	.0	0	.0	0	.0	0	.0	0	.0	0
	0	.0	0	.0	0	.0	0	.0	0	.0	0	.0	0
	0	.0	0	.0	0	.0	0	.0	0	.0	0	.0	0
	0	.0	0	.0	0	.0	0	.0	0	.0	0	.0	0
	0	.0	0	.0	0	.0	0	.0	0	.0	0	.0	0
	0	.0	0	.0	0	.0	0	.0	0	.0	0	.0	0
	100	5.6	8	.4	6	.3	114	6.4	1,594	89.7	70	3.9	1,778
	26	11.2	2	.9	0	.0	28	12.1	193	83.2	11	4.7	232
	74	4.8	6	.4	6	.4	86	5.6	1,401	90.6	59	3.8	1,546
	35	5.6	6	1.0	3	.5	45	7.2	552	88.3	28	4.5	625
	2	3.1	0	.0	1	1.6	3	4.7	58	90.6	3	4.7	64
	33	5.9	6	1.1	2	.4	42	7.5	494	88.1	25	4.5	561
	135	5.6	14	.6	9	.4	159	6.6	2,146	89.3	98	4.1	2,403
	28	9.5	2	.7	1	.3	31	10.5	251	84.8	14	4.7	296
	107	5.1	12	.6	8	.4	128	6.1	1,895	89.9	84	4.0	2,107
	9	3.0	4	1.4	3	1.0	17	5.7	229	77.4	50	16.9	296
	0	.0	0	.0	1	4.3	1	4.3	18	78.3	4	17.4	23
	9	3.3	4	1.5	2	.7	16	5.9	211	77.3	46	16.8	273
	144	5.3	18	.7	12	.4	176	6.5	2,375	88.0	148	5.5	2,699
	28	8.8	2	.6	2	.6	32	10.0	269	84.3	18	5.6	319
	116	4.9	16	.7	10	.4	144	6.1	2,106	88.5	130	5.5	2,380
4 INSTITUTIONS)													
	744	42.0	49	2.8	17	1.0	822	46.4	356	20.1	593	33.5	1,771
	160	56.7	2	.7	2	.7	165	58.5	56	19.5	62	22.0	282
	584	39.2	47	3.2	15	1.0	657	44.1	301	20.2	531	35.7	1,489
	526	62.5	54	6.4	6	.7	605	71.9	132	15.7	104	12.4	841
	75	78.1	1	1.0	0	.0	76	79.2	7	7.3	13	13.5	96
	451	60.5	53	7.1	6	.8	529	71.0	125	16.8	91	12.2	745
	1,270	48.6	103	3.9	23	.9	1,427	54.6	488	18.7	697	26.7	2,612
	235	62.2	3	.8	2	.5	241	63.8	62	16.4	75	19.8	378
	1,035	46.3	100	4.5	21	.9	1,186	53.1	426	19.1	622	27.8	2,234
	30	8.6	19	5.5	4	1.1	54	15.5	63	18.1	231	66.4	348
	10	38.5	0	.0	1	3.8	11	42.3	3	11.5	12	46.2	26
	20	6.2	19	5.9	3	.9	43	13.4	60	18.6	219	68.0	322
	89	6.5	95	6.9	26	1.9	218	15.8	1,004	72.9	156	11.3	1,378
	12	12.8	8	8.5	0	.0	20	21.3	66	70.2	8	8.5	94
	77	6.0	87	6.8	26	2.0	198	15.4	938	73.1	148	11.5	1,284
	119	6.9	114	6.6	30	1.7	272	15.8	1,067	61.8	387	22.4	1,726
	22	18.3	8	6.7	1	.8	31	25.8	69	57.5	20	16.7	120
	97	6.0	106	6.6	29	1.8	241	15.0	998	62.1	367	22.9	1,606
	0	.0	0	.0	0	.0	0	.0	0	.0	0	.0	0
	0	.0	0	.0	0	.0	0	.0	0	.0	0	.0	0
	0	.0	0	.0	0	.0	0	.0	0	.0	0	.0	0
	0	.0	0	.0	0	.0	0	.0	0	.0	0	.0	0
	0	.0	0	.0	0	.0	0	.0	0	.0	0	.0	0
	0	.0	0	.0	0	.0	0	.0	0	.0	0	.0	0
	774	36.5	68	3.2	21	1.0	876	41.3	419	19.8	824	38.9	2,119
	170	55.2	2	.6	3	1.0	176	57.1	58	18.8	74	24.0	308
	604	33.4	66	3.6	18	1.0	700	38.7	361	19.9	750	41.4	1,811
	615	27.7	149	6.7	32	1.4	823	37.1	1,136	51.2	260	11.7	2,219
	87	45.8	9	4.7	0	.0	96	50.5	73	38.4	21	11.1	190
	528	26.0	140	6.9	32	1.6	727	35.8	1,063	52.4	239	11.8	2,029
	1,389	32.0	217	5.0	53	1.2	1,699	39.2	1,555	35.8	1,084	25.0	4,338
	257	51.6	11	2.2	3	.6	272	54.6	131	26.3	95	19.1	498
	1,132	29.5	206	5.4	50	1.3	1,427	37.2	1,424	37.1	989	25.8	3,840
	15	6.0	25	9.9	3	1.2	44	17.5	114	45.2	94	37.3	252
	2	13.3	0	.0	0	.0	2	13.3	9	60.0	4	26.7	15
	13	5.5	25	10.5	3	1.3	42	17.7	105	44.3	90	38.0	237
	1,404	30.6	242	5.3	56	1.2	1,743	38.0	1,669	36.4	1,178	25.7	4,590
	259	50.5	11	2.1	3	.6	274	53.4	140	27.3	99	19.3	513
	1,145	28.1	231	5.7	53	1.3	1,469	36.0	1,529	37.5	1,079	26.5	4,077

TABLE 17 - TOTAL ENROLLMENT IN INSTITUTIONS OF HIGHER EDUCATION FOR SELECTED MAJOR FIELDS OF STUDY AND LEVEL OF ENROLLMENT
BY RACE, ETHNICITY, AND SEX: STATE: 1978

MAJOR FIELD 0900 - ENGINEERING

	AMERICAN INDIAN ALASKAN NATIVE		BLACK NON-HISPANIC		ASIAN OR PACIFIC ISLANDER		HISPANIC		TOTAL MINORITY		WHITE NON-HISPANIC		NON-RESIDENT ALIEN	
	NUMBER	%	NUMBER	%	NUMBER	%	NUMBER	%	NUMBER	%	NUMBER	%	NUMBER	%
FLORIDA (15 INSTITUTIONS)														
UNDERGRADUATES:														
FULL-TIME	10	.1	381	4.6	229	2.8	587	7.1	1,207	14.6	6,653	80.2	432	5.2
FEMALE	1	.1	74	5.1	27	1.9	90	6.2	192	13.3	1,223	84.5	32	2.2
MALE	9	.1	307	4.5	202	3.0	497	7.3	1,015	14.8	5,430	79.3	400	5.8
PART-TIME	21	1.0	178	8.1	101	4.6	245	11.1	545	24.8	1,572	71.5	83	3.8
FEMALE	1	.4	18	8.0	3	1.3	31	13.8	53	23.7	164	73.2	7	3.1
MALE	20	1.0	160	8.1	98	5.0	214	10.8	492	24.9	1,408	71.3	76	3.8
TOTAL	31	.3	559	5.3	330	3.1	832	7.9	1,752	16.7	8,225	78.4	515	4.9
FEMALE	2	.1	92	5.5	30	1.8	121	7.2	245	14.7	1,387	83.0	39	2.3
MALE	29	.3	467	5.3	300	3.4	711	8.1	1,507	17.1	6,838	77.5	476	5.4
GRADUATE:														
FULL-TIME	1	.2	15	2.8	19	3.6	16	3.0	51	9.6	334	62.5	149	27.9
FEMALE	0	.0	0	.0	1	2.2	2	4.3	3	6.5	32	69.6	11	23.9
MALE	1	.2	15	3.1	18	3.7	14	2.9	48	9.8	302	61.9	138	28.3
PART-TIME	1	.2	20	4.2	18	3.8	27	5.6	66	13.8	373	78.0	39	8.2
FEMALE	1	3.7	1	3.7	0	.0	2	7.4	4	14.8	20	74.1	3	11.1
MALE	0	.0	19	4.2	18	4.0	25	5.5	62	13.7	353	78.3	36	8.0
TOTAL	2	.2	35	3.5	37	3.7	43	4.2	117	11.6	707	69.9	188	18.6
FEMALE	1	1.4	1	1.4	1	1.4	4	5.5	7	9.6	52	71.2	14	19.2
MALE	1	.1	34	3.6	36	3.8	39	4.2	110	11.7	655	69.8	174	18.5
PROFESSIONAL:														
FULL-TIME	0	.0	0	.0	0	.0	0	.0	0	.0	0	.0	0	.0
FEMALE	0	.0	0	.0	0	.0	0	.0	0	.0	0	.0	0	.0
MALE	0	.0	0	.0	0	.0	0	.0	0	.0	0	.0	0	.0
PART-TIME	0	.0	0	.0	0	.0	0	.0	0	.0	0	.0	0	.0
FEMALE	0	.0	0	.0	0	.0	0	.0	0	.0	0	.0	0	.0
MALE	0	.0	0	.0	0	.0	0	.0	0	.0	0	.0	0	.0
TOTAL	0	.0	0	.0	0	.0	0	.0	0	.0	0	.0	0	.0
FEMALE	0	.0	0	.0	0	.0	0	.0	0	.0	0	.0	0	.0
MALE	0	.0	0	.0	0	.0	0	.0	0	.0	0	.0	0	.0
UNC+GRAD+PROF:														
FULL-TIME	11	.1	396	4.5	248	2.8	603	6.8	1,258	14.3	6,987	79.2	581	6.6
FEMALE	1	.1	74	5.0	28	1.9	92	6.2	195	13.1	1,255	84.1	43	2.9
MALE	10	.1	322	4.4	220	3.0	511	7.0	1,063	14.5	5,732	78.2	538	7.3
PART-TIME	22	.8	198	7.4	119	4.4	272	10.2	611	22.8	1,945	72.6	122	4.6
FEMALE	2	.8	19	7.6	3	1.2	33	13.1	57	22.7	184	73.3	10	4.0
MALE	20	.8	179	7.4	116	4.8	239	9.8	554	22.8	1,761	72.6	112	4.6
TOTAL	33	.3	594	5.3	367	3.2	875	7.6	1,869	16.2	8,932	77.6	703	6.1
FEMALE	3	.2	93	5.3	31	1.8	125	7.2	252	14.4	1,439	82.5	53	3.0
MALE	30	.3	501	5.3	336	3.4	750	7.7	1,617	16.6	7,493	76.8	650	6.7
UNCLASSIFIED:														
TOTAL	3	.3	72	6.7	10	.9	31	2.9	116	10.9	923	86.3	30	2.8
FEMALE	2	.5	35	8.7	0	.0	10	2.5	47	11.7	351	87.5	3	.7
MALE	1	.1	37	5.5	10	1.5	21	3.1	69	10.3	572	85.6	27	4.0
TOTAL ENROLLMENT:														
TOTAL	36	.3	666	5.3	377	3.0	906	7.2	1,985	15.8	9,855	78.4	733	5.8
FEMALE	5	.2	128	6.0	31	1.4	135	6.3	299	13.9	1,790	83.4	56	2.6
MALE	31	.3	538	5.2	346	3.3	771	7.4	1,686	16.2	8,065	77.3	677	6.5
GEORGIA (25 INSTITUTIONS)														
UNDERGRADUATES:														
FULL-TIME	14	.2	971	11.5	76	.9	95	1.1	1,156	13.6	6,753	79.6	570	6.7
FEMALE	5	.5	198	20.2	11	1.1	10	1.0	224	22.9	732	74.7	24	2.4
MALE	9	.1	773	10.3	65	.9	85	1.1	932	12.4	6,021	80.3	546	7.3
PART-TIME	4	.3	121	8.5	12	.8	9	.6	146	10.2	1,259	88.0	25	1.7
FEMALE	0	.0	20	13.8	1	.7	1	.7	22	15.2	122	84.1	1	.7
MALE	4	.3	101	7.9	11	.9	8	.6	124	9.6	1,137	88.5	24	1.9
TOTAL	18	.2	1,092	11.0	88	.9	104	1.0	1,302	13.1	8,012	80.9	595	6.0
FEMALE	5	.4	218	19.4	12	1.1	11	1.0	246	21.9	854	75.9	25	2.2
MALE	13	.1	874	9.9	76	.9	93	1.1	1,056	12.0	7,158	81.5	570	6.5
GRADUATE:														
FULL-TIME	0	.0	18	3.6	6	1.2	10	2.0	34	6.8	267	53.6	197	39.6
FEMALE	0	.0	5	15.2	1	3.0	2	6.1	8	24.2	17	51.5	8	24.2
MALE	0	.0	13	2.8	5	1.1	8	1.7	26	5.6	250	53.8	189	40.6
PART-TIME	0	.0	8	2.4	7	2.1	0	.0	15	4.5	259	76.8	62	18.7
FEMALE	0	.0	0	.0	1	4.5	0	.0	1	4.5	21	95.5	0	.0
MALE	0	.0	8	2.6	6	1.9	0	.0	14	4.5	234	75.5	62	20.0
TOTAL	0	.0	26	3.1	13	1.6	10	1.2	49	5.9	522	62.9	259	31.2
FEMALE	0	.0	5	9.1	2	3.6	2	3.6	9	16.4	38	69.1	8	14.5
MALE	0	.0	21	2.7	11	1.4	8	1.0	40	5.2	484	62.5	251	32.4
PROFESSIONAL:														
FULL-TIME	0	.0	0	.0	0	.0	0	.0	0	.0	0	.0	0	.0
FEMALE	0	.0	0	.0	0	.0	0	.0	0	.0	0	.0	0	.0
MALE	0	.0	0	.0	0	.0	0	.0	0	.0	0	.0	0	.0

ENROLLMENT IN INSTITUTIONS OF HIGHER EDUCATION FOR SELECTED MAJOR FIELDS OF STUDY AND LEVEL OF ENROLLMENT BY ETHNICITY, AND SEX: STATE, 1978

ENGINEERING

AMER INDIAN NATIVE %	BLACK NON-HISPANIC NUMBER	%	ASIAN OR PACIFIC ISLANDER NUMBER	%	HISPANIC NUMBER	%	TOTAL MINORITY NUMBER	%	WHITE NON-HISPANIC NUMBER	%	NON-RESIDENT ALIEN NUMBER	%	TOTAL NUMBER
CONTINUED													
.0	0	.0	0	.0	0	.0	0	.0	0	.0	0	.0	0
.0	0	.0	0	.0	0	.0	0	.0	0	.0	0	.0	0
.0	0	.0	0	.0	0	.0	0	.0	0	.0	0	.0	0
.0	0	.0	0	.0	0	.0	0	.0	0	.0	0	.0	0
.0	0	.0	0	.0	0	.0	0	.0	0	.0	0	.0	0
.0	0	.0	0	.0	0	.0	0	.0	0	.0	0	.0	0
.2	989	11.0	82	.9	105	1.2	1,190	13.3	7,020	78.2	767	8.5	8,977
.5	203	20.0	12	1.2	12	1.2	232	22.9	749	73.9	32	3.2	1,013
.1	784	9.9	70	.9	93	1.2	958	12.0	6,271	78.7	735	9.2	7,964
.2	129	7.3	19	1.1	9	.5	161	9.1	1,514	85.9	87	4.9	1,762
.0	20	12.0	2	1.2	1	.6	23	13.8	143	85.6	1	.6	167
.3	109	6.8	17	1.1	8	.5	138	8.7	1,371	86.0	86	5.4	1,595
.2	1,118	10.4	101	.9	114	1.1	1,351	12.6	8,534	79.5	854	8.0	10,739
.4	223	18.9	14	1.2	13	1.1	255	21.6	892	75.6	33	2.8	1,180
.1	895	9.4	87	.9	101	1.1	1,096	11.5	7,642	79.9	821	8.6	9,559
.0	13	7.4	1	.6	2	1.1	16	9.1	120	68.2	40	22.7	176
.0	3	11.5	0	.0	1	3.8	4	15.4	21	80.8	1	3.8	26
.0	10	6.7	1	.7	1	.7	12	8.0	99	66.0	39	26.0	150
.2	1,131	10.4	102	.9	116	1.1	1,367	12.5	8,654	79.3	894	8.2	10,915
.4	226	18.7	14	1.2	14	1.2	259	21.5	913	75.7	34	2.8	1,206
.1	905	9.3	88	.9	102	1.1	1,108	11.4	7,741	79.7	860	8.9	9,709
(2 INSTITUTIONS)													
.0	4	.4	819	81.3	10	1.0	833	82.6	100	9.9	75	7.4	1,008
.0	0	.0	111	90.2	0	.0	111	90.2	10	8.1	2	1.6	123
.0	4	.5	708	80.0	10	1.1	722	81.6	90	10.2	73	8.2	885
.0	0	.0	84	81.6	1	1.0	85	82.5	16	15.5	2	1.9	103
.0	0	.0	10	100.0	0	.0	10	100.0	0	.0	0	.0	10
.0	0	.0	74	79.6	1	1.1	75	80.6	16	17.2	2	2.2	93
.0	4	.4	903	81.3	11	1.0	918	82.6	116	10.4	77	6.9	1,111
.0	0	.0	121	91.0	0	.0	121	91.0	10	7.5	2	1.5	133
.0	4	.4	782	80.0	11	1.1	797	81.5	106	10.8	75	7.7	978
.0	1	1.5	39	60.0	2	3.1	42	64.6	16	24.6	7	10.8	65
.0	0	.0	0	.0	0	.0	0	.0	0	.0	0	.0	0
.0	1	1.5	39	60.0	2	3.1	42	64.6	16	24.6	7	10.8	65
.0	0	.0	37	62.7	0	.0	37	62.7	17	28.8	5	8.5	59
.0	0	.0	5	100.0	0	.0	5	100.0	0	.0	0	.0	5
.0	0	.0	32	59.3	0	.0	32	59.3	17	31.5	5	9.3	54
.0	1	.8	76	61.3	2	1.6	79	63.7	33	26.6	12	9.7	124
.0	0	.0	5	100.0	0	.0	5	100.0	0	.0	0	.0	5
.0	1	.8	71	59.7	2	1.7	74	62.2	33	27.7	12	10.1	119
.0	0	.0	0	.0	0	.0	0	.0	0	.0	0	.0	0
.0	0	.0	0	.0	0	.0	0	.0	0	.0	0	.0	0
.0	0	.0	0	.0	0	.0	0	.0	0	.0	0	.0	0
.0	0	.0	0	.0	0	.0	0	.0	0	.0	0	.0	0
.0	0	.0	0	.0	0	.0	0	.0	0	.0	0	.0	0
.0	0	.0	0	.0	0	.0	0	.0	0	.0	0	.0	0
.0	0	.0	0	.0	0	.0	0	.0	0	.0	0	.0	0
.0	0	.0	0	.0	0	.0	0	.0	0	.0	0	.0	0
.0	0	.0	0	.0	0	.0	0	.0	0	.0	0	.0	0
.0	5	.5	858	80.0	12	1.1	875	81.5	116	10.8	82	7.6	1,073
.0	0	.0	111	90.2	0	.0	111	90.2	10	8.1	2	1.6	123
.0	5	.5	747	78.6	12	1.3	764	80.4	106	11.2	80	8.4	950
.0	0	.0	121	74.7	1	.6	122	75.3	33	20.4	7	4.3	162
.0	0	.0	15	100.0	0	.0	15	100.0	0	.0	0	.0	15
.0	0	.0	106	72.1	1	.7	107	72.8	33	22.4	7	4.8	147
.0	5	.4	979	79.3	13	1.1	997	80.7	149	12.1	89	7.2	1,235
.0	0	.0	126	91.3	0	.0	126	91.3	10	7.2	2	1.4	138
.0	5	.5	853	77.8	13	1.2	871	79.4	139	12.7	87	7.9	1,097
.0	0	.0	0	.0	0	.0	0	.0	0	.0	0	.0	0
.0	0	.0	0	.0	0	.0	0	.0	0	.0	0	.0	0
.0	0	.0	0	.0	0	.0	0	.0	0	.0	0	.0	0
.0	5	.4	979	79.3	13	1.1	997	80.7	149	12.1	89	7.2	1,235
.0	0	.0	126	91.3	0	.0	126	91.3	10	7.2	2	1.4	138
.0	5	.5	853	77.8	13	1.2	871	79.4	139	12.7	87	7.9	1,097

MAJOR FIELD 0900 - ENGINEERING

	AMERICAN INDIAN ALASKAN NATIVE		BLACK NON-HISPANIC		ASIAN OR PACIFIC ISLANDER		HISPANIC		TOTAL MINORITY		WHITE NON-HISPANIC		NON-RESIDENT ALIEN		TOTAL
	NUMBER	%	NUMBER	%	NUMBER	%	NUMBER	%	NUMBER	%	NUMBER	%	NUMBER	%	NUMBER
IDAHO		**6 INSTITUTIONS**													
UNDERGRADUATES:															
FULL-TIME	6	.5	3	.2	38	3.0	4	.3	51	4.0	1,181	93.0	38	3.0	1,270
FEMALE	0	.0	1	.8	2	1.5	0	.0	3	2.3	124	95.4	3	2.3	130
MALE	6	.5	2	.2	36	3.2	4	.4	48	4.2	1,057	92.7	35	3.1	1,140
PART-TIME	0	.0	0	.0	1	1.1	2	2.1	3	3.2	92	96.8	0	.0	95
FEMALE	0	.0	0	.0	0	.0	0	.0	0	.0	4	100.0	0	.0	4
MALE	0	.0	0	.0	1	1.1	2	2.2	3	3.3	88	96.7	0	.0	91
TOTAL	6	.4	3	.2	39	2.9	6	.4	54	4.0	1,273	93.3	38	2.8	1,365
FEMALE	0	.0	1	.7	2	1.5	0	.0	3	2.2	128	95.5	3	2.2	134
MALE	6	.5	2	.2	37	3.0	6	.5	51	4.1	1,145	93.0	35	2.8	1,231
GRADUATE:															
FULL-TIME	0	.0	1	1.4	1	1.4	1	1.4	3	4.1	54	73.0	17	23.0	74
FEMALE	0	.0	0	.0	0	.0	0	.0	0	.0	4	80.0	1	20.0	5
MALE	0	.0	1	1.4	1	1.4	1	1.4	3	4.3	50	72.5	16	23.2	69
PART-TIME	0	.0	1	.8	1	.8	0	.0	2	1.6	118	92.2	8	6.3	128
FEMALE	0	.0	0	.0	0	.0	0	.0	0	.0	11	91.7	1	8.3	12
MALE	0	.0	1	.9	1	.9	0	.0	2	1.7	107	92.2	7	6.0	116
TOTAL	0	.0	2	1.0	2	1.0	1	.5	5	2.5	172	85.1	25	12.4	202
FEMALE	0	.0	0	.0	0	.0	0	.0	0	.0	15	88.2	2	11.8	17
MALE	0	.0	2	1.1	2	1.1	1	.5	5	2.7	157	84.9	23	12.4	185
PROFESSIONAL:															
FULL-TIME	0	.0	0	.0	0	.0	0	.0	0	.0	0	.0	0	.0	0
FEMALE	0	.0	0	.0	0	.0	0	.0	0	.0	0	.0	0	.0	0
MALE	0	.0	0	.0	0	.0	0	.0	0	.0	0	.0	0	.0	0
PART-TIME	0	.0	0	.0	0	.0	0	.0	0	.0	0	.0	0	.0	0
FEMALE	0	.0	0	.0	0	.0	0	.0	0	.0	0	.0	0	.0	0
MALE	0	.0	0	.0	0	.0	0	.0	0	.0	0	.0	0	.0	0
TOTAL	0	.0	0	.0	0	.0	0	.0	0	.0	0	.0	0	.0	0
FEMALE	0	.0	0	.0	0	.0	0	.0	0	.0	0	.0	0	.0	0
MALE	0	.0	0	.0	0	.0	0	.0	0	.0	0	.0	0	.0	0
UNG+GRAD+PROF:															
FULL-TIME	6	.4	4	.3	39	2.9	5	.4	54	4.0	1,235	91.9	55	4.1	1,344
FEMALE	0	.0	1	.7	2	1.5	0	.0	3	2.2	128	94.8	4	3.0	135
MALE	6	.5	3	.2	37	3.1	5	.4	51	4.2	1,107	91.6	51	4.2	1,209
PART-TIME	0	.0	1	.4	2	.9	2	.9	5	2.2	210	94.2	8	3.6	223
FEMALE	0	.0	0	.0	0	.0	0	.0	0	.0	15	93.8	1	6.3	16
MALE	0	.0	1	.5	2	1.0	2	1.0	5	2.4	195	94.2	7	3.4	207
TOTAL	6	.4	5	.3	41	2.6	7	.4	59	3.8	1,445	92.2	63	4.0	1,567
FEMALE	0	.0	1	.7	2	1.3	0	.0	3	2.0	143	94.7	5	3.3	151
MALE	6	.4	4	.3	39	2.8	7	.5	56	4.0	1,302	91.9	58	4.1	1,416
UNCLASSIFIED:															
TOTAL	0	.0	0	.0	2	15.4	0	.0	2	15.4	10	76.9	1	7.7	13
FEMALE	0	.0	0	.0	0	.0	0	.0	0	.0	1	100.0	0	.0	1
MALE	0	.0	0	.0	2	16.7	0	.0	2	16.7	9	75.0	1	8.3	12
TOTAL ENROLLMENT:															
TOTAL	6	.4	5	.3	43	2.7	7	.4	61	3.9	1,455	92.1	64	4.1	1,580
FEMALE	0	.0	1	.7	2	1.3	0	.0	3	2.0	144	94.7	5	3.3	152
MALE	6	.4	4	.3	41	2.9	7	.5	58	4.1	1,311	91.8	59	4.1	1,428
ILLINOIS		**(52 INSTITUTIONS)**													
UNDERGRADUATES:															
FULL-TIME	39	.2	1,114	6.7	597	3.6	369	2.2	2,119	12.7	13,474	80.9	1,061	6.4	16,654
FEMALE	0	.0	248	13.2	70	3.7	40	2.1	358	19.0	1,481	78.6	46	2.4	1,885
MALE	39	.3	866	5.9	527	3.6	329	2.2	1,761	11.9	11,993	81.2	1,015	6.9	14,769
PART-TIME	10	.2	343	7.0	130	2.7	84	1.7	567	11.6	4,232	86.5	93	1.9	4,892
FEMALE	3	.1	133	5.0	33	1.2	12	.4	181	6.7	2,497	93.1	4	.1	2,682
MALE	7	.3	210	9.5	97	4.4	72	3.3	386	17.5	1,735	78.5	89	4.0	2,210
TOTAL	49	.2	1,457	6.8	727	3.4	453	2.1	2,686	12.5	17,706	82.2	1,154	5.4	21,546
FEMALE	3	.1	381	8.3	103	2.3	52	1.1	539	11.8	3,978	87.1	50	1.1	4,567
MALE	46	.3	1,076	6.3	624	3.7	401	2.4	2,147	12.6	13,728	80.9	1,104	6.5	16,979
GRADUATE:															
FULL-TIME	1	.1	10	.6	91	5.8	18	1.2	120	7.7	813	52.1	626	40.2	1,559
FEMALE	0	.0	1	1.2	5	5.8	1	1.2	7	8.1	55	64.0	24	27.9	86
MALE	1	.1	9	.6	86	5.8	17	1.2	113	7.7	758	51.5	602	40.9	1,473
PART-TIME	0	.0	34	2.8	126	10.2	6	.5	166	13.5	852	69.2	214	17.4	1,232
FEMALE	0	.0	3	4.2	8	11.3	0	.0	11	15.5	48	67.6	12	16.9	71
MALE	0	.0	31	2.7	118	10.2	6	.5	155	13.4	804	69.3	202	17.4	1,161
TOTAL	1	.0	44	1.6	217	7.8	24	.9	286	10.2	1,665	59.7	840	30.1	2,791
FEMALE	0	.0	4	2.5	13	8.3	1	.6	18	11.5	103	65.6	36	22.9	157
MALE	1	.0	40	1.5	204	7.7	23	.9	268	10.2	1,562	59.3	804	30.5	2,634
PROFESSIONAL:															
FULL-TIME	0	.0	0	.0	0	.0	0	.0	0	.0	0	.0	0	.0	0
FEMALE	0	.0	0	.0	0	.0	0	.0	0	.0	0	.0	0	.0	0
MALE	0	.0	0	.0	0	.0	0	.0	0	.0	0	.0	0	.0	0

ENGINEERING

AMERICAN INDIAN NATIVE %	BLACK NON-HISPANIC NUMBER	%	ASIAN OR PACIFIC ISLANDER NUMBER	%	HISPANIC NUMBER	%	TOTAL MINORITY NUMBER	%	WHITE NON-HISPANIC NUMBER	%	NON-RESIDENT ALIEN NUMBER	%	TOTAL NUMBER
CONTINUED													
.0	0	.0	0	.0	0	.0	0	.0	0	.0	0	.0	0
.0	0	.0	0	.0	0	.0	0	.0	0	.0	0	.0	0
.0	0	.0	0	.0	0	.0	0	.0	0	.0	0	.0	0
.0	0	.0	0	.0	0	.0	0	.0	0	.0	0	.0	0
.0	0	.0	0	.0	0	.0	0	.0	0	.0	0	.0	0
.0	0	.0	0	.0	0	.0	0	.0	0	.0	0	.0	0
.2	1,124	6.2	688	3.8	387	2.1	2,239	12.3	14,287	78.4	1,687	9.3	18,213
.0	249	12.6	75	3.8	41	2.1	365	18.5	1,536	77.9	70	3.6	1,971
.2	875	5.4	613	3.8	346	2.1	1,874	11.5	12,751	78.5	1,617	10.0	16,242
.2	377	6.2	296	4.2	90	1.5	733	12.0	5,084	83.0	307	5.0	6,124
.1	136	4.9	41	1.5	12	.4	192	7.0	2,545	92.4	16	.6	2,753
.2	241	7.1	215	6.4	78	2.3	541	16.0	2,539	75.3	291	8.6	3,371
.2	1,501	6.2	944	3.9	477	2.0	2,972	12.2	19,371	79.6	1,994	8.2	24,337
.1	385	8.1	116	2.5	53	1.1	557	11.8	4,081	86.4	86	1.8	4,724
.2	1,116	5.7	828	4.2	424	2.2	2,415	12.3	15,290	78.0	1,908	9.7	19,613
.2	15	2.4	27	4.3	13	2.1	56	8.9	554	88.5	16	2.6	626
.0	2	1.6	4	3.1	1	.8	7	5.5	118	92.9	2	1.6	127
.2	13	2.6	23	4.6	12	2.4	49	9.8	436	87.4	14	2.8	459
.2	1,516	6.1	971	3.9	490	2.0	3,028	12.1	19,925	79.8	2,010	8.1	24,963
.1	387	8.0	120	2.5	54	1.1	564	11.6	4,199	86.6	88	1.8	4,851
.2	1,129	5.6	851	4.2	436	2.2	2,464	12.3	15,726	78.2	1,922	9.6	20,112
(23 INSTITUTIONS)													
.1	384	3.2	102	.9	104	.9	599	5.1	10,683	90.2	565	4.8	11,847
.0	104	7.6	20	1.5	15	1.1	139	10.2	1,200	87.8	27	2.0	1,366
.1	280	2.7	82	.8	89	.8	460	4.4	9,483	90.5	538	5.1	10,481
.1	57	3.7	4	.3	11	.7	73	4.7	1,450	94.2	16	1.0	1,539
.0	9	7.3	1	.8	1	.8	11	8.9	112	91.1	0	.0	123
.1	48	3.4	3	.2	10	.7	62	4.4	1,338	94.5	16	1.1	1,416
.1	441	3.3	106	.8	115	.9	672	5.0	12,133	90.6	581	4.3	13,386
.0	113	7.6	21	1.4	16	1.1	150	10.1	1,312	88.1	27	1.8	1,489
.1	328	2.8	85	.7	99	.8	522	4.4	10,821	91.0	554	4.7	11,897
.0	2	.2	9	.9	5	.5	16	1.6	611	62.7	347	35.6	974
.0	0	.0	0	.0	0	.0	0	.0	63	77.8	18	22.2	81
.0	2	.2	9	1.0	5	.6	16	1.8	548	61.4	329	36.8	893
.0	2	.7	5	1.8	2	.7	9	3.3	225	82.7	38	14.0	272
.0	0	.0	0	.0	0	.0	0	.0	11	84.6	2	15.4	13
.0	2	.8	5	1.9	2	.8	9	3.5	214	82.6	36	13.9	259
.0	4	.3	14	1.1	7	.6	25	2.0	836	67.1	385	30.9	1,246
.0	0	.0	0	.0	0	.0	0	.0	74	78.7	20	21.3	94
.0	4	.3	14	1.2	7	.6	25	2.2	762	66.1	365	31.7	1,152
.0	0	.0	0	.0	0	.0	0	.0	0	.0	0	.0	0
.0	0	.0	0	.0	0	.0	0	.0	0	.0	0	.0	0
.0	0	.0	0	.0	0	.0	0	.0	0	.0	0	.0	0
.0	0	.0	0	.0	0	.0	0	.0	0	.0	0	.0	0
.0	0	.0	0	.0	0	.0	0	.0	0	.0	0	.0	0
.0	0	.0	0	.0	0	.0	0	.0	0	.0	0	.0	0
.0	0	.0	0	.0	0	.0	0	.0	0	.0	0	.0	0
.0	0	.0	0	.0	0	.0	0	.0	0	.0	0	.0	0
.0	0	.0	0	.0	0	.0	0	.0	0	.0	0	.0	0
.1	386	3.0	111	.9	109	.9	615	4.8	11,294	88.1	912	7.1	12,821
.0	104	7.2	20	1.4	15	1.0	139	9.6	1,263	87.3	45	3.1	1,447
.1	282	2.5	91	.8	94	.8	476	4.2	10,031	88.2	867	7.6	11,374
.1	59	3.3	9	.5	13	.7	82	4.5	1,675	92.5	54	3.0	1,811
.0	9	6.6	1	.7	1	.7	11	8.1	123	90.4	2	1.5	136
.1	50	3.0	8	.5	12	.7	71	4.2	1,552	92.7	52	3.1	1,675
.1	445	3.0	120	.8	122	.8	697	4.8	12,969	88.6	966	6.6	14,632
.0	113	7.1	21	1.3	16	1.0	150	9.5	1,386	87.6	47	3.0	1,583
.1	332	2.5	99	.8	106	.8	547	4.2	11,583	88.8	919	7.0	13,049
.0	6	3.5	7	4.0	4	2.3	17	9.8	145	83.8	11	6.4	173
.0	1	11.1	0	.0	0	.0	1	11.1	8	88.9	0	.0	9
.0	5	3.0	7	4.3	4	2.4	16	9.8	137	83.5	11	6.7	164
.1	451	3.0	127	.8	126	.9	714	4.8	13,114	88.6	977	6.6	14,805
.0	114	7.2	21	1.3	16	1.0	151	9.5	1,394	87.6	47	3.0	1,592
.1	337	2.6	106	.8	110	.8	563	4.3	11,720	88.7	930	7.0	13,213

TABLE 17 - TOTAL ENROLLMENT IN INSTITUTIONS OF HIGHER EDUCATION FOR SELECTED MAJOR FIELDS OF STUDY AND LEVEL OF ENROLLMENT BY RACE, ETHNICITY, AND SEX: STATE, 1978

MAJOR FIELD 0900 - ENGINEERING

	AMERICAN INDIAN ALASKAN NATIVE		BLACK NON-HISPANIC		ASIAN OR PACIFIC ISLANDER		HISPANIC		TOTAL MINORITY		WHITE NON-HISPANIC		NON-RESIDENT ALIEN		T N
	NUMBER	%	NUMBER	%	NUMBER	%	NUMBER	%	NUMBER	%	NUMBER	%	NUMBER	%	
IOWA (11 INSTITUTIONS)															
UNDERGRADUATES:															
FULL-TIME	1	.0	47	1.0	52	1.1	15	.3	115	2.5	4,251	90.7	323	6.9	
FEMALE	0	.0	8	1.8	9	2.1	1	.2	18	4.1	399	91.7	18	4.1	
MALE	1	.0	39	.9	43	1.0	14	.3	97	2.3	3,852	90.6	305	7.2	
PART-TIME	1	.2	7	1.7	7	1.7	0	.0	15	3.7	352	87.6	35	8.7	
FEMALE	0	.0	0	.0	1	1.8	0	.0	1	1.8	52	94.5	2	3.6	
MALE	1	.3	7	2.0	6	1.7	0	.0	14	4.0	300	86.5	33	9.5	
TOTAL	2	.0	54	1.1	59	1.2	15	.3	130	2.6	4,603	90.4	358	7.0	
FEMALE	0	.0	8	1.6	10	2.0	1	.2	19	3.9	451	92.0	20	4.1	
MALE	2	.0	46	1.0	49	1.1	14	.3	111	2.4	4,152	90.2	338	7.3	
GRADUATE:															
FULL-TIME	1	.2	5	1.1	9	1.9	2	.4	17	3.6	242	51.6	210	44.8	
FEMALE	0	.0	1	4.2	1	4.2	0	.0	2	8.3	15	62.5	7	29.2	
MALE	1	.2	4	.9	8	1.8	2	.4	15	3.4	227	51.0	203	45.6	
PART-TIME	0	.0	0	.0	5	1.8	0	.0	5	1.8	192	68.3	84	29.9	
FEMALE	0	.0	0	.0	1	6.3	0	.0	1	6.3	14	87.5	1	6.3	
MALE	0	.0	0	.0	4	1.5	0	.0	4	1.5	178	67.2	83	31.3	
TOTAL	1	.1	5	.7	14	1.9	2	.3	22	2.9	434	57.9	294	39.2	
FEMALE	0	.0	1	2.5	2	5.0	0	.0	3	7.5	29	72.5	8	20.0	
MALE	1	.1	4	.6	12	1.7	2	.3	19	2.7	405	57.0	286	40.3	
PROFESSIONAL:															
FULL-TIME	0	.0	0	.0	0	.0	0	.0	0	.0	0	.0	0	.0	
FEMALE	0	.0	0	.0	0	.0	0	.0	0	.0	0	.0	0	.0	
MALE	0	.0	0	.0	0	.0	0	.0	0	.0	0	.0	0	.0	
PART-TIME	0	.0	0	.0	0	.0	0	.0	0	.0	0	.0	0	.0	
FEMALE	0	.0	0	.0	0	.0	0	.0	0	.0	0	.0	0	.0	
MALE	0	.0	0	.0	0	.0	0	.0	0	.0	0	.0	0	.0	
TOTAL	0	.0	0	.0	0	.0	0	.0	0	.0	0	.0	0	.0	
FEMALE	0	.0	0	.0	0	.0	0	.0	0	.0	0	.0	0	.0	
MALE	0	.0	0	.0	0	.0	0	.0	0	.0	0	.0	0	.0	
UND+GRAD+PROF:															
FULL-TIME	2	.0	52	1.0	61	1.2	17	.3	132	2.6	4,493	87.1	533	10.3	
FEMALE	0	.0	9	2.0	10	2.2	1	.2	20	4.4	414	90.2	25	5.4	
MALE	2	.0	43	.9	51	1.1	16	.3	112	2.4	4,079	86.8	508	10.8	
PART-TIME	1	.1	7	1.0	12	1.8	0	.0	20	2.9	544	79.6	119	17.4	
FEMALE	0	.0	0	.0	2	2.8	0	.0	2	2.8	66	93.0	3	4.2	
MALE	1	.2	7	1.1	10	1.6	0	.0	18	2.9	478	78.1	116	19.0	
TOTAL	3	.1	59	1.0	73	1.2	17	.3	152	2.6	5,037	86.2	652	11.2	
FEMALE	0	.0	9	1.7	12	2.3	1	.2	22	4.2	480	90.6	28	5.3	
MALE	3	.1	50	.9	61	1.1	16	.3	130	2.4	4,557	85.8	624	11.7	
UNCLASSIFIED:															
TOTAL	0	.0	0	.0	0	.0	0	.0	0	.0	41	95.3	2	4.7	
FEMALE	0	.0	0	.0	0	.0	0	.0	0	.0	6	100.0	0	.0	
MALE	0	.0	0	.0	0	.0	0	.0	0	.0	35	94.6	2	5.4	
TOTAL ENROLLMENT:															
TOTAL	3	.1	59	1.0	73	1.2	17	.3	152	2.6	5,078	86.3	654	11.1	
FEMALE	0	.0	9	1.7	12	2.2	1	.2	22	4.1	486	90.7	28	5.2	
MALE	3	.1	50	.9	61	1.1	16	.3	130	2.4	4,592	85.9	626	11.7	
KANSAS (16 INSTITUTIONS)															
UNDERGRADUATES:															
FULL-TIME	11	.2	142	3.0	58	1.2	52	1.1	263	5.6	3,897	83.3	519	11.1	
FEMALE	1	.2	27	6.0	9	2.0	8	1.8	45	10.0	388	85.8	19	4.2	
MALE	10	.2	115	2.7	49	1.2	44	1.0	218	5.2	3,509	83.0	500	11.8	
PART-TIME	5	.7	31	4.5	14	2.0	15	2.2	65	9.4	595	86.5	28	4.1	
FEMALE	2	3.8	3	5.8	2	3.8	0	.0	7	13.5	44	84.6	1	1.9	
MALE	3	.5	28	4.4	12	1.9	15	2.4	58	9.1	551	86.6	27	4.2	
TOTAL	16	.3	173	3.2	72	1.3	67	1.2	328	6.1	4,492	83.7	547	10.2	
FEMALE	3	.6	30	6.0	11	2.2	8	1.6	52	10.3	432	85.7	20	4.0	
MALE	13	.3	143	2.9	61	1.3	59	1.2	276	5.7	4,060	83.5	527	10.8	
GRADUATE:															
FULL-TIME	1	.4	1	.4	3	1.1	0	.0	5	1.8	109	38.5	169	59.7	
FEMALE	0	.0	0	.0	0	.0	0	.0	0	.0	12	63.2	7	36.8	
MALE	1	.4	1	.4	3	1.1	0	.0	5	1.9	97	36.7	162	61.4	
PART-TIME	1	.4	3	.9	8	2.4	2	.6	13	3.9	278	82.5	46	13.6	
FEMALE	0	.0	0	.0	1	5.3	0	.0	1	5.3	16	84.2	2	10.5	
MALE	0	.0	3	.9	7	2.2	2	.6	12	3.8	262	82.4	44	13.8	
TOTAL	1	.2	4	.6	11	1.8	2	.3	18	2.9	387	62.4	215	34.7	
FEMALE	0	.0	0	.0	1	2.6	0	.0	1	2.6	28	73.7	9	23.7	
MALE	1	.2	4	.7	10	1.7	2	.3	17	2.9	359	61.7	206	35.4	
PROFESSIONAL:															
FULL-TIME	0	.0	0	.0	0	.0	0	.0	0	.0	0	.0	0	.0	
FEMALE	0	.0	0	.0	0	.0	0	.0	0	.0	0	.0	0	.0	
MALE	0	.0	0	.0	0	.0	0	.0	0	.0	0	.0	0	.0	

ENGINEERING

AM INDIAN NATIVE %	BLACK NON-HISPANIC NUMBER	%	ASIAN OR PACIFIC ISLANDER NUMBER	%	HISPANIC NUMBER	%	TOTAL MINORITY NUMBER	%	WHITE NON-HISPANIC NUMBER	%	NON-RESIDENT ALIEN NUMBER	%	TOTAL NUMBER
CONTINUED													
.0	0	.0	0	.0	0	.0	0	.0	0	.0	0	.0	0
.0	0	.0	0	.0	0	.0	0	.0	0	.0	0	.0	0
.0	0	.0	0	.0	0	.0	0	.0	0	.0	0	.0	0
.0	0	.0	0	.0	0	.0	0	.0	0	.0	0	.0	0
.0	0	.0	0	.0	0	.0	0	.0	0	.0	0	.0	0
.0	0	.0	0	.0	0	.0	0	.0	0	.0	0	.0	0
.2	143	2.9	61	1.2	52	1.0	268	5.4	4,006	80.7	688	13.9	4,962
.2	27	5.7	9	1.9	8	1.7	45	9.6	400	84.9	26	5.5	471
.2	116	2.6	52	1.2	44	1.0	223	5.0	3,606	80.3	662	14.7	4,491
.5	34	3.3	22	2.1	17	1.7	78	7.6	873	85.2	74	7.2	1,025
2.8	3	4.2	3	4.2	0	.0	8	11.3	60	84.5	3	4.2	71
.3	31	3.2	19	2.0	17	1.6	70	7.3	813	85.2	71	7.4	954
.3	177	3.0	83	1.4	69	1.2	346	5.8	4,879	81.5	762	12.7	5,987
.6	30	5.5	12	2.2	8	1.5	53	9.8	460	84.9	29	5.4	542
.3	147	2.7	71	1.3	61	1.1	293	5.4	4,419	81.2	733	13.5	5,445
.0	4	3.3	1	.8	3	2.5	8	6.6	104	85.2	10	8.2	122
.0	0	.0	1	5.6	0	.0	1	5.6	16	88.9	1	5.6	18
.0	4	3.8	0	.0	3	2.9	7	6.7	88	84.6	9	8.7	104
.3	181	3.0	84	1.4	72	1.2	354	5.8	4,983	81.6	772	12.6	6,109
.5	30	5.4	13	2.3	8	1.4	54	9.6	476	85.0	30	5.4	560
.3	151	2.7	71	1.3	64	1.2	300	5.4	4,507	81.2	742	13.4	5,549
(12 INSTITUTIONS)													
.3	171	4.3	71	1.8	10	.3	263	6.7	3,360	85.3	317	8.0	3,940
.5	29	7.9	9	2.5	0	.0	40	10.9	317	86.4	10	2.7	367
.3	142	4.0	62	1.7	10	.3	223	6.2	3,043	85.2	307	8.6	3,573
.0	28	5.4	7	1.3	5	1.0	40	7.6	438	83.7	45	8.6	523
.0	3	6.3	1	2.1	1	2.1	5	10.4	41	85.4	2	4.2	48
.0	25	5.3	6	1.3	4	.8	35	7.4	397	83.6	43	9.1	475
.2	199	4.5	78	1.7	15	.3	303	6.8	3,798	85.1	362	8.1	4,463
.5	32	7.7	10	2.4	1	.2	45	10.8	358	86.3	12	2.9	415
.2	167	4.1	68	1.7	14	.3	258	6.4	3,440	85.0	350	8.6	4,048
.0	1	.5	2	1.0	2	1.0	5	2.5	129	65.5	63	32.0	197
.0	0	.0	0	.0	0	.0	0	.0	14	87.5	2	12.5	16
.0	1	.6	2	1.1	2	1.1	5	2.8	115	63.5	61	33.7	181
.5	3	1.4	5	2.4	1	.5	10	4.8	165	79.3	33	15.9	208
7.7	0	.0	1	7.7	0	.0	2	15.4	9	69.2	2	15.4	13
.0	3	1.5	4	2.1	1	.5	8	4.1	156	80.0	31	15.9	195
.2	4	1.0	7	1.7	3	.7	15	3.7	294	72.6	96	23.7	405
3.4	0	.0	1	3.4	0	.0	2	6.9	23	79.3	4	13.8	29
.0	4	1.1	6	1.6	3	.8	13	3.5	271	72.1	92	24.5	316
.0	0	.0	0	.0	0	.0	0	.0	0	.0	0	.0	0
.0	0	.0	0	.0	0	.0	0	.0	0	.0	0	.0	0
.0	0	.0	0	.0	0	.0	0	.0	0	.0	0	.0	0
.0	0	.0	0	.0	0	.0	0	.0	0	.0	0	.0	0
.0	0	.0	0	.0	0	.0	0	.0	0	.0	0	.0	0
.0	0	.0	0	.0	0	.0	0	.0	0	.0	0	.0	0
.0	0	.0	0	.0	0	.0	0	.0	0	.0	0	.0	0
.0	0	.0	0	.0	0	.0	0	.0	0	.0	0	.0	0
.0	0	.0	0	.0	0	.0	0	.0	0	.0	0	.0	0
.3	172	4.2	73	1.8	12	.3	268	6.5	3,489	84.3	380	9.2	4,137
.5	29	7.6	9	2.3	0	.0	40	10.4	331	86.4	12	3.1	383
.3	143	3.8	64	1.7	12	.3	228	6.1	3,158	84.1	368	9.8	3,754
.1	31	4.2	12	1.6	6	.8	50	6.8	603	82.5	78	10.7	731
1.6	3	4.9	2	3.3	1	1.6	7	11.5	50	82.0	4	6.6	61
.0	28	4.2	10	1.5	5	.7	43	6.4	553	82.5	74	11.0	670
.2	203	4.2	85	1.7	18	.4	318	6.5	4,092	84.1	458	9.4	4,868
.7	32	7.2	11	2.5	1	.2	47	10.6	381	85.8	16	3.6	444
.2	171	3.9	74	1.7	17	.4	271	6.1	3,711	83.9	442	10.0	4,424
.0	0	.0	2	9.1	0	.0	2	9.1	20	90.9	0	.0	22
.0	0	.0	1	50.0	0	.0	1	50.0	1	50.0	0	.0	2
.0	0	.0	1	5.0	0	.0	1	5.0	19	95.0	0	.0	20
.2	203	4.2	87	1.8	18	.4	320	6.5	4,112	84.1	458	9.4	4,890
.7	32	7.2	12	2.7	1	.2	48	10.8	382	85.7	16	3.6	446
.2	171	3.8	75	1.7	17	.4	272	6.1	3,730	83.9	442	9.9	4,444

TABLE 17 - TOTAL ENROLLMENT IN INSTITUTIONS OF HIGHER EDUCATION FOR SELECTED MAJOR FIELDS OF STUDY AND LEVEL OF ENROLLMENT BY RACE, ETHNICITY, AND SEX: STATE, 1978

MAJOR FIELD 0900 - ENGINEERING

	AMERICAN INDIAN ALASKAN NATIVE		BLACK NON-HISPANIC		ASIAN OR PACIFIC ISLANDER		HISPANIC		TOTAL MINORITY		WHITE NON-HISPANIC		NON-RESIDENT ALIEN	
	NUMBER	%	NUMBER	%	NUMBER	%	NUMBER	%	NUMBER	%	NUMBER	%	NUMBER	%
LOUISIANA (16 INSTITUTIONS)														
UNDERGRADUATES:														
FULL-TIME	8	.1	997	11.0	87	1.0	128	1.4	1,220	13.4	6,613	72.7	1,268	13.9
FEMALE	2	.2	187	21.1	10	1.1	15	1.7	214	24.1	594	66.9	80	9.0
MALE	6	.1	810	9.9	77	.9	113	1.4	1,006	12.2	6,019	73.3	1,188	14.5
PART-TIME	1	.1	89	9.4	5	.5	21	2.2	116	12.2	777	81.7	58	6.1
FEMALE	0	.0	9	11.5	1	1.3	0	.0	10	12.8	66	84.6	2	2.6
MALE	1	.1	80	9.2	4	.5	21	2.4	106	12.1	711	81.4	56	6.4
TOTAL	9	.1	1,086	10.8	92	.9	149	1.5	1,336	13.3	7,390	73.5	1,326	13.2
FEMALE	2	.2	196	20.3	11	1.1	15	1.6	224	23.2	660	68.3	82	8.5
MALE	7	.1	890	9.8	81	.9	134	1.5	1,112	12.2	6,730	74.1	1,244	13.7
GRADUATE:														
FULL-TIME	0	.0	0	.0	2	.9	5	2.3	7	3.3	88	41.1	119	55.6
FEMALE	0	.0	0	.0	0	.0	0	.0	0	.0	8	72.7	3	27.3
MALE	0	.0	0	.0	2	1.0	5	2.5	7	3.4	80	39.4	116	57.1
PART-TIME	0	.0	8	2.7	8	2.7	11	3.7	27	9.0	239	79.4	35	11.6
FEMALE	0	.0	2	12.5	0	.0	0	.0	2	12.5	14	87.5	0	.0
MALE	0	.0	6	2.1	8	2.8	11	3.9	25	8.8	225	78.9	35	12.3
TOTAL	0	.0	8	1.6	10	1.9	16	3.1	34	6.6	327	63.5	154	29.9
FEMALE	0	.0	2	7.4	0	.0	0	.0	2	7.4	22	81.5	3	11.1
MALE	0	.0	6	1.2	10	2.0	16	3.3	32	6.6	305	62.5	151	30.9
PROFESSIONAL:														
FULL-TIME	0	.0	0	.0	0	.0	0	.0	0	.0	0	.0	0	.0
FEMALE	0	.0	0	.0	0	.0	0	.0	0	.0	0	.0	0	.0
MALE	0	.0	0	.0	0	.0	0	.0	0	.0	0	.0	0	.0
PART-TIME	0	.0	0	.0	0	.0	0	.0	0	.0	0	.0	0	.0
FEMALE	0	.0	0	.0	0	.0	0	.0	0	.0	0	.0	0	.0
MALE	0	.0	0	.0	0	.0	0	.0	0	.0	0	.0	0	.0
TOTAL	0	.0	0	.0	0	.0	0	.0	0	.0	0	.0	0	.0
FEMALE	0	.0	0	.0	0	.0	0	.0	0	.0	0	.0	0	.0
MALE	0	.0	0	.0	0	.0	0	.0	0	.0	0	.0	0	.0
UND+GRAD+PROF:														
FULL-TIME	8	.1	997	10.7	89	1.0	133	1.4	1,227	13.2	6,701	71.9	1,387	14.9
FEMALE	2	.2	187	20.8	10	1.1	15	1.7	214	23.8	602	67.0	83	9.2
MALE	6	.1	810	9.6	79	.9	118	1.4	1,013	12.0	6,099	72.5	1,304	15.5
PART-TIME	1	.1	97	7.7	13	1.0	32	2.6	143	11.4	1,016	81.2	93	7.4
FEMALE	0	.0	11	11.7	1	1.1	0	.0	12	12.8	80	85.1	2	2.1
MALE	1	.1	86	7.4	12	1.0	32	2.8	131	11.3	936	80.8	91	7.9
TOTAL	9	.1	1,094	10.4	102	1.0	165	1.6	1,370	13.0	7,717	73.0	1,480	14.0
FEMALE	2	.2	198	19.9	11	1.1	15	1.5	226	22.8	682	68.7	85	8.6
MALE	7	.1	896	9.4	91	1.0	150	1.6	1,144	11.9	7,035	73.5	1,395	14.6
UNCLASSIFIED:														
TOTAL	0	.0	2	5.6	0	.0	0	.0	2	5.6	31	86.1		8.3
FEMALE	0	.0	0	.0	0	.0	0	.0	0	.0	5	100.0		.0
MALE	0	.0	2	6.5	0	.0	0	.0	2	6.5	26	83.9	3	9.7
TOTAL ENROLLMENT:														
TOTAL	9	.1	1,096	10.3	102	1.0	165	1.6	1,372	13.0	7,748	73.1	1,483	14.0
FEMALE	2	.2	198	19.8	11	1.1	15	1.5	226	22.6	687	68.8	85	8.5
MALE	7	.1	898	9.3	91	.9	150	1.6	1,146	11.9	7,061	73.5	1,398	14.6
MAINE (5 INSTITUTIONS)														
UNDERGRADUATES:														
FULL-TIME	6	.4	0	.0	6	.4	4	.3	16	1.1	1,417	98.0	13	.9
FEMALE	0	.0	0	.0	1	.9	0	.0	1	.9	112	97.4	2	1.7
MALE	6	.5	0	.0	5	.4	4	.3	15	1.1	1,305	98.0	11	.8
PART-TIME	0	.0	0	.0	0	.0	0	.0	0	.0	53	100.0	0	.0
FEMALE	0	.0	0	.0	0	.0	0	.0	0	.0	9	100.0	0	.0
MALE	0	.0	0	.0	0	.0	0	.0	0	.0	44	100.0	0	.0
TOTAL	6	.4	0	.0	6	.4	4	.3	16	1.1	1,470	98.1	13	.9
FEMALE	0	.0	0	.0	1	.8	0	.0	1	.8	121	97.6	2	1.6
MALE	6	.4	0	.0	5	.4	4	.3	15	1.1	1,349	98.1	11	.8
GRADUATE:														
FULL-TIME	0	.0	0	.0	0	.0	0	.0	0	.0	32	97.0	1	3.0
FEMALE	0	.0	0	.0	0	.0	0	.0	0	.0	3	100.0	0	.0
MALE	0	.0	0	.0	0	.0	0	.0	0	.0	29	96.7	1	3.3
PART-TIME	0	.0	0	.0	0	.0	0	.0	0	.0	9	100.0	0	.0
FEMALE	0	.0	0	.0	0	.0	0	.0	0	.0	1	100.0	0	.0
MALE	0	.0	0	.0	0	.0	0	.0	0	.0	8	100.0	0	.0
TOTAL	0	.0	0	.0	0	.0	0	.0	0	.0	41	97.6	1	2.4
FEMALE	0	.0	0	.0	0	.0	0	.0	0	.0	4	100.0	0	.0
MALE	0	.0	0	.0	0	.0	0	.0	0	.0	37	97.4	1	2.6
PROFESSIONAL:														
FULL-TIME	0	.0	0	.0	0	.0	0	.0	0	.0	0	.0	0	.0
FEMALE	0	.0	0	.0	0	.0	0	.0	0	.0	0	.0	0	.0
MALE	0	.0	0	.0	0	.0	0	.0	0	.0	0	.0	0	.0

ENGINEERING

INDIAN NATIVE	BLACK NON-HISPANIC		ASIAN OR PACIFIC ISLANDER		HISPANIC		TOTAL MINORITY		WHITE NON-HISPANIC		NON-RESIDENT ALIEN		TOTAL
%	NUMBER	%	NUMBER	%	NUMBER	%	NUMBER	%	NUMBER	%	NUMBER	%	NUMBER

CONTINUED

INDIAN NATIVE %	BLACK #	BLACK %	ASIAN #	ASIAN %	HISP #	HISP %	TOT MIN #	TOT MIN %	WHITE #	WHITE %	NON-RES #	NON-RES %	TOTAL #
.0	0	.0	0	.0	0	.0	0	.0	0	.0	0	.0	0
.0	0	.0	0	.0	0	.0	0	.0	0	.0	0	.0	0
.0	0	.0	0	.0	0	.0	0	.0	0	.0	0	'.0	3
.0	0	.0	0	.0	0	.0	0	.0	0	.0	0	.0	0
.0	0	.0	0	.0	0	.0	0	.0	0	.0	0	.0	0
.0	0	.0	0	.0	0	.0	0	.0	0	.0	0	.0	0
.4	0	.0	6	.4	4	.3	16	1.1	1,449	98.0	14	.9	1,479
.4	0	.0	1	.8	0	.0	1	.8	115	97.5	2	1.7	118
.4	0	.0	5	.4	4	.3	15	1.1	1,334	98.0	12	.9	1,361
.0	0	.0	0	.0	0	.0	0	.0	62	100.0	0	.0	62
.0	0	.0	0	.0	0	.0	0	.0	10	100.0	0	.0	10
.0	0	.0	0	.0	0	.0	0	.0	52	100.0	0	.0	52
.4	0	.0	6	.4	4	.3	16	1.0	1,511	98.1	14	.9	1,541
.0	0	.0	1	.8	0	.0	1	.8	125	97.7	2	1.6	128
.4	0	.0	5	.4	4	.3	15	1.1	1,386	98.1	12	.8	1,413
.0	0	.0	0	.0	0	.0	0	.0	12	100.0	0	.0	12
.0	0	.0	0	.0	0	.0	0	.0	1	100.0	0	.0	1
.0	0	.0	0	.0	0	.0	0	.0	11	100.0	0	.0	11
.4	0	.0	6	.4	4	.3	16	1.0	1,523	98.1	14	.9	1,553
.0	0	.0	1	.8	0	.0	1	.8	126	97.7	2	1.6	129
.4	0	.0	5	.4	4	.3	15	1.1	1,397	98.1	12	.8	1,424

(6 INSTITUTIONS)

INDIAN NATIVE %	BLACK #	BLACK %	ASIAN #	ASIAN %	HISP #	HISP %	TOT MIN #	TOT MIN %	WHITE #	WHITE %	NON-RES #	NON-RES %	TOTAL #
.4	185	5.9	87	2.8	25	.8	309	9.8	2,464	78.5	367	11.7	3,140
.6	47	14.0	13	3.9	1	.3	63	18.8	232	69.3	40	11.9	335
.4	138	4.9	74	2.6	24	.9	246	8.8	2,232	79.6	327	11.7	2,805
.5	20	5.0	8	2.0	5	1.3	35	8.8	328	82.2	36	9.0	359
.0	4	11.4	1	2.9	0	.0	5	14.3	28	80.0	2	5.7	35
.5	16	4.4	7	1.9	5	1.4	30	8.2	300	82.4	34	9.3	364
.4	205	5.8	95	2.7	30	.8	344	9.7	2,792	78.9	403	11.4	3,539
.5	51	13.8	14	3.8	1	.3	68	18.4	260	70.3	42	11.4	370
.4	154	4.9	81	2.6	29	.9	276	8.7	2,532	79.9	361	11.4	3,169
1.1	2	.8	5	1.9	0	.0	10	3.8	160	61.3	91	34.9	261
8.0	0	.0	1	4.0	0	.0	3	12.0	16	64.0	6	24.0	25
.4	2	.8	4	1.7	0	.0	7	3.0	144	61.0	85	36.0	236
.8	17	2.6	10	1.6	6	.9	38	5.9	551	85.8	53	8.3	642
2.6	1	2.6	1	2.6	0	.0	3	7.7	34	87.2	2	5.1	39
.7	16	2.7	9	1.5	6	1.0	35	5.8	517	85.7	51	8.5	603
.9	19	2.1	15	1.7	6	.7	48	5.3	711	78.7	144	15.9	903
4.7	1	1.6	2	3.1	0	.0	6	9.4	50	78.1	8	12.5	64
.6	18	2.1	13	1.5	6	.7	42	5.0	661	78.8	136	16.2	839
.0	0	.0	0	.0	0	.0	0	.0	0	.0	0	.0	0
.0	0	.0	0	.0	0	.0	0	.0	0	.0	0	.0	0
.0	0	.0	0	.0	0	.0	0	.0	0	.0	0	.0	0
.0	0	.0	0	.0	0	.0	0	.0	0	.0	0	.0	0
.0	0	.0	0	.0	0	.0	0	.0	0	.0	0	.0	0
.0	0	.0	0	.0	0	.0	0	.0	0	.0	0	.0	0
.0	0	.0	0	.0	0	.0	0	.0	0	.0	0	.0	0
.0	0	.0	0	.0	0	.0	0	.0	0	.0	0	.0	0
.0	0	.0	0	.0	0	.0	0	.0	0	.0	0	.0	0
.4	187	5.5	92	2.7	25	.7	319	9.4	2,624	77.2	458	13.5	3,401
1.1	47	13.1	14	3.9	1	.3	66	18.3	248	68.9	46	12.8	300
.4	140	4.6	78	2.6	24	.8	253	8.3	2,376	78.1	412	13.5	3,041
.7	37	3.6	18	1.7	11	1.1	73	7.0	879	84.4	89	8.5	1,041
1.4	5	6.8	2	2.7	0	.0	8	10.8	62	83.8	4	5.4	74
.6	32	3.3	16	1.7	11	1.1	65	6.7	817	84.5	85	8.8	967
.5	224	5.0	110	2.5	36	.8	392	8.8	3,503	78.9	547	12.3	4,442
1.2	52	12.0	16	3.7	1	.2	74	17.1	310	71.4	50	11.5	434
.4	172	4.3	94	2.3	35	.9	318	7.9	3,193	79.7	497	12.4	4,008
.0	37	5.8	19	3.0	7	1.1	63	9.9	535	84.4	36	5.7	634
.0	3	6.5	3	6.5	1	2.2	7	15.2	34	73.9	5	10.9	46
.0	34	5.8	16	2.7	6	1.0	56	9.5	501	85.2	31	5.3	588
.4	261	5.1	129	2.5	43	.8	455	9.0	4,038	79.6	583	11.5	5,076
1.0	55	11.5	19	4.0	2	.4	81	16.9	344	71.7	55	11.5	480
.4	206	4.5	110	2.4	41	.9	374	8.1	3,694	80.4	528	11.5	4,595

TABLE 17 - TOTAL ENROLLMENT IN INSTITUTIONS OF HIGHER EDUCATION FOR SELECTED MAJOR FIELDS OF STUDY AND LEVEL OF ENROLLMENT
BY RACE, ETHNICITY, AND SEX: STATE, 1978

MAJOR FIELD 0900 - ENGINEERING

	AMERICAN INDIAN ALASKAN NATIVE		BLACK NON-HISPANIC		ASIAN OR PACIFIC ISLANDER		HISPANIC		TOTAL MINORITY		WHITE NON-HISPANIC		NON-RESIDENT ALIEN	
	NUMBER	%	NUMBER	%	NUMBER	%	NUMBER	%	NUMBER	%	NUMBER	%	NUMBER	%
MASSACHUSETTS (25 INSTITUTIONS)														
UNDERGRADUATES:														
FULL-TIME	57	.3	555	3.1	470	2.7	245	1.4	1,327	7.5	15,349	86.5	1,059	6.0
FEMALE	6	.3	120	6.8	71	4.0	26	1.5	223	12.7	1,434	81.5	103	5.9
MALE	51	.3	435	2.7	399	2.5	219	1.4	1,104	6.9	13,915	87.1	956	6.0
PART-TIME	8	.2	62	1.5	33	.8	31	.8	134	3.3	3,899	95.9	31	.8
FEMALE	1	.2	10	1.8	3	.5	5	.9	19	3.4	530	96.2	2	.4
MALE	7	.2	52	1.5	30	.9	26	.7	115	3.3	3,369	95.9	29	.8
TOTAL	65	.3	617	2.8	503	2.3	276	1.3	1,461	6.7	19,248	88.3	1,090	5.0
FEMALE	7	.3	130	5.6	74	3.2	31	1.3	242	10.5	1,964	85.0	105	4.5
MALE	58	.3	487	2.5	429	2.2	245	1.3	1,219	6.3	17,284	88.7	985	5.1
GRADUATE:														
FULL-TIME	0	.0	44	1.8	77	3.1	23	.9	144	5.8	1,503	60.6	835	33.6
FEMALE	0	.0	10	4.8	11	5.3	3	1.4	24	11.6	144	69.6	39	10.8
MALE	0	.0	34	1.8	66	2.9	20	.9	120	5.3	1,359	59.7	796	35.0
PART-TIME	2	.1	29	1.5	104	5.4	17	.9	152	7.9	1,670	86.8	101	5.3
FEMALE	0	.0	2	1.2	12	7.3	1	.6	15	9.1	143	87.2	6	3.7
MALE	2	.1	27	1.5	92	5.2	16	.9	137	7.8	1,527	86.8	95	5.4
TOTAL	2	.0	73	1.7	181	4.1	40	.9	296	6.7	3,173	72.0	936	21.2
FEMALE	0	.0	12	3.2	23	6.2	4	1.1	39	10.5	287	77.4	45	12.1
MALE	2	.0	61	1.5	158	3.9	36	.9	257	6.4	2,886	71.5	891	22.1
PROFESSIONAL:														
FULL-TIME	0	.0	0	.0	0	.0	0	.0	0	.0	1	100.0	0	.0
FEMALE	0	.0	0	.0	0	.0	0	.0	0	.0	0	.0	0	.0
MALE	0	.0	0	.0	0	.0	0	.0	0	.0	1	100.0	0	.0
PART-TIME	0	.0	0	.0	0	.0	0	.0	0	.0	0	.0	0	.0
FEMALE	0	.0	0	.0	0	.0	0	.0	0	.0	0	.0	0	.0
MALE	0	.0	0	.0	0	.0	0	.0	0	.0	0	.0	0	.0
TOTAL	0	.0	0	.0	0	.0	0	.0	0	.0	1	100.0	0	.0
FEMALE	0	.0	0	.0	0	.0	0	.0	0	.0	0	.0	0	.0
MALE	0	.0	0	.0	0	.0	0	.0	0	.0	1	100.0	0	.0
UND+GRAD+PROF:														
FULL-TIME	57	.3	599	3.0	547	2.7	268	1.3	1,471	7.3	16,853	83.4	1,894	9.4
FEMALE	6	.3	130	6.6	82	4.2	29	1.5	247	12.6	1,578	80.2	142	7.2
MALE	51	.3	469	2.6	465	2.5	239	1.3	1,224	6.7	15,275	83.7	1,752	9.6
PART-TIME	10	.2	91	1.5	137	2.3	48	.8	286	4.8	5,569	93.0	132	2.2
FEMALE	1	.1	12	1.7	15	2.1	6	.6	34	4.8	673	94.1	8	1.1
MALE	9	.2	79	1.5	122	2.3	42	.8	252	4.8	4,896	92.9	124	2.4
TOTAL	67	.3	690	2.6	684	2.6	316	1.2	1,757	6.7	22,422	85.6	2,026	7.7
FEMALE	7	.3	142	5.3	97	3.6	35	1.3	281	10.5	2,251	83.9	150	5.6
MALE	60	.3	548	2.3	587	2.5	281	1.2	1,476	6.3	20,171	85.6	1,876	8.0
UNCLASSIFIED:														
TOTAL	0	.0	6	1.8	15	4.5	2	.6	23	6.9	244	72.8	68	20.3
FEMALE	0	.0	1	2.9	0	.0	0	.0	1	2.9	31	91.2	2	5.9
MALE	0	.0	5	1.7	15	5.0	2	.7	22	7.3	213	70.8	66	21.9
TOTAL ENROLLMENT:														
TOTAL	67	.3	696	2.6	699	2.6	318	1.2	1,780	6.7	22,666	85.4	2,094	7.9
FEMALE	7	.3	143	5.3	97	3.6	35	1.3	282	10.4	2,282	84.0	152	5.6
MALE	60	.3	553	2.3	602	2.5	283	1.2	1,498	6.3	20,384	85.6	1,942	8.2
MICHIGAN (33 INSTITUTIONS)														
UNDERGRADUATES:														
FULL-TIME	62	.3	831	4.3	271	1.4	130	.7	1,294	6.7	16,480	85.7	1,452	7.6
FEMALE	4	.2	198	7.8	42	1.7	15	.6	259	10.3	2,192	86.8	73	2.9
MALE	58	.3	633	3.8	229	1.4	115	.7	1,035	6.2	14,288	85.5	1,379	8.3
PART-TIME	26	.6	355	8.4	54	1.3	63	1.5	498	11.8	3,541	83.7	190	4.5
FEMALE	3	.9	53	16.7	8	2.5	5	1.6	69	21.8	241	76.0	7	2.2
MALE	23	.6	302	7.7	46	1.2	58	1.5	429	11.0	3,300	84.4	183	4.7
TOTAL	88	.4	1,186	5.1	325	1.4	193	.8	1,792	7.6	20,021	85.4	1,642	7.0
FEMALE	7	.2	251	8.8	50	1.8	20	.7	328	11.5	2,433	85.6	80	2.8
MALE	81	.4	935	4.5	275	1.3	173	.8	1,464	7.1	17,588	85.3	1,562	7.6
GRADUATE:														
FULL-TIME	0	.0	26	2.2	67	5.6	8	.7	101	8.5	647	54.2	445	37.3
FEMALE	0	.0	5	7.5	3	4.5	1	1.5	9	13.4	43	64.2	15	22.4
MALE	0	.0	21	1.9	64	5.7	7	.6	92	8.2	604	53.6	430	38.2
PART-TIME	1	.1	35	3.5	62	6.2	2	.2	100	10.0	757	75.7	143	14.3
FEMALE	0	.0	7	11.9	0	.0	0	.0	7	11.9	47	79.7	5	8.5
MALE	1	.1	28	3.0	62	6.6	2	.2	93	9.9	710	75.5	138	14.7
TOTAL	1	.0	61	2.8	129	5.9	10	.5	201	9.2	1,404	64.0	588	26.8
FEMALE	0	.0	12	9.5	3	2.4	1	.8	16	12.7	90	71.4	20	15.9
MALE	1	.0	49	2.4	126	6.1	9	.4	185	9.0	1,314	63.6	568	27.5
PROFESSIONAL:														
FULL-TIME	0	.0	0	.0	0	.0	0	.0	0	.0	0	.0	0	.0
FEMALE	0	.0	0	.0	0	.0	0	.0	0	.0	0	.0	0	.0
MALE	0	.0	0	.0	0	.0	0	.0	0	.0	0	.0	0	.0

ENGINEERING

N INDIAN NATIVE	BLACK NON-HISPANIC		ASIAN OR PACIFIC ISLANDER		HISPANIC		TOTAL MINORITY		WHITE NON-HISPANIC		NON-RESIDENT ALIEN		TOTAL
%	NUMBER	%	NUMBER	%	NUMBER	%	NUMBER	%	NUMBER	%	NUMBER	%	NUMBER

CONTINUED

.0	0	.0	0	.0	0	.0	0	.0	0	.0	0	.0	0
.0	0	.0	0	.0	0	.0	0	.0	0	.0	0	.0	0
.0	0	.0	0	.0	0	.0	0	.0	0	.0	0	.0	0
.0	0	.0	0	.0	0	.0	0	.0	0	.0	0	.0	0
.0	0	.0	0	.0	0	.0	0	.0	0	.0	0	.0	0
.0	0	.0	0	.0	0	.0	0	.0	0	.0	0	.0	0
.3	857	4.2	338	1.7	138	.7	1,395	6.8	17,127	83.9	1,897	9.3	20,419
.2	203	7.8	45	1.7	16	.6	268	10.3	2,235	86.3	88	3.4	2,591
.3	654	3.7	293	1.6	122	.7	1,127	6.3	14,892	83.5	1,809	10.1	17,828
.5	390	7.5	116	2.2	65	1.2	598	11.4	4,298	82.2	333	6.4	5,229
.8	60	16.0	8	2.1	5	1.3	76	20.2	288	76.6	12	3.2	376
.5	330	6.8	108	2.2	60	1.2	522	10.8	4,010	82.6	321	6.6	4,853
.3	1,247	4.9	454	1.8	203	.8	1,993	7.8	21,425	83.5	2,230	8.7	25,648
.2	263	8.9	53	1.8	21	.7	344	11.6	2,523	85.0	100	3.4	2,967
.4	984	4.3	401	1.8	182	.8	1,649	7.3	18,902	83.3	2,130	9.4	22,681
.0	29	8.3	7	2.0	4	1.1	40	11.5	201	57.8	107	30.7	348
.0	7	20.0	0	.0	0	.0	7	20.0	24	68.6	4	11.4	35
.0	22	7.0	7	2.2	4	1.3	33	10.5	177	56.5	103	32.9	313
.3	1,276	4.9	461	1.8	207	.8	2,033	7.8	21,626	83.2	2,337	9.0	25,996
.2	270	9.0	53	1.8	21	.7	351	11.7	2,547	84.8	104	3.5	3,002
.4	1,006	4.4	408	1.8	186	.8	1,682	7.3	19,079	83.0	2,233	9.7	22,994

(25 INSTITUTIONS)

N INDIAN NATIVE	BLACK NON-HISPANIC		ASIAN OR PACIFIC ISLANDER		HISPANIC		TOTAL MINORITY		WHITE NON-HISPANIC		NON-RESIDENT ALIEN		TOTAL
.2	23	.6	97	2.4	15	.4	141	3.6	3,645	92.0	175	4.4	3,961
.6	6	1.8	9	2.7	1	.3	17	5.0	315	92.9	7	2.1	339
.1	17	.5	88	2.4	14	.4	124	3.4	3,330	91.9	168	4.6	3,622
.0	4	.8	9	1.8	1	.2	14	2.8	483	96.8	2	.4	499
.0	0	.0	2	3.7	0	.0	2	3.7	52	96.3	0	.0	54
.0	4	.9	7	1.6	1	.2	12	2.7	431	96.9	2	.4	445
.1	27	.6	106	2.4	16	.4	155	3.5	4,128	92.6	177	4.0	4,460
.3	6	1.5	11	2.8	1	.3	19	4.8	367	93.4	7	1.8	393
.1	21	.5	95	2.3	15	.4	136	3.3	3,761	92.5	170	4.2	4,067
.0	1	.2	20	3.1	10	1.5	31	4.8	441	68.3	174	26.9	646
.0	0	.0	2	5.3	0	.0	2	5.3	32	84.2	4	10.5	38
.0	1	.2	18	3.0	10	1.6	29	4.8	409	67.3	170	28.0	608
.0	0	.0	0	.0	0	.0	0	.0	0	.0	0	.0	0
.0	0	.0	0	.0	0	.0	0	.0	0	.0	0	.0	0
.0	0	.0	0	.0	0	.0	0	.0	0	.0	0	.0	0
.0	1	.2	20	3.1	10	1.5	31	4.8	441	68.3	174	26.9	646
.0	0	.0	2	5.3	0	.0	2	5.3	32	84.2	4	10.5	38
.0	1	.2	18	3.0	10	1.6	29	4.8	409	67.3	170	28.0	608
.0	0	.0	0	.0	0	.0	0	.0	0	.0	0	.0	0
.0	0	.0	0	.0	0	.0	0	.0	0	.0	0	.0	0
.0	0	.0	0	.0	0	.0	0	.0	0	.0	0	.0	0
.0	0	.0	0	.0	0	.0	0	.0	0	.0	0	.0	0
.0	0	.0	0	.0	0	.0	0	.0	0	.0	0	.0	0
.0	0	.0	0	.0	0	.0	0	.0	0	.0	0	.0	0
.1	24	.5	117	2.5	25	.5	172	3.7	4,086	88.7	349	7.6	4,607
.3	6	1.6	11	2.9	1	.3	19	5.0	347	92.0	11	2.9	377
.1	18	.4	106	2.5	24	.6	153	3.6	3,739	88.4	338	8.0	4,230
.0	4	.8	9	1.8	1	.2	14	2.8	483	96.8	2	.4	499
.0	0	.0	2	3.7	0	.0	2	3.7	52	96.3	0	.0	54
.0	4	.9	7	1.6	1	.2	12	2.7	431	96.9	2	.4	445
.1	28	.5	126	2.5	26	.5	186	3.6	4,569	89.5	351	6.9	5,106
.2	6	1.4	13	3.0	1	.2	21	4.9	399	92.6	11	2.6	431
.1	22	.5	113	2.4	25	.5	165	3.5	4,170	89.2	340	7.3	4,675
1.6	1	1.6	0	.0	0	.0	2	3.3	58	95.1	1	1.6	61
.0	0	.0	0	.0	0	.0	0	.0	8	100.0	0	.0	8
1.9	1	1.9	0	.0	0	.0	2	3.8	50	94.3	1	1.9	53
.1	29	.6	126	2.4	26	.5	188	3.6	4,627	89.5	352	6.8	5,167
.2	6	1.4	13	3.0	1	.2	21	4.8	407	92.7	11	2.5	439
.1	23	.5	113	2.4	25	.5	167	3.5	4,220	89.3	341	7.2	4,721

TABLE 17 - TOTAL ENROLLMENT IN INSTITUTIONS OF HIGHER EDUCATION FOR SELECTED MAJOR FIELDS OF STUDY AND LEVEL OF ENROLLMENT BY RACE, ETHNICITY, AND SEX: STATE, 1978

MAJOR FIELD 0900 - ENGINEERING

	AMERICAN INDIAN ALASKAN NATIVE		BLACK NON-HISPANIC		ASIAN OR PACIFIC ISLANDER		HISPANIC		TOTAL MINORITY		WHITE NON-HISPANIC		NON-RESIDENT ALIEN	
	NUMBER	%	NUMBER	%	NUMBER	%	NUMBER	%	NUMBER	%	NUMBER	%	NUMBER	%
MISSISSIPPI (20 INSTITUTIONS)														
UNDERGRADUATES:														
FULL-TIME	1	.0	123	4.4	21	.8	5	.2	150	5.4	2,398	85.9	243	8.7
FEMALE	0	.0	21	9.2	1	.4	1	.4	23	10.1	194	85.1	11	4.8
MALE	1	.0	102	4.0	20	.8	4	.2	127	5.0	2,204	86.0	232	9.1
PART-TIME	1	.3	16	4.3	3	.8	0	.0	20	5.3	347	92.5	8	2.1
FEMALE	0	.0	1	2.6	0	.0	0	.0	1	2.6	38	97.4	0	.0
MALE	1	.3	15	4.5	3	.9	0	.0	19	5.7	309	92.0	8	2.4
TOTAL	2	.1	139	4.4	24	.8	5	.2	170	5.4	2,745	86.7	251	7.9
FEMALE	0	.0	22	8.2	1	.4	1	.4	24	9.0	232	86.9	11	4.1
MALE	2	.1	117	4.0	23	.8	4	.1	146	5.0	2,513	86.7	240	8.3
GRADUATE:														
FULL-TIME	1	.9	3	2.8	0	.0	0	.0	4	3.7	59	54.6	45	41.7
FEMALE	1	50.0	0	.0	0	.0	0	.0	1	50.0	1	50.0	0	.0
MALE	0	.0	3	2.8	0	.0	0	.0	3	2.8	58	54.7	45	42.5
PART-TIME	1	1.0	2	1.9	1	1.0	0	.0	4	3.8	61	58.1	40	38.1
FEMALE	0	.0	0	.0	0	.0	0	.0	0	.0	0	.0	1	100.0
MALE	1	1.0	2	1.9	1	1.0	0	.0	4	3.8	61	58.7	39	37.5
TOTAL	2	.9	5	2.3	1	.5	0	.0	8	3.8	120	56.3	85	39.9
FEMALE	1	33.3	0	.0	0	.0	0	.0	1	33.3	1	33.3	1	33.3
MALE	1	.5	5	2.4	1	.5	0	.0	7	3.3	119	56.7	84	40.0
PROFESSIONAL:														
FULL-TIME	0	.0	0	.0	0	.0	0	.0	0	.0	0	.0	0	.0
FEMALE	0	.0	0	.0	0	.0	0	.0	0	.0	0	.0	0	.0
MALE	0	.0	0	.0	0	.0	0	.0	0	.0	0	.0	0	.0
PART-TIME	0	.0	0	.0	0	.0	0	.0	0	.0	0	.0	0	.0
FEMALE	0	.0	0	.0	0	.0	0	.0	0	.0	0	.0	0	.0
MALE	0	.0	0	.0	0	.0	0	.0	0	.0	0	.0	0	.0
TOTAL	0	.0	0	.0	0	.0	0	.0	0	.0	0	.0	0	.0
FEMALE	0	.0	0	.0	0	.0	0	.0	0	.0	0	.0	0	.0
MALE	0	.0	0	.0	0	.0	0	.0	0	.0	0	.0	0	.0
UND+GRAD+PROF:														
FULL-TIME	2	.1	126	4.3	21	.7	5	.2	154	5.3	2,457	84.8	288	9.9
FEMALE	1	.4	21	9.1	1	.4	1	.4	24	10.4	195	84.8	11	4.8
MALE	1	.0	105	3.9	20	.7	4	.1	130	4.9	2,262	84.8	277	10.4
PART-TIME	2	.4	18	3.8	4	.8	0	.0	24	5.0	408	85.0	48	10.0
FEMALE	0	.0	1	2.5	0	.0	0	.0	1	2.5	38	95.0	1	2.5
MALE	2	.5	17	3.9	4	.9	0	.0	23	5.2	370	84.1	47	10.7
TOTAL	4	.1	144	4.3	25	.7	5	.1	178	5.3	2,865	84.8	336	9.9
FEMALE	1	.4	22	8.1	1	.4	1	.4	25	9.3	233	86.3	12	4.4
MALE	3	.1	122	3.9	24	.8	4	.1	153	4.9	2,632	84.7	324	10.4
UNCLASSIFIED:														
TOTAL	0	.0	0	.0	1	2.9	0	.0	1	2.9	8	23.5	25	73.5
FEMALE	0	.0	0	.0	0	.0	0	.0	0	.0	1	100.0	0	.0
MALE	0	.0	0	.0	1	3.0	0	.0	1	3.0	7	21.2	25	75.8
TOTAL ENROLLMENT:														
TOTAL	4	.1	144	4.2	26	.8	5	.1	179	5.2	2,873	84.2	361	10.6
FEMALE	1	.4	22	8.1	1	.4	1	.4	25	9.2	234	86.3	12	4.4
MALE	3	.1	122	3.9	25	.8	4	.1	154	4.9	2,639	84.0	349	11.1
MISSOURI (11 INSTITUTIONS)														
UNDERGRADUATES:														
FULL-TIME	15	.2	259	3.4	123	1.6	31	.4	428	5.7	6,686	88.6	430	5.7
FEMALE	0	.0	60	6.7	17	1.9	4	.4	81	9.0	779	86.9	36	4.0
MALE	15	.2	199	3.0	106	1.6	27	.4	347	5.2	5,907	88.9	394	5.9
PART-TIME	1	.1	34	4.4	20	2.6	4	.5	59	7.7	674	87.4	38	4.9
FEMALE	0	.0	5	6.7	5	6.7	1	1.3	11	14.7	61	81.3	3	4.0
MALE	1	.1	29	4.2	15	2.2	3	.4	48	6.9	613	88.1	35	5.0
TOTAL	16	.2	293	3.5	143	1.7	35	.4	487	5.9	7,360	88.5	468	5.6
FEMALE	0	.0	65	6.7	22	2.3	5	.5	92	9.5	840	86.5	39	4.0
MALE	16	.2	228	3.1	121	1.6	30	.4	395	5.4	6,520	88.8	429	5.8
GRADUATE:														
FULL-TIME	0	.0	7	1.5	39	8.3	8	1.7	54	11.5	254	53.9	163	34.6
FEMALE	0	.0	0	.0	0	.0	1	2.8	1	2.8	23	63.9	12	33.3
MALE	0	.0	7	1.6	39	9.0	7	1.6	53	12.2	231	53.1	151	34.7
PART-TIME	1	.1	8	.9	44	4.9	11	1.2	64	7.1	722	80.6	110	12.3
FEMALE	0	.0	0	.0	6	12.5	0	.0	6	12.5	35	72.9	7	14.6
MALE	1	.1	8	.9	38	4.5	11	1.3	58	6.8	687	81.0	103	12.1
TOTAL	1	.1	15	1.1	83	6.1	19	1.4	118	8.6	976	71.4	273	20.0
FEMALE	0	.0	0	.0	6	7.1	1	1.2	7	8.3	58	69.0	19	22.6
MALE	1	.1	15	1.2	77	6.0	18	1.4	111	8.7	918	71.6	254	19.8
PROFESSIONAL:														
FULL-TIME	0	.0	0	.0	0	.0	0	.0	0	.0	0	.0	0	.0
FEMALE	0	.0	0	.0	0	.0	0	.0	0	.0	0	.0	0	.0
MALE	0	.0	0	.0	0	.0	0	.0	0	.0	0	.0	0	.0

ENGINEERING

I INDIAN NATIVE		BLACK NON-HISPANIC		ASIAN OR PACIFIC ISLANDER		HISPANIC		TOTAL MINORITY		WHITE NON-HISPANIC		NON-RESIDENT ALIEN		TOTAL
%	NUMBER	%	NUMBER	%	NUMBER	%	NUMBER	%	NUMBER	%	NUMBER	%	NUMBER	%	NUMBER

CONTINUED

.0	0	.0	0	.0	0	.0	0	.0	0	.0	0	.0	0	.0	0
.0	0	.0	0	.0	0	.0	0	.0	0	.0	0	.0	0	.0	0
.0	0	.0	0	.0	0	.0	0	.0	0	.0	0	.0	0	.0	0
.0	0	.0	0	.0	0	.0	0	.0	0	.0	0	.0	0	.0	0
.0	0	.0	0	.0	0	.0	0	.0	0	.0	0	.0	0	.0	0
.0	0	.0	0	.0	0	.0	0	.0	0	.0	0	.0	0	.0	0
.2	266	3.3	162	2.0	39	.5	482	6.0	6,940	86.6	593	7.4	8,015
.0	60	6.4	17	1.8	5	.5	82	8.8	802	86.1	48	5.2	932
.2	206	2.9	145	2.0	34	.5	400	5.6	6,138	86.7	545	7.7	7,083
.1	42	2.5	64	3.8	15	.9	123	7.4	1,396	83.7	148	8.9	1,667
.0	5	4.1	11	8.9	1	.8	17	13.8	96	78.0	10	8.1	123
.1	37	2.4	53	3.4	14	.9	106	6.9	1,300	84.2	138	8.9	1,544
.2	308	3.2	226	2.3	54	.6	605	6.2	8,336	86.1	741	7.7	9,682
.0	65	6.2	28	2.7	6	.6	99	9.4	898	85.1	58	5.5	1,055
.2	243	2.8	198	2.3	48	.6	506	5.9	7,438	86.2	683	7.9	8,627
.0	0	.0	0	.0	0	.0	0	.0	43	95.6	2	4.4	45
.0	0	.0	0	.0	0	.0	0	.0	5	100.0	0	.0	5
.0	0	.0	0	.0	0	.0	0	.0	38	95.0	2	5.0	40
.2	308	3.2	226	2.3	54	.6	605	6.2	8,379	86.1	743	7.6	9,727
.0	65	6.1	28	2.6	6	.6	99	9.3	903	85.2	58	5.5	1,060
.2	243	2.8	198	2.3	48	.6	506	5.8	7,476	86.3	685	7.9	8,667

(2 INSTITUTIONS)

.2	1	.0	10	.5	5	.2	21	1.0	2,131	96.5	56	2.5	2,208
.9	0	.0	2	.9	0	.0	4	1.7	221	96.5	4	1.7	229
.2	1	.1	8	.4	5	.3	17	.9	1,910	96.5	52	2.6	1,979
.0	0	.0	0	.0	0	.0	0	.0	85	98.8	1	1.2	86
.0	0	.0	0	.0	0	.0	0	.0	14	93.3	1	6.7	15
.0	0	.0 .	0	.0	0	.0	0	.0	71	100.0	0	.0	71
.2	1	.0	10	.4	5	.2	21	.9	2,216	96.6	57	2.5	2,294
.8	0	.0	2	.8	0	.0	4	1.6	235	96.3	5	2.0	244
.1	1	.0	8	.4	5	.2	17	.8	1,981	96.6	52	2.5	2,050
3.4	1	1.7	0	.0	0	.0	3	5.2	46	79.3	9	15.5	58
.0	0	.0	0	.0	0	.0	0	.0	4	80.0	1	20.0	5
3.8	1	1.9	0	.0	0	.0	3	5.7	42	79.2	8	15.1	53
.0	0	.0	1	4.0	0	.0	1	4.0	23	92.0	1	4.0	25
.0	0	.0	1	25.0	0	.0	1	25.0	3	75.0	0	.0	4
.0	0	.0	0	.0	0	.0	0	.0	20	95.2	1	4.8	21
2.4	1	1.2	1	1.2	0	.0	4	4.8	69	83.1	10	12.0	83
.0	0	.0	1	11.1	0	.0	1	11.1	7	77.8	1	11.1	9
2.7	1	1.4	0	.0	0	.0	3	4.1	62	83.8	9	12.2	74
.0	0	.0	0	.0	0	.0	0	.0	0	.0	0	.0	0
.0	0	.0	0	.0	0	.0	0	.0	0	.0	0	.0	0
.0	0	.0	0	.0	0	.0	0	.0	0	.0	0	.0	0
.0	0	.0	0	.0	0	.0	0	.0	0	.0	0	.0	0
.0	0	.0	0	.0	0	.0	0	.0	0	.0	0	.0	0
.0	0	.0	0	.0 .	0	.0	0	.0	0	.0	0	.0	0
.3	2	.1	10	.4	5	.2	24	1.1	2,177	96.1	65	2.9	2,266
.9	0	.0	2	.9	0	.0	4	1.7	225	96.2	5	2.1	234
.2	2	.1	8	.4	5	.2	20	1.0	1,952	96.1	60	3.0	2,032
.0	0	.0	1	.9	0	.0	1	.9	108	97.3	2	1.8	111
.0	0	.0	1	5.3	0	.0	1	5.3	17	89.5	1	5.3	19
.0	0	.0	0	.0	0	.0	0	.0	91	98.9	1	1.1	92
.3	2	.1	11	.5	5	.2	25	1.1	2,285	96.1	67	2.8	2,377
.8	0	.0	3	1.2	0	.0	5	2.0	242	95.7	6	2.4	253
.2	2	.1	8	.4	5	.2	20	.9	2,043	96.2	61	2.9	2,124
.0	0	.0	0	.0	0	.0	0	.0	0	.0	0	.0	0
.0	0	.0	0	.0	0	.0	0	.0	0	.0	0	.0	0
.0	0	.0	0	.0	0	.0	0	.0	0	.0	0	.0	0
.3	2	.1	11	.5	5	.2	25	1.1	2,285	96.1	67	2.8	2,377
.8	0	.0	3	1.2	0	.0	5	2.0	242	95.7	6	2.4	253
.2	2	.1	8	.4	5	.2	20	.9	2,043	96.2	61	2.9	2,124

TABLE 17 - TOTAL ENROLLMENT IN INSTITUTIONS OF HIGHER EDUCATION FOR SELECTED MAJOR FIELDS OF STUDY AND LEVEL OF ENROLLMENT BY RACE, ETHNICITY, AND SEX: STATE, 1978

MAJOR FIELD 0900 - ENGINEERING

	AMERICAN INDIAN ALASKAN NATIVE		BLACK NON-HISPANIC		ASIAN OR PACIFIC ISLANDER		HISPANIC		TOTAL MINORITY		WHITE NON-HISPANIC		NON-RESIDENT ALIEN		TO
	NUMBER	%	NUMBER	%	NUMBER	%	NUMBER	%	NUMBER	%	NUMBER	%	NUMBER	%	NU
NEBRASKA (9 INSTITUTIONS)															
UNDERGRADUATES:															
FULL-TIME	5	.2	26	1.2	17	.8	12	.5	60	2.7	1,991	88.6	196	8.7	2
FEMALE	0	.0	3	2.3	3	2.3	1	.8	7	5.3	120	90.2	6	4.5	
MALE	5	.2	23	1.1	14	.7	11	.5	53	2.5	1,871	88.5	190	9.0	2
PART-TIME	2	.4	13	2.3	7	1.3	6	1.1	28	5.0	519	92.8	12	2.1	
FEMALE	0	.0	0	.0	0	.0	0	.0	0	.0	25	96.2	1	3.8	
MALE	2	.4	13	2.4	7	1.3	6	1.1	28	5.3	494	92.7	11	2.1	
TOTAL	7	.2	39	1.4	24	.9	18	.6	88	3.1	2,510	89.5	208	7.4	2
FEMALE	0	.0	3	1.9	3	1.9	1	.6	7	4.4	145	91.2	7	4.4	
MALE	7	.3	36	1.4	21	.8	17	.6	81	3.1	2,365	89.3	201	7.6	2
GRADUATE:															
FULL-TIME	0	.0	0	.0	2	3.4	0	.0	2	3.4	35	59.3	22	37.3	
FEMALE	0	.0	0	.0	0	.0	0	.0	0	.0	3	100.0	0	.0	
MALE	0	.0	0	.0	2	3.6	0	.0	2	3.6	32	57.1	22	39.3	
PART-TIME	0	.0	0	.0	1	1.3	0	.0	1	1.3	70	89.7	7	9.0	
FEMALE	0	.0	0	.0	0	.0	0	.0	0	.0	3	100.0	0	.0	
MALE	0	.0	0	.0	1	1.3	0	.0	1	1.3	67	89.3	7	9.3	
TOTAL	0	.0	0	.0	3	2.2	0	.0	3	2.2	105	76.6	29	21.2	
FEMALE	0	.0	0	.0	0	.0	0	.0	0	.0	6	100.0	0	.0	
MALE	0	.0	0	.0	3	2.3	0	.0	3	2.3	99	75.6	29	22.1	
PROFESSIONAL:															
FULL-TIME	0	.0	0	.0	0	.0	0	.0	0	.0	0	.0	0	.0	
FEMALE	0	.0	0	.0	0	.0	0	.0	0	.0	0	.0	0	.0	
MALE	0	.0	0	.0	0	.0	0	.0	0	.0	0	.0	0	.0	
PART-TIME	0	.0	0	.0	0	.0	0	.0	0	.0	0	.0	0	.0	
FEMALE	0	.0	0	.0	0	.0	0	.0	0	.0	0	.0	0	.0	
MALE	0	.0	0	.0	0	.0	0	.0	0	.0	0	.0	0	.0	
TOTAL	0	.0	0	.0	0	.0	0	.0	0	.0	0	.0	0	.0	
FEMALE	0	.0	0	.0	0	.0	0	.0	0	.0	0	.0	0	.0	
MALE	0	.0	0	.0	0	.0	0	.0	0	.0	0	.0	0	.0	
UND+GRAD+PROF:															
FULL-TIME	5	.2	26	1.1	19	.8	12	.5	62	2.7	2,026	87.9	218	9.5	2
FEMALE	0	.0	3	2.2	3	2.2	1	.7	7	5.1	123	90.4	6	4.4	
MALE	5	.2	23	1.1	16	.7	11	.5	55	2.5	1,903	87.7	212	9.8	2
PART-TIME	2	.3	13	2.0	8	1.3	6	.9	29	4.6	589	92.5	19	3.0	
FEMALE	0	.0	0	.0	0	.0	0	.0	0	.0	28	96.6	1	3.4	
MALE	2	.3	13	2.1	8	1.3	6	1.0	29	4.8	561	92.3	18	3.0	
TOTAL	7	.2	39	1.3	27	.9	18	.6	91	3.1	2,615	88.9	237	8.1	2
FEMALE	0	.0	3	1.8	3	1.8	1	.6	7	4.2	151	91.5	7	4.2	
MALE	7	.3	36	1.3	24	.9	17	.6	84	3.0	2,464	88.7	230	8.3	2
UNCLASSIFIED:															
TOTAL	0	.0	0	.0	0	.0	0	.0	0	.0	15	100.0	0	.0	
FEMALE	0	.0	0	.0	0	.0	0	.0	0	.0	3	100.0	0	.0	
MALE	0	.0	0	.0	0	.0	0	.0	0	.0	12	100.0	0	.0	
TOTAL ENROLLMENT:															
TOTAL	7	.2	39	1.3	27	.9	18	.6	91	3.1	2,630	88.9	237	8.0	2
FEMALE	0	.0	3	1.8	3	1.8	1	.6	7	4.2	154	91.7	7	4.2	
MALE	7	.3	36	1.3	24	.9	17	.6	84	3.0	2,476	88.7	230	8.2	2
NEVADA (2 INSTITUTIONS)															
UNDERGRADUATES:															
FULL-TIME	6	1.0	11	1.9	16	2.7	17	2.9	50	8.6	460	79.0	72	12.4	
FEMALE	0	.0	0	.0	3	5.6	4	7.4	7	13.0	45	83.3	2	3.7	
MALE	6	1.1	11	2.1	13	2.5	13	2.5	43	8.1	415	78.6	70	13.3	
PART-TIME	1	.4	4	1.7	11	4.8	4	1.7	20	8.7	200	87.3	9	3.9	
FEMALE	0	.0	1	4.3	1	4.3	0	.0	2	8.7	21	91.3	0	.0	
MALE	1	.5	3	1.5	10	4.9	4	1.9	18	8.7	179	86.9	9	4.4	
TOTAL	7	.9	15	1.8	27	3.3	21	2.6	70	8.6	660	81.4	81	10.0	
FEMALE	0	.0	1	1.3	4	5.2	4	5.2	9	11.7	66	85.7	2	2.6	
MALE	7	1.0	14	1.9	23	3.1	17	2.3	61	8.3	594	80.9	79	10.8	
GRADUATE:															
FULL-TIME	0	.0	0	.0	1	3.0	0	.0	1	3.0	19	57.6	13	39.4	
FEMALE	0	.0	0	.0	0	.0	0	.0	0	.0	3	100.0	0	.0	
MALE	0	.0	0	.0	1	3.3	0	.0	1	3.3	16	53.3	13	43.3	
PART-TIME	0	.0	0	.0	1	4.0	0	.0	1	4.0	17	68.0	7	28.0	
FEMALE	0	.0	0	.0	0	.0	0	.0	0	.0	2	100.0	0	.0	
MALE	0	.0	0	.0	1	4.3	0	.0	1	4.3	15	65.2	7	30.4	
TOTAL	0	.0	0	.0	2	3.4	0	.0	2	3.4	36	62.1	20	34.5	
FEMALE	0	.0	0	.0	0	.0	0	.0	0	.0	5	100.0	0	.0	
MALE	0	.0	0	.0	2	3.8	0	.0	2	3.8	31	58.5	20	37.7	
PROFESSIONAL:															
FULL-TIME	0	.0	0	.0	0	.0	0	.0	0	.0	0	.0	0	.0	
FEMALE	0	.0	0	.0	0	.0	0	.0	0	.0	0	.0	0	.0	
MALE	0	.0	0	.0	0	.0	0	.0	0	.0	0	.0	0	.0	

ROLLMENT IN INSTITUTIONS OF HIGHER EDUCATION FOR SELECTED MAJOR FIELDS OF STUDY AND LEVEL OF ENROLLMENT
ETHNICITY, AND SEX: STATE, 1978

ENGINEERING

INDIAN NATIVE	BLACK NON-HISPANIC		ASIAN OR PACIFIC ISLANDER		HISPANIC		TOTAL MINORITY		WHITE NON-HISPANIC		NON-RESIDENT ALIEN		TOTAL
%	NUMBER	%	NUMBER	%	NUMBER	%	NUMBER	%	NUMBER	%	NUMBER	%	NUMBER

CONTINUED

%	NUMBER	%	NUMBER	%	NUMBER	%	NUMBER	%	NUMBER	%	NUMBER	%	NUMBER
.0	0	.0	0	.0	0	.0	0	.0	0	.0	0	.0	0
.0	0	.0	0	.0	0	.0	0	.0	0	.0	0	.0	0
.0	0	.0	0	.0	0	.0	0	.0	0	.0	0	.0	0
.0	0	.0	0	.0	0	.0	0	.0	0	.0	0	.0	0
.0	0	.0	0	.0	0	.0	0	.0	0	.0	0	.0	0
.0	0	.0	0	.0	0	.0	0	.0	0	.0	0	.0	0
1.0	11	1.8	17	2.8	17	2.8	51	8.3	479	77.9	85	13.8	615
.0	0	.0	3	5.3	4	7.0	7	12.3	48	84.2	2	3.5	57
1.1	11	2.0	14	2.5	13	2.3	44	7.9	431	77.2	83	14.9	558
.4	4	1.6	12	4.7	4	1.6	21	8.3	217	85.4	16	6.3	294
.0	1	4.0	1	4.0	0	.0	2	8.0	23	92.0	0	.0	25
.4	3	1.3	11	4.8	4	1.7	19	8.3	194	84.7	16	7.0	229
.8	15	1.7	29	3.3	21	2.4	72	8.3	696	80.1	101	11.6	869
.0	1	1.2	4	4.9	4	4.9	9	11.0	71	86.6	2	2.4	82
.9	14	1.8	25	3.2	17	2.2	63	8.0	625	79.4	99	12.6	787
1.4	2	2.9	1	1.4	2	2.9	6	8.7	63	91.3	0	.0	69
.0	1	2.5	1	2.5	2	5.0	4	10.0	36	90.0	0	.0	40
3.4	1	3.4	0	.0	0	.0	2	6.9	27	93.1	0	.0	29
.9	17	1.8	30	3.2	23	2.5	78	8.3	759	80.9	101	10.8	938
.0	2	1.6	5	4.1	6	4.9	13	10.7	107	87.7	2	1.6	122
1.0	15	1.8	25	3.1	17	2.1	65	8.0	652	79.9	99	12.1	816

(5 INSTITUTIONS)

%	NUMBER	%	NUMBER	%	NUMBER	%	NUMBER	%	NUMBER	%	NUMBER	%	NUMBER
.1	11	.8	16	1.2	2	.1	31	2.3	1,249	93.6	55	4.1	1,335
.7	0	.0	1	.7	0	.0	2	1.5	131	96.3	3	2.2	136
.1	11	.9	15	1.3	2	.2	29	2.4	1,118	93.2	52	4.3	1,199
.0	5	3.4	3	2.1	3	2.1	11	7.6	134	92.4	0	.0	145
.0	0	.0	1	4.8	0	.0	1	4.8	20	95.2	0	.0	21
.0	5	4.0	2	1.6	3	2.4	10	8.1	114	91.9	0	.0	124
.1	16	1.1	19	1.3	5	.3	42	2.8	1,383	93.4	55	3.7	1,480
.6	0	.0	2	1.3	0	.0	3	1.9	151	96.2	3	1.9	157
.1	16	1.2	17	1.3	5	.4	39	2.9	1,232	93.1	52	3.9	1,323
1.8	0	.0	7	6.4	0	.0	9	8.3	98	89.9	2	1.8	109
.0	0	.0	3	42.9	0	.0	3	42.9	4	57.1	0	.0	7
2.0	0	.0	4	3.9	0	.0	6	5.9	94	92.2	2	2.0	102
.0	0	.0	0	.0	0	.0	0	.0	20	95.2	1	4.8	21
.0	0	.0	0	.0	0	.0	0	.0	4	100.0	0	.0	4
.0	0	.0	0	.0	0	.0	0	.0	16	94.1	1	5.9	17
1.5	0	.0	7	5.4	0	.0	9	6.9	118	90.8	3	2.3	130
.0	0	.0	3	27.3	0	.0	3	27.3	8	72.7	0	.0	11
1.7	0	.0	4	3.4	0	.0	6	5.0	110	92.4	3	2.5	119
.0	0	.0	0	.0	0	.0	0	.0	0	.0	0	.0	0
.0	0	.0	0	.0	0	.0	0	.0	0	.0	0	.0	0
.0	0	.0	0	.0	0	.0	0	.0	0	.0	0	.0	0
.0	0	.0	0	.0	0	.0	0	.0	0	.0	0	.0	0
.0	0	.0	0	.0	0	.0	0	.0	0	.0	0	.0	0
.0	0	.0	0	.0	0	.0	0	.0	0	.0	0	.0	0
.3	11	.8	23	1.6	2	.1	40	2.8	1,347	93.3	57	3.9	1,444
.7	0	.0	4	2.8	0	.0	5	3.5	135	94.4	3	2.1	143
.2	11	.8	19	1.5	2	.2	35	2.7	1,212	93.2	54	4.2	1,301
.0	5	3.0	3	1.8	3	1.8	11	6.6	154	92.8	1	.6	166
.0	0	.0	1	4.0	0	.0	1	4.0	24	96.0	0	.0	25
.0	5	3.5	2	1.4	3	2.1	10	7.1	130	92.2	1	.7	141
.2	16	1.0	26	1.6	5	.3	51	3.2	1,501	93.2	58	3.6	1,610
.6	0	.0	5	3.0	0	.0	6	3.6	159	94.6	3	1.8	168
.2	16	1.1	21	1.5	5	.3	45	3.1	1,342	93.1	55	3.8	1,442
.0	0	.0	0	.0	0	.0	0	.0	5	100.0	0	.0	5
.0	0	.0	0	.0	0	.0	0	.0	0	.0	0	.0	0
.0	0	.0	0	.0	0	.0	0	.0	5	100.0	0	.0	5
.2	16	1.0	26	1.6	5	.3	51	3.2	1,506	93.3	58	3.6	1,615
.6	0	.0	5	3.0	0	.0	6	3.6	159	94.6	3	1.8	168
.2	16	1.1	21	1.5	5	.3	45	3.1	1,347	93.1	55	3.8	1,447

TABLE 17 - TOTAL ENROLLMENT IN INSTITUTIONS OF HIGHER EDUCATION FOR SELECTED MAJOR FIELDS OF STUDY AND LEVEL OF ENROLLMENT
BY RACE, ETHNICITY, AND SEX: STATE, 1978

MAJOR FIELD 0900 - ENGINEERING

	AMERICAN INDIAN ALASKAN NATIVE		BLACK NON-HISPANIC		ASIAN OR PACIFIC ISLANDER		HISPANIC		TOTAL MINORITY		WHITE NON-HISPANIC		NON-RESIDENT ALIEN	
	NUMBER	%	NUMBER	%	NUMBER	%	NUMBER	%	NUMBER	%	NUMBER	%	NUMBER	%
NEW JERSEY	(	26 INSTITUTIONS)												
UNDERGRADUATES:														
FULL-TIME	7	.1	366	4.6	247	3.1	301	3.8	921	11.7	6,638	84.3	317	4.0
FEMALE	0	.0	54	8.0	32	4.7	32	4.7	118	17.5	542	80.2	16	2.4
MALE	7	.1	312	4.3	215	3.0	269	3.7	803	11.2	6,096	84.7	301	4.2
PART-TIME	3	.2	77	3.9	34	1.7	68	3.4	182	9.1	1,795	90.0	17	.9
FEMALE	0	.0	9	10.0	1	1.1	4	4.4	14	15.6	75	83.3	1	1.1
MALE	3	.2	68	3.6	33	1.7	64	3.4	168	8.8	1,720	90.3	16	.8
TOTAL	10	.1	443	4.5	281	2.8	369	3.7	1,103	11.2	8,433	85.4	334	3.4
FEMALE	0	.0	63	8.2	33	4.3	36	4.7	132	17.2	617	80.5	17	2.2
MALE	10	.1	380	4.2	248	2.7	333	3.7	971	10.7	7,816	85.9	317	3.5
GRADUATE:														
FULL-TIME	1	.2	5	1.0	26	5.1	6	1.2	38	7.5	272	53.6	197	38.9
FEMALE	0	.0	1	1.7	2	3.4	0	.0	3	5.2	47	81.0	8	13.8
MALE	1	.2	4	.9	24	5.3	6	1.3	35	7.8	225	50.1	189	42.1
PART-TIME	2	.1	35	2.4	83	5.7	29	2.0	149	10.3	1,287	89.1	9	.6
FEMALE	0	.0	7	5.1	10	7.4	3	2.2	20	14.7	116	85.3	0	.0
MALE	2	.2	28	2.1	73	5.6	26	2.0	129	9.9	1,171	89.5	9	.7
TOTAL	3	.2	40	2.0	109	5.6	35	1.8	187	9.6	1,559	79.9	206	10.6
FEMALE	0	.0	8	4.1	12	6.2	3	1.5	23	11.9	163	84.0	8	4.1
MALE	3	.2	32	1.8	97	5.5	32	1.8	164	9.3	1,396	79.4	198	11.3
PROFESSIONAL:														
FULL-TIME	0	.0	0	.0	0	.0	0	.0	0	.0	0	.0	0	.0
FEMALE	0	.0	0	.0	0	.0	0	.0	0	.0	0	.0	0	.0
MALE	0	.0	0	.0	0	.0	0	.0	0	.0	0	.0	0	.0
PART-TIME	0	.0	0	.0	0	.0	0	.0	0	.0	0	.0	0	.0
FEMALE	0	.0	0	.0	0	.0	0	.0	0	.0	0	.0	0	.0
MALE	0	.0	0	.0	0	.0	0	.0	0	.0	0	.0	0	.0
TOTAL	0	.0	0	.0	0	.0	0	.0	0	.0	0	.0	0	.0
FEMALE	0	.0	0	.0	0	.0	0	.0	0	.0	0	.0	0	.0
MALE	0	.0	0	.0	0	.0	0	.0	0	.0	0	.0	0	.0
UND+GRAD+PROF:														
FULL-TIME	8	.1	371	4.4	273	3.3	307	3.7	959	11.4	6,910	82.4	514	6.1
FEMALE	0	.0	55	7.5	34	4.6	32	4.4	121	16.5	589	80.2	24	3.3
MALE	8	.1	316	4.1	239	3.1	275	3.6	838	11.0	6,321	82.6	490	6.4
PART-TIME	5	.1	112	3.3	117	3.4	97	2.8	331	9.6	3,082	89.6	26	.8
FEMALE	0	.0	16	7.1	11	4.9	7	3.1	34	15.0	191	84.5	1	.4
MALE	5	.2	96	3.0	106	3.3	90	2.8	297	9.2	2,891	90.0	25	.8
TOTAL	13	.1	483	4.1	390	3.3	404	3.4	1,290	10.9	9,992	84.5	540	4.6
FEMALE	0	.0	71	7.4	45	4.7	39	4.1	155	16.1	780	81.3	25	2.6
MALE	13	.1	412	3.8	345	3.2	365	3.4	1,135	10.4	9,212	84.8	515	4.7
UNCLASSIFIED:														
TOTAL	0	.0	3	2.3	4	3.0	2	1.5	9	6.8	122	91.7	2	1.5
FEMALE	0	.0	0	.0	0	.0	0	.0	0	.0	9	100.0	0	.0
MALE	0	.0	3	2.4	4	3.2	2	1.6	9	7.3	113	91.1	2	1.6
TOTAL ENROLLMENT:														
TOTAL	13	.1	486	4.1	394	3.3	406	3.4	1,299	10.9	10,114	84.6	542	4.5
FEMALE	0	.0	71	7.3	45	4.6	39	4.0	155	16.0	789	81.4	25	2.6
MALE	13	.1	415	3.8	349	3.2	367	3.3	1,144	10.4	9,325	84.9	517	4.7
NEW MEXICO	(	10 INSTITUTIONS)												
UNDERGRADUATES:														
FULL-TIME	56	1.8	37	1.2	36	1.1	670	21.0	799	25.0	2,198	68.9	194	6.1
FEMALE	11	2.7	10	2.4	4	1.0	97	23.7	122	29.8	280	68.5	7	1.7
MALE	45	1.6	27	1.0	32	1.2	573	20.6	677	24.3	1,918	68.9	187	6.7
PART-TIME	5	1.1	4	.9	2	.4	106	23.8	117	26.2	321	72.0	8	1.8
FEMALE	0	.0	1	2.3	0	.0	7	15.9	8	18.2	35	79.5	1	2.3
MALE	5	1.2	3	.7	2	.5	99	24.6	109	27.1	286	71.1	7	1.7
TOTAL	61	1.7	41	1.1	38	1.0	776	21.3	916	25.2	2,519	69.3	202	5.6
FEMALE	11	2.4	11	2.4	4	.9	104	23.0	130	28.7	315	69.5	8	1.8
MALE	50	1.6	30	.9	34	1.1	672	21.1	786	24.7	2,204	69.2	194	6.1
GRADUATE:														
FULL-TIME	0	.0	0	.0	6	2.7	10	4.5	16	7.2	122	55.0	84	37.8
FEMALE	0	.0	0	.0	0	.0	0	.0	0	.0	12	80.0	3	20.0
MALE	0	.0	0	.0	6	2.9	10	4.8	16	7.7	110	53.1	81	39.1
PART-TIME	1	.5	2	1.0	3	1.5	14	7.0	20	10.0	167	83.1	14	7.0
FEMALE	0	.0	0	.0	2	11.1	1	5.6	3	16.7	15	83.3	0	.0
MALE	1	.5	2	1.1	1	.5	13	7.1	17	9.3	152	83.1	14	7.7
TOTAL	1	.2	2	.5	9	2.1	24	5.7	36	8.5	289	68.3	98	23.2
FEMALE	0	.0	0	.0	2	6.1	1	3.0	3	9.1	27	81.8	3	9.1
MALE	1	.3	2	.5	7	1.8	23	5.9	33	8.5	262	67.2	95	24.4
PROFESSIONAL:														
FULL-TIME	0	.0	0	.0	0	.0	0	.0	0	.0	0	.0	0	.0
FEMALE	0	.0	0	.0	0	.0	0	.0	0	.0	0	.0	0	.0
MALE	0	.0	0	.0	0	.0	0	.0	0	.0	0	.0	0	.0

460

ENGINEERING

INDIAN NATIVE	BLACK NON-HISPANIC		ASIAN OR PACIFIC ISLANDER		HISPANIC		TOTAL MINORITY		WHITE NON-HISPANIC		NON-RESIDENT ALIEN		TOTAL
%	NUMBER	%	NUMBER	%	NUMBER	%	NUMBER	%	NUMBER	%	NUMBER	%	NUMBER

CONTINUED

.0	0	.0	0	.0	0	.0	0	.0	0	.0	0	.0	0
.0	0	.0	0	.0	0	.0	0	.0	0	.0	0	.0	0
.0	0	.0	0	.0	0	.0	0	.0	0	.0	0	.0	0
.0	0	.0	0	.0	0	.0	0	.0	0	.0	0	.0	0
.0	0	.0	0	.0	0	.0	0	.0	0	.0	0	.0	0
.0	0	.0	0	.0	0	.0	0	.0	0	.0	0	.0	0
1.6	37	1.1	42	1.2	680	19.9	815	23.9	2,320	68.0	278	8.1	3,413
2.6	10	2.4	4	.9	97	22.9	122	28.8	292	68.9	10	2.4	424
1.5	27	.9	38	1.3	583	19.5	693	23.2	2,028	67.8	268	9.0	2,989
.9	6	.9	5	.8	120	18.5	137	21.2	488	75.4	22	3.4	647
.0	1	1.6	2	3.2	8	12.9	11	17.7	50	80.6	1	1.6	62
1.0	5	.9	3	.5	112	19.1	126	21.5	438	74.9	21	3.6	585
1.5	43	1.1	47	1.2	800	19.7	952	23.4	2,808	69.2	300	7.4	4,060
2.3	11	2.3	6	1.2	105	21.6	133	27.4	342	70.4	11	2.3	486
1.4	32	.9	41	1.1	695	19.4	819	22.9	2,466	69.0	289	8.1	3,574
4.8	5	6.0	0	.0	15	17.9	24	28.6	56	66.7	4	4.8	84
7.7	1	7.7	0	.0	2	15.4	4	30.8	8	61.5	1	7.7	13
4.2	4	5.6	0	.0	13	18.3	20	28.2	48	67.6	3	4.2	71
1.6	48	1.2	47	1.1	815	19.7	976	23.6	2,864	69.1	304	7.3	4,144
2.4	12	2.4	6	1.2	107	21.4	137	27.5	350	70.1	12	2.4	499
1.5	36	1.0	41	1.1	708	19.4	839	23.0	2,514	69.0	292	8.0	3,645

(56 INSTITUTIONS)

.1	706	3.3	871	4.1	501	2.4	2,108	9.9	17,928	84.4	1,211	5.7	21,247
.1	92	4.3	102	4.7	44	2.0	240	11.1	1,867	86.4	55	2.5	2,162
.1	614	3.2	769	4.0	457	2.4	1,868	9.8	16,061	84.2	1,156	6.1	19,085
.1	253	9.1	77	2.8	99	3.6	433	15.5	2,292	82.2	63	2.3	2,788
.6	13	7.7	8	4.5	1	.6	23	13.1	151	85.8	2	1.1	176
.1	240	9.2	69	2.6	98	3.8	410	15.7	2,141	82.0	61	2.3	2,612
.1	959	4.0	948	3.9	600	2.5	2,541	10.6	20,220	84.1	1,274	5.3	24,035
.1	105	4.5	110	4.7	45	1.9	263	11.2	2,018	86.3	57	2.4	2,338
.1	854	3.9	838	3.9	555	2.6	2,278	10.5	18,202	83.9	1,217	5.6	21,697
.0	31	1.2	102	4.1	31	1.2	164	6.6	1,342	53.7	994	39.8	2,500
.0	2	1.2	3	1.8	0	.0	5	3.0	122	72.2	42	24.9	169
.0	29	1.2	99	4.2	31	1.3	159	6.8	1,220	52.3	952	40.8	2,331
.3	36	2.3	99	6.5	17	1.1	156	10.2	1,239	80.9	137	8.9	1,532
.0	3	2.2	5	3.7	2	1.5	10	7.4	117	86.0	9	6.6	136
.3	33	2.4	94	6.7	15	1.1	146	10.5	1,122	80.4	128	9.2	1,396
.1	67	1.7	201	5.0	48	1.2	320	7.9	2,581	64.0	1,131	28.1	4,032
.0	5	1.6	8	2.6	2	.7	15	4.9	239	78.4	51	16.7	305
.1	62	1.7	193	5.2	46	1.2	305	8.2	2,342	62.8	1,080	29.0	3,727
.0	0	.0	0	.0	0	.0	0	.0	0	.0	0	.0	0
.0	0	.0	0	.0	0	.0	0	.0	0	.0	0	.0	0
.0	0	.0	0	.0	0	.0	0	.0	0	.0	0	.0	0
.0	0	.0	0	.0	0	.0	0	.0	0	.0	0	.0	0
.0	0	.0	0	.0	0	.0	0	.0	0	.0	0	.0	0
.0	0	.0	0	.0	0	.0	0	.0	0	.0	0	.0	0
.1	737	3.1	973	4.1	532	2.2	2,272	9.6	19,270	81.1	2,205	9.3	23,747
.1	94	4.0	105	4.5	44	1.9	245	10.5	1,989	85.3	97	4.2	2,331
.1	643	3.0	868	4.1	488	2.3	2,027	9.5	17,281	80.7	2,108	9.8	21,416
.2	289	6.7	176	4.1	116	2.7	589	13.6	3,531	81.7	200	4.6	4,320
.3	16	5.1	13	4.2	3	1.0	33	10.6	268	85.9	11	3.5	312
.2	273	6.8	163	4.1	113	2.8	556	13.9	3,263	81.4	189	4.7	4,008
.1	1,026	3.7	1,149	4.1	648	2.3	2,861	10.2	22,801	81.2	2,405	8.6	28,067
.1	110	4.2	118	4.5	47	1.8	278	10.5	2,257	85.4	108	4.1	2,643
.1	916	3.6	1,031	4.1	601	2.4	2,583	10.2	20,544	80.8	2,297	9.0	25,424
1.5	6	2.9	19	9.3	3	1.5	31	15.1	150	73.2	24	11.7	205
.0	2	13.3	3	20.0	0	.0	5	33.3	8	53.3	2	13.3	15
1.6	4	2.1	16	8.4	3	1.6	26	13.7	142	74.7	22	11.6	190
.1	1,032	3.7	1,168	4.1	651	2.3	2,892	10.2	22,951	81.2	2,429	8.6	28,272
.1	112	4.2	121	4.6	47	1.8	283	10.6	2,265	85.2	110	4.1	2,658
.1	920	3.6	1,047	4.1	604	2.4	2,609	10.2	20,686	80.8	2,319	9.1	25,614

TABLE 17 - TOTAL ENROLLMENT IN INSTITUTIONS OF HIGHER EDUCATION FOR SELECTED MAJOR FIELDS OF STUDY AND LEVEL OF ENROLLMENT BY RACE, ETHNICITY, AND SEX: STATE, 1978

MAJOR FIELD 0900 - ENGINEERING

	AMERICAN INDIAN ALASKAN NATIVE		BLACK NON-HISPANIC		ASIAN OR PACIFIC ISLANDER		HISPANIC		TOTAL MINORITY		WHITE NON-HISPANIC		NON-RESIDENT ALIEN	
	NUMBER	%	NUMBER	%	NUMBER	%	NUMBER	%	NUMBER	%	NUMBER	%	NUMBER	%
NORTH CAROLINA (11 INSTITUTIONS)														
UNDERGRADUATES:														
FULL-TIME	12	.2	1,041	16.3	44	.7	34	.5	1,131	17.7	4,863	76.0	402	6.3
FEMALE	2	.3	173	23.2	7	.9	3	.4	185	24.8	536	71.9	24	3.2
MALE	10	.2	868	15.4	37	.7	31	.5	946	16.7	4,327	76.6	378	6.7
PART-TIME	1	.2	76	12.5	8	1.3	3	.5	88	14.4	498	81.6	24	3.9
FEMALE	0	.0	7	14.6	1	2.1	0	.0	8	16.7	37	77.1	3	6.3
MALE	1	.2	69	12.3	7	1.2	3	.5	80	14.2	461	82.0	21	3.7
TOTAL	13	.2	1,117	15.9	52	.7	37	.5	1,219	17.4	5,361	76.5	426	6.1
FEMALE	2	.3	180	22.7	8	1.0	3	.4	193	24.3	573	72.3	27	3.4
MALE	11	.2	937	15.1	44	.7	34	.5	1,026	16.5	4,788	77.1	399	6.4
GRADUATE:														
FULL-TIME	0	.0	8	2.4	2	.6	2	.6	12	3.6	191	56.5	135	39.9
FEMALE	0	.0	3	8.8	0	.0	0	.0	3	8.8	23	67.6	8	23.5
MALE	0	.0	5	1.6	2	.7	2	.7	9	3.0	168	55.3	127	41.8
PART-TIME	0	.0	12	4.4	9	3.3	1	.4	22	8.1	177	65.1	73	26.8
FEMALE	0	.0	2	8.7	1	4.3	0	.0	3	13.0	16	69.6	4	17.4
MALE	0	.0	10	4.0	8	3.2	1	.4	19	7.6	161	64.7	69	27.7
TOTAL	0	.0	20	3.3	11	1.8	3	.5	34	5.6	368	60.3	208	34.1
FEMALE	0	.0	5	8.8	1	1.8	0	.0	6	10.5	39	68.4	12	21.1
MALE	0	.0	15	2.7	10	1.8	3	.5	28	5.1	329	59.5	196	35.4
PROFESSIONAL:														
FULL-TIME	0	.0	0	.0	0	.0		.0	0	.0	0	.0	0	.0
FEMALE	0	.0	0	.0	0	.0		.0	0	.0	0	.0	0	.0
MALE	0	.0	0	.0	0	.0		.0	0	.0	0	.0	0	.0
PART-TIME	0	.0	0	.0	0	.0		.0	0	.0	0	.0	0	.0
FEMALE	0	.0	0	.0	0	.0		.0	0	.0	0	.0	0	.0
MALE	0	.0	0	.0	0	.0	0	.0	0	.0	0	.0	0	.0
TOTAL	0	.0	0	.0	0	.0		.0	0	.0	0	.0	0	.0
FEMALE	0	.0	0	.0	0	.0		.0	0	.0	0	.0	0	.0
MALE	0	.0	0	.0	0	.0	0	.0	0	.0	0	.0	0	.0
UND+GRAD+PROF:														
FULL-TIME	12	.2	1,049	15.6	46	.7	36	.5	1,143	17.0	5,054	75.1	537	8.0
FEMALE	2	.3	176	22.6	7	.9	3	.4	188	24.1	559	71.8	32	4.1
MALE	10	.2	873	14.7	39	.7	33	.6	955	16.0	4,495	75.5	505	8.5
PART-TIME	1	.1	88	10.0	17	1.9	4	.5	110	12.5	675	76.5	97	11.0
FEMALE	0	.0	9	12.7	2	2.8	0	.0	11	15.5	53	74.6	7	9.9
MALE	1	.1	79	9.7	15	1.8	4	.5	99	12.2	622	76.7	90	11.1
TOTAL	13	.2	1,137	14.9	63	.8	40	.5	1,253	16.5	5,729	75.2	634	8.3
FEMALE	2	.2	185	21.8	9	1.1	3	.4	199	23.4	612	72.0	39	4.6
MALE	11	.2	952	14.1	54	.8	37	.5	1,054	15.6	5,117	75.6	595	8.8
UNCLASSIFIED:														
TOTAL	0	.0	1	50.0	0	.0		.0	1	50.0	0	.0	1	50.0
FEMALE	0	.0	0	.0	0	.0		.0	0	.0	0	.0	0	.0
MALE	0	.0	1	50.0	0	.0	0	.0	1	50.0	0	.0	1	50.0
TOTAL ENROLLMENT:														
TOTAL	13	.2	1,138	14.9	63	.8	40	.5	1,254	16.5	5,729	75.2	635	8.3
FEMALE	2	.2	185	21.8	9	1.1	3	.4	199	23.4	612	72.0	39	4.6
MALE	11	.2	953	14.1	54	.8	37	.5	1,055	16.0	5,117	75.6	596	8.8
NORTH DAKOTA (7 INSTITUTIONS)														
UNDERGRADUATES:														
FULL-TIME	6	.4	6	.4	16	1.0	2	.1	30	1.8	1,606	97.0	20	1.2
FEMALE	1	.8	0	.0	2	1.6	0	.0	3	2.3	126	97.7	0	.0
MALE	5	.3	6	.4	14	.9	2	.1	27	1.8	1,480	96.9	20	1.3
PART-TIME	0	.0	1	3.7	0	.0	0	.0	1	3.7	25	92.6	1	3.7
FEMALE	0	.0	0	.0	0	.0	0	.0	0	.0	4	100.0	0	.0
MALE	0	.0	1	4.3	0	.0	0	.0	1	4.3	21	91.3	1	4.3
TOTAL	6	.4	7	.4	16	1.0	2	.1	31	1.8	1,631	96.9	21	1.2
FEMALE	1	.8	0	.0	2	1.5	0	.0	3	2.3	130	97.7	0	.0
MALE	5	.3	7	.5	14	.9	2	.1	28	1.8	1,501	96.8	21	1.4
GRADUATE:														
FULL-TIME	0	.0	0	.0	1	4.2		.0	1	4.2	14	58.3	9	37.5
FEMALE	0	.0	0	.0	0	.0		.0	0	.0	0	.0	1	100.0
MALE	0	.0	0	.0	1	4.3		.0	1	4.3	14	60.9	8	34.8
PART-TIME	0	.0	0	.0	0	.0		.0	0	.0	19	73.1	7	26.9
FEMALE	0	.0	0	.0	0	.0		.0	0	.0	1	100.0	0	.0
MALE	0	.0	0	.0	0	.0	0	.0	0	.0	18	72.0	7	28.0
TOTAL	0	.0	0	.0	1	2.0	0	.0	1	2.0	33	66.0	16	32.0
FEMALE	0	.0	0	.0	0	.0		.0	0	.0	1	50.0	1	50.0
MALE	0	.0	0	.0	1	2.1	0	.0	1	2.1	32	66.7	15	31.3
PROFESSIONAL:														
FULL-TIME	0	.0	0	.0	0	.0	0	.0	0	.0	0	.0	0	.0
FEMALE	0	.0	0	.0	0	.0	0	.0	0	.0	0	.0	0	.0
MALE	0	.0	0	.0	0	.0	0	.0	0	.0	0	.0	0	.0

ENGINEERING

INDIAN NATIVE %	BLACK NON-HISPANIC NUMBER	%	ASIAN OR PACIFIC ISLANDER NUMBER	%	HISPANIC NUMBER	%	TOTAL MINORITY NUMBER	%	WHITE NON-HISPANIC NUMBER	%	NON-RESIDENT ALIEN NUMBER	%	TOTAL NUMBER
CONTINUED													
.0	0	.0	0	.0	0	.0	0	.0	0	.0	0	.0	0
.0	0	.0	0	.0	0	.0	0	.0	0	.0	0	.0	0
.0	0	.0	0	.0	0	.0	0	.0	0	.0	0	.0	0
.0	0	.0	0	.0	0	.0	0	.0	0	.0	0	.0	0
.0	0	.0	0	.0	0	.0	0	.0	0	.0	0	.0	0
.0	0	.0	0	.0	0	.0	0	.0	0	.0	0	.0	0
.4	6	.4	17	1.0	2	.1	31	1.8	1,620	96.4	29	1.7	1,680
.8	0	.0	2	1.5	0	.0	3	2.3	126	96.9	1	.8	130
.3	6	.4	15	1.0	2	.1	28	1.8	1,494	96.4	28	1.8	1,550
.0	1	1.9	0	.0	0	.0	1	1.9	44	83.0	8	15.1	53
.0	0	.0	0	.0	0	.0	0	.0	5	100.0	0	.0	5
.0	1	2.1	0	.0	0	.0	1	2.1	39	81.3	8	16.7	48
.3	7	.4	17	1.0	2	.1	32	1.8	1,664	96.0	37	2.1	1,733
.7	0	.0	2	1.5	0	.0	3	2.2	131	97.0	1	.7	135
.3	7	.4	15	.9	2	.1	29	1.8	1,533	95.9	36	2.3	1,598
.0	0	.0	1	6.7	0	.0	1	6.7	13	86.7	1	6.7	15
.0	0	.0	0	.0	0	.0	0	.0	2	100.0	0	.0	2
.0	0	.0	1	7.7	0	.0	1	7.7	11	84.6	1	7.7	13
.3	7	.4	18	1.0	2	.1	33	1.9	1,677	95.9	38	2.2	1,746
.7	0	.0	2	1.5	0	.0	3	2.2	133	97.1	1	.7	137
.3	7	.4	16	1.0	2	.1	30	1.9	1,544	95.8	37	2.3	1,611
(54 INSTITUTIONS)													
.2	657	4.2	96	.6	68	.4	848	5.5	13,799	89.0	863	5.6	15,510
.2	137	9.2	12	.8	6	.4	158	10.6	1,286	86.3	47	3.2	1,491
.2	520	3.7	84	.6	62	.4	690	4.9	12,513	89.3	816	5.8	14,019
.2	492	6.0	53	.6	36	.4	598	7.3	7,489	91.5	94	1.1	8,181
.3	56	9.2	6	1.0	2	.3	66	10.9	538	88.5	4	.7	608
.2	436	5.8	47	.6	34	.4	532	7.0	6,951	91.8	90	1.2	7,573
.2	1,149	4.8	149	.6	104	.4	1,446	6.1	21,288	89.9	957	4.0	23,691
.2	193	9.2	18	.9	8	.4	224	10.7	1,824	86.9	51	2.4	2,099
.2	956	4.4	131	.6	96	.4	1,222	5.7	19,464	90.1	906	4.2	21,592
.1	20	1.4	26	1.9	12	.9	60	4.3	724	52.3	599	43.3	1,383
.0	5	5.0	4	4.0	1	1.0	10	10.0	68	68.0	22	22.0	100
.2	15	1.2	22	1.7	11	.9	50	3.9	656	51.1	577	45.0	1,283
.2	22	1.7	35	2.7	11	.8	68	5.2	1,084	83.0	154	11.8	1,306
.0	0	.0	2	2.4	1	1.2	3	3.6	75	90.4	5	6.0	83
.0	22	1.8	33	2.7	10	.8	65	5.2	1,009	82.5	149	12.2	1,223
.1	42	1.6	61	2.3	23	.9	128	4.8	1,808	67.2	753	28.0	2,689
.0	5	2.7	6	3.3	2	1.1	13	7.1	143	78.1	27	14.8	183
.1	37	1.5	55	2.2	21	.8	115	4.6	1,665	66.4	726	29.0	2,506
.0	0	.0	0	.0	0	.0	0	.0	0	.0	0	.0	0
.0	0	.0	0	.0	0	.0	0	.0	0	.0	0	.0	0
.0	0	.0	0	.0	0	.0	0	.0	0	.0	0	.0	0
.0	0	.0	0	.0	0	.0	0	.0	0	.0	0	.0	0
.0	0	.0	0	.0	0	.0	0	.0	0	.0	0	.0	0
.0	0	.0	0	.0	0	.0	0	.0	0	.0	0	.0	0
.0	0	.0	0	.0	0	.0	0	.0	0	.0	0	.0	0
.0	0	.0	0	.0	0	.0	0	.0	0	.0	0	.0	0
.0	0	.0	0	.0	0	.0	0	.0	0	.0	0	.0	0
.2	677	4.0	122	.7	80	.5	908	5.4	14,523	86.0	1,462	8.7	16,893
.2	142	8.9	16	1.0	7	.4	168	10.6	1,354	85.1	69	4.3	1,591
.2	535	3.5	106	.7	73	.5	740	4.8	13,169	86.1	1,393	9.1	15,302
.2	514	5.4	88	.9	47	.5	666	7.0	8,573	90.4	248	2.6	9,487
.3	56	8.1	8	1.2	3	.4	69	10.0	613	88.7	9	1.3	691
.2	458	5.2	80	.9	44	.5	597	6.8	7,960	90.5	239	2.7	8,796
.2	1,191	4.5	210	.8	127	.5	1,574	6.0	23,096	87.6	1,710	6.5	26,380
.2	198	8.7	24	1.1	10	.4	237	10.4	1,967	86.2	78	3.4	2,282
.2	993	4.1	186	.8	117	.5	1,337	5.5	21,129	87.7	1,632	6.8	24,098
.2	17	3.1	14	2.6	4	.7	36	6.6	471	86.4	38	7.0	545
.0	3	4.7	2	3.1	0	.0	5	7.8	58	90.6	1	1.6	64
.2	14	2.9	12	2.5	4	.8	31	6.4	413	85.9	37	7.7	481
.2	1,208	4.5	224	.8	131	.5	1,610	6.0	23,567	87.5	1,748	6.5	26,925
.2	201	8.6	26	1.1	10	.4	242	10.3	2,025	86.3	79	3.4	2,346
.2	1,007	4.1	198	.8	121	.5	1,368	5.6	21,542	87.6	1,669	6.8	24,579

MAJOR FIELD 0900 - ENGINEERING

	AMERICAN INDIAN ALASKAN NATIVE		BLACK NON-HISPANIC		ASIAN OR PACIFIC ISLANDER		HISPANIC		TOTAL MINORITY		WHITE NON-HISPANIC		NON-RESIDENT ALIEN	
	NUMBER	%	NUMBER	%	NUMBER	%	NUMBER	%	NUMBER	%	NUMBER	%	NUMBER	%
OKLAHOMA (21 INSTITUTIONS)														
UNDERGRADUATES:														
FULL-TIME	127	1.9	136	2.0	102	1.5	37	.5	402	5.9	4,691	68.6	1,746	25.5
FEMALE	26	4.2	42	6.8	7	1.1	1	.2	76	12.2	442	71.1	104	16.7
MALE	101	1.6	94	1.5	95	1.5	36	.6	326	5.2	4,249	68.3	1,642	26.4
PART-TIME	23	2.6	44	4.9	10	1.1	5	.6	82	9.1	731	81.2	87	9.7
FEMALE	4	2.9	16	11.0	2	1.4	2	1.4	24	17.4	106	76.8	8	5.8
MALE	19	2.5	28	3.7	8	1.0	3	.4	58	7.6	625	82.0	79	10.4
TOTAL	150	1.9	180	2.3	112	1.4	42	.5	484	6.3	5,422	70.1	1,833	23.7
FEMALE	30	3.9	58	7.6	9	1.2	3	.4	100	13.2	548	72.1	112	14.7
MALE	120	1.7	122	1.7	103	1.5	39	.6	384	5.5	4,874	69.8	1,721	24.7
GRADUATE:														
FULL-TIME	2	.4	6	1.2	9	1.8	2	.4	19	3.9	164	33.6	305	62.5
FEMALE	0	.0	2	7.4	0	.0	0	.0	2	7.4	15	55.6	10	37.0
MALE	2	.4	4	.9	9	2.0	2	.4	17	3.7	149	32.3	295	64.0
PART-TIME	2	.4	8	1.8	3	.7	0	.0	13	2.9	297	65.3	145	31.9
FEMALE	1	2.5	1	2.5	0	.0	0	.0	2	5.0	29	72.5	9	22.5
MALE	1	.2	7	1.7	3	.7	0	.0	11	2.7	268	64.6	136	32.8
TOTAL	4	.4	14	1.5	12	1.3	2	.2	32	3.4	461	48.9	450	47.7
FEMALE	1	1.5	3	4.5	0	.0	0	.0	4	6.0	44	65.7	19	28.4
MALE	3	.3	11	1.3	12	1.4	2	.2	28	3.2	417	47.6	431	49.2
PROFESSIONAL:														
FULL-TIME	0	.0	0	.0	0	.0	0	.0	0	.0	0	.0	0	.0
FEMALE	0	.0	0	.0	0	.0	0	.0	0	.0	0	.0	0	.0
MALE	0	.0	0	.0	0	.0	0	.0	0	.0	0	.0	0	.0
PART-TIME	0	.0	0	.0	0	.0	0	.0	0	.0	0	.0	0	.0
FEMALE	0	.0	0	.0	0	.0	0	.0	0	.0	0	.0	0	.0
MALE	0	.0	0	.0	0	.0	0	.0	0	.0	0	.0	0	.0
TOTAL	0	.0	0	.0	0	.0	0	.0	0	.0	0	.0	0	.0
FEMALE	0	.0	0	.0	0	.0	0	.0	0	.0	0	.0	0	.0
MALE	0	.0	0	.0	0	.0	0	.0	0	.0	0	.0	0	.0
UND+GRAD+PROF:														
FULL-TIME	129	1.8	142	1.9	111	1.5	39	.5	421	5.7	4,855	66.3	2,051	28.0
FEMALE	26	4.0	44	6.8	7	1.1	1	.2	78	12.0	457	70.4	114	17.6
MALE	103	1.5	98	1.5	104	1.6	38	.6	343	5.1	4,398	65.9	1,937	29.0
PART-TIME	25	1.8	52	3.8	13	1.0	5	.4	95	7.0	1,028	75.9	232	17.1
FEMALE	5	2.8	17	9.6	2	1.1	2	1.1	26	14.6	135	75.8	17	9.6
MALE	20	1.7	35	3.0	11	.9	3	.3	69	5.9	893	75.9	215	18.3
TOTAL	154	1.8	194	2.2	124	1.4	44	.5	516	5.9	5,883	67.8	2,283	26.3
FEMALE	31	3.7	61	7.4	9	1.1	3	.4	104	12.6	592	71.6	131	15.8
MALE	123	1.6	133	1.7	115	1.5	41	.5	412	5.2	5,291	67.4	2,152	27.4
UNCLASSIFIED:														
TOTAL	3	3.1	1	1.0	4	4.1	1	1.0	9	9.3	72	74.2	16	16.5
FEMALE	0	.0	0	.0	0	.0	0	.0	0	.0	12	85.7	2	14.3
MALE	3	3.6	1	1.2	4	4.8	1	1.2	9	10.8	60	72.3	14	16.9
TOTAL ENROLLMENT:														
TOTAL	157	1.8	195	2.2	128	1.5	45	.5	525	6.0	5,955	67.8	2,299	26.2
FEMALE	31	3.7	61	7.3	9	1.1	3	.4	104	12.4	604	71.8	133	15.8
MALE	126	1.6	134	1.7	119	1.5	42	.5	421	5.3	5,351	67.4	2,166	27.3
OREGON (14 INSTITUTIONS)														
UNDERGRADUATES:														
FULL-TIME	51	1.2	16	.4	204	4.9	20	.5	291	7.0	3,434	82.3	449	10.8
FEMALE	5	1.3	1	.3	27	7.2	1	.3	34	9.1	310	83.1	29	7.8
MALE	46	1.2	15	.4	177	4.7	19	.5	257	6.8	3,124	82.2	420	11.0
PART-TIME	8	1.3	3	.5	13	2.2	3	.5	27	4.5	540	90.3	31	5.2
FEMALE	0	.0	0	.0	0	.0	0	.0	0	.0	71	98.6	1	1.4
MALE	8	1.5	3	.6	13	2.5	3	.6	27	5.1	469	89.2	30	5.7
TOTAL	59	1.2	19	.4	217	4.5	23	.5	318	6.7	3,974	83.3	480	10.1
FEMALE	5	1.1	1	.2	27	6.1	1	.2	34	7.6	381	85.6	30	6.7
MALE	54	1.2	18	.4	190	4.4	22	.5	284	6.6	3,593	83.0	450	10.4
GRADUATE:														
FULL-TIME	1	.4	0	.0	3	1.1	0	.0	4	1.5	121	44.2	149	54.4
FEMALE	0	.0	0	.0	1	5.3	0	.0	1	5.3	14	73.7	4	21.1
MALE	1	.4	0	.0	2	.8	0	.0	3	1.2	107	42.0	145	56.9
PART-TIME	1	1.5	0	.0	3	4.6	0	.0	4	6.2	48	73.8	13	20.0
FEMALE	0	.0	0	.0	0	.0	0	.0	0	.0	4	100.0	0	.0
MALE	1	1.6	0	.0	3	4.9	0	.0	4	6.6	44	72.1	13	21.3
TOTAL	2	.6	0	.0	6	1.8	0	.0	8	2.4	169	49.9	162	47.8
FEMALE	0	.0	0	.0	1	4.3	0	.0	1	4.3	18	78.3	4	17.4
MALE	2	.6	0	.0	5	1.6	0	.0	7	2.2	151	47.8	158	50.0
PROFESSIONAL														
FULL-TIME	0	.0	0	.0	0	.0	0	.0	0	.0	0	.0	0	.0
FEMALE	0	.0	0	.0	0	.0	0	.0	0	.0	0	.0	0	.0
MALE	0	.0	0	.0	0	.0	0	.0	0	.0	0	.0	0	.0

464

ENGINEERING

INDIAN NATIVE %	BLACK NON-HISPANIC NUMBER	%	ASIAN OR PACIFIC ISLANDER NUMBER	%	HISPANIC NUMBER	%	TOTAL MINORITY NUMBER	%	WHITE NON-HISPANIC NUMBER	%	NON-RESIDENT ALIEN NUMBER	%	TOTAL NUMBER
CONTINUED													
.0	0	.0	0	.0	0	.0	0	.0	0	.0	0	.0	0
.0	0	.0	0	.0	0	.0	0	.0	0	.0	0	.0	0
.0	0	.0	0	.0	0	.0	0	.0	0	.0	0	.0	0
.0	0	.0	0	.0	0	.0	0	.0	0	.0	0	.0	0
.0	0	.0	0	.0	0	.0	0	.0	0	.0	0	.0	0
.0	0	.0	0	.0	0	.0	0	.0	0	.0	0	.0	0
1.2	16	.4	207	4.7	20	.4	295	6.6	3,555	79.9	598	13.4	4,448
1.3	1	.3	28	7.1	1	.3	35	8.9	324	82.7	33	8.4	392
1.2	15	.4	179	4.4	19	.5	260	6.4	3,231	79.7	565	13.9	4,056
1.4	3	.5	16	2.4	3	.5	31	4.7	588	88.7	44	6.6	663
.0	0	.0	0	.0	0	.0	0	.0	75	98.7	1	1.3	76
1.5	3	.5	16	2.7	3	.5	31	5.3	513	87.4	43	7.3	587
1.2	19	.4	223	4.4	23	.5	326	6.4	4,143	81.1	642	12.6	5,111
1.1	1	.2	28	6.0	1	.2	35	7.5	399	85.3	34	7.3	468
1.2	18	.4	195	4.2	22	.5	291	6.3	3,744	80.6	608	13.1	4,643
1.1	3	.9	14	4.0	5	1.4	26	7.5	294	84.5	28	8.0	348
.0	0	.0	2	6.1	0	.0	2	6.1	31	93.9	0	.0	33
1.3	3	1.0	12	3.8	5	1.6	24	7.6	263	83.5	28	8.9	315
1.2	22	.4	237	4.3	28	.5	352	6.4	4,437	81.3	670	12.3	5,459
1.0	1	.2	30	6.0	1	.2	37	7.4	430	85.8	34	6.8	501
1.2	21	.4	207	4.2	27	.5	315	6.4	4,007	80.8	636	12.8	4,958
(65 INSTITUTIONS)													
.1	827	3.6	322	1.4	144	.6	1,312	5.7	21,082	91.7	593	2.6	22,987
.1	191	6.7	42	1.5	20	.7	256	9.0	2,523	89.0	56	2.0	2,835
.1	636	3.2	280	1.4	124	.6	1,056	5.2	18,559	92.1	537	2.7	20,152
.2	196	5.0	22	.6	16	.4	242	6.2	3,631	93.0	33	.8	3,906
.0	16	5.8	2	.7	2	.7	20	7.2	255	91.7	3	1.1	278
.2	180	5.0	20	.6	14	.4	222	6.1	3,376	93.1	30	.8	3,628
.1	1,023	3.8	344	1.3	160	.6	1,554	5.8	24,713	91.9	626	2.3	26,893
.1	207	6.6	44	1.4	22	.7	276	8.9	2,778	89.2	59	1.9	3,113
.1	816	3.4	300	1.3	138	.6	1,278	5.5	21,935	92.2	567	2.4	23,780
.4	16	1.4	23	2.0	15	1.3	59	5.1	655	56.7	442	38.2	1,156
.0	2	2.3	2	2.3	0	.0	4	4.6	64	73.6	19	21.8	87
.5	14	1.3	21	2.0	15	1.4	55	5.1	591	55.3	423	39.6	1,069
.1	43	3.2	63	4.7	14	1.0	122	9.1	1,167	86.8	56	4.2	1,345
.0	4	4.2	6	6.3	1	1.1	11	11.6	84	88.4	0	.0	95
.2	39	3.1	57	4.6	13	1.0	111	8.9	1,083	86.6	56	4.5	1,250
.3	59	2.4	86	3.4	29	1.2	181	7.2	1,822	72.9	498	19.9	2,501
.0	6	3.3	8	4.4	1	.5	15	8.2	148	81.3	19	10.4	182
.3	53	2.3	78	3.4	28	1.2	166	7.2	1,674	72.2	479	20.7	2,319
.0	0	.0	0	.0	0	.0	0	.0	0	.0	0	.0	0
.0	0	.0	0	.0	0	.0	0	.0	0	.0	0	.0	0
.0	0	.0	0	.0	0	.0	0	.0	0	.0	0	.0	0
.0	0	.0	0	.0	0	.0	0	.0	0	.0	0	.0	0
.0	0	.0	0	.0	0	.0	0	.0	0	.0	0	.0	0
.0	0	.0	0	.0	0	.0	0	.0	0	.0	0	.0	0
.1	843	3.5	345	1.4	159	.7	1,371	5.7	21,737	90.0	1,035	4.3	24,143
.1	193	6.6	44	1.5	20	.7	260	8.9	2,587	88.5	75	2.6	2,922
.1	650	3.1	301	1.4	139	.7	1,111	5.2	19,150	90.2	960	4.5	21,221
.2	239	4.6	85	1.6	30	.6	364	6.9	4,798	91.4	89	1.7	5,251
.2	20	5.4	8	2.1	3	.8	31	8.3	339	90.9	3	.8	373
.2	219	4.5	77	1.6	27	.6	333	6.8	4,459	91.4	86	1.8	4,878
.1	1,082	3.7	430	1.5	189	.6	1,735	5.9	26,535	90.3	1,124	3.8	29,394
.1	213	6.5	52	1.6	23	.7	291	8.8	2,926	88.8	78	2.4	3,295
.1	869	3.3	378	1.4	166	.6	1,444	5.5	23,609	90.5	1,046	4.0	26,099
.1	25	2.6	96	10.0	18	1.9	140	14.6	800	83.6	17	1.8	957
.0	6	6.9	6	6.9	2	2.3	14	16.1	71	81.6	2	2.3	87
.1	19	2.2	90	10.3	16	1.8	126	14.5	729	83.8	15	1.7	870
.1	1,107	3.6	526	1.7	207	.7	1,875	6.2	27,335	90.1	1,141	3.8	30,351
.1	219	6.5	58	1.7	25	.7	305	9.0	2,997	88.6	80	2.4	3,382
.1	888	3.3	468	1.7	182	.7	1,570	5.8	24,338	90.2	1,061	3.9	26,969

TABLE 17 - TOTAL ENROLLMENT IN INSTITUTIONS OF HIGHER EDUCATION FOR SELECTED MAJOR FIELDS OF STUDY AND LEVEL OF ENROLLMENT
BY RACE, ETHNICITY, AND SEX: STATE, 1978

MAJOR FIELD 0900 - ENGINEERING

	AMERICAN INDIAN ALASKAN NATIVE		BLACK NON-HISPANIC		ASIAN OR PACIFIC ISLANDER		HISPANIC		TOTAL MINORITY		WHITE NON-HISPANIC		NON-RESIDENT ALIEN	
	NUMBER	%	NUMBER	%	NUMBER	%	NUMBER	%	NUMBER	%	NUMBER	%	NUMBER	%
RHODE ISLAND	**(5 INSTITUTIONS)**													
UNDERGRADUATES:														
FULL-TIME	1	.1	60	4.1	34	2.3	14	1.0	109	7.5	1,238	85.4	103	7.1
FEMALE	0	.0	12	6.5	3	1.6	0	.0	15	8.1	162	87.6	8	4.3
MALE	1	.1	48	3.8	31	2.5	14	1.1	94	7.4	1,076	85.1	95	7.5
PART-TIME	0	.0	9	1.3	1	.1	1	.1	11	1.6	670	98.0	3	.4
FEMALE	0	.0	0	.0	0	.0	0	.0	0	.0	38	100.0	0	.0
MALE	0	.0	9	1.4	1	.2	1	.2	11	1.7	632	97.8	3	.5
TOTAL	1	.0	69	3.2	35	1.6	15	.7	120	5.6	1,908	89.4	106	5.0
FEMALE	0	.0	12	5.4	3	1.3	0	.0	15	6.7	200	89.7	8	3.6
MALE	1	.1	57	3.0	32	1.7	15	.8	105	5.5	1,708	89.4	98	5.1
GRADUATE:														
FULL-TIME	1	.5	2	1.0	5	2.6	0	.0	8	4.1	105	54.1	81	41.8
FEMALE	0	.0	0	.0	0	.0	0	.0	0	.0	7	63.6	4	36.4
MALE	1	.5	2	1.1	5	2.7	0	.0	8	4.4	98	53.6	77	42.1
PART-TIME	0	.0	0	.0	3	3.0	0	.0	3	3.0	83	83.8	13	13.1
FEMALE	0	.0	0	.0	0	.0	0	.0	0	.0	4	100.0	0	.0
MALE	0	.0	0	.0	3	3.2	0	.0	3	3.2	79	83.2	13	13.7
TOTAL	1	.3	2	.7	8	2.7	0	.0	11	3.8	188	64.2	94	32.1
FEMALE	0	.0	0	.0	0	.0	0	.0	0	.0	11	73.3	4	26.7
MALE	1	.4	2	.7	8	2.9	0	.0	11	4.0	177	63.7	90	32.4
PROFESSIONAL:														
FULL-TIME	0	.0	0	.0	0	.0	0	.0	0	.0	0	.0	0	.0
FEMALE	0	.0	0	.0	0	.0	0	.0	0	.0	0	.0	0	.0
MALE	0	.0	0	.0	0	.0	0	.0	0	.0	0	.0	0	.0
PART-TIME	0	.0	0	.0	0	.0	0	.0	0	.0	0	.0	0	.0
FEMALE	0	.0	0	.0	0	.0	0	.0	0	.0	0	.0	0	.0
MALE	0	.0	0	.0	0	.0	0	.0	0	.0	0	.0	0	.0
TOTAL	0	.0	0	.0	0	.0	0	.0	0	.0	0	.0	0	.0
FEMALE	0	.0	0	.0	0	.0	0	.0	0	.0	0	.0	0	.0
MALE	0	.0	0	.0	0	.0	0	.0	0	.0	0	.0	0	.0
UND+GRAD+PROF:														
FULL-TIME	2	.1	62	3.8	39	2.4	14	.9	117	7.1	1,343	81.7	184	11.2
FEMALE	0	.0	12	6.1	3	1.5	0	.0	15	7.7	169	86.2	12	6.1
MALE	2	.1	50	3.5	36	2.5	14	1.0	102	7.0	1,174	81.1	172	11.9
PART-TIME	0	.0	9	1.1	4	.5	1	.1	14	1.8	753	96.2	16	2.0
FEMALE	0	.0	0	.0	0	.0	0	.0	0	.0	42	100.0	0	.0
MALE	0	.0	9	1.2	4	.5	1	.1	14	1.9	711	96.0	16	2.2
TOTAL	2	.1	71	2.9	43	1.8	15	.6	131	5.4	2,096	86.4	200	8.2
FEMALE	0	.0	12	5.0	3	1.3	0	.0	15	6.3	211	88.7	12	5.0
MALE	2	.1	59	2.7	40	1.8	15	.7	116	5.3	1,885	86.1	188	8.6
UNCLASSIFIED:														
TOTAL	0	.0	0	.0	1	100.0	0	.0	1	100.0	0	.0	0	.0
FEMALE	0	.0	0	.0	0	.0	0	.0	0	.0	0	.0	0	.0
MALE	0	.0	0	.0	1	100.0	0	.0	1	100.0	0	.0	0	.0
TOTAL ENROLLMENT:														
TOTAL	2	.1	71	2.9	44	1.8	15	.6	132	5.4	2,096	86.3	200	8.2
FEMALE	0	.0	12	5.0	3	1.3	0	.0	15	6.3	211	88.7	12	5.0
MALE	2	.1	59	2.7	41	1.9	15	.7	117	5.3	1,885	86.1	188	8.6
SOUTH CAROLINA	**(14 INSTITUTIONS)**													
UNDERGRADUATES:														
FULL-TIME	4	.1	376	7.9	26	.5	12	.3	418	8.7	4,266	89.3	95	2.0
FEMALE	0	.0	53	9.3	2	.4	1	.2	56	9.8	511	89.8	2	.4
MALE	4	.1	323	7.7	24	.6	11	.3	362	8.6	3,755	89.2	93	2.2
PART-TIME	1	.3	26	6.6	3	.8	1	.3	31	7.9	355	90.8	5	1.3
FEMALE	0	.0	2	6.5	0	.0	0	.0	2	6.5	29	93.5	0	.0
MALE	1	.3	24	6.7	3	.8	1	.3	29	8.1	326	90.6	5	1.4
TOTAL	5	.1	402	7.8	29	.6	13	.3	449	8.7	4,621	89.4	100	1.9
FEMALE	0	.0	55	9.2	2	.3	1	.2	58	9.7	540	90.0	2	.3
MALE	5	.1	347	7.6	27	.6	12	.3	391	8.6	4,081	89.3	98	2.1
GRADUATE:														
FULL-TIME	0	.0	6	2.4	3	1.2	4	1.6	13	5.1	185	73.1	55	21.7
FEMALE	0	.0	2	.0	0	.0	0	.0	0	.0	26	92.9	2	7.1
MALE	0	.0	6	2.7	3	1.3	4	1.8	13	5.8	159	70.7	53	23.6
PART-TIME	1	.4	3	1.1	3	1.1	0	.0	7	2.7	247	93.6	10	3.8
FEMALE	0	.0	0	.0	1	12.5	0	.0	1	12.5	4	50.0	3	37.5
MALE	1	.4	3	1.2	2	.8	0	.0	6	2.3	243	94.9	7	2.7
TOTAL	1	.2	9	1.7	6	1.2	4	.8	20	3.9	432	83.6	65	12.6
FEMALE	0	.0	0	.0	1	2.8	0	.0	1	2.8	30	83.3	5	13.9
MALE	1	.2	9	1.9	5	1.0	4	.8	19	4.0	402	83.6	60	12.5
PROFESSIONAL:														
FULL-TIME	0	.0	0	.0	0	.0	0	.0	0	.0	0	.0	0	.0
FEMALE	0	.0	0	.0	0	.0	0	.0	0	.0	0	.0	0	.0
MALE	0	.0	0	.0	0	.0	0	.0	0	.0	0	.0	0	.0

ROLLMENT IN INSTITUTIONS OF HIGHER EDUCATION FOR SELECTED MAJOR FIELDS OF STUDY AND LEVEL OF ENROLLMENT
ETHNICITY, AND SEX: STATE, 1978

ENGINEERING

INDIAN NATIVE %	BLACK NON-HISPANIC NUMBER	%	ASIAN OR PACIFIC ISLANDER NUMBER	%	HISPANIC NUMBER	%	TOTAL MINORITY NUMBER	%	WHITE NON-HISPANIC NUMBER	%	NON-RESIDENT ALIEN NUMBER	%	TOTAL NUMBER
CONTINUED													
.0	0	.0	0	.0		.0	0	.0	0	.0		.0	
.0	0	.0	0	.0	0	.0	0	.0	0	.0	0	.0	0
.0	0	.0	0	.0		.0	0	.0	0	.0		.0	
.0	0	.0	0	.0		.0	0	.0	0	.0		.0	
.0	0	.0	0	.0	0	.0	0	.0	0	.0	0	.0	0
.0	0	.0	0	.0		.0	0	.0	0	.0		.0	
.1	382	7.6	29	.6	16	.3	431	8.6	4,451	88.5	150	3.0	5,032
.0	53	8.9	2	.3	1	.2	56	9.4	537	89.9	4	.7	597
.1	329	7.4	27	.6	15	.3	375	8.5	3,914	88.3	146	3.3	4,435
.3	29	4.4	6	.9	1	.2	38	5.8	602	91.9	15	2.3	655
.0	2	5.1	1	2.6	0	.0	3	7.7	33	84.6	3	7.7	39
.3	27	4.4	5	.8	1	.2	35	5.7	569	92.4	12	1.9	616
.1	411	7.2	35	.6	17	.3	469	8.2	5,053	88.9	165	2.9	5,687
.0	55	8.6	3	.5	1	.2	59	9.3	570	89.6	7	1.1	636
.1	356	7.0	32	.6	16	.3	410	8.1	4,483	88.8	158	3.1	5,051
.0	5	9.1	0	.0		.0	5	9.1	49	89.1	1	1.8	55
.0	0	.0	0	.0	0	.0	0	.0	5	100.0	0	.0	5
.0	5	10.0	0	.0		.0	5	10.0	44	88.0	1	2.0	50
.1	416	7.2	35	.6	17	.3	474	8.3	5,102	88.9	166	2.9	5,742
.0	55	8.6	3	.5	1	.2	59	9.2	575	89.7	7	1.1	641
.1	361	7.1	32	.6	16	.3	415	8.1	4,527	88.7	159	3.1	5,101
(3 INSTITUTIONS)													
.7	7	.4	9	.5	5	.3	34	1.8	1,673	90.3	145	7.8	1,852
.0	1	.5	0	.0	0	.0	1	.5	183	95.8	7	3.7	191
.8	6	.4	9	.5	5	.3	33	2.0	1,490	89.7	138	8.3	1,661
.0	0	.0	0	.0	0	.0	0	.0	59	88.1	8	11.9	67
.0	0	.0	0	.0	0	.0	0	.0	5	83.3	1	16.7	6
.0	0	.0	0	.0	0	.0	0	.0	54	88.5	7	11.5	61
.7	7	.4	9	.5	5	.3	34	1.8	1,732	90.3	153	8.0	1,919
.0	1	.5	0	.0	0	.0	1	.5	188	95.4	8	4.1	197
.8	6	.3	9	.5	5	.3	33	1.9	1,544	89.7	145	8.4	1,722
.0	0	.0	0	.0	1	1.0	1	1.0	55	55.6	43	43.4	99
.0	0	.0	0	.0	0	.0	0	.0	4	100.0	0	.0	4
.0	0	.0	0	.0	1	1.1	1	1.1	51	53.7	43	45.3	95
.0	0	.0	0	.0	0	.0	0	.0	29	69.0	13	31.0	42
.0	0	.0	0	.0	0	.0	0	.0	3	100.0	0	.0	3
.0	0	.0	0	.0	0	.0	0	.0	26	66.7	13	33.3	39
.0	0	.0	0	.0	1	.7	1	.7	84	59.6	56	39.7	141
.0	0	.0	0	.0	0	.0	0	.0	7	100.0	0	.0	7
.0	0	.0	0	.0	1	.7	1	.7	77	57.5	56	41.8	134
.0	0	.0	0	.0		.0	0	.0	0	.0		.0	
.0	0	.0	0	.0		.0	0	.0	0	.0		.0	
.0	0	.0	0	.0		.0	0	.0	0	.0		.0	
.0	0	.0	0	.0		.0	0	.0	0	.0		.0	
.0	0	.0	0	.0		.0	0	.0	0	.0		.0	
.0	0	.0	0	.0	0	.0	0	.0	0	.0	0	.0	0
.0	0	.0	0	.0		.0	0	.0	0	.0		.0	
.0	0	.0	0	.0		.0	0	.0	0	.0		.0	
.0	0	.0	0	.0	0	.0	0	.0	0	.0	0	.0	0
.7	7	.4	9	.5		.3	35	1.8	1,728	88.6	188	9.6	1,951
.0	1	.5	0	.0		.3	1	.5	187	95.9	7	3.6	195
.7	6	.3	9	.5		.3	34	1.9	1,541	87.8	181	10.3	1,756
.0	0	.0	0	.0		.0	0	.0	88	80.7	21	19.3	109
.0	0	.0	0	.0		.0	0	.0	8	88.9	1	11.1	9
.0	0	.0	0	.0	0	.0	0	.0	80	80.0	20	20.0	100
.6	7	.3	9	.4		.3	35	1.7	1,816	88.2	209	10.1	2,060
.0	1	.5	0	.0		.0	1	.5	195	95.6	8	3.9	204
.7	6	.3	9	.5	0	.3	34	1.8	1,621	87.3	201	10.6	1,850
.0	0	.0	0	.0		.0	0	.0	3	100.0		.0	3
.0	0	.0	0	.0	0	.0	0	.0	1	100.0	0	.0	1
.0	0	.0	0	.0		.0	0	.0	2	100.0		.0	2
.6	7	.3	9	.4		.3	35	1.7	1,819	88.2	209	10.1	2,063
.0	1	.5	0	.0		.0	1	.5	196	95.6	8	3.9	205
.7	6	.3	9	.5	0	.3	34	1.8	1,623	87.4	201	10.8	1,858

TABLE 17 - TOTAL ENROLLMENT IN INSTITUTIONS OF HIGHER EDUCATION FOR SELECTED MAJOR FIELDS OF STUDY AND LEVEL OF ENROLLMENT BY RACE, ETHNICITY, AND SEX: STATE, 1978

MAJOR FIELD 0900 - ENGINEERING

	AMERICAN INDIAN ALASKAN NATIVE		BLACK NON-HISPANIC		ASIAN OR PACIFIC ISLANDER		HISPANIC		TOTAL MINORITY		WHITE NON-HISPANIC		NON-RESIDENT ALIEN	
	NUMBER	%	NUMBER	%	NUMBER	%	NUMBER	%	NUMBER	%	NUMBER	%	NUMBER	%
TENNESSEE (22 INSTITUTIONS)														
UNDERGRADUATES:														
FULL-TIME	7	.1	1,538	15.4	75	.8	37	.4	1,657	16.6	7,492	74.9	847	8.5
FEMALE	0	.0	341	24.8	11	.8	2	.1	354	25.7	976	70.8	48	3.5
MALE	7	.1	1,197	13.9	64	.7	35	.4	1,303	15.1	6,516	75.6	799	9.3
PART-TIME	7	.2	349	11.8	5	.2	18	.6	379	12.8	2,522	85.4	51	1.7
FEMALE	0	.0	51	10.0	2	.4	2	.4	55	10.8	447	88.0	6	1.2
MALE	7	.3	298	12.2	3	.1	16	.7	324	13.3	2,075	84.9	45	1.8
TOTAL	14	.1	1,887	14.6	80	.6	55	.4	2,036	15.7	10,014	77.3	898	6.9
FEMALE	0	.0	392	20.8	13	.7	4	.2	409	21.7	1,421	75.4	54	2.9
MALE	14	.1	1,495	13.5	67	.6	51	.5	1,627	14.7	8,593	77.7	844	7.6
GRADUATE:														
FULL-TIME	0	.0	2	.4	14	3.1	1	.2	17	3.7	281	61.9	156	34.4
FEMALE	0	.0	0	.0	1	2.3	0	.0	1	2.3	34	79.1	8	18.6
MALE	0	.0	2	.5	13	3.2	1	.2	16	3.9	247	60.1	148	36.0
PART-TIME	0	.0	16	2.0	11	1.4	6	.8	33	4.2	657	82.8	103	13.0
FEMALE	0	.0	2	5.7	1	2.9	1	2.9	4	11.4	27	77.1	4	11.4
MALE	0	.0	14	1.8	10	1.3	5	.7	29	3.8	630	83.1	99	13.1
TOTAL	0	.0	18	1.4	25	2.0	7	.6	50	4.0	938	75.2	259	20.8
FEMALE	0	.0	2	2.6	2	2.6	1	1.3	5	6.4	61	78.2	12	15.4
MALE	0	.0	16	1.4	23	2.0	6	.5	45	3.8	877	75.0	247	21.1
PROFESSIONAL:														
FULL-TIME	0	.0	0	.0	0	.0	0	.0	0	.0	7	87.5	1	12.5
FEMALE	0	.0	0	.0	0	.0	0	.0	0	.0	0	.0	1	100.0
MALE	0	.0	0	.0	0	.0	0	.0	0	.0	7	100.0	0	.0
PART-TIME	0	.0	0	.0	0	.0	0	.0	0	.0	0	.0	0	.0
FEMALE	0	.0	0	.0	0	.0	0	.0	0	.0	0	.0	0	.0
MALE	0	.0	0	.0	0	.0	0	.0	0	.0	0	.0	0	.0
TOTAL	0	.0	0	.0	0	.0	0	.0	0	.0	7	87.5	1	12.5
FEMALE	0	.0	0	.0	0	.0	0	.0	0	.0	0	.0	1	100.0
MALE	0	.0	0	.0	0	.0	0	.0	0	.0	7	100.0	0	.0
UND+GRAD+PROF:														
FULL-TIME	7	.1	1,540	14.7	89	.9	38	.4	1,674	16.0	7,780	74.4	1,004	9.6
FEMALE	0	.0	341	24.0	12	.8	2	.1	355	25.0	1,008	71.0	57	4.0
MALE	7	.1	1,199	13.3	77	.9	36	.4	1,319	14.6	6,772	74.9	947	10.5
PART-TIME	7	.2	365	9.7	16	.4	24	.6	412	11.0	3,179	84.9	154	4.1
FEMALE	0	.0	53	9.8	3	.6	3	.6	59	10.9	474	87.3	10	1.8
MALE	7	.2	312	9.7	13	.4	21	.7	353	11.0	2,705	84.5	144	4.5
TOTAL	14	.1	1,905	13.4	105	.7	62	.4	2,086	14.7	10,959	77.2	1,158	8.2
FEMALE	0	.0	394	20.1	15	.8	5	.3	414	21.1	1,482	75.5	67	3.4
MALE	14	.1	1,511	12.3	90	.7	57	.5	1,672	13.7	9,477	77.4	1,091	8.9
UNCLASSIFIED:														
TOTAL	0	.0	35	32.7	0	.0	0	.0	35	32.7	65	60.7	7	6.5
FEMALE	0	.0	4	16.7	0	.0	0	.0	4	16.7	20	83.3	0	.0
MALE	0	.0	31	37.3	0	.0	0	.0	31	37.3	45	54.2	7	8.4
TOTAL ENROLLMENT:														
TOTAL	14	.1	1,940	13.6	105	.7	62	.4	2,121	14.8	11,024	77.0	1,165	8.1
FEMALE	0	.0	398	20.0	15	.8	5	.3	418	21.0	1,502	75.6	67	3.4
MALE	14	.1	1,542	12.5	90	.7	57	.5	1,703	13.8	9,522	77.3	1,098	8.9
TEXAS (81 INSTITUTIONS)														
UNDERGRADUATES:														
FULL-TIME	70	.3	1,312	5.1	343	1.3	1,816	7.1	3,541	13.8	17,929	70.0	4,139	16.2
FEMALE	5	.2	309	11.8	62	2.4	204	7.8	580	22.1	1,842	70.2	203	7.7
MALE	65	.3	1,003	4.4	281	1.2	1,612	7.0	2,961	12.9	16,087	70.0	3,936	17.1
PART-TIME	33	.5	324	5.1	104	1.6	579	9.1	1,040	16.4	4,986	78.5	327	5.1
FEMALE	1	.2	39	6.4	6	1.0	48	7.9	94	15.5	492	81.3	19	3.1
MALE	32	.6	285	5.0	98	1.7	531	9.2	946	16.5	4,494	78.2	308	5.4
TOTAL	103	.3	1,636	5.1	447	1.4	2,395	7.5	4,581	14.3	22,915	71.7	4,466	14.0
FEMALE	6	.2	348	10.8	68	2.1	252	7.8	674	20.9	2,334	72.3	222	6.9
MALE	97	.3	1,288	4.5	379	1.3	2,143	7.5	3,907	13.6	20,581	71.6	4,244	14.8
GRADUATE:														
FULL-TIME	3	.1	10	.4	109	4.7	40	1.7	162	7.0	1,132	48.9	1,022	44.1
FEMALE	0	.0	1	.7	9	6.6	4	2.9	14	10.2	94	68.6	29	21.2
MALE	3	.1	9	.4	100	4.6	36	1.7	148	6.8	1,038	47.6	993	45.6
PART-TIME	5	.3	33	2.0	36	2.2	51	3.1	125	7.7	1,300	79.6	208	12.7
FEMALE	1	.8	2	1.6	1	.8	3	2.4	7	5.5	104	81.9	16	12.6
MALE	4	.3	31	2.1	35	2.3	48	3.2	118	7.8	1,196	79.4	192	12.7
TOTAL	8	.2	43	1.1	145	3.7	91	2.3	287	7.3	2,432	61.6	1,230	31.1
FEMALE	1	.4	3	1.1	10	3.8	7	2.7	21	8.0	198	75.0	45	17.0
MALE	7	.2	40	1.1	135	3.7	84	2.3	266	7.2	2,234	60.6	1,185	32.2
PROFESSIONAL:														
FULL-TIME	0	.0	0	.0	0	.0	0	.0	0	.0	0	.0	0	.0
FEMALE	0	.0	0	.0	0	.0	0	.0	0	.0	0	.0	0	.0
MALE	0	.0	0	.0	0	.0	0	.0	0	.0	0	.0	0	.0

ENGINEERING

INDIAN NATIVE		BLACK NON-HISPANIC		ASIAN OR PACIFIC ISLANDER		HISPANIC		TOTAL MINORITY		WHITE NON-HISPANIC		NON-RESIDENT ALIEN		TOTAL
%	NUMBER	%	NUMBER	%	NUMBER	%	NUMBER	%	NUMBER	%	NUMBER	%	NUMBER	%	NUMBER

CONTINUED

.0	0	.0	0	.0	0	.0	0	.0	0	.0	0	.0	0	.0	0
.0	0	.0	0	.0	0	.0	0	.0	0	.0	0	.0	0	.0	0
.0	0	.0	0	.0	0	.0	0	.0	0	.0	0	.0	0	.0	0
.0	0	.0	0	.0	0	.0	0	.0	0	.0	0	.0	0	.0	0
.0	0	.0	0	.0	0	.0	0	.0	0	.0	0	.0	0	.0	0
.0	0	.0	0	.0	0	.0	0	.0	0	.0	0	.0	0	.0	0
.3	1,322	4.7	452	1.6	1,856	6.6	3,703	13.3	19,061	68.3	5,161	18.5			27,925
.2	310	11.2	71	2.6	208	7.5	594	21.5	1,936	70.1	232	8.4			2,762
.3	1,012	4.0	381	1.5	1,648	6.5	3,109	12.4	17,125	68.1	4,929	19.6			25,163
.5	357	4.5	140	1.8	630	7.9	1,165	14.6	6,286	78.7	535	6.7			7,986
.3	41	5.6	7	1.0	51	7.0	101	13.8	596	81.4	35	4.8			732
.5	316	4.4	133	1.8	579	8.0	1,064	14.7	5,690	78.4	500	6.9			7,254
.3	1,679	4.7	592	1.6	2,486	6.9	4,868	13.6	25,347	70.6	5,696	15.9			35,911
.2	351	10.0	78	2.2	259	7.4	695	19.9	2,532	72.5	267	7.6			3,494
.3	1,328	4.1	514	1.6	2,227	6.9	4,173	12.9	22,815	70.4	5,429	16.7			32,417
.7	22	3.0	15	2.0	89	12.1	131	17.8	536	72.6	71	9.6			738
1.4	6	8.1	3	4.1	8	10.8	18	24.3	54	73.0	2	2.7			74
.6	16	2.4	12	1.8	81	12.2	113	17.0	482	72.6	69	10.4			664
.3	1,701	4.6	607	1.7	2,575	7.0	4,999	13.6	25,883	70.6	5,767	15.7			36,649
.2	357	10.0	81	2.3	267	7.5	713	20.0	2,586	72.5	269	7.5			3,568
.3	1,344	4.1	526	1.6	2,308	7.0	4,286	13.0	23,297	70.4	5,498	16.6			33,081

(7 INSTITLTIONS)

.4	9	.3	41	1.2	17	.5	82	2.4	2,938	85.2	430	12.5			3,450
1.0	0	.0	6	3.0	1	.5	9	4.5	169	84.9	21	10.6			199
.4	9	.3	35	1.1	16	.5	73	2.2	2,769	85.2	409	12.6			3,251
.4	1	.2	4	.7	10	1.8	17	3.0	522	92.7	24	4.3			563
.0	0	.0	1	3.2	0	.0	1	3.2	28	90.3	2	6.5			31
.4	1	.2	3	.6	10	1.9	16	3.0	494	92.9	22	4.1			532
.4	10	.2	45	1.1	27	.7	99	2.5	3,460	86.2	454	11.3			4,013
.9	0	.0	7	3.0	1	.4	10	4.3	197	85.7	23	10.0			230
.4	10	.3	38	1.0	26	.7	89	2.4	3,263	86.3	431	11.4			3,783
.3	0	.0	8	2.6	1	.3	10	3.3	221	72.0	76	24.8			307
.0	0	.0	1	7.7	0	.0	1	7.7	9	69.2	3	23.1			13
.3	0	.0	7	2.4	1	.3	9	3.1	212	72.1	73	24.8			294
.0	0	.0	6	2.5	0	.0	6	2.5	158	65.8	76	31.7			240
.0	0	.0	1	7.7	0	.0	1	7.7	6	46.2	6	46.2			13
.0	0	.0	5	2.2	0	.0	5	2.2	152	67.0	70	30.8			227
.2	0	.0	14	2.6	1	.2	16	2.9	379	69.3	152	27.8			547
.0	0	.0	2	7.7	0	.0	2	7.7	15	57.7	9	34.6			26
.2	0	.0	12	2.3	1	.2	14	2.7	364	69.9	143	27.4			521
.0	0	.0	0	.0	0	.0	0	.0	0	.0	0	.0			0
.0	0	.0	0	.0	0	.0	0	.0	0	.0	0	.0			0
.0	0	.0	0	.0	0	.0	0	.0	0	.0	0	.0			0
.0	0	.0	0	.0	0	.0	0	.0	0	.0	0	.0			0
.0	0	.0	0	.0	0	.0	0	.0	0	.0	0	.0			0
.0	0	.0	0	.0	0	.0	0	.0	0	.0	0	.0			0
.0	0	.0	0	.0	0	.0	0	.0	0	.0	0	.0			0
.0	0	.0	0	.0	0	.0	0	.0	0	.0	0	.0			0
.0	0	.0	0	.0	0	.0	0	.0	0	.0	0	.0			0
.4	9	.2	49	1.3	18	.5	92	2.4	3,159	84.1	506	13.5			3,757
.9	0	.0	7	3.3	1	.5	10	4.7	178	84.0	24	11.3			212
.4	9	.3	42	1.2	17	.5	82	2.3	2,981	84.1	482	13.6			3,545
.2	1	.1	10	1.2	10	1.2	23	2.9	680	84.7	100	12.5			803
.0	0	.0	2	4.5	0	.0	2	4.5	34	77.3	8	18.2			44
.3	1	.1	8	1.1	10	1.3	21	2.8	646	85.1	92	12.1			759
.4	10	.2	59	1.3	28	.6	115	2.5	3,839	84.2	606	13.3			4,560
.8	0	.0	9	3.5	1	.4	12	4.7	212	82.8	32	12.5			256
.4	10	.2	50	1.2	27	.6	103	2.4	3,627	84.3	574	13.3			4,304
.0	0	.0	0	.0	0	.0	0	.0	1	100.0	0	.0			1
.0	0	.0	0	.0	0	.0	0	.0	0	.0	0	.0			0
.0	0	.0	0	.0	0	.0	0	.0	1	100.0	0	.0			1
.4	10	.2	59	1.3	28	.6	115	2.5	3,840	84.2	606	13.3			4,561
.8	0	.0	9	3.5	1	.4	12	4.7	212	82.8	32	12.5			256
.4	10	.2	50	1.2	27	.6	103	2.4	3,628	84.3	574	13.3			4,305

TABLE 17 - TOTAL ENROLLMENT IN INSTITUTIONS OF HIGHER EDUCATION FOR SELECTED MAJOR FIELDS OF STUDY AND LEVEL OF ENROLLMENT
BY RACE, ETHNICITY, AND SEX: STATE, 1978

MAJOR FIELD 0900 - ENGINEERING

	AMERICAN INDIAN ALASKAN NATIVE		BLACK NON-HISPANIC		ASIAN OR PACIFIC ISLANDER		HISPANIC		TOTAL MINORITY		WHITE NON-HISPANIC		NON-RESIDENT ALIEN		
	NUMBER	%	NUMBER	%	NUMBER	%	NUMBER	%	NUMBER	%	NUMBER	%	NUMBER	%	
VERMONT			3 INSTITUTIONS)												
UNDERGRADUATES:															
FULL-TIME	5	.4	8	.6	3	.2	8	.6	24	1.9	1,138	90.2	100	7.9	
FEMALE	0	.0	3	2.3	1	.8	0	.0	4	3.1	105	82.0	19	14.8	
MALE	5	.4	5	.4	2	.2	8	.7	20	1.8	1,033	91.1	81	7.1	
PART-TIME	0	.0	0	.0	0	.0	0	.0	0	.0	58	100.0	0	.0	
FEMALE	0	.0	0	.0	0	.0	0	.0	0	.0	7	100.0	0	.0	
MALE	0	.0	0	.0	0	.0	0	.0	0	.0	51	100.0	0	.0	
TOTAL	5	.4	8	.6	3	.2	8	.6	24	1.8	1,196	90.6	100	7.6	
FEMALE	0	.0	3	2.2	1	.7	0	.0	4	3.0	112	83.0	19	14.1	
MALE	5	.4	5	.4	2	.2	8	.7	20	1.7	1,084	91.5	81	6.8	
GRADUATE:															
FULL-TIME	0	.0	0	.0	0	.0	0	.0	0	.0	30	78.9	8	21.1	
FEMALE	0	.0	0	.0	0	.0	0	.0	0	.0	0	.0	0	.0	
MALE	0	.0	0	.0	0	.0	0	.0	0	.0	30	78.9	8	21.1	
PART-TIME	0	.0	0	.0	0	.0	0	.0	0	.0	38	95.0	2	5.0	
FEMALE	0	.0	0	.0	0	.0	0	.0	0	.0	7	100.0	0	.0	
MALE	0	.0	0	.0	0	.0	0	.0	0	.0	31	93.9	2	6.1	
TOTAL	0	.0	0	.0	0	.0	0	.0	0	.0	68	87.2	10	12.8	
FEMALE	0	.0	0	.0	0	.0	0	.0	0	.0	7	100.0	0	.0	
MALE	0	.0	0	.0	0	.0	0	.0	0	.0	61	85.9	10	14.1	
PROFESSIONAL:															
FULL-TIME	0	.0	0	.0	0	.0	0	.0	0	.0	0	.0	0	.0	
FEMALE	0	.0	0	.0	0	.0	0	.0	0	.0	0	.0	0	.0	
MALE	0	.0	0	.0	0	.0	0	.0	0	.0	0	.0	0	.0	
PART-TIME	0	.0	0	.0	0	.0	0	.0	0	.0	0	.0	0	.0	
FEMALE	0	.0	0	.0	0	.0	0	.0	0	.0	0	.0	0	.0	
MALE	0	.0	0	.0	0	.0	0	.0	0	.0	0	.0	0	.0	
TOTAL	0	.0	0	.0	0	.0	0	.0	0	.0	0	.0	0	.0	
FEMALE	0	.0	0	.0	0	.0	0	.0	0	.0	0	.0	0	.0	
MALE	0	.0	0	.0	0	.0	0	.0	0	.0	0	.0	0	.0	
UND+GRAD+PROF:															
FULL-TIME	5	.4	8	.6	3	.2	8	.6	24	1.8	1,168	89.8	108	8.3	
FEMALE	0	.0	3	2.3	1	.8	0	.0	4	3.1	105	82.0	19	14.8	
MALE	5	.4	5	.4	2	.2	8	.7	20	1.7	1,063	90.7	89	7.6	
PART-TIME	0	.0	0	.0	0	.0	0	.0	0	.0	96	98.0	2	2.0	
FEMALE	0	.0	0	.0	0	.0	0	.0	0	.0	14	100.0	0	.0	
MALE	0	.0	0	.0	0	.0	0	.0	0	.0	82	97.6	2	2.4	
TOTAL	5	.4	8	.6	3	.2	8	.6	24	1.7	1,264	90.4	110	7.9	
FEMALE	0	.0	3	2.1	1	.7	0	.0	4	2.8	119	83.8	19	13.4	
MALE	5	.4	5	.4	2	.2	8	.6	20	1.6	1,145	91.2	91	7.2	
UNCLASSIFIED:															
TOTAL	0	.0	0	.0	0	.0	0	.0	0	.0	0	.0	0	.0	
FEMALE	0	.0	0	.0	0	.0	0	.0	0	.0	0	.0	0	.0	
MALE	0	.0	0	.0	0	.0	0	.0	0	.0	0	.0	0	.0	
TOTAL ENROLLMENT:															
TOTAL	5	.4	8	.6	3	.2	8	.6	24	1.7	1,264	90.4	110	7.9	
FEMALE	0	.0	3	2.1	1	.7	0	.0	4	2.8	119	83.8	19	13.4	
MALE	5	.4	5	.4	2	.2	8	.6	20	1.6	1,145	91.2	91	7.2	
VIRGINIA			(21 INSTITUTIONS)												
UNDERGRADUATES:															
FULL-TIME	10	.1	290	3.7	139	1.8	22	.3	461	5.8	7,194	91.1	245	3.1	
FEMALE	2	.2	52	5.8	14	1.6	1	.1	69	7.8	808	90.9	12	1.3	
MALE	8	.1	238	3.4	125	1.8	21	.3	392	5.6	6,386	91.1	233	3.3	
PART-TIME	1	.1	53	6.4	15	1.8	8	1.0	77	9.3	740	88.9	15	1.8	
FEMALE	0	.0	2	2.7	2	2.7	2	2.7	6	8.0	69	92.0	0	.0	
MALE	1	.1	51	6.7	13	1.7	6	.8	71	9.4	671	88.6	15	2.0	
TOTAL	11	.1	343	3.9	154	1.8	30	.3	538	6.2	7,934	90.9	260	3.0	
FEMALE	2	.2	54	5.6	16	1.7	3	.3	75	7.8	877	91.0	12	1.2	
MALE	9	.1	289	3.7	138	1.8	27	.3	463	6.0	7,057	90.8	248	3.2	
GRADUATE:															
FULL-TIME	0	.0	8	1.1	27	3.7	0	.0	35	4.8	553	75.4	145	19.8	
FEMALE	0	.0	0	.0	1	1.6	0	.0	1	1.6	51	82.3	10	16.1	
MALE	0	.0	8	1.2	26	3.9	0	.0	34	5.1	502	74.8	135	20.1	
PART-TIME	0	.0	0	.0	16	3.0	0	.0	16	3.0	487	90.9	33	6.2	
FEMALE	0	.0	0	.0	3	9.7	0	.0	3	9.7	26	83.9	2	6.5	
MALE	0	.0	0	.0	13	2.6	0	.0	13	2.6	461	91.3	31	6.1	
TOTAL	0	.0	8	.6	43	3.4	0	.0	51	4.0	1,040	82.0	178	14.0	
FEMALE	0	.0	0	.0	4	4.3	0	.0	4	4.3	77	82.8	12	12.9	
MALE	0	.0	8	.7	39	3.3	0	.0	47	4.0	963	81.9	166	14.1	
PROFESSIONAL:															
FULL-TIME	0	.0	0	.0	0	.0	0	.0	0	.0	0	.0	0	.0	
FEMALE	0	.0	0	.0	0	.0	0	.0	0	.0	0	.0	0	.0	
MALE	0	.0	0	.0	0	.0	0	.0	0	.0	0	.0	0	.0	

470

ROLLMENT IN INSTITUTIONS OF HIGHER EDUCATION FOR SELECTED MAJOR FIELDS OF STUDY AND LEVEL OF ENROLLMENT
ETHNICITY, AND SEX: STATE, 1978

ENGINEERING

INDIAN NATIVE	BLACK NON-HISPANIC		ASIAN OR PACIFIC ISLANDER		HISPANIC		TOTAL MINORITY		WHITE NON-HISPANIC		NON-RESIDENT ALIEN		TOTAL
%	NUMBER	%	NUMBER	%	NUMBER	%	NUMBER	%	NUMBER	%	NUMBER	%	NUMBER
CONTINUED													
.0	0	.0	0	.0	0	.0	0	.0	0	.0	0	.0	0
.0	0	.0	0	.0	0	.0	0	.0	0	.0	0	.0	0
.0	0	.0	0	.0	0	.0	0	.0	0	.0	0	.0	0
.0	0	.0	0	.0	0	.0	0	.0	0	.0	0	.0	0
.0	0	.0	0	.0	0	.0	0	.0	0	.0	0	.0	0
.0	0	.0	0	.0	0	.0	0	.0	0	.0	0	.0	0
.1	298	3.5	166	1.9	22	.3	496	5.7	7,747	89.7	390	4.5	8,633
.2	52	5.5	15	1.6	1	.1	70	7.4	859	90.3	22	2.3	951
.1	246	3.2	151	2.0	21	.3	426	5.5	6,888	89.7	368	4.8	7,682
.1	53	3.9	31	2.3	8	.6	93	6.8	1,227	89.7	48	3.5	1,368
.0	2	1.9	5	4.7	2	1.9	9	8.5	95	89.6	2	1.9	106
.1	51	4.0	26	2.1	6	.5	84	6.7	1,132	89.7	46	3.6	1,262
.1	351	3.5	197	2.0	30	.3	589	5.9	8,974	89.7	438	4.4	10,001
.2	54	5.1	20	1.9	3	.3	79	7.5	954	90.3	24	2.3	1,057
.1	297	3.3	177	2.0	27	.3	510	5.7	8,020	89.7	414	4.6	8,944
.0	2	5.7	0	.0	0	.0	2	5.7	31	88.6	2	5.7	35
.0	1	33.3	0	.0	0	.0	1	33.3	2	66.7	0	.0	3
.0	1	3.1	0	.0	0	.0	1	3.1	29	90.6	2	6.3	32
.1	353	3.5	197	2.0	30	.3	591	5.9	9,005	89.7	440	4.4	10,036
.2	55	5.2	20	1.9	3	.3	80	7.5	956	90.2	24	2.3	1,080
.1	298	3.3	177	2.0	27	.3	511	5.7	8,049	89.7	416	4.6	8,976
(9 INSTITUTIONS)													
.5	58	1.3	324	7.5	24	.6	429	10.0	3,400	79.0	475	11.0	4,304
.4	4	.8	54	11.0	3	.6	63	12.9	404	82.4	23	4.7	490
.4	54	1.4	270	7.1	21	.6	366	9.6	2,996	78.6	452	11.9	3,814
.2	4	.7	35	6.3	5	.9	45	8.2	466	84.4	41	7.4	552
.0	1	1.7	1	1.7	1	1.7	3	5.2	55	94.8	0	.0	58
.2	3	.6	34	6.9	4	.8	42	8.5	411	83.2	41	8.3	494
.5	62	1.3	359	7.4	29	.6	474	9.8	3,866	79.6	516	10.6	4,856
.4	5	.9	55	10.0	4	.7	66	12.0	459	83.8	23	4.2	548
.5	57	1.3	304	7.1	25	.6	408	9.5	3,407	79.1	493	11.4	4,308
.2	4	.7	23	4.1	1	.2	29	5.2	276	49.2	256	45.6	561
.0	1	2.6	3	7.9	0	.0	4	10.5	25	65.8	9	23.7	38
.2	3	.6	20	3.8	1	.2	25	4.8	251	48.0	247	47.2	523
.0	1	.4	19	6.8	1	.4	21	7.6	223	80.2	34	12.2	278
.0	0	.0	3	16.7	0	.0	3	16.7	14	77.8	1	5.6	18
.0	1	.4	16	6.2	1	.4	18	6.9	209	80.4	33	12.7	260
.1	5	.6	42	5.0	2	.2	50	6.0	499	59.5	290	34.6	839
.0	1	1.8	6	10.7	0	.0	7	12.5	39	69.6	10	17.9	56
.1	4	.5	36	4.6	2	.3	43	5.5	460	58.7	280	35.8	783
.0	0	.0	0	.0	0	.0	0	.0	0	.0	0	.0	0
.0	0	.0	0	.0	0	.0	0	.0	0	.0	0	.0	0
.0	0	.0	0	.0	0	.0	0	.0	0	.0	0	.0	0
.0	0	.0	0	.0	0	.0	0	.0	0	.0	0	.0	0
.0	0	.0	0	.0	0	.0	0	.0	0	.0	0	.0	0
.0	0	.0	0	.0	0	.0	0	.0	0	.0	0	.0	0
.0	0	.0	0	.0	0	.0	0	.0	0	.0	0	.0	0
.0	0	.0	0	.0	0	.0	0	.0	0	.0	0	.0	0
.0	0	.0	0	.0	0	.0	0	.0	0	.0	0	.0	0
.5	62	1.3	347	7.1	25	.5	458	9.4	3,676	75.6	731	15.0	4,865
.9	5	.9	57	10.8	3	.6	67	12.7	429	81.3	32	6.1	526
.5	57	1.3	290	6.7	22	.5	391	9.0	3,247	74.9	699	16.1	4,337
.1	5	.6	54	6.5	6	.7	66	8.0	689	83.0	75	9.0	830
.1	1	1.3	4	5.3	1	1.3	6	7.9	69	90.8	1	1.3	76
.1	4	.5	50	6.6	5	.7	60	8.0	620	82.2	74	9.8	754
.4	67	1.2	401	7.0	31	.5	524	9.2	4,365	76.6	806	14.2	5,695
.3	6	1.0	61	10.1	4	.7	73	12.1	498	82.5	33	5.5	604
.5	61	1.2	340	6.7	27	.5	451	8.9	3,867	76.0	773	15.2	5,091
.4	1	.4	14	5.4	0	.0	16	6.2	197	75.8	47	18.1	260
2.7	0	.0	4	10.8	0	.0	5	13.5	31	83.8	1	2.7	37
.0	1	.4	10	4.5	0	.0	11	4.9	166	74.4	46	20.6	223
.4	68	1.1	415	7.0	31	.5	540	9.1	4,562	76.6	853	14.3	5,955
.5	6	.9	65	10.1	4	.6	78	12.2	529	82.5	34	5.3	641
.4	62	1.2	350	6.6	27	.5	462	8.7	4,033	75.9	819	15.4	5,314

TABLE 17 - TOTAL ENROLLMENT IN INSTITUTIONS OF HIGHER EDUCATION FOR SELECTED MAJOR FIELDS OF STUDY AND LEVEL OF ENROLLMENT BY RACE, ETHNICITY, AND SEX: STATE, 1978

MAJOR FIELD 0900 - ENGINEERING

	AMERICAN INDIAN ALASKAN NATIVE		BLACK NON-HISPANIC		ASIAN OR PACIFIC ISLANDER		HISPANIC		TOTAL MINORITY		WHITE NON-HISPANIC		NON-RESIDENT ALIEN	
	NUMBER	%	NUMBER	%	NUMBER	%	NUMBER	%	NUMBER	%	NUMBER	%	NUMBER	%
WEST VIRGINIA (13 INSTITUTIONS)														
UNDERGRADUATES:														
FULL-TIME	3	.1	85	2.4	15	.4	2	.1	105	3.0	3,072	87.5	333	9.5
FEMALE	0	.0	8	2.6	2	.7	0	.0	10	3.3	288	93.8	9	2.9
MALE	3	.1	77	2.4	13	.4	2	.1	95	3.0	2,784	86.9	324	10.1
PART-TIME	3	.7	8	1.8	3	.7	0	.0	14	3.2	408	92.7	18	4.1
FEMALE	1	2.3	2	4.7	1	2.3	0	.0	4	9.3	39	90.7	0	.0
MALE	2	.5	6	1.5	2	.5	0	.0	10	2.5	369	92.9	18	4.5
TOTAL	6	.2	93	2.4	18	.5	2	.1	119	3.0	3,480	88.1	351	8.9
FEMALE	1	.3	10	2.9	3	.9	0	.0	14	4.0	327	93.4	9	2.6
MALE	5	.1	83	2.3	15	.4	2	.1	105	2.9	3,153	87.6	342	9.5
GRADUATE:														
FULL-TIME	1	.6	1	.6	0	.0	1	.6	3	1.7	83	46.4	93	52.0
FEMALE	0	.0	0	.0	0	.0	1	6.7	1	6.7	12	80.0	2	13.3
MALE	1	.6	1	.6	0	.0	0	.0	2	1.2	71	43.3	91	55.5
PART-TIME	2	.6	5	1.5	12	3.5	3	.9	22	6.4	287	83.9	33	9.6
FEMALE	0	.0	1	2.0	0	.0	1	2.0	2	4.1	46	93.9	1	2.0
MALE	2	.7	4	1.4	12	4.1	2	.7	20	6.8	241	82.3	32	10.9
TOTAL	3	.6	6	1.2	12	2.3	4	.8	25	4.8	370	71.0	126	24.2
FEMALE	0	.0	1	1.6	0	.0	2	3.1	3	4.7	58	90.6	3	4.7
MALE	3	.7	5	1.1	12	2.6	2	.4	22	4.8	312	68.3	123	26.9
PROFESSIONAL:														
FULL-TIME	0	.0	0	.0	0	.0	0	.0	0	.0	0	.0	0	.0
FEMALE	0	.0	0	.0	0	.0	0	.0	0	.0	0	.0	0	.0
MALE	0	.0	0	.0	0	.0	0	.0	0	.0	0	.0	0	.0
PART-TIME	0	.0	0	.0	0	.0	0	.0	0	.0	0	.0	0	.0
FEMALE	0	.0	0	.0	0	.0	0	.0	0	.0	0	.0	0	.0
MALE	0	.0	0	.0	0	.0	0	.0	0	.0	0	.0	0	.0
TOTAL	0	.0	0	.0	0	.0	0	.0	0	.0	0	.0	0	.0
FEMALE	0	.0	0	.0	0	.0	0	.0	0	.0	0	.0	0	.0
MALE	0	.0	0	.0	0	.0	0	.0	0	.0	0	.0	0	.0
UND+GRAD+PROF:														
FULL-TIME	4	.1	86	2.3	15	.4	3	.1	108	2.9	3,155	85.5	426	11.5
FEMALE	0	.0	8	2.5	2	.6	1	.3	11	3.4	300	93.2	11	3.4
MALE	4	.1	78	2.3	13	.4	2	.1	97	2.9	2,855	84.8	415	12.3
PART-TIME	5	.6	13	1.7	15	1.9	3	.4	36	4.6	695	88.9	51	6.5
FEMALE	1	1.1	3	3.3	1	1.1	1	1.1	6	6.5	85	92.4	1	1.1
MALE	4	.6	10	1.4	14	2.0	2	.3	30	4.3	610	88.4	50	7.2
TOTAL	9	.2	99	2.2	30	.7	6	.1	144	3.2	3,850	86.1	477	10.7
FEMALE	1	.2	11	2.7	3	.7	2	.5	17	4.1	385	93.0	12	2.9
MALE	8	.2	88	2.2	27	.7	4	.1	127	3.1	3,465	85.4	465	11.5
UNCLASSIFIED:														
TOTAL	0	.0	2	5.3	0	.0	0	.0	2	5.3	33	86.8	3	7.9
FEMALE	0	.0	0	.0	0	.0	0	.0	0	.0	2	100.0	0	.0
MALE	0	.0	2	5.6	0	.0	0	.0	2	5.6	31	86.1	3	8.3
TOTAL ENROLLMENT:														
TOTAL	9	.2	101	2.2	30	.7	6	.1	146	3.2	3,883	86.1	480	10.6
FEMALE	1	.2	11	2.6	3	.7	2	.5	17	4.1	387	93.0	12	2.9
MALE	8	.2	90	2.2	27	.7	4	.1	129	3.2	3,496	85.4	468	11.4
WISCONSIN (15 INSTITUTIONS)														
UNDERGRADUATES:														
FULL-TIME	13	.2	162	1.9	64	.7	49	.6	288	3.4	7,966	92.8	328	3.8
FEMALE	0	.0	33	2.9	6	.5	1	.1	40	3.6	1,072	95.2	14	1.2
MALE	13	.2	129	1.7	58	.8	48	.6	248	3.3	6,894	92.5	314	4.2
PART-TIME	4	.1	36	1.3	5	.2	5	.2	50	1.8	2,775	97.3	27	.9
FEMALE	1	.2	8	1.3	0	.0	0	.0	9	1.4	623	98.6	0	.0
MALE	3	.1	28	1.3	5	.2	5	.2	41	1.8	2,152	96.9	27	1.2
TOTAL	17	.1	198	1.7	69	.6	54	.5	338	3.0	10,741	93.9	355	3.1
FEMALE	1	.1	41	2.3	6	.3	1	.1	49	2.8	1,695	96.4	14	.8
MALE	16	.2	157	1.6	63	.7	53	.5	289	3.0	9,046	93.5	341	3.5
GRADUATE:														
FULL-TIME	1	.1	4	.5	37	4.4	4	.5	46	5.5	458	54.6	335	39.9
FEMALE	0	.0	1	1.6	6	9.7	1	1.6	8	12.9	40	64.5	14	22.6
MALE	1	.1	3	.4	31	4.0	3	.4	38	4.9	418	53.8	321	41.3
PART-TIME	1	.3	2	.5	16	4.1	1	.3	20	5.1	338	86.0	35	8.9
FEMALE	0	.0	0	.0	3	6.7	0	.0	3	6.7	39	86.7	3	6.7
MALE	1	.3	2	.6	13	3.7	1	.3	17	4.9	299	85.9	32	9.2
TOTAL	2	.2	6	.5	53	4.3	5	.4	66	5.4	796	64.6	370	30.0
FEMALE	0	.0	1	.9	9	8.4	1	.9	11	10.3	79	73.8	17	15.9
MALE	2	.2	5	.4	44	3.9	4	.4	55	4.9	717	63.7	353	31.4
PROFESSIONAL:														
FULL-TIME	0	.0	0	.0	0	.0	0	.0	0	.0	0	.0	0	.0
FEMALE	0	.0	0	.0	0	.0	0	.0	0	.0	0	.0	0	.0
MALE	0	.0	0	.0	0	.0	0	.0	0	.0	0	.0	0	.0

ENGINEERING

(INDIAN NATIVE	BLACK NON-HISPANIC		ASIAN OR PACIFIC ISLANDER		HISPANIC		TOTAL MINORITY		WHITE NON-HISPANIC		NON-RESIDENT ALIEN		TOTAL
%	NUMBER	%	NUMBER	%	NUMBER	%	NUMBER	%	NUMBER	%	NUMBER	%	NUMBER

CONTINUED

.0	0	.0	0	.0	0	.0	0	.0	0	.0	0	.0	0
.0	0	.0	0	.0	0	.0	0	.0	0	.0	0	.0	0
.0	0	.0	0	.0	0	.0	0	.0	0	.0	0	.0	0
.0	0	.0	0	.0	0	.0	0	.0	0	.0	0	.0	0
.0	0	.0	0	.0	0	.0	0	.0	0	.0	0	.0	0
.0	0	.0	0	.0	0	.0	0	.0	0	.0	0	.0	0
.1	166	1.8	101	1.1	53	.6	334	3.5	8,424	89.4	663	7.0	9,421
.0	34	2.9	12	1.0	2	.2	48	4.0	1,112	93.6	28	2.4	1,188
.2	132	1.6	89	1.1	51	.6	286	3.5	7,312	88.8	635	7.7	8,233
.2	38	1.2	21	.6	6	.2	70	2.2	3,113	95.9	62	1.9	3,245
.1	8	1.2	3	.4	0	.0	12	1.8	662	97.8	3	.4	677
.2	30	1.2	18	.7	6	.2	58	2.3	2,451	95.4	59	2.3	2,568
.2	204	1.6	122	1.0	59	.5	404	3.2	11,537	91.1	725	5.7	12,666
.1	42	2.3	15	.8	2	.1	60	3.2	1,774	95.1	31	1.7	1,865
.2	162	1.5	107	1.0	57	.5	344	3.2	9,763	90.4	694	6.4	10,801
1.0	2	2.1	3	3.1	0	.0	6	6.2	87	89.7	4	4.1	97
.0	1	14.3	1	14.3	0	.0	2	28.6	3	42.9	2	28.6	7
1.1	1	1.1	2	2.2	0	.0	4	4.4	84	93.3	2	2.2	90
.2	206	1.6	125	1.0	59	.5	410	3.2	11,624	91.1	729	5.7	12,763
.1	43	2.3	16	.9	2	.1	62	3.3	1,777	94.9	33	1.8	1,872
.2	163	1.5	109	1.0	57	.5	348	3.2	9,847	90.4	696	6.4	10,891

(6 INSTITUTIONS)

.4	5	.5	7	.6	8	.7	24	2.2	942	85.1	141	12.7	1,107
.0	0	.0	2	1.9	0	.0	2	1.9	98	95.1	3	2.9	103
.4	5	.5	5	.5	8	2.0	22	2.2	844	84.1	138	13.7	1,004
.0	0	.0	0	.0	2	2.0	2	2.0	90	91.8	6	6.1	98
.0	0	.0	0	.0	0	.0	0	.0	16	100.0	0	.0	16
.0	0	.0	0	.0	2	2.4	2	2.4	74	90.2	6	7.3	82
.3	5	.4	7	.6	10	.8	26	2.2	1,032	85.6	147	12.2	1,205
.0	0	.0	2	1.7	0	.0	2	1.7	114	95.8	3	2.5	119
.4	5	.5	5	.5	10	.9	24	2.2	918	84.5	144	13.3	1,086
.0	0	.0	0	.0	0	.0	0	.0	43	69.4	19	30.6	62
.0	0	.0	0	.0	0	.0	0	.0	4	80.0	1	20.0	5
.0	0	.0	0	.0	0	.0	0	.0	39	68.4	18	31.6	57
.0	0	.0	0	.0	0	.0	0	.0	16	69.6	7	30.4	23
.0	0	.0	0	.0	0	.0	0	.0	2	66.7	1	33.3	3
.0	0	.0	0	.0	0	.0	0	.0	14	70.0	6	30.0	20
.0	0	.0	0	.0	0	.0	0	.0	59	69.4	26	30.6	85
.0	0	.0	0	.0	0	.0	0	.0	6	75.0	2	25.0	8
.0	0	.0	0	.0	0	.0	0	.0	53	68.8	24	31.2	77
.0	0	.0	0	.0	0	.0	0	.0	0	.0	0	.0	0
.0	0	.0	0	.0	0	.0	0	.0	0	.0	0	.0	0
.0	0	.0	0	.0	0	.0	0	.0	0	.0	0	.0	0
.0	0	.0	0	.0	0	.0	0	.0	0	.0	0	.0	0
.0	0	.0	0	.0	0	.0	0	.0	0	.0	0	.0	0
.0	0	.0	0	.0	0	.0	0	.0	0	.0	0	.0	0
.3	5	.4	7	.6	8	.7	24	2.1	985	84.3	160	13.7	1,169
.0	0	.0	2	1.9	0	.0	2	1.9	102	94.4	4	3.7	108
.4	5	.5	5	.5	8	.8	22	2.1	883	83.2	156	14.7	1,061
.0	0	.0	0	.0	2	1.7	2	1.7	106	87.6	13	10.7	121
.0	0	.0	0	.0	0	.0	0	.0	18	94.7	1	5.3	19
.0	0	.0	0	.0	2	2.0	2	2.0	88	86.3	12	11.8	102
.3	5	.4	7	.5	10	.8	26	2.0	1,091	84.6	173	13.4	1,290
.0	0	.0	2	1.6	0	.0	2	1.6	120	94.5	5	3.9	127
.3	5	.4	5	.4	10	.9	24	2.1	971	83.5	168	14.4	1,163
.0	0	.0	0	.0	0	.0	0	.0	7	87.5	1	12.5	8
.0	0	.0	0	.0	0	.0	0	.0	1	100.0	0	.0	1
.0	0	.0	0	.0	0	.0	0	.0	6	85.7	1	14.3	7
.3	5	.4	7	.5	10	.8	26	2.0	1,098	84.6	174	13.4	1,298
.0	0	.0	2	1.6	0	.0	2	1.6	121	94.5	5	3.9	128
.3	5	.4	5	.4	10	.9	24	2.1	977	83.5	169	14.4	1,170

TABLE 17 - TOTAL ENROLLMENT IN INSTITUTIONS OF HIGHER EDUCATION FOR SELECTED MAJOR FIELDS OF STUDY AND LEVEL OF ENROLLMENT BY RACE, ETHNICITY, AND SEX: STATE, 1978

MAJOR FIELD 0900 - ENGINEERING

	AMERICAN INDIAN ALASKAN NATIVE		BLACK NON-HISPANIC		ASIAN OR PACIFIC ISLANDER		HISPANIC		TOTAL MINORITY		WHITE NON-HISPANIC		NON-RESIDENT ALIEN	
	NUMBER	%	NUMBER	%	NUMBER	%	NUMBER	%	NUMBER	%	NUMBER	%	NUMBER	%
THE STATES AND D.C. (987 INSTITUTIONS)														
UNDERGRADUATES:														
FULL-TIME	1,192	.3	17,740	4.9	10,811	3.0	8,330	2.3	38,073	10.6	290,205	81.0	30,102	8.4
FEMALE	129	.3	3,516	9.0	1,416	3.6	913	2.3	5,974	15.3	31,260	80.3	1,695	4.4
MALE	1,063	.3	14,224	4.5	9,395	2.9	7,417	2.3	32,099	10.0	259,025	81.1	28,407	8.9
PART-TIME	483	.6	5,517	6.4	2,576	3.0	3,317	3.9	11,893	13.9	70,896	82.7	2,942	3.4
FEMALE	49	.5	766	7.4	241	2.3	243	2.3	1,299	12.5	8,913	86.0	156	1.5
MALE	434	.6	4,751	6.3	2,335	3.1	3,074	4.1	10,594	14.1	61,983	82.2	2,786	3.7
TOTAL	1,675	.4	23,257	5.2	13,387	3.0	11,647	2.6	49,966	11.2	361,181	81.3	33,044	7.4
FEMALE	178	.4	4,282	8.7	1,657	3.4	1,156	2.3	7,273	14.8	40,173	81.5	1,851	3.8
MALE	1,497	.4	18,975	4.8	11,730	3.0	10,491	2.7	42,693	10.8	321,008	81.3	31,193	7.9
GRADUATE:														
FULL-TIME	43	.1	336	1.1	1,209	4.0	309	1.0	1,897	6.3	16,445	55.0	11,569	38.7
FEMALE	4	.2	57	2.7	84	4.0	20	.9	165	7.8	1,463	69.4	480	22.8
MALE	39	.1	279	1.0	1,125	4.0	289	1.0	1,732	6.2	14,982	53.9	11,089	39.9
PART-TIME	55	.2	566	2.1	1,569	5.9	380	1.4	2,570	9.7	20,515	77.2	3,484	13.1
FEMALE	6	.3	56	3.0	110	5.9	19	1.0	191	10.3	1,505	80.9	165	8.9
MALE	49	.2	510	2.1	1,459	5.9	361	1.5	2,379	9.6	19,010	76.9	3,319	13.4
TOTAL	98	.2	902	1.6	2,778	4.9	689	1.2	4,467	7.9	36,960	65.4	15,053	26.7
FEMALE	10	.3	113	2.8	194	4.9	39	1.0	356	9.0	2,968	74.8	645	16.3
MALE	88	.2	789	1.5	2,584	4.9	650	1.2	4,111	7.8	33,992	64.7	14,408	27.4
PROFESSIONAL:														
FULL-TIME	0	.0	0	.0	0	.0	0	.0	0	.0	8	88.9	1	11.1
FEMALE	0	.0	0	.0	0	.0	0	.0	0	.0	0	.0	1	100.0
MALE	0	.0	0	.0	0	.0	0	.0	0	.0	8	100.0	0	.0
PART-TIME	0	.0	0	.0	0	.0	0	.0	0	.0	0	.0	0	.0
FEMALE	0	.0	0	.0	0	.0	0	.0	0	.0	0	.0	0	.0
MALE	0	.0	0	.0	0	.0	0	.0	0	.0	0	.0	0	.0
TOTAL	0	.0	0	.0	0	.0	0	.0	0	.0	8	88.9	1	11.1
FEMALE	0	.0	0	.0	0	.0	0	.0	0	.0	0	.0	1	100.0
MALE	0	.0	0	.0	0	.0	0	.0	0	.0	8	100.0	0	.0
UNDERGRAD+PROF:														
FULL-TIME	1,235	.3	18,076	4.7	12,020	3.1	8,639	2.2	39,970	10.3	306,738	79.0	41,672	10.7
FEMALE	133	.3	3,573	8.7	1,500	3.7	933	2.3	6,139	15.0	32,723	79.7	2,176	5.3
MALE	1,102	.3	14,503	4.2	10,520	3.0	7,706	2.2	33,831	9.7	274,015	78.9	39,496	11.4
PART-TIME	538	.5	6,083	5.4	4,145	3.7	3,697	3.3	14,463	12.9	91,411	81.4	6,426	5.7
FEMALE	55	.4	822	6.7	351	2.9	262	2.1	1,490	12.2	10,418	85.2	321	2.6
MALE	483	.5	5,261	5.3	3,794	3.8	3,435	3.4	12,973	13.0	80,993	80.9	6,105	6.1
TOTAL	1,773	.4	24,159	4.8	16,165	3.2	12,336	2.5	54,433	10.9	398,149	79.5	48,098	9.6
FEMALE	188	.4	4,395	8.3	1,851	3.5	1,195	2.2	7,629	14.3	43,141	81.0	2,497	4.7
MALE	1,585	.4	19,764	4.4	14,314	3.2	11,141	2.5	46,804	10.5	355,008	79.3	45,601	10.2
UNCLASSIFIED:														
TOTAL	99	.8	566	4.4	724	5.6	530	4.1	1,919	14.8	9,999	76.9	1,082	8.3
FEMALE	9	.5	113	6.5	64	3.7	51	2.9	237	13.6	1,450	83.1	57	3.3
MALE	90	.8	453	4.0	660	5.9	479	4.3	1,682	14.9	8,549	76.0	1,025	9.1
TOTAL ENROLLMENT:														
TOTAL	1,872	.4	24,725	4.8	16,889	3.3	12,866	2.5	56,352	11.0	408,148	79.5	49,180	9.6
FEMALE	197	.4	4,508	8.2	1,915	3.5	1,246	2.3	7,866	14.3	44,591	81.1	2,554	4.6
MALE	1,675	.4	20,217	4.4	14,974	3.3	11,620	2.5	48,486	10.6	363,557	79.3	46,626	10.2
PUERTO RICO (5 INSTITUTIONS)														
UNDERGRADUATES:														
FULL-TIME	0	.0	0	.0	0	.0	3,244	100.0	3,244	100.0	0	.0	0	.0
FEMALE	0	.0	0	.0	0	.0	326	100.0	326	100.0	0	.0	0	.0
MALE	0	.0	0	.0	0	.0	2,918	100.0	2,918	100.0	0	.0	0	.0
PART-TIME	0	.0	0	.0	0	.0	320	100.0	320	100.0	0	.0	0	.0
FEMALE	0	.0	0	.0	0	.0	18	100.0	18	100.0	0	.0	0	.0
MALE	0	.0	0	.0	0	.0	302	100.0	302	100.0	0	.0	0	.0
TOTAL	0	.0	0	.0	0	.0	3,564	100.0	3,564	100.0	0	.0	0	.0
FEMALE	0	.0	0	.0	0	.0	344	100.0	344	100.0	0	.0	0	.0
MALE	0	.0	0	.0	0	.0	3,220	100.0	3,220	100.0	0	.0	0	.0
GRADUATE:														
FULL-TIME	0	.0	0	.0	0	.0	0	.0	0	.0	0	.0	0	.0
FEMALE	0	.0	0	.0	0	.0	0	.0	0	.0	0	.0	0	.0
MALE	0	.0	0	.0	0	.0	0	.0	0	.0	0	.0	0	.0
PART-TIME	0	.0	0	.0	0	.0	49	100.0	49	100.0	0	.0	0	.0
FEMALE	0	.0	0	.0	0	.0	3	100.0	3	100.0	0	.0	0	.0
MALE	0	.0	0	.0	0	.0	46	100.0	46	100.0	0	.0	0	.0
TOTAL	0	.0	0	.0	0	.0	49	100.0	49	100.0	0	.0	0	.0
FEMALE	0	.0	0	.0	0	.0	3	100.0	3	100.0	0	.0	0	.0
MALE	0	.0	0	.0	0	.0	46	100.0	46	100.0	0	.0	0	.0
PROFESSIONAL:														
FULL-TIME	0	.0	0	.0	0	.0	0	.0	0	.0	0	.0	0	.0
FEMALE	0	.0	0	.0	0	.0	0	.0	0	.0	0	.0	0	.0
MALE	0	.0	0	.0	0	.0	0	.0	0	.0	0	.0	0	.0

ENROLLMENT IN INSTITUTIONS OF HIGHER EDUCATION FOR SELECTED MAJOR FIELDS OF STUDY AND LEVEL OF ENROLLMENT
CE, ETHNICITY, AND SEX: STATE, 1978

- ENGINEERING

CAN INDIAN AN NATIVE		BLACK NON-HISPANIC		ASIAN OR PACIFIC ISLANDER		HISPANIC		TOTAL MINORITY		WHITE NON-HISPANIC		NON-RESIDENT ALIEN		TOTAL
ER	%	NUMBER	%	NUMBER	%	NUMBER	%	NUMBER	%	NUMBER	%	NUMBER	%	NUMBER
CONTINUED														
0	.0	0	.0	0	.0	0	.0	0	.0	0	.0	0	.0	0
0	.0	0	.0	0	.0	0	.0	0	.0	0	.0	0	.0	0
0	.0	0	.0	0	.0	0	.0	0	.0	0	.0	0	.0	0
0	.0	0	.0	0	.0	0	.0	0	.0	0	.0	0	.0	0
0	.0	0	.0	0	.0	0	.0	0	.0	0	.0	0	.0	0
0	.0	0	.0	0	.0	0	.0	0	.0	0	.0	0	.0	0
0	.0	0	.0	0	.0	3,244	100.0	3,244	100.0	0	.0	0	.0	3,244
0	.0	0	.0	0	.0	326	100.0	326	100.0	0	.0	0	.0	326
0	.0	0	.0	0	.0	2,918	100.0	2,918	100.0	0	.0	0	.0	2,918
0	.0	0	.0	0	.0	369	100.0	369	100.0	0	.0	0	.0	369
0	.0	0	.0	0	.0	21	100.0	21	100.0	0	.0	0	.0	21
0	.0	0	.0	0	.0	348	100.0	348	100.0	0	.0	0	.0	348
0	.0	0	.0	0	.0	3,613	100.0	3,613	100.0	0	.0	0	.0	3,613
0	.0	0	.0	0	.0	347	100.0	347	100.0	0	.0	0	.0	347
0	.0	0	.0	0	.0	3,266	100.0	3,266	100.0	0	.0	0	.0	3,266
0	.0	0	.0	0	.0	8	100.0	8	100.0	0	.0	0	.0	8
0	.0	0	.0	0	.0	1	100.0	1	100.0	0	.0	0	.0	1
0	.0	0	.0	0	.0	7	100.0	7	100.0	0	.0	0	.0	7
0	.0	0	.0	0	.0	3,621	100.0	3,621	100.0	0	.0	0	.0	3,621
0	.0	0	.0	0	.0	348	100.0	348	100.0	0	.0	0	.0	348
0	.0	0	.0	0	.0	3,273	100.0	3,273	100.0	0	.0	0	.0	3,273
(	1 INSTITLTIONS)													
0	.0	13	76.5	0	.0	0	.0	13	76.5	1	5.9	3	17.6	17
0	.0	0	.0	0	.0	0	.0	0	.0	0	.0	0	.0	0
0	.0	13	76.5	0	.0	0	.0	13	76.5	1	5.9	3	17.6	17
0	.0	0	.0	0	.0	0	.0	0	.0	0	.0	0	.0	0
0	.0	0	.0	0	.0	0	.0	0	.0	0	.0	0	.0	0
0	.0	13	76.5	0	.0	0	.0	13	76.5	1	5.9	3	17.6	17
0	.0	0	.0	0	.0	0	.0	0	.0	0	.0	0	.0	0
0	.0	13	76.5	0	.0	0	.0	13	76.5	1	5.9	3	17.6	17
0	.0	0	.0	0	.0	0	.0	0	.0	0	.0	0	.0	0
0	.0	0	.0	0	.0	0	.0	0	.0	0	.0	0	.0	0
0	.0	0	.0	0	.0	0	.0	0	.0	0	.0	0	.0	0
0	.0	0	.0	0	.0	0	.0	0	.0	0	.0	0	.0	0
0	.0	0	.0	0	.0	0	.0	0	.0	0	.0	0	.0	0
0	.0	0	.0	0	.0	0	.0	0	.0	0	.0	0	.0	0
0	.0	0	.0	0	.0	0	.0	0	.0	0	.0	0	.0	0
0	.0	0	.0	0	.0	0	.0	0	.0	0	.0	0	.0	0
0	.0	0	.0	0	.0	0	.0	0	.0	0	.0	0	.0	0
0	.0	0	.0	0	.0	0	.0	0	.0	0	.0	0	.0	0
0	.0	0	.0	0	.0	0	.0	0	.0	0	.0	0	.0	0
0	.0	0	.0	0	.0	0	.0	0	.0	0	.0	0	.0	0
0	.0	0	.0	0	.0	0	.0	0	.0	0	.0	0	.0	0
0	.0	13	76.5	0	.0	0	.0	13	76.5	1	5.9	3	17.6	17
0	.0	0	.0	0	.0	0	.0	0	.0	0	.0	0	.0	0
0	.0	13	76.5	0	.0	0	.0	13	76.5	1	5.9	3	17.6	17
0	.0	0	.0	0	.0	0	.0	0	.0	0	.0	0	.0	0
0	.0	0	.0	0	.0	0	.0	0	.0	0	.0	0	.0	0
0	.0	13	76.5	0	.0	0	.0	13	76.5	1	5.9	3	17.6	17
0	.0	0	.0	0	.0	0	.0	0	.0	0	.0	0	.0	0
0	.0	13	76.5	0	.0	0	.0	13	76.5	1	5.9	3	17.6	17
0	.0	0	.0	0	.0	0	.0	0	.0	0	.0	0	.0	0
0	.0	0	.0	0	.0	0	.0	0	.0	0	.0	0	.0	0
0	.0	0	.0	0	.0	0	.0	0	.0	0	.0	0	.0	0
0	.0	13	76.5	0	.0	0	.0	13	76.5	1	5.9	3	17.6	17
0	.0	0	.0	0	.0	0	.0	0	.0	0	.0	0	.0	0
0	.0	13	76.5	0	.0	0	.0	13	76.5	1	5.9	3	17.6	17

TABLE 17 - TOTAL ENROLLMENT IN INSTITUTIONS OF HIGHER EDUCATION FOR SELECTED MAJOR FIELDS OF STUDY AND LEVEL OF ENROLLMENT BY RACE, ETHNICITY, AND SEX: STATE, 1978

MAJOR FIELD 0900 - ENGINEERING

OUTLYING AREAS (6 INSTITUTIONS)

	AMERICAN INDIAN ALASKAN NATIVE		BLACK NON-HISPANIC		ASIAN OR PACIFIC ISLANDER		HISPANIC		TOTAL MINORITY		WHITE NON-HISPANIC		NON-RESIDENT ALIEN		TOT
	NUMBER	%	NUMBER	%	NUMBER	%	NUMBER	%	NUMBER	%	NUMBER	%	NUMBER	%	NUM
UNDERGRADUATES:															
FULL-TIME	0	.0	13	.4	0	.0	3,244	99.5	3,257	99.9	1	.0	3	.1	3,
FEMALE	0	.0	0	.0	0	.0	326	100.0	326	100.0	0	.0	0	.0	
MALE	0	.0	13	.4	0	.0	2,918	99.4	2,931	99.9	1	.0	3	.1	2,
PART-TIME	0	.0	0	.0	0	.0	320	100.0	320	100.0	0	.0	0	.0	
FEMALE	0	.0	0	.0	0	.0	18	100.0	18	100.0	0	.0	0	.0	
MALE	0	.0	0	.0	0	.0	302	100.0	302	100.0	0	.0	0	.0	
TOTAL	0	.0	13	.4	0	.0	3,564	99.5	3,577	99.9	1	.0	3	.1	3,
FEMALE	0	.0	0	.0	0	.0	344	100.0	344	100.0	0	.0	0	.0	
MALE	0	.0	13	.4	0	.0	3,220	99.5	3,233	99.9	1	.0	3	.1	3,
GRADUATE:															
FULL-TIME	0	.0	0	.0	0	.0	0	.0	0	.0	0	.0	0	.0	
FEMALE	0	.0	0	.0	0	.0	0	.0	0	.0	0	.0	0	.0	
MALE	0	.0	0	.0	0	.0	0	.0	0	.0	0	.0	0	.0	
PART-TIME	0	.0	0	.0	0	.0	49	100.0	49	100.0	-0	.0	0	.0	
FEMALE	0	.0	0	.0	0	.0	3	100.0	3	100.0	0	.0	0	.0	
MALE	0	.0	0	.0	0	.0	46	100.0	46	100.0	0	.0	0	.0	
TOTAL	0	.0	0	.0	0	.0	49	100.0	49	100.0	0	.0	0	.0	
FEMALE	0	.0	0	.0	0	.0	3	100.0	3	100.0	0	.0	0	.0	
MALE	0	.0	0	.0	0	.0	46	100.0	46	100.0	0	.0	0	.0	
PROFESSIONAL:															
FULL-TIME	0	.0	0	.0	0	.0	0	.0	0	.0	0	.0	0	.0	
FEMALE	0	.0	0	.0	0	.0	0	.0	0	.0	0	.0	0	.0	
MALE	0	.0	0	.0	0	.0	0	.0	0	.0	0	.0	0	.0	
PART-TIME	0	.0	0	.0	0	.0	0	.0	0	.0	0	.0	0	.0	
FEMALE	0	.0	0	.0	0	.0	0	.0	0	.0	0	.0	0	.0	
MALE	0	.0	0	.0	0	.0	0	.0	0	.0	0	.0	0	.0	
TOTAL	0	.0	0	.0	0	.0	0	.0	0	.0	0	.0	0	.0	
FEMALE	0	.0	0	.0	0	.0	0	.0	0	.0	0	.0	0	.0	
MALE	0	.0	0	.0	0	.0	0	.0	0	.0	0	.0	0	.0	
UND+GRAD+PROF:															
FULL-TIME	0	.0	13	.4	0	.0	3,244	99.5	3,257	99.9	1	.0	3	.1	3
FEMALE	0	.0	0	.0	0	.0	326	100.0	326	100.0	0	.0	0	.0	
MALE	0	.0	13	.4	0	.0	2,918	99.4	2,931	99.9	1	.0	3	.1	2
PART-TIME	0	.0	0	.0	0	.0	369	100.0	369	100.0	0	.0	0	.0	
FEMALE	0	.0	0	.0	0	.0	21	100.0	21	100.0	0	.0	0	.0	
MALE	0	.0	0	.0	0	.0	348	100.0	348	100.0	0	.0	0	.0	
TOTAL	0	.0	13	.4	0	.0	3,613	99.5	3,626	99.9	1	.0	3	.1	3
FEMALE	0	.0	0	.0	0	.0	347	100.0	347	100.0	0	.0	0	.0	
MALE	0	.0	13	.4	0	.0	3,266	99.5	3,279	99.9	1	.0	3	.1	3
UNCLASSIFIED:															
TOTAL	0	.0	0	.0	0	.0	8	100.0	8	100.0	0	.0	0	.0	
FEMALE	0	.0	0	.0	0	.0	1	100.0	1	100.0	0	.0	0	.0	
MALE	0	.0	0	.0	0	.0	7	100.0	7	100.0	0	.0	0	.0	
TOTAL ENROLLMENT:															
TOTAL	0	.0	13	.4	0	.0	3,621	99.5	3,634	99.9	1	.0	3	.1	3
FEMALE	0	.0	0	.0	0	.0	348	100.0	348	100.0	0	.0	0	.0	
MALE	0	.0	13	.4	0	.0	3,273	99.5	3,286	99.9	1	.0	3	.1	3

MAJOR FIELD AGGREGATE 0900 (993 INSTITUTIONS)

	AI/AN NUMBER	%	BLACK NUMBER	%	ASIAN/PI NUMBER	%	HISPANIC NUMBER	%	TOTAL MIN. NUMBER	%	WHITE NUMBER	%	NON-RES NUMBER	%	TOT
UNDERGRADUATES:															
FULL-TIME	1,192	.3	17,753	4.9	10,811	3.0	11,574	3.2	41,330	11.4	290,286	80.3	30,105	8.3	361
FEMALE	129	.3	3,516	9.0	1,416	3.6	1,239	3.2	6,300	16.0	31,260	79.6	1,695	4.3	39
MALE	1,063	.3	14,237	4.4	9,395	2.9	10,335	3.2	35,030	10.9	259,026	80.3	28,410	8.8	322
PART-TIME	483	.6	5,517	6.4	2,576	3.0	3,637	4.2	12,213	14.2	70,896	82.4	2,992	3.4	86
FEMALE	49	.5	366	7.4	241	2.3	261	2.5	1,317	12.7	8,913	85.8	156	1.5	10
MALE	434	.6	4,751	6.3	2,335	3.1	3,376	4.5	10,896	14.4	61,983	81.9	2,786	3.7	75
TOTAL	1,675	.4	23,270	5.2	13,387	3.0	15,211	3.4	53,543	12.0	361,182	80.7	33,047	7.4	447
FEMALE	178	.4	4,282	8.6	1,657	3.3	1,500	3.0	7,617	15.3	40,173	80.9	1,851	3.7	49
MALE	1,497	.4	18,988	4.8	11,730	2.9	13,711	3.4	45,926	11.5	321,009	80.6	31,196	7.8	398
GRADUATE:															
FULL-TIME	43	.1	336	1.1	1,209	4.0	309	1.0	1,897	6.3	16,445	55.0	11,569	38.7	29
FEMALE	4	.2	57	2.7	84	4.0	20	.9	165	7.8	1,463	69.4	480	22.8	2
MALE	39	.1	279	1.0	1,125	4.0	289	1.0	1,732	6.2	14,982	53.9	11,089	39.9	27
PART-TIME	55	.2	566	2.1	1,569	5.9	429	1.6	2,619	9.8	20,515	77.1	3,484	13.1	26
FEMALE	6	.3	56	3.0	110	5.9	22	1.2	194	10.4	1,505	80.7	165	8.9	1
MALE	49	.2	510	2.1	1,459	5.9	407	1.6	2,425	9.8	19,010	76.8	3,319	13.4	24
TOTAL	98	.2	902	1.6	2,778	4.9	738	1.3	4,516	8.0	36,960	65.4	15,053	26.6	56
FEMALE	10	.3	113	2.8	194	4.9	42	1.1	359	9.0	2,968	74.7	645	16.2	3
MALE	88	.2	789	1.5	2,584	4.9	696	1.3	4,157	7.9	33,992	64.7	14,408	27.4	5
PROFESSIONAL:															
FULL-TIME	0	.0	0	.0	0	.0	0	.0	0	.0	8	88.9	1	11.1	
FEMALE	0	.0	0	.0	0	.0	0	.0	0	.0	0	.0	1	100.0	
MALE	0	.0	0	.0	0	.0	0	.0	0	.0	8	100.0	0	.0	

TOTAL ENROLLMENT IN INSTITUTIONS OF HIGHER EDUCATION FOR SELECTED MAJOR FIELDS OF STUDY AND LEVEL OF ENROLLMENT BY RACE, ETHNICITY, AND SEX: STATE, 1978

D 0900 - ENGINEERING

AMERICAN INDIAN ALASKAN NATIVE		BLACK NON-HISPANIC		ASIAN OR PACIFIC ISLANDER		HISPANIC		TOTAL MINORITY		WHITE NON-HISPANIC		NON-RESIDENT ALIEN		TOTAL
NUMBER	%	NUMBER	%	NUMBER	%	NUMBER	%	NUMBER	%	NUMBER	%	NUMBER	%	NUMBER

D AGGREGATE 0900 CONTINUED

AL:

0	.0	0	.0	0	.0	0	.0	0	.0	0	.0	0	.0	0
0	.0	0	.0	0	.0	0	.0	0	.0	0	.0	0	.0	0
0	.0	0	.0	0	.0	0	.0	0	.0	0	.0	0	.0	0
0	.0	0	.0	0	.0	0	.0	0	.0	8	88.9	1	11.1	9
0	.0	0	.0	0	.0	0	.0	0	.0	0	.0	1	100.0	1
0	.0	0	.0	0	.0	0	.0	0	.0	8	100.0	0	.0	8

ROF:

1,235	.3	18,089	4.6	12,020	3.1	11,883	3.0	43,227	11.0	306,739	78.3	41,675	10.6	391,641
133	.3	3,573	8.6	1,500	3.6	1,259	3.0	6,465	15.6	32,723	79.1	2,176	5.3	41,364
1,102	.3	14,516	4.1	10,520	3.0	10,624	3.0	36,762	10.5	274,016	78.2	39,499	11.3	350,277
538	.5	6,083	5.4	4,145	3.7	4,066	3.6	14,832	13.2	91,411	81.1	6,426	5.7	112,669
55	.4	822	6.7	351	2.9	283	2.3	1,511	12.3	10,418	85.0	321	2.6	12,250
483	.5	5,261	5.2	3,794	3.8	3,783	3.8	13,321	13.3	80,993	80.7	6,105	6.1	100,419
1,773	.4	24,172	4.8	16,165	3.2	15,949	3.2	58,059	11.5	398,150	78.9	48,101	9.5	504,310
188	.4	4,395	8.2	1,851	3.5	1,542	2.9	7,976	14.9	43,141	80.5	2,497	4.7	53,614
1,585	.4	19,777	4.4	14,314	3.2	14,407	3.2	50,083	11.1	355,009	78.8	45,604	10.1	450,696

EO:

99	.8	566	4.4	724	5.6	538	4.1	1,927	14.8	9,999	76.9	1,082	8.3	13,008
9	.5	113	6.5	64	3.7	52	3.0	238	13.6	1,450	83.1	57	3.3	1,745
90	.8	453	4.0	660	5.9	486	4.3	1,689	15.0	8,549	75.9	1,025	9.1	11,263

LLMENT:

1,872	.4	24,738	4.8	16,889	3.3	16,487	3.2	59,986	11.6	408,149	78.9	49,183	9.5	517,318
197	.4	4,508	8.1	1,915	3.5	1,594	2.9	8,214	14.8	44,591	80.5	2,554	4.6	55,359
1,675	.4	20,230	4.4	14,974	3.2	14,893	3.2	51,772	11.2	363,558	78.7	46,629	10.1	461,959

TABLE 17 - TOTAL ENROLLMENT IN INSTITUTIONS OF HIGHER EDUCATION FOR SELECTED MAJOR FIELDS OF STUDY AND LEVEL OF ENROLLMENT
BY RACE, ETHNICITY, AND SEX: STATE, 1978

MAJOR FIELD 1204 - DENTISTRY

	AMERICAN INDIAN ALASKAN NATIVE		BLACK NON-HISPANIC		ASIAN OR PACIFIC ISLANDER		HISPANIC		TOTAL MINORITY		WHITE NON-HISPANIC		NON-RESIDENT ALIEN		T
	NUMBER	%	NUMBER	%	NUMBER	%	NUMBER	%	NUMBER	%	NUMBER	%	NUMBER	%	N
ALABAMA			1 INSTITUTIONS)												
UNDERGRADUATES:															
FULL-TIME	0	.0	0	.0	0	.0	0	.0	0	.0	0	.0		.0	
FEMALE	0	.0	0	.0	0	.0	0	.0	0	.0	0	.0		.0	
MALE	0	.0	0	.0	0	.0	0	.0	0	.0	0	.0		.0	
PART-TIME	0	.0	0	.0	0	.0	0	.0	0	.0	0	.0		.0	
FEMALE	0	.0	0	.0	0	.0	0	.0	0	.0	0	.0		.0	
MALE	0	.0	0	.0	0	.0	0	.0	0	.0	0	.0	0	.0	
TOTAL	0	.0	0	.0	0	.0	0	.0	0	.0	0	.0		.0	
FEMALE	0	.0	0	.0	0	.0	0	.0	0	.0	0	.0		.0	
MALE	0	.0	0	.0	0	.0	0	.0	0	.0	0	.0	0	.0	
GRADUATE:															
FULL-TIME	0	.0	0	.0	0	.0	0	.0	0	.0	0	.0		.0	
FEMALE	0	.0	0	.0	0	.0	0	.0	0	.0	0	.0		.0	
MALE	0	.0	0	.0	0	.0	0	.0	0	.0	0	.0		.0	
PART-TIME	0	.0	0	.0	0	.0	0	.0	0	.0	0	.0		.0	
FEMALE	0	.0	0	.0	0	.0	0	.0	0	.0	0	.0		.0	
MALE	0	.0	0	.0	0	.0	0	.0	0	.0	0	.0	0	.0	
TOTAL	0	.0	0	.0	0	.0	0	.0	0	.0	0	.0		.0	
FEMALE	0	.0	0	.0	0	.0	0	.0	0	.0	0	.0		.0	
MALE	0	.0	0	.0	0	.0	0	.0	0	.0	0	.0	0	.0	
PROFESSIONAL:															
FULL-TIME	0	.0	16	5.4	7	2.4	0	.0	23	7.8	273	92.2		.0	
FEMALE	0	.0	6	12.8	4	8.5	0	.0	10	21.3	37	78.7		.0	
MALE	0	.0	10	4.0	3	1.2	0	.0	13	5.2	236	94.8		.0	
PART-TIME	0	.0	0	.0	0	.0	0	.0	0	.0	0	.0		.0	
FEMALE	0	.0	0	.0	0	.0	0	.0	0	.0	0	.0		.0	
MALE	0	.0	0	.0	0	.0	0	.0	0	.0	0	.0	0	.0	
TOTAL	0	.0	16	5.4	7	2.4	0	.0	23	7.8	273	92.2		.0	
FEMALE	0	.0	6	12.8	4	8.5	0	.0	10	21.3	37	78.7		.0	
MALE	0	.0	10	4.0	3	1.2	0	.0	13	5.2	236	94.8	0	.0	
UND+GRAD+PROF:															
FULL-TIME	0	.0	16	5.4	7	2.4	0	.0	23	7.8	273	92.2		.0	
FEMALE	0	.0	6	12.8	4	8.5	0	.0	10	21.3	37	78.7		.0	
MALE	0	.0	10	4.0	3	1.2	0	.0	13	5.2	236	94.8		.0	
PART-TIME	0	.0	0	.0	0	.0	0	.0	0	.0	0	.0		.0	
FEMALE	0	.0	0	.0	0	.0	0	.0	0	.0	0	.0		.0	
MALE	0	.0	0	.0	0	.0	0	.0	0	.0	0	.0	0	.0	
TOTAL	0	.0	16	5.4	7	2.4	0	.0	23	7.8	273	92.2		.0	
FEMALE	0	.0	6	12.8	4	8.5	0	.0	10	21.3	37	78.7		.0	
MALE	0	.0	10	4.0	3	1.2	0	.0	13	5.2	236	94.8	0	.0	
UNCLASSIFIED:															
TOTAL	0	.0	0	.0	0	.0	0	.0	0	.0	0	.0		.0	
FEMALE	0	.0	0	.0	0	.0	0	.0	0	.0	0	.0		.0	
MALE	0	.0	0	.0	0	.0	0	.0	0	.0	0	.0	0	.0	
TOTAL ENROLLMENT:															
TOTAL	0	.0	16	5.4	7	2.4	0	.0	23	7.8	273	92.2		.0	
FEMALE	0	.0	6	12.8	4	8.5	0	.0	10	21.3	37	78.7		.0	
MALE	0	.0	10	4.0	3	1.2	0	.0	13	5.2	236	94.8	0	.0	
CALIFORNIA	(		5 INSTITUTIONS)												
UNDERGRADUATES:															
FULL-TIME	0	.0	0	.0	0	.0	0	.0	0	.0	0	.0		.0	
FEMALE	0	.0	0	.0	0	.0	0	.0	0	.0	0	.0		.0	
MALE	0	.0	0	.0	0	.0	0	.0	0	.0	0	.0		.0	
PART-TIME	0	.0	0	.0	0	.0	0	.0	0	.0	0	.0		.0	
FEMALE	0	.0	0	.0	0	.0	0	.0	0	.0	0	.0		.0	
MALE	0	.0	0	.0	0	.0	0	.0	0	.0	0	.0	0	.0	
TOTAL	0	.0	0	.0	0	.0	0	.0	0	.0	0	.0		.0	
FEMALE	0	.0	0	.0	0	.0	0	.0	0	.0	0	.0		.0	
MALE	0	.0	0	.0	0	.0	0	.0	0	.0	0	.0	0	.0	
GRADUATE:															
FULL-TIME	0	.0	0	.0	0	.0	0	.0	0	.0	0	.0		.0	
FEMALE	0	.0	0	.0	0	.0	0	.0	0	.0	0	.0		.0	
MALE	0	.0	0	.0	0	.0	0	.0	0	.0	0	.0		.0	
PART-TIME	0	.0	0	.0	0	.0	0	.0	0	.0	0	.0		.0	
FEMALE	0	.0	0	.0	0	.0	0	.0	0	.0	0	.0		.0	
MALE	0	.0	0	.0	0	.0	0	.0	0	.0	0	.0	0	.0	
TOTAL	0	.0	0	.0	0	.0	0	.0	0	.0	0	.0		.0	
FEMALE	0	.0	0	.0	0	.0	0	.0	0	.0	0	.0		.0	
MALE	0	.0	0	.0	0	.0	0	.0	0	.0	0	.0	0	.0	
PROFESSIONAL:															
FULL-TIME	11	.6	75	3.8	342	17.3	163	8.2	591	29.9	1,351	68.3	35	1	
FEMALE	0	.0	38	12.4	60	19.6	25	8.2	123	40.2	175	57.2	8	2	
MALE	11	.7	37	2.2	282	16.9	138	8.3	468	28.0	1,176	70.4	27	118	

E 17 - TOTAL ENROLLMENT IN INSTITUTIONS OF HIGHER EDUCATION FOR SELECTED MAJOR FIELDS OF STUDY AND LEVEL OF ENROLLMENT
BY RACE, ETHNICITY, AND SEX: STATE, 1978

R FIELD   1204 - DENTISTRY

	AMERICAN INDIAN ALASKAN NATIVE		BLACK NON-HISPANIC		ASIAN OR PACIFIC ISLANDER		HISPANIC		TOTAL MINORITY		WHITE NON-HISPANIC		NON-RESIDENT ALIEN		TOTAL
	NUMBER	%	NUMBER	%	NUMBER	%	NUMBER	%	NUMBER	%	NUMBER	%	NUMBER	%	NUMBER
FORNIA		CONTINUED													
ESSIONAL:															
-TIME	0	.0	1	14.3	0	.0	0	.0	1	14.3	5	71.4	1	14.3	7
EMALE	0	.0	1	50.0	0	.0	0	.0	1	50.0	1	50.0	0	.0	2
MALE	0	.0	0	.0	0	.0	0	.0	0	.0	4	80.0	1	20.0	5
L	11	.6	76	3.8	342	17.2	163	8.2	592	29.8	1,356	68.3	36	1.8	1,984
EMALE	0	.0	39	12.7	60	19.5	25	8.1	124	40.3	176	57.1	8	2.6	308
MALE	11	.7	37	2.2	282	16.8	138	8.2	468	27.9	1,180	70.4	28	1.7	1,676
GRAD+PROF:															
-TIME	11	.6	75	3.8	342	17.3	163	8.2	591	29.9	1,351	68.3	35	1.8	1,977
EMALE	0	.0	38	12.4	60	19.6	25	8.2	123	40.2	175	57.2	8	2.6	306
MALE	11	.7	37	2.2	282	16.9	138	8.3	468	28.0	1,176	70.4	27	1.6	1,671
-TIME	0	.0	1	14.3	0	.0	0	.0	1	14.3	5	71.4	1	14.3	7
EMALE	0	.0	1	50.0	0	.0	0	.0	1	50.0	1	50.0	0	.0	2
MALE	0	.0	0	.0	0	.0	0	.0	0	.0	4	80.0	1	20.0	5
L	11	.6	76	3.8	342	17.2	163	8.2	592	29.8	1,356	68.3	36	1.8	1,984
EMALE	0	.0	39	12.7	60	19.5	25	8.1	124	40.3	176	57.1	8	2.6	308
MALE	11	.7	37	2.2	282	16.8	138	8.2	468	27.9	1,180	70.4	28	1.7	1,676
ASSIFIED:															
L	0	.0	0	.0	0	.0	0	.0	0	.0	0	.0	0	.0	0
EMALE	0	.0	0	.0	0	.0	0	.0	0	.0	0	.0	0	.0	0
MALE	0	.0	0	.0	0	.0	0	.0	0	.0	0	.0	0	.0	0
L ENROLLMENT:															
L	11	.6	76	3.8	342	17.2	163	8.2	592	29.8	1,356	68.3	36	1.8	1,984
EMALE	0	.0	39	12.7	60	19.5	25	8.1	124	40.3	176	57.1	8	2.6	308
MALE	11	.7	37	2.2	282	16.8	138	8.2	468	27.9	1,180	70.4	28	1.7	1,676
RADO	(	1 INSTITUTIONS)													
RGRADUATES:															
-TIME	0	.0	0	.0	0	.0	0	.0	0	.0	0	.0	0	.0	0
EMALE	0	.0	0	.0	0	.0	0	.0	0	.0	0	.0	0	.0	0
MALE	0	.0	0	.0	0	.0	0	.0	0	.0	0	.0	0	.0	0
-TIME	0	.0	0	.0	0	.0	0	.0	0	.0	0	.0	0	.0	0
EMALE	0	.0	0	.0	0	.0	0	.0	0	.0	0	.0	0	.0	0
MALE	0	.0	0	.0	0	.0	0	.0	0	.0	0	.0	0	.0	0
L	0	.0	0	.0	0	.0	0	.0	0	.0	0	.0	0	.0	0
EMALE	0	.0	0	.0	0	.0	0	.0	0	.0	0	.0	0	.0	0
MALE	0	.0	0	.0	0	.0	0	.0	0	.0	0	.0	0	.0	0
UATE:															
-TIME	0	.0	0	.0	0	.0	0	.0	0	.0	0	.0	0	.0	0
EMALE	0	.0	0	.0	0	.0	0	.0	0	.0	0	.0	0	.0	0
MALE	0	.0	0	.0	0	.0	0	.0	0	.0	0	.0	0	.0	0
-TIME	0	.0	0	.0	0	.0	0	.0	0	.0	0	.0	0	.0	0
EMALE	0	.0	0	.0	0	.0	0	.0	0	.0	0	.0	0	.0	0
MALE	0	.0	0	.0	0	.0	0	.0	0	.0	0	.0	0	.0	0
L	0	.0	0	.0	0	.0	0	.0	0	.0	0	.0	0	.0	0
EMALE	0	.0	0	.0	0	.0	0	.0	0	.0	0	.0	0	.0	0
MALE	0	.0	0	.0	0	.0	0	.0	0	.0	0	.0	0	.0	0
ESSIONAL:															
-TIME	0	.0	2	2.0	4	4.0	6	5.9	12	11.9	89	88.1	0	.0	101
EMALE	0	.0	1	7.7	1	7.7	1	7.7	3	23.1	10	76.9	0	.0	13
MALE	0	.0	1	1.1	3	3.4	5	5.7	9	10.2	79	89.8	0	.0	88
-TIME	0	.0	0	.0	0	.0	0	.0	0	.0	0	.0	0	.0	0
EMALE	0	.0	0	.0	0	.0	0	.0	0	.0	0	.0	0	.0	0
MALE	0	.0	0	.0	0	.0	0	.0	0	.0	0	.0	0	.0	0
L	0	.0	2	2.0	4	4.0	6	5.9	12	11.9	89	88.1	0	.0	101
EMALE	0	.0	1	7.7	1	7.7	1	7.7	3	23.1	10	76.9	0	.0	13
MALE	0	.0	1	1.1	3	3.4	5	5.7	9	10.2	79	89.8	0	.0	88
GRAD+PROF:															
-TIME	0	.0	2	2.0	4	4.0	6	5.9	12	11.9	89	88.1	0	.0	101
EMALE	0	.0	1	7.7	1	7.7	1	7.7	3	23.1	10	76.9	0	.0	13
MALE	0	.0	1	1.1	3	3.4	5	5.7	9	10.2	79	89.8	0	.0	88
-TIME	0	.0	0	.0	0	.0	0	.0	0	.0	0	.0	0	.0	0
EMALE	0	.0	0	.0	0	.0	0	.0	0	.0	0	.0	0	.0	0
MALE	0	.0	0	.0	0	.0	0	.0	0	.0	0	.0	0	.0	0
L	0	.0	2	2.0	4	4.0	6	5.9	12	11.9	89	88.1	0	.0	101
EMALE	0	.0	1	7.7	1	7.7	1	7.7	3	23.1	10	76.9	0	.0	13
MALE	0	.0	1	1.1	3	3.4	5	5.7	9	10.2	79	89.8	0	.0	88
ASSIFIED:															
L	0	.0	0	.0	0	.0	0	.0	0	.0	0	.0	0	.0	0
EMALE	0	.0	0	.0	0	.0	0	.0	0	.0	0	.0	0	.0	0
MALE	0	.0	0	.0	0	.0	0	.0	0	.0	0	.0	0	.0	0
L ENROLLMENT:															
L	0	.0	2	2.0	4	4.0	6	5.9	12	11.9	89	88.1	0	.0	101
EMALE	0	.0	1	7.7	1	7.7	1	7.7	3	23.1	10	76.9	0	.0	13
MALE	0	.0	1	1.1	3	3.4	5	5.7	9	10.2	79	89.8	0	.0	88

MAJOR FIELD 1204 - DENTISTRY

	AMERICAN INDIAN ALASKAN NATIVE		BLACK NON-HISPANIC		ASIAN OR PACIFIC ISLANDER		HISPANIC		TOTAL MINORITY		WHITE NON-HISPANIC		NON-RESIDENT ALIEN		TOT
	NUMBER	%	NUMBER	%	NUMBER	%	NUMBER	%	NUMBER	%	NUMBER	%	NUMBER	%	NUM
CONNECTICUT (1 INSTITUTIONS)															
UNDERGRADUATES:															
FULL-TIME	0	.0	0	.0	0	.0	0	.0	0	.0	0	.0		.0	
FEMALE	0	.0	0	.0	0	.0	0	.0	0	.0	0	.0		.0	
MALE	0	.0	0	.0	0	.0	0	.0	0	.0	0	.0		.0	
PART-TIME	0	.0	0	.0	0	.0	0	.0	0	.0	0	.0		.0	
FEMALE	0	.0	0	.0	0	.0	0	.0	0	.0	0	.0		.0	
MALE	0	.0	0	.0	0	.0	0	.0	0	.0	0	.0	0	.0	
TOTAL	0	.0	0	.0	0	.0	0	.0	0	.0	0	.0		.0	
FEMALE	0	.0	0	.0	0	.0	0	.0	0	.0	0	.0		.0	
MALE	0	.0	0	.0	0	.0	0	.0	0	.0	0	.0	0	.0	
GRADUATE:															
FULL-TIME	0	.0	0	.0	0	.0	0	.0	0	.0	0	.0		.0	
FEMALE	0	.0	0	.0	0	.0	0	.0	0	.0	0	.0		.0	
MALE	0	.0	0	.0	0	.0	0	.0	0	.0	0	.0		.0	
PART-TIME	0	.0	0	.0	0	.0	0	.0	0	.0	0	.0		.0	
FEMALE	0	.0	0	.0	0	.0	0	.0	0	.0	0	.0		.0	
MALE	0	.0	0	.0	0	.0	0	.0	0	.0	0	.0	0	.0	
TOTAL	0	.0	0	.0	0	.0	0	.0	0	.0	0	.0		.0	
FEMALE	0	.0	0	.0	0	.0	0	.0	0	.0	0	.0		.0	
MALE	0	.0	0	.0	0	.0	0	.0	0	.0	0	.0	0	.0	
PROFESSIONAL:															
FULL-TIME	0	.0	1	.5	2	1.0	0	.0	3	1.6	188	98.4		.0	
FEMALE	0	.0	0	.0	0	.0	0	.0	0	.0	30	100.0		.0	
MALE	0	.0	1	.6	2	1.2	0	.0	3	1.9	158	98.1		.0	
PART-TIME	0	.0	0	.0	0	.0	0	.0	0	.0	0	.0		.0	
FEMALE	0	.0	0	.0	0	.0	0	.0	0	.0	0	.0		.0	
MALE	0	.0	0	.0	0	.0	0	.0	0	.0	0	.0	0	.0	
TOTAL	0	.0	1	.5	2	1.0	0	.0	3	1.6	188	98.4		.0	
FEMALE	0	.0	0	.0	0	.0	0	.0	0	.0	30	100.0		.0	
MALE	0	.0	1	.6	2	1.2	0	.0	3	1.9	158	98.1	0	.0	
UND+GRAD+PROF:															
FULL-TIME	0	.0	1	.5	2	1.0	0	.0	3	1.6	188	98.4		.0	
FEMALE	0	.0	0	.0	0	.0	0	.0	0	.0	30	100.0		.0	
MALE	0	.0	1	.6	2	1.2	0	.0	3	1.9	158	98.1		.0	
PART-TIME	0	.0	0	.0	0	.0	0	.0	0	.0	0	.0		.0	
FEMALE	0	.0	0	.0	0	.0	0	.0	0	.0	0	.0		.0	
MALE	0	.0	0	.0	0	.0	0	.0	0	.0	0	.0	0	.0	
TOTAL	0	.0	1	.5	2	1.0	0	.0	3	1.6	188	98.4		.0	
FEMALE	0	.0	0	.0	0	.0	0	.0	0	.0	30	100.0		.0	
MALE	0	.0	1	.6	2	1.2	0	.0	3	1.9	158	98.1	0	.0	
UNCLASSIFIED:															
TOTAL	0	.0	0	.0	0	.0	0	.0	0	.0	0	.0		.0	
FEMALE	0	.0	0	.0	0	.0	0	.0	0	.0	0	.0		.0	
MALE	0	.0	0	.0	0	.0	0	.0	0	.0	0	.0	0	.0	
TOTAL ENROLLMENT:															
TOTAL	0	.0	1	.5	2	1.0	0	.0	3	1.6	188	98.4		.0	
FEMALE	0	.0	0	.0	0	.0	0	.0	0	.0	30	100.0		.0	
MALE	0	.0	1	.6	2	1.2	0	.0	3	1.9	158	98.1	0	.0	
DISTRICT OF COLUMBIA (2 INSTITUTIONS)															
UNDERGRADUATES:															
FULL-TIME	0	.0	0	.0	0	.0	0	.0	0	.0	0	.0		.0	
FEMALE	0	.0	0	.0	0	.0	0	.0	0	.0	0	.0		.0	
MALE	0	.0	0	.0	0	.0	0	.0	0	.0	0	.0		.0	
PART-TIME	0	.0	0	.0	0	.0	0	.0	0	.0	0	.0		.0	
FEMALE	0	.0	0	.0	0	.0	0	.0	0	.0	0	.0		.0	
MALE	0	.0	0	.0	0	.0	0	.0	0	.0	0	.0	0	.0	
TOTAL	0	.0	0	.0	0	.0	0	.0	0	.0	0	.0		.0	
FEMALE	0	.0	0	.0	0	.0	0	.0	0	.0	0	.0		.0	
MALE	0	.0	0	.0	0	.0	0	.0	0	.0	0	.0	0	.0	
GRADUATE:															
FULL-TIME	0	.0	0	.0	0	.0	0	.0	0	.0	0	.0		.0	
FEMALE	0	.0	0	.0	0	.0	0	.0	0	.0	0	.0		.0	
MALE	0	.0	0	.0	0	.0	0	.0	0	.0	0	.0		.0	
PART-TIME	0	.0	0	.0	0	.0	0	.0	0	.0	0	.0		.0	
FEMALE	0	.0	0	.0	0	.0	0	.0	0	.0	0	.0		.0	
MALE	0	.0	0	.0	0	.0	0	.0	0	.0	0	.0	0	.0	
TOTAL	0	.0	0	.0	0	.0	0	.0	0	.0	0	.0		.0	
FEMALE	0	.0	0	.0	0	.0	0	.0	0	.0	0	.0		.0	
MALE	0	.0	0	.0	0	.0	0	.0	0	.0	0	.0	0	.0	
PROFESSIONAL:															
FULL-TIME	2	.2	233	23.9	26	2.7	8	.8	269	27.6	639	65.5	67	6.9	
FEMALE	0	.0	69	50.0	5	3.6	2	1.4	76	55.1	43	31.2	19	13.8	
MALE	2	.2	164	19.6	21	2.5	6	.7	193	23.1	596	71.2	48	5.7	

JOR FIELD 1204 - DENTISTRY

	AMERICAN INDIAN ALASKAN NATIVE		BLACK NON-HISPANIC		ASIAN OR PACIFIC ISLANDER		HISPANIC		TOTAL MINORITY		WHITE NON-HISPANIC		NON-RESIDENT ALIEN		TOTAL
	NUMBER	%	NUMBER	%	NUMBER	%	NUMBER	%	NUMBER	%	NUMBER	%	NUMBER	%	NUMBER

STRICT OF COLUMBIA   CONTINUED

OFESSIONAL:

RT-TIME	0	.0	13	76.5	0	.0	1	5.9	14	82.4	0	.0	3	17.6	17
FEMALE	0	.0	4	100.0	0	.0	0	.0	4	100.0	0	.0	0	.0	4
MALE	0	.0	9	69.2	0	.0	1	7.7	10	76.9	0	.0	3	23.1	13
TAL	2	.2	246	24.8	26	2.6	9	.9	283	28.5	639	64.4	70	7.1	992
FEMALE	0	.0	73	51.4	5	3.5	2	1.4	80	56.3	43	30.3	19	13.4	142
MALE	2	.2	173	20.4	21	2.5	7	.8	203	23.9	596	70.1	51	6.0	850
D+GRAD+PROF:															
LL-TIME	2	.2	233	23.9	26	2.7	8	.8	269	27.6	639	65.5	67	6.9	975
FEMALE	0	.0	69	50.0	5	3.6	2	1.4	76	55.1	43	31.2	19	13.8	138
MALE	2	.2	164	19.6	21	2.5	6	.7	193	23.1	596	71.2	48	5.7	837
RT-TIME	0	.0	13	76.5	0	.0	1	5.9	14	82.4	0	.0	3	17.6	17
FEMALE	0	.0	4	100.0	0	.0	0	.0	4	100.0	0	.0	0	.0	4
MALE	0	.0	9	69.2	0	.0	1	7.7	10	76.9	0	.0	3	23.1	13
TAL	2	.2	246	24.8	26	2.6	9	.9	283	28.5	639	64.4	70	7.1	992
FEMALE	0	.0	73	51.4	5	3.5	2	1.4	80	56.3	43	30.3	19	13.4	142
MALE	2	.2	173	20.4	21	2.5	7	.8	203	23.9	596	70.1	51	6.0	850
CLASSIFIED:															
TAL	0	.0	0	.0	0	.0	0	.0	0	.0	0	.0	0	.0	0
FEMALE	0	.0	0	.0	0	.0	0	.0	0	.0	0	.0	0	.0	0
MALE	0	.0	0	.0	0	.0	0	.0	0	.0	0	.0	0	.0	0
TAL ENROLLMENT:															
TAL	2	.2	246	24.8	26	2.6	9	.9	283	28.5	639	64.4	70	7.1	992
FEMALE	0	.0	73	51.4	5	3.5	2	1.4	80	56.3	43	30.3	19	13.4	142
MALE	2	.2	173	20.4	21	2.5	7	.8	203	23.9	596	70.1	51	6.0	850

ORIDA   (1 INSTITUTIONS)

DERGRADUATES:

LL-TIME	0	.0	0	.0	0	.0	0	.0	0	.0	0	.0	0	.0	0
FEMALE	0	.0	0	.0	0	.0	0	.0	0	.0	0	.0	0	.0	0
MALE	0	.0	0	.0	0	.0	0	.0	0	.0	0	.0	0	.0	0
RT-TIME	0	.0	0	.0	0	.0	0	.0	0	.0	0	.0	0	.0	0
FEMALE	0	.0	0	.0	0	.0	0	.0	0	.0	0	.0	0	.0	0
MALE	0	.0	0	.0	0	.0	0	.0	0	.0	0	.0	0	.0	0
TAL	0	.0	0	.0	0	.0	0	.0	0	.0	0	.0	0	.0	0
FEMALE	0	.0	0	.0	0	.0	0	.0	0	.0	0	.0	0	.0	0
MALE	0	.0	0	.0	0	.0	0	.0	0	.0	0	.0	0	.0	0
ADUATE:															
LL-TIME	0	.0	0	.0	0	.0	0	.0	0	.0	0	.0	0	.0	0
FEMALE	0	.0	0	.0	0	.0	0	.0	0	.0	0	.0	0	.0	0
MALE	0	.0	0	.0	0	.0	0	.0	0	.0	0	.0	0	.0	0
RT-TIME	0	.0	0	.0	0	.0	0	.0	0	.0	0	.0	0	.0	0
FEMALE	0	.0	0	.0	0	.0	0	.0	0	.0	0	.0	0	.0	0
MALE	0	.0	0	.0	0	.0	0	.0	0	.0	0	.0	0	.0	0
TAL	0	.0	0	.0	0	.0	0	.0	0	.0	0	.0	0	.0	0
FEMALE	0	.0	0	.0	0	.0	0	.0	0	.0	0	.0	0	.0	0
MALE	0	.0	0	.0	0	.0	0	.0	0	.0	0	.0	0	.0	0
OFESSIONAL:															
LL-TIME	1	.4	5	2.1	1	.4	11	4.6	18	7.5	221	92.1	1	.4	240
FEMALE	0	.0	0	.0	0	.0	4	10.0	4	10.0	35	87.5	1	2.5	40
MALE	1	.5	5	2.5	1	.5	7	3.5	14	7.0	186	93.0	0	.0	200
RT-TIME	0	.0	0	.0	0	.0	0	.0	0	.0	0	.0	0	.0	0
FEMALE	0	.0	0	.0	0	.0	0	.0	0	.0	0	.0	0	.0	0
MALE	0	.0	0	.0	0	.0	0	.0	0	.0	0	.0	0	.0	0
TAL	1	.4	5	2.1	1	.4	11	4.6	18	7.5	221	92.1	1	.4	240
FEMALE	0	.0	0	.0	0	.0	4	10.0	4	10.0	35	87.5	1	2.5	40
MALE	1	.5	5	2.5	1	.5	7	3.5	14	7.0	186	93.0	0	.0	200
D+GRAD+PROF:															
LL-TIME	1	.4	5	2.1	1	.4	11	4.6	18	7.5	221	92.1	1	.4	240
FEMALE	0	.0	0	.0	0	.0	4	10.0	4	10.0	35	87.5	1	2.5	40
MALE	1	.5	5	2.5	1	.5	7	3.5	14	7.0	186	93.0	0	.0	200
RT-TIME	0	.0	0	.0	0	.0	0	.0	0	.0	0	.0	0	.0	0
FEMALE	0	.0	0	.0	0	.0	0	.0	0	.0	0	.0	0	.0	0
MALE	0	.0	0	.0	0	.0	0	.0	0	.0	0	.0	0	.0	0
TAL	1	.4	5	2.1	1	.4	11	4.6	18	7.5	221	92.1	1	.4	240
FEMALE	0	.0	0	.0	0	.0	4	10.0	4	10.0	35	87.5	1	2.5	40
MALE	1	.5	5	2.5	1	.5	7	3.5	14	7.0	186	93.0	0	.0	200
CLASSIFIED:															
TAL	0	.0	0	.0	0	.0	0	.0	0	.0	0	.0	0	.0	0
FEMALE	0	.0	0	.0	0	.0	0	.0	0	.0	0	.0	0	.0	0
MALE	0	.0	0	.0	0	.0	0	.0	0	.0	0	.0	0	.0	0
TAL ENROLLMENT:															
TAL	1	.4	5	2.1	1	.4	11	4.6	18	7.5	221	92.1	1	.4	240
FEMALE	0	.0	0	.0	0	.0	4	10.0	4	10.0	35	87.5	1	2.5	40
MALE	1	.5	5	2.5	1	.5	7	3.5	14	7.0	186	93.0	0	.0	200

TABLE 17 - TOTAL ENROLLMENT IN INSTITUTIONS OF HIGHER EDUCATION FOR SELECTED MAJOR FIELDS OF STUDY AND LEVEL OF ENROLLMENT BY RACE, ETHNICITY, AND SEX: STATE, 1978

MAJOR FIELD 1204 - DENTISTRY

	AMERICAN INDIAN ALASKAN NATIVE		BLACK NON-HISPANIC		ASIAN OR PACIFIC ISLANDER		HISPANIC		TOTAL MINORITY		WHITE NON-HISPANIC		NON-RESIDENT ALIEN		T
	NUMBER	%	NUMBER	%	NUMBER	%	NUMBER	%	NUMBER	%	NUMBER	%	NUMBER	%	N
GEORGIA (2 INSTITUTIONS)															
UNDERGRADUATES:															
FULL-TIME	0	.0	0	.0	0	.0	0	.0	0	.0	0	.0	0	.0	
FEMALE	0	.0	0	.0	0	.0	0	.0	0	.0	0	.0		.0	
MALE	0	.0	0	.0	0	.0	0	.0	0	.0	0	.0		.0	
PART-TIME	0	.0	0	.0	0	.0	0	.0	0	.0	0	.0		.0	
FEMALE	0	.0	0	.0	0	.0	0	.0	0	.0	0	.0	0	.0	
MALE	0	.0	0	.0	0	.0	0	.0	0	.0	0	.0	0	.0	
TOTAL	0	.0	0	.0	0	.0	0	.0	0	.0	0	.0	0	.0	
FEMALE	0	.0	0	.0	0	.0	0	.0	0	.0	0	.0	0	.0	
MALE	0	.0	0	.0	0	.0	0	.0	0	.0	0	.0	0	.0	
GRADUATE:															
FULL-TIME	0	.0	0	.0	0	.0	0	.0	0	.0	0	.0	0	.0	
FEMALE	0	.0	0	.0	0	.0	0	.0	0	.0	0	.0		.0	
MALE	0	.0	0	.0	0	.0	0	.0	0	.0	0	.0		.0	
PART-TIME	0	.0	0	.0	0	.0	0	.0	0	.0	0	.0		.0	
FEMALE	0	.0	0	.0	0	.0	0	.0	0	.0	0	.0	0	.0	
MALE	0	.0	0	.0	0	.0	0	.0	0	.0	0	.0	0	.0	
TOTAL	0	.0	0	.0	0	.0	0	.0	0	.0	0	.0	0	.0	
FEMALE	0	.0	0	.0	0	.0	0	.0	0	.0	0	.0	0	.0	
MALE	0	.0	0	.0	0	.0	0	.0	0	.0	0	.0	0	.0	
PROFESSIONAL:															
FULL-TIME	1	.2	14	2.4	4	.7	4	.7	23	3.9	564	95.8	2	.3	
FEMALE	0	.0	7	13.0	0	.0	2	3.7	9	16.7	45	83.3	0	.0	
MALE	1	.2	7	1.3	4	.7	2	.4	14	2.6	519	97.0	2	.4	
PART-TIME	0	.0	3	50.0	0	.0	0	.0	3	50.0	3	50.0	0	.0	
FEMALE	0	.0	1	100.0	0	.0	0	.0	1	100.0	0	.0	0	.0	
MALE	0	.0	2	40.0	0	.0	0	.0	2	40.0	3	60.0	0	.0	
TOTAL	1	.2	17	2.9	4	.7	4	.7	26	4.4	567	95.3	2	.3	
FEMALE	0	.0	8	14.5	0	.0	2	3.6	10	18.2	45	81.8	0	.0	
MALE	1	.2	9	1.7	4	.7	2	.4	16	3.0	522	96.7	2	.4	
UND+GRAD+PROF:															
FULL-TIME	1	.2	14	2.4	4	.7	4	.7	23	3.9	564	95.8	2	.3	
FEMALE	0	.0	7	13.0	0	.0	2	3.7	9	16.7	45	83.3	0	.0	
MALE	1	.2	7	1.3	4	.7	2	.4	14	2.6	519	97.0	2	.4	
PART-TIME	0	.0	3	50.0	0	.0	0	.0	3	50.0	3	50.0	0	.0	
FEMALE	0	.0	1	100.0	0	.0	0	.0	1	100.0	0	.0	0	.0	
MALE	0	.0	2	40.0	0	.0	0	.0	2	40.0	3	60.0	0	.0	
TOTAL	1	.2	17	2.9	4	.7	4	.7	26	4.4	567	95.3	2	.3	
FEMALE	0	.0	8	14.5	0	.0	2	3.6	10	18.2	45	81.8	0	.0	
MALE	1	.2	9	1.7	4	.7	2	.4	16	3.0	522	96.7	2	.4	
UNCLASSIFIED:															
TOTAL	0	.0	0	.0	0	.0	0	.0	0	.0	0	.0	0	.0	
FEMALE	0	.0	0	.0	0	.0	0	.0	0	.0	0	.0	0	.0	
MALE	0	.0	0	.0	0	.0	0	.0	0	.0	0	.0	0	.0	
TOTAL ENROLLMENT:															
TOTAL	1	.2	17	2.9	4	.7	4	.7	26	4.4	567	95.3	2	.3	
FEMALE	0	.0	8	14.5	0	.0	2	3.6	10	18.2	45	81.8	0	.0	
MALE	1	.2	9	1.7	4	.7	2	.4	16	3.0	522	96.7	2	.4	
ILLINOIS (4 INSTITUTIONS)															
UNDERGRADUATES:															
FULL-TIME	0	.0	0	.0	0	.0	0	.0	0	.0	0	.0		.0	
FEMALE	0	.0	0	.0	0	.0	0	.0	0	.0	0	.0		.0	
MALE	0	.0	0	.0	0	.0	0	.0	0	.0	0	.0		.0	
PART-TIME	0	.0	0	.0	0	.0	0	.0	0	.0	0	.0		.0	
FEMALE	0	.0	0	.0	0	.0	0	.0	0	.0	0	.0		.0	
MALE	0	.0	0	.0	0	.0	0	.0	0	.0	0	.0	0	.0	
TOTAL	0	.0	0	.0	0	.0	0	.0	0	.0	0	.0	0	.0	
FEMALE	0	.0	0	.0	0	.0	0	.0	0	.0	0	.0	0	.0	
MALE	0	.0	0	.0	0	.0	0	.0	0	.0	0	.0	0	.0	
GRADUATE:															
FULL-TIME	0	.0	0	.0	0	.0	0	.0	0	.0	0	.0		.0	
FEMALE	0	.0	0	.0	0	.0	0	.0	0	.0	0	.0		.0	
MALE	0	.0	0	.0	0	.0	0	.0	0	.0	0	.0		.0	
PART-TIME	0	.0	0	.0	0	.0	0	.0	0	.0	0	.0		.0	
FEMALE	0	.0	0	.0	0	.0	0	.0	0	.0	0	.0		.0	
MALE	0	.0	0	.0	0	.0	0	.0	0	.0	0	.0	0	.0	
TOTAL	0	.0	0	.0	0	.0	0	.0	0	.0	0	.0	0	.0	
FEMALE	0	.0	0	.0	0	.0	0	.0	0	.0	0	.0	0	.0	
MALE	0	.0	0	.0	0	.0	0	.0	0	.0	0	.0	0	.0	
PROFESSIONAL:															
FULL-TIME	2	.1	35	2.1	44	2.6	13	.8	94	5.6	1,583	93.7	13	.8	
FEMALE	0	.0	17	7.5	6	2.7	2	.9	25	11.1	199	88.1	2	.9	
MALE	2	.1	18	1.2	38	2.6	11	.8	69	4.7	1,384	94.5	11	.8	

- DENTISTRY

:AN INDIAN IN NATIVE		BLACK NON-HISPANIC		ASIAN OR PACIFIC ISLANDER		HISPANIC		TOTAL MINORITY		WHITE NON-HISPANIC		NON-RESIDENT ALIEN		TOTAL
:R	%	NUMBER	%	NUMBER	%	NUMBER	%	NUMBER	%	NUMBER	%	NUMBER	%	NUMBER
CONTINUED														
0	.0	0	.0	0	.0	0	.0	0	.0	0	.0	0	.0	0
0	.0	0	.0	0	.0	0	.0	0	.0	0	.0	0	.0	0
0	.0	0	.0	0	.0	0	.0	0	.0	0	.0	0	.0	0
2	.1	35	2.1	44	2.6	13	.8	94	5.6	1,583	93.7	13	.8	1,690
0	.0	17	7.5	6	2.7	2	.9	25	11.1	199	88.1	2	.9	220
2	.1	18	1.2	38	2.6	11	.8	69	4.7	1,384	94.5	11	.8	1,464
2	.1	35	4.1	44	2.6	13	.8	94	5.6	1,583	93.7	13	.8	1,690
0	.0	17	7.5	6	2.7	2	.9	25	11.1	199	88.1	2	.9	226
2	.1	18	1.2	38	2.6	11	.8	69	4.7	1,384	94.5	11	.8	1,464
0	.0	0	.0	0	.0	0	.0	0	.0	0	.0	0	.0	0
0	.0	0	.0	0	.0	0	.0	0	.0	0	.0	0	.0	0
2	.1	35	2.1	44	2.6	13	.8	94	5.6	1,583	93.7	13	.8	1,690
0	.0	17	7.5	6	2.7	2	.9	25	11.1	199	88.1	2	.9	226
2	.1	18	1.2	38	2.6	11	.8	69	4.7	1,384	94.5	11	.8	1,464
0	.0	0	.0	0	.0	0	.0	0	.0	0	.0	0	.0	0
0	.0	0	.0	0	.0	0	.0	0	.0	0	.0	0	.0	0
0	.0	0	.0	0	.0	0	.0	0	.0	0	.0	0	.0	0
2	.1	35	2.1	44	2.6	13	.8	94	5.6	1,583	93.7	13	.8	1,690
0	.0	17	7.5	6	2.7	2	.9	25	11.1	199	88.1	2	.9	226
2	.1	18	1.2	38	2.6	11	.8	69	4.7	1,384	94.5	11	.8	1,464
(		1 INSTITUTIONS)												
0	.0	0	.0	0	.0	0	.0	0	.0	0	.0	0	.0	0
0	.0	0	.0	0	.0	0	.0	0	.0	0	.0	0	.0	0
0	.0	0	.0	0	.0	0	.0	0	.0	0	.0	0	.0	0
0	.0	0	.0	0	.0	0	.0	0	.0	0	.0	0	.0	0
0	.0	0	.0	0	.0	0	.0	0	.0	0	.0	0	.0	0
0	.0	0	.0	0	.0	0	.0	0	.0	0	.0	0	.0	0
0	.0	0	.0	0	.0	0	.0	0	.0	0	.0	0	.0	0
0	.0	0	.0	0	.0	0	.0	0	.0	0	.0	0	.0	0
0	.0	0	.0	0	.0	0	.0	0	.0	0	.0	0	.0	0
0	.0	0	.0	0	.0	0	.0	0	.0	0	.0	0	.0	0
0	.0	0	.0	0	.0	0	.0	0	.0	0	.0	0	.0	0
0	.0	0	.0	0	.0	0	.0	0	.0	0	.0	0	.0	0
0	.0	0	.0	0	.0	0	.0	0	.0	0	.0	0	.0	0
0	.0	0	.0	0	.0	0	.0	0	.0	0	.0	0	.0	0
0	.0	0	.0	0	.0	0	.0	0	.0	0	.0	0	.0	0
0	.0	0	.0	0	.0	0	.0	0	.0	0	.0	0	.0	0
0	.0	0	.0	0	.0	0	.0	0	.0	0	.0	0	.0	0
1	.2	5	.9	9	1.7	1	.2	16	3.0	502	94.4	14	2.6	532
0	.0	2	3.2	1	1.6	0	.0	3	4.8	58	92.1	2	3.2	63
1	.2	3	.6	8	1.7	1	.2	13	2.8	444	94.7	12	2.6	469
0	.0	1	1.0	1	1.0	1	1.0	3	3.0	85	85.9	11	11.1	99
0	.0	0	.0	0	.0	0	.0	0	.0	10	83.3	2	16.7	12
0	.0	1	1.1	1	1.1	1	1.1	3	3.4	75	86.2	9	10.3	87
1	.2	6	1.0	10	1.6	2	.3	19	3.0	587	93.0	25	4.0	631
0	.0	2	2.7	1	1.3	0	.0	3	4.0	68	90.7	4	5.3	75
1	.2	4	.7	9	1.6	2	.4	16	2.9	519	93.3	21	3.8	556
1	.2	5	.9	9	1.7	1	.2	16	3.0	502	94.4	14	2.6	532
0	.0	2	3.2	1	1.6	0	.0	3	4.8	58	92.1	2	3.2	63
1	.2	3	.6	8	1.7	1	.2	13	2.8	444	94.7	12	2.6	469
0	.0	1	1.0	1	1.0	1	1.0	3	3.0	85	85.9	11	11.1	99
0	.0	0	.0	0	.0	0	.0	0	.0	10	83.3	2	16.7	12
0	.0	1	1.1	1	1.1	1	1.1	3	3.4	75	86.2	9	10.3	87
1	.2	6	1.0	10	1.6	2	.3	19	3.0	587	93.0	25	4.0	631
0	.0	2	2.7	1	1.3	0	.0	3	4.0	68	90.7	4	5.3	75
1	.2	4	.7	9	1.6	2	.4	16	2.9	519	93.3	21	3.8	556
0	.0	0	.0	0	.0	0	.0	0	.0	0	.0	0	.0	0
0	.0	0	.0	0	.0	0	.0	0	.0	0	.0	0	.0	0
0	.0	0	.0	0	.0	0	.0	0	.0	0	.0	0	.0	0
1	.2	6	1.0	10	1.6	2	.3	19	3.0	587	93.0	25	4.0	631
0	.0	2	2.7	1	1.3	0	.0	3	4.0	68	90.7	4	5.3	75
1	.2	4	.7	9	1.6	2	.4	16	2.9	519	93.3	21	3.8	556

TABLE 17 - TOTAL ENROLLMENT IN INSTITUTIONS OF HIGHER EDUCATION FOR SELECTED MAJOR FIELDS OF STUDY AND LEVEL OF ENROLLMENT
BY RACE, ETHNICITY, AND SEX: STATE, 1978

MAJOR FIELD 1204 - DENTISTRY

	AMERICAN INDIAN ALASKAN NATIVE		BLACK NON-HISPANIC		ASIAN OR PACIFIC ISLANDER		HISPANIC		TOTAL MINORITY		WHITE NON-HISPANIC		NON-RESIDENT ALIEN	
	NUMBER	%	NUMBER	%	NUMBER	%	NUMBER	%	NUMBER	%	NUMBER	%	NUMBER	%
IOWA			**1 INSTITUTIONS)**											
UNDERGRADUATES:														
FULL-TIME	0	.0	0	.0	0	.0	0	.0	0	.0	0	.0		.0
FEMALE	0	.0	0	.0	0	.0	0	.0	0	.0	0	.0		.0
MALE	0	.0	0	.0	0	.0	0	.0	0	.0	0	.0		.0
PART-TIME	0	.0	0	.0	0	.0	0	.0	0	.0	0	.0		.0
FEMALE	0	.0	0	.0	0	.0	0	.0	0	.0	0	.0		.0
MALE	0	.0	0	.0	0	.0	0	.0	0	.0	0	.0	0	.0
TOTAL	0	.0	0	.0	0	.0	0	.0	0	.0	0	.0	0	.0
FEMALE	0	.0	0	.0	0	.0	0	.0	0	.0	0	.0	0	.0
MALE	0	.0	0	.0	0	.0	0	.0	0	.0	0	.0	0	.0
GRADUATE:														
FULL-TIME	0	.0	0	.0	0	.0	0	.0	0	.0	0	.0		.0
FEMALE	0	.0	0	.0	0	.0	0	.0	0	.0	0	.0		.0
MALE	0	.0	0	.0	0	.0	0	.0	0	.0	0	.0		.0
PART-TIME	0	.0	0	.0	0	.0	0	.0	0	.0	0	.0		.0
FEMALE	0	.0	0	.0	0	.0	0	.0	0	.0	0	.0		.0
MALE	0	.0	0	.0	0	.0	0	.0	0	.0	0	.0	0	.0
TOTAL	0	.0	0	.0	0	.0	0	.0	0	.0	0	.0	0	.0
FEMALE	0	.0	0	.0	0	.0	0	.0	0	.0	0	.0	0	.0
MALE	0	.0	0	.0	0	.0	0	.0	0	.0	0	.0	0	.0
PROFESSIONAL:														
FULL-TIME	6	1.6	5	1.3	6	1.6	4	1.0	21	5.5	356	93.2	5	1.3
FEMALE	1	2.0	1	2.0	2	4.0	1	2.0	5	10.0	43	86.0	2	4.0
MALE	5	1.5	4	1.2	4	1.2	3	.9	16	4.8	313	94.3	3	.9
PART-TIME	0	.0	0	.0	0	.0	0	.0	0	.0	0	.0	0	.0
FEMALE	0	.0	0	.0	0	.0	0	.0	0	.0	0	.0	0	.0
MALE	0	.0	0	.0	0	.0	0	.0	0	.0	0	.0	0	.0
TOTAL	6	1.6	5	1.3	6	1.6	4	1.0	21	5.5	356	93.2	5	1.3
FEMALE	1	2.0	1	2.0	2	4.0	1	2.0	5	10.0	43	86.0	2	4.0
MALE	5	1.5	4	1.2	4	1.2	3	.9	16	4.8	313	94.3	3	.9
UND+GRAD+PROF:														
FULL-TIME	6	1.6	5	1.3	6	1.6	4	1.0	21	5.5	356	93.2	5	1.3
FEMALE	1	2.0	1	2.0	2	4.0	1	2.0	5	10.0	43	86.0	2	4.0
MALE	5	1.5	4	1.2	4	1.2	3	.9	16	4.8	313	94.3	3	.9
PART-TIME	0	.0	0	.0	0	.0	0	.0	0	.0	0	.0	0	.0
FEMALE	0	.0	0	.0	0	.0	0	.0	0	.0	0	.0	0	.0
MALE	0	.0	0	.0	0	.0	0	.0	0	.0	0	.0	0	.0
TOTAL	6	1.6	5	1.3	6	1.6	4	1.0	21	5.5	356	93.2	5	1.3
FEMALE	1	2.0	1	2.0	2	4.0	1	2.0	5	10.0	43	86.0	2	4.0
MALE	5	1.5	4	1.2	4	1.2	3	.9	16	4.8	313	94.3	3	.9
UNCLASSIFIED:														
TOTAL	0	.0	0	.0	0	.0	0	.0	0	.0	0	.0	0	.0
FEMALE	0	.0	0	.0	0	.0	0	.0	0	.0	0	.0	0	.0
MALE	0	.0	0	.0	0	.0	0	.0	0	.0	0	.0	0	.0
TOTAL ENROLLMENT:														
TOTAL	6	1.6	5	1.3	6	1.6	4	1.0	21	5.5	356	93.2	5	1.3
FEMALE	1	2.0	1	2.0	2	4.0	1	2.0	5	10.0	43	86.0	2	4.0
MALE	5	1.5	4	1.2	4	1.2	3	.9	16	4.8	313	94.3	3	.9
KENTUCKY			**(2 INSTITUTIONS)**											
UNDERGRADUATES:														
FULL-TIME	0	.0	0	.0	0	.0	0	.0	0	.0	0	.0		.0
FEMALE	0	.0	0	.0	0	.0	0	.0	0	.0	0	.0		.0
MALE	0	.0	0	.0	0	.0	0	.0	0	.0	0	.0		.0
PART-TIME	0	.0	0	.0	0	.0	0	.0	0	.0	0	.0		.0
FEMALE	0	.0	0	.0	0	.0	0	.0	0	.0	0	.0		.0
MALE	0	.0	0	.0	0	.0	0	.0	0	.0	0	.0	0	.0
TOTAL	0	.0	0	.0	0	.0	0	.0	0	.0	0	.0	0	.0
FEMALE	0	.0	0	.0	0	.0	0	.0	0	.0	0	.0	0	.0
MALE	0	.0	0	.0	0	.0	0	.0	0	.0	0	.0	0	.0
GRADUATE:														
FULL-TIME	0	.0	0	.0	0	.0	0	.0	0	.0	0	.0		.0
FEMALE	0	.0	0	.0	0	.0	0	.0	0	.0	0	.0		.0
MALE	0	.0	0	.0	0	.0	0	.0	0	.0	0	.0		.0
PART-TIME	0	.0	0	.0	0	.0	0	.0	0	.0	0	.0		.0
FEMALE	0	.0	0	.0	0	.0	0	.0	0	.0	0	.0		.0
MALE	0	.0	0	.0	0	.0	0	.0	0	.0	0	.0	0	.0
TOTAL	0	.0	0	.0	0	.0	0	.0	0	.0	0	.0	0	.0
FEMALE	0	.0	0	.0	0	.0	0	.0	0	.0	0	.0	0	.0
MALE	0	.0	0	.0	0	.0	0	.0	0	.0	0	.0	0	.0
PROFESSIONAL:														
FULL-TIME	0	.0	13	2.2	3	.5	0	.0	16	2.7	571	96.8	3	.5
FEMALE	0	.0	8	7.4	0	.0	0	.0	8	7.4	99	91.7	1	.9
MALE	0	.0	5	1.0	3	.6	0	.0	8	1.7	472	97.9	2	.4

484

ENROLLMENT IN INSTITUTIONS OF HIGHER EDUCATION FOR SELECTED MAJOR FIELDS OF STUDY AND LEVEL OF ENROLLMENT CE, ETHNICITY, AND SEX: STATE, 1978

- DENTISTRY

CAN INDIAN AN NATIVE		BLACK NON-HISPANIC		ASIAN OR PACIFIC ISLANDER		HISPANIC		TOTAL MINORITY		WHITE NON-HISPANIC		NON-RESIDENT ALIEN		TOTAL
ER	%	NUMBER	%	NUMBER	%	NUMBER	%	NUMBER	%	NUMBER	%	NUMBER	%	NUMBER
CONTINUED														
0	.0	0	.0	0	.0	0	.0	0	.0	0	.0	0	.0	0
0	.0	0	.0	0	.0	0	.0	0	.0	0	.0	0	.0	0
0	.0	0	.0	0	.0	0	.0	0	.0	0	.0	0	.0	0
0	.0	13	2.2	3	.5	0	.0	16	2.7	571	96.8	3	.5	590
0	.0	8	7.4	0	.0	0	.0	8	7.4	99	91.7	1	.9	108
0	.0	5	1.0	3	.6	0	.0	8	1.7	472	97.9	2	.4	482
0	.0	13	2.2	3	.5	0	.0	16	2.7	571	96.8	3	.5	590
0	.0	8	7.4	0	.0	0	.0	8	7.4	99	91.7	1	.9	108
0	.0	5	1.0	3	.6	0	.0	8	1.7	472	97.9	2	.4	482
0	.0	0	.0	0	.0	0	.0	0	.0	0	.0	0	.0	0
0	.0	.0	.0	0	.0	0	.0	0	.0	0	.0	0	.0	0
0	.0	0	.0	0	.0	0	.0	0	.0	0	.0	0	.0	0
0	.0	13	2.2	3	.5	0	.0	16	2.7	571	96.8	3	.5	590
0	.0	8	7.4	0	.0	0	.0	8	7.4	99	91.7	1	.9	108
0	.0	5	1.0	3	.6	0	.0	8	1.7	472	97.9	2	.4	482
0	.0	0	.0	0	.0	0	.0	0	.0	0	.0	0	.0	0
0	.0	0	.0	0	.0	0	.0	0	.0	0	.0	0	.0	0
0	.0	0	.0	0	.0	0	.0	0	.0	0	.0	0	.0	0
0	.0	13	2.2	3	.5	0	.0	16	2.7	571	96.8	3	.5	590
0	.0	8	7.4	0	.0	0	.0	8	7.4	99	91.7	1	.9	108
0	.0	5	1.0	3	.6	0	.0	8	1.7	472	97.9	2	.4	482
(1 INSTITUTIONS)														
0	.0	0	.0	0	.0	0	.0	0	.0	0	.0	0	.0	0
0	.0	0	.0	0	.0	0	.0	0	.0	0	.0	0	.0	0
0	.0	0	.0	0	.0	0	.0	0	.0	0	.0	0	.0	0
0	.0	0	.0	0	.0	0	.0	0	.0	0	.0	0	.0	0
0	.0	0	.0	0	.0	0	.0	0	.0	0	.0	0	.0	0
0	.0	0	.0	0	.0	0	.0	0	.0	0	.0	0	.0	0
0	.0	0	.0	0	.0	0	.0	0	.0	0	.0	0	.0	0
0	.0	0	.0	0	.0	0	.0	0	.0	0	.0	0	.0	0
0	.0	0	.0	0	.0	0	.0	0	.0	0	.0	0	.0	0
0	.0	0	.0	0	.0	0	.0	0	.0	0	.0	0	.0	0
0	.0	0	.0	0	.0	0	.0	0	.0	0	.0	0	.0	0
0	.0	0	.0	0	.0	0	.0	0	.0	0	.0	0	.0	0
0	.0	0	.0	0	.0	0	.0	0	.0	0	.0	0	.0	0
0	.0	0	.0	0	.0	0	.0	0	.0	0	.0	0	.0	0
0	.0	0	.0	0	.0	0	.0	0	.0	0	.0	0	.0	0
1	.3	5	1.4	0	.0	1	.3	7	1.9	355	98.1	0	.0	362
0	.0	1	2.4	0	.0	1	2.4	2	4.9	39	95.1	0	.0	41
1	.3	4	1.2	0	.0	0	.0	5	1.6	316	98.4	0	.0	321
0	.0	0	.0	0	.0	0	.0	0	.0	0	.0	0	.0	0
0	.0	0	.0	0	.0	0	.0	0	.0	0	.0	0	.0	0
0	.0	0	.0	0	.0	0	.0	0	.0	0	.0	0	.0	0
1	.3	5	1.4	0	.0	1	.3	7	1.9	355	98.1	0	.0	362
0	.0	1	2.4	0	.0	1	2.4	2	4.9	39	95.1	0	.0	41
1	.3	4	1.2	0	.0	0	.0	5	1.6	316	98.4	0	.0	321
1	.3	5	1.4	0	.0	1	.3	7	1.9	355	98.1	0	.0	362
0	.0	1	2.4	0	.0	1	2.4	2	4.9	39	95.1	0	.0	41
1	.3	4	1.2	0	.0	0	.0	5	1.6	316	98.4	0	.0	321
0	.0	0	.0	0	.0	0	.0	0	.0	0	.0	0	.0	0
0	.0	0	.0	0	.0	0	.0	0	.0	0	.0	0	.0	0
1	.3	5	1.4	0	.0	1	.3	7	1.9	355	98.1	0	.0	362
0	.0	1	2.4	0	.0	1	2.4	2	4.9	39	95.1	0	.0	41
1	.3	4	1.2	0	.0	0	.0	5	1.6	316	98.4	0	.0	321
0	.0	0	.0	0	.0	0	.0	0	.0	0	.0	0	.0	0
0	.0	0	.0	0	.0	0	.0	0	.0	0	.0	0	.0	0
0	.0	0	.0	0	.0	0	.0	0	.0	0	.0	0	.0	0
1	.3	5	1.4	0	.0	1	.3	7	1.9	355	98.1	0	.0	362
0	.0	1	2.4	0	.0	1	2.4	2	4.9	39	95.1	0	.0	41
1	.3	4	1.2	0	.0	0	.0	5	1.6	316	98.4	0	.0	321

TABLE 17 - TOTAL ENROLLMENT IN INSTITUTIONS OF HIGHER EDUCATION FOR SELECTED MAJOR FIELDS OF STUDY AND LEVEL OF ENROLLMENT BY RACE, ETHNICITY, AND SEX: STATE, 1978

MAJOR FIELD 1204 - DENTISTRY

	AMERICAN INDIAN ALASKAN NATIVE		BLACK NLN-HISPANIC		ASIAN OR PACIFIC ISLANDER		HISPANIC		TOTAL MINORITY		WHITE NON-HISPANIC		NON-RESIDENT ALIEN		TOT
	NUMBER	%	NUMBER	%	NUMBER	%	NUMBER	%	NUMBER	%	NUMBER	%	NUMBER	%	NUM
MARYLAND (1 INSTITUTIONS)															
UNDERGRADUATES:															
FULL-TIME															
FEMALE	0	.0	0	.0	0	.0	0	.0	0	.0	0	.0	0	.0	
MALE	0	.0	0	.0	0	.0	0	.0	0	.0	0	.0	0	.0	
PART-TIME															
FEMALE	0	.0	0	.0	0	.0	0	.0	0	.0	0	.0	0	.0	
MALE	0	.0	0	.0	0	.0	0	.0	0	.0	0	.0	0	.0	
TOTAL	0	.0	0	.0	0	.0	0	.0	0	.0	0	.0	0	.0	
FEMALE	0	.0	0	.0	0	.0	0	.0	0	.0	0	.0	0	.0	
MALE	0	.0	0	.0	0	.0	0	.0	0	.0	0	.0	0	.0	
GRADUATE:															
FULL-TIME															
FEMALE	0	.0	0	.0	0	.0	0	.0	0	.0	0	.0	0	.0	
MALE	0	.0	0	.0	0	.0	0	.0	0	.0	0	.0	0	.0	
PART-TIME															
FEMALE	0	.0	0	.0	0	.0	0	.0	0	.0	0	.0	0	.0	
MALE	0	.0	0	.0	0	.0	0	.0	0	.0	0	.0	0	.0	
TOTAL	0	.0	0	.0	0	.0	0	.0	0	.0	0	.0	0	.0	
FEMALE	0	.0	0	.0	0	.0	0	.0	0	.0	0	.0	0	.0	
MALE	0	.0	0	.0	0	.0	0	.0	0	.0	0	.0	0	.0	
PROFESSIONAL:															
FULL-TIME	0	.0	37	7.0	14	2.7	9	1.7	60	11.4	466	88.6	0	.0	
FEMALE	0	.0	13	15.5	4	4.8	1	1.2	18	21.4	66	78.6	0	.0	
MALE	0	.0	24	5.4	10	2.3	8	1.8	42	9.5	400	90.5	0	.0	
PART-TIME	0	.0	0	.0	0	.0	0	.0	0	.0	2	100.0	0	.0	
FEMALE	0	.0	0	.0	0	.0	0	.0	0	.0	1	100.0	0	.0	
MALE	0	.0	0	.0	0	.0	0	.0	0	.0	1	100.0	0	.0	
TOTAL	0	.0	37	7.0	14	2.7	9	1.7	60	11.4	468	88.6	0	.0	
FEMALE	0	.0	13	15.3	4	4.7	1	1.2	18	21.2	67	78.8	0	.0	
MALE	0	.0	24	5.4	10	2.3	8	1.8	42	9.5	401	90.5	0.	.0	
UND+GRAD+PROF:															
FULL-TIME	0	.0	37	7.0	14	2.7	9	1.7	60	11.4	466	88.6		.0	
FEMALE	0	.0	13	15.5	4	4.8	1	1.2	18	21.4	66	78.6		.0	
MALE	0	.0	24	5.4	10	2.3	8	1.8	42	9.5	400	90.5		.0	
PART-TIME	0	.0	0	.0	0	.0	0	.0	0	.0	2	100.0	0	.0	
FEMALE	0	.0	0	.0	0	.0	0	.0	0	.0	1	100.0	0	.0	
MALE	0	.0	0	.0	0	.0	0	.0	0	.0	1	100.0	0	.0	
TOTAL	0	.0	37	7.0	14	2.7	9	1.7	60	11.4	468	88.6	0	.0	
FEMALE	0	.0	13	15.3	4	4.7	1	1.2	18	21.2	67	78.8	0	.0	
MALE	0	.0	24	5.4	10	2.3	8	1.8	42	9.5	401	90.5	0	.0	
UNCLASSIFIED:															
TOTAL	0	.0	0	.0	0	.0	0	.0	0	.0	0	.0	0	.0	
FEMALE	0	.0	0	.0	0	.0	0	.0	0	.0	0	.0	0	.0	
MALE	0	.0	0	.0	0	.0	0	.0	0	.0	0	.0	0	.0	
TOTAL ENROLLMENT:															
TOTAL	0	.0	37	7.0	14	2.7	9	1.7	60	11.4	468	88.6	0	.0	
FEMALE	0	.0	13	15.3	4	4.7	1	1.2	18	21.2	67	78.8	0	.0	
MALE	0	.0	24	5.4	10	2.3	8	1.8	42	9.5	401	90.5	0	.0	
MASSACHUSETTS (3 INSTITUTIONS)															
UNDERGRADUATES:															
FULL-TIME															
FEMALE	0	.0	0	.0	0	.0	0	.0	0	.0	0	.0	0	.0	
MALE	0	.0	0	.0	0	.0	0	.0	0	.0	0	.0	0	.0	
PART-TIME															
FEMALE	0	.0	0	.0	0	.0	0	.0	0	.0	0	.0	0	.0	
MALE	0	.0	0	.0	0	.0	0	.0	0	.0	0	.0	0	.0	
TOTAL	0	.0	0	.0	0	.0	0	.0	0	.0	0	.0	0	.0	
FEMALE	0	.0	0	.0	0	.0	0	.0	0	.0	0	.0	0	.0	
MALE	0	.0	0	.0	0	.0	0	.0	0	.0	0	.0	0	.0	
GRADUATE:															
FULL-TIME															
FEMALE	0	.0	0	.0	0	.0	0	.0	0	.0	0	.0	0	.0	
MALE	0	.0	0	.0	0	.0	0	.0	0	.0	0	.0	0	.0	
PART-TIME															
FEMALE	0	.0	0	.0	0	.0	0	.0	0	.0	0	.0	0	.0	
MALE	0	.0	0	.0	0	.0	0	.0	0	.0	0	.0	0	.0	
TOTAL	0	.0	0	.0	0	.0	0	.0	0	.0	0	.0	0	.0	
FEMALE	0	.0	0	.0	0	.0	0	.0	0	.0	0	.0	0	.0	
MALE	0	.0	0	.0	0	.0	0	.0	0	.0	0	.0	0	.0	
PROFESSIONAL:															
FULL-TIME	2	.4	16	3.0	22	4.2	10	1.9	50	9.5	460	87.0	19	3.6	
FEMALE	0	.0	7	5.6	9	7.3	2	1.6	18	14.5	100	80.6	6	4.8	
MALE	2	.5	9	2.2	13	3.2	8	2.0	32	7.9	360	88.9	13	3.2	

DENTISTRY

I INDIAN NATIVE	BLACK NON-HISPANIC		ASIAN OR PACIFIC ISLANDER		HISPANIC		TOTAL MINORITY		WHITE NON-HISPANIC		NON-RESIDENT ALIEN		TOTAL
%	NUMBER	%	NUMBER	%	NUMBER	%	NUMBER	%	NUMBER	%	NUMBER	%	NUMBER

CONTINUED

.0	0	.0	0	.0	0	.0	0	.0	0	.0	0	.0	0
.0	0	.0	0	.0	0	.0	0	.0	0	.0	0	.0	0
.0	0	.0	0	.0	0	.0	0	.0	0	.0	0	.0	0
.4	16	3.0	22	4.2	10	1.9	50	9.5	460	87.0	19	3.6	529
.0	7	5.6	9	7.3	2	1.6	18	14.5	100	80.6	6	4.8	124
.5	9	2.2	13	3.2	8	2.0	32	7.9	360	88.9	13	3.2	405
.4	16	3.0	22	4.2	10	1.9	50	9.5	460	87.0	19	3.6	529
.0	7	5.6	9	7.3	2	1.6	18	14.5	100	80.6	6	4.8	124
.5	9	2.2	13	3.2	8	2.0	32	7.9	360	88.9	13	3.2	405
.0	0	.0	0	.0	0	.0	0	.0	0	.0	0	.0	0
.0	0	.0	0	.0	0	.0	0	.0	0	.0	0	.0	0
.0	0	.0	0	.0	0	.0	0	.0	0	.0	0	.0	0
.4	16	3.0	22	4.2	10	1.9	50	9.5	460	87.0	19	3.6	529
.0	7	5.6	9	7.3	2	1.6	18	14.5	100	80.6	6	4.8	124
.5	9	2.2	13	3.2	8	2.0	32	7.9	360	88.9	13	3.2	405
.4	16	3.0	22	4.2	10	1.9	50	9.5	460	87.0	19	3.6	529
.0	7	5.6	9	7.3	2	1.6	18	14.5	100	80.6	6	4.8	124
.5	9	2.2	13	3.2	8	2.0	32	7.9	360	88.9	13	3.2	405

(2 INSTITUTIONS)

.0	0	.0	0	.0	0	.0	0	.0	0	.0	0	.0	0
.0	0	.0	0	.0	0	.0	0	.0	0	.0	0	.0	0
.0	0	.0	0	.0	0	.0	0	.0	0	.0	0	.0	0
.0	0	.0	0	.0	0	.0	0	.0	0	.0	0	.0	0
.0	0	.0	0	.0	0	.0	0	.0	0	.0	0	.0	0
.0	0	.0	0	.0	0	.0	0	.0	0	.0	0	.0	0
.0	0	.0	0	.0	0	.0	0	.0	0	.0	0	.0	0
.0	0	.0	0	.0	0	.0	0	.0	0	.0	0	.0	0
.0	0	.0	0	.0	0	.0	0	.0	0	.0	0	.0	0
.0	0	.0	0	.0	0	.0	0	.0	0	.0	0	.0	0
.0	0	.0	0	.0	0	.0	0	.0	0	.0	0	.0	0
.0	0	.0	0	.0	0	.0	0	.0	0	.0	0	.0	0
.0	0	.0	0	.0	0	.0	0	.0	0	.0	0	.0	0
.0	0	.0	0	.0	0	.0	0	.0	0	.0	0	.0	0
.0	0	.0	0	.0	0	.0	0	.0	0	.0	0	.0	0
.1	46	5.0	7	.8	4	.4	58	6.3	855	93.3	3	.3	916
.0	19	15.1	2	1.6	1	.8	22	17.5	102	81.0	2	1.6	126
.1	27	3.4	5	.6	3	.4	36	4.6	753	95.3	1	.1	790
.0	0	.0	0	.0	0	.0	0	.0	0	.0	0	.0	0
.0	0	.0	0	.0	0	.0	0	.0	0	.0	0	.0	0
.1	46	5.0	7	.8	4	.4	58	6.3	855	93.3	3	.3	916
.0	19	15.1	2	1.6	1	.8	22	17.5	102	81.0	2	1.6	126
.1	27	3.4	5	.6	3	.4	36	4.6	753	95.3	1	.1	790
.1	46	5.0	7	.8	4	.4	58	6.3	855	93.3	3	.3	916
.0	19	15.1	2	1.6	1	.8	22	17.5	102	81.0	2	1.6	126
.1	27	3.4	5	.6	3	.4	36	4.6	753	95.3	1	.1	790
.0	0	.0	0	.0	0	.0	0	.0	0	.0	0	.0	0
.0	0	.0	0	.0	0	.0	0	.0	0	.0	0	.0	0
.0	0	.0	0	.0	0	.0	0	.0	0	.0	0	.0	0
.1	46	5.0	7	.8	4	.4	58	6.3	855	93.3	3	.3	916
.0	19	15.1	2	1.6	1	.8	22	17.5	102	81.0	2	1.6	126
.1	27	3.4	5	.6	3	.4	36	4.6	753	95.3	1	.1	790
.0	0	.0	0	.0	0	.0	0	.0	0	.0	0	.0	0
.0	0	.0	0	.0	0	.0	0	.0	0	.0	0	.0	0
.0	0	.0	0	.0	0	.0	0	.0	0	.0	0	.0	0
.1	46	5.0	7	.8	4	.4	58	6.3	855	93.3	3	.3	916
.0	19	15.1	2	1.6	1	.8	22	17.5	102	81.0	2	1.6	126
.1	27	3.4	5	.6	3	.4	36	4.6	753	95.3	1	.1	790

TABLE 17 - TOTAL ENROLLMENT IN INSTITUTIONS OF HIGHER EDUCATION FOR SELECTED MAJOR FIELDS OF STUDY AND LEVEL OF ENROLLMENT
BY RACE, ETHNICITY, AND SEX: STATE, 1978

MAJOR FIELD 1204 - DENTISTRY

	AMERICAN INDIAN ALASKAN NATIVE		BLACK NON-HISPANIC		ASIAN OR PACIFIC ISLANDER		HISPANIC		TOTAL MINORITY		WHITE NON-HISPANIC		NON-RESIDENT ALIEN	
	NUMBER	%	NUMBER	%	NUMBER	%	NUMBER	%	NUMBER	%	NUMBER	%	NUMBER	%
MINNESOTA (1 INSTITUTIONS)														
UNDERGRADUATES:														
FULL-TIME	0	.0	0	.0	0	.0	0	.0	0	.0	0	.0	0	.0
FEMALE	0	.0	0	.0	0	.0	0	.0	0	.0	0	.0	0	.0
MALE	0	.0	0	.0	0	.0	0	.0	0	.0	0	.0	0	.0
PART-TIME	0	.0	0	.0	0	.0	0	.0	0	.0	0	.0	0	.0
FEMALE	0	.0	0	.0	0	.0	0	.0	0	.0	0	.0	0	.0
MALE	0	.0	0	.0	0	.0	0	.0	0	.0	0	.0	0	.0
TOTAL	0	.0	0	.0	0	.0	0	.0	0	.0	0	.0		.0
FEMALE	0	.0	0	.0	0	.0	0	.0	0	.0	0	.0	0	.0
MALE	0	.0	0	.0	0	.0	0	.0	0	.0	0	.0	0	.0
GRADUATE:														
FULL-TIME	0	.0	0	.0	0	.0	0	.0	0	.0	0	.0	0	.0
FEMALE	0	.0	0	.0	0	.0	0	.0	0	.0	0	.0	0	.0
MALE	0	.0	0	.0	0	.0	0	.0	0	.0	0	.0	0	.0
PART-TIME	0	.0	0	.0	0	.0	0	.0	0	.0	0	.0	0	.0
FEMALE	0	.0	0	.0	0	.0	0	.0	0	.0	0	.0	0	.0
MALE	0	.0	0	.0	0	.0	0	.0	0	.0	0	.0	0	.0
TOTAL	0	.0	0	.0	0	.0	0	.0	0	.0	0	.0	0	.0
FEMALE	0	.0	0	.0	0	.0	0	.0	0	.0	0	.0	0	.0
MALE	0	.0	0	.0	0	.0	0	.0	0	.0	0	.0	0	.0
PROFESSIONAL:														
FULL-TIME	1	.2	4	.7	4	.7	5	.9	14	2.4	555	97.0	3	.5
FEMALE	1	1.5	1	1.5	0	.0	1	1.5	3	4.5	62	93.9	1	1.5
MALE	0	.0	3	.6	4	.8	4	.8	11	2.2	493	97.4	2	.4
PART-TIME	0	.0	0	.0	0	.0	0	.0	0	.0	0	.0	0	.0
FEMALE	0	.0	0	.0	0	.0	0	.0	0	.0	0	.0	0	.0
MALE	0	.0	0	.0	0	.0	0	.0	0	.0	0	.0	0	.0
TOTAL	1	.2	4	.7	4	.7	5	.9	14	2.4	555	97.0	3	.5
FEMALE	1	1.5	1	1.5	0	.0	1	1.5	3	4.5	62	93.9	1	1.5
MALE	0	.0	3	.6	4	.8	4	.8	11	2.2	493	97.4	2	.4
UND+GRAD+PROF:														
FULL-TIME	1	.2	4	.7	4	.7	5	.9	14	2.4	555	97.0	3	.5
FEMALE	1	1.5	1	1.5	0	.0	1	1.5	3	4.5	62	93.9	1	1.5
MALE	0	.0	3	.6	4	.8	4	.8	11	2.2	493	97.4	2	.4
PART-TIME	0	.0	0	.0	0	.0	0	.0	0	.0	0	.0	0	.0
FEMALE	0	.0	0	.0	0	.0	0	.0	0	.0	0	.0	0	.0
MALE	0	.0	0	.0	0	.0	0	.0	0	.0	0	.0	0	.0
TOTAL	1	.2	4	.7	4	.7	5	.9	14	2.4	555	97.0	3	.5
FEMALE	1	1.5	1	1.5	0	.0	1	1.5	3	4.5	62	93.9	1	1.5
MALE	0	.0	3	.6	4	.8	4	.8	11	2.2	493	97.4	2	.4
UNCLASSIFIED:														
TOTAL	0	.0	0	.0	0	.0	0	.0	0	.0	0	.0		.0
FEMALE	0	.0	0	.0	0	.0	0	.0	0	.0	0	.0	0	.0
MALE	0	.0	0	.0	0	.0	0	.0	0	.0	0	.0	0	.0
TOTAL ENROLLMENT:														
TOTAL	1	.2	4	.7	4	.7	5	.9	14	2.4	555	97.0	3	.5
FEMALE	1	1.5	1	1.5	0	.0	1	1.5	3	4.5	62	93.9	1	1.5
MALE	0	.0	3	.6	4	.8	4	.8	11	2.2	493	97.4	2	.4
MISSISSIPPI (1 INSTITUTIONS)														
UNDERGRADUATES:														
FULL-TIME	0	.0	0	.0	0	.0	0	.0	0	.0	0	.0	0	.0
FEMALE	0	.0	0	.0	0	.0	0	.0	0	.0	0	.0	0	.0
MALE	0	.0	0	.0	0	.0	0	.0	0	.0	0	.0	0	.0
PART-TIME	0	.0	0	.0	0	.0	0	.0	0	.0	0	.0	0	.0
FEMALE	0	.0	0	.0	0	.0	0	.0	0	.0	0	.0	0	.0
MALE	0	.0	0	.0	0	.0	0	.0	0	.0	0	.0	0	.0
TOTAL	0	.0	0	.0	0	.0	0	.0	0	.0	0	.0	0	.0
FEMALE	0	.0	0	.0	0	.0	0	.0	0	.0	0	.0	0	.0
MALE	0	.0	0	.0	0	.0	0	.0	0	.0	0	.0	0	.0
GRADUATE:														
FULL-TIME	0	.0	0	.0	0	.0	0	.0	0	.0	0	.0	0	.0
FEMALE	0	.0	0	.0	0	.0	0	.0	0	.0	0	.0	0	.0
MALE	0	.0	0	.0	0	.0	0	.0	0	.0	0	.0	0	.0
PART-TIME	0	.0	0	.0	0	.0	0	.0	0	.0	0	.0	0	.0
FEMALE	0	.0	0	.0	0	.0	0	.0	0	.0	0	.0	0	.0
MALE	0	.0	0	.0	0	.0	0	.0	0	.0	0	.0	0	.0
TOTAL	0	.0	0	.0	0	.0	0	.0	0	.0	0	.0	0	.0
FEMALE	0	.0	0	.0	0	.0	0	.0	0	.0	0	.0	0	.0
MALE	0	.0	0	.0	0	.0	0	.0	0	.0	0	.0	0	.0
PROFESSIONAL:														
FULL-TIME	1	.8	14	11.1	3	2.4	0	.0	18	14.3	108	85.7	0	.0
FEMALE	0	.0	4	33.3	1	8.3	0	.0	5	41.7	7	58.3	0	.0
MALE	1	.9	10	8.8	2	1.8	0	.0	13	11.4	101	88.6	0	.0

DENTISTRY

INDIAN NATIVE	BLACK NON-HISPANIC		ASIAN OR PACIFIC ISLANDER		HISPANIC		TOTAL MINORITY		WHITE NON-HISPANIC		NON-RESIDENT ALIEN		TOTAL
%	NUMBER	%	NUMBER	%	NUMBER	%	NUMBER	%	NUMBER	%	NUMBER	%	NUMBER

CONTINUED

.0	0	.0	0	.0	0	.0	0	.0	0	.0	0	.0	0
.0	0	.0	0	.0	0	.0	0	.0	0	.0	0	.0	0
.0	0	.0	0	.0	0	.0	0	.0	0	.0	0	.0	0
.8	14	11.1	3	2.4	0	.0	18	14.3	108	85.7	0	.0	126
.0	4	33.3	1	8.3	0	.0	5	41.7	7	58.3	0	.0	12
.9	10	8.8	2	1.8	0	.0	13	11.4	101	88.6	0	.0	114
.8	14	11.1	3	2.4	0	.0	18	14.3	108	85.7	0	.0	126
.0	4	33.3	1	8.3	0	.0	5	41.7	7	58.3	0	.0	12
.9	10	8.8	2	1.8	0	.0	13	11.4	101	88.6	0	.0	114
.0	0	.0	0	.0	0	.0	0	.0	0	.0	0	.0	0
.0	0	.0	0	.0	0	.0	0	.0	0	.0	0	.0	0
.0	0	.0	0	.0	0	.0	0	.0	0	.0	0	.0	0
.8	14	11.1	3	2.4	0	.0	18	14.3	108	85.7	0	.0	126
.0	4	33.3	1	8.3	0	.0	5	41.7	7	58.3	0	.0	12
.9	10	8.8	2	1.8	0	.0	13	11.4	101	88.6	0	.0	114
.0	0	.0	0	.0	0	.0	0	.0	0	.0	0	.0	0
.0	0	.0	0	.0	0	.0	0	.0	0	.0	0	.0	0
.0	0	.0	0	.0	0	.0	0	.0	0	.0	0	.0	0
.8	14	11.1	3	2.4	0	.0	18	14.3	108	85.7	0	.0	126
.0	4	33.3	1	8.3	0	.0	5	41.7	7	58.3	0	.0	12
.9	10	8.8	2	1.8	0	.0	13	11.4	101	88.6	0	.0	114

(2 INSTITUTIONS)

.0	0	.0	0	.0	0	.0	0	.0	0	.0	0	.0	0
.0	0	.0	0	.0	0	.0	0	.0	0	.0	0	.0	0
.0	0	.0	0	.0	0	.0	0	.0	0	.0	0	.0	0
.0	0	.0	0	.0	0	.0	0	.0	0	.0	0	.0	0
.0	0	.0	0	.0	0	.0	0	.0	0	.0	0	.0	0
.0	0	.0	0	.0	0	.0	0	.0	0	.0	0	.0	0
.0	0	.0	0	.0	0	.0	0	.0	0	.0	0	.0	0
.0	0	.0	0	.0	0	.0	0	.0	0	.0	0	.0	0
.0	0	.0	0	.0	0	.0	0	.0	0	.0	0	.0	0
.0	0	.0	0	.0	0	.0	0	.0	0	.0	0	.0	0
.0	0	.0	0	.0	0	.0	0	.0	0	.0	0	.0	0
.0	0	.0	0	.0	0	.0	0	.0	0	.0	0	.0	0
.1	18	1.9	32	3.5	15	1.6	66	7.1	847	91.6	12	1.3	925
.0	4	4.4	4	4.4	0	.0	8	8.8	80	87.9	3	3.3	91
.1	14	1.7	28	3.4	15	1.8	58	7.0	767	92.0	9	1.1	834
.0	0	.0	0	.0	0	.0	0	.0	0	.0	0	.0	0
.0	0	.0	0	.0	0	.0	0	.0	0	.0	0	.0	0
.0	0	.0	0	.0	0	.0	0	.0	0	.0	0	.0	0
.1	18	1.9	32	3.5	15	1.6	66	7.1	847	91.6	12	1.3	925
.0	4	4.4	4	4.4	0	.0	8	8.8	80	87.9	3	3.3	91
.1	14	1.7	28	3.4	15	1.8	58	7.0	767	92.0	9	1.1	834
.1	18	1.9	32	3.5	15	1.6	66	7.1	847	91.6	12	1.3	925
.0	4	4.4	4	4.4	0	.0	8	8.8	80	87.9	3	3.3	91
.1	14	1.7	28	3.4	15	1.8	58	7.0	767	92.0	9	1.1	834
.0	0	.0	0	.0	0	.0	0	.0	0	.0	0	.0	0
.0	0	.0	0	.0	0	.0	0	.0	0	.0	0	.0	0
.0	0	.0	0	.0	0	.0	0	.0	0	.0	0	.0	0
.1	18	1.9	32	3.5	15	1.6	66	7.1	847	91.6	12	1.3	925
.0	4	4.4	4	4.4	0	.0	8	8.8	80	87.9	3	3.3	91
.1	14	1.7	28	3.4	15	1.8	58	7.0	767	92.0	9	1.1	834
.0	0	.0	0	.0	0	.0	0	.0	0	.0	0	.0	0
.0	0	.0	0	.0	0	.0	0	.0	0	.0	0	.0	0
.0	0	.0	0	.0	0	.0	0	.0	0	.0	0	.0	0
.1	18	1.9	32	3.5	15	1.6	66	7.1	847	91.6	12	1.3	925
.0	4	4.4	4	4.4	0	.0	8	8.8	80	87.9	3	3.3	91
.1	14	1.7	28	3.4	15	1.8	58	7.0	767	92.0	9	1.1	834

TABLE 17 - TOTAL ENROLLMENT IN INSTITUTIONS OF HIGHER EDUCATION FOR SELECTED MAJOR FIELDS OF STUDY AND LEVEL OF ENROLLMENT BY RACE, ETHNICITY, AND SEX: STATE, 1978

MAJOR FIELD 1204 - DENTISTRY

	AMERICAN INDIAN ALASKAN NATIVE		BLACK NON-HISPANIC		ASIAN OR PACIFIC ISLANDER		HISPANIC		TOTAL MINORITY		WHITE NON-HISPANIC		NON-RESIDENT ALIEN	
	NUMBER	%	NUMBER	%	NUMBER	%	NUMBER	%	NUMBER	%	NUMBER	%	NUMBER	%
NEBRASKA	(	2 INSTITUTIONS)												
UNDERGRADUATES:														
FULL-TIME	0	.0	0	.0	0	.0	0	.0	0	.0	0	.0		.0
FEMALE	0	.0	0	.0	0	.0	0	.0	0	.0	0	.0		.0
MALE	0	.0	0	.0	0	.0	0	.0	0	.0	0	.0		.0
PART-TIME	0	.0	0	.0	0	.0	0	.0	0	.0	0	.0		.0
FEMALE	0	.0	0	.0	0	.0	0	.0	0	.0	0	.0	0	.0
MALE	0	.0	0	.0	0	.0	0	.0	0	.0	0	.0	0	.0
TOTAL	0	.0	0	.0	0	.0	0	.0	0	.0	0	.0		.0
FEMALE	0	.0	0	.0	0	.0	0	.0	0	.0	0	.0	0	.0
MALE	0	.0	0	.0	0	.0	0	.0	0	.0	0	.0	0	.0
GRADUATE:														
FULL-TIME	0	.0	0	.0	0	.0	0	.0	0	.0	0	.0		.0
FEMALE	0	.0	0	.0	0	.0	0	.0	0	.0	0	.0		.0
MALE	0	.0	0	.0	0	.0	0	.0	0	.0	0	.0		.0
PART-TIME	0	.0	0	.0	0	.0	0	.0	0	.0	0	.0		.0
FEMALE	0	.0	0	.0	0	.0	0	.0	0	.0	0	.0		.0
MALE	0	.0	0	.0	0	.0	0	.0	0	.0	0	.0	0	.0
TOTAL	0	.0	0	.0	0	.0	0	.0	0	.0	0	.0		.0
FEMALE	0	.0	0	.0	0	.0	0	.0	0	.0	0	.0	0	.0
MALE	0	.0	0	.0	0	.0	0	.0	0	.0	0	.0	0	.0
PROFESSIONAL:														
FULL-TIME	2	.3	8	1.3	9	1.5	8	1.3	27	4.5	575	95.2	2	.3
FEMALE	0	.0	4	4.8	1	1.2	0	.0	5	6.0	79	94.0	0	.0
MALE	2	.4	4	.8	8	1.5	8	1.5	22	4.2	496	95.4	2	.4
PART-TIME	0	.0	0	.0	0	.0	0	.0	0	.0	2	100.0	0	.0
FEMALE	0	.0	0	.0	0	.0	0	.0	0	.0	0	.0	0	.0
MALE	0	.0	0	.0	0	.0	0	.0	0	.0	2	100.0	0	.0
TOTAL	2	.3	8	1.3	9	1.5	8	1.3	27	4.5	577	95.2	2	.3
FEMALE	0	.0	4	4.8	1	1.2	0	.0	5	6.0	79	94.0	0	.0
MALE	2	.4	4	.8	8	1.5	8	1.5	22	4.2	498	95.4	2	.4
UND+GRAD+PROF:														
FULL-TIME	2	.3	8	1.3	9	1.5	8	1.3	27	4.5	575	95.2	2	.3
FEMALE	0	.0	4	4.8	1	1.2	0	.0	5	6.0	79	94.0	0	.0
MALE	2	.4	4	.8	8	1.5	8	1.5	22	4.2	496	95.4	2	.4
PART-TIME	0	.0	0	.0	0	.0	0	.0	0	.0	2	100.0	0	.0
FEMALE	0	.0	0	.0	0	.0	0	.0	0	.0	0	.0	0	.0
MALE	0	.0	0	.0	0	.0	0	.0	0	.0	2	100.0	0	.0
TOTAL	2	.3	8	1.3	9	1.5	8	1.3	27	4.5	577	95.2	2	.3
FEMALE	0	.0	4	4.8	1	1.2	0	.0	5	6.0	79	94.0	0	.0
MALE	2	.4	4	.8	8	1.5	8	1.5	22	4.2	498	95.4	2	.4
UNCLASSIFIED:														
TOTAL	0	.0	0	.0	0	.0	0	.0	0	.0	0	.0		.0
FEMALE	0	.0	0	.0	0	.0	0	.0	0	.0	0	.0	0	.0
MALE	0	.0	0	.0	0	.0	0	.0	0	.0	0	.0	0	.0
TOTAL ENROLLMENT:														
TOTAL	2	.3	8	1.3	9	1.5	8	1.3	27	4.5	577	95.2	2	.3
FEMALE	0	.0	4	4.8	1	1.2	0	.0	5	6.0	79	94.0	0	.0
MALE	2	.4	4	.8	8	1.5	8	1.5	22	4.2	498	95.4	2	.4
NEW JERSEY	(	2 INSTITUTIONS)												
UNDERGRADUATES:														
FULL-TIME	0	.0	0	.0	0	.0	0	.0	0	.0	0	.0		.0
FEMALE	0	.0	0	.0	0	.0	0	.0	0	.0	0	.0		.0
MALE	0	.0	0	.0	0	.0	0	.0	0	.0	0	.0		.0
PART-TIME	0	.0	0	.0	0	.0	0	.0	0	.0	0	.0		.0
FEMALE	0	.0	0	.0	0	.0	0	.0	0	.0	0	.0		.0
MALE	0	.0	0	.0	0	.0	0	.0	0	.0	0	.0	0	.0
TOTAL	0	.0	0	.0	0	.0	0	.0	0	.0	0	.0		.0
FEMALE	0	.0	0	.0	0	.0	0	.0	0	.0	0	.0		.0
MALE	0	.0	0	.0	0	.0	0	.0	0	.0	0	.0	0	.0
GRADUATE:														
FULL-TIME	0	.0	0	.0	0	.0	0	.0	0	.0	0	.0		.0
FEMALE	0	.0	0	.0	0	.0	0	.0	0	.0	0	.0		.0
MALE	0	.0	0	.0	0	.0	0	.0	0	.0	0	.0		.0
PART-TIME	0	.0	0	.0	0	.0	0	.0	0	.0	0	.0		.0
FEMALE	0	.0	0	.0	0	.0	0	.0	0	.0	0	.0		.0
MALE	0	.0	0	.0	0	.0	0	.0	0	.0	0	.0	0	.0
TOTAL	0	.0	0	.0	0	.0	0	.0	0	.0	0	.0		.0
FEMALE	0	.0	0	.0	0	.0	0	.0	0	.0	0	.0		.0
MALE	0	.0	0	.0	0	.0	0	.0	0	.0	0	.0	0	.0
PROFESSIONAL:														
FULL-TIME	2	.3	36	6.2	5	.9	11	1.9	54	9.2	530	90.8		.0
FEMALE	1	1.3	11	14.3	0	.0	4	5.2	16	20.8	61	79.2		.0
MALE	1	.2	25	4.9	5	1.0	7	1.4	38	7.5	469	92.5	0	.0

490

DENTISTRY

INDIAN NATIVE	BLACK NON-HISPANIC		ASIAN OR PACIFIC ISLANDER		HISPANIC		TOTAL MINORITY		WHITE NON-HISPANIC		NON-RESIDENT ALIEN		TOTAL
%	NUMBER	%	NUMBER	%	NUMBER	%	NUMBER	%	NUMBER	%	NUMBER	%	NUMBER

CONTINUED

INDIAN NATIVE %	BLACK NUMBER	BLACK %	ASIAN NUMBER	ASIAN %	HISP NUMBER	HISP %	TOT MIN NUMBER	TOT MIN %	WHITE NUMBER	WHITE %	ALIEN NUMBER	ALIEN %	TOTAL NUMBER
.0	0	.0	0	.0	0	.0	0	.0	0	.0	0	.0	0
.0	0	.0	0	.0	0	.0	0	.0	0	.0	0	.0	0
.0	0	.0	0	.0	0	.0	0	.0	0	.0	0	.0	0
.3	36	6.2	5	.9	11	1.9	54	9.2	530	90.8	0	.0	584
1.3	11	14.3	0	.0	4	5.2	16	20.8	61	79.2	0	.0	77
.2	25	4.9	5	1.0	7	1.4	38	7.5	469	92.5	0	.0	507
.3	36	6.2	5	.9	11	1.9	54	9.2	530	90.8	0	.0	584
1.3	11	14.3	0	.0	4	5.2	16	20.8	61	79.2	0	.0	77
.2	25	4.9	5	1.0	7	1.4	38	7.5	469	92.5	0	.0	507
.0	0	.0	0	.0	0	.0	0	.0	0	.0	0	.0	0
.0	0	.0	0	.0	0	.0	0	.0	0	.0	0	.0	0
.0	0	.0	0	.0	0	.0	0	.0	0	.0	0	.0	0
.3	36	6.2	5	.9	11	1.9	54	9.2	530	90.8	0	.0	584
1.3	11	14.3	0	.0	4	5.2	16	20.8	61	79.2	0	.0	77
.2	25	4.9	5	1.0	7	1.4	38	7.5	469	92.5	0	.0	507
.0	0	.0	0	.0	0	.0	0	.0	0	.0	0	.0	0
.0	0	.0	0	.0	0	.0	0	.0	0	.0	0	.0	0
.0	0	.0	0	.0	0	.0	0	.0	0	.0	0	.0	0
.3	36	6.2	5	.9	11	1.9	54	9.2	530	90.8	0	.0	584
1.3	11	14.3	0	.0	4	5.2	16	20.8	61	79.2	0	.0	77
.2	25	4.9	5	1.0	7	1.4	38	7.5	469	92.5	0	.0	507

(4 INSTITUTIONS)

INDIAN NATIVE %	BLACK NUMBER	BLACK %	ASIAN NUMBER	ASIAN %	HISP NUMBER	HISP %	TOT MIN NUMBER	TOT MIN %	WHITE NUMBER	WHITE %	ALIEN NUMBER	ALIEN %	TOTAL NUMBER
.0	0	.0	0	.0	0	.0	0	.0	0	.0	0	.0	0
.0	0	.0	0	.0	0	.0	0	.0	0	.0	0	.0	0
.0	0	.0	0	.0	0	.0	0	.0	0	.0	0	.0	0
.0	0	.0	0	.0	0	.0	0	.0	0	.0	0	.0	0
.0	0	.0	0	.0	0	.0	0	.0	0	.0	0	.0	0
.0	0	.0	0	.0	0	.0	0	.0	0	.0	0	.0	0
.0	0	.0	0	.0	0	.0	0	.0	0	.0	0	.0	0
.0	0	.0	0	.0	0	.0	0	.0	0	.0	0	.0	0
.0	0	.0	0	.0	0	.0	0	.0	0	.0	0	.0	0
.0	0	.0	0	.0	0	.0	0	.0	0	.0	0	.0	0
.0	0	.0	0	.0	0	.0	0	.0	0	.0	0	.0	0
.0	0	.0	0	.0	0	.0	0	.0	0	.0	0	.0	0
.0	0	.0	0	.0	0	.0	0	.0	0	.0	0	.0	0
.0	0	.0	0	.0	0	.0	0	.0	0	.0	0	.0	0
.0	0	.0	0	.0	0	.0	0	.0	0	.0	0	.0	0
.0	0	.0	0	.0	0	.0	0	.0	0	.0	0	.0	0
.0	0	.0	0	.0	0	.0	0	.0	0	.0	0	.0	0
.0	0	.0	0	.0	0	.0	0	.0	0	.0	0	.0	0
.1	14	1.0	29	2.0	23	1.6	68	4.7	1,371	94.2	16	1.1	1,455
.0	4	1.9	9	4.2	5	2.3	18	8.3	196	90.7	2	.9	216
.2	10	.8	20	1.6	18	1.5	50	4.0	1,175	94.8	14	1.1	1,239
.0	0	.0	0	.0	0	.0	0	.0	0	.0	0	.0	0
.0	0	.0	0	.0	0	.0	0	.0	0	.0	0	.0	0
.0	0	.0	0	.0	0	.0	0	.0	0	.0	0	.0	0
.1	14	1.0	29	2.0	23	1.6	68	4.7	1,371	94.2	16	1.1	1,455
.0	4	1.9	9	4.2	5	2.3	18	8.3	196	90.7	2	.9	216
.2	10	.8	20	1.6	18	1.5	50	4.0	1,175	94.8	14	1.1	1,239
.1	14	1.0	29	2.0	23	1.6	68	4.7	1,371	94.2	16	1.1	1,455
.0	4	1.9	9	4.2	5	2.3	18	8.3	196	90.7	2	.9	216
.2	10	.8	20	1.6	18	1.5	50	4.0	1,175	94.8	14	1.1	1,239
.0	0	.0	0	.0	0	.0	0	.0	0	.0	0	.0	0
.0	0	.0	0	.0	0	.0	0	.0	0	.0	0	.0	0
.0	0	.0	0	.0	0	.0	0	.0	0	.0	0	.0	0
.1	14	1.0	29	2.0	23	1.6	68	4.7	1,371	94.2	16	1.1	1,455
.0	4	1.9	9	4.2	5	2.3	18	8.3	196	90.7	2	.9	216
.2	10	.8	20	1.6	18	1.5	50	4.0	1,175	94.8	14	1.1	1,239
.0	0	.0	0	.0	0	.0	0	.0	0	.0	0	.0	0
.0	0	.0	0	.0	0	.0	0	.0	0	.0	0	.0	0
.0	0	.0	0	.0	0	.0	0	.0	0	.0	0	.0	0
.1	14	1.0	29	2.0	23	1.6	68	4.7	1,371	94.2	16	1.1	1,455
.0	4	1.9	9	4.2	5	2.3	18	8.3	196	90.7	2	.9	216
.2	10	.8	20	1.6	18	1.5	50	4.0	1,175	94.8	14	1.1	1,239

MAJOR FIELD 1204 - DENTISTRY

	AMERICAN INDIAN ALASKAN NATIVE		BLACK NON-HISPANIC		ASIAN OR PACIFIC ISLANDER		HISPANIC		TOTAL MINORITY		WHITE NON-HISPANIC		NON-RESIDENT ALIEN	
	NUMBER	%	NUMBER	%	NUMBER	%	NUMBER	%	NUMBER	%	NUMBER	%	NUMBER	%
NORTH CAROLINA (1 INSTITUTIONS)														
UNDERGRADUATES:														
FULL-TIME	0	.0	0	.0	0	.0	0	.0	0	.0	0	.0	0	.0
FEMALE	0	.0	0	.0	0	.0	0	.0	0	.0	0	.0	0	.0
MALE	0	.0	0	.0	0	.0	0	.0	0	.0	0	.0	0	.0
PART-TIME	0	.0	0	.0	0	.0	0	.0	0	.0	0	.0	0	.0
FEMALE	0	.0	0	.0	0	.0	0	.0	0	.0	0	.0	0	.0
MALE	0	.0	0	.0	0	.0	0	.0	0	.0	0	.0	0	.0
TOTAL	0	.0	0	.0	0	.0	0	.0	0	.0	0	.0	0	.0
FEMALE	0	.0	0	.0	0	.0	0	.0	0	.0	0	.0	0	.0
MALE	0	.0	0	.0	0	.0	0	.0	0	.0	0	.0	0	.0
GRADUATE:														
FULL-TIME	0	.0	0	.0	0	.0	0	.0	0	.0	0	.0	0	.0
FEMALE	0	.0	0	.0	0	.0	0	.0	0	.0	0	.0	0	.0
MALE	0	.0	0	.0	0	.0	0	.0	0	.0	0	.0	0	.0
PART-TIME	0	.0	0	.0	0	.0	0	.0	0	.0	0	.0	0	.0
FEMALE	0	.0	0	.0	0	.0	0	.0	0	.0	0	.0	0	.0
MALE	0	.0	0	.0	0	.0	0	.0	0	.0	0	.0	0	.0
TOTAL	0	.0	0	.0	0	.0	0	.0	0	.0	0	.0	0	.0
FEMALE	0	.0	0	.0	0	.0	0	.0	0	.0	0	.0	0	.0
MALE	0	.0	0	.0	0	.0	0	.0	0	.0	0	.0	0	.0
PROFESSIONAL:														
FULL-TIME	4	1.2	16	4.8	5	1.5	2	.6	27	8.0	309	92.0	0	.0
FEMALE	2	4.4	6	13.3	2	4.4	0	.0	10	22.2	35	77.8	0	.0
MALE	2	.7	10	3.4	3	1.0	2	.7	17	5.8	274	94.2	0	.0
PART-TIME	0	.0	0	.0	0	.0	0	.0	0	.0	0	.0	0	.0
FEMALE	0	.0	0	.0	0	.0	0	.0	0	.0	0	.0	0	.0
MALE	0	.0	0	.0	0	.0	0	.0	0	.0	0	.0	0	.0
TOTAL	4	1.2	16	4.8	5	1.5	2	.6	27	8.0	309	92.0	0	.0
FEMALE	2	4.4	6	13.3	2	4.4	0	.0	10	22.2	35	77.8	0	.0
MALE	2	.7	10	3.4	3	1.0	2	.7	17	5.8	274	94.2	0	.0
UNG+GRAD+PROF:														
FULL-TIME	4	1.2	16	4.8	5	1.5	2	.6	27	8.0	309	92.0	0	.0
FEMALE	2	4.4	6	13.3	2	4.4	0	.0	10	22.2	35	77.8	0	.0
MALE	2	.7	10	3.4	3	1.0	2	.7	17	5.8	274	94.2	0	.0
PART-TIME	0	.0	0	.0	0	.0	0	.0	0	.0	0	.0	0	.0
FEMALE	0	.0	0	.0	0	.0	0	.0	0	.0	0	.0	0	.0
MALE	0	.0	0	.0	0	.0	0	.0	0	.0	0	.0	0	.0
TOTAL	4	1.2	16	4.8	5	1.5	2	.6	27	8.0	309	92.0	0	.0
FEMALE	2	4.4	6	13.3	2	4.4	0	.0	10	22.2	35	77.8	0	.0
MALE	2	.7	10	3.4	3	1.0	2	.7	17	5.8	274	94.2	0	.0
UNCLASSIFIED:														
TOTAL	0	.0	0	.0	0	.0	0	.0	0	.0	0	.0	0	.0
FEMALE	0	.0	0	.0	0	.0	0	.0	0	.0	0	.0	0	.0
MALE	0	.0	0	.0	0	.0	0	.0	0	.0	0	.0	0	.0
TOTAL ENROLLMENT:														
TOTAL	4	1.2	16	4.8	5	1.5	2	.6	27	8.0	309	92.0	0	.0
FEMALE	2	4.4	6	13.3	2	4.4	0	.0	10	22.2	35	77.8	0	.0
MALE	2	.7	10	3.4	3	1.0	2	.7	17	5.8	274	94.2	0	.0
OHIO (2 INSTITUTIONS)														
UNDERGRADUATES:														
FULL-TIME	0	.0	0	.0	0	.0	0	.0	0	.0	0	.0	0	.0
FEMALE	0	.0	0	.0	0	.0	0	.0	0	.0	0	.0	0	.0
MALE	0	.0	0	.0	0	.0	0	.0	0	.0	0	.0	0	.0
PART-TIME	0	.0	0	.0	0	.0	0	.0	0	.0	0	.0	0	.0
FEMALE	0	.0	0	.0	0	.0	0	.0	0	.0	0	.0	0	.0
MALE	0	.0	0	.0	0	.0	0	.0	0	.0	0	.0	0	.0
TOTAL	0	.0	0	.0	0	.0	0	.0	0	.0	0	.0	0	.0
FEMALE	0	.0	0	.0	0	.0	0	.0	0	.0	0	.0	0	.0
MALE	0	.0	0	.0	0	.0	0	.0	0	.0	0	.0	0	.0
GRADUATE:														
FULL-TIME	0	.0	0	.0	0	.0	0	.0	0	.0	0	.0	0	.0
FEMALE	0	.0	0	.0	0	.0	0	.0	0	.0	0	.0	0	.0
MALE	0	.0	0	.0	0	.0	0	.0	0	.0	0	.0	0	.0
PART-TIME	0	.0	0	.0	0	.0	0	.0	0	.0	0	.0	0	.0
FEMALE	0	.0	0	.0	0	.0	0	.0	0	.0	0	.0	0	.0
MALE	0	.0	0	.0	0	.0	0	.0	0	.0	0	.0	0	.0
TOTAL	0	.0	0	.0	0	.0	0	.0	0	.0	0	.0	0	.0
FEMALE	0	.0	0	.0	0	.0	0	.0	0	.0	0	.0	0	.0
MALE	0	.0	0	.0	0	.0	0	.0	0	.0	0	.0	0	.0
PROFESSIONAL:														
FULL-TIME	0	.0	16	1.6	6	.6	4	.4	26	2.6	965	96.7	7	.7
FEMALE	0	.0	6	4.0	0	.0	1	.7	7	4.7	143	95.3	0	.0
MALE	0	.0	10	1.2	6	.7	3	.4	19	2.2	822	96.9	7	.8

ASIAN OR PACIFIC ISLANDER		HISPANIC		TOTAL MINORITY		WHITE NON-HISPANIC		NON-RESIDENT ALIEN		TOTAL
NUMBER	%	NUMBER	%	NUMBER	%	NUMBER	%	NUMBER	%	NUMBER
0	.0	0	.0	0	.0	1	100.0	0	.0	1
0	.0	0	.0	0	.0	0	.0	0	.0	0
0	.0	0	.0	0	.0	1	100.0	0	.0	1
6	.6	4	.4	26	2.6	966	96.7	7	.7	959
0	.0	1	.7	7	4.7	143	95.3	0	.0	150
6	.7	3	.4	19	2.2	823	96.9	7	.8	849
6	.6	4	.4	26	2.6	965	96.7	7	.7	998
0	.0	1	.7	7	4.7	143	95.3	0	.0	150
6	.7	3	.4	19	2.2	822	96.9	7	.8	848
0	.0	0	.0	0	.0	1	100.0	0	.0	1
0	.0	0	.0	0	.0	0	.0	0	.0	0
0	.0	0	.0	0	.0	1	100.0	0	.0	1
6	.6	4	.4	26	2.6	966	96.7	7	.7	959
0	.0	1	.7	7	4.7	143	95.3	0	.0	150
6	.7	3	.4	19	2.2	823	96.9	7	.8	849
0	.0	0	.0	0	.0	0	.0	0	.0	0
0	.0	0	.0	0	.0	0	.0	0	.0	0
0	.0	0	.0	0	.0	0	.0	0	.0	0
6	.6	4	.4	26	2.6	966	96.7	7	.7	959
0	.0	1	.7	7	4.7	143	95.3	0	.0	150
6	.7	3	.4	19	2.2	823	96.9	7	.8	849
0	.0	0	.0	0	.0	0	.0	0	.0	0
0	.0	0	.0	0	.0	0	.0	0	.0	0
0	.0	0	.0	0	.0	0	.0	0	.0	0
0	.0	0	.0	0	.0	0	.0	0	.0	0
0	.0	0	.0	0	.0	0	.0	0	.0	0
0	.0	0	.0	0	.0	0	.0	0	.0	0
0	.0	0	.0	0	.0	0	.0	0	.0	0
0	.0	0	.0	0	.0	0	.0	0	.0	0
0	.0	0	.0	0	.0	0	.0	0	.0	0
0	.0	0	.0	0	.0	0	.0	0	.0	0
0	.0	0	.0	0	.0	0	.0	0	.0	0
0	.0	0	.0	0	.0	0	.0	0	.0	0
0	.0	0	.0	0	.0	0	.0	0	.0	0
0	.0	0	.0	0	.0	0	.0	0	.0	0
0	.0	0	.0	0	.0	0	.0	0	.0	0
0	.0	0	.0	0	.0	0	.0	0	.0	0
4	1.6	2	.8	18	7.3	228	92.7	0	.0	246
2	10.5	0	.0	4	21.1	15	78.9	0	.0	19
2	.9	2	.9	14	6.2	213	93.8	0	.0	227
0	.0	0	.0	0	.0	0	.0	0	.0	0
0	.0	0	.0	0	.0	0	.0	0	.0	0
0	.0	0	.0	0	.0	0	.0	0	.0	0
4	1.6	2	.8	18	7.3	228	92.7	0	.0	246
2	10.5	0	.0	4	21.1	15	78.9	0	.0	19
2	.9	2	.9	14	6.2	213	93.8	0	.0	227
4	1.6	2	.8	18	7.3	228	92.7	0	.0	246
2	10.5	0	.0	4	21.1	15	78.9	0	.0	19
2	.9	2	.9	14	6.2	213	93.8	0	.0	227
0	.0	0	.0	0	.0	0	.0	0	.0	0
0	.0	0	.0	0	.0	0	.0	0	.0	0
0	.0	0	.0	0	.0	0	.0	0	.0	0
4	1.6	2	.8	18	7.3	228	92.7	0	.0	246
2	10.5	0	.0	4	21.1	15	78.9	0	.0	19
2	.9	2	.9	14	6.2	213	93.8	0	.0	227
0	.0	0	.0	0	.0	0	.0	0	.0	0
0	.0	0	.0	0	.0	0	.0	0	.0	0
0	.0	0	.0	0	.0	0	.0	0	.0	0
4	1.6	2	.8	18	7.3	228	92.7	0	.0	246
2	10.5	0	.0	4	21.1	15	78.9	0	.0	19
2	.9	2	.9	14	6.2	213	93.8	0	.0	227

TABLE 17 -   TOTAL ENROLLMENT IN INSTITUTIONS OF HIGHER EDUCATION FOR SELECTED MAJOR FIELDS OF STUDY AND LEVEL OF ENROLLMENT
             BY RACE, ETHNICITY, AND SEX: STATE: 1978

MAJOR FIELD 1204 - DENTISTRY

	AMERICAN INDIAN ALASKAN NATIVE		BLACK NON-HISPANIC		ASIAN OR PACIFIC ISLANDER		HISPANIC		TOTAL MINORITY		WHITE NON-HISPANIC		NON-RESIDENT ALIEN		TO
	NUMBER	%	NUMBER	%	NUMBER	%	NUMBER	%	NUMBER	%	NUMBER	%	NUMBER	%	NU
OREGON	(	1 INSTITUTIONS)													
UNDERGRADUATES:															
FULL-TIME	0	.0	0	.0	0	.0	0	.0	0	.0	0	.0	0	.0	
FEMALE	0	.0	0	.0	0	.0	0	.0	0	.0	0	.0	0	.0	
MALE	0	.0	0	.0	0	.0	0	.0	0	.0	0	.0	0	.0	
PART-TIME	0	.0	0	.0	0	.0	0	.0	0	.0	0	.0	0	.0	
FEMALE	0	.0	0	.0	0	.0	0	.0	0	.0	0	.0	0	.0	
MALE	0	.0	0	.0	0	.0	0	.0	0	.0	0	.0	0	.0	
TOTAL	0	.0	0	.0	0	.0	0	.0	0	.0	0	.0		.0	
FEMALE	0	.0	0	.0	0	.0	0	.0	0	.0	0	.0	0	.0	
MALE	0	.0	0	.0	0	.0	0	.0	0	.0	0	.0	0	.0	
GRADUATE:															
FULL-TIME	0	.0	0	.0	0	.0	0	.0	0	.0	0	.0	0	.0	
FEMALE	0	.0	0	.0	0	.0	0	.0	0	.0	0	.0	0	.0	
MALE	0	.0	0	.0	0	.0	0	.0	0	.0	0	.0	0	.0	
PART-TIME	0	.0	0	.0	0	.0	0	.0	0	.0	0	.0	0	.0	
FEMALE	0	.0	0	.0	0	.0	0	.0	0	.0	0	.0	0	.0	
MALE	0	.0	0	.0	0	.0	0	.0	0	.0	0	.0	0	.0	
TOTAL	0	.0	0	.0	0	.0	0	.0	0	.0	0	.0	0	.0	
FEMALE	0	.0	0	.0	0	.0	0	.0	0	.0	0	.0	0	.0	
MALE	0	.0	0	.0	0	.0	0	.0	0	.0	0	.0	0	.0	
PROFESSIONAL:															
FULL-TIME	1	.3	6	1.9	12	3.8	8	2.5	27	8.6	287	91.4	0	.0	
FEMALE	0	.0	2	6.1	2	6.1	1	3.0	5	15.2	28	84.8	0	.0	
MALE	1	.4	4	1.4	10	3.6	7	2.5	22	7.8	259	92.2	0	.0	
PART-TIME	0	.0	0	.0	0	.0	0	.0	0	.0	0	.0	0	.0	
FEMALE	0	.0	0	.0	0	.0	0	.0	0	.0	0	.0	0	.0	
MALE	0	.0	0	.0	0	.0	0	.0	0	.0	0	.0	0	.0	
TOTAL	1	.3	6	1.9	12	3.8	8	2.5	27	8.6	287	91.4	0	.0	
FEMALE	0	.0	2	6.1	2	6.1	1	3.0	5	15.2	28	84.8	0	.0	
MALE	1	.4	4	1.4	10	3.6	7	2.5	22	7.8	259	92.2	0	.0	
UNG+GRAD+PROF:															
FULL-TIME	1	.3	6	1.9	12	3.8	8	2.5	27	8.6	287	91.4	0	.0	
FEMALE	0	.0	2	6.1	2	6.1	1	3.0	5	15.2	28	84.8	0	.0	
MALE	1	.4	4	1.4	10	3.6	7	2.5	22	7.8	259	92.2	0	.0	
PART-TIME	0	.0	0	.0	0	.0	0	.0	0	.0	0	.0	0	.0	
FEMALE	0	.0	0	.0	0	.0	0	.0	0	.0	0	.0	0	.0	
MALE	0	.0	0	.0	0	.0	0	.0	0	.0	0	.0	0	.0	
TOTAL	1	.3	6	1.9	12	3.8	8	2.5	27	8.6	287	91.4	0	.0	
FEMALE	0	.0	2	6.1	2	6.1	1	3.0	5	15.2	28	84.8	0	.0	
MALE	1	.4	4	1.4	10	3.6	7	2.5	22	7.8	259	92.2	0	.0	
UNCLASSIFIED:															
TOTAL	0	.0	0	.0	0	.0	0	.0	0	.0	0	.0	0	.0	
FEMALE	0	.0	0	.0	0	.0	0	.0	0	.0	0	.0	0	.0	
MALE	0	.0	0	.0	0	.0	0	.0	0	.0	0	.0	0	.0	
TOTAL ENROLLMENT:															
TOTAL	1	.3	6	1.9	12	3.8	8	2.5	27	8.6	287	91.4	0	.0	
FEMALE	0	.0	2	6.1	2	6.1	1	3.0	5	15.2	28	84.8	0	.0	
MALE	1	.4	4	1.4	10	3.6	7	2.5	22	7.8	259	92.2	0	.0	
PENNSYLVANIA	(	3 INSTITUTIONS)													
UNDERGRADUATES:															
FULL-TIME	0	.0	0	.0	0	.0	0	.0	0	.0	0	.0	0	.0	
FEMALE	0	.0	0	.0	0	.0	0	.0	0	.0	0	.0	0	.0	
MALE	0	.0	0	.0	0	.0	0	.0	0	.0	0	.0	0	.0	
PART-TIME	0	.0	0	.0	0	.0	0	.0	0	.0	0	.0	0	.0	
FEMALE	0	.0	0	.0	0	.0	0	.0	0	.0	0	.0	0	.0	
MALE	0	.0	0	.0	0	.0	0	.0	0	.0	0	.0	0	.0	
TOTAL	0	.0	0	.0	0	.0	0	.0	0	.0	0	.0		.0	
FEMALE	0	.0	0	.0	0	.0	0	.0	0	.0	0	.0		.0	
MALE	0	.0	0	.0	0	.0	0	.0	0	.0	0	.0	0	.0	
GRADUATE:															
FULL-TIME	0	.0	0	.0	0	.0	0	.0	0	.0	0	.0	0	.0	
FEMALE	0	.0	0	.0	0	.0	0	.0	0	.0	0	.0	0	.0	
MALE	0	.0	0	.0	0	.0	0	.0	0	.0	0	.0	0	.0	
PART-TIME	0	.0	0	.0	0	.0	0	.0	0	.0	0	.0	0	.0	
FEMALE	0	.0	0	.0	0	.0	0	.0	0	.0	0	.0	0	.0	
MALE	0	.0	0	.0	0	.0	0	.0	0	.0	0	.0	0	.0	
TOTAL	0	.0	0	.0	0	.0	0	.0	0	.0	0	.0		.0	
FEMALE	0	.0	0	.0	0	.0	0	.0	0	.0	0	.0		.0	
MALE	0	.0	0	.0	0	.0	0	.0	0	.0	0	.0	0	.0	
PROFESSIONAL:															
FULL-TIME	4	.2	42	2.3	25	1.4	14	.8	85	4.7	1,715	94.2	20	1.1	
FEMALE	0	.0	21	7.4	7	2.5	5	1.8	33	11.7	248	87.6	2	.7	
MALE	4	.3	21	1.4	18	1.2	9	.6	52	3.4	1,467	95.4	18	1.2	

NS OF HIGHER EDUCATION FOR SELECTED MAJOR FIELDS OF STUDY AND LEVEL OF ENROLLMENT
TATE, 1978

ASIAN OR C PACIFIC ISLANDER		HISPANIC		TOTAL MINORITY		WHITE NON-HISPANIC		NON-RESIDENT ALIEN		TOTAL
NUMBER	%	NUMBER	%	NUMBER	%	NUMBER	%	NUMBER	%	NUMBER
0	.0	0	.0	0	.0	0	.0	0	.0	0
0	.0	0	.0	0	.0	0	.0	0	.0	0
0	.0	0	.0	0	.0	0	.0	0	.0	0
25	1.4	14	.8	85	4.7	1,715	94.2	20	1.1	1,820
7	2.5	5	1.8	33	11.7	248	87.6	2	.7	283
18	1.2	9	.6	52	3.4	1,467	95.4	18	1.2	1,537
25	1.4	14	.8	85	4.7	1,715	94.2	20	1.1	1,820
7	2.5	5	1.8	33	11.7	248	87.6	2	.7	283
18	1.2	9	.6	52	3.4	1,467	95.4	18	1.2	1,537
0	.0	0	.0	0	.0	0	.0	0	.0	0
0	.0	0	.0	0	.0	0	.0	0	.0	0
0	.0	0	.0	0	.0	0	.0	0	.0	0
25	1.4	14	.8	85	4.7	1,715	94.2	20	1.1	1,820
7	2.5	5	1.8	33	11.7	248	87.6	2	.7	283
18	1.2	9	.6	52	3.4	1,467	95.4	18	1.2	1,537
0	.0	0	.0	0	.0	0	.0	0	.0	0
0	.0	0	.0	0	.0	0	.0	0	.0	0
0	.0	0	.0	0	.0	0	.0	0	.0	0
25	1.4	14	.8	85	4.7	1,715	94.2	20	1.1	1,820
7	2.5	5	1.8	33	11.7	248	87.6	2	.7	283
18	1.2	9	.6	52	3.4	1,467	95.4	18	1.2	1,537
0	.0	0	.0	0	.0	0	.0	0	.0	0
0	.0	0	.0	0	.0	0	.0	0	.0	0
0	.0	0	.0	0	.0	0	.0	0	.0	0
0	.0	0	.0	0	.0	0	.0	0	.0	0
0	.0	0	.0	0	.0	0	.0	0	.0	0
0	.0	0	.0	0	.0	0	.0	0	.0	0
0	.0	0	.0	0	.0	0	.0	0	.0	0
0	.0	0	.0	0	.0	0	.0	0	.0	0
0	.0	0	.0	0	.0	0	.0	0	.0	0
0	.0	0	.0	0	.0	0	.0	0	.0	0
0	.0	0	.0	0	.0	0	.0	0	.0	0
0	.0	0	.0	0	.0	0	.0	0	.0	0
0	.0	0	.0	0	.0	0	.0	0	.0	0
0	.0	0	.0	0	.0	0	.0	0	.0	0
0	.0	0	.0	0	.0	0	.0	0	.0	0
0	.0	0	.0	0	.0	0	.0	0	.0	0
0	.0	0	.0	0	.0	0	.0	0	.0	0
0	.0	0	.0	0	.0	0	.0	0	.0	0
5	.7	3	.4	182	25.1	541	74.5	3	.4	726
1	1.0	0	.0	56	53.3	49	46.7	0	.0	105
4	.6	3	.5	126	20.3	492	79.2	3	.5	621
0	.0	1	16.7	4	66.7	1	16.7	1	16.7	6
0	.0	0	.0	1	100.0	0	.0	0	.0	1
0	.0	1	20.0	3	60.0	1	20.0	1	20.0	5
5	.7	4	.5	186	25.4	542	74.0	4	.5	732
1	.9	0	.0	57	53.8	49	46.2	0	.0	106
4	.6	4	.6	129	20.6	493	78.8	4	.6	626
5	.7	3	.4	182	25.1	541	74.5	3	.4	726
1	1.0	0	.0	56	53.3	49	46.7	0	.0	105
4	.6	3	.5	126	20.3	492	79.2	3	.5	621
0	.0	1	16.7	4	66.7	1	16.7	1	16.7	6
0	.0	0	.0	1	100.0	0	.0	0	.0	1
0	.0	1	20.0	3	60.0	1	20.0	1	20.0	5
5	.7	4	.5	186	25.4	542	74.0	4	.5	732
1	.9	0	.0	57	53.8	49	46.2	0	.0	106
4	.6	4	.6	129	20.6	493	78.8	4	.6	626
0	.0	0	.0	0	.0	0	.0	0	.0	0
0	.0	0	.0	0	.0	0	.0	0	.0	0
0	.0	0	.0	0	.0	0	.0	0	.0	0
5	.7	4	.5	186	25.4	542	74.0	4	.5	732
1	.9	0	.0	57	53.8	49	46.2	0	.0	106
4	.6	4	.6	129	20.6	493	78.8	4	.6	626

MAJOR FIELD 1204 - DENTISTRY

	AMERICAN INDIAN ALASKAN NATIVE		BLACK NON-HISPANIC		ASIAN OR PACIFIC ISLANDER		HISPANIC		TOTAL MINORITY		WHITE NON-HISPANIC		NON-RESIDENT ALIEN		T.
	NUMBER	%	NUMBER	%	NUMBER	%	NUMBER	%	NUMBER	%	NUMBER	%	NUMBER	%	N
TEXAS	(	3 INSTITUTIONS)													
UNDERGRADUATES:															
FULL-TIME	0	.0	0	.0	0	.0	0	.0	0	.0	0	.0	0	.0	
FEMALE	0	.0	0	.0	0	.0	0	.0	0	.0	0	.0	0	.0	
MALE	0	.0	0	.0	0	.0	0	.0	0	.0	0	.0	0	.0	
PART-TIME	0	.0	0	.0	0	.0	0	.0	0	.0	0	.0	0	.0	
FEMALE	0	.0	0	.0	0	.0	0	.0	0	.0	0	.0	0	.0	
MALE	0	.0	0	.0	0	.0	0	.0	0	.0	0	.0	0	.0	
TOTAL	0	.0	0	.0	0	.0	0	.0	0	.0	0	.0	0	.0	
FEMALE	0	.0	0	.0	0	.0	0	.0	0	.0	0	.0	0	.0	
MALE	0	.0	0	.0	0	.0	0	.0	0	.0	0	.0	0	.0	
GRADUATE:															
FULL-TIME	0	.0	0	.0	0	.0	0	.0	0	.0	0	.0	0	.0	
FEMALE	0	.0	0	.0	0	.0	0	.0	0	.0	0	.0	0	.0	
MALE	0	.0	0	.0	0	.0	0	.0	0	.0	0	.0	0	.0	
PART-TIME	0	.0	0	.0	0	.0	0	.0	0	.0	0	.0	0	.0	
FEMALE	0	.0	0	.0	0	.0	0	.0	0	.0	0	.0	0	.0	
MALE	0	.0	0	.0	0	.0	0	.0	0	.0	0	.0	0	.0	
TOTAL	0	.0	0	.0	0	.0	0	.0	0	.0	0	.0	0	.0	
FEMALE	0	.0	0	.0	0	.0	0	.0	0	.0	0	.0	0	.0	
MALE	0	.0	0	.0	0	.0	0	.0	0	.0	0	.0	0	.0	
PROFESSIONAL:															
FULL-TIME	5	.4	26	1.8	19	1.3	71	5.0	121	8.5	1,294	91.4	1	.1	
FEMALE	1	.6	10	5.6	5	2.8	17	9.4	33	18.3	147	81.7	0	.0	
MALE	4	.3	16	1.3	14	1.1	54	4.4	88	7.1	1,147	92.8	1	.1	
PART-TIME	0	.0	0	.0	0	.0	0	.0	0	.0	5	100.0	0	.0	
FEMALE	0	.0	0	.0	0	.0	0	.0	0	.0	2	100.0	0	.0	
MALE	0	.0	0	.0	0	.0	0	.0	0	.0	3	100.0	0	.0	
TOTAL	5	.4	26	1.8	19	1.3	71	5.0	121	8.5	1,299	91.4	1	.1	
FEMALE	1	.5	10	5.5	5	2.7	17	9.3	33	18.1	149	81.9	0	.0	
MALE	4	.3	16	1.3	14	1.1	54	4.4	88	7.1	1,150	92.8	1	.1	
UND+GRAD+PROF:															
FULL-TIME	5	.4	26	1.8	19	1.3	71	5.0	121	8.5	1,294	91.4	1	.1	
FEMALE	1	.6	10	5.6	5	2.8	17	9.4	33	18.3	147	81.7	0	.0	
MALE	4	.3	16	1.3	14	1.1	54	4.4	88	7.1	1,147	92.8	1	.1	
PART-TIME	0	.0	0	.0	0	.0	0	.0	0	.0	5	100.0	0	.0	
FEMALE	0	.0	0	.0	0	.0	0	.0	0	.0	2	100.0	0	.0	
MALE	0	.0	0	.0	0	.0	0	.0	0	.0	3	100.0	0	.0	
TOTAL	5	.4	26	1.8	19	1.3	71	5.0	121	8.5	1,299	91.4	1	.1	
FEMALE	1	.5	10	5.5	5	2.7	17	9.3	33	18.1	149	81.9	0	.0	
MALE	4	.3	16	1.3	14	1.1	54	4.4	88	7.1	1,150	92.8	1	.1	
UNCLASSIFIED:															
TOTAL	0	.0	0	.0	0	.0	0	.0	0	.0	0	.0	0	.0	
FEMALE	0	.0	0	.0	0	.0	0	.0	0	.0	0	.0	0	.0	
MALE	0	.0	0	.0	0	.0	0	.0	0	.0	0	.0	0	.0	
TOTAL ENROLLMENT:															
TOTAL	5	.4	26	1.8	19	1.3	71	5.0	121	8.5	1,299	91.4	1	.1	
FEMALE	1	.5	10	5.5	5	2.7	17	9.3	33	18.1	149	81.9	0	.0	
MALE	4	.3	16	1.3	14	1.1	54	4.4	88	7.1	1,150	92.8	1	.1	
VIRGINIA	(	1 INSTITUTIONS)													
UNDERGRADUATES:															
FULL-TIME	0	.0	0	.0	0	.0	0	.0	0	.0	0	.0	0	.0	
FEMALE	0	.0	0	.0	0	.0	0	.0	0	.0	0,	.0	0	.0	
MALE	0	.0	0	.0	0	.0	0	.0	0	.0	0	.0	0	.0	
PART-TIME	0	.0	0	.0	0	.0	0	.0	0	.0	0	.0	0	.0	
FEMALE	0	.0	0	.0	0	.0	0	.0	0	.0	0	.0	0	.0	
MALE	0	.0	0	.0	0	.0	0	.0	0	.0	0	.0	0	.0	
TOTAL	0	.0	0	.0	0	.0	0	.0	0	.0	0	.0	0	.0	
FEMALE	0	.0	0	.0	0	.0	0	.0	0	.0	0	.0	0	.0	
MALE	0	.0	0	.0	0	.0	0	.0	0	.0	0	.0	0	.0	
GRADUATE:															
FULL-TIME	0	.0	0	.0	0	.0	0	.0	0	.0	0	.0	0	.0	
FEMALE	0	.0	0	.0	0	.0	0	.0	0	.0	0	.0	0	.0	
MALE	0	.0	0	.0	0	.0	0	.0	0	.0	0	.0	0	.0	
PART-TIME	0	.0	0	.0	0	.0	0	.0	0	.0	0	.0	0	.0	
FEMALE	0	.0	0	.0	0	.0	0	.0	0	.0	0	.0	0	.0	
MALE	0	.0	0	.0	0	.0	0	.0	0	.0	0	.0	0	.0	
TOTAL	0	.0	0	.0	0	.0	0	.0	0	.0	0	.0	0	.0	
FEMALE	0	.0	0	.0	0	.0	0	.0	0	.0	0	.0	0	.0	
MALE	0	.0	0	.0	0	.0	0	.0	0	.0	0	.0	0	.0	
PROFESSIONAL:															
FULL-TIME	0	.0	8	1.8	12	2.8	3	.7	23	5.3	412	94.7	0	.0	
FEMALE	0	.0	2	2.4	4	4.8	1	1.2	7	8.4	76	91.6	0	.0	
MALE	0	.0	6	1.7	8	2.3	2	.6	16	4.5	336	95.5	0	.0	

DENTISTRY

INDIAN NATIVE	BLACK NON-HISPANIC		ASIAN OR PACIFIC ISLANDER		HISPANIC		TOTAL MINORITY		WHITE NON-HISPANIC		NON-RESIDENT ALIEN		TOTAL
%	NUMBER	%	NUMBER	%	NUMBER	%	NUMBER	%	NUMBER	%	NUMBER	%	NUMBER
CONTINUED													
.0	0	.0	0	.0	0	.0	0	.0	0	.0	0	.0	0
.0	0	.0	0	.0	0	.0	0	.0	0	.0	0	.0	0
.0	0	.0	0	.0	0	.0	0	.0	0	.0	0	,0	0
.0	8	1.8	12	2.8	3	.7	23	5.3	412	94.7	0	.0	435
.0	2	2.4	4	4.8	1	1.2	7	8.4	76	91.6	0	.0	83
.0	6	1.7	8	2.3	2	.6	16	4.5	336	95.5	0	.0	352
.0	8	1.8	12	2.8	3	.7	23	5.3	412	94.7	0	.0	435
.0	2	2.4	4	4.8	1	1.2	7	8.4	76	91.6	0	.0	83
.0	6	1.7	8	2.3	2	.6	16	4.5	336	95.5	0	.0	352
.0	0	.0	0	.0	0	.0	0	.0	0	.0	0	.0	0
.0	0	.0	0	.0	0	.0	0	.0	0	.0	0	.0	0
.0	0	.0	0	.0	0	.0	0	.0	0	.0	0	.0	0
.0	8	1.8	12	2.8	3	.7	23	5.3	412	94.7	0	.0	435
.0	2	2.4	4	4.8	1	1.2	7	8.4	76	91.6	0	.0	83
.0	6	1.7	8	2.3	2	.6	16	4.5	336	95.5	0	.0	352
.0	0	.0	0	.0	0	.0	0	.0	0	.0	0	.0	0
.0	0	.0	0	.0	0	.0	0	.0	0	.0	0	.0	0
.0	0	.0	0	.0	0	.0	0	.0	0	.0	0	.0	0
.0	8	1.8	12	2.8	3	.7	23	5.3	412	94.7	0	.0	435
.0	2	2.4	4	4.8	1	1.2	7	8.4	76	91.6	0	.0	83
.0	6	1.7	8	2.3	2	.6	16	4.5	336	95.5	0	.0	352
(1 INSTITUTIONS)													
.0	0	.0	0	.0	0	.0	0	.0	0	.0	0	.0	0
.0	0	.0	0	.0	0	.0	0	.0	0	.0	0	.0	0
.0	0	.0	0	.0	0	.0	0	.0	0	.0	0	.0	0
.0	0	.0	0	.0	0	.0	0	.0	0	.0	0	.0	0
.0	0	.0	0	.0	0	.0	0	.0	0	.0	0	.0	0
.0	0	.0	0	.0	0	.0	0	.0	0	.0	0	.0	0
.0	0	.0	0	.0	0	.0	0	.0	0	.0	0	.0	0
.0	0	.0	0	.0	0	.0	0	.0	0	.0	0	.0	0
.0	0	.0.	0	.0	0	.0	0	.0	0	.0	0	.0	0
.0	0	.0	0	.0	0	.0	0	.0	0	.0	0	.0	0
.0	0	.0	0	.0	0	.0	0	.0	0	.0	0	.0	0
.0	0	.0	0	.0	0	.0	0	.0	0	.0	0	.0	0
.0	0	.0	0	.0	0	.0	0	.0	0	.0	0	.0	0
.0	0	.0	0	.0	0	.0	0	.0	0	.0	0	.0	0
.0	0	.0	0	.0	0	.0	0	.0	0	.0	0	.0	0
.3	4	1.0	11	2.8	11	2.8	27	6.8	366	92.4	3	.8	396
.0	1	1.5	1	1.5	1	1.5	3	4.4	64	94.1	1	1.5	68
.3	3	.9	10	3.0	10	3.0	24	7.3	302	92.1	2	.6	328
20.0	0	.0	0	.0	0	.0	1	20.0	4	80.0	0	.0	5
.0	0	.0	0	.0	0	.0	0	.0	0	.0	0	.0	0
20.0	0	.0	0	.0	0	.0	1	20.0	4	80.0	0	.0	5
.5	4	1.0	11	2.7	11	2.7	28	7.0	370	92.3	3	.7	401
.0	1	1.5	1	1.5	1	1.5	3	4.4	64	94.1	1	1.5	68
.6	3	.9	10	3.0	10	3.0	25	7.5	306	91.9	2	.6	333
.3	4	1.0	11	2.8	11	2.8	27	6.8	366	92.4	3	.8	396
.0	1	1.5	1	1.5	1	1.5	3	4.4	64	94.1	1	1.5	68
.3	3	.9	10	3.0	10	3.0	24	7.3	302	92.1	2	.6	328
20.0	0	.0	0	.0	0	.0	1	20.0	4	80.0	0	.0	5
.0	0	.0	0	.0	0	.0	0	.0	0	.0	0	.0	0
20.0	0	.0	0	.0	0	.0	1	20.0	4	80.0	0	.0	5
.5	4	1.0	11	2.7	11	2.7	28	7.0	370	92.3	3	.7	401
.0	1	1.5	1	1.5	1	1.5	3	4.4	64	94.1	1	1.5	68
.6	3	.9	10	3.0	10	3.0	25	7.5	306	91.9	2	.6	333
.0	0	.0	0	.0	0	.0	0	.0	0	.0	0	.0	0
.0	0	.0	0	.0	0	.0	0	.0	0	.0	0	.0	0
.0	0	.0	0	.0	0	.0	0	.0	0	.0	0	.0	0
.5	4	1.0	11	2.7	11	2.7	28	7.0	370	92.3	3	.7	401
.0	1	1.5	1	1.5	1	1.5	3	4.4	64	94.1	1	1.5	68
.6	3	.9	10	3.0	10	3.0	25	7.5	306	91.9	2	.6	333

MAJOR FIELD 1204 - DENTISTRY

	AMERICAN INDIAN ALASKAN NATIVE		BLACK NON-HISPANIC		ASIAN OR PACIFIC ISLANDER		HISPANIC		TOTAL MINORITY		WHITE NON-HISPANIC		NON-RESIDENT ALIEN		T	
	NUMBER	%	NUMBER	%	NUMBER	%	NUMBER	%	NUMBER	%	NUMBER	%	NUMBER	%	N
WEST VIRGINIA	(	1 INSTITUTIONS)														
UNDERGRADUATES:																
FULL-TIME																
FEMALE	0	.0	0	.0	0	.0	0	.0	0	.0	0	.0	0	.0	
MALE	0	.0	0	.0	0	.0	0	.0	0	.0	0	.0	0	.0	
PART-TIME																
FEMALE	0	.0	0	.0	0	.0	0	.0	0	.0	0	.0	0	.0	
MALE	0	.0	0	.0	0	.0	0	.0	0	.0	0	.0	0	.0	
TOTAL																
FEMALE	0	.0	0	.0	0	.0	0	.0	0	.0	0	.0	0	.0	
MALE	0	.0	0	.0	0	.0	0	.0	0	.0	0	.0	0	.0	
GRADUATE:																
FULL-TIME																
FEMALE	0	.0	0	.0	0	.0	0	.0	0	.0	0	.0	0	.0	
MALE	0	.0	0	.0	0	.0	0	.0	0	.0	0	.0	0	.0	
PART-TIME																
FEMALE	0	.0	0	.0	0	.0	0	.0	0	.0	0	.0	0	.0	
MALE	0	.0	0	.0	0	.0	0	.0	0	.0	0	.0	0	.0	
TOTAL																
FEMALE	0	.0	0	.0	0	.0	0	.0	0	.0	0	.0	0	.0	
MALE	0	.0	0	.0	0	.0	0	.0	0	.0	0	.0	0	.0	
PROFESSIONAL:																
FULL-TIME	2	.9	1	.4	0	.0	1	.4	4	1.8	220	98.2	0	.0	
FEMALE	1	5.0	0	.0	0	.0	0	.0	1	5.0	19	95.0	0	.0	
MALE	1	.5	1	.5	0	.0	1	.5	3	1.5	201	98.5	0	.0	
PART-TIME	0	.0	0	.0	0	.0	0	.0	0	.0	14	100.0	0	.0	
FEMALE	0	.0	0	.0	0	.0	0	.0	0	.0	2	100.0	0	.0	
MALE	0	.0	0	.0	0	.0	0	.0	0	.0	12	100.0	0	.0	
TOTAL	2	.8	1	.4	0	.0	1	.4	4	1.7	234	98.3	0	.0	
FEMALE	1	4.5	0	.0	0	.0	0	.0	1	4.5	21	95.5	0	.0	
MALE	1	.5	1	.5	0	.0	1	.5	3	1.4	213	98.6	0	.0	
UND+GRAD+PROF:																
FULL-TIME	2	.9	1	.4	0	.0	1	.4	4	1.8	220	98.2	0	.0	
FEMALE	1	5.0	0	.0	0	.0	0	.0	1	5.0	19	95.0	0	.0	
MALE	1	.5	1	.5	0	.0	1	.5	3	1.5	201	98.5	0	.0	
PART-TIME	0	.0	0	.0	0	.0	0	.0	0	.0	14	100.0	0	.0	
FEMALE	0	.0	0	.0	0	.0	0	.0	0	.0	2	100.0	0	.0	
MALE	0	.0	0	.0	0	.0	0	.0	0	.0	12	100.0	0	.0	
TOTAL	2	.8	1	.4	0	.0	1	.4	4	1.7	234	98.3	0	.0	
FEMALE	1	4.5	0	.0	0	.0	0	.0	1	4.5	21	95.5	0	.0	
MALE	1	.5	1	.5	0	.0	1	.5	3	1.4	213	98.6	0	.0	
UNCLASSIFIED:																
TOTAL	0	.0	0	.0	0	.0	0	.0	0	.0	0	.0	0	.0	
FEMALE	0	.0	0	.0	0	.0	0	.0	0	.0	0	.0	0	.0	
MALE	0	.0	0	.0	0	.0	0	.0	0	.0	0	.0	0	.0	
TOTAL ENROLLMENT:																
TOTAL	2	.8	1	.4	0	.0	1	.4	4	1.7	234	98.3	0	.0	
FEMALE	1	4.5	0	.0	0	.0	0	.0	1	4.5	21	95.5	0	.0	
MALE	1	.5	1	.5	0	.0	1	.5	3	1.4	213	98.6	0	.0	
WISCONSIN	(	1 INSTITUTIONS)														
UNDERGRADUATES:																
FULL-TIME	0	.0	0	.0	0	.0	0	.0	0	.0	0	.0	0	.0	
FEMALE	0	.0	0	.0	0	.0	0	.0	0	.0	0	.0	0	.0	
MALE	0	.0	0	.0	0	.0	0	.0	0	.0	0	.0	0	.0	
PART-TIME	0	.0	0	.0	0	.0	0	.0	0	.0	0	.0	0	.0	
FEMALE	0	.0	0	.0	0	.0	0	.0	0	.0	0	.0	0	.0	
MALE	0	.0	0	.0	0	.0	0	.0	0	.0	0	.0	0	.0	
TOTAL	0	.0	0	.0	0	.0	0	.0	0	.0	0	.0	0	.0	
FEMALE	0	.0	0	.0	0	.0	0	.0	0	.0	0	.0	0	.0	
MALE	0	.0	0	.0	0	.0	0	.0	0	.0	0	.0	0	.0	
GRADUATE:																
FULL-TIME	0	.0	0	.0	0	.0	0	.0	0	.0	0	.0	0	.0	
FEMALE	0	.0	0	.0	0	.0	0	.0	0	.0	0	.0	0	.0	
MALE	0	.0	0	.0	0	.0	0	.0	0	.0	0	.0	0	.0	
PART-TIME	0	.0	0	.0	0	.0	0	.0	0	.0	0	.0	0	.0	
FEMALE	0	.0	0	.0	0	.0	0	.0	0	.0	0	.0	0	.0	
MALE	0	.0	0	.0	0	.0	0	.0	0	.0	0	.0	0	.0	
TOTAL	0	.0	0	.0	0	.0	0	.0	0	.0	0	.0	0	.0	
FEMALE	0	.0	0	.0	0	.0	0	.0	0	.0	0	.0	0	.0	
MALE	0	.0	0	.0	0	.0	0	.0	0	.0	0	.0	0	.0	
PROFESSIONAL:																
FULL-TIME	0	.0	1	.2	3	.5	3	.5	7	1.3	542	98.7	0	.0	
FEMALE	0	.0	0	.0	1	2.0	0	.0	1	2.0	50	98.0	0	.0	
MALE	0	.0	1	.2	2	.4	3	.6	6	1.2	492	98.8	0	.0	

DENTISTRY

INDIAN NATIVE %	BLACK NON-HISPANIC NUMBER	%	ASIAN OR PACIFIC ISLANDER NUMBER	%	HISPANIC NUMBER	%	TOTAL MINORITY NUMBER	%	WHITE NON-HISPANIC NUMBER	%	NON-RESIDENT ALIEN NUMBER	%	TOTAL NUMBER
CONTINUED													
.0	0	.0	0	.0	0	.0	0	.0	7	100.0	0	.0	7
.0	0	.0	0	.0	0	.0	0	.0	0	.0	0	.0	0
.0	0	.0	0	.0	0	.0	0	.0	7	100.0	0	.0	7
.0	1	.2	3	.5	3	.5	7	1.3	549	98.7	0	.0	556
.0	0	.0	1	2.0	0	.0	1	2.0	50	98.0	0	.0	51
.0	1	.2	2	.4	3	.6	6	1.2	499	98.8	0	.0	505
.0	1	.2	3	.5	3	.5	7	1.3	542	98.7	0	.0	549
.0	0	.0	1	2.0	0	.0	1	2.0	50	98.0	0	.0	51
.0	1	.2	2	.4	3	.6	6	1.2	492	98.8	0	.0	498
.0	0	.0	0	.0	0	.0	0	.0	7	100.0	0	.0	7
.0	0	.0	0	.0	0	.0	0	.0	0	.0	0	.0	0
.0	0	.0	0	.0	0	.0	0	.0	7	100.0	0	.0	7
.0	1	.2	3	.5	3	.5	7	1.3	549	98.7	0	.0	556
.0	0	.0	1	2.0	0	.0	1	2.0	50	98.0	0	.0	51
.0	1	.2	2	.4	3	.6	6	1.2	499	98.8	0	.0	505
.0	0	.0	0	.0	0	.0	0	.0	0	.0	0	.0	0
.0	0	.0	0	.0	0	.0	0	.0	0	.0	0	.0	0
.0	0	.0	0	.0	0	.0	0	.0	0	.0	0	.0	0
.0	1	.2	3	.5	3	.5	7	1.3	549	98.7	0	.0	556
.0	0	.0	1	2.0	0	.0	1	2.0	50	98.0	0	.0	51
.0	1	.2	2	.4	3	.6	6	1.2	499	98.8	0	.0	505
(57 INSTITUTIONS)													
.0	0	.0	0	.0	0	.0	0	.0	0	.0	0	.0	0
.0	0	.0	0	.0	0	.0	0	.0	0	.0	0	.0	0
.0	0	.0	0	.0	0	.0	0	.0	0	.0	0	.0	0
.0	0	.0	0	.0	0	.0	0	.0	0	.0	0	.0	0
.0	0	.0	0	.0	0	.0	0	.0	0	.0	0	.0	0
.0	0	.0	0	.0	0	.0	0	.0	0	.0	0	.0	0
.0	0	.0	0	.0	0	.0	0	.0	0	.0	0	.0	0
.0	0	.0	0	.0	0	.0	0	.0	0	.0	0	.0	0
.0	0	.0	0	.0	0	.0	0	.0	0	.0	0	.0	0
.0	0	.0	0	.0	0	.0	0	.0	0	.0	0	.0	0
.0	0	.0	0	.0	0	.0	0	.0	0	.0	0	.0	0
.0	0	.0	0	.0	0	.0	0	.0	0	.0	0	.0	0
.3	898	4.2	675	3.1	418	1.9	2,055	9.5	19,338	89.4	229	1.1	21,622
.2	322	10.6	134	4.4	78	2.6	541	17.8	2,440	80.4	52	1.7	3,033
.3	576	3.1	541	2.9	340	1.8	1,514	8.1	16,898	90.9	177	1.0	18,589
1.2	20	11.7	1	.6	3	1.8	26	15.2	129	75.4	16	9.4	171
.0	7	28.0	0	.0	0	.0	7	28.0	16	64.0	2	8.0	25
1.4	13	8.9	1	.7	3	2.1	19	13.0	113	77.4	14	9.6	146
.3	918	4.2	676	3.1	421	1.9	2,081	9.5	19,467	89.3	245	1.1	21,793
.2	329	10.8	134	4.4	78	2.6	548	17.9	2,456	80.3	54	1.8	3,058
.3	589	3.1	542	2.9	343	1.8	1,533	8.2	17,011	90.8	191	1.0	18,735
.3	898	4.2	675	3.1	418	1.9	2,055	9.5	19,338	89.4	229	1.1	21,622
.2	322	10.6	134	4.4	78	2.6	541	17.8	2,440	80.4	52	1.7	3,033
.3	576	3.1	541	2.9	340	1.8	1,514	8.1	16,898	90.9	177	1.0	18,589
1.2	20	11.7	1	.6	3	1.8	26	15.2	129	75.4	16	9.4	171
.0	7	28.0	0	.0	0	.0	7	28.0	16	64.0	2	8.0	25
1.4	13	8.9	1	.7	3	2.1	19	13.0	113	77.4	14	9.6	146
.3	918	4.2	676	3.1	421	1.9	2,081	9.5	19,467	89.3	245	1.1	21,793
.2	329	10.8	134	4.4	78	2.6	548	17.9	2,456	80.3	54	1.8	3,058
.3	589	3.1	542	2.9	343	1.8	1,533	8.2	17,011	90.8	191	1.0	18,735
.0	0	.0	0	.0	0	.0	0	.0	0	.0	0	.0	0
.0	0	.0	0	.0	0	.0	0	.0	0	.0	0	.0	0
.0	0	.0	0	.0	0	.0	0	.0	0	.0	0	.0	0
.3	918	4.2	676	3.1	421	1.9	2,081	9.5	19,467	89.3	245	1.1	21,793
.2	329	10.8	134	4.4	78	2.6	548	17.9	2,456	80.3	54	1.8	3,058
.3	589	3.1	542	2.9	343	1.8	1,533	8.2	17,011	90.8	191	1.0	18,735

MAJOR FIELD 1204 - DENTISTRY

	AMERICAN INDIAN ALASKAN NATIVE		BLACK NON-HISPANIC		ASIAN OR PACIFIC ISLANDER		HISPANIC		TOTAL MINORITY		WHITE NON-HISPANIC		NON-RESIDENT ALIEN		TOT
	NUMBER	%	NUMBER	%	NUMBER	%	NUMBER	%	NUMBER	%	NUMBER	%	NUMBER	%	NUM
PUERTO RICO	(	1 INSTITUTIONS)													
UNDERGRADUATES:															
FULL-TIME	0	.0	0	.0	0	.0	0	.0	0	.0	0	.0		.0
FEMALE	0	.0	0	.0	0	.0	0	.0	0	.0	0	.0		.0
MALE	0	.0	0	.0	0	.0	0	.0	0	.0	0	.0		.0
PART-TIME	0	.0	0	.0	0	.0	0	.0	0	.0	0	.0		.0
FEMALE	0	.0	0	.0	0	.0	0	.0	0	.0	0	.0		.0
MALE	0	.0	0	.0	0	.0	0	.0	0	.0	0	.0	0	.0
TOTAL	0	.0	0	.0	0	.0	0	.0	0	.0	0	.0		.0
FEMALE	0	.0	0	.0	0	.0	0	.0	0	.0	0	.0		.0
MALE	0	.0	0	.0	0	.0	0	.0	0	.0	0	.0	0	.0
GRADUATE:															
FULL-TIME	0	.0	0	.0	0	.0	0	.0	0	.0	0	.0		.0
FEMALE	0	.0	0	.0	0	.0	0	.0	0	.0	0	.0		.0
MALE	0	.0	0	.0	0	.0	0	.0	0	.0	0	.0		.0
PART-TIME	0	.0	0	.0	0	.0	0	.0	0	.0	0	.0		.0
FEMALE	0	.0	0	.0	0	.0	0	.0	0	.0	0	.0		.0
MALE	0	.0	0	.0	0	.0	0	.0	0	.0	0	.0	0	.0
TOTAL	0	.0	0	.0	0	.0	0	.0	0	.0	0	.0		.0
FEMALE	0	.0	0	.0	0	.0	0	.0	0	.0	0	.0		.0
MALE	0	.0	0	.0	0	.0	0	.0	0	.0	0	.0	0	.0
PROFESSIONAL:															
FULL-TIME	0	.0	0	.0	0	.0	241	100.0	241	100.0	0	.0		.0
FEMALE	0	.0	0	.0	0	.0	82	100.0	82	100.0	0	.0		.0
MALE	0	.0	0	.0	0	.0	159	100.0	159	100.0	0	.0		.0
PART-TIME	0	.0	0	.0	0	.0	0	.0	0	.0	0	.0		.0
FEMALE	0	.0	0	.0	0	.0	0	.0	0	.0	0	.0		.0
MALE	0	.0	0	.0	0	.0	0	.0	0	.0	0	.0	0	.0
TOTAL	0	.0	0	.0	0	.0	241	100.0	241	100.0	0	.0		.0
FEMALE	0	.0	0	.0	0	.0	82	100.0	82	100.0	0	.0		.0
MALE	0	.0	0	.0	0	.0	159	100.0	159	100.0	0	.0	0	.0
UND+GRAD+PROF:															
FULL-TIME	0	.0	0	.0	0	.0	241	100.0	241	100.0	0	.0		.0
FEMALE	0	.0	0	.0	0	.0	82	100.0	82	100.0	0	.0		.0
MALE	0	.0	0	.0	0	.0	159	100.0	159	100.0	0	.0		.0
PART-TIME	0	.0	0	.0	0	.0	0	.0	0	.0	0	.0		.0
FEMALE	0	.0	0	.0	0	.0	0	.0	0	.0	0	.0		.0
MALE	0	.0	0	.0	0	.0	0	.0	0	.0	0	.0	0	.0
TOTAL	0	.0	0	.0	0	.0	241	100.0	241	100.0	0	.0		.0
FEMALE	0	.0	0	.0	0	.0	82	100.0	82	100.0	0	.0		.0
MALE	0	.0	0	.0	0	.0	159	100.0	159	100.0	0	.0	0	.0
UNCLASSIFIED:															
TOTAL	0	.0	0	.0	0	.0	0	.0	0	.0	0	.0		.0
FEMALE	0	.0	0	.0	0	.0	0	.0	0	.0	0	.0		.0
MALE	0	.0	0	.0	0	.0	0	.0	0	.0	0	.0	0	.0
TOTAL ENROLLMENT:															
TOTAL	0	.0	0	.0	0	.0	241	100.0	241	100.0	0	.0		.0
FEMALE	0	.0	0	.0	0	.0	82	100.0	82	100.0	0	.0		.0
MALE	0	.0	0	.0	0	.0	159	100.0	159	100.0	0	.0	0	.0
OUTLYING AREAS	(	1 INSTITUTIONS)													
UNDERGRADUATES:															
FULL-TIME	0	.0	0	.0	0	.0	0	.0	0	.0	0	.0		.0
FEMALE	0	.0	0	.0	0	.0	0	.0	0	.0	0	.0		.0
MALE	0	.0	0	.0	0	.0	0	.0	0	.0	0	.0		.0
PART-TIME	0	.0	0	.0	0	.0	0	.0	0	.0	0	.0		.0
FEMALE	0	.0	0	.0	0	.0	0	.0	0	.0	0	.0		.0
MALE	0	.0	0	.0	0	.0	0	.0	0	.0	0	.0	0	.0
TOTAL	0	.0	0	.0	0	.0	0	.0	0	.0	0	.0		.0
FEMALE	0	.0	0	.0	0	.0	0	.0	0	.0	0	.0		.0
MALE	0	.0	0	.0	0	.0	0	.0	0	.0	0	.0	0	.0
GRADUATE:															
FULL-TIME	0	.0	0	.0	0	.0	0	.0	0	.0	0	.0		.0
FEMALE	0	.0	0	.0	0	.0	0	.0	0	.0	0	.0		.0
MALE	0	.0	0	.0	0	.0	0	.0	0	.0	0	.0		.0
PART-TIME	0	.0	0	.0	0	.0	0	.0	0	.0	0	.0		.0
FEMALE	0	.0	0	.0	0	.0	0	.0	0	.0	0	.0		.0
MALE	0	.0	0	.0	0	.0	0	.0	0	.0	0	.0	0	.0
TOTAL	0	.0	0	.0	0	.0	0	.0	0	.0	0	.0	0	.0
FEMALE	0	.0	0	.0	0	.0	0	.0	0	.0	0	.0	0	.0
MALE	0	.0	0	.0	0	.0	0	.0	0	.0	0	.0	0	.0
PROFESSIONAL:															
FULL-TIME	0	.0	0	.0	0	.0	241	100.0	241	100.0	0	.0		.0
FEMALE	0	.0	0	.0	0	.0	82	100.0	82	100.0	0	.0		.0
MALE	0	.0	0	.0	0	.0	159	100.0	159	100.0	0	.0	0	.0

NS OF HIGHER EDUCATION FOR SELECTED MAJOR FIELDS OF STUDY AND LEVEL OF ENROLLMENT
TATE, 1978

ASIAN OR C PACIFIC ISLANDER		HISPANIC		TOTAL MINORITY		WHITE NON-HISPANIC		NON-RESIDENT ALIEN		TOTAL
NUMBER	%	NUMBER	%	NUMBER	%	NUMBER	%	NUMBER	%	NUMBER
0	.0	0	.0	0	.0	0	.0	0	.0	0
0	.0	0	.0	0	.0	0	.0	0	.0	0
0	.0	0	.0	0	.0	0	.0	0	.0	0
0	.0	241	100.0	241	100.0	0	.0	0	.0	241
0	.0	82	100.0	82	100.0	0	.0	0	.0	82
0	.0	159	100.0	159	100.0	0	.0	0	.0	159
0	.0	241	100.0	241	100.0	0	.0	0	.0	241
0	.0	82	100.0	82	100.0	0	.0	0	.0	82
0	.0	159	100.0	159	100.0	0	.0	0	.0	159
0	.0	0	.0	0	.0	0	.0	0	.0	0
0	.0	0	.0	0	.0	0	.0	0	.0	0
0	.0	0	.0	0	.0	0	.0	0	.0	0
0	.0	241	100.0	241	100.0	0	.0	0	.0	241
0	.0	82	100.0	82	100.0	0	.0	0	.0	82
0	.0	159	100.0	159	100.0	0	.0	0	.0	159
0	.0	0	.0	0	.0	0	.0	0	.0	0
0	.0	0	.0	0	.0	0	.0	0	.0	0
0	.0	0	.0	0	.0	0	.0	0	.0	0
0	.0	241	100.0	241	100.0	0	.0	0	.0	241
0	.0	82	100.0	82	100.0	0	.0	0	.0	82
0	.0	159	100.0	159	100.0	0	.0	0	.0	159

UTIONS)

ASIAN OR C PACIFIC ISLANDER		HISPANIC		TOTAL MINORITY		WHITE NON-HISPANIC		NON-RESIDENT ALIEN		TOTAL
0	.0	0	.0	0	.0	0	.0	0	.0	0
0	.0	0	.0	0	.0	0	.0	0	.0	0
0	.0	0	.0	0	.0	0	.0	0	.0	0
0	.0	0	.0	0	.0	0	.0	0	.0	0
0	.0	0	.0	0	.0	0	.0	0	.0	0
0	.0	0	.0	0	.0	0	.0	0	.0	0
0	.0	0	.0	0	.0	0	.0	0	.0	0
0	.0	0	.0	0	.0	0	.0	0	.0	0
0	.0	0	.0	0	.0	0	.0	0	.0	0
0	.0	0	.0	0	.0	0	.0	0	.0	0
0	.0	0	.0	0	.0	0	.0	0	.0	0
0	.0	0	.0	0	.0	0	.0	0	.0	0
0	.0	0	.0	0	.0	0	.0	0	.0	0
0	.0	0	.0	0	.0	0	.0	0	.0	0
0	.0	0	.0	0	.0	0	.0	0	.0	0
0	.0	0	.0	0	.0	0	.0	0	.0	0
0	.0	0	.0	0	.0	0	.0	0	.0	0
0	.0	0	.0	0	.0	0	.0	0	.0	0
675	3.1	659	3.0	2,296	10.5	19,338	88.5	229	1.0	21,863
134	4.3	160	5.1	623	20.0	2,440	78.3	52	1.7	3,115
541	2.9	499	2.7	1,673	8.9	16,898	90.1	177	.9	18,748
1	.6	3	1.8	26	15.2	129	75.4	16	9.4	171
0	.0	0	.0	7	28.0	16	64.0	2	8.0	25
1	.7	3	2.1	19	13.0	113	77.4	14	9.6	146
676	3.1	662	3.0	2,322	10.5	19,467	88.3	245	1.1	22,034
134	4.3	160	5.1	630	20.1	2,456	78.2	54	1.7	3,140
542	2.9	502	2.7	1,692	9.0	17,011	90.0	191	1.0	18,894
675	3.1	659	3.0	2,296	10.5	19,338	88.5	229	1.0	21,863
134	4.3	160	5.1	623	20.0	2,440	78.3	52	1.7	3,115
541	2.9	499	2.7	1,673	8.9	16,898	90.1	177	.9	18,748
1	.6	3	1.8	26	15.2	129	75.4	16	9.4	171
0	.0	0	.0	7	28.0	16	64.0	2	8.0	25
1	.7	3	2.1	19	13.0	113	77.4	14	9.6	146
676	3.1	662	3.0	2,322	10.5	19,467	88.3	245	1.1	22,034
134	4.3	160	5.1	630	20.1	2,456	78.2	54	1.7	3,140
542	2.9	502	2.7	1,692	9.0	17,011	90.0	191	1.0	18,894
0	.0	0	.0	0	.0	0	.0	0	.0	0
0	.0	0	.0	0	.0	0	.0	0	.0	0
0	.0	0	.0	0	.0	0	.0	0	.0	0
676	3.1	662	3.0	2,322	10.5	19,467	88.3	245	1.1	22,034
134	4.3	160	5.1	630	20.1	2,456	78.2	54	1.7	3,140
542	2.9	502	2.7	1,692	9.0	17,011	90.0	191	1.0	18,894

MAJOR FIELD 1206 - MEDICINE

	AMERICAN INDIAN ALASKAN NATIVE		BLACK NON-HISPANIC		ASIAN OR PACIFIC ISLANDER		HISPANIC		TOTAL MINORITY		WHITE NON-HISPANIC		NON-RESIDENT ALIEN		TO
	NUMBER	%	NUMBER	%	NUMBER	%	NUMBER	%	NUMBER	%	NUMBER	%	NUMBER	%	NU
ALABAMA (4 INSTITUTIONS)															
UNDERGRADUATES:															
FULL-TIME	0	.0	0	.0	0	.0	0	.0	0	.0	0	.0		.0	
FEMALE	0	.0	0	.0	0	.0	0	.0	0	.0	0	.0		.0	
MALE	0	.0	0	.0	0	.0	0	.0	0	.0	0	.0		.0	
PART-TIME	0	.0	0	.0	0	.0	0	.0	0	.0	0	.0		.0	
FEMALE	0	.0	0	.0	0	.0	0	.0	0	.0	0	.0		.0	
MALE	0	.0	0	.0	0	.0	0	.0	0	.0	0	.0	0	.0	
TOTAL	0	.0	0	.0	0	.0	0	.0	0	.0	0	.0		.0	
FEMALE	0	.0	0	.0	0	.0	0	.0	0	.0	0	.0		.0	
MALE	0	.0	0	.0	0	.0	0	.0	0	.0	0	.0	0	.0	
GRADUATE:															
FULL-TIME	0	.0	0	.0	0	.0	0	.0	0	.0	0	.0		.0	
FEMALE	0	.0	0	.0	0	.0	0	.0	0	.0	0	.0		.0	
MALE	0	.0	0	.0	0	.0	0	.0	0	.0	0	.0		.0	
PART-TIME	0	.0	0	.0	0	.0	0	.0	0	.0	0	.0		.0	
FEMALE	0	.0	0	.0	0	.0	0	.0	0	.0	0	.0		.0	
MALE	0	.0	0	.0	0	.0	0	.0	0	.0	0	.0	0	.0	
TOTAL	0	.0	0	.0	0	.0	0	.0	0	.0	0	.0		.0	
FEMALE	0	.0	0	.0	0	.0	0	.0	0	.0	0	.0		.0	
MALE	0	.0	0	.0	0	.0	0	.0	0	.0	0	.0	0	.0	
PROFESSIONAL:															
FULL-TIME	1	.1	43	4.3	7	.7	2	.2	53	5.3	943	94.5	2	.2	
FEMALE	0	.0	15	8.2	2	1.1	1	.5	18	9.8	164	89.6	1	.5	
MALE	1	.1	28	3.4	5	.6	1	.1	35	4.3	779	95.6	1	.1	
PART-TIME	0	.0	0	.0	0	.0	0	.0	0	.0	0	.0	0	.0	
FEMALE	0	.0	0	.0	0	.0	0	.0	0	.0	0	.0	0	.0	
MALE	0	.0	0	.0	0	.0	0	.0	0	.0	0	.0	0	.0	
TOTAL	1	.1	43	4.3	7	.7	2	.2	53	5.3	943	94.5	2	.2	
FEMALE	0	.0	15	8.2	2	1.1	1	.5	18	9.8	164	89.6	1	.5	
MALE	1	.1	28	3.4	5	.6	1	.1	35	4.3	779	95.6	1	.1	
UND+GRAD+PROF:															
FULL-TIME	1	.1	43	4.3	7	.7	2	.2	53	5.3	943	94.5	2	.2	
FEMALE	0	.0	15	8.2	2	1.1	1	.5	18	9.8	164	89.6	1	.5	
MALE	1	.1	28	3.4	5	.6	1	.1	35	4.3	779	95.6	1	.1	
PART-TIME	0	.0	0	.0	0	.0	0	.0	0	.0	0	.0	0	.0	
FEMALE	0	.0	0	.0	0	.0	0	.0	0	.0	0	.0	0	.0	
MALE	0	.0	0	.0	0	.0	0	.0	0	.0	0	.0	0	.0	
TOTAL	1	.1	43	4.3	7	.7	2	.2	53	5.3	943	94.5	2	.2	
FEMALE	0	.0	15	8.2	2	1.1	1	.5	18	9.8	164	89.6	1	.5	
MALE	1	.1	28	3.4	5	.6	1	.1	35	4.3	779	95.6	1	.1	
UNCLASSIFIED:															
TOTAL	0	.0	0	.0	0	.0	0	.0	0	.0	0	.0	0	.0	
FEMALE	0	.0	0	.0	0	.0	0	.0	0	.0	0	.0	0	.0	
MALE	0	.0	0	.0	0	.0	0	.0	0	.0	0	.0	0	.0	
TOTAL ENROLLMENT:															
TOTAL	1	.1	43	4.3	7	.7	2	.2	53	5.3	943	94.5	2	.2	
FEMALE	0	.0	15	8.2	2	1.1	1	.5	18	9.8	164	89.6	1	.5	
MALE	1	.1	28	3.4	5	.6	1	.1	35	4.3	779	95.6	1	.1	
ARIZONA (1 INSTITUTIONS)															
UNDERGRADUATES:															
FULL-TIME	0	.0	0	.0	0	.0	0	.0	0	.0	0	.0		.0	
FEMALE	0	.0	0	.0	0	.0	0	.0	0	.0	0	.0		.0	
MALE	0	.0	0	.0	0	.0	0	.0	0	.0	0	.0		.0	
PART-TIME	0	.0	0	.0	0	.0	0	.0	0	.0	0	.0		.0	
FEMALE	0	.0	0	.0	0	.0	0	.0	0	.0	0	.0		.0	
MALE	0	.0	0	.0	0	.0	0	.0	0	.0	0	.0	0	.0	
TOTAL	0	.0	0	.0	0	.0	0	.0	0	.0	0	.0		.0	
FEMALE	0	.0	0	.0	0	.0	0	.0	0	.0	0	.0		.0	
MALE	0	.0	0	.0	0	.0	0	.0	0	.0	0	.0	0	.0	
GRADUATE:															
FULL-TIME	0	.0	0	.0	0	.0	0	.0	0	.0	0	.0		.0	
FEMALE	0	.0	0	.0	0	.0	0	.0	0	.0	0	.0		.0	
MALE	0	.0	0	.0	0	.0	0	.0	0	.0	0	.0		.0	
PART-TIME	0	.0	0	.0	0	.0	0	.0	0	.0	0	.0		.0	
FEMALE	0	.0	0	.0	0	.0	0	.0	0	.0	0	.0		.0	
MALE	0	.0	0	.0	0	.0	0	.0	0	.0	0	.0	0	.0	
TOTAL	0	.0	0	.0	0	.0	0	.0	0	.0	0	.0		.0	
FEMALE	0	.0	0	.0	0	.0	0	.0	0	.0	0	.0		.0	
MALE	0	.0	0	.0	0	.0	0	.0	0	.0	0	.0	0	.0	
PROFESSIONAL:															
FULL-TIME	1	.3	0	.0	1	.3	6	2.0	8	2.7	289	97.0	1	.3	
FEMALE	0	.0	0	.0	0	.0	2	2.9	2	2.9	65	95.6	1	1.5	
MALE	1	.4	0	.0	1	.4	4	1.7	6	2.6	224	97.4	0	.0	

MEDICINE

INDIAN NATIVE	BLACK NON-HISPANIC		ASIAN OR PACIFIC ISLANDER		HISPANIC		TOTAL MINORITY		WHITE NON-HISPANIC		NON-RESIDENT ALIEN		TOTAL
%	NUMBER	%	NUMBER	%	NUMBER	%	NUMBER	%	NUMBER	%	NUMBER	%	NUMBER

CONTINUED

.0	0	.0	0	.0	1	3.4	1	3.4	28	96.6	0	.0	29
.0	0	.0	0	.0	0	.0	0	.0	12	100.0	0	.0	12
.0	0	.0	0	.0	1	5.9	1	5.9	16	94.1	0	.0	17
.3	0	.0	1	.3	7	2.1	9	2.8	317	96.9	1	.3	327
.0	0	.0	0	.0	2	2.5	2	2.5	77	96.3	1	1.3	80
.4	0	.0	1	.4	5	2.0	7	2.8	240	97.2	0	.0	247
.3	0	.0	1	.3	6	2.0	8	2.7	289	97.0	1	.3	298
.0	0	.0	0	.0	2	2.9	2	2.9	65	95.6	1	1.5	68
.4	0	.0	1	.4	4	1.7	6	2.6	224	97.4	0	.0	230
.0	0	.0	0	.0	1	3.4	1	3.4	28	96.6	0	.0	29
.0	0	.0	0	.0	0	.0	0	.0	12	100.0	0	.0	12
.0	0	.0	0	.0	1	5.9	1	5.9	16	94.1	0	.0	17
.3	0	.0	1	.3	7	2.1	9	2.8	317	96.9	1	.3	327
.0	0	.0	0	.0	2	2.5	2	2.5	77	96.3	1	1.3	80
.4	0	.0	1	.4	5	2.0	7	2.8	240	97.2	0	.0	247
.0	0	.0	0	.0	0	.0	0	.0	0	.0	0	.0	0
.0	0	.0	0	.0	0	.0	0	.0	0	.0	0	.0	0
.0	0	.0	0	.0	0	.0	0	.0	0	.0	0	.0	0
.3	0	.0	1	.3	7	2.1	9	2.8	317	96.9	1	.3	327
.0	0	.0	0	.0	2	2.5	2	2.5	77	96.3	1	1.3	80
.4	0	.0	1	.4	5	2.0	7	2.8	240	97.2	0	.0	247

(1 INSTITUTIONS)

.0	0	.0	0	.0	0	.0	0	.0	0	.0	0	.0	0
.0	0	.0	0	.0	0	.0	0	.0	0	.0	0	.0	0
.0	0	.0	0	.0	0	.0	0	.0	0	.0	0	.0	0
.0	0	.0	0	.0	0	.0	0	.0	0	.0	0	.0	0
.0	0	.0	0	.0	0	.0	0	.0	0	.0	0	.0	0
.0	0	.0	0	.0	0	.0	0	.0	0	.0	0	.0	0
.0	0	.0	0	.0	0	.0	0	.0	0	.0	0	.0	0
.0	0	.0	0	.0	0	.0	0	.0	0	.0	0	.0	0
.0	0	.0	0	.0	0	.0	0	.0	0	.0	0	.0	0
.0	0	.0	0	.0	0	.0	0	.0	0	.0	0	.0	0
.0	0	.0	0	.0	0	.0	0	.0	0	.0	0	.0	0
.0	0	.0	0	.0	0	.0	0	.0	0	.0	0	.0	0
.0	0	.0	0	.0	0	.0	0	.0	0	.0	0	.0	0
.0	0	.0	0	.0	0	.0	0	.0	0	.0	0	.0	0
.0	0	.0	0	.0	0	.0	0	.0	0	.0	0	.0	0
.4	29	5.6	11	2.1	1	.2	43	8.2	479	91.8	0	.0	522
.9	10	9.4	2	1.9	1	.9	14	13.2	92	86.8	0	.0	106
.2	19	4.6	9	2.2	0	.0	29	7.0	387	93.0	0	.0	416
.0	0	.0	0	.0	0	.0	0	.0	0	.0	0	.0	0
.0	0	.0	0	.0	0	.0	0	.0	0	.0	0	.0	0
.0	0	.0	0	.0	0	.0	0	.0	0	.0	0	.0	0
.4	29	5.6	11	2.1	1	.2	43	8.2	479	91.8	0	.0	522
.9	10	9.4	2	1.9	1	.9	14	13.2	92	86.8	0	.0	106
.2	19	4.6	9	2.2	0	.0	29	7.0	387	93.0	0	.0	416
.4	29	5.6	11	2.1	1	.2	43	8.2	479	91.8	0	.0	522
.9	10	9.4	2	1.9	1	.9	14	13.2	92	86.8	0	.0	106
.2	19	4.6	9	2.2	0	.0	29	7.0	387	93.0	0	.0	416
.0	0	.0	0	.0	0	.0	0	.0	0	.0	0	.0	0
.0	0	.0	0	.0	0	.0	0	.0	0	.0	0	.0	0
.0	0	.0	0	.0	0	.0	0	.0	0	.0	0	.0	0
.4	29	5.6	11	2.1	1	.2	43	8.2	479	91.8	0	.0	522
.9	10	9.4	2	1.9	1	.9	14	13.2	92	86.8	0	.0	106
.2	19	4.6	9	2.2	0	.0	29	7.0	387	93.0	0	.0	416
.0	0	.0	0	.0	0	.0	0	.0	0	.0	0	.0	0
.0	0	.0	0	.0	0	.0	0	.0	0	.0	0	.0	0
.0	0	.0	0	.0	0	.0	0	.0	0	.0	0	.0	0
.4	29	5.6	11	2.1	1	.2	43	8.2	479	91.8	0	.0	522
.9	10	9.4	2	1.9	1	.9	14	13.2	92	86.8	0	.0	106
.2	19	4.6	9	2.2	0	.0	29	7.0	387	93.0	0	.0	416

TABLE 17 - TOTAL ENROLLMENT IN INSTITUTIONS OF HIGHER EDUCATION FOR SELECTED MAJOR FIELDS OF STUDY AND LEVEL OF ENROLLMENT
            BY RACE, ETHNICITY, AND SEX: STATE: 1978

MAJOR FIELD 1206 - MEDICINE

	AMERICAN INDIAN ALASKAN NATIVE		BLACK NON-HISPANIC		ASIAN OR PACIFIC ISLANDER		HISPANIC		TOTAL MINORITY		WHITE NON-HISPANIC		NON-RESIDENT ALIEN		TO
	NUMBER	%	NUMBER	%	NUMBER	%	NUMBER	%	NUMBER	%	NUMBER	%	NUMBER	%	NUI
CALIFORNIA	(	12 INSTITUTIONS)													
UNDERGRADUATES:															
FULL-TIME	0	.0	0	.0	0	.0	0	.0	0	.0	0	.0		.0	
FEMALE	0	.0	0	.0	0	.0	0	.0	0	.0	0	.0		.0	
MALE	0	.0	0	.0	0	.0	0	.0	0	.0	0	.0		.0	
PART-TIME	0	.0	0	.0	0	.0	0	.0	0	.0	0	.0		.0	
FEMALE	0	.0	0	.0	0	.0	0	.0	0	.0	0	.0	0	.0	
MALE	0	.0	0	.0	0	.0	0	.0	0	.0	0	.0	0	.0	
TOTAL	0	.0	0	.0	0	.0	0	.0	0	.0	0	.0		.0	
FEMALE	0	.0	0	.0	0	.0	0	.0	0	.0	0	.0	0	.0	
MALE	0	.0	0	.0	0	.0	0	.0	0	.0	0	.0	0	.0	
GRADUATE:															
FULL-TIME	0	.0	0	.0	0	.0	0	.0	0	.0	0	.0		.0	
FEMALE	0	.0	0	.0	0	.0	0	.0	0	.0	0	.0		.0	
MALE	0	.0	0	.0	0	.0	0	.0	0	.0	0	.0		.0	
PART-TIME	0	.0	0	.0	0	.0	0	.0	0	.0	0	.0		.0	
FEMALE	0	.0	0	.0	0	.0	0	.0	0	.0	0	.0		.0	
MALE	0	.0	0	.0	0	.0	0	.0	0	.0	0	.0	0	.0	
TOTAL	0	.0	0	.0	0	.0	0	.0	0	.0	0	.0		.0	
FEMALE	0	.0	0	.0	0	.0	0	.0	0	.0	0	.0		.0	
MALE	0	.0	0	.0	0	.0	0	.0	0	.0	0	.0	0	.0	
PROFESSIONAL:															
FULL-TIME	30	.6	226	4.5	453	9.1	312	6.3	1,021	20.5	3,826	76.9	128	2.6	4
FEMALE	10	.9	89	7.7	115	10.0	64	5.5	278	24.1	843	73.0	34	2.9	1
MALE	20	.5	137	3.6	338	8.8	248	6.5	743	19.5	2,983	78.1	94	2.5	3
PART-TIME	1	.3	9	2.7	11	3.3	2	.6	23	6.9	216	64.7	95	28.4	
FEMALE	0	.0	6	8.2	4	5.5	1	1.4	11	15.1	39	53.4	23	31.5	
MALE	1	.4	3	1.1	7	2.7	1	.4	12	4.6	177	67.8	72	27.6	
TOTAL	31	.6	235	4.4	464	8.7	314	5.9	1,044	19.7	4,042	76.1	223	4.2	5
FEMALE	10	.8	95	7.7	119	9.7	65	5.3	289	23.5	882	71.8	57	4.6	1
MALE	21	.5	140	3.4	345	8.5	249	6.1	755	18.5	3,160	77.4	166	4.1	4
UNG+GRAD+PROF:															
FULL-TIME	30	.6	226	4.5	453	9.1	312	6.3	1,021	20.5	3,826	76.9	128	2.	4
FEMALE	10	.9	89	7.7	115	10.0	64	5.5	278	24.1	843	73.0	34	2.	1
MALE	20	.5	137	3.6	338	8.8	248	6.5	743	19.5	2,983	78.1	94	2.	3
PART-TIME	1	.3	9	2.7	11	3.3	2	.6	23	6.9	216	64.7	95	28.	
FEMALE	0	.0	6	8.2	4	5.5	1	1.4	11	15.1	39	53.4	23	31.	
MALE	1	.4	3	1.1	7	2.7	1	.4	12	4.6	177	67.8	72	27.8	
TOTAL	31	.6	235	4.4	464	8.7	314	5.9	1,044	19.7	4,042	76.1	223	.2	5
FEMALE	10	.8	95	7.7	119	9.7	65	5.3	289	23.5	882	71.8	57	4.6	1
MALE	21	.5	140	3.4	345	8.5	249	6.1	755	18.5	3,160	77.4	166	4.1	4
UNCLASSIFIED:															
TOTAL	0	.0	0	.0	0	.0	0	.0	0	.0	0	.0		.0	
FEMALE	0	.0	0	.0	0	.0	0	.0	0	.0	0	.0		.0	
MALE	0	.0	0	.0	0	.0	0	.0	0	.0	0	.0	0	.0	
TOTAL ENROLLMENT:															
TOTAL	31	.6	235	4.4	464	8.7	314	5.9	1,044	19.7	4,042	76.1	223	4.2	
FEMALE	10	.8	95	7.7	119	9.7	65	5.3	289	23.5	882	71.8	57	4.6	
MALE	21	.3	140	3.4	345	8.5	249	6.1	755	18.5	3,160	77.4	166	4.1	
COLORADO	(	1 INSTITUTIONS)													
UNDERGRADUATES:															
FULL-TIME	0	.0	0	.0	0	.0	0	.0	0	.0	0	.0		.0	
FEMALE	0	.0	0	.0	0	.0	0	.0	0	.0	0	.0		.0	
MALE	0	.0	0	.0	0	.0	0	.0	0	.0	0	.0		.0	
PART-TIME	0	.0	0	.0	0	.0	0	.0	0	.0	0	.0		.0	
FEMALE	0	.0	0	.0	0	.0	0	.0	0	.0	0	.0		.0	
MALE	0	.0	0	.0	0	.0	0	.0	0	.0	0	.0	0	.0	
TOTAL	0	.0	0	.0	0	.0	0	.0	0	.0	0	.0		.0	
FEMALE	0	.0	0	.0	0	.0	0	.0	0	.0	0	.0		.0	
MALE	0	.0	0	.0	0	.0	0	.0	0	.0	0	.0	0	.0	
GRADUATE:															
FULL-TIME	0	.0	0	.0	0	.0	0	.0	0	.0	0	.0		.0	
FEMALE	0	.0	0	.0	0	.0	0	.0	0	.0	0	.0		.0	
MALE	0	.0	0	.0	0	.0	0	.0	0	.0	0	.0		.0	
PART-TIME	0	.0	0	.0	0	.0	0	.0	0	.0	0	.0		.0	
FEMALE	0	.0	0	.0	0	.0	0	.0	0	.0	0	.0		.0	
MALE	0	.0	0	.0	0	.0	0	.0	0	.0	0	.0	0	.0	
TOTAL	0	.0	0	.0	0	.0	0	.0	0	.0	0	.0		.0	
FEMALE	0	.0	0	.0	0	.0	0	.0	0	.0	0	.0		.0	
MALE	0	.0	0	.0	0	.0	0	.0	0	.0	0	.0	0	.0	
PROFESSIONAL:															
FULL-TIME	10	1.9	19	3.6	19	3.6	51	9.7	99	18.9	426	81.1	0	.0	
FEMALE	4	2.9	6	4.4	5	3.6	16	11.7	31	22.6	106	77.4	0	.0	
MALE	6	1.5	13	3.4	14	3.6	35	9.0	68	17.5	320	82.5	0	.0	

ROLLMENT IN INSTITUTIONS OF HIGHER EDUCATION FOR SELECTED MAJOR FIELDS OF STUDY AND LEVEL OF ENROLLMENT
   ETHNICITY, AND SEX: STATE, 1978

MEDICINE

INDIAN NATIVE %	BLACK NON-HISPANIC NUMBER	%	ASIAN OR PACIFIC ISLANDER NUMBER	%	HISPANIC NUMBER	%	TOTAL MINORITY NUMBER	%	WHITE NON-HISPANIC NUMBER	%	NON-RESIDENT ALIEN NUMBER	%	TOTAL NUMBER
CONTINUED													
.0	0	.0	0	.0	0	.0	0	.0	0	.0	0	.0	0
.0	0	.0	0	.0	0	.0	0	.0	0	.0	0	.0	0
.0	0	.0	0	.0	0	.0	0	.0	0	.0	0	.0	0
1.9	19	3.6	19	3.6	51	9.7	99	18.9	426	81.1	0	.0	525
2.9	6	4.4	5	3.6	16	11.7	31	22.6	106	77.4	0	.0	137
1.5	13	3.4	14	3.6	35	9.0	68	17.5	320	82.5	0	.0	38d
1.9	19	3.6	19	3.6	51	9.7	99	18.9	426	81.1	0	.0	525
2.9	6	4.4	5	3.6	16	11.7	31	22.6	106	77.4	0	.0	137
1.5	13	3.4	14	3.6	35	9.0	68	17.5	320	82.5	0	.0	388
.0	0	.0	0	.0	0	.0	0	.0	0	.0	0	.0	0
.0	0	.0	0	.0	0	.0	0	.0	0	.0	0	.0	0
.0	0	.0	0	.0	0	.0	0	.0	0	.0	0	.0	0
1.9	19	3.6	19	3.6	51	9.7	99	18.9	426	81.1	0	.0	525
2.9	6	4.4	5	3.6	16	11.7	31	22.6	106	77.4	0	.0	137
1.5	13	3.4	14	3.6	35	9.0	68	17.5	320	82.5	0	.0	388
.0	0	.0	0	.0	0	.0	0	.0	0	.0	0	.0	0
.0	0	.0	0	.0	0	.0	0	.0	0	.0	0	.0	0
.0	0	.0	0	.0	0	.0	0	.0	0	.0	0	.0	0
1.9	19	3.6	19	3.6	51	9.7	99	18.9	426	81.1	0	.0	525
2.9	6	4.4	5	3.6	16	11.7	31	22.6	106	77.4	0	.0	137
1.5	13	3.4	14	3.6	35	9.0	68	17.5	320	82.5	0	.0	388
(2 INSTITUTIONS)													
.0	0	.0	0	.0	0	.0	0	.0	0	.0	0	.0	0
.0	0	.0	0	.0	0	.0	0	.0	0	.0	0	.0	0
.0	0	.0	0	.0	0	.0	0	.0	0	.0	0	.0	0
.0	0	.0	0	.0	0	.0	0	.0	0	.0	0	.0	0
.0	0	.0	0	.0	0	.0	0	.0	0	.0	0	.0	0
.0	0	.0	0	.0	0	.0	0	.0	0	.0	0	.0	0
.0	0	.0	0	.0	0	.0	0	.0	0	.0	0	.0	0
.0	0	.0	0	.0	0	.0	0	.0	0	.0	0	.0	0
.0	0	.0	0	.0	0	.0	0	.0	0	.0	0	.0	0
.0	0	.0	0	.0	0	.0	0	.0	0	.0	0	.0	0
.0	0	.0	0	.0	0	.0	0	.0	0	.0	0	.0	0
.0	0	.0	0	.0	0	.0	0	.0	0	.0	0	.0	0
.0	0	.0	0	.0	0	.0	0	.0	0	.0	0	.0	0
.0	0	.0	0	.0	0	.0	0	.0	0	.0	0	.0	0
.0	0	.0	0	.0	0	.0	0	.0	0	.0	0	.0	0
.0	0	.0	0	.0	0	.0	0	.0	0	.0	0	.0	0
.0	0	.0	0	.0	0	.0	0	.0	0	.0	0	.0	0
.0	0	.0	0	.0	0	.0	0	.0	0	.0	0	.0	0
.0	51	6.4	21	2.6	38	4.8	110	13.9	665	83.9	18	2.3	753
.0	18	8.2	7	3.2	10	4.5	35	15.9	185	84.1	0	.0	220
.0	33	5.8	14	2.4	28	4.9	75	13.1	480	83.8	18	3.1	573
.0	0	.0	0	.0	0	.0	0	.0	0	.0	0	.0	0
.0	0	.0	0	.0	0	.0	0	.0	0	.0	0	.0	0
.0	0	.0	0	.0	0	.0	0	.0	0	.0	0	.0	0
.0	51	6.4	21	2.6	38	4.8	110	13.9	665	83.9	18	2.3	793
.0	18	8.2	7	3.2	10	4.5	35	15.9	185	84.1	0	.0	220
.0	33	5.8	14	2.4	28	4.9	75	13.1	480	83.8	18	3.1	573
.0	51	6.4	21	2.6	38	4.8	110	13.9	665	83.9	18	2.3	793
.0	18	8.2	7	3.2	10	4.5	35	15.9	185	84.1	0	.0	220
.0	33	5.8	14	2.4	28	4.9	75	13.1	480	83.8	18	3.1	573
.0	0	.0	0	.0	0	.0	0	.0	0	.0	0	.0	0
.0	0	.0	0	.0	0	.0	0	.0	0	.0	0	.0	0
.0	0	.0	0	.0	0	.0	0	.0	0	.0	0	.0	0
.0	51	6.4	21	2.6	38	4.8	110	13.9	665	83.9	18	2.3	793
.0	18	8.2	7	3.2	10	4.5	35	15.9	185	84.1	0	.0	220
.0	33	5.8	14	2.4	28	4.9	75	13.1	480	83.8	18	3.1	573
.0	0	.0	0	.0	0	.0	0	.0	0	.0	0	.0	0
.0	0	.0	0	.0	0	.0	0	.0	0	.0	0	.0	0
.0	0	.0	0	.0	0	.0	0	.0	0	.0	0	.0	0
.0	51	6.4	21	2.6	38	4.8	110	13.9	665	83.9	18	2.3	793
.0	18	8.2	7	3.2	10	4.5	35	15.9	185	84.1	0	.0	220
.0	33	5.8	14	2.4	28	4.9	75	13.1	480	83.8	18	3.1	573

TABLE 17 - TOTAL ENROLLMENT IN INSTITUTIONS OF HIGHER EDUCATION FOR SELECTED MAJOR FIELDS OF STUDY AND LEVEL OF ENROLLMENT BY RACE, ETHNICITY, AND SEX: STATE, 1978

MAJOR FIELD 1206 - MEDICINE

	AMERICAN INDIAN ALASKAN NATIVE		BLACK NON-HISPANIC		ASIAN OR PACIFIC ISLANDER		HISPANIC		TOTAL MINORITY		WHITE NON-HISPANIC		NON-RESIDENT ALIEN	
	NUMBER	%	NUMBER	%	NUMBER	%	NUMBER	%	NUMBER	%	NUMBER	%	NUMBER	%
DISTRICT OF COLUMBIA (3 INSTITUTIONS)														
UNDERGRADUATES:														
FULL-TIME	0	.0	0	.0	0	.0	0	.0	0	.0	0	.0	0	.0
FEMALE	0	.0	0	.0	0	.0	0	.0	0	.0	0	.0	0	.0
MALE	0	.0	0	.0	0	.0	0	.0	0	.0	0	.0	0	.0
PART-TIME	0	.0	0	.0	0	.0	0	.0	0	.0	0	.0	0	.0
FEMALE	0	.0	0	.0	0	.0	0	.0	0	.0	0	.0	0	.0
MALE	0	.0	0	.0	0	.0	0	.0	0	.0	0	.0	0	.0
TOTAL	0	.0	0	.0	0	.0	0	.0	0	.0	0	.0	0	.0
FEMALE	0	.0	0	.0	0	.0	0	.0	0	.0	0	.0	0	.0
MALE	0	.0	0	.0	0	.0	0	.0	0	.0	0	.0	0	.0
GRADUATE														
FULL-TIME	0	.0	0	.0	0	.0	0	.0	0	.0	0	.0	0	.0
FEMALE	0	.0	0	.0	0.	.0	0	.0	0	.0	0	.0	0	.0
MALE	0	.0	0	.0	0	.0	0	.0	0	.0	0	.0	0	.0
PART-TIME	0	.0	0	.0	0	.0	0	.0	0	.0	0	.0	0	.0
FEMALE	0	.0	0	.0	0	.0	0	.0	0	.0	0	.0	0	.0
MALE	0	.0	0	.0	0	.0	0	.0	0	.0	0	.0	0	.0
TOTAL	0	.0	0	.0	0	.0	0	.0	0	.0	0	.0	0	.0
FEMALE	0	.0	0	.0	0	.0	0	.0	0	.0	0	.0	0	.0
MALE	0	.0	0	.0	0	.0	0	.0	0	.0	0	.0	0	.0
PROFESSIONAL:														
FULL-TIME	6	.3	428	22.6	24	1.3	19	1.0	477	25.2	1,363	72.1	50	2.6
FEMALE	2	.4	177	36.2	11	2.2	8	1.6	198	40.5	279	57.1	12	2.5
MALE	4	.3	251	17.9	13	.9	11	.8	279	19.9	1,084	77.4	38	2.7
PART-TIME	0	.0	3	75.0	0	.0	0	.0	3	75.0	0	.0	1	25.0
FEMALE	0	.0	2	100.0	0	.0	0	.0	2	100.0	0	.0	0	.0
MALE	0	.0	1	50.0	0	.0	0	.0	1	50.0	0	.0	1	50.0
TOTAL	6	.3	431	22.8	24	1.3	19	1.0	480	25.3	1,363	72.0	51	2.7
FEMALE	2	.4	179	36.5	11	2.2	8	1.6	200	40.7	279	56.8	12	2.4
MALE	4	.3	252	18.0	13	.9	11	.8	280	20.0	1,084	77.3	39	2.8
UNG+GRAD+PROF:														
FULL-TIME	6	.3	428	22.6	24	1.3	19	1.0	477	25.2	1,363	72.1	50	2.6
FEMALE	2	.4	177	36.2	11	2.2	8	1.6	198	40.5	279	57.1	12	2.5
MALE	4	.3	251	17.9	13	.9	11	.8	279	19.9	1,084	77.4	38	2.7
PART-TIME	0	.0	3	75.0	0	.0	0	.0	3	75.0	0	.0	0	.0
FEMALE	0	.0	2	100.0	0	.0	0	.0	2	100.0	0	.0	1	50.0
MALE	0	.0	1	50.0	0	.0	0	.0	1	50.0	0	.0		
TOTAL	6	.3	431	22.8	24	1.3	19	1.0	480	25.3	1,363	72.0	51	2.7
FEMALE	2	.4	179	36.5	11	2.2	8	1.6	200	40.7	279	56.8	12	2.4
MALE	4	.3	252	18.0	13	.9	11	.8	280	20.0	1,084	77.3	39	2.8
UNCLASSIFIED:														
TOTAL	0	.0	0	.0	0	.0	0	.0	0	.0	0	.0	0	.0
FEMALE	0	.0	0	.0	0	.0	0	.0	0	.0	0	.0	0	.0
MALE	0	.0	0	.0	0	.0	0	.0	0	.0	0	.0	0	.0
TOTAL ENROLLMENT:														
TOTAL	6	.3	431	22.8	24	1.3	19	1.0	480	25.3	1,363	72.0	51	2.7
FEMALE	2	.4	179	36.5	11	2.2	8	1.6	200	40.7	279	56.8	12	2.4
MALE	4	.3	252	18.0	13	.9	11	.8	280	20.0	1,084	77.3	39	2.8
FLORIDA (3 INSTITUTIONS)														
UNDERGRADUATES:														
FULL-TIME	0	.0	0	.0	0	.0	0	.0	0	.0	0	.0	0	.0
FEMALE	0	.0	0	.0	0	.0	0	.0	0	.0	0	.0	0	.0
MALE	0	.0	0	.0	0	.0	0	.0	0	.0	0	.0	0	.0
PART-TIME	0	.0	0	.0	0	.0	0	.0	0	.0	0	.0	0	.0
FEMALE	0	.0	0	.0	0	.0	0	.0	0	.0	0	.0	0	.0
MALE	0	.0	0	.0	0	.0	0	.0	0	.0	0	.0	0	.0
TOTAL	0	.0	0	.0	0	.0	0	.0	0	.0	0	.0	0	.0
FEMALE	0	.0	0	.0	0	.0	0	.0	0	.0	0	.0	0	.0
MALE	0	.0	0	.0	0	.0	0	.0	0	.0	0	.0	0	.0
GRADUATE														
FULL-TIME	0	.0	0	.0	0	.0	0	.0	0	.0	0	.0	0	.0
FEMALE	0	.0	0	.0	0	.0	0	.0	0	.0	0	.0	0	.0
MALE	0	.0	0	.0	0	.0	0	.0	0	.0	0	.0	0	.0
PART-TIME	0	.0	0	.0	0	.0	0	.0	0	.0	0	.0	0	.0
FEMALE	0	.0	0	.0	0	.0	0	.0	0	.0	0	.0	0	.0
MALE	0	.0	0	.0	0	.0	0	.0	0	.0	0	.0	0	.0
TOTAL	0	.0	0	.0	0	.0	0	.0	0	.0	0	.0	0	.0
FEMALE	0	.0	0	.0	0	.0	0	.0	0	.0	0	.0	0	.0
MALE	0	.0	0	.0	0	.0	0	.0	0	.0	0	.0	0	.0
PROFESSIONAL:														
FULL-TIME	3	.2	60	4.6	12	.9	83	6.3	158	12.0	1,154	88.0	0	.0
FEMALE	0	.0	15	5.8	3	1.2	14	5.4	32	12.3	228	87.7	0	.0
MALE	3	.3	45	4.3	9	.9	69	6.6	126	12.0	926	88.0	0	.0

MEDICINE

INDIAN NATIVE	BLACK NON-HISPANIC		ASIAN OR PACIFIC ISLANDER		HISPANIC		TOTAL MINORITY		WHITE NON-HISPANIC		NON-RESIDENT ALIEN		TOTAL
%	NUMBER	%	NUMBER	%	NUMBER	%	NUMBER	%	NUMBER	%	NUMBER	%	NUMBER

CONTINUED

.0	0	.0	0	.0	0	.0	0	.0	0	.0	0	.0	0
.0	0	.0	0	.0	0	.0	0	.0	0	.0	0	.0	0
.0	0	.0	0	.0	0	.0	0	.0	0	.0	0	.0	0
.2	60	4.6	12	.9	83	6.3	158	12.0	1,154	88.0	0	.0	1,312
.0	15	5.8	3	1.2	14	5.4	32	12.3	228	87.7	0	.0	260
.3	45	4.3	9	.9	69	6.6	126	12.0	926	88.0	0	.0	1,052
.2	60	4.6	12	.9	83	6.3	158	12.0	1,154	88.0	0	.0	1,312
.0	15	5.8	3	1.2	14	5.4	32	12.3	228	87.7	0	.0	260
.3	45	4.3	9	.9	69	6.6	126	12.0	926	88.0	0	.0	1,052
.0	0	.0	0	.0	0	.0	0	.0	0	.0	0	.0	0
.0	0	.0	0	.0	0	.0	0	.0	0	.0	0	.0	0
.0	0	.0	0	.0	0	.0	0	.0	0	.0	0	.0	0
.2	60	4.6	12	.9	83	6.3	158	12.0	1,154	88.0	0	.0	1,312
.0	15	5.8	3	1.2	14	5.4	32	12.3	228	87.7	0	.0	260
.3	45	4.3	9	.9	69	6.6	126	12.0	926	88.0	0	.0	1,052
.0	0	.0	0	.0	0	.0	0	.0	0	.0	0	.0	0
.0	0	.0	0	.0	0	.0	0	.0	0	.0	0	.0	0
.0	0	.0	0	.0	0	.0	0	.0	0	.0	0	.0	0
.2	60	4.6	12	.9	83	6.3	158	12.0	1,154	88.0	0	.0	1,312
.0	15	5.8	3	1.2	14	5.4	32	12.3	228	87.7	0	.0	260
.3	45	4.3	9	.9	69	6.6	126	12.0	926	88.0	0	.0	1,052

(2 INSTITUTIONS)

.0	0	.0	0	.0	0	.0	0	.0	0	.0	0	.0	0
.0	0	.0	0	.0	0	.0	0	.0	0	.0	0	.0	0
.0	0	.0	0	.0	0	.0	0	.0	0	.0	0	.0	0
.0	0	.0	0	.0	0	.0	0	.0	0	.0	0	.0	0
.0	0	.0	0	.0	0	.0	0	.0	0	.0	0	.0	0
.0	0	.0	0	.0	0	.0	0	.0	0	.0	0	.0	0
.0	0	.0	0	.0	0	.0	0	.0	0	.0	0	.0	0
.0	0	.0	0	.0	0	.0	0	.0	0	.0	0	.0	0
.0	0	.0	0	.0	0	.0	0	.0	0	.0	0	.0	0
.0	0	.0	0	.0	0	.0	0	.0	0	.0	0	.0	0
.0	0	.0	0	.0	0	.0	0	.0	0	.0	0	.0	0
.0	0	.0	0	.0	0	.0	0	.0	0	.0	0	.0	0
.0	0	.0	0	.0	0	.0	0	.0	0	.0	0	.0	0
.0	0	.0	0	.0	0	.0	0	.0	0	.0	0	.0	0
.0	0	.0	0	.0	0	.0	0	.0	0	.0	0	.0	0
.1	35	3.0	8	.7	14	1.2	58	4.9	1,121	95.0	1	.1	1,180
.0	11	4.7	2	.8	1	.4	14	5.9	222	94.1	0	.0	236
.1	24	2.5	6	.6	13	1.4	44	4.7	899	95.2	1	.1	944
.0	0	.0	0	.0	0	.0	0	.0	0	.0	0	.0	0
.0	0	.0	0	.0	0	.0	0	.0	0	.0	0	.0	0
.1	35	3.0	8	.7	14	1.2	58	4.9	1,121	95.0	1	.1	1,180
.0	11	4.7	2	.8	1	.4	14	5.9	222	94.1	0	.0	236
.1	24	2.5	6	.6	13	1.4	44	4.7	899	95.2	1	.1	944
.1	35	3.0	8	.7	14	1.2	58	4.9	1,121	95.0	1	.1	1,180
.0	11	4.7	2	.8	1	.4	14	5.9	222	94.1	0	.0	236
.1	24	2.5	6	.6	13	1.4	44	4.7	899	95.2	1	.1	944
.0	0	.0	0	.0	0	.0	0	.0	0	.0	0	.0	0
.0	0	.0	0	.0	0	.0	0	.0	0	.0	0	.0	0
.1	35	3.0	8	.7	14	1.2	58	4.9	1,121	95.0	1	.1	1,180
.0	11	4.7	2	.8	1	.4	14	5.9	222	94.1	0	.0	236
.1	24	2.5	6	.6	13	1.4	44	4.7	899	95.2	1	.1	944
.0	0	.0	0	.0	0	.0	0	.0	0	.0	0	.0	0
.0	0	.0	0	.0	0	.0	0	.0	0	.0	0	.0	0
.0	0	.0	0	.0	0	.0	0	.0	0	.0	0	.0	0
.1	35	3.0	8	.7	14	1.2	58	4.9	1,121	95.0	1	.1	1,180
.0	11	4.7	2	.8	1	.4	14	5.9	222	94.1	0	.0	236
.1	24	2.5	6	.6	13	1.4	44	4.7	899	95.2	1	.1	944

TABLE 17 - TOTAL ENROLLMENT IN INSTITUTIONS OF HIGHER EDUCATION FOR SELECTED MAJOR FIELDS OF STUDY AND LEVEL OF ENROLLMENT
BY RACE, ETHNICITY, AND SEX: STATE, 1978

MAJOR FIELD 1206 - MEDICINE

	AMERICAN INDIAN ALASKAN NATIVE		BLACK NON-HISPANIC		ASIAN OR PACIFIC ISLANDER		HISPANIC		TOTAL MINORITY		WHITE NON-HISPANIC		NON-RESIDENT ALIEN		TOT
	NUMBER	%	NUMBER	%	NUMBER	%	NUMBER	%	NUMBER	%	NUMBER	%	NUMBER	%	NUM
HAWAII	(	1 INSTITUTIONS)													
UNDERGRADUATES:															
FULL-TIME	0	.0	0	.0	0	.0	0	.0	0	.0	0	.0	0	.0	
FEMALE	0	.0	0	.0	0	.0	0	.0	0	.0	0	.0	0	.0	
MALE	0	.0	0	.0	0	.0	0	.0	0	.0	0	.0	0	.0	
PART-TIME	0	.0	0	.0	0	.0	0	.0	0	.0	0	.0	0	.0	
FEMALE	0	.0	0	.0	0	.0	0	.0	0	.0	0	.0	0	.0	
MALE	0	.0	0	.0	0	.0	0	.0	0	.0	0	.0	0	.0	
TOTAL	0	.0	0	.0	0	.0	0	.0	0	.0	0	.0	0	.0	
FEMALE	0	.0	0	.0	0	.0	0	.0	0	.0	0	.0	0	.0	
MALE	0	.0	0	.0	0	.0	0	.0	0	.0	0	.0	0	.0	
GRADUATE:															
FULL-TIME	0	.0	0	.0	0	.0	0	.0	0	.0	0	.0	0	.0	
FEMALE	0	.0	0	.0	0	.0	0	.0	0	.0	0	.0	0	.0	
MALE	0	.0	0	.0	0	.0	0	.0	0	.0	0	.0	0	.0	
PART-TIME	0	.0	0	.0	0	.0	0	.0	0	.0	0	.0	0	.0	
FEMALE	0	.0	0	.0	0	.0	0	.0	0	.0	0	.0	0	.0	
MALE	0	.0	0	.0	0	.0	0	.0	0	.0	0	.0	0	.0	
TOTAL	0	.0	0	.0	0	.0	0	.0	0	.0	0	.0	0	.0	
FEMALE	0	.0	0	.0	0	.0	0	.0	0	.0	0	.0	0	.0	
MALE	0	.0	0	.0	0	.0	0	.0	0	.0	0	.0	0	.0	
PROFESSIONAL:															
FULL-TIME	0	.0	0	.0	204	72.6	0	.0	204	72.6	68	24.2	9	3.2	
FEMALE	0	.0	0	.0	45	59.2	0	.0	45	59.2	29	38.2	2	2.6	
MALE	0	.0	0	.0	159	77.6	0	.0	159	77.6	39	19.0	7	3.4	
PART-TIME	0	.0	0	.0	5	71.4	0	.0	5	71.4	2	28.6	0	.0	
FEMALE	0	.0	0	.0	3	75.0	0	.0	3	75.0	1	25.0	0	.0	
MALE	0	.0	0	.0	2	66.7	0	.0	2	66.7	1	33.3	0	.0	
TOTAL	0	.0	0	.0	209	72.6	0	.0	209	72.6	70	24.3	9	3.1	
FEMALE	0	.0	0	.0	48	60.0	0	.0	48	60.0	30	37.5	2	2.5	
MALE	0	.0	0	.0	161	77.4	0	.0	161	77.4	40	19.2	7	3.4	
UND+GRAD+PROF:															
FULL-TIME	0	.0	0	.0	204	72.6	0	.0	204	72.6	68	24.2	9	3.2	
FEMALE	0	.0	0	.0	45	59.2	0	.0	45	59.2	29	38.2	2	2.6	
MALE	0	.0	0	.0	159	77.6	0	.0	159	77.6	39	19.0	7	3.4	
PART-TIME	0	.0	0	.0	5	71.4	0	.0	5	71.4	2	28.6	0	.0	
FEMALE	0	.0	0	.0	3	75.0	0	.0	3	75.0	1	25.0	0	.0	
MALE	0	.0	0	.0	2	66.7	0	.0	2	66.7	1	33.3	0	.0	
TOTAL	0	.0	0	.0	209	72.6	0	.0	209	72.6	70	24.3	9	3.1	
FEMALE	0	.0	0	.0	48	60.0	0	.0	48	60.0	30	37.5	2	2.5	
MALE	0	.0	0	.0	161	77.4	0	.0	161	77.4	40	19.2	7	3.4	
UNCLASSIFIED:															
TOTAL	0	.0	0	.0	0	.0	0	.0	0	.0	0	.0	0	.0	
FEMALE	0	.0	0	.0	0	.0	0	.0	0	.0	0	.0	0	.0	
MALE	0	.0	0	.0	0	.0	0	.0	0	.0	0	.0	0	.0	
TOTAL ENROLLMENT:															
TOTAL	0	.0	0	.0	209	72.6	0	.0	209	72.6	70	24.3	9	3.1	
FEMALE	0	.0	0	.0	48	60.0	0	.0	48	60.0	30	37.5	2	2.5	
MALE	0	.0	0	.0	161	77.4	0	.0	161	77.4	40	19.2	7	3.4	
ILLINOIS	(	8 INSTITUTIONS)													
UNDERGRADUATES:															
FULL-TIME	0	.0	0	.0	0	.0	0	.0	0	.0	0	.0	0	.0	
FEMALE	0	.0	0	.0	0	.0	0	.0	0	.0	0	.0	0	.0	
MALE	0	.0	0	.0	0	.0	0	.0	0	.0	0	.0	0	.0	
PART-TIME	0	.0	0	.0	0	.0	0	.0	0	.0	0	.0	0	.0	
FEMALE	0	.0	0	.0	0	.0	0	.0	0	.0	0	.0	0	.0	
MALE	0	.0	0	.0	0	.0	0	.0	0	.0	0	.0	0	.0	
TOTAL	0	.0	0	.0	0	.0	0	.0	0	.0	0	.0	0	.0	
FEMALE	0	.0	0	.0	0	.0	0	.0	0	.0	0	.0	0	.0	
MALE	0	.0	0	.0	0	.0	0	.0	0	.0	0	.0	0	.0	
GRADUATE:															
FULL-TIME	0	.0	0	.0	0	.0	0	.0	0	.0	0	.0	0	.0	
FEMALE	0	.0	0	.0	0	.0	0	.0	0	.0	0	.0	0	.0	
MALE	0	.0	0	.0	0	.0	0	.0	0	.0	0	.0	0	.0	
PART-TIME	0	.0	0	.0	0	.0	0	.0	0	.0	0	.0	0	.0	
FEMALE	0	.0	0	.0	0	.0	0	.0	0	.0	0	.0	0	.0	
MALE	0	.0	0	.0	0	.0	0	.0	0	.0	0	.0	0	.0	
TOTAL	0	.0	0	.0	0	.0	0	.0	0	.0	0	.0	0	.0	
FEMALE	0	.0	0	.0	0	.0	0	.0	0	.0	0	.0	0	.0	
MALE	0	.0	0	.0	0	.0	0	.0	0	.0	0	.0	0	.0	
PROFESSIONAL:															
FULL-TIME	9	.2	232	5.2	121	2.7	85	1.9	447	10.0	3,991	89.3	31	.7	
FEMALE	1	.1	104	9.8	28	2.6	21	2.0	154	14.5	901	84.9	6	.6	
MALE	8	.2	128	3.8	93	2.7	64	1.9	293	8.6	3,090	90.7	25	.7	

508

ENROLLMENT IN INSTITUTIONS OF HIGHER EDUCATION FOR SELECTED MAJOR FIELDS OF STUDY AND LEVEL OF ENROLLMENT
CE, ETHNICITY, AND SEX: STATE, 1978

- MEDICINE

CAN INDIAN IN NATIVE		BLACK NON-HISPANIC		ASIAN OR PACIFIC ISLANDER		HISPANIC		TOTAL MINORITY		WHITE NON-HISPANIC		NON-RESIDENT ALIEN		TOTAL
EK	%	NUMBER	%	NUMBER	%	NUMBER	%	NUMBER	%	NUMBER	%	NUMBER	%	NUMBER
		CONTINUED												
0	.0	4	20.0	0	.0	3	15.0	7	35.0	13	65.0	0	.0	20
0	.0	0	.0	0	.0	0	.0	0	.0	5	100.0	0	.0	5
0	.0	4	26.7	0	.0	3	20.0	7	46.7	8	53.3	0	.0	15
9	.2	236	5.3	121	2.7	88	2.0	454	10.1	4,004	89.2	31	.7	4,489
1	.1	104	9.8	28	2.6	21	2.0	154	14.4	906	85.0	6	.6	1,066
6	.2	132	3.9	93	2.7	67	2.0	300	8.8	3,098	90.5	25	.7	3,423
9	.2	232	5.2	121	2.7	85	1.9	447	10.0	3,991	89.3	31	.7	4,469
1	.1	104	9.8	28	2.6	21	2.0	154	14.5	901	84.9	6	.6	1,061
B	.2	128	3.8	93	2.7	64	1.9	293	8.6	3,090	90.7	25	.7	3,408
0	.0	4	20.0	0	.0	3	15.0	7	35.0	13	65.0	0	.0	20
0	.0	0	.0	0	.0	0	.0	0	.0	5	100.0	0	.0	5
0	.0	4	26.7	0	.0	3	20.0	7	46.7	8	53.3	0	.0	15
9	.2	236	5.3	121	2.7	88	2.0	454	10.1	4,004	89.2	31	.7	4,489
1	.1	104	9.8	28	2.6	21	2.0	154	14.4	906	85.0	6	.6	1,066
B	.2	132	3.9	93	2.7	67	2.0	300	8.8	3,098	90.5	25	.7	3,423
0	.0	0	.0	0	.0	0	.0	0	.0	0	.0	0	.0	0
0	.0	0	.0	0	.0	0	.0	0	.0	0	.0	0	.0	0
0	.0	0	.0	0	.0	0	.0	0	.0	0	.0	0	.0	0
9	.2	236	5.3	121	2.7	88	2.0	454	10.1	4,004	89.2	31	.7	4,489
1	.1	104	9.8	28	2.6	21	2.0	154	14.4	906	85.0	6	.6	1,066
B	.2	132	3.9	93	2.7	67	2.0	300	8.8	3,098	90.5	25	.7	3,423
(		4 INSTITUTIONS)												
0	.0	0	.0	0	.0	0	.0	0	.0	0	.0	0	.0	0
0	.0	0	.0	0	.0	0	.0	0	.0	0	.0	0	.0	0
0	.0	0	.0	0	.0	0	.0	0	.0	0	.0	0	.0	0
0	.0	0	.0	0	.0	0	.0	0	.0	0	.0	0	.0	0
0	.0	0	.0	0	.0	0	.0	0	.0	0	.0	0	.0	0
0	.0	0	.0	0	.0	0	.0	0	.0	0	.0	0	.0	0
0	.0	0	.0	0	.0	0	.0	0	.0	0	.0	0	.0	0
0	.0	0	.0	0	.0	0	.0	0	.0	0	.0	0	.0	0
0	.0	0	.0	0	.0	0	.0	0	.0	0	.0	0	.0	0
0	.0	0	.0	0	.0	0	.0	0	.0	0	.0	0	.0	0
0	.0	0	.0	0	.0	0	.0	0	.0	0	.0	0	.0	0
0	.0	0	.0	0	.0	0	.0	0	.0	0	.0	0	.0	0
0	.0	0	.0	0	.0	0	.0	0	.0	0	.0	0	.0	0
0	.0	0	.0	0	.0	0	.0	0	.0	0	.0	0	.0	0
0	.0	0	.0	0	.0	0	.0	0	.0	0	.0	0	.0	0
3	.3	18	1.6	11	1.0	5	.4	37	3.3	1,080	95.9	9	.8	1,126
0	.0	8	3.4	3	1.3	2	.9	13	5.6	216	93.1	3	1.3	232
3	.3	10	1.1	8	.9	3	.3	24	2.7	864	96.6	6	.7	894
0	.0	2	3.0	2	3.0	0	.0	4	6.1	62	93.9	0	.0	66
C	.0	1	5.3	0	.0	1	5.3	1	5.3	18	94.7	0	.0	19
0	.0	1	2.1	2	4.3	0	.0	3	6.4	44	93.6	0	.0	47
3	.3	20	1.7	13	1.1	5	.4	41	3.4	1,142	95.8	9	.8	1,192
0	.0	9	3.6	3	1.2	2	.8	14	5.6	234	93.2	3	1.2	251
3	.3	11	1.2	10	1.1	3	.3	27	2.9	908	96.5	6	.6	941
3	.3	18	1.6	11	1.0	5	.4	37	3.3	1,080	95.9	9	.8	1,126
0	.0	8	3.4	3	1.3	2	.9	13	5.6	216	93.1	3	1.3	232
3	.3	10	1.1	8	.9	3	.3	24	2.7	864	96.6	6	.7	894
0	.0	2	3.0	2	3.0	0	.0	4	6.1	62	93.9	0	.0	66
0	.0	1	5.3	0	.0	0	.0	1	5.3	18	94.7	0	.0	19
0	.0	1	2.1	2	4.3	0	.0	3	6.4	44	93.6	0	.0	47
3	.3	20	1.7	13	1.1	5	.4	41	3.4	1,142	95.8	9	.8	1,192
0	.0	9	3.6	3	1.2	2	.8	14	5.6	234	93.2	3	1.2	251
3	.3	11	1.2	10	1.1	3	.3	27	2.9	908	96.5	6	.6	941
0	.0	0	.0	0	.0	0	.0	0	.0	0	.0	0	.0	0
0	.0	0	.0	0	.0	0	.0	0	.0	0	.0	0	.0	0
0	.0	0	.0	0	.0	0	.0	0	.0	0	.0	0	.0	0
3	.3	20	1.7	13	1.1	5	.4	41	3.4	1,142	95.8	9	.8	1,192
0	.0	9	3.6	3	1.2	2	.8	14	5.6	234	93.2	3	1.2	251
3	.3	11	1.2	10	1.1	3	.3	27	2.9	908	96.5	6	.6	941

TABLE 17 - TOTAL ENROLLMENT IN INSTITUTIONS OF HIGHER EDUCATION FOR SELECTED MAJOR FIELDS OF STUDY AND LEVEL OF ENROLLMENT BY RACE, ETHNICITY, AND SEX: STATE, 1978

MAJOR FIELD 1206 - MEDICINE

	AMERICAN INDIAN ALASKAN NATIVE		BLACK NON-HISPANIC		ASIAN OR PACIFIC ISLANDER		HISPANIC		TOTAL MINORITY		WHITE NON-HISPANIC		NON-RESIDENT ALIEN	
	NUMBER	%	NUMBER	%	NUMBER	%	NUMBER	%	NUMBER	%	NUMBER	%	NUMBER	%
IOWA			**2 INSTITUTIONS)**											
UNDERGRADUATES:														
FULL-TIME	0	.0	0	.0	0	.0	0	.0	0	.0	0	.0	0	.0
FEMALE	0	.0	0	.0	0	.0	0	.0	0	.0	0	.0	0	.0
MALE	0	.0	0	.0	0	.0	0	.0	0	.0	0	.0	0	.0
PART-TIME	0	.0	0	.0	0	.0	0	.0	0	.0	0	.0	0	.0
FEMALE	0	.0	0	.0	0	.0	0	.0	0	.0	0	.0	0	.0
MALE	0	.0	0	.0	0	.0	0	.0	0	.0	0	.0	0	.0
TOTAL	0	.0	0	.0	0	.0	0	.0	0	.0	0	.0	0	.0
FEMALE	0	.0	0	.0	0	.0	0	.0	0	.0	0	.0	0	.0
MALE	0	.0	0	.0	0	.0	0	.0	0	.0	0	.0	0	.0
GRADUATE:														
FULL-TIME	0	.0	0	.0	0	.0	0	.0	0	.0	0	.0	0	.0
FEMALE	0	.0	0	.0	0	.0	0	.0	0	.0	0	.0	0	.0
MALE	0	.0	0	.0	0	.0	0	.0	0	.0	0	.0	0	.0
PART-TIME	0	.0	0	.0	0	.0	0	.0	0	.0	0	.0	0	.0
FEMALE	0	.0	0	.0	0	.0	0	.0	0	.0	0	.0	0	.0
MALE	0	.0	0	.0	0	.0	0	.0	0	.0	0	.0	0	.0
TOTAL	0	.0	0	.0	0	.0	0	.0	0	.0	0	.0	0	.0
FEMALE	0	.0	0	.0	0	.0	0	.0	0	.0	0	.0	0	.0
MALE	0	.0	0	.0	0	.0	0	.0	0	.0	0	.0	0	.0
PROFESSIONAL:														
FULL-TIME	12	.7	22	1.3	8	.5	14	.8	56	3.3	1,622	94.1	45	2.6
FEMALE	2	.6	6	1.9	2	.6	2	.6	12	3.8	291	92.1	13	4.1
MALE	10	.7	16	1.1	6	.4	12	.9	44	3.1	1,331	94.6	32	2.3
PART-TIME	0	.0	0	.0	0	.0	0	.0	0	.0	0	.0	0	.0
FEMALE	0	.0	0	.0	0	.0	0	.0	0	.0	0	.0	0	.0
MALE	0	.0	0	.0	0	.0	0	.0	0	.0	0	.0	0	.0
TOTAL	12	.7	22	1.3	8	.5	14	.8	56	3.3	1,622	94.1	45	2.6
FEMALE	2	.6	6	1.9	2	.6	2	.6	12	3.8	291	92.1	13	4.1
MALE	10	.7	16	1.1	6	.4	12	.9	44	3.1	1,331	94.6	32	2.3
UND+GRAD+PROF:														
FULL-TIME	12	.7	22	1.3	8	.5	14	.8	56	3.3	1,622	94.1	45	2.6
FEMALE	2	.6	6	1.9	2	.6	2	.6	12	3.8	291	92.1	13	4.1
MALE	10	.7	16	1.1	6	.4	12	.9	44	3.1	1,331	94.6	32	2.3
PART-TIME	0	.0	0	.0	0	.0	0	.0	0	.0	0	.0	0	.0
FEMALE	0	.0	0	.0	0	.0	0	.0	0	.0	0	.0	0	.0
MALE	0	.0	0	.0	0	.0	0	.0	0	.0	0	.0	0	.0
TOTAL	12	.7	22	1.3	8	.5	14	.8	56	3.3	1,622	94.1	45	2.6
FEMALE	2	.6	6	1.9	2	.6	2	.6	12	3.8	291	92.1	13	4.1
MALE	10	.7	16	1.1	6	.4	12	.9	44	3.1	1,331	94.6	32	2.3
UNCLASSIFIED:														
TOTAL	0	.0	0	.0	0	.0	0	.0	0	.0	0	.0	0	.0
FEMALE	0	.0	0	.0	0	.0	0	.0	0	.0	0	.0	0	.0
MALE	0	.0	0	.0	0	.0	0	.0	0	.0	0	.0	0	.0
TOTAL ENROLLMENT:														
TOTAL	12	.7	22	1.3	8	.5	14	.8	56	3.3	1,622	94.1	45	2.6
FEMALE	2	.6	6	1.9	2	.6	2	.6	12	3.8	291	92.1	13	4.1
MALE	10	.7	16	1.1	6	.4	12	.9	44	3.1	1,331	94.6	32	2.3
KANSAS			**1 INSTITUTIONS)**											
UNDERGRADUATES:														
FULL-TIME	0	.0	0	.0	0	.0	0	.0	0	.0	0	.0	0	.0
FEMALE	0	.0	0	.0	0	.0	0	.0	0	.0	0	.0	0	.0
MALE	0	.0	0	.0	0	.0	0	.0	0	.0	0	.0	0	.0
PART-TIME	0	.0	0	.0	0	.0	0	.0	0	.0	0	.0	0	.0
FEMALE	0	.0	0	.0	0	.0	0	.0	0	.0	0	.0	0	.0
MALE	0	.0	0	.0	0	.0	0	.0	0	.0	0	.0	0	.0
TOTAL	0	.0	0	.0	0	.0	0	.0	0	.0	0	.0	0	.0
FEMALE	0	.0	0	.0	0	.0	0	.0	0	.0	0	.0	0	.0
MALE	0	.0	0	.0	0	.0	0	.0	0	.0	0	.0	0	.0
GRADUATE:														
FULL-TIME	0	.0	0	.0	0	.0	0	.0	0	.0	0	.0	0	.0
FEMALE	0	.0	0	.0	0	.0	0	.0	0	.0	0	.0	0	.0
MALE	0	.0	0	.0	0	.0	0	.0	0	.0	0	.0	0	.0
PART-TIME	0	.0	0	.0	0	.0	0	.0	0	.0	0	.0	0	.0
FEMALE	0	.0	0	.0	0	.0	0	.0	0	.0	0	.0	0	.0
MALE	0	.0	0	.0	0	.0	0	.0	0	.0	0	.0	0	.0
TOTAL	0	.0	0	.0	0	.0	0	.0	0	.0	0	.0	0	.0
FEMALE	0	.0	0	.0	0	.0	0	.0	0	.0	0	.0	0	.0
MALE	0	.0	0	.0	0	.0	0	.0	0	.0	0	.0	0	.0
PROFESSIONAL:														
FULL-TIME	3	.4	16	2.2	8	1.1	9	1.3	36	5.0	678	95.0	0	.0
FEMALE	0	.0	5	3.7	2	1.5	5	3.7	12	8.8	124	91.2	0	.0
MALE	3	.5	11	1.9	6	1.0	4	.7	24	4.2	554	95.8	0	.0

- MEDICINE

CAN INDIAN AN NATIVE		BLACK NON-HISPANIC		ASIAN OR PACIFIC ISLANDER		HISPANIC		TOTAL MINORITY		WHITE NON-HISPANIC		NON-RESIDENT ALIEN		TOTAL
ER	%	NUMBER	%	NUMBER	%	NUMBER	%	NUMBER	%	NUMBER	%	NUMBER	%	NUMBER
CONTINUED														
0	.0	2	9.5	0	.0	0	.0	2	9.5	19	90.5	0	.0	21
0	.0	1	50.0	0	.0	0	.0	1	50.0	1	50.0	0	.0	2
0	.0	1	5.3	0	.0	0	.0	1	5.3	18	94.7	0	.0	19
3	.4	18	2.4	8	1.1	9	1.2	38	5.2	697	94.8	0	.0	735
0	.0	6	4.3	2	1.4	5	3.6	13	9.4	125	90.6	0	.0	138
3	.5	12	2.0	6	1.0	4	.7	25	4.2	572	95.8	0	.0	597
3	.4	16	2.2	8	1.1	9	1.3	36	5.0	678	95.0	0	.0	714
0	.0	5	3.7	2	1.5	5	3.7	12	8.8	124	91.2	0	.0	136
3	.5	11	1.9	6	1.0	4	.7	24	4.2	554	95.8	0	.0	578
0	.0	2	9.5	0	.0	0	.0	2	9.5	19	90.5	0	.0	21
0	.0	1	50.0	0	.0	0	.0	1	50.0	1	50.0	0	.0	2
0	.0	1	5.3	0	.0	0	.0	1	5.3	18	94.7	0	.0	19
3	.4	18	2.4	8	1.1	9	1.2	38	5.2	697	94.8	0	.0	735
0	.0	6	4.3	2	1.4	5	3.6	13	9.4	125	90.6	0	.0	138
3	.5	12	2.0	6	1.0	4	.7	25	4.2	572	95.8	0	.0	597
0	.0	0	.0	0	.0	0	.0	0	.0	0	.0	0	.0	0
0	.0	0	.0	0	.0	0	.0	0	.0	0	.0	0	.0	0
0	.0	0	.0	0	.0	0	.0	0	.0	0	.0	0	.0	0
3	.4	18	2.4	8	1.1	9	1.2	38	5.2	697	94.8	0	.0	735
0	.0	6	4.3	2	1.4	5	3.6	13	9.4	125	90.6	0	.0	138
3	.5	12	2.0	6	1.0	4	.7	25	4.2	572	95.8	0	.0	597
(2 INSTITUTIONS)														
0	.0	0	.0	0	.0	0	.0	0	.0	0	.0	0	.0	0
0	.0	0	.0	0	.0	0	.0	0	.0	0	.0	0	.0	0
0	.0	0	.0	0	.0	0	.0	0	.0	0	.0	0	.0	0
0	.0	0	.0	0	.0	0	.0	0	.0	0	.0	0	.0	0
0	.0	0	.0	0	.0	0	.0	0	.0	0	.0	0	.0	0
0	.0	0	.0	0	.0	0	.0	0	.0	0	.0	0	.0	0
0	.0	0	.0	0	.0	0	.0	0	.0	0	.0	0	.0	0
0	.0	0	.0	0	.0	0	.0	0	.0	0	.0	0	.0	0
0	.0	0	.0	0	.0	0	.0	0	.0	0	.0	0	.0	0
0	.0	0	.0	0	.0	0	.0	0	.0	0	.0	0	.0	0
0	.0	0	.0	0	.0	0	.0	0	.0	0	.0	0	.0	0
0	.0	0	.0	0	.0	0	.0	0	.0	0	.0	0	.0	0
0	.0	0	.0	0	.0	0	.0	0	.0	0	.0	0	.0	0
0	.0	0	.0	0	.0	0	.0	0	.0	0	.0	0	.0	0
0	.0	0	.0	0	.0	0	.0	0	.0	0	.0	0	.0	0
0	.0	0	.0	0	.0	0	.0	0	.0	0	.0	0	.0	0
0	.0	0	.0	0	.0	0	.0	0	.0	0	.0	0	.0	0
0	.0	0	.0	0	.0	0	.0	0	.0	0	.0	0	.0	0
3	.2	30	2.1	70	5.0	10	.7	113	8.1	1,289	91.9	1	.1	1,403
2	.6	6	1.9	18	5.8	3	1.0	29	9.4	280	90.6	0	.0	309
1	.1	24	2.2	52	4.8	7	.6	84	7.7	1,009	92.2	1	.1	1,094
0	.0	0	.0	0	.0	0	.0	0	.0	0	.0	0	.0	0
0	.0	0	.0	0	.0	0	.0	0	.0	0	.0	0	.0	0
0	.0	0	.0	0	.0	0	.0	0	.0	0	.0	0	.0	0
3	.2	30	2.1	70	5.0	10	.7	113	8.1	1,289	91.9	1	.1	1,403
2	.6	6	1.9	18	5.8	3	1.0	29	9.4	280	90.6	0	.0	309
1	.1	24	2.2	52	4.8	7	.6	84	7.7	1,009	92.2	1	.1	1,094
3	.2	30	2.1	70	5.0	10	.7	113	8.1	1,289	91.9	1	.1	1,403
2	.6	6	1.9	18	5.8	3	1.0	29	9.4	280	90.6	0	.0	309
1	.1	24	2.2	52	4.8	7	.6	84	7.7	1,009	92.2	1	.1	1,094
0	.0	0	.0	0	.0	0	.0	0	.0	0	.0	0	.0	0
0	.0	0	.0	0	.0	0	.0	0	.0	0	.0	0	.0	0
3	.2	30	2.1	70	5.0	10	.7	113	8.1	1,289	91.9	1	.1	1,403
2	.6	6	1.9	18	5.8	3	1.0	29	9.4	280	90.6	0	.0	309
1	.1	24	2.2	52	4.8	7	.6	84	7.7	1,009	92.2	1	.1	1,094
0	.0	0	.0	0	.0	0	.0	0	.0	0	.0	0	.0	0
0	.0	0	.0	0	.0	0	.0	0	.0	0	.0	0	.0	0
0	.0	0	.0	0	.0	0	.0	0	.0	0	.0	0	.0	0
3	.2	30	2.1	70	5.0	10	.7	113	8.1	1,289	91.9	1	.1	1,403
2	.6	6	1.9	18	5.8	3	1.0	29	9.4	280	90.6	0	.0	309
1	.1	24	2.2	52	4.8	7	.6	84	7.7	1,009	92.2	1	.1	1,094

TABLE 17 - TOTAL ENROLLMENT IN INSTITUTIONS OF HIGHER EDUCATION FOR SELECTED MAJOR FIELDS OF STUDY AND LEVEL OF ENROLLMENT
BY RACE, ETHNICITY, AND SEX: STATE, 1978

MAJOR FIELD 1206 - MEDICINE

	AMERICAN INDIAN ALASKAN NATIVE		BLACK NON-HISPANIC		ASIAN OR PACIFIC ISLANDER		HISPANIC		TOTAL MINORITY		WHITE NON-HISPANIC		NON-RESIDENT ALIEN		TO NU
	NUMBER	%	NUMBER	%	NUMBER	%	NUMBER	%	NUMBER	%	NUMBER	%	NUMBER	%	
LOUISIANA (2 INSTITUTIONS)															
UNDERGRADUATES:															
FULL-TIME	0	.0	0	.0	0	.0	0	.0	0	.0	0	.0	0	.0	
FEMALE	0	.0	0	.0	0	.0	0	.0	0	.0	0	.0	0	.0	
MALE	0	.0	0	.0	0	.0	0	.0	0	.0	0	.0	0	.0	
PART-TIME	0	.0	0	.0	0	.0	0	.0	0	.0	0	.0	0	.0	
FEMALE	0	.0	0	.0	0	.0	0	.0	0	.0	0	.0	0	.0	
MALE	0	.0	0	.0	0	.0	0	.0	0	.0	0	.0	0	.0	
TOTAL	0	.0	0	.0	0	.0	0	.0	0	.0	0	.0	0	.0	
FEMALE	0	.0	0	.0	0	.0	0	.0	0	.0	0	.0	0	.0	
MALE	0	.0	0	.0	0	.0	0	.0	0	.0	0	.0	0	.0	
GRADUATE:															
FULL-TIME	0	.0	0	.0	0	.0	0	.0	0	.0	0	.0	0	.0	
FEMALE	0	.0	0	.0	0	.0	0	.0	0	.0	0	.0	0	.0	
MALE	0	.0	0	.0	0	.0	0	.0	0	.0	0	.0	0	.0	
PART-TIME	0	.0	0	.0	0	.0	0	.0	0	.0	0	.0	0	.0	
FEMALE	0	.0	0	.0	0	.0	0	.0	0	.0	0	.0	0	.0	
MALE	0	.0	0	.0	0	.0	0	.0	0	.0	0	.0	0	.0	
TOTAL	0	.0	0	.0	0	.0	0	.0	0	.0	0	.0	0	.0	
FEMALE	0	.0	0	.0	0	.0	0	.0	0	.0	0	.0	0	.0	
MALE	0	.0	0	.0	0	.0	0	.0	0	.0	0	.0	0	.0	
PROFESSIONAL:															
FULL-TIME	4	.2	63	3.7	20	1.2	25	1.5	112	6.6	1,582	92.9	8	.5	1
FEMALE	2	.6	22	6.7	4	1.2	6	1.8	34	10.3	295	89.4	1	.3	
MALE	2	.1	41	3.0	16	1.2	19	1.4	78	5.7	1,287	93.8	7	.5	1
PART-TIME	0	.0	0	.0	0	.0	0	.0	0	.0	0	.0	0	.0	
FEMALE	0	.0	0	.0	0	.0	0	.0	0	.0	0	.0	0	.0	
MALE	0	.0	0	.0	0	.0	0	.0	0	.0	0	.0	0	.0	
TOTAL	4	.2	63	3.7	20	1.2	25	1.5	112	6.6	1,582	92.9	8	.5	1
FEMALE	2	.6	22	6.7	4	1.2	6	1.8	34	10.3	295	89.4	1	.3	
MALE	2	.1	41	3.0	16	1.2	19	1.4	78	5.7	1,287	93.8	7	.5	1
UND+GRAD+PROF:															
FULL-TIME	4	.2	63	3.7	20	1.2	25	1.5	112	6.6	1,582	92.9	8	.5	1
FEMALE	2	.6	22	6.7	4	1.2	6	1.8	34	10.3	295	89.4	1	.3	
MALE	2	.1	41	3.0	16	1.2	19	1.4	78	5.7	1,287	93.8	7	.5	1
PART-TIME	0	.0	0	.0	0	.0	0	.0	0	.0	0	.0	0	.0	
FEMALE	0	.0	0	.0	0	.0	0	.0	0	.0	0	.0	0	.0	
MALE	0	.0	0	.0	0	.0	0	.0	0	.0	0	.0	0	.0	
TOTAL	4	.2	63	3.7	20	1.2	25	1.5	112	6.6	1,582	92.9	8	.5	1
FEMALE	2	.6	22	6.7	4	1.2	6	1.8	34	10.3	295	89.4	1	.3	
MALE	2	.1	41	3.0	16	1.2	19	1.4	78	5.7	1,287	93.8	7	.5	1
UNCLASSIFIED:															
TOTAL	0	.0	0	.0	0	.0	0	.0	0	.0	0	.0	0	.0	
FEMALE	0	.0	0	.0	0	.0	0	.0	0	.0	0	.0	0	.0	
MALE	0	.0	0	.0	0	.0	0	.0	0	.0	0	.0	0	.0	
TOTAL ENROLLMENT:															
TOTAL	4	.2	63	3.7	20	1.2	25	1.5	112	6.6	1,582	92.9	8	.5	1
FEMALE	2	.6	22	6.7	4	1.2	6	1.8	34	10.3	295	89.4	1	.3	
MALE	2	.1	41	3.0	16	1.2	19	1.4	78	5.7	1,287	93.8	7	.5	1
MARYLAND (2 INSTITUTIONS)															
UNDERGRADUATES:															
FULL-TIME	0	.0	0	.0	0	.0	0	.0	0	.0	0	.0	0	.0	
FEMALE	0	.0	0	.0	0	.0	0	.0	0	.0	0	.0	0	.0	
MALE	0	.0	0	.0	0	.0	0	.0	0	.0	0	.0	0	.0	
PART-TIME	0	.0	0	.0	0	.0	0	.0	0	.0	0	.0	0	.0	
FEMALE	0	.0	0	.0	0	.0	0	.0	0	.0	0	.0	0	.0	
MALE	0	.0	0	.0	0	.0	0	.0	0	.0	0	.0	0	.0	
TOTAL	0	.0	0	.0	0	.0	0	.0	0	.0	0	.0	0	.0	
FEMALE	0	.0	0	.0	0	.0	0	.0	0	.0	0	.0	0	.0	
MALE	0	.0	0	.0	0	.0	0	.0	0	.0	0	.0	0	.0	
GRADUATE:															
FULL-TIME	0	.0	0	.0	0	.0	0	.0	0	.0	0	.0	0	.0	
FEMALE	0	.0	0	.0	0	.0	0	.0	0	.0	0	.0	0	.0	
MALE	0	.0	0	.0	0	.0	0	.0	0	.0	0	.0	0	.0	
PART-TIME	0	.0	0	.0	0	.0	0	.0	0	.0	0	.0	0	.0	
FEMALE	0	.0	0	.0	0	.0	0	.0	0	.0	0	.0	0	.0	
MALE	0	.0	0	.0	0	.0	0	.0	0	.0	0	.0	0	.0	
TOTAL	0	.0	0	.0	0	.0	0	.0	0	.0	0	.0	0	.0	
FEMALE	0	.0	0	.0	0	.0	0	.0	0	.0	0	.0	0	.0	
MALE	0	.0	0	.0	0	.0	0	.0	0	.0	0	.0	0	.0	
PROFESSIONAL:															
FULL-TIME	1	.1	58	4.8	57	4.8	8	.7	124	10.3	1,066	88.9	9	.8	1
FEMALE	0	.0	21	8.2	16	6.3	0	.0	37	14.5	218	85.2	1	.4	
MALE	1	.1	37	3.9	41	4.3	8	.8	87	9.2	848	89.9	8	.8	

512

- MEDICINE

CAN INDIAN AN NATIVE		BLACK NON-HISPANIC		ASIAN OR PACIFIC ISLANDER		HISPANIC		TOTAL MINORITY		WHITE NON-HISPANIC		NON-RESIDENT ALIEN		TOTAL
ER	%	NUMBER	%	NUMBER	%	NUMBER	%	NUMBER	%	NUMBER	%	NUMBER	%	NUMBER

CONTINUED

0	.0	0	.0	0	.0	0	.0	0	.0	3	100.0	0	.0	3
0	.0	0	.0	0	.0	0	.0	0	.0	0	.0	0	.0	0
0	.0	0	.0	0	.0	0	.0	0	.0	3	100.0	0	.0	3
1	.1	58	4.8	57	4.7	8	.7	124	10.3	1,069	88.9	9	.7	1,202
0	.0	21	8.2	16	6.3	0	.0	37	14.5	218	85.2	1	.4	256
1	.1	37	3.9	41	4.3	8	.8	87	9.2	851	90.0	8	.8	946
1	.1	58	4.8	57	4.8	8	.7	124	10.3	1,066	88.9	9	.8	1,199
0	.0	21	8.2	16	6.3	0	.0	37	14.5	218	85.2	1	.4	256
1	.1	37	3.9	41	4.3	8	.8	87	9.2	848	89.9	8	.8	943
0	.0	0	.0	0	.0	0	.0	0	.0	3	100.0	0	.0	3
0	.0	0	.0	0	.0	0	.0	0	.0	0	.0	0	.0	0
0	.0	0	.0	0	.0	0	.0	0	.0	3	100.0	0	.0	3
1	.1	58	4.8	57	4.7	8	.7	124	10.3	1,069	88.9	9	.7	1,202
0	.0	21	8.2	16	6.3	0	.0	37	14.5	218	85.2	1	.4	256
1	.1	37	3.9	41	4.3	8	.8	87	9.2	851	90.0	8	.8	946
0	.0	0	.0	0	.0	0	.0	0	.0	0	.0	0	.0	0
0	.0	0	.0	0	.0	0	.0	0	.0	0	.0	0	.0	0
0	.0	0	.0	0	.0	0	.0	0	.0	0	.0	0	.0	0
1	.1	58	4.8	57	4.7	8	.7	124	10.3	1,069	88.9	9	.7	1,202
0	.0	21	8.2	16	6.3	0	.0	37	14.5	218	85.2	1	.4	256
1	.1	37	3.9	41	4.3	8	.8	87	9.2	851	90.0	8	.8	946

(5 INSTITUTIONS)

0	.0	0	.0	0	.0	0	.0	0	.0	0	.0	0	.0	0
0	.0	0	.0	0	.0	0	.0	0	.0	0	.0	0	.0	0
0	.0	0	.0	0	.0	0	.0	0	.0	0	.0	0	.0	0
0	.0	0	.0	0	.0	0	.0	0	.0	0	.0	0	.0	0
0	.0	0	.0	0	.0	0	.0	0	.0	0	.0	0	.0	0
0	.0	0	.0	0	.0	0	.0	0	.0	0	.0	0	.0	0
0	.0	0	.0	0	.0	0	.0	0	.0	0	.0	0	.0	0
0	.0	0	.0	0	.0	0	.0	0	.0	0	.0	0	.0	0
0	.0	0	.0	0	.0	0	.0	0	.0	0	.0	0	.0	0
0	.0	0	.0	0	.0	0	.0	0	.0	0	.0	0	.0	0
0	.0	0	.0	0	.0	0	.0	0	.0	0	.0	0	.0	0
0	.0	0	.0	0	.0	0	.0	0	.0	0	.0	0	.0	0
0	.0	0	.0	0	.0	0	.0	0	.0	0	.0	0	.0	0
0	.0	0	.0	0	.0	0	.0	0	.0	0	.0	0	.0	0
0	.0	0	.0	0	.0	0	.0	0	.0	0	.0	0	.0	0
0	.0	0	.0	0	.0	0	.0	0	.0	0	.0	0	.0	0
0	.0	0	.0	0	.0	0	.0	0	.0	0	.0	0	.0	0
2	.1	77	5.3	52	3.6	43	3.0	174	12.0	1,256	86.9	15	1.0	1,445
1	.2	35	8.0	14	3.2	18	4.1	68	15.5	370	84.5	0	.0	438
1	.1	42	4.2	38	3.8	25	2.5	106	10.5	886	88.0	15	1.5	1,007
0	.0	0	.0	0	.0	0	.0	0	.0	0	.0	0	.0	0
0	.0	0	.0	0	.0	0	.0	0	.0	0	.0	0	.0	0
2	.1	77	5.3	52	3.6	43	3.0	174	12.0	1,256	86.9	15	1.0	1,445
1	.2	35	8.0	14	3.2	18	4.1	68	15.5	370	84.5	0	.0	438
1	.1	42	4.2	38	3.8	25	2.5	106	10.5	886	88.0	15	1.5	1,007
2	.1	77	5.3	52	3.6	43	3.0	174	12.0	1,256	86.9	15	1.0	1,445
1	.2	35	8.0	14	3.2	18	4.1	68	15.5	370	84.5	0	.0	438
1	.1	42	4.2	38	3.8	25	2.5	106	10.5	886	88.0	15	1.5	1,007
0	.0	0	.0	0	.0	0	.0	0	.0	0	.0	0	.0	0
0	.0	0	.0	0	.0	0	.0	0	.0	0	.0	0	.0	0
2	.1	77	5.3	52	3.6	43	3.0	174	12.0	1,256	86.9	15	1.0	1,445
1	.2	35	8.0	14	3.2	18	4.1	68	15.5	370	84.5	0	.0	438
1	.1	42	4.2	38	3.8	25	2.5	106	10.5	886	88.0	15	1.5	1,007
0	.0	0	.0	0	.0	0	.0	0	.0	0	.0	0	.0	0
0	.0	0	.0	0	.0	0	.0	0	.0	0	.0	0	.0	0
0	.0	0	.0	0	.0	0	.0	0	.0	0	.0	0	.0	0
2	.1	77	5.3	52	3.6	43	3.0	174	12.0	1,256	86.9	15	1.0	1,445
1	.1	35	8.0	14	3.2	18	4.1	68	15.5	370	84.5	0	.0	438
1	.1	42	4.2	38	3.8	25	2.5	106	10.5	886	88.0	15	1.5	1,007

MAJOR FIELD 1206 - MEDICINE

	AMERICAN INDIAN ALASKAN NATIVE		BLACK NON-HISPANIC		ASIAN OR PACIFIC ISLANDER		HISPANIC		TOTAL MINORITY		WHITE NON-HISPANIC		NON-RESIDENT ALIEN		T
	NUMBER	%	NUMBER	%	NUMBER	%	NUMBER	%	NUMBER	%	NUMBER	%	NUMBER	%	N
MICHIGAN	(	3 INSTITUTIONS)													
UNDERGRADUATES:															
FULL-TIME	0	.0	0	.0	0	.0	0	.0	0	.0	0	.0	0	.0	
FEMALE	0	.0	0	.0	0	.0	0	.0	0	.0	0	.0	0	.0	
MALE	0	.0	0	.0	0	.0	0	.0	0	.0	0	.0	0	.0	
PART-TIME	0	.0	0	.0	0	.0	0	.0	0	.0	0	.0	0	.0	
FEMALE	0	.0	0	.0	0	.0	0	.0	0	.0	0	.0	0	.0	
MALE	0	.0	0	.0	0	.0	0	.0	0	.0	0	.0	0	.0	
TOTAL	0	.0	0	.0	0	.0	0	.0	0	.0	0	.0	0	.0	
FEMALE	0	.0	0	.0	0	.0	0	.0	0	.0	0	.0	0	.0	
MALE	0	.0	0	.0	0	.0	0	.0	0	.0	0	.0	0	.0	
GRADUATE:															
FULL-TIME	0	.0	0	.0	0	.0	0	.0	0	.0	0	.0	0	.0	
FEMALE	0	.0	0	.0	0	.0	0	.0	0	.0	0	.0	0	.0	
MALE	0	.0	0	.0	0	.0	0	.0	0	.0	0	.0	0	.0	
PART-TIME	0	.0	0	.0	0	.0	0	.0	0	.0	0	.0	0	.0	
FEMALE	0	.0	0	.0	0	.0	0	.0	0	.0	0	.0	0	.0	
MALE	0	.0	0	.0	0	.0	0	.0	0	.0	0	.0	0	.0	
TOTAL	0	.0	0	.0	0	.0	0	.0	0	.0	0	.0	0	.0	
FEMALE	0	.0	0	.0	0	.0	0	.0	0	.0	0	.0	0	.0	
MALE	0	.0	0	.0	0	.0	0	.0	0	.0	0	.0	0	.0	
PROFESSIONAL:															
FULL-TIME	11	.4	226	8.4	64	2.4	63	2.3	364	13.5	2,330	86.3	6	.2	
FEMALE	4	.5	98	13.3	19	2.6	17	2.3	138	18.8	596	81.0	2	.3	
MALE	7	.4	128	6.5	45	2.3	46	2.3	226	11.5	1,734	88.3	4	.2	
PART-TIME	0	.0	0	.0	0	.0	0	.0	0	.0	0	.0	0	.0	
FEMALE	0	.0	0	.0	0	.0	0	.0	0	.0	0	.0	0	.0	
MALE	0	.0	0	.0	0	.0	0	.0	0	.0	0	.0	0	.0	
TOTAL	11	.4	226	8.4	64	2.4	63	2.3	364	13.5	2,330	86.3	6	.2	
FEMALE	4	.5	98	13.3	19	2.6	17	2.3	138	18.8	596	81.0	2	.3	
MALE	7	.4	128	6.5	45	2.3	46	2.3	226	11.5	1,734	88.3	4	.2	
UND+GRAG+PROF:															
FULL-TIME	11	.4	226	8.4	64	2.4	63	2.3	364	13.5	2,330	86.3	6	.2	
FEMALE	4	.5	98	13.3	19	2.6	17	2.3	138	18.8	596	81.0	2	.3	
MALE	7	.4	128	6.5	45	2.3	46	2.3	226	11.5	1,734	88.3	4	.2	
PART-TIME	0	.0	0	.0	0	.0	0	.0	0	.0	0	.0	0	.0	
FEMALE	0	.0	0	.0	0	.0	0	.0	0	.0	0	.0	0	.0	
MALE	0	.0	0	.0	0	.0	0	.0	0	.0	0	.0	0	.0	
TOTAL	11	.4	226	8.4	64	2.4	63	2.3	364	13.5	2,330	86.3	6	.2	
FEMALE	4	.5	98	13.3	19	2.6	17	2.3	138	18.8	596	81.0	2	.3	
MALE	7	.4	128	6.5	45	2.3	46	2.3	226	11.5	1,734	88.3	4	.2	
UNCLASSIFIED:															
TOTAL	0	.0	0	.0	0	.0	0	.0	0	.0	0	.0	0	.0	
FEMALE	0	.0	0	.0	0	.0	0	.0	0	.0	0	.0	0	.0	
MALE	0	.0	0	.0	0	.0	0	.0	0	.0	0	.0	0	.0	
TOTAL ENROLLMENT:															
TOTAL	11	.4	226	8.4	64	2.4	63	2.3	364	13.5	2,330	86.3	6	.2	
FEMALE	4	.5	98	13.3	19	2.6	17	2.3	138	18.8	596	81.0	2	.3	
MALE	7	.4	128	6.5	45	2.3	46	2.3	226	11.5	1,734	88.3	4	.2	
MINNESOTA	(	3 INSTITUTIONS)													
UNDERGRADUATES:															
FULL-TIME	0	.0	0	.0	0	.0	0	.0	0	.0	0	.0	0	.0	
FEMALE	0	.0	0	.0	0	.0	0	.0	0	.0	0	.0	0	.0	
MALE	0	.0	0	.0	0	.0	0	.0	0	.0	0	.0	0	.0	
PART-TIME	0	.0	0	.0	0	.0	0	.0	0	.0	0	.0	0	.0	
FEMALE	0	.0	0	.0	0	.0	0	.0	0	.0	0	.0	0	.0	
MALE	0	.0	0	.0	0	.0	0	.0	0	.0	0	.0	0	.0	
TOTAL	0	.0	0	.0	0	.0	0	.0	0	.0	0	.0	0	.0	
FEMALE	0	.0	0	.0	0	.0	0	.0	0	.0	0	.0	0	.0	
MALE	0	.0	0	.0	0	.0	0	.0	0	.0	0	.0	0	.0	
GRADUATE:															
FULL-TIME	0	.0	0	.0	0	.0	0	.0	0	.0	0	.0	0	.0	
FEMALE	0	.0	0	.0	0	.0	0	.0	0	.0	0	.0	0	.0	
MALE	0	.0	0	.0	0	.0	0	.0	0	.0	0	.0	0	.0	
PART-TIME	0	.0	0	.0	0	.0	0	.0	0	.0	0	.0	0	.0	
FEMALE	0	.0	0	.0	0	.0	0	.0	0	.0	0	.0	0	.0	
MALE	0	.0	0	.0	0	.0	0	.0	0	.0	0	.0	0	.0	
TOTAL	0	.0	0	.0	0	.0	0	.0	0	.0	0	.0	0	.0	
FEMALE	0	.0	0	.0	0	.0	0	.0	0	.0	0	.0	0	.0	
MALE	0	.0	0	.0	0	.0	0	.0	0	.0	0	.0	0	.0	
PROFESSIONAL:															
FULL-TIME	13	1.0	32	2.4	12	.9	47	3.6	104	7.9	1,218	92.1	1	.1	
FEMALE	2	.7	13	4.4	2	.7	11	3.8	28	9.6	265	90.4	0	.0	
MALE	11	1.1	19	1.8	10	1.0	36	3.5	76	7.4	953	92.5	1	.1	

MEDICINE

INDIAN NATIVE	BLACK NON-HISPANIC		ASIAN OR PACIFIC ISLANDER		HISPANIC		TOTAL MINORITY		WHITE NON-HISPANIC		NON-RESIDENT ALIEN		TOTAL
%	NUMBER	%	NUMBER	%	NUMBER	%	NUMBER	%	NUMBER	%	NUMBER	%	NUMBER
CONTINUED													
.0	0	.0	0	.0	0	.0	0	.0	0	.0	0	.0	0
.0	0	.0	0	.0	0	.0	0	.0	0	.0	0	.0	0
.0	0	.0	0	.0	0	.0	0	.0	0	.0	0	.0	0
1.0	32	2.4	12	.9	47	3.6	104	7.9	1,218	92.1	1	.1	1,323
.7	13	4.4	2	.7	11	3.8	28	9.6	265	90.4	0	.0	293
1.1	19	1.8	10	1.0	36	3.5	76	7.4	953	92.5	1	.1	1,030
1.0	32	2.4	12	.9	47	3.6	104	7.9	1,218	92.1	1	.1	1,323
.7	13	4.4	2	.7	11	3.8	28	9.6	265	90.4	0	.0	293
1.1	19	1.8	10	1.0	36	3.5	76	7.4	953	92.5	1	.1	1,030
.0	0	.0	0	.0	0	.0	0	.0	0	.0	0	.0	0
.0	0	.0	0	.0	0	.0	0	.0	0	.0	0	.0	0
.0	0	.0	0	.0	0	.0	0	.0	0	.0	0	.0	0
1.0	32	2.4	12	.9	47	3.6	104	7.9	1,218	92.1	1	.1	1,323
.7	13	4.4	2	.7	11	3.8	28	9.6	265	90.4	0	.0	293
1.1	19	1.8	10	1.0	36	3.5	76	7.4	953	92.5	1	.1	1,030
.0	0	.0	0	.0	0	.0	0	.0	0	.0	0	.0	0
.0	0	.0	0	.0	0	.0	0	.0	0	.0	0	.0	0
.0	0	.0	0	.0	0	.0	0	.0	0	.0	0	.0	0
1.0	32	2.4	12	.9	47	3.6	104	7.9	1,218	92.1	1	.1	1,323
.7	13	4.4	2	.7	11	3.8	28	9.6	265	90.4	0	.0	293
1.1	19	1.8	10	1.0	36	3.5	76	7.4	953	92.5	1	.1	1,030
(	1 INSTITUTIONS)												
.0	0	.0	0	.0	0	.0	0	.0	0	.0	0	.0	0
.0	0	.0	0	.0	0	.0	0	.0	0	.0	0	.0	0
.0	0	.0	0	.0	0	.0	0	.0	0	.0	0	.0	0
.0	0	.0	0	.0	0	.0	0	.0	0	.0	0	.0	0
.0	0	.0	0	.0	0	.0	0	.0	0	.0	0	.0	0
.0	0	.0	0	.0	0	.0	0	.0	0	.0	0	.0	0
.0	0	.0	0	.0	0	.0	0	.0	0	.0	0	.0	0
.0	0	.0	0	.0	0	.0	0	.0	0	.0	0	.0	0
.0	0	.0	0	.0	0	.0	0	.0	0	.0	0	.0	0
.0	0	.0	0	.0	0	.0	0	.0	0	.0	0	.0	0
.0	0	.0	0	.0	0	.0	0	.0	0	.0	0	.0	0
.0	0	.0	0	.0	0	.0	0	.0	0	.0	0	.0	0
.0	0	.0	0	.0	0	.0	0	.0	0	.0	0	.0	0
.0	0	.0	0	.0	0	.0	0	.0	0	.0	0	.0	0
.0	0	.0	0	.0	0	.0	0	.0	0	.0	0	.0	0
.2	31	5.1	6	1.0	1	.2	39	6.4	567	93.6	0	.0	606
.8	8	6.3	2	1.6	0	.0	11	8.7	116	91.3	0	.0	127
.0	23	4.8	4	.8	1	.2	28	5.8	451	94.2	0	.0	479
.0	0	.0	0	.0	0	.0	0	.0	1	100.0	0	.0	1
.0	0	.0	0	.0	0	.0	0	.0	0	.0	0	.0	0
.0	0	.0	0	.0	0	.0	0	.0	1	100.0	0	.0	1
.2	31	5.1	6	1.0	1	.2	39	6.4	568	93.6	0	.0	607
.8	8	6.3	2	1.6	0	.0	11	8.7	116	91.3	0	.0	127
.0	23	4.8	4	.8	1	.2	28	5.8	452	94.2	0	.0	480
.2	31	5.1	6	1.0	1	.2	39	6.4	567	93.6	0	.0	606
.8	8	6.3	2	1.6	0	.0	11	8.7	116	91.3	0	.0	127
.0	23	4.8	4	.8	1	.2	28	5.8	451	94.2	0	.0	479
.0	0	.0	0	.0	0	.0	0	.0	1	100.0	0	.0	1
.0	0	.0	0	.0	0	.0	0	.0	0	.0	0	.0	0
.0	0	.0	0	.0	0	.0	0	.0	1	100.0	0	.0	1
.2	31	5.1	6	1.0	1	.2	39	6.4	568	93.6	0	.0	607
.8	8	6.3	2	1.6	0	.0	11	8.7	116	91.3	0	.0	127
.0	23	4.8	4	.8	1	.2	28	5.8	452	94.2	0	.0	480
.0	0	.0	0	.0	0	.0	0	.0	0	.0	0	.0	0
.0	0	.0	0	.0	0	.0	0	.0	0	.0	0	.0	0
.0	0	.0	0	.0	0	.0	0	.0	0	.0	0	.0	0
.2	31	5.1	6	1.0	1	.2	39	6.4	568	93.6	0	.0	607
.8	8	6.3	2	1.6	0	.0	11	8.7	116	91.3	0	.0	127
.0	23	4.8	4	.8	1	.2	28	5.8	452	94.2	0	.0	480

TABLE 17 - TOTAL ENROLLMENT IN INSTITUTIONS OF HIGHER EDUCATION FOR SELECTED MAJOR FIELDS OF STUDY AND LEVEL OF ENROLLMENT
BY RACE, ETHNICITY, AND SEX: STATE, 1978

MAJOR FIELD 1206 - MEDICINE

	AMERICAN INDIAN ALASKAN NATIVE		BLACK NON-HISPANIC		ASIAN OR PACIFIC ISLANDER		HISPANIC		TOTAL MINORITY		WHITE NON-HISPANIC		NON-RESIDENT ALIEN		T
	NUMBER	%	NUMBER	%	NUMBER	%	NUMBER	%	NUMBER	%	NUMBER	%	NUMBER	%	N
MISSOURI (6 INSTITUTIONS)															
UNDERGRADUATES:															
FULL-TIME	0	.0	0	.0	0	.0	0	.0	0	.0	0	.0	0	.0	
FEMALE	0	.0	0	.0	0	.0	0	.0	0	.0	0	.0	0	.0	
MALE	0	.0	0	.0	0	.0	0	.0	0	.0	0	.0	0	.0	
PART-TIME	0	.0	0	.0	0	.0	0	.0	0	.0	0	.0	0	.0	
FEMALE	0	.0	0	.0	0	.0	0	.0	0	.0	0	.0	0	.0	
MALE	0	.0	0	.0	0	.0	0	.0	0	.0	0	.0	0	.0	
TOTAL	0	.0	0	.0	0	.0	0	.0	0	.0	0	.0	0	.0	
FEMALE	0	.0	0	.0	0	.0	0	.0	0	.0	0	.0	0	.0	
MALE	0	.0	0	.0	0	.0	0	.0	0	.0	0	.0	0	.0	
GRADUATE:															
FULL-TIME	0	.0	0	.0	0	.0	0	.0	0	.0	0	.0	0	.0	
FEMALE	0	.0	0	.0	0	.0	0	.0	0	.0	0	.0	0	.0	
MALE	0	.0	0	.0	0	.0	0	.0	0	.0	0	.0	0	.0	
PART-TIME	0	.0	0	.0	0	.0	0	.0	0	.0	0	.0	0	.0	
FEMALE	0	.0	0	.0	0	.0	0	.0	0	.0	0	.0	0	.0	
MALE	0	.0	0	.0	0	.0	0	.0	0	.0	0	.0	0	.0	
TOTAL	0	.0	0	.0	0	.0	0	.0	0	.0	0	.0	0	.0	
FEMALE	0	.0	0	.0	0	.0	0	.0	0	.0	0	.0	0	.0	
MALE	0	.0	0	.0	0	.0	0	.0	0	.0	0	.0	0	.0	
PROFESSIONAL:															
FULL-TIME	17	.6	101	3.3	65	2.2	17	.6	200	6.6	2,804	92.9	13	.4	
FEMALE	6	1.1	43	7.5	21	3.7	5	.9	75	13.2	492	86.3	3	.5	
MALE	11	.4	58	2.4	44	1.8	12	.5	125	5.1	2,312	94.5	10	.4	
PART-TIME	0	.0	0	.0	0	.0	0	.0	0	.0	14	100.0	0	.0	
FEMALE	0	.0	0	.0	0	.0	0	.0	0	.0	3	100.0	0	.0	
MALE	0	.0	0	.0	0	.0	0	.0	0	.0	11	100.0	0	.0	
TOTAL	17	.6	101	3.3	65	2.1	17	.6	200	6.6	2,818	93.0	13	.4	
FEMALE	6	1.0	43	7.5	21	3.7	5	.9	75	13.1	495	86.4	3	.5	
MALE	11	.4	58	2.4	44	1.8	12	.5	125	5.1	2,323	94.5	10	.4	
UND+GRAD+PROF:															
FULL-TIME	17	.6	101	3.3	65	2.2	17	.6	200	6.6	2,804	92.9	13	.4	
FEMALE	6	1.1	43	7.5	21	3.7	5	.9	75	13.2	492	86.3	3	.5	
MALE	11	.4	58	2.4	44	1.8	12	.5	125	5.1	2,312	94.5	10	.4	
PART-TIME	0	.0	0	.0	0	.0	0	.0	0	.0	14	100.0	0	.0	
FEMALE	0	.0	0	.0	0	.0	0	.0	0	.0	3	100.0	0	.0	
MALE	0	.0	0	.0	0	.0	0	.0	0	.0	11	100.0	0	.0	
TOTAL	17	.6	101	3.3	65	2.1	17	.6	200	6.6	2,818	93.0	13	.4	
FEMALE	6	1.0	43	7.5	21	3.7	5	.9	75	13.1	495	86.4	3	.5	
MALE	11	.4	58	2.4	44	1.8	12	.5	125	5.1	2,323	94.5	10	.4	
UNCLASSIFIED:															
TOTAL	0	.0	0	.0	0	.0	0	.0	0	.0	0	.0	0	.0	
FEMALE	0	.0	0	.0	0	.0	0	.0	0	.0	0	.0	0	.0	
MALE	0	.0	0	.0	0	.0	0	.0	0	.0	0	.0	0	.0	
TOTAL ENROLLMENT:															
TOTAL	17	.6	101	3.3	65	2.1	17	.6	200	6.6	2,818	93.0	13	.4	
FEMALE	6	1.0	43	7.5	21	3.7	5	.9	75	13.1	495	86.4	3	.5	
MALE	11	.4	58	2.4	44	1.8	12	.5	125	5.1	2,323	94.5	10	.4	
NEBRASKA (2 INSTITUTIONS)															
UNDERGRADUATES:															
FULL-TIME	0	.0	0	.0	0	.0	0	.0	0	.0	0	.0	0	.0	
FEMALE	0	.0	0	.0	0	.0	0	.0	0	.0	0	.0	0	.0	
MALE	0	.0	0	.0	0	.0	0	.0	0	.0	0	.0	0	.0	
PART-TIME	0	.0	0	.0	0	.0	0	.0	0	.0	0	.0	0	.0	
FEMALE	0	.0	0	.0	0	.0	0	.0	0	.0	0	.0	0	.0	
MALE	0	.0	0	.0	0	.0	0	.0	0	.0	0	.0	0	.0	
TOTAL	0	.0	0	.0	0	.0	0	.0	0	.0	0	.0	0	.0	
FEMALE	0	.0	0	.0	0	.0	0	.0	0	.0	0	.0	0	.0	
MALE	0	.0	0	.0	0	.0	0	.0	0	.0	0	.0	0	.0	
GRADUATE:															
FULL-TIME	0	.0	0	.0	0	.0	0	.0	0	.0	0	.0	0	.0	
FEMALE	0	.0	0	.0	0	.0	0	.0	0	.0	0	.0	0	.0	
MALE	0	.0	0	.0	0	.0	0	.0	0	.0	0	.0	0	.0	
PART-TIME	0	.0	0	.0	0	.0	0	.0	0	.0	0	.0	0	.0	
FEMALE	0	.0	0	.0	0	.0	0	.0	0	.0	0	.0	0	.0	
MALE	0	.0	0	.0	0	.0	0	.0	0	.0	0	.0	0	.0	
TOTAL	0	.0	0	.0	0	.0	0	.0	0	.0	0	.0	0	.0	
FEMALE	0	.0	0	.0	0	.0	0	.0	0	.0	0	.0	0	.0	
MALE	0	.0	0	.0	0	.0	0	.0	0	.0	0	.0	0	.0	
PROFESSIONAL:															
FULL-TIME	4	.4	17	1.8	18	1.9	24	2.5	63	6.5	903	93.1	4	.4	
FEMALE	2	1.0	3	1.5	4	2.1	1	.5	10	5.2	184	94.8	0	.0	
MALE	2	.3	14	1.8	14	1.8	23	3.0	53	6.8	719	92.7	4	.5	

MEDICINE

INDIAN NATIVE %	BLACK NON-HISPANIC NUMBER	%	ASIAN OR PACIFIC ISLANDER NUMBER	%	HISPANIC NUMBER	%	TOTAL MINORITY NUMBER	%	WHITE NON-HISPANIC NUMBER	%	NON-RESIDENT ALIEN NUMBER	%	TOTAL NUMBER
CONTINUED													
.0	0	.0	0	.0	0	.0	0	.0	1	100.0	0	.0	1
.0	0	.0	0	.0	0	.0	0	.0	0	.0	0	.0	0
.0	0	.0	0	.0	0	.0	0	.0	1	100.0	0	.0	1
.4	17	1.8	18	1.9	24	2.5	63	6.5	904	93.1	4	.4	971
1.0	3	1.5	4	2.1	1	.5	10	5.2	184	94.8	0	.0	194
.3	14	1.8	14	1.8	23	3.0	53	6.8	720	92.7	4	.5	777
.4	17	1.8	18	1.9	24	2.5	63	6.5	903	93.1	4	.4	970
1.0	3	1.5	4	2.1	1	.5	10	5.2	184	94.8	0	.0	194
.3	14	1.8	14	1.8	23	3.0	53	6.8	719	92.7	4	.5	776
.0	0	.0	0	.0	0	.0	0	.0	1	100.0	0	.0	1
.0	0	.0	0	.0	0	.0	0	.0	0	.0	0	.0	0
.0	0	.0	0	.0	0	.0	0	.0	1	100.0	0	.0	1
.4	17	1.8	18	1.9	24	2.5	63	6.5	904	93.1	4	.4	971
1.0	3	1.5	4	2.1	1	.5	10	5.2	184	94.8	0	.0	194
.3	14	1.8	14	1.8	23	3.0	53	6.8	720	92.7	4	.5	777
.0	0	.0	0	.0	0	.0	0	.0	0	.0	0	.0	0
.0	0	.0	0	.0	0	.0	0	.0	0	.0	0	.0	0
.0	0	.0	0	.0	0	.0	0	.0	0	.0	0	.0	0
.4	17	1.8	18	1.9	24	2.5	63	6.5	904	93.1	4	.4	971
1.0	3	1.5	4	2.1	1	.5	10	5.2	184	94.8	0	.0	194
.3	14	1.8	14	1.8	23	3.0	53	6.8	720	92.7	4	.5	777
(1 INSTITUTIONS)													
.0	0	.0	0	.0	0	.0	0	.0	0	.0	0	.0	0
.0	0	.0	0	.0	0	.0	0	.0	0	.0	0	.0	0
.0	0	.0	0	.0	0	.0	0	.0	0	.0	0	.0	0
.0	0	.0	0	.0	0	.0	0	.0	0	.0	0	.0	0
.0	0	.0	0	.0	0	.0	0	.0	0	.0	0	.0	0
.0	0	.0	0	.0	0	.0	0	.0	0	.0	0	.0	0
.0	0	.0	0	.0	0	.0	0	.0	0	.0	0	.0	0
.0	0	.0	0	.0	0	.0	0	.0	0	.0	0	.0	0
.0	0	.0	0	.0	0	.0	0	.0	0	.0	0	.0	0
.0	0	.0	0	.0	0	.0	0	.0	0	.0	0	.0	0
.0	0	.0	0	.0	0	.0	0	.0	0	.0	0	.0	0
.0	0	.0	0	.0	0	.0	0	.0	0	.0	0	.0	0
.0	0	.0	0	.0	0	.0	0	.0	0	.0	0	.0	0
.0	0	.0	0	.0	0	.0	0	.0	0	.0	0	.0	0
.0	0	.0	0	.0	0	.0	0	.0	0	.0	0	.0	0
.0	0	.0	0	.0	0	.0	0	.0	0	.0	0	.0	0
.0	0	.0	0	.0	0	.0	0	.0	0	.0	0	.0	0
1.6	9	4.8	8	4.3	6	3.2	26	14.0	160	86.0	0	.0	186
1.8	3	5.5	5	9.1	3	5.5	12	21.8	43	78.2	0	.0	55
1.5	6	4.6	3	2.3	3	2.3	14	10.7	117	89.3	0	.0	131
.0	0	.0	0	.0	0	.0	0	.0	0	.0	0	.0	0
.0	0	.0	0	.0	0	.0	0	.0	0	.0	0	.0	0
.0	0	.0	0	.0	0	.0	0	.0	0	.0	0	.0	0
1.6	9	4.8	8	4.3	6	3.2	26	14.0	160	86.0	0	.0	186
1.8	3	5.5	5	9.1	3	5.5	12	21.8	43	78.2	0	.0	55
1.5	6	4.6	3	2.3	3	2.3	14	10.7	117	89.3	0	.0	131
1.6	9	4.8	8	4.3	6	3.2	26	14.0	160	86.0	0	.0	186
1.8	3	5.5	5	9.1	3	5.5	12	21.8	43	78.2	0	.0	55
1.5	6	4.6	3	2.3	3	2.3	14	10.7	117	89.3	0	.0	131
.0	0	.0	0	.0	0	.0	0	.0	0	.0	0	.0	0
.0	0	.0	0	.0	0	.0	0	.0	0	.0	0	.0	0
.0	0	.0	0	.0	0	.0	0	.0	0	.0	0	.0	0
1.6	9	4.8	8	4.3	6	3.2	26	14.0	160	86.0	0	.0	186
1.8	3	5.5	5	9.1	3	5.5	12	21.8	43	78.2	0	.0	55
1.5	6	4.6	3	2.3	3	2.3	14	10.7	117	89.3	0	.0	131
.0	0	.0	0	.0	0	.0	0	.0	0	.0	0	.0	0
.0	0	.0	0	.0	0	.0	0	.0	0	.0	0	.0	0
.0	0	.0	0	.0	0	.0	0	.0	0	.0	0	.0	0
1.6	9	4.8	8	4.3	6	3.2	26	14.0	160	86.0	0	.0	186
1.8	3	5.5	5	9.1	3	5.5	12	21.8	43	78.2	0	.0	55
1.5	6	4.6	3	2.3	3	2.3	14	10.7	117	89.3	0	.0	131

TABLE 17 - TOTAL ENROLLMENT IN INSTITUTIONS OF HIGHER EDUCATION FOR SELECTED MAJOR FIELDS OF STUDY AND LEVEL OF ENROLLMENT BY RACE, ETHNICITY, AND SEX: STATE, 1978

MAJOR FIELD 1206 - MEDICINE

	AMERICAN INDIAN ALASKAN NATIVE		BLACK NON-HISPANIC		ASIAN OR PACIFIC ISLANDER		HISPANIC		TOTAL MINORITY		WHITE NON-HISPANIC		NON-RESIDENT ALIEN		TOTAL
	NUMBER	%	NUMBER	%	NUMBER	%	NUMBER	%	NUMBER	%	NUMBER	%	NUMBER	%	NUMB
NEW JERSEY	(	1 INSTITUTIONS)													
UNDERGRADUATES:															
FULL-TIME	0	.0	0	.0	0	.0	0	.0	0	.0	0	.0		.0	
FEMALE	0	.0	0	.0	0	.0	0	.0	0	.0	0	.0		.0	
MALE	0	.0	0	.0	0	.0	0	.0	0	.0	0	.0		.0	
PART-TIME	0	.0	0	.0	0	.0	0	.0	0	.0	0	.0		.0	
FEMALE	0	.0	0	.0	0	.0	0	.0	0	.0	0	.0		.0	
MALE	0	.0	0	.0	0	.0	0	.0	0	.0	0	.0	0	.0	
TOTAL	0	.0	0	.0	0	.0	0	.0	0	.0	0	.0		.0	
FEMALE	0	.0	0	.0	0	.0	0	.0	0	.0	0	.0		.0	
MALE	0	.0	0	.0	0	.0	0	.0	0	.0	0	.0	0	.0	
GRADUATE:															
FULL-TIME	0	.0	0	.0	0	.0	0	.0	0	.0	0	.0		.0	
FEMALE	0	.0	0	.0	0	.0	0	.0	0	.0	0	.0		.0	
MALE	0	.0	0	.0	0	.0	0	.0	0	.0	0	.0		.0	
PART-TIME	0	.0	0	.0	0	.0	0	.0	0	.0	0	.0		.0	
FEMALE	0	.0	0	.0	0	.0	0	.0	0	.0	0	.0		.0	
MALE	0	.0	0	.0	0	.0	0	.0	0	.0	0	.0	0	.0	
TOTAL	0	.0	0	.0	0	.0	0	.0	0	.0	0	.0		.0	
FEMALE	0	.0	0	.0	0	.0	0	.0	0	.0	0	.0		.0	
MALE	0	.0	0	.0	0	.0	0	.0	0	.0	0	.0	0	.0	
PROFESSIONAL															
FULL-TIME	0	.0	134	14.7	14	1.5	41	4.5	189	20.8	721	79.2		.0	9
FEMALE	0	.0	56	23.4	8	3.3	12	5.0	76	31.8	163	68.2		.0	2
MALE	0	.0	78	11.6	6	.9	29	4.3	113	16.8	558	83.2		.0	6
PART-TIME	0	.0	1	50.0	0	.0	1	50.0	2	100.0	0	.0		.0	
FEMALE	0	.0	1	100.0	0	.0	0	.0	1	100.0	0	.0		.0	
MALE	0	.0	0	.0	0	.0	1	100.0	1	100.0	0	.0	0	.0	
TOTAL	0	.0	135	14.8	14	1.5	42	4.6	191	20.9	721	79.1		.0	9
FEMALE	0	.0	57	23.8	8	3.3	12	5.0	77	32.1	163	67.9		.0	2
MALE	0	.0	78	11.6	6	.9	30	4.5	114	17.0	558	83.0	0	.0	6
UND+GRAD+PROF:															
FULL-TIME	0	.0	134	14.7	14	1.5	41	4.5	189	20.8	721	79.2		.0	9
FEMALE	0	.0	56	23.4	8	3.3	12	5.0	76	31.8	163	68.2		.0	2
MALE	0	.0	78	11.6	6	.9	29	4.3	113	16.8	558	83.2		.0	6
PART-TIME	0	.0	1	50.0	0	.0	1	50.0	2	100.0	0	.0		.0	
FEMALE	0	.0	1	100.0	0	.0	0	.0	1	100.0	0	.0		.0	
MALE	0	.0	0	.0	0	.0	1	100.0	1	100.0	0	.0	0	.0	
TOTAL	0	.0	135	14.8	14	1.5	42	4.6	191	20.9	721	79.1		.0	9
FEMALE	0	.0	57	23.8	8	3.3	12	5.0	77	32.1	163	67.9		.0	2
MALE	0	.0	78	11.6	6	.9	30	4.5	114	17.0	558	83.0	0	.0	6
UNCLASSIFIED															
TOTAL	0	.0	0	.0	0	.0	0	.0	0	.0	0	.0		.0	
FEMALE	0	.0	0	.0	0	.0	0	.0	0	.0	0	.0		.0	
MALE	0	.0	0	.0	0	.0	0	.0	0	.0	0	.0	0	.0	
TOTAL ENROLLMENT:															
TOTAL	0	.0	135	14.8	14	1.5	42	4.6	191	20.9	721	79.1		.0	9
FEMALE	0	.0	57	23.8	8	3.3	12	5.0	77	32.1	163	67.9		.0	2
MALE	0	.0	78	11.6	6	.9	30	4.5	114	17.0	558	83.0	0	.0	6
NEW MEXICO	(	1 INSTITLTIONS)													
UNDERGRADUATES:															
FULL-TIME	0	.0	0	.0	0	.0	0	.0	0	.0	0	.0		.0	
FEMALE	0	.0	0	.0	0	.0	0	.0	0	.0	0	.0		.0	
MALE	0	.0	0	.0	0	.0	0	.0	0	.0	0	.0		.0	
PART-TIME	0	.0	0	.0	0	.0	0	.0	0	.0	0	.0		.0	
FEMALE	0	.0	0	.0	0	.0	0	.0	0	.0	0	.0		.0	
MALE	0	.0	0	.0	0	.0	0	.0	0	.0	0	.0	0	.0	
TOTAL	0	.0	0	.0	0	.0	0	.0	0	.0	0	.0		.0	
FEMALE	0	.0	0	.0	0	.0	0	.0	0	.0	0	.0		.0	
MALE	0	.0	0	.0	0	.0	0	.0	0	.0	0	.0	0	.0	
GRADUATE:															
FULL-TIME	0	.0	0	.0	0	.0	0	.0	0	.0	0	.0		.0	
FEMALE	0	.0	0	.0	0	.0	0	.0	0	.0	0	.0		.0	
MALE	0	.0	0	.0	0	.0	0	.0	0	.0	0	.0		.0	
PART-TIME	0	.0	0	.0	0	.0	0	.0	0	.0	0	.0		.0	
FEMALE	0	.0	0	.0	0	.0	0	.0	0	.0	0	.0		.0	
MALE	0	.0	0	.0	0	.0	0	.0	0	.0	0	.0	0	.0	
TOTAL	0	.0	0	.0	0	.0	0	.0	0	.0	0	.0		.0	
FEMALE	0	.0	0	.0	0	.0	0	.0	0	.0	0	.0		.0	
MALE	0	.0	0	.0	0	.0	0	.0	0	.0	0	.0	0	.0	
PROFESSIONAL:															
FULL-TIME	6	2.0	2	.7	6	2.0	59	19.7	73	24.3	227	75.7		.0	3
FEMALE	1	1.1	1	1.1	3	3.4	15	17.0	20	22.7	68	77.3		.0	
MALE	5	2.4	1	.5	3	1.4	44	20.8	53	25.0	159	75.0		.0	2

ENROLLMENT IN INSTITUTIONS OF HIGHER EDUCATION FOR SELECTED MAJOR FIELDS OF STUDY AND LEVEL OF ENROLLMENT
CE, ETHNICITY, AND SEX: STATE, 1978

- MEDICINE

		BLACK NON-HISPANIC		ASIAN OR PACIFIC ISLANDER		HISPANIC		TOTAL MINORITY		WHITE NON-HISPANIC		NON-RESIDENT ALIEN		TOTAL
ER	%	NUMBER	%	NUMBER	%	NUMBER	%	NUMBER	%	NUMBER	%	NUMBER	%	NUMBER

CONTINUED

0	.0	0	.0	0	.0	0	.0	0	.0	0	.0	0	.0	0
0	.0	0	.0	0	.0	0	.0	0	.0	0	.0	0	.0	0
0	.0	0	.0	0	.0	0	.0	0	.0	0	.0	0	.0	0
6	2.0	2	.7	6	2.0	59	19.7	73	24.3	227	75.7	0	.0	300
1	1.1	1	1.1	3	3.4	15	17.0	20	22.7	68	77.3	0	.0	88
5	2.4	1	.5	3	1.4	44	20.8	53	25.0	159	75.0	0	.0	212
6	2.0	2	.7	6	2.0	59	19.7	73	24.3	227	75.7	0	.0	300
1	1.1	1	1.1	3	3.4	15	17.0	20	22.7	68	77.3	0	.0	88
5	2.4	1	.5	3	1.4	44	20.8	53	25.0	159	75.0	0	.0	212
0	.0	0	.0	0	.0	0	.0	0	.0	0	.0	0	.0	0
0	.0	0	.0	0	.0	0	.0	0	.0	0	.0	0	.0	0
6	2.0	2	.7	6	2.0	59	19.7	73	24.3	227	75.7	0	.0	300
1	1.1	1	1.1	3	3.4	15	17.0	20	22.7	68	77.3	0	.0	88
5	2.4	1	.5	3	1.4	44	20.8	53	25.0	159	75.0	0	.0	212
0	.0	0	.0	0	.0	0	.0	0	.0	0	.0	0	.0	0
0	.0	0	.0	0	.0	0	.0	0	.0	0	.0	0	.0	0
0	.0	0	.0	0	.0	0	.0	0	.0	0	.0	0	.0	0
6	2.0	2	.7	6	2.0	59	19.7	73	24.3	227	75.7	0	.0	300
1	1.1	1	1.1	3	3.4	15	17.0	20	22.7	68	77.3	0	.0	88
5	2.4	1	.5	3	1.4	44	20.8	53	25.0	159	75.0	0	.0	212

(14 INSTITUTIONS)

0	.0	0	.0	0	.0	0	.0	0	.0	0	.0	0	.0	0
0	.0	0	.0	0	.0	0	.0	0	.0	0	.0	0	.0	0
0	.0	0	.0	0	.0	0	.0	0	.0	0	.0	0	.0	0
0	.0	0	.0	0	.0	0	.0	0	.0	0	.0	0	.0	0
0	.0	0	.0	0	.0	0	.0	0	.0	0	.0	0	.0	0
0	.0	0	.0	0	.0	0	.0	0	.0	0	.0	0	.0	0
0	.0	0	.0	0	.0	0	.0	0	.0	0	.0	0	.0	0
0	.0	0	.0	0	.0	0	.0	0	.0	0	.0	0	.0	0
0	.0	0	.0	0	.0	0	.0	0	.0	0	.0	0	.0	0
0	.0	0	.0	0	.0	0	.0	0	.0	0	.0	0	.0	0
0	.0	0	.0	0	.0	0	.0	0	.0	0	.0	0	.0	0
0	.0	0	.0	0	.0	0	.0	0	.0	0	.0	0	.0	0
0	.0	0	.0	0	.0	0	.0	0	.0	0	.0	0	.0	0
0	.0	0	.0	0	.0	0	.0	0	.0	0	.0	0	.0	0
0	.0	0	.0	0	.0	0	.0	0	.0	0	.0	0	.0	0
8	.1	302	4.2	181	2.5	174	2.4	665	9.2	6,496	89.8	69	1.0	7,230
5	.3	138	7.1	64	3.3	61	3.2	268	13.9	1,653	85.6	11	.6	1,932
3	.1	164	3.1	117	2.2	113	2.1	397	7.5	4,843	91.4	58	1.1	5,296
0	.0	0	.0	0	.0	0	.0	0	.0	0	.0	0	.0	0
0	.0	0	.0	0	.0	0	.0	0	.0	0	.0	0	.0	0
8	.1	302	4.2	181	2.5	174	2.4	665	9.2	6,496	89.8	69	1.0	7,230
5	.3	138	7.1	64	3.3	61	3.2	268	13.9	1,653	85.6	11	.6	1,932
3	.1	164	3.1	117	2.2	113	2.1	397	7.5	4,843	91.4	58	1.1	5,298
8	.1	302	4.2	181	2.5	174	2.4	665	9.2	6,496	89.8	69	1.0	7,230
5	.3	138	7.1	64	3.3	61	3.2	268	13.9	1,653	85.6	11	.6	1,932
3	.1	164	3.1	117	2.2	113	2.1	397	7.5	4,843	91.4	58	1.1	5,298
0	.0	0	.0	0	.0	0	.0	0	.0	0	.0	0	.0	0
0	.0	0	.0	0	.0	0	.0	0	.0	0	.0	0	.0	0
8	.1	302	4.2	181	2.5	174	2.4	665	9.2	6,496	89.8	69	1.0	7,230
5	.3	138	7.1	64	3.3	61	3.2	268	13.9	1,653	85.6	11	.6	1,932
3	.1	164	3.1	117	2.2	113	2.1	397	7.5	4,843	91.4	58	1.1	5,298
0	.0	0	.0	0	.0	0	.0	0	.0	0	.0	0	.0	0
0	.0	0	.0	0	.0	0	.0	0	.0	0	.0	0	.0	0
0	.0	0	.0	0	.0	0	.0	0	.0	0	.0	0	.0	0
8	.1	302	4.2	181	2.5	174	2.4	665	9.2	6,496	89.8	69	1.0	7,230
5	.3	138	7.1	64	3.3	61	3.2	268	13.9	1,653	85.6	11	.6	1,932
3	.1	164	3.1	117	2.2	113	2.1	397	7.5	4,843	91.4	58	1.1	5,298

TABLE 17 - TOTAL ENROLLMENT IN INSTITUTIONS OF HIGHER EDUCATION FOR SELECTED MAJOR FIELDS OF STUDY AND LEVEL OF ENROLLMENT BY RACE, ETHNICITY, AND SEX: STATE, 1978

MAJOR FIELD 1206 - MEDICINE

	AMERICAN INDIAN ALASKAN NATIVE		BLACK NON-HISPANIC		ASIAN OR PACIFIC ISLANDER		HISPANIC		TOTAL MINORITY		WHITE NON-HISPANIC		NON-RESIDENT ALIEN		T
	NUMBER	%	NUMBER	%	NUMBER	%	NUMBER	%	NUMBER	%	NUMBER	%	NUMBER	%	N
NORTH CAROLINA (4 INSTITUTIONS)															
UNDERGRADUATES:															
FULL-TIME	0	.0	0	.0	0	.0	0	.0	0	.0	0	.0	0	.0	
FEMALE	0	.0	0	.0	0	.0	0	.0	0	.0	0	.0	0	.0	
MALE	0	.0	0	.0	0	.0	0	.0	0	.0	0	.0	0	.0	
PART-TIME	0	.0	0	.0	0	.0	0	.0	0	.0	0	.0	0	.0	
FEMALE	0	.0	0	.0	0	.0	0	.0	0	.0	0	.0	0	.0	
MALE	0	.0	0	.0	0	.0	0	.0	0	.0	0	.0	0	.0	
TOTAL	0	.0	0	.0	0	.0	0	.0	0	.0	0	.0	0	.0	
FEMALE	0	.0	0	.0	0	.0	0	.0	0	.0	0	.0	0	.0	
MALE	0	.0	0	.0	0	.0	0	.0	0	.0	0	.0	0	.0	
GRADUATE:															
FULL-TIME	0	.0	0	.0	0	.0	0	.0	0	.0	0	.0	0	.0	
FEMALE	0	.0	0	.0	0	.0	0	.0	0	.0	0	.0	0	.0	
MALE	0	.0	0	.0	0	.0	0	.0	0	.0	0	.0	0	.0	
PART-TIME	0	.0	0	.0	0	.0	0	.0	0	.0	0	.0	0	.0	
FEMALE	0	.0	0	.0	0	.0	0	.0	0	.0	0	.0	0	.0	
MALE	0	.0	0	.0	0	.0	0	.0	0	.0	0	.0	0	.0	
TOTAL	0	.0	0	.0	0	.0	0	.0	0	.0	0	.0	0	.0	
FEMALE	0	.0	0	.0	0	.0	0	.0	0	.0	0	.0	0	.0	
MALE	0	.0	0	.0	0	.0	0	.0	0	.0	0	.0	0	.0	
PROFESSIONAL:															
FULL-TIME	13	.8	125	7.8	13	.8	6	.4	157	9.8	1,425	89.3	14	.9	
FEMALE	3	.7	45	11.1	5	1.2	2	.5	55	13.6	346	85.6	3	.7	
MALE	10	.8	80	6.7	8	.7	4	.3	102	8.6	1,079	90.5	11	.9	
PART-TIME	0	.0	0	.0	0	.0	0	.0	0	.0	1	100.0	0	.0	
FEMALE	0	.0	0	.0	0	.0	0	.0	0	.0	0	.0	0	.0	
MALE	0	.0	0	.0	0	.0	0	.0	0	.0	1	100.0	0	.0	
TOTAL	13	.8	125	7.8	13	.8	6	.4	157	9.8	1,426	89.3	14	.9	
FEMALE	3	.7	45	11.1	5	1.2	2	.5	55	13.6	346	85.6	3	.7	
MALE	10	.8	80	6.7	8	.7	4	.3	102	8.5	1,080	90.5	11	.9	
UNG+GRAD+PROF:															
FULL-TIME	13	.8	125	7.8	13	.8	6	.4	157	9.8	1,425	89.3	14	.9	
FEMALE	3	.7	45	11.1	5	1.2	2	.5	55	13.6	346	85.6	3	.7	
MALE	10	.8	80	6.7	8	.7	4	.3	102	8.6	1,079	90.5	11	.9	
PART-TIME	0	.0	0	.0	0	.0	0	.0	0	.0	1	100.0	0	.0	
FEMALE	0	.0	0	.0	0	.0	0	.0	0	.0	0	.0	0	.0	
MALE	0	.0	0	.0	0	.0	0	.0	0	.0	1	100.0	0	.0	
TOTAL	13	.8	125	7.8	13	.8	6	.4	157	9.8	1,426	89.3	14	.9	
FEMALE	3	.7	45	11.1	5	1.2	2	.5	55	13.6	346	85.6	3	.7	
MALE	10	.8	80	6.7	8	.7	4	.3	102	8.5	1,080	90.5	11	.9	
UNCLASSIFIED:															
TOTAL	0	.0	0	.0	0	.0	0	.0	0	.0	0	.0	0	.0	
FEMALE	0	.0	0	.0	0	.0	0	.0	0	.0	0	.0	0	.0	
MALE	0	.0	0	.0	0	.0	0	.0	0	.0	0	.0	0	.0	
TOTAL ENROLLMENT:															
TOTAL	13	.8	125	7.8	13	.8	6	.4	157	9.8	1,426	89.3	14	.9	
FEMALE	3	.7	45	11.1	5	1.2	2	.5	55	13.6	346	85.6	3	.7	
MALE	10	.8	80	6.7	8	.7	4	.3	102	8.5	1,080	90.5	11	.7	
NORTH DAKOTA (1 INSTITUTIONS)															
UNDERGRADUATES:															
FULL-TIME	0	.0	0	.0	0	.0	0	.0	0	.0	0	.0	0	.0	
FEMALE	0	.0	0	.0	0	.0	0	.0	0	.0	0	.0	0	.0	
MALE	0	.0	0	.0	0	.0	0	.0	0	.0	0	.0	0	.0	
PART-TIME	0	.0	0	.0	0	.0	0	.0	0	.0	0	.0	0	.0	
FEMALE	0	.0	0	.0	0	.0	0	.0	0	.0	0	.0	0	.0	
MALE	0	.0	0	.0	0	.0	0	.0	0	.0	0	.0	0	.0	
TOTAL	0	.0	0	.0	0	.0	0	.0	0	.0	0	.0	0	.0	
FEMALE	0	.0	0	.0	0	.0	0	.0	0	.0	0	.0	0	.0	
MALE	0	.0	0	.0	0	.0	0	.0	0	.0	0	.0	0	.0	
GRADUATE:															
FULL-TIME	0	.0	0	.0	0	.0	0	.0	0	.0	0	.0	0	.0	
FEMALE	0	.0	0	.0	0	.0	0	.0	0	.0	0	.0	0	.0	
MALE	0	.0	0	.0	0	.0	0	.0	0	.0	0	.0	0	.0	
PART-TIME	0	.0	0	.0	0	.0	0	.0	0	.0	0	.0	0	.0	
FEMALE	0	.0	0	.0	0	.0	0	.0	0	.0	0	.0	0	.0	
MALE	0	.0	0	.0	0	.0	0	.0	0	.0	0	.0	0	.0	
TOTAL	0	.0	0	.0	0	.0	0	.0	0	.0	0	.0	0	.0	
FEMALE	0	.0	0	.0	0	.0	0	.0	0	.0	0	.0	0	.0	
MALE	0	.0	0	.0	0	.0	0	.0	0	.0	0	.0	0	.0	
PROFESSIONAL:															
FULL-TIME	9	4.3	0	.0	2	.9	0	.0	11	5.2	200	94.8	0	.0	
FEMALE	1	2.6	0	.0	0	.0	0	.0	1	2.6	38	97.4	0	.0	
MALE	8	4.7	0	.0	2	1.2	0	.0	10	5.8	162	94.2	0	.0	

ROLLMENT IN INSTITUTIONS OF HIGHER EDUCATION FOR SELECTED MAJOR FIELDS OF STUDY AND LEVEL OF ENROLLMENT ETHNICITY, AND SEX: STATE, 1978

MEDICINE

INDIAN NATIVE	BLACK NON-HISPANIC		ASIAN OR PACIFIC ISLANDER		HISPANIC		TOTAL MINORITY		WHITE NON-HISPANIC		NON-RESIDENT ALIEN		TOTAL
%	NUMBER	%	NUMBER	%	NUMBER	%	NUMBER	%	NUMBER	%	NUMBER	%	NUMBER
CONTINUED													
.0	0	.0	0	.0	0	.0	0	.0	2	100.0	0	.0	2
.0	0	.0	0	.0	0	.0	0	.0	0	.0	0	.0	0
.0	0	.0	0	.0	0	.0	0	.0	2	100.0	0	.0	2
4.2	0	.0	2	.9	0	.0	11	5.2	202	94.8	0	.0	213
2.6	0	.0	0	.0	0	.0	1	2.6	38	97.4	0	.0	39
4.6	0	.0	2	1.1	0	.0	10	5.7	164	94.3	0	.0	174
4.3	0	.0	2	.9	0	.0	11	5.2	200	94.8	0	.0	211
2.6	0	.0	0	.0	0	.0	1	2.6	38	97.4	0	.0	39
4.7	0	.0	2	1.2	0	.0	10	5.8	162	94.2	0	.0	172
.0	0	.0	0	.0	0	.0	0	.0	2	100.0	0	.0	2
.0	0	.0	0	.0	0	.0	0	.0	0	.0	0	.0	0
.0	0	.0	0	.0	0	.0	0	.0	2	100.0	0	.0	2
4.2	0	.0	2	.9	0	.0	11	5.2	202	94.8	0	.0	213
2.6	0	.0	0	.0	0	.0	1	2.6	38	97.4	0	.0	39
4.6	0	.0	2	1.1	0	.0	10	5.7	164	94.3	0	.0	174
.0	0	.0	0	.0	0	.0	0	.0	0	.0	0	.0	0
.0	0	.0	0	.0	0	.0	0	.0	0	.0	0	.0	0
.0	0	.0	0	.0	0	.0	0	.0	0	.0	0	.0	0
4.2	0	.0	2	.9	0	.0	11	5.2	202	94.8	0	.0	213
2.6	0	.0	0	.0	0	.0	1	2.6	38	97.4	0	.0	39
4.6	0	.0	2	1.1	0	.0	10	5.7	164	94.3	0	.0	174
(6 INSTITUTIONS)													
.0	0	.0	0	.0	0	.0	0	.0	0	.0	0	.0	0
.0	0	.0	0	.0	0	.0	0	.0	0	.0	0	.0	0
.0	0	.0	0	.0	0	.0	0	.0	0	.0	0	.0	0
.0	0	.0	0	.0	0	.0	0	.0	0	.0	0	.0	0
.0	0	.0	0	.0	0	.0	0	.0	0	.0	0	.0	0
.0	0	.0	0	.0	0	.0	0	.0	0	.0	0	.0	0
.0	0	.0	0	.0	0	.0	0	.0	0	.0	0	.0	0
.0	0	.0	0	.0	0	.0	0	.0	0	.0	0	.0	0
.0	0	.0	0	.0	0	.0	0	.0	0	.0	0	.0	0
.0	0	.0	0	.0	0	.0	0	.0	0	.0	0	.0	0
.0	0	.0	0	.0	0	.0	0	.0	0	.0	0	.0	0
.0	0	.0	0	.0	0	.0	0	.0	0	.0	0	.0	0
.0	0	.0	0	.0	0	.0	0	.0	0	.0	0	.0	0
.0	0	.0	0	.0	0	.0	0	.0	0	.0	0	.0	0
.0	0	.0	0	.0	0	.0	0	.0	0	.0	0	.0	0
.1	144	5.5	35	1.3	19	.7	200	7.7	2,378	91.6	17	.7	2,595
.3	64	9.6	8	1.2	4	.6	78	11.7	587	87.7	4	.6	669
.0	80	4.2	27	1.4	15	.8	122	6.3	1,791	93.0	13	.7	1,926
.0	1	5.9	0	.0	0	.0	1	5.9	16	94.1	0	.0	17
.0	0	.0	0	.0	0	.0	0	.0	4	100.0	0	.0	4
.0	1	7.7	0	.0	0	.0	1	7.7	12	92.3	0	.0	13
.1	145	5.6	35	1.3	19	.7	201	7.7	2,394	91.7	17	.7	2,612
.3	64	9.5	8	1.2	4	.6	78	11.6	591	87.8	4	.6	673
.0	81	4.2	27	1.4	15	.8	123	6.3	1,803	93.0	13	.7	1,939
.1	144	5.5	35	1.3	19	.7	200	7.7	2,378	91.6	17	.7	2,595
.3	64	9.6	8	1.2	4	.6	78	11.7	587	87.7	4	.6	669
.0	80	4.2	27	1.4	15	.8	122	6.3	1,791	93.0	13	.7	1,926
.0	1	5.9	0	.0	0	.0	1	5.9	16	94.1	0	.0	17
.0	0	.0	0	.0	0	.0	0	.0	4	100.0	0	.0	4
.0	1	7.7	0	.0	0	.0	1	7.7	12	92.3	0	.0	13
.1	145	5.6	35	1.3	19	.7	201	7.7	2,394	91.7	17	.7	2,612
.3	64	9.5	8	1.2	4	.6	78	11.6	591	87.8	4	.6	673
.0	81	4.2	27	1.4	15	.8	123	6.3	1,803	93.0	13	.7	1,939
.0	0	.0	0	.0	0	.0	0	.0	0	.0	0	.0	0
.0	0	.0	0	.0	0	.0	0	.0	0	.0	0	.0	0
.0	0	.0	0	.0	0	.0	0	.0	0	.0	0	.0	0
.1	145	5.6	35	1.3	19	.7	201	7.7	2,394	91.7	17	.7	2,612
.3	64	9.5	8	1.2	4	.6	78	11.6	591	87.8	4	.6	673
.0	81	4.2	27	1.4	15	.8	123	6.3	1,803	93.0	13	.7	1,939

TABLE 17 - TOTAL ENROLLMENT IN INSTITUTIONS OF HIGHER EDUCATION FOR SELECTED MAJOR FIELDS OF STUDY AND LEVEL OF ENROLLMENT BY RACE, ETHNICITY, AND SEX: STATE, 1978

MAJOR FIELD 1206 - MEDICINE

	AMERICAN INDIAN ALASKAN NATIVE		BLACK NON-HISPANIC		ASIAN OR PACIFIC ISLANDER		HISPANIC		TOTAL MINORITY		WHITE NON-HISPANIC		NON-RESIDENT ALIEN		TOT
	NUMBER	%	NUMBER	%	NUMBER	%	NUMBER	%	NUMBER	%	NUMBER	%	NUMBER	%	NUM
OKLAHOMA (1 INSTITUTIONS)															
UNDERGRADUATES:															
FULL-TIME															
FEMALE	0	.0	0	.0	0	.0	0	.0	0	.0	0	.0		.0	
MALE	0	.0	0	.0	0	.0	0	.0	0	.0	0	.0		.0	
PART-TIME															
FEMALE	0	.0	0	.0	0	.0	0	.0	0	.0	0	.0		.0	
MALE	0	.0	0	.0	0	.0	0	.0	0	.0	0	.0	0	.0	0
TOTAL															
FEMALE	0	.0	0	.0	0	.0	0	.0	0	.0	0	.0		.0	
MALE	0	.0	0	.0	0	.0	0	.0	0	.0	0	.0	0	.0	0
GRADUATE:															
FULL-TIME															
FEMALE	0	.0	0	.0	0	.0	0	.0	0	.0	0	.0		.0	
MALE	0	.0	0	.0	0	.0	0	.0	0	.0	0	.0		.0	
PART-TIME															
FEMALE	0	.0	0	.0	0	.0	0	.0	0	.0	0	.0		.0	
MALE	0	.0	0	.0	0	.0	0	.0	0	.0	0	.0	0	.0	0
TOTAL															
FEMALE	0	.0	0	.0	0	.0	0	.0	0	.0	0	.0		.0	
MALE	0	.0	0	.0	0	.0	0	.0	0	.0	0	.0	0	.0	0
PROFESSIONAL:															
FULL-TIME	17	2.4	7	1.0	9	1.3	9	1.3	42	6.0	659	93.6	3	.4	
FEMALE	6	4.5	1	.7	2	1.5	2	1.5	11	8.2	123	91.8	0	.0	
MALE	11	1.9	6	1.1	7	1.2	7	1.2	31	5.4	536	94.0	3	.5	
PART-TIME	0	.0	0	.0	0	.0	0	.0	0	.0	0	.0	0	.0	
FEMALE	0	.0	0	.0	0	.0	0	.0	0	.0	0	.0	0	.0	
MALE	0	.0	0	.0	0	.0	0	.0	0	.0	0	.0	0	.0	
TOTAL	17	2.4	7	1.0	9	1.3	9	1.3	42	6.0	659	93.6	3	.4	
FEMALE	6	4.5	1	.7	2	1.5	2	1.5	11	8.2	123	91.8	0	.0	
MALE	11	1.9	6	1.1	7	1.2	7	1.2	31	5.4	536	94.0	3	.5	
UND+GRAD+PROF:															
FULL-TIME	17	2.4	7	1.0	9	1.3	9	1.3	42	6.0	659	93.6	3	.4	
FEMALE	6	4.5	1	.7	2	1.5	2	1.5	11	8.2	123	91.8	0	.0	
MALE	11	1.9	6	1.1	7	1.2	7	1.2	31	5.4	536	94.0	3	.5	
PART-TIME	0	.0	0	.0	0	.0	0	.0	0	.0	0	.0	0	.0	
FEMALE	0	.0	0	.0	0	.0	0	.0	0	.0	0	.0	0	.0	
MALE	0	.0	0	.0	0	.0	0	.0	0	.0	0	.0	0	.0	
TOTAL	17	2.4	7	1.0	9	1.3	9	1.3	42	6.0	659	93.6	3	.4	
FEMALE	6	4.5	1	.7	2	1.5	2	1.5	11	8.2	123	91.8	0	.0	
MALE	11	1.9	6	1.1	7	1.2	7	1.2	31	5.4	536	94.0	3	.5	
UNCLASSIFIED:															
TOTAL	0	.0	0	.0	0	.0	0	.0	0	.0	0	.0	0	.0	
FEMALE	0	.0	0	.0	0	.0	0	.0	0	.0	0	.0	0	.0	
MALE	0	.0	0	.0	0	.0	0	.0	0	.0	0	.0	0	.0	
TOTAL ENROLLMENT:															
TOTAL	17	2.4	7	1.0	9	1.3	9	1.3	42	6.0	659	93.6	3	.4	
FEMALE	6	4.5	1	.7	2	1.5	2	1.5	11	8.2	123	91.8	0	.0	
MALE	11	1.9	6	1.1	7	1.2	7	1.2	31	5.4	536	94.0	3	.5	
OREGON (2 INSTITUTIONS)															
UNDERGRADUATES:															
FULL-TIME															
FEMALE	0	.0	0	.0	0	.0	0	.0	0	.0	0	.0		.0	
MALE	0	.0	0	.0	0	.0	0	.0	0	.0	0	.0		.0	
PART-TIME															
FEMALE	0	.0	0	.0	0	.0	0	.0	0	.0	0	.0		.0	
MALE	0	.0	0	.0	0	.0	0	.0	0	.0	0	.0	0	.0	0
TOTAL															
FEMALE	0	.0	0	.0	0	.0	0	.0	0	.0	0	.0		.0	
MALE	0	.0	0	.0	0	.0	0	.0	0	.0	0	.0	0	.0	0
GRADUATE:															
FULL-TIME															
FEMALE	0	.0	0	.0	0	.0	0	.0	0	.0	0	.0		.0	
MALE	0	.0	0	.0	0	.0	0	.0	0	.0	0	.0		.0	
PART-TIME															
FEMALE	0	.0	0	.0	0	.0	0	.0	0	.0	0	.0		.0	
MALE	0	.0	0	.0	0	.0	0	.0	0	.0	0	.0	0	.0	0
TOTAL															
FEMALE	0	.0	0	.0	0	.0	0	.0	0	.0	0	.0		.0	
MALE	0	.0	0	.0	0	.0	0	.0	0	.0	0	.0	0	.0	0
PROFESSIONAL:															
FULL-TIME	2	.2	4	.4	12	1.2	3	.3	21	2.1	955	96.9	10	1	
FEMALE	2	1.0	1	.5	2	1.0	0	.0	5	2.6	188	96.4	2	1	0
MALE	0	.0	3	.4	10	1.3	3	.4	16	2.0	767	97.0	8	1	110

MEDICINE

INDIAN NATIVE	BLACK NON-HISPANIC		ASIAN OR PACIFIC ISLANDER		HISPANIC		TOTAL MINORITY		WHITE NON-HISPANIC		NON-RESIDENT ALIEN		TOTAL
%	NUMBER	%	NUMBER	%	NUMBER	%	NUMBER	%	NUMBER	%	NUMBER	%	NUMBER
CONTINUED													
.0	0	.0	0	.0	0	.0	0	.0	0	.0	0	.0	0
.0	0	.0	0	.0	0	.0	0	.0	0	.0	0	.0	0
.0	0	.0	0	.0	0	.0	0	.0	0	.0	0	.0	0
.2	4	.4	12	1.2	3	.3	21	2.1	955	96.9	10	1.0	986
1.0	1	.5	2	1.0	0	.0	5	2.6	188	96.4	2	1.0	195
.0	3	.4	10	1.3	3	.4	16	2.0	767	97.0	8	1.0	791
.2	4	.4	12	1.2	3	.3	21	2.1	955	96.9	10	1.0	986
1.0	1	.5	2	1.0	0	.0	5	2.6	188	96.4	2	1.0	195
.0	3	.4	10	1.3	3	.4	16	2.0	767	97.0	8	1.0	791
.0	0	.0	0	.0	0	.0	0	.0	0	.0	0	.0	0
.0	0	.0	0	.0	0	.0	0	.0	0	.0	0	.0	0
.0	0	.0	0	.0	0	.0	0	.0	0	.0	0	.0	0
.2	4	.4	12	1.2	3	.3	21	2.1	955	96.9	10	1.0	986
1.0	1	.5	2	1.0	0	.0	5	2.6	188	96.4	2	1.0	195
.0	3	.4	10	1.3	3	.4	16	2.0	767	97.0	8	1.0	791
.0	0	.0	0	.0	0	.0	0	.0	0	.0	0	.0	0
.0	0	.0	0	.0	0	.0	0	.0	0	.0	0	.0	0
.0	0	.0	0	.0	0	.0	0	.0	0	.0	0	.0	0
.2	4	.4	12	1.2	3	.3	21	2.1	955	96.9	10	1.0	986
1.0	1	.5	2	1.0	0	.0	5	2.6	188	96.4	2	1.0	195
.0	3	.4	10	1.3	3	.4	16	2.0	767	97.0	8	1.0	791
(9 INSTITUTIONS)													
.0	0	.0	0	.0	0	.0	0	.0	0	.0	0	.0	0
.0	0	.0	0	.0	0	.0	0	.0	0	.0	0	.0	0
.0	0	.0	0	.0	0	.0	0	.0	0	.0	0	.0	0
.0	0	.0	0	.0	0	.0	0	.0	0	.0	0	.0	0
.0	0	.0	0	.0	0	.0	0	.0	0	.0	0	.0	0
.0	0	.0	0	.0	0	.0	0	.0	0	.0	0	.0	0
.0	0	.0	0	.0	0	.0	0	.0	0	.0	0	.0	0
.0	0	.0	0	.0	0	.0	0	.0	0	.0	0	.0	0
.0	0	.0	0	.0	0	.0	0	.0	0	.0	0	.0	0
.0	0	.0	0	.0	0	.0	0	.0	0	.0	0	.0	0
.0	0	.0	0	.0	0	.0	0	.0	0	.0	0	.0	0
.0	0	.0	0	.0	0	.0	0	.0	0	.0	0	.0	0
.0	0	.0	0	.0	0	.0	0	.0	0	.0	0	.0	0
.0	0	.0	0	.0	0	.0	0	.0	0	.0	0	.0	0
.0	0	.0	0	.0	0	.0	0	.0	0	.0	0	.0	0
.2	267	4.7	71	1.2	59	1.0	409	7.2	5,262	92.1	41	.7	5,712
.3	110	7.9	26	1.9	17	1.2	157	11.3	1,220	87.6	15	1.1	1,392
.2	157	3.6	45	1.0	42	1.0	252	5.8	4,042	93.6	26	.6	4,320
.0	1	25.0	0	.0	0	.0	1	25.0	3	75.0	0	.0	4
.0	1	50.0	0	.0	0	.0	1	50.0	1	50.0	0	.0	2
.0	0	.0	0	.0	0	.0	0	.0	2	100.0	0	.0	2
.2	268	4.7	71	1.2	59	1.0	410	7.2	5,265	92.1	41	.7	5,716
.3	111	8.0	26	1.9	17	1.2	158	11.3	1,221	87.6	15	1.1	1,394
.2	157	3.6	45	1.0	42	1.0	252	5.8	4,044	93.6	26	.6	4,322
.2	267	4.7	71	1.2	59	1.0	409	7.2	5,262	92.1	41	.7	5,712
.3	110	7.9	26	1.9	17	1.2	157	11.3	1,220	87.6	15	1.1	1,392
.2	157	3.6	45	1.0	42	1.0	252	5.8	4,042	93.6	26	.6	4,320
.0	1	25.0	0	.0	0	.0	1	25.0	3	75.0	0	.0	4
.0	1	50.0	0	.0	0	.0	1	50.0	1	50.0	0	.0	2
.0	0	.0	0	.0	0	.0	0	.0	2	100.0	0	.0	2
.2	268	4.7	71	1.2	59	1.0	410	7.2	5,265	92.1	41	.7	5,716
.3	111	8.0	26	1.9	17	1.2	158	11.3	1,221	87.6	15	1.1	1,394
.2	157	3.6	45	1.0	42	1.0	252	5.8	4,044	93.6	26	.6	4,322
.0	0	.0	0	.0	0	.0	0	.0	0	.0	0	.0	0
.0	0	.0	0	.0	0	.0	0	.0	0	.0	0	.0	0
.0	0	.0	0	.0	0	.0	0	.0	0	.0	0	.0	0
.2	268	4.7	71	1.2	59	1.0	410	7.2	5,265	92.1	41	.7	5,716
.3	111	8.0	26	1.9	17	1.2	158	11.3	1,221	87.6	15	1.1	1,394
.2	157	3.6	45	1.0	42	1.0	252	5.8	4,044	93.6	26	.6	4,322

MAJOR FIELD 1206 - MEDICINE

	AMERICAN INDIAN ALASKAN NATIVE		BLACK NON-HISPANIC		ASIAN OR PACIFIC ISLANDER		HISPANIC		TOTAL MINORITY		WHITE NON-HISPANIC		NON-RESIDENT ALIEN		
	NUMBER	%	NUMBER	%	NUMBER	%	NUMBER	%	NUMBER	%	NUMBER	%	NUMBER	%	

RHODE ISLAND   (1 INSTITUTIONS)

UNDERGRADUATES:															
FULL-TIME	0	.0	0	.0	0	.0	0	.0	0	.0	0	.0	0	.0	
FEMALE	0	.0	0	.0	0	.0	0	.0	0	.0	0	.0	0	.0	
MALE	0	.0	0	.0	0	.0	0	.0	0	.0	0	.0	0	.0	
PART-TIME	0	.0	0	.0	0	.0	0	.0	0	.0	0	.0	0	.0	
FEMALE	0	.0	0	.0	0	.0	0	.0	0	.0	0	.0	0	.0	
MALE	0	.0	0	.0	0	.0	0	.0	0	.0	0	.0	0	.0	
TOTAL	0	.0	0	.0	0	.0	0	.0	0	.0	0	.0	0	.0	
FEMALE	0	.0	0	.0	0	.0	0	.0	0	.0	0	.0	0	.0	
MALE	0	.0	0	.0	0	.0	0	.0	0	.0	0	.0	0	.0	
GRADUATE:															
FULL-TIME	0	.0	0	.0	0	.0	0	.0	0	.0	0	.0	0	.0	
FEMALE	0	.0	0	.0	0	.0	0	.0	0	.0	0	.0	0	.0	
MALE	0	.0	0	.0	0	.0	0	.0	0	.0	0	.0	0	.0	
PART-TIME	0	.0	0	.0	0	.0	0	.0	0	.0	0	.0	0	.0	
FEMALE	0	.0	0	.0	0	.0	0	.0	0	.0	0	.0	0	.0	
MALE	0	.0	0	.0	0	.0	0	.0	0	.0	0	.0	0	.0	
TOTAL	0	.0	0	.0	0	.0	0	.0	0	.0	0	.0	0	.0	
FEMALE	0	.0	0	.0	0	.0	0	.0	0	.0	0	.0	0	.0	
MALE	0	.0	0	.0	0	.0	0	.0	0	.0	0	.0	0	.0	
PROFESSIONAL:															
FULL-TIME	0	.0	14	5.5	11	4.3	5	2.0	30	11.9	219	86.6	4	1.6	
FEMALE	0	.0	5	5.9	9	10.6	0	.0	14	16.5	70	82.4	1	1.2	
MALE	0	.0	9	5.4	2	1.2	5	3.0	16	9.5	149	88.7	3	1.8	
PART-TIME	0	.0	0	.0	0	.0	0	.0	0	.0	0	.0	0	.0	
FEMALE	0	.0	0	.0	0	.0	0	.0	0	.0	0	.0	0	.0	
MALE	0	.0	0	.0	0	.0	0	.0	0	.0	0	.0	0	.0	
TOTAL	0	.0	14	5.5	11	4.3	5	2.0	30	11.9	219	86.6	4	1.6	
FEMALE	0	.0	5	5.9	9	10.6	0	.0	14	16.5	70	82.4	1	1.2	
MALE	0	.0	9	5.4	2	1.2	5	3.0	16	9.5	149	88.7	3	1.8	
UND+GRAD+PROF:															
FULL-TIME	0	.0	14	5.5	11	4.3	5	2.0	30	11.9	219	86.6	4	1.6	
FEMALE	0	.0	5	5.9	9	10.6	0	.0	14	16.5	70	82.4	1	1.2	
MALE	0	.0	9	5.4	2	1.2	5	3.0	16	9.5	149	88.7	3	1.8	
PART-TIME	0	.0	0	.0	0	.0	0	.0	0	.0	0	.0	0	.0	
FEMALE	0	.0	0	.0	0	.0	0	.0	0	.0	0	.0	0	.0	
MALE	0	.0	0	.0	0	.0	0	.0	0	.0	0	.0	0	.0	
TOTAL	0	.0	14	5.5	11	4.3	5	2.0	30	11.9	219	86.6	4	1.6	
FEMALE	0	.0	5	5.9	9	10.6	0	.0	14	16.5	70	82.4	1	1.2	
MALE	0	.0	9	5.4	2	1.2	5	3.0	16	9.5	149	88.7	3	1.8	
UNCLASSIFIED:															
TOTAL	0	.0	0	.0	0	.0	0	.0	0	.0	0	.0	0	.0	
FEMALE	0	.0	0	.0	0	.0	0	.0	0	.0	0	.0	0	.0	
MALE	0	.0	0	.0	0	.0	0	.0	0	.0	0	.0	0	.0	
TOTAL ENROLLMENT:															
TOTAL	0	.0	14	5.5	11	4.3	5	2.0	30	11.9	219	86.6	4	1.6	
FEMALE	0	.0	5	5.9	9	10.6	0	.0	14	16.5	70	82.4	1	1.2	
MALE	0	.0	9	5.4	2	1.2	5	3.0	16	9.5	149	88.7	3	1.8	

SOUTH CAROLINA   (1 INSTITUTIONS)

UNDERGRADUATES:															
FULL-TIME	0	.0	0	.0	0	.0	0	.0	0	.0	0	.0	0	.0	
FEMALE	0	.0	0	.0	0	.0	0	.0	0	.0	0	.0	0	.0	
MALE	0	.0	0	.0	0	.0	0	.0	0	.0	0	.0	0	.0	
PART-TIME	0	.0	0	.0	0	.0	0	.0	0	.0	0	.0	0	.0	
FEMALE	0	.0	0	.0	0	.0	0	.0	0	.0	0	.0	0	.0	
MALE	0	.0	0	.0	0	.0	0	.0	0	.0	0	.0	0	.0	
TOTAL	0	.0	0	.0	0	.0	0	.0	0	.0	0	.0	0	.0	
FEMALE	0	.0	0	.0	0	.0	0	.0	0	.0	0	.0	0	.0	
MALE	0	.0	0	.0	0	.0	0	.0	0	.0	0	.0	0	.0	
GRADUATE:															
FULL-TIME	0	.0	0	.0	0	.0	0	.0	0	.0	0	.0	0	.0	
FEMALE	0	.0	0	.0	0	.0	0	.0	0	.0	0	.0	0	.0	
MALE	0	.0	0	.0	0	.0	0	.0	0	.0	0	.0	0	.0	
PART-TIME	0	.0	0	.0	0	.0	0	.0	0	.0	0	.0	0	.0	
FEMALE	0	.0	0	.0	0	.0	0	.0	0	.0	0	.0	0	.0	
MALE	0	.0	0	.0	0	.0	0	.0	0	.0	0	.0	0	.0	
TOTAL	0	.0	0	.0	0	.0	0	.0	0	.0	0	.0	0	.0	
FEMALE	0	.0	0	.0	0	.0	0	.0	0	.0	0	.0	0	.0	
MALE	0	.0	0	.0	0	.0	0	.0	0	.0	0	.0	0	.0	
PROFESSIONAL:															
FULL-TIME	0	.0	2	3.4	0	.0	0	.0	2	3.4	57	96.6	0	.0	
FEMALE	0	.0	1	14.3	0	.0	0	.0	1	14.3	6	85.7	0	.0	
MALE	0	.0	1	1.9	0	.0	0	.0	1	1.9	51	98.1	0	.0	

ACK ISPANIC	ASIAN OR PACIFIC ISLANDER		HISPANIC		TOTAL MINORITY		WHITE NON-HISPANIC		NON-RESIDENT ALIEN		TOTAL
%	NUMBER	%	NUMBER	%	NUMBER	%	NUMBER	%	NUMBER	%	NUMBER
.0	0	.0	0	.0	0	.0	0	.0	0	.0	0
.0	0	.0	0	.0	0	.0	0	.0	0	.0	0
.0	0	.0	0	.0	0	.0	0	.0	0	.0	0
3.4	0	.0	0	.0	2	3.4	57	96.6	0	.0	59
14.3	0	.0	0	.0	1	14.3	6	85.7	0	.0	7
1.9	0	.0	0	.0	1	1.9	51	98.1	0	.0	52
3.4	0	.0	0	.0	2	3.4	57	96.6	0	.0	59
14.3	0	.0	0	.0	1	14.3	6	85.7	0	.0	7
1.9	0	.0	0	.0	1	1.9	51	98.1	0	.0	52
.0	0	.0	0	.0	0	.0	0	.0	0	.0	0
.0	0	.0	0	.0	0	.0	0	.0	0	.0	0
.0	0	.0	0	.0	0	.0	0	.0	0	.0	0
3.4	0	.0	0	.0	2	3.4	57	96.6	0	.0	59
14.3	0	.0	0	.0	1	14.3	6	85.7	0	.0	7
1.9	0	.0	0	.0	1	1.9	51	98.1	0	.0	52
.0	0	.0	0	.0	0	.0	0	.0	0	.0	0
.0	0	.0	0	.0	0	.0	0	.0	0	.0	0
.0	0	.0	0	.0	0	.0	0	.0	0	.0	0
3.4	0	.0	0	.0	2	3.4	57	96.6	0	.0	59
14.3	0	.0	0	.0	1	14.3	6	85.7	0	.0	7
1.9	0	.0	0	.0	1	1.9	51	98.1	0	.0	52

UTIONS)

ACK ISPANIC	ASIAN OR PACIFIC ISLANDER		HISPANIC		TOTAL MINORITY		WHITE NON-HISPANIC		NON-RESIDENT ALIEN		TOTAL
.0	0	.0	0	.0	0	.0	0	.0	0	.0	0
.0	0	.0	0	.0	0	.0	0	.0	0	.0	0
.0	0	.0	0	.0	0	.0	0	.0	0	.0	0
.0	0	.0	0	.0	0	.0	0	.0	0	.0	0
.0	0	.0	0	.0	0	.0	0	.0	0	.0	0
.0	0	.0	0	.0	0	.0	0	.0	0	.0	0
.0	0	.0	0	.0	0	.0	0	.0	0	.0	0
.0	0	.0	0	.0	0	.0	0	.0	0	.0	0
.0	0	.0	0	.0	0	.0	0	.0	0	.0	0
.0	0	.0	0	.0	0	.0	0	.0	0	.0	0
.0	0	.0	0	.0	0	.0	0	.0	0	.0	0
.0	0	.0	0	.0	0	.0	0	.0	0	.0	0
.0	0	.0	0	.0	0	.0	0	.0	0	.0	0
.0	0	.0	0	.0	0	.0	0	.0	0	.0	0
.0	0	.0	0	.0	0	.0	0	.0	0	.0	0
.0	1	.5	0	.0	1	.5	217	99.5	0	.0	218
.0	0	.0	0	.0	0	.0	41	100.0	0	.0	41
.0	1	.6	0	.0	1	.6	176	99.4	0	.0	177
.0	0	.0	0	.0	0	.0	0	.0	0	.0	0
.0	0	.0	0	.0	0	.0	0	.0	0	.0	0
.0	1	.5	0	.0	1	.5	217	99.5	0	.0	218
.0	0	.0	0	.0	0	.0	41	100.0	0	.0	41
.0	1	.6	0	.0	1	.6	176	99.4	0	.0	177
.0	1	.5	0	.0	1	.5	217	99.5	0	.0	218
.0	0	.0	0	.0	0	.0	41	100.0	0	.0	41
.0	1	.6	0	.0	1	.6	176	99.4	0	.0	177
.0	0	.0	0	.0	0	.0	0	.0	0	.0	0
.0	0	.0	0	.0	0	.0	0	.0	0	.0	0
.0	1	.5	0	.0	1	.5	217	99.5	0	.0	218
.0	0	.0	0	.0	0	.0	41	100.0	0	.0	41
.0	1	.6	0	.0	1	.6	176	99.4	0	.0	177
.0	0	.0	0	.0	0	.0	0	.0	0	.0	0
.0	0	.0	0	.0	0	.0	0	.0	0	.0	0
.0	0	.0	0	.0	0	.0	0	.0	0	.0	0
.0	1	.5	0	.0	1	.5	217	99.5	0	.0	218
.0	0	.0	0	.0	0	.0	41	100.0	0	.0	41
.0	1	.6	0	.0	1	.6	176	99.4	0	.0	177

TABLE 17 - TOTAL ENROLLMENT IN INSTITUTIONS OF HIGHER EDUCATION FOR SELECTED MAJOR FIELDS OF STUDY AND LEVEL OF ENROLLMENT BY RACE, ETHNICITY, AND SEX: STATE, 1978

MAJOR FIELD 1206 - MEDICINE

	AMERICAN INDIAN ALASKAN NATIVE		BLACK NON-HISPANIC		ASIAN OR PACIFIC ISLANDER		HISPANIC		TOTAL MINORITY		WHITE NON-HISPANIC		NON-RESIDENT ALIEN		T
	NUMBER	%	NUMBER	%	NUMBER	%	NUMBER	%	NUMBER	%	NUMBER	%	NUMBER	%	N
TENNESSEE	(	4 INSTITUTIONS)													
UNDERGRADUATES															
FULL-TIME	0	.0	0	.0	0	.0	0	.0	0	.0	0	.0	0	.0	
FEMALE	0	.0	0	.0	0	.0	0	.0	0	.0	0	.0	0	.0	
MALE	0	.0	0	.0	0	.0	0	.0	0	.0	0	.0	0	.0	
PART-TIME	0	.0	0	.0	0	.0	0	.0	0	.0	0	.0	0	.0	
FEMALE	0	.0	0	.0	0	.0	0	.0	0	.0	0	.0	0	.0	
MALE	0	.0	0	.0	0	.0	0	.0	0	.0	0	.0	0	.0	
TOTAL	0	.0	0	.0	0	.0	0	.0	0	.0	0	.0	0	.0	
FEMALE	0	.0	0	.0	0	.0	0	.0	0	.0	0	.0	0	.0	
MALE	0	.0	0	.0	0	.0	0	.0	0	.0	0	.0	0	.0	
GRADUATE															
FULL-TIME	0	.0	0	.0	0	.0	0	.0	0	.0	0	.0	0	.0	
FEMALE	0	.0	0	.0	0	.0	0	.0	0	.0	0	.0	0	.0	
MALE	0	.0	0	.0	0	.0	0	.0	0	.0	0	.0	0	.0	
PART-TIME	0	.0	0	.0	0	.0	0	.0	0	.0	0	.0	0	.0	
FEMALE	0	.0	0	.0	0	.0	0	.0	0	.0	0	.0	0	.0	
MALE	0	.0	0	.0	0	.0	0	.0	0	.0	0	.0	0	.0	
TOTAL	0	.0	0	.0	0	.0	0	.0	0	.0	0	.0	0	.0	
FEMALE	0	.0	0	.0	0	.0	0	.0	0	.0	0	.0	0	.0	
MALE	0	.0	0	.0	0	.0	0	.0	0	.0	0	.0	0	.0	
PROFESSIONAL															
FULL-TIME	5	.3	432	26.7	11	.7	19	1.2	467	28.8	1,137	70.1	17	1.0	
FEMALE	1	.3	135	40.4	2	.6	3	.9	141	42.2	187	56.0	6	1.8	
MALE	4	.3	297	23.1	9	.7	16	1.2	326	25.3	950	73.8	11	.9	
PART-TIME	0	.0	3	100.0	0	.0	0	.0	3	100.0	0	.0	0	.0	
FEMALE	0	.0	1	100.0	0	.0	0	.0	1	100.0	0	.0	0	.0	
MALE	0	.0	2	100.0	0	.0	0	.0	2	100.0	0	.0	0	.0	
TOTAL	5	.3	435	26.8	11	.7	19	1.2	470	28.9	1,137	70.0	17	1.0	
FEMALE	1	.3	136	40.6	2	.6	3	.9	142	42.4	187	55.8	6	1.8	
MALE	4	.3	299	23.2	9	.7	16	1.2	328	25.4	950	73.7	11	.9	
UND+GRAD+PROF															
FULL-TIME	5	.3	432	26.7	11	.7	19	1.2	467	28.8	1,137	70.1	17	1.0	
FEMALE	1	.3	135	40.4	2	.6	3	.9	141	42.2	187	56.0	6	1.8	
MALE	4	.3	297	23.1	9	.7	16	1.2	326	25.3	950	73.8	11	.9	
PART-TIME	0	.0	3	100.0	0	.0	0	.0	3	100.0	0	.0	0	.0	
FEMALE	0	.0	1	100.0	0	.0	0	.0	1	100.0	0	.0	0	.0	
MALE	0	.0	2	100.0	0	.0	0	.0	2	100.0	0	.0	0	.0	
TOTAL	5	.3	435	26.8	11	.7	19	1.2	470	28.9	1,137	70.0	17	1.0	
FEMALE	1	.3	136	40.6	2	.6	3	.9	142	42.4	187	55.8	6	1.8	
MALE	4	.3	299	23.2	9	.7	16	1.2	328	25.4	950	73.7	11	.9	
UNCLASSIFIED															
TOTAL	0	.0	53	70.7	0	.0	0	.0	53	70.7	3	4.0	19	25.3	
FEMALE	0	.0	14	87.5	0	.0	0	.0	14	87.5	1	6.3	1	6.3	
MALE	0	.0	39	66.1	0	.0	0	.0	39	66.1	2	3.4	18	30.5	
TOTAL ENROLLMENT															
TOTAL	5	.3	488	28.7	11	.6	19	1.1	523	30.8	1,140	67.1	36	2.1	
FEMALE	1	.3	150	42.7	2	.6	3	.9	156	44.4	188	53.6	7	2.0	
MALE	4	.3	338	25.1	9	.7	16	1.2	367	27.2	952	70.6	29	2.2	
TEXAS	(	7 INSTITUTIONS)													
UNDERGRADUATES															
FULL-TIME	0	.0	0	.0	0	.0	0	.0	0	.0	0	.0	0	.0	
FEMALE	0	.0	0	.0	0	.0	0	.0	0	.0	0	.0	0	.0	
MALE	0	.0	0	.0	0	.0	0	.0	0	.0	0	.0	0	.0	
PART-TIME	0	.0	0	.0	0	.0	0	.0	0	.0	0	.0	0	.0	
FEMALE	0	.0	0	.0	0	.0	0	.0	0	.0	0	.0	0	.0	
MALE	0	.0	0	.0	0	.0	0	.0	0	.0	0	.0	0	.0	
TOTAL	0	.0	0	.0	0	.0	0	.0	0	.0	0	.0	0	.0	
FEMALE	0	.0	0	.0	0	.0	0	.0	0	.0	0	.0	0	.0	
MALE	0	.0	0	.0	0	.0	0	.0	0	.0	0	.0	0	.0	
GRADUATE															
FULL-TIME	0	.0	0	.0	0	.0	0	.0	0	.0	0	.0	0	.0	
FEMALE	0	.0	0	.0	0	.0	0	.0	0	.0	0	.0	0	.0	
MALE	0	.0	0	.0	0	.0	0	.0	0	.0	0	.0	0	.0	
PART-TIME	0	.0	0	.0	0	.0	0	.0	0	.0	0	.0	0	.0	
FEMALE	0	.0	0	.0	0	.0	0	.0	0	.0	0	.0	0	.0	
MALE	0	.0	0	.0	0	.0	0	.0	0	.0	0	.0	0	.0	
TOTAL	0	.0	0	.0	0	.0	0	.0	0	.0	0	.0	0	.0	
FEMALE	0	.0	0	.0	0	.0	0	.0	0	.0	0	.0	0	.0	
MALE	0	.0	0	.0	0	.0	0	.0	0	.0	0	.0	0	.0	
PROFESSIONAL															
FULL-TIME	6	.2	96	2.6	76	2.1	254	7.0	432	11.9	3,188	87.5	24	.7	
FEMALE	0	.0	36	4.7	26	3.4	53	7.0	115	15.2	638	84.1	6	.8	
MALE	6	.2	60	2.1	50	1.7	201	7.0	317	11.0	2,550	88.4	18	.6	

MEDICINE

INDIAN NATIVE	BLACK NON-HISPANIC		ASIAN OR PACIFIC ISLANDER		HISPANIC		TOTAL MINORITY		WHITE NON-HISPANIC		NON-RESIDENT ALIEN		TOTAL
%	NUMBER	%	NUMBER	%	NUMBER	%	NUMBER	%	NUMBER	%	NUMBER	%	NUMBER

CONTINUED

.0	0	.0	0	.0	0	.0	0	.0	0	.0	0	.0	0
.0	0	.0	0	.0	0	.0	0	.0	0	.0	0	.0	0
.0	0	.0	0	.0	0	.0	0	.0	0	.0	0	.0	0
.2	96	2.6	76	2.1	254	7.0	432	11.9	3,188	87.5	24	.7	3,644
.0	36	4.7	26	3.4	53	7.0	115	15.2	638	84.1	6	.8	759
.2	60	2.1	50	1.7	201	7.0	317	11.0	2,550	88.4	18	.6	2,885
.2	96	2.6	76	2.1	254	7.0	432	11.9	3,188	87.5	24	.7	3,644
.0	36	4.7	26	3.4	53	7.0	115	15.2	638	84.1	6	.8	759
.2	60	2.1	50	1.7	201	7.0	317	11.0	2,550	88.4	18	.6	2,885
.0	0	.0	0	.0	0	.0	0	.0	0	.0	0	.0	0
.0	0	.0	0	.0	0	.0	0	.0	0	.0	0	.0	0
.0	0	.0	0	.0	0	.0	0	.0	0	.0	0	.0	0
.2	96	2.6	76	2.1	254	7.0	432	11.9	3,188	87.5	24	.7	3,644
.0	36	4.7	26	3.4	53	7.0	115	15.2	638	84.1	6	.8	759
.2	60	2.1	50	1.7	201	7.0	317	11.0	2,550	88.4	18	.6	2,885
.0	0	.0	0	.0	0	.0	0	.0	0	.0	0	.0	0
.0	0	.0	0	.0	0	.0	0	.0	0	.0	0	.0	0
.0	0	.0	0	.0	0	.0	0	.0	0	.0	0	.0	0
.2	96	2.6	76	2.1	254	7.0	432	11.9	3,188	87.5	24	.7	3,644
.0	36	4.7	26	3.4	53	7.0	115	15.2	638	84.1	6	.8	759
.2	60	2.1	50	1.7	201	7.0	317	11.0	2,550	88.4	18	.6	2,885

(1 INSTITUTIONS)

.0	0	.0	0	.0	0	.0	0	.0	0	.0	0	.0	0
.0	0	.0	0	.0	0	.0	0	.0	0	.0	0	.0	0
.0	0	.0	0	.0	0	.0	0	.0	0	.0	0	.0	0
.0	0	.0	0	.0	0	.0	0	.0	0	.0	0	.0	0
.0	0	.0	0	.0	0	.0	0	.0	0	.0	0	.0	0
.0	0	.0	0	.0	0	.0	0	.0	0	.0	0	.0	0
.0	0	.0	0	.0	0	.0	0	.0	0	.0	0	.0	0
.0	0	.0	0	.0	0	.0	0	.0	0	.0	0	.0	0
.0	0	.0	0	.0	0	.0	0	.0	0	.0	0	.0	0
.0	0	.0	0	.0	0	.0	0	.0	0	.0	0	.0	0
.0	0	.0	0	.0	0	.0	0	.0	0	.0	0	.0	0
.0	0	.0	0	.0	0	.0	0	.0	0	.0	0	.0	0
.0	0	.0	0	.0	0	.0	0	.0	0	.0	0	.0	0
.0	0	.0	0	.0	0	.0	0	.0	0	.0	0	.0	0
.0	0	.0	0	.0	0	.0	0	.0	0	.0	0	.0	0
1.0	4	1.0	8	2.0	16	4.0	32	8.0	365	91.5	2	.5	399
.0	3	5.4	2	3.6	3	5.4	8	14.3	48	85.7	0	.0	56
1.2	1	.3	6	1.7	13	3.8	24	7.0	317	92.4	2	.6	343
.0	0	.0	0	.0	0	.0	0	.0	0	.0	0	.0	0
.0	0	.0	0	.0	0	.0	0	.0	0	.0	0	.0	0
.0	0	.0	0	.0	0	.0	0	.0	0	.0	0	.0	0
1.0	4	1.0	8	2.0	16	4.0	32	8.0	365	91.5	2	.5	399
.0	3	5.4	2	3.6	3	5.4	8	14.3	48	85.7	0	.0	56
1.2	1	.3	6	1.7	13	3.8	24	7.0	317	92.4	2	.6	343
1.0	4	1.0	8	2.0	16	4.0	32	8.0	365	91.5	2	.5	399
.0	3	5.4	2	3.6	3	5.4	8	14.3	48	85.7	0	.0	56
1.2	1	.3	6	1.7	13	3.8	24	7.0	317	92.4	2	.6	343
.0	0	.0	0	.0	0	.0	0	.0	0	.0	0	.0	0
.0	0	.0	0	.0	0	.0	0	.0	0	.0	0	.0	0
.0	0	.0	0	.0	0	.0	0	.0	0	.0	0	.0	0
1.0	4	1.0	8	2.0	16	4.0	32	8.0	365	91.5	2	.5	399
.0	3	5.4	2	3.6	3	5.4	8	14.3	48	85.7	0	.0	56
1.2	1	.3	6	1.7	13	3.8	24	7.0	317	92.4	2	.6	343
.0	0	.0	0	.0	0	.0	0	.0	0	.0	0	.0	0
.0	0	.0	0	.0	0	.0	0	.0	0	.0	0	.0	0
.0	0	.0	0	.0	0	.0	0	.0	0	.0	0	.0	0
1.0	4	1.0	8	2.0	16	4.0	32	8.0	365	91.5	2	.5	399
.0	3	5.4	2	3.6	3	5.4	8	14.3	48	85.7	0	.0	56
1.2	1	.3	6	1.7	13	3.8	24	7.0	317	92.4	2	.6	343

MAJOR FIELD 1206 - MEDICINE

	AMERICAN INDIAN ALASKAN NATIVE		BLACK NON-HISPANIC		ASIAN OR PACIFIC ISLANDER		HISPANIC		TOTAL MINORITY		WHITE NON-HISPANIC		NON-RESIDENT ALIEN		T(
	NUMBER	%	NUMBER	%	NUMBER	%	NUMBER	%	NUMBER	%	NUMBER	%	NUMBER	%	N(
VERMONT	(	1 INSTITUTIONS)													
UNDERGRADUATES:															
FULL-TIME	0	.0	0	.0	0	.0	0	.0	0	.0	0	.0		.0	
FEMALE	0	.0	0	.0	0	.0	0	.0	0	.0	0	.0		.0	
MALE	0	.0	0	.0	0	.0	0	.0	0	.0	0	.0		.0	
PART-TIME	0	.0	0	.0	0	.0	0	.0	0	.0	0	.0		.0	
FEMALE	0	.0	0	.0	0	.0	0	.0	0	.0	0	.0		.0	
MALE	0	.0	0	.0	0	.0	0	.0	0	.0	0	.0	0	.0	
TOTAL	0	.0	0	.0	0	.0	0	.0	0	.0	0	.0		.0	
FEMALE	0	.0	0	.0	0	.0	0	.0	0	.0	0	.0		.0	
MALE	0	.0	0	.0	0	.0	0	.0	0	.0	0	.0	0	.0	
GRADUATE:															
FULL-TIME	0	.0	0	.0	0	.0	0	.0	0	.0	0	.0		.0	
FEMALE	0	.0	0	.0	0	.0	0	.0	0	.0	0	.0		.0	
MALE	0	.0	0	.0	0	.0	0	.0	0	.0	0	.0		.0	
PART-TIME	0	.0	0	.0	0	.0	0	.0	0	.0	0	.0		.0	
FEMALE	0	.0	0	.0	0	.0	0	.0	0	.0	0	.0		.0	
MALE	0	.0	0	.0	0	.0	0	.0	0	.0	0	.0	0	.0	
TOTAL	0	.0	0	.0	0	.0	0	.0	0	.0	0	.0	0	.0	
FEMALE	0	.0	0	.0	0	.0	0	.0	0	.0	0	.0	0	.0	
MALE	0	.0	0	.0	0	.0	0	.0	0	.0	0	.0	0	.0	
PROFESSIONAL:															
FULL-TIME	0	.0	0	.0	2	.6	0	.0	2	.6	318	98.8	2	.6	
FEMALE	0	.0	0	.0	0	.0	0	.0	0	.0	68	100.0	0	.0	
MALE	0	.0	0	.0	2	.8	0	.0	2	.8	250	98.4	2	.8	
PART-TIME	0	.0	0	.0	0	.0	0	.0	0	.0	0	.0	0	.0	
FEMALE	0	.0	0	.0	0	.0	0	.0	0	.0	0	.0	0	.0	
MALE	0	.0	0	.0	0	.0	0	.0	0	.0	0	.0	0	.0	
TOTAL	0	.0	0	.0	2	.6	0	.0	2	.6	318	98.8	2	.6	
FEMALE	0	.0	0	.0	0	.0	0	.0	0	.0	68	100.0	0	.0	
MALE	0	.0	0	.0	2	.8	0	.0	2	.8	250	98.4	2	.8	
UND+GRAD+PROF:															
FULL-TIME	0	.0	0	.0	2	.6	0	.0	2	.6	318	98.8	2	.6	
FEMALE	0	.0	0	.0	0	.0	0	.0	0	.0	68	100.0	0	.0	
MALE	0	.0	0	.0	2	.8	0	.0	2	.8	250	98.4	2	.8	
PART-TIME	0	.0	0	.0	0	.0	0	.0	0	.0	0	.0	0	.0	
FEMALE	0	.0	0	.0	0	.0	0	.0	0	.0	0	.0	0	.0	
MALE	0	.0	0	.0	0	.0	0	.0	0	.0	0	.0	0	.0	
TOTAL	0	.0	0	.0	2	.6	0	.0	2	.6	318	98.8	2	.6	
FEMALE	0	.0	0	.0	0	.0	0	.0	0	.0	68	100.0	0	.0	
MALE	0	.0	0	.0	2	.8	0	.0	2	.8	250	98.4	2	.8	
UNCLASSIFIED:															
TOTAL	0	.0	0	.0	0	.0	0	.0	0	.0	0	.0	0	.0	
FEMALE	0	.0	0	.0	0	.0	0	.0	0	.0	0	.0	0	.0	
MALE	0	.0	0	.0	0	.0	0	.0	0	.0	0	.0	0	.0	
TOTAL ENROLLMENT:															
TOTAL	0	.0	0	.0	2	.6	0	.0	2	.6	318	98.8	2	.6	
FEMALE	0	.0	0	.0	0	.0	0	.0	0	.0	68	100.0	0	.0	
MALE	0	.0	0	.0	2	.8	0	.0	2	.8	250	98.4	2	.8	
VIRGINIA	(	3 INSTITUTIONS)													
UNDERGRADUATES:															
FULL-TIME	0	.0	0	.0	0	.0	0	.0	0	.0	0	.0		.0	
FEMALE	0	.0	0	.0	0	.0	0	.0	0	.0	0	.0		.0	
MALE	0	.0	0	.0	0	.0	0	.0	0	.0	0	.0		.0	
PART-TIME	0	.0	0	.0	0	.0	0	.0	0	.0	0	.0		.0	
FEMALE	0	.0	0	.0	0	.0	0	.0	0	.0	0	.0		.0	
MALE	0	.0	0	.0	0	.0	0	.0	0	.0	0	.0	0	.0	
TOTAL	0	.0	0	.0	0	.0	0	.0	0	.0	0	.0		.0	
FEMALE	0	.0	0	.0	0	.0	0	.0	0	.0	0	.0		.0	
MALE	0	.0	0	.0	0	.0	0	.0	0	.0	0	.0	0	.0	
GRADUATE:															
FULL-TIME	0	.0	0	.0	0	.0	0	.0	0	.0	0	.0		.0	
FEMALE	0	.0	0	.0	0	.0	0	.0	0	.0	0	.0		.0	
MALE	0	.0	0	.0	0	.0	0	.0	0	.0	0	.0		.0	
PART-TIME	0	.0	0	.0	0	.0	0	.0	0	.0	0	.0		.0	
FEMALE	0	.0	0	.0	0	.0	0	.0	0	.0	0	.0		.0	
MALE	0	.0	0	.0	0	.0	0	.0	0	.0	0	.0	0	.0	
TOTAL	0	.0	0	.0	0	.0	0	.0	0	.0	0	.0		.0	
FEMALE	0	.0	0	.0	0	.0	0	.0	0	.0	0	.0		.0	
MALE	0	.0	0	.0	0	.0	0	.0	0	.0	0	.0	0	.0	
PROFESSIONAL:															
FULL-TIME	1	.1	64	4.5	18	1.3	6	.4	89	6.2	1,332	93.3	6	.4	
FEMALE	0	.0	24	7.4	5	1.5	0	.0	29	9.0	294	90.7	1	.3	
MALE	1	.1	40	3.6	13	1.2	6	.5	60	5.4	1,038	94.1	5	.5	

ROLLMENT IN INSTITUTIONS OF HIGHER EDUCATION FOR SELECTED MAJOR FIELDS OF STUDY AND LEVEL OF ENROLLMENT
ETHNICITY, AND SEA: STATE, 1978

MEDICINE

INDIAN NATIVE	BLACK NON-HISPANIC		ASIAN OR PACIFIC ISLANDER		HISPANIC		TOTAL MINORITY		WHITE NON-HISPANIC		NON-RESIDENT ALIEN		TOTAL
%	NUMBER	%	NUMBER	%	NUMBER	%	NUMBER	%	NUMBER	%	NUMBER	%	NUMBER
CONTINUED													
.0	0	.0	0	.0	0	.0	0	.0	1	100.0	0	.0	1
.0	0	.0	0	.0	0	.0	0	.0	0	.0	0	.0	0
.0	0	.0	0	.0	0	.0	0	.0	1	100.0	0	.0	1
.1	64	4.5	18	1.3	6	.4	89	6.2	1,333	93.3	6	.4	1,428
.0	24	7.4	5	1.5	0	.0	29	9.0	294	90.7	1	.3	324
.1	40	3.6	13	1.2	6	.5	60	5.4	1,039	94.1	5	.5	1,104
.1	64	4.5	18	1.3	6	.4	89	6.2	1,332	93.3	6	.4	1,427
.0	24	7.4	5	1.5	0	.0	29	9.0	294	90.7	1	.3	324
.1	40	3.6	13	1.2	6	.5	60	5.4	1,038	94.1	5	.5	1,103
.0	0	.0	0	.0	0	.0	0	.0	1	100.0	0	.0	1
.0	0	.0	0	.0	0	.0	0	.0	0	.0	0	.0	0
.0	0	.0	0	.0	0	.0	0	.0	1	100.0	0	.0	1
.1	64	4.5	18	1.3	6	.4	89	6.2	1,333	93.3	6	.4	1,428
.0	24	7.4	5	1.5	0	.0	29	9.0	294	90.7	1	.3	324
.1	40	3.6	13	1.2	6	.5	60	5.4	1,039	94.1	5	.5	1,104
.0	0	.0	0	.0	0	.0	0	.0	0	.0	0	.0	0
.0	0	.0	0	.0	0	.0	0	.0	0	.0	0	.0	0
.0	0	.0	0	.0	0	.0	0	.0	0	.0	0	.0	0
.1	64	4.5	18	1.3	6	.4	89	6.2	1,333	93.3	6	.4	1,428
.0	24	7.4	5	1.5	0	.0	29	9.0	294	90.7	1	.3	324
.1	40	3.6	13	1.2	6	.5	60	5.4	1,039	94.1	5	.5	1,104
(1 INSTITUTIONS)													
.0	0	.0	0	.0	0	.0	0	.0	0	.0	0	.0	0
.0	0	.0	0	.0	0	.0	0	.0	0	.0	0	.0	0
.0	0	.0	0	.0	0	.0	0	.0	0	.0	0	.0	0
.0	0	.0	0	.0	0	.0	0	.0	0	.0	0	.0	0
.0	0	.0	0	.0	0	.0	0	.0	0	.0	0	.0	0
.0	0	.0	0	.0	0	.0	0	.0	0	.0	0	.0	0
.0	0	.0	0	.0	0	.0	0	.0	0	.0	0	.0	0
.0	0	.0	0	.0	0	.0	0	.0	0	.0	0	.0	0
.0	0	.0	0	.0	0	.0	0	.0	0	.0	0	.0	0
.0	0	.0	0	.0	0	.0	0	.0	0	.0	0	.0	0
.0	0	.0	0	.0	0	.0	0	.0	0	.0	0	.0	0
.0	0	.0	0	.0	0	.0	0	.0	0	.0	0	.0	0
.0	0	.0	0	.0	0	.0	0	.0	0	.0	0	.0	0
.0	0	.0	0	.0	0	.0	0	.0	0	.0	0	.0	0
.0	0	.0	0	.0	0	.0	0	.0	0	.0	0	.0	0
.3	6	1.0	25	4.1	11	1.8	44	7.2	565	92.6	1	.2	610
.0	2	1.3	8	5.1	3	1.9	13	8.3	143	91.7	0	.0	156
.4	4	.9	17	3.7	8	1.8	31	6.8	422	93.0	1	.2	454
.0	1	1.3	0	.0	0	.0	1	1.3	76	98.7	0	.0	77
.0	0	.0	0	.0	0	.0	0	.0	18	100.0	0	.0	18
.0	1	1.7	0	.0	0	.0	1	1.7	58	98.3	0	.0	59
.3	7	1.0	25	3.6	11	1.6	45	6.6	641	93.3	1	.1	687
.0	2	1.1	8	4.6	3	1.7	13	7.5	161	92.5	0	.0	174
.4	5	1.0	17	3.3	8	1.6	32	6.2	480	93.6	1	.2	513
.3	6	1.0	25	4.1	11	1.8	44	7.2	565	92.6	1	.2	610
.0	2	1.3	8	5.1	3	1.9	13	8.3	143	91.7	0	.0	156
.4	4	.9	17	3.7	8	1.8	31	6.8	422	93.0	1	.2	454
.0	1	1.3	0	.0	0	.0	1	1.3	76	98.7	0	.0	77
.0	0	.0	0	.0	0	.0	0	.0	18	100.0	0	.0	18
.0	1	1.7	0	.0	0	.0	1	1.7	58	98.3	0	.0	59
.3	7	1.0	25	3.6	11	1.6	45	6.6	641	93.3	1	.1	687
.0	2	1.1	8	4.6	3	1.7	13	7.5	161	92.5	0	.0	174
.4	5	1.0	17	3.3	8	1.6	32	6.2	480	93.6	1	.2	513
.0	0	.0	0	.0	0	.0	0	.0	0	.0	0	.0	0
.0	0	.0	0	.0	0	.0	0	.0	0	.0	0	.0	0
.0	0	.0	0	.0	0	.0	0	.0	0	.0	0	.0	0
.3	7	1.0	25	3.6	11	1.6	45	6.6	641	93.3	1	.1	687
.0	2	1.1	8	4.6	3	1.7	13	7.5	161	92.5	0	.0	174
.4	5	1.0	17	3.3	8	1.6	32	6.2	480	93.6	1	.2	513

TABLE 17 - TOTAL ENROLLMENT IN INSTITUTIONS OF HIGHER EDUCATION FOR SELECTED MAJOR FIELDS OF STUDY AND LEVEL OF ENROLLMENT
BY RACE, ETHNICITY, AND SEX: STATE, 1978

MAJOR FIELD 1206 - MEDICINE

	AMERICAN INDIAN ALASKAN NATIVE		BLACK NON-HISPANIC		ASIAN OR PACIFIC ISLANDER		HISPANIC		TOTAL MINORITY		WHITE NON-HISPANIC		NON-RESIDENT ALIEN		T(
	NUMBER	%	NUMBER	%	NUMBER	%	NUMBER	%	NUMBER	%	NUMBER	%	NUMBER	%	N(
WEST VIRGINIA (3 INSTITUTIONS)															
UNDERGRADUATES:															
FULL-TIME	0	.0	0	.0	0	.0	0	.0	0	.0	0	.0	0	.0	
FEMALE	0	.0	0	.0	0	.0	0	.0	0	.0	0	.0	0	.0	
MALE	0	.0	0	.0	0	.0	0	.0	0	.0	0	.0	0	.0	
PART-TIME	0	.0	0	.0	0	.0	0	.0	0	.0	0	.0	0	.0	
FEMALE	0	.0	0	.0	0	.0	0	.0	0	.0	0	.0	0	.0	
MALE	0	.0	0	.0	0	.0	0	.0	0	.0	0	.0	0	.0	
TOTAL	0	.0	0	.0	0	.0	0	.0	0	.0	0	.0	0	.0	
FEMALE	0	.0	0	.0	0	.0	0	.0	0	.0	0	.0	0	.0	
MALE	0	.0	0	.0	0	.0	0	.0	0	.0	0	.0	0	.0	
GRADUATE:															
FULL-TIME	0	.0	0	.0	0	.0	0	.0	0	.0	0	.0	0	.0	
FEMALE	0	.0	0	.0	0	.0	0	.0	0	.0	0	.0	0	.0	
MALE	0	.0	0	.0	0	.0	0	.0	0	.0	0	.0	0	.0	
PART-TIME	0	.0	0	.0	0	.0	0	.0	0	.0	0	.0	0	.0	
FEMALE	0	.0	0	.0	0	.0	0	.0	0	.0	0	.0	0	.0	
MALE	0	.0	0	.0	0	.0	0	.0	0	.0	0	.0	0	.0	
TOTAL	0	.0	0	.0	0	.0	0	.0	0	.0	0	.0	0	.0	
FEMALE	0	.0	0	.0	0	.0	0	.0	0	.0	0	.0	0	.0	
MALE	0	.0	0	.0	0	.0	0	.0	0	.0	0	.0	0	.0	
PROFESSIONAL:															
FULL-TIME	0	.0	5	.8	2	.3	1	.2	8	1.3	593	98.2	3	.5	
FEMALE	0	.0	1	.9	0	.0	1	.9	2	1.8	107	97.3	1	.9	
MALE	0	.0	4	.8	2	.4	0	.0	6	1.2	486	98.4	2	.4	
PART-TIME	0	.0	0	.0	0	.0	0	.0	0	.0	1	100.0	0	.0	
FEMALE	0	.0	0	.0	0	.0	0	.0	0	.0	1	100.0	0	.0	
MALE	0	.0	0	.0	0	.0	0	.0	0	.0	0	.0	0	.0	
TOTAL	0	.0	5	.8	2	.3	1	.2	8	1.3	594	98.2	3	.5	
FEMALE	0	.0	1	.9	0	.0	1	.9	2	1.8	108	97.3	1	.9	
MALE	0	.0	4	.8	2	.4	0	.0	6	1.2	486	98.4	2	.4	
UND+GRAD+PROF:															
FULL-TIME	0	.0	5	.8	2	.3	1	.2	8	1.3	593	98.2	3	.5	
FEMALE	0	.0	1	.9	0	.0	1	.9	2	1.8	107	97.3	1	.9	
MALE	0	.0	4	.8	2	.4	0	.0	6	1.2	486	98.4	2	.4	
PART-TIME	0	.0	0	.0	0	.0	0	.0	0	.0	1	100.0	0	.0	
FEMALE	0	.0	0	.0	0	.0	0	.0	0	.0	1	100.0	0	.0	
MALE	0	.0	0	.0	0	.0	0	.0	0	.0	0	.0	0	.0	
TOTAL	0	.0	5	.8	2	.3	1	.2	8	1.3	594	98.2	3	.5	
FEMALE	0	.0	1	.9	0	.0	1	.9	2	1.8	108	97.3	1	.9	
MALE	0	.0	4	.8	2	.4	0	.0	6	1.2	486	98.4	2	.4	
UNCLASSIFIED:															
TOTAL	0	.0	0	.0	0	.0	0	.0	0	.0	0	.0	0	.0	
FEMALE	0	.0	0	.0	0	.0	0	.0	0	.0	0	.0	0	.0	
MALE	0	.0	0	.0	0	.0	0	.0	0	.0	0	.0	0	.0	
TOTAL ENROLLMENT:															
TOTAL	0	.0	5	.8	2	.3	1	.2	8	1.3	594	98.2	3	.5	
FEMALE	0	.0	1	.9	0	.0	1	.9	2	1.8	108	97.3	1	.9	
MALE	0	.0	4	.8	2	.4	0	.0	6	1.2	486	98.4	2	.4	
WISCONSIN (2 INSTITUTIONS)															
UNDERGRADUATES:															
FULL-TIME	0	.0	0	.0	0	.0	0	.0	0	.0	0	.0	0	.0	
FEMALE	0	.0	0	.0	0	.0	0	.0	0	.0	0	.0	0	.0	
MALE	0	.0	0	.0	0	.0	0	.0	0	.0	0	.0	0	.0	
PART-TIME	0	.0	0	.0	0	.0	0	.0	0	.0	0	.0	0	.0	
FEMALE	0	.0	0	.0	0	.0	0	.0	0	.0	0	.0	0	.0	
MALE	0	.0	0	.0	0	.0	0	.0	0	.0	0	.0	0	.0	
TOTAL	0	.0	0	.0	0	.0	0	.0	0	.0	0	.0	0	.0	
FEMALE	0	.0	0	.0	0	.0	0	.0	0	.0	0	.0	0	.0	
MALE	0	.0	0	.0	0	.0	0	.0	0	.0	0	.0	0	.0	
GRADUATE:															
FULL-TIME	0	.0	0	.0	0	.0	0	.0	0	.0	0	.0	0	.0	
FEMALE	0	.0	0	.0	0	.0	0	.0	0	.0	0	.0	0	.0	
MALE	0	.0	0	.0	0	.0	0	.0	0	.0	0	.0	0	.0	
PART-TIME	0	.0	0	.0	0	.0	0	.0	0	.0	0	.0	0	.0	
FEMALE	0	.0	0	.0	0	.0	0	.0	0	.0	0	.0	0	.0	
MALE	0	.0	0	.0	0	.0	0	.0	0	.0	0	.0	0	.0	
TOTAL	0	.0	0	.0	0	.0	0	.0	0	.0	0	.0	0	.0	
FEMALE	0	.0	0	.0	0	.0	0	.0	0	.0	0	.0	0	.0	
MALE	0	.0	0	.0	0	.0	0	.0	0	.0	0	.0	0	.0	
PROFESSIONAL:															
FULL-TIME	2	.2	57	4.6	17	1.4	37	3.0	113	9.1	1,118	90.5	5	.4	
FEMALE	0	.0	24	8.5	6	2.1	4	1.4	34	12.1	245	87.2	2	.7	
MALE	2	.2	33	3.5	11	1.2	33	3.5	79	8.3	873	91.4	3	.3	

530

MEDICINE

INDIAN NATIVE	BLACK NON-HISPANIC		ASIAN OR PACIFIC ISLANDER		HISPANIC		TOTAL MINORITY		WHITE NON-HISPANIC		NON-RESIDENT ALIEN		TOTAL
%	NUMBER	%	NUMBER	%	NUMBER	%	NUMBER	%	NUMBER	%	NUMBER	%	NUMBER
CONTINUED													
5.6	3	8.3	1	2.8	0	.0	6	16.7	27	75.0	3	8.3	36
.0	0	.0	1	7.7	0	.0	1	7.7	10	76.9	2	15.4	13
8.7	3	13.0	0	.0	0	.0	5	21.7	17	73.9	1	4.3	23
.3	60	4.7	18	1.4	37	2.9	119	9.4	1,145	90.0	8	.6	1,272
.0	24	8.2	7	2.4	4	1.4	35	11.9	255	86.7	4	1.4	294
.4	36	3.7	11	1.1	33	3.4	84	8.6	890	91.0	4	.4	978
.2	57	4.6	17	1.4	37	3.0	113	9.1	1,118	90.5	5	.4	1,236
.0	24	8.5	6	2.1	4	1.4	34	12.1	245	87.2	2	.7	281
.2	33	3.5	11	1.2	33	3.5	79	8.3	873	91.4	3	.3	955
5.6	3	8.3	1	2.8	0	.0	6	16.7	27	75.0	3	8.3	36
.0	0	.0	1	7.7	0	.0	1	7.7	10	76.9	2	15.4	13
8.7	3	13.0	0	.0	0	.0	5	21.7	17	73.9	1	4.3	23
.3	60	4.7	18	1.4	37	2.9	119	9.4	1,145	90.0	8	.6	1,272
.0	24	8.2	7	2.4	4	1.4	35	11.9	255	86.7	4	1.4	294
.4	36	3.7	11	1.1	33	3.4	84	8.6	890	91.0	4	.4	978
.0	0	.0	0	.0	0	.0	0	.0	0	.0	0	.0	0
.0	0	.0	0	.0	0	.0	0	.0	0	.0	0	.0	0
.0	0	.0	0	.0	0	.0	0	.0	0	.0	0	.0	0
.3	60	4.7	18	1.4	37	2.9	119	9.4	1,145	90.0	8	.6	1,272
.0	24	8.2	7	2.4	4	1.4	35	11.9	255	86.7	4	1.4	294
.4	36	3.7	11	1.1	33	3.4	84	8.6	890	91.0	4	.4	978
(136 INSTITUTIONS)													
.0	0	.0	0	.0	0	.0	0	.0	0	.0	0	.0	0
.0	0	.0	0	.0	0	.0	0	.0	0	.0	0	.0	0
.0	0	.0	0	.0	0	.0	0	.0	0	.0	0	.0	0
.0	0	.0	0	.0	0	.0	0	.0	0	.0	0	.0	0
.0	0	.0	0	.0	0	.0	0	.0	0	.0	0	.0	0
.0	0	.0	0	.0	0	.0	0	.0	0	.0	0	.0	0
.0	0	.0	0	.0	0	.0	0	.0	0	.0	0	.0	0
.0	0	.0	0	.0	0	.0	0	.0	0	.0	0	.0	0
.0	0	.0	0	.0	0	.0	0	.0	0	.0	0	.0	0
.0	0	.0	0	.0	0	.0	0	.0	0	.0	0	.0	0
.0	0	.0	0	.0	0	.0	0	.0	0	.0	0	.0	0
.0	0	.0	0	.0	0	.0	0	.0	0	.0	0	.0	0
.0	0	.0	0	.0	0	.0	0	.0	0	.0	0	.0	0
.0	0	.0	0	.0	0	.0	0	.0	0	.0	0	.0	0
.0	0	.0	0	.0	0	.0	0	.0	0	.0	0	.0	0
.0	0	.0	0	.0	0	.0	0	.0	0	.0	0	.0	0
.0	0	.0	0	.0	0	.0	0	.0	0	.0	0	.0	0
.0	0	.0	0	.0	0	.0	0	.0	0	.0	0	.0	0
.3	3,488	5.3	1,794	2.7	1,602	2.4	7,113	10.8	58,312	88.4	569	.9	65,994
.4	1,363	8.9	508	3.3	391	2.6	2,328	15.2	12,837	83.9	131	.9	15,296
.3	2,125	4.2	1,286	2.5	1,211	2.4	4,785	9.4	45,475	89.7	438	.9	50,698
.5	30	4.7	19	3.0	7	1.1	59	9.2	486	75.5	99	15.4	644
.0	13	8.1	8	5.0	1	.6	22	13.8	113	70.6	25	15.6	160
.6	17	3.5	11	2.3	6	1.2	37	7.6	373	77.1	74	15.3	484
.3	3,518	5.3	1,813	2.7	1,609	2.4	7,172	10.8	58,798	88.2	668	1.0	66,638
.4	1,376	8.9	516	3.3	392	2.5	2,350	15.2	12,950	83.8	156	1.0	15,456
.3	2,142	4.2	1,297	2.5	1,217	2.4	4,822	9.4	45,848	89.6	512	1.0	51,182
.3	3,488	5.3	1,794	2.7	1,602	2.4	7,113	10.8	58,312	88.4	569	.9	65,994
.4	1,363	8.9	508	3.3	391	2.6	2,328	15.2	12,837	83.9	131	.9	15,296
.3	2,125	4.2	1,286	2.5	1,211	2.4	4,785	9.4	45,475	89.7	438	.9	50,698
.5	30	4.7	19	3.0	7	1.1	59	9.2	486	75.5	99	15.4	644
.0	13	8.1	8	5.0	1	.6	22	13.8	113	70.6	25	15.6	160
.6	17	3.5	11	2.3	6	1.2	37	7.6	373	77.1	74	15.3	484
.3	3,518	5.3	1,813	2.7	1,609	2.4	7,172	10.8	58,798	88.2	668	1.0	66,638
.4	1,376	8.9	516	3.3	392	2.5	2,350	15.2	12,950	83.8	156	1.0	15,456
.3	2,142	4.2	1,297	2.5	1,217	2.4	4,822	9.4	45,848	89.6	512	1.0	51,182
.0	53	70.7	0	.0	0	.0	53	70.7	3	4.0	19	25.3	75
.0	14	87.5	0	.0	0	.0	14	87.5	1	6.3	1	6.3	16
.0	39	66.1	0	.0	0	.0	39	66.1	2	3.4	18	30.5	59
.3	3,571	5.4	1,813	2.7	1,609	2.4	7,225	10.8	58,801	88.1	687	1.0	66,713
.4	1,390	9.0	516	3.3	392	2.5	2,364	15.3	12,951	83.7	157	1.0	15,472
.3	2,181	4.3	1,297	2.5	1,217	2.4	4,861	9.5	45,850	89.5	530	1.0	51,241

MAJOR FIELD 1206 - MEDICINE

	AMERICAN INDIAN ALASKAN NATIVE		BLACK NON-HISPANIC		ASIAN OR PACIFIC ISLANDER		HISPANIC		TOTAL MINORITY		WHITE NON-HISPANIC		NON-RESIDENT ALIEN		TO
	NUMBER	%	NUMBER	%	NUMBER	%	NUMBER	%	NUMBER	%	NUMBER	%	NUMBER	%	NU
PUERTO RICO	(	2 INSTITUTIONS)													
UNDERGRADUATES:															
FULL-TIME	0	.0	0	.0	0	.0	0	.0	0	.0	0	.0	0	.0	
FEMALE	0	.0	0	.0	0	.0	0	.0	0	.0	0	.0	0	.0	
MALE	0	.0	0	.0	0	.0	0	.0	0	.0	0	.0	0	.0	
PART-TIME	0	.0	0	.0	0	.0	0	.0	0	.0	0	.0	0	.0	
FEMALE	0	.0	0	.0	0	.0	0	.0	0	.0	0	.0	0	.0	
MALE	0	.0	0	.0	0	.0	0	.0	0	.0	0	.0	0	.0	
TOTAL	0	.0	0	.0	0	.0	0	.0	0	.0	0	.0	0	.0	
FEMALE	0	.0	0	.0	0	.0	0	.0	0	.0	0	.0	0	.0	
MALE	0	.0	0	.0	0	.0	0	.0	0	.0	0	.0	0	.0	
GRADUATE:															
FULL-TIME	0	.0	0	.0	0	.0	0	.0	0	.0	0	.0	0	.0	
FEMALE	0	.0	0	.0	0	.0	0	.0	0	.0	0	.0	0	.0	
MALE	0	.0	0	.0	0	.0	0	.0	0	.0	0	.0	0	.0	
PART-TIME	0	.0	0	.0	0	.0	0	.0	0	.0	0	.0	0	.0	
FEMALE	0	.0	0	.0	0	.0	0	.0	0	.0	0	.0	0	.0	
MALE	0	.0	0	.0	0	.0	0	.0	0	.0	0	.0	0	.0	
TOTAL	0	.0	0	.0	0	.0	0	.0	0	.0	0	.0	0	.0	
FEMALE	0	.0	0	.0	0	.0	0	.0	0	.0	0	.0	0	.0	
MALE	0	.0	0	.0	0	.0	0	.0	0	.0	0	.0	0	.0	
PROFESSIONAL:															
FULL-TIME	0	.0	0	.0	0	.0	642	100.0	642	100.0	0	.0	0	.0	
FEMALE	0	.0	0	.0	0	.0	218	100.0	218	100.0	0	.0	0	.0	
MALE	0	.0	0	.0	0	.0	424	100.0	424	100.0	0	.0	0	.0	
PART-TIME	0	.0	0	.0	0	.0	0	.0	0	.0	0	.0	0	.0	
FEMALE	0	.0	0	.0	0	.0	0	.0	0	.0	0	.0	0	.0	
MALE	0	.0	0	.0	0	.0	0	.0	0	.0	0	.0	0	.0	
TOTAL	0	.0	0	.0	0	.0	642	100.0	642	100.0	0	.0	0	.0	
FEMALE	0	.0	0	.0	0	.0	218	100.0	218	100.0	0	.0	0	.0	
MALE	0	.0	0	.0	0	.0	424	100.0	424	100.0	0	.0	0	.0	
UND+GRAD+PROF:															
FULL-TIME	0	.0	0	.0	0	.0	642	100.0	642	100.0	0	.0	0	.0	
FEMALE	0	.0	0	.0	0	.0	218	100.0	218	100.0	0	.0	0	.0	
MALE	0	.0	0	.0	0	.0	424	100.0	424	100.0	0	.0	0	.0	
PART-TIME	0	.0	0	.0	0	.0	0	.0	0	.0	0	.0	0	.0	
FEMALE	0	.0	0	.0	0	.0	0	.0	0	.0	0	.0	0	.0	
MALE	0	.0	0	.0	0	.0	0	.0	0	.0	0	.0	0	.0	
TOTAL	0	.0	0	.0	0	.0	642	100.0	642	100.0	0	.0	0	.0	
FEMALE	0	.0	0	.0	0	.0	218	100.0	218	100.0	0	.0	0	.0	
MALE	0	.0	0	.0	0	.0	424	100.0	424	100.0	0	.0	0	.0	
UNCLASSIFIED:															
TOTAL	0	.0	0	.0	0	.0	0	.0	0	.0	0	.0	0	.0	
FEMALE	0	.0	0	.0	0	.0	0	.0	0	.0	0	.0	0	.0	
MALE	0	.0	0	.0	0	.0	0	.0	0	.0	0	.0	0	.0	
TOTAL ENROLLMENT:															
TOTAL	0	.0	0	.0	0	.0	642	100.0	642	100.0	0	.0	0	.0	
FEMALE	0	.0	0	.0	0	.0	218	100.0	218	100.0	0	.0	0	.0	
MALE	0	.0	0	.0	0	.0	424	100.0	424	100.0	0	.0	0	.0	
OUTLYING AREAS	(	2 INSTITUTIONS)													
UNDERGRADUATES:															
FULL-TIME	0	.0	0	.0	0	.0	0	.0	0	.0	0	.0	0	.0	
FEMALE	0	.0	0	.0	0	.0	0	.0	0	.0	0	.0	0	.0	
MALE	0	.0	0	.0	0	.0	0	.0	0	.0	0	.0	0	.0	
PART-TIME	0	.0	0	.0	0	.0	0	.0	0	.0	0	.0	0	.0	
FEMALE	0	.0	0	.0	0	.0	0	.0	0	.0	0	.0	0	.0	
MALE	0	.0	0	.0	0	.0	0	.0	0	.0	0	.0	0	.0	
TOTAL	0	.0	0	.0	0	.0	0	.0	0	.0	0	.0	0	.0	
FEMALE	0	.0	0	.0	0	.0	0	.0	0	.0	0	.0	0	.0	
MALE	0	.0	0	.0	0	.0	0	.0	0	.0	0	.0	0	.0	
GRADUATE:															
FULL-TIME	0	.0	0	.0	0	.0	0	.0	0	.0	0	.0	0	.0	
FEMALE	0	.0	0	.0	0	.0	0	.0	0	.0	0	.0	0	.0	
MALE	0	.0	0	.0	0	.0	0	.0	0	.0	0	.0	0	.0	
PART-TIME	0	.0	0	.0	0	.0	0	.0	0	.0	0	.0	0	.0	
FEMALE	0	.0	0	.0	0	.0	0	.0	0	.0	0	.0	0	.0	
MALE	0	.0	0	.0	0	.0	0	.0	0	.0	0	.0	0	.0	
TOTAL	0	.0	0	.0	0	.0	0	.0	0	.0	0	.0	0	.0	
FEMALE	0	.0	0	.0	0	.0	0	.0	0	.0	0	.0	0	.0	
MALE	0	.0	0	.0	0	.0	0	.0	0	.0	0	.0	0	.0	
PROFESSIONAL:															
FULL-TIME	0	.0	0	.0	0	.0	642	100.0	642	100.0	0	.0	0	.0	
FEMALE	0	.0	0	.0	0	.0	218	100.0	218	100.0	0	.0	0	.0	
MALE	0	.0	0	.0	0	.0	424	100.0	424	100.0	0	.0	0	.0	

MEDICINE

INDIAN NATIVE %	BLACK NON-HISPANIC NUMBER	%	ASIAN OR PACIFIC ISLANDER NUMBER	%	HISPANIC NUMBER	%	TOTAL MINORITY NUMBER	%	WHITE NON-HISPANIC NUMBER	%	NON-RESIDENT ALIEN NUMBER	%	TOTAL NUMBER
CONTINUED													
.0	0	.0	0	.0	0	.0	0	.0	0	.0	0	.0	0
.0	0	.0	0	.0	0	.0	0	.0	0	.0	0	.0	0
.0	0	.0	0	.0	0	.0	0	.0	0	.0	0	.0	0
.0	0	.0	0	.0	642	100.0	642	100.0	0	.0	0	.0	642
.0	0	.0	0	.0	218	100.0	218	100.0	0	.0	0	.0	218
.0	0	.0	0	.0	424	100.0	424	100.0	0	.0	0	.0	424
.0	0	.0	0	.0	642	100.0	642	100.0	0	.0	0	.0	642
.0	0	.0	0	.0	218	100.0	218	100.0	0	.0	0	.0	218
.0	0	.0	0	.0	424	100.0	424	100.0	0	.0	0	.0	424
.0	0	.0	0	.0	0	.0	0	.0	0	.0	0	.0	0
.0	0	.0	0	.0	0	.0	0	.0	0	.0	0	.0	0
.0	0	.0	0	.0	0	.0	0	.0	0	.0	0	.0	0
.0	0	.0	0	.0	642	100.0	642	100.0	0	.0	0	.0	642
.0	0	.0	0	.0	218	100.0	218	100.0	0	.0	0	.0	218
.0	0	.0	0	.0	424	100.0	424	100.0	0	.0	0	.0	424
.0	0	.0	0	.0	0	.0	0	.0	0	.0	0	.0	0
.0	0	.0	0	.0	0	.0	0	.0	0	.0	0	.0	0
.0	0	.0	0	.0	0	.0	0	.0	0	.0	0	.0	0
.0	0	.0	0	.0	642	100.0	642	100.0	0	.0	0	.0	642
.0	0	.0	0	.0	218	100.0	218	100.0	0	.0	0	.0	218
.0	0	.0	0	.0	424	100.0	424	100.0	0	.0	0	.0	424
E 1206 (138 INSTITUTIONS)													
.0	0	.0	0	.0	0	.0	0	.0	0	.0	0	.0	0
.0	0	.0	0	.0	0	.0	0	.0	0	.0	0	.0	0
.0	0	.0	0	.0	0	.0	0	.0	0	.0	0	.0	0
.0	0	.0	0	.0	0	.0	0	.0	0	.0	0	.0	0
.0	0	.0	0	.0	0	.0	0	.0	0	.0	0	.0	0
.0	0	.0	0	.0	0	.0	0	.0	0	.0	0	.0	0
.0	0	.0	0	.0	0	.0	0	.0	0	.0	0	.0	0
.0	0	.0	0	.0	0	.0	0	.0	0	.0	0	.0	0
.0	0	.0	0	.0	0	.0	0	.0	0	.0	0	.0	0
.0	0	.0	0	.0	0	.0	0	.0	0	.0	0	.0	0
.0	0	.0	0	.0	0	.0	0	.0	0	.0	0	.0	0
.0	0	.0	0	.0	0	.0	0	.0	0	.0	0	.0	0
.0	0	.0	0	.0	0	.0	0	.0	0	.0	0	.0	0
.0	0	.0	0	.0	0	.0	0	.0	0	.0	0	.0	0
.0	0	.0	0	.0	0	.0	0	.0	0	.0	0	.0	0
.0	0	.0	0	.0	0	.0	0	.0	0	.0	0	.0	0
.0	0	.0	0	.0	0	.0	0	.0	0	.0	0	.0	0
.0	0	.0	0	.0	0	.0	0	.0	0	.0	0	.0	0
.3	3,488	5.2	1,794	2.7	2,244	3.4	7,755	11.6	58,312	87.5	569	.9	66,636
.4	1,363	8.8	508	3.3	609	3.9	2,546	16.4	12,837	82.7	131	.8	15,514
.3	2,125	4.2	1,286	2.5	1,635	3.2	5,209	10.2	45,475	89.0	438	.9	51,122
.5	30	4.7	19	3.0	7	1.1	59	9.2	486	75.5	99	15.4	644
.6	13	8.1	8	5.0	1	.6	22	13.8	113	70.6	25	15.6	160
.6	17	3.5	11	2.3	6	1.2	37	7.6	373	77.1	74	15.3	484
.3	3,518	5.2	1,813	2.7	2,251	3.3	7,814	11.6	58,798	87.4	668	1.0	67,280
.4	1,376	8.8	516	3.3	610	3.9	2,568	16.4	12,950	82.6	156	1.0	15,674
.3	2,142	4.2	1,297	2.5	1,641	3.2	5,246	10.2	45,848	88.8	512	1.0	51,606
.3	3,488	5.2	1,794	2.7	2,244	3.4	7,755	11.6	58,312	87.5	569	.9	66,636
.4	1,363	8.8	508	3.3	609	3.9	2,546	16.4	12,837	82.7	131	.8	15,514
.3	2,125	4.2	1,286	2.5	1,635	3.2	5,209	10.2	45,475	89.0	438	.9	51,122
.5	30	4.7	19	3.0	7	1.1	59	9.2	486	75.5	99	15.4	644
.0	13	8.1	8	5.0	1	.6	22	13.8	113	70.6	25	15.6	160
.6	17	3.5	11	2.3	6	1.2	37	7.6	373	77.1	74	15.3	484
.3	3,518	5.2	1,813	2.7	2,251	3.3	7,814	11.6	58,798	87.4	668	1.0	67,280
.4	1,376	8.8	516	3.3	610	3.9	2,568	16.4	12,950	82.6	156	1.0	15,674
.3	2,142	4.2	1,297	2.5	1,641	3.2	5,246	10.2	45,848	88.8	512	1.0	51,606
.0	53	70.7	0	.0	0	.0	53	70.7	3	4.0	19	25.3	75
.0	14	87.5	0	.0	0	.0	14	87.5	1	6.3	1	6.3	16
.0	39	66.1	0	.0	0	.0	39	66.1	2	3.4	18	30.5	59
.3	3,571	5.3	1,813	2.7	2,251	3.3	7,867	11.7	58,801	87.3	687	1.0	67,355
.4	1,390	8.9	516	3.3	610	3.9	2,582	16.5	12,951	82.5	157	1.0	15,690
.3	2,181	4.2	1,297	2.5	1,641	3.2	5,285	10.2	45,850	88.7	530	1.0	51,665

TABLE 17 - TOTAL ENROLLMENT IN INSTITUTIONS OF HIGHER EDUCATION FOR SELECTED MAJOR FIELDS OF STUDY AND LEVEL OF ENROLLMENT
BY RACE, ETHNICITY, AND SEX: STATE, 1978

MAJOR FIELD 1218 - VETERINARY MEDICINE

	AMERICAN INDIAN ALASKAN NATIVE		BLACK NON-HISPANIC		ASIAN OR PACIFIC ISLANDER		HISPANIC		TOTAL MINORITY		WHITE NON-HISPANIC		NON-RESIDENT ALIEN		T(
	NUMBER	%	NUMBER	%	NUMBER	%	NUMBER	%	NUMBER	%	NUMBER	%	NUMBER	%	NU
ALABAMA (2 INSTITUTIONS)															
UNDERGRADUATES:															
FULL-TIME	0	.0	0	.0	0	.0	0	.0	0	.0	0	.0	0	.0	
FEMALE	0	.0	0	.0	0	.0	0	.0	0	.0	0	.0	0	.0	
MALE	0	.0	0	.0	0	.0	0	.0	0	.0	0	.0	0	.0	
PART-TIME	0	.0	0	.0	0	.0	0	.0	0	.0	0	.0	0	.0	
FEMALE	0	.0	0	.0	0	.0	0	.0	0	.0	0	.0	0	.0	
MALE	0	.0	0	.0	0	.0	0	.0	0	.0	0	.0	0	.0	
TOTAL	0	.0	0	.0	0	.0	0	.0	0	.0	0	.0	0	.0	
FEMALE	0	.0	0	.0	0	.0	0	.0	0	.0	0	.0	0	.0	
MALE	0	.0	0	.0	0	.0	0	.0	0	.0	0	.0	0	.0	
GRADUATE:															
FULL-TIME	0	.0	0	.0	0	.0	0	.0	0	.0	0	.0	0	.0	
FEMALE	0	.0	0	.0	0	.0	0	.0	0	.0	0	.0	0	.0	
MALE	0	.0	0	.0	0	.0	0	.0	0	.0	0	.0	0	.0	
PART-TIME	0	.0	0	.0	0	.0	0	.0	0	.0	0	.0	0	.0	
FEMALE	0	.0	0	.0	0	.0	0	.0	0	.0	0	.0	0	.0	
MALE	0	.0	0	.0	0	.0	0	.0	0	.0	0	.0	0	.0	
TOTAL	0	.0	0	.0	0	.0	0	.0	0	.0	0	.0	0	.0	
FEMALE	0	.0	0	.0	0	.0	0	.0	0	.0	0	.0	0	.0	
MALE	0	.0	0	.0	0	.0	0	.0	0	.0	0	.0	0	.0	
PROFESSIONAL:															
FULL-TIME	0	.0	102	15.6	8	1.2	1	.2	111	17.0	525	80.4	17	2.6	
FEMALE	0	.0	50	25.6	2	1.0	0	.0	52	26.7	142	72.8	1	.5	
MALE	0	.0	52	11.4	6	1.3	1	.2	59	12.9	383	83.6	16	3.5	
PART-TIME	0	.0	1	100.0	0	.0	0	.0	1	100.0	0	.0	0	.0	
FEMALE	0	.0	0	.0	0	.0	0	.0	0	.0	0	.0	0	.0	
MALE	0	.0	1	100.0	0	.0	0	.0	1	100.0	0	.0	0	.0	
TOTAL	0	.0	103	15.7	8	1.2	1	.2	112	17.1	525	80.3	17	2.6	
FEMALE	0	.0	50	25.6	2	1.0	0	.0	52	26.7	142	72.8	1	.5	
MALE	0	.0	53	11.5	6	1.3	1	.2	60	13.1	383	83.4	16	3.5	
UND+GRAD+PROF:															
FULL-TIME	0	.0	102	15.6	8	1.2	1	.2	111	17.0	525	80.4	17	2.6	
FEMALE	0	.0	50	25.6	2	1.0	0	.0	52	26.7	142	72.8	1	.5	
MALE	0	.0	52	11.4	6	1.3	1	.2	59	12.9	383	83.6	16	3.5	
PART-TIME	0	.0	1	100.0	0	.0	0	.0	1	100.0	0	.0	0	.0	
FEMALE	0	.0	0	.0	0	.0	0	.0	0	.0	0	.0	0	.0	
MALE	0	.0	1	100.0	0	.0	0	.0	1	100.0	0	.0	0	.0	
TOTAL	0	.0	103	15.7	8	1.2	1	.2	112	17.1	525	80.3	17	2.6	
FEMALE	0	.0	50	25.6	2	1.0	0	.0	52	26.7	142	72.8	1	.5	
MALE	0	.0	53	11.5	6	1.3	1	.2	60	13.1	383	83.4	16	3.5	
UNCLASSIFIED:															
TOTAL	0	.0	0	.0	0	.0	0	.0	0	.0	0	.0	0	.0	
FEMALE	0	.0	0	.0	0	.0	0	.0	0	.0	0	.0	0	.0	
MALE	0	.0	0	.0	0	.0	0	.0	0	.0	0	.0	0	.0	
TOTAL ENROLLMENT:															
TOTAL	0	.0	103	15.7	8	1.2	1	.2	112	17.1	525	80.3	17	2.6	
FEMALE	0	.0	50	25.6	2	1.0	0	.0	52	26.7	142	72.8	1	.5	
MALE	0	.0	53	11.5	6	1.3	1	.2	60	13.1	383	83.4	16	3.5	
CALIFORNIA (1 INSTITUTIONS)															
UNDERGRADUATES:															
FULL-TIME	0	.0	0	.0	0	.0	0	.0	0	.0	0	.0	0	.0	
FEMALE	0	.0	0	.0	0	.0	0	.0	0	.0	0	.0	0	.0	
MALE	0	.0	0	.0	0	.0	0	.0	0	.0	0	.0	0	.0	
PART-TIME	0	.0	0	.0	0	.0	0	.0	0	.0	0	.0	0	.0	
FEMALE	0	.0	0	.0	0	.0	0	.0	0	.0	0	.0	0	.0	
MALE	0	.0	0	.0	0	.0	0	.0	0	.0	0	.0	0	.0	
TOTAL	0	.0	0	.0	0	.0	0	.0	0	.0	0	.0	0	.0	
FEMALE	0	.0	0	.0	0	.0	0	.0	0	.0	0	.0	0	.0	
MALE	0	.0	0	.0	0	.0	0	.0	0	.0	0	.0	0	.0	
GRADUATE:															
FULL-TIME	0	.0	0	.0	0	.0	0	.0	0	.0	0	.0	0	.0	
FEMALE	0	.0	0	.0	0	.0	0	.0	0	.0	0	.0	0	.0	
MALE	0	.0	0	.0	0	.0	0	.0	0	.0	0	.0	0	.0	
PART-TIME	0	.0	0	.0	0	.0	0	.0	0	.0	0	.0	0	.0	
FEMALE	0	.0	0	.0	0	.0	0	.0	0	.0	0	.0	0	.0	
MALE	0	.0	0	.0	0	.0	0	.0	0	.0	0	.0	0	.0	
TOTAL	0	.0	0	.0	0	.0	0	.0	0	.0	0	.0	0	.0	
FEMALE	0	.0	0	.0	0	.0	0	.0	0	.0	0	.0	0	.0	
MALE	0	.0	0	.0	0	.0	0	.0	0	.0	0	.0	0	.0	
PROFESSIONAL:															
FULL-TIME	0	.0	6	1.5	10	2.4	6	1.5	22	5.4	386	94.1	2	.5	
FEMALE	0	.0	3	1.9	4	2.6	2	1.3	9	5.8	145	93.5	1	.6	
MALE	0	.0	3	1.2	6	2.4	4	1.6	13	5.1	241	94.5	1	.4	

VETERINARY MEDICINE

INDIAN NATIVE %	BLACK NON-HISPANIC NUMBER	%	ASIAN OR PACIFIC ISLANDER NUMBER	%	HISPANIC NUMBER	%	TOTAL MINORITY NUMBER	%	WHITE NON-HISPANIC NUMBER	%	NON-RESIDENT ALIEN NUMBER	%	TOTAL NUMBER
CONTINUED													
.0	0	.0	0	.0	0	.0	0	.0	0	.0	0	.0	0
.0	0	.0	0	.0	0	.0	0	.0	0	.0	0	.0	0
.0	0	.0	0	.0	0	.0	0	.0	0	.0	0	.0	0
.0	6	1.5	10	2.4	6	1.5	22	5.4	386	94.1	2	.5	410
.0	3	1.9	4	2.6	2	1.3	9	5.8	145	93.5	1	.6	155
.0	3	1.2	6	2.4	4	1.6	13	5.1	241	94.5	1	.4	255
.0	6	1.5	10	2.4	6	1.5	22	5.4	386	94.1	2	.5	410
.0	3	1.9	4	2.6	2	1.3	9	5.8	145	93.5	1	.6	155
.0	3	1.2	6	2.4	4	1.6	13	5.1	241	94.5	1	.4	255
.0	0	.0	0	.0	0	.0	0	.0	0	.0	0	.0	0
.0	0	.0	0	.0	0	.0	0	.0	0	.0	0	.0	0
.0	0	.0	0	.0	0	.0	0	.0	0	.0	0	.0	0
.0	6	1.5	10	2.4	6	1.5	22	5.4	386	94.1	2	.5	410
.0	3	1.9	4	2.6	2	1.3	9	5.8	145	93.5	1	.6	155
.0	3	1.2	6	2.4	4	1.6	13	5.1	241	94.5	1	.4	255
.0	0	.0	0	.0	0	.0	0	.0	0	.0	0	.0	0
.0	0	.0	0	.0	0	.0	0	.0	0	.0	0	.0	0
.0	0	.0	0	.0	0	.0	0	.0	0	.0	0	.0	0
.0	6	1.5	10	2.4	6	1.5	22	5.4	386	94.1	2	.5	410
.0	3	1.9	4	2.6	2	1.3	9	5.8	145	93.5	1	.6	155
.0	3	1.2	6	2.4	4	1.6	13	5.1	241	94.5	1	.4	255
(1 INSTITUTIONS)													
.0	0	.0	0	.0	0	.0	0	.0	0	.0	0	.0	0
.0	0	.0	0	.0	0	.0	0	.0	0	.0	0	.0	0
.0	0	.0	0	.0	0	.0	0	.0	0	.0	0	.0	0
.0	0	.0	0	.0	0	.0	0	.0	0	.0	0	.0	0
.0	0	.0	0	.0	0	.0	0	.0	0	.0	0	.0	0
.0	0	.0	0	.0	0	.0	0	.0	0	.0	0	.0	0
.0	0	.0	0	.0	0	.0	0	.0	0	.0	0	.0	0
.0	0	.0	0	.0	0	.0	0	.0	0	.0	0	.0	0
.0	0	.0	0	.0	0	.0	0	.0	0	.0	0	.0	0
.0	0	.0	0	.0	0	.0	0	.0	0	.0	0	.0	0
.0	0	.0	0	.0	0	.0	0	.0	0	.0	0	.0	0
.0	0	.0	0	.0	0	.0	0	.0	0	.0	0	.0	0
.0	0	.0	0	.0	0	.0	0	.0	0	.0	0	.0	0
.0	0	.0	0	.0	0	.0	0	.0	0	.0	0	.0	0
.0	0	.0	0	.0	0	.0	0	.0	0	.0	0	.0	0
.0	0	.0	0	.0	0	.0	0	.0	0	.0	0	.0	0
.0	0	.0	0	.0	0	.0	0	.0	0	.0	0	.0	0
.0	0	.0	0	.0	0	.0	0	.0	0	.0	0	.0	0
.2	3	.7	9	2.0	2	.4	15	3.3	443	96.5	1	.2	459
.0	3	2.0	3	2.0	1	.7	7	4.6	144	95.4	0	.0	151
.3	0	.0	6	1.9	1	.3	8	2.6	299	97.1	1	.3	308
.0	0	.0	0	.0	0	.0	0	.0	1	100.0	0	.0	1
.0	0	.0	0	.0	0	.0	0	.0	0	.0	0	.0	0
.0	0	.0	0	.0	0	.0	0	.0	1	100.0	0	.0	1
.2	3	.7	9	2.0	2	.4	15	3.3	444	96.5	1	.2	460
.0	3	2.0	3	2.0	1	.7	7	4.6	144	95.4	0	.0	151
.3	0	.0	6	1.9	1	.3	8	2.6	300	97.1	1	.3	309
.2	3	.7	9	2.0	2	.4	15	3.3	443	96.5	1	.2	459
.0	3	2.0	3	2.0	1	.7	7	4.6	144	95.4	0	.0	151
.3	0	.0	6	1.9	1	.3	8	2.6	299	97.1	1	.3	308
.0	0	.0	0	.0	0	.0	0	.0	1	100.0	0	.0	1
.0	0	.0	0	.0	0	.0	0	.0	0	.0	0	.0	0
.0	0	.0	0	.0	0	.0	0	.0	1	100.0	0	.0	1
.2	3	.7	9	2.0	2	.4	15	3.3	444	96.5	1	.2	460
.0	3	2.0	3	2.0	1	.7	7	4.6	144	95.4	0	.0	151
.3	0	.0	6	1.9	1	.3	8	2.6	300	97.1	1	.3	309
.0	0	.0	0	.0	0	.0	0	.0	0	.0	0	.0	0
.0	0	.0	0	.0	0	.0	0	.0	0	.0	0	.0	0
.0	0	.0	0	.0	0	.0	0	.0	0	.0	0	.0	0
.2	3	.7	9	2.0	2	.4	15	3.3	444	96.5	1	.2	460
.0	3	2.0	3	2.0	1	.7	7	4.6	144	95.4	0	.0	151
.3	0	.0	6	1.9	1	.3	8	2.6	300	97.1	1	.3	309

TABLE 17 - TOTAL ENROLLMENT IN INSTITUTIONS OF HIGHER EDUCATION FOR SELECTED MAJOR FIELDS OF STUDY AND LEVEL OF ENROLLMENT
BY RACE, ETHNICITY, AND SEX: STATE, 1978

MAJOR FIELD 1218 - VETERINARY MEDICINE

	AMERICAN INDIAN ALASKAN NATIVE		BLACK NON-HISPANIC		ASIAN OR PACIFIC ISLANDER		HISPANIC		TOTAL MINORITY		WHITE NON-HISPANIC		NON-RESIDENT ALIEN	
	NUMBER	%	NUMBER	%	NUMBER	%	NUMBER	%	NUMBER	%	NUMBER	%	NUMBER	%
FLORIDA			1 INSTITUTIONS)											
UNDERGRADUATES:														
FULL-TIME	0	.0	0	.0	0	.0	0	.0	0	.0	0	.0	0	.0
FEMALE	0	.0	0	.0	0	.0	0	.0	0	.0	0	.0	0	.0
MALE	0	.0	0	.0	0	.0	0	.0	0	.0	0	.0	0	.0
PART-TIME	0	.0	0	.0	0	.0	0	.0	0	.0	0	.0	0	.0
FEMALE	0	.0	0	.0	0	.0	0	.0	0	.0	0	.0	0	.0
MALE	0	.0	0	.0	0	.0	0	.0	0	.0	0	.0	0	.0
TOTAL	0	.0	0	.0	0	.0	0	.0	0	.0	0	.0	0	.0
FEMALE	0	.0	0	.0	0	.0	0	.0	0	.0	0	.0	0	.0
MALE	0	.0	0	.0	0	.0	0	.0	0	.0	0	.0	0	.0
GRADUATE:														
FULL-TIME	0	.0	0	.0	0	.0	0	.0	0	.0	0	.0	0	.0
FEMALE	0	.0	0	.0	0	.0	0	.0	0	.0	0	.0	0	.0
MALE	0	.0	0	.0	0	.0	0	.0	0	.0	0	.0	0	.0
PART-TIME	0	.0	0	.0	0	.0	0	.0	0	.0	0	.0	0	.0
FEMALE	0	.0	0	.0	0	.0	0	.0	0	.0	0	.0	0	.0
MALE	0	.0	0	.0	0	.0	0	.0	0	.0	0	.0	0	.0
TOTAL	0	.0	0	.0	0	.0	0	.0	0	.0	0	.0	0	.0
FEMALE	0	.0	0	.0	0	.0	0	.0	0	.0	0	.0	0	.0
MALE	0	.0	0	.0	0	.0	0	.0	0	.0	0	.0	0	.0
PROFESSIONAL:														
FULL-TIME	1	.5	1	.5	0	.0	6	3.0	8	4.0	192	96.0	0	.0
FEMALE	0	.0	0	.0	0	.0	1	1.4	1	1.4	68	98.6	0	.0
MALE	1	.8	1	.8	0	.0	5	3.8	7	5.3	124	94.7	0	.0
PART-TIME	0	.0	0	.0	0	.0	0	.0	0	.0	0	.0	0	.0
FEMALE	0	.0	0	.0	0	.0	0	.0	0	.0	0	.0	0	.0
MALE	0	.0	0	.0	0	.0	0	.0	0	.0	0	.0	0	.0
TOTAL	1	.5	1	.5	0	.0	6	3.0	8	4.0	192	96.0	0	.0
FEMALE	0	.0	0	.0	0	.0	1	1.4	1	1.4	68	98.6	0	.0
MALE	1	.8	1	.8	0	.0	5	3.8	7	5.3	124	94.7	0	.0
UNG+GRAD+PROF:														
FULL-TIME	1	.5	1	.5	0	.0	6	3.0	8	4.0	192	96.0	0	.0
FEMALE	0	.0	0	.0	0	.0	1	1.4	1	1.4	68	98.6	0	.0
MALE	1	.8	1	.8	0	.0	5	3.8	7	5.3	124	94.7	0	.0
PART-TIME	0	.0	0	.0	0	.0	0	.0	0	.0	0	.0	0	.0
FEMALE	0	.0	0	.0	0	.0	0	.0	0	.0	0	.0	0	.0
MALE	0	.0	0	.0	0	.0	0	.0	0	.0	0	.0	0	.0
TOTAL	1	.5	1	.5	0	.0	6	3.0	8	4.0	192	96.0	0	.0
FEMALE	0	.0	0	.0	0	.0	1	1.4	1	1.4	68	98.6	0	.0
MALE	1	.8	1	.8	0	.0	5	3.8	7	5.3	124	94.7	0	.0
UNCLASSIFIED:														
TOTAL	0	.0	0	.0	0	.0	0	.0	0	.0	0	.0	0	.0
FEMALE	0	.0	0	.0	0	.0	0	.0	0	.0	0	.0	0	.0
MALE	0	.0	0	.0	0	.0	0	.0	0	.0	0	.0	0	.0
TOTAL ENROLLMENT:														
TOTAL	1	.5	1	.5	0	.0	6	3.0	8	4.0	192	96.0	0	.0
FEMALE	0	.0	0	.0	0	.0	1	1.4	1	1.4	68	98.6	0	.0
MALE	1	.8	1	.8	0	.0	5	3.8	7	5.3	124	94.7	0	.0
GEORGIA			1 INSTITUTIONS)											
UNDERGRADUATES:														
FULL-TIME	0	.0	0	.0	0	.0	0	.0	0	.0	0	.0	0	.0
FEMALE	0	.0	0	.0	0	.0	0	.0	0	.0	0	.0	0	.0
MALE	0	.0	0	.0	0	.0	0	.0	0	.0	0	.0	0	.0
PART-TIME	0	.0	0	.0	0	.0	0	.0	0	.0	0	.0	0	.0
FEMALE	0	.0	0	.0	0	.0	0	.0	0	.0	0	.0	0	.0
MALE	0	.0	0	.0	0	.0	0	.0	0	.0	0	.0	0	.0
TOTAL	0	.0	0	.0	0	.0	0	.0	0	.0	0	.0	0	.0
FEMALE	0	.0	0	.0	0	.0	0	.0	0	.0	0	.0	0	.0
MALE	0	.0	0	.0	0	.0	0	.0	0	.0	0	.0	0	.0
GRADUATE:														
FULL-TIME	0	.0	0	.0	0	.0	0	.0	0	.0	0	.0	0	.0
FEMALE	0	.0	0	.0	0	.0	0	.0	0	.0	0	.0	0	.0
MALE	0	.0	0	.0	0	.0	0	.0	0	.0	0	.0	0	.0
PART-TIME	0	.0	0	.0	0	.0	0	.0	0	.0	0	.0	0	.0
FEMALE	0	.0	0	.0	0	.0	0	.0	0	.0	0	.0	0	.0
MALE	0	.0	0	.0	0	.0	0	.0	0	.0	0	.0	0	.0
TOTAL	0	.0	0	.0	0	.0	0	.0	0	.0	0	.0	0	.0
FEMALE	0	.0	0	.0	0	.0	0	.0	0	.0	0	.0	0	.0
MALE	0	.0	0	.0	0	.0	0	.0	0	.0	0	.0	0	.0
PROFESSIONAL:														
FULL-TIME	3	.9	1	.3	2	.6	0	.0	6	1.8	331	97.9	1	.3
FEMALE	1	.8	0	.0	1	.8	0	.0	2	1.7	116	97.5	1	.8
MALE	2	.9	1	.5	1	.5	0	.0	4	1.8	215	98.2	0	.0

ENROLLMENT IN INSTITUTIONS OF HIGHER EDUCATION FOR SELECTED MAJOR FIELDS OF STUDY AND LEVEL OF ENROLLMENT ETHNICITY, AND SEX: STATE, 1978

VETERINARY MEDICINE

INDIAN NATIVE	BLACK NON-HISPANIC		ASIAN OR PACIFIC ISLANDER		HISPANIC		TOTAL MINORITY		WHITE NON-HISPANIC		NON-RESIDENT ALIEN		TOTAL
%	NUMBER	%	NUMBER	%	NUMBER	%	NUMBER	%	NUMBER	%	NUMBER	%	NUMBER
CONTINUED													
.0	0	.0	0	.0	0	.0	0	.0	3	100.0	0	.0	3
.0	0	.0	0	.0	0	.0	0	.0	0	.0	0	.0	0
.0	0	.0	0	.0	0	.0	0	.0	3	100.0	0	.0	3
.9	1	.3	2	.6	0	.0	6	1.8	334	97.9	1	.3	341
.8	0	.0	1	.8	0	.0	2	1.7	116	97.5	1	.8	119
.9	1	.5	1	.5	0	.0	4	1.8	218	98.2	0	.0	222
.9	1	.3	2	.6	0	.0	6	1.8	331	97.9	1	.3	338
.8	0	.0	1	.8	0	.0	2	1.7	116	97.5	1	.8	119
.9	1	.5	1	.5	0	.0	4	1.8	215	98.2	0	.0	219
.0	0	.0	0	.0	0	.0	0	.0	3	100.0	0	.0	3
.0	0	.0	0	.0	0	.0	0	.0	0	.0	0	.0	0
.0	0	.0	0	.0	0	.0	0	.0	3	100.0	0	.0	3
.9	1	.3	2	.6	0	.0	6	1.8	334	97.9	1	.3	341
.8	0	.0	1	.8	0	.0	2	1.7	116	97.5	1	.8	119
.9	1	.5	1	.5	0	.0	4	1.8	218	98.2	0	.0	222
.0	0	.0	0	.0	0	.0	0	.0	0	.0	0	.0	0
.0	0	.0	0	.0	0	.0	0	.0	0	.0	0	.0	0
.0	0	.0	0	.0	0	.0	0	.0	0	.0	0	.0	0
.9	1	.3	2	.6	0	.0	6	1.8	334	97.9	1	.3	341
.8	0	.0	1	.8	0	.0	2	1.7	116	97.5	1	.8	119
.9	1	.5	1	.5	0	.0	4	1.8	218	98.2	0	.0	222
(1 INSTITUTIONS)													
.0	0	.0	0	.0	0	.0	0	.0	0	.0	0	.0	0
.0	0	.0	0	.0	0	.0	0	.0	0	.0	0	.0	0
.0	0	.0	0	.0	0	.0	0	.0	0	.0	0	.0	0
.0	0	.0	0	.0	0	.0	0	.0	0	.0	0	.0	0
.0	0	.0	0	.0	0	.0	0	.0	0	.0	0	.0	0
.0	0	.0	0	.0	0	.0	0	.0	0	.0	0	.0	0
.0	0	.0	0	.0	0	.0	0	.0	0	.0	0	.0	0
.0	0	.0	0	.0	0	.0	0	.0	0	.0	0	.0	0
.0	0	.0	0	.0	0	.0	0	.0	0	.0	0	.0	0
.0	0	.0	0	.0	0	.0	0	.0	0	.0	0	.0	0
.0	0	.0	0	.0	0	.0	0	.0	0	.0	0	.0	0
.0	0	.0	0	.0	0	.0	0	.0	0	.0	0	.0	0
.0	0	.0	0	.0	0	.0	0	.0	0	.0	0	.0	0
.0	0	.0	0	.0	0	.0	0	.0	0	.0	0	.0	0
.0	0	.0	0	.0	0	.0	0	.0	0	.0	0	.0	0
.3	0	.0	1	.3	0	.0	2	.6	315	99.4	0	.0	317
.9	0	.0	1	.9	0	.0	2	1.7	115	98.3	0	.0	117
.0	0	.0	0	.0	0	.0	0	.0	200	100.0	0	.0	200
.0	0	.0	0	.0	0	.0	0	.0	22	100.0	0	.0	22
.0	0	.0	0	.0	0	.0	0	.0	7	100.0	0	.0	7
.0	0	.0	0	.0	0	.0	0	.0	15	100.0	0	.0	15
.3	0	.0	1	.3	0	.0	2	.6	337	99.4	0	.0	339
.8	0	.0	1	.8	0	.0	2	1.6	122	98.4	0	.0	124
.0	0	.0	0	.0	0	.0	0	.0	215	100.0	0	.0	215
.3	0	.0	1	.3	0	.0	2	.6	315	99.4	0	.0	317
.9	0	.0	1	.9	0	.0	2	1.7	115	98.3	0	.0	117
.0	0	.0	0	.0	0	.0	0	.0	200	100.0	0	.0	200
.0	0	.0	0	.0	0	.0	0	.0	22	100.0	0	.0	22
.0	0	.0	0	.0	0	.0	0	.0	7	100.0	0	.0	7
.0	0	.0	0	.0	0	.0	0	.0	15	100.0	0	.0	15
.3	0	.0	1	.3	0	.0	2	.6	337	99.4	0	.0	339
.8	0	.0	1	.8	0	.0	2	1.6	122	98.4	0	.0	124
.0	0	.0	0	.0	0	.0	0	.0	215	100.0	0	.0	215
.0	0	.0	0	.0	0	.0	0	.0	0	.0	0	.0	0
.0	0	.0	0	.0	0	.0	0	.0	0	.0	0	.0	0
.0	0	.0	0	.0	0	.0	0	.0	0	.0	0	.0	0
.3	0	.0	1	.3	0	.0	2	.6	337	99.4	0	.0	339
.8	0	.0	1	.8	0	.0	2	1.6	122	98.4	0	.0	124
.0	0	.0	0	.0	0	.0	0	.0	215	100.0	0	.0	215

TABLE 17 - TOTAL ENROLLMENT IN INSTITUTIONS OF HIGHER EDUCATION FOR SELECTED MAJOR FIELDS OF STUDY AND LEVEL OF ENROLLMENT BY RACE, ETHNICITY, AND SEX: STATE, 1978

MAJOR FIELD 1218 - VETERINARY MEDICINE

	AMERICAN INDIAN ALASKAN NATIVE		BLACK NON-HISPANIC		ASIAN OR PACIFIC ISLANDER		HISPANIC		TOTAL MINORITY		WHITE NON-HISPANIC		NON-RESIDENT ALIEN		TOT
	NUMBER	%	NUMBER	%	NUMBER	%	NUMBER	%	NUMBER	%	NUMBER	%	NUMBER	%	NUM
INDIANA	1 INSTITUTIONS)														
UNDERGRADUATES:															
FULL-TIME	0	.0	0	.0	0	.0	0	.0	0	.0	0	.0		.0	
FEMALE	0	.0	0	.0	0	.0	0	.0	0	.0	0	.0		.0	
MALE	0	.0	0	.0	0	.0	0	.0	0	.0	0	.0		.0	
PART-TIME	0	.0	0	.0	0	.0	0	.0	0	.0	0	.0		.0	
FEMALE	0	.0	0	.0	0	.0	0	.0	0	.0	0	.0	0	.0	
MALE	0	.0	0	.0	0	.0	0	.0	0	.0	0	.0	0	.0	
TOTAL	0	.0	0	.0	0	.0	0	.0	0	.0	0	.0		.0	
FEMALE	0	.0	0	.0	0	.0	0	.0	0	.0	0	.0	0	.0	
MALE	0	.0	0	.0	0	.0	0	.0	0	.0	0	.0	0	.0	
GRADUATE:															
FULL-TIME	0	.0	0	.0	0	.0	0	.0	0	.0	0	.0		.0	
FEMALE	0	.0	0	.0	0	.0	0	.0	0	.0	0	.0		.0	
MALE	0	.0	0	.0	0	.0	0	.0	0	.0	0	.0		.0	
PART-TIME	0	.0	0	.0	0	.0	0	.0	0	.0	0	.0		.0	
FEMALE	0	.0	0	.0	0	.0	0	.0	0	.0	0	.0	0	.0	
MALE	0	.0	0	.0	0	.0	0	.0	0	.0	0	.0	0	.0	
TOTAL	0	.0	0	.0	0	.0	0	.0	0	.0	0	.0		.0	
FEMALE	0	.0	0	.0	0	.0	0	.0	0	.0	0	.0	0	.0	
MALE	0	.0	0	.0	0	.0	0	.0	0	.0	0	.0	0	.0	
PROFESSIONAL:															
FULL-TIME	0	.0	3	1.2	0	.0	1	.4	4	1.6	254	98.4		.0	
FEMALE	0	.0	3	3.8	0	.0	1	1.3	4	5.0	76	95.0		.0	
MALE	0	.0	0	.0	0	.0	0	.0	0	.0	178	100.0		.0	
PART-TIME	0	.0	0	.0	0	.0	1	3.4	1	3.4	28	96.6		.0	
FEMALE	0	.0	0	.0	0	.0	0	.0	0	.0	8	100.0	0	.0	
MALE	0	.0	0	.0	0	.0	1	4.8	1	4.8	20	95.2	0	.0	
TOTAL	0	.0	3	1.0	0	.0	2	.7	5	1.7	282	98.3		.0	
FEMALE	0	.0	3	3.4	0	.0	1	1.1	4	4.5	84	95.5	0	.0	
MALE	0	.0	0	.0	0	.0	1	.5	1	.5	198	99.5	0	.0	
UND+GRAD+PROF:															
FULL-TIME	0	.0	3	1.2	0	.0	1	.4	4	1.6	254	98.4		.0	
FEMALE	0	.0	3	3.8	0	.0	1	1.3	4	5.0	76	95.0		.0	
MALE	0	.0	0	.0	0	.0	0	.0	0	.0	178	100.0		.0	
PART-TIME	0	.0	0	.0	0	.0	1	3.4	1	3.4	28	96.6		.0	
FEMALE	0	.0	0	.0	0	.0	0	.0	0	.0	8	100.0	0	.0	
MALE	0	.0	0	.0	0	.0	1	4.8	1	4.8	20	95.2	0	.0	
TOTAL	0	.0	3	1.0	0	.0	2	.7	5	1.7	282	98.3		.0	
FEMALE	0	.0	3	3.4	0	.0	1	1.1	4	4.5	84	95.5	0	.0	
MALE	0	.0	0	.0	0	.0	1	.5	1	.5	198	99.5	0	.0	
UNCLASSIFIED:															
TOTAL	0	.0	0	.0	0	.0	0	.0	0	.0	0	.0		.0	
FEMALE	0	.0	0	.0	0	.0	0	.0	0	.0	0	.0	0	.0	
MALE	0	.0	0	.0	0	.0	0	.0	0	.0	0	.0	0	.0	
TOTAL ENROLLMENT:															
TOTAL	0	.0	3	1.0	0	.0	2	.7	5	1.7	282	98.3		.0	
FEMALE	0	.0	3	3.4	0	.0	1	1.1	4	4.5	84	95.5	0	.0	
MALE	0	.0	0	.0	0	.0	1	.5	1	.5	198	99.5	0	.0	
IOWA	1 INSTITUTIONS)														
UNDERGRADUATES:															
FULL-TIME	0	.0	0	.0	0	.0	0	.0	0	.0	0	.0		.0	
FEMALE	0	.0	0	.0	0	.0	0	.0	0	.0	0	.0		.0	
MALE	0	.0	0	.0	0	.0	0	.0	0	.0	0	.0		.0	
PART-TIME	0	.0	0	.0	0	.0	0	.0	0	.0	0	.0		.0	
FEMALE	0	.0	0	.0	0	.0	0	.0	0	.0	0	.0	0	.0	
MALE	0	.0	0	.0	0	.0	0	.0	0	.0	0	.0	0	.0	
TOTAL	0	.0	0	.0	0	.0	0	.0	0	.0	0	.0		.0	
FEMALE	0	.0	0	.0	0	.0	0	.0	0	.0	0	.0	0	.0	
MALE	0	.0	0	.0	0	.0	0	.0	0	.0	0	.0	0	.0	
GRADUATE:															
FULL-TIME	0	.0	0	.0	0	.0	0	.0	0	.0	0	.0		.0	
FEMALE	0	.0	0	.0	0	.0	0	.0	0	.0	0	.0		.0	
MALE	0	.0	0	.0	0	.0	0	.0	0	.0	0	.0		.0	
PART-TIME	0	.0	0	.0	0	.0	0	.0	0	.0	0	.0		.0	
FEMALE	0	.0	0	.0	0	.0	0	.0	0	.0	0	.0	0	.0	
MALE	0	.0	0	.0	0	.0	0	.0	0	.0	0	.0	0	.0	
TOTAL	0	.0	0	.0	0	.0	0	.0	0	.0	0	.0		.0	
FEMALE	0	.0	0	.0	0	.0	0	.0	0	.0	0	.0	0	.0	
MALE	0	.0	0	.0	0	.0	0	.0	0	.0	0	.0	0	.0	
PROFESSIONAL:															
FULL-TIME	1	.2	0	.0	4	.9	1	.2	6	1.3	447	98.7		.0	
FEMALE	0	.0	0	.0	2	1.7	0	.0	2	1.7	118	98.3		.0	
MALE	1	.3	0	.0	2	.6	1	.3	4	1.2	329	98.8	0	.0	

538

VETERINARY MEDICINE

INDIAN NATIVE %	BLACK NON-HISPANIC NUMBER	%	ASIAN OR PACIFIC ISLANDER NUMBER	%	HISPANIC NUMBER	%	TOTAL MINORITY NUMBER	%	WHITE NON-HISPANIC NUMBER	%	NON-RESIDENT ALIEN NUMBER	%	TOTAL NUMBER
CONTINUED													
.0	0	.0	0	.0	0	.0	0	.0	2	100.0	0	.0	2
.0	0	.0	0	.0	0	.0	0	.0	1	100.0	0	.0	1
.0	0	.0	0	.0	0	.0	0	.0	1	100.0	0	.0	1
.2	0	.0	4	.9	1	.2	6	1.3	449	98.7	0	.0	455
.0	0	.0	2	1.7	0	.0	2	1.7	119	98.3	0	.0	121
.3	0	.0	2	.6	1	.3	4	1.2	330	98.8	0	.0	334
.2	0	.0	4	.9	1	.2	6	1.3	447	98.7	0	.0	453
.0	0	.0	2	1.7	0	.0	2	1.7	118	98.3	0	.0	120
.3	0	.0	2	.6	1	.3	4	1.2	329	98.8	0	.0	333
.0	0	.0	0	.0	0	.0	0	.0	2	100.0	0	.0	2
.0	0	.0	0	.0	0	.0	0	.0	1	100.0	0	.0	1
.0	0	.0	0	.0	0	.0	0	.0	1	100.0	0	.0	1
.2	0	.0	4	.9	1	.2	6	1.3	449	98.7	0	.0	455
.0	0	.0	2	1.7	0	.0	2	1.7	119	98.3	0	.0	121
.3	0	.0	2	.6	1	.3	4	1.2	330	98.8	0	.0	334
.0	0	.0	0	.0	0	.0	0	.0	0	.0	0	.0	0
.0	0	.0	0	.0	0	.0	0	.0	0	.0	0	.0	0
.0	0	.0	0	.0	0	.0	0	.0	0	.0	0	.0	0
.2	0	.0	4	.9	1	.2	6	1.3	449	98.7	0	.0	455
.0	0	.0	2	1.7	0	.0	2	1.7	119	98.3	0	.0	121
.3	0	.0	2	.6	1	.3	4	1.2	330	98.8	0	.0	334
(1 INSTITUTIONS)													
.0	0	.0	0	.0	0	.0	0	.0	0	.0	0	.0	0
.0	0	.0	0	.0	0	.0	0	.0	0	.0	0	.0	0
.0	0	.0	0	.0	0	.0	0	.0	0	.0	0	.0	0
.0	0	.0	0	.0	0	.0	0	.0	0	.0	0	.0	0
.0	0	.0	0	.0	0	.0	0	.0	0	.0	0	.0	0
.0	0	.0	0	.0	0	.0	0	.0	0	.0	0	.0	0
.0	0	.0	0	.0	0	.0	0	.0	0	.0	0	.0	0
.0	0	.0	0	.0	0	.0	0	.0	0	.0	0	.0	0
.0	0	.0	0	.0	0	.0	0	.0	0	.0	0	.0	0
.0	0	.0	0	.0	0	.0	0	.0	0	.0	0	.0	0
.0	0	.0	0	.0	0	.0	0	.0	0	.0	0	.0	0
.0	0	.0	0	.0	0	.0	0	.0	0	.0	0	.0	0
.0	0	.0	0	.0	0	.0	0	.0	0	.0	0	.0	0
.0	0	.0	0	.0	0	.0	0	.0	0	.0	0	.0	0
.0	0	.0	0	.0	0	.0	0	.0	0	.0	0	.0	0
.5	4	1.0	3	.7	8	2.0	17	4.2	385	95.8	0	.0	402
.0	1	1.2	0	.0	2	2.4	3	3.5	82	96.5	0	.0	85
.6	3	.9	3	.9	6	1.9	14	4.4	303	95.6	0	.0	317
.0	0	.0	0	.0	0	.0	0	.0	2	100.0	0	.0	2
.0	0	.0	0	.0	0	.0	0	.0	0	.0	0	.0	0
.0	0	.0	0	.0	0	.0	0	.0	2	100.0	0	.0	2
.5	4	1.0	3	.7	8	2.0	17	4.2	387	95.8	0	.0	404
.0	1	1.2	0	.0	2	2.4	3	3.5	82	96.5	0	.0	85
.6	3	.9	3	.9	6	1.9	14	4.4	305	95.6	0	.0	319
.5	4	1.0	3	.7	8	2.0	17	4.2	385	95.8	0	.0	402
.0	1	1.2	0	.0	2	2.4	3	3.5	82	96.5	0	.0	85
.6	3	.9	3	.9	6	1.9	14	4.4	303	95.6	0	.0	317
.0	0	.0	0	.0	0	.0	0	.0	2	100.0	0	.0	2
.0	0	.0	0	.0	0	.0	0	.0	0	.0	0	.0	0
.0	0	.0	0	.0	0	.0	0	.0	2	100.0	0	.0	2
.5	4	1.0	3	.7	8	2.0	17	4.2	387	95.8	0	.0	404
.0	1	1.2	0	.0	2	2.4	3	3.5	82	96.5	0	.0	85
.6	3	.9	3	.9	6	1.9	14	4.4	305	95.6	0	.0	319
.0	0	.0	0	.0	0	.0	0	.0	0	.0	0	.0	0
.0	0	.0	0	.0	0	.0	0	.0	0	.0	0	.0	0
.0	0	.0	0	.0	0	.0	0	.0	0	.0	0	.0	0
.5	4	1.0	3	.7	8	2.0	17	4.2	387	95.8	0	.0	404
.0	1	1.2	0	.0	2	2.4	3	3.5	82	96.5	0	.0	85
.6	3	.9	3	.9	6	1.9	14	4.4	305	95.6	0	.0	319

TABLE 17 - TOTAL ENROLLMENT IN INSTITUTIONS OF HIGHER EDUCATION FOR SELECTED MAJOR FIELDS OF STUDY AND LEVEL OF ENROLLMENT
BY RACE, ETHNICITY, AND SEX: STATE, 1978

MAJOR FIELD 1218 - VETERINARY MEDICINE

	AMERICAN INDIAN ALASKAN NATIVE		BLACK NON-HISPANIC		ASIAN OR PACIFIC ISLANDER		HISPANIC		TOTAL MINORITY		WHITE NON-HISPANIC		NON-RESIDENT ALIEN		TOTAL
	NUMBER	%	NUMBER	%	NUMBER	%	NUMBER	%	NUMBER	%	NUMBER	%	NUMBER	%	NUMBER
LOUISIANA (1 INSTITUTIONS)															
UNDERGRADUATES:															
FULL-TIME	0	.0	0	.0	0	.0	0	.0	0	.0	0	.0	0	.0	0
FEMALE	0	.0	0	.0	0	.0	0	.0	0	.0	0	.0	0	.0	0
MALE	0	.0	0	.0	0	.0	0	.0	0	.0	0	.0	0	.0	0
PART-TIME	0	.0	0	.0	0	.0	0	.0	0	.0	0	.0	0	.0	0
FEMALE	0	.0	0	.0	0	.0	0	.0	0	.0	0	.0	0	.0	0
MALE	0	.0	0	.0	0	.0	0	.0	0	.0	0	.0	0	.0	0
TOTAL	0	.0	0	.0	0	.0	0	.0	0	.0	0	.0	0	.0	0
FEMALE	0	.0	0	.0	0	.0	0	.0	0	.0	0	.0	0	.0	0
MALE	0	.0	0	.0	0	.0	0	.0	0	.0	0	.0	0	.0	0
GRADUATE:															
FULL-TIME	0	.0	0	.0	0	.0	0	.0	0	.0	0	.0	0	.0	0
FEMALE	0	.0	0	.0	0	.0	0	.0	0	.0	0	.0	0	.0	0
MALE	0	.0	0	.0	0	.0	0	.0	0	.0	0	.0	0	.0	0
PART-TIME	0	.0	0	.0	0	.0	0	.0	0	.0	0	.0	0	.0	0
FEMALE	0	.0	0	.0	0	.0	0	.0	0	.0	0	.0	0	.0	0
MALE	0	.0	0	.0	0	.0	0	.0	0	.0	0	.0	0	.0	0
TOTAL	0	.0	0	.0	0	.0	0	.0	0	.0	0	.0	0	.0	0
FEMALE	0	.0	0	.0	0	.0	0	.0	0	.0	0	.0	0	.0	0
MALE	0	.0	0	.0	0	.0	0	.0	0	.0	0	.0	0	.0	0
PROFESSIONAL:															
FULL-TIME	0	.0	2	.7	1	.3	1	.3	4	1.4	287	98.3	1	.3	292
FEMALE	0	.0	0	.0	1	1.3	1	1.3	2	2.5	78	97.5	0	.0	80
MALE	0	.0	2	.9	0	.0	0	.0	2	.9	209	98.6	1	.5	212
PART-TIME	0	.0	0	.0	0	.0	0	.0	0	.0	0	.0	0	.0	0
FEMALE	0	.0	0	.0	0	.0	0	.0	0	.0	0	.0	0	.0	0
MALE	0	.0	0	.0	0	.0	0	.0	0	.0	0	.0	0	.0	0
TOTAL	0	.0	2	.7	1	.3	1	.3	4	1.4	287	98.3	1	.3	292
FEMALE	0	.0	0	.0	1	1.3	1	1.3	2	2.5	78	97.5	0	.0	80
MALE	0	.0	2	.9	0	.0	0	.0	2	.9	209	98.6	1	.5	212
UND+GRAD+PROF:															
FULL-TIME	0	.0	2	.7	1	.3	1	.3	4	1.4	287	98.3	1	.3	292
FEMALE	0	.0	0	.0	1	1.3	1	1.3	2	2.5	78	97.5	0	.0	80
MALE	0	.0	2	.9	0	.0	0	.0	2	.9	209	98.6	1	.5	212
PART-TIME	0	.0	0	.0	0	.0	0	.0	0	.0	0	.0	0	.0	0
FEMALE	0	.0	0	.0	0	.0	0	.0	0	.0	0	.0	0	.0	0
MALE	0	.0	0	.0	0	.0	0	.0	0	.0	0	.0	0	.0	0
TOTAL	0	.0	2	.7	1	.3	1	.3	4	1.4	287	98.3	1	.3	292
FEMALE	0	.0	0	.0	1	1.3	1	1.3	2	2.5	78	97.5	0	.0	80
MALE	0	.0	2	.9	0	.0	0	.0	2	.9	209	98.6	1	.5	212
UNCLASSIFIED:															
TOTAL	0	.0	0	.0	0	.0	0	.0	0	.0	0	.0	0	.0	0
FEMALE	0	.0	0	.0	0	.0	0	.0	0	.0	0	.0	0	.0	0
MALE	0	.0	0	.0	0	.0	0	.0	0	.0	0	.0	0	.0	0
TOTAL ENROLLMENT:															
TOTAL	0	.0	2	.7	1	.3	1	.3	4	1.4	287	98.3	1	.3	292
FEMALE	0	.0	0	.0	1	1.3	1	1.3	2	2.5	78	97.5	0	.0	80
MALE	0	.0	2	.9	0	.0	0	.0	2	.9	209	98.6	1	.5	212
MICHIGAN (1 INSTITUTIONS)															
UNDERGRADUATES:															
FULL-TIME	0	.0	0	.0	0	.0	0	.0	0	.0	0	.0	0	.0	0
FEMALE	0	.0	0	.0	0	.0	0	.0	0	.0	0	.0	0	.0	0
MALE	0	.0	0	.0	0	.0	0	.0	0	.0	0	.0	0	.0	0
PART-TIME	0	.0	0	.0	0	.0	0	.0	0	.0	0	.0	0	.0	0
FEMALE	0	.0	0	.0	0	.0	0	.0	0	.0	0	.0	0	.0	0
MALE	0	.0	0	.0	0	.0	0	.0	0	.0	0	.0	0	.0	0
TOTAL	0	.0	0	.0	0	.0	0	.0	0	.0	0	.0	0	.0	0
FEMALE	0	.0	0	.0	0	.0	0	.0	0	.0	0	.0	0	.0	0
MALE	0	.0	0	.0	0	.0	0	.0	0	.0	0	.0	0	.0	0
GRADUATE:															
FULL-TIME	0	.0	0	.0	0	.0	0	.0	0	.0	0	.0	0	.0	0
FEMALE	0	.0	0	.0	0	.0	0	.0	0	.0	0	.0	0	.0	0
MALE	0	.0	0	.0	0	.0	0	.0	0	.0	0	.0	0	.0	0
PART-TIME	0	.0	0	.0	0	.0	0	.0	0	.0	0	.0	0	.0	0
FEMALE	0	.0	0	.0	0	.0	0	.0	0	.0	0	.0	0	.0	0
MALE	0	.0	0	.0	0	.0	0	.0	0	.0	0	.0	0	.0	0
TOTAL	0	.0	0	.0	0	.0	0	.0	0	.0	0	.0	0	.0	0
FEMALE	0	.0	0	.0	0	.0	0	.0	0	.0	0	.0	0	.0	0
MALE	0	.0	0	.0	0	.0	0	.0	0	.0	0	.0	0	.0	0
PROFESSIONAL:															
FULL-TIME	1	.3	2	.6	1	.3	1	.3	5	1.5	334	98.5	0	.0	339
FEMALE	1	.7	1	.7	0	.0	0	.0	2	1.4	145	98.6	0	.0	147
MALE	0	.0	1	.5	1	.5	1	.5	3	1.6	189	98.4	0	.0	192

VETERINARY MEDICINE

INDIAN NATIVE		BLACK NON-HISPANIC		ASIAN OR PACIFIC ISLANDER		HISPANIC		TOTAL MINORITY		WHITE NON-HISPANIC		NON-RESIDENT ALIEN		TOTAL
%	NUMBER	%	NUMBER	%	NUMBER	%	NUMBER	%	NUMBER	%	NUMBER	%	NUMBER	NUMBER

CONTINUED

.0	0	.0	0	.0	0	.0	0	.0	0	.0	0	.0	0	.0	0
.0	0	.0	0	.0	0	.0	0	.0	0	.0	0	.0	0	.0	0
.0	0	.0	0	.0	0	.0	0	.0	0	.0	0	.0	0	.0	0
.3	2	.6	1	.3	1	.3	5	1.5	334	98.5	0	.0	339
.7	1	.7	0	.0	0	.0	2	1.4	145	98.6	0	.0	147
.0	1	.5	1	.5	1	.5	3	1.6	189	98.4	0	.0	192
.3	2	.6	1	.3	1	.3	5	1.5	334	98.5	0	.0	339
.7	1	.7	0	.0	0	.0	2	1.4	145	98.6	0	.0	147
.0	1	.5	1	.5	1	.5	3	1.6	189	98.4	0	.0	192
.0	0	.0	0	.0	0	.0	0	.0	0	.0	0	.0	0
.0	0	.0	0	.0	0	.0	0	.0	0	.0	0	.0	0
.0	0	.0	0	.0	0	.0	0	.0	0	.0	0	.0	0
.3	2	.6	1	.3	1	.3	5	1.5	334	98.5	0	.0	339
.7	1	.7	0	.0	0	.0	2	1.4	145	98.6	0	.0	147
.0	1	.5	1	.5	1	.5	3	1.6	189	98.4	0	.0	192

(1 INSTITUTIONS)

.0	0	.0	0	.0	0	.0	0	.0	0	.0	0	.0	0
.0	0	.0	0	.0	0	.0	0	.0	0	.0	0	.0	0
.0	0	.0	0	.0	0	.0	0	.0	0	.0	0	.0	0
.0	0	.0	0	.0	0	.0	0	.0	0	.0	0	.0	0
.0	0	.0	0	.0	0	.0	0	.0	0	.0	0	.0	0
.0	0	.0	0	.0	0	.0	0	.0	0	.0	0	.0	0
.0	0	.0	0	.0	0	.0	0	.0	0	.0	0	.0	0
.0	0	.0	0	.0	0	.0	0	.0	0	.0	0	.0	0
.0	0	.0	0	.0	0	.0	0	.0	0	.0	0	.0	0
.0	0	.0	0	.0	0	.0	0	.0	0	.0	0	.0	0
.0	0	.0	0	.0	0	.0	0	.0	0	.0	0	.0	0
.0	0	.0	0	.0	0	.0	0	.0	0	.0	0	.0	0
.0	0	.0	0	.0	0	.0	0	.0	0	.0	0	.0	0
.0	0	.0	0	.0	0	.0	0	.0	0	.0	0	.0	0
.6	0	.0	4	1.3	0	.0	6	1.9	311	98.1	0	.0	317
.8	0	.0	3	2.4	0	.0	4	3.2	120	96.8	0	.0	124
.5	0	.0	1	.5	0	.0	2	1.0	191	99.0	0	.0	193
.0	0	.0	0	.0	0	.0	0	.0	0	.0	0	.0	0
.0	0	.0	0	.0	0	.0	0	.0	0	.0	0	.0	0
.0	0	.0	0	.0	0	.0	0	.0	0	.0	0	.0	0
.6	0	.0	4	1.3	0	.0	6	1.9	311	98.1	0	.0	317
.8	0	.0	3	2.4	0	.0	4	3.2	120	96.8	0	.0	124
.5	0	.0	1	.5	0	.0	2	1.0	191	99.0	0	.0	193
.6	0	.0	4	1.3	0	.0	6	1.9	311	98.1	0	.0	317
.8	0	.0	3	2.4	0	.0	4	3.2	120	96.8	0	.0	124
.5	0	.0	1	.5	0	.0	2	1.0	191	99.0	0	.0	193
.0	0	.0	0	.0	0	.0	0	.0	0	.0	0	.0	0
.0	0	.0	0	.0	0	.0	0	.0	0	.0	0	.0	0
.0	0	.0	0	.0	0	.0	0	.0	0	.0	0	.0	0
.6	0	.0	4	1.3	0	.0	6	1.9	311	98.1	0	.0	317
.8	0	.0	3	2.4	0	.0	4	3.2	120	96.8	0	.0	124
.5	0	.0	1	.5	0	.0	2	1.0	191	99.0	0	.0	193
.0	0	.0	0	.0	0	.0	0	.0	0	.0	0	.0	0
.0	0	.0	0	.0	0	.0	0	.0	0	.0	0	.0	0
.0	0	.0	0	.0	0	.0	0	.0	0	.0	0	.0	0
.6	0	.0	4	1.3	0	.0	6	1.9	311	98.1	0	.0	317
.8	0	.0	3	2.4	0	.0	4	3.2	120	96.8	0	.0	124
.5	0	.0	1	.5	0	.0	2	1.0	191	99.0	0	.0	193

MAJOR FIELD 1218 - VETERINARY MEDICINE

	AMERICAN INDIAN ALASKAN NATIVE		BLACK NON-HISPANIC		ASIAN OR PACIFIC ISLANDER		HISPANIC		TOTAL MINORITY		WHITE NON-HISPANIC		NON-RESIDENT ALIEN		TOT
	NUMBER	%	NUMBER	%	NUMBER	%	NUMBER	%	NUMBER	%	NUMBER	%	NUMBER	%	NUM
MISSISSIPPI	(1 INSTITUTIONS)														
UNDERGRADUATES:															
FULL-TIME	0	.0	0	.0	0	.0	0	.0	0	.0	0	.0	0	.0	
FEMALE	0	.0	0	.0	0	.0	0	.0	0	.0	0	.0	0	.0	
MALE	0	.0	0	.0	0	.0	0	.0	0	.0	0	.0	0	.0	
PART-TIME	0	.0	0	.0	0	.0	0	.0	0	.0	0	.0	0	.0	
FEMALE	0	.0	0	.0	0	.0	0	.0	0	.0	0	.0	0	.0	
MALE	0	.0	0	.0	0	.0	0	.0	0	.0	0	.0	0	.0	
TOTAL	0	.0	0	.0	0	.0	0	.0	0	.0	0	.0		.0	
FEMALE	0	.0	0	.0	0	.0	0	.0	0	.0	0	.0	0	.0	
MALE	0	.0	0	.0	0	.0	0	.0	0	.0	0	.0	0	.0	
GRADUATE:															
FULL-TIME	0	.0	0	.0	0	.0	0	.0	0	.0	0	.0	0	.0	
FEMALE	0	.0	0	.0	0	.0	0	.0	0	.0	0	.0	0	.0	
MALE	0	.0	0	.0	0	.0	0	.0	0	.0	0	.0	0	.0	
PART-TIME	0	.0	0	.0	0	.0	0	.0	0	.0	0-	.0	0	.0	
FEMALE	0	.0	0	.0	0	.0	0	.0	0	.0	0	.0	0	.0	
MALE	0	.0	0	.0	0	.0	0	.0	0	.0	0	.0	0	.0	
TOTAL	0	.0	0	.0	0	.0	0	.0	0	.0	0	.0	0	.0	
FEMALE	0	.0	0	.0	0	.0	0	.0	0	.0	0	.0	0	.0	
MALE	0	.0	0	.0	0	.0	0	.0	0	.0	0	.0	0	.0	
PROFESSIONAL:															
FULL-TIME	0	.0	2	3.6	0	.0	0	.0	2	3.6	53	96.4	0	.0	
FEMALE	0	.0	2	10.5	0	.0	0	.0	2	10.5	17	89.5	0	.0	
MALE	0	.0	0	.0	0	.0	0	.0	0	.0	36	100.0	0	.0	
PART-TIME	0	.0	0	.0	0	.0	0	.0	0	.0	0	.0	0	.0	
FEMALE	0	.0	0	.0	0	.0	0	.0	0	.0	0	.0	0	.0	
MALE	0	.0	0	.0	0	.0	0	.0	0	.0	0	.0	0	.0	
TOTAL	0	.0	2	3.6	0	.0	0	.0	2	3.6	53	96.4		.0	
FEMALE	0	.0	2	10.5	0	.0	0	.0	2	10.5	17	89.5	0	.0	
MALE	0	.0	0	.0	0	.0	0	.0	0	.0	36	100.0	0	.0	
UND+GRAD+PROF:															
FULL-TIME	0	.0	2	3.6	0	.0	0	.0	2	3.6	53	96.4	0	.0	
FEMALE	0	.0	2	10.5	0	.0	0	.0	2	10.5	17	89.5	0	.0	
MALE	0	.0	0	.0	0	.0	0	.0	0	.0	36	100.0	0	.0	
PART-TIME	0	.0	0	.0	0	.0	0	.0	0	.0	0	.0	0	.0	
FEMALE	0	.0	0	.0	0	.0	0	.0	0	.0	0	.0	0	.0	
MALE	0	.0	0	.0	0	.0	0	.0	0	.0	0	.0	0	.0	
TOTAL	0	.0	2	3.6	0	.0	0	.0	2	3.6	53	96.4	0	.0	
FEMALE	0	.0	2	10.5	0	.0	0	.0	2	10.5	17	89.5	0	.0	
MALE	0	.0	0	.0	0	.0	0	.0	0	.0	36	100.0			
UNCLASSIFIED:															
TOTAL	0	.0	0	.0	0	.0	0	.0	0	.0	0	.0	0	.0	
FEMALE	0	.0	0	.0	0	.0	0	.0	0	.0	0	.0	0	.0	
MALE	0	.0	0	.0	0	.0	0	.0	0	.0	0	.0	0	.0	
TOTAL ENROLLMENT:															
TOTAL	0	.0	2	3.6	0	.0	0	.0	2	3.6	53	96.4	0	.0	
FEMALE	0	.0	2	10.5	0	.0	0	.0	2	10.5	17	89.5	0	.0	
MALE	0	.0	0	.0	0	.0	0	.0	0	.0	36	100.0	0	.0	
MISSOURI	(1 INSTITUTIONS)														
UNDERGRADUATES:															
FULL-TIME	0	.0	0	.0	0	.0	0	.0	0	.0	0	.0	0	.0	
FEMALE	0	.0	0	.0	0	.0	0	.0	0	.0	0	.0	0	.0	
MALE	0	.0	0	.0	0	.0	0	.0	0	.0	0	.0	0	.0	
PART-TIME	0	.0	0	.0	0	.0	0	.0	0	.0	0	.0	0	.0	
FEMALE	0	.0	0	.0	0	.0	0	.0	0	.0	0	.0	0	.0	
MALE	0	.0	0	.0	0	.0	0	.0	0	.0	0	.0	0	.0	
TOTAL	0	.0	0	.0	0	.0	0	.0	0	.0	0	.0	0	.0	
FEMALE	0	.0	0	.0	0	.0	0	.0	0	.0	0	.0	0	.0	
MALE	0	.0	0	.0	0	.0	0	.0	0	.0	0	.0	0	.0	
GRADUATE:															
FULL-TIME	0	.0	0	.0	0	.0	0	.0	0	.0	0	.0	0	.0	
FEMALE	0	.0	0	.0	0	.0	0	.0	0	.0	0	.0	0	.0	
MALE	0	.0	0	.0	0	.0	0	.0	0	.0	0	.0	0	.0	
PART-TIME	0	.0	0	.0	0	.0	0	.0	0	.0	0	.0	0	.0	
FEMALE	0	.0	0	.0	0	.0	0	.0	0	.0	0	.0	0	.0	
MALE	0	.0	0	.0	0	.0	0	.0	0	.0	0	.0	0	.0	
TOTAL	0	.0	0	.0	0	.0	0	.0	0	.0	0	.0	0	.0	
FEMALE	0	.0	0	.0	0	.0	0	.0	0	.0	0	.0	0	.0	
MALE	0	.0	0	.0	0	.0	0	.0	0	.0	0	.0	0	.0	
PROFESSIONAL:															
FULL-TIME	2	.7	0	.0	2	.7	1	.3	5	1.7	284	98.3	0	.0	
FEMALE	1	1.2	0	.0	0	.0	0	.0	1	1.2	85	98.8	0	.0	
MALE	1	.5	0	.0	2	1.0	1	.5	4	2.0	199	98.0	0	.0	

VETERINARY MEDICINE

I INDIAN NATIVE	BLACK NON-HISPANIC		ASIAN OR PACIFIC ISLANDER		HISPANIC		TOTAL MINORITY		WHITE NON-HISPANIC		NON-RESIDENT ALIEN		TOTAL
%	NUMBER	%	NUMBER	%	NUMBER	%	NUMBER	%	NUMBER	%	NUMBER	%	NUMBER

CONTINUED

%	NUMBER	%	NUMBER	%	NUMBER	%	NUMBER	%	NUMBER	%	NUMBER	%	NUMBER
.0	0	.0	0	.0	0	.0	0	.0	0	.0	0	.0	0
.0	0	.0	0	.0	0	.0	0	.0	0	.0	0	.0	0
.0	0	.0	0	.0	0	.0	0	.0	0	.0	0	.0	0
.7	0	.0	2	.7	1	.3	5	1.7	284	98.3	0	.0	289
1.2	0	.0	0	.0	0	.0	1	1.2	85	98.8	0	.0	86
.5	0	.0	2	1.0	1	.5	4	2.0	199	98.0	0	.0	203
.7	0	.0	2	.7	1	.3	5	1.7	284	98.3	0	.0	289
1.2	0	.0	0	.0	0	.0	1	1.2	85	98.8	0	.0	86
.5	0	.0	2	1.0	1	.5	4	2.0	199	98.0	0	.0	203
.0	0	.0	0	.0	0	.0	0	.0	0	.0	0	.0	0
.0	0	.0	0	.0	0	.0	0	.0	0	.0	0	.0	0
.7	0	.0	2	.7	1	.3	5	1.7	284	98.3	0	.0	289
1.2	0	.0	0	.0	0	.0	1	1.2	85	98.8	0	.0	86
.5	0	.0	2	1.0	1	.5	4	2.0	199	98.0	0	.0	203
.0	0	.0	0	.0	0	.0	0	.0	0	.0	0	.0	0
.0	0	.0	0	.0	0	.0	0	.0	0	.0	0	.0	0
.0	0	.0	0	.0	0	.0	0	.0	0	.0	0	.0	0
.7	0	.0	2	.7	1	.3	5	1.7	284	98.3	0	.0	289
1.2	0	.0	0	.0	0	.0	1	1.2	85	98.8	0	.0	86
.5	0	.0	2	1.0	1	.5	4	2.0	199	98.0	0	.0	203

(1 INSTITUTIONS)

%	NUMBER	%	NUMBER	%	NUMBER	%	NUMBER	%	NUMBER	%	NUMBER	%	NUMBER
.0	0	.0	0	.0	0	.0	0	.0	0	.0	0	.0	0
.0	0	.0	0	.0	0	.0	0	.0	0	.0	0	.0	0
.0	0	.0	0	.0	0	.0	0	.0	0	.0	0	.0	0
.0	0	.0	0	.0	0	.0	0	.0	0	.0	0	.0	0
.0	0	.0	0	.0	0	.0	0	.0	0	.0	0	.0	0
.0	0	.0	0	.0	0	.0	0	.0	0	.0	0	.0	0
.0	0	.0	0	.0	0	.0	0	.0	0	.0	0	.0	0
.0	0	.0	0	.0	0	.0	0	.0	0	.0	0	.0	0
.0	0	.0	0	.0	0	.0	0	.0	0	.0	0	.0	0
.0	0	.0	0	.0	0	.0	0	.0	0	.0	0	.0	0
.0	0	.0	0	.0	0	.0	0	.0	0	.0	0	.0	0
.0	0	.0	0	.0	0	.0	0	.0	0	.0	0	.0	0
.0	0	.0	0	.0	0	.0	0	.0	0	.0	0	.0	0
.0	0	.0	0	.0	0	.0	0	.0	0	.0	0	.0	0
.0	0	.0	0	.0	0	.0	0	.0	0	.0	0	.0	0
.0	0	.0	0	.0	0	.0	0	.0	0	.0	0	.0	0
.0	0	.0	0	.0	0	.0	0	.0	0	.0	0	.0	0
.0	0	.0	0	.0	0	.0	0	.0	0	.0	0	.0	0
.6	3	1.0	3	1.0	1	.3	9	2.9	299	97.1	0	.0	308
.0	3	2.1	2	1.4	0	.0	5	3.5	136	96.5	0	.0	141
1.2	0	.0	1	.6	1	.6	4	2.4	163	97.6	0	.0	167
.0	0	.0	0	.0	0	.0	0	.0	0	.0	0	.0	0
.0	0	.0	0	.0	0	.0	0	.0	0	.0	0	.0	0
.0	0	.0	0	.0	0	.0	0	.0	0	.0	0	.0	0
.6	3	1.0	3	1.0	1	.3	9	2.9	299	97.1	0	.0	308
.0	3	2.1	2	1.4	0	.0	5	3.5	136	96.5	0	.0	141
1.2	0	.0	1	.6	1	.6	4	2.4	163	97.6	0	.0	167
.6	3	1.0	3	1.0	1	.3	9	2.9	299	97.1	0	.0	308
.0	3	2.1	2	1.4	0	.0	5	3.5	136	96.5	0	.0	141
1.2	0	.0	1	.6	1	.6	4	2.4	163	97.6	0	.0	167
.0	0	.0	0	.0	0	.0	0	.0	0	.0	0	.0	0
.0	0	.0	0	.0	0	.0	0	.0	0	.0	0	.0	0
.6	3	1.0	3	1.0	1	.3	9	2.9	299	97.1	0	.0	308
.0	3	2.1	2	1.4	0	.0	5	3.5	136	96.5	0	.0	141
1.2	0	.0	1	.6	1	.6	4	2.4	163	97.6	0	.0	167
.0	0	.0	0	.0	0	.0	0	.0	0	.0	0	.0	0
.0	0	.0	0	.0	0	.0	0	.0	0	.0	0	.0	0
.0	0	.0	0	.0	0	.0	0	.0	0	.0	0	.0	0
.6	3	1.0	3	1.0	1	.3	9	2.9	299	97.1	0	.0	308
.0	3	2.1	2	1.4	0	.0	5	3.5	136	96.5	0	.0	141
1.2	0	.0	1	.6	1	.6	4	2.4	163	97.6	0	.0	167

TABLE 17 - TOTAL ENROLLMENT IN INSTITUTIONS OF HIGHER EDUCATION FOR SELECTED MAJOR FIELDS OF STUDY AND LEVEL OF ENROLLMENT
BY RACE, ETHNICITY, AND SEX: STATE, 1978

MAJOR FIELD 1218 - VETERINARY MEDICINE

	AMERICAN INDIAN ALASKAN NATIVE		BLACK NON-HISPANIC		ASIAN OR PACIFIC ISLANDER		HISPANIC		TOTAL MINORITY		WHITE NON-HISPANIC		NON-RESIDENT ALIEN		TOT
	NUMBER	%	NUMBER	%	NUMBER	%	NUMBER	%	NUMBER	%	NUMBER	%	NUMBER	%	NUM
OHIO	(	1 INSTITUTIONS)													
UNDERGRADUATES:															
FULL-TIME	0	.0	0	.0	0	.0	0	.0	0	.0	0	.0		.0	
FEMALE	0	.0	0	.0	0	.0	0	.0	0	.0	0	.0		.0	
MALE	0	.0	0	.0	0	.0	0	.0	0	.0	0	.0		.0	
PART-TIME	0	.0	0	.0	0	.0	0	.0	0	.0	0	.0		.0	
FEMALE	0	.0	0	.0	0	.0	0	.0	0	.0	0	.0	0	.0	
MALE	0	.0	0	.0	0	.0	0	.0	0	.0	0	.0	0	.0	
TOTAL	0	.0	0	.0	0	.0	0	.0	0	.0	0	.0		.0	
FEMALE	0	.0	0	.0	0	.0	0	.0	0	.0	0	.0	0	.0	
MALE	0	.0	0	.0	0	.0	0	.0	0	.0	0	.0	0	.0	
GRADUATE:															
FULL-TIME	0	.0	0	.0	0	.0	0	.0	0	.0	0	.0		.0	
FEMALE	0	.0	0	.0	0	.0	0	.0	0	.0	0	.0		.0	
MALE	0	.0	0	.0	0	.0	0	.0	0	.0	0	.0		.0	
PART-TIME	0	.0	0	.0	0	.0	0	.0	0	.0	0	.0		.0	
FEMALE	0	.0	0	.0	0	.0	0	.0	0	.0	0	.0	0	.0	
MALE	0	.0	0	.0	0	.0	0	.0	0	.0	0	.0	0	.0	
TOTAL	0	.0	0	.0	0	.0	0	.0	0	.0	0	.0		.0	
FEMALE	0	.0	0	.0	0	.0	0	.0	0	.0	0	.0	0	.0	
MALE	0	.0	0	.0	0	.0	0	.0	0	.0	0	.0	0	.0	
PROFESSIONAL:															
FULL-TIME	0	.0	4	.9	2	.5	0	.0	6	1.4	431	98.6		.0	
FEMALE	0	.0	2	1.2	2	1.2	0	.0	4	2.4	163	97.6		.0	
MALE	0	.0	2	.7	0	.0	0	.0	2	.7	268	99.3		.0	
PART-TIME	0	.0	0	.0	0	.0	0	.0	0	.0	0	.0		.0	
FEMALE	0	.0	0	.0	0	.0	0	.0	0	.0	0	.0	0	.0	
MALE	0	.0	0	.0	0	.0	0	.0	0	.0	0	.0	0	.0	
TOTAL	0	.0	4	.9	2	.5	0	.0	6	1.4	431	98.6		.0	
FEMALE	0	.0	2	1.2	2	1.2	0	.0	4	2.4	163	97.6		.0	
MALE	0	.0	2	.7	0	.0	0	.0	2	.7	268	99.3	0	.0	
UNC+GRAD+PROF:															
FULL-TIME	0	.0	4	.9	2	.5	0	.0	6	1.4	431	98.6		.0	
FEMALE	0	.0	2	1.2	2	1.2	0	.0	4	2.4	163	97.6		.0	
MALE	0	.0	2	.7	0	.0	0	.0	2	.7	268	99.3		.0	
PART-TIME	0	.0	0	.0	0	.0	0	.0	0	.0	0	.0		.0	
FEMALE	0	.0	0	.0	0	.0	0	.0	0	.0	0	.0	0	.0	
MALE	0	.0	0	.0	0	.0	0	.0	0	.0	0	.0	0	.0	
TOTAL	0	.0	4	.9	2	.5	0	.0	6	1.4	431	98.6		.0	
FEMALE	0	.0	2	1.2	2	1.2	0	.0	4	2.4	163	97.6		.0	
MALE	0	.0	2	.7	0	.0	0	.0	2	.7	268	99.3	0	.0	
UNCLASSIFIED:															
TOTAL	0	.0	0	.0	0	.0	0	.0	0	.0	0	.0		.0	
FEMALE	0	.0	0	.0	0	.0	0	.0	0	.0	0	.0		.0	
MALE	0	.0	0	.0	0	.0	0	.0	0	.0	0	.0	0	.0	
TOTAL ENROLLMENT:															
TOTAL	0	.0	4	.9	2	.5	0	.0	6	1.4	431	98.6		.0	
FEMALE	0	.0	2	1.2	2	1.2	0	.0	4	2.4	163	97.6		.0	
MALE	0	.0	2	.7	0	.0	0	.0	2	.7	268	99.3	0	.0	
OKLAHOMA	(	1 INSTITUTIONS)													
UNDERGRADUATES:															
FULL-TIME	0	.0	0	.0	0	.0	0	.0	0	.0	0	.0		.0	
FEMALE	0	.0	0	.0	0	.0	0	.0	0	.0	0	.0		.0	
MALE	0	.0	0	.0	0	.0	0	.0	0	.0	0	.0		.0	
PART-TIME	0	.0	0	.0	0	.0	0	.0	0	.0	0	.0		.0	
FEMALE	0	.0	0	.0	0	.0	0	.0	0	.0	0	.0		.0	
MALE	0	.0	0	.0	0	.0	0	.0	0	.0	0	.0	0	.0	
TOTAL	0	.0	0	.0	0	.0	0	.0	0	.0	0	.0		.0	
FEMALE	0	.0	0	.0	0	.0	0	.0	0	.0	0	.0		.0	
MALE	0	.0	0	.0	0	.0	0	.0	0	.0	0	.0	0	.0	
GRADUATE:															
FULL-TIME	0	.0	0	.0	0	.0	0	.0	0	.0	0	.0		.0	
FEMALE	0	.0	0	.0	0	.0	0	.0	0	.0	0	.0		.0	
MALE	0	.0	0	.0	0	.0	0	.0	0	.0	0	.0		.0	
PART-TIME	0	.0	0	.0	0	.0	0	.0	0	.0	0	.0		.0	
FEMALE	0	.0	0	.0	0	.0	0	.0	0	.0	0	.0		.0	
MALE	0	.0	0	.0	0	.0	0	.0	0	.0	0	.0	0	.0	
TOTAL	0	.0	0	.0	0	.0	0	.0	0	.0	0	.0		.0	
FEMALE	0	.0	0	.0	0	.0	0	.0	0	.0	0	.0		.0	
MALE	0	.0	0	.0	0	.0	0	.0	0	.0	0	.0	0	.0	
PROFESSIONAL:															
FULL-TIME	4	1.6	1	.4	3	1.2	1	.4	9	3.5	247	96.5		.0	
FEMALE	0	.0	0	.0	1	1.7	0	.0	1	1.7	58	98.3		.0	
MALE	4	2.0	1	.5	2	1.0	1	.5	8	4.1	189	95.9	0	.0	

- VETERINARY MEDICINE

:AN INDIAN :N NATIVE		BLACK NON-HISPANIC		ASIAN OR PACIFIC ISLANDER		HISPANIC		TOTAL MINORITY		WHITE NON-HISPANIC		NON-RESIDENT ALIEN		TOTAL
:R	%	NUMBER	%	NUMBER	%	NUMBER	%	NUMBER	%	NUMBER	%	NUMBER	%	NUMBER

CONTINUED

0	.0	0	.0	0	.0	0	.0	0	.0	0	.0	0	.0	0
0	.0	0	.0	0	.0	0	.0	0	.0	0	.0	0	.0	0
0	.0	0	.0	0	.0	0	.0	0	.0	0	.0	0	.0	0
4	1.6	1	.4	3	1.2	1	.4	9	3.5	247	96.5	0	.0	256
0	.0	0	.0	1	1.7	0	.0	1	1.7	58	98.3	0	.0	59
4	2.0	1	.5	2	1.0	1	.5	8	4.1	189	95.9	0	.0	197
4	1.6	1	.4	3	1.2	1	.4	9	3.5	247	96.5	0	.0	256
0	.0	0	.0	1	1.7	0	.0	1	1.7	58	98.3	0	.0	59
4	2.0	1	.5	2	1.0	1	.5	8	4.1	189	95.9	0	.0	197
0	.0	0	.0	0	.0	0	.0	0	.0	0	.0	0	.0	0
0	.0	0	.0	0	.0	0	.0	0	.0	0	.0	0	.0	0
0	.0	0	.0	0	.0	0	.0	0	.0	0	.0	0	.0	0
4	1.6	1	.4	3	1.2	1	.4	9	3.5	247	96.5	0	.0	256
0	.0	0	.0	1	1.7	0	.0	1	1.7	58	98.3	0	.0	59
4	2.0	1	.5	2	1.0	1	.5	8	4.1	189	95.9	0	.0	197
0	.0	0	.0	0	.0	0	.0	0	.0	0	.0	0	.0	0
0	.0	0	.0	0	.0	0	.0	0	.0	0	.0	0	.0	0
0	.0	0	.0	0	.0	0	.0	0	.0	0	.0	0	.0	0
4	1.6	1	.4	3	1.2	1	.4	9	3.5	247	96.5	0	.0	256
0	.0	0	.0	1	1.7	0	.0	1	1.7	58	98.3	0	.0	59
4	2.0	1	.5	2	1.0	1	.5	8	4.1	189	95.9	0	.0	197

(1 INSTITUTIONS)

0	.0	0	.0	0	.0	0	.0	0	.0	0	.0	0	.0	0
0	.0	0	.0	0	.0	0	.0	0	.0	0	.0	0	.0	0
0	.0	0	.0	0	.0	0	.0	0	.0	0	.0	0	.0	0
0	.0	0	.0	0	.0	0	.0	0	.0	0	.0	0	.0	0
0	.0	0	.0	0	.0	0	.0	0	.0	0	.0	0	.0	0
0	.0	0	.0	0	.0	0	.0	0	.0	0	.0	0	.0	0
0	.0	0	.0	0	.0	0	.0	0	.0	0	.0	0	.0	0
0	.0	0	.0	0	.0	0	.0	0	.0	0	.0	0	.0	0
0	.0	0	.0	0	.0	0	.0	0	.0	0	.0	0	.0	0
0	.0	0	.0	0	.0	0	.0	0	.0	0	.0	0	.0	0
0	.0	0	.0	0	.0	0	.0	0	.0	0	.0	0	.0	0
0	.0	0	.0	0	.0	0	.0	0	.0	0	.0	0	.0	0
0	.0	0	.0	0	.0	0	.0	0	.0	0	.0	0	.0	0
0	.0	0	.0	0	.0	0	.0	0	.0	0	.0	0	.0	0
0	.0	9	2.1	1	.2	3	.7	13	3.0	414	96.7	1	.2	428
0	.0	7	3.7	1	.5	1	.5	9	4.8	177	94.7	1	.5	187
0	.0	2	.8	0	.0	2	.8	4	1.7	237	98.3	0	.0	241
0	.0	0	.0	0	.0	0	.0	0	.0	0	.0	0	.0	0
0	.0	0	.0	0	.0	0	.0	0	.0	0	.0	0	.0	0
0	.0	0	.0	0	.0	0	.0	0	.0	0	.0	0	.0	0
0	.0	9	2.1	1	.2	3	.7	13	3.0	414	96.7	1	.2	428
0	.0	7	3.7	1	.5	1	.5	9	4.8	177	94.7	1	.5	187
0	.0	2	.8	0	.0	2	.8	4	1.7	237	98.3	0	.0	241
0	.0	9	2.1	1	.2	3	.7	13	3.0	414	96.7	1	.2	428
0	.0	7	3.7	1	.5	1	.5	9	4.8	177	94.7	1	.5	187
0	.0	2	.8	0	.0	2	.8	4	1.7	237	98.3	0	.0	241
0	.0	0	.0	0	.0	0	.0	0	.0	0	.0	0	.0	0
0	.0	0	.0	0	.0	0	.0	0	.0	0	.0	0	.0	0
0	.0	0	.0	0	.0	0	.0	0	.0	0	.0	0	.0	0
0	.0	9	2.1	1	.2	3	.7	13	3.0	414	96.7	1	.2	428
0	.0	7	3.7	1	.5	1	.5	9	4.8	177	94.7	1	.5	187
0	.0	2	.8	0	.0	2	.8	4	1.7	237	98.3	0	.0	241
0	.0	0	.0	0	.0	0	.0	0	.0	0	.0	0	.0	0
0	.0	0	.0	0	.0	0	.0	0	.0	0	.0	0	.0	0
0	.0	0	.0	0	.0	0	.0	0	.0	0	.0	0	.0	0
0	.0	9	2.1	1	.2	3	.7	13	3.0	414	96.7	1	.2	428
0	.0	7	3.7	1	.5	1	.5	9	4.8	177	94.7	1	.5	187
0	.0	2	.8	0	.0	2	.8	4	1.7	237	98.3	0	.0	241

MAJOR FIELD 1218 - VETERINARY MEDICINE

	AMERICAN INDIAN ALASKAN NATIVE		BLACK NON-HISPANIC		ASIAN OR PACIFIC ISLANDER		HISPANIC		TOTAL MINORITY		WHITE NON-HISPANIC		NON-RESIDENT ALIEN		TO
	NUMBER	%	NUMBER	%	NUMBER	%	NUMBER	%	NUMBER	%	NUMBER	%	NUMBER	%	NU
TENNESSEE	(	1 INSTITUTIONS)													
UNDERGRADUATES:															
FULL-TIME	0	.0	0	.0	0	.0	0	.0	0	.0	0	.0	0	.0	
FEMALE	0	.0	0	.0	0	.0	0	.0	0	.0	0	.0	0	.0	
MALE	0	.0	0	.0	0	.0	0	.0	0	.0	0	.0	0	.0	
PART-TIME	0	.0	0	.0	0	.0	0	.0	0	.0	0	.0	0	.0	
FEMALE	0	.0	0	.0	0	.0	0	.0	0	.0	0	.0	0	.0	
MALE	0	.0	0	.0	0	.0	0	.0	0	.0	0	.0	0	.0	
TOTAL	0	.0	0	.0	0	.0	0	.0	0	.0	0	.0			
FEMALE	0	.0	0	.0	0	.0	0	.0	0	.0	0	.0	0	.0	
MALE	0	.0	0	.0	0	.0	0	.0	0	.0	0	.0	0	.0	
GRADUATE:															
FULL-TIME	0	.0	0	.0	0	.0	0	.0	0	.0	0	.0		.0	
FEMALE	0	.0	0	.0	0	.0	0	.0	0	.0	0	.0		.0	
MALE	0	.0	0	.0	0	.0	0	.0	0	.0	0	.0		.0	
PART-TIME	0	.0	0	.0	0	.0	0	.0	0	.0	0	.0		.0	
FEMALE	0	.0	0	.0	0	.0	0	.0	0	.0	0	.0		.0	
MALE	0	.0	0	.0	0	.0	0	.0	0	.0	0	.0		.0	
TOTAL	0	.0	0	.0	0	.0	0	.0	0	.0	0	.0			
FEMALE	0	.0	0	.0	0	.0	0	.0	0	.0	0	.0		.0	
MALE	0	.0	0	.0	0	.0	0	.0	0	.0	0	.0		.0	
PROFESSIONAL:															
FULL-TIME	0	.0	1	.6	0	.0	2	1.1	3	1.7	176	98.3		.0	
FEMALE	0	.0	1	1.9	0	.0	1	1.9	2	3.8	50	96.2		.0	
MALE	0	.0	0	.0	0	.0	1	.8	1	.8	126	99.2		.0	
PART-TIME	0	.0	0	.0	0	.0	0	.0	0	.0	0	.0		.0	
FEMALE	0	.0	0	.0	0	.0	0	.0	0	.0	0	.0		.0	
MALE	0	.0	0	.0	0	.0	0	.0	0	.0	0	.0		.0	
TOTAL	0	.0	1	.6	0	.0	2	1.1	3	1.7	176	98.3			
FEMALE	0	.0	1	1.9	0	.0	1	1.9	2	3.8	50	96.2		.0	
MALE	0	.0	0	.0	0	.0	1	.8	1	.8	126	99.2		.0	
UND+GRAD+PROF:															
FULL-TIME	0	.0	1	.6	0	.0	2	1.1	3	1.7	176	98.3	0	.0	
FEMALE	0	.0	1	1.9	0	.0	1	1.9	2	3.8	50	96.2	0	.0	
MALE	0	.0	0	.0	0	.0	1	.8	1	.8	126	99.2	0	.0	
PART-TIME	0	.0	0	.0	0	.0	0	.0	0	.0	0	.0	0	.0	
FEMALE	0	.0	0	.0	0	.0	0	.0	0	.0	0	.0	0	.0	
MALE	0	.0	0	.0	0	.0	0	.0	0	.0	0	.0	0	.0	
TOTAL	0	.0	1	.6	0	.0	2	1.1	3	1.7	176	98.3	0	.0	
FEMALE	0	.0	1	1.9	0	.0	1	1.9	2	3.8	50	96.2	0	.0	
MALE	0	.0	0	.0	0	.0	1	.8	1	.8	126	99.2	0	.0	
UNCLASSIFIED:															
TOTAL	0	.0	0	.0	0	.0	0	.0	0	.0	0	.0	0	.0	
FEMALE	0	.0	0	.0	0	.0	0	.0	0	.0	0	.0	0	.0	
MALE	0	.0	0	.0	0	.0	0	.0	0	.0	0	.0	0	.0	
TOTAL ENROLLMENT:															
TOTAL	0	.0	1	.6	0	.0	2	1.1	3	1.7	176	98.3	0	.0	
FEMALE	0	.0	1	1.9	0	.0	1	1.9	2	3.8	50	96.2	0	.0	
MALE	0	.0	0	.0	0	.0	1	.8	1	.8	126	99.2	0	.0	
TEXAS	(	1 INSTITUTIONS)													
UNDERGRADUATES:															
FULL-TIME	0	.0	0	.0	0	.0	0	.0	0	.0	0	.0	0	.0	
FEMALE	0	.0	0	.0	0	.0	0	.0	0	.0	0	.0	0	.0	
MALE	0	.0	0	.0	0	.0	0	.0	0	.0	0	.0	0	.0	
PART-TIME	0	.0	0	.0	0	.0	0	.0	0	.0	0	.0	0	.0	
FEMALE	0	.0	0	.0	0	.0	0	.0	0	.0	0	.0	0	.0	
MALE	0	.0	0	.0	0	.0	0	.0	0	.0	0	.0	0	.0	
TOTAL	0	.0	0	.0	0	.0	0	.0	0	.0	0	.0	0	.0	
FEMALE	0	.0	0	.0	0	.0	0	.0	0	.0	0	.0	0	.0	
MALE	0	.0	0	.0	0	.0	0	.0	0	.0	0	.0	0	.0	
GRADUATE:															
FULL-TIME	0	.0	0	.0	0	.0	0	.0	0	.0	0	.0	0	.0	
FEMALE	0	.0	0	.0	0	.0	0	.0	0	.0	0	.0	0	.0	
MALE	0	.0	0	.0	0	.0	0	.0	0	.0	0	.0	0	.0	
PART-TIME	0	.0	0	.0	0	.0	0	.0	0	.0	0	.0	0	.0	
FEMALE	0	.0	0	.0	0	.0	0	.0	0	.0	0	.0	0	.0	
MALE	0	.0	0	.0	0	.0	0	.0	0	.0	0	.0	0	.0	
TOTAL	0	.0	0	.0	0	.0	0	.0	0	.0	0	.0	0	.0	
FEMALE	0	.0	0	.0	0	.0	0	.0	0	.0	0	.0	0	.0	
MALE	0	.0	0	.0	0	.0	0	.0	0	.0	0	.0	0	.0	
PROFESSIONAL:															
FULL-TIME	7	1.7	1	.2	1	.2	2	.5	11	2.6	406	97.4	0	.0	
FEMALE	1	.7	0	.0	1	.7	0	.0	2	1.3	148	98.7	0	.0	
MALE	6	2.2	1	.4	0	.0	2	.7	9	3.4	258	96.6	0	.0	

VETERINARY MEDICINE

I INDIAN NATIVE	BLACK NON-HISPANIC		ASIAN OR PACIFIC ISLANDER		HISPANIC		TOTAL MINORITY		WHITE NON-HISPANIC		NON-RESIDENT ALIEN		TOTAL
%	NUMBER	%	NUMBER	%	NUMBER	%	NUMBER	%	NUMBER	%	NUMBER	%	NUMBER
CONTINUED													
.0	0	.0	0	.0	0	.0	0	.0	1	100.0	0	.0	1
.0	0	.0	0	.0	0	.0	0	.0	0	.0	0	.0	0
.0	0	.0	0	.0	0	.0	0	.0	1	100.0	0	.0	1
1.7	1	.2	1	.2	2	.5	11	2.6	407	97.4	0	.0	418
.7	0	.0	1	.7	0	.0	2	1.3	148	98.7	0	.0	150
2.2	1	.4	0	.0	2	.7	9	3.4	259	96.6	0	.0	268
1.7	1	.2	1	.2	2	.5	11	2.6	406	97.4	0	.0	417
.7	0	.0	1	.7	0	.0	2	1.3	148	98.7	0	.0	150
2.2	1	.4	0	.0	2	.7	9	3.4	258	96.6	0	.0	267
.0	0	.0	0	.0	0	.0	0	.0	1	100.0	0	.0	1
.0	0	.0	0	.0	0	.0	0	.0	0	.0	0	.0	0
.0	0	.0	0	.0	0	.0	0	.0	1	100.0	0	.0	1
1.7	1	.2	1	.2	2	.5	11	2.6	407	97.4	0	.0	418
.7	0	.0	1	.7	0	.0	2	1.3	148	98.7	0	.0	150
2.2	1	.4	0	.0	2	.7	9	3.4	259	96.6	0	.0	268
.0	0	.0	0	.0	0	.0	0	.0	0	.0	0	.0	0
.0	0	.0	0	.0	0	.0	0	.0	0	.0	0	.0	0
.0	0	.0	0	.0	0	.0	0	.0	0	.0	0	.0	0
1.7	1	.2	1	.2	2	.5	11	2.6	407	97.4	0	.0	418
.7	0	.0	1	.7	0	.0	2	1.3	148	98.7	0	.0	150
2.2	1	.4	0	.0	2	.7	9	3.4	259	96.6	0	.0	268
(1 INSTITUTIONS)													
.0	0	.0	0	.0	0	.0	0	.0	0	.0	0	.0	0
.0	0	.0	0	.0	0	.0	0	.0	0	.0	0	.0	0
.0	0	.0	0	.0	0	.0	0	.0	0	.0	0	.0	0
.0	0	.0	0	.0	0	.0	0	.0	0	.0	0	.0	0
.0	0	.0	0	.0	0	.0	0	.0	0	.0	0	.0	0
.0	0	.0	0	.0	0	.0	0	.0	0	.0	0	.0	0
.0	0	.0	0	.0	0	.0	0	.0	0	.0	0	.0	0
.0	0	.0	0	.0	0	.0	0	.0	0	.0	0	.0	0
.0	0	.0	0	.0	0	.0	0	.0	0	.0	0	.0	0
.0	0	.0	0	.0	0	.0	0	.0	0	.0	0	.0	0
.0	0	.0	0	.0	0	.0	0	.0	0	.0	0	.0	0
.0	0	.0	0	.0	0	.0	0	.0	0	.0	0	.0	0
.0	0	.0	0	.0	0	.0	0	.0	0	.0	0	.0	0
.0	0	.0	0	.0	0	.0	0	.0	0	.0	0	.0	0
.0	0	.0	0	.0	0	.0	0	.0	0	.0	0	.0	0
.0	1	.3	5	1.6	1	.3	7	2.2	311	97.8	0	.0	318
.0	1	1.0	2	1.9	1	1.0	4	3.8	101	96.2	0	.0	105
.0	0	.0	3	1.4	0	.0	3	1.4	210	98.6	0	.0	213
.0	0	.0	0	.0	0	.0	0	.0	0	.0	0	.0	0
.0	0	.0	0	.0	0	.0	0	.0	0	.0	0	.0	0
.0	0	.0	0	.0	0	.0	0	.0	0	.0	0	.0	0
.0	1	.3	5	1.6	1	.3	7	2.2	311	97.8	0	.0	318
.0	1	1.0	2	1.9	1	1.0	4	3.8	101	96.2	0	.0	105
.0	0	.0	3	1.4	0	.0	3	1.4	210	98.6	0	.0	213
.0	1	.3	5	1.6	1	.3	7	2.2	311	97.8	0	.0	318
.0	1	1.0	2	1.9	1	1.0	4	3.8	101	96.2	0	.0	105
.0	0	.0	3	1.4	0	.0	3	1.4	210	98.6	0	.0	213
.0	0	.0	0	.0	0	.0	0	.0	0	.0	0	.0	0
.0	0	.0	0	.0	0	.0	0	.0	0	.0	0	.0	0
.0	0	.0	0	.0	0	.0	0	.0	0	.0	0	.0	0
.0	1	.3	5	1.6	1	.3	7	2.2	311	97.8	0	.0	318
.0	1	1.0	2	1.9	1	1.0	4	3.8	101	96.2	0	.0	105
.0	0	.0	3	1.4	0	.0	3	1.4	210	98.6	0	.0	213
.0	0	.0	0	.0	0	.0	0	.0	0	.0	0	.0	0
.0	0	.0	0	.0	0	.0	0	.0	0	.0	0	.0	0
.0	0	.0	0	.0	0	.0	0	.0	0	.0	0	.0	0
.0	1	.3	5	1.6	1	.3	7	2.2	311	97.8	0	.0	318
.0	1	1.0	2	1.9	1	1.0	4	3.8	101	96.2	0	.0	105
.0	0	.0	3	1.4	0	.0	3	1.4	210	98.6	0	.0	213

MAJOR FIELD 1218 - VETERINARY MEDICINE

	AMERICAN INDIAN ALASKAN NATIVE		BLACK NON-HISPANIC		ASIAN OR PACIFIC ISLANDER		HISPANIC		TOTAL MINORITY		WHITE NON-HISPANIC		NON-RESIDENT ALIEN	
	NUMBER	%	NUMBER	%	NUMBER	%	NUMBER	%	NUMBER	%	NUMBER	%	NUMBER	%
THE STATES AND D.C. (22 INSTITUTIONS)														
UNDERGRADUATES:														
FULL-TIME	0	.0	0	.0	0	.0	0	.0	0	.0	0	.0	0	.0
FEMALE	0	.0	0	.0	0	.0	0	.0	0	.0	0	.0	0	.0
MALE	0	.0	0	.0	0	.0	0	.0	0	.0	0	.0	0	.0
PART-TIME	0	.0	0	.0	0	.0	0	.0	0	.0	0	.0	0	.0
FEMALE	0	.0	0	.0	0	.0	0	.0	0	.0	0	.0	0	.0
MALE	0	.0	0	.0	0	.0	0	.0	0	.0	0	.0	0	.0
TOTAL	0	.0	0	.0	0	.0	0	.0	0	.0	0	.0	0	.0
FEMALE	0	.0	0	.0	0	.0	0	.0	0	.0	0	.0	0	.0
MALE	0	.0	0	.0	0	.0	0	.0	0	.0	0	.0	0	.0
GRADUATE:														
FULL-TIME	0	.0	0	.0	0	.0	0	.0	0	.0	0	.0	0	.0
FEMALE	0	.0	0	.0	0	.0	0	.0	0	.0	0	.0	0	.0
MALE	0	.0	0	.0	0	.0	0	.0	0	.0	0	.0	0	.0
PART-TIME	0	.0	0	.0	0	.0	0	.0	0	.0	0	.0	0	.0
FEMALE	0	.0	0	.0	0	.0	0	.0	0	.0	0	.0	0	.0
MALE	0	.0	0	.0	0	.0	0	.0	0	.0	0	.0	0	.0
TOTAL	0	.0	0	.0	0	.0	0	.0	0	.0	0	.0	0	.0
FEMALE	0	.0	0	.0	0	.0	0	.0	0	.0	0	.0	0	.0
MALE	0	.0	0	.0	0	.0	0	.0	0	.0	0	.0	0	.0
PROFESSIONAL:														
FULL-TIME	27	.4	146	2.0	60	.8	38	.5	271	3.8	6,831	95.9	23	.3
FEMALE	6	.2	77	3.2	26	1.1	11	.5	120	5.0	2,284	94.9	4	.2
MALE	21	.4	69	1.5	34	.7	27	.6	151	3.2	4,547	96.4	19	.4
PART-TIME	0	.0	1	1.6	0	.0	1	1.6	2	3.3	59	96.7	0	.0
FEMALE	0	.0	0	.0	0	.0	0	.0	0	.0	16	100.0	0	.0
MALE	0	.0	1	2.2	0	.0	1	2.2	2	4.4	43	95.6	0	.0
TOTAL	27	.4	147	2.0	60	.8	39	.5	273	3.8	6,890	95.9	23	.3
FEMALE	6	.2	77	3.2	26	1.1	11	.5	120	5.0	2,300	94.9	4	.2
MALE	21	.4	70	1.5	34	.7	28	.6	153	3.2	4,590	96.4	19	.4
UND+GRAD+PROF:														
FULL-TIME	27	.4	146	2.0	60	.8	38	.5	271	3.8	6,831	95.9	23	.3
FEMALE	6	.2	77	3.2	26	1.1	11	.5	120	5.0	2,284	94.9	4	.2
MALE	21	.4	69	1.5	34	.7	27	.6	151	3.2	4,547	96.4	19	.4
PART-TIME	0	.0	1	1.6	0	.0	1	1.6	2	3.3	59	96.7	0	.0
FEMALE	0	.0	0	.0	0	.0	0	.0	0	.0	16	100.0	0	.0
MALE	0	.0	1	2.2	0	.0	1	2.2	2	4.4	43	95.6	0	.0
TOTAL	27	.4	147	2.0	60	.8	39	.5	273	3.8	6,890	95.9	23	.3
FEMALE	6	.2	77	3.2	26	1.1	11	.5	120	5.0	2,300	94.9	4	.2
MALE	21	.4	70	1.5	34	.7	28	.6	153	3.2	4,590	96.4	19	.4
UNCLASSIFIED:														
TOTAL	0	.0	0	.0	0	.0	0	.0	0	.0	0	.0	0	.0
FEMALE	0	.0	0	.0	0	.0	0	.0	0	.0	0	.0	0	.0
MALE	0	.0	0	.0	0	.0	0	.0	0	.0	0	.0	0	.0
TOTAL ENROLLMENT:														
TOTAL	27	.4	147	2.0	60	.8	39	.5	273	3.8	6,890	95.9	23	.3
FEMALE	6	.2	77	3.2	26	1.1	11	.5	120	5.0	2,300	94.9	4	.2
MALE	21	.4	70	1.5	34	.7	28	.6	153	3.2	4,590	96.4	19	.4
MAJOR FIELD AGGREGATE 1218 (22 INSTITUTIONS)														
UNDERGRADUATES:														
FULL-TIME	0	.0	0	.0	0	.0	0	.0	0	.0	0	.0	0	.0
FEMALE	0	.0	0	.0	0	.0	0	.0	0	.0	0	.0	0	.0
MALE	0	.0	0	.0	0	.0	0	.0	0	.0	0	.0	0	.0
PART-TIME	0	.0	0	.0	0	.0	0	.0	0	.0	0	.0	0	.0
FEMALE	0	.0	0	.0	0	.0	0	.0	0	.0	0	.0	0	.0
MALE	0	.0	0	.0	0	.0	0	.0	0	.0	0	.0	0	.0
TOTAL	0	.0	0	.0	0	.0	0	.0	0	.0	0	.0	0	.0
FEMALE	0	.0	0	.0	0	.0	0	.0	0	.0	0	.0	0	.0
MALE	0	.0	0	.0	0	.0	0	.0	0	.0	0	.0	0	.0
GRADUATE:														
FULL-TIME	0	.0	0	.0	0	.0	0	.0	0	.0	0	.0	0	.0
FEMALE	0	.0	0	.0	0	.0	0	.0	0	.0	0	.0	0	.0
MALE	0	.0	0	.0	0	.0	0	.0	0	.0	0	.0	0	.0
PART-TIME	0	.0	0	.0	0	.0	0	.0	0	.0	0	.0	0	.0
FEMALE	0	.0	0	.0	0	.0	0	.0	0	.0	0	.0	0	.0
MALE	0	.0	0	.0	0	.0	0	.0	0	.0	0	.0	0	.0
TOTAL	0	.0	0	.0	0	.0	0	.0	0	.0	0	.0	0	.0
FEMALE	0	.0	0	.0	0	.0	0	.0	0	.0	0	.0	0	.0
MALE	0	.0	0	.0	0	.0	0	.0	0	.0	0	.0	0	.0
PROFESSIONAL:														
FULL-TIME	27	.4	146	2.0	60	.8	38	.5	271	3.8	6,831	95.9	23	.3
FEMALE	6	.2	77	3.2	26	1.1	11	.5	120	5.0	2,284	94.9	4	.2
MALE	21	.4	69	1.5	34	.7	27	.6	151	3.2	4,547	96.4	19	.4

VETERINARY MEDICINE

INDIAN NATIVE	BLACK NON-HISPANIC		ASIAN OR PACIFIC ISLANDER		HISPANIC		TOTAL MINORITY		WHITE NON-HISPANIC		NON-RESIDENT ALIEN		TOTAL
%	NUMBER	%	NUMBER	%	NUMBER	%	NUMBER	%	NUMBER	%	NUMBER	%	NUMBER

E I2IB CONTINUED

%	NUMBER	%	NUMBER	%	NUMBER	%	NUMBER	%	NUMBER	%	NUMBER	%	NUMBER
.0	1	1.6	0	.0	1	1.6	2	3.3	59	96.7	0	.0	61
.0	0	.0	0	.0	0	.0	0	.0	16	100.0	0	.0	16
.0	1	2.2	0	.0	1	2.2	2	4.4	43	95.6	0	.0	45
.4	147	2.0	60	.8	39	.5	273	3.8	6,890	95.9	23	.3	7,186
.2	77	3.2	26	1.1	11	.5	120	5.0	2,300	94.9	4	.2	2,424
.4	70	1.5	34	.7	28	.6	153	3.2	4,590	96.4	19	.4	4,762
.4	146	2.0	60	.8	38	.5	271	3.8	6,831	95.9	23	.3	7,125
.2	77	3.2	26	1.1	11	.5	120	5.0	2,284	94.9	4	.2	2,408
.4	69	1.5	34	.7	27	.6	151	3.2	4,547	96.4	19	.4	4,717
.0	1	1.6	0	.0	1	1.6	2	3.3	59	96.7	0	.0	61
.0	0	.0	0	.0	0	.0	0	.0	16	100.0	0	.0	16
.0	1	2.2	0	.0	1	2.2	2	4.4	43	95.6	0	.0	45
.4	147	2.0	60	.8	39	.5	273	3.8	6,890	95.9	23	.3	7,186
.2	77	3.2	26	1.1	11	.5	120	5.0	2,300	94.9	4	.2	2,424
.4	70	1.5	34	.7	28	.6	153	3.2	4,590	96.4	19	.4	4,762
.0	0	.0	0	.0	0	.0	0	.0	0	.0	0	.0	0
.0	0	.0	0	.0	0	.0	0	.0	0	.0	0	.0	0
.0	0	.0	0	.0	0	.0	0	.0	0	.0	0	.0	0
.4	147	2.0	60	.8	39	.5	273	3.8	6,890	95.9	23	.3	7,186
.2	77	3.2	26	1.1	11	.5	120	5.0	2,300	94.9	4	.2	2,424
.4	70	1.5	34	.7	28	.6	153	3.2	4,590	96.4	19	.4	4,762

TABLE 17 - TOTAL ENROLLMENT IN INSTITUTIONS OF HIGHER EDUCATION FOR SELECTED MAJOR FIELDS OF STUDY AND LEVEL OF ENROLLMENT
BY RACE, ETHNICITY, AND SEX: STATE, 1978

MAJOR FIELD 1400 - LAW

	AMERICAN INDIAN ALASKAN NATIVE		BLACK NON-HISPANIC		ASIAN OR PACIFIC ISLANDER		HISPANIC		TOTAL MINORITY		WHITE NON-HISPANIC		NON-RESIDENT ALIEN		TOT
	NUMBER	%	NUMBER	%	NUMBER	%	NUMBER	%	NUMBER	%	NUMBER	%	NUMBER	%	NUM
ALABAMA	(	2 INSTITUTIONS)													
UNDERGRADUATES:															
FULL-TIME	0	.0	0	.0	0	.0	0	.0	0	.0	0	.0	0	.0	
FEMALE	0	.0	0	.0	0	.0	0	.0	0	.0	0	.0	0	.0	
MALE	0	.0	0	.0	0	.0	0	.0	0	.0	0	.0	0	.0	
PART-TIME	0	.0	0	.0	0	.0	0	.0	0	.0	0	.0	0	.0	
FEMALE	0	.0	0	.0	0	.0	0	.0	0	.0	0	.0	0	.0	
MALE	0	.0	0	.0	0	.0	0	.0	0	.0	0	.0	0	.0	
TOTAL	0	.0	0	.0	0	.0	0	.0	0	.0	0	.0	0	.0	
FEMALE	0	.0	0	.0	0	.0	0	.0	0	.0	0	.0	0	.0	
MALE	0	.0	0	.0	0	.0	0	.0	0	.0	0	.0	0	.0	
GRADUATE:															
FULL-TIME	0	.0	0	.0	0	.0	0	.0	0	.0	0	.0	0	.0	
FEMALE	0	.0	0	.0	0	.0	0	.0	0	.0	0	.0	0	.0	
MALE	0	.0	0	.0	0	.0	0	.0	0	.0	0	.0	0	.0	
PART-TIME	0	.0	0	.0	0	.0	0	.0	0	.0	0	.0	0	.0	
FEMALE	0	.0	0	.0	0	.0	0	.0	0	.0	0	.0	0	.0	
MALE	0	.0	0	.0	0	.0	0	.0	0	.0	0	.0	0	.0	
TOTAL	0	.0	0	.0	0	.0	0	.0	0	.0	0	.0	0	.0	
FEMALE	0	.0	0	.0	0	.0	0	.0	0	.0	0	.0	0	.0	
MALE	0	.0	0	.0	0	.0	0	.0	0	.0	0	.0	0	.0	
PROFESSIONAL:															
FULL-TIME	0	.0	24	1.9	0	.0	3	.2	27	2.1	1,240	97.6	3	.2	1,
FEMALE	0	.0	9	3.7	0	.0	1	.4	10	4.1	230	95.0	2	.8	
MALE	0	.0	15	1.5	0	.0	2	.2	17	1.7	1,010	98.2	1	.1	1,
PART-TIME	0	.0	0	.0	0	.0	0	.0	0	.0	43	100.0	0	.0	
FEMALE	0	.0	0	.0	0	.0	0	.0	0	.0	2	100.0	0	.0	
MALE	0	.0	0	.0	0	.0	0	.0	0	.0	41	100.0	0	.0	
TOTAL	0	.0	24	1.8	0	.0	3	.2	27	2.1	1,283	97.7	3	.2	1,
FEMALE	0	.0	9	3.7	0	.0	1	.4	10	4.1	232	95.1	2	.8	1,
MALE	0	.0	15	1.4	0	.0	2	.2	17	1.6	1,051	98.3	1	.1	1,
UNC+GRAD+PROF:															
FULL-TIME	0	.0	24	1.9	0	.0	3	.2	27	2.1	1,240	97.6	3	.2	1,
FEMALE	0	.0	9	3.7	0	.0	1	.4	10	4.1	230	95.0	2	.8	
MALE	0	.0	15	1.5	0	.0	2	.2	17	1.7	1,010	98.2	1	.1	1,
PART-TIME	0	.0	0	.0	0	.0	0	.0	0	.0	43	100.0	0	.0	
FEMALE	0	.0	0	.0	0	.0	0	.0	0	.0	2	100.0	0	.0	
MALE	0	.0	0	.0	0	.0	0	.0	0	.0	41	100.0	0	.0	
TOTAL	0	.0	24	1.8	0	.0	3	.2	27	2.1	1,283	97.7	3	.2	1,
FEMALE	0	.0	9	3.7	0	.0	1	.4	10	4.1	232	95.1	2	.8	1,
MALE	0	.0	15	1.4	0	.0	2	.2	17	1.6	1,051	98.3	1	.1	1,
UNCLASSIFIED:															
TOTAL	0	.0	0	.0	0	.0	0	.0	0	.0	0	.0		.0	
FEMALE	0	.0	0	.0	0	.0	0	.0	0	.0	0	.0	0	.0	
MALE	0	.0	0	.0	0	.0	0	.0	0	.0	0	.0	0	.0	
TOTAL ENROLLMENT:															
TOTAL	0	.0	24	1.8	0	.0	3	.2	27	2.1	1,283	97.7	3	.2	1,
FEMALE	0	.0	9	3.7	0	.0	1	.4	10	4.1	232	95.1	2	.8	1,
MALE	0	.0	15	1.4	0	.0	2	.2	17	1.6	1,051	98.3	1	.1	1,
ARIZONA		2 INSTITUTIONS)													
UNDERGRADUATES:															
FULL-TIME	0	.0	0	.0	0	.0	0	.0	0	.0	0	.0	0	.0	
FEMALE	0	.0	0	.0	0	.0	0	.0	0	.0	0	.0	0	.0	
MALE	0	.0	0	.0	0	.0	0	.0	0	.0	0	.0	0	.0	
PART-TIME	0	.0	0	.0	0	.0	0	.0	0	.0	0	.0	0	.0	
FEMALE	0	.0	0	.0	0	.0	0	.0	0	.0	0	.0	0	.0	
MALE	0	.0	0	.0	0	.0	0	.0	0	.0	0	.0	0	.0	
TOTAL	0	.0	0	.0	0	.0	0	.0	0	.0	0	.0	0	.0	
FEMALE	0	.0	0	.0	0	.0	0	.0	0	.0	0	.0	0	.0	
MALE	0	.0	0	.0	0	.0	0	.0	0	.0	0	.0	0	.0	
GRADUATE:															
FULL-TIME	0	.0	0	.0	0	.0	0	.0	0	.0	0	.0	0	.0	
FEMALE	0	.0	0	.0	0	.0	0	.0	0	.0	0	.0	0	.0	
MALE	0	.0	0	.0	0	.0	0	.0	0	.0	0	.0	0	.0	
PART-TIME	0	.0	0	.0	0	.0	0	.0	0	.0	0	.0	0	.0	
FEMALE	0	.0	0	.0	0	.0	0	.0	0	.0	0	.0	0	.0	
MALE	0	.0	0	.0	0	.0	0	.0	0	.0	0	.0	0	.0	
TOTAL	0	.0	0	.0	0	.0	0	.0	0	.0	0	.0	0	.0	
FEMALE	0	.0	0	.0	0	.0	0	.0	0	.0	0	.0	0	.0	
MALE	0	.0	0	.0	0	.0	0	.0	0	.0	0	.0	0	.0	
PROFESSIONAL:															
FULL-TIME	3	.4	1	.1	2	.2	18	2.1	24	2.8	821	96.8	3	.4	
FEMALE	1	.4	0	.0	1	.4	6	2.1	8	2.8	276	97.2	0	.0	
MALE	2	.4	1	.2	1	.2	12	2.1	16	2.8	545	96.6	3	.5	

LAW

INDIAN NATIVE	BLACK NON-HISPANIC		ASIAN OR PACIFIC ISLANDER		HISPANIC		TOTAL MINORITY		WHITE NON-HISPANIC		NON-RESIDENT ALIEN		TOTAL
%	NUMBER	%	NUMBER	%	NUMBER	%	NUMBER	%	NUMBER	%	NUMBER	%	NUMBER
CONTINUED													
.0	0	.0	1	9.1	0	.0	1	9.1	10	90.9	0	.0	11
.0	0	.0	1	20.0	0	.0	1	20.0	4	80.0	0	.0	5
.0	0	.0	0	.0	0	.0	0	.0	6	100.0	0	.0	6
.3	1	.1	3	.3	18	2.1	25	2.9	831	96.7	3	.3	859
.3	0	.0	2	.7	6	2.1	9	3.1	280	96.9	0	.0	289
.4	1	.2	1	.2	12	2.1	16	2.8	551	96.7	3	.5	570
.4	1	.1	2	.2	18	2.1	24	2.8	821	96.8	3	.4	848
.4	0	.0	1	.4	6	2.1	8	2.8	276	97.2	0	.0	284
.4	1	.2	1	.2	12	2.1	16	2.8	545	96.6	3	.5	564
.0	0	.0	1	9.1	0	.0	1	9.1	10	90.9	0	.0	11
.0	0	.0	1	20.0	0	.0	1	20.0	4	80.0	0	.0	5
.0	0	.0	0	.0	0	.0	0	.0	6	100.0	0	.0	6
.3	1	.1	3	.3	18	2.1	25	2.9	831	96.7	3	.3	859
.3	0	.0	2	.7	6	2.1	9	3.1	280	96.9	0	.0	289
.4	1	.2	1	.2	12	2.1	16	2.8	551	96.7	3	.5	570
.0	0	.0	0	.0	0	.0	0	.0	0	.0	0	.0	0
.0	0	.0	0	.0	0	.0	0	.0	0	.0	0	.0	0
.0	0	.0	0	.0	0	.0	0	.0	0	.0	0	.0	0
.3	1	.1	3	.3	18	2.1	25	2.9	831	96.7	3	.3	859
.3	0	.0	2	.7	6	2.1	9	3.1	280	96.9	0	.0	289
.4	1	.2	1	.2	12	2.1	16	2.8	551	96.7	3	.5	570
(2 INSTITUTIONS)													
.0	0	.0	0	.0	0	.0	0	.0	0	.0	0	.0	0
.0	0	.0	0	.0	0	.0	0	.0	0	.0	0	.0	0
.0	0	.0	0	.0	0	.0	0	.0	0	.0	0	.0	0
.0	0	.0	0	.0	0	.0	0	.0	0	.0	0	.0	0
.0	0	.0	0	.0	0	.0	0	.0	0	.0	0	.0	0
.0	0	.0	0	.0	0	.0	0	.0	0	.0	0	.0	0
.0	0	.0	0	.0	0	.0	0	.0	0	.0	0	.0	0
.0	0	.0	0	.0	0	.0	0	.0	0	.0	0	.0	0
.0	0	.0	0	.0	0	.0	0	.0	0	.0	0	.0	0
.0	0	.0	0	.0	0	.0	0	.0	0	.0	0	.0	0
.0	0	.0	0	.0	0	.0	0	.0	0	.0	0	.0	0
.0	0	.0	0	.0	0	.0	0	.0	0	.0	0	.0	0
.0	0	.0	0	.0	0	.0	0	.0	0	.0	0	.0	0
.0	0	.0	0	.0	0	.0	0	.0	0	.0	0	.0	0
.0	0	.0	0	.0	0	.0	0	.0	0	.0	0	.0	0
.0	0	.0	0	.0	0	.0	0	.0	0	.0	0	.0	0
.0	0	.0	0	.0	0	.0	0	.0	0	.0	0	.0	0
.0	0	.0	0	.0	0	.0	0	.0	0	.0	0	.0	0
.4	24	3.5	2	.3	3	.4	32	4.7	646	95.3	0	.0	678
.0	6	4.1	0	.0	1	.7	7	4.8	140	95.2	0	.0	147
.6	18	3.4	2	.4	2	.4	25	4.7	506	95.3	0	.0	531
.6	10	5.5	1	.6	1	.6	12	6.6	169	93.4	0	.0	181
.0	4	7.4	1	1.9	0	.0	5	9.3	49	90.7	0	.0	54
.0	6	4.7	0	.0	1	.8	7	5.5	120	94.5	0	.0	127
.3	34	4.0	3	.3	4	.5	44	5.1	815	94.9	0	.0	859
.0	10	5.0	1	.5	1	.5	12	6.0	189	94.0	0	.0	201
.5	24	3.6	2	.3	3	.5	32	4.9	626	95.1	0	.0	658
.4	24	3.5	2	.3	3	.4	32	4.7	646	95.3	0	.0	678
.0	6	4.1	0	.0	1	.7	7	4.8	140	95.2	0	.0	147
.6	18	3.4	2	.4	2	.4	25	4.7	506	95.3	0	.0	531
.0	10	5.5	1	.6	1	.6	12	6.6	169	93.4	0	.0	181
.0	4	7.4	1	1.9	0	.0	5	9.3	49	90.7	0	.0	54
.0	6	4.7	0	.0	1	.8	7	5.5	120	94.5	0	.0	127
.3	34	4.0	3	.3	4	.5	44	5.1	815	94.9	0	.0	859
.0	10	5.0	1	.5	1	.5	12	6.0	189	94.0	0	.0	201
.5	24	3.6	2	.3	3	.5	32	4.9	626	95.1	0	.0	658
.0	0	.0	0	.0	0	.0	0	.0	0	.0	0	.0	0
.0	0	.0	0	.0	0	.0	0	.0	0	.0	0	.0	0
.0	0	.0	0	.0	0	.0	0	.0	0	.0	0	.0	0
.3	34	4.0	3	.3	4	.5	44	5.1	815	94.9	0	.0	859
.0	10	5.0	1	.5	1	.5	12	6.0	189	94.0	0	.0	201
.5	24	3.6	2	.3	3	.5	32	4.9	626	95.1	0	.0	658

TABLE 17 - TOTAL ENROLLMENT IN INSTITUTIONS OF HIGHER EDUCATION FOR SELECTED MAJOR FIELDS OF STUDY AND LEVEL OF ENROLLMENT
           BY RACE, ETHNICITY, AND SEX: STATE, 1978

MAJOR FIELD 1400 - LAW

	AMERICAN INDIAN ALASKAN NATIVE		BLACK NON-HISPANIC		ASIAN OR PACIFIC ISLANDER		HISPANIC		TOTAL MINORITY		WHITE NON-HISPANIC		NON-RESIDENT ALIEN	
	NUMBER	%	NUMBER	%	NUMBER	%	NUMBER	%	NUMBER	%	NUMBER	%	NUMBER	%
CALIFORNIA (27 INSTITUTIONS)														
UNDERGRADUATES:														
FULL-TIME	0	.0	0	.0	0	.0	0	.0	0	.0	0	.0	0	.0
FEMALE	0	.0	0	.0	0	.0	0	.0	0	.0	0	.0	0	.0
MALE	0	.0	0	.0	0	.0	0	.0	0	.0	0	.0	0	.0
PART-TIME	0	.0	0	.0	0	.0	0	.0	0	.0	0	.0	0	.0
FEMALE	0	.0	0	.0	0	.0	0	.0	0	.0	0	.0	0	.0
MALE	0	.0	0	.0	0	.0	0	.0	0	.0	0	.0	0	.0
TOTAL	0	.0	0	.0	0	.0	0	.0	0	.0	0	.0	0	.0
FEMALE	0	.0	0	.0	0	.0	0	.0	0	.0	0	.0	0	.0
MALE	0	.0	0	.0	0	.0	0	.0	0	.0	0	.0	0	.0
GRADUATE:														
FULL-TIME	0	.0	0	.0	0	.0	0	.0	0	.0	0	.0	0	.0
FEMALE	0	.0	0	.0	0	.0	0	.0	0	.0	0	.0	0	.0
MALE	0	.0	0	.0	0	.0	0	.0	0	.0	0	.0	0	.0
PART-TIME	0	.0	0	.0	0	.0	0	.0	0	.0	0	.0	0	.0
FEMALE	0	.0	0	.0	0	.0	0	.0	0	.0	0	.0	0	.0
MALE	0	.0	0	.0	0	.0	0	.0	0	.0	0	.0	0	.0
TOTAL	0	.0	0	.0	0	.0	0	.0	0	.0	0	.0	0	.0
FEMALE	0	.0	0	.0	0	.0	0	.0	0	.0	0	.0	0	.0
MALE	0	.0	0	.0	0	.0	0	.0	0	.0	0	.0	0	.0
PROFESSIONAL:														
FULL-TIME	74	.5	538	3.8	558	3.9	642	4.5	1,812	12.7	12,345	86.5	119	.8
FEMALE	25	.6	248	5.5	213	4.8	200	4.5	686	15.3	3,757	83.9	33	.7
MALE	49	.5	290	3.0	345	3.5	442	4.5	1,126	11.5	8,588	87.6	86	.9
PART-TIME	35	.7	258	5.2	118	2.4	201	4.0	612	12.2	4,366	87.3	22	.4
FEMALE	12	.7	96	5.9	36	2.2	56	3.4	200	12.3	1,428	87.5	4	.2
MALE	23	.7	162	4.8	82	2.4	145	4.3	412	12.2	2,938	87.2	18	.5
TOTAL	109	.6	796	4.1	676	3.5	843	4.4	2,424	12.6	16,711	86.7	141	.7
FEMALE	37	.6	344	5.6	249	4.1	256	4.2	886	14.5	5,185	84.9	37	.6
MALE	72	.5	452	3.4	427	3.2	587	4.5	1,538	11.7	11,526	87.5	104	.8
UND+GRAD+PROF:														
FULL-TIME	74	.5	538	3.8	558	3.9	642	4.5	1,812	12.7	12,345	86.5	119	.8
FEMALE	25	.6	248	5.5	213	4.8	200	4.5	686	15.3	3,757	83.9	33	.7
MALE	49	.5	290	3.0	345	3.5	442	4.5	1,126	11.5	8,588	87.6	86	.9
PART-TIME	35	.7	258	5.2	118	2.4	201	4.0	612	12.2	4,366	87.3	22	.4
FEMALE	12	.7	96	5.9	36	2.2	56	3.4	200	12.3	1,428	87.5	4	.2
MALE	23	.7	162	4.8	82	2.4	145	4.3	412	12.2	2,938	87.2	18	.5
TOTAL	109	.6	796	4.1	676	3.5	843	4.4	2,424	12.6	16,711	86.7	141	.7
FEMALE	37	.6	344	5.6	249	4.1	256	4.2	886	14.5	5,185	84.9	37	.6
MALE	72	.5	452	3.4	427	3.2	587	4.5	1,538	11.7	11,526	87.5	104	.8
UNCLASSIFIED:														
TOTAL	0	.0	0	.0	0	.0	0	.0	0	.0	0	.0	0	.0
FEMALE	0	.0	0	.0	0	.0	0	.0	0	.0	0	.0	0	.0
MALE	0	.0	0	.0	0	.0	0	.0	0	.0	0	.0	0	.0
TOTAL ENROLLMENT:														
TOTAL	109	.6	796	4.1	676	3.5	843	4.4	2,424	12.6	16,711	86.7	141	.7
FEMALE	37	.6	344	5.6	249	4.1	256	4.2	886	14.5	5,185	84.9	37	.6
MALE	72	.5	452	3.4	427	3.2	587	4.5	1,538	11.7	11,526	87.5	104	.8
COLORADO (3 INSTITUTIONS)														
UNDERGRADUATES:														
FULL-TIME	0	.0	0	.0	0	.0	0	.0	0	.0	0	.0	0	.0
FEMALE	0	.0	0	.0	0	.0	0	.0	0	.0	0	.0	0	.0
MALE	0	.0	0	.0	0	.0	0	.0	0	.0	0	.0	0	.0
PART-TIME	0	.0	0	.0	0	.0	0	.0	0	.0	0	.0	0	.0
FEMALE	0	.0	0	.0	0	.0	0	.0	0	.0	0	.0	0	.0
MALE	0	.0	0	.0	0	.0	0	.0	0	.0	0	.0	0	.0
TOTAL	0	.0	0	.0	0	.0	0	.0	0	.0	0	.0	0	.0
FEMALE	0	.0	0	.0	0	.0	0	.0	0	.0	0	.0	0	.0
MALE	0	.0	0	.0	0	.0	0	.0	0	.0	0	.0	0	.0
GRADUATE:														
FULL-TIME	0	.0	0	.0	0	.0	0	.0	0	.0	0	.0	0	.0
FEMALE	0	.0	0	.0	0	.0	0	.0	0	.0	0	.0	0	.0
MALE	0	.0	0	.0	0	.0	0	.0	0	.0	0	.0	0	.0
PART-TIME	0	.0	0	.0	0	.0	0	.0	0	.0	0	.0	0	.0
FEMALE	0	.0	0	.0	0	.0	0	.0	0	.0	0	.0	0	.0
MALE	0	.0	0	.0	0	.0	0	.0	0	.0	0	.0	0	.0
TOTAL	0	.0	0	.0	0	.0	0	.0	0	.0	0	.0	0	.0
FEMALE	0	.0	0	.0	0	.0	0	.0	0	.0	0	.0	0	.0
MALE	0	.0	0	.0	0	.0	0	.0	0	.0	0	.0	0	.0
PROFESSIONAL:														
FULL-TIME	10	1.0	14	1.4	3	.3	42	4.3	69	7.0	916	92.8	2	.2
FEMALE	4	1.1	4	1.1	2	.5	11	3.0	21	5.8	343	94.2	0	.0
MALE	6	1.0	10	1.6	1	.2	31	5.0	48	7.7	573	92.0	2	.3

552

ROLLMENT IN INSTITUTIONS OF HIGHER EDUCATION FOR SELECTED MAJOR FIELDS OF STUDY AND LEVEL OF ENROLLMENT ETHNICITY, AND SEX: STATE, 1978

LAW

INDIAN NATIVE	BLACK NON-HISPANIC		ASIAN OR PACIFIC ISLANDER		HISPANIC		TOTAL MINORITY		WHITE NON-HISPANIC		NON-RESIDENT ALIEN		TUTAL
%	NUMBER	%	NUMBER	%	NUMBER	%	NUMBER	%	NUMBER	%	NUMBER	%	NUMBER
CONTINUED													
1.4	17	4.9	1	.3	12	3.4	35	10.1	312	89.7	1	.3	348
.0	5	3.7	0	.0	3	2.2	8	5.9	127	93.4	1	.7	136
2.4	12	5.7	1	.5	9	4.2	27	12.7	185	87.3	0	.0	212
1.1	31	2.3	4	.3	54	4.0	104	7.8	1,228	92.0	3	.2	1,335
.8	9	1.8	2	.4	14	2.8	29	5.8	470	94.0	1	.2	500
1.3	22	2.6	2	.2	40	4.8	75	9.0	758	90.8	2	.2	835
1.0	14	1.4	3	.3	42	4.3	69	7.0	916	92.8	2	.2	987
1.1	4	1.1	2	.5	11	3.0	21	5.8	343	94.2	0	.0	364
1.0	10	1.6	1	.2	31	5.0	48	7.7	573	92.0	2	.3	623
1.4	17	4.9	1	.3	12	3.4	35	10.1	312	89.7	1	.3	348
.0	5	3.7	0	.0	3	2.2	8	5.9	127	93.4	1	.7	136
2.4	12	5.7	1	.5	9	4.2	27	12.7	185	87.3	0	.0	212
1.1	31	2.3	4	.3	54	4.0	104	7.8	1,228	92.0	3	.2	1,335
.8	9	1.8	2	.4	14	2.8	29	5.8	470	94.0	1	.2	500
1.3	22	2.6	2	.2	40	4.8	75	9.0	758	90.8	2	.2	835
.0	0	.0	0	.0	0	.0	0	.0	0	.0	0	.0	0
.0	0	.0	0	.0	0	.0	0	.0	0	.0	0	.0	0
.0	0	.0	0	.0	0	.0	0	.0	0	.0	0	.0	0
1.1	31	2.3	4	.3	54	4.0	104	7.8	1,228	92.0	3	.2	1,335
.8	9	1.8	2	.4	14	2.8	29	5.8	470	94.0	1	.2	500
1.3	22	2.6	2	.2	40	4.8	75	9.0	758	90.8	2	.2	835
(3 INSTITUTIONS)													
.0	0	.0	0	.0	0	.0	0	.0	0	.0	0	.0	0
.0	0	.0	0	.0	0	.0	0	.0	0	.0	0	.0	0
.0	0	.0	0	.0	0	.0	0	.0	0	.0	0	.0	0
.0	0	.0	0	.0	0	.0	0	.0	0	.0	0	.0	0
.0	0	.0	0	.0	0	.0	0	.0	0	.0	0	.0	0
.0	0	.0	0	.0	0	.0	0	.0	0	.0	0	.0	0
.0	0	.0	0	.0	0	.0	0	.0	0	.0	0	.0	0
.0	0	.0	0	.0	0	.0	0	.0	0	.0	0	.0	0
.0	0	.0	0	.0	0	.0	0	.0	0	.0	0	.0	0
.0	0	.0	0	.0	0	.0	0	.0	0	.0	0	.0	0
.0	0	.0	0	.0	0	.0	0	.0	0	.0	0	.0	0
.0	0	.0	0	.0	0	.0	0	.0	0	.0	0	.0	0
.0	0	.0	0	.0	0	.0	0	.0	0	.0	0	.0	0
.0	0	.0	0	.0	0	.0	0	.0	0	.0	0	.0	0
.2	44	3.7	5	.4	39	3.3	90	7.6	1,083	91.5	10	.8	1,183
.5	25	6.8	2	.5	15	4.1	44	12.0	320	87.4	2	.5	366
.0	19	2.3	3	.4	24	2.9	46	5.6	763	93.4	8	1.0	817
.0	9	2.1	1	.2	4	1.0	14	3.3	404	96.4	1	.2	419
.0	3	2.5	0	.0	0	.0	3	2.5	117	96.7	1	.8	121
.0	6	2.0	1	.3	4	1.3	11	3.7	287	96.3	0	.0	298
.1	53	3.3	6	.4	43	2.7	104	6.5	1,487	92.8	11	.7	1,602
.4	28	5.7	2	.4	15	3.1	47	9.7	437	89.7	3	.6	487
.0	25	2.2	4	.4	28	2.5	57	5.1	1,050	94.2	8	.7	1,115
.2	44	3.7	5	.4	39	3.3	90	7.6	1,083	91.5	10	.8	1,183
.5	25	6.8	2	.5	15	4.1	44	12.0	320	87.4	2	.5	366
.0	19	2.3	3	.4	24	2.9	46	5.6	763	93.4	8	1.0	817
.0	9	2.1	1	.2	4	1.0	14	3.3	404	96.4	1	.2	419
.0	3	2.5	0	.0	0	.0	3	2.5	117	96.7	1	.8	121
.0	6	2.0	1	.3	4	1.3	11	3.7	287	96.3	0	.0	298
.1	53	3.3	6	.4	43	2.7	104	6.5	1,487	92.8	11	.7	1,602
.4	28	5.7	2	.4	15	3.1	47	9.7	437	89.7	3	.6	487
.0	25	2.2	4	.4	28	2.5	57	5.1	1,050	94.2	8	.7	1,115
.0	0	.0	0	.0	0	.0	0	.0	0	.0	0	.0	0
.0	0	.0	0	.0	0	.0	0	.0	0	.0	0	.0	0
.0	0	.0	0	.0	0	.0	0	.0	0	.0	0	.0	0
.1	53	3.3	6	.4	43	2.7	104	6.5	1,487	92.8	11	.7	1,602
.4	28	5.7	2	.4	15	3.1	47	9.7	437	89.7	3	.6	487
.0	25	2.2	4	.4	28	2.5	57	5.1	1,050	94.2	8	.7	1,115

MAJOR FIELD 1400 - LAW

	AMERICAN INDIAN ALASKAN NATIVE		BLACK NON-HISPANIC		ASIAN OR PACIFIC ISLANDER		HISPANIC		TOTAL MINORITY		WHITE NON-HISPANIC		NON-RESIDENT ALIEN		T
	NUMBER	%	NUMBER	%	NUMBER	%	NUMBER	%	NUMBER	%	NUMBER	%	NUMBER	%	N
DISTRICT OF COLUMBIA (5 INSTITUTIONS)															
UNDERGRADUATES:															
FULL-TIME	0	.0	0	.0	0	.0	0	.0	0	.0	0	.0	0	.0	
FEMALE	0	.0	0	.0	0	.0	0	.0	0	.0	0	.0	0	.0	
MALE	0	.0	0	.0	0	.0	0	.0	0	.0	0	.0	0	.0	
PART-TIME	0	.0	0	.0	0	.0	0	.0	0	.0	0	.0	0	.0	
FEMALE	0	.0	0	.0	0	.0	0	.0	0	.0	0	.0	0	.0	
MALE	0	.0	0	.0	0	.0	0	.0	0	.0	0	.0	0	.0	
TOTAL	0	.0	0	.0	0	.0	0	.0	0	.0	0	.0	0	.0	
FEMALE	0	.0	0	.0	0	.0	0	.0	0	.0	0	.0	0	.0	
MALE	0	.0	0	.0	0	.0	0	.0	0	.0	0	.0	0	.0	
GRADUATE:															
FULL-TIME	0	.0	0	.0	0	.0	0	.0	0	.0	0	.0	0	.0	
FEMALE	0	.0	0	.0	0	.0	0	.0	0	.0	0	.0	0	.0	
MALE	0	.0	0	.0	0	.0	0	.0	0	.0	0	.0	0	.0	
PART-TIME	0	.0	0	.0	0	.0	0	.0	0	.0	0	.0	0	.0	
FEMALE	0	.0	0	.0	0	.0	0	.0	0	.0	0	.0	0	.0	
MALE	0	.0	0	.0	0	.0	0	.0	0	.0	0	.0	0	.0	
TOTAL	0	.0	0	.0	0	.0	0	.0	0	.0	0	.0	0	.0	
FEMALE	0	.0	0	.0	0	.0	0	.0	0	.0	0	.0	0	.0	
MALE	0	.0	0	.0	0	.0	0	.0	0	.0	0	.0	0	.0	
PROFESSIONAL:															
FULL-TIME	5	.1	652	16.2	88	2.2	140	3.5	885	21.9	3,104	77.0	43	1.1	
FEMALE	0	.0	329	20.6	40	2.5	47	2.9	416	26.0	1,168	73.0	16	1.0	
MALE	5	.2	323	13.3	48	2.0	93	3.8	469	19.3	1,936	79.6	27	1.1	
PART-TIME	4	.3	127	9.0	13	.9	34	2.4	178	12.7	1,218	86.6	11	.8	
FEMALE	1	.2	63	10.7	6	1.0	9	1.5	79	13.4	505	85.7	5	.8	
MALE	3	.4	64	7.8	7	.9	25	3.1	99	12.1	713	87.2	6	.7	
TOTAL	9	.2	779	14.3	101	1.9	174	3.2	1,063	19.5	4,322	79.5	54	1.0	
FEMALE	1	.0	392	17.9	46	2.1	56	2.6	495	22.6	1,673	76.4	21	1.0	
MALE	8	.2	387	11.9	55	1.7	118	3.6	568	17.5	2,649	81.5	33	1.0	
UND+GRAD+PROF:															
FULL-TIME	5	.1	652	16.2	88	2.2	140	3.5	885	21.9	3,104	77.0	43	1.1	
FEMALE	0	.0	329	20.6	40	2.5	47	2.9	416	26.0	1,168	73.0	16	1.0	
MALE	5	.2	323	13.3	48	2.0	93	3.8	469	19.3	1,936	79.6	27	1.1	
PART-TIME	4	.3	127	9.0	13	.9	34	2.4	178	12.7	1,218	86.6	11	.8	
FEMALE	1	.2	63	10.7	6	1.0	9	1.5	79	13.4	505	85.7	5	.8	
MALE	3	.4	64	7.8	7	.9	25	3.1	99	12.1	713	87.2	6	.7	
TOTAL	9	.2	779	14.3	101	1.9	174	3.2	1,063	19.5	4,322	79.5	54	1.0	
FEMALE	1	.0	392	17.9	46	2.1	56	2.6	495	22.6	1,673	76.4	21	1.0	
MALE	8	.2	387	11.9	55	1.7	118	3.6	568	17.5	2,649	81.5	33	1.0	
UNCLASSIFIED:															
TOTAL	0	.0	0	.0	0	.0	0	.0	0	.0	0	.0	0	.0	
FEMALE	0	.0	0	.0	0	.0	0	.0	0	.0	0	.0	0	.0	
MALE	0	.0	0	.0	0	.0	0	.0	0	.0	0	.0	0	.0	
TOTAL ENROLLMENT:															
TOTAL	9	.2	779	14.3	101	1.9	174	3.2	1,063	19.5	4,322	79.5	54	1.0	
FEMALE	1	.0	392	17.9	46	2.1	56	2.6	495	22.6	1,673	76.4	21	1.0	
MALE	8	.2	387	11.9	55	1.7	118	3.6	568	17.5	2,649	81.5	33	1.0	
FLORIDA (5 INSTITUTIONS)															
UNDERGRADUATES:															
FULL-TIME	0	.0	0	.0	0	.0	0	.0	0	.0	0	.0	0	.0	
FEMALE	0	.0	0	.0	0	.0	0	.0	0	.0	0	.0	0	.0	
MALE	0	.0	0	.0	0	.0	0	.0	0	.0	0	.0	0	.0	
PART-TIME	0	.0	0	.0	0	.0	0	.0	0	.0	0	.0	0	.0	
FEMALE	0	.0	0	.0	0	.0	0	.0	0	.0	0	.0	0	.0	
MALE	0	.0	0	.0	0	.0	0	.0	0	.0	0	.0	0	.0	
TOTAL	0	.0	0	.0	0	.0	0	.0	0	.0	0	.0	0	.0	
FEMALE	0	.0	0	.0	0	.0	0	.0	0	.0	0	.0	0	.0	
MALE	0	.0	0	.0	0	.0	0	.0	0	.0	0	.0	0	.0	
GRADUATE:															
FULL-TIME	0	.0	0	.0	0	.0	0	.0	0	.0	0	.0	0	.0	
FEMALE	0	.0	0	.0	0	.0	0	.0	0	.0	0	.0	0	.0	
MALE	0	.0	0	.0	0	.0	0	.0	0	.0	0	.0	0	.0	
PART-TIME	0	.0	0	.0	0	.0	0	.0	0	.0	0	.0	0	.0	
FEMALE	0	.0	0	.0	0	.0	0	.0	0	.0	0	.0	0	.0	
MALE	0	.0	0	.0	0	.0	0	.0	0	.0	0	.0	0	.0	
TOTAL	0	.0	0	.0	0	.0	0	.0	0	.0	0	.0	0	.0	
FEMALE	0	.0	0	.0	0	.0	0	.0	0	.0	0	.0	0	.0	
MALE	0	.0	0	.0	0	.0	0	.0	0	.0	0	.0	0	.0	
PROFESSIONAL:															
FULL-TIME	2	.1	118	3.7	7	.2	170	5.3	297	9.2	2,910	90.4	13	.4	
FEMALE	0	.0	33	3.5	1	.1	40	4.3	74	7.9	853	91.6	4	.4	
MALE	2	.1	85	3.7	6	.3	130	5.7	223	9.7	2,057	89.9	9	.4	

LAW

INDIAN NATIVE	BLACK NON-HISPANIC		ASIAN OR PACIFIC ISLANDER		HISPANIC		TOTAL MINORITY		WHITE NON-HISPANIC		NON-RESIDENT ALIEN		TOTAL
%	NUMBER	%	NUMBER	%	NUMBER	%	NUMBER	%	NUMBER	%	NUMBER	%	NUMBER

CONTINUED

%	NUMBER	%	NUMBER	%	NUMBER	%	NUMBER	%	NUMBER	%	NUMBER	%	NUMBER
.8	4	.8	3	.6	19	3.6	30	5.7	495	94.3	0	.0	525
.7	1	.7	0	.0	6	4.1	8	5.4	139	94.6	0	.0	147
.8	3	.8	3	.8	13	3.4	22	5.8	356	94.2	0	.0	378
.2	122	3.3	10	.3	189	5.0	327	8.7	3,405	90.9	13	.3	3,745
.1	34	3.2	1	.1	46	4.3	82	7.6	992	92.0	4	.4	1,078
.2	88	3.3	9	.3	143	5.4	245	9.2	2,413	90.5	9	.3	2,667
.1	118	3.7	7	.2	170	5.3	297	9.2	2,910	90.4	13	.4	3,220
.0	33	3.5	1	.1	40	4.3	74	7.9	853	91.6	4	.4	931
.1	85	3.7	6	.3	130	5.7	223	9.7	2,057	89.9	9	.4	2,289
.8	4	.8	3	.6	19	3.6	30	5.7	495	94.3	0	.0	525
.7	1	.7	0	.0	6	4.1	8	5.4	139	94.6	0	.0	147
.8	3	.8	3	.8	13	3.4	22	5.8	356	94.2	0	.0	378
.2	122	3.3	10	.3	189	5.0	327	8.7	3,405	90.9	13	.3	3,745
.1	34	3.2	1	.1	46	4.3	82	7.6	992	92.0	4	.4	1,078
.2	88	3.3	9	.3	143	5.4	245	9.2	2,413	90.5	9	.3	2,667
.0	0	.0	0	.0	0	.0	0	.0	0	.0	0	.0	0
.0	0	.0	0	.0	0	.0	0	.0	0	.0	0	.0	0
.0	0	.0	0	.0	0	.0	0	.0	0	.0	0	.0	0
.2	122	3.3	10	.3	189	5.0	327	8.7	3,405	90.9	13	.3	3,745
.1	34	3.2	1	.1	46	4.3	82	7.6	992	92.0	4	.4	1,078
.2	88	3.3	9	.3	143	5.4	245	9.2	2,413	90.5	9	.3	2,667

(3 INSTITUTIONS)

%	NUMBER	%	NUMBER	%	NUMBER	%	NUMBER	%	NUMBER	%	NUMBER	%	NUMBER
.0	0	.0	0	.0	0	.0	0	.0	0	.0	0	.0	0
.0	0	.0	0	.0	0	.0	0	.0	0	.0	0	.0	0
.0	0	.0	0	.0	0	.0	0	.0	0	.0	0	.0	0
.0	0	.0	0	.0	0	.0	0	.0	0	.0	0	.0	0
.0	0	.0	0	.0	0	.0	0	.0	0	.0	0	.0	0
.0	0	.0	0	.0	0	.0	0	.0	0	.0	0	.0	0
.0	0	.0	0	.0	0	.0	0	.0	0	.0	0	.0	0
.0	0	.0	0	.0	0	.0	0	.0	0	.0	0	.0	0
.0	0	.0	0	.0	0	.0	0	.0	0	.0	0	.0	0
.0	0	.0	0	.0	0	.0	0	.0	0	.0	0	.0	0
.0	0	.0	0	.0	0	.0	0	.0	0	.0	0	.0	0
.0	0	.0	0	.0	0	.0	0	.0	0	.0	0	.0	0
.0	0	.0	0	.0	0	.0	0	.0	0	.0	0	.0	0
.0	0	.0	0	.0	0	.0	0	.0	0	.0	0	.0	0
.0	0	.0	0	.0	0	.0	0	.0	0	.0	0	.0	0
.1	71	4.3	5	.3	14	.8	92	5.5	1,572	94.4	1	.1	1,665
.4	39	7.8	1	.2	3	.6	45	8.9	458	91.1	0	.0	503
.0	32	2.8	4	.3	11	.9	47	4.0	1,114	95.9	1	.1	1,162
.0	3	3.5	0	.0	0	.0	3	3.5	79	91.9	4	4.7	86
.0	2	13.3	0	.0	0	.0	2	13.3	12	80.0	1	6.7	15
.0	1	1.4	0	.0	0	.0	1	1.4	67	94.4	3	4.2	71
.1	74	4.2	5	.3	14	.8	95	5.4	1,651	94.3	5	.3	1,751
.4	41	7.9	1	.2	3	.6	47	9.1	470	90.7	1	.2	518
.0	33	2.7	4	.3	11	.9	48	3.9	1,181	95.8	4	.3	1,233
.1	71	4.3	5	.3	14	.8	92	5.5	1,572	94.4	1	.1	1,665
.4	39	7.8	1	.2	3	.6	45	8.9	458	91.1	0	.0	503
.0	32	2.8	4	.3	11	.9	47	4.0	1,114	95.9	1	.1	1,162
.0	3	3.5	0	.0	0	.0	3	3.5	79	91.9	4	4.7	86
.0	2	13.3	0	.0	0	.0	2	13.3	12	80.0	1	6.7	15
.0	1	1.4	0	.0	0	.0	1	1.4	67	94.4	3	4.2	71
.1	74	4.2	5	.3	14	.8	95	5.4	1,651	94.3	5	.3	1,751
.4	41	7.9	1	.2	3	.6	47	9.1	470	90.7	1	.2	518
.0	33	2.7	4	.3	11	.9	48	3.9	1,181	95.8	4	.3	1,233
.0	0	.0	0	.0	0	.0	0	.0	0	.0	0	.0	0
.0	0	.0	0	.0	0	.0	0	.0	0	.0	0	.0	0
.0	0	.0	0	.0	0	.0	0	.0	0	.0	0	.0	0
.1	74	4.2	5	.3	14	.8	95	5.4	1,651	94.3	5	.3	1,751
.4	41	7.9	1	.2	3	.6	47	9.1	470	90.7	1	.2	518
.0	33	2.7	4	.3	11	.9	48	3.9	1,181	95.8	4	.3	1,233

TABLE 17 - TOTAL ENROLLMENT IN INSTITUTIONS OF HIGHER EDUCATION FOR SELECTED MAJOR FIELDS OF STUDY AND LEVEL OF ENROLLMENT BY RACE, ETHNICITY, AND SEX: STATE, 1978

MAJOR FIELD 1400 - LAW

	AMERICAN INDIAN ALASKAN NATIVE		BLACK NON-HISPANIC		ASIAN OR PACIFIC ISLANDER		HISPANIC		TOTAL MINORITY		WHITE NON-HISPANIC		NON-RESIDENT ALIEN	
	NUMBER	%	NUMBER	%	NUMBER	%	NUMBER	%	NUMBER	%	NUMBER	%	NUMBER	%
HAWAII (1 INSTITUTIONS)														
UNDERGRADUATES:														
FULL-TIME	0	.0	0	.0	0	.0	0	.0	0	.0	0	.0	0	.0
FEMALE	0	.0	0	.0	0	.0	0	.0	0	.0	0	.0	0	.0
MALE	0	.0	0	.0	0	.0	0	.0	0	.0	0	.0	0	.0
PART-TIME	0	.0	0	.0	0	.0	0	.0	0	.0	0	.0	0	.0
FEMALE	0	.0	0	.0	0	.0	0	.0	0	.0	0	.0	0	.0
MALE	0	.0	0	.0	0	.0	0	.0	0	.0	0	.0	0	.0
TOTAL	0	.0	0	.0	0	.0	0	.0	0	.0	0	.0	0	.0
FEMALE	0	.0	0	.0	0	.0	0	.0	0	.0	0	.0	0	.0
MALE	0	.0	0	.0	0	.0	0	.0	0	.0	0	.0	0	.0
GRADUATE:														
FULL-TIME	0	.0	0	.0	0	.0	0	.0	0	.0	0	.0	0	.0
FEMALE	0	.0	0	.0	0	.0	0	.0	0	.0	0	.0	0	.0
MALE	0	.0	0	.0	0	.0	0	.0	0	.0	0	.0	0	.0
PART-TIME	0	.0	0	.0	0	.0	0	.0	0	.0	0	.0	0	.0
FEMALE	0	.0	0	.0	0	.0	0	.0	0	.0	0	.0	0	.0
MALE	0	.0	0	.0	0	.0	0	.0	0	.0	0	.0	0	.0
TOTAL	0	.0	0	.0	0	.0	0	.0	0	.0	0	.0	0	.0
FEMALE	0	.0	0	.0	0	.0	0	.0	0	.0	0	.0	0	.0
MALE	0	.0	0	.0	0	.0	0	.0	0	.0	0	.0	0	.0
PROFESSIONAL:														
FULL-TIME	0	.0	0	.0	144	76.2	3	1.6	147	77.8	40	21.2	2	1.1
FEMALE	0	.0	0	.0	55	72.4	2	2.6	57	75.0	19	25.0	0	.0
MALE	0	.0	0	.0	89	78.8	1	.9	90	79.6	21	18.6	2	1.8
PART-TIME	0	.0	0	.0	7	53.8	0	.0	7	53.8	6	46.2	0	.0
FEMALE	0	.0	0	.0	5	83.3	0	.0	5	83.3	1	16.7	0	.0
MALE	0	.0	0	.0	2	28.6	0	.0	2	28.6	5	71.4	0	.0
TOTAL	0	.0	0	.0	151	74.8	3	1.5	154	76.2	46	22.8	2	1.0
FEMALE	0	.0	0	.0	60	73.2	2	2.4	62	75.6	20	24.4	0	.0
MALE	0	.0	0	.0	91	75.8	1	.8	92	76.7	26	21.7	2	1.7
UNDGRAD+PROF:														
FULL-TIME	0	.0	0	.0	144	76.2	3	1.6	147	77.8	40	21.2	2	1.1
FEMALE	0	.0	0	.0	55	72.4	2	2.6	57	75.0	19	25.0	0	.0
MALE	0	.0	0	.0	89	78.8	1	.9	90	79.6	21	18.6	2	1.8
PART-TIME	0	.0	0	.0	7	53.8	0	.0	7	53.8	6	46.2	0	.0
FEMALE	0	.0	0	.0	5	83.3	0	.0	5	83.3	1	16.7	0	.0
MALE	0	.0	0	.0	2	28.6	0	.0	2	28.6	5	71.4	0	.0
TOTAL	0	.0	0	.0	151	74.8	3	1.5	154	76.2	46	22.8	2	1.0
FEMALE	0	.0	0	.0	60	73.2	2	2.4	62	75.6	20	24.4	0	.0
MALE	0	.0	0	.0	91	75.8	1	.8	92	76.7	26	21.7	2	1.7
UNCLASSIFIED:														
TOTAL	0	.0	0	.0	0	.0	0	.0	0	.0	0	.0	0	.0
FEMALE	0	.0	0	.0	0	.0	0	.0	0	.0	0	.0	0	.0
MALE	0	.0	0	.0	0	.0	0	.0	0	.0	0	.0	0	.0
TOTAL ENROLLMENT:														
TOTAL	0	.0	0	.0	151	74.8	3	1.5	154	76.2	46	22.8	2	1.0
FEMALE	0	.0	0	.0	60	73.2	2	2.4	62	75.6	20	24.4	0	.0
MALE	0	.0	0	.0	91	75.8	1	.8	92	76.7	26	21.7	2	1.7
ILLINOIS (9 INSTITUTIONS)														
UNDERGRADUATES:														
FULL-TIME	0	.0	0	.0	0	.0	0	.0	0	.0	0	.0	0	.0
FEMALE	0	.0	0	.0	0	.0	0	.0	0	.0	0	.0	0	.0
MALE	0	.0	0	.0	0	.0	0	.0	0	.0	0	.0	0	.0
PART-TIME	0	.0	0	.0	0	.0	0	.0	0	.0	0	.0	0	.0
FEMALE	0	.0	0	.0	0	.0	0	.0	0	.0	0	.0	0	.0
MALE	0	.0	0	.0	0	.0	0	.0	0	.0	0	.0	0	.0
TOTAL	0	.0	0	.0	0	.0	0	.0	0	.0	0	.0	0	.0
FEMALE	0	.0	0	.0	0	.0	0	.0	0	.0	0	.0	0	.0
MALE	0	.0	0	.0	0	.0	0	.0	0	.0	0	.0	0	.0
GRADUATE:														
FULL-TIME	0	.0	0	.0	0	.0	0	.0	0	.0	0	.0	0	.0
FEMALE	0	.0	0	.0	0	.0	0	.0	0	.0	0	.0	0	.0
MALE	0	.0	0	.0	0	.0	0	.0	0	.0	0	.0	0	.0
PART-TIME	0	.0	0	.0	0	.0	0	.0	0	.0	0	.0	0	.0
FEMALE	0	.0	0	.0	0	.0	0	.0	0	.0	0	.0	0	.0
MALE	0	.0	0	.0	0	.0	0	.0	0	.0	0	.0	0	.0
TOTAL	0	.0	0	.0	0	.0	0	.0	0	.0	0	.0	0	.0
FEMALE	0	.0	0	.0	0	.0	0	.0	0	.0	0	.0	0	.0
MALE	0	.0	0	.0	0	.0	0	.0	0	.0	0	.0	0	.0
PROFESSIONAL:														
FULL-TIME	13	.2	173	3.3	44	.8	64	1.2	294	5.5	4,989	94.0	26	.5
FEMALE	7	.5	75	4.8	19	1.2	17	1.1	118	7.6	1,426	91.9	7	.5
MALE	6	.2	98	2.6	25	.7	47	1.3	176	4.7	3,563	94.8	19	.5

RULLMENT IN INSTITUTIONS OF HIGHER EDUCATION FOR SELECTED MAJOR FIELDS OF STUDY AND LEVEL OF ENROLLMENT
ETHNICITY, AND SEX: STATE, 1978

LAW

INDIAN NATIVE	BLACK NON-HISPANIC		ASIAN OR PACIFIC ISLANDER		HISPANIC		TOTAL MINORITY		WHITE NON-HISPANIC		NON-RESIDENT ALIEN		TOTAL
%	NUMBER	%	NUMBER	%	NUMBER	%	NUMBER	%	NUMBER	%	NUMBER	%	NUMBER

CONTINUED

.1	63	4.5	20	1.4	13	.9	97	6.9	1,310	92.8	5	.4	1,412
.3	23	6.1	4	1.1	2	.5	30	8.0	344	91.7	1	.3	375
.0	40	3.9	16	1.5	11	1.1	67	6.5	966	93.2	4	.4	1,037
.2	236	3.5	64	1.0	77	1.1	391	5.8	6,299	93.7	31	.5	6,721
.4	98	5.1	23	1.2	19	1.0	148	7.7	1,770	91.9	8	.4	1,926
.1	138	2.9	41	.9	58	1.2	243	5.1	4,529	94.5	23	.5	4,795
.2	173	3.3	44	.8	64	1.2	294	5.5	4,989	94.0	26	.5	5,309
.5	75	4.8	19	1.2	17	1.1	118	7.6	1,426	91.9	7	.5	1,551
.2	98	2.6	25	.7	47	1.3	176	4.7	3,563	94.8	19	.5	3,758
.1	63	4.5	20	1.4	13	.9	97	6.9	1,310	92.8	5	.4	1,412
.3	23	6.1	4	1.1	2	.5	30	8.0	344	91.7	1	.3	375
.0	40	3.9	16	1.5	11	1.1	67	6.5	966	93.2	4	.4	1,037
.2	236	3.5	64	1.0	77	1.1	391	5.8	6,299	93.7	31	.5	6,721
.4	98	5.1	23	1.2	19	1.0	148	7.7	1,770	91.9	8	.4	1,926
.1	138	2.9	41	.9	58	1.2	243	5.1	4,529	94.5	23	.5	4,795
.0	0	.0	0	.0	0	.0	0	.0	0	.0	0	.0	0
.0	0	.0	0	.0	0	.0	0	.0	0	.0	0	.0	0
.0	0	.0	0	.0	0	.0	0	.0	0	.0	0	.0	0
.2	236	3.5	64	1.0	77	1.1	391	5.8	6,299	93.7	31	.5	6,721
.4	98	5.1	23	1.2	19	1.0	148	7.7	1,770	91.9	8	.4	1,926
.1	138	2.9	41	.9	58	1.2	243	5.1	4,529	94.5	23	.5	4,795

(4 INSTITUTIONS)

.0	0	.0	0	.0	0	.0	0	.0	0	.0	0	.0	0
.0	0	.0	0	.0	0	.0	0	.0	0	.0	0	.0	0
.0	0	.0	0	.0	0	.0	0	.0	0	.0	0	.0	0
.0	0	.0	0	.0	0	.0	0	.0	0	.0	0	.0	0
.0	0	.0	0	.0	0	.0	0	.0	0	.0	0	.0	0
.0	0	.0	0	.0	0	.0	0	.0	0	.0	0	.0	0
.0	0	.0	0	.0	0	.0	0	.0	0	.0	0	.0	0
.0	0	.0	0	.0	0	.0	0	.0	0	.0	0	.0	0
.0	0	.0	0	.0	0	.0	0	.0	0	.0	0	.0	0
.0	0	.0	0	.0	0	.0	0	.0	0	.0	0	.0	0
.0	0	.0	0	.0	0	.0	0	.0	0	.0	0	.0	0
.0	0	.0	0	.0	0	.0	0	.0	0	.0	0	.0	0
.0	0	.0	0	.0	0	.0	0	.0	0	.0	0	.0	0
.0	0	.0	0	.0	0	.0	0	.0	0	.0	0	.0	0
.0	0	.0	0	.0	0	.0	0	.0	0	.0	0	.0	0
.6	99	5.7	7	.4	38	2.2	155	8.9	1,579	90.6	9	.5	1,743
.4	38	7.6	1	.2	9	1.8	50	10.0	449	89.6	2	.4	501
.7	61	4.9	6	.5	29	2.3	105	8.5	1,130	91.0	7	.6	1,242
.7	11	2.6	0	.0	2	.5	16	3.7	400	93.2	13	3.0	429
1.6	4	3.1	0	.0	1	.8	7	5.5	119	93.0	2	1.6	128
.3	7	2.3	0	.0	1	.3	9	3.0	281	93.4	11	3.7	301
.6	110	5.1	7	.3	40	1.8	171	7.9	1,979	91.1	22	1.0	2,172
.6	42	6.7	1	.2	10	1.6	57	9.1	568	90.3	4	.6	629
.6	68	4.4	6	.4	30	1.9	114	7.4	1,411	91.4	18	1.2	1,543
.6	99	5.7	7	.4	38	2.2	155	8.9	1,579	90.6	9	.5	1,743
.4	38	7.6	1	.2	9	1.8	50	10.0	449	89.6	2	.4	501
.7	61	4.9	6	.5	29	2.3	105	8.5	1,130	91.0	7	.6	1,242
.7	11	2.6	0	.0	2	.5	16	3.7	400	93.2	13	3.0	429
1.6	4	3.1	0	.0	1	.8	7	5.5	119	93.0	2	1.6	128
.3	7	2.3	0	.0	1	.3	9	3.0	281	93.4	11	3.7	301
.6	110	5.1	7	.3	40	1.8	171	7.9	1,979	91.1	22	1.0	2,172
.6	42	6.7	1	.2	10	1.6	57	9.1	568	90.3	4	.6	629
.6	68	4.4	6	.4	30	1.9	114	7.4	1,411	91.4	18	1.2	1,543
.0	0	.0	0	.0	0	.0	0	.0	0	.0	0	.0	0
.0	0	.0	0	.0	0	.0	0	.0	0	.0	0	.0	0
.0	0	.0	0	.0	0	.0	0	.0	0	.0	0	.0	0
.6	110	5.1	7	.3	40	1.8	171	7.9	1,979	91.1	22	1.0	2,172
.6	42	6.7	1	.2	10	1.6	57	9.1	568	90.3	4	.6	629
.6	68	4.4	6	.4	30	1.9	114	7.4	1,411	91.4	18	1.2	1,543

TABLE 17 - TOTAL ENROLLMENT IN INSTITUTIONS OF HIGHER EDUCATION FOR SELECTED MAJOR FIELDS OF STUDY AND LEVEL OF ENROLLMENT
BY RACE, ETHNICITY, AND SEX: STATE, 1978

MAJOR FIELD 1400 - LAW

	AMERICAN INDIAN ALASKAN NATIVE		BLACK NON-HISPANIC		ASIAN OR PACIFIC ISLANDER		HISPANIC		TOTAL MINORITY		WHITE NON-HISPANIC		NON-RESIDENT ALIEN		TO
	NUMBER	%	NUMBER	%	NUMBER	%	NUMBER	%	NUMBER	%	NUMBER	%	NUMBER	%	NU
IOWA	(	2 INSTITUTIONS)													
UNDERGRADUATES:															
FULL-TIME	0	.0	0	.0	0	.0	0	.0	0	.0	0	.0	0	.0	
FEMALE	0	.0	0	.0	0	.0	0	.0	0	.0	0	.0	0	.0	
MALE	0	.0	0	.0	0	.0	0	.0	0	.0	0	.0	0	.0	
PART-TIME	0	.0	0	.0	0	.0	0	.0	0	.0	0	.0	0	.0	
FEMALE	0	.0	0	.0	0	.0	0	.0	0	.0	0	.0	0	.0	
MALE	0	.0	0	.0	0	.0	0	.0	0	.0	0	.0	0	.0	
TOTAL	0	.0	0	.0	0	.0	0	.0	0	.0	0	.0	0	.0	
FEMALE	0	.0	0	.0	0	.0	0	.0	0	.0	0	.0	0	.0	
MALE	0	.0	0	.0	0	.0	0	.0	0	.0	0	.0	0	.0	
GRADUATE:															
FULL-TIME	0	.0	0	.0	0	.0	0	.0	0	.0	0	.0	0	.0	
FEMALE	0	.0	0	.0	0	.0	0	.0	0	.0	0	.0	0	.0	
MALE	0	.0	0	.0	0	.0	0	.0	0	.0	0	.0	0	.0	
PART-TIME	0	.0	0	.0	0	.0	0	.0	0	.0	0	.0	0	.0	
FEMALE	0	.0	0	.0	0	.0	0	.0	0	.0	0	.0	0	.0	
MALE	0	.0	0	.0	0	.0	0	.0	0	.0	0	.0	0	.0	
TOTAL	0	.0	0	.0	0	.0	0	.0	0	.0	0	.0	0	.0	
FEMALE	0	.0	0	.0	0	.0	0	.0	0	.0	0	.0	0	.0	
MALE	0	.0	0	.0	0	.0	0	.0	0	.0	0	.0	0	.0	
PROFESSIONAL:															
FULL-TIME	4	.3	31	2.7	7	.6	8	.7	50	4.3	1,107	94.9	9	.8	1
FEMALE	0	.0	9	3.2	3	1.1	0	.0	12	4.3	262	94.6	3	1.1	
MALE	4	.4	22	2.5	4	.4	8	.9	38	4.3	845	95.1	6	.7	
PART-TIME	0	.0	2	8.7	0	.0	1	4.3	3	13.0	20	87.0	0	.0	
FEMALE	0	.0	0	.0	0	.0	0	.0	0	.0	7	100.0	0	.0	
MALE	0	.0	2	12.5	0	.0	1	6.3	3	18.8	13	81.3	0	.0	
TOTAL	4	.3	33	2.8	7	.6	9	.8	53	4.5	1,127	94.8	9	.8	1
FEMALE	0	.0	9	3.2	3	1.1	0	.0	12	4.2	269	94.7	3	1.1	
MALE	4	.4	24	2.7	4	.4	9	1.0	41	4.5	858	94.8	6	.7	
UND+GRAD+PROF:															
FULL-TIME	4	.3	31	2.7	7	.6	8	.7	50	4.3	1,107	94.9	9	.8	1
FEMALE	0	.0	9	3.2	3	1.1	0	.0	12	4.3	262	94.6	3	1.1	
MALE	4	.4	22	2.5	4	.4	8	.9	38	4.3	845	95.1	6	.7	
PART-TIME	0	.0	2	8.7	0	.0	1	4.3	3	13.0	20	87.0	0	.0	
FEMALE	0	.0	0	.0	0	.0	0	.0	0	.0	7	100.0	0	.0	
MALE	0	.0	2	12.5	0	.0	1	6.3	3	18.8	13	81.3	0	.0	
TOTAL	4	.3	33	2.8	7	.6	9	.8	53	4.5	1,127	94.8	9	.8	1
FEMALE	0	.0	9	3.2	3	1.1	0	.0	12	4.2	269	94.7	3	1.1	
MALE	4	.4	24	2.7	4	.4	9	1.0	41	4.5	858	94.8	6	.7	
UNCLASSIFIED:															
TOTAL	0	.0	0	.0	0	.0	0	.0	0	.0	0	.0	0	.0	
FEMALE	0	.0	0	.0	0	.0	0	.0	0	.0	0	.0	0	.0	
MALE	0	.0	0	.0	0	.0	0	.0	0	.0	0	.0	0	.0	
TOTAL ENROLLMENT:															
TOTAL	4	.3	33	2.8	7	.6	9	.8	53	4.5	1,127	94.8	9	.8	1
FEMALE	0	.0	9	3.2	3	1.1	0	.0	12	4.2	269	94.7	3	1.1	
MALE	4	.4	24	2.7	4	.4	9	1.0	41	4.5	858	94.8	6	.7	
KANSAS	(	2 INSTITUTIONS)													
UNDERGRADUATES:															
FULL-TIME	0	.0	0	.0	0	.0	0	.0	0	.0	0	.0	0	.0	
FEMALE	0	.0	0	.0	0	.0	0	.0	0	.0	0	.0	0	.0	
MALE	0	.0	0	.0	0	.0	0	.0	0	.0	0	.0	0	.0	
PART-TIME	0	.0	0	.0	0	.0	0	.0	0	.0	0	.0	0	.0	
FEMALE	0	.0	0	.0	0	.0	0	.0	0	.0	0	.0	0	.0	
MALE	0	.0	0	.0	0	.0	0	.0	0	.0	0	.0	0	.0	
TOTAL	0	.0	0	.0	0	.0	0	.0	0	.0	0	.0	0	.0	
FEMALE	0	.0	0	.0	0	.0	0	.0	0	.0	0	.0	0	.0	
MALE	0	.0	0	.0	0	.0	0	.0	0	.0	0	.0	0	.0	
GRADUATE:															
FULL-TIME	0	.0	0	.0	0	.0	0	.0	0	.0	0	.0	0	.0	
FEMALE	0	.0	0	.0	0	.0	0	.0	0	.0	0	.0	0	.0	
MALE	0	.0	0	.0	0	.0	0	.0	0	.0	0	.0	0	.0	
PART-TIME	0	.0	0	.0	0	.0	0	.0	0	.0	0	.0	0	.0	
FEMALE	0	.0	0	.0	0	.0	0	.0	0	.0	0	.0	0	.0	
MALE	0	.0	0	.0	0	.0	0	.0	0	.0	0	.0	0	.0	
TOTAL	0	.0	0	.0	0	.0	0	.0	0	.0	0	.0	0	.0	
FEMALE	0	.0	0	.0	0	.0	0	.0	0	.0	0	.0	0	.0	
MALE	0	.0	0	.0	0	.0	0	.0	0	.0	0	.0	0	.0	
PROFESSIONAL:															
FULL-TIME	2	.2	22	2.0	3	.3	16	1.5	43	4.0	1,045	96.0	0	.0	1
FEMALE	0	.0	8	3.0	1	.4	4	1.5	13	4.9	250	95.1	0	.0	
MALE	2	.2	14	1.7	2	.2	12	1.5	30	3.6	795	96.4	0	.0	

558

ENROLLMENT IN INSTITUTIONS OF HIGHER EDUCATION FOR SELECTED MAJOR FIELDS OF STUDY AND LEVEL OF ENROLLMENT
, ETHNICITY, AND SEX: STATE, 1978

LAW

INDIAN NATIVE %	BLACK NON-HISPANIC NUMBER	%	ASIAN OR PACIFIC ISLANDER NUMBER	%	HISPANIC NUMBER	%	TOTAL MINORITY NUMBER	%	WHITE NON-HISPANIC NUMBER	%	NON-RESIDENT ALIEN NUMBER	%	TOTAL NUMBER
CONTINUED													
.0	0	.0	1	3.3	2	6.7	3	10.0	27	90.0	0	.0	30
.0	0	.0	1	16.7	0	.0	1	16.7	5	83.3	0	.0	6
.0	0	.0	0	.0	2	8.3	2	8.3	22	91.7	0	.0	24
.2	22	2.0	4	.4	18	1.6	46	4.1	1,072	95.9	0	.0	1,118
.0	8	3.0	2	.7	4	1.5	14	5.2	255	94.8	0	.0	269
.2	14	1.6	2	.2	14	1.6	32	3.8	817	96.2	0	.0	849
.2	22	2.0	3	.3	16	1.5	43	4.0	1,045	96.0	0	.0	1,088
.0	8	3.0	1	.4	4	1.5	13	4.9	250	95.1	0	.0	263
.2	14	1.7	2	.2	12	1.5	30	3.6	795	96.4	0	.0	825
.0	0	.0	1	3.3	2	6.7	3	10.0	27	90.0	0	.0	30
.0	0	.0	1	16.7	0	.0	1	16.7	5	83.3	0	.0	6
.0	0	.0	0	.0	2	8.3	2	8.3	22	91.7	0	.0	24
.2	22	2.0	4	.4	18	1.6	46	4.1	1,072	95.9	0	.0	1,118
.0	8	3.0	2	.7	4	1.5	14	5.2	255	94.8	0	.0	269
.2	14	1.6	2	.2	14	1.6	32	3.8	817	96.2	0	.0	849
.0	0	.0	0	.0	0	.0	0	.0	0	.0	0	.0	0
.0	0	.0	0	.0	0	.0	0	.0	0	.0	0	.0	0
.0	0	.0	0	.0	0	.0	0	.0	0	.0	0	.0	0
.2	22	2.0	4	.4	18	1.6	46	4.1	1,072	95.9	0	.0	1,118
.0	8	3.0	2	.7	4	1.5	14	5.2	255	94.8	0	.0	269
.2	14	1.6	2	.2	14	1.6	32	3.8	817	96.2	0	.0	849
(3 INSTITUTIONS)													
.0	0	.0	0	.0	0	.0	0	.0	0	.0	0	.0	0
.0	0	.0	0	.0	0	.0	0	.0	0	.0	0	.0	0
.0	0	.0	0	.0	0	.0	0	.0	0	.0	0	.0	0
.0	0	.0	0	.0	0	.0	0	.0	0	.0	0	.0	0
.0	0	.0	0	.0	0	.0	0	.0	0	.0	0	.0	0
.0	0	.0	0	.0	0	.0	0	.0	0	.0	0	.0	0
.0	0	.0	0	.0	0	.0	0	.0	0	.0	0	.0	0
.0	0	.0	0	.0	0	.0	0	.0	0	.0	0	.0	0
.0	0	.0	0	.0	0	.0	0	.0	0	.0	0	.0	0
.0	0	.0	0	.0	0	.0	0	.0	0	.0	0	.0	0
.0	0	.0	0	.0	0	.0	0	.0	0	.0	0	.0	0
.0	0	.0	0	.0	0	.0	0	.0	0	.0	0	.0	0
.0	0	.0	0	.0	0	.0	0	.0	0	.0	0	.0	0
.0	0	.0	0	.0	0	.0	0	.0	0	.0	0	.0	0
.0	0	.0	0	.0	0	.0	0	.0	0	.0	0	.0	0
.2	32	2.2	3	.2	5	.3	43	2.9	1,414	96.8	3	.2	1,460
.0	6	1.7	1	.3	0	.0	7	1.9	351	97.5	2	.6	360
.3	26	2.4	2	.2	5	.5	36	3.3	1,063	96.6	1	.1	1,100
1.2	5	5.9	1	1.2	0	.0	7	8.2	78	91.8	0	.0	85
.0	4	15.4	0	.0	0	.0	4	15.4	22	84.6	0	.0	26
1.7	1	1.7	1	1.7	0	.0	3	5.1	56	94.9	0	.0	59
.3	37	2.4	4	.3	5	.3	50	3.2	1,492	96.6	3	.2	1,545
.0	10	2.6	1	.3	0	.0	11	2.8	373	96.6	2	.5	386
.3	27	2.3	3	.3	5	.4	39	3.4	1,119	96.5	1	.1	1,159
.2	32	2.2	3	.2	5	.3	43	2.9	1,414	96.8	3	.2	1,460
.0	6	1.7	1	.3	0	.0	7	1.9	351	97.5	2	.6	360
.3	26	2.4	2	.2	5	.5	36	3.3	1,063	96.6	1	.1	1,100
1.2	5	5.9	1	1.2	0	.0	7	8.2	78	91.8	0	.0	85
.0	4	15.4	0	.0	0	.0	4	15.4	22	84.6	0	.0	26
1.7	1	1.7	1	1.7	0	.0	3	5.1	56	94.9	0	.0	59
.3	37	2.4	4	.3	5	.3	50	3.2	1,492	96.6	3	.2	1,545
.0	10	2.6	1	.3	0	.0	11	2.8	373	96.6	2	.5	386
.3	27	2.3	3	.3	5	.4	39	3.4	1,119	96.5	1	.1	1,159
.0	0	.0	0	.0	0	.0	0	.0	0	.0	0	.0	0
.0	0	.0	0	.0	0	.0	0	.0	0	.0	0	.0	0
.0	0	.0	0	.0	0	.0	0	.0	0	.0	0	.0	0
.3	37	2.4	4	.3	5	.3	50	3.2	1,492	96.6	3	.2	1,545
.0	10	2.6	1	.3	0	.0	11	2.8	373	96.6	2	.5	386
.3	27	2.3	3	.3	5	.4	39	3.4	1,119	96.5	1	.1	1,159

MAJOR FIELD 1400 - LAW

	AMERICAN INDIAN ALASKAN NATIVE		BLACK NON-HISPANIC		ASIAN OR PACIFIC ISLANDER		HISPANIC		TOTAL MINORITY		WHITE NON-HISPANIC		NON-RESIDENT ALIEN		T N
	NUMBER	%	NUMBER	%	NUMBER	%	NUMBER	%	NUMBER	%	NUMBER	%	NUMBER	%	
LOUISIANA (3 INSTITUTIONS)															
UNDERGRADUATES:															
FULL-TIME	0	.0	0	.0	0	.0	0	.0	0	.0	0	.0	0	.0	
FEMALE	0	.0	0	.0	0	.0	0	.0	0	.0	0	.0	0	.0	
MALE	0	.0	0	.0	0	.0	0	.0	0	.0	0	.0	0	.0	
PART-TIME	0	.0	0	.0	0	.0	0	.0	0	.0	0	.0	0	.0	
FEMALE	0	.0	0	.0	0	.0	0	.0	0	.0	0	.0	0	.0	
MALE	0	.0	0	.0	0	.0	0	.0	0	.0	0	.0	0	.0	
TOTAL	0	.0	0	.0	0	.0	0	.0	0	.0	0	.0	0	.0	
FEMALE	0	.0	0	.0	0	.0	0	.0	0	.0	0	.0	0	.0	
MALE	0	.0	0	.0	0	.0	0	.0	0	.0	0	.0	0	.0	
GRADUATE:															
FULL-TIME	0	.0	0	.0	0	.0	0	.0	0	.0	0	.0	0	.0	
FEMALE	0	.0	0	.0	0	.0	0	.0	0	.0	0	.0	0	.0	
MALE	0	.0	0	.0	0	.0	0	.0	0	.0	0	.0	0	.0	
PART-TIME	0	.0	0	.0	0	.0	0	.0	0	.0	0	.0	0	.0	
FEMALE	0	.0	0	.0	0	.0	0	.0	0	.0	0	.0	0	.0	
MALE	0	.0	0	.0	0	.0	0	.0	0	.0	0	.0	0	.0	
TOTAL	0	.0	0	.0	0	.0	0	.0	0	.0	0	.0	0	.0	
FEMALE	0	.0	0	.0	0	.0	0	.0	0	.0	0	.0	0	.0	
MALE	0	.0	0	.0	0	.0	0	.0	0	.0	0	.0	0	.0	
PROFESSIONAL:															
FULL-TIME	2	.2	163	12.6	5	.4	16	1.2	186	14.3	1,103	85.0	8	.6	
FEMALE	0	.0	49	14.2	1	.3	5	1.4	55	15.9	289	83.8	1	.3	
MALE	2	.2	114	12.0	4	.4	11	1.2	131	13.8	814	85.5	7	.7	
PART-TIME	1	.3	24	8.3	0	.0	6	2.1	31	10.7	259	89.3	0	.0	
FEMALE	1	1.0	6	5.9	0	.0	2	2.0	9	8.8	93	91.2	0	.0	
MALE	0	.0	18	9.6	0	.0	4	2.1	22	11.7	166	88.3	0	.0	
TOTAL	3	.2	187	11.8	5	.3	22	1.4	217	13.7	1,362	85.8	8	.5	
FEMALE	1	.2	55	12.3	1	.2	7	1.6	64	14.3	382	85.5	1	.2	
MALE	2	.2	132	11.6	4	.4	15	1.3	153	13.4	980	86.0	7	.6	
UNC+GRAD+PROF:															
FULL-TIME	2	.2	163	12.6	5	.4	16	1.2	186	14.3	1,103	85.0	8	.6	
FEMALE	0	.0	49	14.2	1	.3	5	1.4	55	15.9	289	83.8	1	.3	
MALE	2	.2	114	12.0	4	.4	11	1.2	131	13.8	814	85.5	7	.7	
PART-TIME	1	.3	24	8.3	0	.0	6	2.1	31	10.7	259	89.3	0	.0	
FEMALE	1	1.0	6	5.9	0	.0	2	2.0	9	8.8	93	91.2	0	.0	
MALE	0	.0	18	9.6	0	.0	4	2.1	22	11.7	166	88.3	0	.0	
TOTAL	3	.2	187	11.8	5	.3	22	1.4	217	13.7	1,362	85.8	8	.5	
FEMALE	1	.2	55	12.3	1	.2	7	1.6	64	14.3	382	85.5	1	.2	
MALE	2	.2	132	11.6	4	.4	15	1.3	153	13.4	980	86.0	7	.6	
UNCLASSIFIED:															
TOTAL	0	.0	0	.0	0	.0	0	.0	0	.0	0	.0	0	.0	
FEMALE	0	.0	0	.0	0	.0	0	.0	0	.0	0	.0	0	.0	
MALE	0	.0	0	.0	0	.0	0	.0	0	.0	0	.0	0	.0	
TOTAL ENROLLMENT:															
TOTAL	3	.2	187	11.8	5	.3	22	1.4	217	13.7	1,362	85.8	8	.5	
FEMALE	1	.2	55	12.3	1	.2	7	1.6	64	14.3	382	85.5	1	.2	
MALE	2	.2	132	11.6	4	.4	15	1.3	153	13.4	980	86.0	7	.6	
MAINE (1 INSTITUTIONS)															
UNDERGRADUATES:															
FULL-TIME	0	.0	0	.0	0	.0	0	.0	0	.0	0	.0	0	.0	
FEMALE	0	.0	0	.0	0	.0	0	.0	0	.0	0	.0	0	.0	
MALE	0	.0	0	.0	0	.0	0	.0	0	.0	0	.0	0	.0	
PART-TIME	0	.0	0	.0	0	.0	0	.0	0	.0	0	.0	0	.0	
FEMALE	0	.0	0	.0	0	.0	0	.0	0	.0	0	.0	0	.0	
MALE	0	.0	0	.0	0	.0	0	.0	0	.0	0	.0	0	.0	
TOTAL	0	.0	0	.0	0	.0	0	.0	0	.0	0	.0	0	.0	
FEMALE	0	.0	0	.0	0	.0	0	.0	0	.0	0	.0	0	.0	
MALE	0	.0	0	.0	0	.0	0	.0	0	.0	0	.0	0	.0	
GRADUATE:															
FULL-TIME	0	.0	0	.0	0	.0	0	.0	0	.0	0	.0	0	.0	
FEMALE	0	.0	0	.0	0	.0	0	.0	0	.0	0	.0	0	.0	
MALE	0	.0	0	.0	0	.0	0	.0	0	.0	0	.0	0	.0	
PART-TIME	0	.0	0	.0	0	.0	0	.0	0	.0	0	.0	0	.0	
FEMALE	0	.0	0	.0	0	.0	0	.0	0	.0	0	.0	0	.0	
MALE	0	.0	0	.0	0	.0	0	.0	0	.0	0	.0	0	.0	
TOTAL	0	.0	0	.0	0	.0	0	.0	0	.0	0	.0	0	.0	
FEMALE	0	.0	0	.0	0	.0	0	.0	0	.0	0	.0	0	.0	
MALE	0	.0	0	.0	0	.0	0	.0	0	.0	0	.0	0	.0	
PROFESSIONAL:															
FULL-TIME	0	.0	0	.0	0	.0	0	.0	0	.0	241	100.0	0	.0	
FEMALE	0	.0	0	.0	0	.0	0	.0	0	.0	92	100.0	0	.0	
MALE	0	.0	0	.0	0	.0	0	.0	0	.0	149	100.0	0	.0	

LAW

I INDIAN NATIVE		BLACK NON-HISPANIC		ASIAN OR PACIFIC ISLANDER		HISPANIC		TOTAL MINORITY		WHITE NON-HISPANIC		NON-RESIDENT ALIEN		TOTAL
%	NUMBER	%	NUMBER	%	NUMBER	%	NUMBER	%	NUMBER	%	NUMBER	%	NUMBER	NUMBER

CONTINUED

.0	0	.0	0	.0	0	.0	0	.0	4	100.0	0	.0	4
.0	0	.0	0	.0	0	.0	0	.0	2	100.0	0	.0	2
.0	0	.0	0	.0	0	.0	0	.0	2	100.0	0	.0	2
.0	0	.0	0	.0	0	.0	0	.0	245	100.0	0	.0	245
.0	0	.0	0	.0	0	.0	0	.0	94	100.0	0	.0	94
.0	0	.0	0	.0	0	.0	0	.0	151	100.0	0	.0	151
.0	0	.0	0	.0	0	.0	0	.0	241	100.0	0	.0	241
.0	0	.0	0	.0	0	.0	0	.0	92	100.0	0	.0	92
.0	0	.0	0	.0	0	.0	0	.0	149	100.0	0	.0	149
.0	0	.0	0	.0	0	.0	0	.0	4	100.0	0	.0	4
.0	0	.0	0	.0	0	.0	0	.0	2	100.0	0	.0	2
.0	0	.0	0	.0	0	.0	0	.0	2	100.0	0	.0	2
.0	0	.0	0	.0	0	.0	0	.0	245	100.0	0	.0	245
.0	0	.0	0	.0	0	.0	0	.0	94	100.0	0	.0	94
.0	0	.0	0	.0	0	.0	0	.0	151	100.0	0	.0	151
.0	0	.0	0	.0	0	.0	0	.0	0	.0	0	.0	0
.0	0	.0	0	.0	0	.0	0	.0	0	.0	0	.0	0
.0	0	.0	0	.0	0	.0	0	.0	0	.0	0	.0	0
.0	0	.0	0	.0	0	.0	0	.0	245	100.0	0	.0	245
.0	0	.0	0	.0	0	.0	0	.0	94	100.0	0	.0	94
.0	0	.0	0	.0	0	.0	0	.0	151	100.0	0	.0	151

(2 INSTITUTIONS)

.0	0	.0	0	.0	0	.0	0	.0	0	.0	0	.0	0
.0	0	.0	0	.0	0	.0	0	.0	0	.0	0	.0	0
.0	0	.0	0	.0	0	.0	0	.0	0	.0	0	.0	0
.0	0	.0	0	.0	0	.0	0	.0	0	.0	0	.0	0
.0	0	.0	0	.0	0	.0	0	.0	0	.0	0	.0	0
.0	0	.0	0	.0	0	.0	0	.0	0	.0	0	.0	0
.0	0	.0	0	.0	0	.0	0	.0	0	.0	0	.0	0
.0	0	.0	0	.0	0	.0	0	.0	0	.0	0	.0	0
.0	0	.0	0	.0	0	.0	0	.0	0	.0	0	.0	0
.0	0	.0	0	.0	0	.0	0	.0	0	.0	0	.0	0
.0	0	.0	0	.0	0	.0	0	.0	0	.0	0	.0	0
.0	0	.0	0	.0	0	.0	0	.0	0	.0	0	.0	0
.0	0	.0	0	.0	0	.0	0	.0	0	.0	0	.0	0
.0	0	.0	0	.0	0	.0	0	.0	0	.0	0	.0	0
.0	0	.0	0	.0	0	.0	0	.0	0	.0	0	.0	0
.0	0	.0	0	.0	0	.0	0	.0	0	.0	0	.0	0
.0	0	.0	0	.0	0	.0	0	.0	0	.0	0	.0	0
.0	0	.0	0	.0	0	.0	0	.0	0	.0	0	.0	0
.1	107	7.0	4	.3	6	.4	118	7.8	1,402	92.2	1	.1	1,521
.0	40	8.6	0	.0	4	.9	44	9.5	421	90.5	0	.0	465
.1	67	6.3	4	.4	2	.2	74	7.0	981	92.9	1	.1	1,056
.0	21	8.2	1	.4	1	.4	23	9.0	228	89.4	4	1.6	255
.0	11	12.8	0	.0	1	1.2	12	14.0	72	83.7	2	2.3	86
.0	10	5.9	1	.6	0	.0	11	6.5	156	92.3	2	1.2	169
.1	128	7.2	5	.3	7	.4	141	7.9	1,630	91.8	5	.3	1,776
.0	51	9.3	0	.0	5	.9	56	10.2	493	89.5	2	.4	551
.1	77	6.3	5	.4	2	.2	85	6.9	1,137	92.8	3	.2	1,225
.1	107	7.0	4	.3	6	.4	118	7.8	1,402	92.2	1	.1	1,521
.0	40	8.6	0	.0	4	.9	44	9.5	421	90.5	0	.0	465
.1	67	6.3	4	.4	2	.2	74	7.0	981	92.9	1	.1	1,056
.0	21	8.2	1	.4	1	.4	23	9.0	228	89.4	4	1.6	255
.0	11	12.8	0	.0	1	1.2	12	14.0	72	83.7	2	2.3	86
.0	10	5.9	1	.6	0	.0	11	6.5	156	92.3	2	1.2	169
.1	128	7.2	5	.3	7	.4	141	7.9	1,630	91.8	5	.3	1,776
.0	51	9.3	0	.0	5	.9	56	10.2	493	89.5	2	.4	551
.1	77	6.3	5	.4	2	.2	85	6.9	1,137	92.8	3	.2	1,225
.0	0	.0	0	.0	0	.0	0	.0	0	.0	0	.0	0
.0	0	.0	0	.0	0	.0	0	.0	0	.0	0	.0	0
.0	0	.0	0	.0	0	.0	0	.0	0	.0	0	.0	0
.1	128	7.2	5	.3	7	.4	141	7.9	1,630	91.8	5	.3	1,776
.0	51	9.3	0	.0	5	.9	56	10.2	493	89.5	2	.4	551
.1	77	6.3	5	.4	2	.2	85	6.9	1,137	92.8	3	.2	1,225

TABLE 17 - TOTAL ENROLLMENT IN INSTITUTIONS OF HIGHER EDUCATION FOR SELECTED MAJOR FIELDS OF STUDY AND LEVEL OF ENROLLMENT
BY RACE, ETHNICITY, AND SEX: STATE, 1978

MAJOR FIELD 1400 - LAW

	AMERICAN INDIAN ALASKAN NATIVE		BLACK NON-HISPANIC		ASIAN OR PACIFIC ISLANDER		HISPANIC		TOTAL MINORITY		WHITE NON-HISPANIC		NON-RESIDENT ALIEN		T
	NUMBER	%	NUMBER	%	NUMBER	%	NUMBER	%	NUMBER	%	NUMBER	%	NUMBER	%	N
MASSACHUSETTS (7 INSTITUTIONS)															
UNDERGRADUATES:															
FULL-TIME	0	.0	0	.0	0	.0	0	.0	0	.0	0	.0	0	.0	
FEMALE	0	.0	0	.0	0	.0	0	.0	0	.0	0	.0	0	.0	
MALE	0	.0	0	.0	0	.0	0	.0	0	.0	0	.0	0	.0	
PART-TIME	0	.0	0	.0	0	.0	0	.0	0	.0	0	.0	0	.0	
FEMALE	0	.0	0	.0	0	.0	0	.0	0	.0	0	.0	0	.0	
MALE	0	.0	0	.0	0	.0	0	.0	0	.0	0	.0	0	.0	
TOTAL	0	.0	0	.0	0	.0	0	.0	0	.0	0	.0	0	.0	
FEMALE	0	.0	0	.0	0	.0	0	.0	0	.0	0	.0	0	.0	
MALE	0	.0	0	.0	0	.0	0	.0	0	.0	0	.0	0	.0	
GRADUATE:															
FULL-TIME	0	.0	0	.0	0	.0	0	.0	0	.0	0	.0	0	.0	
FEMALE	0	.0	0	.0	0	.0	0	.0	0	.0	0	.0	0	.0	
MALE	0	.0	0	.0	0	.0	0	.0	0	.0	0	.0	0	.0	
PART-TIME	0	.0	0	.0	0	.0	0	.0	0	.0	0	.0	0	.0	
FEMALE	0	.0	0	.0	0	.0	0	.0	0	.0	0	.0	0	.0	
MALE	0	.0	0	.0	0	.0	0	.0	0	.0	0	.0	0	.0	
TOTAL	0	.0	0	.0	0	.0	0	.0	0	.0	0	.0	0	.0	
FEMALE	0	.0	0	.0	0	.0	0	.0	0	.0	0	.0	0	.0	
MALE	0	.0	0	.0	0	.0	0	.0	0	.0	0	.0	0	.0	
PROFESSIONAL:															
FULL-TIME	14	.2	259	4.6	63	1.1	111	2.0	447	7.9	5,059	89.7	134	2.4	
FEMALE	6	.3	104	5.7	28	1.5	34	1.9	172	9.5	1,620	89.0	28	1.5	
MALE	8	.2	155	4.1	35	.9	77	2.0	275	7.2	3,439	90.0	106	2.8	
PART-TIME	4	.3	18	1.3	5	.4	5	.4	32	2.2	1,385	97.0	11	.8	
FEMALE	2	.5	8	2.0	3	.7	2	.5	15	3.7	392	95.8	2	.5	
MALE	2	.2	10	1.0	2	.2	3	.3	17	1.7	993	97.4	9	.9	
TOTAL	18	.3	277	3.9	68	1.0	116	1.6	479	6.8	6,444	91.2	145	2.1	
FEMALE	8	.4	112	5.0	31	1.4	36	1.6	187	8.4	2,012	90.3	30	1.3	
MALE	10	.2	165	3.4	37	.8	80	1.7	292	6.0	4,432	91.6	115	2.4	
UND+GRAD+PROF:															
FULL-TIME	14	.2	259	4.6	63	1.1	111	2.0	447	7.9	5,059	89.7	134	2.4	
FEMALE	6	.3	104	5.7	28	1.5	34	1.9	172	9.5	1,620	89.0	28	1.5	
MALE	8	.2	155	4.1	35	.9	77	2.0	275	7.2	3,439	90.0	106	2.8	
PART-TIME	4	.3	18	1.3	5	.4	5	.4	32	2.2	1,385	97.0	11	.8	
FEMALE	2	.5	8	2.0	3	.7	2	.5	15	3.7	392	95.8	2	.5	
MALE	2	.2	10	1.0	2	.2	3	.3	17	1.7	993	97.4	9	.9	
TOTAL	18	.3	277	3.9	68	1.0	116	1.6	479	6.8	6,444	91.2	145	2.1	
FEMALE	8	.4	112	5.0	31	1.4	36	1.6	187	8.4	2,012	90.3	30	1.3	
MALE	10	.2	165	3.4	37	.8	80	1.7	292	6.0	4,432	91.6	115	2.4	
UNCLASSIFIED:															
TOTAL	0	.0	0	.0	0	.0	0	.0	0	.0	0	.0	0	.0	
FEMALE	0	.0	0	.0	0	.0	0	.0	0	.0	0	.0	0	.0	
MALE	0	.0	0	.0	0	.0	0	.0	0	.0	0	.0	0	.0	
TOTAL ENROLLMENT:															
TOTAL	18	.3	277	3.9	68	1.0	116	1.6	479	6.8	6,444	91.2	145	2.1	
FEMALE	8	.4	112	5.0	31	1.4	36	1.6	187	8.4	2,012	90.3	30	1.3	
MALE	10	.2	165	3.4	37	.8	80	1.7	292	6.0	4,432	91.6	115	2.4	
MICHIGAN (5 INSTITUTIONS)															
UNDERGRADUATES:															
FULL-TIME	0	.0	0	.0	0	.0	0	.0	0	.0	0	.0	0	.0	
FEMALE	0	.0	0	.0	0	.0	0	.0	0	.0	0	.0	0	.0	
MALE	0	.0	0	.0	0	.0	0	.0	0	.0	0	.0	0	.0	
PART-TIME	0	.0	0	.0	0	.0	0	.0	0	.0	0	.0	0	.0	
FEMALE	0	.0	0	.0	0	.0	0	.0	0	.0	0	.0	0	.0	
MALE	0	.0	0	.0	0	.0	0	.0	0	.0	0	.0	0	.0	
TOTAL	0	.0	0	.0	0	.0	0	.0	0	.0	0	.0	0	.0	
FEMALE	0	.0	0	.0	0	.0	0	.0	0	.0	0	.0	0	.0	
MALE	0	.0	0	.0	0	.0	0	.0	0	.0	0	.0	0	.0	
GRADUATE:															
FULL-TIME	0	.0	0	.0	0	.0	0	.0	0	.0	0	.0	0	.0	
FEMALE	0	.0	0	.0	0	.0	0	.0	0	.0	0	.0	0	.0	
MALE	0	.0	0	.0	0	.0	0	.0	0	.0	0	.0	0	.0	
PART-TIME	0	.0	0	.0	0	.0	0	.0	0	.0	0	.0	0	.0	
FEMALE	0	.0	0	.0	0	.0	0	.0	0	.0	0	.0	0	.0	
MALE	0	.0	0	.0	0	.0	0	.0	0	.0	0	.0	0	.0	
TOTAL	0	.0	0	.0	0	.0	0	.0	0	.0	0	.0	0	.0	
FEMALE	0	.0	0	.0	0	.0	0	.0	0	.0	0	.0	0	.0	
MALE	0	.0	0	.0	0	.0	0	.0	0	.0	0	.0	0	.0	
PROFESSIONAL:															
FULL-TIME	15	.4	216	5.1	22	.5	71	1.7	324	7.6	3,911	91.6	35	.8	
FEMALE	4	.3	99	8.5	7	.6	20	1.7	130	11.2	1,029	88.3	6	.5	
MALE	11	.4	117	3.8	15	.5	51	1.6	194	6.2	2,882	92.8	29	.9	

562

LAW

AMER INDIAN NATIVE %	BLACK NON-HISPANIC NUMBER	%	ASIAN OR PACIFIC ISLANDER NUMBER	%	HISPANIC NUMBER	%	TOTAL MINORITY NUMBER	%	WHITE NON-HISPANIC NUMBER	%	NON-RESIDENT ALIEN NUMBER	%	TOTAL NUMBER
							CONTINUED						
.0	40	7.1	1	.2	1	.2	42	7.5	520	92.5	0	.0	562
.0	14	10.3	0	.0	0	.0	14	10.3	122	89.7	0	.0	136
.0	26	6.1	1	.2	1	.2	28	6.6	398	93.4	0	.0	426
.3	256	5.3	23	.5	72	1.5	366	7.6	4,431	91.7	35	.7	4,832
.3	113	8.7	7	.5	20	1.5	144	11.1	1,151	88.5	6	.5	1,301
.3	143	4.0	16	.5	52	1.5	222	6.3	3,280	92.9	29	.8	3,531
.4	216	5.1	22	.5	71	1.7	324	7.6	3,911	91.6	35	.8	4,270
.3	99	8.5	7	.6	20	1.7	130	11.2	1,029	88.3	6	.5	1,165
.4	117	3.8	15	.5	51	1.6	194	6.2	2,882	92.8	29	.9	3,105
.0	40	7.1	1	.2	1	.2	42	7.5	520	92.5	0	.0	562
.0	14	10.3	0	.0	0	.0	14	10.3	122	89.7	0	.0	136
.0	26	6.1	1	.2	1	.2	28	6.6	398	93.4	0	.0	426
.3	256	5.3	23	.5	72	1.5	366	7.6	4,431	91.7	35	.7	4,832
.3	113	8.7	7	.5	20	1.5	144	11.1	1,151	88.5	6	.5	1,301
.3	143	4.0	16	.5	52	1.5	222	6.3	3,280	92.9	29	.8	3,531
.0	0	.0	0	.0	0	.0	0	.0	0	.0	0	.0	0
.0	0	.0	0	.0	0	.0	0	.0	0	.0	0	.0	0
.0	0	.0	0	.0	0	.0	0	.0	0	.0	0	.0	0
.3	256	5.3	23	.5	72	1.5	366	7.6	4,431	91.7	35	.7	4,832
.3	113	8.7	7	.5	20	1.5	144	11.1	1,151	88.5	6	.5	1,301
.3	143	4.0	16	.5	52	1.5	222	6.3	3,280	92.9	29	.8	3,531
(3 INSTITUTIONS)													
.0	0	.0	0	.0	0	.0	0	.0	0	.0	0	.0	0
.0	0	.0	0	.0	0	.0	0	.0	0	.0	0	.0	0
.0	0	.0	0	.0	0	.0	0	.0	0	.0	0	.0	0
.0	0	.0	0	.0	0	.0	0	.0	0	.0	0	.0	0
.0	0	.0	0	.0	0	.0	0	.0	0	.0	0	.0	0
.0	0	.0	0	.0	0	.0	0	.0	0	.0	0	.0	0
.0	0	.0	0	.0	0	.0	0	.0	0	.0	0	.0	0
.0	0	.0	0	.0	0	.0	0	.0	0	.0	0	.0	0
.0	0	.0	0	.0	0	.0	0	.0	0	.0	0	.0	0
.0	0	.0	0	.0	0	.0	0	.0	0	.0	0	.0	0
.0	0	.0	0	.0	0	.0	0	.0	0	.0	0	.0	0
.0	0	.0	0	.0	0	.0	0	.0	0	.0	0	.0	0
.0	0	.0	0	.0	0	.0	0	.0	0	.0	0	.0	0
.0	0	.0	0	.0	0	.0	0	.0	0	.0	0	.0	0
.0	0	.0	0	.0	0	.0	0	.0	0	.0	0	.0	0
.0	0	.0	0	.0	0	.0	0	.0	0	.0	0	.0	0
.0	0	.0	0	.0	0	.0	0	.0	0	.0	0	.0	0
.0	0	.0	0	.0	0	.0	0	.0	0	.0	0	.0	0
.6	42	1.8	8	.3	17	.7	82	3.5	2,242	96.3	4	.2	2,328
.8	19	2.6	5	.7	5	.7	35	4.7	708	95.2	1	.1	744
.6	23	1.5	3	.2	12	.8	47	3.0	1,534	96.8	3	.2	1,584
.0	0	.0	0	.0	0	.0	0	.0	29	100.0	0	.0	29
.0	0	.0	0	.0	0	.0	0	.0	10	100.0	0	.0	10
.0	0	.0	0	.0	0	.0	0	.0	19	100.0	0	.0	19
.6	42	1.8	8	.3	17	.7	82	3.5	2,271	96.4	4	.2	2,357
.8	19	2.5	5	.7	5	.7	35	4.6	718	95.2	1	.1	754
.6	23	1.4	3	.2	12	.7	47	2.9	1,553	96.9	3	.2	1,603
.6	42	1.8	8	.3	17	.7	82	3.5	2,242	96.3	4	.2	2,328
.8	19	2.6	5	.7	5	.7	35	4.7	708	95.2	1	.1	744
.6	23	1.5	3	.2	12	.8	47	3.0	1,534	96.8	3	.2	1,584
.0	0	.0	0	.0	0	.0	0	.0	29	100.0	0	.0	29
.0	0	.0	0	.0	0	.0	0	.0	10	100.0	0	.0	10
.0	0	.0	0	.0	0	.0	0	.0	19	100.0	0	.0	19
.6	42	1.8	8	.3	17	.7	82	3.5	2,271	96.4	4	.2	2,357
.8	19	2.5	5	.7	5	.7	35	4.6	718	95.2	1	.1	754
.6	23	1.4	3	.2	12	.7	47	2.9	1,553	96.9	3	.2	1,603
.0	0	.0	0	.0	0	.0	0	.0	0	.0	0	.0	0
.0	0	.0	0	.0	0	.0	0	.0	0	.0	0	.0	0
.6	42	1.8	8	.3	17	.7	82	3.5	2,271	96.4	4	.2	2,357
.6	19	2.5	5	.7	5	.7	35	4.6	718	95.2	1	.1	754
.6	23	1.4	3	.2	12	.7	47	2.9	1,553	96.9	3	.2	1,603

TABLE 17 - TOTAL ENROLLMENT IN INSTITUTIONS OF HIGHER EDUCATION FOR SELECTED MAJOR FIELDS OF STUDY AND LEVEL OF ENROLLMENT
BY RACE, ETHNICITY, AND SEX: STATE, 1978

MAJOR FIELD 1400 - LAW

	AMERICAN INDIAN ALASKAN NATIVE		BLACK NON-HISPANIC		ASIAN OR PACIFIC ISLANDER		HISPANIC		TOTAL MINORITY		WHITE NON-HISPANIC		NON-RESIDENT ALIEN		TOT
	NUMBER	%	NUMBER	%	NUMBER	%	NUMBER	%	NUMBER	%	NUMBER	%	NUMBER	%	NUM
MISSISSIPPI	(	2 INSTITUTIONS)													
UNDERGRADUATES:															
FULL-TIME	0	.0	0	.0	0	.0	0	.0	0	.0	0	.0	0	.0	
FEMALE	0	.0	0	.0	0	.0	0	.0	0	.0	0	.0	0	.0	
MALE	0	.0	0	.0	0	.0	0	.0	0	.0	0	.0	0	.0	
PART-TIME	0	.0	0	.0	0	.0	0	.0	0	.0	0	.0	0	.0	
FEMALE	0	.0	0	.0	0	.0	0	.0	0	.0	0	.0	0	.0	
MALE	0	.0	0	.0	0	.0	0	.0	0	.0	0	.0	0	.0	
TOTAL	0	.0	0	.0	0	.0	0	.0	0	.0	0	.0		.0	
FEMALE	0	.0	0	.0	0	.0	0	.0	0	.0	0	.0	0	.0	
MALE	0	.0	0	.0	0	.0	0	.0	0	.0	0	.0	0	.0	
GRADUATE:															
FULL-TIME	0	.0	0	.0	0	.0	0	.0	0	.0	0	.0	0	.0	
FEMALE	0	.0	0	.0	0	.0	0	.0	0	.0	0	.0	0	.0	
MALE	0	.0	0	.0	0	.0	0	.0	0	.0	0	.0	0	.0	
PART-TIME	0	.0	0	.0	0	.0	0	.0	0	.0	0	.0	0	.0	
FEMALE	0	.0	0	.0	0	.0	0	.0	0	.0	0	.0	0	.0	
MALE	0	.0	0	.0	0	.0	0	.0	0	.0	0	.0	0	.0	
TOTAL	0	.0	0	.0	0	.0	0	.0	0	.0	0	.0	0	.0	
FEMALE	0	.0	0	.0	0	.0	0	.0	0	.0	0	.0	0	.0	
MALE	0	.0	0	.0	0	.0	0	.0	0	.0	0	.0	0	.0	
PROFESSIONAL:															
FULL-TIME	0	.0	26	4.0	0	.0	3	.5	29	4.5	615	95.5	0	.0	
FEMALE	0	.0	11	8.0	0	.0	1	.7	12	8.8	125	91.2	0	.0	
MALE	0	.0	15	3.0	0	.0	2	.4	17	3.4	490	96.6	0	.0	
PART-TIME	0	.0	3	1.0	2	.7	0	.0	5	1.7	284	95.9	7	2.4	
FEMALE	0	.0	0	.0	0	.0	0	.0	0	.0	58	89.2	7	10.8	
MALE	0	.0	3	1.3	2	.9	0	.0	5	2.2	226	97.8	0	.0	
TOTAL	0	.0	29	3.1	2	.2	3	.3	34	3.6	899	95.6	7	.7	
FEMALE	0	.0	11	5.4	0	.0	1	.5	12	5.9	183	90.6	7	3.5	
MALE	0	.0	18	2.4	2	.3	2	.3	22	3.0	716	97.0	0	.0	
UNI+GRAD+PROF:															
FULL-TIME	0	.0	26	4.0	0	.0	3	.5	29	4.5	615	95.5	0	.0	
FEMALE	0	.0	11	8.0	0	.0	1	.7	12	8.8	125	91.2	0	.0	
MALE	0	.0	15	3.0	0	.0	2	.4	17	3.4	490	96.6	0	.0	
PART-TIME	0	.0	3	1.0	2	.7	0	.0	5	1.7	284	95.9	7	2.4	
FEMALE	0	.0	0	.0	0	.0	0	.0	0	.0	58	89.2	7	10.8	
MALE	0	.0	3	1.3	2	.9	0	.0	5	2.2	226	97.8	0	.0	
TOTAL	0	.0	29	3.1	2	.2	3	.3	34	3.6	899	95.6	7	.7	
FEMALE	0	.0	11	5.4	0	.0	1	.5	12	5.9	183	90.6	7	3.5	
MALE	0	.0	18	2.4	2	.3	2	.3	22	3.0	716	97.0	0	.0	
UNCLASSIFIED:															
TOTAL	0	.0	0	.0	0	.0	0	.0	0	.0	0	.0	0	.0	
FEMALE	0	.0	0	.0	0	.0	0	.0	0	.0	0	.0	0	.0	
MALE	0	.0	0	.0	0	.0	0	.0	0	.0	0	.0	0	.0	
TOTAL ENROLLMENT:															
TOTAL	0	.0	29	3.1	2	.2	3	.3	34	3.6	899	95.6	7	.7	
FEMALE	0	.0	11	5.4	0	.0	1	.5	12	5.9	183	90.6	7	3.5	
MALE	0	.0	18	2.4	2	.3	2	.3	22	3.0	716	97.0	0	.0	
MISSOURI	(	4 INSTITUTIONS)													
UNDERGRADUATES:															
FULL-TIME	0	.0	0	.0	0	.0	0	.0	0	.0	0	.0	0	.0	
FEMALE	0	.0	0	.0	0	.0	0	.0	0	.0	0	.0	0	.0	
MALE	0	.0	0	.0	0	.0	0	.0	0	.0	0	.0	0	.0	
PART-TIME	0	.0	0	.0	0	.0	0	.0	0	.0	0	.0	0	.0	
FEMALE	0	.0	0	.0	0	.0	0	.0	0	.0	0	.0	0	.0	
MALE	0	.0	0	.0	0	.0	0	.0	0	.0	0	.0	0	.0	
TOTAL	0	.0	0	.0	0	.0	0	.0	0	.0	0	.0	0	.0	
FEMALE	0	.0	0	.0	0	.0	0	.0	0	.0	0	.0	0	.0	
MALE	0	.0	0	.0	0	.0	0	.0	0	.0	0	.0	0	.0	
GRADUATE:															
FULL-TIME	0	.0	0	.0	0	.0	0	.0	0	.0	0	.0	0	.0	
FEMALE	0	.0	0	.0	0	.0	0	.0	0	.0	0	.0	0	.0	
MALE	0	.0	0	.0	0	.0	0	.0	0	.0	0	.0	0	.0	
PART-TIME	0	.0	0	.0	0	.0	0	.0	0	.0	0	.0	0	.0	
FEMALE	0	.0	0	.0	0	.0	0	.0	0	.0	0	.0	0	.0	
MALE	0	.0	0	.0	0	.0	0	.0	0	.0	0	.0	0	.0	
TOTAL	0	.0	0	.0	0	.0	0	.0	0	.0	0	.0	0	.0	
FEMALE	0	.0	0	.0	0	.0	0	.0	0	.0	0	.0	0	.0	
MALE	0	.0	0	.0	0	.0	0	.0	0	.0	0	.0	0	.0	
PROFESSIONAL:															
FULL-TIME	4	.2	70	3.4	16	.8	7	.3	97	4.7	1,942	95.0	5	.2	2
FEMALE	2	.3	34	5.5	7	1.1	2	.3	45	7.3	568	92.5	1	.2	
MALE	2	.1	36	2.5	9	.6	5	.3	52	3.6	1,374	96.1	4	.3	1

- LAW

CAN INDIAN AN NATIVE		BLACK NON-HISPANIC		ASIAN OR PACIFIC ISLANDER		HISPANIC		TOTAL MINORITY		WHITE NON-HISPANIC		NON-RESIDENT ALIEN		TOTAL
ER	%	NUMBER	%	NUMBER	%	NUMBER	%	NUMBER	%	NUMBER	%	NUMBER	%	NUMBER
CONTINUED														
2	1.9	6	5.6	0	.0	0	.0	8	7.4	99	91.7	1	.9	108
0	.0	4	13.3	0	.0	0	.0	4	13.3	26	86.7	0	.0	30
2	2.6	2	2.6	0	.0	0	.0	4	5.1	73	93.6	1	1.3	78
6	.3	76	3.5	16	.7	7	.3	105	4.9	2,041	94.8	6	.3	2,152
2	.3	38	5.9	7	1.1	2	.3	49	7.6	594	92.2	1	.2	644
4	.3	38	2.5	9	.6	5	.3	56	3.7	1,447	96.0	5	.3	1,508
4	.2	70	3.4	16	.8	7	.3	97	4.7	1,942	95.0	5	.2	2,044
2	.3	34	5.5	7	1.1	2	.3	45	7.3	568	92.5	1	.2	614
2	.1	36	2.5	9	.6	5	.3	52	3.6	1,374	96.1	4	.3	1,430
2	1.9	6	5.6	0	.0	0	.0	8	7.4	99	91.7	1	.9	108
0	.0	4	13.3	0	.0	0	.0	4	13.3	26	86.7	0	.0	30
2	2.6	2	2.6	0	.0	0	.0	4	5.1	73	93.6	1	1.3	78
6	.3	76	3.5	16	.7	7	.3	105	4.9	2,041	94.8	6	.3	2,152
2	.3	38	5.9	7	1.1	2	.3	49	7.6	594	92.2	1	.2	644
4	.3	38	2.5	9	.6	5	.3	56	3.7	1,447	96.0	5	.3	1,508
0	.0	0	.0	0	.0	0	.0	0	.0	0	.0	0	.0	0
0	.0	0	.0	0	.0	0	.0	0	.0	0	.0	0	.0	0
0	.0	0	.0	0	.0	0	.0	0	.0	0	.0	0	.0	0
6	.3	76	3.5	16	.7	7	.3	105	4.9	2,041	94.8	6	.3	2,152
2	.3	38	5.9	7	1.1	2	.3	49	7.6	594	92.2	1	.2	644
4	.3	38	2.5	9	.6	5	.3	56	3.7	1,447	96.0	5	.3	1,508
(	1 INSTITUTIONS)													
0	.0	0	.0	0	.0	0	.0	0	.0	0	.0	0	.0	0
0	.0	0	.0	0	.0	0	.0	0	.0	0	.0	0	.0	0
0	.0	0	.0	0	.0	0	.0	0	.0	0	.0	0	.0	0
0	.0	0	.0	0	.0	0	.0	0	.0	0	.0	0	.0	0
0	.0	0	.0	0	.0	0	.0	0	.0	0	.0	0	.0	0
0	.0	0	.0	0	.0	0	.0	0	.0	0	.0	0	.0	0
0	.0	0	.0	0	.0	0	.0	0	.0	0	.0	0	.0	0
0	.0	0	.0	0	.0	0	.0	0	.0	0	.0	0	.0	0
0	.0	0	.0.	0	.0	0	.0	0	.0	0	.0	0	.0	0
0	.0	0	.0	0	.0	0	.0	0	.0	0	.0	0	.0	0
0	.0	0	.0	0	.0	0	.0	0	.0	0	.0	0	.0	0
0	.0	0	.0	0	.0	0	.0	0	.0	0	.0	0	.0	0
0	.0	0	.0	0	.0	0	.0	0	.0	0	.0	0	.0	0
0	.0	0	.0	0	.0	0	.0	0	.0	0	.0	0	.0	0
0	.0	0	.0	0	.0	0	.0	0	.0	0	.0	0	.0	0
0	.0	0	.0	0	.0	0	.0	0	.0	0	.0	0	.0	0
0	.0	0	.0	0	.0	0	.0	0	.0	0	.0	0	.0	0
0	.0	0	.0	0	.0	0	.0	0	.0	0	.0	0	.0	0
0	.0	0	.0	0	.0	0	.0	0	.0	217	99.5	1	.5	218
0	.0	0	.0	0	.0	0	.0	0	.0	64	100.0	0	.0	64
0	.0	0	.0	0	.0	0	.0	0	.0	153	99.4	1	.6	154
0	.0	0	.0	0	.0	0	.0	0	.0	5	100.0	0	.0	5
0	.0	0	.0	0	.0	0	.0	0	.0	3	100.0	0	.0	3
0	.0	0	.0	0	.0	0	.0	0	.0	2	100.0	0	.0	2
0	.0	0	.0	0	.0	0	.0	0	.0	222	99.6	1	.4	223
0	.0	0	.0	0	.0	0	.0	0	.0	67	100.0	0	.0	67
0	.0	0	.0	0	.0	0	.0	0	.0	155	99.4	1	.6	156
0	.0	0	.0	0	.0	0	.0	0	.0	217	99.5	1	.5	218
0	.0	0	.0	0	.0	0	.0	0	.0	64	100.0	0	.0	64
0	.0	0	.0	0	.0	0	.0	0	.0	153	99.4	1	.0	154
0	.0	0	.0	0	.0	0	.0	0	.0	5	100.0	0	.0	5
0	.0	0	.0	0	.0	0	.0	0	.0	3	100.0	0	.0	3
0	.0	0	.0	0	.0	0	.0	0	.0	2	100.0	0	.0	2
0	.0	0	.0	0	.0	0	.0	0	.0	222	99.6	1	.4	223
0	.0	0	.0	0	.0	0	.0	0	.0	67	100.0	0	.0	67
0	.0	0	.0	0	.0	0	.0	0	.0	155	99.4	1	.6	156
0	.0	0	.0	0	.0	0	.0	0	.0	0	.0	0	.0	0
0	.0	0	.0	0	.0	0	.0	0	.0	0	.0	0	.0	0
0	.0	0	.0	0	.0	0	.0	0	.0	0	.0	0	.0	0
0	.0	0	.0	0	.0	0	.0	0	.0	222	99.6	1	.4	223
0	.0	0	.0	0	.0	0	.0	0	.0	67	100.0	0	.0	67
0	.0	0	.0	0	.0	0	.0	0	.0	155	99.4	1	.6	156

MAJOR FIELD 1400 - LAW

	AMERICAN INDIAN ALASKAN NATIVE		BLACK NON-HISPANIC		ASIAN OR PACIFIC ISLANDER		HISPANIC		TOTAL MINORITY		WHITE NON-HISPANIC		NON-RESIDENT ALIEN		T(
	NUMBER	%	NUMBER	%	NUMBER	%	NUMBER	%	NUMBER	%	NUMBER	%	NUMBER	%	N(
NEBRASKA (2 INSTITUTIONS)															
UNDERGRADUATES:															
FULL-TIME	0	.0	0	.0	0	.0	0	.0	0	.0	0	.0	0	.0	
FEMALE	0	.0	0	.0	0	.0	0	.0	0	.0	0	.0	0	.0	
MALE	0	.0	0	.0	0	.0	0	.0	0	.0	0	.0	0	.0	
PART-TIME	0	.0	0	.0	0	.0	0	.0	0	.0	0	.0	0	.0	
FEMALE	0	.0	0	.0	0	.0	0	.0	0	.0	0	.0	0	.0	
MALE	0	.0	0	.0	0	.0	0	.0	0	.0	0	.0	0	.0	
TOTAL	0	.0	0	.0	0	.0	0	.0	0	.0	0	.0	0	.0	
FEMALE	0	.0	0	.0	0	.0	0	.0	0	.0	0	.0	0	.0	
MALE	0	.0	0	.0	0	.0	0	.0	0	.0	0	.0	0	.0	
GRADUATE:															
FULL-TIME	0	.0	0	.0	0	.0	0	.0	0	.0	0	.0	0	.0	
FEMALE	0	.0	0	.0	0	.0	0	.0	0	.0	0	.0	0	.0	
MALE	0	.0	0	.0	0	.0	0	.0	0	.0	0	.0	0	.0	
PART-TIME	0	.0	0	.0	0	.0	0	.0	0	.0	0	.0	0	.0	
FEMALE	0	.0	0	.0	0	.0	0	.0	0	.0	0	.0	0	.0	
MALE	0	.0	0	.0	0	.0	0	.0	0	.0	0	.0	0	.0	
TOTAL	0	.0	0	.0	0	.0	0	.0	0	.0	0	.0	0	.0	
FEMALE	0	.0	0	.0	0	.0	0	.0	0	.0	0	.0	0	.0	
MALE	0	.0	0	.0	0	.0	0	.0	0	.0	0	.0	0	.0	
PROFESSIONAL:															
FULL-TIME	1	.1	18	1.8	3	.3	5	.5	27	2.7	970	97.2	1	.1	
FEMALE	0	.0	6	2.4	1	.4	2	.8	9	3.6	243	96.4	0	.0	
MALE	1	.1	12	1.6	2	.3	3	.4	18	2.4	727	97.5	1	.1	
PART-TIME	0	.0	1	16.7	0	.0	0	.0	1	16.7	5	83.3	0	.0	
FEMALE	0	.0	1	100.0	0	.0	0	.0	1	100.0	0	.0	0	.0	
MALE	0	.0	0	.0	0	.0	0	.0	0	.0	5	100.0	0	.0	
TOTAL	1	.1	19	1.9	3	.3	5	.5	28	2.8	975	97.1	1	.1	
FEMALE	0	.0	7	2.8	1	.4	2	.8	10	4.0	243	96.0	0	.0	
MALE	1	.1	12	1.6	2	.3	3	.4	18	2.4	732	97.5	1	.1	
UND+GRAD+PROF:															
FULL-TIME	1	.1	18	1.8	3	.3	5	.5	27	2.7	970	97.2	1	.1	
FEMALE	0	.0	6	2.4	1	.4	2	.8	9	3.6	243	96.4	0	.0	
MALE	1	.1	12	1.6	2	.3	3	.4	18	2.4	727	97.5	1	.1	
PART-TIME	0	.0	1	16.7	0	.0	0	.0	1	16.7	5	83.3	0	.0	
FEMALE	0	.0	1	100.0	0	.0	0	.0	1	100.0	0	.0	0	.0	
MALE	0	.0	0	.0	0	.0	0	.0	0	.0	5	100.0	0	.0	
TOTAL	1	.1	19	1.9	3	.3	5	.5	28	2.8	975	97.1	1	.1	
FEMALE	0	.0	7	2.8	1	.4	2	.8	10	4.0	243	96.0	0	.0	
MALE	1	.1	12	1.6	2	.3	3	.4	18	2.4	732	97.5	1	.1	
UNCLASSIFIED:															
TOTAL	0	.0	0	.0	0	.0	0	.0	0	.0	0	.0	0	.0	
FEMALE	0	.0	0	.0	0	.0	0	.0	0	.0	0	.0	0	.0	
MALE	0	.0	0	.0	0	.0	0	.0	0	.0	0	.0	0	.0	
TOTAL ENROLLMENT:															
TOTAL	1	.1	19	1.9	3	.3	5	.5	28	2.8	975	97.1	1	.1	
FEMALE	0	.0	7	2.8	1	.4	2	.8	10	4.0	243	96.0	0	.0	
MALE	1	.1	12	1.6	2	.3	3	.4	18	2.4	732	97.5	1	.1	
NEW HAMPSHIRE (1 INSTITUTIONS)															
UNDERGRADUATES:															
FULL-TIME	0	.0	0	.0	0	.0	0	.0	0	.0	0	.0	0	.0	
FEMALE	0	.0	0	.0	0	.0	0	.0	0	.0	0	.0	0	.0	
MALE	0	.0	0	.0	0	.0	0	.0	0	.0	0	.0	0	.0	
PART-TIME	0	.0	0	.0	0	.0	0	.0	0	.0	0	.0	0	.0	
FEMALE	0	.0	0	.0	0	.0	0	.0	0	.0	0	.0	0	.0	
MALE	0	.0	0	.0	0	.0	0	.0	0	.0	0	.0	0	.0	
TOTAL	0	.0	0	.0	0	.0	0	.0	0	.0	0	.0	0	.0	
FEMALE	0	.0	0	.0	0	.0	0	.0	0	.0	0	.0	0	.0	
MALE	0	.0	0	.0	0	.0	0	.0	0	.0	0	.0	0	.0	
GRADUATE:															
FULL-TIME	0	.0	0	.0	0	.0	0	.0	0	.0	0	.0	0	.0	
FEMALE	0	.0	0	.0	0	.0	0	.0	0	.0	0	.0	0	.0	
MALE	0	.0	0	.0	0	.0	0	.0	0	.0	0	.0	0	.0	
PART-TIME	0	.0	0	.0	0	.0	0	.0	0	.0	0	.0	0	.0	
FEMALE	0	.0	0	.0	0	.0	0	.0	0	.0	0	.0	0	.0	
MALE	0	.0	0	.0	0	.0	0	.0	0	.0	0	.0	0	.0	
TOTAL	0	.0	0	.0	0	.0	0	.0	0	.0	0	.0	0	.0	
FEMALE	0	.0	0	.0	0	.0	0	.0	0	.0	0	.0	0	.0	
MALE	0	.0	0	.0	0	.0	0	.0	0	.0	0	.0	0	.0	
PROFESSIONAL:															
FULL-TIME	3	1.2	0	.0	3	1.2	5	2.0	11	4.4	240	95.6	0	.0	
FEMALE	2	13.3	0	.0	2	13.3	1	6.7	5	33.3	10	66.7	0	.0	
MALE	1	.4	0	.0	1	.4	4	1.7	6	2.5	230	97.5	0	.0	

ENROLLMENT IN INSTITUTIONS OF HIGHER EDUCATION FOR SELECTED MAJOR FIELDS OF STUDY AND LEVEL OF ENROLLMENT
CE, ETHNICITY, AND SEX: STATE, 1976

- LAW

	GAN INDIAN AN NATIVE		BLACK NON-HISPANIC		ASIAN OR PACIFIC ISLANDER		HISPANIC		TOTAL MINORITY		WHITE NON-HISPANIC		NON-RESIDENT ALIEN		TUTAL
ER	%	NUMBER	%	NUMBER	%	NUMBER	%	NUMBER	%	NUMBER	%	NUMBER	%	NUMBER
CONTINUED															
0	.0	0	.0	0	.0	0	.0	0	.0	0	.0	0	.0	0
0	.0	0	.0	0	.0	0	.0	0	.0	0	.0	0	.0	0
0	.0	0	.0	0	.0	0	.0	0	.0	0	.0	0	.0	0
3	1.2	0	.0	3	1.2	5	2.0	11	4.4	240	95.6	0	.0	251
2	13.3	0	.0	2	13.3	1	6.7	5	33.3	10	66.7	0	.0	15
1	.4	0	.0	1	.4	4	1.7	6	2.5	230	97.5	0	.0	236
3	1.2	0	.0	3	1.2	5	2.0	11	4.4	240	95.6	0	.0	251
2	13.3	0	.0	2	13.3	1	6.7	5	33.3	10	66.7	0	.0	15
1	.4	0	.0	1	.4	4	1.7	6	2.5	230	97.5	0	.0	236
0	.0	0	.0	0	.0	0	.0	0	.0	0	.0	0	.0	0
0	.0	0	.0	0	.0	0	.0	0	.0	0	.0	0	.0	0
3	1.2	0	.0	3	1.2	5	2.0	11	4.4	240	95.6	0	.0	251
2	13.3	0	.0	2	13.3	1	6.7	5	33.3	10	66.7	0	.0	15
1	.4	0	.0	1	.4	4	1.7	6	2.5	230	97.5	0	.0	236
0	.0	0	.0	0	.0	0	.0	0	.0	0	.0	0	.0	0
0	.0	0	.0	0	.0	0	.0	0	.0	0	.0	0	.0	0
0	.0	0	.0	0	.0	0	.0	0	.0	0	.0	0	.0	0
3	1.2	0	.0	3	1.2	5	2.0	11	4.4	240	95.6	0	.0	251
2	13.3	0	.0	2	13.3	1	6.7	5	33.3	10	66.7	0	.0	15
1	.4	0	.0	1	.4	4	1.7	6	2.5	230	97.5	0	.0	236
(3 INSTITUTIONS)															
0	.0	0	.0	0	.0	0	.0	0	.0	0	.0	0	.0	0
0	.0	0	.0	0	.0	0	.0	0	.0	0	.0	0	.0	0
0	.0	0	.0	0	.0	0	.0	0	.0	0	.0	0	.0	0
0	.0	0	.0	0	.0	0	.0	0	.0	0	.0	0	.0	0
0	.0	0	.0	0	.0	0	.0	0	.0	0	.0	0	.0	0
0	.0	0	.0	0	.0	0	.0	0	.0	0	.0	0	.0	0
0	.0	0	.0	0	.0	0	.0	0	.0	0	.0	0	.0	0
0	.0	0	.0	0	.0	0	.0	0	.0	0	.0	0	.0	J
0	.0	0	.0	0	.0	0	.0	0	.0	0	.0	0	.0	0
0	.0	0	.0	0	.0	0	.0	0	.0	0	.0	0	.0	0
0	.0	0	.0	0	.0	0	.0	0	.0	0	.0	0	.0	0
0	.0	0	.0	0	.0	0	.0	0	.0	0	.0	0	.0	0
0	.0	0	.0	0	.0	0	.0	0	.0	0	.0	0	.0	0
0	.0	0	.0	0	.0	0	.0	0	.0	0	.0	0	.0	0
0	.0	0	.0	0	.0	0	.0	0	.0	0	.0	0	.0	0
0	.0	0	.0	0	.0	0	.0	0	.0	0	.0	0	.0	0
0	.0	0	.0	0	.0	0	.0	0	.0	0	.0	0	.0	0
1	.1	135	7.6	23	1.3	69	3.9	228	12.8	1,559	87.2	0	.0	1,787
0	.0	66	10.2	13	2.0	31	4.8	110	16.9	539	83.1	0	.0	649
1	.1	69	6.1	10	.9	38	3.3	118	10.4	1,020	89.6	0	.0	1,138
3	.3	67	7.5	9	1.0	34	3.8	113	12.6	782	87.4	0	.0	895
2	.7	32	10.9	4	1.4	14	4.8	52	17.7	242	82.3	0	.0	294
1	.2	35	5.8	5	.8	20	3.3	61	10.1	540	89.9	0	.0	601
4	.1	202	7.5	32	1.2	103	3.8	341	12.7	2,341	87.3	0	.0	2,682
2	.2	98	10.4	17	1.8	45	4.8	162	17.2	781	82.8	0	.0	943
2	.1	104	6.0	15	.9	58	3.3	179	10.3	1,560	89.7	0	.0	1,739
1	.1	135	7.6	23	1.3	69	3.9	228	12.8	1,559	87.2	0	.0	1,787
0	.0	66	10.2	13	2.0	31	4.8	110	16.9	539	83.1	0	.0	649
1	.1	69	6.1	10	.9	38	3.3	118	10.4	1,020	89.6	0	.0	1,138
3	.3	67	7.5	9	1.0	34	3.8	113	12.6	782	87.4	0	.0	895
2	.7	32	10.9	4	1.4	14	4.8	52	17.7	242	82.3	0	.0	294
1	.2	35	5.8	5	.8	20	3.3	61	10.1	540	89.9	0	.0	601
4	.1	202	7.5	32	1.2	103	3.8	341	12.7	2,341	87.3	0	.0	2,682
2	.2	98	10.4	17	1.8	45	4.8	162	17.2	781	82.8	0	.0	943
2	.1	104	6.0	15	.9	58	3.3	179	10.3	1,560	89.7	0	.0	1,739
0	.0	0	.0	0	.0	0	.0	0	.0	0	.0	0	.0	0
0	.0	0	.0	0	.0	0	.0	0	.0	0	.0	0	.0	0
0	.0	0	.0	0	.0	0	.0	0	.0	0	.0	0	.0	0
4	.1	202	7.5	32	1.2	103	3.8	341	12.7	2,341	87.3	0	.0	2,682
2	.2	98	10.4	17	1.8	45	4.8	162	17.2	781	82.8	0	.0	943
2	.1	104	6.0	15	.9	58	3.3	179	10.3	1,560	89.7	0	.0	1,739

MAJOR FIELD 1400 - LAW

	AMERICAN INDIAN ALASKAN NATIVE		BLACK NON-HISPANIC		ASIAN OR PACIFIC ISLANDER		HISPANIC		TOTAL MINORITY		WHITE NON-HISPANIC		NON-RESIDENT ALIEN		TOT
	NUMBER	%	NUMBER	%	NUMBER	%	NUMBER	%	NUMBER	%	NUMBER	%	NUMBER	%	NUM
NEW MEXICO (1 INSTITUTIONS)															
UNDERGRADUATES:															
FULL-TIME	0	.0	0	.0	0	.0	0	.0	0	.0	0	.0	0	.0	
FEMALE	0	.0	0	.0	0	.0	0	.0	0	.0	0	.0	0	.0	
MALE	0	.0	0	.0	0	.0	0	.0	0	.0	0	.0	0	.0	
PART-TIME	0	.0	0	.0	0	.0	0	.0	0	.0	0	.0	0	.0	
FEMALE	0	.0	0	.0	0	.0	0	.0	0	.0	0	.0	0	.0	
MALE	0	.0	0	.0	0	.0	0	.0	0	.0	0	.0	0	.0	
TOTAL	0	.0	0	.0	0	.0	0	.0	0	.0	0	.0	0	.0	
FEMALE	0	.0	0	.0	0	.0	0	.0	0	.0	0	.0	0	.0	
MALE	0	.0	0	.0	0	.0	0	.0	0	.0	0	.0	0	.0	
GRADUATE:															
FULL-TIME	0	.0	0	.0	0	.0	0	.0	0	.0	0	.0	0	.0	
FEMALE	0	.0	0	.0	0	.0	0	.0	0	.0	0	.0	0	.0	
MALE	0	.0	0	.0	0	.0	0	.0	0	.0	0	.0	0	.0	
PART-TIME	0	.0	0	.0	0	.0	0	.0	0	.0	0	.0	0	.0	
FEMALE	0	.0	0	.0	0	.0	0	.0	0	.0	0	.0	0	.0	
MALE	0	.0	0	.0	0	.0	0	.0	0	.0	0	.0	0	.0	
TOTAL	0	.0	0	.0	0	.0	0	.0	0	.0	0	.0	0	.0	
FEMALE	0	.0	0	.0	0	.0	0	.0	0	.0	0	.0	0	.0	
MALE	0	.0	0	.0	0	.0	0	.0	0	.0	0	.0	0	.0	
PROFESSIONAL:															
FULL-TIME	15	4.8	5	1.6	4	1.3	88	28.4	112	36.1	198	63.9	0	.0	
FEMALE	6	4.7	2	1.6	3	2.4	31	24.4	42	33.1	85	66.9	0	.0	
MALE	9	4.9	3	1.6	1	.5	57	31.1	70	38.3	113	61.7	0	.0	
PART-TIME	1	7.1	0	.0	1	7.1	2	14.3	4	28.6	10	71.4	0	.0	
FEMALE	0	.0	0	.0	0	.0	1	25.0	1	25.0	3	75.0	0	.0	
MALE	1	10.0	0	.0	1	10.0	1	10.0	3	30.0	7	70.0	0	.0	
TOTAL	16	4.9	5	1.5	5	1.5	90	27.8	116	35.8	208	64.2	0	.0	
FEMALE	6	4.6	2	1.5	3	2.3	32	24.4	43	32.8	88	67.2	0	.0	
MALE	10	5.2	3	1.6	2	1.0	58	30.1	73	37.8	120	62.2	0	.0	
UND+GRAD+PROF:															
FULL-TIME	15	4.8	5	1.6	4	1.3	88	28.4	112	36.1	198	63.9	0	.0	
FEMALE	6	4.7	2	1.6	3	2.4	31	24.4	42	33.1	85	66.9	0	.0	
MALE	9	4.9	3	1.6	1	.5	57	31.1	70	38.3	113	61.7	0	.0	
PART-TIME	1	7.1	0	.0	1	7.1	2	14.3	4	28.6	10	71.4	0	.0	
FEMALE	0	.0	0	.0	0	.0	1	25.0	1	25.0	3	75.0	0	.0	
MALE	1	10.0	0	.0	1	10.0	1	10.0	3	30.0	7	70.0	0	.0	
TOTAL	16	4.9	5	1.5	5	1.5	90	27.8	116	35.8	208	64.2	0	.0	
FEMALE	6	4.6	2	1.5	3	2.3	32	24.4	43	32.8	88	67.2	0	.0	
MALE	10	5.2	3	1.6	2	1.0	58	30.1	73	37.8	120	62.2	0	.0	
UNCLASSIFIED:															
TOTAL	0	.0	0	.0	0	.0	0	.0	0	.0	0	.0	0	.0	
FEMALE	0	.0	0	.0	0	.0	0	.0	0	.0	0	.0	0	.0	
MALE	0	.0	0	.0	0	.0	0	.0	0	.0	0	.0	0	.0	
TOTAL ENROLLMENT:															
TOTAL	16	4.9	5	1.5	5	1.5	90	27.8	116	35.8	208	64.2	0	.0	
FEMALE	6	4.6	2	1.5	3	2.3	32	24.4	43	32.8	88	67.2	0	.0	
MALE	10	5.2	3	1.6	2	1.0	58	30.1	73	37.8	120	62.2	0	.0	
NEW YORK (13 INSTITUTIONS)															
UNDERGRADUATES:															
FULL-TIME	0	.0	0	.0	0	.0	0	.0	0	.0	0	.0	0	.0	
FEMALE	0	.0	0	.0	0	.0	0	.0	0	.0	0	.0	0	.0	
MALE	0	.0	0	.0	0	.0	0	.0	0	.0	0	.0	0	.0	
PART-TIME	0	.0	0	.0	0	.0	0	.0	0	.0	0	.0	0	.0	
FEMALE	0	.0	0	.0	0	.0	0	.0	0	.0	0	.0	0	.0	
MALE	0	.0	0	.0	0	.0	0	.0	0	.0	0	.0	0	.0	
TOTAL	0	.0	0	.0	0	.0	0	.0	0	.0	0	.0	0	.0	
FEMALE	0	.0	0	.0	0	.0	0	.0	0	.0	0	.0	0	.0	
MALE	0	.0	0	.0	0	.0	0	.0	0	.0	0	.0	0	.0	
GRADUATE:															
FULL-TIME	0	.0	0	.0	0	.0	0	.0	0	.0	0	.0	0	.0	
FEMALE	0	.0	0	.0	0	.0	0	.0	0	.0	0	.0	0	.0	
MALE	0	.0	0	.0	0	.0	0	.0	0	.0	0	.0	0	.0	
PART-TIME	0	.0	0	.0	0	.0	0	.0	0	.0	0	.0	0	.0	
FEMALE	0	.0	0	.0	0	.0	0	.0	0	.0	0	.0	0	.0	
MALE	0	.0	0	.0	0	.0	0	.0	0	.0	0	.0	0	.0	
TOTAL	0	.0	0	.0	0	.0	0	.0	0	.0	0	.0	0	.0	
FEMALE	0	.0	0	.0	0	.0	0	.0	0	.0	0	.0	0	.0	
MALE	0	.0	0	.0	0	.0	0	.0	0	.0	0	.0	0	.0	
PROFESSIONAL:															
FULL-TIME	23	.2	331	3.4	69	.7	182	1.9	605	6.3	9,040	93.4	29	.3	9
FEMALE	14	.4	179	5.1	30	.8	69	2.0	292	8.3	3,231	91.5	7	.2	3
MALE	9	.1	152	2.5	39	.6	113	1.8	313	5.1	5,809	94.5	22	.4	6

17 - TOTAL ENROLLMENT IN INSTITUTIONS OF HIGHER EDUCATION FOR SELECTED MAJOR FIELDS OF STUDY AND LEVEL OF ENROLLMENT BY RACE, ETHNICITY, AND SEX: STATE, 1978

FIELD 1400 - LAW

	AMERICAN INDIAN ALASKAN NATIVE		BLACK NON-HISPANIC		ASIAN OR PACIFIC ISLANDER		HISPANIC		TOTAL MINORITY		WHITE NON-HISPANIC		NON-RESIDENT ALIEN		TOTAL
	NUMBER	%	NUMBER	%	NUMBER	%	NUMBER	%	NUMBER	%	NUMBER	%	NUMBER	%	NUMBER
RK		CONTINUED													
SIGNAL:															
IME	1	.1	53	2.9	11	.6	35	1.9	100	5.5	1,713	94.4	2	.1	1,815
ALE	0	.0	27	5.2	1	.2	12	2.3	40	7.7	478	92.3	0	.0	518
ALE	1	.1	26	2.0	10	.8	23	1.8	60	4.6	1,235	95.2	2	.2	1,297
	24	.2	384	3.3	80	.7	217	1.9	705	6.1	10,753	93.6	31	.3	11,489
ALE	14	.3	206	5.1	31	.8	81	2.0	332	8.2	3,709	91.6	7	.2	4,048
ALE	10	.1	178	2.4	49	.7	136	1.8	373	5.0	7,044	94.7	24	.3	7,441
AC+PROF:															
IME	23	.2	331	3.4	69	.7	182	1.9	605	6.3	9,040	93.4	29	.3	9,674
ALE	14	.4	179	5.1	30	.8	69	2.0	292	8.3	3,231	91.5	7	.2	3,530
ALE	9	.1	152	2.5	39	.6	113	1.8	313	5.1	5,809	94.5	22	.4	6,144
IME	1	.1	53	2.9	11	.6	35	1.9	100	5.5	1,713	94.4	2	.1	1,815
ALE	0	.0	27	5.2	1	.2	12	2.3	40	7.7	478	92.3	0	.0	518
ALE	1	.1	26	2.0	10	.8	23	1.8	60	4.6	1,235	95.2	2	.2	1,297
	24	.2	384	3.3	80	.7	217	1.9	705	6.1	10,753	93.6	31	.3	11,489
ALE	14	.3	206	5.1	31	.8	81	2.0	332	8.2	3,709	91.6	7	.2	4,048
ALE	10	.1	176	2.4	49	.7	136	1.8	373	5.0	7,044	94.7	24	.3	7,441
SIFIED:															
	0	.0	0	.0	0	.0	0	.0	0	.0	0	.0	0	.0	0
ALE	0	.0	0	.0	0	.0	0	.0	0	.0	0	.0	0	.0	0
ALE	0	.0	0	.0	0	.0	0	.0	0	.0	0	.0	0	.0	0
ENROLLMENT:															
	24	.2	384	3.3	80	.7	217	1.9	705	6.1	10,753	93.6	31	.3	11,489
ALE	14	.3	206	5.1	31	.8	81	2.0	332	8.2	3,709	91.6	7	.2	4,048
ALE	10	.1	178	2.4	49	.7	136	1.8	373	5.0	7,044	94.7	24	.3	7,441
CAROLINA	(	5 INSTITUTIONS)													
RADUATES:															
IME	0	.0	0	.0	0	.0	0	.0	0	.0	0	.0	0	.0	0
ALE	0	.0	0	.0	0	.0	0	.0	0	.0	0	.0	0	.0	0
ALE	0	.0	0	.0	0	.0	0	.0	0	.0	0	.0	0	.0	0
IME	0	.0	0	.0	0	.0	0	.0	0	.0	0	.0	0	.0	0
ALE	0	.0	0	.0	0	.0	0	.0	0	.0	0	.0	0	.0	0
ALE	0	.0	0	.0	0	.0	0	.0	0	.0	0	.0	0	.0	0
	0	.0	0	.0	0	.0	0	.0	0	.0	0	.0	0	.0	0
ALE	0	.0	0	.0	0	.0	0	.0	0	.0	0	.0	0	.0	0
ALE	0	.0	0	.0	0	.0	0	.0	0	.0	0	.0	0	.0	0
TE:															
IME	0	.0	0	.0	0	.0	0	.0	0	.0	0	.0	0	.0	0
ALE	0	.0	0	.0	0	.0	0	.0	0	.0	0	.0	0	.0	0
ALE	0	.0	0	.0	0	.0	0	.0	0	.0	0	.0	0	.0	0
IME	0	.0	0	.0	0	.0	0	.0	0	.0	0	.0	0	.0	0
ALE	0	.0	0	.0	0	.0	0	.0	0	.0	0	.0	0	.0	0
ALE	0	.0	0	.0	0	.0	0	.0	0	.0	0	.0	0	.0	0
	0	.0	0	.0	0	.0	0	.0	0	.0	0	.0	0	.0	0
ALE	0	.0	0	.0	0	.0	0	.0	0	.0	0	.0	0	.0	0
ALE	0	.0	0	.0	0	.0	0	.0	0	.0	0	.0	0	.0	0
SIGNAL:															
IME	7	.3	189	8.8	6	.3	7	.3	209	9.7	1,935	90.0	7	.3	2,151
ALE	0	.0	56	10.4	0	.0	1	.2	57	10.6	478	89.2	1	.2	536
ALE	7	.4	133	8.2	6	.4	6	.4	152	9.4	1,457	90.2	6	.4	1,615
IME	0	.0	3	25.0	0	.0	0	.0	3	25.0	8	66.7	1	8.3	12
ALE	0	.0	0	.0	0	.0	0	.0	0	.0	5	100.0	0	.0	5
ALE	0	.0	3	42.9	0	.0	0	.0	3	42.9	3	42.9	1	14.3	7
	7	.3	192	8.9	6	.3	7	.3	212	9.8	1,943	89.8	8	.4	2,163
ALE	0	.0	56	10.4	0	.0	1	.2	57	10.5	483	89.3	1	.2	541
ALE	7	.4	136	8.4	6	.4	6	.4	155	9.6	1,460	90.0	7	.4	1,622
AD+PROF:															
IME	7	.3	189	8.8	6	.3	7	.3	209	9.7	1,935	90.0	7	.3	2,151
ALE	0	.0	56	10.4	0	.0	1	.2	57	10.6	478	89.2	1	.2	536
ALE	7	.4	133	8.2	6	.4	6	.4	152	9.4	1,457	90.2	6	.4	1,615
IME	0	.0	3	25.0	0	.0	0	.0	3	25.0	8	66.7	1	8.3	12
ALE	0	.0	0	.0	0	.0	0	.0	0	.0	5	100.0	0	.0	5
ALE	0	.0	3	42.9	0	.0	0	.0	3	42.9	3	42.9	1	14.3	7
	7	.3	192	8.9	6	.3	7	.3	212	9.8	1,943	89.8	8	.4	2,163
ALE	0	.0	56	10.4	0	.0	1	.2	57	10.5	483	89.3	1	.2	541
ALE	7	.4	136	8.4	6	.4	6	.4	155	9.6	1,460	90.0	7	.4	1,622
SIFIED:															
	0	.0	0	.0	0	.0	0	.0	0	.0	0	.0	0	.0	0
ALE	0	.0	0	.0	0	.0	0	.0	0	.0	0	.0	0	.0	0
ALE	0	.0	0	.0	0	.0	0	.0	0	.0	0	.0	0	.0	0
ENROLLMENT:															
	7	.3	192	8.9	6	.3	7	.3	212	9.8	1,943	89.8	8	.4	2,163
ALE	0	.0	56	10.4	0	.0	1	.2	57	10.5	483	89.3	1	.2	541
ALE	7	.4	136	8.4	6	.4	6	.4	155	9.6	1,460	90.0	7	.4	1,622

TABLE 17 - TOTAL ENROLLMENT IN INSTITUTIONS OF HIGHER EDUCATION FOR SELECTED MAJOR FIELDS OF STUDY AND LEVEL OF ENROLLMENT BY RACE, ETHNICITY, AND SEX: STATE, 1978

MAJOR FIELD 1400 - LAW

	AMERICAN INDIAN ALASKAN NATIVE		BLACK NON-HISPANIC		ASIAN OR PACIFIC ISLANDER		HISPANIC		TOTAL MINORITY		WHITE NON-HISPANIC		NON-RESIDENT ALIEN		T(
	NUMBER	%	NUMBER	%	NUMBER	%	NUMBER	%	NUMBER	%	NUMBER	%	NUMBER	%	NU
NORTH DAKOTA (1 INSTITUTIONS)															
UNDERGRADUATES:															
FULL-TIME	0	.0	0	.0	0	.0	0	.0	0	.0	0	.0	0	.0	
FEMALE	0	.0	0	.0	0	.0	0	.0	0	.0	0	.0	0	.0	
MALE	0	.0	0	.0	0	.0	0	.0	0	.0	0	.0	0	.0	
PART-TIME	0	.0	0	.0	0	.0	0	.0	0	.0	0	.0	0	.0	
FEMALE	0	.0	0	.0	0	.0	0	.0	0	.0	0	.0	0	.0	
MALE	0	.0	0	.0	0	.0	0	.0	0	.0	0	.0	0	.0	
TOTAL	0	.0	0	.0	0	.0	0	.0	0	.0	0	.0	0	.0	
FEMALE	0	.0	0	.0	0	.0	0	.0	0	.0	0	.0	0	.0	
MALE	0	.0	0	.0	0	.0	0	.0	0	.0	0	.0	0	.0	
GRADUATE:															
FULL-TIME	0	.0	0	.0	0	.0	0	.0	0	.0	0	.0	0	.0	
FEMALE	0	.0	0	.0	0	.0	0	.0	0	.0	0	.0	0	.0	
MALE	0	.0	0	.0	0	.0	0	.0	0	.0	0	.0	0	.0	
PART-TIME	0	.0	0	.0	0	.0	0	.0	0	.0	0	.0	0	.0	
FEMALE	0	.0	0	.0	0	.0	0	.0	0	.0	0	.0	0	.0	
MALE	0	.0	0	.0	0	.0	0	.0	0	.0	0	.0	0	.0	
TOTAL	0	.0	0	.0	0	.0	0	.0	0	.0	0	.0	0	.0	
FEMALE	0	.0	0	.0	0	.0	0	.0	0	.0	0	.0	0	.0	
MALE	0	.0	0	.0	0	.0	0	.0	0	.0	0	.0	0	.0	
PROFESSIONAL:															
FULL-TIME	1	.4	0	.0	0	.0	0	.0	1	.4	269	99.6	0	.0	
FEMALE	0	.0	0	.0	0	.0	0	.0	0	.0	54	100.0	0	.0	
MALE	1	.5	0	.0	0	.0	0	.0	1	.5	215	99.5	0	.0	
PART-TIME	0	.0	0	.0	0	.0	0	.0	0	.0	2	100.0	0	.0	
FEMALE	0	.0	0	.0	0	.0	0	.0	0	.0	1	100.0	0	.0	
MALE	0	.0	0	.0	0	.0	0	.0	0	.0	1	100.0	0	.0	
TOTAL	1	.4	0	.0	0	.0	0	.0	1	.4	271	99.6	0	.0	
FEMALE	0	.0	0	.0	0	.0	0	.0	0	.0	55	100.0	0	.0	
MALE	1	.5	0	.0	0	.0	0	.0	1	.5	216	99.5	0	.0	
UND+GRAD+PROF:															
FULL-TIME	1	.4	0	.0	0	.0	0	.0	1	.4	269	99.6	0	.0	
FEMALE	0	.0	0	.0	0	.0	0	.0	0	.0	54	100.0	0	.0	
MALE	1	.5	0	.0	0	.0	0	.0	1	.5	215	99.5	0	.0	
PART-TIME	0	.0	0	.0	0	.0	0	.0	0	.0	2	100.0	0	.0	
FEMALE	0	.0	0	.0	0	.0	0	.0	0	.0	1	100.0	0	.0	
MALE	0	.0	0	.0	0	.0	0	.0	0	.0	1	100.0	0	.0	
TOTAL	1	.4	0	.0	0	.0	0	.0	1	.4	271	99.6	0	.0	
FEMALE	0	.0	0	.0	0	.0	0	.0	0	.0	55	100.0	0	.0	
MALE	1	.5	0	.0	0	.0	0	.0	1	.5	216	99.5	0	.0	
UNCLASSIFIED:															
TOTAL	0	.0	0	.0	0	.0	0	.0	0	.0	0	.0	0	.0	
FEMALE	0	.0	0	.0	0	.0	0	.0	0	.0	0	.0	0	.0	
MALE	0	.0	0	.0	0	.0	0	.0	0	.0	0	.0	0	.0	
TOTAL ENROLLMENT:															
TOTAL	1	.4	0	.0	0	.0	0	.0	1	.4	271	99.6	0	.0	
FEMALE	0	.0	0	.0	0	.0	0	.0	0	.0	55	100.0	0	.0	
MALE	1	.5	0	.0	0	.0	0	.0	1	.5	216	99.5	0	.0	
OHIO (10 INSTITUTIONS)															
UNDERGRADUATES:															
FULL-TIME	0	.0	0	.0	0	.0	0	.0	0	.0	0	.0	0	.0	
FEMALE	0	.0	0	.0	0	.0	0	.0	0	.0	0	.0	0	.0	
MALE	0	.0	0	.0	0	.0	0	.0	0	.0	0	.0	0	.0	
PART-TIME	0	.0	0	.0	0	.0	0	.0	0	.0	0	.0	0	.0	
FEMALE	0	.0	0	.0	0	.0	0	.0	0	.0	0	.0	0	.0	
MALE	0	.0	0	.0	0	.0	0	.0	0	.0	0	.0	0	.0	
TOTAL	0	.0	0	.0	0	.0	0	.0	0	.0	0	.0	0	.0	
FEMALE	0	.0	0	.0	0	.0	0	.0	0	.0	0	.0	0	.0	
MALE	0	.0	0	.0	0	.0	0	.0	0	.0	0	.0	0	.0	
GRADUATE:															
FULL-TIME	0	.0	0	.0	0	.0	0	.0	0	.0	0	.0	0	.0	
FEMALE	0	.0	0	.0	0	.0	0	.0	0	.0	0	.0	0	.0	
MALE	0	.0	0	.0	0	.0	0	.0	0	.0	0	.0	0	.0	
PART-TIME	0	.0	0	.0	0	.0	0	.0	0	.0	0	.0	0	.0	
FEMALE	0	.0	0	.0	0	.0	0	.0	0	.0	0	.0	0	.0	
MALE	0	.0	0	.0	0	.0	0	.0	0	.0	0	.0	0	.0	
TOTAL	0	.0	0	.0	0	.0	0	.0	0	.0	0	.0	0	.0	
FEMALE	0	.0	0	.0	0	.0	0	.0	0	.0	0	.0	0	.0	
MALE	0	.0	0	.0	0	.0	0	.0	0	.0	0	.0	0	.0	
PROFESSIONAL:															
FULL-TIME	9	.2	284	5.7	27	.5	42	.8	362	7.2	4,610	92.0	37	.7	
FEMALE	5	.3	124	8.6	11	.8	13	.9	153	10.6	1,277	88.5	13	.9	
MALE	4	.1	160	4.5	16	.4	29	.8	209	5.9	3,333	93.5	24	.7	

570

OR FIELD 1400 - LAW

	AMERICAN INDIAN ALASKAN NATIVE		BLACK NON-HISPANIC		ASIAN OR PACIFIC ISLANDER		HISPANIC		TOTAL MINORITY		WHITE NON-HISPANIC		NON-RESIDENT ALIEN		TOTAL
	NUMBER	%	NUMBER	%	NUMBER	%	NUMBER	%	NUMBER	%	NUMBER	%	NUMBER	%	NUMBER
O CONTINUED															
FESSIONAL:															
T-TIME	5	.4	83	6.5	3	.2	4	.3	95	7.4	1,179	91.9	9	.7	1,283
FEMALE	2	.6	30	8.5	0	.0	0	.0	32	9.1	320	90.7	1	.3	353
MALE	3	.3	53	5.7	3	.3	4	.4	63	6.8	859	92.4	8	.9	930
AL	14	.2	367	5.8	30	.5	46	.7	457	7.3	5,789	92.0	46	.7	6,292
FEMALE	7	.4	154	8.6	11	.6	13	.7	185	10.3	1,597	88.9	14	.8	1,796
MALE	7	.2	213	4.7	19	.4	33	.7	272	6.0	4,192	93.2	32	.7	4,496
+GRAD+PROF:															
L-TIME	9	.2	284	5.7	27	.5	42	.8	362	7.2	4,610	92.0	37	.7	5,009
FEMALE	5	.3	124	8.6	11	.8	13	.9	153	10.6	1,277	88.5	13	.9	1,443
MALE	4	.1	160	4.5	16	.4	29	.8	209	5.9	8,333	93.5	24	.7	3,566
T-TIME	5	.4	83	6.5	3	.2	4	.3	95	7.4	1,179	91.9	9	.7	1,283
FEMALE	2	.6	30	8.5	0	.0	0	.0	32	9.1	320	90.7	1	.3	353
MALE	3	.3	53	5.7	3	.3	4	.4	63	6.8	859	92.4	8	.9	930
AL	14	.2	367	5.8	30	.5	46	.7	457	7.3	5,789	92.0	46	.7	6,292
FEMALE	7	.4	154	8.6	11	.6	13	.7	185	10.3	1,597	88.9	14	.8	1,796
MALE	7	.2	213	4.7	19	.4	33	.7	272	6.0	4,192	93.2	32	.7	4,496
LASSIFIED:															
AL	0	.0	0	.0	0	.0	0	.0	0	.0	0	.0	0	.0	0
FEMALE	0	.0	0	.0	0	.0	0	.0	0	.0	0	.0	0	.0	0
MALE	0	.0	0	.0	0	.0	0	.0	0	.0	0	.0	0	.0	0
AL ENROLLMENT:															
AL	14	.2	367	5.8	30	.5	46	.7	457	7.3	5,789	92.0	46	.7	6,292
FEMALE	7	.4	154	8.6	11	.6	13	.7	185	10.3	1,597	88.9	14	.8	1,796
MALE	7	.2	213	4.7	19	.4	33	.7	272	6.0	4,192	93.2	32	.7	4,496
AHOMA (3 INSTITUTIONS)															
ERGRADUATES:															
L-TIME	0	.0	0	.0	0	.0	0	.0	0	.0	0	.0	0	.0	0
FEMALE	0	.0	0	.0	0	.0	0	.0	0	.0	0	.0	0	.0	0
MALE	0	.0	0	.0	0	.0	0	.0	0	.0	0	.0	0	.0	0
T-TIME	0	.0	0	.0	0	.0	0	.0	0	.0	0	.0	0	.0	0
FEMALE	0	.0	0	.0	0	.0	0	.0	0	.0	0	.0	0	.0	0
MALE	0	.0	0	.0	0	.0	0	.0	0	.0	0	.0	0	.0	0
AL	0	.0	0	.0	0	.0	0	.0	0	.0	0	.0	0	.0	0
FEMALE	0	.0	0	.0	0	.0	0	.0	0	.0	0	.0	0	.0	0
MALE	0	.0	0	.0	0	.0	0	.0	0	.0	0	.0	0	.0	0
OUATE:															
L-TIME	0	.0	0	.0	0	.0	0	.0	0	.0	0	.0	0	.0	0
FEMALE	0	.0	0	.0	0	.0	0	.0	0	.0	0	.0	0	.0	0
MALE	0	.0	0	.0	0	.0	0	.0	0	.0	0	.0	0	.0	0
T-TIME	0	.0	0	.0	0	.0	0	.0	0	.0	0	.0	0	.0	0
FEMALE	0	.0	0	.0	0	.0	0	.0	0	.0	0	.0	0	.0	0
MALE	0	.0	0	.0	0	.0	0	.0	0	.0	0	.0	0	.0	0
AL	0	.0	0	.0	0	.0	0	.0	0	.0	0	.0	0	.0	0
FEMALE	0	.0	0	.0	0	.0	0	.0	0	.0	0	.0	0	.0	0
MALE	0	.0	0	.0	0	.0	0	.0	0	.0	0	.0	0	.0	0
FESSIONAL:															
L-TIME	39	2.5	28	1.8	9	.6	11	.7	87	5.7	1,439	93.9	6	.4	1,532
FEMALE	10	2.5	12	3.0	3	.7	3	.7	28	6.9	377	92.9	1	.2	406
MALE	29	2.6	16	1.4	6	.5	8	.7	59	5.2	1,062	94.3	5	.4	1,126
T-TIME	6	2.8	6	2.8	0	.0	1	.5	13	6.0	199	91.3	6	2.8	218
FEMALE	1	2.1	1	2.1	0	.0	0	.0	2	4.2	44	91.7	2	4.2	48
MALE	5	2.9	5	2.9	0	.0	1	.6	11	6.5	155	91.2	4	2.4	170
AL	45	2.6	34	1.9	9	.5	12	.7	100	5.7	1,638	93.6	12	.7	1,750
FEMALE	11	2.4	13	2.9	3	.7	3	.7	30	6.6	421	92.7	3	.7	454
MALE	34	2.6	21	1.6	6	.5	9	.7	70	5.4	1,217	93.9	9	.7	1,296
+GRAD+PROF:															
L-TIME	39	2.5	28	1.8	9	.6	11	.7	87	5.7	1,439	93.9	6	.4	1,532
FEMALE	10	2.5	12	3.0	3	.7	3	.7	28	6.9	377	92.9	1	.2	406
MALE	29	2.6	16	1.4	6	.5	8	.7	59	5.2	1,062	94.3	5	.4	1,126
T-TIME	6	2.8	6	2.8	0	.0	1	.5	13	6.0	199	91.3	6	2.8	218
FEMALE	1	2.1	1	2.1	0	.0	0	.0	2	4.2	44	91.7	2	4.2	48
MALE	5	2.9	5	2.9	0	.0	1	.6	11	6.5	155	91.2	4	2.4	170
AL	45	2.6	34	1.9	9	.5	12	.7	100	5.7	1,638	93.6	12	.7	1,750
FEMALE	11	2.4	13	2.9	3	.7	3	.7	30	6.6	421	92.7	3	.7	454
MALE	34	2.6	21	1.6	6	.5	9	.7	70	5.4	1,217	93.9	9	.7	1,296
LASSIFIED:															
AL	0	.0	0	.0	0	.0	0	.0	0	.0	0	.0	0	.0	0
FEMALE	0	.0	0	.0	0	.0	0	.0	0	.0	0	.0	0	.0	0
MALE	0	.0	0	.0	0	.0	0	.0	0	.0	0	.0	0	.0	0
AL ENROLLMENT:															
AL	45	2.6	34	1.9	9	.5	12	.7	100	5.7	1,638	93.6	12	.7	1,750
FEMALE	11	2.4	13	2.9	3	.7	3	.7	30	6.6	421	92.7	3	.7	454
MALE	34	2.6	21	1.6	6	.5	9	.7	70	5.4	1,217	93.9	9	.7	1,296

MAJOR FIELD 1400 - LAW

	AMERICAN INDIAN ALASKAN NATIVE		BLACK NON-HISPANIC		ASIAN OR PACIFIC ISLANDER		HISPANIC		TOTAL MINORITY		WHITE NON-HISPANIC		NON-RESIDENT ALIEN		
	NUMBER	%	NUMBER	%	NUMBER	%	NUMBER	%	NUMBER	%	NUMBER	%	NUMBER	%	
OREGON (3 INSTITUTIONS)															
UNDERGRADUATES:															
FULL-TIME	0	.0	0	.0	0	.0	0	.0	0	.0	0	.0	0	.0	
FEMALE	0	.0	0	.0	0	.0	0	.0	0	.0	0	.0	0	.0	
MALE	0	.0	0	.0	0	.0	0	.0	0	.0	0	.0	0	.0	
PART-TIME	0	.0	0	.0	0	.0	0	.0	0	.0	0	.0	0	.0	
FEMALE	0	.0	0	.0	0	.0	0	.0	0	.0	0	.0	0	.0	
MALE	0	.0	0	.0	0	.0	0	.0	0	.0	0	.0	0	.0	
TOTAL	0	.0	0	.0	0	.0	0	.0	0	.0	0	.0	0	.0	
FEMALE	0	.0	0	.0	0	.0	0	.0	0	.0	0	.0	0	.0	
MALE	0	.0	0	.0	0	.0	0	.0	0	.0	0	.0	0	.0	
GRADUATE:															
FULL-TIME	0	.0	0	.0	0	.0	0	.0	0	.0	0	.0	0	.0	
FEMALE	0	.0	0	.0	0	.0	0	.0	0	.0	0	.0	0	.0	
MALE	0	.0	0	.0	0	.0	0	.0	0	.0	0	.0	0	.0	
PART-TIME	0	.0	0	.0	0	.0	0	.0	0	.0	0	.0	0	.0	
FEMALE	0	.0	0	.0	0	.0	0	.0	0	.0	0	.0	0	.0	
MALE	0	.0	0	.0	0	.0	0	.0	0	.0	0	.0	0	.0	
TOTAL	0	.0	0	.0	0	.0	0	.0	0	.0	0	.0	0	.0	
FEMALE	0	.0	0	.0	0	.0	0	.0	0	.0	0	.0	0	.0	
MALE	0	.0	0	.0	0	.0	0	.0	0	.0	0	.0	0	.0	
PROFESSIONAL:															
FULL-TIME	10	.7	21	1.6	42	3.1	15	1.1	88	6.6	1,244	93.3	2	.1	
FEMALE	5	1.3	6	1.5	14	3.5	3	.8	28	7.0	371	93.0	0	.0	
MALE	5	.5	15	1.6	28	3.0	12	1.3	60	6.4	873	93.4	2	.2	
PART-TIME	0	.0	4	1.3	3	.9	4	1.3	11	3.5	307	96.5	0	.0	
FEMALE	0	.0	2	2.1	0	.0	1	1.1	3	3.2	92	96.8	0	.0	
MALE	0	.0	2	.9	3	1.3	3	1.3	8	3.6	215	96.4	0	.0	
TOTAL	10	.6	25	1.5	45	2.7	19	1.2	99	6.0	1,551	93.9	2	.1	
FEMALE	5	1.0	8	1.6	14	2.8	4	.8	31	6.3	463	93.7	0	.0	
MALE	5	.4	17	1.5	31	2.7	15	1.3	68	5.9	1,088	94.0	2	.2	
UNC+GRAD+PROF:															
FULL-TIME	10	.7	21	1.6	42	3.1	15	1.1	88	6.6	1,244	93.3	2	.1	
FEMALE	5	1.3	6	1.5	14	3.5	3	.6	28	7.0	371	93.0	0	.0	
MALE	5	.5	15	1.6	28	3.0	12	1.3	60	6.4	873	93.4	2	.2	
PART-TIME	0	.0	4	1.3	3	.9	4	1.3	11	3.5	307	96.5	0	.0	
FEMALE	0	.0	2	2.1	0	.0	1	1.1	3	3.2	92	96.8	0	.0	
MALE	0	.0	2	.9	3	1.3	3	1.3	8	3.6	215	96.4	0	.0	
TOTAL	10	.6	25	1.5	45	2.7	19	1.2	99	6.0	1,551	93.9	2	.1	
FEMALE	5	1.0	8	1.6	14	2.8	4	.8	31	6.3	463	93.7	0	.0	
MALE	5	.4	17	1.5	31	2.7	15	1.3	68	5.9	1,088	94.0	2	.2	
UNCLASSIFIED:															
TOTAL	0	.0	0	.0	0	.0	0	.0	0	.0	0	.0	0	.0	
FEMALE	0	.0	0	.0	0	.0	0	.0	0	.0	0	.0	0	.0	
MALE	0	.0	0	.0	0	.0	0	.0	0	.0	0	.0	0	.0	
TOTAL ENROLLMENT:															
TOTAL	10	.6	25	1.5	45	2.7	19	1.2	99	6.0	1,551	93.9	2	.1	
FEMALE	5	1.0	8	1.6	14	2.8	4	.8	31	6.3	463	93.7	0	.0	
MALE	5	.4	17	1.5	31	2.7	15	1.3	68	5.9	1,088	94.0	2	.2	
PENNSYLVANIA (5 INSTITUTIONS)															
UNDERGRADUATES:															
FULL-TIME	0	.0	0	.0	0	.0	0	.0	0	.0	0	.0	0	.0	
FEMALE	0	.0	0	.0	0	.0	0	.0	0	.0	0	.0	0	.0	
MALE	0	.0	0	.0	0	.0	0	.0	0	.0	0	.0	0	.0	
PART-TIME	0	.0	0	.0	0	.0	0	.0	0	.0	0	.0	0	.0	
FEMALE	0	.0	0	.0	0	.0	0	.0	0	.0	0	.0	0	.0	
MALE	0	.0	0	.0	0	.0	0	.0	0	.0	0	.0	0	.0	
TOTAL	0	.0	0	.0	0	.0	0	.0	0	.0	0	.0	0	.0	
FEMALE	0	.0	0	.0	0	.0	0	.0	0	.0	0	.0	0	.0	
MALE	0	.0	0	.0	0	.0	0	.0	0	.0	0	.0	0	.0	
GRADUATE:															
FULL-TIME	0	.0	0	.0	0	.0	0	.0	0	.0	0	.0	0	.0	
FEMALE	0	.0	0	.0	0	.0	0	.0	0	.0	0	.0	0	.0	
MALE	0	.0	0	.0	0	.0	0	.0	0	.0	0	.0	0	.0	
PART-TIME	0	.0	0	.0	0	.0	0	.0	0	.0	0	.0	0	.0	
FEMALE	0	.0	0	.0	0	.0	0	.0	0	.0	0	.0	0	.0	
MALE	0	.0	0	.0	0	.0	0	.0	0	.0	0	.0	0	.0	
TOTAL	0	.0	0	.0	0	.0	0	.0	0	.0	0	.0	0	.0	
FEMALE	0	.0	0	.0	0	.0	0	.0	0	.0	0	.0	0	.0	
MALE	0	.0	0	.0	0	.0	0	.0	0	.0	0	.0	0	.0	
PROFESSIONAL:															
FULL-TIME	6	.2	165	4.8	29	.8	40	1.2	240	7.0	3,193	92.6	17	.5	
FEMALE	3	.3	82	6.9	8	.7	14	1.2	107	9.0	1,079	90.4	7	.6	
MALE	3	.1	83	3.7	21	.9	26	1.2	133	5.9	2,114	93.7	10	.4	

ENROLLMENT IN INSTITUTIONS OF HIGHER EDUCATION FOR SELECTED MAJOR FIELDS OF STUDY AND LEVEL OF ENROLLMENT
E, ETHNICITY, AND SEX: STATE, 1978

- LAW

AN INDIAN N NATIVE		BLACK NON-HISPANIC		ASIAN OR PACIFIC ISLANDER		HISPANIC		TOTAL MINORITY		WHITE NON-HISPANIC		NON-RESIDENT ALIEN		TOTAL
R	%	NUMBER	%	NUMBER	%	NUMBER	%	NUMBER	%	NUMBER	%	NUMBER	%	NUMBER

CONTINUED

0	.0	9	9.2	3	3.1	2	2.0	14	14.3	84	85.7	0	.0	98
0	.0	4	10.5	1	2.6	1	2.6	6	15.8	32	84.2	0	.0	38
0	.0	5	8.3	2	3.3	1	1.7	8	13.3	52	86.7	0	.0	60
6	.2	174	4.9	32	.9	42	1.2	254	7.2	3,277	92.4	17	.5	3,548
3	.2	86	7.0	9	.7	15	1.2	113	9.2	1,111	90.3	7	.6	1,231
3	.1	88	3.8	23	1.0	27	1.2	141	6.1	2,166	93.5	10	.4	2,317
6	.2	165	4.8	29	.8	40	1.2	240	7.0	3,193	92.6	17	.5	3,450
3	.3	82	6.9	8	.7	14	1.2	107	9.0	1,079	90.4	7	.6	1,193
3	.1	83	3.7	21	.9	26	1.2	133	5.9	2,114	93.7	10	.4	2,257
0	.0	9	9.2	3	3.1	2	2.0	14	14.3	84	85.7	0	.0	98
0	.0	4	10.5	1	2.6	1	2.6	6	15.8	32	84.2	0	.0	38
0	.0	5	8.3	2	3.3	1	1.7	8	13.3	52	86.7	0	.0	60
6	.2	174	4.9	32	.9	42	1.2	254	7.2	3,277	92.4	17	.5	3,548
3	.2	86	7.0	9	.7	15	1.2	113	9.2	1,111	90.3	7	.6	1,231
3	.1	d8	3.8	23	1.0	27	1.2	141	6.1	2,166	93.5	10	.4	2,317
0	.0	0	.0	0	.0	0	.0	0	.0	0	.0	0	.0	0
0	.0	0	.0	0	.0	0	.0	0	.0	0	.0	0	.0	0
0	.0	0	.0	0	.0	0	.0	0	.0	0	.0	0	.0	0
6	.2	174	4.9	32	.9	42	1.2	254	7.2	3,277	92.4	17	.5	3,54d
3	.2	86	7.0	9	.7	15	1.2	113	9.2	1,111	90.3	7	.6	1,231
3	.1	88	3.8	23	1.0	27	1.2	141	6.1	2,166	93.5	10	.4	2,317

(1 INSTITUTIONS)

0	.0	0	.0	0	.0	0	.0	0	.0	0	.0	0	.0	0
0	.0	0	.0	0	.0	0	.0	0	.0	0	.0	0	.0	0
0	.0	0	.0	0	.0	0	.0	0	.0	0	.0	0	.0	0
0	.0	0	.0	0	.0	0	.0	0	.0	0	.0	0	.0	0
0	.0	0	.0	0	.0	0	.0	0	.0	0	.0	0	.0	0
0	.0	0	.0	0	.0	0	.0	0	.0	0	.0	0	.0	0
0	.0	0	.0	0	.0	0	.0	0	.0	0	.0	0	.0	0
0	.0	0	.0	0	.0	0	.0	0	.0	0	.0	0	.0	0
0	.0	0	.0	0	.0	0	.0	0	.0	0	.0	0	.0	0
0	.0	0	.0	0	.0	0	.0	0	.0	0	.0	0	.0	0
0	.0	0	.0	0	.0	0	.0	0	.0	0	.0	0	.0	0
0	.0	0	.0	0	.0	0	.0	0	.0	0	.0	0	.0	0
0	.0	0	.0	0	.0	0	.0	0	.0	0	.0	0	.0	0
0	.0	0	.0	0	.0	0	.0	0	.0	0	.0	0	.0	0
0	.0	0	.0	0	.0	0	.0	0	.0	0	.0	0	.0	0
0	.0	50	7.5	0	.0	0	.0	50	7.5	618	92.5	0	.0	668
0	.0	13	7.6	0	.0	0	.0	13	7.6	157	92.4	0	.0	170
0	.0	37	7.4	0	.0	0	.0	37	7.4	461	92.6	0	.0	498
0	.0	0	.0	0	.0	0	.0	0	.0	6	100.0	0	.0	6
0	.0	0	.0.	0	.0	0	.0	0	.0	2	100.0	0	.0	2
0	.0	0	.0	0	.0	0	.0	0	.0	4	100.0	0	.0	4
0	.0	50	7.4	0	.0	0	.0	50	7.4	624	92.6	0	.0	674
0	.0	13	7.6	0	.0	0	.0	13	7.6	159	92.4	0	.0	172
0	.0	37	7.4	0	.0	0	.0	37	7.4	465	92.6	0	.0	502
0	.0	50	7.5	0	.0	0	.0	50	7.5	618	92.5	0	.0	668
0	.0	13	7.6	0	.0	0	.0	13	7.6	157	92.4	0	.0	170
0	.0	37	7.4	0	.0	0	.0	37	7.4	461	92.6	0	.0	498
0	.0	0	.0	0	.0	0	.0	0	.0	6	100.0	0	.0	6
0	.0	0	.0	0	.0	0	.0	0	.0	2	100.0	0	.0	2
0	.0	0	.0	0	.0	0	.0	0	.0	4	100.0	0	.0	4
0	.0	50	7.4	0	.0	0	.0	50	7.4	624	92.6	0	.0	674
0	.0	13	7.6	0	.0	0	.0	13	7.6	159	92.4	0	.0	172
0	.0	37	7.4	0	.0	0	.0	37	7.4	465	92.6	0	.0	502
0	.0	0	.0	0	.0	0	.0	0	.0	0	.0	0	.0	0
0	.0	0	.0	0	.0	0	.0	0	.0	0	.0	0	.0	0
0	.0	0	.0	0	.0	0	.0	0	.0	0	.0	0	.0	0
0	.0	50	7.4	0	.0	0	.0	50	7.4	624	92.6	0	.0	674
0	.0	13	7.6	0	.0	0	.0	13	7.6	159	92.4	0	.0	172
0	.0	37	7.4	0	.0	0	.0	37	7.4	465	92.6	0	.0	502

MAJOR FIELD 1400 - LAW

	AMERICAN INDIAN ALASKAN NATIVE		BLACK NON-HISPANIC		ASIAN OR PACIFIC ISLANDER		HISPANIC		TOTAL MINORITY		WHITE NON-HISPANIC		NON-RESIDENT ALIEN		TOT
	NUMBER	%	NUMBER	%	NUMBER	%	NUMBER	%	NUMBER	%	NUMBER	%	NUMBER	%	NUM
SOUTH DAKOTA	(	1 INSTITUTIONS)													
UNDERGRADUATES:															
FULL-TIME	0	.0	0	.0	0	.0	0	.0	0	.0	0	.0		.0	
FEMALE	0	.0	0	.0	0	.0	0	.0	0	.0	0	.0		.0	
MALE	0	.0	0	.0	0	.0	0	.0	0	.0	0	.0		.0	
PART-TIME	0	.0	0	.0	0	.0	0	.0	0	.0	0	.0		.0	
FEMALE	0	.0	0	.0	0	.0	0	.0	0	.0	0	.0		.0	
MALE	0	.0	0	.0	0	.0	0	.0	0	.0	0	.0	0	.0	
TOTAL	0	.0	0	.0	0	.0	0	.0	0	.0	0	.0	0	.0	
FEMALE	0	.0	0	.0	0	.0	0	.0	0	.0	0	.0	0	.0	
MALE	0	.0	0	.0	0	.0	0	.0	0	.0	0	.0	0	.0	
GRADUATE:															
FULL-TIME	0	.0	0	.0	0	.0	0	.0	0	.0	0	.0		.0	
FEMALE	0	.0	0	.0	0	.0	0	.0	0	.0	0	.0		.0	
MALE	0	.0	0	.0	0	.0	0	.0	0	.0	0	.0		.0	
PART-TIME	0	.0	0	.0	0	.0	0	.0	0	.0	0	.0		.0	
FEMALE	0	.0	0	.0	0	.0	0	.0	0	.0	0	.0		.0	
MALE	0	.0	0	.0	0	.0	0	.0	0	.0	0	.0	0	.0	
TOTAL	0	.0	0	.0	0	.0	0	.0	0	.0	0	.0		.0	
FEMALE	0	.0	0	.0	0	.0	0	.0	0	.0	0	.0		.0	
MALE	0	.0	0	.0	0	.0	0	.0	0	.0	0	.0	0	.0	
PROFESSIONAL:															
FULL-TIME	1	.5	0	.0	0	.0	0	.0	1	.5	196	99.5		.0	
FEMALE	0	.0	0	.0	0	.0	0	.0	0	.0	44	100.0		.0	
MALE	1	.7	0	.0	0	.0	0	.0	1	.7	152	99.3		.0	
PART-TIME	0	.0	0	.0	0	.0	0	.0	0	.0	1	100.0		.0	
FEMALE	0	.0	0	.0	0	.0	0	.0	0	.0	0	.0		.0	
MALE	0	.0	0	.0	0	.0	0	.0	0	.0	1	100.0	0	.0	
TOTAL	1	.5	0	.0	0	.0	0	.0	1	.5	197	99.5		.0	
FEMALE	0	.0	0	.0	0	.0	0	.0	0	.0	44	100.0		.0	
MALE	1	.6	0	.0	0	.0	0	.0	1	.6	153	99.4	0	.0	
UND+GRAD+PROF:															
FULL-TIME	1	.5	0	.0	0	.0	0	.0	1	.5	196	99.5		.0	
FEMALE	0	.0	0	.0	0	.0	0	.0	0	.0	44	100.0		.0	
MALE	1	.7	0	.0	0	.0	0	.0	1	.7	152	99.3		.0	
PART-TIME	0	.0	0	.0	0	.0	0	.0	0	.0	1	100.0		.0	
FEMALE	0	.0	0	.0	0	.0	0	.0	0	.0	0	.0		.0	
MALE	0	.0	0	.0	0	.0	0	.0	0	.0	1	100.0	0	.0	
TOTAL	1	.5	0	.0	0	.0	0	.0	1	.5	197	99.5		.0	
FEMALE	0	.0	0	.0	0	.0	0	.0	0	.0	44	100.0		.0	
MALE	1	.6	0	.0	0	.0	0	.0	1	.6	153	99.4	0	.0	
UNCLASSIFIED:															
TOTAL	0	.0	0	.0	0	.0	0	.0	0	.0	0	.0		.0	
FEMALE	0	.0	0	.0	0	.0	0	.0	0	.0	0	.0		.0	
MALE	0	.0	0	.0	0	.0	0	.0	0	.0	0	.0	0	.0	
TOTAL ENROLLMENT:															
TOTAL	1	.5	0	.0	0	.0	0	.0	1	.5	197	99.5		.0	
FEMALE	0	.0	0	.0	0	.0	0	.0	0	.0	44	100.0		.0	
MALE	1	.6	0	.0	0	.0	0	.0	1	.6	153	99.4	0	.0	
TENNESSEE	(	3 INSTITUTIONS)													
UNDERGRADUATES:															
FULL-TIME	0	.0	0	.0	0	.0	0	.0	0	.0	0	.0		.0	
FEMALE	0	.0	0	.0	0	.0	0	.0	0	.0	0	.0		.0	
MALE	0	.0	0	.0	0	.0	0	.0	0	.0	0	.0		.0	
PART-TIME	0	.0	0	.0	0	.0	0	.0	0	.0	0	.0		.0	
FEMALE	0	.0	0	.0	0	.0	0	.0	0	.0	0	.0		.0	
MALE	0	.0	0	.0	0	.0	0	.0	0	.0	0	.0	0	.0	
TOTAL	0	.0	0	.0	0	.0	0	.0	0	.0	0	.0	0	.0	
FEMALE	0	.0	0	.0	0	.0	0	.0	0	.0	0	.0	0	.0	
MALE	0	.0	0	.0	0	.0	0	.0	0	.0	0	.0	0	.0	
GRADUATE:															
FULL-TIME	0	.0	0	.0	0	.0	0	.0	0	.0	0	.0		.0	
FEMALE	0	.0	0	.0	0	.0	0	.0	0	.0	0	.0		.0	
MALE	0	.0	0	.0	0	.0	0	.0	0	.0	0	.0		.0	
PART-TIME	0	.0	0	.0	0	.0	0	.0	0	.0	0	.0		.0	
FEMALE	0	.0	0	.0	0	.0	0	.0	0	.0	0	.0		.0	
MALE	0	.0	0	.0	0	.0	0	.0	0	.0	0	.0	0	.0	
TOTAL	0	.0	0	.0	0	.0	0	.0	0	.0	0	.0		.0	
FEMALE	0	.0	0	.0	0	.0	0	.0	0	.0	0	.0		.0	
MALE	0	.0	0	.0	0	.0	0	.0	0	.0	0	.0	0	.0	
PROFESSIONAL:															
FULL-TIME	1	.1	55	3.5	1	.1	1	.1	58	3.7	1,513	96.2	2	.1	1
FEMALE	0	.0	26	6.0	0	.0	0	.0	26	6.0	407	93.8	1	.2	
MALE	1	.1	29	2.5	1	.1	1	.1	32	2.8	1,106	97.1	1	.1	1

574

ENROLLMENT IN INSTITUTIONS OF HIGHER EDUCATION FOR SELECTED MAJOR FIELDS OF STUDY AND LEVEL OF ENROLLMENT
CE, ETHNICITY, AND SEX: STATE, 1978

- LAW

CAN INDIAN AN NATIVE		BLACK NON-HISPANIC		ASIAN OR PACIFIC ISLANDER		HISPANIC		TOTAL MINORITY		WHITE NON-HISPANIC		NON-RESIDENT ALIEN		TOTAL
ER	%	NUMBER	%	NUMBER	%	NUMBER	%	NUMBER	%	NUMBER	%	NUMBER	%	NUMBER

CONTINUED

0	.0	4	4.0	1	1.0	0	.0	5	5.0	95	95.0	0	.0	100
0	.0	3	9.4	0	.0	0	.0	3	9.4	29	90.6	0	.0	32
0	.0	1	1.5	1	1.5	0	.0	2	2.9	66	97.1	0	.0	68

1	.1	59	3.5	2	.1	1	.1	63	3.8	1,608	96.1	2	.1	1,673
0	.0	29	6.2	0	.0	0	.0	29	6.2	436	93.6	1	.2	466
1	.1	30	2.5	2	.2	1	.1	34	2.8	1,172	97.1	1	.1	1,207

1	.1	55	3.5	1	.1	1	.1	58	3.7	1,513	96.2	2	.1	1,573
0	.0	26	6.0	0	.0	0	.0	26	6.0	407	93.8	1	.2	434
1	.1	29	2.5	1	.1	1	.1	32	2.8	1,106	97.1	1	.1	1,139
0	.0	4	4.0	1	1.0	0	.0	5	5.0	95	95.0	0	.0	100
0	.0	3	9.4	0	.0	0	.0	3	9.4	29	90.6	0	.0	32
0	.0	1	1.5	1	1.5	0	.0	2	2.9	66	97.1	0	.0	68

1	.1	59	3.5	2	.1	1	.1	63	3.8	1,608	96.1	2	.1	1,673
0	.0	29	6.2	0	.0	0	.0	29	6.2	436	93.6	1	.2	466
1	.1	30	2.5	2	.2	1	.1	34	2.8	1,172	97.1	1	.1	1,207

0	.0	0	.0	0	.0	0	.0	0	.0	0	.0	0	.0	0
0	.0	0	.0	0	.0	0	.0	0	.0	0	.0	0	.0	0
0	.0	0	.0	0	.0	0	.0	0	.0	0	.0	0	.0	0

1	.1	59	3.5	2	.1	1	.1	63	3.8	1,608	96.1	2	.1	1,673
0	.0	29	6.2	0	.0	0	.0	29	6.2	436	93.6	1	.2	466
1	.1	30	2.5	2	.2	1	.1	34	2.8	1,172	97.1	1	.1	1,207

(8 INSTITUTIONS)

0	.0	0	.0	0	.0	0	.0	0	.0	0	.0	0	.0	0
0	.0	0	.0	0	.0	0	.0	0	.0	0	.0	0	.0	0
0	.0	0	.0	0	.0	0	.0	0	.0	0	.0	0	.0	0
0	.0	0	.0	0	.0	0	.0	0	.0	0	.0	0	.0	0
0	.0	0	.0	0	.0	0	.0	0	.0	0	.0	0	.0	0
0	.0	0	.0	0	.0	0	.0	0	.0	0	.0	0	.0	0

0	.0	0	.0	0	.0	0	.0	0	.0	0	.0	0	.0	0
0	.0	0	.0	0	.0	0	.0	0	.0	0	.0	0	.0	0
0	.0	0	.0	0	.0	0	.0	0	.0	0	.0	0	.0	0

0	.0	0	.0	0	.0	0	.0	0	.0	0	.0	0	.0	0
0	.0	0	.0	0	.0	0	.0	0	.0	0	.0	0	.0	0
0	.0	0	.0	0	.0	0	.0	0	.0	0	.0	0	.0	0
0	.0	0	.0	0	.0	0	.0	0	.0	0	.0	0	.0	0
0	.0	0	.0	0	.0	0	.0	0	.0	0	.0	0	.0	0

| 0 | .0 | 0 | .0 | 0 | .0 | 0 | .0 | 0 | .0 | 0 | .0 | 0 | .0 | 0 |
| 0 | .0 | 0 | .0 | 0 | .0 | 0 | .0 | 0 | .0 | 0 | .0 | 0 | .0 | 0 |

21	.4	287	5.2	24	.4	417	7.6	749	13.6	4,721	85.9	26	.5	5,496
5	.3	134	8.4	10	.6	97	6.1	246	15.5	1,337	84.2	4	.3	1,587
16	.4	153	3.9	14	.4	320	8.2	503	12.9	3,384	86.6	22	.6	3,909
0	.0	59	5.5	6	.6	56	5.3	121	11.4	927	87.0	18	1.7	1,066
0	.0	18	5.9	2	.7	16	5.3	36	11.8	265	87.2	3	1.0	304
0	.0	41	5.4	4	.5	40	5.2	85	11.2	662	86.9	15	2.0	762

21	.3	346	5.3	30	.5	473	7.2	870	13.3	5,648	86.1	44	.7	6,562
5	.3	152	8.0	12	.6	113	6.0	282	14.9	1,602	84.7	7	.4	1,891
16	.3	194	4.2	18	.4	360	7.7	588	12.6	4,046	86.6	37	.8	4,671

21	.4	287	5.2	24	.4	417	7.6	749	13.6	4,721	85.9	26	.5	5,496
5	.3	134	8.4	10	.6	97	6.1	246	15.5	1,337	84.2	4	.3	1,587
16	.4	153	3.9	14	.4	320	8.2	503	12.9	3,384	86.6	22	.6	3,909
0	.0	59	5.5	6	.6	56	5.3	121	11.4	927	87.0	18	1.7	1,066
0	.0	18	5.9	2	.7	16	5.3	36	11.8	265	87.2	3	1.0	304
0	.0	41	5.4	4	.5	40	5.2	85	11.2	662	86.9	15	2.0	762

21	.3	346	5.3	30	.5	473	7.2	870	13.3	5,648	86.1	44	.7	6,562
5	.3	152	8.0	12	.6	113	6.0	282	14.9	1,602	84.7	7	.4	1,891
16	.3	194	4.2	18	.4	360	7.7	588	12.6	4,046	86.6	37	.8	4,671

0	.0	0	.0	0	.0	0	.0	0	.0	0	.0	0	.0	0
0	.0	0	.0	0	.0	0	.0	0	.0	0	.0	0	.0	0
0	.0	0	.0	0	.0	0	.0	0	.0	0	.0	0	.0	0

21	.3	346	5.3	30	.5	473	7.2	870	13.3	5,648	86.1	44	.7	6,562
5	.3	152	8.0	12	.6	113	6.0	282	14.9	1,602	84.7	7	.4	1,891
16	.3	194	4.2	18	.4	360	7.7	588	12.6	4,046	86.6	37	.8	4,671

MAJOR FIELD 1400 - LAW

	AMERICAN INDIAN ALASKAN NATIVE		BLACK NON-HISPANIC		ASIAN OR PACIFIC ISLANDER		HISPANIC		TOTAL MINORITY		WHITE NON-HISPANIC		NON-RESIDENT ALIEN		TO
	NUMBER	%	NUMBER	%	NUMBER	%	NUMBER	%	NUMBER	%	NUMBER	%	NUMBER	%	NU
UTAH (2 INSTITUTIONS)															
UNDERGRADUATES:															
FULL-TIME	0	.0	0	.0	0	.0	0	.0	0	.0	0	.0	0	.0	
FEMALE	0	.0	0	.0	0	.0	0	.0	0	.0	0	.0	0	.0	
MALE	0	.0	0	.0	0	.0	0	.0	0	.0	0	.0	0	.0	
PART-TIME	0	.0	0	.0	0	.0	0	.0	0	.0	0	.0	0	.0	
FEMALE	0	.0	0	.0	0	.0	0	.0	0	.0	0	.0	0	.0	
MALE	0	.0	0	.0	0	.0	0	.0	0	.0	0	.0	0	.0	
TOTAL	0	.0	0	.0	0	.0	0	.0	0	.0	0	.0	0	.0	
FEMALE	0	.0	0	.0	0	.0	0	.0	0	.0	0	.0	0	.0	
MALE	0	.0	0	.0	0	.0	0	.0	0	.0	0	.0	0	.0	
GRADUATE:															
FULL-TIME	0	.0	0	.0	0	.0	0	.0	0	.0	0	.0	0	.0	
FEMALE	0	.0	0	.0	0	.0	0	.0	0	.0	0	.0	0	.0	
MALE	0	.0	0	.0	0	.0	0	.0	0	.0	0	.0	0	.0	
PART-TIME	0	.0	0	.0	0	.0	0	.0	0	.0	0	.0	0	.0	
FEMALE	0	.0	0	.0	0	.0	0	.0	0	.0	0	.0	0	.0	
MALE	0	.0	0	.0	0	.0	0	.0	0	.0	0	.0	0	.0	
TOTAL	0	.0	0	.0	0	.0	0	.0	0	.0	0	.0	0	.0	
FEMALE	0	.0	0	.0	0	.0	0	.0	0	.0	0	.0	0	.0	
MALE	0	.0	0	.0	0	.0	0	.0	0	.0	0	.0	0	.0	
PROFESSIONAL:															
FULL-TIME	1	.1	6	.7	6	.7	8	1.0	21	2.5	799	96.1	11	1.3	
FEMALE	0	.0	1	.7	0	.0	1	.7	2	1.3	142	95.3	5	3.4	
MALE	1	.1	5	.7	6	.9	7	1.0	19	2.8	657	96.3	6	.9	
PART-TIME	0	.0	0	.0	0	.0	1	8.3	1	8.3	11	91.7	0	.0	
FEMALE	0	.0	0	.0	0	.0	0	.0	0	.0	4	100.0	0	.0	
MALE	0	.0	0	.0	0	.0	1	12.5	1	12.5	7	87.5	0	.0	
TOTAL	1	.1	6	.7	6	.7	9	1.1	22	2.6	810	96.1	11	1.3	
FEMALE	0	.0	1	.7	0	.0	1	.7	2	1.3	146	95.4	5	3.3	
MALE	1	.1	5	.7	6	.9	8	1.2	20	2.9	664	96.2	6	.9	
UNDERGRAD+PROF:															
FULL-TIME	1	.1	6	.7	6	.7	8	1.0	21	2.5	799	96.1	11	1.3	
FEMALE	0	.0	1	.7	0	.0	1	.7	2	1.3	142	95.3	5	3.4	
MALE	1	.1	5	.7	6	.9	7	1.0	19	2.8	657	96.3	6	.9	
PART-TIME	0	.0	0	.0	0	.0	1	8.3	1	8.3	11	91.7	0	.0	
FEMALE	0	.0	0	.0	0	.0	0	.0	0	.0	4	100.0	0	.0	
MALE	0	.0	0	.0	0	.0	1	12.5	1	12.5	7	87.5	0	.0	
TOTAL	1	.1	6	.7	6	.7	9	1.1	22	2.6	810	96.1	11	1.3	
FEMALE	0	.0	1	.7	0	.0	1	.7	2	1.3	146	95.4	5	3.3	
MALE	1	.1	5	.7	6	.9	8	1.2	20	2.9	664	96.2	6	.9	
UNCLASSIFIED :															
TOTAL	0	.0	0	.0	0	.0	0	.0	0	.0	0	.0	0	.0	
FEMALE	0	.0	0	.0	0	.0	0	.0	0	.0	0	.0	0	.0	
MALE	0	.0	0	.0	0	.0	0	.0	0	.0	0	.0	0	.0	
TOTAL ENROLLMENT:															
TOTAL	1	.1	6	.7	6	.7	9	1.1	22	2.6	810	96.1	11	1.3	
FEMALE	0	.0	1	.7	0	.0	1	.7	2	1.3	146	95.4	5	3.3	
MALE	1	.1	5	.7	6	.9	8	1.2	20	2.9	664	96.2	6	.9	
VERMONT (1 INSTITUTIONS)															
UNDERGRADUATES:															
FULL-TIME	0	.0	0	.0	0	.0	0	.0	0	.0	0	.0	0	.0	
FEMALE	0	.0	0	.0	0	.0	0	.0	0	.0	0	.0	0	.0	
MALE	0	.0	0	.0	0	.0	0	.0	0	.0	0	.0	0	.0	
PART-TIME	0	.0	0	.0	0	.0	0	.0	0	.0	0	.0	0	.0	
FEMALE	0	.0	0	.0	0	.0	0	.0	0	.0	0	.0	0	.0	
MALE	0	.0	0	.0	0	.0	0	.0	0	.0	0	.0	0	.0	
TOTAL	0	.0	0	.0	0	.0	0	.0	0	.0	0	.0	0	.0	
FEMALE	0	.0	0	.0	0	.0	0	.0	0	.0	0	.0	0	.0	
MALE	0	.0	0	.0	0	.0	0	.0	0	.0	0	.0	0	.0	
GRADUATE:															
FULL-TIME	0	.0	0	.0	0	.0	0	.0	0	.0	0	.0	0	.0	
FEMALE	0	.0	0	.0	0	.0	0	.0	0	.0	0	.0	0	.0	
MALE	0	.0	0	.0	0	.0	0	.0	0	.0	0	.0	0	.0	
PART-TIME	0	.0	0	.0	0	.0	0	.0	0	.0	0	.0	0	.0	
FEMALE	0	.0	0	.0	0	.0	0	.0	0	.0	0	.0	0	.0	
MALE	0	.0	0	.0	0	.0	0	.0	0	.0	0	.0	0	.0	
TOTAL	0	.0	0	.0	0	.0	0	.0	0	.0	0	.0	0	.0	
FEMALE	0	.0	0	.0	0	.0	0	.0	0	.0	0	.0	0	.0	
MALE	0	.0	0	.0	0	.0	0	.0	0	.0	0	.0	0	.0	
PROFESSIONAL:															
FULL-TIME	0	.0	0	.0	1	.3	0	.0	1	.3	322	99.4	1	.3	
FEMALE	0	.0	0	.0	1	1.1	0	.0	1	1.1	86	97.7	1	1.1	
MALE	0	.0	0	.0	0	.0	0	.0	0	.0	236	100.0	0	.0	

ENROLLMENT IN INSTITUTIONS OF HIGHER EDUCATION FOR SELECTED MAJOR FIELDS OF STUDY AND LEVEL OF ENROLLMENT
E, ETHNICITY, AND SEX, STATE, 1978

- LAW

AN INDIAN N NATIVE		BLACK NON-HISPANIC		ASIAN OR PACIFIC ISLANDER		HISPANIC		TOTAL MINORITY		WHITE NON-HISPANIC		NON-RESIDENT ALIEN		TOTAL
R	%	NUMBER	%	NUMBER	%	NUMBER	%	NUMBER	%	NUMBER	%	NUMBER	%	NUMBER
CONTINUED														
0	.0	0	.0	0	.0	0	.0	0	.0	0	.0	0	.0	0
0	.0	0	.0	0	.0	0	.0	0	.0	0	.0	0	.0	0
0	.0	0	.0	0	.0	0	.0	0	.0	0	.0	0	.0	0
0	.0	0	.0	1	.3	0	.0	1	.3	322	99.4	1	.3	324
0	.0	0	.0	1	1.1	0	.0	1	1.1	86	97.7	1	1.1	88
0	.0	0	.0	0	.0	0	.0	0	.0	236	100.0	0	.0	236
0	.0	0	.0	1	.3	0	.0	1	.3	322	99.4	1	.3	324
0	.0	0	.0	1	1.1	0	.0	1	1.1	86	97.7	1	1.1	88
0	.0	0	.0	0	.0	0	.0	0	.0	236	100.0	0	.0	236
0	.0	0	.0	0	.0	0	.0	0	.0	0	.0	0	.0	0
0	.0	0	.0	0	.0	0	.0	0	.0	0	.0	0	.0	0
0	.0	0	.0	0	.0	0	.0	0	.0	0	.0	0	.0	0
0	.0	0	.0	1	.3	0	.0	1	.3	322	99.4	1	.3	324
0	.0	0	.0	1	1.1	0	.0	1	1.1	86	97.7	1	1.1	88
0	.0	0	.0	0	.0	0	.0	0	.0	236	100.0	0	.0	236
0	.0	0	.0	0	.0	0	.0	0	.0	0	.0	0	.0	0
0	.0	0	.0	0	.0	0	.0	0	.0	0	.0	0	.0	0
0	.0	0	.0	0	.0	0	.0	0	.0	0	.0	0	.0	0
0	.0	0	.0	1	.3	0	.0	1	.3	322	99.4	1	.3	324
0	.0	0	.0	1	1.1	0	.0	1	1.1	86	97.7	1	1.1	88
0	.0	0	.0	0	.0	0	.0	0	.0	236	100.0	0	.0	236
(4 INSTITUTIONS)														
0	.0	0	.0	0	.0	0	.0	0	.0	0	.0	0	.0	0
0	.0	0	.0	0	.0	0	.0	0	.0	0	.0	0	.0	0
0	.0	0	.0	0	.0	0	.0	0	.0	0	.0	0	.0	0
0	.0	0	.0	0	.0	0	.0	0	.0	0	.0	0	.0	0
0	.0	0	.0	0	.0	0	.0	0	.0	0	.0	0	.0	0
0	.0	0	.0	0	.0	0	.0	0	.0	0	.0	0	.0	0
0	.0	0	.0	0	.0	0	.0	0	.0	0	.0	0	.0	0
0	.0	0	.0	0	.0	0	.0	0	.0	0	.0	0	.0	0
0	.0	0	.0	0	.0	0	.0	0	.0	0	.0	0	.0	0
0	.0	0	.0	0	.0	0	.0	0	.0	0	.0	0	.0	0
0	.0	0	.0	0	.0	0	.0	0	.0	0	.0	0	.0	0
0	.0	0	.0	0	.0	0	.0	0	.0	0	.0	0	.0	0
0	.0	0	.0	0	.0	0	.0	0	.0	0	.0	0	.0	0
0	.0	0	.0	0	.0	0	.0	0	.0	0	.0	0	.0	0
0	.0	0	.0	0	.0	0	.0	0	.0	0	.0	0	.0	0
0	.0	0	.0	0	.0	0	.0	0	.0	0	.0	0	.0	0
0	.0	0	.0	0	.0	0	.0	0	.0	0	.0	0	.0	0
0	.0	0	.0	0	.0	0	.0	0	.0	0	.0	0	.0	0
1	.0	91	4.0	5	.2	4	.2	101	4.5	2,155	95.1	11	.5	2,267
1	.2	46	7.4	1	.2	1	.2	49	7.9	569	91.2	6	1.0	624
0	.0	45	2.7	4	.2	3	.2	52	3.2	1,586	96.5	5	.3	1,643
0	.0	1	16.7	0	.0	0	.0	1	16.7	5	83.3	0	.0	6
0	.0	1	33.3	0	.0	0	.0	1	33.3	2	66.7	0	.0	3
0	.0	0	.0	0	.0	0	.0	0	.0	3	100.0	0	.0	3
1	.0	92	4.0	5	.2	4	.2	102	4.5	2,160	95.0	11	.5	2,273
1	.2	47	7.5	1	.2	1	.2	50	8.0	571	91.1	6	1.0	627
0	.0	45	2.7	4	.2	3	.2	52	3.2	1,589	96.5	5	.3	1,646
1	.0	91	4.0	5	.2	4	.2	101	4.5	2,155	95.1	11	.5	2,267
1	.2	46	7.4	1	.2	1	.2	49	7.9	569	91.2	6	1.0	624
0	.0	45	2.7	4	.2	3	.2	52	3.2	1,586	96.5	5	.3	1,643
0	.0	1	16.7	0	.0	0	.0	1	16.7	5	83.3	0	.0	6
0	.0	1	33.3	0	.0	0	.0	1	33.3	2	66.7	0	.0	3
0	.0	0	.0	0	.0	0	.0	0	.0	3	100.0	0	.0	3
1	.0	92	4.0	5	.2	4	.2	102	4.5	2,160	95.0	11	.5	2,273
1	.2	47	7.5	1	.2	1	.2	50	8.0	571	91.1	6	1.0	627
0	.0	45	2.7	4	.2	3	.2	52	3.2	1,589	96.5	5	.3	1,646
0	.0	0	.0	0	.0	0	.0	0	.0	0	.0	0	.0	0
0	.0	0	.0	0	.0	0	.0	0	.0	0	.0	0	.0	0
0	.0	0	.0	0	.0	0	.0	0	.0	0	.0	0	.0	0
1	.0	92	4.0	5	.2	4	.2	102	4.5	2,160	95.0	11	.5	2,273
1	.2	47	7.5	1	.2	1	.2	50	8.0	571	91.1	6	1.0	627
0	.0	45	2.7	4	.2	3	.2	52	3.2	1,589	96.5	5	.3	1,646

MAJOR FIELD 1400 - LAW

	AMERICAN INDIAN ALASKAN NATIVE		BLACK NON-HISPANIC		ASIAN OR PACIFIC ISLANDER		HISPANIC		TOTAL MINORITY		WHITE NON-HISPANIC		NON-RESIDENT ALIEN		TO
	NUMBER	%	NUMBER	%	NUMBER	%	NUMBER	%	NUMBER	%	NUMBER	%	NUMBER	%	NU
WASHINGTON (3 INSTITUTIONS)															
UNDERGRADUATES:															
FULL-TIME	0	.0	0	.0	0	.0	0	.0	0	.0	0	.0		.0	
FEMALE	0	.0	0	.0	0	.0	0	.0	0	.0	0	.0		.0	
MALE	0	.0	0	.0	0	.0	0	.0	0	.0	0	.0		.0	
PART-TIME	0	.0	0	.0	0	.0	0	.0	0	.0	0	.0		.0	
FEMALE	0	.0	0	.0	0	.0	0	.0	0	.0	0	.0	0	.0	
MALE	0	.0	0	.0	0	.0	0	.0	0	.0	0	.0	0	.0	
TOTAL	0	.0	0	.0	0	.0	0	.0	0	.0	0	.0		.0	
FEMALE	0	.0	0	.0	0	.0	0	.0	0	.0	0	.0		.0	
MALE	0	.0	0	.0	0	.0	0	.0	0	.0	0	.0	0	.0	
GRADUATE:															
FULL-TIME	0	.0	0	.0	0	.0	0	.0	0	.0	0	.0		.0	
FEMALE	0	.0	0	.0	0	.0	0	.0	0	.0	0	.0		.0	
MALE	0	.0	0	.0	0	.0	0	.0	0	.0	0	.0		.0	
PART-TIME	0	.0	0	.0	0	.0	0	.0	0	.0	0	.0		.0	
FEMALE	0	.0	0	.0	0	.0	0	.0	0	.0	0	.0		.0	
MALE	0	.0	0	.0	0	.0	0	.0	0	.0	0	.0	0	.0	
TOTAL	0	.0	0	.0	0	.0	0	.0	0	.0	0	.0		.0	
FEMALE	0	.0	0	.0	0	.0	0	.0	0	.0	0	.0		.0	
MALE	0	.0	0	.0	0	.0	0	.0	0	.0	0	.0	0	.0	
PROFESSIONAL:															
FULL-TIME	16	.8	23	1.2	40	2.1	26	1.4	105	5.5	1,789	94.4	2	.1	1
FEMALE	8	1.7	10	2.1	11	2.3	10	2.1	39	8.2	439	91.8	0	.0	
MALE	8	.6	13	.9	29	2.0	16	1.1	66	4.7	1,350	95.2	2	.1	1
PART-TIME	2	.8	2	.8	4	1.7	2	.8	10	4.2	229	95.8	0	.0	
FEMALE	0	.0	1	1.6	2	3.1	1	1.6	4	6.3	60	93.8	0	.0	
MALE	2	1.1	1	.6	2	1.1	1	.6	6	3.4	169	96.6	0	.0	
TOTAL	18	.8	25	1.2	44	2.1	28	1.3	115	5.4	2,018	94.5	2	.1	2
FEMALE	8	1.5	11	2.0	13	2.4	11	2.0	43	7.9	499	92.1	0	.0	
MALE	10	.6	14	.9	31	1.9	17	1.1	72	4.5	1,519	95.4	2	.1	1
UND+GRAD+PROF:															
FULL-TIME	16	.8	23	1.2	40	2.1	26	1.4	105	5.5	1,789	94.4	2	.1	1
FEMALE	8	1.7	10	2.1	11	2.3	10	2.1	39	8.2	439	91.8	0	.0	
MALE	8	.6	13	.9	29	2.0	16	1.1	66	4.7	1,350	95.2	2	.1	1
PART-TIME	2	.8	2	.8	4	1.7	2	.8	10	4.2	229	95.8	0	.0	
FEMALE	0	.0	1	1.6	2	3.1	1	1.6	4	6.3	60	93.8	0	.0	
MALE	2	1.1	1	.6	2	1.1	1	.6	6	3.4	169	96.6	0	.0	
TOTAL	18	.8	25	1.2	44	2.1	28	1.3	115	5.4	2,018	94.5	2	.1	2
FEMALE	8	1.5	11	2.0	13	2.4	11	2.0	43	7.9	499	92.1	0	.0	
MALE	10	.6	14	.9	31	1.9	17	1.1	72	4.5	1,519	95.4	2	.1	1
UNCLASSIFIED:															
TOTAL	0	.0	0	.0	0	.0	0	.0	0	.0	0	.0		.0	
FEMALE	0	.0	0	.0	0	.0	0	.0	0	.0	0	.0		.0	
MALE	0	.0	0	.0	0	.0	0	.0	0	.0	0	.0	0	.0	
TOTAL ENROLLMENT:															
TOTAL	18	.8	25	1.2	44	2.1	28	1.3	115	5.4	2,018	94.5	2	.1	2
FEMALE	8	1.5	11	2.0	13	2.4	11	2.0	43	7.9	499	92.1	0	.0	
MALE	10	.6	14	.9	31	1.9	17	1.1	72	4.5	1,519	95.4	2	.1	1
WEST VIRGINIA (1 INSTITUTIONS)															
UNDERGRADUATES:															
FULL-TIME	0	.0	0	.0	0	.0	0	.0	0	.0	0	.0		.0	
FEMALE	0	.0	0	.0	0	.0	0	.0	0	.0	0	.0		.0	
MALE	0	.0	0	.0	0	.0	0	.0	0	.0	0	.0		.0	
PART-TIME	0	.0	0	.0	0	.0	0	.0	0	.0	0	.0		.0	
FEMALE	0	.0	0	.0	0	.0	0	.0	0	.0	0	.0		.0	
MALE	0	.0	0	.0	0	.0	0	.0	0	.0	0	.0	0	.0	
TOTAL	0	.0	0	.0	0	.0	0	.0	0	.0	0	.0		.0	
FEMALE	0	.0	0	.0	0	.0	0	.0	0	.0	0	.0		.0	
MALE	0	.0	0	.0	0	.0	0	.0	0	.0	0	.0	0	.0	
GRADUATE:															
FULL-TIME	0	.0	0	.0	0	.0	0	.0	0	.0	0	.0		.0	
FEMALE	0	.0	0	.0	0	.0	0	.0	0	.0	0	.0		.0	
MALE	0	.0	0	.0	0	.0	0	.0	0	.0	0	.0		.0	
PART-TIME	0	.0	0	.0	0	.0	0	.0	0	.0	0	.0		.0	
FEMALE	0	.0	0	.0	0	.0	0	.0	0	.0	0	.0		.0	
MALE	0	.0	0	.0	0	.0	0	.0	0	.0	0	.0	0	.0	
TOTAL	0	.0	0	.0	0	.0	0	.0	0	.0	0	.0		.0	
FEMALE	0	.0	0	.0	0	.0	0	.0	0	.0	0	.0		.0	
MALE	0	.0	0	.0	0	.0	0	.0	0	.0	0	.0	0	.0	
PROFESSIONAL:															
FULL-TIME	1	.2	7	1.7	0	.0	1	.2	9	2.2	405	97.8		.0	
FEMALE	0	.0	5	5.6	0	.0	1	1.1	6	6.7	84	93.3	0	.0	
MALE	1	.3	2	.6	0	.0	0	.0	3	.9	321	99.1	0	.0	

D 1400 - LAW

	AMERICAN INDIAN ALASKAN NATIVE		BLACK NON-HISPANIC		ASIAN OR PACIFIC ISLANDER		HISPANIC		TOTAL MINORITY		WHITE NON-HISPANIC		NON-RESIDENT ALIEN		TOTAL
	NUMBER	%	NUMBER	%	NUMBER	%	NUMBER	%	NUMBER	%	NUMBER	%	NUMBER	%	NUMBER
NIA	CONTINUED														
AL:															
	0	.0	0	.0	0	.0	0	.0	0	.0	8	100.0	0	.0	8
	0	.0	0	.0	0	.0	0	.0	0	.0	4	100.0	0	.0	4
	0	.0	0	.0	0	.0	0	.0	0	.0	4	100.0	0	.0	4
	1	.2	7	1.7	0	.0	1	.2	9	2.1	413	97.9	0	.0	422
	0	.0	5	5.3	0	.0	1	1.1	6	6.4	88	93.6	0	.0	94
	1	.3	2	.6	0	.0	0	.0	3	.9	325	99.1	0	.0	328
RGF:															
	1	.2	7	1.7	0	.0	1	.2	9	2.2	405	97.8	0	.0	414
	0	.0	5	5.6	0	.0	1	1.1	6	6.7	84	93.3	0	.0	90
	1	.3	2	.6	0	.0	0	.0	3	.9	321	99.1	0	.0	324
	0	.0	0	.0	0	.0	0	.0	0	.0	8	100.0	0	.0	4
	0	.0	0	.0	0	.0	0	.0	0	.0	4	100.0	0	.0	4
	0	.0	0	.0	0	.0	0	.0	0	.0	4	100.0	0	.0	4
	1	.2	7	1.7	0	.0	1	.2	9	2.1	413	97.9	0	.0	422
	0	.0	5	5.3	0	.0	1	1.1	6	6.4	88	93.6	0	.0	94
	1	.3	2	.6	0	.0	0	.0	3	.9	325	99.1	0	.0	328
ED:															
	0	.0	0	.0	0	.0	0	.0	0	.0	0	.0	0	.0	0
	0	.0	0	.0	0	.0	0	.0	0	.0	0	.0	0	.0	0
	0	.0	0	.0	0	.0	0	.0	0	.0	0	.0	0	.0	0
LLMENT:															
	1	.2	7	1.7	0	.0	1	.2	9	2.1	413	97.9	0	.0	422
	0	.0	5	5.3	0	.0	1	1.1	6	6.4	88	93.6	0	.0	94
	1	.3	2	.6	0	.0	0	.0	3	.9	325	99.1	0	.0	328
(2 INSTITUTIONS)															
ATES:															
	0	.0	0	.0	0	.0	0	.0	0	.0	0	.0	0	.0	0
	0	.0	0	.0	0	.0	0	.0	0	.0	0	.0	0	.0	3
	0	.0	0	.0	0	.0	0	.0	0	.0	0	.0	0	.0	0
	0	.0	0	.0	0	.0	0	.0	0	.0	0	.0	0	.0	0
	0	.0	0	.0	0	.0	0	.0	0	.0	0	.0	0	.0	0
	0	.0	0	.0	0	.0	0	.0	0	.0	0	.0	0	.0	0
	0	.0	0	.0	0	.0	0	.0	0	.0	0	.0	0	.0	0
	0	.0	0	.0	0	.0	0	.0	0	.0	0	.0	0	.0	0
	0	.0	0	.0	0	.0	0	.0	0	.0	0	.0	0	.0	0
	0	.0	0	.0	0	.0	0	.0	0	.0	0	.0	0	.0	0
	0	.0	0	.0	0	.0	0	.0	0	.0	0	.0	0	.0	0
	0	.0	0	.0	0	.0	0	.0	0	.0	0	.0	0	.0	0
	0	.0	0	.0	0	.0	0	.0	0	.0	0	.0	0	.0	0
	0	.0	0	.0	0	.0	0	.0	0	.0	0	.0	0	.0	0
	0	.0	0	.0	0	.0	0	.0	0	.0	0	.0	0	.0	0
AL:															
	14	1.1	36	2.7	8	.6	24	1.8	82	6.2	1,229	93.5	3	.2	1,314
	4	.9	16	3.7	4	.9	11	2.5	35	8.0	400	92.0	0	.0	435
	10	1.1	20	2.3	4	.5	13	1.5	47	5.3	829	94.3	3	.3	879
	1	1.8	1	1.8	0	.0	0	.0	2	3.6	51	92.7	2	3.6	55
	0	.0	0	.0	0	.0	0	.0	0	.0	17	94.4	1	5.6	18
	1	2.7	1	2.7	0	.0	0	.0	2	5.4	34	91.9	1	2.7	37
	15	1.1	37	2.7	8	.6	24	1.8	84	6.1	1,280	93.5	5	.4	1,369
	4	.9	16	3.5	4	.9	11	2.4	35	7.7	417	92.1	1	.2	453
	11	1.2	21	2.3	4	.4	13	1.4	49	5.3	863	94.2	4	.4	916
RGF:															
	14	1.1	36	2.7	8	.6	24	1.8	82	6.2	1,229	93.5	3	.2	1,314
	4	.9	16	3.7	4	.9	11	2.5	35	8.0	400	92.0	0	.0	435
	10	1.1	20	2.3	4	.5	13	1.5	47	5.3	829	94.3	3	.3	879
	1	1.8	1	1.8	0	.0	0	.0	2	3.6	51	92.7	2	3.6	55
	0	.0	0	.0	0	.0	0	.0	0	.0	17	94.4	1	5.6	18
	1	2.7	1	2.7	0	.0	0	.0	2	5.4	34	91.9	1	2.7	37
	15	1.1	37	2.7	8	.6	24	1.8	84	6.1	1,280	93.5	5	.4	1,369
	4	.9	16	3.5	4	.9	11	2.4	35	7.7	417	92.1	1	.2	453
	11	1.2	21	2.3	4	.4	13	1.4	49	5.3	863	94.2	4	.4	916
ED:															
	0	.0	0	.0	0	.0	0	.0	0	.0	0	.0	0	.0	0
	0	.0	0	.0	0	.0	0	.0	0	.0	0	.0	0	.0	0
	0	.0	0	.0	0	.0	0	.0	0	.0	0	.0	0	.0	0
LLMENT:															
	15	1.1	37	2.7	8	.6	24	1.8	84	6.1	1,280	93.5	5	.4	1,369
	4	.9	16	3.5	4	.9	11	2.4	35	7.7	417	92.1	1	.2	453
	11	1.2	21	2.3	4	.4	13	1.4	49	5.3	863	94.2	4	.4	916

MAJOR FIELD 1400 - LAW

	AMERICAN INDIAN ALASKAN NATIVE		BLACK NON-HISPANIC		ASIAN OR PACIFIC ISLANDER		HISPANIC		TOTAL MINORITY		WHITE NON-HISPANIC		NON-RESIDENT ALIEN	
	NUMBER	%	NUMBER	%	NUMBER	%	NUMBER	%	NUMBER	%	NUMBER	%	NUMBER	%
WYOMING	(	1 INSTITUTIONS)												
UNDERGRADUATES:														
FULL-TIME	0	.0	0	.0	0	.0	0	.0	0	.0	0	.0	0	.0
FEMALE	0	.0	0	.0	0	.0	0	.0	0	.0	0	.0	0	.0
MALE	0	.0	0	.0	0	.0	0	.0	0	.0	0	.0	0	.0
PART-TIME	0	.0	0	.0	0	.0	0	.0	0	.0	0	.0	0	.0
FEMALE	0	.0	0	.0	0	.0	0	.0	0	.0	0	.0	0	.0
MALE	0	.0	0	.0	0	.0	0	.0	0	.0	0	.0	0	.0
TOTAL	0	.0	0	.0	0	.0	0	.0	0	.0	0	.0	0	.0
FEMALE	0	.0	0	.0	0	.0	0	.0	0	.0	0	.0	0	.0
MALE	0	.0	0	.0	0	.0	0	.0	0	.0	0	.0	0	.0
GRADUATE:														
FULL-TIME	0	.0	0	.0	0	.0	0	.0	0	.0	0	.0	0	.0
FEMALE	0	.0	0	.0	0	.0	0	.0	0	.0	0	.0	0	.0
MALE	0	.0	0	.0	0	.0	0	.0	0	.0	0	.0	0	.0
PART-TIME	0	.0	0	.0	0	.0	0	.0	0	.0	0	.0	0	.0
FEMALE	0	.0	0	.0	0	.0	0	.0	0	.0	0	.0	0	.0
MALE	0	.0	0	.0	0	.0	0	.0	0	.0	0	.0	0	.0
TOTAL	0	.0	0	.0	0	.0	0	.0	0	.0	0	.0	0	.0
FEMALE	0	.0	0	.0	0	.0	0	.0	0	.0	0	.0	0	.0
MALE	0	.0	0	.0	0	.0	0	.0	0	.0	0	.0	0	.0
PROFESSIONAL:														
FULL-TIME	0	.0	0	.0	1	.5	2	.9	3	1.4	210	98.6	0	.0
FEMALE	0	.0	0	.0	1	1.9	1	1.9	2	3.8	51	96.2	0	.0
MALE	0	.0	0	.0	0	.0	1	.6	1	.6	159	99.4	0	.0
PART-TIME	0	.0	0	.0	0	.0	0	.0	0	.0	1	100.0	0	.0
FEMALE	0	.0	0	.0	0	.0	0	.0	0	.0	1	100.0	0	.0
MALE	0	.0	0	.0	0	.0	0	.0	0	.0	0	.0	0	.0
TOTAL	0	.0	0	.0	1	.5	2	.9	3	1.4	211	98.6	0	.0
FEMALE	0	.0	0	.0	1	1.9	1	1.9	2	3.7	52	96.3	0	.0
MALE	0	.0	0	.0	0	.0	1	.6	1	.6	159	99.4	0	.0
UNG+GRAD+PROF:														
FULL-TIME	0	.0	0	.0	1	.5	2	.9	3	1.4	210	98.6	0	.0
FEMALE	0	.0	0	.0	1	1.9	1	1.9	2	3.8	51	96.2	0	.0
MALE	0	.0	0	.0	0	.0	1	.6	1	.6	159	99.4	0	.0
PART-TIME	0	.0	0	.0	0	.0	0	.0	0	.0	1	100.0	0	.0
FEMALE	0	.0	0	.0	0	.0	0	.0	0	.0	1	100.0	0	.0
MALE	0	.0	0	.0	0	.0	0	.0	0	.0	0	.0	0	.0
TOTAL	0	.0	0	.0	1	.5	2	.9	3	1.4	211	98.6	0	.0
FEMALE	0	.0	0	.0	1	1.9	1	1.9	2	3.7	52	96.3	0	.0
MALE	0	.0	0	.0	0	.0	1	.6	1	.6	159	99.4	0	.0
UNCLASSIFIED:														
TOTAL	0	.0	0	.0	0	.0	0	.0	0	.0	0	.0	0	.0
FEMALE	0	.0	0	.0	0	.0	0	.0	0	.0	0	.0	0	.0
MALE	0	.0	0	.0	0	.0	0	.0	0	.0	0	.0	0	.0
TOTAL ENROLLMENT:														
TOTAL	0	.0	0	.0	1	.5	2	.9	3	1.4	211	98.6	0	.0
FEMALE	0	.0	0	.0	1	1.9	1	1.9	2	3.7	52	96.3	0	.0
MALE	0	.0	0	.0	0	.0	1	.6	1	.6	159	99.4	0	.0
THE STATES AND D.C.	(	175 INSTITUTIONS)												
UNDERGRADUATES:														
FULL-TIME	0	.0	0	.0	0	.0	0	.0	0	.0	0	.0	0	.0
FEMALE	0	.0	0	.0	0	.0	0	.0	0	.0	0	.0	0	.0
MALE	0	.0	0	.0	0	.0	0	.0	0	.0	0	.0	0	.0
PART-TIME	0	.0	0	.0	0	.0	0	.0	0	.0	0	.0	0	.0
FEMALE	0	.0	0	.0	0	.0	0	.0	0	.0	0	.0	0	.0
MALE	0	.0	0	.0	0	.0	0	.0	0	.0	0	.0	0	.0
TOTAL	0	.0	0	.0	0	.0	0	.0	0	.0	0	.0	0	.0
FEMALE	0	.0	0	.0	0	.0	0	.0	0	.0	0	.0	0	.0
MALE	0	.0	0	.0	0	.0	0	.0	0	.0	0	.0	0	.0
GRADUATE:														
FULL-TIME	0	.0	0	.0	0	.0	0	.0	0	.0	0	.0	0	.0
FEMALE	0	.0	0	.0	0	.0	0	.0	0	.0	0	.0	0	.0
MALE	0	.0	0	.0	0	.0	0	.0	0	.0	0	.0	0	.0
PART-TIME	0	.0	0	.0	0	.0	0	.0	0	.0	0	.0	0	.0
FEMALE	0	.0	0	.0	0	.0	0	.0	0	.0	0	.0	0	.0
MALE	0	.0	0	.0	0	.0	0	.0	0	.0	0	.0	0	.0
TOTAL	0	.0	0	.0	0	.0	0	.0	0	.0	0	.0	0	.0
FEMALE	0	.0	0	.0	0	.0	0	.0	0	.0	0	.0	0	.0
MALE	0	.0	0	.0	0	.0	0	.0	0	.0	0	.0	0	.0
PROFESSIONAL:														
FULL-TIME	356	.4	4,457	4.5	1,297	1.3	2,383	2.4	8,493	8.6	90,197	90.9	586	.6
FEMALE	124	.4	1,969	6.5	501	1.7	717	2.4	3,311	11.0	26,678	88.5	154	.5
MALE	232	.3	2,488	3.6	796	1.2	1,666	2.4	5,182	7.5	63,519	91.9	432	.6

17 - TOTAL ENROLLMENT IN INSTITUTIONS OF HIGHER EDUCATION FOR SELECTED MAJOR FIELDS OF STUDY AND LEVEL OF ENROLLMENT BY RACE, ETHNICITY, AND SEX: STATE, 1978

FIELD 1400 - LAW

	AMERICAN INDIAN ALASKAN NATIVE		BLACK NON-HISPANIC		ASIAN OR PACIFIC ISLANDER		HISPANIC		TOTAL MINORITY		WHITE NON-HISPANIC		NON-RESIDENT ALIEN		TOTAL
	NUMBER	%	NUMBER	%	NUMBER	%	NUMBER	%	NUMBER	%	NUMBER	%	NUMBER	%	NUMBER

ATES AND D.C. CONTINUED

SIONAL:
IME	79	.4	914	4.8	217	1.1	443	2.3	1,653	8.6	17,373	90.7	118	.6	19,144
ALE	25	.4	368	6.3	67	1.1	128	2.2	588	10.0	5,260	89.4	33	.6	5,881
ALE	54	.4	546	4.1	150	1.1	315	2.4	1,065	8.0	12,113	91.3	85	.6	13,263
	435	.4	5,371	4.5	1,514	1.3	2,826	2.4	10,146	8.6	107,570	90.8	704	.6	118,420
ALE	149	.4	2,337	6.5	568	1.6	845	2.3	3,899	10.8	31,938	88.7	187	.5	36,024
ALE	286	.3	3,034	3.7	946	1.1	1,981	2.4	6,247	7.6	75,632	91.8	517	.6	82,396

AD+PROF:
IME	356	.4	4,457	4.5	1,297	1.3	2,383	2.4	8,493	8.6	90,197	90.9	586	.6	99,276
ALE	124	.4	1,969	6.5	501	1.7	717	2.4	3,311	11.0	26,678	88.5	154	.5	30,143
ALE	232	.3	2,488	3.6	796	1.2	1,666	2.4	5,182	7.5	63,519	91.9	432	.6	69,133
IME	79	.4	914	4.8	217	1.1	443	2.3	1,653	8.6	17,373	90.7	118	.6	19,144
ALE	25	.4	368	6.3	67	1.1	128	2.2	588	10.0	5,260	89.4	33	.6	5,881
ALE	54	.4	546	4.1	150	1.1	315	2.4	1,065	8.0	12,113	91.3	85	.6	13,263
	435	.4	5,371	4.5	1,514	1.3	2,826	2.4	10,146	8.6	107,570	90.8	704	.6	118,420
ALE	149	.4	2,337	6.5	568	1.6	845	2.3	3,899	10.8	31,938	88.7	187	.5	36,024
ALE	286	.3	3,034	3.7	946	1.1	1,981	2.4	6,247	7.6	75,632	91.8	517	.6	82,396

SIFIED:
	0	.0	0	.0	0	.0	0	.0	0	.0	0	.0	0	.0	0
ALE	0	.0	0	.0	0	.0	0	.0	0	.0	0	.0	0	.0	0
ALE	0	.0	0	.0	0	.0	0	.0	0	.0	0	.0	0	.0	0

ENROLLMENT:
	435	.4	5,371	4.5	1,514	1.3	2,826	2.4	10,146	8.6	107,570	90.8	704	.6	118,420
ALE	149	.4	2,333	6.5	568	1.6	845	2.3	3,899	10.8	31,938	88.7	187	.5	36,024
ALE	286	.3	3,034	3.7	946	1.1	1,981	2.4	6,247	7.6	75,632	91.8	517	.6	82,396

RICO   (2 INSTITUTIONS)

RADUATES:
IME	0	.0	0	.0	0	.0	0	.0	0	.0	0	.0	0	.0	0
ALE	0	.0	0	.0	0	.0	0	.0	0	.0	0	.0	0	.0	0
ALE	0	.0	0	.0	0	.0	0	.0	0	.0	0	.0	0	.0	0
IME	0	.0	0	.0	0	.0	0	.0	0	.0	0	.0	0	.0	0
ALE	0	.0	0	.0	0	.0	0	.0	0	.0	0	.0	0	.0	0
ALE	0	.0	0	.0	0	.0	0	.0	0	.0	0	.0	0	.0	0
	0	.0	0	.0	0	.0	0	.0	0	.0	0	.0	0	.0	0
ALE	0	.0	0	.0	0	.0	0	.0	0	.0	0	.0	0	.0	0
ALE	0	.0	0	.0	0	.0	0	.0	0	.0	0	.0	0	.0	0

TE:
IME	0	.0	0	.0	0	.0	0	.0	0	.0	0	.0	0	.0	0
ALE	0	.0	0	.0	0	.0	0	.0	0	.0	0	.0	0	.0	0
ALE	0	.0	0	.0	0	.0	0	.0	0	.0	0	.0	0	.0	0
IME	0	.0	0	.0	0	.0	0	.0	0	.0	0	.0	0	.0	0
ALE	0	.0	0	.0	0	.0	0	.0	0	.0	0	.0	0	.0	0
ALE	0	.0	0	.0	0	.0	0	.0	0	.0	0	.0	0	.0	0
	0	.0	0	.0	0	.0	0	.0	0	.0	0	.0	0	.0	0
ALE	0	.0	0	.0	0	.0	0	.0	0	.0	0	.0	0	.0	0
ALE	0	.0	0	.0	0	.0	0	.0	0	.0	0	.0	0	.0	0

SIONAL:
IME	0	.0	0	.0	0	.0	538	100.0	538	100.0	0	.0	0	.0	538
ALE	0	.0	0	.0	0	.0	186	100.0	186	100.0	0	.0	0	.0	186
ALE	0	.0	0	.0	0	.0	352	100.0	352	100.0	0	.0	0	.0	352
IME	0	.0	0	.0	0	.0	162	100.0	162	100.0	0	.0	0	.0	162
ALE	0	.0	0	.0	0	.0	41	100.0	41	100.0	0	.0	0	.0	41
ALE	0	.0	0	.0	0	.0	121	100.0	121	100.0	0	.0	0	.0	121
	0	.0	0	.0	0	.0	700	100.0	700	100.0	0	.0	0	.0	700
ALE	0	.0	0	.0	0	.0	227	100.0	227	100.0	0	.0	0	.0	227
ALE	0	.0	0	.0	0	.0	473	100.0	473	100.0	0	.0	0	.0	473

AD+PROF:
IME	0	.0	0	.0	0	.0	538	100.0	538	100.0	0	.0	0	.0	538
ALE	0	.0	0	.0	0	.0	186	100.0	186	100.0	0	.0	0	.0	186
ALE	0	.0	0	.0	0	.0	352	100.0	352	100.0	0	.0	0	.0	352
IME	0	.0	0	.0	0	.0	162	100.0	162	100.0	0	.0	0	.0	162
ALE	0	.0	0	.0	0	.0	41	100.0	41	100.0	0	.0	0	.0	41
ALE	0	.0	0	.0	0	.0	121	100.0	121	100.0	0	.0	0	.0	121
	0	.0	0	.0	0	.0	700	100.0	700	100.0	0	.0	0	.0	700
ALE	0	.0	0	.0	0	.0	227	100.0	227	100.0	0	.0	0	.0	227
ALE	0	.0	0	.0	0	.0	473	100.0	473	100.0	0	.0	0	.0	473

SIFIED:
	0	.0	0	.0	0	.0	0	.0	0	.0	0	.0	0	.0	0
ALE	0	.0	0	.0	0	.0	0	.0	0	.0	0	.0	0	.0	0
ALE	0	.0	0	.0	0	.0	0	.0	0	.0	0	.0	0	.0	0

ENROLLMENT:
	0	.0	0	.0	0	.0	700	100.0	700	100.0	0	.0	0	.0	700
ALE	0	.0	0	.0	0	.0	227	100.0	227	100.0	0	.0	0	.0	227
ALE	0	.0	0	.0	0	.0	473	100.0	473	100.0	0	.0	0	.0	473

MAJOR FIELD 1400 - LAW

	AMERICAN INDIAN ALASKAN NATIVE		BLACK NON-HISPANIC		ASIAN OR PACIFIC ISLANDER		HISPANIC		TOTAL MINORITY		WHITE NON-HISPANIC		NON-RESIDENT ALIEN		TOT
	NUMBER	%	NUMBER	%	NUMBER	%	NUMBER	%	NUMBER	%	NUMBER	%	NUMBER	%	NUM
OUTLYING AREAS (2 INSTITUTIONS)															
UNDERGRADUATES:															
FULL-TIME	0	.0	0	.0	0	.0	0	.0	0	.0	0	.0		.0	
FEMALE	0	.0	0	.0	0	.0	0	.0	0	.0	0	.0		.0	
MALE	0	.0	0	.0	0	.0	0	.0	0	.0	0	.0		.0	
PART-TIME	0	.0	0	.0	0	.0	0	.0	0	.0	0	.0		.0	
FEMALE	0	.0	0	.0	0	.0	0	.0	0	.0	0	.0		.0	
MALE	0	.0	0	.0	0	.0	0	.0	0	.0	0	.0	0	.0	
													0		
TOTAL	0	.0	0	.0	0	.0	0	.0	0	.0	0	.0		.0	
FEMALE	0	.0	0	.0	0	.0	0	.0	0	.0	0	.0		.0	
MALE	0	.0	0	.0	0	.0	0	.0	0	.0	0	.0	0	.0	
													0		
GRADUATE:															
FULL-TIME	0	.0	0	.0	0	.0	0	.0	0	.0	0	.0		.0	
FEMALE	0	.0	0	.0	0	.0	0	.0	0	.0	0	.0		.0	
MALE	0	.0	0	.0	0	.0	0	.0	0	.0	0	.0		.0	
PART-TIME	0	.0	0	.0	0	.0	0	.0	0	.0	0	.0		.0	
FEMALE	0	.0	0	.0	0	.0	0	.0	0	.0	0	.0		.0	
MALE	0	.0	0	.0	0	.0	0	.0	0	.0	0	.0	0	.0	
													0		
TOTAL	0	.0	0	.0	0	.0	0	.0	0	.0	0	.0		.0	
FEMALE	0	.0	0	.0	0	.0	0	.0	0	.0	0	.0		.0	
MALE	0	.0	0	.0	0	.0	0	.0	0	.0	0	.0	0	.0	
													0		
PROFESSIONAL:															
FULL-TIME	0	.0	0	.0	0	.0	538	100.0	538	100.0	0	.0		.0	
FEMALE	0	.0	0	.0	0	.0	186	100.0	186	100.0	0	.0		.0	
MALE	0	.0	0	.0	0	.0	352	100.0	352	100.0	0	.0		.0	
PART-TIME	0	.0	0	.0	0	.0	162	100.0	162	100.0	0	.0		.0	
FEMALE	0	.0	0	.0	0	.0	41	100.0	41	100.0	0	.0		.0	
MALE	0	.0	0	.0	0	.0	121	100.0	121	100.0	0	.0	0	.0	
													0		
TOTAL	0	.0	0	.0	0	.0	700	100.0	700	100.0	0	.0		.0	
FEMALE	0	.0	0	.0	0	.0	227	100.0	227	100.0	0	.0		.0	
MALE	0	.0	0	.0	0	.0	473	100.0	473	100.0	0	.0	0	.0	
													0		
UND+GRAD+PROF:															
FULL-TIME	0	.0	0	.0	0	.0	538	100.0	538	100.0	0	.0		.0	
FEMALE	0	.0	0	.0	0	.0	186	100.0	186	100.0	0	.0		.0	
MALE	0	.0	0	.0	0	.0	352	100.0	352	100.0	0	.0		.0	
PART-TIME	0	.0	0	.0	0	.0	162	100.0	162	100.0	0	.0		.0	
FEMALE	0	.0	0	.0	0	.0	41	100.0	41	100.0	0	.0		.0	
MALE	0	.0	0	.0	0	.0	121	100.0	121	100.0	0	.0	0	.0	
													0		
TOTAL	0	.0	0	.0	0	.0	700	100.0	700	100.0	0	.0		.0	
FEMALE	0	.0	0	.0	0	.0	227	100.0	227	100.0	0	.0		.0	
MALE	0	.0	0	.0	0	.0	473	100.0	473	100.0	0	.0	0	.0	
													0		
UNCLASSIFIED:															
TOTAL	0	.0	0	.0	0	.0	0	.0	0	.0	0	.0		.0	
FEMALE	0	.0	0	.0	0	.0	0	.0	0	.0	0	.0		.0	
MALE	0	.0	0	.0	0	.0	0	.0	0	.0	0	.0	0	.0	
													0		
TOTAL ENROLLMENT:															
TOTAL	0	.0	0	.0	0	.0	700	100.0	700	100.0	0	.0		.0	
FEMALE	0	.0	0	.0	0	.0	227	100.0	227	100.0	0	.0		.0	
MALE	0	.0	0	.0	0	.0	473	100.0	473	100.0	0	.0	0	.0	
													0		
MAJOR FIELD AGGREGATE 1400 (177 INSTITUTIONS)															
UNDERGRADUATES:															
FULL-TIME	0	.0	0	.0	0	.0	0	.0	0	.0	0	.0		.0	
FEMALE	0	.0	0	.0	0	.0	0	.0	0	.0	0	.0		.0	
MALE	0	.0	0	.0	0	.0	0	.0	0	.0	0	.0		.0	
PART-TIME	0	.0	0	.0	0	.0	0	.0	0	.0	0	.0		.0	
FEMALE	0	.0	0	.0	0	.0	0	.0	0	.0	0	.0		.0	
MALE	0	.0	0	.0	0	.0	0	.0	0	.0	0	.0	0	.0	
													0		
TOTAL	0	.0	0	.0	0	.0	0	.0	0	.0	0	.0	0	.0	
FEMALE	0	.0	0	.0	0	.0	0	.0	0	.0	0	.0	0	.0	
MALE	0	.0	0	.0	0	.0	0	.0	0	.0	0	.0	0	.0	
GRADUATE															
FULL-TIME	0	.0	0	.0	0	.0	0	.0	0	.0	0	.0		.0	
FEMALE	0	.0	0	.0	0	.0	0	.0	0	.0	0	.0		.0	
MALE	0	.0	0	.0	0	.0	0	.0	0	.0	0	.0		.0	
PART-TIME	0	.0	0	.0	0	.0	0	.0	0	.0	0	.0		.0	
FEMALE	0	.0	0	.0	0	.0	0	.0	0	.0	0	.0		.0	
MALE	0	.0	0	.0	0	.0	0	.0	0	.0	0	.0	0	.0	
													0		
TOTAL	0	.0	0	.0	0	.0	0	.0	0	.0	0	.0		.0	
FEMALE	0	.0	0	.0	0	.0	0	.0	0	.0	0	.0		.0	
MALE	0	.0	0	.0	0	.0	0	.0	0	.0	0	.0	0	.0	
													0		
PROFESSIONAL:															
FULL-TIME	396	.4	4,457	4.5	1,297	1.3	2,921	2.9	9,031	9.0	90,197	90.4	586	.6	99,
FEMALE	124	.4	1,969	6.5	501	1.7	903	3.0	3,497	11.5	26,678	88.0	154	.5	30,
MALE	232	.3	2,488	3.6	796	1.1	2,018	2.9	5,534	8.0	63,519	91.4	432	.6	69,

7 - TOTAL ENROLLMENT IN INSTITUTIONS OF HIGHER EDUCATION FOR SELECTED MAJOR FIELDS OF STUDY AND LEVEL OF ENROLLMENT
BY RACE, ETHNICITY, AND SEX: STATE, 1978

IELD 1400 - LAW

	AMERICAN INDIAN ALASKAN NATIVE		BLACK NON-HISPANIC		ASIAN OR PACIFIC ISLANDER		HISPANIC		TOTAL MINORITY		WHITE NON-HISPANIC		NON-RESIDENT ALIEN		TOTAL
	NUMBER	%	NUMBER	%	NUMBER	%	NUMBER	%	NUMBER	%	NUMBER	%	NUMBER	%	NUMBER
IELD AGGREGATE 1400 CONTINUED															
IONAL:															
Me	79	.4	914	4.7	217	1.1	605	3.1	1,815	9.4	17,373	90.0	118	.6	19,306
LE	25	.4	368	6.2	67	1.1	169	2.9	629	10.6	5,260	88.8	33	.6	5,922
LE	54	.4	546	4.1	150	1.1	436	3.3	1,186	8.9	12,113	90.5	85	.6	13,384
	435	.4	5,371	4.5	1,514	1.3	3,526	3.0	10,846	9.1	107,570	90.3	704	.6	119,120
LE	149	.4	2,337	6.4	568	1.6	1,072	3.0	4,126	11.4	31,938	88.1	187	.5	36,251
LE	286	.3	3,034	3.7	946	1.1	2,454	3.0	6,720	8.1	75,632	91.3	517	.6	82,869
D+PROF:															
ME	356	.4	4,457	4.5	1,297	1.3	2,921	2.9	9,031	9.0	90,197	90.4	986	.6	99,814
LE	124	.4	1,969	6.5	501	1.7	903	3.0	3,497	11.5	26,678	88.0	154	.5	30,329
LE	232	.3	2,488	3.6	796	1.1	2,018	2.9	5,534	8.0	63,519	91.4	432	.6	69,485
Me	79	.4	914	4.7	217	1.1	605	3.1	1,815	9.4	17,373	90.0	118	.6	19,306
LE	25	.4	368	6.2	67	1.1	169	2.9	629	10.6	5,260	88.8	33	.6	5,922
LE	54	.4	546	4.1	150	1.1	436	3.3	1,186	8.9	12,113	90.5	85	.6	13,384
	435	.4	5,371	4.5	1,514	1.3	3,526	3.0	10,846	9.1	107,570	90.3	704	.6	119,120
LE	149	.4	2,337	6.4	568	1.6	1,072	3.0	4,126	11.4	31,938	88.1	187	.5	36,251
LE	286	.3	3,034	3.7	946	1.1	2,454	3.0	6,720	8.1	75,632	91.3	517	.6	82,869
IFIED:															
	0	.0	0	.0	0	.0	0	.0	0	.0	0	.0	0	.0	0
LE	0	.0	0	.0	0	.0	0	.0	0	.0	0	.0	0	.0	0
LE	0	.0	0	.0	0	.0	0	.0	0	.0	0	.0	0	.0	0
NROLLMENT:															
	435	.4	5,371	4.5	1,514	1.3	3,526	3.0	10,846	9.1	107,570	90.3	704	.6	119,120
LE	149	.4	2,337	6.4	568	1.6	1,072	3.0	4,126	11.4	31,938	88.1	187	.5	36,251
LE	286	.3	3,034	3.7	946	1.1	2,454	3.0	6,720	8.1	75,632	91.3	517	.6	82,869

TABLE 17 - TOTAL ENROLLMENT IN INSTITUTIONS OF HIGHER EDUCATION FOR SELECTED MAJOR FIELDS OF STUDY AND LEVEL OF ENROLLMENT
BY RACE, ETHNICITY, AND SEX: STATE, 1978

MAJOR FIELD 1900 - PHYSICAL SCIENCES

	AMERICAN INDIAN ALASKAN NATIVE		BLACK NON-HISPANIC		ASIAN OR PACIFIC ISLANDER		HISPANIC		TOTAL MINORITY		WHITE NON-HISPANIC		NON-RESIDENT ALIEN		T
	NUMBER	%	NUMBER	%	NUMBER	%	NUMBER	%	NUMBER	%	NUMBER	%	NUMBER	%	N
ALABAMA	(	36 INSTITUTIONS)													
UNDERGRADUATES:															
FULL-TIME	0	.0	178	14.7	3	.2	1	.1	182	15.0	984	81.1	47	3.9	
FEMALE	0	.0	73	23.9	1	.3	1	.3	75	24.5	225	73.5	6	2.0	
MALE	0	.0	105	11.6	2	.2	0	.0	107	11.8	759	83.7	41	4.5	
PART-TIME	0	.0	30	14.4	1	.5	1	.5	32	15.3	174	83.3	3	1.4	
FEMALE	0	.0	11	21.6	0	.0	0	.0	11	21.6	37	72.5	3	5.9	
MALE	0	.0	19	12.0	1	.6	1	.6	21	13.3	137	86.7	0	.0	
TOTAL	0	.0	208	14.6	4	.3	2	.1	214	15.0	1,158	81.4	50	3.5	
FEMALE	0	.0	84	23.5	1	.3	1	.3	86	24.1	262	73.4	9	2.5	
MALE	0	.0	124	11.6	3	.3	1	.1	128	12.0	896	84.1	41	3.8	
GRADUATE:															
FULL-TIME	0	.0	6	3.8	4	2.5	1	.6	11	7.0	104	65.8	43	27.2	
FEMALE	0	.0	4	17.4	1	4.3	0	.0	5	21.7	13	56.5	5	21.7	
MALE	0	.0	2	1.5	3	2.2	1	.7	6	4.4	91	67.4	38	28.1	
PART-TIME	0	.0	10	10.5	2	2.1	0	.0	12	12.6	76	80.0	7	7.4	
FEMALE	0	.0	6	21.4	1	3.6	0	.0	7	25.0	18	64.3	3	10.7	
MALE	0	.0	4	6.0	1	1.5	0	.0	5	7.5	58	86.6	4	6.0	
TOTAL	0	.0	16	6.3	6	2.4	1	.4	23	9.1	180	71.1	50	19.8	
FEMALE	0	.0	10	19.6	2	3.9	0	.0	12	23.5	31	60.8	8	15.7	
MALE	0	.0	6	3.0	4	2.0	1	.5	11	5.4	149	73.8	42	20.8	
PROFESSIONAL:															
FULL-TIME	0	.0	0	.0	0	.0	0	.0	0	.0	0	.0	0	.0	
FEMALE	0	.0	0	.0	0	.0	0	.0	0	.0	0	.0	0	.0	
MALE	0	.0	0	.0	0	.0	0	.0	0	.0	0	.0	0	.0	
PART-TIME	0	.0	0	.0	0	.0	0	.0	0	.0	0	.0	0	.0	
FEMALE	0	.0	0	.0	0	.0	0	.0	0	.0	0	.0	0	.0	
MALE	0	.0	0	.0	0	.0	0	.0	0	.0	0	.0	0	.0	
TOTAL	0	.0	0	.0	0	.0	0	.0	0	.0	0	.0	0	.0	
FEMALE	0	.0	0	.0	0	.0	0	.0	0	.0	0	.0	0	.0	
MALE	0	.0	0	.0	0	.0	0	.0	0	.0	0	.0	0	.0	
UND+GRAD+PROF:															
FULL-TIME	0	.0	184	13.4	7	.5	2	.1	193	14.1	1,088	79.4	90	6.6	
FEMALE	0	.0	77	23.4	2	.6	1	.3	80	24.3	238	72.3	11	3.3	
MALE	0	.0	107	10.3	5	.5	1	.1	113	10.8	850	81.6	79	7.6	
PART-TIME	0	.0	40	13.2	3	1.0	1	.3	44	14.5	250	82.2	10	3.3	
FEMALE	0	.0	17	21.5	1	1.3	0	.0	18	22.8	55	69.6	6	7.6	
MALE	0	.0	23	10.2	2	.9	1	.4	26	11.6	195	86.7	4	1.8	
TOTAL	0	.0	224	13.4	10	.6	3	.2	237	14.1	1,338	79.9	100	6.0	
FEMALE	0	.0	94	23.0	3	.7	1	.2	98	24.0	293	71.8	17	4.2	
MALE	0	.0	130	10.3	7	.6	2	.2	139	11.0	1,045	82.5	83	6.6	
UNCLASSIFIED:															
TOTAL	0	.0	6	9.0	1	1.5	0	.0	7	10.4	54	80.6	6	9.0	
FEMALE	0	.0	4	20.0	0	.0	0	.0	4	20.0	14	70.0	2	10.0	
MALE	0	.0	2	4.3	1	2.1	0	.0	3	6.4	40	85.1	4	8.5	
TOTAL ENROLLMENT:															
TOTAL	0	.0	230	13.2	11	.6	3	.2	244	14.0	1,392	79.9	106	6.1	
FEMALE	0	.0	98	22.9	3	.7	1	.2	102	23.8	307	71.7	19	4.4	
MALE	0	.0	132	10.0	8	.6	2	.2	142	10.8	1,085	82.6	87	6.6	
ALASKA	(	3 INSTITUTIONS)													
UNDERGRADUATES:															
FULL-TIME	2	2.7	0	.0	0	.0	0	.0	2	2.7	72	97.3	0	.0	
FEMALE	1	5.9	0	.0	0	.0	0	.0	1	5.9	16	94.1	0	.0	
MALE	1	1.6	0	.0	0	.0	0	.0	1	1.8	56	98.2	0	.0	
PART-TIME	2	9.1	0	.0	0	.0	0	.0	2	9.1	20	90.9	0	.0	
FEMALE	2	25.0	0	.0	0	.0	0	.0	2	25.0	6	75.0	0	.0	
MALE	0	.0	0	.0	0	.0	0	.0	0	.0	14	100.0	0	.0	
TOTAL	4	4.2	0	.0	0	.0	0	.0	4	4.2	92	95.8	0	.0	
FEMALE	3	12.0	0	.0	0	.0	0	.0	3	12.0	22	88.0	0	.0	
MALE	1	1.4	0	.0	0	.0	0	.0	1	1.4	70	98.6	0	.0	
GRADUATE:															
FULL-TIME	1	2.7	0	.0	1	2.7	0	.0	2	5.4	31	83.8	4	10.8	
FEMALE	1	9.1	0	.0	1	9.1	0	.0	2	18.2	8	72.7	1	9.1	
MALE	0	.0	0	.0	0	.0	0	.0	0	.0	23	88.5	3	11.5	
PART-TIME	0	.0	0	.0	0	.0	0	.0	0	.0	46	92.0	4	8.0	
FEMALE	0	.0	0	.0	0	.0	0	.0	0	.0	10	100.0	0	.0	
MALE	0	.0	0	.0	0	.0	0	.0	0	.0	36	90.0	4	10.0	
TOTAL	1	1.1	0	.0	1	1.1	0	.0	2	2.3	77	88.5	8	9.2	
FEMALE	1	4.8	0	.0	1	4.8	0	.0	2	9.5	18	85.7	1	4.8	
MALE	0	.0	0	.0	0	.0	0	.0	0	.0	59	89.4	7	10.6	
PROFESSIONAL:															
FULL-TIME	0	.0	0	.0	0	.0	0	.0	0	.0	0	.0	0	.0	
FEMALE	0	.0	0	.0	0	.0	0	.0	0	.0	0	.0	0	.0	
MALE	0	.0	0	.0	0	.0	0	.0	0	.0	0	.0	0	.0	

IELD 1900 - PHYSICAL SCIENCES

	AMERICAN INDIAN ALASKAN NATIVE		BLACK NON-HISPANIC		ASIAN OR PACIFIC ISLANDER		HISPANIC		TOTAL MINORITY		WHITE NON-HISPANIC		NON-RESIDENT ALIEN		TOTAL
	NUMBER	%	NUMBER	%	NUMBER	%	NUMBER	%	NUMBER	%	NUMBER	%	NUMBER	%	NUMBER
	CONTINUED														
IONAL:															
ME	0	.0	0	.0	0	.0	0	.0	0	.0	0	.0	0	.0	0
LE	0	.0	0	.0	0	.0	0	.0	0	.0	0	.0	0	.0	0
LE	0	.0	0	.0	0	.0	0	.0	0	.0	0	.0	0	.0	0
	0	.0	0	.0	0	.0	0	.0	0	.0	0	.0	0	.0	0
LE	0	.0	0	.0	0	.0	0	.0	0	.0	0	.0	0	.0	0
LE	0	.0	0	.0	0	.0	0	.0	0	.0	0	.0	0	.0	0
D+PROF:															
ME	3	2.7	0	.0	1	.9	0	.0	4	3.6	103	92.8	4	3.6	111
LE	2	7.1	0	.0	1	3.6	0	.0	3	10.7	24	85.7	1	3.6	28
LE	1	1.2	0	.0	0	.0	0	.0	1	1.2	79	95.2	3	3.6	83
ME	2	2.8	0	.0	0	.0	0	.0	2	2.8	66	91.7	4	5.6	72
LE	2	11.1	0	.0	0	.0	0	.0	2	11.1	16	88.9	0	.0	18
LE	0	.0	0	.0	0	.0	0	.0	0	.0	50	92.6	4	7.4	54
	5	2.7	0	.0	1	.5	0	.0	6	3.3	169	92.3	8	4.4	183
LE	4	8.7	0	.0	1	2.2	0	.0	5	10.9	40	87.0	1	2.2	46
LE	1	.7	0	.0	0	.0	0	.0	1	.7	129	94.2	7	5.1	137
IFIED:															
	0	.0	0	.0	0	.0	0	.0	0	.0	6	100.0	0	.0	6
LE	0	.0	0	.0	0	.0	0	.0	0	.0	1	100.0	0	.0	1
LE	0	.0	0	.0	0	.0	0	.0	0	.0	5	100.0	0	.0	5
NROLLMENT:															
	5	2.6	0	.0	1	.5	0	.0	6	3.2	175	92.6	8	4.2	189
LE	4	8.5	0	.0	1	2.1	0	.0	5	10.6	41	87.2	1	2.1	47
LE	1	.7	0	.0	0	.0	0	.0	1	.7	134	94.4	7	4.9	142
		(	12 INSTITUTIONS)												
ADUATES:															
ME	15	1.1	39	2.8	17	1.2	52	3.8	123	8.9	1,220	88.7	33	2.4	1,376
LE	4	1.4	5	1.7	7	2.4	7	2.4	23	7.9	261	89.4	8	2.7	292
LE	11	1.0	34	3.1	10	.9	45	4.2	100	9.2	959	88.5	25	2.3	1,084
ME	2	.4	7	1.4	6	1.2	21	4.3	36	7.4	439	90.7	9	1.9	484
LE	0	.0	1	.7	1	.7	3	2.1	5	3.5	136	94.4	3	2.1	144
LE	2	.6	6	1.8	5	1.5	18	5.3	31	9.1	303	89.1	6	1.8	340
	17	.9	46	2.5	23	1.2	73	3.9	159	8.5	1,659	89.2	42	2.3	1,860
LE	4	.9	6	1.4	8	1.8	10	2.3	28	6.4	397	91.1	11	2.5	436
LE	13	.9	40	2.8	15	1.1	63	4.4	131	9.2	1,262	88.6	31	2.2	1,424
E:															
ME	0	.0	0	.0	3	1.1	1	.4	4	1.5	225	82.1	45	16.4	274
LE	0	.0	0	.0	0	.0	0	.0	0	.0	30	93.8	2	6.3	32
LE	0	.0	0	.0	3	1.2	1	.4	4	1.7	195	80.6	43	17.8	242
ME	1	.3	0	.0	2	.6	1	.3	4	1.3	281	91.2	23	7.5	308
LE	1	2.9	0	.0	0	.0	0	.0	1	2.9	31	91.2	2	5.9	34
LE	0	.0	0	.0	2	.7	1	.4	3	1.1	250	91.2	21	7.7	274
	1	.2	0	.0	5	.9	2	.3	8	1.4	506	86.9	68	11.7	582
LE	1	1.5	0	.0	0	.0	0	.0	1	1.5	61	92.4	4	6.1	66
LE	0	.0	0	.0	5	1.0	2	.4	7	1.4	445	86.2	64	12.4	516
IONAL:															
ME	0	.0	0	.0	0	.0	0	.0	0	.0	0	.0	0	.0	0
LE	0	.0	0	.0	0	.0	0	.0	0	.0	0	.0	0	.0	0
LE	0	.0	0	.0	0	.0	0	.0	0	.0	0	.0	0	.0	0
ME	0	.0	0	.0	0	.0	0	.0	0	.0	0	.0	0	.0	0
LE	0	.0	0	.0	0	.0	0	.0	0	.0	0	.0	0	.0	0
LE	0	.0	0	.0	0	.0	0	.0	0	.0	0	.0	0	.0	0
	0	.0	0	.0	0	.0	0	.0	0	.0	0	.0	0	.0	0
LE	0	.0	0	.0	0	.0	0	.0	0	.0	0	.0	0	.0	0
LE	0	.0	0	.0	0	.0	0	.0	0	.0	0	.0	0	.0	0
D+PROF:															
ME	15	.9	39	2.4	20	1.2	53	3.2	127	7.7	1,445	87.6	78	4.7	1,650
LE	4	1.2	5	1.5	7	2.2	7	2.2	23	7.1	291	89.8	10	3.1	324
LE	11	.8	34	2.6	13	1.0	46	3.5	104	7.8	1,154	87.0	68	5.1	1,326
ME	3	.4	7	.9	8	1.0	22	2.8	40	5.1	720	90.9	32	4.0	792
LE	1	.6	1	.6	1	.6	3	1.7	6	3.4	167	93.8	5	2.8	178
LE	2	.3	6	1.0	7	1.1	19	3.1	34	5.5	553	90.1	27	4.4	614
	18	.7	46	1.9	28	1.1	75	3.1	167	6.8	2,165	88.7	110	4.5	2,442
LE	5	1.0	6	1.2	8	1.6	10	2.0	29	5.8	458	91.2	15	3.0	502
LE	13	.7	40	2.1	20	1.0	65	3.4	138	7.1	1,707	88.0	95	4.9	1,940
IFIED:															
	5	4.0	21	16.7	0	.0	14	11.1	40	31.7	84	66.7	2	1.6	126
LE	0	.0	0	.0	0	.0	0	.0	0	.0	4	100.0	0	.0	4
LE	5	4.1	21	17.2	0	.0	14	11.5	40	32.8	80	65.6	2	1.6	122
NROLLMENT:															
	23	.9	67	2.6	28	1.1	89	3.5	207	8.1	2,249	87.6	112	4.4	2,568
LE	5	1.0	6	1.2	8	1.6	10	2.0	29	5.7	462	91.3	15	3.0	506
LE	18	.9	61	3.0	20	1.0	79	3.8	178	8.6	1,787	86.7	97	4.7	2,062

MAJOR FIELD 1900 - PHYSICAL SCIENCES

	AMERICAN INDIAN ALASKAN NATIVE		BLACK NON-HISPANIC		ASIAN OR PACIFIC ISLANDER		HISPANIC		TOTAL MINORITY		WHITE NON-HISPANIC		NON-RESIDENT ALIEN	
	NUMBER	%	NUMBER	%	NUMBER	%	NUMBER	%	NUMBER	%	NUMBER	%	NUMBER	%
ARKANSAS (21 INSTITUTIONS)														
UNDERGRADUATES:														
FULL-TIME	4	.5	56	7.1	19	2.4	5	.6	84	10.7	692	88.3	8	1.0
FEMALE	1	.5	20	10.1	3	1.5	2	1.0	26	13.1	170	85.9	2	1.0
MALE	3	.5	36	6.1	16	2.7	3	.5	58	9.9	522	89.1	6	1.0
PART-TIME	0	.0	6	8.1	2	2.7	1	1.4	9	12.2	65	87.8	0	.0
FEMALE	0	.0	2	9.5	0	.0	1	4.8	3	14.3	18	85.7	0	.0
MALE	0	.0	4	7.5	2	3.8	0	.0	6	11.3	47	88.7	0	.0
TOTAL	4	.5	62	7.2	21	2.4	6	.7	93	10.8	757	88.2	8	.9
FEMALE	1	.5	22	10.0	3	1.4	3	1.4	29	13.2	188	85.8	2	.9
MALE	3	.5	40	6.3	18	2.8	3	.5	64	10.0	569	89.0	6	.9
GRADUATE:														
FULL-TIME	1	1.0	1	1.0	0	.0	0	.0	2	2.1	76	79.2	18	18.8
FEMALE	1	7.7	0	.0	0	.0	0	.0	1	7.7	10	76.9	2	15.4
MALE	0	.0	1	1.2	0	.0	0	.0	1	1.2	66	79.5	16	19.3
PART-TIME	0	.0	2	6.5	2	6.5	0	.0	4	12.9	24	77.4	3	9.7
FEMALE	0	.0	1	14.3	2	28.6	0	.0	3	42.9	2	28.6	2	28.6
MALE	0	.0	1	4.2	0	.0	0	.0	1	4.2	22	91.7	1	4.2
TOTAL	1	.8	3	2.4	2	1.6	0	.0	6	4.7	100	78.7	21	16.5
FEMALE	1	5.0	1	5.0	2	10.0	0	.0	4	20.0	12	60.0	4	20.0
MALE	0	.0	2	1.9	0	.0	0	.0	2	1.9	88	82.2	17	15.9
PROFESSIONAL:														
FULL-TIME	0	.0	0	.0	0	.0	0	.0	0	.0	0	.0	0	.0
FEMALE	0	.0	0	.0	0	.0	0	.0	0	.0	0	.0	0	.0
MALE	0	.0	0	.0	0	.0	0	.0	0	.0	0	.0	0	.0
PART-TIME	0	.0	0	.0	0	.0	0	.0	0	.0	0	.0	0	.0
FEMALE	0	.0	0	.0	0	.0	0	.0	0	.0	0	.0	0	.0
MALE	0	.0	0	.0	0	.0	0	.0	0	.0	0	.0	0	.0
TOTAL	0	.0	0	.0	0	.0	0	.0	0	.0	0	.0	0	.0
FEMALE	0	.0	0	.0	0	.0	0	.0	0	.0	0	.0	0	.0
MALE	0	.0	0	.0	0	.0	0	.0	0	.0	0	.0	0	.0
UND+GRAD+PROF:														
FULL-TIME	5	.6	57	6.5	19	2.2	5	.6	86	9.8	768	87.3	26	3.0
FEMALE	2	.9	20	9.5	3	1.4	2	.9	27	12.8	180	85.3	4	1.9
MALE	3	.4	37	5.5	16	2.4	3	.4	59	8.8	588	87.9	22	3.3
PART-TIME	0	.0	8	7.6	4	3.8	1	1.0	13	12.4	89	84.8	3	2.9
FEMALE	0	.0	3	10.7	2	7.1	1	3.6	6	21.4	20	71.4	2	7.1
MALE	0	.0	5	6.5	2	2.6	0	.0	7	9.1	69	89.6	1	1.3
TOTAL	5	.5	65	6.6	23	2.3	6	.6	99	10.1	857	87.0	29	2.9
FEMALE	2	.8	23	9.6	5	2.1	3	1.3	33	13.8	200	83.7	6	2.5
MALE	3	.4	42	5.6	18	2.4	3	.4	66	8.8	657	88.1	23	3.1
UNCLASSIFIED:														
TOTAL	0	.0	4	13.3	0	.0	0	.0	4	13.3	26	86.7	0	.0
FEMALE	0	.0	2	18.2	0	.0	0	.0	2	18.2	9	81.8	0	.0
MALE	0	.0	2	10.5	0	.0	0	.0	2	10.5	17	89.5	0	.0
TOTAL ENROLLMENT:														
TOTAL	5	.5	69	6.8	23	2.3	6	.6	103	10.1	883	87.0	29	2.9
FEMALE	2	.8	25	10.0	5	2.0	3	1.2	35	14.0	209	83.6	6	2.4
MALE	3	.4	44	5.8	18	2.4	3	.4	68	8.9	674	88.1	23	3.0
CALIFORNIA (130 INSTITUTIONS)														
UNDERGRADUATES:														
FULL-TIME	90	.9	320	3.3	767	7.8	424	4.3	1,601	16.4	7,659	78.3	517	5.3
FEMALE	24	.9	127	4.9	247	5.6	114	4.4	512	19.8	1,917	74.3	151	5.9
MALE	66	.9	193	2.7	520	7.2	310	4.3	1,089	15.1	5,742	79.8	366	5.1
PART-TIME	61	1.6	193	5.2	237	6.2	210	5.5	705	18.6	3,013	79.3	80	2.1
FEMALE	18	1.6	71	5.5	92	7.2	52	4.1	233	18.2	1,031	80.4	19	1.5
MALE	43	1.7	126	5.0	145	5.8	158	6.3	472	18.8	1,982	78.8	61	2.4
TOTAL	151	1.1	517	3.8	1,004	7.4	634	4.7	2,306	17.0	10,672	78.6	597	4.4
FEMALE	42	1.1	198	5.1	339	8.8	166	4.3	745	19.3	2,948	76.3	170	4.4
MALE	109	1.1	319	3.3	665	6.8	468	4.8	1,561	16.1	7,724	79.5	427	4.4
GRADUATE:														
FULL-TIME	13	.4	23	.7	142	4.1	42	1.2	220	6.4	2,691	78.0	537	15.6
FEMALE	1	.2	3	.6	41	7.6	3	.6	48	8.9	408	76.0	81	15.1
MALE	12	.4	20	.7	101	3.5	39	1.3	172	5.9	2,283	78.4	456	15.7
PART-TIME	4	.4	8	.8	84	8.4	18	1.8	114	11.4	754	75.2	135	13.5
FEMALE	1	.5	1	.5	23	10.6	2	.9	27	12.4	160	73.4	31	14.2
MALE	3	.4	7	.9	61	7.8	16	2.0	87	11.1	594	75.7	104	13.2
TOTAL	17	.4	31	.7	226	5.1	60	1.3	334	7.5	3,445	77.4	672	15.1
FEMALE	2	.4	4	.5	64	8.5	5	.7	75	9.9	568	75.2	112	14.8
MALE	15	.4	27	.7	162	4.4	55	1.5	259	7.0	2,877	77.8	560	15.2
PROFESSIONAL:														
FULL-TIME	0	.0	0	.0	0	.0	0	.0	0	.0	0	.0	0	.0
FEMALE	0	.0	0	.0	0	.0	0	.0	0	.0	0	.0	0	.0
MALE	0	.0	0	.0	0	.0	0	.0	0	.0	0	.0	0	.0

LD 1900 - PHYSICAL SCIENCES

	AMERICAN INDIAN ALASKAN NATIVE		BLACK NON-HISPANIC		ASIAN OR PACIFIC ISLANDER		HISPANIC		TOTAL MINORITY		WHITE NON-HISPANIC		NON-RESIDENT ALIEN		TOTAL
	NUMBER	%	NUMBER	%	NUMBER	%	NUMBER	%	NUMBER	%	NUMBER	%	NUMBER	%	NUMBER
A	CONTINUED														
NAL:															
	0	.0	0	.0	0	.0	0	.0	0	.0	0	.0	0	.0	0
	0	.0	0	.0	0	.0	0	.0	0	.0	0	.0	0	.0	0
	0	.0	0	.0	0	.0	0	.0	0	.0	0	.0	0	.0	0
	0	.0	0	.0	0	.0	0	.0	0	.0	0	.0	0	.0	0
	0	.0	0	.0	0	.0	0	.0	0	.0	0	.0	0	.0	0
PROF:															
	103	.8	343	2.6	909	6.9	466	3.5	1,821	13.8	10,350	78.3	1,054	8.0	13,225
	25	.8	130	4.2	288	9.2	117	3.8	560	18.0	2,325	74.6	232	7.4	3,117
	78	.8	213	2.1	621	6.1	349	3.5	1,261	12.5	8,025	79.4	822	8.1	10,108
	65	1.4	205	4.3	321	6.7	228	4.7	819	17.1	3,767	78.5	215	4.5	4,801
	19	1.3	72	4.8	115	7.7	54	3.6	260	17.3	1,191	79.3	50	3.3	1,501
	46	1.4	133	4.0	206	6.2	174	5.3	559	16.9	2,576	78.1	165	5.0	3,300
	168	.9	548	3.0	1,230	6.8	694	3.8	2,640	14.6	14,117	78.3	1,269	7.0	18,026
	44	1.0	202	4.4	403	8.7	171	3.7	820	17.8	3,516	76.1	282	6.1	4,618
	124	.9	346	2.6	827	6.2	523	3.9	1,820	13.6	10,601	79.1	987	7.4	13,408
IED:															
	12	1.0	63	5.4	54	4.6	37	3.1	166	14.1	940	79.9	71	6.0	1,177
	1	.2	30	6.9	19	4.3	11	2.5	61	14.0	361	82.6	15	3.4	437
	11	1.5	33	4.5	35	4.7	26	3.5	105	14.2	579	78.2	56	7.6	740
OLLMENT:															
	180	.9	611	3.2	1,284	6.7	731	3.8	2,806	14.6	15,057	78.4	1,340	7.0	19,203
	45	.9	232	4.6	422	8.3	182	3.6	881	17.4	3,877	76.7	297	5.9	5,055
	135	1.0	375	2.7	862	6.1	549	3.9	1,925	13.6	11,180	79.0	1,043	7.4	14,148
	(19 INSTITUTIONS)														
UATES:															
	12	.5	31	1.4	28	1.3	46	2.1	117	5.3	2,009	91.8	63	2.9	2,189
	6	1.1	14	2.6	9	1.6	16	2.9	45	8.2	491	89.6	12	2.2	548
	6	.4	17	1.0	19	1.2	30	1.8	72	4.4	1,518	92.5	51	3.1	1,641
	4	1.1	21	5.5	8	2.1	12	3.2	45	11.8	327	86.1	8	2.1	380
	2	1.8	16	14.0	2	1.8	2	1.8	22	19.3	91	79.8	1	.9	114
	2	.8	5	1.9	6	2.3	10	3.8	23	8.6	236	88.7	7	2.6	266
	16	.6	52	2.0	36	1.4	58	2.3	162	6.3	2,336	90.9	71	2.8	2,569
	8	1.2	30	4.5	11	1.7	18	2.7	67	10.1	582	87.9	13	2.0	662
	8	.4	22	1.2	25	1.3	40	2.1	95	5.0	1,754	92.0	58	3.0	1,907
	1	.2	1	.2	1	.2	1	.2	4	.8	440	88.0	56	11.2	500
	0	.0	0	.0	0	.0	0	.0	0	.0	81	93.1	6	6.9	87
	1	.2	1	.2	1	.2	1	.2	4	1.0	359	86.9	50	12.1	413
	2	.8	1	.4	4	1.5	2	.8	9	3.5	223	85.8	28	10.8	260
	1	2.2	0	.0	1	2.2	0	.0	2	4.4	39	86.7	4	8.9	45
	1	.5	1	.5	3	1.4	2	.9	7	3.3	184	85.6	24	11.2	215
	3	.4	2	.3	5	.7	3	.4	13	1.7	663	87.2	84	11.1	760
	1	.8	0	.0	1	.8	0	.0	2	1.5	120	90.9	10	7.6	132
	2	.3	2	.3	4	.6	3	.5	11	1.8	543	86.5	74	11.8	628
NAL:															
	0	.0	0	.0	0	.0	0	.0	0	.0	0	.0	0	.0	0
	0	.0	0	.0	0	.0	0	.0	0	.0	0	.0	0	.0	0
	0	.0	0	.0	0	.0	0	.0	0	.0	0	.0	0	.0	0
	0	.0	0	.0	0	.0	0	.0	0	.0	0	.0	0	.0	0
	0	.0	0	.0	0	.0	0	.0	0	.0	0	.0	0	.0	0
	0	.0	0	.0	0	.0	0	.0	0	.0	0	.0	0	.0	0
	0	.0	0	.0	0	.0	0	.0	0	.0	0	.0	0	.0	0
PROF:															
	13	.5	32	1.2	29	1.1	47	1.7	121	4.5	2,449	91.1	119	4.4	2,689
	6	.9	14	2.2	9	1.4	16	2.5	45	7.1	572	90.1	18	2.8	635
	7	.3	18	.9	20	1.0	31	1.5	76	3.7	1,877	91.4	101	4.9	2,054
	6	.9	22	3.4	12	1.9	14	2.2	54	8.4	550	85.9	36	5.6	640
	3	1.9	16	10.1	3	1.9	2	1.3	24	15.1	130	81.8	5	3.1	159
	3	.6	6	1.2	9	1.9	12	2.5	30	6.2	420	87.3	31	6.4	481
	19	.6	54	1.6	41	1.2	61	1.8	175	5.3	2,999	90.1	155	4.7	3,329
	9	1.1	30	3.8	12	1.5	18	2.3	69	8.7	702	88.4	23	2.9	794
	10	.4	24	.9	29	1.1	43	1.7	106	4.2	2,297	90.6	132	5.2	2,535
IED:															
	0	.0	4	6.3	1	1.6	4	6.3	9	14.1	54	84.4	1	1.6	64
	0	.0	2	9.5	1	4.8	1	4.8	4	19.0	17	81.0	0	.0	21
	0	.0	2	4.7	0	.0	3	7.0	5	11.6	37	86.0	1	2.3	43
OLLMENT:															
	19	.6	58	1.7	42	1.2	65	1.9	184	5.4	3,053	90.0	156	4.6	3,393
	9	1.1	32	3.9	13	1.6	19	2.3	73	9.0	719	88.2	23	2.8	815
	10	.4	26	1.0	29	1.1	46	1.8	111	4.3	2,334	90.5	133	5.2	2,578

MAJOR FIELD 1900 - PHYSICAL SCIENCES

	AMERICAN INDIAN ALASKAN NATIVE		BLACK NON-HISPANIC		ASIAN OR PACIFIC ISLANDER		HISPANIC		TOTAL MINORITY		WHITE NON-HISPANIC		NON-RESIDENT ALIEN	
	NUMBER	%	NUMBER	%	NUMBER	%	NUMBER	%	NUMBER	%	NUMBER	%	NUMBER	%
CONNECTICUT (18 INSTITUTIONS)														
UNDERGRADUATES:														
FULL-TIME	1	.1	27	2.2	15	1.2	11	.9	54	4.5	1,139	94.1	17	1.4
FEMALE	0	.0	5	1.6	5	1.6	2	.6	12	3.7	304	94.7	5	1.6
MALE	1	.1	22	2.5	10	1.1	9	1.0	42	4.7	835	93.9	12	1.3
PART-TIME	0	.0	6	3.7	1	.6	3	1.9	10	6.2	150	93.2	1	.6
FEMALE	0	.0	1	2.1	0	.0	0	.0	1	2.1	47	97.9	0	.0
MALE	0	.0	5	4.4	1	.9	3	2.7	9	8.0	103	91.2	1	.9
TOTAL	1	.1	33	2.4	16	1.2	14	1.0	64	4.7	1,289	94.0	18	1.3
FEMALE	0	.0	6	1.6	5	1.4	2	.5	13	3.5	351	95.1	5	1.4
MALE	1	.1	27	2.7	11	1.1	12	1.2	51	5.1	938	93.6	13	1.3
GRADUATE:														
FULL-TIME	2	.6	1	.3	5	1.6	4	1.3	12	3.8	244	78.0	57	18.2
FEMALE	0	.0	0	.0	3	5.4	1	1.8	4	7.1	42	75.0	10	17.9
MALE	2	.8	1	.4	2	.8	3	1.2	8	3.1	202	78.6	47	18.3
PART-TIME	0	.0	2	1.0	8	4.0	2	1.0	12	6.0	186	92.5	3	1.5
FEMALE	0	.0	2	3.4	1	1.7	0	.0	3	5.2	54	93.1	1	1.7
MALE	0	.0	0	.0	7	4.9	2	1.4	9	6.3	132	92.3	2	1.4
TOTAL	2	.4	3	.6	13	2.5	6	1.2	24	4.7	430	83.7	60	11.7
FEMALE	0	.0	2	1.8	4	3.5	1	.9	7	6.1	96	84.2	11	9.6
MALE	2	.5	1	.3	9	2.3	5	1.3	17	4.3	334	83.5	49	12.3
PROFESSIONAL:														
FULL-TIME	0	.0	0	.0	0	.0	0	.0	0	.0	0	.0	0	.0
FEMALE	0	.0	0	.0	0	.0	0	.0	0	.0	0	.0	0	.0
MALE	0	.0	0	.0	0	.0	0	.0	0	.0	0	.0	0	.0
PART-TIME	0	.0	0	.0	0	.0	0	.0	0	.0	0	.0	0	.0
FEMALE	0	.0	0	.0	0	.0	0	.0	0	.0	0	.0	0	.0
MALE	0	.0	0	.0	0	.0	0	.0	0	.0	0	.0	0	.0
TOTAL	0	.0	0	.0	0	.0	0	.0	0	.0	0	.0	0	.0
FEMALE	0	.0	0	.0	0	.0	0	.0	0	.0	0	.0	0	.0
MALE	0	.0	0	.0	0	.0	0	.0	0	.0	0	.0	0	.0
UND+GRAD+PROF:														
FULL-TIME	3	.2	28	1.8	20	1.3	15	1.0	66	4.3	1,383	90.8	74	4.9
FEMALE	0	.0	5	1.3	8	2.1	3	.8	16	4.2	346	91.8	15	4.0
MALE	3	.3	23	2.0	12	1.0	12	1.0	50	4.4	1,037	90.5	59	5.1
PART-TIME	0	.0	8	2.2	9	2.5	5	1.4	22	6.1	336	92.8	4	1.1
FEMALE	0	.0	3	2.8	1	.9	0	.0	4	3.8	101	95.3	1	.9
MALE	0	.0	5	2.0	8	3.1	5	2.0	18	7.0	235	91.8	3	1.2
TOTAL	3	.2	36	1.9	29	1.5	20	1.1	88	4.7	1,719	91.2	78	4.1
FEMALE	0	.0	8	1.7	9	1.9	3	.6	20	4.1	447	92.5	16	3.3
MALE	3	.2	28	2.0	20	1.4	17	1.2	68	4.9	1,272	90.7	62	4.4
UNCLASSIFIED:														
TOTAL	0	.0	0	.0	0	.0	0	.0	0	.0	2	100.0	0	.0
FEMALE	0	.0	0	.0	0	.0	0	.0	0	.0	1	100.0	0	.0
MALE	0	.0	0	.0	0	.0	0	.0	0	.0	1	100.0	0	.0
TOTAL ENROLLMENT:														
TOTAL	3	.2	36	1.9	29	1.5	20	1.1	88	4.7	1,721	91.2	78	4.1
FEMALE	0	.0	8	1.7	9	1.9	3	.6	20	4.1	448	92.6	16	3.3
MALE	3	.2	28	2.0	20	1.4	17	1.2	68	4.8	1,273	90.7	62	4.4
DELAWARE (3 INSTITUTIONS)														
UNDERGRADUATES:														
FULL-TIME	1	.3	22	6.5	4	1.2	1	.3	28	8.3	302	89.9	6	1.8
FEMALE	0	.0	12	10.7	0	.0	1	.9	13	11.6	97	86.6	2	1.8
MALE	1	.4	10	4.5	4	1.8	0	.0	15	6.7	205	91.5	4	1.8
PART-TIME	0	.0	0	.0	0	.0	0	.0	0	.0	32	97.0	1	3.0
FEMALE	0	.0	0	.0	0	.0	0	.0	0	.0	8	100.0	0	.0
MALE	0	.0	0	.0	0	.0	0	.0	0	.0	24	96.0	1	4.0
TOTAL	1	.3	22	6.0	4	1.1	1	.3	28	7.6	334	90.5	7	1.9
FEMALE	0	.0	12	10.0	0	.0	1	.8	13	10.8	105	87.5	2	1.7
MALE	1	.4	10	4.0	4	1.6	0	.0	15	6.0	229	92.0	5	2.0
GRADUATE:														
FULL-TIME	0	.0	1	4.8	0	.0	0	.0	1	4.8	15	71.4	5	23.8
FEMALE	0	.0	0	.0	0	.0	0	.0	0	.0	3	50.0	3	50.0
MALE	0	.0	1	6.7	0	.0	0	.0	1	6.7	12	80.0	2	13.3
PART-TIME	0	.0	1	1.6	0	.0	0	.0	1	1.6	59	92.2	4	6.3
FEMALE	0	.0	0	.0	0	.0	0	.0	0	.0	19	95.0	1	5.0
MALE	0	.0	1	2.3	0	.0	0	.0	1	2.3	40	90.9	3	6.8
TOTAL	0	.0	2	2.4	0	.0	0	.0	2	2.4	74	87.1	9	10.6
FEMALE	0	.0	0	.0	0	.0	0	.0	0	.0	22	84.6	4	15.4
MALE	0	.0	2	3.4	0	.0	0	.0	2	3.4	52	88.1	5	8.5
PROFESSIONAL:														
FULL-TIME	0	.0	0	.0	0	.0	0	.0	0	.0	0	.0	0	.0
FEMALE	0	.0	0	.0	0	.0	0	.0	0	.0	0	.0	0	.0
MALE	0	.0	0	.0	0	.0	0	.0	0	.0	0	.0	0	.0

- PHYSICAL SCIENCES

AM INDIAN AN NATIVE		BLACK NON-HISPANIC		ASIAN OR PACIFIC ISLANDER		HISPANIC		TOTAL MINORITY		WHITE NON-HISPANIC		NON-RESIDENT ALIEN		TOTAL
ER	%	NUMBER	%	NUMBER	%	NUMBER	%	NUMBER	%	NUMBER	%	NUMBER	%	NUMBER
CONTINUED														
0	.0	0	.0	0	.0	0	.0	0	.0	0	.0	0	.0	0
0	.0	0	.0	0	.0	0	.0	0	.0	0	.0	0	.0	0
0	.0	0	.0	0	.0	0	.0	0	.0	0	.0	0	.0	0
0	.0	0	.0	0	.0	0	.0	0	.0	0	.0	0	.0	0
0	.0	0	.0	0	.0	0	.0	0	.0	0	.0	0	.0	0
1	.3	23	6.4	4	1.1	1	.3	29	8.1	317	88.8	11	3.1	357
0	.0	12	10.2	0	.0	1	.8	13	11.0	100	84.7	5	4.2	118
1	.4	11	4.6	4	1.7	0	.0	16	6.7	217	90.8	6	2.5	239
0	.0	1	1.0	0	.0	0	.0	1	1.0	91	93.8	5	5.2	97
0	.0	0	.0	0	.0	0	.0	0	.0	27	96.4	1	3.6	28
0	.0	1	1.4	0	.0	0	.0	1	1.4	64	92.8	4	5.8	69
1	.2	24	5.3	4	.9	1	.2	30	6.6	408	89.9	16	3.5	454
0	.0	12	8.2	0	.0	1	.7	13	8.9	127	87.0	6	4.1	146
1	.3	12	3.9	4	1.3	0	.0	17	5.5	281	91.2	10	3.2	308
1	.6	6	3.7	1	.6	1	.6	9	5.6	142	87.7	11	6.8	162
0	.0	2	4.8	0	.0	0	.0	2	4.8	34	81.0	6	14.3	42
1	.8	4	3.3	1	.8	1	.8	7	5.8	108	90.0	5	4.2	120
2	.3	30	4.9	5	.8	2	.3	39	6.3	550	89.3	27	4.4	616
0	.0	14	7.4	0	.0	1	.5	15	8.0	161	85.6	12	6.4	188
2	.5	16	3.7	5	1.2	1	.2	24	5.6	389	90.9	15	3.5	428
DIA (	8 INSTITUTIONS)													
1	.2	274	41.2	15	2.3	11	1.7	301	45.3	250	37.6	114	17.1	665
0	.0	124	48.8	5	2.0	5	2.0	134	52.8	92	36.2	28	11.0	254
1	.2	150	36.5	10	2.4	6	1.5	167	40.6	158	38.4	86	20.9	411
0	.0	62	37.1	3	1.8	7	4.2	72	43.1	64	38.3	31	18.6	167
0	.0	31	47.0	0	.0	0	.0	31	47.0	26	39.4	9	13.6	66
0	.0	31	30.7	3	3.0	7	6.9	41	40.6	38	37.6	22	21.8	101
1	.1	336	40.4	18	2.2	18	2.2	373	44.8	314	37.7	145	17.4	832
0	.0	155	48.4	5	1.6	5	1.6	165	51.6	118	36.9	37	11.6	320
1	.2	181	35.4	13	2.5	13	2.5	208	40.6	196	38.3	108	21.1	512
0	.0	32	14.2	6	2.7	0	.0	38	16.8	81	35.8	107	47.3	226
0	.0	10	18.2	0	.0	0	.0	10	18.2	24	43.6	21	38.2	55
0	.0	22	12.9	6	3.5	0	.0	28	16.4	57	33.3	86	50.3	171
0	.0	35	14.4	6	2.5	3	1.2	44	18.1	159	65.4	40	16.5	243
0	.0	6	10.3	1	1.7	0	.0	7	12.1	43	74.1	8	13.8	58
0	.0	29	15.7	5	2.7	3	1.6	37	20.0	116	62.7	32	17.3	185
0	.0	67	14.3	12	2.6	3	.6	82	17.5	240	51.2	147	31.3	469
0	.0	16	14.2	1	.9	0	.0	17	15.0	67	59.3	29	25.7	113
0	.0	51	14.3	11	3.1	3	.8	65	18.3	173	48.6	118	33.1	356
0	.0	0	.0	0	.0	0	.0	0	.0	0	.0	0	.0	0
0	.0	0	.0	0	.0	0	.0	0	.0	0	.0	0	.0	0
0	.0	0	.0	0	.0	0	.0	0	.0	0	.0	0	.0	0
0	.0	0	.0	0	.0	0	.0	0	.0	0	.0	0	.0	0
0	.0	0	.0	0	.0	0	.0	0	.0	0	.0	0	.0	0
0	.0	0	.0	0	.0	0	.0	0	.0	0	.0	0	.0	0
0	.0	0	.0	0	.0	0	.0	0	.0	0	.0	0	.0	0
0	.0	0	.0	0	.0	0	.0	0	.0	0	.0	0	.0	0
1	.1	306	34.3	21	2.4	11	1.2	339	38.0	331	37.1	221	24.8	891
0	.0	134	43.4	5	1.6	5	1.6	144	46.6	116	37.5	49	15.9	309
1	.2	172	29.6	16	2.7	6	1.0	195	33.5	215	36.9	172	29.6	582
0	.0	97	23.7	9	2.2	10	2.4	116	28.3	223	54.4	71	17.3	410
0	.0	37	29.8	1	.8	0	.0	38	30.6	69	55.6	17	13.7	124
0	.0	60	21.0	8	2.8	10	3.5	78	27.3	154	53.8	54	18.9	286
1	.1	403	31.0	30	2.3	21	1.6	455	35.0	554	42.6	292	22.4	1,301
0	.0	171	39.5	6	1.4	5	1.2	182	42.0	185	42.7	66	15.2	433
1	.1	232	26.7	24	2.8	16	1.8	273	31.5	369	42.5	226	26.0	868
0	.0	7	17.5	0	.0	1	2.5	8	20.0	30	75.0	2	5.0	40
0	.0	4	26.7	0	.0	0	.0	4	26.7	9	60.0	2	13.3	15
0	.0	3	12.0	0	.0	0	.0	0	.0	21	84.0	0	.0	25
1	.1	410	30.6	30	2.2	22	1.6	463	34.5	584	43.5	294	21.9	1,341
0	.0	175	39.1	6	1.3	5	1.1	186	41.5	194	43.3	68	15.2	448
1	.1	235	26.3	24	2.7	17	1.9	277	31.0	390	43.7	226	25.3	893

TABLE 17 - TOTAL ENROLLMENT IN INSTITUTIONS OF HIGHER EDUCATION FOR SELECTED MAJOR FIELDS OF STUDY AND LEVEL OF ENROLLMENT
BY RACE, ETHNICITY, AND SEX: STATE, 1978

MAJOR FIELD 1900 - PHYSICAL SCIENCES

	AMERICAN INDIAN ALASKAN NATIVE		BLACK NON-HISPANIC		ASIAN OR PACIFIC ISLANDER		HISPANIC		TOTAL MINORITY		WHITE NON-HISPANIC		NON-RESIDENT ALIEN	
	NUMBER	%	NUMBER	%	NUMBER	%	NUMBER	%	NUMBER	%	NUMBER	%	NUMBER	%
FLORIDA	(	23 INSTITUTIONS)												
UNDERGRADUATES:														
FULL-TIME	9	.2	172	3.3	41	.8	255	4.9	477	9.1	4,616	88.4	126	2.4
FEMALE	2	.2	55	6.5	13	1.5	90	10.7	160	19.0	665	79.2	15	1.8
MALE	7	.2	117	2.7	28	.6	165	3.8	317	7.2	3,951	90.2	111	2.5
PART-TIME	2	.2	20	2.0	9	.9	71	7.1	102	10.2	883	88.0	18	1.8
FEMALE	0	.0	5	2.6	1	.5	29	14.9	35	17.9	159	81.5	1	.5
MALE	2	.2	15	1.9	8	1.0	42	5.2	67	8.3	724	89.6	17	2.1
TOTAL	11	.2	192	3.1	50	.8	326	5.2	579	9.3	5,499	88.4	144	2.3
FEMALE	2	.2	60	5.8	14	1.4	119	11.5	195	18.8	824	79.6	16	1.5
MALE	9	.2	132	2.5	36	.7	207	4.0	384	7.4	4,675	90.1	128	2.5
GRADUATE:														
FULL-TIME	1	.2	9	1.7	6	1.1	14	2.6	30	5.5	452	83.4	60	11.1
FEMALE	0	.0	2	2.7	1	1.4	3	4.1	6	8.1	63	85.1	5	6.8
MALE	1	.2	7	1.5	5	1.1	11	2.4	24	5.1	389	83.1	55	11.8
PART-TIME	3	1.4	1	.5	7	3.2	6	2.7	17	7.7	191	86.8	12	5.5
FEMALE	0	.0	0	.0	1	4.2	1	4.2	2	8.3	20	83.3	2	8.3
MALE	3	1.5	1	.5	6	3.1	5	2.6	15	7.7	171	87.2	10	5.1
TOTAL	4	.5	10	1.3	13	1.7	20	2.6	47	6.2	643	84.4	72	9.4
FEMALE	0	.0	2	2.0	2	2.0	4	4.1	8	8.2	83	84.7	7	7.1
MALE	4	.6	8	1.2	11	1.7	16	2.4	39	5.9	560	84.3	65	9.8
PROFESSIONAL:														
FULL-TIME	0	.0	0	.0	0	.0	0	.0	0	.0	0	.0	0	.0
FEMALE	0	.0	0	.0	0	.0	0	.0	0	.0	0	.0	0	.0
MALE	0	.0	0	.0	0	.0	0	.0	0	.0	0	.0	0	.0
PART-TIME	0	.0	0	.0	0	.0	0	.0	0	.0	0	.0	0	.0
FEMALE	0	.0	0	.0	0	.0	0	.0	0	.0	0	.0	0	.0
MALE	0	.0	0	.0	0	.0	0	.0	0	.0	0	.0	0	.0
TOTAL	0	.0	0	.0	0	.0	0	.0	0	.0	0	.0	0	.0
FEMALE	0	.0	0	.0	0	.0	0	.0	0	.0	0	.0	0	.0
MALE	0	.0	0	.0	0	.0	0	.0	0	.0	0	.0	0	.0
UND+GRAD+PROF:														
FULL-TIME	10	.2	181	3.1	47	.8	269	4.7	507	8.8	5,068	88.0	186	3.2
FEMALE	2	.2	57	6.2	14	1.5	93	10.2	166	18.2	728	79.6	20	2.2
MALE	8	.2	124	2.6	33	.7	176	3.6	341	7.0	4,340	89.5	166	3.4
PART-TIME	5	.4	21	1.7	16	1.3	77	6.3	119	9.7	1,074	87.8	30	2.5
FEMALE	0	.0	5	2.3	2	.9	30	13.7	37	16.9	179	81.7	3	1.4
MALE	5	.5	16	1.6	14	1.4	47	4.7	82	8.2	895	89.1	27	2.7
TOTAL	15	.2	202	2.9	63	.9	346	5.0	626	9.0	6,142	87.9	216	3.1
FEMALE	2	.2	62	5.5	16	1.4	123	10.9	203	17.9	907	80.1	23	2.0
MALE	13	.2	140	2.4	47	.8	223	3.8	423	7.2	5,235	89.5	193	3.3
UNCLASSIFIED	:													
TOTAL	1	.4	5	1.8	1	.4	16	5.9	23	8.5	209	77.1	39	14.4
FEMALE	0	.0	2	4.8	1	2.4	7	16.7	10	23.8	32	76.2	0	.0
MALE	1	.4	3	1.3	0	.0	9	3.9	13	5.7	177	77.3	39	17.0
TOTAL ENROLLMENT:														
TOTAL	16	.2	207	2.9	64	.9	362	5.0	649	8.9	6,351	87.5	255	3.5
FEMALE	2	.2	64	5.4	17	1.4	130	11.1	213	18.1	939	79.9	23	2.0
MALE	14	.2	143	2.4	47	.8	232	3.8	436	7.2	5,412	89.0	232	3.8
GEORGIA	(	46 INSTITUTIONS)												
UNDERGRADUATES:														
FULL-TIME	3	.1	411	19.9	13	.6	20	1.0	447	21.6	1,536	74.3	85	4.1
FEMALE	0	.0	215	38.7	4	.7	4	.7	223	40.2	318	57.3	14	2.5
MALE	3	.2	196	13.0	9	.6	16	1.1	224	14.8	1,218	80.5	71	4.7
PART-TIME	0	.0	45	12.7	7	2.0	0	.0	52	14.7	296	83.9	5	1.4
FEMALE	0	.0	14	16.7	2	2.4	0	.0	16	19.0	67	79.8	1	1.2
MALE	0	.0	31	11.5	5	1.9	0	.0	36	13.4	229	85.1	4	1.5
TOTAL	3	.1	456	18.8	20	.8	20	.8	499	20.6	1,832	75.7	90	3.7
FEMALE	0	.0	229	35.8	6	.9	4	.6	239	37.4	385	60.3	15	2.3
MALE	3	.2	227	12.7	14	.8	16	.9	260	14.6	1,447	81.2	75	4.2
GRADUATE:														
FULL-TIME	0	.0	35	17.5	1	.5	1	.5	37	18.5	116	58.0	47	23.5
FEMALE	0	.0	11	25.6	0	.0	0	.0	11	25.6	25	58.1	7	16.3
MALE	0	.0	24	15.3	1	.6	1	.6	26	16.6	91	58.0	40	25.5
PART-TIME	0	.0	21	5.9	1	.3	1	.3	23	6.5	281	79.4	50	14.1
FEMALE	0	.0	9	14.8	0	.0	0	.0	9	14.8	45	73.8	7	11.5
MALE	0	.0	12	4.1	1	.3	1	.3	14	4.8	236	80.5	43	14.7
TOTAL	0	.0	56	10.1	2	.4	2	.4	60	10.8	397	71.7	97	17.5
FEMALE	0	.0	20	19.2	0	.0	0	.0	20	19.2	70	67.3	14	13.5
MALE	0	.0	36	8.0	2	.4	2	.4	40	8.9	327	72.7	83	18.4
PROFESSIONAL:														
FULL-TIME	0	.0	0	.0	0	.0	0	.0	0	.0	0	.0	0	.0
FEMALE	0	.0	0	.0	0	.0	0	.0	0	.0	0	.0	0	.0
MALE	0	.0	0	.0	0	.0	0	.0	0	.0	0	.0	0	.0

O - PHYSICAL SCIENCES

ICAN INDIAN KAN NATIVE		BLACK NON-HISPANIC		ASIAN OR PACIFIC ISLANDER		HISPANIC		TOTAL MINORITY		WHITE NCN-HISPANIC		NON-RESIDENT ALIEN		TOTAL
BER	%	NUMBER	%	NUMBER	%	NUMBER	%	NUMBER	%	NUMBER	%	NUMBER	%	NUMBER

CONTINUED

0	.0	0	.0	0	.0	0	.0	0	.0	0	.0		.0	
0	.0	0	.0	0	.0	0	.0	0	.0	0	.0	0	.0	0
0	.0	0	.0	0	.0	0	.0	0	.0	0	.0	0	.0	0

0	.0	0	.0	0	.0	0	.0	0	.0	0	.0		.0	
0	.0	0	.0	0	.0	0	.0	0	.0	0	.0	0	.0	0
0	.0	0	.0	0	.0	0	.0	0	.0	0	.0	0	.0	0

3	.1	446	19.7	14	.6	21	.9	484	21.3	1,652	72.8	132	5.8	2,268
0	.0	226	37.8	4	.7	4	.7	234	39.1	343	57.4	21	3.5	598
3	.2	220	13.2	10	.6	17	1.0	250	15.0	1,309	78.4	111	6.6	1,670
0	.0	66	9.3	8	1.1	1	.1	75	10.6	577	81.6	55	7.8	707
0	.0	23	15.9	2	1.4	0	.0	25	17.2	112	77.2	8	5.5	145
0	.0	43	7.7	6	1.1	1	.2	50	8.9	465	82.7	47	8.4	562

3	.1	512	17.2	22	.7	22	.7	559	18.8	2,229	74.9	187	6	2,975
0	.0	249	33.5	6	.8	4	.5	259	34.9	455	61.2	29	3	743
3	.1	263	11.8	16	.7	18	.8	300	13.4	1,774	79.5	158	71?	2,232

0	.0	6	10.3	0	.0	0	.0	6	10.3	40	69.0	12	20.7	58
0	.0	4	20.0	0	.0	0	.0	4	20.0	14	70.0	2	10.0	20
0	.0	2	5.3	0	.0	0	.0	2	5.3	26	68.4	10	26.3	38

3	.1	518	17.1	22	.7	22	.7	565	18.6	2,269	74.8	199	6.?	3,033
0	.0	253	33.2	6	.8	4	.5	263	34.5	469	61.5	31	4.?	763
3	.1	265	11.7	16	.7	18	.8	302	13.3	1,800	79.3	168	7.?	2,270

(3 INSTITUTIONS)

2	1.2	1	.6	71	43.8	3	1.9	77	47.5	72	44.4	13	8.0	162
0	.0	1	2.7	20	54.1	0	.0	21	56.8	13	35.1	3	8.1	37
2	1.6	0	.0	51	40.8	3	2.4	56	44.8	59	47.2	10	8.0	125
0	.0	1	2.4	26	61.9	4	9.5	31	73.8	10	23.8	1	2.4	42
0	.0	0	.0	5	45.5	4	36.4	9	81.8	2	18.2	0	.0	11
0	.0	1	3.2	21	67.7	0	.0	22	71.0	8	25.8	1	3.2	31

2	1.0	2	1.0	97	47.5	7	3.4	108	52.9	82	40.2	14	6	204
0	.0	1	2.1	25	52.1	4	8.3	30	62.5	15	31.3	3	6	48
2	1.3	1	.6	72	46.2	3	1.9	78	50.0	67	42.9	11	71?	156

0	.0	0	.0	20	19.4	0	.0	20	19.4	77	74.8		5.	103
0	.0	0	.0	5	31.3	0	.0	5	31.3	11	68.8		.	16
0	.0	0	.0	15	17.2	0	.0	15	17.2	66	75.9		.?	87
2	2.1	2	2.1	12	12.4	0	.0	16	16.5	77	79.4	?	?.8	97
2	11.8	0	.0	1	5.9	0	.0	3	17.6	13	76.5	?	5.	17
0	.0	2	2.5	11	13.8	0	.0	13	16.3	64	80.0	3	3.8	80

2	1.0	2	1.0	32	16.0	0	.0	36	18.0	154	77.0	10	5.	200
2	6.1	0	.0	6	18.2	0	.0	8	24.2	24	72.7	1	3.0	33
0	.0	2	1.2	26	15.6	0	.0	28	16.8	130	77.8	?	5.8	167

0	.0	0	.0	0	.0	0	.0	0	.0	0	.0		.0	
0	.0	0	.0	0	.0	0	.0	0	.0	0	.0		.0	
0	.0	0	.0	0	.0	0	.0	0	.0	0	.0		.0	
0	.0	0	.0	0	.0	0	.0	0	.0	0	.0		.0	
0	.0	0	.0	0	.0	0	.0	0	.0	0	.0		.0	
0	.0	0	.0	0	.0	0	.0	0	.0	0	.0	0	.0	0

0	.0	0	.0	0	.0	0	.0	0	.0	0	.0		.0	
0	.0	0	.0	0	.0	0	.0	0	.0	0	.0		.0	
0	.0	0	.0	0	.0	0	.0	0	.0	0	.0	0	.0	0

2	.8	1	.4	91	34.3	3	1.1	97	36.6	149	56.2	19	7.2	265
0	.0	1	1.9	25	47.2	0	.0	26	49.1	24	45.3	3	5.7	53
2	.9	0	.0	66	31.1	3	1.4	71	33.5	125	59.0	16	7.5	212
2	1.4	3	2.2	38	27.3	4	2.9	47	33.8	87	62.6	5	3.6	139
2	7.1	0	.0	6	21.4	4	14.3	12	42.9	15	53.6	1	3.6	28
0	.0	3	2.7	32	28.8	0	.0	35	31.5	72	64.9	4	3.6	111

4	1.0	4	1.0	129	31.9	7	1.7	144	35.6	236	58.4	24	5.9	404
2	2.5	1	1.2	31	38.3	4	4.9	38	46.9	39	48.1	4	4.9	81
2	.6	3	.9	98	30.3	3	.9	106	32.8	197	61.0	20	6.2	323

0	.0	1	100.0	0	.0	0	.0	1	100.0	0	.0		.0	1
0	.0	1	100.0	0	.0	0	.0	1	100.0	0	.0		.0	1
0	.0	0	.0	0	.0	0	.0	0	.0	0	.0	0	.0	0

4	1.0	5	1.2	129	31.9	7	1.7	145	35.8	236	58.3	24	5.9	405
2	2.4	2	2.4	31	37.8	4	4.9	39	47.6	39	47.6	4	4.9	82
2	.6	3	.9	98	30.3	3	.9	106	32.8	197	61.0	20	6.2	323

TABLE 17 - TOTAL ENROLLMENT IN INSTITUTIONS OF HIGHER EDUCATION FOR SELECTED MAJOR FIELDS OF STUDY AND LEVEL OF ENROLLMENT BY RACE, ETHNICITY, AND SEX: STATE: 1978

MAJOR FIELD 1900 - PHYSICAL SCIENCES

	AMERICAN INDIAN ALASKAN NATIVE		BLACK NON-HISPANIC		ASIAN OR PACIFIC ISLANDER		HISPANIC		TOTAL MINORITY		WHITE NON-HISPANIC		NON-RESIDENT ALIEN		T(
	NUMBER	%	NUMBER	%	NUMBER	%	NUMBER	%	NUMBER	%	NUMBER	%	NUMBER	%	NU
IDAHO (8 INSTITUTIONS)															
UNDERGRADUATES:															
FULL-TIME	1	.2	1	.2	6	1.4	0	.0	8	1.8	421	97.2	4	.9	
FEMALE	0	.0	0	.0	1	1.2	0	.0	1	1.2	81	97.6	1	1.2	
MALE	1	.3	1	.3	5	1.4	0	.0	7	2.0	340	97.1	3	.9	
PART-TIME	0	.0	0	.0	1	1.6	1	1.6	2	3.2	60	96.8	0	.0	
FEMALE	0	.0	0	.0	0	.0	0	.0	0	.0	22	100.0	0	.0	
MALE	0	.0	0	.0	1	2.5	1	2.5	2	5.0	38	95.0	0	.0	
TOTAL	1	.2	1	.2	7	1.4	1	.2	10	2.0	481	97.2	4	.8	
FEMALE	0	.0	0	.0	1	1.0	0	.0	1	1.0	103	98.1	1	1.0	
MALE	1	.3	1	.3	6	1.5	1	.3	9	2.3	378	96.9	3	.8	
GRADUATE:															
FULL-TIME	0	.0	1	1.2	5	5.8	0	.0	6	7.0	75	87.2	5	5.8	
FEMALE	0	.0	0	.0	0	.0	0	.0	0	.0	15	86.2	2	11.8	
MALE	0	.0	1	1.4	5	7.2	0	.0	6	8.7	60	87.0	3	4.3	
PART-TIME	0	.0	0	.0	4	5.9	0	.0	4	5.9	61	89.7	3	4.4	
FEMALE	0	.0	0	.0	0	.0	0	.0	0	.0	13	100.0	0	.0	
MALE	0	.0	0	.0	4	7.3	0	.0	4	7.3	48	87.3	3	5.5	
TOTAL	0	.0	1	.6	9	5.8	0	.0	10	6.5	136	88.3	8	5.2	
FEMALE	0	.0	0	.0	0	.0	0	.0	0	.0	28	93.3	2	6.7	
MALE	0	.0	1	.8	9	7.3	0	.0	10	8.1	108	87.1	6	4.8	
PROFESSIONAL:															
FULL-TIME	0	.0	0	.0	0	.0	0	.0	0	.0	0	.0	0	.0	
FEMALE	0	.0	0	.0	0	.0	0	.0	0	.0	0	.0	0	.0	
MALE	0	.0	0	.0	0	.0	0	.0	0	.0	0	.0	0	.0	
PART-TIME	0	.0	0	.0	0	.0	0	.0	0	.0	0	.0	0	.0	
FEMALE	0	.0	0	.0	0	.0	0	.0	0	.0	0	.0	0	.0	
MALE	0	.0	0	.0	0	.0	0	.0	0	.0	0	.0	0	.0	
TOTAL	0	.0	0	.0	0	.0	0	.0	0	.0	0	.0	0	.0	
FEMALE	0	.0	0	.0	0	.0	0	.0	0	.0	0	.0	0	.0	
MALE	0	.0	0	.0	0	.0	0	.0	0	.0	0	.0	0	.0	
UND+GRAD+PROF:															
FULL-TIME	1	.2	2	.4	11	2.1	0	.0	14	2.7	496	95.6	9	1.7	
FEMALE	0	.0	0	.0	1	1.0	0	.0	1	1.0	96	96.0	3	3.0	
MALE	1	.2	2	.5	10	2.4	0	.0	13	3.1	400	95.5	6	1.4	
PART-TIME	0	.0	0	.0	5	3.8	1	.8	6	4.6	121	93.1	3	2.3	
FEMALE	0	.0	0	.0	0	.0	0	.0	0	.0	35	100.0	0	.0	
MALE	0	.0	0	.0	5	5.3	1	1.1	6	6.3	86	90.5	3	3.2	
TOTAL	1	.2	2	.3	16	2.5	1	.2	20	3.1	617	95.1	12	1.8	
FEMALE	0	.0	0	.0	1	.7	0	.0	1	.7	131	97.0	3	2.2	
MALE	1	.2	2	.4	15	2.9	1	.2	19	3.7	486	94.6	9	1.8	
UNCLASSIFIED:															
TOTAL	0	.0	0	.0	1	5.6	0	.0	1	5.6	17	94.4	0	.0	
FEMALE	0	.0	0	.0	0	.0	0	.0	0	.0	5	100.0	0	.0	
MALE	0	.0	0	.0	1	7.7	0	.0	1	7.7	12	92.3	0	.0	
TOTAL ENROLLMENT:															
TOTAL	1	.1	2	.3	17	2.5	1	.1	21	3.1	634	95.1	12	1.8	
FEMALE	0	.0	0	.0	1	.7	0	.0	1	.7	136	97.1	3	2.1	
MALE	1	.2	2	.4	16	3.0	1	.2	20	3.8	498	94.5	9	1.7	
ILLINOIS (58 INSTITUTIONS)															
UNDERGRADUATES:															
FULL-TIME	8	.2	287	7.0	123	3.0	44	1.1	462	11.2	3,526	85.6	133	3.2	
FEMALE	3	.3	141	14.0	31	3.1	19	1.9	194	19.3	704	78.0	27	2.7	
MALE	5	.2	146	4.7	92	3.0	25	.8	268	8.6	2,742	88.0	106	3.4	
PART-TIME	5	.9	64	10.9	16	2.7	11	1.9	96	16.4	480	81.8	11	1.9	
FEMALE	1	.5	34	18.7	5	2.7	6	3.3	46	25.3	132	72.5	4	2.2	
MALE	4	1.0	30	7.4	11	2.7	5	1.2	50	12.3	348	85.9	7	1.7	
TOTAL	13	.3	351	7.5	139	3.0	55	1.2	558	11.9	4,006	85.1	144	3.1	
FEMALE	4	.3	175	14.7	36	3.0	25	2.1	240	20.2	916	77.2	31	2.6	
MALE	9	.3	176	5.0	103	2.9	30	.9	318	9.0	3,090	87.8	113	3.2	
GRADUATE:															
FULL-TIME	1	.1	14	1.0	46	3.2	9	.6	70	4.9	1,094	77.2	253	17.9	
FEMALE	0	.0	1	.5	15	6.8	3	1.4	19	8.6	161	73.2	40	18.2	
MALE	1	.1	13	1.1	31	2.6	6	.5	51	4.3	933	77.9	213	17.8	
PART-TIME	1	.2	22	4.3	26	5.1	3	.6	52	10.1	385	74.9	77	15.0	
FEMALE	1	.8	10	6.3	7	3.8	1	.8	19	15.8	82	68.3	19	15.8	
MALE	0	.0	12	3.0	19	4.8	2	.5	33	8.4	303	76.9	58	14.7	
TOTAL	2	.1	36	1.9	72	3.7	12	.6	122	6.3	1,479	76.6	330	17.1	
FEMALE	1	.3	11	3.2	22	6.5	4	1.2	38	11.2	243	71.5	59	17.4	
MALE	1	.1	25	1.6	50	3.1	8	.5	84	5.3	1,236	77.7	271	17.0	
PROFESSIONAL:															
FULL-TIME	0	.0	0	.0	0	.0	0	.0	0	.0	0	.0	0	.0	
FEMALE	0	.0	0	.0	0	.0	0	.0	0	.0	0	.0	0	.0	
MALE	0	.0	0	.0	0	.0	0	.0	0	.0	0	.0	0	.0	

PHYSICAL SCIENCES

N INDIAN NATIVE	BLACK NON-HISPANIC		ASIAN OR PACIFIC ISLANDER		HISPANIC		TOTAL MINORITY		WHITE NON-HISPANIC		NON-RESIDENT ALIEN		TOTAL
%	NUMBER	%	NUMBER	%	NUMBER	%	NUMBER	%	NUMBER	%	NUMBER	%	NUMBER

CONTINUED

N INDIAN NATIVE %	BLACK NUMBER	%	ASIAN NUMBER	%	HISP NUMBER	%	MINORITY NUMBER	%	WHITE NUMBER	%	ALIEN NUMBER	%	TOTAL NUMBER
.0	0	.0	0	.0	0	.0	0	.0	0	.0	0	.0	0
.0	0	.0	0	.0	0	.0	0	.0	0	.0	0	.0	0
.0	0	.0	0	.0	0	.0	0	.0	0	.0	0	.0	0
.0	0	.0	0	.0	0	.0	0	.0	0	.0	0	.0	0
.0	0	.0	0	.0	0	.0	0	.0	0	.0	0	.0	0
.0	0	.0	0	.0	0	.0	0	.0	0	.0	0	.0	0
.2	301	5.4	169	3.1	53	1.0	532	9.6	4,620	83.4	386	7.0	5,538
.2	142	11.6	46	3.8	22	1.8	213	17.4	945	77.1	67	5.5	1,225
.1	159	3.7	123	2.9	31	.7	319	7.4	3,675	85.2	319	7.4	4,313
.5	86	7.8	42	3.8	14	1.3	148	13.4	865	78.6	88	8.0	1,101
.7	44	14.6	12	4.0	7	2.3	65	21.5	214	70.9	23	7.6	302
.5	42	5.3	30	3.8	7	.9	83	10.4	651	81.5	65	8.1	799
.2	387	5.8	211	3.2	67	1.0	680	10.2	5,485	82.6	474	7.1	6,639
.3	186	12.2	58	3.8	29	1.9	278	18.2	1,159	75.9	90	5.9	1,527
.2	201	3.9	153	3.0	38	.7	402	7.9	4,326	84.6	384	7.5	5,112
.0	10	6.4	7	4.5	4	2.5	21	13.4	133	84.7	3	1.9	157
.0	5	8.2	1	1.6	1	1.6	7	11.5	54	88.5	0	.0	61
.0	5	5.2	6	6.3	3	3.1	14	14.6	79	82.3	3	3.1	96
.2	397	5.8	218	3.2	71	1.0	701	10.3	5,618	82.7	477	7.0	6,796
.3	191	12.0	59	3.7	30	1.9	285	17.9	1,213	76.4	90	5.7	1,588
.2	206	4.0	159	3.1	41	.8	416	8.0	4,405	84.6	387	7.4	5,208

(42 INSTITUTIONS)

N INDIAN NATIVE %	BLACK NUMBER	%	ASIAN NUMBER	%	HISP NUMBER	%	MINORITY NUMBER	%	WHITE NUMBER	%	ALIEN NUMBER	%	TOTAL NUMBER
.1	46	1.8	19	.8	16	.6	84	3.3	2,375	94.0	68	2.7	2,527
.3	17	2.7	5	.8	6	.9	30	4.7	581	91.9	21	3.3	632
.1	29	1.5	14	.7	10	.5	54	2.8	1,794	94.7	47	2.5	1,895
.3	23	5.8	2	.5	6	1.5	32	8.1	360	90.7	5	1.3	397
.0	7	6.8	2	1.9	1	1.0	10	9.7	92	89.3	1	1.0	103
.3	16	5.4	0	.0	5	1.7	22	7.5	268	91.2	4	1.4	294
.1	69	2.4	21	.7	22	.8	116	4.0	2,735	93.5	73	2.5	2,924
.3	24	3.3	7	1.0	7	1.0	40	5.4	673	91.6	22	3.0	735
.1	45	2.1	14	.6	15	.7	76	3.5	2,062	94.2	51	2.3	2,189
.0	2	.3	10	1.3	2	.3	15	1.9	603	78.1	154	19.9	772
.0	0	.0	2	1.6	1	.8	3	2.3	95	73.6	31	24.0	129
.2	2	.3	8	1.2	1	.2	12	1.9	508	79.0	123	19.1	643
.0	6	2.3	5	1.9	2	.8	13	4.9	225	84.6	28	10.5	266
.0	2	3.6	1	1.8	0	.0	3	5.4	50	89.3	3	5.4	56
.0	4	1.9	4	1.9	2	1.0	10	4.8	175	83.3	25	11.9	210
.1	8	.8	15	1.4	4	.4	28	2.7	828	79.8	182	17.5	1,038
.0	2	1.1	3	1.6	1	.5	6	3.2	145	78.4	34	18.4	185
.1	6	.7	12	1.4	3	.4	22	2.6	683	80.1	148	17.4	853
.0	0	.0	0	.0	0	.0	0	.0	13	92.9	1	7.1	14
.0	0	.0	0	.0	0	.0	0	.0	3	75.0	1	25.0	4
.0	0	.0	0	.0	0	.0	0	.0	10	100.0	0	.0	10
.0	0	.0	0	.0	0	.0	0	.0	1	100.0	0	.0	1
.0	0	.0	0	.0	0	.0	0	.0	0	.0	0	.0	0
.0	0	.0	0	.0	0	.0	0	.0	1	100.0	0	.0	1
.0	0	.0	0	.0	0	.0	0	.0	14	93.3	1	6.7	15
.0	0	.0	0	.0	0	.0	0	.0	3	75.0	1	25.0	4
.0	0	.0	0	.0	0	.0	0	.0	11	100.0	0	.0	11
.1	48	1.4	29	.9	18	.5	99	3.0	2,991	90.3	223	6.7	3,313
.3	17	2.2	7	.9	7	.9	33	4.3	679	88.8	53	6.9	765
.1	31	1.2	22	.9	11	.4	66	2.6	2,312	90.7	170	6.7	2,548
.2	29	4.4	7	1.1	8	1.2	45	6.8	586	88.3	33	5.0	664
.0	9	5.7	3	1.9	1	.6	13	8.2	142	89.3	4	2.5	159
.2	20	4.0	4	.8	7	1.4	32	6.3	444	87.9	29	5.7	505
.1	77	1.9	36	.9	26	.7	144	3.6	3,577	89.9	256	6.4	3,977
.2	26	2.8	10	1.1	8	.9	46	5.0	821	88.9	57	6.2	924
.1	51	1.7	26	.9	18	.6	98	3.2	2,756	90.3	199	6.5	3,053
1.4	0	.0	1	1.4	0	.0	2	2.9	63	91.3	4	5.8	69
.0	0	.0	0	.0	0	.0	0	.0	14	93.3	1	6.7	15
1.9	0	.0	1	1.9	0	.0	2	3.7	49	90.7	3	5.6	54
.1	77	1.9	37	.9	26	.6	146	3.6	3,640	90.0	260	6.4	4,046
.2	26	2.8	10	1.1	8	.9	46	5.0	835	88.9	58	6.2	939
.1	51	1.6	27	.9	18	.6	100	3.2	2,805	90.3	202	6.5	3,107

TABLE 17 - TOTAL ENROLLMENT IN INSTITUTIONS OF HIGHER EDUCATION FOR SELECTED MAJOR FIELDS OF STUDY AND LEVEL OF ENROLLMENT BY RACE, ETHNICITY, AND SEX: STATE, 1978

MAJOR FIELD 1900 - PHYSICAL SCIENCES

	AMERICAN INDIAN ALASKAN NATIVE		BLACK NON-HISPANIC		ASIAN OR PACIFIC ISLANDER		HISPANIC		TOTAL MINORITY		WHITE NON-HISPANIC		NON-RESIDENT ALIEN		T	
	NUMBER	%	NUMBER	%	NUMBER	%	NUMBER	%	NUMBER	%	NUMBER	%	NUMBER	%	N	
IOWA (24 INSTITUTIONS)																
UNDERGRADUATES:																
FULL-TIME	2	.2	17	1.6	11	1.1	3	.3	33	3.2	974	94.0	29	2.8		
FEMALE	1	.4	8	2.9	5	1.8	0	.0	14	5.1	254	93.0	5	1.8		
MALE	1	.1	9	1.2	6	.8	3	.4	19	2.5	720	94.4	24	3.1		
PART-TIME	0	.0	1	1.1	1	1.1	0	.0	2	2.2	84	92.3	5	5.5		
FEMALE	0	.0	1	4.5	0	.0	0	.0	1	4.5	20	90.9	1	4.5		
MALE	0	.0	0	.0	1	1.4	0	.0	1	1.4	64	92.8	4	5.8		
TOTAL	2	.2	18	1.6	12	1.1	3	.3	35	3.1	1,058	93.9	34	3.0		
FEMALE	1	.3	9	3.1	5	1.7	0	.0	15	5.1	274	92.9	6	2.0		
MALE	1	.1	9	1.1	7	.8	3	.4	20	2.4	784	94.2	28	3.4		
GRADUATE:																
FULL-TIME	0	.0	2	.5	11	2.5	1	.2	14	3.2	347	79.8	74	17.0		
FEMALE	0	.0	1	1.6	4	6.3	0	.0	5	7.9	44	69.8	14	22.2		
MALE	0	.0	1	.3	7	1.9	1	.3	9	2.4	303	81.5	60	16.1		
PART-TIME	0	.0	3	2.1	1	.7	0	.0	4	2.8	122	86.5	15	10.6		
FEMALE	0	.0	0	.0	1	6.3	0	.0	1	6.3	13	81.3	2	12.5		
MALE	0	.0	3	2.4	0	.0	0	.0	3	2.4	109	87.2	13	10.4		
TOTAL	0	.0	5	.9	12	2.1	1	.2	18	3.1	469	81.4	89	15.5		
FEMALE	0	.0	1	1.3	5	6.3	0	.0	6	7.6	57	72.2	16	20.3		
MALE	0	.0	4	.8	7	1.4	1	.2	12	2.4	412	82.9	73	14.7		
PROFESSIONAL:																
FULL-TIME	0	.0	0	.0	0	.0	0	.0	0	.0	0	.0	0	.0		
FEMALE	0	.0	0	.0	0	.0	0	.0	0	.0	0	.0	0	.0		
MALE	0	.0	0	.0	0	.0	0	.0	0	.0	0	.0	0	.0		
PART-TIME	0	.0	0	.0	0	.0	0	.0	0	.0	0	.0	0	.0		
FEMALE	0	.0	0	.0	0	.0	0	.0	0	.0	0	.0	0	.0		
MALE	0	.0	0	.0	0	.0	0	.0	0	.0	0	.0	0	.0		
TOTAL	0	.0	0	.0	0	.0	0	.0	0	.0	0	.0	0	.0		
FEMALE	0	.0	0	.0	0	.0	0	.0	0	.0	0	.0	0	.0		
MALE	0	.0	0	.0	0	.0	0	.0	0	.0	0	.0	0	.0		
UND+GRAD+PROF:																
FULL-TIME	2	.1	19	1.3	22	1.5	4	.3	47	3.2	1,321	89.8	103	7.0		
FEMALE	1	.3	9	2.7	9	2.7	0	.0	19	5.7	298	88.7	19	5.7		
MALE	1	.1	10	.9	13	1.1	4	.4	28	2.5	1,023	90.1	84	7.4		
PART-TIME	0	.0	4	1.7	2	.9	0	.0	6	2.6	206	88.8	20	8.6		
FEMALE	0	.0	1	2.6	1	2.6	0	.0	2	5.3	33	86.8	3	7.9		
MALE	0	.0	3	1.5	1	.5	0	.0	4	2.1	173	89.2	17	8.8		
TOTAL	2	.1	23	1.4	24	1.4	4	.2	53	3.1	1,527	89.7	123	7.2		
FEMALE	1	.3	10	2.7	10	2.7	0	.0	21	5.6	331	88.5	22	5.9		
MALE	1	.1	13	1.0	14	1.1	4	.3	32	2.4	1,196	90.0	101	7.6		
UNCLASSIFIED:																
TOTAL	0	.0	0	.0	0	.0	0	.0	0	.0	2	100.0	0	.0		
FEMALE	0	.0	0	.0	0	.0	0	.0	0	.0	0	.0	0	.0		
MALE	0	.0	0	.0	0	.0	0	.0	0	.0	2	100.0	0	.0		
TOTAL ENROLLMENT:																
TOTAL	2	.1	23	1.3	24	1.4	4	.2	53	3.1	1,529	89.7	123	7.2		
FEMALE	1	.3	10	2.7	10	2.7	0	.0	21	5.6	331	88.5	22	5.9		
MALE	1	.1	13	1.0	14	1.1	4	.3	32	2.4	1,198	90.0	101	7.6		
KANSAS (35 INSTITUTIONS)																
UNDERGRADUATES:																
FULL-TIME	2	.1	35	2.5	17	1.2	19	1.3	73	5.1	1,256	88.5	91	6.4		
FEMALE	0	.0	12	4.0	4	1.3	6	2.0	22	7.4	269	90.0	8	2.7		
MALE	2	.2	23	2.1	13	1.2	13	1.2	51	4.5	987	88.0	83	7.4		
PART-TIME	1	.5	7	3.6	1	.5	7	3.6	16	8.3	169	88.0	7	3.6		
FEMALE	0	.0	2	3.6	0	.0	5	8.9	7	12.5	49	87.5	0	.0		
MALE	1	.7	5	3.7	1	.7	2	1.5	9	6.6	120	88.2	7	5.1		
TOTAL	3	.2	42	2.6	18	1.1	26	1.6	89	5.5	1,425	88.4	98	6.1		
FEMALE	0	.0	14	3.9	4	1.1	11	3.1	29	8.2	318	89.6	8	2.3		
MALE	3	.2	28	2.2	14	1.1	15	1.2	60	4.8	1,107	88.1	90	7.2		
GRADUATE:																
FULL-TIME	1	.4	2	.7	3	1.1	2	.7	8	2.9	165	60.4	100	36.6		
FEMALE	0	.0	0	.0	0	.0	0	.0	0	.0	21	60.0	14	40.0		
MALE	1	.4	2	.8	3	1.3	2	.8	8	3.4	144	60.5	86	36.1		
PART-TIME	1	.6	3	1.9	0	.0	1	.6	5	3.1	122	75.8	34	21.1		
FEMALE	0	.0	0	.0	0	.0	0	.0	0	.0	21	75.0	7	25.0		
MALE	1	.8	3	2.3	0	.0	1	.8	5	3.8	101	75.9	27	20.3		
TOTAL	2	.5	5	1.2	3	.7	3	.7	13	3.0	287	66.1	134	30.9		
FEMALE	0	.0	0	.0	0	.0	0	.0	0	.0	42	66.7	21	33.3		
MALE	2	.5	5	1.3	3	.8	3	.8	13	3.5	245	66.0	113	30.5		
PROFESSIONAL:																
FULL-TIME	0	.0	0	.0	0	.0	0	.0	0	.0	0	.0	0	.0		
FEMALE	0	.0	0	.0	0	.0	0	.0	0	.0	0	.0	0	.0		
MALE	0	.0	0	.0	0	.0	0	.0	0	.0	0	.0	0	.0		

- PHYSICAL SCIENCES

CAN INDIAN AN NATIVE		BLACK NON-HISPANIC		ASIAN OR PACIFIC ISLANDER		HISPANIC		TOTAL MINORITY		WHITE NON-HISPANIC		NON-RESIDENT ALIEN		TOTAL
ER	%	NUMBER	%	NUMBER	%	NUMBER	%	NUMBER	%	NUMBER	%	NUMBER	%	NUMBER
CONTINUED														
0	.0	0	.0	0	.0	0	.0	0	.0	0	.0	0	.0	0
0	.0	0	.0	0	.0	0	.0	0	.0	0	.0	0	.0	0
0	.0	0	.0	0	.0	0	.0	0	.0	0	.0	0	.0	0
0	.0	0	.0	0	.0	0	.0	0	.0	0	.0	0	.0	0
0	.0	0	.0	0	.0	0	.0	0	.0	0	.0	0	.0	0
0	.0	0	.0	0	.0	0	.0	0	.0	0	.0	0	.0	0
3	.2	37	2.2	20	1.2	21	1.2	81	4.8	1,421	83.9	191	11.3	1,693
0	.0	12	3.6	4	1.2	6	1.8	22	6.6	290	86.8	22	6.6	334
3	.2	25	1.8	16	1.2	15	1.1	59	4.3	1,131	83.2	169	12.4	1,359
2	.6	10	2.8	1	.3	8	2.3	21	5.9	291	82.4	41	11.6	353
0	.0	2	2.4	0	.0	5	6.0	7	8.3	70	83.3	7	8.3	84
2	.7	8	3.0	1	.4	3	1.1	14	5.2	221	82.2	34	12.6	269
5	.2	47	2.3	21	1.0	29	1.4	102	5.0	1,712	83.7	232	11.3	2,046
0	.0	14	3.3	4	1.0	11	2.6	29	6.9	360	86.1	29	6.9	418
5	.3	33	2.0	17	1.0	18	1.1	73	4.5	1,352	83.0	203	12.5	1,628
1	2.3	2	4.5	1	2.3	0	.0	4	9.1	37	84.1	3	6.8	44
0	.0	1	10.0	0	.0	0	.0	1	10.0	8	80.0	1	10.0	10
1	2.9	1	2.9	1	2.9	0	.0	3	8.8	29	85.3	2	5.9	34
6	.3	49	2.3	22	1.1	29	1.4	106	5.1	1,749	83.7	235	11.2	2,090
0	.0	15	3.5	4	.9	11	2.6	30	7.0	368	86.0	30	7.0	428
6	.4	34	2.0	18	1.1	18	1.1	76	4.6	1,381	83.1	205	12.3	1,662
(	20 INSTITUTIONS)													
2	.2	25	2.0	13	1.0	10	.8	50	3.9	1,180	92.5	45	3.5	1,275
0	.0	8	2.5	4	1.3	4	1.3	16	5.1	291	92.4	8	2.5	315
2	.2	17	1.8	9	.9	6	.6	34	3.5	889	92.6	37	3.9	960
1	.5	5	2.3	3	1.4	2	.9	11	5.0	206	93.6	3	1.4	220
0	.0	2	3.9	0	.0	1	2.0	3	5.9	48	94.1	0	.0	51
1	.6	3	1.8	3	1.8	1	.6	8	4.7	158	93.5	3	1.8	169
3	.2	30	2.0	16	1.1	12	.8	61	4.1	1,386	92.7	48	3.2	1,495
0	.0	10	2.7	4	1.1	5	1.4	19	5.2	339	92.6	8	2.2	366
3	.3	20	1.8	12	1.1	7	.6	42	3.7	1,047	92.7	40	3.5	1,129
1	.8	1	.8	9	6.8	2	1.5	13	9.8	100	75.8	19	14.4	132
0	.0	0	.0	2	18.2	0	.0	2	18.2	5	45.5	4	36.4	11
1	.8	1	.8	7	5.8	2	1.7	11	9.1	95	78.5	15	12.4	121
0	.0	0	.0	1	1.3	0	.0	1	1.3	67	84.8	11	13.9	79
0	.0	0	.0	0	.0	0	.0	0	.0	13	100.0	0	.0	13
0	.0	0	.0	1	1.5	0	.0	1	1.5	54	81.8	11	16.7	66
1	.5	1	.5	10	4.7	2	.9	14	6.6	167	79.1	30	14.2	211
0	.0	0	.0	2	8.3	0	.0	2	8.3	18	75.0	4	16.7	24
1	.5	1	.5	8	4.3	2	1.1	12	6.4	149	79.7	26	13.9	187
0	.0	0	.0	0	.0	0	.0	0	.0	0	.0	0	.0	0
0	.0	0	.0	0	.0	0	.0	0	.0	0	.0	0	.0	0
0	.0	0	.0	0	.0	0	.0	0	.0	0	.0	0	.0	0
0	.0	0	.0	0	.0	0	.0	0	.0	0	.0	0	.0	0
0	.0	0	.0	0	.0	0	.0	0	.0	0	.0	0	.0	0
0	.0	0	.0	0	.0 ·	0	.0	0	.0	0	.0	0	.0	0
0	.0	0	.0	0	.0	0	.0	0	.0	0	.0	0	.0	0
0	.0	0	.0	0	.0	0	.0	0	.0	0	.0	0	.0	0
0	.0	0	.0	0	.0	0	.0	0	.0	0	.0	0	.0	0
3	.2	26	1.8	22	1.6	12	.9	63	4.5	1,280	91.0	64	4.5	1,407
0	.0	8	2.5	6	1.8	4	1.2	18	5.5	296	90.8	12	3.7	326
3	.3	18	1.7	16	1.5	8	.7	45	4.2	904	91.0	52	4.8	1,001
1	.3	5	1.7	4	1.3	2	.7	12	4.0	273	91.3	14	4.7	299
0	.0	2	3.1	0	.0	1	1.6	3	4.7	61	95.3	0	.0	64
1	.4	3	1.3	4	1.7	1	.4	9	3.8	212	90.2	14	6.0	235
4	.2	31	1.8	26	1.5	14	.8	75	4.4	1,553	91.0	78	4.6	1,706
0	.0	10	2.6	6	1.5	5	1.3	21	5.4	357	91.5	12	3.1	390
4	.3	21	1.6	20	1.5	9	.7	54	4.1	1,196	90.9	66	5.0	1,316
0	.0	4	11.8	0	.0	0	.0	4	11.8	30	88.2	0	.0	34
0	.0	1	12.5	0	.0	0	.0	1	12.5	7	87.5	0	.0	8
0	.0	3	11.5	0	.0	0	.0	3	11.5	23	88.5	0	.0	26
4	.2	35	2.0	26	1.5	14	.8	79	4.5	1,583	91.0	78	4.5	1,740
0	.0	11	2.8	6	1.5	5	1.3	22	5.5	364	91.5	12	3.0	358
4	.3	24	1.8	20	1.5	9	.7	57	4.2	1,219	90.8	66	4.9	1,342

TABLE 17 - TOTAL ENROLLMENT IN INSTITUTIONS OF HIGHER EDUCATION FOR SELECTED MAJOR FIELDS OF STUDY AND LEVEL OF ENROLLMENT
BY RACE, ETHNICITY, AND SEX: STATE, 1978

MAJOR FIELD 1900 - PHYSICAL SCIENCES

	AMERICAN INDIAN ALASKAN NATIVE		BLACK NON-HISPANIC		ASIAN OR PACIFIC ISLANDER		HISPANIC		TOTAL MINORITY		WHITE NON-HISPANIC		NON-RESIDENT ALIEN		T
	NUMBER	%	NUMBER	%	NUMBER	%	NUMBER	%	NUMBER	%	NUMBER	%	NUMBER	%	N
LOUISIANA (21 INSTITUTIONS)															
UNDERGRADUATES:															
FULL-TIME	0	.0	252	15.6	11	.7	23	1.4	286	17.7	1,264	78.2	66	4.1	
FEMALE	0	.0	105	24.3	6	1.4	6	1.4	117	27.1	300	69.4	15	3.5	
MALE	0	.0	147	12.4	5	.4	17	1.4	169	14.3	964	81.4	51	4.3	
PART-TIME	0	.0	18	9.2	0	.0	0	.0	18	9.2	175	89.3	3	1.5	
FEMALE	0	.0	6	10.0	0	.0	0	.0	6	10.0	52	86.7	2	3.3	
MALE	0	.0	12	8.8	0	.0	0	.0	12	8.8	123	90.4	1	.7	
TOTAL	0	.0	270	14.9	11	.6	23	1.3	304	16.8	1,439	79.4	69	3.8	
FEMALE	0	.0	111	22.6	6	1.2	6	1.2	123	25.0	352	71.5	17	3.5	
MALE	0	.0	159	12.0	5	.4	17	1.3	181	13.7	1,087	82.3	52	3.9	
GRADUATE:															
FULL-TIME	0	.0	2	.6	3	1.0	6	1.9	11	3.5	231	74.5	68	21.9	
FEMALE	0	.0	0	.0	1	1.7	2	3.4	3	5.1	47	79.7	9	15.3	
MALE	0	.0	2	.8	2	.8	4	1.6	8	3.2	184	73.3	59	23.5	
PART-TIME	0	.0	6	7.0	0	.0	2	2.3	8	9.3	71	82.6	7	8.1	
FEMALE	0	.0	3	20.0	0	.0	0	.0	3	20.0	12	80.0	0	.0	
MALE	0	.0	3	4.2	0	.0	2	2.8	5	7.0	59	83.1	7	9.9	
TOTAL	0	.0	8	2.0	3	.8	8	2.0	19	4.8	302	76.3	75	18.9	
FEMALE	0	.0	3	4.1	1	1.4	2	2.7	6	8.1	59	79.7	9	12.2	
MALE	0	.0	5	1.6	2	.6	6	1.9	13	4.0	243	75.5	66	20.5	
PROFESSIONAL:															
FULL-TIME	0	.0	0	.0	0	.0	0	.0	0	.0	0	.0	0	.0	
FEMALE	0	.0	0	.0	0	.0	0	.0	0	.0	0	.0	0	.0	
MALE	0	.0	0	.0	0	.0	0	.0	0	.0	0	.0	0	.0	
PART-TIME	0	.0	0	.0	0	.0	0	.0	0	.0	0	.0	0	.0	
FEMALE	0	.0	0	.0	0	.0	0	.0	0	.0	0	.0	0	.0	
MALE	0	.0	0	.0	0	.0	0	.0	0	.0	0	.0	0	.0	
TOTAL	0	.0	0	.0	0	.0	0	.0	0	.0	0	.0	0	.0	
FEMALE	0	.0	0	.0	0	.0	0	.0	0	.0	0	.0	0	.0	
MALE	0	.0	0	.0	0	.0	0	.0	0	.0	0	.0	0	.0	
UND+GRAD+PROF:															
FULL-TIME	0	.0	254	13.2	14	.7	29	1.5	297	15.4	1,495	77.6	134	7.0	
FEMALE	0	.0	105	21.4	7	1.4	8	1.6	120	24.4	347	70.7	24	4.9	
MALE	0	.0	149	10.4	7	.5	21	1.5	177	12.3	1,148	80.0	110	7.7	
PART-TIME	0	.0	24	8.5	0	.0	2	.7	26	9.2	246	87.2	10	3.5	
FEMALE	0	.0	9	12.0	0	.0	0	.0	9	12.0	64	85.3	2	2.7	
MALE	0	.0	15	7.2	0	.0	2	1.0	17	8.2	182	87.9	8	3.9	
TOTAL	0	.0	278	12.6	14	.6	31	1.4	323	14.6	1,741	78.8	144	6.5	
FEMALE	0	.0	114	20.1	7	1.2	8	1.4	129	22.8	411	72.6	26	4.6	
MALE	0	.0	164	10.0	7	.4	23	1.4	194	11.8	1,330	81.0	118	7.2	
UNCLASSIFIED:															
TOTAL	0	.0	2	8.3	0	*0	0	.0	2	8.3	21	87.5	1	4.2	
FEMALE	0	.0	1	16.7	0	.0	0	.0	1	16.7	5	83.3	0	.0	
MALE	0	.0	1	5.6	0	.0	0	.0	1	5.6	16	88.9	1	5.6	
TOTAL ENROLLMENT:															
TOTAL	0	.0	280	12.5	14	.6	31	1.4	325	14.6	1,762	78.9	145	6.5	
FEMALE	0	.0	115	20.1	7	1.2	8	1.4	130	22.7	416	72.7	26	4.5	
MALE	0	.0	165	9.9	7	.4	23	1.4	195	11.7	1,346	81.1	119	7.2	
MAINE (8 INSTITUTIONS)															
UNDERGRADUATES:															
FULL-TIME	0	.0	1	.4	2	.7	2	.7	5	1.9	260	97.0	3	1.1	
FEMALE	0	.0	0	.0	1	1.6	0	.0	1	1.6	62	96.9	1	1.6	
MALE	0	.0	1	.5	1	.5	2	1.0	4	2.0	198	97.1	2	1.0	
PART-TIME	0	.0	0	.0	0	.0	0	.0	0	.0	11	100.0	0	.0	
FEMALE	0	.0	0	.0	0	.0	0	.0	0	.0	3	100.0	0	.0	
MALE	0	.0	0	.0	0	.0	0	.0	0	.0	8	100.0	0	.0	
TOTAL	0	.0	1	.4	2	.7	2	.7	5	1.8	271	97.1	3	1.1	
FEMALE	0	.0	0	.0	1	1.5	0	.0	1	1.5	65	97.0	1	1.5	
MALE	0	.0	1	.5	1	.5	2	.9	4	1.9	206	97.2	2	.9	
GRADUATE:															
FULL-TIME	0	.0	0	.0	0	.0	0	.0	0	.0	55	90.2	6	9.8	
FEMALE	0	.0	0	.0	0	.0	0	.0	0	.0	11	100.0	0	.0	
MALE	0	.0	0	.0	0	.0	0	.0	0	.0	44	88.0	6	12.0	
PART-TIME	0	.0	0	.0	0	.0	0	.0	0	.0	17	94.4	1	5.6	
FEMALE	0	.0	0	.0	0	.0	0	.0	0	.0	5	83.3	1	16.7	
MALE	0	.0	0	.0	0	.0	0	.0	0	.0	12	100.0	0	.0	
TOTAL	0	.0	0	.0	0	.0	0	.0	0	.0	72	91.1	7	8.9	
FEMALE	0	.0	0	.0	0	.0	0	.0	0	.0	16	94.1	1	5.9	
MALE	0	.0	0	.0	0	.0	0	.0	0	.0	56	90.3	6	9.7	
PROFESSIONAL:															
FULL-TIME	0	.0	0	.0	0	.0	0	.0	0	.0	0	.0	0	.0	
FEMALE	0	.0	0	.0	0	.0	0	.0	0	.0	0	.0	0	.0	
MALE	0	.0	0	.0	0	.0	0	.0	0	.0	0	.0	0	.0	

- PHYSICAL SCIENCES

AMER INDIAN/AK NATIVE NUMBER	%	BLACK NON-HISPANIC NUMBER	%	ASIAN OR PACIFIC ISLANDER NUMBER	%	HISPANIC NUMBER	%	TOTAL MINORITY NUMBER	%	WHITE NON-HISPANIC NUMBER	%	NON-RESIDENT ALIEN NUMBER	%	TOTAL NUMBER
					CONTINUED									
0	.0	0	.0	0	.0	0	.0	0	.0	0	.0	0	.0	0
0	.0	0	.0	0	.0	0	.0	0	.0	0	.0	0	.0	0
0	.0	0	.0	0	.0	0	.0	0	.0	0	.0	0	.0	0
0	.0	0	.0	0	.0	0	.0	0	.0	0	.0	0	.0	0
0	.0	0	.0	0	.0	0	.0	0	.0	0	.0	0	.0	0
0	.0	1	.3	2	.6	2	.6	5	1.5	315	95.7	9	2.7	329
0	.0	0	.0	1	1.3	0	.0	1	1.3	73	97.3	1	1.3	75
0	.0	1	.4	2	.8	0	.0	4	1.6	242	95.3	8	3.1	254
0	.0	0	.0	0	.0	0	.0	0	.0	28	96.6	1	3.4	29
0	.0	0	.0	0	.0	0	.0	0	.0	8	88.9	1	11.1	9
0	.0	0	.0	0	.0	0	.0	0	.0	20	100.0	0	.0	20
0	.0	1	.3	2	.6	2	.6	5	1.4	343	95.8	10	2.8	358
0	.0	0	.0	1	1.2	0	.0	1	1.2	81	96.4	2	2.4	84
0	.0	1	.4	1	.4	2	.7	4	1.5	262	95.6	8	2.9	274
0	.0	0	.0	0	.0	0	.0	0	.0	2	100.0	0	.0	2
0	.0	0	.0	0	.0	0	.0	0	.0	1	100.0	0	.0	1
0	.0	0	.0	0	.0	0	.0	0	.0	1	100.0	0	.0	1
0	.0	1	.3	2	.6	2	.6	5	1.4	345	95.8	10	2.8	360
0	.0	0	.0	1	1.2	0	.0	1	1.2	82	96.5	2	2.4	85
0	.0	1	.4	1	.4	2	.7	4	1.5	263	95.6	8	2.9	275
				(	18 INSTITUTIONS)									
3	.2	128	8.8	36	2.5	20	1.4	187	12.9	1,165	80.4	97	6.7	1,449
0	.0	46	12.4	6	1.6	11	3.0	63	17.0	284	76.8	23	6.2	370
3	.3	82	7.6	30	2.8	9	.8	124	11.5	881	81.6	74	6.9	1,079
1	.5	25	11.5	3	1.4	3	1.4	32	14.7	174	79.8	12	5.5	218
0	.0	9	15.0	2	3.3	1	1.7	12	20.0	44	73.3	4	6.7	60
1	.6	16	10.1	1	.6	2	1.3	20	12.7	130	82.3	8	5.1	158
4	.2	153	9.2	39	2.3	23	1.4	219	13.1	1,339	80.3	109	6.5	1,667
0	.0	55	12.8	8	1.9	12	2.8	75	17.4	328	76.3	27	6.3	430
4	.3	98	7.9	31	2.5	11	.9	144	11.6	1,011	81.7	82	6.6	1,237
2	.4	4	.9	4	.9	5	1.1	15	3.3	364	79.1	81	17.6	460
1	1.4	1	1.4	2	2.7	1	1.4	5	6.8	54	73.0	15	20.3	74
1	.3	3	.8	2	.5	4	1.0	10	2.6	310	80.3	66	17.1	386
0	.0	7	3.1	1	.4	3	1.3	11	4.8	190	83.3	27	11.8	228
0	.0	3	5.5	0	.0	1	1.8	4	7.3	41	74.5	10	18.2	55
0	.0	4	2.3	1	.6	2	1.2	7	4.0	149	86.1	17	9.8	173
2	.3	11	1.6	5	.7	8	1.2	26	3.8	554	80.5	108	15.7	688
1	.8	4	3.1	2	1.6	2	1.6	9	7.0	95	73.6	25	19.4	129
1	.2	7	1.3	3	.5	6	1.1	17	3.0	459	82.1	83	14.8	559
0	.0	0	.0	0	.0	0	.0	0	.0	0	.0	0	.0	0
0	.0	0	.0	0	.0	0	.0	0	.0	0	.0	0	.0	0
0	.0	0	.0	0	.0	0	.0	0	.0	0	.0	0	.0	0
0	.0	0	.0	0	.0	0	.0	0	.0	0	.0	0	.0	0
0	.0	0	.0	0	.0	0	.0	0	.0	0	.0	0	.0	0
0	.0	0	.0	0	.0	0	.0	0	.0	0	.0	0	.0	0
0	.0	0	.0	0	.0	0	.0	0	.0	0	.0	0	.0	0
0	.0	0	.0	0	.0	0	.0	0	.0	0	.0	0	.0	0
0	.0	0	.0	0	.0	0	.0	0	.0	0	.0	0	.0	0
5	.3	132	6.9	40	2.1	25	1.3	202	10.6	1,529	80.1	178	9.3	1,909
1	.2	47	10.6	8	1.8	12	2.7	68	15.3	338	76.1	38	8.6	444
4	.3	85	5.8	32	2.2	13	.9	134	9.1	1,191	81.3	140	9.6	1,465
1	.2	32	7.2	4	.9	6	1.3	43	9.6	364	81.6	39	8.7	446
0	.0	12	10.4	2	1.7	2	1.7	16	13.9	85	73.9	14	12.2	115
1	.3	20	6.0	2	.6	4	1.2	27	8.2	279	84.3	25	7.6	331
6	.3	164	7.0	44	1.9	31	1.3	245	10.4	1,893	80.4	217	9.2	2,355
1	.2	59	10.6	10	1.8	14	2.5	84	15.0	423	75.7	52	9.3	559
5	.3	105	5.8	34	1.9	17	.9	161	9.0	1,470	81.8	165	9.2	1,796
1	.3	31	8.9	7	2.0	4	1.1	43	12.4	289	83.0	16	4.6	348
1	1.0	13	13.0	2	2.0	0	.0	16	16.0	78	78.0	6	6.0	100
0	.0	18	7.3	5	2.0	4	1.6	27	10.9	211	85.1	10	4.0	248
7	.3	195	7.2	51	1.9	35	1.3	288	10.7	2,182	80.7	233	8.6	2,703
2	.3	72	10.9	12	1.8	14	2.1	100	15.2	501	76.0	58	8.8	659
5	.2	123	6.0	39	1.9	21	1.0	188	9.2	1,681	82.2	175	8.6	2,044

MAJOR FIELD 1900 - PHYSICAL SCIENCES

	AMERICAN INDIAN ALASKAN NATIVE		BLACK NON-HISPANIC		ASIAN OR PACIFIC ISLANDER		HISPANIC		TOTAL MINORITY		WHITE NON-HISPANIC		NON-RESIDENT ALIEN		T	
	NUMBER	%	NUMBER	%	NUMBER	%	NUMBER	%	NUMBER	%	NUMBER	%	NUMBER	%	N	
MASSACHUSETTS (41 INSTITUTIONS)																
UNDERGRADUATES:																
FULL-TIME	6	.2	68	1.8	68	1.8	37	1.0	179	4.7	3,529	92.2	118	3.1		
FEMALE	1	.1	29	2.9	19	1.9	13	1.3	62	6.2	913	91.9	18	1.8		
MALE	5	.2	39	1.4	49	1.7	24	.8	117	4.1	2,616	92.3	100	3.5		
PART-TIME	0	.0	3	2.0	2	1.3	2	1.3	7	4.7	140	93.3	3	2.0		
FEMALE	0	.0	1	2.6	0	.0	0	.0	1	2.6	36	94.7	1	2.6		
MALE	0	.0	2	1.8	2	1.8	2	1.8	6	5.4	104	92.9	2	1.8		
TOTAL	6	.2	71	1.8	70	1.8	39	1.0	186	4.7	3,669	92.3	121	3.0		
FEMALE	1	.1	30	2.9	19	1.8	13	1.3	63	6.1	949	92.0	19	1.8		
MALE	5	.2	41	1.4	51	1.7	26	.9	123	4.2	2,720	92.4	102	3.5		
GRADUATE:																
FULL-TIME	1	.1	26	1.7	33	2.1	15	1.0	75	4.8	1,204	77.0	284	18.2		
FEMALE	0	.0	8	3.2	10	4.0	3	1.2	21	8.5	187	75.4	40	16.1		
MALE	1	.1	18	1.4	23	1.7	12	.9	54	4.1	1,017	77.3	244	18.6		
PART-TIME	0	.0	12	2.6	6	1.3	1	.2	19	4.1	407	88.5	34	7.4		
FEMALE	0	.0	5	4.0	1	.8	0	.0	6	4.8	116	92.1	9	3.2		
MALE	0	.0	7	2.1	5	1.5	1	.3	13	3.9	291	87.1	30	9.0		
TOTAL	1	.0	38	1.9	39	1.9	16	.8	94	4.6	1,611	79.6	318	15.7		
FEMALE	0	.0	13	3.5	11	2.9	3	.8	27	7.2	303	81.0	44	11.8		
MALE	1	.1	25	1.5	28	1.7	13	.8	67	4.1	1,308	79.3	274	16.6		
PROFESSIONAL:																
FULL-TIME	0	.0	0	.0	0	.0	0	.0	0	.0	2	100.0	0	.0		
FEMALE	0	.0	0	.0	0	.0	0	.0	0	.0	0	.0	0	.0		
MALE	0	.0	0	.0	0	.0	0	.0	0	.0	2	100.0	0	.0		
PART-TIME	0	.0	0	.0	0	.0	0	.0	0	.0	0	.0	0	.0		
FEMALE	0	.0	0	.0	0	.0	0	.0	0	.0	0	.0	0	.0		
MALE	0	.0	0	.0	0	.0	0	.0	0	.0	0	.0	0	.0		
TOTAL	0	.0	0	.0	0	.0	0	.0	0	.0	2	100.0	0	.0		
FEMALE	0	.0	0	.0	0	.0	0	.0	0	.0	0	.0	0	.0		
MALE	0	.0	0	.0	0	.0	0	.0	0	.0	2	100.0	0	.0		
UND+GRAD+PROF:																
FULL-TIME	7	.1	94	1.7	101	1.9	52	1.0	254	4.7	4,735	87.8	402	7.5		
FEMALE	1	.1	37	3.0	29	2.3	16	1.3	83	6.7	1,100	88.6	58	4.7		
MALE	6	.1	57	1.4	72	1.7	36	.9	171	4.1	3,635	87.6	344	8.3		
PART-TIME	0	.0	15	2.5	8	1.3	3	.5	26	4.3	547	89.7	37	6.1		
FEMALE	0	.0	6	3.7	1	.6	0	.0	7	4.3	152	92.7	5	3.0		
MALE	0	.0	9	2.0	7	1.6	3	.7	19	4.3	395	88.6	32	7.2		
TOTAL	7	.1	109	1.8	109	1.8	55	.9	280	4.7	5,282	88.0	439	7.3		
FEMALE	1	.1	43	3.1	30	2.1	16	1.1	90	6.4	1,252	89.1	63	4.5		
MALE	6	.1	66	1.4	79	1.7	39	.8	190	4.1	4,030	87.7	376	8.2		
UNCLASSIFIED:																
TOTAL	0	.0	0	.0	1	2.6	0	.0	1	2.6	31	81.6	6	15.8		
FEMALE	0	.0	0	.0	1	11.1	0	.0	1	11.1	5	55.6	3	33.3		
MALE	0	.0	0	.0	0	.0	0	.0	0	.0	26	89.7	3	10.3		
TOTAL ENROLLMENT:																
TOTAL	7	.1	109	1.8	110	1.8	55	.9	281	4.7	5,313	88.0	445	7.4		
FEMALE	1	.1	43	3.0	31	2.2	16	1.1	91	6.4	1,257	88.9	66	4.7		
MALE	6	.1	66	1.4	79	1.7	39	.8	190	4.1	4,056	87.7	379	8.2		
MICHIGAN (44 INSTITUTIONS)																
UNDERGRADUATES:																
FULL-TIME	13	.4	100	3.0	33	1.0	22	.7	168	5.0	3,119	92.2	97	2.9		
FEMALE	3	.3	48	5.4	7	.8	8	.9	66	7.4	809	90.3	21	2.3		
MALE	10	.4	52	2.1	26	1.0	14	.6	102	4.1	2,310	92.8	76	3.1		
PART-TIME	6	.8	49	6.2	9	1.1	10	1.3	74	9.4	703	89.3	10	1.3		
FEMALE	1	.4	17	7.4	2	.9	1	.4	21	9.1	207	89.6	3	1.3		
MALE	5	.9	32	5.8	7	1.3	9	1.6	53	9.5	496	89.2	7	1.3		
TOTAL	19	.5	149	3.6	42	1.0	32	.8	242	5.8	3,822	91.6	107	2.6		
FEMALE	4	.4	65	5.8	9	.8	9	.8	87	7.7	1,016	90.2	24	2.1		
MALE	15	.6	84	2.8	33	1.1	23	.8	155	5.1	2,806	92.2	83	2.7		
GRADUATE:																
FULL-TIME	2	.3	7	.9	29	3.8	8	1.1	46	6.1	540	71.6	168	22.3		
FEMALE	0	.0	2	1.8	5	4.4	2	1.8	9	7.9	79	69.3	26	22.8		
MALE	2	.3	5	.8	24	3.8	6	.9	37	5.8	461	72.0	142	22.2		
PART-TIME	0	.0	10	2.7	9	2.4	3	.8	22	5.9	288	77.4	62	16.7		
FEMALE	0	.0	3	4.2	1	1.4	0	.0	4	5.6	57	80.3	10	14.1		
MALE	0	.0	7	2.3	8	2.7	3	1.0	18	6.0	231	76.7	52	17.3		
TOTAL	2	.2	17	1.5	38	3.4	11	1.0	68	6.0	828	73.5	230	20.4		
FEMALE	0	.0	5	2.7	6	3.2	2	1.1	13	7.0	136	73.5	36	19.5		
MALE	2	.2	12	1.3	32	3.4	9	1.0	55	5.8	692	73.5	194	20.6		
PROFESSIONAL:																
FULL-TIME	0	.0	0	.0	0	.0	0	.0	0	.0	0	.0	0	.0		
FEMALE	0	.0	0	.0	0	.0	0	.0	0	.0	0	.0	0	.0		
MALE	0	.0	0	.0	0	.0	0	.0	0	.0	0	.0	0	.0		

NROLLMENT IN INSTITUTIONS OF HIGHER EDUCATION FOR SELECTED MAJOR FIELDS OF STUDY AND LEVEL OF ENROLLMENT
, ETHNICITY, AND SEX: STATE, 1978

PHYSICAL SCIENCES

N INDIAN NATIVE	BLACK NON-HISPANIC		ASIAN OR PACIFIC ISLANDER		HISPANIC		TOTAL MINORITY		WHITE NON-HISPANIC		NON-RESIDENT ALIEN		TOTAL
%	NUMBER	%	NUMBER	%	NUMBER	%	NUMBER	%	NUMBER	%	NUMBER	%	NUMBER
CONTINUED													
.0	0	.0	0	.0	0	.0	0	.0	0	.0	0	.0	0
.0	0	.0	0	.0	0	.0	0	.0	0	.0	0	.0	0
.0	0	.0	0	.0	0	.0	0	.0	0	.0	0	.0	0
.0	0	.0	0	.0	0	.0	0	.0	0	.0	0	.0	0
.0	0	.0	0	.0	0	.0	0	.0	0	.0	0	.0	0
.0	0	.0	0	.0	0	.0	0	.0	0	.0	0	.0	0
.4	107	2.6	62	1.5	30	.7	214	5.2	3,659	88.4	265	6.4	4,138
.4	50	5.0	12	1.2	10	1.0	75	7.4	888	87.9	47	4.7	1,010
.4	57	1.8	50	1.6	20	.6	139	4.4	2,771	88.6	218	7.0	3,128
.5	59	5.1	18	1.6	13	1.1	96	8.3	991	85.5	72	6.2	1,159
.3	20	6.6	3	1.0	1	.3	25	8.3	264	87.4	13	4.3	302
.6	39	4.6	15	1.8	12	1.4	71	8.3	727	84.8	59	6.9	857
.4	166	3.1	80	1.5	43	.8	310	5.9	4,650	87.8	337	6.4	5,297
.3	70	5.3	15	1.1	11	.8	100	7.6	1,152	87.8	60	4.6	1,312
.4	96	2.4	65	1.6	32	.8	210	5.3	3,498	87.8	277	7.0	3,985
.0	3	6.1	1	2.0	0	.0	4	8.2	37	75.5	8	16.3	49
.0	2	14.3	0	.0	0	.0	2	14.3	10	71.4	2	14.3	14
.0	1	2.9	1	2.9	0	.0	2	5.7	27	77.1	6	17.1	35
.4	169	3.2	81	1.5	43	.8	314	5.9	4,687	87.7	345	6.5	5,346
.3	72	5.4	15	1.1	11	.8	102	7.7	1,162	87.6	62	4.7	1,326
.4	97	2.4	66	1.6	32	.8	212	5.3	3,525	87.7	283	7.0	4,020
(38 INSTITUTIONS)													
.2	20	.8	43	1.7	11	.4	78	3.0	2,427	93.8	82	3.2	2,587
.0	5	.8	13	2.2	5	.8	23	3.8	555	92.8	20	3.3	598
.2	15	.8	30	1.5	6	.3	55	2.8	1,872	94.1	62	3.1	1,989
1.9	1	.6	0	.0	1	.6	5	3.2	149	96.1	1	.6	155
.0	0	.0	0	.0	0	.0	0	.0	23	100.0	0	.0	23
2.3	1	.8	0	.0	1	.8	5	3.8	126	95.5	1	.8	132
.3	21	.8	43	1.6	12	.4	83	3.0	2,576	93.9	83	3.0	2,742
.0	5	.8	13	2.1	5	.8	23	3.7	578	93.1	20	3.2	621
.3	16	.8	30	1.4	7	.3	60	2.8	1,998	94.2	63	3.0	2,121
.0	1	.4	3	1.1	0	.0	4	1.5	211	79.6	50	18.9	265
.0	0	.0	0	.0	0	.0	0	.0	36	80.0	9	20.0	45
.0	1	.5	3	1.4	0	.0	4	1.8	175	79.5	41	18.6	220
.0	0	.0	1	16.7	0	.0	1	16.7	4	66.7	1	16.7	6
.0	0	.0	0	.0	0	.0	0	.0	0	.0	0	.0	0
.0	0	.0	1	16.7	0	.0	1	16.7	4	66.7	1	16.7	6
.0	1	.4	4	1.5	0	.0	5	1.8	215	79.3	51	18.8	271
.0	0	.0	0	.0	0	.0	0	.0	36	80.0	9	20.0	45
.0	1	.4	4	1.8	0	.0	5	2.2	179	79.2	42	18.6	226
.0	0	.0	0	.0	0	.0	0	.0	0	.0	0	.0	0
.0	0	.0	0	.0	0	.0	0	.0	0	.0	0	.0	0
.0	0	.0	0	.0	0	.0	0	.0	0	.0	0	.0	0
.0	0	.0	0	.0	0	.0	0	.0	0	.0	0	.0	0
.0	0	.0	0	.0	0	.0	0	.0	0	.0	0	.0	0
.0	0	.0	0	.0	0	.0	0	.0	0	.0	0	.0	0
.0	0	.0	0	.0	0	.0	0	.0	0	.0	0	.0	0
.0	0	.0	0	.0	0	.0	0	.0	0	.0	0	.0	0
.0	0	.0	0	.0	0	.0	0	.0	0	.0	0	.0	0
.1	21	.7	46	1.6	11	.4	82	2.9	2,638	92.5	132	4.6	2,852
.0	5	.8	13	2.0	5	.8	23	3.6	591	91.9	29	4.5	643
.2	16	.7	33	1.5	6	.3	59	2.7	2,047	92.7	103	4.7	2,209
1.9	1	.6	1	.6	1	.6	6	3.7	153	95.0	2	1.2	161
.0	0	.0	0	.0	0	.0	0	.0	23	100.0	0	.0	23
2.2	1	.7	1	.7	1	.7	6	4.3	130	94.2	2	1.4	138
.2	22	.7	47	1.6	12	.4	88	2.9	2,791	92.6	134	4.4	3,013
.0	5	.8	13	2.0	5	.8	23	3.5	614	92.2	29	4.4	666
.3	17	.7	34	1.4	7	.3	65	2.8	2,177	92.8	105	4.5	2,347
.0	1	3.1	0	.0	0	.0	1	3.1	29	90.6	2	6.3	32
.0	0	.0	0	.0	0	.0	0	.0	6	100.0	0	.0	6
.0	1	3.8	0	.0	0	.0	1	3.8	23	88.5	2	7.7	26
.2	23	.8	47	1.5	12	.4	89	2.9	2,820	92.6	136	4.5	3,045
.0	5	.7	13	1.9	5	.7	23	3.4	620	92.3	29	4.3	672
.3	18	.8	34	1.4	7	.3	66	2.8	2,200	92.7	107	4.5	2,373

TABLE 17 - TOTAL ENROLLMENT IN INSTITUTIONS OF HIGHER EDUCATION FOR SELECTED MAJOR FIELDS OF STUDY AND LEVEL OF ENROLLMENT BY RACE, ETHNICITY, AND SEX: STATE: 1978

MAJOR FIELD 1900 - PHYSICAL SCIENCES

	AMERICAN INDIAN ALASKAN NATIVE		BLACK NON-HISPANIC		ASIAN OR PACIFIC ISLANDER		HISPANIC		TOTAL MINORITY		WHITE NON-HISPANIC		NON-RESIDENT ALIEN		T(
	NUMBER	%	NUMBER	%	NUMBER	%	NUMBER	%	NUMBER	%	NUMBER	%	NUMBER	%	N(
MISSISSIPPI (26 INSTITUTIONS)															
UNDERGRADUATES:															
FULL-TIME	2	.2	278	31.4	7	.8	6	.7	293	33.1	578	65.3	14	1.6	
FEMALE	0	.0	116	43.9	3	1.1	0	.0	119	45.1	142	53.8	3	1.1	
MALE	2	.3	162	26.1	4	.6	6	1.0	174	28.0	436	70.2	11	1.8	
PART-TIME	1	1.2	13	16.0	0	.0	0	.0	14	17.3	65	80.2	2	2.5	
FEMALE	0	.0	4	16.7	0	.0	0	.0	4	16.7	19	79.2	1	4.2	
MALE	1	1.8	9	15.0	0	.0	0	.0	10	17.5	46	80.7	1	1.8	
TOTAL	3	.3	291	30.1	7	.7	6	.6	307	31.8	643	66.6	16	1.7	
FEMALE	0	.0	120	41.7	3	1.0	0	.0	123	42.7	161	55.9	4	1.4	
MALE	3	.4	171	25.2	4	.6	6	.9	184	27.1	482	71.1	12	1.8	
GRADUATE:															
FULL-TIME	0	.0	14	14.1	4	4.0	0	.0	18	18.2	72	72.7	9	9.1	
FEMALE	0	.0	4	25.0	0	.0	0	.0	4	25.0	9	56.3	3	18.8	
MALE	0	.0	10	12.0	4	4.8	0	.0	14	16.9	63	75.9	6	7.2	
PART-TIME	0	.0	4	9.8	1	2.4	0	.0	5	12.2	30	73.2	6	14.6	
FEMALE	0	.0	0	.0	0	.0	0	.0	0	.0	8	80.0	2	20.0	
MALE	0	.0	4	12.9	1	3.2	0	.0	5	16.1	22	71.0	4	12.9	
TOTAL	0	.0	18	12.9	5	3.6	0	.0	23	16.4	102	72.9	15	10.7	
FEMALE	0	.0	4	15.4	0	.0	0	.0	4	15.4	17	65.4	5	19.2	
MALE	0	.0	14	12.3	5	4.4	0	.0	19	16.7	85	74.6	10	8.8	
PROFESSIONAL:															
FULL-TIME	0	.0	0	.0	0	.0	0	.0	0	.0	0	.0	0	.0	
FEMALE	0	.0	0	.0	0	.0	0	.0	0	.0	0	.0	0	.0	
MALE	0	.0	0	.0	0	.0	0	.0	0	.0	0	.0	0	.0	
PART-TIME	0	.0	0	.0	0	.0	0	.0	0	.0	0	.0	0	.0	
FEMALE	0	.0	0	.0	0	.0	0	.0	0	.0	0	.0	0	.0	
MALE	0	.0	0	.0	0	.0	0	.0	0	.0	0	.0	0	.0	
TOTAL	0	.0	0	.0	0	.0	0	.0	0	.0	0	.0	0	.0	
FEMALE	0	.0	0	.0	0	.0	0	.0	0	.0	0	.0	0	.0	
MALE	0	.0	0	.0	0	.0	0	.0	0	.0	0	.0	0	.0	
UND+GRAD+PROF:															
FULL-TIME	2	.2	292	29.7	11	1.1	6	.6	311	31.6	650	66.1	23	2.3	
FEMALE	0	.0	120	42.9	3	1.1	0	.0	123	43.9	151	53.9	6	2.1	
MALE	2	.3	172	24.4	8	1.1	6	.9	188	26.7	499	70.9	17	2.4	
PART-TIME	1	.8	17	13.9	1	.8	0	.0	19	15.6	95	77.9	8	6.6	
FEMALE	0	.0	4	11.8	0	.0	0	.0	4	11.8	27	79.4	3	8.8	
MALE	1	1.1	13	14.8	1	1.1	0	.0	15	17.0	68	77.3	5	5.7	
TOTAL	3	.3	309	27.9	12	1.1	6	.5	330	29.8	745	67.4	31	2.8	
FEMALE	0	.0	124	39.5	3	1.0	0	.0	127	40.4	178	56.7	9	2.9	
MALE	3	.4	185	23.4	9	1.1	6	.8	203	25.6	567	71.6	22	2.8	
UNCLASSIFIED:															
TOTAL	0	.0	0	.0	0	.0	1	1.8	1	1.8	47	85.5	7	12.7	
FEMALE	0	.0	0	.0	0	.0	0	.0	0	.0	9	100.0	0	.0	
MALE	0	.0	0	.0	0	.0	1	2.2	1	2.2	38	82.6	7	15.2	
TOTAL ENROLLMENT:															
TOTAL	3	.3	309	26.6	12	1.0	7	.6	331	28.5	792	68.2	38	3.3	
FEMALE	0	.0	124	38.4	3	.9	0	.0	127	39.3	187	57.9	9	2.8	
MALE	3	.4	185	22.1	9	1.1	7	.8	204	24.3	605	72.2	29	3.5	
MISSOURI (31 INSTITUTIONS)															
UNDERGRADUATES:															
FULL-TIME	5	.3	42	2.6	19	1.2	12	.8	78	4.9	1,471	92.2	47	2.9	
FEMALE	0	.0	12	3.7	3	.9	0	.0	15	4.6	305	93.3	7	2.1	
MALE	5	.4	30	2.4	16	1.3	12	.9	63	5.0	1,166	91.9	40	3.2	
PART-TIME	1	.4	16	5.7	9	5.1	4	1.4	25	8.9	253	90.0	3	1.1	
FEMALE	1	1.7	6	10.0	2	3.3	0	.0	9	15.0	51	85.0	0	.0	
MALE	0	.0	10	4.5	2	.9	4	1.8	16	7.2	202	91.4	3	1.4	
TOTAL	6	.3	58	3.1	23	1.2	16	.9	103	5.5	1,724	91.8	50	2.7	
FEMALE	1	.3	18	4.7	5	1.3	0	.0	24	6.2	356	92.0	7	1.8	
MALE	5	.3	40	2.7	18	1.2	16	1.1	79	5.3	1,368	91.8	43	2.9	
GRADUATE:															
FULL-TIME	0	.0	1	.4	16	6.3	4	1.6	21	8.3	173	68.4	59	23.3	
FEMALE	0	.0	0	.0	5	12.8	0	.0	5	12.8	27	69.2	7	17.9	
MALE	0	.0	1	.5	11	5.1	4	1.9	16	7.5	146	68.2	52	24.3	
PART-TIME	0	.0	3	1.7	9	5.1	1	.6	13	7.3	145	81.9	19	10.7	
FEMALE	0	.0	1	2.9	3	8.8	0	.0	4	11.8	25	73.5	5	14.7	
MALE	0	.0	2	1.4	6	4.2	1	.7	9	6.3	120	83.9	14	9.8	
TOTAL	0	.0	4	.9	25	5.8	5	1.2	34	7.9	318	74.0	78	18.1	
FEMALE	0	.0	1	1.4	8	11.0	0	.0	9	12.3	52	71.2	12	16.4	
MALE	0	.0	3	.8	17	4.8	5	1.4	25	7.0	266	74.5	66	18.5	
PROFESSIONAL:															
FULL-TIME	0	.0	0	.0	0	.0	0	.0	0	.0	0	.0	0	.0	
FEMALE	0	.0	0	.0	0	.0	0	.0	0	.0	0	.0	0	.0	
MALE	0	.0	0	.0	0	.0	0	.0	0	.0	0	.0	0	.0	

- PHYSICAL SCIENCES

CAN INDIAN AN NATIVE		BLACK NON-HISPANIC		ASIAN OR PACIFIC ISLANDER		HISPANIC		TOTAL MINORITY		WHITE NON-HISPANIC		NON-RESIDENT ALIEN		TOTAL
ER	%	NUMBER	%	NUMBER	%	NUMBER	%	NUMBER	%	NUMBER	%	NUMBER	%	NUMBER
CONTINUED														
0	.0	0	.0	0	.0	0	.0	0	.0	0	.0	0	.0	0
0	.0	0	.0	0	.0	0	.0	0	.0	0	.0	0	.0	0
0	.0	0	.0	0	.0	0	.0	0	.0	0	.0	0	.0	0
0	.0	0	.0	0	.0	0	.0	0	.0	0	.0	0	.0	0
0	.0	0	.0	0	.0	0	.0	0	.0	0	.0	0	.0	0
0	.0	0	.0	0	.0	0	.0	0	.0	0	.0	0	.0	0
5	.3	43	2.3	35	1.9	16	.9	99	5.4	1,644	88.9	106	5.7	1,849
0	.0	12	3.3	8	2.2	0	.0	20	5.5	332	90.7	14	3.8	366
5	.3	31	2.1	27	1.8	16	1.1	79	5.3	1,312	88.5	92	6.2	1,483
1	.2	19	4.1	13	2.8	5	1.1	38	8.3	398	86.9	22	4.8	458
1	1.1	7	7.4	5	5.3	0	.0	13	13.8	76	80.9	5	5.3	94
0	.0	12	3.3	8	2.2	5	1.4	25	6.9	322	88.5	17	4.7	364
6	.3	62	2.7	48	2.1	21	.9	137	5.9	2,042	88.5	128	5.5	2,307
1	.2	19	4.1	13	2.8	0	.0	33	7.2	408	88.7	19	4.1	460
5	.3	43	2.3	35	1.9	21	1.1	104	5.6	1,634	88.5	109	5.9	1,847
0	.0	0	.0	1	4.5	0	.0	1	4.5	20	90.9	1	4.5	22
0	.0	0	.0	1	12.5	0	.0	1	12.5	7	87.5	0	.0	8
0	.0	0	.0	0	.0	0	.0	0	.0	13	92.9	1	7.1	14
6	.3	62	2.7	49	2.1	21	.9	138	5.9	2,062	88.5	129	5.5	2,329
1	.2	19	4.1	14	3.0	0	.0	34	7.3	415	88.7	19	4.1	468
5	.3	43	2.3	35	1.9	21	1.1	104	5.6	1,647	88.5	110	5.9	1,861
(5 INSTITUTIONS)														
3	.5	0	.0	2	.4	4	.7	9	1.6	545	97.7	4	.7	558
1	.5	0	.0	1	.6	1	.5	3	1.7	176	98.3	0	.0	179
2	.5	0	.0	1	.3	3	.8	6	1.6	369	97.4	4	1.1	379
0	.0	0	.0	0	.0	0	.0	0	.0	53	98.1	1	1.9	54
0	.0	0	.0	0	.0	0	.0	0	.0	13	100.0	0	.0	13
0	.0	0	.0	0	.0	0	.0	0	.0	40	97.6	1	2.4	41
3	.5	0	.0	2	.3	4	.7	9	1.5	598	97.7	5	.8	612
1	.5	0	.0	1	.5	1	.5	3	1.6	189	98.4	0	.0	192
2	.5	0	.0	1	.2	3	.7	6	1.4	409	97.4	5	1.2	420
0	.0	0	.0	0	.0	0	.0	0	.0	55	98.2	1	1.8	56
0	.0	0	.0	0	.0	0	.0	0	.0	6	100.0	0	.0	6
0	.0	0	.0	0	.0	0	.0	0	.0	49	98.0	1	2.0	50
1	1.4	0	.0	2	2.9	0	.0	3	4.3	66	95.7	0	.0	69
1	8.3	0	.0	0	.0	0	.0	1	8.3	11	91.7	0	.0	12
0	.0	0	.0	2	3.5	0	.0	2	3.5	55	96.5	0	.0	57
1	.8	0	.0	2	1.6	0	.0	3	2.4	121	96.8	1	.8	125
1	5.6	0	.0	0	.0	0	.0	1	5.6	17	94.4	0	.0	18
0	.0	0	.0	2	1.9	0	.0	2	1.9	104	97.2	1	.9	107
0	.0	0	.0	0	.0	0	.0	0	.0	0	.0	0	.0	0
0	.0	0	.0	0	.0	0	.0	0	.0	0	.0	0	.0	0
0	.0	0	.0	0	.0	0	.0	0	.0	0	.0	0	.0	0
0	.0	0	.0	0	.0	0	.0	0	.0	0	.0	0	.0	0
0	.0	0	.0	0	.0	0	.0	0	.0	0	.0	0	.0	0
0	.0	0	.0	0	.0	0	.0	0	.0	0	.0	0	.0	0
0	.0	0	.0	0	.0	0	.0	0	.0	0	.0	0	.0	0
0	.0	0	.0	0	.0	0	.0	0	.0	0	.0	0	.0	0
0	.0	0	.0	0	.0	0	.0	0	.0	0	.0	0	.0	0
3	.5	0	.0	2	.3	4	.7	9	1.5	600	97.7	5	.8	614
1	.5	0	.0	1	.5	1	.5	3	1.6	182	98.4	0	.0	185
2	.5	0	.0	1	.2	3	.7	6	1.4	418	97.4	5	1.2	429
1	.8	0	.0	2	1.6	0	.0	3	2.4	119	96.7	1	.8	123
1	4.0	0	.0	0	.0	0	.0	1	4.0	24	96.0	0	.0	25
0	.0	0	.0	2	2.0	0	.0	2	2.0	95	96.9	1	1.0	98
4	.5	0	.0	4	.5	4	.5	12	1.6	719	97.6	6	.8	737
2	1.0	0	.0	1	.5	1	.5	4	1.9	206	98.1	0	.0	210
2	.4	0	.0	3	.6	3	.6	8	1.5	513	97.3	6	1.1	527
0	.0	0	.0	0	.0	0	.0	0	.0	1	100.0	0	.0	1
0	.0	0	.0	0	.0	0	.0	0	.0	1	100.0	0	.0	1
0	.0	0	.0	0	.0	0	.0	0	.0	0	.0	0	.0	0
4	.5	0	.0	4	.5	4	.5	12	1.6	720	97.6	6	.8	738
2	.9	0	.0	1	.5	1	.5	4	1.9	207	98.1	0	.0	211
2	.4	0	.0	3	.6	3	.6	8	1.5	513	97.3	6	1.1	527

MAJOR FIELD 1900 - PHYSICAL SCIENCES

	AMERICAN INDIAN ALASKAN NATIVE		BLACK NON-HISPANIC		ASIAN OR PACIFIC ISLANDER		HISPANIC		TOTAL MINORITY		WHITE NON-HISPANIC		NON-RESIDENT ALIEN		TOTAL
	NUMBER	%	NUMBER	%	NUMBER	%	NUMBER	%	NUMBER	%	NUMBER	%	NUMBER	%	NUM
NEBRASKA (19 INSTITUTIONS)															
UNDERGRADUATES:															
FULL-TIME	0	.0	13	1.8	17	2.4	1	.1	31	4.3	664	92.7	21	2.9	
FEMALE	0	.0	6	4.0	4	2.6	0	.0	10	6.6	137	90.7	4	2.6	
MALE	0	.0	7	1.2	13	2.3	1	.2	21	3.7	527	93.3	17	3.0	
PART-TIME	0	.0	1	1.3	0	.0	1	1.3	2	2.6	75	97.4	0	.0	
FEMALE	0	.0	1	3.8	0	.0	1	3.8	2	7.7	24	92.3	0	.0	
MALE	0	.0	0	.0	0	.0	0	.0	0	.0	51	100.0	0	.0	
TOTAL	0	.0	14	1.8	17	2.1	2	.3	33	4.2	739	93.2	21	2.6	
FEMALE	0	.0	7	4.0	4	2.3	1	.6	12	6.8	161	91.0	4	2.3	
MALE	0	.0	7	1.1	13	2.1	1	.2	21	3.4	578	93.8	17	2.8	
GRADUATE:															
FULL-TIME	0	.0	1	.5	4	2.2	1	.5	6	3.3	143	78.6	33	18.1	
FEMALE	0	.0	0	.0	2	10.0	0	.0	2	10.0	18	90.0	0	.0	
MALE	0	.0	1	.6	2	1.2	1	.6	4	2.5	125	77.2	33	20.4	
PART-TIME	0	.0	0	.0	0	.0	1	1.3	1	1.3	68	86.1	10	12.7	
FEMALE	0	.0	0	.0	0	.0	0	.0	0	.0	18	100.0	0	.0	
MALE	0	.0	0	.0	0	.0	1	1.6	1	1.6	50	82.0	10	16.4	
TOTAL	0	.0	1	.4	4	1.5	2	.8	7	2.7	211	80.8	43	16.5	
FEMALE	0	.0	0	.0	2	5.3	0	.0	2	5.3	36	94.7	0	.0	
MALE	0	.0	1	.4	2	.9	2	.9	5	2.2	175	78.5	43	19.3	
PROFESSIONAL:															
FULL-TIME	0	.0	0	.0	0	.0	0	.0	0	.0	0	.0	0	.0	
FEMALE	0	.0	0	.0	0	.0	0	.0	0	.0	0	.0	0	.0	
MALE	0	.0	0	.0	0	.0	0	.0	0	.0	0	.0	0	.0	
PART-TIME	0	.0	0	.0	0	.0	0	.0	0	.0	0	.0	0	.0	
FEMALE	0	.0	0	.0	0	.0	0	.0	0	.0	0	.0	0	.0	
MALE	0	.0	0	.0	0	.0	0	.0	0	.0	0	.0	0	.0	
TOTAL	0	.0	0	.0	0	.0	0	.0	0	.0	0	.0	0	.0	
FEMALE	0	.0	0	.0	0	.0	0	.0	0	.0	0	.0	0	.0	
MALE	0	.0	0	.0	0	.0	0	.0	0	.0	0	.0	0	.0	
UNG+GRAD+PROF:															
FULL-TIME	0	.0	14	1.6	21	2.3	2	.2	37	4.1	807	89.9	54	6.0	
FEMALE	0	.0	6	3.5	6	3.5	0	.0	12	7.0	155	90.6	4	2.3	
MALE	0	.0	8	1.1	15	2.1	2	.3	25	3.4	652	89.7	50	6.9	
PART-TIME	0	.0	1	.6	0	.0	2	1.3	3	1.9	143	91.7	10	6.4	
FEMALE	0	.0	1	2.3	0	.0	1	2.3	2	4.5	42	95.5	0	.0	
MALE	0	.0	0	.0	0	.0	1	.9	1	.9	101	90.2	10	8.9	
TOTAL	0	.0	15	1.4	21	2.0	4	.4	40	3.8	950	90.1	64	6.1	1
FEMALE	0	.0	7	3.3	6	2.8	1	.5	14	6.5	197	91.6	4	1.9	
MALE	0	.0	8	1.0	15	1.8	3	.4	26	3.1	753	89.7	60	7.2	
UNCLASSIFIED:															
TOTAL	0	.0	0	.0	0	.0	0	.0	0	.0	4	100.0	0	.0	
FEMALE	0	.0	0	.0	0	.0	0	.0	0	.0	1	100.0	0	.0	
MALE	0	.0	0	.0	0	.0	0	.0	0	.0	3	100.0	0	.0	
TOTAL ENROLLMENT:															
TOTAL	0	.0	15	1.4	21	2.0	4	.4	40	3.8	954	90.2	64	6.0	1
FEMALE	0	.0	7	3.2	6	2.8	1	.5	14	6.5	198	91.7	4	1.9	
MALE	0	.0	8	1.0	15	1.8	3	.4	26	3.1	756	89.8	60	7.1	
NEVADA (3 INSTITUTIONS)															
UNDERGRADUATES:															
FULL-TIME	0	.0	3	1.2	4	1.5	6	2.3	13	5.0	228	88.0	18	6.9	
FEMALE	0	.0	1	1.7	0	.0	1	1.7	2	3.4	53	89.8	4	6.8	
MALE	0	.0	2	1.0	4	2.0	5	2.5	11	5.5	175	87.5	14	7.0	
PART-TIME	1	.9	3	2.6	2	1.7	2	1.7	8	7.0	102	88.7	5	4.3	
FEMALE	0	.0	1	2.9	2	5.7	0	.0	3	8.6	29	82.9	3	8.6	
MALE	1	1.3	2	2.5	0	.0	2	2.5	5	6.3	73	91.3	2	2.5	
TOTAL	1	.3	6	1.6	6	1.6	8	2.1	21	5.6	330	88.2	23	6.1	
FEMALE	0	.0	2	2.1	2	2.1	1	1.1	5	5.3	82	87.2	7	7.4	
MALE	1	.4	4	1.4	4	1.4	7	2.5	16	5.7	248	88.6	16	5.7	
GRADUATE:															
FULL-TIME	0	.0	0	.0	1	2.7	0	.0	1	2.7	30	81.1	6	16.2	
FEMALE	0	.0	0	.0	0	.0	0	.0	0	.0	4	66.7	2	33.3	
MALE	0	.0	0	.0	1	3.2	0	.0	1	3.2	26	83.9	4	12.9	
PART-TIME	1	1.5	1	1.5	5	7.5	1	1.5	8	11.9	57	85.1	2	3.0	
FEMALE	0	.0	0	.0	1	12.5	0	.0	1	12.5	7	87.5	0	.0	
MALE	1	1.7	1	1.7	4	6.8	1	1.7	7	11.9	50	84.7	2	3.4	
TOTAL	1	1.0	1	1.0	6	5.8	1	1.0	9	8.7	87	83.7	8	7.7	
FEMALE	0	.0	0	.0	1	7.1	0	.0	1	7.1	11	78.6	2	14.3	
MALE	1	1.1	1	1.1	5	5.6	1	1.1	8	8.9	76	84.4	6	6.7	
PROFESSIONAL:															
FULL-TIME	0	.0	0	.0	0	.0	0	.0	0	.0	0	.0	0	.0	
FEMALE	0	.0	0	.0	0	.0	0	.0	0	.0	0	.0	0	.0	
MALE	0	.0	0	.0	0	.0	0	.0	0	.0	0	.0	0	.0	

- PHYSICAL SCIENCES

AMERICAN INDIAN NATIVE		BLACK NON-HISPANIC		ASIAN OR PACIFIC ISLANDER		HISPANIC		TOTAL MINORITY		WHITE NON-HISPANIC		NON-RESIDENT ALIEN		TOTAL
R	%	NUMBER	%	NUMBER	%	NUMBER	%	NUMBER	%	NUMBER	%	NUMBER	%	NUMBER

CONTINUED

0	.0	0	.0	0	.0	0	.0	0	.0	0	.0	0	.0	0
0	.0	0	.0	0	.0	0	.0	0	.0	0	.0	0	.0	0
0	.0	0	.0	0	.0	0	.0	0	.0	0	.0	0	.0	0
0	.0	0	.0	0	.0	0	.0	0	.0	0	.0	0	.0	0
0	.0	0	.0	0	.0	0	.0	0	.0	0	.0	0	.0	0
0	.0	0	.0	0	.0	0	.0	0	.0	0	.0	0	.0	0
0	.0	3	1.0	5	1.7	6	2.0	14	4.7	258	87.2	24	8.1	296
0	.0	1	1.5	0	.0	1	1.5	2	3.1	57	87.7	6	9.2	65
0	.0	2	.9	5	2.2	5	2.2	12	5.2	201	87.0	18	7.8	231
2	1.1	4	2.2	7	3.8	3	1.6	16	8.8	159	87.4	7	3.8	182
0	.0	1	2.3	3	7.0	0	.0	4	9.3	36	83.7	3	7.0	43
2	1.4	3	2.2	4	2.9	3	2.2	12	8.6	123	88.5	4	2.9	139
2	.4	7	1.5	12	2.5	9	1.9	30	6.3	417	87.2	31	6.5	478
0	.0	2	1.9	3	2.8	1	.9	6	5.6	93	86.1	9	8.3	108
2	.5	5	1.4	9	2.4	8	2.2	24	6.5	324	87.6	22	5.9	370
0	.0	1	3.0	1	3.0	0	.0	2	6.1	31	93.9	0	.0	33
0	.0	0	.0	0	.0	0	.0	0	.0	16	100.0	0	.0	16
0	.0	1	5.9	1	5.9	0	.0	2	11.8	15	88.2	0	.0	17
2	.4	8	1.6	13	2.5	9	1.8	32	6.3	448	87.7	31	6.1	511
0	.0	2	1.6	3	2.4	1	.8	6	4.8	109	87.9	9	7.3	124
2	.5	6	1.6	10	2.6	8	2.1	26	6.7	339	87.6	22	5.7	387

(7 INSTITUTIONS)

0	.0	3	.6	3	.6	2	.4	8	1.5	516	97.4	6	1.1	530
0	.0	0	.0	0	.0	0	.0	0	.0	126	99.2	1	.4	127
0	.0	3	.7	3	.7	2	.5	8	2.0	390	96.8	5	1.2	403
0	.0	0	.0	0	.0	0	.0	0	.0	20	95.2	1	4.8	21
0	.0	0	.0	0	.0	0	.0	0	.0	7	100.0	0	.0	7
0	.0	0	.0	0	.0	0	.0	0	.0	13	92.9	1	7.1	14
0	.0	3	.5	3	.5	2	.4	8	1.5	536	97.3	7	1.3	551
0	.0	0	.0	0	.0	0	.0	0	.0	133	99.3	1	.7	134
0	.0	3	.7	3	.7	2	.5	8	1.9	403	96.6	6	1.4	417
0	.0	1	.9	3	2.6	0	.0	4	3.4	113	96.6	0	.0	117
0	.0	0	.0	1	3.8	0	.0	1	3.8	25	96.2	0	.0	26
0	.0	1	1.1	2	2.2	0	.0	3	3.3	88	96.7	0	.0	91
0	.0	0	.0	0	.0	1	7.1	1	7.1	12	85.7	1	7.1	14
0	.0	0	.0	0	.0	1	25.0	1	25.0	2	50.0	1	25.0	4
0	.0	0	.0	0	.0	0	.0	0	.0	10	100.0	0	.0	10
0	.0	1	.8	3	2.3	1	.8	5	3.8	125	95.4	1	.8	131
0	.0	0	.0	1	3.3	1	3.3	2	6.7	27	90.0	1	3.3	30
0	.0	1	1.0	2	2.0	0	.0	3	3.0	98	97.0	0	.0	101
0	.0	0	.0	0	.0	0	.0	0	.0	0	.0	0	.0	0
0	.0	0	.0	0	.0	0	.0	0	.0	0	.0	0	.0	0
0	.0	0	.0	0	.0	0	.0	0	.0	0	.0	0	.0	0
0	.0	0	.0	0	.0	0	.0	0	.0	0	.0	0	.0	0
0	.0	0	.0	0	.0	0	.0	0	.0	0	.0	0	.0	0
0	.0	0	.0	0	.0	0	.0	0	.0	0	.0	0	.0	0
0	.0	0	.0	0	.0	0	.0	0	.0	0	.0	0	.0	0
0	.0	0	.0	0	.0	0	.0	0	.0	0	.0	0	.0	0
0	.0	0	.0	0	.0	0	.0	0	.0	0	.0	0	.0	0
0	.0	4	.6	6	.9	2	.3	12	1.9	629	97.2	6	.9	647
0	.0	0	.0	1	.7	0	.0	1	.7	151	98.7	1	.7	153
0	.0	4	.8	5	1.0	2	.4	11	2.2	478	96.8	5	1.0	494
0	.0	0	.0	0	.0	1	2.9	1	2.9	32	91.4	2	5.7	35
0	.0	0	.0	0	.0	1	9.1	1	9.1	9	81.8	1	9.1	11
0	.0	0	.0	0	.0	0	.0	0	.0	23	95.8	1	4.2	24
0	.0	4	.6	6	.9	3	.4	13	1.9	661	96.9	8	1.2	682
0	.0	0	.0	1	.6	1	.6	2	1.2	160	97.6	2	1.2	164
0	.0	4	.8	5	1.0	2	.4	11	2.1	501	96.7	6	1.2	518
0	.0	0	.0	0	.0	0	.0	0	.0	0	.0	0	.0	0
0	.0	0	.0	0	.0	0	.0	0	.0	0	.0	0	.0	0
0	.0	0	.0	0	.0	0	.0	0	.0	0	.0	0	.0	0
0	.0	4	.6	6	.9	3	.4	13	1.9	661	96.9	8	1.2	682
0	.0	0	.0	1	.6	1	.6	2	1.2	160	97.6	2	1.2	164
0	.0	4	.8	5	1.0	2	.4	11	2.1	501	96.7	6	1.2	518

TABLE 17 - TOTAL ENROLLMENT IN INSTITUTIONS OF HIGHER EDUCATION FOR SELECTED MAJOR FIELDS OF STUDY AND LEVEL OF ENROLLMENT
BY RACE, ETHNICITY, AND SEX: STATE, 1978

MAJOR FIELD 1900 - PHYSICAL SCIENCES

	AMERICAN INDIAN ALASKAN NATIVE		BLACK NON-HISPANIC		ASIAN OR PACIFIC ISLANDER		HISPANIC		TOTAL MINORITY		WHITE NON-HISPANIC		NON-RESIDENT ALIEN		T
	NUMBER	%	NUMBER	%	NUMBER	%	NUMBER	%	NUMBER	%	NUMBER	%	NUMBER	%	N
NEW JERSEY (31 INSTITUTIONS)															
UNDERGRADUATES:															
FULL-TIME	2	.1	90	5.0	34	1.9	54	3.0	180	10.0	1,589	88.4	29	1.6	
FEMALE	0	.0	52	9.2	17	3.0	21	3.7	90	16.0	466	82.8	7	1.2	
MALE	2	.2	38	3.1	17	1.4	33	2.7	90	7.3	1,123	90.9	22	1.8	
PART-TIME	0	.0	38	5.6	8	1.2	15	2.2	61	9.0	615	90.4	4	.6	
FEMALE	0	.0	16	5.1	7	2.2	5	1.6	28	8.9	287	91.1	0	.0	
MALE	0	.0	22	6.0	1	.3	10	2.7	33	9.0	328	89.9	4	1.1	
TOTAL	2	.1	128	5.2	42	1.7	69	2.8	241	9.7	2,204	88.9	33	1.3	
FEMALE	0	.0	68	7.7	24	2.7	26	3.0	118	13.4	753	85.8	7	.8	
MALE	2	.1	60	3.8	18	1.1	43	2.7	123	7.7	1,451	90.7	26	1.6	
GRADUATE:															
FULL-TIME	0	.0	4	1.0	13	3.2	3	.7	20	4.9	323	79.0	66	16.1	
FEMALE	0	.0	0	.0	4	6.6	2	3.3	6	9.8	50	82.0	5	8.2	
MALE	0	.0	4	1.1	9	2.6	1	.3	14	4.0	273	78.4	61	17.5	
PART-TIME	0	.0	3	1.0	11	3.8	5	1.7	19	6.5	270	92.2	4	1.4	
FEMALE	0	.0	2	2.9	0	.0	0	.0	2	2.9	66	94.3	2	2.9	
MALE	0	.0	1	.4	11	4.9	5	2.2	17	7.6	204	91.5	2	.9	
TOTAL	0	.0	7	1.0	24	3.4	8	1.1	39	5.6	593	84.5	70	10.0	
FEMALE	0	.0	2	1.5	4	3.1	2	1.5	8	6.1	116	88.5	7	5.3	
MALE	0	.0	5	.9	20	3.5	6	1.1	31	5.4	477	83.5	63	11.0	
PROFESSIONAL:															
FULL-TIME	0	.0	0	.0	0	.0	0	.0	0	.0	0	.0	0	.0	
FEMALE	0	.0	0	.0	0	.0	0	.0	0	.0	0	.0	0	.0	
MALE	0	.0	0	.0	0	.0	0	.0	0	.0	0	.0	0	.0	
PART-TIME	0	.0	0	.0	0	.0	0	.0	0	.0	0	.0	0	.0	
FEMALE	0	.0	0	.0	0	.0	0	.0	0	.0	0	.0	0	.0	
MALE	0	.0	0	.0	0	.0	0	.0	0	.0	0	.0	0	.0	
TOTAL	0	.0	0	.0	0	.0	0	.0	0	.0	0	.0	0	.0	
FEMALE	0	.0	0	.0	0	.0	0	.0	0	.0	0	.0	0	.0	
MALE	0	.0	0	.0	0	.0	0	.0	0	.0	0	.0	0	.0	
UNC+GRAD+PROF:															
FULL-TIME	2	.1	94	4.3	47	2.1	57	2.6	200	9.1	1,912	86.6	95	4.3	
FEMALE	0	.0	52	8.3	21	3.4	23	3.7	96	15.4	516	82.7	12	1.9	
MALE	2	.1	42	2.7	26	1.4	34	2.1	104	6.6	1,396	88.2	83	5.2	
PART-TIME	0	.0	41	4.2	19	2.0	20	2.1	80	8.2	885	91.0	8	.8	
FEMALE	0	.0	18	4.7	7	1.8	5	1.3	30	7.8	393	91.7	2	.5	
MALE	0	.0	23	3.9	12	2.0	15	2.6	50	8.5	532	90.5	6	1.0	
TOTAL	2	.1	135	4.2	66	2.1	77	2.4	280	8.8	2,797	88.0	103	3.2	
FEMALE	0	.0	70	6.9	28	2.8	28	2.8	126	12.5	869	86.1	14	1.4	
MALE	2	.1	65	3.0	38	1.8	49	2.3	154	7.1	1,928	88.8	89	4.1	
UNCLASSIFIED:															
TOTAL	0	.0	18	5.3	14	4.1	7	2.0	39	11.4	298	87.1	5	1.5	
FEMALE	0	.0	10	10.4	5	5.2	3	3.1	18	18.8	78	81.3	0	.0	
MALE	0	.0	8	3.3	9	3.7	4	1.6	21	8.5	220	89.4	5	2.0	
TOTAL ENROLLMENT:															
TOTAL	2	.1	153	4.3	80	2.3	84	2.4	319	9.1	3,095	87.9	108	3.1	
FEMALE	0	.0	80	7.2	33	3.0	31	2.8	144	13.0	947	85.7	14	1.3	
MALE	2	.1	73	3.0	47	1.9	53	2.2	175	7.2	2,148	88.9	94	3.9	
NEW MEXICO (11 INSTITUTIONS)															
UNDERGRADUATES:															
FULL-TIME	10	1.3	10	1.3	8	1.1	104	13.8	132	17.5	617	81.6	7	.9	
FEMALE	3	1.7	6	3.5	1	.6	26	15.0	36	20.8	135	78.0	2	1.2	
MALE	7	1.2	4	.7	7	1.2	78	13.4	96	16.5	482	82.7	5	.9	
PART-TIME	4	4.1	2	2.0	0	.0	13	13.3	19	19.4	79	80.6	0	.0	
FEMALE	0	.0	0	.0	0	.0	3	12.5	3	12.5	21	87.5	0	.0	
MALE	4	5.4	2	2.7	0	.0	10	13.5	16	21.6	58	78.4	0	.0	
TOTAL	14	1.6	12	1.4	8	.9	117	13.7	151	17.7	696	81.5	7	.8	
FEMALE	3	1.5	6	3.0	1	.5	29	14.7	39	19.8	156	79.2	2	1.0	
MALE	11	1.7	6	.9	7	1.1	88	13.4	112	17.0	540	82.2	5	.8	
GRADUATE:															
FULL-TIME	0	.0	2	.8	4	1.7	11	4.6	17	7.1	189	79.4	32	13.4	
FEMALE	0	.0	0	.0	0	.0	1	2.7	1	2.7	34	91.9	2	5.4	
MALE	0	.0	2	1.0	4	2.0	10	5.0	16	8.0	155	77.1	30	14.9	
PART-TIME	1	.7	1	.7	2	1.4	1	.7	5	3.5	130	90.9	8	5.6	
FEMALE	0	.0	0	.0	1	3.3	0	.0	1	3.3	26	86.7	3	10.0	
MALE	1	.9	1	.9	1	.9	1	.9	4	3.5	104	92.0	5	4.4	
TOTAL	1	.3	3	.8	6	1.6	12	3.1	22	5.8	319	83.7	40	10.5	
FEMALE	0	.0	0	.0	1	1.5	1	1.5	2	3.0	60	89.6	5	7.5	
MALE	1	.3	3	1.0	5	1.6	11	3.5	20	6.4	259	82.5	35	11.1	
PROFESSIONAL:															
FULL-TIME	0	.0	0	.0	0	.0	0	.0	0	.0	0	.0	0	.0	
FEMALE	0	.0	0	.0	0	.0	0	.0	0	.0	0	.0	0	.0	
MALE	0	.0	0	.0	0	.0	0	.0	0	.0	0	.0	0	.0	

PHYSICAL SCIENCES

INDIAN NATIVE	BLACK NON-HISPANIC		ASIAN OR PACIFIC ISLANDER		HISPANIC		TOTAL MINORITY		WHITE NON-HISPANIC		NON-RESIDENT ALIEN		TOTAL
%	NUMBER	%	NUMBER	%	NUMBER	%	NUMBER	%	NUMBER	%	NUMBER	%	NUMBER
CONTINUED													
.0	0	.0	0	.0	0	.0	0	.0	0	.0	0	.0	0
.0	0	.0	0	.0	0	.0	0	.0	0	.0	0	.0	u
.0	0	.0	0	.0	0	.0	0	.0	0	.0	0	.0	0
.0	0	.0	0	.0	0	.0	0	.0	0	.0	0	.0	0
.0	0	.0	0	.0	0	.0	0	.0	0	.0	0	.0	0
.0	0	.0	0	.0	0	.0	0	.0	0	.0	0	.0	0
1.0	12	1.2	12	1.2	115	11.6	149	15.0	806	81.1	39	3.9	994
1.4	6	2.9	1	.5	27	12.9	37	17.6	169	80.5	4	1.9	210
.9	6	.8	11	1.4	88	11.2	112	14.3	637	81.3	35	4.5	784
2.1	3	1.2	2	.8	14	5.8	24	10.0	209	86.7	8	3.3	241
.0	0	.0	1	1.9	3	5.6	4	7.4	47	87.0	3	5.6	54
2.7	3	1.6	1	.5	11	5.9	20	10.7	162	86.6	5	2.7	187
1.2	15	1.2	14	1.1	129	10.4	173	14.0	1,015	82.2	47	3.8	1,236
1.1	6	2.3	2	.8	30	11.4	41	15.5	216	81.8	7	2.7	264
1.2	9	.9	12	1.2	99	10.2	132	13.6	799	82.3	40	4.1	971
.0	0	.0	0	.0	1	10.0	1	10.0	9	90.0	0	.0	10
.0	0	.0	0	.0	0	.0	0	.0	2	100.0	0	.0	2
.0	0	.0	0	.0	1	12.5	1	12.5	7	87.5	0	.0	8
1.2	15	1.2	14	1.1	130	10.4	174	14.0	1,024	82.2	47	3.8	1,245
1.1	6	2.3	2	.8	30	11.3	41	15.4	218	82.0	7	2.6	266
1.2	9	.9	12	1.2	100	10.2	133	13.6	806	82.3	40	4.1	979
(95 INSTITUTIONS)													
.2	275	4.1	164	2.4	155	2.3	609	9.0	5,990	89.0	134	2.0	6,733
.2	87	5.0	53	3.1	30	1.7	174	10.1	1,531	88.4	26	1.5	1,731
.2	188	3.8	111	2.2	125	2.5	435	8.7	4,459	89.1	108	2.2	5,002
1.1	52	7.3	13	1.8	9	1.3	82	11.5	616	86.3	16	2.2	714
2.8	16	7.4	4	1.9	6	2.8	32	14.9	181	84.2	2	.9	215
.4	36	7.2	9	1.8	3	.6	50	10.0	435	87.2	14	2.8	499
.3	327	4.4	177	2.4	164	2.2	691	9.3	6,606	88.7	150	2.0	7,447
.5	103	5.3	57	2.9	36	1.8	206	10.6	1,712	88.0	28	1.4	1,946
.2	224	4.1	120	2.2	128	2.3	485	8.8	4,894	89.0	122	2.2	5,501
.1	25	1.2	66	3.1	10	.5	103	4.9	1,514	72.0	485	23.1	2,102
.3	2	.6	13	4.1	3	.9	19	6.0	230	74.8	61	19.2	318
.1	23	1.3	53	3.0	7	.4	84	4.7	1,276	71.5	424	23.8	1,784
.2	28	3.5	40	5.0	8	1.0	78	9.7	655	81.1	75	9.3	808
.5	7	3.6	11	5.6	2	1.0	21	10.8	165	84.6	9	4.6	195
.2	21	3.4	29	4.7	6	1.0	57	9.3	490	79.9	66	10.8	613
.1	53	1.8	106	3.6	18	.6	181	6.2	2,169	74.5	560	19.2	2,910
.4	9	1.8	24	4.7	5	1.0	40	7.8	403	78.6	70	13.6	513
.1	44	1.8	82	3.4	13	.5	141	5.9	1,766	73.7	490	20.4	2,397
.0	0	.0	0	.0	0	.0	0	.0	0	.0	0	.0	0
.0	0	.0	0	.0	0	.0	0	.0	0	.0	0	.0	0
.0	0	.0	0	.0	0	.0	0	.0	0	.0	0	.0	0
.0	0	.0	0	.0	0	.0	0	.0	0	.0	0	.0	0
.0	0	.0	0	.0	0	.0	0	.0	0	.0	0	.0	0
.0	0	.0	0	.0	0	.0	0	.0	0	.0	0	.0	0
.0	0	.0	0	.0	0	.0	0	.0	0	.0	0	.0	0
.0	0	.0	0	.0	0	.0	0	.0	0	.0	0	.0	0
.0	0	.0	0	.0	0	.0	0	.0	0	.0	0	.0	0
.2	300	3.4	230	2.6	165	1.9	712	8.1	7,504	84.9	619	7.0	8,835
.2	89	4.3	66	3.2	33	1.6	193	9.4	1,769	86.3	87	4.2	2,049
.2	211	3.1	164	2.4	132	1.9	519	7.6	5,735	84.5	532	7.8	6,786
.7	80	5.3	53	3.5	17	1.1	160	10.5	1,271	83.5	91	6.0	1,522
1.7	23	5.6	15	3.7	8	2.0	53	12.9	346	84.4	11	2.7	410
.3	57	5.1	38	3.4	9	.8	107	9.6	925	83.2	80	7.2	1,112
.3	380	3.7	283	2.7	182	1.8	872	8.4	8,775	84.7	710	6.9	10,357
.5	112	4.6	81	3.3	41	1.7	246	10.0	2,115	86.0	98	4.0	2,459
.2	268	3.4	202	2.6	141	1.8	626	7.9	6,660	84.3	612	7.7	7,898
1.0	1	1.0	1	1.0	3	3.1	6	6.3	86	89.6	4	4.2	96
.0	0	.0	0	.0	1	3.6	1	3.6	26	92.9	1	3.6	28
1.5	1	1.5	1	1.5	2	2.9	5	7.4	60	88.2	3	4.4	68
.3	381	3.6	284	2.7	185	1.8	878	8.4	8,861	84.8	714	6.8	10,453
.5	112	4.5	81	3.3	42	1.7	247	9.9	2,141	86.1	99	4.0	2,487
.2	269	3.4	203	2.5	143	1.8	631	7.9	6,720	84.4	615	7.7	7,946

MAJOR FIELD 1900 - PHYSICAL SCIENCES

	AMERICAN INDIAN ALASKAN NATIVE		BLACK NON-HISPANIC		ASIAN OR PACIFIC ISLANDER		HISPANIC		TOTAL MINORITY		WHITE NON-HISPANIC		NON-RESIDENT ALIEN		
	NUMBER	%	NUMBER	%	NUMBER	%	NUMBER	%	NUMBER	%	NUMBER	%	NUMBER	%	
NORTH CAROLINA	(	38 INSTITUTIONS)													
UNDERGRADUATES															
FULL-TIME	10	.4	191	7.2	32	1.2	15	.6	248	9.4	2,339	88.6	53	2.0	
FEMALE	3	.5	57	9.0	12	1.9	5	.8	77	12.2	547	86.6	8	1.3	
MALE	7	.3	134	6.7	20	1.0	10	.5	171	8.5	1,792	89.2	45	2.2	
PART-TIME	0	.0	26	9.9	2	.8	0	.0	28	10.7	232	88.5	2	.8	
FEMALE	0	.0	9	11.7	1	1.3	0	.0	10	13.0	67	87.0	0	.0	
MALE	0	.0	17	9.2	1	.5	0	.0	18	9.7	165	89.2	2	1.1	
TOTAL	10	.3	217	7.5	34	1.2	15	.5	276	9.5	2,571	88.6	55	1.9	
FEMALE	3	.4	66	9.3	13	1.8	5	.7	87	12.3	614	86.6	8	1.1	
MALE	7	.3	151	6.9	21	1.0	10	.5	189	8.6	1,957	89.2	47	2.1	
GRADUATE:															
FULL-TIME	0	.0	8	1.7	2	.4	0	.0	10	2.2	397	86.3	53	11.5	
FEMALE	0	.0	3	3.2	0	.0	0	.0	3	3.2	81	86.2	10	10.6	
MALE	0	.0	5	1.4	2	.5	0	.0	7	1.9	316	86.3	43	11.7	
PART-TIME	1	.3	13	4.0	6	1.9	4	1.2	24	7.5	263	81.9	34	10.6	
FEMALE	0	.0	2	3.8	3	5.7	0	.0	5	9.4	40	75.5	8	15.1	
MALE	1	.4	11	4.1	3	1.1	4	1.5	19	7.1	223	83.2	26	9.7	
TOTAL	1	.1	21	2.7	8	1.0	4	.5	34	4.4	660	84.5	87	11.1	
FEMALE	0	.0	5	3.4	3	2.0	0	.0	8	5.4	121	82.3	18	12.2	
MALE	1	.2	16	2.5	5	.8	4	.6	26	4.1	539	85.0	69	10.9	
PROFESSIONAL:															
FULL-TIME	0	.0	0	.0	0	.0	0	.0	0	.0	0	.0	0	.0	
FEMALE	0	.0	0	.0	0	.0	0	.0	0	.0	0	.0	0	.0	
MALE	0	.0	0	.0	0	.0	0	.0	0	.0	0	.0	0	.0	
PART-TIME	0	.0	0	.0	0	.0	0	.0	0	.0	0	.0	0	.0	
FEMALE	0	.0	0	.0	0	.0	0	.0	0	.0	0	.0	0	.0	
MALE	0	.0	0	.0	0	.0	0	.0	0	.0	0	.0	0	.0	
TOTAL	0	.0	0	.0	0	.0	0	.0	0	.0	0	.0	0	.0	
FEMALE	0	.0	0	.0	0	.0	0	.0	0	.0	0	.0	0	.0	
MALE	0	.0	0	.0	0	.0	0	.0	0	.0	0	.0	0	.0	
UND+GRAD+PROF:															
FULL-TIME	10	.3	199	6.4	34	1.1	15	.5	258	8.3	2,736	88.3	106	3.4	
FEMALE	3	.4	60	8.3	12	1.7	5	.7	80	11.0	628	86.5	18	2.5	
MALE	7	.3	139	5.9	22	.9	10	.4	178	7.5	2,108	88.8	88	3.7	
PART-TIME	1	.2	39	6.7	8	1.4	4	.7	52	8.9	495	84.9	36	6.2	
FEMALE	0	.0	11	8.5	4	3.1	0	.0	15	11.5	107	82.3	8	6.2	
MALE	1	.2	28	6.2	4	.9	4	.9	37	8.2	388	85.7	28	6.2	
TOTAL	11	.3	238	6.5	42	1.1	19	.5	310	8.4	3,231	87.7	142	3.9	
FEMALE	3	.4	71	8.3	16	1.9	5	.6	95	11.1	735	85.9	26	3.0	
MALE	8	.3	167	5.9	26	.9	14	.5	215	7.6	2,496	88.3	116	4.1	
UNCLASSIFIED:															
TOTAL	0	.0	0	.0	0	.0	0	.0	0	.0	6	85.7	1	14.3	
FEMALE	0	.0	0	.0	0	.0	0	.0	0	.0	1	100.0	0	.0	
MALE	0	.0	0	.0	0	.0	0	.0	0	.0	5	83.3	1	16.7	
TOTAL ENROLLMENT:															
TOTAL	11	.3	238	6.4	42	1.1	19	.5	310	8.4	3,237	87.7	143	3.9	
FEMALE	3	.4	71	8.3	16	1.9	5	.6	95	11.1	736	85.9	26	3.0	
MALE	8	.3	167	5.9	26	.9	14	.5	215	7.6	2,501	88.3	117	4.1	
NORTH DAKOTA	(	10 INSTITUTIONS)													
UNDERGRADUATES:															
FULL-TIME	11	2.9	2	.5	2	.5	2	.5	17	4.5	362	95.3	1	.3	
FEMALE	5	5.7	1	1.1	0	.0	1	1.1	7	8.0	80	92.0	0	.0	
MALE	6	2.0	1	.3	2	.7	1	.3	10	3.4	282	96.2	1	.3	
PART-TIME	0	.0	0	.0	0	.0	0	.0	0	.0	19	100.0	0	.0	
FEMALE	0	.0	0	.0	0	.0	0	.0	0	.0	4	100.0	0	.0	
MALE	0	.0	0	.0	0	.0	0	.0	0	.0	15	100.0	0	.0	
TOTAL	11	2.8	2	.5	2	.5	2	.5	17	4.3	381	95.5	1	.3	
FEMALE	5	5.5	1	1.1	0	.0	1	1.1	7	7.7	84	92.3	0	.0	
MALE	6	1.9	1	.3	2	.6	1	.3	10	3.2	297	96.4	1	.3	
GRADUATE:															
FULL-TIME	0	.0	0	.0	2	3.5	0	.0	2	3.5	46	80.7	9	15.8	
FEMALE	0	.0	0	.0	0	.0	0	.0	0	.0	8	80.0	2	20.0	
MALE	0	.0	0	.0	2	4.3	0	.0	2	4.3	38	80.9	7	14.9	
PART-TIME	0	.0	0	.0	2	2.7	0	.0	2	2.7	59	78.7	14	18.7	
FEMALE	0	.0	0	.0	0	.0	0	.0	0	.0	3	60.0	2	40.0	
MALE	0	.0	0	.0	2	2.9	0	.0	2	2.9	56	80.0	12	17.1	
TOTAL	0	.0	0	.0	4	3.0	0	.0	4	3.0	105	79.5	23	17.4	
FEMALE	0	.0	0	.0	0	.0	0	.0	0	.0	11	73.3	4	26.7	
MALE	0	.0	0	.0	4	3.4	0	.0	4	3.4	94	80.3	19	16.2	
PROFESSIONAL:															
FULL-TIME	0	.0	0	.0	0	.0	0	.0	0	.0	0	.0	0	.0	
FEMALE	0	.0	0	.0	0	.0	0	.0	0	.0	0	.0	0	.0	
MALE	0	.0	0	.0	0	.0	0	.0	0	.0	0	.0	0	.0	

HYSICAL SCIENCES

INDIAN ATIVE %	BLACK NON-HISPANIC		ASIAN OR PACIFIC ISLANDER		HISPANIC		TOTAL MINORITY		WHITE NON-HISPANIC		NON-RESIDENT ALIEN		TOTAL
%	NUMBER	%	NUMBER	%	NUMBER	%	NUMBER	%	NUMBER	%	NUMBER	%	NUMBER

CONTINUED

.0	0	.0	0	.0	0	.0	0	.0	0	.0	0	.0	0
.0	0	.0	0	.0	0	.0	0	.0	0	.0	0	.0	0
.0	0	.0	0	.0	0	.0	0	.0	0	.0	0	.0	0
.0	0	.0	0	.0	0	.0	0	.0	0	.0	0	.0	0
.0	0	.0	0	.0	0	.0	0	.0	0	.0	0	.0	0
.0	0	.0	0	.0	0	.0	0	.0	0	.0	0	.0	0
2.5	2	.5	4	.9	2	.5	19	4.3	408	93.4	10	2.3	437
5.2	1	1.0	0	.0	1	1.0	7	7.2	88	90.7	2	2.1	97
1.8	1	.3	4	1.2	1	.3	12	3.5	320	94.1	8	2.4	340
.0	0	.0	2	2.1	0	.0	2	2.1	78	83.0	14	14.9	94
.0	0	.0	0	.0	0	.0	0	.0	7	77.8	2	22.2	9
.0	0	.0	2	2.4	0	.0	2	2.4	71	83.5	12	14.1	85
2.1	2	.4	6	1.1	2	.4	21	4.0	486	91.5	24	4.5	531
4.7	1	.9	0	.0	1	.9	7	6.6	95	89.6	4	3.8	106
1.4	1	.2	6	1.4	1	.2	14	3.3	391	92.0	20	4.7	425
11.1	0	.0	0	.0	0	.0	1	11.1	8	88.9	0	.0	9
.0	0	.0	0	.0	0	.0	0	.0	5	100.0	0	.0	5
25.0	0	.0	0	.0	0	.0	1	25.0	3	75.0	0	.0	4
2.2	2	.4	6	1.1	2	.4	22	4.1	494	91.5	24	4.4	540
4.5	1	.9	0	.0	1	.9	7	6.3	100	90.1	4	3.6	111
1.6	1	.2	6	1.4	1	.2	15	3.5	394	91.8	20	4.7	429

(66 INSTITUTIONS)

.0	243	5.5	34	.8	12	.3	291	6.5	4,031	90.7	122	2.7	4,444
.0	98	8.7	8	.7	4	.4	110	9.8	999	88.6	19	1.7	1,128
.1	145	4.4	26	.8	8	.2	181	5.5	3,032	91.4	103	3.1	3,316
.3	28	4.5	2	.3	4	.6	36	5.7	583	92.7	10	1.6	629
.0	12	7.9	1	.7	2	1.3	15	9.9	135	88.8	2	1.3	152
.4	16	3.4	1	.2	2	.4	21	4.4	448	93.9	8	1.7	477
.1	271	5.3	36	.7	16	.3	327	6.4	4,614	91.0	132	2.6	5,073
.0	110	8.6	9	.7	6	.5	125	9.8	1,134	88.6	21	1.6	1,280
.1	161	4.2	27	.7	10	.3	202	5.3	3,480	91.7	111	2.9	3,793
.0	41	2.9	16	1.1	11	.8	68	4.8	1,007	71.6	332	23.6	1,407
.0	20	8.3	1	.4	1	.4	22	9.2	153	63.8	65	27.1	240
.0	21	1.8	15	1.3	10	.9	46	3.9	854	73.2	267	22.9	1,167
.2	14	3.1	4	.9	1	.2	20	4.5	379	84.6	49	10.9	448
.0	7	6.2	1	.9	0	.0	8	7.1	94	83.2	11	9.7	113
.3	7	2.1	3	.9	1	.3	12	3.6	285	85.1	38	11.3	335
.1	55	3.0	20	1.1	12	.6	88	4.7	1,386	74.7	381	20.5	1,855
.0	27	7.6	2	.6	1	.3	30	8.5	247	70.0	76	21.5	353
.1	28	1.9	18	1.2	11	.7	58	3.9	1,139	75.8	305	20.3	1,502
.0	0	.0	0	.0	0	.0	0	.0	0	.0	0	.0	0
.0	0	.0	0	.0	0	.0	0	.0	0	.0	0	.0	0
.0	0	.0	0	.0	0	.0	0	.0	0	.0	0	.0	0
.0	0	.0	0	.0	0	.0	0	.0	0	.0	0	.0	0
.0	0	.0	0	.0	0	.0	0	.0	0	.0	0	.0	0
.0	0	.0	0	.0	0	.0	0	.0	0	.0	0	.0	0
.0	0	.0	0	.0	0	.0	0	.0	0	.0	0	.0	0
.0	0	.0	0	.0	0	.0	0	.0	0	.0	0	.0	0
.0	0	.0	0	.0	0	.0	0	.0	0	.0	0	.0	0
.0	284	4.9	50	.9	23	.4	359	6.1	5,038	86.1	454	7.8	5,851
.0	118	8.6	9	.7	5	.4	132	9.6	1,152	84.2	84	6.1	1,368
.0	166	3.7	41	.9	18	.4	227	5.1	3,886	86.7	370	8.3	4,483
.3	42	3.9	6	.6	5	.5	56	5.2	962	89.3	59	5.5	1,077
.0	19	7.2	2	.8	2	.8	23	8.7	229	86.4	13	4.9	265
.4	23	2.8	4	.5	3	.4	33	4.1	733	90.3	46	5.7	812
.1	326	4.7	56	.8	28	.4	415	6.0	6,000	86.6	513	7.4	6,928
.0	137	8.4	11	.7	7	.4	155	9.5	1,381	84.6	97	5.9	1,633
.1	189	3.6	45	.8	21	.4	260	4.9	4,619	87.2	416	7.9	5,295
.0	6	4.3	1	.7	0	.0	7	5.0	131	92.9	3	2.1	141
.0	4	7.5	1	1.9	0	.0	5	9.4	48	90.6	0	.0	53
.0	2	2.3	0	.0	0	.0	2	2.3	83	94.3	3	3.4	88
.1	332	4.7	57	.8	28	.4	422	6.0	6,131	86.7	516	7.3	7,069
.0	141	8.4	12	.7	7	.4	160	9.5	1,429	84.8	97	5.8	1,686
.1	191	3.5	45	.8	21	.4	262	4.9	4,702	87.3	419	7.8	5,383

MAJOR FIELD 1900 - PHYSICAL SCIENCES

	AMERICAN INDIAN ALASKAN NATIVE		BLACK NON-HISPANIC		ASIAN OR PACIFIC ISLANDER		HISPANIC		TOTAL MINORITY		WHITE NON-HISPANIC		NON-RESIDENT ALIEN	
	NUMBER	%	NUMBER	%	NUMBER	%	NUMBER	%	NUMBER	%	NUMBER	%	NUMBER	%
OKLAHOMA (31 INSTITUTIONS)														
UNDERGRADUATES:														
FULL-TIME	44	2.1	42	2.0	27	1.3	17	.8	130	6.2	1,749	83.7	210	10.1
FEMALE	14	2.8	17	3.4	6	1.2	4	.8	41	8.3	422	85.4	31	6.3
MALE	30	1.9	25	1.6	21	1.3	13	.8	89	5.6	1,327	83.2	179	11.2
PART-TIME	11	2.3	12	2.5	6	1.3	3	.6	32	6.8	430	90.9	11	2.3
FEMALE	4	2.3	4	2.3	4	2.3	2	1.2	14	8.1	156	90.2	3	1.7
MALE	7	2.3	8	2.7	2	.7	1	.3	18	6.0	274	91.3	8	2.7
TOTAL	55	2.1	54	2.1	33	1.3	20	.8	162	6.3	2,179	85.1	221	8.6
FEMALE	18	2.7	21	3.1	10	1.5	6	.9	55	8.2	578	86.7	34	5.1
MALE	37	2.0	33	1.7	23	1.2	14	.7	107	5.6	1,601	84.5	187	9.9
GRADUATE:														
FULL-TIME	0	.0	4	2.1	2	1.1	0	.0	6	3.2	131	69.3	52	27.5
FEMALE	0	.0	0	.0	1	4.3	0	.0	1	4.3	13	56.5	9	39.1
MALE	0	.0	4	2.4	1	.6	0	.0	5	3.0	118	71.1	43	25.9
PART-TIME	0	.0	7	3.4	1	.5	1	.5	9	4.3	155	74.5	44	21.2
FEMALE	0	.0	1	2.6	0	.0	0	.0	1	2.6	29	76.3	8	21.1
MALE	0	.0	6	3.5	1	.6	1	.6	8	4.7	126	74.1	36	21.2
TOTAL	0	.0	11	2.8	3	.8	1	.3	15	3.8	286	72.0	96	24.2
FEMALE	0	.0	1	1.6	1	1.6	0	.0	2	3.3	42	68.9	17	27.9
MALE	0	.0	10	3.0	2	.6	1	.3	13	3.9	244	72.6	79	23.5
PROFESSIONAL:														
FULL-TIME	0	.0	0	.0	0	.0	0	.0	0	.0	0	.0	0	.0
FEMALE	0	.0	0	.0	0	.0	0	.0	0	.0	0	.0	0	.0
MALE	0	.0	0	.0	0	.0	0	.0	0	.0	0	.0	0	.0
PART-TIME	0	.0	0	.0	0	.0	0	.0	0	.0	0	.0	0	.0
FEMALE	0	.0	0	.0	0	.0	0	.0	0	.0	0	.0	0	.0
MALE	0	.0	0	.0	0	.0	0	.0	0	.0	0	.0	0	.0
TOTAL	0	.0	0	.0	0	.0	0	.0	0	.0	0	.0	0	.0
FEMALE	0	.0	0	.0	0	.0	0	.0	0	.0	0	.0	0	.0
MALE	0	.0	0	.0	0	.0	0	.0	0	.0	0	.0	0	.0
UNC+GRAD+PROF:														
FULL-TIME	44	1.9	46	2.0	29	1.3	17	.7	136	6.0	1,880	82.5	262	11.5
FEMALE	14	2.7	17	3.3	7	1.4	4	.8	42	8.1	435	84.1	40	7.7
MALE	30	1.7	29	1.6	22	1.2	13	.7	94	5.3	1,445	82.1	222	12.6
PART-TIME	11	1.6	19	2.8	7	1.0	4	.6	41	6.0	585	85.9	55	8.1
FEMALE	4	1.9	5	2.4	4	1.9	2	.9	15	7.1	185	87.7	11	5.2
MALE	7	1.5	14	3.0	3	.6	2	.4	26	5.5	400	85.1	44	9.4
TOTAL	55	2.2	65	2.2	36	1.2	21	.7	177	6.0	2,465	83.3	317	10.7
FEMALE	18	2.5	22	3.0	11	1.5	6	.8	57	7.8	620	85.2	51	7.0
MALE	37	1.7	43	1.9	25	1.1	15	.7	120	5.4	1,845	82.7	266	11.9
UNCLASSIFIED:														
TOTAL	1	1.5	1	1.5	0	.0	1	1.5	3	4.5	61	91.0	3	4.5
FEMALE	0	.0	0	.0	0	.0	1	5.0	1	5.0	19	95.0	0	.0
MALE	1	2.1	1	2.1	0	.0	0	.0	2	4.3	42	89.4	3	6.4
TOTAL ENROLLMENT:														
TOTAL	56	1.9	66	2.2	36	1.2	22	.7	180	5.9	2,526	83.5	320	10.6
FEMALE	18	2.4	22	2.9	11	1.5	7	.9	58	7.8	639	85.4	51	6.8
MALE	38	1.7	44	1.9	25	1.1	15	.7	122	5.4	1,887	82.8	269	11.8
OREGON (23 INSTITUTIONS)														
UNDERGRADUATES:														
FULL-TIME	15	1.0	11	.7	43	2.8	12	.8	81	5.2	1,414	91.0	59	3.8
FEMALE	3	.8	4	1.0	14	3.6	3	.8	24	6.2	354	90.8	12	3.1
MALE	12	1.0	7	.6	29	2.5	9	.8	57	4.9	1,060	91.1	47	4.0
PART-TIME	4	1.5	2	.8	6	2.3	0	.0	12	4.6	245	93.9	4	1.5
FEMALE	2	2.2	0	.0	3	3.3	0	.0	5	5.5	86	94.5	0	.0
MALE	2	1.2	2	1.2	3	1.8	0	.0	7	4.1	159	93.5	4	2.4
TOTAL	19	1.0	13	.7	49	2.7	12	.7	93	5.1	1,659	91.4	63	3.5
FEMALE	5	1.0	4	.8	17	3.5	3	.6	29	6.0	440	91.5	12	2.5
MALE	14	1.0	9	.7	32	2.4	9	.7	64	4.8	1,219	91.4	51	3.8
GRADUATE:														
FULL-TIME	2	.4	1	.2	5	1.0	0	.0	8	1.5	386	73.4	132	25.1
FEMALE	0	.0	0	.0	1	1.0	0	.0	1	1.0	80	80.8	18	18.2
MALE	2	.5	1	.2	4	.9	0	.0	7	1.6	306	71.7	114	26.7
PART-TIME	1	1.1	0	.0	1	1.1	0	.0	2	2.2	78	86.7	10	11.1
FEMALE	1	5.3	0	.0	0	.0	0	.0	1	5.3	17	89.5	1	5.3
MALE	0	.0	0	.0	1	1.4	0	.0	1	1.4	61	85.9	9	12.7
TOTAL	3	.5	1	.2	6	1.0	0	.0	10	1.6	464	75.3	142	23.1
FEMALE	1	.8	0	.0	1	.8	0	.0	2	1.7	97	82.2	19	16.1
MALE	2	.4	1	.2	5	1.0	0	.0	8	1.6	367	73.7	123	24.7
PROFESSIONAL:														
FULL-TIME	0	.0	0	.0	0	.0	0	.0	0	.0	0	.0	0	.0
FEMALE	0	.0	0	.0	0	.0	0	.0	0	.0	0	.0	0	.0
MALE	0	.0	0	.0	0	.0	0	.0	0	.0	0	.0	0	.0

HYSICAL SCIENCES

INDIAN ATIVE	BLACK NON-HISPANIC		ASIAN OR PACIFIC ISLANDER		HISPANIC		TOTAL MINORITY		WHITE NON-HISPANIC		NON-RESIDENT ALIEN		TOTAL
%	NUMBER	%	NUMBER	%	NUMBER	%	NUMBER	%	NUMBER	%	NUMBER	%	NUMBER

CONTINUED

.0	0	.0	0	.0	0	.0	0	.0	0	.0	0	.0	0
.0	0	.0	0	.0	0	.0	0	.0	0	.0	0	.0	0
.0	0	.0	0	.0	0	.0	0	.0	0	.0	0	.0	0
.0	0	.0	0	.0	0	.0	0	.0	0	.0	0	.0	0
.0	0	.0	0	.0	0	.0	0	.0	0	.0	0	.0	0
.0	0	.0	0	.0	0	.0	0	.0	0	.0	0	.0	0
.8	12	.6	48	2.3	12	.6	89	4.3	1,800	86.5	191	9.2	2,080
.6	4	.8	15	3.1	3	.6	25	5.1	434	88.8	30	6.1	489
.9	8	.5	33	2.1	9	.6	64	4.0	1,366	85.9	161	10.1	1,591
1.4	2	.6	7	2.0	0	.0	14	4.0	323	92.0	14	4.0	351
2.7	0	.0	3	2.7	0	.0	6	5.5	103	93.6	1	.9	110
.8	2	.8	4	1.7	0	.0	8	3.3	220	91.3	13	5.4	241
.9	14	.6	55	2.3	12	.5	103	4.2	2,123	87.3	205	8.4	2,431
1.0	4	.7	18	3.0	3	.5	31	5.2	537	89.6	31	5.2	599
.9	10	.5	37	2.0	9	.5	72	3.9	1,586	86.6	174	9.5	1,832
1.2	0	.0	0	.0	0	.0	1	1.2	80	94.1	4	4.7	85
4.2	0	.0	0	.0	0	.0	1	4.2	23	95.8	0	.0	24
.0	0	.0	0	.0	0	.0	0	.0	57	93.4	4	6.6	61
.9	14	.6	55	2.2	12	.5	104	4.1	2,203	87.6	209	8.3	2,516
1.1	4	.6	18	2.9	3	.5	32	5.1	560	89.9	31	5.0	623
.8	10	.5	37	2.0	9	.5	72	3.8	1,643	86.8	178	9.4	1,893

(106 INSTITUTIONS)

.1	312	3.4	168	1.8	31	.3	523	5.8	8,408	92.5	158	1.7	9,089
.2	124	4.6	53	2.0	13	.5	195	7.3	2,465	91.7	27	1.0	2,687
.1	188	2.9	115	1.8	18	.3	328	5.1	5,943	92.8	131	2.0	6,402
.0	48	6.0	9	1.1	6	.7	63	7.9	730	91.0	9	1.1	802
.0	19	8.9	3	1.4	2	.9	24	11.3	188	88.3	1	.5	213
.0	29	4.9	6	1.0	4	.7	39	6.6	542	92.0	8	1.4	589
.1	360	3.6	177	1.8	37	.4	586	5.9	9,138	92.4	167	1.7	9,891
.2	143	4.9	56	1.9	15	.5	219	7.6	2,653	91.5	28	1.0	2,900
.1	217	3.1	121	1.7	22	.3	367	5.2	6,485	92.8	139	2.0	6,991
.2	15	1.5	18	1.8	8	.8	43	4.2	799	78.4	177	17.4	1,019
.0	2	1.3	5	3.2	2	1.3	9	5.7	125	79.6	23	14.6	157
.2	13	1.5	13	1.5	6	.7	34	3.9	674	78.2	154	17.9	862
.5	7	1.7	12	2.9	2	.5	23	5.5	375	89.7	20	4.8	418
.9	0	.0	6	5.5	0	.0	7	6.4	100	90.9	3	2.7	110
.3	7	2.3	6	1.9	2	.6	16	5.2	275	89.3	17	5.5	308
.3	22	1.5	30	2.1	10	.7	66	4.6	1,174	81.7	197	13.7	1,437
.4	2	.7	11	4.1	2	.7	16	6.0	225	84.3	26	9.7	267
.3	20	1.7	19	1.6	8	.7	50	4.3	949	81.1	171	14.6	1,170
.0	0	.0	0	.0	0	.0	0	.0	0	.0	0	.0	0
.0	0	.0	0	.0	0	.0	0	.0	0	.0	0	.0	0
.0	0	.0	0	.0	0	.0	0	.0	0	.0	0	.0	0
.0	0	.0	0	.0	0	.0	0	.0	0	.0	0	.0	0
.0	0	.0	0	.0	0	.0	0	.0	0	.0	0	.0	0
.0	0	.0	0	.0	0	.0	0	.0	0	.0	0	.0	0
.0	0	.0	0	.0	0	.0	0	.0	0	.0	0	.0	0
.0	0	.0	0	.0	0	.0	0	.0	0	.0	0	.0	0
.0	0	.0	0	.0	0	.0	0	.0	0	.0	0	.0	0
.1	327	3.2	186	1.8	39	.4	566	5.6	9,207	91.1	335	3.3	10,108
.2	126	4.4	58	2.0	15	.5	204	7.2	2,590	91.1	50	1.8	2,844
.1	201	2.8	128	1.8	24	.3	362	5.0	6,617	91.1	285	3.9	7,264
.2	55	4.5	21	1.7	8	.7	86	7.0	1,105	90.6	29	2.4	1,220
.3	19	5.9	9	2.8	2	.6	31	9.6	288	89.2	4	1.2	323
.1	36	4.0	12	1.3	6	.7	55	6.1	817	91.1	25	2.8	897
.1	382	3.4	207	1.8	47	.4	652	5.8	10,312	91.0	364	3.2	11,328
.2	145	4.6	67	2.1	17	.5	235	7.4	2,878	90.9	54	1.7	3,167
.1	237	2.9	140	1.7	30	.4	417	5.1	7,434	91.1	310	3.8	8,161
.0	10	2.6	49	12.6	3	.8	62	16.0	318	82.0	8	2.1	388
.0	3	3.8	10	12.7	2	2.5	15	19.0	61	77.2	3	3.8	79
.0	7	2.3	39	12.6	1	.3	47	15.2	257	83.2	5	1.6	309
.1	392	3.3	256	2.2	50	.4	714	6.1	10,630	90.7	372	3.2	11,716
.2	148	4.6	77	2.4	19	.6	250	7.7	2,939	90.5	57	1.8	3,246
.1	244	2.9	179	2.1	31	.4	464	5.5	7,691	90.8	315	3.7	8,470

MAJOR FIELD 1900 - PHYSICAL SCIENCES

	AMERICAN INDIAN ALASKAN NATIVE		BLACK NON-HISPANIC		ASIAN OR PACIFIC ISLANDER		HISPANIC		TOTAL MINORITY		WHITE NON-HISPANIC		NON-RESIDENT ALIEN		TO
	NUMBER	%	NUMBER	%	NUMBER	%	NUMBER	%	NUMBER	%	NUMBER	%	NUMBER	%	
RHODE ISLAND	(	4 INSTITUTIONS)													
UNDERGRADUATES:															
FULL-TIME	0	.0	5	1.4	13	3.6	3	.8	21	5.8	333	91.5	10	2.7	
FEMALE	0	.0	1	1.0	6	6.0	1	1.0	8	8.0	90	90.0	2	2.0	
MALE	0	.0	4	1.5	7	2.7	2	.8	13	4.9	243	92.0	8	3.0	
PART-TIME	1	5.9	1	5.9	0	.0	0	.0	2	11.8	15	88.2	0	.0	
FEMALE	0	.0	0	.0	0	.0	0	.0	0	.0	6	100.0	0	.0	
MALE	1	9.1	1	9.1	0	.0	0	.0	2	18.2	9	81.8	0	.0	
TOTAL	1	.3	6	1.6	13	3.4	3	.8	23	6.0	348	91.3	10	2.6	
FEMALE	0	.0	1	.9	6	5.7	1	.9	8	7.5	96	90.6	2	1.9	
MALE	1	.4	5	1.8	7	2.5	2	.7	15	5.5	252	91.6	8	2.9	
GRADUATE:															
FULL-TIME	0	.0	3	.9	6	1.9	2	.6	11	3.4	250	78.4	58	18.2	
FEMALE	0	.0	1	1.4	0	.0	1	1.4	2	2.9	53	76.8	14	20.3	
MALE	0	.0	2	.8	6	2.4	1	.4	9	3.6	197	78.8	44	17.6	
PART-TIME	1	1.0	1	1.0	1	1.0	0	.0	3	3.0	94	94.0	3	3.0	
FEMALE	0	.0	0	.0	1	3.8	0	.0	1	3.8	24	92.3	1	3.8	
MALE	1	1.4	1	1.4	0	.0	0	.0	2	2.7	70	94.6	2	2.7	
TOTAL	1	.2	4	1.0	7	1.7	2	.5	14	3.3	344	82.1	61	14.6	
FEMALE	0	.0	1	1.1	1	1.1	1	1.1	3	3.2	77	81.1	15	15.8	
MALE	1	.3	3	.9	6	1.9	1	.3	11	3.4	267	82.4	46	14.2	
PROFESSIONAL:															
FULL-TIME	0	.0	0	.0	0	.0	0	.0	0	.0	0	.0	0	.0	
FEMALE	0	.0	0	.0	0	.0	0	.0	0	.0	0	.0	0	.0	
MALE	0	.0	0	.0	0	.0	0	.0	0	.0	0	.0	0	.0	
PART-TIME	0	.0	0	.0	0	.0	0	.0	0	.0	0	.0	0	.0	
FEMALE	0	.0	0	.0	0	.0	0	.0	0	.0	0	.0	0	.0	
MALE	0	.0	0	.0	0	.0	0	.0	0	.0	0	.0	0	.0	
TOTAL	0	.0	0	.0	0	.0	0	.0	0	.0	0	.0	0	.0	
FEMALE	0	.0	0	.0	0	.0	0	.0	0	.0	0	.0	0	.0	
MALE	0	.0	0	.0	0	.0	0	.0	0	.0	0	.0	0	.0	
UND+GRAD+PROF:															
FULL-TIME	0	.0	8	1.2	19	2.8	5	.7	32	4.7	583	85.4	68	10.0	
FEMALE	0	.0	2	1.2	6	3.6	2	1.2	10	5.9	143	84.6	16	9.5	
MALE	0	.0	6	1.2	13	2.5	3	.6	22	4.3	440	85.6	52	10.1	
PART-TIME	2	1.7	2	1.7	1	.9	0	.0	5	4.3	109	93.2	3	2.6	
FEMALE	0	.0	0	.0	1	3.1	0	.0	1	3.1	30	93.8	1	3.1	
MALE	2	2.4	2	2.4	0	.0	0	.0	4	4.7	79	92.9	2	2.4	
TOTAL	2	.3	10	1.3	20	2.5	5	.6	37	4.6	692	86.5	71	8.9	
FEMALE	0	.0	2	1.0	7	3.5	2	1.0	11	5.5	173	86.1	17	8.5	
MALE	2	.3	8	1.3	13	2.2	3	.5	26	4.3	519	86.6	54	9.0	
UNCLASSIFIED:															
TOTAL	0	.0	0	.0	0	.0	0	.0	0	.0	1	100.0	0	.0	
FEMALE	0	.0	0	.0	0	.0	0	.0	0	.0	1	100.0	0	.0	
MALE	0	.0	0	.0	0	.0	0	.0	0	.0	0	.0	0	.0	
TOTAL ENROLLMENT:															
TOTAL	2	.2	10	1.2	20	2.5	5	.6	37	4.6	693	86.5	71	8.9	
FEMALE	0	.0	2	1.0	7	3.5	2	1.0	11	5.4	174	86.1	17	8.4	
MALE	2	.3	8	1.3	13	2.2	3	.5	26	4.3	519	86.6	54	9.0	
SOUTH CAROLINA	(	29 INSTITUTIONS)													
UNDERGRADUATES:															
FULL-TIME	1	.1	189	17.4	8	.7	3	.3	201	18.5	867	80.0	16	1.5	1,
FEMALE	1	.1	72	20.9	4	1.5	1	.4	77	28.7	188	70.1	3	1.1	
MALE	1	.1	117	14.3	4	.5	2	.2	124	15.2	679	83.2	13	1.6	
PART-TIME	0	.0	8	8.5	1	1.1	0	.0	9	9.6	85	90.4	0	.0	
FEMALE	0	.0	3	12.0	0	.0	0	.0	3	12.0	22	88.0	0	.0	
MALE	0	.0	5	7.2	1	1.4	0	.0	6	8.7	63	91.3	0	.0	
TOTAL	1	.1	197	16.7	9	.8	3	.3	210	17.8	952	80.8	16	1.4	1,
FEMALE	0	.0	75	25.6	4	1.4	1	.3	80	27.3	210	71.7	3	1.0	
MALE	1	.1	122	13.8	5	.6	2	.2	130	14.7	742	83.8	13	1.5	
GRADUATE:															
FULL-TIME	0	.0	4	1.6	1	.4	0	.0	5	2.0	217	88.9	22	9.0	
FEMALE	0	.0	2	4.5	1	2.3	0	.0	3	6.8	38	86.4	3	6.8	
MALE	0	.0	2	1.0	0	.0	0	.0	2	1.0	179	89.5	19	9.5	
PART-TIME	0	.0	1	1.4	0	.0	0	.0	1	1.4	65	92.9	4	5.7	
FEMALE	0	.0	1	4.8	0	.0	0	.0	1	4.8	19	90.5	1	4.8	
MALE	0	.0	0	.0	0	.0	0	.0	0	.0	46	93.9	3	6.1	
TOTAL	0	.0	5	1.6	1	.3	0	.0	6	1.9	282	89.8	26	8.3	
FEMALE	0	.0	3	4.6	1	1.5	0	.0	4	6.2	57	87.7	4	6.2	
MALE	0	.0	2	.8	0	.0	0	.0	2	.8	225	90.4	22	8.8	
PROFESSIONAL:															
FULL-TIME	0	.0	0	.0	0	.0	0	.0	0	.0	0	.0	0	.0	
FEMALE	0	.0	0	.0	0	.0	0	.0	0	.0	0	.0	0	.0	
MALE	0	.0	0	.0	0	.0	0	.0	0	.0	0	.0	0	.0	

ENROLLMENT IN INSTITUTIONS OF HIGHER EDUCATION FOR SELECTED MAJOR FIELDS OF STUDY AND LEVEL OF ENROLLMENT
E, ETHNICITY, AND SEX: STATE, 1978

- PHYSICAL SCIENCES

AN INDIAN N NATIVE		BLACK NON-HISPANIC		ASIAN OR PACIFIC ISLANDER		HISPANIC		TOTAL MINORITY		WHITE NON-HISPANIC		NON-RESIDENT ALIEN		TOTAL
R	%	NUMBER	%	NUMBER	%	NUMBER	%	NUMBER	%	NUMBER	%	NUMBER	%	NUMBER
CONTINUED														
0	.0	0	.0	0	.0	0	.0	0	.0	0	.0	0	.0	0
0	.0	0	.0	0	.0	0	.0	0	.0	0	.0	0	.0	0
0	.0	0	.0	0	.0	0	.0	0	.0	0	.0	0	.0	0
0	.0	0	.0	0	.0	0	.0	0	.0	0	.0	0	.0	0
0	.0	0	.0	0	.0	0	.0	0	.0	0	.0	0	.0	0
0	.0	0	.0	0	.0	0	.0	0	.0	0	.0	0	.0	0
1	.1	193	14.5	9	.7	3	.2	206	15.5	1,084	81.6	38	2.9	1,328
0	.0	74	23.7	5	1.6	1	.3	80	25.6	226	72.4	6	1.9	312
1	.1	119	11.7	4	.4	2	.2	126	12.4	898	84.4	32	3.1	1,016
0	.0	9	5.5	1	.6	0	.0	10	6.1	150	91.5	4	2.4	164
0	.0	4	8.7	0	.0	0	.0	4	8.7	41	89.1	1	2.2	46
0	.0	5	4.2	1	.8	0	.0	6	5.1	109	92.4	3	2.5	118
1	.1	202	13.5	10	.7	3	.2	216	14.5	1,234	82.7	42	2.8	1,492
0	.0	78	21.8	5	1.4	1	.3	84	23.5	267	74.6	7	2.0	358
1	.1	124	10.9	5	.4	2	.2	132	11.6	967	85.3	35	3.1	1,134
0	.0	0	.0	0	.0	0	.0	0	.0	8	100.0	0	.0	8
0	.0	0	.0	0	.0	0	.0	0	.0	2	100.0	0	.0	2
0	.0	0	.0	0	.0	0	.0	0	.0	6	100.0	0	.0	6
1	.1	202	13.5	10	.7	3	.2	216	14.4	1,242	82.8	42	2.8	1,500
0	.0	78	21.7	5	1.4	1	.3	84	23.3	269	74.7	7	1.9	360
1	.1	124	10.9	5	.4	2	.2	132	11.6	973	85.4	35	3.1	1,140

(13 INSTITUTIONS)

AN INDIAN N NATIVE		BLACK NON-HISPANIC		ASIAN OR PACIFIC ISLANDER		HISPANIC		TOTAL MINORITY		WHITE NON-HISPANIC		NON-RESIDENT ALIEN		TOTAL
1	.3	2	.6	4	1.2	0	.0	7	2.2	312	97.2	2	.6	321
0	.0	2	2.2	0	.0	0	.0	2	2.2	89	97.8	0	.0	91
1	.4	0	.0	4	1.7	0	.0	5	2.2	223	97.0	2	.9	230
0	.0	0	.0	0	.0	0	.0	0	.0	26	100.0	0	.0	26
0	.0	0	.0	0	.0	0	.0	0	.0	8	100.0	0	.0	8
0	.0	0	.0	0	.0	0	.0	0	.0	18	100.0	0	.0	18
1	.3	2	.6	4	1.2	0	.0	7	2.0	338	97.4	2	.6	347
0	.0	2	2.0	0	.0	0	.0	2	2.0	97	98.0	0	.0	99
1	.4	0	.0	4	1.6	0	.0	5	2.0	241	97.2	2	.8	248
0	.0	0	.0	0	.0	0	.0	0	.0	32	71.1	13	28.9	45
0	.0	0	.0	0	.0	0	.0	0	.0	6	66.7	3	33.3	9
0	.0	0	.0	0	.0	0	.0	0	.0	26	72.2	10	27.8	36
0	.0	0	.0	0	.0	0	.0	0	.0	20	66.7	10	33.3	30
0	.0	0	.0	0	.0	0	.0	0	.0	4	57.1	3	42.9	7
0	.0	0	.0	0	.0	0	.0	0	.0	16	69.6	7	30.4	23
0	.0	0	.0	0	.0	0	.0	0	.0	52	69.3	23	30.7	75
0	.0	0	.0	0	.0	0	.0	0	.0	10	62.5	6	37.5	16
0	.0	0	.0	0	.0	0	.0	0	.0	42	71.2	17	28.8	59
0	.0	0	.0	0	.0	0	.0	0	.0	0	.0	0	.0	0
0	.0	0	.0	0	.0	0	.0	0	.0	0	.0	0	.0	0
0	.0	0	.0	0	.0	0	.0	0	.0	0	.0	0	.0	0
0	.0	0	.0	0	.0	0	.0	0	.0	0	.0	0	.0	0
0	.0	0	.0	0	.0	0	.0	0	.0	0	.0	0	.0	0
0	.0	0	.0	0	.0	0	.0	0	.0	0	.0	0	.0	0
0	.0	0	.0	0	.0	0	.0	0	.0	0	.0	0	.0	0
1	.3	2	.5	4	1.1	0	.0	7	1.9	344	94.0	15	4.1	366
0	.0	2	2.0	0	.0	0	.0	2	2.0	95	95.0	3	3.0	100
1	.4	0	.0	4	1.5	0	.0	5	1.9	249	93.6	12	4.5	266
0	.0	0	.0	0	.0	0	.0	0	.0	46	82.1	10	17.9	56
0	.0	0	.0	0	.0	0	.0	0	.0	12	80.0	3	20.0	15
0	.0	0	.0	0	.0	0	.0	0	.0	34	82.9	7	17.1	41
1	.2	2	.5	4	.9	0	.0	7	1.7	390	92.4	25	5.9	422
0	.0	2	1.7	0	.0	0	.0	2	1.7	107	93.0	6	5.2	115
1	.3	0	.0	4	1.3	0	.0	5	1.6	283	92.2	19	6.2	307
0	.0	0	.0	0	.0	0	.0	0	.0	3	100.0	0	.0	3
0	.0	0	.0	0	.0	0	.0	0	.0	1	100.0	0	.0	1
0	.0	0	.0	0	.0	0	.0	0	.0	2	100.0	0	.0	2
1	.2	2	.5	4	.9	0	.0	7	1.6	393	92.5	25	5.9	425
0	.0	2	1.7	0	.0	0	.0	2	1.7	108	93.1	6	5.2	116
1	.3	0	.0	4	1.3	0	.0	5	1.6	285	92.2	19	6.1	309

TABLE 17 - TOTAL ENROLLMENT IN INSTITUTIONS OF HIGHER EDUCATION FOR SELECTED MAJOR FIELDS OF STUDY AND LEVEL OF ENROLLMENT BY RACE, ETHNICITY, AND SEX: STATE, 1978

MAJOR FIELD 1900 - PHYSICAL SCIENCES

	AMERICAN INDIAN ALASKAN NATIVE		BLACK NON-HISPANIC		ASIAN OR PACIFIC ISLANDER		HISPANIC		TOTAL MINORITY		WHITE NON-HISPANIC		NON-RESIDENT ALIEN	
	NUMBER	%	NUMBER	%	NUMBER	%	NUMBER	%	NUMBER	%	NUMBER	%	NUMBER	%
TENNESSEE (36 INSTITUTIONS)														
UNDERGRADUATES:														
FULL-TIME	1	.1	212	14.4	15	1.0	3	.2	231	15.7	1,200	81.6	39	2.7
FEMALE	1	.3	117	31.1	5	1.3	0	.0	123	32.7	249	66.2	4	1.1
MALE	0	.0	95	8.7	10	.9	3	.3	108	9.9	951	86.9	35	3.2
PART-TIME	0	.0	8	4.5	1	.6	0	.0	9	5.1	168	94.4	1	.6
FEMALE	0	.0	2	6.3	0	.0	0	.0	2	6.3	30	93.8	0	.0
MALE	0	.0	6	4.1	1	.7	0	.0	7	4.8	138	94.5	1	.7
TOTAL	1	.1	220	13.3	16	1.0	3	.2	240	14.6	1,368	83.0	40	2.4
FEMALE	1	.2	119	29.2	5	1.2	0	.0	125	30.6	279	68.4	4	1.0
MALE	0	.0	101	8.1	11	.9	3	.2	115	9.3	1,089	87.8	36	2.9
GRADUATE:														
FULL-TIME	0	.0	33	12.9	4	1.6	0	.0	37	14.5	180	70.6	38	14.9
FEMALE	0	.0	20	39.2	0	.0	0	.0	20	39.2	25	49.0	6	11.8
MALE	0	.0	13	6.4	4	2.0	0	.0	17	8.3	155	76.0	32	15.7
PART-TIME	1	.7	5	3.6	1	.7	0	.0	7	5.1	114	83.2	16	11.7
FEMALE	1	4.0	2	8.0	0	.0	0	.0	3	12.0	18	72.0	4	16.0
MALE	0	.0	3	2.7	1	.9	0	.0	4	3.6	96	85.7	12	10.7
TOTAL	1	.3	38	9.7	5	1.3	0	.0	44	11.2	294	75.0	54	13.8
FEMALE	1	1.3	22	28.9	0	.0	0	.0	23	30.3	43	56.6	10	13.2
MALE	0	.0	16	5.1	5	1.6	0	.0	21	6.6	251	79.4	44	13.9
PROFESSIONAL:														
FULL-TIME	0	.0	0	.0	0	.0	0	.0	0	.0	0	.0	0	.0
FEMALE	0	.0	0	.0	0	.0	0	.0	0	.0	0	.0	0	.0
MALE	0	.0	0	.0	0	.0	0	.0	0	.0	0	.0	0	.0
PART-TIME	0	.0	0	.0	0	.0	0	.0	0	.0	0	.0	0	.0
FEMALE	0	.0	0	.0	0	.0	0	.0	0	.0	0	.0	0	.0
MALE	0	.0	0	.0	0	.0	0	.0	0	.0	0	.0	0	.0
TOTAL	0	.0	0	.0	0	.0	0	.0	0	.0	0	.0	0	.0
FEMALE	0	.0	0	.0	0	.0	0	.0	0	.0	0	.0	0	.0
MALE	0	.0	0	.0	0	.0	0	.0	0	.0	0	.0	0	.0
UND+GRAD+PROF:														
FULL-TIME	1	.1	245	14.2	19	1.1	3	.2	268	15.5	1,380	80.0	77	4.5
FEMALE	1	.2	137	32.1	5	1.2	0	.0	143	33.5	274	64.2	10	2.3
MALE	0	.0	108	8.3	14	1.1	3	.2	125	9.6	1,106	85.2	67	5.2
PART-TIME	1	.3	13	4.1	2	.6	0	.0	16	5.1	282	89.5	17	5.4
FEMALE	1	1.8	4	7.0	0	.0	0	.0	5	8.8	48	84.2	4	7.0
MALE	0	.0	9	3.5	2	.8	0	.0	11	4.3	234	90.7	13	5.0
TOTAL	2	.1	258	12.6	21	1.0	3	.1	284	13.9	1,662	81.5	94	4.6
FEMALE	2	.4	141	29.1	5	1.0	0	.0	148	30.6	322	66.5	14	2.9
MALE	0	.0	117	7.5	16	1.0	3	.2	136	8.7	1,340	86.1	80	5.1
UNCLASSIFIED:														
TOTAL	0	.0	1	10.0	0	.0	0	.0	1	10.0	9	90.0	0	.0
FEMALE	0	.0	0	.0	0	.0	0	.0	0	.0	4	100.0	0	.0
MALE	0	.0	1	16.7	0	.0	0	.0	1	16.7	5	83.3	0	.0
TOTAL ENROLLMENT:														
TOTAL	2	.1	259	12.6	21	1.0	3	.1	285	13.9	1,671	81.5	94	4.6
FEMALE	2	.4	141	28.9	5	1.0	0	.0	148	30.3	326	66.8	14	2.9
MALE	0	.0	118	7.6	16	1.0	3	.2	137	8.8	1,345	86.1	80	5.1
TEXAS (102 INSTITUTIONS)														
UNDERGRADUATES:														
FULL-TIME	18	.3	304	4.5	80	1.2	454	6.8	856	12.7	5,442	81.0	423	6.3
FEMALE	4	.2	120	6.8	31	1.8	141	8.0	296	16.9	1,377	78.6	79	4.5
MALE	14	.3	184	3.7	49	1.0	313	6.3	560	11.3	4,065	81.8	344	6.9
PART-TIME	13	.4	286	8.6	45	1.4	198	6.0	542	16.4	2,702	81.6	68	2.1
FEMALE	9	.7	136	10.8	19	1.5	73	5.8	237	18.8	1,011	80.0	16	1.3
MALE	4	.2	150	7.3	26	1.3	125	6.1	305	14.9	1,691	82.6	52	2.5
TOTAL	31	.3	590	5.9	125	1.2	652	6.5	1,398	13.9	8,144	81.2	491	4.9
FEMALE	13	.4	256	8.5	50	1.7	214	7.1	533	17.7	2,388	79.2	95	3.1
MALE	18	.3	334	4.8	75	1.1	438	6.2	865	12.3	5,756	82.0	396	5.6
GRADUATE:														
FULL-TIME	6	.3	14	.7	47	2.4	22	1.1	89	4.6	1,488	76.5	367	18.9
FEMALE	1	.3	5	1.4	13	3.7	5	1.4	24	6.8	271	77.2	56	16.0
MALE	5	.3	9	.6	34	2.1	17	1.1	65	4.1	1,217	76.4	311	19.5
PART-TIME	7	1.0	16	2.2	19	2.6	17	2.4	59	8.2	585	81.1	77	10.7
FEMALE	5	2.5	3	1.5	6	3.0	4	2.0	18	9.0	168	83.6	15	7.5
MALE	2	.4	13	2.5	13	2.5	13	2.5	41	7.9	417	80.2	62	11.9
TOTAL	13	.5	30	1.1	66	2.5	39	1.5	148	5.6	2,073	77.8	444	16.7
FEMALE	6	1.1	8	1.4	19	3.4	9	1.6	42	7.6	439	79.5	71	12.9
MALE	7	.3	22	1.0	47	2.2	30	1.4	106	5.0	1,634	77.3	373	17.7
PROFESSIONAL:														
FULL-TIME	0	.0	0	.0	0	.0	0	.0	0	.0	0	.0	0	.0
FEMALE	0	.0	0	.0	0	.0	0	.0	0	.0	0	.0	0	.0
MALE	0	.0	0	.0	0	.0	0	.0	0	.0	0	.0	0	.0

ROLLMENT IN INSTITUTIONS OF HIGHER EDUCATION FOR SELECTED MAJOR FIELDS OF STUDY AND LEVEL OF ENROLLMENT
ETHNICITY, AND SEX: STATE, 1978

PHYSICAL SCIENCES

INDIAN NATIVE %	BLACK NON-HISPANIC NUMBER	%	ASIAN OR PACIFIC ISLANDER NUMBER	%	HISPANIC NUMBER	%	TOTAL MINORITY NUMBER	%	WHITE NON-HISPANIC NUMBER	%	NON-RESIDENT ALIEN NUMBER	%	TOTAL NUMBER
CONTINUED													
.0	0	.0	0	.0	0	.0	0	.0	0	.0	0	.0	0
.0	0	.0	0	.0	0	.0	0	.0	0	.0	0	.0	0
.0	0	.0	0	.0	0	.0	0	.0	0	.0	0	.0	0
.0	0	.0	0	.0	0	.0	0	.0	0	.0	0	.0	0
.0	0	.0	0	.0	0	.0	0	.0	0	.0	0	.0	0
.0	0	.0	0	.0	0	.0	0	.0	0	.0	0	.0	0
.3	318	3.7	127	1.5	476	5.5	945	10.9	6,930	80.0	790	9.1	8,665
.2	125	5.9	44	2.1	146	6.9	320	15.2	1,648	78.4	135	6.4	2,103
.3	193	2.9	83	1.3	330	5.0	625	9.5	5,282	80.5	655	10.0	6,562
.5	302	7.5	64	1.6	215	5.3	601	14.9	3,287	81.5	145	3.6	4,033
1.0	139	9.5	25	1.7	77	5.3	255	17.4	1,179	80.5	31	2.1	1,465
.2	163	6.3	39	1.5	138	5.4	346	13.5	2,108	82.1	114	4.4	2,560
.3	620	4.9	191	1.5	691	5.4	1,546	12.2	10,217	80.5	935	7.4	12,698
.5	264	7.4	69	1.9	223	6.3	575	16.1	2,827	79.2	166	4.7	3,568
.3	356	3.9	122	1.3	468	5.1	971	10.6	7,390	80.9	769	8.4	9,130
.3	53	9.0	11	1.9	40	6.8	106	17.9	474	80.2	11	1.9	591
.5	19	9.2	4	1.9	15	7.2	39	18.8	165	79.7	3	1.4	207
.3	34	8.9	7	1.8	25	6.5	67	17.4	309	80.5	8	2.1	384
.3	673	5.1	202	1.5	731	5.5	1,652	12.4	10,691	80.4	946	7.1	13,289
.5	283	7.5	73	1.9	238	6.3	614	16.3	2,992	79.3	169	4.5	3,775
.3	390	4.1	129	1.4	493	5.2	1,038	10.9	7,699	80.9	777	8.2	9,514
(9 INSTITUTIONS)													
.6	3	.2	15	1.2	9	.7	35	2.7	1,206	94.1	41	3.2	1,282
2.1	0	.0	3	1.3	2	.8	10	4.2	216	90.0	14	5.8	240
.3	3	.3	12	1.2	7	.7	25	2.4	990	95.0	27	2.6	1,042
.4	0	.0	0	.0	0	.0	1	.4	233	97.5	5	2.1	239
.0	0	.0	0	.0	0	.0	0	.0	57	98.3	1	1.7	58
.6	0	.0	0	.0	0	.0	1	.6	176	97.2	4	2.2	181
.6	3	.2	15	1.0	9	.6	36	2.4	1,439	94.6	46	3.0	1,521
1.7	0	.0	3	1.0	2	.7	10	3.4	273	91.6	15	5.0	298
.3	3	.2	12	1.0	7	.6	26	2.1	1,166	95.3	31	2.5	1,223
.0	0	.0	2	1.3	1	.7	3	2.0	124	81.0	26	17.0	153
.0	0	.0	0	.0	0	.0	0	.0	9	75.0	3	25.0	12
.0	0	.0	2	1.4	1	.7	3	2.1	115	81.6	23	16.3	141
.0	0	.0	3	1.0	1	.3	4	1.3	261	87.3	34	11.4	299
.0	0	.0	1	3.1	0	.0	1	3.1	26	81.3	5	15.6	32
.0	0	.0	2	.7	1	.4	3	1.1	235	88.0	29	10.9	267
.0	0	.0	5	1.1	2	.4	7	1.5	385	85.2	60	13.3	452
.0	0	.0	1	2.3	0	.0	1	2.3	35	79.5	8	18.2	44
.0	0	.0	4	1.0	2	.5	6	1.5	350	85.8	52	12.7	408
.0	0	.0	0	.0	0	.0	0	.0	0	.0	0	.0	0
.0	0	.0	0	.0	0	.0	0	.0	0	.0	0	.0	0
.0	0	.0	0	.0	0	.0	0	.0	0	.0	0	.0	0
.0	0	.0	0	.0	0	.0	0	.0	0	.0	0	.0	0
.0	0	.0	0	.0	0	.0	0	.0	0	.0	0	.0	0
.0	0	.0	0	.0	0	.0	0	.0	0	.0	0	.0	0
.0	0	.0	0	.0	0	.0	0	.0	0	.0	0	.0	0
.0	0	.0	0	.0	0	.0	0	.0	0	.0	0	.0	0
.0	0	.0	0	.0	0	.0	0	.0	0	.0	0	.0	0
.6	3	.2	17	1.2	10	.7	38	2.6	1,330	92.7	67	4.7	1,435
2.0	0	.0	3	1.2	2	.8	10	4.0	225	89.3	17	6.7	252
.3	3	.3	14	1.2	8	.7	28	2.4	1,105	93.4	50	4.2	1,183
.0	0	.0	3	.6	1	.2	5	.9	494	91.8	39	7.2	538
.0	0	.0	1	1.1	0	.0	1	1.1	83	92.2	6	6.7	90
.2	0	.0	2	.4	1	.2	4	.9	411	91.7	33	7.4	448
.5	3	.2	20	1.0	11	.6	43	2.2	1,824	92.4	106	5.4	1,973
1.5	0	.0	4	1.2	2	.6	11	3.2	308	90.1	23	6.7	342
.2	3	.2	16	1.0	9	.6	32	2.0	1,516	92.9	83	5.1	1,031
.0	0	.0	0	.0	0	.0	0	.0	1	100.0	0	.0	1
.0	0	.0	0	.0	0	.0	0	.0	0	.0	0	.0	0
.0	0	.0	0	.0	0	.0	0	.0	1	100.0	0	.0	1
.5	3	.2	20	1.0	11	.6	43	2.2	1,825	92.5	106	5.4	1,974
1.5	0	.0	4	1.2	2	.6	11	3.2	308	90.1	23	6.7	342
.2	3	.2	16	1.0	9	.6	32	2.0	1,517	93.0	83	5.1	1,032

MAJOR FIELD 1900 - PHYSICAL SCIENCES

	AMERICAN INDIAN ALASKAN NATIVE		BLACK NON-HISPANIC		ASIAN OR PACIFIC ISLANDER		HISPANIC		TOTAL MINORITY		WHITE NON-HISPANIC		NON-RESIDENT ALIEN		TOTAL
	NUMBER	%	NUMBER	%	NUMBER	%	NUMBER	%	NUMBER	%	NUMBER	%	NUMBER	%	NUMBER
VERMONT (9 INSTITUTIONS)															
UNDERGRADUATES:															
FULL-TIME	0	.0	0	.0	1	.2	2	.4	3	.6	469	97.9	7	1.5	
FEMALE	0	.0	0	.0	0	.0	1	.9	1	.9	116	99.1	0	.0	
MALE	0	.0	0	.0	1	.3	1	.3	2	.6	353	97.5	7	1.9	
PART-TIME	0	.0	0	.0	0	.0	0	.0	0	.0	10	100.0	0	.0	
FEMALE	0	.0	0	.0	0	.0	0	.0	0	.0	2	100.0	0	.0	
MALE	0	.0	0	.0	0	.0	0	.0	0	.0	8	100.0	0	.0	
TOTAL	0	.0	0	.0	1	.2	2	.4	3	.6	479	98.0	7	1.4	
FEMALE	0	.0	0	.0	0	.0	1	.8	1	.8	118	99.2	0	.0	
MALE	0	.0	0	.0	1	.3	1	.3	2	.5	361	97.6	7	1.9	
GRADUATE:															
FULL-TIME	0	.0	0	.0	0	.0	0	.0	0	.0	32	97.0	1	3.0	
FEMALE	0	.0	0	.0	0	.0	0	.0	0	.0	7	100.0	0	.0	
MALE	0	.0	0	.0	0	.0	0	.0	0	.0	25	96.2	1	3.8	
PART-TIME	0	.0	0	.0	0	.0	0	.0	0	.0	27	100.0	0	.0	
FEMALE	0	.0	0	.0	0	.0	0	.0	0	.0	4	100.0	0	.0	
MALE	0	.0	0	.0	0	.0	0	.0	0	.0	23	100.0	0	.0	
TOTAL	0	.0	0	.0	0	.0	0	.0	0	.0	59	98.3	1	1.7	
FEMALE	0	.0	0	.0	0	.0	0	.0	0	.0	11	100.0	0	.0	
MALE	0	.0	0	.0	0	.0	0	.0	0	.0	48	98.0	1	2.0	
PROFESSIONAL:															
FULL-TIME	0	.0	0	.0	0	.0	0	.0	0	.0	0	.0	0	.0	
FEMALE	0	.0	0	.0	0	.0	0	.0	0	.0	0	.0	0	.0	
MALE	0	.0	0	.0	0	.0	0	.0	0	.0	0	.0	0	.0	
PART-TIME	0	.0	0	.0	0	.0	0	.0	0	.0	0	.0	0	.0	
FEMALE	0	.0	0	.0	0	.0	0	.0	0	.0	0	.0	0	.0	
MALE	0	.0	0	.0	0	.0	0	.0	0	.0	0	.0	0	.0	
TOTAL	0	.0	0	.0	0	.0	0	.0	0	.0	0	.0	0	.0	
FEMALE	0	.0	0	.0	0	.0	0	.0	0	.0	0	.0	0	.0	
MALE	0	.0	0	.0	0	.0	0	.0	0	.0	0	.0	0	.0	
UND+GRAD+PROF:															
FULL-TIME	0	.0	0	.0	1	.2	2	.4	3	.6	501	97.9	8	1.6	
FEMALE	0	.0	0	.0	0	.0	1	.8	1	.8	123	99.2	0	.0	
MALE	0	.0	0	.0	1	.3	1	.3	2	.5	378	97.4	8	2.1	
PART-TIME	0	.0	0	.0	0	.0	0	.0	0	.0	37	100.0	0	.0	
FEMALE	0	.0	0	.0	0	.0	0	.0	0	.0	6	100.0	0	.0	
MALE	0	.0	0	.0	0	.0	0	.0	0	.0	31	100.0	0	.0	
TOTAL	0	.0	0	.0	1	.2	2	.4	3	.5	538	98.0	8	1.5	
FEMALE	0	.0	0	.0	0	.0	1	.8	1	.8	129	99.2	0	.0	
MALE	0	.0	0	.0	1	.2	1	.2	2	.5	409	97.6	8	1.9	
UNCLASSIFIED:															
TOTAL	0	.0	0	.0	0	.0	0	.0	0	.0	5	100.0	0	.0	
FEMALE	0	.0	0	.0	0	.0	0	.0	0	.0	2	100.0	0	.0	
MALE	0	.0	0	.0	0	.0	0	.0	0	.0	3	100.0	0	.0	
TOTAL ENROLLMENT:															
TOTAL	0	.0	0	.0	1	.2	2	.4	3	.5	543	98.0	8	1.4	
FEMALE	0	.0	0	.0	0	.0	1	.8	1	.8	131	99.2	0	.0	
MALE	0	.0	0	.0	1	.2	1	.2	2	.5	412	97.6	8	1.9	
VIRGINIA (54 INSTITUTIONS)															
UNDERGRADUATES:															
FULL-TIME	2	.1	250	7.3	63	1.8	12	.3	327	9.5	3,056	88.7	61	1.8	3
FEMALE	1	.1	110	9.3	25	2.1	4	.3	140	11.8	1,022	86.5	20	1.7	1
MALE	1	.0	140	6.2	38	1.7	8	.4	187	8.3	2,034	89.9	41	1.8	2
PART-TIME	0	.0	69	7.5	11	1.2	4	.4	84	9.2	826	90.4	4	.4	
FEMALE	0	.0	36	8.6	4	1.0	1	.2	41	9.8	375	89.5	3	.7	
MALE	0	.0	33	6.7	7	1.4	3	.6	43	8.7	451	91.1	1	.2	
TOTAL	2	.0	319	7.3	74	1.7	16	.4	411	9.4	3,882	89.1	65	1.5	4
FEMALE	1	.1	146	9.1	29	1.8	5	.3	181	11.3	1,397	87.3	23	1.4	1
MALE	1	.0	173	6.3	45	1.6	11	.4	230	8.3	2,485	90.1	42	1.5	2
GRADUATE:															
FULL-TIME	0	.0	4	1.0	10	2.4	1	.2	15	3.6	352	85.4	45	10.9	
FEMALE	0	.0	1	1.3	1	1.3	0	.0	2	2.5	76	95.0	2	2.5	
MALE	0	.0	3	.9	9	2.7	1	.3	13	3.9	276	83.1	43	13.0	
PART-TIME	0	.0	8	3.8	9	4.2	0	.0	17	8.0	187	88.2	8	3.8	
FEMALE	0	.0	3	5.9	3	5.9	0	.0	6	11.8	45	88.2	0	.0	
MALE	0	.0	5	3.1	6	3.7	0	.0	11	6.8	142	88.2	8	5.0	
TOTAL	0	.0	12	1.9	19	3.0	1	.2	32	5.1	539	86.4	53	8.5	
FEMALE	0	.0	4	3.1	4	3.1	0	.0	8	6.1	121	92.4	2	1.5	
MALE	0	.0	8	1.6	15	3.0	1	.2	24	4.9	418	84.8	51	10.3	
PROFESSIONAL:															
FULL-TIME	0	.0	0	.0	0	.0	0	.0	0	.0	0	.0	0	.0	
FEMALE	0	.0	0	.0	0	.0	0	.0	0	.0	0	.0	0	.0	
MALE	0	.0	0	.0	0	.0	0	.0	0	.0	0	.0	0	.0	

FIELD 1900 - PHYSICAL SCIENCES

	AMERICAN INDIAN ALASKAN NATIVE		BLACK NON-HISPANIC		ASIAN OR PACIFIC ISLANDER		HISPANIC		TOTAL MINORITY		WHITE NON-HISPANIC		NON-RESIDENT ALIEN		TOTAL
	NUMBER	%	NUMBER	%	NUMBER	%	NUMBER	%	NUMBER	%	NUMBER	%	NUMBER	%	NUMBER
NIA CONTINUED															
SSIONAL:															
TIME	0	.0	0	.0	0	.0	0	.0	0	.0	0	.0	0	.0	0
MALE	0	.0	0	.0	0	.0	0	.0	0	.0	0	.0	0	.0	0
MALE	0	.0	0	.0	0	.0	0	.0	0	.0	0	.0	0	.0	0
	0	.0	0	.0	0	.0	0	.0	0	.0	0	.0	0	.0	0
MALE	0	.0	0	.0	0	.0	0	.0	0	.0	0	.0	0	.0	0
MALE	0	.0	0	.0	0	.0	0	.0	0	.0	0	.0	0	.0	0
RAD+PROF:															
TIME	2	.1	254	6.6	73	1.9	13	.3	342	8.9	3,408	88.4	106	2.7	3,856
MALE	1	.1	111	8.8	26	2.1	4	.3	142	11.3	1,098	87.0	22	1.7	1,262
MALE	1	.0	143	5.5	47	1.8	9	.3	200	7.7	2,310	89.1	84	3.2	2,594
TIME	1	.0	77	6.8	20	1.8	4	.4	101	9.0	1,013	90.0	12	1.1	1,126
MALE	0	.0	39	8.3	7	1.5	1	.2	47	10.0	420	89.4	3	.6	470
MALE	0	.0	38	5.8	13	2.0	3	.5	54	8.2	593	90.4	9	1.4	656
	2	.0	331	6.6	93	1.9	17	.3	443	8.9	4,421	88.7	118	2.4	4,982
MALE	1	.1	150	8.7	33	1.9	5	.3	189	10.9	1,518	87.6	25	1.4	1,732
MALE	1	.0	181	5.6	60	1.8	12	.4	254	7.8	2,903	89.3	93	2.9	3,250
SSIFIED:															
	0	.0	9	29.0	1	3.2	0	.0	10	32.3	21	67.7	0	.0	31
MALE	0	.0	6	46.2	0	.0	0	.0	6	46.2	7	53.8	0	.0	13
MALE	0	.0	3	16.7	1	5.6	0	.0	4	22.2	14	77.8	0	.0	18
ENROLLMENT:															
	2	.0	340	6.8	94	1.9	17	.3	453	9.0	4,442	88.6	118	2.4	5,013
MALE	1	.1	156	8.9	33	1.9	5	.3	195	11.2	1,525	87.4	25	1.4	1,745
MALE	1	.0	184	5.6	61	1.9	12	.4	258	7.9	2,917	89.3	93	2.8	3,268
NGION (14 INSTITUTIONS)															
GRADUATES:															
TIME	7	.4	11	.7	41	2.5	6	.4	65	4.0	1,513	92.4	59	3.6	1,637
MALE	5	1.2	2	.5	12	2.9	2	.5	21	5.2	374	91.9	12	2.9	407
MALE	2	.2	9	.7	29	2.4	4	.3	44	3.6	1,139	92.6	47	3.8	1,230
TIME	2	.9	3	1.3	5	2.2	0	.0	10	4.3	215	92.7	7	3.0	232
MALE	0	.0	0	.0	1	2.1	0	.0	1	2.1	44	93.6	2	4.3	47
MALE	2	1.1	3	1.6	4	2.2	0	.0	9	4.9	171	92.4	5	2.7	185
	9	.5	14	.7	46	2.5	6	.3	75	4.0	1,728	92.5	66	3.5	1,869
MALE	5	1.1	2	.4	13	2.9	2	.4	22	4.8	418	92.1	14	3.1	454
MALE	4	.3	12	.8	33	2.3	4	.3	53	3.7	1,310	92.6	52	3.7	1,415
ATE:															
TIME	3	.4	9	1.3	15	2.1	2	.3	29	4.1	529	74.8	149	21.1	707
MALE	2	1.9	2	1.9	2	1.9	1	1.0	7	6.7	76	73.1	21	20.2	104
MALE	1	.2	7	1.2	13	2.2	1	.2	22	3.6	453	75.1	128	21.2	603
TIME	1	.7	1	.7	5	3.7	0	.0	7	5.2	120	88.9	8	5.9	135
MALE	0	.0	0	.0	0	.0	0	.0	0	.0	8	80.0	2	20.0	10
MALE	1	.8	1	.8	5	4.0	0	.0	7	5.6	112	89.6	6	4.8	125
	4	.5	10	1.2	20	2.4	2	.2	36	4.3	649	77.1	157	18.6	842
MALE	2	1.8	2	1.8	2	1.8	1	.9	7	6.1	84	73.7	23	20.2	114
MALE	2	.3	8	1.1	18	2.5	1	.1	29	4.0	565	77.6	134	18.4	728
SSIONAL:															
TIME	0	.0	0	.0	0	.0	0	.0	0	.0	0	.0	0	.0	0
MALE	0	.0	0	.0	0	.0	0	.0	0	.0	0	.0	0	.0	0
MALE	0	.0	0	.0	0	.0	0	.0	0	.0	0	.0	0	.0	0
TIME	0	.0	0	.0	0	.0	0	.0	0	.0	0	.0	0	.0	0
MALE	0	.0	0	.0	0	.0	0	.0	0	.0	0	.0	0	.0	0
MALE	0	.0	0	.0	0	.0	0	.0	0	.0	0	.0	0	.0	0
	0	.0	0	.0	0	.0	0	.0	0	.0	0	.0	0	.0	0
MALE	0	.0	0	.0	0	.0	0	.0	0	.0	0	.0	0	.0	0
MALE	0	.0	0	.0	0	.0	0	.0	0	.0	0	.0	0	.0	0
RAD+PROF:															
TIME	10	.4	20	.9	56	2.4	8	.3	94	4.0	2,042	87.1	208	8.9	2,344
MALE	7	1.4	4	.8	14	2.7	3	.6	28	5.5	450	88.1	33	6.5	511
MALE	3	.2	16	.9	42	2.3	5	.3	66	3.6	1,592	86.9	175	9.5	1,833
TIME	3	.8	4	1.1	10	2.7	0	.0	17	4.6	335	91.3	15	4.1	367
MALE	0	.0	0	.0	1	1.8	0	.0	1	1.8	52	91.2	4	7.0	57
MALE	3	1.0	4	1.3	9	2.9	0	.0	16	5.2	283	91.3	11	3.5	310
	13	.5	24	.9	66	2.4	8	.3	111	4.1	2,377	87.7	223	8.2	2,711
MALE	7	1.2	4	.7	15	2.6	3	.5	29	5.1	502	88.4	37	6.5	568
MALE	6	.3	20	.9	51	2.4	5	.2	82	3.8	1,875	87.5	186	8.7	2,143
SSIFIED:															
	1	1.0	0	.0	4	4.1	0	.0	5	5.2	87	89.7	5	5.2	97
MALE	1	3.6	0	.0	2	7.1	0	.0	3	10.7	23	82.1	2	7.1	28
MALE	0	.0	0	.0	2	2.9	0	.0	2	2.9	64	92.8	3	4.3	69
ENROLLMENT:															
	14	.5	24	.9	70	2.5	8	.3	116	4.1	2,464	87.7	228	8.1	2,808
MALE	8	1.3	4	.7	17	2.9	3	.5	32	5.4	525	88.1	39	6.5	596
MALE	6	.3	20	.9	53	2.4	5	.2	84	3.8	1,939	87.7	189	8.5	2,212

TABLE 17 - TOTAL ENROLLMENT IN INSTITUTIONS OF HIGHER EDUCATION FOR SELECTED MAJOR FIELDS OF STUDY AND LEVEL OF ENROLLMENT BY RACE, ETHNICITY, AND SEX: STATE, 1978

MAJOR FIELD 1900 - PHYSICAL SCIENCES

	AMERICAN INDIAN ALASKAN NATIVE		BLACK NON-HISPANIC		ASIAN OR PACIFIC ISLANDER		HISPANIC		TOTAL MINORITY		WHITE NON-HISPANIC		NON-RESIDENT ALIEN		T	
	NUMBER	%	NUMBER	%	NUMBER	%	NUMBER	%	NUMBER	%	NUMBER	%	NUMBER	%	N	
WEST VIRGINIA (10 INSTITUTIONS)																
UNDERGRADUATES:																
FULL-TIME	2	.2	21	2.3	10	1.1	1	.1	34	3.7	863	92.8	33	3.5		
FEMALE	1	.5	7	3.2	1	.5	1	.5	10	4.5	206	92.8	6	2.7		
MALE	1	.1	14	2.0	9	1.3	0	.0	24	3.4	657	92.8	27	3.8		
PART-TIME	1	.8	3	2.5	3	2.5	1	.8	8	6.6	113	93.4	0	.0		
FEMALE	0	.0	0	.0	1	2.9	0	.0	1	2.9	34	97.1	0	.0		
MALE	1	1.2	3	3.5	2	2.3	1	1.2	7	8.1	79	91.9	0	.0		
TOTAL	3	.3	24	2.3	13	1.2	2	.2	42	4.0	976	92.9	33	3.1		
FEMALE	1	.4	7	2.7	2	.8	1	.4	11	4.3	240	93.4	6	2.3		
MALE	2	.3	17	2.1	11	1.4	1	.1	31	3.9	736	92.7	27	3.4		
GRADUATE:																
FULL-TIME	1	.8	2	1.7	1	.8	0	.0	4	3.4	89	76.8	26	21.8		
FEMALE	0	.0	0	.0	0	.0	0	.0	0	.0	14	82.4	3	17.6		
MALE	1	1.0	2	2.0	1	1.0	0	.0	4	3.9	75	73.5	23	22.5		
PART-TIME	0	.0	1	1.4	1	1.4	0	.0	2	2.7	69	93.2	3	4.1		
FEMALE	0	.0	0	.0	0	.0	0	.0	0	.0	15	93.8	1	6.3		
MALE	0	.0	1	1.7	1	1.7	0	.0	2	3.4	54	93.1	2	3.4		
TOTAL	1	.5	3	1.6	2	1.0	0	.0	6	3.1	158	81.9	29	19.0		
FEMALE	0	.0	0	.0	0	.0	0	.0	0	.0	29	87.9	4	12.1		
MALE	1	.6	3	1.9	2	1.3	0	.0	6	3.8	129	80.6	25	15.6		
PROFESSIONAL:																
FULL-TIME	0	.0	0	.0	0	.0	0	.0	0	.0	0	.0	0	.0		
FEMALE	0	.0	0	.0	0	.0	0	.0	0	.0	0	.0	0	.0		
MALE	0	.0	0	.0	0	.0	0	.0	0	.0	0	.0	0	.0		
PART-TIME	0	.0	0	.0	0	.0	0	.0	0	.0	0	.0	0	.0		
FEMALE	0	.0	0	.0	0	.0	0	.0	0	.0	0	.0	0	.0		
MALE	0	.0	0	.0	0	.0	0	.0	0	.0	0	.0	0	.0		
TOTAL	0	.0	0	.0	0	.0	0	.0	0	.0	0	.0	0	.0		
FEMALE	0	.0	0	.0	0	.0	0	.0	0	.0	0	.0	0	.0		
MALE	0	.0	0	.0	0	.0	0	.0	0	.0	0	.0	0	.0		
UND+GRAD+PROF:																
FULL-TIME	3	.3	23	2.2	11	1.0	1	.1	38	3.6	952	90.8	59	5.6		
FEMALE	1	.4	7	2.9	1	.4	1	.4	10	4.2	220	92.1	9	3.8		
MALE	2	.2	16	2.0	10	1.2	0	.0	28	3.5	732	90.4	50	6.2		
PART-TIME	1	.5	4	2.1	4	2.1	1	.5	10	5.1	182	93.3	3	1.5		
FEMALE	0	.0	0	.0	1	2.0	0	.0	1	2.0	49	96.1	1	2.0		
MALE	1	.7	4	2.8	3	2.1	1	.7	9	6.3	133	92.4	2	1.4		
TOTAL	4	.3	27	2.2	15	1.2	2	.2	48	3.9	1,134	91.2	62	5.0		
FEMALE	1	.3	7	2.4	2	.7	1	.3	11	3.8	269	92.8	10	3.4		
MALE	3	.3	20	2.1	13	1.4	1	.1	37	3.9	865	90.7	52	5.5		
UNCLASSIFIED:																
TOTAL	0	.0	0	.0	0	.0	0	.0	0	.0	29	100.0	0	.0		
FEMALE	0	.0	0	.0	0	.0	0	.0	0	.0	5	100.0	0	.0		
MALE	0	.0	0	.0	0	.0	0	.0	0	.0	24	100.0	0	.0		
TOTAL ENROLLMENT:																
TOTAL	4	.3	27	2.1	15	1.2	2	.2	48	3.8	1,163	91.4	62	4.9		
FEMALE	1	.3	7	2.4	2	.7	1	.3	11	3.7	274	92.9	10	3.4		
MALE	3	.3	20	2.0	13	1.3	1	.1	37	3.8	889	90.9	52	5.3		
WISCONSIN (27 INSTITUTIONS)																
UNDERGRADUATES:																
FULL-TIME	2	.1	12	.8	12	.8	9	.6	35	2.3	1,472	94.8	45	2.9		
FEMALE	1	.3	5	1.5	4	1.2	1	.3	11	3.4	310	94.5	7	2.1		
MALE	1	.1	7	.6	8	.7	8	.7	24	2.0	1,162	94.9	38	3.1		
PART-TIME	1	.5	3	1.6	0	.0	0	.0	4	2.1	186	97.9	0	.0		
FEMALE	0	.0	2	5.0	0	.0	0	.0	2	5.0	38	95.0	0	.0		
MALE	1	.7	1	.7	0	.0	0	.0	2	1.3	148	98.7	0	.0		
TOTAL	3	.2	15	.9	12	.7	9	.5	39	2.2	1,658	95.2	45	2.6		
FEMALE	1	.3	7	1.9	4	1.1	1	.3	13	3.5	348	94.6	7	1.9		
MALE	2	.1	8	.6	8	.6	8	.6	26	1.9	1,310	95.3	38	2.8		
GRADUATE:																
FULL-TIME	0	.0	7	.9	19	2.4	4	.5	30	3.9	663	85.2	85	10.9		
FEMALE	0	.0	1	.9	5	4.3	2	1.7	8	7.0	89	77.4	18	15.7		
MALE	0	.0	6	.9	14	2.1	2	.3	22	3.3	574	86.6	67	10.1		
PART-TIME	0	.0	0	.0	3	2.4	3	2.4	6	4.7	97	76.4	24	18.9		
FEMALE	0	.0	0	.0	0	.0	0	.0	0	.0	22	84.6	4	15.4		
MALE	0	.0	0	.0	3	3.0	3	3.0	6	5.9	75	74.3	20	19.8		
TOTAL	0	.0	7	.8	22	2.4	7	.8	36	4.0	760	84.0	109	12.0		
FEMALE	0	.0	1	.7	5	3.5	2	1.4	8	5.7	111	78.7	22	15.6		
MALE	0	.0	6	.8	17	2.2	5	.7	28	3.7	649	84.9	87	11.4		
PROFESSIONAL:																
FULL-TIME	0	.0	0	.0	0	.0	0	.0	0	.0	0	.0	0	.0		
FEMALE	0	.0	0	.0	0	.0	0	.0	0	.0	0	.0	0	.0		
MALE	0	.0	0	.0	0	.0	0	.0	0	.0	0	.0	0	.0		

- PHYSICAL SCIENCES

AN INDIAN N NATIVE		BLACK NON-HISPANIC		ASIAN OR PACIFIC ISLANDER		HISPANIC		TOTAL MINORITY		WHITE NON-HISPANIC		NON-RESIDENT ALIEN		TOTAL
R	%	NUMBER	%	NUMBER	%	NUMBER	%	NUMBER	%	NUMBER	%	NUMBER	%	NUMBER
CONTINUED														
0	.0	0	.0	0	.0	0	.0	0	.0	0	.0	0	.0	0
0	.0	0	.0	0	.0	0	.0	0	.0	0	.0	0	.0	0
0	.0	0	.0	0	.0	0	.0	0	.0	0	.0	0	.0	0
0	.0	0	.0	0	.0	0	.0	0	.0	0	.0	0	.0	0
0	.0	0	.0	0	.0	0	.0	0	.0	0	.0	0	.0	0
0	.0	0	.0	0	.0	0	.0	0	.0	0	.0	0	.0	0
2	.1	19	.8	31	1.3	13	.6	65	2.8	2,135	91.6	130	5.6	2,330
1	.2	6	1.4	9	2.0	3	.7	19	4.3	399	90.1	25	5.6	443
1	.1	13	.7	22	1.2	10	.5	46	2.4	1,736	92.0	105	5.6	1,887
1	.3	3	.9	3	.9	3	.9	10	3.2	283	89.3	24	7.6	317
0	.0	2	3.0	0	.0	0	.0	2	3.0	-60	90.9	4	6.1	66
1	.4	1	.4	3	1.2	3	1.2	8	3.2	223	88.8	20	8.0	251
3	.1	22	.8	34	1.3	16	.6	75	2.8	2,418	91.3	154	5.8	2,647
1	.2	8	1.6	9	1.8	3	.6	21	4.1	459	90.2	29	5.7	509
2	.1	14	.7	25	1.2	13	.6	54	2.5	1,959	91.6	125	5.8	2,138
1	2.9	1	2.9	0	.0	1	2.9	3	8.8	30	88.2	1	2.9	34
0	.0	0	.0	0	.0	1	12.5	1	12.5	7	87.5	0	.0	8
1	3.8	1	3.8	0	.0	0	.0	2	7.7	23	88.5	1	3.8	26
4	.1	23	.9	34	1.3	17	.6	78	2.9	2,448	91.3	155	5.8	2,681
1	.2	8	1.5	9	1.7	4	.8	22	4.3	466	90.1	29	5.6	517
3	.1	15	.7	25	1.2	13	.6	56	2.6	1,982	91.6	126	5.8	2,164
(5 INSTITUTIONS)														
1	.3	2	.6	0	.0	2	.6	5	1.6	307	95.3	10	3.1	322
1	1.4	0	.0	0	.0	1	1.4	2	2.7	72	97.3	0	.0	74
0	.0	2	.8	0	.0	1	.4	3	1.2	235	94.8	10	4.0	248
0	.0	0	.0	0	.0	0	.0	0	.0	27	100.0	0	.0	27
0	.0	0	.0	0	.0	0	.0	0	.0	7	100.0	0	.0	7
0	.0	0	.0	0	.0	0	.0	0	.0	20	100.0	0	.0	20
1	.3	2	.6	0	.0	2	.6	5	1.4	334	95.7	10	2.9	349
1	1.2	0	.0	0	.0	1	1.2	2	2.6	79	97.5	0	.0	81
0	.0	2	.7	0	.0	1	.4	3	1.1	255	95.1	10	3.7	268
0	.0	0	.0	0	.0	0	.0	0	.0	86	91.5	8	8.5	94
0	.0	0	.0	0	.0	0	.0	0	.0	11	91.7	1	8.3	12
0	.0	0	.0	0	.0	0	.0	0	.0	75	91.5	7	8.5	82
0	.0	0	.0	0	.0	1	2.5	1	2.5	36	90.0	3	7.5	40
0	.0	0	.0	0	.0	0	.0	0	.0	4	100.0	0	.0	4
0	.0	0	.0	0	.0	1	2.8	1	2.8	32	88.9	3	8.3	36
0	.0	0	.0	0	.0	1	.7	1	.7	122	91.0	11	8.2	134
0	.0	0	.0	0	.0	0	.0	0	.0	15	93.8	1	6.3	16
0	.0	0	.0	0	.0	1	.8	1	.8	107	90.7	10	8.5	118
0	.0	0	.0	0	.0	0	.0	0	.0	0	.0	0	.0	0
0	.0	0	.0	0	.0	0	.0	0	.0	0	.0	0	.0	0
0	.0	0	.0.	0	.0	0	.0	0	.0	0	.0	0	.0	0
0	.0	0	.0	0	.0	0	.0	0	.0	0	.0	0	.0	0
0	.0	0	.0	0	.0	0	.0	0	.0	0	.0	0	.0	0
0	.0	0	.0	0	.0	0	.0	0	.0	0	.0	0	.0	0
0	.0	0	.0	0	.0	0	.0	0	.0	0	.0	0	.0	0
0	.0	0	.0	0	.0	0	.0	0	.0	0	.0	0	.0	0
0	.0	0	.0	0	.0	0	.0	0	.0	0	.0	0	.0	0
1	.2	2	.5	0	.0	2	.5	5	1.2	393	94.5	18	4.3	416
1	1.2	0	.0	0	.0	1	1.2	2	2.3	83	96.5	1	1.2	86
0	.0	2	.6	0	.0	1	.3	3	.9	310	93.9	17	5.2	330
0	.0	0	.0	0	.0	1	1.5	1	1.5	63	94.0	3	4.5	67
0	.0	0	.0	0	.0	0	.0	0	.0	11	100.0	0	.0	11
0	.0	0	.0	0	.0	1	1.8	1	1.8	52	92.9	3	5.4	56
1	.2	2	.4	0	.0	3	.6	6	1.2	456	94.4	21	4.3	483
1	1.0	0	.0	0	.0	1	1.0	2	2.1	94	96.9	1	1.0	97
0	.0	2	.5	0	.0	2	.5	4	1.0	362	93.8	20	5.2	386
0	.0	0	.0	0	.0	0	.0	0	.0	3	75.0	1	25.0	4
0	.0	0	.0	0	.0	0	.0	0	.0	0	.0	0	.0	0
0	.0	0	.0	0	.0	0	.0	0	.0	3	75.0	1	25.0	4
1	.2	2	.4	0	.0	3	.6	6	1.2	459	94.3	22	4.5	487
1	1.0	0	.0.	0	.0	1	1.0	2	2.1	94	96.9	1	1.0	97
0	.0	2	.5	0	.0	2	.5	4	1.0	365	93.6	21	5.4	390

TABLE 17 - TOTAL ENROLLMENT IN INSTITUTIONS OF HIGHER EDUCATION FOR SELECTED MAJOR FIELDS OF STUDY AND LEVEL OF ENROLLMENT BY RACE, ETHNICITY, AND SEX: STATE, 1978

MAJOR FIELD 1900 - PHYSICAL SCIENCES

	AMERICAN INDIAN ALASKAN NATIVE		BLACK NON-HISPANIC		ASIAN OR PACIFIC ISLANDER		HISPANIC		TOTAL MINORITY		WHITE NON-HISPANIC		NON-RESIDENT ALIEN	
	NUMBER	%	NUMBER	%	NUMBER	%	NUMBER	%	NUMBER	%	NUMBER	%	NUMBER	%
THE STATES AND D.C. (1,501 INSTITUTIONS)														
UNDERGRADUATES:														
FULL-TIME	358	.3	5,037	4.9	2,201	2.1	1,973	1.9	9,569	9.3	89,588	87.3	3,491	3.4
FEMALE	105	.4	2,087	8.0	682	2.6	584	2.2	3,458	13.2	21,999	84.1	712	2.7
MALE	253	.3	2,950	3.9	1,519	2.0	1,389	1.8	6,111	8.0	67,589	88.4	2,779	3.6
PART-TIME	140	.7	1,213	6.2	456	2.3	633	3.2	2,442	12.4	16,907	85.7	370	1.9
FEMALE	46	.7	498	8.0	166	2.7	201	3.2	911	14.6	5,258	84.0	87	1.4
MALE	94	.7	715	5.3	290	2.2	432	3.2	1,531	11.4	11,649	86.5	283	2.1
TOTAL	498	.4	6,250	5.1	2,657	2.2	2,606	2.1	12,011	9.8	106,495	87.0	3,861	3.2
FEMALE	151	.5	2,585	8.0	848	2.6	785	2.4	4,369	13.5	27,257	84.1	799	2.5
MALE	347	.4	3,665	4.1	1,809	2.0	1,821	2.0	7,642	8.5	79,238	88.1	3,062	3.4
GRADUATE:														
FULL-TIME	44	.2	364	1.5	606	2.5	194	.8	1,208	4.9	18,961	76.8	4,531	18.3
FEMALE	8	.2	106	2.6	148	3.7	37	.9	299	7.5	3,019	75.4	684	17.1
MALE	36	.2	258	1.2	458	2.2	157	.8	909	4.4	15,942	77.0	3,847	18.6
PART-TIME	34	.3	266	2.5	320	3.0	96	.9	716	6.8	8,733	82.8	1,099	10.4
FEMALE	16	.7	80	3.6	79	3.5	12	.5	187	8.3	1,845	82.3	209	9.3
MALE	18	.2	186	2.2	241	2.9	84	1.0	529	6.4	6,888	82.9	890	10.7
TOTAL	78	.2	630	1.8	926	2.6	290	.8	1,924	5.5	27,694	78.6	5,630	16.0
FEMALE	24	.4	186	3.0	227	3.6	49	.8	486	7.8	4,864	77.9	893	14.3
MALE	54	.2	444	1.5	699	2.4	241	.8	1,438	5.0	22,830	78.7	4,737	16.3
PROFESSIONAL:														
FULL-TIME	0	.0	0	.0	0	.0	0	.0	0	.0	15	93.8	1	6.3
FEMALE	0	.0	0	.0	0	.0	0	.0	0	.0	3	75.0	1	25.0
MALE	0	.0	0	.0	0	.0	0	.0	0	.0	12	100.0	0	.0
PART-TIME	0	.0	0	.0	0	.0	0	.0	0	.0	1	100.0	0	.0
FEMALE	0	.0	0	.0	0	.0	0	.0	0	.0	0	.0	0	.0
MALE	0	.0	0	.0	0	.0	0	.0	0	.0	1	100.0	0	.0
TOTAL	0	.0	0	.0	0	.0	0	.0	0	.0	16	94.1	1	5.9
FEMALE	0	.0	0	.0	0	.0	0	.0	0	.0	3	75.0	1	25.0
MALE	0	.0	0	.0	0	.0	0	.0	0	.0	13	100.0	0	.0
UND+GRAD+PROF:														
FULL-TIME	402	.3	5,401	4.2	2,807	2.2	2,167	1.7	10,777	8.5	108,564	85.2	8,023	6.3
FEMALE	113	.4	2,193	7.3	830	2.8	621	2.1	3,757	12.5	25,021	82.9	1,397	4.6
MALE	289	.3	3,208	3.3	1,977	2.0	1,546	1.6	7,020	7.2	83,543	86.0	6,626	6.8
PART-TIME	174	.6	1,479	4.9	776	2.6	729	2.4	3,158	10.4	25,641	84.7	1,469	4.9
FEMALE	62	.7	578	6.8	245	2.9	213	2.5	1,098	12.9	7,103	83.6	296	3.5
MALE	112	.5	901	4.1	531	2.4	516	2.4	2,060	9.5	18,538	85.1	1,173	5.4
TOTAL	576	.4	6,880	4.4	3,583	2.3	2,896	1.8	13,935	8.8	134,205	85.1	9,492	6.0
FEMALE	175	.5	2,771	7.2	1,075	2.8	834	2.2	4,855	12.6	32,124	83.1	1,693	4.4
MALE	401	.3	4,109	3.5	2,508	2.1	2,062	1.7	9,080	7.6	102,081	85.8	7,799	6.6
UNCLASSIFIED:														
TOTAL	30	.6	277	5.7	160	3.3	138	2.8	605	12.4	4,049	82.7	241	4.9
FEMALE	5	.3	116	7.9	48	3.3	43	2.9	212	14.5	1,203	82.2	49	3.3
MALE	25	.7	161	4.7	112	3.3	95	2.8	393	11.5	2,846	82.9	192	5.6
TOTAL ENROLLMENT:														
TOTAL	606	.4	7,157	4.4	3,743	2.3	3,034	1.9	14,540	8.9	138,254	85.1	9,733	6.0
FEMALE	180	.4	2,887	7.2	1,123	2.8	877	2.2	5,067	12.6	33,327	83.0	1,742	4.3
MALE	426	.3	4,270	3.5	2,620	2.1	2,157	1.8	9,473	7.7	104,927	85.7	7,991	6.5
GUAM (1 INSTITUTIONS)														
UNDERGRADUATES:														
FULL-TIME	0	.0	0	.0	11	55.0	0	.0	11	55.0	4	20.0	5	25.0
FEMALE	0	.0	0	.0	0	.0	0	.0	0	.0	2	100.0	0	.0
MALE	0	.0	0	.0	11	61.1	0	.0	11	61.1	2	11.1	5	27.8
PART-TIME	0	.0	0	.0	1	100.0	0	.0	1	100.0	0	.0	0	.0
FEMALE	0	.0	0	.0	0	.0	0	.0	0	.0	0	.0	0	.0
MALE	0	.0	0	.0	1	100.0	0	.0	1	100.0	0	.0	0	.0
TOTAL	0	.0	0	.0	12	57.1	0	.0	12	57.1	4	19.0	5	23.8
FEMALE	0	.0	0	.0	0	.0	0	.0	0	.0	2	100.0	0	.0
MALE	0	.0	0	.0	12	63.2	0	.0	12	63.2	2	10.5	5	26.3
GRADUATE:														
FULL-TIME	0	.0	0	.0	0	.0	0	.0	0	.0	0	.0	0	.0
FEMALE	0	.0	0	.0	0	.0	0	.0	0	.0	0	.0	0	.0
MALE	0	.0	0	.0	0	.0	0	.0	0	.0	0	.0	0	.0
PART-TIME	0	.0	0	.0	0	.0	0	.0	0	.0	0	.0	0	.0
FEMALE	0	.0	0	.0	0	.0	0	.0	0	.0	0	.0	0	.0
MALE	0	.0	0	.0	0	.0	0	.0	0	.0	0	.0	0	.0
TOTAL	0	.0	0	.0	0	.0	0	.0	0	.0	0	.0	0	.0
FEMALE	0	.0	0	.0	0	.0	0	.0	0	.0	0	.0	0	.0
MALE	0	.0	0	.0	0	.0	0	.0	0	.0	0	.0	0	.0
PROFESSIONAL:														
FULL-TIME	0	.0	0	.0	0	.0	0	.0	0	.0	0	.0	0	.0
FEMALE	0	.0	0	.0	0	.0	0	.0	0	.0	0	.0	0	.0
MALE	0	.0	0	.0	0	.0	0	.0	0	.0	0	.0	0	.0

- PHYSICAL SCIENCES

CAN INDIAN AN NATIVE		BLACK NON-HISPANIC		ASIAN OR PACIFIC ISLANDER		HISPANIC		TOTAL MINORITY		WHITE NON-HISPANIC		NON-RESIDENT ALIEN		TOTAL
ER	%	NUMBER	%	NUMBER	%	NUMBER	%	NUMBER	%	NUMBER	%	NUMBER	%	NUMBER
CONTINUED														
0	.0	0	.0	0	.0	0	.0	0	.0	0	.0	0	.0	0
0	.0	0	.0	0	.0	0	.0	0	.0	0	.0	0	.0	0
0	.0	0	.0	0	.0	0	.0	0	.0	0	.0	0	.0	0
0	.0	0	.0	0	.0	0	.0	0	.0	0	.0	0	.0	0
0	.0	0	.0	0	.0	0	.0	0	.0	0	.0	0	.0	0
0	.0	0	.0	0	.0	0	.0	0	.0	0	.0	0	.0	0
0	.0	0	.0	11	55.0	0	.0	11	55.0	4	20.0	5	25.0	20
0	.0	0	.0	0	.0	0	.0	0	.0	2	100.0	0	.0	2
0	.0	0	.0	11	61.1	0	.0	11	61.1	2	11.1	5	27.8	18
0	.0	0	.0	1	100.0	0	.0	1	100.0	0	.0	0	.0	1
0	.0	0	.0	0	.0	0	.0	0	.0	0	.0	0	.0	0
0	.0	0	.0	1	100.0	0	.0	1	100.0	0	.0	0	.0	1
0	.0	0	.0	12	57.1	0	.0	12	57.1	4	19.0	5	23.8	21
0	.0	0	.0	0	.0	0	.0	0	.0	2	100.0	0	.0	2
0	.0	0	.0	12	63.2	0	.0	12	63.2	2	10.5	5	26.3	19
0	.0	0	.0	0	.0	0	.0	0	.0	0	.0	0	.0	0
0	.0	0	.0	0	.0	0	.0	0	.0	0	.0	0	.0	0
0	.0	0	.0	0	.0	0	.0	0	.0	0	.0	0	.0	0
0·	.0	0	.0	12	57.1	0	.0	12	57.1	4	19.0	5	23.8	21
0	.0	0	.0	0	.0	0	.0	0	.0	2	100.0	0	.0	2
0	.0	0	.0	12	63.2	0	.0	12	63.2	2	10.5	5	26.3	19
(12 INSTITUTIONS)														
0	.0	0	.0	0	.0	588	99.8	588	99.8	1	.2	0	.0	589
0	.0	0	.0	0	.0	201	100.0	201	100.0	0	.0	0	.0	201
0	.0	0	.0	0	.0	387	99.7	387	99.7	1	.3	0	.0	388
0	.0	0	.0	0	.0	99	100.0	99	100.0	0	.0	0	.0	99
0	.0	0	.0	0	.0	31	100.0	31	100.0	0	.0	0	.0	31
0	.0	0	.0	0	.0	68	100.0	68	100.0	0	.0	0	.0	68
0	.0	0	.0	0	.0	687	99.9	687	99.9	1	.1	0	.0	688
0	.0	0	.0	0	.0	232	100.0	232	100.0	0	.0	0	.0	232
0	.0	0	.0	0	.0	455	99.8	455	99.8	1	.2	0	.0	456
0	.0	0	.0	0	.0	10	100.0	10	100.0	0	.0	0	.0	10
0	.0	0	.0	0	.0	2	100.0	2	100.0	0	.0	0	.0	2
0	.0	0	.0	0	.0	8	100.0	8	100.0	0	.0	0	.0	8
0	.0	0	.0	0	.0	10	100.0	10	100.0	0	.0	0	.0	10
0	.0	0	.0	0	.0	2	100.0	2	100.0	0	.0	0	.0	2
0	.0	0	.0	0	.0	8	100.0	8	100.0	0	.0	0	.0	8
0	.0	0	.0	0	.0	20	100.0	20	100.0	0	.0	0	.0	20
0	.0	0	.0	0	.0	4	100.0	4	100.0	0	.0	0	.0	4
0	.0	0	.0	0	.0	16	100.0	16	100.0	0	.0	0	.0	16
0	.0	0	.0	0	.0	0	.0	0	.0	0	.0	0	.0	0
0	.0	0	.0	0	.0	0	.0	0	.0	0	.0	0	.0	0
0	.0	0	.0	0	.0	0	.0	0	.0	0	.0	0	.0	0
0	.0	0	.0	0	.0	0	.0	0	.0	0	.0	0	.0	0
0	.0	0	.0	0	.0	0	.0	0	.0	0	.0	0	.0	0
0	.0	0	.0	0	.0	0	.0	0	.0	0	.0	0	.0	0
0	.0	0	.0	0	.0	0	.0	0	.0	0	.0	0	.0	0
0	.0	0	.0	0	.0	0	.0	0	.0	0	.0	0	.0	0
0	.0	0	.0	0	.0	0	.0	0	.0	0	.0	0	.0	0
0	.0	0	.0	0	.0	598	99.8	598	99.8	1	.2	0	.0	599
0	.0	0	.0	0	.0	203	100.0	203	100.0	0	.0	0	.0	203
0	.0	0	.0	0	.0	395	99.7	395	99.7	1	.3	0	.0	396
0	.0	0	.0	0	.0	109	100.0	109	100.0	0	.0	0	.0	109
0	.0	0	.0	0	.0	33	100.0	33	100.0	0	.0	0	.0	33
0	.0	0	.0	0	.0	76	100.0	76	100.0	0	.0	0	.0	76
0	.0	0	.0	0	.0	707	99.9	707	99.9	1	.1	0	.0	708
0	.0	0	.0	0	.0	236	100.0	236	100.0	0	.0	0	.0	236
0	.0	0	.0	0	.0	471	99.8	471	99.8	1	.2	0	.0	472
0	.0	0	.0	0	.0	15	100.0	15	100.0	0	.0	0	.0	15
0	.0	0	.0	0	.0	10	100.0	10	100.0	0	.0	0	.0	10
0	.0	0	.0	0	.0	5	100.0	5	100.0	0	.0	0	.0	5
0	.0	0	.0	0	.0	722	99.9	722	99.9	1	.1	0	.0	723
0	.0	0	.0	0	.0	246	100.0	246	100.0	0	.0	0	.0	246
0	.0	0	.0	0	.0	476	99.8	476	99.8	1	.2	0	.0	477

TABLE 17 - TOTAL ENROLLMENT IN INSTITUTIONS OF HIGHER EDUCATION FOR SELECTED MAJOR FIELDS OF STUDY AND LEVEL OF ENROLLMENT
           BY RACE, ETHNICITY, AND SEX: STATE, 1978

MAJOR FIELD 1900 - PHYSICAL SCIENCES

	AMERICAN INDIAN ALASKAN NATIVE		BLACK NON-HISPANIC		ASIAN OR PACIFIC ISLANDER		HISPANIC		TOTAL MINORITY		WHITE NON-HISPANIC		NON-RESIDENT ALIEN		T(
	NUMBER	%	NUMBER	%	NUMBER	%	NUMBER	%	NUMBER	%	NUMBER	%	NUMBER	%	N(
VIRGIN ISLANDS (1 INSTITUTIONS)															
UNDERGRADUATES:															
FULL-TIME	0	.0	4	50.0	0	.0	0	.0	4	50.0	0	.0	4	50.0	
FEMALE	0	.0	1	25.0	0	.0	0	.0	1	25.0	0	.0	3	75.0	
MALE	0	.0	3	75.0	0	.0	0	.0	3	75.0	0	.0	1	25.0	
PART-TIME	0	.0	0	.0	0	.0	0	.0	0	.0	0	.0	0	.0	
FEMALE	0	.0	0	.0	0	.0	0	.0	0	.0	0	.0	0	.0	
MALE	0	.0	0	.0	0	.0	0	.0	0	.0	0	.0	0	.0	
TOTAL	0	.0	4	50.0	0	.0	0	.0	4	50.0	0	.0	4	50.0	
FEMALE	0	.0	1	25.0	0	.0	0	.0	1	25.0	0	.0	3	75.0	
MALE	0	.0	3	75.0	0	.0	0	.0	3	75.0	0	.0	1	25.0	
GRADUATE:															
FULL-TIME	0	.0	0	.0	0	.0	0	.0	0	.0	0	.0	0	.0	
FEMALE	0	.0	0	.0	0	.0	0	.0	0	.0	0	.0	0	.0	
MALE	0	.0	0	.0	0	.0	0	.0	0	.0	0	.0	0	.0	
PART-TIME	0	.0	0	.0	0	.0	0	.0	0	.0	0	.0	0	.0	
FEMALE	0	.0	0	.0	0	.0	0	.0	0	.0	0	.0	0	.0	
MALE	0	.0	0	.0	0	.0	0	.0	0	.0	0	.0	0	.0	
TOTAL	0	.0	0	.0	0	.0	0	.0	0	.0	0	.0	0	.0	
FEMALE	0	.0	0	.0	0	.0	0	.0	0	.0	0	.0	0	.0	
MALE	0	.0	0	.0	0	.0	0	.0	0	.0	0	.0	0	.0	
PROFESSIONAL:															
FULL-TIME	0	.0	0	.0	0	.0	0	.0	0	.0	0	.0	0	.0	
FEMALE	0	.0	0	.0	0	.0	0	.0	0	.0	0	.0	0	.0	
MALE	0	.0	0	.0	0	.0	0	.0	0	.0	0	.0	0	.0	
PART-TIME	0	.0	0	.0	0	.0	0	.0	0	.0	0	.0	0	.0	
FEMALE	0	.0	0	.0	0	.0	0	.0	0	.0	0	.0	0	.0	
MALE	0	.0	0	.0	0	.0	0	.0	0	.0	0	.0	0	.0	
TOTAL	0	.0	0	.0	0	.0	0	.0	0	.0	0	.0	0	.0	
FEMALE	0	.0	0	.0	0	.0	0	.0	0	.0	0	.0	0	.0	
MALE	0	.0	0	.0	0	.0	0	.0	0	.0	0	.0	0	.0	
UND+GRAD+PROF:															
FULL-TIME	0	.0	4	50.0	0	.0	0	.0	4	50.0	0	.0	4	50.0	
FEMALE	0	.0	1	25.0	0	.0	0	.0	1	25.0	0	.0	3	75.0	
MALE	0	.0	3	75.0	0	.0	0	.0	3	75.0	0	.0	1	25.0	
PART-TIME	0	.0	0	.0	0	.0	0	.0	0	.0	0	.0	0	.0	
FEMALE	0	.0	0	.0	0	.0	0	.0	0	.0	0	.0	0	.0	
MALE	0	.0	0	.0	0	.0	0	.0	0	.0	0	.0	0	.0	
TOTAL	0	.0	4	50.0	0	.0	0	.0	4	50.0	0	.0	4	50.0	
FEMALE	0	.0	1	25.0	0	.0	0	.0	1	25.0	0	.0	3	75.0	
MALE	0	.0	3	75.0	0	.0	0	.0	3	75.0	0	.0	1	25.0	
UNCLASSIFIED															
TOTAL	0	.0	0	.0	0	.0	0	.0	0	.0	0	.0	0	.0	
FEMALE	0	.0	0	.0	0	.0	0	.0	0	.0	0	.0	0	.0	
MALE	0	.0	0	.0	0	.0	0	.0	0	.0	0	.0	0	.0	
TOTAL ENROLLMENT:															
TOTAL	0	.0	4	50.0	0	.0	0	.0	4	50.0	0	.0	4	50.0	
FEMALE	0	.0	1	25.0	0	.0	0	.0	1	25.0	0	.0	3	75.0	
MALE	0	.0	3	75.0	0	.0	0	.0	3	75.0	0	.0	1	25.0	
OUTLYING AREAS (14 INSTITUTIONS)															
UNDERGRADUATES:															
FULL-TIME	0	.0	4	.6	11	1.8	588	95.3	603	97.7	5	.8	9	1.5	
FEMALE	0	.0	1	.5	0	.0	201	97.1	202	97.6	2	1.0	3	1.4	
MALE	0	.0	3	.7	11	2.7	387	94.4	401	97.8	3	.7	6	1.5	
PART-TIME	0	.0	C	.0	1	1.0	99	99.0	100	100.0	0	.0	0	.0	
FEMALE	0	.0	0	.0	0	.0	31	100.0	31	100.0	0	.0	0	.0	
MALE	0	.0	0	.0	1	1.4	68	98.6	69	100.0	0	.0	0	.0	
TOTAL	0	.0	4	.6	12	1.7	687	95.8	703	98.0	5	.7	9	1.3	
FEMALE	0	.0	1	.4	0	.0	232	97.5	233	97.9	2	.8	3	1.3	
MALE	0	.0	3	.6	12	2.5	455	95.0	470	98.1	3	.6	6	1.3	
GRADUATE:															
FULL-TIME	0	.0	0	.0	0	.0	10	100.0	10	100.0	0	.0	0	.0	
FEMALE	0	.0	0	.0	0	.0	2	100.0	2	100.0	0	.0	0	.0	
MALE	0	.0	0	.0	0	.0	8	100.0	8	100.0	0	.0	0	.0	
PART-TIME	0	.0	0	.0	0	.0	10	100.0	10	100.0	0	.0	0	.0	
FEMALE	0	.0	0	.0	0	.0	2	100.0	2	100.0	0	.0	0	.0	
MALE	0	.0	0	.0	0	.0	8	100.0	8	100.0	0	.0	0	.0	
TOTAL	0	.0	0	.0	0	.0	20	100.0	20	100.0	0	.0	0	.0	
FEMALE	0	.0	0	.0	0	.0	4	100.0	4	100.0	0	.0	0	.0	
MALE	0	.0	0	.0	0	.0	16	100.0	16	100.0	0	.0	0	.0	
PROFESSIONAL:															
FULL-TIME	0	.0	0	.0	0	.0	0	.0	0	.0	0	.0	0	.0	
FEMALE	0	.0	0	.0	0	.0	0	.0	0	.0	0	.0	0	.0	
MALE	0	.0	0	.0	0	.0	0	.0	0	.0	0	.0	0	.0	

HYSICAL SCIENCES

INDIAN ATIVE		BLACK NON-HISPANIC		ASIAN OR PACIFIC ISLANDER		HISPANIC		TOTAL MINORITY		WHITE NON-HISPANIC		NON-RESIDENT ALIEN		TOTAL
%	NUMBER	%	NUMBER	%	NUMBER	%	NUMBER	%	NUMBER	%	NUMBER	%	NUMBER	%	NUMBER

CONTINUED

.0	0	.0	0	.0	0	.0	0	.0	0	.0	0	.0	0	.0	0
.0	0	.0	0	.0	0	.0	0	.0	0	.0	0	.0	0	.0	0
.0	0	.0	0	.0	0	.0	0	.0	0	.0	0	.0	0	.0	0
.0	0	.0	0	.0	0	.0	0	.0	0	.0	0	.0	0	.0	0
.0	0	.0	0	.0	0	.0	0	.0	0	.0	0	.0	0	.0	0
.0	0	.0	0	.0	0	.0	0	.0	0	.0	0	.0	0	.0	0
.0	4	.6	11	1.8	598	95.4	613	97.8	5	.8	9	1.4	627
.0	1	.5	0	.0	203	97.1	204	97.6	2	1.0	3	1.4	209
.0	3	.7	11	2.6	395	94.5	409	97.8	3	.7	6	1.4	418
.0	0	.0	1	.9	109	99.1	110	100.0	0	.0	0	.0	110
.0	0	.0	0	.0	33	100.0	33	100.0	0	.0	0	.0	33
.0	0	.0	1	1.3	76	98.7	77	100.0	0	.0	0	.0	77
.0	4	.5	12	1.6	707	95.9	723	98.1	5	.7	9	1.2	737
.0	1	.4	0	.0	236	97.5	237	97.9	2	.8	3	1.2	242
.0	3	.6	12	2.4	471	95.2	486	98.2	3	.6	6	1.2	495
.0	0	.0	0	.0	15	100.0	15	100.0	0	.0	0	.0	15
.0	0	.0	0	.0	10	100.0	10	100.0	0	.0	0	.0	10
.0	0	.0	0	.0	5	100.0	5	100.0	0	.0	0	.0	5
.0	4	.5	12	1.6	722	96.0	738	98.1	5	.7	9	1.2	752
.0	1	.4	0	.0	246	97.6	247	98.0	2	.8	3	1.2	252
.0	3	.6	12	2.4	476	95.2	491	98.2	3	.6	6	1.2	500

1900 (1,515 INSTITUTIONS)

.3	5,041	4.9	2,212	2.1	2,561	2.5	10,172	9.9	89,593	86.8	3,500	3.4	103,265
.4	2,088	7.9	682	2.6	785	3.0	3,660	13.9	22,001	83.4	715	2.7	26,376
.3	2,953	3.8	1,530	2.0	1,776	2.3	6,512	8.5	67,592	87.9	2,785	3.6	76,889
.7	1,213	6.1	457	2.3	732	3.7	2,542	12.8	16,907	85.3	370	1.9	19,819
.7	498	7.9	166	2.6	232	3.7	942	15.0	5,258	83.6	87	1.4	6,287
.7	715	5.3	291	2.2	500	3.7	1,600	11.8	11,649	86.1	283	2.1	13,532
.4	6,254	5.1	2,669	2.2	3,293	2.7	12,714	10.3	106,500	86.5	3,870	3.1	123,084
.5	2,586	7.9	848	2.6	1,017	3.1	4,602	14.1	27,259	83.5	802	2.5	32,663
.4	3,668	4.1	1,821	2.0	2,276	2.5	8,112	9.0	79,241	87.6	3,068	3.4	90,421
.2	364	1.5	606	2.5	204	.8	1,218	4.9	18,961	76.7	4,531	18.3	24,710
.2	106	2.6	148	3.7	39	1.0	301	7.5	3,019	75.4	684	17.1	4,004
.2	258	1.2	458	2.2	165	.8	917	4.4	15,942	77.0	3,847	18.6	20,706
.3	266	2.5	320	3.0	106	1.0	726	6.9	8,733	82.7	1,099	10.4	10,558
.7	80	3.6	79	3.5	14	.6	189	8.4	1,845	82.3	209	9.3	2,243
.2	184	2.2	241	2.9	92	1.1	537	6.5	6,888	82.8	890	10.7	8,315
.2	630	1.8	926	2.6	310	.9	1,944	5.5	27,694	78.5	5,630	16.0	35,268
.4	186	3.0	227	3.6	53	.8	490	7.8	4,864	77.9	893	14.3	6,247
.2	444	1.5	699	2.4	257	.9	1,454	5.0	22,830	78.7	4,737	16.3	29,021
.0	0	.0	0	.0	0	.0	0	.0	15	93.8	1	6.3	16
.0	0	.0	0	.0	0	.0	0	.0	3	75.0	1	25.0	4
.0	0	.0	0	.0	0	.0	0	.0	12	100.0	0	.0	12
.0	0	.0	0	.0	0	.0	0	.0	1	100.0	0	.0	1
.0	0	.0	0	.0	0	.0	0	.0	0	.0	0	.0	0
.0	0	.0	0	.0	0	.0	0	.0	1	100.0	0	.0	1
.0	0	.0	0	.0	0	.0	0	.0	16	94.1	1	5.9	17
.0	0	.0	0	.0	0	.0	0	.0	3	75.0	1	25.0	4
.0	0	.0	0	.0	0	.0	0	.0	13	100.0	0	.0	13
.3	5,405	4.2	2,818	2.2	2,765	2.2	11,390	8.9	108,569	84.8	8,032	6.3	127,991
.4	2,194	7.2	830	2.7	824	2.7	3,961	13.0	25,023	82.4	1,400	4.6	30,384
.3	3,211	3.3	1,988	2.0	1,941	2.0	7,429	7.6	83,546	85.6	6,632	6.8	97,607
.6	1,479	4.9	777	2.6	838	2.8	3,268	10.8	25,641	84.4	1,469	4.8	30,378
.7	578	6.8	245	2.9	246	2.9	1,131	13.3	7,103	83.3	296	3.5	8,530
.5	901	4.1	532	2.4	592	2.7	2,137	9.8	18,538	84.8	1,173	5.4	21,848
.4	6,884	4.3	3,595	2.3	3,603	2.3	14,658	9.3	134,210	84.7	9,501	6.0	158,369
.4	2,772	7.1	1,075	2.8	1,070	2.7	5,092	13.1	32,126	82.6	1,696	4.4	38,914
.3	4,112	3.4	2,520	2.1	2,533	2.1	9,566	8.0	102,084	85.5	7,805	6.5	119,455
.6	277	5.6	160	3.3	153	3.1	620	12.6	4,049	82.5	241	4.9	4,910
.3	116	7.9	48	3.3	53	3.6	222	15.1	1,203	81.6	49	3.3	1,474
.7	161	4.7	112	3.3	100	2.9	398	11.6	2,846	82.8	192	5.6	3,436
.4	7,161	4.4	3,755	2.3	3,756	2.3	15,278	9.4	138,259	84.7	9,742	6.0	163,279
.4	2,888	7.2	1,123	2.8	1,123	2.8	5,314	13.2	33,329	82.5	1,745	4.3	40,388
.3	4,273	3.5	2,632	2.1	2,633	2.1	9,964	8.1	104,930	85.4	7,997	6.5	122,891

621

MAJOR FIELD 9000 - ALL OTHERS

	AMERICAN INDIAN ALASKAN NATIVE		BLACK NON-HISPANIC		ASIAN OR PACIFIC ISLANDER		HISPANIC		TOTAL MINORITY		WHITE NON-HISPANIC		NON-RESIDENT ALIEN	
	NUMBER	%	NUMBER	%	NUMBER	%	NUMBER	%	NUMBER	%	NUMBER	%	NUMBER	%
ALABAMA	(	57 INSTITUTIONS)												
UNDERGRADUATES:														
FULL-TIME	81	.1	19,954	29.6	161	.2	221	.3	20,417	30.3	46,330	68.8	629	.9
FEMALE	44	.1	12,715	31.1	68	.2	110	.3	12,937	31.6	27,808	67.9	182	.4
MALE	37	.1	7,239	27.4	93	.4	111	.4	7,480	28.3	18,522	70.0	447	1.7
PART-TIME	50	.2	3,876	17.2	56	.2	70	.3	4,052	18.0	18,399	81.8	51	.2
FEMALE	25	.2	2,363	19.0	26	.2	30	.2	2,444	19.7	9,942	80.1	21	.2
MALE	25	.2	1,513	15.0	30	.3	40	.4	1,608	15.9	8,457	83.8	30	.3
TOTAL	131	.1	23,830	26.5	217	.2	291	.3	24,469	27.2	64,729	72.0	680	.8
FEMALE	69	.1	15,078	28.3	94	.2	140	.3	15,381	28.8	37,750	70.8	203	.4
MALE	62	.2	8,752	23.9	123	.3	151	.4	9,088	24.9	26,979	73.8	477	1.3
GRADUATE:														
FULL-TIME	9	.3	501	14.3	18	.5	23	.7	551	15.8	2,830	81.0	111	3.2
FEMALE	1	.1	311	16.4	8	.4	4	.2	324	17.1	1,538	81.2	32	1.7
MALE	8	.5	190	11.9	10	.6	19	1.2	227	14.2	1,292	80.9	79	4.9
PART-TIME	5	.1	1,238	14.3	30	.3	24	.3	1,297	15.0	7,281	84.4	53	.6
FEMALE	5	.1	870	15.5	7	.1	11	.2	893	16.0	4,683	83.7	20	.4
MALE	0	.0	368	12.1	23	.8	13	.4	404	13.3	2,598	85.6	33	1.1
TOTAL	14	.1	1,739	14.3	48	.4	47	.4	1,848	15.2	10,111	83.4	164	1.4
FEMALE	6	.1	1,181	15.8	15	.2	15	.2	1,217	16.2	6,221	83.1	52	.7
MALE	8	.2	558	12.0	33	.7	32	.7	631	13.6	3,890	84.0	112	2.4
PROFESSIONAL:														
FULL-TIME	0	.0	10	6.7	0	.0	0	.0	10	6.7	140	93.3	0	.0
FEMALE	0	.0	5	16.1	0	.0	0	.0	5	16.1	26	83.9	0	.0
MALE	0	.0	5	4.2	0	.0	0	.0	5	4.2	114	95.8	0	.0
PART-TIME	0	.0	0	.0	0	.0	0	.0	0	.0	0	.0	0	.0
FEMALE	0	.0	0	.0	0	.0	0	.0	0	.0	0	.0	0	.0
MALE	0	.0	0	.0	0	.0	0	.0	0	.0	0	.0	0	.0
TOTAL	0	.0	10	6.7	0	.0	0	.0	10	6.7	140	93.3	0	.0
FEMALE	0	.0	5	16.1	0	.0	0	.0	5	16.1	26	83.9	0	.0
MALE	0	.0	5	4.2	0	.0	0	.0	5	4.2	114	95.8	0	.0
UNDERGRAD+PROF:														
FULL-TIME	90	.1	20,465	28.8	179	.3	244	.3	20,978	29.5	49,300	69.4	740	1.0
FEMALE	45	.1	13,031	30.4	76	.2	114	.3	13,266	31.0	29,372	68.5	214	.5
MALE	45	.2	7,434	26.4	103	.4	130	.5	7,712	27.4	19,928	70.6	526	1.9
PART-TIME	55	.2	5,114	16.4	86	.3	94	.3	5,349	17.2	25,680	82.5	104	.3
FEMALE	30	.2	3,233	18.0	33	.2	41	.2	3,337	18.5	14,625	81.2	41	.2
MALE	25	.2	1,881	14.3	53	.4	53	.4	2,012	15.3	11,055	84.2	63	.5
TOTAL	145	.1	25,579	25.0	265	.3	338	.3	26,327	25.8	74,980	73.9	844	.8
FEMALE	75	.1	16,264	26.7	109	.2	155	.3	16,603	27.3	43,997	72.3	255	.4
MALE	70	.2	9,315	22.6	156	.4	183	.4	9,724	23.5	30,983	75.0	589	1.4
UNCLASSIFIED:														
TOTAL	6	.1	1,160	23.7	16	.3	12	.2	1,194	24.4	3,642	74.3	64	1.3
FEMALE	6	.2	782	27.8	10	.4	4	.1	802	28.5	1,996	70.9	16	.6
MALE	0	.0	378	18.1	6	.3	8	.4	392	18.8	1,646	78.9	48	2.3
TOTAL ENROLLMENT:														
TOTAL	151	.1	26,739	25.0	281	.3	350	.3	27,521	25.7	78,622	73.4	908	.8
FEMALE	81	.1	17,046	26.8	119	.2	159	.2	17,405	27.3	45,993	72.2	271	.4
MALE	70	.2	9,693	22.3	162	.4	191	.4	10,116	23.3	32,629	75.2	637	1.5
ALASKA	(	16 INSTITUTIONS)												
UNDERGRADUATES:														
FULL-TIME	652	15.1	180	4.2	83	1.9	44	1.0	959	22.2	3,331	77.1	31	.7
FEMALE	384	16.9	86	3.8	33	1.5	21	.9	524	23.1	1,731	76.3	15	.7
MALE	268	13.1	94	4.6	50	2.4	23	1.1	435	21.2	1,600	78.0	16	.8
PART-TIME	757	7.0	306	3.6	205	1.9	163	1.5	1,511	13.9	9,344	86.0	13	.1
FEMALE	485	7.2	109	2.8	122	1.6	94	1.4	890	13.2	5,820	86.6	10	.1
MALE	272	6.6	197	4.7	83	2.0	69	1.7	621	15.0	3,524	85.0	3	.1
TOTAL	1,409	9.3	486	3.7	288	1.9	207	1.4	2,470	16.3	12,675	83.4	44	.3
FEMALE	869	9.7	275	3.1	155	1.7	115	1.3	1,414	15.7	7,551	84.0	25	.3
MALE	540	8.7	291	4.7	133	2.1	92	1.5	1,056	17.0	5,124	82.7	19	.3
GRADUATE:														
FULL-TIME	4	2.8	7	4.8	1	.7	4	2.8	16	11.0	124	85.5	5	3.4
FEMALE	1	1.3	2	2.7	0	.0	2	2.7	5	6.7	66	88.0	4	5.3
MALE	3	4.3	5	7.1	1	1.4	2	2.9	11	15.7	58	82.9	1	1.4
PART-TIME	31	4.8	26	4.0	13	2.0	8	1.2	78	12.0	571	87.8	1	.2
FEMALE	20	4.9	15	3.7	9	2.2	7	1.7	51	12.6	353	87.2	1	.2
MALE	11	4.5	11	4.5	4	1.6	1	.4	27	11.0	218	89.0	0	.0
TOTAL	35	4.4	33	4.2	14	1.8	12	1.5	94	11.9	695	87.4	6	.8
FEMALE	21	4.4	17	3.5	9	1.9	9	1.9	56	11.7	419	87.3	5	1.0
MALE	14	4.4	16	5.1	5	1.6	3	1.0	38	12.1	276	87.6	1	.3
PROFESSIONAL:														
FULL-TIME	0	.0	0	.0	0	.0	0	.0	0	.0	0	.0	0	.0
FEMALE	0	.0	0	.0	0	.0	0	.0	0	.0	0	.0	0	.0
MALE	0	.0	0	.0	0	.0	0	.0	0	.0	0	.0	0	.0

ENROLLMENT IN INSTITUTIONS OF HIGHER EDUCATION FOR SELECTED MAJOR FIELDS OF STUDY AND LEVEL OF ENROLLMENT, ETHNICITY, AND SEX: STATE, 1978

ALL OTHERS

N INDIAN NATIVE	BLACK NON-HISPANIC		ASIAN OR PACIFIC ISLANDER		HISPANIC		TOTAL MINORITY		WHITE NON-HISPANIC		NON-RESIDENT ALIEN		TOTAL
%	NUMBER	%	NUMBER	%	NUMBER	%	NUMBER	%	NUMBER	%	NUMBER	%	NUMBER
CONTINUED													
.0	0	.0	0	.0	0	.0	0	.0	0	.0	0	.0	0
.0	0	.0	0	.0	0	.0	0	.0	0	.0	0	.0	0
.0	0	.0	0	.0	0	.0	0	.0	0	.0	0	.0	0
.0	0	.0	0	.0	0	.0	0	.0	0	.0	0	.0	0
.0	0	.0	0	.0	0	.0	0	.0	0	.0	0	.0	0
.0	0	.0	0	.0	0	.0	0	.0	0	.0	0	.0	0
14.7	187	4.2	84	1.9	48	1.1	975	21.8	3,455	77.4	36	.8	4,466
16.4	88	3.8	33	1.4	23	1.0	529	22.6	1,797	76.6	19	.8	2,345
12.8	99	4.7	51	2.4	25	1.2	446	21.0	1,658	78.2	17	.8	2,121
6.8	412	3.6	218	1.9	171	1.5	1,509	13.8	9,915	86.1	14	.1	11,518
7.1	204	2.9	131	1.8	101	1.4	941	13.2	6,173	86.6	11	.2	7,125
6.4	208	4.7	87	2.0	70	1.6	648	14.8	3,742	85.2	3	.1	4,393
9.0	599	3.7	302	1.9	219	1.4	2,564	16.0	13,370	83.6	50	.3	15,984
9.4	292	3.1	164	1.7	124	1.3	1,470	15.5	7,970	84.2	30	.3	9,470
8.5	307	4.7	138	2.1	95	1.5	1,094	16.8	5,400	82.9	20	.3	6,514
10.2	259	3.2	122	1.5	106	1.3	1,328	16.2	6,877	83.7	11	.1	8,216
11.0	113	2.4	71	1.5	46	1.0	747	15.9	3,952	84.0	7	.1	4,706
9.2	146	4.2	51	1.5	60	1.7	581	16.6	2,925	83.3	4	.1	3,510
9.4	858	3.5	424	1.8	325	1.3	3,892	16.1	20,247	83.7	61	.3	24,200
9.9	405	2.9	235	1.7	170	1.2	2,217	15.6	11,922	84.1	37	.3	14,176
8.8	453	4.5	189	1.9	155	1.5	1,675	16.7	8,325	83.1	24	.2	10,024
(22 INSTITUTIONS)													
3.5	1,683	3.3	427	.8	4,443	8.8	8,294	16.5	41,425	82.4	549	1.1	50,268
4.0	666	2.6	227	.9	2,021	7.8	3,943	15.2	21,787	84.0	198	.8	25,928
2.9	1,017	4.2	200	.8	2,422	10.0	4,351	17.9	19,638	80.7	351	1.4	24,340
4.2	1,715	3.0	516	.9	7,200	12.6	11,843	20.7	44,629	78.1	635	1.1	57,107
4.3	756	2.4	349	1.1	4,400	13.8	6,868	21.5	24,806	77.5	324	1.0	31,998
4.2	959	3.8	167	.7	2,800	11.2	4,975	19.8	19,823	78.9	311	1.2	25,109
3.9	3,398	3.2	943	.9	11,643	10.8	20,137	18.8	86,054	80.1	1,184	1.1	107,375
4.1	1,422	2.5	576	1.0	6,421	11.1	10,811	18.7	46,593	80.4	522	.9	57,926
3.6	1,976	4.0	367	.7	5,222	10.6	9,326	18.9	39,461	79.8	662	1.3	49,449
1.0	41	1.2	28	.8	92	2.7	194	5.6	3,014	87.7	227	6.6	3,435
1.2	15	.9	16	.9	33	1.9	85	4.9	1,603	91.7	60	3.4	1,748
.7	26	1.5	12	.7	59	3.5	109	6.5	1,411	83.6	167	9.9	1,687
.7	57	.9	30	.5	209	3.5	338	5.6	5,626	93.3	69	1.1	6,033
.8	34	1.0	19	.5	114	3.3	195	5.6	3,232	93.5	29	.8	3,456
.5	23	.9	11	.4	95	3.7	143	5.5	2,394	92.9	40	1.6	2,577
.8	98	1.0	58	.6	301	3.2	532	5.6	8,640	91.3	296	3.1	9,468
.9	49	.9	35	.7	147	2.8	280	5.4	4,835	92.9	89	1.7	5,204
.6	49	1.1	23	.5	154	3.6	252	5.9	3,805	89.2	207	4.9	4,264
.0	0	.0	0	.0	0	.0	0	.0	0	.0	0	.0	0
.0	0	.0	0	.0	0	.0	0	.0	0	.0	0	.0	0
.0	0	.0	0	.0	0	.0	0	.0	0	.0	0	.0	0
.0	0	.0	0	.0	0	.0	0	.0	3	100.0	0	.0	3
.0	0	.0	0	.0	0	.0	0	.0	1	100.0	0	.0	1
.0	0	.0	0	.0	0	.0	0	.0	2	100.0	0	.0	2
.0	0	.0	0	.0	0	.0	0	.0	3	100.0	0	.0	3
.0	0	.0	0	.0	0	.0	0	.0	1	100.0	0	.0	1
.0	0	.0	0	.0	0	.0	0	.0	2	100.0	0	.0	2
3.3	1,724	3.2	455	.8	4,535	8.4	8,488	15.8	44,439	82.7	776	1.4	53,703
3.8	681	2.5	243	.9	2,054	7.4	4,028	14.6	23,390	84.5	258	.9	27,676
2.8	1,043	4.0	212	.8	2,481	9.5	4,460	17.1	21,049	80.9	518	2.0	26,027
3.9	1,772	2.8	546	.9	7,409	11.7	12,181	19.3	50,258	79.6	704	1.1	63,143
3.9	790	2.2	368	1.0	4,514	12.7	7,063	19.9	28,039	79.1	353	1.0	35,455
3.8	982	3.5	178	.6	2,895	10.5	5,118	18.5	22,219	80.2	351	1.3	27,608
3.6	3,496	3.0	1,001	.9	11,944	10.2	20,669	17.7	94,697	81.0	1,480	1.3	116,846
3.9	1,471	2.3	611	1.0	6,568	10.4	11,091	17.6	51,429	81.5	611	1.0	63,131
3.3	2,025	3.8	390	.7	5,376	10.0	9,578	17.8	43,268	80.6	869	1.6	53,715
3.9	231	1.3	96	.6	1,218	7.0	2,228	12.8	15,110	86.7	93	.5	17,431
4.1	106	1.0	34	.3	627	6.2	1,188	11.7	8,948	87.8	55	.5	10,191
3.6	125	1.7	62	.9	591	8.2	1,040	14.4	6,162	85.1	38	.5	7,240
3.7	3,727	2.8	1,097	.8	13,162	9.8	22,897	17.1	109,807	81.8	1,573	1.2	134,277
3.9	1,577	2.2	645	.9	7,195	9.8	12,279	16.7	60,377	82.3	666	.9	73,322
3.4	2,150	3.5	452	.7	5,967	9.8	10,618	17.4	49,430	81.1	907	1.5	60,955

TABLE 17 - TOTAL ENROLLMENT IN INSTITUTIONS OF HIGHER EDUCATION FOR SELECTED MAJOR FIELDS OF STUDY AND LEVEL OF ENROLLMENT BY RACE, ETHNICITY, AND SEX: STATE, 1978

MAJOR FIELD 9000 - ALL OTHERS

	AMERICAN INDIAN ALASKAN NATIVE		BLACK NON-HISPANIC		ASIAN OR PACIFIC ISLANDER		HISPANIC		TOTAL MINORITY		WHITE NON-HISPANIC		NON-RESIDENT ALIEN	
	NUMBER	%	NUMBER	%	NUMBER	%	NUMBER	%	NUMBER	%	NUMBER	%	NUMBER	%
ARKANSAS	(	33 INSTITUTIONS)												
UNDERGRADUATES:														
FULL-TIME	167	.5	6,163	19.0	152	.5	123	.4	6,605	20.4	29,630	79.1	178	.5
FEMALE	77	.4	3,664	19.6	66	.4	63	.3	3,870	20.7	14,771	79.0	68	.4
MALE	90	.7	2,499	18.2	86	.6	60	.4	2,735	20.0	10,859	79.2	110	.8
PART-TIME	85	.8	1,293	12.8	90	.9	44	.4	1,512	15.0	8,550	84.9	8	.1
FEMALE	46	.8	768	12.7	33	.5	23	.4	870	14.4	5,170	85.5	6	.1
MALE	39	1.0	525	13.0	57	1.4	21	.5	642	16.0	3,380	84.0	2	.0
TOTAL	252	.6	7,456	17.6	242	.6	167	.4	8,117	19.1	34,180	80.5	186	.4
FEMALE	123	.5	4,432	17.9	99	.4	86	.3	4,740	19.1	19,941	80.6	74	.3
MALE	129	.7	3,024	17.1	143	.8	81	.5	3,377	19.0	14,239	80.3	112	.6
GRADUATE:														
FULL-TIME	14	1.0	121	8.5	10	.7	11	.8	156	10.9	1,219	85.2	55	3.8
FEMALE	8	1.1	72	10.3	5	.7	5	.7	90	12.9	596	85.4	12	1.7
MALE	6	.8	49	6.7	5	.7	6	.8	66	9.0	623	85.1	43	5.9
PART-TIME	13	.4	291	9.3	16	.5	5	.2	325	10.4	2,792	89.3	8	.3
FEMALE	8	.4	197	9.8	8	.4	2	.1	215	10.7	1,786	89.2	2	.1
MALE	5	.4	94	8.4	8	.7	3	.3	110	9.8	1,006	89.7	6	.5
TOTAL	27	.6	412	9.0	26	.6	16	.4	481	10.6	4,011	88.1	63	1.4
FEMALE	16	.6	269	10.0	13	.5	7	.3	305	11.3	2,382	88.2	14	.5
MALE	11	.6	143	7.7	13	.7	9	.5	176	9.5	1,629	87.9	49	2.6
PROFESSIONAL:														
FULL-TIME	1	.9	3	2.8	0	.0	0	.0	4	3.7	99	92.5	4	3.7
FEMALE	0	.0	0	.0	0	.0	0	.0	0	.0	1	100.0	0	.0
MALE	1	.9	3	2.8	0	.0	0	.0	4	3.8	98	92.5	4	3.8
PART-TIME	0	.0	1	2.9	0	.0	0	.0	1	2.9	34	97.1	0	.0
FEMALE	0	.0	0	.0	0	.0	0	.0	0	.0	0	.0	0	.0
MALE	0	.0	1	2.9	0	.0	0	.0	1	2.9	34	97.1	0	.0
TOTAL	1	.7	4	2.8	0	.0	0	.0	5	3.5	133	93.7	4	2.8
FEMALE	0	.0	0	.0	0	.0	0	.0	0	.0	1	100.0	0	.0
MALE	1	.7	4	2.8	0	.0	0	.0	5	3.5	132	93.6	4	2.8
UND+GRAD+PROF:														
FULL-TIME	182	.5	6,287	18.5	162	.5	134	.4	6,765	19.9	26,948	79.4	237	.7
FEMALE	85	.4	3,736	19.2	71	.4	68	.4	3,960	20.4	15,368	79.2	80	.4
MALE	97	.7	2,551	17.5	91	.6	66	.5	2,805	19.3	11,580	79.6	157	1.1
PART-TIME	98	.7	1,585	12.0	106	.8	49	.4	1,838	13.9	11,376	86.0	16	.1
FEMALE	54	.7	965	12.0	41	.5	25	.3	1,085	13.5	6,956	86.4	8	.1
MALE	44	.8	620	12.0	65	1.3	24	.5	753	14.5	4,420	85.3	8	.2
TOTAL	280	.6	7,872	16.7	268	.6	183	.4	8,603	18.2	38,324	81.2	253	.5
FEMALE	139	.5	4,701	17.1	112	.4	93	.3	5,045	18.4	22,324	81.3	88	.3
MALE	141	.7	3,171	16.1	156	.8	90	.5	3,558	18.0	16,000	81.1	165	.8
UNCLASSIFIED:														
TOTAL	17	.6	269	8.6	46	1.5	10	.3	342	10.9	2,773	88.5	18	.6
FEMALE	9	.5	170	8.7	21	1.1	9	.5	209	10.7	1,739	88.7	13	.7
MALE	8	.7	99	8.4	25	2.1	1	.1	133	11.3	1,034	88.2	5	.4
TOTAL ENROLLMENT:														
TOTAL	297	.6	8,141	16.2	314	.6	193	.4	8,945	17.8	41,097	81.7	271	.5
FEMALE	148	.5	4,871	16.6	133	.5	102	.3	5,254	17.9	24,063	81.8	101	.3
MALE	149	.7	3,270	15.6	181	.9	91	.4	3,691	17.7	17,034	81.5	170	.8
CALIFORNIA	(	248 INSTITUTIONS)												
UNDERGRADUATES:														
FULL-TIME	5,418	1.2	42,279	9.6	31,483	7.2	43,762	10.0	122,942	28.0	304,686	69.5	10,979	2.5
FEMALE	2,837	1.2	22,867	9.8	16,421	7.0	22,043	9.4	64,168	27.4	165,598	70.7	4,441	1.9
MALE	2,581	1.3	19,412	9.5	15,062	7.4	21,719	10.6	58,774	28.7	139,128	68.1	6,538	3.2
PART-TIME	9,156	1.6	55,116	9.8	29,314	5.2	61,215	10.9	154,801	27.5	403,487	71.7	4,506	.8
FEMALE	4,934	1.5	30,736	9.5	15,070	4.7	31,391	9.7	82,131	25.4	238,770	73.9	2,009	.6
MALE	4,222	1.8	24,380	10.2	14,244	5.9	29,824	12.4	72,670	30.3	164,717	68.7	2,497	1.0
TOTAL	14,574	1.5	97,395	9.7	60,797	6.1	104,977	10.5	277,743	27.7	708,173	70.7	15,485	1.5	1,
FEMALE	7,771	1.4	53,603	9.6	31,491	5.7	53,434	9.6	146,299	26.3	404,328	72.6	6,450	1.2
MALE	6,803	1.5	43,792	9.9	29,306	6.6	51,543	11.6	131,444	29.6	303,845	68.4	9,035	2.0
GRADUATE:														
FULL-TIME	181	.6	1,602	5.0	1,376	4.3	1,653	5.2	4,812	15.0	24,287	75.9	2,883	9.0
FEMALE	96	.6	921	5.7	783	4.8	798	4.9	2,598	16.0	12,710	78.1	957	5.9
MALE	85	.5	681	4.3	593	3.8	855	5.4	2,214	14.1	11,577	73.7	1,926	12.3
PART-TIME	372	.9	2,281	5.6	1,880	4.6	2,195	5.4	6,728	16.6	31,840	78.6	1,916	4.7
FEMALE	163	.8	1,384	6.5	1,058	5.0	1,085	5.1	3,690	17.4	16,889	79.5	669	3.1
MALE	209	1.1	897	4.7	822	4.3	1,110	5.8	3,038	15.8	14,951	77.7	1,247	6.5
TOTAL	553	.8	3,883	5.4	3,256	4.5	3,848	5.3	11,540	15.9	56,127	77.5	4,799	6.6
FEMALE	259	.7	2,305	6.1	1,841	4.9	1,883	5.0	6,288	16.8	29,599	78.9	1,626	4.3
MALE	294	.8	1,578	4.5	1,415	4.0	1,965	5.6	5,252	15.0	26,528	75.9	3,173	9.1
PROFESSIONAL:														
FULL-TIME	14	.4	106	3.2	408	12.1	111	3.3	639	19.0	2,600	77.3	124	3.7
FEMALE	6	.6	36	3.9	165	17.8	17	1.8	224	24.2	676	73.1	25	2.7
MALE	8	.3	70	2.9	243	10.0	94	3.9	415	17.0	1,924	78.9	99	4.1

624

ENROLLMENT IN INSTITUTIONS OF HIGHER EDUCATION FOR SELECTED MAJOR FIELDS OF STUDY AND LEVEL OF ENROLLMENT
, ETHNICITY, AND SEX: STATE, 1978

ALL OTHERS

N INDIAN NATIVE %	BLACK NON-HISPANIC NUMBER	%	ASIAN OR PACIFIC ISLANDER NUMBER	%	HISPANIC NUMBER	%	TOTAL MINORITY NUMBER	%	WHITE NON-HISPANIC NUMBER	%	NON-RESIDENT ALIEN NUMBER	%	TOTAL NUMBER
CONTINUED													
.4	31	5.8	25	4.7	21	3.9	79	14.8	440	82.7	13	2.4	532
.0	4	2.3	8	4.7	2	1.2	14	8.1	156	90.7	2	1.2	172
.0	27	7.5	17	4.7	19	5.3	65	18.1	284	78.9	11	3.1	360
.4	137	3.5	433	11.1	132	3.4	718	18.4	3,040	78.0	137	3.5	3,895
.5	40	3.6	173	15.8	19	1.7	238	21.7	832	75.8	27	2.5	1,097
.4	97	3.5	260	9.3	113	4.0	480	17.2	2,208	78.9	110	3.9	2,794
1.2	43,987	9.3	33,267	7.0	45,526	9.6	128,393	27.1	331,573	70.0	13,986	3.0	473,952
1.2	23,824	9.5	17,369	6.9	22,858	9.1	66,990	26.7	178,944	71.2	5,423	2.2	251,357
1.2	20,163	9.1	15,898	7.1	22,668	10.2	61,403	27.6	152,629	68.6	8,563	3.8	222,595
1.6	57,428	9.5	31,219	5.2	63,431	10.5	161,608	26.8	435,767	72.2	6,435	1.1	603,810
1.5	32,124	9.3	16,136	4.7	32,478	9.4	85,835	24.9	255,815	74.3	2,680	.8	344,330
1.7	25,304	9.8	15,083	5.8	30,953	11.9	75,773	29.2	179,952	69.4	3,755	1.4	259,480
1.4	101,415	9.4	64,486	6.0	108,957	10.1	290,001	26.9	767,340	71.2	20,421	1.9	1,077,762
1.3	55,948	9.4	33,505	5.6	55,336	9.3	152,825	25.7	434,759	73.0	8,103	1.4	595,687
1.5	45,467	9.4	30,981	6.4	53,621	11.1	137,176	28.5	332,581	69.0	12,318	2.6	482,075
1.3	13,630	6.2	14,740	6.7	16,625	7.5	47,766	21.6	170,793	77.2	2,780	1.3	221,339
1.2	7,316	6.2	7,273	6.1	7,944	6.7	23,963	20.2	93,781	78.9	1,152	1.0	118,896
1.3	6,314	6.2	7,467	7.3	8,681	8.5	23,803	23.2	77,012	75.2	1,628	1.6	102,443
1.4	115,045	8.9	79,226	6.1	125,582	9.7	337,767	26.0	938,133	72.2	23,201	1.8	1,299,101
1.3	63,264	8.9	40,778	5.7	63,280	8.9	176,788	24.7	528,540	74.0	9,255	1.3	714,503
1.4	51,781	8.9	38,448	6.6	62,302	10.7	160,979	27.5	409,593	70.1	13,946	2.4	584,518
(40 INSTITUTIONS)													
1.0	2,142	3.9	790	1.4	4,020	7.2	7,513	13.5	47,014	84.7	987	1.8	55,514
1.0	971	3.2	424	1.4	1,962	6.5	3,659	12.2	26,138	87.0	249	.8	30,046
1.0	1,171	4.6	366	1.4	2,058	8.1	3,854	15.1	20,876	82.0	738	2.9	25,468
.9	1,053	4.0	264	1.0	1,556	5.9	3,113	11.9	22,794	86.6	325	1.2	26,232
.9	495	3.4	149	1.0	745	5.1	1,515	10.3	13,071	88.8	131	.9	14,717
1.0	558	4.8	115	1.0	811	7.0	1,598	13.9	9,723	84.4	194	1.7	11,515
1.0	3,195	3.9	1,054	1.3	5,576	6.8	10,626	13.0	69,808	85.4	1,312	1.6	81,746
1.0	1,466	3.3	573	1.3	2,707	6.0	5,174	11.6	39,209	87.6	380	.8	44,763
1.0	1,729	4.7	481	1.3	2,869	7.8	5,452	14.7	30,599	82.7	932	2.5	36,983
.4	115	2.4	51	1.1	199	4.2	383	8.1	4,011	85.3	308	6.6	4,702
.4	59	2.4	26	1.0	94	3.8	189	7.6	2,205	88.7	92	3.7	2,486
.4	56	2.5	25	1.1	105	4.7	194	8.8	1,806	81.5	216	9.7	2,216
.4	64	1.7	39	1.0	197	5.1	315	8.2	3,389	88.1	144	3.7	3,848
.6	30	1.4	25	1.2	101	4.7	168	7.7	1,957	90.2	45	2.1	2,170
.2	34	2.0	14	.8	96	5.7	147	8.8	1,432	85.3	99	5.9	1,678
.4	179	2.1	90	1.1	396	4.6	698	8.2	7,400	86.5	452	5.3	8,550
.5	89	1.9	51	1.1	195	4.2	357	7.7	4,162	89.4	137	2.9	4,656
.3	90	2.3	39	1.0	201	5.2	341	8.8	3,238	83.2	315	8.1	3,894
.0	6	1.6	3	.8	7	1.9	16	4.3	349	94.1	6	1.6	371
.0	1	2.1	0	.0	0	.0	1	2.1	47	97.9	0	.0	48
.0	5	1.5	3	.9	7	2.2	15	4.6	302	93.5	6	1.9	323
.0	2	1.2	0	.0	0	.0	2	1.2	159	98.1	1	.6	162
.0	1	2.9	0	.0	0	.0	1	2.9	34	97.1	0	.0	35
.0	1	.8	0	.0	0	.0	1	.8	125	98.4	1	.8	127
.0	8	1.5	3	.6	7	1.3	18	3.4	508	95.3	7	1.3	533
.0	2	2.4	0	.0	0	.0	2	2.4	81	97.6	0	.0	83
.0	6	1.3	3	.7	7	1.6	16	3.6	427	94.9	7	1.6	450
1.0	2,263	3.7	844	1.4	4,226	7.0	7,912	13.1	51,374	84.8	1,301	2.1	60,587
1.0	1,031	3.2	450	1.4	2,056	6.3	3,849	11.8	28,390	87.1	341	1.0	32,580
1.0	1,232	4.0	394	1.4	2,170	7.7	4,063	14.5	22,984	82.1	960	3.4	28,007
.8	1,119	3.7	303	1.0	1,753	5.8	3,430	11.3	26,342	87.1	470	1.6	30,242
.8	526	3.1	174	1.0	846	5.0	1,684	10.0	15,062	89.0	176	1.0	16,922
.9	593	4.5	129	1.0	907	6.8	1,746	13.1	11,280	84.7	294	2.2	13,320
.9	3,382	3.7	1,147	1.3	5,979	6.6	11,342	12.5	77,716	85.6	1,771	1.9	90,829
.9	1,557	3.1	624	1.3	2,902	5.9	5,533	11.2	43,452	87.8	517	1.0	49,502
.9	1,825	4.4	523	1.3	3,077	7.4	5,809	14.1	34,204	82.9	1,254	3.0	41,327
1.3	743	3.6	192	.9	1,915	9.2	3,112	14.9	17,610	84.2	190	.9	20,912
1.2	418	3.6	108	.9	757	6.5	1,425	12.3	10,077	87.1	67	.6	11,569
1.3	325	3.5	84	.9	1,158	12.4	1,687	18.1	7,533	80.6	123	1.3	9,343
1.0	4,125	3.7	1,339	1.2	7,894	7.1	14,454	12.9	95,326	85.3	1,961	1.8	111,741
1.0	1,975	3.2	732	1.2	3,659	6.0	6,958	11.4	53,529	87.7	584	1.0	61,071
1.0	2,150	4.2	607	1.2	4,235	8.4	7,496	14.8	41,797	82.5	1,377	2.7	50,670

MAJOR FIELD 9000 - ALL OTHERS

	AMERICAN INDIAN ALASKAN NATIVE		BLACK NON-HISPANIC		ASIAN OR PACIFIC ISLANDER		HISPANIC		TOTAL MINORITY		WHITE NON-HISPANIC		NON-RESIDENT ALIEN	
	NUMBER	%	NUMBER	%	NUMBER	%	NUMBER	%	NUMBER	%	NUMBER	%	NUMBER	%
CONNECTICUT (44 INSTITUTIONS)														
UNDERGRADUATES:														
FULL-TIME	105	.2	2,694	5.3	466	.9	839	1.6	4,104	8.0	46,345	90.8	575	1.1
FEMALE	51	.2	1,610	5.6	234	.8	444	1.5	2,339	8.1	20,404	91.1	248	.9
MALE	54	.2	1,084	4.9	232	1.1	395	1.8	1,765	8.0	19,941	90.5	327	1.5
PART-TIME	79	.3	1,947	6.6	138	.5	647	2.2	2,811	9.6	26,445	90.2	55	.2
FEMALE	59	.3	1,150	6.8	65	.4	375	2.2	1,649	9.7	15,331	90.1	31	.2
MALE	20	.2	797	6.5	73	.6	272	2.2	1,162	9.4	11,114	90.4	24	.2
TOTAL	184	.2	4,641	5.8	604	.8	1,486	1.8	6,915	8.6	72,790	90.6	630	.8
FEMALE	110	.2	2,760	6.0	299	.6	819	1.8	3,988	8.7	41,735	90.7	279	.6
MALE	74	.2	1,881	5.5	305	.9	667	1.9	2,927	8.5	31,055	90.5	351	1.0
GRADUATE:														
FULL-TIME	4	.1	132	3.0	29	.7	141	3.2	306	7.0	3,713	85.4	327	7.5
FEMALE	2	.1	81	3.6	10	.4	55	2.5	148	6.7	1,969	88.5	107	4.8
MALE	2	.1	51	2.4	19	.9	86	4.1	158	7.4	1,744	82.2	220	10.4
PART-TIME	11	.1	254	2.4	38	.4	105	1.0	408	3.9	9,873	95.1	96	.9
FEMALE	6	.1	128	1.9	22	.3	52	.8	208	3.2	6,357	96.4	32	.5
MALE	5	.1	126	3.3	16	.4	53	1.4	200	5.3	3,516	93.0	64	1.7
TOTAL	15	.1	386	2.6	67	.5	246	1.7	714	4.8	13,586	92.3	423	2.9
FEMALE	8	.1	209	2.4	32	.4	107	1.2	356	4.0	8,326	94.4	139	1.6
MALE	7	.1	177	3.0	35	.6	139	2.4	358	6.1	5,260	89.1	284	4.8
PROFESSIONAL:														
FULL-TIME	2	.6	24	7.4	3	.9	8	2.5	37	11.5	278	86.1	8	2.5
FEMALE	1	.7	3	2.1	2	1.4	3	2.1	9	6.4	129	92.1	2	1.4
MALE	1	.5	21	11.5	1	.5	5	2.7	28	15.3	149	81.4	6	3.3
PART-TIME	0	.0	2	7.7	0	.0	0	.0	2	7.7	19	73.1	5	19.2
FEMALE	0	.0	1	11.1	0	.0	0	.0	1	11.1	7	77.8	1	11.1
MALE	0	.0	1	5.9	0	.0	0	.0	1	5.9	12	70.6	4	23.5
TOTAL	2	.6	26	7.4	3	.9	8	2.3	39	11.2	297	85.1	13	3.7
FEMALE	1	.7	4	2.7	2	1.3	3	2.0	10	6.7	136	91.3	3	2.0
MALE	1	.5	22	11.0	1	.5	5	2.5	29	14.5	161	80.5	10	5.0
UNC+GRAD+PROF:														
FULL-TIME	111	.2	2,850	5.1	498	.9	988	1.8	4,447	8.0	50,336	90.4	910	1.6
FEMALE	54	.2	1,694	5.4	246	.8	502	1.6	2,496	8.0	28,502	90.9	357	1.1
MALE	57	.2	1,156	4.7	252	1.0	486	2.0	1,951	8.0	21,834	89.7	553	2.3
PART-TIME	90	.2	2,203	5.5	176	.4	752	1.9	3,221	8.1	36,337	91.5	156	.4
FEMALE	65	.3	1,279	5.4	87	.4	427	1.8	1,858	7.9	21,695	91.9	64	.3
MALE	25	.2	924	5.7	89	.6	325	2.0	1,363	8.5	14,642	91.0	92	.6
TOTAL	201	.2	5,053	5.3	674	.7	1,740	1.8	7,668	8.0	86,673	90.8	1,066	1.1
FEMALE	119	.2	2,973	5.4	333	.6	929	1.7	4,354	7.9	50,197	91.3	421	.8
MALE	82	.2	2,080	5.1	341	.8	811	2.0	3,314	8.2	36,476	90.2	645	1.6
UNCLASSIFIED:														
TOTAL	44	.3	449	3.5	73	.6	207	1.6	773	6.0	12,082	93.4	80	.6
FEMALE	23	.3	299	3.6	50	.6	111	1.4	483	5.9	7,680	93.6	43	.5
MALE	21	.4	150	3.2	23	.5	96	2.0	290	6.1	4,402	93.1	37	.8
TOTAL ENROLLMENT:														
TOTAL	245	.2	5,502	5.1	747	.6	1,947	1.8	8,441	7.8	98,755	91.2	1,146	1.1
FEMALE	142	.2	3,272	5.2	383	.6	1,040	1.6	4,837	7.7	57,877	91.6	464	.7
MALE	103	.2	2,230	4.9	364	.8	907	2.0	3,604	8.0	40,878	90.5	682	1.5
DELAWARE (9 INSTITUTIONS)														
UNDERGRADUATES:														
FULL-TIME	16	.1	1,317	12.1	35	.3	47	.4	1,415	13.0	9,410	86.1	99	.9
FEMALE	8	.1	780	11.1	25	.4	26	.4	839	11.9	6,171	87.4	48	.7
MALE	8	.2	537	13.9	10	.3	21	.5	576	14.9	3,239	83.8	51	1.3
PART-TIME	5	.2	445	15.7	14	.5	43	1.5	507	17.9	2,303	81.4	18	.6
FEMALE	4	.2	294	16.3	6	.3	32	1.8	336	18.6	1,450	80.5	16	.9
MALE	1	.1	151	14.7	8	.8	11	1.1	171	16.7	853	83.1	2	.2
TOTAL	21	.2	1,762	12.8	49	.4	90	.7	1,922	14.0	11,713	85.2	117	.9
FEMALE	12	.1	1,074	12.1	31	.3	58	.7	1,175	13.3	7,621	86.0	64	.7
MALE	9	.2	688	14.1	18	.4	32	.7	747	15.3	4,092	83.6	53	1.1
GRADUATE:														
FULL-TIME	1	.5	4	2.1	2	1.1	0	.0	7	3.7	163	86.2	19	10.1
FEMALE	0	.0	1	1.0	0	.0	0	.0	1	1.0	93	95.9	3	3.1
MALE	1	1.1	3	3.3	2	2.2	0	.0	6	6.5	70	76.1	16	17.4
PART-TIME	1	.2	17	2.8	1	.2	2	.3	21	3.4	582	94.8	11	1.8
FEMALE	0	.0	13	3.3	1	.3	2	.5	16	4.0	375	94.7	5	1.3
MALE	1	.5	4	1.8	0	.0	0	.0	5	2.3	207	95.0	6	2.8
TOTAL	2	.2	21	2.6	3	.4	2	.4	28	3.5	745	92.8	30	3.7
FEMALE	0	.0	14	2.8	1	.2	2	.4	17	3.4	468	94.9	8	1.6
MALE	2	.6	7	2.3	2	.6	0	.0	11	3.5	277	89.4	22	7.1
PROFESSIONAL:														
FULL-TIME	0	.0	0	.0	0	.0	0	.0	0	.0	0	.0	0	.0
FEMALE	0	.0	0	.0	0	.0	0	.0	0	.0	0	.0	0	.0
MALE	0	.0	0	.0	0	.0	0	.0	0	.0	0	.0	0	.0

ALL OTHERS

INDIAN NATIVE	BLACK NON-HISPANIC		ASIAN OR PACIFIC ISLANDER		HISPANIC		TOTAL MINORITY		WHITE NON-HISPANIC		NON-RESIDENT ALIEN		TOTAL
%	NUMBER	%	NUMBER	%	NUMBER	%	NUMBER	%	NUMBER	%	NUMBER	%	NUMBER
CONTINUED													
.0	0	.0	0	.0	0	.0	0	.0	0	.0	0	.0	0
.0	0	.0	0	.0	0	.0	0	.0	0	.0	0	.0	0
.0	0	.0	0	.0	0	.0	0	.0	0	.0	0	.0	0
.0	0	.0	0	.0	0	.0	0	.0	0	.0	0	.0	0
.0	0	.0	0	.0	0	.0	0	.0	0	.0	0	.0	0
.0	0	.0	0	.0	0	.0	0	.0	0	.0	0	.0	0
.2	1,321	11.9	37	.3	47	.4	1,422	12.8	9,573	86.1	118	1.1	11,113
.1	781	10.9	25	.3	26	.4	840	11.7	6,264	87.5	51	.7	7,155
.2	540	13.6	12	.3	21	.5	582	14.7	3,309	83.6	67	1.7	3,958
.2	462	13.4	15	.4	45	1.3	528	15.3	2,885	83.8	29	.8	3,442
.2	307	14.0	7	.3	34	1.5	352	16.0	1,825	83.0	21	1.0	2,198
.2	155	12.5	8	.6	11	.9	176	14.1	1,060	85.2	8	.6	1,244
.2	1,783	12.3	52	.4	92	.6	1,950	13.4	12,458	85.6	147	1.0	14,555
.1	1,088	11.6	32	.3	60	.6	1,192	12.7	8,089	86.5	72	.8	9,353
.2	695	13.4	20	.4	32	.6	758	14.6	4,369	84.0	75	1.4	5,202
.2	317	9.4	8	.2	21	.6	353	10.5	2,953	87.6	64	1.9	3,370
.3	167	8.6	4	.2	14	.7	191	9.8	1,721	88.5	32	1.6	1,944
.1	150	10.5	4	.3	7	.5	162	11.4	1,232	86.4	32	2.2	1,426
.2	2,100	11.7	60	.3	113	.6	2,303	12.8	15,411	86.0	211	1.2	17,925
.2	1,255	11.1	36	.3	74	.7	1,383	12.2	9,810	86.8	104	.9	11,297
.2	845	12.7	24	.4	39	.6	920	13.9	5,601	84.5	107	1.6	6,628
(15 INSTITUTIONS)													
.4	6,959	32.8	306	1.4	384	1.8	7,733	36.5	12,047	56.8	1,432	6.8	21,212
.3	4,518	35.5	138	1.1	211	1.7	4,904	38.5	7,069	55.6	752	5.9	12,725
.6	2,441	28.8	168	2.0	173	2.0	2,829	33.3	4,978	58.7	680	8.0	8,487
1.2	6,310	67.6	286	3.1	130	1.4	6,839	73.3	1,940	20.8	550	5.9	9,329
.5	4,006	72.2	68	1.2	89	1.6	4,189	75.5	1,033	18.6	324	5.8	5,546
2.3	2,304	60.9	218	5.8	41	1.1	2,650	70.1	907	24.0	226	6.0	3,783
.6	13,269	43.4	592	1.9	514	1.7	14,572	47.7	13,987	45.8	1,982	6.5	30,541
.3	8,524	46.7	206	1.1	300	1.6	9,093	49.8	8,102	44.3	1,076	5.9	18,271
1.1	4,745	38.7	386	3.1	214	1.7	5,479	44.7	5,885	48.0	906	7.4	12,270
.1	815	15.9	57	1.1	66	1.3	943	18.4	3,291	64.3	885	17.3	5,119
.1	528	20.0	21	.8	39	1.5	590	22.3	1,716	65.0	335	12.7	2,641
.1	287	11.6	36	1.5	27	1.1	353	14.2	1,575	63.6	550	22.2	2,478
.2	1,423	16.5	161	1.9	113	1.3	1,714	19.9	6,243	72.6	642	7.5	8,599
.0	954	22.9	73	1.8	58	1.4	1,086	26.1	2,833	68.1	241	5.8	4,160
.4	469	10.6	88	2.0	55	1.2	628	14.1	3,410	76.8	401	9.0	4,439
.2	2,238	16.3	218	1.6	179	1.3	2,657	19.4	9,534	69.5	1,527	11.1	13,718
.0	1,482	21.8	94	1.4	97	1.4	1,676	24.6	4,549	66.9	576	8.5	6,801
.3	756	10.9	124	1.8	82	1.2	961	14.2	4,985	72.1	951	13.7	6,917
.0	94	27.6	1	.3	2	.6	97	28.5	232	68.2	11	3.2	340
.0	16	21.6	1	1.4	0	.0	17	23.0	56	75.7	1	1.4	74
.0	78	29.3	0	.0	2	.8	80	30.1	176	66.2	10	3.8	266
.0	24	25.3	0	.0	1	1.1	25	26.3	69	72.6	1	1.1	95
.0	4	12.5	0	.0	0	.0	4	12.5	27	84.4	1	3.1	32
.0	20	31.7	0	.0	1	1.6	21	33.3	42	66.7	0	.0	63
.0	118	27.1	1	.2	3	.7	122	28.0	301	69.2	12	2.8	435
.0	20	18.9	1	.9	0	.0	21	19.8	83	78.3	2	1.9	106
.0	98	29.8	0	.0	3	.9	101	30.7	218	66.3	10	3.0	329
.3	7,868	29.5	364	1.4	452	1.7	8,773	32.9	15,570	58.4	2,328	8.7	26,671
.3	5,062	32.8	160	1.0	250	1.6	5,511	35.7	8,841	57.3	1,088	7.0	15,440
.4	2,806	25.0	204	1.8	202	1.8	3,262	29.0	6,729	59.9	1,240	11.0	11,231
.7	7,757	43.0	447	2.5	244	1.4	8,578	47.6	8,252	45.8	1,193	6.6	18,023
.3	4,964	51.0	141	1.4	147	1.5	5,279	54.2	3,893	40.0	566	5.8	9,738
1.2	2,793	33.7	306	3.7	97	1.2	3,299	39.8	4,359	52.6	627	7.6	8,285
.5	15,625	35.0	811	1.8	696	1.6	17,351	38.8	23,822	53.3	3,521	7.9	44,694
.3	10,026	39.8	301	1.2	397	1.6	10,790	42.9	12,734	50.6	1,654	6.6	25,178
.8	5,599	28.7	510	2.6	299	1.5	6,561	33.6	11,088	56.8	1,867	9.6	19,516
.4	1,239	16.4	185	2.4	140	1.9	1,591	21.0	5,035	66.6	935	12.4	7,561
.4	732	18.5	94	2.4	93	2.4	933	23.6	2,585	65.5	429	10.9	3,947
.4	507	14.0	91	2.5	47	1.3	658	18.2	2,450	67.8	506	14.0	3,614
.5	16,864	32.3	996	1.9	836	1.6	18,942	36.2	28,857	55.2	4,456	8.5	52,255
.3	10,758	36.9	395	1.4	490	1.7	11,723	40.3	15,319	52.6	2,083	7.2	29,125
.7	6,106	26.4	601	2.6	346	1.5	7,219	31.2	13,538	58.5	2,373	10.3	23,130

MAJOR FIELD 9000 - ALL OTHERS

	AMERICAN INDIAN ALASKAN NATIVE		BLACK NON-HISPANIC		ASIAN OR PACIFIC ISLANDER		HISPANIC		TOTAL MINORITY		WHITE NON-HISPANIC		NON-RESIDENT ALIEN	
	NUMBER	%	NUMBER	%	NUMBER	%	NUMBER	%	NUMBER	%	NUMBER	%	NUMBER	%
FLORIDA (70 INSTITUTIONS)														
UNDERGRADUATES:														
FULL-TIME	373	.3	19,644	14.7	776	.6	9,198	6.9	29,991	22.4	99,712	74.4	4,301	3.2
FEMALE	236	.3	12,745	17.7	386	.5	4,970	6.9	18,337	25.5	52,342	72.7	1,354	1.9
MALE	137	.2	6,899	11.1	390	.6	4,228	6.8	11,654	18.8	47,370	76.4	2,947	4.8
PART-TIME	317	.3	10,938	10.3	720	.7	9,287	8.7	21,262	20.0	84,448	79.2	852	.8
FEMALE	198	.3	6,725	11.1	338	.6	5,109	8.5	12,370	20.5	47,625	78.8	420	.7
MALE	119	.3	4,213	9.1	382	.8	4,178	9.1	8,892	19.3	36,823	79.8	432	.9
TOTAL	690	.3	30,582	12.7	1,496	.6	18,485	7.7	51,253	21.3	184,160	76.6	5,153	2.1
FEMALE	434	.3	19,470	14.7	724	.5	10,079	7.6	30,707	23.2	99,967	75.5	1,774	1.3
MALE	256	.2	11,112	10.3	772	.7	8,406	7.8	20,546	19.0	84,193	77.9	3,379	3.1
GRADUATE:														
FULL-TIME	21	.2	1,251	12.6	81	.8	363	3.7	1,716	17.3	7,864	79.4	329	3.3
FEMALE	6	.1	729	15.2	27	.6	207	4.3	969	20.3	3,730	78.0	85	1.8
MALE	15	.3	522	10.2	54	1.1	156	3.0	747	14.6	4,134	80.7	244	4.8
PART-TIME	15	.2	1,024	11.8	38	.4	309	3.6	1,386	15.9	7,208	82.8	109	1.3
FEMALE	10	.2	737	13.4	26	.5	206	3.8	979	17.8	4,470	81.4	43	.8
MALE	5	.2	287	8.9	12	.4	103	3.2	407	12.7	2,738	85.3	66	2.1
TOTAL	36	.2	2,275	12.2	119	.6	672	3.6	3,102	16.7	15,072	81.0	438	2.4
FEMALE	16	.2	1,466	14.3	53	.5	413	4.0	1,948	19.0	8,200	79.8	128	1.2
MALE	20	.2	809	9.7	66	.8	259	3.1	1,154	13.8	6,872	82.4	310	3.7
PROFESSIONAL:														
FULL-TIME	4	.8	3	.6	3	.6	16	3.2	26	5.2	474	94.8	0	.0
FEMALE	1	.7	1	.7	0	.0	4	2.9	6	4.3	132	95.7	0	.0
MALE	3	.8	2	.6	3	.8	12	3.3	20	5.5	342	94.5	0	.0
PART-TIME	0	.0	1	20.0	0	.0	0	.0	1	20.0	4	80.0	0	.0
FEMALE	0	.0	0	.0	0	.0	0	.0	0	.0	2	100.0	0	.0
MALE	0	.0	1	33.3	0	.0	0	.0	1	33.3	2	66.7	0	.0
TOTAL	4	.8	4	.8	3	.6	16	3.2	27	5.3	478	94.7	0	.0
FEMALE	1	.7	1	.7	0	.0	4	2.9	6	4.3	134	95.7	0	.0
MALE	3	.8	3	.8	3	.8	12	3.3	21	5.8	344	94.2	0	.0
UND+GRAD+PROF:														
FULL-TIME	398	.3	20,898	14.5	860	.6	9,577	6.6	31,733	22.0	108,050	74.8	4,630	3.2
FEMALE	243	.3	13,475	17.5	413	.5	5,181	6.7	19,312	25.1	56,204	73.0	1,439	1.9
MALE	155	.2	7,423	11.0	447	.7	4,396	6.5	12,421	18.4	51,846	76.9	3,191	4.7
PART-TIME	332	.3	11,963	10.4	758	.7	9,596	8.3	22,649	19.6	91,660	79.5	961	.8
FEMALE	208	.3	7,462	11.3	364	.6	5,315	8.1	13,349	20.3	52,097	79.0	463	.7
MALE	124	.3	4,501	9.1	394	.8	4,281	8.7	9,300	18.8	39,563	80.2	498	1.0
TOTAL	730	.3	32,861	12.7	1,618	.6	19,173	7.4	54,382	20.9	199,710	76.6	5,591	2.2
FEMALE	451	.3	20,937	14.7	777	.5	10,496	7.3	32,661	22.9	108,301	75.8	1,902	1.3
MALE	279	.2	11,924	10.2	841	.7	8,677	7.4	21,721	18.6	91,409	78.2	3,689	3.2
UNCLASSIFIED:														
TOTAL	133	.3	3,958	9.5	284	.7	2,995	7.2	7,370	17.7	33,923	81.5	327	.8
FEMALE	77	.3	2,525	10.3	135	.6	1,755	7.2	4,492	18.4	19,823	81.1	135	.6
MALE	56	.3	1,433	8.3	149	.9	1,240	7.2	2,878	16.8	14,100	82.1	192	1.1
TOTAL ENROLLMENT:														
TOTAL	863	.3	36,819	12.2	1,902	.6	22,168	7.4	61,752	20.5	233,633	77.5	5,918	2.0
FEMALE	528	.3	23,462	14.0	912	.5	12,251	7.3	37,153	22.2	128,124	76.6	2,037	1.2
MALE	335	.2	13,357	10.0	990	.7	9,917	7.4	24,599	18.4	105,509	78.7	3,881	2.9
GEORGIA (68 INSTITUTIONS)														
UNDERGRADUATES:														
FULL-TIME	103	.2	15,040	23.7	210	.3	289	.4	16,242	24.6	48,791	74.0	905	1.4
FEMALE	46	.1	9,898	25.5	116	.3	140	.4	10,200	26.3	28,319	72.9	330	.8
MALE	57	.2	5,142	21.2	94	.3	149	.6	6,042	22.3	20,472	75.6	575	2.1
PART-TIME	63	.3	3,494	15.0	101	.4	158	.7	3,816	16.4	19,199	82.6	219	.9
FEMALE	32	.2	2,062	15.3	51	.4	61	.5	2,206	16.4	11,149	82.9	100	.7
MALE	31	.3	1,432	14.6	50	.5	97	1.0	1,610	16.5	8,050	82.3	119	1.2
TOTAL	166	.2	19,134	21.5	311	.3	447	.5	20,058	22.5	67,990	76.2	1,124	1.3
FEMALE	78	.1	11,960	22.9	167	.3	201	.4	12,406	23.7	39,468	75.5	430	.8
MALE	88	.2	7,174	19.5	144	.4	246	.7	7,652	20.8	28,522	77.4	694	1.9
GRADUATE:														
FULL-TIME	6	.1	1,075	18.2	21	.4	15	.3	1,117	18.9	4,534	76.6	271	4.6
FEMALE	2	.1	794	21.6	10	.3	8	.2	814	22.2	2,781	75.8	73	2.0
MALE	4	.2	281	12.5	11	.5	7	.3	303	13.4	1,753	77.8	198	8.8
PART-TIME	15	.1	1,544	15.2	41	.4	19	.2	1,619	16.0	8,350	82.3	171	1.7
FEMALE	10	.1	1,174	16.8	24	.3	8	.1	1,216	17.4	5,694	81.4	83	1.2
MALE	5	.2	370	11.8	17	.5	11	.3	403	12.8	2,656	84.4	88	2.8
TOTAL	21	.1	2,619	16.3	62	.4	34	.2	2,736	17.0	12,884	80.2	442	2.8
FEMALE	12	.1	1,968	18.5	34	.3	16	.2	2,030	19.0	8,475	79.5	156	1.5
MALE	9	.2	651	12.1	28	.5	18	.3	706	13.1	4,409	81.6	286	5.3
PROFESSIONAL:														
FULL-TIME	0	.0	286	16.9	0	.0	5	.3	291	17.2	1,371	81.2	27	1.6
FEMALE	0	.0	42	15.8	0	.0	0	.0	42	15.8	220	83.0	3	1.1
MALE	0	.0	244	17.1	0	.0	5	.4	249	17.5	1,151	80.8	24	1.7

NROLLMENT IN INSTITUTIONS OF HIGHER EDUCATION FOR SELECTED MAJOR FIELDS OF STUDY AND LEVEL OF ENROLLMENT
, ETHNICITY, AND SEX(STATE, 1978

ALL OTHERS

N INDIAN NATIVE	BLACK NON-HISPANIC		ASIAN OR PACIFIC ISLANDER		HISPANIC		TOTAL MINORITY		WHITE NON-HISPANIC		NON-RESIDENT ALIEN		TOTAL
%	NUMBER	%	NUMBER	%	NUMBER	%	NUMBER	%	NUMBER	%	NUMBER	%	NUMBER

CONTINUED

.0	15	11.3	0	.0	0	.0	15	11.3	118	88.7	0	.0	133
.0	1	5.0	0	.0	0	.0	1	5.0	19	95.0	0	.0	20
.0	14	12.4	0	.0	0	.0	14	12.4	99	87.6	0	.0	113
.0	301	16.5	0	.0	5	.3	306	16.8	1,489	81.7	27	1.5	1,822
.0	43	15.1	0	.0	0	.0	43	15.1	239	83.9	3	1.1	285
.0	258	16.8	0	.0	5	.3	263	17.1	1,250	81.3	24	1.6	1,537
.1	17,001	23.1	231	.3	309	.4	17,650	24.0	54,696	74.4	1,203	1.6	73,549
.1	10,734	25.1	126	.3	148	.3	11,056	25.8	31,320	73.2	406	.9	42,782
.2	6,267	20.4	105	.3	161	.5	6,594	21.4	23,376	76.0	797	2.6	30,767
.2	5,053	15.1	142	.4	177	.5	5,450	16.3	27,667	82.6	390	1.2	33,507
.2	3,237	15.8	75	.4	69	.3	3,423	16.7	16,862	82.4	183	.9	20,468
.3	1,816	13.9	67	.5	108	.8	2,027	15.5	10,805	82.9	207	1.6	13,039
.2	22,054	20.6	373	.3	486	.5	23,100	21.6	82,363	76.9	1,593	1.5	107,056
.1	13,971	22.1	201	.3	217	.3	14,479	22.9	48,182	76.2	589	.9	63,250
.2	8,083	18.5	172	.4	269	.6	8,621	19.7	34,181	78.0	1,004	2.3	43,806
.3	1,451	17.6	47	.6	62	.8	1,582	19.2	6,487	78.8	162	2.0	8,231
.3	883	18.9	27	.6	24	.5	948	20.3	3,648	78.1	73	1.6	4,669
.2	568	15.9	20	.6	38	1.1	634	17.8	2,839	79.7	89	2.5	3,562
.2	23,505	20.4	420	.4	548	.5	24,682	21.4	88,850	77.1	1,755	1.5	115,287
.2	14,854	21.9	228	.3	241	.4	15,427	22.7	51,830	76.3	662	1.0	67,919
.2	8,651	18.3	192	.4	307	.6	9,255	19.5	37,020	78.2	1,093	2.3	47,368

(12 INSTITUTIONS)

.3	202	.9	14,997	69.9	662	3.1	15,916	74.2	4,499	21.0	1,027	4.8	21,442
.2	81	.7	7,807	70.7	290	2.6	8,203	74.3	2,355	21.3	484	4.4	11,042
.3	121	1.2	7,190	69.1	372	3.6	7,713	74.2	2,144	20.6	543	5.2	10,400
.2	173	1.5	7,203	64.5	456	4.1	7,849	70.3	3,030	27.1	284	2.5	11,163
.1	71	1.4	3,217	61.4	224	4.3	3,517	67.1	1,586	30.3	135	2.6	5,238
.2	102	1.7	3,986	67.3	232	3.9	4,332	73.1	1,444	24.4	149	2.5	5,925
.2	375	1.2	22,200	68.1	1,118	3.4	23,765	72.9	7,529	23.1	1,311	4.0	32,605
.2	152	.9	11,024	67.7	514	3.2	11,720	72.0	3,941	24.2	619	3.8	16,280
.3	223	1.4	11,176	68.5	604	3.7	12,045	73.8	3,588	22.0	692	4.2	16,325
.0	11	.8	529	38.0	27	1.9	567	40.7	736	52.8	90	6.5	1,393
.0	6	.8	332	42.0	16	2.0	354	44.8	402	50.8	35	4.4	791
.0	5	.8	197	32.7	11	1.8	213	35.4	334	55.5	55	9.1	602
.1	5	.4	463	40.9	14	1.2	483	42.6	591	52.2	59	5.2	1,133
.0	2	.3	264	43.3	6	1.0	272	44.6	316	51.8	22	3.6	610
.2	3	.6	199	38.0	8	1.5	211	40.3	275	52.6	37	7.1	523
.0	16	.6	992	39.3	41	1.6	1,050	41.6	1,327	52.5	149	5.9	2,526
.0	8	.6	596	42.5	22	1.6	626	44.7	718	51.2	57	4.1	1,401
.1	8	.7	396	35.2	19	1.7	424	37.7	609	54.1	92	8.2	1,125
.0	0	.0	0	.0	0	.0	0	.0	0	.0	0	.0	0
.0	0	.0	0	.0	0	.0	0	.0	0	.0	0	.0	0
.0	0	.0	0	.0	0	.0	0	.0	0	.0	0	.0	0
.0	0	.0	0	.0	0	.0	0	.0	0	.0	0	.0	0
.0	0	.0	0	.0	0	.0	0	.0	0	.0	0	.0	0
.0	0	.0	0	.0	0	.0	0	.0	0	.0	0	.0	0
.0	0	.0	0	.0	0	.0	0	.0	0	.0	0	.0	0
.0	0	.0	0	.0	0	.0	0	.0	0	.0	0	.0	0
.0	0	.0	0	.0	0	.0	0	.0	0	.0	0	.0	0
.2	213	.9	15,526	68.0	689	3.0	16,483	72.2	5,235	22.9	1,117	4.9	22,835
.2	87	.7	8,139	68.8	306	2.6	8,557	72.3	2,757	23.3	519	4.4	11,833
.3	126	1.1	7,387	67.1	383	3.5	7,926	72.0	2,478	22.5	598	5.4	11,002
.1	178	1.4	7,666	62.3	470	3.8	8,332	67.8	3,621	29.4	343	2.8	12,296
.1	73	1.2	3,481	59.5	230	3.9	3,789	64.8	1,902	32.5	157	2.7	5,848
.2	105	1.6	4,189	64.9	240	3.7	4,543	70.5	1,719	26.7	186	2.9	6,448
.2	391	1.1	23,192	66.0	1,159	3.3	24,815	70.6	8,856	25.2	1,460	4.2	35,131
.2	160	.9	11,620	65.7	536	3.0	12,346	69.8	4,659	26.4	676	3.8	17,681
.2	231	1.3	11,572	66.3	623	3.6	12,469	71.5	4,197	24.1	784	4.5	17,450
.3	92	2.2	2,369	55.6	139	3.3	2,611	61.2	1,565	36.7	88	2.1	4,264
.1	25	1.0	1,328	55.6	64	2.7	1,420	59.4	926	38.8	43	1.8	2,389
.4	67	3.6	1,041	55.5	75	4.0	1,191	63.5	639	34.1	45	2.4	1,875
.2	483	1.2	25,561	64.9	1,298	3.3	27,426	69.6	10,421	26.5	1,548	3.9	39,395
.2	185	.9	12,948	64.5	600	3.0	13,766	68.6	5,585	27.8	719	3.6	20,070
.3	298	1.5	12,613	65.3	698	3.6	13,660	70.7	4,836	25.0	829	4.3	19,325

MAJOR FIELD 9000 - ALL OTHERS

	AMERICAN INDIAN ALASKAN NATIVE		BLACK NON-HISPANIC		ASIAN OR PACIFIC ISLANDER		HISPANIC		TOTAL MINORITY		WHITE NON-HISPANIC		NON-RESIDENT ALIEN	
	NUMBER	%	NUMBER	%	NUMBER	%	NUMBER	%	NUMBER	%	NUMBER	%	NUMBER	%
IDAHO	(	9 INSTITUTIONS)												
UNDERGRADUATES:														
FULL-TIME	135	.8	114	.7	154	.9	153	.9	556	3.2	16,240	94.9	318	1.9
FEMALE	85	.9	22	.2	77	.8	84	.9	268	2.8	9,246	95.3	187	1.9
MALE	50	.7	92	1.2	77	1.0	69	.9	288	3.9	6,994	94.3	131	1.8
PART-TIME	41	.6	33	.5	40	.6	61	1.0	175	2.8	6,116	96.7	33	.5
FEMALE	30	.6	14	.4	25	.7	31	.8	100	2.7	3,582	96.7	22	.6
MALE	11	.4	19	.7	15	.6	30	1.1	75	2.9	2,534	96.7	11	.4
TOTAL	176	.8	147	.6	194	.8	214	.9	731	3.1	22,356	95.4	351	1.5
FEMALE	115	.9	36	.3	102	.8	115	.9	368	2.7	12,828	95.7	209	1.6
MALE	61	.8	111	1.1	92	.9	99	1.0	363	3.6	9,528	95.0	142	1.4
GRADUATE:														
FULL-TIME	4	.9	4	.9	7	1.5	4	.9	19	4.1	436	93.4	12	2.6
FEMALE	0	.0	1	.5	3	1.4	2	1.0	6	2.9	198	95.2	4	1.9
MALE	4	1.5	3	1.2	4	1.5	2	.8	13	5.0	238	91.9	8	3.1
PART-TIME	10	.6	7	.4	14	.8	19	1.1	50	3.0	1,633	96.8	4	.2
FEMALE	6	.6	4	.4	9	.9	11	1.1	30	2.9	996	97.0	1	.1
MALE	4	.6	3	.5	5	.8	8	1.2	20	3.0	637	96.5	3	.5
TOTAL	14	.6	11	.5	21	1.0	23	1.1	69	3.2	2,069	96.1	16	.7
FEMALE	6	.5	5	.4	12	1.0	13	1.1	36	2.9	1,194	96.7	5	.4
MALE	8	.9	6	.7	9	1.0	10	1.1	33	3.6	875	95.2	11	1.2
PROFESSIONAL:														
FULL-TIME	0	.0	1	.4	2	.8	0	.0	3	1.1	259	98.9	0	.0
FEMALE	0	.0	1	2.1	1	2.1	0	.0	2	4.3	45	95.7	0	.0
MALE	0	.0	0	.0	1	.5	0	.0	1	.5	214	99.5	0	.0
PART-TIME	0	.0	0	.0	0	.0	0	.0	0	.0	8	100.0	0	.0
FEMALE	0	.0	0	.0	0	.0	0	.0	0	.0	3	100.0	0	.0
MALE	0	.0	0	.0	0	.0	0	.0	0	.0	5	100.0	0	.0
TOTAL	0	.0	1	.4	2	.7	0	.0	3	1.1	267	98.9	0	.0
FEMALE	0	.0	1	2.0	1	2.0	0	.0	2	4.0	48	96.0	0	.0
MALE	0	.0	0	.0	1	.5	0	.0	1	.5	219	99.5	0	.0
UND+GRAD+PROF:														
FULL-TIME	139	.8	119	.7	163	.9	157	.9	578	3.2	16,935	94.9	330	1.8
FEMALE	85	.9	24	.2	81	.8	86	.9	276	2.8	9,489	95.3	191	1.9
MALE	54	.7	95	1.2	82	1.0	71	.9	302	3.8	7,446	94.4	139	1.8
PART-TIME	51	.6	40	.5	54	.7	80	1.0	225	2.8	7,757	96.7	37	.5
FEMALE	36	.6	18	.4	34	.7	42	.9	130	2.7	4,581	96.8	23	.5
MALE	15	.5	22	.7	20	.6	38	1.2	95	2.9	3,176	96.7	14	.4
TOTAL	190	.7	159	.6	217	.8	237	.9	803	3.1	24,692	95.5	367	1.4
FEMALE	121	.8	42	.3	115	.8	128	.9	406	2.8	14,070	95.8	214	1.5
MALE	69	.6	117	1.0	102	.9	109	1.0	397	3.6	10,622	95.1	153	1.4
UNCLASSIFIED:														
TOTAL	28	.8	9	.3	45	1.4	32	1.0	114	3.4	3,201	96.5	3	.1
FEMALE	14	.8	2	.1	23	1.3	13	.8	52	3.1	1,649	96.8	3	.2
MALE	14	.9	7	.4	22	1.4	19	1.2	62	3.8	1,552	96.2	0	.0
TOTAL ENROLLMENT:														
TOTAL	218	.7	168	.6	262	.9	269	.9	917	3.1	27,893	95.6	370	1.3
FEMALE	135	.8	44	.3	138	.8	141	.9	458	2.8	15,719	95.9	217	1.3
MALE	83	.6	124	1.0	124	1.0	128	1.0	459	3.6	12,174	95.2	153	1.2
ILLINOIS	(	146 INSTITUTIONS)												
UNDERGRADUATES:														
FULL-TIME	568	.3	31,121	16.0	2,422	1.2	5,024	2.6	39,135	20.1	152,852	78.4	2,921	1.5
FEMALE	300	.3	18,901	17.6	1,277	1.2	2,700	2.5	23,178	21.6	83,169	77.4	1,059	1.0
MALE	268	.3	12,220	14.0	1,145	1.3	2,324	2.7	15,957	18.2	69,683	79.6	1,862	2.1
PART-TIME	836	.5	22,347	13.4	2,014	1.2	4,357	2.6	29,554	17.7	135,025	81.1	1,969	1.2
FEMALE	472	.5	13,674	14.1	1,085	1.1	2,099	2.2	17,330	17.9	78,619	81.2	932	1.0
MALE	364	.5	8,673	12.4	929	1.3	2,258	3.2	12,224	17.5	56,406	81.0	1,037	1.5
TOTAL	1,404	.4	53,468	14.8	4,436	1.2	9,381	2.6	68,689	19.0	287,877	79.6	4,890	1.4
FEMALE	772	.4	32,575	15.9	2,362	1.2	4,799	2.3	40,508	19.8	161,788	79.2	1,991	1.0
MALE	632	.4	20,893	13.3	2,074	1.3	4,582	2.9	28,181	17.9	126,089	80.2	2,899	1.8
GRADUATE:														
FULL-TIME	25	.2	798	6.2	221	1.7	239	1.9	1,283	10.0	10,340	80.3	1,260	9.8
FEMALE	9	.1	491	8.1	106	1.7	114	1.9	720	11.8	4,958	81.3	421	6.9
MALE	16	.2	307	4.5	115	1.7	125	1.8	563	8.3	5,382	79.3	839	12.4
PART-TIME	54	.2	2,195	9.1	324	1.3	291	1.2	2,864	11.8	20,591	85.2	714	3.0
FEMALE	28	.2	1,448	10.9	135	1.0	151	1.1	1,762	13.3	11,246	84.7	273	2.1
MALE	26	.2	747	6.9	189	1.7	140	1.3	1,102	10.1	9,345	85.8	441	4.1
TOTAL	79	.2	2,993	8.1	545	1.5	530	1.4	4,147	11.2	30,931	83.5	1,974	5.3
FEMALE	37	.2	1,939	10.0	241	1.2	265	1.4	2,482	12.8	16,204	83.6	694	3.6
MALE	42	.2	1,054	6.0	304	1.7	265	1.5	1,665	9.4	14,727	83.3	1,280	7.2
PROFESSIONAL:														
FULL-TIME	4	.1	104	2.8	48	1.3	25	.7	181	4.8	3,488	92.7	92	2.4
FEMALE	0	.0	27	4.9	8	1.5	2	.4	37	6.7	503	91.3	11	2.0
MALE	4	.1	77	2.4	40	1.2	23	.7	144	4.5	2,985	93.0	81	2.5

NROLLMENT IN INSTITUTIONS OF HIGHER EDUCATION FOR SELECTED MAJOR FIELDS UF STUDY AND LEVEL OF ENROLLMENT
, ETHNICITY, AND SEX: STATE, 1978

ALL OTHERS

% INDIAN NATIVE	BLACK NON-HISPANIC		ASIAN OR PACIFIC ISLANDER		HISPANIC		TOTAL MINORITY		WHITE NON-HISPANIC		NON-RESIDENT ALIEN		TOTAL
%	NUMBER	%	NUMBER	%	NUMBER	%	NUMBER	%	NUMBER	%	NUMBER	%	NUMBER
CONTINUED													
.0	8	3.3	2	.8	0	.0	10	4.1	225	92.6	8	3.3	243
.0	0	.0	0	.0	0	.0	0	.0	52	98.1	1	1.9	53
.0	8	4.2	2	1.1	0	.0	10	5.3	173	91.1	7	3.7	190
.1	112	2.8	50	1.2	25	.6	191	4.8	3,713	92.7	100	2.5	4,004
.0	27	4.5	8	1.3	2	.3	37	6.1	555	91.9	12	2.0	604
.1	85	2.5	42	1.2	23	.7	154	4.5	3,158	92.9	88	2.6	3,400
.3	32,023	15.1	2,691	1.3	5,288	2.5	40,599	19.2	166,680	78.8	4,273	2.0	211,552
.3	19,419	17.0	1,391	1.2	2,816	2.5	23,935	21.0	88,630	77.7	1,491	1.3	114,056
.3	12,604	12.9	1,300	1.3	2,472	2.5	16,664	17.1	78,050	80.1	2,782	2.9	97,496
.5	24,550	12.9	2,340	1.2	4,648	2.4	32,428	17.0	155,841	81.6	2,691	1.4	190,960
.5	15,122	13.7	1,220	1.1	2,250	2.0	19,092	17.3	89,917	81.6	1,206	1.1	110,215
.5	9,428	11.7	1,120	1.4	2,398	3.0	13,336	16.5	65,924	81.6	1,485	1.8	80,745
.4	56,573	14.1	5,031	1.2	9,936	2.5	73,027	18.1	322,521	80.1	6,964	1.7	402,512
.4	34,541	15.4	2,611	1.2	5,066	2.3	43,027	19.2	178,547	79.6	2,697	1.2	224,271
.4	22,032	12.4	2,420	1.4	4,870	2.7	30,000	16.8	143,974	80.8	4,267	2.4	178,241
.3	6,167	8.8	1,363	2.0	1,759	2.5	9,518	13.6	58,996	84.5	1,307	1.9	69,821
.3	3,741	9.0	765	1.8	932	2.2	5,572	13.3	35,608	85.2	610	1.5	41,790
.3	2,426	8.7	598	2.1	827	3.0	3,946	14.1	23,388	83.4	697	2.5	28,031
.4	62,740	13.3	6,394	1.4	11,695	2.5	82,545	17.5	381,517	80.8	8,271	1.8	472,333
.4	38,282	14.4	3,376	1.3	5,998	2.3	48,599	18.3	214,155	80.5	3,307	1.2	266,061
.4	24,458	11.9	3,018	1.5	5,697	2.8	33,946	16.5	167,362	81.1	4,964	2.4	206,272
(6J INSTITUTIONS)													
.2	4,912	5.7	423	.5	831	1.0	6,333	7.3	78,963	91.6	937	1.1	86,233
.2	2,813	5.8	222	.5	387	.8	3,500	7.2	44,988	92.0	387	.8	48,875
.2	2,099	5.6	201	.5	444	1.2	2,833	7.6	33,975	90.9	550	1.5	37,358
.4	2,801	8.2	163	.5	367	1.1	3,455	10.1	30,609	89.4	181	.5	34,245
.3	1,703	9.1	78	.4	189	1.0	2,023	10.8	16,543	88.6	104	.6	18,670
.5	1,098	7.0	85	.5	170	1.1	1,432	9.2	14,066	90.3	77	.5	15,575
.2	7,713	6.4	586	.5	1,198	1.0	9,788	8.1	109,572	90.9	1,118	.9	120,478
.2	4,516	6.7	300	.4	576	.9	5,523	8.2	61,531	91.1	491	.7	67,545
.3	3,197	6.0	286	.5	622	1.2	4,265	8.1	48,041	90.8	627	1.2	52,933
.3	230	3.4	38	.6	94	1.4	384	5.7	5,585	83.5	720	10.8	6,689
.4	129	4.2	22	.7	35	1.1	198	6.4	2,679	86.3	227	7.3	3,104
.3	101	2.8	16	.4	59	1.6	186	5.2	2,906	81.1	493	13.8	3,585
.2	570	3.9	59	.4	55	.4	709	4.8	13,645	92.5	397	2.7	14,751
.2	385	4.2	31	.3	33	.4	467	5.1	8,463	93.2	153	1.7	9,083
.1	185	3.3	28	.5	22	.4	242	4.3	5,182	91.4	244	4.3	5,668
.2	800	3.7	97	.5	149	.7	1,093	5.1	19,230	89.7	1,117	5.2	21,440
.2	514	4.2	53	.4	68	.6	665	5.5	11,142	91.4	380	3.1	12,187
.2	286	3.1	44	.5	81	.9	428	4.6	8,088	87.4	737	8.0	9,253
.1	28	2.0	9	.6	23	1.6	61	4.3	1,307	92.7	42	3.0	1,410
.0	13	9.0	1	.7	2	1.4	16	11.0	123	84.8	6	4.1	145
.1	15	1.2	8	.6	21	1.7	45	3.6	1,184	93.6	36	2.8	1,265
.0	9	2.7	1	.3	1	.3	11	3.3	321	95.8	3	.9	335
.0	3	5.5	0	.0	0	.0	3	5.5	51	92.7	1	1.8	55
.0	6	2.1	1	.4	1	.4	8	2.9	270	96.4	2	.7	280
.1	37	2.1	10	.6	24	1.4	72	4.1	1,628	93.3	45	2.6	1,745
.0	16	8.0	1	.5	2	1.0	19	9.5	174	87.0	7	3.5	200
.1	21	1.4	9	.6	22	1.4	53	3.4	1,454	94.1	38	2.5	1,545
.2	5,170	5.5	470	.5	948	1.0	6,778	7.2	85,855	91.0	1,699	1.8	94,332
.2	2,955	5.7	245	.5	424	.8	3,714	7.1	47,790	91.7	620	1.2	52,124
.2	2,215	5.8	225	.5	524	1.2	3,064	7.3	38,065	90.2	1,079	2.6	42,208
.3	3,380	6.9	223	.5	423	.9	4,175	8.5	44,575	90.4	581	1.2	49,331
.3	2,091	7.5	109	.4	222	.8	2,493	9.0	25,057	90.1	258	.9	27,808
.4	1,289	6.0	114	.5	201	.9	1,682	7.8	19,518	90.7	323	1.5	21,523
.2	8,550	6.0	693	.5	1,371	1.0	10,953	7.6	130,430	90.8	2,280	1.6	143,663
.2	5,046	6.3	354	.4	646	.8	6,207	7.8	72,847	91.1	878	1.1	79,932
.3	3,504	5.5	339	.5	725	1.1	4,746	7.4	57,583	90.4	1,402	2.2	63,731
.3	733	6.0	80	.7	122	1.0	971	7.9	11,091	90.2	232	1.9	12,294
.3	480	6.4	41	.5	65	.9	612	8.2	6,737	90.3	109	1.5	7,458
.2	253	5.2	39	.8	57	1.2	359	7.4	4,354	90.0	123	2.5	4,836
.2	9,283	6.0	773	.5	1,493	1.0	11,924	7.6	141,521	90.7	2,512	1.6	155,957
.2	5,526	6.3	395	.5	711	.8	6,819	7.8	79,584	91.1	987	1.1	87,390
.3	3,757	5.5	378	.6	782	1.1	5,105	7.4	61,937	90.3	1,525	2.2	68,567

TABLE 17 - TOTAL ENROLLMENT IN INSTITUTIONS OF HIGHER EDUCATION FOR SELECTED MAJOR FIELDS OF STUDY AND LEVEL OF ENROLLMENT BY RACE, ETHNICITY, AND SEX: STATE, 1976

MAJOR FIELD 9000 - ALL OTHERS

	AMERICAN INDIAN ALASKAN NATIVE		BLACK NON-HISPANIC		ASIAN OR PACIFIC ISLANDER		HISPANIC		TOTAL MINORITY		WHITE NON-HISPANIC		NON-RESIDENT ALIEN	
	NUMBER	%	NUMBER	%	NUMBER	%	NUMBER	%	NUMBER	%	NUMBER	%	NUMBER	%
IOWA (60 INSTITUTIONS)														
UNDERGRADUATES:														
FULL-TIME	231	.4	1,643	2.6	334	.5	365	.6	2,573	4.1	59,734	94.3	1,043	1.6
FEMALE	118	.3	673	1.9	157	.4	163	.5	1,111	3.2	33,578	95.6	419	1.2
MALE	113	.4	970	3.4	177	.6	202	.7	1,462	5.2	26,156	92.6	624	2.2
PART-TIME	64	.5	245	1.8	69	.5	89	.7	467	3.5	12,678	95.7	103	.8
FEMALE	40	.5	153	1.9	35	.4	46	.6	274	3.4	7,722	95.9	56	.7
MALE	24	.5	92	1.8	34	.7	43	.8	193	3.7	4,956	95.4	47	.9
TOTAL	295	.4	1,888	2.5	403	.5	454	.6	3,040	4.0	72,412	94.5	1,146	1.5
FEMALE	158	.4	826	1.9	192	.4	209	.5	1,385	3.2	41,300	95.7	475	1.1
MALE	137	.4	1,062	3.2	211	.6	245	.7	1,655	4.9	31,112	93.0	671	2.0
GRADUATE:														
FULL-TIME	8	.2	126	3.6	29	.8	31	.9	194	5.6	2,927	83.8	373	10.7
FEMALE	3	.2	77	5.0	10	.6	14	.9	104	6.7	1,314	85.0	127	8.2
MALE	5	.3	49	2.5	19	1.0	17	.9	90	4.6	1,613	82.8	246	12.6
PART-TIME	14	.2	135	1.9	41	.6	18	.3	208	2.9	6,681	93.1	284	4.0
FEMALE	9	.2	70	1.7	20	.5	8	.2	107	2.6	3,954	94.9	106	2.5
MALE	5	.2	65	2.2	21	.7	10	.3	101	3.4	2,727	90.7	178	5.9
TOTAL	22	.2	261	2.4	70	.7	49	.5	402	3.8	9,608	90.1	657	6.2
FEMALE	12	.2	147	2.6	30	.5	22	.4	211	3.7	5,268	92.2	233	4.1
MALE	10	.2	114	2.3	40	.8	27	.5	191	3.9	4,340	87.6	424	8.6
PROFESSIONAL:														
FULL-TIME	4	.2	6	.3	9	.4	20	1.0	39	1.9	1,815	87.5	221	10.7
FEMALE	1	.4	0	.0	2	.7	4	1.5	7	2.6	246	91.4	16	5.9
MALE	3	.2	6	.3	7	.4	16	.9	32	1.8	1,569	86.9	205	11.4
PART-TIME	0	.0	0	.0	0	.0	0	.0	0	.0	12	100.0	0	.0
FEMALE	0	.0	0	.0	0	.0	0	.0	0	.0	6	100.0	0	.0
MALE	0	.0	0	.0	0	.0	0	.0	0	.0	6	100.0	0	.0
TOTAL	4	.2	6	.3	9	.4	20	1.0	39	1.9	1,827	87.5	221	10.6
FEMALE	1	.4	0	.0	2	.7	4	1.5	7	2.5	252	91.6	16	5.8
MALE	3	.2	6	.3	7	.4	16	.9	32	1.8	1,575	86.9	205	11.3
UNC+GRAD+PROF:														
FULL-TIME	243	.4	1,775	2.6	372	.5	416	.6	2,806	4.1	64,476	93.6	1,637	2.4
FEMALE	122	.4	750	2.0	169	.5	181	.5	1,222	3.3	35,138	95.2	562	1.5
MALE	121	.4	1,025	3.2	203	.6	235	.7	1,584	5.0	29,338	91.7	1,075	3.4
PART-TIME	78	.4	380	1.9	110	.5	107	.5	675	3.3	19,371	94.8	387	1.9
FEMALE	49	.4	223	1.8	55	.4	54	.4	381	3.1	11,682	95.6	162	1.3
MALE	29	.4	151	1.9	55	.7	53	.6	294	3.6	7,689	93.7	225	2.7
TOTAL	321	.4	2,155	2.4	482	.5	523	.6	3,481	3.9	83,847	93.8	2,024	2.3
FEMALE	171	.3	973	2.0	224	.5	235	.5	1,603	3.3	46,820	95.3	724	1.5
MALE	150	.4	1,182	2.9	258	.6	288	.7	1,878	4.7	37,027	92.1	1,300	3.2
UNCLASSIFIED:														
TOTAL	17	.4	62	1.5	10	.2	10	.2	99	2.5	3,824	95.1	98	2.4
FEMALE	10	.4	34	1.3	7	.3	8	.3	59	2.3	2,481	96.1	41	1.6
MALE	7	.5	28	1.9	3	.2	2	.1	40	2.8	1,343	93.3	57	4.0
TOTAL ENROLLMENT:														
TOTAL	338	.4	2,217	2.4	492	.5	533	.6	3,580	3.8	87,671	93.9	2,122	2.3
FEMALE	181	.3	1,007	1.9	231	.4	243	.5	1,662	3.2	49,301	95.3	765	1.5
MALE	157	.4	1,210	2.9	261	.6	290	.7	1,918	4.6	38,370	92.1	1,357	3.3
KANSAS (52 INSTITUTIONS)														
UNDERGRADUATES:														
FULL-TIME	1,089	2.4	2,497	5.4	196	.4	690	1.5	4,472	9.7	40,743	88.4	881	1.9
FEMALE	565	2.1	1,173	4.5	87	.3	342	1.3	2,167	8.2	23,890	90.8	260	1.0
MALE	524	2.6	1,324	6.7	109	.6	348	1.8	2,305	11.7	16,853	85.2	621	3.1
PART-TIME	187	.9	986	4.5	94	.4	291	1.3	1,558	7.1	20,238	92.4	96	.4
FEMALE	92	.7	447	3.5	51	.4	136	1.1	726	5.6	12,122	94.1	28	.2
MALE	95	1.1	539	6.0	43	.5	155	1.7	832	9.2	8,116	90.0	68	.8
TOTAL	1,276	1.9	3,483	5.1	290	.4	981	1.4	6,030	8.9	60,981	89.7	977	1.4
FEMALE	657	1.7	1,620	4.1	138	.4	478	1.2	2,893	7.4	36,012	91.9	288	.7
MALE	619	2.1	1,863	6.5	152	.5	503	1.7	3,137	10.9	24,969	86.7	689	2.4
GRADUATE:														
FULL-TIME	18	.6	119	3.7	23	.7	49	1.5	209	6.6	2,624	82.3	356	11.2
FEMALE	10	.6	66	3.9	15	.9	30	1.8	121	7.2	1,423	85.2	127	7.6
MALE	8	.5	53	3.5	8	.5	19	1.3	88	5.8	1,201	79.1	229	15.1
PART-TIME	36	.3	267	2.5	39	.4	75	.7	417	4.0	9,834	93.9	222	2.1
FEMALE	19	.3	162	2.5	19	.3	35	.5	235	3.6	6,256	95.0	97	1.5
MALE	17	.4	105	2.7	20	.5	40	1.0	182	4.7	3,578	92.1	125	3.2
TOTAL	54	.4	386	2.8	62	.5	124	.9	626	4.6	12,458	91.2	578	4.2
FEMALE	29	.4	228	2.8	34	.4	65	.8	356	4.3	7,679	93.0	224	2.7
MALE	25	.5	158	2.9	28	.5	59	1.1	270	5.0	4,779	88.5	354	6.6
PROFESSIONAL:														
FULL-TIME	0	.0	0	.0	0	.0	0	.0	0	.0	0	.0	0	.0
FEMALE	0	.0	0	.0	0	.0	0	.0	0	.0	0	.0	0	.0
MALE	0	.0	0	.0	0	.0	0	.0	0	.0	0	.0	0	.0

E 17. - TOTAL ENROLLMENT IN INSTITUTIONS OF HIGHER EDUCATION FOR SELECTED MAJOR FIELDS OF STUDY AND LEVEL OF ENROLLMENT BY RACE, ETHNICITY, AND SEX: STATE, 1978

R FIELD 9000 - ALL OTHERS

	AMERICAN INDIAN ALASKAN NATIVE		BLACK NON-HISPANIC		ASIAN OR PACIFIC ISLANDER		HISPANIC		TOTAL MINORITY		WHITE NON-HISPANIC		NON-RESIDENT ALIEN		TOTAL
	NUMBER	%	NUMBER	%	NUMBER	%	NUMBER	%	NUMBER	%	NUMBER	%	NUMBER	%	NUMBER
AS			CONTINUED												
ESSIONAL:															
-TIME	0	.0	0	.0	0	.0	0	.0	0	.0	0	.0	0	.0	0
EMALE	0	.0	0	.0	0	.0	0	.0	0	.0	0	.0	0	.0	0
MALE	0	.0	0	.0	0	.0	0	.0	0	.0	0	.0	0	.0	0
L	0	.0	0	.0	0	.0	0	.0	0	.0	0	.0	0	.0	0
EMALE	0	.0	0	.0	0	.0	0	.0	0	.0	0	.0	0	.0	0
MALE	0	.0	0	.0	0	.0	0	.0	0	.0	0	.0	0	.0	0
GRAD+PROF:															
-TIME	1,107	2.2	2,616	5.3	219	.4	739	1.5	4,681	9.5	43,367	88.0	1,237	2.5	49,285
EMALE	575	2.1	1,239	4.4	102	.4	372	1.3	2,288	8.2	25,313	90.4	387	1.4	27,988
MALE	532	2.5	1,377	6.5	117	.5	367	1.7	2,393	11.2	18,054	84.8	850	4.0	21,297
-TIME	223	.7	1,253	3.9	133	.4	366	1.1	1,975	6.1	30,072	92.9	318	1.0	32,365
EMALE	111	.6	609	3.1	70	.4	171	.9	961	4.9	16,378	94.4	125	.6	19,464
MALE	112	.9	644	5.0	63	.5	195	1.5	1,014	7.9	11,694	90.6	193	1.5	12,901
L	1,330	1.6	3,869	4.7	352	.4	1,105	1.4	6,656	8.2	73,439	89.9	1,555	1.9	81,650
EMALE	686	1.4	1,848	3.9	172	.4	543	1.1	3,249	6.8	43,691	92.1	512	1.1	47,452
MALE	644	1.9	2,021	5.9	180	.5	562	1.6	3,407	10.0	29,748	87.0	1,043	3.0	34,198
ASSIFIED:															
L	87	.9	423	4.5	95	1.0	97	1.0	702	7.4	8,470	89.7	271	2.9	9,443
EMALE	54	1.0	218	4.0	50	.9	58	1.1	380	6.9	5,035	91.4	91	1.7	5,506
MALE	33	.8	205	5.2	45	1.1	39	1.0	322	8.2	3,435	87.2	180	4.6	3,937
L ENROLLMENT:															
L	1,417	1.6	4,292	4.7	447	.5	1,202	1.3	7,358	8.1	81,909	89.9	1,826	2.0	91,093
EMALE	740	1.4	2,066	3.9	222	.4	601	1.1	3,629	6.9	48,726	92.0	603	1.1	52,958
MALE	677	1.8	2,226	5.8	225	.6	601	1.6	3,729	9.8	33,183	87.0	1,223	3.2	38,135
UCKY	(	39 INSTITUTIONS)													
RGRADUATES:															
-TIME	102	.2	4,608	8.6	215	.4	120	.2	5,045	9.4	47,897	89.4	612	1.1	53,554
EMALE	57	.2	2,606	8.2	116	.4	64	.2	2,843	8.9	26,795	90.5	187	.6	31,825
MALE	45	.2	2,002	9.2	99	.5	56	.3	2,202	10.1	19,102	87.9	425	2.0	21,729
-TIME	34	.2	1,203	6.7	58	.3	56	.3	1,351	7.5	16,557	92.2	58	.3	17,966
EMALE	18	.2	738	6.8	31	.3	23	.2	810	7.4	10,070	92.1	35	.3	10,915
MALE	16	.2	465	6.6	27	.4	33	.5	541	7.7	6,487	92.0	23	.3	7,051
L	136	.2	5,811	8.1	273	.4	176	.2	6,396	8.9	64,454	90.1	670	.9	71,520
EMALE	75	.2	3,344	7.8	147	.3	87	.2	3,653	8.5	38,865	90.9	222	.5	42,740
MALE	61	.2	2,467	8.6	126	.4	89	.3	2,743	9.5	25,589	88.9	448	1.6	28,780
UATE:															
-TIME	51	1.7	96	3.2	17	.6	20	.7	184	6.2	2,613	88.3	163	5.5	2,960
EMALE	31	1.8	56	3.3	7	.4	8	.5	102	5.9	1,562	91.1	51	3.0	1,715
MALE	20	1.6	40	3.2	10	.8	12	1.0	82	6.6	1,051	84.4	112	9.0	1,245
-TIME	38	.3	399	3.4	23	.2	21	.2	481	4.1	11,295	95.3	68	.6	11,804
EMALE	24	.3	256	3.1	9	.1	12	.1	301	3.7	7,914	96.1	17	.2	8,232
MALE	14	.4	143	4.0	14	.4	9	.3	180	5.0	3,341	93.5	51	1.4	3,572
L	89	.6	495	3.4	40	.3	41	.3	665	4.5	13,868	93.9	231	1.6	14,764
EMALE	55	.6	312	3.1	16	.2	20	.2	403	4.1	9,476	95.3	68	.7	9,947
MALE	34	.7	183	3.8	24	.5	21	.4	262	5.4	4,392	91.2	163	3.4	4,817
ESSIONAL:															
-TIME	2	.3	12	1.6	0	.0	2	.3	16	2.1	721	96.4	11	1.5	748
EMALE	0	.0	4	5.2	0	.0	1	1.3	5	6.5	72	93.5	0	.0	77
MALE	2	.3	8	1.2	0	.0	1	.1	11	1.6	649	96.7	11	1.6	671
-TIME	3	1.9	6	3.9	0	.0	2	1.3	11	7.1	142	91.6	2	1.3	155
EMALE	0	.0	0	.0	0	.0	0	.0	0	.0	18	94.7	1	5.3	19
MALE	3	2.2	6	4.4	0	.0	2	1.5	11	8.1	124	91.2	1	.7	136
L	5	.6	18	2.0	0	.0	4	.4	27	3.0	863	95.6	13	1.4	903
EMALE	0	.0	4	4.2	0	.0	1	1.0	5	5.2	90	93.8	1	1.0	96
MALE	5	.6	14	1.7	0	.0	3	.4	22	2.7	773	95.8	12	1.5	807
GRAD+PROF:															
-TIME	155	.3	4,716	8.2	232	.4	142	.2	5,245	9.2	51,231	89.5	786	1.4	57,262
EMALE	88	.3	2,666	7.9	123	.4	73	.2	2,950	8.8	30,429	90.5	238	.7	33,617
MALE	67	.3	2,050	8.7	109	.5	69	.3	2,295	9.7	20,802	88.0	548	2.3	23,645
-TIME	75	.3	1,608	5.4	81	.3	79	.3	1,843	6.2	27,954	93.4	128	.4	29,925
EMALE	42	.2	994	5.2	40	.2	35	.2	1,111	5.8	18,002	93.9	53	.3	19,166
MALE	33	.3	614	5.7	41	.4	44	.4	732	6.8	9,952	92.5	75	.7	10,759
L	230	.3	6,324	7.3	313	.4	221	.3	7,088	8.1	79,185	90.8	914	1.0	87,187
EMALE	130	.2	3,660	6.9	163	.3	108	.2	4,061	7.7	48,431	91.8	291	.6	52,783
MALE	100	.3	2,664	7.7	150	.4	113	.3	3,027	8.8	30,754	89.4	623	1.8	34,404
ASSIFIED:															
L	29	.4	378	5.9	31	.5	29	.4	467	7.2	5,923	91.7	66	1.0	6,456
EMALE	21	.5	220	5.6	21	.5	23	.6	285	7.3	3,587	91.9	31	.8	3,903
MALE	8	.3	158	6.2	10	.4	6	.2	182	7.1	2,336	91.5	35	1.4	2,553
L ENROLLMENT:															
L	259	.3	6,702	7.2	344	.4	250	.3	7,555	8.1	85,108	90.9	980	1.0	93,643
EMALE	151	.3	3,880	6.8	184	.3	131	.2	4,346	7.7	52,018	91.8	322	.6	56,686
MALE	108	.3	2,822	7.6	160	.4	119	.3	3,209	8.7	33,090	89.5	658	1.8	36,957

MAJOR FIELD 9000 - ALL OTHERS

	AMERICAN INDIAN ALASKAN NATIVE		BLACK NON-HISPANIC		ASIAN OR PACIFIC ISLANDER		HISPANIC		TOTAL MINORITY		WHITE NON-HISPANIC		NON-RESIDENT ALIEN	
	NUMBER	%	NUMBER	%	NUMBER	%	NUMBER	%	NUMBER	%	NUMBER	%	NUMBER	%
LOUISIANA (31 INSTITUTIONS)														
UNDERGRADUATES:														
FULL-TIME	122	.2	19,180	31.0	252	.4	689	1.1	20,243	32.7	40,479	65.3	1,239	2.0
FEMALE	63	.2	12,234	32.6	122	.3	362	1.0	12,781	34.0	24,262	64.6	519	1.4
MALE	59	.2	6,946	28.5	130	.5	327	1.3	7,462	30.6	16,217	66.5	720	3.0
PART-TIME	48	.3	3,814	20.1	137	.7	360	1.9	4,359	22.9	14,393	75.7	261	1.4
FEMALE	21	.2	2,087	20.2	61	.6	172	1.7	2,341	22.7	7,853	76.0	138	1.3
MALE	27	.3	1,727	19.9	76	.9	188	2.2	2,018	23.2	6,540	75.3	123	1.4
TOTAL	170	.2	22,994	28.4	389	.5	1,049	1.3	24,602	30.4	54,872	67.8	1,500	1.9
FEMALE	84	.2	14,321	29.9	183	.4	534	1.1	15,122	31.6	32,115	67.1	657	1.4
MALE	86	.3	8,673	26.2	206	.6	515	1.6	9,480	28.7	22,757	68.8	843	2.5
GRADUATE:														
FULL-TIME	13	.4	346	10.6	12	.4	50	1.5	421	12.9	2,631	80.3	223	6.8
FEMALE	7	.4	226	13.5	2	.1	26	1.6	261	15.6	1,345	80.3	69	4.1
MALE	6	.4	120	7.5	10	.6	24	1.5	160	10.0	1,286	80.4	154	9.6
PART-TIME	18	.2	2,108	22.2	25	.3	126	1.3	2,277	24.0	7,091	74.8	112	1.2
FEMALE	8	.1	1,657	24.3	9	.1	81	1.2	1,755	25.8	5,008	73.6	43	.6
MALE	10	.4	451	16.9	16	.6	45	1.7	522	19.5	2,083	77.9	69	2.6
TUTAL	31	.2	2,454	19.2	37	.3	176	1.4	2,698	21.2	9,722	76.2	335	2.6
FEMALE	15	.2	1,883	22.2	11	.1	107	1.3	2,016	23.8	6,353	74.9	112	1.3
MALE	16	.4	571	13.4	26	.6	69	1.6	682	16.0	3,369	78.8	223	5.2
PROFESSIONAL:														
FULL-TIME	0	.0	2	5.6	1	2.8	3	8.3	6	16.7	30	83.3	0	.0
FEMALE	0	.0	0	.0	0	.0	0	.0	0	.0	0	.0	0	.0
MALE	0	.0	2	5.6	1	2.8	3	8.3	6	16.7	30	83.3	0	.0
PART-TIME	0	.0	3	30.0	1	10.0	0	.0	4	40.0	6	60.0	0	.0
FEMALE	0	.0	0	.0	0	.0	0	.0	0	.0	3	100.0	0	.0
MALE	0	.0	3	42.9	1	14.3	0	.0	4	57.1	3	42.9	0	.0
TOTAL	0	.0	5	10.9	2	4.3	3	6.5	10	21.7	36	78.3	0	.0
FEMALE	0	.0	0	.0	0	.0	0	.0	0	.0	3	100.0	0	.0
MALE	0	.0	5	11.6	2	4.7	3	7.0	10	23.3	33	76.7	0	.0
UNG+GRAD+PROF:														
FULL-TIME	135	.2	19,528	29.9	265	.4	742	1.1	20,670	31.7	43,140	66.1	1,462	2.2
FEMALE	70	.2	12,460	31.8	124	.3	388	1.0	13,042	33.2	25,607	65.3	588	1.5
MALE	65	.2	7,068	27.1	141	.5	354	1.4	7,628	29.3	17,533	67.3	874	3.4
PART-TIME	66	.2	5,925	20.8	163	.6	486	1.7	6,640	23.3	21,490	75.4	373	1.3
FEMALE	29	.2	3,744	21.8	70	.4	253	1.5	4,096	23.9	12,864	75.0	181	1.1
MALE	37	.3	2,181	19.2	93	.8	233	2.1	2,544	22.4	8,626	75.9	192	1.7
TOTAL	201	.2	25,453	27.1	428	.5	1,228	1.3	27,310	29.1	64,630	68.8	1,835	2.0
FEMALE	99	.2	16,204	28.7	194	.3	641	1.1	17,138	30.4	38,471	68.2	769	1.4
MALE	102	.2	9,249	24.7	234	.6	587	1.6	10,172	27.2	26,159	69.9	1,066	2.9
UNCLASSIFIED:														
TOTAL	11	.2	757	14.9	19	.4	75	1.5	862	17.0	4,138	81.6	72	1.4
FEMALE	7	.2	538	17.1	8	.3	38	1.2	591	18.8	2,511	79.9	42	1.3
MALE	4	.2	219	11.4	11	.6	37	1.9	271	14.1	1,627	84.4	30	1.6
TOTAL ENROLLMENT:														
TOTAL	212	.2	26,210	26.5	447	.5	1,303	1.3	28,172	28.5	68,768	69.6	1,907	1.9
FEMALE	106	.2	16,742	28.1	202	.3	679	1.1	17,729	29.8	40,982	68.9	811	1.4
MALE	106	.3	9,468	24.1	245	.6	624	1.6	10,443	26.6	27,786	70.7	1,096	2.8
MAINE (24 INSTITUTIONS)														
UNDERGRADUATES:														
FULL-TIME	73	.4	111	.6	48	.3	39	.2	271	1.5	17,490	97.9	101	.6
FEMALE	40	.4	43	.4	25	.3	15	.2	123	1.3	9,573	98.4	29	.3
MALE	33	.4	68	.8	23	.3	24	.3	148	1.8	7,917	97.3	72	.9
PART-TIME	24	.9	10	.4	6	.2	2	.1	42	1.5	2,676	98.3	4	.1
FEMALE	17	1.1	5	.3	5	.3	1	.1	28	1.9	1,465	98.1	1	.1
MALE	7	.6	5	.4	1	.1	1	.1	14	1.1	1,211	98.6	3	.2
TOTAL	97	.5	121	.6	54	.3	41	.2	313	1.5	20,166	98.0	105	.5
FEMALE	57	.5	48	.4	30	.3	16	.1	151	1.3	11,038	98.4	30	.3
MALE	40	.4	73	.8	24	.3	25	.3	162	1.7	9,128	97.5	75	.8
GRADUATE:														
FULL-TIME	1	.2	2	.4	2	.4	2	.4	7	1.2	556	97.9	5	.9
FEMALE	1	.4	0	.0	1	.4	1	.4	3	1.4	274	97.5	5	1.4
MALE	0	.0	2	.7	1	.3	1	.3	3	1.4	282	98.3	1	.3
PART-TIME	1	.2	0	.0	0	.0	2	.3	3	.5	601	98.7	5	.8
FEMALE	0	.0	0	.0	0	.0	1	.3	1	.3	369	98.7	4	1.1
MALE	1	.4	0	.0	0	.0	1	.4	2	.9	232	98.7	1	.4
TOTAL	2	.2	2	.2	2	.2	4	.3	10	.8	1,157	98.3	10	.8
FEMALE	1	.2	0	.0	1	.2	2	.3	4	.6	643	98.2	8	1.2
MALE	1	.2	2	.4	1	.2	2	.4	6	1.1	514	98.5	2	.4
PROFESSIONAL:														
FULL-TIME	0	.0	1	1.3	0	.0	1	1.3	2	2.5	77	97.5	0	.0
FEMALE	0	.0	0	.0	0	.0	0	.0	0	.0	17	100.0	0	.0
MALE	0	.0	1	1.6	0	.0	1	1.6	2	3.2	60	96.8	0	.0

BLE 17 - TOTAL ENROLLMENT IN INSTITUTIONS OF HIGHER EDUCATION FOR SELECTED MAJOR FIELDS OF STUDY AND LEVEL OF ENROLLMENT
BY RACE, ETHNICITY, AND SEX: STATE, 1978

JOR FIELD 9000 - ALL OTHERS

	AMERICAN INDIAN ALASKAN NATIVE		BLACK NON-HISPANIC		ASIAN OR PACIFIC ISLANDER		HISPANIC		TOTAL MINORITY		WHITE NON-HISPANIC		NON-RESIDENT ALIEN		TOTAL
	NUMBER	%	NUMBER	%	NUMBER	%	NUMBER	%	NUMBER	%	NUMBER	%	NUMBER	%	NUMBER
INE	CONTINUED														
OFESSIONAL:															
RT-TIME	0	.0	0	.0	0	.0	0	.0	0	.0	8	100.0	0	.0	8
FEMALE	0	.0	0	.0	0	.0	0	.0	0	.0	4	100.0	0	.0	4
MALE	0	.0	0	.0	0	.0	0	.0	0	.0	4	100.0	0	.0	4
TAL	0	.0	1	1.1	0	.0	1	1.1	2	2.3	85	97.7	0	.0	87
FEMALE	0	.0	0	.0	0	.0	0	.0	0	.0	21	100.0	0	.0	21
MALE	0	.0	1	1.5	0	.0	1	1.5	2	3.0	64	97.0	0	.0	66
D+GRAD+PROF:															
LL-TIME	74	.4	114	.6	50	.3	42	.2	280	1.5	18,123	97.9	106	.6	18,509
FEMALE	41	.4	43	.4	26	.3	16	.2	126	1.3	9,864	98.4	33	.3	10,023
MALE	33	.4	71	.8	24	.3	26	.3	154	1.8	8,259	97.3	73	.9	8,486
RT-TIME	25	.7	10	.3	6	.2	4	.1	45	1.3	3,285	98.4	9	.3	3,339
FEMALE	17	.9	5	.3	5	.3	2	.1	29	1.5	1,838	98.2	5	.3	1,872
MALE	8	.5	5	.3	1	.1	2	.1	16	1.1	1,447	98.6	4	.3	1,467
TAL	99	.5	124	.6	56	.3	46	.2	325	1.5	21,408	98.0	115	.5	21,848
FEMALE	58	.5	48	.4	31	.3	18	.2	155	1.3	11,702	98.4	38	.3	11,895
MALE	41	.4	76	.8	25	.3	28	.3	170	1.7	9,706	97.5	77	.8	9,953
CLASSIFIED:															
TAL	15	.2	15	.2	8	.1	4	.0	42	.5	8,124	99.1	32	.4	8,198
FEMALE	4	.1	4	.1	5	.1	3	.1	16	.3	4,744	99.3	19	.4	4,779
MALE	11	.3	11	.3	3	.1	1	.0	26	.8	3,380	98.9	13	.4	3,419
TAL ENROLLMENT:															
TAL	114	.4	139	.5	64	.2	50	.2	367	1.2	29,532	98.3	147	.5	30,046
FEMALE	62	.4	52	.3	36	.2	21	.1	171	1.0	16,446	98.6	57	.3	16,674
MALE	52	.4	87	.7	28	.2	29	.2	196	1.5	13,086	97.9	90	.7	13,372
RYLAND	(	54 INSTITUTIONS)													
OERGRADUATES:															
LL-TIME	169	.2	14,872	20.8	805	1.1	669	.9	16,515	23.0	53,064	74.0	2,088	2.9	71,667
FEMALE	84	.2	9,482	22.8	406	1.0	365	.9	10,337	24.9	30,309	73.0	856	2.1	41,502
MALE	85	.3	5,390	17.9	399	1.3	304	1.0	6,178	20.5	22,755	75.4	1,232	4.1	30,165
RT-TIME	223	.3	12,207	18.4	957	1.4	712	1.1	14,099	21.2	51,707	77.8	626	.9	66,432
FEMALE	119	.3	7,490	19.2	524	1.3	397	1.0	8,530	21.9	30,119	77.2	353	.9	39,002
MALE	104	.4	4,717	17.2	433	1.6	315	1.1	5,569	20.3	21,588	78.7	273	1.0	27,430
TAL	392	.3	27,079	19.6	1,762	1.3	1,381	1.0	30,614	22.2	104,771	75.9	2,714	2.0	138,099
FEMALE	203	.3	16,972	21.1	930	1.2	762	.9	18,867	23.4	60,428	75.1	1,209	1.5	80,504
MALE	189	.3	10,107	17.5	832	1.4	619	1.1	11,747	20.4	44,343	77.0	1,505	2.6	57,595
ADUATE:															
LL-TIME	10	.2	353	7.3	70	1.5	49	1.0	482	10.0	3,900	80.8	445	9.2	4,827
FEMALE	8	.3	238	9.4	39	1.5	32	1.3	317	12.5	2,083	81.9	142	5.6	2,542
MALE	2	.1	115	5.0	31	1.4	17	.7	165	7.2	1,817	79.5	303	13.3	2,285
RT-TIME	35	.3	1,321	12.0	97	.9	77	.7	1,530	13.9	9,216	83.8	254	2.3	11,000
FEMALE	26	.4	935	13.4	61	.9	47	.7	1,069	15.3	5,845	83.5	86	1.2	7,000
MALE	9	.2	386	9.7	36	.9	30	.8	461	11.5	3,371	84.3	168	4.2	4,000
TAL	45	.3	1,674	10.6	167	1.1	126	.8	2,012	12.7	13,116	82.9	699	4.4	15,827
FEMALE	34	.4	1,173	12.3	100	1.0	79	.8	1,386	14.5	7,928	83.1	228	2.4	9,542
MALE	11	.2	501	8.0	67	1.1	47	.7	626	10.0	5,188	82.5	471	7.5	6,285
OFESSIONAL:															
LL-TIME	0	.0	0	.0	0	.0	3	8.6	29	82.9	3	8.6	35		
FEMALE	0	.0	0	.0	0	.0	1	7.1	1	7.1	13	92.9	0	.0	14
MALE	0	.0	.0		0	.0	2	9.5	2	9.5	16	76.2	3	14.3	21
RT-TIME	0	.0	1	16.7	0	.0	0	.0	1	16.7	5	83.3	0	.0	6
FEMALE	0	.0	1	50.0	0	.0	0	.0	1	50.0	1	50.0	0	.0	2
MALE	0	.0	0	.0	0	.0	0	.0	0	.0	4	100.0	0	.0	4
TAL	0	.0	1	2.4	0	.0	3	7.3	4	9.8	34	82.9	3	7.3	41
FEMALE	0	.0	1	6.3	0	.0	1	6.3	2	12.5	14	87.5	0	.0	16
MALE	0	.0	0	.0	0	.0	2	8.0	2	8.0	20	80.0	3	12.0	25
D+GRAD+PROF:															
LL-TIME	179	.2	15,225	19.9	875	1.1	721	.9	17,000	22.2	56,993	74.5	2,536	3.3	76,529
FEMALE	92	.2	9,720	22.1	445	1.0	398	.9	10,655	24.2	32,405	73.6	998	2.3	44,058
MALE	87	.3	5,505	17.0	430	1.3	323	1.0	6,345	19.5	24,588	75.7	1,538	4.7	32,471
RT-TIME	258	.3	13,529	17.5	1,054	1.4	789	1.0	15,630	20.2	60,928	78.7	880	1.1	77,438
FEMALE	145	.3	8,426	18.3	585	1.3	444	1.0	9,600	20.9	35,965	78.2	439	1.0	46,004
MALE	113	.4	5,103	16.2	469	1.5	345	1.1	6,030	19.2	24,963	79.4	441	1.4	31,434
TAL	437	.3	28,754	18.7	1,929	1.3	1,510	1.0	32,630	21.2	117,921	76.6	3,416	2.2	153,967
FEMALE	237	.3	18,146	20.1	1,030	1.1	842	.9	20,255	22.5	68,370	75.9	1,437	1.6	90,062
MALE	200	.3	10,608	16.6	899	1.4	668	1.0	12,375	19.4	49,551	77.5	1,979	3.1	63,905
CLASSIFIED:															
TAL	71	.4	2,849	15.5	286	1.6	152	.8	3,358	18.2	14,364	78.0	686	3.7	18,408
FEMALE	44	.4	1,796	16.9	147	1.4	73	.7	2,060	19.4	8,275	78.0	272	2.6	10,607
MALE	27	.3	1,053	13.5	139	1.8	79	1.0	1,298	16.6	6,089	78.1	414	5.3	7,801
TAL ENROLLMENT:															
TAL	508	.3	31,603	18.3	2,215	1.3	1,662	1.0	35,988	20.9	132,285	76.7	4,102	2.4	172,375
FEMALE	281	.3	19,942	19.8	1,177	1.2	915	.9	22,315	22.2	76,645	76.1	1,709	1.7	100,669
MALE	227	.3	11,661	16.3	1,038	1.4	747	1.0	13,673	19.1	55,640	77.6	2,393	3.3	71,706

MAJOR FIELD 9000 - ALL OTHERS

	AMERICAN INDIAN ALASKAN NATIVE		BLACK NON-HISPANIC		ASIAN OR PACIFIC ISLANDER		HISPANIC		TOTAL MINORITY		WHITE NON-HISPANIC		NON-RESIDENT ALIEN		TOTAL
	NUMBER	%	NUMBER	%	NUMBER	%	NUMBER	%	NUMBER	%	NUMBER	%	NUMBER	%	NUMBER
MASSACHUSETTS	(	111 INSTITUTIONS)													
UNDERGRADUATES:															
FULL-TIME	788	.5	7,025	4.8	1,844	1.3	2,305	1.6	11,962	8.1	132,102	89.9	2,826	1.9	146,890
FEMALE	544	.6	4,204	4.8	963	1.1	1,277	1.5	6,988	8.0	79,089	90.5	1,282	1.5	87,359
MALE	244	.4	2,821	4.7	881	1.5	1,028	1.7	4,974	8.4	53,013	89.1	1,544	2.6	59,531
PART-TIME	166	.6	880	3.3	1,323	5.0	290	1.1	2,659	10.0	23,907	89.5	142	.5	26,708
FEMALE	105	.7	483	3.1	648	4.2	151	1.0	1,387	8.9	14,087	90.7	54	.3	15,528
MALE	61	.5	397	3.6	675	6.0	139	1.2	1,272	11.4	9,820	87.8	88	.8	11,180
TOTAL	954	.5	7,905	4.6	3,167	1.8	2,595	1.5	14,621	8.4	156,009	89.9	2,968	1.7	173,598
FEMALE	649	.6	4,687	4.6	1,611	1.6	1,428	1.4	8,375	8.1	93,176	90.6	1,336	1.3	102,887
MALE	305	.4	3,218	4.6	1,556	2.2	1,167	1.7	6,246	8.8	62,833	88.9	1,632	2.3	70,711
GRADUATE:															
FULL-TIME	25	.2	488	4.0	205	1.7	224	1.8	942	7.7	9,840	81.0	1,373	11.3	12,155
FEMALE	16	.2	263	4.1	102	1.6	108	1.7	489	7.6	5,450	85.0	474	7.4	6,413
MALE	9	.2	225	3.9	103	1.8	116	2.0	453	7.9	4,390	76.5	899	15.7	5,742
PART-TIME	33	.2	485	3.1	148	.9	187	1.2	853	5.5	14,465	92.5	321	2.1	15,639
FEMALE	5	.1	225	2.5	74	.8	84	.9	388	4.3	8,467	94.0	154	1.7	9,029
MALE	28	.4	260	3.9	74	1.1	103	1.6	465	7.0	5,978	90.4	167	2.5	6,610
TOTAL	58	.2	973	3.5	353	1.3	411	1.5	1,795	6.5	24,305	87.4	1,694	6.1	27,794
FEMALE	21	.1	488	3.2	176	1.1	192	1.2	877	5.7	13,937	90.3	628	4.1	15,442
MALE	37	.3	485	3.9	177	1.4	219	1.8	918	7.4	10,368	83.9	1,066	8.6	12,352
PROFESSIONAL:															
FULL-TIME	3	.2	47	2.4	15	.8	12	.6	77	4.0	1,803	94.0	39	2.0	1,919
FEMALE	0	.0	16	2.5	10	1.6	1	.2	27	4.2	608	94.6	8	1.2	643
MALE	3	.2	31	2.4	5	.4	11	.9	50	3.9	1,195	93.7	31	2.4	1,276
PART-TIME	0	.0	4	2.8	0	.0	2	1.4	6	4.2	135	95.1	1	.7	142
FEMALE	0	.0	0	.0	0	.0	0	.0	0	.0	36	100.0	0	.0	36
MALE	0	.0	4	3.8	0	.0	2	1.9	6	5.7	99	93.4	1	.9	106
TOTAL	3	.1	51	2.5	15	.7	14	.7	83	4.0	1,938	94.0	40	1.9	2,061
FEMALE	0	.0	16	2.4	10	1.5	1	.1	27	4.0	644	94.8	8	1.2	679
MALE	3	.2	35	2.5	5	.4	13	.9	56	4.1	1,294	93.6	32	2.3	1,382
UND+GRAD+PROF:															
FULL-TIME	816	.5	7,560	4.7	2,064	1.3	2,541	1.6	12,981	8.1	143,745	89.3	4,238	2.6	160,964
FEMALE	560	.6	4,483	4.7	1,075	1.1	1,386	1.5	7,504	7.9	85,147	90.2	1,764	1.9	94,415
MALE	256	.4	3,077	4.6	989	1.5	1,155	1.7	5,477	8.2	58,598	88.1	2,474	3.7	66,549
PART-TIME	199	.5	1,369	3.2	1,471	3.5	479	1.1	3,518	8.3	38,507	90.6	464	1.1	42,489
FEMALE	110	.4	708	2.9	722	2.9	235	1.0	1,775	7.2	22,610	91.9	208	.8	24,593
MALE	89	.5	661	3.7	749	4.2	244	1.4	1,743	9.7	15,897	88.8	256	1.4	17,896
TOTAL	1,015	.5	8,929	4.4	3,535	1.7	3,020	1.5	16,499	8.1	182,252	89.6	4,702	2.3	203,453
FEMALE	670	.6	5,191	4.4	1,797	1.5	1,621	1.4	9,279	7.8	107,757	90.5	1,972	1.7	119,008
MALE	345	.4	3,738	4.4	1,738	2.1	1,399	1.7	7,220	8.5	74,495	88.2	2,730	3.2	84,445
UNCLASSIFIED:															
TOTAL	155	.3	1,360	2.3	473	.8	610	1.0	2,598	4.3	56,105	93.9	1,035	1.7	59,738
FEMALE	88	.3	801	2.3	286	.8	356	1.0	1,531	4.5	32,187	94.1	494	1.4	34,212
MALE	67	.3	559	2.2	187	.7	254	1.0	1,067	4.2	23,918	93.7	541	2.1	25,526
TOTAL ENROLLMENT:															
TOTAL	1,170	.4	10,289	3.9	4,008	1.5	3,630	1.4	19,097	7.3	238,357	90.6	5,737	2.2	263,191
FEMALE	758	.5	5,992	3.9	2,083	1.4	1,977	1.3	10,810	7.1	139,944	91.3	2,466	1.6	153,220
MALE	412	.4	4,297	3.9	1,925	1.8	1,653	1.5	8,287	7.5	98,413	89.5	3,271	3.0	109,971
MICHIGAN	(	85 INSTITUTIONS)													
UNDERGRADUATES:															
FULL-TIME	855	.5	18,104	11.1	1,123	.7	1,862	1.1	21,944	13.4	139,176	85.1	2,483	1.5	163,603
FEMALE	454	.5	11,367	12.4	566	.6	986	1.1	13,373	14.6	77,097	84.3	967	1.1	91,437
MALE	401	.6	6,737	9.3	557	.8	876	1.2	8,571	11.9	62,079	86.0	1,516	2.1	72,166
PART-TIME	1,019	.7	14,981	10.9	837	.6	2,393	1.7	19,230	14.0	117,586	85.6	520	.4	137,336
FEMALE	537	.7	8,741	12.1	400	.6	1,177	1.6	10,855	15.0	61,367	84.7	241	.3	72,463
MALE	482	.7	6,240	9.0	437	.7	1,216	1.9	8,375	12.9	56,219	86.7	279	.4	64,873
TOTAL	1,874	.6	33,085	11.0	1,960	.7	4,255	1.4	41,174	13.7	256,762	85.3	3,003	1.0	300,939
FEMALE	991	.6	20,108	12.3	966	.6	2,163	1.3	24,228	14.8	138,464	84.5	1,208	.7	163,900
MALE	883	.6	12,977	9.5	994	.7	2,092	1.5	16,946	12.4	118,298	86.3	1,795	1.3	137,039
GRADUATE:															
FULL-TIME	44	.4	1,068	8.9	165	1.4	190	1.6	1,467	12.3	9,260	77.3	1,248	10.4	11,975
FEMALE	26	.4	696	11.1	79	1.3	87	1.4	888	14.2	5,020	80.1	357	5.7	6,265
MALE	18	.3	372	6.5	86	1.5	103	1.8	579	10.1	4,240	74.3	891	15.6	5,710
PART-TIME	82	.3	1,696	7.0	147	.6	189	.8	2,114	8.7	21,528	88.5	688	2.8	24,330
FEMALE	47	.3	1,206	7.8	82	.5	111	.7	1,446	9.3	13,787	88.7	305	2.0	15,538
MALE	35	.4	490	5.6	65	.7	78	.9	668	7.6	7,741	88.0	383	4.4	8,792
TOTAL	126	.3	2,764	7.6	312	.9	379	1.0	3,581	9.9	30,788	84.8	1,936	5.3	36,305
FEMALE	73	.3	1,902	8.7	161	.7	198	.9	2,334	10.7	18,807	86.3	662	3.0	21,803
MALE	53	.4	862	5.9	151	1.0	181	1.2	1,247	8.6	11,981	82.6	1,274	8.8	14,502
PROFESSIONAL:															
FULL-TIME	1	.1	50	3.6	27	2.0	24	1.7	102	7.4	970	70.1	312	22.5	1,384
FEMALE	0	.0	0	.0	5	3.3	3	2.0	8	5.3	98	64.5	46	30.3	152
MALE	1	.1	50	4.1	22	1.8	21	1.7	94	7.6	872	70.8	266	21.6	1,232

ALL OTHERS

INDIAN NATIVE	BLACK NON-HISPANIC		ASIAN OR PACIFIC ISLANDER		HISPANIC		TOTAL MINORITY		WHITE NON-HISPANIC		NON-RESIDENT ALIEN		TOTAL
%	NUMBER	%	NUMBER	%	NUMBER	%	NUMBER	%	NUMBER	%	NUMBER	%	NUMBER
CONTINUED													
.0	8	5.3	3	2.0	6	4.0	17	11.3	112	74.7	21	14.0	150
.0	0	.0	1	8.3	1	8.3	2	16.7	9	75.0	1	8.3	12
.0	8	5.8	2	1.4	5	3.6	15	10.9	103	74.6	20	14.5	138
.1	58	3.8	30	2.0	30	2.0	119	7.8	1,082	70.5	333	21.7	1,534
.0	0	.0	6	3.7	4	2.4	10	6.1	107	65.2	47	28.7	164
.1	58	4.2	24	1.8	26	1.9	109	8.0	975	71.2	286	20.9	1,370
.5	19,222	10.9	1,315	.7	2,076	1.2	23,513	13.3	149,406	84.4	4,043	2.3	176,962
.5	12,063	12.3	650	.7	1,076	1.1	14,269	14.6	82,215	84.0	1,370	1.4	97,854
.5	7,159	9.0	665	.8	1,000	1.3	9,244	11.7	67,191	84.9	2,673	3.4	79,108
.7	16,685	10.3	987	.6	2,588	1.6	21,361	13.2	139,226	86.0	1,229	.8	161,816
.7	9,947	11.3	483	.5	1,289	1.5	12,303	14.0	75,163	85.4	547	.6	88,013
.7	6,738	9.1	504	.7	1,299	1.8	9,058	12.3	64,063	86.8	682	.9	73,803
.6	35,907	10.6	2,302	.7	4,664	1.4	44,874	13.2	288,632	85.2	5,272	1.6	338,778
.6	22,010	11.8	1,133	.6	2,365	1.3	26,572	14.3	157,378	84.7	1,917	1.0	185,867
.6	13,897	9.1	1,169	.8	2,299	1.5	18,302	12.0	131,254	85.8	3,355	2.2	152,911
.8	3,847	18.6	288	1.4	188	.9	4,490	21.7	15,995	77.4	183	.9	20,668
.9	2,347	19.3	94	.8	115	.9	2,663	21.9	9,437	77.6	61	.5	12,161
.7	1,500	17.6	194	2.3	73	.9	1,827	21.5	6,558	77.1	122	1.4	8,507
.6	39,754	11.1	2,590	.7	4,852	1.3	49,364	13.7	304,627	84.7	5,455	1.5	359,446
.6	24,357	12.3	1,227	.6	2,480	1.3	29,235	14.8	166,815	84.2	1,978	1.0	198,028
.6	15,397	9.5	1,363	.8	2,372	1.5	20,129	12.5	137,812	85.4	3,477	2.2	161,418
(63 INSTITUTIONS)													
.8	1,274	1.6	499	.6	379	.5	2,772	3.4	77,156	95.0	1,284	1.6	81,212
.8	611	1.3	252	.5	202	.4	1,424	3.0	45,433	96.0	449	.9	47,306
.8	663	2.0	247	.7	177	.5	1,348	4.0	31,723	93.6	835	2.5	33,906
.4	330	.9	264	.8	113	.3	894	2.4	33,982	97.1	176	.5	35,012
.4	145	.7	128	.6	62	.3	425	2.0	20,430	97.5	96	.5	20,951
.4	185	1.3	136	1.0	51	.4	429	3.1	13,552	96.4	80	.6	14,061
.7	1,604	1.4	763	.7	492	.4	3,626	3.1	111,138	95.6	1,460	1.3	116,224
.7	756	1.1	380	.6	264	.4	1,849	2.7	65,863	96.5	545	.8	68,257
.7	848	1.8	383	.8	228	.5	1,777	3.7	45,275	94.4	915	1.9	47,967
.4	120	1.9	83	1.3	67	1.0	297	4.6	5,539	86.3	584	9.1	6,420
.3	60	2.0	35	1.2	28	.9	133	4.4	2,737	90.2	164	5.4	3,034
.5	60	1.8	48	1.4	39	1.2	164	4.8	2,802	82.8	420	12.4	3,386
.2	16	.3	27	.4	12	.2	65	1.0	6,215	98.4	39	.6	6,319
.2	9	.3	13	.4	11	.3	40	1.1	3,524	98.7	8	.2	3,572
.1	7	.3	14	.5	1	.0	25	.9	2,691	98.0	31	1.1	2,747
.3	136	1.1	110	.9	79	.6	362	2.8	11,754	92.3	623	4.9	12,739
.3	69	1.0	48	.7	39	.6	173	2.6	6,261	94.8	172	2.6	6,606
.3	67	1.1	62	1.0	40	.7	189	3.1	5,493	89.6	451	7.4	6,133
.0	2	.1	5	.3	1	.1	8	.5	1,535	97.2	37	2.3	1,580
.0	1	.4	0	.0	0	.0	1	.4	216	96.4	7	3.1	224
.0	1	.1	5	.4	1	.1	7	.5	1,319	97.3	30	2.2	1,356
.6	1	.6	2	.0	0	.0	2	1.1	170	97.1	3	1.7	175
.0	0	.0	0	.0	0	.0	0	.0	54	100.0	0	.0	54
.8	1	.8	0	.0	0	.0	2	1.7	116	95.9	3	2.5	121
.1	3	.2	5	.3	1	.1	10	.6	1,705	97.2	40	2.3	1,755
.0	1	.4	0	.0	0	.0	1	.4	270	97.1	7	2.5	278
.1	2	.1	5	.3	1	.1	9	.6	1,435	97.2	33	2.2	1,477
.7	1,396	1.6	587	.7	447	.5	3,077	3.4	84,230	94.4	1,905	2.1	89,212
.7	672	1.3	287	.6	230	.5	1,558	3.1	48,386	95.7	620	1.2	50,564
.7	724	1.9	300	.8	217	.6	1,519	3.9	35,844	92.7	1,285	3.3	38,648
.4	347	.8	291	.7	125	.3	921	2.2	40,367	97.3	218	.5	41,506
.4	154	.6	141	.6	73	.3	465	1.9	24,008	97.7	104	.4	24,577
.4	193	1.1	150	.9	52	.3	456	2.7	16,359	96.6	114	.7	16,929
.6	1,743	1.3	878	.7	572	.4	3,998	3.1	124,597	95.3	2,123	1.6	130,718
.6	826	1.1	428	.6	303	.4	2,023	2.7	72,394	96.3	724	1.0	75,141
.6	917	1.6	450	.8	269	.5	1,975	3.6	52,203	93.9	1,399	2.5	55,577
.6	191	1.3	62	.4	61	.4	405	2.7	14,020	95.1	317	2.2	14,742
.6	86	1.0	40	.5	24	.3	200	2.4	8,021	95.6	169	2.0	8,390
.6	105	1.7	22	.3	37	.6	205	3.2	5,999	94.4	148	2.3	6,352
.6	1,934	1.3	940	.6	633	.4	4,403	3.0	138,617	95.3	2,440	1.7	145,460
.6	912	1.1	468	.6	327	.4	2,223	2.7	80,415	96.3	893	1.1	83,531
.6	1,022	1.7	472	.8	306	.5	2,180	3.5	58,202	94.0	1,547	2.5	61,929

MAJOR FIELD 9000 - ALL OTHERS

	AMERICAN INDIAN ALASKAN NATIVE		BLACK NON-HISPANIC		ASIAN OR PACIFIC ISLANDER		HISPANIC		TOTAL MINORITY		WHITE NON-HISPANIC		NON-RESIDENT ALIEN	
	NUMBER	%	NUMBER	%	NUMBER	%	NUMBER	%	NUMBER	%	NUMBER	%	NUMBER	%
MISSISSIPPI	(	45 INSTITUTIONS)												
UNDERGRADUATES:														
FULL-TIME	64	.2	16,855	36.4	108	.2	54	.1	17,101	36.9	28,979	62.6	236	.5
FEMALE	48	.2	9,873	36.4	60	.2	29	.1	10,010	36.9	17,050	62.8	83	.3
MALE	36	.2	6,982	36.4	48	.3	25	.1	7,091	37.0	11,929	62.2	153	.8
PART-TIME	123	1.0	2,463	20.3	64	.5	23	.2	2,673	22.0	9,479	78.0	5	.0
FEMALE	78	1.1	1,598	21.6	23	.3	10	.1	1,709	23.1	5,678	76.9	1	.0
MALE	45	.9	865	18.1	41	.9	13	.3	964	20.2	3,801	79.7	4	.1
TOTAL	207	.4	19,318	33.0	172	.3	77	.1	19,774	33.8	38,458	65.8	241	.4
FEMALE	126	.4	11,471	33.2	83	.2	39	.1	11,719	33.9	22,728	65.8	84	.2
MALE	81	.3	7,847	32.8	89	.4	38	.2	8,055	33.6	15,730	65.7	157	.7
GRADUATE:														
FULL-TIME	1	.1	416	21.4	9	.5	4	.2	430	22.1	1,474	75.7	43	2.2
FEMALE	0	.0	258	25.6	5	.5	1	.1	264	26.2	728	72.2	17	1.7
MALE	1	.1	158	16.8	4	.4	3	.3	166	17.7	746	79.5	26	2.8
PART-TIME	14	.3	1,469	30.5	33	.7	3	.1	1,519	31.6	3,256	67.7	36	.7
FEMALE	11	.4	1,059	33.7	12	.4	3	.1	1,085	34.6	2,046	65.2	7	.2
MALE	3	.2	410	24.5	21	1.3	0	.0	434	25.9	1,210	72.3	29	1.7
TOTAL	15	.2	1,885	27.9	42	.6	7	.1	1,949	28.8	4,730	70.0	79	1.2
FEMALE	11	.3	1,317	31.8	17	.4	4	.1	1,349	32.5	2,774	66.9	24	.6
MALE	4	.2	568	21.8	25	1.0	3	.1	600	23.0	1,956	74.9	55	2.1
PROFESSIONAL:														
FULL-TIME	0	.0	0	.0	0	.0	0	.0	0	.0	0	.0	0	.0
FEMALE	0	.0	0	.0	0	.0	0	.0	0	.0	0	.0	0	.0
MALE	0	.0	0	.0	0	.0	0	.0	0	.0	0	.0	0	.0
PART-TIME	1	20.0	4	80.0	0	.0	0	.0	5	100.0	0	.0	0	.0
FEMALE	1	20.0	4	80.0	0	.0	0	.0	5	100.0	0	.0	0	.0
MALE	0	.0	0	.0	0	.0	0	.0	0	.0	0	.0	0	.0
TOTAL	1	20.0	4	80.0	0	.0	0	.0	5	100.0	0	.0	0	.0
FEMALE	1	20.0	4	80.0	0	.0	0	.0	5	100.0	0	.0	0	.0
MALE	0	.0	0	.0	0	.0	0	.0	0	.0	0	.0	0	.0
UND+GRAD+PROF:														
FULL-TIME	85	.2	17,271	35.8	117	.2	58	.1	17,531	36.3	30,453	63.1	279	.6
FEMALE	48	.2	10,131	36.0	65	.2	30	.1	10,274	36.5	17,778	63.2	100	.4
MALE	37	.2	7,140	35.5	52	.3	28	.1	7,257	36.1	12,675	63.0	179	.9
PART-TIME	138	.8	3,936	23.2	97	.6	26	.2	4,197	24.7	12,735	75.0	41	.2
FEMALE	90	.9	2,661	25.3	35	.3	13	.1	2,799	26.6	7,724	73.3	8	.1
MALE	48	.7	1,275	19.8	62	1.0	13	.2	1,398	21.7	5,011	77.8	33	.5
TOTAL	223	.3	21,207	32.5	214	.3	84	.1	21,728	33.3	43,188	66.2	320	.5
FEMALE	138	.4	12,792	33.1	100	.3	43	.1	13,073	33.8	25,502	65.9	108	.3
MALE	85	.3	8,415	31.7	114	.4	41	.2	8,655	32.6	17,686	66.6	212	.8
UNCLASSIFIED:														
TOTAL	45	1.1	906	22.9	32	.8	3	.1	986	24.9	2,924	73.9	46	1.2
FEMALE	22	1.2	384	21.2	4	.2	1	.1	411	22.7	1,379	76.3	18	1.0
MALE	23	1.1	522	24.3	28	1.3	2	.1	575	26.8	1,545	71.9	28	1.3
TOTAL ENROLLMENT:														
TOTAL	268	.4	22,113	32.0	246	.4	87	.1	22,714	32.8	46,112	66.6	366	.5
FEMALE	160	.4	13,176	32.5	104	.3	44	.1	13,484	33.3	26,881	66.4	126	.3
MALE	108	.4	8,937	31.1	142	.5	43	.1	9,230	32.2	19,231	67.0	240	.8
MISSOURI	(	82 INSTITUTIONS)												
UNDERGRADUATES:														
FULL-TIME	250	.3	7,488	8.8	511	.6	587	.7	8,836	10.3	75,604	88.5	1,000	1.2
FEMALE	113	.2	4,281	9.1	219	.5	255	.5	4,868	10.3	42,105	89.1	301	.6
MALE	137	.4	3,207	8.4	292	.8	332	.9	3,968	10.4	33,499	87.8	699	1.8
PART-TIME	130	.3	5,281	13.2	250	.6	432	1.1	6,093	15.3	33,544	84.1	237	.6
FEMALE	69	.3	3,254	14.5	132	.6	192	.9	3,647	16.2	18,682	83.2	126	.6
MALE	61	.4	2,027	11.6	118	.7	240	1.4	2,446	14.0	14,862	85.3	111	.6
TOTAL	380	.3	12,769	10.2	761	.6	1,019	.8	14,929	11.9	109,148	87.1	1,237	1.0
FEMALE	182	.3	7,535	10.8	351	.5	447	.6	8,515	12.2	60,787	87.2	427	.6
MALE	198	.4	5,234	9.4	410	.7	572	1.0	6,414	11.5	48,361	87.0	810	1.5
GRADUATE:														
FULL-TIME	12	.2	389	7.2	86	1.6	32	.6	519	9.6	4,519	83.2	392	7.2
FEMALE	5	.2	210	8.4	31	1.2	9	.4	255	10.2	2,101	84.4	132	5.3
MALE	7	.2	179	6.1	55	1.9	23	.8	264	9.0	2,418	82.2	260	8.8
PART-TIME	22	.2	640	5.9	275	2.5	66	.6	1,003	9.2	9,726	89.0	201	1.8
FEMALE	11	.2	430	7.1	38	.6	37	.6	516	8.5	5,518	90.6	55	.9
MALE	11	.2	210	4.3	237	4.9	29	.6	487	10.1	4,208	86.9	146	3.0
TOTAL	34	.2	1,029	6.3	361	2.2	98	.6	1,522	9.3	14,245	87.1	593	3.6
FEMALE	16	.2	640	7.5	69	.8	46	.5	771	9.0	7,619	88.8	187	2.2
MALE	18	.2	389	5.0	292	3.8	52	.7	751	9.6	6,626	85.1	406	5.2
PROFESSIONAL:														
FULL-TIME	6	.2	60	2.0	30	1.0	4	.1	100	3.4	2,769	94.1	73	2.5
FEMALE	0	.0	20	5.0	1	.3	0	.0	21	5.3	369	92.7	8	2.0
MALE	6	.2	40	1.6	29	1.1	4	.2	79	3.1	2,400	94.3	65	2.6

ALL OTHERS

INDIAN NATIVE	BLACK NON-HISPANIC		ASIAN OR PACIFIC ISLANDER		HISPANIC		TOTAL MINORITY		WHITE NON-HISPANIC		NON-RESIDENT ALIEN		TOTAL
%	NUMBER	%	NUMBER	%	NUMBER	%	NUMBER	%	NUMBER	%	NUMBER	%	NUMBER
CONTINUED													
.0	6	2.2	8	2.9	5	1.8	19	6.8	255	91.4	5	1.8	279
.0	2	5.1	5	12.8	0	.0	7	17.9	32	82.1	0	.0	39
.0	4	1.7	3	1.3	5	2.1	12	5.0	223	92.9	5	2.1	240
.2	66	2.0	38	1.2	9	.3	119	3.7	3,024	93.9	78	2.4	3,221
.0	22	5.0	6	1.4	0	.0	28	6.4	401	91.8	8	1.8	437
.2	44	1.6	32	1.1	9	.3	91	3.3	2,623	94.2	70	2.5	2,784
.3	7,937	8.5	627	.7	623	.7	9,455	10.1	82,892	88.4	1,465	1.6	93,812
.2	4,511	9.0	251	.5	264	.5	5,144	10.3	44,575	88.9	441	.9	50,160
.3	3,426	7.8	376	.9	359	.8	4,311	9.9	38,317	87.8	1,024	2.3	43,652
.3	5,927	11.6	533	1.0	503	1.0	7,115	13.9	43,525	85.2	443	.9	51,083
.3	3,686	12.9	175	.6	229	.8	4,170	14.6	24,232	84.8	181	.6	28,583
.3	2,241	10.0	358	1.6	274	1.2	2,945	13.1	19,293	85.7	262	1.2	22,500
.3	13,864	9.6	1,160	.8	1,126	.8	16,570	11.4	126,417	87.2	1,908	1.3	144,895
.3	8,197	10.4	426	.5	493	.6	9,314	11.8	68,807	87.4	622	.8	78,743
.3	5,667	8.6	734	1.1	633	1.0	7,256	11.0	57,610	87.1	1,286	1.9	66,152
.5	3,188	16.3	186	.8	199	.9	4,288	18.4	18,907	81.2	97	.4	23,292
.4	2,195	16.9	89	.7	82	.6	2,422	18.6	10,528	81.0	43	.3	12,993
.6	1,593	15.5	97	.9	117	1.1	1,866	18.1	8,379	81.4	54	.5	10,299
.3	17,652	10.5	1,346	.8	1,325	.8	20,858	12.4	145,324	86.4	2,005	1.2	168,187
.3	10,392	11.3	515	.6	575	.6	11,736	12.8	79,335	86.5	665	.7	91,736
.4	7,260	9.5	831	1.1	750	1.0	9,122	11.9	65,989	86.3	1,340	1.8	76,451
(13 INSTITUTIONS)													
3.3	64	.5	47	.4	45	.3	602	4.5	12,715	94.9	83	.6	13,400
3.6	25	.3	13	.2	20	.3	337	4.4	7,378	95.3	30	.4	7,745
3.0	39	.7	34	.6	25	.4	265	4.7	5,337	94.4	53	.9	5,655
3.6	16	.7	9	.4	21	.9	131	5.5	2,216	93.9	14	.6	2,361
3.8	7	.5	3	.2	12	.8	79	5.3	1,416	94.2	8	.5	1,503
3.3	9	1.0	6	.7	9	1.0	52	6.1	800	93.2	6	.7	858
3.4	80	.5	56	.4	66	.4	733	4.7	14,931	94.7	97	.6	15,761
3.6	32	.3	16	.2	32	.3	416	4.5	8,794	95.1	38	.4	9,248
3.0	48	.7	40	.6	34	.5	317	4.9	6,137	94.2	59	.9	6,513
2.9	2	.4	2	.4	0	.0	19	3.6	496	95.0	7	1.3	522
2.4	0	.0	1	.3	0	.0	8	2.8	278	95.9	4	1.4	290
3.4	2	.9	1	.4	0	.0	11	4.7	218	94.0	3	1.3	232
1.0	2	.2	3	.3	4	.4	19	2.0	934	97.1	9	.9	962
1.5	0	.0	2	.4	1	.2	11	2.1	510	96.8	6	1.1	527
.5	2	.5	1	.2	3	.7	8	1.8	424	97.5	3	.7	435
1.7	4	.3	5	.3	4	.3	38	2.6	1,430	96.4	16	1.1	1,484
1.8	0	.0	3	.4	1	.1	19	2.3	788	96.5	10	1.2	817
1.5	4	.6	2	.3	3	.4	19	2.8	642	96.3	6	.9	667
.0	0	.0	0	.0	0	.0	0	.0	0	.0	0	.0	0
.0	0	.0	0	.0	0	.0	0	.0	0	.0	0	.0	0
.0	0	.0	0	.0	0	.0	0	.0	0	.0	0	.0	0
.0	0	.0	0	.0	0	.0	0	.0	0	.0	0	.0	0
.0	0	.0	0	.0	0	.0	0	.0	0	.0	0	.0	0
.0	0	.0	0	.0	0	.0	0	.0	0	.0	0	.0	0
.0	0	.0	0	.0	0	.0	0	.0	0	.0	0	.0	0
.0	0	.0	0	.0	0	.0	0	.0	0	.0	0	.0	0
.0	0	.0	0	.0	0	.0	0	.0	0	.0	0	.0	0
3.3	66	.5	49	.4	45	.3	621	4.5	13,211	94.9	90	.6	13,922
3.6	25	.3	14	.2	20	.2	345	4.3	7,656	95.3	34	.4	8,035
3.0	41	.7	35	.6	25	.4	276	4.7	5,555	94.4	56	1.0	5,887
2.9	18	.5	12	.4	25	.8	150	4.5	3,150	94.8	23	.7	3,323
3.2	7	.3	5	.2	13	.6	90	4.4	1,926	94.9	14	.7	2,030
2.3	11	.9	7	.5	12	.9	60	4.6	1,224	94.7	9	.7	1,293
3.2	84	.5	61	.4	70	.4	771	4.5	16,361	94.9	113	.7	17,245
3.5	32	.3	19	.2	33	.3	435	4.3	9,582	95.2	48	.5	10,065
2.9	52	.7	42	.6	37	.5	336	4.7	6,779	94.4	65	.9	7,180
7.6	57	1.9	8	.3	30	1.0	327	10.7	2,712	88.4	28	.9	3,067
9.2	19	1.0	5	.3	25	1.4	220	11.9	1,615	87.3	14	.8	1,849
5.0	38	3.1	3	.2	5	.4	107	8.8	1,097	90.1	14	1.1	1,218
3.9	141	.7	69	.3	100	.5	1,098	5.4	19,073	93.9	141	.7	20,312
4.4	51	.4	24	.2	58	.5	655	5.5	11,197	94.0	62	.5	11,914
3.2	90	1.1	45	.5	42	.5	443	5.3	7,876	93.8	79	.9	8,390

MAJOR FIELD 9000 - ALL OTHERS

	AMERICAN INDIAN ALASKAN NATIVE		BLACK NON-HISPANIC		ASIAN OR PACIFIC ISLANDER		HISPANIC		TOTAL MINORITY		WHITE NON-HISPANIC		NON-RESIDENT ALIEN		TO
	NUMBER	%	NUMBER	%	NUMBER	%	NUMBER	%	NUMBER	%	NUMBER	%	NUMBER	%	NU
NEBRASKA (31 INSTITUTIONS)															
UNDERGRADUATES:															
FULL-TIME	136	.4	1,079	3.2	153	.5	327	1.0	1,695	5.0	31,503	93.7	424	1.3	33
FEMALE	69	.4	487	2.6	82	.4	186	1.0	824	4.5	17,541	94.8	137	.7	18
MALE	67	.4	592	3.9	71	.5	141	.9	871	5.8	13,962	92.3	287	1.9	15
PART-TIME	73	.4	785	4.7	77	.5	209	1.2	1,144	6.8	15,500	92.8	73	.4	16
FEMALE	33	.4	367	3.9	44	.5	115	1.2	559	6.0	8,700	93.6	34	.4	9
MALE	40	.5	418	5.6	33	.4	94	1.3	585	7.8	6,800	91.7	39	.5	7
TOTAL	209	.4	1,864	3.7	230	.5	536	1.1	2,839	5.6	47,083	93.4	497	1.0	50
FEMALE	102	.4	854	3.1	126	.5	301	1.1	1,383	5.0	26,241	94.4	171	.6	27
MALE	107	.5	1,010	4.5	104	.5	235	1.0	1,456	6.4	20,842	92.1	326	1.4	22
GRADUATE:															
FULL-TIME	7	.6	29	2.3	12	1.0	16	1.3	64	5.2	1,104	89.4	67	5.4	1
FEMALE	3	.5	9	1.5	9	1.5	6	1.0	27	4.6	554	93.4	12	2.0	
MALE	4	.6	20	3.1	3	.5	10	1.6	37	5.8	550	85.7	55	8.6	
PART-TIME	6	.1	98	2.3	19	.4	28	.6	151	3.5	4,130	95.9	26	.6	4
FEMALE	2	.1	62	2.4	11	.4	9	.3	84	3.2	2,501	96.3	13	.5	2
MALE	4	.2	36	2.1	8	.5	19	1.1	67	3.9	1,637	95.3	13	.8	1
TOTAL	13	.2	127	2.3	31	.6	44	.8	215	3.9	5,242	94.5	93	1.7	5
FEMALE	5	.2	71	2.2	20	.6	19	.5	111	3.5	3,055	95.7	25	.8	3
MALE	8	.3	56	2.4	11	.5	29	1.2	104	4.4	2,187	92.7	68	2.9	2
PROFESSIONAL:															
FULL-TIME	0	.0	5	2.3	9	4.1	1	.5	15	6.8	200	90.9	5	2.3	
FEMALE	0	.0	1	1.2	2	2.4	0	.0	3	3.5	81	95.3	1	1.2	
MALE	0	.0	4	3.0	7	5.2	1	.7	12	8.9	119	88.1	4	3.0	
PART-TIME	0	.0	0	.0	0	.0	0	.0	0	.0	8	100.0	0	.0	
FEMALE	0	.0	0	.0	0	.0	0	.0	0	.0	3	100.0	0	.0	
MALE	0	.0	0	.0	0	.0	0	.0	0	.0	5	100.0	0	.0	
TOTAL	0	.0	5	2.2	9	3.9	1	.4	15	6.6	208	91.2	5	2.2	
FEMALE	0	.0	1	1.1	2	2.3	0	.0	3	3.4	84	95.5	1	1.1	
MALE	0	.0	4	2.9	7	5.0	1	.7	12	8.6	124	88.6	4	2.9	
UND+GRAD+PROF:															
FULL-TIME	143	.4	1,113	3.2	174	.5	344	1.0	1,774	5.1	32,807	93.5	496	1.4	35
FEMALE	72	.4	497	2.6	93	.5	192	1.0	854	4.5	18,176	94.8	150	.8	19
MALE	71	.4	616	3.9	81	.5	152	1.0	920	5.8	14,631	92.0	346	2.2	15
PART-TIME	79	.4	883	4.2	96	.5	237	1.1	1,295	6.1	19,726	93.4	99	.5	21
FEMALE	35	.3	429	3.6	55	.5	124	1.0	643	5.4	11,204	94.2	47	.4	11
MALE	44	.5	454	4.9	41	.4	113	1.2	652	7.1	8,522	92.4	52	.6	9
TOTAL	222	.4	1,996	3.6	270	.5	581	1.0	3,069	5.5	52,533	93.5	595	1.1	56
FEMALE	107	.3	926	3.0	148	.5	316	1.0	1,497	4.8	29,380	94.5	197	.6	31
MALE	115	.5	1,070	4.3	122	.5	265	1.1	1,572	6.3	23,153	92.2	398	1.6	25
UNCLASSIFIED:															
TOTAL	19	.4	59	1.2	36	.7	25	.5	139	2.8	4,856	96.5	38	.7	5
FEMALE	14	.4	30	.9	15	.5	14	.4	73	2.2	3,192	97.4	13	.4	3
MALE	5	.4	29	1.7	21	1.2	11	.6	66	3.8	1,664	94.8	25	1.4	1
TOTAL ENROLLMENT:															
TOTAL	241	.4	2,055	3.4	306	.5	606	1.0	3,208	5.4	57,389	93.7	633	1.0	61
FEMALE	121	.4	956	2.8	163	.5	330	1.0	1,570	4.6	32,572	94.8	210	.6	34
MALE	120	.4	1,099	4.1	143	.5	276	1.0	1,638	6.1	24,817	92.3	423	1.6	26
NEVADA (6 INSTITUTIONS)															
UNDERGRADUATES:															
FULL-TIME	81	1.2	376	5.8	102	1.6	168	2.6	727	11.2	5,684	87.4	91	1.4	6
FEMALE	53	1.6	166	5.1	43	1.3	67	2.1	329	10.1	2,904	89.1	26	.8	3
MALE	28	.9	210	6.5	59	1.8	101	3.1	398	12.3	2,780	85.7	65	2.0	3
PART-TIME	124	1.0	484	3.8	127	1.0	239	1.9	974	7.7	11,710	92.0	48	.4	12
FEMALE	65	1.0	236	3.6	60	.9	114	1.8	475	7.3	5,999	92.4	19	.3	6
MALE	59	.9	248	4.0	67	1.1	125	2.0	499	8.0	5,711	91.5	29	.5	6
TOTAL	205	1.1	860	4.5	229	1.2	407	2.1	1,701	9.0	17,394	90.4	139	.7	1
FEMALE	118	1.2	402	4.1	103	1.1	181	1.9	804	8.2	8,903	91.3	45	.5	
MALE	87	.9	458	4.8	126	1.3	226	2.4	897	9.5	8,491	89.5	94	1.0	
GRADUATE:															
FULL-TIME	2	.8	6	2.4	2	.8	4	1.6	14	5.7	227	92.7	4	1.6	
FEMALE	0	.0	3	2.1	1	.7	2	1.4	6	4.2	135	93.8	3	2.1	
MALE	2	2.0	3	3.0	1	1.0	2	2.0	8	7.9	92	91.1	1	1.0	
PART-TIME	7	.8	36	4.2	4	.5	20	2.3	67	7.9	780	91.5	5	.6	
FEMALE	3	.5	24	4.3	3	.5	11	2.0	41	7.4	515	92.5	1	.2	
MALE	4	1.4	12	4.1	1	.3	9	3.1	26	8.8	265	89.8	4	1.4	
TOTAL	9	.8	42	3.8	6	.5	24	2.2	81	7.4	1,007	91.8	9	.8	1
FEMALE	3	.4	27	3.9	4	.6	13	1.9	47	6.7	650	92.7	4	.6	
MALE	6	1.5	15	3.8	2	.5	11	2.8	34	8.6	357	90.2	5	1.3	
PROFESSIONAL:															
FULL-TIME	0	.0	0	.0	0	.0	0	.0	0	.0	0	.0	0	.0	
FEMALE	0	.0	0	.0	0	.0	0	.0	0	.0	0	.0	0	.0	
MALE	0	.0	0	.0	0	.0	0	.0	0	.0	0	.0	0	.0	

ALL OTHERS

INDIAN NATIVE	BLACK NON-HISPANIC		ASIAN OR PACIFIC ISLANDER		HISPANIC		TOTAL MINORITY		WHITE NON-HISPANIC		NON-RESIDENT ALIEN		TOTAL
%	NUMBER	%	NUMBER	%	NUMBER	%	NUMBER	%	NUMBER	%	NUMBER	%	NUMBER
CONTINUED													
.0	C	.0	0	.0	0	.0	0	.0	0	.0	0	.0	0
.0	0	.0	0	.0	0	.0	0	.0	0	.0	0	.0	0
.0	U	.0	0	.0	0	.0	0	.0	0	.0	0	.0	0
.0	0	.0	0	.0	0	.0	0	.0	0	.0	0	.0	0
.0	0	.0	0	.0	0	.0	0	.0	0	.0	0	.0	0
.0	0	.0	0	.0	0	.0	0	.0	0	.0	0	.0	0
1.2	382	5.7	104	1.5	172	2.5	741	11.0	5,911	87.6	95	1.4	6,747
1.6	169	5.0	44	1.3	69	2.0	335	9.8	3,039	89.3	29	.9	3,403
.9	213	6.4	60	1.8	103	3.1	406	12.1	2,872	85.9	66	2.0	3,344
1.0	920	3.8	131	1.0	259	1.9	1,041	7.7	12,490	91.9	53	.4	13,584
1.0	266	3.7	63	.9	125	1.8	516	7.3	6,514	92.4	20	.3	7,050
1.0	260	4.0	68	1.0	134	2.1	525	8.0	5,976	91.5	33	.5	6,534
1.1	402	4.4	235	1.2	431	2.1	1,782	8.8	18,401	90.5	148	.7	20,331
1.2	425	4.1	107	1.0	194	1.9	851	8.1	9,553	91.4	49	.5	10,453
.9	473	4.8	128	1.3	237	2.4	931	9.4	8,848	89.0	99	1.0	9,878
1.1	570	7.5	102	1.4	262	3.5	1,017	13.5	6,532	86.5	1	.0	7,550
1.0	206	6.9	45	1.2	98	2.5	447	11.6	3,398	88.4	1	.0	3,846
1.2	304	8.2	57	1.5	164	4.4	570	15.4	3,134	84.6	0	.0	3,704
1.1	1,472	5.3	337	1.2	693	2.5	2,799	10.0	24,933	89.4	149	.5	27,881
1.1	695	4.9	152	1.1	292	2.0	1,298	9.1	12,951	90.6	50	.3	14,299
1.0	777	5.7	185	1.4	401	3.0	1,501	11.1	11,982	88.2	99	.7	13,582
(20 INSTITUTIONS)													
.3	444	2.3	58	.3	69	.4	628	3.3	18,200	95.2	284	1.5	19,112
.3	177	1.7	25	.2	29	.3	260	2.5	9,879	96.7	78	.8	10,217
.3	267	3.0	33	.4	40	.4	368	4.1	8,321	93.5	206	2.3	8,895
.1	14	.5	6	.2	5	.2	27	.9	2,866	99.0	3	.1	2,896
.1	4	.2	4	.2	3	.2	13	.7	1,799	99.2	1	.1	1,813
.0	10	.9	2	.2	2	.2	14	1.3	1,067	98.5	2	.2	1,083
.3	458	2.1	64	.3	74	.3	655	3.0	21,066	95.7	287	1.3	22,008
.3	181	1.5	29	.2	32	.3	273	2.3	11,678	97.1	79	.7	12,030
.3	277	2.8	35	.4	42	.4	382	3.8	9,388	94.1	208	2.1	9,978
.3	2	.6	3	1.0	1	.3	7	2.3	299	96.1	5	1.6	311
.6	0	.0	1	.6	1	.6	3	1.9	153	97.5	1	.6	157
.0	2	1.3	2	1.3	0	.0	4	2.6	146	94.8	4	2.6	154
.0	2	.3	0	.0	5	.7	7	1.0	697	98.4	4	.6	708
.0	1	.2	0	.0	3	.6	4	.8	497	99.2	0	.0	501
.0	1	.5	0	.0	2	1.0	3	1.4	200	96.6	4	1.9	207
.1	4	.4	3	.3	6	.6	14	1.4	996	97.7	9	.9	1,019
.2	1	.2	1	.2	4	.6	7	1.1	650	98.8	1	.2	658
.0	3	.8	2	.6	2	.6	7	1.9	346	95.8	8	2.2	361
.0	0	.0	0	.0	0	.0	0	.0	0	.0	0	.0	0
.0	0	.0	0	.0	0	.0	0	.0	0	.0	0	.0	0
.0	0	.0	0	.0	0	.0	0	.0	0	.0	0	.0	0
.0	0	.0	0	.0	0	.0	0	.0	0	.0	0	.0	0
.0	0	.0	0	.0	0	.0	0	.0	0	.0	0	.0	0
.0	C	.0	0	.0	0	.0	0	.0	0	.0	0	.0	0
.0	0	.0	0	.0	0	.0	0	.0	0	.0	0	.0	0
.0	0	.0	0	.0	0	.0	0	.0	0	.0	0	.0	0
.0	0	.0	0	.0	0	.0	0	.0	0	.0	0	.0	0
.3	446	2.3	61	.3	70	.4	635	3.3	18,499	95.2	289	1.5	19,423
.3	177	1.7	26	.3	30	.3	263	2.5	10,032	96.7	79	.8	10,374
.3	269	3.0	35	.4	40	.4	372	4.1	8,467	93.6	210	2.3	9,049
.1	16	.4	6	.2	10	.3	34	.9	3,563	98.9	7	.2	3,604
.1	5	.2	4	.2	6	.3	17	.7	2,296	99.2	1	.0	2,314
.0	11	.9	2	.2	4	.3	17	1.3	1,267	98.2	6	.5	1,290
.3	462	2.0	67	.3	80	.3	669	2.9	22,062	95.8	296	1.3	23,027
.3	182	1.4	30	.2	36	.3	280	2.2	12,328	97.2	80	.6	12,688
.3	280	2.7	37	.4	44	.4	389	3.8	9,734	94.1	216	2.1	10,339
.3	7	.2	11	.4	9	.3	36	1.2	3,067	98.7	3	.1	3,106
.3	1	.0	6	.3	6	.3	20	1.0	1,983	99.0	0	.0	2,003
.2	6	.5	5	.5	3	.3	16	1.5	1,084	98.3	3	.3	1,103
.3	469	1.8	78	.3	89	.3	705	2.7	25,129	96.2	299	1.1	26,133
.3	183	1.2	36	.2	42	.3	300	2.0	14,311	97.4	80	.5	14,691
.3	286	2.5	42	.4	47	.4	405	3.5	10,818	94.5	219	1.9	11,442

TABLE 17 - TOTAL ENROLLMENT IN INSTITUTIONS OF HIGHER EDUCATION FOR SELECTED MAJOR FIELDS OF STUDY AND LEVEL OF ENROLLMENT BY RACE, ETHNICITY, AND SEX: STATE, 1978

MAJOR FIELD 9000 - ALL OTHERS

	AMERICAN INDIAN ALASKAN NATIVE		BLACK NON-HISPANIC		ASIAN OR PACIFIC ISLANDER		HISPANIC		TOTAL MINORITY		WHITE NON-HISPANIC		NON-RESIDENT ALIEN		TO
	NUMBER	%	NUMBER	%	NUMBER	%	NUMBER	%	NUMBER	%	NUMBER	%	NUMBER	%	NU

NEW JERSEY   (63 INSTITUTIONS)

UNDERGRADUATES:
FULL-TIME	262	.2	13,661	12.9	871	.8	5,470	5.2	20,264	19.2	83,838	79.5	1,397	1.3	105
FEMALE	161	.3	8,883	14.6	508	.8	3,334	5.5	12,886	21.2	47,419	77.9	539	.9	60
MALE	101	.2	4,778	10.7	363	.8	2,136	4.8	7,378	16.5	36,419	81.6	858	1.9	44
PART-TIME	131	.2	5,741	10.8	507	1.0	1,683	3.2	8,062	15.1	44,916	84.3	283	.5	53
FEMALE	75	.2	3,622	11.2	314	1.0	963	3.0	4,974	15.4	27,161	84.1	173	.5	32
MALE	56	.3	2,119	10.1	193	.9	720	3.4	3,088	14.7	17,755	84.7	110	.5	20

TOTAL	393	.2	19,402	12.2	1,378	.9	7,153	4.5	28,326	17.8	128,754	81.1	1,680	1.1	158
FEMALE	236	.3	12,505	13.4	822	.9	4,297	4.6	17,860	19.2	74,580	80.1	712	.8	93
MALE	157	.2	6,897	10.5	556	.8	2,856	4.4	10,466	16.0	54,174	82.6	988	1.5	65

GRADUATE:
FULL-TIME	8	.2	254	5.7	70	1.6	85	1.9	417	9.4	3,340	75.6	663	15.0	4
FEMALE	6	.3	159	8.2	37	1.9	43	2.2	245	12.6	1,548	79.5	153	7.9	1
MALE	2	.1	95	3.8	33	1.3	42	1.7	172	7.0	1,792	72.4	510	20.6	2
PART-TIME	18	.1	1,026	5.8	176	1.0	432	2.4	1,652	9.4	15,726	89.1	275	1.6	17
FEMALE	10	.1	678	6.3	80	.7	268	2.5	1,036	9.7	9,556	89.4	102	1.0	10
MALE	8	.1	348	5.0	96	1.4	164	2.4	616	8.9	6,170	88.7	173	2.5	6

TOTAL	26	.1	1,280	5.8	246	1.1	517	2.3	2,069	9.4	19,066	86.4	938	4.2	22
FEMALE	16	.1	837	6.6	117	.9	311	2.5	1,281	10.1	11,104	87.8	255	2.0	12
MALE	10	.1	443	4.7	129	1.4	206	2.2	788	8.4	7,962	84.4	683	7.2	9

PROFESSIONAL:
FULL-TIME	2	.2	42	4.1	7	.7	8	.8	59	5.8	928	90.9	34	3.3	1
FEMALE	0	.0	9	5.5	3	1.8	0	.0	12	7.3	150	91.5	9	1.2	
MALE	2	.2	33	3.9	4	.5	8	.9	47	5.5	778	90.8	32	3.7	
PART-TIME	0	.0	12	9.4	2	1.6	1	.8	15	11.8	111	87.4	1	.8	
FEMALE	0	.0	2	3.0	0	.0	0	.0	2	3.0	64	97.0	0	.0	
MALE	0	.0	10	16.4	2	3.3	1	1.6	13	21.3	47	77.0	1	1.6	

TOTAL	2	.2	54	4.7	9	.8	9	.8	74	6.4	1,039	90.5	35	3.0	1
FEMALE	0	.0	11	4.8	3	1.3	0	.0	14	6.1	214	93.0	2	.9	
MALE	2	.2	43	4.7	6	.7	9	1.0	60	6.5	825	89.9	33	3.6	

UND+GRAD+PROF:
FULL-TIME	272	.2	13,957	12.6	948	.9	5,563	5.0	20,740	18.7	88,106	79.4	2,094	1.9	110
FEMALE	167	.3	9,051	14.4	548	.9	3,377	5.4	13,143	20.9	49,117	78.0	694	1.1	62
MALE	105	.2	4,906	10.2	400	.8	2,186	4.6	7,597	15.8	38,989	81.3	1,400	2.9	47
PART-TIME	149	.2	6,779	9.5	685	1.0	2,116	3.0	9,729	13.7	60,753	85.5	559	.8	71
FEMALE	85	.2	4,302	10.0	394	.9	1,231	2.9	6,012	14.0	36,781	85.4	275	.6	43
MALE	64	.2	2,477	8.9	291	1.0	885	3.2	3,717	13.3	23,972	85.7	284	1.0	27

TOTAL	421	.2	20,736	11.4	1,633	.9	7,679	4.2	30,469	16.7	148,859	81.8	2,653	1.5	181
FEMALE	252	.2	13,353	12.6	942	.9	4,608	4.3	19,155	18.1	85,898	81.0	969	.9	106
MALE	169	.2	7,383	9.7	691	.8	3,071	4.0	11,314	14.9	62,961	82.9	1,684	2.2	75

UNCLASSIFIED:
TOTAL	121	.2	4,613	8.5	594	1.1	1,594	3.0	6,922	12.8	46,604	80.4	435	.8	53
FEMALE	42	.1	2,771	9.3	318	1.1	893	3.0	4,024	13.4	25,713	85.9	184	.6	29
MALE	79	.3	1,842	7.7	276	1.1	701	2.9	2,898	12.1	20,891	86.9	251	1.0	24

TOTAL ENROLLMENT:
TOTAL	542	.2	25,349	10.7	2,227	.9	9,273	3.9	37,391	15.8	195,463	82.8	3,088	1.3	235
FEMALE	294	.2	16,124	11.9	1,260	.9	5,501	4.0	23,179	17.1	111,611	82.1	1,153	.8	135
MALE	248	.2	9,225	9.2	967	1.0	3,772	3.8	14,212	14.2	83,852	83.9	1,935	1.9	99

NEW MEXICO   (19 INSTITUTIONS)

UNDERGRADUATES:
FULL-TIME	924	4.7	570	2.9	130	.7	5,462	27.9	7,086	36.1	12,376	63.1	144	.7	19
FEMALE	553	5.1	236	2.2	58	.5	3,046	28.2	3,893	36.0	6,862	63.5	55	.5	10
MALE	371	4.2	334	3.8	72	.8	2,416	27.5	3,193	36.3	5,514	62.7	89	1.0	8
PART-TIME	343	4.7	137	1.9	45	.6	1,856	25.3	2,381	32.4	4,937	67.2	29	.4	7
FEMALE	234	5.3	65	1.5	27	.6	1,165	26.5	1,491	34.0	2,880	65.6	18	.4	4
MALE	109	3.7	72	2.4	18	.6	691	23.4	890	30.1	2,057	69.5	11	.4	2

TOTAL	1,267	4.7	707	2.6	175	.6	7,318	27.2	9,467	35.1	17,313	64.2	173	.6	26
FEMALE	787	5.2	301	2.0	85	.6	4,211	27.7	5,384	35.4	9,742	64.1	73	.5	15
MALE	480	4.1	406	3.5	90	.8	3,107	26.4	4,083	34.7	7,571	64.4	100	.9	11

GRADUATE:
FULL-TIME	45	2.9	23	1.5	13	.9	281	18.4	362	23.7	1,062	69.5	105	6.9	1
FEMALE	31	3.9	9	1.1	5	.6	134	16.6	179	22.2	598	74.3	28	3.5	
MALE	14	1.9	14	1.9	8	1.1	147	20.3	183	25.3	464	64.1	77	10.6	
PART-TIME	61	2.2	53	1.9	14	.5	563	20.4	691	25.0	2,032	73.5	42	1.5	2
FEMALE	30	1.9	30	1.9	10	.6	280	17.7	350	22.1	1,216	76.9	16	1.0	1
MALE	31	2.6	23	1.9	4	.3	283	23.9	341	28.8	816	69.0	26	2.2	1

TOTAL	106	2.5	76	1.8	27	.6	844	19.7	1,053	24.5	3,094	72.1	147	3.4	4
FEMALE	61	2.6	39	1.6	15	.6	414	17.3	529	22.2	1,814	76.0	44	1.8	2
MALE	45	2.4	37	1.9	12	.6	430	22.5	524	27.5	1,280	67.1	103	5.4	1

PROFESSIONAL:
FULL-TIME	0	.0	0	.0	0	.0	0	.0	0	.0	0	.0	0	.0	
FEMALE	0	.0	0	.0	0	.0	0	.0	0	.0	0	.0	0	.0	
MALE	0	.0	0	.0	0	.0	0	.0	0	.0	0	.0	0	.0	

FIELD 9000 - ALL OTHERS

	AMERICAN INDIAN ALASKAN NATIVE		BLACK NON-HISPANIC		ASIAN OR PACIFIC ISLANDER		HISPANIC		TOTAL MINORITY		WHITE NON-HISPANIC		NON-RESIDENT ALIEN		TOTAL
	NUMBER	%	NUMBER	%	NUMBER	%	NUMBER	%	NUMBER	%	NUMBER	%	NUMBER	%	NUMBER

EXICU   CONTINUED

SSIONAL:
TIME	0	.0	0	.0	0	.0	0	.0	0	.0	0	.0	0	.0	0
MALE	0	.0	0	.0	0	.0	0	.0	0	.0	0	.0	0	.0	0
MALE	0	.0	0	.0	0	.0	0	.0	0	.0	0	.0	0	.0	0
	0	.0	0	.0	0	.0	0	.0	0	.0	0	.0	0	.0	0
MALE	0	.0	0	.0	0	.0	0	.0	0	.0	0	.0	0	.0	0
MALE	0	.0	0	.0	0	.0	0	.0	0	.0	0	.0	0	.0	0

RAD+PROF:
TIME	969	4.6	593	2.8	143	.7	5,743	27.2	7,448	35.2	13,438	63.6	249	1.2	21,135
MALE	584	5.0	245	2.1	63	.5	3,180	27.4	4,072	35.1	7,460	64.2	83	.7	11,615
MALE	385	4.0	348	3.7	80	.8	2,563	26.9	3,376	35.5	5,978	62.8	166	1.7	9,520
TIME	404	4.0	190	1.9	59	.6	2,419	23.9	3,072	30.4	6,969	68.9	71	.7	10,112
MALE	264	4.4	95	1.6	37	.6	1,445	24.2	1,841	30.8	4,096	68.6	34	.6	5,971
MALE	140	3.4	95	2.3	22	.5	974	23.5	1,231	29.7	2,873	69.4	37	.9	4,141
	1,373	4.4	783	2.5	202	.6	8,162	26.1	10,520	33.7	20,407	65.3	320	1.0	31,247
MALE	848	4.8	340	1.9	100	.6	4,625	26.3	5,913	33.6	11,556	65.7	117	.7	17,586
MALE	525	3.8	443	3.2	102	.7	3,537	25.9	4,607	33.7	8,851	64.8	203	1.5	13,661

SSIFIED:
	499	6.0	153	1.8	56	.7	1,615	19.3	2,323	27.7	6,004	71.6	59	.7	8,386
MALE	334	6.6	73	1.4	29	.6	976	19.2	1,412	27.8	3,638	71.7	21	.4	5,071
MALE	165	5.0	80	2.4	27	.8	639	19.3	911	27.5	2,366	71.4	38	1.1	3,315

ENROLLMENT:
	1,872	4.7	936	2.4	258	.7	9,777	24.7	12,843	32.4	26,411	66.6	379	1.0	39,633
MALE	1,182	5.2	413	1.8	129	.6	5,601	24.7	7,325	32.3	15,194	67.1	138	.6	22,657
MALE	690	4.1	523	3.1	129	.8	4,176	24.6	5,518	32.5	11,217	66.1	241	1.4	16,976

URK   (264 INSTITUTIONS)

GRADUATES:
TIME	2,369	13.0	54,546	13.0	8,347	2.0	27,494	6.5	92,756	22.1	322,176	76.6	5,504	1.3	420,436
MALE	1,168	.5	34,457	15.1	4,074	1.8	15,970	7.0	55,669	24.4	170,363	74.6	2,215	1.0	228,247
MALE	1,201	.6	20,089	10.5	4,273	2.2	11,524	6.0	37,087	19.3	151,813	79.0	3,289	1.7	192,189
TIME	735	.6	17,084	14.8	2,022	1.6	6,733	5.8	26,574	23.0	88,003	76.2	886	.8	115,463
MALE	347	.5	11,581	17.2	1,062	1.6	3,692	5.5	16,682	24.7	50,318	74.6	463	.7	67,463
MALE	388	.8	5,503	11.5	960	2.0	3,041	6.3	9,892	20.6	37,685	78.5	423	.9	48,000
	3,104	.6	71,630	13.4	10,369	1.9	34,227	6.4	119,330	22.3	410,179	76.5	6,390	1.2	535,899
MALE	1,515	.5	46,038	15.6	5,136	1.7	19,662	6.6	72,351	24.5	220,681	74.6	2,678	.9	295,710
MALE	1,589	.7	25,592	10.7	5,233	2.2	14,565	6.1	46,979	19.6	189,498	78.9	3,712	1.5	240,189

ATE:
TIME	110	.4	1,818	5.9	611	2.0	972	3.2	3,511	11.4	24,570	80.1	2,591	8.4	30,672
MALE	43	.3	1,095	6.7	285	1.7	531	3.2	1,954	11.9	13,550	82.9	850	5.2	16,354
MALE	67	.5	723	5.0	326	2.3	441	3.1	1,557	10.9	11,020	77.0	1,741	12.2	14,318
TIME	203	.4	3,660	6.9	1,339	2.5	1,748	3.3	6,950	13.1	44,738	84.2	1,439	2.7	53,123
MALE	91	.3	2,431	7.6	631	2.0	1,103	3.5	4,256	13.4	26,909	84.5	675	2.1	31,840
MALE	112	.5	1,229	5.8	708	3.3	645	3.0	2,694	12.7	17,829	83.8	760	3.6	21,283
	313	.5	5,478	6.5	1,950	2.3	2,720	3.2	10,461	12.5	69,308	82.7	4,026	4.8	83,795
MALE	134	.3	3,526	7.3	916	1.9	1,634	3.4	6,210	12.9	40,459	84.0	1,525	3.2	48,194
MALE	179	.5	1,952	5.5	1,034	2.9	1,086	3.1	4,251	11.9	28,049	81.0	2,501	7.0	35,601

SSIONAL:
TIME	1	.0	66	3.3	11	.5	23	1.1	101	5.0	1,889	93.4	32	1.6	2,022
MALE	0	.0	21	5.3	4	1.0	4	1.0	29	7.3	367	92.2	2	.5	398
MALE	1	.1	45	2.8	7	.4	19	1.2	72	4.4	1,522	93.7	30	1.8	1,624
TIME	0	.0	22	22.9	1	1.0	3	3.1	26	27.1	70	72.9	0	.0	96
MALE	0	.0	3	11.1	0	.0	2	7.4	5	18.5	22	81.5	0	.0	27
MALE	0	.0	19	27.5	1	1.4	1	1.4	21	30.4	48	69.6	0	.0	69
	1	.0	88	4.2	12	.6	26	1.2	127	6.0	1,959	92.5	32	1.5	2,118
MALE	0	.0	24	5.6	4	.9	6	1.4	34	8.0	389	91.5	2	.5	425
MALE	1	.1	64	3.8	8	.5	20	1.2	53	5.5	1,570	92.7	30	1.8	1,693

RAD+PROF:
TIME	2,440	.5	56,430	12.5	8,969	2.0	28,489	6.3	96,368	21.3	348,035	76.9	8,127	1.8	453,130
MALE	1,211	.5	35,573	14.5	4,363	1.8	16,505	6.7	57,652	23.5	184,280	75.2	3,067	1.3	244,959
MALE	1,269	.6	20,857	10.0	4,606	2.2	11,984	5.8	38,716	18.6	164,355	79.0	5,060	2.4	208,131
TIME	938	.6	20,766	12.3	3,362	2.0	8,484	5.0	33,550	19.9	132,811	78.7	2,321	1.4	168,682
MALE	438	.4	14,015	14.1	1,693	1.7	4,797	4.8	20,943	21.1	77,249	77.8	1,138	1.1	99,330
MALE	500	.7	6,751	9.7	1,669	2.4	3,687	5.3	12,607	18.2	55,562	80.1	1,183	1.7	69,352
	3,418	.5	77,196	12.4	12,331	2.0	36,973	5.9	129,918	20.9	481,446	77.4	10,448	1.7	621,812
MALE	1,649	.5	49,588	14.4	6,056	1.8	21,302	6.2	78,595	22.8	261,529	76.0	4,205	1.2	344,329
MALE	1,769	.6	27,608	9.9	6,275	2.3	15,671	5.6	51,323	18.5	219,917	79.3	6,243	2.2	277,483

SSIFIED:
	564	.5	10,028	8.2	4,010	1.6	4,292	3.5	16,894	13.8	104,639	85.2	1,295	1.1	122,828
MALE	358	.5	6,333	8.9	991	1.4	2,426	3.4	10,108	14.2	60,447	84.9	658	.9	71,213
MALE	206	.4	3,695	7.2	1,019	2.0	1,866	3.6	6,786	13.1	44,192	85.6	637	1.2	51,615

ENROLLMENT:
	3,982	.5	87,224	11.7	14,341	1.9	41,265	5.5	146,812	19.7	586,085	78.7	11,743	1.6	744,640
MALE	2,007	.5	55,921	13.5	7,047	1.7	23,728	5.7	88,703	21.3	321,976	77.5	4,863	1.2	415,542
MALE	1,975	.6	31,303	9.5	7,294	2.2	17,537	5.3	58,109	17.7	264,109	80.3	6,880	2.1	329,098

TABLE 17 - TOTAL ENROLLMENT IN INSTITUTIONS OF HIGHER EDUCATION FOR SELECTED MAJOR FIELDS OF STUDY AND LEVEL OF ENROLLMENT
BY RACE, ETHNICITY, AND SEX: STATE, 1978

MAJOR FIELD 9000 - ALL OTHERS

	AMERICAN INDIAN ALASKAN NATIVE		BLACK NON-HISPANIC		ASIAN OR PACIFIC ISLANDER		HISPANIC		TOTAL MINORITY		WHITE NON-HISPANIC		NON-RESIDENT ALIEN		T
	NUMBER	%	NUMBER	%	NUMBER	%	NUMBER	%	NUMBER	%	NUMBER	%	NUMBER	%	NU
NORTH CAROLINA (119 INSTITUTIONS)															
UNDERGRADUATES:															
FULL-TIME	1,341	.8	28,491	21.7	486	.4	465	.4	30,483	23.2	99,967	76.2	781	.6	131
FEMALE	633	.9	16,587	22.8	211	.3	235	.3	17,666	24.3	54,705	75.3	277	.4	72
MALE	408	.7	11,904	20.3	275	.5	230	.4	12,817	21.9	45,262	77.3	504	.9	58
PART-TIME	370	.8	7,771	17.8	152	.3	180	.4	8,472	19.4	34,991	80.3	101	.2	43
FEMALE	189	.9	3,871	18.3	84	.4	62	.3	4,206	19.9	16,905	79.9	54	.3	21
MALE	181	.8	3,899	17.4	68	.3	118	.5	4,266	19.0	18,086	80.7	47	.2	22
TOTAL	1,711	.8	36,261	20.7	638	.4	645	.4	38,955	22.3	134,958	77.2	882	.5	174
FEMALE	822	.9	20,458	21.8	295	.3	297	.3	21,872	23.3	71,610	76.3	331	.4	93
MALE	589	.7	15,803	19.5	343	.4	348	.4	17,083	21.1	63,348	78.2	551	.7	80
GRADUATE:															
FULL-TIME	16	.3	397	7.8	28	.6	29	.6	470	9.2	4,392	86.4	223	4.4	5
FEMALE	9	.3	240	8.9	13	.5	21	.8	283	10.5	2,331	86.4	85	3.1	2
MALE	7	.3	157	6.6	15	.6	8	.3	187	7.8	2,061	86.4	138	5.8	2
PART-TIME	36	.5	1,425	18.5	17	.2	19	.2	1,497	19.4	6,118	79.3	98	1.3	7
FEMALE	18	.4	980	19.5	5	.1	11	.2	1,014	20.2	3,960	79.0	41	.8	5
MALE	18	.7	445	16.5	12	.4	8	.3	483	17.9	2,158	80.0	57	2.1	2
TOTAL	52	.4	1,822	14.2	45	.4	48	.4	1,967	15.4	10,510	82.1	321	2.5	12
FEMALE	27	.4	1,220	15.8	18	.2	32	.4	1,297	16.8	6,291	81.6	126	1.6	7
MALE	25	.3	602	11.8	27	.5	16	.3	670	13.2	4,219	83.0	195	3.8	5
PROFESSIONAL:															
FULL-TIME	0	.0	37	10.2	0	.0	1	.3	38	10.5	320	88.4	4	1.1	
FEMALE	0	.0	9	8.7	0	.0	1	1.0	10	9.6	91	87.5	3	2.9	
MALE	0	.0	28	10.9	0	.0	0	.0	28	10.9	229	88.8	1	.4	
PART-TIME	0	.0	2	7.7	0	.0	0	.0	2	7.7	22	84.6	2	7.7	
FEMALE	0	.0	1	5.9	0	.0	0	.0	1	5.9	15	88.2	1	5.9	
MALE	0	.0	1	11.1	0	.0	0	.0	1	11.1	7	77.8	1	11.1	
TOTAL	0	.0	39	10.1	0	.0	1	.3	40	10.3	342	88.1	6	1.5	
FEMALE	0	.0	10	8.3	0	.0	1	.8	11	9.1	106	87.6	4	3.3	
MALE	0	.0	29	10.9	0	.0	0	.0	29	10.9	236	88.4	2	.7	
UNDERGRAD+PROF:															
FULL-TIME	1,057	.8	28,925	21.2	514	.4	495	.4	30,991	22.7	104,679	76.6	1,008	.7	136
FEMALE	642	.9	16,836	22.3	224	.3	257	.3	17,959	23.8	57,127	75.7	365	.5	75
MALE	415	.7	12,089	19.7	290	.5	238	.4	13,032	21.3	47,552	77.7	643	1.1	61
PART-TIME	406	.8	9,197	17.9	169	.3	199	.4	9,971	19.4	41,131	80.2	201	.4	51
FEMALE	207	.8	4,852	18.5	89	.3	73	.3	5,221	19.9	20,880	79.7	96	.4	26
MALE	199	.8	4,345	17.3	80	.3	126	.5	4,750	18.9	20,251	80.7	105	.4	25
TOTAL	1,463	.8	38,122	20.3	683	.4	694	.4	40,962	21.8	145,810	77.6	1,209	.6	187
FEMALE	849	.8	21,688	21.3	313	.3	330	.3	23,180	22.8	78,007	76.7	461	.5	101
MALE	614	.7	16,434	19.0	370	.4	364	.4	17,782	20.6	67,803	78.5	748	.9	86
UNCLASSIFIED:															
TOTAL	206	1.1	2,635	13.5	107	.5	114	.6	3,062	15.7	16,367	83.7	133	.7	19
FEMALE	147	1.2	1,728	13.9	57	.5	56	.4	1,988	15.9	10,432	83.6	52	.4	12
MALE	59	.8	907	12.8	50	.7	58	.8	1,074	15.1	5,935	83.7	81	1.1	7
TOTAL ENROLLMENT:															
TOTAL	1,669	.8	40,757	19.6	790	.4	808	.4	44,024	21.2	162,177	78.1	1,342	.6	207
FEMALE	996	.9	23,416	20.5	370	.3	386	.3	25,168	22.1	88,439	77.5	513	.4	114
MALE	673	.7	17,341	18.6	420	.4	422	.5	18,856	20.2	73,738	78.9	829	.9	93
NORTH DAKOTA (16 INSTITUTIONS)															
UNDERGRADUATES:															
FULL-TIME	640	3.5	99	.5	39	.2	29	.2	807	4.5	17,107	94.8	133	.7	18
FEMALE	367	3.6	26	.3	20	.2	14	.1	427	4.2	9,684	95.2	66	.6	10
MALE	273	3.5	73	.9	19	.2	15	.2	380	4.8	7,423	94.3	67	.9	7
PART-TIME	188	12.4	6	.4	5	.3	5	.3	204	13.5	1,308	86.3	4	.3	1
FEMALE	123	12.2	3	.3	5	.5	4	.4	135	13.4	874	86.4	2	.2	1
MALE	65	12.9	3	.6	0	.0	1	.2	69	13.7	434	85.9	2	.4	
TOTAL	828	4.2	105	.5	44	.2	34	.2	1,011	5.2	18,415	94.1	137	.7	19
FEMALE	490	4.4	29	.3	25	.2	18	.2	562	5.0	10,558	94.4	68	.6	11
MALE	338	4.0	76	.9	19	.2	16	.2	449	5.4	7,857	93.8	69	.8	8
GRADUATE:															
FULL-TIME	1	.3	4	1.3	4	1.3	0	.0	9	3.0	261	86.4	32	10.6	
FEMALE	1	.7	3	2.2	2	1.4	0	.0	6	4.3	117	84.2	16	11.5	
MALE	0	.0	1	.6	2	1.2	0	.0	3	1.8	144	88.3	16	9.8	
PART-TIME	10	1.5	4	.6	2	.3	4	.6	20	3.0	645	95.3	12	1.8	
FEMALE	7	2.3	0	.0	1	.3	1	.3	9	3.0	285	95.6	4	1.3	
MALE	3	.9	4	1.1	1	.3	3	.8	11	2.9	360	95.0	8	2.1	
TOTAL	11	1.1	8	.8	6	.6	4	.4	29	3.0	906	92.5	44	4.5	
FEMALE	8	1.8	3	.7	3	.7	1	.2	15	3.4	402	92.0	20	4.6	
MALE	3	.6	5	.9	3	.6	3	.6	14	2.6	504	93.0	24	4.4	
PROFESSIONAL:															
FULL-TIME	0	.0	0	.0	0	.0	0	.0	0	.0	0	.0	0	.0	
FEMALE	0	.0	0	.0	0	.0	0	.0	0	.0	0	.0	0	.0	
MALE	0	.0	0	.0	0	.0	0	.0	0	.0	0	.0	0	.0	

ALL OTHERS

INDIAN NATIVE	BLACK NON-HISPANIC		ASIAN OR PACIFIC ISLANDER		HISPANIC		TOTAL MINORITY		WHITE NON-HISPANIC		NON-RESIDENT ALIEN		TOTAL
%	NUMBER	%	NUMBER	%	NUMBER	%	NUMBER	%	NUMBER	%	NUMBER	%	NUMBER

CONTINUED

.0	0	.0	0	.0	0	.0	0	.0	0	.0	0	.0	0
.0	0	.0	0	.0	0	.0	0	.0	0	.0	0	.0	0
.0	0	.0	0	.0	0	.0	0	.0	0	.0	0	.0	0
.0	0	.0	0	.0		.0	0	.0	0	.0	0	.0	0
.0	0	.0	0	.0	0	.0	0	.0	0	.0	0	.0	0
.0	0	.0	0	.0	0	.0	0	.0	0	.0	0	.0	0
3.5	103	.6	43	.2	29	.2	816	4.4	17,368	94.7	165	.9	18,349
3.6	29	.3	22	.2	14	.1	433	4.2	9,801	95.0	82	.8	10,316
3.4	74	.9	21	.3	15	.2	383	4.8	7,567	94.2	83	1.0	8,033
9.0	10	.5	7	.3	9	.4	224	10.2	1,953	89.1	16	.7	2,193
9.9	3	.2	6	.5	5	.4	144	11.0	1,159	88.5	6	.5	1,309
7.7	7	.8	1	.1	4	.5	80	9.0	794	89.8	10	1.1	884
4.1	113	.6	50	.2	38	.2	1,040	5.1	19,321	94.1	181	.9	20,542
4.3	32	.3	28	.2	19	.2	577	5.0	10,960	94.3	88	.8	11,625
3.8	81	.9	22	.2	19	.2	463	5.2	8,361	93.8	93	1.0	8,917
3.0	5	.2	7	.3	2	.1	77	3.7	2,021	95.8	11	.5	2,109
2.4	3	.2	2	.2	1	.1	37	2.9	1,223	96.5	8	.6	1,268
3.8	2	.2	5	.6	1	.1	40	4.8	798	94.9	3	.4	841
4.0	118	.5	57	.3	40	.2	1,117	4.9	21,342	94.2	192	.8	22,651
4.1	35	.3	30	.2	20	.2	614	4.8	12,183	94.5	96	.7	12,893
3.8	83	.9	27	.3	20	.2	503	5.2	9,159	93.9	96	1.0	9,758

(128 INSTITUTIONS)

.3	17,323	10.1	721	.4	1,125	.7	19,767	11.5	149,987	87.5	1,623	.9	171,377
.5	10,522	10.9	408	.4	611	.6	11,974	12.4	83,639	87.0	568	.6	96,181
.5	6,801	9.0	313	.4	514	.7	7,793	10.4	66,348	88.2	1,055	1.4	75,196
.2	8,066	11.3	323	.5	496	.7	9,044	12.7	61,546	86.6	497	.7	71,087
.2	5,308	12.3	195	.5	292	.7	5,881	13.7	36,830	85.6	304	.7	43,015
.3	2,758	9.8	128	.5	204	.7	3,163	11.3	24,716	88.0	193	.7	28,072
.3	25,369	10.5	1,044	.4	1,621	.7	28,811	11.9	211,533	87.2	2,120	.9	242,464
.4	15,830	11.4	603	.4	903	.6	17,855	12.8	120,469	86.5	872	.6	139,196
.2	9,559	9.3	441	.4	718	.7	10,956	10.6	91,064	88.2	1,248	1.2	103,268
.4	1,066	7.7	80	.6	147	1.1	1,342	9.7	11,490	83.3	957	6.9	13,789
.3	598	6.3	37	.5	72	1.0	727	10.1	6,161	85.3	338	4.7	7,226
.4	468	7.1	43	.7	75	1.1	615	9.4	5,329	81.2	619	9.4	6,563
.2	1,548	7.5	78	.4	76	.4	1,742	8.4	18,678	90.4	249	1.2	20,669
.2	1,022	7.8	52	.4	46	.4	1,143	8.7	11,844	90.4	109	.8	13,096
.2	526	6.9	26	.3	30	.4	599	7.9	6,834	90.2	140	1.8	7,573
.3	2,614	7.6	158	.5	223	.6	3,084	9.0	30,168	87.6	1,206	3.5	34,458
.2	1,820	8.0	89	.4	118	.6	1,870	9.2	18,005	88.6	447	2.2	20,322
.3	994	7.0	69	.5	105	.7	1,214	8.6	12,163	80.0	759	5.4	14,136
11.5	92	4.4	8	.4	8	.4	351	16.7	1,732	82.3	22	1.0	2,105
7.7	25	7.2	3	.9	2	.6	57	16.3	290	83.1	2	.6	349
12.3	67	3.8	5	.3	6	.3	294	16.7	1,442	82.1	20	1.1	1,756
3.9	5	6.6	0	.0	0	.0	8	10.5	68	89.5	0	.0	76
9.1	2	9.1	0	.0	0	.0	4	18.2	18	81.8	0	.0	22
1.9	3	5.6	0	.0	0	.0	4	7.4	50	92.6	0	.0	54
11.3	97	4.4	8	.4		.4	359	16.4	1,800	82.5	22	1.0	2,181
7.8	27	7.3	3	.8	8	.5	61	16.4	308	83.0	2	.5	371
12.0	70	3.9	5	.3		.3	298	16.5	1,492	82.4	20	1.1	1,810
.5	18,481	9.9	809	.4	1,280	.7	21,460	11.5	163,209	87.2	2,602	1.4	187,271
.5	11,145	10.7	448	.4	685	.7	12,758	12.3	90,090	86.8	908	.9	103,756
.5	7,336	8.8	301	.4	595	.7	8,702	10.4	73,119	87.6	1,694	2.0	83,515
.2	9,819	10.5	401	.4	572	.6	10,794	11.8	80,292	87.4	746	.8	91,832
.2	6,332	11.3	247	.4	338	.6	7,028	12.5	48,692	86.7	413	.7	56,133
.3	3,287	9.2	154	.4	234	.7	3,766	10.5	31,600	88.5	333	.9	35,699
.4	28,100	10.1	1,210	.4	1,852	.7	32,254	11.6	243,501	87.2	3,348	1.2	279,103
.4	17,477	10.9	695	.4	1,023	.6	19,786	12.4	138,782	86.8	1,321	.8	159,889
.4	10,623	8.9	515	.4	829	.7	12,468	10.5	104,719	87.8	2,027	1.7	119,214
.4	1,934	6.7	183	.6	95	.3	2,319	8.0	26,491	91.3	211	.7	29,021
.4	1,197	7.0	94	.5	54	.3	1,408	8.2	15,661	91.2	99	.6	17,168
.4	737	6.2	89	.8	41	.3	911	7.7	10,830	91.4	112	.9	11,853
.4	30,034	9.7	1,393	.5	1,947	.6	34,573	11.2	269,992	87.6	3,559	1.2	308,124
.4	18,674	10.5	789	.4	1,077	.6	21,194	12.0	154,443	87.2	1,420	.8	177,057
.4	11,360	8.7	604	.5	870	.7	13,379	10.2	115,549	88.2	2,139	1.6	131,067

MAJOR FIELD 9000 - ALL OTHERS

	AMERICAN INDIAN ALASKAN NATIVE		BLACK NON-HISPANIC		ASIAN OR PACIFIC ISLANDER		HISPANIC		TOTAL MINORITY		WHITE NON-HISPANIC		NON-RESIDENT ALIEN	
	NUMBER	%	NUMBER	%	NUMBER	%	NUMBER	%	NUMBER	%	NUMBER	%	NUMBER	%
UKLAHOMA	(	42 INSTITUTIONS)												
UNDERGRADUATES:														
FULL-TIME	2,522	4.5	4,133	7.4	370	.7	421	.8	7,446	13.3	46,407	83.1	1,985	3.6
FEMALE	1,462	4.8	2,160	7.0	163	.5	192	.6	3,977	13.0	26,231	85.5	471	1.5
MALE	1,060	4.2	1,973	7.8	207	.8	229	.9	3,469	13.8	20,176	80.2	1,514	6.0
PART-TIME	907	3.3	2,019	7.4	216	.8	311	1.1	3,453	12.7	23,190	85.2	575	2.1
FEMALE	552	3.6	1,092	7.0	111	.7	147	.9	1,902	12.3	13,409	86.5	189	1.2
MALE	355	3.0	927	7.9	105	.9	164	1.4	1,551	13.2	9,781	83.5	386	3.3
TOTAL	3,429	4.1	6,152	7.4	586	.7	732	.9	10,899	13.1	69,597	83.8	2,560	3.1
FEMALE	2,014	4.4	3,252	7.0	274	.6	339	.7	5,079	12.7	39,640	85.8	660	1.4
MALE	1,415	3.8	2,900	7.9	312	.8	393	1.1	5,020	13.6	29,957	81.2	1,900	5.2
GRADUATE:														
FULL-TIME	91	3.2	126	4.5	11	.4	23	.8	251	8.9	2,179	77.4	386	13.7
FEMALE	50	3.8	72	5.5	5	.4	12	.9	139	10.6	1,047	79.9	125	9.5
MALE	41	2.7	54	3.6	6	.4	11	.7	112	7.4	1,132	75.2	261	17.3
PART-TIME	207	3.1	285	4.3	28	.4	33	.5	553	8.3	5,908	88.9	183	2.8
FEMALE	122	3.1	174	4.4	19	.5	13	.3	328	8.2	3,608	90.3	59	1.5
MALE	85	3.2	111	4.2	9	.3	20	.8	225	8.5	2,300	86.8	124	4.7
TOTAL	298	3.2	411	4.3	39	.4	56	.6	804	8.5	8,087	85.5	569	6.0
FEMALE	172	3.2	246	4.6	24	.5	25	.5	467	8.8	4,655	87.7	184	3.5
MALE	126	3.0	165	4.0	15	.4	31	.7	337	8.1	3,432	82.6	385	9.3
PROFESSIONAL:														
FULL-TIME	5	1.6	4	1.3	2	.6	1	.3	12	3.8	306	96.2	0	.0
FEMALE	0	.0	2	3.7	1	1.9	0	.0	3	5.6	51	94.4	0	.0
MALE	5	1.9	2	.8	1	.4	1	.4	9	3.4	255	96.6	0	.0
PART-TIME	0	.0	0	.0	0	.0	0	.0	0	.0	62	100.0	0	.0
FEMALE	0	.0	0	.0	0	.0	0	.0	0	.0	10	100.0	0	.0
MALE	0	.0	0	.0	0	.0	0	.0	0	.0	52	100.0	0	.0
TOTAL	5	1.3	4	1.1	2	.5	1	.3	12	3.2	368	96.8	0	.0
FEMALE	0	.0	2	3.1	1	1.6	0	.0	3	4.7	61	95.3	0	.0
MALE	5	1.6	2	.6	1	.3	1	.3	9	2.8	307	97.2	0	.0
UNDERGRAD+PROF:														
FULL-TIME	2,618	4.4	4,263	7.2	383	.6	445	.8	7,709	13.1	48,892	82.9	2,371	4.0
FEMALE	1,512	4.7	2,234	7.0	169	.5	204	.6	4,119	12.9	27,329	85.3	596	1.9
MALE	1,106	4.1	2,029	7.5	214	.8	241	.9	3,590	13.3	21,563	80.1	1,775	6.6
PART-TIME	1,114	3.3	2,364	6.8	244	.7	344	1.0	4,006	11.8	29,160	86.0	758	2.2
FEMALE	674	3.5	1,266	6.5	130	.7	160	.8	2,230	11.4	17,027	87.3	248	1.3
MALE	440	3.1	1,038	7.2	114	.8	184	1.3	1,776	12.3	12,133	84.1	510	3.5
TOTAL	3,732	4.0	6,567	7.1	627	.7	789	.8	11,715	12.6	78,052	84.0	3,129	3.4
FEMALE	2,186	4.2	3,500	6.8	299	.6	364	.7	6,349	12.3	44,356	86.0	844	1.6
MALE	1,546	3.7	3,067	7.4	328	.8	425	1.0	5,366	13.0	33,696	81.5	2,285	5.5
UNCLASSIFIED:														
TOTAL	322	4.0	275	3.4	27	.3	47	.6	671	8.3	7,232	88.9	228	2.8
FEMALE	215	4.5	145	3.0	13	.3	27	.6	400	8.4	4,293	90.0	77	1.6
MALE	107	3.2	130	3.9	14	.4	20	.6	271	8.1	2,939	87.4	151	4.5
TOTAL ENROLLMENT:														
TOTAL	4,054	4.0	6,842	6.8	654	.6	836	.8	12,386	12.3	85,284	84.4	3,357	3.3
FEMALE	2,401	4.3	3,645	6.5	312	.6	391	.7	6,749	12.0	48,649	86.4	921	1.6
MALE	1,653	3.7	3,197	7.2	342	.8	445	1.0	5,637	12.6	36,635	81.9	2,436	5.4
OREGON	(	41 INSTITUTIONS)												
UNDERGRADUATES:														
FULL-TIME	650	1.2	808	1.5	1,236	2.4	655	1.2	3,349	6.4	48,022	91.4	1,143	2.2
FEMALE	339	1.2	321	1.2	648	2.4	328	1.2	1,636	5.9	25,427	92.4	444	1.6
MALE	311	1.2	467	1.9	588	2.4	327	1.3	1,713	6.9	22,595	90.4	699	2.8
PART-TIME	360	1.1	385	1.2	690	2.1	457	1.4	1,892	5.7	30,546	92.0	532	1.6
FEMALE	203	1.1	184	1.0	358	1.9	242	1.3	987	5.4	17,183	93.1	277	1.5
MALE	157	1.1	201	1.4	332	2.3	215	1.5	905	6.2	13,363	92.0	255	1.8
TOTAL	1,010	1.2	1,193	1.4	1,926	2.3	1,112	1.3	5,241	6.1	78,568	91.9	1,675	2.0
FEMALE	542	1.2	505	1.1	1,006	2.2	570	1.2	2,623	5.7	42,610	92.7	721	1.6
MALE	468	1.2	688	1.7	920	2.3	542	1.4	2,618	6.6	35,958	91.0	954	2.4
GRADUATE:														
FULL-TIME	28	.8	48	1.4	63	1.8	30	.9	169	4.8	2,851	81.6	476	13.6
FEMALE	16	.9	19	1.1	37	2.2	12	.7	84	4.9	1,455	85.3	166	9.7
MALE	12	.7	29	1.6	26	1.5	18	1.0	85	4.7	1,396	77.9	310	17.3
PART-TIME	9	.3	30	1.1	41	1.6	25	1.0	105	4.0	2,415	92.5	92	3.5
FEMALE	6	.4	13	.8	20	1.3	10	.7	49	3.2	1,455	94.9	30	2.0
MALE	3	.3	17	1.6	21	1.9	15	1.4	56	5.2	960	89.1	62	5.8
TOTAL	37	.6	78	1.3	104	1.7	55	.9	274	4.5	5,266	86.2	568	9.3
FEMALE	22	.7	32	1.0	57	1.8	22	.7	133	4.1	2,910	89.8	196	6.1
MALE	15	.5	46	1.6	47	1.6	33	1.2	141	4.9	2,356	82.1	372	13.0
PROFESSIONAL:														
FULL-TIME	1	.2	4	.6	42	6.3	1	.2	48	7.2	599	90.2	17	2.6
FEMALE	0	.0	0	.0	14	19.4	0	.0	14	19.4	57	79.2	1	1.4
MALE	1	.2	4	.7	28	4.7	1	.2	34	5.7	542	91.0	16	2.7

ALL OTHERS

INDIAN NATIVE		BLACK NON-HISPANIC		ASIAN OR PACIFIC ISLANDER		HISPANIC		TOTAL MINORITY		WHITE NON-HISPANIC		NON-RESIDENT ALIEN		TOTAL
%	NUMBER	%	NUMBER	%	NUMBER	%	NUMBER	%	NUMBER	%	NUMBER	%	NUMBER	%	NUMBER

CONTINUED

.7	0	.0	3	2.1	1	.7	5	3.4	139	95.2	2	1.4	146
.0	0	.0	1	25.0	0	.0	1	25.0	3	75.0	0	.0	4
.7	0	.0	2	1.4	1	.7	4	2.8	136	95.8	2	1.4	142

.2	4	.5	45	5.6	2	.2	53	6.5	738	91.1	19	2.3	810
.0	0	.0	15	19.7	0	.0	15	19.7	60	78.9	1	1.3	76
.3	4	.5	30	4.1	2	.3	38	5.2	678	92.4	18	2.5	734

1.2	860	1.5	1,341	2.4	686	1.2	3,566	6.3	51,472	90.8	1,636	2.9	56,674
1.2	340	1.2	699	2.4	340	1.2	1,734	5.9	26,939	92.0	611	2.1	29,284
1.2	520	1.9	642	2.3	346	1.3	1,832	6.7	24,533	89.6	1,025	3.7	27,390
1.0	415	1.2	734	2.1	483	1.4	2,002	5.6	33,100	92.6	626	1.8	35,728
1.0	197	1.0	379	1.9	252	1.3	1,037	5.2	18,641	93.3	307	1.5	19,985
1.0	218	1.4	355	2.3	231	1.5	965	6.1	14,459	91.8	319	2.0	15,743

1.1	1,275	1.4	2,075	2.2	1,169	1.3	5,568	6.0	84,572	91.5	2,262	2.4	92,402
1.1	533	1.1	1,078	2.2	592	1.2	2,771	5.6	45,580	92.5	918	1.9	49,269
1.1	736	1.7	997	2.3	577	1.3	2,797	6.5	38,992	90.4	1,344	3.1	43,133

.9	140	.6	302	1.4	205	.9	848	3.8	20,986	95.1	240	1.1	22,074
.8	64	.5	161	1.2	105	.8	439	3.3	12,698	96.1	79	.6	13,216
1.0	76	.9	141	1.6	100	1.1	409	4.6	8,288	93.6	161	1.8	8,858

1.1	1,415	1.2	2,377	2.1	1,374	1.2	6,416	5.6	105,558	92.2	2,502	2.2	114,476
1.1	601	1.0	1,239	2.0	697	1.1	3,210	5.1	58,278	93.3	997	1.6	62,485
1.1	814	1.6	1,138	2.2	677	1.3	3,206	6.2	47,280	90.9	1,505	2.9	51,991

(172 INSTITUTIONS)

.1	14,729	8.4	940	.5	1,349	.8	17,255	9.9	156,429	89.3	1,391	.8	175,075
.1	9,238	9.0	511	.5	785	.8	10,674	10.4	91,786	89.1	571	.6	103,031
.1	5,491	7.6	429	.6	564	.8	6,581	9.1	64,643	89.7	820	1.1	72,044
.2	6,590	12.7	329	.6	585	1.1	7,606	14.7	44,123	85.1	145	.3	51,874
.2	4,330	13.6	185	.6	384	1.2	4,957	15.6	26,811	84.2	60	.2	31,828
.2	2,260	11.3	144	.7	201	1.0	2,649	13.2	17,312	86.4	85	.4	20,046

.1	21,319	9.4	1,269	.6	1,934	.9	24,861	11.0	200,552	88.4	1,536	.7	226,949
.1	13,568	10.1	696	.5	1,169	.9	15,631	11.6	118,597	87.9	631	.5	134,859
.2	7,751	8.4	573	.6	765	.8	9,230	10.0	81,955	89.0	905	1.0	92,090

.3	503	4.9	138	1.4	122	1.2	794	7.8	9,004	78.8	1,364	13.4	10,162
.3	314	6.2	70	1.4	68	1.3	466	9.2	4,239	84.1	334	6.6	5,039
.3	189	3.7	68	1.3	54	1.1	328	6.4	3,765	73.5	1,030	20.1	5,123
.1	595	4.6	146	.7	101	.5	1,271	5.9	20,163	93.1	224	1.0	21,658
.1	648	5.1	83	.7	62	.5	803	6.3	11,779	93.1	64	.5	12,646
.2	347	3.9	63	.7	39	.4	468	5.2	8,384	93.0	160	1.8	9,012

.2	1,498	4.7	284	.9	223	.7	2,065	6.5	28,167	88.5	1,588	5.0	31,820
.1	962	5.4	153	.9	130	.7	1,269	7.2	16,018	90.6	398	2.3	17,685
.3	536	3.8	131	.9	93	.7	796	5.6	12,149	85.9	1,190	8.4	14,135

.0	56	2.2	21	.8	15	.6	92	3.6	2,463	95.1	36	1.4	2,591
.0	13	3.4	8	2.1	6	1.5	27	7.0	303	91.0	8	2.1	308
.0	43	2.0	13	.6	9	.4	65	3.0	2,110	95.8	28	1.3	2,203
.0	13	6.5	2	1.0	2	1.0	17	8.5	182	91.0	1	.5	200
.0	5	8.6	1	1.7	1	1.7	7	12.1	51	87.9	0	.0	58
.0	8	5.6	1	.7	1	.7	10	7.0	131	92.3	1	.7	142

.0	69	2.5	23	.8	17	.6	109	3.9	2,645	94.8	37	1.3	2,791
.0	18	4.0	9	2.0	7	1.6	34	7.6	404	90.6	8	1.8	446
.0	51	2.2	14	.6	10	.4	75	3.2	2,241	95.6	29	1.2	2,345

.1	15,288	8.1	1,099	.6	1,486	.8	18,141	9.7	166,896	88.9	2,791	1.5	187,828
.1	9,565	8.8	589	.5	859	.8	11,167	10.3	96,378	86.9	913	.8	108,458
.1	5,723	7.2	510	.6	627	.8	6,974	8.8	70,518	88.8	1,878	2.4	79,370
.2	7,598	10.3	477	.6	688	.9	8,894	12.1	64,468	87.4	370	.5	73,732
.2	4,983	11.2	269	.6	447	1.0	5,767	13.0	38,641	86.6	124	.3	44,532
.2	2,615	9.0	208	.7	241	.8	3,127	10.7	25,827	88.4	246	.8	29,200

.2	22,886	8.7	1,576	.6	2,174	.8	27,035	10.3	231,364	88.5	3,161	1.2	261,560
.1	14,548	9.5	858	.6	1,306	.9	16,934	11.1	135,019	88.3	1,037	.7	152,990
.2	8,338	7.7	718	.7	868	.8	10,101	9.3	96,345	88.7	2,124	2.0	108,570

.2	3,119	6.3	412	.8	354	.7	4,300	8.1	45,121	91.2	347	.7	49,468
.2	1,856	6.6	182	.7	194	.7	2,280	8.2	25,513	91.3	155	.6	27,948
.3	1,263	5.9	230	1.1	160	.7	1,720	8.0	19,608	91.1	192	.9	21,520

.2	26,005	8.4	1,988	.6	2,528	.8	31,035	10.0	276,485	88.9	3,508	1.1	311,028
.1	16,404	9.1	1,040	.6	1,500	.8	19,214	10.6	160,532	86.7	1,192	.7	180,938
.2	9,601	7.4	948	.7	1,028	.8	11,821	9.1	115,953	89.1	2,316	1.8	130,090

MAJOR FIELD 9000 - ALL OTHERS

	AMERICAN INDIAN ALASKAN NATIVE		BLACK NON-HISPANIC		ASIAN OR PACIFIC ISLANDER		HISPANIC		TOTAL MINORITY		WHITE NON-HISPANIC		NON-RESIDENT ALIEN		TO
	NUMBER	%	NUMBER	%	NUMBER	%	NUMBER	%	NUMBER	%	NUMBER	%	NUMBER	%	NU
RHODE ISLAND (12 INSTITUTIONS)															
UNDERGRADUATES:															
FULL-TIME	50	.2	694	3.0	181	.8	169	.7	1,094	4.7	21,756	94.0	289	1.2	23
FEMALE	34	.3	362	2.8	112	.8	93	.7	621	4.6	12,750	94.5	120	.9	13
MALE	16	.2	312	3.2	69	.7	76	.8	473	4.9	9,006	93.3	169	1.8	9
PART-TIME	17	.3	102	2.0	15	.3	25	.5	159	3.1	4,860	95.9	51	1.0	5
FEMALE	10	.4	52	2.0	8	.3	13	.5	83	3.2	2,465	95.8	25	1.0	2
MALE	7	.3	50	2.0	7	.3	12	.5	76	3.0	2,395	95.9	26	1.0	2
TOTAL	67	.2	796	2.8	196	.7	194	.7	1,253	4.4	26,616	94.4	340	1.2	28
FEMALE	44	.3	434	2.7	120	.7	106	.7	704	4.4	15,215	94.7	145	.9	16
MALE	23	.2	362	3.0	76	.6	88	.7	549	4.5	11,401	93.9	195	1.6	12
GRADUATE:															
FULL-TIME	6	.4	28	2.0	14	1.0	12	.8	60	4.2	1,224	86.6	130	9.2	1
FEMALE	4	.6	15	2.2	4	.6	5	.7	28	4.0	630	90.6	37	5.3	
MALE	2	.3	13	1.8	10	1.4	7	1.0	32	4.5	594	82.6	93	12.9	
PART-TIME	6	.3	25	1.2	10	.5	10	.5	51	2.4	2,044	94.9	58	2.7	2
FEMALE	4	.3	16	1.2	6	.5	6	.5	32	2.4	1,271	95.5	28	2.1	1
MALE	2	.2	9	1.1	4	.5	4	.5	19	2.3	773	94.0	30	3.6	
TOTAL	12	.3	53	1.5	24	.7	22	.6	111	3.1	3,268	91.6	188	5.3	3
FEMALE	8	.4	31	1.5	10	.5	11	.5	60	3.0	1,901	93.8	65	3.2	2
MALE	4	.3	22	1.4	14	.9	11	.7	51	3.3	1,367	88.7	123	8.0	1
PROFESSIONAL:															
FULL-TIME	0	.0	0	.0	0	.0	0	.0	0	.0	0	.0	0	.0	
FEMALE	0	.0	0	.0	0	.0	0	.0	0	.0	0	.0	0	.0	
MALE	0	.0	0	.0	0	.0	0	.0	0	.0	0	.0	0	.0	
PART-TIME	0	.0	0	.0	0	.0	0	.0	0	.0	0	.0	0	.0	
FEMALE	0	.0	0	.0	0	.0	0	.0	0	.0	0	.0	0	.0	
MALE	0	.0	0	.0	0	.0	0	.0	0	.0	0	.0	0	.0	
TOTAL	0	.0	0	.0	0	.0	0	.0	0	.0	0	.0	0	.0	
FEMALE	0	.0	0	.0	0	.0	0	.0	0	.0	0	.0	0	.0	
MALE	0	.0	0	.0	0	.0	0	.0	0	.0	0	.0	0	.0	
UNDGRAD+PROF:															
FULL-TIME	56	.2	722	2.9	195	.8	181	.7	1,154	4.7	22,980	93.6	419	1.7	24
FEMALE	38	.3	397	2.8	116	.8	98	.7	649	4.6	13,380	94.3	157	1.1	14
MALE	18	.2	325	3.1	79	.8	83	.8	505	4.9	9,600	92.6	262	2.5	10
PART-TIME	23	.3	127	1.8	25	.3	35	.5	210	2.9	6,904	95.6	109	1.5	7
FEMALE	14	.4	68	1.7	14	.4	19	.5	115	2.9	3,736	95.7	93	1.4	3
MALE	9	.3	59	1.8	11	.3	16	.5	95	2.9	3,168	95.5	56	1.7	3
TOTAL	79	.2	849	2.7	220	.7	216	.7	1,364	4.3	29,884	94.0	528	1.7	31
FEMALE	52	.3	465	2.6	130	.7	117	.6	764	4.2	17,116	94.6	210	1.2	18
MALE	27	.2	384	2.8	90	.7	99	.7	600	4.4	12,768	93.3	318	2.3	13
UNCLASSIFIED:															
TOTAL	25	.2	295	2.4	60	.5	43	.4	423	3.5	11,670	96.0	65	.5	12
FEMALE	11	.1	164	2.2	31	.4	27	.4	233	3.1	7,351	96.5	30	.4	7
MALE	14	.3	131	2.9	29	.6	16	.4	190	4.2	4,319	95.0	35	.8	4
TOTAL ENROLLMENT:															
TOTAL	104	.2	1,144	2.6	280	.6	259	.6	1,787	4.1	41,554	94.6	593	1.3	43
FEMALE	63	.2	629	2.4	161	.6	144	.6	997	3.9	24,467	95.2	240	.9	25
MALE	41	.2	515	2.8	119	.7	115	.6	790	4.3	17,087	93.7	353	1.9	18
SOUTH CAROLINA (58 INSTITUTIONS)															
UNDERGRADUATES:															
FULL-TIME	63	.1	15,170	25.4	246	.4	149	.2	15,628	26.2	43,761	73.2	356	.6	59
FEMALE	24	.1	8,493	26.8	114	.4	58	.2	8,689	27.5	22,855	72.2	101	.3	31
MALE	39	.1	6,677	23.8	132	.5	91	.3	6,939	24.7	20,906	74.4	255	.9	28
PART-TIME	41	.2	5,166	24.3	97	.5	58	.3	5,362	25.3	15,800	74.4	72	.3	21
FEMALE	15	.1	2,633	26.1	46	.5	22	.2	2,716	26.9	7,357	72.8	25	.3	10
MALE	26	.2	2,533	22.7	51	.5	36	.3	2,646	23.8	8,443	75.8	46	.4	11
TOTAL	104	.1	20,336	25.1	343	.4	207	.3	20,990	25.9	59,561	73.6	428	.5	80
FEMALE	39	.1	11,126	26.7	160	.4	80	.2	11,405	27.3	30,212	72.4	127	.3	41
MALE	65	.2	9,210	23.5	183	.5	127	.3	9,585	24.4	29,349	74.8	301	.8	39
GRADUATE:															
FULL-TIME	4	.2	154	9.2	8	.5	7	.4	173	10.4	1,426	85.5	69	4.1	1
FEMALE	3	.3	101	11.5	2	.2	5	.6	111	12.6	746	84.9	22	2.5	
MALE	1	.1	53	6.7	6	.8	2	.3	62	7.9	680	86.2	47	6.0	
PART-TIME	6	.1	1,102	14.9	8	.1	15	.2	1,131	14.8	6,480	84.9	22	.3	7
FEMALE	3	.1	807	15.0	4	.1	10	.2	824	15.3	4,551	84.5	10	.2	5
MALE	3	.1	295	13.1	4	.2	5	.2	307	13.7	1,929	85.8	12	.5	2
TOTAL	10	.1	1,256	13.5	16	.2	22	.2	1,304	14.0	7,906	85.0	91	1.0	9
FEMALE	6	.1	908	14.5	6	.1	15	.2	935	14.9	5,297	84.6	32	.5	6
MALE	4	.1	348	11.5	10	.3	7	.2	369	12.2	2,609	85.9	59	1.9	3
PROFESSIONAL:															
FULL-TIME	2	.1	36	2.5	4	.3	4	.3	46	3.2	1,336	93.0	54	3.8	1
FEMALE	2	.8	10	4.1	0	.0	1	.3	13	5.3	216	88.9	14	5.8	
MALE	0	.0	26	2.2	4	.3	3	.3	33	2.8	1,120	93.9	40	3.4	1

OR FIELD 9000 - ALL OTHERS

	AMERICAN INDIAN ALASKAN NATIVE		BLACK NON-HISPANIC		ASIAN OR PACIFIC ISLANDER		HISPANIC		TOTAL MINORITY		WHITE NON-HISPANIC		NON-RESIDENT ALIEN		TOTAL
	NUMBER	%	NUMBER	%	NUMBER	%	NUMBER	%	NUMBER	%	NUMBER	%	NUMBER	%	NUMBER
TH CAROLINA CONTINUED															
FESSIONAL:															
T-TIME	0	.0	3	5.6	0	.0	0	.0	3	5.6	50	92.6	1	1.9	54
FEMALE	0	.0	0	.0	0	.0	0	.0	0	.0	15	100.0	0	.0	15
MALE	0	.0	3	7.7	0	.0	0	.0	3	7.7	35	89.7	1	2.6	39
AL	2	.1	39	2.6	4	.3	4	.3	49	3.3	1,386	93.0	55	3.7	1,490
FEMALE	2	.8	10	3.9	0	.0	1	.4	13	5.0	231	89.5	14	5.4	258
MALE	0	.0	29	2.4	4	.3	3	.2	36	2.9	1,155	93.8	41	3.3	1,232
+GRAD+PROF:															
L-TIME	69	.1	15,360	24.4	258	.4	160	.3	15,847	25.2	46,523	74.0	479	.8	62,849
FEMALE	29	.1	8,604	26.3	116	.4	64	.2	8,813	26.9	23,817	72.7	137	.4	32,767
MALE	40	.1	6,756	22.5	142	.5	96	.3	7,034	23.4	22,706	75.5	342	1.1	30,082
T-TIME	47	.2	6,271	21.7	105	.4	73	.3	6,496	22.5	22,330	77.2	95	.3	28,921
FEMALE	18	.1	3,440	22.2	50	.3	32	.2	3,540	22.8	11,923	76.9	36	.2	15,499
MALE	29	.2	2,831	21.1	55	.4	41	.3	2,956	22.0	10,407	77.5	59	.4	13,422
AL	116	.1	21,631	23.6	363	.4	233	.3	22,343	24.3	68,853	75.0	574	.6	91,770
FEMALE	47	.1	12,044	25.0	166	.3	96	.2	12,353	25.6	35,740	74.0	173	.4	48,266
MALE	69	.2	9,587	22.0	197	.5	137	.3	9,990	23.0	33,113	76.1	401	.9	43,504
LASSIFIED:															
AL	14	.3	914	17.5	28	.5	18	.3	974	18.6	4,181	80.0	68	1.3	5,223
FEMALE	9	.3	553	17.5	12	.4	7	.2	581	18.4	2,526	80.1	48	1.5	3,155
MALE	5	.2	361	17.5	16	.8	11	.5	393	19.0	1,655	80.0	20	1.0	2,068
AL ENROLLMENT:															
AL	130	.1	22,545	23.2	391	.4	251	.3	23,317	24.0	73,034	75.3	642	.7	96,993
FEMALE	56	.1	12,597	24.5	178	.3	103	.2	12,934	25.2	38,266	74.4	221	.4	51,421
MALE	74	.2	9,948	21.8	213	.5	148	.3	10,383	22.8	34,768	76.3	421	.9	45,572
TH DAKOTA (17 INSTITUTIONS)															
ERGRADUATES:															
L-TIME	408	2.7	122	.8	49	.3	21	.1	600	4.0	14,164	95.4	82	.6	14,846
FEMALE	219	2.5	36	.4	21	.2	9	.1	285	3.3	8,325	96.3	35	.4	8,645
MALE	189	3.0	86	1.4	28	.5	12	.2	315	5.1	5,839	94.2	47	.8	6,201
T-TIME	125	8.8	8	.6	21	1.5	2	.1	156	11.0	1,251	88.4	8	.6	1,415
FEMALE	79	8.5	6	.6	14	1.5	2	.2	101	10.8	828	88.8	3	.3	932
MALE	46	9.5	2	.4	7	1.4	0	.0	55	11.4	423	87.6	5	1.0	483
AL	533	3.3	130	.8	70	.4	23	.1	756	4.6	15,415	94.8	90	.6	16,261
FEMALE	298	3.1	42	.4	35	.4	11	.1	386	4.0	9,153	95.6	38	.4	9,577
MALE	235	3.5	88	1.3	35	.5	12	.2	370	5.5	6,262	93.7	52	.8	6,684
JUATE:															
L-TIME	23	6.3	1	.3	1	.3	1	.3	26	7.1	325	88.6	16	4.4	367
FEMALE	9	5.7	0	.0	0	.0	0	.0	9	5.7	143	90.5	6	3.8	158
MALE	14	6.7	1	.5	1	.5	1	.5	17	8.1	182	87.1	10	4.8	209
I-TIME	2	.2	2	.2	1	.1	0	.0	5	.6	838	99.1	3	.4	846
FEMALE	1	.2	1	.2	0	.0	0	.0	2	.4	483	99.6	0	.0	485
MALE	1	.3	1	.3	1	.3	0	.0	3	.8	355	98.3	3	.8	361
AL	25	2.1	3	.2	2	.2	1	.1	31	2.6	1,163	95.9	19	1.6	1,213
FEMALE	10	1.6	1	.2	0	.0	0	.0	11	1.7	626	97.4	6	.9	643
MALE	15	2.6	2	.4	2	.4	1	.2	20	3.5	537	94.2	13	2.3	570
FESSIONAL:															
L-TIME	0	.0	1	1.2	0	.0	1	1.2	2	2.5	64	79.0	15	18.5	81
FEMALE	0	.0	0	.0	0	.0	0	.0	0	.0	7	77.8	2	22.2	9
MALE	0	.0	1	1.4	0	.0	1	1.4	2	2.8	57	79.2	13	18.1	72
I-TIME	0	.0	0	.0	0	.0	0	.0	0	.0	8	80.0	2	20.0	10
FEMALE	0	.0	0	.0	0	.0	0	.0	0	.0	2	66.7	1	33.3	3
MALE	0	.0	0	.0	0	.0	0	.0	0	.0	6	85.7	1	14.3	7
AL	0	.0	1	1.1	0	.0	1	1.1	2	2.2	72	79.1	17	18.7	91
FEMALE	0	.0	0	.0	0	.0	0	.0	0	.0	9	75.0	3	25.0	12
MALE	0	.0	1	1.3	0	.0	1	1.3	2	2.5	63	79.7	14	17.7	79
+GRAD+PROF:															
L-TIME	431	2.8	124	.8	50	.3	23	.2	628	4.1	14,553	95.2	113	.7	15,294
FEMALE	228	2.6	36	.4	21	.2	9	.1	294	3.3	8,475	96.2	43	.5	8,812
MALE	203	3.1	88	1.4	29	.4	14	.2	334	5.2	6,078	93.8	70	1.1	6,482
I-TIME	127	5.6	10	.4	22	1.0	2	.1	161	7.1	2,097	92.3	13	.6	2,271
FEMALE	80	5.6	7	.5	14	1.0	2	.1	103	7.3	1,313	92.5	4	.3	1,420
MALE	47	5.5	3	.4	8	.9	0	.0	58	6.8	784	92.1	9	1.1	851
AL	558	3.2	134	.8	72	.4	25	.1	789	4.5	16,650	94.8	126	.7	17,565
FEMALE	308	3.0	43	.4	35	.3	11	.1	397	3.9	9,788	95.7	47	.5	10,232
MALE	250	3.4	91	1.2	37	.5	14	.2	392	5.3	6,862	93.6	79	1.1	7,333
LASSIFIED:															
AL	157	5.5	3	.1	2	.1	6	.2	168	5.9	2,673	93.6	14	.5	2,855
FEMALE	115	6.6	2	.1	1	.1	1	.1	119	6.9	1,605	92.7	7	.4	1,731
MALE	42	3.7	1	.1	1	.1	5	.4	49	4.4	1,068	95.0	7	.6	1,124
AL ENROLLMENT:															
AL	715	3.5	137	.7	74	.4	31	.2	957	4.7	19,323	94.6	140	.7	20,420
FEMALE	423	3.5	45	.4	36	.3	12	.1	516	4.3	11,393	95.2	54	.5	11,963
MALE	292	3.5	92	1.1	38	.4	19	.2	441	5.2	7,930	93.8	86	1.0	8,457

MAJOR FIELD 9000 - ALL OTHERS

	AMERICAN INDIAN ALASKAN NATIVE		BLACK NON-HISPANIC		ASIAN OR PACIFIC ISLANDER		HISPANIC		TOTAL MINORITY		WHITE NON-HISPANIC		NON-RESIDENT ALIEN		TO
	NUMBER	%	NUMBER	%	NUMBER	%	NUMBER	%	NUMBER	%	NUMBER	%	NUMBER	%	NU
TENNESSEE (69 INSTITUTIONS)															
UNDERGRADUATES:															
FULL-TIME	111	.1	13,444	17.4	219	.3	275	.4	14,049	18.1	62,591	80.7	880	1.1	77
FEMALE	62	.1	8,324	18.9	112	.3	139	.3	8,637	19.6	35,131	79.7	334	.8	44
MALE	49	.1	5,120	19.3	107	.3	136	.4	5,412	16.2	27,420	82.1	546	1.6	33
PART-TIME	58	.2	3,341	10.8	89	.3	111	.4	3,599	11.6	27,222	87.8	196	.6	31
FEMALE	37	.2	2,130	11.5	48	.3	63	.3	2,278	12.3	16,188	87.2	105	.6	18
MALE	21	.2	1,211	9.7	41	.3	48	.4	1,321	10.6	11,034	88.7	91	.7	12
TOTAL	169	.2	16,785	15.5	308	.3	386	.4	17,648	16.3	89,773	82.7	1,076	1.0	108
FEMALE	99	.2	10,454	16.7	160	.3	202	.3	10,915	17.4	51,319	81.9	439	.7	62
MALE	70	.2	6,331	13.8	148	.3	184	.4	6,733	14.7	38,454	83.9	637	1.4	45
GRADUATE:															
FULL-TIME	14	.4	309	7.8	27	.7	16	.4	366	9.3	3,254	82.4	331	8.4	3
FEMALE	8	.4	192	9.0	19	.9	9	.4	228	10.6	1,809	84.4	106	4.9	2
MALE	6	.3	117	6.5	8	.4	7	.4	138	7.6	1,445	79.9	225	12.4	1
PART-TIME	8	.1	666	9.3	20	.3	12	.2	706	9.8	6,335	88.0	157	2.2	7
FEMALE	5	.1	453	10.0	5	.1	9	.2	472	10.5	3,985	88.3	55	1.2	4
MALE	3	.1	213	7.9	15	.6	3	.1	234	8.7	2,350	87.5	102	3.8	2
TOTAL	22	.2	975	8.7	47	.4	28	.3	1,072	9.6	9,589	86.0	488	4.4	11
FEMALE	13	.2	645	9.7	24	.4	18	.3	700	10.5	5,794	87.1	161	2.4	6
MALE	9	.2	330	7.3	23	.5	10	.2	372	8.3	3,795	84.4	327	7.3	4
PROFESSIONAL:															
FULL-TIME	0	.0	41	4.1	5	.5	0	.0	46	4.6	950	94.8	6	.6	1
FEMALE	0	.0	11	4.4	1	.4	0	.0	12	4.9	160	92.5	1	.6	
MALE	0	.0	30	3.6	4	.5	0	.0	34	4.1	790	95.3	5	.6	
PART-TIME	0	.0	0	.0	0	.0	0	.0	0	.0	93	97.9	2	2.1	
FEMALE	0	.0	0	.0	0	.0	0	.0	0	.0	3	100.0	0	.0	
MALE	0	.0	0	.0	0	.0	0	.0	0	.0	90	97.8	2	2.2	
TOTAL	0	.0	41	3.7	5	.5	0	.0	46	4.2	1,043	95.1	8	.7	1
FEMALE	0	.0	11	6.3	1	.4	0	.0	12	6.8	163	92.6	1	.6	
MALE	0	.0	30	3.3	4	.4	0	.0	34	3.7	880	95.5	7	.8	
UND+GRAD+PROF:															
FULL-TIME	125	.2	13,794	16.7	251	.3	291	.4	14,461	17.5	66,755	81.0	1,217	1.5	82
FEMALE	70	.2	8,527	18.4	132	.3	148	.3	8,877	19.1	37,100	79.9	441	1.0	46
MALE	55	.2	5,267	14.6	119	.3	143	.4	5,584	15.5	29,655	82.3	776	2.2	36
PART-TIME	66	.2	4,007	10.5	109	.3	123	.3	4,305	11.2	33,650	87.8	355	.9	36
FEMALE	42	.2	2,583	11.2	53	.2	72	.3	2,750	11.9	20,176	87.4	160	.7	23
MALE	24	.2	1,424	9.4	56	.4	51	.3	1,555	10.2	13,474	88.5	195	1.3	15
TOTAL	191	.2	17,801	14.7	360	.3	414	.3	18,766	15.5	100,405	83.2	1,572	1.3	120
FEMALE	112	.2	11,110	16.0	185	.3	220	.3	11,627	16.7	57,276	82.4	601	.9	69
MALE	79	.2	6,691	13.1	175	.3	194	.4	7,139	13.9	43,129	84.2	971	1.9	51
UNCLASSIFIED:															
TOTAL	54	.4	2,240	15.7	75	.5	35	.2	2,404	16.9	11,475	80.5	380	2.7	14
FEMALE	18	.2	1,433	17.1	40	.5	17	.2	1,506	18.0	6,647	79.5	212	2.5	8
MALE	36	.6	807	13.7	35	.6	18	.3	898	15.2	4,828	81.9	168	2.9	5
TOTAL ENROLLMENT:															
TOTAL	245	.2	20,041	14.8	435	.3	449	.3	21,170	15.7	111,880	82.9	1,952	1.4	135
FEMALE	128	.2	12,543	16.1	225	.3	237	.3	13,133	16.9	63,923	82.1	813	1.0	77
MALE	117	.2	7,498	13.1	210	.4	212	.4	8,037	14.1	47,957	83.9	1,139	2.0	57
TEXAS (144 INSTITUTIONS)															
UNDERGRADUATES:															
FULL-TIME	694	.3	23,198	10.7	1,331	.6	30,533	14.0	55,756	25.6	156,565	71.9	9,402	2.5	217
FEMALE	358	.3	12,907	10.7	669	.6	16,149	13.4	30,083	25.0	88,854	73.7	1,635	1.4	120
MALE	336	.3	10,291	10.6	662	.7	14,384	14.8	25,673	26.4	67,711	69.7	3,767	3.9	97
PART-TIME	709	.5	16,738	11.5	1,207	.8	22,176	15.3	40,830	28.1	102,748	70.8	1,579	1.1	145
FEMALE	344	.4	8,458	10.9	634	.8	11,128	14.3	20,564	26.5	56,280	72.5	780	1.0	77
MALE	365	.5	8,280	12.3	573	.8	11,048	16.4	20,266	30.0	46,468	68.8	759	1.2	67
TOTAL	1,403	.4	39,936	11.0	2,538	.7	52,709	14.5	96,586	26.6	259,313	71.5	6,981	1.9	362
FEMALE	702	.4	21,365	10.8	1,303	.7	27,277	13.8	50,647	25.6	145,134	73.2	2,415	1.2	198
MALE	701	.4	18,571	11.3	1,235	.7	25,432	15.4	45,939	27.9	114,179	69.3	4,566	2.8	164
GRADUATE:															
FULL-TIME	62	.4	866	5.4	274	1.7	851	5.3	2,053	12.9	12,522	78.6	1,351	8.5	15
FEMALE	22	.3	513	6.7	118	1.5	404	5.2	1,057	13.7	6,167	80.0	485	6.3	7
MALE	40	.5	353	4.3	156	1.9	447	5.4	996	12.1	6,355	77.3	866	10.5	8
PART-TIME	116	.4	2,535	8.9	204	.7	2,954	10.3	5,809	20.3	22,098	77.4	659	2.3	28
FEMALE	52	.3	1,632	9.5	117	.7	1,685	9.8	3,486	20.2	13,536	78.4	235	1.4	17
MALE	64	.4	903	8.0	87	.8	1,269	11.2	2,323	20.5	8,562	75.7	424	3.7	11
TOTAL	178	.4	3,401	7.6	478	1.1	3,805	8.6	7,862	17.7	34,620	77.8	2,010	4.5	44
FEMALE	74	.3	2,145	8.6	235	.9	2,089	8.4	4,543	18.2	19,703	78.9	720	2.9	24
MALE	104	.5	1,256	6.4	243	1.2	1,716	8.8	3,319	17.0	14,917	76.4	1,290	6.6	19
PROFESSIONAL:															
FULL-TIME	3	.2	37	2.6	12	.8	65	4.5	117	8.2	1,238	86.5	77	5.4	1
FEMALE	1	.2	5	2.1	2	.8	11	4.6	19	8.0	206	86.6	13	5.5	
MALE	2	.2	32	2.7	10	.8	54	4.5	98	8.2	1,032	86.4	64	5.4	1

NROLLMENT IN INSTITUTIONS OF HIGHER EDUCATION FOR SELECTED MAJOR FIELDS OF STUDY AND LEVEL OF ENROLLMENT, ETHNICITY, AND SEX: STATE, 1978

ALL OTHERS

N INDIAN NATIVE %	BLACK NON-HISPANIC NUMBER	%	ASIAN OR PACIFIC ISLANDER NUMBER	%	HISPANIC NUMBER	%	TOTAL MINORITY NUMBER	%	WHITE NON-HISPANIC NUMBER	%	NON-RESIDENT ALIEN NUMBER	%	TOTAL NUMBER
CONTINUED													
.8	16	6.2	0	.0	9	3.5	27	10.4	226	87.3	6	2.3	259
.0	3	4.2	0	.0	4	5.6	7	9.9	64	90.1	0	.0	71
1.1	13	6.9	0	.0	5	2.7	20	10.6	162	86.2	6	3.2	168
.3	53	3.1	12	.7	74	4.4	144	8.5	1,464	86.6	83	4.9	1,691
.3	8	2.6	2	.6	15	4.9	26	8.4	270	87.4	13	4.2	309
.3	45	3.3	10	.7	59	4.3	118	8.5	1,194	86.4	70	5.1	1,382
.3	24,101	10.3	1,617	.7	31,449	13.4	57,926	24.6	170,325	72.5	6,830	2.9	235,081
.3	13,425	10.4	789	.6	16,564	12.9	31,159	24.2	95,227	74.1	2,133	1.7	128,519
.3	10,676	10.0	828	.8	14,885	14.0	26,767	25.1	75,098	70.5	4,697	4.4	106,562
.5	19,289	11.1	1,411	.8	25,139	14.4	46,666	26.8	125,072	71.9	2,244	1.3	173,982
.4	10,093	10.6	751	.8	12,817	13.5	24,057	25.3	69,880	73.6	1,015	1.1	94,952
.5	9,198	11.6	660	.8	12,322	15.6	22,609	28.6	55,192	69.8	1,229	1.6	79,030
.4	43,390	10.6	3,028	.7	56,588	13.8	104,592	25.6	295,397	72.2	9,074	2.2	409,063
.3	23,518	10.5	1,540	.7	29,381	13.1	55,216	24.7	165,107	73.9	3,148	1.4	223,471
.4	19,872	10.7	1,488	.8	27,207	14.7	49,376	26.6	130,290	70.2	5,926	3.2	185,592
.5	2,786	9.2	239	.8	4,224	13.9	7,415	24.4	22,514	74.0	486	1.6	30,415
.4	1,412	9.2	125	.8	1,674	10.9	3,279	21.4	11,827	77.3	188	1.2	15,294
.6	1,374	9.1	114	.8	2,550	16.9	4,136	27.4	10,687	70.7	298	2.0	15,121
.4	46,176	10.5	3,267	.7	60,812	13.8	112,007	25.5	317,911	72.3	9,560	2.2	439,478
.4	24,930	10.4	1,665	.7	31,055	13.0	58,495	24.5	176,934	74.1	3,336	1.4	238,765
.5	21,246	10.6	1,602	.8	29,757	14.8	53,512	26.7	140,977	70.2	6,224	3.1	200,713
(12 INSTITUTIONS)													
1.5	281	.7	812	1.9	500	1.2	2,232	5.3	37,620	89.6	2,045	4.9	41,897
1.5	106	.5	455	2.0	235	1.0	1,124	5.0	20,276	90.2	1,089	4.8	22,489
1.6	175	.9	357	1.8	265	1.4	1,108	5.7	17,344	89.4	956	4.9	19,408
.7	71	.4	175	1.1	300	1.9	664	4.2	15,094	94.9	150	.9	15,908
.8	25	.3	95	1.2	116	1.4	299	3.7	7,621	95.2	82	1.0	8,002
.7	46	.6	80	1.0	184	2.3	365	4.6	7,473	94.5	68	.9	7,906
1.3	352	.6	987	1.7	800	1.4	2,896	5.0	52,714	91.2	2,195	3.8	57,805
1.3	131	.4	550	1.8	351	1.2	1,423	4.7	27,897	91.5	1,171	3.8	30,491
1.3	221	.8	437	1.6	449	1.6	1,473	5.4	24,817	90.9	1,024	3.7	27,314
1.3	18	.7	32	1.3	33	1.3	117	4.6	2,174	86.1	233	9.2	2,524
1.6	4	.4	17	1.6	15	1.4	53	5.1	913	87.4	79	7.6	1,045
1.1	14	.9	15	1.0	18	1.2	64	4.3	1,261	85.3	154	10.4	1,479
.4	14	.5	42	1.6	25	1.0	92	3.5	2,341	90.2	163	6.3	2,596
.4	10	.8	21	1.7	14	1.2	50	4.1	1,101	90.9	60	5.0	1,211
.4	4	.3	21	1.5	11	.8	42	3.0	1,240	89.5	103	7.4	1,385
.9	32	.6	74	1.4	58	1.1	209	4.1	4,515	88.2	396	7.7	5,120
1.0	14	.6	38	1.7	29	1.3	103	4.6	2,014	89.3	139	6.2	2,256
.8	18	.6	36	1.3	29	1.0	106	3.7	2,501	87.3	257	9.0	2,864
.0	0	.0	0	.0	0	.0	0	.0	0	.0	0	.0	0
.0	0	.0	0	.0	0	.0	0	.0	0	.0	0	.0	0
.0	0	.0	0	.0	0	.0	0	.0	0	.0	0	.0	0
.0	0	.0	0	.0	0	.0	0	.0	0	.0	0	.0	0
.0	0	.0	0	.0	0	.0	0	.0	0	.0	0	.0	0
.0	0	.0	0	.0	0	.0	0	.0	0	.0	0	.0	0
.0	0	.0	0	.0	0	.0	0	.0	0	.0	0	.0	0
.0	0	.0	0	.0	0	.0	0	.0	0	.0	0	.0	0
.0	0	.0	0	.0	0	.0	0	.0	0	.0	0	.0	0
1.5	299	.7	844	1.9	533	1.2	2,349	5.3	39,794	89.6	2,278	5.1	44,421
1.5	110	.5	472	2.0	250	1.1	1,177	5.0	21,189	90.0	1,168	5.0	23,534
1.6	189	.9	372	1.8	283	1.4	1,172	5.6	18,605	89.1	1,110	5.3	20,887
.7	85	.5	217	1.2	325	1.8	756	4.1	17,435	94.2	313	1.7	18,504
.7	35	.4	116	1.3	130	1.4	349	3.8	8,722	94.7	142	1.5	9,213
.7	50	.5	101	1.1	195	2.1	407	4.4	8,713	93.8	171	1.8	9,291
1.3	384	.6	1,001	1.7	858	1.4	3,105	4.9	57,229	90.9	2,591	4.1	62,925
1.3	145	.4	588	1.8	380	1.2	1,526	4.7	29,911	91.3	1,310	4.0	32,747
1.3	239	.8	473	1.6	478	1.6	1,579	5.2	27,318	90.3	1,281	4.2	30,178
.2	3	.3	13	1.3	4	.4	22	2.2	846	85.1	126	12.7	994
.4	1	.2	8	1.5	0	.0	11	2.1	480	90.4	40	7.5	531
.0	2	.4	5	1.1			11	2.4	366	79.0	86	18.6	463
1.3	387	.7	1,074	1.7	862	1.4	3,127	4.9	58,075	90.9	2,717	4.3	63,919
1.2	146	.4	596	1.8	380	1.1	1,537	4.6	30,391	91.3	1,350	4.1	33,278
1.3	241	.8	478	1.6	482	1.6	1,590	5.2	27,684	90.3	1,367	4.5	30,641

MAJOR FIELD 9000 - ALL OTHERS

	AMERICAN INDIAN ALASKAN NATIVE		BLACK NON-HISPANIC		ASIAN OR PACIFIC ISLANDER		HISPANIC		TOTAL MINORITY		WHITE NON-HISPANIC		NON-RESIDENT ALIEN	
	NUMBER	%	NUMBER	%	NUMBER	%	NUMBER	%	NUMBER	%	NUMBER	%	NUMBER	%
VERMONT	(	20 INSTITUTIONS)												
UNDERGRADUATES:														
FULL-TIME	30	.2	243	1.7	38	.3	89	.6	400	2.9	13,375	96.2	131	.9
FEMALE	18	.2	145	1.7	22	.3	56	.6	241	2.8	8,414	96.5	65	.7
MALE	12	.2	98	1.9	16	.3	33	.6	159	3.1	4,961	95.7	66	1.3
PART-TIME	2	.1	4	.2	0	.0	2	.1	8	.3	2,541	99.6	2	.1
FEMALE	0	.0	3	.2	0	.0	2	.1	5	.3	1,775	99.7	1	.1
MALE	2	.3	1	.1	0	.0	0	.0	3	.4	766	99.5	1	.1
TOTAL	32	.2	247	1.5	38	.2	91	.6	408	2.5	15,916	96.7	133	.8
FEMALE	18	.2	148	1.4	22	.2	58	.6	246	2.3	10,189	97.0	66	.6
MALE	14	.2	99	1.7	16	.3	33	.6	162	2.7	5,727	96.2	67	1.1
GRADUATE:														
FULL-TIME	1	.1	29	3.4	7	.8	15	1.7	52	6.1	765	89.1	42	4.9
FEMALE	0	.0	13	2.5	5	.9	6	1.1	24	4.5	489	92.4	16	3.0
MALE	1	.3	16	4.8	2	.6	9	2.7	28	8.5	276	83.6	26	7.9
PART-TIME	1	.1	4	.4	0	.0	0	.0	5	.5	929	96.2	32	3.3
FEMALE	0	.0	3	.5	0	.0	0	.0	3	.5	622	97.0	16	2.5
MALE	1	.3	1	.3	0	.0	0	.0	2	.6	307	94.5	16	4.9
TOTAL	2	.1	33	1.8	7	.4	15	.8	57	3.1	1,694	92.8	74	4.1
FEMALE	0	.0	16	1.4	5	.4	6	.5	27	2.3	1,111	95.0	32	2.7
MALE	2	.3	17	2.6	2	.3	9	1.4	30	4.6	583	89.0	42	6.4
PROFESSIONAL:														
FULL-TIME	0	.0	0	.0	0	.0	0	.0	0	.0	0	.0	0	.0
FEMALE	0	.0	0	.0	0	.0	0	.0	0	.0	0	.0	0	.0
MALE	0	.0	0	.0	0	.0	0	.0	0	.0	0	.0	0	.0
PART-TIME	0	.0	0	.0	0	.0	0	.0	0	.0	0	.0	0	.0
FEMALE	0	.0	0	.0	0	.0	0	.0	0	.0	0	.0	0	.0
MALE	0	.0	0	.0	0	.0	0	.8	0	.0	0	.0	0	.0
TOTAL	0	.0	0	.0	0	.0	0	.0	0	.0	0	.0		.0
FEMALE	0	.0	0	.0	0	.0	0	.0	0	.0	0	.0	0	.0
MALE	0	.0	0	.0	0	.0	0	.0	0	.0	0	.0	0	.0
UND+GRAD+PROF:														
FULL-TIME	31	.2	272	1.8	45	.3	104	.7	452	3.1	14,140	95.8	173	1.2
FEMALE	18	.2	158	1.7	27	.3	62	.7	265	2.9	8,903	96.3	81	.9
MALE	13	.2	114	2.1	18	.3	42	.8	187	3.4	5,237	94.9	92	1.7
PART-TIME	3	.1	8	.2	0	.0	2	.1	13	.4	3,470	98.7	34	1.0
FEMALE	0	.0	6	.2	0	.0	2	.1	8	.3	2,397	99.0	17	.7
MALE	3	.3	2	.2	0	.0	0	.0	5	.5	1,073	98.0	17	1.6
TOTAL	34	.2	280	1.5	45	.2	106	.6	465	2.5	17,610	96.3	207	1.1
FEMALE	18	.2	164	1.4	27	.2	64	.5	273	2.3	11,300	96.8	98	.8
MALE	16	.2	116	1.8	16	.3	42	.6	192	2.9	6,310	95.4	109	1.6
UNCLASSIFIED:														
TOTAL	2	.1	5	.2	1	.0	3	.1	11	.4	2,906	93.7	185	0
FEMALE	1	.1	2	.1	1	.1	1	.1	5	.3	1,652	96.9	48	.18
MALE	1	.1	3	.2	0	.0	2	.1	6	.4	1,254	89.8	137	9.8
TOTAL ENROLLMENT:														
TOTAL	36	.2	285	1.3	46	.2	109	.5	476	2.2	20,516	95.9	392	1.8
FEMALE	19	.1	166	1.2	28	.2	65	.5	278	2.1	12,952	96.8	146	1.1
MALE	17	.2	119	1.5	18	.2	44	.5	198	2.5	7,564	94.5	246	3.1
VIRGINIA	(	68 INSTITUTIONS)												
UNDERGRADUATES:														
FULL-TIME	173	.2	15,149	17.5	588	.7	386	.4	16,296	18.8	69,465	80.3	751	.9
FEMALE	102	.2	9,447	18.4	324	.6	219	.4	10,092	19.6	40,975	79.6	379	.7
MALE	71	.2	5,702	16.3	264	.8	167	.5	6,204	17.7	28,490	81.2	372	1.1
PART-TIME	76	.3	5,176	17.6	286	1.0	170	.6	5,708	19.4	23,657	80.3	109	.4
FEMALE	46	.3	2,675	16.9	156	1.0	83	.5	2,960	18.7	12,829	81.0	59	.4
MALE	30	.2	2,501	18.4	130	1.0	87	.6	2,748	20.2	10,828	79.5	46	.3
TOTAL	249	.2	20,325	17.5	874	.8	556	.5	22,004	19.0	93,122	80.3	896	.7
FEMALE	148	.2	12,122	18.0	480	.7	302	.4	13,052	19.4	53,804	80.0	438	.7
MALE	101	.2	8,203	16.8	394	.8	254	.5	8,952	18.4	39,318	80.8	418	.9
GRADUATE:														
FULL-TIME	6	.1	559	11.4	28	.6	22	.4	615	12.5	4,130	84.0	174	3.5
FEMALE	2	.1	308	11.9	14	.5	12	.5	336	12.9	2,196	84.5	67	2.6
MALE	4	.2	251	10.8	14	.6	10	.4	279	12.0	1,934	83.4	107	4.6
PART-TIME	15	.2	1,178	13.7	34	.4	32	.4	1,259	14.7	1,263	84.7	54	.6
FEMALE	8	.1	845	14.9	13	.2	23	.4	889	15.6	4,766	83.8	29	.5
MALE	7	.2	333	11.5	21	.7	9	.3	370	12.8	2,497	86.3	25	.9
TOTAL	21	.2	1,737	12.9	62	.5	54	.4	1,874	13.9	11,393	84.4	228	1.7
FEMALE	10	.1	1,153	13.9	27	.3	35	.4	1,225	14.8	6,962	84.1	96	1.2
MALE	11	.2	584	11.2	35	.7	19	.4	649	12.5	4,431	85.0	132	2.5
PROFESSIONAL:														
FULL-TIME	0	.0	2	1.1	0	.0	0	.0	2	1.1	184	98.4	1	.5
FEMALE	0	.0	0	.0	0	.0	0	.0	0	.0	33	100.0	0	.0
MALE	0	.0	2	1.3	0	.0	0	.0	2	1.3	151	98.1	1	.6

ALL OTHERS

N INDIAN NATIVE		BLACK NON-HISPANIC		ASIAN OR PACIFIC ISLANDER		HISPANIC		TOTAL MINORITY		WHITE NON-HISPANIC		NON-RESIDENT ALIEN		TOTAL
%	NUMBER	%	NUMBER	%	NUMBER	%	NUMBER	%	NUMBER	%	NUMBER	%	NUMBER	%	NUMBER
CONTINUED														
.0	0	.0	0	.0	0	.0	0	.0	0	.0	30	100.0	0	.0	30
.0	0	.0	0	.0	0	.0	0	.0	0	.0	5	100.0	0	.0	5
.0	0	.0	0	.0	0	.0	0	.0	0	.0	25	100.0	0	.0	25
.0	2	.9	0	.0	0	.0	2	.9	214	98.6	1	.5	217
.0	0	.0	0	.0	0	.0	0	.0	38	100.0	0	.0	38
.0	2	1.1	0	.0	0	.0	2	1.1	176	98.3	1	.6	179
.2	15,710	17.1	616	.7	408	.4	16,913	18.5	73,779	80.5	926	1.0	91,618
.2	9,755	18.0	338	.6	231	.4	10,428	19.3	43,204	79.9	446	.8	54,078
.2	5,955	15.9	278	.7	177	.5	6,485	17.3	30,575	81.4	480	1.3	37,540
.2	6,354	16.7	320	.8	202	.5	6,967	18.3	30,950	81.3	159	.4	38,076
.3	3,520	16.3	169	.8	106	.5	3,849	17.9	17,600	81.7	88	.4	21,537
.2	2,834	17.1	151	.9	96	.6	3,118	18.9	13,350	80.7	71	.4	16,539
.2	22,064	17.0	936	.7	610	.5	23,880	18.4	104,729	80.8	1,085	.8	129,694
.2	13,275	17.6	507	.7	337	.4	14,277	18.9	60,804	80.4	534	.7	75,615
.2	8,789	16.3	429	.8	273	.5	9,603	17.8	43,925	81.2	551	1.0	54,079
.3	8,509	11.9	1,096	1.5	590	.8	10,401	14.5	60,552	84.4	797	1.1	71,750
.3	5,124	12.1	583	1.4	310	.7	6,156	14.6	35,731	84.6	361	.9	42,248
.2	3,385	11.5	513	1.7	280	.9	4,245	14.4	24,821	84.1	436	1.5	29,502
.2	30,573	15.2	2,032	1.0	1,200	.6	34,281	17.0	165,281	82.0	1,882	.9	201,444
.3	18,399	15.6	1,090	.9	647	.5	20,433	17.3	96,535	81.9	895	.8	117,863
.2	12,174	14.6	942	1.1	553	.7	13,848	16.6	68,746	82.3	987	1.2	83,581
(49 INSTITUTIONS)														
1.5	3,142	3.2	2,992	3.0	1,336	1.4	8,905	9.0	86,253	87.6	3,302	3.4	98,460
1.6	1,362	2.7	1,590	3.2	590	1.2	4,322	8.6	44,633	89.0	1,188	2.4	50,143
1.4	1,780	3.7	1,402	2.9	746	1.5	4,583	9.5	41,620	86.1	2,114	4.4	48,317
1.4	762	3.2	627	2.6	360	1.5	2,089	8.7	21,331	89.1	508	2.1	23,928
1.6	345	2.5	341	2.5	170	1.2	1,070	7.9	12,265	90.0	291	2.1	13,626
1.2	417	4.0	286	2.8	190	1.8	1,019	9.9	9,066	88.0	217	2.1	10,302
1.5	3,904	3.2	3,619	3.0	1,696	1.4	10,994	9.0	107,584	87.9	3,810	3.1	122,388
1.6	1,707	2.7	1,931	3.0	760	1.2	5,392	8.5	56,898	89.2	1,479	2.3	63,769
1.3	2,197	3.7	1,688	2.9	936	1.6	5,602	9.6	50,686	86.5	2,331	4.0	58,619
.9	119	2.6	140	3.1	72	1.6	371	8.1,	3,834	83.6	383	8.3	4,588
.7	61	2.5	76	3.1	20	.8	174	7.1	2,108	86.6	153	6.3	2,435
1.1	58	2.7	64	3.0	52	2.4	197	9.2	1,726	80.2	230	10.7	2,153
.9	97	2.7	84	2.3	38	1.0	253	7.0	3,039	83.9	329	9.1	3,621
1.2	49	2.5	41	2.1	17	.9	130	6.7	1,723	88.3	98	5.0	1,951
.7	48	2.9	43	2.6	21	1.3	123	7.4	1,316	78.8	231	13.8	1,670
.9	216	2.6	224	2.7	110	1.3	624	7.6	6,873	83.7	712	8.7	8,209
.9	110	2.5	117	2.7	37	.8	304	6.9	3,831	87.3	251	5.7	4,386
.9	106	2.8	107	2.8	73	1.9	320	8.4	3,042	79.6	461	12.1	3,823
.0	0	.0	2	7.7	1	3.8	3	11.5	23	88.5	0	.0	26
.0	0	.0	2	7.7	1	3.8	3	11.5	23	88.5	0	.0	26
.0	0	.0	0	.0	0	.0	0	.0	0	.0	0	.0	0
.0	0	.0	0	.0	0	.0	0	.0	2	100.0	0	.0	2
.0	0	.0	0	.0	0	.0	0	.0	2	100.0	0	.0	2
.0	0	.0	0	.0	0	.0	0	.0	0	.0	0	.0	0
.0	0	.0	2	7.1	1	3.6	3	10.7	25	89.3	0	.0	28
.0	0	.0	2	7.1	1	3.6	3	10.7	25	89.3	0	.0	28
.0	0	.0	0	.0	0	.0	0	.0	0	.0	0	.0	0
1.4	3,261	3.2	3,134	3.0	1,409	1.4	9,279	9.0	90,110	87.4	3,685	3.6	103,074
1.5	1,423	2.7	1,668	3.2	611	1.2	4,499	8.6	46,764	88.9	1,341	2.5	52,604
1.3	1,838	3.6	1,466	2.9	798	1.6	4,780	9.5	43,346	85.9	2,344	4.6	50,470
1.4	859	3.1	711	2.6	398	1.4	2,342	8.5	24,372	88.5	837	3.0	27,551
1.5	394	2.5	382	2.5	187	1.2	1,200	7.7	13,990	89.8	389	2.5	15,579
1.1	465	3.9	329	2.7	211	1.8	1,142	9.5	10,382	86.7	448	3.7	11,972
1.4	4,120	3.2	3,845	2.9	1,807	1.4	11,621	8.9	114,482	87.6	4,522	3.5	130,625
1.5	1,817	2.7	2,050	3.0	798	1.2	5,699	8.4	60,754	89.1	1,730	2.5	68,183
1.3	2,303	3.7	1,795	2.9	1,009	1.6	5,922	9.5	53,728	86.0	2,792	4.5	62,442
1.2	1,701	1.5	1,839	1.6	1,637	1.4	6,603	5.8	104,856	91.4	3,273	2.9	114,732
1.3	808	1.2	1,154	1.7	877	1.3	3,722	5.5	62,222	91.7	1,924	2.8	67,868
1.2	893	1.9	685	1.5	760	1.6	2,881	6.1	42,634	91.0	1,349	2.9	46,864
1.3	5,821	2.4	5,684	2.3	3,444	1.4	18,224	7.4	219,338	89.4	7,795	3.2	245,357
1.4	2,625	1.9	3,204	2.4	1,675	1.2	9,421	6.9	122,976	90.4	3,654	2.7	136,051
1.2	3,196	2.9	2,480	2.3	1,769	1.6	8,803	8.1	96,362	88.2	4,141	3.8	109,306

TABLE 17 - TOTAL ENROLLMENT IN INSTITUTIONS OF HIGHER EDUCATION FOR SELECTED MAJOR FIELDS OF STUDY AND LEVEL OF ENROLLMENT
BY RACE, ETHNICITY, AND SEX: STATE, 1978

MAJOR FIELD 9000 - ALL OTHERS

	AMERICAN INDIAN ALASKAN NATIVE		BLACK NON-HISPANIC		ASIAN OR PACIFIC ISLANDER		HISPANIC		TOTAL MINORITY		WHITE NON-HISPANIC		NON-RESIDENT ALIEN	
	NUMBER	%	NUMBER	%	NUMBER	%	NUMBER	%	NUMBER	%	NUMBER	%	NUMBER	%
WEST VIRGINIA (27 INSTITUTIONS)														
UNDERGRADUATES:														
FULL-TIME	64	.2	1,622	5.6	84	.3	63	.2	1,833	6.3	26,937	93.0	200	.7
FEMALE	37	.2	789	4.7	35	.2	31	.2	892	5.3	15,817	94.3	63	.4
MALE	27	.2	833	6.8	49	.4	32	.3	941	7.7	11,120	91.2	137	1.1
PART-TIME	71	.6	429	3.6	42	.3	22	.2	564	4.7	11,412	95.1	25	.2
FEMALE	54	.7	270	3.6	24	.3	13	.2	361	4.8	7,187	95.1	12	.2
MALE	17	.4	159	3.6	18	.4	9	.2	203	4.6	4,225	95.1	13	.3
TOTAL	135	.3	2,051	5.0	126	.3	85	.2	2,397	5.9	38,349	93.6	225	.5
FEMALE	91	.4	1,059	4.4	59	.2	44	.2	1,253	5.1	23,004	94.5	75	.3
MALE	44	.3	992	6.0	67	.4	41	.2	1,144	6.9	15,345	92.2	150	.9
GRADUATE:														
FULL-TIME	4	.3	24	1.7	20	1.4	4	.3	52	3.6	1,317	90.9	80	5.5
FEMALE	2	.3	11	1.5	7	.9	1	.1	21	2.8	697	92.6	35	4.6
MALE	2	.3	13	1.9	13	1.9	3	.4	31	4.5	620	89.1	45	6.5
PART-TIME	31	.4	206	2.6	25	.3	10	.1	272	3.5	7,527	95.9	47	.6
FEMALE	20	.4	133	2.5	13	.2	6	.1	172	3.2	5,110	96.4	19	.4
MALE	11	.4	73	2.9	12	.5	4	.2	100	3.9	2,417	95.0	28	1.1
TOTAL	35	.4	230	2.5	45	.5	14	.2	324	3.5	8,844	95.1	127	1.4
FEMALE	22	.4	144	2.4	20	.3	7	.1	193	3.2	5,807	95.9	54	.9
MALE	13	.4	86	2.7	25	.8	7	.2	131	4.0	3,037	93.7	73	2.3
PROFESSIONAL:														
FULL-TIME	0	.0	0	.0	0	.0	0	.0	0	.0	0	.0		.0
FEMALE	0	.0	0	.0	0	.0	0	.0	0	.0	0	.0		.0
MALE	0	.0	0	.0	0	.0	0	.0	0	.0	0	.0		.0
PART-TIME	0	.0	0	.0	0	.0	0	.0	0	.0	0	.0		.0
FEMALE	0	.0	0	.0	0	.0	0	.0	0	.0	0	.0		.0
MALE	0	.0	0	.0	0	.0	0	.0	0	.0	0	.0	0	.0
TOTAL	0	.0	0	.0	0	.0	0	.0	0	.0	0	.0		.0
FEMALE	0	.0	0	.0	0	.0	0	.0	0	.0	0	.0		.0
MALE	0	.0	0	.0	0	.0	0	.0	0	.0	0	.0	0	.0
UND+GRAD+PROF:														
FULL-TIME	68	.2	1,646	5.4	104	.3	67	.2	1,885	6.2	28,254	92.9	280	.9
FEMALE	39	.2	800	4.6	42	.2	32	.2	913	5.2	16,514	94.2	98	.6
MALE	29	.2	846	6.6	62	.5	35	.3	972	7.5	11,740	91.1	182	1.4
PART-TIME	102	.5	635	3.2	67	.3	32	.2	836	4.2	18,939	95.4	72	.4
FEMALE	74	.6	403	3.1	37	.3	19	.1	533	4.1	12,297	95.6	31	.2
MALE	28	.4	232	3.3	30	.4	13	.2	303	4.3	6,642	95.1	41	.6
TOTAL	170	.3	2,281	4.5	171	.3	99	.2	2,721	5.4	47,193	93.9	352	.7
FEMALE	113	.4	1,203	4.0	79	.3	51	.2	1,446	4.8	28,811	94.8	129	.4
MALE	57	.3	1,078	5.4	92	.5	48	.2	1,275	6.4	18,382	92.5	223	1.1
UNCLASSIFIED:														
TOTAL	11	.2	163	2.9	27	.5	14	.2	215	3.8	5,484	95.9	19	.3
FEMALE	8	.2	82	2.3	10	.3	7	.2	107	3.0	3,431	96.7	9	.3
MALE	3	.1	81	3.7	17	.8	7	.3	108	5.0	2,053	94.6	10	.5
TOTAL ENROLLMENT:														
TOTAL	181	.3	2,444	4.4	198	.4	113	.2	2,936	5.2	52,677	94.1	371	.7
FEMALE	121	.4	1,285	3.8	89	.3	58	.2	1,553	4.6	32,242	95.0	138	.4
MALE	60	.3	1,159	5.3	109	.5	55	.2	1,383	6.3	20,435	92.7	233	1.1
WISCONSIN (57 INSTITUTIONS)														
UNDERGRADUATES:														
FULL-TIME	685	.6	3,482	3.3	588	.5	905	.8	5,660	5.3	100,343	93.8	935	.9
FEMALE	384	.7	1,971	3.3	299	.5	447	.8	3,101	5.3	55,479	94.2	306	.5
MALE	301	.6	1,511	3.1	289	.6	458	1.0	2,559	5.3	44,864	93.4	629	1.3
PART-TIME	209	.5	2,249	5.6	249	.6	414	1.0	3,121	7.7	37,249	92.0	125	.3
FEMALE	125	.6	1,380	6.2	142	.6	186	.8	1,833	8.3	20,260	91.5	39	.2
MALE	84	.5	869	4.7	107	.6	228	1.2	1,288	7.0	16,989	92.5	86	.5
TOTAL	894	.6	5,731	3.9	837	.6	1,319	.9	8,781	6.0	137,592	93.3	1,060	.7
FEMALE	509	.6	3,351	4.1	441	.5	633	.8	4,934	6.1	75,739	93.5	345	.4
MALE	385	.6	2,380	3.6	396	.6	686	1.0	3,847	5.6	61,853	93.1	715	1.1
GRADUATE:														
FULL-TIME	28	.5	207	3.4	93	1.5	103	1.7	431	7.2	4,911	81.7	669	11.1
FEMALE	16	.5	112	3.7	42	1.4	50	1.7	220	7.3	2,587	85.8	208	6.9
MALE	12	.4	95	3.2	51	1.7	53	1.8	211	7.0	2,324	77.6	461	15.4
PART-TIME	18	.3	160	2.5	41	.6	47	.7	266	4.1	6,119	94.1	115	1.8
FEMALE	13	.3	107	2.6	25	.6	30	.7	175	4.3	3,843	94.6	46	1.1
MALE	5	.2	53	2.2	16	.7	17	.7	91	3.7	2,276	93.4	69	2.8
TOTAL	46	.4	367	2.9	134	1.1	150	1.2	697	5.6	11,030	88.2	784	6.3
FEMALE	29	.4	219	3.1	67	.9	80	1.1	395	5.6	6,430	90.8	254	3.6
MALE	17	.3	148	2.7	67	1.2	70	1.3	302	5.6	4,600	84.7	530	9.8
PROFESSIONAL:														
FULL-TIME	0	.0	2	.7	0	.0	8	3.0	10	3.7	255	95.1	3	1.1
FEMALE	0	.0	0	.0	0	.0	0	.0	0	.0	11	100.0	0	.0
MALE	0	.0	2	.8	0	.0	8	3.1	10	3.9	244	94.9	3	1.2

ALL OTHERS

Y INDIAN NATIVE	BLACK NON-HISPANIC		ASIAN OR PACIFIC ISLANDER		HISPANIC		TOTAL MINORITY		WHITE NON-HISPANIC		NON-RESIDENT ALIEN		TOTAL
%	NUMBER	%	NUMBER	%	NUMBER	%	NUMBER	%	NUMBER	%	NUMBER	%	NUMBER

CONTINUED

.0	0	.0	0	.0	0	.0	0	.0	25	100.0	0	.0	25
.0	0	.0	0	.0	0	.0	0	.0	11	100.0	0	.0	11
.0	0	.0	0	.0	0	.0	0	.0	14	100.0	0	.0	14

.0	2	.7	0	.0	8	2.7	10	3.4	280	95.6	3	1.0	293
.0	0	.0	0	.0	0	.0	0	.0	22	100.0	0	.0	22
.0	2	.7	0	.0	8	3.0	10	3.7	258	95.2	3	1.1	271

.6	3,691	3.3	681	.6	1,016	.9	6,101	5.4	105,509	93.2	1,607	1.4	113,217
.6	2,083	3.4	341	.6	497	.8	3,321	5.4	58,077	93.8	514	.8	61,912
.6	1,608	3.1	340	.7	519	1.0	2,780	5.4	47,432	92.5	1,093	2.1	51,305
.5	2,409	5.1	290	.6	461	1.0	3,387	7.2	43,393	92.3	240	.5	47,020
.5	1,487	5.7	167	.6	216	.8	2,008	7.7	24,114	92.0	85	.3	26,207
.4	922	4.4	123	.6	245	1.2	1,379	6.6	19,279	92.6	155	.7	20,813

.6	6,100	3.8	971	.6	1,477	.9	9,488	5.9	148,902	92.9	1,847	1.2	160,237
.6	3,570	4.1	508	.6	713	.8	5,329	6.0	82,191	93.3	599	.7	88,119
.6	2,530	3.5	463	.6	764	1.1	4,159	5.8	66,711	92.5	1,248	1.7	72,118

1.6	932	4.1	199	.9	185	.8	1,684	7.4	20,852	91.8	178	.8	22,714
1.9	432	3.5	93	.8	97	.8	848	7.0	11,251	92.3	88	.7	12,187
1.3	500	4.7	106	1.0	88	.8	836	7.9	9,601	91.2	90	.9	10,527

.7	7,032	3.8	1,170	.6	1,662	.9	11,172	6.1	169,754	92.8	2,025	1.1	182,951
.8	4,002	4.0	601	.6	810	.8	6,177	6.2	93,442	93.2	687	.7	100,306
.7	3,030	3.7	569	.7	852	1.0	4,995	6.0	76,312	92.3	1,338	1.6	82,645

(8 INSTITUTIONS)

1.6	130	1.9	40	.6	129	1.9	405	5.9	6,329	92.7	95	1.4	6,829
1.7	43	1.1	18	.5	73	1.9	200	5.2	3,647	94.1	28	.7	3,875
1.4	87	2.9	22	.7	56	1.9	205	6.9	2,682	90.8	67	2.3	2,954
.4	56	1.6	19	.5	106	3.0	195	5.5	3,340	94.1	15	.4	3,550
.5	25	1.1	11	.5	49	2.2	96	4.4	2,086	95.3	7	.3	2,189
.2	31	2.3	8	.6	57	4.2	99	7.3	1,254	92.1	8	.6	1,361

1.2	186	1.8	59	.6	235	2.3	600	5.8	9,669	93.2	110	1.1	10,379
1.3	68	1.1	29	.5	122	2.0	296	4.9	5,733	94.5	35	.6	6,064
1.0	118	2.7	30	.7	113	2.6	304	7.0	3,936	91.2	75	1.7	4,315

.0	3	1.0	1	.3	4	1.4	8	2.7	263	90.1	21	7.2	292
.0	3	2.3	0	.0	2	1.6	5	3.9	122	94.6	2	1.6	129
.0	0	.0	1	.6	2	1.2	3	1.8	141	86.5	19	11.7	163
.8	1	.4	4	1.6	2	.8	9	3.5	231	90.2	16	6.3	256
.5	0	.0	3	1.4	0	.0	4	1.8	207	95.0	7	3.2	218
2.6	1	2.6	1	2.6	2	5.3	5	13.2	24	63.2	9	23.7	38

.4	4	.7	5	.9	6	1.1	17	3.1	494	90.1	37	6.8	548
.3	3	.9	3	.9	2	.6	9	2.6	329	94.8	9	2.6	347
.5	1	.5	2	1.0	4	2.0	8	4.0	165	82.1	28	13.9	201

.0	0	.0	0	.0	0	.0	0	.0	0	.0	0	.0	
.0	0	.0	0	.0	0	.0	0	.0	0	.0	0	.0	
.0	0	.0	0	.0	0	.0	0	.0	0	.0	0	.0	
.0	0	.0	0	.0	0	.0	0	.0	0	.0	0	.0	
.0	0	.0	0	.0	0	.0	0	.0	0	.0	0	.0	0
.0	0	.0	0	.0	0	.0	0	.0	0	.0	0	.0	0

.0	0	.0	0	.0	0	.0	0	.0	0	.0	0	.0	
.0	0	.0	0	.0	0	.0	0	.0	0	.0	0	.0	0
.0	0	.0	0	.0	0	.0	0	.0	0	.0	0	.0	0

1.5	133	1.9	41	.6	133	1.9	413	5.8	6,592	92.6	116	1.6	7,121
1.6	46	1.1	18	.4	75	1.9	205	5.1	3,769	94.1	30	.7	4,004
1.3	87	2.8	23	.7	58	1.9	208	6.7	2,823	90.6	86	2.8	3,117
.4	57	1.5	23	.6	108	2.8	204	5.4	3,571	93.8	31	.8	3,806
.5	25	1.0	14	.6	49	2.0	100	4.2	2,293	95.3	14	.6	2,407
.3	32	2.3	9	.6	59	4.2	104	7.4	1,278	91.4	17	1.2	1,399

1.1	190	1.7	64	.6	241	2.2	617	5.6	10,163	93.0	147	1.3	10,927
1.2	71	1.1	32	.5	124	1.9	305	4.8	6,062	94.6	44	.7	6,411
1.0	119	2.6	32	.7	117	2.6	312	6.9	4,101	90.8	103	2.3	4,516

.4	5	.1	10	.3	42	1.1	74	1.9	3,836	97.8	11	.3	3,921
.5	3	.1	2	.1	27	1.2	44	1.9	2,289	97.7	9	.4	2,342
.3	2	.1	8	.5	15	.9	30	1.9	1,547	98.0	2	.1	1,579

.9	195	1.3	74	.5	283	1.9	691	4.7	13,999	94.3	158	1.1	14,848
1.0	74	.8	34	.4	151	1.7	349	4.0	8,351	95.4	53	.6	8,753
.8	121	2.0	40	.7	132	2.2	342	5.6	5,648	92.7	105	1.7	6,095

MAJOR FIELD 9000 - ALL OTHERS

	AMERICAN INDIAN ALASKAN NATIVE NUMBER	%	BLACK NON-HISPANIC NUMBER	%	ASIAN OR PACIFIC ISLANDER NUMBER	%	HISPANIC NUMBER	%	TOTAL MINORITY NUMBER	%	WHITE NON-HISPANIC NUMBER	%	NON-RESIDENT ALIEN NUMBER	%	TO NU
THE STATES AND D.C. (2,973 INSTITUTIONS)															
UNDERGRADUATES:															
FULL-TIME	29,030	.7	461,661	11.3	79,488	1.9	155,433	3.8	725,612	17.8	3,293,229	80.6	69,112	1.7	4,087
FEMALE	16,082	.7	276,174	12.1	41,029	1.8	82,448	3.6	415,733	18.2	1,840,011	80.6	26,174	1.1	2,281
MALE	12,948	.7	185,487	10.3	38,459	2.1	72,985	4.0	309,879	17.2	1,453,218	80.5	42,938	2.4	1,806
PART-TIME	21,819	1.0	237,526	10.6	52,518	2.3	127,041	5.7	438,904	19.6	1,785,502	79.6	17,953	.8	2,242
FEMALE	12,066	.9	138,819	10.9	26,691	2.1	66,301	5.2	243,877	19.1	1,021,518	80.2	8,746	.7	1,274
MALE	9,753	1.0	98,707	10.2	25,827	2.7	60,740	6.3	195,027	20.1	763,984	78.9	9,207	1.0	968
TOTAL	50,849	.8	699,187	11.0	132,006	2.1	282,474	4.5	1,164,516	18.4	5,078,731	80.2	87,065	1.4	6,330
FEMALE	28,148	.8	414,993	11.7	67,720	1.9	148,749	4.2	659,610	18.5	2,861,529	80.5	34,920	1.0	3,556
MALE	22,701	.8	284,194	10.2	64,286	2.3	133,725	4.8	504,906	18.2	2,217,202	79.9	52,145	1.9	2,774
GRADUATE:															
FULL-TIME	1,183	.4	16,825	6.3	4,852	1.8	6,499	2.4	29,359	11.0	214,450	80.3	23,086	8.6	266
FEMALE	588	.4	10,144	7.5	2,502	1.8	3,187	2.3	16,421	12.1	112,054	82.4	7,442	5.5	135
MALE	595	.5	6,681	5.1	2,350	1.8	3,312	2.5	12,938	9.9	102,396	78.2	15,644	11.9	130
PART-TIME	1,816	.4	34,686	7.3	6,342	1.3	10,544	2.2	53,388	11.3	408,299	86.4	10,933	2.3	472
FEMALE	947	.3	23,503	8.2	3,213	1.1	5,895	2.1	33,558	11.7	248,191	86.8	4,224	1.5	285
MALE	869	.5	11,183	6.0	3,129	1.7	4,649	2.5	19,830	10.6	160,108	85.4	6,709	3.6	186
TOTAL	2,999	.4	51,511	7.0	11,194	1.5	17,043	2.3	82,747	11.2	622,749	84.2	34,019	4.6	739
FEMALE	1,535	.4	33,647	8.0	5,715	1.4	9,082	2.2	49,979	11.8	360,245	85.4	11,666	2.8	421
MALE	1,464	.5	17,864	5.6	5,479	1.7	7,961	2.5	32,768	10.3	262,504	82.6	22,353	7.0	317
PROFESSIONAL:															
FULL-TIME	249	.8	1,270	3.5	687	1.9	404	1.1	2,660	7.2	32,833	89.2	1,316	3.6	36
FEMALE	39	.6	292	4.5	236	3.6	64	1.0	631	9.7	5,693	87.5	182	2.8	6
MALE	260	.9	978	3.2	451	1.5	340	1.1	2,029	6.7	27,140	89.6	1,134	3.7	30
PART-TIME	13	.3	199	5.3	48	1.3	54	1.4	314	8.4	3,341	89.5	80	2.1	3
FEMALE	3	.3	37	4.2	16	1.8	10	1.1	66	7.5	803	91.4	10	1.1	
MALE	10	.4	162	5.7	32	1.1	44	1.5	248	8.7	2,538	88.9	70	2.5	2
TOTAL	312	.8	1,469	3.6	735	1.8	458	1.1	2,974	7.3	36,174	89.2	1,396	3.4	40
FEMALE	42	.6	329	4.5	252	3.4	74	1.0	697	9.4	6,496	88.0	192	2.6	7
MALE	270	.8	1,140	3.4	483	1.5	384	1.2	2,277	6.9	29,678	89.5	1,204	3.6	33
UND+GRAD+PROF:															
FULL-TIME	30,512	.7	479,756	10.9	85,027	1.9	162,336	3.7	757,631	17.3	3,540,512	80.6	93,514	2.1	4,391
FEMALE	16,709	.7	286,610	11.8	43,767	1.8	85,699	3.5	432,785	17.9	1,957,758	80.8	33,798	1.4	2,424
MALE	13,803	.7	193,146	9.8	41,260	2.1	76,637	3.9	324,846	16.5	1,582,754	80.5	59,716	3.0	1,967
PART-TIME	23,648	.9	272,411	10.0	58,908	2.2	137,639	5.1	492,606	18.1	2,197,142	80.8	28,966	1.1	2,718
FEMALE	13,016	.8	162,359	10.4	29,920	1.9	72,206	4.6	277,501	17.8	1,270,512	81.4	12,980	.8	1,560
MALE	10,632	.9	110,052	9.5	28,988	2.5	65,433	5.7	215,105	18.4	926,630	80.0	15,986	1.4	1,157
TOTAL	54,160	.8	752,167	10.6	143,935	2.0	299,975	4.2	1,250,237	17.6	5,737,654	80.7	122,480	1.7	7,110
FEMALE	29,725	.7	448,969	11.3	73,687	1.8	157,905	4.0	710,286	17.8	3,228,270	81.0	46,778	1.2	3,985
MALE	24,435	.8	303,198	9.7	70,248	2.2	142,070	4.5	539,951	17.3	2,509,384	80.3	75,702	2.4	3,125
UNCLASSIFIED:															
TOTAL	10,909	.9	86,434	7.0	26,600	2.3	42,236	3.4	168,179	13.6	1,049,409	84.9	17,888	1.4	1,235
FEMALE	6,366	.9	50,884	7.2	14,713	2.1	21,159	3.0	93,122	13.2	605,873	85.6	8,393	1.2	707
MALE	4,543	.9	35,550	6.7	13,887	2.6	21,077	4.0	75,057	14.2	443,536	84.0	9,495	1.8	528
TOTAL ENROLLMENT:															
TOTAL	65,069	.8	838,601	10.0	172,535	2.1	342,211	4.1	1,418,416	17.0	6,787,063	81.3	140,368	1.7	8,345
FEMALE	36,091	.8	499,853	10.7	88,400	1.9	179,064	3.8	803,408	17.1	3,834,143	81.7	55,171	1.2	4,692
MALE	28,978	.8	338,748	9.3	84,135	2.3	163,147	4.5	615,008	16.8	2,952,920	80.8	85,197	2.3	3,653
AMERICAN SAMOA (1 INSTITUTIONS)															
UNDERGRADUATES:															
FULL-TIME	0	.0	0	.0	286	97.6	0	.0	286	97.6	7	2.4	0	.0	
FEMALE	0	.0	0	.0	139	99.3	0	.0	139	99.3	1	.7	0	.0	
MALE	0	.0	0	.0	147	96.1	0	.0	147	96.1	6	3.9	0	.0	
PART-TIME	0	.0	0	.0	303	89.1	0	.0	303	89.1	37	10.9	0	.0	
FEMALE	0	.0	0	.0	153	86.4	0	.0	153	86.4	24	13.6	0	.0	
MALE	0	.0	0	.0	150	92.0	0	.0	150	92.0	13	8.0	0	.0	
TOTAL	0	.0	0	.0	589	93.0	0	.0	589	93.0	44	7.0	0	.0	
FEMALE	0	.0	0	.0	292	92.1	0	.0	292	92.1	25	7.9	0	.0	
MALE	0	.0	0	.0	297	94.0	0	.0	297	94.0	19	6.0	0	.0	
GRADUATE:															
FULL-TIME	0	.0	0	.0	0	.0	0	.0	0	.0	0	.0	0	.0	
FEMALE	0	.0	0	.0	0	.0	0	.0	0	.0	0	.0	0	.0	
MALE	0	.0	0	.0	0	.0	0	.0	0	.0	0	.0	0	.0	
PART-TIME	0	.0	0	.0	0	.0	0	.0	0	.0	0	.0	0	.0	
FEMALE	0	.0	0	.0	0	.0	0	.0	0	.0	0	.0	0	.0	
MALE	0	.0	0	.0	0	.0	0	.0	0	.0	0	.0	0	.0	
TOTAL	0	.0	0	.0	0	.0	0	.0	0	.0	0	.0	0	.0	
FEMALE	0	.0	0	.0	0	.0	0	.0	0	.0	0	.0	0	.0	
MALE	0	.0	0	.0	0	.0	0	.0	0	.0	0	.0	0	.0	
PROFESSIONAL:															
FULL-TIME	0	.0	0	.0	0	.0	0	.0	0	.0	0	.0	0	.0	
FEMALE	0	.0	0	.0	0	.0	0	.0	0	.0	0	.0	0	.0	
MALE	0	.0	0	.0	0	.0	0	.0	0	.0	0	.0	0	.0	

IELD 9000 - ALL OTHERS

	AMERICAN INDIAN ALASKAN NATIVE		BLACK NON-HISPANIC		ASIAN OR PACIFIC ISLANDER		HISPANIC		TOTAL MINORITY		WHITE NON-HISPANIC		NON-RESIDENT ALIEN		TOTAL
	NUMBER	%	NUMBER	%	NUMBER	%	NUMBER	%	NUMBER	%	NUMBER	%	NUMBER	%	NUMBER
N SAMOA	**CONTINUED**														
IONAL:															
ME	0	.0	0	.0	0	.0	0	.0	0	.0	0	.0	0	.0	0
LE	0	.0	0	.0	0	.0	0	.0	0	.0	0	.0	0	.0	0
LE	0	.0	0	.0	0	.0	0	.0	0	.0	0	.0	0	.0	0
	0	.0	0	.0	0	.0	0	.0	0	.0	0	.0	0	.0	0
LE	0	.0	0	.0	0	.0	0	.0	0	.0	0	.0	0	.0	0
LE	0	.0	0	.0	0	.0	0	.0	0	.0	0	.0	0	.0	C
D+PROF:															
ME	0	.0	0	.0	286	97.6	0	.0	286	97.6	7	2.4	0	.0	293
LE	0	.0	C	.0	139	99.3	0	.0	139	99.3	1	.7	0	.0	140
LE	0	.0	0	.0	147	96.1	0	.0	147	96.1	6	3.9	0	.0	153
ME	0	.0	0	.0	303	89.1	0	.0	303	89.1	37	10.9	0	.0	340
LE	0	.0	0	.0	153	86.4	0	.0	153	86.4	24	13.6	0	.0	177
LE	0	.0	0	.0	150	92.0	0	.0	150	92.0	13	8.0	0	.0	163
	0	.0	0	.0	589	93.0	0	.0	589	93.0	44	7.0	0	.0	633
LE	0	.0	0	.0	292	92.1	0	.0	292	92.1	25	7.9	0	.0	317
LE	0	.0	0	.0	297	94.0	0	.0	297	94.0	19	6.0	0	.0	316
IFIED:															
	0	.0	0	.0	0	.0	0	.0	0	.0	0	.0	0	.0	0
LE	0	.0	0	.0	0	.0	0	.0	0	.0	0	.0	0	.0	0
LE	0	.0	0	.0	0	.0	0	.0	0	.0	0	.0	0	.0	0
NROLLMENT:															
	0	.0	0	.0	589	93.0	0	.0	589	93.0	44	7.0	0	.0	633
LE	0	.0	0	.0	292	92.1	0	.0	292	92.1	25	7.9	0	.0	317
LE	0	.0	0	.0	297	94.0	0	.0	297	94.0	19	6.0	0	.0	316
ONE	**(1 INSTITUTIONS)**														
ADUATES:															
ME	0	.0	44	10.5	0	.0	132	31.4	176	41.9	244	58.1	0	.0	420
LE	0	.0	25	10.5	0	.0	70	29.5	95	40.1	142	59.9	0	.0	237
LE	0	.0	19	10.4	0	.0	62	33.9	81	44.3	102	55.7	0	.0	183
ME	0	.0	0	.0	0	.0	0	.0	0	.0	0	.0	0	.0	0
LE	0	.0	0	.0	0	.0	0	.0	0	.0	0	.0	0	.0	0
LE	0	.0	0	.0	0	.0	0	.0	0	.0	0	.0	0	.0	0
	0	.0	44	10.5	0	.0	132	31.4	176	41.9	244	58.1	0	.0	420
LE	0	.0	25	10.5	0	.0	70	29.5	95	40.1	142	59.9	0	.0	237
LE	0	.0	19	10.4	0	.0	62	33.9	81	44.3	102	55.7	0	.0	183
E:															
ME	0	.0	0	.0	0	.0	0	.0	0	.0	0	.0	0	.0	0
LE	0	.0	0	.0	0	.0	0	.0	0	.0	0	.0	0	.0	0
LE	0	.0	0	.0	0	.0	0	.0	0	.0	0	.0	0	.0	0
ME	0	.0	0	.0	0	.0	0	.0	0	.0	0	.0	0	.0	0
LE	0	.0	0	.0	0	.0	0	.0	0	.0	0	.0	0	.0	0
LE	0	.0	0	.0	0	.0	0	.0	0	.0	0	.0	0	.0	0
	0	.0	0	.0	0	.0	0	.0	0	.0	0	.0	0	.0	0
LE	0	.0	0	.0	0	.0	0	.0	0	.0	0	.0	0	.0	0
IONAL:															
ME	0	.0	0	.0	0	.0	0	.0	0	.0	0	.0	0	.0	0
LE	0	.0	0	.0	0	.0	0	.0	0	.0	0	.0	0	.0	0
LE	0	.0	0	.0	0	.0	0	.0	0	.0	0	.0	0	.0	0
ME	0	.0	0	.0	0	.0	0	.0	0	.0	0	.0	0	.0	0
LE	0	.0	0	.0	0	.0	0	.0	0	.0	0	.0	0	.0	0
LE	0	.0	0	.0	0	.0	0	.0	0	.0	0	.0	0	.0	0
	0	.0	0	.0	0	.0	0	.0	0	.0	0	.0	0	.0	0
LE	0	.0	0	.0	0	.0	0	.0	0	.0	0	.0	0	.0	0
D+PROF:															
ME	0	.0	44	10.5	0	.0	132	31.4	176	41.9	244	58.1	0	.0	420
LE	0	.0	25	10.5	0	.0	70	29.5	95	40.1	142	59.9	0	.0	237
LE	0	.0	19	10.4	0	.0	62	33.9	81	44.3	102	55.7	0	.0	183
ME	0	.0	0	.0	0	.0	0	.0	0	.0	0	.0	0	.0	0
LE	0	.0	0	.0	0	.0	0	.0	0	.0	0	.0	0	.0	0
LE	0	.0	0	.0	0	.0	0	.0	0	.0	0	.0	0	.0	0
	0	.0	44	10.5	0	.0	132	31.4	176	41.9	244	58.1	0	.0	420
LE	0	.0	25	10.5	0	.0	70	29.5	95	40.1	142	59.9	0	.0	237
LE	0	.0	19	10.4	0	.0	62	33.9	81	44.3	102	55.7	0	.0	183
IFIED:															
	0	.0	125	10.3	0	.0	372	30.5	497	40.8	721	59.2	0	.0	1,218
LE	0	.0	70	10.3	0	.0	211	30.9	281	41.2	401	58.8	0	.0	682
LE	0	.0	55	10.3	0	.0	161	30.0	216	40.3	320	59.7	0	.0	536
NROLLMENT:															
	0	.0	169	10.3	0	.0	504	30.8	673	41.1	965	58.9	0	.0	1,638
LE	0	.0	95	10.3	0	.0	281	30.6	376	40.9	543	59.1	0	.0	919
LE	0	.0	74	10.3	0	.0	223	31.0	297	41.3	422	58.7	0	.0	719

TABLE 17 - TOTAL ENROLLMENT IN INSTITUTIONS OF HIGHER EDUCATION FOR SELECTED MAJOR FIELDS OF STUDY AND LEVEL OF ENROLLMENT BY RACE, ETHNICITY, AND SEX: STATE, 1978

MAJOR FIELD 9000 - ALL OTHERS

	AMERICAN INDIAN ALASKAN NATIVE		BLACK NON-HISPANIC		ASIAN OR PACIFIC ISLANDER		HISPANIC		TOTAL MINORITY		WHITE NON-HISPANIC		NON-RESIDENT ALIEN	
	NUMBER	%	NUMBER	%	NUMBER	%	NUMBER	%	NUMBER	%	NUMBER	%	NUMBER	%
GUAM (1 INSTITUTIONS)														
UNDERGRADUATES:														
FULL-TIME	7	.6	11	.9	917	74.5	28	2.3	963	78.2	159	12.9	109	8.9
FEMALE	3	.4	6	.8	575	78.3	10	1.4	594	80.9	100	13.6	40	5.4
MALE	4	.8	5	1.0	342	68.8	18	3.6	369	74.2	59	11.9	69	13.9
PART-TIME	3	.2	14	1.1	897	73.0	19	1.5	933	76.0	271	22.1	24	2.0
FEMALE	1	.2	8	1.5	404	74.7	7	1.3	420	77.6	110	20.3	11	2.0
MALE	2	.3	6	.9	493	71.8	12	1.7	513	74.7	161	23.4	13	1.9
TOTAL	10	.4	25	1.0	1,814	73.8	47	1.9	1,896	77.1	430	17.5	133	5.4
FEMALE	4	.3	14	1.1	979	76.8	17	1.3	1,014	79.5	210	16.5	51	4.0
MALE	6	.5	11	.9	835	70.5	30	2.5	882	74.5	220	18.6	82	6.9
GRADUATE:														
FULL-TIME	0	.0	0	.0	9	75.0	0	.0	9	75.0	3	25.0	0	.0
FEMALE	0	.0	0	.0	5	71.4	0	.0	5	71.4	2	28.6	0	.0
MALE	0	.0	0	.0	4	80.0	0	.0	4	80.0	1	20.0	0	.0
PART-TIME	0	.0	0	.0	106	46.5	10	4.4	116	50.9	112	49.1	0	.0
FEMALE	0	.0	0	.0	89	57.8	10	6.5	99	64.3	55	35.7	0	.0
MALE	0	.0	0	.0	17	23.0	0	.0	17	23.0	57	77.0	0	.0
TOTAL	0	.0	0	.0	115	47.9	10	4.2	125	52.1	115	47.9	0	.0
FEMALE	0	.0	0	.0	94	58.4	10	6.2	104	64.6	57	35.4	0	.0
MALE	0	.0	0	.0	21	26.6	0	.0	21	26.6	58	73.4	0	.0
PROFESSIONAL:														
FULL-TIME	0	.0	0	.0	0	.0	0	.0	0	.0	0	.0	0	.0
FEMALE	0	.0	0	.0	0	.0	0	.0	0	.0	0	.0	0	.0
MALE	0	.0	0	.0	0	.0	0	.0	0	.0	0	.0	0	.0
PART-TIME	0	.0	0	.0	0	.0	0	.0	0	.0	0	.0	0	.0
FEMALE	0	.0	0	.0	0	.0	0	.0	0	.0	0	.0	0	.0
MALE	0	.0	0	.0	0	.0	0	.0	0	.0	0	.0	0	.0
TOTAL	0	.0	0	.0	0	.0	0	.0	0	.0	0	.0	0	.0
FEMALE	0	.0	0	.0	0	.0	0	.0	0	.0	0	.0	0	.0
MALE	0	.0	0	.0	0	.0	0	.0	0	.0	0	.0	0	.0
UND+GRAD+PROF:														
FULL-TIME	7	.6	11	.9	926	74.5	28	2.3	972	78.2	162	13.0	109	8.8
FEMALE	3	.4	6	.8	580	78.3	10	1.3	599	80.8	102	13.8	40	5.4
MALE	4	.8	5	1.0	346	68.9	18	3.6	373	74.3	60	12.0	69	13.7
PART-TIME	3	.2	14	1.0	1,003	68.9	29	2.0	1,049	72.0	383	26.3	24	1.6
FEMALE	1	.1	8	1.2	493	70.9	17	2.4	519	74.7	165	23.7	11	1.6
MALE	2	.3	6	.8	510	67.0	12	1.6	530	69.6	218	28.6	13	1.7
TOTAL	10	.4	25	.9	1,929	71.5	57	2.1	2,021	74.9	545	20.2	133	4.9
FEMALE	4	.3	14	1.0	1,073	74.7	27	1.9	1,118	77.9	267	18.6	51	3.6
MALE	6	.5	11	.9	856	67.8	30	2.4	903	71.5	278	22.0	82	6.5
UNCLASSIFIED:														
TOTAL	0	.0	0	.0	0	.0	0	.0	0	.0	0	.0	0	.0
FEMALE	0	.0	0	.0	0	.0	0	.0	0	.0	0	.0	0	.0
MALE	0	.0	0	.0	0	.0	0	.0	0	.0	0	.0	0	.0
TOTAL ENROLLMENT:														
TOTAL	10	.4	25	.9	1,929	71.5	57	2.1	2,021	74.9	545	20.2	133	4.9
FEMALE	4	.3	14	1.0	1,073	74.7	27	1.9	1,118	77.9	267	18.6	51	3.6
MALE	6	.5	11	.9	856	67.8	30	2.4	903	71.5	278	22.0	82	6.5
PUERTO RICO (30 INSTITUTIONS)														
UNDERGRADUATES:														
FULL-TIME	0	.0	10	.0	0	.0	57,522	99.6	57,532	99.6	166	.3	39	.1
FEMALE	0	.0	2	.0	0	.0	37,097	99.7	37,099	99.7	101	.3	18	.0
MALE	0	.0	8	.0	0	.0	20,425	99.5	20,433	99.6	65	.3	21	.1
PART-TIME	0	.0	0	.0	0	.0	13,379	99.7	13,379	99.7	37	.3	5	.0
FEMALE	0	.0	0	.0	0	.0	8,509	99.7	8,509	99.7	22	.3	3	.0
MALE	0	.0	0	.0	0	.0	4,870	99.7	4,870	99.7	15	.3	2	.0
TOTAL	0	.0	10	.0	0	.0	70,901	99.6	70,911	99.7	203	.3	44	.1
FEMALE	0	.0	2	.0	0	.0	45,606	99.7	45,608	99.7	123	.3	21	.0
MALE	0	.0	8	.0	0	.0	25,295	99.6	25,303	99.6	80	.3	23	.1
GRADUATE:														
FULL-TIME	0	.0	0	.0	0	.0	1,321	89.6	1,321	89.6	149	10.1	4	.3
FEMALE	0	.0	0	.0	0	.0	901	91.1	901	91.1	85	8.6	3	.3
MALE	0	.0	0	.0	0	.0	420	86.6	420	86.6	64	13.2	1	.2
PART-TIME	0	.0	0	.0	0	.0	1,889	96.4	1,889	96.4	68	3.5	2	.1
FEMALE	0	.0	0	.0	0	.0	1,152	95.9	1,152	95.9	48	4.0	1	.1
MALE	0	.0	0	.0	0	.0	737	97.2	737	97.2	20	2.6	1	.1
TOTAL	0	.0	0	.0	0	.0	3,210	93.5	3,210	93.5	217	6.3	6	.2
FEMALE	0	.0	0	.0	0	.0	2,053	93.7	2,053	93.7	133	6.1	4	.2
MALE	0	.0	0	.0	0	.0	1,157	93.1	1,157	93.1	84	6.8	2	.2
PROFESSIONAL:														
FULL-TIME	0	.0	0	.0	0	.0	9	100.0	9	100.0	0	.0	0	.0
FEMALE	0	.0	0	.0	0	.0	6	100.0	6	100.0	0	.0	0	.0
MALE	0	.0	0	.0	0	.0	3	100.0	3	100.0	0	.0	0	.0

- ALL OTHERS

AN INDIAN N NATIVE		BLACK NON-HISPANIC		ASIAN OR PACIFIC ISLANDER		HISPANIC		TOTAL MINORITY		WHITE NON-HISPANIC		NON-RESIDENT ALIEN		TOTAL
R	%	NUMBER	%	NUMBER	%	NUMBER	%	NUMBER	%	NUMBER	%	NUMBER	%	NUMBER

CONTINUED

0	.0	0	.0	0	.0		.0		.0		.0		.0	0
0	.0	0	.0	0	.0	0	.0	0	.0	0	.0	0	.0	0
0	.0	0	.0	0	.0	0	.0	0	.0	0	.0	0	.0	0

0	.0	0	.0	0	.0	9	100.0	9	100.0		.0	0	.0	
0	.0	0	.0	0	.0	6	100.0	9	100.0	0	.0	0	.0	
0	.0	0	.0	0	.0	3	100.0		100.0	0	.0	0	.0	0

0	.0	10	.0	0	.0	58,852	99.4	58,862	99.4	315	.5	43	.1	59,220
0	.0	2	.0	0	.0	38,004	99.5	38,006	99.5	186	.5	21	.1	38,213
0	.0	8	.0	0	.0	20,848	99.2	20,856	99.3	129	.6	22	.1	21,007
0	.0	0	.0	0	.0	15,268	99.3	15,268	99.3	105	.7	7	.0	15,380
0	.0	0	.0	0	.0	9,661	99.2	9,661	99.2	70	.7	4	.0	9,735
0	.0	0	.0	0	.0	5,607	99.3	5,607	99.3	35	.6	3	.1	5,645

0	.0	10	.0	0	.0	74,120	99.4	74,130	99.4	420	.6	50	.1	74,600
0	.0	2	.0	0	.0	47,665	99.4	47,667	99.4	256	.5	25	.1	47,948
0	.0	8	.0	0	.0	26,455	99.3	26,463	99.3	164	.6	25	.1	26,652

0	.0	0	.0	0	.0	3,173	100.0	3,173	100.0	1	.0		.0	3,174
0	.0	0	.0	0	.0	1,817	99.9	1,817	99.9	1	.1	0	.0	1,818
0	.0	0	.0	0	.0	1,356	100.0	1,356	100.0	0	.0	0	.0	1,356

0	.0	10	.0	0	.0	77,293	99.4	77,303	99.4	421	.6	50	.1	77,774
0	.0	2	.0	0	.0	49,482	99.4	49,484	99.4	257	.5	25	.1	49,766
0	.0	8	.0	0	.0	27,811	99.3	27,819	99.3	164	.6	25	.1	28,008

(1 INSTITUTIONS)

0	.0	0	.0	221	100.0		.0	221	100.0		.0		.0	221
0	.0	0	.0	78	100.0		.0	78	100.0		.0		.0	78
0	.0	0	.0	143	100.0		.0	143	100.0		.0		.0	143
0	.0	0	.0	3	100.0		.0	3	100.0		.0		.0	3
0	.0	0	.0	0			.0	0	.0		.0		.0	0
0	.0	0	.0	3	100.0	0	.0	3	100.0	0	.0	0	.0	3

0	.0	0	.0	224	100.0		.0	224	100.0		.0		.0	224
0	.0	0	.0	78	100.0	0	.0	78	100.0	0	.0	0	.0	78
0	.0	0	.0	146	100.0	0	.0	146	100.0	0	.0	0	.0	146

0	.0	0	.0	0	.0		.0		.0		.0		.0	
0	.0	0	.0	0	.0		.0		.0		.0		.0	
0	.0	0	.0	0	.0		.0		.0		.0		.0	
0	.0	0	.0	0	.0		.0		.0		.0		.0	
0	.0	0	.0	0	.0		.0		.0		.0		.0	
0	.0	0	.0	0	.0	0	.0	0	.0	0	.0	0	.0	0

0	.0	0	.0	0	.0		.0		.0		.0		.0	
0	.0	0	.0	0	.0	0	.0	0	.0	0	.0	0	.0	0
0	.0	0	.0	0	.0		.0		.0	0	.0		.0	

0	.0	0	.0	0	.0		.0		.0		.0		.0	
0	.0	0	.0	0	.0		.0		.0		.0		.0	
0	.0	0	.0	0	.0		.0		.0		.0		.0	
0	.0	0	.0	0	.0		.0		.0		.0		.0	
0	.0	0	.0	0	.0	0	.0	0	.0	0	.0	0	.0	0

| 0 | .0 | 0 | .0 | 0 | .0 | | .0 | | .0 | | .0 | | .0 | |
| 0 | .0 | 0 | .0 | 0 | .0 · | 0 | .0 | 0 | .0 | 0 | .0 | 0 | .0 | 0 |

0	.0	0	.0	221	100.0		.0	221	100.0		.0		.0	221
0	.0	0	.0	78	100.0		.0	78	100.0		.0		.0	78
0	.0	0	.0	143	100.0		.0	143	100.0		.0		.0	143
0	.0	0	.0	3	100.0		.0	3	100.0		.0		.0	3
0	.0	0	.0	0			.0	0	.0		.0		.0	0
0	.0	0	.0	3	100.0	0	.0	3	100.0	0	.0	0	.0	3

0	.0	0	.0	224	100.0		.0	224	100.0		.0		.0	224
0	.0	0	.0	78	100.0	0	.0	78	100.0	0	.0	0	.0	78
0	.0	0	.0	146	100.0	0	.0	146	100.0	0	.0	0	.0	146

0	.0	0	.0	115	100.0		.0	115	100.0		.0		.0	115
0	.0	0	.0	32	100.0	0	.0	32	100.0	0	.0	0	.0	32
0	.0	0	.0	83	100.0		.0	83	100.0		.0		.0	83

0	.0	0	.0	339	100.0		.0	339	100.0		.0	0	.0	339
0	.0	0	.0	110	100.0	0	.0	110	100.0	0	.0	0	.0	110
0	.0	0	.0	229	100.0		.0	229	100.0		.0	0	.0	229

MAJOR FIELD 9000 - ALL OTHERS

	AMERICAN INDIAN ALASKAN NATIVE		BLACK NON-HISPANIC		ASIAN OR PACIFIC ISLANDER		HISPANIC		TOTAL MINORITY		WHITE NON-HISPANIC		NON-RESIDENT ALIEN	
	NUMBER	%	NUMBER	%	NUMBER	%	NUMBER	%	NUMBER	%	NUMBER	%	NUMBER	%
VIRGIN ISLANDS (1 INSTITUTIONS)														
UNDERGRADUATES:														
FULL-TIME	0	.0	190	62.5	1	.3	15	4.9	206	67.8	21	6.9	77	25.3
FEMALE	0	.0	160	65.6	1	.4	12	4.9	173	70.9	12	4.9	59	24.2
MALE	0	.0	30	50.0	0	.0	3	5.0	33	55.0	9	15.0	18	30.0
PART-TIME	0	.0	0	.0	0	.0	0	.0	0	.0	0	.0	0	.0
FEMALE	0	.0	0	.0	0	.0	0	.0	0	.0	0	.0	0	.0
MALE	0	.0	0	.0	0	.0	0	.0	0	.0	0	.0	0	.0
TOTAL	0	.0	190	62.5	1	.3	15	4.9	206	67.8	21	6.9	77	25.3
FEMALE	0	.0	160	65.6	1	.4	12	4.9	173	70.9	12	4.9	59	24.2
MALE	0	.0	30	50.0	0	.0	3	5.0	33	55.0	9	15.0	18	30.0
GRADUATE:														
FULL-TIME	0	.0	0	.0	0	.0	0	.0	0	.0	0	.0	0	.0
FEMALE	0	.0	0	.0	0	.0	0	.0	0	.0	0	.0	0	.0
MALE	0	.0	0	.0	0	.0	0	.0	0	.0	0	.0	0	.0
PART-TIME	0	.0	28	65.1	0	.0	1	2.3	29	67.4	14	32.6	0	.0
FEMALE	0	.0	19	57.6	0	.0	1	3.0	20	60.6	13	39.4	0	.0
MALE	0	.0	9	90.0	0	.0	0	.0	9	90.0	1	10.0	0	.0
TOTAL	0	.0	28	65.1	0	.0	1	2.3	29	67.4	14	32.6	0	.0
FEMALE	0	.0	19	57.6	0	.0	1	3.0	20	60.6	13	39.4	0	.0
MALE	0	.0	9	90.0	0	.0	0	.0	9	90.0	1	10.0	0	.0
PROFESSIONAL:														
FULL-TIME	0	.0	0	.0	0	.0	0	.0	0	.0	0	.0	0	.0
FEMALE	0	.0	0	.0	0	.0	0	.0	0	.0	0	.0	0	.0
MALE	0	.0	0	.0	0	.0	0	.0	0	.0	0	.0	0	.0
PART-TIME	0	.0	0	.0	0	.0	0	.0	0	.0	0	.0	0	.0
FEMALE	0	.0	0	.0	0	.0	0	.0	0	.0	0	.0	0	.0
MALE	0	.0	0	.0	0	.0	0	.0	0	.0	0	.0	0	.0
TOTAL	0	.0	0	.0	0	.0	0	.0	0	.0	0	.0	0	.0
FEMALE	0	.0	0	.0	0	.0	0	.0	0	.0	0	.0	0	.0
MALE	0	.0	0	.0	0	.0	0	.0	0	.0	0	.0	0	.0
UND+GRAD+PROF:														
FULL-TIME	0	.0	190	62.5	1	.3	15	4.9	206	67.8	21	6.9	77	25.3
FEMALE	0	.0	160	65.6	1	.4	12	4.9	173	70.9	12	4.9	59	24.2
MALE	0	.0	30	50.0	0	.0	3	5.0	33	55.0	9	15.0	18	30.0
PART-TIME	0	.0	28	65.1	0	.0	1	2.3	29	67.4	14	32.6	0	.0
FEMALE	0	.0	19	57.6	0	.0	1	3.0	20	60.6	13	39.4	0	.0
MALE	0	.0	9	90.0	0	.0	0	.0	9	90.0	1	10.0	0	.0
TOTAL	0	.0	218	62.8	1	.3	16	4.6	235	67.7	35	10.1	77	22.2
FEMALE	0	.0	179	64.6	1	.4	13	4.7	193	69.7	25	9.0	59	21.3
MALE	0	.0	39	55.7	0	.0	3	4.3	42	60.0	10	14.3	18	25.7
UNCLASSIFIED:														
TOTAL	0	.0	1,027	81.4	10	.8	67	5.3	1,104	87.5	128	10.2	29	2.3
FEMALE	0	.0	703	82.4	4	.5	43	5.0	750	87.9	84	9.8	19	2.2
MALE	0	.0	324	79.4	6	1.5	24	5.9	354	86.8	44	10.8	10	2.5
TOTAL ENROLLMENT:														
TOTAL	0	.0	1,245	77.4	11	.7	83	5.2	1,339	83.3	163	10.1	106	6.6
FEMALE	0	.0	882	78.1	5	.4	56	5.0	943	83.5	109	9.6	78	6.9
MALE	0	.0	363	75.9	6	1.3	27	5.6	396	82.8	54	11.3	28	5.9
OUTLYING AREAS (35 INSTITUTIONS)														
UNDERGRADUATES:														
FULL-TIME	7	.0	255	.4	1,425	2.4	57,697	95.8	59,384	98.6	597	1.0	225	.4
FEMALE	3	.0	193	.5	793	2.1	37,189	96.2	38,178	98.8	356	.9	117	.3
MALE	4	.0	62	.3	632	2.9	20,508	95.1	21,206	98.4	241	1.1	108	.5
PART-TIME	3	.0	14	.1	1,203	8.0	13,398	89.4	14,618	97.5	345	2.3	29	.2
FEMALE	1	.0	8	.1	557	6.0	8,516	92.0	9,082	98.2	156	1.7	14	.2
MALE	2	.0	6	.1	646	11.3	4,882	85.1	5,536	96.4	189	3.3	15	.3
TOTAL	10	.0	269	.4	2,628	3.5	71,095	94.5	74,002	98.4	942	1.3	254	.3
FEMALE	4	.0	201	.4	1,350	2.8	45,705	95.4	47,260	98.7	512	1.1	131	.3
MALE	6	.0	68	.2	1,278	4.7	25,390	93.0	26,742	98.0	430	1.6	123	.5
GRADUATE:														
FULL-TIME	0	.0	0	.0	9	.6	1,321	88.9	1,330	89.5	152	10.2	4	.3
FEMALE	0	.0	0	.0	5	.5	901	90.5	906	91.0	87	8.7	3	.3
MALE	0	.0	0	.0	4	.8	420	85.7	424	86.5	65	13.3	1	.2
PART-TIME	0	.0	28	1.3	106	4.8	1,900	85.2	2,034	91.2	194	8.7	2	.1
FEMALE	0	.0	19	1.4	89	6.4	1,163	83.8	1,271	91.6	116	8.4	1	.1
MALE	0	.0	9	1.1	17	2.0	737	87.5	763	90.6	78	9.3	1	.1
TOTAL	0	.0	28	.8	115	3.1	3,221	86.7	3,364	90.5	346	9.3	6	.2
FEMALE	0	.0	19	.8	94	3.9	2,064	86.6	2,177	91.3	203	8.5	4	.2
MALE	0	.0	9	.7	21	1.6	1,157	86.9	1,187	89.1	143	10.7	2	.2
PROFESSIONAL:														
FULL-TIME	0	.0	0	.0	0	.0	9	100.0	9	100.0	0	.0	0	.0
FEMALE	0	.0	0	.0	0	.0	6	100.0	6	100.0	0	.0	0	.0
MALE	0	.0	0	.0	0	.0	3	100.0	3	100.0	0	.0	0	.0

OLLMENT IN INSTITUTIONS OF HIGHER EDUCATION FOR SELECTED MAJOR FIELDS OF STUDY AND LEVEL OF ENROLLMENT
ETHNICITY, AND SEX: STATE, 1978

LL OTHERS

INDIAN ATIVE %	BLACK NON-HISPANIC NUMBER	%	ASIAN OR PACIFIC ISLANDER NUMBER	%	HISPANIC NUMBER	%	TOTAL MINORITY NUMBER	%	WHITE NON-HISPANIC NUMBER	%	NON-RESIDENT ALIEN NUMBER	%	TOTAL NUMBER
CONTINUED													
.0	0	.0	0	.0	0	.0	0	.0	0	.0	0	.0	0
.0	0	.0	0	.0	0	.0	0	.0	0	.0	0	.0	0
.0	0	.0	0	.0	0	.0	0	.0	0	.0	0	.0	0
.0	0	.0	0	.0	9	100.0	9	100.0	0	.0	0	.0	9
.0	0	.0	0	.0	6	100.0	6	100.0	0	.0	0	.0	6
.0	0	.0	0	.0	3	100.0	3	100.0	0	.0	0	.0	3
.0	255	.4	1,434	2.3	59,027	95.7	60,723	98.4	749	1.2	229	.4	61,701
.0	193	.5	798	2.0	38,096	96.1	39,090	98.6	443	1.1	120	.3	39,653
.0	62	.3	636	2.9	20,931	94.9	21,633	98.1	306	1.4	109	.5	22,048
.0	42	.2	1,309	7.6	15,298	88.8	16,652	96.7	539	3.1	31	.2	17,222
.0	27	.3	646	6.1	9,679	91.0	10,353	97.3	272	2.6	13	.1	10,640
.0	15	.2	663	10.1	5,619	85.4	6,299	95.7	267	4.1	16	.2	6,582
.0	297	.4	2,743	3.5	74,325	94.2	77,375	98.0	1,288	1.6	260	.3	78,923
.0	220	.4	1,444	2.9	47,775	95.0	49,443	98.3	715	1.4	135	.3	50,293
.0	77	.3	1,299	4.5	26,550	92.7	27,932	97.6	573	2.0	125	.4	28,630
.0	1,152	20.0	125	2.2	3,612	62.6	4,889	84.8	850	14.7	29	.5	5,768
.0	773	22.8	36	1.1	2,071	61.2	2,880	85.1	486	14.4	19	.6	3,385
.0	379	15.9	89	3.7	1,541	64.7	2,009	84.3	364	15.3	10	.4	2,383
.0	1,449	1.7	2,868	3.4	77,937	92.0	82,264	97.1	2,138	2.5	289	.3	84,691
.0	993	1.8	1,480	2.8	49,846	92.9	52,323	97.5	1,201	2.2	154	.3	53,678
.0	456	1.5	1,388	4.5	28,091	90.6	29,941	96.5	937	3.0	135	.4	31,013
E 9000 (3,008 INSTITUTIONS)													
.7	461,916	11.1	80,913	2.0	213,130	5.1	784,996	18.9	3,293,826	79.4	69,337	1.7	4,148,159
.7	276,367	11.9	41,822	1.8	119,637	5.2	453,911	19.6	1,840,367	79.3	26,291	1.1	2,320,569
.7	185,549	10.2	39,091	2.1	93,493	5.1	331,085	18.1	1,453,459	79.5	43,046	2.4	1,827,590
1.0	237,540	10.5	53,721	2.4	140,439	6.2	453,522	20.1	1,785,847	79.1	17,982	.8	2,257,351
.9	138,827	10.8	27,248	2.1	74,817	5.8	252,959	19.7	1,021,679	79.6	8,760	.7	1,283,393
1.0	98,713	10.1	26,473	2.7	65,622	6.7	200,563	20.6	764,173	78.5	9,222	.9	973,958
.8	699,456	10.9	134,634	2.1	353,569	5.5	1,238,518	19.3	5,079,673	79.3	87,319	1.4	6,405,510
.8	415,194	11.5	69,070	1.9	194,454	5.4	706,870	19.6	2,862,041	79.4	35,051	1.0	3,603,962
.8	284,262	10.1	65,564	2.3	159,115	5.7	531,648	19.0	2,217,632	79.2	52,268	1.9	2,801,548
.4	16,825	6.3	4,861	1.8	7,820	2.9	30,689	11.4	214,602	80.0	23,090	8.6	268,381
.4	10,144	7.4	2,507	1.8	4,088	3.0	17,327	12.7	112,141	81.9	7,445	5.4	136,913
.5	6,681	5.1	2,354	1.8	3,732	2.8	13,362	10.2	102,441	77.9	15,645	11.9	131,448
.4	34,714	7.3	6,448	1.4	12,444	2.6	55,422	11.7	408,493	86.0	10,935	2.3	474,850
.3	23,522	8.2	3,302	1.1	7,058	2.5	34,829	12.1	246,307	86.4	4,225	1.5	287,361
.5	11,192	6.0	3,146	1.7	5,386	2.9	20,593	11.0	160,186	85.4	6,710	3.6	187,489
.4	51,539	6.9	11,309	1.5	20,264	2.7	86,111	11.6	623,095	83.8	34,025	4.6	743,231
.4	33,666	7.9	5,809	1.4	11,146	2.6	52,156	12.3	360,448	85.0	11,670	2.8	424,274
.5	17,873	5.6	5,500	1.7	9,118	2.9	33,955	10.6	262,647	82.3	22,355	7.0	318,957
.8	1,270	3.4	687	1.9	413	1.1	2,669	7.2	32,833	89.2	1,316	3.6	36,818
.6	292	4.5	236	3.6	70	1.1	637	9.8	5,693	87.4	182	2.8	6,512
.9	978	3.2	451	1.5	343	1.1	2,032	6.7	27,140	89.6	1,134	3.7	30,306
.3	199	5.3	48	1.3	54	1.4	314	8.4	3,341	89.5	80	2.1	3,735
.3	37	4.2	16	1.8	10	1.1	66	7.5	803	91.4	10	1.1	879
.4	162	5.7	32	1.1	44	1.5	248	8.7	2,538	88.9	70	2.5	2,856
.8	1,469	3.6	735	1.8	467	1.2	2,983	7.4	36,174	89.2	1,396	3.4	40,553
.6	329	4.5	252	3.4	80	1.1	703	9.5	6,496	87.9	192	2.6	7,391
.6	1,140	3.4	483	1.5	387	1.2	2,280	6.9	29,678	89.5	1,204	3.6	33,162
.7	480,011	10.8	86,461	1.9	221,363	5.0	818,354	18.4	3,541,261	79.5	93,743	2.1	4,453,358
.7	286,803	11.6	44,565	1.8	123,795	5.0	471,875	19.2	1,958,201	79.5	33,918	1.4	2,463,994
.7	193,208	9.7	41,896	2.1	97,568	4.9	346,479	17.4	1,583,060	79.6	59,825	3.0	1,989,364
.8	272,453	10.0	60,217	2.2	152,937	5.6	509,258	18.6	2,197,681	80.3	28,997	1.1	2,735,936
.8	162,386	10.3	30,566	1.9	81,885	5.2	287,054	18.3	1,270,704	80.7	12,995	.8	1,571,633
.9	110,067	9.5	29,651	2.5	71,052	6.1	221,404	19.0	926,897	79.6	16,002	1.4	1,164,303
.8	752,464	10.5	146,678	2.0	374,300	5.2	1,327,612	18.5	5,738,942	79.8	122,740	1.7	7,189,294
.7	449,189	11.1	75,131	1.9	205,680	5.1	759,729	18.8	3,228,985	80.0	46,913	1.2	4,035,627
.8	303,275	9.6	71,547	2.3	168,620	5.3	567,883	18.0	2,509,957	79.6	75,827	2.4	3,153,667
.9	87,586	7.1	28,725	2.3	45,848	3.7	173,068	13.9	1,050,259	84.6	17,917	1.4	1,241,244
.9	51,657	7.3	14,749	2.1	23,230	3.3	96,002	13.5	606,359	85.3	8,412	1.2	710,773
.9	35,929	6.8	13,976	2.6	22,618	4.3	77,066	14.5	443,900	83.7	9,505	1.8	530,471
.8	840,050	10.0	175,403	2.1	420,148	5.0	1,500,680	17.8	6,789,201	80.5	140,657	1.7	8,430,538
.8	500,846	10.6	89,880	1.9	228,910	4.8	855,731	18.0	3,835,344	80.8	55,325	1.2	4,746,400
.8	339,204	9.2	85,523	2.3	191,238	5.2	644,949	17.5	2,953,857	80.2	85,332	2.3	3,684,138

MAJOR FIELD 9999 - SUMMARY

	AMERICAN INDIAN ALASKAN NATIVE		BLACK NON-HISPANIC		ASIAN OR PACIFIC ISLANDER		HISPANIC		TOTAL MINORITY		WHITE NON-HISPANIC		NON-RESIDENT ALIEN	
	NUMBER	%	NUMBER	%	NUMBER	%	NUMBER	%	NUMBER	%	NUMBER	%	NUMBER	%
ALABAMA (58 INSTITUTIONS)														
UNDERGRADUATES:														
FULL-TIME	104	.1	27,076	26.2	297	.3	344	.3	27,821	26.9	73,884	71.4	1,709	1.7
FEMALE	50	.1	16,092	30.7	111	.2	136	.3	16,389	31.3	35,780	68.2	271	.5
MALE	54	.1	10,984	21.5	186	.4	208	.4	11,432	22.4	38,104	74.8	1,438	2.8
PART-TIME	67	.2	5,010	15.3	97	.3	104	.3	5,278	16.1	27,397	83.6	104	.3
FEMALE	33	.2	2,903	18.2	39	.2	40	.3	3,015	18.9	12,899	80.9	33	.2
MALE	34	.2	2,107	12.5	58	.3	64	.4	2,263	13.4	14,498	86.1	71	.4
TOTAL	171	.1	32,086	23.6	394	.3	448	.3	33,099	24.3	101,281	74.4	1,813	1.3
FEMALE	83	.1	18,995	27.8	150	.2	176	.3	19,404	28.4	48,679	71.2	304	.4
MALE	88	.1	13,091	19.3	244	.4	272	.4	13,695	20.2	52,602	77.6	1,509	2.2
GRADUATE:														
FULL-TIME	12	.2	613	11.7	51	1.0	29	.6	705	13.4	4,188	79.8	356	6.8
FEMALE	1	.0	354	16.1	14	.6	4	.2	373	16.9	1,765	80.0	67	3.0
MALE	11	.4	259	8.5	37	1.2	25	.8	332	10.9	2,423	79.6	289	9.5
PART-TIME	6	.1	1,449	13.5	48	.4	30	.3	1,533	14.3	9,026	84.1	178	1.7
FEMALE	5	.1	966	15.9	9	.1	11	.2	991	16.3	5,031	83.0	41	.7
MALE	1	.0	483	10.3	39	.8	19	.4	542	11.6	3,995	85.5	137	2.9
TOTAL	18	.1	2,062	12.9	99	.6	59	.4	2,238	14.0	13,214	82.7	534	3.3
FEMALE	6	.1	1,320	16.0	23	.3	15	.2	1,364	16.5	6,796	82.2	108	1.3
MALE	12	.2	742	9.6	76	1.0	44	.6	874	11.3	6,418	83.2	426	5.5
PROFESSIONAL:														
FULL-TIME	1	.0	195	5.8	22	.7	6	.2	224	6.7	3,121	92.7	22	.7
FEMALE	0	.0	85	12.2	8	1.1	2	.3	95	13.6	599	85.8	4	.6
MALE	1	.0	110	4.1	14	.5	4	.1	129	4.8	2,522	94.5	18	.7
PART-TIME	0	.0	1	2.3	0	.0	0	.0	1	2.3	43	97.7	0	.0
FEMALE	0	.0	0	.0	0	.0	0	.0	0	.0	2	100.0	0	.0
MALE	0	.0	1	2.4	0	.0	0	.0	1	2.4	41	97.6	0	.0
TOTAL	1	.0	196	5.7	22	.6	6	.2	225	6.6	3,164	92.8	22	.6
FEMALE	0	.0	85	12.1	8	1.1	2	.3	95	13.6	601	85.9	4	.6
MALE	1	.0	111	4.1	14	.5	4	.1	130	4.8	2,563	94.5	18	.7
UND+GRAD+PROF:														
FULL-TIME	117	.1	27,884	24.9	370	.3	379	.3	28,750	25.7	81,193	72.5	2,087	1.9
FEMALE	51	.1	16,531	29.9	133	.2	142	.3	16,857	30.5	38,144	68.9	342	.6
MALE	66	.1	11,353	20.0	237	.4	237	.4	11,893	21.0	43,049	75.9	1,745	3.1
PART-TIME	73	.2	6,460	14.8	145	.3	134	.3	6,812	15.6	36,466	83.7	282	.6
FEMALE	38	.2	3,869	17.6	48	.2	51	.2	4,006	18.2	17,932	81.5	74	.3
MALE	35	.2	2,591	12.0	97	.5	83	.4	2,806	13.0	18,534	86.0	208	1.0
TOTAL	190	.1	34,344	22.1	515	.3	513	.3	35,562	22.9	117,659	75.6	2,369	1.5
FEMALE	89	.1	20,400	26.4	181	.2	193	.2	20,863	27.0	56,076	72.5	416	.5
MALE	101	.1	13,944	17.8	334	.4	320	.4	14,699	18.8	61,583	78.7	1,953	2.5
UNCLASSIFIED:														
TOTAL	6	.1	1,316	22.0	19	.3	12	.2	1,353	22.6	4,551	76.0	85	1.4
FEMALE	6	.2	867	27.1	11	.3	4	.1	888	27.7	2,296	71.7	19	.6
MALE	0	.0	449	16.1	8	.3	8	.3	465	16.7	2,255	80.9	66	2.4
TOTAL ENROLLMENT:														
TOTAL	196	.1	35,660	22.1	534	.3	525	.3	36,915	22.8	122,210	75.6	2,454	1.5
FEMALE	95	.1	21,267	26.4	192	.2	197	.2	21,751	27.0	58,372	72.5	435	.5
MALE	101	.1	14,393	17.8	342	.4	328	.4	15,164	18.7	63,838	78.8	2,019	2.5
ALASKA (16 INSTITUTIONS)														
UNDERGRADUATES:														
FULL-TIME	729	13.9	197	3.7	105	2.0	49	.9	1,080	20.5	4,142	78.7	41	.8
FEMALE	422	16.4	90	3.5	39	1.5	23	.9	574	22.4	1,979	77.1	15	.6
MALE	307	11.4	107	4.0	66	2.4	26	1.0	506	18.8	2,163	80.3	26	1.0
PART-TIME	784	6.9	405	3.6	216	1.9	168	1.5	1,573	13.8	9,805	86.1	15	.1
FEMALE	503	7.2	200	2.9	126	1.8	96	1.4	925	13.2	6,049	86.6	11	.2
MALE	281	6.4	205	4.7	90	2.0	72	1.6	648	14.7	3,756	85.2	4	.1
TOTAL	1,513	9.1	602	3.6	321	1.9	217	1.3	2,653	15.9	13,947	83.7	56	.3
FEMALE	925	9.7	290	3.0	165	1.7	119	1.2	1,499	15.7	8,028	84.0	26	.3
MALE	588	8.3	312	4.4	156	2.2	98	1.4	1,154	16.2	5,919	83.3	30	.4
GRADUATE:														
FULL-TIME	5	2.0	8	3.2	3	1.2	4	1.6	20	8.0	212	85.1	17	6.8
FEMALE	2	1.9	2	1.9	1	.9	2	1.9	7	6.6	94	88.7	5	4.7
MALE	3	2.1	6	4.2	2	1.4	2	1.4	13	9.1	118	82.5	12	8.4
PART-TIME	34	3.8	30	3.3	16	1.8	9	1.0	89	9.9	800	89.2	8	.9
FEMALE	22	4.7	15	3.2	10	2.1	7	1.5	54	11.6	411	88.2	1	.2
MALE	12	2.8	15	3.5	6	1.4	2	.5	35	8.1	389	90.3	7	1.6
TOTAL	39	3.4	38	3.3	19	1.7	13	1.1	109	9.5	1,012	88.3	25	2.2
FEMALE	24	4.2	17	3.0	11	1.9	9	1.6	61	10.7	505	88.3	6	1.0
MALE	15	2.6	21	3.7	8	1.4	4	.7	48	8.4	507	88.3	19	3.3
PROFESSIONAL:														
FULL-TIME	0	.0	0	.0	0	.0	0	.0	0	.0	0	.0	0	.0
FEMALE	0	.0	0	.0	0	.0	0	.0	0	.0	0	.0	0	.0
MALE	0	.0	0	.0	0	.0	0	.0	0	.0	0	.0	0	.0

ROLLMENT IN INSTITUTIONS OF HIGHER EDUCATION FOR SELECTED MAJOR FIELDS UF STUDY AND LEVEL OF ENROLLMENT
ETHNICITY, AND SEX: STATE, 1978

SUMMARY

INDIAN NATIVE		BLACK NON-HISPANIC		ASIAN OR PACIFIC ISLANDER		HISPANIC		TOTAL MINORITY		WHITE NON-HISPANIC		NON-RESIDENT ALIEN		TOTAL
%	NUMBER	%	NUMBER	%	NUMBER	%	NUMBER	%	NUMBER	%	NUMBER	%	NUMBER	NUMBER

CONTINUED

.0	0	.0	0	.0	0	.0	0	.0	0	.0	0	.0	0	0
.0	0	.0	0	.0	0	.0	0	.0	0	.0	0	.0	0	0
.0	0	.0	0	.0	0	.0	0	.0	0	.0	0	.0	0	0

.0	0	.0	0	.0	0	.0	0	.0	0	.0	0	.0	0	0
.0	0	.0	0	.0	0	.0	0	.0	0	.0	0	.0	0	0
.0	0	.0	0	.0	0	.0	0	.0	0	.0	0	.0	0	0

13.3	205	3.7	108	2.0	53	1.0	1,100	20.0	4,354	79.0	58	1.1	5,512
15.9	92	3.4	40	1.5	25	.9	981	21.7	2,073	77.5	20	.7	2,674
10.9	113	4.0	68	2.4	28	1.0	519	18.3	2,281	80.4	38	1.3	2,838
6.7	435	3.5	232	1.9	177	1.4	1,662	13.5	10,605	86.3	23	.2	12,290
7.0	215	2.9	136	1.8	103	1.4	979	13.1	6,460	86.7	12	.2	7,451
6.1	220	4.5	96	2.0	74	1.5	683	14.1	4,145	85.7	11	.2	4,839

8.7	640	3.6	340	1.9	230	1.3	2,762	15.5	14,959	84.0	81	.5	17,802
9.4	307	3.0	176	1.7	128	1.3	1,560	15.4	8,533	84.3	32	.3	10,125
7.9	333	4.3	164	2.1	102	1.3	1,202	15.7	6,426	83.7	49	.6	7,677

10.7	265	3.1	133	1.6	107	1.3	1,416	16.6	7,121	83.3	12	.1	8,549
11.6	114	2.3	78	1.6	46	.9	807	16.4	4,097	83.4	7	.1	4,911
9.4	151	4.2	55	1.5	61	1.7	609	16.7	3,024	83.1	5	.1	3,638

9.3	905	3.4	473	1.8	337	1.3	4,178	15.9	22,080	83.8	93	.4	26,351
10.1	421	2.8	254	1.7	174	1.2	2,367	15.7	12,630	84.0	39	.3	15,036
8.4	484	4.3	219	1.9	163	1.4	1,811	16.0	9,450	83.5	54	.5	11,315

(23 INSTITUTIONS)

2.8	2,183	2.9	723	1.0	5,692	7.6	10,709	14.2	63,096	83.9	1,398	1.9	75,203
3.6	824	2.5	332	1.0	2,420	7.3	4,775	14.4	28,152	84.7	293	.9	33,220
2.2	1,359	3.2	391	.9	3,272	7.8	5,934	14.1	34,944	83.2	1,105	2.6	41,983
3.8	2,073	3.0	675	1.0	8,119	11.9	13,436	19.7	53,959	79.1	808	1.2	68,203
4.0	900	2.5	423	1.2	4,776	13.2	7,554	20.8	28,336	78.2	354	1.0	36,244
3.5	1,173	3.7	252	.8	3,343	10.5	5,882	18.4	25,623	80.2	454	1.4	31,959

3.3	4,256	3.0	1,398	1.0	13,811	9.6	24,145	16.8	117,055	81.6	2,206	1.5	143,406
3.8	1,724	2.5	755	1.1	7,196	10.4	12,329	17.7	56,488	81.3	647	.9	69,464
2.7	2,532	3.4	643	.9	6,615	8.9	11,816	16.0	60,567	81.9	1,559	2.1	73,942

.6	50	.8	52	.9	115	1.9	256	4.2	5,081	84.0	709	11.7	6,046
1.1	19	.9	23	1.1	41	1.9	107	5.0	1,957	90.7	94	4.4	2,158
.4	31	.8	29	.7	74	1.9	149	3.8	3,124	80.3	615	15.8	3,888
.8	66	.8	62	.8	231	2.9	411	5.1	7,374	92.1	224	2.8	8,009
.8	36	.9	20	.5	117	3.1	204	5.3	3,576	93.5	43	1.1	3,823
.5	30	.7	42	1.0	114	2.7	207	4.9	3,798	90.7	181	4.3	4,186

.6	116	.8	114	.8	346	2.5	667	4.7	12,455	88.6	933	6.6	14,055
.9	55	.9	43	.7	158	2.6	311	5.2	5,533	92.5	137	2.3	5,981
.4	61	.8	71	.9	188	2.3	356	4.4	6,922	85.7	796	9.9	8,074

.3	1	.1	3	.3	24	2.1	32	2.8	1,110	96.9	4	.3	1,146
.3	0	.0	1	.3	8	2.3	10	2.8	341	96.9	1	.3	352
.4	1	.1	2	.3	16	2.0	22	2.8	769	96.9	3	.4	794
.0	0	.0	1	2.3	1	2.3	2	4.7	41	95.3	0	.0	43
.0	0	.0	1	5.6	0	.0	1	5.6	17	94.4	0	.0	18
.0	0	.0	0	.0	1	4.0	1	4.0	24	96.0	0	.0	25

.3	1	.1	4	.3	25	2.1	34	2.9	1,151	96.8	4	.3	1,189
.3	0	.0	2	.5	8	2.2	11	3.0	358	96.8	1	.3	370
.4	1	.1	2	.2	17	2.1	23	2.8	793	96.8	3	.4	819

2.6	2,234	2.7	778	.9	5,831	7.1	10,997	13.3	69,287	84.1	2,111	2.6	82,395
3.4	843	2.4	356	1.0	2,469	6.9	4,892	13.7	30,450	85.2	388	1.1	35,730
2.0	1,391	3.0	422	.9	3,362	7.2	6,105	13.1	38,837	83.2	1,723	3.7	46,665
3.4	2,139	2.8	738	1.0	8,351	11.0	13,849	18.2	61,374	80.5	1,032	1.4	76,259
3.7	936	2.3	444	1.1	4,893	12.2	7,759	19.4	31,929	79.7	397	1.0	40,085
3.1	1,203	3.3	294	.8	3,458	9.6	6,090	16.8	29,445	81.4	635	1.8	36,170

3.0	4,373	2.8	1,516	1.0	14,182	8.9	24,846	15.7	130,661	82.4	3,143	2.0	158,650
3.6	1,779	2.3	800	1.1	7,362	9.7	12,651	16.7	62,379	82.3	785	1.0	75,815
2.5	2,594	3.1	716	.9	6,820	8.2	12,195	14.7	68,282	82.4	2,358	2.8	82,835

4.1	267	1.5	98	1.5	1,283	7.1	2,383	13.3	15,468	86.1	111	.6	17,962
4.3	113	1.1	35	.3	660	6.3	1,259	12.1	9,089	87.4	57	.5	10,405
3.8	154	2.0	63	.8	623	8.2	1,124	14.9	6,379	84.4	54	.7	7,557

3.1	4,640	2.6	1,614	.9	15,465	8.8	27,229	15.4	146,129	82.7	3,254	1.8	176,612
3.7	1,892	2.2	835	1.0	8,022	9.3	13,910	16.1	71,468	82.9	842	1.0	86,220
2.6	2,748	3.0	779	.9	7,443	8.2	13,319	14.7	74,661	82.6	2,412	2.7	90,392

TABLE 17 - TOTAL ENROLLMENT IN INSTITUTIONS OF HIGHER EDUCATION FOR SELECTED MAJOR FIELDS OF STUDY AND LEVEL OF ENROLLMENT
BY RACE, ETHNICITY, AND SEX: STATE, 1978

MAJOR FIELD 9999 - SUMMARY

	AMERICAN INDIAN ALASKAN NATIVE		BLACK NON-HISPANIC		ASIAN OR PACIFIC ISLANDER		HISPANIC		TOTAL MINORITY		WHITE NON-HISPANIC		NON-RESIDENT ALIEN	
	NUMBER	%	NUMBER	%	NUMBER	%	NUMBER	%	NUMBER	%	NUMBER	%	NUMBER	%
ARKANSAS (34 INSTITUTIONS)														
UNDERGRADUATES:														
FULL-TIME	265	.5	8,332	17.2	278	.6	173	.4	9,048	18.7	38,927	80.3	486	1.0
FEMALE	105	.4	4,713	19.6	93	.4	75	.3	4,986	20.7	18,979	78.9	91	.4
MALE	160	.7	3,619	14.8	185	.8	98	.4	4,062	16.6	19,948	81.7	395	1.6
PART-TIME	119	.9	1,559	12.4	104	.8	54	.4	1,836	14.6	10,766	85.3	16	.1
FEMALE	67	.9	908	12.7	38	.5	31	.4	1,044	14.6	6,122	85.4	6	.1
MALE	52	1.0	651	12.0	66	1.2	23	.4	792	14.5	4,644	85.3	10	.2
TOTAL	384	.6	9,891	16.2	382	.6	227	.4	10,884	17.8	49,693	81.4	502	.8
FEMALE	172	.6	5,621	18.0	131	.4	106	.3	6,030	19.3	25,101	80.4	97	.3
MALE	212	.7	4,270	14.3	251	.8	121	.4	4,854	16.3	24,592	82.4	405	1.4
GRADUATE:														
FULL-TIME	21	1.0	142	6.5	17	.8	15	.7	195	8.9	1,807	82.9	179	8.2
FEMALE	10	1.2	79	9.2	7	.8	5	.6	101	11.7	735	85.5	24	2.8
MALE	11	.8	63	4.8	10	.8	10	.8	94	7.1	1,072	81.2	155	11.7
PART-TIME	17	.5	322	8.8	21	.6	5	.1	365	10.0	3,259	89.2	28	.8
FEMALE	9	.4	213	9.9	11	.5	2	.1	235	11.0	1,902	88.8	6	.3
MALE	8	.5	109	7.2	10	.7	3	.2	130	8.6	1,357	89.9	22	1.5
TOTAL	38	.7	464	8.0	38	.7	20	.3	560	9.6	5,066	86.9	207	3.5
FEMALE	19	.6	292	9.7	18	.6	7	.2	336	11.2	2,637	87.8	30	1.0
MALE	19	.7	172	6.1	20	.7	13	.5	224	7.9	2,429	85.8	177	6.3
PROFESSIONAL:														
FULL-TIME	6	.5	56	4.3	13	1.0	4	.3	79	6.0	1,224	93.6	4	.3
FEMALE	1	.4	16	6.3	2	.8	2	.8	21	8.3	233	91.7	0	.0
MALE	5	.5	40	3.8	11	1.0	2	.2	58	5.5	991	94.1	4	.4
PART-TIME	0	.0	11	5.1	1	.5	1	.5	13	6.0	203	94.0	0	.0
FEMALE	0	.0	4	7.4	1	1.9	0	.0	5	9.3	49	90.7	0	.0
MALE	0	.0	7	4.3	0	.0	1	.6	8	4.9	154	95.1	0	.0
TOTAL	6	.4	67	4.4	14	.9	5	.3	92	6.0	1,427	93.7	4	.3
FEMALE	1	.3	20	6.5	3	1.0	2	.6	26	8.4	282	91.6	0	.0
MALE	5	.4	47	3.9	11	.9	3	.2	66	5.4	1,145	94.2	4	.3
UND+GRAD+PROF:														
FULL-TIME	292	.6	8,530	16.4	308	.6	192	.4	9,322	17.9	41,958	80.8	669	1.3
FEMALE	116	.5	4,808	19.1	102	.4	82	.3	5,108	20.3	19,947	79.2	115	.5
MALE	176	.7	3,722	13.9	206	.8	110	.4	4,214	15.7	22,011	82.2	554	2.1
PART-TIME	136	.8	1,892	11.5	126	.8	60	.4	2,214	13.4	14,228	86.3	44	.3
FEMALE	76	.8	1,125	12.0	50	.5	33	.4	1,284	13.7	8,073	86.2	12	.1
MALE	60	.8	767	10.8	76	1.1	27	.4	930	13.1	6,155	86.5	32	.4
TOTAL	428	.6	10,422	15.2	434	.6	252	.4	11,536	16.9	56,186	82.1	713	1.0
FEMALE	192	.6	5,933	17.2	152	.4	115	.3	6,392	18.5	28,020	81.1	127	.4
MALE	236	.7	4,489	13.2	282	.8	137	.4	5,144	15.2	28,166	83.1	586	1.7
UNCLASSIFIED:														
TOTAL	20	.5	318	8.2	58	1.5	15	.4	411	10.6	3,447	88.8	25	.6
FEMALE	12	.5	190	8.4	21	.9	10	.4	233	10.2	2,028	89.1	14	.6
MALE	8	.5	128	8.0	37	2.3	5	.3	178	11.1	1,419	88.2	11	.7
TOTAL ENROLLMENT:														
TOTAL	448	.6	10,740	14.9	492	.7	267	.4	11,947	16.5	59,633	82.5	738	1.0
FEMALE	204	.6	6,123	16.6	173	.5	125	.3	6,625	18.0	30,048	81.6	141	.4
MALE	244	.7	4,617	13.0	319	.9	142	.4	5,322	15.0	29,585	83.3	597	1.7
CALIFORNIA (261 INSTITUTIONS)														
UNDERGRADUATES:														
FULL-TIME	6,959	1.2	52,425	8.9	46,182	7.8	53,951	9.1	159,517	26.9	411,029	69.4	21,706	3.7
FEMALE	3,394	1.2	27,335	9.6	21,774	7.6	25,556	9.0	78,059	27.4	200,438	70.3	6,637	2.3
MALE	3,565	1.2	25,090	8.2	24,408	7.9	28,395	9.2	81,458	26.5	210,591	68.6	15,069	4.9
PART-TIME	10,679	1.6	63,946	9.6	36,376	5.5	69,479	10.4	180,480	27.1	479,461	71.9	6,892	1.0
FEMALE	5,620	1.5	34,364	9.5	17,675	4.8	34,588	9.4	92,647	25.3	270,904	74.0	2,586	.7
MALE	5,059	1.7	29,182	9.7	18,701	6.2	34,891	11.6	87,833	29.2	208,557	69.4	4,306	1.4
TOTAL	17,638	1.4	116,371	9.2	82,558	6.6	123,430	9.8	339,997	27.0	890,490	70.7	28,598	2.3 1,
FEMALE	9,014	1.4	62,099	9.5	39,449	6.1	60,144	9.2	170,706	26.2	471,342	72.4	9,223	1.4
MALE	8,624	1.4	54,272	8.6	43,109	7.1	63,286	10.4	169,291	27.9	419,148	69.0	19,375	3.2
GRADUATE:														
FULL-TIME	247	.5	1,960	3.7	2,624	5.0	2,059	3.9	6,890	13.0	38,426	72.7	7,504	14.2
FEMALE	111	.4	1,030	5.0	1,094	5.3	884	4.3	3,119	15.1	16,022	77.5	1,535	7.4
MALE	136	.4	930	2.9	1,530	4.8	1,175	3.7	3,771	11.7	22,404	69.7	5,969	18.6
PART-TIME	447	.7	2,340	4.5	3,569	5.9	2,600	4.3	9,356	15.4	47,638	78.2	3,928	6.4
FEMALE	182	.7	1,475	5.7	1,405	5.4	1,153	4.5	4,215	16.3	20,652	79.9	970	3.8
MALE	265	.8	1,265	3.6	2,164	6.2	1,447	4.1	5,141	14.7	26,986	76.9	2,958	8.4
TOTAL	694	.6	4,700	4.1	6,193	5.4	4,659	4.1	16,246	14.3	86,064	75.7	11,432	10.1
FEMALE	293	.6	2,505	5.4	2,499	5.4	2,037	4.4	7,334	15.8	36,674	78.8	2,505	5.4
MALE	401	.6	2,195	3.3	3,694	5.5	2,622	3.9	8,912	13.3	49,390	73.5	8,927	13.3
PROFESSIONAL:														
FULL-TIME	129	.5	951	3.8	1,771	7.1	1,234	4.9	4,085	16.3	20,508	82.0	408	1.6
FEMALE	41	.6	414	5.9	557	7.9	308	4.4	1,320	18.8	5,596	79.7	101	1.4
MALE	88	.5	537	3.0	1,214	6.8	926	5.1	2,765	15.4	14,912	82.9	307	1.7

SUMMARY

INDIAN NATIVE %	BLACK NON-HISPANIC NUMBER	%	ASIAN OR PACIFIC ISLANDER NUMBER	%	HISPANIC NUMBER	%	TOTAL MINORITY NUMBER	%	WHITE NON-HISPANIC NUMBER	%	NON-RESIDENT ALIEN NUMBER	%	TOTAL NUMBER
CONTINUED													
.6	299	5.1	154	2.6	224	3.8	715	12.2	5,027	85.6	132	2.2	5,874
.6	107	5.7	48	2.6	59	3.1	226	12.0	1,624	86.4	30	1.6	1,880
.7	192	4.8	106	2.7	165	4.1	489	12.2	3,403	85.2	102	2.6	3,994
.5	1,250	4.0	1,925	6.2	1,458	4.7	4,800	15.5	25,535	82.7	540	1.7	30,875
.6	521	5.9	605	6.8	367	4.1	1,546	17.4	7,220	81.2	131	1.5	8,897
.5	729	3.3	1,320	6.0	1,091	5.0	3,254	14.8	18,315	83.3	409	1.9	21,978
1.1	55,336	8.3	50,577	7.5	57,244	8.5	170,492	25.4	469,963	70.1	29,618	4.4	670,073
1.1	28,779	9.2	23,425	7.5	26,748	8.6	82,498	20.4	222,056	71.0	8,273	2.6	312,827
1.1	26,557	7.4	27,152	7.6	30,496	8.5	87,994	24.6	247,907	69.4	21,345	6.0	357,246
1.5	66,985	9.1	40,099	5.5	72,303	9.9	190,551	26.0	532,126	72.5	10,952	1.5	733,629
1.5	36,346	9.2	19,128	4.9	35,800	9.1	97,088	24.7	293,180	74.4	3,586	.9	393,854
1.6	30,639	9.0	20,971	6.2	36,503	10.7	93,463	27.5	238,946	70.3	7,366	2.2	339,775
1.3	122,321	8.7	90,676	6.5	129,547	9.2	361,043	25.7	1,002,089	71.4	40,570	2.9	1,403,702
1.3	65,125	9.2	42,953	6.0	62,548	8.9	179,586	25.4	515,236	72.9	11,859	1.7	706,681
1.3	57,196	8.2	48,123	6.9	66,999	9.6	181,457	26.0	486,853	69.8	28,711	4.1	697,021
1.2	14,916	6.1	16,389	6.7	18,083	7.4	52,448	21.4	188,780	77.0	3,920	1.6	245,148
1.2	7,853	6.1	7,838	6.1	8,438	6.6	25,655	20.1	100,669	78.8	1,432	1.1	127,756
1.3	7,063	6.0	8,551	7.3	9,645	8.2	26,793	22.8	88,111	75.1	2,488	2.1	117,392
1.3	137,237	8.3	107,065	6.5	147,630	9.0	413,491	25.1	1,190,869	72.2	44,490	2.7	1,648,850
1.3	72,978	8.7	50,391	6.0	70,986	8.5	205,241	24.6	615,905	73.8	13,291	1.6	834,437
1.3	64,259	7.9	56,674	7.0	76,644	9.4	208,250	25.6	574,964	70.6	31,199	3.8	814,413
(41 INSTITUTIONS)													
.8	2,524	3.0	1,222	1.5	4,741	5.7	9,197	11.0	72,625	86.8	1,863	2.2	83,685
1.0	1,128	2.9	558	1.5	2,177	5.7	4,233	11.0	33,726	86.0	364	.9	38,323
.7	1,396	3.1	664	1.5	2,564	5.7	4,964	10.9	38,899	85.8	1,499	3.3	45,362
.9	1,156	3.8	318	1.0	1,714	5.6	3,454	11.4	26,570	87.4	393	1.3	30,417
.8	541	3.4	171	1.1	785	4.9	1,633	10.1	14,329	89.0	147	.9	16,109
.9	615	4.3	147	1.0	929	6.5	1,821	12.7	12,241	85.6	246	1.7	14,308
.9	3,680	3.2	1,540	1.3	6,455	5.7	12,651	11.1	99,195	86.9	2,256	2.0	114,102
.9	1,669	3.1	729	1.3	2,962	5.4	5,866	10.8	48,055	88.3	511	.9	54,432
.8	2,011	3.4	811	1.4	3,493	5.9	6,785	11.4	51,140	85.7	1,745	2.9	59,670
.3	149	1.9	87	1.1	221	2.7	482	6.0	6,742	83.9	813	10.1	8,037
.3	68	2.1	34	1.1	96	3.0	208	6.5	2,841	89.3	134	4.2	3,183
.3	81	1.7	53	1.1	125	2.6	274	5.6	3,901	80.4	679	14.0	4,854
.4	74	1.4	58	1.1	210	3.9	364	6.8	4,680	87.8	284	5.3	5,328
.3	32	1.5	30	1.2	103	4.1	179	7.1	2,296	90.7	57	2.3	2,532
.3	42	1.5	28	1.0	107	3.8	185	6.6	2,384	85.3	227	8.1	2,796
.4	223	1.7	145	1.1	431	3.2	846	6.3	11,422	85.5	1,097	8.2	13,365
.4	100	1.7	64	1.1	199	3.5	387	6.0	5,137	89.9	191	3.3	5,715
.3	123	1.6	81	1.1	232	3.0	459	6.0	6,285	82.2	906	11.8	7,650
.9	44	1.8	38	1.6	108	4.4	211	8.6	2,223	91.0	9	.4	2,443
1.1	15	2.1	11	1.5	29	4.1	63	8.8	650	91.2	0	.0	713
1.8	29	1.7	27	1.6	79	4.6	148	8.6	1,573	90.9	9	.5	1,730
1.0	19	3.7	1	.2	12	2.3	37	7.2	472	92.4	2	.4	511
1.0	6	3.5	0	.0	3	1.8	9	5.3	161	94.2	1	.6	171
1.5	13	3.8	1	.3	9	2.6	28	8.2	311	91.5	1	.3	340
.9	63	2.1	39	1.3	120	4.1	248	8.4	2,695	91.2	11	.4	2,954
.9	21	2.4	11	1.2	32	3.6	72	8.1	811	91.7	1	.1	884
.9	42	2.0	28	1.4	88	4.3	176	8.5	1,804	91.0	10	.5	2,070
.8	2,317	2.9	1,347	1.4	5,070	5.4	9,890	10.5	81,590	86.6	2,685	2.9	94,165
.9	1,211	2.9	603	1.4	2,302	5.5	4,504	10.7	37,217	88.2	498	1.2	42,219
.7	1,506	2.9	744	1.4	2,768	5.3	5,386	10.4	44,373	85.4	2,187	4.2	51,946
.8	1,249	3.4	377	1.0	1,936	5.3	3,855	10.6	31,722	87.5	679	1.9	36,256
.8	579	3.1	201	1.1	891	4.7	1,821	9.7	16,786	89.2	205	1.1	18,812
.8	670	3.8	176	1.0	1,045	6.0	2,034	11.7	14,936	85.6	474	2.7	17,444
.8	3,966	3.0	1,724	1.3	7,006	5.4	13,745	10.5	113,312	86.9	3,364	2.6	130,421
.8	1,190	2.9	804	1.3	3,193	5.2	6,325	10.4	54,003	88.5	703	1.2	61,031
.7	2,176	3.1	920	1.3	3,813	5.5	7,420	10.7	59,309	85.5	2,661	3.8	69,390
1.2	784	3.6	201	.9	1,975	9.0	3,227	14.7	18,508	84.4	203	.9	21,938
1.2	431	3.6	110	.9	772	6.5	1,457	12.2	10,430	87.2	69	.6	11,956
1.2	353	3.5	91	.9	1,203	12.1	1,770	17.7	8,078	80.9	134	1.3	9,982
.9	4,750	3.1	1,925	1.3	8,981	5.9	16,972	11.1	131,820	86.5	3,567	2.3	152,359
.9	2,221	3.0	914	1.3	3,965	5.4	7,782	10.7	64,433	88.3	772	1.1	72,987
.8	2,529	3.2	1,011	1.3	5,016	6.3	9,190	11.6	67,387	84.9	2,795	3.5	79,372

TABLE 17 - TOTAL ENROLLMENT IN INSTITUTIONS OF HIGHER EDUCATION FOR SELECTED MAJOR FIELDS OF STUDY AND LEVEL OF ENROLLMENT BY RACE, ETHNICITY, AND SEX: STATE, 1978

MAJOR FIELD 9999 - SUMMARY

	AMERICAN INDIAN ALASKAN NATIVE		BLACK NON-HISPANIC		ASIAN OR PACIFIC ISLANDER		HISPANIC		TOTAL MINORITY		WHITE NON-HISPANIC		NON-RESIDENT ALIEN	
	NUMBER	%	NUMBER	%	NUMBER	%	NUMBER	%	NUMBER	%	NUMBER	%	NUMBER	%
CONNECTICUT (47 INSTITUTIONS)														
UNDERGRADUATES:														
FULL-TIME	136	.2	3,658	5.0	674	.9	1,178	1.6	5,646	7.7	67,128	91.0	968	1.3
FEMALE	60	.2	1,986	5.4	309	.8	565	1.5	2,920	7.9	33,595	91.2	316	.9
MALE	76	.2	1,672	4.9	365	1.0	613	1.7	2,726	7.4	33,533	90.8	652	1.8
PART-TIME	97	.2	2,649	6.7	193	.5	835	2.1	3,774	9.6	35,527	90.2	90	.2
FEMALE	68	.3	1,498	7.1	89	.4	452	2.1	2,107	10.0	19,006	89.9	39	.2
MALE	29	.2	1,151	6.3	104	.6	383	2.1	1,667	9.1	16,521	90.6	51	.3
TOTAL	233	.2	6,307	5.6	867	.8	2,013	1.8	9,420	8.3	102,655	90.7	1,058	.9
FEMALE	128	.2	3,484	6.0	398	.7	1,017	1.8	5,027	8.7	52,601	90.7	355	.6
MALE	105	.2	2,823	5.1	469	.9	996	1.8	4,393	8.0	50,054	90.8	703	1.3
GRADUATE:														
FULL-TIME	9	.1	169	2.6	64	1.0	168	2.6	410	6.4	5,459	84.6	582	9.0
FEMALE	5	.2	92	3.3	26	.9	62	2.2	185	6.6	2,487	88.4	142	5.0
MALE	4	.1	77	2.1	38	1.0	106	2.9	225	6.2	2,972	81.7	440	12.1
PART-TIME	14	.1	408	2.5	87	.5	157	.9	666	4.0	15,695	95.0	167	1.0
FEMALE	8	.1	166	2.0	39	.5	61	.7	274	3.3	7,907	96.2	36	.4
MALE	6	.1	242	2.9	48	.6	96	1.2	392	4.7	7,788	93.7	131	1.6
TOTAL	23	.1	577	2.5	151	.7	325	1.4	1,076	4.7	21,154	92.1	749	3.3
FEMALE	13	.1	258	2.3	65	.6	123	1.1	459	4.2	10,394	94.2	178	1.6
MALE	10	.1	319	2.7	86	.7	202	1.7	617	5.2	10,760	90.1	571	4.8
PROFESSIONAL:														
FULL-TIME	4	.2	120	4.8	31	1.2	85	3.4	240	9.6	2,214	88.9	36	1.4
FEMALE	3	.4	46	6.1	11	1.5	28	3.7	88	11.6	664	87.8	4	.5
MALE	1	.1	74	4.3	20	1.2	57	3.3	152	8.8	1,550	89.4	32	1.8
PART-TIME	0	.0	11	2.5	1	.2	4	.9	16	3.6	423	95.1	6	1.3
FEMALE	0	.0	4	3.1	0	.0	0	.0	4	3.1	124	95.4	2	1.5
MALE	0	.0	7	2.2	1	.3	4	1.3	12	3.8	299	94.9	4	1.3
TOTAL	4	.1	131	4.5	32	1.1	89	3.0	256	8.7	2,637	89.8	42	1.4
FEMALE	3	.3	50	5.6	11	1.2	28	3.2	92	10.4	788	88.9	6	.7
MALE	1	.0	81	4.0	21	1.0	61	3.0	164	8.0	1,849	90.2	36	1.8
UNG+GRAD+PROF:														
FULL-TIME	149	.2	3,947	4.8	769	.9	1,431	1.7	6,296	7.6	74,801	90.5	1,586	1.9
FEMALE	68	.2	2,124	5.3	346	.9	655	1.6	3,193	7.9	36,746	91.0	462	1.1
MALE	81	.2	1,823	4.3	423	1.0	776	1.8	3,103	7.3	38,055	90.0	1,124	2.7
PART-TIME	111	.2	3,068	5.4	281	.5	996	1.8	4,456	7.9	51,645	91.6	263	.5
FEMALE	76	.3	1,668	5.7	128	.4	513	1.7	2,385	8.1	27,037	91.7	77	.3
MALE	35	.1	1,400	5.2	153	.6	483	1.8	2,071	7.7	24,608	91.6	186	.7
TOTAL	260	.2	7,015	5.0	1,050	.8	2,427	1.7	10,752	7.7	126,446	90.9	1,849	1.3
FEMALE	144	.2	3,792	5.4	474	.7	1,168	1.7	5,578	8.0	63,783	91.2	539	.8
MALE	116	.2	3,223	4.7	576	.8	1,259	1.8	5,174	7.5	62,663	90.6	1,310	1.9
UNCLASSIFIED:														
TOTAL	47	.4	456	3.4	87	.7	213	1.6	803	6.0	12,497	93.4	84	.6
FEMALE	24	.4	302	3.6	51	.6	113	1.4	490	5.9	7,800	93.6	46	.6
MALE	23	.5	154	3.1	36	.7	100	2.0	313	6.2	4,697	93.0	38	.8
TOTAL ENROLLMENT:														
TOTAL	307	.2	7,471	4.9	1,137	.7	2,640	1.7	11,555	7.6	138,943	91.2	1,933	1.3
FEMALE	168	.2	4,094	5.2	525	.7	1,281	1.6	6,068	7.8	71,583	91.5	585	.7
MALE	139	.2	3,377	4.6	612	.8	1,359	1.8	5,487	7.4	67,360	90.8	1,348	1.8
DELAWARE (10 INSTITUTIONS)														
UNDERGRADUATES:														
FULL-TIME	23	.1	2,327	12.1	64	.3	80	.4	2,494	13.0	16,475	85.8	226	1.2
FEMALE	10	.1	1,296	12.5	37	.4	40	.4	1,383	13.3	8,903	85.9	83	.8
MALE	13	.1	1,031	11.7	27	.3	40	.5	1,111	12.6	7,572	85.8	143	1.6
PART-TIME	10	.2	737	14.0	30	.6	67	1.3	844	16.0	4,396	83.4	31	.6
FEMALE	5	.2	449	16.1	12	.4	44	1.6	510	18.3	2,257	81.0	21	.8
MALE	5	.2	288	11.6	18	.7	23	.9	334	13.5	2,139	86.1	10	.4
TOTAL	33	.1	3,064	12.5	94	.4	147	.6	3,338	13.6	20,871	85.3	257	1.1
FEMALE	15	.1	1,745	13.3	49	.4	84	.6	1,893	14.4	11,160	84.8	104	.8
MALE	18	.2	1,319	11.7	45	.4	63	.6	1,445	12.8	9,711	85.9	153	1.4
GRADUATE:														
FULL-TIME	1	.3	16	4.7	2	.6	0	.0	19	5.5	283	82.3	42	12.2
FEMALE	0	.0	3	2.2	0	.0	0	.0	3	2.2	123	91.8	8	6.0
MALE	1	.5	13	6.2	2	1.0	0	.0	16	7.6	160	76.2	34	16.2
PART-TIME	1	.1	41	3.6	6	.5	4	.4	52	4.6	1,040	91.5	45	4.0
FEMALE	0	.0	16	3.0	1	.2	3	.6	20	3.8	496	94.3	10	1.9
MALE	1	.2	25	4.1	5	.8	1	.2	32	5.2	544	89.0	35	5.7
TOTAL	2	.1	57	3.8	8	.5	4	.3	71	4.8	1,323	89.3	87	5.9
FEMALE	0	.0	19	2.9	1	.2	3	.5	23	3.5	619	93.8	18	2.7
MALE	2	.2	38	4.6	7	.9	1	.1	48	5.8	704	85.7	69	8.4
PROFESSIONAL:														
FULL-TIME	0	.0	0	.0	0	.0	0	.0	0	.0	0	.0	0	.0
FEMALE	0	.0	0	.0	0	.0	0	.0	0	.0	0	.0	0	.0
MALE	0	.0	0	.0	0	.0	0	.0	0	.0	0	.0	0	.0

ROLLMENT IN INSTITUTIONS OF HIGHER EDUCATION FOR SELECTED MAJOR FIELDS OF STUDY AND LEVEL OF ENROLLMENT
ETHNICITY, AND SEX: STATE, 1978

SUMMARY

INDIAN NATIVE	BLACK NON-HISPANIC		ASIAN OR PACIFIC ISLANDER		HISPANIC		TOTAL MINORITY		WHITE NON-HISPANIC		NON-RESIDENT ALIEN		TOTAL
%	NUMBER	%	NUMBER	%	NUMBER	%	NUMBER	%	NUMBER	%	NUMBER	%	NUMBER
CONTINUED													
.0	0	.0	0	.0	0	.0	0	.0	0	.0	0	.0	0
.0	0	.0	0	.0	0	.0	0	.0	0	.0	0	.0	0
.0	0	.0	0	.0	0	.0	0	.0	0	.0	0	.0	0
.0	0	.0	0	.0	0	.0	0	.0	0	.0	0	.0	0
.0	0	.0	0	.0	0	.0	0	.0	0	.0	0	.0	0
.0	0	.0	0	.0	0	.0	0	.0	0	.0	0	.0	0
.1	2,343	12.0	66	.3	80	.4	2,513	12.9	16,758	85.8	268	1.4	19,539
.1	1,299	12.4	37	.4	40	.4	1,386	13.2	9,026	85.9	91	.9	10,503
.2	1,044	11.6	29	.3	40	.4	1,127	12.5	7,732	85.6	177	2.0	9,036
.2	778	12.1	36	.6	71	1.1	896	14.0	5,436	84.8	76	1.2	6,408
.2	465	14.0	13	.4	47	1.4	530	16.0	2,753	83.1	31	.9	3,314
.2	313	10.1	23	.7	24	.8	366	11.8	2,683	86.7	45	1.5	3,094
.1	3,121	12.0	102	.4	151	.6	3,409	13.1	22,194	85.5	344	1.3	25,947
.1	1,764	12.8	50	.4	87	.6	1,916	13.9	11,779	85.3	122	.9	13,817
.2	1,357	11.2	52	.4	64	.5	1,493	12.3	10,415	85.9	222	1.8	12,130
.2	365	7.3	23	.5	30	.6	429	8.6	4,396	88.4	146	2.9	4,971
.3	184	7.0	10	.4	16	.6	217	8.3	2,342	89.7	52	2.0	2,611
.2	181	7.7	13	.6	14	.6	212	9.0	2,054	87.0	94	4.0	2,360
.1	3,486	11.3	125	.4	181	.6	3,838	12.4	26,590	86.0	490	1.6	30,918
.1	1,948	11.9	60	.4	103	.6	2,133	13.0	14,121	86.0	174	1.1	16,428
.2	1,538	10.6	65	.4	78	.5	1,705	11.8	12,469	86.1	316	2.2	14,490
(16 INSTITUTIONS)													
.4	10,915	35.9	486	1.6	510	1.7	12,032	39.5	15,308	50.3	3,091	10.2	30,431
.3	6,348	39.2	192	1.2	253	1.6	6,837	42.2	8,182	50.5	1,170	7.2	16,189
.5	4,567	32.1	294	2.1	257	1.8	5,195	36.5	7,126	50.0	1,921	13.5	14,242
1.2	9,351	67.2	462	3.3	188	1.4	10,172	73.2	2,772	19.9	961	6.9	13,905
.4	5,622	73.1	91	1.2	113	1.5	5,859	76.2	1,361	17.7	471	6.1	7,691
2.2	3,729	60.0	371	6.0	75	1.2	4,313	69.4	1,411	22.7	490	7.9	6,214
.7	20,266	45.7	948	2.1	698	1.6	22,204	50.1	18,080	40.8	4,052	9.1	44,336
.3	11,970	50.1	283	1.2	366	1.5	12,696	53.2	9,543	40.0	1,641	6.9	23,880
1.1	8,296	40.6	665	3.3	332	1.6	9,508	46.5	8,537	41.7	2,411	11.8	20,456
.1	1,122	15.7	111	1.6	96	1.3	1,336	18.7	4,218	58.9	1,606	22.4	7,160
.1	655	20.4	33	1.0	48	1.5	739	23.0	2,021	62.9	455	14.2	3,215
.1	467	11.8	78	2.0	48	1.2	597	15.1	2,197	55.7	1,151	29.2	3,945
.3	1,898	14.1	344	2.6	183	1.4	2,464	18.3	9,924	73.8	1,063	7.9	13,451
.1	1,140	21.6	100	1.9	66	1.2	1,311	24.8	3,658	69.3	312	5.9	5,281
.4	758	9.3	244	3.0	117	1.4	1,153	14.1	6,266	76.7	751	9.2	8,170
.2	3,020	14.7	455	2.2	279	1.4	3,800	18.4	14,142	68.6	2,669	12.9	20,611
.1	1,395	21.1	133	1.6	114	1.3	2,050	24.1	5,679	66.8	767	9.0	8,496
.3	1,225	10.1	322	2.7	165	1.4	1,750	14.4	8,463	69.9	1,902	15.7	12,115
.2	1,407	19.4	139	1.9	169	2.3	1,728	23.9	5,338	73.8	171	2.4	7,237
.1	591	25.7	57	2.5	57	2.5	707	30.7	1,546	67.2	48	2.1	2,301
.2	816	16.5	82	1.7	112	2.3	1,021	20.7	3,792	76.8	123	2.5	4,936
.3	167	11.0	13	.9	36	2.4	220	14.4	1,287	84.5	16	1.1	1,523
.2	73	11.0	6	1.0	9	1.4	89	14.2	532	84.8	6	1.0	627
.3	94	10.5	7	.8	27	3.0	131	14.6	755	84.3	10	1.1	896
.2	1,574	18.0	152	1.7	205	2.3	1,948	22.2	6,625	75.6	187	2.1	8,760
.1	664	22.7	63	2.2	66	2.3	796	27.2	2,078	71.0	54	1.8	2,928
.2	910	19.6	89	1.5	139	2.4	1,152	19.8	4,547	78.0	133	2.3	5,832
.3	13,444	30.0	736	1.6	775	1.7	15,096	33.7	24,864	55.5	4,868	10.9	44,828
.2	7,594	35.0	282	1.3	358	1.6	8,283	38.2	11,749	54.1	1,673	7.7	21,705
.4	5,850	25.3	454	2.0	417	1.8	6,813	29.5	13,115	56.7	3,195	13.8	23,123
.7	11,416	39.5	819	2.8	407	1.4	12,856	44.5	13,983	48.4	2,040	7.1	28,879
.3	6,835	50.3	197	1.4	188	1.4	7,259	53.4	5,551	40.8	789	5.8	13,599
1.1	4,581	30.0	622	4.1	219	1.4	5,597	36.6	8,432	55.2	1,251	8.2	15,280
.5	24,860	33.7	1,555	2.1	1,182	1.6	27,952	37.9	38,847	52.7	6,908	9.4	73,707
.2	14,429	40.9	479	1.4	546	1.5	15,542	44.0	17,300	49.0	2,462	7.0	35,304
.7	10,431	27.2	1,076	2.8	636	1.7	12,410	32.3	21,547	56.1	4,446	11.6	38,403
.4	1,340	16.5	214	2.6	147	1.8	1,732	21.4	5,321	65.7	1,047	12.9	8,100
.4	786	19.2	96	2.3	94	2.3	992	24.3	2,657	65.0	438	10.7	4,087
.4	554	13.8	118	2.9	53	1.3	740	18.4	2,664	66.4	609	15.2	4,013
.5	26,200	32.0	1,769	2.2	1,329	1.6	29,684	36.3	44,168	54.0	7,955	9.7	81,807
.3	15,215	38.6	575	1.5	640	1.6	16,534	42.0	19,957	50.7	2,900	7.4	39,391
.7	10,985	25.9	1,194	2.8	689	1.6	13,150	31.0	24,211	57.1	5,059	11.9	42,416

MAJOR FIELD 9999 - SUMMARY

	AMERICAN INDIAN ALASKAN NATIVE		BLACK NON-HISPANIC		ASIAN OR PACIFIC ISLANDER		HISPANIC		TOTAL MINORITY		WHITE NON-HISPANIC		NON-RESIDENT ALIEN	
	NUMBER	%	NUMBER	%	NUMBER	%	NUMBER	%	NUMBER	%	NUMBER	%	NUMBER	%
FLORIDA (77 INSTITUTIONS)														
UNDERGRADUATES:														
FULL-TIME	559	.3	23,876	13.2	1,306	.7	11,979	6.6	37,720	20.8	138,123	76.1	5,649	3.1
FEMALE	262	.3	14,481	17.0	510	.6	5,850	6.9	21,103	24.8	62,341	73.3	1,576	1.9
MALE	297	.3	9,395	9.7	796	.8	6,129	6.4	16,617	17.2	75,782	78.6	4,073	4.2
PART-TIME	357	.3	11,653	9.8	902	.8	10,662	9.0	23,574	19.9	93,918	79.2	1,072	.9
FEMALE	208	.3	6,967	10.9	367	.6	5,571	8.7	13,113	20.5	50,380	78.8	458	.7
MALE	149	.3	4,686	8.6	535	1.0	5,091	9.3	10,461	19.2	43,538	79.7	614	1.1
TOTAL	916	.3	35,529	11.8	2,208	.7	22,641	7.5	61,294	20.4	232,041	77.3	6,721	2.2
FEMALE	470	.3	21,448	14.4	877	.6	11,421	7.7	34,216	23.0	112,721	75.7	2,034	1.4
MALE	446	.3	14,081	9.3	1,331	.9	11,220	7.4	27,078	17.9	119,320	79.0	4,687	3.1
GRADUATE:														
FULL-TIME	27	.2	1,394	10.0	155	1.1	520	3.7	2,096	15.0	10,994	78.8	867	6.2
FEMALE	6	.1	766	13.7	42	.8	240	4.3	1,054	18.8	4,384	78.4	154	2.8
MALE	21	.3	628	7.5	113	1.4	280	3.3	1,042	12.5	6,610	79.0	713	8.5
PART-TIME	26	.2	1,214	9.5	92	.7	469	3.7	1,801	14.0	10,803	84.2	229	1.8
FEMALE	12	.2	795	12.6	35	.6	252	4.0	1,094	17.4	5,147	81.7	58	.9
MALE	14	.2	419	6.4	57	.9	217	3.3	707	10.8	5,656	86.6	171	2.6
TOTAL	53	.2	2,608	9.7	247	.9	989	3.7	3,897	14.5	21,797	81.4	1,096	4.1
FEMALE	18	.2	1,561	15.1	77	.6	492	4.1	2,148	18.1	9,531	80.2	212	1.8
MALE	35	.2	1,047	7.0	170	1.1	497	3.3	1,749	11.7	12,266	82.3	884	5.9
PROFESSIONAL:														
FULL-TIME	11	.2	187	3.4	23	.4	286	5.2	507	9.3	4,951	90.5	14	.3
FEMALE	1	.1	49	3.4	4	.3	63	4.4	117	8.1	1,316	91.5	5	.3
MALE	10	.2	138	3.4	19	.5	223	5.5	390	9.7	3,635	90.1	9	.2
PART-TIME	4	.6	5	.9	3	.6	19	3.6	31	5.8	499	94.2	0	.0
FEMALE	1	.7	1	.7	0	.0	6	4.0	8	5.4	141	94.6	0	.0
MALE	3	.8	4	1.0	3	.8	13	3.4	23	6.0	358	94.0	0	.0
TOTAL	15	.2	192	3.2	26	.4	305	5.1	538	9.0	5,450	90.8	14	.2
FEMALE	2	.1	50	3.2	4	.3	69	4.3	125	7.9	1,457	91.8	5	.3
MALE	13	.3	142	3.2	22	.5	236	5.3	413	9.4	3,993	90.4	9	.2
UND+GRAD+PROF:														
FULL-TIME	597	.3	25,457	12.7	1,484	.7	12,785	6.4	40,323	20.1	154,068	76.7	6,530	3.3
FEMALE	269	.3	15,296	16.6	556	.6	6,153	6.7	22,274	24.2	68,041	73.9	1,735	1.9
MALE	328	.3	10,161	9.3	928	.9	6,632	6.1	18,049	16.6	86,027	79.0	4,795	4.4
PART-TIME	387	.3	12,872	9.8	997	.8	11,150	8.5	25,406	19.3	105,220	79.8	1,301	1.0
FEMALE	221	.3	7,763	11.0	402	.6	5,829	8.3	14,215	20.2	55,668	79.1	516	.7
MALE	166	.3	5,109	8.3	595	1.0	5,321	8.6	11,191	18.2	49,552	80.5	785	1.3
TOTAL	984	.3	38,329	11.5	2,481	.7	23,935	7.2	65,729	19.7	259,288	77.9	7,831	2.4
FEMALE	490	.3	23,059	14.2	958	.6	11,982	7.4	36,489	22.5	123,709	76.2	2,251	1.4
MALE	494	.3	15,270	9.0	1,523	.9	11,953	7.0	29,240	17.2	135,579	79.6	5,580	3.3
UNCLASSIFIED:														
TOTAL	138	.3	4,113	9.3	307	.7	3,080	7.0	7,638	17.3	36,185	81.8	429	1.0
FEMALE	79	.3	2,598	10.3	141	.6	1,785	7.0	4,603	18.2	20,598	81.3	144	.6
MALE	59	.3	1,515	8.0	166	.9	1,295	6.8	3,035	16.1	15,587	82.4	285	1.5
TOTAL ENROLLMENT:														
TOTAL	1,122	.3	42,442	11.3	2,788	.7	27,015	7.2	73,367	19.5	295,473	78.4	8,260	2.2
FEMALE	569	.3	25,657	13.7	1,099	.6	13,767	7.3	41,092	21.9	144,307	76.8	2,395	1.3
MALE	553	.3	16,785	8.9	1,689	.9	13,248	7.0	32,275	17.0	151,166	79.9	5,865	3.1
GEORGIA (72 INSTITUTIONS)														
UNDERGRADUATES:														
FULL-TIME	141	.1	22,352	21.8	397	.4	523	.5	23,413	22.8	37,140	75.3	1,947	1.9
FEMALE	56	.1	12,883	25.5	173	.3	187	.4	13,299	26.4	36,677	72.7	447	.9
MALE	85	.2	9,469	18.2	224	.4	336	.6	10,114	19.4	40,463	77.7	1,500	2.9
PART-TIME	79	.2	4,871	14.0	158	.5	215	.6	5,323	15.3	29,278	83.9	281	.8
FEMALE	39	.2	2,700	15.2	70	.4	76	.4	2,885	16.3	14,730	83.1	114	.6
MALE	40	.2	2,171	12.7	88	.5	139	.8	2,438	14.2	14,548	84.8	167	1.0
TOTAL	220	.2	27,223	19.8	555	.4	738	.5	28,736	20.9	106,418	77.5	2,228	1.6
FEMALE	95	.1	15,583	22.9	243	.4	263	.4	16,184	23.7	51,407	75.4	561	.8
MALE	125	.2	11,640	16.8	312	.5	475	.7	12,552	18.1	55,011	79.5	1,667	2.4
GRADUATE:														
FULL-TIME	9	.1	1,400	15.3	55	.6	35	.4	1,499	16.4	6,868	75.3	756	8.3
FEMALE	3	.1	933	21.3	21	.5	10	.2	967	22.0	3,292	75.0	131	3.0
MALE	6	.1	467	9.9	34	.7	25	.5	532	11.2	3,576	75.6	625	13.2
PART-TIME	20	.2	1,716	13.4	61	.5	24	.2	1,821	14.2	10,648	83.1	340	2.7
FEMALE	10	.2	1,233	16.2	30	.4	9	.1	1,282	16.8	6,221	81.7	109	1.4
MALE	10	.2	483	9.3	31	.6	15	.3	539	10.4	4,427	85.2	231	4.4
TOTAL	29	.1	3,116	14.2	116	.5	59	.3	3,320	15.1	17,516	79.9	1,096	5.0
FEMALE	13	.1	2,166	18.0	51	.4	19	.2	2,249	18.7	9,513	79.3	240	2.0
MALE	16	.2	950	9.6	65	.7	40	.4	1,071	10.8	8,003	80.6	856	8.6
PROFESSIONAL:														
FULL-TIME	7	.1	407	7.5	19	.4	37	.7	470	8.6	4,959	90.8	32	.6
FEMALE	3	.3	99	8.4	4	.3	6	.5	112	9.5	1,061	90.1	4	.3
MALE	4	.1	308	7.2	15	.4	31	.7	358	8.4	3,898	91.0	28	.7

SUMMARY

INDIAN NATIVE	BLACK NON-HISPANIC		ASIAN OR PACIFIC ISLANDER		HISPANIC		TOTAL MINORITY		WHITE NON-HISPANIC		NON-RESIDENT ALIEN		TOTAL
%	NUMBER	%	NUMBER	%	NUMBER	%	NUMBER	%	NUMBER	%	NUMBER	%	NUMBER
CONTINUED													
.0	21	9.2	0	.0	0	.0	21	9.2	203	89.0	4	1.8	228
.0	4	11.1	0	.0	0	.0	4	11.1	31	86.1	1	2.8	36
.0	17	8.9	0	.0	0	.0	17	8.9	172	89.6	3	1.6	192
.1	428	7.5	19	.3	37	.7	491	8.6	5,162	90.7	36	.6	5,689
.2	103	8.5	4	.3	6	.5	116	9.6	1,092	90.0	5	.4	1,213
.1	325	7.3	15	.3	31	.7	375	8.4	4,070	90.9	31	.7	4,476
.1	24,159	20.6	471	.4	595	.5	25,382	21.7	88,967	76.0	2,735	2.3	117,084
.1	13,915	24.9	198	.4	203	.4	14,378	25.7	41,030	73.3	582	1.0	55,990
.1	10,244	16.8	273	.4	392	.6	11,004	18.0	47,937	78.5	2,153	3.5	61,094
.2	6,608	13.8	219	.5	239	.5	7,165	15.0	40,129	83.7	625	1.3	47,919
.2	3,937	15.5	100	.4	85	.3	4,171	16.4	20,982	82.7	224	.9	25,377
.2	2,671	11.8	119	.5	154	.7	2,994	13.3	19,147	84.9	401	1.8	22,542
.2	30,767	18.6	690	.4	834	.5	32,547	19.7	129,096	78.2	3,360	2.0	165,003
.1	17,852	21.9	298	.4	288	.4	18,549	22.8	62,012	76.2	806	1.0	81,367
.2	12,915	15.4	392	.5	546	.7	13,998	16.7	67,084	80.2	2,554	3.1	83,636
.3	1,722	17.5	94	.5	72	.7	1,874	19.0	7,730	78.4	260	2.6	9,864
.3	1,030	19.5	28	.5	28	.5	1,101	20.8	4,106	77.5	88	1.7	5,295
.2	692	15.1	26	.6	44	1.0	773	16.9	3,624	79.3	172	3.8	4,569
.2	32,489	18.6	744	.4	906	.5	34,421	19.7	136,826	78.2	3,620	2.1	174,867
.1	18,882	21.8	326	.4	316	.4	19,650	22.7	66,118	76.3	894	1.0	86,662
.2	13,607	15.4	418	.5	590	.7	14,771	16.7	70,708	80.2	2,726	3.1	88,205
(12 INSTITUTIONS)													
.2	233	.9	17,840	65.7	717	2.8	18,849	73.6	5,388	21.0	1,366	5.3	25,603
.2	95	.8	8,801	70.6	308	2.5	9,230	74.1	2,644	21.2	587	4.7	12,461
.3	138	1.1	9,039	68.8	409	3.1	9,619	73.2	2,744	20.9	779	5.9	13,142
.1	369	2.8	7,868	59.3	520	3.9	8,776	66.2	4,184	31.6	297	2.2	13,257
.1	75	1.3	3,410	60.5	233	4.1	3,725	66.1	1,768	31.4	141	2.5	5,634
.2	294	3.9	4,458	58.5	287	3.8	5,051	66.3	2,416	31.7	156	2.0	7,623
.2	602	1.5	25,708	66.2	1,237	3.2	27,625	71.1	9,572	24.6	1,663	4.3	38,860
.2	170	.9	12,211	67.5	541	3.0	12,955	71.6	4,412	24.4	728	4.0	18,095
.2	432	2.1	13,497	65.0	696	3.4	14,670	70.6	5,160	24.8	935	4.5	20,765
.0	16	.8	763	37.9	35	1.7	814	40.9	1,040	51.7	157	7.8	2,011
.0	6	.6	397	42.0	16	1.7	419	44.3	479	50.7	47	5.0	945
.0	10	.9	366	34.3	19	1.8	395	37.1	561	52.6	110	10.3	1,066
.2	9	.5	760	42.1	20	1.1	793	43.9	918	50.9	94	5.2	1,805
.4	2	.3	326	42.7	7	.9	338	44.3	396	51.9	29	3.8	763
.1	7	.7	434	41.7	13	1.2	455	43.7	522	50.1	65	6.2	1,042
.1	25	.7	1,523	39.9	55	1.4	1,607	42.1	1,958	51.3	251	6.6	3,816
.1	8	.5	723	42.3	23	1.3	757	44.3	875	51.2	76	4.4	1,708
.0	17	.8	800	38.0	32	1.5	850	40.3	1,083	51.4	175	8.3	2,108
.0	0	.0	348	74.0	3	.6	351	74.7	108	23.0	11	2.3	470
.0	0	.0	100	65.8	2	1.3	102	67.1	48	31.6	2	1.3	152
.0	0	.0	248	78.0	1	.3	249	78.3	60	18.9	9	2.8	318
.0	0	.0	12	60.0	0	.0	12	60.0	8	40.0	0	.0	20
.0	0	.0	8	80.0	0	.0	8	80.0	2	20.0	0	.0	10
.0	0	.0	4	40.0	0	.0	4	40.0	6	60.0	0	.0	10
.0	0	.0	360	73.5	3	.6	363	74.1	116	23.7	11	2.2	490
.0	0	.0	108	66.7	2	1.2	110	67.9	50	30.9	2	1.2	162
.0	0	.0	252	76.8	1	.3	253	77.1	66	20.1	9	2.7	328
.2	249	.9	18,951	67.5	755	2.7	20,014	71.3	6,536	23.3	1,534	5.5	28,084
.2	101	.7	9,298	68.6	326	2.4	9,751	71.9	3,171	23.4	636	4.7	13,558
.2	148	1.0	9,653	66.5	429	3.0	10,263	70.7	3,365	23.2	898	6.2	14,526
.2	378	2.5	8,640	57.3	540	3.6	9,581	63.5	5,110	33.9	391	2.6	15,082
.2	77	1.2	3,744	58.4	240	3.7	4,071	63.5	2,166	33.8	170	2.7	6,407
.1	301	3.5	4,896	56.4	300	3.5	5,510	63.5	2,944	33.9	221	2.5	8,675
.2	627	1.5	27,591	63.9	1,295	3.0	29,595	68.6	11,646	27.0	1,925	4.5	43,166
.2	178	.9	13,042	65.3	566	2.8	13,822	69.2	5,337	26.7	806	4.0	19,965
.2	449	1.9	14,549	62.7	729	3.1	15,773	68.0	6,309	27.2	1,119	4.8	23,201
.3	93	2.1	2,405	55.0	141	3.2	2,650	60.7	1,631	37.3	88	2.0	4,369
.1	26	1.1	1,347	55.1	64	2.6	1,440	58.9	960	39.3	43	1.8	2,443
.4	67	3.5	1,058	54.9	77	4.0	1,210	62.8	671	34.8	45	2.3	1,926
.2	720	1.5	29,996	63.1	1,436	3.0	32,245	67.8	13,277	27.9	2,013	4.2	47,535
.2	204	.9	14,389	64.2	630	2.8	15,262	68.1	6,297	28.1	849	3.8	22,408
.2	516	2.1	15,607	62.1	806	3.2	16,983	67.6	6,980	27.8	1,164	4.6	25,127

MAJOR FIELD 9999 - SUMMARY

	AMERICAN INDIAN ALASKAN NATIVE		BLACK NON-HISPANIC		ASIAN OR PACIFIC ISLANDER		HISPANIC		TOTAL MINORITY		WHITE NON-HISPANIC		NON-RESIDENT ALIEN	
	NUMBER	%	NUMBER	%	NUMBER	%	NUMBER	%	NUMBER	%	NUMBER	%	NUMBER	%
IDAHO (9 INSTITUTIONS)														
UNDERGRADUATES:														
FULL-TIME	161	.7	139	.6	280	1.1	204	.8	784	3.2	23,409	95.0	448	1.8
FEMALE	91	.8	26	.2	111	.9	106	.9	334	2.8	11,242	95.4	211	1.8
MALE	70	.5	113	.9	169	1.3	98	.8	450	3.5	12,167	94.7	237	1.8
PART-TIME	46	.6	35	.5	54	.7	78	1.0	213	2.8	7,417	96.7	30	.5
FEMALE	35	.8	15	.4	29	.7	39	.9	118	2.8	4,129	96.7	24	.6
MALE	11	.3	20	.6	25	.7	39	1.1	95	2.8	3,288	96.8	14	.4
TOTAL	207	.6	174	.5	334	1.0	282	.9	997	3.1	30,826	95.4	486	1.5
FEMALE	126	.8	41	.3	140	.9	145	.9	452	2.8	15,371	95.7	235	1.5
MALE	81	.5	133	.8	194	1.2	137	.8	545	3.4	15,455	95.1	251	1.5
GRADUATE:														
FULL-TIME	5	.5	9	.9	17	1.8	8	.8	39	4.0	862	89.3	64	6.6
FEMALE	1	.4	1	.4	4	1.4	2	.7	8	2.8	263	92.6	13	4.6
MALE	4	.6	8	1.2	13	1.9	6	.9	31	4.6	599	88.0	51	7.5
PART-TIME	12	.6	8	.4	21·	1.0	19	.9	60	2.8	2,071	96.2	21	1.0
FEMALE	7	.6	4	.4	9	.8	11	1.0	31	2.8	1,070	96.9	3	.3
MALE	5	.5	4	.4	12	1.1	8	.8	29	2.8	1,001	95.5	18	1.7
TOTAL	17	.5	17	.5	38	1.2	27	.9	99	3.2	2,933	94.1	85	2.7
FEMALE	8	.6	5	.4	13	.9	13	.9	39	2.8	1,333	96.0	16	1.2
MALE	9	.5	12	.7	25	1.4	14	.8	60	3.5	1,600	92.5	69	4.0
PROFESSIONAL:														
FULL-TIME	0	.0	1	.4	2	.8	0	.0	3	1.1	259	98.9	0	.0
FEMALE	0	.0	1	2.1	1	2.1	0	.0	2	4.3	45	95.7	0	.0
MALE	0	.0	0	.0	1	.5	0	.0	1	.5	214	99.5	0	.0
PART-TIME	0	.0	0	.0	0	.0	0	.0	0	.0	8	100.0	0	.0
FEMALE	0	.0	0	.0	0	.0	0	.0	0	.0	3	100.0	0	.0
MALE	0	.0	0	.0	0	.0	0	.0	0	.0	5	100.0	0	.0
TOTAL	0	.0	1	.4	2	.7	0	.0	3	1.1	267	98.9	0	.0
FEMALE	0	.0	1	2.0	1	2.0	0	.0	2	4.0	48	96.0	0	.0
MALE	0	.0	0	.0	1	.5	0	.0	1	.5	219	99.5	0	.0
UND+GRAD+PROF:														
FULL-TIME	166	.6	149	.6	299	1.2	212	.8	826	3.2	24,530	94.8	512	2.0
FEMALE	92	.8	28	.2	116	1.0	108	.9	344	2.8	11,550	95.3	224	1.8
MALE	74	.5	121	.9	183	1.3	104	.8	482	3.5	12,980	94.6	288	2.1
PART-TIME	58	.6	43	.4	75	.8	97	1.0	273	2.8	9,496	96.6	59	.6
FEMALE	42	.8	19	.4	38	.7	50	.9	149	2.8	5,202	96.7	27	.5
MALE	16	.4	24	.5	37	.8	47	1.1	124	2.8	4,294	96.5	32	.7
TOTAL	224	.6	192	.5	374	1.0	309	.9	1,099	3.1	34,026	95.3	571	1.6
FEMALE	134	.8	47	.3	154	.9	158	.9	493	2.8	16,752	95.7	251	1.4
MALE	90	.5	145	.8	220	1.2	151	.8	606	3.3	17,274	94.9	320	1.8
UNCLASSIFIED:														
TOTAL	30	.8	9	.3	50	1.4	32	.9	121	3.4	3,434	96.5	4	.1
FEMALE	14	.8	2	.1	24	1.3	13	.7	53	3.0	1,732	96.9	3	.2
MALE	16	.9	7	.4	26	1.5	19	1.1	68	3.8	1,702	96.1	1	.1
TOTAL ENROLLMENT:														
TOTAL	254	.6	201	.5	424	1.1	341	.9	1,220	3.1	37,460	95.4	575	1.5
FEMALE	148	.8	49	.3	178	.9	171	.9	546	2.8	18,484	95.9	254	1.3
MALE	106	.5	152	.8	246	1.2	170	.9	674	3.4	18,976	95.0	321	1.6
ILLINOIS (154 INSTITUTIONS)														
UNDERGRADUATES:														
FULL-TIME	754	.3	39,619	14.5	4,058	1.5	6,349	2.3	50,780	18.6	217,513	79.5	5,235	1.9
FEMALE	359	.3	23,684	17.8	1,794	1.4	3,172	2.4	29,009	21.8	102,424	77.1	1,442	1.1
MALE	395	.3	15,935	11.3	2,264	1.6	3,177	2.3	21,771	15.5	115,089	81.8	3,793	2.7
PART-TIME	913	.5	26,262	13.9	2,331	1.2	4,798	2.5	34,304	18.2	152,322	80.7	2,205	1.2
FEMALE	502	.5	16,020	14.9	1,191	1.1	2,255	2.1	19,968	18.5	86,834	80.6	992	.9
MALE	411	.5	10,242	12.6	1,140	1.4	2,543	3.1	14,336	17.7	65,488	80.8	1,213	1.5
TOTAL	1,667	.4	65,881	14.2	6,389	1.4	11,147	2.4	85,084	18.4	369,835	80.0	7,440	1.6
FEMALE	861	.4	39,704	16.5	2,985	1.2	5,427	2.3	48,977	20.4	189,258	78.6	2,434	1.0
MALE	806	.4	26,177	11.8	3,404	1.5	5,720	2.6	36,107	16.3	180,577	81.5	5,006	2.3
GRADUATE:														
FULL-TIME	34	.2	1,032	4.8	507	2.3	311	1.4	1,884	8.7	16,802	77.5	2,996	13.8
FEMALE	10	.1	569	7.2	174	2.2	131	1.7	884	11.1	6,401	80.7	650	8.2
MALE	24	.2	463	3.4	333	2.4	180	1.3	1,000	7.3	10,401	75.7	2,346	17.1
PART-TIME	76	.2	2,915	8.0	738	2.0	378	1.0	4,107	11.3	30,963	85.3	1,239	3.4
FEMALE	37	.2	1,739	10.6	230	1.4	177	1.1	2,183	13.3	13,890	84.6	351	2.1
MALE	39	.2	1,176	5.9	508	2.6	201	1.0	1,924	9.7	17,073	85.9	888	4.5
TOTAL	110	.2	3,947	6.8	1,245	2.1	689	1.2	5,991	10.3	47,765	82.4	4,235	7.3
FEMALE	47	.2	2,308	9.5	404	1.7	308	1.3	3,067	12.6	20,291	83.3	1,001	4.1
MALE	63	.2	1,639	4.9	841	2.5	381	1.1	2,924	8.7	27,474	81.7	3,234	9.6
PROFESSIONAL:														
FULL-TIME	29	.2	544	3.5	258	1.7	187	1.2	1,018	6.5	14,366	92.4	162	1.0
FEMALE	9	.3	223	6.4	62	1.8	42	1.2	336	9.6	3,144	89.7	26	.7
MALE	20	.2	321	2.7	196	1.6	145	1.2	682	5.7	11,222	93.2	136	1.1

SUMMARY

INDIAN NATIVE	BLACK NON-HISPANIC		ASIAN OR PACIFIC ISLANDER		HISPANIC		TOTAL MINORITY		WHITE NON-HISPANIC		NON-RESIDENT ALIEN		TOTAL
%	NUMBER	%	NUMBER	%	NUMBER	%	NUMBER	%	NUMBER	%	NUMBER	%	NUMBER

CONTINUED

%	NUMBER	%	NUMBER	%	NUMBER	%	NUMBER	%	NUMBER	%	NUMBER	%	NUMBER
.1	75	4.4	22	1.3	16	.9	114	6.7	1,570	92.5	13	.8	1,697
.2	23	5.2	4	.9	2	.5	30	6.8	408	92.7	2	.5	440
.0	52	4.1	18	1.4	14	1.1	84	6.7	1,162	92.4	11	.9	1,257
.2	619	3.6	280	1.6	203	1.2	1,132	6.6	15,936	92.4	175	1.0	17,243
.3	246	6.2	66	1.7	44	1.1	366	9.3	3,552	90.0	28	.7	3,946
.2	373	2.8	214	1.6	159	1.2	766	5.8	12,384	93.1	147	1.1	13,297
.3	41,195	13.3	4,823	1.6	6,847	2.2	53,682	17.3	248,681	80.0	8,393	2.7	310,756
.3	24,476	17.0	2,030	1.4	3,345	2.3	30,229	20.9	111,969	77.6	2,118	1.5	144,316
.3	16,719	10.0	2,793	1.7	3,502	2.1	23,453	14.1	136,712	82.1	6,275	3.8	166,440
.4	29,252	12.9	3,091	1.4	5,192	2.3	38,525	17.0	184,855	81.5	3,457	1.5	226,837
.4	17,782	14.3	1,425	1.1	2,634	2.0	22,181	17.8	101,132	81.1	1,345	1.1	124,658
.4	11,470	11.2	1,666	1.6	2,758	2.7	16,344	16.0	83,723	81.9	2,112	2.1	102,179
.3	70,447	13.1	7,914	1.5	12,039	2.2	92,207	17.2	433,536	80.6	11,850	2.2	537,593
.3	42,258	15.7	3,455	1.3	5,779	2.1	52,410	19.5	213,101	79.2	3,463	1.3	268,974
.3	28,189	10.5	4,459	1.7	6,260	2.3	39,797	14.8	220,435	82.1	8,387	3.1	268,619
.3	6,389	8.7	1,477	2.0	1,870	2.5	9,981	13.5	62,423	84.6	1,415	1.9	73,819
.3	3,851	8.8	798	1.8	969	2.2	5,757	13.2	37,254	85.3	639	1.5	43,650
.4	2,538	8.4	679	2.3	901	3.0	4,224	14.0	25,169	83.4	776	2.6	30,169
.3	76,836	12.6	9,391	1.5	13,909	2.3	102,188	16.7	495,959	81.1	13,265	2.2	611,412
.3	46,109	14.7	4,253	1.4	6,748	2.2	58,167	18.6	250,355	80.1	4,102	1.3	312,624
.3	30,327	10.3	5,138	1.7	7,161	2.4	44,021	14.7	245,604	82.2	9,163	3.1	298,788

(66 INSTITUTIONS)

%	NUMBER	%	NUMBER	%	NUMBER	%	NUMBER	%	NUMBER	%	NUMBER	%	NUMBER
.2	6,996	5.3	688	.5	1,197	.9	9,097	6.9	120,004	91.6	1,973	1.5	131,074
.1	3,760	6.1	321	.5	510	.8	4,678	7.6	56,736	91.6	545	.9	61,959
.2	3,236	4.7	367	.5	687	1.0	4,419	6.4	63,268	91.5	1,428	2.1	69,115
.3	3,445	8.0	195	.5	467	1.1	4,250	9.8	38,826	89.6	244	.6	43,320
.3	2,017	9.3	98	.5	232	1.1	2,407	11.1	19,227	88.4	124	.6	21,758
.4	1,428	6.6	97	.4	235	1.1	1,843	8.5	19,599	90.9	120	.6	21,562
.2	10,441	6.0	883	.5	1,664	1.0	13,347	7.7	158,830	91.1	2,217	1.3	174,394
.2	5,777	6.9	419	.5	742	.9	7,085	8.5	75,963	90.7	669	.8	83,717
.2	4,664	5.1	464	.5	922	1.0	6,262	6.9	82,867	91.4	1,548	1.7	90,677
.3	290	2.7	68	.8	120	1.1	532	5.0	8,582	80.9	1,500	14.1	10,614
.5	150	3.9	37	1.0	40	1.0	246	6.4	3,291	85.2	324	8.4	3,861
.2	140	2.1	51	.8	80	1.2	286	4.2	5,291	78.4	1,176	17.4	6,753
.2	644	3.6	91	.5	70	.4	834	4.6	16,653	92.4	532	3.0	18,019
.2	402	4.1	38	.4	35	.4	495	5.0	9,167	93.2	178	1.8	9,840
.1	242	3.0	53	.6	35	.4	339	4.1	7,486	91.5	354	4.3	8,179
.2	934	3.3	179	.6	190	.7	1,366	4.8	25,235	88.1	2,032	7.1	28,633
.3	552	4.0	75	.5	75	.5	741	5.4	12,458	90.9	502	3.7	13,701
.2	382	2.6	104	.7	115	.8	625	4.2	12,777	85.6	1,530	10.2	14,932
.3	153	3.0	37	.7	68	1.3	274	5.3	4,775	93.2	77	1.5	5,126
.2	64	6.2	7	.7	14	1.4	87	8.4	932	90.1	15	1.5	1,034
.3	89	2.2	30	.7	54	1.3	187	4.6	3,843	93.9	62	1.5	4,092
.3	23	2.4	4	.4	5	.5	35	3.6	897	93.5	27	2.8	959
.9	8	3.6	0	.0	1	.5	11	5.0	206	92.8	5	2.3	222
.1	15	2.0	4	.5	4	.5	24	3.3	691	93.8	22	3.0	737
.3	176	2.9	41	.7	73	1.2	309	5.1	5,672	93.2	104	1.7	6,085
.3	72	5.7	7	.6	15	1.2	98	7.8	1,138	90.6	20	1.6	1,256
.3	104	2.2	34	.7	58	1.2	211	4.4	4,534	93.9	84	1.7	4,829
.2	7,439	5.1	813	.6	1,385	.9	9,903	6.7	133,361	90.8	3,550	2.4	146,814
.2	3,974	5.9	365	.5	564	.8	5,011	7.5	60,959	91.2	884	1.3	66,854
.2	3,465	4.3	448	.6	821	1.0	4,892	6.1	72,402	90.5	2,666	3.3	79,960
.2	4,112	6.6	290	.5	542	.9	5,119	8.2	56,376	90.5	803	1.3	62,298
.3	2,427	7.6	136	.4	268	.8	2,913	9.2	28,600	89.9	307	1.0	31,820
.3	1,685	5.5	154	.5	274	.9	2,206	7.2	27,776	91.1	496	1.6	30,478
.2	11,551	5.5	1,103	.5	1,927	.9	15,022	7.2	189,737	90.7	4,353	2.1	209,112
.2	6,401	6.5	501	.5	832	.8	7,924	8.0	89,559	90.8	1,191	1.2	98,674
.2	5,150	4.7	602	.5	1,095	1.0	7,098	6.4	100,178	90.7	3,162	2.9	110,438
.3	826	6.0	102	.7	134	1.0	1,105	8.1	12,300	89.9	274	2.0	13,679
.4	535	6.6	44	.5	68	.8	676	8.4	7,258	90.1	121	1.5	8,055
.2	291	5.2	58	1.0	66	1.2	429	7.6	5,042	89.7	153	2.7	5,624
.2	12,377	5.6	1,205	.5	2,061	.9	16,127	7.2	202,037	90.7	4,627	2.1	222,791
.2	6,936	6.5	545	.5	900	.8	8,600	8.1	96,817	90.7	1,312	1.2	106,729
.2	5,441	4.7	660	.6	1,161	1.0	7,527	6.5	105,220	90.7	3,315	2.9	116,062

TABLE 17 - TOTAL ENROLLMENT IN INSTITUTIONS OF HIGHER EDUCATION FOR SELECTED MAJOR FIELDS OF STUDY AND LEVEL OF ENROLLMENT
         BY RACE, ETHNICITY, AND SEX: STATE, 1978

MAJOR FIELD 9999 - SUMMARY

	AMERICAN INDIAN ALASKAN NATIVE		BLACK NON-HISPANIC		ASIAN OR PACIFIC ISLANDER		HISPANIC		TOTAL MINORITY		WHITE NON-HISPANIC		NON-RESIDENT ALIEN		TO
	NUMBER	%	NUMBER	%	NUMBER	%	NUMBER	%	NUMBER	%	NUMBER	%	NUMBER	%	NU
IOWA	(	62 INSTITUTIONS)													
UNDERGRADUATES:															
FULL-TIME	267	.3	2,098	2.4	482	.5	440	.5	3,287	3.7	83,901	94.4	1,688	1.9	88
FEMALE	136	.3	843	2.0	208	.5	182	.4	1,369	3.2	41,062	95.6	931	1.2	42
MALE	131	.3	1,255	2.7	274	.6	258	.6	1,918	4.2	42,839	93.3	1,157	2.5	45
PART-TIME	79	.5	309	1.9	98	.6	96	.6	582	3.6	15,306	95.4	163	1.0	16
FEMALE	48	.5	174	1.9	43	.5	49	.5	314	3.5	8,638	95.8	68	.8	9
MALE	31	.4	135	1.9	55	.8	47	.7	268	3.8	6,668	94.8	95	1.4	7
TOTAL	346	.3	2,407	2.3	580	.6	536	.5	3,869	3.7	99,207	94.5	1,851	1.8	104
FEMALE	184	.4	1,017	2.0	251	.5	231	.4	1,683	3.2	49,700	95.6	599	1.2	51
MALE	162	.3	1,390	2.6	329	.6	305	.6	2,186	4.1	49,507	93.5	1,252	2.4	52
GRADUATE:															
FULL-TIME	9	.2	149	2.7	63	1.2	36	.7	257	4.7	4,381	80.4	814	14.9	5
FEMALE	3	.2	86	4.4	19	1.0	16	.8	124	6.4	1,639	84.3	181	9.3	1
MALE	6	.2	63	1.8	44	1.3	20	.6	133	3.8	2,742	78.2	633	18.0	3
PART-TIME	16	.2	145	1.7	51	.6	20	.2	232	2.7	7,831	91.6	488	5.7	8
FEMALE	10	.2	71	1.6	24	.5	9	.2	114	2.6	4,183	94.6	126	2.8	4
MALE	6	.1	74	1.8	27	.7	11	.3	118	2.9	3,648	88.4	362	8.8	4
TOTAL	25	.2	294	2.1	114	.8	56	.4	489	3.5	12,212	87.2	1,302	9.3	14
FEMALE	13	.2	157	2.5	43	.7	25	.4	238	3.7	5,822	91.4	307	4.8	6
MALE	12	.2	137	1.8	71	.9	31	.4	251	3.3	6,390	83.7	995	13.0	7
PROFESSIONAL:															
FULL-TIME	27	.5	64	1.1	34	.6	47	.8	172	3.0	5,347	92.2	280	4.8	5
FEMALE	4	.4	16	1.6	11	1.1	7	.7	38	3.7	960	93.0	34	3.3	1
MALE	23	.4	48	1.0	23	.5	40	.8	134	2.8	4,387	92.0	246	5.2	4
PART-TIME	0	.0	2	5.4	0	.0	1	2.7	3	8.1	34	91.9	0	.0	
FEMALE	0	.0	0	.0	0	.0	0	.0	0	.0	14	100.0	0	.0	
MALE	0	.0	2	8.7	0	.0	1	4.3	3	13.0	20	87.0	0	.0	
TOTAL	27	.5	66	1.1	34	.6	48	.8	175	3.0	5,381	92.2	280	4.8	5
FEMALE	4	.4	16	1.5	11	1.1	7	.7	38	3.6	974	93.1	34	3.3	1
MALE	23	.4	50	1.0	23	.5	41	.9	137	2.9	4,407	92.0	246	5.1	4
UND+GRAD+PROF:															
FULL-TIME	303	.3	2,311	2.3	579	.6	523	.5	3,716	3.7	93,629	93.5	2,782	2.8	100
FEMALE	143	.3	945	2.1	238	.5	205	.4	1,531	3.3	43,661	95.0	746	1.6	45
MALE	160	.3	1,366	2.5	341	.6	318	.6	2,185	4.0	49,968	92.2	2,036	3.8	54
PART-TIME	95	.4	456	1.9	149	.6	117	.5	817	3.3	23,171	94.0	651	2.6	24
FEMALE	58	.4	245	1.8	67	.5	58	.4	428	3.2	12,835	95.4	194	1.4	13
MALE	37	.3	211	1.9	82	.7	59	.5	389	3.5	10,336	92.4	457	4.1	11
TOTAL	398	.3	2,767	2.2	728	.6	640	.5	4,533	3.6	116,800	93.6	3,433	2.8	124
FEMALE	201	.3	1,190	2.0	305	.5	263	.4	1,959	3.3	56,496	95.1	940	1.6	59
MALE	197	.3	1,577	2.4	423	.6	377	.6	2,574	3.9	60,304	92.2	2,493	3.8	65
UNCLASSIFIED:															
TOTAL	17	.4	66	1.5	11	.2	10	.2	104	2.4	4,206	95.3	105	2.4	4
FEMALE	10	.4	35	1.3	7	.3	8	.3	60	2.2	2,664	96.2	45	1.6	2
MALE	7	.4	31	1.9	4	.2	2	.1	44	2.7	1,542	93.7	60	3.6	1
TOTAL ENROLLMENT:															
TOTAL	415	.3	2,833	2.2	739	.6	650	.5	4,637	3.6	121,006	93.7	3,538	2.7	129
FEMALE	211	.3	1,225	2.0	312	.5	271	.4	2,019	3.2	59,160	95.2	985	1.6	62
MALE	204	.3	1,608	2.4	427	.6	379	.6	2,618	3.9	61,846	92.3	2,553	3.8	67
KANSAS	(	52 INSTITUTIONS)													
UNDERGRADUATES:															
FULL-TIME	1,197	1.7	3,437	4.9	360	.5	1,002	1.4	5,996	8.5	62,926	88.8	1,932	2.7	70
FEMALE	606	1.8	1,500	4.5	135	.4	432	1.3	2,673	8.0	30,475	90.9	378	1.1	33
MALE	591	1.6	1,937	5.2	225	.6	570	1.5	3,323	8.9	32,451	86.9	1,554	4.2	37
PART-TIME	228	1.8	1,316	4.9	124	.5	423	1.6	2,091	7.8	24,694	91.6	160	.6	26
FEMALE	105	.7	596	4.0	63	.4	196	1.3	960	6.4	13,944	93.3	43	.3	14
MALE	123	1.0	720	6.0	61	.5	227	1.9	1,131	9.4	10,750	89.6	117	1.0	11
TOTAL	1,425	1.5	4,753	4.9	484	.5	1,425	1.5	8,087	8.3	87,620	89.6	2,092	2.1	97
FEMALE	711	1.5	2,096	4.3	198	.4	628	1.3	3,633	7.5	44,419	91.6	421	.9	48
MALE	714	1.4	2,657	5.4	286	.6	797	1.6	4,454	9.0	43,201	87.6	1,671	3.4	49
GRADUATE:															
FULL-TIME	26	.5	139	2.9	36	.8	60	1.3	261	5.5	3,658	76.8	847	17.8	4
FEMALE	10	.5	73	3.7	18	.9	32	1.6	133	6.7	1,657	83.4	198	10.0	1
MALE	16	.6	66	2.4	18	.6	28	1.0	128	4.6	2,001	72.0	649	23.4	2
PART-TIME	41	.3	285	2.3	61	.5	90	.7	477	3.9	11,268	92.8	401	3.3	12
FEMALE	19	.3	167	2.4	24	.3	37	.5	247	3.5	6,593	94.6	132	1.9	6
MALE	22	.4	118	2.3	37	.7	53	1.0	230	4.4	4,675	90.4	269	5.2	5
TOTAL	67	.4	424	2.5	97	.6	150	.9	738	4.4	14,926	88.3	1,248	7.4	16
FEMALE	29	.3	240	2.7	42	.5	69	.8	380	4.2	8,250	92.1	330	3.7	8
MALE	38	.5	184	2.3	55	.7	81	1.0	358	4.5	6,676	84.0	918	11.5	7
PROFESSIONAL:															
FULL-TIME	7	.3	42	1.9	14	.6	33	1.5	96	4.4	2,108	95.6	0	.0	2
FEMALE	0	.0	14	2.9	3	.6	11	2.3	28	5.8	456	94.2	0	.0	
MALE	7	.4	28	1.6	11	.6	22	1.3	68	4.0	1,652	96.0	0	.0	1

672

SUMMARY

INDIAN NATIVE		BLACK NON-HISPANIC		ASIAN OR PACIFIC ISLANDER		HISPANIC		TOTAL MINORITY		WHITE NON-HISPANIC		NON-RESIDENT ALIEN		TOTAL
%	NUMBER	%	NUMBER	%	NUMBER	%	NUMBER	%	NUMBER	%	NUMBER	%	NUMBER	%	NUMBER

CONTINUED

.0	2	3.8	1	1.9	2	3.8	5	9.4	48	90.6	0	.0	53
.0	1	12.5	1	12.5	0	.0	2	25.0	6	75.0	0	.0	8
.0	1	2.2	0	.0	2	4.4	3	6.7	42	93.3	0	.0	45
.3	44	1.9	15	.7	35	1.6	101	4.5	2,156	95.5	0	.0	2,257
.0	15	3.0	4	.8	11	2.2	30	6.1	462	93.9	0	.0	492
.4	29	1.6	11	.6	24	1.4	71	4.0	1,694	96.0	0	.0	1,765
1.6	3,618	4.6	410	.5	1,095	1.4	6,353	8.2	68,692	88.3	2,779	3.6	77,824
1.7	1,587	4.4	156	.4	475	1.3	2,834	7.9	32,588	90.5	576	1.6	35,998
1.5	2,031	4.9	254	.6	620	1.5	3,519	8.4	36,104	86.3	2,203	5.3	41,826
.7	1,603	4.1	186	.5	515	1.3	2,573	6.6	36,010	92.0	561	1.4	39,144
.6	764	3.5	88	.4	233	1.1	1,209	5.5	20,543	93.7	175	.8	21,927
.8	839	4.9	98	.6	282	1.6	1,364	7.9	15,467	89.8	386	2.2	17,217
1.3	5,221	4.5	596	.5	1,610	1.4	8,926	7.6	104,702	89.5	3,340	2.9	116,968
1.3	2,351	4.1	244	.4	708	1.2	4,043	7.0	53,131	91.7	751	1.3	57,925
1.3	2,870	4.9	352	.6	902	1.5	4,883	8.3	51,571	87.3	2,589	4.4	59,043
.9	472	4.6	108	1.0	108	1.0	778	7.5	9,276	89.6	301	2.9	10,355
.9	234	4.0	55	.9	60	1.0	403	6.9	5,327	91.3	102	1.7	5,832
.8	238	5.3	53	1.2	48	1.1	375	8.3	3,949	87.3	199	4.4	4,523
1.2	5,693	4.5	704	.6	1,718	1.3	9,704	7.6	113,978	89.5	3,641	2.9	127,323
1.2	2,585	4.1	299	.5	768	1.2	4,446	7.0	58,458	91.7	853	1.3	63,757
1.3	3,108	4.9	405	.6	950	1.5	5,258	8.3	55,520	87.3	2,788	4.4	63,566

(42 INSTITUTIONS)

.2	6,310	8.0	427	.5	197	.3	7,076	9.0	70,186	89.4	1,232	1.6	78,494
.2	3,359	8.4	177	.4	86	.2	3,696	9.3	35,808	90.1	259	.7	39,763
.2	2,951	7.6	250	.6	111	.3	3,380	8.7	34,378	88.8	973	2.5	38,731
.2	1,580	6.7	83	.4	82	.3	1,788	7.6	21,627	91.9	118	.5	23,533
.2	935	7.1	38	.3	35	.3	1,029	7.8	12,172	91.9	38	.3	13,239
.2	645	6.3	45	.4	47	.5	759	7.4	9,455	91.8	80	.8	10,294
.2	7,890	7.7	510	.5	279	.3	8,864	8.7	91,813	90.0	1,350	1.3	102,027
.2	4,294	8.1	215	.4	121	.2	4,725	8.9	47,980	90.5	297	.6	53,002
.2	3,596	7.3	295	.6	158	.3	4,139	8.4	43,833	89.4	1,053	2.1	49,025
1.6	102	2.5	48	1.2	29	.7	243	6.0	3,458	85.4	350	8.6	4,051
1.9	57	3.0	15	.8	10	.5	118	6.1	1,725	89.9	76	4.0	1,919
1.3	45	2.1	33	1.5	19	.9	125	5.9	1,733	81.3	274	12.9	2,132
.3	429	3.3	45	.3	28	.2	548	4.2	12,490	94.7	157	1.2	13,195
.3	266	3.1	15	.2	13	.2	321	3.8	8,172	95.9	28	.3	8,521
.4	163	3.5	30	.6	15	.3	227	4.9	4,318	92.4	129	2.8	4,674
.6	531	3.1	93	.5	57	.3	791	4.6	15,948	92.5	507	2.9	17,246
.6	323	3.1	30	.3	23	.2	439	4.2	9,897	94.8	104	1.0	10,440
.7	208	3.1	63	.9	34	.5	352	5.2	6,051	88.9	403	5.9	6,806
.2	87	2.1	76	1.8	17	.4	188	4.5	3,995	95.1	18	.4	4,201
.2	24	2.8	19	2.2	4	.5	49	5.7	802	93.9	3	.4	854
.2	63	1.9	57	1.7	13	.4	139	4.2	3,193	95.4	15	.4	3,347
1.7	11	4.6	1	.4	2	.8	18	7.5	220	91.7	2	.8	240
.0	4	8.9	0	.0	0	.0	4	8.9	40	88.9	1	2.2	45
2.1	7	3.6	1	.5	2	1.0	14	7.2	180	92.3	1	.5	195
.3	98	2.2	77	1.7	19	.4	206	4.6	4,215	94.9	20	.5	4,441
.2	28	3.1	19	2.1	4	.4	53	5.9	842	93.7	4	.4	899
.3	70	2.0	58	1.6	15	.4	153	4.3	3,373	95.2	16	.5	3,542
.2	6,499	7.5	551	.6	243	.3	7,507	8.7	77,639	89.5	1,600	1.8	86,746
.3	3,440	8.1	211	.5	100	.2	3,863	9.1	38,335	90.1	338	.8	42,536
.2	3,059	6.9	340	.8	143	.3	3,644	8.2	39,304	88.9	1,262	2.9	44,210
.2	2,020	5.5	129	.3	112	.3	2,354	6.4	34,337	92.9	277	.7	36,968
.2	1,205	5.5	53	.2	48	.2	1,354	6.2	20,384	93.5	67	.3	21,805
.3	815	5.4	76	.5	64	.4	1,000	6.6	13,953	92.0	210	1.4	15,163
.2	8,519	6.9	680	.5	355	.3	9,861	8.0	111,976	90.5	1,877	1.5	123,714
.2	4,645	7.2	264	.4	148	.2	5,217	8.1	58,719	91.3	405	.6	64,341
.2	3,874	6.5	416	.7	207	.3	4,644	7.8	53,257	89.7	1,472	2.5	59,373
.4	401	5.8	34	.5	36	.5	500	7.2	6,376	91.8	69	1.0	6,945
.5	226	5.5	23	.6	26	.6	296	7.2	3,765	92.0	32	.8	4,093
.3	175	6.1	10	.4	10	.4	204	7.2	2,611	91.5	37	1.3	2,852
.3	8,920	6.8	714	.5	391	.3	10,361	7.9	118,352	90.6	1,946	1.5	130,659
.3	4,871	7.1	287	.4	174	.3	5,513	8.1	62,484	91.3	437	.6	68,434
.2	4,049	6.5	427	.7	217	.3	4,848	7.8	55,868	89.8	1,509	2.4	62,225

TABLE 17 - TOTAL ENROLLMENT IN INSTITUTIONS OF HIGHER EDUCATION FOR SELECTED MAJOR FIELDS OF STUDY AND LEVEL OF ENROLLMENT
BY RACE, ETHNICITY, AND SEX: STATE, 1978

MAJOR FIELD 9999 - SUMMARY

	AMERICAN INDIAN ALASKAN NATIVE		BLACK NON-HISPANIC		ASIAN OR PACIFIC ISLANDER		HISPANIC		TOTAL MINORITY		WHITE NON-HISPANIC		NON-RESIDENT ALIEN		TOT
	NUMBER	%	NUMBER	%	NUMBER	%	NUMBER	%	NUMBER	%	NUMBER	%	NUMBER	%	NUM
LOUISIANA	(	32 INSTITUTIONS)													
UNDERGRADUATES:															
FULL-TIME	164	.2	25,408	25.6	447	.5	1,188	1.2	27,207	27.5	68,347	69.0	3,519	3.6	99,
FEMALE	78	.2	15,253	30.9	180	.4	530	1.1	16,041	32.5	32,390	65.7	879	1.8	49,
MALE	86	.2	10,155	20.4	267	.5	658	1.3	11,166	22.4	35,957	72.3	2,640	5.3	49,
PART-TIME	70	.3	4,959	19.0	177	.7	486	1.9	5,692	21.8	20,026	76.7	377	1.4	26,
FEMALE	36	.3	2,643	19.7	80	.6	226	1.7	2,985	22.3	10,235	76.5	163	1.2	13,
MALE	34	.3	2,316	18.2	97	.8	260	2.0	2,707	21.3	9,791	77.0	214	1.7	12,
TOTAL	234	.2	30,367	24.3	624	.5	1,674	1.3	32,899	26.3	88,373	70.6	3,896	3.1	125,
FEMALE	114	.2	17,896	28.5	260	.4	756	1.2	19,026	30.3	42,625	68.0	1,042	1.7	62,
MALE	120	.2	12,471	20.0	364	.6	918	1.5	13,873	22.2	45,748	73.2	2,854	4.6	62,
GRADUATE:															
FULL-TIME	18	.3	389	7.4	31	.6	85	1.6	523	10.0	4,085	77.8	640	12.2	5,
FEMALE	8	.4	246	11.4	5	.2	37	1.7	296	13.8	1,725	80.3	128	6.0	2,
MALE	10	.3	143	4.6	26	.8	48	1.5	227	7.3	2,360	76.2	512	16.5	3,
PART-TIME	19	.2	2,191	19.6	39	.3	150	1.3	2,399	21.4	8,574	76.6	214	1.9	11,
FEMALE	8	.1	1,692	23.6	11	.2	87	1.2	1,798	25.1	5,319	74.2	50	.7	7,
MALE	11	.3	499	12.4	28	.7	63	1.6	601	15.0	3,295	81.0	164	4.1	4,
TOTAL	37	.2	2,580	15.7	70	.4	235	1.4	2,922	17.8	12,659	77.0	854	5.2	16,
FEMALE	16	.2	1,938	20.8	16	.2	124	1.3	2,094	22.5	7,044	75.6	178	1.9	9,
MALE	21	.3	642	9.0	54	.8	111	1.6	828	11.6	5,615	78.9	676	9.5	7,
PROFESSIONAL:															
FULL-TIME	7	.2	235	6.4	27	.7	46	1.2	315	8.5	3,357	91.0	17	.5	3,
FEMALE	2	.3	72	9.0	6	.8	13	1.6	93	11.7	701	88.1	2	.3	
MALE	5	.2	163	5.6	21	.7	33	1.1	222	7.7	2,656	91.8	15	.5	2,
PART-TIME	1	.3	27	9.0	1	.3	6	2.0	35	11.7	265	88.3	0	.0	
FEMALE	1	1.0	6	5.7	0	.0	2	1.9	9	8.6	96	91.4	0	.0	
MALE	0	.0	21	10.8	1	.5	4	2.1	26	13.3	169	86.7	0	.0	
TOTAL	8	.2	262	6.6	28	.7	52	1.3	350	8.8	3,622	90.8	17	.4	3,
FEMALE	3	.3	78	8.7	6	.7	15	1.7	102	11.3	797	88.5	2	.2	
MALE	5	.2	184	6.0	22	.7	37	1.2	248	8.0	2,825	91.5	15	.5	3,
UNDG+GRAD+PROF:															
FULL-TIME	189	.2	26,032	24.1	505	.5	1,319	1.2	28,045	26.0	75,789	70.2	4,176	3.9	108,
FEMALE	88	.2	15,571	29.8	191	.4	580	1.1	16,430	31.4	34,816	66.6	1,009	1.9	52,
MALE	101	.2	10,461	16.8	314	.6	739	1.3	11,615	20.8	40,973	73.5	3,167	5.7	55,
PART-TIME	90	.2	7,177	19.1	217	.6	642	1.7	8,126	21.6	28,865	76.8	591	1.6	37,
FEMALE	45	.2	4,341	21.0	91	.4	315	1.5	4,792	23.2	15,650	75.8	213	1.0	20,
MALE	45	.3	2,836	16.8	126	.7	327	1.9	3,334	19.7	13,215	78.1	378	2.2	16,
TOTAL	279	.2	33,209	22.8	722	.5	1,961	1.3	36,171	24.8	104,654	71.9	4,767	3.3	145,
FEMALE	133	.2	19,912	27.3	282	.4	895	1.2	21,222	29.1	50,466	69.2	1,222	1.7	72,
MALE	146	.2	13,297	18.3	440	.6	1,066	1.5	14,949	20.6	54,188	74.6	3,545	4.9	72,
UNCLASSIFIED:															
TOTAL	11	.2	798	14.5	22	.4	77	1.4	908	16.4	4,532	82.1	81	1.5	5,
FEMALE	7	.2	557	16.8	9	.3	39	1.2	612	18.4	2,668	80.3	44	1.3	3,
MALE	4	.2	241	11.0	13	.6	38	1.7	296	15.3	1,864	84.8	37	1.7	2,
TOTAL ENROLLMENT:															
TOTAL	290	.2	34,007	22.5	744	.5	2,038	1.3	37,079	24.5	109,186	72.3	4,848	3.2	151,
FEMALE	140	.2	20,469	26.9	291	.4	934	1.2	21,834	28.6	53,134	69.7	1,266	1.7	76,
MALE	150	.2	13,538	18.1	453	.6	1,104	1.5	15,245	20.4	56,052	74.9	3,582	4.8	74,
MAINE	(	27 INSTITUTIONS)													
UNDERGRADUATES:															
FULL-TIME	108	.4	141	.5	85	.3	65	.2	399	1.5	25,672	97.9	153	.6	26,
FEMALE	54	.4	54	.4	32	.3	22	.2	162	1.3	12,209	98.1	44	.4	12,
MALE	54	.4	87	.6	53	.4	43	.3	237	1.7	13,463	97.5	109	.8	13,
PART-TIME	29	.7	16	.4	8	.2	6	.2	59	1.5	3,912	98.4	4	.1	3,
FEMALE	19	1.0	7	.4	6	.3	3	.2	35	1.9	1,853	98.1	1	.1	1,
MALE	10	.5	9	.4	2	.1	3	.1	24	1.2	2,059	98.7	3	.1	2,
TOTAL	137	.5	157	.5	93	.3	71	.2	458	1.5	29,584	98.0	157	.5	30,
FEMALE	73	.5	61	.4	38	.3	25	.2	197	1.4	14,062	98.3	45	.3	14,
MALE	64	.4	96	.6	55	.3	46	.3	261	1.6	15,522	97.7	112	.7	15,
GRADUATE:															
FULL-TIME	1	.1	2	.2	2	.2	4	.4	9	1.0	885	97.3	16	1.8	
FEMALE	1	.3	0	.0	1	.3	1	.3	3	.9	339	98.0	4	1.2	
MALE	0	.0	2	.4	1	.2	3	.5	6	1.1	546	96.8	12	2.1	
PART-TIME	1	.1	1	.1	0	.0	2	.2	4	.5	803	98.6	7	.9	
FEMALE	0	.0	0	.0	0	.0	1	.2	1	.2	412	98.6	5	1.2	
MALE	1	.3	1	.3	0	.0	1	.3	3	.8	391	98.7	2	.5	
TOTAL	2	.1	3	.2	2	.1	6	.3	13	.8	1,688	97.9	23	1.3	1,
FEMALE	1	.1	0	.0	1	.1	2	.3	4	.5	751	98.3	9	1.2	
MALE	1	.1	3	.3	1	.1	4	.4	9	.9	937	97.6	14	1.5	
PROFESSIONAL:															
FULL-TIME	0	.0	1	.3	0	.0	1	.3	2	.6	318	99.4	0	.0	
FEMALE	0	.0	0	.0	0	.0	0	.0	0	.0	109	100.0	0	.0	
MALE	0	.0	1	.5	0	.0	1	.5	2	.9	209	99.1	0	.0	

SUMMARY

INDIAN NATIVE	BLACK NON-HISPANIC		ASIAN OR PACIFIC ISLANDER		HISPANIC		TOTAL MINORITY		WHITE NON-HISPANIC		NON-RESIDENT ALIEN		TOTAL
%	NUMBER	%	NUMBER	%	NUMBER	%	NUMBER	%	NUMBER	%	NUMBER	%	NUMBER
CONTINUED													
.0	0	.0	0	.0	0	.0	0	.0	12	100.0	0	.0	12
.0	0	.0	0	.0	0	.0	0	.0	6	100.0	0	.0	6
.0	0	.0	0	.0	0	.0	0	.0	6	100.0	0	.0	6
.0	1	.3	0	.0	1	.3	2	.6	330	99.4	0	.0	332
.0	0	.0	0	.0	0	.0	0	.0	115	100.0	0	.0	115
.0	1	.5	0	.0	1	.5	2	.9	215	99.1	0	.0	217
.4	144	.5	87	.3	70	.3	410	1.5	26,875	97.9	169	.6	27,454
.4	54	.4	33	.3	23	.2	165	1.3	12,657	98.3	48	.4	12,870
.4	90	.6	54	.4	47	.3	245	1.7	14,218	97.5	121	.8	14,584
.8	17	.4	8	.2	8	.2	63	1.3	4,727	98.5	11	.2	4,801
.8	7	.3	6	.3	4	.2	36	1.6	2,271	98.2	6	.3	2,313
.4	10	.4	2	.1	4	.2	27	1.1	2,456	98.7	5	.2	2,488
.4	161	.5	95	.3	78	.2	473	1.5	31,602	98.0	180	.6	32,255
.5	61	.4	39	.3	27	.2	201	1.3	14,928	98.3	54	.4	15,183
.4	100	.6	56	.3	51	.3	272	1.6	16,674	97.7	126	.7	17,012
.2	22	.2	14	.2	4	.0	57	.6	9,116	99.0	32	.3	9,205
.1	5	.1	6	.1	3	.1	20	.4	5,272	99.3	19	.4	5,311
.3	17	.4	8	.2	1	.0	37	1.0	3,844	98.7	13	.3	3,894
.4	183	.4	109	.3	82	.2	530	1.3	40,718	98.2	212	.5	41,460
.4	66	.3	45	.2	30	.1	221	1.1	20,200	98.6	73	.4	20,494
.4	117	.6	64	.3	52	.2	309	1.5	20,518	97.9	139	.7	20,966
(54 INSTITUTIONS)													
.2	18,357	19.4	1,180	1.2	880	.9	20,644	21.8	70,634	74.7	3,219	3.4	94,497
.2	11,216	22.9	533	1.1	437	.9	12,284	25.0	35,623	72.6	1,167	2.4	49,074
.3	7,141	15.7	647	1.4	443	1.0	8,360	18.4	35,011	77.1	2,052	4.5	45,423
.3	13,605	18.3	1,051	1.4	777	1.0	15,682	21.1	57,680	77.6	790	1.1	74,152
.3	8,240	19.5	563	1.3	418	1.0	9,351	22.1	32,589	77.0	406	1.0	42,346
.4	5,365	16.9	488	1.5	359	1.1	6,331	19.9	25,091	78.9	384	1.2	31,806
.3	31,962	19.0	2,231	1.3	1,657	1.0	36,326	21.5	128,314	76.1	4,003	2.4	168,649
.2	19,456	21.3	1,096	1.2	855	.9	21,635	23.7	68,212	74.6	1,573	1.7	91,420
.3	12,506	16.2	1,135	1.5	802	1.0	14,691	19.0	60,102	77.8	2,436	3.2	77,229
.4	452	6.9	95	1.4	64	1.0	628	9.6	5,201	79.3	729	11.1	6,558
.4	278	9.3	48	1.6	36	1.2	373	12.5	2,428	81.3	186	6.2	2,987
.2	174	4.9	47	1.3	28	.8	255	7.1	2,773	77.7	543	15.2	3,571
.3	1,611	11.1	136	.9	97	.7	1,889	13.0	12,208	84.0	441	3.0	14,538
.4	1,056	13.4	71	.9	51	.6	1,206	15.3	6,542	83.1	121	1.5	7,869
.3	555	8.3	65	1.0	46	.7	683	10.2	5,666	85.0	320	4.8	6,669
.3	2,063	9.8	231	1.1	161	.8	2,517	11.9	17,409	82.5	1,170	5.5	21,096
.4	1,334	12.3	119	1.1	87	.8	1,579	14.5	8,970	82.6	307	2.8	10,856
.2	729	7.1	112	1.1	74	.7	938	9.2	8,439	82.4	863	8.4	10,240
.1	202	6.2	75	2.3	26	.8	305	9.3	2,963	90.3	13	.4	3,281
.0	74	9.0	20	2.4	6	.7	100	12.2	718	87.7	1	.1	819
.1	128	5.2	55	2.2	20	.8	205	8.3	2,245	91.2	12	.5	2,462
.0	22	8.3	1	.4	1	.4	24	9.0	238	89.5	4	1.5	266
.0	12	13.5	0	.0	1	1.1	11	14.6	74	83.1	2	2.2	89
.0	10	5.6	1	.6	0	.0	11	6.2	164	92.7	2	1.1	177
.1	224	6.3	76	2.1	27	.8	329	9.3	3,201	90.2	17	.5	3,547
.0	86	9.5	20	2.2	7	.8	113	12.4	792	87.2	3	.3	908
.1	138	5.2	56	2.1	20	.8	216	8.2	2,409	91.3	14	.5	2,639
.2	19,011	18.2	1,350	1.3	970	.9	21,577	20.7	78,798	75.5	3,961	3.8	104,336
.2	11,568	21.9	601	1.1	479	.9	12,757	24.1	38,769	73.3	1,354	2.6	52,880
.3	7,443	14.5	749	1.5	491	1.0	8,820	17.1	40,029	77.8	2,607	5.1	51,456
.3	15,238	17.1	1,188	1.3	875	1.0	17,595	19.8	70,126	78.8	1,235	1.4	88,956
.3	9,308	18.5	634	1.3	470	.9	10,570	21.0	39,205	77.9	529	1.1	50,304
.4	5,930	15.3	554	1.4	405	1.0	7,025	18.2	30,921	80.0	706	1.8	38,652
.3	34,249	17.7	2,538	1.3	1,845	1.0	39,172	20.3	148,924	77.0	5,196	2.7	193,292
.3	20,876	20.2	1,235	1.2	949	.9	23,327	22.6	77,974	75.6	1,883	1.8	103,184
.3	13,373	14.6	1,303	1.4	896	1.0	15,845	17.6	70,950	78.7	3,313	3.7	90,108
.4	3,201	15.1	330	1.6	175	.8	3,785	17.9	16,554	78.2	824	3.9	21,163
.4	1,958	17.1	161	1.4	80	.7	2,246	19.7	8,866	77.6	312	2.7	11,424
.3	1,243	12.8	169	1.7	95	1.0	1,539	15.8	7,688	78.9	512	5.3	9,739
.3	37,450	17.5	2,868	1.3	2,020	.9	42,957	20.0	165,478	77.2	6,020	2.8	214,455
.3	22,834	19.9	1,396	1.2	1,029	.9	25,573	22.3	86,840	75.8	2,195	1.9	114,608
.3	14,410	14.6	1,472	1.5	991	1.0	17,384	17.4	78,638	78.8	3,825	3.8	99,847

TABLE 17 - TOTAL ENROLLMENT IN INSTITUTIONS OF HIGHER EDUCATION FOR SELECTED MAJOR FIELDS OF STUDY AND LEVEL OF ENROLLMENT
BY RACE, ETHNICITY, AND SEX: STATE, 1978

MAJOR FIELD 9999 - SUMMARY

	AMERICAN INDIAN ALASKAN NATIVE		BLACK NON-HISPANIC		ASIAN OR PACIFIC ISLANDER		HISPANIC		TOTAL MINORITY		WHITE NON-HISPANIC		NON-RESIDENT ALIEN	
	NUMBER	%	NUMBER	%	NUMBER	%	NUMBER	%	NUMBER	%	NUMBER	%	NUMBER	%
MASSACHUSETTS	**(119 INSTITUTIONS)**													
UNDERGRADUATES:														
FULL-TIME	962	.4	9,381	4.4	2,959	1.4	3,140	1.5	16,442	7.6	194,271	90.1	4,894	2.3
FEMALE	586	.5	5,277	4.8	1,344	1.2	1,612	1.5	8,819	8.1	98,767	90.3	1,736	1.6
MALE	376	.4	4,104	3.9	1,615	1.5	1,528	1.4	7,623	7.2	95,504	89.9	3,158	3.0
PART-TIME	213	.4	1,511	3.1	1,410	2.9	502	1.0	3,636	7.6	44,106	91.9	246	.5
FEMALE	127	.5	794	3.3	670	2.8	244	1.0	1,835	7.6	22,072	92.0	85	.4
MALE	86	.4	717	3.0	740	3.1	258	1.1	1,801	7.5	22,094	91.8	161	.7
TOTAL	1,175	.4	10,892	4.1	4,369	1.7	3,642	1.4	20,078	7.6	238,437	90.4	5,140	1.9
FEMALE	713	.5	6,071	4.6	2,014	1.5	1,856	1.4	10,654	8.0	120,839	90.6	1,821	1.4
MALE	462	.4	4,821	3.7	2,355	1.8	1,786	1.4	9,424	7.2	117,598	90.2	3,319	2.5
GRADUATE:														
FULL-TIME	35	.2	731	3.3	439	2.0	337	1.5	1,542	7.0	17,491	78.9	3,148	14.2
FEMALE	19	.2	337	3.9	161	1.9	137	1.6	654	7.6	7,287	84.7	666	7.7
MALE	16	.1	394	2.9	278	2.0	200	1.5	888	6.5	10,204	75.2	2,482	18.3
PART-TIME	42	.2	617	2.5	320	1.3	232	1.0	1,211	5.0	22,615	92.8	545	2.2
FEMALE	7	.1	263	2.4	108	1.0	91	.8	469	4.2	10,529	94.1	191	1.7
MALE	35	.3	354	2.7	212	1.6	141	1.1	742	5.6	12,086	91.7	354	2.7
TOTAL	77	.2	1,348	2.9	759	1.6	569	1.2	2,753	5.9	40,106	86.2	3,693	7.9
FEMALE	26	.1	600	3.0	269	1.4	228	1.2	1,123	5.7	17,816	90.0	857	4.3
MALE	51	.2	748	2.8	490	1.8	341	1.3	1,630	6.1	22,290	83.3	2,836	10.6
PROFESSIONAL:														
FULL-TIME	21	.2	399	4.1	153	1.6	176	1.8	749	7.7	8,722	90.1	207	2.1
FEMALE	7	.2	162	5.2	61	2.0	55	1.8	285	9.2	2,779	89.5	42	1.4
MALE	14	.2	237	3.6	92	1.4	121	1.8	464	7.1	5,943	90.4	165	2.5
PART-TIME	4	.3	22	1.4	5	.3	7	.4	38	2.4	1,520	96.8	12	.8
FEMALE	2	.4	8	1.8	3	.7	2	.4	15	3.4	428	96.2	2	.4
MALE	2	.2	14	1.2	2	.2	5	.4	23	2.0	1,092	97.1	10	.9
TOTAL	25	.2	421	3.7	158	1.4	183	1.6	787	7.0	10,242	91.1	219	1.9
FEMALE	9	.3	170	4.8	64	1.8	57	1.6	300	8.4	3,207	90.3	44	1.2
MALE	16	.2	251	3.3	94	1.2	126	1.6	487	6.3	7,035	91.4	175	2.3
UND+GRAD+PROF:														
FULL-TIME	1,018	.4	10,511	4.2	3,551	1.4	3,653	1.5	18,733	7.6	220,484	89.1	8,249	3.3
FEMALE	612	.5	5,776	4.8	1,566	1.3	1,804	1.5	9,758	8.1	108,833	89.9	2,444	2.0
MALE	406	.3	4,735	3.7	1,985	1.6	1,849	1.5	8,975	7.1	111,651	88.3	5,805	4.6
PART-TIME	259	.4	2,150	2.9	1,735	2.3	741	1.0	4,885	6.6	68,301	92.3	803	1.1
FEMALE	136	.4	1,065	3.0	781	2.2	337	.9	2,319	6.5	33,029	92.7	278	.8
MALE	123	.3	1,085	2.8	954	2.5	404	1.1	2,566	6.7	35,272	91.9	525	1.4
TOTAL	1,277	.4	12,661	3.9	5,286	1.6	4,394	1.4	23,618	7.3	288,785	89.8	9,052	2.8
FEMALE	748	.5	6,841	4.4	2,347	1.5	2,141	1.4	12,077	7.7	141,862	90.6	2,722	1.7
MALE	529	.3	5,820	3.5	2,939	1.8	2,253	1.4	11,541	7.0	146,923	89.2	6,330	3.8
UNCLASSIFIED:														
TOTAL	158	.3	1,436	2.3	522	.8	638	1.0	2,754	4.4	59,039	93.6	1,252	2.0
FEMALE	88	.2	834	2.4	301	.9	368	1.0	1,591	4.5	33,282	94.0	533	1.5
MALE	70	.3	602	2.2	221	.8	270	1.0	1,163	4.2	25,757	93.2	719	2.6
TOTAL ENROLLMENT:														
TOTAL	1,435	.4	14,097	3.7	5,808	1.5	5,032	1.3	26,372	6.9	347,824	90.5	10,304	2.7
FEMALE	836	.4	7,675	4.0	2,648	1.4	2,509	1.3	13,668	7.1	175,144	91.2	3,255	1.7
MALE	599	.3	6,422	3.3	3,160	1.6	2,523	1.3	12,704	6.6	172,680	89.7	7,049	3.7
MICHIGAN	**(96 INSTITUTIONS)**													
UNDERGRADUATES:														
FULL-TIME	1,108	.5	23,459	9.9	1,706	.7	2,477	1.0	28,750	12.1	203,084	85.8	4,884	2.1
FEMALE	538	.5	14,281	12.4	731	.6	1,215	1.1	16,765	14.5	97,557	84.4	1,255	1.1
MALE	570	.5	9,178	7.6	975	.8	1,262	1.0	11,985	9.9	105,527	87.1	3,629	3.0
PART-TIME	1,151	.7	17,464	10.5	1,026	.6	2,917	1.8	22,558	13.6	142,989	85.9	836	.5
FEMALE	590	.7	10,029	11.7	469	.5	1,461	1.7	12,549	14.7	72,633	85.0	289	.3
MALE	561	.7	7,435	9.2	557	.7	1,456	1.8	10,009	12.4	70,356	87.0	547	.7
TOTAL	2,259	.6	40,923	10.2	2,732	.7	5,394	1.3	51,308	12.7	346,073	85.9	5,720	1.4
FEMALE	1,128	.6	24,310	12.1	1,200	.6	2,676	1.3	29,314	14.6	170,190	84.7	1,544	.8
MALE	1,131	.6	16,613	8.2	1,532	.8	2,718	1.3	21,994	10.9	175,883	87.0	4,176	2.1
GRADUATE:														
FULL-TIME	58	.3	1,197	6.7	311	1.7	234	1.3	1,800	10.1	13,654	76.5	2,386	13.4
FEMALE	29	.4	742	10.0	103	1.4	95	1.3	969	13.1	5,958	80.5	476	6.4
MALE	29	.3	455	4.4	208	2.0	139	1.3	831	8.0	7,696	73.7	1,910	18.3
PART-TIME	88	.3	1,958	6.3	276	.9	216	.7	2,538	8.2	27,314	88.2	1,113	3.6
FEMALE	47	.3	1,307	7.7	102	.6	114	.7	1,570	9.3	14,954	88.5	367	2.2
MALE	41	.3	651	4.6	174	1.2	102	.7	968	6.9	12,360	87.8	740	5.3
TOTAL	146	.3	3,155	6.5	587	1.2	450	.9	4,338	8.9	40,968	83.9	3,499	7.2
FEMALE	76	.3	2,049	8.4	205	.8	209	.9	2,539	10.5	20,912	86.1	843	3.5
MALE	70	.3	1,106	4.5	382	1.6	241	1.0	1,799	7.3	20,056	81.8	2,656	10.8
PROFESSIONAL:														
FULL-TIME	29	.4	540	5.6	121	1.3	163	1.7	853	8.9	8,400	87.4	356	3.7
FEMALE	9	.4	217	9.3	33	1.4	41	1.8	300	12.9	1,970	84.7	56	2.4
MALE	20	.3	323	4.4	88	1.2	122	1.7	553	7.6	6,430	88.3	300	4.1

SUMMARY

INDIAN NATIVE %	BLACK NON-HISPANIC NUMBER	BLACK NON-HISPANIC %	ASIAN OR PACIFIC ISLANDER NUMBER	ASIAN OR PACIFIC ISLANDER %	HISPANIC NUMBER	HISPANIC %	TOTAL MINORITY NUMBER	TOTAL MINORITY %	WHITE NON-HISPANIC NUMBER	WHITE NON-HISPANIC %	NON-RESIDENT ALIEN NUMBER	NON-RESIDENT ALIEN %	TOTAL NUMBER
CONTINUED													
.0	48	6.7	4	.6	7	1.0	59	8.3	632	88.8	21	2.9	712
.0	14	9.5	1	.7	1	.7	16	10.8	131	88.5	1	.7	148
.0	34	6.0	3	.5	6	1.1	43	7.6	501	88.8	20	3.5	564
.3	586	5.7	125	1.2	170	1.6	912	8.8	9,032	87.5	377	3.7	10,321
.4	231	9.3	34	1.4	42	1.7	316	12.8	2,101	84.9	57	2.3	2,474
.3	357	4.5	91	1.2	128	1.6	596	7.6	6,931	88.3	320	4.1	7,847
.5	25,196	9.5	2,138	.8	2,874	1.1	31,403	11.9	225,138	85.2	7,626	2.9	264,167
.5	15,240	12.2	867	.7	1,351	1.1	18,034	14.4	105,485	84.2	1,787	1.4	125,306
.4	9,956	7.2	1,271	.9	1,523	1.1	13,369	9.6	119,653	86.2	5,839	4.2	138,861
.6	19,470	9.8	1,306	.7	3,140	1.6	25,155	12.7	170,935	86.3	1,970	1.0	198,060
.6	11,350	11.1	572	.6	1,576	1.5	14,135	13.8	87,718	85.6	657	.6	102,510
.6	8,120	8.5	734	.8	1,564	1.6	11,020	11.5	83,217	87.1	1,313	1.4	95,550
.5	44,666	9.7	3,444	.7	6,014	1.3	56,558	12.2	396,073	85.7	9,596	2.1	462,227
.5	26,590	11.7	1,439	.6	2,927	1.3	32,169	14.1	193,203	84.8	2,444	1.1	227,816
.5	18,076	7.7	2,005	.9	3,087	1.3	24,389	10.4	202,870	86.5	7,152	3.1	234,411
.8	4,295	18.6	319	1.4	207	.9	4,999	21.7	17,746	76.9	320	1.4	23,065
.8	2,614	19.9	100	.8	122	.9	2,947	22.5	10,105	77.0	70	.5	13,122
.7	1,681	16.9	219	2.2	85	.9	2,052	20.6	7,641	76.8	250	2.5	9,943
.5	48,561	10.1	3,763	.8	6,221	1.3	61,557	12.7	413,819	85.3	9,916	2.0	485,292
.5	29,204	12.1	1,539	.6	3,049	1.3	35,116	14.6	203,308	84.4	2,514	1.0	240,938
.5	19,757	8.1	2,224	.9	3,172	1.3	26,441	10.8	210,511	86.2	7,402	3.0	244,354
(65 INSTITUTIONS)													
.6	1,548	1.4	804	.7	479	.4	3,545	3.2	106,440	95.1	1,939	1.7	111,924
.7	704	1.2	351	.6	238	.4	1,682	3.0	54,131	96.0	579	1.0	56,392
.6	844	1.5	453	.8	241	.4	1,863	3.4	52,309	94.2	1,360	2.4	55,532
.4	363	.9	302	.8	126	.3	946	2.4	37,609	97.1	187	.5	38,742
.4	153	.7	144	.6	64	.3	453	2.0	21,793	97.5	97	.4	22,343
.4	210	1.3	158	1.0	62	.4	493	3.0	15,816	96.4	90	.5	16,359
.6	1,911	1.3	1,106	.7	605	.4	4,491	3.0	144,049	95.6	2,126	1.4	150,666
.6	857	1.1	495	.6	302	.4	2,135	2.7	75,924	96.4	676	.9	78,735
.5	1,054	1.5	611	.8	303	.4	2,356	3.3	68,125	94.7	1,450	2.0	71,931
.4	133	1.4	134	1.4	84	.9	384	4.1	7,933	84.5	1,075	11.4	9,392
.4	62	1.7	44	1.2	30	.8	148	4.0	3,356	89.7	238	6.4	3,742
.4	71	1.3	90	1.6	54	1.0	236	4.2	4,577	81.0	837	14.8	5,650
.2	19	.3	37	.5	13	.2	81	1.1	7,170	98.1	56	.8	7,307
.2	9	.2	13	.3	11	.3	40	1.1	3,722	98.6	11	.3	3,773
.1	10	.3	24	.7	2	.1	41	1.2	3,448	97.6	45	1.3	3,534
.3	152	.9	171	1.0	97	.6	465	2.8	15,103	90.4	1,131	6.8	16,669
.3	71	.9	57	.8	41	.5	188	2.5	7,078	94.2	249	3.3	7,515
.3	81	.9	114	1.2	56	.6	277	3.0	8,025	87.4	882	9.6	9,184
.5	80	1.3	33	.5	70	1.1	214	3.5	5,861	95.8	45	.7	6,120
.7	34	2.3	10	.7	17	1.2	71	4.9	1,371	94.5	9	.6	1,451
.4	46	1.0	23	.5	53	1.1	143	3.1	4,490	96.2	36	.8	4,669
.5	1	.5	0	.0	0	.0	2	1.0	199	97.5	3	1.5	204
.0	0	.0	0	.0	0	.0	0	.0	64	100.0	0	.0	64
.7	1	.7	0	.0	0	.0	2	1.4	135	96.4	3	2.1	140
.5	81	1.3	33	.5	70	1.1	216	3.4	6,060	95.8	48	.8	6,324
.7	34	2.2	10	.7	17	1.1	71	4.7	1,935	94.7	9	.6	1,515
.5	47	1.0	23	.5	53	1.1	145	3.0	4,625	96.2	39	.8	4,809
.6	1,761	1.4	971	.8	633	.5	4,143	3.3	120,234	94.3	3,059	2.4	127,436
.7	800	1.3	405	.7	285	.5	1,901	3.1	58,858	95.6	826	1.3	61,585
.6	961	1.5	566	.9	348	.5	2,242	3.4	61,376	93.2	2,233	3.4	65,851
.4	383	.8	339	.7	139	.3	1,029	2.2	44,978	97.2	246	.5	46,253
.4	162	.6	157	.6	75	.3	493	1.9	25,579	97.7	108	.4	26,180
.3	221	1.1	182	.9	64	.3	536	2.7	19,399	96.6	138	.7	20,073
.5	2,144	1.2	1,310	.8	772	.4	5,172	3.0	165,212	95.1	3,305	1.9	173,689
.6	962	1.1	562	.6	360	.4	2,394	2.7	84,437	96.2	934	1.1	87,765
.5	1,182	1.4	748	.9	412	.5	2,778	3.2	80,775	94.0	2,371	2.8	85,924
.6	197	1.3	70	.5	62	.4	424	2.8	14,622	95.0	352	2.3	15,398
.6	88	1.0	43	.5	24	.3	206	2.4	8,247	95.6	171	2.0	8,624
.6	109	1.6	27	.4	38	.6	218	3.2	6,375	94.1	181	2.7	6,774
.6	2,341	1.2	1,380	.7	834	.4	5,596	3.0	179,834	95.1	3,657	1.9	189,087
.6	1,050	1.1	605	.6	384	.4	2,600	2.7	92,684	96.2	1,105	1.1	96,389
.5	1,291	1.4	775	.8	450	.5	2,996	3.2	87,150	94.0	2,552	2.8	92,698

MAJOR FIELD 9999 - SUMMARY

	AMERICAN INDIAN ALASKAN NATIVE		BLACK NON-HISPANIC		ASIAN OR PACIFIC ISLANDER		HISPANIC		TOTAL MINORITY		WHITE NON-HISPANIC		NON-RESIDENT ALIEN	
	NUMBER	%	NUMBER	%	NUMBER	%	NUMBER	%	NUMBER	%	NUMBER	%	NUMBER	%
MISSISSIPPI (46 INSTITUTIONS)														
UNDERGRADUATES:														
FULL-TIME	108	.2	22,526	33.4	180	.3	82	.1	22,896	34.0	43,841	65.1	617	.9
FEMALE	60	.2	13,174	37.3	88	.2	31	.1	13,353	37.8	21,888	61.9	120	.3
MALE	48	.2	9,352	29.2	92	.3	51	.2	9,543	29.8	21,953	68.6	497	1.6
PART-TIME	134	.9	2,947	19.0	79	.5	30	.2	3,190	20.6	12,273	79.3	21	.1
FEMALE	84	1.0	1,859	21.2	25	.3	14	.2	1,982	22.6	6,783	77.4	4	.0
MALE	50	.7	1,088	16.2	54	.8	16	.2	1,208	18.0	5,490	81.8	17	.3
TOTAL	242	.3	25,473	30.8	259	.3	112	.1	26,086	31.5	56,114	67.7	638	.8
FEMALE	144	.3	15,033	34.1	113	.3	45	.1	15,335	34.7	28,671	65.0	124	.3
MALE	98	.3	10,440	27.0	146	.4	67	.2	10,751	27.8	27,443	70.9	514	1.3
GRADUATE:														
FULL-TIME	2	.1	514	18.2	23	.8	5	.2	544	19.2	2,082	73.6	202	7.1
FEMALE	1	.1	297	24.8	5	.4	2	.2	305	25.4	852	71.1	42	3.5
MALE	1	.1	217	13.3	18	1.1	3	.2	239	14.7	1,230	75.5	160	9.8
PART-TIME	17	.3	1,586	27.5	45	.8	6	.1	1,654	28.6	3,994	69.2	126	2.2
FEMALE	13	.4	1,110	33.1	15	.4	3	.1	1,141	34.0	2,196	65.4	19	.6
MALE	4	.2	476	19.7	30	1.2	3	.1	513	21.2	1,798	74.4	107	4.4
TOTAL	19	.2	2,100	24.4	68	.8	11	.1	2,198	25.6	6,076	70.6	328	3.8
FEMALE	14	.3	1,407	30.9	20	.4	5	.1	1,446	31.7	3,048	66.9	61	1.3
MALE	5	.1	693	17.1	48	1.2	6	.1	752	18.6	3,028	74.8	267	6.6
PROFESSIONAL:														
FULL-TIME	2	.1	73	5.1	9	.6	4	.3	88	6.1	1,343	93.9	0	.0
FEMALE	1	.3	25	8.5	3	1.0	1	.3	30	10.2	265	89.8	0	.0
MALE	1	.1	48	4.2	6	.5	3	.3	58	5.1	1,078	94.9	0	.0
PART-TIME	1	.3	7	2.3	2	.7	0	.0	10	3.3	288	94.4	7	2.3
FEMALE	1	1.4	4	5.7	0	.0	0	.0	5	7.1	58	82.9	7	10.0
MALE	0	.0	3	1.3	2	.9	0	.0	5	2.1	230	97.9	0	.0
TOTAL	3	.2	80	4.6	11	.6	4	.2	98	5.6	1,631	94.0	7	.4
FEMALE	2	.5	29	7.9	3	.8	1	.3	35	9.6	323	88.5	7	1.9
MALE	1	.1	51	3.7	8	.6	3	.2	63	4.6	1,308	95.4	0	.0
UND+GRAD+PROF:														
FULL-TIME	112	.2	23,113	32.3	212	.3	91	.1	23,528	32.9	47,266	66.0	819	1.1
FEMALE	62	.2	13,496	36.6	96	.3	34	.1	13,688	37.1	23,005	62.4	162	.4
MALE	50	.1	9,617	27.7	116	.3	57	.2	9,840	28.3	24,261	69.8	657	1.9
PART-TIME	152	.7	4,540	21.1	126	.6	36	.2	4,854	22.5	16,555	76.8	154	.7
FEMALE	98	.8	2,973	24.4	40	.3	17	.1	3,128	25.6	9,037	74.1	30	.2
MALE	54	.6	1,567	16.7	86	.9	19	.2	1,726	18.4	7,518	80.3	124	1.3
TOTAL	264	.3	27,653	29.7	338	.4	127	.1	28,382	30.5	63,821	68.5	973	1.0
FEMALE	160	.3	16,469	33.6	136	.3	51	.1	16,816	34.3	32,042	65.3	192	.4
MALE	104	.2	11,184	25.3	202	.5	76	.2	11,566	26.2	31,779	72.0	781	1.8
UNCLASSIFIED:														
TOTAL	45	1.0	934	21.6	35	.8	4	.1	1,018	23.6	3,213	74.5	84	1.9
FEMALE	22	1.1	410	20.8	5	.3	1	.1	438	22.3	1,511	76.8	18	.9
MALE	23	1.0	524	22.3	30	1.3	3	.1	580	24.7	1,702	72.5	66	2.8
TOTAL ENROLLMENT:														
TOTAL	309	.3	28,587	29.3	373	.4	131	.1	29,400	30.2	67,034	68.8	1,057	1.1
FEMALE	182	.4	16,879	33.1	141	.3	52	.1	17,254	33.8	33,553	65.8	210	.4
MALE	127	.3	11,708	25.2	232	.5	79	.2	12,146	26.1	33,481	72.0	847	1.8
MISSOURI (84 INSTITUTIONS)														
UNDERGRADUATES:														
FULL-TIME	336	.3	9,197	7.8	778	.7	767	.6	11,078	9.4	105,603	89.2	1,761	1.5
FEMALE	132	.2	5,049	8.9	297	.5	306	.5	5,784	10.2	50,678	89.1	424	.7
MALE	204	.3	4,148	6.7	481	.8	461	.7	5,294	8.6	54,925	89.2	1,337	2.2
PART-TIME	192	.3	5,395	12.5	304	.7	491	1.1	6,742	14.5	39,400	84.8	313	.7
FEMALE	80	.3	3,478	14.1	153	.6	208	.8	3,919	15.8	20,689	83.6	142	.6
MALE	72	.3	2,317	10.7	151	.7	283	1.3	2,823	13.0	18,711	86.2	171	.8
TOTAL	488	.3	14,992	9.1	1,082	.7	1,258	.8	17,820	10.8	145,003	87.9	2,074	1.3
FEMALE	212	.3	8,527	10.4	450	.6	514	.6	9,703	11.9	71,367	87.4	566	.7
MALE	276	.3	6,465	7.8	632	.8	744	.9	8,117	9.7	73,636	88.4	1,508	1.8
GRADUATE:														
FULL-TIME	16	.2	503	6.1	200	2.4	60	.7	779	9.4	6,696	81.0	794	9.6
FEMALE	6	.2	238	7.8	49	1.6	12	.4	305	10.0	2,529	83.2	207	6.8
MALE	10	.2	265	5.1	151	2.9	48	.9	474	9.1	4,167	79.7	587	11.2
PART-TIME	30	.2	791	5.1	368	2.4	95	.6	1,284	8.2	13,889	89.2	399	2.6
FEMALE	12	.2	471	6.7	61	.9	40	.6	584	8.3	6,384	90.5	85	1.2
MALE	18	.2	320	3.8	307	3.6	55	.6	700	8.2	7,515	88.1	314	3.7
TOTAL	46	.2	1,294	5.4	568	2.4	155	.6	2,063	9.6	20,595	86.3	1,193	5.0
FEMALE	18	.2	709	7.0	110	1.1	52	.5	889	8.8	8,913	88.3	292	2.9
MALE	28	.2	585	4.3	458	3.3	103	.7	1,174	8.5	11,682	84.9	901	6.5
PROFESSIONAL:														
FULL-TIME	30	.3	250	2.7	145	1.6	44	.5	469	5.1	8,648	93.8	103	1.1
FEMALE	9	.5	102	5.8	33	1.9	7	.4	151	8.6	1,594	90.6	15	.9
MALE	21	.3	148	2.0	112	1.5	37	.5	318	4.3	7,054	94.6	88	1.2

ENROLLMENT IN INSTITUTIONS OF HIGHER EDUCATION FOR SELECTED MAJOR FIELDS OF STUDY AND LEVEL OF ENROLLMENT
ETHNICITY, AND SEX: STATE, 1978

SUMMARY

INDIAN NATIVE	BLACK NON-HISPANIC		ASIAN OR PACIFIC ISLANDER		HISPANIC		TOTAL MINORITY		WHITE NON-HISPANIC		NON-RESIDENT ALIEN		TOTAL
%	NUMBER	%	NUMBER	%	NUMBER	%	NUMBER	%	NUMBER	%	NUMBER	%	NUMBER

CONTINUED

%	NUMBER	%	NUMBER	%	NUMBER	%	NUMBER	%	NUMBER	%	NUMBER	%	NUMBER
.5	12	3.0	8	2.0	5	1.2	27	6.7	369	91.8	6	1.5	402
.0	4	8.3	5	6.9	0	.0	11	15.3	61	84.7	0	.0	72
.6	4	1.8	3	.9	5	1.5	16	4.8	308	93.3	6	1.8	330
.3	262	2.7	153	1.6	49	.5	496	5.2	9,017	93.7	109	1.1	9,622
.5	108	5.9	38	2.1	7	.4	162	8.8	1,695	90.3	15	.8	1,832
.3	154	2.0	115	1.5	42	.5	334	4.3	7,362	94.5	94	1.2	7,790
.3	9,950	7.3	1,123	.8	871	.6	12,326	9.1	120,947	89.0	2,658	2.0	135,931
.2	5,389	8.7	379	.6	325	.5	6,240	10.1	54,801	88.8	646	1.0	61,687
.3	4,561	6.1	744	1.0	546	.7	6,086	8.2	66,146	89.1	2,012	2.7	74,244
.3	6,598	10.6	680	1.1	591	.9	8,053	12.9	53,608	86.0	718	1.1	62,439
.3	3,955	12.4	219	.7	248	.8	4,514	14.2	27,134	85.1	227	.7	31,875
.3	2,643	8.6	461	1.5	343	1.1	3,539	11.6	26,534	86.8	491	1.6	30,564
.3	16,544	8.3	1,803	.9	1,462	.7	20,379	10.3	174,615	88.0	3,376	1.7	198,370
.3	9,344	10.0	598	.6	573	.6	10,754	11.5	81,935	87.6	873	.9	93,562
.3	7,204	6.9	1,205	1.1	889	.8	9,625	9.2	92,680	88.4	2,503	2.4	104,808
.5	3,804	16.1	192	.8	202	.9	4,313	18.3	19,184	81.3	102	.4	23,599
.4	2,204	16.8	93	.7	84	.6	2,437	18.6	10,043	81.1	44	.3	13,124
.6	1,600	15.3	99	.9	118	1.1	1,876	17.9	8,541	81.5	58	.6	10,475
.3	20,352	9.2	1,995	.9	1,664	.7	24,692	11.1	193,799	87.3	3,478	1.6	221,969
.3	11,548	10.8	691	.6	657	.6	13,191	12.4	92,578	86.8	917	.9	106,686
.3	8,804	7.6	1,304	1.1	1,007	.9	11,501	10.0	101,221	87.8	2,561	2.2	115,283

(13 INSTITUTIONS)

%	NUMBER	%	NUMBER	%	NUMBER	%	NUMBER	%	NUMBER	%	NUMBER	%	NUMBER
2.3	80	.4	78	.3	74	.3	742	3.3	21,570	95.9	189	.8	22,501
2.9	29	.3	21	.2	31	.3	386	3.7	10,110	95.9	41	.4	10,537
1.7	51	.4	57	.5	43	.4	356	3.0	11,460	95.8	148	1.2	11,964
3.2	18	.6	13	.4	24	.8	155	4.9	2,970	94.3	23	.7	3,146
3.5	9	.5	4	.2	13	.7	87	4.9	1,671	94.5	10	.6	1,768
2.8	9	.7	9	.7	11	.8	68	4.9	1,299	94.1	13	.9	1,380
2.4	98	.4	91	.4	98	.4	897	3.5	24,540	95.7	212	.8	25,649
3.0	38	.3	25	.2	44	.4	473	3.8	11,781	95.7	51	.4	12,305
1.8	60	.4	66	.5	54	.4	424	3.2	12,759	95.6	161	1.2	13,344
2.3	3	.4	2	.3	1	.1	24	3.0	748	94.3	21	2.6	793
2.4	0	.0	1	.3	0	.0	9	2.7	317	95.2	7	2.1	333
2.2	3	.7	1	.2	1	.2	15	3.3	431	93.7	14	3.0	460
.9	2	.2	6	.5	4	.3	24	1.8	1,272	97.2	12	.9	1,308
1.7	0	.0	3	.5	1	.2	14	2.3	576	96.6	6	1.0	596
.3	2	.3	3	.4	3	.4	10	1.4	696	97.8	6	.8	712
1.4	5	.2	8	.4	5	.2	48	2.3	2,020	96.1	33	1.6	2,101
1.9	0	.0	4	.4	1	.1	23	2.5	893	96.1	13	1.4	929
1.0	5	.4	4	.3	4	.3	25	2.1	1,127	96.2	20	1.7	1,172
.0	0	.0	0	.0	0	.0	0	.0	217	99.5	1	.5	218
.0	0	.0	0	.0	0	.0	0	.0	64	100.0	0	.0	64
.0	0	.0	0	.0	0	.0	0	.0	153	99.4	1	.6	154
.0	0	.0	0	.0	0	.0	0	.0	5	100.0	0	.0	5
.0	0	.0	0	.0	0	.0	0	.0	3	100.0	0	.0	3
.0	0	.0	0	.0	0	.0	0	.0	2	100.0	0	.0	2
.0	0	.0	0	.0	0	.0	0	.0	222	99.6	1	.4	223
.0	0	.0	0	.0	0	.0	0	.0	67	100.0	0	.0	67
.0	0	.0	0	.0	0	.0	0	.0	155	99.4	1	.6	156
2.2	83	.4	80	.3	75	.3	766	3.3	22,535	95.8	211	.9	23,512
2.9	29	.3	22	.2	31	.3	395	3.6	10,491	95.9	48	.4	10,934
1.7	54	.4	58	.5	44	.4	371	2.9	12,044	95.8	163	1.3	12,578
2.5	20	.4	19	.4	28	.6	179	4.0	4,247	95.2	35	.8	4,461
3.0	9	.4	7	.3	14	.6	101	4.3	2,250	95.1	16	.7	2,367
2.0	11	.5	12	.6	14	.7	78	3.7	1,997	95.4	19	.9	2,094
2.3	103	.4	99	.4	103	.4	945	3.4	26,782	95.7	246	.9	27,973
2.9	38	.3	29	.2	45	.3	496	3.7	12,741	95.8	64	.5	13,301
1.7	65	.4	70	.5	58	.4	449	3.1	14,041	95.7	182	1.2	14,672
7.4	57	1.8	8	.3	30	1.0	327	10.4	2,775	88.7	28	.9	3,130
9.1	19	1.0	5	.3	25	1.3	220	11.7	1,639	87.5	14	.7	1,873
4.9	38	3.0	3	.2	5	.4	107	8.5	1,136	90.4	14	1.1	1,257
2.8	160	.5	107	.3	133	.4	1,272	4.1	29,557	95.0	274	.9	31,103
3.7	53	.4	34	.2	70	.4	716	4.7	14,380	94.8	78	.5	15,174
2.0	103	.6	73	.5	63	.4	556	3.5	15,177	95.3	196	1.2	15,929

MAJOR FIELD 9999 - SUMMARY

	AMERICAN INDIAN ALASKAN NATIVE		BLACK NON-HISPANIC		ASIAN OR PACIFIC ISLANDER		HISPANIC		TOTAL MINORITY		WHITE NON-HISPANIC		NON-RESIDENT ALIEN		TOT
	NUMBER	%	NUMBER	%	NUMBER	%	NUMBER	%	NUMBER	%	NUMBER	%	NUMBER	%	NUM
NEBRASKA (31 INSTITUTIONS)															
UNDERGRADUATES:															
FULL-TIME	166	.4	1,355	2.9	253	.5	415	.9	2,189	4.7	43,818	93.5	853	1.8	46,
FEMALE	78	.4	593	2.7	105	.5	208	1.0	984	4.5	20,662	94.7	182	.8	21,
MALE	88	.4	762	3.0	148	.6	207	.8	1,205	4.8	23,156	92.5	671	2.7	25,
PART-TIME	80	.4	890	4.5	94	.5	239	1.2	1,303	6.6	18,212	92.8	104	.5	19,
FEMALE	34	.3	409	4.1	48	.5	121	1.2	612	6.1	9,422	93.5	41	.4	10,
MALE	46	.5	481	5.0	46	.5	118	1.2	691	7.2	8,790	92.1	63	.7	9,
TOTAL	246	.4	2,245	3.4	347	.5	654	1.0	3,492	5.3	62,030	93.3	957	1.4	66,
FEMALE	112	.4	1,002	3.1	153	.5	329	1.0	1,596	5.0	30,084	94.3	223	.7	31,
MALE	134	.4	1,243	3.6	194	.6	325	.9	1,896	5.5	31,946	92.4	734	2.1	34,
GRADUATE:															
FULL-TIME	7	.4	37	1.9	26	1.3	20	1.0	90	4.6	1,664	85.3	196	10.1	1,
FEMALE	3	.4	10	1.4	12	1.7	7	1.0	32	4.5	660	92.3	23	3.2	
MALE	4	.3	27	2.2	14	1.1	13	1.1	58	4.7	1,004	81.3	173	14.0	1,
PART-TIME	7	.1	107	2.0	30	.6	34	.6	178	3.4	4,976	94.9	87	1.7	5,
FEMALE	2	.1	63	2.3	15	.5	9	.3	89	3.2	2,672	96.0	21	.8	2,
MALE	5	.2	44	1.8	15	.6	25	1.0	89	3.6	2,304	93.7	66	2.7	2,
TOTAL	14	.2	144	2.0	56	.8	54	.8	268	3.7	6,640	92.3	283	3.9	7,
FEMALE	5	.2	73	2.1	27	.8	16	.5	121	3.5	3,332	95.3	44	1.3	3,
MALE	9	.2	71	1.9	29	.8	38	1.0	147	4.0	3,308	89.6	239	6.5	3,
PROFESSIONAL:															
FULL-TIME	7	.3	48	1.7	39	1.4	38	1.4	132	4.7	2,656	94.9	12	.4	2,
FEMALE	2	.3	14	2.3	8	1.3	3	.5	27	4.4	588	95.5	1	.2	
MALE	5	.2	34	1.6	31	1.4	35	1.6	105	4.8	2,068	94.7	11	.5	2,
PART-TIME	0	.0	1	5.6	0	.0	0	.0	1	5.6	17	94.4	0	.0	
FEMALE	0	.0	1	25.0	0	.0	0	.0	1	25.0	3	75.0	0	.0	
MALE	0	.0	0	.0	0	.0	0	.0	0	.0	14	100.0	0	.0	
TOTAL	7	.2	49	1.7	39	1.4	38	1.3	133	4.7	2,673	94.9	12	.4	2,
FEMALE	2	.3	15	2.4	8	1.3	3	.5	28	4.5	591	95.3	1	.2	
MALE	5	.2	34	1.5	31	1.4	35	1.6	105	4.8	2,082	94.7	11	.5	2,
UND+GRAD+PROF:															
FULL-TIME	180	.3	1,440	2.8	318	.6	473	.9	2,411	4.7	48,138	93.3	1,061	2.1	51,
FEMALE	83	.4	617	2.7	125	.5	218	.9	1,043	4.5	21,910	94.6	206	.9	23,
MALE	97	.3	823	2.9	193	.7	255	.9	1,368	4.8	26,228	92.2	855	3.0	28,
PART-TIME	87	.3	998	4.0	124	.5	273	1.1	1,482	6.0	23,205	93.3	191	.8	24,
FEMALE	36	.3	473	3.7	63	.5	130	1.0	702	5.5	12,097	94.1	62	.5	12,
MALE	51	.4	525	4.4	61	.5	143	1.2	780	6.5	11,108	92.4	129	1.1	12,
TOTAL	267	.3	2,438	3.2	442	.6	746	1.0	3,893	5.1	71,343	93.3	1,252	1.6	76,
FEMALE	119	.3	1,090	3.0	188	.5	348	1.0	1,745	4.8	34,007	94.4	268	.7	36,
MALE	148	.4	1,348	3.3	254	.6	398	1.0	2,148	5.3	37,336	92.3	984	2.4	40,
UNCLASSIFIED:															
TOTAL	19	.4	67	1.3	37	.7	29	.6	152	2.9	5,013	96.3	38	.7	5,
FEMALE	14	.4	33	1.0	15	.4	16	.5	78	2.3	3,243	97.3	13	.4	3,
MALE	5	.3	34	1.8	22	1.2	13	.7	74	4.0	1,770	94.7	25	1.3	1,
TOTAL ENROLLMENT:															
TOTAL	286	.4	2,505	3.1	479	.6	775	1.0	4,045	5.0	76,356	93.5	1,290	1.6	81,
FEMALE	133	.4	1,123	2.9	203	.5	364	.9	1,823	4.6	37,250	94.7	281	.7	39,
MALE	153	.4	1,382	3.3	276	.7	411	1.0	2,222	5.2	39,106	92.4	1,009	2.4	42,
NEVADA (6 INSTITUTIONS)															
UNDERGRADUATES:															
FULL-TIME	116	1.2	464	5.0	159	1.7	233	2.5	972	10.4	8,116	87.1	234	2.5	9,
FEMALE	67	1.7	191	4.8	65	1.6	85	2.1	408	10.2	3,552	88.5	55	1.4	4,
MALE	49	.9	273	5.1	94	1.8	148	2.8	564	10.6	4,564	86.0	179	3.4	5,
PART-TIME	164	1.1	513	3.5	168	1.1	291	2.0	1,136	7.7	13,506	91.7	88	.6	14,
FEMALE	92	1.3	245	3.4	74	1.0	137	1.9	548	7.5	6,715	92.0	32	.4	7,
MALE	72	1.0	268	3.6	94	1.3	154	2.1	588	7.9	6,791	91.3	56	.8	7,
TOTAL	280	1.2	977	4.1	327	1.4	524	2.2	2,108	8.8	21,622	89.9	322	1.3	24,
FEMALE	159	1.4	436	3.9	139	1.2	222	2.0	956	8.5	10,267	90.8	87	.8	11,
MALE	121	.9	541	4.2	188	1.5	302	2.4	1,152	9.0	11,355	89.1	235	1.8	12,
GRADUATE:															
FULL-TIME	2	.5	7	1.6	7	1.6	4	.9	20	4.7	367	86.4	38	8.9	
FEMALE	0	.0	3	1.6	3	1.6	2	1.1	8	4.4	164	90.1	10	5.5	
MALE	2	.8	4	1.6	4	1.6	2	.8	12	4.9	203	83.5	28	11.5	
PART-TIME	9	.8	38	3.4	14	1.2	23	2.0	84	7.4	1,021	90.4	24	2.1	1,
FEMALE	3	.5	24	4.0	4	.7	11	1.8	42	6.9	558	92.1	6	1.0	
MALE	6	1.1	14	2.7	10	1.9	12	2.3	42	8.0	463	88.5	18	3.4	
TOTAL	11	.7	45	2.9	21	1.4	27	1.7	104	6.7	1,388	89.3	62	4.0	1,
FEMALE	3	.4	27	3.4	7	.9	13	1.6	50	6.3	722	91.6	16	2.0	
MALE	8	1.0	18	2.3	14	1.8	14	1.8	54	7.0	666	86.9	46	6.0	
PROFESSIONAL:															
FULL-TIME	0	.0	0	.0	0	.0	0	.0	0	.0	0	.0	0	.0	
FEMALE	0	.0	0	.0	0	.0	0	.0	0	.0	0	.0	0	.0	
MALE	0	.0	0	.0	0	.0	0	.0	0	.0	0	.0	0	.0	

SUMMARY

INDIAN NATIVE	BLACK NON-HISPANIC		ASIAN OR PACIFIC ISLANDER		HISPANIC		TOTAL MINORITY		WHITE NON-HISPANIC		NON-RESIDENT ALIEN		TOTAL
%	NUMBER	%	NUMBER	%	NUMBER	%	NUMBER	%	NUMBER	%	NUMBER	%	NUMBER

CONTINUED

.0	0	.0	0	.0	0	.0	0	.0	0	.0	0	.0	0
.0	0	.0	0	.0	0	.0	0	.0	0	.0	0	.0	0
.0	0	.0	0	.0	0	.0	0	.0	0	.0	0	.0	0
.0	0	.0	0	.0	0	.0	0	.0	0	.0	0	.0	0
.0	0	.0	0	.0	0	.0	0	.0	0	.0	0	.0	0
.0	0	.0	0	.0	0	.0	0	.0	0	.0	0	.0	0
1.2	471	4.8	166	1.7	237	2.4	992	10.2	8,483	87.0	272	2.8	9,747
1.6	194	4.6	68	1.6	87	2.1	416	9.9	3,716	88.5	65	1.5	4,197
.9	277	5.0	98	1.8	150	2.7	576	10.4	4,767	85.9	207	3.7	5,550
1.1	551	3.5	182	1.1	314	2.0	1,220	7.7	14,527	91.6	112	.7	15,859
1.2	269	3.4	78	1.0	148	1.9	590	7.5	7,273	92.1	38	.5	7,901
1.0	282	3.5	104	1.3	166	2.1	630	7.9	7,254	91.2	74	.9	7,958
1.1	1,022	4.0	348	1.4	551	2.2	2,212	8.6	23,010	89.9	384	1.5	25,606
1.3	463	3.8	146	1.2	235	1.9	1,006	8.3	10,989	90.8	103	.9	12,098
1.0	559	4.1	202	1.5	316	2.3	1,206	8.9	12,021	89.0	281	2.1	13,508
1.1	575	7.2	111	1.4	270	3.4	1,042	13.1	6,890	86.9	1	.0	7,933
1.0	267	6.6	47	1.2	100	2.5	453	11.2	3,589	88.8	1	.0	4,043
1.2	308	7.9	64	1.6	170	4.4	589	15.1	3,301	84.9	0	.0	3,890
1.1	1,597	4.8	459	1.4	821	2.4	3,254	9.7	29,900	89.1	385	1.1	33,539
1.2	730	4.5	193	1.2	335	2.1	1,459	9.0	14,578	90.3	104	.6	16,141
1.0	867	5.0	266	1.5	486	2.8	1,795	10.3	15,322	88.1	281	1.6	17,398

(24 INSTITUTIONS)

.2	556	1.9	94	.3	214	.7	937	3.2	28,037	95.2	487	1.7	29,461
.2	197	1.4	33	.2	44	.3	307	2.3	13,167	96.8	126	.9	13,600
.3	359	2.3	61	.4	170	1.1	630	4.0	14,870	93.8	361	2.3	15,861
.0	33	.6	12	.2	25	.4	72	1.3	5,549	98.6	8	.1	5,629
.1	8	.3	5	.2	6	.2	21	.8	2,702	99.2	1	.0	2,724
.0	25	.9	7	.2	19	.7	51	1.8	2,847	98.0	7	.2	2,905
.2	589	1.7	106	.3	239	.7	1,009	2.9	33,586	95.7	495	1.4	35,090
.2	205	1.3	38	.2	50	.3	328	2.0	15,869	97.2	127	.8	16,324
.2	384	2.0	68	.4	189	1.0	681	3.6	17,717	94.4	368	2.0	18,766
.3	18	1.6	21	1.9	4	.4	46	4.1	1,058	94.7	13	1.2	1,117
.3	5	1.5	10	2.9	1	.3	17	5.0	322	94.2	3	.9	342
.3	13	1.7	11	1.4	3	.4	29	3.7	736	95.0	10	1.3	775
.0	12	.7	5	.3	4	.4	23	1.4	1,584	98.1	8	.5	1,615
.0	3	.5	1	.2	4	.6	8	1.2	646	98.5	2	.3	656
.0	9	.9	4	.4	2	.2	15	1.6	938	97.8	6	.6	959
.1	30	1.1	26	1.0	10	.4	69	2.5	2,642	96.7	21	.8	2,732
.1	8	.8	11	1.1	5	.5	25	2.5	968	97.0	5	.5	998
.1	22	1.3	15	.9	5	.3	44	2.5	1,674	96.5	16	.9	1,734
1.4	9	2.1	11	2.5	37	8.5	400	91.5	0	.0	437
4.3	3	4.3	7	10.0	4	5.7	17	24.3	53	75.7	0	.0	70
.8	6	1.6	4	1.1	7	1.9	20	5.4	347	94.6	0	.0	367
.0	0	.0	0	.0	0	.0	0	.0	0	.0	0	.0	0
.0	0	.0	0	.0	0	.0	0	.0	0	.0	0	.0	0
.0	0	.0	0	.0	0	.0	0	.0	0	.0	0	.0	0
1.4	9	2.1	11	2.5	11	2.5	37	8.5	400	91.5	0	.0	437
4.3	3	4.3	7	10.0	4	5.7	17	24.3	53	75.7	0	.0	70
.8	6	1.6	4	1.1	7	1.9	20	5.4	347	94.6	0	.0	367
.3	583	1.9	126	.4	229	.7	1,020	3.3	29,495	95.1	500	1.6	31,015
.3	205	1.5	50	.4	49	.3	341	2.4	13,542	96.6	129	.9	14,012
.3	378	2.2	76	.4	180	1.1	679	4.0	15,953	93.8	371	2.2	17,003
.0	45	.6	17	.2	31	.4	95	1.3	7,133	98.5	16	.2	7,244
.1	11	.3	6	.2	10	.3	29	.9	3,348	99.1	3	.1	3,380
.0	34	.9	11	.3	21	.5	66	1.7	3,785	98.0	13	.3	3,864
.2	628	1.6	143	.4	260	.7	1,115	2.9	36,628	95.7	516	1.3	38,259
.2	216	1.2	56	.3	99	.3	370	2.1	16,890	97.1	132	.8	17,392
.2	412	2.0	87	.4	201	1.0	745	3.6	19,738	94.6	384	1.8	20,867
.3	7	.2	12	.4	9	.3	37	1.1	3,250	98.8	3	.1	3,290
.3	1	.0	7	.3	6	.3	21	1.0	2,070	99.0	0	.0	2,091
.2	6	.5	5	.4	3	.3	16	1.3	1,180	98.4	3	.3	1,199
.2	635	1.5	155	.4	269	.6	1,152	2.8	39,878	96.0	519	1.2	41,549
.2	217	1.1	63	.3	65	.3	391	2.0	18,960	97.3	132	.7	19,483
.2	418	1.9	92	.4	204	.9	761	3.4	20,918	94.8	387	1.8	22,066

681

MAJOR FIELD 9999 - SUMMARY

	AMERICAN INDIAN ALASKAN NATIVE		BLACK NON-HISPANIC		ASIAN OR PACIFIC ISLANDER		HISPANIC		TOTAL MINORITY		WHITE NON-HISPANIC		NON-RESIDENT ALIEN	
	NUMBER	%	NUMBER	%	NUMBER	%	NUMBER	%	NUMBER	%	NUMBER	%	NUMBER	%
NEW JERSEY	(	63 INSTITUTIONS)												
UNDERGRADUATES:														
FULL-TIME	334	.2	16,434	11.4	1,402	1.0	6,734	4.7	24,904	17.2	117,699	81.4	2,009	1.4
FEMALE	189	.3	10,176	14.0	652	.9	3,783	5.2	14,800	20.3	57,445	78.8	669	.9
MALE	145	.2	6,258	8.7	750	1.0	2,951	4.1	10,104	14.1	60,254	84.0	1,340	1.9
PART-TIME	152	.2	6,922	10.2	657	1.0	2,103	3.1	9,834	14.5	57,730	85.0	382	.6
FEMALE	83	.2	4,244	11.1	377	1.0	1,109	2.9	5,813	15.1	32,352	84.3	207	.5
MALE	69	.2	2,678	9.1	280	.9	994	3.4	4,021	13.6	25,378	85.8	175	.6
TOTAL	486	.2	23,356	11.0	2,059	1.0	8,837	4.2	34,738	16.3	175,429	82.5	2,391	1.1
FEMALE	272	.2	14,420	13.0	1,029	.9	4,892	4.4	20,613	18.5	89,797	80.7	876	.8
MALE	214	.2	8,936	8.8	1,030	1.0	3,945	3.9	14,125	13.9	85,632	84.6	1,515	1.5
GRADUATE:														
FULL-TIME	10	.1	309	4.5	142	2.1	106	1.6	567	8.3	5,264	77.1	995	14.6
FEMALE	7	.3	172	6.8	55	2.2	47	1.9	281	11.1	2,059	81.4	188	7.4
MALE	3	.1	137	3.2	87	2.0	59	1.4	286	6.7	3,205	74.6	807	18.8
PART-TIME	23	.1	1,259	5.1	376	1.5	517	2.1	2,175	8.8	22,233	89.7	377	1.5
FEMALE	10	.1	760	6.1	123	1.0	285	2.3	1,178	9.5	11,084	89.5	117	.9
MALE	13	.1	499	4.0	253	2.0	232	1.9	997	8.0	11,149	89.9	260	2.1
TOTAL	33	.1	1,568	5.0	518	1.6	623	2.0	2,742	8.7	27,497	87.0	1,372	4.3
FEMALE	17	.1	932	6.3	178	1.2	332	2.2	1,459	9.8	13,143	88.2	305	2.0
MALE	16	.1	636	3.8	340	2.0	291	1.7	1,283	7.7	14,354	85.9	1,067	6.4
PROFESSIONAL:														
FULL-TIME	5	.1	347	8.1	49	1.1	129	3.0	530	12.3	3,738	86.9	34	.8
FEMALE	1	.1	142	12.6	24	2.1	47	4.2	214	19.0	913	80.9	2	.2
MALE	4	.1	205	6.5	25	.8	82	2.6	316	10.0	2,825	89.0	32	1.0
PART-TIME	3	.3	80	7.8	11	1.1	36	3.5	130	12.7	893	87.2	1	.1
FEMALE	2	.6	35	9.7	4	1.1	14	3.9	55	15.2	306	84.8	0	.0
MALE	1	.2	45	6.8	7	1.1	22	3.3	75	11.3	587	88.5	1	.2
TOTAL	8	.2	427	8.0	60	1.1	165	3.1	660	12.4	4,631	87.0	35	.7
FEMALE	3	.2	177	11.9	28	1.9	61	4.1	269	18.1	1,219	81.8	2	.1
MALE	5	.1	250	6.5	32	.8	104	2.7	391	10.2	3,412	88.9	33	.9
UND+GRAD+PROF:														
FULL-TIME	349	.2	17,090	11.0	1,593	1.0	6,969	4.5	26,001	16.7	126,701	81.4	3,038	2.0
FEMALE	197	.3	10,490	13.7	731	1.0	3,877	5.1	15,295	20.0	60,417	78.9	859	1.1
MALE	152	.2	6,600	8.3	862	1.1	3,092	3.9	10,706	13.5	66,284	83.7	2,179	2.8
PART-TIME	178	.2	8,261	8.8	1,044	1.1	2,656	2.8	12,139	12.9	80,856	86.2	760	.8
FEMALE	95	.2	5,039	9.9	504	1.0	1,408	2.8	7,046	13.8	43,742	85.6	324	.6
MALE	83	.2	3,222	7.6	540	1.3	1,248	2.9	5,093	11.9	37,114	87.0	436	1.0
TOTAL	527	.2	25,351	10.2	2,637	1.1	9,625	3.9	38,140	15.3	207,557	83.2	3,798	1.5
FEMALE	292	.2	15,529	12.2	1,235	1.0	5,285	4.1	22,341	17.5	104,159	81.6	1,183	.9
MALE	235	.2	9,822	8.1	1,402	1.2	4,340	3.6	15,799	13.0	103,398	84.9	2,615	2.1
UNCLASSIFIED:														
TOTAL	132	.2	5,428	9.2	654	1.1	1,692	2.9	7,906	13.4	50,438	85.8	443	.8
FEMALE	49	.2	3,269	10.3	339	1.1	929	2.9	4,586	14.5	26,910	84.9	184	.6
MALE	83	.3	2,159	8.0	315	1.2	763	2.8	3,320	12.2	23,528	86.8	259	1.0
TOTAL ENROLLMENT:														
TOTAL	659	.2	30,779	10.0	3,291	1.1	11,317	3.7	46,046	14.9	257,995	83.7	4,241	1.4
FEMALE	341	.2	18,798	11.8	1,574	1.0	6,214	3.9	26,927	16.9	131,069	82.2	1,367	.9
MALE	318	.2	11,981	8.0	1,717	1.2	5,103	3.4	19,119	12.8	126,926	85.2	2,874	1.9
NEW MEXICO	(	19 INSTITUTIONS)												
UNDERGRADUATES:														
FULL-TIME	1,205	3.9	787	2.6	232	.8	7,984	26.1	10,208	33.3	19,899	64.9	531	1.7
FEMALE	689	4.9	293	2.1	84	.6	3,832	27.3	4,898	34.9	9,065	64.5	83	.6
MALE	516	3.1	494	3.0	148	.9	4,152	25.0	5,310	32.0	10,834	65.3	448	2.7
PART-TIME	395	4.1	184	1.9	59	.6	2,517	26.1	3,155	32.7	6,438	66.8	47	.5
FEMALE	262	5.0	82	1.6	34	.6	1,418	26.9	1,796	34.1	3,447	65.5	22	.4
MALE	133	3.0	102	2.3	25	.6	1,099	25.1	1,359	31.1	2,991	68.4	25	.6
TOTAL	1,600	4.0	971	2.4	291	.7	10,501	26.1	13,363	33.2	26,337	65.4	578	1.4
FEMALE	951	4.9	375	1.9	118	.6	5,250	27.2	6,694	34.7	12,512	64.8	105	.5
MALE	649	3.1	596	2.8	173	.8	5,251	25.0	6,669	31.8	13,825	65.9	473	2.3
GRADUATE:														
FULL-TIME	51	2.0	28	1.1	28	1.1	331	13.2	438	17.4	1,763	70.1	315	12.5
FEMALE	32	3.3	9	.9	8	.8	139	14.3	188	19.4	746	76.9	36	3.7
MALE	19	1.2	19	1.2	20	1.3	192	12.4	250	16.2	1,017	65.8	279	18.0
PART-TIME	65	1.8	61	1.7	24	.7	608	16.8	758	21.0	2,766	76.5	94	2.6
FEMALE	30	1.7	31	1.7	15	.8	288	16.3	364	20.5	1,385	78.2	23	1.3
MALE	35	1.9	30	1.6	9	.5	320	17.3	394	21.3	1,381	74.8	71	3.8
TOTAL	116	1.9	89	1.5	52	.8	939	15.3	1,196	19.5	4,529	73.8	409	6.7
FEMALE	62	2.3	40	1.5	23	.8	427	15.6	552	20.1	2,131	77.7	59	2.2
MALE	54	1.6	49	1.4	29	.9	512	15.1	644	19.0	2,398	70.7	350	10.3
PROFESSIONAL:														
FULL-TIME	21	3.4	7	1.1	10	1.6	147	24.1	185	30.3	425	69.7	0	.0
FEMALE	7	3.3	3	1.4	6	2.8	46	21.4	62	28.8	153	71.2	0	.0
MALE	14	3.5	4	1.0	4	1.0	101	25.6	123	31.1	272	68.9	0	.0

FIELD 9999 - SUMMARY

	AMERICAN INDIAN ALASKAN NATIVE		BLACK NON-HISPANIC		ASIAN OR PACIFIC ISLANDER		HISPANIC		TOTAL MINORITY		WHITE NON-HISPANIC		NON-RESIDENT ALIEN		TOTAL
	NUMBER	%	NUMBER	%	NUMBER	%	NUMBER	%	NUMBER	%	NUMBER	%	NUMBER	%	NUMBER
EXICO		CONTINUED													
SSIONAL:															
TIME	1	7.1	0	.0	1	7.1	2	14.3	4	28.6	10	71.4	0	.0	14
MALE	0	.0	0	.0	0	.0	1	25.0	1	25.0	3	75.0	0	.0	4
MALE	1	10.0	0	.0	1	10.0	1	10.0	3	30.0	7	70.0	0	.0	10
	22	3.5	7	1.1	11	1.8	149	23.9	189	30.3	435	69.7	0	.0	624
MALE	7	3.2	3	1.4	6	2.7	47	21.5	63	28.8	156	71.2	0	.0	219
MALE	15	3.7	4	1.0	5	1.2	102	25.2	126	31.1	279	68.9	0	.0	405
RAD+PROF:															
TIME	1,277	3.8	822	2.4	270	.8	8,462	25.1	10,831	32.1	22,087	65.4	846	2.5	33,764
MALE	728	4.8	305	2.0	98	.6	4,017	26.4	5,148	33.8	9,964	65.4	119	.8	15,231
MALE	549	3.0	517	2.8	172	.9	4,445	24.0	5,683	30.7	12,123	65.4	727	3.9	18,533
TIME	461	3.5	245	1.8	84	.6	3,127	23.6	3,917	29.5	9,214	69.4	141	1.1	13,272
MALE	292	4.1	113	1.6	49	.7	1,707	24.2	2,161	30.7	4,835	68.7	45	.6	7,041
MALE	169	2.7	132	2.1	35	.6	1,420	22.8	1,756	28.2	4,379	70.3	96	1.5	6,231
	1,738	3.7	1,067	2.3	354	.8	11,589	24.6	14,748	31.4	31,301	66.5	987	2.1	47,036
MALE	1,020	4.6	418	1.9	147	.7	5,724	25.7	7,309	32.8	14,799	66.4	164	.7	22,272
MALE	718	2.9	649	2.6	207	.8	5,865	23.7	7,439	30.0	16,502	66.6	823	3.3	24,764
SSIFIED:															
	507	5.8	162	1.9	57	.7	1,688	19.4	2,414	27.8	6,197	71.4	70	.8	8,681
MALE	339	6.6	75	1.5	29	.6	994	19.2	1,437	27.8	3,703	71.7	24	.5	5,164
MALE	168	4.8	87	2.5	28	.8	694	19.7	977	27.8	2,494	70.9	46	1.3	3,517
ENROLLMENT:															
	2,245	4.0	1,229	2.2	411	.7	13,277	23.8	17,162	30.8	37,498	67.3	1,057	1.9	55,717
MALE	1,359	5.0	493	1.8	176	.6	6,718	24.5	8,746	31.9	18,502	67.4	188	.7	27,436
MALE	886	3.1	736	2.6	235	.8	6,559	23.2	8,416	29.8	18,996	67.2	869	3.1	28,281
ORK		(286 INSTITLTIONS)													
GRADUATES:															
TIME	2,613	.5	61,479	11.6	10,931	2.1	30,921	5.8	105,944	20.0	415,226	78.4	8,520	1.6	529,690
MALE	1,255	.5	37,794	14.3	4,950	1.9	17,412	6.6	61,411	23.2	200,960	75.8	2,772	1.0	265,143
MALE	1,358	.5	23,685	9.0	5,981	2.3	13,509	5.1	44,533	16.8	214,266	81.0	5,748	2.2	264,547
TIME	824	.6	19,971	14.2	2,487	1.8	7,868	5.6	31,150	22.2	107,849	76.9	1,204	.9	140,203
MALE	390	.5	12,891	16.8	1,256	1.6	4,111	5.3	18,648	24.2	57,716	75.1	539	.7	76,903
MALE	434	.7	7,680	11.2	1,231	1.9	3,757	5.9	12,502	19.8	50,133	79.2	665	1.1	63,300
	3,437	.5	81,450	12.2	13,418	2.0	38,789	5.8	137,094	20.5	523,075	78.1	9,724	1.5	669,893
MALE	1,645	.5	50,685	14.8	6,206	1.8	21,523	6.3	80,059	23.4	258,676	75.6	3,311	1.0	342,046
MALE	1,792	.5	30,765	9.4	7,212	2.2	17,266	5.3	57,035	17.4	264,399	80.6	6,413	2.0	327,847
ATE:															
TIME	138	.3	2,258	5.0	1,096	2.4	1,146	2.5	4,630	10.3	35,250	77.9	5,336	11.8	45,224
MALE	47	.2	1,261	6.3	404	2.0	560	2.8	2,272	11.3	16,590	82.6	1,232	6.1	20,094
MALE	91	.4	997	4.0	692	2.8	586	2.3	2,366	9.4	18,660	74.3	4,104	16.3	25,130
TIME	263	.4	4,609	6.2	2,053	2.8	2,141	2.9	9,066	12.2	63,291	84.8	2,235	3.0	74,592
MALE	112	.3	2,301	7.1	840	2.2	1,218	3.2	4,871	12.9	32,141	84.9	852	2.3	37,864
MALE	151	.4	1,908	5.2	1,213	3.3	923	2.5	4,195	11.4	31,150	84.8	1,383	3.8	36,728
	401	.3	6,867	5.7	3,149	2.6	3,287	2.7	13,704	11.4	98,541	82.2	7,571	6.3	119,816
MALE	159	.3	3,962	6.8	1,244	2.1	1,778	3.1	7,143	12.3	48,731	84.1	2,084	3.6	57,958
MALE	242	.4	2,905	4.7	1,905	3.1	1,509	2.4	6,561	10.6	49,810	80.5	5,487	8.9	61,858
SSIONAL:															
TIME	36	.2	716	3.5	293	1.4	403	1.9	1,448	7.0	19,095	92.3	146	.7	20,689
MALE	19	.3	345	5.5	109	1.8	139	2.2	612	9.8	5,583	89.8	22	.4	6,217
MALE	17	.1	371	2.6	184	1.3	264	1.8	836	5.8	13,512	93.4	124	.9	14,472
TIME	1	.1	75	3.9	12	.6	38	2.0	126	6.6	1,783	93.3	2	.1	1,911
MALE	0	.0	30	5.5	1	.2	14	2.6	45	8.3	500	91.7	0	.0	545
MALE	1	.1	45	3.3	11	.8	24	1.8	81	5.9	1,283	93.9	2	.1	1,366
	37	.2	791	3.5	305	1.3	441	2.0	1,574	7.0	20,878	92.4	148	.7	22,600
MALE	19	.3	375	5.5	110	1.6	153	2.3	657	9.7	6,083	90.0	22	.3	6,762
MALE	18	.1	416	2.6	195	1.2	288	1.8	917	5.8	14,795	93.4	126	.8	15,838
RAD+PROF:															
TIME	2,787	.5	64,453	10.8	12,320	2.1	32,470	5.5	112,030	18.8	469,571	78.8	14,002	2.4	595,603
MALE	1,321	.5	39,400	13.5	5,463	1.9	18,111	6.2	64,295	22.1	223,133	76.6	4,026	1.4	291,454
MALE	1,466	.5	25,053	8.2	6,857	2.3	14,359	4.7	47,735	15.7	246,438	81.0	9,976	3.3	304,149
TIME	1,088	.5	24,655	11.4	4,552	2.1	10,047	4.6	40,342	18.6	172,923	79.8	3,441	1.6	216,706
MALE	502	.4	15,622	13.5	2,097	1.8	5,343	4.6	23,564	20.4	90,357	78.4	1,391	1.2	115,312
MALE	586	.6	9,033	8.9	2,455	2.4	4,704	4.6	16,778	16.5	82,566	81.4	2,050	2.0	101,394
	3,875	.5	89,108	11.0	16,872	2.1	42,517	5.2	152,372	18.8	642,494	79.1	17,443	2.1	812,309
MALE	1,823	.4	55,022	13.5	7,560	1.9	23,454	5.8	87,859	21.6	313,490	77.1	5,417	1.3	406,766
MALE	2,052	.5	34,086	8.4	9,312	2.3	19,063	4.7	64,513	15.9	329,004	81.1	12,026	3.0	405,943
SSIFIED:															
	572	.5	10,274	8.1	2,130	1.7	4,408	3.5	17,384	13.7	107,994	85.2	1,383	1.1	126,761
MALE	360	.5	6,455	8.9	1,032	1.4	2,482	3.4	10,329	14.2	61,751	84.9	677	.9	72,757
MALE	212	.4	3,819	7.1	1,098	2.0	1,926	3.6	7,055	13.1	46,243	85.6	706	1.3	54,004
ENROLLMENT:															
	4,447	.5	99,382	10.6	19,002	2.0	46,925	5.0	169,756	18.1	750,488	79.9	18,826	2.0	939,070
MALE	2,183	.5	61,477	12.8	8,592	1.8	25,936	5.4	98,188	20.5	375,241	78.3	6,094	1.3	479,523
MALE.	2,264	.5	37,905	8.2	10,410	2.3	20,989	4.6	71,568	15.6	375,247	81.7	12,732	2.8	459,547

MAJOR FIELD 9999 - SUMMARY

	AMERICAN INDIAN ALASKAN NATIVE		BLACK NON-HISPANIC		ASIAN OR PACIFIC ISLANDER		HISPANIC		TOTAL MINORITY		WHITE NON-HISPANIC		NON-RESIDENT ALIEN	
	NUMBER	%	NUMBER	%	NUMBER	%	NUMBER	%	NUMBER	%	NUMBER	%	NUMBER	%
NORTH CAROLINA	(	126 INSTITUTIONS)												
UNDERGRADUATES:														
FULL-TIME	1,192	.7	38,450	22.3	667	.4	617	.4	40,926	23.8	129,491	75.3	1,638	1.0
FEMALE	710	.8	21,105	24.4	271	.3	287	.3	22,373	25.8	63,866	73.7	405	.5
MALE	482	.6	17,345	20.3	396	.5	330	.4	18,553	21.7	65,625	76.8	1,233	1.4
PART-TIME	395	.8	8,443	17.8	170	.4	198	.4	9,206	19.4	38,186	80.3	159	.3
FEMALE	197	.9	4,208	18.6	90	.4	70	.3	4,565	20.1	18,049	79.6	68	.3
MALE	198	.8	4,235	17.0	80	.3	128	.5	4,641	18.7	20,137	81.0	91	.4
TOTAL	1,587	.7	46,893	21.4	837	.4	815	.4	50,132	22.8	167,677	76.4	1,797	.8
FEMALE	907	.8	25,313	23.2	361	.3	357	.3	26,938	24.6	81,915	74.9	473	.4
MALE	680	.6	21,580	19.6	476	.4	458	.4	23,194	21.0	85,762	77.8	1,324	1.2
GRADUATE:														
FULL-TIME	20	.2	547	6.8	50	.6	44	.5	661	8.2	6,820	84.9	556	6.9
FEMALE	12	.3	315	9.0	21	.6	27	.8	375	10.7	2,980	85.4	135	3.9
MALE	8	.2	232	5.1	29	.6	17	.4	286	6.3	3,840	84.5	421	9.3
PART-TIME	41	.4	1,567	15.7	53	.5	30	.3	1,691	17.0	7,933	79.7	334	3.4
FEMALE	19	.3	1,042	18.7	18	.3	14	.3	1,093	19.6	4,417	79.2	67	1.2
MALE	22	.5	525	12.0	35	.8	16	.4	598	13.6	3,516	80.3	267	6.1
TOTAL	61	.3	2,114	11.7	103	.6	74	.4	2,352	13.1	14,753	82.0	890	4.9
FEMALE	31	.3	1,357	15.0	39	.4	41	.5	1,468	16.2	7,397	81.6	202	2.2
MALE	30	.3	757	8.5	64	.7	33	.4	884	9.9	7,356	82.4	688	7.7
PROFESSIONAL:														
FULL-TIME	24	.5	367	8.3	24	.5	16	.4	431	9.7	3,989	89.7	25	.6
FEMALE	5	.5	116	10.7	7	.6	4	.4	132	12.1	950	87.2	7	.6
MALE	19	.6	251	7.5	17	.5	12	.4	299	8.9	3,039	90.6	18	.5
PART-TIME	0	.0	5	12.8	0	.0	0	.0	5	12.8	31	79.5	3	7.7
FEMALE	0	.0	1	4.5	0	.0	0	.0	1	4.5	20	90.9	1	4.5
MALE	0	.0	4	23.5	0	.0	0	.0	4	23.5	11	64.7	2	11.8
TOTAL	24	.5	372	8.3	24	.5	16	.4	436	9.7	4,020	89.7	28	.6
FEMALE	5	.5	117	10.5	7	.6	4	.4	133	12.0	970	87.3	8	.7
MALE	19	.6	255	7.6	17	.5	12	.4	303	9.0	3,050	90.4	20	.6
UND+GRAD+PROF:														
FULL-TIME	1,236	.7	39,364	21.3	741	.4	677	.4	42,018	22.8	140,300	76.0	2,219	1.2
FEMALE	727	.8	21,536	23.6	299	.3	318	.3	22,880	25.1	67,796	74.3	547	.6
MALE	509	.5	17,828	19.1	442	.5	359	.4	19,138	20.5	72,504	77.7	1,672	1.8
PART-TIME	436	.8	10,015	17.4	223	.4	228	.4	10,902	18.9	46,150	80.2	496	.9
FEMALE	216	.8	5,251	18.6	108	.4	84	.3	5,659	20.0	22,486	79.5	136	.5
MALE	220	.8	4,764	16.3	115	.4	144	.5	5,243	17.9	23,664	80.9	360	1.2
TOTAL	1,672	.7	49,379	20.4	964	.4	905	.4	52,920	21.9	186,450	77.0	2,715	1.1
FEMALE	943.	.8	26,787	22.4	407	.3	402	.3	28,539	23.9	90,282	75.5	683	.6
MALE	729	.6	22,592	18.4	557	.5	503	.4	24,381	19.9	96,168	78.5	2,032	1.7
UNCLASSIFIED:														
TOTAL	206	1.0	2,657	13.5	108	.5	117	.6	3,088	15.7	16,471	83.6	139	.7
FEMALE	147	1.2	1,736	13.9	57	.5	57	.5	1,997	16.0	10,468	83.6	53	.4
MALE	59	.8	921	12.8	51	.7	60	.8	1,091	15.2	6,003	83.6	86	1.2
TOTAL ENROLLMENT:														
TOTAL	1,878	.7	52,036	19.9	1,072	.4	1,022	.4	56,008	21.4	202,921	77.5	2,854	1.1
FEMALE	1,090	.8	28,523	21.6	464	.4	459	.3	30,536	23.1	100,750	76.3	736	.6
MALE	788	.6	23,513	18.1	608	.5	563	.4	25,472	19.6	102,171	78.7	2,118	1.6
NORTH DAKOTA	(	16 INSTITUTIONS)												
UNDERGRADUATES:														
FULL-TIME	794	3.1	145	.6	73	.3	43	.2	1,055	4.1	24,697	95.2	178	.7
FEMALE	456	3.8	41	.3	26	.2	20	.2	543	4.5	11,509	94.9	71	.6
MALE	338	2.4	104	.8	47	.3	23	.2	512	3.7	13,188	95.5	107	.8
PART-TIME	198	11.1	8	.4	5	.3	5	.3	216	12.1	1,564	87.6	5	.3
FEMALE	131	11.7	3	.3	5	.4	4	.4	143	12.8	970	87.0	2	.2
MALE	67	10.0	5	.7	0	.0	1	.1	73	10.9	594	88.7	3	.4
TOTAL	992	3.6	153	.6	78	.3	48	.2	1,271	4.6	26,261	94.8	183	.7
FEMALE	587	4.4	44	.3	31	.2	24	.2	686	5.2	12,479	94.3	73	.6
MALE	405	2.8	109	.8	47	.3	24	.2	585	4.0	13,782	95.2	110	.8
GRADUATE:														
FULL-TIME	1	.2	5	.8	9	1.5	0	.0	15	2.5	485	82.3	89	15.1
FEMALE	1	.5	3	1.6	3	1.6	0	.0	7	3.8	156	83.9	23	12.4
MALE	0	.0	2	.5	6	1.5	0	.0	8	2.0	329	81.6	66	16.4
PART-TIME	10	1.0	5	.5	8	.8	4	.4	27	2.8	875	91.6	53	5.5
FEMALE	7	2.1	0	.0	2	.6	1	.3	10	3.0	314	94.9	7	2.1
MALE	3	.5	5	.8	6	1.0	3	.5	17	2.7	561	89.9	46	7.4
TOTAL	11	.7	10	.6	17	1.1	4	.3	42	2.7	1,360	88.1	142	9.2
FEMALE	8	1.5	3	.6	5	1.0	1	.2	17	3.3	470	90.9	30	5.8
MALE	3	.3	7	.7	12	1.2	3	.3	25	2.4	890	86.7	112	10.9
PROFESSIONAL:														
FULL-TIME	10	2.1	0	.0	2	.4	0	.0	12	2.5	469	97.5	0	.0
FEMALE	1	1.1	0	.0	0	.0	0	.0	1	1.1	92	98.9	0	.0
MALE	9	2.3	0	.0	2	.5	0	.0	11	2.8	377	97.2	0	.0

FIELD 9999 - SUMMARY

	AMERICAN INDIAN ALASKAN NATIVE		BLACK NON-HISPANIC		ASIAN OR PACIFIC ISLANDER		HISPANIC		TOTAL MINORITY		WHITE NON-HISPANIC		NON-RESIDENT ALIEN		TOTAL
	NUMBER	%	NUMBER	%	NUMBER	%	NUMBER	%	NUMBER	%	NUMBER	%	NUMBER	%	NUMBER
AKOTA	CONTINUED														
IONAL:															
ME	0	.0	0	.0	0	.0	0	.0	0	.0	4	100.0	0	.0	4
LE	0	.0	0	.0	0	.0	0	.0	0	.0	1	100.0	0	.0	1
LE	0	.0	0	.0	0	.0	0	.0	0	.0	3	100.0	0	.0	3
LE	10	2.1	0	.0	2	.4	0	.0	12	2.5	473	97.5	0	.0	485
LE	1	1.1	0	.0	0	.0	0	.0	1	1.1	93	98.9	0	.0	94
LE	9	2.3	0	.0	2	.5	0	.0	11	2.8	380	97.2	0	.0	391
D+PROF:															
ME	805	3.0	150	.6	84	.3	43	.2	1,082	4.0	25,651	95.0	267	1.0	27,000
LE	458	3.7	44	.4	29	.2	20	.2	551	4.4	11,757	94.8	94	.8	12,402
LE	347	2.4	106	.7	55	.4	23	.2	531	3.6	13,894	95.2	173	1.2	14,598
ME	208	7.6	13	.5	13	.5	9	.3	243	8.9	2,443	89.0	58	2.1	2,744
LE	138	9.5	3	.2	7	.5	5	.3	153	10.6	1,285	88.8	9	.6	1,447
LE	70	5.4	10	.8	6	.5	4	.3	90	6.9	1,158	89.3	49	3.8	1,297
	1,013	3.4	163	.5	97	.3	52	.2	1,325	4.5	28,094	94.5	325	1.1	29,744
LE	596	4.3	47	.3	36	.3	25	.2	704	5.1	13,042	94.2	103	.7	13,849
LE	417	2.6	116	.7	61	.4	27	.2	621	3.9	15,052	94.7	222	1.4	15,895
IFIED:															
	68	2.6	6	.2	8	.3	2	.1	84	3.3	2,485	96.3	12	.5	2,581
LE	34	2.5	3	.2	2	.1	1	.1	40	3.0	1,302	96.4	8	.6	1,350
LE	34	2.8	3	.2	6	.5	1	.1	44	3.6	1,183	96.1	4	.3	1,231
NROLLMENT:															
	1,081	3.3	169	.5	105	.3	54	.2	1,409	4.4	30,579	94.6	337	1.0	32,325
LE	630	4.1	50	.3	38	.3	26	.2	744	4.9	14,344	94.4	111	.7	15,199
LE	451	2.6	119	.7	67	.4	28	.2	665	3.9	16,235	94.8	226	1.3	17,126
(133 INSTITUTIONS)															
ADUATES:															
ME	724	.3	24,295	9.8	1,063	.4	1,469	.6	27,551	11.1	216,323	87.5	3,278	1.3	247,152
LE	482	.4	13,850	11.6	528	.4	727	.6	15,587	13.0	103,365	86.3	814	.7	119,766
LE	242	.2	10,445	8.2	535	.4	742	.6	11,964	9.4	112,958	88.7	2,464	1.9	127,386
ME	237	.2	11,813	10.8	504	.5	675	.6	13,229	12.1	94,878	87.1	803	.7	108,910
LE	122	.2	7,331	12.5	277	.5	382	.7	8,112	13.9	49,895	85.4	414	.7	58,421
LE	115	.2	4,482	8.9	227	.4	293	.6	5,117	10.1	44,983	89.1	389	.8	50,489
	961	.3	36,108	10.1	1,567	.4	2,144	.6	40,780	11.5	311,201	87.4	4,081	1.1	356,062
LE	604	.3	21,181	11.9	805	.5	1,109	.6	23,699	13.3	153,260	86.0	1,228	.7	178,187
LE	357	.2	14,927	8.4	762	.4	1,035	.6	17,081	9.6	157,941	88.8	2,853	1.6	177,875
E:															
ME	60	.3	1,385	6.7	168	.8	198	1.0	1,811	8.8	16,442	80.0	2,295	11.2	20,54d
LE	22	.3	731	8.4	56	.6	87	1.0	896	10.3	7,301	83.9	500	5.7	8,697
LE	38	.3	654	5.5	112	.9	111	.9	915	7.7	9,141	77.1	1,795	15.1	11,851
ME	44	.2	1,767	6.1	168	.6	108	.4	2,087	7.2	26,453	90.9	559	1.9	29,059
LE	24	.2	1,078	7.3	69	.5	53	.4	1,224	8.3	13,456	90.8	147	1.0	14,827
LE	20	.1	689	4.8	99	.7	55	.4	863	6.0	12,997	91.1	412	2.9	14,272
	104	.2	3,152	6.3	336	.7	306	.6	3,898	7.9	42,895	86.4	2,854	5.7	49,647
LE	46	.2	1,809	7.7	125	.5	140	.6	2,120	9.0	20,757	88.2	647	2.8	23,524
LE	58	.2	1,343	5.1	211	.8	166	.6	1,778	6.8	22,138	84.7	2,207	8.4	26,123
IONAL:															
ME	254	2.3	540	4.8	78	.7	73	.7	945	8.5	10,116	90.8	83	.7	11,144
LE	34	1.2	221	8.0	24	.9	20	.7	299	10.8	2,460	88.6	19	.7	2,778
LE	220	2.6	319	3.8	54	.6	53	.6	646	7.7	7,656	91.5	64	.8	8,366
ME	8	.6	89	6.5	3	.2	4	.3	104	7.6	1,204	91.8	9	.7	1,317
LE	4	1.1	32	8.4	0	.0	0	.0	36	9.5	342	90.2	1	.3	379
LE	4	.4	57	5.7	3	.3	4	.4	68	6.8	922	92.4	8	.8	998
	262	2.1	629	5.0	81	.6	77	.6	1,049	8.4	11,380	90.9	92	.7	12,521
LE	38	1.2	253	8.0	24	.8	20	.6	335	10.6	2,802	88.8	20	.6	3,157
LE	224	2.4	376	4.0	57	.6	57	.6	714	7.6	8,578	91.6	72	.8	9,364
D+PROF:															
ME	1,038	.4	26,220	9.4	1,309	.5	1,740	.6	30,307	10.9	242,881	87.1	5,656	2.0	278,844
LE	538	.4	14,802	11.3	608	.5	834	.6	16,782	12.8	113,126	86.2	1,333	1.0	131,241
LE	500	.3	11,418	7.7	701	.5	906	.6	13,525	9.2	129,755	87.9	4,323	2.9	147,603
ME	289	.2	13,669	9.8	675	.5	787	.6	15,420	11.1	122,595	88.0	1,371	1.0	139,386
LE	150	.2	8,441	11.5	346	.5	435	.6	9,372	12.7	63,693	86.5	562	.8	73,627
LE	139	.2	5,228	8.0	329	.5	352	.5	6,048	9.2	58,902	89.6	809	1.2	65,759
	1,327	.3	39,889	9.5	1,984	.5	2,527	.6	45,727	10.9	365,476	87.4	7,027	1.7	418,230
LE	688	.3	23,243	11.3	954	.5	1,269	.6	26,154	12.8	176,819	86.3	1,895	.9	204,868
LE	639	.3	16,646	7.8	1,030	.5	1,258	.6	19,573	9.2	188,657	88.4	5,132	2.4	213,362
IFIED:															
	108	.3	2,207	6.8	211	.7	112	.3	2,638	8.1	29,488	91.0	277	.9	32,403
LE	63	.3	1,347	7.3	104	.6	59	.3	1,573	8.5	16,892	91.0	102	.5	18,567
LE	45	.3	860	6.2	107	.8	53	.4	1,065	7.7	12,596	91.0	175	1.3	13,836
NROLLMENT:															
	1,435	.3	42,096	9.3	2,195	.5	2,639	.6	48,365	10.7	394,964	87.6	7,304	1.6	450,633
LE	751	.3	24,590	11.0	1,058	.5	1,328	.6	27,727	12.4	193,711	86.7	1,997	.9	223,435
LE	684	.3	17,506	7.7	1,137	.5	1,311	.6	20,638	9.1	201,253	88.6	5,307	2.3	227,198

TABLE 17 - TOTAL ENROLLMENT IN INSTITUTIONS OF HIGHER EDUCATION FOR SELECTED MAJOR FIELDS OF STUDY AND LEVEL OF ENROLLMENT BY RACE, ETHNICITY, AND SEX: STATE, 1978

MAJOR FIELD 9999 - SUMMARY

	AMERICAN INDIAN ALASKAN NATIVE		BLACK NON-HISPANIC		ASIAN OR PACIFIC ISLANDER		HISPANIC		TOTAL MINORITY		WHITE NON-HISPANIC		NON-RESIDENT ALIEN	
	NUMBER	%	NUMBER	%	NUMBER	%	NUMBER	%	NUMBER	%	NUMBER	%	NUMBER	%
OKLAHOMA (43 INSTITUTIONS)														
UNDERGRADUATES:														
FULL-TIME	3,406	3.9	5,628	6.5	656	.8	640	.7	10,330	11.9	71,577	82.5	4,870	5.6
FEMALE	1,836	4.6	2,858	7.2	242	.6	265	.7	5,201	13.1	33,792	84.9	810	2.0
MALE	1,570	3.3	2,770	5.9	414	.9	375	.8	5,129	10.9	37,785	80.4	4,060	8.6
PART-TIME	1,180	3.3	2,577	7.1	283	.8	394	1.1	4,434	12.2	30,970	85.6	792	2.2
FEMALE	700	3.6	1,375	7.0	134	.7	183	.9	2,392	12.2	16,949	86.5	242	1.2
MALE	480	2.9	1,202	7.2	149	.9	211	1.3	2,042	12.3	14,021	84.4	550	3.3
TOTAL	4,586	3.7	8,205	6.7	939	.8	1,034	.8	14,764	12.0	102,547	83.4	5,662	4.6
FEMALE	2,536	4.3	4,233	7.1	376	.6	448	.8	7,593	12.8	50,741	85.4	1,052	1.8
MALE	2,050	3.2	3,972	6.2	563	.9	586	.9	7,171	11.3	51,806	81.5	4,610	7.2
GRADUATE:														
FULL-TIME	105	2.2	153	3.1	36	.7	29	.6	323	6.6	3,294	67.6	1,257	25.8
FEMALE	54	3.3	83	5.1	9	.5	12	.7	158	9.6	1,251	76.4	229	14.0
MALE	51	1.6	70	2.2	27	.8	17	.5	165	5.1	2,043	63.1	1,028	31.8
PART-TIME	229	2.6	352	4.0	42	.5	40	.5	663	7.6	7,622	86.8	492	5.6
FEMALE	127	2.9	196	4.5	21	.5	13	.3	357	8.2	3,923	89.7	92	2.1
MALE	102	2.3	156	3.5	21	.5	27	.6	306	6.9	3,699	84.0	400	9.1
TOTAL	334	2.4	505	3.7	78	.6	69	.5	986	7.2	10,916	80.0	1,749	12.8
FEMALE	181	3.0	279	4.6	30	.5	25	.4	515	8.6	5,174	86.1	321	5.3
MALE	153	2.0	226	3.0	48	.6	44	.6	471	6.2	5,742	75.1	1,428	18.7
PROFESSIONAL:														
FULL-TIME	72	2.4	45	1.5	27	.9	24	.8	168	5.5	2,879	94.2	9	.3
FEMALE	16	2.4	17	2.5	9	1.3	5	.7	47	7.0	624	92.9	1	.1
MALE	56	2.3	28	1.2	18	.8	19	.8	121	5.1	2,255	94.6	8	.3
PART-TIME	6	2.1	6	2.1	0	.0	1	.4	13	4.6	261	93.2	6	2.1
FEMALE	1	1.7	1	1.7	0	.0	0	.0	2	3.4	54	93.1	2	3.4
MALE	5	2.3	5	2.3	0	.0	1	.5	11	5.0	207	93.2	4	1.8
TOTAL	78	2.4	51	1.5	27	.8	25	.7	181	5.4	3,140	94.1	15	.4
FEMALE	17	2.3	18	2.5	9	1.2	5	.7	49	6.7	678	92.9	3	.4
MALE	61	2.3	33	1.3	18	.7	20	.8	132	5.1	2,462	94.5	12	.5
UND+GRAD+PROF:														
FULL-TIME	3,583	3.8	5,826	6.2	719	.8	693	.7	10,821	11.4	77,750	82.1	6,136	6.5
FEMALE	1,906	4.5	2,958	7.0	260	.6	282	.7	5,406	12.8	35,667	84.7	1,040	2.5
MALE	1,677	3.2	2,868	5.5	459	.7	411	.8	5,415	10.3	42,083	80.0	5,096	9.7
PART-TIME	1,415	3.1	2,935	6.5	325	.7	435	1.0	5,110	11.3	38,853	85.9	1,290	2.9
FEMALE	828	3.4	1,572	6.5	155	.6	196	.8	2,751	11.5	20,926	87.1	336	1.4
MALE	587	2.8	1,363	6.4	170	.8	239	1.1	2,359	11.1	17,927	84.4	954	4.5
TOTAL	4,998	3.6	8,761	6.3	1,044	.7	1,128	.8	15,931	11.4	116,603	83.3	7,426	5.3
FEMALE	2,734	4.1	4,530	6.9	415	.6	478	.7	8,157	12.3	56,593	85.6	1,376	2.1
MALE	2,264	3.1	4,231	5.7	629	.9	650	.9	7,774	10.5	60,010	81.3	6,050	8.2
UNCLASSIFIED:														
TOTAL	353	3.7	329	3.5	42	.4	57	.6	781	8.3	8,382	88.8	274	2.9
FEMALE	228	4.3	169	3.2	18	.3	32	.6	447	8.5	4,739	89.9	85	1.6
MALE	125	3.0	160	3.8	24	.6	25	.6	334	8.0	3,643	87.4	189	4.5
TOTAL ENROLLMENT:														
TOTAL	5,351	3.6	9,090	6.1	1,086	.7	1,185	.8	16,712	11.2	124,985	83.7	7,700	5.2
FEMALE	2,962	4.1	4,699	6.6	433	.6	510	.7	8,604	12.1	61,332	85.9	1,461	2.0
MALE	2,389	3.1	4,391	5.6	653	.8	675	.9	8,108	10.4	63,653	81.6	6,239	8.0
OREGON (43 INSTITUTIONS)														
UNDERGRADUATES:														
FULL-TIME	890	1.2	1,022	1.4	1,897	2.6	792	1.1	4,601	6.3	66,144	90.8	2,082	2.9
FEMALE	418	1.2	398	1.2	869	2.6	365	1.1	2,050	6.1	30,972	92.1	593	1.8
MALE	472	1.2	624	1.6	1,028	2.6	427	1.1	2,551	6.5	35,172	89.7	1,489	3.8
PART-TIME	393	1.1	423	1.1	775	2.1	481	1.3	2,072	5.6	34,126	92.7	600	1.6
FEMALE	214	1.1	197	1.0	392	2.0	250	1.3	1,053	5.3	18,590	93.3	283	1.4
MALE	179	1.1	226	1.3	383	2.3	231	1.4	1,019	6.0	15,536	92.1	317	1.9
TOTAL	1,283	1.2	1,445	1.3	2,672	2.4	1,273	1.2	6,673	6.1	100,270	91.5	2,682	2.4
FEMALE	632	1.2	595	1.1	1,261	2.4	615	1.1	3,103	5.8	49,562	92.6	876	1.6
MALE	651	1.2	850	1.5	1,411	2.5	658	1.2	3,570	6.4	50,708	90.4	1,806	3.2
GRADUATE:														
FULL-TIME	42	.7	62	1.1	95	1.7	38	.7	237	4.1	4,515	78.7	984	17.2
FEMALE	18	.8	20	.9	47	2.1	15	.7	100	4.5	1,862	84.7	236	10.7
MALE	24	.7	42	1.2	48	1.4	23	.7	137	3.9	2,653	75.0	748	21.1
PART-TIME	15	.4	33	.9	72	2.0	28	.8	148	4.2	3,225	91.6	149	4.2
FEMALE	7	.4	15	.8	27	1.5	10	.6	59	3.3	1,673	94.7	35	2.0
MALE	8	.5	18	1.0	45	2.6	18	1.0	89	5.1	1,552	88.4	114	6.5
TOTAL	57	.6	95	1.0	167	1.8	66	.7	385	4.2	7,740	83.6	1,133	12.2
FEMALE	25	.6	35	.9	74	1.9	25	.6	159	4.0	3,535	89.2	271	6.8
MALE	32	.6	60	1.1	93	1.8	41	.8	226	4.3	4,205	79.4	862	16.3
PROFESSIONAL:														
FULL-TIME	14	.4	35	1.1	108	3.3	27	.8	184	5.6	3,085	93.5	29	.9
FEMALE	7	1.0	9	1.3	32	4.6	4	.6	52	7.4	644	92.1	3	.4
MALE	7	.3	26	1.0	76	2.9	23	.9	132	5.1	2,441	93.9	26	1.0

SUMMARY

INDIAN NATIVE	BLACK NON-HISPANIC		ASIAN OR PACIFIC ISLANDER		HISPANIC		TOTAL MINORITY		WHITE NON-HISPANIC		NON-RESIDENT ALIEN		TOTAL
%	NUMBER	%	NUMBER	%	NUMBER	%	NUMBER	%	NUMBER	%	NUMBER	%	NUMBER
CONTINUED													
.2	4	.9	6	1.3	5	1.1	16	3.4	446	96.1	2	.4	464
.0	2	2.0	1	1.0	1	1.0	4	4.0	95	96.0	0	.0	99
.3	2	.5	5	1.4	4	1.1	12	3.3	351	96.2	2	.5	365
.4	39	1.0	114	3.0	32	.9	200	5.3	3,531	93.9	31	.8	3,762
.9	11	1.4	33	4.1	5	.6	56	7.0	739	92.6	3	.4	798
.3	28	.9	81	2.7	27	.9	144	4.9	2,792	94.2	28	.9	2,964
1.2	1,119	1.4	2,100	2.6	857	1.0	5,022	6.1	73,744	90.1	3,095	3.8	81,861
1.2	427	1.2	948	2.6	384	1.1	2,202	6.0	33,478	91.7	832	2.3	36,512
1.1	692	1.5	1,152	2.5	473	1.0	2,820	6.2	40,266	88.8	2,263	5.0	45,349
1.0	400	1.1	853	2.1	514	1.3	2,236	5.5	37,797	92.7	751	1.8	40,784
1.0	214	1.0	420	1.9	261	1.2	1,116	5.1	20,358	93.4	318	1.5	21,792
1.0	246	1.3	433	2.3	253	1.3	1,120	5.9	17,439	91.8	433	2.3	18,992
1.1	1,579	1.3	2,953	2.4	1,371	1.1	7,258	5.9	111,541	90.9	3,846	3.1	122,645
1.1	641	1.1	1,368	2.3	645	1.1	3,318	5.7	53,036	92.3	1,150	2.0	58,304
1.1	938	1.5	1,585	2.5	726	1.1	3,940	6.1	57,705	89.7	2,696	4.2	64,341
.9	149	.6	350	1.5	218	.9	928	3.9	22,435	94.6	341	1.4	23,704
.8	68	.5	176	1.3	108	.8	465	3.4	13,215	95.9	96	.7	13,776
1.0	81	.8	174	1.8	110	1.1	463	4.7	9,220	92.9	245	2.5	9,928
1.1	1,728	1.2	3,303	2.3	1,589	1.1	8,186	5.6	133,976	91.5	4,187	2.9	146,349
1.1	709	1.0	1,544	2.1	753	1.0	3,783	5.2	67,051	93.0	1,246	1.7	72,080
1.1	1,019	1.4	1,759	2.4	836	1.1	4,403	5.9	66,925	90.1	2,941	4.0	74,269
(177 INSTITUTIONS)													
.1	19,952	7.1	1,859	.7	1,842	.7	23,996	8.6	253,080	90.5	2,706	1.0	279,782
.1	11,570	8.6	806	.6	949	.7	13,503	10.0	120,260	89.4	791	.6	134,554
.1	8,382	5.8	1,053	.7	893	.6	10,493	7.2	132,820	91.5	1,915	1.3	145,228
.2	8,934	11.5	439	.6	782	1.0	10,302	13.3	66,931	86.4	263	.3	77,496
.2	5,474	12.9	232	.5	464	1.1	6,244	14.7	36,144	85.1	97	.2	42,485
.2	3,460	9.9	207	.6	318	.9	4,058	11.6	30,787	87.9	166	.5	35,011
.1	28,886	8.1	2,298	.6	2,624	.7	34,298	9.6	320,011	89.6	2,969	.8	357,278
.1	17,044	9.6	1,038	.6	1,413	.8	19,747	11.2	156,404	88.3	888	.5	177,039
.1	11,842	6.6	1,260	.7	1,211	.7	14,551	8.1	163,607	90.8	2,081	1.2	180,239
.3	653	3.8	269	1.6	204	1.2	1,175	6.8	13,611	78.7	2,514	14.5	17,300
.3	366	5.5	97	1.5	92	1.4	576	8.7	5,572	84.4	452	6.8	6,600
.3	287	2.7	172	1.6	112	1.0	599	5.6	8,039	75.1	2,062	19.3	10,700
.2	1,182	4.0	274	.9	133	.4	1,639	5.5	27,496	93.0	440	1.5	29,575
.1	691	4.9	110	.8	65	.5	882	6.2	13,168	93.1	91	.6	14,141
.2	491	3.2	164	1.1	68	.4	757	4.9	14,328	92.8	349	2.3	15,434
.2	1,835	3.9	543	1.2	337	.7	2,814	6.0	41,107	87.7	2,954	6.3	46,875
.2	1,057	5.1	207	1.0	157	.8	1,458	7.0	18,740	90.4	543	2.6	20,741
.2	778	3.0	336	1.3	180	.7	1,356	5.2	22,367	85.6	2,411	9.2	26,134
.2	539	3.8	147	1.0	131	.9	839	6.0	13,047	93.2	115	.8	14,001
.2	233	6.8	50	1.5	43	1.2	333	9.7	3,077	89.4	33	1.0	3,443
.1	306	2.9	97	.9	88	.8	506	4.8	9,970	94.4	82	.8	10,558
.0	23	7.6	5	1.7	4	1.3	32	10.6	269	89.1	1	.3	302
.0	10	10.2	2	2.0	2	2.0	14	14.3	84	85.7	0	.0	98
.0	13	6.4	3	1.5	2	1.0	18	8.8	185	90.7	1	.5	204
.2	562	3.9	152	1.1	135	.9	871	6.1	13,316	93.1	116	.8	14,303
.2	243	6.9	52	1.5	45	1.3	347	9.8	3,161	89.3	33	.9	3,541
.1	319	3.0	100	.9	90	.8	524	4.9	10,155	94.4	83	.8	10,762
.1	21,144	6.8	2,275	.7	2,177	.7	26,010	8.4	279,738	89.9	5,335	1.7	311,083
.1	12,169	8.4	953	.7	1,084	.7	14,412	10.0	128,909	89.2	1,276	.9	144,597
.1	8,975	5.4	1,322	.8	1,093	.7	11,598	7.0	150,829	90.6	4,059	2.4	166,486
.2	10,139	9.4	718	.7	919	.9	11,973	11.2	94,696	88.2	704	.7	107,373
.2	6,175	10.9	344	.6	531	.9	7,140	12.6	49,396	87.1	188	.3	56,724
.2	3,964	7.8	374	.7	388	.8	4,833	9.5	45,300	89.4	516	1.0	50,649
.1	31,283	7.5	2,993	.7	3,096	.7	37,983	9.1	374,434	89.5	6,039	1.4	418,456
.1	18,344	9.1	1,297	.6	1,615	.8	21,552	10.7	178,305	88.6	1,464	.7	201,321
.1	12,939	6.0	1,696	.8	1,481	.7	16,431	7.6	196,129	90.3	4,575	2.1	217,135
.2	3,304	6.2	579	1.1	379	.7	4,383	8.2	48,454	91.0	388	.7	53,225
.2	1,946	6.7	210	.7	199	.7	2,405	8.3	26,504	91.2	166	.6	29,075
.3	1,358	5.6	369	1.5	180	.7	1,978	8.2	21,950	90.9	222	.9	24,150
.2	34,587	7.3	3,572	.7	3,475	.7	42,366	9.0	422,888	89.7	6,427	1.4	471,681
.2	20,290	8.8	1,507	.7	1,814	.8	23,957	10.4	204,809	88.9	1,630	.7	230,396
.2	14,297	5.9	2,065	.9	1,661	.7	18,409	7.6	218,079	90.4	4,797	2.0	241,285

MAJOR FIELD 9999 - SUMMARY

	AMERICAN INDIAN ALASKAN NATIVE		BLACK NON-HISPANIC		ASIAN OR PACIFIC ISLANDER		HISPANIC		TOTAL MINORITY		WHITE NON-HISPANIC		NON-RESIDENT ALIEN	
	NUMBER	%	NUMBER	%	NUMBER	%	NUMBER	%	NUMBER	%	NUMBER	%	NUMBER	%
RHODE ISLAND	(	13 INSTITUTIONS)												
UNDERGRADUATES:														
FULL-TIME	62	.2	1,383	3.7	290	.8	233	.6	1,968	5.3	34,506	93.3	528	1.4
FEMALE	36	.2	629	3.6	143	.8	107	.6	915	5.2	16,535	93.9	156	.9
MALE	26	.1	754	3.9	147	.8	126	.6	1,053	5.4	17,971	92.7	372	1.9
PART-TIME	19	.3	150	2.0	22	.3	39	.5	230	3.0	7,303	96.2	58	.8
FEMALE	11	.3	67	2.0	9	.3	16	.5	103	3.1	3,194	96.1	26	.8
MALE	8	.2	83	1.9	13	.3	23	.5	127	3.0	4,109	96.3	32	.7
TOTAL	81	.2	1,533	3.4	312	.7	272	.6	2,198	4.9	41,809	93.8	586	1.3
FEMALE	47	.2	696	3.3	152	.7	123	.6	1,018	4.9	19,729	94.3	182	.9
MALE	34	.1	837	3.5	160	.7	149	.6	1,180	5.0	22,080	93.3	404	1.7
GRADUATE:														
FULL-TIME	7	.3	41	1.8	34	1.5	14	.6	96	4.1	1,921	82.4	313	13.4
FEMALE	4	.4	18	2.0	5	.6	6	.7	33	3.7	801	89.2	64	7.1
MALE	3	.2	23	1.6	29	2.0	8	.6	63	4.4	1,120	78.2	249	17.4
PART-TIME	8	.2	42	1.1	30	.8	17	.5	97	2.6	3,529	95.1	85	2.3
FEMALE	4	.2	20	1.2	10	.6	8	.5	42	2.5	1,609	95.7	31	1.8
MALE	4	.2	22	1.1	20	1.0	9	.4	55	2.7	1,920	94.6	54	2.7
TOTAL	15	.2	83	1.4	64	1.1	31	.5	193	3.2	5,450	90.2	398	6.6
FEMALE	8	.3	38	1.5	15	.6	14	.5	75	2.9	2,410	93.4	95	3.7
MALE	7	.2	45	1.3	49	1.4	17	.5	118	3.4	3,040	87.8	303	8.8
PROFESSIONAL:														
FULL-TIME	0	.0	14	5.5	11	4.3	5	2.0	30	11.9	219	86.6	4	1.6
FEMALE	0	.0	5	5.9	9	10.6	0	.0	14	16.5	70	82.4	1	1.2
MALE	0	.0	9	5.4	2	1.2	5	3.0	16	9.5	149	88.7	3	1.8
PART-TIME	0	.0	0	.0	0	.0	0	.0	0	.0	0	.0	0	.0
FEMALE	0	.0	0	.0	0	.0	0	.0	0	.0	0	.0	0	.0
MALE	0	.0	0	.0	0	.0	0	.0	0	.0	0	.0	0	.0
TOTAL	0	.0	14	5.5	11	4.3	5	2.0	30	11.9	219	86.6	4	1.6
FEMALE	0	.0	5	5.9	9	10.6	0	.0	14	16.5	70	82.4	1	1.2
MALE	0	.0	9	5.4	2	1.2	5	3.0	16	9.5	149	88.7	3	1.8
UNC+GRAD+PROF:														
FULL-TIME	69	.2	1,438	3.6	335	.8	252	.6	2,094	5.3	36,646	92.6	845	2.1
FEMALE	40	.2	652	3.5	157	.8	113	.6	962	5.2	17,406	93.6	221	1.2
MALE	29	.1	786	3.7	178	.8	139	.7	1,132	5.4	19,240	91.6	624	3.0
PART-TIME	27	.2	192	1.7	52	.5	56	.5	327	2.9	10,832	95.8	143	1.3
FEMALE	15	.3	87	1.7	19	.4	24	.5	145	2.9	4,803	96.0	57	1.1
MALE	12	.2	105	1.7	33	.5	32	.5	182	2.9	6,029	95.7	86	1.4
TOTAL	96	.2	1,630	3.2	387	.8	308	.6	2,421	4.8	47,478	93.3	988	1.9
FEMALE	55	.2	739	3.1	176	.7	137	.6	1,107	4.7	22,209	94.1	278	1.2
MALE	41	.2	891	3.3	211	.8	171	.6	1,314	4.8	25,269	92.6	710	2.6
UNCLASSIFIED:														
TOTAL	25	.2	357	2.8	62	.5	43	.3	487	3.8	12,114	95.6	65	.5
FEMALE	11	.1	188	2.4	32	.4	27	.3	258	3.3	7,501	96.3	30	.4
MALE	14	.3	169	3.5	30	.6	16	.3	229	4.7	4,613	94.6	35	.7
TOTAL ENROLLMENT:														
TOTAL	121	.2	1,987	3.1	449	.7	351	.6	2,908	4.6	59,592	93.8	1,053	1.7
FEMALE	66	.2	927	3.0	208	.7	164	.5	1,365	4.3	29,710	94.7	308	1.0
MALE	55	.2	1,060	3.3	241	.7	187	.6	1,543	4.8	29,882	92.9	745	2.3
SOUTH CAROLINA	(	61 INSTITUTIONS)												
UNDERGRADUATES:														
FULL-TIME	78	.1	19,403	23.9	335	.4	199	.2	20,015	24.7	60,446	74.6	597	.7
FEMALE	28	.1	10,703	28.0	151	.4	68	.2	10,950	28.7	27,127	71.0	120	.3
MALE	50	.1	8,700	20.3	184	.4	131	.3	9,065	21.1	33,319	77.7	477	1.1
PART-TIME	44	.2	5,846	23.7	112	.5	74	.3	6,076	24.7	18,491	75.0	80	.3
FEMALE	15	.1	2,822	25.4	51	.5	24	.2	2,912	26.2	8,163	73.5	28	.3
MALE	29	.2	3,024	22.3	61	.5	50	.4	3,164	23.4	10,328	76.3	52	.4
TOTAL	122	.1	25,249	23.9	447	.4	273	.3	26,091	24.7	78,937	74.7	677	.6
FEMALE	43	.1	13,525	27.4	202	.4	92	.2	13,862	28.1	35,290	71.6	148	.3
MALE	79	.1	11,724	20.8	245	.4	181	.3	12,229	21.7	43,647	77.4	529	.9
GRADUATE:														
FULL-TIME	4	.1	179	6.3	14	.5	15	.5	212	7.4	2,458	86.0	189	6.6
FEMALE	3	.3	107	9.4	3	.3	5	.4	118	10.4	983	86.3	38	3.3
MALE	1	.1	72	4.2	11	.6	10	.6	94	5.5	1,475	85.8	151	8.8
PART-TIME	8	.1	1,136	12.5	21	.2	22	.2	1,187	13.0	7,876	86.4	56	.6
FEMALE	3	.1	820	14.4	8	.1	12	.2	843	14.8	4,824	84.8	19	.3
MALE	5	.1	316	9.2	13	.4	10	.3	344	10.0	3,052	88.9	37	1.1
TOTAL	12	.1	1,315	11.0	35	.3	37	.3	1,399	11.7	10,334	86.3	245	2.0
FEMALE	6	.1	927	13.6	11	.2	17	.2	961	14.1	5,807	85.1	57	.8
MALE	6	.1	388	7.5	24	.5	20	.4	438	8.5	4,527	87.9	188	3.6
PROFESSIONAL:														
FULL-TIME	2	.1	88	4.1	4	.2	4	.2	98	4.5	2,011	93.0	54	2.5
FEMALE	2	.5	24	5.7	0	.0	1	.2	27	6.4	379	90.2	14	3.3
MALE	0	.0	64	3.7	4	.2	3	.2	71	4.1	1,632	93.6	40	2.3

LO 9999 - SUMMARY

	AMERICAN INDIAN ALASKAN NATIVE		BLACK NON-HISPANIC		ASIAN OR PACIFIC ISLANDER		HISPANIC		TOTAL MINORITY		WHITE NON-HISPANIC		NON-RESIDENT ALIEN		TOTAL
	NUMBER	%	NUMBER	%	NUMBER	%	NUMBER	%	NUMBER	%	NUMBER	%	NUMBER	%	NUMBER
OLINA CONTINUED															
NAL:															
	0	.0	3	5.0	0	.0	0	.0	3	5.0	56	93.3	1	1.7	60
	0	.0	0	.0	0	.0	0	.0	0	.0	17	100.0	0	.0	17
	0	.0	3	7.0	0	.0	0	.0	3	7.0	39	90.7	1	2.3	43
	2	.1	91	4.1	4	.2	4	.2	101	4.5	2,067	93.0	55	2.5	2,223
	2	.5	24	5.5	0	.0	1	.2	27	6.2	396	90.6	14	3.2	437
	0	.0	67	3.8	4	.2	3	.2	74	4.1	1,671	93.6	41	2.3	1,786
PROF:															
	84	.1	19,670	22.9	353	.4	218	.3	20,325	23.6	64,915	75.4	840	1.0	86,080
	33	.1	10,834	27.3	154	.4	74	.2	11,095	27.9	28,489	71.7	172	.4	39,756
	51	.1	8,836	19.1	199	.4	144	.3	9,230	19.9	36,426	78.0	668	1.4	46,324
	52	.2	6,985	20.6	133	.4	96	.3	7,266	21.5	26,423	78.1	137	.4	33,826
	18	.1	3,642	21.7	59	.4	36	.2	3,755	22.3	13,004	77.4	47	.3	16,806
	34	.2	3,343	19.6	74	.4	60	.4	3,511	20.6	13,419	78.8	90	.5	17,020
	136	.1	26,655	22.2	486	.4	314	.3	27,591	23.0	91,338	76.2	977	.8	119,906
	51	.1	14,476	25.6	213	.4	110	.2	14,850	26.3	41,493	73.4	219	.4	56,562
	85	.1	12,179	19.2	273	.4	204	.3	12,741	20.1	49,845	78.7	758	1.2	63,344
IED:															
	14	.2	970	17.1	33	.6	18	.3	1,035	18.2	4,573	80.4	81	1.4	5,689
	9	.3	577	17.4	13	.4	7	.2	606	18.3	2,664	80.2	50	1.5	3,320
	5	.2	393	16.6	20	.8	11	.5	429	18.1	1,909	80.6	31	1.3	2,369
OLLMENT:															
	150	.1	27,625	22.0	519	.4	332	.3	28,626	22.8	95,911	76.4	1,058	.8	125,595
	60	.1	15,053	25.1	226	.4	117	.2	15,456	25.8	44,157	73.7	269	.4	59,882
	90	.1	12,572	19.1	293	.4	215	.3	13,170	20.0	51,754	78.8	789	1.2	65,713
OTA (18 INSTITUTIONS)															
DATES:															
	607	2.6	311	1.3	83	.3	280	1.2	1,281	5.4	22,167	93.4	280	1.2	23,728
	320	2.9	56	.5	29	.3	34	.3	439	4.0	10,429	95.5	51	.5	10,919
	287	2.2	255	2.0	54	.4	246	1.9	842	6.6	11,738	91.6	229	1.8	12,809
	143	8.0	9	.5	21	1.2	3	.2	176	9.9	1,584	89.1	18	1.0	1,778
	93	8.9	6	.6	14	1.3	2	.2	115	11.0	930	88.7	4	.4	1,049
	50	6.9	3	.4	7	1.0	1	.1	61	8.4	654	89.7	14	1.9	729
	750	2.9	320	1.3	104	.4	283	1.1	1,457	5.7	23,751	93.1	298	1.2	25,506
	413	3.5	62	.5	43	.4	36	.3	554	4.6	11,359	94.9	55	.5	11,968
	337	2.5	258	1.9	61	.4	247	1.8	903	6.7	12,392	91.5	243	1.8	13,538
	23	3.8	1	.2	1	.2	2	.4	27	4.4	500	81.7	85	13.9	612
	9	4.7	0	.0	0	.0	0	.0	9	4.7	172	90.5	9	4.7	190
	14	3.3	1	.2	1	.2	2	.5	18	4.3	328	77.7	76	18.0	422
	3	.2	2	.2	1	.1	0	.0	6	.5	1,246	97.2	30	2.3	1,282
	1	.2	1	.2	0	.0	0	.0	2	.4	551	99.1	3	.5	556
	2	.3	1	.1	1	.1	0	.0	4	.6	695	95.7	27	3.7	726
	26	1.4	3	.2	2	.1	2	.1	33	1.7	1,746	92.2	115	6.1	1,894
	10	1.3	1	.1	0	.0	0	.0	11	1.5	723	96.9	12	1.6	746
	16	1.4	2	.2	2	.2	2	.2	22	1.9	1,023	89.1	103	9.0	1,148
NAL:															
	1	.2	1	.2	1	.2	1	.2	4	.8	477	96.2	15	3.0	496
	0	.0	0	.0	0	.0	0	.0	0	.0	92	97.9	2	2.1	94
	1	.2	1	.2	1	.2	1	.2	4	1.0	385	95.8	13	3.2	402
	0	.0	0	.0	0	.0	0	.0	0	.0	9	81.8	2	18.2	11
	0	.0	0	.0	0	.0	0	.0	0	.0	2	66.7	1	33.3	3
	0	.0	0	.0.	0	.0	0	.0	0	.0	7	87.5	1	12.5	8
	1	.2	1	.2	1	.2	1	.2	4	.8	486	95.9	17	3.4	507
	0	.0	0	.0	0	.0	0	.0	0	.0	94	96.9	3	3.1	97
	1	.2	1	.2	1	.2	1	.2	4	1.0	392	95.6	14	3.4	410
PROF:															
	631	2.5	313	1.3	85	.3	283	1.1	1,312	5.3	23,144	93.2	380	1.5	24,836
	329	2.9	56	.5	29	.3	34	.3	448	4.0	10,693	95.4	62	.6	11,203
	302	2.2	257	1.9	56	.4	249	1.8	864	6.3	12,451	91.3	318	2.3	13,633
	146	4.8	11	.4	22	.7	3	.1	182	5.9	2,839	92.4	50	1.6	3,071
	94	5.8	7	.4	14	.9	2	.1	117	7.3	1,483	92.2	8	.5	1,608
	52	3.6	4	.3	8	.5	1	.1	65	4.4	1,356	92.7	42	2.9	1,463
	777	2.8	324	1.2	107	.4	286	1.0	1,494	5.4	25,983	93.1	430	1.5	27,907
	423	3.3	63	.5	43	.3	36	.3	565	4.4	12,176	95.0	70	.5	12,811
	354	2.3	261	1.7	64	.4	250	1.7	929	6.2	13,807	91.5	360	2.4	15,096
IED:															
	157	5.2	6	.2	2	.1	7	.2	172	5.7	2,838	93.8	14	.5	3,024
	115	6.3	4	.2	1	.1	1	.1	121	6.7	1,685	92.9	7	.4	1,813
	42	3.5	2	.2	1	.1	6	.5	51	4.2	1,153	95.2	7	.6	1,211
OLLMENT:															
	934	3.0	330	1.1	109	.4	293	.9	1,666	5.4	28,821	93.2	444	1.4	30,931
	538	3.7	67	.5	44	.3	37	.3	686	4.7	13,861	94.8	77	.5	14,624
	396	2.4	263	1.6	65	.4	256	1.6	980	6.0	14,960	91.7	367	2.3	16,307

TABLE 17 - TOTAL ENROLLMENT IN INSTITUTIONS OF HIGHER EDUCATION FOR SELECTED MAJOR FIELDS OF STUDY AND LEVEL OF ENROLLMENT
BY RACE, ETHNICITY, AND SEX: STATE, 1978

MAJOR FIELD 9999 - SUMMARY

	AMERICAN INDIAN ALASKAN NATIVE		BLACK NON-HISPANIC		ASIAN OR PACIFIC ISLANDER		HISPANIC		TOTAL MINORITY		WHITE NON-HISPANIC		NON-RESIDENT ALIEN	
	NUMBER	%	NUMBER	%	NUMBER	%	NUMBER	%	NUMBER	%	NUMBER	%	NUMBER	%
TENNESSEE	(		76 INSTITUTIONS)											
UNDERGRADUATES:														
FULL-TIME	150	.1	21,020	17.9	398	.3	399	.3	21,967	18.8	92,877	79.3	2,269	1.9
FEMALE	78	.1	11,890	20.9	158	.3	160	.3	12,286	21.6	44,173	77.5	902	.9
MALE	72	.1	9,130	15.2	240	.4	239	.4	9,681	16.1	48,704	81.0	1,767	2.9
PART-TIME	77	.2	4,525	10.9	114	.3	154	.4	4,870	11.7	36,355	87.6	275	.7
FEMALE	42	.2	2,630	11.7	61	.3	78	.3	2,811	12.5	19,613	87.0	121	.5
MALE	35	.2	1,895	10.0	53	.3	76	.4	2,059	10.9	16,742	88.3	154	.8
TOTAL	227	.1	25,545	16.1	512	.3	553	.3	26,837	16.9	129,232	81.5	2,544	1.6
FEMALE	120	.2	14,520	18.3	219	.3	238	.3	15,097	19.0	63,786	80.2	623	.8
MALE	107	.1	11,025	13.9	293	.4	315	.4	11,740	14.8	65,446	82.7	1,921	2.4
GRADUATE:														
FULL-TIME	17	.3	400	6.9	62	1.1	26	.4	505	8.7	4,625	79.6	678	11.7
FEMALE	9	.4	241	9.4	27	1.1	10	.4	287	11.2	2,129	82.9	152	5.9
MALE	8	.2	159	4.9	35	1.1	16	.5	218	6.7	2,496	77.0	526	16.2
PART-TIME	12	.1	775	7.7	44	.5	23	.2	856	8.5	8,826	87.9	364	3.6
FEMALE	7	.1	498	9.9	10	.2	13	.3	528	10.5	4,428	87.9	83	1.6
MALE	5	.1	277	5.5	36	.7	10	.2	328	6.6	4,398	87.8	281	5.6
TOTAL	29	.2	1,175	7.4	108	.7	49	.3	1,361	8.6	13,451	84.8	1,042	6.6
FEMALE	16	.2	739	9.7	37	.5	23	.3	815	10.7	6,557	86.2	235	3.1
MALE	13	.2	436	5.3	71	.9	26	.3	546	6.6	6,894	83.6	807	9.8
PROFESSIONAL:														
FULL-TIME	9	.2	700	13.2	22	.4	25	.5	756	14.3	4,511	85.1	32	.6
FEMALE	1	.1	228	20.0	4	.4	4	.4	237	20.8	896	78.5	9	.8
MALE	8	.2	472	11.4	18	.4	21	.5	519	12.5	3,615	87.0	23	.6
PART-TIME	1	.5	9	4.4	1	.5	1	.5	12	5.9	189	92.6	3	1.5
FEMALE	0	.0	5	13.5	0	.0	0	.0	5	13.5	32	86.5	0	.0
MALE	1	.6	4	2.4	1	.6	1	.6	7	4.2	157	94.0	3	1.8
TOTAL	10	.2	709	12.9	23	.4	26	.5	768	14.0	4,700	85.4	35	.6
FEMALE	1	.1	233	19.8	4	.3	4	.3	242	20.5	928	78.7	9	.8
MALE	9	.2	476	11.0	19	.4	22	.5	526	12.2	3,772	87.2	26	.6
UND+GRAD+PROF:														
FULL-TIME	176	.1	22,120	17.3	482	.4	450	.4	23,228	18.1	102,013	79.6	2,979	2.3
FEMALE	88	.1	12,359	20.4	189	.3	174	.3	12,810	21.1	47,198	77.8	663	1.1
MALE	88	.1	9,761	14.5	293	.4	276	.4	10,418	15.4	54,815	81.1	2,316	3.4
PART-TIME	90	.2	5,309	10.3	161	.3	178	.3	5,738	11.1	45,370	87.7	642	1.2
FEMALE	49	.2	3,133	11.3	71	.3	91	.3	3,344	12.1	24,073	87.2	204	.7
MALE	41	.2	2,176	9.0	90	.4	87	.4	2,394	9.9	21,297	88.3	438	1.8
TOTAL	266	.1	27,429	15.2	643	.4	628	.3	28,966	16.1	147,383	81.9	3,621	2.0
FEMALE	137	.2	15,492	17.5	260	.3	265	.3	16,154	18.3	71,271	80.7	867	1.0
MALE	129	.1	11,937	13.0	383	.4	363	.4	12,812	14.0	76,112	83.0	2,754	3.0
UNCLASSIFIED:														
TOTAL	54	.4	2,427	16.5	76	.5	35	.2	2,592	17.6	11,692	79.6	413	2.8
FEMALE	16	.2	1,504	17.6	40	.5	17	.2	1,577	18.5	6,741	79.0	214	2.5
MALE	38	.6	923	15.0	36	.6	18	.3	1,015	16.5	4,951	80.3	199	3.2
TOTAL ENROLLMENT:														
TOTAL	320	.2	29,856	15.3	719	.4	663	.3	31,558	16.2	159,075	81.7	4,034	2.1
FEMALE	153	.2	16,996	17.6	300	.3	282	.3	17,731	18.3	78,012	80.6	1,081	1.1
MALE	167	.2	12,860	13.1	419	.4	381	.4	13,827	14.1	81,063	82.9	2,953	3.0
TEXAS	(		147 INSTITUTIONS)											
UNDERGRADUATES:														
FULL-TIME	1,015	.3	32,276	9.5	2,433	.7	40,831	12.0	76,555	22.5	250,754	73.7	12,867	3.8
FEMALE	466	.3	17,308	10.8	1,082	.7	19,638	12.3	38,494	24.1	118,663	74.2	2,677	1.7
MALE	549	.3	14,968	8.3	1,351	.7	21,193	11.8	38,061	21.1	132,091	73.2	10,190	5.7
PART-TIME	923	.5	21,745	11.0	1,791	.9	27,620	14.0	52,079	26.4	143,019	72.4	2,415	1.2
FEMALE	430	.4	11,258	11.1	936	.9	13,468	13.3	26,092	25.7	74,443	73.3	966	1.0
MALE	493	.5	10,487	10.9	855	.9	14,152	14.7	25,987	27.1	68,576	71.4	1,449	1.5
TOTAL	1,938	.4	54,021	10.0	4,224	.8	68,451	12.7	128,634	23.9	393,773	73.2	15,282	2.8
FEMALE	896	.3	28,566	10.9	2,018	.8	33,106	12.7	64,586	24.7	193,106	73.9	3,643	1.4
MALE	1,042	.4	25,455	9.2	2,206	.8	35,345	12.8	64,048	23.2	200,667	72.6	11,639	4.2
GRADUATE:														
FULL-TIME	85	.3	1,057	3.8	612	2.2	1,093	4.0	2,847	10.3	20,674	75.0	4,033	14.6
FEMALE	26	.3	570	5.6	200	2.0	461	4.5	1,257	12.3	8,152	79.7	815	8.0
MALE	59	.3	487	2.8	412	2.4	632	3.6	1,590	9.2	12,522	72.3	3,218	18.6
PART-TIME	160	.4	2,905	7.4	339	.9	3,428	8.8	6,832	17.4	30,917	79.0	1,409	3.6
FEMALE	66	.3	1,777	8.9	149	.7	1,790	8.9	3,782	18.9	15,892	79.3	357	1.8
MALE	94	.5	1,128	5.9	190	1.0	1,638	8.6	3,050	15.9	15,025	78.6	1,052	5.5
TOTAL	245	.4	3,962	5.9	951	1.4	4,521	6.8	9,679	14.5	51,591	77.3	5,442	8.2
FEMALE	92	.3	2,347	7.8	349	1.2	2,251	7.4	5,039	16.7	24,044	79.5	1,172	3.9
MALE	153	.4	1,615	4.4	602	1.7	2,270	6.2	4,640	12.7	27,547	75.4	4,270	11.7
PROFESSIONAL:														
FULL-TIME	42	.3	447	3.6	132	1.1	809	6.5	1,430	11.5	10,887	87.4	128	1.0
FEMALE	8	.3	185	6.3	44	1.5	178	6.1	415	14.2	2,476	85.0	23	.8
MALE	34	.4	262	2.8	88	.9	631	6.6	1,015	10.7	8,371	88.2	105	1.1

690

SUMMARY

N INDIAN NATIVE	BLACK NON-HISPANIC		ASIAN OR PACIFIC ISLANDER		HISPANIC		TOTAL MINORITY		WHITE NON-HISPANIC		NON-RESIDENT ALIEN		TOTAL
%	NUMBER	%	NUMBER	%	NUMBER	%	NUMBER	%	NUMBER	%	NUMBER	%	NUMBER

CONTINUED

.2	75	5.6	6	.5	65	4.9	148	11.1	1,159	87.1	24	1.8	1,331
.0	21	5.6	2	.5	20	5.3	43	11.4	331	87.8	3	.8	377
.2	54	5.7	4	.4	45	4.7	105	11.0	828	86.8	21	2.2	954

.3	522	3.8	138	1.0	874	6.4	1,578	11.5	12,006	87.4	152	1.1	13,736
.2	206	6.3	46	1.4	198	6.0	458	13.9	2,807	85.3	26	.8	3,291
.3	316	3.0	92	.9	676	6.5	1,120	10.7	9,199	88.1	126	1.2	10,445

.3	33,780	8.9	3,177	.8	42,733	11.2	80,832	21.3	282,275	74.3	17,028	4.5	380,135
.3	18,063	10.4	1,326	.8	20,277	11.7	40,166	23.2	129,291	74.7	3,515	2.0	172,972
.3	15,717	7.6	1,851	.9	22,456	10.8	40,666	19.6	152,984	73.8	13,513	6.5	207,163
.5	24,725	10.4	2,136	.9	31,113	13.1	59,059	24.8	175,095	73.6	3,848	1.6	238,002
.4	13,056	10.7	1,087	.9	15,278	12.5	29,917	24.5	90,666	74.4	1,326	1.1	121,909
.5	11,669	10.1	1,049	.9	15,835	13.6	29,142	25.1	84,429	72.7	2,522	2.2	116,093

.4	58,505	9.5	5,313	.9	73,846	11.9	139,891	22.6	457,370	74.0	20,876	3.4	618,137
.3	31,119	10.6	2,413	.8	35,555	12.1	70,083	23.8	219,957	74.6	4,841	1.6	294,881
.4	27,386	8.5	2,900	.9	38,291	11.8	69,808	21.6	237,413	73.4	16,035	5.0	323,256

.5	3,573	9.4	365	1.0	5,108	13.5	9,246	24.4	27,959	73.8	662	1.7	37,867
.4	1,833	10.1	193	1.1	1,955	10.8	4,060	22.3	13,900	76.4	224	1.2	18,184
.6	1,740	8.8	172	.9	3,153	16.0	5,186	26.3	14,059	71.4	438	2.2	19,683

.4	62,078	9.5	5,678	.9	78,954	12.0	149,137	22.7	485,329	74.0	21,538	3.3	656,004
.3	32,952	10.5	2,606	.8	37,510	12.0	74,143	23.7	233,857	74.7	5,065	1.6	313,065
.4	29,126	8.5	3,072	.9	41,444	12.1	74,994	21.9	251,472	73.3	16,473	4.8	342,939

(14 INSTITLTIONS)

1.3	349	.6	1,069	1.9	642	1.1	2,779	4.9	51,343	89.9	2,978	5.2	57,100
1.4	124	.5	541	2.1	279	1.1	1,311	5.1	23,278	90.0	1,263	4.9	25,852
1.1	225	.7	528	1.7	363	1.2	1,468	4.7	28,065	89.8	1,715	5.5	31,248
.7	95	.5	214	1.0	405	1.9	861	4.1	19,807	94.8	219	1.0	20,887
.8	36	.4	102	1.1	136	1.5	345	3.8	8,539	95.1	99	1.1	8,983
.6	59	.5	112	.9	269	2.3	516	4.3	11,268	94.7	120	1.0	11,904

1.1	444	.6	1,283	1.6	1,047	1.3	3,640	4.7	71,150	91.2	3,197	4.1	77,987
1.3	160	.5	643	1.8	415	1.2	1,656	4.8	31,817	91.3	1,362	3.9	34,835
1.0	284	.7	640	1.5	632	1.5	1,984	4.6	39,333	91.1	1,835	4.3	43,152

.9	18	.4	49	1.2	37	.9	141	3.4	3,504	85.7	442	10.8	4,087
1.4	4	.3	18	1.5	15	1.2	54	4.4	1,080	87.7	97	7.9	1,231
.7	14	.5	31	1.1	22	.8	87	3.0	2,424	84.9	345	12.1	2,856
.3	15	.4	54	1.5	31	.8	111	3.0	3,208	87.7	341	9.3	3,660
.4	10	.7	24	1.7	16	1.2	55	4.0	1,222	89.1	95	6.9	1,372
.3	5	.2	30	1.3	15	.7	56	2.4	1,986	86.8	246	10.8	2,288

.6	33	.4	103	1.3	68	.9	252	3.3	6,712	86.6	783	10.1	7,747
.8	14	.5	42	1.6	31	1.2	109	4.2	2,302	88.4	192	7.4	2,603
.5	19	.4	61	1.2	37	.7	143	2.8	4,410	85.7	591	11.5	5,144

.4	10	.8	14	1.1	24	2.0	53	4.3	1,164	94.6	13	1.1	1,230
.0	4	2.0	2	1.0	4	2.0	10	4.9	190	92.7	5	2.4	205
.5	6	.6	12	1.2	20	2.0	43	4.2	974	95.0	8	.8	1,025
.0	0	.0	0	.0	1	8.3	1	8.3	11	91.7	0	.0	12
.0	0	.0	0	.0	0	.0	0	.0	4	100.0	0	.0	4
.0	0	.0	0	.0	1	12.5	1	12.5	7	87.5	0	.0	8

.4	10	.8	14	1.1	25	2.0	54	4.3	1,175	94.6	13	1.0	1,242
.0	4	1.9	2	1.0	4	1.9	10	4.8	194	92.8	5	2.4	209
.5	6	.6	12	1.2	21	2.0	44	4.3	981	95.0	8	.8	1,033

1.2	377	.6	1,132	1.8	703	1.1	2,973	4.8	56,011	89.7	3,433	5.5	62,417
1.1	132	.5	561	2.1	298	1.1	1,375	5.0	24,548	90.0	1,365	5.0	27,288
1.2	245	.7	571	1.6	405	1.2	1,598	4.5	31,463	89.6	2,068	5.9	35,129
.6	110	.4	268	1.1	437	1.8	973	4.0	23,026	93.8	560	2.3	24,559
.7	46	.4	126	1.2	152	1.5	400	3.9	9,765	94.3	194	1.9	10,359
.6	64	.5	142	1.0	285	2.0	573	4.0	13,261	93.4	366	2.6	14,200

1.1	407	.6	1,400	1.6	1,140	1.3	3,946	4.5	79,037	90.9	3,993	4.6	86,976
1.2	178	.5	687	1.8	450	1.2	1,775	4.7	34,313	91.1	1,559	4.1	37,647
.9	309	.6	713	1.4	690	1.4	2,171	4.4	44,724	90.7	2,434	4.9	49,329

1.0	9	.4	34	1.7	29	1.4	93	4.6	1,792	89.0	128	6.4	2,013
2.1	6	.6	23	2.3	10	1.0	60	5.9	920	90.2	40	3.9	1,020
.0	3	.3	11	1.1	19	1.9	33	3.3	872	87.8	88	8.9	993

1.1	496	.6	1,434	1.6	1,169	1.3	4,039	4.5	80,829	90.8	4,121	4.6	88,989
1.2	184	.5	710	1.8	460	1.2	1,835	4.7	35,233	91.1	1,599	4.1	38,667
.9	312	.6	724	1.4	709	1.4	2,204	4.4	45,596	90.6	2,522	5.0	50,322

MAJOR FIELD 9999 - SUMMARY

	AMERICAN INDIAN ALASKAN NATIVE		BLACK NON-HISPANIC		ASIAN OR PACIFIC ISLANDER		HISPANIC		TOTAL MINORITY		WHITE NON-HISPANIC		NON-RESIDENT ALIEN	
	NUMBER	%	NUMBER	%	NUMBER	%	NUMBER	%	NUMBER	%	NUMBER	%	NUMBER	%
VERMONT (21 INSTITUTIONS)														
UNDERGRADUATES:														
FULL-TIME	40	.2	278	1.4	50	.2	122	.6	490	2.4	19,471	95.9	337	1.7
FEMALE	19	.2	158	1.5	26	.2	66	.6	269	2.5	10,324	96.5	101	.9
MALE	21	.2	120	1.2	24	.2	56	.6	221	2.3	9,147	95.2	236	2.5
PART-TIME	3	.1	5	.2	0	.0	3	.1	11	.4	2,992	99.5	3	.1
FEMALE	0	.0	3	.2	0	.0	2	.1	5	.3	1,953	99.7	1	.1
MALE	3	.3	2	.2	0	.0	1	.1	6	.6	1,039	99.2	2	.2
TOTAL	43	.2	283	1.2	50	.2	125	.5	501	2.1	22,463	96.4	340	1.5
FEMALE	19	.2	161	1.3	26	.2	68	.5	274	2.2	12,277	97.0	102	.8
MALE	24	.2	122	1.1	24	.2	57	.5	227	2.1	10,186	95.6	238	2.2
GRADUATE:														
FULL-TIME	2	.2	34	3.0	7	.6	17	1.5	60	5.3	994	88.6	68	6.1
FEMALE	0	.0	16	2.7	5	.8	6	1.0	27	4.5	552	91.7	23	3.8
MALE	2	.4	18	3.5	2	.4	11	2.1	33	6.3	442	85.0	45	8.7
PART-TIME	1	.1	11	.9	1	.1	2	.2	15	1.2	1,216	95.6	41	3.2
FEMALE	0	.0	7	.9	1	.1	0	.0	8	1.1	720	96.5	18	2.4
MALE	1	.2	4	.8	0	.0	2	.4	7	1.3	496	94.3	23	4.4
TOTAL	3	.1	45	1.9	8	.3	19	.8	75	3.1	2,210	92.3	109	4.6
FEMALE	0	.0	23	1.7	6	.4	6	.4	35	2.6	1,272	94.4	41	3.0
MALE	3	.3	22	2.1	2	.2	13	1.2	40	3.8	938	89.7	68	6.5
PROFESSIONAL:														
FULL-TIME	0	.0	0	.0	3	.5	0	.0	3	.5	640	99.1	3	.5
FEMALE	0	.0	0	.0	1	.6	0	.0	1	.6	154	98.7	1	.6
MALE	0	.0	0	.0	2	.4	0	.0	2	.4	486	99.2	2	.4
PART-TIME	0	.0	0	.0	0	.0	0	.0	0	.0	0	.0	0	.0
FEMALE	0	.0	0	.0	0	.0	0	.0	0	.0	0	.0	0	.0
MALE	0	.0	0	.0	0	.0	0	.0	0	.0	0	.0	0	.0
TOTAL	0	.0	0	.0	3	.5	0	.0	3	.5	640	99.1	3	.5
FEMALE	0	.0	0	.0	1	.6	0	.0	1	.6	154	98.7	1	.6
MALE	0	.0	0	.0	2	.4	0	.0	2	.4	486	99.2	2	.4
UND+GRAD+PROF:														
FULL-TIME	42	.2	312	1.4	60	.3	139	.6	553	2.5	21,105	95.6	408	1.8
FEMALE	19	.2	174	1.5	32	.3	72	.6	297	2.6	11,030	96.3	125	1.1
MALE	23	.2	138	1.3	28	.3	67	.6	256	2.4	10,075	94.9	283	2.7
PART-TIME	4	.1	16	.4	1	.0	5	.1	26	.6	4,208	98.4	44	1.0
FEMALE	0	.0	10	.4	1	.0	2	.1	13	.5	2,673	98.8	19	.7
MALE	4	.3	6	.4	0	.0	3	.2	13	.8	1,535	97.6	25	1.6
TOTAL	46	.2	328	1.2	61	.2	144	.5	579	2.2	25,313	96.1	452	1.7
FEMALE	19	.1	164	1.3	33	.2	74	.5	310	2.2	13,703	96.8	144	1.0
MALE	27	.2	144	1.2	28	.2	70	.6	269	2.2	11,610	95.3	308	2.5
UNCLASSIFIED:														
TOTAL	2	.1	5	.2	2	.1	3	.1	12	.4	3,036	93.9	185	5.7
FEMALE	1	.1	2	.1	2	.1	1	.1	6	.3	1,720	97.0	48	2.7
MALE	1	.1	3	.2	0	.0	2	.1	6	.4	1,316	90.2	137	9.4
TOTAL ENROLLMENT:														
TOTAL	48	.2	333	1.1	63	.2	147	.5	591	2.0	28,349	95.8	637	2.2
FEMALE	20	.1	186	1.2	35	.2	75	.5	316	2.0	15,423	96.8	192	1.2
MALE	28	.2	147	1.1	28	.2	72	.5	275	2.0	12,926	94.7	445	3.3
VIRGINIA (71 INSTITUTIONS)														
UNDERGRADUATES:														
FULL-TIME	219	.2	20,474	16.4	1,001	.8	541	.4	22,235	17.8	101,477	81.1	1,339	1.1
FEMALE	121	.2	12,068	18.5	472	.7	275	.4	12,936	19.9	51,631	79.3	509	.8
MALE	98	.2	8,406	14.0	529	.9	266	.4	9,299	15.5	49,846	83.1	830	1.4
PART-TIME	89	.2	6,135	16.7	361	1.0	222	.6	6,807	18.6	29,704	81.0	159	.4
FEMALE	53	.3	3,069	16.5	187	1.0	101	.5	3,410	18.4	15,082	81.2	75	.4
MALE	36	.2	3,066	16.9	174	1.0	121	.7	3,397	18.8	14,622	80.8	84	.5
TOTAL	308	.2	26,609	16.5	1,362	.8	763	.5	29,042	18.0	131,181	81.1	1,498	.9
FEMALE	174	.2	15,137	18.1	659	.8	376	.4	16,346	19.5	66,713	79.8	584	.7
MALE	134	.2	11,472	14.7	703	.9	387	.5	12,696	16.3	64,468	82.6	914	1.2
GRADUATE:														
FULL-TIME	7	.1	635	7.7	90	1.1	28	.3	760	9.2	7,023	85.0	478	5.8
FEMALE	2	.1	329	9.8	23	.7	13	.4	367	10.9	2,894	86.1	102	3.0
MALE	5	.1	306	6.2	67	1.4	15	.3	393	8.0	4,129	84.3	376	7.7
PART-TIME	19	.2	1,291	11.0	85	.7	43	.4	1,438	12.3	10,171	86.8	111	.9
FEMALE	8	.1	887	14.1	25	.4	25	.4	945	15.0	5,317	84.5	33	.5
MALE	11	.2	404	7.4	60	1.1	18	.3	493	9.1	4,854	89.5	78	1.4
TOTAL	26	.1	1,926	9.6	175	.9	71	.4	2,198	11.0	17,194	86.1	589	2.9
FEMALE	10	.1	1,216	12.6	48	.5	38	.4	1,312	13.6	8,211	85.0	135	1.4
MALE	16	.2	710	6.9	127	1.2	33	.3	886	8.6	8,983	87.0	454	4.4
PROFESSIONAL:														
FULL-TIME	2	.0	165	3.8	35	.8	13	.3	215	5.0	4,083	94.6	18	.4
FEMALE	1	.1	72	6.8	10	.9	2	.2	85	8.0	972	91.4	7	.7
MALE	1	.0	93	2.9	25	.8	11	.3	130	4.0	3,111	95.7	11	.3

ENROLLMENT IN INSTITUTIONS OF HIGHER EDUCATION FOR SELECTED MAJOR FIELDS OF STUDY AND LEVEL OF ENROLLMENT
, ETHNICITY, AND SEX: STATE, 1978

SUMMARY

N INDIAN NATIVE	BLACK NON-HISPANIC		ASIAN OR PACIFIC ISLANDER		HISPANIC		TOTAL MINORITY		WHITE NON-HISPANIC		NON-RESIDENT ALIEN		TOTAL
%	NUMBER	%	NUMBER	%	NUMBER	%	NUMBER	%	NUMBER	%	NUMBER	%	NUMBER
CONTINUED													
.0	1	2.7	0	.0	0	.0	1	2.7	36	97.3	0	.0	37
.0	1	12.5	0	.0	0	.0	1	12.5	7	87.5	0	.0	8
.0	0	.0	0	.0	0	.0	0	.0	29	100.0	0	.0	29
.0	106	3.8	35	.8	13	.3	216	5.0	4,119	94.6	18	.4	4,353
.1	73	6.8	10	.9	2	.2	86	8.0	979	91.3	7	.7	1,072
.0	93	2.8	25	.8	11	.3	130	4.0	3,140	95.7	11	.3	3,281
.2	21,274	15.5	1,126	.8	582	.4	23,210	16.9	112,583	81.8	1,835	1.3	137,624
.2	12,469	17.9	505	.7	290	.4	13,388	19.3	55,497	79.8	618	.9	69,503
.2	8,805	12.9	621	.9	292	.4	9,822	14.4	57,086	83.8	1,217	1.8	68,125
.2	7,427	15.3	446	.9	265	.5	8,246	17.0	39,911	82.4	270	.6	48,427
.2	3,957	15.9	212	.9	126	.5	4,356	17.5	20,406	82.1	108	.4	24,870
.2	3,470	14.7	234	1.0	139	.6	3,890	16.5	19,505	82.8	162	.7	23,557
.2	28,701	15.4	1,572	.8	847	.5	31,456	16.9	152,494	82.0	2,105	1.1	186,055
.2	16,426	17.4	717	.8	416	.4	17,744	18.8	75,903	80.4	726	.8	94,373
.2	12,275	13.4	855	.9	431	.5	13,712	15.0	76,591	83.5	1,379	1.5	91,682
.3	8,616	11.9	1,098	1.5	594	.8	10,517	14.5	60,985	84.3	811	1.1	72,313
.3	5,169	12.2	583	1.4	311	.7	6,204	14.6	35,912	84.5	366	.9	42,482
.2	3,447	11.6	515	1.7	283	.9	4,313	14.5	25,073	84.1	445	1.5	29,831
.2	37,317	14.4	2,670	1.0	1,441	.6	41,973	16.2	213,479	82.6	2,916	1.1	258,368
.2	21,595	15.8	1,300	.9	727	.5	23,948	17.5	111,815	81.7	1,092	.8	136,855
.2	15,722	12.9	1,370	1.1	714	.6	18,025	14.8	101,664	83.7	1,824	1.5	121,513
(49 INSTITUTIONS)													
1.3	3,397	2.9	3,776	3.3	1,439	1.2	10,147	8.8	101,363	87.5	4,269	3.7	115,779
1.5	1,443	2.6	1,822	3.3	620	1.1	4,697	8.5	49,100	89.1	1,333	2.4	55,130
1.2	1,954	3.2	1,954	3.2	819	1.4	5,450	9.0	52,263	86.2	2,936	4.8	60,649
1.3	830	3.1	755	2.8	374	1.4	2,317	8.7	23,668	89.0	602	2.3	26,587
1.5	361	2.5	378	2.6	174	1.2	1,133	7.9	12,911	90.0	306	2.1	14,350
1.1	469	3.8	377	3.1	200	1.6	1,184	9.7	10,757	87.9	296	2.4	12,237
1.3	4,227	3.0	4,531	3.2	1,813	1.3	12,464	8.8	125,031	87.8	4,871	3.4	142,366
1.5	1,804	2.6	2,200	3.2	794	1.1	5,830	8.4	62,011	89.3	1,639	2.4	69,480
1.2	2,423	3.3	2,331	3.2	1,019	1.4	6,634	9.1	63,020	86.5	3,232	4.4	72,886
.7	172	2.1	246	3.0	94	1.1	566	6.8	6,628	79.8	1,109	13.4	8,303
.6	76	2.4	109	3.4	23	.7	228	7.1	2,736	85.6	231	7.2	3,195
.7	96	1.9	137	2.7	71	1.4	338	6.6	3,892	76.2	878	17.2	5,108
.7	123	2.3	149	2.8	44	.8	355	6.6	4,589	85.4	427	8.0	5,371
1.0	52	2.3	49	2.1	19	.8	143	6.2	2,040	89.1	106	4.6	2,289
.5	71	2.3	100	3.2	25	.8	212	6.9	2,549	82.7	321	10.4	3,082
.7	295	2.2	395	2.9	138	1.0	921	6.7	11,217	82.0	1,536	11.2	13,674
.8	128	2.3	158	2.9	42	.8	371	6.8	4,776	87.1	337	6.1	5,484
.6	167	2.0	237	2.9	96	1.2	550	6.7	6,441	78.6	1,199	14.6	8,190
.6	34	1.0	83	2.6	50	1.5	186	5.7	3,054	94.1	6	.2	3,246
1.0	14	1.7	24	2.9	16	1.9	62	7.4	770	92.4	1	.1	833
.5	20	.8	59	2.4	34	1.4	124	5.1	2,284	94.7	5	.2	2,413
.9	3	.9	4	1.2	2	.6	12	3.7	311	96.3	0	.0	323
.0	1	1.2	2	2.4	1	1.2	4	4.8	80	95.2	0	.0	84
1.3	2	.8	2	.8	1	.4	8	3.3	231	96.7	0	.0	239
.6	37	1.0	87	2.4	52	1.5	198	5.5	3,365	94.3	6	.2	3,569
.9	15	1.6	26	2.8	17	1.9	66	7.2	850	92.7	1	.1	917
.5	22	.8	61	2.3	35	1.3	132	5.0	2,515	94.8	5	.2	2,652
1.3	3,603	2.8	4,105	3.2	1,583	1.2	10,899	8.6	111,045	87.2	5,384	4.2	127,328
1.4	1,533	2.6	1,955	3.3	659	1.1	4,987	8.4	52,606	88.9	1,565	2.6	59,158
1.4	2,070	3.0	2,150	3.2	924	1.4	5,912	8.7	58,439	85.7	3,819	5.6	68,170
1.2	956	3.0	908	2.8	420	1.3	2,684	8.3	28,568	88.5	1,029	3.2	32,281
1.5	414	2.5	429	2.6	194	1.2	1,280	7.7	15,031	89.9	412	2.5	16,723
1.0	542	3.5	479	3.1	226	1.5	1,404	9.0	13,537	87.0	617	4.0	15,558
1.3	4,559	2.9	5,013	3.1	2,003	1.3	13,583	8.5	139,613	87.5	6,413	4.0	159,609
1.4	1,947	2.6	2,384	3.1	853	1.1	6,267	8.3	67,637	89.1	1,977	2.6	75,881
1.1	2,612	3.1	2,629	3.1	1,150	1.4	7,316	8.7	71,976	86.0	4,436	5.3	83,728
1.2	1,711	1.5	1,874	1.6	1,638	1.4	6,653	5.8	105,670	91.3	3,367	2.9	119,690
1.3	810	1.2	1,169	1.7	877	1.3	3,741	5.5	62,472	91.7	1,936	2.8	68,149
1.1	901	1.9	705	1.5	761	1.6	2,912	6.1	43,198	90.9	1,431	3.0	47,541
1.2	6,270	2.3	6,887	2.5	3,641	1.3	20,236	7.4	245,283	89.1	9,780	3.6	275,299
1.4	2,757	1.9	3,553	2.5	1,730	1.2	10,008	6.9	130,109	90.3	3,913	2.7	144,030
1.1	3,513	2.7	3,334	2.5	1,911	1.5	10,228	7.8	115,174	87.7	5,867	4.5	131,269

MAJOR FIELD 9999 - SUMMARY

	AMERICAN INDIAN ALASKAN NATIVE		BLACK NON-HISPANIC		ASIAN OR PACIFIC ISLANDER		HISPANIC		TOTAL MINORITY		WHITE NON-HISPANIC		NON-RESIDENT ALIEN	
	NUMBER	%	NUMBER	%	NUMBER	%	NUMBER	%	NUMBER	%	NUMBER	%	NUMBER	%
WEST VIRGINIA (28 INSTITUTIONS)														
UNDERGRADUATES:														
FULL-TIME	93	.2	2,195	4.9	154	.3	98	.2	2,540	5.7	41,156	92.7	697	1.6
FEMALE	42	.2	974	4.7	50	.2	37	.2	1,103	5.3	19,634	94.2	110	.5
MALE	51	.2	1,221	5.2	104	.4	61	.3	1,437	6.1	21,522	91.4	587	2.5
PART-TIME	80	.5	595	4.0	54	.4	25	.2	754	5.0	14,168	94.6	55	.4
FEMALE	57	.7	343	3.9	28	.3	14	.2	442	5.1	8,253	94.8	15	.2
MALE	23	.4	252	4.0	26	.4	11	.2	312	5.0	5,915	94.4	40	.6
TOTAL	173	.3	2,790	4.7	208	.4	123	.2	3,294	5.5	55,324	93.2	752	1.3
FEMALE	99	.3	1,317	4.5	78	.3	51	.2	1,545	5.2	27,887	94.3	125	.4
MALE	74	.2	1,473	4.9	130	.4	72	.2	1,749	5.9	27,437	92.0	627	2.1
GRADUATE:														
FULL-TIME	7	.3	29	1.3	31	1.4	7	.3	74	3.4	1,865	84.7	262	11.9
FEMALE	2	.2	12	1.3	10	1.1	3	.3	27	3.0	825	91.4	51	5.6
MALE	5	.4	17	1.3	21	1.6	4	.3	47	3.6	1,040	80.1	211	16.3
PART-TIME	36	.4	239	2.6	52	.6	15	.2	342	3.7	8,805	95.2	104	1.1
FEMALE	21	.4	146	2.6	17	.3	7	.1	191	3.4	5,431	96.2	24	.4
MALE	15	.4	93	2.6	35	1.0	8	.2	151	4.2	3,374	93.6	80	2.2
TOTAL	43	.4	268	2.3	83	.7	22	.2	416	3.6	10,670	93.2	366	3.2
FEMALE	23	.4	158	2.4	27	.4	10	.2	218	3.3	6,256	95.5	75	1.1
MALE	20	.4	110	2.2	56	1.1	12	.2	198	4.0	4,414	90.0	291	5.9
PROFESSIONAL:														
FULL-TIME	3	.2	13	1.0	2	.2	3	.2	21	1.7	1,218	98.1	3	.2
FEMALE	1	.5	6	2.7	0	.0	2	.9	9	4.1	210	95.5	1	.5
MALE	2	.2	7	.7	2	.2	1	.1	12	1.2	1,008	98.6	2	.2
PART-TIME	0	.0	0	.0	0	.0	0	.0	0	.0	23	100.0	0	.0
FEMALE	0	.0	0	.0	0	.0	0	.0	0	.0	7	100.0	0	.0
MALE	0	.0	0	.0	0	.0	0	.0	0	.0	16	100.0	0	.0
TOTAL	3	.2	13	1.0	2	.2	3	.2	21	1.7	1,241	98.1	3	.2
FEMALE	1	.4	6	2.6	0	.0	2	.9	9	4.0	217	95.6	1	.4
MALE	2	.2	7	.7	2	.2	1	.1	12	1.2	1,024	98.7	2	.2
UND+GRAD+PROF:														
FULL-TIME	103	.2	2,237	4.7	187	.4	108	.2	2,635	5.5	44,239	92.5	962	2.0
FEMALE	45	.2	992	4.5	60	.3	42	.2	1,139	5.2	20,669	94.1	162	.7
MALE	58	.2	1,245	4.8	127	.5	66	.3	1,496	6.0	23,570	91.1	800	3.1
PART-TIME	116	.4	834	3.4	106	.4	40	.2	1,096	4.5	22,996	94.8	159	.7
FEMALE	78	.5	489	3.4	45	.3	21	.1	633	4.4	13,691	95.3	39	.3
MALE	38	.4	345	3.5	61	.6	19	.2	463	4.7	9,305	94.1	120	1.2
TOTAL	219	.3	3,071	4.3	293	.4	148	.2	3,731	5.2	67,235	93.3	1,121	1.6
FEMALE	123	.3	1,481	4.1	105	.3	63	.2	1,772	4.9	34,360	94.6	201	.6
MALE	96	.3	1,590	4.4	188	.5	85	.2	1,959	5.5	32,875	91.9	920	2.6
UNCLASSIFIED:														
TOTAL	14	.2	196	2.8	28	.4	19	.3	257	3.7	6,641	96.0	22	.3
FEMALE	8	.2	98	2.5	10	.3	8	.2	124	3.1	3,832	96.6	9	.2
MALE	6	.2	98	3.3	18	.6	11	.4	133	4.5	2,809	95.1	13	.4
TOTAL ENROLLMENT:														
TOTAL	233	.3	3,267	4.1	321	.4	167	.2	3,988	5.0	73,876	93.5	1,143	1.4
FEMALE	131	.3	1,579	3.9	115	.3	71	.2	1,896	4.7	38,192	94.8	210	.5
MALE	102	.3	1,688	4.4	206	.5	96	.2	2,092	5.4	35,684	92.2	933	2.4
WISCONSIN (62 INSTITUTIONS)														
UNDERGRADUATES:														
FULL-TIME	806	.6	4,296	3.0	766	.5	1,110	.8	6,978	4.8	136,453	94.0	1,667	1.1
FEMALE	435	.6	2,326	3.3	351	.5	493	.7	3,605	5.1	66,411	94.3	433	.6
MALE	371	.5	1,970	2.6	415	.6	617	.8	3,373	4.5	70,042	93.8	1,234	1.7
PART-TIME	229	.5	2,492	5.0	278	.6	460	.9	3,459	6.9	46,284	92.7	171	.3
FEMALE	131	.5	1,470	5.8	156	.6	199	.8	1,956	7.8	23,221	92.1	43	.2
MALE	98	.4	1,022	4.1	122	.5	261	1.1	1,503	6.1	23,063	93.4	128	.5
TOTAL	1,035	.5	6,788	3.5	1,044	.5	1,570	.8	10,437	5.4	182,737	93.7	1,838	.9
FEMALE	566	.6	3,796	4.0	507	.5	692	.7	5,561	5.8	89,632	93.7	476	.5
MALE	469	.5	2,992	3.0	537	.5	878	.9	4,876	4.9	93,105	93.7	1,362	1.4
GRADUATE:														
FULL-TIME	37	.4	270	2.7	193	1.9	129	1.3	629	6.3	7,886	79.0	1,472	14.7
FEMALE	19	.5	136	3.5	66	1.7	59	1.5	280	7.3	3,248	84.5	318	8.3
MALE	18	.3	134	2.2	127	2.1	70	1.1	349	5.7	4,638	75.5	1,154	18.8
PART-TIME	21	.2	185	2.0	86	.9	67	.7	359	3.9	8,641	93.7	218	2.4
FEMALE	13	.3	112	2.4	34	.7	32	.7	191	4.1	4,357	94.5	63	1.4
MALE	8	.2	73	1.6	52	1.1	35	.8	168	3.6	4,284	93.0	155	3.4
TOTAL	58	.3	455	2.4	279	1.5	196	1.0	988	5.1	16,527	86.1	1,690	8.8
FEMALE	32	.4	248	2.9	100	1.2	91	1.1	471	5.6	7,605	89.9	381	4.5
MALE	26	.2	207	1.9	179	1.7	105	1.0	517	4.8	8,922	83.0	1,309	12.2
PROFESSIONAL:														
FULL-TIME	16	.5	96	2.9	28	.8	72	2.1	212	6.3	3,144	93.4	11	.3
FEMALE	4	.5	40	5.1	11	1.4	15	1.9	70	9.0	706	90.7	2	.3
MALE	12	.5	56	2.2	17	.7	57	2.2	142	5.5	2,438	94.2	9	.3

LE 17 - TOTAL ENROLLMENT IN INSTITUTIONS OF HIGHER EDUCATION FOR SELECTED MAJOR FIELDS OF STUDY AND LEVEL OF ENROLLMENT
BY RACE, ETHNICITY, AND SEX: STATE, 1978

OR FIELD 9999 - SUMMARY

	AMERICAN INDIAN ALASKAN NATIVE		BLACK NON-HISPANIC		ASIAN OR PACIFIC ISLANDER		HISPANIC		TOTAL MINORITY		WHITE NON-HISPANIC		NON-RESIDENT ALIEN		TOTAL
	NUMBER	%	NUMBER	%	NUMBER	%	NUMBER	%	NUMBER	%	NUMBER	%	NUMBER	%	NUMBER

CONSIN   CONTINUED

FESSIONAL:
T-TIME	3	2.4	4	3.3	1	.8	0	.0	8	6.5	110	89.4	5	4.1	123
FEMALE	0	.0	0	.0	1	2.4	0	.0	1	2.4	38	90.5	3	7.1	42
MALE	3	3.7	4	4.9	0	.0	0	.0	7	8.6	72	88.9	2	2.5	81

AL	19	.5	100	2.9	29	.8	72	2.1	220	6.3	3,254	93.2	16	.5	3,490
FEMALE	4	.5	40	4.9	12	1.5	15	1.8	71	8.7	744	90.7	5	.6	820
MALE	15	.6	60	2.2	17	.6	57	2.1	149	5.6	2,510	94.0	11	.4	2,670

+GRAD+PROF:
L-TIME	859	.5	4,662	2.9	987	.6	1,311	.8	7,819	4.9	147,483	93.1	3,150	2.0	158,452
FEMALE	458	.6	2,502	3.3	428	.6	567	.8	3,955	5.3	70,365	93.7	753	1.0	75,073
MALE	401	.5	2,160	2.6	559	.7	744	.9	3,864	4.6	77,118	92.5	2,397	2.9	83,379
T-TIME	253	.4	2,681	4.5	365	.6	527	.9	3,826	6.5	55,035	92.9	394	.7	59,255
FEMALE	144	.5	1,582	5.3	191	.6	231	.8	2,148	7.2	27,616	92.4	109	.4	29,873
MALE	109	.4	1,099	3.7	174	.6	296	1.0	1,678	5.7	27,419	93.3	285	1.0	29,382

AL	1,112	.5	7,343	3.4	1,352	.6	1,838	.8	11,645	5.3	202,518	93.0	3,544	1.6	217,707
FEMALE	602	.6	4,084	3.9	619	.6	798	.8	6,103	5.8	97,981	93.4	862	.8	104,946
MALE	510	.5	3,259	2.9	733	.7	1,040	.9	5,542	4.9	104,537	92.7	2,682	2.4	112,761

LASSIFIED:
AL	375	1.6	978	4.1	207	.9	191	.8	1,751	7.4	21,726	91.8	200	.8	23,677
FEMALE	228	1.8	458	3.7	96	.8	100	.8	882	7.0	11,541	92.2	93	.7	12,516
MALE	147	1.3	520	4.7	111	1.0	91	.8	869	7.8	10,185	91.3	107	1.0	11,161

AL ENROLLMENT:
AL	1,487	.6	8,321	3.4	1,559	.6	2,029	.8	13,396	5.5	224,244	92.9	3,744	1.6	241,384
FEMALE	830	.7	4,542	3.9	715	.6	898	.8	6,985	5.9	109,522	93.2	955	.8	117,462
MALE	657	.5	3,779	3.0	844	.7	1,131	.9	6,411	5.2	114,722	92.6	2,789	2.3	123,922

MING   (8 INSTITUTIONS)

ERGRADUATES:
L-TIME	121	1.1	161	1.5	63	.6	176	1.7	521	4.9	9,807	92.2	304	2.9	10,632
FEMALE	76	1.5	47	1.0	30	.6	91	1.9	244	5.0	4,626	94.2	41	.8	4,911
MALE	45	.8	114	2.0	33	.6	85	1.5	277	4.8	5,181	90.6	263	4.6	5,721
T-TIME	14	.3	59	1.4	19	.5	121	3.0	213	5.2	3,842	94.2	23	.6	4,078
FEMALE	11	.4	26	1.1	11	.4	59	2.4	107	4.3	2,355	95.4	7	.3	2,469
MALE	3	.2	33	2.1	8	.5	62	3.9	106	6.6	1,487	92.4	16	1.0	1,609

AL	135	.9	220	1.5	82	.6	297	2.0	734	5.0	13,649	92.8	327	2.2	14,710
FEMALE	87	1.2	73	1.0	41	.6	150	2.0	351	4.8	6,981	94.6	48	.7	7,380
MALE	48	.7	147	2.0	41	.6	147	2.0	383	5.2	6,668	91.0	279	3.8	7,330

QUATE:
L-TIME	0	.0	3	.5	1	.2	4	.6	8	1.3	559	88.3	66	10.4	633
FEMALE	0	.0	3	1.6	0	.0	2	1.0	5	2.6	179	93.7	7	3.7	191
MALE	0	.0	0	.0	1	.2	2	.5	3	.7	380	86.0	59	13.3	442
T-TIME	3	.7	1	.2	4	1.0	4	1.0	12	2.9	366	88.0	38	9.1	416
FEMALE	1	.4	0	.0	3	1.2	0	.0	4	1.6	229	94.2	10	4.1	243
MALE	2	1.2	1	.6	1	.6	4	2.3	8	4.6	137	79.2	28	16.2	173

AL	3	.3	4	.4	5	.5	8	.8	20	1.9	925	88.2	104	9.9	1,049
FEMALE	1	.2	3	.7	3	.7	2	.5	9	2.1	408	94.0	17	3.9	434
MALE	2	.3	1	.2	2	.3	6	1.0	11	1.8	517	84.1	87	14.1	615

FESSIONAL:
L-TIME	0	.0	0	.0	1	.5	2	.9	3	1.4	210	98.6	0	.0	213
FEMALE	0	.0	0	.0	1	1.9	1	1.9	2	3.8	51	96.2	0	.0	53
MALE	0	.0	0	.0	0	.0	1	.6	1	.6	159	99.4	0	.0	160
T-TIME	0	.0	0	.0	0	.0	0	.0	0	.0	1	100.0	0	.0	1
FEMALE	0	.0	0	.0	0	.0	0	.0	0	.0	1	100.0	0	.0	1
MALE	0	.0	0	.0	0	.0	0	.0	0	.0	0	.0	0	.0	0

AL	0	.0	0	.0	1	.5	2	.9	3	1.4	211	98.6	0	.0	214
FEMALE	0	.0	0	.0	1	1.9	1	1.9	2	3.7	52	96.3	0	.0	54
MALE	0	.0	0	.0	0	.0	1	.6	1	.6	159	99.4	0	.0	160

+GRAD+PROF:
L-TIME	121	1.1	164	1.4	65	.6	182	1.6	532	4.6	10,576	92.1	370	3.2	11,478
FEMALE	76	1.5	50	1.0	31	.6	94	1.8	251	4.9	4,856	94.2	48	.9	5,155
MALE	45	.7	114	1.8	34	.5	88	1.4	281	4.4	5,720	90.5	322	5.1	6,323
T-TIME	17	.4	60	1.3	23	.5	125	2.8	225	5.0	4,209	93.6	61	1.4	4,495
FEMALE	12	.4	26	1.0	14	.5	59	2.2	111	4.1	2,585	95.3	17	.6	2,713
MALE	5	.3	34	1.9	9	.5	66	3.7	114	6.4	1,624	91.1	44	2.5	1,782

AL	138	.9	224	1.4	88	.6	307	1.9	757	4.7	14,785	92.6	431	2.7	15,973
FEMALE	88	1.1	76	1.0	45	.6	153	1.9	362	4.6	7,441	94.6	65	.8	7,868
MALE	50	.6	148	1.8	43	.5	154	1.9	395	4.9	7,344	90.6	366	4.5	8,105

LASSIFIED:
AL	18	.5	5	.1	10	.3	42	1.1	75	1.9	3,870	97.7	15	.4	3,960
FEMALE	12	.5	3	.1	2	.1	27	1.1	44	1.9	2,298	97.7	9	.4	2,351
MALE	6	.4	2	.1	8	.5	15	.9	31	1.9	1,572	97.7	6	.4	1,609

AL ENROLLMENT:
AL	156	.8	229	1.1	98	.5	349	1.8	832	4.2	18,655	93.6	446	2.2	19,933
FEMALE	100	1.0	79	.8	47	.5	180	1.8	406	4.0	9,739	95.3	74	.7	10,219
MALE	56	.6	150	1.5	51	.5	169	1.7	426	4.4	8,916	91.8	372	3.8	9,714

MAJOR FIELD 9999 - SUMMARY

	AMERICAN INDIAN ALASKAN NATIVE		BLACK NON-HISPANIC		ASIAN OR PACIFIC ISLANDER		HISPANIC		TOTAL MINORITY		WHITE NON-HISPANIC		NON-RESIDENT ALIEN	
	NUMBER	%	NUMBER	%	NUMBER	%	NUMBER	%	NUMBER	%	NUMBER	%	NUMBER	%
THE STATES AND D.C.	**(3,123 INSTITUTIONS)**													
UNDERGRADUATES:														
FULL-TIME	36,192	.6	600,904	10.4	113,790	2.0	196,452	3.4	947,338	16.4	4,716,593	81.4	129,651	2.2
FEMALE	18,782	.7	342,272	12.1	52,738	1.9	96,345	3.4	510,137	18.1	2,273,042	80.6	36,128	1.3
MALE	17,410	.6	258,632	8.7	61,052	2.1	100,107	3.4	437,201	14.7	2,443,551	82.2	93,523	3.1
PART-TIME	25,215	.9	286,601	10.3	64,048	2.3	148,506	5.4	524,370	18.9	2,222,406	80.2	25,218	.9
FEMALE	13,599	.9	163,054	11.0	30,944	2.1	74,790	5.0	282,387	19.0	1,195,011	80.3	10,506	.7
MALE	11,616	.9	123,547	9.6	33,104	2.6	73,716	5.7	241,983	18.8	1,027,395	80.0	14,712	1.1
TUTAL	61,407	.7	887,505	10.4	177,838	2.1	344,958	4.0	1,471,708	17.2	6,938,999	81.0	154,869	1.8
FEMALE	32,381	.8	505,326	11.7	83,682	1.9	171,135	4.0	792,524	18.4	3,468,053	80.5	46,634	1.1
MALE	29,026	.7	382,179	9.0	94,156	2.2	173,823	4.1	679,184	15.9	3,470,946	81.5	108,235	2.5
GRADUATE:														
FULL-TIME	1,540	.4	20,985	4.9	9,267	2.2	8,325	2.0	40,117	9.5	331,006	78.1	52,953	12.5
FEMALE	678	.4	11,633	6.8	3,567	2.1	3,581	2.1	19,459	11.4	139,381	82.0	11,166	6.6
MALE	862	.3	9,352	3.7	5,700	2.2	4,744	1.9	20,658	8.1	191,625	75.4	41,787	16.4
PART-TIME	2,245	.3	40,886	6.3	11,345	1.8	12,730	2.0	67,206	10.4	559,795	86.5	20,415	3.2
FEMALE	1,062	.3	25,580	7.8	4,315	1.3	6,365	1.9	37,322	11.4	283,459	86.8	5,647	1.7
MALE	1,183	.4	15,306	4.8	7,030	2.2	6,365	2.0	29,884	9.3	276,336	86.1	14,768	4.6
TUTAL	3,785	.4	61,871	5.	20,612	1.9	21,055	2.0	107,323	10.0	890,801	83.1	73,368	6.8
FEMALE	1,740	.4	37,213	7	7,882	1.6	9,946	2.0	56,781	11.4	422,840	85.2	16,813	3.4
MALE	2,045	.4	24,658	4.8	12,730	2.2	11,109	1.9	50,542	8.8	467,961	81.4	56,555	9.8
PROFESSIONAL:														
FULL-TIME	975	.4	10,260	4.4	4,515	2.0	4,845	2.1	20,595	8.9	207,912	89.9	2,730	1.2
FEMALE	242	.4	4,024	7.0	1,406	2.4	1,261	2.2	6,933	12.1	50,067	87.0	526	.9
MALE	733	.4	6,236	3.6	3,109	1.8	3,584	2.1	13,662	7.9	157,845	90.9	2,204	1.3
PART-TIME	97	.4	1,164	4.9	285	1.2	508	2.1	2,054	8.6	21,394	90.0	314	1.3
FEMALE	28	.4	425	6.1	91	1.3	139	2.0	683	9.8	6,208	89.2	71	1.0
MALE	69	.4	739	4.4	194	1.2	369	2.2	1,371	8.2	15,186	90.4	243	1.4
TUTAL	1,072	.4	11,424	4.5	4,800	1.9	5,353	2.1	22,649	8.9	229,306	89.9	3,044	1.2
FEMALE	270	.4	4,449	6.9	1,497	2.3	1,400	2.2	7,616	11.8	56,275	87.3	597	.9
MALE	802	.4	6,975	3.7	3,303	1.7	3,953	2.1	15,033	7.9	173,031	90.8	2,447	1.3
UND+GRAD+PROF:														
FULL-TIME	38,707	.6	632,149	9.8	127,572	2.0	209,622	3.3	1,008,050	15.6	5,255,511	81.5	185,334	2.9
FEMALE	19,702	.6	357,929	11.7	57,711	1.9	101,187	3.3	536,529	17.6	2,462,490	80.8	47,820	1.6
MALE	19,005	.6	274,220	8.1	69,861	2.1	108,435	3.2	471,521	13.9	2,793,021	82.1	137,514	4.0
PART-TIME	27,557	.8	328,651	9.5	75,678	2.2	161,744	4.7	593,630	17.2	2,803,595	81.4	45,947	1.3
FEMALE	14,689	.8	189,059	10.4	35,350	1.9	81,294	4.5	320,392	17.6	1,484,678	81.5	16,224	.9
MALE	12,868	.8	139,592	8.6	40,328	2.5	80,450	5.0	273,238	16.8	1,318,917	81.3	29,723	1.8
TUTAL	66,264	.7	960,800	9.7	203,250	2.1	371,366	3.8	1,601,680	16.2	8,059,106	81.5	231,281	2.3
FEMALE	34,391	.7	546,988	11.2	93,061	1.9	182,481	3.7	856,921	17.6	3,947,168	81.1	64,044	1.3
MALE	31,873	.6	413,812	8.2	110,189	2.2	188,885	3.4	744,759	14.8	4,111,938	81.8	167,237	3.3
UNCLASSIFIED:														
TUTAL	11,558	.9	92,880	7.0	31,332	2.4	45,455	3.4	181,265	13.7	1,120,824	84.7	20,985	1.6
FEMALE	6,647	.9	54,087	7.3	15,640	2.1	22,244	3.0	98,618	13.3	632,877	85.5	9,011	1.2
MALE	4,911	.8	38,793	6.7	15,732	2.7	23,211	4.0	82,647	14.2	487,947	83.8	11,974	2.1
TOTAL ENROLLMENT:														
TUTAL	77,822	.7	1,053,680	9.4	234,622	2.1	416,821	3.7	1,782,945	15.9	9,179,930	81.9	252,266	2.2
FEMALE	41,038	.7	601,075	10.7	108,701	1.9	204,725	3.7	955,539	17.0	4,580,045	81.7	73,055	1.3
MALE	36,784	.7	452,605	8.1	125,921	2.2	212,096	3.8	827,406	14.8	4,599,885	82.0	179,211	3.2
AMERICAN SAMOA	**(1 INSTITUTIONS)**													
UNDERGRADUATES:														
FULL-TIME		.0	0	.0	367	97.6	0	.0	367	97.6	9	2.4	0	.0
FEMALE		.0	0	.0	186	98.4	0	.0	186	98.4	3	1.6	0	.0
MALE		.0	0	.0	181	96.8	0	.0	181	96.8	6	3.2	0	.0
PART-TIME		.0	1	.2	414	91.0	0	.0	415	91.2	40	8.8	0	.0
FEMALE	0	.0	1	.4	231	89.5	0	.0	232	89.9	26	10.1	0	.0
MALE	0	.0	0	.0	183	92.9	0	.0	183	92.9	14	7.1	0	.0
TUTAL		.0	1	.1	781	94.0	0	.0	782	94.1	49	5.9	0	.0
FEMALE	0	.0	1	.2	417	93.3	0	.0	418	93.5	29	6.5	0	.0
MALE	0	.0	0	.0	364	94.8	0	.0	364	94.8	20	5.2	0	.0
GRADUATE:														
FULL-TIME		.0		.0	0	.0	0	.0	0	.0	0	.0	0	.0
FEMALE		.0		.0	0	.0	0	.0	0	.0	0	.0	0	.0
MALE		.0		.0	0	.0	0	.0	0	.0	0	.0	0	.0
PART-TIME		.0		.0	0	.0	0	.0	0	.0	0	.0	0	.0
FEMALE	0	.0	0	.0	0	.0	0	.0	0	.0	0	.0	0	.0
MALE	0	.0	0	.0	0	.0	0	.0	0	.0	0	.0	0	.0
TOTAL		.0		.0	0	.0	0	.0	0	.0	0	.0	0	.0
FEMALE	0	.0	0	.0	0	.0	0	.0	0	.0	0	.0	0	.0
PROFESSIONAL:														
FULL-TIME		.0		.0	0	.0	0	.0	0	.0	0	.0	0	.0
FEMALE	0	.0	0	.0	0	.0	0	.0	0	.0	0	.0	0	.0
MALE	0	.0	0	.0	0	.0	0	.0	0	.0	0	.0	0	.0

ENROLLMENT IN INSTITUTIONS OF HIGHER EDUCATION FOR SELECTED MAJOR FIELDS OF STUDY AND LEVEL OF ENROLLMENT
E, ETHNICITY, AND SEX: STATE, 1978

- SUMMARY

AN INDIAN N NATIVE		BLACK NON-HISPANIC		ASIAN OR PACIFIC ISLANDER		HISPANIC		TOTAL MINORITY		WHITE NON-HISPANIC		NON-RESIDENT ALIEN		TOTAL
R	%	NUMBER	%	NUMBER	%	NUMBER	%	NUMBER	%	NUMBER	%	NUMBER	%	NUMBER
CONTINUED														
0	.0	0	.0	0	.0	0	.0	0	.0	0	.0	0	.0	0
0	.0	0	.0	0	.0	0	.0	0	.0	0	.0	0	.0	0
0	.0	0	.0	0	.0	0	.0	0	.0	0	.0	0	.0	0
0	.0	0	.0	0	.0	0	.0	0	.0	0	.0	0	.0	0
0	.0	0	.0	0	.0	0	.0	0	.0	0	.0	0	.0	0
0	.0	0	.0	0	.0	0	.0	0	.0	0	.0	0	.0	0
0	.0	0	.0	367	97.6	0	.0	367	97.6	9	2.4	0	.0	376
0	.0	0	.0	186	98.4	0	.0	186	98.4	3	1.6	0	.0	189
0	.0	0	.0	181	96.8	0	.0	181	96.8	6	3.2	0	.0	187
0	.0	1	.2	414	91.0	0	.0	415	91.2	40	8.8	0	.0	455
0	.0	1	.4	231	89.5	0	.0	232	89.9	26	10.1	0	.0	258
0	.0	0	.0	183	92.9	0	.0	183	92.9	14	7.1	0	.0	197
0	.0	1	.1	781	94.0	0	.0	782	94.1	49	5.9	0	.0	831
0	.0	1	.2	417	93.3	0	.0	418	93.5	29	6.5	0	.0	447
0	.0	0	.0	364	94.8	0	.0	364	94.8	20	5.2	0	.0	384
0	.0	0	.0	0	.0	0	.0	0	.0	0	.0	0	.0	0
0	.0	0	.0	0	.0	0	.0	0	.0	0	.0	0	.0	0
0	.0	0	.0	0	.0	0	.0	0	.0	0	.0	0	.0	0
0	.0	1	.1	781	94.0	0	.0	782	94.1	49	5.9	0	.0	831
0	.0	1	.2	417	93.3	0	.0	418	93.5	29	6.5	0	.0	447
0	.0	0	.0	364	94.8	0	.0	364	94.8	20	5.2	0	.0	384
(1 INSTITUTIONS)														
0	.0	44	10.5	0	.0	132	31.4	176	41.9	244	58.1	0	.0	420
0	.0	25	10.5	0	.0	70	29.5	95	40.1	142	59.9	0	.0	237
0	.0	19	10.4	0	.0	62	33.9	81	44.3	102	55.7	0	.0	183
0	.0	0	.0	0	.0	0	.0	0	.0	0	.0	0	.0	0
0	.0	0	.0	0	.0	0	.0	0	.0	0	.0	0	.0	0
0	.0	0	.0	0	.0	0	.0	0	.0	0	.0	0	.0	0
0	.0	44	10.5	0	.0	132	31.4	176	41.9	244	58.1	0	.0	420
0	.0	25	10.5	0	.0	70	29.5	95	40.1	142	59.9	0	.0	237
0	.0	19	10.4	0	.0	62	33.9	81	44.3	102	55.7	0	.0	183
0	.0	0	.0	0	.0	0	.0	0	.0	0	.0	0	.0	0
0	.0	0	.0	0	.0	0	.0	0	.0	0	.0	0	.0	0
0	.0	0	.0	0	.0	0	.0	0	.0	0	.0	0	.0	0
0	.0	0	.0	0	.0	0	.0	0	.0	0	.0	0	.0	0
0	.0	0	.0	0	.0	0	.0	0	.0	0	.0	0	.0	0
0	.0	0	.0	0	.0	0	.0	0	.0	0	.0	0	.0	0
0	.0	0	.0	0	.0	0	.0	0	.0	0	.0	0	.0	0
0	.0	0	.0	0	.0	0	.0	0	.0	0	.0	0	.0	0
0	.0	0	.0	0	.0	0	.0	0	.0	0	.0	0	.0	0
0	.0	0	.0	0	.0	0	.0	0	.0	0	.0	0	.0	0
0	.0	0	.0	0	.0	0	.0	0	.0	0	.0	0	.0	0
0	.0	0	.0	0	.0	0	.0	0	.0	0	.0	0	.0	0
0	.0	44	10.5	0	.0	132	31.4	176	41.9	244	58.1	0	.0	420
0	.0	25	10.5	0	.0	70	29.5	95	40.1	142	59.9	0	.0	237
0	.0	19	10.4	0	.0	62	33.9	81	44.3	102	55.7	0	.0	183
0	.0	44	10.5	0	.0	132	31.4	176	41.9	244	58.1	0	.0	420
0	.0	25	10.5	0	.0	70	29.5	95	40.1	142	59.9	0	.0	237
0	.0	19	10.4	0	.0	62	33.9	81	44.3	102	55.7	0	.0	183
0	.0	125	10.3	0	.0	372	30.5	497	40.8	721	59.2	0	.0	1,218
0	.0	70	10.3	0	.0	211	30.9	281	41.2	401	58.8	0	.0	682
0	.0	55	10.3	0	.0	161	30.0	216	40.3	320	59.7	0	.0	536
0	.0	169	10.3	0	.0	504	30.8	673	41.1	965	58.9	0	.0	1,638
0	.0	95	10.3	0	.0	281	30.6	376	40.9	543	59.1	0	.0	919
0	.0	74	10.3	0	.0	223	31.0	297	41.3	422	58.7	0	.0	719

TABLE 17 - TOTAL ENROLLMENT IN INSTITUTIONS OF HIGHER EDUCATION FOR SELECTED MAJOR FIELDS OF STUDY AND LEVEL OF ENROLLMENT BY RACE, ETHNICITY, AND SEX: STATE, 1978

MAJOR FIELD 9999 - SUMMARY

	AMERICAN INDIAN ALASKAN NATIVE		BLACK NON-HISPANIC		ASIAN OR PACIFIC ISLANDER		HISPANIC		TOTAL MINORITY		WHITE NON-HISPANIC		NON-RESIDENT ALIEN	
	NUMBER	%	NUMBER	%	NUMBER	%	NUMBER	%	NUMBER	%	NUMBER	%	NUMBER	%
GUAM (1 INSTITUTIONS)														
UNDERGRADUATES:														
FULL-TIME	7	.4	12	.7	1,153	71.8	36	2.2	1,208	75.2	213	13.3	185	11.5
FEMALE	3	.3	7	.8	707	77.5	13	1.4	730	80.0	120	13.2	62	6.8
MALE	4	.6	5	.7	446	64.3	23	3.3	478	68.9	93	13.4	123	17.7
PART-TIME	4	.3	16	1.2	989	73.0	22	1.6	1,031	76.1	297	21.9	27	2.0
FEMALE	1	.2	9	1.5	439	74.7	8	1.4	457	77.7	119	20.2	12	2.0
MALE	3	.4	7	.9	550	71.7	14	1.8	574	74.8	178	23.2	15	2.0
TOTAL	11	.4	28	.9	2,142	72.3	58	2.0	2,239	75.6	510	17.2	212	7.2
FEMALE	4	.3	16	1.1	1,146	76.4	21	1.4	1,187	79.1	239	15.9	74	4.9
MALE	7	.5	12	.8	996	68.2	37	2.5	1,052	72.0	271	18.5	138	9.4
GRADUATE:														
FULL-TIME	0	.0	0	.0	10	76.9	0	.0	10	76.9	3	23.1	0	.0
FEMALE	0	.0	0	.0	5	71.4	0	.0	5	71.4	2	28.6	0	.0
MALE	0	.0	0	.0	5	83.3	0	.0	5	83.3	1	16.7	0	.0
PART-TIME	0	.0	0	.0	108	46.2	11	4.7	119	50.9	115	49.1	0	.0
FEMALE	0	.0	0	.0	89	57.4	11	7.1	100	64.5	55	35.5	0	.0
MALE	0	.0	0	.0	19	24.1	0	.0	19	24.1	60	75.9	0	.0
TOTAL	0	.0	0	.0	118	47.8	11	4.5	129	52.2	118	47.8	0	.0
FEMALE	0	.0	0	.0	94	58.0	11	6.8	105	64.8	57	35.2	0	.0
MALE	0	.0	0	.0	24	28.2	0	.0	24	28.2	61	71.8	0	.0
PROFESSIONAL:														
FULL-TIME	0	.0	0	.0	0	.0	0	.0	0	.0	0	.0	0	.0
FEMALE	0	.0	0	.0	0	.0	0	.0	0	.0	0	.0	0	.0
MALE	0	.0	0	.0	0	.0	0	.0	0	.0	0	.0	0	.0
PART-TIME	0	.0	0	.0	0	.0	0	.0	0	.0	0	.0	0	.0
FEMALE	0	.0	0	.0	0	.0	0	.0	0	.0	0	.0	0	.0
MALE	0	.0	0	.0	0	.0	0	.0	0	.0	0	.0	0	.0
TOTAL	0	.0	0	.0	0	.0	0	.0	0	.0	0	.0	0	.0
FEMALE	0	.0	0	.0	0	.0	0	.0	0	.0	0	.0	0	.0
MALE	0	.0	0	.0	0	.0	0	.0	0	.0	0	.0	0	.0
UND+GRAD+PROF:														
FULL-TIME	7	.4	12	.7	1,163	71.8	36	2.2	1,218	75.2	216	13.3	185	11.4
FEMALE	3	.3	7	.8	712	77.5	13	1.4	735	80.0	122	13.3	62	6.7
MALE	4	.6	5	.7	451	64.4	23	3.3	483	69.0	94	13.4	123	17.6
PART-TIME	4	.3	16	1.0	1,097	69.0	33	2.1	1,150	72.4	412	25.9	27	1.7
FEMALE	1	.1	9	1.2	528	71.1	19	2.6	557	75.0	174	23.4	12	1.6
MALE	3	.4	7	.8	569	67.3	14	1.7	593	70.1	238	28.1	15	1.8
TOTAL	11	.3	28	.9	2,260	70.4	69	2.2	2,368	73.8	628	19.6	212	6.6
FEMALE	4	.2	16	1.0	1,240	74.6	32	1.9	1,292	77.7	296	17.8	74	4.5
MALE	7	.5	12	.8	1,020	66.0	37	2.4	1,076	69.6	332	21.5	138	8.9
UNCLASSIFIED:														
TOTAL	0	.0	0	.0	0	.0	0	.0	0	.0	0	.0	0	.0
FEMALE	0	.0	0	.0	0	.0	0	.0	0	.0	0	.0	0	.0
MALE	0	.0	0	.0	0	.0	0	.0	0	.0	0	.0	0	.0
TOTAL ENROLLMENT:														
TOTAL	11	.3	28	.9	2,260	70.4	69	2.2	2,368	73.8	628	19.6	212	6.6
FEMALE	4	.2	16	1.0	1,240	74.6	32	1.9	1,292	77.7	296	17.8	74	4.5
MALE	7	.5	12	.8	1,020	66.0	37	2.4	1,076	69.6	332	21.5	138	8.9
PUERTO RICO (34 INSTITUTIONS)														
UNDERGRADUATES:														
FULL-TIME	0	.0	10	.0	1	.0	94,550	99.6	94,561	99.7	272	.3	60	.1
FEMALE	0	.0	2	.0	1	.0	54,288	99.7	54,291	99.7	150	.3	30	.1
MALE	0	.0	8	.0	0	.0	40,262	99.6	40,270	99.6	122	.3	30	.1
PART-TIME	0	.0	0	.0	0	.0	19,528	99.7	19,528	99.7	60	.3	5	.0
FEMALE	0	.0	0	.0	0	.0	11,118	99.7	11,118	99.7	32	.3	3	.0
MALE	0	.0	0	.0	0	.0	8,410	99.6	8,410	99.6	28	.3	2	.0
TOTAL	0	.0	10	.0	1	.0	114,078	99.6	114,089	99.7	332	.3	65	.1
FEMALE	0	.0	2	.0	1	.0	65,406	99.7	65,409	99.7	182	.3	33	.1
MALE	0	.0	8	.0	0	.0	48,672	99.6	48,680	99.6	150	.3	32	.1
GRADUATE:														
FULL-TIME	0	.0	0	.0	0	.0	1,508	90.6	1,508	90.6	149	9.0	7	.4
FEMALE	0	.0	0	.0	0	.0	968	91.7	968	91.7	85	8.0	3	.3
MALE	0	.0	0	.0	0	.0	540	88.8	540	88.8	64	10.5	4	.7
PART-TIME	0	.0	0	.0	0	.0	2,602	97.3	2,602	97.3	69	2.6	4	.1
FEMALE	0	.0	0	.0	0	.0	1,356	96.5	1,356	96.5	48	3.4	1	.1
MALE	0	.0	0	.0	0	.0	1,246	98.1	1,246	98.1	21	1.7	3	.2
TOTAL	0	.0	0	.0	0	.0	4,110	94.7	4,110	94.7	218	5.0	11	.3
FEMALE	0	.0	0	.0	0	.0	2,324	94.4	2,324	94.4	133	5.4	4	.2
MALE	0	.0	0	.0	0	.0	1,786	95.1	1,786	95.1	85	4.5	7	.4
PROFESSIONAL:														
FULL-TIME	0	.0	0	.0	0	.0	1,430	100.0	1,430	100.0	0	.0	0	.0
FEMALE	0	.0	0	.0	0	.0	492	100.0	492	100.0	0	.0	0	.0
MALE	0	.0	0	.0	0	.0	938	100.0	938	100.0	0	.0	0	.0

R FIELD 9999 - SUMMARY

	AMERICAN INDIAN ALASKAN NATIVE		BLACK NON-HISPANIC		ASIAN OR PACIFIC ISLANDER		HISPANIC		TOTAL MINORITY		WHITE NON-HISPANIC		NON-RESIDENT ALIEN		TOTAL
	NUMBER	%	NUMBER	%	NUMBER	%	NUMBER	%	NUMBER	%	NUMBER	%	NUMBER	%	NUMBER
TO RICO	CONTINUED														
ESSIONAL:															
-TIME	0	.0	0	.0	0	.0	162	100.0	162	100.0	0	.0	0	.0	162
EMALE	0	.0	0	.0	0	.0	41	100.0	41	100.0	0	.0	0	.0	41
MALE	0	.0	0	.0	0	.0	121	100.0	121	100.0	0	.0	0	.0	121
L	0	.0	0	.0	0	.0	1,592	100.0	1,592	100.0	0	.0	0	.0	1,592
EMALE	0	.0	0	.0	0	.0	533	100.0	533	100.0	0	.0	0	.0	533
MALE	0	.0	0	.0	0	.0	1,059	100.0	1,059	100.0	0	.0	0	.0	1,059
GRAD+PROF:															
-TIME	0	.0	10	.0	1	.0	97,488	99.5	97,499	99.5	421	.4	67	.1	97,987
EMALE	0	.0	2	.0	1	.0	55,748	99.5	55,751	99.5	235	.4	33	.1	56,019
MALE	0	.0	8	.0	0	.0	41,740	99.5	41,748	99.5	186	.4	34	.1	41,968
-TIME	0	.0	0	.0	0	.0	22,292	99.4	22,292	99.4	129	.6	9	.0	22,430
EMALE	0	.0	0	.0	0	.0	12,515	99.3	12,515	99.3	80	.6	4	.0	12,599
MALE	0	.0	0	.0	0	.0	9,777	99.5	9,777	99.5	49	.5	5	.1	9,831
L	0	.0	10	.0	1	.0	119,780	99.5	119,791	99.5	550	.5	76	.1	120,417
EMALE	0	.0	2	.0	1	.0	68,263	99.5	68,266	99.5	315	.5	37	.1	68,618
MALE	0	.0	8	.0	0	.0	51,517	99.5	51,525	99.5	235	.5	39	.1	51,799
ASSIFIED:															
L	0	.0	0	.0	0	.0	3,549	100.0	3,549	100.0	1	.0	0	.0	3,550
EMALE	0	.0	0	.0	0	.0	1,989	99.9	1,989	99.9	1	.1	0	.0	1,990
MALE	0	.0	0	.0	0	.0	1,560	100.0	1,560	100.0	0	.0	0	.0	1,560
L ENROLLMENT:															
L	0	.0	10	.0	1	.0	123,329	99.5	123,340	99.5	551	.4	76	.1	123,967
EMALE	0	.0	2	.0	1	.0	70,252	99.5	70,255	99.5	316	.4	37	.1	70,608
MALE	0	.0	8	.0	0	.0	53,077	99.5	53,085	99.5	235	.4	39	.1	53,359
T TERRITORY	(	1 INSTITUTIONS)													
RGRADUATES:															
-TIME	0	.0	0	.0	248	100.0	0	.0	248	100.0	0	.0	0	.0	248
EMALE	0	.0	0	.0	88	100.0	0	.0	88	100.0	0	.0	0	.0	88
MALE	0	.0	0	.0	160	100.0	0	.0	160	100.0	0	.0	0	.0	160
-TIME	0	.0	0	.0	3	100.0	0	.0	3	100.0	0	.0	0	.0	3
EMALE	0	.0	0	.0	0	.0	0	.0	0	.0	0	.0	0	.0	0
MALE	0	.0	0	.0	3	100.0	0	.0	3	100.0	0	.0	0	.0	3
L	0	.0	0	.0	251	100.0	0	.0	251	100.0	0	.0	0	.0	251
EMALE	0	.0	0	.0	88	100.0	0	.0	88	100.0	0	.0	0	.0	88
MALE	0	.0	0	.0	163	100.0	0	.0	163	100.0	0	.0	0	.0	163
UATE:															
-TIME	0	.0	0	.0	0	.0	0	.0	0	.0	0	.0	0	.0	0
EMALE	0	.0	0	.0	0	.0	0	.0	0	.0	0	.0	0	.0	0
MALE	0	.0	0	.0	0	.0	0	.0	0	.0	0	.0	0	.0	0
-TIME	0	.0	0	.0	0	.0	0	.0	0	.0	0	.0	0	.0	0
EMALE	0	.0	0	.0	0	.0	0	.0	0	.0	0	.0	0	.0	0
MALE	0	.0	0	.0	0	.0	0	.0	0	.0	0	.0	0	.0	0
L	0	.0	0	.0	0	.0	0	.0	0	.0	0	.0	0	.0	0
EMALE	0	.0	0	.0	0	.0	0	.0	0	.0	0	.0	0	.0	0
MALE	0	.0	0	.0	0	.0	0	.0	0	.0	0	.0	0	.0	0
ESSIONAL:															
-TIME	0	.0	0	.0	0	.0	0	.0	0	.0	0	.0	0	.0	0
EMALE	0	.0	0	.0	0	.0	0	.0	0	.0	0	.0	0	.0	0
MALE	0	.0	0	.0	0	.0	0	.0	0	.0	0	.0	0	.0	0
-TIME	0	.0	0	.0	0	.0	0	.0	0	.0	0	.0	0	.0	0
EMALE	0	.0	0	.0	0	.0	0	.0	0	.0	0	.0	0	.0	0
MALE	0	.0	0	.0	0	.0	0	.0	0	.0	0	.0	0	.0	0
L	0	.0	0	.0	0	.0	0	.0	0	.0	0	.0	0	.0	0
EMALE	0	.0	0	.0	0	.0	0	.0	0	.0	0	.0	0	.0	0
MALE	0	.0	0	.0	0	.0	0	.0	0	.0	0	.0	0	.0	0
GRAD+PROF:															
-TIME	0	.0	0	.0	248	100.0	0	.0	248	100.0	0	.0	0	.0	248
EMALE	0	.0	0	.0	88	100.0	0	.0	88	100.0	0	.0	0	.0	88
MALE	0	.0	0	.0	160	100.0	0	.0	160	100.0	0	.0	0	.0	160
-TIME	0	.0	0	.0	3	100.0	0	.0	3	100.0	0	.0	0	.0	3
EMALE	0	.0	0	.0	0	.0	0	.0	0	.0	0	.0	0	.0	0
MALE	0	.0	0	.0	3	100.0	0	.0	3	100.0	0	.0	0	.0	3
L	0	.0	0	.0	251	100.0	0	.0	251	100.0	0	.0	0	.0	251
EMALE	0	.0	0	.0	88	100.0	0	.0	88	100.0	0	.0	0	.0	88
MALE	0	.0	0	.0	163	100.0	0	.0	163	100.0	0	.0	0	.0	163
ASSIFIED:															
L	0	.0	0	.0	115	100.0	0	.0	115	100.0	0	.0	0	.0	115
EMALE	0	.0	0	.0	32	100.0	0	.0	32	100.0	0	.0	0	.0	32
MALE	0	.0	0	.0	83	100.0	0	.0	83	100.0	0	.0	0	.0	83
L ENROLLMENT:															
L	0	.0	0	.0	366	100.0	0	.0	366	100.0	0	.0	0	.0	366
EMALE	0	.0	0	.0	120	100.0	0	.0	120	100.0	0	.0	0	.0	120
MALE	0	.0	0	.0	246	100.0	0	.0	246	100.0	0	.0	0	.0	246

TABLE 17 - TOTAL ENROLLMENT IN INSTITUTIONS OF HIGHER EDUCATION FOR SELECTED MAJOR FIELDS OF STUDY AND LEVEL OF ENROLLMENT BY RACE, ETHNICITY, AND SEX: STATE, 1978

MAJOR FIELD 9999 - SUMMARY

	AMERICAN INDIAN ALASKAN NATIVE		BLACK NON-HISPANIC		ASIAN OR PACIFIC ISLANDER		HISPANIC		TOTAL MINORITY		WHITE NON-HISPANIC		NON-RESIDENT ALIEN	
	NUMBER	%	NUMBER	%	NUMBER	%	NUMBER	%	NUMBER	%	NUMBER	%	NUMBER	%

VIRGIN ISLANDS   (1 INSTITUTIONS

	NUMBER	%	NUMBER	%	NUMBER	%	NUMBER	%	NUMBER	%	NUMBER	%	NUMBER	%
UNDERGRADUATES:														
FULL-TIME	0	.0	311	60.4	1	.2	27	5.2	339	65.8	51	9.9	125	24.3
FEMALE	0	.0	237	64.2	1	.3	18	4.9	256	69.4	22	6.0	91	24.7
MALE	0	.0	74	50.7	0	.0	9	6.2	83	56.8	29	19.9	34	23.3
PART-TIME	0	.0	0	.0	0	.0	0	.0	0	.0	0	.0	0	.0
FEMALE	0	.0	0	.0	0	.0	0	.0	0	.0	0	.0	0	.0
MALE	0	.0	0	.0	0	.0	0	.0	0	.0	0	.0	0	.0
TOTAL	0	.0	311	60.4	1	.2	27	5.2	339	65.8	51	9.9	125	24.3
FEMALE	0	.0	237	64.2	1	.3	18	4.9	256	69.4	22	6.0	91	24.7
MALE	0	.0	74	50.7	0	.0	9	6.2	83	56.8	29	19.9	34	23.3
GRADUATE:														
FULL-TIME	0	.0	0	.0	0	.0	0	.0	0	.0	0	.0	0	.0
FEMALE	0	.0	0	.0	0	.0	0	.0	0	.0	0	.0	0	.0
MALE	0	.0	0	.0	0	.0	0	.0	0	.0	0	.0	0	.0
PART-TIME	0	.0	47	65.3	1	1.4	2	2.8	50	69.4	20	27.8	2	2.8
FEMALE	0	.0	29	65.9	0	.0	1	2.3	30	68.2	14	31.8	0	.0
MALE	0	.0	18	64.3	1	3.6	1	3.6	20	71.4	6	21.4	2	7.1
TOTAL	0	.0	47	65.3	1	1.4	2	2.8	50	69.4	20	27.8	2	2.8
FEMALE	0	.0	29	65.9	0	.0	1	2.3	30	68.2	14	31.8	0	.0
MALE	0	.0	18	64.3	1	3.6	1	3.6	20	71.4	6	21.4	2	7.1
PROFESSIONAL:														
FULL-TIME	0	.0	0	.0	0	.0	0	.0	0	.0	0	.0	0	.0
FEMALE	0	.0	0	.0	0	.0	0	.0	0	.0	0	.0	0	.0
MALE	0	.0	0	.0	0	.0	0	.0	0	.0	0	.0	0	.0
PART-TIME	0	.0	0	.0	0	.0	0	.0	0	.0	0	.0	0	.0
FEMALE	0	.0	0	.0	0	.0	0	.0	0	.0	0	.0	0	.0
MALE	0	.0	0	.0	0	.0	0	.0	0	.0	0	.0	0	.0
TOTAL	0	.0	0	.0	0	.0	0	.0	0	.0	0	.0	0	.0
FEMALE	0	.0	0	.0	0	.0	0	.0	0	.0	0	.0	0	.0
MALE	0	.0	0	.0	0	.0	0	.0	0	.0	0	.0	0	.0
UND+GRAD+PROF:														
FULL-TIME	0	.0	311	60.4	1	.2	27	5.2	339	65.8	51	9.9	125	24.3
FEMALE	0	.0	237	64.2	1	.3	18	4.9	256	69.4	22	6.0	91	24.7
MALE	0	.0	74	50.7	0	.0	9	6.2	83	56.8	29	19.9	34	23.3
PART-TIME	0	.0	47	65.3	1	1.4	2	2.8	50	69.4	20	27.8	2	2.8
FEMALE	0	.0	29	65.9	0	.0	1	2.3	30	68.2	14	31.8	0	.0
MALE	0	.0	18	64.3	1	3.6	1	3.6	20	71.4	6	21.4	2	7.1
TOTAL	0	.0	358	61.0	2	.3	29	4.9	389	66.3	71	12.1	127	21.6
FEMALE	0	.0	266	64.4	1	.2	19	4.6	286	69.2	36	8.7	91	22.0
MALE	0	.0	92	52.9	1	.6	10	5.7	103	59.2	35	20.1	36	20.7
UNCLASSIFIED:														
TOTAL	0	.0	1,027	81.4	10	.8	67	5.3	1,104	67.5	128	10.2	29	2.3
FEMALE	0	.0	703	82.4	4	.5	43	5.0	750	87.9	84	9.8	19	2.2
MALE	0	.0	324	79.4	6	1.5	24	5.9	354	86.8	44	10.8	10	2.5
TOTAL ENROLLMENT:														
TOTAL	0	.0	1,385	74.9	12	.6	96	5.2	1,493	80.8	199	10.8	156	8.4
FEMALE	0	.0	969	76.5	5	.4	62	4.9	1,036	81.8	120	9.5	110	8.7
MALE	0	.0	416	71.5	7	1.2	34	5.8	457	78.5	79	13.6	46	7.9

OUTLYING AREAS   (39 INSTITUTIONS)

	NUMBER	%	NUMBER	%	NUMBER	%	NUMBER	%	NUMBER	%	NUMBER	%	NUMBER	%
UNDERGRADUATES:														
FULL-TIME	7	.0	377	.4	1,770	1.8	94,745	96.6	96,899	98.8	789	.8	370	.4
FEMALE	3	.0	271	.5	983	1.7	54,389	96.7	55,646	98.9	437	.8	183	.3
MALE	4	.0	106	.3	787	1.9	40,356	96.6	41,253	98.7	352	.8	187	.4
PART-TIME	4	.0	17	.1	1,406	6.6	19,550	91.3	20,977	98.0	397	1.9	32	.1
FEMALE	1	.0	10	.1	670	5.6	11,126	92.7	11,807	98.4	177	1.5	15	.1
MALE	3	.0	7	.1	736	7.8	8,424	89.6	9,170	97.5	220	2.3	17	.2
TOTAL	11	.0	394	.3	3,176	2.7	114,295	95.7	117,876	98.7	1,186	1.0	402	.3
FEMALE	4	.0	281	.4	1,653	2.4	65,515	96.0	67,453	98.8	614	.9	198	.3
MALE	7	.0	113	.2	1,523	3.0	48,780	95.3	50,423	98.5	572	1.1	204	.4
GRADUATE:														
FULL-TIME	0	.0	0	.0	10	.6	1,508	89.9	1,518	90.5	152	9.1	7	.4
FEMALE	0	.0	0	.0	5	.5	968	91.1	973	91.5	87	8.2	3	.3
MALE	0	.0	0	.0	5	.8	540	87.9	545	88.8	65	10.6	4	.7
PART-TIME	0	.0	47	1.6	109	3.7	2,615	87.7	2,771	93.0	204	6.8	6	.2
FEMALE	0	.0	29	1.8	89	5.5	1,368	85.3	1,486	92.6	117	7.3	1	.1
MALE	0	.0	18	1.3	20	1.5	1,247	90.6	1,285	93.3	87	6.3	5	.4
TOTAL	0	.0	47	1.0	119	2.6	4,123	88.5	4,289	92.1	356	7.6	13	.3
FEMALE	0	.0	29	1.1	94	3.5	2,336	87.0	2,459	92.2	204	7.6	4	.1
MALE	0	.0	18	.9	25	1.3	1,787	89.8	1,830	91.9	152	7.6	9	.5
PROFESSIONAL:														
FULL-TIME	0	.0	0	.0	0	.0	1,430	100.0	1,430	100.0	0	.0	0	.0
FEMALE	0	.0	0	.0	0	.0	492	100.0	492	100.0	0	.0	0	.0
MALE	0	.0	0	.0	0	.0	938	100.0	938	100.0	0	.0	0	.0

UMMARY

INDIAN ATIVE	BLACK NON-HISPANIC		ASIAN OR PACIFIC ISLANDER		HISPANIC		TOTAL MINORITY		WHITE NON-HISPANIC		NON-RESIDENT ALIEN		TOTAL
%	NUMBER	%	NUMBER	%	NUMBER	%	NUMBER	%	NUMBER	%	NUMBER	%	NUMBER

CONTINUED

%	NUMBER	%	NUMBER	%	NUMBER	%	NUMBER	%	NUMBER	%	NUMBER	%	NUMBER
.0	0	.0	0	.0	162	100.0	162	100.0	0	.0	0	.0	162
.0	0	.0	0	.0	41	100.0	41	100.0	0	.0	0	.0	41
.0	0	.0	0	.0	121	100.0	121	100.0	0	.0	0	.0	121
.0	0	.0	0	.0	1,592	100.0	1,592	100.0	0	.0	0	.0	1,592
.0	0	.0	0	.0	533	100.0	533	100.0	0	.0	0	.0	533
.0	0	.0	0	.0	1,059	100.0	1,059	100.0	0	.0	0	.0	1,059
.0	377	.4	1,780	1.8	97,683	96.6	99,847	98.7	941	.9	377	.4	101,165
.0	271	.5	988	1.7	55,849	96.6	57,111	98.8	524	.9	186	.3	57,821
.0	106	.2	792	1.8	41,834	96.5	42,736	98.6	417	1.0	191	.4	43,344
.0	64	.3	1,515	6.2	22,327	90.9	23,910	97.4	601	2.4	38	.2	24,549
.0	39	.3	759	5.6	12,535	91.9	13,334	97.7	294	2.2	16	.1	13,644
.0	25	.2	756	6.9	9,792	89.8	10,576	97.0	307	2.8	22	.2	10,905
.0	441	.4	3,295	2.6	120,010	95.5	123,757	98.4	1,542	1.2	415	.3	125,714
.0	310	.4	1,747	2.4	68,384	95.7	70,445	98.6	818	1.1	202	.3	71,465
.0	131	.2	1,548	2.9	51,626	95.2	53,312	98.3	724	1.3	213	.4	54,249
.0	1,152	18.8	125	2.0	3,988	64.9	5,265	85.7	850	13.8	29	.5	6,144
.0	773	21.7	36	1.0	2,243	63.1	3,052	85.8	486	13.7	19	.5	3,557
.0	379	14.7	89	3.4	1,745	67.5	2,213	85.5	364	14.1	10	.4	2,587
.0	1,593	1.2	3,420	2.6	123,998	94.0	129,022	97.8	2,392	1.8	444	.3	131,858
.0	1,083	1.4	1,783	2.4	70,627	94.1	73,497	98.0	1,304	1.7	221	.3	75,022
.0	510	.9	1,637	2.9	53,371	93.9	55,525	97.7	1,088	1.9	223	.4	56,836

9999 (3,162 INSTITUTIONS

%	NUMBER	%	NUMBER	%	NUMBER	%	NUMBER	%	NUMBER	%	NUMBER	%	NUMBER
.6	601,281	10.2	115,560	2.0	291,197	4.9	1,044,237	17.7	4,717,382	80.1	130,021	2.2	5,891,640
.7	342,543	11.9	53,721	1.8	150,734	5.2	565,783	19.7	2,273,479	79.1	36,311	1.3	2,875,573
.6	258,738	8.6	61,839	2.1	140,463	4.7	478,454	15.9	2,443,903	81.0	93,710	3.1	3,016,067
.9	286,618	10.3	65,454	2.3	168,056	6.0	545,347	19.5	2,222,803	79.6	25,250	.9	2,793,400
.9	163,064	10.9	31,614	2.1	85,916	5.7	294,194	19.6	1,195,188	79.7	10,521	.7	1,499,903
.9	123,554	9.6	33,840	2.6	82,140	6.4	251,153	19.4	1,027,615	79.4	14,729	1.1	1,293,497
.7	887,899	10.2	181,014	2.1	459,253	5.3	1,589,584	18.3	6,940,185	79.9	155,271	1.8	8,685,040
.7	505,607	11.6	85,335	2.0	236,650	5.4	859,977	19.7	3,468,667	79.3	46,832	1.1	4,375,476
.7	382,292	8.9	95,679	2.2	222,603	5.2	729,607	16.9	3,471,518	80.6	108,439	2.5	4,309,564
.4	20,985	4.9	9,277	2.2	9,833	2.3	41,635	9.8	331,158	77.8	52,960	12.4	425,753
.4	11,633	6.8	3,572	2.1	4,549	2.7	20,432	11.9	139,468	81.5	11,169	6.5	171,069
.3	9,352	3.7	5,705	2.2	5,284	2.1	21,203	8.3	191,690	75.3	41,791	16.4	254,684
.3	40,933	6.3	11,454	1.8	15,345	2.4	69,977	10.8	559,999	86.1	20,421	3.1	650,397
.3	25,609	7.8	4,404	1.3	7,733	2.4	38,808	11.8	283,576	86.4	5,648	1.7	328,032
.4	15,324	4.8	7,050	2.2	7,612	2.4	31,169	9.7	276,423	85.7	14,773	4.6	322,365
.4	61,918	5.8	20,731	1.9	25,178	2.3	111,612	10.4	891,157	82.8	73,381	6.8	1,076,150
.3	37,242	7.5	7,976	1.6	12,282	2.5	59,240	11.9	423,044	84.8	16,817	3.4	499,101
.4	24,676	4.3	12,755	2.2	12,896	2.2	52,372	9.1	468,113	81.1	56,564	9.8	577,049
.4	10,260	4.4	4,515	1.9	6,275	2.7	22,025	9.5	207,912	89.4	2,730	1.2	232,667
.4	4,024	6.9	1,406	2.4	1,753	3.0	7,425	12.8	50,067	86.3	526	.9	58,018
.4	6,236	3.6	3,109	1.8	4,522	2.6	14,600	8.4	157,845	90.4	2,204	1.3	174,649
.4	1,164	4.9	285	1.2	670	2.8	2,216	9.3	21,394	89.4	314	1.3	23,924
.4	425	6.1	91	1.3	180	2.6	724	10.3	6,208	88.6	71	1.0	7,003
.4	739	4.4	194	1.1	490	2.9	1,492	8.8	15,186	89.7	243	1.4	16,921
.4	11,424	4.5	4,800	1.9	6,945	2.7	24,241	9.4	229,306	89.4	3,044	1.2	256,591
.4	4,449	6.8	1,497	2.3	1,933	3.0	8,149	12.5	56,275	86.5	597	.9	65,021
.4	6,975	3.6	3,303	1.7	5,012	2.6	16,092	8.4	173,031	90.3	2,447	1.3	191,570
.6	632,526	9.7	129,352	2.0	307,305	4.7	1,107,897	16.9	5,256,452	80.3	185,711	2.8	6,550,060
.6	358,200	11.5	58,699	1.9	157,036	5.1	593,640	19.1	2,463,014	79.3	48,006	1.5	3,104,600
.6	274,326	8.0	70,653	2.1	150,269	4.4	514,257	14.9	2,793,438	81.1	137,705	4.0	3,445,400
.8	328,715	9.5	77,193	2.2	184,071	5.3	617,540	17.8	2,804,196	80.9	45,985	1.3	3,467,721
.8	189,098	10.3	36,109	2.0	93,829	5.1	333,726	18.2	1,484,972	80.9	16,240	.9	1,834,938
.8	139,617	8.6	41,084	2.5	90,242	5.5	283,814	17.4	1,319,224	80.8	29,745	1.8	1,632,783
.7	961,241	9.6	206,545	2.1	491,376	4.9	1,725,437	17.2	8,060,648	80.5	231,696	2.3	10,017,781
.7	547,298	11.1	94,808	1.9	250,865	5.1	927,366	18.8	3,947,986	79.9	64,246	1.3	4,939,598
.6	413,943	8.2	111,737	2.2	240,511	4.7	798,071	15.7	4,112,662	81.0	167,450	3.3	5,078,183
.9	94,032	7.1	31,497	2.4	49,443	3.7	186,530	14.0	1,121,674	84.4	21,014	1.6	1,329,218
.9	54,860	7.4	15,676	2.1	24,487	3.3	101,670	13.7	633,363	85.1	9,030	1.2	744,063
.8	39,172	6.7	15,821	2.7	24,956	4.3	84,860	14.5	488,311	83.4	11,984	2.0	585,155
.7	1,055,273	9.3	238,042	2.1	540,819	4.8	1,911,967	16.8	9,182,322	80.9	252,710	2.2	11,346,999
.7	602,158	10.6	110,484	1.9	275,352	4.8	1,029,036	18.1	4,581,349	80.6	73,276	1.3	5,683,661
.6	453,115	8.0	127,558	2.3	265,467	4.7	882,931	15.6	4,600,973	81.2	179,434	3.2	5,663,338

TABLE 18 - COMPARISIONS OF ENROLLMENT IN INSTITUTIONS OF HIGHER EDUCATION FOR SELECTED FIELDS OF STUDY AND LEVEL OF ENROLLMENT
BY RACE, ETHNICITY AND SEX: STATE 1974, 1976, 1978

MAJOR FIELD 0100 - AGRICULTURE AND NATURAL RESOURCES

	AMERICAN INDIAN ALASKAN NATIVE		BLACK NON-HISPANIC		ASIAN OR PACIFIC ISLANDER		HISPANIC		TOTAL MINORITY		WHITE NON-HISPANIC		TOT
	NUMBER	%	NUMBER	%	NUMBER	%	NUMBER	%	NUMBER	%	NUMBER	%	NUMB
ALABAMA · · · · · · · · · · ·													
FEMALE													
1974 (14 INSTITUTIONS)	0	.0	116	51.1	2	.9	0	.0	118	52.0	109	48.0	2
1976 (22 INSTITUTIONS)	1	.3	130	35.8	2	.5	0	.0	141	36.6	244	63.4	3
% CHANGE 1974 TO 1976	100.0		19.0		.0		.0		19.5		123.9		69.6
1978 (22 INSTITUTIONS)	0	.0	137	32.2	3	.7	1	.2	141	33.1	285	66.9	4
% CHANGE 1976 TO 1978	- 100.0		- .7		50.0		100.0		.0		16.8		10.6
MALE													
1974 (14 INSTITUTIONS)	3	.2	384	25.1	1	.1	4	.3	392	25.7	1,135	74.3	1,5
1976 (22 INSTITUTIONS)	3	.2	383	19.2	1	.1	0	.0	387	19.4	1,604	80.6	1,9
% CHANGE 1974 TO 1976	.0		- .3		.0		- 100.0		- 1.3		41.3		30.4
1978 (22 INSTITUTIONS)	0	.0	229	14.6	12	.8	7	.4	248	15.8	1,318	84.2	1,5
% CHANGE 1976 TO 1978	- 100.0		- 40.2		1100.0		100.0		- 35.9		- 17.8		- 21.3
ALASKA · · · · · · · · · · ·													
FEMALE													
1974 (0 INSTITUTIONS)	0	.0	0	.0	0	.0	0	.0	0	.0	0	.0	
1976 (1 INSTITUTIONS)	4	80.0	0	.0	0	.0	0	.0	4	80.0	1	20.0	
% CHANGE 1974 TO 1976	100.0		.0		.0		.0		100.0		100.0		100.0
1978 (1 INSTITUTIONS)	0	.0	0	.0	1	2.1	0	.0	1	2.1	46	97.9	
% CHANGE 1976 TO 1978	- 100.0		.0		100.0		.0		- 75.0		4500.0		840.0
MALE													
1974 (0 INSTITUTIONS)	0	.0	0	.0	0	.0	0	.0	0	.0	0	.0	
1976 (1 INSTITUTIONS)	4	18.2	0	.0	0	.0	0	.0	4	18.2	18	81.8	
% CHANGE 1974 TO 1976	100.0		.0		.0		.0		100.0		100.0		100.0
1978 (1 INSTITUTIONS)	5	2.8	1	.6	2	1.1	0	.0	8	4.5	171	95.5	1
% CHANGE 1976 TO 1978	25.0		100.0		100.0		.0		100.0		850.0		713.6
ARIZONA · · · · · · · · · · ·													
FEMALE													
1974 (10 INSTITUTIONS)	3	.8	1	.3	1	.3	4	1.1	9	2.5	351	97.5	3
1976 (9 INSTITUTIONS)	7	.8	2	.2	6	.6	24	2.6	39	4.2	886	95.8	9
% CHANGE 1974 TO 1976	133.3		100.0		500.0		500.0		333.3		152.4		156.9
1978 (11 INSTITUTIONS)	11	1.0	3	.3	4	.4	26	2.3	44	3.9	1,072	96.1	1,1
% CHANGE 1976 TO 1978	57.1		50.0		- 33.3		8.3		12.8		21.0		20.6
MALE													
1974 (10 INSTITUTIONS)	22	1.7	4	.3	7	.5	39	3.0	72	5.6	1,221	94.4	1,2
1976 (9 INSTITUTIONS)	34	1.7	7	.3	9	.4	65	3.2	115	5.6	1,943	94.4	2,0
% CHANGE 1974 TO 1976	54.5		75.0		28.6		66.7		59.7		59.1		59.2
1978 (11 INSTITUTIONS)	23	1.2	8	.4	7	.4	58	3.0	96	5.0	1,824	95.0	1,9
% CHANGE 1976 TO 1978	- 32.4		14.3		- 22.2		- 10.8		- 16.5		- 6.1		- 6.7
ARKANSAS · · · · · · · · · ·													
FEMALE													
1974 (8 INSTITUTIONS)	0	.0	4	3.3	0	.0	0	.0	4	3.3	119	96.7	1
1976 (8 INSTITUTIONS)	0	.0	5	2.1	2	.8	1	.4	8	3.3	233	96.7	2
% CHANGE 1974 TO 1976	.0		25.0		100.0		100.0		100.0		95.8		95.9
1978 (8 INSTITUTIONS)	0	.0	16	5.0	0	.0	0	.0	16	5.0	302	95.0	3
% CHANGE 1976 TO 1978	.0		220.0		- 100.0		- 100.0		100.0		29.6		32.0
MALE													
1974 (8 INSTITUTIONS)	5	.3	66	4.4	1	.1	5	.3	77	5.2	1,413	94.8	1,4
1976 (8 INSTITUTIONS)	8	.5	67	4.2	2	.1	2	.1	79	5.0	1,510	95.0	1,5
% CHANGE 1974 TO 1976	60.0		1.5		100.0		- 60.0		2.6		6.9		6.6
1978 (8 INSTITUTIONS)	14	.9	62	4.0	4	.3	6	.4	86	5.6	1,456	94.4	1,5
% CHANGE 1976 TO 1978	75.0		- 7.5		100.0		200.0		8.9		- 3.6		- 3.0

RE AND NATURAL RESOURCES

ICAN INDIAN SKAN NATIVE		BLACK NON-HISPANIC		ASIAN OR PACIFIC ISLANDER		HISPANIC		TOTAL MINORITY		WHITE NON-HISPANIC		TOTAL
NUMBER	%	NUMBER	%	NUMBER	%	NUMBER	%	NUMBER	%	NUMBER	%	NUMBER
62	1.0	119	2.0	189	3.2	174	2.9	544	9.2	5,380	90.8	5,924
150	1.9	97	1.3	278	3.6	270	3.5	795	10.3	6,940	89.7	7,735
141.9		- 18.5		47.1		55.2		46.1		29.0		30.6
108	1.7	86	1.4	285	4.5	209	3.3	688	10.8	5,678	89.2	6,366
28.0		- 11.3		2.5		- 22.6		- 13.5		- 18.2		- 17.7
217	1.4	263	1.7	464	3.0	739	4.8	1,683	11.0	13,644	89.0	15,327
400	2.3	496	2.9	545	3.2	1,326	7.8	2,767	16.2	14,334	83.8	17,101
84.3		88.6		17.5		79.4		64.4		5.1		11.6
203	1.8	182	1.6	445	3.9	710	6.2	1,540	13.4	9,920	86.6	11,460
49.3		- 63.3		- 18.3		- 46.5		- 44.3		- 30.8		- 33.0
2	.2	4	.5	5	.6	5	.6	16	1.9	843	98.1	859
3	.3	5	.6	5	.6	7	.8	20	2.3	864	97.7	884
50.0		25.0		.0		40.0		25.0		2.5		2.9
3	.3	1	.1	6	.6	9	.9	19	1.9	962	98.1	981
.0		- 80.0		20.0		28.6		- 5.0		11.3		11.0
8	.3	9	.3	19	.7	25	1.0	61	2.4	2,516	97.6	2,577
7	.3	5	.2	17	.7	35	1.4	64	2.6	2,382	97.4	2,446
12.5		- 44.4		- 10.5		40.0		4.9		- 5.3		- 5.1
5	.2	5	.2	16	.7	42	1.8	68	2.9	2,247	97.1	2,315
28.6		.0		- 5.9		20.0		6.3		- 5.7		- 5.4
0	.0	4	.9	1	.2	4	.9	9	2.1	423	97.9	432
0	.0	6	.9	2	.3	3	.4	11	1.6	665	98.4	676
.0		50.0		100.0		- 25.0		22.2		57.2		56.5
0	.0	2	.3	8	1.2	2	.3	12	1.9	632	98.1	644
.0		- 66.7		300.0		- 33.3		9.1		- 5.0		- 4.7
1	.2	6	1.0	2	.3	4	.7	13	2.1	602	97.9	615
0	.0	7	.9	0	.0	2	.3	9	1.2	753	98.8	762
100.0		16.7		- 100.0		- 50.0		- 30.8		25.1		23.9
3	.4	6	.9	3	.4	9	1.3	21	3.0	684	97.0	705
100.0		- 14.3		100.0		350.0		133.3		- 9.2		- 7.5
0	.0	2	1.1	0	.0	0	.0	2	1.1	172	98.9	174
0	.0	1	.3	0	.0	0	.0	1	.3	287	99.7	288
.0		- 50.0		.		.0		- 50.0		66.9		65.5
0	.0	8	2.7	0	.0	0	.0	8	2.7	289	97.3	297
.0		700.0		.0		.0		700.0		.7		3.1
0	.0	20	4	1	.2	0	.0	21	5.1	392	94.9	413
1	.2	15	2.8	1	.2	0	.0	17	3.3	502	96.7	519
100.0		- 25.0		.0		.0		- 19.0		28.1		25.7
1	.2	35	7.0	1	.2	0	.0	37	7.4	461	92.6	498
.0		133.3		.0		.0		117.6		- 8.2		- 4.0

TABLE 18 - COMPARISIONS OF ENROLLMENT IN INSTITUTIONS OF HIGHER EDUCATION FOR SELECTED FIELDS OF STUDY AND LEVEL OF ENRO BY RACE, ETHNICITY AND SEX: STATE 1974, 1976, 1978

MAJOR FIELD 0100 - AGRICULTURE AND NATURAL RESOURCES

	AMERICAN INDIAN ALASKAN NATIVE		BLACK NON-HISPANIC		ASIAN OR PACIFIC ISLANDER		HISPANIC		TOTAL MINORITY		WHITE NON-HISPANIC	
	NUMBER	%	NUMBER	%	NUMBER	%	NUMBER	%	NUMBER	%	NUMBER	%
DISTRICT OF COLUMBIA. . . .												
FEMALE												
1974 (1 INSTITUTIONS)	0	.0	54	85.7	0	.0	2	3.2	56	88.9	7	11.1
1976 (1 INSTITUTIONS)	0	.0	89	89.0	2	2.0	3	3.0	94	94.0	6	6.0
% CHANGE 1974 TO 1976	.0		64.8		100.0		50.0		67.9		- 14.3	
1978 (2 INSTITUTIONS)	0	.0	65	92.9	0	.0	0	.0	65	92.9	5	7.1
% CHANGE 1976 TO 1978	.0		- 27.0		- 100.0		- 100.0		- 30.9		- 16.7	
MALE												
1974 (1 INSTITUTIONS)	0	.0	91	87.5	1	1.0	2	1.9	94	90.4	10	9.6
1976 (1 INSTITUTIONS)	0	.0	164	95.9	0	.0	5	2.9	169	98.8	2	1.2
% CHANGE 1974 TO 1976	.0		80.2		- 100.0		150.0		79.8		- 80.0	
1978 (2 INSTITUTIONS)	3	2.8	88	80.7	10	9.2	0	.0	101	92.7	8	7.3
% CHANGE 1976 TO 1978	100.0		- 46.3		100.0		- 100.0		- 40.2		300.0	
FLORIDA												
FEMALE												
1974 (22 INSTITUTIONS)	1	.2	53	8.6	7	1.1	22	3.6	83	13.4	536	86.6
1976 (2 INSTITUTIONS)	1	.2	6	1.1	4	.7	4	.7	15	2.7	533	97.3
% CHANGE 1974 TO 1976	.0		- 88.7		- 42.9		- 81.8		- 81.9		- .6	
1978 (4 INSTITUTIONS)	1	.2	16	2.5	5	.8	8	1.2	30	4.7	614	95.3
% CHANGE 1976 TO 1978	.0		166.7		25.0		100.0		100.0		15.2	
MALE												
1974 (22 INSTITUTIONS)	10	.6	62	4.0	43	2.8	31	2.0	146	9.5	1,395	90.5
1976 (2 INSTITUTIONS)	2	.2	15	1.4	2	.2	26	2.1	45	4.1	1,045	95.9
% CHANGE 1974 TO 1976	- 80.0		- 75.8		- 95.3		- 16.1		- 69.2		- 25.1	
1978 (4 INSTITUTIONS)	2	.2	62	5.3	7	.6	39	3.4	110	9.5	1,050	90.5
% CHANGE 1976 TO 1978	.0		313.3		250.0		50.0		144.4		.5	
GEORGIA												
FEMALE												
1974 (16 INSTITUTIONS)	2	.8	3	1.2	3	1.2	1	.4	9	3.5	248	96.5
1976 (19 INSTITUTIONS)	1	.2	9	2.1	1	.2	1	.2	12	2.8	417	97.2
% CHANGE 1974 TO 1976	- 50.0		200.0		- 66.7		.0		33.3		68.1	
1978 (22 INSTITUTIONS)	0	.0	17	3.3	3	.6	2	.4	22	4.2	498	95.8
% CHANGE 1976 TO 1978	- 100.0		88.9		200.0		100.0		83.3		19.4	
MALE												
1974 (16 INSTITUTIONS)	5	.3	121	8.1	3	.2	10	.7	139	9.3	1,352	90.7
1976 (19 INSTITUTIONS)	11	.6	119	6.4	1	.1	7	.4	138	7.5	1,709	92.5
% CHANGE 1974 TO 1976	120.0		- 1.7		- 66.7		- 30.0		- .7		26.4	
1978 (22 INSTITUTIONS)	3	.2	60	3.3	4	.2	13	.7	80	4.3	1,763	95.7
% CHANGE 1976 TO 1978	- 72.7		- 49.6		300.0		85.7		- 42.0		3.2	
HAWAII.												
FEMALE												
1974 (0 INSTITUTIONS)	0	.0	0	.0	0	.0	0	.0	0	.0	0	.0
1976 (2 INSTITUTIONS)	0	.0	2	1.0	144	69.9	0	.0	146	70.9	60	29.1
% CHANGE 1974 TO 1976	.0		100.0		100.0		.0		100.0		100.0	
1978 (2 INSTITUTIONS)	0	.0	2	1.0	134	64.1	2	1.0	138	66.0	71	34.0
% CHANGE 1976 TO 1978	.0		.0		- 6.9		100.0		- 5.5		18.3	
MALE												
1974 (0 INSTITUTIONS)	0	.0	0	.0	0	.0	0	.0	0	.0	0	.0
1976 (2 INSTITUTIONS)	0	.0	9	1.5	398	67.5	16	2.7	423	71.7	167	28.3
% CHANGE 1974 TO 1976	.0		100.0		100.0		100.0		100.0		100.0	
1978 (2 INSTITUTIONS)	0	.0	3	.6	303	62.0	9	1.8	315	64.4	174	35.6
% CHANGE 1976 TO 1978	.0		- 66.7		- 23.9		- 43.8		- 25.5		4.2	

E AND NATURAL RESOURCES

ICAN INDIAN SKAN NATIVE		BLACK NON-HISPANIC		ASIAN OR PACIFIC ISLANDER		HISPANIC		TOTAL MINORITY		WHITE NON-HISPANIC		TOTAL
NUMBER	%	NUMBER	%	NUMBER	%	NUMBER	%	NUMBER	%	NUMBER	%	NUMBER
0	.0	0	.0	3	2.2	0	.0	8	2.2	136	97.8	139
1	.4	0	.0	6	2.3	2	.8		3.4	252	96.6	261
100.0		.0		100.0		100.0		200.0		85.3		87.8
1	.3	0	.0	4	1.2	1	.3	6	1.8	336	98.2	342
.0		.0		- 33.3		- 50.0		- 33.3		33.3		31.0
5	.4	3	.3	11	1.0	5	.4	24	2.1	1,128	97.9	1,152
5	.4	4	.3	11	.9	7	.5	27	2.1	1,263	97.9	1,290
.0		33.3		.0		40.0		12.5		12.0		12.0
5	.5	1	.1	4	.4	1	.1	11	1.0	1,072	99.0	1,083
.0		- 75.0		- 63.6		- 85.7		- 59.3		- 15.1		- 16.0
1	.2	3	.5	7	1.1	4	.6	15	2.4	607	97.6	622
4	.4	6	.5	9	.8	6	.5	25	2.2	1,097	97.8	1,122
300.0		100.0		28.6		50.0		66.7		80.7		80.4
6	.5	11	.9	14	1.2	4	.3	35	3.0	1,151	97.0	1,186
50.0		83.3		55.6		- 33.3		40.0		4.9		5.7
6	.2	17	.6	7	.2	10	.3	40	1 3	2,985	98.7	3,025
7	.2	28	.7	20	.5	20	.5	75	1t9	3,813	98.1	3,888
16.7		64.7		185.7		100.0		87.5		27.7		28.5
18	.5	23	.7	18	.5	16	.5	75	2.2	3,266	97.8	3,341
157.1		- 17.9		- 10.0		- 20.0		.0		- 14.3		- 14.1
2	.3	11	1.5	5	.7	2	.3	20	2.8	695	97.2	715
0	.0	7	.8	1	.1	0	.0	8	.9	874	99.1	882
100.0		- 36.4		- 80.0		- 100.0		- 60.0		25.8		23.4
0	.0	5	.5	4	.4	2	.2	11	1.1	962	98.9	973
.0		- 28.6		300.0		100.0		37.5		10.1		10.3
1	.0	17	.7	11	.4	19	.7	48	1.9	2,501	98.1	2,549
5	.2	11	.4	3	.1	3	.1	22	.8	2,635	99.2	2,657
400.0		- 35.3		- 72.7		- 84.2		- 54.2		5.4		4.2
0	.0	3	.1	3	.1	5	.2	11	.5	2,329	99.5	2,340
100.0		- 72.7		.0		66.7		- 50.0		- 11.6		- 11.9
2	.6	6	1.8	4	1.2	1	.3	13	3.9	322	96.1	335
0	.0	3	.5	0	.0	1	.2	4	.7	581	99.3	585
100.0		- 50.0		- 100.0		.0		- 69.2		80.4		74.6
0	.0	4	.6	2	.3	1	.1	7	1.0	675	99.0	682
.0		33.3		100.0		.0		75.0		16.2		16.6
2	.1	7	.3	3	.1	2	.1	14	.6	2,337	99.4	2,351
3	.1	8	.3	5	.2	2	.0	17	.6	2,699	99.4	2,716
50.0		14.3		66.7		- 50.0		21.4		15.5		15.5
1	.0	12	.4	11	.4	4	.1	28	.9	3,066	99.1	3,094
66.7		50.0		120.0		300.0		64.7		13.6		13.9

MAJOR FIELD 0100 - AGRICULTURE AND NATURAL RESOURCES

	AMERICAN INDIAN ALASKAN NATIVE		BLACK NON-HISPANIC		ASIAN OR PACIFIC ISLANDER		HISPANIC		TOTAL MINORITY		WHITE NON-HISPANIC	
	NUMBER	%	NUMBER	%	NUMBER	%	NUMBER	%	NUMBER	%	NUMBER	%
KANSAS.												
FEMALE												
1974 (15 INSTITUTIONS)	2	.6	1	.3	1	.3	1	.3	5	1.5	338	98.5
1976 (19 INSTITUTIONS)	12	2.0	1	.2	0	.0	4	.7	17	2.9	570	97.1
% CHANGE 1974 TO 1976	500.0		.0		- 100.0		300.0		240.0		68.6	
1978 (20 INSTITUTIONS)	3	.5	3	.5	1	.2	11	1.8	18	3.0	581	97.0
% CHANGE 1976 TO 1978	- 75.0		200.0		100.0		175.0		5.9		1.9	
MALE												
1974 (15 INSTITUTIONS)	6	.3	5	.2	17	.8	8	.4	36	1.8	1,981	98.2
1976 (19 INSTITUTIONS)	42	1.6	10	.4	6	.2	13	.5	71	2.8	2,491	97.2
% CHANGE 1974 TO 1976	600.0		100.0		- 64.7		62.5		97.2		25.7	
1978 (20 INSTITUTIONS)	15	.6	7	.3	3	.1	21	.9	46	1.9	2,404	98.1
% CHANGE 1976 TO 1978	- 64.3		- 30.0		- 50.0		61.5		- 35.2		- 3.5	-
KENTUCKY.												
FEMALE												
1974 (7 INSTITUTIONS)	4	.8	1	.2	0	.0	2	.4	7	1.4	491	98.6
1976 (9 INSTITUTIONS)	0	.0	4	.6	2	.3	1	.1	7	1.0	691	99.0
% CHANGE 1974 TO 1976	- 100.0		300.0		100.0		- 50.0		.0		40.7	
1978 (9 INSTITUTIONS)	7	1.0	4	.6	6	.8	2	.3	19	2.6	701	97.4
% CHANGE 1976 TO 1978	100.0		.0		200.0		100.0		171.4		1.4	
MALE												
1974 (7 INSTITUTIONS)	4	.2	12	.6	10	.5	1	.1	27	1.4	1,958	98.6
1976 (9 INSTITUTIONS)	8	.4	19	1.0	6	.3	4	.2	37	1.9	1,911	98.1
% CHANGE 1974 TO 1976	100.0		58.3		- 40.0		300.0		37.0		- 2.4	
1978 (9 INSTITUTIONS)	4	.2	15	.9	14	.9	4	.2	37	2.2	1,609	97.8
% CHANGE 1976 TO 1978	- 50.0		- 21.1		133.3		.0		.0		- 15.8	-
LOUISIANA												
FEMALE												
1974 (12 INSTITUTIONS)	1	.2	7	1.6	1	.2	1	.2	10	2.3	421	97.7
1976 (12 INSTITUTIONS)	0	.0	13	1.9	3	.4	7	1.0	23	3.4	652	96.6
% CHANGE 1974 TO 1976	- 100.0		85.7		200.0		600.0		130.0		54.9	
1978 (12 INSTITUTIONS)	2	.3	31	4.4	1	.1	5	.7	39	5.6	659	94.4
% CHANGE 1976 TO 1978	100.0		138.5		- 66.7		- 28.6		69.6		1.1	
MALE												
1974 (12 INSTITUTIONS)	4	.1	86	3.1	6	.2	14	.5	110	3.9	2,690	96.1
1976 (12 INSTITUTIONS)	2	.1	118	4.7	4	.2	11	.4	135	5.3	2,400	94.7
% CHANGE 1974 TO 1976	- 50.0		37.2		- 33.3		- 21.4		22.7		- 10.8	-
1978 (12 INSTITUTIONS)	1	.1	119	6.0	5	.3	15	.8	140	7.1	1,839	92.9
% CHANGE 1976 TO 1978	- 50.0		.8		25.0		36.4		3.7		- 23.4	-
MAINE												
FEMALE												
1974 (4 INSTITUTIONS)	1	.4	0	.0	0	.0	0	.0	1	.4	233	99.6
1976 (2 INSTITUTIONS)	1	.3	0	.0	0	.0	0	.0	1	.3	319	99.7
% CHANGE 1974 TO 1976	.0		.0		.0		.0		.0		36.9	
1978 (3 INSTITUTIONS)	1	.2	1	.2	1	.2	3	.6	6	1.3	466	98.7
% CHANGE 1976 TO 1978	.0		100.0		100.0		100.0		500.0		46.1	
MALE												
1974 (4 INSTITUTIONS)	4	.4	1	.1	1	.1	0	.0	6	.6	924	99.4
1976 (2 INSTITUTIONS)	4	.5	0	.0	1	.1	0	.0	5	.6	804	99.4
% CHANGE 1974 TO 1976	.0		- 100.0		.0		.0		- 16.7		- 13.0	-
1978 (3 INSTITUTIONS)	3	.3	2	.2	1	.1	3	.3	9	.9	1,037	99.1
% CHANGE 1976 TO 1978	- 25.0		100.0		.0		100.0		80.0		29.0	

RE AND NATURAL RESOURCES

ICAN INDIAN SKAN NATIVE		BLACK NON-HISPANIC		ASIAN OR PACIFIC ISLANDER		HISPANIC		TOTAL MINORITY		WHITE NON-HISPANIC		TOTAL
NUMBER	%	NUMBER	%	NUMBER	%	NUMBER	%	NUMBER	%	NUMBER	%	NUMBER
2	.6	4	1.2	4	1.2	2	.6	12	3.6	326	96.4	338
4	.7	11	1.8	7	1.2	4	.7	26	4.3	580	95.7	606
100.0		175.0		75.0		100.0		116.7		77.9		79.3
0	.0	14	2.3	7	1.1	5	.8	26	4.2	592	95.8	618
100.0		27.3		.0		25.0		.0		2.1		2.0
9	1.2	33	4.4	13	1.7	9	1.2	64	8.6	680	91.4	744
10	1.0	24	2.5	10	1.0	6	.6	50	5.2	911	94.8	961
11.1		- 27.3		- 23.1		- 33.3		- 21.9		34.0		29.2
3	.4	26	3.1	8	.9	4	.5	41	4.8	808	95.2	849
70.0		8.3		- 20.0		- 33.3		- 18.0		- 11.3		- 11.7
8	1.2	3	.5	1	.2	2	.3	14	2 2	636	97.8	650
2	.2	3	.3	4	.5	9	1.0	18	211	841	97.9	859
75.0		.0		300.0		350.0		28.6		32.2		32.2
4	.2	21	1.2	20	1.2	12	.7	57	3.3	1,645	96.7	1,702
100.0		600.0		400.0		33.3		216.7		95.6		98.1
7	.6	8	.6	2	.2	3	.2	20	1.6	1,244	98.4	1,264
4	.3	9	.6	5	.3	7	.5	25	1.9	1,446	98.3	1,471
42.9		12.5		150.0		133.3		25.0		16.2		16.4
6	.3	24	1.4	24	1.4	16	.9	70	4.0	1,700	96.0	1,770
50.0		166.7		360.0		128.6		180.0		17.6		20.3
1	.1	25	1.9	12	.9	4	.3	42	3.2	1,266	96.8	1,308
3	.2	39	2.0	12	.6	6	.3	60	3.1	1,868	96.9	1,928
200.0		56.0		.0		50.0		42.9		47.6		47.4
5	.3	36	2.0	11	.6	3	.2	55	3.1	1,711	96.9	1,766
66.7		- 7.7		- 8.3		- 50.0		- 8.3		- 8.4		- 8.4
14	.3	81	1.9	23	.5	13	.3	131	3.1	4,141	96.9	4,272
14	.3	77	1.6	19	.4	18	.4	128	2.7	4,544	97.3	4,672
.0		- 4.9		- 17.4		38.5		- 2.3		9.7		9.4
9	.2	52	1.4	18	.5	18	.5	97	2.6	3,571	97.4	3,668
35.7		- 32.5		- 5.3		.0		- 24.2		- 21.4		- 21.5
4	1.1	1	.3	17	4.7	2	.6	24	6.7	334	93.3	358
2	.3	2	.3	11	1.6	0	.0	15	2.2	675	97.8	690
50.0		100.0		- 35.3		- 100.0		- 37.5		102.1		92.7
3	.4	3	.4	5	.6	3	.4	14	1.8	765	98.2	779
50.0		50.0		- 54.5		100.0		- 6.7		13.3		12.9
15	.9	9	.5	50	3.0	1	.1	75	4.5	1,579	95.5	1,654
11	.5	13	.6	41	1.9	6	.3	71	3.2	2,124	96.8	2,195
26.7		44.4		- 18.0		500.0		- 5.3		34.5		32.7
9	.4	7	.3	17	.8	7	.3	40	1.9	2,051	98.1	2,091
18.2		- 46.2		- 58.5		16.7		- 43.7		- 3.4		- 4.7

TABLE 18 - COMPARISIONS OF ENROLLMENT IN INSTITUTIONS OF HIGHER EDUCATION FOR SELECTED FIELDS OF STUDY AND LEVEL OF ENROLLME
BY RACE, ETHNICITY AND SEX: STATE 1974, 1976, 1978

MAJOR FIELD 0100 - AGRICULTURE AND NATURAL RESOURCES

	AMERICAN INDIAN ALASKAN NATIVE		BLACK NON-HISPANIC		ASIAN OR PACIFIC ISLANDER		HISPANIC		TOTAL MINORITY		WHITE NON-HISPANIC	
	NUMBER	%	NUMBER	%	NUMBER	%	NUMBER	%	NUMBER	%	NUMBER	%
MISSISSIPPI · · · · · · · ·												
FEMALE												
1974 (15 INSTITUTIONS)	0	.0	5	5.1	0	.0	2	2.0	7	7.1	92	92.9
1976 (16 INSTITUTIONS)	1	.4	13	5.6	0	.0	0	.0	14	6.0	218	94.0
% CHANGE 1974 TO 1976	100.0		160.0		.0		- 100.0		100.0		137.0	
1978 (19 INSTITUTIONS)	1	.3	99	28.1	2	.6	0	.0	102	29.0	250	71.0
% CHANGE 1976 TO 1978	.0		661.5		100.0		.0		628.6		14.7	
MALE												
1974 (15 INSTITUTIONS)	3	.2	101	6.2	4	.2	1	.1	109	6.7	1,514	93.3
1976 (16 INSTITUTIONS)	1	.1	173	10.0	2	.1	0	.0	176	10.2	1,555	89.8
% CHANGE 1974 TO 1976	- 66.7		71.3		- 50.0		- 100.0		61.5		2.7	
1978 (19 INSTITUTIONS)	0	.0	282	18.5	4	.3	1	.1	287	18.8	1,239	81.2
% CHANGE 1976 TO 1978	- 100.0		63.0		100.0		100.0		63.1		- 20.3	-
MISSOURI · · · · · · · · ·												
FEMALE												
1974 (12 INSTITUTIONS)	1	.2	9	1.8	1	.2	1	.2	12	2.3	501	97.7
1976 (15 INSTITUTIONS)	1	.1	15	2.0	3	.4	3	.4	22	2.9	744	97.1
% CHANGE 1974 TO 1976	.0		66.7		200.0		200.0		83.3		48.5	
1978 (11 INSTITUTIONS)	0	.0	24	2.8	5	.6	1	.1	30	3.5	831	96.5
% CHANGE 1976 TO 1978	- 100.0		60.0		66.7		- 66.7		36.4		11.7	
MALE												
1974 (12 INSTITUTIONS)	7	.2	32	1.1	0	.0	5	.2	44	1.5	2,906	98.5
1976 (15 INSTITUTIONS)	9	.3	50	1.5	7	.2	8	.2	74	2.2	3,324	97.8
% CHANGE 1974 TO 1976	28.6		56.3		100.0		60.0		68.2		14.4	
1978 (11 INSTITUTIONS)	9	.3	42	1.4	14	.5	12	.4	77	2.6	2,886	97.4
% CHANGE 1976 TO 1978	.0		- 16.0		100.0		50.0		4.1		- 13.2	-
MONTANA · · · · · · · · · ·												
FEMALE												
1974 (3 INSTITUTIONS)	4	1.6	0	.0	0	.0	0	.0	4	1.6	250	98.4
1976 (3 INSTITUTIONS)	4	1.0	0	.0	1	.3	0	.0	5	1.3	376	98.7
% CHANGE 1974 TO 1976	.0		.0		100.0		.0		25.0		50.4	
1978 (3 INSTITUTIONS)	0	.0	0	.0	0	.0	3	.6	3	.6	504	99.4
% CHANGE 1976 TO 1978	- 100.0		.0		- 100.0		100.0		- 40.0		34.0	
MALE												
1974 (3 INSTITUTIONS)	10	.7	3	.2	4	.3	3	.2	20	1.5	1,352	98.5
1976 (3 INSTITUTIONS)	22	1.5	4	.3	5	.3	4	.3	35	2.3	1,480	97.7
% CHANGE 1974 TO 1976	120.0		33.3		25.0		33.3		75.0		9.5	
1978 (3 INSTITUTIONS)	17	1.2	1	.1	2	.1	3	.2	23	1.7	1,369	98.3
% CHANGE 1976 TO 1978	- 22.7		- 75.0		- 60.0		- 25.0		- 34.3		- 7.5	-
NEBRASKA · · · · · · · · ·												
FEMALE												
1974 (5 INSTITUTIONS)	0	.0	0	.0	0	.0	1	.7	1	.7	145	99.3
1976 (4 INSTITUTIONS)	0	.0	0	.0	0	.0	0	.0	0	.0	207	100.0
% CHANGE 1974 TO 1976	.0		.0		.0		- 100.0		- 100.0		42.8	
1978 (8 INSTITUTIONS)	0	.0	2	.5	0	.0	0	.0	2	.5	373	99.5
% CHANGE 1976 TO 1978	.0		100.0		.0		.0		100.0		80.2	
MALE												
1974 (5 INSTITUTIONS)	0	.0	3	.2	6	.4	4	.3	13	1.0	1,331	99.0
1976 (4 INSTITUTIONS)	1	.1	3	.2	6	.5	8	.6	18	1.4	1,312	98.6
% CHANGE 1974 TO 1976	100.0		.0		.0		100.0		38.5		- 1.4	-
1978 (8 INSTITUTIONS)	4	.2	4	.2	5	.3	10	.6	23	1.3	1,705	98.7
% CHANGE 1976 TO 1978	300.0		33.3		- 16.7		25.0		27.8		30.0	

D 0100 – AGRICULTURE AND NATURAL RESOURCES

	AMERICAN INDIAN ALASKAN NATIVE		BLACK NON-HISPANIC		ASIAN OR PACIFIC ISLANDER		HISPANIC		TOTAL MINORITY		WHITE NON-HISPANIC		TOTAL
	NUMBER	%	NUMBER	%	NUMBER	%	NUMBER	%	NUMBER	%	NUMBER	%	NUMBER
. . . .													
1 INSTITUTIONS)	1	1.1	0	.0	0	.0	0	.0	1	1.1	91	98.9	92
3 INSTITUTIONS)	3	1.3	0	.0	0	.0	2	.9	5	2.1	230	97.9	235
1974 TO 1976	200.0		.0		.0		100.0		400.0		152.7		155.4
2 INSTITUTIONS)	0	.0	0	.0	1	.5	3	1.5	4	2.0	201	98.0	205
1976 TO 1978	- 100.0		.0		100.0		50.0		- 20.0		- 12.6		- 12.8
1 INSTITUTIONS)	7	1.9	2	.5	4	1.1	4	1.1	17	4.6	351	95.4	368
3 INSTITUTIONS)	8	1.3	4	.8	5	.9	5	.9	22	4.2	505	95.8	527
1974 TO 1976	14.3		100.0		25.0		25.0		29.4		43.9		43.2
2 INSTITUTIONS)	5	1.5	6	1.8	4	1.2	3	.9	18	5.4	316	94.6	334
1976 TO 1978	- 37.5		50.0		- 20.0		- 40.0		- 18.2		- 37.4		- 36.6
IRE													
1 INSTITUTIONS)	0	.0	0	.0	2	.5	0	.0	2	.5	364	99.5	366
2 INSTITUTIONS)	0	.0	0	.0	0	.0	2	.5	2	.5	429	99.5	431
1974 TO 1976	.0		.0		- 100.0		100.0		.0		17.9		17.8
2 INSTITUTIONS)	0	.0	0	.0	0	.0	1	.2	1	.2	417	99.8	418
1976 TO 1978	.0		.0		.0		- 50.0		- 50.0		- 2.8		- 3.0
1 INSTITUTIONS)	2	.4	1	.2	0	.0	0	.0	3	.6	532	99.4	535
2 INSTITUTIONS)	1	.2	1	.2	1	.2	1	.2	4	.7	568	99.3	572
1974 TO 1976	- 50.0		.0		100.0		100.0		33.3		6.8		6.9
2 INSTITUTIONS)	1	.2	0	.0	1	.2	1	.2	3	.6	459	99.4	462
1976 TO 1978	.0		- 100.0		.0		.0		- 25.0		- 19.2		- 19.2
. . . .													
2 INSTITUTIONS)	0	.0	10	2.1	10	2.1	3	.6	23	4.9	450	95.1	473
3 INSTITUTIONS)	0	.0	12	2.0	5	.8	4	.7	21	3.6	568	96.4	589
1974 TO 1976	.0		20.0		- 50.0		33.3		8.7		26.2		24.5
4 INSTITUTIONS)	0	.0	9	1.6	5	.9	5	.9	19	3.4	533	96.6	552
1976 TO 1978	.0		- 25.0		.0		25.0		- 9.5		- 6.2		- 6.3
2 INSTITUTIONS)	0	.0	20	1.8	23	2.0	11	1.0	54	4.8	1,072	95.2	1,126
3 INSTITUTIONS)	0	.0	13	1.6	10	1.2	13	1.6	36	4.4	773	95.6	809
1974 TO 1976	.0		- 35.0		- 56.5		18.2		- 33.3		- 27.9		- 28.2
4 INSTITUTIONS)	1	.1	12	1.7	11	1.6	8	1.2	32	4.7	655	95.3	687
1976 TO 1978	100.0		- 7.7		10.0		- 38.5		- 11.1		- 15.3		- 15.1
. . . .													
8 INSTITUTIONS)	5	2.4	0	.0	0	.0	12	5.8	17	8.2	190	91.8	207
8 INSTITUTIONS)	13	3.9	0	.0	2	.6	43	13.0	58	17.5	273	82.5	331
1974 TO 1976	160.0		.0		100.0		258.3		241.2		43.7		59.9
8 INSTITUTIONS)	10	2.7	0	.0	1	.3	44	12.1	55	15.1	309	84.9	364
1976 TO 1978	- 23.1		.0		- 50.0		2.3		- 5.2		13.2		10.0
8 INSTITUTIONS)	25	2.5	1	.1	7	.7	120	12.2	153	15.5	833	84.5	986
8 INSTITUTIONS)	32	2.7	6	.5	10	.8	193	16.1	241	20.1	959	79.9	1,200
1974 TO 1976	28.0		500.0		42.9		60.8		57.5		15.1		21.7
8 INSTITUTIONS)	24	2.4	3	.3	3	.3	186	18.9	216	22.0	767	78.0	983
1976 TO 1978	- 25.0		- 50.0		- 70.0		- 3.6		- 10.4		- 20.0		- 18.1

TABLE 18 - COMPARISIONS OF ENROLLMENT IN INSTITUTIONS OF HIGHER EDUCATION FOR SELECTED FIELDS OF STUDY AND LEVEL OF ENROLLMENT
BY RACE, ETHNICITY AND SEX: STATE 1974, 1976, 1978

MAJOR FIELD 0100 - AGRICULTURE AND NATURAL RESOURCES

	AMERICAN INDIAN ALASKAN NATIVE		BLACK NON-HISPANIC		ASIAN OR PACIFIC ISLANDER		HISPANIC		TOTAL MINORITY		WHITE NON-HISPANIC		T
	NUMBER	%	NUMBER	%	NUMBER	%	NUMBER	%	NUMBER	%	NUMBER	%	NU
NEW YORK.													
FEMALE													
1974 (5 INSTITUTIONS)	2	.5	6	1.4	5	1.2	1	.2	14	3.3	414	96.7	
1976 (5 INSTITUTIONS)	0	.0	16	1.9	9	1.0	10	1.2	35	4.1	823	95.9	
% CHANGE 1974 TO 1976	- 100.0		166.7		80.0		900.0		150.0		98.8		100
1978 (5 INSTITUTIONS)	5	.5	25	2.6	31	3.2	14	1.4	75	7.8	892	92.2	
% CHANGE 1976 TO 1978	100.0		56.3		244.4		40.0		114.3		8.4		12
MALE													
1974 (5 INSTITUTIONS)		.2	16	.8	5	.3	3	.2	27	1.4	1,893	98.6	1
1976 (5 INSTITUTIONS)	9	.5	34	2.0	7	.4	13	.8	63	3.8	1,598	96.2	1
% CHANGE 1974 TO 1976	200.0		112.5		40.0		333.3		133.3		- 15.6		- 13
1978 (5 INSTITUTIONS)	6	.3	51	2.6	43	2.2	41	2.1	141	7.2	1,805	92.8	1
% CHANGE 1976 TO 1978	- 33.3		50.0		514.3		215.4		123.8		13.0	·	17
NORTH CAROLINA.													
FEMALE													
1974 (11 INSTITUTIONS)	0	.0	20	4.5	0	.0	1	.2	21	.7	427	95.3	
1976 (8 INSTITUTIONS)	1	.2	46	7.9	0	.0	1	.2	48	8.3	531	91.7	
% CHANGE 1974 TO 1976	100.0		130.0		.0		.0		128.6		24.4		29
1978 (5 INSTITUTIONS)	1	.2	41	7.1	1	.2	3	.5	46	7.9	533	92.1	
% CHANGE 1976 TO 1978	.0		- 10.9		100.0		200.0		- 4.2		.4		
MALE													
1974 (11 INSTITUTIONS)	3	.2	57	3.0	0	.2	0	.5	72	3.8	1,803	96.2	1
1976 (8 INSTITUTIONS)	5	.2	166	7.8	0	.2	4	.2	180	8.4	1,958	91.6	2
% CHANGE 1974 TO 1976	66.7		191.2		66.7		- 55.6		150.0		8.6		14
1978 (5 INSTITUTIONS)	2	.1	137	9.4	7	.5	7	.5	153	10.5	1,298	89.5	1
% CHANGE 1976 TO 1978	- 60.0		- 17.5		40.0		75.0		- 15.0		- 33.7		- 32
NORTH DAKOTA.													
FEMALE													
1974 (3 INSTITUTIONS)	1	1.5	0	.0	0	.0	0	.0	1	1.5	64	98.5	
1976 (5 INSTITUTIONS)	0	.0	0	.0	0	.0	0	.0	0	.0	183	100.0	
% CHANGE 1974 TO 1976	- 100.0		.0		.0		.0		- 100.0		185.9		181
1978 (6 INSTITUTIONS)	2	.8	0	.0	0	.0	0	.0	2	.8	252	99.2	
% CHANGE 1976 TO 1978	100.0		.0		.0		.0		100.0		37.7		38
MALE													
1974 (3 INSTITUTIONS)	2	.3	1	.1	1	.1	0	.0	4	.6	706	99.4	
1976 (5 INSTITUTIONS)	2	.2	1	.1	3	.2	2	.2	8	.6	1,231	99.4	1
% CHANGE 1974 TO 1976	.0		.0		200.0		100.0		100.0		74.4		74
1978 (6 INSTITUTIONS)	6	.5	2	.2	1	.1	0	.0	9	.7	1,229	99.3	1
% CHANGE 1976 TO 1978	200.0		100.0		- 66.7		- 100.0		12.5		- .2		
OHIO.													
FEMALE													
1974 (4 INSTITUTIONS)	1	.2	2	.4	0	.0	1	.2	4	.8	509	99.2	
1976 (14 INSTITUTIONS)	0	.0	55	2.4	8	.3	6	.3	69	3.0	2,219	97.0	2
% CHANGE 1974 TO 1976	- 100.0		2650.0		100.0		500.0		1625.0		336.0		346
1978 (18 INSTITUTIONS)	3	.3	9	.8	2	.2	4	.4	18	1.6	1,120	98.4	1
% CHANGE 1976 TO 1978	100.0		- 83.6		- 75.0		- 33.3		- 73.9		- 49.5		- 50
MALE													
1974 (4 INSTITUTIONS)	0	.0	5	.2	7	.3	0	.0	12	.5	2,273	99.5	2
1976 (14 INSTITUTIONS)	2	.1	20	.6	17	.5	9	.3	48	1.5	3,177	98.5	3
% CHANGE 1974 TO 1976	100.0		300.0		142.9		100.0		300.0		39.8		41
1978 (18 INSTITUTIONS)	6	.3	19	.8	7	.3	9	.4	41	1.7	2,351	98.3	2
% CHANGE 1976 TO 1978	200.0		- 5.0		- 58.8		.0		- 14.6		- 26.0		- 25

RE AND NATURAL RESOURCES

ICAN INDIAN SKAN NATIVE		BLACK NON-HISPANIC		ASIAN OR PACIFIC ISLANDER		HISPANIC		TOTAL MINORITY		WHITE NON-HISPANIC		TOTAL
NUMBER	%	NUMBER	%	NUMBER	%	NUMBER	%	NUMBER	%	NUMBER	%	NUMBER
7	3.9	1	.6	0	.0	0	.0	8	4.4	172	95.6	180
14	2.8	4	.8	3	.6	3	.6	24	4.8	471	95.2	495
100.0		300.0		100.0		100.0		200.0		173.8		175.0
15	2.5	9	1.5	3	.5	4	.7	31	5.1	575	94.9	606
7.1		125.0		.0		33.3		29.2		22.1		22.4
46	2.2	34	1.6	9	.4	10	.5	99	4.7	2,009	95.3	2,108
60	2.1	35	1.3	24	.9	16	.6	135	4.8	2,663	95.2	2,798
30.4		2.9		166.7		60.0		36.4		32.6		32.7
42	1.9	25	1.1	11	.5	12	.5	90	4.0	2,152	96.0	2,242
30.0		- 28.6		- 54.2		- 25.0		- 33.3		- 19.2		- 19.9
5	.8	0	.0	5	.8	6	1.0	16	2.7	584	97.3	600
7	.8	2	.2	4	.4	1	.1	14	1.6	882	98.4	896
40.0		100.0		- 20.0		- 83.3		- 12.5		51.0		49.3
10	1.2	1	.1	9	1.1	1	.1	21	2.5	811	97.5	832
42.9		- 50.0		125.0		.0		50.0		- 8.0		- 7.1
12	.6	7	.3	35	1.7	13	.6	67	3.3	1,989	96.7	2,056
15	.6	4	.2	20	.9	13	.6	52	2.2	2,296	97.8	2,348
25.0		- 42.9		- 42.9		.0		- 22.4		15.4		14.2
30	1.5	11	.6	26	1.3	8	.4	75	3.9	1,866	96.1	1,941
100.0		175.0		30.0		- 38.5		44.2		- 18.7		- 17.3
0	.0	4	.4	2	.2	3	.3	9	.9	1,043	99.1	1,052
0	.0	12	.9	6	.5	2	.2	20	1.5	1,280	98.5	1,300
.0		200.0		200.0		- 33.3		122.2		22.7		23.6
4	.1	50	1.8	26	1.0	4	.1	84	3.1	2,634	96.9	2,718
100.0		316.7		333.3		100.0		320.0		105.8		109.1
5	.2	22	.7	4	.1	5	.2	36	1.1	3,123	98.9	3,159
3	.1	19	.6	1	.0	8	.2	31	.9	3,328	99.1	3,359
40.0		- 13.6		- 75.0		60.0		- 13.9		6.6		6.3
8	.2	84	1.8	11	.2	13	.3	116	2.5	4,462	97.5	4,578
166.7		342.1		1000.0		62.5		274.2		34.1		36.3
0	.0	0	.0	0	.0	2	1.0	2	1.0	205	99.0	207
0	.0	0	.0	1	.3	1	.3	2	.6	354	99.4	356
.0		.0		100.0		- 50.0		.0		72.7		72.0
2	.5	0	.0	1	.3	1	.3	4	1.1	375	98.9	379
100.0		.0		.0		.0		100.0		5.9		6.5
1	.2	4	.6	2	.3	4	.6	11	1.7	644	98.3	655
2	.3	4	.6	1	.1	2	.3	9	1.3	664	98.7	673
100.0		.0		- 50.0		- 50.0		- 18.2		3.1		2.7
1	.2	1	.2	2	.3	1	.2	5	.9	572	99.1	577
50.0		- 75.0		100.0		- 50.0		- 44.4		- 13.9		- 14.3

TABLE 18 - COMPARISIONS OF ENROLLMENT IN INSTITUTIONS OF HIGHER EDUCATION FOR SELECTED FIELDS OF STUDY AND LEVEL OF ENROLLME
          BY RACE, ETHNICITY AND SEX: STATE 1974, 1976, 1978

MAJOR FIELD 0100 - AGRICULTURE AND NATURAL RESOURCES

	AMERICAN INDIAN ALASKAN NATIVE		BLACK NON-HISPANIC		ASIAN OR PACIFIC ISLANDER		HISPANIC		TOTAL MINORITY		WHITE NON-HISPANIC	
	NUMBER	%	NUMBER	%	NUMBER	%	NUMBER	%	NUMBER	%	NUMBER	%
SOUTH CAROLINA.												
FEMALE												
1974 (1 INSTITUTIONS)	0	.0	0	.0	0	.0	0	.0	0	.0	111	100.0
1976 (2 INSTITUTIONS)	0	.0	2	.9	0	.0	0	.0	2	.9	228	99.1
% CHANGE 1974 TO 1976	.0		100.0		.0		.0		100.0		105.4	
1978 (2 INSTITUTIONS)	0	.0	1	.4	1	.4	0	.0	2	.7	278	99.3
% CHANGE 1976 TO 1978	.0		- 50.0		100.0		.0		.0		21.9	
MALE												
1974 (1 INSTITUTIONS)	1	.2	3	.5	3	.5	0	.0	7	1.2	598	98.8
1976 (2 INSTITUTIONS)	2	.3	2	.3	3	.5	1	.2	8	1.2	651	98.8
% CHANGE 1974 TO 1976	100.0		- 33.3		.0		100.0		14.3		8.9	
1978 (2 INSTITUTIONS)	1	.2	3	.5	0	.0	1	.2	5	.8	587	99.2
% CHANGE 1976 TO 1978	- 50.0		50.0		- 100.0		.0		- 37.5		- 9.8	-
SOUTH DAKOTA.												
FEMALE												
1974 (2 INSTITUTIONS)	1	1.2	0	.0	0	.0	0	.0	1	1.2	81	98.8
1976 (3 INSTITUTIONS)	0	.0	0	.0	0	.0	0	.0	0	.0	130	100.0
% CHANGE 1974 TO 1976	- 100.0		.0		.0		.0		- 100.0		60.5	
1978 (3 INSTITUTIONS)	0	.0	0	.0	0	.0	0	.0	0	.0	132	100.0
% CHANGE 1976 TO 1978	.0		.0		.0		.0		.0		1.5	
MALE												
1974 (2 INSTITUTIONS)	6	.6	0	.0	0	.0	0	.0	6	.6	990	99.4
1976 (3 INSTITUTIONS)	3	.3	1	.1	0	.0	0	.0	4	.4	895	99.6
% CHANGE 1974 TO 1976	- 50.0		100.0		.0		.0		- 33.3		- 9.6	
1978 (3 INSTITUTIONS)	2	.2	0	.0	0	.0	0	.0	2	.2	880	99.8
% CHANGE 1976 TO 1978	- 33.3		- 100.0		.0		.0		- 50.0		- 1.7	-
TENNESSEE												
FEMALE												
1974 (12 INSTITUTIONS)	0	.0	201	42.7	0	.0	1	.2	202	42.9	269	57.1
1976 (14 INSTITUTIONS)	2	.3	18	3.1	1	.2	1	.2	22	3.8	551	96.2
% CHANGE 1974 TO 1976	100.0		- 91.0		100.0		.0		- 89.1		104.8	
1978 (13 INSTITUTIONS)	1	.2	24	3.7	5	.8	1	.2	31	4.8	618	95.2
% CHANGE 1976 TO 1978	- 50.0		33.3		400.0		.0		40.9		12.2	
MALE												
1974 (12 INSTITUTIONS)	4	.2	379	17.9	0	.0	0	.0	383	18.0	1,739	82.0
1976 (14 INSTITUTIONS)	4	.2	101	4.6	0	.0	0	.0	105	4.7	2,111	95.3
% CHANGE 1974 TO 1976	.0		- 73.4		.0		.0		- 72.6		21.4	
1978 (13 INSTITUTIONS)	2	.1	137	6.6	8	.4	2	.1	149	7.2	1,920	92.8
% CHANGE 1976 TO 1978	- 50.0		35.6		100.0		100.0		41.9		- 9.0	-
TEXAS												
FEMALE												
1974 (46 INSTITUTIONS)	14	1.2	7	.6	6	.5	23	2.0	50	4.4	1,090	95.6
1976 (58 INSTITUTIONS)	27	1.4	40	2.1	1	.1	26	1.4	94	4.9	1,819	95.1
% CHANGE 1974 TO 1976	92.9		471.4		- 83.3		13.0		88.0		66.9	
1978 (56 INSTITUTIONS)	9	.4	30	1.2	7	.3	51	2.0	97	3.8	2,457	96.2
% CHANGE 1976 TO 1978	- 66.7		- 25.0		600.0		96.2		3.2		35.1	
MALE												
1974 (46 INSTITUTIONS)	104	1.3	144	1.8	31	.4	216	2.6	495	6.1	7,667	93.9
1976 (58 INSTITUTIONS)	68	.8	161	1.8	22	.3	258	2.9	509	5.8	8,283	94.2
% CHANGE 1974 TO 1976	- 34.6		11.8		- 29.0		19.4		2.8		8.0	
1978 (56 INSTITUTIONS)	30	.4	180	2.3	40	.5	288	3.7	538	6.9	7,279	93.1
% CHANGE 1976 TO 1978	- 55.9		11.8		81.8		11.6		5.7		- 12.1	-

COMPARISIONS OF ENROLLMENT IN INSTITUTIONS OF HIGHER EDUCATION FOR SELECTED FIELDS OF STUDY AND LEVEL OF ENROLLMENT
BY RACE, ETHNICITY AND SEX: STATE 1974, 1976, 1978

D 0100 — AGRICULTURE AND NATURAL RESOURCES

	AMERICAN INDIAN ALASKAN NATIVE		BLACK NON-HISPANIC		ASIAN OR PACIFIC ISLANDER		HISPANIC		TOTAL MINORITY		WHITE NON-HISPANIC		TOTAL
	NUMBER	%	NUMBER	%	NUMBER	%	NUMBER	%	NUMBER	%	NUMBER	%	NUMBER
· · · · · · · · · ·													
5 INSTITUTIONS)	0	.0	1	.3	4	1.3	1	.3	6	2.0	298	98.0	304
6 INSTITUTIONS)	2	.4	2	.4	5	1.1	3	.6	12	2.6	453	97.4	465
1974 TO 1976	100.0		100.0		25.0		200.0		100.0		52.0		53.0
4 INSTITUTIONS)	4	1.0	2	.5	4	1.0	1	.2	11	2.7	398	97.3	409
1976 TO 1978	100.0		.0		- 20.0		- 66.7		- 8.3		- 12.1		- 12.0
5 INSTITUTIONS)	7	.4	2	.1	6	.4	8	.5	23	1.5	1,536	98.5	1,559
6 INSTITUTIONS)	7	.4	4	.3	4	.3	10	.6	25	1.6	1,541	98.4	1,566
1974 TO 1976	.0		100.0		- 33.3		25.0		8.7		.3		.4
4 INSTITUTIONS)	2	.2	4	.3	9	.7	9	.7	24	1.9	-1,233	98.1	1,257
1976 TO 1978	- 71.4		.0		125.0		- 10.0		- 4.0		- 20.0		- 19.7
· · · · · · · · · ·													
2 INSTITUTIONS)	0	.0	1	.5	0	.0	0	.0	1	.5	209	99.5	210
2 INSTITUTIONS)	0	.0	3	.8	0	.0	2	.5	5	1.3	385	98.7	390
1974 TO 1976	.0		200.0		.0		100.0		400.0		84.2		85.7
4 INSTITUTIONS)	0	.0	2	.4	0	.0	0	.0	2	.4	450	99.6	452
1976 TO 1978	.0		- 33.3		.0		- 100.0		- 60.0		16.9		15.9
2 INSTITUTIONS)	0	.0	0	.0	0	.0	0	.0	0	.0	481	100.0	481
2 INSTITUTIONS)	1	.2	1	.2	1	.2	0	.0	3	.6	540	99.4	543
1974 TO 1976	100.0		100.0		100.0		.0		100.0		12.3		12.9
4 INSTITUTIONS)	0	.0	0	.0	0	.0	0	.0	0	.0	657	100.0	657
1976 TO 1978	- 100.0		- 100.0		- 100.0		.0		- 100.0		21.7		21.0
· · · · · · · · · ·													
5 INSTITUTIONS)	0	.0	12	2.3	2	.4	1	.2	15	2.8	518	97.2	533
7 INSTITUTIONS)	0	.0	15	1.5	2	.2	2	.2	19	1.9	957	98.1	976
1974 TO 1976	.0		25.0		.0		100.0		26.7		84.7		83.1
6 INSTITUTIONS)	2	.2	12	1.2	3	.3	3	.3	20	1.9	1,016	98.1	1,036
1976 TO 1978	100.0		- 20.0		50.0		50.0		5.3		6.2		6.1
5 INSTITUTIONS)	0	.0	69	4.4	6	.4	3	.2	78	5.0	1,480	95.0	1,558
7 INSTITUTIONS)	0	.0	65	3.7	7	.4	1	.1	73	4.2	1,680	95.8	1,753
1974 TO 1976	.0		- 5.8		16.7		- 66.7		- 6.4		13.5		12.5
6 INSTITUTIONS)	0	.0	31	1.9	7	.4	0	.0	38	2.3	1,600	97.7	1,638
1976 TO 1978	.0		- 52.3		.0		- 100.0		- 47.9		- 4.8		- 6.6
· · · · · · · · · ·													
8 INSTITUTIONS)	2	.5	2	.5	10	2.	0	.0	14	.%	398	96.6	412
3 INSTITUTIONS)	1	.2	2	.4	9	1.8	1	.2	13	3.8	486	97.4	499
1974 TO 1976	- 50.0		.0		- 10.0		100.0		- 7.1		22.1		21.1
4 INSTITUTIONS)	4	.7	2	.3	11	1.8	4	.7	21	3.4	588	96.6	609
1976 TO 1978	300.0		.0		22.2		300.0		61.5		21.0		22.0
8 INSTITUTIONS)	20	1.0	12	.6	51	2.5	9	.4	92	4.6	1,916	95.4	2,008
3 INSTITUTIONS)	15	.8	10	.6	35	2.0	7	.4	67	3.8	1,719	96.2	1,786
1974 TO 1976	- 25.0		- 16.7		- 31.4		- 22.2		- 27.2		- 10.3		- 11.1
4 INSTITUTIONS)	13	.7	8	.4	35	1.9	8	.4	64	3.6	1,738	96.4	1,802
1976 TO 1978	- 13.3		- 20.0		.0		14.3		- 4.5		1.1		.9

TABLE 18 - COMPARISIONS OF ENROLLMENT IN INSTITUTIONS OF HIGHER EDUCATION FOR SELECTED FIELDS OF STUDY AND LEVEL OF ENROLLM
BY RACE, ETHNICITY AND SEX: STATE 1974, 1976, 1978

MAJOR FIELD 0100 - AGRICULTURE AND NATURAL RESOURCES

	AMERICAN INDIAN ALASKAN NATIVE		BLACK NON-HISPANIC		ASIAN OR PACIFIC ISLANDER		HISPANIC		TOTAL MINORITY		WHITE NON-HISPANIC	
	NUMBER	%	NUMBER	%	NUMBER	%	NUMBER	%	NUMBER	%	NUMBER	%
WEST VIRGINIA												
FEMALE												
1974 (4 INSTITUTIONS)	0	.0	0	.0	2	1.3	0	.0	2	1.3	155	98.7
1976 (3 INSTITUTIONS)	0	.0	2	.7	0	.0	1	.4	3	1.1	281	98.9
% CHANGE 1974 TO 1976	.0		100.0		- 100.0		100.0		50.0		81.3	
1978 (3 INSTITUTIONS)	0	.0	3	.7	2	.5	1	.2	6	1.4	437	98.6
% CHANGE 1976 TO 1978	.0		50.0		100.0		.0		100.0		55.5	
MALE												
1974 (4 INSTITUTIONS)	0	.0	6	.6	3	.3	2	.2	11	1.1	1,034	98.9
1976 (3 INSTITUTIONS)	0	.0	10	1.2	12	1.4	0	.0	22	2.5	844	97.5
% CHANGE 1974 TO 1976	.0		66.7		300.0		- 100.0		100.0		- 18.4	-
1978 (3 INSTITUTIONS)	9	.7	15	1.2	0	.0	20	1.6	44	3.5	1,203	96.5
% CHANGE 1976 TO 1978	100.0		50.0		- 100.0		100.0		100.0		42.5	
WISCONSIN												
FEMALE												
1974 (5 INSTITUTIONS)	2	.3	2	.3	4	.5	1	.1	9	1.1	789	98.9
1976 (13 INSTITUTIONS)	6	.4	3	.2	1	.1	10	.7	20	1.3	1,473	98.7
% CHANGE 1974 TO 1976	200.0		50.0		- 75.0		900.0		122.2		86.7	
1978 (13 INSTITUTIONS)	8	.6	1	.1	0	.0	3	.2	12	.8	1,439	99.2
% CHANGE 1976 TO 1978	33.3		- 66.7		- 100.0		- 70.0		- 40.0		- 2.3	
MALE												
1974 (5 INSTITUTIONS)	11	.3	11	.3	8	.2	14	.4	44	1.1	3,926	98.9
1976 (13 INSTITUTIONS)	14	.2	14	.2	8	.1	17	.3	53	.9	5,701	99.1
% CHANGE 1974 TO 1976	27.3		27.3		.0		21.4		20.5		45.2	
1978 (13 INSTITUTIONS)	29	.7	15	.3	12	.3	14	.3	70		4,228	98.4
% CHANGE 1976 TO 1978	107.1		7.1		50.0		- 17.6		32.1		- 25.8	
WYOMING												
FEMALE												
1974 (6 INSTITUTIONS)	0	.0	0	.0	0	.0	0	.0	0	.0	120	100.0
1976 (6 INSTITUTIONS)	1	.5	0	.0	1	.5	0	.0	2	1.0	201	99.0
% CHANGE 1974 TO 1976	100.0		.0		100.0		.0		100.0		67.5	
1978 (5 INSTITUTIONS)	2	1.1	0	.0	0	.0	1	.5	3	1.6	187	98.4
% CHANGE 1976 TO 1978	100.0		.0		- 100.0		100.0		50.0		- 7.0	-
MALE												
1974 (6 INSTITUTIONS)	13	1.8	1	.1	1	.1	2	.3	17	2.4	693	97.6
1976 (6 INSTITUTIONS)	2	.3	1	.1	2	.3	3	.4	8	1.2	660	98.8
% CHANGE 1974 TO 1976	- 84.6		.0		100.0		50.0		- 52.9		- 4.8	-
1978 (5 INSTITUTIONS)	1	.2	0	.0	2	.4	2	.4	5	.9	561	99.1
% CHANGE 1976 TO 1978	- 50.0		- 100.0		.0		- 33.3		- 37.5		- 15.0	-
THE STATES AND D.C.												
FEMALE												
1974 (490 INSTITUTIONS)	144	.6	705	2.8	316	1.3	293	1.2	1,458	5.8	23,532	94.2
1976 (573 INSTITUTIONS)	279	.7	711	1.8	563	1.4	477	1.2	2,030	5.2	36,888	94.8
% CHANGE 1974 TO 1976	93.8		.9		78.2		62.8		39.2		56.8	
1978 (566 INSTITUTIONS)	238	.6	832	2.0	645	1.6	464	1.1	2,179	5.3	39,308	94.7
% CHANGE 1976 TO 1978	- 14.7		17.0		14.6		- 2.7		7.3		6.6	
MALE												
1974 (490 INSTITUTIONS)	640	.6	2,241	2.3	919	.9	1,390	1.4	5,190	5.2	94,219	94.8
1976 (573 INSTITUTIONS)	873	.8	2,515	2.2	1,325	1.2	2,176	1.9	6,889	6.2	105,026	93.8
% CHANGE 1974 TO 1976	36.4		12.2		44.2		44.2		32.7		11.5	
1978 (566 INSTITUTIONS)	587	.6	2,105	2.1	1,205	1.2	1,666	1.7	5,563	5.7	92,845	94.3
% CHANGE 1976 TO 1978	- 32.8		- 16.3		- 9.1		- 9.1		- 19.2		- 11.6	-

TURE AND NATURAL RESOURCES

ERICAN INDIAN LASKAN NATIVE		BLACK NON-HISPANIC		ASIAN OR PACIFIC ISLANDER		HISPANIC		TOTAL MINORITY		WHITE NON-HISPANIC		TOTAL
NUMBER	%	NUMBER	%	NUMBER	%	NUMBER	%	NUMBER	%	NUMBER	%	NUMBER
0	.0	0	.0	0	.0	0	.0	0	.0	0	.0	0
0	.0	0	.0	0	.0	0	.0	0	.0	1	100.0	1
	.0		.0		.0		.0		.0		100.0	100.0
0	.0	0	.0	0	.0	0	.0	0	.0	0	.0	0
	.0		.0		.0		.0		.0	-	100.0	- 100.0
0	.0	0	.0	5	.0	0	.0	5	.0	0	.0	0
					62.5				62.5	3	37.5	8
	.0		.0		100.0		.0		100.0		100.0	100.0
0	.0	0	.0	8	88.9	0	.0	8	88.9	1	11.1	9
	.0		.0		60.0		.0		60.0	-	66.7	12.5
0	.0	0	.0	0	.0	0	.0	0	.0	0	.0	0
						160	100.0	160	100.0			160
	.0		.0		.0		100.0		100.0		.0	100.0
0	.0	0	.0	0	.0	245	100.0	245	100.0	0	.0	245
	.0		.0		.0		53.1		53.1		.0	53.1
0	.0	0	.0	0	.0	0	.0	0	.0	0	.0	0
						571	100.0	571	100.0			571
	.0		.0		.0		100.0		100.0		.0	100.0
0	.0	0	.0	0	.0	721	100.0	721	100.0	0	.0	721
	.0		.0		.0		26.3		26.3		.0	26.3
0	.0	0	.0	0	.0	0	.0	0	.0	0	.0	0
0	.0	0	.0	0	.0	0	.0	0	.0	0	.0	0
	.0		.0		.0		.0		.0		.0	.0
0	.0	1	50.0	0	.0	0	.0	1	50.0	1	50.0	2
	.0		100.0		.0		.0		100.0		100.0	100.0
0	.0	0	.0	0	.0	0	.0	0	.0	0	.0	0
0	.0	0	.0	0	.0	0	.0	0	.0	0	.0	0
	.0		.0		.0		.0		.0		.0	.0
0	.0	0	.0	0	.0	0	.0	0	.0	0	.0	0
	.0		.0		.0		.0		.0		.0	.0
0	.0	0	.0	0	.0	0	.0	0	.0	0	.0	0
						160	99.4	160	99.4	1	.6	161
	.0		.0		.0		100.0		100.0		100.0	100.0
0	.0	1	.4	0	.0	245	99.2	246	99.6	1	.4	247
	.0		100.0		.0		53.1		53.8		.0	53.4
0	.0	0	.0	0	.0	0	.0	0	.0	0	.0	0
0	.0	0	.0	5	.9	571	98.6	576	99.5	3	.5	579
	.0		.0		100.0		100.0		100.0		100.0	100.0
0	.0	0	.0	8	1.1	721	98.8	729	99.9	1	.1	730
	.0		.0		60.0		60.0		26.6	-	66.7	26.1

MAJOR FIELD 0100 - AGRICULTURE AND NATURAL RESOURCES

	AMERICAN INDIAN ALASKAN NATIVE		BLACK NON-HISPANIC		ASIAN OR PACIFIC ISLANDER		HISPANIC		TOTAL MINORITY		WHITE NON-HISPANIC	
	NUMBER	%	NUMBER	%	NUMBER	%	NUMBER	%	NUMBER	%	NUMBER	%
MAJOR FIELD AGGREGATE 0100.												
FEMALE												
1974 (490 INSTITUTIONS)	144	.6	705	2.8	316	1.3	293	1.2	1,458	5.8	23,532	94.2
1976 (575 INSTITUTIONS)	279	.7	711	1.8	563	1.4	637	1.6	2,190	5.6	36,889	94.4
% CHANGE 1974 TO 1976	93.8		.9		78.2		117.4		50.2		56.8	
1978 (569 INSTITUTIONS)	238	.6	833	2.0	645	1.5	709	1.7	2,425	5.8	39,309	94.2
% CHANGE 1976 TO 1978	- 14.7		17.2		14.6		11.3		10.7		6.6	
MALE												
1974 (490 INSTITUTIONS)	640	.6	2,241	2.3	919	.9	1,390	1.4	5,190	5.2	94,219	94.8
1976 (575 INSTITUTIONS)	873	.8	2,515	2.2	1,330	1.2	2,747	2.4	7,465	6.6	105,029	93.4	1
% CHANGE 1974 TO 1976	36.4		12.2		44.7		44.7		43.8		11.5	
1978 (569 INSTITUTIONS)	587	.6	2,105	2.1	1,213	1.2	2,387	2.4	6,292	6.3	92,846	93.7
% CHANGE 1976 TO 1978	- 32.8		- 16.3		- 8.8		- 8.8		- 15.7		- 11.6	-

ENROLLMENT IN INSTITUTIONS OF HIGHER EDUCATION FOR SELECTED FIELDS OF STUDY AND LEVEL OF ENROLLMENT [B]Y AND SEX: STATE 1974, 1976, 1978

[ARCHITEC]TURE AND ENVIRONMENTAL DESIGN

[AMER]ICAN INDIAN [ALA]SKAN NATIVE		BLACK NON-HISPANIC		ASIAN OR PACIFIC ISLANDER		HISPANIC		TOTAL MINORITY		WHITE NON-HISPANIC		TOTAL
NUMBER	%	NUMBER	%	NUMBER	%	NUMBER	%	NUMBER	%	NUMBER	%	NUMBER
0	.0	0	.0	0	.0	1	.8	1	.8	126	99.2	127
1	.7	23	15.1	1	.7	0	.0	25	16.4	127	83.6	152
100.0		100.0		100.0		- 100.0		2400.0		.8		19.7
0	.0	20	9.3	2	.9	1	.5	23	10.7	192	89.3	215
100.0		- 13.0		100.0		100.0		- 8.0		51.2		41.4
0	.0	9	1.2	4	.5	7	.9	20	2.6	747	97.4	767
0	.0	116	11.9	2	.2	1	.1	119	12.2	854	87.8	973
.0		1188.9		- 50.0		- 85.7		495.0		14.3		26.9
1	.1	121	12.5	3	.3	1	.1	126	13.0	842	87.0	968
100.0		4.3		50.0		.0		5.9		- 1.4		- .5
0	.0	1	.4	2	.8	7	2.7	10	3.9	249	96.1	259
0	.0	1	.6	1	.6	5	3.1	7	4.3	156	95.7	163
.0		.0		- 50.0		- 28.6		- 30.0		- 37.3		- 37.1
2	.5	1	.3	4	1.0	13	3.4	20	5.2	362	94.8	382
100.0		.0		300.0		160.0		185.7		132.1		134.4
9	.8	14	1.3	20	1.9	52	4.9	95	8.9	975	91.1	1,070
7	.7	11	1.2	15	1.6	43	4.6	76	8.1	859	91.9	935
22.2		- 21.4		- 25.0		- 17.3		- 20.0		- 11.9		- 12.6
9	.9	10	1.0	16	1.6	47	4.8	82	8.3	904	91.7	986
28.6		- 9.1		6.7		9.3		7.9		5.2		5.5
2	6.7	0	.0	0	.0	1	3.3	3	10.0	27	90.0	30
0	.0	2	4.9	3	7.3	0	.0	5	12.2	36	87.8	41
100.0		100.0		100.0		- 100.0		66.7		33.3		36.7
0	.0	1	2.1	2	4.3	0	.0	3	6.4	44	93.6	47
.0		- 50.0		- 33.3		.0		- 40.0		22.2		14.6
5	1.5	3	.9	1	.3	4	1.2	13	3.8	331	96.2	344
2	.4	8	1.7	1	.2	1	.2	12	2.6	452	97.4	464
60.0		166.7		.0		- 75.0		- 7.7		36.6		34.9
3	.8	13	3.4	4	1.1	1	.3	21	5.5	359	94.5	380
50.0		62.5		300.0		.0		75.0		- 20.6		- 18.1
18	1.0	94	5.5	82	4.8	88	5.1	282	16.4	1,436	83.6	1,718
28	1.0	113	4.2	168	6.2	130	4.8	439	16.3	2,255	83.7	2,694
55.6		20.2		104.9		47.7		55.7		57.0		56.8
21	1.0	76	3.6	196	9.2	115	5.4	408	19.1	1,729	80.9	2,137
25.0		- 32.7		16.7		- 11.5		- 7.1		- 23.3		- 20.7
62	.9	394	5.5	521	7.2	713	9.9	1,690	23.4	5,521	76.6	7,211
71	.9	371	4.7	574	7.2	824	10.4	1,840	23.1	6,111	76.9	7,951
14.5		- 5.8		10.2		15.6		8.9		10.7		10.3
74	1.3	277	4.7	529	9.0	570	9.7	1,450	24.6	4,446	75.4	5,896
4.2		- 25.3		- 7.8		- 30.8		- 21.2		- 27.2		- 25.8

TABLE 18 - COMPARISIONS OF ENROLLMENT IN INSTITUTIONS OF HIGHER EDUCATION FOR SELECTED FIELDS OF STUDY AND LEVEL OF ENROLLMENT
BY RACE, ETHNICITY AND SEX: STATE 1974, 1976, 1978

MAJOR FIELD 0200 - ARCHITECTURE AND ENVIRONMENTAL DESIGN

	AMERICAN INDIAN ALASKAN NATIVE		BLACK NON-HISPANIC		ASIAN OR PACIFIC ISLANDER		HISPANIC		TOTAL MINORITY		WHITE NON-HISPANIC		T
	NUMBER	%	NUMBER	%	NUMBER	%	NUMBER	%	NUMBER	%	NUMBER	%	NU
COLORADO.													
FEMALE													
1974 (4 INSTITUTIONS)	0	.0	7	5.1	5	3.6	1	.7	13	9.5	124	90.5	
1976 (7 INSTITUTIONS)	0	.0	4	2.2	4	2.2	2	1.1	10	5.5	171	94.5	
% CHANGE 1974 TO 1976	.0		- 42.9		- 20.0		100.0		- 23.1		37.9		32
1978 (5 INSTITUTIONS)	0	.0	6	2.5	2	.8	3	1.3	11	4.6	227	95.4	
% CHANGE 1976 TO 1978	.0		50.0		- 50.0		50.0		10.0		32.7		31
MALE													
1974 (4 INSTITUTIONS)	1	.2	9	1.5	6	1.0	13	2.1	29	4.7	588	95.3	
1976 (7 INSTITUTIONS)	3	.5	10	1.8	9	1.6	11	1.9	33	5.8	532	94.2	
% CHANGE 1974 TO 1976	200.0		11.1		50.0		- 15.4		13.8		- 9.5		- 8
1978 (5 INSTITUTIONS)	1	.2	5	.9	12	2.2	9	1.7	27	5.0	513	95.0	
% CHANGE 1976 TO 1978	- 66.7		- 50.0		33.3		- 18.2		- 18.2		- 3.6		- 4
CONNECTICUT													
FEMALE													
1974 (1 INSTITUTIONS)	0	.0	4	8.0	1	2.0	1	2.0	6	12.0	44	88.0	
1976 (5 INSTITUTIONS)	0	.0	2	3.4	0	.0	1	1.7	3	5.2	55	94.8	
% CHANGE 1974 TO 1976	.0		- 50.0		- 100.0		.0		- 50.0		25.0		16
1978 (4 INSTITUTIONS)	2	1.9	4	3.8	2	1.9	3	2.9	11	10.6	93	89.4	
% CHANGE 1976 TO 1978	100.0		100.0		100.0		200.0		266.7		69.1		79
MALE													
1974 (1 INSTITUTIONS)	0	.0	4	2.6	2	1.3	1	.6	7	4.5	148	95.5	
1976 (5 INSTITUTIONS)	0	.0	7	2.3	0	.0	0	.0	7	2.3	299	97.7	
% CHANGE 1974 TO 1976	.0		75.0		- 100.0		- 100.0		.0		102.0		97
1978 (4 INSTITUTIONS)	0	.0	9	3.1	6	2.1	11	3.8	26	9.1	260	90.9	
% CHANGE 1976 TO 1978	.0		28.6		100.0		100.0		271.4		- 13.0		- 6
DELAWARE.													
FEMALE													
1974 (0 INSTITUTIONS)	0	.0	0	.0	0	.0	0	.0	0	.0	0	.0	
1976 (3 INSTITUTIONS)	0	.0	3	10.3	1	3.4	0	.0	4	13.8	25	86.2	
% CHANGE 1974 TO 1976	.0		100.0		100.0		.0		100.0		100.0		100
1978 (3 INSTITUTIONS)	0	.0	2	5.7	1	2.9	0	.0	3	8.6	32	91.4	
% CHANGE 1976 TO 1978	.0		- 33.3		.0		.0		- 25.0		28.0		20
MALE													
1974 (0 INSTITUTIONS)	0	.0	0	.0	0	.0	0	.0	0	.0	0	.0	
1976 (3 INSTITUTIONS)	0	.0	17	10.1	0	.0	1	.6	18	10.7	150	89.3	
% CHANGE 1974 TO 1976	.0		100.0		.0		100.0		100.0		100.0		100
1978 (3 INSTITUTIONS)	1	.5	15	7.5	1	.5	2	1.0	19	9.5	181	90.5	
% CHANGE 1976 TO 1978	100.0		- 11.8		100.0		100.0		5.6		20.7		19
DISTRICT OF COLUMBIA. . . .													
FEMALE													
1974 (2 INSTITUTIONS)	0	.0	31	36.5	4	4.7	9	10.6	44	51.8	41	48.2	
1976 (4 INSTITUTIONS)	0	.0	80	38.1	3	1.4	5	2.4	88	41.9	122	58.1	
% CHANGE 1974 TO 1976	.0		158.1		- 25.0		- 44.4		100.0		197.6		147
1978 (5 INSTITUTIONS)	0	.0	61	32.6	2	1.1	6	3.2	69	36.9	118	63.1	
% CHANGE 1976 TO 1978	.0		- 23.8		- 33.3		20.0		- 21.6		- 3.3		- 11
MALE													
1974 (2 INSTITUTIONS)	1	.2	186	32.3	22	3.8	17	3.0	226	39.2	350	60.8	
1976 (4 INSTITUTIONS)	2	.4	226	45.0	13	2.6	9	1.8	250	49.8	252	50.2	
% CHANGE 1974 TO 1976	100.0		21.5		- 40.9		- 47.1		10.6		- 28.0		- 12
1978 (5 INSTITUTIONS)	2	.4	186	41.2	10	2.2	13	2.9	211	46.7	241	53.3	
% CHANGE 1976 TO 1978	.0		- 17.7		- 23.1		44.4		- 15.6		- 4.4		- 10

718

COMPARISIONS OF ENROLLMENT IN INSTITUTIONS OF HIGHER EDUCATION FOR SELECTED FIELDS OF STUDY AND LEVEL OF ENROLLMENT
BY RACE, ETHNICITY AND SEX: STATE 1974, 1976, 1978

D 0200 - ARCHITECTURE AND ENVIRONMENTAL DESIGN

	AMERICAN INDIAN ALASKAN NATIVE		BLACK NON-HISPANIC		ASIAN OR PACIFIC ISLANDER		HISPANIC		TOTAL MINORITY		WHITE NON-HISPANIC		TOTAL
	NUMBER	%	NUMBER	%	NUMBER	%	NUMBER	%	NUMBER	%	NUMBER	%	NUMBER
19 INSTITUTIONS)	1	.2	18	2.9	3	.5	33	5.3	55	8.9	563	91.1	618
5 INSTITUTIONS)	0	.0	9	1.6	8	1.4	47	8.2	64	11.1	512	88.9	576
1974 TO 1976	- 100.0		- 50.0		166.7		42.4		16.4		- 9.1		- 6.8
6 INSTITUTIONS)	0	.0	28	4.1	5	.7	64	9.4	97	14.2	587	85.8	684
1976 TO 1978	.0		211.1		- 37.5		36.2		51.6		14.6		18.8
19 INSTITUTIONS)	6	.3	67	3.0	15	.7	163	7.3	251	11.3	1,978	88.7	2,229
5 INSTITUTIONS)	3	.2	61	3.7	26	1.6	184	11.1	274	16.6	1,379	83.4	1,653
1974 TO 1976	- 50.0		- 9.0		73.3		12.9		9.2		- 30.3		- 25.8
6 INSTITUTIONS)	3	.2	81	4.7	34	2.0	210	12.2	328	19.0	1,394	81.0	1,722
1976 TO 1978	.0		32.8		30.8		14.1		19.7		1.1		4.2
8 INSTITUTIONS)	0	.0	10	5.6	0	.0	2	1.1	12	6.8	165	93.2	177
11 INSTITUTIONS)	0	.0	19	8.4	0	.0	4	1.8	23	10.2	203	89.8	226
1974 TO 1976	.0		90.0		.0		100.0		91.7		23.0		27.7
10 INSTITUTIONS)	1	.4	13	4.9	4	1.5	5	1.9	23	8.6	243	91.4	266
1976 TO 1978	100.0		- 31.6		100.0		25.0		.0		19.7		17.7
8 INSTITUTIONS)	3	.3	34	3.2	7	.7	7	.7	51	4.8	1,018	95.2	1,069
11 INSTITUTIONS)	2	.2	49	4.9	6	.6	14	1.4	71	7.2	921	92.8	992
1974 TO 1976	- 33.3		44.1		- 14.3		100.0		39.2		- 9.5		- 7.2
10 INSTITUTIONS)	0	.0	42	4.5	4	.4	14	1.5	60	6.4	872	93.6	932
1976 TO 1978	- 100.0		- 14.3		- 33.3		.0		- 15.5		- 5.3		- 6.0
0 INSTITUTIONS)	0	.0	0	.0	0	.0	0	.0	0	.0	0	.0	0
1 INSTITUTIONS)	0	.0	0	.0	27	64.3	0	.0	27	64.3	15	35.7	42
1974 TO 1976	.0		.0		100.0		.0		100.0		100.0		100.0
1 INSTITUTIONS)	0	.0	0	.0	29	59.2	0	.0	29	59.2	20	40.8	49
1976 TO 1978	.0		.0		7.4		.0		7.4		33.3		16.7
0 INSTITUTIONS)	0	.0	0	.0	0	.0	0	.0	0	.0	0	.0	0
1 INSTITUTIONS)	0	.0	0	.0	102	80.3	1	.8	103	81.1	24	18.9	127
1974 TO 1976	.0		.0		100.0		100.0		100.0		100.0		100.0
1 INSTITUTIONS)	0	.0	0	.0	89	70.1	2	1.6	91	71.7	36	28.3	127
1976 TO 1978	.0		.0		- 12.7		100.0		- 11.7		50.0		.0
3 INSTITUTIONS)	0	.0	0	.0	1	1.4	1	1.4	2	2.7	72	97.3	74
3 INSTITUTIONS)	0	.0	0	.0	2	2.6	1	1.3	3	3.8	75	96.2	78
1974 TO 1976	.0		.0		100.0		.0		50.0		4.2		5.4
3 INSTITUTIONS)	0	.0	0	.0	0	.0	1	1.1	1	1.1	92	98.9	93
1976 TO 1978	.0		.0		- 100.0		.0		- 66.7		22.7		19.2
3 INSTITUTIONS)	2	.6	2	.6	8	2.4	4	1.2	16	4.8	317	95.2	333
3 INSTITUTIONS)	3	.8	2	.6	8	2.2	3	.8	16	4.4	345	95.6	361
1974 TO 1976	50.0		.0		.0		- 25.0		.0		8.8		8.4
3 INSTITUTIONS)	0	.0	2	.5	10	2.5	2	.5	14	3.5	383	96.5	397
1976 TO 1978	- 100.0		.0		25.0		- 33.3		- 12.5		11.0		10.0

MAJOR FIELD 0200 - ARCHITECTURE AND ENVIRONMENTAL DESIGN

	AMERICAN INDIAN ALASKAN NATIVE		BLACK NON-HISPANIC		ASIAN OR PACIFIC ISLANDER		HISPANIC		TOTAL MINORITY		WHITE NON-HISPANIC	
	NUMBER	%	NUMBER	%	NUMBER	%	NUMBER	%	NUMBER	%	NUMBER	%
ILLINOIS........												
FEMALE												
1974 (13 INSTITUTIONS)	0	.0	31	5.9	6	1.1	2	.4	39	7.	486	92.6
1976 (18 INSTITUTIONS)	1	.2	35	5.7	15	2.5	8	1.3	59	9.?	551	90.3
% CHANGE 1974 TO 1976	100.0		12.9		150.0		300.0		51.3		13.4	
1978 (18 INSTITUTIONS)	1	.1	44	5.8	21	2.8	11	1.5	77	10.2	681	89.8
% CHANGE 1976 TO 1978	.0		25.7		40.0		37.5		30.5		23.6	
MALE												
1974 (13 INSTITUTIONS)	1	.0	104	4.2	63	2.5	35	1 4	203	8.1	2,294	91.9
1976 (18 INSTITUTIONS)	8	.3	124	5.2	66	2.8	53	2±2	249	10.5	2,132	89.5
% CHANGE 1974 TO 1976	500.0		19.2		4.8		51.4		22.7		- 7.1	-
1978 (18 INSTITUTIONS)	7	.3	160	7.7	57	2.7	73	3.5	297	14.3	1,778	85.7
% CHANGE 1976 TO 1978	16.7		29.0		- 13.6		37.7		19.3		- 16.6	-
INDIANA												
FEMALE												
1974 (8 INSTITUTIONS)	0	.0	9	4.8	1	.5	1	.5	11	5.8	178	94.2
1976 (6 INSTITUTIONS)	0	.0	2	.8	1	.4	2	.8	5	1.9	259	98.1
% CHANGE 1974 TO 1976	.0		- 77.8		.0		100.0		- 54.5		45.5	
1978 (5 INSTITUTIONS)	0	.0	6	1.7	2	.6	5	1.4	13	3.7	336	96.3
% CHANGE 1976 TO 1978	.0		200.0		100.0		150.0		160.0		29.7	
MALE												
1974 (8 INSTITUTIONS)	2	.3	17	2.7	4	.6		1.0	29	4.7	591	95.3
1976 (6 INSTITUTIONS)	3	.4	12	1.5	5	.6	8	1.0	28	3.6	753	96.4
% CHANGE 1974 TO 1976	50.0		- 29.4		25.0		33.3		- 3.4		27.4	
1978 (5 INSTITUTIONS)	0	.0	21	2.6	8	1.0	11	1.3	40	4.9	775	95.1
% CHANGE 1976 TO 1978	- 100.0		75.0		60.0		37.5		42.9		2.9	
IOWA.........												
FEMALE												
1974 (3 INSTITUTIONS)	0	.0	1	.9	1	.9	0	.0	2	1.7	115	98.3
1976 (6 INSTITUTIONS)	1	.7	3	2.1	2	1.4	0	.0	6	4.1	139	95.9
% CHANGE 1974 TO 1976	100.0		200.0		100.0		.0		200.0		20.9	
1978 (6 INSTITUTIONS)	1	.2	6	1.2	2	.4	1	.2	10	1.9	507	98.1
% CHANGE 1976 TO 1978	.0		100.0		.0		100.0		66.7		264.7	2
MALE												
1974 (3 INSTITUTIONS)	1	.1	11	1.2	2	.2	2	.2	16	1.7	906	98.3
1976 (6 INSTITUTIONS)	1	.1	15	1.6	2	.2	5	.5	23	2.5	903	97.5
% CHANGE 1974 TO 1976	.0		36.4		.0		150.0		43.8		- .3	
1978 (6 INSTITUTIONS)	0	.0	19	2.1	3	.3	1	.1	23	2.5	888	97.5
% CHANGE 1976 TO 1978	- 100.0		26.7		50.0		- 80.0		.0		- 1.7	-
KANSAS..........												
FEMALE												
1974 (7 INSTITUTIONS)	2	1.2	6	3.6	2	1.2	2	1.2	12	7.2	154	92.8
1976 (10 INSTITUTIONS)	2	.8	12	4.7	1	.4	3	1.2	18	7.0	240	93.0
% CHANGE 1974 TO 1976	.0		100.0		- 50.0		50.0		50.0		55.8	
1978 (8 INSTITUTIONS)	1	.3	9	2.9	2	.7	5	1.6	17	5.6	289	94.4
% CHANGE 1976 TO 1978	- 50.0		- 25.0		100.0		66.7		- 5.6		20.4	
MALE												
1974 (7 INSTITUTIONS)	5	.3	24	1.7	13	.9	8	.6	50	3.5	1,391	96.5
1976 (10 INSTITUTIONS)	25	1.9	40	3.1	6	.5	9	.7	80	6.1	1,229	93.9
% CHANGE 1974 TO 1976	400.0		66.7		- 53.8		12.5		60.0		- 11.6	-
1978 (8 INSTITUTIONS)	9	.7	40	3.2	7	.6	16	1.3	72	5.7	1,189	94.3
% CHANGE 1976 TO 1978	- 64.0		.0		16.7		77.8		- 10.0		- 3.3	-

TURE AND ENVIRONMENTAL DESIGN

AMERICAN INDIAN ALASKAN NATIVE		BLACK NON-HISPANIC		ASIAN OR PACIFIC ISLANDER		HISPANIC		TOTAL MINORITY		WHITE NON-HISPANIC		TOTAL
NUMBER	%	NUMBER	%	NUMBER	%	NUMBER	%	NUMBER	%	NUMBER	%	NUMBER
0	.0	2	1.5	0	.0	0	.0	2	1.5	133	98.5	135
0	.0	8	4.1	1	.5	0	.0	9	4.6	187	95.4	196
.0		300.0		100.0		.0		350.0		40.6		45.2
1	.5	3	1.4	1	.5	0	.0	5	2.3	209	97.7	214
100.0		- 62.5		.0		.0		- 44.4		11.8		9.2
0	.0	9	1.8	5	1.0	1	.2	15	3.0	478	97.0	493
1	.2	7	1.7	4	.9	1	.2	13	3.1	409	96.9	422
100.0		- 22.2		- 20.0		.0		- 13.3		- 14.4		- 14.4
1	.3	7	1.9	8	2.2	1	.3	17	4.6	350	95.4	367
.0		.0		100.0		.0		30.8		- 14.4		- 13.0
1	.3	13	3.3	1	.3	6	1 5	21	5.3	373	94.7	394
1	.2	21	3.3	3	.5	8	113	33	5.3	595	94.7	628
.0		61.5		200.0		33.3		57.1		59.5		59.4
1	.2	29	4.5	0	.0	15	2.3	45	6.9	603	93.1	648
.0		38.1		- 100.0		87.5		36.4		1.3		3.2
7	.4	52	3.2	4	.2	25	1 5	88	5.4	1,532	94.6	1,620
5	.3	59	3.7	10	.6	26	116	100	6.2	1,509	93.8	1,609
28.6		13.5		150.0		4.0		13.6		- 1.5		- .7
8	.5	73	4.6	9	.6	35	2.2	125	7.9	1,464	92.1	1,589
60.0		23.7		- 10.0		34.6		25.0		- 3.0		- 1.2
0	.0	7	11.5	4	6.6	0	.0	11	18.0	50	82.0	61
0	.0	22	17.7	3	2.4	2	1.6	27	21.8	97	78.2	124
.0		214.3		- 25.0		100.0		145.5		94.0		103.3
1	.5	26	13.3	4	2.1	0	.0	31	15.9	164	84.1	195
100.0		18.2		33.3		- 100.0		14.8		69.1		57.3
2	.7	34	12.4	10	3.6	5	1.8	51	18.6	223	81.4	274
0	.0	47	15.8	5	1.7	4	1.3	56	18.8	242	81.2	298
100.0		38.2		- 50.0		20.0		9.8		8.5		8.8
0	.0	26	11.1	2	.9	7	3.0	35	15.0	199	85.0	234
.0		- 44.7		- 60.0		75.0		- 37.5		- 17.8		- 21.5
0	.0	30	7.1	5	1.2	8	1.9	43	10.2	380	89.8	423
2	.4	27	5.6	12	2.5	4	.8	45	9.3	437	90.7	482
100.0		- 10.0		140.0		- 50.0		4.7		15.0		13.9
2	.3	30	4.7	14	2.2	9	1.4	55	8.7	579	91.3	634
.0		11.1		16.7		125.0		22.2		32.5		31.5
4	.6	34	5.0	6	.9	11	1.6	55	8.1	625	91.9	680
6	.6	41	4.3	13	1.4	24	2.5	84	8.9	864	91.1	948
50.0		20.6		116.7		118.2		52.7		38.2		39.4
7	.8	38	4.2	35	3.9	20	2.2	100	11.0	807	89.0	907
16.7		- 7.3		169.2		- 16.7		19.0		- 6.6		- 4.3

MAJOR FIELD 0200 - ARCHITECTURE AND ENVIRONMENTAL DESIGN

	AMERICAN INDIAN ALASKAN NATIVE		BLACK NON-HISPANIC		ASIAN OR PACIFIC ISLANDER		HISPANIC		TOTAL MINORITY		WHITE NON-HISPANIC	
	NUMBER	%	NUMBER	%	NUMBER	%	NUMBER	%	NUMBER	%	NUMBER	%
MICHIGAN.												
FEMALE												
1974 (14 INSTITUTIONS)	2	.6	37	10.9	5	1.5		.6	46	13.5	294	86.5
1976 (21 INSTITUTIONS)	1	.2	31	7.1	5	1.2	7	1.6	44	10.1	390	89.9
% CHANGE 1974 TO 1976	- 50.0		- 16.2		.0		250.0		- 4.3		32.7	
1978 (21 INSTITUTIONS)	3	.5	49	8.1	12	2.0	11	1.8	75	12.4	532	87.6
% CHANGE 1976 TO 1978	200.0		58.1		140.0		57.1		70.5		36.4	
MALE												
1974 (14 INSTITUTIONS)	6	.3	144	6.6	18	.8	22	1.0	190	8.7	2,003	91.3
1976 (21 INSTITUTIONS)	12	.5	162	6.6	28	1.1	31	1.3	233	9.4	2,235	90.6
% CHANGE 1974 TO 1976	100.0		12.5		55.6		40.9		22.6		11.6	
1978 (21 INSTITUTIONS)	5	.2	158	6.5	36	1.5	41	1.7	240	9.9	2,176	90.1
% CHANGE 1976 TO 1978	- 58.3		- 2.5		28.6		32.3		3.0		- 2.6	-
MINNESOTA												
FEMALE												
1974 (6 INSTITUTIONS)	3	.6	5	1.1	7	1.5	3	.6	18	3.8	458	96.2
1976 (16 INSTITUTIONS)	2	.5	5	1.3	4	1.0	0	.0	11	2.8	389	97.3
% CHANGE 1974 TO 1976	- 33.3		.0		- 42.9		- 100.0		- 38.9		- 15.1	-
1978 (19 INSTITUTIONS)	1	.2	2	.5	6	1.4	0	.0	9	2.1	418	97.9
% CHANGE 1976 TO 1978	- 50.0		- 60.0		50.0		.0		- 18.2		7.5	
MALE												
1974 (6 INSTITUTIONS)	7	.7	10	1.0	34	3.3	1	.1	52	5.0	985	95.0
1976 (16 INSTITUTIONS)	4	.4	10	1.0	28	2.7	4	.4	46	4.4	1,001	95.6
% CHANGE 1974 TO 1976	- 42.9		.0		- 17.6		300.0		- 11.5		1.6	
1978 (19 INSTITUTIONS)	3	.3	10	1.1	21	2.3	5	.6	39	4.3	864	95.7
% CHANGE 1976 TO 1978	- 25.0		.0		- 25.0		25.0		- 15.2		- 13.7	-
MISSISSIPPI												
FEMALE												
1974 (8 INSTITUTIONS)	0	.0	1	2.9	1	2.9	0	.0	2	5.7	33	94.3
1976 (12 INSTITUTIONS)	1	1.4	3	4.3	1	1.4	0	.0	5	7.2	64	92.8
% CHANGE 1974 TO 1976	100.0		200.0		.0		.0		150.0		93.9	
1978 (16 INSTITUTIONS)	1	.4	7	3.1	1	.4	0	.0	9	3.9	220	96.1
% CHANGE 1976 TO 1978	.0		133.3		.0		.0		80.0		243.8	
MALE												
1974 (8 INSTITUTIONS)	4	1.4	9	3.2	4	1.4	0	.0	17	6.1	263	93.9
1976 (12 INSTITUTIONS)	1	.2	20	3.6	1	.2	0	.0	22	4.0	526	96.0
% CHANGE 1974 TO 1976	- 75.0		122.2		- 75.0		.0		29.4		100.0	
1978 (16 INSTITUTIONS)	1	.2	24	4.5	2	.4	1	.2	28	5.3	501	94.7
% CHANGE 1976 TO 1978	.0		20.0		100.0		100.0		27.3		- 4.8	-
MISSOURI												
FEMALE												
1974 (5 INSTITUTIONS)	0	.0	5	4.7	0	.0	2	1.9	7	6.5	100	93.5
1976 (6 INSTITUTIONS)	0	.0	6	5.0	2	1.7	0	.0	8	6.6	113	93.4
% CHANGE 1974 TO 1976	.0		20.0		100.0		- 100.0		14.3		13.0	
1978 (4 INSTITUTIONS)	0	.0	9	6.1	6	4.1	2	1.4	17	11.5	131	88.5
% CHANGE 1976 TO 1978	.0		50.0		200.0		100.0		112.5		15.9	
MALE												
1974 (5 INSTITUTIONS)	0	.0	14	3.9	6	1.7	3	.8	23	6.5	333	93.5
1976 (6 INSTITUTIONS)	2	.6	13	4.0	5	1.5	3	.9	23	7.0	306	93.0
% CHANGE 1974 TO 1976	100.0		- 7.1		- 16.7		.0		.0		- 8.1	-
1978 (4 INSTITUTIONS)	1	.4	6	2.4	11	4.4	5	2.0	23	9.2	227	90.8
% CHANGE 1976 TO 1978	- 50.0		- 53.8		120.0		66.7		.0		- 25.8	-

COMPARISIONS OF ENROLLMENT IN INSTITUTIONS OF HIGHER EDUCATION FOR SELECTED FIELDS OF STUDY AND LEVEL OF ENROLLMENT
BY RACE, ETHNICITY AND SEX: STATE 1974, 1976, 1978

D 0200 - ARCHITECTURE AND ENVIRONMENTAL DESIGN

	AMERICAN INDIAN ALASKAN NATIVE		BLACK NON-HISPANIC		ASIAN OR PACIFIC ISLANDER		HISPANIC		TOTAL MINORITY		WHITE NON-HISPANIC		TOTAL
	NUMBER	%	NUMBER	%	NUMBER	%	NUMBER	%	NUMBER	%	NUMBER	%	NUMBER
. . . .													
1 INSTITUTIONS)	0	.0	0	.0	0	.0	0	.0	0	.0	24	100.0	24
1 INSTITUTIONS)	1	2.9	0	.0	0	.0	0	.0	1	2.9	34	97.1	35
1974 TO 1976	100.0		.0		.0		.0		100.0		41.7		45.8
1 INSTITUTIONS)	1	2.4	0	.0	0	.0	0	.0	1	2.4	41	97.6	42
1976 TO 1978	.0		.0		.0		.0		.0		20.6		20.0
1 INSTITUTIONS)	1	.4	0	.0	2	.7	1	.4	4	1.4	275	98.6	279
1 INSTITUTIONS)	0	.0	1	.3	0	.0	1	.3	2	.7	303	99.3	305
1974 TO 1976	- 100.0		100.0		- 100.0		.0		- 50.0		10.2		9.3
1 INSTITUTIONS)	2	.8	0	.0	0	.0	0	.0	2	.8	258	99.2	260
1976 TO 1978	100.0		- 100.0		.0		- 100.0		.0		- 14.9		- 14.8
. . . .													
1 INSTITUTIONS)	0	.0	0	.0	0	.0	0	.0	0	.0	38	100.0	38
5 INSTITUTIONS)	0	.0	1	1.7	1	1.7	1	1.7	3	5.0	57	95.0	60
1974 TO 1976	.0		100.0		100.0		100.0		100.0		50.0		57.9
4 INSTITUTIONS)	0	.0	0	.0	0	.0	0	.0	0	.0	79	100.0	79
1976 TO 1978	.0		- 100.0		- 100.0		- 100.0		- 100.0		38.6		31.7
1 INSTITUTIONS)	1	.2	4	.9	5	1.1	6	1.4	16	3.7	422	96.3	438
5 INSTITUTIONS)	0	.0	6	1.0	6	1.0	3	.5	15	2.6	557	97.4	572
1974 TO 1976	- 100.0		50.0		20.0		- 50.0		- 6.3		32.0		30.6
4 INSTITUTIONS)	2	.4	9	1.7	4	.7	6	1.1	21	3.9	514	96.1	535
1976 TO 1978	100.0		50.0		- 33.3		100.0		40.0		- 7.7		- 6.5
IRE													
2 INSTITUTIONS)	0	.0	0	.0	0	.0	0	.0	0	.0	11	100.0	11
2 INSTITUTIONS)	0	.0	0	.0	0	.0	0	.0	0	.0	19	100.0	19
1974 TO 1976	.0		.0		.0		.0		.0		72.7		72.7
3 INSTITUTIONS)	0	.0	0	.0	0	.0	0	.0	0	.0	23	100.0	23
1976 TO 1978	.0		.0		.0		.0		.0		21.1		21.1
2 INSTITUTIONS)	0	.0	0	.0	0	.0	0	.0	0	.0	25	100.0	25
2 INSTITUTIONS)	0	.0	1	1.3	0	.0	0	.0	1	1.3	78	98.7	79
1974 TO 1976	.0		100.0		.0		.0		100.0		212.0		216.0
3 INSTITUTIONS)	0	.0	0	.0	0	.0	1	2.4	1	2.4	41	97.6	42
1976 TO 1978	.0		- 100.0		.0		100.0		.0		- 47.4		- 46.8
. . . .													
7 INSTITUTIONS)	0	.0	104	25.6	3	.7	6	1.5	113	27.8	294	72.2	407
5 INSTITUTIONS)	0	.0	15	7.1	0	.0	3	1.4	18	8.5	193	91.5	211
1974 TO 1976	.0		- 85.6		- 100.0		- 50.0		- 84.1		- 34.4		- 48.2
8 INSTITUTIONS)	1	.2	54	9.3	9	1.5	12	2.1	76	13.1	506	86.9	582
1976 TO 1978	100.0		260.0		100.0		300.0		322.2		162.2		175.8
7 INSTITUTIONS)	1	.1	76	8.9	5	.6	23	2.7	105	12.2	753	87.8	858
5 INSTITUTIONS)	0	.0	45	5.3	13	1.5	47	5.5	105	12.3	752	87.7	857
1974 TO 1976	- 100.0		- 40.8		160.0		104.3		.0		- .1		- .1
8 INSTITUTIONS)	2	.2	51	5.0	18	1.8	38	3.7	109	10.6	915	89.4	1,024
1976 TO 1978	100.0		13.3		38.5		- 19.1		3.8		21.7		19.5

TABLE 18 — COMPARISIONS OF ENROLLMENT IN INSTITUTIONS OF HIGHER EDUCATION FOR SELECTED FIELDS OF STUDY AND LEVEL OF ENROLLME
BY RACE, ETHNICITY AND SEX: STATE 1974, 1976, 1978

MAJOR FIELD 0200 — ARCHITECTURE AND ENVIRONMENTAL DESIGN

	AMERICAN INDIAN ALASKAN NATIVE		BLACK NON-HISPANIC		ASIAN OR PACIFIC ISLANDER		HISPANIC		TOTAL MINORITY		WHITE NON-HISPANIC	
	NUMBER	%	NUMBER	%	NUMBER	%	NUMBER	%	NUMBER	%	NUMBER	%
NEW MEXICO.........												
FEMALE												
1974 (1 INSTITUTIONS)	2	2.7	0	.0	1	1.4	2	2.7	5	6.8	68	93.2
1976 (4 INSTITUTIONS)	1	1.3	2	2.5	1	1.3	13	16.3	17	21.3	63	78.8
% CHANGE 1974 TO 1976	- 50.0		100.0		.0		550.0		240.0		- 7.4	
1978 (2 INSTITUTIONS)	1	1.5	2	3.0	0	.0	14	20.9	17	25.4	50	74.6
% CHANGE 1976 TO 1978	.0		.0		- 100.0		7.7		.0		- 20.6	-
MALE												
1974 (1 INSTITUTIONS)	12	2.9	4	1.0	3	.7	59	14.3	78	18.8	336	81.2
1976 (4 INSTITUTIONS)	0	.0	1	.3	2	.5	78	20.1	81	20.8	308	79.2
% CHANGE 1974 TO 1976	- 100.0		- 75.0		- 33.3		32.2		3.8		- 8.3	-
1978 (2 INSTITUTIONS)	3	1.0	2	.7	2	.7	67	22.3	74	24.6	227	75.4
% CHANGE 1976 TO 1978	100.0		100.0		.0		- 14.1		- 8.6		- 26.3	-
NEW YORK..........												
FEMALE												
1974 (15 INSTITUTIONS)	2	.2	39	4.2	29	3.2	20	2.2	90	9.8	830	90.2
1976 (20 INSTITUTIONS)	2	.1	87	3.9	59	2.7	53	2.4	201	9.1	2,004	90.9
% CHANGE 1974 TO 1976	.0		123.1		103.4		165.0		123.3		141.4	
1978 (19 INSTITUTIONS)	2	.1	86	5.7	76	5.1	55	3.7	219	14.6	1,284	85.4
% CHANGE 1976 TO 1978	.0		- 1.1		28.8		3.8		9.0		- 35.9	-
MALE												
1974 (15 INSTITUTIONS)	2	.1	189	5.6	145	4.3	109	3.2	445	13.1	2,959	86.9
1976 (20 INSTITUTIONS)	7	.2	326	8.1	126	3.1	194	4.8	653	16.3	3,355	83.7
% CHANGE 1974 TO 1976	250.0		72.5		- 13.1		78.0		46.7		13.4	
1978 (19 INSTITUTIONS)	19	.5	239	6.6	106	2.9	. 185	5.1	549	15.1	3,083	84.9
% CHANGE 1976 TO 1978	171.4		- 26.7		- 15.9		- 4.6		- 15.9		- 8.1	-
NORTH CAROLINA.......												
FEMALE												
1974 (5 INSTITUTIONS)	0	.0	22	8.1	1	.4	0	.0	23	8.5	247	91.5
1976 (9 INSTITUTIONS)	0	.0	20	8.5	0	.0	0	.0	20	8.5	216	91.5
% CHANGE 1974 TO 1976	.0		- 9.1		- 100.0		.0		- 13.0		- 12.6	-
1978 (7 INSTITUTIONS)	0	.0	23	8.3	2	.7	2	.7	27	9.8	249	90.2
% CHANGE 1976 TO 1978	.0		15.0		100.0		100.0		35.0		15.3	
MALE												
1974 (5 INSTITUTIONS)	1	.1	46	6.2	2	.3	4	.5	53	7.1	694	92.9
1976 (9 INSTITUTIONS)	0	.0	38	5.1	3	.4	2	.3	43	5.8	699	94.2
% CHANGE 1974 TO 1976	- 100.0		- 17.4		50.0		- 50.0		- 18.9		.7	
1978 (7 INSTITUTIONS)	0	.0	46	7.6	3	.5	5	.8	54	8.9	554	91.1
% CHANGE 1976 TO 1978	.0		21.1		.0		150.0		25.6		- 20.7	-
NORTH DAKOTA........												
FEMALE												
1974 (1 INSTITUTIONS)	0	.0	0	.0	0	.0	0	.0	0	.0	27	100.0
1976 (1 INSTITUTIONS)	0	.0	0	.0	0	.0	0	.0	0	.0	32	100.0
% CHANGE 1974 TO 1976	.0		.0		.0		.0		.0		18.5	
1978 (2 INSTITUTIONS)	0	.0	0	.0	0	.0	0	.0	0	.0	75	100.0
% CHANGE 1976 TO 1978	.0		.0		.0		.0		.0		134.4	
MALE												
1974 (1 INSTITUTIONS)	1	.4	0	.0	0	.0	0	.0	1	.4	250	99.6
1976 (1 INSTITUTIONS)	2	.7	2	.7	0	.0	0	.0	4	1.3	300	98.7
% CHANGE 1974 TO 1976	100.0		100.0		.0		.0		300.0		20.0	
1978 (2 INSTITUTIONS)	2	.7	2	.7	2	.7	3	1.1	9	3.3	265	96.7
% CHANGE 1976 TO 1978	.0		.0		100.0		100.0		125.0		- 11.7	-

TURE AND ENVIRONMENTAL DESIGN

RICAN INDIAN ASKAN NATIVE		BLACK NON-HISPANIC		ASIAN OR PACIFIC ISLANDER		HISPANIC		TOTAL MINORITY		WHITE NON-HISPANIC		TOTAL
NUMBER	%	NUMBER	%	NUMBER	%	NUMBER	%	NUMBER	%	NUMBER	%	NUMBER
0	.0	54	18.5	2	.7	1	.3	57	19.5	235	80.5	292
0	.0	34	6.1	2	.4	5	.9	41	7.4	512	92.6	553
...0		- 37.0		.0		400.0		- 28.1		117.9		89.4
3	.5	30	4.6	4	.6	8	1.2	45	7.0	601	93.0	646
100.0		- 11.8		100.0		60.0		9.8		17.4		16.8
1	.0	72	3.5	10	.5	3	.1	86	4.2	1,944	95.8	2,030
0	.0	81	3.9	12	.6	6	.3	99	4.7	2,002	95.3	2,101
100.0		12.5		20.0		100.0		15.1		3.0		3.5
5	.2	77	3.6	11	.5	8	.4	101	4.8	2,012	95.2	2,113
100.0		- 4.9		- 8.3		33.3		2.0		.5		.6
4	6.0	1	1.5	0	.0	2	3 0	7	10.4	60	89.6	67
2	2.1	11	11.5	1	1.0	1	110	15	15.6	81	84.4	96
50.0		1000.0		100.0		- 50.0		114.3		35.0		43.3
4	3.5	6	5.3	3	2.7	1	.9	14	12.4	99	87.6	113
100.0		- 45.5		200.0		.0		- 6.7		22.2		17.7
16	2.0	23	2.8	7	.9	3	.4	49	6.0	769	94.0	818
19	2.5	27	3.5	9	1.2	3	.4	58	7.6	710	92.4	768
18.8		17.4		28.6		.0		18.4		- 7.7		- 6.1
13	2.0	9	1.4	11	1.7	4	.6	37	5.8	604	94.2	641
31.6		- 66.7		22.2		33.3		- 36.2		- 14.9		- 16.5
7	2.0	2	.6	3	.9	1	.3	13	3.8	329	96.2	342
6	1.8	2	.6	12	3.6	1	.3	21	6.3	314	93.7	335
14.3		.0		300.0		.0		61.5		- 4.6		- 2.0
6	1.8	1	.3	10	3.0	0	.0	17	5.2	313	94.8	330
.0		- 50.0		- 16.7		- 100.0		- 19.0		- .3		- 1.5
20	1.9	7	.7	32	3.0	5	.5	64	6.0	1,008	94.0	1,072
7	.8	16	1.7	29	3.1	17	1.8	69	7.4	863	92.6	932
65.0		128.6		- 9.4		240.0		7.8		- 14.4		- 13.1
9	1.2	4	.6	24	3.3	11	1.5	48	6.6	676	93.4	724
28.6		- 75.0		- 17.2		- 35.3		- 30.4		- 21.7		- 22.3
0	.0	19	6.0	3	.9	7	2.2	29	9.2	287	90.8	316
1	.2	19	4.0	8	1.7	3	.6	31	6.6	440	93.4	471
100.0		.0		166.7		- 57.1		6.9		53.3		49.1
0	.0	31	6.2	9	1.8	5	1.0	45	9.0	454	91.0	499
100.0		63.2		12.5		66.7		45.2		3.2		5.9
3	.2	58	4.1	13	.9	8	.6	82	5.7	1,347	94.3	1,429
5	.3	134	7.3	18	1.0	16	.9	173	9.5	1,651	90.5	1,824
66.7		131.0		38.5		100.0		111.0		22.6		27.6
5	.3	138	7.8	17	1.0	13	.7	173	9.7	1,602	90.3	1,775
.0		3.0		- 5.6		- 18.8		.0		- 3.0		- 2.7

TABLE 18 - COMPARISIONS OF ENROLLMENT IN INSTITUTIONS OF HIGHER EDUCATION FOR SELECTED FIELDS OF STUDY AND LEVEL OF ENROLLMENT
BY RACE, ETHNICITY AND SEX: STATE 1974, 1976, 1978

MAJOR FIELD 0200 - ARCHITECTURE AND ENVIRONMENTAL DESIGN

	AMERICAN INDIAN ALASKAN NATIVE		BLACK NON-HISPANIC		ASIAN OR PACIFIC ISLANDER		HISPANIC		TOTAL MINORITY		WHITE NON-HISPANIC		TO
	NUMBER	%	NUMBER	%	NUMBER	%	NUMBER	%	NUMBER	%	NUMBER	%	NUM
RHODE ISLAND.													
FEMALE													
1974 (2 INSTITUTIONS)	0	.0	1	.9	1	.9	0	.0	2	1.7	115	98.3	
1976 (2 INSTITUTIONS)	0	.0	5	3.6	0	.0	3	2.2	8	5.8	130	94.2	
% CHANGE 1974 TO 1976	.0		400.0		- 100.0		100.0		300.0		13.0		17.
1978 (5 INSTITUTIONS)	0	.0	5	2.8	1	.6	1	.6	7	3.9	174	96.1	
% CHANGE 1976 TO 1978	.0		.0		100.0		- 66.7		- 12.5		33.8		31.
MALE													
1974 (2 INSTITUTIONS)	0	.0	7	2.3	3	1.0	1	.3	11	3.6	291	96.4	
1976 (2 INSTITUTIONS)	0	.0	9	3.7	0	.0	3	1.2	12	4.9	234	95.1	
% CHANGE 1974 TO 1976	.0		28.6		- 100.0		200.0		9.1		- 19.6		- 18.
1978 (5 INSTITUTIONS)	1	.2	21	3.6	9	1.5	2	.3	33	5.6	554	94.4	
% CHANGE 1976 TO 1978	100.0		133.3		100.0		- 33.3		175.0		136.8		138.
SOUTH CAROLINA.													
FEMALE													
1974 (1 INSTITUTIONS)	0	.0	1	2.2	0	.0	0	.0	1	2.2	45	97.8	
1976 (2 INSTITUTIONS)	0	.0	5	4.2	0	.0	0	.0	5	4.2	113	95.8	
% CHANGE 1974 TO 1976	.0		400.0		.0		.0		400.0		151.1		156.
1978 (2 INSTITUTIONS)	0	.0	3	2.2	0	.0	0	.0	3	2.2	136	97.8	
% CHANGE 1976 TO 1978	.0		- 40.0		.0		.0		- 40.0		20.4		17.
MALE													
1974 (1 INSTITUTIONS)	2	.4	6	1.1	2	.4	2	.4	12	2.	520	97.7	
1976 (2 INSTITUTIONS)	1	.2	9	2.0	1	.2	2	.5	13	2.9	430	97.1	
% CHANGE 1974 TO 1976	- 50.0		50.0		- 50.0		.0		8.3		- 17.3		- 16.
1978 (2 INSTITUTIONS)	0	.0	5	1.4	1	.3	3	.8	9	2.5	354	97.5	
% CHANGE 1976 TO 1978	- 100.0		- 44.4		.0		50.0		- 30.8		- 17.7		- 18.
SOUTH DAKOTA.													
FEMALE													
1974 (1 INSTITUTIONS)	0	.0	0	.0	0	.0	0	.0	0	.0	2	100.0	
1976 (2 INSTITUTIONS)	0	.0	0	.0	0	.0	0	.0	0	.0	9	100.0	
% CHANGE 1974 TO 1976	.0		.0		.0		.0		.0		350.0		350.
1978 (1 INSTITUTIONS)	0	.0	0	.0	0	.0	0	.0	0	.0	7	100.0	
% CHANGE 1976 TO 1978	.0		.0		.0		.0		.0		- 22.2		- 22.
MALE													
1974 (1 INSTITUTIONS)	0	.0	0	.0	0	.0	0	.0	0	.0	34	100.0	
1976 (2 INSTITUTIONS)	2	7.1	0	.0	0	.0	0	.0	2	7.1	26	92.9	
% CHANGE 1974 TO 1976	100.0		.0		.0		.0		100.0		- 23.5		- 17.
1978 (1 INSTITUTIONS)	0	.0	0	.0	0	.0	0	.0	0	.0	17	100.0	
% CHANGE 1976 TO 1978	- 100.0		.0		.0		.0		- 100.0		- 34.6		- 39.
TENNESSEE													
FEMALE													
1974 (5 INSTITUTIONS)	0	.0	4	4.3	1	1.1	0	.0	5	5.4	88	94.6	
1976 (9 INSTITUTIONS)	0	.0	12	8.7	1	.7	0	.0	13	9.4	125	90.6	
% CHANGE 1974 TO 1976	.0		200.0		.0		.0		160.0		42.0		48.
1978 (7 INSTITUTIONS)	0	.0	14	7.6	0	.0	0	.0	14	7.6	171	92.4	
% CHANGE 1976 TO 1978	.0		16.7		- 100.0		.0		7.7		36.8		34.
MALE													
1974 (5 INSTITUTIONS)	1	.1	18	2.5	0	.0	0	.0	19	2.6	711	97.4	
1976 (9 INSTITUTIONS)	2	.3	31	4.1	2	.3	4	.5	39	5.1	725	94.9	
% CHANGE 1974 TO 1976	100.0		72.2		100.0		100.0		105.3		2.0		4.
1978 (7 INSTITUTIONS)	1	.2	22	3.5	2	.3	7	1.1	32	5.1	596	94.9	
% CHANGE 1976 TO 1978	- 50.0		- 29.0		.0		75.0		- 17.9		- 17.8		- 17.

726

TURE AND ENVIRONMENTAL DESIGN

RICAN INDIAN ASKAN NATIVE		BLACK NON-HISPANIC		ASIAN OR PACIFIC ISLANDER		HISPANIC		TOTAL MINORITY		WHITE NON-HISPANIC		TOTAL
NUMBER	%	NUMBER	%	NUMBER	%	NUMBER	%	NUMBER	%	NUMBER	%	NUMBER
2	.4	7	1.3	3	.5	35	6.3	47	5	508	91.5	555
5	.6	16	1.8	6	.7	52	6.0	79	9.1	787	90.9	866
150.0		128.6		100.0		48.6		68.1		54.9		56.0
3	.3	45	4.1	8	.7	65	6.0	121	11.1	967	88.9	1,088
40.0		181.3		33.3		25.0		53.2		22.9		25.6
34	1.0	65	2.0	29	.9	241	7.	369	11.3	2,911	88.8	3,280
42	1.0	116	2.7	25	.6	370	8.8	553	12.7	3,789	87.3	4,342
23.5		78.5		- 13.8		53.5		49.9		30.2		32.4
17	.4	199	4.5	43	1.0	407	9.2	666	15.1	3,757	84.9	4,423
59.5		71.6		72.0		10.0		20.4		- .8		1.9
0	.0	0	.0	2	.6	0	.0	2	.6	340	99.4	342
1	.2	2	.4	6	1.3	2	.4	11	2.4	454	97.6	465
100.0		100.0		200.0		100.0		450.0		33.5		36.0
0	.0	1	1.9	0	.0	2	3.8	3	5.8	49	94.2	52
100.0		- 50.0		- 100.0		.0		- 72.7		- 89.2		- 88.8
1	.2	4	.8	9	1.8	7	1.4	21	4 3	467	95.7	488
3	.4	1	.1	10	1.4	10	1.4	24	3:3	694	96.7	718
200.0		- 75.0		11.1		42.9		14.3		48.6		47.1
1	.5	0	.0	1	.5	0	.0	2	1.0	204	99.0	206
66.7		- 100.0		- 90.0		- 100.0		- 91.7		- 70.6		- 71.3
0	.0	0	.0	0	.0	0	.0	0	.0	26	100.0	26
0	.0	0	.0	0	.0	0	.0	0	.0	0	.0	0
.0		.0		.0		.0		.0		- 100.0		- 100.0
0	.0	0	.0	1	4.8	0	.0	1	4.8	20	95.2	21
.0		.0		100.0		.0		100.0		100.0		100.0
0	.0	0	.0	0	.0	0	.0	0	.0	129	100.0	129
0	.0	0	.0	0	.0	0	.0	0	.0	0	.0	0
.0		.0		.0		.0		.0		- 100.0		- 100.0
0	.0	0	.0	0	.0	1	1.1	1	1.1	94	98.9	95
.0		.0		.0		100.0		100.0		100.0		100.0
0	.0	10	3.9	2	.8	0	.0	12	4.6	247	95.4	259
0	.0	18	4.5	7	1.8	1	.3	26	6.6	370	93.4	396
.0		80.0		250.0		100.0		116.7		49.8		52.9
0	.0	35	7.7	4	.9	0	.0	39	8.6	416	91.4	455
.0		94.4		- 42.9		- 100.0		50.0		12.4		14.9
2	.1	122	8.0	6	.4	6	.4	136	9 0	1,382	91.0	1,518
0	.0	116	8.6	11	.8	5	.4	132	9:8	1,216	90.2	1,348
100.0		- 4.9		83.3		- 16.7		- 2.9		- 12.0		- 11.2
0	.0	109	9.6	7	.6	3	.3	119	10.5	1,019	89.5	1,138
.0		- 6.0		- 36.4		- 40.0		- 9.8		- 16.2		- 15.6

TABLE 18 - COMPARISONS OF ENROLLMENT IN INSTITUTIONS OF HIGHER EDUCATION FOR SELECTED FIELDS OF STUDY AND LEVEL OF ENROLLMENT BY RACE, ETHNICITY AND SEX: STATE 1974, 1976, 1978

MAJOR FIELD 0200 - ARCHITECTURE AND ENVIRONMENTAL DESIGN

	AMERICAN INDIAN ALASKAN NATIVE		BLACK NON-HISPANIC		ASIAN OR PACIFIC ISLANDER		HISPANIC		TOTAL MINORITY		WHITE NON-HISPANIC		TOT
	NUMBER	%	NUMBER	%	NUMBER	%	NUMBER	%	NUMBER	%	NUMBER	%	NUMB
WASHINGTON.													
FEMALE													
1974 (7 INSTITUTIONS)	0	.0	9	4.9	6	3.3	2	1.1	17	9.3	165	90.7	1
1976 (4 INSTITUTIONS)	2	.8	11	4.2	11	4.2	1	.4	25	9.6	235	90.4	2
% CHANGE 1974 TO 1976	100.0		22.2		83.3		- 50.0		47.1		42.4		42.9
1978 (4 INSTITUTIONS)	2	.8	5	2.0	14	5.7	0	.0	21	8.5	226	91.5	2
% CHANGE 1976 TO 1978	.0		- 54.5		27.3		- 100.0		- 16.0		- 3.8		- 5.0
MALE													
1974 (7 INSTITUTIONS)	4	.5	27	3.3	39	4.8	8	1.0	78	9.7	730	90.3	8
1976 (4 INSTITUTIONS)	6	.7	21	2.4	53	6.0	6	.7	86	9.7	800	90.3	8
% CHANGE 1974 TO 1976	50.0		- 22.2		35.9		- 25.0		10.3		9.6		9.7
1978 (4 INSTITUTIONS)	1	.1	15	2.1	47	6.4	4	.5	67	9.2	663	90.8	7
% CHANGE 1976 TO 1978	- 83.3		- 28.6		- 11.3		- 33.3		- 22.1		- 17.1		- 17.6
WEST VIRGINIA													
FEMALE													
1974 (1 INSTITUTIONS)	0	.0	0	.0	0	.0	0	.0	0	.0	16	100.0	
1976 (1 INSTITUTIONS)	0	.0	0	.0	0	.0	0	.0	0	.0	41	100.0	
% CHANGE 1974 TO 1976	.0		.0		.0		.0		.0		156.3		156.3
1978 (2 INSTITUTIONS)	0	.0	2	2.9	0	.0	0	.0	2	2.9	67	97.1	
% CHANGE 1976 TO 1978	.0		100.0		.0		.0		100.0		63.4		68.3
MALE													
1974 (1 INSTITUTIONS)	1	1.1	1	1.1	0	.0	0	.0	2	2.2	88	97.8	
1976 (1 INSTITUTIONS)	0	.0	0	.0	0	.0	0	.0	0	.0	159	100.0	1
% CHANGE 1974 TO 1976	- 100.0		- 100.0		.0		.0		- 100.0		80.7		76.7
1978 (2 INSTITUTIONS)	0	.0	1	.6	1	.6	0	.0	2	1.2	161	98.8	1
% CHANGE 1976 TO 1978	.0		100.0		100.0		.0		100.0		1.3		2.5
WISCONSIN													
FEMALE													
1974 (4 INSTITUTIONS)	0	.0	8	3.6	2	.9	4	1.8	14	6.3	208	93.7	2
1976 (4 INSTITUTIONS)	1	.3	7	2.0	1	.3	1	.3	10	2.8	341	97.2	3
% CHANGE 1974 TO 1976	100.0		- 12.5		- 50.0		- 75.0		- 28.6		63.9		58.1
1978 (5 INSTITUTIONS)	0	.0	3	.8	2	.5	4	1.0	9	2.3	377	97.7	3
% CHANGE 1976 TO 1978	- 100.0		- 57.1		100.0		300.0		- 10.0		10.6		10.0
MALE													
1974 (4 INSTITUTIONS)	3	.4	21	2.5	5	.6	7	.8	36	4.3	795	95.7	8
1976 (4 INSTITUTIONS)	3	.5	10	1.7	7	1.2	7	1.2	27	4.7	547	95.3	5
% CHANGE 1974 TO 1976	.0		- 52.4		40.0		.0		- 25.0		- 31.2		- 30.9
1978 (5 INSTITUTIONS)	4	.9	10	2.2	4	.9	7	1.5	25	5.4	435	94.6	4
% CHANGE 1976 TO 1978	33.3		.0		- 42.9		.0		- 7.4		- 20.5		- 19.9
WYOMING													
FEMALE													
1974 (0 INSTITUTIONS)	0	.0	0	.0	0	.0	0	.0	0	.0	0	.0	
1976 (0 INSTITUTIONS)	0	.0	0	.0	0	.0	0	.0	0	.0	0	.0	
% CHANGE 1974 TO 1976	.0		.0		.0		.0		.0		.0		.0
1978 (1 INSTITUTIONS)	0	.0	0	.0	0	.0	0	.0	0	.0	0	.0	
% CHANGE 1976 TO 1978	.0		.0		.0		.0		.0		.0		.0
MALE													
1974 (0 INSTITUTIONS)	0	.0	0	.0	0	.0	0	.0	0	.0	0	.0	
1976 (0 INSTITUTIONS)	0	.0	0	.0	0	.0	0	.0	0	.0	0	.0	
% CHANGE 1974 TO 1976	.0		.0		.0		.0		.0		.0		
1978 (1 INSTITUTIONS)	0	.0	0	.0	0	.0	0	.0	0	.0	1	100.0	
% CHANGE 1976 TO 1978	.0		.0		.0		.0		.0		100.0		100.0

CTURE AND ENVIRONMENTAL DESIGN

ERICAN INDIAN LASKAN NATIVE		BLACK NON-HISPANIC		ASIAN OR PACIFIC ISLANDER		HISPANIC		TOTAL MINORITY		WHITE NON-HISPANIC		TOTAL
NUMBER	%	NUMBER	%	NUMBER	%	NUMBER	%	NUMBER	%	NUMBER	%	NUMBER
46	.4	593	5.4	190	1.7	250	2.3	1,079	9.9	9,811	90.1	10,890
62	.4	698	4.6	384	2.5	369	2.4	1,513	9.9	13,783	90.1	15,296
34.8		17.7		102.1		47.6		40.2		40.5		40.5
62	.4	778	4.7	463	2.8	439	2.7	1,742	10.5	14,792	89.5	16,534
.0		11.5		20.6		19.0		15.1		7.3		8.1
235	.5	1,934	4.1	1,092	2.3	1,593	3.4	4,854	10.3	42,437	89.7	47,291
258	.5	2,419	4.8	1,256	2.5	2,034	4.0	5,967	11.8	44,485	88.2	50,452
9.8		25.1		15.0		15.0		22.9		4.8		6.7
223	.5	2,302	5.0	1,230	2.7	1,873	4.1	5,628	12.3	40,255	87.7	45,883
- 13.6		- 4.8		- 2.1		- 2.1		- 5.7		- 9.5		- 9.1
0	.0	0	.0	0	.0	0	.0	0	.0	0	.0	0
0	.0	0	.0	0	.0	189	100.0	189	100.0	0	.0	189
.0		.0		.0		100.0		100.0		.0		100.0
0	.0	0	.0	0	.0	64	100.0	64	100.0	0	.0	64
.0		.0		.0		- 66.1		- 66.1		.0		- 66.1
0	.0	0	.0	0	.0	0	.0	0	.0	0	.0	0
0	.0	0	.0	0	.0	709	100.0	709	100.0	0	.0	709
.0		.0		.0		100.0		100.0		.0		100.0
0	.0	0	.0	0	.0	201	100.0	201	100.0	0	.0	201
.0		.0		.0		- 71.7		- 71.7		.0		- 71.7
0	.0	0	.0	0	.0	0	.0	0	.0	0	.0	0
0	.0	0	.0	0	.0	189	100.0	189	100.0	0	.0	189
.0		.0		.0		100.0		100.0		.0		100.0
0	.0	0	.0	0	.0	64	100.0	64	100.0	0	.0	64
.0		.0		.0		- 66.1		- 66.1		.0		- 66.1
0	.0	0	.0	0	.0	0	.0	0	.0	0	.0	0
0	.0	0	.0	0	.0	709	100.0	709	100.0	0	.0	709
.0		.0		.0		.0		100.0		.0		100.0
0	.0	0	.0	0	.0	201	100.0	201	100.0	0	.0	201
.0		.0		.0		.0		- 71.7		.0		- 71.7
46	.4	593	5.4	190	1.7	250	2.3	1,079	9.9	9,811	90.1	10,890
62	.4	698	4.5	384	2.5	558	3.6	1,702	11.0	13,783	89.0	15,485
34.8		17.7		102.1		123.2		57.7		40.5		42.2
62	.4	778	4.7	463	2.8	503	3.0	1,806	10.9	14,792	89.1	16,598
.0		11.5		20.6		- 9.9		6.1		7.3		7.2
235	.5	1,934	4.1	1,092	2.3	1,593	3.4	4,854	10.3	42,437	89.7	47,291
258	.5	2,419	4.7	1,256	2.5	2,743	5.4	6,676	13.0	44,485	87.0	51,161
9.8		25.1		15.0		15.0		37.5		4.8		8.2
223	.5	2,302	5.0	1,230	2.7	2,074	4.5	5,829	12.6	40,255	87.4	46,084
- 13.6		- 4.8		- 2.1		- 2.1		- 12.7		- 9.5		- 9.9

MAJOR FIELD 0500 - BUSINESS AND MANAGEMENT

	AMERICAN INDIAN ALASKAN NATIVE		BLACK NON-HISPANIC		ASIAN OR PACIFIC ISLANDER		HISPANIC		TOTAL MINORITY		WHITE NON-HISPANIC	
	NUMBER	%	NUMBER	%	NUMBER	%	NUMBER	%	NUMBER	%	NUMBER	%
ALABAMA · · · · · · · · · · ·												
FEMALE												
1974 (41 INSTITUTIONS)	10	.2	1,426	30.2	26	.6	11	.2	1,473	31.2	3,250	68.8
1976 (51 INSTITUTIONS)	9	.1	2,803	31.7	20	.2	14	.2	2,846	32.2	6,004	67.8
% CHANGE 1974 TO 1976	- 10.0		96.6		- 23.1		27.3		93.2		84.7	
1978 (52 INSTITUTIONS)	10	.1	3,200	26.1	29	.2	21	.2	3,260	26.6	9,007	73.4
% CHANGE 1976 TO 1978	11.1		14.2		45.0		50.0		14.5		50.0	
MALE												
1974 (41 INSTITUTIONS)	37	.3	1,984	14.3	80	.6	58	.4	2,159	15.5	11,728	84.5
1976 (51 INSTITUTIONS)	22	.1	3,213	16.8	37	.2	41	.2	3,313	17.3	15,868	82.7
% CHANGE 1974 TO 1976	- 40.5		61.9		- 53.8		- 29.3		53.5		35.3	
1978 (52 INSTITUTIONS)	18	.1	2,913	14.5	40	.2	56	.3	3,027	15.0	17,097	85.0
% CHANGE 1976 TO 1978	- 18.2		- 9.3		8.1		36.6		- 8.6		7.7	
ALASKA · · · · · · · · · · ·												
FEMALE												
1974 (0 INSTITUTIONS)	0	.0	0	.0	0	.0	0	.0	0	.0	0	.0
1976 (1 INSTITUTIONS)	11	91.7	0	.0	0	.0	0	.0	11	91.7	1	8.3
% CHANGE 1974 TO 1976	100.0		.0		.0		.0		100.0		100.0	
1978 (10 INSTITUTIONS)	79	13.9	13	2.3	14	2.5	2	.4	108	19.0	459	81.0
% CHANGE 1976 TO 1978	618.2		100.0		100.0		100.0		881.8		5800.0		4
MALE												
1974 (0 INSTITUTIONS)	0	.0	0	.0	0	.0	0	.0	0	.0	0	.0
1976 (1 INSTITUTIONS)	15	88.2	0	.0	0	.0	0	.0	15	88.2	2	11.8
% CHANGE 1974 TO 1976	100.0		.0		.0		.0		100.0		100.0	
1978 (10 INSTITUTIONS)	43	9.7	21	4.7	11	2.5	7	1.6	82	18.4	363	81.6
% CHANGE 1976 TO 1978	186.7		100.0		100.0		100.0		446.7		8050.0		2
ARIZONA · · · · · · · · · · ·												
FEMALE												
1974 (15 INSTITUTIONS)	68	2.0	76	2.3	35	1.0	228	6.8	407	12.2	2,937	87.8
1976 (15 INSTITUTIONS)	159	2.3	226	3.3	65	1.0	511	7.5	961	14.2	5,808	85.8
% CHANGE 1974 TO 1976	133.8		197.4		85.7		124.1		136.1		97.8	
1978 (18 INSTITUTIONS)	239	2.7	278	3.2	145	1.7	690	7.9	1,352	15.5	7,386	84.5
% CHANGE 1976 TO 1978	50.3		23.0		123.1		35.0		40.7		27.2	
MALE												
1974 (15 INSTITUTIONS)	127	1.2	218	2.1	73	.7	747	7.1	1,165	11.0	9,380	89.0
1976 (15 INSTITUTIONS)	136	1.0	329	2.4	105	.8	861	6.2	1,431	10.3	12,483	89.7
% CHANGE 1974 TO 1976	7.1		50.9		43.8		15.3		22.8		33.1	
1978 (18 INSTITUTIONS)	135	.9	400	2.8	137	1.0	841	5.9	1,513	10.6	12,794	89.4
% CHANGE 1976 TO 1978	- .7		21.6		30.5		- 2.3		5.7		2.5	
ARKANSAS · · · · · · · · · ·												
FEMALE												
1974 (19 INSTITUTIONS)	13	.6	328	15.5	4	.2	3	.1	348	16.4	1,773	83.6
1976 (23 INSTITUTIONS)	7	.2	784	22.1	15	.4	8	.2	814	22.9	2,741	77.1
% CHANGE 1974 TO 1976	- 46.2		139.0		275.0		166.7		133.9		54.6	
1978 (24 INSTITUTIONS)	46	.8	1,068	19.6	20	.4	12	.2	1,146	21.0	4,301	79.0
% CHANGE 1976 TO 1978	557.1		36.2		33.3		50.0		40.8		56.9	
MALE												
1974 (19 INSTITUTIONS)	31	.6	462	8.5	10	.2	14	.3	517	9.5	4,912	90.5
1976 (23 INSTITUTIONS)	26	.4	652	10.5	16	.3	8	.1	702	11.3	5,524	88.7
% CHANGE 1974 TO 1976	- 16.1		41.1		60.0		- 42.9		35.8		12.5	
1978 (24 INSTITUTIONS)	49	.7	965	12.9	40	.5	21	.3	1,075	14.4	6,405	85.6
% CHANGE 1976 TO 1978	88.5		48.0		150.0		162.5		53.1		15.9	

SS AND MANAGEMENT

MERICAN INDIAN ALASKAN NATIVE		BLACK NON-HISPANIC		ASIAN OR PACIFIC ISLANDER		HISPANIC		TOTAL MINORITY		WHITE NON-HISPANIC		TOTAL
NUMBER	%	NUMBER	%	NUMBER	%	NUMBER	%	NUMBER	%	NUMBER	%	NUMBER
413	.9	6,434	13.9	2,537	5.5	3,376	7 3	12,760	27.5	33,635	72.5	46,395
864	1.2	7,674	11.1	4,479	6.5	5,822	8 4	18,839	27.2	50,506	72.8	69,345
109.2		19.3		76.5		72.5		47.6		50.2		49.5
960	1.4	7,376	10.4	5,662	8.0	5,488	7.8	19,486	27.6	51,236	72.4	70,722
11.1		- 3.9		26.4		- 5.7		3.4		1.4		2.0
759	.8	8,182	8.7	4,202	4.5	5,922	6.3	19,065	20.2	75,116	79.8	94,181
1,190	1.1	8,318	7.7	6,526	6.0	7,656	7.1	23,690	21.8	84,774	78.2	108,464
56.8		1.7		55.3		29.3		24.3		12.9		15.2
989	1.1	7,226	7.8	6,853	7.4	6,220	6.7	21,288	23.1	70,942	76.9	92,230
- 16.9		- 13.1		5.0		- 18.8		- 10.1		- 16.3		- 15.0
29	.8	143	4.0	50	1.4	183	5.1	405	11.2	3,210	88.8	3,615
42	.8	128	2.4	65	1.2	286	5.4	521	9.8	4,817	90.2	5,338
44.8		- 10.5		30.0		56.3		28.6		50.1		47.7
51	.9	117	2.1	90	1.6	171	3.0	429	7.5	5,271	92.5	5,700
21.4		- 8.6		38.5		- 40.2		- 17.7		9.4		6.8
48	.5	215	2.1	105	1.0	360	3.5	728	7.1	9,530	92.9	10,258
56	.5	238	2.1	113	1.0	476	4.1	883	7.6	10,689	92.4	11,572
16.7		10.7		7.6		32.2		21.3		12.2		12.8
51	.5	189	1.9	111	1.1	297	2.9	648	6.4	9,443	93.6	10,091
- 8.9		- 20.6		- 1.8		- 37.6		- 26.6		- 11.7		- 12.8
3	.1	168	6.6	22	.9	46	1.8	239	9.3	2,320	90.7	2,559
0	.0	200	4.7	24	.6	36	.8	260	6.1	4,037	93.9	4,297
- 100.0		19.0		9.1		- 21.7		8.8		74.0		67.9
20	.2	670	6.4	80	.8	183	1.7	953	9.0	9,584	91.0	10,537
100.0		235.0		233.3		408.3		266.5		137.4		145.2
6	.1	323	3.1	56	.5	111	1.1	496	4.8	9,764	95.2	10,260
9	.1	299	2.6	42	.4	79	.7	429	3.7	11,293	96.3	11,722
50.0		- 7.4		- 25.0		- 28.8		- 13.5		15.7		14.2
25	.2	774	4.9	81	.5	234	1.5	1,114	7.1	14,598	92.9	15,712
177.8		158.9		92.9		196.2		159.7		29.3		34.0
0	.0	154	12.4	1	.1	2	.2	157	12.7	1,081	87.3	1,238
2	.1	410	19.9	29	1.4	23	1.1	464	22.5	1,594	77.5	2,058
100.0		166.2		2800.0		1050.0		195.5		47.5		66.2
4	.1	614	16.5	16	.4	26	.7	660	17.7	3,068	82.3	3,728
100.0		49.8		- 44.8		13.0		42.2		92.5		81.1
0	.0	272	11.1	5	.2	4	.2	281	11.4	2,175	88.6	2,456
1	.0	522	15.8	29	.9	17	.5	569	17.2	2,737	82.8	3,306
100.0		91.9		480.0		325.0		102.5		25.8		34.6
5	.1	493	13.6	15	.4	22	.6	535	14.8	3,081	85.2	3,616
400.0		- 5.6		- 48.3		29.4		- 6.0		12.6		9.4

TABLE 18 - COMPARISIONS OF ENROLLMENT IN INSTITUTIONS OF HIGHER EDUCATION FOR SELECTED FIELDS OF STUDY AND LEVEL OF ENROLLMENT
BY RACE, ETHNICITY AND SEX: STATE 1974, 1976, 1978

MAJOR FIELD 0500 - BUSINESS AND MANAGEMENT

	AMERICAN INDIAN ALASKAN NATIVE		BLACK NON-HISPANIC		ASIAN OR PACIFIC ISLANDER		HISPANIC		TOTAL MINORITY		WHITE NON-HISPANIC		TOTAL
	NUMBER	%	NUMBER	%	NUMBER	%	NUMBER	%	NUMBER	%	NUMBER	%	NUMBER
DISTRICT OF COLUMBIA. . . .													
FEMALE													
1974 (9 INSTITUTIONS)	1	.1	879	53.6	13	.8	7	.4	900	54.9	740	45.1	1,640
1976 (11 INSTITUTIONS)	7	.2	2,013	60.7	66	2.0	37	1.1	2,123	64.0	1,192	36.0	3,315
% CHANGE 1974 TO 1976	600.0		129.0		407.7		428.6		135.9		61.1		102.1
1978 (12 INSTITUTIONS)	18	.4	2,762	59.6	70	1.5	50	1.1	2,900	62.6	1,736	37.4	4,636
% CHANGE 1976 TO 1978	157.1		37.2		6.1		35.1		36.6		45.6		39.8
MALE													
1974 (9 INSTITUTIONS)	13	.3	1,434	33.5	36	.8	30	.7	1,513	35.3	2,772	64.7	4,285
1976 (11 INSTITUTIONS)	17	.3	1,907	34.2	132	2.4	75	1.3	2,131	38.2	3,444	61.8	5,575
% CHANGE 1974 TO 1976	30.8		33.0		266.7		150.0		40.8		24.2		30.1
1978 (12 INSTITUTIONS)	55	.9	2,023	33.8	196	3.3	95	1.6	2,369	39.6	3,615	60.4	5,984
% CHANGE 1976 TO 1978	223.5		6.1		48.5		26.7		11.2		5.0		7.3
FLORIDA													
FEMALE													
1974 (50 INSTITUTIONS)	· 14	.2	963	14.2	39	.6	261	3.9	1,277	18.9	5,483	81.1	6,760
1976 (32 INSTITUTIONS)	10	.1	1,333	16.4	56	.7	637	7.8	2,036	25.0	6,104	75.0	8,140
% CHANGE 1974 TO 1976	- 28.6		38.4		43.6		144.1		59.4		11.3		20.4
1978 (37 INSTITUTIONS)	29	.3	1,677	14.7	98	.9	952	8.3	2,756	24.2	8,649	75.8	11,405
% CHANGE 1976 TO 1978	190.0		25.8		75.0		49.5		35.4		41.7		40.1
MALE													
1974 (50 INSTITUTIONS)	33	.1	1,575	6.6	96	.4	582	2.4	2,286	9.5	21,745	90.5	24,031
1976 (32 INSTITUTIONS)	40	.2	2,126	8.6	108	.4	1,182	4.8	3,456	13.9	21,344	86.1	24,800
% CHANGE 1974 TO 1976	21.2		35.0		12.5		103.1		51.2		- 1.8		3.2
1978 (37 INSTITUTIONS)	145	.6	2,225	8.6	205	.8	1,572	6.1	4,147	16.1	21,622	83.9	25,769
% CHANGE 1976 TO 1978	262.5		4.7		89.8		33.0		20.0		1.3		3.9
GEORGIA													
FEMALE													
1974 (47 INSTITUTIONS)	7	.1	1,563	28.1	25	.4	13	.2	1,608	28.9	3,951	71.1	5,559
1976 (52 INSTITUTIONS)	17	.2	2,236	25.4	34	.4	16	.2	2,303	26.2	6,489	73.8	8,792
% CHANGE 1974 TO 1976	142.9		43.1		36.0		23.1		43.2		64.2		58.2
1978 (57 INSTITUTIONS)	12	.1	2,660	22.2	46	.4	32	.3	2,750	22.9	9,247	77.1	11,997
% CHANGE 1976 TO 1978	- 29.4		19.0		35.3		100.0		19.4		42.5		36.5
MALE													
1974 (47 INSTITUTIONS)	32	.2	2,437	13.7	81	.5	44	.2	2,594	14.6	15,146	85.4	17,740
1976 (52 INSTITUTIONS)	38	.2	2,687	14.7	94	.5	48	.3	2,867	15.7	15,376	84.3	18,243
% CHANGE 1974 TO 1976	18.8		10.3		16.0		9.1		10.5		1.5		2.8
1978 (57 INSTITUTIONS)	23	.1	2,913	15.5	71	.4	85	.5	3,092	16.5	15,683	83.5	18,775
% CHANGE 1976 TO 1978	- 39.5		8.4		- 24.5		77.1		7.8		2.0		2.9
HAWAII.													
FEMALE													
1974 (0 INSTITUTIONS)	0	.0	0	.0	0	.0	0	.0	0	.0	0	.0	0
1976 (4 INSTITUTIONS)	0	.0	3	.3	815	77.6	19	1.8	837	79.7	213	20.3	1,050
% CHANGE 1974 TO 1976	.0		100.0		100.0		100.0		100.0		100.0		100.0
1978 (5 INSTITUTIONS)	2	.2	11	.9	856	69.3	17	1.4	886	71.7	349	28.3	1,235
% CHANGE 1976 TO 1978	100.0		266.7		5.0		- 10.5		5.9		63.8		17.6
MALE													
1974 (0 INSTITUTIONS)	0	.0	0	.0	0	.0	0	.0	0	.0	0	.0	0
1976 (4 INSTITUTIONS)	26	1.2	11	.5	1,323	62.3	24	1.1	1,384	65.2	739	34.8	2,123
% CHANGE 1974 TO 1976	100.0		100.0		100.0		100.0		100.0		100.0		100.0
1978 (5 INSTITUTIONS)	1	.0	203	7.6	1,090	41.0	70	2.6	1,364	51.4	1,292	48.6	2,656
% CHANGE 1976 TO 1978	- 96.2		1745.5		- 17.6		191.7		- 1.4		74.8		25.1

SS AND MANAGEMENT

MERICAN INDIAN ALASKAN NATIVE		BLACK NON-HISPANIC		ASIAN OR PACIFIC ISLANDER		HISPANIC		TOTAL MINORITY		WHITE NON-HISPANIC		TOTAL
NUMBER	%	NUMBER	%	NUMBER	%	NUMBER	%	NUMBER	%	NUMBER	%	NUMBER
5	.7	3	.4	13	1.9	30	4.3	51	7.3	646	92.7	697
15	1.1	3	.2	19	1.3	17	1.2	54	3.8	1,356	96.2	1,410
200.0		.0		46.2		- 43.3		5.9		109.9		102.3
12	.6	4	.2	27	1.5	28	1.5	71	3.8	1,781	96.2	1,852
- 20.0		33.3		42.1		64.7		31.5		31.3		31.3
11	.5	15	.7	29	1.3	48	2.2	103	4.7	2,091	95.3	2,194
14	.5	31	1.1	54	1.8	42	1.4	141	4.8	2,799	95.2	2,940
27.3		106.7		86.2		- 12.5		36.9		33.9		34.0
10	.3	15	.5	40	1.3	30	.9	95	3.0	3,082	97.0	3,177
- 28.6		- 51.6		- 25.9		- 28.6		- 32.6		10.1		8.1
25	.2	3,865	28.9	220	1.6	221	1.7	4,331	32.4	9,044	67.6	13,375
42	.2	3,067	15.2	240	1.2	348	1.7	3,697	18.3	16,473	81.7	20,170
68.0		- 20.6		9.1		57.5		- 14.6		82.1		50.8
73	.3	5,924	22.1	322	1.2	420	1.6	6,739	25.1	20,078	74.9	26,817
73.8		93.2		34.2		20.7		82.3		21.9		33.0
48	.1	3,705	9.8	355	.9	391	1.0	4,499	11.9	33,220	88.1	37,719
61	.1	2,952	7.0	532	1.3	623	1.5	4,168	9.9	38,134	90.1	42,302
27.1		- 20.3		49.9		59.3		- 7.4		14.8		12.2
103	.2	3,906	9.4	600	1.4	558	1.3	5,167	12.4	36,548	87.6	41,715
68.9		32.3		12.8		- 10.4		24.0		- 4.2		- 1.4
10	.3	300	7.8	19	.5	49	1.3	378	9.8	3,467	90.2	3,845
16	.2	687	8.2	37	.4	73	.9	813	9.7	7,582	90.3	8,395
60.0		129.0		94.7		49.0		115.1		118.7		118.3
22	.2	1,087	9.2	62	.5	119	1.0	1,290	11.0	10,480	89.0	11,770
37.5		58.2		67.6		63.0		58.7		38.2		40.2
33	.2	688	4.5	47	.3	147	1.0	915	6.0	14,402	94.0	15,317
36	.2	936	4.6	71	.4	156	.8	1,199	5.9	19,053	94.1	20,252
9.1		36.0		51.1		6.1		31.0		32.3		32.2
39	.2	1,089	5.2	80	.4	167	.8	1,375	6.6	19,499	93.4	20,874
8.3		16.3		12.7		7.1		14.7		2.3		3.1
3	.2	58	3.8	7	.5	3	.2	71	4.6	1,461	95.4	1,532
2	.1	85	3.3	10	.4	10	.4	107	4.1	2,492	95.9	2,599
- 33.3		46.6		42.9		233.3		50.7		70.6		69.6
18	.3	137	2.4	31	.5	14	.2	200	3.4	5,619	96.6	5,819
800.0		61.2		210.0		40.0		86.9		125.5		123.9
6	.1	151	2.2	22	.3	23	.3	202	3.0	6,511	97.0	6,713
11	.2	155	2.6	17	.3	18	.3	201	3.3	5,844	96.7	6,045
83.3		2.6		- 22.7		- 21.7		.5		- 10.2		- 10.0
17	.2	213	2.3	37	.4	33	.4	300	3.2	8,944	96.8	9,244
54.5		37.4		117.6		83.3		49.3		53.0		52.9

TABLE 18 - COMPARISIONS OF ENROLLMENT IN INSTITUTIONS OF HIGHER EDUCATION FOR SELECTED FIELDS OF STUDY AND LEVEL OF ENROLLMENT BY RACE, ETHNICITY AND SEX: STATE 1974, 1976, 1978

MAJOR FIELD 0500 - BUSINESS AND MANAGEMENT

	AMERICAN INDIAN ALASKAN NATIVE		BLACK NON-HISPANIC		ASIAN OR PACIFIC ISLANDER		HISPANIC		TOTAL MINORITY		WHITE NON-HISPANIC		T
	NUMBER	%	NUMBER	%	NUMBER	%	NUMBER	%	NUMBER	%	NUMBER	%	NU
KANSAS.													
FEMALE													
1974 (36 INSTITUTIONS)	9	.3	145	5.1	13	.5	26	.9	193	6.8	2,646	93.2	2
1976 (41 INSTITUTIONS)	199	4.1	306	6.3	14	.3	45	.9	564	11.6	4,290	88.4	4
% CHANGE 1974 TO 1976	2111.1		111.0		7.7		73.1		192.2		62.1		71
1978 (41 INSTITUTIONS)	33	.5	381	5.7	40	.6	97	1.5	551	8.3	6,079	91.7	6
% CHANGE 1976 TO 1978	- 83.4		24.5		185.7		115.6		- 2.3		41.7		36
MALE													
1974 (36 INSTITUTIONS)	24	.3	236	3.0	33	.4	90	1.2	383	4 9	7,435	95.1	7
1976 (41 INSTITUTIONS)	122	1.4	421	5.0	31	.4	117	1.4	691	8:2	7,725	91.8	8
% CHANGE 1974 TO 1976	408.3		78.4		- 6.1		30.0		80.4		3.9		7
1978 (41 INSTITUTIONS)	52	.5	550	5.5	50	.5	173	1.7	825	8.2	9,206	91.8	10
% CHANGE 1976 TO 1978	- 57.4		30.6		61.3		47.9		19.4		19.2		19
KENTUCKY.													
FEMALE													
1974 (19 INSTITUTIONS)	6	.2	231	7.9	7	.2	3	.1	247	8.5	2,664	91.5	2
1976 (28 INSTITUTIONS)	14	.3	533	11.3	18	.4	20	.4	585	12.4	4,114	87.6	4
% CHANGE 1974 TO 1976	133.3		130.7		157.1		566.7		136.8		54.4		61
1978 (31 INSTITUTIONS)	10	.1	857	11.3	35	.5	27	.4	929	12.2	6,680	87.8	7
% CHANGE 1976 TO 1978	- 28.6		60.8		94.4		35.0		58.8		62.4		61
MALE													
1974 (19 INSTITUTIONS)	34	.4	436	4.7	36	.4	22	.2	530	5 7	8,722	94.3	9
1976 (28 INSTITUTIONS)	13	.1	908	8.0	33	.3	24	.2	978	816	10,332	91.4	11
% CHANGE 1974 TO 1976	- 63.9		108.3		- 8.3		9.1		84.5		18.5		22
1978 (31 INSTITUTIONS)	17	.1	883	7.2	66	.5	43	.4	1,009	8.3	11,180	91.7	12
% CHANGE 1976 TO 1978	30.8		- 2.8		100.0		79.2		3.2		8.2		7
LOUISIANA													
FEMALE													
1974 (23 INSTITUTIONS)	11	.2	2,116	34.8	19	.3	42	.7	2,188	36.0	3,897	64.0	6
1976 (25 INSTITUTIONS)	10	.1	3,103	33.0	48	.5	118	1.3	3,279	34.8	6,137	65.2	9
% CHANGE 1974 TO 1976	- 9.1		46.6		152.6		181.0		49.9		57.5		54
1978 (27 INSTITUTIONS)	22	.2	2,838	26.7	55	.5	156	1.5	3,071	28.8	7,574	71.2	10
% CHANGE 1976 TO 1978	120.0		- 8.5		14.6		32.2		- 6.3		23.4		13
MALE													
1974 (23 INSTITUTIONS)	16	.1	2,156	17.6	52	.4	95	.8	2,319	19.0	9,917	81.0	12
1976 (25 INSTITUTIONS)	20	.1	2,841	20.0	53	.4	147	1.0	3,061	21.6	11,138	78.4	14
% CHANGE 1974 TO 1976	25.0		31.8		1.9		54.7		32.0		12.3		16
1978 (27 INSTITUTIONS)	19	.1	2,388	17.1	55	.4	175	1.2	2,637	18.8	11,365	81.2	14
% CHANGE 1976 TO 1978	- 5.0		- 15.9		3.8		19.0		- 13.9		2.0		- 1
MAINE													
FEMALE													
1974 (9 INSTITUTIONS)	1	.3	9	3.0	0	.0	0	.0	10	3.3	289	96.7	
1976 (15 INSTITUTIONS)	12	.7	15	.9	4	.2	2	.1	33	1.9	1,702	98.1	1
% CHANGE 1974 TO 1976	1100.0		66.7		100.0		100.0		230.0		488.9		480
1978 (15 INSTITUTIONS)	16	.7	6	.3	5	.2	5	.2	32	1.4	2,315	98.6	2
% CHANGE 1976 TO 1978	33.3		- 60.0		25.0		150.0		- 3.0		36.0		35
MALE													
1974 (9 INSTITUTIONS)	4	.2	28	1.5	2	.1	19	1.0	53	2.8	1,869	97.2	1
1976 (15 INSTITUTIONS)	13	.4	31	.9	4	.1	14	.4	62	1.7	3,579	98.3	3
% CHANGE 1974 TO 1976	225.0		10.7		100.0		- 26.3		17.0		91.5		89
1978 (15 INSTITUTIONS)	15	.4	19	.5	18	.5	13	.4	65	1.8	3,608	98.2	3
% CHANGE 1976 TO 1978	15.4		- 38.7		350.0		- 7.1		4.8		.8		

E 18 - COMPARISIONS OF ENROLLMENT IN INSTITUTIONS OF HIGHER EDUCATION FOR SELECTED FIELDS OF STUDY AND LEVEL OF ENROLLMENT BY RACE, ETHNICITY AND SEX: STATE 1974, 1976, 1978

R FIELD 0500 - BUSINESS AND MANAGEMENT

	AMERICAN INDIAN ALASKAN NATIVE		BLACK NON-HISPANIC		ASIAN OR PACIFIC ISLANDER		HISPANIC		TOTAL MINORITY		WHITE NON-HISPANIC		TOTAL
	NUMBER	%	NUMBER	%	NUMBER	%	NUMBER	%	NUMBER	%	NUMBER	%	NUMBER
LAND...........													
ALE													
74 (20 INSTITUTIONS)	18	.7	708	26.2	62	2.3	13	.5	801	29.7	1,899	70.3	2,700
76 (17 INSTITUTIONS)	17	.4	1,525	36.9	60	1.5	16	.4	1,618	39.1	2,515	60.9	4,133
CHANGE 1974 TO 1976	- 5.6		115.4		- 3.2		23.1		102.0		32.4		53.1
78 (33 INSTITUTIONS)	21	.2	2,323	26.9	102	1.2	64	.7	2,510	29.0	6,135	71.0	8,645
CHANGE 1976 TO 1978	23.5		52.3		70.0		300.0		55.1		143.9		109.2
E													
74 (20 INSTITUTIONS)	65	.7	998	11.4	92	1.0	58	.7	1,213	13.8	7,550	86.2	8,763
76 (17 INSTITUTIONS)	40	.4	1,524	15.8	61	.6	49	.5	1,674	17.3	7,979	82.7	9,653
CHANGE 1974 TO 1976	- 38.5		52.7		- 33.7		- 15.5		38.0		5.7		10.2
78 (33 INSTITUTIONS)	39	.3	2,185	15.3	145	1.0	108	.8	2,477	17.4	11,767	82.6	14,244
CHANGE 1976 TO 1978	- 2.5		43.4		137.7		120.4		48.0		47.5		47.6
ACHUSETTS........													
ALE													
74 (40 INSTITUTIONS)	35	.5	323	4.5	81	1.1	61	.8	500	6.9	6,696	93.1	7,196
76 (58 INSTITUTIONS)	65	.4	974	5.3	188	1.0	196	1.1	1,423	7.7	16,987	92.3	18,410
CHANGE 1974 TO 1976	85.7		201.5		132.1		221.3		184.6		153.7		155.8
78 (58 INSTITUTIONS)	46	.2	1,104	4.6	248	1.0	351	1.5	1,749	7.2	22,376	92.8	24,125
CHANGE 1976 TO 1978	- 29.2		13.3		31.9		79.1		22.9		31.7		31.0
E													
74 (40 INSTITUTIONS)	57	.2	617	2.5	179	.7	144	.6	997	4.0	24,149	96.0	25,146
76 (58 INSTITUTIONS)	127	.3	1,160	3.1	261	.7	308	.8	1,856	4.9	35,944	95.1	37,800
CHANGE 1974 TO 1976	122.8		88.0		45.8		113.9		86.2		48.8		50.3
78 (58 INSTITUTIONS)	86	.2	1,066	2.8	283	.7	320	.8	1,755	4.6	36,405	95.4	38,160
CHANGE 1976 TO 1978	- 32.3		- 8.1		8.4		3.9		- 5.4		1.3		1.0
IGAN..........													
ALE													
74 (56 INSTITUTIONS)	40	.5	1,234	14.9	74	.9	52	.6	1,400	16.9	6,874	83.1	8,274
76 (60 INSTITUTIONS)	109	.5	2,799	13.9	187	.9	161	.8	3,256	16.1	16,942	83.9	20,198
CHANGE 1974 TO 1976	172.5		126.8		152.7		209.6		132.6		146.5		144.1
78 (65 INSTITUTIONS)	110	.4	3,919	13.2	149	.5	443	1.5	4,621	15.5	25,156	84.5	29,777
CHANGE 1976 TO 1978	.9		40.0		- 20.3		175.2		41.9		48.5		47.4
E													
74 (56 INSTITUTIONS)	90	.3	1,886	7.0	153	.6	148	.5	2,277	8.4	24,774	91.6	27,051
76 (60 INSTITUTIONS)	151	.4	2,690	7.8	224	.6	224	.7	3,289	9.8	31,074	90.4	34,363
CHANGE 1974 TO 1976	67.8		42.6		46.4		51.4		44.4		25.4		27.0
78 (65 INSTITUTIONS)	137	.4	2,547	7.0	196	.5	378	1.0	3,258	9.0	33,075	91.0	36,333
CHANGE 1976 TO 1978	- 9.3		- 5.3		- 12.5		68.8		- .9		6.4		5.7
ESOTA..........													
ALE													
74 (21 INSTITUTIONS)	15	.9	34	2.0	11	.6	5	.3	65	3.8	1,661	96.2	1,726
76 (37 INSTITUTIONS)	24	.6	51	1.2	42	1.0	10	.2	127	3.0	4,116	97.0	4,243
CHANGE 1974 TO 1976	60.0		50.0		281.8		100.0		95.4		147.8		145.8
78 (41 INSTITUTIONS)	23	.4	71	1.1	63	1.0	22	.3	179	2.7	6,382	97.3	6,561
CHANGE 1976 TO 1978	- 4.2		39.2		50.0		120.0		40.9		55.1		54.6
E													
74 (21 INSTITUTIONS)	35	.4	79	1.0	76	.9	19	.2	209	2.6	7,801	97.4	8,010
76 (37 INSTITUTIONS)	50	.4	126	1.1	87	.8	20	.2	283	2.4	11,273	97.6	11,556
CHANGE 1974 TO 1976	42.9		59.5		14.5		5.3		35.4		44.5		44.3
78 (41 INSTITUTIONS)	43	.3	151	1.1	64	.5	34	.3	292	2.2	13,036	97.8	13,328
CHANGE 1976 TO 1978	- 14.0		19.8		- 26.4		70.0		3.2		15.6		15.3

TABLE 18 - COMPARISIONS OF ENROLLMENT IN INSTITUTIONS OF HIGHER EDUCATION FOR SELECTED FIELDS OF STUDY AND LEVEL OF ENROLLME
             BY RACE, ETHNICITY AND SEX: STATE 1974, 1976, 1978

MAJOR FIELD 0500 - BUSINESS AND MANAGEMENT

	AMERICAN INDIAN ALASKAN NATIVE		BLACK NON-HISPANIC		ASIAN OR PACIFIC ISLANDER		HISPANIC		TOTAL MINORITY		WHITE NON-HISPANIC	
	NUMBER	%	NUMBER	%	NUMBER	%	NUMBER	%	NUMBER	%	NUMBER	%
MISSISSIPPI												
FEMALE												
1974 (33 INSTITUTIONS)	1	.0	1,586	41.5	15	.4	0	.0	1,602	41.9	2,223	58.1
1976 (34 INSTITUTIONS)	7	.1	2,732	43.9	14	.2	1	.0	2,754	44.2	3,470	55.8
% CHANGE 1974 TO 1976	600.0		72.3		- 6.7		100.0		71.9		56.1	
1978 (36 INSTITUTIONS)	16	.2	2,603	36.6	24	.3	5	.1	2,648	37.2	4,462	62.8
% CHANGE 1976 TO 1978	128.6		- 4.7		71.4		400.0		- 3.8		28.6	
MALE												
1974 (33 INSTITUTIONS)	4	.1	1,433	19.1	28	.4	5	.1	1,470	19.6	6,034	80.4
1976 (34 INSTITUTIONS)	12	.1	1,992	22.8	42	.5	7	.1	2,053	23.5	6,692	76.5
% CHANGE 1974 TO 1976	200.0		39.0		50.0		40.0		39.7		10.9	
1978 (36 INSTITUTIONS)	9	.1	1,757	19.9	33	.4	15	.2	1,814	20.5	7,021	79.5
% CHANGE 1976 TO 1978	- 25.0		- 11.8		- 21.4		114.3		- 11.6		4.9	
MISSOURI												
FEMALE												
1974 (37 INSTITUTIONS)	6	.1	569	12.7	16	.4	30	.7	621	13.9	3,855	86.1
1976 (43 INSTITUTIONS)	21	.3	679	9.8	33	.5	32	.5	765	11.0	6,197	89.0
% CHANGE 1974 TO 1976	250.0		19.3		106.3		6.7		23.2		60.8	
1978 (35 INSTITUTIONS)	28	.3	863	9.3	66	.7	52	.6	1,009	10.9	8,264	89.1
% CHANGE 1976 TO 1978	33.3		27.1		100.0		62.5		31.9		33.4	
MALE												
1974 (37 INSTITUTIONS)	42	.3	957	6.4	68	.5	97	.7	1,164	7.8	13,696	92.2
1976 (43 INSTITUTIONS)	62	.4	992	5.7	89	.5	90	.5	1,233	7.1	16,168	92.9
% CHANGE 1974 TO 1976	47.6		3.7		30.9		- 7.2		5.9		18.0	
1978 (35 INSTITUTIONS)	47	.3	1,024	5.9	105	.6	123	.7	1,299	7.4	16,192	92.6
% CHANGE 1976 TO 1978	- 24.2		3.2		18.0		36.7		5.4		.1	
MONTANA												
FEMALE												
1974 (6 INSTITUTIONS)	31	4.4	4	.6	4	.6	3	.4	42	5.9	668	94.1
1976 (9 INSTITUTIONS)	77	6.0	4	.3	3	.2	5	.4	89	6.9	1,204	93.1
% CHANGE 1974 TO 1976	148.4		.0		- 25.0		66.7		111.9		80.2	
1978 (9 INSTITUTIONS)	23	1.4	4	.2	4	.2	6	.4	37	2.2	1,640	97.8
% CHANGE 1976 TO 1978	- 70.1		.0		33.3		20.0		- 58.4		36.2	
MALE												
1974 (6 INSTITUTIONS)	45	2.2	19	.9	12	.6	6	.3	82	3.9	2,000	96.1
1976 (9 INSTITUTIONS)	40	1.8	33	1.5	10	.5	4	.2	87	3.9	2,121	96.1
% CHANGE 1974 TO 1976	- 11.1		73.7		- 16.7		- 33.3		6.1		6.1	
1978 (9 INSTITUTIONS)	18	.7	10	.4	12	.5	6	.2	46	1.9	2,401	98.1
% CHANGE 1976 TO 1978	- 55.0		- 69.7		20.0		50.0		- 47.1		13.2	
NEBRASKA												
FEMALE												
1974 (18 INSTITUTIONS)	5	.3	43	2.4	9	.5	9	.5	66	3.7	1,707	96.3
1976 (18 INSTITUTIONS)	7	.3	136	6.6	13	.6	24	1.2	180	8.7	1,881	91.3
% CHANGE 1974 TO 1976	40.0		216.3		44.4		166.7		172.7		10.2	
1978 (20 INSTITUTIONS)	9	.3	126	4.4	14	.5	23	.8	172	6.0	2,677	94.0
% CHANGE 1976 TO 1978	28.6		- 7.4		7.7		- 4.2		- 4.4		42.3	
MALE												
1974 (18 INSTITUTIONS)	7	.1	137	2.3	15	.3	42	.7	201	3.4	5,661	96.6
1976 (18 INSTITUTIONS)	12	.2	252	4.3	18	.3	50	.9	332	5.7	5,521	94.3
% CHANGE 1974 TO 1976	71.4		83.9		20.0		19.0		65.2		- 2.5	-
1978 (20 INSTITUTIONS)	13	.2	168	2.8	34	.6	54	.9	269	4.5	5,664	95.5
% CHANGE 1976 TO 1978	8.3		- 33.3		88.9		8.0		19.0		2.6	

MAJOR FIELD 0500 - BUSINESS AND MANAGEMENT

	AMERICAN INDIAN ALASKAN NATIVE		BLACK NON-HISPANIC		ASIAN OR PACIFIC ISLANDER		HISPANIC		TOTAL MINORITY		WHITE NON-HISPANIC		TOTAL
	NUMBER	%	NUMBER	%	NUMBER	%	NUMBER	%	NUMBER	%	NUMBER	%	NUMBER
NEVADA.													
FEMALE													
1974 (3 INSTITUTIONS)	6	2.0	12	3.9	13	4.3	6	2.0	37	12.2	267	87.8	304
1976 (5 INSTITUTIONS)	35	2.4	74	5.1	32	2.2	28	1.9	169	11.6	1,293	88.4	1,462
% CHANGE 1974 TO 1976	483.3		516.7		146.2		366.7		356.8		384.3		380.9
1978 (4 INSTITUTIONS)	41	3.4	29	2.4	25	2.1	31	2.6	126	10.6	1,065	89.4	1,191
% CHANGE 1976 TO 1978	17.1		- 60.8		- 21.9		10.7		- 25.4		- 17.6		- 18.5
MALE													
1974 (3 INSTITUTIONS)	23	1.7	44	3.3	52	3.9	26	2.0	145	11.0	1,178	89.0	1,323
1976 (5 INSTITUTIONS)	25	1.1	95	4.0	40	1.7	47	2.0	207	8.8	2,145	91.2	2,352
% CHANGE 1974 TO 1976	8.7		115.9		- 23.1		80.8		42.8		82.1		77.8
1978 (4 INSTITUTIONS)	22	1.1	61	3.1	38	1.9	51	2.6	172	8.7	1,811	91.3	1,983
% CHANGE 1976 TO 1978	- 12.0		- 35.8		- 5.0		8.5		- 16.9		- 15.6		- 15.7
NEW HAMPSHIRE													
FEMALE													
1974 (9 INSTITUTIONS)	0	.0	14	2.5	1	.2	7	1.3	22	4.0	529	96.0	551
1976 (18 INSTITUTIONS)	1	.0	28	1.2	6	.3	10	.4	45	2.0	2,233	98.0	2,278
% CHANGE 1974 TO 1976	100.0		100.0		500.0		42.9		104.5		322.1		313.4
1978 (18 INSTITUTIONS)	2	.1	24	.7	9	.3	14	.4	49	1.5	3,161	98.5	3,210
% CHANGE 1976 TO 1978	100.0		- 14.3		50.0		40.0		8.9		41.6		40.9
MALE													
1974 (9 INSTITUTIONS)	10	.3	55	1.8	5	.2	37	1.2	107	.5	2,976	96.5	3,083
1976 (18 INSTITUTIONS)	8	.1	54	.9	11	.2	188	3.1	261	4.3	5,825	95.7	6,086
% CHANGE 1974 TO 1976	- 20.0		- 1.8		120.0		408.1		143.9		95.7		97.4
1978 (18 INSTITUTIONS)	9	.1	97	1.4	16	.2	140	2.0	262	3.8	6,641	96.2	6,903
% CHANGE 1976 TO 1978	12.5		79.6		45.5		- 25.5		.4		14.0		13.4
NEW JERSEY.													
FEMALE													
1974 (36 INSTITUTIONS)	14	.2	1,063	16.7	74	1.2	249	3.9	1,400	22.0	4,959	78.0	6,359
1976 (37 INSTITUTIONS)	33	.3	1,492	12.7	86	.7	332	2.8	1,943	16.6	9,762	83.4	11,705
% CHANGE 1974 TO 1976	135.7		40.4		16.2		33.3		38.8		96.9		84.1
1978 (40 INSTITUTIONS)	35	.2	1,986	13.1	133	.9	438	2.9	2,592	17.1	12,560	82.9	15,152
% CHANGE 1976 TO 1978	6.1		33.1		54.7		31.9		33.4		28.7		29.4
MALE													
1974 (36 INSTITUTIONS)	24	.1	1,620	7.0	232	1.0	550	2.4	2,426	10.5	20,700	89.5	23,126
1976 (37 INSTITUTIONS)	39	.2	1,662	6.5	218	.9	518	2.0	2,437	9.5	23,167	90.5	25,604
% CHANGE 1974 TO 1976	62.5		2.6		- 6.0		- 5.8		.5		11.9		10.7
1978 (40 INSTITUTIONS)	37	.1	1,777	6.9	227	.9	627	2.4	2,668	10.4	23,038	89.6	25,706
% CHANGE 1976 TO 1978	- 5.1		6.9		4.1		21.0		9.5		- .6		.4
NEW MEXICO.													
FEMALE													
1974 (15 INSTITUTIONS)	44	3.4	26	2.0	7	.5	355	27.6	432	33.5	856	66.5	1,288
1976 (15 INSTITUTIONS)	82	4.4	36	1.9	11	.6	552	29.5	681	36.4	1,191	63.6	1,872
% CHANGE 1974 TO 1976	86.4		38.5		57.1		55.5		57.6		39.1		45.3
1978 (15 INSTITUTIONS)	107	4.3	38	1.5	23	.9	712	28.9	880	35.8	1,581	64.2	2,461
% CHANGE 1976 TO 1978	30.5		5.6		109.1		29.0		29.2		32.7		31.5
MALE													
1974 (15 INSTITUTIONS)	63	2.0	90	2.8	23	.7	774	24.2	950	29.7	2,248	70.3	3,198
1976 (15 INSTITUTIONS)	50	1.5	116	3.4	23	.6	961	28.2	1,147	33.7	2,258	66.3	3,405
% CHANGE 1974 TO 1976	- 20.6		28.9		- 13.0		24.2		20.7		.4		6.5
1978 (15 INSTITUTIONS)	69	1.9	128	3.6	29	.8	990	27.5	1,216	33.8	2,378	66.2	3,594
% CHANGE 1976 TO 1978	38.0		10.3		45.0		3.0		6.0		5.3		5.6

TABLE. 18 - COMPARISIONS OF ENROLLMENT IN INSTITUTIONS OF HIGHER EDUCATION FOR SELECTED FIELDS OF STUDY AND LEVEL OF ENROLLMENT BY RACE, ETHNICITY AND SEX: STATE 1974, 1976, 1978

MAJOR FIELD 0500 — BUSINESS AND MANAGEMENT

	AMERICAN INDIAN ALASKAN NATIVE		BLACK NON-HISPANIC		ASIAN OR PACIFIC ISLANDER		HISPANIC		TOTAL MINORITY		WHITE NON-HISPANIC		TOTAL
	NUMBER	%	NUMBER	%	NUMBER	%	NUMBER	%	NUMBER	%	NUMBER	%	NUMBER
NEW YORK.............													
FEMALE													
1974 (87 INSTITUTIONS)	26	.2	1,292	11.2	410	3.5	334	2.9	2,062	17.8	9,502	82.2	11,564
1976 (104 INSTITUTIONS)	49	.2	2,652	11.0	620	2.6	740	3.1	4,061	16.8	20,070	83.2	24,131
% CHANGE 1974 TO 1976	88.5		105.3		51.2		121.6		96.9		111.2		108.7
1978 (121 INSTITUTIONS)	110	.3	4,055	10.3	835	2.1	1,510	3.8	6,510	16.6	32,805	83.4	39,315
% CHANGE 1976 TO 1978	124.5		52.9		34.7		104.1		60.3		63.5		62.9
MALE													
1974 (87 INSTITUTIONS)	84	.2	2,673	5.7	867	1.8	1,093	2.3	4,717	10.0	42,238	90.0	46,955
1976 (104 INSTITUTIONS)	133	.2	3,512	6.4	1,028	1.9	1,397	2.8	6,070	11.1	48,522	88.9	54,592
% CHANGE 1974 TO 1976	58.3		31.4		18.6		27.8		28.7		14.9		16.3
1978 (121 INSTITUTIONS)	152	.2	4,110	6.6	1,237	2.0	1,870	3.0	7,369	11.9	54,663	88.1	62,032
% CHANGE 1976 TO 1978	14.3		17.0		20.3		33.9		21.4		12.7		13.6
NORTH CAROLINA.......													
FEMALE													
1974 (49 INSTITUTIONS)	35	.8	2,099	48.2	6	.1	5	.1	2,145	49.3	2,207	50.7	4,352
1976 (53 INSTITUTIONS)	49	.6	3,283	41.9	9	.1	14	.2	3,355	42.8	4,477	57.2	7,832
% CHANGE 1974 TO 1976	40.0		56.4		50.0		180.0		56.4		102.9		80.0
1978 (57 INSTITUTIONS)	54	.5	3,976	36.6	30	.3	32	.3	4,092	37.6	6,777	62.4	10,869
% CHANGE 1976 TO 1978	10.2		21.1		233.3		128.6		22.0		51.4		38.8
MALE													
1974 (49 INSTITUTIONS)	58	.5	2,835	22.9	21	.2	34	.3	2,948	23.8	9,423	76.2	12,371
1976 (53 INSTITUTIONS)	65	.4	3,261	21.9	30	.2	32	.2	3,388	22.7	11,505	77.3	14,893
% CHANGE 1974 TO 1976	12.1		15.0		42.9		− 5.9		14.9		22.1		20.4
1978 (57 INSTITUTIONS)	52	.3	4,078	24.1	48	.3	53	.3	4,231	25.0	12,706	75.0	16,937
% CHANGE 1976 TO 1978	− 20.0		25.1		60.0		65.6		24.9		10.4		13.7
NORTH DAKOTA........													
FEMALE													
1974 (10 INSTITUTIONS)	18	4.2	1	.2	0	.0	0	.0	19	4	406	95.5	425
1976 (12 INSTITUTIONS)	40	4.7	3	.4	3	.4	0	.0	46	5.4	807	94.6	853
% CHANGE 1974 TO 1976	122.2		200.0		100.0		.0		142.1		98.8		100.7
1978 (13 INSTITUTIONS)	84	6.0	10	.7	5	.4	5	.4	104	7.4	1,299	92.6	1,403
% CHANGE 1976 TO 1978	110.0		233.3		66.7		100.0		126.1		61.0		64.5
MALE													
1974 (10 INSTITUTIONS)	23	1.	17	.9	4	.2	1	.1	45	2.5	1,755	97.5	1,800
1976 (12 INSTITUTIONS)	23	1.8	11	.5	2	.1	10	.4	46	2.0	2,203	98.0	2,249
% CHANGE 1974 TO 1976	.0		− 35.3		− 50.0		900.0		2.2		25.5		24.9
1978 (13 INSTITUTIONS)	44	1.5	20	.7	6	.2	2	.1	72	2.5	2,792	97.5	2,864
% CHANGE 1976 TO 1978	91.3		81.8		200.0		− 80.0		56.5		26.7		27.3
OHIO.............													
FEMALE													
1974 (70 INSTITUTIONS)	24	.2	1,636	16.9	49	.5	53	.5	1,762	18.2	7,935	81.8	9,697
1976 (84 INSTITUTIONS)	37	.2	3,345	17.1	81	.4	77	.4	3,540	18.1	15,973	81.9	19,513
% CHANGE 1974 TO 1976	54.2		104.5		65.3		45.3		100.9		101.3		101.2
1978 (95 INSTITUTIONS)	70	.2	4,954	15.0	165	.5	176	.5	5,365	16.2	27,687	83.8	33,052
% CHANGE 1976 TO 1978	89.2		48.1		103.7		128.6		51.6		73.3		69.4
MALE													
1974 (70 INSTITUTIONS)	72	.2	2,706	8.1	116	.3	91	.3	2,985	.8	30,585	91.1	33,570
1976 (84 INSTITUTIONS)	54	.1	3,794	8.9	161	.4	144	.3	4,153	8.8	38,440	90.2	42,593
% CHANGE 1974 TO 1976	− 25.0		40.2		38.8		58.2		39.1		25.7		26.9
1978 (95 INSTITUTIONS)	68	.1	4,325	9.1	175	.4	208	.4	4,776	10.0	42,887	90.0	47,663
% CHANGE 1976 TO 1978	25.9		14.0		8.7		44.4		15.0		11.6		11.9

NROLLMENT IN INSTITUTIONS OF HIGHER EDUCATION FOR SELECTED FIELDS OF STUDY AND LEVEL OF ENROLLMENT
Y AND SEX: STATE 1974, 1976, 1978

AND MANAGEMENT

ICAN INDIAN SKAN NATIVE		BLACK NON-HISPANIC		ASIAN OR PACIFIC ISLANDER		HISPANIC		TOTAL MINORITY		WHITE NON-HISPANIC		TOTAL
NUMBER	%	NUMBER	%	NUMBER	%	NUMBER	%	NUMBER	%	NUMBER	%	NUMBER
257	4.1	511	8.2	27	.4	25	.4	820	13.1	5,427	86.9	6,247
415	4.4	862	9.1	82	.9	73	.8	1,432	15.2	8,005	84.8	9,437
61.5		68.7		203.7		192.0		74.6		47.5		51.1
377	4.0	755	8.0	70	.7	79	.8	1,281	13.5	8,202	86.5	9,483
9.2		- 12.4		- 14.6		8.2		- 10.5		2.5		.5
341	2.4	733	5.3	48	.3	77	.6	1,199	8.6	12,724	91.4	13,923
431	2.7	1,131	7.2	120	.8	119	.8	1,801	11.4	13,988	88.6	15,789
26.4		54.3		150.0		54.5		50.2		9.9		13.4
385	2.8	828	6.0	99	.7	100	.7	1,412	10.2	12,439	89.8	13,851
10.7		- 26.8		- 17.5		- 16.0		- 21.6		- 11.1		- 12.3
25	1.0	32	1.3	60	2.5	5	.2	122	5.1	2,293	94.9	2,415
32	.8	59	1.5	109	2.8	15	.4	215	5.6	3,637	94.4	3,852
28.0		84.4		81.7		200.0		76.2		58.6		59.5
58	1.1	80	1.6	180	3.5	38	.7	356	6.9	4,773	93.1	5,129
81.3		35.6		65.1		153.3		65.6		31.2		33.2
68	1.1	102	1 7	141	2.3	37	.6	348	5.6	5,818	94.4	6,166
50	.7	112	1#5	173	2.3	62	.8	397	5.3	7,071	94.7	7,468
26.5		9.8		22.7		67.6		14.1		21.5		21.1
75	.9	122	1.5	226	2.7	66	.8	489	5.9	7,752	94.1	8,241
50.0		8.9		30.6		6.5		23.2		9.6		10.4
14	.2	539	7.5	32	.4	17	.2	602	8.3	6,618	91.7	7,220
15	.1	2,028	11.0	96	.5	199	1.1	2,338	12.6	16,145	87.4	18,483
7.1		276.3		200.0		1070.6		288.4		144.0		156.0
48	.2	2,810	9.6	172	.6	158	.5	3,188	10.9	26,023	89.1	29,211
220.0		38.6		79.2		- 20.6		36.4		61.2		58.0
102	.3	1,129	3 1	101	.3	105	.3	1,437	3.9	35,072	96.1	36,509
49	.1	2,379	11	184	.4	268	.6	2,880	6.2	43,776	93.8	46,656
52.0		110.7		82.2		155.2		100.4		24.8		27.8
60	.1	2,794	5.5	247	.5	258	.5	3,359	6.6	47,442	93.4	50,801
22.4		17.4		34.2		- 3.7		16.6		8.4		8.9
2	.1	80	4.9	8	.5	10	.6	100	6.1	1,537	93.9	1,637
2	.1	148	6#8	20	.9	57	2.6	227	10.4	1,964	89.6	2,191
.0		85.0		150.0		470.0		127.0		27.8		33.8
1	.0	239	6.3	5	.1	12	.3	257	6.7	3,555	93.3	3,812
50.0		61.5		- 75.0		- 78.9		13.2		81.0		74.0
6	.1	132	2.3	12	.2	24	.4	174	3.1	5,521	96.9	5,695
32	.4	384	4.7	37	.4	70	.9	523	6.4	7,707	93.6	8,230
433.3		190.9		208.3		191.7		200.6		39.6		44.5
4	.0	406	4.7	36	.4	38	.4	484	5.6	8,182	94.4	8,666
87.5		5.7		- 2.7		- 45.7		- 7.5		6.2		5.3

TABLE 18 - COMPARISIONS OF ENROLLMENT IN INSTITUTIONS OF HIGHER EDUCATION FOR SELECTED FIELDS OF STUDY AND LEVEL OF ENROLLME
BY RACE, ETHNICITY AND SEX: STATE 1974, 1976, 1978

MAJOR FIELD 0500 - BUSINESS AND MANAGEMENT

	AMERICAN INDIAN ALASKAN NATIVE		BLACK NON-HISPANIC		ASIAN OR PACIFIC ISLANDER		HISPANIC		TOTAL MINORITY		WHITE NON-HISPANIC	
	NUMBER	%	NUMBER	%	NUMBER	%	NUMBER	%	NUMBER	%	NUMBER	%
SOUTH CAROLINA.												
FEMALE												
1974 (23 INSTITUTIONS)	1	.1	543	33.5	1	.1	2	.1	547	33.7	1,076	66.3
1976 (32 INSTITUTIONS)	1	.0	945	32.0	3	.1	2	.1	951	32.2	1,998	67.8
% CHANGE 1974 TO 1976	.0		74.0		200.0		.0		73.9		85.7	
1978 (36 INSTITUTIONS)	3	.1	1,941	36.5	29	.5	6	.1	1,979	37.2	3,334	62.8
% CHANGE 1976 TO 1978	200.0		105.4		866.7		200.0		108.1		66.9	
MALE												
1974 (23 INSTITUTIONS)	1	.0	664	11.5	3	.1	7	.1	675	11.7	5,079	88.3
1976 (32 INSTITUTIONS)	2	.0	1,028	14.5	5	.1	14	.2	1,049	14.8	6,051	85.2
% CHANGE 1974 TO 1976	100.0		54.8		66.7		100.0		55.4		19.1	
1978 (36 INSTITUTIONS)	8	.1	1,850	18.3	30	.3	37	.4	1,925	19.0	8,186	81.0
% CHANGE 1976 TO 1978	300.0		80.0		500.0		164.3		83.5		35.3	
SOUTH DAKOTA.												
FEMALE												
1974 (14 INSTITUTIONS)	9	2.4	0	.0	0	.0	0	.0	9	2.4	359	97.6
1976 (13 INSTITUTIONS)	57	5.1	11	1.0	11	1.0	6	.5	85	7.5	1,042	92.5
% CHANGE 1974 TO 1976	533.3		100.0		100.0		100.0		844.4		190.3	
1978 (15 INSTITUTIONS)	113	6.3	18	1.0	7	.4	25	1.4	163	9.0	1,644	91.0
% CHANGE 1976 TO 1978	98.2		63.6		- 36.4		316.7		91.8		57.8	
MALE												
1974 (14 INSTITUTIONS)	29	1.4	20	1.0	1	.0	6	.3	56	2.7	2,047	97.3
1976 (13 INSTITUTIONS)	24	.6	28	.7	8	.2	3	.1	63	1.7	3,675	98.3
% CHANGE 1974 TO 1976	- 17.2		40.0		700.0		- 50.0		12.5		79.5	
1978 (15 INSTITUTIONS)	82	2.1	162	4.2	9	.2	230	5.9	483	12.4	3,413	87.6
% CHANGE 1976 TO 1978	241.7		478.6		12.5		7566.7		666.7		- 7.1	
TENNESSEE												
FEMALE												
1974 (42 INSTITUTIONS)	6	.1	749	16.3	9	.2	9	.2	773	16.8	3,833	83.2
1976 (47 INSTITUTIONS)	10	.1	1,950	23.7	39	.5	14	.2	2,013	24.5	6,206	75.5
% CHANGE 1974 TO 1976	66.7		160.3		333.3		55.6		160.4		61.9	
1978 (54 INSTITUTIONS)	19	.2	3,119	24.8	35	.3	30	.2	3,203	25.4	9,398	74.6
% CHANGE 1976 TO 1978	90.0		59.9		- 10.3		114.3		59.1		51.4	
MALE												
1974 (42 INSTITUTIONS)	18	.1	823	6.2	24	.2	27	.2	892	6.7	12,447	93.3
1976 (47 INSTITUTIONS)	22	.1	2,213	13.3	66	.4	24	.1	2,325	13.9	14,356	86.1
% CHANGE 1974 TO 1976	22.2		168.9		175.0		- 11.1		160.7		15.3	
1978 (54 INSTITUTIONS)	18	.1	2,720	15.3	57	.3	61	.3	2,856	16.1	14,915	83.9
% CHANGE 1976 TO 1978	- 18.2		22.9		- 13.6		154.2		22.8		3.9	
TEXAS												
FEMALE												
1974 (105 INSTITUTIONS)	64	.3	2,525	11.7	128	.6	1,710	7.9	4,427	20.5	17,176	79.5
1976 (118 INSTITUTIONS)	178	.5	5,068	14.0	273	.8	3,671	10.1	9,190	25.3	27,080	74.7
% CHANGE 1974 TO 1976	178.1		100.7		113.3		114.7		107.6		57.7	
1978 (118 INSTITUTIONS)	147	.3	6,099	12.5	597	1.2	4,803	9.8	11,646	23.8	37,323	76.2
% CHANGE 1976 TO 1978	- 17.4		20.3		118.7		30.8		26.7		37.8	
MALE												
1974 (105 INSTITUTIONS)	225	.4	3,449	6.3	264	.5	4,756	8.7	8,694	15.9	46,125	84.1
1976 (118 INSTITUTIONS)	271	.4	5,490	8.5	370	.6	6,860	10.6	12,991	20.1	51,666	79.9
% CHANGE 1974 TO 1976	20.4		59.2		40.2		44.2		49.4		12.0	
1978 (118 INSTITUTIONS)	184	.3	4,842	7.6	491	.8	6,353	10.0	11,870	18.7	51,504	81.3
% CHANGE 1976 TO 1978	- 32.1		- 11.8		32.7		- 7.4		- 8.6		- .3	-

ABLE 18 - COMPARISIONS OF ENROLLMENT IN INSTITUTIONS OF HIGHER EDUCATION FOR SELECTED FIELDS OF STUDY AND LEVEL OF ENROLLMENT BY RACE, ETHNICITY AND SEX: STATE 1974, 1976, 1978

AJOR FIELD 0500 - BUSINESS AND MANAGEMENT

	AMERICAN INDIAN ALASKAN NATIVE		BLACK NON-HISPANIC		ASIAN OR PACIFIC ISLANDER		HISPANIC		TOTAL MINORITY		WHITE NON-HISPANIC		TOTAL
	NUMBER	%	NUMBER	%	NUMBER	%	NUMBER	%	NUMBER	%	NUMBER	%	NUMBER
TAH													
FEMALE													
1974 (7 INSTITUTIONS)	5	.3	6	.4	17	1.1	17	1.1	45	3.0	1,454	97.0	1,499
1976 (13 INSTITUTIONS)	75	2.1	11	.3	45	1.2	63	1.7	194	5.4	3,411	94.6	3,605
% CHANGE 1974 TO 1976	1400.0		83.3		164.7		270.6		331.1		134.6		140.5
1978 (14 INSTITUTIONS)	54	1.6	28	.9	80	2.4	63	1.9	225	6.9	3,059	93.1	3,284
% CHANGE 1976 TO 1978	- 28.0		154.5		77.8		.0		16.0		- 10.3		- 8.9
MALE													
1974 (7 INSTITUTIONS)	20	.4	24	.4	50	.9	48	.8	142	2.5	5,513	97.5	5,655
1976 (13 INSTITUTIONS)	29	.4	41	.6	93	1.3	89	1.2	252	3.5	7,004	96.5	7,256
% CHANGE 1974 TO 1976	45.0		70.8		86.0		85.4		77.5		27.0		28.3
1978 (14 INSTITUTIONS)	33	.4	42	.5	118	1.3	136	1.6	329	3.8	8,414	96.2	8,743
% CHANGE 1976 TO 1978	13.8		2.4		26.9		52.8		30.6		20.1		20.5
ERMONT													
FEMALE													
1974 (7 INSTITUTIONS)	1	.5	1	.5	0	.0	0	.0	2	1.0	195	99.0	197
1976 (11 INSTITUTIONS)	9	1.0	6	.7	0	.0	5	.6	20	2.3	859	97.7	879
% CHANGE 1974 TO 1976	800.0		500.0		.0		100.0		900.0		340.5		346.2
1978 (13 INSTITUTIONS)	1	.1	13	1.2	3	.3	6	.5	23	2.1	1,084	97.9	1,107
% CHANGE 1976 TO 1978	- 88.9		116.7		100.0		20.0		15.0		26.2		25.9
MALE													
1974 (7 INSTITUTIONS)	7	.7	15	1.4	0	.0	5	.5	27	2 6	1,028	97.4	1,055
1976 (11 INSTITUTIONS)	7	.4	30	1.8	1	.1	8	.5	46	2±7	1,648	97.3	1,694
% CHANGE 1974 TO 1976	.0		100.0		100.0		60.0		70.4		60.3		60.6
1978 (13 INSTITUTIONS)	5	.3	19	1.0	2	.1	15	.8	41	2.2	1,852	97.8	1,893
% CHANGE 1976 TO 1978	- 28.6		- 36.7		100.0		87.5		- 10.9		12.4		11.7
IRGINIA													
FEMALE													
1974 (52 INSTITUTIONS)	13	.3	1,462	32.2	29	.6	17	.4	1,521	33.5	3,013	66.5	4,534
1976 (56 INSTITUTIONS)	12	.2	2,215	30.2	43	.6	19	.3	2,289	31.2	5,039	68.8	7,328
% CHANGE 1974 TO 1976	- 7.7		51.5		48.3		11.8		50.5		67.2		61.6
1978 (57 INSTITUTIONS)	19	.2	2,504	23.5	103	1.0	50	.5	2,676	25.2	7,961	74.8	10,637
% CHANGE 1976 TO 1978	58.3		13.0		139.5		163.2		16.9		58.0		45.2
MALE													
1974 (52 INSTITUTIONS)	39	.3	1,877	15.5	60	.5	38	.3	2,014	16.7	10,059	83.3	12,073
1976 (56 INSTITUTIONS)	24	.2	2,551	17.1	73	.5	48	.3	2,696	18.1	12,192	81.9	14,888
% CHANGE 1974 TO 1976	- 38.5		35.9		21.7		26.3		33.9		21.2		23.3
1978 (57 INSTITUTIONS)	22	.1	2,541	15.8	119	.7	83	.5	2,765	17.2	13,283	82.8	16,048
% CHANGE 1976 TO 1978	- 8.3		.4		63.0		72.9		2.6		8.9		7.8
ASHINGTON													
FEMALE													
1974 (18 INSTITUTIONS)	11	.7	41	2.6	177	11.2	9	.6	238	15.0	1,348	85.0	1,586
1976 (13 INSTITUTIONS)	21	.9	67	3.0	107	4.8	17	.8	212	9.5	2,023	90.5	2,235
% CHANGE 1974 TO 1976	90.9		63.4		- 39.5		88.9		- 10.9		50.1		40.9
1978 (16 INSTITUTIONS)	19	.6	87	2.8	158	5.2	21	.7	285	9.3	2,779	90.7	3,064
% CHANGE 1976 TO 1978	- 9.5		29.9		47.7		23.5		34.4		37.4		37.1
MALE													
1974 (18 INSTITUTIONS)	29	.5	119	2.0	221	3.6	32	.5	401	6.6	5,680	93.4	6,081
1976 (13 INSTITUTIONS)	42	.7	109	1.9	176	3.1	22	.4	349	6.2	5,256	93.8	5,605
% CHANGE 1974 TO 1976	44.8		- 8.4		- 20.4		- 31.3		- 13.0		- 7.5		- 7.8
1978 (16 INSTITUTIONS)	44	.7	171	2.6	228	3.5	44	.7	487	7.4	6,117	92.6	6,604
% CHANGE 1976 TO 1978	4.8		56.9		29.5		100.0		39.5		16.4		17.8

MAJOR FIELD 0500 - BUSINESS AND MANAGEMENT

	AMERICAN INDIAN ALASKAN NATIVE		BLACK NON-HISPANIC		ASIAN OR PACIFIC ISLANDER		HISPANIC		TOTAL MINORITY		WHITE NON-HISPANIC	
	NUMBER	%	NUMBER	%	NUMBER	%	NUMBER	%	NUMBER	%	NUMBER	%
WEST VIRGINIA												
FEMALE												
1974 (19 INSTITUTIONS)	3	.2	91	7.2	2	.2	1	.1	97	7.6	1,174	92.4
1976 (21 INSTITUTIONS)	3	.1	152	6.2	21	.8	9	.4	185	7.5	2,286	92.5
% CHANGE 1974 TO 1976	.0		67.0		950.0		800.0		90.7		94.7	
1978 (22 INSTITUTIONS)	6	.1	242	5.8	15	.4	5	.1	268	6.4	3,900	93.6
% CHANGE 1976 TO 1978	100.0		59.2		- 28.6		- 44.4		44.9		70.6	
MALE												
1974 (19 INSTITUTIONS)	12	.2	281	5.1	8	.1	14	.3	315	5.7	5,207	94.3
1976 (21 INSTITUTIONS)	6	.1	352	5.8	28	.5	12	.2	398	6.5	5,688	93.5
% CHANGE 1974 TO 1976	- 50.0		25.3		250.0		- 14.3		26.3		9.2	
1978 (22 INSTITUTIONS)	17	.2	362	4.7	44	.6	11	.1	434	5.6	7,299	94.4
% CHANGE 1976 TO 1978	183.3		2.8		57.1		- 8.3		9.0		28.3	
WISCONSIN												
FEMALE												
1974 (23 INSTITUTIONS)	9	.4	116	4.5	16	.6	13	.5	154	6.0	2,415	94.0
1976 (33 INSTITUTIONS)	40	.6	237	3.3	30	.4	45	.6	352	4.8	6,920	95.2
% CHANGE 1974 TO 1976	344.4		104.3.		87.5		246.2		128.6		186.5	
1978 (39 INSTITUTIONS)	40	.4	406	4.1	47	.5	47	.5	540	5.5	9,354	94.5
% CHANGE 1976 TO 1978	.0		71.3		56.7		4.4		53.4		35.2	
MALE												
1974 (23 INSTITUTIONS)	28	.2	274	2.2	28	.2	41	.3	371	3.0	11,915	97.0
1976 (33 INSTITUTIONS)	46	.2	334	2.0	47	.3	81	.5	508	3.1	16,075	96.9
% CHANGE 1974 TO 1976	64.3		21.9		67.9		97.6		36.9		34.9	
1978 (39 INSTITUTIONS)	36	.2	459	2.6	77	.4	116	.7	688	3.9	17,142	96.1
% CHANGE 1976 TO 1978	- 21.7		37.4		63.8		43.2		35.4		6.6	
WYOMING												
FEMALE												
1974 (7 INSTITUTIONS)	5	1.5	4	1.2	6	1.8	17	5.1	32	9.6	303	90.4
1976 (6 INSTITUTIONS)	11	2.3	3	.6	10	2.0	6	1.2	30	6.1	458	93.9
% CHANGE 1974 TO 1976	120.0		- 25.0		66.7		- 64.7		- 6.3		51.2	
1978 (6 INSTITUTIONS)	6	.8	5	.7	8	1.1	25	3.3	44	5.8	710	94.2
% CHANGE 1976 TO 1978	- 45.5		66.7		- 20.0		316.7		46.7		55.0	
MALE												
1974 (7 INSTITUTIONS)	3	.5	7	1.1	4	.7	20	3.3	34	5.6	577	94.4
1976 (6 INSTITUTIONS)	2	.2	17	1.5	2	.2	18	1.6	39	3.5	1,077	96.5
% CHANGE 1974 TO 1976	- 33.3		142.9		- 50.0		- 10.0		14.7		86.7	
1978 (6 INSTITUTIONS)	0	.0	22	2.2	3	.3	21	2.1	46	4.7	932	95.3
% CHANGE 1976 TO 1978	- 100.0		29.4		50.0		16.7		17.9		- 13.5	-
THE STATES AND D.C.												
FEMALE												
1974 (1569 INSTITUTIONS)	1,371	.6	36,205	15.6	4,394	1.9	7,538	3.2	49,508	21.3	182,959	78.7
1976 (1820 INSTITUTIONS)	2,972	.7	59,184	14.3	8,335	2.0	14,441	3.5	84,932	20.5	329,843	79.5
% CHANGE 1974 TO 1976	116.8		63.5		89.7		91.6		71.6		80.3	
1978 (1941 INSTITUTIONS)	3,366	.6	76,111	13.4	11,107	2.0	17,762	3.1	108,346	19.1	458,025	80.9
% CHANGE 1976 TO 1978	13.3		28.6		33.3		23.0		27.6		38.9	
MALE												
1974 (1569 INSTITUTIONS)	2,894	.4	50,332	7.3	8,228	1.2	17,069	2.5	78,523	11.3	614,015	88.7
1976 (1820 INSTITUTIONS)	3,794	.5	66,050	7.9	13,005	1.6	23,355	2.8	106,204	12.7	730,944	87.3
% CHANGE 1974 TO 1976	31.1		31.2		58.1		58.1		35.3		19.0	
1978 (1941 INSTITUTIONS)	3,629	.4	70,252	8.0	14,230	1.6	23,260	2.7	111,371	12.8	761,716	87.2
% CHANGE 1976 TO 1978	- 4.3		6.4		9.4		9.4		4.9		4.2	

AND MANAGEMENT

ICAN INDIAN SKAN NATIVE		BLACK NON-HISPANIC		ASIAN OR PACIFIC ISLANDER		HISPANIC		TOTAL MINORITY		WHITE NON-HISPANIC		TOTAL
NUMBER	%	NUMBER	%	NUMBER	%	NUMBER	%	NUMBER	%	NUMBER	%	NUMBER
0	.0	0	.0	0	.0	0	.0	0	.0	0	.0	0
0	.0	8	.0	138	97.9	0	.0	138	97.9	3	2.1	141
	.0		.0		100.0		.0		100.0		100.0	100.0
0	.0	1	.8	125	96.2	0	.0	126	96.9	4	3.1	130
	.0		100.0	-	9.4		.0	-	8.7		33.3	- 7.8
0	.0	0	.0	0	.0	0	.0	0	.0	0	.0	0
0	.0	0	.0	100	97.1	0	.0	100	97.1	3	2.9	103
	.0		.0		100.0		.0		100.0		100.0	100.0
0	.0	0	.0	67	98.5	0	.0	67	98.5	1	1.5	68
	.0		.0	-	33.0		.0	-	33.0	-	66.7	- 34.0
0	.0	0	.0	0	.0	0	.0	0	.0	0	.0	0
0	.0	13	9.7	0	.0	33	24.6	46	34.3	88	65.7	134
	.0		100.0		.0		100.0		100.0		100.0	100.0
0	.0	0	.0	0	.0	0	.0	0	.0	0	.0	0
	.0	-	100.0		.0	-	100.0	-	100.0	-	100.0	- 100.0
0	.0	0	.0	0	.0	0	.0	0	.0	0	.0	0
0	.0	13	9.2	0	.0	36	25.4	49	34.5	93	65.5	142
	.0		100.0		.0		100.0		100.0		100.0	100.0
0	.0	0	.0	0	.0	0	.0	0	.0	0	.0	0
	.0	-	100.0		.0	-	100.0	-	100.0	-	100.0	- 100.0
0	.0	0	.0	0	.0	0	.0	0	.0	0	.0	0
3	1.2	0	.0	200	80.6	5	2.0	208	83.9	40	16.1	248
100.0			.0		100.0		100.0		100.0		100.0	100.0
0	.0	1	.6	159	87.8	4	2.2	164	90.6	17	9.4	181
100.0			100.0	-	20.5	-	20.0	-	21.2	-	57.5	- 27.0
0	.0	0	.0	0	.0	0	.0	0	.0	0	.0	0
5	1.6	0	.0	222	70.9	19	6.1	246	78.6	67	21.4	313
100.0			.0		100.0		100.0		100.0		100.0	100.0
1	.6	1	.6	130	74.3	6	3.4	138	78.9	37	21.1	175
80.0			100.0	-	41.4	-	68.4	-	43.9	-	44.8	- 44.1
0	.0	0	.0	0	.0	0	.0	0	.0	0	.0	0
0	.0	0	.0	0	.0	6,233	100.0	6,233	100.0	0	.0	6,233
	.0		.0		.0		100.0		100.0		.0	100.0
0	.0	0	.0	1	.0	15,276	99.7	15,277	99.7	40	.3	15,317
	.0		.0		100.0		145.1		145.1		100.0	145.7
0	.0	0	.0	0	.0	0	.0	0	.0	0	.0	0
0	.0	0	.0	0	.0	7,360	100.0	7,360	100.0	0	.0	7,360
	.0		.0		.0		100.0		100.0		.0	100.0
0	.0	0	.0	0	.0	16,310	99.7	16,310	99.7	55	.3	16,365
	.0		.0		.0		121.6		121.6		100.0	122.4

TABLE 18 - COMPARISIONS OF ENROLLMENT IN INSTITUTIONS OF HIGHER EDUCATION FOR SELECTED FIELDS OF STUDY AND LEVEL OF ENROLLM
         BY RACE, ETHNICITY AND SEX: STATE 1974, 1976, 1978

MAJOR FIELD 0500 - BUSINESS AND MANAGEMENT

	AMERICAN INDIAN ALASKAN NATIVE		BLACK NON-HISPANIC		ASIAN OR PACIFIC ISLANDER		HISPANIC		TOTAL MINORITY		WHITE NON-HISPANIC	
	NUMBER	%	NUMBER	%	NUMBER	%	NUMBER	%	NUMBER	%	NUMBER	%
TRUST TERRITORY												
FEMALE												
1974 (0 INSTITUTIONS)	0	.0	0	.0	0	.0	0	.0	0	.0	0	.0
1976 (1 INSTITUTIONS)	0	.0	0	.0	3	100.0	0	.0	3	100.0	0	.0
% CHANGE 1974 TO 1976	.0		.0		100.0		.0		100.0		.0	
1978 (1 INSTITUTIONS)	0	.0	0	.0	10	100.0	0	.0	10	100.0	0	.0
% CHANGE 1976 TO 1978	.0		.0		233.3		.0		233.3		.0	
MALE												
1974 (0 INSTITUTIONS)	0	.0	0	.0	0	.0	0	.0	0	.0	0	.0
1976 (1 INSTITUTIONS)	0	.0	0	.0	15	100.0	0	.0	15	100.0	0	.0
% CHANGE 1974 TO 1976	.0		.0		100.0		.0		100.0		.0	
1978 (1 INSTITUTIONS)	0	.0	0	.0	17	100.0	0	.0	17	100.0	0	.0
% CHANGE 1976 TO 1978	.0		.0		13.3		.0		13.3		.0	
VIRGIN ISLANDS.												
FEMALE												
1974 (0 INSTITUTIONS)	0	.0	0	.0	0	.0	0	.0	0	.0	0	.0
1976 (1 INSTITUTIONS)	0	.0	60	83.3	0	.0	8	11.1	68	94.4	4	5.6
% CHANGE 1974 TO 1976	.0		100.0		.0		100.0		100.0		100.0	
1978 (1 INSTITUTIONS)	0	.0	73	88.0	0	.0	6	7.2	79	95.2	4	4.8
% CHANGE 1976 TO 1978	.0		21.7		.0		- 25.0		16.2		.0	
MALE												
1974 (0 INSTITUTIONS)	0	.0	0	.0	0	.0	0	.0	0	.0	0	.0
1976 (1 INSTITUTIONS)	0	.0	30	69.8	0	.0	5	11.6	35	81.4	8	18.6
% CHANGE 1974 TO 1976	.0		100.0		.0		100.0		100.0		100.0	
1978 (1 INSTITUTIONS)	0	.0	33	60.0	1	1.8	5	9.1	39	70.9	16	29.1
% CHANGE 1976 TO 1978	.0		10.0		100.0		.0		11.4		100.0	
OUTLYING AREAS.												
FEMALE												
1974 (0 INSTITUTIONS)	0	.0	0	.0	0	.0	0	.0	0	.0	0	.0
1976 (15 INSTITUTIONS)	3	.0	73	1.1	341	5.0	6,279	91.9	6,696	98.0	135	2.0
% CHANGE 1974 TO 1976	100.0		100.0		100.0		100.0		100.0		100.0	
1978 (32 INSTITUTIONS)	0	.0	75	.5	295	1.9	15,286	97.2	15,656	99.6	65	.4
% CHANGE 1976 TO 1978	- 100.0		2.7		- 13.5		143.4		133.8		- 51.9	
MALE												
1974 (0 INSTITUTIONS)	0	.0	0	.0	0	.0	0	.0	0	.0	0	.0
1976 (15 INSTITUTIONS)	5	.1	43	.5	337	4.2	7,420	93.0	7,805	97.9	171	2.1
% CHANGE 1974 TO 1976	100.0		100.0		100.0		100.0		100.0		100.0	
1978 (32 INSTITUTIONS)	1	.0	34	.2	215	1.3	16,321	97.8	16,571	99.3	109	.7
% CHANGE 1976 TO 1978	- 80.0		- 20.9		- 36.2		- 36.2		112.3		- 36.3	
MAJOR FIELD AGGREGATE 0500.												
FEMALE												
1974 (1569 INSTITUTIONS)	1,371	.6	36,205	15.6	4,394	1.9	7,538	3.2	49,508	21.3	182,959	78.7
1976 (1835 INSTITUTIONS)	2,975	.7	59,257	14.1	8,676	2.1	20,720	4.9	91,628	21.7	329,978	78.3
% CHANGE 1974 TO 1976	117.0		63.7		97.5		174.9		85.1		80.4	
1978 (1973 INSTITUTIONS)	3,366	.6	76,186	13.1	11,402	2.0	33,048	5.7	124,002	21.3	458,090	78.7
% CHANGE 1976 TO 1978	13.1		28.6		31.4		59.5		35.3		38.8	
MALE												
1974 (1569 INSTITUTIONS)	2,894	.4	50,332	7.3	8,228	1.2	17,069	2.5	78,523	11.3	614,015	88.7
1976 (1835 INSTITUTIONS)	3,799	.4	66,093	7.8	13,342	1.6	30,775	3.6	114,009	13.5	731,115	86.5
% CHANGE 1974 TO 1976	31.3		31.3		62.2		62.2		45.2		19.1	
1978 (1973 INSTITUTIONS)	3,630	.4	70,286	7.9	14,445	1.6	39,581	4.4	127,942	14.4	761,825	85.6
% CHANGE 1976 TO 1978	- 4.4		6.3		8.3		8.3		12.2		4.2	

DIAN TIVE	BLACK NON-HISPANIC		ASIAN OR PACIFIC ISLANDER		HISPANIC		TOTAL MINORITY		WHITE NON-HISPANIC		TOTAL
%	NUMBER	%	NUMBER	%	NUMBER	%	NUMBER	%	NUMBER	%	NUMBER
.0	3	30.0	0	.0	0	.0	3	30.0	7	70.0	10
.0	3	8.8	0	.0	0	.0	3	8.8	31	91.2	34
	.0		.0		.0		.0		342.9		240.0
.0	6	12.8	4	8.5	0	.0	10	21.3	37	78.7	47
	100.0		100.0		.0		233.3		19.4		38.2
.0	8	3.9	0	.0	0	.0	8	3.9	197	96.1	205
.0	9	3.7	4	1.7	0	.0	13	5.4	228	94.6	241
	12.5		100.0		.0		62.5		15.7		17.6
.0	10	4.0	3	1.2	0	.0	13	5.2	236	94.8	249
	11.1	-	25.0		.0		.0		3.5		3.3
.0	3	7.7	0	.0	0	.0	3	7.7	36	92.3	39
.0	0	.0	0	.0	0	.0	0	.0	0	.0	0
-	100.0		.0		.0	-	100.0	-	100.0	-	100.0
.0	0	.0	0	.0	0	.0	0	.0	0	.0	0
	.0		.0		.0		.0		.0		.0
.0	1	2.0	0	.0	0	.0	1	2.0	50	98.0	51
.0	0	.0	0	.0	0	.0	0	.0	0	.0	0
-	100.0		.0		.0	-	100.0	-	100.0	-	100.0
.0	0	.0	0	.0	0	.0	0	.0	0	.0	0
	.0		.0		.0		.0		.0		.0
.9	16	3.6	31	7.0	34	7.7	85	19.2	357	80.8	442
.9	24	11.2	34	15.8	14	6.5	74	34.4	141	65.6	215
	50.0		9.7	-	58.8	, -	12.9	-	60.5	-	51.4
.0	39	13.0	60	20.0	25	8.3	124	41.3	176	58.7	300
	62.5		76.5		78.6		67.6		24.9		39.5
.7	66	4.4	143	9.4	99	6.5	318	21.0	1,197	79.0	1,515
1.3	40	3.1	214	16.5	118	9.1	389	30.1	905	69.9	1,294
	-	39.4		49.7		19.2		22.3	-	24.4	-	14.6
.7	37	2.2	282	17.1	138	8.4	468	28.4	1,180	71.6	1,648
	7.5		31.8		16.9		20.3		30.4		27.4
.0	0	.0	0	.0	1	25.0	1	25.0	3	75.0	4
.0	1	12.5	0	.0	1	12.5	2	25.0	6	75.0	8
	100.0		.0		.0		100.0		100.0		100.0
.0	1	7.7	1	7.7	1	7.7	3	23.1	10	76.9	13
	.0		100.0		.0		50.0		66.7		62.5
2.2	0	.0	2	4.3	4	8.7	7	15.2	39	84.8	46
.0	1	1.1	4	4.5	8	9.0	13	14.6	76	85.4	89
	100.0		100.0		100.0		85.7		94.9		93.5
.0	1	1.1	3	3.4	5	5.7	9	10.2	79	89.8	88
	.0	-	25.0	-	37.5	-	30.8		3.9	-	1.1

745

TABLE 18 - COMPARISIONS OF ENROLLMENT IN INSTITUTIONS OF HIGHER EDUCATION FOR SELECTED FIELDS OF STUDY AND LEVEL OF ENROLLMENT
BY RACE, ETHNICITY AND SEX: STATE 1974, 1976, 1978

MAJOR FIELD 1204 - DENTISTRY

	AMERICAN INDIAN ALASKAN NATIVE		BLACK NON-HISPANIC		ASIAN OR PACIFIC ISLANDER		HISPANIC		TOTAL MINORITY		WHITE NON-HISPANIC		TOTAL
	NUMBER	%	NUMBER	%	NUMBER	%	NUMBER	%	NUMBER	%	NUMBER	%	NUMBER
CONNECTICUT · · · · · · · ·													
FEMALE													
1974 (1 INSTITUTIONS)	0	.0	2	10.5	0	.0	0	.0	2	10.5	17	89.5	19
1976 (1 INSTITUTIONS)	0	.0	2	7.7	0	.0	0	.0	2	7.7	24	92.3	26
% CHANGE 1974 TO 1976	.0		.0		.0		.0		.0		41.2		36.8
1978 (1 INSTITUTIONS)	0	.0	0	.0	0	.0	0	.0	0	.0	30	100.0	30
% CHANGE 1976 TO 1978	.0		- 100.0		.0		.0		- 100.0		25.0		15.4
MALE													
1974 (1 INSTITUTIONS)	0	.0	1	.9	0	.0	0	.0	1	.9	106	99.1	107
1976 (1 INSTITUTIONS)	0	.0	2	1.4	2	1.4	0	.0	4	2.8	139	97.2	143
% CHANGE 1974 TO 1976	.0		100.0		100.0		.0		300.0		31.1		33.6
1978 (1 INSTITUTIONS)	0	.0	1	.6	2	1.2	0	.0	3	1.9	158	98.1	161
% CHANGE 1976 TO 1978	.0		- 50.0		.0		.0		- 25.0		13.7		12.6
DISTRICT OF COLUMBIA. · · ·													
FEMALE													
1974 (2 INSTITUTIONS)	0	.0	61	74.4	0	.0	0	.0	61	74.4	21	25.6	82
1976 (2 INSTITUTIONS)	0	.0	55	57.9	2	2.1	3	3.2	60	63.2	35	36.8	95
% CHANGE 1974 TO 1976	.0		- 9.8		100.0		100.0		- 1.6		66.7		15.9
1978 (2 INSTITUTIONS)	0	.0	73	59.3	5	4.1	2	1.6	80	65.0	43	35.0	123
% CHANGE 1976 TO 1978	.0		32.7		150.0		- 33.3		33.3		22.9		29.5
MALE													
1974 (2 INSTITUTIONS)	0	.0	230	27.0	13	1.5	4	.5	247	29.0	604	71.0	851
1976 (2 INSTITUTIONS)	2	.3	159	20.8	18	2.3	7	.9	186	24.3	580	75.7	766
% CHANGE 1974 TO 1976	100.0		- 30.9		38.5		75.0		- 24.7		- 4.0		- 10.0
1978 (2 INSTITUTIONS)	2	.3	173	21.7	21	2.6	7	.9	203	25.4	596	74.6	799
% CHANGE 1976 TO 1978	.0		8.8		16.7		.0		9.1		2.8		4.3
FLORIDA · · · · · · · · · ·													
FEMALE													
1974 (8 INSTITUTIONS)	0	.0	1	4.3	0	.0	1	4.3	2	8.7	21	91.3	23
1976 (1 INSTITUTIONS)	0	.0	1	4.5	0	.0	1	4.5	2	9.1	20	90.9	22
% CHANGE 1974 TO 1976	.0		.0		.0		.0		.0		- 4.8		- 4.3
1978 (1 INSTITUTIONS)	0	.0	0	.0	0	.0	4	10.3	4	10.3	35	89.7	39
% CHANGE 1976 TO 1978	.0		- 100.0		.0		300.0		100.0		75.0		77.3
MALE													
1974 (8 INSTITUTIONS)	0	.0	4	3.1	0	.0	4	3.1	8	6.1	123	93.9	131
1976 (1 INSTITUTIONS)	1	.6	2	1.3	0	.0	9	5.7	12	7.5	147	92.5	159
% CHANGE 1974 TO 1976	100.0		- 50.0		.0		125.0		50.0		19.5		21.4
1978 (1 INSTITUTIONS)	1	.5	5	2.5	1	.5	7	3.5	14	7.0	186	93.0	200
% CHANGE 1976 TO 1978	.0		150.0		100.0		- 22.2		16.7		26.5		25.8
GEORGIA · · · · · · · · · ·													
FEMALE													
1974 (8 INSTITUTIONS)	0	.0	5	11.6	0	.0	0	.0	5	11.6	38	88.4	43
1976 (2 INSTITUTIONS)	0	.0	7	14.0	0	.0	1	2.0	8	16.0	42	84.0	50
% CHANGE 1974 TO 1976	.0		40.0		.0		100.0		60.0		10.5		16.3
1978 (2 INSTITUTIONS)	0	.0	8	14.5	0	.0	2	3.6	10	18.2	45	81.8	55
% CHANGE 1976 TO 1978	.0		14.3		.0		100.0		25.0		7.1		10.0
MALE													
1974 (8 INSTITUTIONS)	2	.3	20	3.1	7	1.1	4	.6	33	5.2	607	94.8	640
1976 (2 INSTITUTIONS)	0	.0	16	2.8	5	.9	2	.3	23	4.0	550	96.0	573
% CHANGE 1974 TO 1976	- 100.0		- 20.0		- 28.6		- 50.0		- 30.3		- 9.4		- 10.5
1978 (2 INSTITUTIONS)	1	.2	9	1.7	4	.7	2	.4	16	3.0	522	97.0	538
% CHANGE 1976 TO 1978	100.0		- 43.8		- 20.0		.0		- 30.4		- 5.1		- 6.1

ELD 1204 - DENTISTRY

	AMERICAN INDIAN ALASKAN NATIVE		BLACK NON-HISPANIC		ASIAN OR PACIFIC ISLANDER		HISPANIC		TOTAL MINORITY		WHITE NON-HISPANIC		TOTAL
	NUMBER	%	NUMBER	%	NUMBER	%	NUMBER	%	NUMBER	%	NUMBER	%	NUMBER
. . . .													
1 INSTITUTIONS)	0	.0	0	.0	0	.0	0	.0	0	.0	3	100.0	3
0 INSTITUTIONS)	0	.0	0	.0	0	.0	0	.0	0	.0	0	.0	0
GE 1974 TO 1976	.0		.0		.0		.0		.0		- 100.0		- 100.0
0 INSTITUTIONS)	0	.0	0	.0	0	.0	0	.0	0	.0	0	.0	0
GE 1976 TO 1978	.0		.0		.0		.0		.0		.0		.0
1 INSTITUTIONS)	0	.0	2	9.5	0	.0	1	4.8	3	14.3	18	85.7	21
0 INSTITUTIONS)	0	.0	0	.0	0	.0	0	.0	0	.0	0	.0	0
GE 1974 TO 1976	.0		- 100.0		.0		- 100.0		- 100.0		- 100.0		- 100.0
0 INSTITUTIONS)	0	.0	0	.0	0	.0	0	.0	0	.0	0	.0	0
GE 1976 TO 1978	.0		.0		.0		.0		.0		.0		.0
. . . .													
6 INSTITUTIONS)	1	1.2	6	7.4	3	3.7	3	3.7	13	16.0	68	84.0	81
4 INSTITUTIONS)	0	.0	10	5.9	7	4.1	4	2.4	21	12.4	148	87.6	169
GE 1974 TO 1976	- 100.0		66.7		133.3		33.3		61.5		117.6		108.6
4 INSTITUTIONS)	0	.0	17	7.6	6	2.7	2	.9	25	11.2	199	88.8	224
GE 1976 TO 1978	.0		70.0		- 14.3		- 50.0		19.0		34.5		32.5
6 INSTITUTIONS)	0	.0	22	1.5	46	3.2	7	.5	75	5.2	1,363	94.8	1,438
4 INSTITUTIONS)	5	.3	16	1.1	48	3.4	8	.6	77	5.4	1,352	94.6	1,429
GE 1974 TO 1976	100.0		- 27.3		4.3		14.3		2.7		- .8		- .6
4 INSTITUTIONS)	2	.1	18	1.2	38	2.6	11	.8	69	4.7	1,384	95.3	1,453
GE 1976 TO 1978	- 60.0		12.5		- 20.8		37.5		- 10.4		2.4		1.7
. . . .													
4 INSTITUTIONS)	0	.0	1	2.9	0	.0	0	.0	1	2.9	33	97.1	34
5 INSTITUTIONS)	1	1.6	2	3.1	0	.0	0	.0	3	4.7	61	95.3	64
GE 1974 TO 1976	100.0		100.0		.0		.0		200.0		84.8		88.2
1 INSTITUTIONS)	0	.0	2	2.8	1	1.4	0	.0	3	4.2	68	95.8	71
GE 1976 TO 1978	- 100.0		.0		100.0		.0		.0		11.5		10.9
4 INSTITUTIONS)	1	.2	6	1.1	4	.8	1	.2	12	2.	519	97.7	531
5 INSTITUTIONS)	1	.2	5	.9	3	.5	5	.9	14	2.5	548	97.5	562
GE 1974 TO 1976	.0		- 16.7		- 25.0		400.0		16.7		5.6		5.8
1 INSTITUTIONS)	1	.2	4	.7	9	1.7	2	.4	16	3.0	519	97.0	535
GE 1976 TO 1978	.0		- 20.0		200.0		- 60.0		14.3		- 5.3		- 4.8
. 1													
1 INSTITUTIONS)	0	.0	1	2.0	0	.0	0	.0	1	2.0	49	98.0	50
1 INSTITUTIONS)	0	.0	2	4.8	1	2.4	0	.0	3	7.1	39	92.9	42
GE 1974 TO 1976	.0		100.0		100.0		.0		200.0		- 20.4		- 16.0
1 INSTITUTIONS)	1	2.1	1	2.1	2	4.2	1	2.1	5	10.4	43	89.6	48
GE 1976 TO 1978	100.0		- 50.0		100.0		100.0		66.7		10.3		14.3
1 INSTITUTIONS)	2	.4	3	.6	1	.2	0	.0	6	1.1	536	98.9	542
1 INSTITUTIONS)	3	.9	6	1.9	2	.6	3	.9	14	4.3	308	95.7	322
GE 1974 TO 1976	50.0		100.0		100.0		100.0		133.3		- 42.5		- 40.6
1 INSTITUTIONS)	5	1.5	4	1.2	4	1.2	3	.9	16	4.9	313	95.1	329
GE 1976 TO 1978	66.7		- 33.3		100.0		.0		14.3		1.6		2.2

TABLE 18 - COMPARISIONS OF ENROLLMENT IN INSTITUTIONS OF HIGHER EDUCATION FOR SELECTED FIELDS OF STUDY AND LEVEL OF ENROLLME
         BY RACE, ETHNICITY AND SEX: STATE 1974, 1976, 1978

MAJOR FIELD 1204 - DENTISTRY

	AMERICAN INDIAN ALASKAN NATIVE		BLACK NON-HISPANIC		ASIAN OR PACIFIC ISLANDER		HISPANIC		TOTAL MINORITY		WHITE NON-HISPANIC	
	NUMBER	%	NUMBER	%	NUMBER	%	NUMBER	%	NUMBER	%	NUMBER	%
KANSAS.												
FEMALE												
1974 (5 INSTITUTIONS)	1	1.0	3	2.9	0	.0	1	1.0	5	4.8	100	95.2
1976 (0 INSTITUTIONS)	0	.0	0	.0	0	.0	0	.0	0	.0	0	.0
% CHANGE 1974 TO 1976	- 100.0		- 100.0		.0		- 100.0		- 100.0		- 100.0	-
1978 (0 INSTITUTIONS)	0	.0	0	.0	0	.0	0	.0	0	.0	0	.0
% CHANGE 1976 TO 1978	.0		.0		.0		.0		.0		.0	
MALE												
1974 (0 INSTITUTIONS)	0	.0	1	5.0	0	.0	1	5.0	2	10.0	18	90.0
1976 (0 INSTITUTIONS)	0	.0	0	.0	0	.0	0	.0	0	.0	0	.0
% CHANGE 1974 TO 1976	.0		- 100.0		.0		- 100.0		- 100.0		- 100.0	-
1978 (0 INSTITUTIONS)	0	.0	0	.0	0	.0	0	.0	0	.0	0	.0
% CHANGE 1976 TO 1978	.0		.0		.0		.0		.0		.0	
KENTUCKY.												
FEMALE												
1974 (2 INSTITUTIONS)	0	.0	2	5.3	0	.0	0	.0	2	5.3	36	94.7
1976 (2 INSTITUTIONS)	0	.0	6	8.7	0	.0	0	.0	6	8.7	63	91.3
% CHANGE 1974 TO 1976	.0		200.0		.0		.0		200.0		75.0	
1978 (2 INSTITUTIONS)	0	.0	8	7.5	0	.0	0	.0	8	7.5	99	92.5
% CHANGE 1976 TO 1978	.0		33.3		.0		.0		33.3		57.1	
MALE												
1974 (2 INSTITUTIONS)	3	.6	12	2.5	3	.6	2	.4	20	4.1	467	95.9
1976 (2 INSTITUTIONS)	1	.2	7	1.4	1	.2	1	.2	10	2.0	489	98.0
% CHANGE 1974 TO 1976	- 66.7		- 41.7		- 66.7		- 50.0		- 50.0		4.7	
1978 (2 INSTITUTIONS)	0	.0	5	1.0	3	.6	0	.0	8	1.7	472	98.3
% CHANGE 1976 TO 1978	- 100.0		- 28.6		200.0		- 100.0		- 20.0		- 3.5	-
LOUISIANA												
FEMALE												
1974 (1 INSTITUTIONS)	0	.0	1	5.9	0	.0	0	.0	1	5.9	16	94.1
1976 (1 INSTITUTIONS)	0	.0	1	3.6	0	.0	0	.0	1	3.6	27	96.4
% CHANGE 1974 TO 1976	.0		.0		.0		.0		.0		68.8	
1978 (1 INSTITUTIONS)	0	.0	1	2.4	0	.0	1	2.4	2	4.9	39	95.1
% CHANGE 1976 TO 1978	.0		.0		.0		100.0		100.0		44.4	
MALE												
1974 (1 INSTITUTIONS)	0	.0	2	.6	0	.0	2	.6	4	1.2	337	98.8
1976 (1 INSTITUTIONS)	0	.0	3	.9	0	.0	0	.0	3	.9	337	99.1
% CHANGE 1974 TO 1976	.0		50.0		.0		- 100.0		- 25.0		.0	
1978 (1 INSTITUTIONS)	1	.3	4	1.2	0	.0	0	.0	5	1.6	316	98.4
% CHANGE 1976 TO 1978	100.0		33.3		.0		.0		66.7		- 6.2	
MARYLAND.												
FEMALE												
1974 (2 INSTITUTIONS)	0	.0	6	15.8	3	7.9	0	.0	9	23.7	29	76.3
1976 (1 INSTITUTIONS)	0	.0	12	21.4	2	3.6	1	1.8	15	26.8	41	73.2
% CHANGE 1974 TO 1976	.0		100.0		- 33.3		100.0		66.7		41.4	
1978 (1 INSTITUTIONS)	0	.0	13	15.3	4	4.7	1	1.2	18	21.2	67	78.8
% CHANGE 1976 TO 1978	.0		8.3		100.0		.0		20.0		63.4	
MALE												
1974 (2 INSTITUTIONS)	2	.4	31	6.4	1	.2	0	.0	34	7.0	454	93.0
1976 (1 INSTITUTIONS)	0	.0	24	5.1	4	.8	4	.8	32	6.8	440	93.2
% CHANGE 1974 TO 1976	- 100.0		- 22.6		300.0		100.0		- 5.9		- 3.1	-
1978 (1 INSTITUTIONS)	0	.0	24	5.4	10	2.3	8	1.8	42	9.5	401	90.5
% CHANGE 1976 TO 1978	.0		.0		150.0		100.0		31.3		- 8.9	-

COMPARISIONS OF ENROLLMENT IN INSTITUTIONS OF HIGHER EDUCATION FOR SELECTED FIELDS OF STUDY AND LEVEL OF ENROLLMENT
BY RACE, ETHNICITY AND SEX: STATE 1974, 1976, 1978

D 1204 - DENTISTRY

	AMERICAN INDIAN ALASKAN NATIVE		BLACK NON-HISPANIC		ASIAN OR PACIFIC ISLANDER		HISPANIC		TOTAL MINORITY		WHITE NON-HISPANIC		TOTAL
	NUMBER	%	NUMBER	%	NUMBER	%	NUMBER	%	NUMBER	%	NUMBER	%	NUMBER
TTS													
3 INSTITUTIONS)	0	.0	9	10.3	5	5.7	4	4.6	18	20.7	69	79.3	87
3 INSTITUTIONS)	2	1.5	8	6.0	5	3.7	2	1.5	17	12.7	117	87.3	134
1974 TO 1976	100.0		- 11.1		.0		- 50.0		- 5.6		69.6		54.0
3 INSTITUTIONS)	0	.0	7	5.9	9	7.6	2	1.7	18	15.3	100	84.7	118
1976 TO 1978	- 100.0		- 12.5		80.0		.0		5.9		- 14.5		- 11.9
3 INSTITUTIONS)	2	.2	30	3.7	36	4.4	10	1.2	78	9.5	739	90.5	817
3 INSTITUTIONS)	4	.7	11	2.0	14	2.6	3	.5	32	5.8	517	94.2	549
1974 TO 1976	100.0		- 63.3		- 61.1		- 70.0		- 59.0		- 30.0		- 32.8
3 INSTITUTIONS)	2	.5	9	2.3	13	3.3	8	2.0	32	8.2	360	91.8	392
1976 TO 1978	- 50.0		- 18.2		- 7.1		166.7		.0		- 30.4		- 28.6
. . . .													
8 INSTITUTIONS)	1	1.3	12	15.4	0	.0	0	.0	13	16.7	65	83.3	78
2 INSTITUTIONS)	0	.0	18	17.3	1	1.0	0	.0	19	18.3	85	81.7	104
1974 TO 1976	- 100.0		50.0		100.0		.0		46.2		30.8		33.3
2 INSTITUTIONS)	0	.0	19	15.3	2	1.6	1	.8	22	17.7	102	82.3	124
1976 TO 1978	.0		5.6		100.0		100.0		15.8		20.0		19.2
8 INSTITUTIONS)	0	.0	45	5.3	2	.2	3	.4	50	5.8	806	94.2	856
2 INSTITUTIONS)	2	.3	42	5.6	5	.7	1	.1	50	6.7	695	93.3	745
1974 TO 1976	100.0		- 6.7		150.0		- 66.7		.0		- 13.8		- 13.0
2 INSTITUTIONS)	1	.1	27	3.4	5	.6	3	.4	36	4.6	753	95.4	789
1976 TO 1978	- 50.0		- 35.7		.0		200.0		- 28.0		8.3		5.9
. . . .													
2 INSTITUTIONS)	1	2.4	3	7.1	0	.0	0	.0	4	9.5	38	90.5	42
1 INSTITUTIONS)	0	.0	0	.0	0	.0	0	.0	0	.0	41	100.0	41
1974 TO 1976	- 100.0		- 100.0		.0		.0		- 100.0		7.9		2.4
1 INSTITUTIONS)	1	1.5	1	1.5	0	.0	1	1.5	3	4.6	62	95.4	65
1976 TO 1978	100.0		100.0		.0		100.0		100.0		51.2		58.5
2 INSTITUTIONS)	5	.9	4	.7	3	.5	4	.7	16	2.7	569	97.3	585
1 INSTITUTIONS)	1	.2	3	.6	5	.9	6	1.1	15	2.8	515	97.2	530
1974 TO 1976	- 80.0		- 25.0		66.7		50.0		- 6.3		- 9.5		- 9.4
1 INSTITUTIONS)	0	.0	3	.6	4	.8	4	.8	11	2.2	493	97.8	504
1976 TO 1978	- 100.0		.0		- 20.0		- 33.3		- 26.7		- 4.3		- 4.9
. . . .													
7 INSTITUTIONS)	0	.0	0	.0	0	.0	1	9.1	1	9.1	10	90.9	11
1 INSTITUTIONS)	0	.0	1	25.0	0	.0	0	.0	1	25.0	3	75.0	4
1974 TO 1976	.0		100.0		.0		- 100.0		.0		- 70.0		- 63.6
1 INSTITUTIONS)	0	.0	4	33.3	1	8.3	0	.0	5	41.7	7	58.3	12
1976 TO 1978	.0		300.0		100.0		.0		400.0		133.3		200.0
7 INSTITUTIONS)	0	.0	0	.0	0	.0	0	.0	0	.0	22	100.0	22
1 INSTITUTIONS)	1	2.2	2	4.4	1	2.2	0	.0	4	8.9	41	91.1	45
1974 TO 1976	100.0		100.0		100.0		.0		100.0		86.4		104.5
1 INSTITUTIONS)	1	.9	10	8.8	2	1.8	0	.0	13	11.4	101	88.6	114
1976 TO 1978	.0		400.0		100.0		.0		225.0		146.3		153.3

TABLE 18 - COMPARISIONS OF ENROLLMENT IN INSTITUTIONS OF HIGHER EDUCATION FOR SELECTED FIELDS OF STUDY AND LEVEL OF ENROLLMENT
BY RACE, ETHNICITY AND SEX: STATE 1974, 1976, 1978

MAJOR FIELD 1204 - DENTISTRY

		AMERICAN INDIAN ALASKAN NATIVE		BLACK NON-HISPANIC		ASIAN OR PACIFIC ISLANDER		HISPANIC		TOTAL MINORITY		WHITE NON-HISPANIC		T
		NUMBER	%	NUMBER	%	NUMBER	%	NUMBER	%	NUMBER	%	NUMBER	%	NU
MISSOURI.														
FEMALE														
1974 (	2 INSTITUTIONS)	0	.0	5	13.5	0	.0	1	2.7		16.2	31	83.8	
1976 (	2 INSTITUTIONS)	1	1.7	2	3.4	4	6.9	1	1.7	8	13.8	50	86.2	
% CHANGE 1974 TO 1976		100.0		- 60.0		100.0		.0		33.3		61.3		56
1978 (	2 INSTITUTIONS)	0	.0	4	4.5	4	4.5	0	.0	8	9.1	80	90.9	
% CHANGE 1976 TO 1978		- 100.0		100.0		.0		- 100.0		.0		60.0		51
MALE														
1974 (	2 INSTITUTIONS)	3	.3	11	1.2	8	.9	10	1.1	32	3.5	891	96.5	
1976 (	2 INSTITUTIONS)	1	.1	16	1.9	16	1.9	9	1.1	42	5.1	785	94.9	
% CHANGE 1974 TO 1976		- 66.7		45.5		100.0		- 10.0		31.3		- 11.9		- 10
1978 (	2 INSTITUTIONS)	1	.1	14	1.7	28	3.4	15	1.8	58	7.0	767	93.0	
% CHANGE 1976 TO 1978		.0		- 12.5		75.0		66.7		38.1		- 2.3		-
NEBRASKA.														
FEMALE														
1974 (	1 INSTITUTIONS)	0	.0	0	.0	1	9.1	0	.0	1	9.1	10	90.9	
1976 (	3 INSTITUTIONS)	0	.0	2	6.5	1	3.2	0	.0	3	9.7	28	90.3	
% CHANGE 1974 TO 1976		.0		100.0		.0		.0		200.0		180.0		181
1978 (	2 INSTITUTIONS)	0	.0	4	4.8	1	1.2	0	.0	5	6.0	79	94.0	
% CHANGE 1976 TO 1978		.0		100.0		.0		.0		66.7		182.1		171
MALE														
1974 (	1 INSTITUTIONS)	0	.0	11	4.3	8	3.1	3	1.2	22	8.6	234	91.4	
1976 (	3 INSTITUTIONS)	4	.8	9	1.7	6	1.1	6	1.1	25	4.7	502	95.3	
% CHANGE 1974 TO 1976		100.0		- 18.2		- 25.0		100.0		13.6		114.5		105
1978 (	2 INSTITUTIONS)	2	.4	4	.8	8	1.5	8	1.5	22	4.2	498	95.8	
% CHANGE 1976 TO 1978		- 50.0		- 55.6		33.3		33.3		- 12.0		- .8		- 1
NEW JERSEY.														
FEMALE														
1974 (	1 INSTITUTIONS)	0	.0	0	.0	0	.0	0	.0	0	.0	22	100.0	
1976 (	1 INSTITUTIONS)	0	.0	1	3.3	0	.0	1	3.3	2	6.7	28	93.3	
% CHANGE 1974 TO 1976		.0		100.0		.0		100.0		100.0		27.3		36
1978 (	2 INSTITUTIONS)	1	1.3	11	14.3	0	.0	4	5.2	16	20.8	61	79.2	
% CHANGE 1976 TO 1978		100.0		1000.0		.0		300.0		700.0		117.9		156
MALE														
1974 (	1 INSTITUTIONS)	0	.0	10	3.4	3	1.0	2	.7	15	5.1	281	94.9	
1976 (	1 INSTITUTIONS)	0	.0	8	2.7	3	1.0	2	.7	13	4.4	285	95.6	
% CHANGE 1974 TO 1976		.0		- 20.0		.0		.0		- 13.3		1.4		
1978 (	2 INSTITUTIONS)	1	.2	25	4.9	5	1.0	7	1.4	38	7.5	469	92.5	
% CHANGE 1976 TO 1978		100.0		212.5		66.7		250.0		192.3		64.6		70
NEW YORK.														
FEMALE														
1974 (	4 INSTITUTIONS)	0	.0	6	6.5	2	2.2	2	2.2	10	10.9	82	89.1	
1976 (	4 INSTITUTIONS)	0	.0	7	4.9	1	.7	2	1.4	10	7.0	132	93.0	
% CHANGE 1974 TO 1976		.0		16.7		- 50.0		.0		.0		61.0		54
1978 (	4 INSTITUTIONS)	0	.0	4	1.9	9	4.2	5	2.3	18	8.4	196	91.6	
% CHANGE 1976 TO 1978		.0		- 42.9		800.0		150.0		80.0		48.5		50
MALE														
1974 (	4 INSTITUTIONS)	0	.0	29	2.2	11	.9	9	.7	49	3.8	1,241	96.2	1
1976 (	4 INSTITUTIONS)	1	.1	15	1.3	27	2.4	15	1.3	58	5.1	1,087	94.9	1
% CHANGE 1974 TO 1976		100.0		- 48.3		145.5		66.7		18.4		- 12.4		- 11
1978 (	4 INSTITUTIONS)	2	.2	10	.8	20	1.6	18	1.5	50	4.1	1,175	95.9	1
% CHANGE 1976 TO 1978		100.0		- 33.3		- 25.9		20.0		- 13.6		8.1		

ENROLLMENT IN INSTITUTIONS OF HIGHER EDUCATION FOR SELECTED FIELDS OF STUDY AND LEVEL OF ENROLLMENT
TY AND SEX: STATE 1974, 1976, 1978

RICAN INDIAN ASKAN NATIVE		BLACK NON-HISPANIC		ASIAN OR PACIFIC ISLANDER		HISPANIC		TOTAL MINORITY		WHITE NON-HISPANIC		TOTAL
NUMBER	%	NUMBER	%	NUMBER	%	NUMBER	%	NUMBER	%	NUMBER	%	NUMBER
0	.0	2	8.7	0	.0	0	.0	2	8.7	21	91.3	23
2	4.9	5	12.2	1	2.4	0	.0	8	19.5	33	80.5	41
·100.0		150.0		100.0		.0		300.0		57.1		78.3
2	4.4	6	13.3	2	4.4	0	.0	10	22.2	35	77.8	45
.0		20.0		100.0		.0		25.0		6.1		9.8
0	.0	6	1.9	0	.0	2	.6	8	2.5	314	97.5	322
2	.7	9	3.1	1	.3	3	1.0	15	5.2	272	94.8	287
100.0		50.0		100.0		50.0		87.5		- 13.4		- 10.9
2	.7	10	3.4	3	1.0	2	.7	17	5.8	274	94.2	291
.0		11.1		200.0		- 33.3		13.3		.7		1.4
0	.0	4	12.5	0	.0	0	.0	4	12.5	28	87.5	32
0	.0	5	4.6	3	2.8	3	2.8	11	10.1	98	89.9	109
.0		25.0		100.0		100.0		175.0		250.0		240.6
0	.0	6	4.0	0	.0	1	.7	7	4.7	143	95.3	150
.0		20.0		- 100.0		- 66.7		- 36.4		45.9		37.6
2	.5	8	1.9	8	1.9	2	.5	20	4.7	406	95.3	426
0	.0	9	1.1	15	1.8	1	.1	25	3.0	816	97.0	841
100.0		12.5		87.5		- 50.0		25.0		101.0		97.4
0	.0	10	1.2	6	.7	3	.4	19	2.3	823	97.7	842
.0		11.1		- 60.0		200.0		- 24.0		.9		.1
0	.0	0	.0	0	.0	0	.0	0	.0	13	100.0	13
0	.0	0	.0	0	.0	0	.0	0	.0	0	.0	0
.0		.0		.0		.0		.0		- 100.0		- 100.0
0	.0	2	10.5	2	10.5	0	.0	4	21.1	15	78.9	19
.0		100.0		100.0		.0		100.0		100.0		100.0
7	7.1	3	3.0	0	.0	1	1.0	11	11.1	88	88.9	99
0	.0	0	.0	0	.0	0	.0	0	.0	0	.0	0
100.0		- 100.0		.0		- 100.0		- 100.0		- 100.0		- 100.0
7	3.1	3	1.3	2	.9	2	.9	14	6.2	213	93.8	227
100.0		100.0		100.0		100.0		100.0		100.0		100.0
0	.0	0	.0	2	9.5	2	9.5	4	19.0	17	81.0	21
0	.0	1	3.7	3	11.1	1	3.7	5	18.5	22	81.5	27
.0		100.0		50.0		- 50.0		25.0		29.4		28.6
0	.0	2	6.1	2	6.1	1	3.0	5	15.2	28	84.8	33
.0		100.0		- 33.3		.0		.0		27.3		22.2
4	1.2	2	.6	14	˙4+2	3	.9	23	6.8	314	93.2	337
3	1.0	6	2.1	11	3.8	6	2.1	26	9.1	260	90.9	286
25.0		200.0		- 21.4		100.0		13.0		- 17.2		- 15.1
1	.4	4	1.4	10	3.6	7	2.5	22	7.8	259	92.2	281
66.7		- 33.3		- 9.1		16.7		- 15.4		.4		- 1.7

MAJOR FIELD 1204 - DENTISTRY

	AMERICAN INDIAN ALASKAN NATIVE		BLACK NON-HISPANIC		ASIAN OR PACIFIC ISLANDER		HISPANIC		TOTAL MINORITY		WHITE NON-HISPANIC		TO
	NUMBER	%	NUMBER	%	NUMBER	%	NUMBER	%	NUMBER	%	NUMBER	%	NUM
PENNSYLVANIA.													
FEMALE													
1974 (2 INSTITUTIONS)	0	.0	7	5.4	1	.8	0	.0	8	6.5	116	93.5	
1976 (3 INSTITUTIONS)	0	.0	8	3.8	3	1.4	5	2.4	16	7.6	194	92.4	
% CHANGE 1974 TO 1976	.0		14.3		200.0		100.0		100.0		67.2		69.
1978 (3 INSTITUTIONS)	0	.0	21	7.5	7	2.5	5	1.8	33	11.7	248	88.3	
% CHANGE 1976 TO 1978	.0		162.5		133.3		.0		106.3		27.8		33.
MALE													
1974 (2 INSTITUTIONS)	2	.2	32	2.5	6	.5	2	.2	42	3.3	1,242	96.7	1,
1976 (3 INSTITUTIONS)	4	.3	28	1.8	26	1.7	18	1.2	76	5.0	1,449	95.0	1,
% CHANGE 1974 TO 1976	100.0		- 12.5		333.3		800.0		81.0		16.7		18.
1978 (3 INSTITUTIONS)	4	.3	21	1.4	18	1.2	9	.6	52	3.4	1,467	96.6	1,
% CHANGE 1976 TO 1978	.0		- 25.0		- 30.8		- 50.0		- 31.6		1.2		- .
SOUTH CAROLINA.													
FEMALE													
1974 (1 INSTITUTIONS)	0	.0	0	.0	0	.0	0	.0	0	.0	7	100.0	
1976 (1 INSTITUTIONS)	1	11.1	0	.0	0	.0	0	.0	1	11.1	8	88.9	
% CHANGE 1974 TO 1976	100.0		.0		.0		.0		100.0		14.3		28.
1978 (0 INSTITUTIONS)	0	.0	0	.0	0	.0	0	.0	0	.0	0	.0	
% CHANGE 1976 TO 1978	- 100.0		.0		.0		.0		- 100.0		- 100.0		- 100.
MALE													
1974 (1 INSTITUTIONS)	0	.0	1	.6	0	.0	0	.0	1	.6	154	99.4	
1976 (1 INSTITUTIONS)	0	.0	6	3.8	0	.0	0	.0	6	3.8	151	96.2	
% CHANGE 1974 TO 1976	.0		500.0		.0		.0		500.0		- 1.9		1.
1978 (0 INSTITUTIONS)	0	.0	0	.0	0	.0	0	.0	0	.0	0	.0	
% CHANGE 1976 TO 1978	.0		- 100.0		.0		.0		- 100.0		- 100.0		- 100.
TENNESSEE													
FEMALE													
1974 (5 INSTITUTIONS)	0	.0	23	52.3	0	.0	2	4.5	25	56.8	19	43.2	
1976 (2 INSTITUTIONS)	0	.0	37	62.7	0	.0	1	1.7	38	64.4	21	35.6	
% CHANGE 1974 TO 1976	.0		60.9		.0		- 50.0		52.0		10.5		34.
1978 (2 INSTITUTIONS)	0	.0	56	52.8	1	.9	0	.0	57	53.8	49	46.2	
% CHANGE 1976 TO 1978	.0		51.4		100.0		- 100.0		50.0		133.3		79.
MALE													
1974 (5 INSTITUTIONS)	0	.0	130	19.1	3	.4	1	.1	134	19.7	546	80.3	
1976 (2 INSTITUTIONS)	1	.2	111	19.2	3	.5	5	.9	120	20.7	459	79.3	
% CHANGE 1974 TO 1976	100.0		- 14.6		.0		400.0		- 10.4		- 15.9		- 14.
1978 (2 INSTITUTIONS)	4	.6	117	18.8	4	.6	4	.6	129	20.7	493	79.3	
% CHANGE 1976 TO 1978	300.0		5.4		33.3		- 20.0		7.5		7.4		7.
TEXAS													
FEMALE													
1974 (24 INSTITUTIONS)	2	1.2	10	6.1	1	.6	18	10.9	31	18.8	134	81.2	
1976 (3 INSTITUTIONS)	0	.0	5	4.5	3	2.7	12	10.7	20	17.9	92	82.1	
% CHANGE 1974 TO 1976	- 100.0		- 50.0		200.0		- 33.3		- 35.5		- 31.3		- 32.
1978 (3 INSTITUTIONS)	1	.5	10	5.5	5	2.7	17	9.3	33	18.1	149	81.9	
% CHANGE 1976 TO 1978	100.0		100.0		66.7		41.7		65.0		62.0		62.
MALE													
1974 (24 INSTITUTIONS)	4	.3	15	1.1	10	.7	118	8.5	147	10.5	1,248	89.5	1,
1976 (3 INSTITUTIONS)	3	.3	11	.9	14	1.2	44	3.8	72	6.2	1,092	93.8	1,
% CHANGE 1974 TO 1976	- 25.0		- 26.7		40.0		- 62.7		- 51.0		- 12.5		- 16.
1978 (3 INSTITUTIONS)	4	.3	16	1.3	14	1.1	54	4.4	88	7.1	1,150	92.9	1,
% CHANGE 1976 TO 1978	33.3		45.5		.0		22.7		22.2		5.3		6.

ELD 1204 - DENTISTRY

	AMERICAN INDIAN ALASKAN NATIVE		BLACK NON-HISPANIC		ASIAN OR PACIFIC ISLANDER		HISPANIC		TOTAL MINORITY		WHITE NON-HISPANIC		TOTAL
	NUMBER	%	NUMBER	%	NUMBER	%	NUMBER	%	NUMBER	%	NUMBER	%	NUMBER
. . . .													
2 INSTITUTIONS)	0	.0	0	.0	0	.0	0	.0	0	.0	3	100.0	3
0 INSTITUTIONS)	0	.0	0	.0	0	.0	0	.0	0	.0	0	.0	0
GE 1974 TO 1976	.0		.0		.0		.0		.0		- 100.0		- 100.0
0 INSTITUTIONS)	0	.0	0	.0	0	.0	0	.0	0	.0	0	.0	0
GE 1976 TO 1978	.0		.0		.0		.0		.0		.0		.0
2 INSTITUTIONS)	0	.0	0	.0	0	.0	1	2.3	1	2.3	43	97.7	44
0 INSTITUTIONS)	0	.0	0	.0	0	.0	0	.0	0	.0	0	.0	0
GE 1974 TO 1976	.0		.0		.0		- 100.0		- 100.0		- 100.0		- 100.0
0 INSTITUTIONS)	0	.0	0	.0	0	.0	0	.0	0	.0	0	.0	0
GE 1976 TO 1978	.0		.0		.0		.0		.0		.0		.0
. . . .													
3 INSTITUTIONS)	0	.0	0	.0	0	.0	0	.0	0	.0	23	100.0	23
1 INSTITUTIONS)	0	.0	6	12.0	1	2.0	1	2.0	8	16.0	42	84.0	50
GE 1974 TO 1976	.0		100.0		100.0		100.0		100.0		82.6		117.4
1 INSTITUTIONS)	0	.0	2	2.4	4	4.8	1	1.2	7	8.4	76	91.6	83
GE 1976 TO 1978	.0		- 66.7		300.0		.0		- 12.5		81.0		66.0
3 INSTITUTIONS)	0	.0	3	.7	0	.0	0	.0	3	.7	399	99.3	402
1 INSTITUTIONS)	0	.0	7	1.8	6	1.6	1	.3	14	3.6	371	96.4	385
GE 1974 TO 1976	.0		133.3		100.0		100.0		366.7		- 7.0		- 4.2
1 INSTITUTIONS)	0	.0	6	1.7	8	2.3	2	.6	16	4.5	336	95.5	352
GE 1976 TO 1978	.0		- 14.3		33.3		100.0		14.3		- 9.4		- 8.6
ON.													
1 INSTITUTIONS)	0	.0	0	.0	1	4.2	0	.0	1	4.2	23	95.8	24
1 INSTITUTIONS)	0	.0	1	1.8	2	3.6	2	3.6	5	8.9	51	91.1	56
GE 1974 TO 1976	.0		100.0		100.0		100.0		400.0		121.7		133.3
1 INSTITUTIONS)	0	.0	1	1.5	1	1.5	1	1.5	3	4.5	64	95.5	67
GE 1976 TO 1978	.0		.0		- 50.0		- 50.0		- 40.0		25.5		19.6
1 INSTITUTIONS)	0	.0	3	.9	16	4.7	5	1.5	24	7.0	319	93.0	343
1 INSTITUTIONS)	2	.6	5	1.5	16	4.9	14	4.3	37	11.4	287	88.6	324
GE 1974 TO 1976	100.0		66.7		.0		180.0		54.2		- 10.0		- 5.5
1 INSTITUTIONS)	2	.6	3	.9	10	3.0	10	3.0	25	7.6	306	92.4	331
GE 1976 TO 1978	.0		- 40.0		- 37.5		- 28.6		- 32.4		6.6		2.2
GINIA													
1 INSTITUTIONS)	0	.0	0	.0	1	9.1	0	.0	1	9.1	10	90.9	11
1 INSTITUTIONS)	0	.0	0	.0	1	5.3	0	.0	1	5.3	18	94.7	19
GE 1974 TO 1976	.0		.0		.0		.0		.0		80.0		72.7
1 INSTITUTIONS)	1	4.5	0	.0	0	.0	0	.0	1	4.5	21	95.5	22
GE 1976 TO 1978	100.0		.0		- 100.0		.0		.0		16.7		15.8
1 INSTITUTIONS)	0	.0	3	1.2	0	.0	0	.0	3	1.2	243	98.8	246
1 INSTITUTIONS)	0	.0	1	.4	2	.9	0	.0	3	1.3	222	98.7	225
GE 1974 TO 1976	.0		- 66.7		100.0		.0		.0		- 8.6		- 8.5
1 INSTITUTIONS)	1	.5	1	.5	0	.0	1	.5	3	1.4	213	98.6	216
GE 1976 TO 1978	100.0		.0		- 100.0		100.0		.0		- 4.1		- 4.0

TABLE 18 - COMPARISIONS OF ENROLLMENT IN INSTITUTIONS OF HIGHER EDUCATION FOR SELECTED FIELDS OF STUDY AND LEVEL OF ENROLLME BY RACE, ETHNICITY AND SEX: STATE 1974, 1976, 1978

MAJOR FIELD 1204 - DENTISTRY

	AMERICAN INDIAN ALASKAN NATIVE		BLACK NON-HISPANIC		ASIAN OR PACIFIC ISLANDER		HISPANIC		TOTAL MINORITY		WHITE NON-HISPANIC	
	NUMBER	%	NUMBER	%	NUMBER	%	NUMBER	%	NUMBER	%	NUMBER	%
WISCONSIN												
FEMALE												
1974 (1 INSTITUTIONS)	0	.0	0	.0	1	3.2	0	.0	1	3.2	30	96.8
1976 (1 INSTITUTIONS)	0	.0	0	.0	1	2.0	0	.0	1	2.0	48	98.0
% CHANGE 1974 TO 1976	.0		.0		.0		.0		.0		60.0	
1978 (1 INSTITUTIONS)	0	.0	0	.0	1	2.0	0	.0	1	2.0	50	98.0
% CHANGE 1976 TO 1978	.0		.0		.0		.0		.0		4.2	
MALE												
1974 (1 INSTITUTIONS)	0	.0	2	.4	0	.0	3	.6	5	1.0	502	99.0
1976 (1 INSTITUTIONS)	0	.0	1	.2	2	.4	4	.8	7	1.4	490	98.6
% CHANGE 1974 TO 1976	.0		- 50.0		100.0		33.3		40.0		- 2.4	-
1978 (1 INSTITUTIONS)	0	.0	1	.2	2	.4	3	.6	6	1.2	499	98.8
% CHANGE 1976 TO 1978	.0		.0		.0		- 25.0		- 14.3		1.8	
WYOMING												
FEMALE												
1974 (1 INSTITUTIONS)	0	.0	0	.0	0	.0	0	.0	0	.0	20	100.0
1976 (0 INSTITUTIONS)	0	.0	0	.0	0	.0	0	.0	0	.0	0	.0
% CHANGE 1974 TO 1976	.0		.0		.0		.0		.0		- 100.0	-
1978 (0 INSTITUTIONS)	0	.0	0	.0	0	.0	0	.0	0	.0	0	.0
% CHANGE 1976 TO 1978	.0		.0		.0		.0		.0		.0	
MALE												
1974 (1 INSTITUTIONS)	0	.0	0	.0	1	3.7	0	.0	1	3.7	26	96.3
1976 (0 INSTITUTIONS)	0	.0	0	.0	0	.0	0	.0	0	.0	0	.0
% CHANGE 1974 TO 1976	.0		.0		- 100.0		.0		- 100.0		- 100.0	-
1978 (0 INSTITUTIONS)	0	.0	0	.0	0	.0	0	.0	0	.0	0	.0
% CHANGE 1976 TO 1978	.0		.0		.0		.0		.0		.0	
THE STATES AND D.C.												
FEMALE												
1974 (155 INSTITUTIONS)	10	.5	192	9.9	52	2.7	70	3.6	324	16.6	1,625	83.4
1976 (60 INSTITUTIONS)	9	.4	233	10.8	76	3.5	56	2.6	374	17.3	1,789	82.7
% CHANGE 1974 TO 1976	- 10.0		21.4		46.2		- 20.0		15.4		10.1	
1978 (57 INSTITUTIONS)	7	.2	329	11.0	134	4.5	78	2.6	548	18.2	2,456	81.8
% CHANGE 1976 TO 1978	- 22.2		41.2		76.3		39.3		46.5		37.3	
MALE												
1974 (155 INSTITUTIONS)	50	.3	757	4.0	349	1.9	308	1.6	1,464	7.8	17,262	92.2
1976 (60 INSTITUTIONS)	59	.3	478	3.3	478	2.7	303	1.7	1,430	8.0	16,395	92.0
% CHANGE 1974 TO 1976	18.0		- 22.1		37.0		37.0		- 2.3		- 5.0	-
1978 (57 INSTITUTIONS)	59	.3	589	3.2	542	2.9	343	1.8	1,533	8.3	17,011	91.7
% CHANGE 1976 TO 1978	.0		- .2		13.4		13.4		7.2		3.8	
PUERTO RICO												
FEMALE												
1974 (0 INSTITUTIONS)	0	.0	0	.0	0	.0	0	.0	0	.0	0	.0
1976 (1 INSTITUTIONS)	5	8.6	0	.0	0	.0	53	91.4	58	100.0	0	.0
% CHANGE 1974 TO 1976	100.0		.0		.0		100.0		100.0		.0	
1978 (1 INSTITUTIONS)	0	.0	0	.0	0	.0	82	100.0	82	100.0	0	.0
% CHANGE 1976 TO 1978	- 100.0		.0		.0		54.7		41.4		.0	
MALE												
1974 (0 INSTITUTIONS)	0	.0	0	.0	0	.0	0	.0	0	.0	0	.0
1976 (1 INSTITUTIONS)	12	7.4	0	.0	0	.0	150	92.0	162	99.4	1	.6
% CHANGE 1974 TO 1976	100.0		.0		.0		100.0		100.0		100.0	
1978 (1 INSTITUTIONS)	0	.0	0	.0	0	.0	159	100.0	159	100.0	0	.0
% CHANGE 1976 TO 1978	- 100.0		.0		.0		6.0		- 1.9		- 100.0	-

TABLE 18 — COMPARISIONS OF ENROLLMENT IN INSTITUTIONS OF HIGHER EDUCATION FOR SELECTED FIELDS OF STUDY AND LEVEL OF ENROLLMENT
BY RACE, ETHNICITY AND SEX: STATE 1974, 1976, 1978

MAJOR FIELD 1204 — DENTISTRY

	AMERICAN INDIAN ALASKAN NATIVE		BLACK NON-HISPANIC		ASIAN OR PACIFIC ISLANDER		HISPANIC		TOTAL MINORITY		WHITE NON-HISPANIC		TOTAL
	NUMBER	%	NUMBER	%	NUMBER	%	NUMBER	%	NUMBER	%	NUMBER	%	NUMBER
OUTLYING AREAS.													
FEMALE													
1974 (0 INSTITUTIONS)	0	.0	0	.0	0	.0	0	.0	0	.0	0	.0	0
1976 (1 INSTITUTIONS)	5	8.6	0	.0	0	.0	53	91.4	58	100.0	0	.0	58
% CHANGE 1974 TO 1976	100.0		.0		.0		100.0		100.0		.0		100.0
1978 (1 INSTITUTIONS)	0	.0	0	.0	0	.0	82	100.0	82	100.0	0	.0	82
% CHANGE 1976 TO 1978	− 100.0		.0		.0		54.7		41.4		.0		41.4
MALE													
1974 (0 INSTITUTIONS)	0	.0	0	.0	0	.0	0	.0	0	.0	0	.0	0
1976 (1 INSTITUTIONS)	12	7.4	0	.0	0	.0	150	92.0	162	99.4	1	.6	163
% CHANGE 1974 TO 1976	100.0		.0		.0		.0		100.0		100.0		100.0
1978 (1 INSTITUTIONS)	0	.0	0	.0	0	.0	159	100.0	159	100.0	0	.0	159
% CHANGE 1976 TO 1978	− 100.0		.0		.0		.0		− 1.9		− 100.0		− 2.5
MAJOR FIELD AGGREGATE 1204.													
FEMALE													
1974 (155 INSTITUTIONS)	10	.5	192	9.9	52	2.7	70	3.6	324	16.6	1,625	83.4	1,949
1976 (61 INSTITUTIONS)	14	.6	233	10.5	76	3.4	109	4.9	432	19.5	1,789	80.5	2,221
% CHANGE 1974 TO 1976	40.0		21.4		46.2		55.7		33.3		10.1		14.0
1978 (58 INSTITUTIONS)	7	.2	329	10.7	134	4.3	160	5.2	630	20.4	2,456	79.6	3,086
% CHANGE 1976 TO 1978	− 50.0		41.2		76.3		46.8		45.8		37.3		38.9
MALE													
1974 (155 INSTITUTIONS)	50	.3	757	4.0	349	1.9	308	1.6	1,464	7.8	17,262	92.2	18,726
1976 (61 INSTITUTIONS)	71	.4	590	3.3	478	2.7	453	2.5	1,592	8.9	16,396	91.1	17,988
% CHANGE 1974 TO 1976	42.0		− 22.1		37.0		37.0		8.7		− 5.0		− 3.9
1978 (58 INSTITUTIONS)	59	.3	589	3.1	542	2.9	502	2.7	1,692	9.0	17,011	91.0	18,703
% CHANGE 1976 TO 1978	− 16.9		− .2		13.4		13.4		6.3		3.8		4.0

TABLE 18 - COMPARISIONS OF ENROLLMENT IN INSTITUTIONS OF HIGHER EDUCATION FOR SELECTED FIELDS OF STUDY AND LEVEL OF ENROLLMENT BY RACE, ETHNICITY AND SEX: STATE 1974, 1976, 1978

MAJOR FIELD 1206 - MEDICINE

	AMERICAN INDIAN ALASKAN NATIVE		BLACK NON-HISPANIC		ASIAN OR PACIFIC ISLANDER		HISPANIC		TOTAL MINORITY		WHITE NON-HISPANIC		TO
	NUMBER	%	NUMBER	%	NUMBER	%	NUMBER	%	NUMBER	%	NUMBER	%	NUM
ALABAMA													
FEMALE													
1974 (9 INSTITUTIONS)	0	.0	13	8.8	0	.0	8	.0	13	8.8	134	91.2	
1976 (4 INSTITUTIONS)	0	.0	8	7.3	1	.9	8	.0	9	8.2	101	91.8	
% CHANGE 1974 TO 1976	.0		- 38.5		100.0		.0		- 30.8		- 24.6		- 25.
1978 (4 INSTITUTIONS)	0	.0	15	8.2	2	1.1	1	.5	18	9.9	164	90.1	
% CHANGE 1976 TO 1978	.0		87.5		100.0		100.0		100.0		62.4		65.
MALE													
1974 (9 INSTITUTIONS)	0	.0	29	4.4	1	.2	8	.0	30	4.5	636	95.5	
1976 (4 INSTITUTIONS)	0	.0	26	4.8	6	1.1	8	.0	32	5.9	508	94.1	
% CHANGE 1974 TO 1976	.0		- 10.3		500.0		.0		6.7		- 20.1		- 18.
1978 (4 INSTITUTIONS)	1	.1	28	3.4	5	.6	1	.1	35	4.3	779	95.7	
% CHANGE 1976 TO 1978	100.0		7.7		- 16.7		100.0		9.4		53.3		50.
ARIZONA													
FEMALE													
1974 (3 INSTITUTIONS)	1	1.4	1	1.4	1	1.4	2	2.9	5	7.2	64	92.8	
1976 (1 INSTITUTIONS)	1	1.2	0	.0	0	.0	1	1.2	2	2.4	83	97.6	
% CHANGE 1974 TO 1976	.0		- 100.0		- 100.0		- 50.0		- 60.0		29.7		23.
1978 (1 INSTITUTIONS)	0	.0	0	.0	0	.0	2	2.5	2	2.5	77	97.5	
% CHANGE 1976 TO 1978	- 100.0		.0		.0		100.0		.0		- 7.2		- 7.
MALE													
1974 (3 INSTITUTIONS)	2	.9	0	.0	5	2.2	10	4.3	17	7.4	213	92.6	
1976 (1 INSTITUTIONS)	2	1.0	1	.5	2	1.0	7	3.6	12	6.1	185	93.9	
% CHANGE 1974 TO 1976	.0		100.0		- 60.0		- 30.0		- 29.4		- 13.1		- 14.
1978 (1 INSTITUTIONS)	1	.4	0	.0	1	.4	5	2.0	7	2.8	240	97.2	
% CHANGE 1976 TO 1978	- 50.0		- 100.0		- 50.0		- 28.6		- 41.7		29.7		25.
ARKANSAS													
FEMALE													
1974 (5 INSTITUTIONS)	0	.0	20	10.4	1	.5	8	.0	21	10.9	172	89.1	
1976 (1 INSTITUTIONS)	1	1.2	6	7.1	0	.0	8	.0	7	8.2	78	91.8	
% CHANGE 1974 TO 1976	100.0		- 70.0		- 100.0		.0		- 66.7		- 54.7		- 56.
1978 (1 INSTITUTIONS)	1	.9	10	9.4	2	1.9	1	.9	14	13.2	92	86.8	
% CHANGE 1976 TO 1978	.0		66.7		100.0		100.0		100.0		17.9		24.
MALE													
1974 (5 INSTITUTIONS)	0	.0	31	4.6	6	.9	2	.3	39	5.8	630	94.2	
1976 (1 INSTITUTIONS)	0	.0	13	3.3	8	2.0	1	.3	22	5.5	376	94.5	
% CHANGE 1974 TO 1976	.0		- 58.1		33.3		- 50.0		- 43.6		- 40.3		- 40.
1978 (1 INSTITUTIONS)	1	.2	19	4.6	9	2.2	0	.0	29	7.0	387	93.0	
% CHANGE 1976 TO 1978	100.0		46.2		12.5		- 100.0		31.8		2.9		4.
CALIFORNIA													
FEMALE													
1974 (29 INSTITUTIONS)	12	1.0	81	7.0	55	4.7	50	4.3	198	17.1	960	82.9	1,
1976 (8 INSTITUTIONS)	7	.8	56	6.2	69	7.7	51	5.7	183	20.4	715	79.6	
% CHANGE 1974 TO 1976	- 41.7		- 30.9		25.5		2.0		- 7.6		- 25.5		- 22.
1978 (12 INSTITUTIONS)	10	.9	95	8.1	119	10.2	65	5.6	289	24.7	882	75.3	1,
% CHANGE 1976 TO 1978	42.9		69.6		72.5		27.5		57.9		23.4		30.
MALE													
1974 (29 INSTITUTIONS)	29	.9	151	4.5	207	6.1	237	7.0	624	18.5	2,744	81.5	3,
1976 (8 INSTITUTIONS)	19	.7	161	5.8	240	8.6	240	8.6	660	23.7	2,125	76.3	2,
% CHANGE 1974 TO 1976	- 34.5		6.6		15.9		1.3		5.8		- 22.6		- 17.
1978 (12 INSTITUTIONS)	21	.5	140	3.6	345	8.8	249	6.4	755	19.3	3,160	80.7	3,
% CHANGE 1976 TO 1978	10.5		- 13.0		43.8		3.8		14.4		48.7		40.

COMPARISIONS OF ENROLLMENT IN INSTITUTIONS OF HIGHER EDUCATION FOR SELECTED FIELDS OF STUDY AND LEVEL OF ENROLLMENT BY RACE, ETHNICITY AND SEX: STATE 1974, 1976, 1978

D 1206 - MEDICINE

	AMERICAN INDIAN ALASKAN NATIVE		BLACK NON-HISPANIC		ASIAN OR PACIFIC ISLANDER		HISPANIC		TOTAL MINORITY		WHITE NON-HISPANIC		TOTAL
	NUMBER	%	NUMBER	%	NUMBER	%	NUMBER	%	NUMBER	%	NUMBER	%	NUMBER
1 INSTITUTIONS)	3	2.9	13	12.6	5	4.9	9	8.7	30	29.1	73	70.9	103
2 INSTITUTIONS)	2	1.5	8	5.9	7	5.1	13	9.6	30	22.1	106	77.9	136
1974 TO 1976	- 33.3		- 38.5		40.0		44.4		.0		45.2		32.0
1 INSTITUTIONS)	4	2.9	6	4.4	5	3.6	16	11.7	31	22.6	106	77.4	137
1976 TO 1978	100.0		- 25.0		- 28.6		23.1		3.3		.0		.7
1 INSTITUTIONS)	8	1.9	12	2.9	8	1.9	19	4.5	47	11.2	371	88.8	418
2 INSTITUTIONS)	6	1.6	12	3.2	11	2.9	33	8.8	62	16.4	315	83.6	377
1974 TO 1976	- 25.0		.0		37.5		73.7		31.9		- 15.1		- 9.8
1 INSTITUTIONS)	6	1.5	13	3.4	14	3.6	35	9.0	68	17.5	320	82.5	388
1976 TO 1978	.0		8.3		27.3		6.1		.9.7		1.6		2.9
T													
2 INSTITUTIONS)	0	.0	11	8.2	6	4.5	1	.7	18	13.4	116	86.6	134
2 INSTITUTIONS)	0	.0	9	4.7	5	2.6	2	1.0	16	8.4	175	91.6	191
1974 TO 1976	.0		- 18.2		- 16.7		100.0		- 11.1		50.9		42.5
2 INSTITUTIONS)	0	.0	18	8.2	7	3.2	10	4.5	35	15.9	185	84.1	220
1976 TO 1978	.0		100.0		40.0		400.0		118.8		5.7		15.2 ·
2 INSTITUTIONS)	1	.2	41	8.8	11	2.4	6	1.3	59	12.7	407	87.3	466
2 INSTITUTIONS)	1	.2	43	8.8	15	3.1	12	2.5	71	14.5	417	85.5	488
1974 TO 1976	.0		4.9		36.4		100.0		20.3		2.5		4.7
2 INSTITUTIONS)	0	.0	33	5.9	14	2.5	28	5.0	75	13.5	480	86.5	555
1976 TO 1978	- 100.0		- 23.3		- 6.7		133.3		5.6		15.1		13.7
F COLUMBIA. . . .		.											
3 INSTITUTIONS)	0	.0	132	34.5	4	1.0	0	.0	136	35.5	247	64.5	383
3 INSTITUTIONS)	0	.0	146	36.1	4	1.0	1	.2	151	37.4	253	62.6	404
1974 TO 1976	.0		10.6		.0		100.0		11.0		2.4		5.5
3 INSTITUTIONS)	2	.4	179	37.4	11	2.3	8	1.7	200	41.8	279	58.2	479
1976 TO 1978	100.0		22.6		175.0		700.0		32.5		10.3		18.6
3 INSTITUTIONS)	3	.2	263	17.8	27	1.8	15	1.0	308	20.8	1,170	79.2	1,478
3 INSTITUTIONS)	2	.2	201	15.1	21	1.6	13	1.0	237	17.8	1,093	82.2	1,330
1974 TO 1976	- 33.3		- 23.6		- 22.2		- 13.3		- 23.1		- 6.6		- 10.0
3 INSTITUTIONS)	4	.3	252	18.5	13	1.0	11	.8	280	20.5	1,084	79.5	1,364
1976 TO 1978	100.0		25.4		- 38.1		- 15.4		18.1		- .8		2.6
....													
15 INSTITUTIONS)	1	.1	56	7.7	4	.6	46	6.3	107	14.7	619	85.3	726
3 INSTITUTIONS)	0	.0	17	8.3	0	.0	9	4.4	26	12.7	178	87.3	204
1974 TO 1976	- 100.0		- 69.6		- 100.0		- 80.4		- 75.7		- 71.2		- 71.9
3 INSTITUTIONS)	0	.0	15	5.8	3	1.2	14	5.4	32	12.3	228	87.7	260
1976 TO 1978	.0		- 11.8		100.0		55.6		23.1		28.1		27.5
15 INSTITUTIONS)	1	.1	59	3.8	7	.5	68	4.4	135	8.8	1,407	91.2	1,542
3 INSTITUTIONS)	2	.2	42	4.4	8	.8	61	6.4	113	11.9	835	88.1	948
1974 TO 1976	100.0		- 28.8		14.3		- 10.3		- 16.3		- 40.7		- 38.5
3 INSTITUTIONS)	3	.3	45	4.3	9	.9	69	6.6	126	12.0	926	88.0	1,052
1976 TO 1978	50.0		7.1		12.5		13.1		11.5		10.9		11.0

TABLE 18 - COMPARISONS OF ENROLLMENT IN INSTITUTIONS OF HIGHER EDUCATION FOR SELECTED FIELDS OF STUDY AND LEVEL OF ENROLLMENT
BY RACE, ETHNICITY AND SEX: STATE 1974, 1976, 1978

MAJOR FIELD 1206 - MEDICINE

	AMERICAN INDIAN ALASKAN NATIVE		BLACK NON-HISPANIC		ASIAN OR PACIFIC ISLANDER		HISPANIC		TOTAL MINORITY		WHITE NON-HISPANIC		TO NUM
	NUMBER	%	NUMBER	%	NUMBER	%	NUMBER	%	NUMBER	%	NUMBER	%	
GEORGIA													
FEMALE													
1974 (9 INSTITUTIONS)	1	.6	10	5.8	0	.0	1	.6	12	6.9	161	93.1	
1976 (2 INSTITUTIONS)	0	.0	11	5.3	1	.5	0	.0	12	5.8	196	94.2	
% CHANGE 1974 TO 1976	- 100.0		10.0		100.0		- 100.0		.0		21.7		20.
1978 (2 INSTITUTIONS)	0	.0	11	4.7	2	.8	1	.4	14	5.9	222	94.1	
% CHANGE 1976 TO 1978	.0		.0		100.0		100.0		16.7		13.3		13.
MALE													
1974 (9 INSTITUTIONS)	2	.2	42	4.1	12	1.2	3	.3	59	5.8	958	94.2	1,
1976 (2 INSTITUTIONS)	0	.0	24	2.5	5	.5	2	.2	31	3.2	937	96.8	
% CHANGE 1974 TO 1976	- 100.0		- 42.9		- 58.3		- 33.3		- 47.5		- 2.2		- 4.
1978 (2 INSTITUTIONS)	1	.1	24	2.5	6	.6	13	1.4	44	4.7	899	95.3	
% CHANGE 1976 TO 1978	100.0		.0		20.0		550.0		41.9		- 4.1		- 2.
HAWAII													
FEMALE													
1974 (0 INSTITUTIONS)	0	.0	0	.0	0	.0	0	.0	0	.0	0	.0	
1976 (1 INSTITUTIONS)	0	.0	0	.0	42	58.3	0	.0	42	58.3	30	41.7	
% CHANGE 1974 TO 1976	.0		.0		100.0		.0		100.0		100.0		100.
1978 (1 INSTITUTIONS)	0	.0	0	.0	48	61.5	0	.0	48	61.5	30	38.5	
% CHANGE 1976 TO 1978	.0		.0		14.3		.0		14.3		.0		8.
MALE													
1974 (0 INSTITUTIONS)	0	.0	0	.0	0	.0	0	.0	0	.0	0	.0	
1976 (1 INSTITUTIONS)	1	.5	0	.0	166	79.0	0	.0	167	79.5	43	20.5	
% CHANGE 1974 TO 1976	100.0		.0		100.0		.0		100.0		100.0		100.
1978 (1 INSTITUTIONS)	0	.0	0	.0	161	80.1	0	.0	161	80.1	40	19.9	
% CHANGE 1976 TO 1978	- 100.0		.0		3.0		.0		- 3.6		- 7.0		- 4.
IDAHO													
FEMALE													
1974 (2 INSTITUTIONS)	0	.0	0	.0	1	5.9	0	.0	1	5.9	16	94.1	
1976 (0 INSTITUTIONS)	0	.0	0	.0	0	.0	0	.0	0	.0	0	.0	
% CHANGE 1974 TO 1976	.0		.0		- 100.0		.0		- 100.0		- 100.0		- 100.
1978 (0 INSTITUTIONS)	0	.0	0	.0	0	.0	0	.0	0	.0	0	.0	
% CHANGE 1976 TO 1978	.0		.0		.0		.0		.0		.0		
MALE													
1974 (2 INSTITUTIONS)	0	.0	0	.0	0	.0	2	5.4	2	5.4	35	94.6	
1976 (0 INSTITUTIONS)	0	.0	0	.0	0	.0	0	.0	0	.0	0	.0	
% CHANGE 1974 TO 1976	.0		.0		.0		- 100.0		- 100.0		- 100.0		- 100.
1978 (0 INSTITUTIONS)	0	.0	0	.0	0	.0	0	.0	0	.0	0	.0	
% CHANGE 1976 TO 1978	.0		.0		.0		.0		.0		.0		
ILLINOIS													
FEMALE													
1974 (10 INSTITUTIONS)	3	.4	87	11.8	19	2.6	21	2.8	130	17.6	608	82.4	
1976 (9 INSTITUTIONS)	1	.1	91	10.3	20	2.3	16	1.8	128	14.5	754	85.5	
% CHANGE 1974 TO 1976	- 66.7		4.6		5.3		- 23.8		- 1.5		24.0		19.
1978 (8 INSTITUTIONS)	1	.1	104	9.8	28	2.6	21	2.0	154	14.5	906	85.5	1,
% CHANGE 1976 TO 1978	.0		14.3		40.0		31.3		20.3		20.2		20.
MALE													
1974 (10 INSTITUTIONS)	8	.2	191	5.7	54	1.6	39	1.2	292	8.7	3,054	91.3	3,
1976 (9 INSTITUTIONS)	7	.2	137	4.6	79	2.6	49	1.6	272	9.1	2,718	90.9	2,
% CHANGE 1974 TO 1976	- 12.5		- 28.3		46.3		25.6		- 6.8		- 11.0		- 10.
1978 (8 INSTITUTIONS)	8	.2	132	3.9	93	2.7	67	2.0	300	8.8	3,098	91.2	3,
% CHANGE 1976 TO 1978	14.3		- 3.6		17.7		36.7		10.3		14.0		13.

COMPARISIONS OF ENROLLMENT IN INSTITUTIONS OF HIGHER EDUCATION FOR SELECTED FIELDS OF STUDY AND LEVEL OF ENROLLMENT
BY RACE, ETHNICITY AND SEX: STATE 1974, 1976, 1978

D 1206 - MEDICINE

	AMERICAN INDIAN ALASKAN NATIVE		BLACK NON-HISPANIC		ASIAN OR PACIFIC ISLANDER		HISPANIC		TOTAL MINORITY		WHITE NON-HISPANIC		TOTAL
	NUMBER	%	NUMBER	%	NUMBER	%	NUMBER	%	NUMBER	%	NUMBER	%	NUMBER
. . . .													
5 INSTITUTIONS)	0	.0	1	.5	0	.0	1	.5	2	1.1	180	98.9	182
5 INSTITUTIONS)	0	.0	9	3.7	2	.8	1	.4	12	4.9	232	95.1	244
1974 TO 1976	.0		800.0		100.0		.0		500.0		28.9		34.1
4 INSTITUTIONS)	0	.0	9	3.6	3	1.2	2	.8	14	5.6	234	94.4	248
1976 TO 1978	.0		.0		50.0		100.0		16.7		.9		1.6
5 INSTITUTIONS)	2	.2	12	1.3	2	.2	4	.4	20	2.2	899	97.8	919
5 INSTITUTIONS)	1	.1	25	2.5	5	.5	6	.6	37	3.7	954	96.3	991
1974 TO 1976	- 50.0		108.3		150.0		50.0		85.0		6.1		7.8
4 INSTITUTIONS)	3	.3	11	1.2	10	1.1	3	.3	27	2.9	908	97.1	935
1976 TO 1978	200.0		- 56.0		100.0		- 50.0		- 27.0		- 4.8		- 5.7
. . . .													
2 INSTITUTIONS)	1	.5	7	3.3	3	1.4	1	.5	12	5.6	203	94.4	215
1 INSTITUTIONS)	1	.6	4	2.4	2	1.2	0	.0	7	4.1	162	95.9	169
1974 TO 1976	.0		- 42.9		- 33.3		- 100.0		- 41.7		- 20.2		- 21.4
2 INSTITUTIONS)	2	.7	6	2.0	2	.7	2	.7	12	4.0	291	96.0	303
1976 TO 1978	100.0		50.0		.0		100.0		71.4		79.6		79.3
2 INSTITUTIONS)	0	.0	10	1.0	6	.6	6	.6	22	2.	945	97.7	967
1 INSTITUTIONS)	5	.5	16	1.7	2	.2	5	.5	28	3.8	917	97.0	945
1974 TO 1976	100.0		60.0		- 66.7		- 16.7		27.3		- 3.0		- 2.3
2 INSTITUTIONS)	10	.7	16	1.2	6	.4	12	.9	44	3.2	1,331	96.8	1,375
1976 TO 1978	100.0		.0		200.0		140.0		57.1		45.1		45.5
. . . .													
9 INSTITUTIONS)	0	.0	0	.0	0	.0	0	.0	0	.0	63	100.0	63
1 INSTITUTIONS)	0	.0	4	3.3	0	.0	0	.0	4	3.3	117	96.7	121
1974 TO 1976	.0		100.0		.0		.0		100.0		85.7		92.1
1 INSTITUTIONS)	0	.0	6	4.3	2	1.4	5	3.6	13	9.4	125	90.6	138
1976 TO 1978	.0		50.0		100.0		100.0		225.0		6.8		14.0
9 INSTITUTIONS)	0	.0	6	.3	2	1.1	1	.5	9	4.9	173	95.1	182
1 INSTITUTIONS)	4	.9	19	4.1	4	.9	5	1.1	32	6.8	436	93.2	468
1974 TO 1976	100.0		216.7		100.0		400.0		255.6		152.0		157.1
1 INSTITUTIONS)	3	.5	12	2.0	6	1.0	4	.7	25	4.2	572	95.8	597
1976 TO 1978	- 25.0		- 36.8		50.0		- 20.0		- 21.9		31.2		27.6
. . . .													
2 INSTITUTIONS)	1	.7	6	4.3	0	.0	0	.0	7	5.0	133	95.0	140
2 INSTITUTIONS)	2	1.0	5	2.4	0	.0	1	.5	8	3.8	202	96.2	210
1974 TO 1976	100.0		- 16.7		.0		100.0		14.3		51.9		50.0
2 INSTITUTIONS)	2	.6	6	1.9	18	5.8	3	1.0	29	9.4	280	90.6	309
1976 TO 1978	.0		20.0		100.0		200.0		262.5		38.6		47.1
2 INSTITUTIONS)	2	.3	19	2.7	8	1.1	1	.1	30	4.3	675	95.7	705
2 INSTITUTIONS)	2	.3	14	1.9	4	.5	0	.0	20	2.6	736	97.4	756
1974 TO 1976	.0		- 26.3		- 50.0		- 100.0		- 33.3		9.0		7.2
2 INSTITUTIONS)	1	.1	24	2.2	52	4.8	7	.6	84	7.7	1,009	92.3	1,093
1976 TO 1978	- 50.0		71.4		1200.0		100.0		320.0		37.1		44.6

TABLE 18 - COMPARISIONS OF ENROLLMENT IN INSTITUTIONS OF HIGHER EDUCATION FOR SELECTED FIELDS OF STUDY AND LEVEL OF ENROLLMENT BY RACE, ETHNICITY AND SEX: STATE 1974, 1976, 1978

MAJOR FIELD 1206 - MEDICINE

	AMERICAN INDIAN ALASKAN NATIVE		BLACK NON-HISPANIC		ASIAN OR PACIFIC ISLANDER		HISPANIC		TOTAL MINORITY		WHITE NON-HISPANIC		TOTAL
	NUMBER	%	NUMBER	%	NUMBER	%	NUMBER	%	NUMBER	%	NUMBER	%	NUMBER
LOUISIANA													
FEMALE													
1974 (3 INSTITUTIONS)	0	.0	7	6.7	1	1.0	0	.0	8	7.6	97	92.4	105
1976 (2 INSTITUTIONS)	0	.0	14	5.4	3	1.2	3	1.2	20	7.7	239	92.3	259
% CHANGE 1974 TO 1976	.0		100.0		200.0		100.0		150.0		146.4		146.7
1978 (2 INSTITUTIONS)	2	.6	22	6.7	4	1.2	6	1.8	34	10.3	295	89.7	329
% CHANGE 1976 TO 1978	100.0		57.1		33.3		100.0		70.0		23.4		27.0
MALE													
1974 (3 INSTITUTIONS)	0	.0	20	2.8	5	.7	4	.6	29	4.1	676	95.9	705
1976 (2 INSTITUTIONS)	0	.0	15	1.2	3	.2	9	.7	27	2.1	1,229	97.9	1,256
% CHANGE 1974 TO 1976	.0		- 25.0		- 40.0		125.0		- 6.9		81.8		78.2
1978 (2 INSTITUTIONS)	2	.1	41	3.0	16	1.2	19	1.4	78	5.7	1,287	94.3	1,365
% CHANGE 1976 TO 1978	100.0		173.3		433.3		111.1		188.9		4.7		8.7
MARYLAND													
FEMALE													
1974 (3 INSTITUTIONS)	0	.0	39	16.8	10	4.3	0	.0	49	21.1	183	78.9	232
1976 (2 INSTITUTIONS)	0	.0	22	8.7	11	4.4	0	.0	33	13.1	219	86.9	252
% CHANGE 1974 TO 1976	.0		- 43.6		10.0		.0		- 32.7		19.7		8.6
1978 (2 INSTITUTIONS)	0	.0	21	8.2	16	6.3	0	.0	37	14.5	218	85.5	255
% CHANGE 1976 TO 1978	.0		- 4.5		45.5		.0		12.1		- .5		1.2
MALE													
1974 (3 INSTITUTIONS)	3	.3	57	6.1	11	1.2	4	.4	75	8.0	865	92.0	940
1976 (2 INSTITUTIONS)	0	.0	31	3.3	18	1.9	1	.1	50	5.4	878	94.6	928
% CHANGE 1974 TO 1976	- 100.0		- 45.6		63.6		- 75.0		- 33.3		1.5		- 1.3
1978 (2 INSTITUTIONS)	1	.1	37	3.9	41	4.4	8	.9	87	9.3	851	90.7	938
% CHANGE 1976 TO 1978	100.0		19.4		127.8		700.0		74.0		- 3.1		1.1
MASSACHUSETTS													
FEMALE													
1974 (5 INSTITUTIONS)	1	.2	62	12.0	14	2.7	11	2.1	88	17.0	429	83.0	517
1976 (5 INSTITUTIONS)	5	.8	58	9.1	29	4.6	20	3.2	112	17.7	522	82.3	634
% CHANGE 1974 TO 1976	400.0		- 6.5		107.1		81.8		27.3		21.7		22.6
1978 (5 INSTITUTIONS)	1	.2	35	8.0	14	3.2	18	4.1	68	15.5	370	84.5	438
% CHANGE 1976 TO 1978	- 80.0		- 39.7		- 51.7		- 10.0		- 39.3		- 29.1		- 30.9
MALE													
1974 (5 INSTITUTIONS)	6	.4	88	5.9	58	3.9	14	.9	166	11.2	1,318	88.8	1,484
1976 (5 INSTITUTIONS)	13	.9	82	5.6	39	2.6	26	1.8	160	10.8	1,316	89.2	1,476
% CHANGE 1974 TO 1976	116.7		- 6.8		- 32.8		85.7		- 3.6		- .2		- .5
1978 (5 INSTITUTIONS)	1	.1	42	4.2	38	3.8	25	2.5	106	10.7	886	89.3	992
% CHANGE 1976 TO 1978	- 92.3		- 48.8		- 2.6		- 3.8		- 33.8		- 32.7		- 32.8
MICHIGAN													
FEMALE													
1974 (10 INSTITUTIONS)	2	.3	82	12.0	11	1.6	10	1.5	105	15.3	581	84.7	686
1976 (3 INSTITUTIONS)	2	.3	86	13.7	12	1.9	15	2.4	115	18.3	513	81.7	628
% CHANGE 1974 TO 1976	.0		4.9		9.1		50.0		9.5		- 11.7		- 8.5
1978 (3 INSTITUTIONS)	4	.5	98	13.4	19	2.6	17	2.3	138	18.8	596	81.2	734
% CHANGE 1976 TO 1978	100.0		14.0		58.3		13.3		20.0		16.2		16.9
MALE													
1974 (10 INSTITUTIONS)	8	.3	182	7.1	32	1.2	28	1.1	250	9.7	2,318	90.3	2,568
1976 (3 INSTITUTIONS)	13	.7	146	7.9	27	1.5	43	2.3	229	12.4	1,620	87.6	1,849
% CHANGE 1974 TO 1976	62.5		- 19.8		- 15.6		53.6		- 8.4		- 30.1		- 28.0
1978 (3 INSTITUTIONS)	7	.4	128	6.5	45	2.3	46	2.3	226	11.5	1,734	88.5	1,960
% CHANGE 1976 TO 1978	- 46.2		- 12.3		66.7		7.0		- 1.3		7.0		6.0

COMPARISIONS OF ENROLLMENT IN INSTITUTIONS OF HIGHER EDUCATION FOR SELECTED FIELDS OF STUDY AND LEVEL OF ENROLLMENT BY RACE, ETHNICITY AND SEX: STATE 1974, 1976, 1978

D 1206 - MEDICINE

	AMERICAN INDIAN ALASKAN NATIVE		BLACK NON-HISPANIC		ASIAN OR PACIFIC ISLANDER		HISPANIC		TOTAL MINORITY		WHITE NON-HISPANIC		TOTAL
	NUMBER	%	NUMBER	%	NUMBER	%	NUMBER	%	NUMBER	%	NUMBER	%	NUMBER
· · · · · · · · ·													
4 INSTITUTIONS)	1	.4	11	4.2	6	2.3	10	3.8	28	10.8	232	89.2	260
3 INSTITUTIONS)	0	.0	11	4.8	2	.9	6	2.6	19	8.3	210	91.7	229
1974 TO 1976	- 100.0		.0		- 66.7		- 40.0		- 32.1		- 9.5		- 11.9
3 INSTITUTIONS)	2	.7	13	4.4	2	.7	11	3.8	28	9.6	265	90.4	293
1976 TO 1978	100.0		18.2		.0		83.3		47.4		26.2		27.9
4 INSTITUTIONS)	6	.3	25	1.3	9	.5	14	.7	54	2.7	1,921	97.3	1,975
3 INSTITUTIONS)	4	.4	26	2.5	5	.5	25	2.4	60	5.9	964	94.1	1,024
1974 TO 1976	- 33.3		4.0		- 44.4		78.6		11.1		- 49.8		- 48.2
3 INSTITUTIONS)	11	1.1	19	1.8	10	1.0	36	3.5	76	7.4	953	92.6	1,029
1976 TO 1978	175.0		- 26.9		100.0		44.0		26.7		- 1.1		.5
I · · · · · · ·													
8 INSTITUTIONS)	0	.0	10	12.0	1	1.2	0	.0	11	13.3	72	86.7	83
2 INSTITUTIONS)	1	.8	13	10.1	2	1.6	1	.8	17	13.2	112	86.8	129
1974 TO 1976	100.0		30.0		100.0		100.0		54.5		55.6		55.4
1 INSTITUTIONS)	1	.8	8	6.3	2	1.6	0	.0	11	8.7	116	91.3	127
1976 TO 1978	.0		- 38.5		.0		- 100.0		- 35.3		3.6		- 1.6
8 INSTITUTIONS)	0	.0	25	5.0	7	1.4	2	.4	34	6.8	463	93.2	497
2 INSTITUTIONS)	0	.0	30	4.4	9	1.3	3	.4	42	6.1	647	93.9	689
1974 TO 1976	.0		20.0		28.6		50.0		23.5		39.7		38.6
1 INSTITUTIONS)	0	.0	23	4.8	4	.8	1	.2	28	5.8	452	94.2	480
1976 TO 1978	.0		- 23.3		- 55.6		- 66.7		- 33.3		- 30.1		- 30.3
· · · · · · · · ·													
4 INSTITUTIONS)	2	.5	44	11.1	7	1.8	3	.8	56	14.1	340	85.9	396
4 INSTITUTIONS)	1	.3	37	9.6	5	1.3	1	.3	44	11.5	340	88.5	384
1974 TO 1976	- 50.0		- 15.9		- 28.6		- 66.7		- 21.4		.0		- 3.0
6 INSTITUTIONS)	6	1.1	43	7.5	21	3.7	5	.9	75	13.2	495	86.8	570
1976 TO 1978	500.0		16.2		320.0		400.0		70.5		45.6		48.4
4 INSTITUTIONS)	4	.2	89	5.4	14	.9	5	.3	112	6.8	1,527	93.2	1,639
4 INSTITUTIONS)	4	.3	62	4.3	17	1.2	4	.3	87	6.0	1,370	94.0	1,457
1974 TO 1976	.0		- 30.3		21.4		- 20.0		- 22.3		- 10.3		- 11.1
6 INSTITUTIONS)	11	.4	58	2.4	44	1.8	12	.5	125	5.1	2,323	94.9	2,448
1976 TO 1978	175.0		- 6.5		158.8		200.0		43.7		69.6		68.0
· · · · · · · · ·													
1 INSTITUTIONS)	0	.0	0	.0	0	.0	0	.0	0	.0	3	100.0	3
0 INSTITUTIONS)	0	.0	0	.0	0	.0	0	.0	0	.0	0	.0	0
1974 TO 1976	.0		.0		.0		.0		.0		- 100.0		- 100.0
0 INSTITUTIONS)	0	.0	0	.0	0	.0	0	.0	0	.0	0	.0	0
1976 TO 1978	.0		.0		.0		.0		.0		.0		.0
1 INSTITUTIONS)	0	.0	0	.0	0	.0	0	.0	0	.0	7	100.0	7
0 INSTITUTIONS)	0	.0	0	.0	0	.0	0	.0	0	.0	0	.0	0
1974 TO 1976	.0		.0		.0		.0		.0		- 100.0		- 100.0
0 INSTITUTIONS)	0	.0	0	.0	0	.0	0	.0	0	.0	0	.0	0
1976 TO 1978	.0		.0		.0		.0		.0		.0		.0

TABLE 18 - COMPARISIONS OF ENROLLMENT IN INSTITUTIONS OF HIGHER EDUCATION FOR SELECTED FIELDS OF STUDY AND LEVEL OF ENROLLMENT
         BY RACE, ETHNICITY AND SEX: STATE 1974, 1976, 1978

MAJOR FIELD 1206 - MEDICINE

	AMERICAN INDIAN ALASKAN NATIVE		BLACK NON-HISPANIC		ASIAN OR PACIFIC ISLANDER		HISPANIC		TOTAL MINORITY		WHITE NON-HISPANIC		T
	NUMBER	%	NUMBER	%	NUMBER	%	NUMBER	%	NUMBER	%	NUMBER	%	NU
NEBRASKA													
FEMALE													
1974 (3 INSTITUTIONS)	3	2.1	5	3.5	2	1.4	0	.0	10	7.0	133	93.0	
1976 (3 INSTITUTIONS)	0	.0	3	2.0	3	2.0	0	.0	6	4.0	143	96.0	
% CHANGE 1974 TO 1976	- 100.0		- 40.0		50.0		.0		- 40.0		7.5		4
1978 (2 INSTITUTIONS)	2	1.0	3	1.5	4	2.1	1	.5	10	5.2	184	94.8	
% CHANGE 1976 TO 1978	100.0		.0		33.3		100.0		66.7		28.7		30
MALE													
1974 (3 INSTITUTIONS)	3	.3	18	1.7	16	1.5	8	.7	45	4.2	1,031	95.8	1
1976 (3 INSTITUTIONS)	5	.6	18	2.3	14	1.8	17	2.2	54	7.0	722	93.0	
% CHANGE 1974 TO 1976	66.7		.0		- 12.5		112.5		20.0		- 30.0		- 27
1978 (2 INSTITUTIONS)	2	.3	14	1.8	14	1.8	23	3.0	53	6.9	720	93.1	
% CHANGE 1976 TO 1978	- 60.0		- 22.2		.0		35.3		- 1.9		.3	.	-
NEW HAMPSHIRE													
FEMALE													
1974 (1 INSTITUTIONS)	2	5.7	2	5.7	0	.0	1	2.9	5	14.3	30	85.7	
1976 (1 INSTITUTIONS)	1	2.0	3	5.9	1	2.0	2	3.9	7	13.7	44	86.3	
% CHANGE 1974 TO 1976	- 50.0		50.0		100.0		100.0		40.0		46.7		45
1978 (1 INSTITUTIONS)	1	1.8	3	5.5	5	9.1	3	5.5	12	21.8	43	78.2	
% CHANGE 1976 TO 1978	.0		.0		400.0		50.0		71.4		- 2.3		7
MALE													
1974 (1 INSTITUTIONS)	5	4.0	6	4.8	0	.0	2	1.6	13	10.3	113	89.7	
1976 (1 INSTITUTIONS)	3	2.1	10	6.9	2	1.4	4	2.8	19	13.2	125	86.8	
% CHANGE 1974 TO 1976	- 40.0		66.7		100.0		100.0		46.2		10.6		14
1978 (1 INSTITUTIONS)	2	1.5	6	4.6	3	2.3	3	2.3	14	10.7	117	89.3	
% CHANGE 1976 TO 1978	- 33.3		- 40.0		50.0		- 25.0		- 26.3		- 6.4		- 9
NEW JERSEY													
FEMALE													
1974 (1 INSTITUTIONS)	0	.0	32	31.7	0	.0	2	2.0	34	33.7	67	66.3	
1976 (1 INSTITUTIONS)	1	.5	49	22.7	3	1.4	10	4.6	63	29.2	153	70.8	
% CHANGE 1974 TO 1976	100.0		53.1		100.0		400.0		85.3		128.4		113
1978 (1 INSTITUTIONS)	0	.0	57	23.8	8	3.3	12	5.0	77	32.1	163	67.9	
% CHANGE 1976 TO 1978	- 100.0		16.3		166.7		20.0		22.2		6.5		11
MALE													
1974 (1 INSTITUTIONS)	0	.0	40	10.8	2	.5	8	2.2	50	13.4	322	86.6	
1976 (1 INSTITUTIONS)	1	.2	71	11.9	7	1.2	25	4.2	104	17.4	494	82.6	
% CHANGE 1974 TO 1976	100.0		77.5		250.0		212.5		108.0		53.4		60
1978 (1 INSTITUTIONS)	0	.0	78	11.6	6	.9	30	4.5	114	17.0	558	83.0	
% CHANGE 1976 TO 1978	- 100.0		9.9		- 14.3		20.0		9.6		13.0		12
NEW MEXICO													
FEMALE													
1974 (2 INSTITUTIONS)	2	3.2	1	1.6	0	.0	8	12.7	11	17.5	52	82.5	
1976 (1 INSTITUTIONS)	3	3.5	1	1.2	2	2.4	12	14.1	18	21.2	67	78.8	
% CHANGE 1974 TO 1976	50.0		.0		100.0		50.0		63.6		28.8		34
1978 (1 INSTITUTIONS)	1	1.1	1	1.1	3	3.4	15	17.0	20	22.7	68	77.3	
% CHANGE 1976 TO 1978	- 66.7		.0		50.0		25.0		11.1		1.5		3
MALE													
1974 (2 INSTITUTIONS)	6	2.6	3	1.3	1	.4	37	15.9	47	20.2	186	79.8	
1976 (1 INSTITUTIONS)	4	1.9	1	.5	1	.5	38	18.3	44	21.2	164	78.8	
% CHANGE 1974 TO 1976	- 33.3		- 66.7		.0		2.7		- 6.4		- 11.8		- 10
1978 (1 INSTITUTIONS)	5	2.4	1	.5	3	1.4	44	20.8	53	25.0	159	75.0	
% CHANGE 1976 TO 1978	25.0		.0		200.0		15.8		20.5		- 3.0		1

TABLE 18 - COMPARISIONS OF ENROLLMENT IN INSTITUTIONS OF HIGHER EDUCATION FOR SELECTED FIELDS OF STUDY AND LEVEL OF ENROLLMENT
BY RACE, ETHNICITY AND SEX: STATE 1974, 1976, 1978

MAJOR FIELD 1206 - MEDICINE

	AMERICAN INDIAN ALASKAN NATIVE		BLACK NON-HISPANIC		ASIAN OR PACIFIC ISLANDER		HISPANIC		TOTAL MINORITY		WHITE NON-HISPANIC		TOTAL
	NUMBER	%	NUMBER	%	NUMBER	%	NUMBER	%	NUMBER	%	NUMBER	%	NUMBER
NEW YORK.													
FEMALE													
1974 (11 INSTITUTIONS)	3	.2	117	9.6	35	2.9	18	1.5	173	14.1	1,052	85.9	1,225
1976 (12 INSTITUTIONS)	5	.3	159	9.4	44	2.6	46	2.7	254	15.1	1,429	84.9	1,683
% CHANGE 1974 TO 1976	66.7		35.9		25.7		155.6		46.8		35.8		37.4
1978 (14 INSTITUTIONS)	5	.3	138	7.2	64	3.3	61	3.2	268	14.0	1,653	86.0	1,921
% CHANGE 1976 TO 1978	.0		- 13.2		45.5		32.6		5.5		15.7		14.1
MALE													
1974 (11 INSTITUTIONS)	1	.0	202	4.4	92	2.0	76	1.7	371	8.1	4,191	91.9	4,562
1976 (12 INSTITUTIONS)	1	.0	205	4.4	112	2.4	93	2.0	411	8.7	4,298	91.3	4,709
% CHANGE 1974 TO 1976	.0		1.5		21.7		22.4		10.8		2.6		3.2
1978 (14 INSTITUTIONS)	3	.1	164	3.1	117	2.2	113	2.2	397	7.6	4,843	92.4	5,240
% CHANGE 1976 TO 1978	200.0		- 20.0		4.5		21.5		- 3.4		12.7		11.3
NORTH CAROLINA.													
FEMALE													
1974 (6 INSTITUTIONS)	1	.4	20	7.8	1	.4	2	.8	24	9.3	233	90.7	257
1976 (3 INSTITUTIONS)	3	.9	45	13.8	2	.6	3	.9	53	16.2	274	83.8	327
% CHANGE 1974 TO 1976	200.0		125.0		100.0		50.0		120.8		17.6		27.2
1978 (4 INSTITUTIONS)	3	.7	45	11.2	5	1.2	2	.5	55	13.7	346	86.3	401
% CHANGE 1976 TO 1978	.0		.0		150.0		- 33.3		3.8		26.3		22.6
MALE													
1974 (6 INSTITUTIONS)	4	.4	42	3.8	5	.5	2	.2	53	4.8	1,052	95.2	1,105
1976 (3 INSTITUTIONS)	14	1.3	83	7.6	5	.5	1	.1	103	9.4	995	90.6	1,098
% CHANGE 1974 TO 1976	250.0		97.6		.0		- 50.0		94.3		- 5.4		- .6
1978 (4 INSTITUTIONS)	10	.8	80	6.8	8	.7	4	.3	102	8.6	1,080	91.4	1,182
% CHANGE 1976 TO 1978	- 28.6		- 3.6		60.0		300.0		- 1.0		8.5		7.7
NORTH DAKOTA.													
FEMALE													
1974 (1 INSTITUTIONS)	1	4.5	0	.0	0	.0	0	.0	1	4.5	21	95.5	22
1976 (1 INSTITUTIONS)	2	5.7	1	2.9	0	.0	0	.0	3	8.6	32	91.4	35
% CHANGE 1974 TO 1976	100.0		100.0		.0		.0		200.0		52.4		59.1
1978 (1 INSTITUTIONS)	1	2.6	0	.0	0	.0	0	.0	1	2.6	38	97.4	39
% CHANGE 1976 TO 1978	- 50.0		- 100.0		.0		.0		- 66.7		18.8		11.4
MALE													
1974 (1 INSTITUTIONS)	5	3.4	0	.0	0	.0	0	.0	5	3.4	141	96.6	146
1976 (1 INSTITUTIONS)	7	4.0	0	.0	0	.0	0	.0	7	4.0	167	96.0	174
% CHANGE 1974 TO 1976	40.0		.0		.0		.0		40.0		18.4		19.2
1978 (1 INSTITUTIONS)	8	4.6	0	.0	2	1.1	0	.0	10	5.7	164	94.3	174
% CHANGE 1976 TO 1978	14.3		.0		100.0		.0		42.9		- 1.8		.0
OHIO.													
FEMALE													
1974 (5 INSTITUTIONS)	0	.0	35	8.0	4	.9	0	.0	39	8.9	397	91.1	436
1976 (5 INSTITUTIONS)	1	.2	51	9.9	7	1.4	3	.6	62	12.0	455	88.0	517
% CHANGE 1974 TO 1976	100.0		45.7		75.0		100.0		59.0		14.6		18.6
1978 (6 INSTITUTIONS)	2	.3	64	9.6	8	1.2	4	.6	78	11.7	591	88.3	669
% CHANGE 1976 TO 1978	100.0		25.5		14.3		33.3		25.8		29.9		29.4
MALE													
1974 (5 INSTITUTIONS)	1	.1	105	5.7	15	.8	7	.4	128	6.9	1,728	93.1	1,856
1976 (5 INSTITUTIONS)	1	.1	95	5.3	27	1.5	11	.6	134	7.5	1,658	92.5	1,792
% CHANGE 1974 TO 1976	.0		- 9.5		80.0		57.1		4.7		- 4.1		- 3.4
1978 (6 INSTITUTIONS)	0	.0	81	4.2	27	1.4	15	.8	123	6.4	1,803	93.6	1,926
% CHANGE 1976 TO 1978	- 100.0		- 14.7		.0		36.4		- 8.2		8.7		7.5

TABLE 18 - COMPARISIONS OF ENROLLMENT IN INSTITUTIONS OF HIGHER EDUCATION FOR SELECTED FIELDS OF STUDY AND LEVEL OF ENROLLME
BY RACE, ETHNICITY AND SEX: STATE 1974, 1976, 1978

MAJOR FIELD 1206 - MEDICINE

	AMERICAN INDIAN ALASKAN NATIVE		BLACK NON-HISPANIC		ASIAN OR PACIFIC ISLANDER		HISPANIC		TOTAL MINORITY		WHITE NON-HISPANIC	
	NUMBER	%	NUMBER	%	NUMBER	%	NUMBER	%	NUMBER	%	NUMBER	%
OKLAHOMA												
FEMALE												
1974 (9 INSTITUTIONS)	7	4.6	3	2.0	1	.7	2	1.3	13	8.6	138	91.4
1976 (2 INSTITUTIONS)	5	4.2	3	2.5	1	.8	0	.0	9	7.6	109	92.4
% CHANGE 1974 TO 1976	- 28.6		.0		.0		- 100.0		- 30.8		- 21.0	-
1978 (1 INSTITUTIONS)	6	4.5	1	.7	2	1.5	2	1.5	11	8.2	123	91.8
% CHANGE 1976 TO 1978	20.0		- 66.7		100.0		100.0		22.2		12.8	
MALE												
1974 (9 INSTITUTIONS)	21	3.3	12	1.9	3	.5	9	1.4	45	7.0	598	93.0
1976 (2 INSTITUTIONS)	9	1.3	9	1.3	3	.4	3	.4	24	3.4	674	96.6
% CHANGE 1974 TO 1976	- 57.1		- 25.0		.0		- 66.7		- 46.7		12.7	
1978 (1 INSTITUTIONS)	11	1.9	6	1.1	7	1.2	7	1.2	31	5.5	536	94.5
% CHANGE 1976 TO 1978	22.2		- 33.3		133.3		133.3		29.2		- 20.5	-
OREGON.												
FEMALE												
1974 (3 INSTITUTIONS)	0	.0	1	1.2	1	1.2	0	.0	2	2.4	81	97.6
1976 (1 INSTITUTIONS)	2	2.4	2	2.4	1	1.2	0	.0	5	5.9	80	94.1
% CHANGE 1974 TO 1976	100.0		100.0		.0		.0		150.0		- 1.2	
1978 (2 INSTITUTIONS)	2	1.0	1	.5	2	1.0	0	.0	5	2.6	188	97.4
% CHANGE 1976 TO 1978	.0		- 50.0		100.0		.0		.0		135.0	
MALE												
1974 (3 INSTITUTIONS)	2	.5	2	.5	10	2.3	1	.2	15	3.5	419	96.5
1976 (1 INSTITUTIONS)	1	.3	0	.0	13	3.4	0	.0	14	3.7	365	96.3
% CHANGE 1974 TO 1976	- 50.0		- 100.0		30.0		- 100.0		- 6.7		- 12.9	-
1978 (2 INSTITUTIONS)	0	.0	3	.4	10	1.3	3	.4	16	2.0	767	98.0
% CHANGE 1976 TO 1978	- 100.0		100.0		- 23.1		100.0		14.3		110.1	
PENNSYLVANIA.												
FEMALE												
1974 (6 INSTITUTIONS)	3	.4	50	6.5	8	1.0	5	.6	66	8.5	708	91.5
1976 (7 INSTITUTIONS)	2	.2	100	9.2	19	1.7	20	1.8	141	12.9	949	87.1
% CHANGE 1974 TO 1976	- 33.3		100.0		137.5		300.0		113.6		34.0	
1978 (9 INSTITUTIONS)	4	.3	111	8.0	26	1.9	17	1.2	158	11.5	1,221	88.5
% CHANGE 1976 TO 1978	100.0		11.0		36.8		- 15.0		12.1		28.7	
MALE												
1974 (6 INSTITUTIONS)	0	.0	138	5.3	17	.7	16	.6	171	6.6	2,435	93.4
1976 (7 INSTITUTIONS)	4	.1	151	4.8	43	1.4	39	1.2	237	7.6	2,894	92.4
% CHANGE 1974 TO 1976	100.0		9.4		152.9		143.8		38.6		18.9	
1978 (9 INSTITUTIONS)	8	.2	157	3.7	45	1.0	42	1.0	252	5.9	4,044	94.1
% CHANGE 1976 TO 1978	100.0		4.0		4.7		7.7		6.3		39.7	
RHODE ISLAND.												
FEMALE												
1974 (1 INSTITUTIONS)	0	.0	0	.0	2	3.9	0	.0	2	3.9	49	96.1
1976 (1 INSTITUTIONS)	0	.0	1	1.4	5	6.8	0	.0	6	8.2	67	91.8
% CHANGE 1974 TO 1976	.0		100.0		150.0		.0		200.0		36.7	
1978 (1 INSTITUTIONS)	0	.0	5	6.0	9	10.7	0	.0	14	16.7	70	83.3
% CHANGE 1976 TO 1978	.0		400.0		80.0		.0		133.3		4.5	
MALE												
1974 (1 INSTITUTIONS)	0	.0	1	.7	0	.0	0	.0	1	.7	151	99.3
1976 (1 INSTITUTIONS)	0	.0	6	3.4	2	1.1	1	.6	9	5.0	170	95.0
% CHANGE 1974 TO 1976	.0		500.0		100.0		100.0		800.0		12.6	
1978 (1 INSTITUTIONS)	0	.0	9	5.5	2	1.2	5	3.0	16	9.7	149	90.3
% CHANGE 1976 TO 1978	.0		50.0		.0		400.0		77.8		- 12.4	-

COMPARISIONS OF ENROLLMENT IN INSTITUTIONS OF HIGHER EDUCATION FOR SELECTED FIELDS OF STUDY AND LEVEL OF ENROLLMENT BY RACE, ETHNICITY AND SEX: STATE 1974, 1976, 1978

D 1206 - MEDICINE

	AMERICAN INDIAN ALASKAN NATIVE		BLACK NON-HISPANIC		ASIAN OR PACIFIC ISLANDER		HISPANIC		TOTAL MINORITY		WHITE NON-HISPANIC		TOTAL
	NUMBER	%	NUMBER	%	NUMBER	%	NUMBER	%	NUMBER	%	NUMBER	%	NUMBER
LINA........													
1 INSTITUTIONS)	0	.0	5	6.8	0	.0	0	.0	3	6.8	68	93.2	73
1 INSTITUTIONS)	0	.0	5	5.2	0	.0	0	.0		5.2	91	94.8	96
1974 TO 1976	.0		.0		.0		.0		.0		33.8		31.5
1 INSTITUTIONS)	0	.0	1	14.3	0	.0	0	.0	1	14.3	6	85.7	7
1976 TO 1978	.0		- 80.0		.0		.0		- 80.0		- 93.4		- 92.7
1 INSTITUTIONS)	0	.0	23	4.0	0	.0	0	.0	23	4.0	549	96.0	572
1 INSTITUTIONS)	0	.0	26	4.7	1	.2	0	.0	27	4.9	521	95.1	548
1974 TO 1976	.0		13.0		100.0		.0		17.4		- 5.1		- 4.2
1 INSTITUTIONS)	0	.0	1	1.9	0	.0	0	.0	1	1.9	51	98.1	52
1976 TO 1978	.0		- 96.2		- 100.0		.0		- 96.3		- 90.2		- 90.5
TA........													
1 INSTITUTIONS)	0	.0	0	.0	0	.0	0	.0	0	.0	18	100.0	18
1 INSTITUTIONS)	0	.0	0	.0	0	.0	0	.0	0	.0	33	100.0	33
1974 TO 1976	.0		.0		.0		.0		.0		83.3		83.3
1 INSTITUTIONS)	0	.0	0	.0	0	.0	0	.0	0	.0	41	100.0	41
1976 TO 1978	.0		.0		.0		.0		.0		24.2		24.2
1 INSTITUTIONS)	0	.0	0	.0	0	.0	0	.0	0	.0	110	100.0	110
1 INSTITUTIONS)	0	.0	0	.0	0	.0	0	.0	0	.0	172	100.0	172
1974 TO 1976	.0		.0		.0		.0		.0		56.4		56.4
1 INSTITUTIONS)	0	.0	0	.0	1	.6	0	.0	1	.6	176	99.4	177
1976 TO 1978	.0		.0		100.0		.0		100.0		2.3		2.9
....													
6 INSTITUTIONS)	1	.4	102	39.4	1	.4	0	.0	104	40.2	155	59.8	259
3 INSTITUTIONS)	2	.7	124	45.4	3	1.1	2	.7	131	48.0	142	52.0	273
1974 TO 1976	100.0		21.6		200.0		100.0		26.0		- 8.4		5.4
4 INSTITUTIONS)	1	.3	150	43.6	2	.6	3	.9	156	45.3	188	54.7	344
1976 TO 1978	- 50.0		21.0		- 33.3		50.0		19.1		32.4		26.0
6 INSTITUTIONS)	1	.1	279	21.8	2	.2	4	.3	286	22.4	993	77.6	1,279
3 INSTITUTIONS)	3	.3	279	25.1	6	.5	14	1.3	302	27.1	811	72.9	1,113
1974 TO 1976	200.0		.0		200.0		250.0		5.6		- 18.3		- 13.0
4 INSTITUTIONS)	3	.3	338	25.6	9	.7	16	1.2	367	27.8	952	72.2	1,319
1976 TO 1978	33.3		21.1		50.0		14.3		21.5		17.4		18.5
....													
30 INSTITUTIONS)	5	.6	44	5.1	13	1.5	77	8.9	139	16.1	727	83.9	866
6 INSTITUTIONS)	1	.2	32	5.6	12	2.1	37	6.5	82	14.3	491	85.7	573
1974 TO 1976	- 80.0		- 27.3		- 7.7		- 51.9		- 41.0		- 32.5		- 33.8
7 INSTITUTIONS)	0	.0	36	4.8	26	3.5	53	7.0	115	15.3	638	84.7	753
1976 TO 1978	- 100.0		12.5		116.7		43.2		40.2		29.9		31.4
30 INSTITUTIONS)	10	.3	90	2.5	41	1.1	279	7.6	420	11.5	3,246	88.5	3,666
6 INSTITUTIONS)	4	.2	56	2.2	35	1.4	162	6.4	257	10.2	2,273	89.8	2,530
1974 TO 1976	- 60.0		- 37.8		- 14.6		- 41.9		- 38.8		- 30.0		- 31.0
7 INSTITUTIONS)	6	.2	60	2.1	50	1.7	201	7.0	317	11.1	2,550	88.9	2,867
1976 TO 1978	50.0		7.1		42.9		24.1		23.3		12.2		13.3

TABLE 18 — COMPARISIONS OF ENROLLMENT IN INSTITUTIONS OF HIGHER EDUCATION FOR SELECTED FIELDS OF STUDY AND LEVEL OF ENROLLMENT BY RACE, ETHNICITY AND SEX: STATE 1974, 1976, 1978

MAJOR FIELD 1206 — MEDICINE

	AMERICAN INDIAN ALASKAN NATIVE		BLACK NON-HISPANIC		ASIAN OR PACIFIC ISLANDER		HISPANIC		TOTAL MINORITY		WHITE NON-HISPANIC		TOTAL
	NUMBER	%	NUMBER	%	NUMBER	%	NUMBER	%	NUMBER	%	NUMBER	%	NUMBER
UTAH.													
FEMALE													
1974 (3 INSTITUTIONS)	1	1.1	1	1.1	2	2.3	2	2.3	6	9	81	93.1	87
1976 (1 INSTITUTIONS)	0	.0	1	2.0	2	3.9	2	3.9	6	18	46	90.2	51
% CHANGE 1974 TO 1976	- 100.0		.0		.0		.0		- 16.7		- 43.2		- 41.4
1978 (1 INSTITUTIONS)	0	.0	3	5.4	2	3.6	3	5.4	8	14.3	48	85.7	56
% CHANGE 1976 TO 1978	.0		200.0		.0		50.0		60.0		4.3		9.8
MALE													
1974 (3 INSTITUTIONS)	4	.9	0	.0	6	1.4	20	4.6	30	9	408	93.2	438
1976 (1 INSTITUTIONS)	3	.9	1	.3	7	2.0	14	4.1	25	8	319	92.7	344
% CHANGE 1974 TO 1976	- 25.0		100.0		16.7		- 30.0		- 16.7		- 21.8		- 21.5
1978 (1 INSTITUTIONS)	4	1.2	1	.3	6	1.8	13	3.8	24	7.0	317	93.0	341
% CHANGE 1976 TO 1978	33.3		.0		- 14.3		- 7.1		- 4.0		.6		.9
VERMONT													
FEMALE													
1974 (1 INSTITUTIONS)	0	.0	2	4.0	0	.0	0	.0	2	4.0	48	96.0	50
1976 (1 INSTITUTIONS)	0	.0	0	.0	0	.0	0	.0	0	.0	73	100.0	73
% CHANGE 1974 TO 1976	.0		- 100.0		.0		.0		- 100.0		52.1		46.0
1978 (1 INSTITUTIONS)	0	.0	0	.0	0	.0	0	.0	0	.0	68	100.0	68
% CHANGE 1976 TO 1978	.0		.0		.0		.0		.0		- 6.8		- 6.8
MALE													
1974 (1 INSTITUTIONS)	0	.0	1	.4	2	.7	0	.0	3	1.1	265	98.9	268
1976 (1 INSTITUTIONS)	0	.0	1	.4	1	.4	0	.0	2	.8	252	99.2	254
% CHANGE 1974 TO 1976	.0		.0		- 50.0		.0		- 33.3		- 4.9		- 5.2
1978 (1 INSTITUTIONS)	0	.0	0	.0	2	.8	0	.0	2	.8	250	99.2	252
% CHANGE 1976 TO 1978	.0		- 100.0		100.0		.0		.0		- .8		- .8
VIRGINIA													
FEMALE													
1974 (5 INSTITUTIONS)	0	.0	12	7.1	2	1.2	0	.0	14	8.2	156	91.8	170
1976 (3 INSTITUTIONS)	0	.0	23	8.7	4	1.5	0	.0	27	10.2	237	89.8	264
% CHANGE 1974 TO 1976	.0		91.7		100.0		.0		92.9		51.9		55.3
1978 (3 INSTITUTIONS)	0	.0	24	7.4	5	1.5	0	.0	29	9.0	294	91.0	323
% CHANGE 1976 TO 1978	.0		4.3		25.0		.0		7.4		24.1		22.3
MALE													
1974 (5 INSTITUTIONS)	0	.0	38	3.9	3	.3	0	.0	41	4.2	928	95.8	969
1976 (3 INSTITUTIONS)	0	.0	41	4.1	8	.8	2	.2	51	5.1	944	94.9	995
% CHANGE 1974 TO 1976	.0		7.9		166.7		100.0		24.4		1.7		2.7
1978 (3 INSTITUTIONS)	1	.1	40	3.6	13	1.2	6	.5	60	5.5	1,039	94.5	1,099
% CHANGE 1976 TO 1978	100.0		- 2.4		62.5		200.0		17.6		10.1		10.5
WASHINGTON													
FEMALE													
1974 (1 INSTITUTIONS)	0	.0	3	3.8	5	6.3	1	1.3	9	11.4	70	88.6	79
1976 (1 INSTITUTIONS)	0	.0	1	.7	6	4.2	2	1.4	9	6.3	135	93.8	144
% CHANGE 1974 TO 1976	.0		- 66.7		20.0		100.0		.0		92.9		82.3
1978 (1 INSTITUTIONS)	0	.0	2	1.1	8	4.6	3	1.7	13	7.5	161	92.5	174
% CHANGE 1976 TO 1978	.0		100.0		33.3		50.0		44.4		19.3		20.8
MALE													
1974 (1 INSTITUTIONS)	2	.6	12	3.3	18	5.0	9	2.5	41	11.4	320	88.6	361
1976 (1 INSTITUTIONS)	4	.9	14	3.2	23	5.2	8	1.8	49	11.1	394	88.9	443
% CHANGE 1974 TO 1976	100.0		16.7		27.8		- 11.1		19.5		23.1		22.7
1978 (1 INSTITUTIONS)	2	.4	5	1.0	17	3.3	8	1.6	32	6.3	480	93.8	512
% CHANGE 1976 TO 1978	- 50.0		- 64.3		- 26.1		.0		- 34.7		21.8		15.6

ICAN INDIAN SKAN NATIVE		BLACK NON-HISPANIC		ASIAN OR PACIFIC ISLANDER		HISPANIC		TOTAL MINORITY		WHITE NON-HISPANIC		TOTAL
NUMBER	%	NUMBER	%	NUMBER	%	NUMBER	%	NUMBER	%	NUMBER	%	NUMBER
0	.0	0	.0	1	2.8	0	.0	1	2.8	35	97.2	36
0	.0	1	1.8	0	.0	0	.0	1	1.8	54	98.2	55
	.0		100.0	-	100.0		.0		.0		54.3	52.8
0	.0	1	.9	0	.0	1	.9	2	1.8	108	98.2	110
	.0		.0		.0		100.0		100.0		100.0	100.0
0	.0	4	1.3	0	.0	1	.3	5	1 7	293	98.3	298
0	.0	2	.7	1	.3	0	.0	3	1±0	287	99.0	290
	.0	-	50.0		100.0	-	100.0	-	40.0	-	2.0	- 2.7
0	.0	4	.8	2	.4	0	.0	6	1.2	486	98.8	492
	.0		100.0		100.0		.0		100.0		69.3	69.7
0	.0	3	1.6	2	1.1	1	.5	6	.2	180	96.8	186
0	.0	12	4.8	4	1.6	0	.0	16	8.4	234	93.6	250
	.0		300.0		100.0	-	100.0		166.7		30.0	34.4
0	.0	24	8.3	7	2.4	4	1.4	35	12.1	255	87.9	290
	.0		100.0		75.0		100.0		118.8		9.0	16.0
0	.0	26	2.9	7	.8	7	.8	40	4.4	867	95.6	907
4	.4	37	4.1	6	.7	20	2.2	67	7.3	846	92.7	913
100.0		42.3		-	14.3	185.7		67.5		-	2.4	.7
4	.4	36	3.7	11	1.1	33	3.4	84	8.6	890	91.4	974
	.0	-	2.7		83.3		65.0		25.4		5.2	6.7
0	.0	0	.0	0	.0	0	.0	0	.0	2	100.0	2
0	.0	0	.0	0	.0	0	.0	0	.0	0	.0	0
	.0		.0		.0		.0		.0	-	100.0	- 100.0
0	.0	0	.0	0	.0	0	.0	0	.0	0	.0	0
	.0		.0		.0		.0		.0		.0	.0
0	.0	0	.0	0	.0	0	.0	0	.0	6	100.0	6
0	.0	0	.0	0	.0	0	.0	0	.0	0	.0	0
	.0		.0		.0		.0		.0	-	100.0	- 100.0
0	.0	0	.0	0	.0	0	.0	0	.0	0	.0	0
	.0		.0		.0		.0		.0		.0	.0
58	.5	1,131	9.5	229	1.9	285	2 4	1,703	14.3	10,187	85.7	11,890
52	.4	1,232	9.6	336	2.6	280	2±2	1,900	14.9	10,875	85.1	12,775
10.3		8.9		46.7		-	1.8	11.6		6.8		7.4
66	.4	1,390	9.1	516	3.4	392	2.6	2,364	15.4	12,951	84.6	15,315
26.9		12.8		53.6		40.0		24.4		19.1		19.9
150	.3	2,394	5.0	732	1.5	970	2.0	4,246	8.8	43,764	91.2	48,010
154	.3	2,232	5.0	1,011	2.3	997	2.2	4,394	9.9	40,164	90.1	44,558
2.7		-	6.8	38.1		38.1		3.5		-	8.2	- 7.2
166	.3	2,181	4.3	1,297	2.6	1,217	2.4	4,861	9.6	45,850	90.4	50,711
7.8		-	2.3	28.3		28.3		10.6		14.2		13.8

MAJOR FIELD 1206 - MEDICINE

	AMERICAN INDIAN ALASKAN NATIVE		BLACK NON-HISPANIC		ASIAN OR PACIFIC ISLANDER		HISPANIC		TOTAL MINORITY		WHITE NON-HISPANIC	
	NUMBER	%	NUMBER	%	NUMBER	%	NUMBER	%	NUMBER	%	NUMBER	%
PUERTO RICO												
FEMALE												
1974 (0 INSTITUTIONS)	0	.0	0	.0	0	.0	0	.0	0	.0	0	.0
1976 (1 INSTITUTIONS)	18	12.1	0	.0	0	.0	130	87.2	148	99.3	1	.7
% CHANGE 1974 TO 1976	100.0		.0		.0		100.0		100.0		100.0	
1978 (2 INSTITUTIONS)	0	.0	0	.0	0	.0	218	100.0	218	100.0	0	.0
% CHANGE 1976 TO 1978	- 100.0		.0		.0		67.7		47.3		- 100.0	
MALE												
1974 (0 INSTITUTIONS)	0	.0	0	.0	0	.0	0	.0	0	.0	0	.0
1976 (1 INSTITUTIONS)	33	9.1	0	.0	0	.0	322	89.2	355	98.3	6	1.7
% CHANGE 1974 TO 1976	100.0		.0		.0		100.0		100.0		100.0	
1978 (2 INSTITUTIONS)	0	.0	0	.0	0	.0	424	100.0	424	100.0	0	.0
% CHANGE 1976 TO 1978	- 100.0		.0		.0		31.7		19.4		- .100.0	
OUTLYING AREAS.												
FEMALE												
1974 (0 INSTITUTIONS)	0	.0	0	.0	0	.0	0	.0	0	.0	0	.0
1976 (1 INSTITUTIONS)	18	12.1	0	.0	0	.0	130	87.2	148	99.3	1	.7
% CHANGE 1974 TO 1976	100.0		.0		.0		100.0		100.0		100.0	
1978 (2 INSTITUTIONS)	0	.0	0	.0	0	.0	218	100.0	218	100.0	0	.0
% CHANGE 1976 TO 1978	- 100.0		.0		.0		67.7		47.3		- 100.0	
MALE												
1974 (0 INSTITUTIONS)	0	.0	0	.0	0	.0	0	.0	0	.0	0	.0
1976 (1 INSTITUTIONS)	33	9.1	0	.0	0	.0	322	89.2	355	98.3	6	1.7
% CHANGE 1974 TO 1976	100.0		.0		.0		.0		100.0		100.0	
1978 (2 INSTITUTIONS)	0	.0	0	.0	0	.0	424	100.0	424	100.0	0	.0
% CHANGE 1976 TO 1978	- 100.0		.0		.0		.0		19.4		- 100.0	
MAJOR FIELD AGGREGATE 1206.												
FEMALE												
1974 (246 INSTITUTIONS)	58	.5	1,131	9.5	229	1.9	285	2.4	1,703	14.3	10,187	85.7
1976 (125 INSTITUTIONS)	70	.5	1,232	9.5	336	2.6	410	3.2	2,048	15.8	10,876	84.2
% CHANGE 1974 TO 1976	20.7		8.9		46.7		43.9		20.3		6.8	
1978 (138 INSTITUTIONS)	66	.4	1,390	8.9	516	3.3	610	3.9	2,582	16.6	12,951	83.4
% CHANGE 1976 TO 1978	- 5.7		12.8		53.6		48.8		26.1		19.1	
MALE												
1974 (246 INSTITUTIONS)	150	.3	2,394	5.0	732	1.5	970	2.0	4,246	8.8	43,764	91.2
1976 (125 INSTITUTIONS)	187	.4	2,232	5.0	1,011	2.3	1,319	2.9	4,749	10.6	40,170	89.4
% CHANGE 1974 TO 1976	24.7		- 6.8		38.1		38.1		11.8		- 8.2	-
1978 (138 INSTITUTIONS)	166	.3	2,181	4.3	1,297	2.5	1,641	3.2	5,285	10.3	45,850	89.7
% CHANGE 1976 TO 1978	- 11.2		- 2.3		28.3		28.3		11.3		14.1	

Y MEDICINE

ICAN INDIAN SKAN NATIVE		BLACK NON-HISPANIC		ASIAN OR PACIFIC ISLANDER		HISPANIC		TOTAL MINORITY		WHITE NON-HISPANIC		TOTAL
NUMBER	%	NUMBER	%	NUMBER	%	NUMBER	%	NUMBER	%	NUMBER	%	NUMBER
0	.0	31	36.5	0	.0	2	2.4	33	38.8	52	61.2	85
0	.0	31	24.4	0	.0	1	.8	32	25.2	95	74.8	127
.0		.0		.0		- 50.0		- 3.0		82.7		49.4
0	.0	50	25.8	2	1.0	0	.0	52	26.8	142	73.2	194
.0		61.3		100.0		- 100.0		62.5		49.5		52.8
0	.0	147	25.0	4	.7	5	.9	156	26.5	432	73.5	588
0	.0	58	11.8	0	.0	5	1.0	63	12.8	429	87.2	492
.0		- 60.5		- 100.0		.0		- 59.6		- .7		- 16.3
0	.0	53	12.0	6	1.4	1	.2	60	13.5	383	86.5	443
.0		- 8.6		100.0		- 80.0		- 4.8		- 10.7		- 10.0
0	.0	0	.0	0	.0	0	.0	0	.0	12	100.0	12
0	.0	0	.0	0	.0	0	.0	0	.0	0	.0	0
.0		.0		.0		.0		.0		- 100.0		- 100.0
0	.0	0	.0	0	.0	0	.0	0	.0	0	.0	0
.0		.0		.0		.0		.0		.0		.0
0	.0	0	.0	0	.0	0	.0	0	.0	27	100.0	27
0	.0	0	.0	0	.0	0	.0	0	.0	0	.0	0
.0		.0		.0		.0		.0		- 100.0		- 100.0
0	.0	0	.0	0	.0	0	.0	0	.0	0	.0	0
.0		.0		.0		.0		.0		.0		.0
5	1.4	8	2.2	12	3.3	12	3.	37	10.1	330	89.9	367
0	.0	2	1.9	4	3.8	3	2.8	9	8.7	95	91.3	104
100.0		- 75.0		- 66.7		- 75.0		- 75.7		- 71.2		- 71.7
0	.0	3	1.9	4	2.6	2	1.3	9	5.8	145	94.2	154
.0		50.0		.0		- 33.3		.0		52.6		48.1
5	.9	7	1.3	13	2.4	18	3.3	43	7.9	501	92.1	544
3	1.1	4	1.4	8	2.9	6	2.2	21	7.6	255	92.4	276
40.0		- 42.9		- 38.5		- 66.7		- 51.2		- 49.1		- 49.3
0	.0	3	1.2	6	2.4	4	1.6	13	5.1	241	94.9	254
100.0		- 25.0		- 25.0		- 33.3		- 38.1		- 5.5		- 8.0
3	.6	6	1.1	14	2.6	6	1.1	29	5.4	511	94.6	540
0	.0	1	1.1	1	1.1	0	.0	2	2.3	86	97.7	88
100.0		- 83.3		- 92.9		- 100.0		- 93.1		- 83.2		- 83.7
0	.0	3	2.0	3	2.0	1	.7	7	4.6	144	95.4	151
.0		200.0		200.0		100.0		250.0		67.4		71.6
3	.3	4	.4	14	1.5	7	.7	28	2.9	925	97.1	953
1	.3	0	.0	3	1.0	0	.0	4	1.4	282	98.6	286
66.7		- 100.0		- 78.6		- 100.0		- 85.7		- 69.5		- 70.0
1	.3	0	.0	6	1.9	1	.3	8	2.6	300	97.4	308
.0		.0		100.0		100.0		100.0		6.4		7.7

MAJOR FIELD 1210 - VETERINARY MEDICINE

	AMERICAN INDIAN ALASKAN NATIVE		BLACK NON-HISPANIC		ASIAN OR PACIFIC ISLANDER		HISPANIC		TOTAL MINORITY		WHITE NON-HISPANIC		TOTAL
	NUMBER	%	NUMBER	%	NUMBER	%	NUMBER	%	NUMBER	%	NUMBER	%	NUMBER
FLORIDA													
FEMALE													
1974 (10 INSTITUTIONS)	0	.0	3	3.5	0	.0	0	.0	3	3.5	82	96.5	85
1976 (1 INSTITUTIONS)	0	.0	0	.0	0	.0	0	.0	0	.0	13	100.0	13
% CHANGE 1974 TO 1976	.0		-100.0		.0		.0		-100.0		-84.1		-84.7
1978 (1 INSTITUTIONS)	0	.0	0	.0	0	.0	1	1.4	1	1.4	68	98.6	69
% CHANGE 1976 TO 1978	.0		.0		.0		100.0		100.0		423.1		430.8
MALE													
1974 (10 INSTITUTIONS)	0	.0	6	4.0	0	.0	1	.7	7	4.7	143	95.3	150
1976 (1 INSTITUTIONS)	0	.0	0	.0	0	.0	2	7.4	2	7.4	25	92.6	27
% CHANGE 1974 TO 1976	.0		-100.0		.0		100.0		-71.4		-82.5		-82.0
1978 (1 INSTITUTIONS)	1	.8	1	.8	0	.0	5	3.8	7	5.3	124	94.7	131
% CHANGE 1976 TO 1978	100.0		100.0		.0		150.0		250.0		396.0		385.2
GEORGIA													
FEMALE													
1974 (9 INSTITUTIONS)	1	1.1	1	1.1	0	.0	1	1.1	3	3.3	89	96.7	92
1976 (1 INSTITUTIONS)	1	1.0	1	1.0	1	1.0	1	1.0	4	4.0	96	96.0	100
% CHANGE 1974 TO 1976	.0		.0		100.0		.0		33.3		7.9		8.7
1978 (1 INSTITUTIONS)	1	.8	0	.0	1	.8	0	.0	2	1.7	116	98.3	118
% CHANGE 1976 TO 1978	.0		-100.0		.0		-100.0		-50.0		20.8		18.0
MALE													
1974 (9 INSTITUTIONS)	2	.6	0	.0	0	.0	1	.3	3	.9	321	99.1	324
1976 (1 INSTITUTIONS)	3	1.3	1	.4	0	.0	1	.4	5	2.2	226	97.8	231
% CHANGE 1974 TO 1976	50.0		100.0		.0		.0		66.7		-29.6		-28.7
1978 (1 INSTITUTIONS)	2	.9	1	.5	1	.5	0	.0	4	1.8	218	98.2	222
% CHANGE 1976 TO 1978	-33.3		.0		100.0		-100.0		-20.0		-3.5		-3.9
IDAHO													
FEMALE													
1974 (1 INSTITUTIONS)	0	.0	0	.0	0	.0	0	.0	0	.0	6	100.0	6
1976 (0 INSTITUTIONS)	0	.0	0	.0	0	.0	0	.0	0	.0	0	.0	0
% CHANGE 1974 TO 1976	.0		.0		.0		.0		.0		-100.0		-100.0
1978 (0 INSTITUTIONS)	0	.0	0	.0	0	.0	0	.0	0	.0	0	.0	0
% CHANGE 1976 TO 1978	.0		.0		.0		.0		.0		.0		.0
MALE													
1974 (1 INSTITUTIONS)	1	6.3	0	.0	1	6.3	0	.0	2	12.5	14	87.5	16
1976 (0 INSTITUTIONS)	0	.0	0	.0	0	.0	0	.0	0	.0	0	.0	0
% CHANGE 1974 TO 1976	-100.0		.0		-100.0		.0		-100.0		-100.0		-100.0
1978 (0 INSTITUTIONS)	0	.0	0	.0	0	.0	0	.0	0	.0	0	.0	0
% CHANGE 1976 TO 1978	.0		.0		.0		.0		.0		.0		.0
ILLINOIS.													
FEMALE													
1974 (3 INSTITUTIONS)	0	.0	0	.0	3	3.2	0	.0	3	3.2	92	96.8	95
1976 (1 INSTITUTIONS)	1	1.1	0	.0	1	1.1	0	.0	2	2.1	93	97.9	95
% CHANGE 1974 TO 1976	100.0		.0		-66.7		.0		-33.3		1.1		.0
1978 (1 INSTITUTIONS)	1	.8	0	.0	1	.8	0	.0	2	1.6	122	98.4	124
% CHANGE 1976 TO 1978	.0		.0		.0		.0		.0		31.2		30.5
MALE													
1974 (3 INSTITUTIONS)	2	.6	1	.3	0	.0	3	.9	6	1.8	331	98.2	337
1976 (1 INSTITUTIONS)	2	.8	0	.0	0	.0	1	.4	3	1.3	235	98.7	238
% CHANGE 1974 TO 1976	.0		-100.0		.0		-66.7		-50.0		-29.0		-29.4
1978 (1 INSTITUTIONS)	0	.0	0	.0	0	.0	0	.0	0	.0	215	100.0	215
% CHANGE 1976 TO 1978	-100.0		.0		.0		-100.0		-100.0		-8.5		-9.7

Y MEDICINE

ICAN INDIAN SKAN NATIVE		BLACK NON-HISPANIC		ASIAN OR PACIFIC ISLANDER		HISPANIC		TOTAL MINORITY		WHITE NON-HISPANIC		TOTAL
NUMBER	%	NUMBER	%	NUMBER	%	NUMBER	%	NUMBER	%	NUMBER	%	NUMBER
0	.0	0	.0	0	.0	0	.0	0	.0	76	100.0	76
0	.0	1	1.3	0	.0	1	1.3	2	2.6	74	97.4	76
	.0		100.0		.0		100.0		100.0	-	2.6	.0
0	.0	3	3.4	0	.0	1	1.1	4	4.5	84	95.5	88
	.0		200.0		.0		.0		100.0		13.5	15.8
0	.0	1	.4	0	.0	0	.0	1	.4	239	99.6	240
0	.0	1	.5	0	.0	0	.0	1	.5	211	99.5	212
	.0		.0		.0		.0		.0	-	11.7	- 11.7
0	.0	0	.0	0	.0	1	.5	1	.5	198	99.5	199
	.0	-	100.0		.0		100.0		.0	-	6.2	- 6.1
0	.0	0	.0	0	.0	0	.0	0	.0	85	100.0	85
0	.0	0	.0	0	.0	0	.0	0	.0	0	.0	0
	.0		.0		.0		.0		.0	-	100.0	- 100.0
0	.0	0	.0	2	1.7	0	.0	2	1.7	119	98.3	121
	.0		.0		100.0		.0		100.0		100.0	100.0
0	.0	0	.0	0	.0	0	.0	0	.0	317	100.0	317
0	.0	0	.0	0	.0	0	.0	0	.0	0	.0	0
	.0		.0		.0		.0		.0	-	100.0	- 100.0
1	.3	0	.0	2	.6	1	.3	4	1.2	330	98.8	334
	100.0		.0		100.0		100.0		100.0		100.0	100.0
0	.0	2	.6	0	.0	0	.0	2	.6	346	99.4	348
3	4.8	0	.0	2	3.2	0	.0	5	8.1	57	91.9	62
	100.0	-	100.0		100.0		.0		150.0	-	83.5	- 82.2
0	.0	1	1.2	0	.0	2	2.4	3	3.5	82	96.5	85
	100.0		100.0	-	100.0		100.0	-	40.0		43.9	37.1
3	.3	9	1.0	4	.4	5	.5	21	2.3	908	97.7	929
27	8.2	4	1.2	5	1.5	4	1.2	40	12.1	290	87.9	330
	800.0	-	55.6		25.0	-	20.0		90.5	-	68.1	- 64.5
2	.6	3	.9	3	.9	6	1.9	14	4.4	305	95.6	319
	92.6	-	25.0	-	40.0		50.0	-	65.0		5.2	- 3.3
0	.0	0	.0	0	.0	0	.0	0	.0	22	100.0	22
0	.0	0	.0	1	1.9	0	.0	1	1.9	52	98.1	53
	.0		.0		100.0		.0		100.0		136.4	140.9
0	.0	0	.0	1	1.3	1	1.3	2	2.5	78	97.5	80
	.0		.0		.0		100.0		100.0		50.0	50.9
0	.0	1	1.6	0	.0	0	.0	1	1.6	61	98.4	62
0	.0	1	.6	0	.0	0	.0	1	.6	155	99.4	156
	.0		.0		.0		.0		.0		154.1	151.6
0	.0	2	.9	0	.0	0	.0	2	.9	209	99.1	211
	.0		100.0		.0		.0		100.0		34.8	35.3

MAJOR FIELD 1218 - VETERINARY MEDICINE

	AMERICAN INDIAN ALASKAN NATIVE		BLACK NON-HISPANIC		ASIAN OR PACIFIC ISLANDER		HISPANIC		TOTAL MINORITY		WHITE NON-HISPANIC	
	NUMBER	%	NUMBER	%	NUMBER	%	NUMBER	%	NUMBER	%	NUMBER	%
MAINE												
FEMALE												
1974 (1 INSTITUTIONS)	0	.0	0	.0	0	.0	0	.0	0	.0	9	100.0
1976 (0 INSTITUTIONS)	0	.0	0	.0	0	.0	0	.0	0	.0	0	.0
% CHANGE 1974 TO 1976	.0		.0		.0		.0		.0		- 100.0	-
1978 (0 INSTITUTIONS)	0	.0	0	.0	0	.0	0	.0	0	.0	0	.0
% CHANGE 1976 TO 1978	.0		.0		.0		.0		.0		.0	
MALE												
1974 (1 INSTITUTIONS)	0	.0	0	.0	0	.0	0	.0	0	.0	13	100.0
1976 (0 INSTITUTIONS)	0	.0	0	.0	0	.0	0	.0	0	.0	0	.0
% CHANGE 1974 TO 1976	.0		.0		.0		.0		.0		- 100.0	-
1978 (0 INSTITUTIONS)	0	.0	0	.0	0	.0	0	.0	0	.0	0	.0
% CHANGE 1976 TO 1978	.0		.0		.0		.0		.0		.0	
MICHIGAN.												
FEMALE												
1974 (9 INSTITUTIONS)	0	.0	9	1.3	3	.4	1	.1	13	1.9	673	98.1
1976 (1 INSTITUTIONS)	2	1.5	3	2.3	0	.0	0	.0	5	3.8	128	96.2
% CHANGE 1974 TO 1976	100.0		- 66.7		- 100.0		- 100.0		- 61.5		- 81.0	-
1978 (1 INSTITUTIONS)	1	.7	1	.7	0	.0	0	.0	2	1.4	145	98.6
% CHANGE 1976 TO 1978	- 50.0		- 66.7		.0		.0		- 60.0		13.3	
MALE												
1974 (9 INSTITUTIONS)	4	.5	4	.5	0	.0	1	.1	9	1.2	770	98.8
1976 (1 INSTITUTIONS)	0	.0	0	.0	0	.0	0	.0	0	.0	200	100.0
% CHANGE 1974 TO 1976	- 100.0		- 100.0		.0		- 100.0		- 100.0		- 74.0	-
1978 (1 INSTITUTIONS)	0	.0	1	.5	1	.5	1	.5	3	1.6	189	98.4
% CHANGE 1976 TO 1978	.0		100.0		100.0		100.0		100.0		- 5.5	-
MINNESOTA												
FEMALE												
1974 (2 INSTITUTIONS)	1	1.4	0	.0	1	1.4	0	.0	2	2.8	69	97.2
1976 (1 INSTITUTIONS)	0	.0	0	.0	2	2.2	0	.0	2	2.2	91	97.8
% CHANGE 1974 TO 1976	- 100.0		.0		100.0		.0		.0		31.9	
1978 (1 INSTITUTIONS)	1	.8	0	.0	3	2.4	0	.0	4	3.2	120	96.8
% CHANGE 1976 TO 1978	100.0		.0		50.0		.0		100.0		31.9	
MALE												
1974 (2 INSTITUTIONS)	4	1.4	0	.0	2	.7	0	.0	6	2.1	278	97.9
1976 (1 INSTITUTIONS)	1	.5	0	.0	0	.0	0	.0	1	.5	203	99.5
% CHANGE 1974 TO 1976	- 75.0		.0		- 100.0		.0		- 83.3		- 27.0	-
1978 (1 INSTITUTIONS)	1	.5	0	.0	1	.5	0	.0	2	1.0	191	99.0
% CHANGE 1976 TO 1978	.0		.0		100.0		.0		100.0		- 5.9	-
MISSISSIPPI												
FEMALE												
1974 (8 INSTITUTIONS)	0	.0	0	.0	0	.0	0	.0	0	.0	17	100.0
1976 (0 INSTITUTIONS)	0	.0	0	.0	0	.0	0	.0	0	.0	0	.0
% CHANGE 1974 TO 1976	.0		.0		.0		.0		.0		- 100.0	-)
1978 (1 INSTITUTIONS)	0	.0	2	10.5	0	.0	0	.0	2	10.5	17	89.5
% CHANGE 1976 TO 1978	.0		100.0		.0		.0		100.0		100.0	
MALE												
1974 (8 INSTITUTIONS)	0	.0	1	2.4	0	.0	0	.0	1	2.4	40	97.6
1976 (0 INSTITUTIONS)	0	.0	0	.0	0	.0	0	.0	0	.0	0	.0
% CHANGE 1974 TO 1976	.0		- 100.0		.0		.0		- 100.0		- 100.0	-)
1978 (1 INSTITUTIONS)	0	.0	0	.0	0	.0	0	.0	0	.0	36	100.0
% CHANGE 1976 TO 1978	.0		.0		.0		.0		.0		100.0	)

TABLE 18 - COMPARISIONS OF ENROLLMENT IN INSTITUTIONS OF HIGHER EDUCATION FOR SELECTED FIELDS OF STUDY AND LEVEL OF ENROLLMENT BY RACE, ETHNICITY AND SEX: STATE 1974, 1976, 1978

MAJOR FIELD 1218 - VETERINARY MEDICINE

	AMERICAN INDIAN ALASKAN NATIVE		BLACK NON-HISPANIC		ASIAN OR PACIFIC ISLANDER		HISPANIC		TOTAL MINORITY		WHITE NON-HISPANIC		TOTAL
	NUMBER	%	NUMBER	%	NUMBER	%	NUMBER	%	NUMBER	%	NUMBER	%	NUMBER
MISSOURI··········													
FEMALE													
1974 (1 INSTITUTIONS)	0	.0	0	.0	0	.0	0	.0	0	.0	38	100.0	38
1976 (1 INSTITUTIONS)	0	.0	0	.0	0	.0	0	.0	0	.0	61	100.0	61
% CHANGE 1974 TO 1976		.0		.0		.0		.0		.0		60.5	60.5
1978 (1 INSTITUTIONS)	1	1.2	0	.0	0	.0	0	.0	1	1.2	85	98.8	86
% CHANGE 1976 TO 1978	100.0			.0		.0		.0	100.0		39.3		41.0
MALE													
1974 (1 INSTITUTIONS)	0	.0	0	.0	0	.0	0	.0	0	.0	240	100.0	240
1976 (1 INSTITUTIONS)	2	.9	0	.0	1	.5	0	.0	3	1.4	216	98.6	219
% CHANGE 1974 TO 1976	100.0			.0	100.0			.0	100.0		-	10.0	- 8.8
1978 (1 INSTITUTIONS)	1	.5	0	.0	2	1.0	1	.5	4	2.0	199	98.0	203
% CHANGE 1976 TO 1978	- 50.0			.0	100.0		100.0		33.3		-	7.9	- 7.3
MONTANA··········													
FEMALE													
1974 (1 INSTITUTIONS)	2	6.1	0	.0	0	.0	0	.0	2	6.1	31	93.9	33
1976 (0 INSTITUTIONS)	0	.0	0	.0	0	.0	0	.0	0	.0	0	.0	0
% CHANGE 1974 TO 1976	- 100.0			.0		.0		.0	- 100.0		- 100.0		- 100.0
1978 (0 INSTITUTIONS)	0	.0	0	.0	0	.0	0	.0	0	.0	0	.0	0
% CHANGE 1976 TO 1978		.0		.0		.0		.0		.0		.0	.0
MALE													
1974 (1 INSTITUTIONS)	0	.0	0	.0	0	.0	0	.0	0	.0	88	100.0	88
1976 (0 INSTITUTIONS)	0	.0	0	.0	0	.0	0	.0	0	.0	0	.0	0
% CHANGE 1974 TO 1976		.0		.0		.0		.0		.0	- 100.0		- 100.0
1978 (0 INSTITUTIONS)	0	.0	0	.0	0	.0	0	.0	0	.0	0	.0	0
% CHANGE 1976 TO 1978		.0		.0		.0		.0		.0		.0	.0
NEBRASKA··········													
FEMALE													
1974 (1 INSTITUTIONS)	0	.0	0	.0	0	.0	0	.0	0	.0	4	100.0	4
1976 (1 INSTITUTIONS)	0	.0	0	.0	0	.0	0	.0	0	.0	3	100.0	3
% CHANGE 1974 TO 1976		.0		.0		.0		.0		.0	- 25.0		- 25.0
1978 (0 INSTITUTIONS)	0	.0	0	.0	0	.0	0	.0	0	.0	0	.0	0
% CHANGE 1976 TO 1978		.0		.0		.0		.0		.0	- 100.0		- 100.0
MALE													
1974 (1 INSTITUTIONS)	0	.0	0	.0	0	.0	0	.0	0	.0	10	100.0	10
1976 (1 INSTITUTIONS)	0	.0	0	.0	0	.0	0	.0	0	.0	5	100.0	5
% CHANGE 1974 TO 1976		.0		.0		.0		.0		.0	- 50.0		- 50.0
1978 (0 INSTITUTIONS)	0	.0	0	.0	0	.0	0	.0	0	.0	0	.0	0
% CHANGE 1976 TO 1978		.0		.0		.0		.0		.0	- 100.0		- 100.0
NEW YORK··········													
FEMALE													
1974 (1 INSTITUTIONS)	0	.0	3	6.5	0	.0	0	.0	3	6.5	43	93.5	46
1976 (1 INSTITUTIONS)	0	.0	4	4.2	0	.0	0	.0	4	4.2	92	95.8	96
% CHANGE 1974 TO 1976		.0	33.3			.0		.0	33.3		114.0		108.7
1978 (1 INSTITUTIONS)	0	.0	3	2.1	2	1.4	0	.0	5	3.5	136	96.5	141
% CHANGE 1976 TO 1978		.0	- 25.0		100.0			.0	25.0		47.8		46.9
MALE													
1974 (1 INSTITUTIONS)	0	.0	0	.0	0	.0	1	.5	1	.5	187	99.5	188
1976 (1 INSTITUTIONS)	0	.0	1	.5	1	.5	1	.5	3	1.6	184	98.4	187
% CHANGE 1974 TO 1976		.0	100.0		100.0			.0	200.0		-	1.6	- .5
1978 (1 INSTITUTIONS)	2	1.2	0	.0	1	.6	1	.6	4	2.4	163	97.6	167
% CHANGE 1976 TO 1978	100.0		- 100.0			.0		.0	33.3		-	11.4	- 10.7

TABLE 18 - COMPARISIONS OF ENROLLMENT IN INSTITUTIONS OF HIGHER EDUCATION FOR SELECTED FIELDS OF STUDY AND LEVEL OF ENROLLM
BY RACE, ETHNICITY AND SEX: STATE 1974, 1976, 1978

MAJOR FIELD   1218 - VETERINARY MEDICINE

		AMERICAN INDIAN ALASKAN NATIVE		BLACK NON-HISPANIC		ASIAN OR PACIFIC ISLANDER		HISPANIC		TOTAL MINORITY		WHITE NON-HISPANIC	
		NUMBER	%	NUMBER	%	NUMBER	%	NUMBER	%	NUMBER	%	NUMBER	%
OHIO.............													
FEMALE													
1974 (	2 INSTITUTIONS)	1	.7	1	.7	0	.0	0	.0	2	1.5	132	98.5
1976 (	1 INSTITUTIONS)	1	.6	1	.6	0	.0	0	.0	2	1.2	167	98.8
% CHANGE 1974 TO 1976		.0		.0		.0		.0		.0		26.5	
1978 (	1 INSTITUTIONS)	0	.0	2	1.2	2	1.2	0	.0	4	2.4	163	97.6
% CHANGE 1976 TO 1978		- 100.0		100.0		100.0		.0		100.0		- 2.4	
MALE													
1974 (	2 INSTITUTIONS)	1	.2	2	.4	0	.0	1	.2	4	.9	456	99.1
1976 (	1 INSTITUTIONS)	1	.3	2	.6	0	.0	1	.3	4	1.1	354	98.9
% CHANGE 1974 TO 1976		.0		.0		.0		.0		.0		- 22.4	-
1978 (	1 INSTITUTIONS)	0	.0	2	.7	0	.0	0	.0	2	.7	268	99.3
% CHANGE 1976 TO 1978		- 100.0		.0		.0		- 100.0		- 50.0		- 24.3	.
OKLAHOMA..........													
FEMALE													
1974 (	7 INSTITUTIONS)	1	1.5	0	.0	0	.0	1	1.5	2	3.0	64	97.0
1976 (	1 INSTITUTIONS)	1	2.1	0	.0	0	.0	1	2.1	2	4.3	45	95.7
% CHANGE 1974 TO 1976		.0		.0		.0		.0		.0		- 29.7	-
1978 (	1 INSTITUTIONS)	0	.0	0	.0	1	1.7	0	.0	1	1.7	58	98.3
% CHANGE 1976 TO 1978		- 100.0		.0		100.0		- 100.0		- 50.0		28.9	
MALE													
1974 (	7 INSTITUTIONS)	8	2.8	2	.7	0	.0	3	1.0	13	4.5	275	95.5
1976 (	1 INSTITUTIONS)	2	1.0	0	.0	1	.5	2	1.0	5	2.5	197	97.5
% CHANGE 1974 TO 1976		- 75.0		- 100.0		100.0		- 33.3		- 61.5		- 28.4	-
1978 (	1 INSTITUTIONS)	4	2.0	1	.5	2	1.0	1	.5	8	4.1	189	95.9
% CHANGE 1976 TO 1978		100.0		100.0		100.0		- 50.0		60.0		- 4.1	-
OREGON............													
FEMALE													
1974 (	1 INSTITUTIONS)	0	.0	0	.0	0	.0	0	.0	0	.0	6	100.0
1976 (	0 INSTITUTIONS)	0	.0	0	.0	0	.0	0	.0	0	.0	0	.0
% CHANGE 1974 TO 1976		.0		.0		.0		.0		.0		- 100.0	-
1978 (	0 INSTITUTIONS)	0	.0	0	.0	0	.0	0	.0	0	.0	0	.0
% CHANGE 1976 TO 1978		.0		.0		.0		.0		.0		.0	
MALE													
1974 (	1 INSTITUTIONS)	0	.0	0	.0	1	3.2	0	.0	1	3.2	30	96.8
1976 (	0 INSTITUTIONS)	0	.0	0	.0	0	.0	0	.0	0	.0	0	.0
% CHANGE 1974 TO 1976		.0		.0		- 100.0		.0		- 100.0		- 100.0	-
1978 (	0 INSTITUTIONS)	0	.0	0	.0	0	.0	0	.0	0	.0	0	.0
% CHANGE 1976 TO 1978		.0		.0		.0		.0		.0		.0	
PENNSYLVANIA........													
FEMALE													
1974 (	1 INSTITUTIONS)	0	.0	5	3.5	0	.0	1	.7	6	4.3	135	95.7
1976 (	1 INSTITUTIONS)	0	.0	5	2.9	0	.0	2	1.2	7	4.1	164	95.9
% CHANGE 1974 TO 1976		.0		.0		.0		100.0		16.7		21.5	
1978 (	1 INSTITUTIONS)	0	.0	7	3.8	1	.5	1	.5	9	4.8	177	95.2
% CHANGE 1976 TO 1978		.0		40.0		100.0		- 50.0		28.6		- 7.9	
MALE													
1974 (	1 INSTITUTIONS)	0	.0	2	.8	0	.0	1	.4	3	1.2	247	98.8
1976 (	1 INSTITUTIONS)	1	.4	2	.8	0	.0	0	.0	3	1.3	235	98.7
% CHANGE 1974 TO 1976		100.0		.0		.0		- 100.0		.0		- 4.9	-
1978 (	1 INSTITUTIONS)	0	.0	2	.8	0	.0	2	.8	4	1.7	237	98.3
% CHANGE 1976 TO 1978		- 100.0		.0		.0		100.0		33.3		.9	

Y MEDICINE

ICAN INDIAN SKAN NATIVE		BLACK NON-HISPANIC		ASIAN OR PACIFIC ISLANDER		HISPANIC		TOTAL MINORITY		WHITE NON-HISPANIC		TOTAL
NUMBER	%	NUMBER	%	NUMBER	%	NUMBER	%	NUMBER	%	NUMBER	%	NUMBER
0	.0	0	.0	0	.0	0	.0	0	.0	35	100.0	35
0	.0	0	.0	0	.0	0	.0	0	.0	12	100.0	12
.0		.0		.0		.0		.0		- 65.7		- 65.7
0	.0	1	1.9	0	.0	1	1.9	2	3.8	50	96.2	52
.0		100.0		.0		100.0		100.0		316.7		333.3
0	.0	1	.9	0	.0	0	.0	1	.9	111	99.1	112
0	.0	0	.0	0	.0	0	.0	0	.0	28	100.0	28
.0		- 100.0		.0		.0		- 100.0		- 74.8		- 75.0
0	.0	0	.0	0	.0	1	.8	1	.8	126	99.2	127
.0		.0		.0		100.0		100.0		350.0		353.6
0	.0	0	.0	0	.0	1	.6	1	.6	159	99.4	160
0	.0	0	.0	1	.9	0	.0	1	.9	110	99.1	111
.0		.0		100.0		- 100.0		.0		- 30.8		- 30.6
1	.7	0	.0	1	.7	0	.0	2	1.3	148	98.7	150
100.0		.0		.0		.0		100.0		34.5		35.1
0	.0	1	.2	0	.0	5	.8	6	1.0	593	99.0	599
10	3.2	0	.0	0	.0	0	.0	10	3.2	302	96.8	312
100.0		- 100.0		.0		- 100.0		66.7		- 49.1		- 47.9
6	2.2	1	.4	0	.0	2	.7	9	3.4	259	96.6	268
40.0		100.0		.0		100.0		- 10.0		- 14.2		- 14.1
0	.0	0	.0	0	.0	0	.0	0	.0	32	100.0	32
0	.0	0	.0	0	.0	0	.0	0	.0	0	.0	0
.0		.0		.0		.0		.0		- 100.0		- 100.0
0	.0	0	.0	0	.0	0	.0	0	.0	0	.0	0
.0		.0		.0		.0		.0		.0		.0
0	.0	1	.9	0	.0	0	.0	1	.9	113	99.1	114
0	.0	0	.0	0	.0	0	.0	0	.0	0	.0	0
.0		- 100.0		.0		.0		- 100.0		- 100.0		- 100.0
0	.0	0	.0	0	.0	0	.0	0	.0	0	.0	0
.0		.0		.0		.0		.0		.0		.0
0	.0	0	.0	0	.0	0	.0	0	.0	0	.0	0
0	.0	0	.0	0	.0	0	.0	0	.0	0	.0	0
.0		.0		.0		.0		.0		.0		.0
0	.0	0	.0	0	.0	0	.0	0	.0	0	.0	0
.0		.0		.0		.0		.0		.0		.0
0	.0	0	.0	0	.0	0	.0	0	.0	1	100.0	1
0	.0	0	.0	0	.0	0	.0	0	.0	0	.0	0
.0		.0		.0		.0		.0		- 100.0		- 100.0
0	.0	0	.0	0	.0	0	.0	0	.0	0	.0	0
.0		.0		.0		.0		.0		.0		.0

MAJOR FIELD 1218 - VETERINARY MEDICINE

	AMERICAN INDIAN ALASKAN NATIVE		BLACK NON-HISPANIC		ASIAN OR PACIFIC ISLANDER		HISPANIC		TOTAL MINORITY		WHITE NON-HISPANIC	
	NUMBER	%	NUMBER	%	NUMBER	%	NUMBER	%	NUMBER	%	NUMBER	%
WASHINGTON.												
FEMALE												
1974 (2 INSTITUTIONS)	1	1.0	1	1.0	3	3.0	0	.0	5	5.0	96	95.0
1976 (1 INSTITUTIONS)	0	.0	2	2.4	2	2.4	1	1.2	5	6.0	78	94.0
% CHANGE 1974 TO 1976	- 100.0		100.0		- 33.3		100.0		.0		- 18.8	-
1978 (1 INSTITUTIONS)	0	.0	1	1.0	2	1.9	1	1.0	4	3.8	101	96.2
% CHANGE 1976 TO 1978	.0		- 50.0		.0		.0		- 20.0		29.5	
MALE												
1974 (2 INSTITUTIONS)	4	1.4	1	.4	8	2.9	1	.4	14	5.0	264	95.0
1976 (1 INSTITUTIONS)	1	.5	0	.0	2	1.0	1	.5	4	1.9	205	98.1
% CHANGE 1974 TO 1976	- 75.0		- 100.0		- 75.0		.0		- 71.4		- 22.3	-
1978 (1 INSTITUTIONS)	0	.0	0	.0	3	1.4	0	.0	3	1.4	210	98.6
% CHANGE 1976 TO 1978	- 100.0		.0		50.0		- 100.0		- 25.0		2.4	
WYOMING												
FEMALE												
1974 (1 INSTITUTIONS)	0	.0	0	.0	0	.0	0	.0	0	.0	0	.0
1976 (0 INSTITUTIONS)	0	.0	0	.0	0	.0	0	.0	0	.0	0	.0
% CHANGE 1974 TO 1976	.0		.0		.0		.0		.0		.0	
1978 (0 INSTITUTIONS)	0	.0	0	.0	0	.0	0	.0	0	.0	0	.0
% CHANGE 1976 TO 1978	.0		.0		.0		.0		.0		.0	
MALE												
1974 (1 INSTITUTIONS)	0	.0	0	.0	0	.0	0	.0	0	.0	2	100.0
1976 (0 INSTITUTIONS)	0	.0	0	.0	0	.0	0	.0	0	.0	0	.0
% CHANGE 1974 TO 1976	.0		.0		.0		.0		.0		- 100.0	-
1978 (0 INSTITUTIONS)	0	.0	0	.0	0	.0	0	.0	0	.0	0	.0
% CHANGE 1976 TO 1978	.0		.0		.0		.0		.0		.0	
MAJOR FIELD AGGREGATE 1218.												
FEMALE												
1974 (126 INSTITUTIONS)	15	.4	70	2.1	36	1.1	25	.7	146	4.3	3,246	95.7
1976 (21 INSTITUTIONS)	9	.5	51	3.0	15	.9	10	.6	85	5.0	1,612	95.0
% CHANGE 1974 TO 1976	- 40.0		- 27.1		- 58.3		- 60.0		- 41.8		- 50.3	-
1978 (22 INSTITUTIONS)	6	.2	77	3.2	26	1.1	11	.5	120	5.0	2,300	95.0
% CHANGE 1976 TO 1978	- 33.3		51.0		73.3		10.0		41.2		42.7	
MALE												
1974 (126 INSTITUTIONS)	37	.4	191	2.3	47	.6	53	.6	328	4.0	7,934	96.0
1976 (21 INSTITUTIONS)	54	1.2	74	1.7	21	.5	24	.5	173	3.9	4,237	96.1
% CHANGE 1974 TO 1976	45.9		- 61.3		- 55.3		- 55.3		- 47.3		- 46.6	-
1978 (22 INSTITUTIONS)	21	.4	70	1.5	34	.7	28	.6	153	3.2	4,590	96.8
% CHANGE 1976 TO 1978	- 61.1		- 5.4		61.9		61.9		- 11.6		8.3	

ICAN INDIAN SKAN NATIVE		BLACK NON-HISPANIC		ASIAN OR PACIFIC ISLANDER		HISPANIC		TOTAL MINORITY		WHITE NON-HISPANIC		TOTAL
NUMBER	%	NUMBER	%	NUMBER	%	NUMBER	%	NUMBER	%	NUMBER	%	NUMBER
0	.0	15	8.5	0	.0	0	.0	15	8.5	161	91.5	176
0	.0	23	11.5	0	.0	0	.0	23	11.5	177	88.5	200
.0		53.3		.0		.0		53.3		9.9	.	13.6
0	.0	9	3.7	0	.0	1	.4	10	4.1	232	95.9	242
.0	-	60.9		.0		100.0	-	56.5		31.1		21.0
0	.0	65	4.5	0	.0	5	.3	70	8	1,374	95.2	1,444
1	.1	55	5.3	0	.0	2	.2	58	6	983	94.4	1,041
100.0	-	15.4		.0	-	60.0	-	17.1	-	28.5	-	27.9
0	.0	15	1.4	0	.0	2	.2	17	1.6	1,051	98.4	1,068
100.0	-	72.7		.0		.0	-	70.7		6.9		2.6
4	1.3	6	1.9	2	.6	23	7.5	35	11.4	273	88.6	308
0	.0	1	.4	2	.8	9	3.5	12	4.7	244	95.3	256
100.0	-	83.3		.0	-	60.9	-	65.7	-	10.6	-	16.9
1	.3	0	.0	2	.7	6	2.1	9	3.1	280	96.9	289
100.0	-	100.0		.0	-	33.3	-	25.0		14.8		12.9
3	.3	19	1.9	8	.8	78	7.9	108	10.9	881	89.1	989
0	.0	2	.4	4	.7	15	2.8	21	3.9	513	96.1	534
100.0	-	89.5	-	50.0	-	80.8	-	80.6	-	41.8	-	46.0
2	.4	1	.2	1	.2	12	2.1	16	2.8	551	97.2	567
100.0	-	50.0	-	75.0	-	20.0	-	23.8	-	7.4		6.2
3	2.3	14	10.9	0	.0	0	.0	17	13.3	111	86.7	128
3	1.5	11	5.6	1	.5	1	.5	16	8.2	179	91.8	195
.0	-	21.4		100.0		100.0	-	5.9		61.3		52.3
0	.0	10	5.0	1	.5	1	.5	12	6.0	189	94.0	201
100.0	-	9.1		.0		.0	-	25.0		5.6		3.1
22	3.2	28	4.0	0	.0	1	.1	51	7.	647	92.7	698
4	.6	30	4.6	1	.2	2	.3	37	5.8	622	94.4	659
81.8		7.1		100.0		100.0	-	27.5	-	3.9	-	5.6
3	.5	24	3.6	2	.3	3	.5	32	4.9	626	95.1	658
25.0	-	20.0		100.0		50.0	-	13.5		.6	-	.2
33	.7	567	11.7	171	3.5	279	5.7	1,050	21.6	3,810	78.4	4,860
42	.8	324	6.0	231	4.3	214	4.0	811	15.0	4,598	85.0	5,409
27.3	-	42.9	.	35.1	-	23.3	-	22.8		20.7		11.3
37	.6	344	5.7	249	4.1	256	4.2	886	14.6	5,185	85.4	6,071
11.9		6.2		7.8		19.6		9.2		12.8		12.2
92	.6	1,044	7.2	424	2.9	1,156	8.0	2,716	18.8	11,746	81.2	14,462
92	.7	463	3.4	410	3.0	573	4.3	1,538	11.4	11,937	88.6	13,475
.0	-	55.7	-	3.3	-	50.4	-	43.4		1.6	-	6.8
72	.6	452	3.5	427	3.3	587	4.5	1,538	11.8	11,526	88.2	13,064
21.7	-	2.4		4.1		2.4		.0	-	3.4	-	3.1

TABLE 18 - COMPARISIONS OF ENROLLMENT IN INSTITUTIONS OF HIGHER EDUCATION FOR SELECTED FIELDS OF STUDY AND LEVEL OF ENROLLMENT
          BY RACE, ETHNICITY AND SEX: STATE 1974, 1976, 1978

MAJOR FIELD 1400 - LAW

	AMERICAN INDIAN ALASKAN NATIVE		BLACK NON-HISPANIC		ASIAN OR PACIFIC ISLANDER		HISPANIC		TOTAL MINORITY		WHITE NON-HISPANIC		TOTAL
	NUMBER	%	NUMBER	%	NUMBER	%	NUMBER	%	NUMBER	%	NUMBER	%	NUMBER
COLORADO													
FEMALE													
1974 (5 INSTITUTIONS)	0	.0	6	5.0	2	1.7	4	3.	12	10.0	108	90.0	120
1976 (3 INSTITUTIONS)	1	.2	5	1.2	3	.7	10	2.4	19	4.6	398	95.4	417
% CHANGE 1974 TO 1976	100.0		- 16.7		50.0		150.0		58.3		268.5		247.5
1978 (3 INSTITUTIONS)	4	.8	9	1.8	2	.4	14	2.8	29	5.8	470	94.2	499
% CHANGE 1976 TO 1978	300.0		80.0		- 33.3		40.0		52.6		18.1		19.7
MALE													
1974 (5 INSTITUTIONS)	4	1.0	15	3.9	3	.8	32	8.3	54	14.1	330	85.9	384
1976 (3 INSTITUTIONS)	3	.3	18	2.0	3	.3	38	4.2	62	6.9	834	93.1	896
% CHANGE 1974 TO 1976	- 25.0		20.0		.0		18.8		14.8		152.7		133.3
1978 (3 INSTITUTIONS)	11	1.3	22	2.6	2	.2	40	4.8	75	9.0	758	91.0	833
% CHANGE 1976 TO 1978	266.7		22.2		- 33.3		5.3		21.0		- 9.1		- 7.0
CONNECTICUT													
FEMALE													
1974 (2 INSTITUTIONS)	0	.0	18	6.4	1	.4	7	1.1	22	7.8	261	92.2	283
1976 (2 INSTITUTIONS)	1	.3	29	7.9	3	.8	7	1.9	40	10.9	327	89.1	367
% CHANGE 1974 TO 1976	100.0		61.1		200.0		133.3		81.8		25.3		29.7
1978 (3 INSTITUTIONS)	2	.4	28	5.8	2	.4	15	3.1	47	9.7	437	90.3	484
% CHANGE 1976 TO 1978	100.0		- 3.4		- 33.3		114.3		17.5		33.6		31.9
MALE													
1974 (2 INSTITUTIONS)	3	.3	47	5.1	3	.3	15	1.6	68	7	845	92.6	913
1976 (2 INSTITUTIONS)	2	.2	37	4.4	4	.5	14	1.7	57	6.8	780	93.2	837
% CHANGE 1974 TO 1976	- 33.3		- 21.3		33.3		- 6.7		- 16.2		- 7.7		- 8.3
1978 (3 INSTITUTIONS)	0	.0	25	2.3	4	.4	28	2.5	57	5.1	1,050	94.9	1,107
% CHANGE 1976 TO 1978	- 100.0		- 32.4		.0		100.0		.0		34.6		32.3
DISTRICT OF COLUMBIA. . . .													
FEMALE													
1974 (5 INSTITUTIONS)	5	.3	251	17.4	6	.4	30	2.1	292	20.3	1,149	79.7	1,441
1976 (5 INSTITUTIONS)	4	.2	314	16.0	42	2.1	37	1.9	397	20.3	1,561	79.7	1,958
% CHANGE 1974 TO 1976	- 20.0		25.1		600.0		23.3		36.0		35.9		35.9
1978 (5 INSTITUTIONS)	1	.0	392	18.1	46	2.1	56	2.6	495	22.8	1,673	77.2	2,168
% CHANGE 1976 TO 1978	- 75.0		24.8		9.5		51.4		24.7		7.2		10.7
MALE													
1974 (5 INSTITUTIONS)	5	.1	396	9.1	37	.8	81	1.9	519	11.9	3,845	88.1	4,364
1976 (5 INSTITUTIONS)	8	.2	399	9.9	53	1.3	103	2.6	563	14.0	3,463	86.0	4,026
% CHANGE 1974 TO 1976	60.0		.8		43.2		27.2		8.5		- 9.9		- 7.7
1978 (5 INSTITUTIONS)	8	.2	387	12.0	55	1.7	118	3.7	568	17.7	2,649	82.3	3,217
% CHANGE 1976 TO 1978	.0		- 3.0		3.8		14.6		.9		- 23.5		- 20.1
FLORIDA													
FEMALE													
1974 (29 INSTITUTIONS)	1	.1	59	6.5	0	.0	42	4.6	102	11.2	811	88.8	913
1976 (5 INSTITUTIONS)	0	.0	26	3.0	2	.2	27	3.1	55	6.3	813	93.7	868
% CHANGE 1974 TO 1976	- 100.0		- 55.9		100.0		- 35.7		- 46.1		.2		4.9
1978 (5 INSTITUTIONS)	1	.1	34	3.2	1	.1	46	4.3	82	7.6	992	92.4	1,074
% CHANGE 1976 TO 1978	100.0		30.8		- 50.0		70.4		49.1		22.0		23.7
MALE													
1974 (29 INSTITUTIONS)	5	.1	146	3.6	6	.1	88	2.2	245	6.0	3,834	94.0	4,079
1976 (5 INSTITUTIONS)	7	.2	80	2.7	6	.2	95	3.2	188	6.4	2,738	93.6	2,926
% CHANGE 1974 TO 1976	40.0		- 45.2		.0		8.0		- 23.3		- 28.6		- 28.3
1978 (5 INSTITUTIONS)	5	.2	88	3.3	9	.3	143	5.4	245	9.2	2,413	90.8	2,658
% CHANGE 1976 TO 1978	- 28.6		10.0		50.0		50.5		30.3		- 11.9		- 9.2

1400 - LAW

	AMERICAN INDIAN ALASKAN NATIVE		BLACK NON-HISPANIC		ASIAN OR PACIFIC ISLANDER		HISPANIC		TOTAL MINORITY		WHITE NON-HISPANIC		TOTAL
	NUMBER	%	NUMBER	%	NUMBER	%	NUMBER	%	NUMBER	%	NUMBER	%	NUMBER
. . . .													
15 INSTITUTIONS)	0	.0	26	6.9	1	.3	3	.8	30	8.0	346	92.0	376
3 INSTITUTIONS)	1	.3	29	7.3	0	.0	3	.8	33	8.3	366	91.7	399
1974 TO 1976	100.0		11.5		- 100.0		.0		10.0		5.8		6.1
3 INSTITUTIONS)	2	.4	41	7.9	1	.2	3	.6	47	9.1	470	90.9	517
1976 TO 1978	100.0		41.4		100.0		.0		42.4		28.4		29.6
15 INSTITUTIONS)	5	.3	50	3.1	3	.2	7	.4	65	4.1	1,529	95.9	1,594
3 INSTITUTIONS)	1	.1	30	2.5	5	.4	7	.6	43	3.6	1,158	96.4	1,201
1974 TO 1976	- 80.0		- 40.0		66.7		.0		- 33.8		- 24.3		- 24.7
3 INSTITUTIONS)	0	.0	33	2.7	4	.3	11	.9	48	3.9	1,181	96.1	1,229
1976 TO 1978	- 100.0		10.0		- 20.0		57.1		11.6		2.0		2.3
. . . .													
0 INSTITUTIONS)	0	.0	0	.0	0	.0	0	.0	0	.0	0	.0	0
1 INSTITUTIONS)	0	.0	0	.0	47	70.1	1	1.5	48	71.6	19	28.4	67
1974 TO 1976	.0		.0		100.0		100.0		100.0		100.0		100.0
1 INSTITUTIONS)	0	.0	0	.0	60	73.2	2	2.4	62	75.6	20	24.4	82
1976 TO 1978	.0		.0		27.7		100.0		29.2		5.3		22.4
0 INSTITUTIONS)	0	.0	0	.0	0	.0	0	.0	0	.0	0	.0	0
1 INSTITUTIONS)	0	.0	0	.0	83	65.4	0	.0	83	65.4	44	34.6	127
1974 TO 1976	.0		.0		100.0		.0		100.0		100.0		100.0
1 INSTITUTIONS)	0	.0	0	.0	91	77.1	1	.8	92	78.0	26	22.0	118
1976 TO 1978	.0		.0		9.6		100.0		10.8		- 40.9		- 7.1
. . . .													
2 INSTITUTIONS).	0	.0	0	.0	0	.0	1	2.3	1	2.3	42	97.7	43
1 INSTITUTIONS)	0	.0	0	.0	0	.0	0	.0	0	.0	49	100.0	49
1974 TO 1976	.0		.0		.0		- 100.0		- 100.0		16.7		14.0
0 INSTITUTIONS)	0	.0	0	.0	0	.0	0	.0	0	.0	0	.0	0
1976 TO 1978	.0		.0		.0		.0		.0		- 100.0		- 100.0
2 INSTITUTIONS)	1	.4	1	.4	4	1.6	1	.4	7	2.8	242	97.2	249
1 INSTITUTIONS)	1	.5	0	.0	0	.0	1	.5	2	1.0	208	99.0	210
1974 TO 1976	.0		- 100.0		- 100.0		.0		- 71.4		- 14.0		- 15.7
0 INSTITUTIONS)	0	.0	0	.0	0	.0	0	.0	0	.0	0	.0	0
1976 TO 1978	- 100.0		.0		.0		- 100.0		- 100.0		- 100.0		- 100.0
. . . .													
15 INSTITUTIONS)	2	.2	149	11.5	13	1.0	27	2.1	191	14.7	1,105	85.3	1,296
9 INSTITUTIONS)	3	.2	116	6.7	16	.9	19	1.1	154	8.9	1,575	91.1	1,729
1974 TO 1976	50.0		- 22.1		23.1		- 29.6		- 19.4		42.5		33.4
9 INSTITUTIONS)	8	.4	98	5.1	23	1.2	19	1.0	148	7.7	1,770	92.3	1,918
1976 TO 1978	166.7		- 15.5		43.8		.0		- 3.9		12.4		10.9
15 INSTITUTIONS)	7	.1	309	6.3	19	.4	68	1.4	403	8.2	4,513	91.8	4,916
9 INSTITUTIONS)	12	.2	189	3.7	32	.6	85	1.7	318	6.2	4,815	93.8	5,133
1974 TO 1976	71.4		- 38.8		68.4		25.0		- 21.1		6.7		4.4
9 INSTITUTIONS)	6	.1	138	2.9	41	.9	58	1.2	243	5.1	4,529	94.9	4,772
1976 TO 1978	- 50.0		- 27.0		28.1		- 31.8		- 23.6		- 5.9		- 7.0

MAJOR FIELD 1400 - LAW

	AMERICAN INDIAN ALASKAN NATIVE		BLACK NON-HISPANIC		ASIAN OR PACIFIC ISLANDER		HISPANIC		TOTAL MINORITY		WHITE NON-HISPANIC	
	NUMBER	%	NUMBER	%	NUMBER	%	NUMBER	%	NUMBER	%	NUMBER	%
INDIANA												
FEMALE												
1974 (9 INSTITUTIONS)	0	.0	24	6.8	1	.3	4	1.1	29	8.2	326	91.8
1976 (7 INSTITUTIONS)	2	.4	45	8.0	1	.2	11	2.0	59	10.5	505	89.5
% CHANGE 1974 TO 1976	100.0		87.5		.0		175.0		103.4		54.9	
1978 (4 INSTITUTIONS)	4	.6	42	6.7	1	.2	10	1.6	57	9.1	568	90.9
% CHANGE 1976 TO 1978	100.0		- 6.7		.0		- 9.1		- 3.4		12.5	
MALE												
1974 (9 INSTITUTIONS)	4	.3	63	4.4	4	.3	23	1.6	94	6.6	1,332	93.4
1976 (7 INSTITUTIONS)	8	.5	76	4.9	2	.1	31	2.0	117	7.5	1,441	92.5
% CHANGE 1974 TO 1976	100.0		20.6		- 50.0		34.8		24.5		8.2	
1978 (4 INSTITUTIONS)	10	.7	68	4.5	6	.4	30	2.0	114	7.5	1,411	92.5
% CHANGE 1976 TO 1978	25.0		- 10.5		200.0		- 3.2		- 2.6		- 2.1	-
IOWA												
FEMALE												
1974 (2 INSTITUTIONS)	0	.0	12	6.3	1	.5	1	.5	14	7.3	177	92.7
1976 (2 INSTITUTIONS)	1	.4	13	5.8	0	.0	3	1.3	17	7.5	209	92.5
% CHANGE 1974 TO 1976	100.0		8.3		- 100.0		200.0		21.4		18.1	
1978 (2 INSTITUTIONS)	0	.0	9	3.2	3	1.1	0	.0	12	4.3	269	95.7
% CHANGE 1976 TO 1978	- 100.0		- 30.8		100.0		- 100.0		- 29.4		28.7	
MALE												
1974 (2 INSTITUTIONS)	0	.0	16	1.5	7	.7	9	.9	32	3.0	1,022	97.0
1976 (2 INSTITUTIONS)	2	.2	23	2.6	5	.6	11	1.3	41	4.7	829	95.3
% CHANGE 1974 TO 1976	100.0		43.8		- 28.6		22.2		28.1		- 18.9	-
1978 (2 INSTITUTIONS)	4	.4	24	2.7	4	.4	9	1.0	41	4.6	858	95.4
% CHANGE 1976 TO 1978	100.0		4.3		- 20.0		- 18.2		.0		3.5	
KANSAS												
FEMALE												
1974 (15 INSTITUTIONS)	0	.0	5	4.7	0	.0	3	2.8	8	7.5	99	92.5
1976 (2 INSTITUTIONS)	0	.0	10	4.5	0	.0	1	.4	11	4.9	212	95.1
% CHANGE 1974 TO 1976	.0		100.0		.0		- 66.7		37.5		114.1	
1978 (2 INSTITUTIONS)	0	.0	8	3.0	2	.7	4	1.5	14	5.2	255	94.8
% CHANGE 1976 TO 1978	.0		- 20.0		100.0		300.0		27.3		20.3	
MALE												
1974 (15 INSTITUTIONS)	1	.2	22	4.6	4	.8	6	1.3	33	7.0	441	93.0
1976 (2 INSTITUTIONS)	6	.7	17	2.0	3	.4	7	.8	33	4.0	800	96.0
% CHANGE 1974 TO 1976	500.0		- 22.7		- 25.0		16.7		.0		81.4	
1978 (2 INSTITUTIONS)	2	.2	14	1.6	2	.2	14	1.6	32	3.8	817	96.2
% CHANGE 1976 TO 1978	- 66.7		- 17.6		- 33.3		100.0		- 3.0		2.1	
KENTUCKY												
FEMALE												
1974 (5 INSTITUTIONS)	0	.0	13	3.5	2	.5	0	.0	15	4.0	358	96.0
1976 (3 INSTITUTIONS)	1	.3	12	3.1	2	.5	0	.0	15	3.9	367	96.1
% CHANGE 1974 TO 1976	100.0		- 7.7		.0		.0		.0		2.5	
1978 (3 INSTITUTIONS)	0	.0	10	2.6	1	.3	0	.0	11	2.9	373	97.1
% CHANGE 1976 TO 1978	- 100.0		- 16.7		- 50.0		.0		- 26.7		1.6	
MALE												
1974 (5 INSTITUTIONS)	2	.1	41	2.3	3	.2	1	.1	47	2.6	1,730	97.4
1976 (3 INSTITUTIONS)	2	.1	40	3.0	4	.3	3	.2	49	3.6	1,298	96.4
% CHANGE 1974 TO 1976	.0		- 2.4		33.3		200.0		4.3		- 25.0	-
1978 (3 INSTITUTIONS)	4	.3	27	2.3	3	.3	5	.4	39	3.4	1,119	96.6
% CHANGE 1976 TO 1978	100.0		- 32.5		- 25.0		66.7		- 20.4		- 13.8	-

ROLLMENT IN INSTITUTIONS OF HIGHER EDUCATION FOR SELECTED FIELDS OF STUDY AND LEVEL OF ENROLLMENT
AND SEX: STATE 1974, 1976, 1978

ICAN INDIAN SKAN NATIVE		BLACK NON-HISPANIC		ASIAN OR PACIFIC ISLANDER		HISPANIC		TOTAL MINORITY		WHITE NON-HISPANIC		TOTAL
NUMBER	%	NUMBER	%	NUMBER	%	NUMBER	%	NUMBER	%	NUMBER	%	NUMBER
1	.2	38	9.4	1	.2	5	1.2	45	11.1	341	88.9	406
7	1.2	52	8.9	5	.9	4	.7	68	11.7	515	88.3	583
600.0		36.8		400.0		- 20.0		51.1		42.7		43.6
1	.2	55	12.3	1	.2	7	1.6	64	14.3	382	85.7	446
85.7		5.8		- 80.0		75.0		- 5.9		- 25.8		- 23.5
6	.3	152	7.1	13	.6	19	.9	190	8.9	1,949	91.1	2,139
6	.3	147	7.4	7	.4	17	.9	177	8.9	1,810	91.1	1,987
.0		- 3.3		- 46.2		- 10.5		- 6.8		- 7.1		- 7.1
2	.2	132	11.7	4	.4	15	1.3	153	13.5	980	86.5	1,133
66.7		- 10.2		- 42.9		- 11.8		- 13.6		- 45.9		- 43.0
0	.0	1	1.8	0	.0	0	.0	1	1.8	54	98.2	55
0	.0	0	.0	0	.0	0	.0	0	.0	64	100.0	64
.0		- 100.0		.0		.0		- 100.0		18.5		16.4
0	.0	0	.0	0	.0	0	.0	0	.0	94	100.0	94
.0		.0		.0		.0		.0		46.9		46.9
0	.0	1	.4	0	.0	0	.0	1	.6	167	99.4	168
0	.0	0	.0	0	.0	0	.0	0	.0	192	100.0	192
.0		- 100.0		.0		.0		- 100.0		15.0		14.3
0	.0	0	.0	0	.0	0	.0	0	.0	151	100.0	151
.0		.0		.0		.0		.0		- 21.4		- 21.4
2	.9	39	17.0	0	.0	0	.0	41	17.9	188	82.1	229
0	.0	52	11.0	2	.4	2	.4	56	11.9	415	88.1	471
100.0		33.3		100.0		100.0		36.6		120.7		105.7
0	.0	51	9.3	0	.0	5	.9	56	10.2	493	89.8	549
.0		- 1.9		- 100.0		150.0		.0		18.8		16.6
0	.0	89	13.3	3	.4	6	.9	98	14.6	573	85.4	671
0	.0	97	7.3	4	.3	2	.1	103	7.7	1,233	92.3	1,336
.0		9.0		33.3		- 66.7		5.1		115.2		99.1
1	.1	77	6.3	5	.4	2	.2	85	7.0	1,137	93.0	1,222
100.0		- 20.6		25.0		.0		- 17.5		- 7.8		- 8.5
1	.1	71	4.5	22	1.4	11	.7	105	6.7	1,460	93.3	1,565
10	.5	94	4.7	22	1.1	23	1.1	149	7.4	1,872	92.6	2,021
900.0		32.4		.0		109.1		41.9		28.2		29.1
8	.4	112	5.1	31	1.4	36	1.6	187	8.5	2,012	91.5	2,199
20.0		19.1		40.9		56.5		25.5		7.5		8.8
17	.3	211	3.3	41	.6	55	.9	324	5.1	6,091	94.9	6,415
8	.1	169	3.0	41	.7	72	1.3	290	5.2	5,267	94.8	5,557
52.9		- 19.9		.0		30.9		- 10.5		- 13.5		- 13.4
10	.2	165	3.5	37	.8	80	1.7	292	6.2	4,432	93.8	4,724
25.0		- 2.4		- 9.8		11.1		.7		- 15.9		- 15.0

TABLE 18 - COMPARISIONS OF ENROLLMENT IN INSTITUTIONS OF HIGHER EDUCATION FOR SELECTED FIELDS OF STUDY AND LEVEL OF ENROLLME
BY RACE, ETHNICITY AND SEX: STATE 1974, 1976, 1978

MAJOR FIELD 1400 - LAW

	AMERICAN INDIAN ALASKAN NATIVE		BLACK NON-HISPANIC		ASIAN OR PACIFIC ISLANDER		HISPANIC		TOTAL MINORITY		WHITE NON-HISPANIC	
	NUMBER	%	NUMBER	%	NUMBER	%	NUMBER	%	NUMBER	%	NUMBER	%
MICHIGAN............												
FEMALE												
1974 (18 INSTITUTIONS)	3	.4	90	11.7	2	.3	4	.5	99	12.9	667	87.1
1976 (5 INSTITUTIONS)	1	.1	118	11.5	2	.2	13	1.3	134	13.0	893	87.0
% CHANGE 1974 TO 1976	- 66.7		31.1		.0		225.0		35.4		33.9	
1978 (5 INSTITUTIONS)	4	.3	113	8.7	7	.5	20	1.5	144	11.1	1,151	88.9
% CHANGE 1976 TO 1978	300.0		- 4.2		250.0		53.8		7.5		28.9	
MALE												
1974 (18 INSTITUTIONS)	10	.3	192	5.5	11	.3	54	1.6	267	7.7	3,208	92.3
1976 (5 INSTITUTIONS)	10	.3	192	5.3	15	.4	43	1.2	260	7.1	3,377	92.9
% CHANGE 1974 TO 1976	.0		.0		36.4		- 20.4		- 2.6		5.3	
1978 (5 INSTITUTIONS)	11	.3	143	4.1	16	.5	52	1.5	222	6.3	3,280	93.7
% CHANGE 1976 TO 1978	10.0		- 25.5		6.7		20.9		- 14.6		- 2.9	-
MINNESOTA.........												
FEMALE												
1974 (9 INSTITUTIONS)	2	.5	11	2.7	2	.5	1	.2	16	3.9	398	96.1
1976 (3 INSTITUTIONS)	2	.3	14	2.1	1	.2	2	.3	19	2.9	642	97.1
% CHANGE 1974 TO 1976	.0		27.3		- 50.0		100.0		18.8		61.3	
1978 (3 INSTITUTIONS)	6	.8	19	2.5	5	.7	5	.7	35	4.6	718	95.4
% CHANGE 1976 TO 1978	200.0		35.7		400.0		150.0		84.2		11.8	
MALE												
1974 (9 INSTITUTIONS)	7	.5	22	1.5	6	.4	11	.8	46	3.2	1,397	96.8
1976 (3 INSTITUTIONS)	7	.4	26	1.5	3	.2	8	.5	44	2.5	1,710	97.5
% CHANGE 1974 TO 1976	.0		18.2		- 50.0		- 27.3		- 4.3		22.4	
1978 (3 INSTITUTIONS)	9	.6	23	1.4	3	.2	12	.8	47	2.9	1,553	97.1
% CHANGE 1976 TO 1978	28.6		- 11.5		.0		50.0		6.8		- 9.2	-
MISSISSIPPI........												
FEMALE												
1974 (14 INSTITUTIONS)	0	.0	10	10.5	0	.0	0	.0	10	10.5	85	89.5
1976 (2 INSTITUTIONS)	3	1.8	18	10.5	0	.0	1	.6	22	12.9	149	87.1
% CHANGE 1974 TO 1976	100.0		80.0		.0		100.0		120.0		75.3	
1978 (2 INSTITUTIONS)	0	.0	11	5.6	0	.0	1	.5	12	6.2	183	93.8
% CHANGE 1976 TO 1978	- 100.0		- 38.9		.0		.0		- 45.5		22.8	
MALE												
1974 (14 INSTITUTIONS)	0	.0	21	3.3	0	.0	0	.0	21	3.3	608	96.7
1976 (2 INSTITUTIONS)	2	.2	33	3.3	1	.1	0	.0	36	3.6	956	96.4
% CHANGE 1974 TO 1976	100.0		57.1		100.0		.0		71.4		57.2	
1978 (2 INSTITUTIONS)	0	.0	18	2.4	2	.3	2	.3	22	3.0	716	97.0
% CHANGE 1976 TO 1978	- 100.0		- 45.5		100.0		100.0		- 38.9		- 25.1	-
MISSOURI..........												
FEMALE												
1974 (7 INSTITUTIONS)	1	.3	30	7.6	3	.8	2	.5	36	9.1	361	90.9
1976 (4 INSTITUTIONS)	1	.2	43	8.0	4	.7	3	.6	51	9.5	487	90.5
% CHANGE 1974 TO 1976	.0		43.3		33.3		50.0		41.7		34.9	
1978 (4 INSTITUTIONS)	2	.3	38	5.9	7	1.1	2	.3	49	7.6	594	92.4
% CHANGE 1976 TO 1978	100.0		- 11.6		75.0		- 33.3		- 3.9		22.0	
MALE												
1974 (7 INSTITUTIONS)	4	.2	70	3.8	15	.8	7	.4	96	5.2	1,762	94.8
1976 (4 INSTITUTIONS)	2	.1	63	3.8	6	.4	4	.2	75	4.6	1,565	95.4
% CHANGE 1974 TO 1976	- 50.0		- 10.0		- 60.0		- 42.9		- 21.9		- 11.2	-
1978 (4 INSTITUTIONS)	4	.3	38	2.5	9	.6	5	.3	56	3.7	1,447	96.3
% CHANGE 1976 TO 1978	100.0		- 39.7		50.0		25.0		- 25.3		- 7.5	-

ENROLLMENT IN INSTITUTIONS OF HIGHER EDUCATION FOR SELECTED FIELDS OF STUDY AND LEVEL OF ENROLLMENT
TY AND SEX: STATE 1974, 1976, 1978

RICAN INDIAN ASKAN NATIVE		BLACK NON-HISPANIC		ASIAN OR PACIFIC ISLANDER		HISPANIC		TOTAL MINORITY		WHITE NON-HISPANIC		TOTAL
NUMBER	%	NUMBER	%	NUMBER	%	NUMBER	%	NUMBER	%	NUMBER	%	NUMBER
0	.0	0	.0	0	.0	0	.0	0	.0	24	100.0	24
0	.0	0	.0	0	.0	0	.0	0	.0	46	100.0	46
.0		.0		.0		.0		.0		91.7		91.7
0	.0	0	.0	0	.0	0	.0	0	.0	67	100.0	67
.0		.0		.0		.0		.0		45.7		45.7
0	.0	0	.0	0	.0	0	.0	0	.0	178	100.0	178
2	1.2	0	.0	0	.0	0	.0	2	1.2	168	98.8	170
100.0		.0		.0		.0		100.0		- 5.6		- 4.5
0	.0	0	.0	0	.0	0	.0	0	.0	155	100.0	155
100.0		.0		.0		.0		- 100.0		- 7.7		- 8.8
0	.0	6	6.9	0	.0	1	1.1	7	8.0	80	92.0	87
0	.0	7	3.7	0	.0	1	.5	8	4.2	183	95.8	191
.0		16.7		.0		.0		14.3		128.8		119.5
0	.0	7	2.8	1	.4	2	.8	10	4.0	243	96.0	253
.0		.0		100.0		100.0		25.0		32.8		32.5
1	.2	12	2.2	0	.0	1	.2	14	2.6	523	97.4	537
1	.1	11	1.5	4	.5	2	.3	18	2.4	732	97.6	750
.0		- 8.3		100.0		100.0		28.6		40.0		39.7
1	.1	12	1.6	2	.3	3	.4	18	2.4	732	97.6	750
.0		9.1		- 50.0		50.0		.0		.0		.0
0	.0	1	4.2	0	.0	1	4.2	2	8.3	22	91.7	24
0	.0	0	.0	0	.0	0	.0	0	.0	0	.0	0
.0		- 100.0		.0		- 100.0		- 100.0		- 100.0		- 100.0
0	.0	0	.0	0	.0	0	.0	0	.0	0	.0	0
.0		.0		.0		.0		.0		.0		.0
0	.0	1	1.2	0	.0	3	3.6	4	4.8	80	95.2	84
0	.0	0	.0	0	.0	0	.0	0	.0	0	.0	0
.0		- 100.0		.0		- 100.0		- 100.0		- 100.0		- 100.0
0	.0	0	.0	0	.0	0	.0	0	.0	0	.0	0
.0		.0		.0		.0		.0		.0		.0
0	.0	0	.0	0	.0	0	.0	0	.0	0	.0	0
0	.0	0	.0	0	.0	0	.0	0	.0	0	.0	0
.0		.0		.0		.0		.0		.0		.0
2	13.3	0	.0	2	13.3	1	6.7	5	33.3	10	66.7	15
100.0		.0		100.0		100.0		100.0		100.0		100.0
0	.0	0	.0	0	.0	0	.0	0	.0	0	.0	0
0	.0	0	.0	0	.0	0	.0	0	.0	0	.0	0
.0		.0		.0		.0		.0		.0		.0
1	.4	0	.0	1	.4	4	1.7	6	2.5	230	97.5	236
100.0		.0		100.0		100.0		100.0		100.0		100.0

MAJOR FIELD 1400 - LAW

	AMERICAN INDIAN ALASKAN NATIVE		BLACK NON-HISPANIC		ASIAN OR PACIFIC ISLANDER		HISPANIC		TOTAL MINORITY		WHITE NON-HISPANIC		TOTAL
	NUMBER	%	NUMBER	%	NUMBER	%	NUMBER	%	NUMBER	%	NUMBER	%	NUMBER
NEW JERSEY.........													
FEMALE													
1974 (3 INSTITUTIONS)	3	.5	68	11.7	5	.9	16	2.8	92	15.9	487	84.1	579
1976 (3 INSTITUTIONS)	1	.1	80	10.8	8	1.1	25	3.4	114	15.4	624	84.6	738
% CHANGE 1974 TO 1976	- 66.7		17.6		60.0		56.3		23.9		28.1		27.5
1978 (3 INSTITUTIONS)	2	.2	98	10.4	17	1.8	45	4.8	162	17.2	781	82.8	943
% CHANGE 1976 TO 1978	100.0		22.5		112.5		80.0		42.1		25.2		27.8
MALE													
1974 (3 INSTITUTIONS)	2	.1	177	10.8	6	.4	61	3.7	246	15.0	1,399	85.0	1,645
1976 (3 INSTITUTIONS)	4	.2	111	6.4	8	.5	65	3.8	188	10.8	1,545	89.2	1,733
% CHANGE 1974 TO 1976	100.0		- 37.3		33.3		6.6		- 23.6		10.4		5.3
1978 (3 INSTITUTIONS)	2	.1	104	6.0	15	.9	58	3.3	179	10.3	1,560	89.7	1,739
% CHANGE 1976 TO 1978	- 50.0		- 6.3		87.5		- 10.8		- 4.8		1.0		.3
NEW MEXICO.........													
FEMALE													
1974 (3 INSTITUTIONS)	4	4.3	2	2.2	2	2.2	8	8.6	16	17.2	77	82.8	93
1976 (1 INSTITUTIONS)	5	4.4	3	2.7	1	.9	15	13.3	24	21.2	89	78.8	113
% CHANGE 1974 TO 1976	25.0		50.0		- 50.0		87.5		50.0		15.6		21.5
1978 (1 INSTITUTIONS)	6	4.6	2	1.5	3	2.3	32	24.4	43	32.8	88	67.2	131
% CHANGE 1976 TO 1978	20.0		- 33.3		200.0		113.3		79.2		- 1.1		15.9
MALE													
1974 (3 INSTITUTIONS)	11	3.6	6	2.0	6	2.0	61	19.9	84	27.5	222	72.5	306
1976 (1 INSTITUTIONS)	8	3.7	6	2.7	2	.9	68	31.1	84	38.4	135	61.6	219
% CHANGE 1974 TO 1976	- 27.3		.0		- 66.7		11.5		.0		- 39.2		- 28.4
1978 (1 INSTITUTIONS)	10	5.2	3	1.6	2	1.0	58	30.1	73	37.8	120	62.2	193
% CHANGE 1976 TO 1978	25.0		- 50.0		.0		- 14.7		- 13.1		- 11.1		- 11.9
NEW YORK..........													
FEMALE													
1974 (14 INSTITUTIONS)	0	.0	65	4.1	12	.8	21	1.3	98	6.1	1,496	93.9	1,594
1976 (13 INSTITUTIONS)	5	.2	165	5.0	39	1.2	59	1.8	268	8.1	3,061	91.9	3,329
% CHANGE 1974 TO 1976	100.0		153.8		225.0		181.0		173.5		104.6		108.8
1978 (13 INSTITUTIONS)	14	.3	206	5.1	31	.8	81	2.0	332	8.2	3,709	91.8	4,041
% CHANGE 1976 TO 1978	180.0		24.8		- 20.5		37.3		23.9		21.2		21.4
MALE													
1974 (14 INSTITUTIONS)	11	.2	162	2.6	25	.4	73	1.2	271	4.3	5,995	95.7	6,266
1976 (13 INSTITUTIONS)	12	.1	213	2.5	95	1.1	140	1.7	460	5.5	7,919	94.5	8,379
% CHANGE 1974 TO 1976	9.1		31.5		280.0		91.8		69.7		32.1		33.7
1978 (13 INSTITUTIONS)	10	.1	178	2.4	49	.7	136	1.8	373	5.0	7,044	95.0	7,417
% CHANGE 1976 TO 1978	- 16.7		- 16.4		- 48.4		- 2.9		- 18.9		- 11.0		- 11.5
NORTH CAROLINA.......													
FEMALE													
1974 (8 INSTITUTIONS)	1	.3	66	19.2	2	.6	0	.0	69	20.1	274	79.9	343
1976 (5 INSTITUTIONS)	2	.5	64	14.6	0	.0	2	.5	68	15.5	371	84.5	439
% CHANGE 1974 TO 1976	100.0		- 3.0		- 100.0		100.0		- 1.4		35.4		28.0
1978 (5 INSTITUTIONS)	0	.0	56	10.4	0	.0	1	.2	57	10.6	483	89.4	540
% CHANGE 1976 TO 1978	- 100.0		- 12.5		.0		- 50.0		- 16.2		30.2		23.0
MALE													
1974 (8 INSTITUTIONS)	6	.4	161	10.2	2	.1	7	.4	176	11.1	1,410	88.9	1,586
1976 (5 INSTITUTIONS)	4	.3	130	8.5	0	.0	8	.5	142	9.3	1,383	90.7	1,525
% CHANGE 1974 TO 1976	- 33.3		- 19.3		- 100.0		14.3		- 19.3		- 1.9		- 3.8
1978 (5 INSTITUTIONS)	7	.4	136	8.4	6	.4	6	.4	155	9.6	1,460	90.4	1,615
% CHANGE 1976 TO 1978	75.0		4.6		100.0		- 25.0		9.2		5.6		5.9

ENROLLMENT IN INSTITUTIONS OF HIGHER EDUCATION FOR SELECTED FIELDS OF STUDY AND LEVEL OF ENROLLMENT
ITY AND SEX: STATE 1974, 1976, 1978

ERICAN INDIAN LASKAN NATIVE		BLACK NON-HISPANIC		ASIAN OR PACIFIC ISLANDER		HISPANIC		TOTAL MINORITY		WHITE NON-HISPANIC		TOTAL
NUMBER	%	NUMBER	%	NUMBER	%	NUMBER	%	NUMBER	%	NUMBER	%	NUMBER
0	.0	0	.0	0	.0	0	.0	0	.0	38	100.0	38
0	.0	0	.0	0	.0	0	.0	0	.0	51	100.0	51
	.0		.0		.0		.0		.0		34.2	34.2
0	.0	0	.0	0	.0	0	.0	0	.0	55	100.0	55
	.0		.0		.0		.0		.0		7.8	7.8
0	.0	0	.0	0	.0	0	.0	0	.0	210	100.0	210
0	.0	1	.5	0	.0	0	.0	1	.5	191	99.5	192
	.0		100.0		.0		.0		100.0	-	9.0	- 8.6
1	.5	0	.0	0	.0	0	.0	1	.5	216	99.5	217
100.0		- 100.0			.0		.0		.0		13.1	13.0
1	.1	67	8.2	2	.2	4	.5	74	9.1	740	90.9	814
3	.2	116	8.0	10	.7	9	.6	138	9.5	1,316	90.5	1,454
200.0		73.1		400.0		125.0		86.5		77.8		78.6
7	.4	154	8.6	11	.6	13	.7	185	10.4	1,597	89.6	1,782
133.3		32.8		10.0		44.4		34.1		21.4		22.6
10	.3	213	5.6	11	.3	21	.5	255	6.7	3,571	93.3	3,826
9	.2	203	4.5	19	.4	38	.8	269	6.0	4,218	94.0	4,487
10.0		- 4.7		72.7		81.0		5.5		18.1		17.3
7	.2	213	4.8	19	.4	33	.7	272	6.1	4,192	93.9	4,464
- 22.2		4.9		.0		- 13.2		1.1		- .6		- .5
9	3.1	4	1.4	1	.3	0	.0	14	4.8	276	95.2	290
15	4.0	9	2.4	2	.5	4	1.1	30	7.9	349	92.1	379
66.7		125.0		100.0		100.0		114.3		26.4		30.7
11	2.4	13	2.9	3	.7	3	.7	30	6.7	421	93.3	451
- 26.7		44.4		50.0		- 25.0		.0		20.6		19.0
48	3.0	24	1.5	3	.2	5	.3	80	4.9	1,541	95.1	1,621
36	2.4	15	1.0	6	.4	5	.3	62	4.2	1,412	95.8	1,474
- 25.0		- 37.5		100.0		.0		- 22.5		- 8.4		- 9.1
34	2.6	21	1.6	6	.5	9	.7	70	5.4	1,217	94.6	1,287
5.6		40.0		.0		80.0		12.9		- 13.8		- 12.7
2	.6	10	2.8	9	2.5	1	.3	22	6.2	333	93.8	355
4	1.0	4	1.0	5	1.2	1	.2	14	3.5	387	96.5	401
100.0		- 60.0		- 44.4		.0		- 36.4		16.2		13.0
5	1.0	8	1.6	14	2.8	4	.8	31	6.3	463	93.7	494
25.0		100.0		180.0		300.0		121.4		19.6		23.2
7	.5	19	1.4	16	1.2	5	.4	47	3.4	1,318	96.6	1,365
4	.3	11	.9	27	2.3	6	.7	50	4.3	1,125	95.7	1,175
- 42.9		- 42.1		68.8		60.0		6.4		- 14.6		- 13.9
5	.4	17	1.5	31	2.7	15	1.3	68	5.9	1,088	94.1	1,156
25.0		54.5		14.8		87.5		36.0		- 3.3		- 1.6

TABLE 18 - COMPARISIONS OF ENROLLMENT IN INSTITUTIONS OF HIGHER EDUCATION FOR SELECTED FIELDS OF STUDY AND LEVEL OF ENROLLMENT
BY RACE, ETHNICITY AND SEX: STATE 1974, 1976, 1978

MAJOR FIELD 1400 - LAW

	AMERICAN INDIAN ALASKAN NATIVE		BLACK NON-HISPANIC		ASIAN OR PACIFIC ISLANDER		HISPANIC		TOTAL MINORITY		WHITE NON-HISPANIC		T
	NUMBER	%	NUMBER	%	NUMBER	%	NUMBER	%	NUMBER	%	NUMBER	%	NU
PENNSYLVANIA.........													
FEMALE													
1974 (10 INSTITUTIONS)	.2	.3	48	7.5	3	.5	5	.8	58	9.1	580	90.9	
1976 (5 INSTITUTIONS)	2	.2	73	6.5	9	.8	9	.8	93	8.2	1,036	91.8	1
% CHANGE 1974 TO 1976	.0		52.1		200.0		80.0		60.3		78.6		77
1978 (5 INSTITUTIONS)	3	.2	86	7.0	9	.7	15	1.2	113	9.2	1,111	90.8	1
% CHANGE 1976 TO 1978	50.0		17.8		.0		66.7		21.5		7.2		A
MALE													
1974 (10 INSTITUTIONS)	1	.0	114	4.5	12	.5	27	1.1	154	6.	2,354	93.9	2
1976 (5 INSTITUTIONS)	2	.1	103	4.1	27	1.1	39	1.6	171	6.♭	2,315	93.1	2
% CHANGE 1974 TO 1976	100.0		- 9.6		125.0		44.4		11.0		- 1.7		-
1978 (5 INSTITUTIONS)	3	.1	88	3.8	23	1.0	27	1.2	141	6.1	2,166	93.9	2
% CHANGE 1976 TO 1978	50.0		- 14.6		- 14.8		- 30.0		- 17.5		- 6.4		- 7
SOUTH CAROLINA.......													
FEMALE													
1974 (1 INSTITUTIONS)	0	.0	4	3.5	0	.0	0	.0	4	3.5	109	96.5	
1976 (1 INSTITUTIONS)	0	.0	13	8.2	0	.0	0	.0	13	8.2	145	91.8	
% CHANGE 1974 TO 1976	.0		225.0		.0		.0		225.0		33.0		39
1978 (1 INSTITUTIONS)	0	.0	13	7.6	0	.0	0	.0	13	7.6	159	92.4	
% CHANGE 1976 TO 1978	.0		.0		.0		.0		.0		9.7		8
MALE													
1974 (1 INSTITUTIONS)	0	.0	22	2.7	0	.0	0	.0	22	2.7	781	97.3	
1976 (1 INSTITUTIONS)	1	.1	29	4.3	0	.0	1	.1	31	4.6	638	95.4	
% CHANGE 1974 TO 1976	100.0		31.8		.0		100.0		40.9		- 18.3		- 16
1978 (1 INSTITUTIONS)	0	.0	37	7.4	0	.0	0	.0	37	7.4	465	92.6	
% CHANGE 1976 TO 1978	- 100.0		27.6		.0		- 100.0		19.4		- 27.1		- 25
SOUTH DAKOTA........													
FEMALE													
1974 (2 INSTITUTIONS)	2	5.1	0	.0	0	.0	0	.0	2	5.1	37	94.9	
1976 (1 INSTITUTIONS)	0	.0	0	.0	0	.0	1	2.2	1	2.2	45	97.8	
% CHANGE 1974 TO 1976	- 100.0		.0		.0		100.0		- 50.0		21.6		17
1978 (1 INSTITUTIONS)	0	.0	0	.0	0	.0	0	.0	0	.0	44	100.0	
% CHANGE 1976 TO 1978	.0		.0		.0		- 100.0		- 100.0		- 2.2		- 4
MALE													
1974 (2 INSTITUTIONS)	1	.6	0	.0	0	.0	1	.6	2	1.1	177	98.9	
1976 (1 INSTITUTIONS)	0	.0	0	.0	0	.0	0	.0	0	.0	157	100.0	
% CHANGE 1974 TO 1976	- 100.0		.0		.0		- 100.0		- 100.0		- 11.3		- 12
1978 (1 INSTITUTIONS)	1	.6	0	.0	0	.0	0	.0	1	.6	153	99.4	
% CHANGE 1976 TO 1978	100.0		.0		.0		.0		100.0		- 2.5		- 1
TENNESSEE													
FEMALE													
1974 (6 INSTITUTIONS)	1	.4	20	7.2	1	.4	0	.0	22	7.9	255	92.1	
1976 (3 INSTITUTIONS)	1	.3	30	8.0	2	.5	1	.3	34	9.1	339	90.9	
% CHANGE 1974 TO 1976	.0		50.0		100.0		100.0		54.5		32.9		34
1978 (3 INSTITUTIONS)	0	.0	29	6.2	0	.0	0	.0	29	6.2	436	93.8	
% CHANGE 1976 TO 1978	- 100.0		- 3.3		- 100.0		- 100.0		- 14.7		28.6		24
MALE													
1974 (6 INSTITUTIONS)	0	.0	37	2.5	2	.1	1	.1	40	2.7	1,467	97.3	1
1976 (3 INSTITUTIONS)	2	.2	34	2.7	1	.1	1	.1	38	3.0	1,227	97.0	1
% CHANGE 1974 TO 1976	100.0		- 8.1		- 50.0		.0		- 5.0		- 16.4		- 16
1978 (3 INSTITUTIONS)	1	.1	30	2.5	2	.2	1	.1	34	2.8	1,172	97.2	1
% CHANGE 1976 TO 1978	- 50.0		- 11.8		100.0		.0		- 10.5		- 4.5		- 4

ERICAN INDIAN LASKAN NATIVE		BLACK NON-HISPANIC		ASIAN OR PACIFIC ISLANDER		HISPANIC		TOTAL MINORITY		WHITE NON-HISPANIC		TOTAL
NUMBER	%	NUMBER	%	NUMBER	%	NUMBER	%	NUMBER	%	NUMBER	!!	NUMBER
3	.3	81	6.9	5	.4	84	7.2	173	14.8	995	85.2	1,168
3	.5	103	7.1	13	.9	74	5.1	197	13.7	1,244	86.3	1,441
133.3		27.2		160.0		- 11.9		13.9		25.0		23.4
5	.3	152	8.1	12	.6	113	6.0	282	15.0	1,602	85.0	1,884
· 28.6		47.6		- 7.7		52.7		43.1		28.8		30.7
27	.4	280	4.6	12	.2	456	7.5	775	12.7	5,337	87.3	6,112
16	.4	204	4.5	15	.3	293	6.5	528	11.7	3,967	88.3	4,495
- 40.7		- 27.1		25.0		- 35.7		- 31.9		- 25.7		- 26.5
16	.3	194	4.2	18	.4	360	7.8	588	12.7	4,046	87.3	4,634
.0		- 4.9		20.0		22.9		11.4		2.0		3.1
0	.0	3	1.9	0	.0	2	1.3	5	3.2	150	96.8	155
0	.0	1	.9	0	.0	1	.9	2	1.7	114	98.3	116
.0		- 66.7		.0		- 50.0		- 60.0		- 24.0		- 25.2
0	.0	1	.7	0	.0	1	.7	2	1.4	146	98.6	148
.0		.0		.0		.0		.0		28.1		27.6
7	.7	9	.9	8	.8	16	1 6	40	4.1	932	95.9	972
5	.7	3	.4	4	.5	11	115	23	3.1	710	96.9	733
- 28.6		- 66.7		- 50.0		- 31.3		- 42.5		- 23.8		- 24.6
1	.1	5	.7	6	.9	8	1.2	20	2.9	664	97.1	684
· 80.0		66.7		50.0		- 27.3		- 13.0		- 6.5		- 6.7
0	.0	0	.0	0	.0	0	.0		.0	0	.0	0
0	.0	0	.0	0	.0	2	4.1	2	4.1	47	95.9	49
.0		.0		.0		100.0		100.0		100.0		100.0
0	.0	0	.0	1	1.1	0	.0	1	1.1	86	98.9	87
.0		.0		100.0		- 100.0		- 50.0		83.0		77.6
0	.0	0	.0	0	.0	0	.0	0	.0	0	.0	0
0	.0	1	.4	0	.0	1	.4	2	.7	280	99.3	282
.0		100.0		.0		100.0		100.0		100.0		100.0
'0	.0	0	.0	0	.0	0	.0	0	.0	236	100.0	236
.0		- 100.0		.0		- 100.0		- 100.0		- 15.7		- 16.3
0	.0	23	7.2	0	.0	0	.0	23	7.2	296	92.8	319
0	.0	27	6.0	0	.0	1	.2	28	6.2	423	93.8	451
.0		17.4		.0		100.0		21.7		42.9		41.4
1	.2	47	7.6	1	.2	1	.2	50	8.1	571	91.9	621
100.0		74.1		100.0		.0		78.6		35.0		37.7
0	.0	60	3.3	2	.1	1	.1	63	3 5	1,731	96.5	1,794
0	.0	54	3.0	3	.2	3	.2	60	3¦4	1,714	96.6	1,774
.0		- 10.0		50.0		200.0		- 4.8		- 1.0		- 1.1
0	.0	45	2.7	4	.2	3	.2	52	3.2	1,589	96.8	1,641
.0		- 16.7		33.3		.0		- 13.3		- 7.3		- 7.5

TABLE 18 — COMPARISIONS OF ENROLLMENT IN INSTITUTIONS OF HIGHER EDUCATION FOR SELECTED FIELDS OF STUDY AND LEVEL OF ENROLLME
BY RACE, ETHNICITY AND SEX: STATE 1974, 1976, 1978

MAJOR FIELD 1400 — LAW

	AMERICAN INDIAN ALASKAN NATIVE		BLACK NON—HISPANIC		ASIAN OR PACIFIC ISLANDER		HISPANIC		TOTAL MINORITY		WHITE NON—HISPANIC	
	NUMBER	%	NUMBER	%	NUMBER	%	NUMBER	%	NUMBER	%	NUMBER	%
WASHINGTON.												
FEMALE												
1974 (9 INSTITUTIONS)	5	1.3	11	2.8	8	2.0	2	.5	26	6.6	369	93.4
1976 (3 INSTITUTIONS)	5	1.0	7	1.5	12	2.5	6	1.3	30	6.3	447	93.7
% CHANGE 1974 TO 1976	.0		- 36.4		50.0		200.0		15.4		21.1	
1978 (3 INSTITUTIONS)	8	1.5	11	2.0	13	2.4	11	2.0	43	7.9	499	92.1
% CHANGE 1976 TO 1978	60.0		57.1		8.3		83.3		43.3		11.6	
MALE												
1974 (9 INSTITUTIONS)	11	.5	35	1.7	30	1.5	16	.8	92	4.6	1,918	95.4
1976 (3 INSTITUTIONS)	12	.7	16	.9	32	1.8	15	.8	75	4.1	1,738	95.9
% CHANGE 1974 TO 1976	9.1		- 54.3		6.7		- 6.3		- 18.5		- 9.4	-
1978 (3 INSTITUTIONS)	10	.6	14	.9	31	1.9	17	1.1	72	4.5	1,519	95.5
% CHANGE 1976 TO 1978	- 16.7		- 12.5		- 3.1		13.3		- 4.0		- 12.6	-
WEST VIRGINIA												
FEMALE												
1974 (1 INSTITUTIONS)	0	.0	1	1.8	0	.0	0	.0	1	1.8	54	98.2
1976 (1 INSTITUTIONS)	0	.0	3	3.9	1	1.3	0	.0	4	5.2	73	94.8
% CHANGE 1974 TO 1976	.0		200.0		100.0		.0		300.0		35.2	
1978 (1 INSTITUTIONS)	0	.0	5	5.3	0	.0	1	1.1	6	6.4	88	93.6
% CHANGE 1976 TO 1978	.0		66.7		- 100.0		100.0		50.0		20.5	
MALE												
1974 (1 INSTITUTIONS)	0	.0	1	.4	1	.4	1	.4	3	1.1	268	98.9
1976 (1 INSTITUTIONS)	0	.0	10	3.4	1	.3	0	.0	11	3.8	279	96.2
% CHANGE 1974 TO 1976	.0		900.0		.0		- 100.0		266.7		4.1	
1978 (1 INSTITUTIONS)	1	.3	2	.6	0	.0	0	.0	3	.9	325	99.1
% CHANGE 1976 TO 1978	100.0		- 80.0		- 100.0		.0		- 72.7		16.5	
WISCONSIN												
FEMALE												
1974 (3 INSTITUTIONS)	1	.3	12	4.0	0	.0	4	1.3	17	5.6	286	94.4
1976 (2 INSTITUTIONS)	2	.5	15	4.1	2	.5	5	1.4	24	6.6	340	93.4
% CHANGE 1974 TO 1976	100.0		25.0		100.0		25.0		41.2		18.9	
1978 (2 INSTITUTIONS)	4	.9	16	3.5	4	.9	11	2.4	35	7.7	417	92.3
% CHANGE 1976 TO 1978	100.0		6.7		100.0		120.0		45.8		22.6	
MALE												
1974 (3 INSTITUTIONS)	6	.6	47	4.5	1	.1	10	1.0	64	6.2	976	93.8
1976 (2 INSTITUTIONS)	7	.7	30	3.1	6	.6	10	1.0	53	5.6	900	94.4
% CHANGE 1974 TO 1976	16.7		- 36.2		500.0		.0		- 17.2		- 7.8	-
1978 (2 INSTITUTIONS)	11	1.2	21	2.3	4	.4	13	1.4	49	5.4	863	94.6
% CHANGE 1976 TO 1978	57.1		- 30.0		- 33.3		30.0		- 7.5		- 4.1	-
WYOMING												
FEMALE												
1974 (3 INSTITUTIONS)	0	.0	0	.0	0	.0	0	.0	0	.0	39	100.0
1976 (1 INSTITUTIONS)	0	.0	0	.0	0	.0	0	.0	0	.0	49	100.0
% CHANGE 1974 TO 1976	.0		.0		.0		.0		.0		25.6	
1978 (1 INSTITUTIONS)	0	.0	0	.0	1	1.9	1	1.9	2	3.7	52	96.3
% CHANGE 1976 TO 1978	.0		.0		100.0		100.0		100.0		6.1	
MALE												
1974 (3 INSTITUTIONS)	0	.0	2	1.0	2	1.0	0	.0	4	2.0	196	98.0
1976 (1 INSTITUTIONS)	1	.6	1	.6	0	.0	0	.0	2	1.2	159	98.8
% CHANGE 1974 TO 1976	100.0		- 50.0		- 100.0		.0		- 50.0		- 18.9	-
1978 (1 INSTITUTIONS)	0	.0	0	.0	0	.0	1	.6	1	.6	159	99.4
% CHANGE 1976 TO 1978	- 100.0		- 100.0		.0		100.0		- 50.0		.0	

ICAN INDIAN SKAN NATIVE		BLACK NON-HISPANIC		ASIAN OR PACIFIC ISLANDER		HISPANIC		TOTAL MINORITY		WHITE NON-HISPANIC		TOTAL
NUMBER	%	NUMBER	%	NUMBER	%	NUMBER	%	NUMBER	%	NUMBER	%	NUMBER
92	.4	1,947	8.6	280	1.2	592	2.6	2,911	12.9	19,728	87.1	22,639
135	.4	2,069	6.7	490	1.6	607	2.0	3,301	10.7	27,415	89.3	30,716
46.7		6.3		75.0		2.5		13.4		39.0	·	35.7
149	.4	2,337	6.5	568	1.6	845	2.4	3,899	10.9	31,938	89.1	35,837
10.4		13.0		15.9		39.2		18.1		16.5		16.7
347	.4	4,402	4.9	753	.8	2,489	2.7	7,991	8.8	82,650	91.2	90,641
310	.4	3,372	3.8	942	1.1	1,841	2.1	6,465	7.4	81,485	92.6	87,950
10.7	−	23.4		25.1		25.1	−	19.1	−	1.4	−	3.0
286	.3	3,034	3.7	946	1.2	1,981	2.4	6,247	7.6	75,632	92.4	81,879
7.7	−	10.0		.4		.4	−	3.4	−	7.2	−	6.9
0	.0	0	.0	0	.0	0	.0	0	.0	0	.0	0
0	.0	0	.0	0	.0	260	100.0	260	100.0	0	.0	260
.0		.0		.0		100.0		100.0		.0		100.0
0	.0	0	.0	0	.0	227	100.0	227	100.0	0	.0	227
.0		.0		.0		−	12.7	−	12.7	.0		− 12.7
0	.0	0	.0	0	.0	0	.0	0	.0	0	.0	0
0	.0	0	.0	0	.0	630	100.0	630	100.0	0	.0	630
.0		.0		.0		100.0		100.0		.0		100.0
0	.0	0	.0	0	.0	473	100.0	473	100.0	0	.0	473
.0		.0		.0		−	24.9	−	24.9	.0		− 24.9
0	.0	0	.0	0	.0	0	.0	0	.0	0	.0	0
0	.0	0	.0	0	.0	260	100.0	260	100.0	0	.0	260
.0		.0		.0		100.0		100.0		.0		100.0
0	.0	0	.0	0	.0	227	100.0	227	100.0	0	.0	227
.0		.0		.0		−	12.7	−	12.7	.0		− 12.7
0	.0	0	.0	0	.0	0	.0	0	.0	0	.0	0
0	.0	0	.0	0	.0	630	100.0	630	100.0	0	.0	630
.0		.0		.0		.0		100.0		.0		100.0
0	.0	0	.0	0	.0	473	100.0	473	100.0	0	.0	473
.0		.0		.0		−	24.9	−	24.9	.0		− 24.9
92	.4	1,947	8.6	280	1.2	592	2.6	2,911	12.9	19,728	87.1	22,639
135	.4	2,069	6.7	490	1.6	867	2.8	3,561	11.5	27,415	88.5	30,976
46.7		6.3		75.0		46.5		22.3		39.0		36.8
149	.4	2,337	6.5	568	1.6	1,072	3.0	4,126	11.4	31,938	88.6	36,064
10.4		13.0		15.9		23.6		15.9		16.5		16.4
347	.4	4,402	4.9	753	.8	2,489	2.7	7,991	8.8	82,650	91.2	90,641
310	.3	3,372	3.8	942	1.1	2,471	2.8	7,095	8.0	81,485	92.0	88,580
10.7	−	23.4		25.1		25.1	−	11.2	−	1.4	−	2.3
286	.3	3,034	3.7	946	1.1	2,454	3.0	6,720	8.2	75,632	91.8	82,352
7.7	−	10.0		.4		.4	−	5.3	−	7.2	−	7.0

TABLE 19 — TOTAL ENROLLMENT OF UNDERGRADUATES BY CLASS LEVEL IN INSTITUTIONS OF HIGHER EDUCATION BY RACE, ETHNICITY AND SEX:
STATE AND NATION, 1978

	AMERICAN INDIAN ALASKAN NATIVE		BLACK NON-HISPANIC		ASIAN OR PACIFIC ISLANDER		HISPANIC		TOTAL MINORITY		WHITE NON-HISPANIC		NON-RESIDENT ALIEN	
	NUMBER	%	NUMBER	%	NUMBER	%	NUMBER	%	NUMBER	%	NUMBER	%	NUMBER	%
ALABAMA (58 INSTITUTIONS)														
UNDERGRADUATE:														
FIRST YR	86	.1	16,395	25.8	151	.2	190	.3	16,822	26.4	46,117	72.4	726	1.1
FEMALE	43	.1	9,846	29.7	56	.2	78	.2	10,023	30.2	23,005	69.4	142	.4
MALE	43	.1	6,549	21.5	95	.3	112	.4	6,799	22.3	23,112	75.8	584	1.9
SECOND YR	48	.1	7,813	24.1	117	.4	99	.3	8,077	24.9	23,901	73.7	462	1.4
FEMALE	23	.1	4,591	28.6	49	.3	37	.2	4,700	29.3	11,279	70.2	78	.5
MALE	25	.2	3,222	19.7	68	.4	62	.4	3,377	20.6	12,622	77.0	384	2.3
THIRD YR	20	.1	4,132	20.7	69	.3	80	.4	4,301	21.6	15,353	76.9	302	1.5
FEMALE	10	.1	2,391	24.7	21	.2	30	.3	2,452	25.3	7,180	74.2	51	.5
MALE	10	.1	1,741	16.9	48	.5	50	.5	1,849	18.0	8,173	79.6	251	2.4
FOURTH YR	17	.1	3,746	18.6	57	.3	79	.4	3,899	19.4	15,910	79.0	323	1.6
FEMALE	7	.1	2,167	22.9	24	.3	31	.3	2,229	23.5	7,215	76.1	33	.3
MALE	10	.1	1,579	14.8	33	.3	48	.5	1,670	15.7	8,695	81.6	290	2.7
TOTAL	171	.1	32,086	23.6	394	.3	448	.3	33,099	24.3	101,281	74.4	1,813	1.3
FEMALE	83	.1	18,995	27.8	150	.2	176	.3	19,404	28.4	48,679	71.2	304	.4
MALE	88	.1	13,091	19.3	244	.4	272	.4	13,695	20.2	52,602	77.6	1,509	2.2
ALASKA (14 INSTITUTIONS)														
UNDERGRADUATE:														
FIRST YR	1,188	8.9	500	3.8	250	1.9	186	1.4	2,124	16.0	11,129	89.8	34	.3
FEMALE	715	9.2	237	3.1	135	1.7	107	1.4	1,194	15.4	6,547	84.3	21	.3
MALE	473	8.6	263	4.8	115	2.1	79	1.4	930	16.8	4,582	82.9	13	.2
SECOND YR	221	13.5	51	3.1	37	2.3	13	.8	322	19.7	1,303	79.6	11	.7
FEMALE	146	16.7	26	3.0	11	1.3	6	.7	189	21.7	682	78.2	1	.1
MALE	75	9.8	25	3.3	26	3.4	7	.9	133	17.4	621	81.3	10	1.3
THIRD YR	63	6.8	31	3.3	20	2.1	14	1.5	128	13.7	801	85.9	3	.3
FEMALE	41	7.9	18	3.5	12	2.3	4	.8	75	14.5	443	85.5	0	.0
MALE	22	5.3	13	3.1	8	1.9	10	2.4	53	12.8	358	86.5	3	.7
FOURTH YR	41	5.1	20	2.5	14	1.7	4	.5	79	9.9	714	89.1	8	1.0
FEMALE	23	5.7	9	2.2	7	1.7	2	.5	41	10.2	356	88.8	4	1.0
MALE	18	4.5	11	2.8	7	1.8	2	.5	38	9.5	358	89.5	4	1.0
TOTAL	1,513	9.1	602	3.6	321	1.9	217	1.3	2,653	15.9	13,947	83.7	56	.3
FEMALE	925	9.7	290	3.0	165	1.7	119	1.2	1,499	15.7	8,028	84.0	26	.3
MALE	588	8.3	312	4.4	156	2.2	98	1.4	1,154	16.2	5,919	83.3	30	.4
ARIZONA (22 INSTITUTIONS)														
UNDERGRADUATE:														
FIRST YR	2,823	3.6	2,699	3.4	799	1.0	9,300	11.8	15,621	19.8	62,228	78.7	1,198	1.5
FEMALE	1,706	4.2	1,125	2.8	474	1.2	5,429	13.3	8,734	21.5	31,523	77.4	446	1.1
MALE	1,117	2.9	1,574	4.1	325	.8	3,871	10.1	6,887	18.0	30,705	80.1	752	2.0
SECOND YR	1,494	4.1	1,075	3.0	331	.9	3,091	8.5	5,991	16.6	29,613	81.8	595	1.6
FEMALE	748	4.5	399	2.4	169	1.0	1,203	7.2	2,519	15.1	14,005	84.1	126	.8
MALE	746	3.8	676	3.5	162	.8	1,888	9.7	3,472	17.8	15,608	79.8	469	2.4
THIRD YR	162	1.2	253	1.8	141	1.0	713	5.1	1,269	9.1	12,469	89.2	245	1.8
FEMALE	90	1.4	115	1.8	64	1.0	310	4.9	579	9.2	5,686	90.1	45	.7
MALE	72	.9	138	1.8	77	1.0	403	5.3	690	9.0	6,783	88.4	200	2.6
FOURTH YR	201	1.4	229	1.6	127	.9	707	5.0	1,264	8.9	12,745	89.9	168	1.2
FEMALE	110	1.9	85	1.5	48	.8	254	4.4	497	8.6	5,274	90.9	30	.5
MALE	91	1.1	144	1.7	79	.9	453	5.4	767	9.2	7,471	89.2	138	1.6
TOTAL	4,680	3.3	4,256	3.0	1,398	1.0	13,811	9.6	24,145	16.8	117,055	81.6	2,206	1.5	1
FEMALE	2,654	3.8	1,724	2.5	755	1.1	7,196	10.4	12,329	17.7	56,488	81.3	647	.9
MALE	2,026	2.7	2,532	3.4	643	.9	6,615	8.9	11,816	16.0	60,567	81.9	1,559	2.1
ARKANSAS (34 INSTITUTIONS)														
UNDERGRADUATE:														
FIRST YR	229	.8	5,506	18.4	218	.7	139	.5	6,092	20.3	23,726	79.1	168	.6
FEMALE	114	.8	3,240	20.0	74	.5	69	.4	3,497	21.6	12,650	78.2	39	.2
MALE	115	.8	2,266	16.4	144	1.0	70	.5	2,595	18.8	11,076	80.3	129	.9
SECOND YR	80	.6	1,962	14.4	69	.5	37	.3	2,148	15.8	11,333	83.3	119	.9
FEMALE	30	.4	1,085	15.8	21	.3	15	.2	1,151	16.7	5,702	82.9	25	.4
MALE	50	.7	877	13.0	48	.7	22	.3	997	14.8	5,631	83.8	94	1.4
THIRD YR	41	.5	1,205	14.1	53	.6	14	.2	1,313	15.3	7,138	83.3	123	1.4
FEMALE	14	.3	625	15.5	18	.4	4	.1	661	16.4	3,343	83.1	21	.5
MALE	27	.6	580	12.8	35	.8	10	.2	652	14.3	3,795	83.4	102	2.2
FOURTH YR	34	.4	1,218	13.7	42	.5	37	.4	1,331	14.9	7,496	84.0	92	1.0
FEMALE	14	.3	671	16.2	18	.4	18	.4	721	17.4	3,406	82.3	12	.3
MALE	20	.4	547	11.4	24	.5	19	.4	610	12.8	4,090	85.6	80	1.7
TOTAL	384	.6	9,891	16.2	382	.6	227	.4	10,884	17.8	49,693	81.4	502	.8
FEMALE	172	.6	5,621	18.0	131	.4	106	.3	6,030	19.3	25,101	80.4	97	.3
MALE	212	.7	4,270	14.3	251	.8	121	.4	4,854	16.3	24,592	82.4	405	1.4

ABLE 19 - TOTAL ENROLLMENT OF UNDERGRADUATES BY CLASS LEVEL IN INSTITUTIONS OF HIGHER EDUCATION BY RACE, ETHNICITY AND SEX: STATE AND NATION, 1978

	AMERICAN INDIAN ALASKAN NATIVE		BLACK NON-HISPANIC		ASIAN OR PACIFIC ISLANDER		HISPANIC		TOTAL MINORITY		WHITE NON-HISPANIC		NON-RESIDENT ALIEN		TOTAL
	NUMBER	%	NUMBER	%	NUMBER	%	NUMBER	%	NUMBER	%	NUMBER	%	NUMBER	%	NUMBER
ALIFORNIA (226 INSTITUTIONS)															
NDERGRADUATE:															
FIRST YR	11,179	1.5	78,163	10.8	43,047	5.9	79,859	11.0	212,248	29.3	499,354	68.8	13,916	1.9	725,518
FEMALE	5,921	1.5	42,422	10.8	21,014	5.	40,440	10.3	109,797	28.0	277,683	70.8	4,731	1.2	392,211
MALE	5,258	1.6	35,741	10.7	22,033	6.8	39,419	11.8	102,451	30.7	221,671	66.5	9,185	2.8	333,307
ECOND YR	3,860	1.3	24,120	8.3	19,836	6.8	25,686	8.9	73,502	25.3	210,152	72.5	6,377	2.2	290,031
FEMALE	1,917	1.3	12,394	8.5	9,269	6.4	11,792	8.1	35,372	24.3	108,172	74.3	2,099	1.4	145,643
MALE	1,943	1.3	11,726	8.1	10,567	7.3	13,894	9.6	38,130	26.4	101,980	70.6	4,278	3.0	144,388
THIRD YR	1,224	1.	7,270	5.9	9,883	.1	9,446	7.7	27,823	22.7	90,253	73.7	4,383	3.6	122,459
FEMALE	568	1.0	3,890	6.6	4,795	8.1	4,384	7.4	13,637	23.0	44,216	74.7	1,314	2.2	59,167
MALE	656	1.0	3,380	5.3	5,088	8.0	5,062	8.0	14,186	22.4	46,037	72.7	3,069	4.8	63,292
OURTH YR	1,375	1.1	6,818	5.6	9,792	8.1	8,439	7.	26,424	21.8	90,731	74.9	3,922	3.2	121,077
FEMALE	608	1.1	3,393	6.3	4,371	8.1	3,528	6.5	11,900	21.9	41,271	76.1	1,079	2.0	54,250
MALE	767	1.1	3,425	5.1	5,421	8.1	4,911	7.8	14,524	21.7	49,460	74.0	2,843	4.3	66,827
OTAL	17,638	1.	116,371	2	82,558	.6	123,430	9.8	339,997	27.0	890,490	70.7	28,598	2.3	1,259,085
FEMALE	9,014	1.	62,099	5	39,449	.1	60,144	9.2	170,706	26.2	471,342	72.4	9,223	1.4	651,271
MALE	8,624	1.4	54,272	8.9	43,109	8.1	63,286	10.4	169,291	27.9	419,148	69.0	19,375	3.2	607,814
OLORADO (39 INSTITUTIONS)															
NDERGRADUATE:															
FIRST YR	578	1.1	1,939	3	664	1.3	3,336	.3	6,517	12.4	45,022	85.5	1,141	2.2	52,680
FEMALE	306	1.1	911	3	302	1.1	1,623	6.1	3,142	11.8	23,217	87.2	272	1.0	26,631
MALE	272	1.0	1,028	3.8	362	1.4	1,713	6.6	3,375	13.0	21,805	83.7	869	3.3	26,049
ECOND YR	183	.7	903	3	373	1.4	1,528	5.8	2,987	11.4	22,731	86.5	554	2.1	26,272
FEMALE	92	.8	349	2.4	184	1.5	613	5.1	1,238	10.4	10,592	88.7	111	.9	11,941
MALE	91	.6	554	3.9	189	1.3	915	6.4	1,749	12.2	12,139	84.7	443	3.1	14,331
THIRD YR	108	.6	409	2.5	234	1.4	773	4.6	1,524	9.2	14,856	89.3	255	1.5	16,635
FEMALE	57	.7	200	2.6	113	1.5	353	4.6	723	9.3	6,971	89.9	60	.8	7,754
MALE	51	.6	209	2.4	121	1.4	420	4.7	801	9.0	7,885	88.8	195	2.2	8,881
OURTH YR	107	.6	429	2.3	269	1.5	818	4.4	1,623	8.8	16,586	89.6	306	1.7	18,515
FEMALE	51	.6	209	2.6	130	1.6	373	4.6	763	9.4	7,275	89.7	68	.8	8,106
MALE	56	.5	220	2.1	139	1.3	445	4.3	860	8.3	9,311	89.5	238	2.3	10,409
OTAL	976	.9	3,680	3.2	1,540	1.3	6,455	5.7	12,651	11.1	99,195	86.9	2,256	2.0	114,102
FEMALE	506	.9	1,669	3.1	729	1.3	2,962	5.4	5,866	10.8	48,055	88.3	511	.9	54,432
MALE	470	.8	2,011	3.4	811	1.4	3,493	5.9	6,785	11.4	51,140	85.7	1,745	2.9	59,670
ONNECTICUT (44 INSTITUTIONS)															
NDERGRADUATE:															
FIRST YR	137	.2	3,517	6.4	396	.7	1,126	2.1	5,176	9.4	49,178	89.7	460	.8	54,814
FEMALE	80	.3	2,007	6.9	176	.6	608	2.1	2,871	9.8	26,221	89.6	158	.5	29,250
MALE	57	.2	1,510	5.9	220	.9	518	2.0	2,305	9.0	22,957	89.8	302	1.2	25,564
ECOND YR	53	.2	1,597	5	219	.8	499	1.8	2,368	8.7	24,681	90.3	287	1.0	27,336
FEMALE	23	.2	870	6	107	.8	253	1.8	1,253	9.1	12,448	90.2	92	.7	13,793
MALE	30	.2	727	5.8	112	.8	246	1.8	1,115	8.2	12,233	90.3	195	1.4	13,543
THIRD YR	25	.2	648	4.	144	.9	196	1.2	1,013	6.3	15,012	92.7	169	1.0	16,194
FEMALE	14	.2	332	4.0	63	.8	84	1.1	493	6.4	7,158	92.8	61	.8	7,712
MALE	11	.1	316	3.9	81	1.0	112	1.3	520	6.1	7,854	92.6	108	1.3	8,482
OURTH YR	18	.1	545	3.7	108	.7	192	1.	863	5.8	13,784	93.2	142	1.0	14,789
FEMALE	11	.2	275	3.8	52	.7	72	1.	410	5.7	6,774	93.7	44	.6	7,228
MALE	7	.1	270	3.6	56	.7	120	1.8	453	6.0	7,010	92.7	98	1.3	7,561
OTAL	233	.2	6,307	5.6	867	.8	2,013	1.	9,420	8.3	102,655	90.7	1,058	.9	113,133
FEMALE	128	.2	3,484	6.0	398	.7	1,017	1.	5,027	8.7	52,601	90.7	355	.6	57,983
MALE	105	.2	2,823	5.1	469	.9	996	1.8	4,393	8.0	50,054	90.8	703	1.3	55,150
ELAWARE (10 INSTITUTIONS)															
NDERGRADUATE:															
FIRST YR	22	.2	1,968	16.7	48	.4	97	.8	2,135	18.2	9,530	81.1	93	.8	11,758
FEMALE	11	.2	1,147	17.7	20	.3	49	.8	1,227	19.0	5,193	80.4	42	.6	6,462
MALE	11	.2	821	15.5	28	.5	48	.9	908	17.1	4,337	81.9	51	1.0	5,296
ECOND YR	4	.1	543	1.1	23	.4	15	.3	585	10.8	4,742	87.8	71	1.3	5,398
FEMALE	1	.0	308	10.5	14	.5	8	.3	331	11.3	2,573	87.9	23	.8	2,927
MALE	3	.1	235	9.5	9	.4	7	.3	254	10.3	2,169	87.8	48	1.9	2,471
THIRD YR	5	.1	302	7	13	.3	22	.6	342	9.0	3,413	89.7	49	1.3	3,804
FEMALE	3	.1	152	7	10	.5	16	.8	181	8.9	1,830	90.2	17	.8	2,028
MALE	2	.1	150	8.4	3	.2	6	.3	161	9.1	1,583	89.1	32	1.8	1,776
OURTH YR	2	.1	251	7.2	10	.3	13	.4	276	7.9	3,186	90.9	44	1.3	3,506
FEMALE	0	.0	138	7.9	5	.3	11	.6	154	8.9	1,564	89.5	22	1.3	1,740
MALE	2	.1	113	6.4	5	.3	2	.1	122	6.9	1,622	91.8	22	1.2	1,766
OTAL	33	.1	3,064	12.5	94	.4	147	.6	3,338	13.6	20,871	85.3	257	1.1	24,466
FEMALE	15	.1	1,745	13.3	49	.4	84	.6	1,893	14.4	11,160	84.8	104	.8	13,157
MALE	18	.2	1,319	11.7	45	.4	63	.6	1,445	12.8	9,711	85.9	153	1.4	11,309

TABLE 19 - TOTAL ENROLLMENT OF UNDERGRADUATES BY CLASS LEVEL IN INSTITUTIONS OF HIGHER EDUCATION BY RACE, ETHNICITY AND SEX: STATE AND NATION, 1978

	AMERICAN INDIAN ALASKAN NATIVE		BLACK NON-HISPANIC		ASIAN OR PACIFIC ISLANDER		HISPANIC		TOTAL MINORITY		WHITE NON-HISPANIC		NON-RESIDENT ALIEN		TOTAL
	NUMBER	%	NUMBER	%	NUMBER	%	NUMBER	%	NUMBER	%	NUMBER	%	NUMBER	%	NUMBER
DISTRICT OF COLUMBIA (13 INSTITUTIONS)															
UNDERGRADUATE:															
FIRST YR	156	.8	11,295	56.5	476	2.4	317	1.6	12,244	61.2	5,975	29.9	1,785	8.9	20,004
FEMALE	38	.3	6,791	61.5	146	1.3	164	1.5	7,139	64.7	3,157	28.6	739	6.7	11,035
MALE	118	1.3	4,504	50.2	330	3.7	153	1.7	5,105	56.9	2,818	31.4	1,046	11.7	8,969
SECOND YR	55	.6	3,298	38.2	185	2.1	134	1.6	3,672	42.6	4,138	48.0	818	9.5	8,628
FEMALE	17	.4	1,933	41.5	48	1.0	61	1.3	2,059	44.2	2,263	48.5	340	7.3	4,662
MALE	38	1.0	1,365	34.4	137	3.5	73	1.8	1,613	40.7	1,875	47.3	478	12.1	3,966
THIRD YR	39	.5	2,775	34.2	152	1.9	134	1.6	3,100	38.2	4,280	52.7	743	9.1	8,123
FEMALE	10	.2	1,620	38.0	52	1.2	78	1.8	1,760	41.3	2,225	52.2	278	6.5	4,263
MALE	29	.8	1,155	29.9	100	2.6	56	1.5	1,340	34.7	2,055	53.2	465	12.0	3,860
FOURTH YR	42	.6	2,898	38.2	135	1.8	113	1.5	3,188	42.1	3,687	48.6	706	9.3	7,581
FEMALE	12	.3	1,626	41.5	37	.9	63	1.6	1,738	44.3	1,898	48.4	284	7.2	3,920
MALE	30	.8	1,272	34.7	98	2.7	50	1.4	1,450	39.6	1,789	48.9	422	11.5	3,661
TOTAL	292	.7	20,266	45.7	948	2.1	698	1.6	22,204	50.1	18,080	40.8	4,052	9.1	44,336
FEMALE	77	.3	11,970	50.1	283	1.2	366	1.5	12,696	53.2	9,543	40.0	1,641	6.9	23,880
MALE	215	1.1	8,296	40.6	665	3.3	332	1.6	9,508	46.5	8,537	41.7	2,411	11.8	20,456
FLORIDA (74 INSTITUTIONS)															
UNDERGRADUATE:															
FIRST YR	584	.4	19,198	13.1	992	.7	11,568	7.9	32,342	22.1	110,515	75.5	3,500	2.4	146,357
FEMALE	317	.4	11,726	15.3	451	.6	6,077	7.9	18,571	24.2	56,933	74.3	1,111	1.5	76,615
MALE	267	.4	7,472	10.7	541	.8	5,491	7.9	13,771	19.7	53,582	76.8	2,389	3.4	69,742
SECOND YR	229	.3	9,120	11.8	556	.7	5,561	7.2	15,466	20.0	60,096	77.6	1,840	2.4	77,402
FEMALE	112	.3	5,628	14.6	223	.6	2,818	7.3	8,781	22.8	29,209	75.8	539	1.4	38,529
MALE	117	.3	3,492	9.0	333	.9	2,743	7.1	6,685	17.2	30,887	79.5	1,301	3.3	38,873
THIRD YR	53	.1	4,057	9.6	391	.9	2,937	7.0	7,438	17.6	33,968	80.5	779	1.8	42,185
FEMALE	20	.1	2,273	12.0	126	.7	1,329	7.0	3,748	19.8	14,996	79.0	233	1.2	18,977
MALE	33	.1	1,784	7.7	265	1.1	1,608	6.9	3,690	15.9	18,972	81.7	546	2.4	23,208
FOURTH YR	50	.1	3,154	9.2	269	.8	2,575	7.5	6,048	17.7	27,462	80.5	602	1.8	34,112
FEMALE	21	.1	1,821	12.3	77	.5	1,197	8.1	3,116	21.0	11,583	78.0	151	1.0	14,850
MALE	29	.2	1,333	6.9	192	1.0	1,378	7.2	2,932	15.2	15,879	82.4	451	2.3	19,262
TOTAL	916	.3	35,529	11.8	2,208	.7	22,641	7.5	61,294	20.4	232,041	77.3	6,721	2.2	300,056
FEMALE	470	.3	21,448	14.4	877	.6	11,421	7.7	34,216	23.0	112,721	75.7	2,034	1.4	148,971
MALE	446	.3	14,081	9.3	1,331	.9	11,220	7.4	27,078	17.9	119,320	79.0	4,687	3.1	151,085
GEORGIA (68 INSTITUTIONS)															
UNDERGRADUATE:															
FIRST YR	110	.2	13,231	22.0	210	.3	351	.6	13,902	23.1	45,334	75.3	958	1.6	60,194
FEMALE	54	.2	7,745	25.1	108	.3	131	.4	8,038	26.0	22,605	73.2	248	.8	30,891
MALE	56	.2	5,486	18.7	102	.3	220	.8	5,864	20.0	22,729	77.6	710	2.4	29,303
SECOND YR	64	.2	6,344	18.9	140	.4	173	.5	6,721	20.0	26,271	78.2	584	1.7	33,576
FEMALE	23	.1	3,498	21.2	51	.3	57	.3	3,629	22.0	12,755	77.2	138	.8	16,522
MALE	41	.2	2,846	16.7	89	.5	116	.7	3,092	18.1	13,516	79.3	446	2.6	17,054
THIRD YR	22	.1	3,835	18.0	108	.5	107	.5	4,072	19.1	16,846	79.2	362	1.7	21,280
FEMALE	11	.1	2,189	21.2	42	.4	35	.3	2,277	22.1	7,930	77.0	98	1.0	10,305
MALE	11	.1	1,646	15.0	66	.6	72	.7	1,795	16.4	8,916	81.2	264	2.4	10,975
FOURTH YR	24	.1	3,813	17.1	97	.4	107	.5	4,041	18.1	17,967	80.5	324	1.5	22,332
FEMALE	7	.1	2,151	20.6	42	.4	40	.4	2,240	21.5	8,117	77.8	77	.7	10,434
MALE	17	.1	1,662	14.0	55	.5	67	.6	1,801	15.1	9,850	82.8	247	2.1	11,898
TOTAL	220	.2	27,223	19.8	555	.4	738	.5	28,736	20.9	106,418	77.5	2,228	1.6	137,382
FEMALE	95	.1	15,583	22.9	243	.4	263	.4	16,184	23.7	51,407	75.4	561	.8	68,152
MALE	125	.2	11,640	16.8	312	.5	475	.7	12,552	18.1	55,011	79.5	1,667	2.4	69,230
HAWAII (12 INSTITUTIONS)															
UNDERGRADUATE:															
FIRST YR	43	.2	399	2.2	11,588	62.7	754	4.1	12,784	69.2	4,925	26.7	758	4.1	18,467
FEMALE	21	.2	108	1.2	5,691	65.0	342	3.9	6,162	70.3	2,257	25.8	343	3.9	8,762
MALE	22	.2	291	3.0	5,897	60.8	412	4.2	6,622	68.2	2,668	27.5	415	4.3	9,705
SECOND YR	17	.2	136	1.3	7,132	70.0	350	3.4	7,635	74.9	2,113	20.7	445	4.4	10,193
FEMALE	5	.1	37	.8	3,134	70.3	147	3.3	3,323	74.6	941	21.1	191	4.3	4,455
MALE	12	.2	99	1.7	3,998	69.7	203	3.5	4,312	75.1	1,172	20.4	254	4.4	5,738
THIRD YR	12	.3	33	.7	3,179	66.4	65	1.4	3,289	68.7	1,227	25.6	269	5.6	4,785
FEMALE	4	.2	11	.5	1,592	67.7	26	1.1	1,633	69.4	608	25.9	111	4.7	2,352
MALE	8	.3	22	.9	1,587	65.2	39	1.6	1,656	68.1	619	25.4	158	6.5	2,433
FOURTH YR	6	.1	34	.6	3,809	70.3	68	1.3	3,917	72.3	1,307	24.1	191	3.5	5,415
FEMALE	3	.1	14	.6	1,794	71.0	26	1.0	1,837	72.7	606	24.0	83	3.3	2,526
MALE	3	.1	20	.7	2,015	69.7	42	1.5	2,080	72.0	701	24.3	108	3.7	2,889
TOTAL	78	.2	602	1.5	25,708	66.2	1,237	3.2	27,625	71.1	9,572	24.6	1,663	4.3	38,860
FEMALE	33	.2	170	.9	12,211	67.5	541	3.0	12,955	71.6	4,412	24.4	728	4.0	18,095
MALE	45	.2	432	2.1	13,497	65.0	696	3.4	14,670	70.6	5,160	24.8	935	4.5	20,765

TAL ENROLLMENT OF UNDERGRADUATES BY CLASS LEVEL IN INSTITUTIONS OF HIGHER EDUCATION BY RACE, ETHNICITY AND SEX: ATE AND NATION, 1978

ERICAN INDIAN LASKAN NATIVE		BLACK NON-HISPANIC		ASIAN OR PACIFIC ISLANDER		HISPANIC		TOTAL MINORITY		WHITE NON-HISPANIC		NON-RESIDENT ALIEN		TOTAL
UMBER	%	NUMBER	%	NUMBER	%	NUMBER	%	NUMBER	%	NUMBER	%	NUMBER	%	NUMBER
(9 INSTITUTIONS)														
139	.8	91	.6	164	1.0	174	1.1	568	3.4	15,686	94.8	289	1.7	16,543
84	1.0	25	.3	79	.9	95	1.1	283	3.3	8,160	95.0	147	1.7	8,590
55	.7	66	.8	85	1.1	79	1.0	285	3.6	7,526	94.6	142	1.8	7,953
42	.5	36	.4	65	.8	68	.8	211	2.6	7,816	95.7	136	1.7	8,163
26	.6	8	.2	19	.5	34	.8	87	2.1	4,014	96.1	75	1.8	4,176
16	.4	28	.7	46	1.2	34	.9	124	3.1	3,802	95.4	61	1.5	3,987
14	.4	34	.9	53	1.5	18	.5	119	3.3	3,499	95.9	32	.9	3,650
9	.5	7	.4	21	1.3	8	.5	45	2.7	1,603	96.9	6	.4	1,654
5	.3	27	1.4	32	1.6	10	.5	74	3.7	1,896	95.0	26	1.3	1,996
12	.3	13	.3	52	1.3	22	.6	99	2.5	3,825	96.8	29	.7	3,953
7	.4	1	.1	21	1.3	8	.5	37	2.3	1,594	97.3	7	.4	1,638
5	.2	12	.5	31	1.3	14	.6	62	2.7	2,231	96.4	22	1.0	2,315
207	.6	174	.5	334	1.0	282	.9	997	3.1	30,826	95.4	486	1.5	32,309
126	.8	41	.3	140	.9	145	.9	452	2.8	15,371	95.7	235	1.5	16,058
81	.5	133	.8	194	1.2	137	.8	545	3.4	15,455	95.1	251	1.5	16,251
(135 INSTITUTIONS)														
1,103	.4	38,535	15.3	3,325	1.3	6,610	2.6	49,573	19.6	198,721	78.7	4,121	1.6	252,415
592	.4	23,152	17.0	1,602	1.2	3,255	2.4	28,601	21.0	106,384	78.0	1,412	1.0	136,397
511	.4	15,383	13.3	1,723	1.5	3,355	2.9	20,972	18.1	92,337	79.6	2,709	2.3	116,018
318	.3	17,377	16.5	1,473	1.4	2,671	2.5	21,839	20.8	81,775	77.8	1,511	1.4	105,125
159	.3	10,445	19.5	700	1.3	1,285	2.4	12,589	23.5	40,526	75.6	492	.9	53,607
159	.3	6,932	13.5	773	1.5	1,386	2.7	9,250	18.0	41,249	80.1	1,019	2.0	51,518
117	.2	5,364	10.4	742	1.4	934	1.8	7,157	13.9	43,501	84.5	837	1.6	51,495
53	.2	3,278	13.4	319	1.3	461	1.9	4,111	16.8	20,059	82.1	255	1.0	24,425
64	.2	2,086	7.7	423	1.6	473	1.7	3,046	11.3	23,442	86.6	582	2.1	27,070
129	.2	4,605	8.6	849	1.6	932	1.7	6,515	12.2	45,838	86.0	971	1.8	53,324
57	.2	2,829	10.8	364	1.4	426	1.6	3,676	14.0	22,289	84.9	275	1.0	26,240
72	.3	1,776	6.6	485	1.8	506	1.9	2,839	10.5	23,549	86.9	696	2.6	27,084
1,667	.4	65,881	14.2	6,389	1.4	11,147	2.4	85,084	18.4	369,835	80.0	7,440	1.6	462,359
861	.4	39,704	16.5	2,985	1.2	5,427	2.3	48,977	20.4	189,258	78.6	2,434	1.0	240,669
806	.4	26,177	11.8	3,404	1.5	5,720	2.6	36,107	16.3	180,577	81.5	5,006	2.3	221,690
(60 INSTITUTIONS)														
146	.2	5,157	7.6	344	.5	752	1.1	6,399	9.4	60,821	89.2	990	1.5	68,210
61	.2	2,982	8.6	163	.5	369	1.1	3,575	10.3	30,712	88.8	309	.9	34,596
85	.3	2,175	6.5	181	.5	383	1.1	2,824	8.4	30,109	89.6	681	2.0	33,614
125	.3	2,856	6.1	259	.6	460	1.0	3,700	7.9	42,638	91.0	536	1.1	46,874
48	.2	1,500	6.8	126	.6	202	.9	1,876	8.6	19,893	90.7	155	.7	21,924
77	.3	1,356	5.4	133	.5	258	1.0	1,824	7.3	22,745	91.2	381	1.5	24,950
41	.1	1,343	4.4	133	.4	251	.8	1,768	5.8	28,211	93.0	355	1.2	30,334
19	.1	746	5.2	60	.4	102	.7	927	6.5	13,214	92.7	115	.8	14,256
22	.1	597	3.7	73	.5	149	.9	841	5.2	14,997	93.3	240	1.5	16,078
47	.2	1,085	3.7	147	.5	201	.7	1,480	5.1	27,160	93.7	336	1.2	28,976
19	.1	549	4.2	70	.5	69	.5	707	5.5	12,144	93.8	90	.7	12,941
28	.2	536	3.3	77	.5	132	.8	773	4.8	15,016	93.6	246	1.5	16,035
359	.2	10,441	6.0	883	.5	1,664	1.0	13,347	7.7	158,830	91.1	2,217	1.3	174,394
147	.2	5,777	6.9	419	.5	742	.9	7,085	8.5	75,963	90.7	609	.8	83,717
212	.2	4,664	5.1	464	.5	922	1.0	6,262	6.9	82,867	91.4	1,548	1.7	90,677
(50 INSTITUTIONS)														
196	.4	1,219	2.6	263	.6	287	.6	1,965	4.2	44,336	94.3	717	1.5	47,018
102	.4	500	2.1	114	.5	122	.5	838	3.5	22,971	95.5	247	1.0	24,056
94	.4	719	3.1	149	.6	165	.7	1,127	4.9	21,365	93.0	470	2.0	22,962
92	.4	578	2.2	149	.6	129	.5	948	3.6	24,631	94.5	474	1.8	26,053
54	.4	249	1.9	63	.5	55	.4	421	3.3	12,255	95.6	142	1.1	12,818
38	.3	329	2.5	86	.6	74	.6	527	4.0	12,376	93.5	332	2.5	13,235
36	.2	354	2.2	79	.5	66	.4	535	3.3	15,481	94.6	343	2.1	16,359
18	.2	158	2.1	36	.5	31	.4	243	3.2	7,333	95.4	108	1.4	7,684
18	.2	196	2.3	43	.5	35	.4	292	3.4	8,148	93.9	235	2.7	8,675
22	.1	256	1.7	89	.6	54	.3	421	2.7	14,759	95.2	317	2.0	15,497
10	.1	110	1.5	38	.5	23	.3	181	2.4	7,141	96.2	102	1.4	7,424
12	.1	146	1.8	51	.6	31	.4	240	3.0	7,618	94.4	215	2.7	8,073
346	.3	2,407	2.3	580	.6	536	.5	3,869	3.7	99,207	94.5	1,851	1.8	104,927
184	.4	1,017	2.0	251	.5	231	.4	1,683	3.2	49,700	95.6	599	1.2	51,982
162	.3	1,390	2.6	329	.6	305	.6	2,186	4.1	49,507	93.5	1,252	2.4	52,945

TABLE 19 - TOTAL ENROLLMENT OF UNDERGRADUATES BY CLASS LEVEL IN INSTITUTIONS OF HIGHER EDUCATION BY RACE, ETHNICITY AND SEX
STATE AND NATION, 1978

	AMERICAN INDIAN ALASKAN NATIVE		BLACK NON-HISPANIC		ASIAN OR PACIFIC ISLANDER		HISPANIC		TOTAL MINORITY		WHITE NON-HISPANIC		NON-RESIDENT ALIEN	
	NUMBER	%	NUMBER	%	NUMBER	%	NUMBER	%	NUMBER	%	NUMBER	%	NUMBER	%
KANSAS (52 INSTITUTIONS)														
UNDERGRADUATE:														
FIRST YR	930	2.2	2,552	5.9	207	.5	717	1.7	4,406	10.2	37,980	87.8	853	2.0
FEMALE	462	2.1	1,122	5.0	80	.4	332	1.5	1,996	8.9	20,287	90.3	184	.8
MALE	468	2.3	1,430	6.9	127	.6	385	1.9	2,410	11.6	17,693	85.2	669	3.2
SECOND YR	307	1.3	1,181	4.9	113	.5	316	1.3	1,917	8.0	21,448	89.7	551	2.3
FEMALE	157	1.3	513	4.3	49	.4	140	1.2	859	7.3	10,885	92.0	93	.8
MALE	150	1.2	668	5.5	64	.5	176	1.5	1,058	8.8	10,563	87.4	458	3.8
THIRD YR	97	.7	525	3.6	84	.6	190	1.3	896	6.2	13,179	91.5	324	2.3
FEMALE	53	.8	248	3.7	40	.6	77	1.1	418	6.2	6,271	92.8	67	1.0
MALE	44	.6	277	3.6	44	.6	113	1.5	478	6.3	6,908	90.4	257	3.4
FOURTH YR	91	.6	495	3.0	80	.5	202	1.2	868	5.3	15,013	92.4	364	2.2
FEMALE	39	.5	213	2.9	29	.4	79	1.1	360	4.9	6,976	94.1	77	1.0
MALE	52	.6	282	3.2	51	.6	123	1.4	508	5.8	8,037	91.0	287	3.2
TOTAL	1,425	1.5	4,753	4.9	484	.5	1,425	1.5	8,087	8.3	87,620	89.6	2,092	2.1
FEMALE	711	1.5	2,096	4.3	198	.4	628	1.3	3,633	7.5	44,419	91.6	421	.9
MALE	714	1.4	2,657	5.4	286	.6	797	1.6	4,454	9.0	43,201	87.6	1,671	3.4
KENTUCKY (39 INSTITUTIONS)														
UNDERGRADUATE:														
FIRST YR	100	.2	4,207	9.3	181	.4	116	.3	4,604	10.2	40,115	88.6	570	1.3
FEMALE	54	.2	2,386	9.7	46	.3	47	.2	2,553	10.3	21,983	89.0	152	.6
MALE	46	.2	1,821	8.8	115	.6	69	.3	2,051	10.0	18,132	88.0	418	2.0
SECOND YR	41	.2	1,786	7.5	232	1.0	67	.3	2,126	8.9	21,430	89.7	323	1.4
FEMALE	19	.2	958	7.7	109	.9	32	.3	1,118	9.0	11,295	90.6	59	.5
MALE	22	.2	828	7.3	123	1.1	35	.3	1,008	8.8	10,135	88.8	264	2.3
THIRD YR	17	.1	1,026	6.2	51	.3	55	.3	1,149	6.9	15,222	91.7	223	1.3
FEMALE	10	.1	511	6.3	26	.3	24	.3	571	7.0	7,531	92.4	45	.6
MALE	7	.1	515	6.1	25	.3	31	.4	578	6.8	7,691	91.1	178	2.1
FOURTH YR	27	.2	871	5.4	46	.3	41	.3	985	6.1	15,046	92.5	234	1.4
FEMALE	12	.2	439	5.7	14	.2	18	.2	483	6.3	7,171	93.2	41	.5
MALE	15	.2	432	5.0	32	.4	23	.3	502	5.9	7,875	91.9	193	2.3
TOTAL	185	.2	7,890	7.7	510	.5	279	.3	8,864	8.7	91,813	90.0	1,350	1.3
FEMALE	95	.2	4,294	8.1	215	.4	121	.2	4,725	8.9	47,980	90.5	297	.6
MALE	90	.2	3,596	7.3	295	.6	158	.3	4,139	8.4	43,833	89.4	1,053	2.1
LOUISIANA (30 INSTITUTIONS)														
UNDERGRADUATE:														
FIRST YR	131	.2	14,752	26.7	283	.5	788	1.4	15,954	28.9	37,850	68.6	1,391	2.5
FEMALE	70	.2	8,591	30.5	118	.4	369	1.3	9,148	32.5	18,530	65.9	458	1.6
MALE	61	.2	6,161	22.8	165	.6	419	1.5	6,806	25.2	19,320	71.4	933	3.4
SECOND YR	49	.2	6,281	23.5	138	.5	367	1.4	6,835	25.6	19,005	71.1	881	3.3
FEMALE	18	.1	3,713	27.8	66	.5	150	1.1	3,947	29.6	9,179	68.8	209	1.6
MALE	31	.2	2,568	19.2	72	.5	217	1.6	2,888	21.6	9,826	73.4	672	5.0
THIRD YR	25	.1	4,295	21.7	87	.4	236	1.2	4,643	23.4	14,361	72.4	825	4.2
FEMALE	13	.1	2,621	26.7	31	.3	112	1.1	2,777	28.2	6,873	69.9	184	1.9
MALE	12	.1	1,674	16.7	56	.6	124	1.2	1,866	18.7	7,488	74.9	641	6.4
FOURTH YR	29	.1	5,039	21.5	116	.5	283	1.2	5,467	23.3	17,157	73.2	799	3.4
FEMALE	13	.1	2,971	26.1	45	.4	125	1.1	3,154	27.7	8,043	70.6	191	1.7
MALE	16	.1	2,068	17.2	71	.6	158	1.3	2,313	19.2	9,114	75.7	608	5.1
TOTAL	234	.2	30,367	24.3	624	.5	1,674	1.3	32,899	26.3	88,373	70.6	3,896	3.1
FEMALE	114	.2	17,896	28.5	260	.4	756	1.2	19,026	30.3	42,625	68.0	1,042	1.7
MALE	120	.2	12,471	20.0	364	.6	918	1.5	13,873	22.2	45,748	73.2	2,854	4.6
MAINE (27 INSTITUTIONS)														
UNDERGRADUATE:														
FIRST YR	52	.4	62	.5	35	.3	27	.2	176	1.5	11,761	98.0	62	.5
FEMALE	37	.6	20	.3	14	.2	9	.2	80	1.4	5,823	98.4	15	.3
MALE	15	.2	42	.7	21	.3	18	.3	96	1.6	5,938	97.6	47	.8
SECOND YR	48	.6	42	.5	29	.4	16	.2	135	1.6	8,035	97.8	43	.5
FEMALE	23	.6	17	.4	12	.3	6	.2	58	1.5	3,852	98.2	13	.3
MALE	25	.6	25	.6	17	.4	10	.2	77	1.6	4,183	97.5	30	.7
THIRD YR	21	.4	22	.5	14	.3	10	.2	67	1.4	4,737	98.1	26	.5
FEMALE	8	.4	7	.3	5	.2	5	.2	25	1.2	2,095	98.6	5	.2
MALE	13	.5	15	.6	9	.3	5	.2	42	1.6	2,642	97.7	21	.8
FOURTH YR	16	.3	31	.6	15	.3	18	.3	80	1.6	5,051	97.9	26	.5
FEMALE	5	.2	17	.7	7	.3	5	.2	34	1.5	2,292	98.0	12	.5
MALE	11	.4	14	.5	8	.3	13	.5	46	1.6	2,759	97.9	14	.5
TOTAL	137	.5	157	.5	93	.3	71	.2	458	1.5	29,584	98.0	157	.5
FEMALE	73	.5	61	.4	38	.3	25	.2	197	1.4	14,062	98.3	45	.3
MALE	64	.4	96	.6	55	.3	46	.3	261	1.6	15,522	97.7	112	.7

	AMERICAN INDIAN ALASKAN NATIVE		BLACK NON-HISPANIC		ASIAN OR PACIFIC ISLANDER		HISPANIC		TOTAL MINORITY		WHITE NON-HISPANIC		NON-RESIDENT ALIEN		TOTAL
	NUMBER	%	NUMBER	%	NUMBER	%	NUMBER	%	NUMBER	%	NUMBER	%	NUMBER	%	NUMBER
MARYLAND (52 INSTITUTIONS)															
UNDERGRADUATE:															
FIRST YR	265	.3	20,727	22.0	1,256	1.3	961	1.0	23,209	24.6	68,940	73.2	2,042	2.2	94,191
FEMALE	132	.2	12,754	24.0	606	1.1	507	1.0	13,999	26.4	38,200	72.0	842	1.6	53,041
MALE	133	.3	7,973	19.4	650	1.6	454	1.1	9,210	22.4	30,740	74.7	1,200	2.9	41,150
SECOND YR	77	.2	5,913	16.7	532	1.5	398	1.1	6,920	19.5	27,583	77.8	945	2.7	35,448
FEMALE	40	.2	3,617	19.1	277	1.5	205	1.1	4,139	21.8	14,511	76.4	332	1.7	18,982
MALE	37	.2	2,296	13.9	255	1.5	193	1.2	2,781	16.9	13,072	79.4	613	3.7	16,466
THIRD YR	51	.3	3,043	15.3	228	1.1	162	.8	3,484	17.5	15,898	79.9	521	2.6	19,903
FEMALE	18	.2	1,802	18.1	109	1.1	78	.8	2,007	20.1	7,778	77.9	198	2.0	9,983
MALE	33	.3	1,241	12.5	119	1.2	84	.8	1,477	14.9	8,120	81.9	323	3.3	9,920
FOURTH YR	83	.4	2,279	11.9	215	1.1	136	.7	2,713	14.2	15,893	83.2	501	2.6	19,107
FEMALE	38	.4	1,283	13.6	104	1.1	65	.7	1,490	15.8	7,723	82.0	201	2.1	9,414
MALE	45	.5	996	10.3	111	1.1	71	.7	1,223	12.6	8,170	84.3	300	3.1	9,693
TOTAL	476	.3	31,962	19.0	2,231	1.3	1,657	1.0	36,326	21.5	128,314	76.1	4,009	2.4	168,649
FEMALE	228	.2	19,456	21.3	1,096	1.2	855	.9	21,635	23.7	68,212	74.6	1,573	1.7	91,420
MALE	248	.3	12,506	16.2	1,135	1.5	802	1.0	14,691	19.0	60,102	77.8	2,436	3.2	77,229
MASSACHUSETTS (111 INSTITUTIONS)															
UNDERGRADUATE:															
FIRST YR	537	.5	4,799	4.6	1,810	1.7	1,659	1.6	8,805	8.4	93,593	89.8	1,858	1.8	104,256
FEMALE	317	.6	2,599	4.7	797	1.4	899	1.6	4,612	8.3	50,072	90.4	709	1.3	55,393
MALE	220	.5	2,200	4.5	1,013	2.1	760	1.6	4,193	8.6	43,521	89.1	1,149	2.4	48,863
SECOND YR	398	.6	2,706	3.9	1,216	1.8	950	1.4	5,270	7.7	62,107	90.5	1,231	1.3	68,608
FEMALE	288	.8	1,541	4.3	625	1.8	512	1.4	2,966	8.4	32,057	90.3	461	1.3	35,484
MALE	110	.3	1,165	3.5	591	1.8	438	1.3	2,304	7.0	30,050	90.7	770	2.3	33,124
THIRD YR	94	.2	1,698	3.8	735	1.6	526	1.2	3,053	6.8	40,936	91.0	1,005	2.2	44,994
FEMALE	44	.2	968	4.6	328	1.6	220	1.0	1,560	7.4	19,152	91.1	314	1.5	21,026
MALE	50	.2	730	3.0	407	1.7	306	1.3	1,493	6.2	21,784	90.9	691	2.9	23,968
FOURTH YR	146	.3	1,689	3.7	608	1.3	507	1.1	2,950	6.4	41,801	91.3	1,046	2.3	45,797
FEMALE	64	.3	963	4.5	264	1.2	225	1.1	1,516	7.1	19,558	91.3	337	1.6	21,411
MALE	82	.3	726	3.0	344	1.4	282	1.2	1,434	5.9	22,243	91.2	709	2.9	24,386
TOTAL	1,175	.4	10,892	4.1	4,369	1.7	3,642	1.4	20,078	7.6	238,437	90.4	5,140	1.9	263,655
FEMALE	713	.5	6,071	4.6	2,014	1.5	1,856	1.4	10,654	8.0	120,839	90.6	1,821	1.4	133,314
MALE	462	.4	4,821	3.7	2,355	1.8	1,786	1.4	9,424	7.2	117,598	90.2	3,319	2.5	130,341
MICHIGAN (92 INSTITUTIONS)															
UNDERGRADUATE:															
FIRST YR	1,415	.7	24,206	12.2	1,402	.7	3,408	1.7	30,431	15.3	166,147	83.6	2,180	1.1	198,758
FEMALE	727	.7	14,485	14.1	630	.6	1,725	1.7	17,567	17.1	84,745	82.4	557	.5	102,869
MALE	688	.7	9,721	10.1	772	.8	1,683	1.8	12,864	13.4	81,402	84.9	1,623	1.7	95,889
SECOND YR	504	.5	9,964	9.5	662	.6	1,173	1.1	12,303	11.7	91,633	87.0	1,359	1.3	105,295
FEMALE	245	.5	5,994	11.4	308	.6	578	1.1	7,125	13.5	45,151	85.7	380	.7	52,656
MALE	259	.5	3,970	7.5	354	.7	595	1.1	5,178	9.8	46,482	88.3	979	1.9	52,639
THIRD YR	174	.3	3,703	7.4	364	.7	451	.9	4,692	9.3	44,649	88.9	902	1.8	50,243
FEMALE	89	.4	2,118	9.1	146	.6	212	.9	2,565	11.0	20,436	87.9	243	1.0	23,244
MALE	85	.3	1,585	5.9	218	.8	239	.9	2,127	7.9	24,213	89.7	659	2.4	26,999
FOURTH YR	166	.3	3,050	6.2	304	.6	362	.7	3,882	8.0	43,644	89.4	1,279	2.6	48,805
FEMALE	67	.3	1,713	7.7	116	.5	161	.7	2,057	9.2	19,858	89.1	364	1.6	22,279
MALE	99	.4	1,337	5.0	188	.7	201	.8	1,825	6.9	23,786	89.7	915	3.4	26,526
TOTAL	2,259	.6	40,923	10.2	2,732	.7	5,394	1.3	51,308	12.7	346,073	85.9	5,720	1.4	403,101
FEMALE	1,128	.6	24,310	12.1	1,200	.6	2,676	1.3	29,314	14.6	170,190	84.7	1,544	.8	201,048
MALE	1,131	.6	16,613	8.2	1,532	.8	2,718	1.3	21,994	10.9	175,883	87.0	4,176	2.1	202,053
MINNESOTA (55 INSTITUTIONS)															
UNDERGRADUATE:															
FIRST YR	424	.7	820	1.3	321	.5	251	.4	1,816	2.9	59,836	95.9	725	1.2	62,377
FEMALE	240	.7	366	1.1	147	.4	121	.4	874	2.5	33,194	96.7	242	.7	34,310
MALE	184	.7	454	1.6	174	.6	130	.5	942	3.4	26,642	94.9	483	1.7	28,067
SECOND YR	218	.6	481	1.3	290	.8	147	.4	1,136	3.0	36,135	95.8	457	1.2	37,728
FEMALE	115	.6	220	1.1	143	.7	82	.4	560	2.8	19,074	96.5	142	.7	19,776
MALE	103	.6	261	1.5	147	.8	65	.4	576	3.2	17,061	95.0	315	1.8	17,952
THIRD YR	105	.4	320	1.3	254	1.0	93	.4	772	3.1	23,340	95.1	433	1.8	24,545
FEMALE	59	.5	147	1.2	106	.9	44	.4	356	2.9	11,649	96.0	126	1.0	12,131
MALE	46	.4	173	1.4	148	1.2	49	.4	416	3.4	11,691	94.0	307	2.5	12,414
FOURTH YR	122	.5	290	1.1	241	.9	114	.4	767	2.9	24,738	95.1	511	2.0	26,016
FEMALE	67	.5	124	1.0	99	.8	55	.4	345	2.8	12,007	95.9	166	1.3	12,518
MALE	55	.4	166	1.2	142	1.1	59	.4	422	3.1	12,731	94.3	345	2.6	13,498
TOTAL	869	.6	1,911	1.3	1,106	.7	605	.4	4,491	3.0	144,049	95.6	2,126	1.4	150,666
FEMALE	481	.6	857	1.1	495	.6	302	.4	2,135	2.7	75,924	96.4	676	.9	78,735
MALE	388	.5	1,054	1.5	611	.8	303	.4	2,356	3.3	68,125	94.7	1,450	2.0	71,931

TABLE 19 - TOTAL ENROLLMENT OF UNDERGRADUATES BY CLASS LEVEL IN INSTITUTIONS OF HIGHER EDUCATION BY RACE, ETHNICITY AND SEX: STATE AND NATION, 1978

	AMERICAN INDIAN ALASKAN NATIVE		BLACK NON-HISPANIC		ASIAN OR PACIFIC ISLANDER		HISPANIC		TOTAL MINORITY		WHITE NON-HISPANIC		NON-RESIDENT ALIEN		TOTAL
	NUMBER	%	NUMBER	%	NUMBER	%	NUMBER	%	NUMBER	%	NUMBER	%	NUMBER	%	NUMBER
MISSISSIPPI (45 INSTITUTIONS)															
UNDERGRADUATE:															
FIRST YR	142	.4	11,840	31.2	126	.3	47	.1	12,155	32.1	25,525	67.3	245	.6	37,925
FEMALE	90	.4	6,958	33.4	52	.2	23	.1	7,123	34.2	13,638	65.5	51	.2	20,812
MALE	52	.3	4,882	28.5	74	.4	24	.1	5,032	29.4	11,887	69.5	194	1.1	17,113
SECOND YR	48	.2	6,616	33.1	59	.3	24	.1	6,747	33.7	13,067	65.4	172	.9	20,006
FEMALE	24	.2	3,917	36.8	27	.3	5	.0	3,973	37.4	6,634	62.4	27	.3	10,634
MALE	24	.3	2,699	28.8	32	.3	19	.2	2,774	29.6	6,453	68.9	145	1.5	9,372
THIRD YR	38	.3	3,327	26.2	33	.3	23	.2	3,421	26.9	9,183	72.2	116	.9	12,720
FEMALE	21	.3	1,931	30.1	15	.2	11	.2	1,978	30.9	4,412	68.9	18	.3	6,408
MALE	17	.3	1,396	22.1	18	.3	12	.2	1,443	22.9	4,771	75.6	98	1.6	6,312
FOURTH YR	14	.1	3,690	30.3	41	.3	18	.1	3,763	30.9	8,319	68.3	105	.9	12,187
FEMALE	9	.1	2,227	35.5	19	.3	6	.1	2,261	36.0	3,987	63.5	28	.4	6,276
MALE	5	.1	1,463	24.8	22	.4	12	.2	1,502	25.4	4,332	73.3	77	1.3	5,911
TOTAL	242	.3	25,473	30.8	259	.3	112	.1	26,086	31.5	56,114	67.7	638	.8	82,838
FEMALE	144	.3	15,033	34.1	113	.3	45	.1	15,335	34.7	28,671	65.0	124	.3	44,130
MALE	98	.3	10,440	27.0	146	.4	67	.2	10,751	27.8	27,443	70.9	514	1.3	38,708
MISSOURI (70 INSTITUTIONS)															
UNDERGRADUATE:															
FIRST YR	230	.3	8,489	11.4	460	.6	646	.9	9,825	13.2	63,651	85.6	923	1.2	74,399
FEMALE	117	.3	4,973	12.7	207	.5	269	.7	5,566	14.2	33,253	85.1	275	.7	39,094
MALE	113	.3	3,516	10.0	253	.7	377	1.1	4,259	12.1	30,398	86.1	648	1.8	35,305
SECOND YR	109	.5	3,306	8.9	227	.6	305	.8	3,947	10.7	32,593	88.2	416	1.1	36,956
FEMALE	47	.3	1,833	10.1	96	.5	128	.7	2,104	11.6	15,928	87.8	107	.6	18,139
MALE	62	.3	1,473	7.8	131	.7	177	.9	1,843	9.8	16,665	88.6	309	1.6	18,817
THIRD YR	91	.4	1,692	6.7	176	.7	156	.6	2,115	8.4	22,800	90.3	331	1.3	25,246
FEMALE	33	.3	934	7.9	63	.5	61	.5	1,091	9.2	10,637	90.0	85	.7	11,813
MALE	58	.4	758	5.6	113	.8	95	.7	1,024	7.6	12,163	90.5	246	1.8	13,433
FOURTH YR	58	.2	1,505	5.3	219	.8	151	.5	1,933	6.8	25,959	91.7	404	1.4	28,296
FEMALE	15	.1	787	6.3	84	.7	56	.4	942	7.5	11,549	91.7	99	.8	12,590
MALE	43	.3	718	4.6	135	.9	95	.6	991	6.3	14,410	91.7	305	1.9	15,706
TOTAL	488	.3	14,992	9.1	1,082	.7	1,258	.8	17,820	10.8	145,003	87.9	2,074	1.3	164,897
FEMALE	212	.3	8,527	10.4	450	.6	514	.6	9,703	11.9	71,367	87.4	566	.7	81,636
MALE	276	.3	6,465	7.8	632	.8	744	.9	8,117	9.7	73,636	88.4	1,508	1.8	83,261
MONTANA (13 INSTITUTIONS)															
UNDERGRADUATE:															
FIRST YR	359	3.5	38	.4	41	.4	46	.5	484	4.8	9,628	94.5	75	.7	10,187
FEMALE	220	4.3	18	.3	12	.2	20	.4	270	5.2	4,881	94.4	20	.4	5,171
MALE	139	2.8	20	.4	29	.6	26	.5	214	4.3	4,747	94.6	55	1.1	5,016
SECOND YR	100	1.8	28	.5	13	.2	19	.3	160	2.9	5,323	96.4	40	.7	5,523
FEMALE	57	2.1	8	.3	4	.1	11	.4	80	3.0	2,596	96.5	14	.5	2,690
MALE	43	1.5	20	.7	9	.3	8	.3	80	2.8	2,727	96.3	26	.9	2,833
THIRD YR	67	1.5	15	.3	17	.4	14	.3	113	2.5	4,372	96.6	42	.9	4,527
FEMALE	42	2.0	7	.3	4	.2	5	.2	58	2.7	2,060	96.9	7	.3	2,125
MALE	25	1.0	8	.3	13	.5	9	.4	55	2.3	2,312	96.3	35	1.5	2,402
FOURTH YR	84	1.6	17	.3	20	.4	19	.4	140	2.6	5,217	96.4	55	1.0	5,412
FEMALE	47	2.0	5	.2	5	.2	8	.3	65	2.8	2,244	96.8	10	.4	2,319
MALE	37	1.2	12	.4	15	.5	11	.4	75	2.4	2,973	96.1	45	1.5	3,093
TOTAL	610	2.4	98	.4	91	.4	98	.4	897	3.5	24,540	95.7	212	.8	25,649
FEMALE	366	3.0	38	.3	25	.2	44	.4	473	3.8	11,781	95.7	51	.4	12,305
MALE	244	1.8	60	.4	66	.5	54	.4	424	3.2	12,759	95.6	161	1.2	13,344
NEBRASKA (31 INSTITUTIONS)															
UNDERGRADUATE:															
FIRST YR	136	.4	1,287	4.1	167	.5	387	1.2	1,977	6.2	29,424	92.7	346	1.1	31,747
FEMALE	65	.4	613	3.9	83	.5	206	1.3	967	6.1	14,849	93.4	89	.6	15,905
MALE	71	.4	674	4.3	84	.5	181	1.1	1,010	6.4	14,575	92.0	257	1.6	15,842
SECOND YR	58	.4	437	3.0	70	.5	126	.9	691	4.7	13,778	93.5	268	1.8	14,737
FEMALE	20	.3	172	2.5	31	.4	61	.9	284	4.1	6,560	95.1	57	.8	6,901
MALE	38	.5	265	3.4	39	.5	65	.8	407	5.2	7,218	92.1	211	2.7	7,836
THIRD YR	33	.3	309	3.0	55	.5	80	.8	477	4.6	9,679	93.4	204	2.0	10,360
FEMALE	17	.4	124	2.6	17	.4	37	.8	195	4.1	4,500	95.0	42	.9	4,737
MALE	16	.3	185	3.3	38	.7	43	.8	282	5.0	5,179	92.1	162	2.9	5,623
FOURTH YR	19	.2	212	2.2	55	.6	61	.6	347	3.6	9,149	95.0	139	1.4	9,635
FEMALE	10	.2	93	2.1	22	.5	25	.6	150	3.4	4,175	95.8	35	.8	4,360
MALE	9	.2	119	2.3	33	.6	36	.7	197	3.7	4,974	94.3	104	2.0	5,275
TOTAL	246	.4	2,245	3.4	347	.5	654	1.0	3,492	5.3	62,030	93.3	957	1.4	66,479
FEMALE	112	.4	1,002	3.1	153	.5	329	1.0	1,596	5.0	30,084	94.3	223	.7	31,903
MALE	134	.4	1,243	3.6	194	.6	325	.9	1,896	5.5	31,946	92.4	734	2.1	34,576

ICAN INDIAN SKAN NATIVE		BLACK NON-HISPANIC		ASIAN OR PACIFIC ISLANDER		HISPANIC		TOTAL MINORITY		WHITE NON-HISPANIC		NON-RESIDENT ALIEN		TOTAL
BER	%	NUMBER	%	NUMBER	%	NUMBER	%	NUMBER	%	NUMBER	%	NUMBER	%	NUMBER
(6 INSTITUTIONS)														
161	1.1	609	4.1	165	1.1	304	2.0	1,239	8.3	13,541	91.1	86	.6	14,866
92	1.3	294	4.0	79	1.1	137	1.9	602	8.3	6,656	91.4	26	.4	7,284
69	.9	315	4.2	86	1.1	167	2.2	637	8.4	6,885	90.8	60	.8	7,582
81	1.9	206	4.9	83	2.0	133	3.2	503	12.0	3,637	86.5	66	1.6	4,206
44	2.3	79	4.1	32	1.7	51	2.7	206	10.8	1,697	88.7	11	.6	1,914
37	1.6	127	5.5	51	2.2	82	3.6	297	13.0	1,940	84.6	55	2.4	2,292
15	.7	81	3.6	32	1.4	36	1.6	164	7.3	1,998	89.2	78	3.5	2,240
9	.9	27	2.8	8	.8	12	1.2	56	5.7	895	91.9	23	2.4	974
6	.5	54	4.3	24	1.9	24	1.9	108	8.5	1,103	87.1	55	4.3	1,266
23	.8	81	3.0	47	1.7	51	1.9	202	7.4	2,446	89.3	92	3.4	2,740
14	1.2	36	3.2	20	1.8	22	1.9	92	8.1	1,019	89.5	27	2.4	1,138
9	.6	45	2.8	27	1.7	29	1.8	110	6.9	1,427	89.1	65	4.1	1,602
280	1.2	977	4.1	327	1.4	524	2.2	2,108	8.8	21,622	89.9	322	1.3	24,052
159	1.4	436	3.9	139	1.2	222	2.0	956	8.5	10,267	90.8	87	.8	11,310
121	.9	541	4.2	188	1.5	302	2.4	1,152	9.0	11,355	89.1	235	1.8	12,742
(23 INSTITUTIONS)														
36	.3	189	1.3	42	.3	91	.6	358	2.5	13,605	95.5	277	1.9	14,240
14	.2	52	.8	15	.2	23	.3	104	1.6	6,503	97.4	72	1.1	6,679
22	.3	137	1.8	27	.4	68	.9	254	3.4	7,102	93.9	205	2.7	7,561
12	.1	113	1.3	29	.3	39	.4	193	2.2	8,420	96.5	111	1.3	8,724
7	.2	31	.7	9	.2	10	.2	57	1.4	4,053	97.9	29	.7	4,139
5	.1	82	1.8	20	.4	29	.6	136	3.0	4,367	95.2	82	1.8	4,585
11	.2	140	2.3	16	.3	61	1.0	228	3.7	5,873	95.5	50	.8	6,151
5	.2	61	2.2	5	.2	10	.4	81	3.0	2,626	96.3	19	.7	2,726
6	.2	79	2.3	11	.3	51	1.5	147	4.3	3,247	94.8	31	.9	3,425
16	.3	147	2.5	19	.3	48	.8	230	3.8	5,688	95.2	57	1.0	5,975
9	.3	61	2.2	9	.3	7	.3	86	3.1	2,687	96.7	7	.3	2,780
7	.2	86	2.7	10	.3	41	1.3	144	4.5	3,001	93.9	50	1.6	3,195
75	.2	589	1.7	106	.3	239	.7	1,009	2.9	33,586	95.7	495	1.4	35,090
35	.2	205	1.3	38	.2	50	.3	328	2.0	15,869	97.2	127	.8	16,324
40	.2	384	2.0	68	.4	189	1.0	681	3.6	17,717	94.4	368	2.0	18,766
(58 INSTITUTIONS)														
235	.2	14,081	13.3	1,035	1.0	4,964	4.7	20,315	19.1	84,965	80.0	945	.9	106,225
131	.2	8,548	15.0	551	1.0	2,765	4.8	11,995	21.0	44,661	78.3	390	.7	57,046
104	.2	5,533	11.3	484	1.0	2,199	4.5	8,320	16.9	40,304	82.0	555	1.1	49,179
115	.2	5,161	10.7	444	.9	1,859	3.9	7,579	15.8	39,880	83.0	571	1.2	48,030
69	.3	3,318	13.1	200	.8	1,058	4.2	4,654	18.3	20,553	80.9	213	.8	25,420
46	.2	1,843	8.2	235	1.0	801	3.5	2,925	12.9	19,327	85.5	358	1.6	22,610
64	.2	2,273	7.6	300	1.0	1,103	3.7	3,740	12.5	25,856	86.2	404	1.3	30,000
32	.2	1,380	9.4	136	.9	576	3.9	2,124	14.5	12,443	84.7	127	.9	14,694
32	.2	893	5.8	164	1.1	527	3.4	1,616	10.6	13,413	87.6	277	1.8	15,306
72	.3	1,841	6.5	280	1.0	911	3.2	3,104	11.0	24,728	87.4	471	1.7	28,303
40	.3	1,174	8.3	133	.9	493	3.5	1,840	13.0	12,140	85.9	146	1.0	14,126
32	.2	667	4.7	147	1.0	418	2.9	1,264	8.9	12,588	88.8	325	2.3	14,177
486	.2	23,356	11.0	2,059	1.0	8,837	4.2	34,738	16.3	175,429	82.5	2,391	1.1	212,558
272	.2	14,420	13.0	1,029	.9	4,892	4.4	20,613	18.5	89,797	80.7	276	.8	111,286
214	.2	8,936	8.8	1,030	1.0	3,945	3.9	14,125	13.9	85,632	84.6	1,515	1.5	101,272
(19 INSTITUTIONS)														
755	4.5	468	2.8	120	.7	4,702	27.7	6,045	35.7	10,715	63.2	195	1.2	16,955
450	5.3	172	2.0	56	.7	2,477	29.4	3,155	37.5	5,209	61.9	54	.6	8,418
305	3.6	296	3.5	64	.7	2,225	26.1	2,890	33.9	5,506	64.5	141	1.7	8,537
449	4.2	255	2.4	81	.8	2,929	27.6	3,714	35.0	6,732	63.4	171	1.6	10,617
261	5.1	108	2.1	27	.5	1,457	28.2	1,853	35.9	3,288	63.6	26	.5	5,167
188	3.4	147	2.7	54	1.0	1,472	27.0	1,861	34.1	3,444	63.2	145	2.7	5,450
210	3.4	126	2.0	52	.8	1,500	24.1	1,888	30.3	4,243	68.0	105	1.7	6,236
137	4.7	53	1.8	24	.8	731	25.0	945	32.3	1,966	67.2	14	.5	2,925
73	2.2	73	2.2	28	.8	769	23.2	943	28.5	2,277	68.8	91	2.7	3,311
186	2.9	122	1.9	38	.6	1,370	21.2	1,716	26.5	4,647	71.8	107	1.7	6,470
103	3.7	42	1.5	11	.4	585	20.9	741	26.5	2,049	73.2	11	.4	2,801
83	2.3	80	2.2	27	.7	785	21.4	975	26.6	2,598	70.8	96	2.6	3,669
600	4.0	971	2.4	291	.7	10,501	26.1	13,363	33.2	26,337	65.4	578	1.4	40,278
951	4.9	375	1.9	118	.6	5,250	27.2	6,694	34.7	12,512	64.8	105	.5	19,311
649	3.1	596	2.8	173	.8	5,251	25.0	6,669	31.8	13,825	65.9	473	2.3	20,967

TABLE 19 - TOTAL ENROLLMENT OF UNDERGRADUATES BY CLASS LEVEL IN INSTITUTIONS OF HIGHER EDUCATION BY RACE, ETHNICITY AND SEX
STATE AND NATION, 1978

	AMERICAN INDIAN ALASKAN NATIVE		BLACK NON-HISPANIC		ASIAN OR PACIFIC ISLANDER		HISPANIC		TOTAL MINORITY		WHITE NON-HISPANIC		NON-RESIDENT ALIEN	
	NUMBER	%	NUMBER	%	NUMBER	%	NUMBER	%	NUMBER	%	NUMBER	%	NUMBER	%
NEW YORK (259 INSTITUTIONS)														
UNDERGRADUATE:														
FIRST YR	1,730	.6	42,951	14.7	5,822	2.0	21,592	7.4	72,095	24.7	216,032	74.0	3,618	1.2
FEMALE	853	.6	27,247	17.6	2,672	1.7	12,212	7.9	42,984	27.8	110,470	71.4	1,208	.8
MALE	877	.6	15,704	11.5	3,150	2.3	9,380	6.8	29,111	21.2	105,562	77.0	2,410	1.8
SECOND YR	973	.5	19,844	11.2	3,275	1.8	9,346	5.3	33,438	18.8	141,662	79.8	2,330	1.3
FEMALE	439	.5	12,150	13.6	1,564	1.7	5,162	5.8	19,315	21.6	69,486	77.5	807	.9
MALE	534	.6	7,694	8.8	1,711	1.9	4,184	4.8	14,123	16.1	72,176	82.2	1,523	1.7
THIRD YR	393	.4	10,335	9.5	2,332	2.1	4,367	4.0	17,427	16.0	89,396	82.2	1,912	1.8
FEMALE	182	.3	6,256	11.6	1,080	2.0	2,363	4.4	9,881	18.3	43,280	80.4	692	1.3
MALE	211	.4	4,079	7.4	1,252	2.3	2,004	3.7	7,546	13.7	46,116	84.0	1,220	2.2
FOURTH YR	341	.4	8,320	9.0	1,989	2.2	3,484	3.8	14,134	15.4	75,985	82.6	1,864	2.0
FEMALE	171	.4	5,032	11.5	890	2.0	1,786	4.1	7,879	17.9	35,440	80.7	604	1.4
MALE	170	.4	3,288	6.8	1,099	2.3	1,698	3.5	6,255	13.0	40,545	84.4	1,260	2.6
TOTAL	3,437	.5	81,450	12.2	13,418	2.0	38,789	5.8	137,094	20.5	523,075	78.1	9,724	1.5
FEMALE	1,645	.5	50,685	14.8	6,206	1.8	21,523	6.3	80,059	23.4	258,676	75.6	3,311	1.0
MALE	1,792	.5	30,765	9.4	7,212	2.2	17,266	5.3	57,035	17.4	264,399	80.6	6,413	2.0
NORTH CAROLINA (125 INSTITUTIONS)														
UNDERGRADUATE:														
FIRST YR	1,003	.9	26,965	23.2	500	.4	503	.4	28,971	25.0	86,320	74.4	805	.7
FEMALE	572	1.0	14,546	24.8	212	.4	216	.4	15,546	26.5	42,771	73.0	253	.4
MALE	431	.7	12,419	21.6	288	.5	287	.5	13,425	23.3	43,549	75.7	552	1.0
SECOND YR	289	.6	9,761	20.3	146	.3	138	.3	10,334	21.5	37,210	77.6	432	.9
FEMALE	164	.7	4,997	21.9	72	.3	60	.3	5,293	23.2	17,456	76.4	96	.4
MALE	125	.5	4,764	19.0	74	.3	78	.3	5,041	20.1	19,754	78.6	336	1.3
THIRD YR	143	.5	5,028	18.1	107	.4	86	.3	5,364	19.3	22,168	79.7	298	1.1
FEMALE	86	.6	2,885	20.6	42	.3	41	.3	3,054	21.8	10,914	77.8	64	.5
MALE	57	.4	2,143	15.5	65	.5	45	.3	2,310	16.7	11,254	81.6	234	1.7
FOURTH YR	152	.5	5,139	18.5	84	.3	88	.3	5,463	19.7	21,979	79.3	262	.9
FEMALE	85	.6	2,885	20.8	35	.3	40	.3	3,045	21.9	10,774	77.6	60	.4
MALE	67	.5	2,254	16.3	49	.4	48	.3	2,418	17.5	11,205	81.0	202	1.5
TOTAL	1,587	.7	46,893	21.4	837	.4	815	.4	50,132	22.8	167,677	76.4	1,797	.8
FEMALE	907	.8	25,313	23.2	361	.3	357	.3	26,938	24.6	81,915	74.9	473	.4
MALE	680	.6	21,580	19.6	476	.4	458	.4	23,194	21.0	85,762	77.8	1,324	1.2
NORTH DAKOTA (16 INSTITUTIONS)														
UNDERGRADUATE:														
FIRST YR	596	5.3	72	.6	35	.3	25	.2	728	6.4	10,562	93.1	50	.4
FEMALE	346	6.3	21	.4	13	.2	12	.2	392	7.1	5,087	92.4	27	.5
MALE	250	4.3	51	.9	22	.4	13	.2	336	5.8	5,475	93.8	23	.4
SECOND YR	219	2.9	34	.6	16	.2	4	.1	273	3.7	7,097	95.5	60	.8
FEMALE	129	3.7	9	.3	10	.3	2	.1	150	4.3	3,322	95.1	22	.6
MALE	90	2.3	25	.6	6	.2	2	.1	123	3.1	3,775	95.9	38	1.0
THIRD YR	106	2.6	22	.5	13	.3	13	.3	154	3.8	3,896	95.3	38	.9
FEMALE	68	3.4	6	.3	2	.1	8	.4	84	4.2	1,895	95.1	14	.7
MALE	38	1.8	16	.8	11	.5	5	.2	70	3.3	2,001	95.5	24	1.1
FOURTH YR	71	1.5	25	.5	14	.3	6	.1	116	2.4	4,706	96.9	35	.7
FEMALE	44	2.0	8	.4	6	.3	2	.1	60	2.7	2,175	96.9	10	.4
MALE	27	1.0	17	.7	8	.3	4	.2	56	2.1	2,531	96.9	25	1.0
TOTAL	992	3.6	153	.6	78	.3	48	.2	1,271	4.6	26,261	94.8	183	.7
FEMALE	587	4.4	44	.3	31	.2	24	.2	686	5.2	12,479	94.3	73	.6
MALE	405	2.8	109	.8	47	.3	24	.2	585	4.0	13,782	95.2	110	.8
OHIO (124 INSTITUTIONS)														
UNDERGRADUATE:														
FIRST YR	583	.3	20,840	11.9	828	.5	1,177	.7	23,428	13.3	150,395	85.5	2,021	1.1
FEMALE	382	.4	12,643	13.6	452	.5	649	.7	14,126	15.2	78,230	84.1	677	.7
MALE	201	.2	8,197	9.9	376	.5	528	.6	9,302	11.2	72,165	87.1	1,344	1.6
SECOND YR	207	.2	8,862	10.6	338	.4	582	.7	9,989	11.9	73,107	87.0	894	1.1
FEMALE	120	.3	5,135	12.3	172	.4	283	.7	5,710	13.6	35,897	85.8	243	.6
MALE	87	.2	3,727	8.8	166	.4	299	.7	4,279	10.2	37,210	88.3	651	1.5
THIRD YR	99	.2	3,587	7.1	216	.4	226	.4	4,128	8.2	45,624	90.7	561	1.1
FEMALE	68	.3	1,934	8.4	93	.4	105	.5	2,200	9.6	20,609	89.8	143	.6
MALE	31	.1	1,653	6.0	123	.4	121	.4	1,928	7.0	25,015	91.4	418	1.5
FOURTH YR	72	.2	2,819	6.1	185	.4	159	.3	3,235	7.0	42,075	91.6	605	1.3
FEMALE	34	.2	1,469	7.2	88	.4	72	.4	1,663	8.2	18,524	91.0	165	.8
MALE	38	.1	1,350	5.3	97	.4	87	.3	1,572	6.1	23,551	92.1	440	1.7
TOTAL	961	.3	36,108	10.1	1,567	.4	2,144	.6	40,780	11.4	311,201	87.4	4,081	1.1
FEMALE	604	.3	21,181	11.9	805	.5	1,109	.6	23,699	13.3	153,260	86.0	1,228	.7
MALE	357	.2	14,927	8.4	762	.4	1,035	.6	17,081	9.6	157,941	88.8	2,853	1.6

ICAN INDIAN SKAN NATIVE BER	%	BLACK NON-HISPANIC NUMBER	%	ASIAN OR PACIFIC ISLANDER NUMBER	%	HISPANIC NUMBER	%	TOTAL MINORITY NUMBER	%	WHITE NON-HISPANIC NUMBER	%	NON-RESIDENT ALIEN NUMBER	%	TOTAL NUMBER
(42 INSTITUTIONS)														
273	4.1	4,256	7.7	488	.9	536	1.0	7,553	13.6	45,257	81.6	2,626	4.7	55,436
334	4.7	2,317	8.1	229	.8	243	.9	4,123	14.4	23,956	83.8	498	1.7	28,577
939	3.5	1,939	7.2	259	1.0	293	1.1	3,430	12.8	21,301	79.3	2,128	7.9	26,859
122	3.5	2,082	6.5	211	.7	287	.9	3,702	11.6	26,804	83.9	1,451	4.5	31,957
425	4.1	1,031	6.8	66	.4	121	.8	1,843	12.2	13,049	86.2	242	1.6	15,134
497	3.0	1,051	6.2	145	.9	166	1.0	1,859	11.1	13,755	81.8	1,209	7.2	16,823
551	3.2	958	5.5	131	.8	113	.7	1,753	10.1	14,718	84.9	858	5.0	17,329
273	3.5	461	5.9	47	.6	47	.6	828	10.5	6,873	87.3	175	2.2	7,876
278	2.9	497	5.3	84	.9	66	.7	925	9.8	7,845	83.0	683	7.2	9,453
640	3.5	909	5.0	109	.6	98	.5	1,756	9.6	15,768	86.4	727	4.0	18,251
304	3.9	424	5.4	34	.4	37	.5	799	10.2	6,863	88.0	137	1.8	7,799
336	3.2	485	4.6	75	.7	61	.6	957	9.2	8,905	85.2	590	5.6	10,452
586	3.7	8,205	6.7	939	.8	1,034	.8	14,764	12.0	102,547	83.4	5,662	4.6	122,973
536	4.3	4,233	7.1	376	.6	448	.8	7,593	12.8	50,741	85.4	1,052	1.8	59,386
050	3.2	3,972	6.2	563	.9	586	.9	7,171	11.3	51,806	81.5	4,610	7.2	63,587
(39 INSTITUTIONS)														
768	1.2	872	1.4	1,447	2.3	809	1.3	3,896	6.2	57,969	91.6	1,424	2.2	63,289
405	1.3	377	1.2	699	2.2	404	1.3	1,885	5.9	29,666	92.4	540	1.7	32,091
363	1.2	495	1.6	748	2.4	405	1.3	2,011	6.4	28,303	90.7	884	2.8	31,198
256	1.2	273	1.3	529	2.5	237	1.1	1,295	6.1	19,444	91.2	573	2.7	21,312
119	1.2	108	1.1	235	2.3	117	1.2	579	5.7	9,375	92.6	167	1.7	10,121
137	1.2	165	1.5	294	2.6	120	1.1	716	6.4	10,069	90.0	406	3.6	11,191
134	1.1	161	1.4	336	2.8	122	1.0	753	6.4	10,737	90.7	354	3.0	11,844
55	1.0	63	1.1	154	2.8	49	.9	321	5.9	5,068	92.4	98	1.8	5,487
79	1.2	98	1.5	182	2.9	73	1.1	432	6.8	5,669	89.2	256	4.0	6,357
125	.9	139	1.1	360	2.7	105	.8	729	5.5	12,120	92.0	331	2.5	13,180
53	.9	47	.8	173	3.0	45	.8	318	5.4	5,453	93.3	71	1.2	5,842
72	1.0	92	1.3	187	2.5	60	.8	411	5.6	6,667	90.9	260	3.5	7,338
283	1.2	1,445	1.3	2,672	2.4	1,273	1.2	6,673	6.1	100,270	91.5	2,682	2.4	109,625
632	1.2	595	1.1	1,261	2.4	615	1.1	3,103	5.8	49,562	92.6	876	1.6	53,541
651	1.2	850	1.5	1,411	2.5	658	1.2	3,570	6.4	50,708	90.4	1,806	3.2	56,084
(157 INSTITUTIONS)														
240	.2	15,509	10.1	1,036	.7	1,264	.8	18,049	11.7	134,980	87.5	1,176	.8	154,205
133	.2	9,444	11.7	515	.6	715	.9	10,807	13.4	69,638	86.2	373	.5	80,818
107	.1	6,065	8.3	521	.7	549	.7	7,242	9.9	65,342	89.0	803	1.1	73,387
117	.1	7,405	8.5	567	.6	635	.7	8,724	10.0	78,104	89.2	735	.8	87,563
64	.2	4,367	10.3	251	.6	333	.8	5,015	11.8	37,362	87.7	219	.5	42,596
53	.1	3,038	6.8	316	.7	302	.7	3,709	8.2	40,742	90.6	516	1.1	44,967
69	.1	3,181	5.5	353	.6	365	.6	3,968	6.8	53,875	92.3	522	.9	58,365
28	.1	1,729	6.3	143	.5	187	.7	2,087	7.6	25,087	91.8	144	.5	27,318
41	.1	1,452	4.7	210	.7	178	.6	1,881	6.1	28,788	92.7	378	1.2	31,047
64	.1	2,791	4.9	342	.6	360	.6	3,557	6.2	53,052	92.8	536	.9	57,145
27	.1	1,504	5.7	129	.5	178	.7	1,838	7.0	24,317	92.4	152	.6	26,307
37	.1	1,287	4.2	213	.7	182	.6	1,719	5.6	28,735	93.2	384	1.2	30,838
490	.1	28,886	8.1	2,298	.6	2,624	.7	34,298	9.6	320,011	89.6	2,969	.8	357,278
252	.1	17,044	9.6	1,038	.6	1,413	.8	19,747	11.2	156,404	88.3	888	.5	177,039
238	.1	11,842	6.6	1,260	.7	1,211	.7	14,551	8.1	163,607	90.8	2,081	1.2	180,239
(13 INSTITUTIONS)														
35	.2	652	4.0	122	.7	106	.6	915	5.6	15,245	93.4	171	1.0	16,331
20	.3	322	4.1	71	.9	49	.6	462	5.9	7,335	93.5	49	.6	7,846
15	.2	330	3.9	51	.6	57	.7	453	5.3	7,910	93.2	122	1.4	8,485
17	.1	403	3.2	91	.7	81	.6	592	4.7	11,764	94.1	150	1.2	12,506
12	.2	185	3.0	44	.7	35	.6	276	4.5	5,769	94.8	41	.7	6,086
5	.1	218	3.4	47	.7	46	.7	316	4.9	5,995	93.4	109	1.7	6,420
13	.2	224	2.9	62	.8	48	.6	347	4.5	7,315	94.1	112	1.4	7,774
7	.2	94	2.6	21	.6	21	.6	143	4.0	3,413	94.8	44	1.2	3,600
6	.1	130	3.1	41	1.0	27	.6	204	4.9	3,902	93.5	68	1.6	4,174
16	.2	254	3.2	37	.5	37	.5	344	4.3	7,485	93.8	153	1.9	7,982
8	.2	95	2.8	16	.5	18	.5	137	4.0	3,212	94.6	48	1.4	3,397
8	.2	159	3.5	21	.5	19	.4	207	4.5	4,273	93.2	105	2.3	4,585
81	.2	1,533	3.4	312	.7	272	.6	2,198	4.9	41,809	93.8	586	1.3	44,593
47	.2	696	3.3	152	.7	123	.6	1,018	4.9	19,729	94.3	182	.9	20,929
34	.1	837	3.5	160	.7	149	.6	1,180	5.0	22,080	93.3	404	1.7	23,664

	AMERICAN INDIAN ALASKAN NATIVE		BLACK NON-HISPANIC		ASIAN OR PACIFIC ISLANDER		HISPANIC		TOTAL MINORITY		WHITE NON-HISPANIC		NON-RESIDENT ALIEN	
	NUMBER	%	NUMBER	%	NUMBER	%	NUMBER	%	NUMBER	%	NUMBER	%	NUMBER	%
SOUTH CAROLINA (60 INSTITUTIONS)														
UNDERGRADUATE:														
FIRST YR	70	.1	13,553	25.7	285	.5	152	.3	14,060	26.7	38,309	72.7	343	.7
FEMALE	20	.1	7,322	29.6	129	.5	54	.2	7,525	30.4	17,149	69.3	79	.3
MALE	50	.2	6,231	22.3	156	.6	98	.4	6,535	23.4	21,160	75.7	264	.9
SECOND YR	25	.1	6,469	24.4	87	.3	65	.2	6,646	25.1	19,721	74.4	142	.5
FEMALE	9	.1	3,032	25.9	43	.4	19	.2	3,103	26.6	8,553	73.2	29	.2
MALE	16	.1	3,437	23.2	44	.3	46	.3	3,543	23.9	11,168	75.3	113	.8
THIRD YR	18	.1	2,553	19.1	42	.3	28	.2	2,641	19.7	10,638	79.4	122	.9
FEMALE	9	.1	1,563	23.7	14	.2	11	.2	1,597	24.2	4,986	75.5	19	.3
MALE	9	.1	990	14.6	28	.4	17	.3	1,044	15.4	5,652	83.1	103	1.5
FOURTH YR	9	.1	2,674	20.4	33	.3	28	.2	2,744	21.0	10,269	78.5	70	.5
FEMALE	5	.1	1,608	25.7	16	.3	8	.1	1,637	26.2	4,602	73.5	21	.3
MALE	4	.1	1,066	15.6	17	.2	20	.3	1,107	16.2	5,667	83.1	49	.7
TOTAL	122	.1	25,249	23.9	447	.4	273	.3	26,091	24.7	78,937	74.7	677	.6
FEMALE	43	.1	13,525	27.4	202	.4	92	.2	13,862	28.1	35,290	71.6	148	.3
MALE	79	.1	11,724	20.8	245	.4	181	.3	12,229	21.7	43,647	77.4	529	.9
SOUTH DAKOTA (17 INSTITUTIONS)														
UNDERGRADUATE:														
FIRST YR	474	4.9	151	1.5	34	.3	139	1.4	798	8.2	8,879	90.9	92	.9
FEMALE	272	5.6	37	.8	9	.2	21	.4	339	7.0	4,486	92.5	27	.6
MALE	202	4.1	114	2.3	25	.5	118	2.4	459	9.3	4,393	89.3	65	1.3
SECOND YR	140	2.2	75	1.2	30	.5	57	.9	302	4.8	5,877	94.3	55	.9
FEMALE	80	2.7	8	.3	14	.5	6	.2	108	3.6	2,891	96.2	5	.2
MALE	60	1.9	67	2.1	16	.5	51	1.6	194	6.0	2,986	92.4	50	1.5
THIRD YR	75	1.6	58	1.2	29	.6	45	.9	207	4.4	4,463	93.8	86	1.8
FEMALE	34	1.6	15	.7	14	.7	5	.2	68	3.3	2,012	96.2	11	.5
MALE	41	1.5	43	1.6	15	.6	40	1.5	139	5.2	2,451	92.0	75	2.8
FOURTH YR	61	1.3	36	.8	11	.2	42	.9	150	3.2	4,532	95.5	65	1.4
FEMALE	27	1.3	2	.1	6	.3	4	.2	39	1.9	1,970	97.5	12	.6
MALE	34	1.2	34	1.2	5	.2	38	1.4	111	4.1	2,562	94.0	53	1.9
TOTAL	750	2.9	320	1.3	104	.4	283	1.1	1,457	5.7	23,751	93.1	298	1.2
FEMALE	413	3.5	62	.5	43	.4	36	.3	554	4.6	11,359	94.9	55	.5
MALE	337	2.5	258	1.9	61	.5	247	1.8	903	6.7	12,392	91.5	243	1.8
TENNESSEE (74 INSTITUTIONS)														
UNDERGRADUATE														
FIRST YR	119	.2	13,928	18.2	243	.3	284	.4	14,574	19.1	60,600	79.4	1,172	1.5
FEMALE	69	.2	7,863	19.7	106	.3	123	.3	8,161	20.5	31,410	78.8	297	.7
MALE	50	.1	6,065	16.6	137	.4	161	.4	6,413	17.6	29,190	80.0	875	2.4
SECOND YR	44	.1	5,582	15.9	105	.3	130	.4	5,861	16.7	28,708	81.7	578	1.6
FEMALE	21	.1	3,186	18.5	46	.3	60	.3	3,313	19.3	13,738	79.9	142	.8
MALE	23	.1	2,396	13.3	59	.3	70	.4	2,548	14.2	14,970	83.4	436	2.4
THIRD YR	36	.2	3,069	13.7	81	.4	67	.3	3,253	14.6	18,729	83.9	352	1.6
FEMALE	17	.2	1,762	16.1	32	.3	29	.3	1,840	16.8	9,014	82.4	81	.7
MALE	19	.2	1,307	11.5	49	.4	38	.3	1,413	12.4	9,715	85.2	271	2.4
FOURTH YR	28	.1	2,966	12.0	83	.3	72	.3	3,149	12.7	21,195	85.5	442	1.8
FEMALE	13	.1	1,709	14.8	35	.3	26	.2	1,783	15.5	9,624	83.6	103	.9
MALE	15	.1	1,257	9.5	48	.4	46	.3	1,366	10.3	11,571	87.2	339	2.6
TOTAL	227	.1	25,545	16.1	512	.3	553	.3	26,837	16.9	129,232	81.5	2,544	1.6
FEMALE	120	.2	14,520	18.3	219	.3	238	.3	15,097	19.0	63,786	80.2	623	.8
MALE	107	.1	11,025	13.9	293	.4	315	.4	11,740	14.8	65,446	82.7	1,921	2.4
TEXAS (139 INSTITUTIONS)														
UNDERGRADUATE:														
FIRST YR	1,077	.4	31,727	11.5	2,286	.8	39,100	14.2	74,190	26.9	193,859	70.4	7,244	2.6
FEMALE	521	.4	17,014	12.2	1,152	.8	19,738	14.2	38,425	27.7	98,659	71.0	1,877	1.4
MALE	556	.4	14,713	10.8	1,134	.8	19,362	14.2	35,765	26.2	95,200	69.8	5,367	3.9
SECOND YR	368	.3	10,867	9.6	846	.7	14,975	13.2	27,056	23.8	83,428	73.4	3,216	2.8
FEMALE	167	.3	5,597	10.5	398	.7	6,719	12.6	12,881	24.1	39,855	74.6	689	1.3
MALE	201	.3	5,270	8.7	448	.7	8,256	13.7	14,175	23.5	43,573	72.3	2,527	4.2
THIRD YR	230	.3	5,524	7.9	436	.6	6,799	9.7	12,989	18.5	55,073	78.4	2,202	3.1
FEMALE	97	.3	2,938	8.9	189	.6	3,223	9.7	6,447	19.4	26,216	79.0	504	1.5
MALE	133	.4	2,586	7.0	247	.7	3,576	9.6	6,542	17.6	28,857	77.8	1,698	4.6
FOURTH YR	263	.3	5,903	7.5	656	.8	7,577	9.7	14,399	18.4	61,413	78.3	2,620	3.3
FEMALE	111	.3	3,017	8.4	279	.8	3,426	9.6	6,833	19.1	28,376	79.3	573	1.6
MALE	152	.4	2,886	6.8	377	.9	4,151	9.7	7,566	17.7	33,037	77.5	2,047	4.8
TOTAL	1,938	.4	54,021	10.0	4,224	.8	68,451	12.7	128,634	23.9	393,773	73.2	15,282	2.8
FEMALE	896	.3	28,566	10.9	2,018	.8	33,106	12.7	64,586	24.7	193,106	73.9	3,643	1.4
MALE	1,042	.4	25,455	9.2	2,206	.8	35,345	12.8	64,048	23.2	200,667	72.6	11,639	4.2

TABLE 19 - TOTAL ENROLLMENT OF UNDERGRADUATES BY CLASS LEVEL IN INSTITUTIONS OF HIGHER EDUCATION BY RACE, ETHNICITY AND SEX: STATE AND NATION, 1978

	AMERICAN INDIAN ALASKAN NATIVE		BLACK NON-HISPANIC		ASIAN OR PACIFIC ISLANDER		HISPANIC		TOTAL MINORITY		WHITE NON-HISPANIC		NON-RESIDENT ALIEN		TOTAL
	NUMBER	%	NUMBER	%	NUMBER	%	NUMBER	%	NUMBER	%	NUMBER	%	NUMBER	%	NUMBER
UTAH			**13 INSTITUTIONS)**												
UNDERGRADUATE:															
FIRST YR	491	1.3	223	.6	533	1.4	571	1.5	1,818	4.8	34,413	91.7	1,279	3.4	37,510
FEMALE	266	1.5	84	.5	246	1.4	223	1.3	819	4.7	16,075	92.2	548	3.1	17,442
MALE	225	1.1	139	.7	287	1.4	348	1.7	999	5.0	18,338	91.4	731	3.6	20,068
SECOND YR	198	1.3	80	.5	280	1.8	201	1.3	759	4.8	14,200	90.3	759	4.8	15,718
FEMALE	83	1.2	31	.4	156	2.2	79	1.1	349	4.9	6,421	90.6	314	4.4	7,084
MALE	115	1.3	49	.6	124	1.4	122	1.4	410	4.7	7,779	90.1	445	5.2	8,634
THIRD YR	90	.7	69	.6	211	1.7	110	.9	480	4.0	11,039	91.0	616	5.1	12,135
FEMALE	46	.9	22	.4	108	2.0	51	.9	227	4.2	4,845	90.2	302	5.6	5,374
MALE	44	.7	47	.7	103	1.5	59	.9	253	3.7	6,194	91.6	314	4.6	6,761
FOURTH YR	87	.7	72	.6	259	2.1	165	1.3	583	4.6	11,498	91.1	543	4.3	12,624
FEMALE	43	.9	23	.5	133	2.7	62	1.3	261	5.3	4,476	90.7	198	4.0	4,935
MALE	44	.6	49	.6	126	1.6	103	1.3	322	4.2	7,022	91.3	345	4.5	7,689
TOTAL	866	1.1	444	.6	1,283	1.6	1,047	1.3	3,640	4.7	71,150	91.2	3,197	4.1	77,987
FEMALE	438	1.3	160	.5	643	1.8	415	1.2	1,656	4.8	31,817	91.3	1,362	3.9	34,835
MALE	428	1.0	284	.7	640	1.5	632	1.5	1,984	4.6	39,333	91.1	1,835	4.3	43,152
VERMONT			**20 INSTITUTIONS)**												
UNDERGRADUATE:															
FIRST YR	15	.2	84	1.0	19	.2	39	.4	157	1.8	8,401	96.8	121	1.4	8,679
FEMALE	7	.1	44	.9	11	.2	24	.5	86	1.8	4,747	97.1	58	1.2	4,891
MALE	8	.2	40	1.1	8	.2	15	.4	71	1.9	3,654	96.5	63	1.7	3,788
SECOND YR	12	.2	79	1.1	17	.2	33	.5	141	2.0	6,666	96.4	106	1.5	6,913
FEMALE	7	.2	47	1.2	7	.2	17	.4	78	2.0	3,795	97.6	17	.4	3,890
MALE	5	.2	32	1.1	10	.3	16	.5	63	2.1	2,871	95.0	89	2.9	3,023
THIRD YR	6	.2	60	1.5	6	.2	40	1.0	112	2.8	3,780	95.4	72	1.8	3,964
FEMALE	3	.2	32	1.6	3	.2	21	1.1	59	3.0	1,910	96.5	11	.6	1,980
MALE	3	.2	28	1.4	3	.2	19	1.0	53	2.7	1,870	94.3	61	3.1	1,984
FOURTH YR	10	.3	60	1.6	8	.2	13	.3	91	2.4	3,616	96.5	41	1.1	3,748
FEMALE	2	.1	38	2.0	5	.3	6	.3	51	2.7	1,825	96.5	16	.8	1,892
MALE	8	.4	22	1.2	3	.2	7	.4	40	2.2	1,791	96.5	25	1.3	1,856
TOTAL	43	.2	283	1.2	50	.2	125	.5	501	2.1	22,463	96.4	340	1.5	23,304
FEMALE	19	.2	161	1.3	26	.2	68	.5	274	2.2	12,277	97.0	102	.8	12,653
MALE	24	.2	122	1.1	24	.2	57	.5	227	2.1	10,186	95.6	238	2.2	10,651
VIRGINIA			**(66 INSTITUTIONS)**												
UNDERGRADUATE:															
FIRST YR	154	.2	12,981	18.5	639	.9	336	.5	14,110	20.1	55,447	79.0	592	.8	70,149
FEMALE	91	.2	7,441	20.1	302	.8	159	.4	7,993	21.6	28,752	77.7	246	.7	36,991
MALE	63	.2	5,540	16.7	337	1.0	177	.5	6,117	18.4	26,695	80.5	346	1.0	33,158
SECOND YR	67	.2	6,425	15.5	437	1.1	207	.5	7,136	17.3	33,779	81.7	410	1.0	41,325
FEMALE	40	.2	3,577	17.1	195	.9	100	.5	3,912	18.7	16,804	80.5	162	.8	20,878
MALE	27	.1	2,848	13.9	242	1.2	107	.5	3,224	15.8	16,975	83.0	248	1.2	20,447
THIRD YR	37	.1	3,639	13.6	163	.6	121	.5	3,960	14.8	22,466	84.2	268	1.0	26,694
FEMALE	24	.2	2,101	15.3	100	.7	60	.4	2,285	16.6	11,402	82.8	90	.7	13,777
MALE	13	.1	1,538	11.9	63	.5	61	.5	1,675	13.0	11,064	85.7	178	1.4	12,917
FOURTH YR	50	.2	3,564	15.1	123	.5	99	.4	3,836	16.3	19,489	82.7	228	1.0	23,553
FEMALE	19	.2	2,018	16.8	62	.5	57	.5	2,156	18.0	9,755	81.3	86	.7	11,997
MALE	31	.3	1,546	13.4	61	.5	42	.4	1,680	14.5	9,734	84.2	142	1.2	11,556
TOTAL	308	.2	26,609	16.5	1,362	.8	763	.5	29,042	18.0	131,181	81.1	1,498	.9	161,721
FEMALE	174	.2	15,137	18.1	659	.8	376	.4	16,346	19.5	66,713	79.8	584	.7	83,643
MALE	134	.2	11,472	14.7	703	.9	387	.5	12,696	16.3	64,468	82.6	914	1.2	78,078
WASHINGTON			**(49 INSTITUTIONS)**												
UNDERGRADUATE:															
FIRST YR	1,090	1.6	2,350	3.4	2,000	2.9	1,063	1.5	6,503	9.4	60,666	87.3	2,337	3.4	69,506
FEMALE	592	1.7	971	2.8	981	2.8	461	1.3	3,005	8.6	31,057	88.9	855	2.4	34,917
MALE	498	1.4	1,379	4.0	1,019	2.9	602	1.7	3,498	10.1	29,609	85.6	1,482	4.3	34,589
SECOND YR	457	1.3	997	2.9	1,066	3.1	410	1.2	2,930	8.5	30,128	87.4	1,404	4.1	34,462
FEMALE	253	1.5	432	2.6	513	3.1	175	1.0	1,373	8.2	14,845	88.9	474	2.8	16,692
MALE	204	1.1	565	3.2	553	3.1	235	1.3	1,557	8.8	15,283	86.0	930	5.2	17,770
THIRD YR	190	1.0	483	2.5	770	3.9	189	1.0	1,632	8.3	17,417	88.6	605	3.1	19,654
FEMALE	102	1.1	226	2.5	364	4.0	91	1.0	783	8.6	8,148	89.6	158	1.7	9,089
MALE	88	.8	257	2.4	406	3.8	98	.9	849	8.0	9,269	87.7	447	4.2	10,565
FOURTH YR	156	.8	397	2.1	695	3.7	151	.8	1,399	7.5	16,820	89.7	525	2.8	18,744
FEMALE	85	1.0	175	2.0	342	3.9	67	.8	669	7.6	7,961	90.7	152	1.7	8,782
MALE	71	.7	222	2.2	353	3.6	84	.8	730	7.3	8,859	88.9	373	3.7	9,962
TOTAL	1,893	1.3	4,227	3.0	4,531	3.2	1,813	1.3	12,464	8.8	125,031	87.8	4,871	3.4	142,366
FEMALE	1,032	1.5	1,804	2.6	2,200	3.2	794	1.1	5,830	8.4	62,011	89.3	1,639	2.4	69,480
MALE	861	1.2	2,423	3.3	2,331	3.2	1,019	1.4	6,634	9.1	63,020	86.5	3,232	4.4	72,886

TABLE 19 - TOTAL ENROLLMENT OF UNDERGRADUATES BY CLASS LEVEL IN INSTITUTIONS OF HIGHER EDUCATION BY RACE, ETHNICITY AND SEX: STATE AND NATION, 1978

	AMERICAN INDIAN ALASKAN NATIVE		BLACK NON-HISPANIC		ASIAN OR PACIFIC ISLANDER		HISPANIC		TOTAL MINORITY		WHITE NON-HISPANIC		NON-RESIDENT ALIEN		TOTAL
	NUMBER	%	NUMBER	%	NUMBER	%	NUMBER	%	NUMBER	%	NUMBER	%	NUMBER	%	NUMBER
WEST VIRGINIA (26 INSTITUTIONS)															
UNDERGRADUATE:															
FIRST YR	109	.4	1,303	4.8	99	.4	49	.2	1,560	5.7	25,528	93.4	242	.9	27,330
FEMALE	63	.4	672	4.7	43	.3	20	.1	798	5.5	13,547	94.2	43	.3	14,388
MALE	46	.4	631	4.9	56	.4	29	.2	762	5.9	11,981	92.6	199	1.5	12,942
SECOND YR	32	.2	661		54	.4	40	.3	787	5 7	12,936	93.1	176	1.3	13,899
FEMALE	21	.3	313	4.8	21	.3	18	.3	373	5 5	6,365	93.9	38	.6	6,776
MALE	11	.2	348	4.8	33	.5	22	.3	414	5.8	6,571	92.3	138	1.9	7,123
THIRD YR	20	.2	410	.5	27	.3	9	.1	466	5 1	8,481	93.0	174	1.9	9,121
FEMALE	13	.3	161	.7	8	.2	4	.1	186	4 3	4,123	95.2	22	.5	4,331
MALE	7	.1	249	5.2	19	.4	5	.1	280	5.8	4,358	91.0	152	3.2	4,790
FOURTH YR	12	.1	416	.6	28	.3	25	.3	481	5 3	8,379	92.9	160	1.8	9,020
FEMALE	2	.0	171	.2	6	.1	9	.2	188	4 6	3,852	94.8	22	.5	4,062
MALE	10	.2	245	4.9	22	.4	16	.3	293	5.9	4,527	91.3	138	2.8	4,958
TOTAL	173	.3	2,790	4.7	208	.4	123	.2	3,294	5 5	55,324	93.2	752	1.3	59,370
FEMALE	99	.3	1,317	4.5	78	.3	51	.2	1,545	5.2	27,887	94.3	125	.4	29,557
MALE	74	.2	1,473	4.9	130	.4	72	.2	1,749	5.9	27,437	92.0	627	2.1	29,813
WISCONSIN (57 INSTITUTIONS)															
UNDERGRADUATE:															
FIRST YR	647	.7	4,059	4.4	522	.6	826	.9	6,054	6 6	84,700	92.7	591	.6	91,345
FEMALE	356	.8	2,348	5.1	276	.6	369	.8	3,349	7 3	42,674	92.4	164	.4	46,187
MALE	291	.6	1,711	3.8	246	.5	457	1.0	2,705	6.0	42,026	93.1	427	.9	45,158
SECOND YR	183	.4	1,480	3.	240	.5	351	.8	2,254	0	42,216	94.1	404	.9	44,874
FEMALE	97	.4	784	3.	102	.5	156	.7	1,139	3	20,289	94.1	131	.6	21,559
MALE	86	.4	696	3.8	138	.6	195	.8	1,115	5.8	21,927	94.0	273	1.2	23,315
THIRD YR	116	.4	655	2.3	142	.5	187	.7	1,100	3	26,518	94.7	378	1.4	27,996
FEMALE	64	.5	355	2.6	67	.5	88	.7	574	4.2	12,746	95.1	84	.6	13,404
MALE	52	.4	300	2.1	75	.5	99	.7	526	3.6	13,772	94.4	294	2.0	14,592
FOURTH YR	89	.3	594	1.9	140	.5	206	.7	1,029	3 3	29,303	95.1	465	1.5	30,797
FEMALE	49	.3	309	2.1	62	.4	79	.5	499	3 4	13,923	95.9	97	.7	14,519
MALE	40	.2	285	1.8	78	.5	127	.8	530	3.3	15,380	94.5	368	2.3	16,278
TOTAL	1,035	.5	6,788	3.5	1,044	.5	1,570	.8	10,437	.	182,737	93.7	1,838	.9	195,012
FEMALE	566	.6	3,796	4.0	507	.5	692	.7	5,561	.	89,632	93.7	476	.5	95,669
MALE	469	.5	2,992	3.0	537	.5	878	.9	4,876	5.0	93,105	93.7	1,362	1.4	99,343
WYOMING (8 INSTITUTIONS)															
UNDERGRADUATE:															
FIRST YR	95	1.3	112	1.5	40	.5	152	2.1	399	5.5	6,824	93.4	86	1.2	7,309
FEMALE	64	1.6	36	.9	17	.4	72	1.8	189	4.8	3,692	94.6	21	.5	3,902
MALE	31	.9	76	2.2	23	.7	80	2.3	210	6.2	3,132	91.9	65	1.9	3,407
SECOND YR	27	.7	69	1.8	25	.7	93	2.5	214	.	3,510	92.6	66	1 7	3,790
FEMALE	18	.9	23	1.2	12	.6	54	2.7	107	.6	1,879	94.2	9	.5	1,995
MALE	9	.5	46	2.6	13	.7	39	2.2	107	5.8	1,631	90.9	57	3.2	1,795
THIRD YR	6	.4	25	1.6	10	.6	28	1.8	69	.	1,454	91.2	72	4 5	1,595
FEMALE	3	.4	8	1.2	8	1.2	15	2.2	34	.	632	93.1	13	1 9	679
MALE	3	.3	17	1.9	2	.2	13	1.4	35	3.8	822	89.7	59	6.4	916
FOURTH YR	7	.3	14	.7	7	.3	24	1.2	52	2.	1,861	92.3	103	5.1	2,016
FEMALE	2	.2	6	.7	4	.5	9	1.1	21	2.6	778	96.8	5	.6	804
MALE	5	.4	8	.7	3	.2	15	1.2	31	2.6	1,083	89.4	98	8.1	1,212
TOTAL	135	.9	220	1.5	82	.6	297	2.0	734	.0	13,649	92.8	327	2.2	14,710
FEMALE	87	1.2	73	1.0	41	.6	150	2.0	351	.8	6,981	95.2	48	.7	7,380
MALE	48	.7	147	2.0	41	.6	147	2.0	383	5.2	6,668	91.0	279	3.8	7,330
THE STATES AND D.C. (2,903 INSTITUTIONS)															
UNDERGRADUATE:															
FIRST YR	36,196	.9	501,526	12.0	87,564	2.1	202,883	4.8	828,169	19.8	3,294,259	78.6	69,617	1.7	4,192,045
FEMALE	19,749	.9	288,664	13.1	42,253	1.9	104,651	4.8	455,317	20.7	1,721,103	78.3	22,383	1.0	2,198,803
MALE	16,447	.8	212,862	10.7	45,311	2.3	98,232	4.9	372,852	18.7	1,573,156	79.0	47,234	2.4	1,993,242
SECOND YR	14,252	.7	203,733	10.0	43,542	2 1	77,254	3.8	338,781	16.6	1,665,121	81.6	36,366	1.8	2,040,268
FEMALE	7,326	.7	114,371	11.3	20,133	2.0	36,588	3.6	178,418	17.7	821,773	81.3	10,647	1.1	1,010,838
MALE	6,926	.7	89,362	8.7	23,409	2.3	40,666	4.0	160,363	15.6	843,348	81.9	25,719	2.5	1,029,430
THIRD YR	5,427	.5	94,681	8.1	23,359	2.0	33,429	2.9	156,896	13.4	990,421	84.5	24,440	2 1	1,171,757
FEMALE	2,710	.5	53,555	9.6	10,896	1.9	15,889	2.8	83,050	14.8	469,292	83.9	6,959	112	559,301
MALE	2,717	.4	41,126	6.7	12,463	2.0	17,540	2.9	73,846	12.1	521,129	85.1	17,481	2.9	612,456
FOURTH YR	5,532	.5	87,565	7.5	23,373	2.0	31,392	2.7	147,862	12.7	909,198	85.2	24,446	2.1	1,161,506
FEMALE	2,596	.5	48,736	9.1	10,400	1.9	14,007	2.6	75,739	14.1	455,885	84.7	6,645	1.2	538,269
MALE	2,936	.5	38,829	6.2	12,973	2.1	17,385	2.8	72,123	11.6	533,313	85.6	17,801	2.9	623,237
TOTAL	61,407	.7	887,505	10.4	177,838	2.1	344,958	4.0	1,471,708	17.2	6,938,999	81.0	154,869	1.8	8,565,576
FEMALE	32,381	.8	505,326	11.7	83,682	1.9	171,135	4.0	792,524	18.4	3,468,053	80.5	46,634	1.1	4,307,211
MALE	29,026	.7	382,179	9.0	94,156	2.2	173,823	4.1	679,184	15.9	3,470,946	81.5	108,235	2.5	4,258,365

ICAN INDIAN SKAN NATIVE		BLACK NON-HISPANIC		ASIAN OR PACIFIC ISLANDER		HISPANIC		TOTAL MINORITY		WHITE NON-HISPANIC		NON-RESIDENT ALIEN		TOTAL
BER	%	NUMBER	%	NUMBER	%	NUMBER	%	NUMBER	%	NUMBER	%	NUMBER	%	NUMBER
	(	1 INSTITUTIONS)												
0	.0	1	.2	576	92.3	0	.0	577	92.5	47	7.5	0	.0	624
0	.0	1	.3	316	91.3	0	.0	317	91.6	29	8.4	0	.0	346
0	.0	0	.0	260	93.5	0	.0	260	93.5	18	6.5	0	.0	278
0	.0	0	.0	205	99.0	0	.0	205	99.0	2	1.0	0	.0	207
0	.0	0	.0	101	100.0	0	.0	101	100.0	0	.0	0	.0	101
0	.0	0	.0	104	98.1	0	.0	104	98.1	2	1.9	0	.0	106
0	.0	0	.0	0	.0	0	.0	0	.0	0	.0	0	.0	0
0	.0	0	.0	0	.0	0	.0	0	.0	0	.0	0	.0	0
0	.0	0	.0	0	.0	0	.0	0	.0	0	.0	0	.0	0
0	.0	0	.0	0	.0	0	.0	0	.0	0	.0	0	.0	0
0	.0	0	.0	0	.0	0	.0	0	.0	0	.0	0	.0	0
0	.0	0	.0	0	.0	0	.0	0	.0	0	.0	0	.0	0
0	.0	1	.1	781	94.0	0	.0	782	94.1	49	5.9	0	.0	831
0	.0	1	.2	417	93.3	0	.0	418	93.5	29	6.5	0	.0	447
0	.0	0	.0	364	94.8	0	.0	364	94.8	20	5.2	0	.0	384
	(	1 INSTITUTIONS)												
0	.0	28	10.6	0	.0	83	31.4	111	42.0	153	58.0	0	.0	264
0	.0	16	10.6	0	.0	51	33.8	67	44.4	84	55.6	0	.0	151
0	.0	12	10.6	0	.0	32	28.3	44	38.9	69	61.1	0	.0	113
0	.0	15	9.9	0	.0	48	31.8	63	41.7	88	58.3	0	.0	151
0	.0	8	9.6	0	.0	19	22.9	27	32.5	56	67.5	0	.0	83
0	.0	7	10.3	0	.0	29	42.6	36	52.9	32	47.1	0	.0	68
0	.0	1	20.0	0	.0	1	20.0	2	40.0	3	60.0	0	.0	5
0	.0	1	33.3	0	.0	0	.0	1	33.3	2	66.7	0	.0	3
0	.0	0	.0	0	.0	1	50.0	1	50.0	1	50.0	0	.0	2
0	.0	0	.0	0	.0	0	.0	0	.0	0	.0	0	.0	0
0	.0	0	.0	0	.0	0	.0	0	.0	0	.0	0	.0	0
0	.0	0	.0	0	.0	0	.0	0	.0	0	.0	0	.0	0
0	.0	44	10.5	0	.0	132	31.4	176	41.9	244	58.1	0	.0	420
0	.0	25	10.5	0	.0	70	29.5	95	40.1	142	59.9	0	.0	237
0	.0	19	10.4	0	.0	62	33.9	81	44.3	102	55.7	0	.0	183
	(	1 INSTITUTIONS)												
8	.5	13	.8	1,250	77.0	22	1.4	1,293	79.6	221	13.6	110	6.8	1,624
2	.2	5	.6	667	81.9	10	1.2	684	84.0	89	10.9	41	5.0	814
6	.7	8	1.0	583	72.0	12	1.5	609	75.2	132	16.3	69	8.5	810
1	.2	7	1.2	429	70.9	23	3.8	460	76.0	102	16.9	43	7.1	605
0	.0	6	1.9	239	76.4	4	1.3	249	79.6	53	16.9	11	3.5	313
1	.3	1	.3	190	65.1	19	6.5	211	72.3	49	16.8	32	11.0	292
1	.3	5	1.3	256	65.6	6	1.5	268	68.7	90	23.1	32	8.2	390
1	.5	3	1.5	133	66.2	3	1.5	140	69.7	51	25.4	10	5.0	201
0	.0	2	1.1	123	65.1	3	1.6	128	67.7	39	20.6	22	11.6	189
1	.3	3	.9	207	60.5	7	2.0	218	63.7	97	28.4	27	7.9	342
1	.6	2	1.2	107	62.2	4	2.3	114	66.3	46	26.7	12	7.0	172
0	.0	1	.6	100	58.8	3	1.8	104	61.2	51	30.0	15	8.8	170
11	.4	28	.9	2,142	72.3	58	2.0	2,239	75.6	510	17.2	212	7.2	2,961
4	.3	16	1.1	1,146	76.4	21	1.4	1,187	79.1	239	15.9	74	4.9	1,500
7	.5	12	.8	996	68.2	37	2.5	1,052	72.0	271	18.5	138	9.4	1,461
	(	33 INSTITUTIONS)												
0	.0	3	.0	1	.0	50,271	99.6	50,275	99.6	183	.4	27	.1	50,485
0	.0	1	.0	1	.0	29,064	99.6	29,066	99.6	100	.3	12	.0	29,178
0	.0	2	.0	0	.0	21,207	99.5	21,209	99.5	83	.4	15	.1	21,307
0	.0	6	.0	0	.0	28,343	99.7	28,349	99.7	65	.2	20	.1	28,434
0	.0	1	.0	0	.0	16,182	99.7	16,183	99.7	35	.2	13	.1	16,231
0	.0	5	.0	0	.0	12,161	99.7	12,166	99.7	30	.2	7	.1	12,203
0	.0	1	.0	0	.0	17,477	99.7	17,478	99.7	50	.3	10	.1	17,538
0	.0	0	.0	0	.0	10,153	99.7	10,153	99.7	29	.3	3	.0	10,185
0	.0	1	.0	0	.0	7,324	99.6	7,325	99.6	21	.3	7	.1	7,353
0	.0	0	.0	0	.0	17,987	99.8	17,987	99.8	34	.2	8	.0	18,029
0	.0	0	.0	0	.0	10,007	99.8	10,007	99.8	18	.2	5	.0	10,030
0	.0	0	.0	0	.0	7,980	99.8	7,980	99.8	16	.2	3	.0	7,999
0	.0	10	.0	1	.0	114,078	99.6	114,089	99.7	332	.3	65	.1	114,486
0	.0	2	.0	1	.0	65,406	99.7	65,409	99.7	182	.3	33	.1	65,624
0	.0	8	.0	0	.0	48,672	99.6	48,680	99.6	150	.3	32	.1	48,862

TABLE 19 - TOTAL ENROLLMENT OF UNDERGRADUATES BY CLASS LEVEL IN INSTITUTIONS OF HIGHER EDUCATION BY RACE, ETHNICITY AND SEX:
STATE AND NATION, 1978

	AMERICAN INDIAN ALASKAN NATIVE		BLACK NON-HISPANIC		ASIAN OR PACIFIC ISLANDER		HISPANIC		TOTAL MINORITY		WHITE NON-HISPANIC		NON-RESIDENT ALIEN	
	NUMBER	%	NUMBER	%	NUMBER	%	NUMBER	%	NUMBER	%	NUMBER	%	NUMBER	%
TRUST TERRITORY (1 INSTITUTIONS)														
UNDERGRADUATE:														
FIRST YR	0	.0	0	.0	134	100.0	0	.0	134	100.0	0	.0	0	.0
FEMALE	0	.0	0	.0	48	100.0	0	.0	48	100.0	0	.0	0	.0
MALE	0	.0	0	.0	86	100.0	0	.0	86	100.0	0	.0	0	.0
SECOND YR	0	.0	0	.0	117	100.0	0	.0	117	100.0	0	.0	0	.0
FEMALE	0	.0	0	.0	40	100.0	0	.0	40	100.0	0	.0	0	.0
MALE	0	.0	0	.0	77	100.0	0	.0	77	100.0	0	.0	0	.0
THIRD YR	0	.0	0	.0	0	.0	0	.0	0	.0	0	.0	0	.0
FEMALE	0	.0	0	.0	0	.0	0	.0	0	.0	0	.0	0	.0
MALE	0	.0	0	.0	0	.0	0	.0	0	.0	0	.0	0	.0
FOURTH YR	0	.0	0	.0	0	.0	0	.0	0	.0	0	.0	0	.0
FEMALE	0	.0	0	.0	0	.0	0	.0	0	.0	0	.0	0	.0
MALE	0	.0	0	.0	0	.0	0	.0	0	.0	0	.0	0	.0
TOTAL	0	.0	0	.0	251	100.0	0	.0	251	100.0	0	.0	0	.0
FEMALE	0	.0	0	.0	88	100.0	0	.0	88	100.0	0	.0	0	.0
MALE	0	.0	0	.0	163	100.0	0	.0	163	100.0	0	.0	0	.0
VIRGIN ISLANDS (1 INSTITUTIONS)														
UNDERGRADUATE:														
FIRST YR	0	.0	121	55.8	1	.5	13	6.0	135	62.2	23	10.6	59	27.2
FEMALE	0	.0	96	59.3	1	.6	9	5.6	106	65.4	9	5.6	47	29.0
MALE	0	.0	25	45.5	0	.0	4	7.3	29	52.7	14	25.5	12	21.8
SECOND YR	0	.0	96	62.7	0	.0	9	5.9	105	68.6	20	13.1	28	18.3
FEMALE	0	.0	73	66.4	0	.0	6	5.5	79	71.8	9	8.2	22	20.0
MALE	0	.0	23	53.5	0	.0	3	7.0	26	60.5	11	25.6	6	14.0
THIRD YR	0	.0	51	65.4	0	.0	3	3.8	54	69.2	5	6.4	19	24.4
FEMALE	0	.0	32	66.7	0	.0	1	2.1	33	68.8	3	6.3	12	25.0
MALE	0	.0	19	63.3	0	.0	2	6.7	21	70.0	2	6.7	7	23.3
FOURTH YR	0	.0	43	64.2	0	.0	2	3.0	45	67.2	3	4.5	19	28.4
FEMALE	0	.0	36	73.5	0	.0	2	4.1	38	77.6	1	2.0	10	20.4
MALE	0	.0	7	38.9	0	.0	0	.0	7	38.9	2	11.1	9	50.0
TOTAL	0	.0	311	60.4	1	.2	27	5.2	339	65.8	51	9.9	125	24.3
FEMALE	0	.0	237	64.2	1	.3	18	4.9	256	69.4	22	6.0	91	24.7
MALE	0	.0	74	50.7	0	.0	9	6.2	83	56.8	29	19.9	34	23.3
OUTLYING AREAS (38 INSTITUTIONS)														
UNDERGRADUATE:														
FIRST YR	8	.0	166	.3	1,962	3.7	50,389	94.5	52,525	98.5	627	1.2	196	.4
FEMALE	2	.0	119	.4	1,033	3.4	29,134	94.9	30,288	98.7	311	1.0	100	.3
MALE	6	.0	47	.2	929	4.1	21,255	93.8	22,237	98.2	316	1.4	96	.4
SECOND YR	1	.0	124	.4	751	2.5	28,423	95.8	29,299	98.8	277	.9	91	.3
FEMALE	0	.0	88	.5	380	2.3	16,211	96.0	16,679	98.6	153	.9	46	.3
MALE	1	.0	36	.3	371	2.9	12,212	95.5	12,620	98.7	124	1.0	45	.4
THIRD YR	1	.0	58	.3	256	1.4	17,487	97.1	17,802	98.8	148	.8	61	.3
FEMALE	1	.0	36	.3	133	1.3	10,157	97.3	10,327	98.9	85	.8	25	.2
MALE	0	.0	22	.3	123	1.6	7,330	96.8	7,475	98.7	63	.8	36	.5
FOURTH YR	1	.0	46	.2	207	1.1	17,996	97.6	18,250	99.0	134	.7	54	.3
FEMALE	1	.0	38	.4	107	1.0	10,013	97.7	10,159	99.1	65	.6	27	.3
MALE	0	.0	8	.1	100	1.2	7,983	97.5	8,091	98.8	69	.8	27	.3
TOTAL	11	.0	394	.3	3,176	2.7	114,295	95.7	117,876	98.7	1,186	1.0	402	.3	1
FEMALE	4	.0	281	.4	1,653	2.4	65,515	96.0	67,453	98.8	614	.9	198	.3
MALE	7	.0	113	.2	1,523	3.0	48,780	95.3	50,423	98.5	572	1.1	204	.4
NATION TOTAL (2,941 INSTITUTIONS)														
UNDERGRADUATE:														
FIRST YR	36,204	.9	501,692	11.8	89,526	2.1	253,272	6.0	880,694	20.7	3,294,886	77.6	69,813	1.6	4.2
FEMALE	19,751	.9	288,783	13.0	43,286	1.9	133,785	6.0	485,605	21.8	1,721,414	77.2	22,483	1.0	2.2
MALE	16,453	.8	212,909	10.6	46,240	2.3	119,487	5.9	395,089	19.6	1,573,472	78.1	47,330	2.3	2.6
SECOND YR	14,253	.7	203,857	9.8	44,293	2.1	105,677	5.1	368,080	17.8	1,665,398	80.5	36,457	1.	2.6
FEMALE	7,326	.7	114,459	11.1	20,513	2.0	52,799	5.1	195,097	19.0	821,926	80.0	10,693	1.	1.0
MALE	6,927	.7	89,398	8.6	23,780	2.3	52,878	5.1	172,983	16.6	843,472	80.9	25,764	2.	1.6
THIRD YR	5,428	.5	94,739	8.0	23,615	2.0	50,916	4.3	174,698	14.7	990,569	83.3	24,501	2.1	1.1
FEMALE	2,711	.5	53,591	9.4	11,029	1.9	26,046	4.6	93,377	16.4	469,377	82.4	6,984	1.2	5
MALE	2,717	.4	41,148	6.6	12,586	2.0	24,870	4.0	81,321	13.1	521,192	84.1	17,517	2.8	6
FOURTH YR	5,533	.5	87,611	7.4	23,580	2.0	49,388	4.2	166,112	14.1	989,332	83.8	24,500	2.1	1.1
FEMALE	2,597	.5	48,774	8.9	10,507	1.9	24,020	4.4	85,898	15.7	455,950	83.1	6,672	1.2	5
MALE	2,936	.5	38,837	6.2	13,073	2.1	25,368	4.0	80,214	12.7	533,382	84.5	17,828	2.8	6
TOTAL	61,418	.7	887,899	10.2	181,014	2.1	459,253	5.3	1,589,584	18.3	6,940,185	79.9	155,271	1.8	4.4
FEMALE	32,385	.7	505,607	11.6	85,335	2.0	236,650	5.4	859,977	19.7	3,468,667	79.3	46,832	111	4.3
MALE	29,033	.7	382,292	8.9	95,679	2.2	222,603	5.2	729,607	16.9	3,471,518	80.6	108,439	2.5	4.3

	AMERICAN INDIAN ALASKAN NATIVE		BLACK NON-HISPANIC		ASIAN OR PACIFIC ISLANDER		HISPANIC		TOTAL MINORITY		WHITE NON-HISPANIC		NON-RESIDENT ALIEN		TOTAL
	NUMBER	%	NUMBER	%	NUMBER	%	NUMBER	%	NUMBER	%	NUMBER	%	NUMBER	%	NUMBER
ALABAMA			18 INSTITUTIONS)												
GRADUATE:															
FIRST YR	16	.2	1,339	12.7	39	.4	40	.4	1,434	13.6	8,896	84.2	235	2.2	10,565
FEMALE	5	.1	834	15.1	13	.2	11	.2	863	15.6	4,631	83.6	43	.8	5,537
MALE	11	.2	505	10.0	26	.5	29	.6	571	11.4	4,265	84.8	192	3.8	5,028
OVER 1 YR	2	.0	723	13.3	60	1.1	19	.4	804	14.8	4,318	79.7	299	5.5	5,421
FEMALE	1	.0	486	17.8	10	.4	4	.1	501	18.3	2,165	79.3	65	2.4	2,731
MALE	1	.0	237	8.8	50	1.9	15	.6	303	11.3	2,153	80.0	234	8.7	2,690
TOTAL	18	.1	2,062	12.9	99	.6	59	.4	2,238	14.0	13,214	82.7	534	3.3	15,986
FEMALE	6	.1	1,320	16.0	23	.3	15	.2	1,364	16.5	6,796	82.2	108	1.3	8,268
MALE	12	.2	742	9.6	76	1.0	44	.6	674	11.3	6,418	83.2	426	5.5	7,718
ALASKA			7 INSTITUTIONS)												
GRADUATE:															
FIRST YR	22	3.7	24	4.	8	1 3	6	1.0	60	10.1	521	87.3	16	2.7	597
FEMALE	13	4.4	10	2.0	6	2.0	4	1.4	33	11.2	257	87.1	5	1.7	295
MALE	9	3.0	14	4.6	2	.7	2	.7	27	8.9	264	87.4	11	3.6	302
OVER 1 YR	17	3.1	14	2.	11	2.0	7	1.3	49	8.9	491	89.4	9	1.6	549
FEMALE	11	4.0	7	2.	5	1.8	5	1.8	28	10.1	248	89.5	1	.4	277
MALE	6	2.2	7	2.8	6	2.2	2	.7	21	7.7	243	89.3	8	2.9	272
TOTAL	39	3.4	38	3.3	19	1.	13	1.1	109	9.5	1,012	88.3	25	2.2	1,146
FEMALE	24	4.2	17	3.0	11	1.7	9	1.6	61	10.7	505	88.3	6	1.0	572
MALE	15	2.6	21	3.7	8	1.6	4	.7	48	8.4	507	88.3	19	3.3	574
ARIZONA			4 INSTITUTIONS)												
GRADUATE:															
FIRST YR	32	.5	40	.6	53	.8	133	2.1	258	4.1	5,583	88.6	460	7.3	6,301
FEMALE	22	.8	18	.7	24	.9	64	2.4	128	4.9	2,429	92.6	65	2.5	2,622
MALE	10	.3	22	.6	29	.8	69	1.9	130	3.5	3,154	85.7	395	10.7	3,679
OVER 1 YR	59	.8	76	1.0	61	.8	213	2.7	409	5.3	6,872	88.6	473	6.1	7,754
FEMALE	33	1.0	37	1.1	19	.6	94	2.8	183	5.4	3,104	92.4	72	2.1	3,359
MALE	26	.6	39	.9	42	1.0	119	2.7	226	5.1	3,768	85.7	401	9.1	4,395
TOTAL	91	.6	116	.8	114	.8	346	2.5	667	4.7	12,455	88.6	933	6.6	14,055
FEMALE	55	.9	55	.9	43	.7	158	2.6	311	5.2	5,533	92.5	137	2.3	5,981
MALE	36	.4	61	.8	71	.9	188	2.3	356	4.4	6,922	85.7	796	9.9	8,074
ARKANSAS			11 INSTITUTIONS)												
GRADUATE:															
FIRST YR	20	.6	308	8.7	13	.4	10	.3	351	10.0	3,102	88.0	74	2.1	3,527
FEMALE	10	.5	198	9.8	6	.3	4	.2	218	10.8	1,785	88.5	14	.7	2,017
MALE	10	.7	110	7.3	7	.5	6	.4	133	8.8	1,317	87.2	60	4.0	1,510
OVER 1 YR	18	.8	156	6.8	25	1.1	10	.4	209	9.1	1,964	85.2	133	5.8	2,306
FEMALE	9	.9	94	9.5	12	1.2	3	.3	118	12.0	852	86.4	16	1.6	986
MALE	9	.7	62	4.7	13	1.0	7	.5	91	6.9	1,112	84.2	117	8.9	1,320
TOTAL	38	.7	464	.0	38	.7	20	.3	560	9.6	5,066	86.9	207	3.5	5,833
FEMALE	19	.6	292	8.7	18	.6	7	.2	336	11.2	2,637	87.8	30	1.0	3,003
MALE	19	.7	172	8.1	20	.7	13	.5	224	7.9	2,429	85.8	177	6.3	2,830
CALIFORNIA			111 INSTITUTIONS)												
GRADUATE:															
FIRST YR	530	.7	3,262	4.5	4,128	.7	3,244	4.5	11,164	15.5	54,623	75.9	6,199	8.6	71,986
FEMALE	230	.7	1,839	5.7	1,755	.4	1,484	4.6	5,308	16.3	25,665	78.9	1,547	4.8	32,520
MALE	300	.8	1,423	3.6	2,373	8.0	1,760	4.5	5,856	14.8	28,958	73.4	4,652	11.8	39,466
OVER 1 YR	164	.4	1,438	3	2,065	4.9	1,415	3.4	5,082	12.2	31,439	75.3	5,233	12.5	41,754
FEMALE	63	.5	666	4.4	744	5.3	553	4.0	2,026	14.5	11,009	78.7	958	6.8	13,993
MALE	101	.4	772	2.8	1,321	4.8	862	3.1	3,056	11.0	20,430	73.6	4,275	15.4	27,761
TOTAL	694	.6	4,700	.	6,193	5.4	4,659	4.1	16,246	14.3	86,064	75.7	11,432	10.1	113,742
FEMALE	293	.6	2,505	4.	2,499	5.4	2,037	4.4	7,334	15.8	36,674	78.8	2,505	5.4	46,513
MALE	401	.6	2,195	5.4	3,694	5.5	2,622	3.9	8,912	13.3	49,390	73.5	8,927	13.3	67,229
COLORADO			16 INSTITUTIONS)												
GRADUATE:															
FIRST YR	32	.4	134	1 7	86	1 1	297	3.8	549	7.0	6,706	85.1	627	8.0	7,882
FEMALE	17	.5	66	1.8	42	1.2	141	3.9	266	7.4	3,189	88.9	131	3.7	3,586
MALE	15	.3	68	1.6	44	1.0	156	3.6	283	6.6	3,517	81.9	496	11.5	4,296
OVER 1 YR	15	.3	89	1.	59	1.1	134	2.4	297	5.4	4,716	86.0	470	8.6	5,483
FEMALE	7	.3	34	1.6	22	1.0	58	2.7	121	5.7	1,948	91.5	60	2.8	2,129
MALE	8	.2	55	1.6	37	1.1	76	2.3	176	5.2	2,768	82.5	410	12.2	3,354
TOTAL	47	.4	223	1 7	145	1.1	431	3.2	846	6.3	11,422	85.5	1,097	8.2	13,365
FEMALE	24	.4	100	.17	64	1.1	199	3.5	387	6.8	5,137	89.9	191	3.3	5,715
MALE	23	.3	123	1.6	81	1.1	232	3.0	459	6.0	6,285	82.2	906	11.8	7,650

TABLE 20 - TOTAL ENROLLMENT OF GRADUATES BY CLASS LEVEL IN INSTITUTIONS OF HIGHER EDUCATION BY RACE, ETHNICITY AND SEX: STATE AND NATION, 1978

	AMERICAN INDIAN ALASKAN NATIVE		BLACK NON-HISPANIC		ASIAN OR PACIFIC ISLANDER		HISPANIC		TOTAL MINORITY		WHITE NON-HISPANIC		NON-RESIDENT ALIEN	
	NUMBER	%	NUMBER	%	NUMBER	%	NUMBER	%	NUMBER	%	NUMBER	%	NUMBER	%
CONNECTICUT (20 INSTITUTIONS)														
GRADUATE:														
FIRST YR	17	.1	378	2.6	83	.6	141	1.0	619	4.3	13,527	93.2	364	2.5
FEMALE	9	.1	179	2.3	42	.5	67	.9	297	3.9	7,324	95.0	86	1.1
MALE	8	.1	199	2.9	41	.6	74	1.1	322	4.7	6,203	91.2	278	4.1
OVER 1 YR	6	.1	199	2.	68	.8	184	2.2	457	5.4	7,627	90.1	385	4 5
FEMALE	4	.1	79	2.	23	.7	56	1.7	162	4.9	3,070	92.4	92	2 8
MALE	2	.0	120	2.3	45	.9	128	2.5	295	5.7	4,557	88.6	293	5±7
TOTAL	23	.1	577	2 5	151	.7	325	1.4	1,076	4.7	21,154	92.1	749	3
FEMALE	13	.1	258	2 3	65	.6	123	1.1	459	4.2	10,394	94.2	178	1
MALE	10	.1	319	2±7	86	.7	202	1.7	617	5.2	10,760	90.1	571	4±8
DELAWARE (2 INSTITUTIONS)														
GRADUATE:														
FIRST YR	2	.3	30	5.	6	.8	1	.1	39	4.9	704	88.9	49	6 2
FEMALE	0	.0	15	4 8	1	.3	1	.3	17	4.5	350	92.8	10	2 7
MALE	2	.5	15	3±8	5	1.2	0	.0	22	5.3	354	85.3	39	914
OVER 1 YR		.0	27	3.9	2	.3	3	.4	32	4.6	619	89.8	38	-5 5
FEMALE		.0	4	1.4	0	.0	2	.7	6	2.1	269	95.1	8	2 8
MALE	8	.0	23	5.7	2	.5	1	.2	26	6.4	350	86.2	30	7±4
TOTAL	2	.1	57	3	8	.5	4	.5	71	4.8	1,323	89.3	87	5.9
FEMALE	0	.0	19	2 8	1	.2	3	.5	23	3.5	619	93.8	18	2.7
MALE	2	.2	38	4±8	7	.9	1	.1	48	5.8	704	85.7	69	8.4
DISTRICT OF COLUMBIA (12 INSTITUTIONS)														
GRADUATE:														
FIRST YR	28	.3	1,500	13.4	221	2.0	153	1.	1,902	17.0	7,994	71.5	1,283	11.5
FEMALE	8	.2	820	18.7	62	1.4	57	1.	947	21.6	3,087	70.3	356	8.1
MALE	20	.3	680	10.0	159	2.3	96	1.4	955	14.1	4,907	72.3	927	13.7
OVER 1 YR	18	.1	1,520	16.1	234	2.5	126	1	1,898	20.1	6,148	65.2	1,386	14.7
FEMALE	0	.0	975	23.7	71	1.7	57	1	1,103	26.9	2,592	63.1	411	10.0
MALE	18	.3	545	10.2	163	3.1	69	1±8	795	14.9	3,556	66.8	975	18.3
TOTAL	46	.2	3,020	14.7	455	2.2	279	1 4	3,800	18.4	14,142	68.6	2,669	12.9
FEMALE	8	.1	1,795	21.1	133	1.6	114	1±3	2,050	24.1	5,679	66.8	767	9.0
MALE	38	.3	1,225	10.1	322	2.7	165	1.4	1,750	14.4	8,463	69.9	1,902	15.7
FLORIDA (24 INSTITUTIONS)														
GRADUATE:														
FIRST YR	27	.2	1,504	9.9	112	.7	631	4.2	2,274	15.0	12,312	81.1	591	3.
FEMALE	10	.1	945	13.1	37	.5	319	4.4	1,311	18.2	5,779	80.0	132	1.9
MALE	17	.2	559	7.0	75	.9	312	3.9	963	12.1	6,533	82.1	459	5.8
OVER 1 YR	26	.2	1,104	9.5	135	1.2	358	3.1	1,623	14.0	9,485	81.7	505	4.3
FEMALE	8	.2	616	13.2	40	.9	173	3.7	837	17.9	3,752	80.4	80	1.7
MALE	18	.3	488	7.0	95	1.4	185	2.7	786	11.3	5,733	82.6	425	6.1
TOTAL	53	.2	2,608	9.7	247	.9	989	3.7	3,897	14.5	21,797	81.4	1,096	4
FEMALE	18	.2	1,561	13.1	77	.6	492	4.1	2,148	18.1	9,531	80.2	212	1
MALE	35	.2	1,047	7.0	170	1.1	497	3.3	1,749	11.7	12,266	82.3	884	5±8
GEORGIA (26 INSTITUTIONS)														
GRADUATE:														
FIRST YR	20	.2	1,913	14.4	69	.5	36	.3	2,038	15.4	10,647	80.3	577	4.4
FEMALE	9	.1	1,369	17.5	33	.4	11	.1	1,422	18.2	6,251	79.8	156	2.0
MALE	11	.2	544	10.0	36	.7	25	.5	616	11.3	4,396	80.9	421	7.7
OVER 1 YR	9	.1	1,203	13.9	47	.5	23	.3	1,282	14.8	6,869	79.2	519	6.
FEMALE	4	.1	797	19.1	18	.4	8	.2	827	19.8	3,262	78.2	84	2.0
MALE	5	.1	406	9.0	29	.6	15	.3	455	10.1	3,607	80.2	435	9.8
TOTAL	29	.1	3,116	14.2	116	.5	59	.3	3,320	15.1	17,516	79.9	1,096	5
FEMALE	13	.1	2,166	18.0	51	.4	19	.2	2,249	18.7	9,513	79.3	240	2 0
MALE	16	.2	950	9.6	65	.7	40	.4	1,071	10.8	8,003	80.6	856	8±8
HAWAII (2 INSTITUTIONS)														
GRADUATE:														
FIRST YR	0	.0	7	.6	441	40.6	14	1 3	462	42.5	566	52.1	59	4
FEMALE	0	.0	1	.2	235	44.4	8	1 5	244	46.1	268	50.7	17	2
MALE	0	.0	6	1.1	206	36.9	6	1±1	218	39.1	298	53.4	42	±15
OVER 1 YR	4	.1	18	.7	1,082	39.6	41	1 5	1,148	42.0	1,392	51.0	192	7.
FEMALE	3	.3	7	.6	488	41.4	15	123	513	43.5	607	51.5	59	5.0
MALE	1	.1	11	.7	594	38.3	26	1.7	632	40.8	785	50.6	133	8.0
TOTAL	4	.1	25	.7	1,523	39.9	55	1.4	1,607	42.1	1,958	51.3	251	6
FEMALE	3	.2	8	.5	723	42.3	23	1.3	757	44.3	875	51.2	76	4
MALE	1	.0	17	.8	800	38.0	32	1.5	850	40.3	1,083	51.4	175	±13

TOTAL ENROLLMENT OF GRADUATES BY CLASS LEVEL IN INSTITUTIONS OF HIGHER EDUCATION BY RACE, ETHNICITY AND SEX: STATE AND NATION, 1978

AMERICAN INDIAN ALASKAN NATIVE		BLACK NON-HISPANIC		ASIAN OR PACIFIC ISLANDER		HISPANIC		TOTAL MINORITY		WHITE NON-HISPANIC		NON-RESIDENT ALIEN		TOTAL
NUMBER	%	NUMBER	%	NUMBER	%	NUMBER	%	NUMBER	%	NUMBER	%	NUMBER	%	NUMBER
(5 INSTITUTIONS)														
14	.7	12	.6	32	1.6	23	1.2	81	4.1	1,892	94.9	21	1.1	1,994
6	.6	4	.4	12	1.2	10	1.0	32	3.1	1,004	96.4	5	.5	1,041
8	.8	8	.8	20	2.1	13	1.4	49	5.1	888	93.2	16	1.7	953
3	.3	5	.4	6	.5	4	.4	18	1.6	1,041	92.7	64	5.7	1,123
2	.6	1	.3	1	.3	3	.9	7	2.0	329	94.8	11	3.2	347
1	.1	4	.5	5	.6	1	.1	11	1.4	712	91.8	53	6.8	776
17	.5	17	.5	38	1.2	27	.9	99	3.2	2,933	94.1	85	2.7	3,117
8	.6	5	.4	13	.9	13	.9	39	2.8	1,333	96.0	16	1.2	1,388
9	.9	12	.7	25	1.4	14	.8	60	3.5	1,600	92.5	69	4.0	1,729
(60 INSTITUTIONS)														
71	.2	2,820	7.9	718	2.0	433	1.2	4,042	11.3	29,358	82.3	2,266	6.4	35,666
34	.2	1,690	10.2	248	1.5	215	1.3	2,187	13.3	13,689	83.0	621	3.8	16,497
37	.2	1,130	5.9	470	2.5	218	1.1	1,855	9.7	15,669	81.7	1,645	8.6	19,169
39	.2	1,127	5.0	527	2.4	256	1.1	1,949	8.7	18,407	82.5	1,969	8.8	22,325
13	.2	618	7.9	156	2.0	93	1.2	880	11.2	6,602	84.0	380	4.8	7,862
26	.2	509	3.5	371	2.6	163	1.1	1,069	7.4	11,805	81.6	1,589	11.0	14,463
110	.2	3,947	6.8	1,245	2.1	689	1.2	5,991	10.3	47,765	82.4	4,235	7.3	57,991
47	.2	2,308	9.5	404	1.7	308	1.3	3,067	12.6	20,291	83.3	1,001	4.1	24,359
63	.2	1,639	4.9	841	2.5	381	1.1	2,924	8.7	27,474	81.7	3,234	9.6	33,632
(31 INSTITUTIONS)														
41	.2	712	3.6	114	.6	115	.6	982	5.0	17,766	89.7	1,059	5.3	19,807
29	.3	426	4.1	48	.5	56	.5	559	5.4	9,469	91.8	289	2.8	10,317
12	.1	286	3.0	66	.7	59	.6	423	4.5	8,297	87.4	770	8.1	9,490
22	.2	222	2.5	65	.7	75	.8	384	4.4	7,469	84.6	973	11.0	8,826
10	.3	126	3.7	27	.8	19	.6	182	5.4	2,989	88.3	213	6.3	3,384
12	.2	96	1.8	38	.7	56	1.0	202	3.7	4,480	82.3	760	14.0	5,442
63	.2	934	3.3	179	.6	190	.7	1,366	4.8	25,235	88.1	2,032	7.1	28,633
39	.3	552	4.0	75	.5	75	.5	741	5.4	12,458	90.9	502	3.7	13,701
24	.2	382	2.6	104	.7	115	.8	625	4.2	12,777	85.6	1,530	10.2	14,932
(12 INSTITUTIONS)														
9	.1	127	2.1	40	.7	-30	.5	206	3.4	5,533	90.6	370	6.1	6,109
5	.2	79	2.6	15	.5	14	.5	113	3.7	2,845	93.0	101	3.3	3,059
4	.1	48	1.6	25	.8	16	.5	93	3.0	2,688	88.1	269	8.8	3,050
16	.2	167	2.1	74	.9	26	.3	283	3.6	6,679	84.6	932	11.8	7,894
8	.2	78	2.4	28	.8	11	.3	125	3.8	2,977	90.0	206	6.2	3,308
8	.2	89	1.9	46	1.0	15	.3	158	3.4	3,702	80.7	726	15.8	4,586
25	.2	294	2.1	114	.8	56	.4	489	3.5	12,212	87.2	1,302	9.3	14,003
13	.2	157	2.5	43	.7	25	.4	238	3.7	5,822	91.4	307	4.8	6,367
12	.2	137	1.8	71	.9	31	.4	251	3.3	6,390	83.7	995	13.0	7,636
(10 INSTITUTIONS)														
23	.3	201	2.4	55	.6	65	.8	344	4.1	7,577	89.4	554	6.5	8,475
14	.3	112	2.3	28	.6	29	.6	183	3.7	4,545	93.0	157	3.2	4,885
9	.3	89	2.5	27	.8	36	1.0	161	4.5	3,032	84.5	397	11.1	3,590
44	.5	223	2.6	42	.5	85	1.0	394	4.7	7,349	87.1	694	8.2	8,437
15	.4	128	3.1	14	.3	40	1.0	197	4.8	3,705	90.9	173	4.2	4,075
29	.7	95	2.2	28	.6	45	1.0	197	4.5	3,644	83.5	521	11.9	4,362
67	.4	424	2.5	97	.6	150	.9	738	4.4	14,926	88.3	1,248	7.4	16,912
29	.3	240	2.7	42	.5	69	.8	380	4.2	8,250	92.1	330	3.7	8,960
38	.5	184	2.3	55	.7	81	1.0	358	4.5	6,676	84.0	918	11.5	7,952
(16 INSTITUTIONS)														
81	.7	371	3.2	70	.6	39	.3	561	4.9	10,580	92.5	301	2.6	11,442
52	.7	230	3.2	22	.3	14	.2	318	4.5	6,740	94.7	57	.8	7,115
29	.7	141	3.3	48	1.1	25	.6	243	5.6	3,840	88.7	244	5.6	4,327
29	.5	160	2.8	23	.4	18	.3	230	4.0	5,368	92.5	206	3.5	5,804
11	.3	93	2.8	8	.2	9	.3	121	3.6	3,157	94.9	47	1.4	3,325
18	.7	67	2.7	15	.6	9	.4	109	4.4	2,211	89.2	159	6.4	2,479
110	.6	531	3.1	93	.5	57	.3	791	4.6	15,948	92.5	507	2.9	17,246
63	.6	323	3.1	30	.3	23	.2	439	4.2	9,897	94.8	104	1.0	10,440
47	.7	208	3.1	63	.9	34	.5	352	5.2	6,051	88.9	403	5.9	6,806

TABLE 20 - TOTAL ENROLLMENT OF GRADUATES BY CLASS LEVEL IN INSTITUTIONS OF HIGHER EDUCATION BY RACE, ETHNICITY AND SEX: STATE AND NATION, 1978

	AMERICAN INDIAN ALASKAN NATIVE		BLACK NON-HISPANIC		ASIAN OR PACIFIC ISLANDER		HISPANIC		TOTAL MINORITY		WHITE NON-HISPANIC		NON-RESIDENT ALIEN	
	NUMBER	%	NUMBER	%	NUMBER	%	NUMBER	%	NUMBER	%	NUMBER	%	NUMBER	%
LOUISIANA (19 INSTITUTIONS)														
GRADUATE:														
FIRST YR	23	.3	1,097	12.1	47	.5	161	1.8	1,328	14.6	7,373	81.0	400	4.4
FEMALE	10	.2	824	15.6	13	.2	88	1.7	935	17.7	4,258	80.4	100	1.9
MALE	13	.3	273	7.2	34	.9	73	1.9	393	10.3	3,115	81.8	300	7.9
OVER 1 YR	14	.2	1,483	20.2	23	.3	74	1.0	1,594	21.7	5,286	72.1	454	6.2
FEMALE	6	.1	1,114	27.7	3	.1	36	.9	1,159	28.8	2,786	69.3	78	1.9
MALE	8	.2	369	11.1	20	.6	38	1.1	435	13.1	2,500	75.5	376	11.4
TOTAL	37	.2	2,580	15.7	70	.4	235	1.4	2,922	17.8	12,659	77.0	854	5.2
FEMALE	16	.2	1,938	20.8	16	.2	124	1.3	2,094	22.5	7,044	75.6	178	1.9
MALE	21	.3	642	9.0	54	.8	111	1.6	828	11.6	5,615	78.9	676	9.5
MAINE (4 INSTITUTIONS)														
GRADUATE:														
FIRST YR	0	.0	0	.0	1	.1	3	.4	4	.5	749	98.9	4	.5
FEMALE	0	.0	0	.0	0	.0	1	.3	1	.3	328	99.7	0	.0
MALE	0	.0	0	.0	1	.2	2	.5	3	.7	421	98.4	4	.9
OVER 1 YR	2	.2	3	.3	1	.1	3	.3	9	.9	939	97.1	19	2.0
FEMALE	1	.2	0	.0	1	.2	1	.2	3	.7	423	97.2	9	2.1
MALE	1	.2	3	.6	0	.0	2	.4	6	1.1	516	97.0	10	1.9
TOTAL	2	.1	3	.2	2	.1	6	.3	13	.8	1,688	97.9	23	1.3
FEMALE	1	.1	0	.0	1	.1	2	.3	4	.5	751	98.3	9	1.2
MALE	1	.1	3	.3	1	.1	4	.4	9	.9	937	97.6	14	1.5
MARYLAND (27 INSTITUTIONS)														
GRADUATE:														
FIRST YR	38	.3	1,124	9.8	115	1.0	85	.7	1,362	11.9	9,551	83.7	504	4.4
FEMALE	27	.4	761	12.4	60	1.0	46	.8	894	14.6	5,093	83.1	144	2.3
MALE	11	.2	363	6.9	55	1.0	39	.7	468	8.9	4,458	84.3	360	6.8
OVER 1 YR	24	.2	939	9.7	116	1.2	76	.8	1,155	11.9	7,858	81.2	666	6.9
FEMALE	12	.3	573	12.1	59	1.2	41	.9	665	14.5	3,877	82.1	163	3.4
MALE	12	.2	366	7.4	57	1.2	35	.7	470	9.5	3,981	80.4	503	10.2
TOTAL	62	.3	2,063	9.8	231	1.1	161	.8	2,517	11.9	17,409	82.5	1,170	5.5
FEMALE	39	.4	1,334	12.3	119	1.1	87	.8	1,579	14.5	8,970	82.6	307	2.8
MALE	23	.2	729	7.1	112	1.1	74	.7	938	9.2	8,439	82.4	863	8.4
MASSACHUSETTS (51 INSTITUTIONS)														
GRADUATE:														
FIRST YR	27	.1	560	2.9	333	1.7	220	1.1	1,140	5.8	17,048	86.9	1,428	7.3
FEMALE	10	.1	282	3.0	115	1.2	97	1.0	504	5.4	8,443	90.8	354	3.8
MALE	17	.2	278	2.7	218	2.1	123	1.2	636	6.2	8,605	83.4	1,074	10.4
OVER 1 YR	50	.2	788	2.9	426	1.6	349	1.3	1,613	6.0	23,058	85.6	2,265	8.4
FEMALE	16	.2	318	3.0	154	1.5	131	1.2	619	5.9	9,373	89.3	503	4.8
MALE	34	.2	470	2.9	272	1.7	218	1.3	994	6.0	13,685	83.2	1,762	10.7
TOTAL	77	.2	1,348	2.9	759	1.6	569	1.2	2,753	5.9	40,106	86.2	3,693	7.9
FEMALE	26	.1	600	3.0	269	1.4	228	1.2	1,123	5.7	17,816	90.0	857	4.3
MALE	51	.2	748	2.8	490	1.8	341	1.3	1,630	6.1	22,290	83.3	2,836	10.6
MICHIGAN (28 INSTITUTIONS)														
GRADUATE:														
FIRST YR	98	.3	2,103	6.6	351	1.1	272	.9	2,824	8.9	26,841	84.6	2,074	6.5
FEMALE	44	.3	1,421	8.7	131	.8	136	.8	1,732	10.6	14,139	86.1	544	3.3
MALE	54	.4	682	4.5	220	1.4	136	.9	1,092	7.1	12,702	82.9	1,530	10.0
OVER 1 YR	48	.3	1,052	6.2	236	1.4	178	1.0	1,514	8.9	14,127	82.8	1,425	8.3
FEMALE	32	.4	628	8.0	74	.9	73	.9	807	10.2	6,773	86.0	299	3.8
MALE	16	.2	424	4.6	162	1.8	105	1.1	707	7.7	7,354	80.0	1,126	12.3
TOTAL	146	.3	3,155	6.5	587	1.2	450	.9	4,338	8.9	40,968	83.9	3,499	7.2
FEMALE	76	.3	2,049	8.4	205	.8	209	.9	2,539	10.5	20,912	86.1	843	3.5
MALE	70	.3	1,106	4.5	382	1.6	241	1.0	1,799	7.3	20,056	81.8	2,656	10.8
MINNESOTA (17 INSTITUTIONS)														
GRADUATE:														
FIRST YR	22	.2	63	.6	89	.8	55	.5	229	2.0	10,638	93.9	465	4.1
FEMALE	11	.2	30	.5	35	.6	22	.4	98	1.8	5,391	96.4	106	1.9
MALE	11	.2	33	.6	54	.9	33	.6	131	2.3	5,247	91.5	359	6.3
OVER 1 YR	23	.4	89	1.7	82	1.5	42	.8	236	4.4	4,465	83.2	666	12.4
FEMALE	8	.4	41	2.1	22	1.1	19	1.0	90	4.7	1,687	87.9	143	7.4
MALE	15	.4	48	1.4	60	1.7	23	.7	146	4.2	2,778	80.6	523	15.2
TOTAL	45	.3	152	.9	171	1.0	97	.6	465	2.8	15,103	90.4	1,131	6.8
FEMALE	19	.3	71	.9	57	.8	41	.5	188	2.5	7,078	94.2	249	3.3
MALE	26	.3	81	.9	114	1.2	56	.6	277	3.0	8,025	87.4	882	9.6

TABLE 20 — TOTAL ENROLLMENT OF GRADUATES BY CLASS LEVEL IN INSTITUTIONS OF HIGHER EDUCATION BY RACE, ETHNICITY AND SEX: STATE AND NATION, 1978

	AMERICAN INDIAN ALASKAN NATIVE		BLACK NON-HISPANIC		ASIAN OR PACIFIC ISLANDER		HISPANIC		TOTAL MINORITY		WHITE NON-HISPANIC		NON-RESIDENT ALIEN		TOTAL
	NUMBER	%	NUMBER	%	NUMBER	%	NUMBER	%	NUMBER	%	NUMBER	%	NUMBER	%	NUMBER
MISSISSIPPI (12 INSTITUTIONS)															
GRADUATE:															
FIRST YR	14	.2	1,840	25.9	48	.8	6	.1	1,608	27.1	4,095	69.0	233	3.9	5,936
FEMALE	10	.3	1,033	31.4	15	.5	3	.1	1,061	32.3	2,178	66.2	50	1.5	3,289
MALE	4	.2	507	19.2	33	1.2	3	.1	547	20.7	1,917	72.4	183	6.9	2,647
OVER 1 YR	5	.2	560	21.0	20	.8	5	.2	590	22.1	1,981	74.3	95	3.6	2,666
FEMALE	4	.3	374	29.5	5	.4	2	.2	385	30.4	870	68.7	11	.9	1,266
MALE	1	.1	186	13.3	15	1.1	3	.2	205	14.6	1,111	79.4	84	6.0	1,400
TOTAL	19	.2	2,100	24.4	68	.8	11	.1	2,198	25.6	6,076	70.6	328	3.8	8,602
FEMALE	14	.3	1,407	30.9	20	.4	5	.1	1,446	31.7	3,048	66.9	61	1.3	4,555
MALE	5	.1	693	17.1	48	1.2	6	.1	752	18.6	3,028	74.8	267	6.6	4,047
MISSOURI (30 INSTITUTIONS)															
GRADUATE:															
FIRST YR	27	.2	884	5.7	215	1.4	113	.7	1,239	8.0	13,762	88.4	574	3.7	15,575
FEMALE	10	.1	475	6.9	71	1.0	37	.5	593	8.6	6,175	89.1	161	2.3	6,929
MALE	17	.2	409	4.7	144	1.7	76	.9	646	7.5	7,587	87.8	413	4.8	8,646
OVER 1 YR	19	.2	410	5.0	353	4.3	42	.5	824	10.0	6,833	82.6	619	7.5	8,276
FEMALE	8	.3	234	7.4	39	1.2	15	.5	296	9.4	2,738	86.5	131	4.1	3,165
MALE	11	.2	176	3.4	314	6.1	27	.5	528	10.3	4,095	80.1	488	9.5	5,111
TOTAL	46	.2	1,294	5.4	568	2.4	155	.6	2,063	8.6	20,595	86.3	1,193	5.0	23,851
FEMALE	18	.2	709	7.0	110	1.1	52	.5	889	8.8	8,913	88.3	292	2.9	10,094
MALE	28	.2	585	4.3	458	3.3	103	.7	1,174	8.5	11,682	84.9	901	6.5	13,757
MONTANA (7 INSTITUTIONS)															
GRADUATE:															
FIRST YR	14	1.0	0	.0	3	.2	3	.2	22	1.6	1,356	97.1	19	1.4	1,397
FEMALE	10	1.5	0	.0	1	.1	1	.1	12	1.8	656	97.2	7	1.0	675
MALE	4	.6	2	.3	2	.3	2	.3	10	1.4	700	97.0	12	1.7	722
OVER 1 YR	16	2.3	3	.4	5	.7	2	.3	26	3.7	664	94.3	14	2.0	704
FEMALE	8	3.1	0	.0	3	1.2	0	.0	11	4.3	237	93.3	6	2.4	254
MALE	8	1.8	3	.7	2	.4	2	.4	15	3.3	427	94.9	8	1.8	450
TOTAL	30	1.4	5	.2	8	.4	5	.2	48	2.3	2,020	96.1	33	1.6	2,101
FEMALE	18	1.9	0	.0	4	.4	1	.1	23	2.5	893	96.1	13	1.4	929
MALE	12	1.0	5	.4	4	.3	4	.3	25	2.1	1,127	96.2	20	1.7	1,172
NEBRASKA (8 INSTITUTIONS)															
GRADUATE:															
FIRST YR	6	.2	104	2.9	26	.7	22	.6	158	4.5	3,262	92.4	112	3.2	3,532
FEMALE	2	.1	62	3.2	16	.8	8	.4	88	4.5	1,834	94.3	23	1.2	1,945
MALE	4	.3	42	2.6	10	.6	14	.9	70	4.4	1,428	90.0	89	5.6	1,587
OVER 1 YR	8	.2	40	1.1	30	.8	32	.9	110	3.0	3,378	92.3	171	4.7	3,659
FEMALE	3	.2	11	.7	11	.7	8	.5	33	2.1	1,498	96.5	21	1.4	1,552
MALE	5	.2	29	1.4	19	.9	24	1.1	77	3.7	1,880	89.2	150	7.1	2,107
TOTAL	14	.2	144	2.0	56	.8	54	.8	268	3.7	6,640	92.3	283	3.9	7,191
FEMALE	5	.1	73	2.1	27	.8	16	.5	121	3.5	3,332	95.3	44	1.3	3,497
MALE	9	.2	71	1.9	29	.8	38	1.0	147	4.0	3,308	89.6	239	6.5	3,694
NEVADA (2 INSTITUTIONS)															
GRADUATE:															
FIRST YR	7	.8	40	4.5	10	1.1	18	2.0	75	8.4	789	88.8	25	2.8	889
FEMALE	2	.4	25	5.2	4	.8	8	1.7	39	8.1	433	90.2	8	1.7	480
MALE	5	1.2	15	3.7	6	1.5	10	2.4	36	8.8	356	87.0	17	4.2	409
OVER 1 YR	4	.6	5	.8	11	1.7	9	1.4	29	4.4	599	90.1	37	5.6	665
FEMALE	1	.3	2	.6	3	1.0	5	1.6	11	3.6	289	93.8	8	2.6	308
MALE	3	.8	3	.8	8	2.2	4	1.1	18	5.0	310	86.8	29	8.1	357
TOTAL	11	.7	45	2.9	21	1.4	27	1.7	104	6.7	1,388	89.3	62	4.0	1,554
FEMALE	3	.4	27	3.4	7	.9	13	1.6	50	6.3	722	91.6	16	2.0	788
MALE	8	1.0	18	2.3	14	1.8	14	1.8	54	7.0	666	86.9	46	6.0	766
NEW HAMPSHIRE (7 INSTITUTIONS)															
GRADUATE:															
FIRST YR	2	.2	15	1.3	10	.9	4	.3	31	2.7	1,122	96.7	7	.6	1,160
FEMALE	1	.2	7	1.3	6	1.1	2	.4	16	3.0	511	96.6	3	.6	530
MALE	1	.2	8	1.3	4	.6	2	.4	15	2.4	611	97.0	4	.6	630
OVER 1 YR	1	.1	15	1.0	16	1.0	6	.4	38	2.4	1,520	96.7	14	.9	1,572
FEMALE	0	.0	1	.2	5	1.1	3	.6	9	1.9	457	97.6	2	.4	468
MALE	1	.1	14	1.3	11	1.0	3	.3	29	2.6	1,063	96.3	12	1.1	1,104
TOTAL	3	.1	30	1.1	26	1.0	10	.4	69	2.5	2,642	96.7	21	.8	2,732
FEMALE	1	.1	8	.8	11	1.1	5	.5	25	2.5	968	97.0	5	.5	998
MALE	2	.1	22	1.3	15	.9	5	.3	44	2.5	1,674	96.5	16	.9	1,734

	AMERICAN INDIAN ALASKAN NATIVE		BLACK NON-HISPANIC		ASIAN OR PACIFIC ISLANDER		HISPANIC		TOTAL MINORITY		WHITE NON-HISPANIC		NON-RESIDENT ALIEN	
	NUMBER	%	NUMBER	%	NUMBER	%	NUMBER	%	NUMBER	%	NUMBER	%	NUMBER	%
NEW JERSEY (27 INSTITUTIONS)														
GRADUATE:														
FIRST YR	18	.1	687	4.9	226	1.6	307	2.2	1,238	8.8	12,341	87.5	528	3.7
FEMALE	9	.1	408	5.9	83	1.2	148	2.1	648	9.4	6,126	88.9	115	1.7
MALE	9	.1	279	3.9	143	2.0	159	2.2	590	8.2	6,215	86.1	413	5.7
OVER 1 YR	15	.1	881	5.0	292	1.7	316	1.8	1,504	8.6	15,156	86.6	844	4.8
FEMALE	8	.1	524	6.5	95	1.2	184	2.3	811	10.1	7,017	87.5	190	2.4
MALE	7	.1	357	3.8	197	2.1	132	1.4	693	7.3	8,139	85.8	654	6.9
TOTAL	33	.1	1,568	5.0	518	1.6	623	2.0	2,742	8.7	27,497	87.0	1,372	4.3
FEMALE	17	.1	932	6.3	178	1.2	332	2.2	1,459	9.8	13,143	88.2	305	2.0
MALE	16	.1	636	3.8	340	2.0	291	1.7	1,283	7.7	14,354	85.9	1,067	6.4
NEW MEXICO (7 INSTITUTIONS)														
GRADUATE:														
FIRST YR	25	1.4	29	1.6	14	.8	312	17.2	380	21.0	1,279	70.7	151	8.3
FEMALE	15	1.8	14	1.7	5	.6	141	17.0	175	21.1	634	76.4	21	2.5
MALE	10	1.0	15	1.5	9	.9	171	17.4	205	20.9	645	65.8	130	13.3
OVER 1 YR	91	2.1	60	1.4	38	.9	627	14.5	816	18.9	3,250	75.2	258	6.0
FEMALE	47	2.5	26	1.4	18	.9	286	15.0	377	19.7	1,497	78.3	38	2.0
MALE	44	1.8	34	1.4	20	.8	341	14.1	439	18.2	1,753	72.7	220	9.1
TOTAL	116	1.9	89	1.5	52	.8	939	15.3	1,196	19.5	4,529	73.8	409	6.7
FEMALE	62	2.3	40	1.5	23	.8	427	15.6	552	20.1	2,131	77.7	59	2.2
MALE	54	1.6	49	1.4	29	.9	512	15.1	644	19.0	2,398	70.7	350	10.3
NEW YORK (128 INSTITUTIONS)														
GRADUATE:														
FIRST YR	222	.4	3,825	6.3	1,514	2.5	1,817	3.0	7,378	12.2	49,733	82.3	3,314	5.5
FEMALE	83	.3	2,249	7.3	604	2.0	1,062	3.5	3,998	13.0	25,733	83.7	1,006	3.3
MALE	139	.5	1,576	5.3	910	3.1	755	2.5	3,380	11.4	24,000	80.8	2,308	7.8
OVER 1 YR	179	.3	3,042	5.1	1,635	2.8	1,470	2.5	6,326	10.7	48,808	82.2	4,257	7.2
FEMALE	76	.3	1,713	6.3	640	2.4	716	2.6	3,145	11.6	22,998	84.5	1,078	4.0
MALE	103	.3	1,329	4.1	995	3.1	754	2.3	3,181	9.9	25,810	80.2	3,179	9.9
TOTAL	401	.3	6,867	5.7	3,149	2.6	3,287	2.7	13,704	11.4	98,541	82.2	7,571	6.3
FEMALE	159	.3	3,962	6.8	1,244	2.1	1,778	3.1	7,143	12.3	48,731	84.1	2,084	3.6
MALE	242	.4	2,905	4.7	1,905	3.1	1,509	2.4	6,561	10.6	49,810	80.5	5,487	8.9
NORTH CAROLINA (15 INSTITUTIONS)														
GRADUATE:														
FIRST YR	42	.4	1,329	14.1	43	.5	29	.3	1,443	15.4	7,548	80.3	403	4.3
FEMALE	22	.4	834	16.4	18	.4	19	.4	893	17.5	4,096	80.4	103	2.0
MALE	20	.5	495	11.5	25	.6	10	.2	550	12.8	3,452	80.2	300	7.0
OVER 1 YR	19	.2	785	9.1	60	.7	45	.5	909	10.6	7,205	83.8	487	5.7
FEMALE	9	.2	523	13.2	21	.5	22	.6	575	14.5	3,301	83.0	99	2.5
MALE	10	.2	262	5.7	39	.8	23	.5	334	7.2	3,904	84.4	388	8.4
TOTAL	61	.3	2,114	11.7	103	.6	74	.4	2,352	13.1	14,753	82.0	890	4.9
FEMALE	31	.3	1,357	15.0	39	.4	41	.5	1,468	16.2	7,397	81.6	202	2.2
MALE	30	.3	757	8.5	64	.7	33	.4	884	9.9	7,356	82.4	688	7.7
NORTH DAKOTA (3 INSTITUTIONS)														
GRADUATE:														
FIRST YR	6	.7	6	.7	9	1.1	2	.2	23	2.8	731	88.9	68	8.3
FEMALE	6	1.8	2	.6	3	.9	0	.0	11	3.4	291	89.0	25	7.6
MALE	0	.0	4	.8	6	1.2	2	.4	12	2.4	440	88.9	43	8.7
OVER 1 YR	5	.7	4	.6	8	1.1	2	.3	19	2.6	629	87.1	74	10.2
FEMALE	2	1.1	1	.5	2	1.1	1	.5	6	3.2	179	94.2	5	2.6
MALE	3	.6	3	.6	6	1.1	1	.2	13	2.4	450	84.6	69	13.0
TOTAL	11	.7	10	.6	17	1.1	4	.3	42	2.7	1,360	88.1	142	9.2
FEMALE	8	1.5	3	.6	5	1.0	1	.2	17	3.3	470	90.9	30	5.8
MALE	3	.3	7	.7	12	1.2	3	.3	25	2.4	890	86.7	112	10.9
OHIO (57 INSTITUTIONS)														
GRADUATE:														
FIRST YR	63	.2	1,602	6.1	174	.7	146	.6	1,985	7.5	23,210	88.1	1,150	4.4
FEMALE	31	.2	982	7.2	74	.5	74	.5	1,161	8.5	12,192	89.3	300	2.2
MALE	32	.3	620	4.9	100	.8	72	.6	824	6.5	11,018	86.8	850	6.7
OVER 1 YR	41	.2	1,550	6.7	162	.7	160	.7	1,913	8.2	19,636	84.4	1,704	7.3
FEMALE	15	.2	827	8.4	51	.5	66	.7	959	9.7	8,536	86.7	347	3.5
MALE	26	.2	723	5.4	111	.8	94	.7	954	7.1	11,100	82.8	1,357	10.1
TOTAL	104	.2	3,152	6.3	336	.7	306	.6	3,898	7.9	42,895	86.4	2,854	5.7
FEMALE	46	.2	1,809	7.7	125	.5	140	.6	2,120	9.0	20,757	88.2	647	2.8
MALE	58	.2	1,343	5.1	211	.8	166	.6	1,778	6.8	22,138	84.7	2,207	8.4

TOTAL ENROLLMENT OF GRADUATES BY CLASS LEVEL IN INSTITUTIONS OF HIGHER EDUCATION BY RACE, ETHNICITY AND SEX:
STATE AND NATION, 1978

AMERICAN INDIAN ALASKAN NATIVE		BLACK NON-HISPANIC		ASIAN OR PACIFIC ISLANDER		HISPANIC		TOTAL MINORITY		WHITE NON-HISPANIC		NON-RESIDENT ALIEN		TOTAL
NUMBER	%	NUMBER	%	NUMBER	%	NUMBER	%	NUMBER	%	NUMBER	%	NUMBER	%	NUMBER
(14 INSTITUTIONS)														
88	3.0	109	3.8	13	.4	11	.4	221	7.6	2,336	80.6	341	11.8	2,898
53	3.8	61	4.4	4	.3	6	.4	124	8.9	1,194	85.5	79	5.7	1,397
35	2.3	48	3.2	9	.6	5	.3	97	6.5	1,142	76.1	262	17.5	1,501
246	2.3	396	3.7	65	.6	58	.5	765	7.1	8,580	79.8	1,408	13.1	10,753
128	2.8	218	4.7	26	.6	19	.4	391	8.5	3,980	86.3	242	5.2	4,613
118	1.9	178	2.9	39	.6	39	.6	374	6.1	4,600	74.9	1,166	19.0	6,140
334	2.4	505	3.7	78	.6	69	.5	986	7.2	10,916	80.0	1,749	12.8	13,651
181	3.0	279	4.6	30	.5	25	.4	515	8.6	5,174	86.1	321	5.3	6,010
153	2.0	226	3.0	48	.6	44	.6	471	6.2	5,742	75.1	1,428	18.7	7,641
(20 INSTITUTIONS)														
36	.6	54	.9	101	1.6	41	.6	232	3.7	5,392	85.2	701	11.1	6,325
18	.6	18	.6	44	1.5	15	.5	95	3.3	2,579	90.3	181	6.3	2,855
18	.5	36	1.0	57	1.6	26	.7	137	3.9	2,813	81.1	520	15.0	3,470
21	.7	41	1.4	66	2.3	25	.9	153	5.2	2,348	80.1	432	14.7	2,933
7	.6	17	1.5	30	2.7	10	.9	64	5.8	956	86.1	90	8.1	1,110
14	.8	24	1.3	36	2.0	15	.8	89	4.9	1,392	76.4	342	18.8	1,823
57	.6	95	1.0	167	1.8	66	.7	385	4.2	7,740	83.6	1,133	12.2	9,258
25	.6	35	.9	74	1.9	25	.6	159	4.0	3,535	89.2	271	6.8	3,965
32	.6	60	1.1	93	1.8	41	.8	226	4.3	4,205	79.4	862	16.3	5,293
A (77 INSTITUTIONS)														
72	.2	1,220	3.9	333	1.1	226	.7	1,851	6.0	27,798	89.9	1,266	4.1	30,915
28	.2	718	5.0	121	.8	112	.8	979	6.9	13,028	91.4	244	1.7	14,251
44	.3	502	3.0	212	1.3	114	.7	872	5.2	14,770	88.6	1,022	6.1	16,664
27	.2	615	3.9	210	1.3	111	.7	963	6.0	13,309	83.4	1,688	10.6	15,960
9	.1	339	5.2	86	1.3	45	.7	479	7.4	5,712	88.0	299	4.6	6,490
18	.2	276	2.9	124	1.3	66	.7	484	5.1	7,597	80.2	1,389	14.7	9,470
99	.2	1,835	3.9	543	1.2	337	.7	2,814	6.0	41,107	87.7	2,954	6.3	46,875
37	.2	1,057	5.1	207	1.0	157	.8	1,458	7.0	18,740	90.4	543	2.6	20,741
62	.2	778	3.0	336	1.3	180	.7	1,356	5.2	22,367	85.6	2,411	9.2	26,134
NO (7 INSTITUTIONS)														
6	.2	39	1.5	25	1.0	15	.6	85	3.3	2,297	90.4	160	6.3	2,542
3	.3	16	1.4	5	.4	7	.6	31	2.8	1,052	93.6	41	3.6	1,124
3	.2	23	1.6	20	1.4	8	.6	54	3.8	1,245	87.8	119	8.4	1,418
9	.3	44	1.3	39	1.1	16	.5	108	3.1	3,153	90.1	238	6.8	3,499
5	.3	22	1.5	10	.7	7	.5	44	3.0	1,358	93.3	54	3.7	1,456
4	.2	22	1.1	29	1.4	9	.4	64	3.1	1,795	87.9	184	9.0	2,043
15	.2	83	1.4	64	1.1	31	.5	193	3.2	5,450	90.2	398	6.6	6,041
8	.3	38	1.5	15	.6	14	.5	75	2.9	2,410	93.4	95	3.7	2,580
7	.2	45	1.3	49	1.4	17	.5	118	3.4	3,040	87.8	303	8.8	3,461
LINA (14 INSTITUTIONS)														
7	.1	1,043	12.1	24	.3	28	.3	1,102	12.8	7,427	86.0	107	1.2	8,636
3	.1	747	14.5	5	.1	12	.2	767	14.9	4,360	84.5	30	.6	5,157
4	.1	296	8.5	19	.5	16	.5	335	9.6	3,067	88.2	77	2.2	3,479
5	.1	272	8.1	11	.3	9	.3	297	8.9	2,907	87.0	138	4.1	3,342
3	.2	180	10.8	6	.4	5	.3	194	11.6	1,447	86.8	27	1.6	1,668
2	.1	92	5.5	5	.3	4	.2	103	6.2	1,460	87.2	111	6.6	1,674
12	.1	1,315	11.0	35	.3	37	.3	1,399	11.7	10,334	86.3	245	2.0	11,978
6	.1	927	13.6	11	.2	17	.2	961	14.1	5,807	85.1	57	.8	6,825
6	.1	388	7.5	24	.5	20	.4	438	8.5	4,527	87.9	188	3.6	5,153
TA (6 INSTITUTIONS)														
3	.2	0	.0	0	.0	1	.1	4	.3	1,250	93.5	83	6.2	1,337
3	.5	0	.0	0	.0	0	.0	3	.5	554	97.9	9	1.6	566
0	.0	0	.0	0	.0	1	.1	1	.1	696	90.3	74	9.6	771
23	4.1	3	.5	2	.4	1	.2	29	5.2	496	89.0	32	5.7	557
7	3.9	1	.6	0	.0	0	.0	8	4.4	169	93.9	3	1.7	180
16	4.2	2	.5	2	.5	1	.3	21	5.6	327	86.7	29	7.7	377
26	1.4	3	.2	2	.1	2	.1	33	1.7	1,746	92.2	115	6.1	1,894
10	1.3	1	.1	0	.0	0	.0	11	1.5	723	96.9	12	1.6	746
16	1.4	2	.2	2	.2	2	.2	22	1.9	1,023	89.1	103	9.0	1,148

TABLE 20 – TOTAL ENROLLMENT OF GRADUATES BY CLASS LEVEL IN INSTITUTIONS OF HIGHER EDUCATION BY RACE, ETHNICITY AND SEX: STATE AND NATION, 1978

	AMERICAN INDIAN ALASKAN NATIVE		BLACK NON-HISPANIC		ASIAN OR PACIFIC ISLANDER		HISPANIC		TOTAL MINORITY		WHITE NON-HISPANIC		NON-RESIDENT ALIEN	
	NUMBER	%	NUMBER	%	NUMBER	%	NUMBER	%	NUMBER	%	NUMBER	%	NUMBER	%
TENNESSEE (18 INSTITUTIONS)														
GRADUATE:														
FIRST YR	18	.2	814	7.9	50	.5	33	.3	915	8.8	8,887	85.8	552	5.3
FEMALE	10	.2	531	10.1	25	.5	15	.3	581	11.0	4,567	86.7	122	2.3
MALE	8	.2	283	5.6	25	.5	18	.4	334	6.6	4,320	85.0	430	8.5
OVER 1 YR	11	.2	361	6.6	58	1.1	16	.3	446	8.1	4,564	83.0	490	8.9
FEMALE	6	.3	208	8.9	12	.5	8	.3	234	10.0	1,990	85.2	113	4.8
MALE	5	.2	153	4.8	46	1.5	8	.3	212	6.7	2,574	81.4	377	11.9
TOTAL	29	.2	1,175	7.4	108	.7	49	.3	1,361	8.6	13,451	84.8	1,042	6.6
FEMALE	16	.2	739	9.7	37	.5	23	.3	815	10.7	6,557	86.2	235	3.1
MALE	13	.2	436	5.3	71	.9	26	.3	546	6.6	6,894	83.6	807	9.8
TEXAS (56 INSTITUTIONS)														
GRADUATE:														
FIRST YR	159	.4	2,739	6.8	523	1.3	2,928	7.3	6,349	15.8	31,101	77.2	2,815	7.0
FEMALE	59	.3	1,605	8.1	227	1.1	1,561	7.9	3,452	17.4	15,711	79.2	678	3.4
MALE	100	.5	1,134	5.6	296	1.4	1,367	6.7	2,897	14.2	15,390	75.4	2,137	10.5
OVER 1 YR	85	.3	1,210	4.7	423	1.7	1,365	5.3	3,083	12.0	19,966	78.0	2,543	9.9
FEMALE	33	.3	738	7.3	120	1.2	596	5.9	1,487	14.8	8,103	80.5	476	4.7
MALE	52	.3	472	3.0	303	2.0	769	5.0	1,596	10.3	11,863	76.4	2,067	13.3
TOTAL	245	.4	3,962	5.9	951	1.4	4,521	6.8	9,679	14.5	51,591	77.3	5,442	8.2
FEMALE	92	.3	2,347	7.8	349	1.2	2,251	7.4	5,039	16.7	24,044	79.5	1,172	3.9
MALE	153	.4	1,615	4.4	602	1.7	2,270	6.2	4,640	12.7	27,547	75.6	4,270	11.7
UTAH (4 INSTITUTIONS)														
GRADUATE:														
FIRST YR	16	.6	8	.3	31	1.2	21	.8	76	3.0	2,263	88.2	228	8.9
FEMALE	7	.9	2	.2	11	1.4	9	1.1	29	3.6	723	89.0	60	7.4
MALE	9	.5	6	.3	20	1.1	12	.7	47	2.7	1,540	87.7	168	9.6
OVER 1 YR	32	.6	25	.5	72	1.4	47	.9	176	3.4	4,449	85.9	555	10.7
FEMALE	15	.8	12	.7	31	1.7	22	1.2	80	4.5	1,579	88.2	132	7.4
MALE	17	.5	13	.4	41	1.2	25	.7	96	2.8	2,870	84.7	423	12.5
TOTAL	48	.6	33	.4	103	1.3	68	.9	252	3.3	6,712	86.4	783	10.1
FEMALE	22	.8	14	.5	42	1.6	31	1.2	109	4.2	2,302	88.4	192	7.4
MALE	26	.5	19	.4	61	1.2	37	.7	143	2.8	4,410	85.7	591	11.5
VERMONT (11 INSTITUTIONS)														
GRADUATE:														
FIRST YR	3	.2	25	1.6	4	.3	13	.8	45	2.9	1,453	93.1	62	4.0
FEMALE	0	.0	13	1.5	3	.3	4	.4	20	2.2	851	95.4	21	2.4
MALE	3	.4	12	1.8	1	.1	9	1.3	25	3.7	602	90.1	41	6.1
OVER 1 YR	0	.0	20	2.4	4	.5	6	.7	30	3.4	757	90.8	47	5.6
FEMALE	0	.0	10	2.2	3	.7	2	.4	15	3.3	421	92.3	20	4.4
MALE	0	.0	10	2.6	1	.3	4	1.1	15	4.0	336	88.9	27	7.1
TOTAL	3	.1	45	1.9	8	.3	19	.8	75	3.1	2,210	92.3	109	4.6
FEMALE	0	.0	23	1.7	6	.4	6	.4	35	2.6	1,272	94.4	41	3.0
MALE	3	.3	22	2.1	2	.2	13	1.2	40	3.8	938	89.7	68	6.5
VIRGINIA (21 INSTITUTIONS)														
GRADUATE:														
FIRST YR	18	.1	1,102	8.2	100	.7	58	.4	1,278	9.5	11,841	88.2	303	2.3
FEMALE	6	.1	706	10.3	26	.4	33	.5	771	11.2	6,008	87.5	86	1.3
MALE	12	.2	396	6.0	74	1.1	25	.4	507	7.7	5,833	89.0	217	3.3
OVER 1 YR	8	.1	658	10.4	70	1.1	11	.2	747	11.8	5,323	83.8	283	4.5
FEMALE	4	.2	381	14.4	17	.6	3	.1	405	15.4	2,184	82.8	49	1.9
MALE	4	.1	277	7.5	53	1.4	8	.2	342	9.2	3,139	84.5	234	6.3
TOTAL	26	.1	1,926	9.6	175	.9	71	.4	2,198	11.0	17,194	86.1	569	2.9
FEMALE	10	.1	1,216	12.6	48	.5	38	.4	1,312	13.6	8,211	85.0	135	1.4
MALE	16	.2	710	6.9	127	1.2	33	.3	886	8.6	8,983	87.0	454	4.4
WASHINGTON (16 INSTITUTIONS)														
GRADUATE:														
FIRST YR	53	.6	207	2.3	284	3.1	84	.9	628	6.9	7,524	83.2	888	9.8
FEMALE	24	.6	104	2.6	121	3.1	30	.8	279	7.1	3,444	87.5	212	5.4
MALE	29	.6	103	2.0	163	3.2	54	1.1	349	6.8	4,080	79.9	676	13.2
OVER 1 YR	40	.9	88	1.9	111	2.4	54	1.2	293	6.3	3,693	79.7	648	14.0
FEMALE	19	1.2	24	1.5	37	2.4	12	.8	92	5.9	1,332	86.0	125	8.1
MALE	21	.7	64	2.1	74	2.4	42	1.4	201	6.5	2,361	76.5	523	17.0
TOTAL	93	.7	295	2.2	395	2.9	138	1.0	921	6.7	11,217	82.0	1,536	11.2
FEMALE	43	.8	128	2.3	158	2.9	42	.8	371	6.8	4,776	87.1	337	6.1
MALE	50	.6	167	2.0	237	2.9	96	1.2	550	6.7	6,441	78.6	1,199	14.6

TABLE 20 - TOTAL ENROLLMENT OF GRADUATES BY CLASS LEVEL IN INSTITUTIONS OF HIGHER EDUCATION BY RACE, ETHNICITY AND SEX: STATE AND NATION, 1978

	AMERICAN INDIAN ALASKAN NATIVE		BLACK NON-HISPANIC		ASIAN OR PACIFIC ISLANDER		HISPANIC		TOTAL MINORITY		WHITE NON-HISPANIC		NON-RESIDENT ALIEN		TOTAL
	NUMBER	%	NUMBER	%	NUMBER	%	NUMBER	%	NUMBER	%	NUMBER	%	NUMBER	%	NUMBER
WEST VIRGINIA (5 INSTITUTIONS)															
GRADUATE:															
FIRST YR	17	.2	172	2.2	44	.6	12	.2	245	3.2	7,163	93.2	274	3.	7,682
FEMALE	9	.2	106	2.4	14	.3	6	.1	135	3.0	4,311	95.7	59	1.6	4,505
MALE	8	.3	66	2.1	30	.9	6	.2	110	3.5	2,852	89.8	215	6.8	3,177
OVER 1 YR	26	.7	96	2.5	39	1.0	10	.3	171	4.5	3,507	93.0	92	2.	3,770
FEMALE	14	.7	52	2.5	13	.6	4	.2	83	4.1	1,945	95.2	16	.	2,044
MALE	12	.7	44	2.5	26	1.5	6	.3	88	5.1	1,562	90.5	76	4.8	1,726
TOTAL	43	.4	268	2.3	83	.7	22	.2	416	3.6	10,670	93.2	366	3.2	11,452
FEMALE	23	.4	158	2.4	27	.4	10	.2	218	3.3	6,256	95.5	75	1.1	6,549
MALE	20	.4	110	2.2	56	1.1	12	.2	198	4.0	4,414	90.0	291	5.9	4,903
WISCONSIN (22 INSTITUTIONS)															
GRADUATE:															
FIRST YR	37	.3	298	2.5	113	1.0	114	1.0	562	4.7	10,557	89.0	741	6.2	11,860
FEMALE	22	.4	172	3.0	43	.7	60	1.0	297	5.1	5,295	91.5	192	3.3	5,784
MALE	15	.2	126	2.1	70	1.2	54	.9	265	4.4	5,262	86.6	549	9.0	6,076
OVER 1 YR	21	.3	157	2.1	166	2.3	82	1.1	426	5.8	5,970	81.3	949	12.9	7,345
FEMALE	10	.4	76	2.8	57	2.1	31	1.2	174	6.5	2,310	86.4	189	7.1	2,673
MALE	11	.2	81	1.7	109	2.3	51	1.1	252	5.4	3,660	78.3	760	16.3	4,672
TOTAL	58	.3	455	2.4	279	1.5	196	1.0	988	5.1	16,527	86.1	1,690	8.8	19,205
FEMALE	32	.4	248	2.9	100	1.2	91	1.1	471	5.6	7,605	89.9	381	4.5	8,457
MALE	26	.2	207	1.9	179	1.7	105	1.0	517	4.8	8,922	83.0	1,309	12.2	10,748
WYOMING (1 INSTITUTIONS)															
GRADUATE:															
FIRST YR	0	.0	0	.0	0	.0	0	.0	0	.0	113	88.3	15	11.7	128
FEMALE	0	.0	0	.0	0	.0	0	.0	0	.0	38	92.7	3	7.3	41
MALE	0	.0	0	.0	0	.0	0	.0	0	.0	75	86.2	12	13.8	87
OVER 1 YR	3	.3	4	.4	5	.5	8	.9	20	2.2	812	88.2	89	9.7	921
FEMALE	1	.3	3	.8	3	.8	2	.5	9	2.3	370	94.1	14	3.6	393
MALE	2	.4	1	.2	2	.4	6	1.1	11	2.1	442	83.7	75	14.2	528
TOTAL	3	.3	4	.4	5	.5	8	.8	20	1.9	925	88.2	104	9.	1,049
FEMALE	1	.2	3	.7	3	.7	2	.5	9	2.1	408	94.0	17	3.9	434
MALE	2	.3	1	.2	2	.3	6	1.0	11	1.8	517	84.1	87	14.9	615
THE STATES AND D.C. (1,128 INSTITUTIONS)															
GRADUATE:															
FIRST YR	2,172	.4	37,522	6.1	11,161	1.8	12,571	2.0	63,426	10.3	516,717	84.0	35,100	5.7	615,243
FEMALE	1,021	.3	23,043	6.5	4,532	1.5	6,272	2.1	34,868	11.4	261,533	85.7	8,879	2.9	305,280
MALE	1,151	.4	14,479	4.7	6,629	2.1	6,299	2.0	28,558	9.2	255,184	82.3	26,221	8.5	309,963
OVER 1 YR	1,612	.3	24,170	5.3	9,441	2.1	8,254	1.8	43,477	9.6	373,479	82.1	38,181	.4	455,137
FEMALE	719	.4	14,037	7.4	3,343	1.8	3,578	1.9	21,677	11.4	161,029	84.5	7,916	4.2	190,622
MALE	893	.3	10,133	3.8	6,098	2.3	4,676	1.8	21,800	8.2	212,450	80.3	30,265	11.4	264,515
TOTAL	3,785	.4	61,871	5.8	20,612	1.9	21,055	2.0	107,323	10.0	890,801	83.1	73,368	6.8	1,071,492
FEMALE	1,740	.4	37,213	7.5	7,882	1.6	9,946	2.0	56,781	11.4	422,840	85.2	16,813	3.4	496,434
MALE	2,045	.4	24,658	4.3	12,730	2.2	11,109	1.9	50,542	8.8	467,961	81.4	56,555	9.8	575,058
GUAM (1 INSTITUTIONS)															
GRADUATE:															
FIRST YR	0	.0	0	.0	56	51.4	11	10.1	67	61.5	42	38.5	0	.0	109
FEMALE	0	.0	0	.0	48	51.6	11	11.8	59	63.4	34	36.6	0	.0	93
MALE	0	.0	0	.0	8	50.0	0	.0	8	50.0	8	50.0	0	.0	16
OVER 1 YR	0	.0	0	.0	62	44.9	0	.0	62	44.9	76	55.1	0	.0	138
FEMALE	0	.0	0	.0	46	66.7	0	.0	46	66.7	23	33.3	0	.0	69
MALE	0	.0	0	.0	16	23.2	0	.0	16	23.2	53	76.8	0	.0	69
TOTAL	0	.0	0	.0	118	47.8	11	4.5	129	52.2	118	47.8	0	.0	247
FEMALE	0	.0	0	.0	94	58.0	11	6.8	105	64.8	57	35.2	0	.0	162
MALE	0	.0	0	.0	24	28.2	0	.0	24	28.2	61	71.8	0	.0	85
PUERTO RICO (9 INSTITUTIONS)															
GRADUATE:															
FIRST YR	0	.0	0	.0	0	.0	1,573	92.6	1,573	92.6	122	7.2	3	.2	1,698
FEMALE	0	.0	0	.0	0	.0	966	92.4	966	92.4	78	7.5	1	.1	1,045
MALE	0	.0	0	.0	0	.0	607	93.0	607	93.0	44	6.7	2	.3	653
OVER 1 YR	0	.0	0	.0	0	.0	2,537	96.1	2,537	96.1	96	3.6	8	.3	2,641
FEMALE	0	.0	0	.0	0	.0	1,358	95.9	1,358	95.9	55	3.9	3	.2	1,416
MALE	0	.0	0	.0	0	.0	1,179	96.2	1,179	96.2	41	3.3	5	.4	1,225
TOTAL	0	.0	0	.0	0	.0	4,110	94.7	4,110	94.7	218	5.0	1	.3	4,339
FEMALE	0	.0	0	.0	0	.0	2,324	94.4	2,324	94.4	133	5.4	1	.2	2,461
MALE	0	.0	0	.0	0	.0	1,786	95.1	1,786	95.1	85	4.5	1	.4	1,878

TABLE 20 - TOTAL ENROLLMENT OF GRADUATES BY CLASS LEVEL IN INSTITUTIONS OF HIGHER EDUCATION BY RACE, ETHNICITY AND SEX: STATE AND NATION, 1978

	AMERICAN INDIAN ALASKAN NATIVE		BLACK NON-HISPANIC		ASIAN OR PACIFIC ISLANDER		HISPANIC		TOTAL MINORITY		WHITE NON-HISPANIC		NON-RESIDENT ALIEN	
	NUMBER	%	NUMBER	%	NUMBER	%	NUMBER	%	NUMBER	%	NUMBER	%	NUMBER	%
VIRGIN ISLANDS	(	1 INSTITUTIONS)												
GRADUATE:														
FIRST YR	0	.0	22	59.5	1	2.7	2	5.4	25	67.6	10	27.0	2	5.4
FEMALE	0	.0	10	66.7	0	.0	1	6.7	11	73.3	4	26.7	0	.0
MALE	0	.0	12	54.5	1	4.5	1	4.5	14	63.6	6	27.3	2	9.1
OVER 1 YR	0	.0	25	71.4	0	.0	0	.0	25	71.4	10	28.6	0	.0
FEMALE	0	.0	19	65.5	0	.0	0	.0	19	65.5	10	34.5	0	.0
MALE	0	.0	6	100.0	0	.0	0	.0	6	100.0	0	.0	0	.0
TOTAL	0	.0	47	65.3	1	1.4	2	2.8	50	69.4	20	27.8	2	2.8
FEMALE	0	.0	29	65.9	0	.0	1	2.3	30	68.2	14	31.8	0	.0
MALE	0	.0	18	64.3	1	3.6	1	3.6	20	71.4	6	21.4	2	7.1
OUTLYING AREAS	(	11 INSTITUTIONS)												
GRADUATE:														
FIRST YR	0	.0	22	1.2	57	3.1	1,586	86.0	1,665	90.3	174	9.4	5	.3
FEMALE	0	.0	10	.9	48	4.2	978	84.8	1,036	89.9	116	10.1	1	.1
MALE	0	.0	12	1.7	9	1.3	608	88.0	629	91.0	58	8.4	4	.6
OVER 1 YR	0	.0	25	.9	62	2.2	2,537	90.2	2,624	93.2	182	6.5	8	.3
FEMALE	0	.0	19	1.3	46	3.0	1,358	89.7	1,423	94.0	88	5.8	3	.2
MALE	0	.0	6	.5	16	1.2	1,179	90.7	1,201	92.4	94	7.2	5	.4
TOTAL	0	.0	47	1.0	119	2.6	4,123	88.5	4,289	92.1	356	7.6	13	.3
FEMALE	0	.0	29	1.1	94	3.5	2,336	87.6	2,459	92.2	204	7.6	4	.1
MALE	0	.0	18	.9	25	1.3	1,787	89.8	1,830	91.9	152	7.6	9	.5
NATION TOTAL	(	1,139 INSTITUTIONS)												
GRADUATE:														
FIRST YR	2,172	.4	37,544	6.1	11,218	1.8	14,157	2.3	65,091	10.5	516,891	83.8	35,105	5.7
FEMALE	1,021	.3	23,053	7.5	4,580	1.5	7,250	2.4	35,904	11.7	261,649	85.4	8,880	2.9
MALE	1,151	.4	14,491	4.7	6,638	2.1	6,907	2.2	29,187	9.4	255,242	82.2	26,225	8.4
OVER 1 YR	1,612	.4	24,195	5.3	9,503	2.1	10,791	2.4	46,101	10.1	373,661	81.6	38,189	8.3
FEMALE	719	.4	14,056	7.3	3,389	1.8	4,936	2.6	23,100	12.0	161,117	83.9	7,919	4.1
MALE	893	.3	10,139	3.8	6,114	2.3	5,855	2.2	23,001	8.7	212,544	80.0	30,270	11.4
TOTAL	3,785	.4	61,918	5.8	20,731	1.9	25,178	2.3	111,612	10.4	891,157	82.8	73,381	6.8	1,
FEMALE	1,740	.3	37,242	7.5	7,976	1.6	12,282	2.5	59,240	11.9	423,044	84.8	16,817	3.4
MALE	2,045	.4	24,676	4.3	12,755	2.2	12,896	2.2	52,372	9.1	468,113	81.1	56,564	9.8

APPENDIX A

SURVEY REPORT FORM

DEPARTMENT OF HEALTH, EDUCATION, AND WELFARE OFFICE OF EDUCATION WASHINGTON, D.C. 20202 HIGHER EDUCATION GENERAL INFORMATION SURVEY **OPENING FALL ENROLLMENT IN HIGHER EDUCATION, 1974**	PLEASE READ INSTRUCTIONS BEFORE COMPLETING THIS FORM	OMB NO. 51-R0738 APPROVAL EXPIRES: 6/30/75 1. INSTITUTION CODE NUMBER 2. DUE DATE November 1, 1974

Items 1, 3, 4, 5, and 6 MUST be completed by all institutions. If applicable, complete items 7 and 8. Submit a separate survey form for each of the campuses or branch campuses of the institution. If it is impossible to provide separate data for any branch campus, and the data for that branch must be included in the parent institution's report, indicate this in item 8 below. Return the completed form to the U.S. Office of Education, National Center for Educational Statistics, ATTENTION: Room 2164-HEGIS, 400 Maryland Avenue, SW., Washington, D.C. 20202, or your HEGIS coordinator.

3. NAME AND MAILING ADDRESS OF INSTITUTION OR CAMPUS COVERED BY THIS REPORT (Include city, State, and ZIP code)	4. NAME AND TITLE OF RESPONDENT
	5. TELEPHONE NUMBER OF RESPONDENT (Area code, local number and extension)

6. THE INSTITUTION COVERED BY THIS REPORT IS (Check only one)

(a) ☐ A SINGLE-CAMPUS INSTITUTION

(b) ☐ A MAIN CAMPUS ("Parent" institution) WITH ONE OR MORE BRANCH CAMPUSES AND/OR OTHER CAMPUSES (Specify in item 8 below)

(c) ☐ A BRANCH CAMPUS OF A PARENT INSTITUTION (Write the name of parent institution below)

(d) ☐ ONE OF THE ADMINISTRATIVELY EQUAL CAMPUSES OF A MULTI-CAMPUS INSTITUTION

7. IF THE INSTITUTION COVERED BY THIS REPORT IS INCLUDED IN AN "INSTITUTIONAL SYSTEM", WRITE THE NAME OF THE SYSTEM BELOW.

8. PARENT INSTITUTIONS (As checked in item 6b) SHOULD LIST THE NAMES OF ALL THEIR BRANCH CAMPUSES BELOW. USE THE FIRST COLUMN TO SHOW WHETHER DATA FOR ANY OF THESE UNITS ARE INCLUDED WITH THE DATA FOR THE "PARENT" IN THIS REPORT.

ARE DATA FOR THIS UNIT INCLUDED IN THIS REPORT?	NAME OF BRANCH CAMPUS AND/OR OTHER CAMPUS	ADDRESS (City, State, and ZIP code)
☐ YES ☐ NO		
☐ YES ☐ NO	Data shown on the form are for the aggregate United States	
☐ YES ☐ NO		

DEFINITIONS

MULTI-CAMPUS INSTITUTION. An organization bearing a resemblance to an institutional system, but unequivocally designated as a single institution with either of two organizational structures: (1) an institution having two or more campuses responsible to a central administration (which central administration may or may not be located on one of the administratively equal campuses) or (2) an institution having a main campus with one or more branch campuses attached to it.

MAIN CAMPUS. In those institutions comprised of a main campus and one or more branch campuses, the main campus (sometimes called the parent institution) is usually the location of the core, primary, or most comprehensive program. Unless the institution-wide or central administrative office for such institutions is reported to be at a different location, the main campus is also the location of the central administrative office.

BRANCH CAMPUS. A campus of an institution of higher education which is organized on a relatively permanent basis (i.e., has a relatively permanent administration), which offers an organized program or programs of work of at least 2 years (as opposed to courses), and which is located in a community different from that in which its parent institution is located. To be considered in a community different from that of the parent institution, a branch shall be located beyond a reasonable commuting distance from the main campus of the parent institution.

INSTITUTIONAL SYSTEM. A complex of two or more institutions of higher education, each separately organized or independently complete, under the control or supervision of a single administrative body.

OE FORM 2300-2.3, 3/74   REPLACES OE FORM 2300-2.3, 3/73, WHICH IS OBSOLETE.

NAME OF INSTITUTION				INSTITUTION CODE NUMBER		DUE DATE	

PLEASE read the instructions and definitions on the next page before completing this questionnaire.	LINE NO.	HEADCOUNT					FULL-TIME EQUIVALENT OF PART-TIME HEADCOUNT (6)
		MEN		WOMEN			
ALL STUDENTS ENROLLED (resident and extension)		FULL-TIME (1)	PART-TIME (2)	FULL-TIME (3)	PART-TIME (4)	TOTAL (5)	
A. FIRST-TIME STUDENTS (entering freshmen)							
1. IN BACHELOR's-DEGREE-CREDIT PROGRAMS (Also included on line 04 below)	01	761,682	220,406	665,498	227,867	1,875,453	170,255
2. IN NON-BACHELOR'S-DEGREE-CREDIT PROGRAMS (Also included on line 04 below)	02	144,848	129,049	124,723	118,796	517,416	91,236
B. UNDERGRADUATES							
1. LOWER DIVISION UNDERGRADUATES							
a. In Bachelor's-Degree-Credit programs (Includes students reported on line 01 above)	03	1,797,301	694,211	1,465,558	673,264	4,630,334	522,307
b. In Non-Bachelor's-Degree-Credit Programs (Includes students reported on line 02 above)	04	313,934	344,943	304,572	248,207	1,211,656	239,235
2. UPPER DIVISION UNDERGRADUATES	05	1,040,242	231,041	813,162	180,190	2,264,635	166,291
3. TOTAL UNDERGRADUATES (sum of lines 03, 04, and 05)	06	3,151,477	1,270,195	2,526,927	1,158,026	8,106,625	927,820
C. UNCLASSIFIED STUDENTS	07	71,663	313,033	45,238	352,817	782,751	224,073
D. FIRST-PROFESSIONAL STUDENTS	08	180,291	15,770	37,884	4,121	238,066	9,471
E. GRADUATE STUDENTS	09	276,304	388,320	152,685	376,788	1,194,097	283,199
F. GRAND TOTAL-ALL STUDENTS IN SURVEY (sum of lines 06 through 09)	10	3,679,735	1,987,318	2,762,734	1,891,752	10,321,539	1,444,096

IF THE EDUCATIONAL PROGRAM AT YOUR INSTITUTION HAS CHANGED DURING THE PAST YEAR SO THAT THIS YEAR'S FALL ENROLLMENT REPORT IS SIGNIFICANTLY DIFFERENT FROM THE REPORT SUBMITTED IN FALL 1973, PLEASE EXPLAIN THE DIFFERENCES.

PLEASE READ THE FOLLOWING INSTRUCTIONS AND DEFINITIONS BEFORE COMPLETING THIS FORM. DETACH THIS PORTION AND RETURN THE COMPLETED FORM TO THE U.S. OFFICE OF EDUCATION, NATIONAL CENTER FOR EDUCATIONAL STATISTICS, ATTENTION: ROOM 2164-HEGIS, 400 MARYLAND AVENUE, SW., WASHINGTON, D.C. 20202, OR YOUR HEGIS COORDINATOR.

DEFINITIONS

FULL-TIME-EQUIVALENT ENROLLMENT data requested on this year's form are for **PART-TIME STUDENTS** only. Report FTE's as **WHOLE** numbers only.

FIRST-TIME STUDENTS – Entering freshmen who have not previously attended **ANY** college. Include students who attended college for the first-time in the summer of 1973. Also include students who entered with advanced standing *(college credits earned before graduation from high school).*

BACHELOR'S-DEGREE-CREDIT PROGRAMS – Any work creditable toward a bachelor's degree. In 2-year institutions, those programs from which the credits earned are transferable to a bachelor's degree program.

NON-BACHELOR'S-DEGREE-CREDIT PROGRAMS – Organized occupational curriculums of less than four years, primarily in the vocational and technical fields, not chiefly creditable toward a bachelor's degree. Normally terminal and result in formal recognition such as a certificate or diploma.

LOWER DIVISION – In 4-year institutions, includes freshmen and sophomores in bachelor's degree programs. In 2-year institutions, includes students in associate degree programs. Also includes, in all levels of institutions, students in terminal-occupational programs of one, two, or three years that result in formal recognition below the baccalaureate.

UPPER DIVISION – Students who have completed the sophomore year and typically are enrolled in a 4- or 5-year bachelor's degree program. *(Students in professional programs of 6 or more years should generally be included on line 08).*

UNCLASSIFIED STUDENTS – Not candidates for a degree or other formal award, although taking courses in regular classes with other students. This category includes students who cannot be classified by academic level as well as students who already have degrees but who are taking additional courses at the same degree level or lower; this also applies to students with degrees below the baccalaureate at 2-year institutions.

FIRST-PROFESSIONAL STUDENTS – Students enrolled in a professional school or program which required at least 2 academic years of college work for entrance and a total of at least 6 years for a degree. Report only students in those first-professional degree programs in the fields of medicine, law, and theology specified in Part A of OE Form 2300-2.5. Students Enrolled for Advanced Degrees. Students in programs requiring only 4 or 5 years beyond high school should be reported as undergraduates.

GRADUATE STUDENTS – Students who hold the bachelor's or first-professional degree, or equivalent, and are taking work at the graduate level.

FULL-TIME STUDENTS – Those whose academic load – coursework or other required activity – is at least 75% of the normal full-time load.

NORMAL FULL-TIME LOAD – Usually determined by dividing the total number of credits required for completing the program by the number of terms normally required to obtain them.

INSTRUCTIONS

NOTE: Listings of data for individual institutions are regularly included in published reports of this survey.

Proofread the completed report before returning it to the U.S. Office of Education.

This report should include only college-level students taking work creditable toward a bachelor's or higher degree or some other formal recognition below the baccalaureate.

If you need clarification of any item on the questionnaire, please call **Mr. George H. Wade**, U.S. Office of Education, (202) 245-8392. in Washington, D.C.

If exact counts are lacking for a particular category of students that should be reported, include an estimate for that group.

Do **NOT** fill out separate forms for extension centers. Only campuses with their own FICE code numbers should be reported on separate questionnaire. Extension students should be reported on the form for the main campus.

COMPLETE THIS FORM as soon as detailed enrollment breakdowns are available, but no later than November 1, 1974.

PLEASE RETURN YOUR ENROLLMENT DATA ON ONE OF THE ORIGINAL COPIES OF THE FORM SENT TO YOU. DO NOT SEND PHOTOSTATIC COPIES. ADDITIONAL COPIES OF THE FORM WILL BE SENT ON REQUEST

Do **NOT** include in this report:

(a) Students in noncredit adult education courses.

(b) Students taking courses at home by mail, radio, or television.

(c) Students enrolled only for "short courses."

(d) Auditors.

(e) Students studying abroad.

(f) Students in any branch campus or extension center in a foreign country.

(g) High school students taking college courses.

OE FORM 2300-2.3, 3/74 (Instructions)

DEPARTMENT OF HEALTH, EDUCATION, AND WELFARE EDUCATION DIVISION WASHINGTON, D.C. 20202 HIGHER EDUCATION GENERAL INFORMATION SURVEY (HEGIS XI) **FALL ENROLLMENT AND COMPLIANCE REPORT OF** **INSTITUTIONS OF HIGHER EDUCATION, 1976**	**PLEASE READ INSTRUCTIONS BEFORE COMPLETING THIS FORM.**	FORM APPROVED OMB NO. 51-R0738
		1. INSTITUTION CODE NUMBER
		2. DUE DATE **Not later than December 15, 1976**

NOTICE: This report is mandatory only for those institutions subject to the requirements of Title VI of the Civil Rights Act of 1964 and Title IX of the Education Amendments of 1972. For the other institutions, it is voluntary. See page 2 for further information.

When the survey form has been completed, please return it either directly to Department of Health, Education, and Welfare, Education Division, National Center for Education Statistics, ATTN: Room 2164-HEGIS, 400 Maryland Avenue, SW., Washington, D.C. 20202, or to the HEGIS coordinator, if there is a HEGIS coordinator in your State.

Please supply all the identifying information requested on this page.

3. NAME AND MAILING ADDRESS OF INSTITUTION OR CAMPUS COVERED BY THIS REPORT (include city, State, and ZIP code)	4. NAME AND TITLE OF RESPONDENT
	5. TELEPHONE NUMBER OF RESPONDENT (area code, local number, and extension)

PLEASE NOTE THAT EACH INSTITUTION, BRANCH, CAMPUS OR OTHER ENTITY SEPARATELY CERTIFIED BY THE ACCREDITATION AND INSTITUTIONAL ELIGIBILITY UNIT OF THE U.S. OFFICE OF EDUCATION, WITH IT'S OWN FICE CODE, AND LISTED SEPARATELY IN THE EDUCATION DIRECTORY - HIGHER EDUCATION, SHOULD BE REPORTED ON A SEPARATE SURVEY FORM AND NOT INCLUDED OR COMBINED WITH ANY OTHER SUCH CERTIFIED UNIT. BRANCHES, CAMPUSES, AND OTHER ORGANIZATIONAL ENTITIES NOT SEPARATELY CERTIFIED SHOULD BE INCLUDED WITH THE APPROPRIATE INSTITUTION OR BRANCH REPORT. IF SUCH ARE INCLUDED IN THIS REPORT, PLEASE LIST THEM BELOW.

ARE DATA FOR THIS UNIT INCLUDED IN THIS REPORT?	NAME OF BRANCH AND/OR OTHER CAMPUS	ADDRESS (city, State, and ZIP code)
☐ YES ☐ NO		
☐ YES ☐ NO		
☐ YES ☐ NO		

6. IF THE EDUCATIONAL ORGANIZATION OR ENTITY COVERED BY THIS SURVEY REPORT IS PART OF A MULTI-CAMPUS INSTITUTION, OR PART OF A SYSTEM OF INSTITUTIONS, PLEASE ENTER THE NAME OF THE INSTITUTION OR SYSTEM BELOW.
IF NOT APPLICABLE, CHECK HERE ➡ ☐

DEFINITIONS

MULTI-CAMPUS INSTITUTION. An organization bearing a resemblance to an institutional system, but unequivocally designated as a single institution with either of two organizational structures: (1) an institution having two or more campuses responsible to a central administration (which central administration may or may not be located on one of the administratively equal campuses) or (2) an institution having a main campus with one or more branch campuses attached to it.

MAIN CAMPUS. In those institutions comprised of a main campus and one or more branch campuses, the main campus (sometimes called the parent institution) is usually the location of the core, primary, or most comprehensive program. Unless the institution-wide central administrative office for such institutions is reported to be a different location, the main campus is also the location of the central administrative office.

BRANCH CAMPUS. A campus of an institution of higher education which is organized on a relatively permanent basis (i.e., has a relatively permanent administration), which offers an organized program or programs of work of at least 2 years (as opposed to courses), and which is located in a community different from that in which its parent institution is located. To be considered in a community different from that of the parent institution, a branch shall be located beyond a reasonable commuting distance from the main campus of the parent institution.

INSTITUTIONAL SYSTEM. A complex of two or more institutions of higher education, each separately organized or independently complete, under the control or supervision of a single administrative body.

OE FORM 2300-2.3, 3/76   PREVIOUS EDITIONS OF THIS FORM ARE OBSOLETE.

VOLUNTARY VERSUS REQUIRED REPORTING

This survey constitutes an integral part of the comprehensive system of statistics on higher education collected by the National Center for Education Statistics *(NCES)* as part of the Higher Education General Information Survey *(HEGIS)*.

In recent years, for the purpose of enforcing compliance with Federal regulations implementing civil rights laws applicable to institutions of higher education, the Office for Civil Rights *(OCR)* has been collecting similar enrollment data on a mandatory basis.

In order to lighten the burden on reporting institutions by eliminating the considerable duplication of effort in reporting enrollment data to two separate agencies, the two surveys have been combined into this single questionnaire and integrated into the HEGIS program for 1976.

Completion of this questionnaire is mandatory for all institutions of higher education which receive, are applicants for, or expect to be applicants for Federal financial assistance as defined in the Department of Health, Education and Welfare *(HEW)* regulation implementing Title VI *(45 CFR 80.13)*, or as defined in any HEW regulation implementing Title IX. *(See also the Instructions for completing this questionnaire.)*

Those institutions to which the regulations **do not apply** are not required to complete this questionnaire. However, it is hoped that institutions not subject to these provisions will voluntarily complete the entire survey--or at least the Summary page--in order that the data may represent the entire universe of higher education. **As a minimum** NCES requests that institutions complete columns 13 through 16 on the Summary page in order to enable NCES to continue to provide basic enrollment data serving the needs and interests of the higher education community.

INSTRUCTIONS AND DEFINITIONS

OTE. The card that forms the back cover of this report is for the convenience of respondents in providing preliminary data for a pre-publication release. The bottom half of the card is a self-mailer that can be detached without loosening the pages of the report.

GENERAL INSTRUCTIONS

·ead the completed report before returning it to the National Center ·ucation Statistics.

·port should include only college-level students taking work creditable ·d a bachelor's or higher degree or some other formal recognition below ·ccalaureate.

·ct counts are lacking for a particular category of students that should ·orted, include an estimate for that group.

·OT fill out separate forms for extension centers. Only campuses with ·own FICE code numbers should be reported on separate questionnaires. ·sion students should be reported on the form for the main campus.

·OT include in this report:

·) Students in noncredit adult education courses.

·) Students taking courses at home by mail, radio, or television.

·) Students enrolled only for "short courses."

·) Auditors.

·) Students studying abroad if their enrollment at the reporting institu-·n is only an administrative record and the fee is only nominal.

·) Students in any branch campus or extension center in a foreign ·untry.

·) High school students taking college courses.

·) Students known to be enrolled concurrently at another college or ·iversity, if the latter will report their enrollment *(to avoid double-·unting)*. Normally, the institution that will eventually grant the de-·ree should report the student's enrollment.

TE. No matter what the calendar system, report on this questionnaire ·· those students enrolled and only those credit-hours being earned dur-·the FALL TERM.

·u need CLARIFICATION of any item on the questionnaire that per-· to fall enrollment, please call the Survey Director, Mr. George H. ·e, NCES, (202) 245-8392, in Washington, D.C. 20202. Any questions ·erning the racial/ethnic categories or major fields of study should be ·ted to Mrs. Rose Brock, Office for Civil Rights, (202) 245-1788, in ·ington, D.C. 20201.

·OR FIELDS OF STUDY AND CORRESPONDING MAJOR FIELD ·ES.

·listing below identifies selected categories of major fields of study, and ·corresponding codes. These were taken directly from the **HEGIS Tax-·ny of Instructional Programs in Higher Education** and aggregated into the ·s listed. The field name and corresponding code number have been pre-·ted in the upper left-hand corner of each page. If your institution has no ·ents enrolled in any of the designated fields, check the box as indicated.

·) – Agriculture and Natural Resources
·) – Architecture and Environmental Design
·) – Biological Sciences
·) – Business and Management
·) – Engineering
·4 – Dentistry
·5 – Medicine
·8 – Veterinary Medicine
·) – Law
·) – Physical Sciences
·0 – All other *(fields not included above and undecided/undeclared)*
·9 – Summary *(total enrollment)*. In addition to separate reports for each of the major fields or sub-fields listed above, complete the Summary

report which aggregates the enrollment data on the individual field reports.

Columns 15 and 16 will be completed ONLY for the Summary re-port. Individual reports will NOT show data in columns 15 and 16.

FILING INSTRUCTIONS – COMPLIANCE REQUIREMENTS.

Title VI of the Civil Rights Act of 1964 requires that recipients of Federal financial assistance offer their benefits and services without regard to race, color, or national origin. Title IX of the Education Amendments of 1972 requires that the benefits and services of federally assisted educational pro-grams and activities be offered, with certain exceptions, nondiscriminatori-ly on the basis of sex. This report is one indicator utilized by the Office for Civil Rights in carrying out its responsibilities to verify compliance with Title VI and Title IX. Also applicable are Section 799-A, Part H, Title VII and Section 845, Part C, Title VIII of the Public Health Service Act of 1972.

This report is to be filed by all institutions of higher education which receive, are applicants for, or expect to be applicants for Federal financial assistance as defined in the Department of Health, Education, and Welfare Regulation implementing Title VI *(45 CFR 80.13)*, or as defined in any Department of Health, Education, and Welfare Regulation implementing Title IX. If your institution does not fall into any of these categories, please inform us of this fact.

Section 80.6(b) of the Regulation implementing Title VI, set forth below, and similar provisions of the Title VI Regulations of other Federal agencies, authorize collection of this information:
    80.6 Compliance information
        (b) Compliance reports***

Each recipient shall keep such records and submit to the responsible De-partment official or his designee timely, complete and accurate compli-ance reports at such times, and in such form and containing such infor-mation, as the responsible Department official or his designee may deter-mine to be necessary to enable him to ascertain whether the recipient has complied or is complying with this part. For example, recipients should have available for the Department racial and ethnic data showing the extent to which members of minority groups are beneficiaries of and participants in federally-assisted programs. In the case of any program under which a primary recipient extends Federal financial assistance to any other recipient, such other recipient shall also submit such compli-ance reports to the primary recipient as may be necessary to enable the primary recipient to carry out its obligations under this part.

Each institution of higher education, as well as each separately certified branch campus *(with its own FICE code number)* that is subject to the HEW civil rights regulations cited above is required to complete a separate compli-ance report for certain selected major fields *(listed below)* as indicated in the upper left-hand corner of each page.

RACIAL/ETHNIC CATEGORIES.

The following five racial/ethnic categories are utilized in the survey:

    Black Non-Hispanic
    American Indian or Alaskan Native
    Asian or Pacific Islander
    Hispanic
    White Non-Hispanic

In addition, non-resident aliens, i.e., those members of the aforementioned groups who have not been admitted to the United States for permanent residence, should be separately identified as a sixth category; the non-resi-dent aliens are not separately requested by racial/ethnic group, but only in totals.

The definitions for these categories are:

    Non-resident alien. A person who is not a citizen of the United States and who is in this country on a temporary basis and does not have the right to remain indefinitely. Resident aliens, non-citizens who have been lawfully admitted for permanent residence *(and who hold a "green card," Form I-151),* are to be reported in the appropriate racial/ethnic categories along with United States citizens. Nonresident aliens are to be reported separately, in the columns provided, rather than in any of the five racial/ethnic categories which follow.

Black, non-Hispanic. A person having origins in any of the black racial groups *(except those of Hispanic origin).*

American Indian or Alaskan Native. A person having origins in any of the original peoples of North America.

Asian or Pacific Islander. A person having origins in any of the original peoples of the Far East, Southeast Asia, or the Pacific Islands. This area includes, for example, China, Japan, Korea, the Philippine Islands, and Samoa.

Hispanic. A person of Mexican, Puerto Rican, Cuban, Central or South American, or other Spanish culture or origin, regardless of race.

White, non-Hispanic. A person having origins in any of the original peoples of Europe, North Africa, the Middle East or the Indian subcontinent *(except those of Hispanic origin).*

Racial/ethnic designations as used in this survey do not denote scientific definitions of anthropological origins. For the purpose of this report, a student may be included in the group to which he or she appears to belong, identifies with, or is regarded in the community as belonging. However, no person may be counted in more than one racial/ethnic group.

The manner of collecting the racial/ethnic information is left to the discretion of the institution provided that the system which is established results in reasonably accurate data. One acceptable method is a properly controlled system of post-enrollment self-identification by students. If a self-identification method is utilized, a verification procedure to ascertain the completeness and accuracy of student submissions should also be employed where feasible. In order to provide reasonably accurate data, the institution may require students to complete a questionnaire and/or identify themselves by name or otherwise when providing information. The fact that the information is being gathered to comply with Title VI of the Civil Rights Act of 1964 and Title IX of the Education Amendments of 1972 may be disseminated in the manner and to the extent that the administration deems appropriate.

DEFINITIONS

UNDERGRADUATES. Students enrolled in a 4- or 5-year bachelor's degree program, in an associate degree program, or in a vocational or technical program that is normally terminal and results in formal recognition below the baccalaureate.

CLASS LEVEL. Whether first-year, second-year, etc., should be determined in a logical, consistent, and identifiable way. Usually, a student's class level would be based on the proportion of total requirements he has obtained toward the completion of the degree program in which he is enrolled, according to the number of years normally required to obtain them.

FIRST-TIME FRESHMEN. Entering freshmen who have not previously attended ANY college. Include students enrolled in the fall term who attended college for the first time in the summer of 1976. Also include students who entered with advanced standing *(college credits earned before graduation from high school)* at the freshman level.

OTHER FIRST-YEAR. First-year students who entered the institution before the summer of 1976.

UNCLASSIFIED STUDENTS. Not candidates for a degree or other formal award, although taking courses in regular classes with other students.

UNDERGRADUATE LEVEL. Includes but is not limited to undergraduates who cannot be classified by class standing; for example, new transfer students. Also included are students who already have bachelor's degrees or awards below the baccalaureate but are taking courses at the same level

TOTAL
CREDITS
ENROLLED
FOR

(16)

9999 – Sur
(to.

ALL STUDE
(resident

1. NAME OF INSTITUTION

2. INSTITUTION CODE NUMBER

3. DUE DATE Not later than December 15, 1976

0100 — Agriculture and Natural Resources

check, if no students in this field □

ALL STUDENTS ENROLLED (resident and extension)	LINE NO.	NON-RESIDENT ALIEN MEN (1)	WOMEN (2)	BLACK NON-HISPANIC MEN (3)	WOMEN (4)	AMERICAN INDIAN OR ALASKAN NATIVE MEN (5)	WOMEN (6)	ASIAN OR PACIFIC ISLANDER MEN (7)	WOMEN (8)	HISPANIC MEN (9)	WOMEN (10)	WHITE NON-HISPANIC MEN (11)	WOMEN (12)	TOTAL (sum of columns (1) through (12)) MEN (13)	WOMEN (14)
ALL STUDENTS ENROLLED	01														
I. FULL-TIME STUDENTS															
A. Undergraduates, total	02														
1. First-time freshmen	03														
2. Other first-year	04														
3. Second-year	05														
4. Third-year	06														
5. Fourth-year and beyond	07														
B. Unclassified students, total	08														
1. Undergraduate level	09														
2. Postbaccalaureate level	10														
C. First-professional students	11														
D. Graduate students, total	12														
1. First-year	13														
2. Beyond the first year	14														
TOTAL FULL-TIME STUDENTS															
II. PART-TIME STUDENTS															
A. Undergraduates, total	15														
1. First-time freshmen	16														
2. Other first-year	17														
3. Second-year	18														
4. Third-year	19														
5. Fourth-year and beyond	20														
B. Unclassified students, total	21														
1. Undergraduate level	22														
2. Postbaccalaureate level	23														
C. First-professional students	24														
D. Graduate students, total	25														
1. First-year	26														
2. Beyond the first year	27														
TOTAL PART-TIME STUDENTS	28														
III. GRAND TOTAL, ALL STUDENTS	29														

6

CERTIFICATION

I CERTIFY that the information given above is complete, true, and correct to the best of my knowledge and belief. (A willfully false statement is punishable by law, U.S. Code, Title 18, Section 1001.)

NAME OF PERSON FURNISHING INFORMATION

SIGNATURE

TITLE

TELEPHONE — AREA CODE NUMBER — EXTENSION

DATE

OE FORM 2300-2.3, 3/76   PREVIOUS EDITIONS OF THIS FORM ARE OBSOLETE.

1. NAME OF INSTITUTION	2. INSTITUTION CODE NUMBER	3. DUE DATE Not later than December 15, 1976	FORM APPROVED OMB NO. 51-R0738

0200 – Architecture and Environmental Design

check, if no students in this field ☐

ALL STUDENTS ENROLLED (resident and extension)	LINE NO.	NON-RESIDENT ALIEN		BLACK NON-HISPANIC		AMERICAN INDIAN OR ALASKAN NATIVE		ASIAN OR PACIFIC ISLANDER		HISPANIC		WHITE NON-HISPANIC		TOTAL (sum of columns (1) through (12))	
		MEN (1)	WOMEN (2)	MEN (3)	WOMEN (4)	MEN (5)	WOMEN (6)	MEN (7)	WOMEN (8)	MEN (9)	WOMEN (10)	MEN (11)	WOMEN (12)	MEN (13)	WOMEN (14)
I. FULL-TIME STUDENTS															
A. Undergraduates, total	01														
1. First-time freshmen	02														
2. Other first-year	03														
3. Second-year	04														
4. Third-year	05														
5. Fourth-year and beyond	06														
B. Unclassified students, total	07														
1. Undergraduate level	08														
2. Postbaccalaureate level	09														
C. First-professional students	10														
D. Graduate students, total	11														
1. First-year	12														
2. Beyond the first year	13														
TOTAL FULL-TIME STUDENTS	14														
II. PART-TIME STUDENTS															
A. Undergraduates, total	15														
1. First-time freshmen	16														
2. Other first-year	17														
3. Second-year	18														
4. Third-year	19														
5. Fourth-year and beyond	20														
B. Unclassified students, total	21														
1. Undergraduate level	22														
2. Postbaccalaureate level	23														
C. First-professional students	24														
D. Graduate students, total	25														
1. First-year	26														
2. Beyond the first year	27														
TOTAL PART-TIME STUDENTS	28														
III. GRAND TOTAL, ALL STUDENTS	29														

CERTIFICATION	NAME OF PERSON FURNISHING INFORMATION		TITLE		DATE

I CERTIFY that the information given above is complete, true, and correct to the best of my knowledge and belief. (A willfully false statement is punishable by law, U.S. Code, Title 18, Section 1001.)

SIGNATURE

AREA CODE NUMBER   TELEPHONE   EXTENSION

OE FORM 2300-2.3, 3/76   PREVIOUS EDITIONS OF THIS FORM ARE OBSOLETE.

0500 – Business and Management

check, if no students in this field ☐

ALL STUDENTS ENROLLED (resident and extension)	LINE NO.	NON-RESIDENT ALIEN		BLACK NON-HISPANIC		AMERICAN INDIAN OR ALASKAN NATIVE		ASIAN OR PACIFIC ISLANDER		HISPANIC		WHITE NON-HISPANIC		TOTAL (sum of columns (1) through (12))	
		MEN (1)	WOMEN (2)	MEN (3)	WOMEN (4)	MEN (5)	WOMEN (6)	MEN (7)	WOMEN (8)	MEN (9)	WOMEN (10)	MEN (11)	WOMEN (12)	MEN (13)	WOMEN (14)
I. FULL-TIME STUDENTS															
A. Undergraduates, total	01														
1. First-time freshmen	02														
2. Other first-year	03														
3. Second-year	04														
4. Third-year	05														
5. Fourth-year and beyond	06														
B. Unclassified students, total	07														
1. Undergraduate level	08														
2. Postbaccalaureate level	09														
C. First-professional students	10														
D. Graduate students, total	11														
1. First-year	12														
2. Beyond the first year	13														
TOTAL FULL-TIME STUDENTS	14														
II. PART-TIME STUDENTS															
A. Undergraduates, total	15														
1. First-time freshmen	16														
2. Other first-year	17														
3. Second-year	18														
4. Third-year	19														
5. Fourth-year and beyond	20														
B. Unclassified students, total	21														
1. Undergraduate level	22														
2. Postbaccalaureate level	23														
C. First-professional students	24														
D. Graduate students, total	25														
1. First-year	26														
2. Beyond the first year	27														
TOTAL PART-TIME STUDENTS	28														
III. GRAND TOTAL, ALL STUDENTS	29														

9

CERTIFICATION

NAME OF PERSON FURNISHING INFORMATION | TITLE

I CERTIFY that the information given above is complete, true, and correct to the best of my knowledge and belief. (A willfully false statement is punishable by law, U.S. Code, Title 18, Section 1001.)

SIGNATURE

AREA CODE NUMBER | TELEPHONE | EXTENSION | DATE

III. GRAND TOTAL,
ALL STUDENTS

CEI

I CERTIFY that the
plete, true, and corre
and belief. (A willful
by law, U.S. Code, Ti

1. NAME OF INSTITUTION   2. INSTITUTION CODE NUMBER   3. DUE DATE Not later than December 15, 1976.

1206 — Medicine

ALL STUDENTS ENROLLED (resident and extension)   check, if no students in this field ☐

	LINE NO.	NON-RESIDENT ALIEN MEN (1)	NON-RESIDENT ALIEN WOMEN (2)	BLACK NON-HISPANIC MEN (3)	BLACK NON-HISPANIC WOMEN (4)	AMERICAN INDIAN OR ALASKAN NATIVE MEN (5)	AMERICAN INDIAN OR ALASKAN NATIVE WOMEN (6)	ASIAN OR PACIFIC ISLANDER MEN (7)	ASIAN OR PACIFIC ISLANDER WOMEN (8)	HISPANIC MEN (9)	HISPANIC WOMEN (10)	WHITE NON-HISPANIC MEN (11)	WHITE NON-HISPANIC WOMEN (12)	TOTAL (sum of columns (1) through (12)) MEN (13)	TOTAL WOMEN (14)
I. FULL-TIME STUDENTS															
A. Undergraduates, total	01														
1. First-time freshmen	02														
2. Other first-year	03														
3. Second-year	04														
4. Third-year	05														
5. Fourth-year and beyond	06														
B. Unclassified students, total	07														
1. Undergraduate level	08														
2. Postbaccalaureate level	09														
C. First-professional students	10														
D. Graduate students, total	11														
1. First-year	12														
2. Beyond the first year	13														
TOTAL FULL-TIME STUDENTS	14														
II. PART-TIME STUDENTS															
A. Undergraduates, total	15														
1. First-time freshmen	16														
2. Other first-year	17														
3. Second-year	18														
4. Third-year	19														
5. Fourth-year and beyond	20														
B. Unclassified students, total	21														
1. Undergraduate level	22														
2. Postbaccalaureate level	23														
C. First-professional students	24														
D. Graduate students, total	25														
1. First-year	26														
2. Beyond the first year	27														
TOTAL PART-TIME STUDENTS	28														
III. GRAND TOTAL, ALL STUDENTS	29														

CERTIFICATION

I CERTIFY that the information given above is complete, true, and correct to the best of my knowledge and belief. (A willfully false statement is punishable by law, U.S. Code, Title 18, Section 1001.)

NAME OF PERSON FURNISHING INFORMATION

SIGNATURE   TITLE   DATE

TELEPHONE   AREA CODE   NUMBER   EXTENSION

HE FORM 2300-2.3, 3/76   PREVIOUS EDITIONS OF THIS FORM ARE OBSOLETE.

12

1. NAME OF INSTITUTION		2. INSTITUTION CODE NUMBER	3. DUE DATE Not later than December 15, 1976	FORM APPROVED OMB NO. 51-R0738

1218 – Veterinary Medicine

check, if no students in this field ☐

ALL STUDENTS ENROLLED (resident and extension)	LINE NO.	NON-RESIDENT ALIEN		BLACK NON-HISPANIC		AMERICAN INDIAN OR ALASKAN NATIVE		ASIAN OR PACIFIC ISLANDER		HISPANIC		WHITE NON-HISPANIC		TOTAL (sum of columns (1) through (12))	
		MEN (1)	WOMEN (2)	MEN (3)	WOMEN (4)	MEN (5)	WOMEN (6)	MEN (7)	WOMEN (8)	MEN (9)	WOMEN (10)	MEN (11)	WOMEN (12)	MEN (13)	WOMEN (14)
I. FULL-TIME STUDENTS															
A. Undergraduates, total	01														
1. First-time freshmen	02														
2. Other first-year	03														
3. Second-year	04														
4. Third-year	05														
5. Fourth-year and beyond	06														
B. Unclassified students, total	07														
1. Undergraduate level	08														
2. Postbaccalaureate level	09														
C. First-professional students	10														
D. Graduate students, total	11														
1. First-year	12														
2. Beyond the first year	13														
TOTAL FULL-TIME STUDENTS	14														
II. PART-TIME STUDENTS															
A. Undergraduates, total	15														
1. First-time freshmen	16														
2. Other first-year	17														
3. Second-year	18														
4. Third-year	19														
5. Fourth-year and beyond	20														
B. Unclassified students, total	21														
1. Undergraduate level	22														
2. Postbaccalaureate level	23														
C. First-professional students	24														
D. Graduate students, total	25														
1. First-year	26														
2. Beyond the first year	27														
TOTAL PART-TIME STUDENTS	28														
III. GRAND TOTAL, ALL STUDENTS	29														

CERTIFICATION

I CERTIFY that the information given above is complete, true, and correct to the best of my knowledge and belief. (A willfully false statement is punishable by law, U.S. Code, Title 18, Section 1001.)

NAME OF PERSON FURNISHING INFORMATION | TITLE

SIGNATURE | DATE

AREA CODE | NUMBER | EXTENSION

TELEPHONE

PREVIOUS EDITIONS OF THIS FORM ARE OBSOLETE.

1900 – Physical Sciences

check, if no students in this field ☐

ALL STUDENTS ENROLLED (resident and extension)	LINE NO.	NON-RESIDENT ALIEN		BLACK NON-HISPANIC		AMERICAN INDIAN OR ALASKAN NATIVE		ASIAN OR PACIFIC ISLANDER		HISPANIC		WHITE NON-HISPANIC		TOTAL (sum of columns (1) through (12))	
		MEN (1)	WOMEN (2)	MEN (3)	WOMEN (4)	MEN (5)	WOMEN (6)	MEN (7)	WOMEN (8)	MEN (9)	WOMEN (10)	MEN (11)	WOMEN (12)	MEN (13)	WOMEN (14)
I. FULL-TIME STUDENTS	01														
A. Undergraduates, total	02														
1. First-time freshmen	03														
2. Other first-year	04														
3. Second-year	05														
4. Third-year	06														
5. Fourth-year and beyond	07														
B. Unclassified students, total	08														
1. Undergraduate level	09														
2. Postbaccalaureate level	10														
C. First-professional students	11														
D. Graduate students, total	12														
1. First-year	13														
2. Beyond the first year	14														
TOTAL FULL-TIME STUDENTS	15														
II. PART-TIME STUDENTS	16														
A. Undergraduates, total	17														
1. First-time freshmen	18														
2. Other first-year	19														
3. Second-year	20														
4. Third-year	21														
5. Fourth-year and beyond	22														
B. Unclassified students, total	23														
1. Undergraduate level	24														
2. Postbaccalaureate level	25														
C. First-professional students	26														
D. Graduate students, total	27														
1. First-year	28														
2. Beyond the first year	29														
TOTAL PART-TIME STUDENTS	28														
III. GRAND TOTAL, ALL STUDENTS	29														

CERTIFICATION

I CERTIFY that the information given above is complete, true, and correct to the best of my knowledge and belief. (A willfully false statement is punishable by law, U.S. Code, Title 18, Section 1001.)

NAME OF PERSON FURNISHING INFORMATION

SIGNATURE

TITLE

TELEPHONE

AREA CODE   NUMBER   EXTENSION

DATE

OE FORM 2300-2.3, 3/76   PREVIOUS EDITIONS OF THIS FORM ARE OBSOLETE.

15

1. NAME OF INSTITUTION

2. INSTITUTION CODE NUMBER

3. DUE DATE
Not later than December 15, 1976

9000 — All other

check, if no students in this field ☐

ALL STUDENTS ENROLLED (resident and extension)	LINE NO.	NON-RESIDENT ALIEN		BLACK NON-HISPANIC		AMERICAN INDIAN OR ALASKAN NATIVE		ASIAN OR PACIFIC ISLANDER		HISPANIC		WHITE NON-HISPANIC		TOTAL (sum of columns (1) through (12))	
		MEN (1)	WOMEN (2)	MEN (3)	WOMEN (4)	MEN (5)	WOMEN (6)	MEN (7)	WOMEN (8)	MEN (9)	WOMEN (10)	MEN (11)	WOMEN (12)	MEN (13)	WOMEN (14)
I. FULL-TIME STUDENTS															
A. Undergraduates, total	01														
1. First-time freshmen	02														
2. Other first-year	03														
3. Second-year	04														
4. Third-year	05														
5. Fourth-year and beyond	06														
B. Unclassified students, total	07														
1. Undergraduate level	08														
2. Postbaccalaureate level	09														
C. First-professional students	10														
D. Graduate students, total	11														
1. First-year	12														
2. Beyond the first year	13														
TOTAL FULL-TIME STUDENTS	14														
II. PART-TIME STUDENTS															
A. Undergraduates, total	15														
ime freshmen	16														
2. Other first-year	17														
3. Second-year	18														
4. Third-year	19														
5. Fourth-year and beyond	20														
B. Unclassified students, total	21														
1. Undergraduate level	22														
2. Postbaccalaureate level	23														
C. First-professional students	24														
D. Graduate students, total	25														
1. First-year	26														
2. Beyond the first year	27														
TOTAL PART-TIME STUDENTS	28														
III. GRAND TOTAL, ALL STUDENTS	29														

CERTIFICATION

I CERTIFY that the information given above is complete, true, and correct to the best of my knowledge and belief. (A willfully false statement is punishable by law, U.S. Code, Title 18, Section 1001.)

NAME OF PERSON FURNISHING INFORMATION

TITLE

SIGNATURE

TELEPHONE
AREA CODE   NUMBER   EXTENSION

DATE

OE FORM 2300-2.3, 3/76   PREVIOUS EDITIONS OF THIS FORM ARE OBSOLETE.

16

DEPARTMENT OF HEALTH, EDUCATION, AND WELFARE
EDUCATION DIVISION
WASHINGTON, D.C. 20202

HIGHER EDUCATION GENERAL INFORMATION SURVEY (HEGIS XIII)

PLEASE READ INSTRUCTIONS BEFORE COMPLETING THIS FORM.	FORM APPROVED OMB NO. 51—R0738
	1. INSTITUTION CODE NUMBER
	2. DUE DATE
	Not later than November 15, 1978

FALL ENROLLMENT AND COMPLIANCE REPORT OF INSTITUTIONS OF HIGHER EDUCATION, 1978

NOTICE: This report is mandatory only for those institutions subject to the requirements of Title VI of the Civil Rights Act of 1964 and Title IX of the Education Amendments of 1972. For the other institutions, it is voluntary. See page 2 for further information.

Please supply all the identifying information requested on this page. When the survey form has been completed, please return it either directly to Department of Health, Education, and Welfare, Education Division, National Center for Education Statistics, ATTN: Room 3073 HEGIS, 400 Maryland Avenue, SW, Washington, D.C. 20202, or to the HEGIS coordinator, if there is a HEGIS coordinator in your State.

3. NAME AND MAILING ADDRESS OF INSTITUTION OR CAMPUS COVERED BY THIS REPORT (include city, State, and ZIP code)

4. NAME AND TITLE OF RESPONDENT

5. TELEPHONE NUMBER OF RESPONDENT (area code, local number, and extension)

6. PLEASE NOTE THAT EACH INSTITUTION, BRANCH, CAMPUS OR OTHER ENTITY SEPARATELY CERTIFIED BY THE ACCREDITATION AND INSTITUTIONAL ELIGIBILITY UNIT OF THE U.S. OFFICE OF EDUCATION, WITH IT'S OWN FICE CODE, AND LISTED SEPARATELY IN THE EDUCATION DIRECTORY - HIGHER EDUCATION, SHOULD BE REPORTED ON A SEPARATE SURVEY FORM AND NOT INCLUDED OR COMBINED WITH ANY OTHER SUCH CERTIFIED UNIT. BRANCHES, CAMPUSES, AND OTHER ORGANIZATIONAL ENTITIES NOT SEPARATELY CERTIFIED SHOULD BE INCLUDED WITH THE APPROPRIATE INSTITUTION OR BRANCH REPORT. IF SUCH ARE INCLUDED IN THIS REPORT, PLEASE LIST THEM BELOW.

ARE DATA FOR THIS UNIT INCLUDED IN THIS REPORT?	NAME OF BRANCH AND/OR OTHER CAMPUS	ADDRESS (city, State, and ZIP code)
☐ YES ☐ NO		
☐ YES ☐ NO		
☐ YES ☐ NO		

7. IF THE EDUCATIONAL ORGANIZATION OR ENTITY COVERED BY THIS SURVEY REPORT IS PART OF A MULTI-CAMPUS INSTITUTION, OR PART OF A SYSTEM OF INSTITUTIONS, PLEASE ENTER THE NAME OF THE INSTITUTION OR SYSTEM BELOW. IF NOT APPLICABLE, CHECK HERE ➤ ☐

DEFINITIONS

MULTI-CAMPUS INSTITUTION. An organization bearing a resemblance to an institutional system, but unequivocally designated as a single institution with either of two organizational structures: (1) an institution having two or more campuses responsible to a central administration (which central administration may or may not be located on one of the administratively equal campuses) or (2) an institution having a main campus with one or more branch campuses attached to it.

MAIN CAMPUS. In those institutions comprised of a main campus and one or more branch campuses, the main campus (sometimes called the parent institution) is usually the location of the core, primary, or most comprehensive program. Unless the institution-wide or central administrative office for such institutions is reported to be at a different location, the main campus is also the location of the central administrative office.

BRANCH CAMPUS. A campus of an institution of higher education which is organized on a relatively permanent basis (i.e., has a relatively permanent administration), which offers an organized program or programs of work of at least 2 years (as opposed to courses), and which is located in a community different from that in which its parent institution is located. To be considered in a community different from that of the parent institution, a branch shall be located beyond a reasonable commuting distance from the main campus of the parent institution.

INSTITUTIONAL SYSTEM. A complex of two or more institutions of higher education, each separately organized or independently complete, under the control or supervision of a single administrative body.

OE FORM 2300-2.3, 7/78 (FM Control No. 56)   REPLACES OE FORM 2300-2.3, 4/77, WHICH IS OBSOLETE

VOLUNTARY VERSUS REQUIRED REPORTING

This survey constitutes an integral part of the comprehensive system of statistics on higher education collected by the National Center for Education Statistics *(NCES)* as part of the Higher Education General Information Survey *(HEGIS)*.

In recent years, for the purpose of enforcing compliance with Federal regulations implementing civil rights laws applicable to institutions of higher education, the Office for Civil Rights *(OCR)* has been collecting similar enrollment data on a mandatory basis.

In order to lighten the burden on reporting institutions by eliminating the considerable duplication of effort in reporting enrollment data to two separate agencies, the two surveys have been combined into this single questionnaire and integrated into the HEGIS program.

Completion of this questionnaire is mandatory for all institutions of higher education which receive, are applicants for, or expect to be applicants for Federal financial assistance as defined in the Department of Health, Education and Welfare *(HEW)* regulation implementing Title VI *(45 CFR 80.13)*, or as defined in any HEW regulation implementing Title IX. *(See also the Instructions for completing this questionnaire.)*

Those institutions to which the regulations **do not apply** are not required to complete this questionnaire. However, it is hoped that institutions not subject to these provisions will voluntarily complete the entire survey--or at least the Summary page--in order that the data may represent the entire universe of higher education. **As a minimum** NCES requests that institutions complete columns 13 through 15 on the Summary page in order to enable NCES to continue to provide basic enrollment data serving the needs and interests of the higher education community.

INSTRUCTIONS AND DEFINITIONS

NOTE. The card that forms the back cover of this report is for the convenience of respondents in providing preliminary data for a pre-publication release. The bottom half of the card is a self-mailer that can be detached without loosening the pages of the report.

GENERAL INSTRUCTIONS

Proofread the completed report before returning it to the National Center for Education Statistics.

This report should include only college-level students taking work creditable toward a bachelor's or higher degree or some other formal recognition below the baccalaureate.

If exact counts are lacking for a particular category of students that should be reported, include an estimate for that group.

Do NOT fill out separate forms for extension centers. Only campuses with their own FICE code numbers should be reported on separate questionnaires. Extension students should be reported on the form for the main campus.

Do NOT include in this report:

(a) Students in noncredit adult education courses.

(b) Students taking courses at home by mail, radio, or television.

(c) Students enrolled only for "short courses."

(d) Auditors.

(e) Students studying abroad if their enrollment at the reporting institution is only an administrative record and the fee is only nominal.

(f) Students in any branch campus or extension center in a foreign country.

(g) High school students taking college courses.

(h) Students known to be enrolled concurrently at another college or university, if the latter will report their enrollment *(to avoid double-counting)*. Normally, the institution that will eventually grant the degree should report the student's enrollment.

NOTE. No matter what the calendar system, report on this questionnaire only those students enrolled and only those credit-hours being earned during the FALL TERM.

If you need CLARIFICATION of any item on the questionnaire that pertains to fall enrollment, please call the Survey Director, Dr. Andrew J. Pepin, NCES, (202) 245-8392, in Washington, D.C. 20202. Any questions concerning the racial/ethnic categories or major fields of study should be directed to Ms. Carol Campbell, Office for Civil Rights, (202) 245-7420, in Washington, D.C. 20201.

MAJOR FIELDS OF STUDY AND CORRESPONDING MAJOR FIELD CODES.

The listing below identifies selected categories of major fields of study, and their corresponding codes. These were taken directly from the HEGIS Taxonomy of Instructional Programs in Higher Education and aggregated into the fields listed. The field name and corresponding code number have been pre-printed in the upper left-hand corner of each page. If your institution has no students enrolled in any of the designated fields, check the box as indicated. Students enrolled in the fields of Dentistry, Medicine, Veterinary Medicine and Law are not to be reported as undergraduate or graduate students but only as First-Professional students. Students in these programs requiring only 4 or 5 years beyond high school should be reported as undergraduates in the appropriate fields.

0100 – Agriculture and Natural Resources
0200 – Architecture and Environmental Design
0400 – Biological Sciences
0500 – Business and Management
0900 – Engineering
1204 – Dentistry
1206 – Medicine
1218 – Veterinary Medicine
1400 – Law
1900 – Physical Sciences

OE FORM 2300-2.3, 7/78 *(FM Control No. 56)*

9000 - All other *(fields not included above and undecided/undeclared)*
9999 – Summary *(total enrollment)*. In addition to separate reports for each of the major fields or sub-fields listed above, complete the Summary report which aggregates the enrollment data on the individual field reports.

Column 15 will be completed ONLY for the Summary report. Individual reports will NOT show data in column 15.

FILING INSTRUCTIONS – COMPLIANCE REQUIREMENTS.

Title VI of the Civil Rights Act of 1964 requires that recipients of Federal financial assistance offer their benefits and services without regard to race, color, or national origin. Title IX of the Education Amendments of 1972 requires that the benefits and services of federally assisted educational programs and activities be offered, with certain exceptions, nondiscriminatorily on the basis of sex. This report is one indicator utilized by the Office for Civil Rights in carrying out its responsibilities to verify compliance with Title VI and Title IX. Also applicable are Section 799-A, Part H, Title VII and Section 845, Part C, Title VIII of the Public Health Service Act of 1972.

This report is to be filed by all institutions of higher education which receive, are applicants for, or expect to be applicants for Federal financial assistance as defined in the Department of Health, Education, and Welfare Regulation implementing Title VI *(45 CFR 80.13)*, or as defined in any Department of Health, Education, and Welfare Regulation implementing Title IX. If your institution does not fall into any of these categories, please inform us of this fact.

Section 80.6(b) of the Regulation implementing Title VI, set forth below, and similar provisions of the Title VI Regulations of other Federal agencies, authorize collection of this information:

    80.6 Compliance information
      (b) Compliance reports***

Each recipient shall keep such records and submit to the responsible Department official or his designee timely, complete and accurate compliance reports at such times, and in such form and containing such information, as the responsible Department official or his designee may determine to be necessary to enable him to ascertain whether the recipient has complied or is complying with this part. For example, recipients should have available for the Department racial and ethnic data showing the extent to which members of minority groups are beneficiaries of and participants in federally-assisted programs. In the case of any program under which a primary recipient extends Federal financial assistance to any other recipient, such other recipient shall also submit such compliance reports to the primary recipient as may be necessary to enable the primary recipient to carry out its obligations under this part.

Each institution of higher education, as well as each separately certified branch campus *(with its own FICE code number)* that is subject to the HEW civil rights regulations cited above is required to complete a separate compliance report for certain selected major fields *(listed below)* as indicated in the upper left-hand corner of each page.

RACIAL/ETHNIC CATEGORIES.

The following five racial/ethnic categories are utilized in the survey:

    Black Non-Hispanic
    American Indian or Alaskan Native
    Asian or Pacific Islander
    Hispanic
    White Non-Hispanic

In addition, non-resident aliens, i.e., those members of the aforementioned groups who have not been admitted to the United States for permanent residence, should be separately identified as a sixth category; the non-resident aliens are not separately requested by racial/ethnic group, but only in totals.

The definitions for these categories are:

    Non-resident alien. A person who is not a citizen of the United States and who is in this country on a temporary basis and does not

3   REPLACES OE FORM 2300-2.3, 4/77, WHICH IS OBSOLET

have the right to remain indefinitely. Resident aliens, non-citizens who have been lawfully admitted for permanent residence *(and who hold a "green card," Form I-151)*, are to be reported in the appropriate racial/ethnic categories along with United States citizens. Non-resident aliens are to be reported separately, in the columns provided, rather than in any of the five racial/ethnic categories which follow.

Black Non-Hispanic. A person having origins in any of the black racial groups of Africa.

American Indian or Alaskan Native. A person having origins in any of the original peoples of North America, and who maintains cultural identification through tribal affiliation or community recognition.

Asian or Pacific Islander. A person having origins in any of the original peoples of the Far East, Southeast Asia, the Indian subcontinent, or the Pacific Islands. This area includes, for example, China, India, Japan, Korea, the Philippine Islands, and Samoa.

Hispanic. A person of Mexican, Puerto Rican, Cuban, Central or South American or other Spanish culture or origin, regardless of race.

White Non-Hispanic. A person having origins in any of the original peoples of Europe, North Africa, or in the Middle East.

Racial/ethnic designations as used in this survey do not denote scientific definitions of anthropological origins. For the purpose of this report, a student may be included in the group to which he or she appears to belong, identifies with, or is regarded in the community as belonging. However, no person may be counted in more than one racial/ethnic group.

The manner of collecting the racial/ethnic information is left to the discretion of the institution provided that the system which is established results in reasonably accurate data. One acceptable method is a properly controlled system of post-enrollment self-identification by students. If a self-identification method is utilized, a verification procedure to ascertain the completeness and accuracy of student submissions should also be employed where feasible. In order to provide reasonably accurate data, the institution may require students to complete a questionnaire and/or identify themselves by name or otherwise when providing information. The fact that the information is being gathered to comply with Title VI of the Civil Rights Act of 1964 and Title IX of the Education Amendments of 1972 may be disseminated in the manner and to the extent that the administration deems appropriate.

DEFINITIONS

UNDERGRADUATES. Students enrolled in a 4- or 5-year bachelor's degree program, in an associate degree program, or in a vocational or technical program that is normally terminal and results in formal recognition below the baccalaureate.

CLASS LEVEL. Whether first-year, second-year, etc., should be determined in a logical, consistent, and identifiable way. Usually, a student's class level would be based on the proportion of total requirements he has obtained toward the completion of the degree program in which he is enrolled, according to the number of years normally required to obtain them.

FIRST-TIME FRESHMEN. Entering freshmen who have not previously attended ANY college. Include students enrolled in the fall term who attended college for the first time in the summer of 1978. Also include students who entered with advanced standing *(college credits earned before graduation from high school)* at the freshman level.

1. NAME OF INSTITUTION

IM APPROVED 3 NO. 51—R073B

9999 — Summary (total enrollment)

ALL STUDENTS ENROLLED (resident and extension)	LINE NO.	NON-RESIDENT ALIEN		BLACK NON-HISPANIC		AMERICAN INDIAN OR ALASKAN NATIVE		ASIAN OR PACIFIC ISLANDER		HISPANIC		WHITE NON-HISPANIC		TOTAL (sum of columns (1) through (12))		FTE OF PART-TIME
		MEN (1)	WOMEN (2)	MEN (3)	WOMEN (4)	MEN (5)	WOMEN (6)	MEN (7)	WOMEN (8)	MEN (9)	WOMEN (10)	MEN (11)	WOMEN (12)	MEN (13)	WOMEN (14)	(15)
I. FULL-TIME STUDENTS																
A. Undergraduates, total	01															
1. First-time freshmen	02															
2. Other first-year	03															
3. Second-year	04															
4. Third-year	05															
5. Fourth-year and beyond	06															
B. Unclassified students, total	07															
1. Undergraduate level	08															
2. Postbaccalaureate level	09															
C. First-professional students	10															
D. Graduate students, total	11															
1. First-year	12															
2. Beyond the first year	13															
TOTAL FULL-TIME STUDENTS	14															
II. PART-TIME STUDENTS																
A. Undergraduates, total	15															
1. First-time freshmen	16															
2. Other first-year	17															
3. Second-year	18															
4. Third-year	19															
5. Fourth-year and beyond	20															
B. Unclassified students, total	21															
1. Undergraduate level	22															
2. Postbaccalaureate level	23															
C. First-professional students	24															
D. Graduate students, total	25															
1. First-year	26															
2. Beyond the first year	27															
TOTAL PART-TIME STUDENTS	28															
III. GRAND TOTAL, ALL STUDENTS	29															

CERTIFICATION

I CERTIFY that the information given above is complete, true, and correct to the best of my knowledge and belief. (A willfully false statement is punishable by law, U.S. Code, Title 18, Section 1001.)

NAME OF PERSON FURNISHING INFORMATION

TITLE

SIGNATURE

DATE

TELEPHONE — AREA CODE | NUMBER | EXTENSION

OE FORM 2300-2.3, 7/78 (FM Control No. 56)   REPLACES OE FORM 2300-2.3, 4/77, WHICH IS OBSOLETE

1. NAME OF INSTITUTION

2. INSTITUTION CODE NUMBER

3. DUE DATE
Not later than
November 15, 1978

0200 — Architecture and Environmental Design

check, if no students in this field ☐

ALL STUDENTS ENROLLED (resident and extension)	LINE NO.	NON-RESIDENT ALIEN		BLACK NON-HISPANIC		AMERICAN INDIAN OR ALASKAN NATIVE		ASIAN OR PACIFIC ISLANDER		HISPANIC		WHITE NON-HISPANIC		TOTAL (sum of columns (1) through (12))	
		MEN (1)	WOMEN (2)	MEN (3)	WOMEN (4)	MEN (5)	WOMEN (6)	MEN (7)	WOMEN (8)	MEN (9)	WOMEN (10)	MEN (11)	WOMEN (12)	MEN (13)	WOMEN (14)
I. FULL-TIME STUDENTS															
A. Undergraduates, total	01														
1. First-time freshmen	02														
2. Other first-year	03														
3. Second-year	04														
4. Third-year	05														
5. Fourth-year and beyond	06														
B. Unclassified students, total	07														
1. Undergraduate level	08														
2. Postbaccalaureate level	09														
C. First-professional students	10														
D. Graduate students, total	11														
1. First-year	12														
2. Beyond the first year	13														
TOTAL FULL-TIME STUDENTS	14														
II. PART-TIME STUDENTS															
A. Undergraduates, total	15														
1. First-time freshmen	16														
2. Other first-year	17														
3. Second-year	18														
4. Third-year	19														
5. Fourth-year and beyond	20														
B. Unclassified students, total	21														
1. Undergraduate level	22														
2. Postbaccalaureate level	23														
C. First-professional students	24														
D. Graduate students, total	25														
1. First-year	26														
2. Beyond the first year	27														
TOTAL PART-TIME STUDENTS	28														
III. GRAND TOTAL, ALL STUDENTS	29														

CERTIFICATION

I CERTIFY that the information given above is complete, true, and correct to the best of my knowledge and belief. (A willfully false statement is punishable by law, U.S. Code, Title 18, Section 1001.)

NAME OF PERSON FURNISHING INFORMATION

TITLE

SIGNATURE

DATE

TELEPHONE

AREA CODE | NUMBER | EXTENSION

OE FORM 2300-2.3, 7/78 (FM Control No. 56)   REPLACES OE FORM 2300-2.3, 4/77, WHICH IS OBSOLETE

FORM APPROVED
OMB NO. 51–R0738

1. NAME OF INSTITUTION

2. INSTITUTION CODE NUMBER

3. DUE DATE Not later than November 15, 1978

0400 — Biological Sciences

check, if no students in this field ☐

ALL STUDENTS ENROLLED (resident and extension)	LINE NO.	NON-RESIDENT ALIEN		BLACK NON-HISPANIC		AMERICAN INDIAN OR ALASKAN NATIVE		ASIAN OR PACIFIC ISLANDER		HISPANIC		WHITE NON-HISPANIC		TOTAL (sum of columns (1) through (12))	
		MEN (1)	WOMEN (2)	MEN (3)	WOMEN (4)	MEN (5)	WOMEN (6)	MEN (7)	WOMEN (8)	MEN (9)	WOMEN (10)	MEN (11)	WOMEN (12)	MEN (13)	WOMEN (14)
I. FULL-TIME STUDENTS															
A. Undergraduates, total	01														
1. First-time freshmen	02														
2. Other first-year	03														
3. Second-year	04														
4. Third-year	05														
5. Fourth-year and beyond	06														
B. Unclassified students, total	07														
1. Undergraduate level	08														
2. Postbaccalaureate level	09														
C. First-professional students	10														
D. Graduate students, total	11														
1. First-year	12														
2. Beyond the first year	13														
TOTAL FULL-TIME STUDENTS	14														
II. PART-TIME STUDENTS															
A. Undergraduates, total	15														
1. First-time freshmen	16														
2. Other first-year	17														
3. Second-year	18														
4. Third-year	19														
5. Fourth-year and beyond	20														
B. Unclassified students, total	21														
1. Undergraduate level	22														
2. Postbaccalaureate level	23														
C. First-professional students	24														
D. Graduate students, total	25														
1. First-year	26														
2. Beyond the first year	27														
TOTAL PART-TIME STUDENTS	28														
III. GRAND TOTAL, ALL STUDENTS	29														

CERTIFICATION

I CERTIFY that the information given above is complete, true, and correct to the best of my knowledge and belief. (A willfully false statement is punishable by law, U.S. Code, Title 18, Section 1001.)

NAME OF PERSON FURNISHING INFORMATION | TITLE

SIGNATURE | DATE

AREA CODE | TELEPHONE NUMBER | EXTENSION

OE FORM 2300-2.3, 7/78 (HM Control No. 56)   REPLACES OE FORM 2300-2.3, 4/77, WHICH IS OBSOLETE

0500 — Business and Management

check, if no students in this field ☐

ALL STUDENTS ENROLLED (resident and extension)	LINE NO.	NON-RESIDENT ALIEN		BLACK NON-HISPANIC		AMERICAN INDIAN OR ALASKAN NATIVE		ASIAN OR PACIFIC ISLANDER		HISPANIC		WHITE NON-HISPANIC		TOTAL (sum of columns (1) through (12))	
		MEN (1)	WOMEN (2)	MEN (3)	WOMEN (4)	MEN (5)	WOMEN (6)	MEN (7)	WOMEN (8)	MEN (9)	WOMEN (10)	MEN (11)	WOMEN (12)	MEN (13)	WOMEN (14)
I. FULL-TIME STUDENTS															
A. Undergraduates, total	01														
1. First-time freshmen	02														
2. Other first-year	03														
3. Second-year	04														
4. Third-year	05														
5. Fourth-year and beyond	06														
B. Unclassified students, total	07														
1. Undergraduate level	08														
2. Postbaccalaureate level	09														
C. First-professional students	10														
D. Graduate students, total	11														
1. First-year	12														
2. Beyond the first year	13														
TOTAL FULL-TIME STUDENTS	14														
II. PART-TIME STUDENTS															
A. Undergraduates, total	15														
1. First-time freshmen	16														
2. Other first-year	17														
3. Second-year	18														
4. Third-year	19														
5. Fourth-year and beyond	20														
B. Unclassified students, total	21														
1. Undergraduate level	22														
2. Postbaccalaureate level	23														
C. First-professional students	24														
D. Graduate students, total	25														
1. First-year	26														
2. Beyond the first year	27														
TOTAL PART-TIME STUDENTS	28														
III. GRAND TOTAL, ALL STUDENTS	29														

CERTIFICATION

I CERTIFY that the information given above is complete, true, and correct to the best of my knowledge and belief. (A willfully false statement is punishable by law, U.S. Code, Title 18, Section 1001.)

NAME OF PERSON FURNISHING INFORMATION | TITLE

SIGNATURE   DATE

TELEPHONE   AREA CODE | NUMBER | EXTENSION

OE FORM 2300-2.3, 7/78 (FM Control No. 56)   REPLACES OE FORM 2300-2.3, 4/77, WHICH IS OBSOLETE

9

| 1. NAME OF INSTITUTION | 2. INSTITUTION CODE NUMBER | 3. DUE DATE Not later than November 15, 1978 | FORM APPROVED OMB NO 51-R0738 |

0900— Engineering
check if no students in this field ☐

ALL STUDENTS ENROLLED (resident and extension)	LINE NO.	NON-RESIDENT ALIEN		BLACK NON-HISPANIC		AMERICAN INDIAN OR ALASKAN NATIVE		ASIAN OR PACIFIC ISLANDER		HISPANIC		WHITE-NON-HISPANIC		TOTAL (sum of columns (1) through (12))	
		MEN (1)	WOMEN (2)	MEN (3)	WOMEN (4)	MEN (5)	WOMEN (6)	MEN (7)	WOMEN (8)	MEN (9)	WOMEN (10)	MEN (11)	WOMEN (12)	MEN (13)	WOMEN (14)
I. FULL-TIME STUDENTS															
A. Undergraduates, total	01														
1. First-time freshmen	02														
2. Other first-year	03														
3. Second-year	04														
4. Third-year	05														
5. Fourth-year and beyond	06														
B. Unclassified students, total	07														
1. Undergraduate level	08														
2. Postbaccalaureate level	09														
C. First-professional students	10														
D. Graduate students, total	11														
1. First-year	12														
2. Beyond the first year	13														
TOTAL FULL-TIME STUDENTS	14														
II. PART-TIME STUDENTS															
A. Undergraduates, total	15														
1. First-time freshmen	16														
2. Other first-year	17														
3. Second-year	18														
4. Third-year	19														
5. Fourth-year and beyond	20														
B. Unclassified students, total	21														
1. Undergraduate level	22														
2. Postbaccalaureate level	23														
C. First-professional students	24														
D. Graduate students, total	25														
1. First year	26														
2. Beyond the first year	27														
TOTAL PART-TIME STUDENTS	28														
III. GRAND TOTAL ALL STUDENTS	29														

CERTIFICATION

I CERTIFY that the information given above is complete, true, and correct to the best of my knowledge and belief. (A willfully false statement is punishable by law, U.S. Code, Title 18, Section 1001.)

| NAME OF PERSON FURNISHING INFORMATION | TITLE |

SIGNATURE

| TELEPHONE | DATE |
| AREA CODE | NUMBER | EXTENSION |

FORM APPROVED OMB NO. 51-R0738

1. NAME OF INSTITUTION

2. INSTITUTION CODE NUMBER

3. DUE DATE — Not later than November 15, 1978

1204 – Dentistry

check, if no students in this field ☐

ALL STUDENTS ENROLLED (resident and extension)	LINE NO.	NON-RESIDENT ALIEN		BLACK NON-HISPANIC		AMERICAN INDIAN OR ALASKAN NATIVE		ASIAN OR PACIFIC ISLANDER		HISPANIC		WHITE NON-HISPANIC		TOTAL (sum of columns (1) through (12))	
		MEN (1)	WOMEN (2)	MEN (3)	WOMEN (4)	MEN (5)	WOMEN (6)	MEN (7)	WOMEN (8)	MEN (9)	WOMEN (10)	MEN (11)	WOMEN (12)	MEN (13)	WOMEN (14)
I. FULL-TIME STUDENTS															
A. Undergraduates, total	01														
1. First-time freshmen	02														
2. Other first-year	03														
3. Second-year	04														
4. Third-year	05														
5. Fourth-year and beyond	06														
B. Unclassified students, total	07														
1. Undergraduate level	08														
2. Postbaccalaureate level	09														
C. First-professional students	10														
D. Graduate students, total	11														
1. First-year	12														
2. Beyond the first year	13														
TOTAL FULL-TIME STUDENTS	14														
II. PART-TIME STUDENTS															
A. Undergraduates, total	15														
1. First-time freshmen	16														
2. Other first-year	17														
3. Second-year	18														
4. Third-year	19														
5. Fourth-year and beyond	20														
B. Unclassified students, total	21														
1. Undergraduate level	22														
2. Postbaccalaureate level	23														
C. First-professional students	24														
D. Graduate students, total	25														
1. First-year	26														
2. Beyond the first year	27														
TOTAL PART-TIME STUDENTS	28														
III. GRAND TOTAL, ALL STUDENTS	29														

CERTIFICATION

I CERTIFY that the information given above is complete, true, and correct to the best of my knowledge and belief. (A willfully false statement is punishable by law, U.S. Code, Title 18, Section 1001.)

NAME OF PERSON FURNISHING INFORMATION	TITLE
SIGNATURE	DATE
AREA CODE NUMBER — TELEPHONE EXTENSION	

OE FORM 2300-2.3, 7/78 (FM Control No. 56)   REPLACES OE FORM 2300-2.3, 4/77, WHICH IS OBSOLETE

1. NAME OF INSTITUTION		2. INSTITUTION CODE NUMBER	3. DUE DATE Not later than November 15, 1978		FORM APPROVED OMB NO. 51-R0738

1206 – Medicine

check, if no students in this field ☐

ALL STUDENTS ENROLLED (resident and extension)	LINE NO.	NON-RESIDENT ALIEN		BLACK NON-HISPANIC		AMERICAN INDIAN OR ALASKAN NATIVE		ASIAN OR PACIFIC ISLANDER		HISPANIC		WHITE NON-HISPANIC		TOTAL (sum of columns (1) through (12))	
		MEN (1)	WOMEN (2)	MEN (3)	WOMEN (4)	MEN (5)	WOMEN (6)	MEN (7)	WOMEN (8)	MEN (9)	WOMEN (10)	MEN (11)	WOMEN (12)	MEN (13)	WOMEN (14)
I. FULL-TIME STUDENTS															
A. Undergraduates, total	01														
1. First-time freshmen	02														
2. Other first-year	03														
3. Second-year	04														
4. Third-year	05														
5. Fourth-year and beyond	06														
B. Unclassified students, total	07														
1. Undergraduate level	08														
2. Postbaccalaureate level	09														
C. First-professional students	10														
D. Graduate students, total	11														
1. First-year	12														
2. Beyond the first year	13														
TOTAL FULL-TIME STUDENTS	14														
II. PART-TIME STUDENTS															
A. Undergraduates, total	15														
1. First-time freshmen	16														
2. Other first-year	17														
3. Second-year	18														
4. Third-year	19														
5. Fourth-year and beyond	20														
B. Unclassified students, total	21														
1. Undergraduate level	22														
2. Postbaccalaureate level	23														
C. First-professional students	24														
D. Graduate students, total	25														
1. First-year	26														
2. Beyond the first year	27														
TOTAL PART-TIME STUDENTS	28														
III. GRAND TOTAL, ALL STUDENTS	29														

CERTIFICATION

I CERTIFY that the information given above is complete, true, and correct to the best of my knowledge and belief. (A willfully false statement is punishable by law, U.S. Code, Title 18, Section 1001.)

NAME OF PERSON FURNISHING INFORMATION	TITLE	
SIGNATURE		DATE
	AREA CODE	TELEPHONE NUMBER / EXTENSION

OE FORM 2300-2.3, 7/78 (FM Control No. 56)   REPLACES OE FORM 2300-2.3, 4/77, WHICH IS OBSOLETE

1. NAME OF INSTITUTION | **2. INSTITUTION CODE NUMBER** | **3. DUE DATE** Not later than November 15, 1978 | **FORM APPROVED** OMB NO. 51-R0738

SIGNATURE (...to the best of my knowledge...)

ALL STUDENTS ENROLLED (resident and extension)	LINE NO.	NON-RESIDENT ALIEN		BLACK NON-HISPANIC		AMERICAN INDIAN OR ALASKAN NATIVE		ASIAN OR PACIFIC ISLANDER		HISPANIC		WHITE NON-HISPANIC		TOTAL (sum of columns (1) through (12))	
		MEN (1)	WOMEN (2)	MEN (3)	WOMEN (4)	MEN (5)	WOMEN (6)	MEN (7)	WOMEN (8)	MEN (9)	WOMEN (10)	MEN (11)	WOMEN (12)	MEN (13)	WOMEN (14)
1218 — Veterinary Medicine — check, if no students in this field ☐															
I. FULL-TIME STUDENTS															
A. Undergraduates, total	01														
1. First-time freshmen	02														
2. Other first-year	03														
3. Second-year	04														
4. Third-year	05														
5. Fourth-year and beyond	06														
B. Unclassified students, total	07														
1 Undergraduate level	08														
2 Postbaccalaureate level	09														
C. First-professional students	10														
D. Graduate students, total	11														
1. First-year	12														
2. Beyond the first year	13														
TOTAL FULL-TIME STUDENTS	14														
II. PART-TIME STUDENTS															
A. Undergraduates, total	15														
1. First-time freshmen	16														
2. Other first-year	17														
3. Second-year	18														
4. Third-year	19														
5. Fourth-year and beyond	20														
B. Unclassified students, total	21														
1. Undergraduate level	22														
2. Postbaccalaureate level	23														
C. First-professional students	24														
D. Graduate students, total	25														
1. First-year	26														
2. Beyond the first year	27														
TOTAL PART-TIME STUDENTS	28														
III. GRAND TOTAL ALL STUDENTS	29														

CERTIFICATION

I CERTIFY that the information given above is complete, true, and correct to the best of my knowledge and belief. (A willfully false statement is punishable by law, U.S. Code, Title 18, Section 1001.)

NAME OF PERSON FURNISHING INFORMATION | TITLE

SIGNATURE | DATE

AREA CODE NUMBER | TELEPHONE | EXTENSION

OE FORM 2300-2.3, 7/78 (FM Control No. 56) — REPLACES OE FORM 2300-2.3, 4/77, WHICH IS OBSOLETE

| IR | HISPANIC | WHI |
| R | | HI |

II. PART-TIME STUDENT

A. Undergraduates, tota
  1. First-time freshme
  2. Other first-year
  3. Second-year
  4. Third-year
  5. Fourth-year and be
B. Unclassified students, 1
  1. Undergraduate level
  2. Postbaccalaureate le
C. First-professional stude

CERTIFICATION

I CERTIFY that the information given above is complete, true, and correct to the best of my knowledge and belief. (A willfully false statement is punishable by law, U.S. Code, Title 18, Section 1001.)

OE FORM 2300-2.3, 7/78 (FM Con

HING INFORMATION | TITLE

DATE

AREA CODE | NUMBER | EXTENSION

TELEPHONE

A.
L. FUL
A. U

B
1. L.
2. P
C. Frst
D Grad
1. F.
2. B
TOTAL
15
II PAR
A. U

B

C.

DEPARTMENT OF HEALTH, EDUCATION, AND WELFARE
EDUCATION DIVISION
WASHINGTON, D.C. 20202
HIGHER EDUCATION GENERAL INFORMATION SURVEY (HEGIS XIII)

FALL ENROLLMENT IN HIGHER EDUCATION, 1978

NAME AND MAILING ADDRESS OF INSTITUTION OR CAMPUS COVERED BY THIS
REPORT *(include city, State, and ZIP code)*

PLEASE NOTE THAT EACH INSTITUTION, BRANCH, CAMPUS OR OTHER ENTITY SEPARATELY CERTIFIED BY THE ACCREDITATION AND
INSTITUTIONAL ELIGIBILITY UNIT OF THE U.S. OFFICE OF EDUCATION, WITH IT'S OWN **FICE** CODE, AND LISTED SEPARATELY IN THE
EDUCATION DIRECTORY - HIGHER EDUCATION, SHOULD BE REPORTED ON A SEPARATE SURVEY FORM AND NOT INCLUDED OR COMBINED
WITH ANY OTHER SUCH CERTIFIED UNIT. BRANCHES, CAMPUSES, AND OTHER ORGANIZATIONAL ENTITIES NOT SEPARATELY CERTIFIED
SHOULD BE INCLUDED WITH THE APPROPRIATE INSTITUTION OR BRANCH REPORT. IF SUCH ARE INCLUDED IN THIS REPORT, PLEASE
LIST THEM BELOW.

OE FORM 2300-2.3, 7/78 *(FM Control No. 56)*   REPLACES OE FORM 2300-2.3, 4/77, WHICH IS OBSOLETE

DEPARTMENT OF
HEALTH, EDUCATION, AND WELFARE
ASSISTANT SECRETARY FOR EDUCATION
NATIONAL CENTER FOR EDUCATION STATISTICS
WASHINGTON, D.C. 20202

OFFICIAL BUSINESS
PENALTY FOR PRIVATE USE, $300

POSTAGE AND FEES PAID
U.S. DEPARTMENT OF H.E.W.
HEW 395

Department of Health, Education, and Welfare
Assistant Secretary for Education
National Center for Education Statistics
ATTENTION: Room 3073-HEGIS
Washington, D.C. 20202

Each fall since 1972, the National Center for Education Statistics has issued early estimates of enrollment in higher education consisting of tabulations of selected items of data for all institutions in the fall enrollment survey. These estimates have been extremely useful for planners within the institutions, State legislatures, Congress, and other interested persons in the higher education community. We ask that you submit the same information again for fall 1978, using this card to transmit the data to the National Center for Education Statistics.

Please complete every item on this card. Refer to the INSTRUCTIONS for definitions and other needed information. Provide final data when possible. Otherwise, if you find it necessary to make estimates, please make a notation to that effect on the card.

When completed, detach the self-addressed, postage-paid half of the card and mail it. Retain the other half for your files.

DEPARTMENT OF HEALTH, EDUCATION, AND WELFARE EDUCATION DIVISION WASHINGTON, D.C. 20202 HIGHER EDUCATION GENERAL INFORMATION SURVEY (HEGIS XIII) **FALL ENROLLMENT IN HIGHER EDUCATION, 1978**	These data are preliminary. Detach this portion and mail it to Assistant Secretary for Education. No envelope or postage required. Please read instructions before completing this card.	FORM APPROVED OMB NO. 51-R0738
		DUE DATE Not later than October 15, 1978
		INSTITUTION CODE NUMBER

NAME AND MAILING ADDRESS OF INSTITUTION OR CAMPUS COVERED BY THIS REPORT *(include city, State, and ZIP code)*	NAME AND TITLE OF RESPONDENT
	TELEPHONE NUMBER OF RESPONDENT *(area code, local number, and extension)*

PLEASE NOTE THAT EACH INSTITUTION, BRANCH, CAMPUS OR OTHER ENTITY SEPARATELY CERTIFIED BY THE ACCREDITATION AND INSTITUTIONAL ELIGIBILITY UNIT OF THE U.S. OFFICE OF EDUCATION, WITH IT'S OWN **FICE** CODE, AND LISTED SEPARATELY IN THE **EDUCATION DIRECTORY - HIGHER EDUCATION**, SHOULD BE REPORTED ON A SEPARATE SURVEY FORM AND NOT INCLUDED OR COMBINED WITH ANY OTHER SUCH CERTIFIED UNIT. BRANCHES, CAMPUSES, AND OTHER ORGANIZATIONAL ENTITIES NOT SEPARATELY CERTIFIED SHOULD BE INCLUDED WITH THE APPROPRIATE INSTITUTION OR BRANCH REPORT. IF SUCH ARE INCLUDED IN THIS REPORT, PLEASE LIST THEM BELOW.

ARE DATA FOR THIS UNIT INCLUDED IN THIS REPORT?	NAME OF BRANCH AND/OR OTHER CAMPUS	ADDRESS *(city, State, and ZIP code)*
☐ YES ☐ NO		
☐ YES ☐ NO		

	MEN		WOMEN		TOTAL *(sum of columns (1) through (4))*	TOTAL *(first-time freshmen)*
	FULL-TIME *(1)*	PART-TIME *(2)*	FULL-TIME *(3)*	PART-TIME *(4)*	*(5)*	*(6)*
ALL STUDENTS ENROLLED						

OE FORM 2300-2.3A, 7/78 *(FM Control No. 56)*   REPLACES OE FORM 2300-2.3A, 4/77, WHICH IS OBSOLETE   GPO 932 847

APPENDIX D
TECHNICAL NOTES

Discrepancies in total enrollment between this publication and the National Center for Education Statistics publications are due to the differences between the Office for Civil Rights' mandatory reporting requirements and the National Center for Education Statistics' voluntary reporting requirements.

The Office for Civil Rights does not survey military institutions or proprietary schools, or schools not receiving Federal financial assistance.

Definitions of "type of institution, or highest level of offering" used in this publication :

Two year institutions	Four year institutions
Junior colleges	Four- or five-year baccalaureate
Community colleges	First professional degree
Technical institutes	Master's
Normal schools offering at least a two-year	Beyond master's but less than doctorate
program of college level studies	Doctorate
	Undergraduate non-degree granting
	Graduate non-degree granting
	Post doctoral research only

Definitions of "control of institution" are:

Public	Private
Federal	Independent, non-profit
State	Affiliated with religious groups
Local	
State and Local	
State-related	

*U.S. GOVERNMENT PRINTING OFFICE: 1981-0-727-718/1681

U.S. Department of Education
Washington, D.C. 20202

. . . .

OFFICIAL BUSINESS

401

FOURTH CLASS - BOOK
Mr. Don W. Draughon
Documents Expediting Project
Exchange and Gift Division
Library of Congress
Washington, D.C.   20540

Pkg 6 of 6

U.S. DEPARTMENT OF EDUCATION/Office for Civil Rights

Lightning Source UK Ltd.
Milton Keynes UK
UKHW012137180219
337529UK00012B/1354/P